THE LAW OF CONTRACT

THE LAW OF CONTRACT

THIRTEENTH EDITION

by

EDWIN PEEL, B.C.L., M.A.

Professor of Law
Fellow of Keble College, Oxford
Solicitor & Consultant,
Clifford Chance LLP

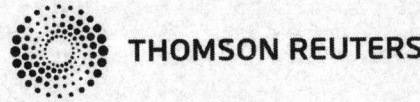

SWEET & MAXWELL   THOMSON REUTERS

First edition 1962
Second edition 1966
Third edition 1970
Fourth edition 1975
Fifth edition 1979
Sixth edition 1983
Seventh edition 1987
Eighth edition 1991
Ninth edition 1995
Tenth edition 1999
Eleventh edition 2003
Twelfth edition 2007
Reprinted 2010

Published in 2011 by Sweet & Maxwell, 100 Avenue Road, London, NW3 3PF
Part of Thomson Reuters (Professional) UK Limited
(Registered in England & Wales, Company No 1679046. Registered Office
and address for service: Aldgate House, 33 Aldgate High Street, London, EC3N 1DL)

Typeset by Interactive Sciences Ltd, Gloucester
Printed and bound by CPI Group (UK) Ltd, Croydon, CR0 4YY

For further information on our products and services, visit
www.sweetandmaxwell.co.uk

ISBN: 978 1 847039 217

No natural forests were destroyed to make this product, only farmed
timber was used and replanted.

CIP catalogue record for this book is available from the British Library.

Crown copyright material is reproduced with the permission of the Controller
of HMSO and the Queen's Printer for Scotland.

PREFACE TO THE THIRTEENTH EDITION

Since the last edition the courts have been as busy as ever, but both Parliaments, UK and European, have been mercifully quiet, at least so far as the law of contract is concerned. If one starts with legislation, perhaps the most significant development is the coming into force of most of the provisions of the Companies Act 2006 which were incorporated in the text in the last edition. On that occasion, readers were warned generally that it would be necessary to check whether the provisions referred to had come into force. In the present edition, it may be assumed that any provision of the 2006 Act to which reference is made *has* come into force unless the contrary is stated. The same applies to any other references to legislation. The Bribery Act 2010 and the Equality Act 2010 are significant developments in their own right, but their impact on this book is limited. An account has also been given of the changes which will be introduced by the Third Parties (Rights against Insurers) Act 2010.

The most significant of the statutory instruments to have been made are the Consumer Protection from Unfair Trading Regulations 2008, giving effect to The Unfair Commercial Practices Directive, but, for the reasons given in the text, their impact upon the law of contract is fairly minimal. Among other developments at the European level which are noted are the work to produce a Draft Common Frame of Reference and the prospects for an "optional instrument".

Any relative inactivity so far as legislation is concerned has been more than made up for by judicial development. In total, over 350 new cases are referred to in the text, but with re-writing and judicious pruning of the footnotes, the overall length of the text is almost identical to the previous edition.

It has been a particularly busy time at the highest level in the House of Lords and its successor, the Supreme Court. The very significant contribution to the development of the law of contract made in particular by Lord Hoffmann is acknowledged, following his retirement from the bench, by highlighting three decisions in which he played a prominent role. First, in giving the judgment of the Judicial Committee of the Privy Council in *Attorney General of Belize v Belize Telecom Ltd* he advocated a potentially broader approach to the test for terms implied in fact. Whether, in practice, the approach advocated is one which is broader than the tests previously applied is open to debate, but it is one which has been endorsed in this edition and this has led to a significant re-writing of the relevant section of chapter 6. Secondly, in *The Achilleas*, along with Lord Hope (and, possibly, Lord Walker) he introduced a "reformulation" of the test of remoteness. Some doubts are expressed about the utility of this particular development, but it has raised important questions about the fundamental nature of the test of remoteness, if not the law of contract generally, and an attempt to deal with those questions has led to a major re-writing of the section on remoteness in chapter 20. Overall, chapter 20 has seen the most significant revision in the light of other developments in the law relating to damages, some of which are noted below. Thirdly, in *Chartbrook Ltd v Persimmon Homes Ltd*, to the surprise of some, the House of Lords declined the invitation to abrogate the rule excluding evidence of the parties' pre-contractual negotiations as an aid to the interpretation of the contract. The surprise was perhaps compounded by the simultaneous re-affirmation of Lord Hoffmann's "re-statement" of the principles of inter-pretation in *Investors Compensation Scheme Ltd v West Bromwich Building Society* which heralded the sort of "purposive interpretation" seen in the actual decision in *Chartbrook* and which may be thought to lend support to the admission of evidence of the parties' negotiations, where relevant. That said, it may be noted that in two very recent decisions (*Kookmin Bank v Rainy Sky SA* (see especially Patten L.J.) and *ING Bank NV v Ros Roca SA*) the Court of Appeal has appeared concerned to put a limit on the extent to which "purposive interpretation" is permissible. These developments are all considered in chapter 6.

Other decisions of the House of Lords, or Supreme Court, of particular note are the following: *Cobbe v Yeoman's Row Management Ltd* and *Thorner v Major* (proprietary estoppel, chapter 3); *In re Sigma Finance Corporation* (interpretation, chapter 6); *Sempra Metals Ltd v Commissioners of Inland Revenue* (loss of interest as damages, chapter 20); *Office of Fair Trading v Abbey National Plc* (Unfair Terms in Consumer Contracts Regulations 1999, chapter 7); *Radmacher v Granatino* (ante-nuptial agreements, chapter 11); *Stone & Rolls Ltd v Moore Stephens* (illegality, chapter 11); and *RTS Flexible Systems Ltd v Molkerei Alois Müller GmbH & Co KG* (contractual intention, chapters 2 and 4). A further judgment of the Privy Council, in *Pell Frischmann Engineering Ltd v Bow Valley Iran Ltd*, has made a telling contribution to the development of the award of what now seems commonly to be referred to as "*Wrotham Park* damages" (chapter 20).

In addition to the two cases cited above, among the most significant of the decisions of the Court of Appeal to be covered in this edition are the following: *The Sea Angel* (frustration, chapter 19); *Safeway Stores Ltd v Twigger* (illegality, chapter 11); *Collier v P & M.J. Wright (Holdings) Ltd* (promissory estoppel, chapter 3); *Stocznia Gdynia SA v Gearbulk Holdings Ltd* (termination for breach, chapter 18); *Parabola Investments Ltd v Browallia Cal Ltd* (fraudulent mis-representation, chapter 9); *Supershield Ltd v Siemens Building Technologies FE Ltd* (remoteness, chapter 20); *The Reborn* (implied terms, chapter 6); *Tekdata Inter-connections Ltd v Amphenol* (battle of the forms, chapter 2); *Milner v Carnival Plc* (damages for loss of enjoyment, chapter 20); *Benedetti v Sawiris* (*quantum meruit*, chapter 22); and *Sibthorpe v Southwark L.B.C.* (champerty, chapter 11).

At first instance, the masterly analysis by Christopher Clarke J. in *Raiffeisen Zentralbank Osterreich AG v Royal Bank of Scotland Plc* of many of the difficult issues to arise in a claim of misrepresentation has resulted in numerous references to this decision in chapter 9. Other decisions at first instance of particular interest include *Guido van der Garde BV v Force India Formula One Ltd* and *The Mamola Challenger* (damages, chapter 20) and *The Harriette N* (mistake, chapter 8).

I have attempted to give an account of the law as at 1 June 2011, though it has been possible to add one or two later citations to the footnotes, where appropriate, at the proofs stage.

Most of the work on this edition was done during a period of leave and I am grateful in this regard to the Faculty of Law in Oxford and to the Warden and Fellows of Keble College. That work was supported by two excellent research assistants: Carmine Conte, who helped in the search for and collation of the decisions of the courts; and Paul Wee who helped with the updating of the references to legislation. My thanks to them both and also to Adrian Briggs, James Edelman, John Cartwright and Andrew Burrows who have been kind enough in the intervening years since the last edition to discuss, sometimes at length, some of the issues which are covered in this edition. I am also very grateful to Oke Odudu who once again kindly reviewed the section on competition in chapter 11 (Illegality). The publication of this edition was made possible by the very hard work done by Sweet & Maxwell and, with apologies to those whom I am not able to identify individually, I should like to thank, in particular, Nicola Thurlow, Steven Warriner, Mat Beal and Zoe Haynes.

As with the last edition, my greatest thanks is reserved for my wife, Helen, and my children, Emily and Charlotte, for their kindness, support and patience, particularly when the demands of the task have taken more of my time than it is fair to have asked them to give up. I now have the opportunity to make up that lost time.

Edwin Peel
Oxford, 7 July 2011.

CONTENTS

TABLE OF CASES

TABLE OF STATUTES

TABLE OF STATUTORY INSTRUMENTS

TABLE OF EUROPEAN LEGISLATION

CHAPTER ONE

INTRODUCTION

Contract as enforceable agreement. A contract is an agreement giving rise   **1–001**
to obligations which are enforced or recognised by law. The factor which distinguishes contractual from other legal obligations is that they are based on the
agreement of the contracting parties. This proposition remains generally true,
even though it is subject to a number of important qualifications.

The objective principle.[1] The first such qualification is that the law is often   **1–002**
concerned with the objective appearance, rather than with the actual fact, of
agreement: a person is bound "whatever [his] real intention may be", if "a
reasonable man would believe that he was assenting to the terms proposed by the
other party and that other party upon that belief enters into a contract with him".[2]
This objective principle is based on the needs of commercial convenience. Considerable uncertainty would result if A, after inducing B reasonably to believe that
he (A) had agreed to certain terms, could then escape liability merely by showing
that he had no "real intention" to enter into that agreement. The principle is an
important one; but it would be wrong to say that the law of contract has no
concern at all with actual agreement. This would put too much emphasis on the
exceptional situation; for in most cases, the appearance corresponds with the fact
of agreement. And the principle is not purely objective: A is not bound merely
because "a reasonable man would believe that he was assenting to the terms
proposed by the other party". In particular, there will be no contract if (in spite
of the objective appearance of agreement) B *actually knows* that A in fact has *no*
intention to contract with him, or to contract on the terms alleged.[3]
    A subjective element thus qualifies the objective principle; and this follows from
the purpose of that principle, which is to protect B from the prejudice which he
might suffer as a result of relying on a false appearance of agreement. There is
clearly no need in this way to protect a party who knows that the objective
appearance does not correspond with reality.[4] It also follows from the purpose of
the objective principle that it will not apply where A's apparent assent is based on
a mistake induced by B's negligence.[5] More generally, it may be said that the
objective principle applies only where serious inconvenience would be caused by
allowing a party to rely on his "real intention". In the interests of convenience the
law may sometimes hold that there is a contract although there was not even the

---

[1] Friedmann, 119 L.Q.R. 68.

[2] *Smith v Hughes* (1871) L.R. 6 QB 597 at 607; see below, para.8–047; Howarth 100 L.Q.R. 265;
Vorster 103 L.Q.R. 274; Howarth 103 L.Q.R. 527; Goddard 7 *Legal Studies*, 263; de Moor 106 L.Q.R.
632.

[3] e.g. below, paras 2–002—2–003, 8–050.

[4] For the further question whether the objective principle protects the "other party" where he has
no view on the question whether the objective appearance corresponded with reality, see below,
para.2–003.

[5] e.g. below, paras 8–052, 8–067; cf. *Norwich Union Fire Insurance Society Ltd v Price* [1934] A.C. 455
at 463.

objective appearance of an agreement.[6] It does not follow that the law is not concerned with any sort of agreement at all: to allege that this was the position "would introduce into the law of contract a novel heresy".[7]

1–003   **Standards of behaviour imposed on the parties.** The idea that contractual obligations are based on agreement must, secondly, be qualified because contracting parties are normally expected to observe certain standards of behaviour. These are the result of terms implied by law[8] into certain types of contract, for example, into contracts for the sale of goods or of employment. The parties may be able to vary or exclude some such terms by contrary agreement; but unless they do so they are bound by many duties to which they have not expressly agreed and of which they may have never thought. Agreement is not the *sole* factor which determines the legal effects of a contract once it is shown to exist. But it remains an important factor. For example, the intention of the parties (objectively ascertained) determines whether a statement made at the time of contracting has contractual force or is a mere representation[9]; and it determines whether a term which is not expressly stated in the contract should be implied in fact, i.e. because the parties must have intended to incorporate it.[10]

It has been suggested that in such cases the courts only *say* that the intention of the parties is the determining factor, but really apply rules based on various considerations of policy unconnected with that intention.[11] But a bare assertion that the relevant judgments do not mean what they say should not be accepted unless it is supported by argument. Such an argument can, perhaps, be based on the history of the doctrine of frustration, under which contracting parties may be discharged from liability by supervening events[12]: e.g. where such events make performance impossible. The doctrine was at one time justified by saying that the parties had impliedly agreed to be discharged in such circumstances; but many lawyers now prefer to say that the parties are discharged by operation of law, whether they would have agreed to discharge or not. This may be true; but the intention of the parties cannot for that reason be wholly disregarded. Before holding that parties are discharged, the court must find out what they contracted about: they may have deliberately taken the risk of supervening impossibility. The court must decide whether the parties contracted about a certainty or about a possibility; and it does so by ascertaining, as best it can, their intentions in the matter.

1–004   **Freedom of contract.** The idea that contractual obligations are based on agreement must, thirdly, be qualified in relation to the scope of the principle of freedom of contract.[13] In the nineteenth century, judges took the view that persons of full capacity should in general be allowed to make what contracts they liked: the law only interfered on fairly specific grounds such as misrepresentation, undue

---

[6] See below, para.2–055.

[7] *The Hannah Blumenthal* [1983] 1 A.C. 854 at 916–917.

[8] See below, para.6–041 et seq.

[9] See below, para.9–043.

[10] See below, para.6–032.

[11] Atiyah, *An Introduction to the Law of Contract*, 5th edn, (Oxford University Press, 1995), pp.20–21. (The point was more emphatically put in the 1st edn at pp.13, 103, and is somewhat less emphatically put in the 6th edn (by Smith) at 16.)

[12] See below, Ch.19.

[13] For an historical account, see Atiyah, *The Rise and Fall of Freedom of Contract*, (Oxford University Press).

influence or illegality.[14] It did not interfere merely because one party was economically more powerful than the other and so able to drive a hard bargain. This attitude became particularly important when the courts recognised the validity of standard form contracts[15] drawn up by one party on terms designed to protect its interests at the expense of those of the other. This practice of contracting on standard terms is now very common; and it is arguable that a customer who contracts on such standard terms has them imposed on him, and does not really "agree" to them at all. This argument is particularly strong where standard terms are used by a monopoly supplier, or where all suppliers in a particular field use the same standard terms. The customer's only choice may then be between accepting those terms or doing without the goods or services in question; and often he cannot in practice do without. On the other hand, exact equality of bargaining power is probably rare; and there can be much dispute as to the precise degree of pressure which makes the difference between consent reluctantly given and a state of mind which cannot properly be described as consent at all. The amount of pressure which can be brought to bear on the customer does not depend solely on the respective wealth and power of the parties, but also on market conditions. In a buyer's market, an insistent private customer may be able to induce a normally powerful supplier to modify his standard terms, rather than lose a sale; while in a seller's market a customer may be ready to agree to any terms which the seller puts forward, or be willing to take his chance on the contents of any document put forward by the seller. A person may also agree to contract on a set of terms although he does not know in detail what they provide, e.g. where parties contract on terms settled by a trade association, or where a person takes employment on terms negotiated between employers and a trade union.[16] In such cases the parties would not deny that they *had* agreed to the terms, whatever they might be.

Imbalance of bargaining power. Important inroads on the principle of freedom of contract have been made by legislation passed to redress some real or supposed imbalance of bargaining power. For example, the contents of many contracts of employment are now regulated in some detail by legislation.[17] Under other statutes, terms are compulsorily implied into contracts and cannot be excluded by contrary agreement[18]; while the validity of standard form contracts is subject to severe legislative restrictions, especially in contracts between a commercial supplier of goods or services and a consumer.[19] In all these cases the main relationship between the parties is still based on agreement, but many of the obligations arising out of it are imposed or regulated by law.   1–005

Doubtful cases. There are cases in which the law plays so large, and the agreement of parties so small, a part that it becomes doubtful whether the relationship can still be called contractual. The agreement of the parties may create a status, such as marriage, the main legal incidents of which are fixed by law and cannot be varied by the parties at all.[20] Sometimes, the terms on which a   1–006

---

[14] See below, Chs 9, 10, 11.
[15] See below, Ch.7.
[16] See below, para.7–005.
[17] See, e.g. Employment Rights Act 1996, s.86; National Minimum Wage Act 1998; Employment Relations Act 1999; Employment Act 2002; Employment Relations Act 2004; Employment Act 2008.
[18] e.g. Equality Act 2010, ss.66, 144; cf. National Minimum Wage Act 1998, s.49.
[19] See below, para.7–049 et seq.
[20] The parties "contract into the package which the law of the land lays down": *Radmacher v Granatino* [2010] UKSC 42; [2011] 1 A.C. 534 at [132].

person is employed (especially in the public service) are governed in part by legislation; and in one such case it was said that a claim under the "statutory scheme of employment"[21] could not "be dealt with as though it were an ordinary master and servant claim in which the rights of the parties were regulated solely by contract".[22] Similarly, a member of the armed forces is not in any contractual relationship with the Crown, even if he enlists voluntarily.[23] In a number of further borderline cases, the fact that many of the terms of the relationship are settled by law has not of itself been regarded as decisive. Thus on the one hand the relationship between a general medical practitioner and the health authority in whose area he worked under the National Health Service is not a contractual one.[24] On the other hand, it has been said that a consultant appointed to a post at a hospital under the National Health Service, works under "an ordinary contract between master and servant," although it is one with a "strong statutory flavour",[25] as it is governed by regulations made under statutory powers and having the force of law.

1–007   **Freedom not to contract.** In the cases so far considered the parties are free to decide whether or not to enter into the relationship (though the law may fix some or all of its incidents); but there are other cases in which the law to some extent restricts even this freedom. At common law a common innkeeper may be liable criminally[26] or in tort[27] for refusing, without sufficient excuse, to accommodate a guest. Injunctions may be granted and damages awarded against persons whose withholding of supplies from, for example, distributors, amounts to an abuse of a dominant position, contrary to EC or UK competition law.[28] A person may be forbidden to refuse to contract by legislation aimed to prevent discrimination on grounds of age, disability, gender reassignment, marriage and civil partnership, pregnancy and maternity, race, religion or belief, sex or sexual orientation.[29] It is unlawful to refuse a person employment "because he is, or is not, a member

---

[21] *Barber v Manchester Regional Hospital Board* [1958] 1 W.L.R. 181 at 196.

[22] *Barber*'s case, above; for the effect of this distinction on remedies, see below, para.21–036. See also: *Johnson v Unisys Ltd* [2001] UKHL 13; [2003] 1 A.C. 518 (below, para.20–083); *Gisda Cyf v Barratt* [2010] UKSC 41; [2010] I.R.L.R. 1073.

[23] See *Grant v S of S for India* (1877) 2 C.P.D. 445; *Leaman v R.* [1920] 3 KB 663; dicta in *Owners of SS Raphael v Brandy* [1911] A.C. 413 at 415 perhaps suggest the contrary.

[24] *Roy v Kensington and Chelsea and Westminster Family Practice Committee* [1992] 1 A.C. 624.

[25] *Barber*'s case, above; cf. the position of school teachers under Education Act 2002, s.122.

[26] See *R. v Ivens* (1835) 7 C. & P. 213.

[27] *Constantine v Imperial Hotels Ltd* [1944] K.B. 693.

[28] *Garden Cottage Foods Ltd v Milk Marketing Board* [1984] A.C. 130; below, para.11–108.

[29] See, generally, the Equality Act 2010. Where the parties have entered into a contract any term of it is unenforceable against a person in so far as it constitutes, promotes or provides for treatment of that or another person that is of a description prohibited by the Act (s.142(1)). See also Human Rights Act 1998, s.1 and Sch.1, Pt I, Art.14. By virtue of s.6, this provision makes unlawful only the activities of a "public authority" (including a court: s.6(3)(a)) and the question to what extent the Act gives rise to rights between private persons (the question of so-called "horizontal effect") remains as yet unresolved: see, e.g. Buxton, 116 L.Q.R. 48; Wade, 116 L.Q.R. 217; Hunt, 116 L.Q.R. 423; Bamforth, 117 L.Q.R. 34; [1999] C.L.J. 159; *Campbell v Mirror Group Newspapers Ltd* [2004] UKHL 22; [2004] 2 A.C. 457. Such rights could also be affected in consequence of judicial declarations of incompatibility of other legislation with the Convention (to which the Act gives the force of law) under s.4 of the Act, but only in relation to contracts entered after the Act came into force: *Wilson v First County Trust Ltd* [2003] UKHL 40; [2004] 1 A.C. 816 (also indicating that the Act has no retrospective effect for the purpose of s.6). For a detailed consideration of the potential impact of the 1998 Act on the law of contract, see *Chitty on Contracts*, edited by Beale, 30th edn, (London: Sweet & Maxwell, 2010), Vol.1, paras 1–035—1–066.

of a trade union"[30]; and compensation is payable to a person who is excluded from a trade union (except on one of a number of specified grounds).[31] In these cases a relationship which results from some degree of legal compulsion may nevertheless be regarded as contractual, because the parties still have considerable freedom to regulate its incidents. But there are other cases in which a relationship created by legal compulsion is clearly not contractual. A person whose property is compulsorily acquired against his will does not make a contract with the acquiring authority even though he receives compensation[32]; a patient who is treated in a hospital under the National Health Service is not considered to make a contract with the hospital authority[33]; nor does one to whom medicines are supplied under the Service make a contract to buy them, even if he pays a prescription charge[34]; and at common law, a person who posted a letter or parcel did not make a contract with the Post Office[35]; and the relations that now arise between such a person and a "universal [postal] service provider" appears similarly to be governed, not by contract, but by a scheme made under statute.[36] The borderline between the two classes of cases is by no means clearly defined: it is, for example, doubtful whether there is a contract between a patient and his doctor or dentist under the National Health Service. In the case of arrangements for the supply of gas, electricity or water, there may be a contract even though the supplier is bound by statute to make the supply, so long as the terms on which the supply is made are not also determined by legislation so as to leave no scope for bargaining between the supplier and the customer.[37]

Two key questions: agreement and enforceability. In spite of the above 1–008 qualifications, it remains broadly true that the law of contract is concerned with

---

[30] Trade Union and Labour Relations (Consolidation) Act 1992, s.137(1)(a); cf. Trade Union and Labour Relations (Consolidation) Act 1992, s.138(1)(a); under s.140 the remedy (in the last resort) is by way of compensation. cf. Human Rights Act 1998, s.1 and Sch.1, Pt I, Art.11; but see above, fn.30.

[31] Trade Union and Labour Relations (Consolidation) Act 1992, ss.174–177, as substituted by Trade Union and Employment Rights Act 1993, s.14.

[32] See *Sovmots Investments Ltd v S of S for the Environment* [1977] Q.B. 411 at 443, affirmed [1979] A.C. 144 without reference to this point. If a price is agreed after notice to treat, there is said to be a "statutory contract": *Munton v GLC* [1976] 1 W.L.R. 649. Even where this is not the case, the transaction may be regarded as a contract for the purpose of a particular statute: *Ridge Nominees v IRC* [1962] Ch. 376.

[33] *Allen v Bloomsbury Health Authority* [1993] 1 All E.R. 651.

[34] See *Pfizer Corp v Ministry of Health* [1965] A.C. 512; *Appleby v Sleep* [1968] 1 W.L.R. 948; *Re Medicaments Reference* [1970] 1 W.L.R. 1339.

[35] *Whitfield v Lord Le Despencer* (1778) Cowp. 754 at 764.

[36] Postal Services Act 2000, s.89; for exclusion and limitation of liability, see Postal Services Act 2000, ss.90, 91 (to be amended by the Postal Services Act 2011, Sch.12, Pt I, paras 23–26 (not yet in force)).

[37] See, e.g., Electricity Act 1989, ss.16 and 17 (as substituted by Utilities Act 2000, s.44) and Electricity Act 1989, Sch.6 (as substituted by Utilities Act 2000, s.51 and Sch.4). The repeal of s.18 of the 1989 Act by s.45 of the 2000 Act, abolishing charges by reference to tariffs, appears to undermine the reasoning of *Norweb Plc v Dixon* [1995] 1 W.L.R. 635, that there was no contract between the supplier and a "tariff" customer; see also the 2000 Act, s.108 and Sch.7, para.23(2): supplier deemed to have contracted with former tariff customers. The position appears to be the same with regard to the supply of gas: see the repeal by s.89 of the 2000 Act of Gas Act 1986, s.10(2), which appears to have assumed that there was no contract between the supplier and a domestic customer. In the case of water supplies, the relations between suppliers and domestic consumers appear to remain non-contractual as even the terms of such supply are regulated by legislation: see Water Industry Act 1991, ss.53, 54; contrast Water Industry Act 1991, ss.55, 56 (terms of *bulk* supply to be determined by agreement or by the Director); see also Water Industry Act 1999 and Water Act 2003.

the circumstances in which agreements are legally binding. Thus it deals mainly with the two questions of agreement and legal effects or enforceability. The rules relating to offer and acceptance,[38] for instance, deal with the process of reaching agreement. Those relating to consideration and contractual intention[39] concern the requirements which must normally be satisfied before an agreement will be legally enforced; while the rules relating to misrepresentation, duress, undue influence and illegality[40] deal with the effect of special factors on account of which the law may refuse to enforce agreements which would, apart from such factors, be binding. The rules which limit the contractual capacity of certain individuals[41] are based partly on the view that certain classes of persons cannot form the requisite contractual intention, and partly on the view that it is undesirable to enforce agreements against them. The rules relating to mistake are based partly on the view that there is no agreement when the parties are at cross-purposes on a fundamental point,[42] and partly on the view that an agreement has no legal effect if both parties were under a fundamental mistake as to the subject-matter.[43] The rules relating to the contents of a contract, performance, breach and frustration[44] are again partly based on the agreement between the parties, and partly on rules of law which determine the precise legal effect of that agreement.

1–009   **Other topics.** The bulk of the law of contract is concerned with the questions of agreement and legal enforceability; but a number of other topics also call for discussion. Thus the rules relating to plurality, third parties, assignment and agency[45] determine who is bound by, and entitled to the benefit of, a contract. The rules relating to remedies[46] assume the existence of an enforceable agreement, and deal with the methods of, and limits on, enforcement. These are in principle determined by law. Thus the agreement of the parties does not determine whether a contract is to be enforced specifically, or only by an award of damages; though that agreement may be relevant in determining the precise amount of damages which will be awarded for a breach of contract.

1–010   **Remedies: protection of the "expectation" interest.** Remedies for breach of contract are discussed in Chapters 20 and 21; but one fundamental point relating to them must be made at this stage. Such remedies might attempt to do one of two things. First, they might attempt to put the injured party into the position in which he would have been if the contract *had never been made*. This would require the party in breach to restore anything that he had received under the contract, and also to compensate the injured party for any loss that he had suffered by acting in reliance on the contract. Such remedies are said to protect the injured party's *restitution* and *reliance* interests.[47] But remedies for breach of contract go beyond the pursuit of these objectives. Their distinguishing feature is that they seek to put the injured party into the position in which he would have

---

[38] See below, Ch.2.
[39] See below, Chs 3, 4.
[40] See below, Chs 9–11.
[41] See below, Ch.12.
[42] See below, Ch.8, para.8–033 et seq.
[43] See below, Ch.8, para.8–002 et seq.
[44] See below, Chs 6, 17, 18, 19.
[45] See below, Chs 13–16.
[46] See below, Chs 20–21.
[47] See below, para.20–027 et seq.

been if the contract *had been performed*.[48] If, for example, a seller agrees to sell goods for less than they are worth, and then fails to deliver them, he must compensate the buyer for not having received goods which are worth more than he had agreed to pay for them. Conversely, if a buyer contracts to buy goods for more than they are worth, and then fails to pay for them, he is liable for the agreed price[49]: it is quite immaterial that the value of the goods with which the seller has parted was lower than that price. What the law does in these cases is to protect the injured party's *expectation* or *performance* interest.[50] Sometimes it does so directly, by actually ordering the party in breach to perform his part of the contract.[51] Sometimes it does so indirectly by ordering him to pay the injured party damages for *loss of his bargain*.

The result of awarding damages on this basis is to compensate the injured party, not because he is worse off than he was before the contract was made, but because the other party has failed to make him better off.[52] The law of contract takes this position in response to the needs of commercial certainty. The protection of the expectation interest promotes stability and furthers one of the central purposes of the law of contract in providing the legal framework required for commercial relations.

A European law of contract. The account which is given in this book is an account of the English law of contract, but the content of that law is, in some respects, EU law, as a result of its implementation in accordance with the Treaty obligations of the United Kingdom.[53] There have also been a number of projects aimed at developing common principles of European contract law,[54] but the prospect of a European Contract Code seems unlikely[55] and these projects have, as yet, not greatly influenced the development of domestic English law.

1–011

---

[48] See below, para.20–022 et seq.
[49] Assuming that the conditions stated at paras 21–005—21–015, below, are satisfied.
[50] See below, para.20–022 et seq.
[51] See below, para.21–016 et seq.
[52] *South Australian Asset Management Corp v York Montague Ltd* [1997] A.C. 191 at 216.
[53] e.g. the Unfair Terms in Consumer Contracts Regulations 1999 (SI 1999/2083) implementing Dir.93/13; below, para.7–095.
[54] See, e.g. Lando and Beale, *Principles of European Contract Law Parts I and II*; Study Group on a European Civil Code and Research Group on EC Private Law (Acquis Group), *Principles, Definitions and Model Rules of European Private Law: Draft Common Frame of Reference*; Jansen & Zimmerman [2010] C.L.J. 98.
[55] For proposals for an optional instrument, see the European Commission's Green Paper on policy options for progress towards a European Contract Law for consumers and businesses, Com (2010) 348 final (July 1, 2010); Whittaker 2011/3 *European Review of Contract Law* 1.

CHAPTER TWO

AGREEMENT[1]

2–001   The first requisite of a contract is that the parties should have reached agreement. Generally speaking, an agreement is made when one party accepts an offer made by the other. Further requirements are that the agreement must be certain and final; and special problems arise from conditional agreements.

1. OFFER

(a) Offer Defined

2–002   **The objective test.** An offer is an expression of willingness to contract on specified terms, made with the intention that it is to become binding as soon as it is accepted by the person to whom it is addressed.[2] Under the objective test of

---

[1] Winfield 55 L.Q.R. 499; Nussbaum 36 Col.L.Rev. 920.
[2] e.g. *Storer v Manchester CC* [1974] 1 W.L.R. 1403; contrast *Crest Nicholson (Londinium) Ltd v Akaria Investments Ltd* [2010] EWCA Civ 1331.

agreement,[3] an apparent intention to be bound may suffice, i.e. the alleged offeror (A) may be bound if his words or conduct[4] are such as to induce a reasonable person to believe that he intends to be bound, even though in fact he has no such intention.[5] This was, for example, held to be the case where a solicitor who had been instructed by his client to settle a claim for $155,000 by mistake offered to settle it for the higher sum of £150,000.[6] Similarly, if A offers to sell a book to B for £10 and B accepts the offer, A cannot escape liability merely by showing that his actual intention was to offer the book to B for £20, or that he intended the offer to relate to a book different from that specified in the offer.[7]

The offeree's state of mind. Whether A is actually bound by an acceptance 2–003 of his apparent offer depends on the state of mind of the alleged offeree (B); to this extent, the test is not purely objective.[8] With regard to B's state of mind, there are three possibilities. First, B actually believes that A intends to be bound: here the objective test is satisfied so that B can hold A to his apparent offer even though A did not, subjectively, have the requisite intention.[9] The general view is that there is no further requirement that A must also be aware of B's state of mind.[10] Secondly, B knows that, in spite of the objective appearance, A does not have the requisite intention: here A is not bound; the objective test does not apply in favour of B as he knows the truth about A's actual intention.[11] Thirdly, B has simply not formed any view about A's intention, so that B neither believes that A has the requisite intention nor knows that A does not have this intention: this situation has given rise to a conflict of judicial opinion. One view is that A is not bound: in other words, the objective test is satisfied only if A's conduct is such as to induce a reasonable person to believe that A had the requisite intention *and* if B actually held that belief.[12] The opposing view is that (in our third situation) A is bound: in other words, the objective test is satisfied if A's words or conduct would induce a reasonable person to believe that A had the requisite intention, so long as B does

---

[3] See above, para.1–002; *First Energy (UK) Ltd v Hungarian International Bank Ltd* [1993] 2 Lloyd's Rep. 195 at 201; *Ignazio Messina & Co v Polskie Linie Oceaniczne* [1995] 2 Lloyd's Rep. 566 at 571; *Bowerman v Association of British Travel Agents Ltd* [1995] N.L.J. 1815.

[4] For offers made by conduct, see below, at fnn.16–24; *The Aramis* [1989] 1 Lloyd's Rep. 213 (where the objective test was not satisfied) *G Percy Trentham Ltd v Archital Luxfer Ltd* [1993] 1 Lloyd's Rep. 25 at 27.

[5] *Maple Leaf Macro Volatility Master Fund v Rouvroy* [2009] EWCA Civ 1334 at [10], [17].

[6] *OT Africa Line Ltd v Vickers Plc* [1996] 1 Lloyd's Rep. 700; cf. *Moran v University College Salford (No.2)*, The Times, November 23, 1993.

[7] cf. *Centrovincial Estates Plc v Merchant Investors Assurance Co Ltd* [1983] Com.L.R. 158; cited with approval in *Whittaker v Campbell* [1984] Q.B. 318 at 327; and in *OT Africa Line Ltd v Vickers Plc* [1996] 1 Lloyd's Rep. 700 at 702.

[8] *The Hannah Blumenthal* [1983] 1 A.C. 854 at 924.

[9] *The Splendid Sun* [1981] 1 Q.B. 694, as explained in *The Hannah Blumenthal*, above; *The Multibank Holsatia* [1988] 2 Lloyd's Rep. 486 at 493.

[10] The suggestion that A must be aware of B's state of mind was made by Lord Diplock in *The Hannah Blumenthal* [1983] 1 A.C. 854 at 916 but Lord Brightman's contrary view, expressed in [1983] 1 A.C. 854 at 924 has been generally preferred: see *The Multibank Holsatia*, above, at 492.

[11] See above, para.1–002; *Ignazio Messina & Co v Polskie Linie Oceaniczne* [1995] 2 Lloyd's Rep. 566 at 571; *OT Africa Line Ltd v Vickers Plc* [1996] 1 Lloyd's Rep. 700 at 703; and see the authorities cited in fn.13, below.

[12] *The Hannah Blumenthal*, fn.8 above, as interpreted in *The Leonidas D* [1985] 1 W.L.R. 925; Beatson 102 L.Q.R. 19; Atiyah 102 L.Q.R. 392; *The Agrabele* [1987] 2 Lloyd's Rep. 223, esp. at 235; cf. *Cie Française d'Importation, SA v Deutsche Continental Handelsgesellschaft* [1985] 2 Lloyd's Rep. 592 at 597; *Amherst v James Walker Goldsmith and Silversmith Ltd* [1983] Ch. 305.

not actually know that A does *not* have any such intention.[13] This latter view no doubt facilitates proof of agreement, but it is hard to see why B should be protected in the situation to which it refers. Where B has no positive belief in A's (apparent) intention to be bound, he cannot be prejudiced by acting in reliance on it; and the purpose of the objective test is simply to protect B from the risk of suffering such prejudice.[14] The test embodies a principle of convenience; it is not based on any inherent superiority of objective over subjective criteria. It is therefore submitted that the objective test should not apply to our third situation since in it B's state of mind is such that there is no risk of his suffering any prejudice as a result of the objective appearance of A's intention.[15]

2–004   **Conduct as an offer.** An offer may be addressed either to an individual, or to a group of persons, or to the world at large; and it may be made expressly or by conduct. At common law, a person who had contracted to sell goods and tendered different goods (or a different quantity) might be considered to make an offer by conduct to sell the goods which he had tendered.[16] It seems that an offer to sell can still be made in this way, though by legislation against "inertia selling" the dispatch of goods without any prior request from the recipient may amount to a gift to him, rather than to an offer to sell.[17]

2–005   **Inactivity as an offer by conduct.** A number of cases raise the further question whether the "conduct" from which an offer may be inferred can take the form of inactivity. The issue in these cases was whether an agreement to submit a dispute to arbitration could be said to have been "abandoned" where, over a long period of time, neither party had taken any steps in the arbitration proceedings.[18] Such a question could also arise in the context of the alleged abandonment of some other type of right or remedy.[19] The arbitration cases indicate that, when inactivity is combined with other circumstances (such as destruction of relevant files),[20] it may, on the objective test, amount to an offer of abandonment, even though those

---

[13] *The Golden Bear* [1987] 1 Lloyd's Rep. 330 at 341 (doubted on another point at para.2–043, below); this view was approved in *The Antclizo* [1987] 2 Lloyd's Rep. 130 at 143 but doubted in [1987] 2 Lloyd's Rep. 130 at 147 (affd. [1988] 1 W.L.R. 603 without reference to the point); and *semble* in *Floating Dock Ltd v Hong Kong and Shanghai Bank Ltd* [1986] 1 Lloyd's Rep. 65 at 77; *The Multibank Holsatia* [1988] 2 Lloyd's Rep. 486 at 492 ("at least did not conflict with [B's] subjective understanding"); *The Maritime Winner* [1989] 2 Lloyd's Rep. 506 at 515 (using similar language).

[14] See above, para.1–002.

[15] *Maple Leaf Macro Volatility Master Fund v Rouvroy* [2009] EWHC 257 (Comm); [2009] 1 Lloyd's Rep. 475 at [228] (affd. [2009] EWCA Civ 1334).

[16] *Hart v Mills* (1846) 15 L.J.Ex. 200; below, para.2–018; cf. *Steven v Bromley & Son* [1919] 2 K.B. 722; *The Saronikos* [1986] 2 Lloyd's Rep. 277.

[17] Consumer Protection (Distance Selling) Regulations 2000 (SI 2000/2334) (implementing Dir.97/7 ([1997] O.J. L144/19)), regs 22 (amending Unsolicited Goods and Services Act 1971) and 24 (as amended by SI 2008/1277, Sch.2 para.96). For further amendments to the Unsolicited Goods and Services Act 1971, see: SI 2005/55 and SI 2005/148.

[18] The arbitrators have a statutory power to dismiss claims for want of prosecution (Arbitration Act 1996, s.41(3)), but that power may be excluded by agreement (Arbitration Act 1996, s.41(2)).

[19] cf. *Amherst Ltd v James Walker Goldsmith & Silversmith Ltd* [1983] Ch. 305; *Collin v Duke of Westminster* [1985] Q.B. 581; *MSC Mediterranean Shipping Co SA v BRE Metro Ltd* [1985] 2 Lloyd's Rep. 239.

[20] *The Splendid Sun* [1981] Q.B. 694, as explained in *The Hannah Blumenthal* [1983] 1 A.C. 854 (though this explanation was doubted in *Cie Française d'Importation, SA v Deutsche Conti Handelsgesellschaft* [1985] 2 Lloyd's Rep. 592 at 599); *Tracomin SA v Anton C Nielsen* [1984] 2 Lloyd's Rep. 195; *The Multibamk Holsatia* [1988] 2 Lloyd's Rep. 486; for the question whether such an offer can be *accepted* by inactivity, see below, para.2–043.

other circumstances would not, of themselves, constitute evidence from which an offer could be inferred. But when inactivity stands alone, it is unlikely[21] to have this effect, for it is equivocal and explicable on other grounds, such as inertia or forgetfulness, or the simple tactical consideration that the party alleged to have made the offer does not wish to re-activate his opponent's counter claims.[22] Consequently, it will not normally suffice to induce a reasonable person in the position of the other party to believe that an offer is being made[23]; and the mere fact that the other party nevertheless had this belief cannot suffice to turn the former party's inactivity into such an offer.[24]

(b) Offer Distinguished from Invitation to Treat

A test of intention. When parties negotiate with a view to making a contract, many preliminary communications may pass between them before a definite offer is made. One party may simply respond to a request for information (e.g. by stating the price at which he might be prepared to sell a house[25]), or he may make such a request (e.g. where he asks a prospective supplier whether he can supply goods suitable for his purpose).[26] That party is then said to make an "invitation to treat": he does not make an offer but invites the other party to do so.[27] The question whether a statement is an offer or an invitation to treat depends primarily on the intention with which it was made. It follows from the nature of an offer as described above[28] that a statement is not an offer if it in terms negatives the maker's intention to be bound on acceptance: for example, if it expressly provides that he is *not* to be bound merely by the other party's notification of assent, but only when he himself has signed the document in which the statement is contained.[29] Apart from this type of case, the wording is not conclusive. A statement may be an invitation to treat, although it contains the word "offer";[30] as, for example, in *Datec Electronic Holdings Ltd v United Parcels Service Ltd*[31] where an "offer" of carriage subject to certain restrictions was regarded as an invitation to

2–006

---

[21] *Unisys International Services Ltd v Eastern Counties Newspapers Group Ltd* [1991] 1 Lloyd's Rep. 538 at 553; cf. *The Boucraa* [1994] 1 A.C. 486 at 521, describing the "abandonment" approach as "largely useless in practice".

[22] *Unysis* case, above, at 553.

[23] *The Leonidas D* [1985] 1 W.L.R. 925; *Cie Française d'Importation, etc. SA v Deutsche Conti Handelsgesellschaft* [1985] 2 Lloyd's Rep. 592; *The Antclizo* [1988] 1 W.L.R. 603; *contra, The Golden Bear* [1987] 1 Lloyd's Rep. 330 (sed quaere: the decision was in part based on the decision at first instance in *The Agrabele* [1985] 2 Lloyd's Rep. 496, but this was reversed on appeal: [1987] 2 Lloyd's Rep. 223); *The Ermoupolis* [1990] 1 Lloyd's Rep. 160 at 166; see also below, para.2–047.

[24] *The Antclizo* [1988] 1 W.L.R. 603; Davenport, 104 L.Q.R. 493.

[25] *Harvey v Facey* [1893] A.C. 552; *Gibson v Manchester CC* [1979] 1 W.L.R. 294; cf. *The Barranduna* [1985] 2 Lloyd's Rep. 419; *Michael Gerson (Leasing) Ltd v Wilkinson* [2000] Q.B. 514 at 530.

[26] *Interfoto Picture Library Ltd v Stiletto Visual Programmes Ltd* [1989] Q.B. 433 at 436; cf. Electronic Commerce (EC Directive) Regulations 2002 (SI 2002/2013), reg.12: in electronic trading (e.g. on a website) an " 'order' may be, but need not be, the contractual offer . . . " for certain purposes specified in those Regulations.

[27] *Photolibrary Group Ltd v Burda Senator Verlag GmbH* [2008] EWHC 1343 (QB), [2008] 2 All E.R. (Comm) 811, at [63]–[64] where, because of a course of dealing between the parties, either analysis was "viable".

[28] See above, para.2–002, fn.2.

[29] *Financings Ltd v Stimson* [1962] 1 W.L.R. 1184.

[30] *Spencer v Harding* (1870) L.R. 5 C.P. 561; *Clifton v Palumbo* [1944] 2 All E.R. 497.

[31] [2007] UKHL 23; [2007] 1 W.L.R. 1325.

treat. Had it been regarded as an offer in the strict sense, there would have been no contract when the shipper tendered goods that did not comply with the restrictions. The correct analysis was that the shipper made the offer which was accepted by conduct by the carrier and the non-conformity of the goods affected the nature of the contractual regime, e.g. the carrier was entitled to refuse to collect the goods, or to suspend carriage, neither of which it did prior to the loss of the goods. Conversely, a statement may be an offer although it is expressed to be an "acceptance",[32] or requests the person to whom it is addressed to *make* an "offer".[33]

2–007   **Prima facie rules of law.** The distinction between an offer and an invitation to treat is often hard to draw as it depends on the elusive criterion of intention. But there are certain stereotyped situations in which the distinction is determined, at least prima facie, by rules of law. It may be possible to displace these rules by evidence of contrary intention, but in the absence of such evidence they will determine the distinction between offer and invitation to treat, and they will do so without reference to the intention (actual or even objectively ascertained) of the maker of the statement. The most commonly encountered examples are discussed in the following paragraphs.

2–008   **Auction sales.** At an auction sale, the general rule is that the offer is made by the bidder and accepted by the auctioneer when he signifies his acceptance in the customary manner, e.g. by fall of the hammer.[34] Before acceptance the bidder may withdraw his bid and the auctioneer may withdraw the goods. It seems, moreover, that the offer made by each bidder lapses[35] as soon as a higher bid is made. Thus if a higher bid is made and withdrawn the auctioneer can no longer accept the next highest.

When property is put up for auction subject to a reserve price, there is no contract if the auctioneer by mistake purports to accept a bid lower than the reserve price.[36] Where the auction is without reserve, there is no contract *of sale* between the highest bidder and the *owner* of the property if the auctioneer refuses to accept the highest bid. But it has been held that the *auctioneer* is in such a case liable on a separate, or collateral, contract between him and the highest bidder that the sale will be without reserve.[37] Although a mere advertisement of an auction is not an offer to hold it,[38] the actual request for bids seems to be an offer by the auctioneer that he will on the owner's behalf accept the highest bid; and this offer is accepted by the bidding.[39]

---

[32] *Bigg v Boyd Gibbins Ltd* [1971] 1 W.L.R. 913.

[33] *Harvela Investments Ltd v Royal Trust Co of Canada (CI) Ltd* [1986] A.C. 207.

[34] Sale of Goods Act 1979, s.57(2); *British Car Auctions Ltd v Wright* [1972] 1 W.L.R. 1519.

[35] See below, para.2–062.

[36] *McManus v Fortescue* [1907] 2 K.B. 1; on a sale of land, it must be expressly stated whether the sale is with reserve or not: Sale of Land by Auction Act 1867, s.5.

[37] *Warlow v Harrison* (1859) 1 E. & E. 309; cf. *Barry v Davies* [2001] 1 W.L.R. 1962. *Contra, Fenwick v Macdonald, Fraser & Co Ltd* (1904) 6 F. (Ct. of Sess.) 850; Slade 68 L.Q.R. 238; Gower 68 L.Q.R. 457; Slade 69 L.Q.R. 21.

[38] *Harris v Nickerson* (1873) L.R. 8 Q.B. 286.

[39] The question whether there is any consideration for the auctioneer's undertaking is discussed below, para.3–162.

Shop display. The general rule is that a display of price-marked goods in a   2–009
shop window[40] or on the shelves of a self-service shop[41] is not an offer to sell goods
but is an invitation to a customer to make an offer to buy which the retailer may
accept or reject. Similar principles would seem to apply where a supplier of goods
or services indicates their availability on a website: that is, the offer would seem to
come from the customer (e.g. when he clicks the appropriate "button") and it is
then open to the supplier to accept or reject that offer.[42] There is judicial support
for the view that an indication of the price at which petrol is to be sold at a filling
station is likewise an invitation to treat,[43] the offer to buy being made by the
customer and accepted by the seller's conduct in putting the petrol into the tank,[44]
but in the now more common situation in which the station operates a self-service
system, it seems more likely that the seller is making an offer which is accepted by
the customer when he fills up his tank.[45]

The general rule relating to shop and similar displays is well established, but the
reasons given for it are not entirely convincing. One argument is that if the display
were regarded as an offer, the retailer might be exposed to many actions for
damages if more customers purported to accept than his stock could satisfy.[46] But
such an offer could be construed as one which automatically expired when the
retailer's stock was exhausted: this would probably be in keeping with the common
expectation of both retailer and customer. It has also been said that, if a display in
a self-service shop were an offer, the undesirable result would follow that the
customer would be bound to buy as soon as he picked up the goods to examine
them.[47] But if the display were an offer, it could be argued that there was no
acceptance until the customer did some less equivocal act, such as presenting the
goods for payment.[48]

It may be asked whether the general rule might sometimes cause injustice.
Customers may be induced by a window display to believe that they will be able
to buy goods at exceptionally low prices and to wait outside the shop for many
hours in reliance on that belief. Is it right to allow the retailer to go back on such
a statement at the very moment when the customer demands the goods? It seems
that the special terms of a display, or the circumstances in which it is made, may
be evidence of intention to be bound and so displace the prima facie rule that the
display is not an offer: thus in one case a notice in a shop window stating that "We
will beat any TV ... price by £20 on the spot" was described as "a continuing
offer".[49] The customer might, indeed, still lose his bargain since the offer could
be withdrawn at any time before it was accepted[50]; but if it is so withdrawn the

---

[40] *Timothy v Simpson* (1834) 6 C. & P. 499; *Fisher v Bell* [1961] 1 Q.B. 394; contrast *Wiles v Maddison*
[1943] 1 All E.R. 315 at 317.
[41] *Pharmaceutical Society of Great Britain v Boots Cash Chemists Ltd* [1952] 2 Q.B. 795; [1953] 1 Q.B.
401; Unger 16 M.L.R. 369; and cf. *Lacis v Cashmarts Ltd* [1969] 2 Q.B. 400; *Davies v Leighton* [1978]
Crim.L.R. 575.
[42] See below, para.2–016 for what *constitutes* an acceptance, and para.2–034, fn.197 for the *time* of
acceptance, in such cases.
[43] *Esso Petroleum v Commissioners of Customs & Excise* [1976] 1 W.L.R. 1 at 5, 6, 11; *Richardson v
Worrall* [1985] S.T.C. 693 at 717.
[44] *Re Charge Card Services* [1989] Ch. 497 at 512.
[45] cf. below, para.2–011, fn.62.
[46] *Esso Petroleum* case above, fn.43, at 11.
[47] *Boots Case* [1952] 2 Q.B. 795 at 802.
[48] See *Lasky v Economic Grocery Stores* 65 N.E. 2d 305. (1946).
[49] *R. v Warwickshire CC Ex p. Johnson* [1993] A.C. 583 at 588.
[50] See below, para.2–058.

person displaying the notice may incur criminal liability under legislation passed
for the protection of consumers.[51]

2–010   **Advertisements of unilateral contracts.** Advertisements of rewards for the
return of lost or stolen property, or for information leading to the arrest or
conviction of the perpetrator of a crime,[52] are invariably treated as offers: the
intention to be bound is inferred from the fact that no further bargaining is
expected to result from them. The same is true of other advertisements of
unilateral contracts.[53] Thus in *Carlill v Carbolic Smoke Ball Co*,[54] an advertisement
promising to pay £100 to any user of a carbolic smoke ball who caught influenza
was held to be an offer. The intention to be bound[55] was made particularly clear
by the statement that the advertisers had deposited £1,000 in their bank "shewing
our sincerity". A case nearer the borderline was *Bowerman v Association of British
Travel Agents Ltd*[56] where a package holiday had been booked with a tour operator
who was a member of the defendant association (ABTA). A notice displayed on the
tour operator's premises stated, inter alia, that in the event of the financial failure
of an ABTA member before commencement of the holiday, "ABTA arranges for
you to be reimbursed the money you have paid for your holiday". A majority of
the Court of Appeal held that these words constituted an offer from ABTA since,
on the objective test,[57] they would reasonably be regarded as such by a member of
the public booking a holiday with an ABTA member.

2–011   **Advertisements of bilateral contracts.** Such advertisements are not usually
held to be offers since they often lead to further bargaining, and since the
advertiser may legitimately wish, before becoming bound, to assure himself that
the other party is able to perform his part of any contract which may result. Thus
a newspaper advertisement that goods are for sale is not an offer[58]; an advertisement that a scholarship examination will be held is not an offer to a candidate[59];
and the circulation of a price-list by a wine merchant is only an invitation to
treat.[60] The same is probably true of a menu displayed, or handed to a customer,
in a restaurant.[61] On the other hand, a notice at the entrance to an automatic car
park may be an offer which can be accepted by driving in[62] and a display of deck
chairs for *hire* has been held to be an offer.[63] No useful purpose is served by

---

[51] Consumer Protection from Unfair Trading Regulations 2008 (SI 2008/1277), reg.3(4)(d); Sch.1,
para.6.
[52] e.g. *Gibbons v Proctor* (1891) 64 L.T. 594; *Williams v Carwardine* (1833) 5 C. & P. 566; 4 B. & Ad.
621; below, para.2–048.
[53] See below, para.2–051, for the meaning of "unilateral contracts".
[54] [1893] 1 Q.B. 256.
[55] Contrast *Lambert v Lewis* [1982] A.C. 225 at 262, per Stephenson L.J. (affirmed [1982] A.C. 271
without reference to this point).
[56] [1996] C.L.C. 451.
[57] See above, para.2–002.
[58] *Partridge v Crittenden* [1968] 1 W.L.R. 1204; contrast *Lefkowitz v Great Minneapolis Surplus Stores*
86 N.W. 2d 689 (1957).
[59] *Rooke v Dawson* [1895] 1 Ch. 480.
[60] *Grainger & Sons v Gough* [1896] A.C. 325; quaere whether a price-list sent on request to a single
customer could be an offer.
[61] cf. *Guildford v Lockyer* [1975] Crim.L.R. 236.
[62] *Thornton v Shoe Lane Parking Ltd* [1971] 2 Q.B. 163 at 169. cf. *University of Edinburgh v Onifade*
2005 S.L.T. (Sh Ct) 63.
[63] *Chapelton v Barry Urban DC* [1940] 1 K.B. 532.

attempting to reconcile all the cases on this subject, since the question is one of intention in each case.[64]

Timetables and passenger tickets. There is a remarkable diversity of views   2–012
on the question just when a contract is made between a carrier and an intending passenger. It has been said that rail carriers make offers by issuing advertisements stating the times at and conditions under which trains would run[65]; and that a road carrier makes offers to intending passengers by the act of running buses.[66] Such offers could be accepted by an indication on the part of the passenger that he wished to travel, e.g. by applying for a ticket or getting on the bus. Another view is that the carrier makes the offer at a later stage, by issuing the ticket; and that this offer is accepted by the passenger's retention of the ticket without objection,[67] or (even later) by claiming the accommodation offered in the ticket.[68] On this view the passenger makes no more than an invitation to treat when he asks for the ticket to be issued to him; and the offer contained in the ticket may be made to, and accepted by, the passenger even though the fare is paid by a third party (e.g. the passenger's employer[69]). Where the booking is made in advance, through a travel agent, yet a third view has been expressed: that the contract is concluded when the carrier indicates, even before issuing the ticket, that he "accepts" the booking[70] or when he issues the ticket.[71] On this view, it is the passenger who makes the offer. The authorities yield no single rule: one can only say that the exact time of contracting depends in each case on the wording of the relevant document and on the circumstances in which it was issued.

Tenders. At common law, a statement that goods are to be sold by tender is not   2–013
normally an offer, so that the person making the statement is not bound to sell to the person making the highest tender.[72] Similarly a statement inviting tenders for the supply of goods or for the execution of works is not normally an offer.[73] The offer comes from the person who submits the tender and there is no contract until the person asking for the tenders accepts[74] one of them. The preparation of a tender may involve considerable expense; but the tenderer normally incurs this at his own risk. The position is different where the person who invites the tenders states in the invitation that he binds himself to accept the highest offer to buy[75] (or,

---

[64] Contrast *Harvey v Facey* [1893] A.C. 552 with *Philip & Co v Knoblauch* 1907 S.C. 994.

[65] *Denton v GN Ry* (1856) 5 E. & B. 860; *Thompson v LM&S Ry* [1930] 1 K.B. 41 at 47.

[66] *Wilkie v LPTB* [1947] 1 All E.R. 258 at 259.

[67] *Thornton v Shoe Lane Parking Ltd* [1971] 2 Q.B. 163 at 169; *Cockerton v Naviera Aznar SA* [1960] 2 Lloyd's Rep. 450. Such acceptance would be by conduct rather than by silence: cf. below, para.2–047.

[68] *MacRobertson-Miller Airline Service v Commissioner of State Taxation* (1975) 8 A.L.R. 131; the principle resembles that stated in *Heskell v Continental Express Ltd* [1950] 1 All E.R. 1033 at 1037 in relation to carriage of goods by sea.

[69] *Hobbs v L&SW Ry* (1875) L.R. 10 Q.B. 111 at 119, as explained in the *MacRobertson-Miller* case, above, at 147.

[70] *The Eagle* [1977] 2 Lloyd's Rep. 70; *The Dragon* [1979] 1 Lloyd's Rep. 257 (affirmed [1980] 2 Lloyd's Rep. 415); *Oceanic Sun Line Special Shipping Co v Fay* (1988) 165 C.L.R. 97; cf. *The Anwar al Sabar* [1980] 2 Lloyd's Rep. 261 at 263 (carriage of goods by sea).

[71] *The Mikhail Lermontov* [1991] 2 Lloyd's Rep. 155 at 159, reversed on other grounds: *Baltic Shipping Co v Dillon* (1993) 176 C.L.R. 344.

[72] *Spencer v Harding* (1870) L.R. 5 C.P. 561.

[73] ibid. at 564.

[74] See below, para.2–022.

[75] *Spencer v Harding*, above, at 563.

as the case may be, the lowest offer to sell or to provide the specified services[76]).
In such cases, the invitation may be regarded *either* as itself an offer *or* as an
invitation to submit offers coupled with an undertaking to accept the highest (or,
as the case may be, the lowest) offer; and the contract is concluded as soon as the
highest offer to buy (or lowest offer to sell, etc.) is communicated.[77] There is also
an intermediate possibility. This is illustrated by a case[78] in which an invitation to
submit tenders was sent by a local authority to seven selected parties; the
invitation stated that tenders submitted after a specified deadline would not be
considered. It was held that the authority was contractually bound to consider
(though not to accept[79]) a tender submitted before the deadline.

The common law position stated above is in some situations modified by
legislation, for example by regulations[80] which give effect to EC Council Directives, the object of which is to prevent discrimination in the award of major
contracts for public works, supplies and services in one Member State against
nationals of another Member State. These regulations restrict the freedom of the
body seeking tenders to decide which tender it will accept and provide a remedy
in damages for a person who has made a tender and is prejudiced by breach of the
rules.

2–014   **Sales of shares.** A company which, in commercial language,[81] makes an "offer
to the public", asking them to subscribe for shares in it, does not in law offer to
sell the shares. It invites members of the public to apply for them, reserving the
right to decide how many (if any) to allot to each applicant.[82] But where a company
makes a "rights" issue of shares to its existing shareholders, entitling each
shareholder to buy a number of new shares in proportion to the shares he already
holds, the letter informing the shareholder of his rights is regarded as an offer.[83]
This letter will set out the precise rights of each shareholder, thus showing an
intention on the part of the company to be bound, if the shareholder takes up his
rights.

(c) Where and When an Offer Takes Effect

2–015   In one sense an offer cannot take effect until it is received, for until the offeree
knows about it he can take no action in reliance on it. But for the purpose of
determining whether a contract can be sued on in a particular court it has been
held that an offer sent through the post was made *where* it was posted.[84] The

---

[76] See *William Lacey (Hounslow) Ltd v Davis* [1957] 1 W.L.R. 932 at 939; cf. *MJB Enterprises Ltd v Defence Construction Ltd* (1999) 15 Const.L.J. 455 (Supreme Court of Canada).

[77] *Harvela Investments Ltd v Royal Trust of Canada (CI) Ltd* [1986] A.C. 207 at 224–225.

[78] *Blackpool and Fylde Aero Club Ltd v Blackpool BC* [1990] 1 W.L.R. 1195. No decision was reached on the quantum of damages: as to this, see below, para.20–060.

[79] cf. *Fairclough Building v Port Talbot BC* (1992) 62 B.L.R. 82.

[80] Public Contracts Regulations 2006 (SI 2006/5); Utilities Contracts Regulations 2006 (SI 2006/6); On the scope of the former, see: *Brent LBC v Risk Managment Partners Ltd* [2011] UKSC 7; [2011] 2 W.L.R. 166.

[81] And in the terminology of Companies Act 2006, ss.755, 756 and of Financial Services and Markets Act 2000, s.102(B), as inserted by Prospectus Regulations 2005 (SI 2005/1433), Sch.1.

[82] e.g. *Harris' Case* (1872) L.R. 7 Ch.App. 587; *National Westminster Bank Plc v IRC* [1995] 1 A.C. 119 at 126; cf. *Wallace's Case* [1900] 2 Ch. 671; *Rust v Abbey Life Ins Co* [1979] 2 Lloyd's Rep. 335.

[83] *Jackson v Turquand* (1869) L.R. 4 H.L. 305.

[84] *Taylor v Jones* (1871) 1 C.P.D. 87.

question *when* such an offer was made may also arise for the purpose of determining whether the offer has expired by lapse of time[85] before it was accepted. In *Adams v Lindsell*[86] an offer to sell wool was made by a letter which was misdirected. The letter reached the offerees two days late; and they immediately posted an acceptance which was held binding because the delay arose "entirely from the mistake of the [offerors]".[87] From this emphasis on the offerors' fault, it seems that the decision might have gone the other way if the delay had been due to some other factor, e.g. to an accident in the post. In such a case the time for acceptance probably runs from the moment at which the letter would, but for such accident, have reached the offeree's address. Even where the delay is due to the offeror's fault, the offer may have lapsed before its receipt by the offeree. Obviously, the offer could not be accepted if it reached the offeree only after the date expressly specified in it as the last date for acceptance. The position is probably the same where it is clear to the offeree that there has been such a long delay in the transmission of the offer as to make it obvious to the offeree that the offer was "stale" when it reached him.

2. ACCEPTANCE

(a) Acceptance Defined

An objective test. An acceptance is a final and unqualified expression of assent   2–016
to the terms of an offer. The objective test of agreement applies to an acceptance no less than to an offer.[88] On this test, the mere acknowledgment that an offer has been received would not be an acceptance; nor would a person to whom an offer to sell goods had been made accept it merely by replying that it was his "intention to place an order"[89] or by asking for an invoice.[90] But an "acknowledgment" may by its express terms or, in a particular context by implication, contain a statement that the sender agreed to the terms of the offer and that he was therefore accepting it: this might, for example, be the effect of an "acknowledgment" of a customer's order in website trading.[91] Where the offer makes alternative proposals, the reply must make it clear to which of them the assent is directed. In one case an offer to build a freight terminal was made by a tender quoting in the alternative a fixed price and a price varying with the cost of labour and materials. The offeree purported to accept "your tender" and it was held that there was no contract as there was no way of telling which price term had been accepted.[92]

Continuing negotiations. When parties carry on lengthy negotiations, it may   2–017
be hard to say exactly when an offer has been made and accepted. As negotiations progress, each party may make concessions or new demands and the parties may in the end dispute whether they had ever agreed at all. The court must then look

---

[85] See below, para.2–064.

[86] (1818) 1 B. & Ald. 681.

[87] ibid. at 683.

[88] See above, para.2–002; *Inland Revenue Commissioners v Fry* [2001] S.T.C. 1715 at [6, 7]; *University of Edinburgh v Onifade* 2005 S.L.T. (Sh Ct) 63 at [6].

[89] *OTM Ltd v Hydranautics* [1981] 2 Lloyd's Rep. 211 at 214.

[90] *Michael Gerson (Leasing) Ltd v Wilkinson* [2000] Q.B. 514 at 530.

[91] In the Electronic Commerce (EC Directive) Regulations 2002 (SI 2002/2013) (implementing most of the EC Directive 2000/31 on Electronic Commerce ([2000] O.J. L178/1)), reg.11, the words "acknowledge" and "acknowledgement" seem to be used in this sense.

[92] *Peter Lind & Co Ltd v Mersey Docks & Harbour Board* [1972] 2 Lloyd's Rep. 234.

at the whole correspondence and decide whether, on its true construction, the parties had agreed to the same terms. If so, there is a contract even though both parties, or one of them, had reservations not expressed in the correspondence.[93] In *Allianz Insurance Co (Egypt) v Aigaion Insurance Co SA*[94] an insurance slip was e-mailed by the reinsured without a warranty that the parties had previously agreed, but the appearance of "finality" in the reinsurer's e-mailed reply meant that it took effect as an acceptance and there was a contract which omitted the warranty.[95]

The court will be particularly anxious to conclude that there was a contract where the performance which was the subject-matter of the negotiations has actually been rendered. In one such case, a building sub-contract was held to have come into existence (even though the parties had not yet reached agreement when the contractor began the work) as during its progress outstanding matters were resolved by further negotiations.[96] The contract may then be given retrospective effect so as to cover acts done before the final agreement was reached.[97]

Businessmen do not, any more than the courts, find it easy to say precisely when they have reached agreement, and may continue to negotiate after they appear to have agreed to the same terms. The court will then look at the entire course of the negotiations to decide whether an apparently unqualified acceptance did in fact conclude the agreement.[98] If it did, the fact that the parties continued negotiations after this point will not normally affect the existence of the contract[99]; it will do so only if the continuation of the negotiations can be construed as an agreement to rescind the contract. A fortiori, the binding force of an oral contract is not affected or altered merely by the fact that, after its conclusion, one party sends to the other a document containing terms significantly different from those which had been orally agreed.[100]

2–018   **Acceptance by conduct.** An offer may be accepted by conduct, e.g. by supplying or despatching goods in response to an offer to buy them,[101] or by

---

[93] *Kennedy v Lee* (1817) 3 Mer. 441; cf. *Cie de Commerce v Parkinson Stove Co* [1953] 2 Lloyd's Rep. 487; *Thorensen Car Ferries Ltd v Weymouth Portland BC* [1977] 2 Lloyd's Rep. 614; *The Bay Ridge* [1999] 2 All E.R. (Comm) 306.

[94] [2008] EWCA Civ 1455; [2008] 2 C.L.C. 1013.

[95] Given the earlier agreement of the parties to include the warranty, Rix L.J. queried why there had been no plea of rectification (see below, para.8–059 et seq.): [2008] EWCA Civ 1455; [2008] 2 C.L.C. 1013 at [37].

[96] *G Percy Trentham Ltd v Archital Luxfer Ltd* [1993] 1 Lloyd's Rep. 25; cf. *RTS Flexible Systems Ltd v Molkerei Alois Müller GmbH & Co KG* [2010] UKSC 14; [2010] 1 W.L.R. 753. The *Peter Lind* case, above, fn.92, shows that the factor of performance of the work is not decisive, though it may (as in that case) give rise to a restitutionary claim: see below, para.22–021.

[97] *G Percy Trentham Ltd v Archital Luxfer Ltd* [1993] 1 Lloyd's Rep. 25 at 27.

[98] *Hussey v Horne-Payne* (1878) 4 App.Cas. 311; *Bristol, Cardiff & Swansea Aerated Bread Co v Maggs* (1890) 44 Ch.D. 616; *British Guiana Credit Corp v Da Silva* [1965] 1 W.L.R. 248; *Container Transport International Inc v Oceanus Mutual, etc. Association* [1984] 1 Lloyd's Rep. 476; *Pagnan SpA v Feed Products Ltd* [1987] 2 Lloyd's Rep. 601 at 619; *Ignazio Messina & Co v Polskie Linie Oceaniczne* [1995] 2 Lloyd's Rep. 566; cf. in the context of rescinding the contract: *Drake Insurance Plc v Provident Insurance Plc* [2003] EWCA Civ 1834; [2004] Q.B. 601 at [100].

[99] *Perry v Suffields Ltd* [1916] 2 Ch. 187; *Davies v Sweet* [1962] 2 Q.B. 300; *Cranleigh Precision Engineering Ltd v Bryant* [1965] 1 W.L.R. 1293; *The Good Helmsman* [1981] 1 Lloyd's Rep. 377 at 409, 416; *Maple Leaf Macro Volatility Master Fund v Rouvroy* [2009] EWHC 257 (Comm); [2009] 1 Lloyd's Rep. 475 at [230]; affirmed [2009] EWCA Civ 1334, without reference to this point.

[100] *Jayaar Impex Ltd v Toaken Group Ltd* [1996] 2 Lloyd's Rep. 437.

[101] *Harvey v Johnston* (1848) 6 C.B. 295 at 305; cf. *Steven v Bromley & Son* [1919] 2 K.B. 722 at 728; *Interfoto Picture Library Ltd v Stiletto Visual Programmes Ltd* [1989] Q.B. 433 at 436; *Re Charge Card Services* [1989] Ch. 497 at 512.

beginning to render services in response to an offer in the form of a request for them.[102] Similarly, an offer to supply goods (made by sending them to the offeree) can be accepted by using them.[103] Conduct will, however, only have this effect if the offeree did the act with the intention (ascertained in accordance with the objective principle[104]) of accepting the offer.[105] Thus a buyer's taking delivery of goods after the conclusion of an oral contract of sale will not amount to his acceptance of written terms which differ significantly from those orally agreed and which are sent to him by the seller after the making of that contract but before taking delivery.[106] That conduct is then referable to the oral contract rather than to the attempted later variation. Nor is a company's offer to insure a car accepted by taking the car out on the road, if there is evidence that the driver intended to insure with another company.[107] A fortiori, there is no acceptance where the offeree's conduct clearly indicates an intention to reject the offer. This was the position in a Scottish case where a notice on a package containing computer software stated that opening the package would indicate acceptance of the terms on which the supply was made, and the customer returned the package unopened.[108]

Where it is alleged that an offer has been made, or accepted, by conduct it is often hard to say exactly what terms have been agreed. The difficulty may be so great as to lead to the conclusion that no agreement was reached at all.[109] But the court has considerable power to resolve uncertainties. If the offer is silent as to the rate of payment the court may imply a term that a reasonable amount should be paid.[110] Or the court may import into the contract the terms of another contract between the parties, or of a draft agreement between them,[111] or even of a contract between one of them and a third party.[112]

Acceptance must be unqualified. A communication may fail to take effect as an acceptance because it attempts to vary the terms of the offer. Thus an offer to sell 1,200 tons of iron is not accepted by a reply asking for 800 tons[113]; an offer to pay a *fixed* price for building work is not accepted by a promise to do the work for

2–019

---

[102] *The Kurnia Dewi* [1997] 1 Lloyd's Rep. 533; *Datec Electronic Holdings Ltd v United Parcels Service Ltd* [2007] UKHL 23; [2007] 1 W.L.R. 1325: above, para.2–006.

[103] *Weatherby v Banham* (1832) 5 C. & P. 228; or even by using part of the goods: cf. *Hart v Mills* (1846) 15 L.J.Ex. 200. It is assumed that the goods are not "unsolicited" within legislation against "inertia selling": see above, fn.17.

[104] See above, para.2–002.

[105] In the context of employment contracts, see: *Khatri v Cooperatieve Centrale Raiffeisen-Boerenleenbank BA* [2010] EWCA Civ 397; [2010] I.R.L.R. 715 at [51].

[106] *Jayaar Impex Ltd v Toaken Group Ltd* [1992] 2 Lloyd's Rep. 437.

[107] *Taylor v Allon* [1966] 1 Q.B. 304. cf. in another context, *Re Leyland Daf Ltd* [1994] 4 All E.R. 300, affirmed sub nom. *Powdrill v Watson* [1995] 2 A.C. 394.

[108] *Beta Computers (Europe) v Adobe Systems (Europe) Ltd* (1996) S.L.T. 604; even opening the package would not necessarily be an acceptance so as to incorporate the printed terms: see Tapper in *Consensus ad Idem, Essays in the Law of Contract in Honour of Guenter Treitel* (Rose, ed.), pp.287–288.

[109] *Capital Finance Co Ltd v Bray* [1964] 1 W.L.R. 323.

[110] Sale of Goods Act 1979, s.8(2); Supply of Goods and Services Act 1982, s.15(1); cf. *Steven v Bromley & Son*, above; see below, para.2–086.

[111] e.g. *Brogden v Metropolitan Ry* (1877) 2 App.Cas. 666; contrast *D&M Trailers (Halifax) Ltd v Stirling* [1978] R.T.R. 468; *Jayaar Impex Ltd v Toaken Ltd* [1996] 2 Lloyd's Rep. 437 (above, fn.106).

[112] e.g. *Pyrene Co Ltd v Scindia Navigation Co Ltd* [1954] 2 Q.B. 402; see below, para.14–072.

[113] *Tinn v Hoffmann & Co* (1873) 29 L.T. 271; cf. *Jordan v Norton* (1838) 4 M. & W. 155; *Harrison v Battye* [1975] 1 W.L.R. 58.

a *variable* price[114]; an offer to *supply* goods is not accepted by an "order" for their "supply and installation".[115] Nor, generally, is an offer accepted by a reply which varies one of its other terms (e.g. that specifying the time of performance)[116] or by a reply which is intended to introduce an entirely new term.[117] Such replies are not acceptances but counter-offers[118] which the original offeror can accept or reject.

The requirement that the acceptance must be unqualified does not, however, mean that there must be precise *verbal* correspondence between offer and acceptance.[119] An acceptance could be effective even though it departed from the wording of the offer by making express some term which the law would in any case imply.[120] And a reply which adds some new provision by way of indulgence to the offeror (e.g. one allowing him to postpone payment) may be an acceptance. Conversely, an acceptance in which the acceptor asks for extra time to pay may be effective, so long as he makes it clear that he is prepared to perform in accordance with the terms of the offer even if his request is refused. The question is whether what has been introduced would have been regarded by a reasonable offeror as introducing a new term into the bargain rather than acceptance of the offer.[121] It is also possible for a communication which introduces a new term to amount at the same time to a firm acceptance and also to a further offer relating to the same subject-matter but emanating from the original offeree. In such a case, there will be a contract on the terms of the original offer, but none on the terms of the new offer unless that is, in turn, accepted.[122]

After parties have reached agreement, the offer and acceptance may be set out in formal documents. The purpose of such documents may be merely to record the agreed terms[123]; and where one of the documents performs this function accurately while the other fails to do so, the discrepancy between them will not prevent the formation of a contract. In such a case, the court can rectify[124] the document which fails to record the agreed terms, and a contract will be on those terms.[125]

---

[114] *North West Leicestershire DC v East Midlands Housing Assocn* [1981] 1 W.L.R. 1396.

[115] *Butler Machine Tool Co Ltd v Ex-Cell-O Corp (England) Ltd* [1979] 1 W.L.R. 401.

[116] ibid.; *North West Leicestershire DC v East Midlands Housing Association* [1981] 1 W.L.R. 1396; cf. *Brinkibon Ltd v Stahag Stahl und Stahlwarenhandelsgesellschaft mbH* [1983] 2 A.C. 34.

[117] *Jackson v Turquand* (1869) L.R. 4 H.L. 305; *Northland Aircraft Ltd v Dennis Ferranti Meters Ltd* (1970) 114 S.J. 845; *Bircham & Co Nominees (No.2) Ltd v Worrell Holdings Ltd* [2001] EWCA Civ 725; (2001) 82 P. & C.R. 427 at [11]. Statements which are *not* intended to add new terms do not vitiate the acceptance: *Simpson v Hughes* (1897) 66 L.J.Ch. 334; *Butler Machine Tool Co Ltd v Ex-Cell-O Corp (England) Ltd* [1979] 1 W.L.R. 401.

[118] *Jones v Daniel* [1894] 2 Ch. 332; *Von Hartzfeld-Wildenburg v Alexander* [1912] 1 Ch. 284; *Lark v Outhwaite* [1991] 2 Lloyd's Rep. 132 at 139.

[119] *Midgulf International Ltd v Group Chimique Tunisien* [2010] EWCA Civ 66; [2010] 2 Lloyd's Rep. 543 at [45].

[120] *Lark v Outhwaite*, above, at 139.

[121] *G Percy Trentham Ltd v Archital Luxfer Ltd* [1993] 1 Lloyd's Rep. 25 at 28; *Maple Leaf Macro Volatility Master Fund v Rouvroy* [2009] EWHC 257 (Comm); [2009] 1 Lloyd's Rep. 475 at [247] (affd. [2009] EWCA Civ 1334); *Midgulf International Ltd v Group Chimique Tunisien* [2010] EWCA Civ 66; [2010] 2 Lloyd's Rep. 543 at [45].

[122] *The Master Stelios* [1983] 1 Lloyd's Rep. 356.

[123] e.g. *OTM Ltd v Hydranautics* [1981] 2 Lloyd's Rep. 211 at 215; cf. below, para.2–089.

[124] See below, para.8–059.

[125] *Domb v Isoz* [1980] Ch. 548.

The battle of forms. The prevalent use of printed contract forms by one or   2–020
both parties has given rise to problems with regard to the rule that the acceptance
must correspond to the offer. Two situations call for discussion.

First, A may make an offer to B by asking for a supply of goods or services. B
may reply that he is willing to supply the goods or services on B's terms. Prima
facie, B's statement is a counter-offer which A is free to accept or reject, and he
may accept it by accepting the goods or services. If he does so, there is a contract
between A and B which is governed by B's terms.[126]

Secondly, *each* party may purport to contract with reference to his own set of
standard terms and these terms may conflict. In *BRS v Arthur V Crutchley Ltd*[127]
the claimants delivered a consignment of whisky to the defendants for storage.
Their driver handed the defendants a delivery note purporting to incorporate the
claimants' "conditions of carriage". The note was stamped by the defendants:
"Received under [the defendants'] conditions". It was held that this amounted to
a counter-offer which the claimants had accepted by handing over the goods, and
the contract therefore incorporated the defendants' and not the claimants' conditions.

The *Butler Machine Tool* case. The decision in *Crutchley* gave some support   2–021
to the so-called "last shot" doctrine: i.e. to the view that, where conflicting
communications are exchanged, each is a counter-offer so that if a contract results
at all (e.g. from an acceptance by conduct) it must be on the terms of the final
document in the series leading to the conclusion of the contract.[128] But this view
requires some modification in the light of *Butler Machine Tool Co Ltd v Ex-Cell-O
Corp (England) Ltd.*[129] In that case sellers offered to supply a machine for a
specified sum. The offer was expressed to be subject to certain terms and
conditions, including a "price-escalation clause", by which the amount payable by
the buyers was to depend on "prices ruling upon date of delivery". In reply, the
buyers placed an order for the machine on a form setting out their own terms and
conditions, which differed from those of the sellers in containing no price-
escalation clause and in various other respects.[130] It also contained a tear-off slip
to be signed by the sellers and returned to the buyers, stating that the sellers
accepted the order "on the terms and conditions stated therein". The sellers did
so sign the slip and returned it with a letter saying that they were "entering" the
order "in accordance with" their offer. This communication from the sellers was
held to be an acceptance of the buyers' counter-offer[131] so that the resulting
contract was on the buyers' terms, and the sellers were not entitled to the benefit

---

[126] A may challenge the incorporation of B's terms on grounds which are considered below:
para.7–004 et seq.
[127] [1968] 1 W.L.R. 811; cf. *OTM Ltd v Hydranautics* [1981] 2 Lloyd's Rep. 211; *Muirhead v
Industrial Tank Specialities Ltd* [1986] Q.B. 507 at 530.
[128] As in *Zambia Steel & Building Supplies Ltd v James Clark & Eaton Ltd* [1986] 2 Lloyd's Rep.
225.
[129] [1979] 1 W.L.R. 401, esp. at 405; Adams 95 L.Q.R. 481; Rawlings 42 M.L.R. 715. See also
Tekdata Interconnections Ltd v Amphenol [2009] EWCA Civ 1209; [2010] 1 Lloyd's Rep. 357 where the
Court of Appeal acknowledged that the multiple relationships established in a long-term supply chain
might indicate that the parties did not intend to contract on the terms found to apply as a consequence
of the "battle of the forms" rules, but held that this was not made out on the facts of the case.
[130] See above, para.2–018, fnn.115 and 116.
[131] per Lawton and Buckley L.JJ.; Lord Denning M.R. also uses this analysis, but prefers the
alternative approach of considering "the documents . . . as a whole": see at 405 and cf. below,
para.2–075.

of the price-escalation clause. The sellers' reply to the buyers' order did not prevail (though it was the "last shot" in the series) because the reference in it to the original offer was not made for the purpose of reiterating all the terms of that offer, but only for the purpose of identifying the subject-matter.[132] It would, however, have been possible for the sellers to have turned their final communication into a counter-offer by explicitly referring in it, not only to the subject-matter of the original offer, but also to all its other terms. In that case no contract would have been concluded, since the buyers had made it clear before the machine was delivered that they did not agree to the "price-escalation" clause.[133]

Thus it is possible by careful draftsmanship to avoid losing the battle of forms, but not (if the other party is equally careful) to win it. In the *Butler Machine Tool* case, for example, the sellers' conditions included one by which their terms were to "prevail over any terms and conditions in Buyer's order"; but this failed (in consequence of the terms of the buyers' counter-offer) to produce the effect desired by the sellers. The most that the draftsman can be certain of achieving is the stalemate situation in which there is no contract at all, or no contract on either parties' terms.[134] Such a conclusion will often be inconvenient,[135] though where the goods are nevertheless delivered it may lead to a liability on the part of the buyers to pay a reasonable price.[136]

2–022   **Acceptance of tenders.** The submission of a tender normally amounts to an offer,[137] and the effect of an "acceptance" of the tender depends on the interpretation of the documents. Where, for example, a tender is submitted for the construction of a building, acceptance will normally create a binding contract unless it is expressly stipulated that there is to be no contract until certain formal documents have been executed.[138] But where a tender is made for an indefinite amount, e.g. for the supply of "such quantities (not exceeding 1,000 tons) as you may order" the person to whom the tender is submitted does not incur any liability merely by "accepting" it. He becomes liable only when he places an order for the goods[139]; and he is not bound to place any order at all (unless he has expressly or by necessary implication[140] indicated in his invitation for tenders that he would do so).[141] Once an order has been placed, the party who has submitted the tender is bound to fulfil it.[142] Whether he can withdraw before an order has been placed, or avoid liability with regard to future orders, depends on the interpretation of the tender. If it merely means "I will supply such quantities as

---

[132] cf. *Allianz Insurance Co (Egypt)v Aigaion Insurance Co SA* [2008] EWCA Civ 1455; [2008] 2 C.L.C. 1013: an e-mail stating that insurance cover was provided "as we had quoted" did not extend to a warranty which the reinsurer intended to include because the words were followed by "i.e." and what was then stated were only the rates for the cover: see above, para.2–017, text to fn.95.

[133] At 406, per Lawton L.J.

[134] *GHSP Inc v AB Electronic Ltd* [2010] EWHC 1828 (Comm); cf. *Matter of Doughboy Industries Inc* 233 N.Y.S. 2d. 488 at 490 (1962): "The buyer and seller accomplished a legal equivalent to the irresistible force colliding with the immoveable object".

[135] It seems to have been rejected for this reason in *Johnson Matthey Bankers Ltd v State Trading Corp of India* [1984] 1 Lloyd's Rep. 427.

[136] cf. *Peter Lind & Co Ltd v Mersey Docks & Harbour Board* [1972] 2 Lloyd's Rep. 234; above, para.2–016; McKendrick, 8 O.J.L.S. 197.

[137] See above, para.2–013.

[138] See below, para.2–089.

[139] *Percival v London County Council AsylumCommittee* (1918) 87 L.J.K.B. 677.

[140] e.g. *Sylvan Crest Sand & Gravel Co v US* 150 F. 2d. 642 (1945).

[141] cf. *Harvela Investments Ltd v Royal Trust Co of Canada (CI) Ltd* [1986] A.C. 207.

[142] *Great Northern Ry v Witham* (1873) L.R. 9 C.P. 16.

you may order" he can withdraw before a definite order is placed.[143] But he will
not be entitled to withdraw if the tender means "I hereby bind myself to execute
any orders which you may place", and if there is some consideration for this
undertaking.[144]

Acceptance by tender. An invitation for tenders may, exceptionally, amount to   2–023
an offer, e.g. where the person issuing the invitation binds himself to accept the
highest tender to buy (or the lowest tender to sell).[145] The acceptance then takes
the form of the submission of a tender; but difficulties can arise where several
tenders are made and one (or more) of them takes the form of a so-called
"referential bid". In *Harvela Investments Ltd v Royal Trust Co of Canada (CI)
Ltd*[146] an invitation for the submission of "offers" to buy shares was addressed to
two persons; it stated that the prospective sellers bound themselves to accept the
"highest offer". One of the persons to whom the invitation was addressed made
a bid of a fixed sum while the other submitted a "referential bid" undertaking to
pay either a fixed sum or a specified amount in excess of the bid made by the other,
whichever was the higher amount. It was held that this "referential bid" was
ineffective and that the submission of the other bid had concluded the contract.
The House of Lords stressed that the bids were, by the terms of the invitation, to
be confidential, so that neither bidder would know the amount bid by the other.
In these circumstances the object of the invitation, which was to ascertain the
highest amount which each of the persons to whom it was addressed was willing
to pay, would have been defeated by allowing it to be accepted by a "referential
bid".

(b) Communication of Acceptance

(i) *General rule*

Acceptance must be communicated to the offeror. The general rule is that   2–024
an acceptance has no effect until it is communicated to the offeror.[147] One reason
for this rule is the difficulty of proving an uncommunicated decision to accept "for
the Devil himself knows not the intent of a man".[148] But this is not the sole reason
for the rule, which applies even where the fact of acceptance could be proved with
perfect certainty,[149] e.g. where a company resolves to accept an application for
shares, records the resolution, but does not communicate it to the applicant[150];
where a person decides to accept an offer to sell goods to him and instructs his
bank to pay the seller, but neither he nor the bank gives notice of this fact to the

---

[143] *Great Northern Ry v Witham* (1873) L.R. 9 C.P. 16 at 19.
[144] *Percival v London County Council Asylum Committee* (1918) 87 L.J.K.B. 677; cf. *Miller v F A Sadd
& Son Ltd* [1981] 3 All E.R. 265; below, para.3–160.
[145] See above, para.2–013.
[146] [1986] A.C. 207.
[147] *M'Iver v Richardson* (1813) 1 M. & S. 557; *Ex p. Stark* [1897] 1 Ch. 575; *Holwell Securities Ltd
v Hughes* [1974] 1 W.L.R. 155 at 157; *The Leonidas D* [1985] 1 W.L.R. 925 at 937.
[148] *Anon.* (1478) Y.B. 17 Edw. IV Pasch, f.1–pl.2, cited in Fifoot, *History & Sources of the Common
Law*, p.253.
[149] *Kennedy v Thomassen* [1929] 1 Ch. 426; *Brogden v Metropolitan Ry* (1877) 2 App.Cas. 666 at
692.
[150] *Best's Case* (1865) 2 D.J. & S. 650; cf. *Gunn's Case* (1867) L.R. 3 Ch.App. 40.

seller[151]; or where a person communicates the acceptance only to his own agent.[152] The main reason for the rule is that it could cause hardship to an offeror if he were bound without knowing that his offer had been accepted. It follows that there can be a contract if the offeror knows of the acceptance although it was not brought to his notice *by the offeree*.[153] However, there will be no contract if the communication is made by a third party without the authority of the offeree in circumstances indicating that the offeree's decision to accept was not yet regarded by him as irrevocable.[154]

For an acceptance to be "communicated" it must normally be brought to the notice of the offeror. Thus if an oral acceptance is "drowned by an aircraft flying overhead" or is spoken into a telephone after the line has gone dead, or is so indistinct that the offeror does not hear it, there is no contract.[155] The requirement of "communication" may, however, sometimes be satisfied even though the acceptance has not actually come to the notice of the offeror: e.g. where a written notice of acceptance is left at his address.[156]

In a number of cases, contrary to the general rule, an acceptance is, or may be, effective although it is not communicated to the offeror.

(ii) *Exceptional cases*

2–025   **Communication to offeror's agent.** The effect of giving an acceptance to the agent of the offeror depends on the nature of the agent's authority.[157] If the agent has authority to *receive* the acceptance, it takes effect as soon as it is communicated to him, e.g. if acceptance of an offer made by a company is communicated to its managing director. But if the agent is only authorised to *transmit* the acceptance to the offeror, it may not take effect until the offeror receives it, e.g. if a written acceptance is given to a messenger.

2–026   **Offeror's fault.** An offeror may be precluded from denying that he received the acceptance if "it is his own fault that he did not get it", e.g. "if the listener on the telephone does not catch the words of acceptance, but nevertheless does not . . . ask for them to be repeated"[158]; or if the acceptance is sent during business hours by telex but is simply not read by anyone in the offeror's office when it is there transcribed on his machine.[159] If such a message is received out of business hours, it probably takes effect at the beginning of the next business day.[160]

2–027   **Terms of offer.** An offer may expressly or impliedly waive the requirement that acceptance must be communicated.[161] This is often the case where an offer invites acceptance by conduct. Thus where an offer to sell goods is made by

---

[151] *Brinkibon v Stahag Stahl und Stahlwarenhandelsgesellschaft mbH* [1983] 2 A.C. 34.

[152] *Hebb's Case* (1867) L.R. 4 Eq. 9; *Kennedy v Thomassen* [1929] 1 Ch. 426.

[153] *Bloxham's Case* (1864) 33 Beav. 529; (1864) 4 D.J. & S. 447; *Levita's Case* (1867) L.R. 3 Ch.App. 36.

[154] This seems to be the best explanation of *Powell v Lee* (1908) 99 L.T. 284.

[155] *Entores Ltd v Miles Far East Corp* [1955] 2 Q.B. 327 at 332.

[156] cf. below, para.2–058.

[157] *Henthorn v Fraser* [1892] 2 Ch. 27 at 33.

[158] *Entores Ltd v Miles Far East Corp* [1955] 2 Q.B. 327 at 333.

[159] cf. *The Brimnes* [1975] Q.B. 929.

[160] *The Pamela* [1995] 2 Lloyd's Rep. 249 at 252; *The Petr Schmidt* [1998] 2 Lloyd's Rep. 1.

[161] *Argo Fund Ltd v Essar Steel Ltd* [2005] EWHC 600 (Comm); [2005] 2 Lloyd's Rep. 203 at [53], affirmed [2006] EWCA Civ 241; [2006] 2 Lloyd's Rep. 134, without reference to this point.

sending them to the offeree, it may be accepted by simply using them without communicating this fact to the offeror.[162] Similarly, it seems that, where an offer to buy goods is made by asking the seller to supply them, it may be accepted by simply despatching the goods to the buyer.[163] And a tenant can accept an offer of a new tenancy by simply staying on the premises.[164]

Unilateral contracts. Communication of acceptance is scarcely ever required   2–028
in the case of an offer of a unilateral contract.[165] Thus in *Carlill v Carbolic Smoke Ball Co*,[166] the court rejected the argument that the claimant should have notified the defendants of her acceptance of their offer before starting to use the smoke ball. Similarly, where a reward is offered for the return of lost property the finder need not notify the owner in advance of his acceptance: he can accept by finding and returning the thing; and once he has found it the owner probably cannot withdraw.[167] Again, the contract which arises[168] between a bank which has issued a credit card to one of its customers and the retailer to whom the customer presents the card has been described as unilateral,[169] so that the bank's offer can be accepted by the retailer's dealing with the customer even before that acceptance is communicated to the bank.[170]

(iii) *Acceptance by post*[171]

There are many possible solutions to the problem: when does a posted accep-   2–029
tance take effect? Such an acceptance could take effect when it is actually communicated to the offeror, when it arrives at his address, when it should, in the ordinary course of post, have reached him, or when it is posted. As the following discussion will show, each of these solutions is open to objections on the grounds of convenience or justice. This is particularly true where the acceptance is lost or delayed in the post.[172]

The posting rule. What is usually[173] called the general rule is that a postal   2–030
acceptance takes effect when the letter of acceptance is posted.[174] For this purpose a letter is posted when it is in the control of the Post Office,[175] or of one of its

---

[162] *Weatherby v Banham* (1832) 5 C. & P. 228; *cf. Minories Finance Ltd v Afribank Nigeria Ltd* [1995] 1 Lloyd's Rep. 134 at 140; and see above, para.2–004, fn.16.

[163] cf. American Uniform Commercial Code (hereinafter referred to as U.C.C.), s.2–206(1)(b); *The Kurnia Dewi* [1997] 1 Lloyd's Rep. 553 at 559.

[164] *Roberts v Hayward* (1828) 3 C. & P. 432; but not if the tenant disclaims the intention to accept: *Glossop v Ashley* [1921] 2 K.B. 451.

[165] For the meaning of "unilateral contract," see below, para.2–051.

[166] [1893] 1 Q.B. 256; see above, para.2–010.

[167] See below, paras 2–053—2–057.

[168] See below, para.3–024.

[169] *First Sport Ltd v Barclays Bank Plc* [1993] 1 W.L.R. 1229 at 1234.

[170] ibid. at 1234–1235.

[171] Gardner 12 O.J.L.S. 170.

[172] See, e.g., below, after fn.182.

[173] But see below, para.2–035.

[174] *Henthorn v Fraser* [1892] 2 Ch. 27 33; *Adams v Lindsell* (1818) 1 B. & Ald. 681; cf. *Bruner v Moore* [1904] 1 Ch. 305 (telegram); *Stevenson, Jacques & Co v McLean* (1880) 5 Q.B.D. 346; *Cowan v O'Connor* (1888) 20 Q.B.D. 640 (place of acceptance).

[175] *Brinkibon Ltd v Stahag Stahl und Stahlwarenhandelsgesellschaft mbH* [1983] 2 A.C. 34 at 41; the "Post Office" here refers to the provider of the universal postal service under Postal Services Act 2000, by whatever name that provider may from time to time be known.

employees authorised to receive letters: handing a letter to a postman authorised to *deliver* letters is not posting.[176]

2–031   **Reasons for the rule.** Various reasons for the rule have been suggested. One is that the offeror must be considered as making the offer all the time that his offer is in the post, and that therefore the agreement between the parties is complete as soon as the acceptance is posted.[177] But this does not explain why posting has any significance at all: any other proof of intention to accept would equally well show that the parties were in agreement. Another suggested reason for the rule is that, if it did not exist,

> "no contract could ever be completed by the post. For if the [offerors] were not bound by their offer when accepted by the [offerees] till the answer was received, then the [offerees] ought not to be bound till after they had received the notification that the [offerors] had received their answer and assented to it. And so it might go on *ad infinitum*".[178]

But it would be perfectly possible to hold that the acceptance took effect when it came to the notice of the offeror, whether the offeree knew of this or not. Such a rule would not result in an infinity of letters. Yet another suggested reason for the rule is that the Post Office is the common agent of both parties, and that communication to this agent immediately completes the contract.[179] But the contents of a sealed letter cannot realistically be said to have been communicated to the Post Office, which in any case is at most an agent to *transmit* the acceptance, and not to *receive* it.[180] Finally, it has been suggested that the rule minimises difficulties of proof: it is said to be easier to prove that a letter has been posted than that it has been received. But this depends in each case on the efficiency with which the parties keep records of incoming and outgoing letters.[181]

The rule is in truth an arbitrary one, little better or worse than its competitors. When negotiations are conducted by post, one of the parties may be prejudiced if a posted acceptance is lost or delayed; for the offeree may believe that there is a contract and the offeror that there is none, and each may act in reliance on his belief. The posting rule favours the offeree, and is sometimes justified on the ground that an offeror who chooses to start negotiations by post takes the risk of delay and accidents in the post; or on the ground that the offeror can protect himself by expressly stipulating that he is not to be bound until actual receipt of the acceptance.[182] Neither justification is wholly satisfactory, for the negotiations may have been started by the offeree[183]; and the offer may be made on a form provided by the offeree,[184] in which case he, and not the offeror, will for practical

---

[176] *Re London & Northern Bank* [1900] 1 Ch. 220.

[177] *Henthorn v Fraser* [1892] 2 Ch. 27 at 31.

[178] *Adams v Lindsell* (1818) 1 B. & Ald. 681 at 683. This case is usually considered to be one of the early leading authorities in support of the "general rule"; but in fact the court does not mention the *posting* of the *acceptance* at all.

[179] *Household, etc. Insurance Co Ltd v Grant* (1879) 4 Ex.D. 216 at 220.

[180] *Henthorn v Fraser* [1892] 2 Ch. 27 at 33; See above, para.2–025.

[181] See Winfield 55 L.Q.R. 509.

[182] *Household, etc. Insurance Co Ltd v Grant* (1879) 4 Ex.D. 216 at 223.

[183] It is often hard to tell which party is offeror and which is offeree, especially if the final offer was a counter-offer (see above, para.2–019).

[184] See below, para.2–042.

purposes be in control of its terms. The rule does, however, serve a possibly useful function in limiting the offeror's power to withdraw his offer at will[185]: it makes a posted acceptance binding although that acceptance only reaches the offeror after a previously posted withdrawal reaches the offeree.[186]

Must be reasonable to use post. The posting rule only applies when it is   2–032
reasonable to use the post as a means of communicating acceptance. Generally an offer made in a letter sent by post may be so accepted; but it may be reasonable to accept by post even though the offer was not sent in this way. In *Henthorn v Fraser*[187] the mere fact that the parties lived at a distance justified acceptance by post of an oral offer. It would not normally be reasonable to reply by a posted letter to an offer made by telex,[188] email or telephone. Nor would it be reasonable to accept by post if the acceptor knew that the postal service was disrupted.[189]

Terms of the offer. The posting rule can be excluded by the terms of the offer.   2–033
This may be so even though the offer does not expressly provide when the acceptance is to take effect. In *Holwell Securities Ltd v Hughes*[190] an offer to sell a house was made in the form of an option expressed "to be exercisable by notice in writing to the Intending Vendor ... ". Such a notice was posted but did not arrive. It was held that there was no contract of sale as the terms of the offer, on their true construction, required the acceptance to be actually communicated.

Instantaneous and electronic communications.[191] The posting rule does   2–034
not apply to acceptances made by some instantaneous mode of communication, e.g. by telephone or by telex.[192] Such acceptances are therefore governed by the general rule that they must have been communicated to the offeror.[193] The reason why the rule does not apply in such cases is that the acceptor will often know at once that his attempt to communicate was unsuccessful,[194] so that it is up to him to make a proper communication. But a person who accepts by letter which goes astray may not know of the loss or delay until it is too late to make another communication. Fax messages seem to occupy an intermediate position. The sender will usually know at once if his message has not been received at all, and where this is the position the message should not amount to an effective acceptance. But if the message is received in such a form that it is wholly or partly illegible, the sender is unlikely to know this at once, and it is suggested an acceptance sent by fax might well be effective in such circumstances.[195] The same

---

[185] See below, para.2–058. In countries in which the acceptance is only effective when communicated a similar result is often reached by legally limiting the offeror's power to withdraw his offer.
[186] See below, para.2–058.
[187] [1892] 2 Ch. 27.
[188] cf. *Quenerduaine v Cole* (1883) 32 W.R. 185 (telegram).
[189] *Bal v Van Staden* [1902] T.S. 128.
[190] [1974] 1 W.L.R. 155; cf. *New Hart Builders Ltd v Brindley* [1975] Ch. 342.
[191] Nolan, in Burrows & Peel (eds.), *Contract Formation and Parties.*
[192] *Entores Ltd v Miles Far East Corp* [1955] 2 Q.B. 327; *Brinkibon Ltd v Stahag Stahl und Stahlwarenhandelsgesellschaft mbH* [1983] 2 A.C. 34; cf. *Gill & Duffus Landauer Ltd v London Export Corp GmbH* [1982] 2 Lloyd's Rep. 627.
[193] See, above, para.2–024; the exceptions set out in paras 2–025—2–027 may also apply, but not the exception in the form of the posting rule.
[194] See the *Entores* case, above, at 333 and the *Brinkibon* case, above, at 43.
[195] In *JSC Zestafoni Nikoladze Ferroalloy Plant v Ronly Holdings Ltd* [2004] EWHC 245 (Comm); [2004] 2 Lloyd's Rep. 335 at [75] a fax was regarded as a form of instantaneous communication; the issue was *where* acceptance had taken effect, not *whether* it had done so, and there was no consideration of the latter of the two situations considered in the text.

principles should apply to other forms of electronic communication such as email[196] or web–site trading[197]: here again the effects of unsuccessful attempts to communicate should depend on whether the sender of the message knows (or has the means of knowing) at once of any failure in communication.

2–035 **Applications of the posting rule.** Discussions of this subject sometimes start by stating the "general rule" that an acceptance takes effect when posted, and then proceed to deduce various "consequences" from this rule. In fact few, if any, judges or writers have been prepared to follow all these deductions to their logical conclusions; and it would be more accurate to admit that there is no single or universal rule which determines the effect of a posted acceptance.[198] The effect of such an acceptance has to be considered *as against* various competing factors, such as withdrawal of the offer, loss or delay of the acceptance, subsequent revocation of the acceptance, previous rejection of the offer and so forth. Obviously, a rule laid down in a case concerning the effect of a posted acceptance as against a withdrawal of the offer is no real guide to the solution of the problem whether such an acceptance is effective as against a subsequent revocation of the acceptance. The English cases in fact only support three "consequences" of the posting rule. The first (and probably the most important[199]) is that a posted acceptance prevails over a previously posted withdrawal of the offer which had not yet reached the offeree when the acceptance was posted.[200] A second, and more controversial,[201] application of the rule is that an acceptance takes effect on posting even though it never reaches the offeror because it is lost through an accident in the post,[202] and the same rule probably applies where the acceptance is merely delayed through such an accident.[203] Thirdly, the contract is taken to have been made at the *time* of posting so as to take priority over another contract affecting the subject-matter made after the original acceptance had been posted but before it had reached the offeror.[204] Whether a posted acceptance should take effect against

---

[196] *The Eastern Navigator* [2005] EWHC 3020 (Comm); [2006] 1 Lloyd's Rep. 537 at [29]–[31]. For various possible times at which an email can be said to have been *received*, see Law Commission, *Electronic Commerce: Formal Requirements in Electronic Communications* (December 2001) §3.56; the present question is whether such a message may be effective *before* it is received. The Electronic Commerce (EC Directive) Regulations 2002 (SI 2002/2013), which implement most of EC Directive 2000/31 on Electronic Commerce [2000] O.J. L178/1, provide that the formal requirements contained in regs.9 and 11 do not apply to "contracts concluded exclusively by electronic mail or by equivalent individual communications": regs 9(4) and 11(3).

[197] The Law Commission paper (above, fn.196) §3.37 regards "clicking on a website button" as satisfying the requirement of *signature* but does not state whether it is an offer or an acceptance, or specify *when* it takes effect. Art.11.1 of the Directive on Electronic Commerce (above) states that "the order and acknowledgement are deemed to be received when the parties to whom they are addressed are able to access them"; and almost identical language is used in reg.11(2)(a) of the Regulations cited in fn.196, above. But this form of words does not of itself answer the question whether the contract may not be concluded even before that time.

[198] See Evans 15 I.C.L.Q. 553.

[199] See above, para.2–031 text to fn.186.

[200] *Harris' Case* (1872) L.R. 7 Ch.App. 587; *Byrne & Co v Leon van Tienhoven* (1880) 5 C.P.D. 344; *Henthorn v Fraser* [1892] 2 Ch. 27; *Re London & Northern Bank* [1900] 1 Ch. 200.

[201] See above, para.2–029.

[202] *Household, etc. Insurance v Grant* (1879) 4 Ex.D. 216, overruling *British and American Telegraph Co v Colson* (1871) L.R. 6 Ex. 108.

[203] See *Dunlop v Higgins* (1848) 1 H.L.C. 381, which would probably be followed in England though it is expressly restricted (at 402) to Scots law.

[204] *Potter v Sanders* (1846) 6 Hare 1.

other competing factors is a question of policy and convenience.[205] The posting rule will not apply where it would lead to "manifest inconvenience and absurdity".[206] Its scope is determined by practical considerations rather than by "deductions" from a "general" rule.

Misdirected acceptance. A letter of acceptance may be lost or delayed 2–036 because it bears a wrong, or an incomplete, address. Normally, such misdirection will be due to the carelessness of the offeree and the posting rule should not apply to such cases.[207] Even if an offeror can be said to take the risk of accidents in the post, it would be unreasonable to impose on him the further risk of the offeree's carelessness. It does not follow that a misdirected acceptance should necessarily take effect when received. For such a rule may actually favour the careless acceptor, e.g. when an offer is made to sell "at the market price prevailing when this offer is accepted," and the market falls after the misdirected acceptance has been posted. Moreover, the misdirection may be due to the fault of the offeror himself,[208] e.g. if he makes the offer in a letter on which his own address is incompletely or illegibly written, or if he uses an out-of-date letter-head.[209] The better rule, therefore, seems to be that a misdirected acceptance takes effect (if at all) at the time which is least favourable to the party responsible for the misdirection.[210]

Garbled messages. A message may be garbled as a result of some inaccuracy 2–037 in transmission for which the sender is not responsible. This problem used to arise in the case of telegraphed messages and could still arise from the use of now more common modes of communication: e.g. where an electronic message was corrupted in transmission without any fault on the part of the sender; and the discussion of garbled telegraphic messages in (and arising from) the older authorities may provide some guidance to the solution of such problems. In one such case, it was held that an offeror was not bound by a telegraphed offer which was garbled so as to indicate that he was placing an order for a different quantity of goods from that which he wished to buy.[211] But there is no English authority on the question whether an offeror would be bound where it was the acceptance rather than the offer which was garbled in this way. It is submitted that if the offeree sends a message of acceptance in words corresponding to the offer, then (so long as it was reasonable for the offeree to accept in this way), the offeror would be bound by the acceptance and would not be entitled to treat it as a counter-offer. If an offeror takes the risk of such accidents in the post as loss or delay, he should similarly take the risk of errors in the transmission of a message; for in each case the offeree will have no means of knowing that something has gone wrong until it is too late to make another, proper, communication.[212]

---

[205] *Brinkibon Ltd v Stahag Stahl und Stahlwarenhandelsgesellschaft mbH* [1983] 2 A.C. 34 at 41; *Gill & Duffus Landauer Ltd v London Export Corp GmbH* [1982] 2 Lloyd's Rep. 627 at 631.

[206] *Holwell Securities Ltd v Hughes* [1974] 1 W.L.R. 157 at 161.

[207] *LJ Korbetis v Transgrain Shipping BV* [2005] EWHC 1345 (QB).

[208] Fault of one party may not be the effective cause of the misdirection if the resulting error is obvious to the other party.

[209] cf. *Townsend's Case* (1871) L.R. 13 Eq. 148.

[210] *LJ Korbetis v Transgrain Shipping BV* [2005] EWHC 1345 (QB) at [15].

[211] *Henkel v Pape* (1870) L.R. 6 Ex. 7.

[212] cf. above, para.2–031.

2–038   **Revocation of posted acceptance.** An offeree may, after posting an acceptance, attempt to revoke it by a later communication which reaches the offeror
before, or at the same time as, the acceptance. There is no English authority on the
effectiveness of such a revocation. One view is that the revocation has no effect,
since, once a contract has been concluded by posting of the acceptance, it cannot
be dissolved by the unilateral act of one party.[213] But this argument has little to
commend it if (as has been suggested above) it is undesirable to resolve what are
really issues of policy by making "logical" deductions from some "general" rule
as to the effect of posted acceptances. As a matter of policy, the issue is whether
the offeror would be unjustly prejudiced by allowing the offeree to rely on the
subsequent revocation. On the one hand, it can be argued that the offeror cannot
be prejudiced by such revocation as he had no right to have his offer accepted and
as he cannot have relied on its having been accepted before he knew of the
acceptance. Against this, it can be argued that, once the acceptance has been
posted, the offeror can no longer withdraw his offer,[214] and that reciprocity
demands that the offeree should likewise be held to his acceptance. For if the
offeree could revoke the acceptance he would be able, without risk to himself, to
speculate at the expense of the offeror.[215] He could post his acceptance early in the
morning of a working day and could, if the market moved against him, revoke his
acceptance the same afternoon, while the offeror had no similar freedom of action.
It has been suggested[216] that the offeror should take this risk just as much as he
takes the risk of loss or delay; but here again it is submitted that while the offeror
may take the risk of accidents in the post, he should not have to take risks due
entirely to the conduct of the offeree.

So far, it has been assumed that it is in the offeror's interest to uphold the
contract. But to hold the acceptance binding as soon as it was posted, in spite of
an overtaking communication purporting to revoke it, might cause hardship to the
offeror. This is particularly true where he had acted in reliance on the revocation.
Suppose that A offers to sell B a car. After posting a letter of acceptance, B sends
an overtaking email, telling A to ignore that letter. On receipt of the email, A sells
the car to C. Could B change his mind yet again, and claim damages from A?
There are several ways of avoiding such an unjust result. The first is to say that
there had once been a contract but that it was later rescinded by mutual consent:
B's email was an offer to release A, which A accepted by conduct; communication
of such acceptance could be deemed to have been waived. The second is to regard
B's email as a repudiation amounting to a breach of contract; and to say that, by
"accepting" the breach, A has put an end to his obligations under the contract.[217]
This analysis is preferable from A's point of view if the sale to C is for a lower

---

[213] *Morrison v Thoelke* 155 So. 2d 889 (1963); *A to Z Bazaars (Pty) Ltd v Minister of Agriculture* (1974) (4) S.A. 392(C) (Turpin, [1975] C.L.J. 25); cf. *Wenckheim v Arndt* (N.Z.) 1 J.R. 73 (1873), contrast *Dick v US* (1949) 113 Ct.Cl.94, 82 F.Supp. 326; *Dunmore v Alexander* (1830) 9 Shaw 190. See generally Hudson 82. L.Q.R. 169. cf. *Kinch v Bullard* [1999] 1 W.L.R. 423 (no withdrawal by sender of notice which, by virtue of Law of Property Act 1925, s.196(3), had taken effect on being left at a person's place of abode).

[214] See above, para.2–031.

[215] cf. *LJ Korbetis v Transgrain Shipping BV* [2005] EWHC 1345 (Q.B.) at [11], dealing with a similar possible outcome in the case of a misdirected acceptance.

[216] Hudson 82 L.Q.R. 169, who also argues that the offeror can protect himself by stipulating that he is not to be bound till the acceptance reaches him, or that the offeree is to be bound as soon as he posts the acceptance.

[217] See below, para.18–010.

price than that to B, for it would enable A to claim the difference from B as damages.[218]

Consumer's right to cancel distance contracts. A contract made by (for   2–039
example) exchange of letters, faxes or emails or by website trading falls within the
definition of a "distance contract" within the Consumer Protection (Distance
Selling) Regulations 2000 if it is one for the supply of goods or services by a
commercial supplier to a consumer.[219] The Regulations do not specify when such
a contract is made[220]; but if it has been made, they give the consumer the right to
cancel it[221] by notice within a cancellation period specified in the Regulations (e.g.
of seven working days from the consumer's receipt of the goods which have been
supplied under it).[222] The contract, if so cancelled, is as a general rule "treated as
if it had not been made"[223] but this general rule is qualified in various ways.[224] The
effect of the exercise of the right to cancel is therefore not the same as the effect
of saying that no contract has been concluded by (e.g.) exchange of letters under
the common law rules of offer and acceptance discussed above; on the contrary,
the very concept of the consumer's "right to cancel" is based on the assumption
that, as a matter of common law, a contract has come into existence. The *supplier*
has no right to cancel under the Regulations, so that the question whether he has
entered into the contract continues to be governed by the common law rules.

(c) Prescribed Method of Acceptance

Offeror not generally bound by another method. Where an offer states   2–040
that it can only be accepted in a specified way, the offeror is not, in general, bound
unless acceptance is made in that way. Thus if the offeror asks for the acceptance
to be sent to a particular place an acceptance sent elsewhere will not bind him[225];
nor, if he asks for an acceptance in writing, will he be bound by one that is oral.[226]
The rule is particularly strict where the offer is contained in an option.[227] The

---

[218] See below, para.17–079 et seq. cf. *Kinch v Bullard*, above, fn.213, where the withdrawal held ineffective against the addressee was said (at 430–431) to be effective against the sender.

[219] SI 2000/2334 (as amended) (implementing Dir.97/7); for definitions of "distance contract", "consumer" and "supplier", see reg.3; for a list of methods of communication by which such a contract may be made, see SI 2000/2334, Sch.1. For contracts to which only part of the Regulations apply, see reg.6. cf. Financial Services (Distant Marketing) Regulations 2004 (SI 2004/2095) (implementing Dir.2002/65); Cancellation of Contracts made in a Consumer's Home or Place of Work etc. Regulations 2008 (SI 2008/1816) (implementing Dir.85/577).

[220] This is also true of the Electronic Commerce (EC Directive) Regulations 2002 (implementing Dir.2000/31), below, para.5–027). The latter merely provides that in the case of, for example, a contract made on a website, "the order and the acknowledgement of receipt [of the order] will be deemed to be received when the parties to whom they are addressed are able to access them" (reg.11(2)(a)). The effect of acknowledgement of receipt of an order falls to be determined as a matter of common law: see the definition of acceptance at para.2–016, above. The provision of reg.11(2)(a) quoted in this note does *not*, in any event, apply to "contracts concluded exclusively by exchange of electronic mail or by equivalent individual communications": reg.11(3).

[221] reg.10.

[222] reg.11(2).

[223] reg.10(2).

[224] See, e.g. reg.13 (exceptions to right to cancel); reg.17 (dealing with restoration of goods to the supplier after cancellation).

[225] *Frank v Knight* (1937) O.Q.P.D. 113; cf. *Eliason v Henshaw* (1819) 4 Wheat. 225.

[226] *Financings Ltd v Stimson* [1962] 1 W.L.R. 1184 at 1186. Contrast *Hitchens v General Guarantee Corp* [2001] EWCA Civ 359; *The Times*, March 13, 2001.

[227] *Holwell Securities Ltd v Hughes* [1974] 1 W.L.R. 157.

offeror will, however, be bound if he acquiesces in the different mode of acceptance and so waives the stipulated mode. Alternatively, a contract may be concluded if the purported acceptance (which is ineffective as such for failure to comply with the stipulated method) can be regarded as a counter-offer and if that counter-offer is then accepted by the counter-offeree.[228] Since such acceptance may be effected by conduct,[229] the contract may be concluded without any further communication between the parties after the original, ineffective, acceptance.

2–041   **Equally effective alternative method.** Where the offeror prescribes a method of acceptance, he usually does so with some particular object in view, e.g. to secure a speedy acceptance, or one which will prevent disputes from arising as to the terms of the agreement. An acceptance which accomplishes that object just as well as, or better than, the stipulated method may, by way of exception to the general rule, bind the offeror.[230] For the purpose of this exception, it must first be determined what object the offeror had in view. If he says "reply by letter sent by return of post" this may simply mean "reply quickly": the words may "fix the time for acceptance and not the manner of accepting."[231] If so, a reply by email would suffice. But such a reply would not suffice if the offer meant "reply quickly and by letter, I do not like emails as they are often obscure".

2–042   **Prescribed method waived.** An offeror can waive any requirement as to the form of acceptance if the stipulation as to form is solely for its benefit.[232] But if the stipulation is for the benefit of both parties it must be clear that both parties have waived the stipulation.[233] Stipulations as to the mode of acceptance may also be made for the protection and benefit of the *offeree*, e.g. where a customer submits a proposal to enter into a hire-purchase agreement; or where an offer is made on a form of tender provided by the offeree. If the offeree accepts in some other way, this will often be evidence that he has waived the stipulation; and it is submitted that the acceptance ought to be treated as effective unless it can be shown that failure to use the stipulated mode has prejudiced the offeror.[234]

(d) Acceptance by Silence

2–043   **Offeree generally not bound.** An offer may specify, not that it *must*, but that it *may*, be accepted in a particular way. In cases of this kind, particular difficulty arises from provisions to the effect that the offeree may accept by silence. As a general rule, an offeree who simply does nothing on receipt of an offer which states

---

[228] *Wettern Electric Ltd v Welsh Development Agency* [1983] Q.B. 796.

[229] As in the *Wettern Electric* case, above; provided, however, that such conduct is accompanied by the requisite contractual intention: see *Harvela Investments Ltd v Royal Trust Co of Canada (CI) Ltd* [1986] A.C. 207; and below, para.4–026.

[230] *Manchester Diocesan Council for Education v Commercial and General Investments Ltd* [1970] 1 W.L.R. 242.

[231] *Tinn v Hoffmann & Co* (1873) 29 L.T. 271 at 278; *Manchester Diocesan Council for Education v Commercial & General Investments Ltd*, above; cf. *Edmund Murray v PSB Foundations* (1992) 33 Con.L.R. 1.

[232] *MSM Consulting Ltd v Tanzania* [2009] EWHC 121 (QB); 123 Con L.R. 154 at [120].

[233] ibid. cf. *The Botnica* [2006] EWHC 1360 (Comm).

[234] See *Robophone Facilities v Blank* [1966] 1 W.L.R. 1423; *Carlyle Finance Ltd v Pallas Industrial Finance Ltd* [1999] 1 All E.R. (Comm) 659 at 670 (approving reasoning identical with that in the text above); cf. the *Manchester Diocesan* case, above, fn.230. From this point of view, these cases are, it is submitted, to be preferred to *Financings Ltd v Stimson* [1962] 1 W.L.R. 1184.

that it may be accepted by silence is not bound. In *Felthouse v Bindley*[235] an uncle offered to buy his nephew's horse by a letter in which he said: "If I hear no more about him, I shall consider the horse mine." Later, the horse was, by mistake, included in an auction sale of the nephew's property. The uncle sued the auctioneer for damages for the conversion of the horse. It was held that, at the time of the auction, there was no contract for the sale of the horse to the uncle because:

> "The uncle had no right to impose upon the nephew the sale of his horse . . . unless he chose to comply with the condition of writing to repudiate the offer . . . "[236]

The reason for the rule is that it is, in general, undesirable to impose the trouble and expense of rejecting an offer on an offeree who does not wish to accept it.[237]

The question whether silence can amount to an acceptance binding the offeree has also arisen in the cases, already discussed, in which the issue was whether an agreement to abandon an earlier agreement to submit a claim to arbitration could be inferred from inactivity, in the form of long delay in prosecuting the claim.[238] In these cases, it had been held that, even if one party's inactivity could be regarded as an offer to abandon the arbitration,[239] the mere silence or inactivity[240] of the other did not normally amount to an acceptance. For one thing, such inactivity was often[241] equivocal,[242] being explicable on other grounds (such as forgetfulness). For another, acceptance could not, as a matter of law, be inferred from silence alone[243] "save in the most exceptional circumstances".[244]

Offeree exceptionally bound? As the above reference to "exceptional circumstances" suggests, there may be exceptions to the general rule that an offeree is not bound by silence. If the offer has been solicited by the offeree, the argument that he should not be put to the trouble of rejecting it loses much of its force,[245]   2–044

---

[235] (1862) 11 C.B. (N.S.) 869, affirmed (1863) New Rep. 401; Miller 35 M.L.R. 489. cf. *Financial Techniques (Planning Services) v Hughes* [1981] I.R.L.R. 32 at 35.

[236] At 875.

[237] The evidence in *Felthouse v Bindley* that the nephew did in fact wish to sell the horse to the uncle means that the actual decision is hard to support, but this is no criticism of the general rule laid down.

[238] See above, para.2–005.

[239] ibid.

[240] For acceptance by silence *and conduct*, see below, para.2–047.

[241] But not always: see below, fn.249.

[242] e.g. *Jayaar Impex Ltd v Toaken Group Ltd* [1996] 2 Lloyd's Rep. 437 at 445.

[243] *The Leonidas D* [1985] 1 W.L.R. 925 at 927; *Rafsanjan Pistachio Producers Co-operative v Bank Leumi (UK) Plc* [1992] 1 Lloyd's Rep. 513 at 542; *The Gas Enterprise* [1993] 2 Lloyd's Rep. 352 at 357 (affirmed [1993] 2 Lloyd's Rep. 352 at 364, without reference to this point).

[244] *The Leonidas D*, above, at 927; *Vitol SA v Norelf Ltd* [1996] A.C. 800 at 812. Such "exceptional circumstances" may be illustrated by *The Splendid Sun* [1981] Q.B. 694 (where acceptance may have been by conduct: below, para.2–047) though this case is hard to reconcile with *The Leonidas D*, above; cf. *Cie Française d'Importation v Deutsche Continental Handelsgesellschaft* [1985] 2 Lloyd's Rep. 592 at 598. *The Golden Bear* [1987] 1 Lloyd's Rep. 330 is hard to reconcile with these cases and was apparently doubted in *The Antclizo* [1987] 2 Lloyd's Rep. 130 at 147 (affirmed [1988] 1 W.L.R. 603).

[245] cf. *Rust v Abbey Life Ins Co* [1979] 2 Lloyd's Rep. 335.

especially if the offer is made on a form provided by the offeree[246] and that form stipulates that silence may amount to acceptance.[247] Again, if there is a course of dealing between the parties, the offeror may be led to suppose that silence amounts to acceptance: e.g. where a retailer's offers to buy goods from a wholesaler have in the past been accepted as a matter of course by the despatch of the goods in question.[248] In such a case it may not be unreasonable to require the offeree to give notice of his rejection of the offer, especially if the offeror, in reliance on his belief that the goods would be delivered in the usual way, had forborne from seeking an alternative supply. On a somewhat similar principle, one party's wrongful repudiation of a contract may be accepted by the other party's failure to take such further steps in the performance of that contract as he would have been expected to take, if he were treating the contract as still in force.[249]

There may also be "an express undertaking or implied obligation to speak"[250] arising out of the course of negotiations between the parties, e.g. "where the offeree himself indicates that an offer is to be taken as accepted if he does not indicate the contrary by an ascertainable time",[251] particularly if the parties are "sorting out details against the background of a concluded contract."[252] Failure to perform such an "obligation to speak" could enable the *offeror* to treat that failure as an acceptance by silence. But it is not normally open to the *offeree* to treat his own silence (in breach of his "duty to speak") as an acceptance.[253] This course would be open to him only in situations such as that in *Felthouse v Bindley*,[254] in which the offeror had indicated (usually in the terms of the offer) that he would treat silence as an acceptance.

There is also the possibility that silence may constitute an acceptance by virtue of the custom of the trade or business in question.[255]

2–045 **Alternative liability of the offeree.** Even where silence of the offeree does not amount to an acceptance, it is arguable that he might be liable on a different basis. In *Spiro v Lintern* it was said that:

"If A sees B acting in the mistaken belief that A is under some binding obligation to him and in a manner consistent only with such an obligation, which would be to B's disadvantage if A were thereafter to deny the obligation, A is under a duty to B to disclose the non-existence of the supposed obligation."[256]

---

[246] cf. above, para.2–042.
[247] As in *Alexander Hamilton Institute v Jones* 234 Ill. App. (1924).
[248] As in *Cole-McIntyre-Norfleet Co v Holloway* 141 Tenn. 679; 214 S.W. 87 (1919).
[249] *Vitol SA v Norelf Ltd* [1996] A.C. 800; see below, para.18–009.
[250] *The Agrabele* [1985] 2 Lloyd's Rep. 496 at 509, per Evans J., whose statement of the relevant legal principles was approved on appeal, though the actual decision was reversed on the facts: [1987] 2 Lloyd's Rep. 223 at 225. The case would now be governed by Arbitration Act 1996, s.41(3): see above, para.2–005.
[251] *Re Selectmove* [1995] 1 W.L.R. 474 at 478 (where the point was left open).
[252] *The Harriette N* [2008] EWHC 2257; [2008] 2 Lloyd's Rep. 685 at [70], citing *Pagnan SpA v Feed Products Ltd* [1987] 2 Lloyd's Rep. 601 at 614.
[253] *Yona International Ltd v La Réunion Française* [1996] 2 Lloyd's Rep. 84 at 110.
[254] See above, para.2–043, further discussed below.
[255] *Minories Finance Ltd v Afribank Nigeria Ltd* [1995] 1 Lloyd's Rep. 134.
[256] [1973] 1 W.L.R. 1002 at 1011.

Although this statement was made with reference to wholly different circumstances,[257] it could also be applied to certain cases in which an offeror had, to the offeree's knowledge,[258] acted in reliance on the belief that his offer had been accepted by silence.[259] The liability of the offeree would then be based on a kind of estoppel.[260] The application of this doctrine to cases of alleged acceptance by silence gives rise to the difficulty that an estoppel can only arise out of a "clear and unequivocal"[261] representation, and that such a representation cannot generally be inferred from mere inactivity.[262] But this general rule does not preclude the application of the doctrine of estoppel to exceptional cases of the kind here under discussion, in which there are special circumstances which give rise to a "duty to speak", and in which it would be unconscionable for the party under that duty to deny that a contract had come into existence.[263]

Offeror bound? There is some authority for saying that the offeror cannot, any   2–046
more than the offeree, be bound where the offeree simply remains silent in response to the offer,[264] and the case is not one of the exceptional ones discussed above[265] in which an offer can be accepted by silence. But the object of the general rule laid down in *Felthouse v Bindley*[266] is to protect *the offeree* from having to incur the trouble and expense of rejecting the offer so as to avoid being bound. No such argument can normally be advanced for protecting the offeror. He may indeed be left in doubt on the question whether his offer has been accepted; but this is not a matter about which he can legitimately complain where he has drawn up his offer in terms which permit (and even encourage) acceptance by silence.[267] Thus the uncle in *Felthouse v Bindley* might have been bound if the nephew had resolved to accept the offer and had, in reliance on its terms, forborne from attempting to dispose of the horse elsewhere. This possibility has been judicially doubted,[268] but in the case in which the doubt was raised it was not an express term of the offer that silence would be regarded as acceptance. Where the offeror has expressly formulated his offer in such terms, it is submitted that the offeree's silence in response to the offer should be capable of binding the offeror.

---

[257] See below, para.16–028.
[258] See *Yona International Ltd v La Réunion Française* [1996] 2 Lloyd's Rep. 84 at 107 (where this requirement was not satisfied).
[259] If the offeror, to the offeree's knowledge, actually performs in accordance with his offer and so confers a benefit on the offeree, the solution in this type of case may be to make the offeree restore the benefit rather than to hold him to an obligation to perform his part of a contract to which he had never agreed: Burrows, *The Law of Restitution* (3rd edn) at 334–339.
[260] See below, paras 3–090, 9–156; cf. (in another context) *The Stolt Loyalty* [1993] 2 Lloyd's Rep. 281 at 289–291, affirmed [1995] 1 Lloyd's Rep. 598, without reference to this point. The case would not be one of estoppel by convention (below, para.3–094), for such estoppel is based on an *agreed* assumption of fact, while in cases of the present kind the question is whether there was any agreement.
[261] See below, paras 3–081, 9–156.
[262] See below, para.3–082.
[263] Cf. *AC Yule & Son Ltd v Speedwell Roofing & Cladding Ltd* [2007] EWHC 1360 (TCC); [2007] B.L.R. 499 (obligation to respond to adjudicator's requests under the Housing Grants, Construction and Regeneration Act 1996 Pt II).
[264] *Fairline Shipping Corp v Adamson* [1975] Q.B. 180 at 189.
[265] At para.2–044.
[266] See above, para.2–043.
[267] This reasoning would not apply where the terms of the offer had been drawn up by the *offeree*: cf. above, para.2–042.
[268] *Fairline Shipping Corp v Adamson* [1975] Q.B. 180 at 189.

It is settled that a creditor can accept his debtor's offer to give additional security for a debt by simply forbearing to sue for the debt.[269] If such forbearance can be regarded as silence, this rule supports the view that acceptance by silence can bind the offeror. Another possible explanation of the rule is that a creditor who forbears accepts by conduct[270] rather than by silence.

2–047   **Silence and conduct.** In *Roberts v Hayward*[271] a tenant accepted his landlord's offer of a new tenancy at an increased rent by simply staying on the premises. It was held that he had accepted the landlord's offer by silence; but it seems better to say that he accepted by conduct and that the landlord waived notice of acceptance.[272] Similarly an offer made *to* a landowner to occupy land under a licence containing specified terms may be accepted by the landowner's permitting the offeror to occupy the land.[273] An offeree is not, for the present purpose, "silent" merely because his acceptance is not expressed in words.[274] The possibility of acceptance by conduct is, yet again, illustrated by the arbitration cases already mentioned,[275] according to which, an offer of abandonment can be accepted by reacting to it, not merely by inactivity,[276] but also by some further conduct: e.g. by closing or disposing of relevant files.[277]

In *Rust v Abbey Life Ins Co*[278] the claimant applied and paid for a "property bond" which was allocated to her on the terms of the defendants' usual policy of insurance. After having retained this document for some seven months, she claimed the return of her payment, alleging that no contract had been concluded. The claim was rejected on the ground that her application was an offer which had been accepted by issue of the policy. But it was further held that, even if the policy constituted a counter-offer, this counter-offer had been accepted by "the conduct of the [claimant] in doing and saying nothing for seven months . . . ".[279] Thus mere inaction was said to be sufficient to constitute acceptance; and it seems to have amounted to no more than silence in spite of having been described as "conduct". The conclusion that it amounted to acceptance can, however, be justified in the circumstances. The negotiations had been started by the claimant[280] (the counter-offeree), and in view of this fact it was reasonable for the defendants to infer from her long silence that she had accepted the terms of the policy which had been sent to her and which she must be "taken to have examined".[281] The case thus falls within one of the suggested exceptions[282] to the general rule that an offeree is not bound by silence.

---

[269] See below, para.3–040.
[270] See above, para.2–018.
[271] (1828) 3 C. & P. 432.
[272] cf. above, para.2–027.
[273] *Wettern Electric Ltd v Welsh Development Agency* [1983] Q.B. 796.
[274] *Aspinall's Club Ltd v Al Zayat* [2007] EWCA Civ 1001 at [30].
[275] See above, para.2–043.
[276] ibid. cf. *Collin v Duke of Westminster* [1985] Q.B. 581.
[277] See *The Splendid Sun* [1981] Q.B. 694 at 712, 713 ("closed their files"); cf. *The Splendid Sun* [1981] Q.B. 694 at 706 ("did so act"); *The Multibank Holsatia* [1988] 2 Lloyd's Rep. 486 at 493 (where the offeree had destroyed relevant files, so that the case was not one of mere inaction).
[278] [1979] 2 Lloyd's Rep. 335.
[279] ibid., affirming [1978] 2 Lloyd's Rep. 386 at 393.
[280] cf. above, para.2–038 and *Vitol SA v Norelf Ltd* [1996] A.C. 800; above, para.2–044.
[281] Contrast *Yona International Ltd v La Réunion Française* [1996] 2 Lloyd's Rep. 84 at 110; *Cooper v National Westminster Bank Plc* [2009] EWHC 3035 (QB); [2010] 1 Lloyd's Rep. 490.
[282] See above, para.2–044.

(e) Acceptance in Ignorance of Offer

Generally ineffective. The general view is that acceptance in ignorance of an   **2–048**
offer cannot create a contract since the parties must *reach* agreement: it is not
enough that their wishes happen to coincide: the act or promise constituting the
acceptance must be "given in exchange for the offer".[283] The same reasoning
applies where a person once knew of the offer but had at the time of the alleged
acceptance forgotten it.[284] Thus it has been held in other jurisdictions that a
person who gives information for which a reward has been offered cannot claim
the reward unless at the time of giving it he knew of the offer of reward.[285] The
English case of *Gibbons v Proctor*[286] is sometimes thought to support the contrary
view, but can be explained on the ground that the claimant did know of the offer
of reward by the time the information was given on his behalf to the person named
in the advertisement.

In the reward cases just considered, it is hard to see what prejudice the offeror
would suffer if he had to pay the reward to someone who had complied with the
terms of the offer without being aware of it. The reasons for holding that there is
no contract in such a case seem to be largely doctrinal; but more practical
difficulties can arise where the acts alleged to amount to an acceptance can not
only confer rights on the actor, but also deprive him of rights[287] or impose duties
on him. This last possibility may be illustrated by reference to *Upton Rural DC v
Powell*[288] where the defendant, whose house was on fire, telephoned the Upton
police and asked for "the fire brigade". He was entitled to the service of the
Pershore fire brigade free of charge as he lived in its district; but the police called
the Upton fire brigade, in the belief that the defendant lived in that district. The
latter fire brigade for a time shared this belief and thought "that they were
rendering gratuitous services in their own area". It was held that the defendant
was contractually bound to pay for these services. But even if the defendant's
telephone call was an offer, it is hard to see how the Upton brigade's services,
given with no thought of reward, could be an acceptance. It would have been
better to give the claimants a restitutionary remedy than to hold that there was a
contract.[289] The case was concerned only with the rights of the fire brigade, but
the fire brigade could also have owed more extensive duties as contractors than as
volunteers. It may well be hard to subject a person who reasonably thinks that he
is a volunteer to the more stringent duties of a contractor.[290]

Cross-offers. The requirement that the offeree must know of the offer at the   **2–049**
time of the alleged acceptance also accounts for the rule that there is no contract
if two persons make identical cross-offers, neither party knowing of the other's

---

[283] *R. v Clarke* (1927) 40 C.L.R. 227 at 233; *Tracomin SA v Anton C Nielsen* [1984] 2 Lloyd's Rep.
195 at 203; *Lark v Outhwaite* [1991] 2 Lloyd's Rep. 132 at 140.
[284] ibid. at 241.
[285] *Bloom v American Swiss Watch Co* (1915) A.D. 100; the American authorities are divided: see
Corbin, *Contracts*, para.59.
[286] (1891) 64 L.T. 594, sub nom. *Gibson v Proctor* 55 J.P. 616. See Hudson, 84 L.Q.R. 513.
[287] e.g. *Tracomin SA v Anton C Nielsen* [1984] 2 Lloyd's Rep. 195 at 203.
[288] [1942] 1 All E.R. 220; Mitchell, 12 J.C.L. 78.
[289] cf. Burrows, *The Law of Restitution* (3rd edn), at 241–242; *The Sibohelle* [2011] EWHC 1150
(Comm) at [44].
[290] cf. *BSC v Cleveland Bridge & Engineering Co Ltd* [1984] 1 All E.R. 504 at 510. Quaere what the
position should be where one party thinks that he is giving or getting a gratuitous service while the
other thinks that he is contracting.

offer when he makes his own, e.g. if A writes to B offering to sell B his car for
£5,000 and B simultaneously writes to A offering to buy the car for £5,000. If no
further communication took place in such a case, the parties might well be in
doubt as to whether there was indeed a contract between them; and the view that
"cross offers are not an acceptance of each other"[291] can be supported on the
ground that it tends to promote certainty.

2–050   **Motive for acceptance.** A person who knows of the offer may do the act
required for acceptance with some motive other than that of accepting the offer.
In *Williams v Carwardine*[292] the defendant offered a reward of £20 to anyone who
gave information leading to the conviction of the murderers of Walter Carwardine.
The claimant knew of the offer, and, thinking that she had not long to live, signed
a "voluntary statement to ease my conscience, and in hopes of forgiveness
hereafter". This statement resulted in the conviction of the murderers. It was held
that the claimant had brought herself within the terms of the offer and was
entitled to the reward. Patteson J. said: "We cannot go into the (claimant's)
motives".[293] Similarly, in *Carlill v Carbolic Smoke Ball Co*[294] the claimant recovered the £100, although her predominant motive in using the smoke ball was
(presumably) to avoid catching influenza. But in the Australian case of *R. v
Clarke*[295] a reward had been offered for information leading to the arrest and
conviction of the murderers of two police officers. Clarke, who knew of the offer
and was himself suspected of the crime, gave such information. He admitted that
he had done so to clear himself of the charge, and with no thought of claiming the
reward. His claim for the reward failed as he had not given the information "in
exchange for the offer".[296] It seems that an act which is *wholly* motivated by factors
other than the existence of the offer cannot amount to an acceptance,[297] but if the
existence of the offer plays some part, however small, in inducing a person to do
the required act, there is a valid acceptance of the offer.

(f) Acceptance in Unilateral Contracts

2–051   **Classification.** An offer of a unilateral contract is made when one party
promises to pay the other a sum of money[298] if the other will do (or forbear from
doing) something without making any promise to that effect: e.g. when one person
promises to pay another £100 if he will walk from London to York,[299] or give up
smoking for a year.[300] The contract which arises in these cases is called "unilateral" because it arises without the offeree's having made any counter-promise to
perform the required act or forbearance; it is contrasted with a bilateral contract,
in which each party undertakes an obligation and in which acceptance, as a general

[291] *Tinn v Hoffmann & Co* (1873) 29 L.T. 271 at 278.
[292] (1833) 5 C. & P. 566; 4 B. & Ad. 621; it must be assumed that the claimant knew of the offer: *Carlill v Carbolic Smoke Ball Co Ltd* [1892] 2 Q.B. at 489, fn.2.
[293] 4 B. & Ad. at 623.
[294] [1893] 1 Q.B. 256, above, para.2–010.
[295] (1927) 40 C.L.R. 227; contrast *Simonds v US* 308 F. 2d 160 (1962).
[296] At 233.
[297] *Lark v Outhwaite* [1991] 2 Lloyd's Rep. 132 at 140.
[298] Or to do some other act, or to forbear from doing something. In the text we shall deal only with the most common case of a promise to pay money.
[299] An old example: *Rogers v Snow* (1573) Dalison 94; cf. *Great Northern Ry v Witham* (1873) L.R. 9 C.P. 16 at 19.
[300] cf. *Hamer v Sidway* 124 N.Y. 538 (1881).

rule, takes the form of a communication by the offeree of his counter-promise. The distinction between the two types of contract sometimes gives rise to difficulty,[301] because a contract may be in its inception unilateral, but become bilateral in the course of its performance.[302] For example, A may promise to pay B £1,000 for some service (such as repainting A's house) which B does not promise to render. Here B would not be liable if he did nothing; but once he began the work (e.g. by stripping off the old paint) he might be held to have impliedly promised[303] to complete it, so that at this stage the contract would become bilateral[304] and both parties would be bound by it.

General rules as to acceptance. Once a promise is classified as an offer of a   **2–052** unilateral contract, a number of rules apply to the acceptance of such an offer. First, the offer can be accepted by fully performing the required act or forbearance.[305] Secondly, there is no need to give advance notice of acceptance to the offeror.[306] And thirdly, the offer can, like all other offers, be withdrawn before it has been accepted. But there is much dispute as to the exact stage at which the offer is "accepted" so as to deprive the offeror of the power of withdrawal.

Acceptance by part performance. It is probable that the offer can be   **2–053** accepted *only* by some performance and not by a counter-promise to walk to York, or to give up smoking; for such a counter-promise would not be what the offeror had bargained for. Thus the offeror could still withdraw after such a counter-promise had been made. It is less clear whether the offeror can still withdraw after the offeree has *partly* performed the required act or forbearance, e.g. if he has walked half way to York or refrained from smoking for six months. The first problem (which will be discussed here) is whether the offeree has at this stage accepted the offer; the second (to be discussed in Ch.3[307]) is whether he has provided consideration for the offeror's promise.

According to one view, there is no contract until the required act or forbearance has been completed, and this is said to give effect to the intention of the parties, each of whom intends, until then, to reserve a *locus poenitentiae*.[308] But in most cases[309] it is unlikely that the offeree intends to expose himself to the risk of

---

[301] See generally Llewellyn 48 Yale L.J. 1, 799.

[302] cf. *The Eurymedon* [1975] A.C. 154 at 167–8 ("a bargain initially unilateral but capable of becoming mutual"): see further para.14–063, below.

[303] According to a dictum in *Little v Courage Ltd* (1995) 70 P. & C.R. 469 at 475, terms which impose legal obligations cannot be implied into a unilateral contract; but this view would not preclude such a contract from becoming bilateral after it had originally come into existence. See further para.6–037, below.

[304] See *The Unique Mariner* [1979] 2 Lloyd's Rep. 37 at 51–52; *The Kurnia Dewi* [1997] 1 Lloyd's Rep. 553 at 559; contrast *BSC v Cleveland Bridge & Engineering Co Ltd* [1984] 1 All E.R. 504 at 510–511 where such an implied promise was negatived by the fact that the terms of a bilateral contract were still under negotiation and were never agreed. It is not clear whether the situation discussed in *Offord v Davies* (1862) 12 C.B.N.S. 748 at 753 falls into the category of a unilateral or bilateral contract.

[305] See *Daulia Ltd v Four Millbank Nominees Ltd* [1978] Ch. 231 at 238; cf. *Harvela Investments Ltd v Royal Trust of Canada (CI) Ltd* [1986] A.C. 207 at 224.

[306] *Carlill v Carbolic Smoke Ball Co* [1893] 1 Q.B. 256; *Bowerman v Association of British Travel Agents* [1995] N.L.J. 1815.

[307] See below, para.3–158.

[308] Wormser in *Selected Readings on the Law of Contracts*, p.307; but for the same writer's later views see 3 Jl.Leg.Educ. 146.

[309] For a possible exception, see below, para.2–056.

withdrawal when he has partly performed and is willing and able[310] to complete performance for the sake of securing the promised benefit.[311] The general view is that it would cause hardship to the offeree to allow the offeror to withdraw in such a case; and most writers try to find some reason for saying that part-performance prevents the offeror from withdrawing the offer. One possibility is to say that the offeror makes two offers: (1) the principal offer and (2) a collateral one to keep the principal offer open once performance has begun; this latter offer is accepted by beginning to perform.[312] But this analysis is artificial: it is more realistic to say that the principal offer itself is accepted by beginning to perform.[313] It has been objected that this cannot simply be asserted but must be explained.[314] The explanation appears to be that acceptance is no more (or less) than an unqualified expression of assent to the terms of the offer by words or conduct; and that the question whether an inference of such assent can be drawn from part-performance is simply one of fact. The sight of a man walking northwards from London may or may not suggest that he does so in response to an offer to pay him £100 if he reaches York, but, if his conduct does clearly suggest this, there is no theoretical difficulty in saying that he has accepted the offer. Factual difficulties might, of course, arise in distinguishing between commencement of performance and mere preparation to perform. Thus it is probable that an offer of a reward for the return of lost property could still be withdrawn after someone had spent time looking for the property without success, but not after he had actually found it and was in the process of returning it to the owner.

Support for the above view is provided by *Errington v Errington*[315] where a father bought a house subject to a mortgage, allowed his son and daughter-in-law to live in it, and told them that, if they paid the mortgage instalments, the house would be theirs when the mortgage was paid off. The couple started to live in the house and paid some of the mortgage instalments; but they did not bind themselves to go on making the payments. It was held that this arrangement amounted to a contract which could not, after the father's death, be revoked by his personal representatives. Denning L.J. said:

> "The father's promise was a unilateral contract—a promise of the house in return for their act of paying the instalments. It could not be revoked by him once the couple entered on performance of the act, but it would cease to bind him if they left it incomplete and unperformed, which they have not done."[316]

---

[310] It is assumed that performance remains within the offeree's power. If not, the offeror can withdraw: see *Morrison SS Co v The Crown* (1924) 20 Ll.L.R. 283.

[311] Lord Diplock in the *Harvela* case [1986] A.C. 207 at 224 can be read as depriving the offeror of the power to withdraw as soon as his offer is *communicated* (i.e. before any performance); but in that case the offeree had completely performed the required act by making the requested bid.

[312] McGoveney, *Selected Readings*, p.300.

[313] Pollock, *Principles of Contract* (13th edn), p.19; Ballantine, *Selected Readings*, p.312.

[314] McGoveney, above.

[315] [1952] 1 K.B. 290. The reasoning of this case was doubted, but not on this point, in *National Provincial Bank Ltd v Ainsworth* [1965] A.C. 1175 at 1239–1240, 1251–1252 and in *Ashburn Anstalt v Arnold* [1989] Ch. 1 at 17 (overruled on another point in *Prudential Assurance Co Ltd v London Residuary Body* [1992] A.C. 386).

[316] [1952] 1 K.B. 290 at 295. cf. *Soulsbury v Soulsbury* [2007] EWCA Civ 969; [2008] 2 W.L.R. 834 at [50] (where performance had been completed); *Schweppe v Harper* [2008] EWCA Civ 442 at [46]: "Where there is an offer to pay for the performance of a certain task, part performance can produce a contract under which that offer cannot be withdrawn", per Waller L.J., dissenting.

Continuing guarantees. The view that part-performance of a unilateral 2–054
contract can amount to an acceptance is further supported by the law relating to
continuing guarantees. These may be divisible, where each advance constitutes a
separate transaction; or indivisible, e.g. where, on A's admission to an association,
B guarantees all liabilities that A may incur as a member of the association.[317] If
the guarantee is divisible, it can be revoked at any time with regard to future
advances[318]; but an indivisible guarantee cannot be revoked after the creditor has
begun to act on it by giving credit to the principal debtor.[319] This rule applies even
though the contract of guarantee is unilateral in the sense that the creditor has not
made any promise to the guarantor (in return for the guarantee) to give credit to
the debtor.

Bankers' irrevocable credits. This subject is more fully explained in Ch.3.[320] 2–055
Here it need only be said that the essence of the system is that a bank, on the
instruction of its customer (usually a buyer of goods) notifies a third person
(usually the seller) that it has opened an irrevocable credit in his favour, promising
to pay him a stipulated sum if he will present certain specified documents to the
bank. The general view is that the bank cannot revoke the promise once it has been
notified to the seller; and, as the seller makes no promise *to the bank*, this result is
sometimes explained in terms of a unilateral contract between these parties. In
most cases there will be some act of part-performance by the seller, e.g. in shipping
the goods so as to procure the required documents. But the bank's promise is
regarded as binding as soon as it is notified to the seller, i.e. before he has done any
act in response to it. The binding force of such irrevocable credits is not, therefore,
easily explicable in terms of acceptance of an offer.

Estate agents' contracts. Where an estate agent is engaged to negotiate the 2–056
sale of a house, it is arguable that his client's promise to pay a commission on sale
gives rise to a unilateral contract, for in one case of this kind it was said that "No
obligation is imposed on the agent to do anything."[321] It is settled that the client
(the offeror) can, without liability, revoke his instructions before a claim to
commission has accrued, in spite of the fact that the agent (the offeree) has made
considerable efforts to find a purchaser.[322] Hence these cases could be said to
support the view that an offer of a unilateral contract can be withdrawn after part-
performance by the offeree. But the better explanation is that this is one of the
exceptional cases in which, on the true construction of the offer, a *locus poenitentiae*
is reserved to the client even after part-performance by the agent. This view is
supported by the fact that the right to revoke instructions exists even where the
contract is bilateral because the agent has, expressly or by implication, made some
promise: e.g. one to use his best endeavours to effect a sale[323] or one to bear
advertising expenses.[324] Such promises have been found to exist where the agent

---

[317] As in *Lloyd's v Harper* (1880) 16 Ch.D. 290.
[318] As in *Offord v Davies* (1862) 12 C.B.N.S. 748.
[319] *Lloyd's v Harper*, above.
[320] See below, para.3–159.
[321] *Luxor (Eastbourne) Ltd v Cooper* [1941] A.C. 108 at 124. In fact the agent often does undertake
to do something; see below, fnn.323, 324. See generally Murdoch (1975) 91 L.Q.R. 357.
[322] See below, para.16–087.
[323] *Christopher v Essig* [1958] W.N. 461; *John McCann & Co v Pow* [1974] 1 W.L.R. 1643 at
1647.
[324] cf. *Bentall, Horsley & Baldry v Vicary* [1931] 1 K.B. 253.

has been appointed "sole agent", but in practice they are commonly made by other agents as well. A "sole agent" is entitled to damages if the client sells through another agent,[325] but not if he simply revokes his instructions or sells "privately", without the help of any agent at all.[326] These rules apply irrespective of the unilateral or bilateral nature of the contract; so that the estate agency cases shed little, if any, light on the question of acceptance by part-performance of unilateral contracts.

2–057   **Extent of recovery.** Where a unilateral contract takes the shape of a promise to pay a sum of money, it is generally assumed that the promisee must either get nothing or the full sum. But this seems unnecessarily inflexible. If the promisee has walked half way to York before the offer is withdrawn, it is arguable that he should desist and recover damages.[327] This may take the form of a discounted payment of the sum promised to reflect the fact that he may not have completed performance.[328]

3. TERMINATION OF OFFER

(a) Withdrawal

2–058   **Communication to offeree generally required.** As a general rule, an offer can be withdrawn at any time before it is accepted.[329] It is not withdrawn merely by acting inconsistently with it, e.g. by disposing of the subject-matter.[330] Notice of the withdrawal must be given and must actually reach the offeree[331]: mere posting will not suffice. In *Byrne & Co v Leon van Tienhoven*[332] an offer to sell tinplates was posted in Cardiff on October 1 and reached the offerees in New York on October 11, and they immediately accepted it by a telegram which they confirmed by a letter of October 15. Meanwhile, the offerors had on October 8 posted a letter withdrawing their offer, but that letter of withdrawal did not reach the offerees until October 20. It was held that there was a contract since the withdrawal had not been communicated when the offer was accepted. Thus there was a contract in spite of the fact that the parties were demonstrably not in agreement, for when the offerees first knew of the offer, the offerors had already ceased to intend to deal with the offerees. The rule is based on convenience; for

---

[325] *Hampton & Sons Ltd v George* [1939] 3 All E.R. 627; *Christopher v Essig* [1958] W.N. 461; below, para.16–090.

[326] See below, para.16–090.

[327] Unless the promisee has a "substantial or legitimate interest" in going on, this may be the law under the principles laid down in *White & Carter (Councils) Ltd v McGregor* [1962] A.C. 413; below, para.21–012.

[328] *Schweppe v Harper* [2008] EWCA Civ 442 at [53] (per Waller L.J., dissenting. The 'loss of a chance' analysis adopted was particularly apt since complete performance depended on the conduct of third parties: see para.2–060 below).

[329] *Routledge v Grant* (1828) 4 Bing 653; *Offord v Davies* (1862) 12 C.B.N.S. 748; *Scammell v Dicker* [2001] 1 W.L.R. 631; *Bircham & Co Nominees (No.2) v Worrell Holdings* [2001] EWCA Civ 775; (2001) 82 P. & C.R. 472 at [24], [35].

[330] *Adams v Lindsell* (1818) 1 B. & Ald. 681; *Stevenson, Jacques & Co v McLean* (1880) 5 Q.B.D. 346; contrary dicta in *Dickinson v Dodds* (1876) 2 Ch.D. 463 at 472 would no longer be followed.

[331] An initial offer may be withdrawn by making a further offer depending on the nature of the two offers and the circumstances in which they were made: *Pickfords Ltd v Celestica Ltd* [2003] EWCA Civ 1741 at [17].

[332] (1880) 5 C.P.D. 344. Under Consumer Credit Act 1974, s.69(1)(ii) and (7) posting is, exceptionally, sufficient (as is "transmission" of an electronic communication: SI 2004/3236).

no one could rely on a postal offer if it could be withdrawn by a letter already posted but not yet received.

Communication need not come from offeror. Although withdrawal must   2–059
be communicated to the offeree, it need not be communicated by the offeror. It is sufficient if the offeree knows from any reliable source that the offeror no longer intends to contract with him. Thus in *Dickinson v Dodds*[333] it was held that an offer to sell land could not be accepted after the offeror had, to the offeree's knowledge, decided to sell the land to a third party. The decision is based on the fact that there is in such a case no agreement between the parties. But this would be equally true if the offeree did not know of the withdrawal at all when he accepted the offer: yet in that case there is normally[334] a contract.[335] The rule that communication of withdrawal need not come from the offeror can be a regrettable source of uncertainty. It puts on the offeree the possibly difficult task of deciding whether his source of information is reliable, and it may also make it hard for him to tell exactly when the offer was withdrawn. In *Dickinson v Dodds*, for example, it is not clear whether this occurred when the offeree realised that the defendant had (a) sold the land to the third party, or (b) begun to negotiate with the third party, or (c) simply decided not to sell to the claimant. Certainty would be promoted if the rule were that the withdrawal must be communicated by the offeror, as well as to the offeree.

Exceptions. The general rule that the withdrawal must be "brought to the   2–060
mind of"[336] the offeree is subject to a number of exceptions. First, the require-
ment cannot be taken quite literally where an offer is made to a company whose mail is received, opened and sorted in different offices and then distributed to be dealt with in various departments. Is a letter withdrawing such an offer communi-
cated when it is received, or when it is opened, or when it is actually read by the responsible officer?[337] In the interests of certainty it would probably be held that communication took place when the letter was "opened in the ordinary course of business or would have been so opened if the ordinary course was followed."[338] Secondly (as the concluding words of the passage just quoted suggest) the general rule may be displaced by the conduct of the offeree. A withdrawal which had reached the offeree would be effective even though he had simply failed to read it after it had reached him: this would be the position where a withdrawal by fax or email reached the offeree's office during business hours[339] even though it was not actually read by the offeree or by any of his staff till the next day.[340] Of course the withdrawal would not be effective in such a case, if it had been sent to the offeree at a time when he and all responsible members of his staff were, to the offeror's

---

[333] (1876) 2 Ch.D. 463; cf. *Cartwright v Hoogstoel* (1911) 105 L.T. 628.

[334] i.e. subject to the exceptions stated in the following paragraph.

[335] *Byrne & Co v Leon van Tienhoven* (1880) 5 C.P.D. 344, above, fn.332.

[336] *Henthorn v Fraser* [1892] 2 Ch. 27 at 32.

[337] cf. *Curtice v London Bank* [1908] 1 K.B. 291 at 300–301 (notice to countermand a cheque).

[338] *Eaglehill Ltd v J Needham (Builders) Ltd* [1973] A.C. 992 at 1011, discussing notice of dishonour of a cheque; *The Pamela* [1995] 2 Lloyd's Rep. 249 at 252; cf. *The Pendrecht* [1980] 2 Lloyd's Rep. 56 at 66 (telex notice of arbitration); *The Eastern Navigator* [2005] EWHC 3020 (Comm); [2006] 1 Lloyd's Rep. 537 (email notice of arbitration).

[339] For the effect of such messages when sent *out* of business hours, see above, para.2–026. But see the comment in fn.341 below.

[340] cf. *The Brimnes* [1975] Q.B. 929 (notice withdrawing ship from charterparty).

knowledge, away on holiday or on other business.[341] A third exception to the requirement that a withdrawal must be actually communicated relates to offers made to the public, e.g. of rewards for information leading to the arrest of the perpetrator of a crime. As it is impossible for the offeror to ensure that the notice of withdrawal comes to the attention of everyone who knew of the offer, it seems to be enough for him to take reasonable steps to bring the withdrawal to the attention of such persons, even though it does not in fact come to the attention of them all.[342]

2–061   **Revival of a withdrawn offer.** An attempt to accept an offer which has been withdrawn is ineffective as an acceptance, but it may amount to a new offer on the same terms as the withdrawn offer which can be accepted by the conduct of the original offeror.[343]

(b) Rejection

2–062   An offer is terminated by rejection.[344] An attempt to accept an offer on new terms, not contained in the offer, may be a rejection of the offer accompanied by a counter-offer.[345] An offeree who makes such an attempt cannot later accept the original offer.[346] A communication from the offeree *may* be construed as a counter-offer (and hence as a rejection) even though it takes the form of a question as to the offeror's willingness to vary the terms of the offer.[347] But such a communication is not *necessarily* a counter-offer: it may be a mere inquiry[348] or request for information made without any intention of rejecting the terms of the offer. Whether the communication is a counter-offer or a request for information depends on the intention, objectively ascertained,[349] with which it was made. If, for example, an offer is made to sell a house at a specified price, an inquiry whether the intending vendor is prepared to reduce the price will not amount to a rejection if the inquiry is "merely exploratory."[350]

2–063   **Rejection must be communicated to offeror.** It seems that a rejection has no effect unless it is actually communicated to the offeror. There is no ground of convenience for holding that it should take effect when posted. The offeree will not act in reliance on it as he derives no rights or liabilities from it; and the offeror will not know that he is free from the offer until the rejection is actually communicated to him. Hence, if a letter of rejection is overtaken by an acceptance sent by e-mail there should be a contract, provided that the offeree has made his final intention clear to the offeror. But once the rejection had reached the offeror

---

[341] cf. *Brinkibon Ltd v Stahag Stahl und Stahlwarenhandelsgesellschaft mbH* [1983] 2 A.C. 34 at 42 (communication of acceptance). Quaere how strictly such a principle should be applied now when so many communications are by e-mail and the proliferation of remote devices for their transmission has blurred the line between "business" and "non-business" hours.
[342] *Shuey v US* 92 U.S. 73 (1875).
[343] *Pickfords Ltd v Celestica Ltd* [2003] EWCA Civ 1741 at [26].
[344] *Tinn v Hoffmann & Co* (1873) 29 L.T. 271 at 278.
[345] See above, para.2–020.
[346] *Hyde v Wrench* (1840) 3 Beav. 334.
[347] See the treatment in *Tinn v Hoffman* (1873) 29 L.T. 271 at 278 of the claimant's letter of November 27.
[348] *Stevenson Jacques & Co v Maclean* (1880) 5 Q.B.D. 346 at 349.
[349] See above, para.2–002.
[350] *Gibson v Manchester CC* [1979] 1 W.L.R. 294 at 302.

he should not be bound by an acceptance posted after the rejection and also reaching the offeror after the rejection. To hold the offeror bound,[351] merely because the acceptance was *posted* before the rejection had reached him, could expose him to hardship, particularly when he had acted on the rejection, e.g. by disposing elsewhere of the subject-matter. If the offeree has posted a rejection and then wishes, after all, to accept the offer, he should ensure that his subsequently-posted acceptance actually comes to the notice of the offeror before the latter receives the rejection.

(c) Lapse of Time

An offer which is expressly stated to last for a fixed time cannot be accepted after that time; and an offer which stipulates for acceptance "by return" (of post) must normally[352] be accepted either by a return postal communication or by some other, no less expeditious method. An offer which contains no express provision limiting its duration terminates after lapse of a reasonable time.[353] What is a reasonable time depends on such circumstances as the nature of the subject-matter and the means used to communicate the offer. Thus an offer to sell a perishable thing, or one whose price is liable to sudden fluctuations, would determine after a short time. The same is true of an offer made by telegram[354] or by some other, at least equally speedy, means of communication such as e-mail.   2–064

Extension of reasonable time. The period that would normally constitute a reasonable time for acceptance may be extended if the conduct of the offeree within that period indicates an intention to accept and this is known to the offeror. Such conduct would often of itself amount to acceptance, but this possibility may be ruled out by the terms of the offer, which may require the acceptance to be by written notice sent to a specified address.[355] In such a case the offeree's conduct, though it could not *amount* to an acceptance, could nevertheless prolong the time for giving a proper notice of acceptance. For the offeree's conduct to have this effect, it must be known to the offeror; for if this were not the case the offeror might reasonably suppose that the offer had not been accepted within the normal period of time, and act in reliance on that belief: e.g. by disposing elsewhere of the subject-matter.   2–065

(d) Occurrence of Condition

An offer which expressly provides that it is to terminate on the occurrence of some condition cannot be accepted after that condition has occurred; and such a provision may also be implied. If an offer to buy or hire-purchase goods is made after the offeror has examined them, it may be an implied term of the offer that they should at the time of acceptance still be in substantially the same state as that   2–066

---

[351] Under the "posting rule", above, para.2–030.

[352] See above, para.2–040.

[353] *Ramsgate Victoria Hotel Co Ltd v Montefiore* (1866) L.R. 1 Ex. 109; *Cemco Leasing SpA v Rediffusion Ltd* [1987] F.T.L.R. 201; *L.J. Korbetis v Transgrain Shipping BV* [2005] EWHC 1345 (QB).

[354] *Quenerduaine v Cole* (1883) 32 W.R. 185.

[355] As in *Manchester Diocesan Council for Education v Commercial and General Investments Ltd* [1970] 1 W.L.R. 241.

in which they were when the offer was made. Such an offer cannot be accepted after the goods have been seriously damaged.[356] On the same principle, it is submitted that the offer which is made by bidding at an auction by implication provides that it is to lapse as soon as a higher bid is made.[357]

(e) Death

2–067	One possible view is that the death of either party terminates the offer, as the parties can no longer reach agreement.[358] But there may be a contract in spite of a demonstrable lack of agreement if to hold the contrary would cause serious inconvenience.[359] In accordance with this principle, it is submitted that the death of either party should not of itself terminate the offer except in the case of such "personal" contracts as are discharged by the death of either party.[360]

2–068	**Death of offeror.** The effect of the death of the offeror has been considered in a number of cases concerning continuing guarantees. In general, a continuing guarantee, e.g. of a bank overdraft, is divisible[361]: it is a continuing offer by the guarantor, accepted from time to time as the banker makes loans to his customer. Each loan is a separate acceptance, turning the offer pro tanto into a binding contract. It seems that such a guarantee is not terminated merely by the death of the guarantor.[362] But it is terminated if the bank knows that the guarantor has died and that his personal representatives have no power under his will to continue the guarantee[363]; or if for some other reason it is inequitable for the bank to charge the guarantor's estate.[364] If the guarantee expressly provides that it can be terminated only by notice given by the guarantor *or his personal representatives*, the death of the guarantor, even if known to the bank, will not terminate the guarantee: express notice must be given.[365]

2–069	**Death of offeree.** Two cases have some bearing on the effect of the death of the offeree. In *Reynolds v Atherton*[366] an offer to sell shares was made in 1911 "to the directors of" a company. An attempt to accept the offer was made in 1919 by the survivors of the persons who were directors in 1911 and by the personal representatives of those who had since died. The purported acceptance was held to be ineffective; and Warrington L.J. said obiter that an offer "made to a living person who ceases to be a living person before the offer is accepted . . . is no longer an offer at all". The actual ground for the decision, however, was that the offer had, on its true construction, been made to the directors of the company for the time

---

[356] *Financings Ltd v Stimson* [1962] 1 W.L.R. 1184; cf. *Canning v Farquhar* (1885) 16 Q.B.D. 722; *Looker v Law Union & Rock Ins Co Ltd* [1928] 1 K.B. 554

[357] See above, para.2–008.

[358] *Dickinson v Dodds* (1876) 2 Ch.D. 463 at 475.

[359] See above, para.2–058.

[360] e.g. contracts of employment or agency: below, para.16–106. In such cases the legal effects of saying that the offer was terminated, so that there was never any contract, is likely to differ from those of saying that there had been a contract which had been discharged: e.g. Law Reform (Frustrated Contracts) Act 1943 could apply to the latter, but not to the former, situation.

[361] See above, para.2–054.

[362] *Bradbury v Morgan* (1862) 1 H. & C. 249; *Coulthart v Clementson* (1879) 5 Q.B.D. 42 at 46.

[363] *Coulthart v Clementson* (1879) 5 Q.B.D. 42.

[364] *Harris v Fawcett* (1873) L.R. 8 Ch.App. 866.

[365] *Re Silvester* [1895] 1 Ch. 573.

[366] (1921) 125 L.T. 690, affirmed (1922) 127 L.T. 189.

being, and not to those who happened to hold office in 1911. In *Kennedy v Thomassen*[367] an offer to buy annuities was accepted by the solicitors of the annuitant after she had, without the solicitors' knowledge, died. This acceptance was held to be ineffective on the grounds that the solicitors' authority was terminated by their client's death and that the acceptance was made under a mistake.[368] Neither case supports the view that an offer can never be accepted after the offeree's death. It is submitted that, where an offer related to a contract which was not "personal",[369] it might, on its true construction, be held to have been made to the offeree or to his executors, and that such an offer could be accepted after the death of the original offeree.

(f) Supervening Incapacity

Mental incapacity. If an offeror subsequently lacked mental capacity he would not be bound by an acceptance made after this fact had become known to the offeree, or after the offeror's property had been made subject to the control of the court. But the other party would be bound; and an offer made to a person who later lacked mental capacity could be accepted so as to bind the other party. These rules can readily be deduced from the law as to contracts with persons who lack mental capacity.[370]   2–070

Companies governed by the Companies Act 2006. Such a company may lose its capacity to do an act by altering its articles of association.[371] The general rule is that acts done by the company can no longer be called into question on the ground that the company lacked capacity to do them by reason of anything in its constitution[372]; and that, in favour of a person dealing with the company in good faith, the power of the board of directors to bind the company, or to authorise others to do so, is deemed to be free of any limitation under the company's constitution.[373] But a member of the company may bring proceedings to restrain the doing of acts beyond the powers of the directors, except where such acts are done in fulfilment of legal obligations arising from previous acts of the company.[374] The effect of these provisions must be considered on offers made *to* and *by* the company.   2–071

Company as offeree. A company may receive an offer to enter into a contract and then alter its articles of association so as to deprive itself of the capacity to enter into that contract. If it nevertheless accepts the offer, the acceptance is effective in favour of a person who deals with the company in good faith; but before the company has accepted the offer, the directors can be restrained from doing so in proceedings brought by one of its members.   2–072

---

[367] [1929] 1 Ch. 426.
[368] cf. below, para.8–008.
[369] See above, at fn.360.
[370] See below, para.12–052 et seq.
[371] See below, para.12–067.
[372] Companies Act 2006, s.39(1) (modified rules apply to companies which are charities: ss.39(2), 42); below, para.12–068, fn.225.
[373] ibid., s.40(1) (modified rules apply to companies which are charities: ss.40(6), 42; and transactions with directors and their associates: ss.40(6), 41); below, para.12–069.
[374] ibid., s.40(4).

2–073   **Company as offeror.** A company may make an offer to enter into a contract and then alter its articles of association so as to deprive itself of the capacity to enter into that contract. An acceptance of that offer is nevertheless effective in favour of a person dealing with the company in good faith; but it is not entirely clear whether in this situation a member of the company could take proceedings to prevent the conclusion of the contract by the directors. Such proceedings lie only to restrain "the doing of an act"[375] by the directors and since the relevant act (i.e. the making of the offer) would already have been done when the company still had capacity to do it, there seems to be nothing for the member to restrain, unless holding the offer open could be described as a continuing act.

Of course, the company itself could normally withdraw the offer and would be likely to do so in pursuance of the policy which had led it to change its articles of association. But this possibility would not be open to the company where it had bound itself not to withdraw the offer, i.e. where it had granted a legally enforceable option[376]; and in such a case a member could not take proceedings to prevent the conclusion of the contract since such proceedings cannot be taken "in respect of an act to be done in fulfilment of a legal obligation arising from a previous act of the company"[377]: i.e. from the grant of the option.

2–074   **Other corporations.**[378] Companies may also be incorporated by Royal Charter or by special legislation. Charter corporations have the legal capacity of a natural person so that an alteration of the charter would not affect the validity of an offer or acceptance made by the corporation.[379] The legal capacity of corporations incorporated by special statute is governed by the statute, and acts not within that capacity are ultra vires[380] and void. An alteration of the statute could therefore prevent the company from accepting an offer made to it, and from being bound by the acceptance of an offer made by it, where the offer was made before the alteration came into effect. In practice, the problem is likely to be dealt with in the statute which changes the capacity of the corporation.

4. SPECIAL CASES

2–075   In some situations already discussed, the analysis of agreement into offer and acceptance gives rise to considerable difficulty,[381] and in others, to be discussed in this section, such analysis is impossible or highly artificial.[382] For this reason, it has been suggested that the analysis is "out of date"[383] and that "you should look at the correspondence as a whole and at the conduct of the parties and see therefrom

---

[375] ibid., s.40(4).
[376] For legally enforceable options, see below, para.3–160.
[377] Companies Act 2006, s.40(4).
[378] Problems of the kind here under discussion cannot arise with regard to limited liability partnerships incorporated under the Limited Liability Partnerships Act 2000 as they have "unlimited capacity" (s.1(3)).
[379] See below, para.12–064; but members of a corporation could bring proceedings to restrain the conclusion of the contract: ibid.
[380] See below, para.12–071.
[381] See above, paras 2–007, 2–017, 2–020.
[382] *Gibson v Manchester CC* [1978] 1 W.L.R. 520 at 523, reversed [1979] 1 W.L.R. 294; cf. *The Eurymedon* [1975] A.C. 154 at 167.
[383] *Butler Machine Tool Co Ltd v Ex-Cell-O Corp (England) Ltd* [1979] 1 W.L.R. 401 at 404; cf. *Interfoto Picture Library Ltd v Stiletto Visual Programmes Ltd* [1989] Ch. 433 at 443.

whether the parties have come to an agreement".[384] The objection to this view, however, is that it provides too little guidance for the courts (or for the legal advisers of the parties) in determining whether agreement has been reached. For this reason, the situations to be discussed below are best regarded as exceptions[385] to a general requirement of offer and acceptance. This approach is supported by cases in which it has been held that there was no contract precisely because there was no offer and acceptance[386]; and by those in which the terms of a contract have been held to depend on the analysis of the negotiation into offer, counter-offer and acceptance.[387] That said, the offer and acceptance analysis does not require "rigorous compliance" and the "the court will, if appropriate, assess a person's conduct over a period and decide whether its cumulative effect is that he has evinced an intention to make the contract."[388]

Multipartite agreements. In *The Satanita*[389] the claimant and the defendant entered their yachts for a regatta. Each signed a letter, addressed to the secretary of the club which organised the regatta, undertaking to obey certain rules during the race. It was held that there was a contract between all the competitors on the terms of the undertaking, though it is not clear whether the contract was made when the competitors entered their yachts or when they actually began to race. In either event, it is difficult to analyse the transaction into offer and acceptance.[390] If the contract was made when the yachts were entered, one would have to say that the entry of the first competitor was an offer and that the entry of the next was an acceptance of that offer and (simultaneously) an offer to yet later competitors; but this view is artificial and unworkable even in theory unless each competitor knew of the existence of previous ones. It would also lead to the conclusion that entries which were put in the post together were cross-offers and thus not binding on each other.[391] If the contract was made when the race began, then it seems that each competitor simultaneously agreed to terms proposed by the officers of the club, and not that each proposed an identical set of terms amounting at the same time to an offer to the others and to an acceptance of the offers at that instant made by them. Even if the second view of the facts could be taken, the "offers" and "acceptances" would all occur at the same moment. Thus they would be cross-offers and would not create a contract. The competitors, no doubt, reached agreement, but they did not do so by a process which can be analysed into offer and acceptance. Similar reasoning would seem to apply to the contract which

2–076

---

[384] *Gibson v Manchester CC* [1978] 1 W.L.R. 520 at 523, reversed [1979] 1 W.L.R. 294.

[385] *Gibson v Manchester CC* [1979] 1 W.L.R. 294 at 297; *G Percy Trentham v Archital Luxfer Ltd* [1993] 1 Lloyd's Rep. 25 at 27, 29–30; *Tekdata Interconnections Ltd v Amphenol* [2009] EWCA Civ 1209; [2010] 1 Lloyd's Rep. 357 at [25].

[386] *The Kapetan Markos NL (No.2)* [1987] 2 Lloyd's Rep. 323 at 331 ("What was the mechanism for offer and acceptance?"); cf. *The Good Helmsman* [1981] 1 Lloyd's Rep. 377 at 409; *The Aramis* [1989] 1 Lloyd's Rep. 213; Treitel [1989] L.M.C.L.Q. 162. The "offer and acceptance" analysis was also regarded as decisive in many of the arbitration cases discussed at para.2–005, above, though it was viewed with scepticism in *The Multibank Holsatia* [1988] 2 Lloyd's Rep. 486 at 491 and in *The Maritime Winner* [1989] 2 Lloyd's Rep. 506 at 515.

[387] e.g. The "battle of forms" cases discussed at paras 2–020—2–021, above.

[388] *Maple Leaf Macro Volatility Master Fund v Rouvroy* [2009] EWHC 257 (Comm); [2009] 1 Lloyd's Rep. 475 at [242], affirmed [2009] EWCA Civ 1334.

[389] [1895] P. 248; affirmed sub nom. *Clarke v Dunraven* [1897] A.C. 59; Phillips 92 L.Q.R. 499.

[390] cf. *Kingscroft Ins Co Ltd v Nissan Fire and Marine Ins Co Ltd* [2000] 1 All E.R. (Comm) 272 at 291 (admission of new members to an existing insurance pool analysed in terms of offer and acceptance).

[391] See above, para.2–049.

governs the legal relations between members of an unincorporated associa-tion.[392]

The above discussion is based on the assumption that all the parties to the alleged multilateral contract were willing to agree to the same terms. Where one of the negotiating parties had refused to accept one of the terms of the proposed contract, no multilateral contract would arise between that party and any of the others, unless the others agreed to be bound to that party on terms excluding the one rejected by him.[393]

2–077 **Reference to third party.** Where two negotiating parties reach deadlock, they may ask a third party to break it. If both simultaneously assent to a solution proposed by him, there is a contract, but it is again impossible to say which party has made the offer and which the acceptance.[394] The same is true where the parties negotiate through a single broker who eventually obtains their consent to the same terms.[395]

5. CERTAINTY

2–078 An agreement is not a binding contract if it lacks certainty, either because it is too vague or because it is obviously incomplete.[396]

(a) Vagueness

2–079 **Agreements too vague to enforce.** An agreement may be so vague that no definite meaning can be given to it without adding new terms. Thus in *G Scammell & Nephew Ltd v Ouston*[397] the House of Lords held that an agreement to buy goods "on hire-purchase" was too vague to be enforced, since there were many kinds of hire-purchase agreements in widely different terms, so that it was impossible to say on which terms the parties intended to contract. Similarly, agreements "subject to war clause",[398] "subject to strike and lockout clause",[399] and "subject to force majeure conditions"[400] have been held too vague, there being no evidence in any of the cases of a customary or usual form of such clauses or conditions.[401] Similar reasoning has sometimes been applied where agreements were made subject to the "satisfaction" of one party.[402] The problems arising from such provisions are discussed later in this chapter.[403] But the courts do not expect commercial documents to be drafted with strict precision, and will, particularly if

[392] See *Artistic Upholstery Ltd v Art Forma (Furniture) Ltd* [1999] 4 All E.R. 277 at 285; though breach of the rules by one member may not, on their true construction, be actionable in damages at the suit of another: *Anderton v Rowland, The Times*, November 5, 1999.
[393] *Azov Shipping Co v Baltic Shipping Co* [1999] 2 Lloyd's Rep. 159 at 165.
[394] Pollock, *Principles of Contract* (13th edn), p.5.
[395] *Pagnan SpA v Feed Products Ltd* [1987] 2 Lloyd's Rep. 601 at 616.
[396] Fridman 76 L.Q.R. 521.
[397] [1941] A.C. 251.
[398] *Bishop & Baxter Ltd v Anglo-Eastern Trading Co* [1944] K.B. 12.
[399] *Love & Stewart Ltd v S Instone & Co* (1917) 33 T.L.R. 475.
[400] *British Electrical Industries Ltd v Patley Pressings Ltd* [1953] 1 W.L.R. 280.
[401] For further illustrations, see below, para.2–080.
[402] *Stabilad Ltd v Stephens & Carter Ltd (No.2)* [1999] 2 All E.R. (Comm) 651 at 659.
[403] See below, para.2–108.

the parties have acted on an agreement,[404] do their best to avoid striking it down on the ground that it is too vague.[405]

Custom and trade usage. Apparent vagueness can be resolved by custom. **2–080** Thus a contract to load coal at Grimsby "on the terms of the usual colliery guarantee" was upheld on proof of the terms usually contained in such guarantees at Grimsby.[406] It has similarly been held that an undertaking to grant a lease of a shop "in prime position" was not too uncertain to be enforced since the phrase was commonly used by persons dealing with shop property, so that its meaning could be determined by expert evidence.[407] And courts often enforce commercial contracts expressed in abbreviations whose meaning is certain and notorious.

Reasonableness. In *Hillas & Co Ltd v Arcos Ltd*,[408] an agreement for the sale **2–081** of timber "of fair specification", was made between persons well acquainted with the timber trade. The agreement was upheld as the standard of reasonableness could be applied to make the otherwise vague phrase certain since the words of the contract imported some objective standard for assessing the quality of the goods to be supplied. The case should be contrasted with one in which a supplier of clothing to a retail chain alleged that there was an implied contract between them not to terminate their long-standing relationship except on reasonable notice. One ground for rejecting the claim was that there were "no objective criteria by which the court could assess what would be reasonable either as to quantity or price."[409]

Duty to resolve uncertainty. An agreement containing a vague phrase may be **2–082** binding because one party is under a duty to resolve the uncertainty. In one case an agreement to sell goods provided for delivery "free on board . . . good Danish port". It was held that the agreement was not too vague: it amounted to a good contract under which the buyer was bound to select the port of shipment.[410]

---

[404] *Brown v Gould* [1972] Ch. 53 at 57–58; *Tito v Waddell (No.2)* [1977] Ch. 106 at 314; *Sudbrook Trading Estate Ltd v Eggleton* [1983] 1 A.C. 444; *The Mercedes Envoy* [1995] 2 Lloyd's Rep. 559 at 564.

[405] "Void for uncertainty is a last resort conclusion": *Shaw v Lighthousexpress* Ltd [2010] EWCA Civ at [21]. See also: *Rahcassi Shipping Co v Blue Star Line* [1969] 1 Q.B. 173; *Nea Agrex SA v Baltic Shipping Co Ltd* [1976] Q.B. 933; *Deutsche Schachtbau-und-Tiefbohrgesellschaft mbH v Ras Al Khairah National Oil Co* [1990] 1 A.C. 295 at 306, reversed on other grounds: [1990] 1 A.C. 295 at 329 et seq; *Scammell v Dicker* [2005] EWCA Civ 405; [2005] 3 All E.R. 838 at [31]; *Schweppe v Harper* [2008] EWCA Civ 442 at [75], [82]; *Durham Tees Valley Airport Ltd v Bmibaby Ltd* [2010] EWCA Civ 485; [2011] 1 Lloyd's Rep. 68.

[406] *Shamrock SS Co v Storey & Co* (1899) 81 L.T. 413; cf. *Hart v Hart* (1881) 18 Ch.D. 670; *Baynham v Philips Electronics (UK) Ltd*, The Times, July 19, 1995.

[407] *Ashburn Anstalt v Arnold* [1989] Ch. 1 at 27, overruled on another ground in *Prudential Assurance Co Ltd v London Residuary Body* [1992] A.C. 386.

[408] (1932) 147 L.T. 503 (and see below, para.2–095); *Sweet & Maxwell Ltd v Universal News Services Ltd* [1964] 2 Q.B. 699; cf. *Greater London Council v Connolly* [1970] 2 Q.B. 100; *Finchbourne Ltd v Rodrigues* [1976] 3 All E.R. 581; *Scammell v Dicker* [2005] EWCA Civ 405; [2005] 3 All E.R. 838; *Bear Stearns Bank Plc v Forum Global Equity Ltd* [2007] EWHC 1576 (Comm) at [64]; *Furmans Electrical Contractors Ltd v Elecref Ltd* [2009] EWCA Civ 170 at [33].

[409] *Baird Textile Holdings Ltd v Marks & Spencer Plc* [2001] EWCA Civ 274; [2002] 1 All E.R. (Comm) 737 at [30]. cf. *Schweppe v Harper* [2008] EWCA Civ 442 at [72] ("reasonable finance" too uncertain).

[410] *David T Boyd & Co v Louis Louca* [1973] 1 Lloyd's Rep. 209; cf. *Siew Soon Wah v Yong Tong Hong* [1973] A.C. 831; *Pagnan SpA v Feed Products Ltd* [1987] 2 Lloyd's Rep. 601; *Bulk Trading Co Ltd v Zenziper Grains and Feedstuffs* [2001] 1 Lloyd's Rep. 357 (seller's duty to specify place of delivery under f.o.t. contract).

2–083   **Meaningless and self-contradictory phrases.** The court will make considerable efforts to give meaning to an apparently meaningless phrase[411]; but, even where these efforts fail, the presence of such phrases does not necessarily vitiate the agreement. In *Nicolene Ltd v Simmonds*[412] steel bars were bought on terms which were certain except for a clause that the sale was subject to "the usual conditions of acceptance". There being no such usual conditions, it was held that the phrase was meaningless, but that this did not vitiate the whole contract: the words were severable and could be ignored. A self-contradictory clause can be treated in the same way.[413] Thus where an arbitration clause provided for arbitration of "any dispute" in London and of "any other dispute" in Moscow the court disregarded the clause and determined the dispute itself.[414] Such cases show that the question whether a meaningless phrase vitiates the contract, or can be ignored, depends on the importance which the parties may be considered to have attached to it. If it is simply verbiage, not intended to add anything to an otherwise complete agreement, or if it relates to a matter of relatively minor importance, it can be ignored. But if the parties intend it to govern some vital aspect of their relationship, its vagueness will vitiate the entire agreement.

(b) Incompleteness

2–084   An agreement may be incomplete because the parties have left important points unsettled,[415] or because the agreement they have reached expressly requires further agreement to be reached on points as yet left open.[416]

(i) *Agreement in principle only*[417]

2–085   **No contract if agreement incomplete in important respect.** Parties may reach agreement on essential matters of principle, but leave important points unsettled, so that their agreement is incomplete.[418] There is, for example, no contract if an agreement for a lease fails to specify the date on which the term is to commence.[419] Similarly, an agreement for the sale of land by instalments is not a binding contract if it provides for conveyance of "a proportionate part" as each instalment of the price is paid but fails to specify which part was to be conveyed on each payment.[420]

---

[411] *The Tropwind* [1982] 1 Lloyd's Rep. 232.

[412] [1953] 1 Q.B. 543; discussed in *Heisler v Anglo-Dal Ltd* [1954] 1 W.L.R. 1273; cf. *Slater v Raw, The Times*, October 15, 1977; *The Scaptrade* [1981] 2 Lloyd's Rep. 425 at 432, affirmed without reference to this point [1983] 2 A.C. 694.

[413] *Scammell v Dicker* [2005] EWCA Civ 405; [2005] 3 All E.R. 838 at [31].

[414] *E R J Lovelock v Exportles* [1968] 1 Lloyd's Rep. 163; cf. *The Star Texas* [1993] 2 Lloyd's Rep. 445.

[415] See paras 2–085—2–087.

[416] See paras 2–088—2–102.

[417] Lücke 3 Adelaide L.Rev. 46.

[418] *Bols Distilleries BV v Superior Yacht Services Ltd* [2006] UKPC 45; [2007] 1 W.L.R. 12; *Cobbe v Yeoman's Row Management Ltd* [2008] UKHL 55; [2008] 1 W.L.R. 1752 (below, para.3–127); *Whittle Movers Ltd v Hollywood Express Ltd* [2009] EWCA Civ 1189; [2009] 2 C.L.C. 771 at [14].

[419] *Harvey v Pratt* [1965] 1 W.L.R. 1025.

[420] *Bushwall Properties Ltd v Vortex Properties Ltd* [1976] 1 W.L.R. 591; cf. *Hadley v Kemp* [1999] E.M.L.R. 589 at 628; *London & Regional Investments Ltd v TBI Plc Belfast International Airport Ltd* [2002] EWCA Civ 355.

Not all details necessarily required. On the other hand, the agreement does 2–086
not have to be worked out in meticulous detail.[421] Under the Sale of Goods Act
1979, an agreement for the sale of goods may be binding as soon as the parties have
agreed to buy and sell, where the remaining details can be determined by the
standard of reasonableness or by law. Even failure to fix the price is not necessarily
fatal in such a case. Section 8(2) of the Act provides that, if no price is determined
by the contract, a reasonable price must be paid. Under s.15(1) of the Supply of
Goods and Services Act 1982, a reasonable sum must similarly be paid where a
contract for the supply of services fails to fix the remuneration to be paid for
them.[422] These statutory provisions assume that the agreement amounts to a
contract in spite of its failure to fix the price or remuneration. The very fact that
the parties have not reached agreement on this vital point may indicate that there
is *no* contract, e.g. because the price or remuneration is to be fixed by further
agreement.[423] In such a case, the statutory provisions for payment of a reasonable
sum do not apply. There may, however, be a claim for payment of such a sum at
common law: e.g., where work is done in the belief that there was a contract or in
the expectation that the negotiations between the parties would result in the
conclusion of a contract.[424] Such liability arises in restitution, in spite of the fact
that there was *no* contract. It follows that the party doing the work, though he is
entitled to a reasonable sum, is not liable in damages, e.g. for failing to do the work
within a reasonable time.[425] If the claim arose under a contract by virtue of s.15(1)
of the 1982 Act, the party doing the work would be both entitled and liable.

Even an agreement for the sale of land dealing only with the barest essentials
may be regarded as complete if that was the clear intention of the parties. Thus in
Perry v Suffields Ltd[426] an offer to sell a public house with vacant possession for
£7,000 was accepted without qualification. It was held that there was a binding
contract, in spite of the fact that many important points such as the date of
completion[427] and the question of paying a deposit, were left open.[428] In another
case[429] a buyer and seller of corn feed pellets had reached agreement on the
"cardinal terms of the deal: product, price, quantity, period of shipment, range of
loading ports and governing contract terms".[430] The agreement was held to have
contractual force even though the parties had not yet reached agreement on a
number of other important points, such as the loading port,[431] the rate of loading
and certain payments (other than the price) which might in certain events become
due under the contract. In all these cases, the courts took the view that the parties
intended to be bound at once in spite of the fact that further significant terms were

---

[421] *First Energy (UK) Ltd v Hungarian International Bank Ltd* [1993] 2 Lloyd's Rep. 195 at 205; *Bear Stearns Bank Plc v Forum Global Equity Ltd* [2007] EWHC 1576 (Comm).
[422] cf. at common law, *Way v Latilla* [1937] 3 All E.R. 759; *The Tropwind* [1982] 1 Lloyd's Rep. 232; *Michael Elliott & Partners v UK Land* [1991] 1 E.G.L.R. 39; *Furmans Electrical Contractors Ltd v Elecref Ltd* [2009] EWCA Civ 170 at [32]; and see, as to agents' commissions, below, para.16–084.
[423] e.g. *May & Butcher v R.* [1934] 2 K.B. 17n.; *Courtney & Fairbairn Ltd v Tolaini Bros (Hotels) Ltd* [1975] 1 W.L.R. 297; Dugdale and Lowe, [1976] J.B.L. 312; *Chamberlain v Boodle & King* [1982] 1 W.L.R. 1443n; *Russell Bros (Paddington) Ltd v John Elliott Management Ltd* (1995) 11 Const. L.J. 377.
[424] See below, para.22–021.
[425] *BSC v Cleveland Bridge & Engineering Co Ltd* [1984] 1 All E.R. 504.
[426] [1916] 2 Ch. 187; *Elias v George Sahely & Co (Barbados) Ltd* [1982] 3 All E.R. 801.
[427] cf. *Storer v Manchester CC* [1974] 1 W.L.R. 1403.
[428] For the resolution of such points, see below, para.2–090.
[429] *Pagnan SpA v Feed Products Ltd* [1987] 2 Lloyd's Rep. 601.
[430] ibid. at 611.
[431] cf. above, para.2–084, fn.410.

to be agreed later;[432] and that even their failure to reach such agreement would not invalidate the contract unless without such agreement the contract was unworkable or too uncertain[433] to be enforced.

2–087   **Further agreement needed for continued operation of contract.** A distinction must be drawn between cases in which agreement on such matters as the price is required for the making, and those in which it is required for the *continued operation*, of a contract. The latter possibility is illustrated by a case[434] in which an agreement for the supply of services for 10 years fixed the fee to be paid only for the first of those two years. On the parties' failure to fix the fee in later years, it was held that they had intended to enter into a 10-year contract and that a term was to be implied into that contract for payment of a reasonable fee in those later years.

(ii) *Agreements "subject to contract"*

2–088   An agreement may be made "subject to contract". Such an agreement is incomplete until the details of a formal contract have been settled and approved by the parties.[435] But even when the terms of the formal contract have been agreed, there is no binding contract until the parties have gone through the procedure necessary to indicate that the agreement is no longer "subject to contract", e.g. in contracts for the sale of land by private treaty, when there has been an "exchange of contracts".[436] Before the "exchange", there is no uncertainty as to the terms of the agreement, but there is no contract because neither party intends to be legally bound until the "exchange of contracts" takes place. Since the principal effect of the stipulation that an agreement is "subject to contract" is to negate the intention of the parties to be bound, it is dealt with in further detail in Ch.4.[437]

(iii) *Execution of formal document required*

2–089   One possible effect of a stipulation that an agreement is to be embodied in a formal written document is that the agreement is regarded by the parties as incomplete, or as not intended to be legally binding,[438] until the terms of the

---

[432] cf. *RTS Flexible Systems Ltd v Molkerei Alois Müller GbmH* [2010] UKSC 14, [2010] 1 W.L.R. 753 at [45].

[433] See above, para.2–079.

[434] *Mamidoil-Jetoil Arab Petroleum Co SA v Okta Crude Oil Refinery AD* [2001] EWCA Civ 406; [2001] 2 Lloyd's Rep. 76. For further proceedings arising out of the same contract, see [2003] 1 Lloyd's Rep. 1; below, para.2–095.

[435] *Winn v Bull* (1877) 7 Ch.D. 29. cf. *The Junior K* [1988] 2 Lloyd's Rep. 583; (sale of ship and charterparty intended to be "subject to details" not binding before details settled); *The CPC Gallia* [1994] 1 Lloyd's Rep. 68; Debattista [1985] L.M.C.L.Q. 241; *Drake Scull Engineering Ltd v Higgs & Hill (Northern) Ltd* (1995) 11 Const.L.J. 214; *Regalian Properties Plc v London Dockland Development Corp* [1995] 1 W.L.R. 212; contrast *Prudential Assurance Co Ltd v Mount Eden Land Co Ltd* [1997] 1 E.G.L.R. 37 (consent to alterations given by landlord "subject to licence" held effective as the consent was a unilateral act, so that no question of agreement arose).

[436] See below, para.4–007.

[437] See below, para.4–006 et seq.

[438] *BSC v Cleveland Bridge & Engineering Co Ltd* [1984] 1 All E.R. 504; *Ignazio Messina Co v Polskie Linie Oceaniczne* [1995] 2 Lloyd's Rep. 566; *Petromec Inc v Petroleo Brasileiro SA Petrobas* [2005] EWCA Civ 891; [2006] 1 Lloyd's Rep. 161 at [74]–[77]; *Diamond Build Ltd v Clapham Park Homes Ltd* [2008] EWHC 1439 (TCC); 119 Con L.R. 32 (where the parties remained bound only by a letter of intent as a result).

formal document are agreed and the document is duly executed in accordance with the terms of the preliminary agreement (e.g. by signature).[439] A second possibility is that such a document is intended only as a solemn record of an already complete and binding agreement[440]: for example, a contract of insurance is generally regarded as complete as soon as the insurer initials a slip setting out the main terms of the contract, even though the execution of a formal policy is contemplated.[441] The question whether an agreement which expressly requires the execution of a formal document is incomplete depends on the purpose of the requirement in each case[442]; and there is no point multiplying examples.[443]

Even where, under the principles here stated, the agreement has no contractual force, a party to it may be liable on other grounds: e.g. under a separate preliminary contract coming into existence when one party begins to render services requested by the other and entitling the former to a reasonable remuneration for those services[444]; or under a constructive trust.[445]

(iv) *Terms left open*

Parties may be reluctant to commit themselves to a rigid long-term contract, particularly when prices and other factors affecting performance are likely to fluctuate. They therefore attempt sometimes to introduce an element of flexibility into the agreement; a number of devices which have been used for this purpose call for discussion.   **2–090**

Terms "to be agreed". One possibility is to provide that certain matters (such as prices, quantities or delivery dates) are to be agreed later, or from time to time. The question whether the resulting agreement is a binding contract then depends primarily on the intention of the parties; and inferences as to this intention may   **2–091**

---

[439] *Okura & Co Ltd v Navara Shipping Corp SA* [1982] 2 Lloyd's Rep. 537; cf. *New England Reinsurance Corp v Messaghios Insurance Co SA* [1992] 2 Lloyd's Rep. 251; *Thoresen & Co (Bangkok) Ltd v Fathom Marine Co* [2004] EWHC 167; [2004] 1 Lloyd's Rep. 622; *Investec Bank (UK) Ltd v Zulman* [2010] EWCA Civ 536; *Grant v Bragg* [2009] EWCA Civ 1228; [2010] 1 All E.R. (Comm) 1166; *Whittle Movers Ltd v Hollywood Express Ltd* [2009] EWCA Civ 1189; [2009] 2 C.L.C. 771.

[440] *Rossiter v Miller* (1878) 3 App.Cas. 1124; cf. *Filby v Hounsell* [1896] 2 Ch. 737; *Branca v Cobarro* [1947] K.B. 854; *E R Ives Investments Ltd v High* [1967] 2 Q.B. 379; *The Blankenstein* [1985] 1 W.L.R. 435; *The Anemone* [1987] 1 Lloyd's Rep. 547; *Jayaar Impex Ltd v Toaken Group Ltd* [1996] 2 Lloyd's Rep. 437; *Harvey Shopfitters Ltd v ADI Ltd* [2003] EWCA Civ 1752; [2004] 2 All E.R. 982; *Bryen & Langley Ltd v Boston* [2005] EWCA Civ 973; [2005] C.I.L.L. 2261; *Maple Leaf Macro Volatility Master Fund v Rouvroy* [2009] EWCA Civ 1334 at [16].

[441] *Ionides v Pacific Insurance Co* (1871) L.R. 6 Q.B. 674 at 684; *General Reinsurance Corp v Forsakringsaktiebolaget Fennia Patria* [1983] Q.B. 856; *Youell v Bland Welch & Co Ltd* [1992] 2 Lloyd's Rep. 127 at 140–141; *HIH Casualty & General Insurance Ltd v New Hampshire Insurance* [2001] EWCA Civ 735; [2001] 2 Lloyd's Rep. 161 at [86]–[87].

[442] *Von Hatzfeldt-Wildenburg v Alexander* [1912] 1 Ch. 284 at 288–289; *Immingham Storage Co Ltd v Clear Plc* [2011] EWCA Civ 89.

[443] For an extensive survey of the authorities and the considerations to be derived from them, see *Benourad v Compass Group Plc* [2010] EWHC 1882 (QB) at [106].

[444] *The Kurnia Dewi* [1997] 1 Lloyd's Rep. 553; cf. *Galliard Homes Ltd v Jarvis Interiors* [2000] C.L.C. 411, where the incomplete agreement expressly provided for such a remuneration in the events which happened.

[445] *Banner Homes Ltd v Luff Development Ltd* [2000] Ch. 372 (party to joint venture agreement, which lacked contractual force, acquiring proposed subject-matter for himself); contrast *London & Regional Investments Ltd v TBI Plc Belfast International Airport Ltd* [2002] EWCA Civ 355 (where such an agreement was expressly "subject to contract": see below, para.4–006 et seq.).

be drawn both from the importance of the matter left over for further agreement, and from the extent to which the parties have acted on the agreement.

2–092 **Agreements found to be unenforceable.** Sometimes such agreements have no contractual force. In *May & Butcher v R.*[446] an agreement for the sale of tentage provided that the price, dates of payment and manner of delivery should be agreed from time to time. The House of Lords held that the agreement was incomplete as it left vital matters still to be settled. Had the agreement simply been silent on these points, they could perhaps have been settled in accordance with the provisions of the Sale of Goods Act 1979[447]; or by the standard of reasonableness[448]; but the parties showed that this was not their intention by providing that such points were to be settled by further agreement between them. It has similarly been held that a lease at "a rent to be agreed" was not a binding contract.[449] In these cases, the most natural inference to be drawn from the fact that the parties left such an important matter as the price to be settled by further agreement was that they did not intend to be bound until they had agreed on the price. Even where the points left outstanding are of relatively minor importance, there will be no contract if it appears from the words used or other circumstances that the parties did not intend to be bound until agreement on these points had been reached.[450] A fortiori they are not bound by a term requiring outstanding points to be agreed if that term forms part of an agreement which is itself not binding because it was made without any intention of entering into contractual relations.[451]

2–093 **Agreements found to be enforceable.** Where it can be inferred that the parties intended to be bound immediately, in spite of the provision requiring further agreement, a binding contract can be created at once[452]; for the courts are "reluctant to hold void for uncertainty any provision that was intended to have legal effect".[453] This judicial attitude is illustrated by *Foley v Classique Coaches Ltd.*[454] The claimant owned a petrol-filling station and adjoining land. He sold the land to the defendants on condition that they should enter into an agreement to buy petrol for the purpose of their motor-coach business exclusively from him. This agreement was duly executed, but the defendants broke it, and argued that it was incomplete because it provided that the petrol should be bought "at a price agreed by the parties from time to time". The Court of Appeal rejected this

[446] [1934] 2 K.B. 17n.; cf. *British Homophone Ltd v Kunz* (1935) 152 L.T. 589; *The Shamah* [1981] 1 Lloyd's Rep. 40 at 83; *The Good Helmsman* [1981] 1 Lloyd's Rep. 377 at 409; *The Gudermes* [1985] 2 Lloyd's Rep. 623; *Grow With Us Ltd v Green Thumb (UK) Ltd* [2006] EWCA Civ 1201 at [29], where it was found there was not even an *agreement* to agree.
[447] See above, para.2–086.
[448] cf. *Mamidoil-Jetoil Greek Petroleum SA v Okta Crude Oil Refinery AD* [2001] EWCA Civ 406; [2001] 2 Lloyd's Rep. 76, esp. at [73]; *Malcolm v Chancellor, Masters & Scholars of the University of Oxford, The Times,* December 19, 1990.
[449] *King's Motors (Oxford) Ltd v Lax* [1970] 1 W.L.R. 426; cf. *King v King* (1981) 41 P. & C.R. 311 (rent review clause).
[450] *The Gladys* [1994] 2 Lloyd's Rep. 402; *Ignazio Messina & Co v Polskie Linie Oceaniczne* [1995] 2 Lloyd's Rep. 566.
[451] *Orion Insurance Plc v Sphere Drake Insurance Plc* [1992] 1 Lloyd's Rep. 239.
[452] *Pagnan SpA v Freed Products Ltd* [1987] 2 Lloyd's Rep. 601.
[453] *Brown v Gould* [1972] Ch. 53 at 57–58; cf. *Smith v Morgan* [1971] 1 W.L.R. 803 at 807; *Snelling v John G Snelling Ltd* [1973] 1 Q.B. 87 at 93; *Queensland Electricity Generating Board v New Hope Colliery Pty Ltd* [1989] 1 Lloyd's Rep. 205 at 210.
[454] [1934] 2 K.B. 1.

argument and held that, in default of agreement, a reasonable price must be paid.[455] *May & Butcher v R.*[456] was distinguished on a number of grounds: the agreement in *Foley*'s case was contained in a stamped document; it was believed by both parties to be binding and had been acted upon for a number of years; it contained an arbitration clause in a somewhat unusual form which was construed to apply "to any failure to agree as to the price"[457]; and it formed part of a larger bargain under which the defendants had acquired the land at a price which was no doubt fixed on the assumption that they would be bound to buy all their petrol from the claimant.[458] While none of these factors in itself is conclusive,[459] their cumulative effect seems to be sufficient to distinguish the two cases.[460]

Thus an agreement is not incomplete *merely* because it calls for some further agreement between the parties:

"Even if certain terms of economic or other significance to the parties have not been finalised, an objective appraisal of their words and conduct may lead to the conclusion that they did not intend agreement of such terms to be a pre-condition to a concluded and legally binding agreement."[461]

Even the parties' later failure to agree on the matters left outstanding will vitiate the contract only if it makes the agreement "unworkable or void for uncertainty."[462] Often, the failure will not have this effect, for it may be possible to resolve the uncertainty in one of the ways already discussed, e.g. by applying the standard of reasonableness[463]; or by regarding the matter to be negotiated as of such subsidiary importance[464] as not to negative the intention of the parties to be bound by the more significant terms to which they have agreed.[465] There can be no doubt as to the commercial convenience of this approach. Commercial agreements are often intended to be binding in principle even though the parties are not at the time able or willing to settle all the details. For example, contracts of

---

[455] cf. *British Bank for Foreign Trade v Novinex* [1949] 1 K.B. 623; *Beer v Bowden* [1981] 1 W.L.R. 522; *Thomas Bates & Son Ltd v Wyndham's (Lingerie) Ltd* [1981] 1 W.L.R. 505 at 518–519; *The Tropwind* [1982] 1 Lloyd's Rep. 232 at 236; *Voest Alpine Intertrading GmbH v Chevron International Oil Co Ltd* [1987] 2 Lloyd's Rep. 547; *Global Container Lines Ltd v State Black Sea Shipping Co* [1999] 1 Lloyd's Rep. 127 at 155; *Mamidoil-Jetoil* case above, fn.434.

[456] See above, at fn.446.

[457] [1934] 2 K.B. 1 at 10; the clause covered disputes as to "the *subject matter or* construction of this agreement," while the arbitration clause in *May & Butcher v R.* covered "disputes with reference to or arising out of this agreement." For the distinction between the two forms of clause, see *Heyman v Darwins* [1942] A.C. 356 at 382, 392; cf. also *Vosper Thornycroft Ltd v Ministry of Defence* [1976] 1 Lloyd's Rep. 58; *Queensland Electricity Generating Board v New Hope Collieries Pty Ltd* [1989] 1 Lloyd's Rep. 205.

[458] Scrutton L.J. said at 7 that he was glad to decide in favour of the claimant "because I do not regard the [defendants'] contention as an honest one".

[459] R.S.T.C. 49 L.Q.R. 316.

[460] *Foley*'s case was approved by the House of Lords in *G Scammell & Nephew Ltd v Ouston* [1941] A.C. 251.

[461] *RTS Flexible Systems Ltd v Molkerei Alois Müller GmbH & Co KG* [2010] UKSC 14; [2010] 1 W.L.R. 753 at [45], per Lord Clarke; cf. *Wilson Smithett & Cape (Sugar) Ltd v Bangladesh Sugar & Food Industries Ltd* [1986] 1 Lloyd's Rep. 378 at 386.

[462] *Pagnan SpA v Feed Products Ltd* [1987] 2 Lloyd's Rep. 601 at 619; *Bear Stearns Bank Plc v Forum Global Equity Ltd* [2007] EWHC 1576 (Comm) at [155].

[463] See above para.2–081; or by imposing on one party the duty to resolve the uncertainty: para.2–082, fn.410; *Pagnan SpA v Feed Products Ltd*, above.

[464] Though this point is not decisive: see above para.2–092, fn.450.

[465] *Nelson v Stewart* (1991) S.L.R. 523.

insurance may be made "at a premium to be arranged" when immediate cover is required but there is no time to go into all the details at once: such agreements are perfectly valid and a reasonable premium must be paid.[466] All this is not to say that the courts will hold parties bound when they have not yet reached substantial agreement[467]; but once they have reached such agreement it is not necessarily fatal that some points (even important ones) remain to be settled by further negotiation.

2–094   **Options and rights of pre-emption.** An option to purchase land "at a price to be agreed" is not a binding contract[468]; but such an option must be distinguished from a "right of pre-emption" by which a landowner agrees to give the purchaser the right to buy "at a figure to be agreed" should the landowner wish to sell.[469] An *option* has at least some of the characteristics of an offer[470] in that it can become a contract of sale when the purchaser accepts it by exercising the option; and it cannot have this effect where it fails to specify the price. A *right of pre-emption* is not itself an offer[471] but an undertaking to make an offer in certain specified future circumstances. An agreement conferring such a right is therefore not void for uncertainty merely because it fails to specify the price. It obliges the landowner to offer the land to the purchaser at the price at which he is prepared to sell; and if the purchaser accepts that offer there is no uncertainty as to price.[472] This is so even though the parties have described the right as an "option" when its true legal nature is that of a right of pre-emption.[473]

2–095   **Criteria specified in the agreement.** An agreement may fail to specify matters such as price or quality but lay down *criteria* for determining those matters. For example, in *Hillas & Co Ltd v Arcos Ltd*[474] an option to buy timber was held binding even though it did not specify the price, since it provided for the price to be calculated by reference to an official price list. Even a provision that hire under a charterparty was in specified events to be "equitably decreased by an amount to be mutually agreed" has been held sufficiently certain to be enforced:

---

[466] *Gliksten & Son Ltd v State Assurance Co* (1922) 10 Ll.L.Rep. 604; cf. Marine Insurance Act 1906, s.31(2); contrast *American Airline Inc v Hope* [1973] 1 Lloyd's Rep. 233, affirmed [1974] 2 Lloyd's Rep. 301 ("at an additional premium *and geographical area* to be agreed").

[467] See *Shackleford's Case* (1866) L.R. 1 Ch.App. 567; *Loftus v Roberts* (1902) 18 T.L.R. 532; *The Intra Transporter* [1986] 2 Lloyd's Rep. 132; *Pagnan SpA v Granaria BV* [1986] 2 Lloyd's Rep. 547; *Alfred McAlpine Construction Ltd v Panatown Ltd* [2001] EWCA Civ 485; (2001) 67 Con.L.R. 224 at [35].

[468] See *Brown v Gould* [1972] Ch. 52 (where, however, the option was binding for the reason stated below, fn.474).

[469] *Pritchard v Briggs* [1980] Ch. 339. For the purposes of the Landlord and Tenants (Covenants) Act 1995, "'option' includes a right of first refusal:" s.1(6).

[470] See below, para.3–160; *Bircham & Co Nominees (No.2) Ltd v Worrell Holdings Ltd* [2001] EWCA Civ 775; (2001) P. & C.R. 427 at [41].

[471] *Bircham & Co Nominees (No.2) Ltd v Worrell Holdings Ltd* [2001] EWCA Civ 775; (2001) P. & C.R. 427 at [16], [23]; *Tiffany Investments Ltd v Bircham & Co Nominees (No.2) Ltd* [2003] EWCA Civ 1759; [2004] 2 P. & C.R. 10.

[472] *Smith v Morgan* [1971] 1 W.L.R. 803; cf. *Snelling v John G Snelling* [1973] 1 Q.B. 87 at 93; *Miller v Lakefield Estates Ltd* [1988] 1 E.G.L.R. 212 (where some doubts were expressed about *Smith v Morgan*).

[473] See *Fraser v Thames Television Ltd* [1984] Q.B. 44.

[474] (1932) 147 L.T. 503; cf. *Miller v F A Sadd & Son Ltd* [1981] 3 All E.R. 265; *Mamidoil-Jetoil Greek Petroleum Company SA v Okta Crude Oil Refinery AD* [2003] 1 Lloyd's Rep. 1 at [161]–[165]; *Brown v Gould* [1972] Ch. 53 (option to renew a lease "at a rent to be fixed having regard to the market value of the premises")

it was said that "equitably" meant "fairly and reasonably"[475] and that a "purely objective standard has been prescribed."[476] Where, on the other hand, an agreement provided for payment of a fixed percentage of the "open market value" of shares in a *private* company, it was held that these words did not provide a sufficiently precise criterion since there was more than one formula for calculating the market value of shares in such a company.[477]

Machinery specified in the agreement. Alternatively, the agreement may provide *machinery* for resolving matters originally left open. Perhaps the most striking illustration of this possibility is provided by cases in which such matters are to be resolved by the decision of one party, but clear words are required to achieve that result[478] and the power which is conferred is limited by an implied term that it must not be exercised "dishonestly, for an improper purpose, capriciously or arbitrarily".[479] Similarly, an arbitration clause can validly provide for the arbitration to take place at one of two or more places to be selected by one of the parties.[480] Agreements are a fortiori not incomplete merely because they provide that outstanding points shall be determined by arbitration,[481] or by the courts,[482] or by the valuation of a third party.[483] The Sale of Goods Act 1979 provides that if the third party "cannot or does not make the valuation, the agreement is avoided"[484]; but an agreement is not necessarily ineffective merely because the agreed machinery fails to work. In *Sudbrook Trading Estate Ltd v Eggleton*[485] a lease gave the tenant the option to purchase the premises "at such price as may be agreed upon by two Valuers, one to be nominated by" each party. The landlord having refused to appoint a valuer, the House of Lords held that the option did not fail for uncertainty. It amounted, on its true construction, to an agreement to sell at a reasonable price to be determined by the valuers; and the stipulation that each

2–096

---

[475] *The Didymi* [1988] 2 Lloyd's Rep. 108 at 116, 118.

[476] ibid. at 117. Contrast *Willis Management (Isle of Man) Ltd v Cable & Wireless Plc* [2005] EWCA Civ 806; [2005] 2 Lloyd's Rep. 597 (parties agreed that one would take a "fair" share of losses incurred by the other, but the evidence indicated that parties meant fair share *to be agreed*).

[477] *Gillatt v Sky Television Ltd (Formerly Sky Television Plc)* [2000] 1 All E.R. (Comm) 461.

[478] *Lombard Tricity Finance Ltd v Paton* [1989] 1 All E.R. 918; *Esso Petroleum Company v Addison* [2003] EWHC 1730 (Comm); *Amberley UK Ltd v West Sussex County Council* [2011] EWCA Civ 11.

[479] *The Product Star (No.2)* [1993] 1 Lloyd's Rep. 397; *Paragon Finance Ltd v Nash* [2001] EWCA Civ 1466; [2001] 2 All E.R. (Comm) 1025 at [36]; *cf. Cantor Fitzgerald International v Horkulak* [2004] EWCA Civ 1287; [2005] I.C.R. 402 at [48]; *Lymington Marina Ltd v Macnamara* [2007] EWCA Civ; [2007] N.P.C. 27; *Socimer International Bank Ltd v Standard Bank London Ltd* [2008] EWCA Civ 116; [2008] 1 Lloyd's Rep. 558 at [110]: *Do-Buy 95 Ltd v National Westminster Bank Plc* [2010] EWHC 2862 (QB), at [37]. Contrast *GX Networks Ltd v Greenland* [2010] EWCA Civ 784; [2010] I.R.L.R. 991 (discretion to be exercised "by exception only").

[480] *The Star Texas* [1993] 2 Lloyd's Rep. 445.

[481] *Arcos Ltd v Aronson* (1930) 36 Ll.L.R. 108; cf. *Thomas Bates & Son Ltd v Wyndham's (Lingerie) Ltd* [1981] 1 W.L.R. 505, where a lease was rectified (below, para.8–059) to include such a clause; *Queensland Electricity Generating Board v New Hope Collieries Pty Ltd* [1989] 1 Lloyd's Rep. 205.

[482] *Alstom Signalling Ltd v Jarvis Facilities Ltd* [2004] EWHC 1232 (TCC); 95 Con L.R. 55. It is not every incomplete agreement which can be saved by referral to the courts. In *Alstom* agreement had been reached "in principle" and the outstanding term was described as "inessential", so that the contract was enforceable in accordance with the principles discussed in para.2–093.

[483] As in *Heathrow Airport Ltd v Thames Water Utilities Ltd* [2009] EWCA Civ 992.

[484] Sale of Goods Act 1979, s.9(1); cf. *Pym v Campbell* (1856) 6 E. & B. 370.

[485] [1983] 1 A.C. 444; Robertshaw 46 M.L.R. 493.

party should nominate one of the valuers was merely "subsidiary and inessential".[486] So long as the agreed machinery (which fails to operate) is of this character,[487] the court can substitute other machinery: e.g., it can itself fix the price with the aid of expert evidence. This is so not only where the agreed machinery fails because of one party's refusal to operate it,[488] but also where it fails for some other reason, such as the refusal of a designated valuer to make the valuation.[489]

(v) *Facts to be ascertained*

2–097   An agreement is not ineffective on the ground of uncertainty merely because the facts on which its operation depend are not known when it is made: the requirement of certainty is satisfied if those facts become ascertainable and are ascertained (without the need for further negotiation) after the making of the agreement.[490]

(vi) *Contract to make a contract*

2–098   In some cases of incomplete agreements it is said that there is a "contract to make a contract", or an "agreement to agree". This expression may refer to a number of different situations.

2–099   **Agreement to execute formal document.** One possibility is that the parties may agree to execute a formal document incorporating terms on which they have previously agreed. Such a provision does not deprive the agreement of contractual force.[491] For example, in *Morton v Morton*[492] an agreement "to enter into a separation deed containing the following clauses" (of which a summary was then given) was held to be a binding contract. The grant of an option to purchase can similarly be described as a contract by which one party binds himself to enter into a further contract if the other so elects; and neither of these contracts is void for uncertainty.[493]

2–100   **Agreement to negotiate.**[494] A further possibility is that the parties have simply agreed to negotiate. In spite of dicta to the contrary,[495] it has been held that a mere agreement to negotiate is not a contract "because it is too uncertain to have

---

[486] *Re Malpass (Deceased)* [1985] Ch. 42 at 50; *Tito v Waddell (No.2)* [1977] Ch. 106 at 314; *The Didymi* [1988] 2 Lloyd's Rep. 108 at 115.

[487] i.e. not if it is "an integral and essential part of the definition of the payments to be made": *Gillatt v Sky Television Ltd (Formerly Sky Television Plc)* [2000] 1 All E.R. (Comm) 461 at 479.

[488] As in the *Sudbrook* case, above. cf. *Cream Holdings Ltd v Davenport* [2010] EWHC 3096 (Ch).

[489] As in *Re Malpas*, above.

[490] *Welsh Development Agency v Export Finance Ltd* [1992] B.C.L.C. 148.

[491] Subject to statutory exceptions: see Consumer Credit Act 1974, s.59.

[492] [1942] 1 All E.R. 273.

[493] See *The Messiniaki Bergen* [1983] 1 Lloyd's Rep. 424 at 426; and below para.3–160 for various views as to the nature of an option.

[494] Peel, in Burrows & Peel (eds), *Contract Formation and Parties.*

[495] *Chillingworth v Esche* [1924] 1 Ch. 97 at 113; *Hillas & Co Ltd v Arcos Ltd* (1932) 147 L.T. 503 at 515. See F.P. 48 L.Q.R. 141; F.W. McC. 48 L.Q.R. 310; Williams 6 M.L.R. 81.

any binding force."[496] It therefore does not impose any obligation to negotiate, or to use best endeavours to reach agreement,[497] or to accept proposals that "with hindsight appear to be reasonable".[498]

Where an agreement is too uncertain to be enforced, this defect cannot be cured by implying into it a term to the effect that the parties must continue to negotiate in good faith. In *Walford v Miles*,[499] an agreement under which the seller agreed not to negotiate with any third party (a "lock-out" agreement) during negotiations for the sale of a business lacked sufficient certainty because it failed to specify any time limit; and the House of Lords unanimously rejected the argument that a term should be implied requiring the vendors to continue to negotiate in good faith with the purchasers for so long as the vendors continued to desire to sell, since such a term was itself too uncertain to be enforced.[500] The uncertainty lay in the fact that the alleged duty was "inherently inconsistent with the position of a negotiating party"[501] who must normally[502] be free to advance his own interests during the negotiations. The point is well illustrated by the facts of *Walford v Miles* itself, where the defendants had agreed subject to contract to sell a property to the purchasers for £2 million and had (in breach of the ineffective "lock-out" agreement) sold it to a third party for exactly that sum, and the purchasers then claimed damages of £1 million on the basis that the property was (by reason of facts known to them but not the defendants) worth £3 million. If a duty to negotiate in good faith exists, it must be equally incumbent on both parties, so that it can hardly require a vendor to agree to sell a valuable property for only two-thirds of its true value when the facts affecting that value are known to the purchaser and not disclosed (as good faith would seem to require[503]) to the vendor. The actual result in *Walford v Miles* (in which the purchasers recovered the sum of £700 in respect of their wasted expenses as damages for misrepresentation,[504]

---

[496] *Courtney & Fairbairn Ltd v Tolaini Bros (Hotels) Ltd* [1975] 1 W.L.R. 297 at 301; cf. *Von Hatzfeldt-Wildenburg v Alexander* [1912] 1 Ch. 284 at 249; *Mallozzi v Carapelli SpA* [1976] 1 Lloyd's Rep. 407; *The Scaptrade* [1981] 2 Lloyd's Rep. 425 at 432 (affirmed without reference to this point [1983] 2 A.C. 694); *Paul Smith Ltd v H & S International Holdings Inc* [1991] 2 Lloyd's Rep. 127 at 131; *Mamidoil-Jetoil Greek Petroleum SA v Okta Crude Oil Refining AD* [2001] EWCA Civ 406; [2001] 2 Lloyd's Rep. 76 at [53], [59].

[497] *The Scaptrade*, (above, fn.496) [1981] 2 Lloyd's Rep. at 432; *The Junior K* [1988] 2 Lloyd's Rep. 583. Contra. in the U.S., *Hoffman v Red Owl Stores Inc* 133 N.W. 2d. 267 (1965).

[498] *Pagnan SpA v Granaria BV* [1985] 1 Lloyd's Rep. 256 at 270; affirmed [1986] 2 Lloyd's Rep. 547.

[499] [1992] 2 A.C. 128; Neill 108 L.Q.R. 405.

[500] An agreement will not be too uncertain if a temporal limit can be implied which is not tied to the parties' obligation to negotiate: *Compere Associates Ltd v Halsey* [2004] EWHC 1317 (Ch), cf. *JSD Corporation Pte Ltd v Al Waha Capital PJSC* [2009] EWHC 3376 (Ch) where the "lock-out" could be terminated for "default" and this was held to include any failure to observe a "non-binding" undertaking to negotiate (alternatively, the lock-out lasted for a reasonable time).

[501] [1992] 2 A.C. 128 at 138; cf. *Surrey CC v Bredero Homes Ltd* [1993] 1 W.L.R. 1361 at 1368; *Baird Textile Holdings Ltd v Marks and Spencer Plc* [2001] EWCA Civ 274; [2002] 1 All E.R. (Comm) 737 at [68].

[502] For an exception, see *Re Debtors (Nos 4449 and 4450 of 1998)* [1999] 1 All E.R. (Comm) 149 at 158 (Lloyd's bound to negotiate in good faith with its names as it was "performing functions in the public interest within a statutory framework").

[503] In the *DCFR*, para.I–103(1) "the expression 'good faith and fair dealing' refers to a standard of conduct characterised by honesty, openness and consideration for the interests of the other party to the transaction or relationship in question." (Research Group on the Existing EC Private Law (Acquis Group), *Principles, Definitions and Model Rules of European Private Law: Draft Common Frame of Reference (DCFR)*.

[504] See [1992] 2 A.C. 128 at 136. In some circumstances, a quantum meruit may be awarded to reflect the value of work done by the claimant before negotiations have broken down: *Cobbe v Yeoman's Row Management Ltd* [2008] UKHL 55; [2008] 1 W.L.R. 1752; below, para.22–021.

but not the £1 million which they claimed as damages for breach of contract[505])
seems with respect, to be entirely appropriate on the facts, especially because the
vendors reasonably believed themselves to be protected from liability in the
principal negotiation by the phrase "subject to contract".

In *Petromec Inc v Petroleo Brasileiro SA Petrobas*,[506] Longmore L.J. appeared to
support the suggestion[507] that the House of Lords might reconsider the decision
in *Walford v Miles*, but held (obiter) that in any event the decision may not rule out
the enforceability of an *express* agreement to negotiate in good faith in a contract
which was otherwise enforceable, i.e it was not a "bare" agreement to negotiate.[508]
He did not consider as "insurmountable" the objection that it is impossible to
assess any loss caused by breach of an obligation to negotiate.[509] He drew an
analogy with claims which are allowed for the loss of a chance,[510] e.g. assessing
whether legal proceedings would have succeeded if they had not been negligently
conducted by the defendant solicitor in breach of contract.[511] The difficulty with
this analogy is that the "chance", in the present context, depends on the conduct
of the other contracting party[512] and here a different principle comes into play.
Where a contract entitles the party in breach to perform in alternative ways,
damages are, as a general rule, assessed on the assumption that he would have
performed in the way that is least burdensome to himself and least beneficial to the
other party.[513] In this regard, it may be noted that even if a party is subject to a
binding obligation to negotiate, he is not in breach if he fails to reach agreement
on the grounds of commercial self-interest.[514]

2–101   **Agreement to use "best" or "reasonable" endeavours.** In *Walford v Miles*
Lord Ackner, with whom all the other members of the House agreed, described as
"unsustainable" the view expressed in an American case[515]

---

[505] See [1992] 2 A.C. 128 at 135.

[506] *Petromec Inc v Petroleo Brasileiro SA Petrobas* [2005] EWCA Civ 891; [2006] 1 Lloyd's Rep.
161.

[507] [2005] EWCA Civ 891; [2006] 1 Lloyd's Rep. 161 at [121]. The suggestion had been made by
Lord Steyn, writing extra-judicially: 113 L.Q.R. 433 at 439. See also: Berg 119 L.Q.R. 357.

[508] The parties expressly agreed to negotiate the "reasonable cost" of an upgrade to a vessel. There
may be no uncertainty in agreeing "cost", or a "fair price"; the courts can make a finding as to what
that might be, in the absence of the parties' agreement (see para.2–086). But Longmore L.J. also
thought that the court could make a finding as to an element of "uplift" by way of profit on the basis
of the obligation to negotiate in good faith. cf. *Butters v BBC Worldwide Ltd* [2009] EWHC 1954
(Comm) at [148]–[151], affirmed [2009] EWCA Civ 1160; [2010] Ch. 347 without reference to this
point; *Gold Group Properties Ltd v BDW Trading Ltd* [2010] EWHC 1632 (TCC) at [87]; *Dhanani v
Crasnianski* [2011] EWHC 926 (Comm) at [104].

[509] At [118].

[510] An approach adopted in the context of breach of a "lock-out" agreement in *Dandara Holdings Ltd
v Co-operative Retail Services Ltd* [2004] EWHC 1476 (Ch) (no damages awarded).

[511] See para.20–060, below.

[512] Whereas in the example given it depends on a third party, i.e. the court.

[513] See para.20–070, below. This appears to have been acknowledged by Bingham L.J. in the Court
of Appeal in *Walford v Miles* (1991) 62 P & CR 410 at 423: "The [claimants] are entitled to be placed
in the same position as if the defendants had performed their obligation, *albeit in the manner most
favourable to themselves.*" (emphasis added). cf. *Jones v Ricoh UK Ltd* [2010] EWHC 1743 (Ch) at
[77]–[78].

[514] *Phillips Petroleum Co UK Ltd v Enron Europe Ltd* (1997) C.L.C. 329. cf. *Berkeley Community
Villages Ltd v Pullen* [2007] EWHC 1330 (Ch); [2007] 24 E.G. 169 at [97]; *Gold Group Properties Ltd
v BDW Trading Ltd* [2010] EWHC 1632 (TCC) at [91].

[515] *Channel Home Centers Division of Grace Retail Corp v Grossman* 795 F.2d 291 (1986).

"that an agreement to negotiate in good faith is synonymous with an agreement to use best endeavours and, as the latter is enforceable so is the former".[516]

He went on to say that

"the reason why an agreement to negotiate, like an agreement to agree, is unenforceable is simply because it lacks the necessary certainty. The same does not apply to an agreement to use best endeavours".[517]

It seems clear that Lord Ackner's reference to an "agreement to use best endeavours" was not intended to indicate any different approach when the term "best endeavours" is used in conjunction with an agreement to negotiate, or an agreement to agree. It is taken to refer to an agreement to use best endeavours in the *performance* of a contract, e.g. where an admitted contract between A and B requires A to use his best endeavours to make a computer software system supplied by A work,[518] or procure C to enter into a contract with B,[519] rather than in seeking the *formation* of a contract.[520] There is no doubt that terms such as the former can impose a legal obligation on A,[521] as indeed can an obligation to act in good faith.[522] But where the question is whether any contract has come into existence, a number of decisions support the view that an express agreement to use best or reasonable endeavours to agree on the terms of a contract is no more than an agreement to negotiate, lacking contractual force.[523]

It may be that, while an agreement to use best endeavours could be interpreted as referring to the *machinery* of negotiation, one to negotiate in good faith is more plausibly interpreted as referring to its *substance*. A promise to use best endeavours might, for example, oblige a party to make himself available for negotiations, or at least not (e.g. by deliberately failing to pick up his telephone) to prevent the other

---

[516] [1992] 2 A.C. 128 at 138.
[517] ibid.
[518] An obligation of reasonable efforts may be implied to indicate the degree of obligation on the parties, or one of them, to bring about a condition precedent upon which the existence of the main contract depends, e.g. obtaining planning permission, or procuring an export licence: see para.2–110, below.
[519] cf. *Rae Lambert v HTV Cymru (Wales) Ltd* [1998] F.S.R. 87.
[520] *Little v Courage* (1995) 70 P. & C.R. 469 at 475 (based on earlier dicta of Goff L.J. in *IBM United Kingdom Ltd v Rockware Glass Ltd* [1980] F.S.R. 335 at 348, and *Bower v Bantam Investments Ltd* [1972] 1 W.L.R. 1120.
[521] See *Watford Electronics Ltd v Sanderson Ltd* [2001] EWCA Civ 317; [2001] 1 All E.R. (Comm) 696 at [45]. For the meaning of "best endeavours", see: *Sheffield District Railway Co v Great Central Railway Co* (1911) 27 T.L.R. 471; *IBM United Kingdom Ltd v Rockware Glass Ltd,* above fn.520 at 339, 343; *Yewbelle Ltd v London Green Developments* Ltd [2007] EWCA Civ 475; [2007] 23 E.G. 164; *Rhodia International Holdings Ltd v Huntsman International LLC* [2007] EWHC 292 (Comm); [2007] 2 Lloyd's Rep. 325 at [33]–[35] (on the difference between "best" and "reasonable endeavours"). See also: *CPC Group Ltd v Qatari Diar Real Estate Investment Co Ltd* [2010] EWHC 1535; [2010] N.P.C. 74 where the parties agreed to act "in the utmost good faith" and "to use all reasonable but commercially prudent endeavours".
[522] *Berkeley Community Villages Ltd v Pullen* [2007] EWHC 1330 (Ch); [2007] 24 E.G. 169; *Gold Group Properties Ltd v BDW Trading Ltd* [2010] EWHC 1632 (TCC).
[523] *Little v Courage* (1995) 70 P. & C.R. 469 at 475; *London & Regional Investments Ltd v TBI Plc Belfast International Airport Ltd* [2002] EWCA Civ 355 at [39]; *Multiplex Constructions UK Ltd v Cleveland Bridge UK Ltd* [2006] EWHC 1341 (TCC), affirmed [2007] EWCA Civ 443, without reference to this point.

from communicating with him.[524] A promise to negotiate in good faith, on the other hand, would oblige a party not to take unreasonable or exorbitant positions during the negotiations; and it is the difficulty of giving precise content to this obligation, while maintaining each party's freedom to pursue his own interests, that makes such a promise too uncertain to be enforced.

2–102   **Obligation to negotiate outstanding details.** In *Walford v Miles* the principal agreement was not legally binding because it was subject to contract, and the lock-out agreement was not legally binding because it specified no dates.[525] The case does not exclude the possibility that a different conclusion may be reached where the parties have reached agreement on all essential points so as to show that they do intend to be legally bound by the agreement, but have left other points open. The court may then imply a term that they are to negotiate in good faith so as to settle outstanding details which are to be incorporated in the formal document setting out the full terms of the contract between them[526] and, a fortiori, an express term to this effect may also be enforceable.[527]

6. CONDITIONAL AGREEMENTS

(a) Classification

2–103   **Different meanings of "condition".** An agreement is conditional if its operation depends on an event which is not certain to occur. Discussions of this topic are made difficult by the fact that in the law of contract the word "condition" bears many senses: it is "a chameleon-like word which takes on its meaning from its surroundings."[528] At this stage, we are concerned with only one of these meanings; but to clear the ground it is necessary to draw a number of preliminary distinctions.

2–104   **Promissory and contingent conditions.** The word "condition" may refer either to an *event*, or to a *term* of a contract (as in the phrase "conditions of sale"). Where "condition" refers to an event, that event may be either an occurrence which neither party undertakes to bring about, or the performance by one party of his undertaking. The first possibility is illustrated by a contract by which A is to work for B, and B is to pay A £50, "if it rains tomorrow". Here the obligations of both parties are contingent on the happening of the specified event which may therefore be described as a *contingent* condition. The second possibility is illustrated by the ordinary case in which A agrees to work for B at a weekly wage payable at the end of the week. Here the contract is immediately binding on both parties, but B is not liable to pay until A has performed his promise to work. Such

---

[524] Example based on *Nissho Iwai Petroleum Co Inc v Cargill International SA* [1993] 1 Lloyd's Rep. 80, where such conduct was held to amount to a breach of a party's duty to co-operate in the *performance* (not in the *formation*) of a contract. cf. *Re Debtors (Nos 4449 and 4450 of 1998)* [1999] 1 All E.R. (Comm) 149 at 158 (implied obligation to use "best endeavours" to conclude an agreement required the party "not unreasonably to frustrate" its conclusion).
[525] See below, para.4–011.
[526] *Donwin Productions Ltd v EMI Films Ltd, The Times*, March 9, 1984 (not cited in *Walford v Miles* [1992] 2 A.C. 128).
[527] *Petromec Inc v Petroleo Brasileiro SA Petrobas* [2005] EWCA Civ 891; [2006] 1 Lloyd's Rep. 161, above, fn.506; Peel, above fn.494 querying whether there is an enforceable *obligation* to negotiate outstanding details.
[528] *The Varenna* [1984] Q.B. 599 at 618.

performance is a condition of B's liability, and, as A has promised to render it, the condition may be described as *promissory*.[529] In this chapter our concern is with contingent conditions;[530] promissory conditions will be discussed in Chs 17 and 18.[531]

Contingent conditions may be precedent or subsequent. A condition is precedent if it provides that the contract is not to be binding until the specified event occurs. It is subsequent if it provides that a previously binding contract is to determine on the occurrence of the event: e.g. where A contracts to pay an allowance to B until B marries.[532]

(b) Degrees of Obligation

No duty to render principal performance. Where an agreement is subject   2–105
to a contingent condition precedent, there is, before the occurrence of the condition, no duty on either party to render the principal performance promised by him: e.g. a seller is not bound to deliver and a buyer is not bound to pay. Nor, in such a case, does either party undertake that the condition will occur. But an agreement subject to such a condition may impose some degree of obligation on the parties or on one of them. Whether it has this effect, and if so what degree of obligation is imposed, depends on the true construction of the term specifying the condition.[533]

Parties free to withdraw. One possibility is that, before the event occurs, each   2–106
party is free to withdraw from the agreement. In *Pym v Campbell*[534] an agreement for the sale of a patent was executed, but the parties at the same time agreed that it should not "be the agreement" unless a third party approved of the invention. He did not approve, and it was held that the buyer was not liable for refusing to perform. The written agreement was "not an agreement at all".[535] If this is taken literally, either party could have withdrawn even before the third party had given his opinion.

Parties cannot withdraw. A second possibility is that, before the event   2–107
occurs, the main obligations have not accrued; but that, so long as the event can still occur, one (or both) of the parties cannot withdraw. Thus in *Smith v Butler*[536] A bought land from B on condition that a loan to B (secured by a mortgage on the premises) would be transferred to A.[537] It was held that A could not withdraw

---

[529] *Total Gas Marketing Ltd v Arco British Ltd* [1998] 2 Lloyd's Rep. 209 at 215, 218; *UR Power GmbH v Kuok Oils and Grains Pte Ltd* [2009] EWHC 1940 (Comm); [2009] 2 Lloyd's Rep. 495 at [14]–[15].

[530] A contingent condition precedent may take the form of the fulfilment of a warranty, e.g. in a compromise agreement, the employee's warranty that he has not committed a repudiatory breach of the employment contract: *Collidge v Freeport Plc* [2008] EWCA Civ 485; [2008] I.R.L.R. 697.

[531] See below, paras 17–015—17–018, 18–039—18–060.

[532] cf. *Brown v Knowsley BC* [1986] I.R.L.R. 102; *Jameson v CEGB* [2000] 1 A.C. 455 at 477.

[533] For special difficulties where the condition precedent is implied, see *Bentworth Finance Ltd v Lubert* [1968] 1 Q.B. 680; Carnegie, 31 M.L.R. 78.

[534] (1856) 6 E. & B. 370.

[535] ibid. at 374.

[536] [1900] 1 Q.B. 694; cf. *Felixstowe Dock & Ry Co v British Transport Docks Bd* [1976] 2 Lloyd's Rep. 656; *Alan Estates Ltd v W G Stores Ltd* [1982] Ch. 511 at 520.

[537] On agreements "subject to finance" see Coote 40 Conv. (N.S.) 37; Furmston 3 O.J.L.S. 438, discussing *Meehan v Jones* (1982) 149 C.L.R. 571.

before the time fixed for completion: he was bound to wait until then to see whether B could arrange the transfer. However, if it becomes clear that the condition has not occurred, or that it can no longer occur, within the time specified in the contract, the parties will be under no further obligations under the contract.[538] In such a case, the effect of the non-occurrence of the condition is that the parties are "no longer bound"[539] by the contract, or that the contract is "discharged."[540] What the parties have called a "condition precedent" can thus operate as, or have the effect of, a condition subsequent.[541]

2–108   **Parties must not prevent occurrence of condition.** A third possibility is that, before the event occurs, the main obligations have not accrued; but that in the meantime neither party must do anything to prevent the occurrence of the event. Thus in *Mackay v Dick*[542] an excavating machine was sold on condition that it could excavate at a specified rate on the buyer's property. The buyer's refusal to provide facilities for a proper trial was held to be a breach. Similarly, the seller would have been in breach, had he refused to subject the machine to a proper test. The same principle is illustrated by a case[543] in which a professional footballer was transferred for a fee, part of which was to be paid only after he had scored 20 goals. Before he had done so, the new club dropped him from their first team, and they were held to be in breach as they had not given the player a reasonable opportunity to score the 20 goals.

The duty not to prevent the occurrence of the condition has been explained as resting on an implied term and this explanation limits the scope of the duty in a number of ways. For example, the implied term may only be to the effect that a party will not *prevent* fulfilment of the condition, so that he is not in breach simply by doing nothing[544]; or that he will not *deliberately* prevent the occurrence of the condition[545]; or (even more narrowly) that he will not *wrongfully* do so.[546] The latter type of implication may allow a party to engage in certain kinds of deliberate prevention but not in others: e.g. it may allow a company which has promised an employee the opportunity of earning a bonus to deprive him of that opportunity by going out of business, but not by simply dismissing him, before the bonus has become due.[547]

2–109   **Approval of one party.** The sort of implied term referred to in the previous paragraph can be excluded by an express contrary provision[548]; in particular, by a provision making the operation of a contract dependent on the "satisfaction" of

[538] *North Sea Energy Holdings NV v Petroleum Authority of Thailand* [1997] 2 Lloyd's Rep. 418 at 428–429 (affirmed on other grounds [1999] 1 Lloyd's Rep. 483).

[539] *Total Gas Marketing Ltd v Arco British Ltd* [1998] 2 Lloyd's Rep. 209 at 215.

[540] ibid. at 218.

[541] ibid. at 221, 224.

[542] (1881) 6 App.Cas. 251; cf. *Shipping Corp of India v Naviera Letasa* [1976] 1 Lloyd's Rep. 132; *CIA Barca de Panama SA v George Wimpey & Co Ltd* [1980] 1 Lloyd's Rep. 598; contrast *North Sea Energy Holdings NV v Petroleum Authority of Thailand* [1999] 1 Lloyd's Rep. 483 (duty to co-operate in bringing about the event negatived by terms of the contract).

[543] *Bournemouth & Boscombe Athletic FC v Manchester United FC, The Times*, May 22, 1980. cf. *CEL Group Ltd v Nedlloyd Lines UK Ltd* [2003] EWCA Civ 1716; [2004] 1 Lloyd's Rep. 381 at [21]–[22]; *Luxor (Eastbourne) Ltd v Cooper* [1940] A.C. 108, below, para.16–087.

[544] *Taylor v Rive Droite Music Ltd* [2005] EWCA Civ 1300; [2006] E.M.L.R. 4 at [160].

[545] See *Blake & Co v Sohn* [1969] 1 W.L.R. 1412.

[546] See *Thompson v ASDA-MFI Group Plc* [1988] Ch. 241.

[547] Example based on *Thompson v ASDA-MFI Group Plc*, above and below, para.16–087.

[548] See *Micklefield v SAC Technology Ltd* [1990] 1 W.L.R. 1002.

one party with the subject-matter or other aspects relating to the other's perform-ance.[549] Thus it has been held that there was no contract where a house was bought "subject to satisfactory mortgage"[550]; and where a boat was bought "subject to satisfactory survey"[551] it was held that the buyer was not bound if he expressed his dissatisfaction,[552] in spite of the fact that such expression was a deliberate act on his part which prevented the occurrence of the condition. The same is true where goods are bought on approval and the buyer does not approve them,[553] and where an offer of employment is made "subject to satisfactory references," and the prospective employer does not regard the references as satisfactory.[554] There is some apparent conflict in the authorities on the question whether the law imposes any restriction on the freedom of action of the party on whose satisfaction the operation of the contract depends. In one case[555] a proposed royalty agreement relating to the use by a manufacturer of an invention was "subject to detailed evaluation of production and marketing feasibility" by the manufacturer. It was held that his discretion whether to enter into the contract was "unfettered by any obligation to act reasonably or in good faith"[556] and that, as his satisfaction had not been communicated[557] to the other party, the agreement had not acquired contractual force. On the other hand, where a ship was sold "subject to satisfactory completion of two trial voyages" it was said that such a stipulation was to be construed as "subject to bona fides".[558] The distinction between the two lines of cases turns, ultimately, on the construction of the agreement.[559] Even if this requires the discretion to be exercised in good faith, it does not follow that it must be exercised reasonably: the matter may be left to the relevant party's "subjective decision".[560] It has also been held that the party on whose satisfaction the operation of the contract depends must at least provide facilities for, or not impede, the inspection referred to in the agreement.[561] Of course if the result of the inspection is unsatisfactory, the principal obligation of the contract will not take effect.[562]

One party under duty to use reasonable efforts. A fourth possibility is that, before the event occurs, the main obligations have not accrued but that one of the 2–110

---

[549] *Schweppe v Harper* [2008] EWCA Civ 442 at [70].

[550] *Lee-Parker v Izett (No.2)* [1975] 1 W.L.R. 775; distinguished in *Janmohammed v Hassam, The Times*, June 10, 1976.

[551] *Astra Trust Ltd v Adams & Williams* [1969] 1 Lloyd's Rep. 81; doubted in *The Merak* [1976] 2 Lloyd's Rep. 250 at 254 and in *Ee v Kahar* (1979) 40 P. & C.R. 223.

[552] But if the buyer declared his satisfaction the seller would be bound even though the survey was not objectively satisfactory: *Graham v Pitkin* [1992] 1 W.L.R. 403 at 405.

[553] cf. Sale of Goods Act 1979, s.18, r.4.

[554] *Wishart v National Association of Citizens' Advice Bureaux* [1990] I.C.R. 794.

[555] *Stabilad Ltd v Stephens & Carter (No.2)* [1999] 2 All E.R. (Comm) 651.

[556] ibid. at 662.

[557] For the requirement of communication, see *Stabilad Ltd v Stephens & Carter (No.2)* [1999] 2 All E.R. (Comm) 651 at 660; the requirement may be satisfied by conduct from which satisfaction can be inferred, e.g. where a buyer of goods on approval retains them without notifying rejection for more than the stipulated or a reasonable time: Sale of Goods Act 1999, s.18, r.4(b).

[558] *The John S Darbyshire* [1977] 2 Lloyd's Rep. 457 at 464; cf. *BV Oliehandel Jongkind v Coastal International Ltd* [1983] 2 Lloyd's Rep. 463; contrast *The Junior K* [1988] 2 Lloyd's Rep. 583 at 589 (where the words were held to negative contractual intention). See also *El Awadi v Bank of Credit & Commerce International SA* [1990] 1 Q.B. 606 at 619; and in an analogous context, *The Product Star (No.2)* [1993] 1 Lloyd's Rep. 397 at 404 (above, para.2–096, text to fn.479).

[559] *Schweppe v Harper* [2008] EWCA Civ 442 at [71].

[560] *Stabilad Ltd v Stephens & Carter Ltd (No.2)* [1999] 2 All E.R. (Comm) 651 at 659.

[561] *The Merak* [1976] 2 Lloyd's Rep. 250; cf. *Ee v Kahar* (1979) 40 P. & C.R. 223.

[562] As in *The John S Darbyshire* [1977] 2 Lloyd's Rep. 457.

parties undertakes to use reasonable efforts to bring the event about (without absolutely undertaking that his efforts will succeed). This construction was applied, for instance, where land was sold subject to the condition that the purchaser should obtain planning permission to use the land as a transport depot: he was bound to make reasonable efforts to obtain the permission, but he was free from liability when those efforts failed.[563] Similarly, where goods are sold "subject to export (or import) licence", the party whose duty it is to obtain the licence[564] does not prima facie promise absolutely that a licence will be obtained,[565] but only undertakes to make reasonable efforts to that end.[566] The principal obligations to buy and sell will not take effect if no licence is obtained[567]; but if the party who should have made reasonable efforts has failed to do so he will be liable in damages,[568] unless he can show that any such efforts, which he should have made would (if made) have necessarily been unsuccessful.[569]

2–111   **Effect of failure to perform.** It will be seen that in cases falling within the second, third and fourth categories discussed above, a distinction must be drawn between two types of obligation: the principal obligation of each party (e.g. to buy and sell) and a subsidiary obligation, i.e. one not to withdraw, not to prevent occurrence of the condition, or to make reasonable efforts to bring it about. One view is that the party who fails to perform the subsidiary obligation is to be treated as if the condition had occurred; and that he is then liable on the principal obligation. Thus in *Mackay v Dick*[570] the buyer was held liable *for the price*; but there was no discussion as to the remedy. In principle it seems wrong to hold him so liable, for such a result ignores the possibility that the machine might have failed to come up to the standard required by the contract, even if proper facilities for trial had been provided. It is submitted that the correct result in cases of this kind is to award *damages* for breach of the subsidiary obligation: in assessing such damages, the court can take into account the possibility that the condition might not have occurred, even if there had been no such breach.[571] To hold the party in breach liable for the full performance promised by him, on the fiction that the

---

[563] *Hargreaves Transport Ltd v Lynch* [1969] 1 W.L.R. 215 (condition not satisfied); *Richard West & Partners (Inverness) Ltd v Dick* [1969] 2 Ch. 424 (similar condition satisfied); contrast *Tesco Stores Ltd v Gibson* (1970) 214 E.G. 835 (no obligation on purchaser to apply for planning permission).

[564] As to which party has this duty, see *H O Brandt & Co v H N Morris & Co* [1917] 2 K.B. 784; *A V Pound & Co v M W Hardy & Co* [1956] A.C. 588.

[565] The prima facie rule may be excluded by express words which do, on their true construction, impose an absolute duty; e.g. *Peter Cassidy Seed Co Ltd v Osuustukkukauppa* [1957] 1 W.L.R. 273; *C Czarnikow Ltd v Centrala Handlu Zagranicznego "Rolimpex"* [1979] A.C. 351 at 371; *Pagnan SpA v Tradax Ocean Transport SA* [1987] 3 All E.R. 565; Yates and Carter 1 J.C.L. 57.

[566] *Re Anglo-Russian Merchant Traders and John Batt & Co (London) Ltd* [1917] 2 K.B. 679; *Coloniale Import-Export v Loumidis & Sons* [1978] 2 Lloyd's Rep. 560; *Gamerco SA v ICM Fair Warning (Agency) Ltd* [1995] 1 W.L.R. 1226 at 1231. Where the contract is expressly subject to the approval of a public authority, there may not even be a duty to make reasonable efforts to secure that approval: see *Gyllenhammar Partners International v Sour Brodegradevna Industria* [1989] 2 Lloyd's Rep. 403.

[567] *Charles H Windschuegl Ltd v Alexander Pickering & Co Ltd* (1950) 84 Ll.L. Rep 89 at 92–93; *Brauer & Co (Great Britain) Ltd v James Clark (Brush Materials) Ltd* [1952] 2 All E.R. 497 at 501.

[568] e.g. *Malik v Central European Trading Agency* [1974] 1 Lloyd's Rep. 279; *Agroexport v Cie. Européenne de Céréales* [1974] 1 Lloyd's Rep. 499.

[569] See Benjamin's *Sale of Goods* (8th edn), para.18–370; *Overseas Buyers Ltd v Granadex SA* [1980] 2 Lloyd's Rep. 608 at 612.

[570] (1881) 6 App.Cas. 251; above, para.2–108.

[571] *Bournemouth & Boscombe Athletic FC v Manchester United FC, The Times*, May 22, 1980; cf. *The Blankenstein* [1985] 1 W.L.R. 435 (below, para.18–016); *Alpha Trading Ltd v Dunshaw-Patten Ltd* [1981] Q.B. 290; *George Moundreas & Co SA v Navimpex Centrala Navala* [1985] 2 Lloyd's Rep. 515.

condition had occurred, seems to introduce into this branch of the law a punitive element that is inappropriate to a contractual action.[572] The most recent authorities rightly hold that such a doctrine of "fictional fulfilment" of a condition does not form part of English law.[573]

Conditions for the benefit of one party. Where a condition is inserted entirely for the benefit of one party, that party may waive the condition.[574] He can then sue[575] and be sued[576] on the contract as if the condition had occurred. Obviously this rule does not apply to cases falling within the first of the categories discussed above, in which there is no contract at all before the condition occurs.

2–112

---

[572] cf. below, para.20–020.

[573] *Thompson v ASDA-MFI Group Plc* [1988] Ch. 241 at 266 (where the condition was said at 251 to be subsequent); *Little v Courage Ltd* (1995) 70 P. & C.R. 469 at 474.

[574] *Irwin v Wilson* [2011] EWHC 326 (Ch).

[575] *Wood Preservation Ltd v Prior* [1969] 1 W.L.R. 1077; contrast *Heron Garages Properties Ltd v Moss* [1974] 1 W.L.R. 148.

[576] *McKillop v McMullan* [1979] N.I. 85.

CHAPTER THREE

CONSIDERATION[1]

---

[1] Shatwell 1 Sydney L.R. 289; Sutton, *Consideration Reconsidered*.

1. INTRODUCTION

(a) General

General rule. In English law, a promise is not, as a general rule, binding as a   3–001
contract unless it is either made in a deed[2] or supported by some "consideration".
The purpose of the requirement of consideration is to put some legal limits on the
enforceability of agreements even where they are intended to be legally binding[3]
and are not vitiated by some factor such as mistake, misrepresentation, duress or
illegality.[4] The existence of such limits is not a peculiarity of English law: e.g. in
some civil law countries certain promises which in England are not binding for
"want of consideration" cannot be enforced unless they are made in some special
form, e.g. by a notarised writing.[5] The view was, indeed, put forward at one time
that consideration was only evidence of the intention of the parties to be bound,
and that (at any rate in the case of certain commercial contracts), such evidence
could equally well be furnished by writing.[6] But the view that agreements (other
than those contained in deeds) were binding without consideration merely because
they were in writing was rejected in England over 200 years ago,[7] though it has
been revived as a proposal for law reform.[8] The present position therefore is that
English law limits the enforceability of agreements (not in deeds) by reference to
a complex and multifarious body of rules known as "the doctrine of consideration".

Reciprocity. This doctrine is based on the idea of reciprocity: "something of   3–002
value in the eye of the law"[9] must be given for a promise in order to make it
enforceable as a contract. An informal gratuitous promise therefore does not
amount to a contract.[10] A person or body to whom a promise of a gift is made from
purely sentimental or charitable motives gives nothing for the promise; and the
claims of such a promisee are less compelling than those of a person who has given
(or promised) some return for the promise.[11] The invalidity of informal gratuitous
promises of this kind can also be supported on the ground that their enforcement
could prejudice third parties such as creditors of the promisor.[12] Such promises,
too, may be rashly made[13]; and the requirements of executing a deed or giving
value provide at least some protection against this danger.

Promises struck down for want of consideration. The doctrine of con-   3–003
sideration has, however, also struck at many promises which were not "gratuitous"
in any ordinary or commercial sense. These applications of the doctrine were

---

[2] See below, para.3–170.
[3] See below, Ch.4.
[4] See below, Chs 8–11.
[5] See generally von Mehren 72 Harv.L.Rev. 1009.
[6] *Pillans v Van Mierop* (1765) 3 Burr. 1663.
[7] *Rann v Hughes* (1778) 7 T.R. 350n.; 4 Bro. P.C. 27.
[8] See below, para.3–175.
[9] *Thomas v Thomas* (1842) 2 Q.B. 851 at 859.
[10] *Re Hudson* (1885) 54 L.J. Ch. 811; *Williams v Roffey Bros & Nicholls(Contractors) Ltd* [1991] 1
Q.B. 1 at 19.
[11] cf. Eisenberg 47 U. of Chi.L.Rev. 1; 85 Cal.L.Rev. 821.
[12] *Eastwood v Kenyon* (1840) 11 A. & E. 438 at 451.
[13] *Beaton v McDivitt* (1988) 13 N.S.W.L.R. 162 at 170. It is often easier to promise to make a gift
than actually to make one.

brought within its scope by stressing that consideration had to be not merely "something of value", but "something of value *in the eye of the law*".[14] The law in certain cases refused to recognise the "value" of acts or promises which might well be regarded as valuable by a layman. This refusal was based on many disparate policies; so that "promises without consideration" included many different kinds of transactions which, at first sight, had little in common. It is this fact which is the cause of the very great complexity of the doctrine; and which has also led to its occasional unwarranted extensions and hence to demands for reform of the law.[15]

(b) Definitions

3–004   **Benefit and detriment.** The traditional definition of consideration concentrates on the requirement that "something of value" must be given and accordingly states that consideration is either some detriment to the promisee (in that he may give value) or some benefit to the promisor (in that he may receive value).[16] Usually, this detriment and benefit are merely the same thing looked at from different points of view. Thus payment by a buyer is consideration for the seller's promise to deliver and can be described as a detriment to the buyer or as a benefit to the seller; and conversely delivery by a seller is consideration for the buyer's promise to pay and can be described either as a detriment to the seller or as a benefit to the buyer. These statements relate to the consideration *for the promise of each party* looked at separately. For example, the seller suffers a "detriment" when he delivers the goods and this enables him to enforce the buyer's promise to pay the price. It is quite irrelevant that the seller has made a good bargain and so gets a benefit from the performance of the contract. What the law is concerned with is the consideration *for a promise*—not the consideration *for a contract*.

3–005   **Either benefit or detriment sufficient.** Under the traditional definition it is sufficient if there is either a detriment to the promisee or a benefit to the promisor. Thus detriment to the promisee suffices even though the promisor does not benefit[17]: e.g. where A guarantees B's bank overdraft and the promisee bank suffers detriment by advancing money to B, then A is bound by his promise, even though he gets no benefit from the advance to B. One view, indeed, was that "Detriment to the promisee is of the essence of the doctrine, and benefit to the promisor is, when it exists, merely an accident".[18] But the view that benefit to the promisor is, on its own, sufficient to satisfy the requirement of consideration is supported by a number of cases[19] in which promises were enforced on the ground

---

[14] See above, at fn.9; below, para.3–006.

[15] See below, para.3–175.

[16] *Currie v Misa* (1875) L.R. 10 Ex. 153 at 162. See also *Barber v Fox* (1682) 2 Wms. Saund. 134n.(e); *Cooke v Oxley* (1790) 3 T.R. 653 at 654; *Bainbridge v Firmstone* (1838) 8 A. & E. 743 at 744; *Thomas v Thomas* (1842) 2 Q.B. 851 at 859; *Bolton v Madden* (1873) L.R. 9 Q.B. 55 at 56; *Gore v Van der Lann* [1967] 2 Q.B. 31 at 42; *Midland Bank & Trust Co Ltd v Green* [1981] A.C. 513 at 531; *Guiness Mahon & Co Ltd v Kensington & Chelsea Royal BC* [1999] Q.B. 215 at 236; *Modahl v British Athletics Federation Ltd* [2001] EWCA Civ 1447; [2002] 1 W.L.R. 1192 at [50]; cf. [2002] 1 W.L.R. 1192 at [103].

[17] *O'Sullivan v Management Agency & Music Ltd* [1985] Q.B. 428 at 459; *Re Dale* [1994] Ch. 31 at 38; cf. *Gill & Duffus SA v Rionda Futures Ltd* [1994] 2 Lloyd's Rep. 67 at 82.

[18] Holdsworth, *History of English Law*, Vol.8, p.11.

[19] e.g. below, paras 3–025, 3–043 et seq., 3–105, 3–109.

that such a benefit had been conferred, even though there was no apparent detriment to the promisee.

Benefit and detriment may be factual or legal. The traditional definition   3–006
of consideration lacks precision because the key notions of "benefit" and "detriment" are used in at least two senses. They may refer, first, to any act[20] which is of some value, or, secondly, only to acts, the performance of which is not already legally due from the promisee. In the first sense, there is consideration if a benefit or detriment is *in fact* obtained or suffered. When the words are used in the second sense this factual benefit or detriment is disregarded, and a notion of what may be called legal benefit or detriment is substituted. Under this notion, the promisee may provide consideration by doing anything that he was not legally bound to do, whether or not it actually occasions a detriment to him or confers a benefit on the promisor; while conversely, he may provide no consideration by doing only what he was legally bound to do, however much this may in fact occasion a detriment to him or confer a benefit on the promisor. The English courts have not consistently adopted either of these senses of the words "benefit" and "detriment." In some of the situations to be discussed in this chapter, factual benefit is stressed[21] even though legal detriment may also have been present; while in others the absence of a legal detriment or benefit has in the past been regarded as decisive.[22] One more recent authority[23] regards factual benefit to the promisor as sufficient in one such situation, even in the absence of a legal benefit to him or of a legal detriment to the promisee and it is possible (though far from certain) that this approach may spread to at least some[24] of the situations in which the courts have in the past insisted on legal benefit or detriment.

Other definitions. The traditional definition of consideration in terms of   3–007
benefit and detriment is sometimes regarded as unsatisfactory. One cause of dissatisfaction is that it is thought to be wrong to talk of benefit and detriment when both parties expect to, and actually may, benefit from the contract. But this reasoning falls, with respect, into the error of treating the subject-matter of the definition as the consideration *for a contract*,[25] when the definition is actually concerned with the consideration *for a promise*.[26] Another cause of dissatisfaction is the artificial reasoning that is sometimes necessary to accommodate decided cases within the traditional definition. Sir Frederick Pollock has, accordingly, described consideration as simply "the price for which the promise is bought".[27] This statement has been approved in the House of Lords[28]; but if it is to be regarded as a definition of consideration it is defective in being so vague as to give no help in determining whether consideration exists on a given set of facts. A view

---

[20] Or forbearance, or promise to do or to forbear. For the sake of simplicity references in the text are confined to the doing of an act.
[21] e.g. in *Bolton v Madden* (1873) L.R. 9 Q.B. 55, below, para.3–025.
[22] e.g. in some of the existing duty cases discussed at para.3–048, below.
[23] *Williams v Roffey Bros & Nicholls (Contractors) Ltd* [1991] 1 Q.B. 1, below, para.3–050.
[24] e.g. to the variation cases discussed below, paras 3–062—3–065; but probably not to the forbearance to sue cases discussed below, paras 3–066—3–068.
[25] There are traces of this approach in *Williams v Roffey Bros & Nicholls (Contractors) Ltd* [1991] 1 Q.B. 1 at 23: "If both parties benefit from an agreement it is not necessary that each also suffered a detriment."
[26] See above, para.3–004.
[27] *Principles of Contract* (13th edn), p.133.
[28] *Dunlop Pneumatic Tyre Co Ltd v Selfridge Ltd* [1915] A.C. 847 at 855.

which leads to even more uncertainty is that consideration "*means* a reason for the enforcement of promises"[29]—that reason being simply "the justice of the case".[30] But "the justice of the case" is in almost all the decided cases highly debatable, so that the suggested definition provides no basis for formulating a coherent legal doctrine.[31] A modification of the suggested definition, describing consideration as "a reason for the recognition of an obligation",[32] is open to the same objection. Of course the traditional definition does not provide complete (or even a very high degree of) certainty. But it does state the doctrine in a way which gives some basis for predicting the course of future decisions; and it has more support in the authorities than any other definition. For these reasons it will be used in this chapter.

3–008   **Mutual promises.** So far we have discussed performance by one party as consideration for the promise of the other: e.g. payment by a buyer as the consideration for the seller's promise to deliver, or delivery by a seller as consideration for the buyer's promise to pay. It is, however, also well settled that mutual promises can be consideration for each other. Hence if a seller promises to deliver goods in six months' time and the buyer to pay for them on delivery, there is an immediately binding contract from which neither party can withdraw, though, of course, performance cannot be claimed till the appointed time. Implied, no less than express, promises can constitute consideration for each other.[33]

Some difficulty has been felt in explaining the rule that mutual promises can be consideration for each other. At first sight, it might seem that the mere giving of a promise was not a detriment, nor its receipt a benefit, so as to make the counter-promise binding. It will not do to say that the person making the promise suffers a detriment because he is legally bound to perform it; for if this assumption is made about one of the promises, it must also be made of the other, so that the "explanation" assumes the very point in issue. Probably the reason for the rule is simpler. A person who makes a commercial promise expects to have to perform it (and is in fact under considerable pressure to do so). Correspondingly, one who receives such a promise expects it to be kept. These expectations, which can exist even where the promise is not legally enforceable,[34] are based on commercial morality, and can properly be called a detriment and a benefit; hence they satisfy the requirement of consideration in the case of mutual promises. But there must, at least, be a counter-promise from the promisee: "A promise does not become contractually binding simply because the making of the promise is potentially advantageous to the promisor".[35]

---

[29] Atiyah, *Consideration in Contracts: A Fundamental Restatement* (Canberra, 1971), p.60. For an earlier, similar statement, see Llewellyn 40 Yale L.J. at 741 (1931)—"any sufficient justification for court enforcement"; but he makes no attempt to suggest that this actually is the law. For criticism of Atiyah's views, see Treitel 50 A.L.J. 439. cf.*Colonia Versicherung AG v Amoco Oil Co* [1995] 1 Lloyd's Rep. 570 at 577 (affirmed [1997] 1 Lloyd's Rep. 261, without reference to this point) where the words "(a) the reason for and (b) ample consideration for" a payment clearly treat these concepts as distinct.

[30] Atiyah (above, fn.29), pp.52, 58.

[31] cf.the description of a similar concept as "potentially very confusing" in *Guiness Mahon & Co Ltd v Kensington & Chelsea Royal BC* [1999] Q.B. 215 at 236.

[32] Atiyah, *Essays in Contract*, pp.179, 183.

[33] *The Aramis* [1989] 1 Lloyd's Rep. 213 at 225. But a mere proposal falling short of a promise does not suffice: *The Kaliningrad and Nadezhda Krupskaya* [1997] 2 Lloyd's Rep. 35 at 39.

[34] cf. *Lipkin Gorman v Karpnale Ltd* 2 A.C. 548 at 581.

[35] *Ashia Centur v Barker Gillette LLP* [2011] EWHC 148 (QB) at [20].

As a general rule a promise is regarded as consideration for a counter-promise only if its performance would also have been so regarded.[36] It follows that a mere promise to accept a gift cannot be consideration for the promise to make it. Similarly, we shall see that a debtor who actually pays part of a debt does not thereby provide consideration for the creditor's promise to release the balance[37] and the position is exactly the same if the debtor *promises* part-payment in return for the creditor's counter-promise to accept the part-payment in full settlement.

Invented consideration. Normally, a party enters into a contract with a view to obtaining the consideration provided by the other: e.g. the buyer wants the goods and the seller the price. In the United States it has been said that this is essential, and that "Nothing is consideration that is not regarded as such by both parties."[38] But English courts do not insist on this requirement and often regard an act or forbearance as the consideration for a promise even though it may not have been the object of the promisor to secure it,[39] or the promisee may not have consciously realised that he was giving what was, in fact, consideration.[40] They may also regard the possibility of some prejudice to the promisee as a detriment without regard to the question whether it has in fact been suffered.[41] These practices may be called "inventing consideration", and the temptation to adopt one or the other of them is particularly strong when the act or forbearance which was actually bargained for cannot be regarded as consideration for some reason which is thought to be technical and without merit. In such cases the practice of inventing consideration may help to make the operation of the doctrine of consideration more acceptable; but the practice may also be criticised[42] on the ground that it gives the courts a wide discretion to hold promises binding (or not) as they please. Thus the argument that the promisee *might* have suffered prejudice by acting in reliance on a promise is in some cases made a basis of decision,[43] while in others precisely the same argument is rejected.[44] The courts have not been very consistent in the exercise of this discretion and its existence is a source of considerable uncertainty in this branch of the law.

3–009

---

[36] *Thorp v Thorp* (1702) 12 Mod.445 at 449; *Re Dale* [1994] Ch. 31 at 38.

[37] See below, para.3–100.

[38] *Philpot v Gruninger* (1872) 14 Wall 570 at 577; Restatement, *Contracts*, para.75(1); Restatement 2d, *Contracts*, para.71(1) and (2); Corbin, *Contracts*, para.172, is more sceptical. Restatement 2d, *Contracts*, para.72 also supports the converse proposition, namely that anything is consideration if it is bargained for, even if there is no element of benefit or detriment; but this is subject to important exceptions, especially where what is bargained for is the performance of an existing duty or the settlement of an invalid claim: paras 73, 74; as to these topics, see below, paras 3–036—3–039, 3–043—3–055.

[39] See, e.g. below, paras 3–031—3–032, 3–163—3–165; cf. *Pollway Ltd v Abdullah* [1974] 1 W.L.R. 493, discussed by Zuckerman 38 M.L.R. 384; Thornely [1975] C.L.J. 26; *The Alev* [1989] 2 Lloyd's Rep. 138 at 147; *Moran v University College Salford (No.2)*, The Times, November 23, 1993.

[40] *Pitts v Jones* [2007] EWCA Civ 1301; [2008] Q.B. 76.

[41] e.g. below, fn.43.

[42] Holmes, *The Common Law*, p.292. In the U.S. there is less need to invent consideration because of the existence of a broad doctrine of promissory estoppel: see below, para.3–093.

[43] *Shadwell v Shadwell* (1860) 9 C.B.(N.S.) 159 at 174: the consideration was said by Erle C.J. to consist of the possibility that the promisor "*may* have made a most material change in his position . . . ".

[44] In *Offord v Davies* (1862) 12 C.B.(N.S.) 748: the argument of counsel (at 750) that "the plaintiff *might* have altered his position in consequence of the guarantee" was rejected, Erle C.J. being again a member of the court. cf. also below, fn.144 and fn.150, for refusal to "invent" consideration.

3–010   **Motive and consideration.** In *Thomas v Thomas*[45] a testator shortly before his
death expressed a desire that his widow should during her life have the house in
which he lived, or £100. After his death, his executors "in consideration of such
desire" promised to convey the house to the widow during her life or for so long
as she should continue a widow, "provided nevertheless and it is hereby further
agreed" that she should pay £1 per annum towards the ground rent, and keep the
house in repair. In an action by the widow for breach of this promise, the
consideration for it was stated to be the widow's promise to pay and repair. An
objection that the declaration omitted to state part of the consideration, namely
the testator's desire, was rejected. Patteson J. said:

> "Motive is not the same thing with consideration. Consideration means
> something which is of value in the eye of the law, moving from the [claim-
> ant]."[46]

This remark should not be misunderstood: a common motive for making a
promise is the desire to obtain the consideration; and an act or forbearance on the
part of the promisee may fail to constitute consideration precisely because it was
not the promisor's motive to secure it: e.g. where A promises to give B £1,000 and
B thereupon buys a diamond ring. What Patteson J. meant was that a motive for
promising does not amount to consideration unless two further conditions are
satisfied, viz: (i) that the thing secured in exchange for the promise is "of some
value in the eye of the law"[47]; and (ii) that it moves from the promisee.[48]
Consideration and motive are not opposites; the former concept is a subdivision
of the latter. The consideration for a promise is (unless it is nominal or invented)[49]
always a motive for promising; but a motive for making a promise is not necessarily
consideration for it in law. Thus the testator's desire in *Thomas v Thomas* was a
motive for the executors' promise, but not part of the consideration for it. The
widow's promise to pay and repair was another motive for the executors' promise
and did constitute the consideration.

3–011   **Consideration and condition.** *Thomas v Thomas* also illustrates the difference
between consideration and condition[50]: the claimant's remaining a widow was not
part of the consideration but a condition of her entitlement to enforce the
executors' promise. Similarly, in *Carlill v Carbolic Smoke Ball Co*[51] the claimant
provided consideration for the defendants' promise by using the smoke-ball; but
her catching influenza was only a condition of her entitlement to enforce that
promise. In these cases, the promisee can be said to have performed the condition,
but such performance was not requested by the promisor.[52] Where the promisee's
performance of the condition is (or can reasonably be regarded as having been) so

---

[45] (1842) 2 Q.B. 851.
[46] ibid. at 859. cf. *Hadley v Kemp* [1999] E.M.L.R. 589 at 625.
[47] See below, paras 3–027—3–055.
[48] See below, paras 3–023—3–026.
[49] See above, para.3–009, below, para.3–014. In *Thomas v Thomas* the consideration may not have
been adequate, but it was not nominal: cf. below, para.3–015, and *Westminster CC v Duke of Westminster*
[1991] 4 All E.R. 136 at 146 (reversed in part on other grounds (1992) 24 H.L.R. 572).
[50] i.e. a *contingent* condition: see above, para.2–104.
[51] [1893] 1 Q.B. 256; above, para.2–010.
[52] cf. *Dickinson v Abel* [1969] 1 W.L.R. 295.

requested, it can constitute consideration[53]: e.g. where A promised B to convey a plot of land to B if B built a house on it, B could enforce the promise after he had built the house.[54]

Limited effects of promises without consideration. A promise that is not   3–012
supported by consideration may nevertheless give rise to certain legal effects. In particular, English law places certain restrictions on the revocability of a promise where the promisee has acted on it in a way that the promisor could have anticipated but had not requested; and it may give a remedy against a promisor who would be unjustly enriched if he were allowed freely to revoke his promise after such action in reliance on it by the promisee. These limited legal effects of promises without consideration will be discussed later in this chapter[55]: here it is only necessary to emphasise that they do not give such promises the full consequences of binding contracts. Thus the restrictions on their revocability may be only temporary[56] and breach of the promise may not entitle the injured party to the full loss of bargain damages normally awarded for breach of contract,[57] or may not entitle him to them as of right.[58] Only a promise supported by consideration (or one made in a deed) has these full contractual effects. The limited effects of promises without consideration may therefore have mitigated some of the rigours of the strict doctrine; but they have not eliminated consideration as an essential requirement of a binding contract.[59]

2. ADEQUACY

(a) Consideration Need Not Be Adequate

Under the doctrine of consideration, a promise has no contractual force unless   3–013
some value has been given for it. But the courts do not, in general, ask whether adequate value has been given,[60] or whether the agreement is harsh or one-sided.[61] The reason for this is not that the courts *cannot* value the promise of each party: they have to do just this when assessing damages.[62] It is rather that they *should not* interfere with the bargain actually made by the parties. The fact that a person pays "too much" or "too little" for a thing may be evidence of fraud or mistake, or induce the court to imply a term as to the quality of the subject-matter or be relevant to the question whether a contract has been frustrated.[63] But it does not of itself affect the validity of the contract. This state of the law sometimes causes

---

[53] cf. *Ellis v Chief Adjudication Officer* [1998] 1 F.L.R. 184.

[54] See *Raffaele v Raffaele* [1962] W.A.R. 29; Allan 79 L.Q.R. 239; cf. *Re Soames* (1897) 13 T.L.R. 439; *Errington v Errington* [1952] 1 K.B. 290 (above, para.2–053); *The Castle Alpha* [1989] 2 Lloyd's Rep. 383 at 387.

[55] See below, paras 3–076—3–093, 3–111—3–152.

[56] See below, paras 3–086, 3–113—3–115, 3–135—3–137.

[57] See above, para.1–010, below, Ch.20.

[58] See below, para.3–143.

[59] See below, para.3–088.

[60] *Haigh v Brooks* (1840) 10 A. & E. 309 at 320; *Wild v Tucker* [1914] 3 K.B. 36 at 39; cf. *Langdale v Danby* [1982] 1 W.L.R. 1123; *Brady v Brady* [1989] A.C. 755 at 775; Barton 103 L.Q.R. 118. The principle is recognised and, in general, preserved by Unfair Terms in Consumer Contracts Regulations 1999 (SI 1999/2083), reg.6(2)(b), below, para.7–105.

[61] *Gaumont-British Pictures Corp v Alexander* [1936] 2 All E.R. 1686; *Midland Bank & Trust Co Ltd v Green* [1981] A.C. 513 at 532. cf. below, para.10–044, fn.280.

[62] See below, para.20–021 et seq.

[63] e.g. in the coronation cases, below, paras 19–041—19–043.

dissatisfaction, e.g. when it is alleged that "excessive" profits have been made out of government contracts[64] or when, in times of scarcity, it is said that "excessive" prices are charged for goods or services or accommodation. Such problems are, however, more appropriately dealt with by special legislation or by administrative measures than by the ordinary process of civil litigation. The courts are not well equipped to develop a system of price-control, and their refusal, as a general rule, to concern themselves with the adequacy of consideration is a reflection of this fact. At the same time, the general rule is subject to a number of exceptions, to be discussed later in this book.[65] These indicate that the courts are (even where the legislature has not intervened) by no means insensitive to the problem of unequal bargains; but in none of them is a promise held invalid *merely* because adequate value for it has not been given. Some additional factor is required to bring a case within one of the exceptions: e.g. the existence of a relationship in which one party is able to take an unfair advantage of the other. The general rule remains that "no bargain will be upset which is the result of the ordinary interplay of forces".[66]

(b) Nominal Consideration

3–014   **Sufficiency of nominal consideration.** The rule that consideration need not be adequate makes it possible to evade the doctrine of consideration, in the sense that a gratuitous promise can be made binding by means of a nominal considera-tion, e.g. £1 for the promise of valuable property, or a peppercorn for a substantial sum of money. Such cases are merely extreme applications of the rule that the courts will not judge the adequacy of consideration.[67] If, however, it appears on the face of the agreement that the consideration must as a matter of arithmetic be worth less than the performance of the counter-promise, there would seem to be no contract: e.g. if A promised to pay B £100 in return for £1 to be simultaneously paid by B. It is assumed in the example that both sums are simply to be paid in legal tender. An agreement to exchange a specific coin or coins of a particular description for a sum of money greater than their face value (e.g. 20 shilling pieces bearing the date 1900 for £100) would be a good contract. The same would be true of an agreement to pay a sum in one currency in exchange for one payable in another, and of an agreement to pay a larger sum tomorrow in exchange for a smaller sum paid today.

Where an agreement is legally binding on the ground that it is supported by nominal consideration, the doctrine of consideration does not serve its main purpose, of distinguishing between gratuitous and onerous promises. But the law has no settled policy against enforcing all gratuitous promises. It refuses to enforce

---

[64] See [1964] Public Law 391; cf. Turpin 31 M.L.R. 241.

[65] See below, fn.69, paras 10–042—10–044, 11–079, 21–031; Waddams 39 M.L.R. 393; Tiplady 46 M.L.R. 601. See also *Bankway Properties Ltd v Penfold Dunsford* [2001] EWCA Civ 538; [2001] 1 W.L.R. 1369 where a provision for rent increase in a shorthold tenancy far beyond the amount which (as the landlord knew) the tenant could possibly pay was held to be unenforceable as being inconsistent with the intention of the parties to create an assured tenancy.

[66] *Lloyds Bank Ltd v Bundy* [1975] Q.B. 326 at 336, per Lord Denning M.R.

[67] Atiyah, *Essays in Contract*, p.194 argues that there is no logical connection between the two rules, relying on the fact that in many of the United States the courts recognise the principle that consideration need not be adequate, while rejecting the device of nominal consideration. The answer to this argument lies in Holmes' aphorism (The *Common Law*, p.1) that "the life of the law has not been logic: it has been experience": American courts which reject the device of nominal consideration do so on policy grounds which have nothing to do with logic.

only *informal* gratuitous promises; and the deliberate use of a nominal consideration can be regarded as a form to make a gratuitous promise binding. In some cases
it may, indeed, be undesirable to give nominal consideration the same legal effect
as substantial consideration; but these cases are best dealt with by special rules.[68]
Such rules are particularly necessary where the promise can cause prejudice to
third parties. For example, the danger that company promoters might use the
device of nominal consideration to the prejudice of shareholders is avoided by
imposing fiduciary duties on the promoters.[69]

Nominal distinguished from inadequate consideration. It is not normally   3–015
necessary to distinguish between "nominal" and "inadequate" consideration,
since both equally suffice to make a promise binding. The need to draw the
distinction may, however, arise in some of the exceptional cases[70] in which the law
treats promises or transfers supported only by nominal consideration differently
from those supported by consideration which is substantial or "valuable" (even
though it may be inadequate).

One view is that a nominal consideration is one which is of only token value,[71]
while an inadequate consideration is one which has substantial value even though
it is manifestly less than that of the performance promised or rendered in return.
A second view is that

> " 'Nominal consideration' and a 'nominal sum' appear . . . , as terms of art,
> to refer to a sum or consideration which can be mentioned as consideration
> but is not necessarily paid."[72]

This was the view of Lord Wilberforce in *Midland Bank & Trust Co Ltd v Green*,[73]
where a husband sold a farm, said to be worth £40,000, to his wife for £500. It
was held that the wife was, for the purposes of the Land Charges Act 1925, s.13(2),
a "purchaser for money or money's worth" so that the sale to her prevailed over
an unregistered option to purchase the land, which had been granted to one of the
couple's sons.[74] It was not necessary to decide whether the consideration for the
sale was nominal but Lord Wilberforce said that he would have had "great
difficulty" in so holding; and that "To equate 'nominal' with 'inadequate' or even
'grossly inadequate' consideration would embark the law on inquiries which I
cannot think were ever intended by Parliament"[75]: i.e. inquiries into the adequacy
of the price. On the facts of the case the £500 was in fact paid and was more than

---

[68] Thus a nominal consideration was disregarded in *Milroy v Lord* (1862) 4 D.F. & J. 264, discussed
below, para.15–029 and for the purposes of the Law of Property Act 1925, "'valuable consideration'
. . . does not include a nominal consideration in money"; s.205(1)(xxi).

[69] See below, para.9–148. For other ways of protecting third parties from being prejudiced by
contracts made for inadequate consideration see Insolvency Act 1986, ss.238, 339, 423; Trustee Act
1925, s.13; Local Government Act 1972, s.123(2); Inheritance (Provisions for Family and Dependants)
Act 1975, ss.10(2)(b), 10(5)(b), 11(2)(c); cf. Companies Act 2006, ss.190, 593–594.

[70] See above, at fnn.68 and 69.

[71] This seems to be the sense in which 10s. was described as "nominal" consideration (for the
assignment of a debt) in *Turner v Forwood* [1951] 1 All E.R. 746.

[72] *Midland Bank & Trust Co Ltd v Green* [1981] A.C. 513 at 532.

[73] See above.

[74] For later successful proceedings by the son against his parents in conspiracy see [1982] Ch.
529.

[75] [1981] A.C. 513 at 532. In other legislative contexts such an inquiry may be intended: e.g. by use
of the phrase "full and valuable consideration" in Inheritance (Provision for Family and Dependants)
Act 1975, s.1(3).

a mere token, so that the consideration was not nominal on either of the two views stated above. But if the stated consideration had been only £1, or a peppercorn, it is submitted that it would have been nominal even if it had been paid, or delivered, in accordance with the intention of the parties. So to hold would not lead to enquiries as to the adequacy of consideration; for the distinction between a consideration that is a mere token and one that is inadequate (or even grossly inadequate) is, it is submitted, clear as a matter of common sense. Thus where the question was whether a lease amounted to a "disposition . . . for a nominal consideration"[76] it was said that "Any substantial value—that is, a value of more than, say, £5 . . . will prevent [the] disposition from being for a nominal considera-tion".[77] Such an approach gives rise to no more difficulty than the concept of a consideration which is "mentioned as a consideration but . . . not necessarily paid". That test would presumably make the question whether consideration was nominal turn on the intention of the parties; and, in the present context, this would be an even more elusive than usual criterion, since no guidance could be obtained from the terms of the contract, those terms being, in cases of this kind, often deliberately drafted so as to conceal the true nature of the transaction.

(c) Attitude of Equity

3–016   Equity recognised the general rule that the validity of a contract could not be challenged merely on the ground of inadequacy of consideration.[78] But it some-times refused specific performance, or set a contract aside, or even reopened it (i.e. varied its terms) on the ground that adequate value had not been given to a party who was thought to need special protection.[79] Equity also refuses to aid a "volunteer"—i.e. a person who has given no substantial consideration but can nonetheless enforce a promise at law because it was made in a deed or supported by nominal consideration.[80] It was evidently thought that even such formal gratuitous promises did not deserve the same degree of enforcement as those for which substantial value had been given, and so the equitable remedy of specific performance is not available in respect of such a promise.[81]

3. PAST CONSIDERATION

3–017   **General rule.** The consideration for a promise must be given in return for the promise. If A makes a present of a car to B and a year later B promises to pay A £500 there is no consideration for B's promise as A did not give B the car in return for it. This reasoning often applies where there is an interval of time between an act and the promise said to have been given in return for it. The alleged consideration is then said to be "past consideration" and therefore bad.[82] Thus if a thing is guaranteed *after* it has been sold there is no consideration for the guarantee.[83] Similarly, a promise to pay a sum of money may be made to an

---

[76] Within Law of Property Act 1925, s.84(7).
[77] *Westminster CC v Duke of Westminster* [1991] 4 All E.R. 136 at 146, reversed in part on another ground (1992) 24 H.L.R. 572.
[78] See, e.g. *Cheale v Kenward* (1858) 3 D. & J. 27; *Townend v Toker* (1866) L.R. 1 Ch.App. 446.
[79] *Tennent v Tennents* (1870) L.R. 2 Sc. & Div. 6 at 9; below, paras 10–042—10–044, 21–031.
[80] *Jefferys v Jefferys* (1841) Cr. & Ph. 138.
[81] See below, para.21–045.
[82] *Dent v Bennett* (1839) 4 My. & Cr. 269; *Eastwood v Kenyon* (1840) 11 A. & E. 438.
[83] *Thorner v Field* (1612) 1 Bulst.120; *Roscorla v Thomas* (1842) 3 Q.B. 234.

employee after his retirement or to an agent after the termination of the agency. If the sole consideration for the promise is the service previously rendered by the employee or agent under the terminated contract, it will be a past consideration so that the promise will not be contractually binding.[84] It will be so binding only if some consideration, other than the past service, has been provided by the promisee. Such other consideration may consist in his giving up rights which are outstanding (or are in good faith believed to be outstanding) under the original contract,[85] or in his promising or accomplishing some other act or forbearance not due from him under the original contract: e.g. in his validly promising not to compete with the promisor.[86]

When consideration is past. In determining whether consideration is past, the court is not, it is submitted, bound to apply a strictly chronological test. If the consideration and the promise are substantially one transaction, the exact order in which these events occur is not decisive.[87] A manufacturer's "guarantee" may be given to a customer after he has bought the goods. But the consideration for the guarantee would not be past if the sale and the giving of the "guarantee" were in substance a single transaction,[88] as they would be if the customer at the time of the sale thought that he was buying a guaranteed product.[89] The question whether consideration is past is one of fact: the wording of the agreement is not decisive. Thus in *Re McArdle*[90] a promise made "in consideration of your carrying out" certain work was held to be gratuitous as the work had already been done. Conversely, a promise made "in consideration of your having today advanced . . . £750" has been held binding on proof that the advance was made at the same time as the promise.[91]

3–018

Past consideration as good consideration. A past act can be consideration for a promise if three conditions are satisfied: the act must have been done at the request of the promisor[92]; it must have been understood that payment would be made; and the payment, if it had been promised in advance, must have been legally recoverable.[93] In such a case the promisee is, quite apart from the subsequent promise, entitled to a reasonable sum for his services by way of a quantum meruit. The promise can be regarded either as fixing the amount of that sum[94] or as

3–019

---

[84] cf. *Simpson v John Reynolds* [1975] 1 W.L.R. 617; *Murray v Goodhews* [1978] 1 W.L.R. 489.

[85] e.g. *Bell v Lever Bros Ltd* [1932] A.C. 161 (where the value of the rights given up in return for the payment was uncertain in amount since it included not only future salary but also possible future commission).

[86] cf. *Wyatt v Kreglinger and Fernau* [1933] 1 K.B. 793.

[87] *Thornton v Jenkyns* (1840) 1 Man. & G. 166; *Tanner v Moore* (1846) 9 Q.B. 1; *Westminster CC v Duke of Westminster* [1991] 4 All E.R. 136 at 145, reversed in part on another ground (1992) 24 H.L.R. 572.

[88] cf. *Classic Maritime Inc v Lion Diversified Holdings Berhad* [2009] EWHC 1142 (Comm); [2010] 1 Lloyd's Rep. 59.

[89] Where the guarantee is a "consumer guarantee" within the Sale and Supply of Goods to Consumers Regulations 2002 (SI 2002/3045, reg.15, implementing Dir.1999/44, Art.7), it binds the guarantor by force of this legislation without the need for the consumer to prove consideration.

[90] [1951] Ch. 669.

[91] *Goldshede v Swan* (1847) 1 Ex. 154. The burden of proving that the consideration was not past is on the person seeking to enforce the promise: *Savage v Uwechia* [1961] 1 W.L.R. 455.

[92] *Southwark LBC v Logan* (1996) 8 Admin.L.R. 315.

[93] *Re Casey's Patents* [1892] 1 Ch. 104 at 115–116; cf. *Lampleigh v Brathwaite* (1615) Hob. 105.

[94] *Kennedy v Broun* (1863) 13 C.B.(N.S.) 677 at 740; *Rondel v Worsley* [1969] 1 A.C. 191 at 236, 278, 287.

being given in consideration of the promisee's releasing his claim for such a payment. On the other hand, a past service which was not done at the request of the promisor, or one for which payment was not expected, or one for which payment, though expected, is not legally recoverable, is no consideration for a subsequent promise to pay for it.[95]

The consideration for a promise by A can consist not only of a past *act* done by B at A's request, but also of an earlier *promise* made by B at A's request. Thus in *Pao On v Lau Yiu Long*[96] the claimants had promised the defendants that for one year they would not sell certain shares in a company of which the defendants were the principal shareholders. This promise had been made at the request of the defendants, who were anxious to prevent the value of their own holding from being depressed by a sudden sale of the claimants' shares. Later, the defendants gave the claimants a guarantee in which they promised to indemnify the claimants against any loss which they might suffer if, during the year, the shares fell in value.[97] The Privy Council rejected the argument that the consideration for the guarantee was past.[98] The claimants' promise not to sell the shares was good consideration for the guarantee; for although that promise had been made before the guarantee was given, it had been made at the defendants' request and on the understanding that the claimants were, in return for making it, to receive some form of protection against the risk (to which the promise exposed them) of a fall in the value of those shares.

3–020   **Antecedent debt.** In a number of cases it has been held that the mere existence of an antecedent debt does not constitute "value" for a *transfer* by the debtor as it amounts only to past consideration.[99] These cases are not directly concerned with the question whether such an antecedent debt can constitute consideration for a later *promise* by the debtor: e.g. for one to pay higher interest or to pay early. But they may, by analogy, support the view that, where the only possible consideration for such a promise is an antecedent debt owed by the promisor to the promisee, then such consideration is past, so that the promise is not contractually binding.[100] In practice, however, the creditor (i.e. the promisee) will often provide consideration for such a promise by forbearing, on the strength of it, to sue for the debt.[101]

3–021   **Moral obligation.** It is clear that the moral obligation to perform a promise, once made, cannot provide consideration for it, since this would "annihilate the necessity for any consideration at all."[102] Nor is consideration provided by any antecedent moral obligation. Thus in *Eastwood v Kenyon*[103] the guardian of a young girl had raised a loan to pay for her maintenance and education, and to improve her estate. After she had come of age and married, her husband promised the guardian to pay the amount of the loan. The court dismissed the guardian's

---

[95] *Kennedy v Broun*, above; *Rondel v Worsley*, above.

[96] [1980] A.C. 614.

[97] This guarantee replaced an earlier agreement which was less favourable to the claimants.

[98] For the further argument that the consideration was no more than the promise to perform an existing contractual duty, see below, para.3–055.

[99] *Roger v Comptoir d'Escompte de Paris* (1869) L.R. 2 C.P. 393; *Re Barker's Estate* (1875) 44 L.J. Ch. 487; *Wigan v English & Scottish Law Life Assurance Society* [1909] 1 Ch. 291.

[100] e.g. *Hopkinson v Logan* (1839) 5 M. & W. 241 (promise fixing date of payment).

[101] See below, para.3–072.

[102] *Eastwood v Kenyon* (1840) 11 A. & E. 438 at 450.

[103] (1840) 11 A. & E. 438.

action on this promise; the mere existence of the antecedent moral obligation to reimburse the guardian did not amount to consideration for the husband's promise.[104]

Statutory exceptions. There are two exceptions to the rule that past consideration is no consideration. First, an "antecedent debt or liability" is good consideration for a bill of exchange.[105] Secondly, the Limitation Act 1980[106] provides that, where a debtor in a writing signed by him[107] "acknowledges" a debt, it shall be deemed to have accrued on and not before the date of the acknowledgment. An "acknowledgment" need not take the form of a promise[108]; but if it does take this form the promise can extend the period of limitation even though the only consideration for it was the antecedent debt, and thus past. Further acknowledgments made within such an extended period or periods have the same effect.[109] But once the debt has become statute-barred the right to sue for it cannot be revived by any subsequent acknowledgment[110]: to this extent, the old "moral obligation" theory as applied to statute-barred debts[111] has been reversed.

3–022

4. CONSIDERATION MUST MOVE FROM THE PROMISEE

Promisee must provide consideration. The rule that consideration must "move from the promisee"[112] means that a person to whom a promise was made can enforce it only if he himself provided the consideration for it. He has no such right if the consideration moved from a third party. Thus if A promises B to pay £10,000 to B if C will paint A's house, and C does so, B cannot enforce A's promise (unless, of course, B had procured, or undertaken to procure, C to do the work). The promisee need not, however, provide the whole consideration for the promise: thus he can enforce a promise, the consideration for which was provided partly by himself and partly by his agent or partner or by some other co-promisee.[113]

3–023

---

[104] A number of earlier cases supported the theory that an antecedent "moral" obligation would suffice where it was derived from a previous obligation of the promisor which was not enforceable because it suffered from a specific legal defect. *Eastwood v Kenyon* did not purport to overrule the "moral obligation" theory in this narrow sense and it has been applied since (*Roscorla v Thomas* (1842) 3 Q.B. 234 at 237; *Flight v Reed* (1863) 1 H. & C. 703 (mentioned with approval by Scrutton L.J. in *J Evans & Co v Heathcote* [1918] 1 K.B. 418 at 437)), but its scope has been restricted and the label has become unfashionable.

[105] Bills of Exchange Act 1882, s.27(1)(b). Such consideration is not *necessarily* past: it might consist of forbearance of the creditor to sue for the debt or in his treating the bill as conditional payment: see *Currie v Misa* (1875) L.R. 10 Ex. 153 and cf. below, para.3–034.

[106] s.29(5).

[107] Limitation Act 1980, s.30(1).

[108] *Lia Oil SA v ERG Petroli* [2007] EWHC 505 (Comm); [2007] 2 Lloyd's Rep. 509. An admission of liability suffices: *Surrendra Overseas Ltd v Government of Sri Lanka* [1977] 1 W.L.R. 565; *Bradford & Bingley Plc v Rashid* [2006] UKHL 37; [2006] 1 W.L.R. 2066; cf. *Re Overmark Smith Warden Ltd* [1982] 1 W.L.R. 1195. Contrast: *Revenue & Customs Commissioners v Benchdollar* [2009] EWHC 1310 (Ch); [2010] 1 All E.R. 174 (denial of liability).

[109] Limitation Act 1980, s.29(7)

[110] ibid.

[111] *Hyeling v Hastings* (1699) 1 Ld. Raym. 389.

[112] *Barber v Fox* (1682) 2 Wms.Saund. 134, n.(e); *Thomas v Thomas* (1842) 2 Q.B. 851 at 859; *Tweddle v Atkinson* (1861) 1 B. & S. 393 at 398, 399; cf. *Dickinson v Abel* [1969] 1 W.L.R. 295.

[113] *Jones v Robinson* (1847) 1 Ex. 454; *Fleming v Bank of New Zealand* [1900] A.C. 577. For the position where the *whole* consideration is provided by a co-promisee, see below, para.13–034.

3–024   **Consideration need not move to promisor.** While consideration must move from the promisee, it need not move to the promisor.[114] It follows that the requirement of consideration may be satisfied where the promisee suffers some detriment at the promisor's request, but confers no corresponding benefit on the promisor. Thus the promisee may provide consideration by giving up a job[115] or the tenancy of a flat,[116] even though no direct benefit results to the promisor from these acts. Consideration may also move from the promisee without moving to the promisor where the promisee at the promisor's request confers a benefit on a third party, e.g. by entering into a contract with the third party.[117] This possibility is illustrated by the case in which goods are bought and paid for by the use of a debit card or credit card. The issuer of the card makes a promise to the supplier of the goods that the supplier will be paid; and the supplier provides consideration for this promise by supplying the goods to the customer.[118] In the case of the credit card transaction, there is also consideration in the shape of the discount allowed by the supplier of the goods to the issuer of the card: this is both a detriment to the supplier and a benefit to the issuer.[119]

3–025   **Benefit to promisor sufficient.** The requirement that consideration must move from the promisee at first sight supports the view that the essence of consideration is detriment to the promisee. But the requirement may be satisfied, even though the promisee in fact suffers no detriment, if he confers a benefit on the promisor, or on a third party at the promisor's request. This possibility is illustrated by *Edmonds v Lawson*,[120] where the relationship between a pupil barrister and the members of the chambers at which she had accepted an offer of pupillage was held to be contractual even though she paid no pupillage fee. The requirement of consideration was satisfied in that her (and other pupils') agreement to accept pupillage "provide[d] a pool of selected candidates who can be expected to compete with each other for recruitment as tenants",[121] and in that "chambers may see an advantage in developing close relationships with pupils who plan to practise as employed barristers or overseas".[122] Both these factors stress the benefit to the promisors (the members of the chambers), moving from the promisee (the pupil barrister) even though no detriment was suffered by her.

The view that consideration can move from the promisee though he in fact suffers no detriment is supported by two further rules to be discussed later in this chapter. The first is that performance of an existing contractual duty (or a promise to perform such a duty) can constitute consideration if it benefits the promisor[123]: this benefit "moves" from the promisee in that it is conferred by him, even though

---

[114] *Re Wyvern Developments Ltd* [1974] 1 W.L.R. 1097; cf. *Barclays Bank Plc v Weeks, Legg & Dean* [1998] 3 All E.R. 213 at 220–221.

[115] *Jones v Padavatton* [1969] 1 W.L.R. 628.

[116] *Tanner v Tanner* [1975] 1 W.L.R. 1346; contrast *Horrocks v Forray* [1976] 1 W.L.R. 230; *Coombes v Smith* [1986] 1 W.L.R. 808.

[117] See *International Petroleum Refining Supply Ltd v Caleb Brett & Son Ltd* [1980] 1 Lloyd's Rep. 569 at 594 (where the promisor benefited indirectly since promisor and third party were associated companies); cf. also *The Chemical Venture* [1993] 1 Lloyd's Rep. 509 at 522.

[118] See *R. v Lambie* [1982] A.C. 449; *Re Charge Card Services Ltd* [1987] Ch. 150, affirmed [1989] Ch. 497.

[119] *Customs & Excise Commissioners v Diner's Club Ltd* [1989] 1 W.L.R. 1196 at 1207.

[120] [2000] Q.B. 501. cf. *Horton v Higham* [2004] EWCA Civ 941; [2004] 3 All E.R. 863 at [21]; *Bolton v Madden* (1873) L.R. 9 Q.B. 55.

[121] [2000] Q.B. 501 at 515.

[122] ibid. at 515.

[123] See below, paras 3–049, 3–054—3–055.

it may cause him no detriment[124] in the sense that he was already bound to do the acts in question. The second is that a composition agreement between a debtor and his creditors is binding because it benefits the creditors[125]; and this benefit can be said to "move" from the debtor in that his co-operation is essential to the making and performance of the composition agreement. It could be said that the debtor suffers a legal detriment by signing the agreement when he is not bound to do so. But the rule is not based on this invented consideration.[126] It is based on benefit to the promisors.[127]

Contracts (Rights of Third Parties) Act 1999. Under this Act, a term in a   3–026
contract between A (the promisor) and B (the promisee) is, in specified conditions, enforceable by a third party, C, against A. The Act is more fully discussed in Ch.14[128]; the only points to be made here are that C is not prevented from enforcing the term by the fact that no consideration for A's promise moved from him,[129] and that C's right to enforce that promise can be described as a quasi-exception to the rule that consideration must move from the promisee.[130] It is not a true exception to the rule since in the case put the promisee is B, who must provide consideration for A's promise.

5. CONSIDERATION MUST BE OF SOME VALUE

(a) Must be of Economic Value

An act, forbearance or promise will amount to consideration only if the law   3–027
recognises that it has some economic value. It may have such value even though the value cannot be precisely quantified. But "natural affection of itself is not a sufficient consideration",[131] and the same is true of other merely sentimental motives for promising. This is the reason why in *Thomas v Thomas*[132] the desire of the testator that his widow should live in his house was not part of the consideration for the executors' promise that she might do so. Similar reasoning may also explain the decision in *White v Bluett*[133] that a son had not provided consideration (for his father's promise not to sue him on a promissory note) by promising not to bore his father with complaints.

(b) Illusory Consideration

Promise impossible to perform. A promise may appear to be made for some   3–028
consideration which is illusory and which must therefore be disregarded. One such situation can arise when the alleged consideration consists of a promise, the

---

[124] *Williams v Roffey Bros & Nicholls (Contractors) Ltd* [1991] 1 Q.B. 1 at 16.
[125] See below, para.3–109.
[126] See above, para.3–009. The creditors do not bargain for the debtor's signature but for a dividend. If the debtor's signature were the consideration it could equally well be so regarded in a composition with a single creditor, but this would be contrary to *Foakes v Beer* (1884) 9 App.Cas. 605; below, para.3–100.
[127] See below, para.3–100.
[128] See below, para.14–090 et seq.
[129] Law Com. No.242 (on which the Act is based), §6.8.
[130] See below, para.14–099.
[131] *Bret v JS* (1600) Cro.Eliz.756; *Mansukhani v Sharkey* [1992] 2 E.G.L.R. 105.
[132] (1842) 2 Q.B. 851; above, para.3–011.
[133] (1853) 23 L.J.Ex. 36.

performance of which is, to the knowledge of both parties, impossible. For example, a promise by A to pay B £100 in return for B's promise to let A have all the wine in B's cellar would probably be regarded as a gratuitous promise if, when the promise was made, both A and B knew[134] that there was no wine in the cellar. The position would be different if B's promise were to deliver the *future* contents of the cellar. In that case, A would be buying the chance of the cellar's containing wine[135]; and the value of that chance would be illusory only if the question whether any wine was to be put into the cellar had been left entirely to B's discretion.[136]

3–029   **Promisee would have accomplished act or forbearance in any event.** A second situation in which consideration would be illusory is where the promisee would have accomplished the act or forbearance anyway, even if the promise had not been made. This will be the position if A promises B, who has religious objections to smoking, £5 if he will not smoke for a week. Since "it is no consideration to refrain from a course of conduct which it was never intended to pursue",[137] such a promise would not be legally binding. But where the promise provided *an* inducement for the act or forbearance, the requirement of consideration would be satisfied even though there were also other inducements operating on the mind of the promisee.[138] It seems that the burden of proving that the requested act or forbearance would have been accomplished, even if the promise had not been made, is on the promisor.[139]

3–030   **Promise of performance at the discretion of the promisor.**[140] Consideration would again be illusory where it was alleged to consist of a promise the terms of which left performance entirely to the discretion of the promisor.[141] A person does not provide consideration by promising to do something "if I feel like it", or "unless I change my mind"; and the same principle may apply in analogous cases. Thus a promise may be illusory if it is accompanied by a clause effectively excluding all liability of the promisor for breach.[142] And a promise to buy "so much coal as I may decide to order" would be an illusory consideration for the seller's counter-promise to deliver, which could therefore not be enforced.[143] On the other hand, if the promise were to buy "so much of the coal *that I require* as

---

[134] There could be a good contract if the parties were in doubt on this point: see *Smith v Harrison* (1857) 26 L.J. Ch. 412.

[135] cf. *Brady v Brady* [1989] A.C. 755 at 774 ("at the date of the promise").

[136] See below at fn.141.

[137] *Arrale v Costain Civil Engineering Ltd* [1976] 1 Lloyd's Rep. 98 at 106; cf. *Colchester BC v Smith* [1991] Ch. 448 at 489, affirmed on other grounds [1992] Ch. 421; *Birmingham City Council v Forde* [2009] EWHC 12 (QB); [2009] 1 W.L.R. 2732 at [96].

[138] *Brikom Investments Ltd v Carr* [1979] Q.B. 467 at 490.

[139] *Well Barn Farming Ltd v Backhouse* [2005] EWHC 1520 (Ch); [2005] 3 E.G.L.R. 109 at [47]. cf. the analogous rule in cases of "proprietary estoppel" (below, para.3–133): *Greasley v Cook* [1980] 1 W.L.R. 1306; and misrepresentation (below, para.9–027): *Smith v Chadwick* (1884) 9 App.Cas. 187 at 196.

[140] "Promisor" here refers to the person making the promise which is claimed to amount to consideration, though he is the promisee so far as the enforcement of the counter-promise, for which he is said to have provided consideration, is concerned.

[141] *Stabilad Ltd v Stephens & Carter Ltd (No.2)* [1999] 2 All E.R. (Comm) 651 at 659. Such promises may also give rise to problems of contractual intention: see below, para.4–017.

[142] See below, para.7–031.

[143] See *Wickham & Burton Coal Co v Farmer's Lumber Co* 189, 179 N.W. 417 (1923); for an exception, see *Citadel Ins Co v Atlantic Union Ins Co* [1982] 2 Lloyd's Rep. 543; below, para.3–161.

I may order from you", the court could give reality to the promise by implying a term into it to the effect that at least a reasonable part of any requirements which the promisor actually turned out to have must be ordered from the promisee. Equally a buyer would provide consideration by promising to buy from the seller "*all* the coal I require"; for in such a case, even if the buyer does not promise to have any requirements, he does at least give a definite undertaking not to deal with anybody else.[144] Similarly, a promise which is subject to cancellation by A may nevertheless constitute consideration for a counter-promise from B where A's power to cancel is limited by the express terms of the promise, e.g. where it can be exercised only within a specified time. Such a limitation on the power to cancel may also be implied, so that (e.g.) A could not cancel after B had begun to perform his counter-promise. A's promise would then constitute consideration, so that B would be liable if he failed to complete the performance. Finally, the objection that a promise amounts only to illusory consideration on the grounds here discussed can be removed if the promise is performed: such actual performance can constitute consideration even though the person who has rendered it was not legally obliged to render it.[145]

(c) Trivial Acts or Objects

Acts of very small value. Since consideration need not be adequate, acts or omissions of very small value can be consideration.[146] Thus it has been said that the act of executing a deed could be consideration for a promise to pay money although the deed was void[147]; that to show a person a document was consideration[148]; that the grant of permission to cut back undergrowth was consideration for the grant of a licence to occupy land[149]; and that the mere act of conducting negotiations can satisfy the requirement of consideration, even though that act does not commit the promisee to bringing the negotiations to a successful conclusion.[150]   3–031

Objects of trifling value. On the same principle, objects of trifling value can constitute consideration. In *Chappell & Co Ltd v Nestlé Co Ltd*,[151] chocolate manufacturers sold gramophone records for 1s. 6d. plus three wrappers of their 6d.bars of chocolate. It was held that the delivery of the wrappers formed part of   3–032

---

[144] The validity of "requirement" contracts is assumed in such cases as *Metropolitan Electric Supply Co v Ginder* [1901] 2 Ch. 799 and *Dominion Coal Co Ltd v Dominion Steel & Iron Co Ltd* [1909] A.C. 293. Similarly, a contract by a manufacturer to sell his entire output to a particular buyer is binding even though he does not bind himself to have any output: see, e.g. *Donnell v Bennett* (1883) 22 Ch.D. 835; Howard 2 U. of Tas.L.R. 446; Adams 94 L.Q.R. 73. For the possible illegality of such promises, see below, paras 11–092 et seq.

[145] *Cambridge Nutrition Ltd v BBC* [1990] 3 All E.R. 523 at 538; *Stabilad Ltd v Stephens & Carter Ltd (No.2)* [1999] 2 All E.R. (Comm) 651 at 660.

[146] *Gilbert v Ruddeard* (1608) 3 Dy. 272b (n); cf. *Denton v GN Ry* (1856) 5 E. & B. 860.

[147] *Westlake v Adams* (1858) 5 C.B.(N.S.) 248.

[148] *Sturlyn v Albany* (1587) Cro.Eliz. 67; *March v Culpepper* (1628) Cro.Car. 70. Contrast *Re Charge Card Services Ltd* [1987] Ch. 150 at 164, affirmed [1989] Ch. 497 (production of charge card and signature of voucher not the consideration for a supply of goods, evidently because such "consideration" would be blatantly "invented": above, para.3–009).

[149] *Well Barn Farming Ltd v Backhouse* [2005] EWHC 1520 (Ch); [2005] 3 E.G.L.R. 109 at [45].

[150] *Sepong Engineering Construction Co v Formula One Management Ltd* [2000] 1 Lloyd's Rep. 602 at 611; but damages for breach of the resulting contract would probably be no more than nominal: cf. below, para.20–060.

[151] [1960] A.C. 87.

the consideration, though the wrappers were of little value and were in fact thrown away. If the delivery of the wrappers formed part of the consideration it could, presumably, have formed the whole of the consideration, so that a promise to deliver records for wrappers alone would have been binding. This case should be contrasted with *Lipkin Gorman v Karpnale Ltd*,[152] where gaming chips supplied by a gaming club to one of its members (and then lost by the member in the course of the gaming) were held not to constitute consideration for the money which the member had paid for them.[153] One reason for this view appears to have been that "the chips themselves were worthless"[154]; but this is equally true of the wrappers in the *Chappell* case. Another seems to have been that the chips "remained the property of the club"[155]; but this again would not of itself be decisive, for the transfer of possession (no less than that of ownership) can constitute consideration.[156] A third reason for the view that the chips were not consideration for the money may be that the parties did not so regard the transaction: they regarded the chips as merely "a convenient mechanism for facilitating gambling",[157] and the case may be one in which the court refused to "invent" consideration[158] (by regarding something as consideration which was not so regarded by the parties) even though this course was technically open to it. This refusal appears to have been based on the context in which the question arose. The issue was not whether the club could sue the member on any promise made by him: it arose because the money paid by the member to the club had been stolen; and the club, which had received the money in good faith, argued that it had given valuable consideration for it, so as to defeat the true owner's claim for the return of the money. This explanation of the case derives some support from Lord Goff's discussion of a hypothetical case of tokens supplied by a department store in exchange for cash. He said that "by receiving the money in these circumstances the store does not *for present purposes* give valuable consideration for it"[159]; yet he also accepted that (in the store example) "an independent contract is made for the chips when the customer originally obtains them at the cash desk".[160] The question whether a party has provided consideration may thus receive one answer when it arises for the purpose of determining the enforceability of a promise, and a different and narrower one when it arises for the purpose of determining whether a transaction has adversely affected the rights of an innocent third party.[161] It was the desire to protect the victim of the theft which led the House of Lords in the *Lipkin Gorman* case to reject the (no doubt somewhat technical) argument that the chips constituted consideration for the money.

The *Lipkin Gorman* case gives rise to further difficulty because the chips were supplied on the terms that they could be used, not only for gaming, but also to purchase refreshments at the club. There was no evidence of their having been

---

[152] [1991] 2 A.C. 548.

[153] It was necessary to consider whether the chips amounted to valuable consideration because the club could not simply rely on the wagering contract with the member since it was "null and void" under s.18 of Gaming Act 1845; but see now the reforms contained in the Gambling Act 2005: para.11–011 below.

[154] *Lipkin Gorman*'s case at 561.

[155] ibid. and see 575.

[156] *Bainbridge v Firmstone* (1838) 8 A. & E. 743.

[157] *Lipkin Gorman*'s case, at 575.

[158] See above, para.3–009.

[159] *Lipkin Gorman*'s case, at 577; italics supplied; cf. above, para.3–007.

[160] ibid. at 576.

[161] See above, para.3–001.

used for this purpose,[162] but Lord Templeman said that "neither the power to buy refreshments nor the exercise of that power could constitute consideration for the receipt [by the club] of £154,693", (the sum lost by the member of the club).[163] One possible interpretation of this passage is that the supply of refreshments could not constitute consideration for £154,693 since the disparity in value was too great; but this would be inconsistent with the principle that consideration need not be adequate. It is submitted that the preferable explanation of Lord Templeman's statement is that the chips were simply "treated as currency"[164] in the club and could be used for a variety of transactions. The reason why the supply of refreshments was not consideration for the face value of the chips lost at play was simply that these transactions were entirely separate ones.

(d) Gift of Onerous Property

A promise to give away onerous property is binding if the donee promises in return to discharge obligations attached to it. Thus a promise to give away a leasehold house is binding if the donee promises to perform the donor's covenants under the lease, e.g. to repair, to insure and to pay rent[165]; a promise to give away a freehold house is binding if the donee promises to pay outstanding mortgage instalments or other charges[166]; and a promise to give away partly paid-up shares in a company is binding if the donee promises to pay further calls which may be made on the shares.[167]   3–033

(e) Compromise and Forbearance to Sue[168]

(i) *Valid claims*

Promise to release a valid claim is good consideration. A promise not to enforce a valid claim is clearly good consideration for a promise given in return.[169] If, for example, A is injured by the admitted negligence of B, they can validly compromise the claim, A's promise not to sue B constituting the consideration for B's promise to pay the agreed compensation. Similarly, a creditor to whom a sum of money has become due may promise to give the debtor extra time to pay in return for the debtor's promise to pay higher interest or to give additional security. In such a case there is good consideration for the debtor's promise: he benefits by getting extra time to pay, while the creditor suffers a detriment in that he is, for a time, kept out of his money.[170] There is such benefit to the debtor and detriment   3–034

---

[162] *Lipkin Gorman's* case, at 569.

[163] ibid. at 567.

[164] ibid. at 561.

[165] *Price v Jenkins* (1877) 5 Ch.D. 619; *Westminster CC v Duke of Westminster* [1991] 4 All E.R. 136, reversed in part on other grounds (1992) 24 H.L.R. 572.

[166] *Merritt v Merritt* [1970] 1 W.L.R. 1121.

[167] *Cheale v Kenward* (1858) 3 D. & J. 27.

[168] This part is not concerned with the settlement of legal proceedings under CPR Pt 36. Such agreements are sui generis and need not have contractual force, though in the vast majority of cases they will also amount to contracts (*Orton v Collins* [2007] EWHC 803 (Ch); [2007] 1 W.L.R. 2953 at [60]) for the reasons which are explained in this part.

[169] e.g. *Greene v Church Commissioners for England* [1974] Ch. 467; *The Attika Hope* [1988] 1 Lloyd's Rep. 439 at 442 (forbearance to sue third party).

[170] *Crowther v Farrer* (1850) 15 Q.B. 677.

to the creditor even if the creditor promises to forbear for only a limited time; and if no time is specified, the court will infer that he undertook to forbear for a reasonable time.[171] The principles just stated apply, not only to a promise not to enforce a claim, but also to a promise to abandon a good defence[172]; and to a promise to abandon a particular remedy, e.g. to one to abandon arbitration proceedings.[173]

3–035   **Protection of promisor on other grounds.** Although a promise to release a valid claim is thus supported by consideration, the court may protect the party granting the release on other grounds. This possibility is illustrated by *Bank of Credit and Commerce International SA v Ali*[174] where an employee, on being dismissed for redundancy, promised in return for certain payments to release all claims against the employers "of whatever nature that exist or may exist". At the time of the release, claims for "stigma damages" were believed not to be available to employees for breach of their employment contracts, but the availability of such claims established by a later decision of the House of Lords.[175] It was held by the House of Lords in the present case that the general words of the release (quoted above) were not sufficiently clear to show "that the parties intended to provide for the release of rights and surrender of claims which they could never have had in contemplation at all".[176] It is implicit in this reasoning that the possibility of releasing such a claim is not ruled out as a matter of law: the court is simply "slow to infer that a party intended to surrender rights and claims of which he was unaware and could not have been aware".[177] The crucial point in *Ali*'s case seems to have been that *neither* party could have been aware of the possibility that the employee might, in law, have had a claim for stigma damages. If the *employer* had been aware of this possibility, it is far from clear that the employee would have succeeded on the issue of *construction*. There is, however, the further possibility that the amount of a settlement may be affected by the fact that

> "the party to whom the release was given [B] knew that the other party [A] had or might have a claim [beyond the one he thought he was releasing] *and knew also* that the other party was ignorant of this".[178]

B's taking the release "without disclosing the existence of the claim or possible claim" would then be "unacceptable sharp practice"[179] and there is judicial support for the view that the law should on this ground grant relief to A,[180] i.e. allow him to pursue the claim which he had unwittingly abandoned.

---

[171] *Payne v Wilson* (1827) 7 B. & C. 423; *Oldershaw v King* (1857) 2 H. & N. 517.

[172] See *Banque de l'Indochine v J H Rayner(Mincing Lane)Ltd* [1983] Q.B. 711.

[173] *The Leonidas D* [1985] 1 W.L.R. 925 at 933, where there was no such abandonment: see above, para.2–005.

[174] [2001] UKHL 8; [2002] 1 A.C. 251.

[175] *Malik v Bank of Credit and Commerce International* [1998] A.C. 20; below, para.20–092.

[176] [2002] 1 A.C. 251 at [19]; *Satyam Computer Services Ltd v Upaid Systems Ltd* [2008] EWCA Civ 487; [2008] 2 C.L.C. 864 (applied to 'fraud-based claims'). Contrast *Mostcash Plc v Fluor Ltd* [2002] EWCA Civ 975; [2002] B.L.R. 411; *Priory Caring Services Ltd v Capita Property Services Ltd* [2010] EWCA Civ 226; 129 Con L.R. 81.

[177] [2002] 1 A.C. 251 at [10]. Lord Hoffmann dissented.

[178] ibid. at [32], italics supplied.

[179] ibid. In *Ali*'s case there was no such knowledge on B's part.

[180] ibid. per Lord Nicholls. Lord Bingham left the point open: [20]; Lord Hoffmann preferred to confine it to general releases: [69]–[70].

(ii) *Invalid and doubtful claims*

Claims known to be invalid. It used to be thought that a promise by A not   3–036
to enforce a claim which was invalid was no consideration for a promise given by
B in return, since B, if he was not liable, did not benefit from A's promise not to
sue him, while A lost nothing by giving up a worthless right.[181] This reasoning
still applies where the sole[182] consideration provided by A is his forbearance to
enforce a claim which is clearly invalid and which he either knows to be invalid or
does not believe to be valid.[183]

Doubtful claims. Where the claim is doubtful in law, a promise to abandon it   3–037
involves the possibility of detriment to the potential claimant and of benefit to the
other party. Such a promise is therefore good consideration for a counter-promise
given by the latter party: e.g. for one to pay a sum of money to the party promising
to abandon the claim.[184]

Claims wrongly believed to be valid. A promise by A to abandon a claim is   3–038
also good consideration for a counter-promise made by B, even though A's claim
is *clearly* bad in law, if it is believed by A to be a valid one.[185] One reason which
has been given for this rule is that otherwise "in no case of a doubtful claim could
a compromise be enforced"[186]; but this does not explain why the rule applies
where A's claim is not merely "doubtful" but *clearly* bad. Another suggested
reason for the rule is that A suffers detriment because "he gives up what he
believes to be a right of action"[187]; but, in general, consideration must be
something of value, not something believed to be of value. In fact A would be
worse off, if he did not forbear, for he would lose his action and the costs. A
further suggestion is that A suffers detriment in that it becomes more difficult to
get up his case, the longer he waits[188]; this is a possible detriment (even though his
action is bound to fail) as the failure may be more expensive than it would have
been, had he sued promptly. A may also suffer detriment if as a result of the
agreement he loses the right to sue a third party who is liable on the original cause
of action.[189]A's forbearance can also be said to confer a benefit on B since "instead
of being annoyed with an action, he [B] escapes from the vexations incident to
it".[190] There is some difficulty in relying on this benefit as the consideration for

---

[181] *Jones v Ashburnham* (1804) 4 East 455.

[182] The position is different where there is also other consideration: *The Siboen and the Sibotre* [1976]
1 Lloyd's Rep. 293 at 334.

[183] This seems to be the basis of the observation made by Lord Saville in *Borrelli v Ting* [2010]
UKPC 21; [2010] Bus. L.R. 1718 at [41].

[184] *Haigh v Brooks* (1839) 10 A. & E. 309; cf. *Colchester BC v Smith* [1992] Ch. 421; *Colonia
Versicherung AG v Amoco Oil Co* [1995] 1 Lloyd's Rep. 570 at 577 (affirmed [1997] 1 Lloyd's Rep. 261,
without reference to this point).

[185] *Cook v Wright* (1861) 1 B. & S. 559; *Callisher v Bischoffsheim* (1870) L.R. 5 Q.B. 449; *Holsworthy
Urban DC v Holsworthy Rural DC* [1907] 2 Ch. 62; cf. *Horton v Horton* [1961] 1 Q.B. 215; *Freedman
v Union Group Plc* [1997] E.G.C.S. 28.

[186] *Callisher v Bischoffsheim*, above, at 451.

[187] ibid. at 452.

[188] *Cook v Wright*, above, at 569.

[189] ibid. at 569–570.

[190] *Callisher v Bischoffsheim*, above, at 452; cf. *Pitt v PHH Asset Management Ltd* [1994] 1 W.L.R. 327
at 332, but in this case it is not clear that the party forbearing in fact believed in the validity of his claim.
See also *Mousaka Inc v Goldon Seagull Maritime Inc* [2002] 1 Lloyd's Rep. 797 at [14] ("commercial
benefit").

B's counter-promise, since it may also exist where A's claim is *known* to be bad, in which case the compromise is not binding.[191] Perhaps this last rule is based on public policy rather than on want of consideration. As Tindal C.J. said in *Wade v Simeon*[192]:

> "It is almost *contra bonos mores* and certainly contrary to the principles of natural justice that a man should institute proceedings against another when he is conscious that he has no good cause of action".

If compromises of such claims were upheld, improper pressure might be brought to bear on persons who "owed" void debts.

The rule that a promise by A to abandon a claim which is clearly bad, but believed to be valid, is good consideration for a counter-promise from B is subject to a number of safeguards.[193] There must be a "reasonable claim",[194] (i.e. one made on reasonable grounds) and A must honestly believe that his claim had at any rate a fair chance of success.[195] And he must show that he seriously intended to enforce the claim.[196]

The cases in the present group all concern claims the validity of which was doubtful in law. It seems that the same rules apply where the claim was doubtful because of a dispute about the facts. A settlement based on a simple *mistake* of fact made by both parties might be void for mistake.[197] But it will not be void on this ground where both parties knowingly take the risk that the actual facts may turn out to be different from the facts as they were supposed to be. This element of risk is always present when parties negotiate a settlement on disputed facts.

3–039   **Executed compromises.** The preceding discussion is concerned with the enforceability of an agreement to compromise a claim. Different problems can arise after such an agreement has been *performed*, generally by payment of the amount which one party has agreed to pay under the compromise. Even if, under the rules discussed above, there was no consideration for that party's promise, he will not be entitled to the return of the payment if it was made "to close the transaction"[198]: in such a case the payment is treated as if it were an executed gift.[199] To give rise to a claim for repayment, it will be necessary to establish other circumstances than lack of consideration: e.g. that the payment was made under duress.[200]

(iii) *Actual forbearance*

3–040   **As evidence of an implied promise to forbear.** A person may forbear from enforcing a claim without expressly promising to do so. The question then arises

---

[191] See above, fn.183.

[192] (1846) 2 C.B. 548 at 564; cf. *Edwards v Baugh* (1843) 11 M. & W. 641 at 646.

[193] It is not entirely clear whether the validity of a compromise is subject to any duty to disclose facts which would enable B to resist the claim: see below, para.9–146.

[194] *Cook v Wright*, above, at 569.

[195] *Callisher v Bishchoffsheim*, above, at 452.

[196] *Cook v Wright*, above, at 569; *The Proodos C* [1980] 2 Lloyd's Rep. 287 at 392.

[197] e.g. *Gloyne v Richardson* [2001] EWCA Civ 716; [2001] 2 B.C.L.C. 669 at [39]; below, Ch.8; Andrews [1989] L.M.C.L.Q. 431; *Grains & Fourrages SA v Huyton* [1997] 1 Lloyd's Rep. 628.

[198] *Woolwich Equitable BS v IRC (No.2)* [1993] A.C. 70 at 165.

[199] ibid., citing *Maskell v Horner* [1915] 3 K.B. 106 at 120.

[200] See below, para.10–002 et seq.

whether this actual forbearance is consideration for some promise or act of the other party, for example for a promise by him to give security, or for giving the security. Sometimes actual forbearance may be evidence of an implied promise to forbear.[201] Thus the acceptance of a cheque in payment of a debt may be evidence of a promise not to sue the debtor so long as the cheque is not dishonoured, or at least for a reasonable time.[202]

Where there is no promise to forbear. Even where no promise to forbear   3-041
(express or implied) has been made, an actual forbearance may constitute consideration. In *Alliance Bank v Broom*[203] the defendant owed £22,000 to his bank, which pressed him to give some security. He promised to do so, but the bank made no counter-promise not to sue him. It was held that there was consideration for the defendant's promise as the bank had given, and the defendant received, "some degree of forbearance".[204] On the other hand, in *Miles v New Zealand Alford Estate Co*[205] a company had bought land and then became dissatisfied with the purchase. The vendor later promised to make certain payments to the company, and it was alleged that the consideration for this promise was the company's forbearance to take proceedings to rescind the contract. A majority of the Court of Appeal held that there was no consideration for the vendor's promise as no proceedings to rescind were ever intended; and Cotton L.J. added that "it must be shown that there was something which would bind the company not to institute proceedings".[206] Bowen L.J. dissented from this proposition,[207] relying on *Alliance Bank v Broom*; but it may be possible to reconcile the cases by reference to the types of claim forborne. A bank to which £22,000 is owed is virtually certain to take steps to enforce its claim, but a dissatisfied purchaser of land is much less certain to take proceedings for rescission. It may, therefore, be reasonable to say that an actual forbearance can amount to consideration in relation to the former type of claim, but that a promise to forbear is necessary where it is problematical whether the claim will ever be enforced at all. A promise to forbear is also, of course, necessary where that is what the debtor bargains for.

Where the consideration consists of a *promise* to forbear which specifies no time the creditor must forbear for a reasonable time.[208] There is no such requirement where the consideration consists of *actual forbearance*: here it is enough that the debtor had "a certain amount of forbearance".[209]

The promise to be enforced must have been induced by the forbear-   3-042
ance. A forbearance amounts to consideration only for a promise or performance that is induced by it. In *Wigan v English & Scottish Law Life Assurance Society*[210] a debtor executed a mortgage of an insurance policy in favour of his creditor. It

---

[201] *Re Wyvern Developments Ltd* [1974] 1 W.L.R. 1097; *Thornton Springer v NEM Insurance Co Ltd* [2000] 2 All E.R. 489 at 516.
[202] *Baker v Walker* (1845) 14 M. & W. 465; *Elkington v Cooke-Hill* (1914) 30 T.L.R. 670.
[203] (1864) 2 Dr. & Sm. 289; cf. also *Brikom Investments Ltd v Carr* [1979] Q.B. 467 at 490.
[204] ibid. at 292.
[205] (1886) 32 Ch.D. 267; cf. *Hunter v Bradford Property Trust Ltd*, 1970 S.L.T. 173.
[206] ibid. at 285.
[207] ibid. at 291; his view was approved by Lord Macnaghten in *Fullerton v Provincial Bank of Ireland* [1903] A.C. 309 at 314.
[208] See above, para.3–034.
[209] *Alliance Bank v Broom* (1864) 2 Dr. & Sm. 289 at 292; *R v H.M. Attorney General for England and Wales* [2003] UKPC 22; [2003] E.M.L.R. 24 at [31]–[32].
[210] [1909] 1 Ch. 291: cf. above, para.3–020.

was held that the creditor, who knew nothing of the mortgage, had not provided consideration for it merely by having forborne to sue for his antecedent debt. But Parker J. added[211] that the creditor would have provided consideration if he had been told of the mortgage and if, "on the strength of" it, he had actually forborne to sue for the debt. The crucial question, therefore, is whether the creditor has forborne "on the strength of" the debtor's act or promise. He will clearly have done so where the debtor has *expressly* requested the forbearance[212] but in *Alliance Bank v Broom*[213] the bank's forbearance was held to constitute consideration even though the defendant had not expressly requested it. The case has been explained on the ground that the debtor had impliedly requested forbearance.[214] But where the forbearance is not requested either expressly or by implication, it is no consideration. In *Combe v Combe*[215] a husband during divorce proceedings promised to pay his wife an annual allowance. In an action to enforce this promise, the wife argued, inter alia, that she had given consideration for it by forbearing to apply to the court for a maintenance order. But her argument was rejected as she had not forborne at the husband's request.[216]

(f) Performance of Existing Duty[217]

3–043   Much difficulty arises in determining whether a person who does, or promises to do, what he was already under a legal duty to do thereby provides consideration for a promise made to him. As he was already legally bound to do the act, he suffers no legal detriment.[218] But he may suffer a factual detriment if he actually does the act: this may be more troublesome to him than to pay damages. The promisor may also get a factual benefit, as damages might not fully compensate him for the loss which he would suffer if the duty were broken. Denning L.J. has therefore said that the performance of an existing duty, or the promise to perform it, was of itself good consideration.[219] This radical view has not been accepted; but the requirement of consideration in this group of cases has been mitigated by recognising that it can be satisfied where the promisee has conferred a factual (as opposed to a legal) benefit on the promisor.[220]

(i) Duty imposed by law

3–044   **Public Policy.** One group of cases denies the enforceability of a promise made in return for the promise to perform, or the performance of, a duty imposed by law (as opposed to one imposed by contract). Thus a public officer cannot enforce a promise to pay him money for doing his duty as such,[221] and generally a person

---

[211] At 298.

[212] *Crears v Hunter* (1887) 19 Q.B.D. 341 at 344.

[213] (1864) 2 Dr. & Sm. 289.

[214] *Fullerton v Provincial Bank of Ireland* [1903] A.C. 309 at 313.

[215] [1951] 2 K.B. 215.

[216] Quaere whether such a request should not have been implied.

[217] Davis 6 C.L.J. 202; Reynolds and Treitel 7 Malaya Law Rev. 1; Aivazian, Trebilcock & Penny 22 Osgoode Hall L.J. 173; Hooley [1991] J.B.L. 195; Halson 107 L.Q.R. 649.

[218] See above, para.3–006.

[219] *Ward v Byham* [1956] 1 W.L.R. 496 at 498; *Williams v Williams* [1957] 1 W.L.R. 148 at 151.

[220] See below, paras 3–049, 3–054—3–055.

[221] *Wathen v Sandys* (1811) 2 Camp. 640; *Morris v Burdett* (1808) 1 Camp. 218; *Bilke v Havelock* (1813) 3 Camp. 374; *Morgan v Palmer* (1825) 2 B. & C. 729 at 736.

does not provide consideration by forbearing to engage in a course of conduct that is criminal.[222] Enforcement of such promises would tend to encourage an undesirable form of extortion; and it is this ground of public policy, rather than want of consideration, that accounts for most of the authorities in this group.

Performance of the duty as consideration. Promises to pay rewards for   3–045
information that might lead to the arrest of a felon were often enforced[223] though, till 1968, a person who had such information was bound to communicate it to the police, and indeed committed an offence[224] if he failed to do so. Public policy was not offended by the enforcement of such promises, as they might induce people to look for the information and so promote the interests of justice. These cases show that an act may constitute consideration even though there is a public duty to do it. The contrary view is, indeed, supported by *Collins v Godefroy*[225] where an attorney who had been subpoenaed to give evidence was promised a guinea a day for attendance. This was held to be "a promise without consideration" as he was already bound to attend. But the reasoning is hard to reconcile with the reward cases just mentioned; and the actual decision has long ceased to represent the practice in such cases.[226] A subpoena must be accompanied by a tender of "conduct money"[227]; this includes the reasonable expenses of attending the trial, and, in certain cases, compensation for loss of time. Expert witnesses can validly contract for payment[228]; and it seems that all witnesses who attend in a professional capacity, whether they are strictly expert witnesses or not, are entitled to compensation for loss of time.

Other consideration. A person can provide consideration by doing, or prom-   3–046
ising, *more* than he is by law obliged to do. Thus in *Glasbrook Bros Ltd v Glamorgan CC*[229] mine-owners who feared violence from strikers asked, and promised to pay, for a greater degree of police protection than the police reasonably thought necessary. It was held that the police authority had provided consideration for this promise by giving the extra protection, and that accordingly the promise was enforceable. The position in cases of this kind is now regulated by statute. Section 25(1) of the Police Act 1996 provides that payment can be claimed for "special police services" rendered at the "request" of the person requiring them. Such a request can be implied from conduct, e.g. where a person organises an event which cannot safely take place without such special services. On this reasoning, a football club has been held liable to a police authority for the cost of

---

[222] *Brown v Brine* (1875) L.R. 1 Ex.D.5 (forbearance to commit criminal libel).

[223] *England v Davidson* (1840) 11 A. & E. 856; *Neville v Kelly* (1862) 12 C.B.(N.S) 740; *Bent v Wakefield and Barnsley Union Bank* (1878) 4 C.P.D. 1.

[224] i.e. misprision of felony: *Sykes v DPP* [1962] A.C. 528. This offence was abolished by Criminal Law Act 1967, s.1, and replaced with the offence of concealing a relevant offence created by s.5(1) of that Act: below, para.11–046.

[225] (1831) 1 B. & Ad. 950; cf. *Thorensen Car Ferries Ltd v Weymouth Portland BC* [1977] 2 Lloyd's Rep. 614 at 619.

[226] *Re Working Men's Mutual Society* (1882) 21 Ch.D. 831; *Chamberlain v Stoneham* (1889) 24 Q.B.D. 113.

[227] Senior Courts Act 1981, s.36(4).

[228] *Goulden v White Barca* [2000] 1 W.L.R. 167.

[229] [1925] A.C. 270; cf. *Thorensen Car Ferries v Weymouth Portland BC* [1977] 2 Lloyd's Rep. 614 at 619 (A's promise to *make use* of B's services for which he was under a legal duty to *pay* held to constitute consideration for B's counter-promise).

policing matches played on its ground.[230] Such liability arises irrespective of contract.[231]

In *Ward v Byham*[232] the father of an illegitimate child promised to pay its mother £1 per week "providing you can prove that [the child] is well looked after and happy, and also that she is allowed to decide for herself whether or not she wishes to come and live with you". The mother began to look after the child, and it was held that she could enforce the father's promise although she was under a statutory duty to maintain the child. One basis of the decision is that the mother had provided consideration by showing that she had made the child happy, etc.: in this way she can be said to have done more than she was required by law to do, and to have conferred a factual benefit on the father or on the child,[233] even though she may not have suffered any detriment.[234] But if a son's promise not to bore his father is not good consideration,[235] it is hard to see why a mother's promise to make her child happy should stand on a different footing. There is, with respect, force in Denning L.J.'s view, that the mother provided consideration by merely performing her legal duty to support the child. There was certainly no ground of public policy for refusing to enforce the promise.

(ii) *Duty imposed by contract with promisor*

3–047   When A was bound by contract with B to do, or to forbear from doing, something, the law at one time took the view that A's performance of that duty (or his promise to perform it) was no consideration for a new promise by B. Later authority has qualified that view but the extent of the qualification remains uncertain.[236]

3–048   **Cases in which there was no consideration.** The view that there was no consideration for B's new promise was first established in cases in which seamen who had bound themselves to serve for a voyage were promised higher wages by the masters of their ships if they performed their duty by working the ships home. It was held that these promises were not binding. Originally this conclusion was based on the ground of public policy that the enforcement of such promises might lead the men to refuse to perform their original contracts unless they were

---

[230] *Harris v Sheffield United FC Ltd* [1988] Q.B. 77. Contrast *Reading Festival Ltd v West Yorkshire Police Authority* [2006] EWCA Civ 524; [2006] L.L.R. 583 where a music festival was organised in such a way that the organisers had not made a "request" for the "special services" said to have been provided by the police; cf. *Chief Constable of Greater Manchester v Wigan Athletic Football Club* [2008] EWCA 1449; [2009] 1 W.L.R. 1580.

[231] This submission is retained notwithstanding the observations of Scott-Baker L.J., in the *Reading Festival* case, above at [50] that: "it is very difficult to see how s.25(1) can operate absent a contract". Since the police have a discretion over how they provide the services requested (*Reading Festival* case at [21]), the most that can be said is that there must be an agreement "in broad terms" (*Reading Festival* case at [21]).

[232] [1956] 1 W.L.R. 496.

[233] Consideration need not move to the promisor (the father); above, para.3–024.

[234] *Williams v Roffey Bros & Nicholls (Contractors) Ltd* [1991] 1 Q.B. 1 at 13.

[235] *White v Bluett* (1853) 23 L.J. Ex. 36; above, para.3–027.

[236] *WRN Ltd v Ayris* [2008] EWHC 1080 (QB); [2008] I.R.L.R. 889 at [46] (still referring to the fact that it is "well-established that such (i.e. a promise to perform an existing contract) will not, in law, constitute consideration").

promised extra pay.[237] But according to one of the reports of *Stilk v Myrick*[238] such reasoning was doubted in that case, where the claim for extra pay was instead rejected on the ground that the men had provided no consideration by doing only what they were already bound to do; and this is the explanation of such cases which is now commonly accepted.[239] On the same principle, a promise to pay an extra charge for the carriage of goods to the agreed destination cannot be enforced by the carrier[240]; and a debtor's promise to pay in stated instalments a debt that is already due is no consideration for the creditor's promise not to take bankruptcy proceedings in respect of the debt.[241]

The public policy explanation of the rule, stated above, was always open to the objection that it was based on a danger that was not more than hypothetical: in the cases on seamen's wages, for example, there was no evidence of any refusal on the men's part to perform their original contracts. Even where there is such evidence, the argument is much reduced in importance now that the law has come to recognise that such a refusal may amount to economic duress.[242] Where the refusal *does* amount to duress, a promise induced by it can be avoided (and money paid in pursuance of it be recovered back) on that ground.[243] This is true even where the promise *is* supported by consideration: for example, because the promisee has undertaken, not merely to perform his duties under the original contract, but also to render some additional performance.[244] If, on the other hand, the promisee's refusal to perform the original contract does *not* amount to duress, it has been held that the promise cannot be impugned merely on the ground that the refusal amounted to an abuse by the promisee of a dominant bargaining position.[245] To allow a promise to be invalidated on this ground alone would introduce an intermediate category of promises unfairly obtained; and this would (in the words of Lord Scarman) "be unhelpful because it would render the law uncertain".[246]

The now more generally held view is that the new promises in the present group of cases are unenforceable for want of consideration; and the reason for this view seems to have been that the promisee suffered no legal detriment[247] in performing what was already due from him, nor did the promisor receive any legal benefit in receiving what was already due to him.[248] But this reasoning takes no account of the fact that the promisee may in fact suffer a detriment: for example,

---

[237] *Harris v Watson* (1791) Peake 102; cf. *Scotson v Pegg* (1861) 6 H. & N. 295 at 299.

[238] That in (1809) 2 Camp. 317; the other report, in 6 Esp. 129, does not mention consideration and makes the decision turn on public policy. Both grounds are stated in *Harris v Carter* (1854) 3 E. & B. 559.

[239] *Swain v West(Butchers)Ltd* [1936] 1 All E.R. 224; *The Atlantic Baron* [1979] Q.B. 705 at 712; *Pao On v Lau Yiu Long* [1980] A.C. 614 at 633; *Sybron Corp v Rochem Ltd* [1984] Ch. 112 at 129; *The Alev* [1989] 1 Lloyd's Rep. 138 at 147.

[240] *The Proodos C* [1980] 2 Lloyd's Rep. 390; cf. *Atlas Express Ltd v Kafco (Importers and Distributors) Ltd* [1989] Q.B. 833.

[241] *Vanbergen v St Edmund's Properties Ltd* [1933] 2 K.B. 223. On the enforceability of other arrangements for the payment of existing debts, see below para.3–100 et seq.

[242] See below, para.10–005.

[243] As in *The Universe Sentinel* [1983] 1 A.C. 366; *B & S Contracts & Designs v Victor Green Publications* [1984] I.C.R. 419; *Atlas Express Ltd v Kafco(Importers and Distributors)Ltd* [1989] Q.B. 833, below para.10–005.

[244] e.g. *The Atlantic Baron* [1979] Q.B. 705; below, fn.263; *The Alev* [1989] 1 Lloyd's Rep. 138.

[245] *Pao On v Lau Yiu Long* [1980] A.C. 614 at 632.

[246] ibid. at 634. This statement was made in a case involving three parties, but it is of general application: *Williams v Roffey Bros & Nicholls (Contractors) Ltd* [1991] 1 Q.B. 1 at 15.

[247] See above, para.3–004.

[248] *Technip-Coflexip SA v Tube Tech International Ltd* [2005] EWCA Civ 1369; 106 Co [64].

the wages that a seaman could earn elsewhere may exceed those that he would earn under the original contract together with the damages that he would have to pay for breaking it. Conversely, the promisor may in fact benefit from the actual performance of what was legally due to him: in *Stilk v Myrick* the master got his ship home and this may well have been worth more to him than any damages that he could have recovered from the crew.

3–049 **Factual benefit to promisor.** The foregoing discussion shows that a new promise by B in consideration of A's performing his duty to B under an earlier contract between them is not necessarily obtained by duress; and that A's performance of the duty may in fact benefit B. Where both these conditions are satisfied, it has been held that A can enforce B's new promise.

3–050 *Williams v Roffey Bros.* In *Williams v Roffey Bros & Nicholls (Contractors) Ltd*[249] B had engaged A as carpentry sub-contractor, for the purpose of performing a contract between B and X to refurbish a number of flats. The amount payable by B to A under the subcontract was £20,000 but B later promised to make extra payments to A, who undertook no additional obligation in return.[250] B made this new promise because B's own surveyor recognised that the originally agreed sum of £20,000 was too low, and because B feared that A (who was in financial difficulties) would not be able to complete his work on time, and so expose B to penalties for delay under his contract with X. It was held that B's promise to make the extra payments to A was supported by consideration in the shape of the "practical benefits"[251] obtained by B from A's performance of his duties under the original contract between them.[252] Since no allegation of duress on A's part had been made by B, the new promise by B to pay extra could not be avoided on this ground. There had been no threat by A to break his original contract; indeed, the initiative for the agreement containing the promise of extra pay seems to have come from B.

3–051 **Reconciling the cases.** The element of factual benefit which was stressed in the *Williams* case has also been regarded as consideration where a person performs (or promises to perform) a contractual duty owed to a third party[253]; and the *Williams* case is to be welcomed in bringing the two-party cases in line with those involving three parties.[254] But it is by no means clear how the case is, from this

---

[249] [1991] 1 Q.B. 1; Adams and Brownsword 53 M.L.R. 536; Hird and Blair [1996] J.B.L. 254.

[250] The payments under the original contract were found to be due in unspecified instalments while those i̶ ̶he new promise were due as each flat was completed, but no attempt was made to argue th̶ ̶e in the times when payment was due *might* have been to A's disadvantage and therefore ̶ ̶ration. There is perhaps a hint to this effect in Russell L.J.'s judgment at 19. Similar ̶ ̶asis of *Anangel Atlas Compania Naviera SA v Ishikawajima-Harima Heavy Industries* ̶ ̶0] 2 Lloyd's Rep. 526.

̶ ̶ at 11; cf. [1991] 1 Q.B. 1 at 19, 23. See also *Simon Container Machinery Ltd v* ̶ ̶1998] 2 Lloyd's Rep. 428 at 435; *Horwood v Land of Leather Ltd* [2010] EWHC ̶.L.C. 423 at [41].

̶ ̶cure the whole of this benefit, but this was because B's wrongful failure to ̶ ̶stified A's refusal to continue with the work.

̶ ̶—3–055.

̶ ̶para.3–048 the distinction was ignored: no one even asked whether the ̶ ̶romisor (the master) or with a third party (the shipowner). It is clear ̶ ̶ the action was brought against the master. cf. also *Turner v Owen* ̶ ̶acts & Designs v Victor Green Publications Ltd* [1984] I.C.R. 419.

point of view, to be reconciled with *Stilk v Myrick* and with the line of more recent decisions which have followed that case.[255] As has been suggested above, the master in *Stilk v Myrick* also obtained a factual benefit (in getting his ship home); and such a factual benefit will very often be obtained by B where he secures actual performance from A (as opposed to having to sue him for non-performance of the original contract).

In the *Williams* case, *Stilk v Myrick* was not overruled; indeed Purchas L.J. described it as a "pillar stone of the law of contract".[256] But he added that the case might be differently decided today[257]; while Glidewell L.J. said that the present decision did not "contravene" but did "refine and limit"[258] the principle of the earlier case; and Russell L.J. said that the "rigid approach" to consideration in *Stilk v Myrick* was "no longer necessary or desirable."[259] The conclusion which may tentatively be drawn from these statements is that the factual benefit to B in securing A's performance of the earlier contract will normally suffice to constitute consideration. The insistence in the earlier cases on the stricter requirement of legal benefit or detriment is no longer justified (if it ever was) by the need to protect B from the undue pressure that A might exert by refusing to perform his original contract; for this need can now be met by the expanding concept of duress. This provides a more satisfactory solution of the present problem since it invalidates promises only where actual duress is established.[260] Where this is not the case, and the promisee has in fact conferred a benefit on the promisor by performing the original contract, then the requirement of consideration is satisfied and there seems to be no good reason for refusing to enforce the new promise.

Other consideration. The promisee may provide other consideration for the new promise by doing, or promising to do, more than he was bound by the original contract to do.[261] Thus a seaman is entitled to extra wages if, during the voyage, he is promoted and so undertakes additional duties.[262] The same principle was applied where shipbuilders claimed an increase in the agreed price for a supertanker on the ground that the currency in which that price was to be paid had been devalued. The contract required the builders to give a performance guarantee, and it was held that they had provided consideration for the prospective owners' promise to pay the price increase by making a corresponding increase in their performance guarantee.[263]

3–052

---

[255] See above, para.3–048. See also *South Caribbean Trading Ltd v Trafigura Beheer BV* [2004] EWHC 2676; [2005] 1 Lloyd's Rep. 128 at [107], where Colman J. (obiter) would not have followed the *Williams* case, but for the fact it was binding on him.

[256] [1991] 1 Q.B. 1 at 20.

[257] ibid. at 21. But he was not prepared to accept *Watkins v Carrig* 21 A 2d. 591 (1941), where a contractor who had agreed to do excavating work unexpectedly struck hard rock and was held entitled to enforce a promise to pay nine times the originally agreed sum. That case was said not to represent English law in *The Atlantic Baron* [1979] Q.B. 705 at 714, cf. also *Finland SS Co Ltd v Felixstowe Dock Ry Co* [1980] 2 Lloyd's Rep. 390.

[258] [1991] 1 Q.B. 1 at 16.

[259] ibid. at 18.

[260] *Adam Opel GmbH v Mitras Automotive (UK)* Ltd [2008] EWHC 3205 (QB); [2088] C.I.L.L. 2561 at [42]. Colman J.'s view in *Trafigura Beheer*, above fn.255 at [109] that duress "precludes" reliance on any factual benefit is, with respect, open to doubt. Whether there has been any consideration and whether the resulting contract is voidable for duress are quite separate issues; to run them together runs the risk of confusing the issues, as in *Stilk v Myrick*.

[261] *Horwood v Land of Leather Ltd* [2010] EWHC 546 (Comm); [2010] 1 C.L.C. 423 at [39]–[40].

[262] *Hanson v Royden* (1867) L.R. 3 C.P. 47.

[263] *The Atlantic Baron* [1979] Q.B. 705; Coote [1980] C.L.J. 40; Adams 42 M.L.R. 557; *Birmingham City Council v Forde* [2009] EWHC 12 (QB); [2009] 1 W.L.R. 2732 at [83].

The promisee similarly provides other consideration where, before the new promise is made, circumstances arise which justify his refusal to perform the original contract. Thus the crew of a ship may be justified in refusing to complete a voyage because so many of their fellows have deserted that completion will involve hazards of a kind not originally contemplated. If they are induced to go on by a promise of extra pay, they do something which they were not bound to do, and can recover the extra pay.[264] The same principle applies where the contract is determined by notice or by mutual consent. Thus a promise to pay an employee higher wages after he has lawfully determined his contract by notice is binding. Or the parties might agree to rescind the contract and substitute a new one, at a higher rate of pay[265]; though such a transaction might be hard to distinguish from a simple promise to pay higher wages for continuing to work under the original contract.[266] If the original contract is void, voidable or unenforceable, performance of the work specified would, it seems, be consideration for a promise of extra pay; and if the original contract was in fact good but was believed to be defective, then the new promise might be binding on the analogy of the rule that forbearance to litigate an invalid claim may amount to consideration.[267] A final possibility is that the contract may provide, expressly or by implication, for revision of pay scales from time to time; and in such a case an agreement to pay higher (or to accept lower) wages would clearly be binding.[268]

(iii) *Duty imposed by contract with a third party*

3–053   Two problems arise under this heading. The first is whether, if A is under a contractual duty to B, the *performance* of this duty can constitute consideration for a promise made to A by C. The second is whether A's *promise* to perform his contractual duty to B can constitute consideration for a counter-promise made to A by C.[269]

3–054   **Performance of the duty.** The view that performance of a contractual duty owed to a third party can constitute consideration for a promise is supported by *The Eurymedon*.[270] A (a firm of stevedores) had unloaded goods from B's ship.

---

[264] *Hartley v Ponsonby* (1857) 7 E. & B. 872; *O'Neil v Armstrong, Mitchell & Co* [1895] 2 Q.B. 418; *Palace Shipping Co v Caine* [1907] A.C. 386; *Liston v SS Carpathian (Owners)* [1915] 2 K.B. 42.

[265] See *Schwartzreich v Bauman-Basch Inc* 131 N.E. 887 (1921); Dekoven 35 U. of Chi.L. Rev. 173.

[266] cf. below, paras 3–062, 5–030.

[267] See above, paras 3–036—3–038; *E. Hulton & Co v Chadwick Taylor Ltd* (1918) 34 T.L.R. 230 at 231.

[268] e.g. *Pepper & Hope v Daish* [1980] I.R.L.R. 13; cf. *Lombard Tricity Finance Ltd v Paton* [1989] 1 All E.R. 98 (credit agreement providing for increases in interest rates to be made by lender).

[269] There is no doubt that C's promise to perform a duty owed by B to A (or the performance of such a promise) can constitute consideration for a promise (express or implied) by A to C: see, e.g. *Brandt v Liverpool SN Co* [1924] 1 K.B. 575; *The Aramis* [1989] 1 Lloyd's Rep. 213 at 225 (where C's claim failed for want of contractual intention: below, para.4–021).

[270] [1975] A.C. 154; followed in *The New York Star* [1981] 1 W.L.R. 138 and *The Antwerpen* [1994] 1 Lloyd's Rep. 213; cf. *The Mahkutai* [1996] A.C. 650 at 664. See also the earlier decisions in *Scotson v Pegg* (1861) 6 H. & N. 295; *Chichester v Cobb* (1866) 14 L.T. 433 and *Shadwell v Shadwell* (1860) 9 C.B.(N.S.) 159 which also lend support, but in which the reasoning employed is not wholly conclusive.

Some of these belonged to C who, for present purposes,[271] may be taken to have promised A not to sue him for damaging the goods. It was held that A had provided consideration for this promise by unloading the goods even if he was already bound[272] by a contract with B to unload them.

Promise to perform the duty. It was at one time thought that a mere promise   3–055
to perform a contractual duty owed to a third party could not constitute consideration. Thus in *Jones v Waite*[273] it was said that a promise by A to C that A will pay
a debt owed by A to B is no consideration for a promise made by C to A. This view
seems to be based on the idea that A suffers no (legal) detriment by promising to
pay a debt that he was already bound to pay; nor did it appear that C gained any
benefit as a result of the promise. It is, however, possible for C to gain such a
benefit:[274] for example, where C promises A some benefit in return for A's promise
not to carry out his intention of breaking a contract with B, a company in which
C has an interest. This was the position in *Pao On v Lau Yiu Long*[275] where A,
having entered into a contract with a company (B), refused to perform it unless C,
who were shareholders in the company, guaranteed A against loss which might be
incurred as a result of the performance of one of the terms of that contract. The
guarantee was given in consideration of A's promise to perform their contractual
obligations to the company; and was held binding[276] on the ground that "A
promise to perform, or the performance of, a pre-existing contractual obligation to
a third party can be valid consideration".[277] This view seems, with respect, to be
preferable to that expressed in *Jones v Waite*; for the guarantee was certainly not
gratuitous in a commercial sense.

It will, of course, be open to the promisor to avoid liability if he can show that
the promisee's refusal to perform the contract with the third party amounted to
duress[278] not merely with regard to the third party, but also with regard to the
promisor himself.

6. RESCISSION AND VARIATION

A contract may be rescinded or varied by subsequent agreement. The object of   3–056
rescission is to release the parties from the contract, while that of variation is to
alter some term of the contract. Such subsequent agreements give rise to problems
of consideration, which will be discussed here, and to problems of form, to be
discussed in Ch.5. One aspect of the consideration problem has already been dealt
with in our discussion of the question whether the performance by A of his
obligations under the old contract could be consideration for a new promise from

---

[271] For a discussion of this point, see below, paras 14–062—14–068.
[272] A question may arise as to whether A has indeed performed or begun to perform his contract with B: *The Rigoletto* [2000] 2 Lloyd's Rep. 532 at 542–545.
[273] (1839) 5 Bing. N.C. 341, 351, affirmed on another ground (1842) 9 Cl. & F. 107; contrast *Morton v Burn* (1837) 7 A. & E. 19 (promise to pay assignee).
[274] This seems to be acknowledged in *Aviva Life & Pensions UK Ltd v Strand Street Properties Ltd* [2010] EWCA Civ 444, in the opening lines of para.[50] but it is not explained precisely what was the benefit to the promisee.
[275] [1980] A.C. 614.
[276] For rejection of the argument that the consideration was past, see above, para.3–019.
[277] [1980] A.C. 614 at 632. cf. *Scotson v Pegg* (1861) 6 H. & N. 295 at 301; *The Eurymedon*, above, at 183.
[278] See above, para.3–048.

B.[279] Our present problem is whether there is consideration for a promise by B to accept in discharge of A's obligations some performance *other* than that originally undertaken by A, or to grant A a total release from the contract. Even if there is no such consideration B's subsequent promise may, nevertheless, have some limited legal effect either as a waiver or in equity.[280]

(a) Rescission

3–057   **Both parties have outstanding rights.** An agreement to rescind a contract will generate its own consideration whenever each party has outstanding rights under the contract against the other. This is most obviously true where the contract is wholly executory and neither party is in breach.[281] Thus a contract for the sale of goods to be delivered and paid for on a future day can be rescinded by mutual consent at any time before the day fixed for performance. A contract can similarly be rescinded by agreement after both parties have broken it.[282] And a partly executed contract can be rescinded by agreement so long as there are outstanding obligations on both sides: thus a lease for seven years can be rescinded by mutual consent after it has run for three years. In all these cases there is consideration for the rescission in that each party promises to give up his rights against the other under the original contract.[283] It is, of course, essential, that *each* party should make such a promise.[284] If only one party does so, the other making no counter-promise, the former party's promise will be "entirely unilateral and unsupported by any consideration".[285]

3–058   **One party has outstanding rights.** An agreement to rescind a contract may also fail to generate its own consideration (and so lack contractual force) where only one party has outstanding rights under the contract. This will often be the position where the contract has been wholly executed by that party. Suppose that goods are sold and delivered but not paid for, and the parties then agree to "rescind" the contract. If the agreement means that the buyer is to return the goods and to be released from his liability to pay the price, there is good consideration for the promise of each party. But if it simply means that the buyer is not to pay the price, it is a gratuitous promise by the seller.[286] Conversely, goods may be sold, delivered and paid for, but turn out to be defective. Here an agreement to "rescind" would be a gratuitous promise if it simply released the seller from his liability under the original contract for the defects. This is what is meant by the statement that rescission after breach requires separate consideration.[287]

That statement must, however, be qualified where the contract is a continuing one, such as one to deliver goods by instalments. An agreement to "rescind" such

[279] See above, paras 3–047—3–055.
[280] See below, paras 3–066—3–093; 3–111—3–118.
[281] *Foster v Dawber* (1851) Ex. 839 at 850; cf. *The Trado* [1982] 1 Lloyd's Rep. 157.
[282] e.g. *Morris v Baron & Co* [1918] A.C. 1.
[283] cf. *Argo Fund Ltd v Essar Steel Ltd* [2005] EWHC 600 (Comm); [2005] 2 Lloyd's Rep. 203 at [51], affirmed on other grounds [2006] EWCA Civ 241; [2006] 2 Lloyd's Rep. 134.
[284] *Ogilvy & Mather Ltd v Silverado Blue Ltd* [2007] EWHC 1285 (QB) at [21].
[285] *Collin v Duke of Westminster* [1985] Q.B. 581 at 598.
[286] *Commissioner of Stamp Duties v Bone* [1977] A.C. 511 at 519. ("A debt can only be truly released and extinguished by agreement for valuable consideration or under seal.").
[287] *Atlantic Shipping & Trading Ltd v Louis Dreyfus & Co* [1922] 2 A.C. 250 at 262.

a contract after one defective instalment had been delivered and paid for would not be a gratuitous release of the seller from his liability for the defects, for he would be giving up his rights to have future instalments accepted and paid for. It is only where the defect is of such a kind as to give the buyer the right as a matter of law to treat the contract as repudiated[288] that the seller may be said to give up nothing in return for the buyer's promise not to sue for the defect. Even in such a case, however, this result would not necessarily follow; for so long as the seller in good faith believed that the contract remained binding he would provide consideration by forbearing to enforce it.[289]

The need for separate consideration: accord and satisfaction. Where the rescinding agreement does not generate its own consideration, it must be supported by separate consideration: there must, in technical language, be not only accord but also satisfaction. Thus a buyer of goods may agree to release a seller who has become liable in damages for non-delivery, if the seller will pay him £50. The agreement to release the seller is the accord; payment of the £50 is the satisfaction.[290] On payment of the £50, the seller is released from his liability in damages. 3–059

Executory accord. It was formerly said that an executory accord, i.e. one which had not yet been followed by satisfaction, had no effect: that it neither released the party in breach nor gave the other party any new right of action.[291] But it is settled that an executory accord can be enforced by the party to whom the satisfaction was offered,[292] and it may release the party by whom it was offered if that party's *promise* to perform his part of the accord has, on the true construction of the accord, been accepted by the injured party in discharge of his original cause of action.[293] Even where the injured party has not accepted the wrongdoer's promise in settlement of the cause of action, a question can arise as to the time at which the accord takes effect. In the absence of an express provision in it on the point, the accord releases the original cause of action at the time of the accord,[294] subject only to the implied condition subsequent[295] that it will be retrospectively avoided on the wrongdoer's failure to perform it in accordance with its terms. On such failure, the original liability will therefore revive. The parties may, of course, also agree to make performance of the accord a condition precedent to discharge. If they do so, the party originally in breach will not be discharged by the accord so long as it remains executory; he will be discharged only on giving the agreed satisfaction.[296] 3–060

---

[288] See below, Ch.18

[289] See above, paras 3–036—3–038.

[290] *British-Russian Gazette Ltd v Associated Newspapers Ltd* [1933] 2 K.B. 616 at 643. Mere acceptance of a cheque sent in full settlement is not conclusive evidence of such an agreement: *Stour Valley Builders v Stuart, The Times*, February 23, 1993, following *Day v McLea* [1889] 2 Q.B. 610; *Inland Revenue Commissioners v Fry* [2001] S.T.C. 1715 at [12]. See also *Clarke v Nationwide BS* (1998) 76 P. & C.R. D5 (acceptance of cheque sent "as a gesture of goodwill" not an accord).

[291] *Bayley v Homan* (1837) 3 Bing.N.C. 915; cf. *Morris v Baron & Co* [1918] A.C. 1 at 36.

[292] *Henderson v Stobart* (1850) 5 Ex. 99.

[293] *Elton Cop Dyeing Co v Broadbent & Son Ltd* (1919) 89 L.J.K.B. 186; cf. *Cartwright v Cooke* (1832) 3 B. & Ad. 701; *Crowther v Farrer* (1850) 15 Q.B. 677.

[294] *Jameson v CEGB* [2000] 1 A.C. 455 at 477, where the original liability arose in tort; and see para.13–013, below.

[295] ibid.; for the distinction between conditions precedent and subsequent, see above, para.2–104.

[296] cf. *Johnson v Davies* [1999] Ch. 117 at 128 (a case, not of accord and satisfaction at common law, but of a "voluntary arrangement" under the Insolvency Act 1986, Pt VIII).

3–061   **Accord without satisfaction.** There is one long-established exception to the rule that accord without satisfaction does not discharge a contract after breach. If the holder of a bill of exchange or promissory note at or after its maturity absolutely, unconditionally and in writing renounces his rights against any person liable on the bill or note, the latter is discharged.[297] The exception provides a comparatively simple way of evading the general rule: the creditor can take a bill or note in satisfaction of the debt and then renounce it.

(b) Variation

3–062   **Variation amounting to rescission.** A variation of a contract may amount to a rescission of the old contract followed by the making of a new one relating to the same subject-matter. The question whether there is consideration for the rescission then depends on the principles just discussed.[298] If there is consideration for the rescission there is also consideration for the new promises. "The same consideration which existed for the old agreement is imported into the new agreement, which is substituted for it."[299]

3–063   **Variation benefiting either party.** The parties may agree to vary their contract in a way that can benefit either party. Such a variation again normally generates its own consideration. This is the position if a lease is varied by altering the date on which notice of termination can be given[300]; or if a contract of sale is varied by altering the agreed delivery date,[301] or the currency in which payment is to be made.[302] In the latter case, it would make no difference that the new currency was later devalued in relation to the old, for at the time of the variation it could not be certain how the two currencies would move in relation to each other: hence either party *might* benefit from the variation. If a variation is, taken as a whole, capable of benefiting either party, the requirement of consideration will be satisfied even though a particular term of the variation is for the sole benefit of one.[303] A variation does not, however, generate its own consideration if, though capable of benefiting either party, it is in fact made wholly for the benefit of one. For example, a variation as to the place at which a debt is to be paid may benefit either party and thus provide consideration for a promise by the creditor to accept part payment in full settlement. But it will not have this effect if it is introduced solely for the benefit of the debtor.[304] Similarly, an agreement to reduce the quantity of goods to be delivered and paid for under a contract for the sale of

---

[297] Bills of Exchange Act 1882, s.62.
[298] See above, paras 3–057—3–061.
[299] *Stead v Dawber* (1839) 10 A. & E. 57 at 66.
[300] *Fenner v Blake* [1900] 1 Q.B. 427.
[301] *South Caribbean Trading Ltd v Trafigura Beheer BV* [2004] EWHC 2676; [2005] 1 Lloyd's Rep. 128.
[302] *W J Alan & Co Ltd v El Nasr Export & Import Co* [1972] 2 Q.B. 189; *Woodhouse AC Israel Cocoa Ltd SA v Nigerian Produce Marketing Co* [1972] A.C. 741 at 757.
[303] *Ficom SA v Sociedad Cadex Ltda* [1980] 2 Lloyd's Rep. 118 at 132.
[304] *Vanbergen v St. Edmund's Properties Ltd* [1933] 2 K.B. 233; cf. *Continental Grain Export Corp v STM Grain Ltd* [1979] 2 Lloyd's Rep. 460 at 476.

goods may benefit either party; but if it is made purely for the seller's convenience it will not be consideration for the buyer's promise to accept the smaller quantity; nor conversely.[305]

Variation benefiting one party. The parties may agree to vary the contract in a way that can confer a legal benefit[306] on only one party. In some situations, it is settled that such a variation does not generate its own consideration: thus a promise by a creditor to accept part payment of a debt in full settlement is not binding unless it is supported by some separate consideration.[307] Such separate consideration could be provided by some further variation which may benefit the creditor: for example, by a debtor's promise to make the part payment *before* the day when the debt becomes due.[308] In other situations, it is arguable[309] that the variation may be supported by consideration if, though capable of conferring a legal benefit on only one party, it can also confer a factual benefit[310] on the other, e.g. where a buyer's promise to pay more than the originally agreed price secures eventual delivery when strict insistence on the original contract would have led to nothing but litigation.

3–064

Variation before contract concluded. There is the apparently paradoxical possibility that the parties may agree to vary a contract even before that contract has been concluded. This may be the position where A and B negotiate on the basis of formal documents and A represents that the proposed contract will be on terms less favourable to himself than those set out in the documents. If the documents are nevertheless executed without alteration, the representation may then be enforceable as a collateral contract. The consideration for the promise contained in A's representation is provided by B when he executes the documents (and so enters into the principal contract) at the request of A and in reliance on the representation. In *Brikom Investments Ltd v Carr*[311] landlords of blocks of flats, negotiated with their tenants for the sale of long leases of the flats on terms requiring the tenants to contribute to the cost of (inter alia) roof maintenance. At the time of the negotiations, the roof was in need of repairs, and the landlords promised to execute these "at our own cost". It was held that one of the tenants had provided consideration for this promise by executing the agreement for the lease, and the lease itself; and that the promise was accordingly binding as a collateral contract.[312] It followed that the landlords could not enforce the term in the lease under which the tenant would (but for the collateral contract) have been liable to contribute to the cost of the roof repairs.[313] Greater difficulty would have arisen if the tenant had already executed the documents *before* the landlord's

3–065

---

[305] *Vanbergen v St. Edmund's Properties Ltd* [1933] 2 K.B. 233
[306] See above, para.3–006.
[307] See below, para.3–100.
[308] See below, para.3–105.
[309] On the analogy of the reasoning of *Williams v Roffey Bros & Nicholls (Contractors) Ltd* [1991] 1 Q.B. 1, above, para.3–050.
[310] See above, para.3–006.
[311] [1979] Q.B. 467.
[312] cf. *Business Environment Bow Lane Ltd v Deanwater Estates* [2007] EWCA Civ 622; [2007] 32 E.G. 90, where no collateral contract was found to exist.
[313] This was agreed by all members of the Court of Appeal. For other grounds for the decision, see below, paras 3–110, 3–115.

promise had been made,[314] for in that case the execution of the documents would have been past consideration.[315] The tenants could, however, have succeeded, even in such a case, on an alternative ground. The landlords had been guilty of unreasonable delay in executing the repairs, and the tenants would, by forbearing to take proceedings in respect of that breach,[316] have provided consideration for the landlords' promise to bear the cost of the repairs.

(c) Waiver[317]

(i) *At common law*

3–066   Where a party promises to relinquish some or all of his rights under a contract, he is sometimes said to have "waived" those rights. Unfortunately, however, "the word 'waiver' . . . covers a variety of situations different in their legal nature. . . . "[318] Of the many senses in which it is used, three are relevant to the present discussion.[319]

3–067   **To mean rescission.** Sometimes "waiver" means total rescission of the contract: "The waiver spoken of in the case is an entire abandonment and dissolution of the contract."[320] This usage assumes that the rescission is supported by consideration.[321] It has been judicially criticised so far as it refers to a purported release without consideration. "To say that a claim is to be waived is incorrect. If a right has accrued, it must be released or discharged by deed or upon consideration."[322]

3–068   **To mean variation.** Sometimes, "waiver" refers to a variation which is supported by consideration and is therefore binding as a contract.[323] It is also used to refer to a variation which, though supported by consideration, is for some other reason *not* contractually binding. This usage occurs in the context of the rule that a contract which is required to be in, or evidenced in, writing can be rescinded but

---

[314] According to Lord Denning M.R. at 480 "some of the tenants" had *already* signed agreements for leases when the representations were made; but that does not seem to have been the position with regard to any of the cases before the court (see the grounds of appeal as stated at 472–473 of the report).

[315] See above, para.3–017.

[316] See [1979] Q.B. 467 at 490; cf. above, para.3–040. Delay in *executing* the repairs was a breach irrespective of the question of who was to *pay* for them.

[317] Ewart, *Waiver Distributed*; Wilben and Villiers, *Waiver Variation and Estoppel*; Cheshire and Fifoot 63 L.Q.R. 283; Stoljar 35 Can.Bar.Rev. 485; Dugdale and Yates 39 M.L.R. 681; Phipps 123 L.Q.R. 286.

[318] *The Laconia* [1977] A.C. 850 at 871; cf. *The Kanchenjunga* [1990] 1 Lloyd's Rep. 391 at 397; *The Happy Day* [2002] EWCA Civ 1068, [2002] 2 Lloyd's Rep. 487 at [64].

[319] For further senses, see below para.18–076 et seq.

[320] *Price v Dyer* (1810) 17 Ves. 356 at 364.

[321] See above, para.3–057.

[322] *Atlantic Shipping & Trading Co Ltd v Louis Dreyfus & Co* [1922] 2 A.C. 250 at 262; cf. *The Ion* [1980] 2 Lloyd's Rep. 245 at 249.

[323] *Semble*, this is the sense in which the word is used by Roskill and Cumming-Bruce L.JJ. in *Brikom Investments Ltd v Carr* [1979] Q.B. 467 at 488, 491; for the consideration for the "waiver", see above para.3–065; cf. *Shamsher Jute Mills Ltd v Sethia (London) Ltd* [1987] 2 Lloyd's Rep. 388 at 392; *Royal Boskalis Westminster NV v Mountain* [1997] 2 All E.R. 929, where the "waiver", i.e. variation, was not binding because it was vitiated by duress and illegality.

not varied orally.[324] In such cases, the ineffective oral variation is sometimes referred to as a "waiver", so as to contrast it with an effective rescission followed by the making of a substituted contract on new terms: "There was no fresh agreement . . . which can be regarded as having been substituted for the original written contract. There was nothing more than a waiver by the defendants of a delivery by the plaintiff in [the originally stipulated month]".[325]

To mean forbearance. A variation may not be contractually binding for want   3–069
of consideration or of contractual intention, or because it fails to comply with a legal requirement that it must be in, or evidenced in, writing.[326] It may never-theless have certain limited legal effects, which are sometimes said to arise because one party has "waived" his rights. To distinguish such arrangements from con-tractually binding variations, they will here be referred to as "forbearances".[327] Their effects are as follows.

Party requesting forbearance. The party requesting the forbearance cannot   3–070
refuse to accept the varied performance. Thus, if a seller at the request of the buyer delivers late, the buyer cannot refuse to accept on the ground that delivery was made after the time specified in the original contract.[328]

Varied performance made and accepted. If the varied performance is   3–071
actually made and accepted, neither party can claim damages on the ground that performance was not in accordance with the original contract. Thus, in the above example the seller who delivers late, or the buyer who takes delivery late, is not liable in damages. But if the contract is not performed at all, the damages are assessed on the footing that the breach took place at the end of the extended period.[329]

Party granting forbearance. The cases that give rise to the greatest difficulty   3–072
are those in which the party *granting* the forbearance refuses to perform, or to accept performance, in accordance with it. Suppose, for example, that a buyer agrees, at the seller's request, to accept late delivery. The buyer cannot then claim damages for the seller's failure to deliver within the contract period[330]; but a further set of problems can arise if, after expiry of that period but within the extended period, the seller tenders delivery, and the buyer refuses to accept it. One possible view is that the seller cannot derive rights from a forbearance which is not binding as a contract, and that therefore he is not entitled to damages for the buyer's refusal to take delivery within the extended, but outside the original, contract period. A claim for such damages was accordingly rejected in *Plevins v Downing*,[331] where the agreement to extend the delivery dates had no contractual force since it was oral when it should, as the law then stood, have been evidenced

---

[324] See below, paras 5–030—5–034.
[325] *Hickman v Haynes* (1875) L.R. 10 C.P. 598 at 604.
[326] See below, paras 5–030—5–034.
[327] cf. *The Kanchenjunga* [1990] 1 Lloyd's Rep. 391 at 397.
[328] *Hickman v Haynes*, above; *Levey & Co v Goldberg* [1922] 1 K.B. 688; cf. *British and Beningtons Ltd v NW Cachar Tea Co* [1923] A.C. 48.
[329] *Ogle v Vane* (1868) L.R. 3 Q.B. 272.
[330] cf. *The Kanchenjunga* [1989] 1 Lloyd's Rep. 354 at 358, affirmed [1990] 1 Lloyd's Rep. 391.
[331] (1876) 1 C.P.D. 220.

in writing and since it was probably unsupported by consideration, having been made at the request, and for the sole benefit, of the seller.[332]

But in many cases the party for whose benefit the forbearance was granted was allowed to enforce the contract in accordance with the new terms. In *Hartley v Hymans*[333] a buyer of cotton agreed to allow the seller to make late delivery. It was held that he was liable in damages for peremptorily refusing to take delivery after the period originally specified in the contract had expired. Similarly, a party may acquiesce in a method of payment other than that specified in the contract so as to indicate that the new method is to become the "accepted method."[334] He cannot then refuse to perform his part simply because the other party has not performed his obligation to pay strictly in accordance with the terms originally agreed[335]; nor can he peremptorily require performance strictly in accordance with those terms.[336] In these cases it is sometimes said that there is no variation of the contract, but only a variation of the mode of performance; or that there is no variation, but only a waiver[337] in the sense of forbearance.

3–073   **Forbearance distinguished from variation supported by consideration.** Such a forbearance differs from a variation which is supported by consideration in that it does not *irrevocably* alter the rights of the parties under the original contract. The party granting the forbearance *can generally retract it*, provided that he gives reasonable notice of his intention to do so to the party for whose benefit it was granted.[338] Thus, in *Charles Rickards Ltd v Oppenhaim*[339] a contract for the sale of a car provided for delivery on March 20. The car was not delivered on that day but the buyer continued to press for delivery and finally told the seller on June 29 that he must have the car by July 25 at the latest. It was held that the buyer could not have refused peremptorily to accept the car merely because the original delivery date had gone by, as he had continued to press for delivery; but that he could refuse on the seller's failure to comply with a notice to deliver within a reasonable time. Here the notice did give the seller a reasonable time to deliver, so that the buyer was justified in refusing to take the car after July 25. A fortiori, the buyer could have refused to take delivery if the original delivery date had been

---

[332] See above, para.3–063.

[333] [1920] 3 K.B. 475; cf. *Tyers v Rosedale & Ferryhill Iron Co* (1875) L.R. 10 Ex. 195; *Besseller Waechter Glover & Co v South Derwent Coal Ltd* [1938] 1 K.B. 408; and see *Leather Cloth Co v Hieronimus* (1874–75) L.R. 10 Q.B. 140 (variation of route of shipment).

[334] *The Scaptrade* [1981] 2 Lloyd's Rep. 425 at 431 (where this requirement was not satisfied), affirmed [1983] 2 A.C. 694, without reference to this point; *Hazel v Akhtar* [2001] EWCA Civ 1883, *The Times*, January 7, 2002 (landlord tolerating habitually late payment of rent).

[335] *Panoutsos v Raymond Hadley Corp of NY* [1917] 2 K.B. 473; *Tankexpress A/S v Cie Financière Belge des Petroles, SA* [1949] A.C. 76; *Plasticmoda Soc v Davidsons (Manchester) Ltd* [1952] 1 Lloyd's Rep. 527.

[336] *Mitas v Hymans* [1951] 2 T.L.R. 1215.

[337] e.g. in *Plevins v Downing* (1876) 1 C.P.D. 220 at 225; *Besseller Waechter Glover & Co v South Derwent Coal Co Ltd* [1938] 1 K.B. 408 at 416; *The Kanchenjunga* [1990] 1 Lloyd's Rep. 391 at 397–398.

[338] *Banning v Wright* [1972] 1 W.L.R. 972 at 981; *Ficom SA v Sociedad Cadex Ltda.*[1980] 2 Lloyd's Rep. 118 at 131; *Bremer Handelsgesellschaft mbH v Raiffeisen Hauptgenossenschaft EG* [1982] 1 Lloyd's Rep. 599.

[339] [1950] 1 K.B. 616; cf. *Cape Asbestos Co Ltd v Lloyds Bank Ltd* [1921] W.N. 274 at 276; *Bird v Hildage* [1948] 1 K.B. 91; *State Trading Corp of India v Cie Française d'Importation et de Distribution* [1983] 2 Lloyd's Rep. 679 at 681.

extended only for a fixed time and if delivery had not been made by the end of that time.[340]

Forbearance made irrevocable by subsequent events. A forbearance may, however, become irrevocable as a result of subsequent events: for example if a buyer indicates that he is willing to accept goods of a different quality from those contracted for, and the seller, in reliance on that assurance, so conducts himself as to put it out of his power to supply goods of the contract quality within the contract period.[341]

3–074

The intention of the parties. The distinction between a forbearance and a variation is sometimes said to depend on the intention of the parties[342]: a statement is a forbearance if the party making it intends to reserve a power to retract; but a variation if he intends permanently to abandon his rights under the contract. The courts were, however, anxious to avoid the unjust effects of the rules as to variations that were not contractually binding for lack of consideration or failure to comply with formal requirements. Hence they often interpreted a subsequent agreement as a forbearance, so as to give it at least some legal effects.

3–075

(ii) *In equity*[343]

The shortcomings of forbearance. The common law rules as to waiver in the sense of forbearance are defective in two ways. First, they rest on the tenuous distinction between forbearance and variation, which can be deduced from the judgments, but does not provide any very solid basis for distinguishing between the actual decisions. It is hard to see, for instance, why the buyer in *Plevins v Downing*[344] was allowed to reject late delivery, while the buyer in *Hartley v Hymans*[345] was not allowed to do so. Secondly, the common law rules produced the paradoxical result that, the more a party purported to bind himself by a subsequent agreement, the less he was likely to be bound. An attempt permanently to renounce a right would be a variation, and ineffective for want of writing or consideration. But an attempt to suspend a right would be effective, to a limited extent, as a forbearance.

3–076

Equity's solution: "equitable", or "promissory" estoppel. Equity devised a more satisfactory approach to the problem by concentrating, not on the intention of the party granting the forbearance, but on the conduct of that party and on its effect on the position of the other party. The leading case is *Hughes v Metropolitan Ry*,[346] where a landlord had given his tenant notice requiring him to do repairs within six months. During the six months he began to negotiate with the tenant

3–077

---

[340] cf. *Nichimen Corp v Gatoil Overseas Inc* [1987] 2 Lloyd's Rep. 46, where similar fixed term extensions were granted by a seller.
[341] *Toepfer v Warinco AG* [1978] 2 Lloyd's Rep. 569 at 576; *The Bunge Saga Lima* [2005] EWHC 244 (Comm); [2005] 2 Lloyd's Rep. 1 at [31].
[342] *Stead v Dawber* (1839) 10 A. & E. 57 at 64.
[343] Denning 15 M.L.R. 1; Wilson 67 L.Q.R. 330; Sheridan 15 M.L.R. 325; Gordon [1963] C.L.J. 222; Wilson [1965] C.L.J. 93; Thompson [1983] C.L.J. 257; Spence, *Protecting Reliance*.
[344] (1876) 1 C.P.D. 220; above, para.3–072.
[345] [1920] 3 K.B. 475; above, para.3–072.
[346] (1877) 2 App.Cas. 439.

for the purchase of his lease. When the negotiations broke down, he immediately claimed to forfeit the lease on the ground that the tenant had not done the repairs. The claim was rejected, Lord Cairns saying that if one party leads the other "to suppose that the strict rights arising under the contract will not be enforced, or will be kept in suspense or held in abeyance, the person who otherwise might have enforced those rights will not be allowed to enforce them where it would be inequitable having regard to the dealings which have thus taken place between the parties".[347] The landlord had by his conduct led the tenant to suppose that during the negotiations he would not enforce his right to forfeit. Hence he could not forfeit immediately the negotiations broke down: he had to give the tenant a reasonable time from that date to do the repairs. This equitable doctrine can now be applied to arrangements which might formerly have been regarded as variations ineffective at common law for want of consideration.[348] For reasons to be discussed later in this chapter[349] the doctrine is often (if somewhat misleadingly) referred to as "equitable" or "promissory" estoppel.

3–078   **Relationships within the doctrine.** The rights which the equitable doctrine prevents a promisor or representor from enforcing normally arise out of a contract between him and the other party. But the doctrine can also apply where the relationship giving rise to rights and duties is non-contractual: e.g. to prevent the enforcement of a liability imposed by statute[350]; or to prevent a man from ejecting a woman, with whom he had been cohabiting, from the family home.[351] On the other hand, it has been said that the doctrine "has no application as between a landowner and a trespasser".[352] Hence the mere fact that a landowner has for some time failed or neglected to enforce his rights against a trespasser does not prevent him from later doing so without notice.

3–079   **The need for a pre-existing legal relationship.** It has been suggested that the doctrine can apply even where, before the making of the promise or representation, there is no legal relationship of any kind between the parties[353]; or where there is only a putative contract between them: e.g. where the promisee is induced to believe that a contract into which he had undoubtedly entered was between him and the promisor, when in fact it was between the promisee and another person.[354] But it is submitted that these suggestions mistake the nature of the doctrine, which is to restrict the enforcement by the promisor of previously existing rights against the promisee. Such rights can arise only out of a legal relationship existing between these parties before the making of the promise or representation. To

---

[347] (1877) 2 App.Cas. 439 at 448. cf. *Smith v Lawson* (1998) 75 P. & C.R. 466, below para.3–090.

[348] e.g. *Charles Rickards Ltd v Oppenhaim* [1950] K.B. 616 (where both common law and equitable principles were applied).

[349] See below, para.3–090.

[350] *Durham Fancy Goods Ltd v Michael Jackson (Fancy Goods) Ltd* [1968] 2 Q.B. 839. Contrast *Evans v Amicus Healthcare Ltd* [2004] EWCA Civ 727; [2005] Fam. 1 at [120].

[351] *Maharaj v Chand* [1986] A.C. 898.

[352] *Morris v Tarrant* [1971] 2 Q.B. 143 at 160; cf. *Burrows v Brent LBC* [1996] 1 W.L.R. 1448 at 1458, where no attempt was made to invoke the doctrine in favour of a "tolerated trespasser".

[353] See *Evenden v Guildford City FC* [1975] Q.B. 917 at 924, 926; cf. in Australia, *Waltons Stores (Interstate) Ltd v Maher* (1988) 164 C.L.R. 387; below, para.3–093.

[354] *The Henrik Sif* [1982] 1 Lloyd's Rep. 456 at 466; the actual decision can perhaps be explained as one of liability for actionable non-disclosure: below, para.9–151.

apply the doctrine where there was no such relationship would contravene the rule (to be discussed below) that the doctrine creates no new rights.[355]

Requirements. The operation of the doctrine is subject to the requirements   **3–080** set out in the paragraphs below.[356] The burden of proving the necessary facts is on the promisee.[357]

A "clear" or "unequivocal" promise or representation. There must be a   **3–081** promise (or an assurance or representation in the nature of a promise[358]) which is intended to affect the legal relationship between the parties[359] and which indicates that the promisor will not insist on his strict legal rights,[360] arising out of that relationship, against the promisee. Here, as elsewhere,[361] the law applies an objective test. It is enough if the promise induces the promisee reasonably to believe that the other party will not insist on his strict legal rights.[362] A mere threat to do something is not sufficient, nor, probably, is a representation or promise by a person that he *will* enforce a legal right: thus the doctrine does not apply where A tells B that he will exercise his right to cancel a contract between them unless by a specified date B has paid sums due under the contract to A.[363]

The promise or representation must be "clear" or "unequivocal," or "precise and unambiguous."[364] This requirement seems to have originated in the law relating to estoppel by representation[365] and it is now frequently stated in relation to "waiver"[366] and "promissory estoppel."[367] It does not mean that the promise or representation must be express[368]: in *Hughes v Metropolitan Ry*[369] itself the

---

[355] See below, para.3–088; *Baird Textile Holdings Ltd v Marks & Spencer Plc* [2001] EWCA Civ 274; [2002] 1 All E.R. (Comm) 737 at [89] apparently doubting some of the reasoning in *The Henrik Sif* above, but not the outcome since there was undoubtedly "a legal relationship . . . whoever were the parties thereto" (though the difficulty remains that the first defendants, against whom the doctrine was said to operate, were not parties to that relationship).

[356] Paras 3–081—3–085.

[357] *Habib Bank Ltd v Tufail* [2006] EWCA Civ 374 at [21]; cf. proprietary estoppel: below, para.3–133.

[358] *James v Heim Galleries* (1980) 256 E.G. 819 at 821; *Collin v Duke of Westminster* [1985] Q.B. 581 at 595.

[359] *Spence v Shell* (1980) 256 E.G. 55 at 63; *Central London Property Trust Ltd v High Trees House Ltd* [1947] K.B. 130 at 134; *Baird Textile Holdings Ltd v Marks & Spencer Plc*, above, fn.355, at [94].

[360] Or that he will not rely on an available defence: cf. below, paras 3–088, 9–157.

[361] See above, paras 1–002, 2–002.

[362] *Bremer Handelsgesellschaft mbH v Vanden Avenne-Izegem PVBA* [1978] 2 Lloyd's Rep. 109 at 126; *Bremer Handelsgesellschaft mbH v Mackprang Jr* [1979] 1 Lloyd's Rep. 221 (both these cases concerned "waiver"; cf. below, fn.366).

[363] *Drexel Burnham Lambert International NV v El Nasr* [1986] 1 Lloyd's Rep. 356.

[364] It has been said that it is sufficient if "the corpus of the representation should partake of that requirement": *ING Bank NV v Ros Roca SA* [2011] EWCA Civ 353 at [100].

[365] *Low v Bouverie* [1891] 3 Ch. 82 at 106; *Woodhouse AC Israel Cocoa Ltd SA v Nigerian Produce Marketing Co Ltd* [1972] A.C. 741; *The Shackleford* [1978] 2 Lloyd's Rep. 155 at 159; below, para.9–156.

[366] *The Laconia* [1977] A.C. 850 at 871; *The Rio Sun* [1981] 2 Lloyd's Rep. 489 and [1982] 1 Lloyd's Rep. 404; for the analogy between waiver and the equitable doctrine here under discussion, see above, para.3–076; below, para.3–091.

[367] *BP Exploration Co (Libya) Ltd v Hunt (No.2)* [1979] 1 W.L.R. 783 at 812 (affirmed [1983] 2 A.C. 352, without reference to this point); *The Post Chaser* [1981] 2 Lloyd's Rep. 695 at 700; *The Scaptrade* [1983] Q.B. 529 at 534–535 (affirmed [1983] A.C. 694, without reference to this point); *Goldsworthy v Brickell* [1987] Ch. 378 at 410; *The Zenovia* [2009] EWHC 739 (Comm); [2009] 2 Lloyd's Rep. 139 at [29]–[34].

[368] *Spence v Shell* (1980) 256 E.G. 55 at 63.

[369] (1877) 2 App.Cas. 439; cf. *The Post Chaser* [1981] 2 Lloyd's Rep. 695 at 700.

landlord made no express promise that he would not enforce his right to forfeit the lease; but an implication of such a promise fairly arose from the course of the negotiations between the parties. There is some support for the view that the promise must have the same degree of certainty as would be needed to give it contractual effect if it were supported by consideration.[370] Thus if the statement could not have contractual effect because it was too vague,[371] or if it was insufficiently precise to amount to an offer,[372] or if it does not amount to an unqualified acceptance,[373] it will not bring the equitable doctrine into operation.[374]

The purpose of the requirement that the promise or representation must be "clear" or "unequivocal" is to prevent a party from losing his legal rights merely because he has granted some indulgence by failing throughout to insist on strict performance of a contract[375]; or because he has offered some concession in the course of negotiations for the settlement of a dispute arising out of the contract[376] or merely because he has declared his willingness to continue such negotiations.[377] Thus the requirement was not satisfied where one of the parties to such negotiations throughout insisted on strict compliance with the terms of the contract.[378] Nor was it satisfied where he accepted less than that to which he was entitled but did so subject to an express reservation of his rights.[379] Failure, in the course of negotiations of this kind, to object to a defect or deficiency in performance is likewise insufficient if the injured party did not know and could not reasonably have known of it[380] or if full performance remained possible and continued to be demanded by that party.[381] On the other hand, failure to object to a known defect or deficiency within a reasonable time of its discovery[382] may be regarded as an unequivocal indication of the injured party's intention not to insist on his strict legal rights.[383] The position seems to be the same where the defect or deficiency,

---

[370] *The Winson* [1980] 2 Lloyd's Rep. 213 at 222, reversed on other grounds [1982] A.C. 939; *Drexel Burnham Lambert International NV v El Nasr* [1986] 1 Lloyd's Rep. 357; *Baird Textile Holdings Ltd v Marks & Spencer* [2001] EWCA Civ 274; [2002] 1 All E.R. (Comm) 737 at [38], [54]; cf. above, para.2–078 for the requirement of certainty.

[371] See above, para.2–079.

[372] See above, para.2–002.

[373] *Azov Shipping Co v Baltic Shipping Co* [1999] 2 Lloyd's Rep. 159 at 173 (a case of estoppel by representation: see below, para.9–156). For the requirement of an "unqualified" acceptance, see above, para.2–019.

[374] *The Winson* [1980] 2 Lloyd's Rep. 213 at 223, reversed on other grounds [1982] A.C. 939.

[375] *The Scaptrade* [1981] 2 Lloyd's Rep. 425 at 431; [1983] Q.B. 529 at 535 affirmed [1983] 2 A.C. 694; cf. *Cape Asbestos Co Ltd v Lloyds Bank Ltd* [1921] W.N. 274 at 276; *Bremer Handelsgesellschaft mbH v Bunge Corp* [1983] 1 Lloyd's Rep. 476. And see the comment of Longmore L.J. in *Collier v P & M.J. Wright (Holdings) Ltd* [2007] EWCA Civ 1329; [2008] 1 W.L.R. 643 at [48] (considered below, para.3–115).

[376] cf. *London & Clydebank Properties v HM Investment Co* [1993] E.G.C.S. 63.

[377] *Seechurn v Ace Insurance SA* [2002] EWCA Civ 67; [2002] 2 Lloyd's Rep. 390, esp. at [55].

[378] *V Berg & Son Ltd v Vanden Avenne-Izegem PVBA* [1977] 1 Lloyd's Rep. 500; cf. *Edm J M Mertens & Co PVBA v Veevoeder Import Export Vimex BV* [1979] 2 Lloyd's Rep. 372.

[379] *Finagrain SA Geneva v P. Kruse Hamburg* [1976] 2 Lloyd's Rep. 508; cf. *Cook Industries Inc v Meunerie Liègeois SA* [1981] 1 Lloyd's Rep. 359 at 368; *Peter Cremer v Granaria BV* [1981] 2 Lloyd's Rep. 583; cf. *The Winson* [1980] 2 Lloyd's Rep. 213 (as to which see fn.374, above).

[380] *Avimex SA v Dewulf & Cie* [1979] 2 Lloyd's Rep. 57.

[381] *The Mihalios Xilas* [1979] W.L.R. 1018; *The Post Chaser* [1981] 2 Lloyd's Rep. 695 at 700.

[382] See *The Laconia* [1977] A.C. 850 (where retention of an under-payment accepted without authority by the payee's bank was held not to amount to a waiver); *The Superhulls Cover Case (No.2)* [1990] 2 Lloyd's Rep. 431 (where the deficiency was not known).

[383] e.g. *Bremer Handelsgesellschaft mbH v Vanden Avenne-Izegem PVBA* [1978] 2 Lloyd's Rep. 109; *Hazel v Akhtar* [2001] EWCA Civ 1883; [2002] P. & C.R. 17; *Argo Systems FZE v Liberty Insurance (PTE)* [2011] EWHC 301 (Comm).

though not actually known to the injured party, was obvious or could have been discovered by him, if he had taken reasonable steps.[384] But where more than one matter is in dispute between the parties, "emphatic reliance upon some important disputed point does not by itself . . . imply any unequivocal representation that compliance with other parts of the bargain is thereby waived".[385]

Silence and inaction. Although a promise or representation may be made by conduct, mere inactivity will not normally suffice for the present purpose since "it is difficult to imagine how silence and inaction can be anything but equivocal".[386] Unless the law took this view, mere failure to assert a contractual right could lead to its loss; and the courts have on a number of occasions rejected this clearly undesirable conclusion. Thus it has been held that there is "no ground for saying that mere delay, however lengthy, destroys the contractual right"[387]; and that the mere failure to prosecute a claim regarded by both parties as hopeless did not amount to a promise to abandon it.[388] The only circumstances in which "silence and inaction" can have this effect are the exceptional ones (discussed elsewhere in this book[389]) in which the law imposes a duty to disclose facts or to clarify a legal relationship and the party under the duty fails to perform it.[390]   3–082

Reliance. The requirement of reliance means that the promise or representation must in some way have influenced the conduct of the party to whom it was made. Although the promise need not form the sole inducement,[391] it must (it is submitted) be *some* inducement. Hence the requirement would not be satisfied if it could be shown that the other party's conduct was not influenced by the promise at all,[392] so that he was not in any way prejudiced by it.[393] But if this is a matter of "mere speculation",[394] or if the promise or representation "was one of the   3–083

---

[384] See *Bremer Handelsgesellschaft mbH v C. Mackprang Jr* [1979] 1 Lloyd's Rep. 221, where there was a division of opinion on the point in the Court of Appeal. Contrast, for a different type of waiver, below, para.18–076.

[385] *The Athos* [1983] 1 Lloyd's Rep. 127 at 135; *Rafsanjan Pistachio Producers Co-operative v Bank Leumi (UK) Plc* [1992] 1 Lloyd's Rep. 513 at 542.

[386] *The Leonidas D* [1985] 1 W.L.R. 925 at 937; cf. *Cook Industries v Tradax Export SA* [1983] 1 Lloyd's Rep. 327 at 332 (affirmed [1985] 2 Lloyd's Rep. 454); *The August P Leonhardt* [1985] 2 Lloyd's Rep. 28 at 33; *The Superhulls Cover Case (No.2)* [1990] 2 Lloyd's Rep. 431 at 452; and see above, para.2–005.

[387] *Amherst v James Walker Goldsmith & Silversmith Ltd* [1983] Ch. 305 at 315; cf., in another context, *The Nai Genova* [1984] 1 Lloyd's Rep. 353 at 365.

[388] *Collin v Duke of Westminster* [1985] Q.B. 581.

[389] See below, para.9–130 et seq., above, para.2–047; *Petrotrade Inc v Stinnes Handel GmbH* [1995] 1 Lloyd's Rep. 142 at 151, where the statement that there may be a representation by "conduct (including silence)" refers to the exceptional situations described in the text above. In the context of estoppel by convention, where it may be sufficient that one party has "acquiesced" in the mistaken view of another, the line between silence and conduct may be somewhat blurred: below, para.3–095.

[390] cf. *ING Bank NV v Ros Roca SA* [2011] EWCA Civ 353 in which the comments of Rix L.J. that there may be a "duty to speak" should be seen in the context of what was, if anything, an estoppel by convention, notwithstanding his preference for viewing it as promissory estoppel: below para.3–095.

[391] cf. below, para.9–021.

[392] See *Raiffeisen Hauptgenossenschaft v Louis Dreyfus & Co* [1981] 1 Lloyd's Rep. 345 at 352; *Cook Industries Ltd v Meunerie Liègeois SA* [1981] 1 Lloyd's Rep. 359 at 368; *The Scaptrade* [1983] Q.B. 529 at 536, affirmed [1983] 2 A.C. 694, without reference to this point; *Lark v Outhwaite* [1991] 2 Lloyd's Rep. 132 at 142; *The Nerarno* [1996] 1 Lloyd's Rep. 1.

[393] *Ets Soules & Cie v International Trade Development Co Ltd* [1980] 1 Lloyd's Rep. 129; *The Multibank Holsatia* [1988] 2 Lloyd's Rep. 486 at 493.

[394] *Brikom Investments Ltd v Carr* [1979] Q.B. 467 at 482.

factors . . . relied upon",[395] it would form a sufficient inducement. In other words, where the promisee has, after the promise, conducted himself in the way intended by the promisor, it will be up to the promisor to establish that the conduct was not induced by the promise.[396]

3-084   **Detriment?** There is sometimes said to be a further requirement, namely that the promisee must have suffered some "detriment" in reliance on the promise.[397] This may mean that the promisee must have done something which he was not previously bound to do and as a result have suffered loss, e.g. by incurring expenditure in reliance on the promise. The alleged requirement of "detriment" in this sense is based on the analogy of estoppel by representation.[398] But that analogy is (as we shall see)[399] inexact; and the equitable doctrine can clearly operate even though there is no "detriment" in this sense.[400] It is enough if the promisee has altered his position in reliance on the promise so that it would be inequitable to allow the promisor to act inconsistently with it.[401] Thus the requirement can be satisfied if the promisee has forborne from taking steps to safeguard his legal position (as in *Hughes v Metropolitan Ry*[402] itself); or if he has performed or made efforts to perform the original obligation as altered by the promise (e.g. where a seller who has been promised extra time for delivery continues to make efforts to perform after the originally agreed delivery date has gone by).

3-085   **Inequitable.** It must be "inequitable" for the promisor to go back on the promise. This requirement cannot be defined with anything approaching precision, but the underlying idea is that the promisee must have acted in reliance on the promise in one of the ways just described, so that he can no longer be restored to the position in which he was before he took such action.[403] If the promisee can be restored to that position, it will not be inequitable for the promisor to go back on the promise. In one case[404] the promisor re-asserted his strict legal rights only two days after the promise had been made. It was held that this was not "inequitable", since the promisee had not, in this short period, suffered any prejudice: he could be, and was, restored to exactly the position in which he had been before the promise was made. Sometimes, moreover, extraneous circumstances will justify the promisor in going back on the promise without notice. In

---

[395] *Brikom Investments Ltd v Carr* [1979] Q.B. 467 at 490 (per Cumming-Bruce L.J., whose decision was based on the different ground discussed above, para.3–065). cf. *Steria Ltd v Hutchinson* [2006] EWCA Civ 1551; [2007] I.C.R. 445 at [117] ("a significant factor").

[396] cf. the similar rule in cases of "proprietary estoppel" stated below, para.3–133.

[397] e.g. *Fontana NV v Mautner* (1979) 254 E.G. 199; *Meng Long Development Pte v Jip Hong Trading Co Pte Ltd* [1985] A.C. 511 at 524. cf. Wilson 67 L.Q.R. 344.

[398] See below, para.9–156; *Carr v L & NW Ry* (1875) L.R. 10 C.P. 310 at 317.

[399] See below, para.3–090.

[400] *W J Alan & Co Ltd v El Nasr Export & Import Co* [1972] 2 Q.B. 189 at 213.

[401] *The Post Chaser* [1981] 2 Lloyd's Rep. 695 at 701; *The Superhulls Cover Case (No.2)* [1990] 2 Lloyd's Rep. 431 at 454; *Steria Ltd v Hutchinson* [2006] EWCA Civ 1551 at [73], but contrast [95]. cf. *Seechurn v Ace Insurance SA* [2002] EWCA Civ 67; [2002] 2 Lloyd's Rep. 390 at [25], leaving open the question whether further "detriment" is required.

[402] (1877) 2 App.Cas. 439; above, para.3–077.

[403] *Maharaj v Chand* [1986] A.C. 898; *The Bunge Saga Lima* [2005] EWHC 244; [2005] 2 Lloyd's Rep. 1 at [31].

[404] *The Post Chaser* [1981] 2 Lloyd's Rep. 693; cf. *Bremer Handelsgesellschaft mbH v Bunge Corp* [1983] 1 Lloyd's Rep. 476 at 484; *Bremer Handelsgesellschaft mbH v Deutsche-Conti Handelsgesellschaft mbH* [1983] 1 Lloyd's Rep. 689; *The Trado* [1982] 1 Lloyd's Rep. 157 at 160; *Transatlantico de Commercial SA v Incrobasa Industrial e Commercio Brazileira SA* [1995] 1 Lloyd's Rep. 215 at 219.

Williams v Stern[405] the claimant gave the defendant a bill of sale of furniture as security for a loan; the bill entitled the defendant to seize the furniture if the claimant defaulted in paying instalments due under it. When the fourteenth instalment became due, the claimant asked for extra time, and the defendant said that he "would not look to a week". Three days later he seized the furniture because he had heard that the claimant's landlord intended to distrain it for arrears of rent. It was held that the defendant's seizure was justified. There was no consideration for his promise to give time, nor did *Hughes v Metropolitan Ry*[406] apply. Brett L.J. said:

"Has there been any misconduct on the part of the defendant? I think not: it appears that a distress by the (claimant's) landlord was threatened; and under those circumstances I do not blame the defendant for changing his mind."[407]

His conduct was not "inequitable". It may not be inequitable for the promisor to go back on the promise if it was obtained by the unjustifiable conduct of the promisee.[408]

Effect generally suspensory. The equitable doctrine, like the common law   3–086
doctrine of waiver,[409] does not extinguish, but only suspends, rights. In *Hughes v Metropolitan Ry* the landlord was not forever prevented from enforcing the covenant: he could have enforced it on giving reasonable notice requiring the tenant to do the repairs.[410] This aspect of the doctrine was stressed in *Tool Metal Manufacturing Co Ltd v Tungsten Electric Co Ltd*,[411] where a licence for the use of a patent provided that the licensees should pay "compensation" if they manufactured more than a stated number of articles incorporating the patent. In 1942 the owners of the patent agreed to suspend the obligation to pay "compensation" until a new agreement was made. They later gave notice to end the suspension. It was held that they were once again entitled to the payments after the expiry of a reasonable time from the giving of notice. The reason for this rule is that, in equity, the effect of the representation is to give the court a discretion to do what is equitable in all the circumstances[412]; and in the cases just discussed it would not be equitable (or in accordance with the intention of the parties) wholly to extinguish the representor's (or promisor's) rights.

---

[405] (1879) 5 Q.B.D. 409.

[406] (1877) 2 App.Cas. 439; above, para.3–077.

[407] At 413; cf. also *Southwark LBC v Logan* (1996) 8 Admin.L.R. 315.

[408] *South Caribbean Trading Ltd v Trafigura Beheer BV* [2004] EWHC 2676; [2005] 1 Lloyd's Rep. 128. See also: *D & C Builders v Rees* [1966] 2 Q.B. 617 at 626; *Tonkin v UK Insurance Ltd* [2006] EWHC 1120 (TCC); 107 Con. L.R. 107 at [206] (no estoppel where promisee actively (and, possibly, passively) misled the promisor).

[409] i.e. in the sense of forbearance, above, para.3–069.

[410] No reference to this point was made in *Smith v Lawson* (1998) 75 P. & C.R. 446 (below, para.3–089), probably because no attempt was made by the promisor to give notice of any intention to resume his strict legal rights.

[411] [1955] 1 W.L.R. 761; cf. *Banning v Wright* [1972] 1 W.L.R. 972 at 981; *The Post Chaser* [1981] 2 Lloyd's Rep. 695 at 701; *The Kanchenjunga* [1990] 1 Lloyd's Rep 391 at 399; *Hazel v Akhtar* [2001] EWCA Civ 1883; [2002] P. & C.R. 17 at [43].

[412] *Roebuck v Mungovin* [1994] 2 A.C. 224 at 235.

3-087   **Extinctive effect brought about by subsequent events.** Subsequent events may, in exceptional circumstances, give the doctrine an extinctive effect. They can, most obviously, lead to this result where they make it impossible for the promisee to perform his original obligation. In *Birmingham & District Land Co v L & NW Ry*[413] a building lease bound the tenant to build by 1885. The lessor agreed to suspend this obligation; but in 1886, while the suspension was still in force, the land was compulsorily acquired by a railway company, so that performance of the tenant's obligation became impossible. The tenant recovered statutory compensation from the railway company on the footing that the building lease was still binding; but clearly his obligation to build was wholly extinguished. Even where performance of the original obligation has not become literally impossible, the doctrine may sometimes have an extinctive effect. For example, in *Ogilvy v Hope-Davies*[414] a vendor of land indicated on August 15 that he would not insist on the contractual completion date of August 30. It was held that no question of reinstating the contractual completion date could arise "because the time was far too short".[415] The doctrine has an extinctive effect in such cases because subsequent events, or the passage of time, though not making performance of the original obligation impossible, have made it highly inequitable to require such performance even after reasonable notice.[416]

3-088   **Creates no new rights.** The equitable doctrine prevents the enforcement of existing rights, but it does not create entirely new rights or extend the scope of existing ones. This was decided in *Combe v Combe*,[417] where a husband during divorce proceedings promised to pay £100 per annum to his wife who, in reliance on this promise, forbore from applying to the court for maintenance. This forbearance did not constitute consideration for the husband's promise.[418] It was held that the equitable doctrine did not entitle the wife to recover the promised payments; nor is there any support in English cases for the view that it could create a cause of action in the narrower sense of "limiting recovery to reliance loss".[419]

The view that the doctrine gave rise to no new rights came to be associated with its description as a kind of estoppel (known as "promissory estoppel"[420]) and hence with the rule, established in relation to another kind of estoppel (known as "estoppel by representation"[421]), that "you cannot found a cause of action on an

---

[413] (1888) 40 Ch.D. 268. cf. *Durham Fancy Goods Ltd v Michael Jackson (Fancy Goods) Ltd* [1968] 2 Q.B. 839.

[414] [1976] 1 All E.R. 683; *The Ion* [1980] 2 Lloyd's Rep. 245; *Voest Alpine Intertrading GmbH v Chevron International Oil Co* [1987] 2 Lloyd's Rep. 547 at 560.

[415] *Ogilvy v Hope-Davies* [1976] 1 All E.R. 683 at 696.

[416] See *Maharaj v Chand* [1986] A.C. 898; cf. *W J Alan & Co Ltd v El Nasr Export & Import Co* [1972] Q.B. 189 (where the actual decision was that there was a variation supported by consideration: above, para.3–063); *The Bunge Saga Lima* [2005] EWHC 244 (Comm); [2005] 2 Lloyd's Rep. 1 at [31].

[417] [1951] 2 K.B. 215. The point had been foreshadowed in *Central London Property Trust Ltd v High Trees House Ltd* [1947] K.B. 130 at 134.

[418] See above, para.3–042.

[419] *Baird Textile Holdings Ltd v Marks & Spencer Plc* [2001] EWCA Civ 274; [2002] 1 All E.R. (Comm) 737 at [99]; for the difficulty of distinguishing in that case between reliance and expectation loss, see [2002] 1 All E.R. (Comm) 737 at [81], [82]; for the distinction in general, see below, paras 20–022—20–027.

[420] See above, para.3–077.

[421] See below, para.9–156.

estoppel".[422] It will be submitted below[423] that the analogy between the two kinds of estoppel is (to say the least) imperfect and that it does not satisfactorily account for the rule that "promissory estoppel" gives rise to no new rights. The more plausible explanation for this restriction on the scope of the equitable doctrine is that the restriction is needed to prevent that doctrine from coming into head–on collision with the rules which lay down the requirements for the creation of a binding contract. The significant point in the present context is that the restriction preserves consistency between the equitable doctrine and the rule that a promise is not binding as a contract unless it is supported by consideration or made in a deed.[424] *Combe v Combe* has likewise been relied on in support of the view that the equitable doctrine could not give rise to a cause of action on a promise which lacked contractual force for want, not of consideration, but of certainty and contractual intention.[425] There seems, with respect, to be no reason in principle for distinguishing for the present purpose between promises which lack contractual effect for want of consideration and those which lack such effect for some other reason: the danger of collision between the equitable principle and the requirements for the creation of a contract exists, whatever the reason may be why a particular promise lacks contractual force.[426]

The view that the equitable doctrine does not create new causes of action seems to have been doubted[427] or ignored[428] by dicta in later cases; but the promises in these cases created new rights on the orthodox ground that they were supported by consideration.[429] *Combe v Combe* therefore still stands as the leading English[430]

---

[422] *Low v Bouverie* [1891] 3 Ch. 82 at 101; cf. *Low v Bouverie* [1891] 3 Ch. 82 at 105; below, para.9–156.

[423] See below, para.3–090.

[424] This appears to be the point that Denning L.J. had in mind in *Combe v Combe* [1951] 2 K.B. 215 at 219 when he said that he did not want the equitable principle to be "stretched too far lest it be endangered". cf. *Brikom Investments Ltd v Carr* [1979] Q.B. 467 at 486; *Tool Metal Manufacturing Co Ltd v Tungsten Electric Co Ltd* [1955] 1 W.L.R. 761 at 764; contrast *Vaughan v Vaughan* [1953] Q.B. 762 at 768; Denning 15 M.L.R. 1.

[425] *Baird Textile Holdings Ltd v Marks & Spencer Plc*, above, fn.419, where *Combe v Combe* is cited at [34], and [87] in support of the view stated in the text above; though an alternative explanation for the result in the *Baird* case may be that, in the absence of certainty or contractual intention, the *requirements* for the operation of the equitable doctrine are simply not satisfied (above para.3–081), so that no question can arise as to its *effects*.

[426] In *Azov Shipping Co v Baltic Shipping Co* [1999] 2 Lloyd's Rep. 159 at 175 it is suggested that the rule that promissory estoppel gives rise to no cause of action "is limited to the protection of consideration" and has "no general application in the field of estoppel". The estoppel there under discussion was estoppel by representation, and the suggestion is, with respect, hard to reconcile with the statements in *Low v Bouverie* [1891] 3 Ch. 82 at 101, 105 referred to in fn.422 above. Similar difficulty arises from the more tentative suggestion in *Thornton Springer v NEM Insurance Ltd* [2000] 2 All E.R. 489 at 519 that estoppel could lead to the "enforcement of the promise" where no contract was concluded for want of acceptance of an offer, though not where there was no contract for want of consideration. The former situation is one of estoppel by convention (as to which see below, para.3–094); and it is also, with respect, hard to see why one answer should be given to the question whether the rule in *Combe v Combe* applies where the promise lacks contractual force for want of consideration and a different one where it lacks such force for want of an effective acceptance.

[427] *Re Wyvern Developments Ltd* [1974] 1 W.L.R. 1097 at 1104–1105; Atiyah 38 M.L.R. 65 and see Allan 79 L.Q.R. 238. The point was left open in *The Henrik Sif* [1982] 1 Lloyd's Rep. 456 at 466–468 (as to which see above, fn.355).

[428] *Evenden v Guildford City FC* [1975] Q.B. 917 at 924, 926; Napier [1976] C.L.J. 38; and see next note.

[429] e.g. *Secretary of State for Employment v Globe Elastic Thread Co Ltd* [1980] A.C. 506, overruling *Evenden's* case, above. Lord Wilberforce remarked at 518 that "To convert this [contract] into an estoppel is to turn the doctrine of promissory estoppel . . . upside down."

[430] For other jurisdictions, see below, para.3–093.

authority for the proposition that the doctrine creates no new rights and this proposition has been reaffirmed in a number of later cases.[431]

It appears to follow from this proposition that the equitable doctrine would not enable employees in a case like *Stilk v Myrick*[432] to recover the extra pay which they had been promised. It could, indeed, be argued[433] that in such a case the cause of action was the original contract of employment and that the subsequent agreement fell within the principle stated by Denning L.J. in *Combe v Combe* that consideration was not necessary for the "modification or discharge"[434] of a contract where the conditions required for the operation of the equitable doctrine were otherwise satisfied. This argument may derive some judicial support from a dictum that promissory estoppel "may enlarge the effect of an agreement"[435]; for this could mean that a promise of extra pay on facts such as those of *Stilk v Myrick* could create a cause of action even though it was not supported by consideration. This view is, however, hard to reconcile with the treatment of *Stilk v Myrick* in *Williams v Roffey Bros*[436] and with the fact that the decision in the latter case was based, not on estoppel,[437] but on the ground that the promise of extra pay there was supported by consideration. It is submitted that, when in *Combe v Combe* Denning L.J. used the phrase "modification or discharge" he had in mind a modification which *reduced* a party's obligations.[438] To apply it to a case in which it had the effect of *increasing* them necessarily amounts to giving the other party a new cause of action on a promise for which he has not provided any consideration; and *Combe v Combe* decides that this is not the effect of the equitable doctrine here under discussion.[439] A cause of action on a promise unsupported by consideration could, however, arise under other equitable doctrines: e.g. under the doctrine of "proprietary estoppel" to be discussed later in this chapter.[440]

3–089   **"Shield" and not a "sword".** The essentially defensive nature of the equitable doctrine here under discussion is sometimes expressed by saying that it operates as a shield and not as a sword.[441] In other words, its normal effect is merely to protect the promisee against enforcement of the original obligation. But the metaphor is apt to mislead,[442] for the equitable doctrine can assist a claimant no less than a defendant. For example, a creditor may threaten to seize property on

---

[431] *Argy Trading Development Co Ltd v Lapid Developments Ltd* [1977] 1 W.L.R. 444 at 457; *The Proodos C* [1980] 2 Lloyd's Rep. 390 at 394; *Brikom Investments Ltd v Seaford* [1981] 1 W.L.R. 863; cf. *Taylor Fashions Ltd v Liverpool Victoria Trustees Co Ltd* [1982] Q.B. 133 at 152; *Baird Textile Holdings Ltd v Marks & Spencer Plc*, above, fn.425.

[432] (1809) 2 Camp. 317; 6 Esp. 129; above, para.3–048.

[433] See *Hiscox v Outhwaite (No.3)* [1991] 2 Lloyd's Rep. 524 at 535.

[434] [1951] 2 K.B. 215 at 219.

[435] *Baird Textile Holdings Ltd v Marks & Spencer Plc* [2001] EWCA Civ 274; [2002] 1 All E.R. (Comm) 737 at [88].

[436] *Williams v Roffey Bros & Nicholls (Contractors) Ltd* [1991] 1 Q.B. 1; above, para.3–050.

[437] Though there are references to estoppel in that case at 13 ("not yet fully developed") and 17–18 (this reference seems to be to estoppel by convention, the relevance of which to the case is doubted at para.3–097, fn.525, below).

[438] As in *Central London Property Trust Ltd v High Trees House Ltd* [1947] K.B. 130; below para.3–112, this being the case under discussion in *Combe v Combe*, above, at 219.

[439] *The Proodos C* [1980] 2 Lloyd's Rep. 390.

[440] See below, para.3–118 et seq., especially para.3–149.

[441] *Combe v Combe* [1951] 2 K.B. 215 at 224; *The Proodos C* [1980] 2 Lloyd's Rep. 390 at 391 ("time-honoured phrase"); *Lark v Outhwaite* [1991] 2 Lloyd's Rep. 132 at 142.

[442] *Azov Shipping Co v Baltic Shipping Co* [1999] 2 Lloyd's Rep. 159 at 175 ("largely inaccurate"); *Baird Textile Holdings Ltd v Marks & Spencer Plc* [2001] EWCA Civ 274; [2001] 1 All E.R. (Comm) 737 at [52] ("misleading aphorism").

which a debt is secured, after having indicated that he would not insist on punctual payment. In such a case the debtor will, if the requirements of the equitable doctrine are satisfied, be able to restrain the creditor's threatened seizure by injunction.[443] Similarly, a seller may tender goods after the originally agreed delivery date, in reliance on the buyer's promise to accept late delivery. If the buyer without justification refuses to accept the delivery, the seller will be entitled to damages.[444]

The equitable doctrine can also assist the promisee as claimant in that it may prevent the promisor from relying on a defence which would, but for the promise, have been available to him: e.g. the defence that a claim which the promisee has made against him is time-barred,[445] or that the claim has been satisfied,[446] or that the contractual document suffers from some minor formal defect, the effect of which is not specified by the statute imposing the formal requirement.[447] In such cases, the doctrine will, once again, enable the promisee to win an action which, but for the doctrine, he would have lost. But the promisee's cause of action will have arisen independently of the promise which brought the equitable doctrine into operation: the effect of the doctrine is merely to prevent the promisor from relying on some circumstance which would, if the promise had not been made, *have destroyed the promisee's original cause of action*. This situation must be distinguished from that in which the promisor's "defence" is that (apart from the promise) the promisee's alleged *cause of action never existed at all*. It is submitted that the equitable doctrine should not prevent the promisor from relying on a "defence" of this kind. If the doctrine were allowed to operate in this way, it would give the promisee a new cause of action based on the promise, even though the promise was not supported by consideration; and such a result would be inconsistent with the essentially defensive nature of the doctrine.[448]

This doctrine may also, somewhat paradoxically, deprive a promisee of a defence. This was the position in *Smith v Lawson*[449] where a lessor told the lessee that he would not trouble to collect the small rent which the lessee had previously paid. It was held that the lessee's rent-free occupation did not amount to adverse possession since the lessor was precluded by the doctrine of promissory estoppel from obtaining possession on the ground of non-payment of rent and that therefore the lessee could not rely on her occupation to defeat the lessor's claim for a declaration that he remained freehold owner of the land.

Analogy with estoppel by representation. The equitable doctrine has certain features in common with the doctrine of estoppel by representation.[450] Each

3–090

---

[443] Such a claim would have succeeded in *Williams v Stern* (1879) 5 Q.B.D. 409 (above, para.3–085), if the creditor's conduct had been "inequitable."

[444] cf. *Hartley v Hymans* [1920] 3 K.B. 475, applying the corresponding doctrine of common law forbearance (above, para.3–069); *Johnson v Gore-Wood* [2002] 2 A.C. 1 at 40–41. And see Jackson 81 L.Q.R. 223.

[445] See *The Ion* [1980] 2 Lloyd's Rep. 245; *Hazel v Akhtar* [2002] EWCA Civ 1883; *The Times*, January 7, 2002 at [25]. *Commonwealth of Australia v Verwayen* (1990) 170 C.L.R. 394 (discussed by Spence 107 L.Q.R. 221) can be explained on this ground: see *Baird Textile Holdings Ltd v Marks & Spencer Plc*, above, fn.435 at [98].

[446] cf. below, para.9–156.

[447] *Shah v Shah* [2001] EWCA Civ 527; [2001] 4 All E.R. 138 at [31] (a case of estoppel by representation).

[448] cf. the criticism (above, para.3–079) of *The Henrik Sif* [1982] 1 Lloyd's Rep. 456.

[449] (1998) 75 P. & C.R. 466.

[450] See below, para.9–156.

is based on a representation followed by reliance on the part of the representee, and each is defensive in nature in that neither is capable in itself of giving rise to new rights. But there are also many differences between estoppel by representation and the equitable doctrine, even though the latter is now often referred to as a kind of estoppel.[451] These differences are reflected in the statement of Millett L.J. that

> "the attempt . . . to demonstrate that all estoppels . . . are now subsumed in the single and all-embracing estoppel by representation and that they are all governed by the same principle[452] [has] never won general acceptance".[453]

The various kinds of estoppel discussed in this chapter[454] are linked only by the broadest of general principles, that a person's taking of inconsistent positions is in some situations to be discouraged by law; in this sense it can be said that "unconscionability . . . provides the link between them".[455] But they nevertheless have "separate requirements and different terrains of application"[456] and therefore "cannot be accommodated within a single formula".[457] An important difference between the two types of estoppel at this stage under discussion relates to the nature of the representations required to bring them into operation. A representation of *intention* or a *promise* suffices for the purpose of the equitable doctrine; for this reason, and because the doctrine was developed in equity, it is often referred to as "promissory" or "equitable" estoppel.[458] True estoppel by representation, on the other hand, cannot be based on a representation of intention, but only on one of *existing fact*.[459] This rule was laid down in *Jorden v Money*,[460] where it was held

---

[451] Below, fn.471.

[452] The reference seems to be to Lord Denning M.R.'s statement in *Amalgamated Investment & Property Co Ltd v Texas Commerce International Bank Ltd* [1982] 2 Q.B. 73 at 122 ("one general principle shorn of limitations") which is cited with apparent approval by Lord Bingham in *Johnson v Gore Wood & Co* [2002] 2 A.C. 1 at 33.

[453] *First National Bank Plc v Thompson* [1996] Ch. 231 at 236; cf. *The Indian Endurance (No.2)* [1998] A.C. 878 at 913; dicta in *Baird Textile Holdings Ltd v Marks & Spencer Plc* [2001] EWCA Civ 274; [2002] 1 All E.R. (Comm) 737 at [38], [50], [83], [84] perhaps incline in the other direction.

[454] i.e. estoppel by representation (below, para.9–156), promissory estoppel (discussed here), estoppel by convention (below, para.3–094 et seq.) and proprietary estoppel (below, para.3–118 et seq.). See also the "contractual estoppel" which appears to have been accepted in the context of claims for misrepresentation: below, para.9–117.

[455] *Johnson v Gore Wood & Co* [2002] 2 A.C. 1 at 41.

[456] *The Indian Endurance (No.2)* [1998] A.C. 878 at 914; cf. *Donegal International Ltd v Zambia* [2007] EWHC 197; [2007] 1 Lloyd's Rep. 397 at [495].

[457] *Johnson v Gore Wood & Co* [2002] 2 A.C. 1 at 41. See also: *Steria Ltd v Hutchinson* [2006] EWCA Civ 1551 at [92], per Neuberger L.J. See McFarlane in Burrows & Peel (eds.), *Contract Formation and Parties* who decries the idea even of a unitary doctrine of *promissory* estoppel.

[458] e.g. *Woodhouse AC Israel Cocoa Ltd v Nigerian Produce Marketing Co Ltd* [1972] A.C. 741 at 758; *The Post Chaser* [1981] 2 Lloyd's Rep. 695 at 700; *The Kanchenjunga* [1990] 1 Lloyd's Rep. 391 at 398; *Roebuck v Mungovin* [1994] 2 A.C. 224 at 235. Contrast *Brikom Investments Ltd v Carr* [1979] Q.B. 467 at 485, 489, where Roskill L.J. prefers to refer simply to the principle of *Hughes v Metropolitan Ry* (1877) 2 App.Cas. 439.

[459] "Fact" is used here in contradistinction to a promise of future conduct; in *Steria Ltd v Hutchinson* [2006] EWCA Civ 1551 at [89] Neuberger L.J. thought it "realistic" not to suggest that a claim would fail if the representation was one of *law*: see further below, para.3–096.

[460] (1854) 5 H.L.C. 185; criticised by Jackson 81 L.Q.R. 84; cf. Halliwell 5 L.S. 15. For more recent statements of the rule that there must be a representation of fact, see *Argy Trading Development Co Ltd v Lapid Development Ltd* [1977] 1 W.L.R. 444 at 450; *TCB Ltd v Gray* [1986] Ch. 621 at 634, affirmed [1987] Ch. 458; *Roebuck v Mungovin* [1994] 2 A.C. 224 at 235; so-called "estoppel by convention" (below, para.3–094) is similarly based on an assumption as to an *existing* state of fact or (at least to some extent) of "law": see below, para.3–096.

that a representation by a creditor that he *would not* enforce a bond did not give rise to such an estoppel. This difference between estoppel by representation and the equitable doctrine cannot be explained by saying that the requirement of a representation of existing fact did not exist in equity but only at common law.[461] *Jorden v Money* was an appeal from the Court of Appeal in Chancery and was, no less than *Hughes v Metropolitan Ry*,[462] decided on equitable principles; and the requirement of a representation of existing fact is stated in many equity cases.[463] There are, moreover, other significant differences between the two doctrines. The equitable doctrine may operate even though there is no such "detriment" as is required to bring the doctrine of estoppel by representation into play.[464] And the effect of the equitable doctrine is only to suspend rights,[465] while estoppel by representation, where it operates, has a permanent effect. There is, finally, a difference in the legal nature of the two doctrines. Estoppel by representation prevents a party from establishing *facts*: i.e. from alleging that the facts represented by him are untrue, even where that is actually the case.[466] The equitable doctrine, by contrast, has nothing to do with proof of facts; it is concerned with the *legal effects* of a promise. There was, for example, no dispute about facts, in *Hughes v Metropolitan Ry*[467]: the issue was not whether the repairs had been done or whether the landlord had promised or represented that he would not forfeit the lease; it was simply whether he was (to some extent, at least) bound by that promise.

Analogy with waiver. It is submitted that the characteristics just described indicate that the equitable doctrine is not truly analogous with estoppel by representation. As Denning J. (a leading proponent of the modern equitable doctrine) has pointed out, the authorities which support it "although they are said to be cases of estoppel, are not really such".[468] The doctrine has closer affinities with the common law rules of waiver in the sense of forbearance: both are based on promises, or representations of intention; both are suspensive (rather than extinctive) in effect and both are concerned with the legal effects of promises rather than with proof of disputed facts. The main difference between them is that the equitable doctrine avoids the difficulties encountered at common law in distinguishing between a variation and a forbearance.[469]

3–091

---

[461] Estoppel by representation of fact (below, para.9–156) was recognised at common law at least as long ago as *Freeman v Cooke* (1848) 2 Ex. 654; but sometimes this form of estoppel is confusingly referred to as "equitable estoppel": e.g. in *Lombard North Central Plc v Stobart* [1990] Tr.L.R. 105 at 107.

[462] (1877) 2 App.Cas. 439; above, para.3–077.

[463] *Pigott v Stratton* (1859) 1 D.F. & J. 33 at 51; *Maddison v Alderson* (1883) 8 App.Cas. 467 at 473; *Chadwick v Manning* [1896] A.C. 231 at 238.

[464] See above, para.3–084.

[465] See above, para.3–086.

[466] This point accounts for the rule that estoppel *by representation* does not give rise to a cause of action: below para.9–156. If, e.g. A represents to B that B's goods are in C's possession, the fact that A is estopped from denying the truth of that representation does not turn A into a bailee of those goods. The rule that *promissory* estoppel does not give rise to a cause of action is based on different grounds explained at para.3–088, above.

[467] (1877) 2 App. Cas. 439; above, para.3–077; similarly, in *Central London Property Trust Ltd v High Trees House Ltd* [1947] K.B. 130 (below, para.3–112) there was no dispute about facts.

[468] *Central London Property Trust Ltd v High Trees House Ltd* [1947] K.B. 130 at 134; below, para.3–112.

[469] See above, paras 3–072—3–075.

There is much judicial support for these submissions. Lord Pearson has said that "promissory estoppel" was "far removed from the familiar estoppel by representation of fact and seems... to be more like waiver of contractual rights".[470] In many later cases "waiver" and "promissory estoppel" (or the rule in *Hughes v Metropolitan Ry*)[471] are treated as substantially similar doctrines.[472] The two expressions have been judicially described as "two ways of saying exactly the same thing"[473]; and, although the use of terminology has not been wholly consistent,[474] the courts often use the two expressions interchangeably when discussing situations in which it is alleged that one party has indicated that he will not enforce his strict legal rights against the other. This usage indicates that the equitable doctrine is more closely akin to waiver (in the sense of forbearance) than to true estoppel by representation of fact.

3–092   **Distinguished from promises supported by consideration.** Under the equitable doctrine, certain limited effects are given to a promise without consideration. But it is nevertheless in the interests of the promisee to show, if he can, that he did provide consideration so that the promise amounted to a contractually binding variation. Such proof will free him from the many rules that restrict the scope of the equitable doctrine: he need not then show that he has "relied" on the promise, or that it would be "inequitable" for the other party to go back on it; the variation will permanently affect the rights of the promisor and not merely suspend them (unless it is expressed so as to have only a temporary effect); and a contractual variation can not only reduce or extinguish existing rights but also create new ones. Where parties agree to modify an existing contract, the equitable doctrine (and its common law counterpart of waiver) may have reduced, but they have by no means eliminated, the practical importance of the doctrine of consideration.

3–093   **Other jurisdictions.** The English view that the doctrine of promissory estoppel gives rise to no cause of action has not been followed in other common law jurisdictions. In the United States, a similar doctrine has long been regarded as being capable of creating new rights, though both the existence and the content of the resulting rights are matters for the discretion of the courts.[475] A line of Australian cases likewise supports the view that promises or representations which, for want of consideration or of contractual intention, lack contractual force, may nevertheless be enforceable as if they were binding contracts.

---

[470] *Woodhouse AC Israel Cocoa Ltd v Nigerian Produce Marketing Co Ltd* [1972] A.C. 741 at 762.

[471] (1877) 2 App.Cas.439; above, para.3–077.

[472] *Finagrain SA Geneva v P. Kruse Hamburg* [1976] 2 Lloyd's Rep. 508 at 534; *Brikom Investments Ltd v Carr* [1979] Q.B. 467 at 488, 489, 490; *Bremer Handelsgesellschaft mbH v Bunge Corp* [1983] 1 Lloyd's Rep. 476 at 484; *BICC Ltd v Burndy Corp* [1985] Ch. 232 at 253; *The Chemical Venture* [1993] 1 Lloyd's Rep. 509 at 521.

[473] *Prosper Homes v Hambro's Bank Executor & Trustee Co* (1979) 39 P. & C.R. 395 at 401; *The Nerarno* [1996] 1 Lloyd's Rep. 1 at 6.

[474] For suggestions that "waiver" may be distinguishable from the equitable doctrine, see *W J Alan & Co Ltd v El Nasr Export Co* [1972] 2 Q.B. 189 at 212; *The Ion* [1980] 2 Lloyd's Rep. 245 at 249–250; *Brikom Investments Ltd v Carr* [1979] Q.B. 467 at 485, 489 (perhaps because there the "waiver" amounted to a variation supported by consideration).

[475] *Restatement*, Contracts §90 and *Restatement 2d*, Contracts §90. In English law, the need to use the doctrine to give rise to a cause of action is less acute than in the US, where the courts are less ready than the English courts to "invent" consideration (above, para.3–009).

The leading Australian case is *Waltons Stores (Interstate) Ltd v Maher*,[476] where A, a prospective lessor of business premises, did demolition and building work on the premises while the agreement for the lease lacked contractual force because it was still subject to contract[477]; he had done so to meet the prospective lessee's (B's) requirements and on the assumption, of which B must have known, that a binding contract would come into existence. B withdrew from the agreement (relying on his solicitor's advice that he was not bound by it); and it was held that he was estopped from denying that a contract had come into existence and that the agreement for the lease was therefore specifically enforceable against him.[478] The reasoning of the High Court is complex, but the basis of the decision appears to be that B had knowingly induced A to believe that a binding contract would come into existence by exchange of contracts[479] and to act in reasonable reliance on that belief.

In English law, such reliance is, in appropriate circumstances, capable of giving rise to a variety of remedies, even where the promise or representation which induces it lacks contractual force. Sometimes the remedy may be the enforcement of the promise according to its terms, as in cases of proprietary estoppel (to be discussed later in this chapter)[480]; sometimes it may be an award of the reasonable value of work done in the belief that a contract had, or would, come into existence.[481] Neither of these remedies would have been available in the *Waltons Stores* case since proprietary estoppel does not arise where work is done on the promisee's (rather than on the promisor's) land[482] and a claim for the reasonable value of the claimant's work is not available where he is aware of the fact that no binding agreement has come into existence and so takes the risk that the negotiations may fail.[483] Even where the second of these objections can be overcome (e.g. on the ground that the work was done at the request of the promisor or as a result of his assurance that an exchange of contracts would take place) it does not follow that the appropriate remedy is enforcement of the contract in its terms: if the basis of the Australian doctrine is reliance induced by the promisor, compensation for reliance loss would appear to be the more appropriate remedy.[484] The Australian doctrine also gives rise to the difficulties that there appear to be no clear limits to its scope, and that this lack of clarity is a regrettable source of uncertainty. The doctrine is, moreover, hard to reconcile with a number of fundamental principles of English law, such as the non-enforceability of informal gratuitous promises (even if relied on)[485] and the rule that there is no right to damages for a wholly

---

[476] (1988) 164 C.L.R. 387; Duthie 104 L.Q.R. 362; Sutton 1 J.C.L. 205.

[477] See above, para.2–088.

[478] The remedy awarded was damages in lieu of specific performance.

[479] For this requirement, see below, para.4–007.

[480] e.g. in *Dillwyn v Llewelyn* (1862) 4 D.F. & G. 517; below, para.3–130.

[481] e.g. in *William Lacey (Hounslow) Ltd v Davis* [1957] 1 W.L.R. 932; *Countrywide Communications Ltd v ICL Pathways Ltd* [2000] C.L.C. 325; *Cobbe v Yeoman's Row Management Ltd* [2008] UKHL 55; [2008] 1 W.L.R. 1752; cf. below, para.22–021.

[482] See below, para.3–128.

[483] *Regalian Properties Plc v London Dockland Development Corp* [1995] 1 W.L.R. 212.

[484] In *Waltons Stores* the enforcement of the contract is explained as the minimum equity needed to protect the claimant's reliance, whereas only consideration can *guarantee* such enforcement; cf. *Commonwealth of Australia v Verwayen* (1990) 179 C.L.R. 394 at 501: "Often the only way to prevent the promisee suffering detriment will be to enforce the promise". But in *Giumelli v Giumelli* (1999) 196 C.L.R. 101 the High Court of Australia expressly rejected the argument that relief should be limited to the reversal of the detriment suffered by the claimant.

[485] See above, para.3–003.

innocent non-contractual misrepresentation.[486] While on the facts of some of the cases in which the Australian doctrine has been applied the same conclusions would probably be reached in English law on other grounds,[487] the broad doctrine remains, in the present context, inconsistent with the view that the English doctrine of promissory estoppel does not give rise to a cause of action in the sense of entitling the promisee to enforce a promise in its terms, even though it was unsupported by consideration. It is true that other forms of estoppel, such as proprietary estoppel, may produce this result; but the scope of that doctrine is limited in many important ways[488] and the law would present an incongruous appearance if those limits could be outflanked simply by invoking the broader Australian doctrine.

3–094   **Distinguished from estoppel by convention.** Estoppel by convention may arise where both parties to a transaction "act on an assumed state of facts or law,[489] the assumption being either shared by both or made by one and acquiesced in by the other".[490] The parties are then precluded from denying the truth of that assumption, if it would be unjust or "unconscionable"[491] to allow them (or one of them) to go back on it.[492] Such an estoppel differs from estoppel by representation and from promissory estoppel[493] in that it does not depend on any "clear and unequivocal" *representation* or *promise*.[494] It can arise where the assumption was based on a mistake spontaneously made by the party relying on it, and acquiesced in by the other party,[495] though the common assumption of the parties, objectively

---

[486] e.g. *Oscar Chess Ltd v Williams* [1957] 1 W.L.R. 370; below, para.9–073.

[487] See, e.g. *Commonwealth of Australia v Verwayen* (1990) 179 C.L.R. 394, which could be explained in English law on the ground stated in fn.445 above.

[488] e.g. by the requirements that the promisee must believe that legal rights have been, or will be, created in his favour, and that these are rights in or over the promisor's land: see below, para.3–128.

[489] See below, para.3–096.

[490] *The Indian Endurance (No.2)* [1998] A.C. 878 at 913; for qualification of this formulation, see *The Vistafjord* [1988] 2 Lloyd's Rep. 343 at 351; and see *Shearson Lehman Hutton Inc v Maclaine Watson & Co Ltd* [1989] 2 Lloyd's Rep. 570 at 596; *ING Bank NV v Ros Roca SA* [2011] EWCA Civ 353 at [61]–[65]. Dawson 9 *Legal Studies* 16.

[491] *Crédit Suisse v Borough Council of Allerdale* [1995] 2 Lloyd's Rep. 315 at 367–370, affirmed on other grounds [1997] Q.B. 362.

[492] *The Vistafjord* [1988] 2 Lloyd's Rep. 343 at 352; *Hiscox v Outhwaite* [1992] 1 A.C. 562, affirmed on other grounds [1992] 1 A.C. 562 at 585; *The Indian Endurance (No.2)* [1998] A.C. 878 at 913.

[493] cf. above, para.3–090 for the distinction between various kinds of estoppel.

[494] *Troop v Gibson* (1986) 277 E.G. 1134; *Baird Textile Holdings Ltd v Marks & Spencer Plc* [2001] EWCA Civ 274; [2002] 1 All E.R. (Comm) 737 at [84]. Where reliance is placed on an *implied* representation, it may be a matter of interpretation whether it amounts to a representation of fact (in which case estoppel by convention may apply), or a promissory representation (in which case promissory estoppel may apply): *ING Bank NV v Ros Roca SA* [2011] EWCA Civ 353 at [86] per Rix L.J.

[495] The "acquiescence" by one party which can lead to the finding of a shared assumption should be distinguished from estoppel *by acquiescence* which may arise where the owner of property fails to take steps to make his title to property known: *Moorgate Mercantile Co v Twitchings* [1977] A.C. 890 at 903; *The Indian Endurance (No.2)* [1998] A.C. 878 at 913; nonetheless, it seems clear that the "acquiescence" necessary for estoppel by convention may consist primarily (but not, it is submitted, exclusively) of silence on the part of the party estopped: *The Lutetian* [1982] 2 Lloyd's Rep. 140 at 158; *Spring Finance Ltd v HS Real Co LLC* [2009] EWHC 3580 (Comm) at [51]; *ING Bank NV v Ros Roca SA* [2011] EWCA Civ 353 at [87] ("relevant, although not necessarily vital" that the party estopped had a "duty to speak"); see also [95].

assessed,[496] must itself be "unambiguous and unequivocal".[497] Estoppel by convention has also been said to arise out of an express agreement by which the parties had compromised a disputed claim[498]; but where such a compromise is supported by consideration in accordance with the principles discussed earlier in this chapter[499] it is binding as a contract,[500] so that there is, it is submitted, no need to rely on estoppel by convention in order to establish the facts in dispute.

Requirements of estoppel by convention. Estoppel by convention was   3–095 discussed in *Amalgamated Investment & Property Co Ltd v Texas Commerce International Bank Ltd*,[501] where A had negotiated with the X Bank for a loan to B (one of A's subsidiaries) for the purpose of acquiring and developing a property in the Bahamas. It was agreed that the loan was to be secured by a mortgage on that property and also by a guarantee from A. In the guarantee, A promised the X Bank, in consideration of the Bank's giving credit to B, to "pay you . . . all moneys . . . due . . . *to you*" from B. This was an inappropriate form of words since the loan to B was made, not directly by the X Bank, but by one of its subsidiaries, the Y Bank, with money provided by the X Bank: hence, if the guarantee were read literally, it would not apply to the loan since no money was due from B to the X Bank. The Court of Appeal, however, took the view that this literal interpretation would defeat the intention of the parties, and held that, on its true construction, the guarantee applied to the loan made by the Y Bank.[502] But even if the guarantee did not, on its true construction, produce this result, A was estopped from denying that the guarantee covered the loan by the Y Bank, since, when negotiating the loan, A and the X Bank had assumed that the guarantee did cover it; and since the X Bank continued subsequently to act on that assumption[503] in granting various indulgences to A in respect of the loan to B and of another loan made directly by the X Bank to A. It made no difference that the assumption was not induced by any representation made by A but originated in the X Bank's own mistake: the estoppel was not one by representation but by convention.[504] The same principle was applied in *The Vistafjord*[505] where an agreement for the charter of a cruise ship had been negotiated by agents on behalf of the owners. Both the agents and the owners throughout believed that commission on this transaction would be payable under an earlier agreement but, on its true construction, this

---

[496] See *ING Bank NV v Ros Roca SA* [2011] EWCA Civ 353 at [84] where the comments of Rix L.J. that the party to be estopped did not share the assumption "internally" is noted so as to support a preferred analysis of promissory estoppel. It is submitted that, for the purpose of estoppel by convention, what matters is whether there was a shared assumption "externally and objectively".

[497] *Smithkline Beecham Plc v Apotex Europe Ltd* [2006] EWCA Civ 658; [2007] Ch. 71 at [102]. cf. *Commercial Union Assurance Plc v Sun Alliance Assurance Group Plc* [1992] 1 Lloyd's Rep. 475 at 481.

[498] *Colchester BC v Smith* [1992] Ch. 421 at 434.

[499] See above, para.3–034.

[500] *Colchester BC v Smith*, above, at 435.

[501] [1982] Q.B. 84.

[502] cf. on the issue of construction, *TCB Ltd v Gray* [1987] Ch. 458; *Bank of Scotland v Wright* [1990] B.C.C. 663.

[503] Contrast *Crédit Suisse v Borough Council of Allerdale* [1996] 2 Lloyd's Rep. 315 at 367, where this requirement was not satisfied as the conduct of the party alleged to be estopped had not "influenced the mind" of the other party; affirmed on other grounds [1997] Q.B. 362.

[504] cf. *The Leila* [1985] 2 Lloyd's Rep. 172; and see below, fn.510.

[505] [1988] 2 Lloyd's Rep. 343; *Thornton Springer v NEM Insurance Co Ltd* [2000] 2 All E.R. 489 at 516–518; cf. also *Kenneth Allison Ltd v AE Limehouse & Co* [1992] 2 A.C. 105 at 127, per Lord Goff.

agreement gave no such rights to the agents. It was held that estoppel by convention precluded the owners from relying on the true construction of the earlier agreement, so that the agents were justified in retaining the amount of the commission out of sums received by them from the charterers.

To give rise to an estoppel by convention, the mistaken assumption of the party claiming the benefit of the estoppel must, however, have been shared or acquiesced in by the party alleged to be estopped; and both parties must have conducted themselves on the basis of such a shared assumption[506]: the estoppel

> "requires communications to pass across the line between the parties. It is not enough that each of two parties acts on an assumption not communicated to the other".[507]

Such communication may be effected by the conduct[508] of one party, known to the other.[509] But no estoppel by convention arose where each party spontaneously made a different mistake and there was no subsequent conduct by the party alleged to be estopped from which any acquiescence in the other party's mistaken assumption could be inferred.[510] Nor can a party (A) invoke such an estoppel to prevent the other (B) from denying facts alleged to have been agreed between A and B if A has later withdrawn from that agreement; for in the light of A's withdrawal it is no longer unjust to allow B to rely on the true state of affairs.[511]

3–096   **Assumption of law?** It is often said that the assumption giving rise to an estoppel by convention can be one of "fact or law".[512] The point of reference to "law" in this formulation appears to be to include within the scope of the doctrine assumptions about the construction of a contract[513]; for, since the construction of a contract is often said to be a matter of "law",[514] all such assumptions would be excluded from the scope of the doctrine (and its scope be unduly narrowed) if it did not include at least an assumption of this kind. The question whether estoppel by convention could be based on assumptions of "law" in a wider sense was the subject of conflicting views in *Johnson v Gore-Wood & Co.*[515] In that case a company had brought a claim for professional negligence against a firm of solicitors who were told that a further claim based on the same negligence would

---

[506] *Thor Navigation Inc v Ingosstrakh Insurance* [2005] EWHC 19 (Comm); [2005] 1 Lloyd's Rep. 547 at [66]; *Commission for the New Towns v Terrace Hill (Stockton)* [2007] EWHC 3094 (Ch) at [64].

[507] *The Captain Gregos (No.2)* [1990] 2 Lloyd's Rep. 395 at 405, following *The August P Leonhardt* [1985] 2 Lloyd's Rep. 28 at 35; *Hiscox v Outhwaite (No.3)* [1991] 2 Lloyd's Rep. 524 at 533; *The Indian Endurance (No.2)* [1998] A.C. 878 at 913.

[508] See fn.495, above.

[509] As in *The Vistafjord* [1988] 2 Lloyd's Rep. 343 at 351 ("very clear conduct crossing the line ... of which the other party was fully cognisant").

[510] *The August P Leonhardt* [1985] 2 Lloyd's Rep. 28, reversing [1984] 1 Lloyd's Rep. 332, which had been followed in *The Leila*, above, fn.504. The status of *The Leila* is therefore in doubt but the two cases can be reconciled on the ground that in *The Leila* there was the subsequent conduct referred to in the text.

[511] *Gloyne v Richardson* [2001] EWCA Civ 716; [2001] 2 B.C.L.C. 669 at [41].

[512] *Amalgamated Investment* case [1982] 2 Q.B. 84 at 122, 126; *The Vistafjord* [1988] 2 Lloyd's Rep. 343 at 351; *Shearson Lehman Hutton Inc v Maclaine Watson & Co Ltd* [1989] 2 Lloyd's Rep. 570 at 596; *The Indian Endurance (No.2)* [1988] A.C. 878 at 913.

[513] Such an assumption could also be called one of "private right" and hence of fact: *André & Cie SA v Ets Michel Blanc & Fils* [1979] 2 Lloyd's Rep. 427 at 431, 432.

[514] See below, para.19–120; *Carmichael v National Power Plc* [1999] 1 W.L.R. 2042 at 2049.

[515] [2002] 2 A.C. 1.

be made against them by the company's managing director. The company's claim was settled on terms which limited some of the director's personal claims against the solicitor and when the director later brought other claims against the solicitors, it was held that this was not an abuse of process. Lord Bingham based this conclusion in part[516] on estoppel by convention: in his view, the terms of the settlement were based on the common assumption that it would not be an abuse of process for the director to pursue the claims which he had in fact brought; and it would be unfair to allow the solicitors to go back on this assumption. All the members of the House of Lords agreed with Lord Bingham's conclusion that there was no abuse of process; but Lord Goff was "reluctant to proceed on estoppel by convention"[517] as the common assumption was in his view one of law, a type of assumption which in his view did not give rise to this form of estoppel. Support for the view that estoppel by convention can be based on a common assumption of law is admittedly based only on dicta[518]; but it is arguable that those dicta gain support from cases concerned with mistakes (and possibly misrepresentations) of law. In these fields, the distinction between matters of "law" and of "fact" proved hard to draw and appears to have been rejected.[519] On the other hand, the extension of estoppel by convention to *all* common assumptions of "law" could undermine the security of commercial transactions by allowing a party to resist enforcement merely on account of an assumption as to the *legal effect* of a contract the terms or meaning of which were not in dispute; and this is a type of assumption which, on the authorities, does not give rise to such an estoppel.[520]

Effect of estoppel by convention. The effect of this form of estoppel is to preclude a party from denying the agreed or common assumption of fact or as to the meaning of a document[521] or (at least to the extent suggested above[522]) of law. One such assumption may be that a particular promise has been made[523]: thus it is possible to describe the result in the *Amalgamated Investment & Property* case by saying that A was estopped from denying that it had promised the X Bank to repay any sum left unpaid by B to the Y Bank. But, although estoppel by convention may thus take effect in relation to a promise, it is quite different in its legal nature from promissory estoppel. In cases of promissory estoppel, the promisor or representor is not estopped from denying that the promise or representation *has been made*: on the contrary, this must be proved to establish that kind of estoppel, which is concerned with the *legal effects* of a promise that has been shown to exist. Where, on the other hand, the requirements of estoppel by convention are satisfied, then this type of estoppel operates to prevent a party from

3–097

---

[516] See [2002] 2 A.C. 1 at 33–34 for an alternative ground for Lord Bingham's decision. Lords Cooke and Hutton agreed with Lord Bingham on the "abuse of process" point but without referring to estoppel by convention.

[517] [2002] 2 A.C. 1 at 40.

[518] See above, fn.27.

[519] Certainly, in the case of mistake (see para.8–022), and possibly, in the case of misrepresentation (see para.9–013). In *Steria Ltd v Hutchinson* [2006] EWCA Civ 1551; [2007] I.C.R. 445 at [89], in the context of estoppel by representation, Neuberger L.J. thought it "realistic" not to suggest that a claim would fail if the representation was one of law.

[520] See below, para.3–099.

[521] *Amalgamated Investment & Property* case [1982] 2 Q.B. 84 at 126, 130.

[522] See above, para.3–096.

[523] Such an assumption is one of fact (and not as to the future).

denying a *fact*,[524] i.e. that the assumed promise *has been made*, or that a promise contains the assumed term: it does not specify the *legal effects* of the assumed promise or term.[525] In the *Amalgamated Investment & Property* case, once A was estopped from denying the *existence* of the promise described above, no question arose as to its legal *validity*. There could be no doubt that that promise was supported by consideration[526]: this was provided by the X Bank in making funds available to the Y Bank to enable it to make a loan to B, and in inducing the Y Bank to make that loan.[527] Where the assumed promise is one that would, if actually made, have been unsupported by consideration, both types of estoppel can, however, operate in the same case: estoppel by convention to establish the existence of the promise, and promissory estoppel to determine its legal effect.[528]

Estoppel by convention does not operate prospectively, so that "once the common assumption is revealed to be erroneous the estoppel will not apply to future dealings".[529] The parties are, however, entitled to a reasonable time to react to the discovery of the true state of affairs.[530] What constitutes a reasonable time will be determined by the need to avoid the unconscionable consequences which is the basis of the estoppel itself.

3–098   **Whether estoppel by convention can create new rights.** We have seen that promissory estoppel does not "create new causes of action where none existed before"[531]; and the same principle applies to estoppel by representation.[532] Estoppel by convention resembles estoppel by representation in that it can prevent a party from denying existing *facts*, and one would therefore expect estoppel by convention to operate only where its effect was defensive in substance. The question whether estoppel by convention is so limited was discussed in the *Amalgamated Investment & Property* case where, however, it was not necessary to decide the point. The action was brought because the X Bank had sought to apply money due from it to A under another transaction in discharge of A's alleged liability under A's guarantee of B's debt. Hence the effect of the estoppel was to provide the X Bank with a defence to A's claim for a declaration that it was not entitled to apply the money in that way. Eveleigh L.J. said: "I do not think that the bank could have succeeded in a claim on the guarantee itself."[533] Brandon L.J.

---

[524] In this respect its legal nature resembles that of estoppel by representation: see above, para.3–090.

[525] *The Vistafjord* [1988] 2 Lloyd's Rep. 343 at 351 ("not dependent on contract but on common assumption"). For this reason the citation in *Williams v Roffey Bros & Nicholls (Contractors) Ltd* [1991] 1 Q.B. 1 at 17–18 of the *Amalgamated Investment & Property* case seems, with respect, to be of doubtful relevance. In the *Williams* case there was no doubt that the promise had been made; and the actual decision was that it was supported by consideration and thus binding contractually: above, para.3–050.

[526] This was also true in *The Vistafjord* [1988] 2 Lloyd's Rep. 343; above, para.3–095.

[527] It is enough that consideration moved from the promisee (the X Bank): above, para.3–023.

[528] e.g. (apparently) *Troop v Gibson* (1986) 277 E.G. 1134.

[529] *Hiscox v Outhwaite* [1992] A.C. 562 at 575, per Lord Donaldson M.R. (affirmed *Hiscox v Outhwaite* [1992] A.C. 562 at 585 on other grounds); *Phillip Collins Ltd v Davis* [2000] 3 All E.R. 808 at 823; *Centrica Plc v Premier Power Ltd* [2006] EWHC 3068 (Comm) at [136]. Where the common assumption is made prior to the contract, which is entered into on that basis, the estoppel will operate throughout the period of the contract: *The Vistafjord* [1988] 2 Lloyd's Rep. 343; *Centrica Plc v Premier Power Ltd* [2006] EWHC 3068 (Comm) at [136]

[530] *London Borough of Hillingdon v ARC Ltd* [2000] EWCA Civ 191 at [64]; *Revenue & Customs Commissioners v Benchdollar* [2009] EWHC 1310 (Ch); [2010] 1 All E.R. 174

[531] *Combe v Combe* [1951] 2 K.B. 215 at 219; above, para.3–088.

[532] See above, para.3–090; below, para.9–156.

[533] [1982] Q.B. 84 at 126.

seems to have taken the view that the bank could have sued on the guarantee, but to have based that view on the ground that the loan agreement between A and the X Bank imposed an obligation on A to give the guarantee: hence it was that agreement, and not the estoppel, which would have given rise to the X Bank's cause of action, if it had sued on the guarantee.[534] Lord Denning M.R. expressed the principle of estoppel by convention in such a way as to enable it to give rise to a cause of action[535]; but he was alone in stating the principle so broadly.[536] In *The Vistafjord*[537] the estoppel similarly operated defensively. This factor was not stressed in the judgments, but there is no suggestion in them that in this respect estoppel by convention differs from estoppel by representation, which does not, of itself, give rise to a cause of action.[538] It is indeed possible for estoppel by convention (as it is for promissory estoppel[539] and estoppel by representation) to deprive the defendant of a *defence* and so to enable the claimant to win an action which otherwise he would have lost[540]; but even in such cases the estoppel does not create the cause of action, for the *facts giving rise to* the cause of action exist independently of the estoppel.[541] No other authority squarely supports the view that estoppel by convention can, of itself, create a new cause of action; and the present position seems to be that it cannot, any more than promissory estoppel or estoppel by representation, produce this effect.[542]

Invalidity of assumed term. A party is not liable on the basis of estoppel by convention where the alleged agreement would, if concluded, have been ineffective for want of contractual intention,[543] where necessary,[544] or on account of a   3–099

---

[534] [1982] Q.B. 84 at 132. Approved in *Dumford Trading AG v OAO Atlantrybflot* [2005] EWCA Civ 24; [2005] 1 Lloyd's Rep. 289 at [39]. For a different interpretation of Brandon L.J.'s judgment, see *Baird Textile Holdings Ltd v Marks & Spencer Plc* [2001] EWCA Civ 274; [2002] 1 All E.R. (Comm) 737 at [84]. The alleged estoppel in the *Baird* case was regarded at first instance as one "by convention" (at [20]) but it is far from clear whether the Court of Appeal so regarded it.

[535] [1982] Q.B. 84 at 122. A similar view may be hinted at in *Williams v Roffey Bros & Nicholls (Contractors) Ltd* [1991] 1 Q.B. 1 at 17–18; but see above, fn.525.

[536] *Keen v Holland* [1984] 1 W.L.R. 251 at 261–262. In *Wilson Bowden Properties Ltd v Milner & Bardon* [1996] C.L.Y. 1229 the cause of action arose out of the undisputed contract and not out of the estoppel.

[537] [1988] 2 Lloyd's Rep. 343; above, para.3–095. In *Shearson Lehman Hutton Inc v Maclaine Watson & Co Ltd* [1989] 2 Lloyd's Rep. 570 the estoppel would likewise (if supported on the facts) have operated defensively.

[538] See below, para.9–156.

[539] See above, para.3–089.

[540] e.g. *The Amazonia* [1990] 1 Lloyd's Rep. 238; *Revenue & Customs Commissioners v Benchdollar* [2009] EWHC 1310 (Ch); [2010] 1 All E.R. 174. For the possibility that estoppel by convention may deprive a party of a defence, see also *Azov Shipping Co v Baltic Shipping Co* [1999] 1 Lloyd's Rep. 159 at 175–176; *semble* this is subject to the limitation discussed with regard to promissory estoppel at para.3–088, above.

[541] cf. *Cheverny Consulting Ltd v Whitehead Mann Ltd* [2007] EWHC 3130 (Comm) at [108]; *Johnson v Gore Wood & Co* [2002] 2 A.C. 1 (above, para.3–096) where the cause of action was based on negligence but the estoppel helped to dispose of the defendants' objection that the action to enforce that claim was an abuse of process.

[542] *Baird Textile Holdings Ltd v Marks & Spencer Plc* [2001] EWCA Civ 274; [2002] 1 All E.R. (Comm) 73; *White v Riverside Housing Association Ltd* [2005] EWCA Civ 1385; [2006] H.L.R. 15 (though this limit on the estoppel was noted with "regret" by Sir Peter Gibson and Auld L.J.); *Smithkline Beecham Plc v Apotex Europe Ltd* [2006] EWCA Civ 658; [2007] Ch. 71 at [112]; Contrast dicta in *Thornton Springer v NEM Insurance Co Ltd* [2000] 2 All E.R. 489 at 516–518.

[543] *Orion Insurance Plc v Sphere Drake Insurance* [1992] 1 Lloyd's Rep. 239.

[544] *Revenue & Customs Commissioners v Benchdollar* [2009] EWHC 1310 (Ch); [2010] 1 All E.R. 174, at [52] (estoppel arising out of non-contractual dealings).

formal defect[545] (other than a minor one[546]) or where the term in respect of which such an estoppel is alleged to operate would, if actually incorporated in the contract, have been invalid[547]; nor does such an estoppel prevent a party from relying on the true legal effect (as opposed to the meaning[548]) of an admitted contract merely because the parties have entered into it under a mistaken view as to that effect.[549]

(d) Part Payment of a Debt

(i) *General rule*

3–100   **Part payment of a debt is no consideration.** The general rule of common law is that a creditor is not bound by an undertaking to accept part payment in full settlement of a debt. An accrued debt can be discharged only by accord and satisfaction.[550] A promise by the debtor to pay part of the debt provides no consideration for the accord, as it is merely a promise to perform part of an existing duty owed to the creditor. And the actual part payment is no satisfaction under the rule in *Pinnel's* case that "Payment of a lesser sum on the day in satisfaction of a greater sum cannot be any satisfaction for the whole."[551] This rule was approved by the House of Lords in *Foakes v Beer*.[552] Mrs Beer had obtained a judgment against Dr Foakes for £2,090 19s. Sixteen months later Dr Foakes asked for time to pay. Thereupon the parties entered into a written agreement[553] under which Mrs Beer undertook not to take "any proceedings whatsoever" on the judgment, in consideration of an immediate payment by Dr Foakes of £500 and on condition[554] of his paying specified instalments "until the whole of the said sum of £2,090 19s. shall have been paid and satisfied". Some five years later, when Dr Foakes had paid £2,090 19s., Mrs Beer claimed £360[555] for interest on the judgment debt. The House of Lords upheld her claim, and the actual decision does not appear to be unjust; for it seems that Mrs Beer intended only to give Dr Foakes time to pay, and not to forgive interest.[556]

---

[545] *Yaxley v Gotts* [2000] Ch. 162 at 182. For potential liability based on proprietary estoppel, where an agreement does not comply with the requirements of Law of Property (Miscellaneous Provisions) Act 1989, s.2(1), see below, para.5–011.

[546] cf. *Shah v Shah* [2001] EWCA Civ 527; [2002] Q.B. 35 at [31] (deed signed but not in presence of attesting witness); contrast *Shah v Shah* [2001] EWCA Civ 527; [2002] Q.B. 35 at [28] (deed not signed at all). The case was one of estoppel by representation.

[547] See *Keen v Holland* [1984] 1 W.L.R. 251; *Godden Merthyr Tydfil Housing Association* (1997) 74 P. & C.R. D1; contrast *The Amazonia* [1990] 1 Lloyd's Rep. 238 (illegality under foreign law).

[548] See above, para.3–096.

[549] *Keen v Holland*, above, fn.547; cf. *The Nile Rhapsody* [1992] 2 Lloyd's Rep. 399 at 408, affirmed on another ground [1994] 1 Lloyd's Rep. 382.

[550] See above, para.3–059.

[551] (1602) 5 Co.Rep. 117a; *Cumber v Wane* (1721) 1 Stra. 426; *McManus v Bark* (1870) L.R. 5 Ex. 65; *Underwood v Underwood* [1894] P. 204; *Tilney Engineering v Admos Knitting Machinery* [1987] 2 C.L. 21; *Re Broderick* (1986) 6 N.I.J.B. 36.

[552] (1884) 9 App.Cas. 605; Dixon, *Jesting Pilate*, 159–165.

[553] Drawn up by Dr Foakes' solicitor: (1884) 9 App.Cas. 625.

[554] Dr Foakes made no promise to pay the instalments.

[555] *Beer v Foakes* (1883) 11 Q.B.D. 221 at 222.

[556] Lords Fitzgerald and Watson thought that the agreement did not, on its true construction, cover interest. Lords Selborne and Blackburn sympathised with this view but felt unable to adopt it as the operative part of the document was too "clear" to be controlled by the recitals.

Criticism. The rule in *Pinnel*'s case may sometimes have served the useful   3–101
purpose of protecting a creditor against a debtor who had too ruthlessly exploited
the tactical advantage of being a potential defendant in litigation.[557] For example,
in *D & C Builders Ltd v Rees*[558] the claimants had done building work for the
defendant and had presented an account of which some £482 was outstanding. Six
months after payment had first been demanded, the defendant's wife (acting on
his behalf) offered the claimants £300 in full settlement. They accepted this offer
as they were in desperate straits financially; and there was some evidence that the
defendant's wife knew this.[559] It was held that the claimants were entitled to the
balance; and a majority[560] of the Court of Appeal based their decision on the rule
in *Pinnel*'s case. On the other hand, it is arguable that the function of protecting
the creditor in such a situation is now satisfactorily performed by the expanding
concept of economic duress,[561] while the rule in *Pinnel*'s case is open to two main
objections.

First, it applies to all agreements to accept part payment of debts in full
settlement, even though some such agreements are perfectly fair and reasonable
transactions.[562]

Secondly, as Lord Blackburn said in *Foakes v Beer*, part payment is often in fact
more beneficial to the creditor than strict insistence on his full legal rights.[563] A
factual benefit[564] of a similar kind has been accepted as sufficient consideration for
a promise to make an extra payment for the performance of an existing contractual
duty owed by the promisee to the promisor[565]; and the law would be more
consistent, as well as more satisfactory in its practical operation, if it adopted the
same approach to cases of part payment of a debt. Agreements of the kind here
under discussion would then be binding unless they had been made under duress.
But the rule in *Foakes v Beer* is open to challenge only in the House of Lords.[566]
In the meantime, its operation is mitigated by limitations on its scope at common
law and by evasions of it in equity.

(ii) *Common law limitations*

Disputed claims. The general rule does not apply where the creditor's claim   3–102
(or its amount) is disputed in good faith.[567] In such cases, the value of the claim

---

[557] As Dr Foakes appears to have done. Kelly 27 M.L.R. 540, argues that there is consideration in
giving up this advantage, as there is in the compromise of a disputed claim. This may be so, but a
compromise is only binding if there is a bona fide dispute as to liability (above, para.3–036) and there
was no such dispute in *Foakes v Beer*.

[558] [1966] 2 Q.B. 617; Chorley 29 M.L.R. 165; Cornish 29 M.L.R. 428.

[559] ibid. at 622.

[560] Lord Denning M.R. based his decision on a different ground: see below, para.3–117.

[561] cf. above, para.3–050 and below, para.10–005.

[562] e.g. on the facts of *Central London Property Trust Ltd v High Trees House Ltd* [1947] K.B. 130;
below, para.3–112.

[563] (1884) 9 App.Cas. 605 at 617–620.

[564] See above, para.3–006.

[565] *Williams v Roffey Bros & Nicholls (Contractors) Ltd* [1991] 1 Q.B. 1; above, para.3–050.

[566] *Re Selectmove Ltd* [1995] 1 W.L.R. 474; Peel 110 L.Q.R. 353; *Collier v P & M.J. Wright (Holdings
) Ltd* [2007] EWCA Civ 1329; [2008] 1 W.L.R. 643; *Birmingham City Council v Forde* [2009] EWHC
12 (QB); [2009] 1 W.L.R. 2732 at [89].

[567] *Cooper v Parker* (1885) 15 C.B. 822; *Re Warren* (1884) 53 L.J. Ch. 1016; *Anangel Atlas Compania
Naviera SA v Ishikawajima Harima Heavy Industries Co Ltd (No.2)* [1990] 2 Lloyd's Rep. 526 at 544;
for other consideration in this case, see [1990] 2 Lloyd's Rep. 526 at 545 and below, para.3–106; *Huyton
SA v Peter Cremer GmbH* [1999] 1 Lloyd's Rep. 620 at 629.

is doubtful and the debtor accordingly provides consideration by paying something, even though it is less than the amount claimed. It makes no difference that the amount paid is small in relation to the amount claimed, or that the creditor has a good chance of succeeding on the claim; for the law will not generally investigate the adequacy of consideration.[568] Where the defendant admits liability for less than the amount claimed, payment of the smaller sum is no consideration for the claimant's promise to accept that payment in full settlement of the larger claim. The rule in *Foakes v Beer* applies since, once a binding admission has been made to pay the smaller sum, the payment of it amounts to no more than the performance of what, at that stage, is legally due from the defendant.[569]

3–103   **Unliquidated claims.** The general rule applies only if the original claim is also a "liquidated" one, i.e. a claim for a fixed sum of money, such as one for money lent or for the agreed price of goods[570] or services. It does not apply to "unliquidated" claims[571] such as claims for damages or for a reasonable remuneration (where none is fixed by the contract). In such cases, the claim is of uncertain value; and even if the overwhelming probability is that it is worth more than the sum paid, the possibility that it may be worth less suffices to satisfy the requirement of consideration. An originally unliquidated claim may later become liquidated by act of the parties. For example, in *D & C Builders v Rees*[572] it does not seem that the contract fixed the price of the work to be done by the claimants. When they presented their account they had only an unliquidated claim (for a reasonable remuneration); and if at this stage they had accepted £300 in full settlement they would not have been protected by the rule in *Foakes v Beer*. That rule only became applicable because the defendant had, by retaining the account without protest, impliedly agreed that it correctly stated the sum due, and so turned the claim into a liquidated one.

3–104   **Partly liquidated claims.** A creditor may have two claims against the same debtor, one of them liquidated and the other unliquidated; or a single claim which is partly liquidated and partly unliquidated. A promise by the creditor to release the *whole* claim will not be binding if the debtor pays no more than the liquidated amount and if his liability to pay this amount is undisputed. For example, in *Arrale v Costain Civil Engineering Ltd*[573] an employee was injured at work. Legislation in force at the place of work gave him an undisputed right against the employers to a fixed lump sum of £490 and it was assumed that he also had a common law right to sue the employers in tort for unliquidated damages.[574] It was held that any

---

[568] See above, para.3–013. But the fact that the sum received is much smaller than that claimed may be evidence that the recipient has not accepted it in full settlement: *Rustenburg Platinum Mines Ltd v Pan Am* [1979] 1 Lloyd's Rep. 19.

[569] *Ferguson v Davies* [1997] 1 All E.R. 315, per Henry L.J.; Evans L.J.'s judgment is based on the ground that, as a matter of construction, the claimant had not accepted the smaller sum in full settlement. Aldous L.J. agreed with both the other judgments.

[570] A claim may be "liquidated" even though it is disputed and even though the dispute relates to its amount: e.g. where it is for the price of goods and the buyer alleges short delivery: *The New Vanguard* [1994] 1 W.L.R. 1634.

[571] *Wilkinson v Byers* (1834) 1 A. & E. 106; *Ibberson v Neck* (1886) 2 T.L.R. 427.

[572] [1966] 2 Q.B. 617; above, para.3–101.

[573] [1976] 1 Lloyd's Rep. 98; cf. *Rustenburg Platinum Mines Ltd v Pan Am* [1979] 1 Lloyd's Rep 19 at 24.

[574] cf. below, para.6–041.

promise[575] which he might have made not to pursue the common law claim was not made binding by the employers' payment of the £490. They had not provided any consideration for such a promise since, in making that payment, they merely did what they were already bound to do.[576]

Variations in debtor's performance. Consideration for a creditor's promise   3–105
to accept part payment in full settlement can be provided by the debtor's doing an act that he was not previously bound by the contract to do.[577] For example, payment of a smaller sum at the creditor's request before the due day is good consideration for a promise to forego the balance, since it is a benefit to the creditor to receive (and a corresponding detriment to the debtor to make) such early payment.[578] The same applies, mutatis mutandis, where payment of a smaller sum is made at the creditor's request at a place different from that originally fixed for payment,[579] or in a different currency.[580] Again, payment of a smaller sum accompanied at the creditor's request by the delivery of a chattel is good consideration for a promise to forego the balance:

> "The gift of a horse, hawk or robe, etc., in satisfaction is good. For it shall be
> intended that a horse, hawk or robe, etc., might be more beneficial than the
> money . . . ".[581]

Other benefit to creditor. We have seen that a promise to pay a supplier of   3–106
services more than the agreed sum for performing his part of the contract can be supported by consideration in the form of a benefit in fact obtained by the other party as a result of his obtaining the promised performance.[582] Conversely, a promise by the supplier to accept less than the agreed sum may be supported by a similar consideration. The mere receipt of the smaller sum cannot, indeed, constitute the consideration: that possibility is precluded by *Foakes v Beer*.[583] But the performance by the debtor of *other* obligations under the contract may confer such a benefit on the creditor and so satisfy the requirement of consideration. This possibility is illustrated by the *Anangel Atlas*[584] case, where a shipbuilder's promise to reduce the price which the buyers had agreed to pay was held to have been supported by consideration, and one way in which the buyers had provided consideration was by accepting delivery on the day fixed for such acceptance. Even if the buyers were already bound to take delivery on that day, they had conferred

---

[575] Lord Denning M.R. and Stephenson L.J. took the view that no such promise had been made.
[576] Per Stephenson and Geoffrey Lane L.JJ. Lord Denning M.R. based his decision on a different ground: below, para.3–117.
[577] e.g. *Re William Porter & Co* [1937] 2 All E.R. 361: *Ledingham v Bermejo Estancia Co Ltd* [1947] 2 All E.R. 748.
[578] *Pinnel's* case, above, para.3–100.
[579] ibid.
[580] cf. above, para.3–063.
[581] *Pinnel's* case, above. Many cases formerly supported the view that part payment by a negotiable instrument, made at the request of the creditor and accepted by him in full settlement, discharged the debt. But these cases were overruled in *D & C Builders Ltd v Rees* [1966] 2 Q.B. 617.
[582] *Williams v Roffey Bros & Nicholls (Contractors) Ltd* [1991] 1 Q.B. 1; above, para.3–050.
[583] (1884) 9 App.Cas. 605; above, para.3–100; *Collier v P & M.J. Wright (Holdings) Ltd* [2007] EWCA Civ 1329; [2008] 1 W.L.R. 643.
[584] *Anangel Atlas Compania Naviera SA v Ishikawajima-Harima Heavy Industries Co Ltd (No.2)* [1990] 2 Lloyd's Rep. 526. For other consideration in that case, in the form of reducing "a previously ill-defined understanding" to "precise terms," and so settling a potential dispute, see [1990] 2 Lloyd's Rep. 526 at 544.

a benefit on the shipbuilder by so doing since they were "core customers"[585] and their refusal to take delivery might have led other actual or potential customers to cancel (or not to place) orders.

3–107   **Forbearance to enforce cross-claim.** The debtor may have a cross-claim against the creditor; and forbearance to enforce such a claim can constitute consideration for the creditor's promise to accept part payment in full settlement. For example, where a landlord promises to accept part payment of rent in full settlement, the tenant may provide consideration for this promise by forbearing to sue the landlord for breach of the latter's obligation to keep the premises in repair.[586]

3–108   **Part payment by third party.** Part payment by a third party, if accepted by the creditor in full settlement of the debtor's liability,[587] is a good defence to a later action by the creditor against the debtor for the balance.[588] It is generally agreed that this rule does not depend on any contract between debtor and creditor, so that it can apply even though no promise was made to the debtor and no consideration moved from him. The rule has therefore been explained on other grounds. One such ground is that it would be a fraud on the third party to allow the creditor to sue the debtor for the balance of the debt.[589] The difficulty with this reasoning is that the mere breach of a promise does not usually amount to fraud at common law; it only has this effect if the promisor had no intention of performing the promise when he made it.[590] A second reason for the rule is that the court will not help the creditor to break his contract with the third party by allowing him to recover the balance of the debt from the debtor. On the contrary, it has been held that where A (the creditor) contracts with B (the third party) not to sue C (the debtor), and A nevertheless does sue C, B can intervene so as to obtain a stay of the action.[591] A third explanation is suggested by *Hirachand Punamchand v Temple*,[592] where the defendant was indebted to the claimant on a promissory note. The claimant accepted a smaller sum from the defendant's father in full settlement. It was held that he could not later sue the defendant for the balance of the debt, because the promissory note was extinct: the position was the same as if the note had been cancelled.[593] This reasoning again does not depend on any contract between the claimant and the defendant, for the cancellation of a promissory note can release a person liable on it irrespective of contract and without consideration.[594] Under the Contracts (Rights of Third Parties) Act 1999, the debtor may also, if the requirements of the Act are satisfied,[595] be able to take the benefit of any term in the contract between the creditor and the person making the payment which may exclude the debtor's liability for the balance; and he will be able to do

---

[585] [1990] 2 Lloyd's Rep. 526 at 544.
[586] *Brikom Investments Ltd v Carr* [1979] Q.B. 467; as explained above, para.3–065.
[587] See below, para.17–007 for this requirement.
[588] *Welby v Drake* (1825) 1 C. & P. 557; *Cook v Lister* (1863) 13 C.B.(N.S.) 543 at 595.
[589] See the authorities cited in fn.588, above.
[590] See below, para.9–010.
[591] *Snelling v John G Snelling Ltd* [1973] 1 Q.B. 87, distinguishing *Gore v Van der Lann* [1967] 2 Q.B. 31, where no promise was made not to sue C; cf. *South West Trains Ltd v Wightman*, *The Times*, January 14, 1998.
[592] [1911] 2 K.B. 330.
[593] At 336. cf. in the case of joint debts, the reasoning of *Johnson v Davies* [1999] Ch. 117 at 130.
[594] See above, para.3–061.
[595] See below, para.14–090 et seq.

so without having to show that he provided any consideration for the creditor's promise to accept the part payment in full settlement.[596]

Composition agreements. A debtor who cannot pay all his creditors in full   3–109
may be able to induce them to agree with himself and each other to accept a dividend in full settlement of their claims.[597] A creditor who has accepted a dividend under such an agreement cannot sue the debtor for the balance of his original demand.[598] If the debtor fails to pay the agreed dividend, the original debt revives.[599]

One reason why such composition agreements are binding is again said to be that a creditor who sued for the balance of his debt would commit a fraud on the others.[600] On this view it is unnecessary to look for any consideration moving from the debtor. Alternatively, there is consideration for the creditors' promise to forgo the balance since each creditor benefits from the arrangement: he is certain to get some payment, while in the scramble for priority which would take place if there were no composition agreement he might get nothing at all.[601]

Collateral contract. An agreement to accept part payment of a debt in full   3–110
settlement may take effect as a collateral contract if the requirements of contractual intention and consideration are satisfied. This was the position in *Brikom Investments Ltd v Carr*[602] where a tenant's liability to contribute to the maintenance costs of a block of flats was held to have been reduced by a collateral contract under which the landlord undertook to execute certain roof repairs at his own expense.[603] The landlord's claim for contribution in this case was probably unliquidated; but the principle seems to be equally applicable where a creditor enters into a collateral contract to accept part payment in full settlement of a liquidated claim.

(iii) *Equitable evasion*

The common law limitations can (with one exception[604]) be explained on the   3–111
ground that there was, in the situations covered by them, some consideration for the creditor's promise to accept the part payment in full settlement. They assume the continued existence of the general, if often inconvenient, rule that, in the absence of such consideration, the creditor's promise was not binding. Equity has gone further in attempting to evade that rule even where there was no consideration for the creditor's promise.

---

[596] See above, para.3–026, below, para.14–099. For the purposes of the Act, it is the debtor who is the "third party".

[597] Deeds of Arrangement Act 1914 (repealed in part by Insolvency Act 1985, s.235 and Sch.10, Pt III and amended by Insolvency Act 1986, s.439(2)); Insolvency Act 1986, Pts I and VIII.

[598] *Good v Cheesman* (1831) 2 B. & Ad. 328; *Boyd v Hind* (1857) 1 H. & N. 938; the bare *agreement* to pay a dividend may operate as satisfaction, if the parties so intend: *Bradley v Gregory* (1810) 2 Camp. 383.

[599] *Evans v Powis* (1847) 1 Ex. 601.

[600] *Wood v Roberts* (1818) 2 Stark. 417; *Cook v Lister* (1863) 13 C.B.(N.S.) 543 at 595.

[601] *Good v Cheesman* (1831) 2 B. & Ad. 328 at 334; *Garrard v Woolner* (1832) 8 Bing. 258 at 265.

[602] [1979] Q.B. 467. cf. *Business Environment Bow Lane Ltd v Deanwater Estates* [2007] EWCA Civ 622; [2007] 32 E.G. 90

[603] For the consideration supporting this promise, see above para.3–065; for other grounds for the decision, see below, para.3–115.

[604] i.e. cases of part payment by a third party: above, para.3–108.

3–112   **Equitable forbearance, or "promissory estoppel".** Under the equitable doctrine of *Hughes v Metropolitan Ry*[605] a promise by a contracting party not to enforce his legal rights has (even where it is not supported by consideration) at least a limited effect in equity. Before 1946, this doctrine had not been applied where a creditor's promise to accept part payment of a debt in full settlement was not supported by any consideration moving from the debtor. Such an extension of the rule seemed to be barred by *Foakes v Beer*.[606] The possibility of making the extension was, however, suggested in *Central London Property Trust Ltd v High Trees House Ltd*.[607] In 1937 a block of flats had been let to the defendants for 99 years at a rent of £2,500 per annum. In 1940 the landlords agreed to reduce the annual rent to £1,250 as many of the flats were unlet because of war time conditions. After the end of the war, the landlords demanded the full rent for the last two quarters of 1945 and Denning J. upheld their claim on the ground that, as a matter of construction, the 1940 agreement was intended to apply only while the war time conditions lasted. But he also said that the landlords would have been precluded by the equitable doctrine of *Hughes v Metropolitan Ry*[608] from suing for the full rent for the period which *was* covered by the 1940 agreement. He added:

> "The logical consequence no doubt is that a promise to accept a smaller sum, if acted upon, is binding notwithstanding the absence of consideration."[609]

The requirements and effects of the equitable doctrine have already been discussed.[610] Three points give rise to particular difficulty in its application to cases of part payment of a debt.

3–113   **Effect generally suspensory.** The first difficulty is to reconcile the remarks of Denning J. in the *High Trees* case with *Foakes v Beer*.[611] If the claimant in *Foakes v Beer* could go back on her promise not to ask for interest, why could not the landlords in the *High Trees* case go back on their promise not to ask for the full rent in, say, 1941, when war time difficulties of letting still prevailed? One possibility is to say that "that aspect was not considered in *Foakes v Beer*"[612] which was decided without reference to equity, and is therefore "no longer valid"[613]; but this is unsatisfactory, as the rule that part payment of a debt was no discharge was clearly recognised in equity.[614] Another possibility, and one which does less violence to the authorities, is to say that the creditor's right to the balance of his

---

[605] (1877) 2 App.Cas.439; above, para.3–077.
[606] (1884) 9 App.Cas.605; above, para.3–100.
[607] [1947] K.B. 130; Denning 15 M.L.R. 1; Wilson 67 L.Q.R. 330; Sheridan 15 M.L.R. 325; Bennion 16 M.L.R. 441; Guest 30 A.L.J. 187; Turner 1 N.Z.U.L.R. 185; Campbell 1 N.Z.U.L.R. 232.
[608] See above, para.3–077.
[609] [1947] K.B. 130 at 134; cf. *Combe v Combe* [1951] 2 K.B. 215 at 220.
[610] See above, paras 3–077—3–093.
[611] (1884) 9 App.Cas.605; above, para.3–100.
[612] *High Trees* case, above, at p.146; this sentence does not occur in any of the other reports of the case ([1947] L.J.R. 77; (1946) 175 L.T. 333; (1946) 62 T.L.R. 557; [1956] 1 All E.R. 256n.) The argument, with respect, lacks plausibility since *Hughes v Metropolitan Ry*, above, fn.605, had been decided only seven years before *Foakes v Beer* and Lords Selborne and Blackburn heard the appeals in both cases.
[613] *Arrale v Costain Civil Engineering Ltd* [1976] 1 Lloyd's Rep. 98 at 102.
[614] *Bidder v Bridges* (1887) 37 Ch.D. 406; *Re Warren* (1884) 53 L.J.Ch. 1016.

debt is not extinguished but only suspended.[615] This is generally the sole consequence of the principle in *Hughes v Metropolitan Ry*[616] and in the present context it would give effect to the intention of the parties where the purpose of the arrangements was to give the debtor extra time to pay,[617] rather than to extinguish part of the debt. Of course, where the intention is to extinguish, and not merely to suspend, the creditor's right to the balance, the suggestion that the creditor is permanently bound by his promise not to sue for the balance[618] may seem to be an attractive one.[619] But such an extension of the principle of *Hughes v Metropolitan Ry* would require the overruling of *Foakes v Beer*. It is, no doubt, with such difficulties in mind that Lord Hailsham L.C. has said that the *High Trees* principle "may need to be reviewed and reduced to a coherent body of doctrine by the courts".[620]

Effect on periodic payments. For the present the better view is that the principle only suspends rights; but the meaning of this statement is not entirely clear where the debtor is under a continuing obligation to make a series of payments, e.g. of rent under a lease,[621] or of royalties under a licence to use a patent,[622] or of instalments under a hire-purchase agreement.[623] In such cases the statement may mean one of two things: first, that the creditor is entitled to payment in full only of amounts which fall due *after* the expiry of a reasonable notice of the retraction of his promise[624]; or, secondly, that he is then entitled, not only to future payments in full, but also to the unpaid balance of *past* ones. Of course the second of these views might sometimes be at variance with the intention of the parties at the time of the promise.[625] On the other hand it is hard to see why a debtor whose liability accrues from time to time should, for the present purpose, be in a more favourable position than one whose liability is to pay a single lump sum; nor is it clear which of the two views should apply where a debtor who owed a lump sum undertook to pay it off in instalments and the

3–114

---

[615] *Ajayi v R T Briscoe (Nig) Ltd* [1964] 1 W.L.R. 1326 at 1330; Unger 28 M.L.R. 231; cf. *Re Venning* [1947] W.N. 196; Gordon [1963] C.L.J. 222, arguing that the equitable principle is limited to relief against forfeiture. But see Wilson [1965] C.L.J. 93.

[616] See above, para.3–086.

[617] e.g. in *Ajayi v R T Briscoe (Nig) Ltd*, above: see fn.615. This seems also to have been the position in *Foakes v Beer*, above.

[618] Originally made by Lord Denning in the *High Trees* case at 134 and repeated by him in *D & C Builders Ltd v Rees* [1966] 2 Q.B. 617 at 624. cf. *W J Alan & Co Ltd v El Nasr Export & Import Co* [1972] 2 Q.B. 189 at 213; and [1972] 2 Q.B. 189 at 218, 220; but in that case there was consideration: above, para.3–063.

[619] Provided that there was no duress: cf. above, para.3–049.

[620] *Woodhouse AC Israel Cocoa Ltd v Nigerian Produce Marketing Co Ltd* [1972] A.C. 741 at 758; cf. *Baird Textile Holdings Ltd v Marks & Spencer Plc* [2001] EWCA Civ 274; [2002] 1 All E.R. (Comm) 737 at [48] ("not yet fully developed").

[621] As in the *High Trees* case.

[622] As in the *Tool Metal* case [1955] 1 W.L.R. 761; above, para.3–086.

[623] As in *Ajayi v R T Briscoe (Nig) Ltd* [1964] 1 W.L.R. 1326.

[624] *Banning v Wright* [1972] 1 W.L.R. 972 at 981; cf. *W J Alan & Co Ltd v El Nasr Export & Import Co* [1972] 2 Q.B. 189 at 213. This view is apparently regarded as correct in the *Tool Metal* case, above; but the case is not conclusive as the liability of the licensee to make the payments *during* the suspension period was not directly considered by the House of Lords.

[625] This would be so in cases like the *High Trees* and *Tool Metal* cases—but not in a case like *Ajayi v R T Briscoe (Nig) Ltd*, above, fn.615 as the promise there "was not intended to be irrevocable": *Meng Long Development Pte Ltd v Jip Hong Trading Pte Ltd* [1985] A.C. 511 at 524. *J T Sydenham & Co Ltd v Enichem Elastometers Ltd* [1989] 1 E.G.L.R. 257 at 260 (discussed by Cartwright [1990] C.L.J. 13) purports to give the "estoppel" an extinctive effect; but the amount of rent due in that case was in dispute, so that the actual decision is explicable on the ground stated at para.3–102, above.

creditor first made, and then gave reasonable notice revoking, a promise to accept reduced instalments. In such a case, it is at least arguable that the intention of the creditor is only to give extra time for payment. Hence the total debt remains due, and the only effect of the promise is to extend the period over which it is to be repaid.[626]

3–115   **Exceptional cases where creditor's rights extinguished.** There may, however, be exceptional cases where the creditor's right is wholly extinguished. We have seen that a forbearance cannot be retracted where subsequent events, or the passage of time, make it highly inequitable[627] to require performance of the original obligation, even after reasonable notice. This principle could be applied to cases of the present kind, so that the creditor's right to the balance might be extinguished if, in reliance on that promise, the debtor had undertaken new commitments in relation to the subject-matter: e.g. if the tenant in the *High Trees* case had used the rebate to modernise the flats.[628]

The creditor's right was also held to have been wholly extinguished in *Brikom Investments Ltd v Carr*.[629] In that case, long leases of flats provided that the tenants should pay (inter alia) contributions in respect of certain expenses incurred by the landlords on repairs. During negotiations leading to the execution of the leases, the landlords had promised to put the roof into repair "at our own cost". This was held to amount to a collateral contract[630] with one of the original tenants, precluding the landlords from enforcing against her the provision in the lease requiring her to contribute to the cost of the roof repairs. It was further held that claims for contributions to the cost of those repairs could not be made against assignees and sub-assignees of original tenants, even though there were no collateral contracts with these persons. Lord Denning M.R. based this conclusion on the *High Trees* principle which, in his view, was available not only between the original parties, but also in favour of, and against, their assigns.[631] The extinctive effect of the principle in these circumstances can perhaps be supported on the ground that the original tenants, the assignees and the sub-assignees had all, in reliance on the landlord's promise, undertaken fresh commitments by entering into long leases of the flats. Alternatively, the case can be treated, not as one of "promissory estoppel",[632] but as one of "waiver".[633] The latter expression here seems to refer to a variation supported by consideration[634]; for the consideration provided by the tenants[635] could equally support the landlords' promise whether that promise was regarded as a collateral contract[636] or as a variation of the principal contract itself. On this interpretation of the case, it is possible to account for the extinctive effect of the landlord's promise even on the liability of the

---

[626] *Hardwick v Johnson* [1978] 1 W.L.R. 683 (where the creditor was said at 699 to have agreed to "postpone" the debtor's obligation to pay instalments).

[627] See above, para.3–087.

[628] cf. Mitchell 2 Univ. of Western Australia Annual Law Review 245 at 251. The principle is somewhat similar to that which underlies the defence of "change of position" in an action for the recovery of money paid; Burrows, *The Law of Restitution* (3rd edn), pp.524–550.

[629] [1979] Q.B. 467.

[630] See above, para.3–065.

[631] [1979] Q.B. 467 at 484–485.

[632] ibid. at 485, 491.

[633] ibid. at 488, 490.

[634] cf. above, para.3–063.

[635] See above, para.3–065.

[636] See above, para.3–065.

assignees and sub-assignees. The variation was supported by consideration and so extinguished the liability of the original tenants to contribute to the cost of the repairs in question; and once it had been so extinguished it was not revived on assignment of the leases.

In *Collier v P & M.J. Wright (Holdings) Ltd*[637]it was alleged[638] that the defendant had promised the claimant that if he paid one-third of a debt for which the claimant and his two partners were jointly and severally liable, the defendant would not pursue the claimant for the balance. The claimant paid the one-third share and the Court of Appeal held that he had a sufficiently real prospect of success in relying on promissory estoppel to defeat the defendant's claim for the balance that they should set aside a statutory demand and allow the matter to proceed to trial. After reviewing the cases, most notably the *High Trees* case and *D & C Builders Ltd v Rees*,[639] Arden L.J. summed up her conclusion as follows:[640]

> "The facts of this case demonstrate that, if (1) a debtor offers to pay part only of the amount he owes; (2) the creditor voluntarily accepts that offer, and (3) in reliance on the creditor's acceptance the debtor pays that part of the amount he owes in full, the creditor will, by virtue of the doctrine of promissory estoppel, be bound to accept that sum in full and final satisfaction of the whole debt. For him to resile will of itself be inequitable. In addition, in these circumstances, the promissory estoppel has the effect of extinguishing the creditor's right to the balance of the debt. This part of our law originated in the brilliant obiter dictum of Denning J, as he was, in the *High Trees* case. To a significant degree it achieves in practical terms the recommendation of the Law Revision Committee chaired by Lord Wright MR in 1937."

A notable feature of this statement of principle is that there is nothing exceptional, beyond the actual payment of part of the debt,[641] which would seem to merit giving to the defendant's promise an extinctive effect. Such a result may well achieve the recommendation of the Law Revision Committee,[642] but it is also inconsistent with *Foakes v Beer*. If that ruling is no longer to prevail, it would be preferable if that was achieved by a ruling of the Supreme Court, or by legislation, at the earliest opportunity and along the lines suggested above, rather than an equitable evasion of uncertain scope.

---

[637] [2007] EWCA Civ 1329; [2008] 1 W.L.R. 643.

[638] Longmore L.J. thought (at [45]) that it was only just arguable that the statements made by the defendant amounted to a promise of permanent surrender of the right to the balance of the debt. He noted that, if Lord Denning's dictum was to be applied more widely it is "all the more important that agreements which are said to forego a creditor's rights on a permanent basis should not be too benevolently construed" (at [48]).

[639] [1966] 2 Q.B. 617

[640] At [42].

[641] This requirement has led to the suggestion that the decision in *Collier v Wright* and other cases relying on factual benefit (e.g. *Williams v Roffey Bros & Nicholls (Contractors) Ltd* [1991] 1 Q.B. 1) might be better analysed as turning on the creation of a unilateral contract: Chen-Wishart, in Burrows & Peel, *Contract Formation and Parties*; cf. McFarlane, in Burrows & Peel, *Contract Formation and Parties*.

[642] The Committee also recommended that the full debt could be discharged by a promise to pay the lesser sum but that if the new agreement was not performed, the original debt revived (Sixth Interim Report on the Statute of Frauds and the Doctrine of Consideration, Cmnd. 5449, para.35).

3–116   **Reliance.** One difficulty which has been felt about the *High Trees* case is that a tenant who is bound to pay £2,500 per annum for 99 years suffers no "detriment", in the sense in which that word is used in the law of estoppel,[643] by paying half that rent for part of the period. Ingenious attempts have been made to find some "detriment" in the case[644]; but Lord Denning himself has said extra judicially that there was none.[645] Nor is the requirement mentioned in the *High Trees* case itself, or in later statements of the principle.[646] And if such "detriment" is not necessary for the purpose of the rule in *Hughes v Metropolitan Ry*[647] it is hard to see why it should be necessary for the purpose of its offshoot, the *High Trees* rule. All that is necessary is that the tenant should have acted in reliance on the promise in such a way as to make it inequitable for the landlord to act inconsistently with it. This requirement was satisfied on the facts of the *High Trees* case, no less than on those of *Hughes v Metropolitan Ry*.

3–117   **Inequitable.** When the debtor makes the part payment in reliance on the creditor's promise, it becomes prima facie "inequitable" for the creditor peremptorily to go back on his promise.[648] But other circumstances may indicate that it would not be "inequitable" for the creditor to reassert his claim for the full amount[649]: this would, for example, be the position where the debtor had failed to perform his promise to pay the smaller amount.[650] It has been suggested that another such circumstance may be the conduct of the debtor in obtaining the promise. Thus in *D & C Builders Ltd v Rees*[651] Lord Denning M.R. held that the *High Trees* principle did not apply because the builders' promise to accept £300 in full settlement of their claim for £482 had been obtained by taking undue advantage of their desperate financial position. The difficulty with this reasoning is that most debtors who offer part payment in full settlement try to exert some form of "pressure" against their creditors. The law now recognises that it is possible for such pressure to amount to duress[652]; and where it has this effect the promise should clearly not bring the *High Trees* principle into operation. Where, on the other hand, there is no duress, the operation of the *High Trees* principle should not be excluded merely because it could be said that the creditor's promise had, in some sense, been "improperly obtained." Such an intermediate category between promises obtained by duress and those not so obtained should, here as elsewhere,[653] be rejected as "unhelpful because it would make the law uncertain".[654]

---

[643] cf. above, para.3–084.

[644] e.g. Wilson 67 L.Q.R. 330 at p.344.

[645] 15 M.L.R. 1 at pp.6–8.

[646] e.g. in *Combe v Combe* [1951] 2 K.B. 215 at 220. See also above, para.3–085 et seq.

[647] See above, para.3–085.

[648] See the passage quoted from Arden L.J. in *Collier v P & M.J. Wright (Holdings) Ltd* [2007] EWCA Civ 1329; [2008] 1 W.L.R. 643, above.

[649] cf. above, para.3–085.

[650] cf. *Re Selectmove* [1995] 1 W.L.R. 474 at 481, where the debtor's promise was not to pay *less* but to pay *late*; and see *Burrows v Brent LBC* [1996] 1 W.L.R. 1448, where the decision was based on lack of contractual intention so that neither consideration nor the equitable doctrine was discussed.

[651] [1966] 2 Q.B. 617. Winder 82 L.Q.R. 165; above, para.3–101. cf. *Arrale v Costain Civil Engineering Ltd* [1976] 1 Lloyd's Rep. 98 at 102.

[652] See above, paras 3–049—3–050; below, para.10–005.

[653] See above, para.3–055.

[654] *Pao On v Lau Yiu Long* [1980] A.C. 614 at 634; cf. *Huyton SA v Peter Cremer GmbH* [1999] 1 Lloyd's Rep 620, where the requirement of consideration was satisfied (above, para.3–102) but there was no duress (below, para.10–005).

7. PROPRIETARY ESTOPPEL

Proprietary estoppel is said to arise in certain situations in which a person has   3–118
done acts in reliance on the belief that he has, or that he will acquire, rights in or
over another's land. Usually, but not invariably, these acts consist of erecting
buildings on, or making other improvements to, the land in question. Where the
requirements of proprietary estoppel are satisfied, the landowner is precluded
from denying the existence of the rights in question, and may indeed be compelled
to grant them. Because the estoppel precludes him from denying the existence of
rights in property, it has come to be known as "proprietary estoppel". It is
distinct[655] from promissory estoppel, both in the conditions which must be
satisfied before it comes into operation and in its effects. But under both doctrines
some legal effects are given to promises which are not contractually binding for
want of consideration; and it is this aspect[656] of proprietary estoppel which calls
for discussion in the present chapter.

(a) Nature and Scope of the Doctrine

Proprietary estoppel operates in a variety of cases so disparate that it has been   3–119
described as "an amalgam of doubtful utility."[657] The cases can be divided broadly
into two categories.

Acquiescence. In the first, one person acts under a mistake as to the existence   3–120
or as to the extent of his rights in or over another's land. Even though the
landowner did not induce the mistake, he might be prevented from taking
advantage of it, particularly if he "stood by" knowing of the mistake, or actively
encouraged the mistaken party to act in reliance on his mistaken belief.[658] These
cases of so-called "acquiescence"[659] do not raise any questions as to the
enforceability of promises and therefore do not call for further discussion in this
chapter.[660]

Encouragement. In the second group of cases, there is not merely "acquies-   3–121
cence" by the landowner, but "encouragement"[661]: that is, conduct by the landowner, or a representation by him, from which a promise to the other party (the
promisee) can be inferred[662] to the effect that the promisee has a legally enforceable[663] interest in the land or that one will be created in his favour. If the other

---

[655] See below, para.3–147.
[656] For wider discussions, see Davies 8 Sydney L.Rev. 200 and 7 Adelaide L.Rev. 200; Moriarty 100
L.Q.R. 376; Smith in *Consensus ad Idem: Essays in the Law of Contract in Honour of Guenter Treitel* (ed.
Rose), p.235.
[657] *Amalgamated Investment & Property Co Ltd v Texas Commerce International Bank Ltd* [1982] Q.B.
84 at 103.
[658] *Willmott v Barber* (1880) 15 Ch.D. 96; cf. *Taylor Fashions Ltd v Liverpool Victoria Trustees Co Ltd*
[1982] Q.B. 133; *Blue Haven Enterprises Ltd v Dulcie* [2006] UKPC 17 (where the landowner had taken
appropriate steps to notify the claimant of his interest in the land).
[659] ibid. at 105.
[660] Nor do they call for discussion in Ch.8, since the mistake is not one that prevents the formation
of a contract, or is alleged to do so.
[661] *Ramsden v Dyson* (1866) L.R. 1 H.L. 129 at 170. Contrast *Attorney-General of Hong Kong v
Humphreys Estate (Queen's Gardens)* [1987] A.C. 114, where there was no encouragement.
[662] See *Lloyds Bank Plc v Rosset* [1991] 1 A.C. 107; *Keelwalk Properties Ltd v Waller* [2002] EWCA
Civ 1076; (2002) 33 E.G. 95 at [63] (where this requirement was not satisfied).
[663] See *Coombes v Smith* [1986] 1 W.L.R. 808 (where there was no belief in the existence of a *legally
enforceable* right); cf. *Brinnand v Ewens* (1987) 19 H.L.R. 415.

party acts in reliance on such a promise, the question will arise to what extent the promise can be enforced, even though it may not be supported by consideration, or fail to satisfy the other requirements (such as those of certainty or form[664]) of a binding contract.

3–122   **Unjust enrichment.** In some cases, the promisee's reliance takes the form of his making improvements to the promisor's land.[665] The most obvious explanation of such cases is that in them the landowner would be unjustly enriched if he were allowed to disregard his promise and to take back the land after he had induced the promisee to make improvements to it. This explanation is, perhaps, reflected in statements found in some cases that the liability is based on "an implied or constructive trust."[666] But the discussion which follows will show that the doctrine can apply even where there is no enrichment of the kind just described, or indeed of any kind at all.[667] Unjust enrichment therefore cannot provide a complete explanation of the doctrine.

3–123   **Contract.** In other cases the rights of a person who had expended money on the property of another have been explained as being based on contract[668]; and often such an explanation was sufficiently plausible to make reliance on a doctrine of proprietary estoppel unnecessary.[669] A unilateral contract to transfer an interest in land has been held to arise out of a promise to make the transfer if the promisee would pay instalments due under a mortgage on the house[670]; it can equally arise out of a promise to make the transfer if the promisee will make improvements to the land, or indeed do any other act.[671] But not all cases of proprietary estoppel can be explained as depending on contract.[672] Promises in cases of this kind are often made in a family context, without contractual intention, or the promise may lack consideration because the party relying on the estoppel made no counter-promise and so incurred no obligation, and the arrangement was not one in which it would be in accordance with the intention of the parties to treat it as a unilateral contract.[673] The terms of the alleged contract may also be too vague to satisfy the

---

[664] See, e.g. below, fn.666.

[665] See below, para.3–130.

[666] *Sen v Headley* [1991] Ch. 425 at 440; *Cobbe v Yeoman's Row Management Ltd* [2008] UKHL 55; [2008] 1 W.L.R. 1752 (Lord Scott). For the relationship between proprietary estoppel and constructive trust, see: *Kinane v Mackie-Conteh* [2005] EWCA Civ 45; discussed below, para.5–011 in the context of Law of Property (Miscellaneous Provisions) Act 1989, s.2(5).

[667] *Canadian Pacific Railway v The King* [1931] A.C. 414; *Armstrong v Sheppard & Short* [1959] 2 Q.B. 384.

[668] e.g. *Plimmer v Mayor of Wellington* (1884) 9 App.Cas. 699 as explained in *Canadian Pacific Railway v The King* [1931] A.C. 414 at 428; *Eves v Eves* [1975] 1 W.L.R. 1338; *Tanner v Tanner* [1975] 1 W.L.R. 1346; cf. *Re Sharpe* [1980] 1 W.L.R. 219 at 224; and see *E R Ives Investments Ltd v High* [1967] 2 Q.B. 379 (where there was a contract between the defendant and the claimant's predecessor in title).

[669] See *Lloyds Bank Plc v Carrick* [1996] 4 All E.R. 632; *Oxley v Hiscock* [2004] EWCA Civ 546; [2005] Fam 211 at [35]. Contrast *Yaxley v Gotts* [2000] Ch. 162 at 179, where there was *no* such contract but, at most, an agreement lacking contractual force.

[670] *Errington v Errington* [1952] 1 Q.B. 290; see above, para.2–053, fn.315, for authorities doubting this case on other points.

[671] e.g. *Tanner v Tanner* [1975] 1 W.L.R. 1346.

[672] cf. *Beaton v McDivitt* (1988) 13 N.S.W. L.R. 162 at 170–171.

[673] *J T Developments v Quinn* (1991) 62 P. & C.R. 33.

requirement of certainty,[674] or there may have been a failure to comply with the stringent formal requirements for the making of contracts for the disposition of interests in land.[675]

(b) Requirements

Summary. The doctrine of proprietary estoppel is based on three main 3–124 elements: "a representation or assurance made to the claimant; reliance on it by the claimant, and detriment to the claimant in consequence of his (reasonable) reliance."[676] These requirements are considered in more detail below, but while they are considered separately for ease of analysis it is important to bear in mind that proprietary estoppel "cannot be treated as subdivided into three or four watertight compartments".[677] Each of the requirements may, to some extent, influence the other and reliance and detriment, in particular, are often intertwined: "In the end the court must look at the matter in the round."[678]

(i) *Representation or Assurance*

Kinds of promises capable of giving rise to a proprietary estoppel. A 3–125 promise may give rise to a proprietary estoppel even though it is not express but is implied: e.g. from the fact that the parties acted on the common assumption that one of them was to have the right to reside on the other's property.[679] The promise must be of such a kind that it is reasonable for the promisee to rely on it and the promisor must have intended the promisee would so rely on it[680]; and it must induce the promisee to believe that a legal right has been, or will be, created in his favour; though there is no further requirement that this belief must be legally well founded.[681]

The representation or assurance must be "clear enough". It seems that 3–126 the representation or assurance relied upon need not be "clear and unequivocal" in the sense in which that requirement is understood for promissory estoppel, or

---

[674] See above, para.2–078. See *Gillett v Holt* [2001] Ch. 210 at 230; *Banner Homes Group Plc v Luff Developments Ltd* [2000] Ch. 372; *Jennings v Rice* [2002] EWCA Civ 159; [2003] 1 F.L.R. 501 at [10], [49], [50]. *Crabb v Arun DC* [1976] Ch. 179; Atiyah 92 L.Q.R. 174; Millett 92 L.Q.R. 342; Duncanson 39 M.L.R. 268.

[675] Law of Property (Miscellaneous Provisions) Act 1989, s.2(1)–(3): see below, para.5–008. Previously the contract could be *made* informally, but Law of Property Act 1925, s.40 (now repealed) had required either a note or memorandum in writing as evidence of the contract, or "part performance" of the contract. The latter requirement could be satisfied by the conduct of the promisee giving rise to proprietary estoppel. cf. the reference to "part performance" in *Dillwyn v Llewelyn* (1862) 4 D.F. & G. 517 at 521.

[676] *Thorner v Major* [2009] UKHL 18; [2009] 1 W.L.R. 776, at [29].

[677] *Gillett v Holt* [2001] Ch. 210 at 228.

[678] ibid.; cf. Gardner, *An Introduction to Land Law* (2007), at 101.

[679] e.g. *Re Sharpe* [1980] 1 W.L.R. 219.

[680] *Gillett v Holt* [2001] Ch. 210 at 228. It seems that, as is the case with the promisee's reliance, the intention of the promisor is assessed objectively, but that this will be satisfied, save for "exceptional cases", whenever it is found that the promisee's reliance was reasonable: *Thorner v Major* [2009] UKHL 18; [2009] 1 W.L.R. 776 at [78].

[681] ibid. at 229.

estoppel by representation.[682] Given the various, and in particular the non-commercial, contexts in which proprietary estoppel can arise, it has been stated that the relevant assurance must be "clear enough".[683] This appears to mean an assurance which in all the circumstances "one might reasonably expect to be relied upon by the person to whom it was made."[684] For example, in *Thorner v Major*[685] the claimant did substantial work on the promisor's farm and was found to have done so on the basis of the promisor's assurance that he would inherit "the farm".[686] That assurance was not derived from any express representation, but was "a matter of implication and inference from indirect statements and conduct".[687] It also seems that an assurance may be "clear enough" even if it is ambiguous. If the requirements for proprietary estoppel are otherwise satisfied, the fact that the assurance may have more than one possible meaning should not deprive the claimant of relief, but such relief may be based on the interpretation of the assurance which is least beneficial to the claimant.[688]

3–127   **"Certain interest in land"**. There can normally be no belief on the part of the promisee that a legal right has been, or will be, created in his favour, and hence no proprietary estoppel, if the promise expressly disclaims legal effect: e.g. in *Attorney-General of Hong Kong v Humphreys Estates (Queen's Gardens)*[689] it was held that no proprietary estoppel arose out of an agreement for the transfer of a number of flats "subject to contract", it being well known that the effect of these words was to negative the intention to be legally bound.[690] The promisee may have formed "the confident and not unreasonable hope"[691] that the promise would not be withdrawn; but no *belief* to this effect had been encouraged[692] by the promisor or relied on by the promisee.

Such reasoning is not confined to cases where the parties have expressly agreed "subject to contract". In *Cobbe v Yeoman's Row Management Ltd*,[693] the parties had reached an agreement "in principle" that if the claimant obtained planning permission for land owned by the defendant, the defendant would sell the land to

---

[682] Above, para.3–081. Though this seems to be what is required by Lord Scott in *Cobbe v Yeoman's Row Management Ltd* [2008] UKHL 55; [2008] 1 W.L.R. 1752, a view which is consistent with his narrow view of the scope of proprietary estoppel: fn.696 below.

[683] *Thorner v Major* [2009] UKHL 18; [2009] 1 W.L.R. 776 at [56] per Lord Walker, who acknowledged the "question-begging formulation". See also Lord Rodger at [26], Lord Neuberger at [84].

[684] *Walton v Walton*, April 14, 1994 (unreported) at [16] per Hoffmann L.J., cited by Lord Walker above, fn.683.

[685] [2009] UKHL 18; [2009] 1 W.L.R. 776.

[686] On the identity of "the farm", see below para.3–132.

[687] [2008] EWCA Civ 732, CA at [65] per Lloyd L.J. Both parties were described as "taciturn and undemonstrative" ([2008] UKHL 55; [2008] 1 W.L.R. 1752 at [59]), which seems to have added weight to the few words and gestures which did pass between them.

[688] *Thorner v Major* [2009] UKHL 18; [2009] 1 W.L.R. 776, per Lord Neuberger.

[689] [1987] 1 A.C. 114; the case was said in *Waltons Stores (Interstate) Ltd v Maher* (1988) 164 C.L.R. 387 at 404 to be "not a case of proprietary estoppel" but (apparently) one of *promissory* estoppel. cf. *Saloman v Akiens* [1993] 1 E.G.L.R. 10 (no proprietary estoppel arising from agreement "subject to lease"); *Pridean Ltd v Forest Taverns* (1998) P. & C.R. 477 (no proprietary estoppel arising from work done during negotiations which failed to lead to a contract); *Secretary of State for Transport v Christos* [2003] EWCA Civ 1073; [2004] 1 P. & C.R. 17; cf. *Gonthier v Orange Contract Scaffolding Ltd* [2003] EWCA Civ 873; *Spring Finance Ltd v HS Real Co LLC* [2011] EWHC 57 (Comm) at [57].

[690] See below, para.4–006.

[691] [1987] 1 A.C. 114 at 124.

[692] cf. above, para.3–121; *Brinnand v Ewens* (1987) 19 H.L.R. 415.

[693] [2008] UKHL 55; [2008] 1 W.L.R. 1752; Getzler 125 L.Q.R. 196.

the claimant for development for an upfront price and a share of the proceeds of sale of the developed land. The claimant did the work necessary and obtained the permission, but the defendant insisted on re-opening the terms of the agreement. The House of Lords held that, even if the defendant had behaved unconscionably,[694] the claimant had not satisfied the requirements for proprietary estoppel (nor a constructive trust).[695] As Lord Scott explained,[696] the reason why, in a "subject to contract" case, a proprietary estoppel cannot arise is because the expectation of the claimant is speculative; similarly, in *Cobbe* the claimant's expectation was "always speculative"[697] because he knew that his agreement with the claimant was not legally enforceable, either for lack of certainty because key terms were still to be negotiated,[698] or because of non-compliance with the formalities required for contracts for an interest in land.[699] The claimant lacked the expectation of a "certain interest in land",[700] or as Lord Walker put it, "conscious reliance on honour alone will not give rise to an estoppel".[701] At one point, Lord Walker stated that the claimant must believe that the assurance was "binding and irrevocable",[702] a requirement that would deprive proprietary estoppel of much of its utility, but it seems clear from the immediately following decision of the House of Lords that a proprietary estoppel did arise in *Thorner v Major*[703] that this requirement is not to be understood literally; rather it emphasises that it is not enough to "hope, or even to have a confident expectation, that the person who has given assurances will do the proper thing."[704]

The different outcomes in *Cobbe* and *Thorner v Major* may be explained in large part by the different contexts in which any assurance was said to have been given[705]; in particular, as a sophisticated commercial property developer the claimant in *Cobbe* knew that there was no legally binding contract and he took the risk that the defendant might exercise the option she had of re-opening the terms of the agreement in principle.[706] But the context—commercial or non-commercial—is not decisive. Thus where a landowner promised her part-time

---

[694] Lord Scott described the defendant's behaviour as "unconscionable" (at [36]). Lord Walker described it as "unattractive", but not "unconscionable" (at [92]).

[695] He was, however, entitled to a quantum meruit: [2008] UKHL 55; [2008] 1 W.L.R. 1752 at [42]; cf. *Walsh v Singh* [2009] EWHC 3219 (Ch); [2010] 1 F.L.R. 1658 at [65]; below, para.22–021.

[696] At [25]. The result in *Cobbe* is entirely consistent with the reasoning employed in the *Humphreys Estates* case and with the requirements for proprietary estoppel as previously understood, but Lord Scott also took a very narrow view of the doctrine, seeing it as only operating to bar the defendant from asserting some fact (or mixed matters of fact and law) that would stand in the way of a right claimed by the claimant. This view, which equates proprietary estoppel with estoppel by representation and denies its operation as an independent source of rights, was not shared by the other members of the House of Lords in *Cobbe* and is implicitly rejected by the reasoning of the majority of the Law Lords in *Thorner v Major* (in which Lord Scott preferred an analysis based on constructive trust): McFarlane and Robertson 125 L.Q.R. 535.

[697] *Cobbe*, above at [27].

[698] cf. *Kirker v Ridley* unreported, December 17, 2008, Ch D.

[699] See below, para.5–008.

[700] *Taylor Fashions Ltd v Liverpool Victoria Trustees Co Ltd* [1982] Q.B. 133 at 144 per Oliver J. The necessary certainty is as to the nature of the interest in the land; there need not be certainty as to the precise extent of the property which is the subject of the estoppel: *Thorner v Major* [2009] UKHL 18; [2009] 1 W.L.R. 776 at [94], [98] per Lord Neuberger. See below, para.3–132.

[701] *Cobbe*, above at [81].

[702] ibid. at [66].

[703] [2009] UKHL 18; [2009] 1 W.L.R. 776.

[704] *Cobbe*, above at [65]; McFarlane and Robertson 125 L.Q.R. 535.

[705] See Lord Walker in *Cobbe*, above at [68].

[706] But not the risk of not even being paid for his services: above, fn.695.

gardener to leave him her house in her will but told him "not to count his chickens before they were hatched," it was held that no proprietary estoppel arose when, after having made a will in his favour, she then revoked it and made another leaving the property to someone else: in these circumstances it was not unconscionable for the landowner to revoke the promise.[707]

The position is the same where the promise, even though it does not in terms reserve a power of revocation, is in its nature revocable and this is a matter of common knowledge so that the promisee must be taken to have been aware of the risk of its being revoked. This will often be the position where the promise is one to make a will in favour of the promisee; but it does not follow as a matter of law that such a promise cannot give rise to proprietary estoppel. In *Gillett v Holt*[708] the claimant had worked for nearly 40 years in the defendant's farming business in reliance on the defendant's frequently repeated promises to leave him the bulk of his estate, and had in various other ways relied on those promises. It was held that the promises were "more than a statement of revocable intention",[709] and that they were capable of giving rise, and did give rise, to a proprietary estoppel.

3–128   **Rights in or over the property of the promisor.** The rights which the promisee believes to have been created must, as a general rule, be rights in or over the property of the promisor.[710] A representation by a planning authority to the effect that a landowner does not need permission to carry out development on his *own* land is not capable of giving rise to a proprietary estoppel.[711] The promisor may, however, make two promises, of which the first relates to the promisor's land while the second relates to that of the promisee; and the two promises may be so closely linked as to form in substance a single transaction. If the doctrine of proprietary estoppel applies to that transaction as a whole, then it can provide the promisee with a remedy in respect of the second promise even though that promise, standing alone, could not have given rise to proprietary estoppel because it related only to the promisee's land. In one case,[712] for example, A promised B (1) to sell blackacre to B to enable B to build on it, and (2) to buy whiteacre from B so that B could pay for the building operations on blackacre. B carried out the building work envisaged in the first of A's promises and it was held that the doctrine of proprietary estoppel provided B with a remedy in respect of the second promise (which had no contractual force), even though that promise related only to B's land. But it was recognised that the doctrine could not have applied to the second promise if it had stood alone and not formed part of a transaction also relating to A's land.[713] It could not, for example, have applied if A had simply made a non-contractual promise to B to buy whiteacre from B, knowing that B intended to use the proceeds of the sale to buy shares from C, and if B had then entered into a contract to that effect with C. Normally, the doctrine applies to promises to *grant* rights in land *to* the promisee[714]; it only applies to promises to

---

[707] *Taylor v Dickens* [1998] F.L.R. 806, as explained in *Gillett v Holt* [2001] Ch. 210 at 227.

[708] [2001] Ch. 210.

[709] ibid. at 228.

[710] *Newport CC v Charles* [2008] EWCA 1541; [2009] 1 W.L.R. 1884.

[711] *Western Fish Products Ltd v Penwith DC* [1981] 2 All E.R. 204 (decided in 1978); cf. *Lloyd's Bank Plc v Carrick* [1996] 4 All E.R. 632 (above, fn.669).

[712] *Salvation Army Trustee Co v West Yorks Metropolitan CC* (1981) 41 P. & C.R. 179.

[713] ibid. at 191. The case was approved but distinguished in *Attorney-General of Hong Kong v Humphreys Estate (Queen's Gardens)* [1987] A.C. 114 at 126–127.

[714] For the possibility that the doctrine may *prevent* A from asserting rights in B's property against C, a purchaser of that property: see *J S Bloor (Measham) Ltd v Calcott (No.2)* (2002) 9 E.G. 222.

acquire such rights *from* him where they are inextricably linked with promises of the former kind.

Subject-matter of the promise. The question whether a promise can give   3–129
rise to a proprietary estoppel where its subject-matter is property of some kind other than land remains an open one.[715] Even if the doctrine is extended to such promises, its scope will in one respect remain narrower than that of so-called promissory estoppel[716]: the promise must relate to the acquisition of an interest in the property which is the subject-matter of the promise. It is not enough that the promise should in some other way relate to property: e.g. the doctrine of proprietary estoppel would not apply on the facts of *Central London Property Trust v High Trees House Ltd*.[717]

(ii) *Reliance*

Expenditure on another's land. In *Dillwyn v Llewelyn*[718] a father executed a   3–130
memorandum "presenting" a named estate to his son "for the purpose of furnishing himself with a dwelling house". The son spent £14,000 in building a house on the land; and it was held (after the father's death) that he was entitled to have the fee simple of the estate conveyed to him. Many latter cases similarly give some degree of legal enforceability to a promise by a landowner in reliance on which the promisee has spent money on making improvements to the promisor's land:[719] e.g. where A built a bungalow on B's land in reliance on B's promise that A could stay there for the rest of his life[720]; where A spent money on extending or improving B's house in reliance on a similar promise by B[721]; and where, in reliance on such a promise, A actually did the work of improvement him- or herself.[722]

Other acts done in reliance on the promise. Improvement to the promisor's   3–131
land is not a necessary condition for the operation of proprietary estoppel. The doctrine can apply also where the promisee has conferred some other benefit on the promisor[723] and even where no benefit at all is received by the promisor. The

---

[715] For the view that proprietary estoppel is limited to cases where the subject-matter of the promise is land, see *Baird Textile Holdings Ltd v Marks & Spencer Plc* [2001] EWCA Civ 274; [2001] 1 All E.R. (Comm) 737 at [97]. cf. *Strover v Strover* [2005] EWHC 860 (proprietary estoppel applied in relation to a life insurance policy, in a case of "acquiescence"); *Fisher v Brooker* [2009] UKHL 41, [2009] 1 W.L.R. 1764 (copyright, but also a case of "acquiescence"). In *Cobbe v Yeoman's Row Management Ltd* [2008] UKHL 55; [2008] 1 W.L.R. 1752 at [14] Lord Scott stated that it was "in principle, equally available in relation to chattels or choses in action"; cf. *Kirker v Ridley* unreported, December 17, 2008, Ch D (shares).

[716] See above, paras 3–076—3–092.

[717] [1947] K.B. 130; above, para.3–112.

[718] *Dillwyn v Llewelyn* (1862) 4 D.F. & G. 517; Allan 79 L.Q.R. 238.

[719] *Voyce v Voyce* (1991) 62 P. & C.R. 290;

[720] *Inwards v Baker* [1965] 2 Q.B. 29.

[721] *Hussey v Palmer* [1972] 1 W.L.R. 1286; *Pascoe v Turner* [1979] 1 W.L.R. 431.

[722] *Eves v Eves* [1975] 1 W.L.R. 1338.

[723] e.g. *Greasley v Cooke* [1980] 1 W.L.R. 1306; *Jennings v Rice* [2002] EWCA Civ 159; [2003] 1 F.L.R. (below, para.3–143); cf. *Plimmer v Mayor of Wellington* (1884) 9 App.Cas. 699 and *E R Ives Investments Ltd v High* [1967] 2 Q.B. 379 (where the landowner benefited from improvements to his land but also—and more significantly—in other ways); *Grant v Edwards* [1986] Ch. 638 at 657; *Stallion v Albert Stallion Holdings (Great Britain) Ltd* [2009] EWHC 1950 (Ch); [2010] 2 F.L.R. 78; Contrast *Howard v Jones* (1988) 19 Fam. L. 231 (contribution to running cost of *another* property insufficient).

doctrine operated in the absence of any expenditure on the promisor's land in *Crabb v Arun DC*.[724] In that case A (a local authority) by its conduct represented to B that B had a right of way from his land over adjoining land owned by A. In reliance on that representation, B sold part of his own land, so that the only access from the remainder to the nearest public highway was by means of the right of way across A's land. It was held that B had a right to cross A's land for the purpose of access to his retained land. Detrimental reliance by the promisee here gave rise to a proprietary estoppel even though no benefit was conferred on the promisor.[725]

3–132   **Whether reliance must relate to specific property.** The authorities are divided on the question whether, to give rise to a proprietary estoppel, the reliance must relate to identifiable property. According to one case, the promisee's conduct must relate to "some specific asset" in which an interest is claimed; so that proprietary estoppel did not arise merely because B rendered services to A in the expectation of receiving some indeterminate benefit under A's will.[726] But in another case reliance on a similar expectation (induced by A's promise) was held sufficient even though it did not relate to any "particular property".[727] The latter case can perhaps be explained on the ground that the promise did to some extent identify the property.[728] It is submitted that the view that the promise must relate to identified or identifiable property is to be preferred[729]; for, without some such limitation on its scope, the doctrine of proprietary estoppel could extend to any promise on which the promisee had relied to his detriment. Such a very broad doctrine would be fundamentally inconsistent with the doctrine of consideration[730] and, indeed, with the rule that the doctrine of *promissory* estoppel gives rise to no new rights.[731] While the property in question must be identified, or identifiable, the "precise extent of the property" need not be "strictly defined in every case".[732] Thus, in *Thorner v Major*, considered above, the claimant was given the assurance that he would inherit the farm "as it existed from time to time".[733] Lord Neuberger drew an analogy with a floating charge: "the property the subject of the equity could be conceptually identified from the moment the equity came into existence, but its precise extent fell to be determined when the equity crystallised, namely on (the promisor's) death."[734]

3–133   **Burden of proof.** Where a promise has been made which is capable of inducing reliance, and which is in fact followed by such reliance, the question may arise whether the promise actually did induce the reliance. It seems that the burden on

---

[724] [1976] Ch. 179. In *Waltons Stores (Interstate) Ltd v Maher* (1988) 64 C.L.R. 387 at 403 *Crabb*'s case was described as one of "promissory estoppel"; but the requirements of that doctrine (in particular, the requirement of a pre-existing legal relationship: above, para.3–079) were not satisfied in *Crabb*'s case, and the effect of the estoppel differed from promissory estoppel in giving rise to a new right: cf. above, para.3–088.

[725] cf. *Hammersmith & Fulham BC v Top Shop Centres Ltd* [1990] Ch. 237.

[726] *Layton v Martin* [1986] 2 F.L.R. 277.

[727] *Re Basham* [1986] 1 W.L.R. 1498 at 1508.

[728] By referring to the promisor's cottage. In *Gillett v Holt* [2001] Ch. 210 the property was likewise identified, if not very precisely; cf. *Jennings v Rice*, above, fn.723 at [50], where the promise again related in part to the promisor's house.

[729] *Thorner v Major* [2009] UKHL 18; [2009] 1 W.L.R. 776 at [61] per Lord Walker.

[730] See, e.g. above, para.3–001.

[731] See above, para.3–088.

[732] *Thorner v Major* [2009] UKHL 18; [2009] 1 W.L.R. 776 at [98] per Lord Neuberger.

[733] ibid. at [95].

[734] ibid.

this issue is on the promisor: that is, it is up to the promisor, in order to escape liability, to show that the promisee would have done the acts in question anyway, even if the promise had not been made.[735] The position appears to be different where a proprietary estoppel arises because both parties have acted under a mistake as to their rights in the land.[736] Here it seems to be up to the party relying on the proprietary estoppel to show that his conduct in relation to the property was in fact induced by his belief that he had an interest in it.[737]

(iii) *Detriment*

The promisee must have relied on the promise or representation to his detri-   3–134
ment.[738] The requirement has been doubted[739] but in the absence of any such reliance it is hard to see why failure to perform a merely gratuitous promise should be regarded as giving rise to any legal liability. The element of detrimental reliance is necessary to satisfy "the essential test of unconscionability"[740] on which the operation of proprietary estoppel depends; and the existence of the requirement is further supported by the rules (to be discussed below) as to the revocability of the promise.[741] The detriment must be "substantial", i.e. such as to make it "unjust or inequitable to allow the assurance to be disregarded"[742]; and the question whether it has this character is to be judged "as at the moment when the person who has given the assurance seeks to go back on it".[743] Where the promisee's reliance on the promise results in both a benefit and a detriment, they must be weighed together; if the detriment is not outweighed by any benefit, a proprietary estoppel will still arise.[744]

(c) Effects of the Doctrine

(i) *Revocability*

By the terms of the promise. Proprietary estoppel will not arise at all where   3–135
the promise to confer a benefit on the promisee is revocable in the sense that it

---

[735] *Greasley v Cooke*, above; cf. *Grant v Edwards* [1986] Ch. 638; *Re Basham* [1986] 1 W.L.R. 1498; *Hammersmith & Fulham BC v Top Shop Centres Ltd* [1990] Ch. 237; *Thompson v Foy* [2009] EWHC 1076 (Ch). But see the doubts expressed by Neuberger L.J. in *Steria Ltd v Hutchinson* [2006] EWCA Civ 1551 at [131].

[736] See above, para.3–120.

[737] *Taylor Fashions Ltd v Liverpool Victoria Trustees Co Ltd* [1982] Q.B. 133; cf. *Coombes v Smith* [1986] 1 W.L.R. 808.

[738] *Greasley v Cooke* [1980] 1 W.L.R. 1306; *Taylor Fashions Ltd v Liverpool Victoria Trustees Co Ltd* [1982] Q.B. 133; *Grant v Edwards* [1986] Ch. 638 at 657; cf. *Lloyds Bank Plc v Rosset* [1991] 1 A.C. 107 at 132; *Henry v Henry* [2010] UKPC 3; [2010] 1 All E.R. 988. The fact that there was no such reliance was one reason why the claim based on proprietary estoppel failed in *Western Fish Products Ltd v Penwith DC*, above: see [1981] 2 All E.R. 204 at 217; in *Attorney-General of Hong Kong v Humphreys Estate (Queen's Gardens)* [1987] A.C. 114; and in *Jennings v Rice* [2002] EWCA Civ 159; [2003] 1 F.L.R. 501 at [21], [49].

[739] By Lord Denning M.R. in *Greasley v Cooke*, above, at 1311. The argument may be influenced by the analogy of promissory estoppel (see above, para.3–084); but the two doctrines are distinct: below, para.3–147.

[740] *Gillett v Holt* [2001] Ch. 210 at 232; *Jennings v Rice* [2002] EWCA Civ 159; [2003] 1 F.L.R. 501 at [21], [49]; *Fisher v Brooker* [2009] UKHL 41; [2009] 1 W.L.R. 1764 at [63].

[741] See below, para.3–135.

[742] *Gillett v Holt*, above, fn.740 at 232.

[743] ibid.

[744] *Henry v Henry* [2010] UKPC 3; [2010] 1 All E.R. 988; cf. *Fisher v Brooker* [2009] UKHL 41; [2009] 1 W.L.R. 1764.

reserves a power to the promisor wholly to deprive the promisee of that benefit.[745] But even where the promise does not allow the promisor to do this, and so is capable of giving rise to a proprietary estoppel, the extent of the promisee's rights under the estoppel may be limited by terms of the promise giving the promisor a power of putting an end to those rights. Thus if the landowner promises to allow the promisee to stay on the land "until I decide to sell", then the promisee cannot, merely by spending money on improvements to the land, acquire any right to stay there for a longer period.[746]

3–136   **Promise revoked before acted upon by promisee.** Even where the promise is not expressed to be revocable, it can be revoked before the promisee has acted on it. Thus in *Dillwyn v Llewelyn*[747] the father could have revoked his promise before the son had started to build on the land[748] and in *Crabb v Arun DC*[749] the promise to grant a right of way could have been revoked before the promisee had, by selling off part of his land, made it impossible for himself to obtain access to the retained land except by means of the promised right of way. In this respect proprietary estoppel resembles so-called promissory estoppel (under which promises are similarly revocable[750]) and differs from contractually binding promises which are not revocable unless they expressly or impliedly so provide.

3–137   **Promise revoked after acted upon by promise.** The cases of proprietary estoppel assume that once the promisee has acted on the representation, he cannot be restored to his original position. Where he has made improvements to land, this will generally be the case. Where a restoration of the status quo is physically possible, it seems that a promise giving rise to a proprietary estoppel could be revoked even after the promisee had acted on it, provided that the promisor in fact restored the promisee to the position in which he was before he had acted in reliance on the promise. A promise which has given rise to proprietary estoppel may also be none the less revocable, because the court considers it appropriate in this way to limit the effects to be given to the promise.[751]

(ii) *Operation of proprietary estoppel*

3–138   Where the conditions required to give rise to a proprietary estoppel have been satisfied, the effect of the doctrine is said to be to confer an "equity" on the promisee. Two further questions then arise: namely, what is the extent of that "equity", and what are the remedies for its enforcement.[752] In practice these questions tend to merge into each other; but an attempt to deal with them in turn will be made in the following discussion.

3–139   **Extent of the equity.** At one extreme, the promisee may be entitled to conveyance of the fee simple in the property which is the subject-matter of the

---

[745] See above, para.3–125.

[746] *E & L Berg Homes v Gray* (1979) 253 E.G. 473.

[747] (1862) D.F. & G. 517; above, para.3–130.

[748] cf. *Pascoe v Turner* [1979] 1 W.L.R. 431 at 435.

[749] [1976] Ch. 179; above, para.3–131; cf. *Thorner v Major* [2009] UKHL 18; [2009] 1 W.L.R. 776 at [20].

[750] See above, para.3–086.

[751] See below, fn.760.

[752] *Crabb v Arun DC* [1976] Ch. 179 at 193, per Scarman L.J.

promise, as in *Dillwyn v Llewelyn*.[753] On the other hand, in *Inwards v Baker*,[754] where a son had also built a house for himself at his father's suggestion on the latter's land, the result of the estoppel was only to entitle the son to occupy the house for life. Similar results were reached in a number of later cases in which the promisee made improvements to the promisor's property (or otherwise acted to his detriment) in reliance on a promise, or common understanding, that the promisee would be entitled to reside there for as long as he or she wished to do so[755]; or for some shorter period: e.g. until her children had left school[756]; or that a lease of the premises, to which the promise related, would be granted to him[757]; or that he would be entitled to a charge over the property.[758] *Dillwyn v Llewelyn* can be reconciled with these cases by reference to the terms of the respective promises, which may be expressed either as an outright gift of the property or merely as an assurance that the promisee would be entitled to reside in the property for the specified period. Another way of giving effect to a promise of the latter kind is by the grant of a long, non-assignable lease at a nominal rent, on terms that ensured that the right of occupation was personal to the promisee.[759] In other cases, not concerned with rights of personal occupation but with the right to keep and use structures on promisor's land, the promisee has been held entitled only to a revocable licence.[760]

Equity binding on third party donee. Where the circumstances are such as   3–140
to give rise to an estoppel against the landowner, the estoppel is equally available against a third party who claims later to have obtained title to the land by way of gift from the landowner.[761] It may also be available against a third party who has purchased the property with the requisite degree of notice.[762]

The estoppel may operate conditionally. The estoppel may operate condi-   3–141
tionally where the promisee has acted in reliance on the promise but the terms of the promise show that the promisor did not intend to give up his title gratuitously. This was the position in *Lim Teng Huan v Ang Swee Chuan*[763] where A built a house on land jointly owned by him and L, who had agreed that he was to have no title to the house and would exchange his share in the land for other land. The arrangement had no contractual force as the other land was not identified with sufficient certainty; and it was held that L was estopped from asserting title to the house but that he was entitled to be compensated for the loss of his share in the land. In *Thorner v Major*[764] the farm was awarded to the claimant subject to his

[753] (1862) D.F. & G. 517; *Durant v Heritage* [1994] E.G.C.S. 134; or, in the exceptional cases discussed at fnn.712 and 714, to orders enforcing the promises made in those cases.
[754] [1965] 2 Q.B. 29; Maudsley, 81 L.Q.R. 183.
[755] *Jones v Jones* [1977] 1 W.L.R. 438; *Re Sharpe* [1980] 1 W.L.R. 219; *Greasley v Cooke* [1980] 1 W.L.R. 1306.
[756] *Tanner v Tanner* [1975] 1 W.L.R. 1346 (where there was a contract: cf. above, para.3–123); *Yaxley v Gotts* [2000] Ch. 162 (where the remedy was based on constructive trust).
[757] *J T Developments v Quinn* (1991) 62 P. & C.R. 33.
[758] *McGuane v Welch* [2008] EWCA Civ 785, [2008] 2 P. & C. R. 24 at [47].
[759] *Griffiths v Williams* [1978] E.G. Digest of Cases 919; cf. *Jones v Jones* [1977] 1 W.L.R. 438.
[760] *Canadian Pacific Railway v The King* [1931] A.C. 414; *Armstrong v Sheppard & Short* [1959] Q.B. 384.
[761] *Voyce v Voyce* (1991) 62 P. & C.R. 290; *Clark v Clark* [2006] EWHC 275; [2006] 1 F.C.R. 421.
[762] *Henry v Henry* [2010] UKPC 3; [2010] 1 All E.R. 988.
[763] [1991] 1 W.L.R. 113.
[764] [2009] UKHL 18; [2009] 1 W.L.R. 776.

indemnifying the promisor's personal representatives against the payment of inheritance tax related to the farm.

3–142   **Rights of access.** Where the promise is one to allow the promisee access to his own land over that of the promisor, the effect of the proprietary estoppel will be to entitle the promisee to an easement or licence on terms.[765] Such terms, if not agreed between the parties, may be imposed by the court: they can specify the extent of the permitted user as well as any payment that the promisee may be required to make for the exercise of the right.[766] However, an order for such payment was held not to be appropriate in one case, because the promisor had already obtained other benefits under the agreement.[767] It may also be inappropriate for other reasons, as the following discussion of the promisee's remedy will show.

3–143   **Remedy: a flexible, principled approach.** The remedy in cases of proprietary estoppel is "extremely flexible", its object being "to do what is equitable in all the circumstances".[768] Although the court thus has a considerable discretion with regard to the remedy in cases of proprietary estoppel, that discretion is not a "completely unfettered"[769] one and a "principled approach"[770] must be taken to its exercise.[771] In giving effect to the "equity" account must be taken, not only of the claimant's expectations, "but also of the extent of his detrimental reliance"[772]; and "there must be proportionality between the expectation and the detriment".[773] For the purpose of achieving such "proportionality" regard must be had to the degree of precision of the promise giving rise to the expectation. Where this amounts to an assurance that an interest in specific property will be transferred in return for specified acts, then an order for the specific enforcement of that promise (once the acts have been done) may be the appropriate remedy.[774] Where, on the other hand, the terms of the promise are less precise, amounting only to an assurance that some indeterminate benefit will be conferred on the promisee, so that the expectations reasonably arising from it are, at least objectively, uncertain, then the court will not give effect in full to expectations which the promisee may in fact have formed if they are "uncertain or extravagant or out of all proportion to the detriment which the claimant has suffered".[775] In such cases, compensation in money is likely to be the more appropriate remedy. That compensation must be proportionate to the detriment, but need not be its precise equivalent[776]: the fact that the detriment was incurred in response to a promise indicating (though in vague terms) some higher level of recompense is also to be taken into account.

---

[765] *E R Ives Investments Ltd v High* [1967] 2 Q.B. 379; *Crabb v Arun DC* [1976] Ch. 179.

[766] *Crabb v Arun DC* [1976] Ch. 179 at 199.

[767] *E R Ives Investments Ltd v High* [1967] 2 Q.B. 379.

[768] *Roebuck v Mungovin* [1994] 2 A.C. 224 at 235; cf. the remedy granted in *Gillett v Holt* [2001] Ch. 210.

[769] *Jennings v Rice* [2002] EWCA Civ 159; [2003] 1 F.L.R. 501 at [43].

[770] ibid.

[771] Gardner 115 L.Q.R. 438; 122 L.Q.R. 492.

[772] *Jennings v Rice*, above at [49].

[773] ibid. at [36]; cf. ibid. at [56]; *Fisher v Brooker* [2009] UKHL 41, [2009] 1 W.L.R. 1764 at [11].

[774] ibid. at [45].

[775] ibid. at [50].

[776] ibid. at [51].

The balancing of such factors is illustrated by *Jennings v Rice*[777] where the claimant had worked as gardener-handyman for an elderly widow for some 17 years without pay and had also provided personal care for her in the years of increasing frailty towards the end of her life. He had done so in response to her statements that "he would be alright" and that "all this will be yours one day".[778] The latter statement referred to her house and its contents, valued on her death at £435,000 out of a total estate of £1.285 million. The Court of Appeal upheld an award of £200,000 as being properly proportionate to the detriment suffered by the claimant in reliance on the assurances given to him.[779] Where the estoppel is based on a finding that the detriment suffered by the promise outweighed any benefit,[780] the benefit received may nonetheless be reflected in the award of less than the full expectation created by the promise.[781] The inherent flexibility of proprietary estoppel is also capable of dealing with any changes to the property in question which may have occurred between the time that the promise was made and the time when it is to take effect, e.g. upon the promisor's death. In *Thorner v Major*,[782] the effect of such changes was that the farm had increased slightly in size, but conversely it may have been necessary for the promisor to sell half the farm to fund his care into old age.[783] Such changes, and the reasons for them, can be taken into account in the remedy to be awarded.

The conduct of the promisor. Apart from the terms of the promise and the extent of the promisee's reliance on them, the court may also take into account the conduct of the promisor after the facts giving rise to the estoppel. Thus in *Crabb v Arun DC*[784] the defendants acted without warning in blocking the claimants' access to his land. In view of this "high-handedness"[785] and the resulting loss to the claimant, he was not required to make the payment that would otherwise have been a condition of the exercise of the right of way. Similarly, in *Pascoe v Turner*[786] a proprietary estoppel arose when a man told a woman with whom he had formerly cohabited that the house in which they had lived was hers, and she later spent some £230 of her limited resources on repairs and improvements to it. The Court of Appeal relied on the man's "ruthlessness"[787] in seeking to evict the promisee as a ground for ordering him to convey the fee simple to her. The submission that she should have no more than an irrevocable licence to occupy the house was rejected since this would not protect her against a bona fide purchaser from the promisor. The result seems, with respect, unduly punitive; and intermediate possibilities (such as granting the promisee a long lease[788]) were not put before the court.

3–144

---

[777] See above, at fn.769. cf. *Evans v HSBC Trust Co (UK) Ltd* [2005] W.T.L.R. 1299; *Clark v Clark* [2006] EWHC 275 (Ch); [2006] 1 F.C.R. 421.

[778] At [9].

[779] cf. *Munt v Beasley* [2006] EWCA Civ 370 at [45].

[780] See above, para.3–134.

[781] *Henry v Henry* [2010] UKPC 3; [2010] 1 All E.R. 988.

[782] [2009] UKHL 18; [2009] 1 W.L.R. 776.

[783] ibid. at [19], [65].

[784] [1976] Ch. 179.

[785] ibid. at 199; cf. ibid. at 189.

[786] [1979] 1 W.L.R. 431; Sufrin 42 M.L.R. 574.

[787] At 439; cf. the reference in *Gillett v Holt* [2001] Ch. 210 at 235 to the promisee's "bitter humiliation" on being summarily dismissed and made the subject of a police investigation for allegations of dishonesty which the promisor made no attempt to justify at the trial of the civil action.

[788] As in *Griffiths v Williams* [1978] E.G. Digest of Cases 919.

3–145   **Rights of occupation, or compensation?** *Pascoe v Turner* illustrates the
possibility that the grant of an irrevocable licence to remain on the property may
constitute an unsatisfactory remedy because it will not adequately secure the
promisee's possession. It may also be unsatisfactory on account of its inflexibility:
thus in *Inwards v Baker*[789] the remedy would have been of no use to the promisee,
had he wanted to move elsewhere; nor would his dependants have had any remedy
had he died shortly after completing the house. In such cases a remedy by way of
compensation in money would be more satisfactory for the promisee; and it would
also have the advantage for the promisor that dealing with the property would not
be impeded for an indefinite time.[790] Such a remedy was granted in *Dodsworth v
Dodsworth*[791] where the promisees spent £700 on improvements to the promisor's
bungalow in reliance on an implied promise (not intended to have contractual
force) that they could live there as if it were their home. The Court of Appeal held
that to give the promisees a right of occupation for an indefinite time would confer
on them a greater interest than had been contemplated by the parties; and that the
most appropriate remedy was to repay them their outlay on improvements.
Compensation in money will also be the more appropriate remedy where, as a
practical matter, the promise which gives rise to the estoppel cannot be specifically
enforced; e.g. where its performance would involve occupation of premises by, and
co-operation between, members of a family who later quarrel,[792] or between a
couple whose relationship has broken down.[793] Where there is evidence that the
improved property has increased in value by reason of market fluctuations, it is
submitted that the amount recoverable by the promisee should be increased
correspondingly; conversely it should be reduced where the market value of the
property has declined.[794]

In *Dodsworth v Dodsworth*[795] the court awarded compensation even though,
when the action was brought, the promisee was still in possession of the improved
property. More commonly this form of remedy is granted where the promisee is
no longer in possession, having either left voluntarily[796] or been lawfully ejected as
a result of legal proceedings.[797] Where the promisee has been wrongly ordered to
give up possession, compensation in money is similarly available,[798] though in such
a case the court may alternatively order the promisee to be put back into
possession of the premises.[799] The compensation has been assessed in a variety of
ways: at the cost of improvements made with the promisee's money[800]; at a
proportionate interest in the property[801]; or at the reasonable value of the right of

---

[789] [1965] 2 Q.B. 29.
[790] cf. criticisms of the law by Browne-Wilkinson J. in *Re Sharpe* [1980] 1 W.L.R. 219 at 226.
[791] [1973] E.G. Digest of Cases 233; cf. *Campbell v Griffin* [2001] EWCA Civ 990; [2001] W.T.L.R.
981; *Jennings v Rice* [2002] EWCA Civ 159; [2003] 1 F.L.R. 501; *Evans v HSBC Trust Co (UK) Ltd*
[2005] W.T.L.R. 1299.
[792] *Burrows and Burrows v Sharp* (1991) 23 H.L.R. 82; cf. *Baker v Baker* (1993) 25 H.L.R. 408 (where
the action was for damages).
[793] *Clough v Kelly* (1996) 72 P. & C.R. D22.
[794] cf. *Cheese v Thomas* [1994] 1 W.L.R. 129, a case of undue influence.
[795] [1973] E.G. Digest of Cases 233.
[796] As in *Hussey v Palmer* [1972] 1 W.L.R. 1286 and *Eves v Eves* [1975] 1 W.L.R. 1338.
[797] As in *Plimmer v Mayor of Wellington* (1884) 9 App.Cas. 699.
[798] *Tanner v Tanner* [1975] 1 W.L.R. 1346 (where there was a contract).
[799] ibid.
[800] *Hussey v Palmer* [1972] 1 W.L.R. 1286; *Burrows and Burrows v Sharp* (1991) 23 H.L.R. 82.
[801] *Eves v Eves* [1975] 1 W.L.R. 1338.

occupation, based (presumably) on the cost to the promisee of equivalent alternative accommodation.[802] The flexibility of the remedy also enables the court to combine monetary compensation with specific relief: e.g. in *Gillett v Holt*[803] the promisee was awarded part of the property to which the promise referred, together with a cash payment to compensate him for his exclusion from the farming business on that property.

Balance of hardship. The court may, finally, deny the promisee a remedy where, on balance, greater hardship would be produced by giving effect to the promise than by allowing the promisor to go back on it. This was the position in *Sledmore v Dalby*,[804] where the promisee had contributed to major improvements to the property but at the time of the proceedings had already enjoyed 20 years' rent-free occupation and was gainfully employed, while the promisor was a widow living on social security benefits. The promisee's claim to be entitled to a licence for life to stay in the house was in these circumstances rejected and the promisor was held entitled to possession.

3–146

(iii) *Proprietary and promissory estoppels contrasted*[805]

Common features. Proprietary and promissory estoppels have a number of points in common. Both can arise from promises[806]; consideration is not, while action in reliance is, a necessary condition for their operation[807]; and both are, within limits, revocable.[808] But there are also important differences between the two doctrines.[809]

3–147

Proprietary estoppel narrower than promissory estoppel. The scope of proprietary estoppel is in two respects narrower than that of promissory estoppel. First, proprietary estoppel is restricted to promises relating to property (generally the land) of another. Promissory estoppel may, on the other hand, arise (if other necessary conditions are satisfied[810]) out of *any* promise that strict legal rights will not be enforced: there is no need for those rights to relate to land or other property. Secondly, proprietary estoppel requires the promisee to have acted to his detriment,[811] while promissory estoppel may operate even though the promisee merely performs a pre-existing duty and so suffers no detriment in the sense of

3–148

---

[802] *Tanner v Tanner* [1975] 1 W.L.R. 1346; *Baker v Baker* (1993) 25 H.L.R. 408.

[803] [2001] Ch. 210.

[804] (1996) 72 P. & C.R. 196; *Evans v HSBC Trust Co (UK) Ltd* [2005] W.T.L.R. 1299 (where the potential hardship to be taken into account was that caused to a relative of the promisor); cf. *Henry v Henry* [2010] UKPC 3; [2010] 1 All E.R. 988, above fn.744.

[805] Evans [1988] Conv. 346.

[806] See above, paras 3–081, 3–090, 3–112, 3–121. For use of the expression "promissory estoppel" see above, para.3–090.

[807] See above, paras 3–083, 3–112, 3–134.

[808] See above, paras 3–086, 3–113, 3–135.

[809] In *Cobbe v Yeoman's Row Management Ltd* [2008] UKHL 55; [2008] 1 W.L.R. 1752 Lord Scott (at [14]) described proprietary estoppel as a "sub-species" of promissory estoppel, a view which may be thought consistent with his very narrow conception of proprietary estoppel: see above, fn.696. In *Thorner v Major* [2009] UKHL 18; [2009] 1 W.L.R. 776, Lord Walker (at [67]) had "some difficulty" with Lord Scott's observation, a view which may, in turn, be consistent with his implicit rejection of Lord Scott's narrow conception.

[810] See above, paras 3–081—3–085, 3–111—3–117.

[811] See above, para.3–134.

doing something that he was not previously bound to do.[812] This difference between the two doctrines follows from the fact that promissory estoppel is (unlike proprietary estoppel) concerned only with the variation or abandonment of rights arising out of a pre-existing legal relationship between promisor and promisee.

3–149 **Proprietary estoppel wider than promissory estoppel.** On the other hand, the scope of proprietary estoppel is in two respects wider than that of promissory estoppel. First, promissory estoppel arises only out of a representation or promise that is "clear" or "precise and unambiguous".[813] Proprietary estoppel, on the other hand, can arise where there is no actual promise at all:[814] e.g. in cases of "acquiescence" where one party makes improvements to another's land under a mistake[815] and the other either knows of the mistake[816] or seeks to take unconscionable advantage of it.[817] Even in cases of "encouragement" the requirement of a "clear" representation may not be the same as the requirement for promissory estoppel.[818]

3–150 **Proprietary estoppel can give rise to a cause of action.** Secondly (and more significantly), while promissory estoppel is essentially defensive in nature,[819] proprietary estoppel can give rise to a cause of action.[820] The promisee is not merely entitled to raise the estoppel as a defence to an action of trespass or to a claim for possession: the court can make an order for the land to be conveyed to him,[821] or for compensation,[822] or for such other remedy as appropriate.[823] Although the authorities support this second distinction between the two kinds of estoppel, they do not make any attempt to explain or justify it. It is submitted that the explanation is in part historical and terminological. Proprietary estoppel was originally explained in terms of *acquiescence*[824] or *encouragement*.[825] Hence no conflict with the requirement that *promises* must be supported by consideration was perceived; or where it was perceived the facts were said to give rise to a contract.[826] Promissory estoppel, on the other hand, dealt principally with the renegotiation of contracts; it obviously depended on giving binding effect to promises, and it did so in the context of releases and variations, in which the common law requirement of consideration had long been established.[827] The rule that promissory estoppel gives rise to no cause of action was evolved to prevent

---

[812] See above, para.3–084.

[813] See above, para.3–081.

[814] *Thorner v Major* [2009] UKHL 18; [2009] 1 W.L.R. 776: "the classic example of proprietary estoppel is based on silence and inaction" per Lord Neuberger (at [84]); cf. Lord Walker at [54]–[55].

[815] See above, paras 3–120.

[816] *Willmott v Barber* (1880) 15 Ch.D. 96 at 105 (the claim in that case failed as the party against whom it was made did not know of the extent of his own rights or of the other party's mistake).

[817] *Taylor Fashions Ltd v Liverpool Victoria Trustees Co Ltd* [1982] Q.B. 133.

[818] See above, para.3–126.

[819] See above, paras 3–086—3–088.

[820] *Crabb v Arun DC* [1976] Ch. 179 at 187; *Taylor Fashions Ltd v Liverpool Victoria Trustees Co Ltd* [1982] Q.B. 133 at 148; *Thorner v Major* [2009] UKHL 18; [2009] 1 W.L.R. 776 at [61].

[821] e.g. *Dillwyn v Llewelyn* (1862) 4 D.F. & G. 517.

[822] e.g. *Eves v Eves* [1975] 1 W.L.R. 1338.

[823] See above, paras 3–143—3–146.

[824] *Willmott v Barber* (1880) 15 Ch.D. 96 at 105.

[825] *Ramsden v Dyson* (1866) L.R. 1 H.L. 129 at 170.

[826] *Dillwyn v Llewelyn* (1862) 4 D.F. & G. 517 at 522; above, paras 3–130—3–131.

[827] See above, paras 3–056—3–065.

what would otherwise be an obvious conflict between the doctrines of promissory estoppel and consideration. In cases of proprietary estoppel there was no such conflict where liability was based on "acquiescence"; and where it was based on "encouragement" the conflict, though sometimes real enough, was at least less obvious. There are, moreover, two aspects of proprietary estoppel which help to justify the distinction. These are that the acts done by the promisee are not ones which he was under any previous legal obligation to perform; and that generally their effect would be to unjustly enrich the promisor if he were allowed to go back on his promise.[828] In these respects, the facts on which proprietary estoppel is based provide more compelling grounds for relief than those commonly found in cases of promissory estoppel.

Common basis: unconscionability. While the two doctrines are in these respects distinct it can also be argued that they have a common basis, namely that it would be unconscionable for the promisor to go back on his promise after the promisee has acted on it; and that the precise labels to be attached to them are "immaterial".[829] It is perhaps for these reasons that the distinction between the two kinds of estoppel was described as "not . . . helpful" by Scarman L.J. in *Crabb v Arun DC*.[830] That decision was, in a later case, said to illustrate "the virtual equation of promissory estoppel and proprietary estoppel",[831] perhaps because it extended the operation of proprietary estoppel beyond the situations originally within its scope, namely those in which the promisor would be unjustly enriched by the work done by the promisee on the land unless some legal effect were given to the promise. Nevertheless it is submitted that the doctrines are distinct in the respects stated above.[832] Attempts to unite them by posing "simply" the question whether it would be "unconscionable"[833] for the promisor to go back on his promise are, for reasons given earlier in this chapter,[834] unhelpful[835]; and they are also open to the objection that they provide no basis on which a legal doctrine capable of yielding predictable results can be developed.

3–151

(iv) *Proprietary estoppel and contract contrasted*

We have seen that some cases which have been said to support the doctrine of proprietary estoppel can be explained on the alternative basis that there was a

3–152

---

[828] See the reference to the landowner's "profit" in *Ramsden v Dyson* (1866) L.R. 1 H.L. 129 at 141 and cf. above, para.3–131.

[829] *Taylor Fashions Ltd v Liverpool Victoria Trustees Co Ltd* [1982] Q.B. 133 at 153, where, however, a distinction is also drawn between "promissory estoppel" and the principle in *Ramsden v Dyson* (1866) L.R. 1 H.L. 129 (i.e. proprietary estoppel).

[830] [1976] Ch. 179 at 193.

[831] *Taylor Fashions Ltd v Liverpool Victoria Trustees Co Ltd* [1982] Q.B. 133 at 153; cf. also above, fn.738.

[832] At fnn.820–830.

[833] *Taylor Fashions Ltd v Liverpool Victoria Trustees Co Ltd* [1982] Q.B. 133 at 155; cf. *Amalgamated Investment & Property Co Ltd v Texas Commerce International Bank Ltd* [1982] Q.B. 84 at 104, 122.

[834] See above, para.3–090.

[835] *Haslemere Estates Ltd v Baker* [1982] 1 W.L.R. 1109 at 1119; cf. *Cobbe v Yeoman's Row Management Ltd* [2008] UKHL 55; [2008] 1 W.L.R. 1752 at [28], [46]. Dicta emphasising the flexibility of the *remedy* (above, para.3–143) must be read subject to the requirement to adopt a "principle approach" (above, para.3–143) to this aspect of the doctrine; and they should, in any event, not be taken to refer also to *conditions of liability*.

contract between the parties.[836] But this explanation will not cover all the cases; for proprietary estoppel can operate even though the conditions required for the creation of a contract are not satisfied. The need to discuss the doctrine in this chapter arises precisely because a promise can give rise to a proprietary estoppel even though it is not supported by consideration; and a promise can also give rise to such an estoppel even though it cannot take effect as a contract because it is not sufficiently certain or because it fails to comply with formal requirements. Moreover, the effect of a proprietary estoppel differs from that of a contract. Sometimes, indeed, the result of a proprietary estoppel is to give effect to the promise in the terms in which it was made[837]; but such a result does not follow as of right. We have seen that the promisee's rights may depend, not only on the terms of the promise and on the extent to which he has acted on it, but also on the subsequent conduct of the promisor. Thus in *Crabb v Arun DC* the promisee would have had to make some payment not only for the right of way but for the "high-handedness"[838] of the promisor. The rights arising under a binding contract are fixed at its formation and not subject to such variation in the light of the court's approval or disapproval of the subsequent conduct of one of the parties. For this reason, and because proprietary estoppel may be revocable,[839] it will generally be more advantageous to a party to show the existence of a binding contract (if he can) than to rely on a proprietary estoppel.

8. SPECIAL CASES

(a) Defective Promises[840]

3–153   Mutual promises are generally consideration for each other,[841] but difficulty is sometimes felt in treating a promise as consideration for another if the first promise suffered from some defect by reason of which it was not legally binding. The law on this topic is based more on expediency than on any supposedly logical deductions which might be drawn from the doctrine of consideration. The question whether a defective promise can constitute consideration for a counter-promise depends on the policy of the rule of law making the former promise defective.

3–154   **Policy considerations.** One group of cases concerns contracts made between persons, one of whom lacks contractual capacity.[842] A minor can enforce a promise made to him under such a contract, even though the only consideration for that promise is his own promise, which does not bind him by reason of his minority.[843] The same rule applies to contracts with persons who lack mental capacity.[844] The reason for these rules is that it is the policy of the law to protect the person under the incapacity, and not the other party, who is therefore not allowed to rely on that incapacity. A contrasting group of cases concerns promises which are illegal.

---

[836] See above, para.3–131.
[837] e.g. *Dillwyn v Llewelyn* (1862) 4 D.F. & G. 517.
[838] [1976] Ch. 179 at 199.
[839] See above, para.3–135.
[840] Treitel 77 L.Q.R. 83.
[841] See above, para.3–008.
[842] See Ch.12 below.
[843] *Holt v Ward Clarencieux* (1732) 2 Stra. 937.
[844] See below, para.12–052 et seq.

Obviously the illegal promise cannot be enforced; and if both promises are illegal
the consequence that neither can be enforced follows from the policy of the
invalidating rule rather than from the fact that an illegal promise cannot constitute
consideration.[845] But in some cases of illegal contracts the illegality affects the
promise or promises of only one party: this is, for example, often the position
where the contract is in restraint of trade. In such a case, the party who makes the
illegal promise cannot enforce the counter-promise (e.g. to pay a sum of money)
if the illegal promise constitutes the sole consideration for the counter-promise.[846]
Indeed, the position is the same if the illegal promise is the *main* consideration for
the counter-promise, even though there was also some other consideration for
it.[847] The reason for this rule lies in the policy of the law to discourage illegal
bargains.

Performance of defective promise. Where a defective *promise* does not   3–155
amount to consideration its *performance* can nevertheless sometimes provide
consideration for the counter-promise. For example, a mere promise to negotiate
has no contractual force[848] and so cannot constitute consideration for a counter-
promise; but actually carrying on the negotiations can satisfy the requirement of
consideration.[849] A similar principle accounts for the rule that a victim of misrepresentation, duress or undue influence can sue but not be sued: by suing, he
affirms the contract, makes his own promise binding on himself, and so supplies
consideration for the other party's promise. But where the promise of one party
is illegal, even its performance does not entitle that party to enforce the counter-
promise,[850] for the law must not give him any incentive to perform the illegal
promise.

Promise defective by statute. Where one of the promises is defective by   3–156
statute, the terms of the statute may solve the problem whether the person giving
the defective promise can sue on the counter-promise.[851] Thus a party who gives
a promise which is defective under s.4 of the Statute of Frauds 1677, or under s.34
of the Matrimonial Causes Act 1973, may, in spite of not being bound by that
promise, be entitled to enforce the counter-promise[852]; and this may be so even
though for other purposes (such as the validity of a disposition) a promise,
precisely because it is defective by statute, does amount to consideration.[853] Where
a statute invalidates a promise but does not provide for the effect of its invalidity
on the other party's promise, it seems that the invalid promise is not good

---

[845] As suggested in *Nerot v Wallace* (1789) 3 T.R. 17 at 23.

[846] e.g. *Wyatt v Kreglinger & Fernau* [1933] 1 K.B. 793.

[847] See *Goodinson v Goodinson* [1954] 2 Q.B. 118; the actual decision is obsolete in view of
Matrimonial Causes Act 1973, s.34.

[848] See above, para.2–100.

[849] *Sepong Engineering Construction Co Ltd v Formula One Management Ltd* [2000] 1 Lloyd's Rep. 602
at 611, where it was also said that damages for breach of the resulting contract would be no more than
nominal: below, para.20–060.

[850] e.g. *Wyatt v Kreglinger & Fernall* [1933] 1 K.B. 793.

[851] See *Laythoarp v Bryant* (1836) 2 Bing.N.C. 735.

[852] See below, paras 5–018, 11–048. For more elaborate provisions of this kind, see Financial Services
and Markets Act 2000, ss.20, 26–30.

[853] *Re Kumar* [1993] 1 W.L.R. 224, where a void promise was held not to constitute consideration
for the purpose of protecting third parties under Insolvency Act 1986, s.339.

consideration[854]; but, unless the promise is illegal, the party giving it can sue on the counter-promise if he actually performs his own promise.[855]

3–157   **Both promises defective by statute.** A statute may also invalidate *both* promises: this was formerly the position with regard to wagering contracts which were "null and void" under s.18 of the Gaming Act 1845.[856] Performance of one such promise clearly would not make the other enforceable[857]; but the question whether performance of the void promise could constitute consideration might also arise in another context, e.g. in the context of the question whether the performance amounted to consideration for the purpose of a rule of law by which a transfer or disposition of property was effective only if made for valuable consideration. This was the question which arose in *Lipkin Gorman v Karpnale Ltd*,[858] where stolen money was used by the thief for gambling at a club of which he was a member, and it was held that the club had not received the money for valuable consideration so as to be entitled, as against the owner of the money, to retain it. We have already noted that the club did not provide consideration for the payment by exchanging the money for gaming chips.[859] The present point is that the club did not provide consideration for the payments made to it by the member by allowing him to gamble and promising to pay, or actually paying him, the amount of any bets which he had won. The club's *promise* to pay did not amount to consideration since it was, at that time, void under s.18 of the 1845 Act.

(b) Unilateral Contracts[860]

3–158   In the case of a unilateral contract the promisee clearly provides consideration if he completes the required act or forbearance (such as walking to York or not smoking for a year).[861] This amounts in law to a detriment to the promisee; and the promisor may also obtain a benefit: e.g. where he promises a reward for the return of lost property and it is actually returned to him. But it has been suggested that if the promisee has begun, but not yet completed, the required act or forbearance the promisor can still withdraw. At this stage, there is said to be no consideration for the promise, since the promisee is not bound to complete performance.[862] But it may in law be detriment to walk part of the way to York, or to forbear from smoking for part of the year. Questions of fact may, indeed, arise in determining whether performance has actually begun, particularly where the stipulated performance was a forbearance; but if an actual forbearance *to sue* can constitute good

---

[854] *Clayton v Jennings* (1760) 2 W.Bl. 706.

[855] This, it is submitted, is the best justification for *Rajbenback v Mamon* [1955] 1 Q.B. 283; see 77 L.Q.R. 95. For another view, see Unger 19 M.L.R. 99.

[856] Repealed by s.334 of the Gambling Act 2005. Under s.335(1) "[t]he fact that a contract relates to gambling shall not prevent its enforcement", but such a contract may be unlawful for other reasons (see para.11–010 below) and the text which follows in this paragraph deals generally with the position when both promises are defective.

[857] cf. above, at fn.850.

[858] [1991] 2 A.C. 548.

[859] See above, para.3–032.

[860] See above, para.2–051 et seq.

[861] See above, para.2–052; *Marshall v N M Financial Management Ltd* [1997] 1 W.L.R. 1527 at 1533. For controversy whether the act must be "requested" by the promisor in cases of unilateral contracts, see A.L.G. 67 L.Q.R. 456; Smith 69 L.Q.R. 99; A.L.G. 69 L.Q.R. 106.

[862] Wormser, in *Selected Readings on the Law of Contracts*, at p.307; but for the same writer's later views, see 3 Jl.Leg.Educ. 146.

consideration,[863] it must in principle be possible to tell when a forbearance has begun. Thus commencement of performance (whether of an act or of a forbearance) may provide consideration for the promise and so deprive the promisor of the power to withdraw it. Of course, the promisor's liability to pay the amount promised (e.g. the £100 for walking to York) does not accrue before the promisee has fully performed the required act or forbearance. The present point is merely that, after part performance by the promisee, the promisor cannot withdraw his promise with impunity.[864]

It has been suggested that a unilateral contract may be made as soon as the offer is received by the offeree[865]; and this could be interpreted to mean that the contract was binding even before the offeree had acted on the offer in any way. But at this stage the offeree has clearly not provided any consideration, and in the case in which the suggestion was made no problem of consideration arose as the offeree had completed the required act[866] before any attempt to withdraw the offer was made. Except in the case of bankers' irrevocable credits (to be discussed below), the better view is that an offer of a unilateral contract is not binding on receipt, but only when the offeree has begun to render the required performance.

(c) Bankers' Irrevocable Credits

Contracts for the international sale of goods often provide for payment by irrevocable credit.[867] The buyer instructs his bank to open an irrevocable credit in favour of the seller; and the bank then notifies the seller that such a credit has been opened in his favour, and that he will be paid, usually when he tenders specified shipping documents to the bank. The general view is that the bank is bound by this arrangement and is not entitled to withdraw simply because the shipping documents have not yet been tendered.[868] But it is very doubtful whether at this stage there is any consideration, moving from the seller, for the bank's promise to him.[869] If (as seems probable) this view also represents the law, it is best regarded as an exception to the doctrine of consideration.[870]   **3–159**

(d) Firm Offers

Revocable unless supported by consideration. A "firm" offer is one containing a promise not to revoke it for a specified time. Such a promise is not binding unless the offeree has provided some consideration for it. Thus in   **3–160**

---

[863] See above, para.3–040.

[864] *Schweppe v Harper* [2008] EWCA Civ 444 at [42]

[865] *Harvela Investments Ltd v Royal Trust Co of Canada (CI) Ltd* [1986] 1 A.C. 207 at 224 ("when the invitation was received").

[866] By submitting the requested bid: cf. above, para.2–022.

[867] See generally *Guaranty Trust Co of NY v Hannay* [1918] 2 K.B. 623 at 659.

[868] *W J Alan & Co Ltd v El Nasr Export & Import Co* [1972] 2 Q.B. 189 at 208; cf. [1972] 2 Q.B. 189 at 218; *Trendtex Trading Corp v Central Bank of Nigeria* [1977] Q.B. 529 at 551; *The American Accord* [1983] 1 A.C. 168 at 183.

[869] cf. *Raiffeisen Zentralbank Osterreich Attorney-General v China Marine Bunker (Petrochina) Co Ltd* [2006] EWHC 212; [2006] All E.R. (D) 37 at [31] (collecting bank entitled to sue *buyer* under irrevocable payment undertaking: consideration from the bank "may be said to be provided by the recognised financial role of the bank in the transaction in making funds available").

[870] cf. in the US, U.C.C. ss.5–105.

Dickinson v Dodds[871] it was held that an offer to sell land "to be left over until Friday"[872] could be withdrawn on Thursday. Consideration for such a promise is most obviously provided if the offeree pays (or promises to pay) a sum of money for it and so buys an option.[873] It may also be provided by some other promise: e.g. in the case of an offer to sell a house, the offeree may provide consideration for the offeror's promise to hold the offer open, by promising to apply for a mortgage on the house; and, in the case of an offer to buy shares, the offeree may provide consideration for the offeror's promise not to revoke the offer for a specified time, by promising not to dispose of those shares elsewhere during that time.

The performance of the offeree's promises in such cases could likewise provide consideration for the offeror's promise to keep the offer open. In one case a vendor of land entered into a so-called "lock-out" agreement[874] by which he promised a prospective purchaser not to consider other offers if that purchaser would exchange contracts within two weeks; and it was said that "the promise by the [purchaser] to get on by limiting himself to just two weeks"[875] constituted consideration for the vendor's promise not to consider other offers. Such a "lock out" promise is not strictly a firm offer since it does not prevent the vendor from deciding not to sell at all; but the reasoning quoted above could apply to the case of a firm offer. On the facts of the case from which it is taken, the reasoning gives rise to some difficulty since it does not appear that the purchaser there made any *promise* to exchange contracts within two weeks. It seems more plausible to say that the vendor's promise had become binding as a unilateral contract under which the purchaser had provided consideration by actually making efforts to meet the deadline, even though he had not promised to do so.

Similar reasoning can apply if a seller of land promises to keep an offer open for a month, asking the buyer during that period to raise the necessary money. If the buyer makes efforts to that end (without actually promising to do so) it is arguable that he has by part performance accepted the seller's offer of a unilateral contract to keep the principal offer open. On the other hand the equitable doctrine of *Hughes v Metropolitan Ry*[876] will not avail the offeree since it does not create new causes of action where none existed before.[877] Nor does it seem likely that an

---

[871] (1876) 2 Ch.D. 463; cf. *Routledge v Grant* (1828) 4 Bing. 653; *Head v Diggon* (1828) 3 M. & Ry. 97.

[872] Quaere whether this meant that the offer would not be withdrawn before Friday, or only that it should lapse on Friday and not before. The latter interpretation was given to a stipulation that an offer should be "open all Monday" in *Stevenson, Jacques & Co v McLean* (1880) 6 Q.B.D. 346.

[873] The legal characteristics of such an option have been variously described: (1) as a contract: *Greene v Church Commissioners for England* [1974] Ch. 467 at 476, 478; though not one of sale: *Chippenham Golf Club v North Wilts Rural DC* (1992) 64 P. & C.R. 527; (2) as a transaction which, even though it is not a contract, gives rise to an interest in property: *Re Button's Lease* [1964] Ch. 263 at 270–271; *Armstrong & Holmes Ltd v Holmes* [1994] 1 All E.R. 826; (3) as a unilateral contract: *United Scientific Holdings Ltd v Burnley BC* [1978] A.C. 904 at 945; *Little v Courage Ltd* (1995) 70 P. & C.R. 469 at 474; (4) as a conditional contract: *Bircham & Co Nominees (No.2) Ltd v Worrell Holdings Ltd* [2001] EWCA Civ 773; (2001) 82 P. & C.R. 427 at [45]; (5) as "an irrevocable offer which only matures into a bilateral contract upon its due exercise": *Re Gray* [2004] EWHC 1538 (Ch); [2005] 1 W.L.R. 815 at [25]; and (6) as being sui generis: *Spiro v Glencrown Properties* [1991] Ch. 537 at 544. And see Mowbray 74 L.Q.R. 242; Lücke 3 Adelaide L.Rev. 200.

[874] See below, para.4–011.

[875] *Pitt v PHH Asset Management Ltd* [1994] 1 W.L.R. 327 at 332; MacMillan [1993] C.L.J. 392; for other consideration in this case, see above, para.3–038; *Tye v House* [1997] 2 E.G.L.R. 171.

[876] (1877) 2 App.Cas.439; above, para.3–077.

[877] See above, para.3–088.

offeree who suffers loss as a result of the withdrawal of the offer will be able to claim damages in tort[878] for misrepresentation.[879]

Criticism. The rule in *Dickinson v Dodds* can lead to inconvenience, so much 3–161 so that there are some situations in which it has been said that "the market would disdain"[880] to take the point that there was no consideration for a promise to keep an offer open. In the case of certain international sales, the rule is rejected by the Vienna Convention on Contracts for the International Sale of Goods.[881] It is also subject to a common law exception in the law of insurance where an underwriter who initials a slip under an "open cover" arrangement is regarded as making a "standing offer" which the insured can accept from time to time by making "declarations" under it. The underwriter's commitment is regarded as binding even though there is no consideration for his implied promise not to revoke the "standing offer".[882] But even with these mitigations, the rule can still cause hardship to an offeree who has acted in reliance on the assurance that the offer will be kept open for a stated time. Such hardship can, for example, arise where a builder submits a tender in reliance on offers from sub-contractors, expressed to remain "firm" for a fixed period,[883] and those offers are withdrawn within that period but after his tender has been accepted. On the other hand, the rule does sometimes provide necessary protection for the offeror: e.g. when an offer is made by a customer on a form provided by a supplier and expressed to be irrevocable; or when the period of irrevocability is not specified so that the offeror is left subject to an indefinite obligation without acquiring any corresponding right. Any further development of the law on the point will require a balancing of these conflicting factors.[884]

(e) Auction Sales Without Reserve[885]

Where goods are put up for auction without reserve, there is no contract *of sale* 3–162 if the auctioneer refuses to knock the goods down to the highest bidder; but the auctioneer is liable to the highest bidder on a separate promise that the sale will be without reserve.[886] It is arguable that there is no consideration for this promise

---

[878] cf. *Holman Construction Ltd v Delta Timber Co Ltd* [1972] N.Z.L.R. 1081; and see *Blackpool and Fylde Aero Club Ltd v Blackpool BC* [1990] 1 W.L.R. 1195 at 1202.

[879] i.e. under *Hedley Byrne & Co Ltd v Heller & Partners Ltd* [1964] A.C. 465; below, para.9–033.

[880] *Jaglom v Excess Insurance Co Ltd* [1972] 2 Q.B. 250 at 258; cf. *County Ltd v Girozentrale Securities* [1996] 3 All E.R. 834 at 837. For the view that the statement in *Jaglom*'s case was not an offer, but an acceptance (and binding as such), see *General Reinsurance Corp v Forsakringsaktiebolaget Fennia Patria* [1983] Q.B. 856 at 863–864.

[881] Art.16(2); cf.U.C.C. s.2–205, limiting the period of irrevocability to three months on the theory that unlimited irrevocability could unreasonably prejudice the offeror.

[882] *Citadel Insurance Co v Atlantic Union Insurance Co* [1982] 2 Lloyd's Rep. 543 at 546.

[883] For conflicting American authorities, see *James Baird Co v Gimbel Bros* 64 F. 2d. 344 (1933); *Drennan v Star Paving Co* 51 Cal. 2d.409, 333 p.2d.757 (1958). For a review of Canadian authorities, see *Northern Construction Co v Gloge Heating & Plumbing* [1986] 2 W.W.R. 649, holding a sub-contractor bound by his offer.

[884] See Law Commission, Working Paper 60 (1975).

[885] See also above, para.2–008.

[886] *Warlow v Harrison* (1859) 1 E. & E. 309; approved in *Harris v Nickerson* (1873) L.R. 8 Q.B. 286 at 288; *Johnston v Boyes* [1899] 2 Ch. 73 at 77.

as the highest bidder is not bound by his unaccepted bid.[887] But it has been held that the bidder suffers a detriment by bidding on the strength of the promise, for he runs the risk of being bound by a contract of sale[888]; and the auctioneer benefits as the bidding is driven up.[889] Hence there is consideration for the separate promise, and it makes no difference to the auctioneer's liability *on this promise* that he would not be liable if he did not put the goods up for sale at all (since an advertisement of an auction is not an offer to hold it)[890] or that there was no contract *of sale* because of his refusal to accept the highest bid.[891]

(f) Novation of Partnership Debts

3–163   When the composition of a partnership changes, it is usual to arrange that liability for the debts owed by the existing partners should be transferred by novation[892] to the new partners. Two situations may be considered.

3–164   **Retirement and admission of new partner.** A and B are in partnership; A retires and C is admitted as a new partner; it is agreed between A, B and C, and the creditors of the old firm of A and B, that A shall cease to be liable for the firm's debts, and that C shall undertake such liability. The result is that the creditors can sue C[893] and can no longer sue A. They provide consideration for C's promise to pay by abandoning their claim against A; and A provides consideration for their promise to release him by procuring a substitute debtor, C.

3–165   **Retirement without admission of new partner.** A and B are in partnership; A retires; it is agreed between A, B and the creditors of the firm that A shall cease to be liable and that B shall be solely liable. It seems that the creditors cannot sue A, but it is hard to see what consideration moves from him. In one case it was said that there was consideration in that a remedy against a single debtor might be easier to enforce than one against several, all of whom are solvent[894]; thus the creditors benefit by the release of A. This is a possible, if invented[895] consideration.[896]

(g) Gratuitous Bailments

3–166   **Bailment for the benefit of the bailee.** A gratuitous bailment may be for the benefit of either the bailee or the bailor. The first possibility is illustrated by

---

[887] For discussion of this point, see Slade 68 L.Q.R. 238; Gower 68 L.Q.R.457; Slade 69 L.Q.R. 21.

[888] An "invented" consideration: see above, para.3–009.

[889] *Barry v Davies* [2000] 1 W.L.R. 1962 at 1967.

[890] *Harris v Nickerson* (1873) L.R. 8 Q.B. 286; above, para.2–008.

[891] See above, para.2–008.

[892] See below, para.15–003; cf. Partnership Act 1890, s.17(3).

[893] cf. *Re Burton Marsden Douglas* [2004] EWHC 593; [2004] 3 All E.R. 2322 where two new partners could not be sued because there had been no agreement to novate and no consideration from the creditor since there was no promise to release the original partner.

[894] *Lyth v Ault* (1852) 7 Ex. 669; *Thompson v Percival* (1834) 5 B. & Ad. 925 is based on reasoning which is obsolete after *D & C Builders Ltd v Rees* [1967] 2 Q.B. 617.

[895] See above, para.3–009.

[896] cf. *Re Burton Marsden Douglas* [2004] EWHC 593 (Ch), [2004] 3 All E.R. 222 (no novation where A incurred a debt *as an individual* and then went into partnership with B and C).

Bainbridge v Firmstone[897] where the defendant asked for, and received, permission from the claimant to weigh two boilers belonging to the claimant. In performing this operation, the defendant damaged the boilers; and he was held liable for breach of his promise to return them in good condition. The court rejected the argument that, as the defendant was not paid to weigh, or look after, the boilers, there was no consideration for his promise. Patteson J. said:

> "I suppose the defendant thought he had some benefit; at any rate there is a detriment to the (claimant) from his parting with the possession for even so short a time."[898]

It is more doubtful whether there would be any consideration moving from the defendant for any promise by the claimant to allow the defendant to have possession of the boilers. A mere promise by the defendant to return the boilers might not suffice as it would only be a promise to perform a duty imposed by law on all bailees; but a promise to repair the boilers or to improve them in some way would probably be regarded as consideration moving from the defendant.[899]

Bailment for the benefit of the bailor. The second possibility arises where A undertakes the safekeeping of B's chattel without reward. Here B's parting with the possession is hardly a detriment to him; and A's duty to look after the thing[900] does not arise out of a contractual promise made by him but is imposed by the general law. It follows that A's *only* duty is that imposed by the law.[901] Thus A is under no obligation before he actually receives the thing; and if he promised to do anything which went beyond the duty imposed by law (e.g. to keep the thing in repair) he would be bound by this promise only if B had provided some consideration for it apart from the delivery of the chattel.[902] To constitute such consideration, it is not necessary to show that A profited from the transaction; thus it is enough if B reimburses (or promises to reimburse) any expenses that A has incurred for the purpose of performing his promise.[903]

3–167

(h) Gratuitous Services

No liability in contract. Normally, a promise to render services without reward is not binding contractually as no consideration for it is provided by the promisee. For example, where A gratuitously promises B to insure B's property but fails to do so, A is not liable to B for breach of contract if the property is lost or damaged.[904] It may sometimes be possible to find consideration in an indirect

3–168

---

[897] (1838) 8 A. & E. 743.

[898] ibid. at 744.

[899] cf. *Verrall v Farnes* [1966] 1 W.L.R. 1254, a case relating to land; followed in *Mitton v Farrow* (1980) 255 E.G. 449.

[900] For this duty see *Coggs v Bernard* (1703) 2 Ld.Raym. 909; *Mitchell v Ealing LBC* [1979] Q.B. 1; *Port Swettenham Authority v T W Wu & Co* [1979] A.C. 580 at 590.

[901] *Morris v C W Martin Ltd* [1966] 1 Q.B. 716 at 731.

[902] cf. *Charnock v Liverpool Corp* [1968] 1 W.L.R. 1498; below, para.14–007. The *scope* of A's duty imposed by law may nonetheless take into account "promises" which are made, e.g. as to the mode of safekeeping: *Yearworth v North Bristol NHS Trust* [2009] EWCA Civ 37; [2010] Q.B. 1 (Trust liable in bailment for failing to keep semen frozen).

[903] *CCC Films (London) Ltd v Impact Quadrant Films Ltd* [1985] Q.B. 16 at 27.

[904] *Argy Trading & Development Co Ltd v Lapid Developments Ltd* [1977] 1 W.L.R. 444.

benefit which the promisor obtains from the arrangement: e.g. in the form of favourable publicity.[905]

3–169   **Liability in tort.** Even where the promise is not supported by consideration, the promisor may be liable in tort for negligence if he renders the gratuitous services but does so without due care and so causes loss. A banker who gives a negligent credit reference may be liable on this ground even though he makes no charge to the person to whom the information is given.[906] Similarly, where A gratuitously promised B to insure B's property and did so negligently, so that the policy did not cover the loss which occurred, A was held liable to B in tort.[907] In one case, a person was even held liable in tort for negligently giving free advice to a friend in connection with the purchase of a second-hand car which turned out to be seriously defective.[908]

In the cases just considered, the defendant was guilty of the negligent *performance* of a gratuitous service. In tort there is generally no liability for *non-performance*, i.e. "for pure omission",[909] but where there has been an "assumption of responsibility" by the defendant, upon which the claimant has relied,[910] a duty of care may be owed and it has been said that such liability covers "acts of omission, as well as acts of commission".[911] While therefore it has been said that to impose liability in tort for simply doing nothing after having promised to render services gratuitously "would be inconsistent with fundamental principle",[912] it seems that, in some cases, such a promise may be enforceable in negligence.

9. PROMISES IN DEEDS

3–170   **Requirements for a deed.** Consideration is not necessary for the validity of a promise in a deed. The binding force of such a promise does not depend on contract at all. Thus it can take effect although the person in whose favour it was made did not know of it.[913] To take effect as a deed, an instrument must make it

---

[905] cf. *De la Bere v Pearson* [1908] 1 K.B. 280 at 287.

[906] See *Hedley Byrne & Co Ltd v Heller & Partners Ltd* [1964] A.C. 465; cf. below, para.9–033.

[907] *Wilkinson v Coverdale* (1793) 1 Esp. 75.

[908] *Chaudhry v Prabhakar* [1989] 1 W.L.R. 29 where the defendant conceded that he owed a duty of care to the claimant and two members of the Court of Appeal seem to have regarded this concession as correct; Brown [1989] L.M.C.L.Q. 148. Contrast *Henderson v Merrett Syndicates Ltd* [1995] 2 A.C. 145 at 181, suggesting that there may be no liability in respect of services rendered on "an informal occasion."

[909] *Outram v Academy Plastics Ltd* [2001] I.C.R. 367 at 372. A fortiori, there is no liability in tort for pure omission where *no* promise has been made: see *Reid v Rush & Tompkins Group Plc* [1990] 1 W.L.R. 212 and *Van Oppen v Clerk to the Bedford Charity Trustees* [1990] 1 W.L.R. 235.

[910] See, further, para.9–036.

[911] *White v Jones* [1995] 2 A.C. 207 at 268, 295 (where the solicitor was under a duty to act under his contract with the testator: see, further, para.14–052 et seq.); *Lennon v Metropolitan Police Commissioner* [2004] EWCA Civ 130; [2004] 1 W.L.R. 2594 at [21] (where the *Outram* case, above, fn.909, was distinguished (at [33]) on the basis that there had been no express or implied assumption of responsibility). Quaere whether the wrongful conduct in *Lennon* was one of "omission", or "commission". cf. *Van Oppen v Clerk to the Bedford Charity Trustees* [1990] 1 W.L.R. 235 at 260.

[912] *The Zephyr* [1985] 2 Lloyd's Rep. 529 at 538, disapproving the contrary view expressed by Hobhouse J. at first instance ([1984] 1 Lloyd's Rep. 58 at 85), but his view appears to be approved by a later Court of Appeal (*Goshawk Dedicated Ltd v Tyser & Co* [2006] EWCA Civ 54) in support of an "implied contract" between an insurance broker and an underwriter: "Although that case (*The Zephyr*) was brought in tort, the language is as close to contract as it is possible to go" (at [65]).

[913] *Hall v Palmer* (1844) 3 Hare 532; *Macedo v Stroud* [1922] 2 A.C. 330.

clear on its face that it is intended to be a deed[914] and must be validly executed as
such.[915] At common law, execution of an instrument as a deed had to be under
seal, but in many cases the requirement of sealing has been abolished by legislation.[916] Sealing is no longer necessary in the case of an instrument executed as a
deed by an individual.[917] To be validly executed as a deed, such an instrument[918]
must be signed[919] by or at the direction of the person making it in the presence of
one attesting witness if it is signed by that person or of two such witnesses if it is
signed at his direction[920]; it must also be delivered.[921] Sealing is also no longer
necessary for the execution of a deed by a company incorporated under the
Companies Acts: a document signed by two "authorized signatories",[922] or by a
director of the company in the presence of a witness who attests the signature has
the same effect as if executed under the common seal of the company[923]; and (even
if the company has no common seal[924]) a document executed by the company
which makes it clear on its face that it is intended to be a deed has effect upon
delivery as a deed.[925] Similar rules apply to charities incorporated under the
Charities Act 1993.[926] Under the system of electronic conveyancing made possible
by the Land Registration Act 2002, certain electronic documents relating to the
transfer of interests in land[927] are to be regarded as deeds "for the purposes of any
enactment".[928]

Sealing. The common law requirement of sealing, where it is still required, has   3–171
been laxly interpreted. There need be no actual seal: it is enough if the document

---

[914] *HSBC Trust Co(UK) Ltd v Quinn* [2007] EWHC 1543 (Ch).

[915] Law of Property (Miscellaneous Provisions) Act 1989, s.1(2), as amended by Regulatory Reform
(Execution of Deeds and Documents) Order 2005 (SI 2005/1906), art.7(3). The requirement to make
clear the intention to create a deed is separate from the requirement of valid execution; such intention
is not made clear merely because the instrument has been executed under seal: Law of Property
(Miscellaneous Provisions) Act 1989, s.1(2A), as inserted by the 2005 Order, art.8. The 2005 Order,
which gives effect to the principal recommendations of the Law Commission (Law Com. No.253) has
also introduced new provisions to the 1989 Act "clarifying" the application of these requirements
where an instrument is executed by one person on behalf of another: ss.1(2)(b) and 4(A).

[916] In addition to the provisions referred to below, the requirement of sealing has been somewhat
attenuated for corporations aggregate (but not corporations sole): Law of Property Act 1925, s.74(1) as
substituted by Regulatory Reform (Execution of Deeds and Documents) Order 2005 (SI 2005/1906),
art.3.

[917] 1989 Act, above, s.1(1)(b).

[918] On what is, and is not, permissible to produce the instrument in accordance with the requirements in s.1(3), see *R. (on the application of Mercury Tax Group Ltd) v Revenue and Customs
Commissioners* [2008] EWHC 2721; [2009] S.T.C. 743 at [40].

[919] Making one's mark suffices: Law of Property (Miscellaneous Provisions) Act 1989, s.1(4).

[920] Law of Property (Miscellaneous Provisions) Act 1989, s.1(3)(a). In *Shah v Shah* [2001] EWCA
Civ 527; [2001] 4 All E.R. 138 it was held that, though the requirement of signing was "fundamental"
(at [28]), the requirement of the attesting witness' presence at the time of the signature was not; and
that the maker of the instrument could be estopped from denying that the latter requirement was
satisfied where, by delivering the instrument, he had unambiguously represented that the instrument
had been validly executed.

[921] Law of Property (Miscellaneous Provisions) Act 1989, s.1(3)(b).

[922] As defined by Companies Act 2006, s.44(3).

[923] ibid. s.44(4). This provision (formerly Companies Act 1985, s.36(A)(4)) can apply where a
document purporting to be sealed is not properly sealed: *OTV Birwelco Ltd v Technical & General
Guarantee Co* [2002] EWHC 2240 (TCC); [2002] 4 All E.R. 668 at [70]; cf. *Williams v Redcard Ltd*
[2011] EWCA Civ 466.

[924] ibid. s.45(1).

[925] ibid. s.46(1).

[926] Charities Act 1993, ss.50, 60.

[927] See below, para.5–008.

[928] Land Registration Act 2002, s.91(5).

indicates where the seal is meant to be, and is signed with the intention of executing it as a deed.[929]

3–172   **Delivery.** Delivery does not mean transfer of possession, but conduct indicating that the person who has executed the deed intends to be bound by it.[930] Delivery can be effected by giving the deed to the beneficiary, or to a third person to hold for him, but it is perfectly possible for the grantor to "deliver" the deed and yet keep possession of it.[931] In the case of both a corporation aggregate[932] and a company incorporated under the Companies Act 2006,[933] a document is presumed to be delivered upon its being executed,[934] unless a contrary intention appears. Similar rules apply to charities incorporated under the Charities Act 1993.[935]

3–173   **Delivered as an escrow.** A document may be executed as a deed and delivered with the intention that it is to take effect only on the occurrence of some condition. The document is then said to be delivered as an escrow.[936] It will become effective as a deed only if the condition occurs; though it may then relate back to the date of the original delivery. For example, if the document is a lease, rent under it is payable from that date, unless the document specifies some other date.[937] Even before the occurrence of the condition, the document has some legal effect; it cannot be revoked by the grantor so long as it remains possible for the condition to occur.[938] The document will, however, cease to have this effect if the condition fails to occur within the time specified for its occurrence by the document.[939] Where no such time is specified, a term is likely to be implied that the condition must be fulfilled within a reasonable time.[940]

It is sometimes difficult to distinguish between a deed which has not been delivered at all and one which has been delivered as an escrow.[941] The distinction depends on the intention of the grantor. If he reserves an overriding power to recall the deed at his discretion, it is not delivered as an escrow but is simply an undelivered deed.[942]

---

[929] *First National Securities Ltd v Jones* [1978] Ch. 109; Hoath 43 M.L.R. 415. Contrast *TCB Ltd v Gray* [1987] Ch. 48; *Rushingdale SA v Byblos Bank SAL* 1985 P.C.C. 342.

[930] *Xenos v Wickham* (1866) L.R. 2 H.L. 296; cf. *Beesly v Hallwood Estates Ltd* [1960] 1 W.L.R. 549 at 562, affirmed [1961] Ch. 105; *Vincent v Premo Enterprises (Voucher Sales) Ltd* [1969] 2 Q.B. 609; Yale [1970] C.L.J. 52.

[931] *Doe v Knight* (1826) 5 B. & C. 671.

[932] Law of Property Act 1925, s.74(A)(2), as inserted by Regulatory Reform (Execution of Deeds and Documents) Order 2005 (SI 2005/1906), art.4.

[933] Companies Act 2006, s.46(2).

[934] The requirements for valid execution still differ as between the two: above, para.3–170.

[935] Charities Act 1993, s.60(7) and (8).

[936] See, e.g. *Davy Offshore Ltd v Emerald Field Contracting Ltd* [1992] 2 Lloyd's Rep. 142 at 155.

[937] *Alan Estates Ltd v W G Stores Ltd* [1982] Ch. 511.

[938] ibid. at 520–521 and 527 rejecting a dictum in *Terrapin International Investments v IRC* [1976] 1 W.L.R. 665 at 669 that before the condition is fulfilled the escrow has "no effect whatsoever"; cf. above, para.2–106.

[939] *Glessing v Green* [1975] 1 W.L.R. 863.

[940] *Alan Estates Ltd v W G Stores Ltd* [1982] Ch. 511 at 520.

[941] See *Vincent v Premo Enterprises (Voucher Sales) Ltd* [1969] 2 Q.B. 609; *Kingston v Ambrian Investments Ltd* [1975] 1 W.L.R. 161.

[942] *Windsor Refrigerator Co Ltd v Branch Nominees Ltd* [1961] Ch. 88 at 102; actual decision reversed on other grounds [1961] Ch. 375; cf. *Silver Queen Maritime Ltd v Persia Petroleum Services Plc* [2010] EWHC 2867 (QB).

10. PROPOSALS FOR REFORM

Criticism.[943] The doctrine of consideration has attracted much criticism on   3–174
general and on particular grounds. It has been said that the doctrine is an historical
accident; that foreign systems do without it; and that it can easily be evaded, e.g.
by the device of nominal consideration.[944] But these criticisms fail to come to grips
with the fundamental question: whether it is desirable to enforce informal gratuitous promises. So long as the rights and interests of third parties are adequately
protected,[945] the enforcement of such promises may do no harm. On the other
hand, English law does recognise, in the deed, a perfectly safe and relatively simple
means of making gratuitous promises binding. Many such promises are in fact
made by deed for tax purposes; and for this reason the legal enforceability of
promises to give money to charitable institutions presents no serious problem in
England.[946] Moreover, the small amount of extra effort, which the execution of a
deed requires the promisor to make, may be a useful safeguard against rash
promises.[947] The availability of the deed does not solve the problem of action in
reliance on an *informal* gratuitous promise; but where there is such action the
court may be able to invent consideration, or to give at least some effect to the
promise under the doctrine of waiver or in equity.[948]

The doctrine can also cause inconvenience where the law for some reason treats
a promise as not being supported by consideration even though the parties
reasonably regard it as having been made for value.[949] This is particularly true in
the existing duty cases, and in the cases on part payment of a debt. In those cases
the doctrine of consideration may indeed at one time have performed a useful
function in protecting a promisor against undue pressure or other undesirable
conduct on the part of the promisee.[950] But this function is now more satisfactorily
provided by the expanding notion of duress,[951] and the authorities have recognised
this point, by holding that the requirement of consideration can be satisfied by the
performance of, or the promise to perform, an existing duty, even if it causes no
legal detriment to the promisee, so long as it results in a factual benefit to the
promisor.[952] On the other hand, the function of the doctrine in providing protection against the different risk of being bound by rashly made gratuitous promises
remains an important one and must be taken into account in formulating proposals
for reform.

Proposals for reform. A number of such proposals were made in 1937 by the   3–175
Law Revision Committee.[953] Detailed discussion of these proposals no longer

---

[943] *Gay Choon Ing v Loh Sze Ti Terence Peter* [2009] 2 S.L.R. 332 at [92]–[118].

[944] See above, para.3–014.

[945] cf. above, para.3–013; *Eastwood v Kenyon* (1840) 11 A. & E. 438 at 450 and *Horrocks v Forray*
[1976] 1 W.L.R. 230 (where a finding that there was no consideration helped to protect the creditors
of the alleged promisor).

[946] There appear to be only two reported cases in which such claims failed for want of consideration;
Re Hudson (1885) 54 L.J.Ch. 811 and *Re Cory* (1912) 29 T.L.R. 18.

[947] cf. below, para.5–002.

[948] See above, paras 3–009, 3–076—3–092, 3–111—3–117.

[949] e.g. above, paras 3–043—3–052, 3–100—3–101.

[950] See above, paras 3–044, 3–100.

[951] See above, para.3–048; below, para.10–005.

[952] *Pao On v Lau Yiu Long* [1980] A.C. 614; above, para.3–055; *Williams v Roffey Bros & Nicholls
(Contractors) Ltd* [1991] 1 Q.B. 1; above, para.3–050.

[953] 6th Interim Report, Cmnd.5449; Hamson 54 L.Q.R. 233; Hays 41 Col.L.Rev. 849; Chloros 17
I.C.L.Q. 137; Beatson [1992] C.L.P. 1.

seems to be appropriate since some of them have been overtaken by later develop-ments in the law[954] and since proposals for reform, if now revived, would no doubt differ substantially[955] from those made in 1937. Two central questions remain: first, whether the law should protect the promisor and third parties by retaining restrictions on the enforceability of gratuitous promises; and secondly, to what extent the law should protect a promisee who has reasonably acted in reliance on a promise which is not supported by consideration. So far as the second question is concerned, the present law amounts to a compromise solution,[956] giving the promisee *some* remedy on the ground of such reliance. This compromise could be carried further[957] by providing that the promisee, while not necessarily entitled in full to the promised performance,[958] should at least be compensated to the extent to which he has been prejudiced as a result of his reliance on the promise.[959]

---

[954] e.g. in the cases on existing duties as consideration, on promissory estoppel and on proprietary estoppel.

[955] Contrast the Committee's recommendations that "firm offers" should be binding with the more sophisticated proposals, on this subject in Law Commission Working Paper 60 (1975), above, para.3–161.

[956] See above, paras 3–076—3–152.

[957] e.g. by allowing "promissory estoppel" (above, para.3–090) to give rise to a cause of action or by extending the categories of cases covered by proprietary estoppel (above, para.3–118).

[958] The qualification would not preclude such enforcement at the discretion of the court, as at present in cases of proprietary estoppel: above, para.3–143.

[959] cf. para.3–093, above, and *Restatements, Contracts*, §90. Restatement 2d, *Contracts*, §90 imposes somewhat less stringent conditions and concludes: "The remedy . . . may be limited as justice requires."

CHAPTER FOUR

CONTRACTUAL INTENTION

An agreement, though supported by consideration, is not binding as a contract   **4–001** if it was made without any intention of creating legal relations.

1. ILLUSTRATIONS

(a) Mere Puffs

A statement inducing a contract may be so vague, or so clearly one of opinion,   **4–002** that the law refuses to give it any contractual effect.[1] Even a statement that is perfectly precise may nevertheless not be binding if the court considers that it was not seriously meant.[2] Thus in in *Lambert v Lewis*[3] a manufacturer stated in promotional literature that his product was "foolproof" and that it "required no maintenance". These statements did not give rise to a contract between the manufacturer and a dealer (who had bought the product from an intermediary) as they were "not intended to be, nor were they, acted on as being express warranties".[4]

(b) Other Statements Inducing a Contract

A statement inducing a person to enter into a contract may be *either* "mere   **4–003** representation" *or* a term of the contract. The distinction between these categories turns on the intention with which the statement was made.[5] In most cases on this subject the question is merely as to the *contents* of a contract which is proved or admitted to exist. But sometimes the test of intention determines the very existence of the contract itself. This happens when a statement inducing a

---

[1] See below, paras 9–007—9–008.

[2] *Weeks v Tybald* (1605) Noy 11; cf. *Dalrymple v Dalrymple* (1811) 2 Hag.Con. 54 at 105.

[3] [1982] A.C. 225; affirmed, so far as the manufacturer's liability was concerned, but on other grounds, [1982] A.C. 225 at 271.

[4] ibid. at 262; contrast *Carlill v Carbolic Smoke Ball Co Ltd* [1893] 1 Q.B. 256 and *Bowerman v Association of British Travel Agents* [1995] N.L.J. 1815; above, para.2–010. cf. Sale of Goods Act 1979, s.14(2D); Supply of Goods and Services Act 1983, s.4(2B).

[5] See below, para.9–045 et seq.

principal contract for some reason cannot take effect as one of its terms, but only as a collateral contract.[6] In *Heilbut, Symons & Co v Buckleton*[7] the claimant said to the defendants' manager that he understood the defendants to be "bringing out a rubber company." The manager replied that they were, on the strength of which statement the claimant applied for, and was allotted, shares in the company. It turned out not to be a rubber company and the claimant alleged that the defendants had warranted that it was a rubber company. It was held that nothing said by the defendants' manager was intended to have contractual effect.

"Not only the terms of such contracts, but the existence of an *animus contrahendi* on the part of all the parties to them must be clearly shewn".[8]

It follows that a statement made in the course of negotiations will not take effect as a collateral contract where the terms of the main contract show that the parties did not intend the statement to have such effect.[9] This may, for example, be the position where the main contract contains an "entire agreement" clause which shows that statements made in the course of negotiations are to "have no contractual force".[10]

(c) Intention Expressly Negatived

4–004   An agreement has no contractual force if it expressly negatives the intention to be legally bound.[11] It is a question of construction whether a particular provision has this effect.[12]

4–005   **Honour clauses.** In *Rose & Frank Co v J R Crompton & Bros Ltd*[13] an agency agreement provided:

---

[6] See below, paras 5–009, 6–029, 9–051, 14–006—14–008. Under Sale and Supply of Goods to Consumers Regulations 2002 (SI 2002/3045), reg.15(1), a "consumer guarantee" given on the sale or supply of goods to a consumer "takes effect as a contractual obligation owed by the guarantor"; it seems so to take effect by force of the Regulations, without regard to the issue of contractual intention.

[7] [1913] A.C. 30; *IBA v EMI Electronics Ltd* (1980) 14 Build. L.R. 1; cf. *Strover v Harrington* [1988] Ch. 390 at 410. The Regulations referred to above, fn.6, would not apply on facts such as those of any of the cases cited in this note.

[8] At 47; *Unit Construction Co Ltd v Liverpool Corp* (1972) 221 E.G. 459; *The Kapetan Markos NL (No.2)* [1987] 2 Lloyd's Rep. 323 at 332. For possible effects of Misrepresentation Act 1967, s.2 on such statements, see below, para.9–052.

[9] *Business Environment Bow Lane Ltd v Deanwater Estates* [2007] EWCA Civ 622; [2007] 32 E.G. 90.

[10] *Inntrepreneur Pub Co (GL) v East Crown Ltd* [2000] 2 Lloyd's Rep. 611 at 614; cf. *White v Bristol Rugby Club Ltd* [2002] I.R.L.R. 204; *Cheverny Consulting Ltd v Whitehead Mann Ltd* [2005] EWHC 243; [2006] EWCA Civ 1303 (where the "agreement" made entire was held to include a side-letter executed simultaneously with the main contract; for further proceedings, but not on this point: [2007] EWHC 3130 (Comm)); *Lloyd v MGL (Rugby) Ltd* [2007] EWCA Civ 153; (2007) 22 E.G. 162 (entire agreement clause did not prevent reliance on the parties' "understanding" for the purpose of proprietary estoppel) .

[11] e.g. *Broadwick Financial Services Ltd v Spencer* [2002] EWCA Civ 35; [2002] 1 All E.R. (Comm) 446 at [27].

[12] *R. v Lord Chancellor's Departments Ex p. Nangle* [1991] I.C.R. 743.

[13] [1925] A.C. 445; [1923] 2 K.B. 261; *County Ltd v Girozentrale Securities* [1996] 3 All E.R. 834; cf. similar provisions in football pool coupons: *Jones v Vernon's Pools* [1938] 2 All E.R. 464; *Appleson v Littlewoods* [1939] 1 All E.R. 464. In Scotland, it has been argued that such honour clauses in football coupons may be unreasonable and hence ineffective: *Ferguson v Littlewoods Pools* [1997] S.L.T. 309 at 314–315.

"This arrangement is not entered into, nor is this memorandum written, as a formal or legal agreement, and shall not be subject to legal jurisdiction in the Law Courts ... but is only a definite expression and record of the purpose and intention of the ... parties concerned, to which they each honourably pledge themselves ...."

These words were held to negative contractual intention, so that the agreement did not amount to a legally binding contract. On the other hand, contractual intention was not negatived where an arbitration clause in a reinsurance contract provided that "this treaty shall be interpreted as an honourable engagement rather than as a legal obligation ... ". The contract as a whole was clearly intended to be legally binding and the purpose of the words quoted was merely to free the arbitrator "to some extent from strict legal rules"[14] in interpreting the agreement.

Agreement subject to contract. An agreement may be made "subject to   4–006
contract", either expressly,[15] or by implication.[16] Such an agreement is incomplete until the details of a formal contract have been settled and approved by the parties.[17] But even when the terms of the formal contract have been agreed, there is no binding contract until the parties have gone through the procedure necessary to indicate that the agreement is no longer "subject to contract",[18] e.g. in contracts for the sale of land by private treaty,[19] when there has been an "exchange of contracts".[20] Before the "exchange", there is no uncertainty as to the terms of the agreement, but there is no contract because neither party intends to be legally bound until the "exchange of contracts" takes place.

Exchange of contracts. Contracts for the sale of land must satisfy certain   4–007
formal requirements. Each party must sign a document containing all the terms which have been expressly agreed[21]; and the requirement of exchange traditionally refers to the handing over by each party to the other of one of these documents, or to their despatch by post; if the later method is adopted, the process is completed on the receipt of the second of the posted documents.[22] This state of the law, which enables either party with impunity to go back on a concluded agreement prior to exchange, has been described as "a social and moral blot on the

---

[14] *Home Insurance Co v Administratia Asigurarilor* [1983] 2 Lloyd's Rep. 674 at 677; cf. *Overseas Union Ins Ltd v International Ins Ltd* [1988] 2 Lloyd's Rep. 65; *Home & Overseas Ins Co Ltd v Mentor Ins (UK) Ltd* [1989] 1 Lloyd's Rep. 473.

[15] Without needing to use the words "subject to contract" as such: *RTS Flexible Systems Ltd v Molkerei Alois Müller GmbH & Co KG* [2010] UKSC 14; [2010] 1 W.L.R. 753.

[16] *Moria v Bednash* [2011] EWHC 839 (Ch).

[17] See above, para.2–088.

[18] *Rose & Frank Co v J R Crompton & Bros Ltd* [1923] 2 K.B. 261 at 294.

[19] Such agreements are usually made "subject to contract", but not always: *Storer v Manchester CC* [1974] 1 W.L.R. 1403; *Tweddell v Henderson* [1975] 1 W.L.R. 1496 at 1501–1502.

[20] *Eccles v Bryant & Pollock* [1948] Ch. 93; cf. *Coope v Ridout* [1921] 1 Ch. 291; *Chillingworth v Esche* [1924] 1 Ch. 97; *Raingold v Bromley* [1931] 2 Ch. 307; *D'Silva v Lister House Development Ltd* [1971] Ch. 17; *Bolton MBC v Torkington* [2003] EWCA Civ 1634; [2004] Ch. 66 at [53].

[21] Law of Property (Miscellaneous Provisions) Act 1989, s.2(1), (3). This is dealt with in more detail below, para.5–008.

[22] See *Commission for the New Towns v Cooper (Great Britain) Ltd* [1995] Ch. 259 at 285, 289; cf. [1995] Ch. 259 at 293, 295. No doubt the mechanics of "exchange" will be suitably modified when the proposed system of electronic conveyancing is brought into operation on the making of Orders under Land Registration Act 2002.

law"[23]; and the courts have been prepared to mitigate the strictness of the requirement of "exchange of contracts". Thus it has been held that the exchange may be effected by telephone or telex[24]; that certain technical slips in the process may be disregarded[25]; that exchange is not necessary where the parties use the same solicitor[26]; and (in Australia) that where the two parts do not match precisely there may nevertheless be a contract, the discrepancy being remedied by rectification.[27]

4–008   **Waiving subject to contract.** The parties may also create a binding contract by a subsequent agreement to remove the effect of the words "subject to contract," thus indicating their intention henceforth to be legally bound.[28] The court will "not lightly so hold",[29] but while any such agreement to waive reliance must be "unequivocal", it need not be express if it can be inferred from communications between the parties and the conduct of one party known to the other.[30] In *RTS Flexible Systems Ltd v Molkerei Alois Müller GmbH & Co KG*[31] the parties negotiated for a contract for the installation of a packaging line on the basis of certain terms, one of which stated that "it shall not become effective until each party has executed a counterpart and exchanged it with the other." No execution or exchange had taken place, but the Supreme Court found that the parties were nonetheless bound. The "striking features" of the case were that essentially all the terms had been agreed,[32] substantial works had been carried out[33] and the agreement was "varied" in important respects.

4–009   **Liability on other grounds.** Subsequent conduct may also give rise to liability on other grounds: where one party to the agreement encourages the other to believe that he will not withdraw, and the other acts to his detriment in reliance on that belief, the former may be liable on the basis of "proprietary estoppel".[34]

---

[23] *Cohen v Nessdale* [1981] 3 All E.R. 118 at 128 (affirmed [1982] 2 All E.R. 97); cf. Law Com. No.65.

[24] *Domb v Isoz* [1980] Ch. 548.

[25] *Harrison v Battye* [1975] 1 W.L.R. 58.

[26] *Smith v Mansi* [1963] 1 W.L.R. 26; exchange is also unnecessary in the case of a deed, which takes effect as soon as it has been duly executed (below, paras 3–170—3–173): *Vincent v Premo Enterprises Ltd* [1969] 2 Q.B. 609; *D'Silva v Lister House Development Ltd* [1971] Ch. 17.

[27] *Sindel v Georgio* (1984) 1454 C.L.R. 661; for rectification see below, para.8–059 et seq.

[28] *Law v Jones* [1974] Ch. 112, as explained in *Daulia v Four Millbank Nominees* [1978] Ch. 231 at 250; *Cohen v Nessdale* [1981] 3 All E.R. 118 at 127; [1982] 2 All E.R. 97 at 104; see also *Tiverton Estates Ltd v Wearwell* [1975] Ch. 146. In the context of settlement agreements, see: *Jirehouse Capital v Beller* [2009] EWHC 2538 (Ch); cf. *Morgan Walker Solicitors LLP v Zurich Professional and Financial Lines* [2010] EWHC 1532 (Ch).

[29] *RTS Flexible Systems Ltd v Molkerei Alois Müller GmbH & Co KG* [2010] UKSC 14; [2010] 1 W.L.R. 753 at [56].

[30] [2010] 1 W.L.R. 753 at [67].

[31] ibid.

[32] The Supreme Court found that the parties were bound to those terms which had been agreed. The trial judge had found there was a simple contract for a price and no more ([2008] EWHC 1087 (TCC)); the Court of Appeal had found that there was no contract at all ([2009] EWCA Civ 26; [2009] B.L.R. 181).

[33] Initially under a letter of intent, but the parties agreed that that had expired; cf. *Diamond Build Ltd v Clapham Park Homes Ltd* [2008] EWHC 1439 (TCC); 119 Con L.R. 32 where the parties' failure to execute the required formal contract meant that they continued to be bound by the terms of a letter of intent: see below, para.4–018.

[34] See the discussion at para.3–127, above of *Attorney-General of Hong Kong v Humphreys Estate (Queen's Gardens)* [1987] A.C. 114; cf. *Cobbe v Yeoman's Row Management Ltd* [2008] UKHL 55; [2008] 1 W.L.R. 1752 at [25]–[26].

If no contract is formed, but one party has done work which has benefited the other, a quantum meruit may be awarded to the party which has done the work.[35]

Exceptions to the requirement. In "a very strong and exceptional context"[36] the court may infer that the parties intended to be legally bound when executing the original document, even though it is expressed to be "subject to contract". This was held to be the position where a document containing these words laid down an elaborate timetable, imposed a duty on the purchaser to approve the draft contract (subject only to reasonable amendments) and required him then to exchange contracts.[37] In these exceptional circumstances, the words "subject to contract" were taken merely to mean that the parties had not yet settled all the details of the transaction and therefore not to negative the intention to be bound.

Agreements for the sale of land by auction or by tender are not normally made "subject to contract". The intention of the parties in such cases is to enter into a binding contract as soon as an offer to buy has been accepted. In one case[38] of a sale by tender, the words "subject to contract" were, by a clerical error, typed on one of the contractual documents. In these highly exceptional circumstances,[39] the words were held to be meaningless, so that there was a binding contract.[40]

Collateral contract. A party's freedom to withdraw from an agreement "subject to contract" may also be restricted by a collateral contract. For example, a vendor who has agreed to sell land "subject to contract" may, either at the same time or subsequently, undertake not to negotiate for the sale of the land with a third party. Such a collateral agreement (sometimes called a "lock-out" agreement) must satisfy the requirement of certainty[41] and in *Walford v Miles*[42] it was held that this requirement had not been satisfied where the agreement failed to specify the time for which the vendor's freedom to negotiate with third parties was to be restricted. But in a later case[43] it was held that a vendor's promise not to negotiate with third parties *for two weeks* was sufficient to satisfy the requirement of certainty and so to give rise to a collateral contract.[44]

Other phrases. The words "ex gratia" in a promise to make a payment to a dismissed employee have been held not to negative contractual intention: they merely mean that the employers did not admit any pre-existing liability to make

4–010

4–011

4–012

---

[35] See para.2–021 below.

[36] *Alpenstow Ltd v Regalian Properties Ltd* [1985] 1 W.L.R. 721 at 730; Harpum [1986] C.L.J. 356.

[37] ibid.

[38] *Michael Richard Properties Ltd v St Saviour's Parish* [1975] 3 All E.R. 416; Emery [1976] C.L.J. 28.

[39] See also *Munton v GLC* [1976] 1 W.L.R. 649.

[40] *Westway Homes v Moore* (1991) 63 P. & C.R. 480.

[41] See above, para.2–078.

[42] [1992] 2 A.C. 128. See further para.2–100, above.

[43] *Pitt v PHH Asset Management Ltd* [1993] 1 W.L.R. 327; cf. *Tye v House* [1997] 2 E.G.L.R. 171; *JSD Corporation Pte Ltd v Al Waha Capital PJSC* [2009] EWHC 3376 (Ch) where the court found the criteria necessary to determine that the lock out would last for a reasonable time.

[44] For the consideration for this promise, see below, para.3–160.

the payment.[45] Contractual intention was likewise not negatived where a ship-owner, during negotiations for a charterparty said: "we are fixed in good faith".[46] If these words had any effect, they amounted merely to a "collateral under-standing"[47] that account should be taken of damage to the vessel, of which both shipowner and charterer were aware.

(d) Social and Domestic Arrangements

4–013　　**Social arrangements.** Many social arrangements do not amount to contracts because they are not intended to be legally binding.

> "The ordinary example is where two parties agree to take a walk together, or where there is an offer and an acceptance of hospitality."[48]

Similarly it has been held that the winner of a competition held by a golf club could not sue for his prize where "no one concerned with that competition ever intended that there should be any legal results flowing from the conditions posted and the acceptance by the competitor of those conditions"[49]; that the rules of a competition organised by a "jalopy club" for charitable purposes did not have contractual force[50]; that "car pool" and similar arrangements between friends or neighbours did not amount to contracts even though one party contributed to the running costs of the other's vehicle[51]; that an agreement between members of a group of friends relating to musical performances by the group was not intended to have contractual effect[52]; and that the provision of free residential accommoda-tion for close friends did not amount to a contract as it was an act of bounty, done without any intention to enter into legal relations.[53]

4–014　　**Domestic arrangements.** For the same reason, many domestic arrangements lack contractual force. In *Balfour v Balfour*[54] a husband who worked abroad promised to pay an allowance of £30 per month to his wife, who had to stay in England on medical grounds. The wife's attempt to enforce this promise by action failed for two reasons: she had not provided any consideration, and the parties did not intend the arrangement to be legally binding. On the second ground alone, most domestic arrangements between husband and wife are not contracts. Atkin L.J. said:

---

[45] *Edwards v Skyways Ltd* [1964] 1 W.L.R. 349; it was admitted that there was consideration moving from the employee.

[46] *The Mercedes Envoy* [1995] 2 Lloyd's Rep. 559.

[47] ibid. at 612.

[48] *Balfour v Balfour* [1919] 2 K.B. 571 at 578; *Rose & Frank Co v J R Crompton & Bros Ltd* [1923] 2 K.B. 261 at 293; *Wyatt v Kreglinger & Fernau* [1933] 1 K.B. 793 at 806. In addition to the examples following, see also: *Coward v MIB* [1963] 1 Q.B. 259.

[49] *Lens v Devonshire Club, The Times,* December 4, 1914; referred to in *Wyatt*'s case, above, from which the quotation in the text is taken.

[50] *White v Blackmore* [1972] 2 Q.B. 651.

[51] *Coward v MIB* [1963] 1 Q.B. 259; overruled, but not on the issue of contractual intention, in *Albert v MIB* [1972] A.C. 301; *Buckpitt v Oates* [1968] 1 All E.R. 1145.

[52] *Hadley v Kemp* [1999] E.M.L.R. 589 at 623.

[53] *Heslop v Burns* [1974] 1 W.L.R. 1241.

[54] [1919] 2 K.B. 571; Hedley 5 O.J.L.S. 391.

"Those agreements, or many of them, do not result in contracts at all . . .
even though there may be what as between other parties would constitute
consideration for the agreement . . . . They are not contracts . . . because
the parties did not intend that they should be attended by legal consequences."[55]

It has been said that the facts of *Balfour v Balfour* "stretched that doctrine to its
limits"[56]; but the doctrine itself has not been judicially questioned and the cases
provide many other instances of its application.[57] It does not of course prevent a
husband from making a binding contract with his wife:[58] he can be her tenant[59];
and binding separation agreements are often made when husband and wife agree
to live apart.[60] More generally, it has been stated that "there is nothing to stop a
husband and wife from making legally binding arrangements, whether by contract
or settlement, to regulate their property and affairs", as opposed to agreements for
"housekeeping or personal allowances" of the type exemplified by *Balfour v
Balfour*.[61]

Parents and children. Such issues of contractual intention can also arise   4–015
between parents and children. An informal promise by a parent to pay a child an
allowance during study is not normally a contract, though it may become one, if,
for example, it is part of a bargain made to induce the child to give up some
occupation so as to enter on some particular course of study.[62] Similarly, where a
mother bought a house as a residence for her son and daughter-in-law on the
terms that they should pay her £7 per week to pay off the purchase price, this was
held to amount to a contractual licence which the mother could not revoke so long
as either of the young couple kept up the payments.[63] Conversely, it has been held
that the gift of a flat by a mother to her daughter on condition that the daughter
should look after the mother there did not amount to a contract because it was not
intended to have contractual force.[64]

Persons sharing a common household. The principle of *Balfour v Balfour*   4–016
can also apply where persons other than husband and wife share a common
household. While that household is an ongoing concern, many arrangements will
be made about running it from day to day, and it is unlikely that these will be
intended to be legally binding. But this may not be true of the financial terms

---

[55] At 627.
[56] *Pettitt v Pettitt* [1970] A.C. 777 at 816.
[57] e.g. *Gage v King* [1961] 1 Q.B. 188; *Spellman v Spellman* [1961] 1 W.L.R. 921; cf. *Lloyds Bank Plc v Rosset* [1991] 1 A.C. 107.
[58] *Synge v Synge* [1894] 1 Q.B. 466; cf. *Jennings v Brown* (1842) 9 M. & W. 496.
[59] *Pearce v Merriman* [1904] 1 K.B. 80; contrast *Morris v Tarrant* [1971] 2 Q.B. 143.
[60] e.g. *Merrit v Merrit* [1970] 1 W.L.R. 1211; *Tanner v Tanner* [1975] 1 W.L.R. 1346 (where the parties were not married) as explained in *Horrocks v Forray* [1976] 1 W.L.R. 230; cf. below paras 11–048—11–050.
[61] *Radmacher v Granatino* [2010] UKSC 42; [2011] A.C. 534 at [142], per Baroness Hale, said in the context of a pre-nuptial agreement where the principal issue was whether its enforcement would be contrary to public policy: below, para.11–049.
[62] See *Jones v Padavatton* [1969] 1 W.L.R. 328 at 333; cf. *Shadwell v Shadwell* (1860) 9 C.B. N.S. 159.
[63] *Hardwick v Johnson* [1978] 1 W.L.R. 683, per Roskill and Browne L.JJ.; Lord Denning M.R. thought that there was no contract but reached the same conclusion on other grounds; cf. *Collier v Holinshead* (1984) 272 E.G. 941.
[64] *Ellis v Chief Adjudication Officer* [1998] 1 F.L.R. 184 at 188.

which form the basis on which the household was established. In one case a young couple were induced to sell their house, and move in with their elderly relations, by the latter's promise to leave them a share of the proposed joint home. The argument that this promise was not intended to be legally binding was rejected as the young couple would not have taken the important step of selling their own house on the faith of a merely social arrangement.[65] In another case of this kind,[66] the fact that the promisee had helped to improve the property was relied on to support the conclusion that an express or implied promise, giving her an interest in the property, had contractual force. Formal requirements for contracts for the disposition of interests in land[67] make it unlikely that such an arrangement could now take effect as such a contract, but legal effect could be given to it by holding that it had taken effect by way of constructive trust.[68]

In view of the informality of many house-sharing arrangements, it may be hard in a particular case to say just what obligation is created. In *Hussey v Palmer*[69] the claimant spent £600 on having a room added to her son-in-law's house, on the understanding that she could live there for the rest of her life. When she left voluntarily, about a year later, it was held that there was no contract *of loan* in respect of the £600[70] but there probably was a contract to allow her to live in the room for the rest of her life.

An agreement between persons who share a common household may have nothing to do with the management of the household. In *Simpkins v Pays*[71] three ladies who lived in the same house took part in a fashion competition run by a newspaper, agreeing to pool their entries and to share the prize which any entry might win; and the agreement to share was held to be legally binding.

(e) Agreements Giving Wide Discretion to One Party

4–017   Contractual intention may be negatived where the terms of a promise leave its performance entirely to the discretion of the promisor.[72] In *Taylor v Brewer*[73] the claimant agreed to do work for a committee who resolved that he should receive "such remuneration . . . as should be deemed right." His claim for a reasonable remuneration for work done failed: the promise to pay was "merely an engagement of honour".[74] This case is now more often distinguished than followed,[75] but its reasoning would still be followed if the wording made it clear that the promise was

---

[65] *Parker v Clark* [1960] 1 W.L.R. 286; cf. *Schaefer v Schuhman* [1972] 1 W.L.R. 1286; *Lee* 88 L.Q.R. 320; *Tanner v Tanner* [1975] 1 W.L.R. 1346. Contrast *Horrocks v Forray* [1976] 1 W.L.R. 320 and *Coombes v Smith* [1986] 1 W.L.R. 808.
[66] *Eves v Eves* [1975] 1 W.L.R. 1338 at 1345, per Browne L.J. and Brightman J.
[67] Law of Property (Miscellaneous Provisions) Act 1989, s.2; below, para.5–008.
[68] The formal requirements imposed by the 1989 Act (above, fn.67) do not apply to "the creation or operation of . . . constructive trusts": s.2(5).
[69] [1972] 1 W.L.R. 1286.
[70] But she recovered the £600 on equitable grounds; cf. *Re Sharpe* [1980] 1 W.L.R. 219, where there was both a loan and an equitable right in the lender, and *Briggs v Rowan* [1991] E.G.C.S. 6.
[71] [1955] 1 W.L.R. 975.
[72] cf. above, para.3–030 for the question whether such a promise can constitute consideration for a counter-promise.
[73] (1813) 1 M. & S. 290; cf. *Shallcross v Wright* (1850) 12 Beav. 558; *Robinson v Commissioners of Customs & Excise, The Times*, April 28, 2000.
[74] 1 M. & S. at p.291.
[75] See below, para.16–084; cf. *Re Brand Estates* [1936] 3 All E.R. 374.

not intended to be legally binding.[76] A fortiori, there is no contract where performance by *each* party was left to that party's discretion.[77] Where, however, an agreement is clearly intended to have contractual effect, there is judicial support for the view that a discretion conferred by it on one party is subject to an implied term that it will not be exercised "dishonestly, for an improper purpose, capriciously or arbitrarily".[78]

An agreement may give one party discretion to terminate. That party will not be bound if his promise means "I will only perform if I do not change my mind." But the power to terminate may be inserted only as a safeguard in certain eventualities which are not exhaustively stated: e.g. a contract for the sale of land may entitle the vendor to terminate if the purchaser persists in some requisition or objection which the vendor is "unable *or unwilling* to satisfy." In such a case there is a contract and, again, the court will control the exercise of the power to terminate by insisting that the vendor must not terminate "arbitrarily, or capriciously, or unreasonably. Much less can he act in bad faith."[79]

(f) Letters of Intent or of Comfort[80]

An issue of contractual intention may arise where parties in the course of negotiations exchange "letters of intent" or where one party gives to the other a "letter of comfort".[81] The terms of such documents may negative contractual intention.[82] This was, for example, held to be the case where a company had issued a "letter of comfort" to a lender in respect of a loan to one of its subsidiaries.[83] The letter stated that "it is our policy that [the subsidiary] is at all times in a position to meet its liabilities in respect of the loan." This was interpreted to be no more than a statement of the company's present policy: it was not an undertaking that the policy would not be changed, since neither party had intended the statement to take effect as a contractual promise. On the other hand, where the language of such a document does not in terms negative contractual intention, it is open to the courts to hold the parties bound by the document; and they will, in particular, be inclined to do so where the parties have acted on the document for a long period of time or have expended considerable sums of money in reliance on it.[84] The fact that the parties envisage that the letter is to be superseded by a later,

4–018

---

[76] cf. *Re Richmond Gate Property Co Ltd* [1965] 1 W.L.R. 335; below, para.16–084.

[77] *Carmichael v National Power Plc* [1999] 1 W.L.R. 2042. cf. *Prater v Cornwall CC* [2006] EWCA Civ 102; [2006] I.C.R. 731 (no contract in discretionary "arrangement" for referral of pupils for teaching, but each referral accepted constituted a contract).

[78] See below, para.2–096, and the cases cited in fn.479.

[79] *Selkirk v Romar Investments Ltd* [1963] 1 W.L.R. 1415 at 1422. For the possible effects of Unfair Contract Terms Act 1977, s.3(2)(b)(ii) and of Unfair Terms in Consumer Contracts Regulations 1999 (esp. Sch.2, para.1(c)), see below, paras 7–068, 7–111.

[80] Furmston, in Burrows and Peel (eds.), *Contract Formation and Parties*.

[81] *Associated British Ports v Ferryways NV* [2009] EWCA Civ 189; [2009] 1 Lloyd's Rep. 595: while the label used by the parties is "not necessarily determinative" (at [24]), "a document expressed to be a letter of comfort will usually not give rise to legal obligations" (at [27]).

[82] *Snelling v John G Snelling Ltd* [1973] Q.B. 87; cf. *Montreal Gas Co v Vesey* [1900] A.C. 595; *BSC v Cleveland Bridge & Engineering Ltd* [1984] 1 All E.R. 504; *Monk Construction v Norwich Union Life Assurance Society* (1992) 62 B.L.R. 107.

[83] *Kleinwort Benson Ltd v Malaysian Mining Corp* [1989] 1 W.L.R. 379; Reynolds 104 L.Q.R. 353; Davenport [1988] L.M.C.L.Q. 290; Ayres and Moore [1989] L.M.C.L.Q. 281; Tyree 2 J.C.L. 279.

[84] cf. *Turriff Construction Ltd v Regalia Knitting Mills* (1971) 22 E.G. 169; *Wilson Smithett & Cape (Sugar) Ltd v Bangladesh Sugar and Food Industries Ltd* [1986] 1 Lloyd's Rep. 378; *Chemco Leasing SpA v Rediffusion* [1987] 1 F.T.L.R. 201.

more formal, contractual document does not, of itself, prevent it from taking effect as a contract.[85]

(g) Collective Agreements

4–019   Agreements as to rates of wages and conditions of work are commonly reached after collective bargaining between trade unions and employers or associations of employers. The general common law view was that such collective agreements were prima facie not intended to be legally binding[86] as between the trade unions and the employers.[87] The Trade Union and Labour Relations (Consolidation) Act 1992 goes further in providing that a collective agreement[88] is *"conclusively* presumed not to have been intended by the parties to be a legally enforceable contract" unless it is in writing and expressly provides the contrary (in which case the agreement is conclusively presumed to have been intended by the parties to be a legally enforceable contract).[89] To displace the presumption that a collective agreement is not intended to be a legally binding contract, the agreement must provide that it was intended to be *legally* binding. The presumption is not displaced by a statement that the parties shall be "bound" by the agreement, for this may mean that they are to be bound in honour only.[90]

(h) Other Cases

4–020   The cases in which there is no intention to create legal relations cannot be exhaustively classified. Contractual intention may be negatived by many factors other than those listed above: e.g. by evidence that "the agreement was a goodwill agreement ... made without any intention of creating legal relations"[91]; that it was a sham, made with "no intention ... to create legal relations"[92]; that the parties had not yet completed the contractual negotiations[93]; and, where a landlord had agreed not to enforce an order for possession against a tenant who had fallen into arrears with her rent, it was held that the parties "plainly did not intend"[94] the agreement to have contractual force, but intended it merely to turn the tenant into a "tolerated trespasser".[95]

---

[85] See above, para.2–099; *Diamond Build Ltd v Clapham Park Homes Ltd* [2008] EWHC 1439 (TCC); 119 Con L.R. 32.

[86] *Ford Motor Co Ltd v AEF* [1969] 1 W.L.R. 339.

[87] For the position between employer and employee where the terms of a collective agreement are incorporated in individual contracts of employment, see below, para.6–047.

[88] As defined by s.178(1) and (2) of the 1992 Act.

[89] s.179(1) and (2); *The Universe Sentinel* [1983] A.C. 366 at 380. cf. *Cheall v APEX* [1983] 1 A.C. 180 at 189 (inter-union agreement); provisions making collective agreements legally binding are said to be rare: see *Commission of the European Communities v United Kingdom* [1984] I.C.R. 192 at 195.

[90] *NCB v NUM* [1986] I.C.R. 736.

[91] *Orion Ins Co Plc v Sphere Drake Ins Plc* [1990] 1 Lloyd's Rep. 465 at 505, affirmed [1992] 1 Lloyd's Rep. 239; cf. *County Ltd v Girozentrale Securities* [1996] 3 All E.R. 834 at 837; *Clarke v Nationwide Building Society* (1998) 76 P. & C.R. D5.

[92] *The Ocean Enterprise* [1997] 1 Lloyd's Rep. 449 at 484; *Hitch v Stokes* [2001] EWCA Civ 63; [2001] S.T.C. 214.

[93] *The Bay Ridge* [1999] 2 All E.R. (Comm) 306 at 329.

[94] *Burrows v Brent LBC* [1996] 1 W.L.R. 1448 at 1454. cf. *Stirling v Leadenhall Residential 2 Ltd* [2001] EWCA Civ 1011; [2002] 1 W.L.R. 499.

[95] *Burrows v Brent LBC* [1996] 1 W.L.R. 1448 at 1455.

Intention to enter into a new contract. A number of cases support the view   4–021
that an arrangement which was believed simply to give effect to pre-existing rights
was not a contract because the parties had no intention to enter into a *new*
contract[96]; this may be true even where the contract giving rise to those rights had
been discharged, so long as the parties believed that it was still in existence.[97] But
contractual intention is not negatived where the conduct of the parties to an earlier
contract makes it clear that they intended not merely to give effect to that contract
but also to enter into a new contract containing additional terms[98]; nor is contractual intention necessarily negatived where the conduct of only *one* party to the
alleged new contract consisted of his performance of an earlier contract between
him and a third party.[99]

Intention negatived by context. The context in which an agreement is made   4–022
may negative contractual intention.[100] It has been said that the appointment of a
minister of a church did not give rise to a contract as the relationship was not one
"in which the parties intended to create legal relations between themselves so as
to make the agreement . . . enforceable in the courts".[101] But in the context of
statutory protection for employees, it is now recognised "that employment
arrangements between a church and its ministers should not lightly be taken as
intended to have no legal effect and, in consequence, its ministers denied this
protection."[102] Whether there is a contract therefore depends on the facts of each
individual case.[103]

At one time, it was thought that the relationship between the Crown and one of
its civil servants was not contractual because the Crown did not, when the
relationship was entered into, have the necessary contractual intention.[104] But in
one of the cases which supported that view it was said that there was evidence that
the Crown was reconsidering its position on the point[105]; and it has been held[106]
that the requirement of contractual intention was satisfied in spite of the fact that
the terms of appointment stated that "a civil servant does not have a contract of
employment" but rather "a letter of appointment". These words were not sufficient to turn a relationship which, apart from them, had all the characteristics of
a contract into one which was binding in honour only. It has been said that a police
constable was a person who "holds an office and is not therefore strictly an

---

[96] *Beesly v Hallwood Estates Ltd* [1960] 1 W.L.R. 549 at 558, affirmed on other grounds [1961] Ch.
105; cf. *Harvela Investments Ltd v Royal Trust Co of Canada (CI) Ltd* [1986] A.C. 207. See also *The
Aramis* [1989] 1 Lloyd's Rep. 213, Treitel [1989] L.M.C.L.Q. 162; *The Gudermes* [1993] 1 Lloyd's Rep.
311; *The Happy Day* [2002] EWCA Civ 1068; [2002] 2 Lloyd's Rep. 487 at [63]; *James v Greenwich
LBC* [2008] EWCA Civ 35; [2008] I.C.R. 545 at [23].
[97] *G F Sharp & Co v McMillan* [1998] I.R.L.R. 632.
[98] *The Amazonia* [1990] 1 Lloyd's Rep. 238 at 241–242; cf. the *Stirling* case, above, fn.94, where a
new tenancy was held to arise on the parties' agreement to *increase* the rent.
[99] *Pyrene v Scindia Navigation Co Ltd* [1954] 2 Q.B. 402; *The Eurymedon* [1975] A.C. 514; cf. *Halifax
Building Society v Edell* [1992] Ch. 436.
[100] *Rederiaktiebolaget Amphitrite v R.* [1921] 2 K.B. 500 at 503.
[101] *President of the Methodist Conference v Parfitt* [1984] Q.B. 368 at 378.
[102] *Percy v Board of National Mission of Scotland* [2005] UKHL 73; [2006] 2 A.C. 28 at [26].
[103] *New Testament Church of God v Stewart* [2007] EWCA Civ 1044; [2008] I.R.L.R. 134; *Moore v
President of the Methodist Conference* March 15, 2011, EAT.
[104] See *R. v Civil Service Appeal Board Ex p. Bruce* [1988] I.C.R. 649, affirmed on other grounds
[1989] I.C.R. 171; *McLaren v Home Office* [1990] I.C.R. 824.
[105] *R. v Civil Service Appeal Board Ex p. Bruce*, above at 659.
[106] *R. v Lord Chancellor's Department Ex p. Nangle* [1991] I.C.R. 743; cf. Trade Unions and Labour
Relations (Consolidation) Act 1992, ss.62(7), 245: "deemed [for certain purposes] to constitute a
contract".

employee"[107]; and that there is "no contract between a police officer and a chief constable".[108] But it does not follow that the relationship is binding in honour only: the resulting relationship is "closely analogous to a contract of employment"[109] so that duties analogous to those arising out of such a contract may be owed to the constable.

4–023   **Intention negatived by vagueness.** The use of deliberately vague language was held to negative contractual intention where a property developer reached an "understanding" with a firm of solicitors to employ them in connection with a proposed development, but neither side entered into a definite commitment.[110] The assumption was that the parties had reached agreement, and it was the lack of contractual intention which prevented that agreement from having legal effect. Vagueness may also be a ground for concluding that the parties had never reached agreement at all.[111] This issue is separate from that of contractual intention, which strictly speaking concerns only the *effect* of an agreement which is first shown to exist. But the two issues are related in borderline cases in which the question whether an agreement exists depends on the degree of vagueness or on whether the vagueness can be resolved, e.g. by applying the standard of reasonableness; for in such cases "the absence of any intention to create legal relations"[112] may be a ground for holding that no agreement ever came into existence.[113]

4–024   **Statements made in jest or anger.** The fact that a statement was made in jest or anger may also negative contractual intention. Thus in *Licenses Ins Corp v Lawson*[114] the defendant was a director of two companies, A and B. The former company held shares in the latter and resolved, in the defendant's absence, to sell them. At a later meeting this resolution was rescinded after a heated discussion during which the defendant said that he would make good any loss which A might suffer if it kept the shares in B. It was held that the defendant was not liable on this undertaking. Nobody at the meeting regarded it as a contract; it was not recorded as such in the minute book; and the defendant's fellow-directors at most thought that he was bound in honour.

4–025   **Free travel pass.** There are conflicting decisions on the question whether the issue and acceptance of a free travel pass amounts to a contract. In *Wilkie v LPTB*[115] it was held that such a pass issued by a transport undertaking to one of its own employees did not amount to a contract. But the contrary conclusion was reached in *Gore v Van der Lann*[116] where the pass was issued to an old age

---

[107] *White v Chief Constable of the South Yorkshire Police* [1999] A.C. 455 at 481.

[108] ibid. at 497. Nor is there between a GP and a Health Authority: *Essex Strategic HA v David-John* [2004] I.C.R. 112

[109] ibid.; see also *Waters v Commissioner of Police to the Metropolis* [2000] 1 W.L.R. 1607 at 1616.

[110] *J H Milner & Son v Percy Bilton Ltd* [1966] 1 W.L.R. 1582; cf. *Baird Textile Holdings Ltd v Marks & Spencer Plc* [2001] EWCA Civ 274; [2002] 1 All E.R. (Comm) 737 at [10], [46], [47], [73], [76]. See also: *Vaughan v Vaughan* [1953] 1 Q.B. 762 at 765; cf. *Jones v Padavatton* [1969] 1 W.L.R. 328; *Windeler v Whitehall* [1990] 2 F.L.R. 505.

[111] See above, para.2–079.

[112] *Baird Textile Holdings Ltd v Marks & Spencer Plc*, above, fn.110 at [30]; and see above, para.2–081.

[113] *Judge v Crown Leisure Ltd* [2005] EWCA Civ 571; [2005] I.R.L.R. 823 at [9], [24].

[114] (1896) 12 T.L.R. 501.

[115] [1947] 1 All E.R. 258.

[116] [1967] 2 Q.B. 31.

pensioner. This conclusion was based on the ground that an application for the pass had been made on a form couched in contractual language; and *Wilkie*'s case was distinguished on the ground that the pass there was issued to the employee "as a matter of course . . . as one of the privileges attaching to his employment".[117] But as the pass in *Gore*'s case was issued expressly on the "understanding" that it constituted only a licence subject to conditions the distinction seems, with respect, to be a tenuous one.

(i) Proof of Contractual Intention

The question of contractual intention is, in the last resort, one of fact.[118] In deciding it, a distinction must be drawn between implied and express agreements.[119] Claims based on *implied* agreements are approached on the basis that "contracts are not lightly to be implied" and that the court must therefore be able "to conclude with confidence that . . . the parties intended to create contractual relations".[120] The burden of proof on this issue is on the proponent of the implied contract, and in a number of cases claims or defences based on implied contracts have been rejected precisely on the ground that contractual intention had not been shown by that party to exist.[121] But where a claim is based on a proved or admitted *express* agreement the courts do not require, in addition, proof that parties to an ordinary commercial relationship actually intended to be bound. On the contrary, the onus of proving that there was no such intention "is on the party who asserts that no legal effect was intended, and the onus is a heavy one".[122] In deciding whether the onus has been discharged, the courts will be influenced by the importance of the agreement to the parties, and by the fact that one of them has acted in reliance on it.[123] Contractual intention is not negatived merely by the fact that the parties were companies in the same group and that the terms of their agreement "might not in practice be strictly enforced between them".[124]

4–026

---

[117] [1967] 2 Q.B. 31 at 41.

[118] See *Zakhem International Construction Ltd v Nippon Kohan KK* [1987] 2 Lloyd's Rep. 596.

[119] For judicial recognition of the distinction, see *Baird Textile Holdings Ltd v Marks & Spencer Plc* [2001] EWCA Civ 274; [2002] 1 All E.R. (Comm) 737 at [61]; *Modahl v British Athletics Federation Ltd* [2001] EWCA Civ 1447; [2002] 1 W.L.R. 1477 at [102] (where the burden of proof referred to at fn.121, below, was held to have been discharged).

[120] *Blackpool and Fylde Aero Club v Blackpool BC* [1990] 1 W.L.R. 1195 at 1202; cf. the *Baird Textile* case, above, fn.119, at [20], [21], [30], [62]; *Tilson v Alstom Transport* [2010] EWCA Civ 1308.

[121] *The Aramis* [1989] 1 Lloyds Rep. 213; *The Gudermes* [1993] 1 Lloyd's Rep. 311; in these cases rights and liabilities under shipping documents may now arise by virtue of Carriage of Goods by Sea Act 1992, ss.2, 3. See also: *Greville v Venables* [2007] EWCA Civ 878 at [38]–[40]; *Whittle Movers Ltd v Hollywood Express Ltd* [2009] EWCA Civ 1189; [2009] 2 C.L.C. 771; *JD Cleverly Ltd v Family Finance Ltd* [2010] EWCA Civ 1477; cf. *Goshawk Dedicated Ltd v Tyser & Co Ltd* [2006] EWCA Civ 54; [2006] 1 Lloyd's Rep. 566 at [66], where there was a finding of an implied contract.

[122] *Edwards v Skyways Ltd* [1964] 1 W.L.R. 349 at 355; cf. *The Zephyr* [1985] 2 Lloyd's Rep. 529 at 537 (disapproving [1984] 1 Lloyd's Rep. 58 at 63–64); *Yani Haryanto v ED & F Man (Sugar) Ltd* [1986] 2 Lloyd's Rep. 44; *Orion Ins Co Plc v Sphere Drake Ins Plc* [1992] 1 Lloyd's Rep. 239 at 263 (where the burden was discharged); *Mamidoil-Jetoil Greek Petroleum Co SA v Okta Oil Refinery AD* [2003] 1 Lloyd's Rep. 1 at [159].

[123] See above, para.4–016; *Kingswood Estate Co Ltd v Anderson* [1963] 2 Q.B. 169; *Maple Leaf Macro Volatility Master Fund v Rouvroy* [2009] EWCA Civ 1334 at [21].

[124] *The Marine Star (No.2)* [1994] 2 Lloyd's Rep. 629 at 632, reversed on other grounds [1996] 2 Lloyd's Rep. 383.

4–027   **Objective test.** The test of contractual intention is normally an objective one,[125] so that where, for example, an agreement for the sale of a house is *not* "subject to contract",[126] both parties are likely to be bound even though one of them subjectively believed that he would not be bound till the usual exchange of contracts had taken place.[127] But the objective test is here (as elsewhere)[128] subject to the limitation that it does not apply in favour of a party who knows the truth. Thus in the example just given the party who did not intend to be bound would not be bound if his state of mind was actually known to the other party.[129] Nor could a party who did not in fact intend to be bound invoke the objective test so as to hold the other party to the contract[130]: to apply that test in such a case would pervert its purpose, which is to protect a party who has relied on the objective appearance of consent from the prejudice which he would suffer if the *other* party could escape liability on the ground that he had no real intention to be bound. The incidence of the burden of proof and the objective test may explain two controversial decisions, in each of which there was a difference of opinion on the issue of contractual intention.

4–028   *Esso v Mardon.* The first is *Esso Petroleum Ltd v Commissioners of Customs and Excise.*[131] Esso supplied garages with tokens called "World Cup coins", instructing them to give away one coin with every four gallons of petrol sold. The scheme was advertised by Esso and also on posters displayed by the garages. By a majority of four to one, the House of Lords held that there was no "sale" of the coins; but the majority was equally divided on the question whether there was any contract at all with regard to the coins. Those who thought that there was a contract[132] relied on the incidence of the burden of proof, and on the point that "Esso envisaged a bargain of some sort between the garage proprietor and the motorist".[133] But this point relates rather to the intention of Esso than to that of the alleged contracting parties. With regard to *their* intention, it is submitted that the more realistic view is that contractual intention was negatived by the language of the advertisements (in which the coins were said to be "going free"), and by the minimal value of the coins.

4–029   *Evans v Merzario.* The second case is *J Evans & Son (Portsmouth) Ltd v Andrea Merzario Ltd.*[134] The representative of a firm of forwarding agents told a customer, with whom the firm had long dealt, that henceforth his goods would be packed in containers and assured him that these would be carried *under* deck.

---

[125] See above, paras 1–002, 2–002; *Ignazio Messina & Co v Polskie Linie Oceaniczne* [1995] 2 Lloyd's Rep. 566 at 579; *Bowerman v Association of British Travel Agents* [1995] N.L.J. 1815; *Edmonds v Lawson* [2000] Q.B. 501; *Baird Textile Holdings Ltd v Marks & Spencer Plc* [2001] EWCA Civ 274; [2002] 1 All E.R. (Comm) 737; *Maple Leaf Macro Volatility Master Fund v Rouvroy* [2009] EWCA Civ 1334 at [17].

[126] See above, para.4–006.

[127] *Tweddell v Henderson* [1975] 1 W.L.R. 1496; *Storer v Manchester CC* [1974] 1 W.L.R. 1403 at 1408.

[128] See above, para.2–003.

[129] *Pateman v Pay* (1974) 263 E.G. 467.

[130] *Lark v Outhwaite* [1991] 2 Lloyd's Rep. 132 at 141.

[131] [1976] 1 W.L.R. 1; Atiyah 39 M.L.R. 335.

[132] Lords Simon and Wilberforce. Lord Fraser, who dissented on the main issue, took the same view.

[133] [1976] 1 W.L.R. 1 at 6.

[134] [1976] 1 W.L.R. 1078; Adams 40 M.L.R. 227; cf. *El Awadi v Bank of Credit and Commerce International* [1990] 1 Q.B. 606 at 617.

About a year later, such a container was carried *on* deck and lost. At first instance,[135] Kerr J. held that the promise was not intended to be legally binding since it was made in the course of a courtesy call, not related to any particular transaction, and indefinite with regard to its future duration. The Court of Appeal, however, held[136] that the promise did have contractual force, relying principally on the importance attached by the customer to the carriage of his goods under deck, and on the fact that he would not have agreed to the new mode of carriage but for the promise. The case is no doubt a borderline one, but it is submitted that Kerr J.'s view accords more closely with the objective test of contractual intention. In most cases, that test prevents the *promisor* from relying on his subjective intention not to enter into a contractual undertaking. But it should equally prevent the *promisee's* subjective intention (if not known to the promisor) from being decisive. The Court of Appeal appears with respect to have attached too much weight to the customer's subjective state of mind, and too little weight to the circumstances in which the promise was made.

2. INTENTION AND CONSIDERATION

No requirement of positive intention? In the US, the view has been put forward by Williston[137] that "the common law does not require any positive intention to create a legal obligation as an element of contract". No one disputes that an agreement is not a contract if the parties expressly provide that it is not to be legally binding. But it is said that an agreement containing no such provision will generally be a contract although no positive intention to create a legal obligation existed in the minds of the parties. This theory can be interpreted in two ways.   **4–030**

The first interpretation simply emphasises the rule as to burden of proof (as applied to express promises) and the objective test, stated above.[138] Thus Williston says: **4–031**

> "If, under the circumstances, a reasonable person would understand[139] the words used as importing that the speaker promised to do something if given a requested exchange therefor, it is immaterial what intention the offeror may have had."

This statement is no doubt true in the case of an ordinary commercial contract; but it is harder to apply where words are spoken in jest or in anger.[140] Williston admits that there is no contract in such cases; and this admission can perhaps be explained on the ground that a person to whom a promise is made in *obvious* jest or anger would know that it was not intended to be binding, so that the objective test would not be satisfied. Another difficulty is that Williston's test is, if taken quite literally, wide enough to cover ordinary social and domestic arrangements. Williston sees no reason why these "should not create a contract, if the requisites

---

[135] [1975] 1 Lloyd's Rep. 162.

[136] [1976] 1 W.L.R. 1078.

[137] Williston, *Contracts*, s.21; Tuck 21 Can.B.Rev. 123; Shatwell 1 Sydney L.R. 293; Unger 19 M.L.R. 96; Hedley 5 O.J.L.S. 391.

[138] See above, paras 4–026—4–029.

[139] See *Edwards v Skyways Ltd* [1964] 1 W.L.R. 349 at 356 for the difficulties which may arise in determining this question, especially where one of the parties is a corporation.

[140] See above, para.4–024.

for the formation of a contract exist". No doubt it is possible that in exceptional circumstances and by use of clear words acceptance of an invitation to a party could create a contract. But would it do so *merely* because "the speaker promised to do something if given a requested exchange therefor?" Would acceptance of an invitation to a "bring a bottle party" normally create a contract? And can Williston's view be reconciled with the "car pool" cases[141] mentioned above?

4–032   The second, and more extreme, version of the theory is that there is no requirement of contractual intention at all. A promise is binding if it is supported by consideration; nothing else is necessary. Social and domestic arrangements are not contracts, even if they involve reciprocal promises or performances, because the promise of one party is not given as the price for the other's: there is no bargain. "The family circle differs from the market place in that it is not the setting for bargaining but for an exchange of gifts or gratuitous services".[142] This is said to be the true basis of *Balfour v Balfour*.[143] But this view merely makes the requirement of intention part of the definition of consideration: one cannot tell whether mutual promises constitute a bargain or an "exchange of gifts" without regard to the intention of the parties. Nor can one on this view explain why mere puffs or statements made in jest or anger do not give rise to contractual obligations; why a defendant who concedes that there was consideration has any case left to argue on the issue of intention[144] or why there was no contract in *Heilbut, Symons & Co v Buckleton*[145]; and why claims or defences based on implied contracts have been rejected precisely because contractual intention had not been established.[146] It is finally inconsistent with a number of cases in which there was agreement and consideration,[147] and the conclusion that the agreement did not amount to a contract was based solely on the ground that the parties did not intend that it should give rise to legal relations between them.

4–033   **Intention required as a matter of English law.** It is submitted that neither version of the theory is satisfactory. Many of the decisions discussed in this chapter are expressly based on the absence of an intention to create legal relations, and cannot be satisfactorily explained in any other way. They show that such intention is recognised by English law as a separate requirement for the formation of contracts.[148]

---

[141] See above, para.4–013.

[142] Unger, above, fn.137; cf. Hepple [1970] C.L.J. 122.

[143] [1919] 2 K.B. 571.

[144] As in *Edwards v Skyways Ltd* [1964] 1 W.L.R. 349; cf. *Re Beaumont* [1980] Ch. 444 at 453, recognising that consideration may be provided "under a contract *or otherwise*".

[145] [1913] A.C. 30; above, para.4–003.

[146] See above, para.4–026.

[147] e.g. *President of the Methodist Conference v Parfitt* [1984] Q.B. 368 at 378; *R. v Civil Service Appeal Board Ex p. Bruce* [1988] I.C.R. 649 at 659, 665 (affirmed on other grounds [1989] I.C.R. 171); *The Aramis* [1989] 1 Lloyd's Rep. 213.

[148] For recent judicial support for this view, see *Baird Textile Holdings Ltd v Marks & Spencer Plc* [2001] EWCA Civ 274; [2002] 1 All E.R. (Comm) 737 at [30], [59].

CHAPTER FIVE

FORM

1. GENERAL RULE

Form and consideration. A legal system is said to require that a contract shall   5–001
be made in a certain form if it lays down the manner in which the conclusion of
the contract must be marked or recorded. In modern legal systems, such formal
requirements generally consist of writing, sometimes with additional requirements, e.g. those of a deed or (in some countries) of authentication by a notary. It
has even been said that consideration is a form,[1] but more usually "form" refers
to requirements which have nothing to do with the contents of an agreement. In
this sense consideration is not generally a form, though the giving of a peppercorn
to make a gratuitous promise binding might be so regarded.[2]

Form as a necessary requirement. Form may be *sufficient* to make a promise   5–002
binding, as we have seen in discussing the effect of a gratuitous promise made in
a deed.[3] But in this chapter we shall discuss cases in which form is a *necessary*
requirement which must be satisfied (granted that there is agreement, consideration and contractual intention) before the contract is fully effective. Such a
requirement may serve one or more of several purposes. First, it promotes
certainty, as it is usually relatively easy to tell whether the required form has been
used. A requirement of writing also simplifies the problem of ascertaining the
contents of the agreement. Secondly, form has a cautionary effect: a person may
hesitate longer before executing a deed than he would before making an oral
promise. Thirdly, form has a protective function: it is used to protect the weaker
party to a contractual relationship by ensuring that he is provided with a written
record of the terms of the contract.[4] Both the second and the third purposes of

---

[1] Holmes, *The Common Law*, p.273: "Consideration is a form as much as a seal." See also Fuller 41
Col.L.Rev. 799.
[2] See *The Alev* [1989] 1 Lloyd's Rep. 138 at 147.
[3] See above, para.3–170.
[4] See, e.g., Employment Rights Act 1996, ss.1, 2–4; Landlord and Tenant Act 1985, s.4.

form are illustrated by the elaborate formal requirements that protect a debtor under certain consumer credit agreements. He must be given a document to be signed by him inside a "signature box"; this must contain a notice warning him that he is signing a consumer credit agreement. A similar box must contain a notice telling him of his statutory right of cancellation.[5] It is scarcely fanciful to suggest that these boxes fulfil in a modern context some of the functions formerly performed by use of the seal. Form may finally serve what has been called a "channelling" purpose[6]: that is, the use of a certain form may help to distinguish one type of transaction from another.

5–003   **General rule: no formality required.** Form has, on the other hand, the disadvantage that it is time-consuming and clumsy and that it is a source of technical pitfalls. Even the relatively simple requirement of writing is open to these objections and has therefore been regarded as inconvenient from a commercial point of view. Thus the general rule is that contracts can be made quite informally.[7]

2. STATUTORY EXCEPTIONS

5–004   The general rule is subject to many exceptions. These now all depend on legislation dealing with specific types of contracts. Some such contracts must be made by deed, some must be in writing, and others must be evidenced by a note or memorandum in writing. No attempt can be made in this book to give a complete list of these exceptions. A few illustrations must suffice; after these have been discussed, an attempt will be made to consider the impact on this subject of contracting by electronic means.

(a) Contracts which must be made by Deed

5–005   **Lease for more than three years.** A lease for more than three years must be made by deed.[8] If it is not so made, it is "void for the purpose of creating a legal estate".[9] But it operates in equity as an agreement for a lease,[10] which can be specifically enforced if it complies with the formal requirements (to be discussed below)[11] for contracts for the disposition of interests in land. Thus between the parties to the lease lack of a deed is not fatal. But, unless the tenant has registered the lease as a land-charge or, in the case of registered land, is in actual occupation, he can be turned out by a third party to whom the landlord has sold the land.[12]

---

[5] Consumer Credit (Agreements) Regulations (SI 1983/1553), as amended; cf. Consumer Protection (Distance Selling) Regulations 2000 (SI 2000/2334), regs 7 and 8, as amended by Consumer Protection (Distance Selling) (Amendment) Regulations 2005 (SI 2005/689); these Regulations implement Dir.97/7/EC.

[6] Von Mehren 72 H.L.R. 1009 at 1017.

[7] *Beckham v Drake* (1841) 9 M.& W. 79 at 92.

[8] Law of Property Act 1925, ss.52, 54(2).

[9] ibid., s.52.

[10] *Walsh v Lonsdale* (1882) 21 Ch.D. 9.

[11] Below, para.5–008.

[12] At present under Law of Property Act 1925, s.199(1)(i); Land Registration Act 2002, Sch.3, para.2.

(b) Contracts which must be in Writing

(i) *Bills of exchange, etc*

Under nineteenth-century legislation, contracts which must be in writing **5–006** include bills of exchange, promissory notes[13] and bills of sale.[14] A bill of sale is void unless it is in writing in the statutory form.[15] But if the sort of promise which is normally contained in a bill of exchange or promissory note is made orally, it can result in a perfectly valid contract. The contract is not invalid[16] but will not have the legal and commercial characteristics[17] of a bill or note.

(ii) *Consumer credit agreements*

Under the Consumer Credit Act 1974,[18] regulated consumer credit agreements, **5–007** and certain other agreements[19] are "not properly executed"[20] unless certain formalities are complied with. A regulated consumer credit agreement is one by which a creditor provides an individual debtor with credit[21] of any amount.[22] Both parties must sign a document in the form prescribed by government regulations.[23] This must legibly set out all the express terms of the contract[24] and contain a notice of the debtor's statutory right to cancel during the "cooling off" period (where this applies),[25] as well as certain other information.[26] A copy must also be given to the debtor.[27]

An agreement which is not properly executed can be enforced *against the debtor* "on an order of the court only".[28] In the absence of such an order, no restitutionary remedy is available against the borrower at common law since the award of such a remedy to the lender would be inconsistent with the legislative scheme that, in the case of an improperly executed document, "subject to the enforcement powers of the court, the debtor should not have to pay".[29] An application for an enforcement order shall be dismissed only if the court considers it just to do so.[30] In this regard, the court has a wide discretion. It can take into account the prejudice caused to the debtor and the degree of culpability of the creditor[31]; order enforcement conditionally or subject to variations[32]; or reduce the amount payable

---

[13] Bills of Exchange Act 1882, ss.3(1), 17(2).
[14] Bills of Sale Act 1878 (Amendment) Act 1882.
[15] ibid.
[16] *Hitchens v General Guarantee Corp* [2001] EWCA Civ 359; *The Times*, March 13, 2001.
[17] See below, paras 15–046—15–049.
[18] As amended by Consumer Credit Act 2006.
[19] Such as consumer hire agreements (s.15) and security instruments (s.105).
[20] s.61(1).
[21] As defined by s.9.
[22] s.8(1); certain agreements are exempt under ss.16–16C of the 1974 Act.
[23] s.61(1)(a); for exceptions, see s.74; cf. above, para.5–002.
[24] s.61(1)(b) and (c).
[25] s.64(5); for "cooling off" periods, see below, para.10–046.
[26] Consumer Credit Act 1974, s.55(1).
[27] ss.62, 63.
[28] s.65(1). The defective agreement is thus unenforceable only and not void: *R. v Modupe* [1991] C.C.L.R. 29.
[29] *Dimond v Lovell* [2002] 1 A.C. 384 at 398.
[30] s.127(1).
[31] s.127(1)(i).
[32] s.127(1)(ii).

by the debtor.[33] This flexible approach, together with the repeal of provisions which had completely prevented the grant of an order for certain formal defects,[34] goes far to meet the objection that formal requirements can give rise to unmeritorious defences based on technical slips.

(iii) *Contracts for the sale or disposition of an interest in land*

5–008   **Requirements.** Under s.2 of the Law of Property (Miscellaneous Provisions) Act 1989, most contracts for the sale or disposition of an interest in land[35] must be "made in writing".[36] All the terms[37] expressly[38] agreed by the parties must be incorporated in the document (or in each document, where contracts are exchanged).[39] The terms may be incorporated either by being set out in the document, or by reference.[40] The document (or documents) must also be signed "by or on behalf of"[41] each party[42] to the contract.[43] For this purpose "signed" should be given the meaning which "the ordinary man would understand it to

---

[33] s.127(2); *National Guardian Mortgage Corp v Wilks* [1993] C.C.L.R. 1.

[34] s.127(3) and (4) which are repealed by Consumer Credit Act 2006, s.15.

[35] As defined in Law of Property (Miscellaneous Provisions) Act 1989, s.2(6); for application to mortgages, see *United Bank of Kuwait v Sahib* [1997] Ch. 107, not cited in *Target Holdings Ltd v Priestley* (2000) 79 P. & C.R. 305, where s.2 was held not to apply to the disposition itself, as opposed to the contract for the disposition; cf. *McLaughlin v Duffill* [2008] EWCA Civ 1627; [2010] Ch. 1; *Helden v Strathmore Ltd* [2011] EWCA Civ 542 at [27]. A "lock-out" agreement is not within the section: *Pitt v PHH Asset Management Ltd* [1993] 1 W.L.R. 327 (contrast *Lane v Robinson* [2010] EWCA Civ 384 at [11]). Nor is a compromise agreement which merely "relates" to the sale of land: *Nweze v Nwoko* [2004] EWCA Civ 379; [2004] 2 P. & C.R. 33, or trivial dispositions of land consciously made pursuant to an informal boundary agreement: *Joyce v Rigolli* [2004] EWCA Civ 79; [2004] All E.R. (D) 203, or a settlement under CPR Pt 36 which requires the sale or other disposition of an interest in land: *Orton v Collins* [2007] EWHC 803 (Ch); [2007] 1 W.L.R. 2953. But see also: *Kilcarne Holdings Ltd v Targetfollow* [2004] EWHC 2547; [2005] 2 P & C.R. 8 at [203] (a contract for the sale of land cannot escape s.2 "merely because it is wrapped up in an alleged partnership" (affirmed [2005] EWCA Civ 1355, without consideration of this point)).

[36] s.2(1). In the case of electronic conveyancing this may be satisfied through the use of certain qualifying electronic documents: Land Registration Act 2002, s.91.

[37] See *Enfield LBC v Arajah* [1995] E.G.C.S. 164 (where only the *main* terms were set out in the document).

[38] The inclusion of any implied terms is not required (and would be curious if it were): *Markham v Paget* [1908] 1 Ch 697.

[39] Law of Property (Miscellaneous Provisions) Act 1989, s.2(1). An agreement reached in pre-exchange correspondence between the parties will not satisfy s.2(1) where no single document contains all the terms expressly agreed or is signed by both parties; nor will such correspondence amount to an "exchange" since this process refers to exchange of the formal documents described at para.4–007, above: see *Commission for the New Towns v Cooper (Great Britain) Ltd* [1995] Ch. 259 at 285, 293 disapproving the concession to the contrary which had apparently been accepted in *Hooper v Sherman* [1995] C.L.Y. 840.

[40] s.2(2); *Courtney v Corp Ltd* [2006] EWCA Civ 518; cf. *Record v Bell* [1991] 1 W.L.R. 853, where this requirement was not satisfied, but there was a collateral contract (below, fn.52).

[41] Signature by an agent who is liable and entitled under the contract suffices: *Braymist v Wise Finance Co Ltd* [2002] EWCA Civ 127; [2002] 2 All E.R. 333; below, para.16–073.

[42] s.2(3). In the case of an option to purchase, the agreement granting the option is within the section, but the notice exercising it is not, and so does not have to be signed by the vendor: *Spiro v Glencrown Properties Ltd* [1991] Ch. 537.

[43] For a somewhat relaxed application of this requirement in the context of execution by or on behalf of a company under the Companies Act 2006, s.44(2), see *Williams v Redcard Ltd* [2011] EWCA Civ 466.

have", which appears to require that the parties must write their own names with their own hands upon the document.[44] It is no longer satisfied (as it was under earlier legislation superseded by s.2 of the 1989 Act[45]) by merely typing a party's name and address on the document,[46] but it is enough that a party has written his initials, provided it is clear that he intended to authenticate all the terms.[47] The requirement of writing does not apply to short leases for less than three years, to sales at public auctions or to transactions in certain forms of investment securities (e.g. unit trust investing in land).[48]

Failure to include all terms Where the document fails to include *all* the terms on which the parties are alleged to have orally agreed, a number of possibilities call for discussion. If the failure was due to the parties' having *deliberately* omitted the term from the written document, then it will not be a term expressly agreed so as to form part of the contract, so that its omission will not affect the validity of the contract as set out in the document.[49] If the failure was due to a mistake in recording those terms,[50] it may be possible to rectify the document, i.e. to bring it into line with what was actually agreed.[51] If the failure is due to some other cause, it is sometimes possible to treat the omitted term as a separate or "collateral" contract, independent of the (main) contract set out in the document,[52] which will then satisfy the requirements of s.2. The omitted term cannot, however, be so treated if it is intended to form part of the main contract[53]: e.g. if it is so "interwoven with the substance of the transaction"[54] as to form an essential part of it; for to treat a document as sufficient even though it omitted such a term would be inconsistent with the statutory requirement that the document must incorporate all the expressly agreed terms. It seems that a term can for the present purpose be treated as a collateral contract only if it was intended to take effect as an independent contract, separate from that set out in the document. If it can be so treated, two consequences follow. First, a document which omits the term can nevertheless satisfy the statutory requirement of incorporating *all* the express terms of the main contract. Secondly, the collateral

5–009

---

[44] *Firstpost Homes Ltd v Johnson* [1995] 1 W.L.R. 1567, at 1576 citing with approval: *Goodman v J Eban Ltd* [1954] 1 Q.B. 550 at 561.

[45] i.e. Law of Property Act 1925, s.40.

[46] *Firstpost Homes Ltd v Johnson*, above, fn.44. cf. the requirements for contracts of guarantee under the Statute of Frauds 1677, s.4: para.5–013, below.

[47] *Newell v Tarrant* [2004] EWHC 772.

[48] s.2(5).

[49] *Grossman v Hooper* [2001] EWCA Civ 615; [2001] 2 E.G.L.R. 82. This might be achieved by an appropriately drafted entire agreement clause: *North Eastern Properties Ltd v Coleman* [2010] EWCA Civ 277; [2010] 1 W.L.R. 2715.

[50] But not if it was the result of an express agreement to omit the terms: *Oun v Ahmad* [2008] EWHC 545 (Ch); [2008] 13 E.G. 149; cf. *Helden v Strathmore Ltd* [2011] EWCA Civ 542 at [29].

[51] See *Commission for the New Towns v Cooper (GB) Ltd* [1995] Ch. 259. For the conditions in which rectification is available, see below, para.8–059 et seq.; the possibility of rectification is recognised by Law of Property (Miscellaneous Provisions) Act 1989, s.2(4), which provides that the contract is deemed to come into being at such time as may be specified in the court order rectifying the document. See also Law Com. No.164, para.5.6.

[52] e.g. *Record v Bell* [1991] 1 W.L.R. 853.

[53] *Grossman v Hooper*, above, fn.49, at [21].

[54] *Preece v Lewis* (1963) 186 E.G. 113, decided under Law of Property Act 1925, s.40 but, *semble*, equally applicable under Law of Property (Miscellaneous Provisions) Act 1989, s.2(1); see also Law Com. No.164, paras 5.7, 5.8.

contract is binding, even if oral, so long as it is not itself one which is required to be in writing,[55] and so long as evidence of it is admissible under the parol evidence rule.[56]

5–010   **Effect of non-compliance.** The effect of the requirement that it must be "made in writing" is that a contract for the sale or other disposition of an interest in land does not come into existence if the parties fail to comply with the statutory formal requirements. This could cause hardship where one party has partly performed[57] such a contract, or otherwise acted in reliance on it, e.g. by making improvements to the land in question. But such hardship can be avoided by other judicially developed doctrines, such as proprietary estoppel or constructive trust.[58]

5–011   **Proprietary estoppel and constructive trusts.** Under these doctrines, the court may make an order for the transfer of the land to the party who has acted in reliance on the contract.[59] But the remedy is limited in various ways[60] and does not necessarily lead to enforcement of the contract as such.[61] Thus, while they may play a role similar to that of "part performance",[62] the position of the party who has acted in reliance on the defective contract is now less favourable than it was before the 1989 Act.[63] Section 2(5) of the 1989 Act states only that nothing in s.2 "affects the creation or operation of resulting, implied or constructive trusts". This has led to the view that a "mere (proprietary) estoppel, unassociated with a constructive trust" cannot be relied upon.[64] The preferable view, it is submitted, is that the saving provision in s.2(5) should not be so limited, since it was the retention of the very flexibility of proprietary estoppel which was contemplated.[65]

---

[55] *Angell v Duke* (1875) L.R. 10 Q.B. 174 (and see next note); *Record v Bell* [1991] 1 W.L.R. 853; *Business Environment Bow Lane Ltd v Deanwater Estates* [2007] EWCA Civ 622; [2007] 32 E.G. 90.

[56] See below, para.6–028; in *Angell v Duke*, above, the evidence of the collateral contract was later rejected under the parol evidence rule: (1875) 32 L.T. 320.

[57] s.2 has been held not to apply where the contract has been fully performed: *Tootal Clothing v Guinea Properties Management* (1992) 64 P. & C.R. 452.

[58] See below, para.5–011. In some cases, a restitutionary remedy may be available, e.g. a quantum meruit: *Cobbe v Yeoman's Row Management Ltd* [2008] UKHL 55; [2008] 1 W.L.R. 1752; below, para.22–021. For other potentially available restituionary remedies, see *Chitty on Contracts* (30th edn, 2008) at paras 4–084-4–087.

[59] See above, para.3–139.

[60] See above, para.3–139; cf. also above, para.3–143.

[61] See above, para.3–152.

[62] *Kinane v Mackie-Conteh* [2005] EWCA Civ 45; [2005] 6 E.G. 140 at [32].

[63] Under Law of Property Act 1925, s.40 (re-enacting part of s.4 of the Statute of Frauds 1677 and now repealed) failure to comply with the statutory requirement of written evidence only made the contract unenforceable; and "part performance" (below, para.5–026) enabled the party so performing to enforce the contract.

[64] *Kinane v Mackie-Conteh* [2005] EWCA Civ 45; [2005] 6 E.G. 140 at [40], per Neuberger L.J; *Cobbe v Yeoman's Row Management Ltd* [2008] UKHL 55; [2008] 1 W.L.R. 1752 at [29] per Lord Scott; *Thorner v Major* [2009] UKHL 18; [2009] 1 W.L.R. 776 at [96] per Lord Neuberger; cf. *Lancashire Mortgage Corp Ltd v Scottish and Newcastle Plc* [2007] EWCA Civ 684 at [55]; *McGuane v Welch* [2008] EWCA Civ 785; (2008) 40 E.G. 178 at [37].

[65] Law Com. No.164, paras 4.3, 5.4 and 5.5; *Whittaker v Kinnear* [2011] EWHC 1479 (Ch) at [30]. Other forms of estoppel are likely to fail: *Yaxley v Gotts* [2000] Ch. 162 at 182; *Eyestorm Ltd v Hoptonacre Homes Ltd* [2007] EWCA Civ 1366 at [51].

(c) Contracts which must be Evidenced in Writing

(i) *In general*

Some statutes do not require contracts to be *made* in writing, but only to be **5–012** *evidenced* by a written document. A contract of marine insurance, for example, is "inadmissible in evidence" unless it is embodied in a marine policy signed by the insurer.[66] This is not a requirement of the making or validity of such a contract: it is enough if the policy is executed *after* the making of the contract. Other statutory provisions are less exacting; they are satisfied if there is merely a "note or memorandum" in writing. The Statute of Frauds 1677 applied this requirement to six classes of contracts. Its object was to prevent fraudulent claims based on perjured evidence; but it sometimes gave rise to technical defences which had little merit, so that it was restrictively interpreted by the courts. This process can be illustrated by reference to contracts of guarantee, the only type of contract to which the formal requirements imposed by the Statute still apply.

(ii) *Contracts of guarantee*

Definition. Section 4 of the Statute of Frauds provides: "No action shall be **5–013** brought . . . whereby to charge the defendant upon any special promise to answer for the debt, default or miscarriage of another person" unless there is written evidence of the promise. This provision applies whether the liability guaranteed is contractual or tortious.[67] It applies only where the defendant's promise to pay the debt is made to the creditor. It does not apply where that promise is made to the debtor.[68] In addition, it does not apply in the cases discussed in paras 5–014 to 5–016.

Guarantee or indemnity? The Statute applies to a guarantee, but not to an **5–014** indemnity. A guarantee is a promise to pay another's debt if he fails to pay.[69] An indemnity is a promise to indemnify the creditor against loss arising out of the principal contract.[70] In the case of a guarantee the liability of the principal debtor is primary and that of the guarantor only secondary; thus if for some reason the principal debtor is not liable, the guarantor is not liable either. A promise to indemnify creates primary liability which arises even though the promisee has no enforceable rights under the principal contract.[71]

It follows from the nature of a guarantee that there can be no guarantee if there never was a principal debtor: e.g. if A promises to pay B for doing work for C, which C has not ordered so that C is not liable to pay B for it.[72] Nor is a contract a guarantee if there once was a principal debtor, but if the whole object of the new contract is that his liability should cease and the liability of the new promisor be substituted for it. Thus a promise by a father to pay his son's creditor, if the

---

[66] Marine Insurance Act 1906, ss.22 and 24.
[67] *Kirkham v Marter* (1819) 2 B. & Ald. 613.
[68] *Eastwood v Kenyon* (1840) 11 A. & E. 438.
[69] *Lep Air Services v Rolloswin Investments Ltd* [1973] A.C. 331.
[70] *Birkmyr v Darnell* (1704) 1 Salk. 27; *Argo Caribbean Group v Lewis* [1976] 2 Lloyd's Rep. 289; cf. below, para.9–141.
[71] *Yeoman Credit Ltd v Latter* [1961] 1 W.L.R. 828.
[72] *Lakeman v Mountstephen* (1874) L.R. 7 H.L. 17.

creditor will release the son, is an indemnity.[73] But a promise may be an indemnity in spite of the fact that there is a principal debtor whose liability continues. This is the position if the person making the promise undertakes not merely to pay if the principal debtor fails to do so, but "to put the [creditor] in funds in any event".[74]

It can hardly be said that there is less danger of perjury in the case of an indemnity than in the case of a guarantee. The distinction between them has accordingly been criticised for having "raised many hair-splitting distinctions of exactly that kind which bring the law into hatred, ridicule and contempt by the public".[75] It can only be explained historically as a device for restricting the scope of the Statute of Frauds.

5–015   **Part of larger transaction.** The Statute applies to a guarantee which stands alone but not to one which is part of a larger transaction. It did not, for example, apply where the defendant introduced clients to a firm of stockbrokers on the terms that he was to receive half the commissions earned, and to pay half the losses incurred, by the stockbrokers on transactions with such clients.[76] The promise to pay losses was enforceable, though oral, as it formed part of a larger transaction in which the defendant was interested otherwise than as guarantor. Similarly the guarantee given by a *del credere* agent is not within the Statute. Such an agent guarantees the solvency of the third party between whom and his principal he makes a contract: that is, he promises the principal to pay if the third party does not. The main object of a *del credere* agency is to enable the principal to sell and the agent to earn his commission: "Though it may terminate in a liability to pay the debt of another, that is not the immediate object for which the consideration is given."[77] On the wording of the Statute, it is hard to justify the special treatment of these cases. Perhaps it could be said that such promises are more likely to be made than purely disinterested guarantees: hence there is less danger of perjury.

5–016   **Protection of property.** A guarantee is not within the Statute if it is given to protect some proprietary interest of the guarantor. Thus A may buy goods from B which are held by C as security for a debt owed by B to C. If A induces C to deliver the goods to him by promising to pay B's debt in case B does not pay it, A's promise is not within the Statute.[78] The main object of A's promise is said to be to protect his own property and not to guarantee B's debt. This rule may again be justified on the ground that such promises are more likely to be made than purely disinterested guarantees. But if this is so, it is hard to see why the rule is restricted to cases in which the interest is strictly proprietary. The rule has, for example, been held not to apply where the guarantee was given to protect the assets of a company in which the guarantor was a substantial shareholder or

---

[73] *Goodman v Chase* (1818) 1 B. & Ald. 297.

[74] *Guild & Co v Conrad* [1894] 2 Q.B. 885 at 892; cf. *Thomas v Cook* (1828) 8 B. & C. 728; *Wildes v Dudlow* (1874) L.R. 19 Eq. 198; *Re Hoyle* [1893] 1 Ch. 84.

[75] *Yeoman Credit Ltd v Latter* [1961] 1 W.L.R. 828 at 835; *Associated British Ports v Ferryways NV* [2009] EWCA Civ 189; [2009] 1 Lloyd's Rep. 595 at [1] (an "old chestnut" which is "technical and inconvenient", where the issue was not form, but the effect of a variation to the underlying debt (discharge in the case of a guarantee)).

[76] *Sutton & Co v Grey* [1894] 1 Q.B. 285. cf. *Pitts v Jones* [2007] EWCA Civ 1301; [2008] Q.B. 76 (where the argument failed).

[77] *Couturier v Hastie* (1852) 8 Ex. 40 at 56, reversed on another point: (1856) 5 H.L.C. 673; below, para.8–009.

[78] *Fitzgerald v Dressler* (1859) 7 C.B.(N.S.) 374.

debenture holder.[79] It was said that to enforce an oral guarantee in such a case would amount to repealing the Statute.[80] But this is also true where the interest protected is a strictly proprietary one.

Criticism. So many subtle distinctions have been drawn to whittle away the   5–017
application of the Statute to contracts of guarantee that it seems a pity that this part of the Statute has not been replaced by legislation which more effectively furthers its purpose of protecting guarantors. The requirement of written evidence is scarcely an effective means of providing such protection, since it can be satisfied by a standard form of guarantee drafted by a bank to protect its own interests rather than those of the guarantor.[81] Even if the requirement of written evidence did protect the guarantor, it would not do so very effectively, for it can fairly easily be evaded by drawing up the contract as one of indemnity.

Type of evidence required. Contracts within the Statute of Frauds must be   5–018
evidenced by a signed note or memorandum in writing. The exact nature of the evidence required was not specified by the Statute, but the following rules were later laid down by Parliament and by the courts. Many of the relevant cases concern contracts to which the Statute no longer applies; but the principles to be derived from them still apply, where appropriate, to contracts of guarantee.

Parties. The memorandum must identify the parties by naming or describing   5–019
them,[82] and state the capacity in which they contract.[83] It may sufficiently describe the parties without actually naming them. For example, a party can even be sufficiently described by a pronoun.[84]

Consideration. The memorandum of guarantee need not state the considera-   5–020
tion for the guarantee.[85]

Terms. The memorandum must contain all the material terms of the con-   5–021
tract.[86] There is some authority for the view that if a term has been omitted from the memorandum the claimant may waive the term if it is solely for his benefit and not of major importance, and enforce the contract without the term.[87] Conversely, if the omitted term is for the benefit of the defendant, the claimant may be able to enforce the contract on agreeing to perform it.[88]

---

[79] *Harburg India Rubber Comb Co v Martin* [1902] 1 K.B. 778; *Davys v Buswell* [1913] 2 K.B. 47; *The Anemone* [1987] 1 Lloyd's Rep. 547.

[80] *Harburg* case, above, at 787.

[81] See below, para.7–046. In relation to regulated agreements, statutory protection is provided by Consumer Credit Act 1974, Pt VIII and s.127, as amended by Consumer Credit Act 2006: above, para.5–007.

[82] *Williams v Jordan* (1877) 6 Ch.D. 517 ("Sir" not sufficient); *Re Lindrea* (1913) 109 L.T. 623 (first name sufficient); cf. *UCB Corporate Services Ltd v Clyde & Co* [2000] 2 All E.R. (Comm) 257 where the guarantor was not named or otherwise identified.

[83] *Vandenbergh v Spooner* (1866) L.R. 1 Ex. 316; *Newell v Radford* (1867) L.R. 3 C.P. 52; *Dewar v Mintoft* [1912] 2 K.B. 373.

[84] *Carr v Lynch* [1900] 1 Ch. 613.

[85] Mercantile Law Amendment Act 1856, s.3.

[86] *Hawkins v Price* [1947] Ch. 645; cf. *Marshall v Berridge* (1881) 19 Ch.D. 233; *MP Services v Lawyer* (1996) P. & C.R. D49.

[87] *North v Loomes* [1919] 1 Ch. 378; *Beckett v Nurse* [1948] 1 K.B. 535. The point was not argued in *Tweddell v Henderson* [1975] 1 W.L.R. 1496.

[88] *Martin v Pycroft* (1852) 2 D.M. & G. 785; *Scott v Bradley* [1971] Ch. 850 (refusing to follow *Burgess v Cox* [1951] Ch. 383 on this point).

5–022   **Signature.** The memorandum must be signed by the party to be charged or by his agent lawfully authorised to sign for him. The requirement that the memorandum must be "signed" is liberally interpreted. A party need not sign his full name: initials will do.[89] The signature may be printed,[90] and may be in any part of the document, not necessarily at the bottom.[91] It may be put on the document before the contract was made so long as it is "recognised" at the time of contracting. Thus a form printed before the contract is made and bearing one party's name is "signed" by that party if he at the time of contracting submits it to the other party for signature: he thereby "recognises" his own "signature".[92] These rules are lax, but a document is not signed by a party merely because his name occurs somewhere within it: the signature must authenticate the whole document. Thus if a memorandum is headed "Articles of Agreement between A & B" and concludes "As witness our hands . . . " the parties must actually subscribe: the mention of their names at the beginning is clearly not intended as a signature.[93] Similarly, where the terms of a guarantee are set out in an email, the memorandum thereby created[94] is not "signed" if the guarantor's name appears only in the address box and was added by the internet service provider.[95] The implication is that it is "signed" if the name is set out in the text of the email since it can then be taken as intended to give authenticity to the document.[96] A party is not considered to have signed a document merely because he adds his signature to it as witness to the signature of the other party.[97]

The writing need be signed only by "the party to be charged". Thus the contract can be enforced against a party who has signed by one who has not.[98]

5–023   **Memorandum need not be prepared as such.** The memorandum need not be prepared for the purpose of satisfying the statutory requirements of written evidence. A writing which comes into existence before an action is brought[99] on the contract will suffice so long as it acknowledges or recognises the existence of the contract.[100] Thus an offer signed by one party and orally accepted by the other,[101] a recital or disposition in a will,[102] a letter written by one of the parties

---

[89] *Chichester v Cobb* (1866) 14 L.T. 433; *Hill v Hill* [1947] Ch. 231 at 240.

[90] *Schneider v Norris* (1814) 2 M. & S. 286; cf. *Godwin v Francis* (1870) L.R. 5 C.P. 295 (telegram).

[91] *Ogilvie v Foljambe* (1817) 3 Mer. 53; *Durrell v Evans* (1862) 1 H. & C. 174; *Evans v Hoare* [1892] 1 Q.B. 593.

[92] *Schneider v Norris*, above; *Evans v Hoare*, above; *Leeman v Stocks* [1951] Ch. 941.

[93] *Hubert v Treherne* (1842) 3 Man. & G. 743.

[94] See text to fn.106, below.

[95] *Pereira Fernandes SA v Mehta* [2006] EWHC 813; [2006] 1 W.L.R. 1543; cf. *Lindsay v O'Loughnane* [2010] EWHC 529 at [95].

[96] *Golden Ocean Group Ltd v Salgaocar Mining Industries PVT* [2011] EWHC 56 (Comm) at [104].

[97] *Gosbell v Archer* (1835) 1 A. & E. 500.

[98] *Laythoarp v Bryant* (1836) 2 Bing.N.C. 735; cf. *The Maria D* [1992] 1 A.C. 21 (signature by agent sufficient although he was not liable on the main contract); as to specific performance, see below, para.21–032.

[99] See *Lucas v Dixon* (1889) 22 Q.B.D. 357; *Farr, Smith & Co v Messers* [1928] 1 K.B. 397.

[100] *Tweddell v Henderson* [1975] 1 W.L.R. 1496.

[101] *Reuss v Picksley* (1866) L.R. 1 Ex. 342; *Lever v Koffler* [1901] 1 Ch. 543; *Parker v Clark* [1960] 1 W.L.R. 286. cf. *Pereira Fernandes SA v Mehta*, below, fn.106.

[102] *Re Hoyle* [1893] 1 Ch. 84; *Schaefer v Schuhmann* [1972] A.C. 572; contrast *Maddison v Alderson* (1883) 8 App.Cas. 467, where there was probably no contract at all.

to his own agent[103] and pleadings in a previous action between different parties[104] have been held sufficient. A letter repudiating liability is a sufficient memorandum if it admits the terms of the contract but denies the construction put upon them by the other party; but not if it denies that a contract was ever made on the terms alleged.[105] Where the essential terms of a guarantee are set out in an email and the offer contained therein is accepted orally, the email constitutes a sufficient note or memorandum in writing for the purpose of the 1677 Act.[106]

Joinder of documents. Where no single document fully records the transac-   5–024
tion it may be possible to produce a sufficient memorandum by joining together two or more documents.[107] Joinder is, in the first place, possible where one document expressly or impliedly *refers* to another transaction. If that transaction is also recorded in a document, and that document was in existence when the first was signed[108] the two documents can be joined.[109] Joinder may be effected via an intermediate document: e.g. where the first sets out the terms of the guarantee, the second referred to those terms and the third (which is signed by the guarantor) refers to the second.[110] Even where there is no express reference in one document to the other, they can be joined if, on placing them side by side, it becomes obvious without the aid of oral evidence that they are connected.[111] It seems that the original and the photocopy of a document (one signed by one party and the other by the other) could be joined on this ground.[112] But if the document signed by the defendant contains no reference to another document or transaction, and if the connection between the two documents can be established only by oral evidence, joinder is not permitted.[113]

Effect of non-compliance. Failure to comply with the requirements just   5–025
described does not make the contract void, but only unenforceable.[114] The contract can be *made* orally, but it can be enforced by action only if a note or memorandum of it exists, signed by the party against whom enforcement is sought. As the contract is not void, money paid or property transferred under it

---

[103] *Gibson v Holland* (1865) L.R. 1 C.P. 1.

[104] *Grindell v Bass* [1920] 2 Ch. 487. The position is probably different where reliance is placed on pleadings in an earlier action between the *same* parties; *Hardy v Elphick* [1974] Ch. 65.

[105] See *Buxton v Rust* (1872) L.R. 7 Ex. 279; *Thirkell v Cambi* [1919] 2 K.B. 591; cf. *Dobell v Hutchison* (1835) 3 A. & E. 355.

[106] *Pereira Fernandes SA v Mehta* [2006] EWHC 813; [2006] 1 W.L.R. 1543. And see the note following.

[107] A chain of e-mails may suffice: *Golden Ocean Group Ltd v Salgaocar Mining Industries PVT* [2011] EWHC 56 (Comm).

[108] For recognition of, and an exception to, this requirement, see *Re Danish Bacon Co Ltd v Staff Pension Fund* [1971] 1 W.L.R. 248, a case arising under Law of Property Act 1925, s.53(1)(c).

[109] *Long v Millar* (1879) 4 C.P.D. 450; cf. *Reading Trust Ltd v Spero* [1930] 1 K.B. 492; *Holiday Credit Ltd v Erol* [1977] 1 W.L.R. 704; *Elias v George Sahely & Co (Barbados) Ltd* [1983] 1 A.C. 646, where joinder is said at 655 to be possible even though the second document has no contractual force.

[110] *Moat Financial Services v Wilkinson* [2005] EWCA Civ 1253.

[111] *Sheers v Thimbleby* (1879) 13 T.L.R. 451; cf. *Burgess v Cox* [1951] Ch. 383 (disapproved on another point in *Scott v Bradley* [1971] Ch. 850).

[112] *Stokes v Whicher* [1920] 1 Ch. 411 at 419 (top and carbon copies).

[113] *Timmins v Moreland Street Property Co* [1958] Ch. 110; cf. *Boydell v Drummond* (1809) 11 East 192; contrast *Stokes v Whicher* [1920] 1 Ch. 411.

[114] *Leroux v Brown* (1852) 12 C.B. 801; *Elias v George Sahely & Co (Barbados) Ltd* [1983] 1 A.C. 646 at 650.

cannot be recovered back merely because the contract is not evidenced in writing.[115] For example, a guarantor could not recover back from the creditor money which he had paid or property which he had deposited under a guarantee of which there was no sufficient note or memorandum. Similarly, a security given for the guarantor's performance would not be void merely because the guarantee was unenforceable: thus an action could be brought on a cheque given to the creditor in payment of sums due from the debtor.[116]

5–026   **Equitable evasion.** When contracts for the sale or other disposition of land were merely required to be *evidenced* in writing, equity would allow the contract to be enforced by a party who had wholly or partly performed on the strength of it, in spite of the lack of a proper note or memorandum.[117] The requirement that such contracts must now be *made* in writing rules out the doctrine of part performance, since there can be no part performance of a non-existent contract.[118] The same doctrine is very unlikely to apply to a guarantee even though it is only required to be *evidenced* in writing,[119] since it is restricted to contracts which are specifically enforceable which, barring unusual circumstances, is not the case with a guarantee.[120] In addition, any part performance by the creditor is likely to be referable to his contract with the debtor, rather than the guarantee.[121]

In *Actionstrength Ltd v International Glass Engineering SpA*[122] the House of Lords did not rule out that the estoppel principle which underpins the doctrine of part performance might be applied to contracts of guarantee. If, however, as in that case, the estoppel is said to be based merely on the features which attend the giving of every guarantee, i.e. a representation in the form of the oral guarantee and reliance in the form of the creditor's indulgence of the debtor, the guarantor cannot be prevented from invoking the statute: "To admit an estoppel on these grounds would be to repeal the Statute."[123] "Something more" is required,[124] but it is a little difficult to see what might suffice. If, for example, the guarantor is required to represent expressly that it will not invoke the Statute, the parties' minds must surely be sufficiently aware of its requirements as to ensure that they are met.

A contract of guarantee may be the subject of rectification[125] and there is no limit as such to the terms which may be rectified, but it has been said that the court may need to consider the extrinsic evidence that is presented to it for these purposes with particular care since to do otherwise risks undermining the protection that the statute was intended to confer.[126]

(d) Formal Requirements and Electronic Documents

5–027   **Contracts made electronically.** Many problems arise in determining whether the formal requirement of "writing", or of a "document", or of a

---

[115] *Thomas v Brown* (1876) 1 Q.B.D. 714.
[116] *Low v Fry* (1935) 152 L.T. 585.
[117] See the discussion on pp.144–146 of the 7th edition of this book.
[118] Notwithstanding a dictum to the contrary in *Singh v Beggs* (1996) 71 P. & C.R. 120 at 122.
[119] The point was left open in *The Anemone* [1987] 1 Lloyd's Rep. 546 at 557.
[120] [2003] UKHL 17; [2003] 2 A.C. 541.
[121] ibid. at [48].
[122] ibid. at [48].
[123] ibid. at [26].
[124] ibid. at [35].
[125] See below, para.8–059 et seq.
[126] *Fairstate Ltd v General Enterprise and Management Ltd* [2010] EWHC 3072 (QB).

"signature" are satisfied in the case of contracts made electronically. The Law Commission has advised[127] that where commercial contracts are made by email or by trading on a website, the requirement of writing[128] will normally be satisfied,[129] though this will not be true of electronic data interchange[130]: the distinction is based on the point that in the first two of these situations, but not in the third, the terms of the transaction will be produced (on screen or in printed out copies) in visible form.[131] It has also been held that electronically stored information can, in law, constitute a "document".[132] The requirement of "signature" *can* likewise be satisfied in the case of electronic documents: e.g. by a digital signature, by typing a name into an electronic document or even by clicking on a website button.[133] Whether the requirement is *actually* so satisfied depends in these cases on the common law test of what constitutes a signature: i.e. on whether the act in question was done with the intention of authenticating the electronic document.[134] Under s.7 of the Electronic Communications Act 2000, "electronic signatures" are admissible in evidence; but this provision does not specify the *effect* of such signatures, which continues to depend on the common law "authentication" test stated above. Section 8 of the Act also empowers the appropriate Minister by order to modify existing legislation (such as the legislation discussed in this chapter) so as to authorise the use of electronic communications for the purpose of (inter alia)

> "the doing of anything which under . . . such [legislation] is required to be or may be authorised by a person's signature or seal, or is required to be delivered as a deed or witnessed."[135]

The Law Commission has (with respect) rightly advised that, since electronic communications will in most cases be capable of satisfying the requirements of writing and signature, legislation of the kind envisaged by s.8 "is not only unnecessary but risky";[136] legislation should be attempted only where it was "context specific",[137] i.e. where it was needed to create "absolute certainty"[138] in some particular context.[139] Article 9 of the Directive of the European Parliament and Council on Electronic Commerce[140] (the Electronic Commerce Directive

---

[127] In its paper on *Electronic Commerce: Formal Requirements in Commercial Contracts* (December 2001).

[128] Within Interpretation Act 1978, Sch.1.

[129] A view which is endorsed by the decisions in *Pereira Fernandes SA v Mehta* [2006] EWHC 813; [2006] 1 W.L.R. 1543 and *Golden Ocean Group Ltd v Salgaocar Mining Industries PVT* [2011] EWHC 56 (Comm); above, paras 5–022—5–023.

[130] Law Commission, above, fn.127, §§3.9, 3.23.

[131] ibid. §§3.14, 3.20.

[132] *Victor Chandler International v Customs & Excise Commissioners* [2000] 1 W.L.R. 1296.

[133] Law Commission, above, fn.127, §§3.31–3.34, 3.36, 3.39. See *Golden Ocean Group Ltd v Salgaocar Mining Industries PVT* [2011] EWHC 56 (Comm); above, para.5–022.

[134] cf. above, para.5–022.

[135] s.8(2)(c).

[136] Law Commission, above, fn.127, §3.43: general provisions might be inappropriate for specific legislative requirements of form.

[137] ibid. §3.43.

[138] ibid.

[139] e.g. that of electronic conveyancing: above, para.5–008.

[140] Dir.2000/31.

2000) obliges Member States to "ensure that their legal system allows contracts to be concluded by electronic means" and that

> "the legal requirements applicable to the contractual process neither create obstacles for the use of electronic contracts nor result in such contracts being deprived of their legal effectiveness on account of their having been made by electronic means".[141]

Legislation to implement Art.9 will not be necessary[142] where present formal requirements of writing and signature can (as will commonly be the case) be satisfied by electronic means; the need for it is likely to arise where statutory requirements can be satisfied only by the use of paper documents: e.g. where legislation requires one party to send specified contractual particulars to the other by post.[143] The obligations imposed by Art.9 are, moreover, subject to a number of exceptions, the most important of which, in the present context, relate to (1) "contracts that create or transfer rights in real estate, except for rental rights"[144]; and (2) "contracts of suretyship granted on collateral securities furnished by persons acting outside their trade, business or profession".[145] If, and so far as, the UK chooses to rely on these exceptions, it will not (so far as they permit) be required to modify existing legislation imposing formal requirements on contracts for the sale of interests in land and on contracts of guarantee and will, moreover, be free to impose further formal requirements on such contracts where they are made electronically. It follows that, to this extent, the provisions for the use of electronic documents made under the Land Registration Act 2002[146] will not need to comply with Art.9; and that nothing in that Article prevents the UK from imposing legislative restrictions on the efficacy of electronic contracts of guarantee of the kind there specified. The latter point is of some general interest in relation to what we have called the cautionary and protective functions of form[147]: if a guarantor could incur liability by simply clicking on the appropriate part of a website, then these functions would lose much of their efficacy,[148] at least if the guarantor were a person skilled in the use of this technology.

3. FORMAL REQUIREMENTS FOR RESCISSION AND VARIATION

5–028   So far this Chapter has dealt with formal requirements for the making, proof or enforceability of a contract. It is finally necessary to consider the impact of form where a contract which complies with such a requirement, or which is (though it

---

[141] Art.9.1.

[142] Parts of Dir.2000/13 (but not Art.9) are implemented by the Electronic Commerce (EC Directive) Regulations 2002 (SI 2002/2013).

[143] This was previously the requirement under Consumer Credit Act 1974, ss.63(3), 64(2), which now refer to sending by an "appropriate method": inserted by Consumer Credit Act 1974 (Electronic Communications) Order 2004 (SI 2004/3236) which also inserts s.176A setting out the requirements for electronic transmission of documents.

[144] Art.9.2(a).

[145] Art.9.2(c). Art.9.2(b) also allows Member States to retain requirements of notarial attestation for contracts within the Directive: cf. Recital 36 and Art.6.5(d).

[146] See above, para.5–008.

[147] See above, para.5–002.

[148] Law Commission, above, fn.127, §3.46.

is not required to be) made by deed or in writing, is rescinded or varied by subsequent agreement of the parties.[149] Our present concern is with formal requirements for such agreements. They also give rise to problems of consideration, which have been discussed in Ch.3.[150]

(a) Rescission

The general principle is that formal requirements which apply to the making of   5–029
a contract do not apply to its rescission by mutual consent. For example, a contract of guarantee can be rescinded orally[151]; and the same appears to be true of a contract for the disposition of an interest in land.[152] Somewhat greater difficulty arises where the rescinding agreement is itself a contract which is subject to formal requirements. Suppose, for example, that A in writing guarantees X's debt to B and that the guarantee is later rescinded by an oral agreement by which A guarantees Y's debt to B. The oral agreement is a valid contract[153] so that the guarantee of X's debt is rescinded, but B cannot enforce[154] the guarantee of Y's debt since that guarantee is not evidenced in writing. The position is less certain where the original contract is one which must be *made* (and not merely evidenced) in writing and where the rescinding agreement is also such a contract: e.g. where both agreements are contracts for the disposition of an interest in land and the first does, but the second does not, comply with the formalities required for the making of such contracts.[155] The second agreement is not itself a valid contract to make the new disposition; and one possible view is that that agreement, not having been properly "made",[156] is totally ineffective and so cannot operate even to rescind the first. An alternative (and, it is submitted, a preferable) view is that the second agreement is merely ineffective as a contract for the disposition of an interest in land. On this view, it can nevertheless amount to an agreement, supported by good consideration,[157] to rescind the first contract.[158] Hence the first contract is rescinded but the second is not binding.

At common law, a deed could only be rescinded by deed, but this rule did not apply in equity, which now prevails.[159]

---

[149] Our concern here is with this type of rescission. Formal requirements are sometimes imposed where a contract is "rescinded" *without* the consent of a party because of his failure in performance: below, para.18–063, fn.425.

[150] See above, paras 3–056—3–065.

[151] *Close Bros Ltd v Pearce* [2011] EWHC 298 (QB); cf. *Morris v Baron & Co* [1918] A.C. 1.

[152] Law of Property (Miscellaneous Provisions) Act 1989, s.2(1) (above, para.5–008) provides that such a contract shall be "*made* in writing" and says nothing about how it can be *unmade*. cf. *McCausland v Duncan Lawrie Ltd* [1997] 1 W.L.R. 38 at 48 ("rescission . . . may well be capable of being done otherwise than in writing").

[153] See above, para.5–025.

[154] See *Morris v Baron & Co*, above fn.151; *Goman v Salisbury* (1648) 1 Vern. 240.

[155] See above, fn.152.

[156] Law of Property (Miscellaneous Provisions) Act 1989, s.2(1).

[157] See above, para.3–062.

[158] The mere rescission of a contract for the disposition of an interest in land does not itself appear to amount to a "disposition": see the definition of "disposition" in Law of Property Act 1925, s.205(1)(ii), incorporated into Law of Property (Miscellaneous Provisions) Act 1989 by s.2(6) of the latter Act.

[159] *Berry v Berry* [1929] 2 K.B. 316 at 319.

(b) Variation

5–030   Difficult problems used to frequently arise out of oral variations of contracts which had to be evidenced in writing. Many of the cases concerned contracts which no longer need to be so evidenced, or which must now be made in writing[160]; but the rules laid down in them continue to apply to contracts which still have to be in, or evidenced in, writing.[161]

5–031   **Oral variation unenforceable.** An oral variation of a contract which had to be evidenced in writing could be regarded as a rescission of the old contract, followed by the making of a new one affecting the same subject-matter. If so, the old contract was effectively rescinded, but the new one could not be enforced for want of writing.[162] Alternatively, it could be said that the parties had simply tried to vary a term of, or to add one to, the original contract. If so, the original contract remained in force, but the variation, being oral, could not be enforced by action.[163] In this sense, a contract which had to be *evidenced in writing* could not be varied orally. For example, a written guarantee may provide that the guarantor is to be liable only if the creditor gives him notice of the debtor's default within one week of its occurrence. If the guarantor then says orally that he will not insist on this requirement, that oral variation does not have contractual force.[164] The position is the same where a contract which must be *made* in writing is varied in a way that does not satisfy the statutory formal requirements, e.g. where a contract for the sale of land[165] which was made in a document signed by both parties is varied in a material respect by an exchange of letters each of which is signed by only one party. In one case[166] such a variation substituted an earlier completion date for that specified in the original contract; and it was held that the vendor could not insist on the earlier date.

5–032   **Variation or rescission of original agreement?** In the above examples, the result would have been the same if the subsequent oral agreement had been regarded as a rescission: the guarantor or purchaser would not have been *liable* on the original contract because it was rescinded, nor under the new agreement because it was oral. But the distinction between (on the one hand) a rescission followed by a new agreement and (on the other) a variation would have been crucial if an attempt had been made, not to enforce the subsequent agreement, but to assert rights under the original one.[167] Had the subsequent agreement been a rescission, such an attempt would have failed. Had it been a variation, the attempt would prima facie have succeeded since the original agreement would have

---

[160] Law of Property (Miscellaneous Provisions) Act 1989, s.2(1).

[161] See above, paras 5–006—5–026.

[162] *Morris v Baron & Co* [1918] A.C. 1; *Tyers v Rosedale & Ferryhill Iron Co Ltd* (1875) L.R. 10 Ex. 195.

[163] But it may provide a defence: *Re a Debtor (No.517 of 1991)*, *The Times*, November 25, 1991.

[164] Example based on *Goss v Nugent* (1835) 5 B. & Ad. 58, where the contract was one for the disposition of an interest in land which then required only to be evidenced (not made) in writing.

[165] Law of Property (Miscellaneous Provisions) Act 1989, s.2; above, para.5–008.

[166] *McCausland v Duncan Lawrie Ltd* [1997] 1 W.L.R. 38. cf. *EyestormLtd v Hoptonacre Homes Ltd* [2007] EWCA Civ 1366.

[167] e.g. if in *Goss v Nugent*, above, fn.164, the *purchaser* had been suing to enforce the original contract.

remained in force,[168] and the subsequent oral agreement would not have been effective to vary it, though it might have had some effect as a waiver (in the sense of forbearance), or in equity,[169] if the necessary requirements[170] for invoking these doctrines were satisfied.[171]

Test for determining whether variation or rescission. Whether a sub-   5–033
sequent agreement is a rescission or a variation depends on the extent to which it departs from the original contract. It is a rescission if it alters the original contract in some essential way; but if it does not go "to the very root of the original contract"[172] it is only a variation. The distinction is one of degree. In *Morris v Baron & Co*[173] a dispute arising out of a contract for the sale of goods (which then had to be evidenced in writing) was orally compromised: it was agreed that the buyer should have extra time to pay and that he should have an option whether he would take the goods not yet delivered. This compromise was held to be a rescission as it dealt with an essential matter, the quantity of goods to be delivered. On the other hand, alterations in the place and time of delivery have been held to be variations only, so that the original contracts could still be enforced.[174]

Informal variation of contracts in writing but not as required by law.   5–034
The foregoing discussion concerns contracts which are subject to some formal requirement imposed by law. If, however, a contract which is not subject to any such legal requirement merely happens to have been executed in writing or by deed, it can be varied informally. At common law, indeed, a deed could not be varied except by another deed; but this rule did not apply in equity which now prevails. Accordingly it was held in *Berry v Berry*[175] that a separation agreement which had been made by deed (though there was no legal requirement for it to be so made) could be varied by a subsequent agreement that was not made by deed. Later cases apply this rule where the original contract *was* by law required to be made by deed.[176] These decisions are hard to reconcile with the reasoning of cases which hold that a contract required to be evidenced or made in writing cannot be varied orally.[177] They are best explained on the ground that, though the variations were not contractually binding, they nevertheless had a limited effect under the rules of waiver in the sense of forbearance,[178] or in equity.[179]

---

[168] *Robinson v Page* (1826) 3 Russ. 114; *Tyers v Rosedale & Ferryhill Iron Co Ltd* (1875) L.R. 10 Ex. 195.

[169] See above, para.3–066 et seq.

[170] See above, paras 3–080—3–085.

[171] *McCausland v Duncan Lawrie Ltd* [1997] 1 W.L.R. 38 at 49–50.

[172] *British and Beningtons Ltd v NW Cachar Tea Co* [1923] A.C. 48 at 68.

[173] [1918] A.C. 1: criticised as introducing a "formalistic approach", best confined to questions of form, in *Samuel v Wadlow* [2007] EWCA Civ 155 at [46].

[174] e.g. the *British and Beningtons* case, above; *Hickman v Haynes* (1875) L.R. 10 C.P. 598; *The Arawa* [1980] 2 Lloyd's Rep. 135; cf. *United Dominions Corp (Jamaica) Ltd v Shoucair* [1969] 1 A.C. 340 (temporary variation in rate of interest held not to amount to rescission of a mortgage).

[175] [1929] 2 K.B. 316.

[176] *Plymouth Corp v Harvey* [1971] 1 W.L.R. 549 (lease for seven years), and possibly *Mitas v Hyams* [1951] 2 T.L.R. 1215 (where the length of the lease is not stated).

[177] e.g. *Morris v Baron & Co* [1918] A.C. 1; *McCausland v Duncan Lawrie Ltd* [1997] 1 W.L.R. 38.

[178] See above, para.3–069.

[179] See above, para.3–076 et seq.

5–035   **Clauses prohibiting oral amendment.** A contract may contain a term stipulating that it cannot be modified or varied unless in writing. Such terms cannot entirely prevent an oral variation since "there is no reason why the contract, including the clause requiring variations to be in writing, could not have been varied orally."[180] It is, ultimately, a question of the intention of the parties.

---

[180] *Westbrook Resources Ltd v Globe Metallurgical Inc* [2009] EWCA Civ 310; [2009] 2 Lloyd's Rep. 224 at [13]; *I-Way Ltd v World Online Telecom Ltd* [2002] EWCA Civ 413 at [9]; *Spring Finance Ltd v HS Real Co LLC* [2009] EWHC 3580 (Comm) at [36]; [2011] EWHC 57 (Comm) at [53] ("court would be likely to require strong evidence before reaching such a finding"). Contrast: *United Bank Ltd v Asif*, February 11, 2000, CA.

THE CONTENTS OF A CONTRACT

The contents of a contract depend primarily on the words used by the parties **6–001**
in entering into the contract: these make up its express terms. A contract may, in
addition, contain terms which are not expressly stated, but which are implied,
either because that is found to be the intention of the parties, or by operation of
law, or by custom or usage.

1. EXPRESS TERMS

Where a contract is made orally, the ascertainment of its terms raises in the first **6–002**
place the pure question of fact: what did the parties say? Once this has been
determined, a further question can arise as to the meaning of the words used. In
answering this question, the court applies the objective test of agreement.[1] Under
that test, a party cannot enforce the contract in the sense which he gave to the
words, if that sense differs from the one which the other party reasonably gave to
them.[2] Further problems of ascertaining or proving express terms and their
meaning can arise where the contract is, or appears to have been, reduced to
writing.

(a) Joinder of Documents

Incorporation by express reference. The terms of a contract may be con- **6–003**
tained in more than one document. One of these may expressly refer to another,
e.g. where a contract is made subject to standard terms settled by a trade
association. Those terms are then incorporated by reference into the contract; if
there are several editions of the standard terms, the contract is prima facie taken

---

[1] See above, paras 1–002, 2–002.
[2] See below, para.6–006 et seq.

to refer to the most recent edition.[3] It may also incorporate amendments validly made by the association.[4]

6–004   **Conflicting documents.** The parties may purport to incorporate one document in another by express reference, not realising that the terms of the two documents conflict. Where there is an *inconsistency* between negotiated terms and incorporated standard terms, it is the former which will prevail,[5] subject to any overriding provision in the standard terms.[6] It has been said that the inconsistency must be "clear and direct".[7] It is not enough if one term "*qualifies or modifies*" the effect of another[8] and the court should ask whether a "reasonable commercial construction of the whole [contract] can reconcile two provisions (whether typed or printed)."[9] In *Pagnan SpA v Tradax Ocean Transportation SA*[10] the special conditions in an fob contract were said to "prevail in so far as they may be inconsistent" with the printed clauses of GAFTA 119 which was incorporated into the contract. The special conditions required the sellers "to provide for export certificate", whereas one of the terms of GAFTA 119 provided that "in case of prohibition of export (etc.) . . . this contract or any unfulfilled portion thereof shall be cancelled." It was held that the two terms could be reconciled on the basis that the sellers were to provide for the export certificate, but, in case of prohibition of export by the government, the unfulfilled portion of the contract was to be cancelled. This did not deprive the special condition of effect. If the certificate was not provided for as a result of oversight, or error, or possibly simply because the authorities failed to issue it, the sellers would have been liable.

6–005   **Incorporation without express reference.** A contract may be contained in several documents even though one does not expressly refer to the other. Suppose, for example, that a series of dealings takes place under a "master contract", a separate document being executed each time an individual contract is made. All these contracts may be subject to the master contract, even though they do not refer to it.[11] Similarly, a policy of insurance can be read together with the rules of the mutual insurance society which had issued it,[12] although the policy does not expressly refer to the rules[13]; and a contract to purchase securities may be held to incorporate the terms of a prospectus on the faith of which they were bought.[14] A

---

[3] *Smith v South Wales Switchgear Ltd* [1978] 1 W.L.R. 165.

[4] *Shearson Lehman Hutton Inc v Maclaine Watson & Co* [1989] 2 Lloyd's Rep. 570 at 589; cf. *The Marinor* [1996] 1 Lloyd's Rep. 301.

[5] *Adamastos Shipping Co v Anglo-Saxon Petroleum* [1959] A.C. 133; *The Leonidas* [2001] 1 Lloyd's Rep. 533, at 536; *The Starsin* [2003] UKHL 12; [2004] 1 A.C. 715; *The Eternity* [2009] 1 Lloyds Rep. 107 at 113.

[6] *Northwest Regional Metropolitan Hospital Board v TA Bickerton & Sons Ltd* [1970] 1 W.L.R. 607, at 617; *Fenice Investments Inc v Jerram Falkus Construction Ltd* [2009] EWHC 3272 (TCC); 128 Con L.R. 124.

[7] *The Eternity* [2009] 1 Lloyds Rep. 107 at 113.

[8] *Pagnan SpA v Tradax Ocean Transportation SA* [1987] 2 Lloyd's Rep. 342 at 350.

[9] *The Leonidas* [2001] 1 Lloyd's Rep. 533 at 536.

[10] [1987] 2 Lloyd's Rep. 342. cf. *The Leonidas* [2001] 1 Lloyd's Rep. 533; *The Northgate* [2007] EWHC 2796 (Comm); [2008] 1 Lloyd's Rep. 511; *The Lowlands Orchid* [2009] EWHC 2883 (Comm); [2010] 1 Lloyd's Rep 317; *Société Générale v Geys* [2011] EWCA Civ 307 at [29]–[30].

[11] *Panorama Developments (Guildford) Ltd v Fidelis Furnishing Fabrics Ltd* [1971] 2 Q.B. 711.

[12] *Edwards v Aberayron Insurance Society Ltd* (1876) 1 Q.B.D. 563.

[13] For difficulties relating to joinder where contracts have to be evidenced in writing, see above, para.5–024.

[14] *Jacobs v Batavia & General Plantations Trust Ltd* [1924] 1 Ch. 287, affirmed [1924] 2 Ch. 329; another possible explanation of the case is that there was a collateral contract: below, para.6–029.

chain of emails may also be read together even if a later email does not expressly refer back to the earlier emails.[15] Such incorporation without express reference appears to depend on the intention of the parties, determined in accordance with the objective test of agreement.

(b) Interpretation[16]

It has been noted for comment[17] that previous editions of this book did not contain a section on the interpretation of contracts generally.[18] It is now included to acknowledge the influence of Lord Hoffmann's summary of the general principles of interpretation in *Investors Compensation Scheme Ltd v West Bromwich Building Society*,[19] but such acknowledgement is still comparatively short.[20] The reason for this is provided by Lord Goff, writing extra-judicially, who noted that it is neither "easy", nor "helpful" to consider cases on the construction of contracts, since they depend so much on the particular words of the contract[21] (and, one might now add, the "background" against which they were used[22]). It is nevertheless possible to give some indication of the general principles and the broad approach of the courts, which has altered over time.   **6–006**

The significance of Lord Hoffmann's "re-statement". It is quite common to see what Lord Hoffmann described as his "summary" of the principles of interpretation referred to as a "re-statement".[23] He himself was not advocating a radical change in the approach of the courts since, as he pointed out,[24] a "fundamental change" had already overtaken this branch of the law as a result of a number of earlier cases.[25] What his "re-statement" appears to have done, however, is to make more prominent the impact of that fundamental change. Certainly it now seems customary for the consideration of any issue of interpretation which arises in a case to begin with a reminder of the principles he set out.[26]   **6–007**

The basic principle. The first of those principles is that: **6–008**

"Interpretation is the ascertainment of the meaning which the document would convey to a reasonable person having all the knowledge which would

---

[15] *Golden Ocean Group Ltd v Salgaocar Mining Industries PVT* [2011] EWHC 56 (Comm).

[16] Lewison, *The Interpretation of Contracts* (4th edn); McMeel, *The Construction of Contracts* (2nd edn); Staughton [1999] C.L.J. 303; McLauchlan (2000) 19 N.Z.U.L.R. 147; McMeel 119 L.Q.R. 272; Nicholls 121 L.Q.R. 577; Berg 122 L.Q.R. 354; Spigelman 81 A.L.J. 322.

[17] See, e.g. Burrows, in Burrows & Peel (eds) *Contract Terms*.

[18] Particular aspects of interpretation are considered elsewhere, e.g. the admissibility of extrinsic evidence as an aid to construction (see below, para.6–021) and the rules relating to the construction of exemption clauses (see below, para.7–014 et seq.).

[19] [1998] 1 W.L.R. 896 at 912–913.

[20] For a detailed account, see *Chitty on Contracts* (30th edn), para.12–041 et seq.

[21] [1984] L.M.C.L.Q. 382 at 385.

[22] See below, para.6–010.

[23] Further "re-stated" in *Chartbrook Ltd v Persimmon Homes Ltd* [2009] UKHL 38; [2009] A.C. 1101; for an excellent summary, see *Scottish Widows and Life Assurance Society v BGC International* [2011] EWHC 729 (Ch) at [17].

[24] [1998] 1 W.L.R. 896 at 912.

[25] In particular, *Prenn v Simmonds* [1971] 1 W.L.R. 1382 at 1384–1386 and *Reardon Smith Line Ltd v Yngvar Hansen-Tangen* [1976] 1 W.L.R. 989.

[26] In addition to the five principles considered in the following paragraphs, Lord Hoffmann also referred to the discarding of the "old intellectual baggage of 'legal' interpretation" ([1998] 1 W.L.R. 896 at 912); the extent to which this may have been intended to refer to the principle(s) of *contra proferentem* is considered below, para.7–016.

reasonably have been available to the parties in the situation in which they were at the time of the contract."[27]

In the later case of *The Starsin* he refined this basic principle so as to refer to the

> "reasonable person having all the background knowledge *which is reasonably available to the person or class of persons to whom the document is addressed.*"[28]

Thus, in *The Starsin*, the document in question was a bill of lading and it was appropriate to ask what meaning it would have conveyed to the merchants or bankers to whom it was addressed and who would rely on it in their dealings.[29] More generally, in the commercial context, the approach taken is "that a business sense will be given to business documents".[30]

6–009   **An objective approach.** It is clear from the first basic principle that the document setting out the parties' agreement must be interpreted objectively; it is not a question of what one party actually intended, or what the other party actually understood to have been intended, but rather what a reasonable person in the position of the parties would have understood the words to mean.[31] That this is the approach to interpretation is generally accepted, but what is more controversial is how the objective meaning is to be arrived at; in particular, to what extent does it depend on the words in the document, or the context in which they were used?

6–010   **What matters most: the words used, or the "background"?** The knowledge reasonably available to the parties at the time of the contract is sometimes referred to as the "background", or "the matrix of facts".[32] In the second of his principles, Lord Hoffmann explained that:

> "Subject to the requirement that it should have been reasonably available to the parties and to the exception to be mentioned next, it includes absolutely anything which would have affected the way in which the language of the document would have been understood by a reasonable man."[33]

The exception to which Lord Hoffmann refers is the non-admissibility of the "previous negotiations of the parties and their declarations of subjective intent."[34]

---

[27] [1998] 1 W.L.R. 896 at 912.

[28] [2004] 1 A.C. 715 at [73] (emphasis added); cf. *Rennie v Westbury Homes (Holdings) Ltd* [2007] EWCA Civ 1401.

[29] Lord Steyn emphasised that the bill should be read in the way in which a reasonable person "versed in the shipping trade" would read it: [2004] 1 A.C. 715 at [45]; Peel 120 L.Q.R. 11.

[30] *Glynn v Margetson & Co* [1893] A.C. 351 at 359; approved by Lord Bingham in *The Starsin*, above, fn.28 at [10]; *Mannai Investment Co Ltd v Eagle Star Life Assurance Co Ltd* [1997] A.C. 749 at 771.

[31] *Deutsche Geonossenschaftsbank v Burnhope* [1995] 1 W.L.R. 1580 at 1587; cf. below, paras 1–002, 2–002.

[32] *Prenn v Simmonds* [1971] 1 W.L.R. 1382 at 1384, per Lord Wilberforce. Since the *ICS* case it has become customary to refer to the "background".

[33] [1998] 1 W.L.R. 896 at 912–913.

[34] ibid. at 913.

This is dealt with below.[35] In the later case of *BCCI v Ali*[36] Lord Hoffmann felt it necessary to stress both that the "background" only included "absolutely anything" which a reasonable person would have regarded as *relevant* and that the "primary source for understanding what the parties meant is their language interpreted in accordance with conventional usage".[37] The short answer to the question at the start of this paragraph is, therefore, that one begins with the words used by the parties and confers on them their meaning in conventional usage, unless there is anything in the "background" to indicate that some other meaning would have been conveyed to the reasonable person.[38] In this regard, Lord Hoffmann also stressed, in the *ICS* case, that one does "not easily accept that people have made linguistic mistakes, particularly in formal documents".[39]

A more "purposive" approach. The approach which the courts have taken to interpretation has been described at different stages as a "literal" approach,[40] or a "purposive" approach.[41] This can be misleading since the literal approach was never entirely literal and nor is the purposive approach entirely purposive.[42] What can be said, notwithstanding his clarification in the *BCCI* case as to the primacy of the language used by the parties, is that Lord Hoffmann's re-statement appears to have promoted, or confirmed, a *more* purposive approach to the interpretation of contracts.[43]   6–011

The obvious difficulty with the purposive approach is that what may strike one judge as purposive interpretation may strike another as the re-writing of the contract. This is most clearly demonstrated in *Kookmin Bank v Rainy Sky SA*.[44] The claimants were entitled to a refund under a shipbuilding contract if the

---

[35] See below, para.6–022.

[36] [2001] UKHL 8; [2002] 1 A.C. 251.

[37] ibid. at [39].

[38] But it is not a case of "interpreting" the agreement first and then looking at the surrounding circumstances: "The interpretative exercise is the single exercise taking into account the factual matrix", *Bright Asset Ltd v Lewis* [2011] EWCA Civ 122 at [28].

[39] [1998] 1 W.L.R. 896 at 913. Where it is submitted that the court should depart from the definition of a term provided by the contract itself, it has been said that nothing short of an absurd result will do if the term is applied as defined: *City Inn Jersey Ltd v Ten Trinity Square Ltd* [2008] EWCA Civ 156; (2008) 10 E.G. 167 at [8].

[40] Said to be exemplified by the observations of Cozens Hardy M.R. in *Lovell and Christmas Ltd v Wall* (1911) 104 L.T. 85; cf. *Shore v Wilson* (1842) 9 Cl. & Fin. 355 at 365.

[41] See, e.g. *Reardon Smith Line Ltd v Yngvar Hansen-Tangen* [1976] 1 W.L.R. 989 at 995–996, per Lord Wilberforce.

[42] *Charter Reinsurance Co Ltd v Fagan* [1997] AC 313 at 326 and 350; *Petromec Inc v Petroleo Brasileiro SA Petrobras* [2005] EWCA Civ 891; [2006] 1 Lloyd's Rep. 121 at [23]. See also *Prenn v Simmonds* [1971] 1 W.L.R. 1382 and the observation of Lord Wilberforce (at 1384) that: "there is no need to appeal here to any modern, anti-literal, tendencies, for Lord Blackburn's well-known judgment in *River Wear Commissioners v Adamson* (1877) 2 App. Cas. 743, 763 provides ample warrant for a liberal approach"; cf. Lord Steyn's example of an entirely literal approach taken from *The Works of William Paley* in *Sirius International Ins Co v FAI General Ins Ltd* [2004] UKHL 54; [2004] 1 W.L.R. 3251 at [19].

[43] Lord Steyn has been particularly supportive of such a move: *Deutsche Geonossenschaftsbank v Burnhope* [1995] 1 W.L.R. 1580 at 1589; *Lord Napier and Ettrick v R F Kershaw Ltd* [1999] 1 W.L.R. 756 at 763; *Mannai Investment Co Ltd v Eagle Star Life Assurance Co Ltd* [1997] A.C. 749 at 770; *Total Gas Marketing Ltd v Arco British Ltd* [1998] 2 Lloyd's Rep. 209 at 221; *Sirius International Ins Co v FAI General Ins Ltd* [2004] UKHL 54; [2004] 1 W.L.R. 3251. Not all agree with the new so-called "purposive" approach: see, e.g. Staughton [1999] C.L.J. 303, and a number of CA decisions referred to therein.

[44] [2010] EWCA Civ 582; 130 Con L.R. 19; Davies 127 L.Q.R. 185; cf. *Barclays Plc v HHY Luxembourg SARL* [2010] EWCA Civ 1248.

contract was terminated, or there was an "insolvency event". They claimed a refund for an insolvency event and sought recovery from the defendant bank under a guarantee given in support of the refund. The guarantee referred to "all such sums due to [the claimant] under the Contract", but also referred only to the claimant's entitlement to a refund on "termination" and not for an insolvency event. The defendant argued that the guarantee therefore only extended to a refund payable on termination. The arguments from textual interpretation were fairly evenly divided.[45] Tuckey L.J. preferred the interpretation advanced by the claimants that the guarantee was intended to cover an insolvency event: "No credible commercial reason has been advanced as to why the parties (or the [claimant's] financiers) should have agreed to this [i.e. to exclude a refund payable upon an event of insolvency]. On the contrary, it makes no commercial sense."[46] By contrast, Patten L.J. preferred the interpretation put forward by the bank:[47] " . . . merely to say that no credible commercial reason has been advanced for the limited scope of the bond does, in my view, put us in real danger of substituting our own judgment of the commerciality of the transaction for that of those who were actually party to it."[48]

6–012   **Something wrong with the language.** It is, perhaps, the fourth and fifth of the principles set out by Lord Hoffmann which have been largely responsible for any shift in emphasis when it comes to interpretation: "The background may not merely enable the reasonable man to choose between the possible meaning of words which are ambiguous[49] but even (as occasionally happens in ordinary life) to conclude that the parties must, for whatever reason, have used the wrong words or syntax", or "that something must have gone wrong with the language".[50] In this latter regard, in the later case of *Chartbrook Ltd v Persimmon Homes Ltd*,[51] Lord Hoffmann went on to say that there is no "limit to the amount of red ink or verbal arrangement or correction which the court is allowed. All that is required is that it should be clear that something has gone wrong with the language and that it should be clear what a reasonable person would have understood the parties to have meant."[52]

---

[45] Both Tuckey L.J. and Patten L.J. considered the provisions of the shipbuilding contract which dealt with the requirement to put in place the guarantee but drew different conclusions from them.
[46] at [30].
[47] The bank prevailed as a result of the judgment of Thorpe L.J. who found himself in "the invidious position of expressing a decisive opinion in a field that is completely foreign" (at [53]).
[48] at [51]. A view which echoes that of Lord Lloyd in the *ICS* case, below fn.54 and of Lord Walker in *In re Sigma Finance Corporation* [2009] UKSC 2; [2010] 1 All E.R. 571 at [44], and Rix L.J. in *ING Bank NV v Ros Roca SA* [2011] EWCA Civ 353 at [110]: see below, para.6–012, text to fn.57.
[49] The purposive approach does not require, as a premise, that there should be any ambiguity in the conventional meaning of the words used: "Subsequent decisions have made plain that the factual matrix should always be considered, *even if the wording is unambiguous and sensible*", *Fitzroy Robinson Ltd v Mentmore Towers Ltd* [2009] EWHC 1552 (TCC) at [28] (emphasis added), citing *Egan v Static Control Components (Europe) Ltd* [2004] EWCA Civ 392; [2004] 2 Lloyd's Rep. 429. Contrast Lord Hope in *Multi-link Leisure Developments Ltd v North Lanarkshire Council* [2010] UKSC 47 at [11]: "Words should not be added which are not there, and words which are there should not be changed, taken out or moved from the place in the clause where they have been put by the parties. It may be necessary to do some of these things at a later stage to make sense of the language. But this *should not be done until it has become clear that the language the parties actually used creates an ambiguity which cannot be solved otherwise*." (emphasis added).
[50] [1998] 1 W.L.R. 896 at 913. cf. *The Antaios* [1985] A.C. 191 at 201.
[51] [2009] UKHL 38; [2009] A.C. 1101
[52] ibid. at [25]. See below, para.8–060, fn.339.

Thus, in the *ICS* case itself,[53] a number of investors, having been compensated by the Investors Compensation Scheme for the mis-selling of certain financial products, assigned to the Scheme any claims they had against the parties who were involved, including the building society which had provided the necessary funds by way of a mortgage on the investors' homes. In the assignment there was a reservation of "any claim (whether sounding in rescission for undue influence or otherwise) that you have or may have against (the building society) in which you claim an abatement of sums which you would otherwise have to pay to that society in respect of sums borrowed". The "natural and ordinary", or "literal", meaning of this reservation prevented the Scheme from bringing any proceedings against the building society. However, according to Lord Hoffmann it was clear from the background that all the reservation in question was intended to do was to reserve for the investors the right to rescind the mortgages they had taken out with the building society; any reference to abatement was limited to the effects of rescission, i.e. unwinding the mortgage, and was not intended to cover free-standing claims for damages. The words which should have been used and which were therefore found to have been intended were: "any claim sounding in rescission (whether for undue influence or otherwise)". This interpretation did not command the full support of the House of Lords,[54] and it has been suggested that it is indicative of an approach to interpretation which may leave little or no room for the doctrine of rectification.[55] It is, at the very least, a clear indication of the extent to which the courts are willing to adopt an interpretation which is most consistent with what appears to be the "purpose" of the document in question.[56]

It has been said that the distinction which the courts have to be wary of is that between a contract which "carries its own error within its own terms, as understood in context" where a purposive interpretation is permissible even to the extent of correcting the language used, and a contract which "will work perfectly sensibly in the context in which it was made, but it contains a flaw in that it does not provide for all eventualities". In relation to the latter it is not for the courts to remake the contract "on the basis of what the courts consider would have been reasonable, or more sensible, for the contract to have said".[57] This is not an easy distinction to draw, as demonstrated by the *Kookmin Bank* case, above.

(c) The Parol Evidence Rule

(i) *Statement of the rule*

The parol evidence rule states that evidence cannot be admitted (or, even if admitted, cannot be used) to add to, vary or contradict a written instrument.[58] In   6–013

---

[53] cf. a similar rearrangement of the wording of the relevant clause in *Chartbrook*, above fn.51.

[54] Lord Lloyd dissented, on the basis that the result favoured by the majority amounted to impermissible "creative interpretation": [1998] 1 W.L.R. 896 at 904.

[55] Burrows, in Burrows & Peel (eds), *Contract Terms*; Buxton [2010] C.L.J. 253 (also taking into account the later decision in *Chartbrook Ltd v Persimmon Homes Ltd* [2009] UKHL 38; [2009] A.C. 1101). On rectification, see below, para.8–059 et seq.

[56] See also: *HIH Casualty & General Insurance v Chase Manhattan Bank* [2003] UKHL 6; [2003] 2 Lloyd's Rep 61, discussed below, para.7–035; *Egan v Static Control Components (Europe) Ltd* [2004] EWCA Civ 392; [2004] 2 Lloyd's Rep. 429; *Barclays plc v HHY Luxembourg SARL* [2010] EWCA Civ 1248.

[57] *ING Bank NV v Ros Roca SA* [2011] EWCA Civ 353 at [110].

[58] *Jacobs v Batavia & General Plantations Trust Ltd* [1924] 1 Ch. 287 at 295; *Rabin v Gerson Berger Association Ltd* [1986] 1 W.L.R. 526 at 531, 537; *Orion Ins Co v Sphere Drake Ins Plc* [1992] 1 Lloyd's Rep. 239 at 273.

relation to contracts, the rule means that, where a contract has been reduced to writing, neither party can rely on extrinsic evidence of terms alleged to have been agreed, i.e. on evidence not contained in the document. Although the rule is generally stated as applying to *parol* evidence, it applies just as much to other forms of extrinsic evidence. Of course, if a contractual document incorporates another document by reference, evidence of the second document is admissible, but the rule prevents a party from relying on evidence that is extrinsic to both documents.[59]

There are obvious grounds of convenience for the application of the parol evidence rule to contracts: certainty is promoted by holding that parties who have reduced a contract to writing should be bound by the writing and by the writing alone.[60] On the other hand, the parol evidence rule will commonly be invoked where a dispute arises after the time of contracting as to what was actually said at that time; and in such cases one of the parties could feel aggrieved if evidence on the point was excluded merely because the disputed term was not set out in the contractual document.[61] Evidence extrinsic to the document is therefore admitted in a number of situations (to be discussed below) which fall outside the scope of the rule.

(ii) *Cases in which extrinsic evidence is admissible*

6–014   **Written agreement not the whole agreement.** When a contract is reduced to writing, there is a presumption that the writing was intended to include all the terms of the contract; but this presumption is rebuttable.[62] If the written document was not intended to set out all the terms on which the parties had actually agreed, extrinsic evidence is admissible. It seems that a document which is intended simply to form a record of a previously concluded contract will prima facie be a mere memorandum[63]; while a document the execution of which marks the actual conclusion of a contract is more likely to be taken to contain all the terms of the contract.[64]

It has been argued that the right of a party to rely on extrinsic evidence in the present group of cases turns the parol evidence rule (as applied to contracts) into "no more than a circular statement".[65] For if the rule applies only where the written document is intended to contain *all* the terms of the contract, evidence of other terms would be useless even if admitted (since they would not form part of the contract); while the rule never prevents a party from relying on evidence of terms which *were* intended to be part of the contract. Accordingly, on this view,

---

[59] *Jacobs v Batavia & General Plantations Trust Ltd*, above.

[60] *Rabin v Gerson Berger Association Ltd* [1986] 1 W.L.R. 526 at 534, 537; *AIB Group Plc v Martin* [2001] UKHL 63; [2002] 1 W.L.R. 94 at [4].

[61] Contrast *AIB Group Plc v Martin*, above, at [4] with ibid. at [44] on the question whether this was the position in that case.

[62] *Gillespie Bros & Co v Cheney, Eggar & Co* [1896] 2 Q.B. 59 at 62.

[63] e.g. *Allen v Pink* (1838) 4 M. & W. 140; cf. *J Evans & Son (Portsmouth) Ltd v Andrea Merzario* [1976] 1 W.L.R. 1078 at 1083; *The Riza and Sun* [1997] 2 Lloyd's Rep. 314 at 319–320. This view would account for the special position of bills of lading: as to this see *The Ardennes* [1951] 1 K.B. 55; but for the need to protect third parties to whom such documents are transferred, see *Leduc v Ward* (1888) 20 Q.B.D. 475; *Carver on Bills of Lading* (2nd edn, 2005), paras 3–004 to 3–009.

[64] *Hutton v Watling* [1948] Ch. 398 at 404.

[65] Law Commission Report on *The Parol Evidence Rule* (Law Com. No.154), para.2.7; Marston [1986] C.L.J. 192; *Prince Jefri Bolkiah v Brunei Darussalam* [2007] UKPC 63 at [47].

no injustice is caused by the operation of the rule.[66] There is much force in this view in cases in which, at the time of contracting, both parties actually shared a common intention with regard to the term in question. But in most cases in which the rule is invoked this is not the position: the dispute arises precisely because the parties had different intentions, and one alleges, while the other denies, that terms not set out in the document were intended to form part of the contract. In such cases, the court will attach importance to the appearance of the document: if it *looks* like a complete contract to one of the parties taking a reasonable view of it, then the rule will prevent the other party from relying on extrinsic evidence to show that the contract also contained other terms.[67]

This result has been described as being simply an application of the objective test of agreement[68]; but, even if it can be so regarded, it is such a common and frequently recurring application of this test as to amount to an independent rule. In cases of the present kind, moreover, the law goes beyond the normal objective test. That test normally requires the party relying on it to prove that he reasonably believed that the other party was contracting on the terms alleged.[69] Where a document *looks* like a complete contract, the party relying on it does not have to prove that he had such a belief: he can rely on a presumption to that effect which it is up to the other party to rebut.[70] As laymen are known to attach greater importance than the law does to writing in a contractual context, it will be hard for the party relying on extrinsic evidence to rebut the presumption that the written document was an exclusive record of the terms agreed. Moreover, the objective test normally prevents a party from relying on his "private but uncommunicated intention as to what was to be agreed".[71] The presumption which applies in the case of an apparently complete contractual document goes beyond this: it prevents a party from relying on evidence of intention that was not "private and uncommunicated" at all, but simply not recorded in the document.

For these reasons, it is submitted that the admissibility of extrinsic evidence, where it is proved that the document was not in fact intended to contain all the terms of the contract, does not turn the rule into a merely "circular statement".[72] Whether it also supports the conclusion that the rule is not one that "could lead to evidence being unjustly excluded"[73] is perhaps more doubtful. The primary purpose of the rule, like that of the objective test of agreement, is to promote certainty, sometimes even at the expense of justice.[74] Where the parties have brought into being an apparently complete contractual document, the rejection of evidence of extrinsic terms that were actually agreed may cause injustice to the party relying on those terms, while the reception of such evidence may cause injustice to the other party, if he reasonably believed that the document formed an

---

[66] Law Com. No.154, above; and see also para.1.7. See, to similar effect, the willingness of the courts to allow in terms notwithstanding the inclusion of an entire agreement clause: *Cheverny Consulting Ltd v Whitehead Mann Ltd* [2005] EWHC 243; [2006] EWCA Civ 1303.

[67] Wedderburn [1959] C.L.J. 58, 62.

[68] Law Com. No.154, above, paras 2.14, 2.17; cf. *National Westminster Bank Plc v Binney* [2011] EWHC 694 (QB) at [14].

[69] See above, paras 1–002, 2–002.

[70] See above, fn.62.

[71] Law Com. No.154, above, para.2.14; cf. above, para.4–027.

[72] cf. the authorities cited in fn.58, above.

[73] Law Com. No.154, para.2.7.

[74] *AIB Group Plc v Martin* [2001] UKHL 63; [2002] 1 W.L.R. 94 at [4].

exclusive record of the contract.[75] The question is which, on balance, is the greater injustice. Where the evidence is rejected because the party relying on it cannot overcome the presumption arising from the fact that the document *looks* like a complete contract, the greater injustice would appear to lie in the exclusion of the evidence; for the presumption seems to be based on the nature and form of the document, rather than on any actual belief of the party relying on it, that it formed an exclusive record of the contract.[76]

6–015   **Validity.** The rule prevents a party from relying on extrinsic evidence only as to the *contents* of the contract, and not as to its *validity*. Such evidence can therefore be used to establish the presence or absence of consideration or of contractual intention,[77] or some invalidating cause such as incapacity, misrepresentation, mistake[78] or *non est factum*.[79] Evidence has similarly been held admissible to show that provisions in an agreement purporting to be a licence to occupy a room (as opposed to a lease of it) were a "mere sham"[80] in that they had failed to state the parties' true intention and had been inserted simply in an attempt to evade the Rent Act.

6–016   **Implied terms.** The rule prevents a party from relying on extrinsic evidence only as to the express terms of the contract. Where the contract is silent on a matter on which a term is normally implied by law, parol evidence may be given to support, or to rebut, the usual implication. Thus a buyer of coal can show that he made known to the seller the particular purpose for which he required the coal, so as to raise the implication that he relied on the seller's skill and judgment.[81] Conversely, a person who takes out a policy of marine insurance can show that the insurer knew the ship to be unseaworthy, and so negative the usual implied warranty of seaworthiness.[82]

6–017   **Oral warranties.** Where parties enter into a written contract of sale, the rule would prima facie prevent the buyer from relying on evidence of oral undertakings as to the quality of the subject-matter; but this application of the rule is subject to two qualifications. First, an exclusion clause contained in a written contract can be overridden by an express oral warranty given at the time of sale.[83] Secondly, an oral statement of fact may operate as a misrepresentation in spite of its purported incorporation into the contract as a warranty[84]; and where this is the case, the oral

---

[75] For the rejection of evidence in such circumstances, see *Hutton v Watling* [1948] Ch. 398 at 404; and cf. *Rabin v Gerson Berger Association Ltd* [1986] 1 W.L.R. 526 where the rule was applied to a declaration of trust but said at 536 to apply to contracts.

[76] The Law Commission had, before publishing the Report referred to in fn.65, above, provisionally recommended the abolition of the rule: Law Commission Working Paper No.76 (1976).

[77] *Clever v Kirkman* (1876) 33 L.T. 672; *Kleinwort Benson Ltd v Malaysian Mining Corp* [1989] 1 W.L.R. 379 at 392; *Carmichael v National Power Plc* [1999] 1 W.L.R. 2042; *Ove Arup & Partners International Ltd v Mirant Asia-Pacific (Hong Kong) Construction Ltd* [2003] EWCA Civ 1729; [2004] B.L.R. 75

[78] *Campbell Discount Co v Gall* [1961] 1 Q.B. 431 reversed on other points, by Consumer Credit Act 1974, s.56 and by *Branwhite v Worcester Works Finance Ltd* [1969] 1 A.C. 552; below, paras 16–006, 22–013.

[79] *Roe v R A Naylor Ltd* (1918) 87 L.J.K.B. 958 at 964; below, para.8–076.

[80] *AG Securities v Vaughan* [1990] 1 A.C. 417 at 469, 475; cf. *Chase Manhattan Equities Ltd v Goodman* [1991] B.C.L.C. 897.

[81] *Gillespie Bros & Co v Cheney, Eggar & Co* [1896] 2 Q.B. 59.

[82] *Burges v Wickham* (1863) 3 B. & S. 669; Blackburn J. dissented on this point.

[83] See below, para.7–040.

[84] Misrepresentation Act 1967, s.1(a); below, para.9–091.

statement can be used as evidence, not of the contents of the contract, but of an invalidating cause.

Operation of the contract. Extrinsic evidence can be used to show that the **6–018** contract does not yet operate, or that it has ceased to operate. Thus in *Pym v Campbell*[85] a written agreement for the sale of a patent was drawn up, and evidence was admitted of an oral stipulation that the agreement should not *become operative* until a third party had approved of the invention. It seems from the reasoning of the court that evidence of an oral stipulation that the agreement should *cease to bind* if the third party disapproved of the invention would not have been admissible. On the other hand, evidence is admissible to show that a written contract has been varied or rescinded.[86] It is not easy to deduce from the purpose of the parol evidence rule why evidence should be admissible in the first and third, but not in the second of these cases.

Evidence as to parties. Extrinsic evidence can be used to identify the parties[87] **6–019** and to show in what capacities the parties contracted.[88] Where a person contracts ostensibly as principal, evidence is admissible to prove that he really acted as another's agent so as to entitle the latter to sue[89] unless such evidence contradicts the express description of the agent in the contract.[90] As the ostensible contracting party is in such cases personally liable even if he acted as agent, the evidence would not normally relieve him from liability. But in *Wake v Harrop*[91] an agent signed a charterparty on behalf of the charterer, but so as to make himself personally liable. He did so after an oral agreement with the shipowner that he should not be personally liable. It was held that the agent could rely on the oral agreement, if not at law, at any rate by way of equitable defence. Conversely, where a person contracted on the face of the document as agent, evidence was held to be admissible of his contemporaneous statements that he intended to undertake personal liability.[92]

Defence to specific performance. Failure to perform an oral promise may be **6–020** available as a defence when the party who made it claims specific performance of the written agreement.[93] Alternatively, in such a case, the court may have a discretion to order specific performance on the terms that the claimant performs the oral undertaking.[94] Where, as in the authorities which support these propositions, the contract was one for the disposition of an interest in land, it now

---

[85] (1856) 6 E. & B. 370.

[86] *Morris v Baron & Co* [1918] A.C. 1; *Goss v Nugent* (1833) 5 B. & Ad. 58 at 65. It does not, of course, follow from the admissibility of evidence of a variation that the variation can be enforced: as to this, see above, para.5–028 et seq.

[87] *OTV Birwelco Ltd v Technical & General Guarantee Co Ltd* [2002] EWHC 2240 (TCC); [2002] 4 All E.R. 668 at [14]; *Gastronome (UK) Ltd v Anglo-Dutch Meats (UK) Ltd* [2006] EWCA Civ 1233; [2006] 2 Lloyd's Rep 587 at [16]–[17]; cf. *Shogun Finance v Hudson* [2003] UKHL 62; [2004] 1 A.C. 919; discussed below, para.8–039 et seq.

[88] *Newell v Radford* (1867) L.R. 3 C.P. 52; cf. *The Riza and Sun* [1997] 2 Lloyd's Rep. 314 at 320; *Manches LLP v Freer* [2006] EWHC 991 at [12].

[89] *Humfrey v Dale* (1857) 7 E. & B. 266, affirmed (1858) E.B. & E. 1004; *Internaut Shipping GmbH v Fercometal SARL* [2003] EWCA Civ 812; [2003] 2 Lloyd's Rep. 430 at [56] (evidence to show no agency).

[90] See para.16–057.

[91] (1861) 6 H. & N. 768, affirmed 1 H. & C. 202.

[92] *Sun Alliance Pensions Life & Investment Services Ltd v RJL* [1991] 2 Lloyd's Rep. 410.

[93] *Martin v Pycroft* (1852) 2 D.M. & G. 785, 795; cf. *Scott v Bradley* [1971] Ch. 850.

[94] See *London & Birmingham Ry v Winter* (1840) Cr. & Ph. 57.

generally has to be made in writing by incorporating *all* its express terms in a contractual document.[95] Failure to incorporate the oral promise would therefore prevent the contract from coming into existence,[96] and would lead to the dismissal of a claim (whether for specific performance or for damages) on that ground, unless the promise could be said to take effect only as a collateral contract.[97] But the reasoning of the older authorities would still apply where specific performance was sought of a contract which was in fact in writing, even though there was no legal requirement to this effect.[98]

6–021   **Aid to interpretation.** It has been said that where the words of the contract are "clear", extrinsic evidence cannot be used to explain their meaning,[99] unless they have a special meaning by custom.[100] Extrinsic evidence could, on the other hand, be used to explain words or phrases which are ambiguous,[101] or which, if taken literally, make no sense,[102] or conflict with others in the same document,[103] as well as technical terms. This restricted approach to the admissibility of extrinsic evidence must now be reassessed in light of the second of the principles of interpretation "re-stated" by Lord Hoffmann in the *ICS* case.[104] Subject to the first of the exceptions to be mentioned below, he was of the view that the "background" against which the meaning of a document should be ascertained includes "absolutely anything"[105] which would have affected the way the language used would have been understood by a reasonable person. Furthermore, there is no prior requirement that the language used should have been ambiguous.[106] Rather than regarding extrinsic evidence as generally inadmissible, subject to exceptions under which it is admissible, the present approach appears to be to regard it as generally admissible, subject only to exceptions under which it is inadmissible.

6–022   **Pre-contractual negotiations.**[107] The first of those exceptions is referred to by Lord Hoffmann as "the previous negotiations of the parties and their declarations of subjective intent".[108] The exclusion of such evidence has been the subject of considerable criticism[109] and it has been argued that the more relevant question is the *weight* to be given to evidence of previous negotiations rather than its

---

[95] Law of Property (Miscellaneous Provisions) Act 1989, s.2(1); above, para.5–008.

[96] See above, para.5–088.

[97] See above, para.5–088; below, para.6–029.

[98] e.g. if it was a lease for less than three years (above, para.5–008) or a contract for the sale of "unique" goods (below, para.21–023).

[99] *Bank of New Zealand v Simpson* [1900] A.C. 182 at 189.

[100] See below, para.6–026.

[101] *Bank of New Zealand v Simpson* [1900] A.C. 182; cf. *Pao On v Lau Yiu Long* [1980] A.C. 614 at 631; *Forsikringsaktieselskapet Vesta v Butcher* [1989] A.C. 852 at 909–910; *Shearson Lehman Hutton Inc v Maclaine Watson & Co Ltd* [1989] 2 Lloyd's Rep. 570 at 591.

[102] *The Sounion* [1987] 1 Lloyd's Rep. 230 ("grates and stoves" on ships which no longer carried such implements).

[103] e.g. *Mannai Investment Co Ltd v Eagle Star Life Assurance Co* [1997] A.C. 749; *BOC Group Plc v Centeon LLC* [1999] 1 All E.R. (Comm) 970 at 979.

[104] *Investors Compensation Scheme Ltd v West Bromwich Building Society* [1998] 1 W.L.R. 896; discussed above, para.6–006 et seq.

[105] i.e. anything relevant: see above, para.6–010.

[106] See above, fn.49.

[107] Mitchell 26 J.C.L. 134.

[108] [1998] 1 W.L.R. 896.

[109] McMeel 119 L.Q.R. 272; Nicholls 121 L.Q.R. 577; McLauchlan (2009) 31 Sydney Law Review 5.

admissibility,[110] e.g. there is clearly nothing to be gained from the admission of the parties' declarations of subjective intent.[111] Nonetheless, the exclusion of such evidence as an aid to the interpretation of a written contract was confirmed by the House of Lords in *Chartbrook Ltd v Persimmon Homes Ltd*.[112] In the leading speech, Lord Hoffmann accepted that the admission of such evidence would not be inconsistent with the objective theory of interpretation since there will be cases in which it would be relevant by throwing light upon what the parties would reasonably have been taken to have meant by the language which they adopted to express their agreement (in other words, if the courts only took into account evidence of any real weight[113]). He supported its continued exclusion on pragmatic grounds, i.e. that since in most cases such evidence would be irrelevant, it would create greater uncertainty and add to the cost of advice, litigation or arbitration to admit it in every case in the hope of finding something relevant. He also acknowledged that its admission could prejudice third parties, such as assignees, who would not have taken part in the negotiations (though as he also pointed out they may not be familiar with the "background" to the contract, which is admissible[114]).

The continued exclusion of the previous negotiations of the parties is, in part, based on the difficulty the courts would face in drawing the distinction between evidence that would assist in determining the intention of the parties, objectively ascertained, and evidence of their declarations of subjective intent. But by continuing to exclude such evidence altogether, the courts have to grapple with other, possibly equally, difficult distinctions. For example, in *Chartbrook* Lord Hoffmann acknowledged that evidence of previous negotiations may be admitted to "establish that a fact which may be relevant as background was known to the parties".[115] The continued exclusion of previous negotiations is also a little more difficult given the emphasis now on interpreting the language used in light of the "commercial purpose"[116] of the contract in question. It seems that it is necessary to

> "distinguish between admissible background evidence relating to the nature and object of the contractual venture and inadmissible evidence of the terms for which each party was contending in the course of negotiations."[117]

---

[110] McKendrick, in Worthington (ed.) *Commercial Law and Commercial Practice; Proforce Recruit Ltd v The Rugby Group Ltd* [2006] EWCA Civ 69 at [33]–[36]; Berg 122 L.Q.R. 354.

[111] *Prenn v Simmonds* [1971] 1 W.L.R. 1381 at 1385; *Pritchard v Briggs* [1980] Ch. 338; *The Good Helmsman* [1981] 1 Lloyd's Rep. 377 at 416; *The Scaptrade* [1981] 2 Lloyd's Rep. 425 at 432, affirmed [1983] 2 A.C. 694, without reference to this point; *AIB Group Plc v Martin* [2001] UKHL 63; [2001] 1 W.L.R. 99 at [4].

[112] [2009] UKHL 38; [2009] A.C. 1101; McLauchlan [2011] L.M.C.L.Q. 30.

[113] In *Chartbrook*, such evidence took the form of an earlier letter which, if interpreted objectively, was consistent with the interpretation put forward by the defendant and which ultimately prevailed, albeit without the aid of the said letter, as a result of the purposive approach which the House of Lords took to the clause in question.

[114] At [40]; cf. *National Bank of Sharjah v Dellborg* [1997] EWCA Civ 2070 per Saville L.J.

[115] At [42]. Expert evidence may be admitted to establish what the parties knew or believed at the time of the contract: *Pink Floyd Music Ltd v EMI Records Ltd* [2010] EWCA Civ 1429. There is no further bar to admission where the contract takes the form of a settlement agreement and the negotiations were conducted "without predjudice"; the rules applicable to contracts generally apply and no more: *Oceanbulk Shipping & Trading SA v TMT Asia Ltd* [2010] UKSC 44; [2010] 3 W.L.R. 1424.

[116] *Reardon Smith Line Ltd v Yngvar Hansen-Tangen* [1976] 1 W.L.R. 989 at 995–996.

[117] *The Tychi (No.2)* [2001] 2 Lloyd's Rep 403 at [29]; cf. *IRC v Raphael* [1935] A.C. 96 at 142; *Prenn v Simmonds* [1971] 1 W.L.R. 1382 at 1385; *Youell v Bland Welch & Co Ltd* [1992] 2 Lloyd's Rep. 127 at 133; *Bank of Scotland v Dunedin Property Investment Co Ltd* 1998 S.C. 657.

This may be a particularly difficult distinction to draw.[118] Lord Hoffmann was of the opinion that the risk of any injustice, i.e. of holding the parties to a contract which they did not intend had their intention been objectively assessed with the benefit of evidence of previous negotiations, should be met by admitting such evidence for the purpose of rectification,[119] or estoppel by convention.[120]

6–023   **Prior contract.** Evidence of a prior *contract* between the parties may be admissible as part of the "background"[121] surrounding the contract in issue, though if that contract was intended to supersede the prior one, then evidence of the prior contract is either inadmissible[122] or, even if admissible, "of little relevance".[123]

6–024   **"Private dictionary".** As an exception to the rule excluding evidence of previous negotiations, such evidence is admissible under the "private dictionary principle", i.e. to show that the parties placed on certain words or phrases in their contract an unconventional meaning, or gave meaning to a phrase that has no conventional meaning.[124] But this exception does not apply in a case where the court has to decide between two perfectly conventional meanings. If evidence of negotiations was admissible to aid the court's choice in such a case, it would negate the exclusionary rule itself.[125]

6–025   **Subsequent conduct.** A second exception to the admissibility of extrinsic evidence as an aid to interpretation, not in fact mentioned by Lord Hoffmann in his "re-statement", is that evidence of the *conduct* of the parties *after* the making of the contract will not be admitted. For if such evidence were admitted the undesirable result might follow

"that a contract meant one thing the day it was signed but, by reason of subsequent events, meant something different a month or a year later".[126]

---

[118] *Excelsior Group Productions Ltd v Yorkshire Television Ltd* [2009] EWHC 1751 (Comm) at [24] ("a line so fine it almost vanishes").

[119] See below, para.8–059 et seq. Whether its admission for the purposes of rectification would be any the less prejudicial to an assignee has been questioned: Berg 124 L.Q.R. 6; below, para.8–072.

[120] As in *ING Bank NV v Ros Roca SA* [2011] EWCA Civ 353. See generally above, para.3–094 et seq.

[121] *Egan v Static Control Components (Europe) Ltd* [2004] EWCA Civ 392; [2004] 2 Lloyd's Rep. 429 at [35]; *KPMG v Network Rail Infrastructure Ltd* [2007] EWCA Civ 363; [2007] Bus L.R. 1336; cf. *HIH Casualty & General Insurance Ltd v New Hampshire Insurance Co* [2001] 2 All E.R. (Comm) 39; [2001] EWCA Civ 735 at [83]; *St Ivel Ltd v Wincanton Group Ltd* [2008] EWCA Civ 1286.

[122] *Youell v Bland Welch & Co Ltd* [1992] 2 Lloyd's Rep. 127 at 141.

[123] *HIH Casualty* case, above, fn.121, at [83].

[124] *Proforce Recruit Ltd v The Rugby Group Ltd* [2006] EWCA Civ 69 (meaning of "preferred supplier status"), for further proceedings, see: [2007] EWHC 1621 (QB); cf. *The Pacific Colocotronis* [1981] 2 Lloyd's Rep. 40; *Jones v Bright Capital Ltd* [2006] EWHC 3151 (Ch). It may be doubted whether this is an exception to the rule excluding evidence of previous negotiations since "it does not matter whether the evidence of usage by the parties was in the course of negotiations or on any other occasion", *Chartbrook* above fn.112 at [45] per Lord Hoffmann.

[125] See Lord Hoffmann's criticism, in *Chartbrook* (at [47]), of *The Karen Oltmann* [1976] 2 Lloyd's Rep. 708.

[126] *James Miller & Partners v Whitworth Street Estates (Manchester) Ltd* [1970] A.C. 583 at 603, 606; *Wickman Ltd v Schuler AG* [1974] A.C. 325; cf. *Houlder Bros & Co Ltd v Commissioners of Public Works* [1908] A.C. 276 at 285; And see the submission in *HLB Kidsons v Lloyd's Underwriters subscribing to Lloyd's policy No. 621/PK1D00101* [2008] EWCA Civ 1206 at [28]–[29] that "the reaction of professional people in the industry at the time [is] relevant to the objective question of construction of the documents in issue"; not endorsed by the Court of Appeal and treated with caution in *Sattar v Sattar* [2009] EWHC 279 (Ch) at [37].

Such evidence may be admissible to show whether there was a contract[127] and what the terms of the contract were,[128] or that the written terms were a "mere sham",[129] or that the contract had been varied by subsequent agreement,[130] or to raise an estoppel[131]; but it cannot be used to elucidate the original meaning of the contract.[132]

To prove custom. Evidence of custom is admissible "to annex incidents to **6–026** written contracts[133] in matters with respect to which they are silent".[134] It is generally said that the evidence can be used to add to, but not to contradict, the written contract.[135] Thus the evidence cannot be used where the custom, if actually written into the contract, would make it "insensible or inconsistent".[136] For example, where a charterparty provided that expenses of discharging should be borne by the *charterer* "as customary", a custom that they were to be borne by the *shipowner* was held to be inconsistent with the charterparty[137]; and where a bill of lading provided for "freight payable in London" this was held to be inconsistent with a custom that it was payable *in advance* in London.[138] But where a bill of lading provided for freight at a specified rate, evidence of a customary deduction of interest was held merely to add to the contract since the discount was calculated on the contract rate of freight.[139] In such borderline cases, the distinction between customs which add to and those which contradict the written contract is largely one of emphasis.

Custom can also be used as an aid to interpretation.[140] For this purpose, evidence of custom is admissible even though it contradicts the ordinary meaning of the words used in the contract, e.g. to show that "1,000 rabbits" meant "1,200 rabbits."[141]

To identify the subject-matter. Extrinsic evidence is admissible to identify **6–027** the subject-matter of a contract: e.g. to show that "your wool" meant not only wool produced by the claimant but also wool produced on a neighbouring farm.[142]

---

[127] *E.D. & F.Man Commodity Advisers Ltd v Fluxo-Cane Overseas Ltd* [2009] EWCA Civ 406 at [20]–[21].

[128] *Ferguson v Dawson & Partners (Contractors) Ltd* [1976] 1 W.L.R. 1213; *Carmichael v National Power Plc* [1999] 1 W.L.R. 2042 at 2050–2051; cf. above, para.6–014.

[129] See above, fn.80.

[130] *McCausland v Duncan Lawrie Ltd* [1997] 1 W.L.R. 38 at 49.

[131] *James Miller & Partners Ltd v Whitworth Street Estates (Manchester) Ltd* [1970] A.C. 583 at 611, 615; cf. *Amalgamated Investment & Property Co Ltd v Texas Commerce International Bank Ltd* [1982] Q.B. 84 at 119; below, para.3–094.

[132] For criticism, see fn.109 above.

[133] Including those made by deed: *Wigglesworth v Dallison* (1779) 1 Doug. 201.

[134] *Hutton v Warren* (1836) 1 M. & W. 466 at 475.

[135] *Phillips v Syndicate 992 Gunner* [2003] EWHC 48; [2004] Lloyd's Rep I.R. 426 at [25].

[136] *Humfrey v Dale* 7 E. & B. 266, 275, affirmed (1858) E.B. & E. 1004.

[137] *Palgrave Brown & Son Ltd v SS Turid (Owners)* [1922] 1 A.C. 397; cf. *Mowbray Robinson & Co v Rosser* (1922) 91 L.J.K.B. 524.

[138] *Krall v Burnett* (1877) 25 W.R. 305; advance freight would be payable even though the ship failed to reach the contractual destination: below, para.19–109.

[139] *Brown v Byrne* (1854) 3 E. & B. 703.

[140] e.g. *Norden Steam Co v Dempsey* (1876) 1 C.P.D. 654; Evidence of "market practice" may be admitted by way of expert evidence: *Crema v Cenkos Securities Plc* [2010] EWCA Civ 1444 (where the evidence was entirely inconclusive).

[141] *Smith v Wilson* (1832) 3 B. & Ad. 728.

[142] *Macdonald v Longbottom* (1859) 1 E. & E. 977. cf. *Compagnie Noga d'Importation et d'Exportation SA v Abacha (No.4)* [2003] EWCA Civ 24; [2003] 2 All E.R. (Comm) 915.

Similarly, such evidence is admissible to define the extent of a party's obligations under a contract: e.g. to show that a contract to pump oil out of a stranded tanker obliged the party rendering the service to take away only so much oil as was necessary to avert the risk of pollution[143]; or to show whether a guarantee related to one debt only or was a continuing one[144]; or to which of a number of transactions a guarantee related.[145]

6–028   **Rectification.** A document may be meant to record a previous oral agreement, but fail accurately to do so. Such a document can sometimes be rectified, i.e. brought into line with the previous oral agreement.[146] When this is done evidence of the previous oral agreement must inevitably be admitted. This does not mean that a party can claim rectification merely by alleging that terms which were in fact agreed were not incorporated in the document. The remedy of rectification is based on a *mistake* in the recording of a previous oral agreement.[147] In most of the cases in which the parol evidence rule is invoked the parties make no such mistake: they know perfectly well that the extrinsic term is not incorporated in the document, so that rectification is not available.

6–029   **Collateral agreements.** Even where extrinsic evidence cannot be used to vary, add to or contradict the terms of a written agreement, it may be possible to show that the parties made two related contracts, one written and the other oral. In *Mann v Nunn*[148] the claimant orally agreed to take a lease of the defendant's premises if the defendant would first do certain repairs. A written agreement was later executed, but did not refer to the defendant's promise to do the repairs. The claimant was nonetheless able to enforce this promise. "The parol agreement neither alters nor adds to the written one, but is an independent agreement."[149]

Thus evidence is admissible if it proves an "independent agreement"; but it is often hard to say whether the evidence has this effect or whether it varies, or adds to, the terms of the main contract. The test seems to be whether the evidence relates to a term which would go to the essence of the whole transaction: if so, it cannot be regarded as evidence of a collateral contract and will be inadmissible.[150]

In *Mann v Nunn* the lease contained no provisions as to putting the premises in repair, so that the landlord's promise merely *added* to it. According to two later cases, evidence of a collateral contract is inadmissible if it *varies* or *contradicts* a term actually set out in the main written contract. In the first,[151] a lease of a furnished house specified the furniture to be included. Evidence of a collateral

---

[143] *The Pacific Colocotronis* [1981] 2 Lloyd's Rep. 40; cf. *Essex CC v Ellam* [1989] 2 All E.R. 494 (evidence admissible as to legal nature of payments made under covenant).
[144] *Heffield v Meadows* (1869) L.R. 4 C.P. 595.
[145] *Perrylease Ltd v Imecar Ltd* [1988] 1 W.L.R. 463.
[146] See below, para.8–059 et seq.
[147] See below, para.8–059; cf. *Rabin v Gerson Berger Association Ltd* [1986] 1 W.L.R. 526 at 534; *The Riza and Sun* [1997] 2 Lloyd's Rep. 314 at 320.
[148] (1874) 30 L.T. 526; cf. *Walker Property Investments (Brighton) Ltd v Walker* (1947) 177 L.T. 204.
[149] *Mann v Nunn*, above, at 527. For other requirements of collateral contracts, see above, paras 4–003, 5–009, below, 9–051—9–052.
[150] e.g. *The Nile Rhapsody* [1992] 2 Lloyd's Rep. 399 at 407, affirmed [1994] 1 Lloyd's Rep. 382; *Mitchill v Lath* 160 N.E. 646 (1928). cf. in the context of formal requirements above, para.5–009.
[151] *Angell v Duke* (1875) 32 L.T. 320; for previous proceedings in this case, see (1875) L.R. 10 Q.B. 174; above, para.5–009.

agreement, made before the lease, to put in more furniture, was held inadmissible. In the second,[152] rent under a lease was payable quarterly in advance. Evidence of a collateral agreement allowing the tenant (in effect) to pay the rent in arrear was similarly held inadmissible.

On the other hand, in *City & Westminster Properties (1934) Ltd v Mudd*[153] a lease contained a covenant to use the premises for business purposes only. The tenant had been induced to sign it by an oral assurance that the lessors would not object to his continuing to reside on the premises (as he had done in the past). In spite of the fact that this assurance contradicted the lease, evidence of it was held admissible to prove a collateral contract. The case is hard to distinguish from the cases discussed above[154]; and it is arguable that evidence of a collateral contract should not, any more than evidence of custom,[155] be allowed to contradict the main written contract. But evidence of custom is meant to elucidate the meaning of the written document itself, and it could hardly do this by introducing contradictory terms. Evidence of a collateral agreement is not meant to determine the content or meaning of a written document, but to give effect to an independent agreement. There is no compelling reason why this agreement should not contradict the written document.

It can be argued that the collateral contract device largely destroys the parol evidence rule, especially if *Mudd*'s case is right. But some limitations on this device are imposed by the requirements that a statement operates as a collateral contract only if intended to be legally binding and supported by separate consideration.[156] Such consideration will often be provided by the promisee's act of entering into the main contract.[157] But this act could not be consideration for the collateral promise if that promise was made *after* the conclusion of the main contract; for in that case the consideration would be past and hence of no effect in law.[158]

Consideration. In *Turner v Forwood*[159] a person assigned a debt due to him   **6–030** from a company to one of its directors by a deed stated to have been made for a nominal consideration. It was held that evidence was admissible to show that there was a substantial consideration for the assignment.[160] This evidence did not really contradict the deed as the nominal consideration was mentioned only as a matter of form.[161] Where an agreement states a substantial consideration, evidence of *additional* consideration is also admissible, so long as it does not contradict that stated in the written agreement.[162]

---

[152] *Henderson v Arthur* [1907] 1 K.B. 10.

[153] [1959] Ch. 129; cf. *Couchman v Hill* [1947] K.B. 554, where one reason for the decision was that the oral warranty was a collateral contract; and *Brikom Investments Ltd v Carr* [1979] Q.B. 467 (above, para.3–065), where no point as to admissibility of evidence seems to have been taken.

[154] The fact that the tenant actually *refused* to sign the lease until he was given the oral assurance may distinguish *Mudd*'s case from *Angell v Duke* and *Henderson v Arthur*, above, at fnn.151, 152.

[155] See above, para.6–026.

[156] See above, para.3–065; below, para.9–051.

[157] e.g. in *City of Westminster Properties (1934) Ltd v Mudd* [1959] Ch. 129.

[158] See above, para.3–017.

[159] [1951] 1 All E.R. 746.

[160] cf. above, para.3–015.

[161] i.e. to avoid the implication of a use: *Cross and Tapper on Evidence* (12th edn), at 684.

[162] *Pao On v Lau Yiu Long* [1980] A.C. 614 at 631.

2. IMPLIED TERMS[163]

6–031　　Implied terms may be divided into three main groups. The first consists of terms implied in fact, that is, terms which were not expressly set out in the contract, but which it is found that the parties must have intended to include. The second consists of terms imported by operation of law. The third consists of terms implied by custom.

(a) Terms Implied in Fact[164]

(i) *A broad approach?*

6–032　　**A question of interpretation.** As will be seen below, the courts have developed a number of tests, and take into account a number of factors, to determine whether a term of the contract may be implied in fact, i.e. one that is necessary to give effect to the intention of the parties. That the process involved is one of giving effect to the intention of the parties means that there has always been a certain affinity between this form of implication and the interpretation of the express terms to which the parties have agreed.[165] In *Attorney General of Belize v Belize Telecom Ltd*[166] Lord Hoffmann, giving the judgment of the Judicial Committee of the Privy Council, went perhaps a little further. He referred to the tests, or factors, which the courts have employed to determine whether a term should be implied in fact, as summarised by Lord Simon in *BP Refinery (Westernport) Pty Ltd v Shire of Hastings*:[167]

> "(1) it must be reasonable and equitable;[168] (2) it must be necessary to give business efficacy to the contract, so that no term will be implied if the contract is effective without it;[169] (3) it must be so obvious that 'it goes without saying';[170] (4) it must be capable of clear expression;[171] (5) it must not contradict any express term of the contract[172]".

Each of these tests, or factors, will be considered in further detail below, but Lord Hoffmann stressed that they are not a series of "independent tests" each of which have to be surmounted; rather they are "a collection of different ways in which judges have tried to express the central idea that the proposed implied term must spell out what the contract actually means, or in which they have explained why

---

[163] Lücke 5 Adelaide L.Rev. 31.

[164] Kramer [2004] C.L.J. 384.

[165] *Trollope & Colls Ltd v North West Metropolitan Regional Hospital Board* [1973] 1 W.L.R. 601, 609; *Luxor (Eastbourne) Ltd v Cooper* [1941] A.C. 108 at 130 per Lord Wright ("what is in question in all these cases is the interpretation of a particular contract"); *Equitable Life Assurance Society v Hyman* [2002] 1 A.C. 408 at 459. And see the earlier observation of Lord Hoffmann in *Banque Bruxelles Lambert SA v Eagle Star Insurance Co Ltd* [1997] A.C. 191, at 212E that the process of implication "is one of construction of the agreement as a whole in its commercial setting".

[166] [2009] UKPC 10; [2009] 1 W.L.R. 1988; Davies [2010] L.M.C.L.Q. 140; Macdonald 26 J.C.L. 97.

[167] (1978) 52 A.L.J.R. 20 at 26, PC. Lord Simon acknowledged that these tests "may overlap": see further, below para.6–036.

[168] See below, para.6–038.

[169] See below, para.6–035.

[170] See below, para.6–034.

[171] See below, para.6–039.

[172] See below, para.6–039.

they did not think that it did so".[173] In his opinion there is "only one question":[174] if the implied term is included "is that what the instrument,[175] read as a whole against the relevant background, would reasonably be understood to mean?"[176]

It may be that in any consideration of whether to imply a term in fact, the courts will now choose to begin with the statement of principle established by Lord Hoffmann in the *Belize Telecom* case,[177] just as it is customary to begin the process of interpretation by setting out his "re-statement" in the *ICS* case.[178] As in the case of interpretation, it does not appear that Lord Hoffmann was suggesting the need for any fundamental change of approach from the courts. It has been said that he "rebases the doctrine of implied terms within the principles of contractual interpretation", thus imposing a "superstructure of interpretation"[179] on the conditions necessary for the implication of terms, but that "nothing in that approach affects those conditions".[180] It is too early to tell if that view is entirely correct, but even if it is, adopting a broader approach based on interpretation may help to resolve some of the difficulties which are referred to below.[181]

A strict test. One reason why Lord Hoffmann's broader approach is unlikely 6–033 to herald a fundamental change in the outcome of the cases before the courts is because he also affirmed that terms are not lightly to be implied. If a contract does not expressly provide for what is to happen when some event occurs, the "most usual inference in such a case is that nothing is to happen" and "[i]f the event has caused loss to one or other of the parties, the loss lies where it falls".[182] In this respect there remains a fundamental difference between interpretation and the implication of terms in fact:[183]

---

[173] [2009] UKPC 10; [2009] 1 W.L.R. 1988 at [27].

[174] Although he had earlier referred to "*every case* in which it is said that some provision ought to be implied in an instrument" (at [21]) it seems clear that Lord Hoffmann, in context, was concerned with terms implied in fact; the question which he poses would not necessarily produce the "right" answer in cases where terms have been implied in law, since the process of implication involved in such cases is based on considerations other than the intention of the parties: see below, para.6–041.

[175] The instrument in the *Belize Telecom* case was the articles of association of a company, but it is clear that Lord Hoffmann intended the approach advocated to apply to any written instrument, including a contract.

[176] [2009] UKPC 10; [2009] 1 W.L.R. 1988 at [21]. In this sense: "the implication of the term is not an addition to the instrument. It only spells out what the instrument means", [2009] 1 W.L.R. 1988 at [18].

[177] *The Reborn* [2009] EWCA Civ 531; [2009] 2 Lloyd's Rep. 538 at [8]; *Inta Navigation Ltd v Ranch Investments Ltd* [2009] EWHC 1216; [2010] 1 Lloyd's Rep 74 at [42] in which Lord Hoffmann's opinion in the Privy Council is described as another "re-statement"; *Chantry Estates (South East) Ltd v Anderson* [2010] EWCA Civ 316; 130 Con L.R. 11 at [14]; *Durham CC v Beazer Homes Ltd* [2010] EWCA Civ 1175 at [23].

[178] See above, para.6–007.

[179] Counsel's description in *Groveholt Ltd v Hughes* below fn.180.

[180] *Groveholt Ltd v Hughes* [2010] EWCA Civ 538 at [45]; cf. *The Reborn* [2009] EWCA Civ 531; [2009] 2 Lloyd's Rep. 639.

[181] Whatever approach is adopted, the courts are ultimately concerned with the allocation of a risk which the parties have not expressly allocated for themselves. The decision of the court may be easier to reach than to explain: "Lord Mansfield is supposed to have said, in effect, that it is easier for a judge to get the answer right than it is for him to give sound reasons for his correct answer. In a sense, this is one of those areas of the law which puts me in mind of that dictum", *The Reborn* [2009] EWCA Civ 531; [2009] 2 Lloyd's Rep. 538 at [47] per Rix L.J.

[182] [2009] UKPC 10; [2009] 1 W.L.R. 1988 at [27]; cf. *The Kos* [2010] EWCA Civ 772; [2010] 2 Lloyd's Rep. 409 at [17].

[183] *Philips Electronique Grand Public SA v BSkyB Ltd* [1995] E.M.L.R. 472 at 480 per Bingham M.R. (emphasis added); cf. *Legal & General Assurance Society Ltd v Expeditors International (UK) Ltd* [2007] EWCA Civ 7; (2007) 5 E.G. 307 at [47].

"The courts' usual role in contractual interpretation is, by resolving ambiguities or reconciling apparent inconsistencies, to attribute the true meaning to the language in which the parties themselves have expressed their contract. The implication of contract terms involves *a different and altogether more ambitious undertaking*: the interpolation of terms to deal with matters for which, ex hypothesi, the parties themselves have made no provision. It is because the implication of terms is potentially so intrusive that the law imposes strict constraints on the exercise of this extraordinary power."

(ii) *Tests*

6–034   **Officious bystander.** One test for the implication of a term in fact is the "officious bystander" test. This has been stated by MacKinnon L.J. as follows:

"*Prima facie* that which in any contract is left to be implied and need not be expressed is something so obvious that it goes without saying; so that, if while the parties were making their bargain, an officious bystander were to suggest some express provision for it in the agreement, they would testily suppress him with a common 'Oh, of course!' "[184]

For example, in one case[185] a vendor of land undertook that, if he later *sold* certain adjoining land, he would give the purchaser the "first refusal" of it. A term was implied to prevent the vendor from defeating the purchaser's expectation by disposing of the land to a third party by way of *gift*.

Although the officious bystander test is framed by reference to how the parties would respond to the suggested term, the requirement that the implied term must "go without saying" is just one way of determining what the parties, *as reasonable persons*, would understand the contract to mean.[186] The process of implication in fact is an objective one; it "is not critically dependent on proof of an actual intention of the parties."[187] As a consequence, a term may be implied even if, at the time of the contract, one of the parties might have answered the question that such an implied term *"goes without saying"* with the answer "could you please explain that again?"[188] But just as the state of *knowledge* of the parties may be relevant to the "background" for the purpose of interpretation,[189] it is also

---

[184] *Shirlaw v Southern Foundries (1926) Ltd* [1939] 2 K.B. 206 at 227 (affirmed [1940] A.C. 701); cf. *Comptoir Commercial Anversois v Power, Son & Co* [1920] 1 K.B. 868 at 899–900.

[185] *Gardner v Coutts & Co* [1968] 1 W.L.R. 173; cf. *Bournemouth & Boscombe Athletic FC v Manchester United FC, The Times,* May 22, 1980; *Fraser v Thames Television Ltd* [1984] Q.B. 44 at 57; *Independiente Ltd v Music Trading Online (HK) Ltd* [2007] EWCA Civ 111; [2008] 1 W.L.R. 608 (term implied into settlement agreement that defendant would not breach undertaking given to the court pursuant to the settlement).

[186] *Attorney General of Belize v Belize Telecom Ltd* [2009] UKPC 10; [2009] 1 W.L.R. 1988 at [25].

[187] *Equitable Life Assurance Society v Hyman* [2002] 1 A.C. 408 at 459; cf. *BP Refinery (Westernport) Pty Ltd v Shire of Hastings* (1978) 52 A.L.J.R. 20 at 26, PC.

[188] *Attorney General of Belize v Belize Telecom Ltd* [2009] UKPC 10; [2009] 1 W.L.R. 1988 at [25]; cf. *Greene Wood & McLean LLP v Templeton Insurance Ltd* [2009] EWCA Civ 65; [2009] 1 W.L.R. 2013 at [15]. Or even with the answer "no": *Arla Foods UK PLc v Barnes* [2008] EWHC 2851 (Ch); [2009] B.C.L.C. 699 at [59].

[189] See above fn.115.

relevant to implication in fact.[190] In *K C Sethia (1944) Ltd v Partabmull Ramesh-war*[191] sellers of Indian jute to Italian buyers could not perform their contract because they failed to obtain a quota for shipment to Italy. They argued that the contract was impliedly "subject to quota", and one reason why the argument was rejected was that the buyers did not know that the sellers had no quota for Italy.

Similarly, the courts will not conclude that the parties, as reasonable persons, would have agreed to the proposed term if it is clear that it is something about which they have divergent views.[192] For example, in *Luxor (Eastbourne) Ltd v Cooper*[193] the defendant had employed an estate agent to sell two cinemas and promised to pay him a commission "on completion of sale". Before the agent had effected a sale, the defendant sold the cinemas himself. It was held that no term could be implied to the effect that the defendant should not (except for good cause) refuse to sell to a person introduced by the agent. While Viscount Simon stated that he was not satisfied that "the *vendor* would acquiesce",[194] his conclusion is consistent with the objective nature of the test for implication since he later stated that "upon the true construction" of the contract, the agent took the risk of the defendant not being willing to conclude the sale with the person introduced by the agent.[195]

Business efficacy test. A second test for the implication of a term in fact is   6–035
that of "business efficacy." Lord Wright has described such a term as one

> "of which it can be predicated that 'it goes without saying,' some term not
> expressed but necessary to give the transaction such business efficacy as the
> parties must have intended".[196]

It is sometimes also said that all implied terms are subject to a requirement of "necessity",[197] as if that were an additional requirement, but in the present context[198] "necessity" seems to be no more than a part of (or perhaps an alternative to[199]) the "business efficacy"[200] test as stated by Lord Wright.[201] In *The*

---

[190] *McCutcheon v David MacBrayne Ltd* [1964] 1 W.L.R. 125 at 128, 134; cf. *Spring v NASDS* [1956] 1 W.L.R. 585 at 599; *Wilson v Best Travel* [1993] 3 All E.R. 353.

[191] [1950] 1 All E.R. 51 (affirmed [1951] 2 Lloyd's Rep. 89).

[192] *Attica Sea Carriers Corp v Ferrostaal Poseidon Bulk Reederei GmbH* [1976] 1 Lloyd's Rep. 250; *Frobisher (Second Investments) Ltd v Kiloran Trust Co Ltd* [1980] 1 W.L.R. 425; *Nutting v Baldwin* [1995] 1 W.L.R. 201 at 211.

[193] [1941] A.C. 108; cf. *Shell UK Ltd v Lostock Garages Ltd* [1976] 1 W.L.R. 1187; Russell 40 M.L.R. 582; *Lonrho v Shell Petroleum Co* [1981] Com.L.R. 74 (affirmed [1981] 2 All E.R. 456, without reference to the point); *The Good Luck* [1989] 2 Lloyd's Rep. 238 at 273 (reversed on other grounds [1992] 1 A.C. 233); *The Gudermes* [1993] 1 Lloyd's Rep. 311 at 323.

[194] ibid. at 117.

[195] ibid. at 118; cf. at 137 per Lord Wright: "what it is sought to imply is based on an intention *imputed* to the parties from their actual circumstances" (emphasis added).

[196] ibid. at 137; cf. *Comptoir Commercial Anversois v Power, Son & Co* [1920] 1 K.B. 868 at 899–900; *The Star Texas* [1993] 2 Lloyd's Rep. 444 at 451; Burrows 3 N.Z.U.L.R. 121.

[197] ibid. at 125; *Hughes v Greenwich LBC* [1994] A.C. 170 at 179; *Baker v Black Sea & Baltic Ins Co Ltd* [1998] 1 W.L.R. 974 at 980 (but see [1998] 1 W.L.R. 974 at 978).

[198] It is perhaps best confined to a role in contradistinction to reasonableness: below, para.6–038, fn.217.

[199] See *Cox v Bankside* [1995] 2 Lloyd's Rep. 436 at 466.

[200] See above at fn.196; cf. *Friend's Provident Life Office v Hillier Parker May & Rowden* [1995] 4 All E.R. 260 at 279 ("business necessity").

[201] *Concord Trust v The Law Debenture Trust Corp* [2005] UKHL 27; [2005] 1 W.L.R. 1591 at [37].

Moorcock[202] the defendants owned a wharf and made a contract to allow the claimants to unload their ship at the wharf. The ship was damaged by settling at low water on a ridge of hard ground. It was held that the defendants were liable for this damage as they were in breach of an implied term that they would take reasonable care to see that the berth was safe. As Bowen L.J. said: "In business transactions such as this, what the law desires to effect by the implication is to give such business efficacy to the transaction as must have been intended at all events by both parties who are businessmen."[203]

As Lord Hoffmann stated in the *Belize Telecom* case, there is a danger in detaching the phrase "necessary to give business efficacy" from the basic process of construction of the instrument: the contract "may work perfectly well in the sense that both parties can perform their express obligations, but the consequences would contradict what a reasonable person would understand the contract to mean".[204] For example, in *The Reborn*[205] the parties entered into a voyage charter-party with a named loading port under the express terms of which the owner warranted that the vessel would comply with all "restrictions" of the port.[206] The hull of the vessel was penetrated by a hidden underwater projection and it was claimed by the owner that there was an implied warranty on the part of the charterer to nominate a safe berth, so that it was the charterer who was liable for damage done to the vessel. The Court of Appeal held that no such term was to be implied and reached that conclusion, in part, by posing the question: "is the proposed implied term necessary to make the contract work?"[207] However, the contract could "work" either by leaving the loss with the owner, if there was no implied term, or by imposing liability on the charterer, if there was an implied term. By contrast, if one posed the question of what the charterparty could reasonably be understood to mean, when read against the relevant background, as the Court of Appeal also did,[208] i.e. whether the charterers agreed to take the risk of unsafety at the berth from hidden dangers, the answer to that was "no". The implied term contended for was not necessary to "to give effect to the reasonable expectations of the parties."[209]

6–036   **Relationship between the two tests.** The relationship between the "officious bystander" and "business efficacy" tests is not entirely clear.[210] But as has been noted above, the tests employed by the courts "may overlap"[211] and if they are to be regarded merely as different ways in which the courts establish, or express their conclusion as to, what the contract would reasonably be understood to mean, the

---

[202] (1889) 14 P.D. 64.
[203] ibid. at 68 (emphasis added).
[204] [2009] UKPC 10; [2009] 1 W.L.R. 1988 at [23].
[205] [2009] EWCA Civ 531; [2009] 2 Lloyd's Rep. 639.
[206] i.e. risks arising from the specifications and restrictions of the berth.
[207] [2009] EWCA Civ 531; [2009] 2 Lloyd's Rep. 639 at [18]
[208] ibid. at [45].
[209] *Equitable Life Assurance Society v Hyman* [2002] 1 A.C. 408 at 459 per Lord Steyn.
[210] For the view that both tests must be satisfied, see: *Stubbs v Trower Still and King* [1987] I.R.L.R. 321 at 324; *McAuley v Bristol CC* [1992] Q.B. 134 at 147; *Association of British Travel Agents v British Airways Plc* [2000] 1 Lloyd's Rep. 169 at 175, affirmed [2000] 2 Lloyd's Rep. 209. For the view that it is sufficient to satisfy either test, see: *The Manifest Lipkowy* [1989] 2 Lloyd's Rep. 138 at 143 and 144; cf. *The Kurnia Dewi* [1997] 1 Lloyd's Rep. 553 at 559; *Clarion Ltd v National Provident Association* [2000] 1 W.L.R. 1888 at 1896.
[211] See above fn.167; cf. *Lymington Marina Ltd v Macnamara* [2007] EWCA Civ 151; [2007] 2 All E.R. Comm 285 at [37], [44]; *Adler v Ananhall Advisory & Consultancy Services Ltd* [2009] EWCA Civ 586.

precise relationship between them may be regarded as a somewhat sterile debate. It seems therefore, to be the case that satisfaction of either the "officious bystander" or the "business efficacy" test will suffice for the implication of a term in fact.[212]

Unilateral contracts. It has been said that it is "impossible to imply terms **6–037** (. . . which impose legal obligations) . . . into a unilateral contract"[213]; for, where such an implied term would impose obligations on both parties,[214] it would destroy the unilateral nature of the contract. But it is not obvious why such reasoning should preclude the implication of a term which imposed an obligation only on the *promisor*. Nor does the reasoning exclude the possibility of implying a term which imposed an obligation on the *promisee* in cases (of the kind discussed in Ch.2[215]) in which an originally unilateral contract becomes bilateral in the course of its performance.

(iii) *Factors to be taken into account*

Reasonableness. As noted above, the term to be implied "must be reasonable **6–038** and equitable",[216] but reasonableness alone will not suffice.[217] The fact that a particular implication is reasonable may be evidence that the parties, as reasonable persons, would have agreed to it; if so, the "officious bystander test" is satisfied,[218] and the same fact may help to satisfy the "business efficacy" test.[219] But even if the relevant question is now formulated in the broad terms advocated by Lord Hoffmann, the courts will not imply a term in fact merely because it would be reasonable to do so[220]; "they will not . . . improve the contract which the parties have made for themselves, however desirable the improvement might be".[221]

Other factors. It follows from the nature of the process of implication in fact **6–039** that a term cannot be implied in fact if it actually conflicts with the express terms

---

[212] *Greene Wood & McLean LLP v Templeton Insurance Ltd* [2009] EWCA Civ 65; [2009] 1 W.L.R. 2013 at [15].

[213] *Little v Courage Ltd* (1995) 70 P. & C.R. 469 at 474.

[214] The only term which, in *Little v Courage Ltd*, the court was prepared to imply (or to read into the contract as a matter of construction) did not impose any obligation on either party: see below, para.18–072.

[215] See above, para.2–051.

[216] *Young & Marten Ltd v McManus Childs Ltd* [1969] 1 A.C. 454 at 465; *Liverpool CC v Irwin* [1977] A.C. 239 at 262; *Wong Mee Wan v Kwan Kin Travel Services Ltd* [1996] 1 W.L.R. 38 at 46–47.

[217] *Liverpool CC v Irwin* [1977] A.C. 239 at 266: "The touchstone is always necessity and not merely reasonableness".

[218] *Paragon Finance Ltd v Nash* [2001] EWCA Civ 1466; [2002] 1 W.L.R. 685 at [36].

[219] *Weldon v GRE Linked Life Assurance Ltd* [2000] 2 All E.R. (Comm) 914 at 919.

[220] *Reigate v Union Manufacturing Co (Ramsbottom) Ltd* [1918] 1 K.B. 592 at 605; *Lupton v Potts* [1969] 1 W.L.R. 1749; *Liverpool CC v Irwin* [1977] A.C. 239; *Duke of Westminster v Guild* [1985] Q.B. 688 at 698; *McAuley v Bristol CC* [1992] Q.B. 134 at 146; *Friends Provident Life & Pensions Ltd v Sirius International Ins* [2005] EWCA Civ 601; [2005] 2 Lloyd's Rep. 517 at [32]. cf. Lord Simonds' warning in *Scruttons Ltd v Midland Silicones Ltd* [1962] A.C. 446 at 467 that the process of implication is one "against the abuse of which the courts must keep constant guard".

[221] *Trollope & Colls Ltd v NW Metropolitan Hospital Board* [1973] 1 W.L.R. 601 at 609; *cf. Philips Electronique Grand Public SA v British Sky Broadcasting Ltd* [1995] 1 E.M.L.R. 472; *Johnson v Davies* [1999] Ch.117 at 128.

of the contract.[222] The courts are also reluctant to imply such a term "where the parties have entered into a carefully drafted written contract containing detailed terms agreed between them"[223]; or where it is essential that contracts of a particular type "should operate in accordance with the terms which appear on their face", e.g. the financial undertakings used in connection with international commerce.[224] The alleged implication must not be too vague,[225] and it must be possible to formulate its content with "adequate precision".[226]

(iv) Examples

6–040   As will be seen below, the defining feature of terms implied in law is that they are implied into all contracts of a particular type. By contrast, terms are implied in fact on the basis of the circumstances of individual contracts. Nevertheless, the same, or similar, circumstances may be repeated and it is on this basis that there is some value in noting some of the leading examples of terms which may be implied in fact,[227] bearing in mind that it does not follow that the courts will always imply the terms in question just because the case before them shares the same broad features.[228] Thus, the courts may imply a term that the parties will "co-operate" to ensure performance where they have agreed that "something shall be done which cannot effectively be done unless both concur in doing it"[229]; similarly, that one party will not do anything "of his own motion" to put an end to any state of circumstances on which the performance of the contract depends.[230] Where the contract confers rights on one party subject to the consent of other, the court may imply a term that such consent must not be withheld arbitrarily or

---

[222] Duke of Westminster v Guild [1985] Q.B. 688 at 700. cf. Johnstone v Bloomsbury Health Authority [1992] Q.B. 333, per Legatt L.J. and Browne-Wilkinson V.C.; Port of Tilbury (London) Ltd v Stora Enso Transport & Distribution Ltd [2009] EWCA Civ 16; [2009] 1 Lloyd's Rep. 391 at [26]; Lancore Services Ltd v Barclays Bank Plc [2010] EWCA Civ 752; [2010] 1 All E.R. 763 at [28].

[223] Shell UK Ltd v Lostock Garages Ltd [1976] 1 W.L.R. 1187 at 1200; Duke of Westminster v Guild [1985] Q.B. 688; BDW Trading Ltd v JM Rowe Investments Ltd [2011] EWCA Civ 548 at [39]; contrast Associated Japanese Bank (International) v Crédit du Nord SA [1989] 1 W.L.R. 255; The Maira (No.3) [1988] 2 Lloyd's Rep. 126, reversed on other grounds [1990] 1 A.C. 637. A term implied in fact may not be excluded by an entire agreement clause: The Helene Knutsen [2003] EWHC 1964; [2003] 2 Lloyd's Rep. 686 at [27]; contrast fn.299, below.

[224] Uzinterimpex JSC v Standard Bank Plc [2008] EWCA Civ 819; [2008] 2 Lloyd's Rep. 456 at [23].

[225] Shell UK Ltd v Lostock Garages Ltd [1976] 1 W.L.R. 1187; cf. Paul Smith Ltd v H & S International Holdings Inc [1991] 2 Lloyd's Rep. 127 at 131; Walford v Miles [1992] 2 A.C. 128 (above, para.2–100); Yorkshire Water Services Ltd v Sun Alliance & London Insurance Plc [1997] 2 Lloyd's Rep. 21 at 31–32; Socimer International Bank Ltd v Standard Bank London Ltd [2008] EWCA Civ 116; [2008] 1 Lloyd's Rep. 558 at [110].

[226] Luxor (Eastbourne) Ltd v Cooper [1941] A.C. 108 at 117; BP Refinery (Westernport) Pty Ltd v Shire of Hastings, above fn.171; Ashmore v Corp of Lloyd's (No.2) [1992] 2 Lloyd's Rep. 620 at 628.

[227] No distinction is drawn in the illustrations which follow between terms which were implied on the basis of the business efficacy test and those which were implied on the basis of the officious bystander test.

[228] Ashmore v Corp of Lloyd's (No.2) [1992] 2 Lloyd's Rep. 620 at 631.

[229] Mackay v Dick (1881) 6 App. Cas. 251 at 263; Luxor (Eastbourne) Ltd v Cooper [1941] A.C. 108 at 117; General Trading Co (Holdings) Ltd v Richmond Corp Ltd [2008] EWHC 1479; [2008] 2 Lloyd's Rep. 475 at [87].

[230] Though such a term may be regarded as one imposed by operation of law: see below, para.6–044.

unreasonably,[231] and where a contract is subject to a condition precedent, a term may be implied that neither party must do anything to prevent the occurrence of the event,[232] or that one party must use reasonable efforts to bring the event about.[233]

It is clear that contracts with commission agents "do not follow a single pattern"[234] and the courts have refused to imply a term that the principal would not, by going out of business, deprive the agent of a chance of earning his commission.[235] On the other hand, where a seller's agent had negotiated a sale of particular goods, a term was implied that the seller would not, by breaking that contract of sale, deprive the agent of his right to commission.[236] This implied term made the seller liable to the agent only if he broke one particular contract of sale, without otherwise restricting his freedom to go out of business.

(b) Terms Implied in Law[237]

Many of the obligations arising out of particular types of contracts are, at any rate presumptively, determined by rules of law; and some such obligations are said to be the result of implied terms.[238] For example, in a contract of employment the employee impliedly undertakes that he is reasonably skilled,[239] that he will faithfully serve his employer[240] and not act against the employer's interests,[241] and that he will indemnify his employer against liabilities incurred by the employer as a result of his wrongful acts.[242] The employer, for his part, impliedly undertakes that he will not require the employee to do any unlawful act,[243] that he will provide safe premises,[244] that he will take reasonable care not to endanger the employee's health[245]; and that he will not without reasonable cause conduct himself so as to destroy or seriously damage the relationship of trust and confidence between

6–041

---

[231] *Eastleigh BC v Town Quay Developments Ltd* [2009] EWCA Civ 1391; cf. *Lymington Marina Ltd v Macnamara* [2007] EWCA Civ; [2007] N.P.C. 27. See further the cases discussed above, para.2–096, fn.479.

[232] See above, para.2–108.

[233] See above, para.2–110.

[234] *Luxor (Eastbourne) Ltd v Cooper* [1941] A.C. 108 at 119.

[235] *Rhodes v Forwood* (1876) 1 App.Cas. 256; cf. *Hamlyn & Co v Wood* [1891] 2 Q.B. 488; *Sun Alliance Pensions Life & Investment Services Ltd v RJL* [1991] 2 Lloyd's Rep. 410. Contrast cases in which the principal has *expressly* promised to stay in business: *Reigate's Case* [1918] 1 K.B. 592; cf. *Ogdens Ltd v Nelson* [1905] A.C. 109.

[236] *Alpha Trading Ltd v Dunshaw-Patten* [1981] Q.B. 290; below, para.16–090. Contrast *The Manifest Lipkowy* [1989] 2 Lloyd's Rep. 138 where it was held that no such term could be implied in an arrangement between a seller and the *buyer's* agent that the commission was to be deducted from the proceeds of sale.

[237] Peden 117 L.Q.R. 190.

[238] There is no scope for an implication of this kind where the contract does not fall within any "particular generic type": *Clarion Ltd v National Provident Association* [2000] 2 All E.R. 265 at 273; [2000] 1 W.L.R. 1888 at 1897; Phang [1993] J.B.L. 242; [1994] J.B.L. 255.

[239] *Harmer v Cornelius* (1858) 5 C.B.(N.S.) 236.

[240] *Hivac Ltd v Park Royal Scientific Instruments Ltd* [1946] Ch. 169; cf. *Faccenda Chicken Ltd v Fowler* [1987] Ch. 117.

[241] *Wessex Dairies Ltd v Smith* [1935] 2 K.B. 80; *Sanders v Parry* [1967] 1 W.L.R. 753.

[242] *Lister v Romford Ice & Cold Storage Co Ltd* [1957] A.C. 555; below, para.6–044.

[243] *Gregory v Ford* [1951] 1 All E.R. 121.

[244] *Matthews v Kuwait Bechtel Corp* [1959] 2 Q.B. 57; Webber (1959) 22 M.L.R. 521; Jolowicz [1959] C.L.J. 163. See also Employer's Liability (Defective Equipment) Act 1969.

[245] *Johnstone v Bloomsbury Area Health Authority* [1992] 2 Q.B. 333.

himself and the employee.[246] Similarly, a party instructed to act in a professional capacity assumes an obligation to exercise the skill and care which is to be expected of a reasonably competent member of the profession; he does not normally impliedly guarantee a specified result.[247] In some cases, however, the particular circumstances may show that, in addition, a warranty has been given in relation to some part of the service provided.[248] A term implied in law can generally[249] be excluded by a contrary agreement.[250]

Many terms which are implied in law have been put into statutory form. For example, a number of important terms implied into contracts for the sale of goods are stated in ss.12 to 15 of the Sale of Goods Act 1979, and similar terms are implied by statute into hire-purchase agreements,[251] other contracts for the supply of goods[252] and contracts for the supply of services.[253] The power to exclude these terms is now severely restricted by legislation.[254]

Detailed discussion of the terms implied by law into particular types of contracts will be found in specialist works on such contracts. But points of general interest arise out of the distinction between terms implied in fact and terms implied in law, and out of the legal nature of terms of the latter kind.

6–042   **Terms implied in law distinguished from terms implied in fact.** The implication of a term in fact is based on the inference that the parties intended to incorporate the term into their contract,[255] but no such inference is necessary for the implication of a term in law.[256] This point can be illustrated in a number of ways. Some statutory implied terms, such as the implied term as to fitness for a particular purpose set out in s.14(3) of the Sale of Goods Act 1979, are extremely complex. If an officious bystander tried to read, and explain, this subsection to a chemist and an intending buyer of a hot-water bottle, he might be testily suppressed, but scarcely with a common "of course". And the question whether any, and if so what, term is to be implied at common law often turns on distinctions which are so subtle that they can scarcely be based on the intention of the parties, even on an objective basis.[257] The question whether any, and if so what, term should be implied in law is often decided exclusively by the citation of earlier

[246] *Malik v BCCI* [1998] A.C. 20.

[247] See, e.g., in the context of surgery: *Eyre v Measday* [1986] 1 All E.R. 488; *Thake v Maurice* [1986] Q.B. 644; below, para.17–068.

[248] *Platform Funding Ltd v Bank of Scotland Plc* [2008] EWCA Civ 930; [2009] 2 W.L.R. 1016.

[249] i.e. subject to exceptions such as those discussed at paras 7–059—7–060, 7–070, 7–102, below.

[250] e.g. *The Berge Sund* [1993] 2 Lloyd's Rep. 453; *The Spiros C* [2000] 2 Lloyd's Rep. 319 at 335.

[251] Supply of Goods (Implied Terms) Act 1973, ss.8–11.

[252] Supply of Goods and Services Act 1982, ss.2–5, 7–10.

[253] ibid., ss.13–14.

[254] See below, para.7–059 et seq.

[255] This is true though the implication of even such terms may be a question of "law" in the sense of an *inference* based on primary facts: see *O'Brien v Associated Fire Alarms* [1968] 1 W.L.R. 1916.

[256] *The Dadomar General TJ Park* [1986] 2 Lloyd's Rep. 68 at 70; *McAuley v Bristol CC* [1992] Q.B. 134 at 147; *Ashmore v Corp of Lloyd's (No.2)* [1992] 2 Lloyd's Rep. 620 at 626; *McClory v Post Office* [1992] I.C.R. 758 at 764; *Scally v Southern Health & Social Services Board* [1992] 1 A.C. 294 at 307; *Timeload Ltd v British Telecommunications Plc* [1995] E.M.L.R. 459 at 467; *Equitable Life Assurance Society v Hyman* [2002] 1 A.C. 408 at 459.

[257] See, e.g. the contrast between *Young & Marten Ltd v McManus Childs Ltd* [1969] 1 A.C. 454 and *Gloucestershire CC v Richardson* [1969] 1 A.C. 480.

cases.[258] This is done to determine an issue of "pure law"[259] and not to ascertain the intention of the parties.

A test of policy and not of necessity. The implication of a term in law is   6–043 simply a way of specifying some of the duties which prima facie arise out of certain types of contracts, or, as it has been put, "legal incidents of those . . . kinds of contractual relationship".[260] In deciding whether to imply a term in law, the courts are guided by general policy considerations affecting the type of contract in question[261]; and to this extent considerations of reasonableness and fairness may enter into the implication of such terms.[262] It has been suggested that, even in this type of case, the test of implication is "necessity, not reasonableness".[263] If appropriate at all[264] necessity in this context has a different shade of meaning from that which it has in formulations of the business efficacy test.[265] The House of Lords has distinguished

> "between the search for an implied term *necessary* to give business efficacy to a particular contract and the search, based on wider considerations, for a term which the law will imply as a *necessary* incident of a definable category of contractual relationship".[266]

In accordance with this test, it has for example been held that it was an implied term in a contract of employment that the employer should inform the employees of steps which they were entitled to take to enhance their pension rights.[267] Such an implication was not necessary to give business efficacy to any individual employment contract, but it was a necessary aspect of employment relationships of the type before the court.[268] It is submitted that such decisions are clearly based on considerations of "justice and policy"[269] and there is much to be said for abandoning "the elusive concept of necessity".[270] Decisions on such policy issues are not helped by distinguishing between what is reasonable and what is necessary;

---

[258] e.g. *Yeoman Credit Ltd v Apps* [1962] 2 Q.B. 508.

[259] *Malik v BCCI* [1998] A.C. 20 at 46.

[260] *Mears v Safecar Securities Ltd* [1983] Q.B. 54 at 78; cf. *Liverpool City Council v Irwin* [1977] A.C. 239; MacIntyre [1977] C.L.J. 15; *Johnstone v Bloomsbury Health Authority* [1992] Q.B. 333 at 343; *Johnson v CEGB* [2000] 1 A.C. 455 at 477–478.

[261] *The Star Texas* [1993] 2 Lloyd's Rep. 445; *Crossley v Faithful & Gould Holdings* Ltd [2004] EWCA Civ 293; [2004] I.R.L.R. 377 at [36]. Peden 117 L.Q.R. 459, 467–475.

[262] *Crossley*, above, fn.261; cf. *Re Charge Card Services Ltd* [1989] Ch. 497 at 513; *The Spiros C* [2000] 2 Lloyd's Rep. 319 at 333; *Galaxy Energy International Ltd v Bayoil SA* [2001] 1 Lloyd's Rep. 512 at [27].

[263] *Scally v Southern Health and Social Services Board* [1992] 1 A.C. 294 at 307; cf. *Tai Hing Cotton Mill Ltd v Liu Chong Hing Bank Ltd* [1986] A.C. 80 at 104–105: *Spring v Guardian Insurance Plc* [1995] 2 A.C. 296 at 339, 354; *Reid v Rush & Tompkins Group Plc* [1990] 1 W.L.R. 212 at 220.

[264] *Timeload Ltd v British Telecommunications Ltd* [1995] E.M.L.R. 459 at 467.

[265] *Baker v Black Sea & Baltic General Insurance Co* [1998] 1 W.L.R. 974 at 980.

[266] *Scally v Southern Health & Social Services Board* [1992] 1 A.C. 294 at 307 (emphasis added); *Malik v BCCI* [1998] A.C. 20 at 45; cf. *The Foresight Driller II* [1995] 1 Lloyd's Rep. 251 at 266, treating "general principle" and "business efficacy" as *separate* grounds for implying a term.

[267] *Scally* above, fn.266.

[268] It is not an implied term of *any* contract of employment that the employer will take reasonable care for the economic well-being of his employee, whatever form that might take: *Crossley v Faithful & Gould Holdings* Ltd [2004] EWCA Civ 293; [2004] I.R.L.R. 377.

[269] *The Star Texas*, above, fn.261 at 491.

[270] *Crossley v Faithful & Gould Holdings* Ltd [2004] EWCA Civ 293; [2004] I.R.L.R. 377 at [36], though Dyson L.J. more cautiously suggested it is better to "focus" on policy rather than necessity.

in the context of terms implied in law, the distinction appears to be no more than one of degree. The principle that reasonableness is not of itself a ground for implying a term is entirely appropriate when the court is being asked to imply a term *in fact* into an individual contract,[271] but is, it is submitted, not one which should preclude the implication of terms *in law* into contracts of a particular type.

6–044   **Imposition of a legal duty.** In many cases of the kind under consideration, the same process can with equal plausibility be described either as the implication of a term in law or as the imposition of a legal duty. In one case concerning a landlord's duty to repair the outside of the premises the court indiscriminately refers to an "implied term" and to an "implied obligation"[272] which must be "imposed on"[273] the landlord. Where a term is imposed in law, the two processes are, as a practical matter, indistinguishable. It is, for example, commonly said that a landlord *impliedly covenants* that his tenant shall have quiet possession, and that the tenant is under an *obligation* not to commit waste. One could just as well say that the landlord was under an obligation to let the tenant have quiet possession, and that the tenant impliedly covenanted not to commit waste. Again, it is said that if a party enters into an arrangement which can take effect only if a given state of circumstances continues, he impliedly promises not to put an end to it.[274] But in a case in which this rule was applied, Lord Atkin said:

> "Personally I should not so much base the law on an implied term, as on a positive rule of the law of contract that conduct of either promisor or promisee which can be said to amount to himself 'of his motion' bringing about the impossibility of performance is in itself a breach."[275]

This point would not be worth stressing if the true nature of the inquiry before the court were not sometimes obscured by the use of the expression "implied term" to refer to the imposition of a legal duty, and by the failure to distinguish between terms implied in fact and terms implied in law. In *Lister v Romford Ice and Cold Storage Co Ltd*[276] a lorry driver injured a third party by negligent driving in the course of his employment. The third party recovered damages from the employers, who obtained judgment for an indemnity from the driver on the ground that he had broken the implied term in the contract of employment to drive with proper care.[277] The driver in turn argued that the contract also contained an implied promise by the employers. This was formulated in various ways: as a promise to indemnify the driver against liability to third parties if the

---

[271] See above, para.6–038.

[272] *Barrett v Lounava (1982) Ltd* [1990] 1 Q.B. 348 at 359; cf. *Scally v Southern Health & Social Services Board* [1992] 1 A.C. 294 at 307B ("terms which the law will imply"), 307D ("necessary . . . to imply an obligation").

[273] ibid. at 358; cf. *Spring v Guardian Ins Plc* [1995] 2 A.C. 296 at 353 ("imposing a duty").

[274] *Stirling v Maitland* (1864) 5 B. & S. 840; *CEL Group Ltd v Nedlloyd Lines UK* Ltd [2003] EWCA Civ 1716; [2004] 1 Lloyd's Rep. 381 at [11].

[275] *Southern Foundries (1926) Ltd v Shirlaw* [1940] A.C. 701 at 717; cf. *Nisho Iwai Petroleum Co Inc v Cargill International SA* [1993] 1 Lloyd's Rep. 80; *The Energy Progress* [1993] 1 Lloyd's Rep. 355; *Spring v Guardian Ins* [1995] 2 A.C. 296 at 320.

[276] [1957] A.C. 555.

[277] Employers' insurers have agreed not to make such claims against employees, so that the decision has little practical effect. For an unsuccessful attempt by a third party to claim the indemnity, see *Morris v Ford Motor Co Ltd* [1973] Q.B. 792.

employers were insured, or if they were required by law to be insured, or if they ought as reasonable and prudent persons to have been insured. The House of Lords, by a majority, held that no such term could be implied. Some of the reasons given by the majority are reasons against the implication of a term *in fact*. The implication was not "precise and obvious"[278]; it was not necessary to give business efficacy to the contract[279]; and it was not clear that both parties, as reasonable persons, would have agreed to it.[280] But many terms implied *in law* would fail to pass these tests. Whether such terms should be implied is not a question of intention, but one of policy: "*Should* one imply [the alleged] term . . . ?"[281] In fact the House of Lords in *Lister*'s case was to a large extent concerned with considerations of policy. The argument that seems to have weighed most heavily with the majority was that it would be undesirable to allow a driver to recover an indemnity from his employer as he might then drive less carefully. Considerations of this kind always influence the implication of terms in law; but they have nothing to do with the intention of the parties, and hence with the implication of terms in fact.

The distinction between the two types of implication is clearly drawn in the later case of *Reid v Rush & Tompkins Group Plc*,[282] where an employee was injured, while working abroad, as a result of the fault of a third party who could not be traced. He argued that his contract of employment contained an implied term obliging his employers to warn him to insure against such risks; but the argument was rejected on two separate grounds. First, no such term *could* be implied in fact since it would not have been agreed by the parties. And secondly, no such term *should* be implied in law by the court as the exact scope of such an implication raised issues of policy which could be resolved only by the legislature.[283] It is, conversely, possible for both tests to support the conclusion that a term should be implied,[284] in which case the implication can be said to arise both in fact and in law.

There are, however, also cases in which, though no term can be implied in fact, it may be desirable to attach certain "legal incidents"[285] to a contract, or, in other words, to impose a legal duty. This point has sometimes been overlooked,[286] so that it was occasionally held that no terms *should* be implied in law merely because none *could* be implied in fact. But such reasoning would now be inconsistent with *Liverpool City Council v Irwin*.[287] The House of Lords there held that it was an

---

[278] [1957] A.C. 555 at 574.

[279] ibid. at 583.

[280] ibid. at 578.

[281] *Rockeagle Ltd v Alsop Wilkinson* [1992] Ch. 47 at 51.

[282] [1990] 1 W.L.R. 212.

[283] The decision in this case has to some extent been overtaken by subsequent decisions (such as the *Scally* case, above, fn.272) in which the courts have, in certain restricted circumstances, implied a term whose effect is to impose a duty on the employer to safeguard his employee's economic interests: *Crossley v Faithful & Gould Holdings* Ltd [2004] EWCA Civ 293; [2004] I.R.L.R. 377 at [46].

[284] See *The Island Archon* [1994] 2 Lloyd's Rep. 227 at 237, where Evans L.J. regards the implication as justified "first by business efficacy" (i.e. in fact: above, para.6–035) and "secondly . . . [as] an implication of law." cf. *St Albans City and District Council v International Computers Ltd* [1996] 4 All E.R. 481.

[285] Above, fn.260.

[286] e.g. in *Abbott v Sullivan* [1952] 1 K.B. 189 where, it is submitted, a term might well have been implied in law (though on the principle stated at fn.192, above, none could be implied in fact). *The Aramis* [1989] 1 Lloyd's Rep. 213 is open to criticism on similar grounds: see Treitel [1989] L.M.C.L.Q. 162. cf. *John v Rees* [1970] Ch. 345 where a term was implied in law.

[287] [1977] A.C. 239; MacIntyre [1977] C.L.J. 15; *Duke of Westminster v Guild* [1985] Q.B. 688 at 697–698; *Sim v Rotherham MBC* [1987] Ch. 216 at 245.

implied term of a lease of a maisonette in a Council block that the landlord should take reasonable care to keep the common parts of the block in a reasonable state of repair. The term was clearly not implied in fact: the "officious bystander" test was not satisfied[288]; nor was the implication necessary to give business efficacy to the contract.[289] The implication arose because the nature of the relationship made it desirable to place some obligation on the landlord as to the maintenance of the common parts of the premises. It amounted to the imposition of a legal duty, in spite of the fact that no term could be implied in fact.[290]

6-045   **Doubtful cases: party relying on his own breach.**[291] Sometimes it is not clear whether a particular term is implied in fact or in law. It has been said that in the absence of a contrary intention "it is to be presumed that it was not the intention of the parties that either party should be entitled to rely upon his own breaches of his primary obligations as bringing the contract to an end",[292] or to obtain some benefit under it. In the case in which this dictum appears it is referred to as "the well known rule of construction" which, in the light of the *Belize Telecom* case may suggest that it should be viewed as a term implied in fact,[293] but it also appears to have the "status of a rule of law which is imposed upon the parties to a contract almost regardless of what they have agreed".[294] In practice, it is probably something of a hybrid in that it "can be excluded or modified by the terms of the contract and . . . its scope in any particular case will depend upon the construction of the relevant agreement".[295]

(c) Terms Implied by Custom or Trade Usage

6-046   **Custom.** We have seen that evidence of custom is admissible to add to, but not to contradict, a *written* contract.[296] Further, *any* contract (whether written or not) may be deemed to incorporate any relevant and notorious[297] custom of the market, trade or locality in which it is made,[298] unless the custom is inconsistent with the express (or necessarily implied) terms, or with the nature, of the contract.[299] In cases of such inconsistency the custom is said to be "unreasonable", and binds a party only if he knew of it. A custom which is "reasonable" binds both parties,

---

[288] At pp.283–290. This was also the position in *Barrett v Lounava (1982) Ltd* [1990] 1 Q.B. 348 (where a term was nevertheless implied in law).

[289] [1977] A.C. 239 at 255.

[290] cf. *McAuley v Bristol CC* [1992] Q.B. 134.

[291] See also the analogous rule that that one party will not do anything "of his own motion" to put an end to any state of circumstances on which the performance of the contract depends: above, fn.230 and fn.274.

[292] *Cheall v APEX* [1983] 2 A.C. 180 at 189; below, para.18–005

[293] In *BDW Trading Ltd v JM Rowe Investments Ltd* [2011] EWCA Civ 548 at [34] Patten L.J. refers to "the *implication of a term* embodying the own wrong principle" (emphasis added) and also prays in aid the principles set out by Lord Hoffmann in the *Belize Telecom* case, above; cf. *Extra MSA Services Cobham Ltd v Accor UK Economy Hotels Ltd* [2011] EWHC 775 (Ch).

[294] *BDW Trading case*, above at [31].

[295] ibid.

[296] See above, para.6–026.

[297] See *Turner v Royal Bank of Scotland* [1999] 2 All E.R. (Comm) 664, where this requirement was not satisfied.

[298] At the date it was made: see *Phillips v Syndicate 992 Gunner* [2003] EWHC 1084; [2004] Lloyd's Rep I.R. 426 at [24].

[299] Such inconsistency was one ground why the alleged custom was not incorporated in the contract in *Danowski v Henry Moore Foundation* [1996] E.M.L.R. 364. An appropriately drafted entire agreement clause may exclude an implied term based on custom or usage: *The Helene Knutsen* [2003] EWHC 1964; [2003] 2 Lloyd's Rep. 686.

whether they knew of it or not.[300] It is sometimes said that the incorporation of custom into a contract is based on the presumed intention of the parties,[301] but the question whether a custom binds depends on whether it is "reasonable", and this question can give rise to complex issues of law and fact which are more akin to the process of implication in law.[302]

Collective agreements. The terms of collective agreements between trade   **6–047** unions and employers may be incorporated in the employment contracts of individual employees by express reference,[303] or by being acted on over a period of time.[304] Between employer and union, such agreements normally have no contractual force because they are not intended to be legally binding.[305] But when their terms are incorporated in individual contracts of employment, those terms can, if so intended,[306] become legally binding between employer and employee.[307] It has, moreover, been suggested that the terms of collective agreements may be incorporated in contracts of employment as "crystallised custom".[308] The "custom" may be incorporated even in contracts with employees who are not members of the union which has negotiated the agreement, so long as there is some evidence of intention to incorporate it.[309] Once the terms of the collective agreement have been incorporated in the contract of employment, the employee can enforce rights under that contract, even after the collective agreement itself has, as between the union and the employer, been brought to an end.[310]

Trade usage. Terms may also be implied by trade usage.[311] For example, where   **6–048** the owner of a crane hired it out to a contractor who was also engaged in the same business, it was held that the hirer was bound by the owner's usual terms though these were not actually communicated at the time of contracting.[312] They were, however, based on a model supplied by a trade association; and references in the judgment to the fact that they were reasonable and prevalent in the trade[313] suggest that they were incorporated on a principle similar to that which applies to customary terms.

---

[300] *Reynolds v Smith* (1893) 9 T.L.R. 494; for other illustrations, see below, para.16–019.

[301] e.g. in *Produce Brokers Co Ltd v Olympia Oil & Cake Co Ltd* [1916] 1 A.C. 314 at 324; cf. *Garratt v Mirror Group Newspapers Ltd* [2011] EWCA Civ 425 at [45]–[46].

[302] cf. *The Maira (No.3)* [1990] 1 A.C. 637 at 681.

[303] *Hooker v Lange, Bell & Co* [1937] 4 L.J.N.C.C.R. 199; *Camden Exhibition & Display Ltd v Lynott* [1966] 1 Q.B. 555.

[304] *NCB v Galley* [1958] 1 W.L.R. 16.

[305] See above, para.4–019.

[306] *NCB v NUM* [1986] I.C.R. 736; *Kaur v MG Rover Group Ltd* [2004] EWCA Civ 1507; [2005] I.R.L.R. 40; *Malone v British Airways Plc* [2010] EWCA Civ 1225.

[307] *Robertson v British Gas Corp* [1983] I.C.R. 351; *Marley v Forward Trust Group* [1986] I.C.R. 891; *Alexander v Standard Telephone and Cables Ltd* [1990] I.C.R. 291 at 303 (where the intention was later found to have been negatived: see [1991] I.R.L.R. 286); *Keeley v Fosroc International Ltd* [2006] EWCA Civ 1277; [2006] I.R.L.R. 961.

[308] Kahn-Freund in Flanders & Clegg (eds), *The System of Industrial Relations in Great Britain*, Ch.2, p.58.

[309] *Young v Canadian Northern Ry* [1931] A.C. 83.

[310] *Gibbons v Associated British Ports Authority* [1985] I.R.L.R. 376.

[311] See *Baker v Black Sea & Baltic General Ins Co Ltd* [1998] 2 All E.R. 833 for proof of such usage.

[312] *British Crane Hire Corp Ltd v Ipswich Plant Hire Ltd* [1975] Q.B. 303; *Harlow & Jones Ltd v American Express Bank Ltd* [1990] 2 Lloyd's Rep. 343. And see generally Hoggett (1970) 33 M.L.R. 518.

[313] [1975] Q.B. 303 at 311, 313; contrast *Salsi v Jetspeed* [1977] 2 Lloyd's Rep. 57 (where there was no evidence of usage).

EXEMPTION CLAUSES & UNFAIR TERMS[1]

7–001   **The use and abuse of standard form contracts.** Contractual terms are often set out in standard forms which are used for all contracts of the same kind, and are only varied so far as the circumstances of each contract require. Such terms may be settled by a trade association for use by its members for contracting with each other or with members of the outside public. One object of these standard forms is simply to save time. Standard form contracts are also a device for allocating contractual risks: they can be used to determine in advance who is to bear the expense of insuring against those risks[2]; and they also facilitate the quotation of differential rates: e.g. where a carrier's form provides for goods to be carried either at his or at the customer's risk, and the charge is adjusted accordingly. Between businessmen bargaining at arm's length such uses of standard forms can be perfectly legitimate[3]; and this may be true even where the party to whom the standard terms are presented is a private consumer who has or is likely

---

[1] Coote, *Exception Clauses.*

[2] See *Photo Production Ltd v Securicor Transport Ltd* [1980] A.C. 827 at 843, 851; cf. *A Schroeder Music Publishing Co Ltd v Macaulay* [1974] 1 W.L.R. 308 at 316.

[3] See *Photo Production* case, above, at 851; *Ailsa Craig Fishing Co Ltd v Malvern Fishing Co Ltd* [1983] 1 W.L.R. 964 at 966; *Rohlig (UK) Ltd v Rock Unique Ltd* [2011] EWCA Civ 18 at [16].

to have insured against the loss which has occurred.[4] But a less defensible object of the use of standard terms has been the exploitation or abuse of the superior bargaining power of commercial suppliers when contracting with such consumers. The supplier could draft the standard terms in ways highly favourable to himself, both by means of clauses which *excluded* or *limited his liability* (exemption clauses) for failure to perform or for defective performance, and by provisions which *conferred rights* on him under the contract.

In cases concerning exemption clauses, the courts were to a considerable extent able to redress the balance in favour of the parties prejudicially affected by standard form contracts; but they were less inclined to do so where standard terms conferred rights on the supplier. In both fields, legislative intervention has become increasingly important. The most important legislative provisions are contained in the Unfair Contract Terms Act 1977,[5] and in the Unfair Terms in Consumer Contracts Regulations 1999.[6] The 1977 Act deals almost exclusively with exemption clauses; it makes some such clauses ineffective and subjects others to a requirement of reasonableness. The 1999 Regulations deal with standard terms in contracts between commercial sellers and suppliers on the one hand and consumers on the other, and provide that such terms do not bind the consumer if they are "unfair." In a significant number of cases, however, standard form contracts are not affected by these legislative provisions[7] and continue to be governed by rules of common law. These rules therefore still call for discussion, even though many of the cases from which they are derived would now be differently decided under those legislative provisions,[8] or under other legislation to be described later in this chapter.[9] For the most part, the common law rules are concerned with the efficacy of exemption clauses; but it will be necessary also to consider the common law approach to other types of standard terms.

The control of terms in non-standard form. Some of the controls on the   7–002
use of exemption clauses and other unfair terms which are considered in this chapter are not confined to standard form contracts. They may be applied even to fully negotiated terms, including terms agreed by two commercial parties.[10] Where they do apply, the fact that the terms have been negotiated or that the parties are of equal bargaining power will militate in favour of their enforceability, e.g. where the issue is the reasonableness of a term under the 1977 Act.

1. EXEMPTION CLAUSES AT COMMON LAW

A party who wishes to rely on a clause excluding or limiting liability[11] must   7–003
show that the clause has been incorporated in the contract, and also that, on its true construction, it covers both the breach which has occurred and the resulting

---

[4] e.g. in the car park cases, such as *Hollins v J Davy Ltd* [1963] 1 Q.B. 844. Contrast *Mendelssohn v Normand Ltd* [1970] 1 Q.B. 177 (where luggage stolen from a parked car did not belong to the owner of the car).

[5] See below, paras 7–050—7–094.

[6] See below, paras 7–095—7–122.

[7] See below, paras 7–088—7–094, 7–117.

[8] See above at fnn.5 and 6.

[9] See below, paras 7–123—7–126.

[10] e.g. the rules of construction considered at para.7–014 and certain of the controls under the 1977 Act, e.g. s.2 (clauses excluding or limiting liability for negligence): below, paras 7–057, 7–065.

[11] For the distinction between these and certain other kinds of clauses, see below, paras 7–018—7–021.

loss or damage. These two requirements are not confined to exemption clauses and some of the cases which are dealt with in this section have been concerned with analogous terms, such as indemnity clauses. The extent to which incorporation and construction may be used to control terms not analogous to exemption clauses, e.g. terms defining the parties' rights, is considered in the next section.

(a) Incorporation in the Contract

(i) *Signature*

7–004   A person who signs a contractual document is bound by its terms even though he has not read them. In *L'Estrange v F Graucob Ltd*[12] the proprietress of a café bought an automatic cigarette vending machine. She signed, but did not read, a sales agreement which contained an exemption clause "in regrettably small print".[13] It was held that she was bound by the clause, so that she could not rely on defects in the machine, either as a defence to a claim for part of the price, or as entitling her to damages. It would have made no difference had she been a foreigner who could not read English.[14] A party is, however, bound by terms of which he was unaware only if the document which he has signed was one which could reasonably have been expected to contain contractual terms. Where, for example, a hirer of machinery together with a driver had signed weekly time-sheets, it was held that he was not bound by terms printed on these sheets since their purpose was merely to record the hours worked and not to vary the terms of the earlier oral contract of hire.[15] It has been further suggested that "in some extreme circumstances even signature might not be enough", so that a term which was "particularly onerous or unusual" would not be incorporated unless, in addition to the signature, steps were taken to draw the attention of the signer[16] to such a term.[17]

(ii) *Notice*[18]

7–005   If the exemption clause is set out, or referred to,[19] in a document which is simply handed by one party to the other, or displayed where the contract is made, it will be incorporated in the contract only if the latter party either knew that the document contained (or was likely to contain) such a clause,[20] or if reasonable

---

[12] [1934] 2 K.B. 394; *Levison v Patent Steam Cleaning Co Ltd* [1978] Q.B. 69; for criticism, see *McCutcheon v David MacBrayne Ltd* [1964] 1 W.L.R. 125 at 133; cf. Spencer [1973] C.L.J. 104; Samek 52 Can.Bar Rev. 351.

[13] ibid. at 405.

[14] *The Luna* [1920] P. 22; cf. *Barclays Bank Plc v Schwartz, The Times*, August 2, 1995. The signer might be able to rely on the doctrine of *non est factum* (below, para.8–076), but if this applied there would be no contract at all.

[15] *Grogan v Robin Meredith Plant Hire, The Times*, February 20, 1996; cf. below, at fn.21.

[16] i.e. in accordance with the requirements stated at para.7–009, below.

[17] *Ocean Chemical Transport Inc v Exnor Craggs Ltd* [2000] 1 Lloyd's Rep. 446 at 454; *Amiri Flight Authority v BAE Systems Plc* [2003] EWCA Civ 1447; [2003] 2 Lloyd's Rep. 767 at [14]–[16]. But see the doubts expressed in *HIH Casualty & General Insurance Ltd v New Hampshire Insurance Co* [2001] EWCA Civ 735; [2001] 2 Lloyds Rep.161 at [209]; *Do-Buy 95 Ltd v National Westminster Bank Plc* [2010] EWHC 2862 (QB) at [91].

[18] Clarke [1976] C.L.J. 451.

[19] cf. above, para.6–003; below, para.7–008.

[20] *Lacey's Footwear (Wholesale) Ltd v Bowler Insurance Ltd* [1997] 2 Lloyd's Rep. 369 at 378.

notice of its existence is given to that party. Whether such notice has been given depends on the following factors.

Nature of the document. An exemption clause is not incorporated in the   7–006
contract if the document in which it is set out (or referred to) is not intended to
have contractual force: e.g. if the document is a mere receipt for payment.[21] On the
other hand, the mere fact that a document is called a "receipt" will not prevent it
from having contractual effect.[22] A document will have such effect if the party
to whom it was handed knew that it was intended to be a contractual document or
if it was handed to him in such circumstances as to give him reasonable notice of
the fact that it contained conditions.[23] It will also be contractual if it is obvious to
a reasonable person that it must have been intended to have this effect. This will
be the case if the document is of a kind that generally contains contractual terms.[24]
Whether a document falls into this class depends on current commercial practice,
which may vary from time to time.[25]

Degree of notice. The party relying on the exemption clause need not show   7–007
that he actually brought it to the notice of the other party, but only that he took
reasonable steps to do so. The test is whether the former party took such
steps[26]—not whether the latter should, in the exercise of reasonable caution, have
discovered or read the clause.[27] Where the clause is printed on a ticket, it is not
enough to show that the party to whom it was handed knew that there was writing
on the ticket,[28] for the writing might not have been intended to have contractual
effect. Nor is one party's reference in a telephone conversation to his own standard
terms sufficient notice of those terms if the other party has no knowledge or means
of knowledge of them.[29] The question whether adequate notice has been given
turns principally on two factors: the steps taken to give notice and the nature of
the exempting conditions.

Steps taken to give notice. Where the notice is contained in a contractual   7–008
document it is normally sufficient for the exempting condition to be prominently
set out or referred to on the face of the document. In *Thompson v LM & S Ry*[30]
the claimant asked her niece to buy a railway excursion ticket for her. The ticket
(which cost 2s. 7d.) had on its face the words "see back" and on the back a
statement that it was issued subject to the conditions set out in the company's time
tables, which could be bought for 6d. These conditions included an exemption
clause. The claimant could not read the words on the ticket as she was illiterate;
and the jury found that the defendants had not taken reasonable steps to bring the

---

[21] *Chapelton v Barry Urban DC* [1940] 1 K.B. 532; cf. *The Eagle* [1977] 2 Lloyd's Rep. 70; Clarke [1978] C.L.J. 22.
[22] *Harling v Eddy* [1951] 2 K.B. 739 at 746; *Parker v South Eastern Ry* (1877) 2 C.P.D. 416.
[23] *Watkins v Rymill* (1883) 10 Q.B.D. 178.
[24] *Nunan v Southern Ry* [1923] 2 K.B. 703 at 707; *Thompson v London, Midland & Scottish Ry* [1930] 1 K.B. 41 at 46.
[25] For changing views on the status of railway cloakroom tickets, contrast *Parker v South Eastern Ry*, above, fn.22, at 424 with *Alexander v Railway Executive* [1951] 2 K.B. 882 at 886.
[26] *Parker v SE Ry* above, fn.22 at 424; cf. *Burnett v Westminster Bank Ltd* [1966] 1 Q.B. 742.
[27] ibid. at 416.
[28] This was the majority view in *Parker v SE Ry*, above. Bramwell L.J. dissented on this point.
[29] *Jayaar Impex Ltd v Toaken Group Ltd* [1996] 2 Lloyd's Rep. 437.
[30] [1930] 1 K.B. 41; cf. *Hood v Anchor Line* [1918] A.C. 837; *O'Brien v MGN Ltd* [2001] EWCA Civ 1279; [2002] C.L.C. 33.

conditions to the claimant's notice. But the Court of Appeal held that there was no evidence to support this finding as the notice was clear and the ticket was a common form contractual document. Hence the exemption clause was held to be incorporated in the contract. The case is an extreme one since the time table cost nearly a fifth of the fare paid by the claimant and was evidently a volume of some size, the exemption clause being set out on its 552nd page.[31] The likelihood of its being bought (let alone read) by an excursion passenger was, to say the least, remote; and it seems probable that the steps taken to incorporate the clause would not now be regarded as sufficient.[32] The principle that such a clause can be incorporated by reference[33] nevertheless seems to be a sound one.[34] Many common contractual documents would become impossibly bulky if that principle were to be rejected.

On the other hand, the clause is unlikely to be incorporated if there are no words on the face of the document drawing attention to it,[35] or if words on the front of the document refer to terms on the back but the back is blank (only the front having been transmitted by fax),[36] or if the words are made illegible by a date stamp,[37] or if the exemption clause is buried in a mass of advertisements.[38]

In *Thompson*'s case, the illiteracy of the claimant was treated as immaterial; but the position would probably be different where the party relying on the clause knew or should have known of the other party's disability. In an earlier case[39] some reliance was placed on the fact that the other party was a steerage passenger and so could not have been expected to read clauses in small print. Extra steps may have to be taken to bring the notice home to a person suffering from a *known* disability: e.g. translating it to a party who is known not to understand the language in which it is expressed, if such a step is reasonably practicable.[40] A person trying to incorporate the terms of a document should, however, beware of translating only part of it; for by doing this he may suggest that the rest is of no importance and so be unable to rely on it.[41]

7–009   **Nature of the clause.** The more unusual or unexpected a particular term is, the higher will be the degree of notice required to incorporate it. If the clause is of such a nature that the party adversely affected would not normally expect it, then the other party will not be able to incorporate it by simply handing over or displaying a document containing the clause. He must go further and "make it conspicuous"[42] or take other special steps to draw attention to it. For example, a person who drives his car into a car park might expect to find in his contract a

---

[31] [1930] 1 K.B. 41 at 46.
[32] cf. *The Mikhail Lermontov* [1990] 1 Lloyd's Rep. 579 at 594, affirmed [1991] 2 Lloyd's Rep. 155 though reversed on other grounds: sub nom. *Baltic Shipping Co v Dillon* (1993) 176 C.L.R. 344.
[33] cf. *Smith v South Wales Switchgear Ltd* [1978] 1 W.L.R. 165 (indemnity clause).
[34] *Sukuman Ltd v Commonwealth Secretariat* [2006] EWHC 304; [2006] 2 Lloyd's Rep. 53.
[35] *Henderson v Stevenson* (1875) L.R. 2 Sc. & Div. 470; *Richardson, Spence & Co v Rowntree* [1894] A.C. 217. As to the form of words needed on the face of the document, compare *J Murphy & Sons Ltd v Johnston Precast Ltd* [2008] EWHC 3024 (TCC) with *Rooney v CSE Bournemouth Ltd* [2010] EWCA Civ 1364.
[36] *Poseidon Freight Forwarding Co Ltd v Davies Turner Southern Ltd* [1996] 2 Lloyd's Rep. 388. cf. *J Murphy & Sons Ltd v Johnston Precast Ltd* [2008] EWHC 3024 (TCC).
[37] *Sugar v London, Midland & Scottish Ry* [1941] 1 All E.R. 172.
[38] *Stephen v International Sleeping Car Co Ltd* (1903) 19 T.L.R. 620.
[39] *Richardson, Spence & Co v Rowntree* [1894] A.C. 217.
[40] *Geier v Kujawa, Weston & Warne Bros Transport* [1970] 1 Lloyd's Rep. 364.
[41] *H Glynn (Covent Garden) Ltd v Wittleder* [1959] 2 Lloyd's Rep. 409.
[42] *Crooks v Allen* (1870) 5 Q.B.D. 38 at 40.

clause excluding the proprietor's liability for loss of or damage to the car. But in *Thornton v Shoe Lane Parking Ltd*[43] the car park ticket referred to a condition purporting to exclude liability for *personal injury*.[44] It was held that adequate notice of this condition had not been given, even though the steps taken by the proprietor might have been sufficient to incorporate the more usual clauses excluding or limiting liability for property damage. As Denning L.J. had said in an earlier case:

> "Some clauses I have seen would need to be printed in red ink on the face of the document with a red hand pointing to it before the notice could be held to be sufficient."[45]

Time of notice. The steps required to give notice of an exemption clause must be taken before or at the time of contracting. In *Olley v Marlborough Court*[46] the claimant booked a room in the defendants' hotel. She later saw a notice in her bedroom exempting the defendants from liability for articles lost or stolen unless handed to the management for safe custody. It was held that, as the contract had been made at the reception desk when the defendants agreed to accept the claimant as a guest and as the notice in the bedroom could not have been seen by the claimant until later, its terms were not incorporated in the contract.   **7–010**

(iii) *Course of dealing*

The need for a consistent course of dealing. Parties may for some time have dealt with each other on terms that exempted one of them from liability and that were usually incorporated by signature or notice. On the occasion in question, however, the usual document may by some oversight not have been handed over or signed at the time of contracting; and the question then arises whether the usual exemption clause is nevertheless incorporated in that particular transaction. A negative answer to this question was suggested by Lord Devlin in *McCutcheon v David MacBrayne Ltd* where he said: "Previous dealings are relevant only if they prove knowledge of the terms, *actual and not constructive, and consent to them.*"[47] But this view is inconsistent with at least one earlier case[48]; and the House of Lords has held that if there has been a long consistent course of dealing on terms incorporating an exemption clause, then those terms may apply to a particular transaction even though in relation to it the usual steps to incorporate the clause   **7–011**

---

[43] [1971] 2 Q.B. 163; cf. *The Eagle* [1977] 2 Lloyd's Rep. 70; *Interfoto Picture Library Ltd v Stiletto Visual Programmes Ltd* [1989] Q.B. 433, discussed at para.7–047, below; *AEG UK Ltd v Logic Resource Ltd* [1996] C.L.C. 265; Chandler and Holland 104 L.Q.R. 359; Macdonald [1988] J.B.L. 375 and 8 *Legal Studies* 48.

[44] Where the injury is caused *by negligence* such a provision is now ineffective: below, paras 7–057, 7–111.

[45] *J Spurling Ltd v Bradshaw* [1956] 1 W.L.R. 461 at 466. Contrast *Ocean Chemical Transport Inc v Exnor Cragg Ltd* [2000] 1 Lloyd's Rep. 446 at 454 ("neither onerous nor unusual"); *O'Brien v MGN Ltd* [2001] EWCA Civ 1279; [2002] C.L.C. 33 at [21] (term not "onerous or outlandish").

[46] [1949] 1 K.B. 532; cf. *The Eagle* [1977] 2 Lloyd's Rep. 70; *Oceanic Sun Line Special Shipping Co v Fay* (1988) 165 C.L.R. 197.

[47] [1964] 1 W.L.R. 125 at 134 (emphasis added).

[48] *J Spurling Ltd v Bradshaw* [1956] 1 W.L.R. 461.

have not been taken.[49] Of course the terms will not apply if the transaction in question was not part of a *consistent* course of dealing[50]; if the transactions were spread over a long period of time and their number was so small that they could not be said to give rise to a course of dealing[51]; if the steps necessary to incorporate the clause had never been taken at any stage of the dealings between the parties[52]; or if the terms of each transaction in the series had been separately negotiated and expressly agreed between the parties.[53]

7–012   **Attempt to alter terms after a course of dealing.** The fact that there has been a long course of dealing may also be relevant to the degree of notice required when the party claiming the benefit of a clause seeks to alter it to his own advantage. As the other party is reasonably entitled to assume that the course of dealing is continuing on the accustomed terms, it seems that special steps would have to be taken to draw his attention to any such alteration.[54]

7–013   **Trade custom.** The course of dealing referred to in the present discussion is one between the parties to the contract.[55] A term may also be implied into a contract because of a general course of dealing amounting to a trade custom or usage.[56] Such an implication can arise even though the parties to the particular contract in question have not previously dealt with each other.

(b) Construction

7–014   Under this heading we shall first discuss the general principle that exemption clauses are construed *contra proferentem*; we shall then consider the application of that principle to cases in which a party relies on an exemption clause to protect him from liability for particularly serious breaches or for negligence.

---

[49] *Hardwick Game Farm v Suffolk Agricultural, etc. Association* [1969] 2 A.C. 31 at 90, 104, 105, 113, 130; and see *SIAT di dal Ferro v Tradax Overseas SA* [1978] 2 Lloyd's Rep. 470, affirmed [1980] 1 Lloyd's Rep. 53; *George Mitchell (Chesterhall) Ltd v Finney Lock Seeds Ltd* [1983] Q.B. 284 at 295, affirmed [1983] 2 A.C. 803, without reference to this point; *Circle Freight International Ltd v Mideast & Gulf Exports Ltd* [1988] 2 Lloyd's Rep. 427.

[50] *McCutcheon v David MacBrayne Ltd*, above, fn.47, can be explained on the ground that the parties contracted sometimes on one set of terms and sometimes on another. cf. *Mendelssohn v Normand Ltd* [1970] 1 Q.B. 177.

[51] On this question, contrast *Hollier v Rambler Motors (AMC) Ltd* [1972] 2 Q.B. 71 (three or four transactions in five years not sufficient) and *Metaalhandel JA Magnum BV v Ardfields Transport Ltd* [1988] 1 Lloyd's Rep. 197 at 203 ("isolated affairs") with *The Havprins* [1983] 2 Lloyd's Rep. 356 at 362 (three transactions in five years sufficient, though incorporation was "not by course of dealing alone") and with the *Hardwick Game Farm* case, above, fn.49, (three or four contracts a month for three years held to be sufficient).

[52] *Smith v Taylor* [1966] 2 Lloyd's Rep. 231.

[53] *Johnson Matthey Bankers Ltd v State Trading Corp of India* [1984] 1 Lloyd's Rep. 427 at 433.

[54] See *Pancommerce Co SA v Veecheema BV* [1983] 2 Lloyd's Rep. 304 at 305 ("in bold type"); and contrast *Burnett v Westminster Bank Ltd* [1966] 1 Q.B. 742 with *Re Bond Worth Ltd* [1980] Ch. 228.

[55] Or between one of them and a group of companies to which the other belongs, as in the *SIAT* case, above, fn.49, and in *The Raphael* [1982] 2 Lloyd's Rep. 42.

[56] *British Crane Hire Corp Ltd v Ipswich Plant Hire Ltd* [1975] Q.B. 303; above, para.6–048. The dispute concerned an indemnity clause, but the principle seems equally applicable to exemption clauses: cf. *Smith v South Wales Switchgear Ltd* [1978] 1 W.L.R. 165; *Ofir Scheps v Fine Art Logistic Ltd* [2007] EWHC 541 (QB); *Matrix Europe Ltd v Uniserve Holdings Ltd* [2009] EWHC 919 (Comm).

(i) *Contra proferentem*[57]

Statement of the rule, or rules. *Contra proferentem* may be used to describe   7–015
what are, in fact, two rules of construction. The first is that, in case of doubt,
wording in a contract is to be construed against a party who seeks to rely on it in
order to diminish or exclude his "basic obligation, or any common law duty which
arises apart from contract".[58] The second is that: "again in case of doubt, wording
is to be construed against the party who proposed it for inclusion in the contract".[59] In practice, both rules are likely to apply to an exemption clause since it
seeks to diminish or exclude one party's obligations and it will usually have been
inserted in the contract for the benefit[60] of the party seeking to rely upon it. Both
rules are said to apply when there is an ambiguity in the wording of the clause in
question. That is certainly true of the second rule. It is a rule of "last resort"[61] and
"can only apply if a document, properly interpreted, admits of doubt."[62] The
same is not necessarily true of the first rule which applies specifically to exemption
clauses. As will be seen in some of the examples considered below, the wording of
such a clause may appear unambiguous on its face. It is only when one considers
the obligation which it is claimed to diminish or exclude that there may be thought
to be some doubt as to the intention of the parties.[63] The better explanation of the
first rule may therefore be that *any* exemption clause falls to be construed *contra
proferentem*, but that if it is unambiguously worded its meaning may be clear.[64]
Normally, however, the court will express its conclusion in terms that the *contra
proferentem* rule does *not apply* if the clause has a clear meaning.[65] It is with the
first rule that the remainder of this part is principally concerned.

Does the rule still apply? In his re-statement of the principles of inter-   7–016
pretation in the *ICS* case,[66] Lord Hoffmann commented that "almost all the old

---

[57] Peel, in Burrows & Peel (eds), *Contract Terms*.

[58] *Youell v Bland Welch & Co Ltd* [1992] 2 Lloyd's Rep. 127 at 134.

[59] ibid. See to similar effect the comments of Staughton L.J. in *Pera Shipping Corp v Petroship SA*
[1984] 2 Lloyd's Rep. 363 at 365.

[60] It is not enough that the relevant clause was put forward *on behalf* of one of the parties. It must
be shown that it was put forward for his *benefit*: *Royal and Sun Alliance Ins Plc v Dornoch Ltd* [2004]
EWHC 803; [2004] Lloyd's Rep I.R. 815 at [82] (affirmed [2005] EWCA Civ 238; [2005] All ER (D)
160 (Mar)).

[61] *The Olympic Brilliance* [1982] 2 Lloyd's Rep 205 at 208; *McGeown v Direct Travel Insurance* [2003]
EWCA Civ 1606; [2004] 1 All E.R. (Comm) 609; *Pilkington UK Ltd v CGU Ins Plc* [2004] EWCA Civ
23; [2004] B.L.R. 97 at [53]. As a consequence, it is only in a rare case that it "may assist in the final
solution": *Tektrol Ltd v Ins Co of Hanover Ltd* [2005] EWCA Civ 845; [2005] 2 Lloyd's Rep 701 at
[8].

[62] *Static Control Components (Europe) Ltd v Egan* [2004] EWCA Civ 392; [2004] 2 Lloyd's Rep 429
at [37]; *Cattles Plc v Welcome Financial Services Ltd* [2010] EWCA Civ 599; [2010] 2 Lloyd's Rep. 514
at [43], [48]; *Bright Asset Ltd v Lewis* [2011] EWCA Civ 122 at [29].

[63] cf. *Pratt v Aigaion Insurance Co SA* [2008] EWCA Civ 1314; [2009] 1 Lloyd's Rep. 225 at [25]
where, in the context of an insurance warranty, there was said to be an ambiguity in the seemingly
unambiguous phrase "at all times".

[64] See *Frans Maas (UK) Ltd v Samsung Electronics (UK) Ltd* [2004] EWHC 1502; [2004] 2 Lloyd's
Rep 251, where Gross J. appeared to see no contradiction in his interpretation of a limitation clause
by starting with the *contra proferentem* rule (at [138]) and concluding that the "language" of the clause
was "clear" (at [141]).

[65] *Price Waterhouse v University of Keele* [2004] EWCA Civ 583; [2004] P.N.L.R. 43 at [26], per
Arden L.J., but contrast Buxton L.J. at [35].

[66] *Investors Compensation Scheme Ltd v West Bromwich Building Society* [1998] 1 W.L.R. 896. See,
further, para.6–006 et seq.

intellectual baggage of 'legal' interpretation had been discarded".[67] His further comments in a later case[68] may indicate that one example of "legal interpretation" which he had in mind was *contra proferentem*.[69] It is clear, however, that cases decided since the *ICS* case have continued to apply the rule.[70] Indeed, it has been referred to as the "dominant principle" in the interpretation of "clauses by which a party seeks to relieve itself from legal liability."[71] Nonetheless, it may to some extent be subsumed within the general principles of interpretation, in the sense that it is merely "helpful guidance on the proper approach to interpretation".[72] Seen within the context of interpretation generally, *contra proferentem* is, therefore, a question of emphasis: "the degree of strictness appropriate to be applied" will depend upon the extent to which the exemption clause in question involves "departure from the implied obligations".[73] The extent of the departure may be determined by the exemption clause itself operating from a common starting point, e.g. a clause which merely seeks to limit liability will be construed less strictly than one which purports to exclude it altogether.[74] Alternatively, the extent of the departure may be determined by how far the same clause has to go from each starting point, e.g. whether it is relied upon to exclude or limit liability for breach of contract, or negligence,[75] or fraud.[76]

7–017   **"Consequential loss"** The approach of the courts to the meaning of "consequential loss" can be seen as an example of *contra proferentem*. In a series of rulings,[77] some of which post-date Lord Hoffmann's restatement of the principles of interpretation in the *ICS* case,[78] the courts have held that, in the context of an

---

[67] [1998] 1 W.L.R. 896 at 912G.

[68] *Bank of Credit and Commerce International SA v Ali* [2001] UKHL 8; [2002] 1 A.C. 251.

[69] He certainly meant to refer at least to the particularly strained approach to the construction of exemption clauses which was rejected after the passing of the Unfair Contract Terms Act 1977: see para.7–024, below; cf. *Tradigrain SA v Intertek Testing Services Canada Ltd* [2007] EWCA Civ 154 at [46]. By dint of authority, some examples of this particularly strained approach continue to survive, e.g. that liability for breach of the implied conditions under the Sale of Goods Act 1979 can only be excluded by an express reference to "conditions": *The Mercini Lady* [2010] EWCA Civ 1145, applying *Wallis, Son & Wells v Pratt & Haynes* [1911] A.C. 394; *Henry Kendall & Sons v. William Lillico & Sons* [1969] 2 A.C. 31.

[70] Some of them feature in the examples below. See also: *The Starsin* [2004] 1 A.C. 715 at [144]; *Dairy Containers Ltd v Tasman Orient Line CV* [2004] UKPC 22; [2004] 2 All E.R. (Comm) 667 at [12].

[71] *William Hare Ltd v Shepherd Construction Ltd* [2010] EWCA Civ 283, 130 Con L.R. 1 at [18].

[72] *HIH Casualty & General Ins Ltd v Chase Manhattan Bank* [2003] UKHL 6; [2003] 2 Lloyd's Rep 61 at [11], per Lord Bingham (said in the context of the "*Canada Steamship* rules" which are considered below, para.7–034).

[73] *Photo Production Ltd v Securicor Transport Ltd* [1980] A.C. 827 at 850; *Whitecap Leisure Ltd v John H Rundle Ltd* [2008] EWCA Civ 429; [2008] 2 Lloyd's Rep. 216 at [20].

[74] See below, para.7–018.

[75] See below, para.7–034.

[76] See below, para.7–042.

[77] *Millar's Machinery Co Ltd v David Way & Son* (1935) 40 Comm Cas 204; *Saint Line Ltd v Richardsons Westgarth Ltd* [1940] 2 KB 99; *Croudace Construction Ltd v Cawood's Concrete Products Ltd* [1978] 2 Lloyd's Rep 55; *British Sugar plc v NEI Power Projects Ltd* (1998) 87 BLR 42; *Deepak v. ICI* [1999] 1 Lloyd's Rep 387; *BHP Petroleum Ltd v British Steel plc* [1999] 2 Lloyd's Rep 583 (affirmed in part, [2000] 2 Lloyd's Rep 277); *Hotel Services Ltd v Hilton International Hotels (UK) Ltd* [2000] BLR 235; *Pegler Ltd v Wang (UK) Ltd* [2000] BLR 218; *Watford Electronics Ltd v Sanderson CFL Ltd* [2001] EWCA Civ 317; [2001] BLR 218; *GB Gas Holdings Ltd v Accenture (UK) Ltd* [2010] EWCA Civ 912; and the additional cases referred to in fn.81 below.

[78] But note the reservation of Lord Hoffmann as to the correctness of the interpretation in these cases: *Caledonia North Sea Ltd v BT Plc* [2002] UKHL 4; [2002] 1 Lloyd's Rep 553 at [100]; below fn.83.

exemption clause, the term "consequential loss"[79] refers to losses which would be recoverable only under the "second limb" of the test for remoteness laid down in *Hadley v Baxendale*.[80] It is an interpretation which is not free from difficulty,[81] and it departs from the meaning usually given to "consequential loss" in the law of damages generally, i.e. losses going beyond the "normal measure, such as profits lost or expenses incurred through the breach (of contract)".[82] Such a departure is best explained by the *contra proferentem* rule. If the meaning which is given to "consequential loss" in the law of damages generally was to be applied to the interpretation of exemption clauses, it would then include, for example, all lost profits. But if that is the intention of the parties, it is very easy to use a form of words which leave no room for doubt. If the reason why a simpler and more obvious form of words is not used is because, as one suspects, the other party may not agree to it, this rather proves the point: it must be clear that the parties really intended to forego that to which they would otherwise be entitled.[83]

Clauses limiting liability. Although the *contra proferentem* rule applies to all 7–018 exemption clauses, the courts do not apply it with the same rigour to clauses which merely limit liability as they do to those which purport to exclude it[84]; for while it is thought to be "inherently improbable" that the injured party will agree to a total exclusion of the other party's liability, "there is no such high degree of improbability that he would agree to a limitation of . . . liability."[85]

Liquidated damages. Exclusion and limitation clauses must be distinguished 7–019 from clauses that fix damages in advance,[86] e.g. a demurrage clause under which a charterer is required to pay a sum for each day he detains the ship for loading or unloading beyond the time allowed under the charterparty. In the *Suisse Atlantique* case[87] demurrage was fixed at $1,000 per day and one ground for the decision that it was enforceable, even though its *effect* was to limit the liability of the charterer, was that the *purpose* of the demurrage clause was not to limit damages but rather to fix in advance the damages payable in the event of certain

---

[79] It is customary to see it used as part of the composite term "indirect or consequential loss"; "indirect" does not appear to add anything, or at least the point has not yet been taken.

[80] See below, para.20–100. Recent developments in the law of remoteness (below, para.20–110) do not appear to have affected this interpretation.

[81] *BHP Petroleum Ltd v British Steel plc* [1999] 2 Lloyd's Rep 583 at 597–600 (affirmed in part [2000] 2 Lloyd's Rep 277). And see the difference of opinion between Rix J. in the *BHP* case and Andrew Smith J. in *Ease Faith Ltd v Leonis Marine Management Ltd* [2006] EWHC 232; [2006] 1 Lloyd's Rep. 673 on the effect of words such as "or *any other* indirect or consequential (loss)"; cf. Clarke J in *Tsavliris v OSA Marine Ltd*, January 19, 1996; *Ferryways NV v Associated British Ports* [2008] 1 Lloyd's Rep. 639; *BSkyB Ltd v HP Enterprise Services UK Ltd* [2010] EWHC 86 (TCC); *Markerstudy Insurance Co Ltd v Endsleigh Insurance Services Ltd* [2010] EWHC 281 (Comm).

[82] *McGregor on Damages* (18th edn), para.1–036.

[83] The fact that the meaning of "consequential loss" in an exemption clause is now so well established will make any challenge to that meaning in the Supreme Court somewhat difficult. How could it be said that the parties intended it to mean anything else? Is this a case where any change to its meaning could only be given effect *in futuro*?

[84] *Ailsa Craig Fishing Co v Malvern Fishing Co Ltd* [1983] 1 W.L.R. 964; Palmer 45 M.L.R. 327; *George Mitchell (Chesterhall) Ltd v Finney Lock Seeds Ltd* [1983] 2 A.C. 803 at 814; *BHP Petroleum Ltd v British Steel Plc* [2000] 2 All E.R. (Comm) 133 at 149; [2000] 2 All E.R. (Comm) 133 at 143 is more sceptical.

[85] *Ailsa Craig* case, above, at 970.

[86] See below, para.20–130 et seq.

[87] *Suisse Atlantique Societe d'Armement SA v NV Rotterdamsche Kolen Centrale* [1967] 1 A.C. 361.

breaches.[88] Under a limitation clause the owners would have recovered such loss as they could prove, with an upper limit of $1,000 per day. Under the demurrage clause they were entitled to $1,000 per day even if they could not prove any loss at all, or only a smaller loss. In the circumstances, the clause operated to limit the liability of the charterers; but it differed from a limitation clause in that it was capable of benefiting either party. Therefore there was less need to apply strict rules of construction to it.

7–020   **Arbitration clauses.** The lesser need for the application of strict rules of construction is also true of arbitration clauses.[89] Although such clauses may be said to exclude a remedy (in restricting a party's right to sue on the contract in a court of law),[90] their main purpose is not to deprive a party of rights to compensation, but to set up machinery for determining these rights. The same is true of a clause which merely prevents a party from asserting his rights by some specified procedure: e.g. by way of set-off (as opposed to cross-action).[91]

7–021   **Duty defining clauses.** Clauses which assume that there has been a breach and exclude or limit liability may be distinguished from those which define a contracting party's duty.[92] For example, a building contract may provide for completion by a fixed date and contain an "exception" for delays caused by strikes. This may only be another way of saying that the builder will complete by the agreed date, if strikes do not prevent him from doing so: he is under no higher duty.[93] In these cases, failure to complete on the day named is *not a breach at all*.[94] On the other hand, a clause which provided that a builder was not to be liable for loss or damage due to his defective workmanship would be an exemption clause, for it would be absurd to suppose that a building contract should impose no duty at all with respect to the standard of workmanship.[95] This is all the more obvious where the clause only limits, and does not wholly exclude, liability. The rule of strict construction applies to exemption clauses, but it has been said that it does not apply to clauses which merely define the duties of a contracting party.[96] In borderline cases the distinction between the two types of clauses will not be easy to draw[97]; but one important test is whether the events in which a clause is expressed to operate are beyond the control of the party relying on it. If they are,

---

[88] [1967] 1 A.C. 361 at 395, 421, 435–436.

[89] *Woolf v Collis Removal Service* [1948] 1 K.B. 11.

[90] See below, para.11–050.

[91] *The Fedora* [1986] 2 Lloyd's Rep. 441; cf. *Barclays Bank Plc v Kingston* [2006] EWHC 533 (QB); [2006] 2 Lloyd's Rep. 59 at [28]–[29]; but the *contra proferentem* rule (above, para.7–015) was applied to such a clause in *Connaught Restaurants Ltd v Indoor Leisure Ltd* [1994] 1 W.L.R. 501 and in *Esso Petroleum Ltd v Milton* [1997] 1 W.L.R. 938.

[92] See *The London Lion* [1980] 2 Lloyd's Rep. 456 at 468; *The Saudi Prince* [1988] 1 Lloyd's Rep. 1.

[93] *Semble*, the position is the same under Unfair Contract Terms Act 1977, s.3(2)(b)(i). See further, below, para.7–068.

[94] *The Angelia* [1973] 1 W.L.R. 210 at 230, disapproved, but on another point, in *The Nema* [1982] A.C. 724; below, para.19–068.

[95] cf. in another context, *The Union Amsterdam* [1982] 2 Lloyd's Rep. 432 at 436.

[96] *The Angelia*, above, at 231; *Kenyon Son & Craven Ltd v Baxter Hoare & Co* [1971] 1 W.L.R. 519 at 522; cf. *The Gudermes* [1993] 1 Lloyd's Rep. 311 at 328 (oil to be carried on a ship known to have no means of heating it).

[97] In the context of misrepresentation, the distinction between a "duty defining clause" and a disguised exclusion clause is regarded as a question of "substance" rather than "form": see, e.g. para.9–117. See generally, Coote, *Exception Clauses*.

the clause is likely to be regarded as a provision defining the contractual duty rather than as an exemption clause.[98]

The rule applied in favour of the wrongdoer. The *contra proferentem* rule is   **7–022**
intended to protect the injured party but it may sometimes paradoxically have the opposite effect. For example, where an exemption clause is subject to a legislative requirement of reasonableness, it may, on a narrow construction of its words, satisfy that requirement while, on a wider construction, it would not have done so. If the narrow construction suffices to protect the alleged wrongdoer, it will be in his interest to rely on that construction to prevent the clause from being struck down for unreasonableness.[99]

Burden of proof. As a general rule, the burden of proving that a claim falls   **7–023**
within the scope of an exemption clause falls on the party who seeks to rely upon it.[100]

An exemption clause may, as a matter of construction, be held not to cover certain serious breaches,[101] and it may be alleged that the loss which has been suffered is due to such a breach. The question then arises whether it is up to the claimant to show that the breach which has occurred was of this kind or whether it is up to the defendant to show that the loss was not due to a breach of this kind (but to one that is covered by the clause). This question has arisen in a number of cases in which goods were lost by a bailee to whom they had been entrusted for storage, carriage or cleaning. On the one hand, it can be argued that the bailee should not have the burden of proving that the loss was not due to the serious breach alleged, as it is notoriously difficult to prove a negative. On the other hand the bailee will generally be in a better position than the bailor to know how the goods were lost; and that the bailor should not have the burden of proving facts peculiarly accessible to the other party. After some conflict in the authorities, the latter argument has prevailed, so that the burden is on the bailee to show that the breach was not so serious as to fall outside the scope of the exemption clause.[102]

The cases just discussed all concern breaches by bailees of their duty with regard to the safekeeping of the goods. They do not necessarily apply where the breach consists of delay in performance and is alleged to be serious because of its *consequences*.[103] In such cases it is probably the claimant who has the burden of proving that the delay is so serious as not to be covered by the clause. This is consistent with the principle of the bailment cases; for the consequences of the breach on the claimant's position would be a matter peculiarly within *his* (rather than the defendant's) knowledge.

---

[98] *The Angelia*, above, at 231; contrast *Blackburn v Liverpool, etc. SN Co* [1902] 1 K.B. 290 ("exception" expressly including negligence).

[99] As in *Watford Electronics Ltd v Sanderson Ltd* [2001] EWCA Civ 317; [2001] B.L.R. 143. For a legislative provision which is designed to prevent this paradox from arising, see Unfair Terms in Consumer Contracts Regulations 1999 (SI 1999/2083), reg.7(2), below, para.7–118.

[100] *The Glendarroch* [1894] P. 226 at 231; *Pegler Ltd v Wang (UK) Ltd* [2000] B.L.R. 218 at 227.

[101] See below, para.7–026 et seq.

[102] *Levison v Patent Steam Cleaning Co Ltd* [1978] Q.B. 68. See also *J Spurling Ltd v Bradshaw* [1956] 1 W.L.R. 461 at 466, 470; and cf. *United Fresh Meat Co Ltd v Charterhouse Cold Storage Ltd* [1974] 2 Lloyd's Rep. 286 (deterioration of goods in a warehouse); Handford 38 M.L.R. 577; Males [1978] C.L.J. 24. The normal rule as to burden of proof in such cases may be reversed by the terms of the contract: see *Thames Tideway Properties Ltd v Serfaty* [1999] 2 Lloyd's Rep. 110.

[103] e.g. in cases like the *Suisse Atlantique* case [1967] 1 A.C. 361; above, para.7–019.

7–024   **The rise and fall of the doctrine of fundamental breach.**[104] Prior to the Unfair Contract Terms Act 1977, the decisions of the courts contained examples of particularly strained construction in favour of the claimant, principally in an attempt to produce a degree of consumer protection. In some cases, where there was no room even for a strained construction, the courts appeared to go further and introduce a substantive rule that no exemption clause, however worded, could be relied upon to escape a particularly serious breach of contract—often referred to as "fundamental breach".[105] In the *Suisse Atlantique* case,[106] the House of Lords had denied the existence of such a rule but did so in language which suggested that it was significant that the claimant had affirmed the contract. This left room for a further argument that the effect of a fundamental breach was to bring the contract to an end and, with it, the exemption clause relied upon by the defendant.[107] This fallacious argument,[108] and any suggestion of the existence of a substantive rule, was finally laid to rest by the House of Lords in *Photo Production Ltd v Securicor Transport Ltd*.[109] Lord Diplock confirmed[110] that the effect of electing to terminate a contract for breach is not to bring *the contract* to an end. The parties are released from performance of any future "primary" obligations,[111] but the contract itself continues, including any exemption clause.[112] Whether the clause applies to the "secondary" obligation of the party in breach to provide a remedy is purely a matter of construction.[113]

7–025   **Fundamental terms.** In addition to the concept of "fundamental breach", statements can also be found in earlier cases in support of the existence of a category of "fundamental terms".[114] To the extent that this was just a way of describing terms the breach of which would always be so serious that an exemption

---

[104] Grunfeld 24 M.L.R. 62; Guest 77 L.Q.R. 98; Reynolds 79 L.Q.R. 534; Devlin [1966] C.L.J. 192.

[105] See, e.g., *Karsales (Harrow) Ltd v Wallis* [1956] 1 W.L.R. 936; *Yeoman Credit Ltd v Apps* [1962] 2 Q.B. 508; *Charterhouse Credit Co Ltd v Tolly* [1963] 2 Q.B. 683.

[106] *Suisse Atlantique Société d'Armement Maritime SA v NV Rotterdamsche Kolen Centrale* [1967] 1 A.C. 361.

[107] See, e.g., *Harbutts "Plasticine" Ltd v Wayne Tank Co Ltd* [1970] 1 Q.B. 447; *Kenyon Son and Craven Ltd v Baxter Hoare & Co Ltd* [1971] 1 W.L.R. 519; *Levison v Patent Steam Cleaning Co Ltd* [1978] Q.B. 69. See below, para.7–032.

[108] There is little doubt that the fallacy of the argument was well known to its chief proponent, Lord Denning, but that he persisted in it in order to ensure a degree of consumer protection while at the same time pressing Parliament to provide substantive controls. Where he can, perhaps, be criticised is in his application of the doctrine of fundamental breach to an entirely commercial contract: *Harbutts "Plasticine" Ltd v Wayne Tank Co Ltd*, above, fn.107.

[109] [1980] A.C. 827; Guest 96 L.Q.R. 342; Sealy [1980] C.L.J. 252; Nicol & Rawlings 43 M.L.R. 567): see below, para.7–032. See also *George Mitchell (Chesterhall) Ltd v Finney Lock Seeds Ltd* [1983] 2 A.C. 803 at 813; cf in Canada: *Tercon Contractors Ltd v British Columbia* (2010) 315 D.L.R. (4th) 385; McInnes 126 L.Q.R. 365.

[110] The true effect of termination of a contract for breach had previously been clearly and accurately summarised by Lord Porter in *Heyman v Darwins Ltd* [1942] A.C. 356; below, para.18–010.

[111] i.e. those obligations which would have accrued *after* the date of termination; below, para.18–010.

[112] This is confirmed by s.9 of UCTA, which states that neither termination nor affirmation shall affect the application of the Act; below, para.7–085. Since s.9 is confined to clauses which fall within the Act, it is the continuing effect of the decision in the *Photo Production* case which prevents the re-emergence of the doctrine of fundamental breach in contracts which fall outside the scope of the Act.

[113] See below, para.7–026 et seq.

[114] *Smeaton Hanscomb & Co Ltd v Sassoon I Setty & Co (No.1)* [1953] 1 W.L.R. 1468 at 1470; *R W Green Ltd v Cade Bros Farms* [1978] 1 Lloyd's Rep. 602.

clause would have no application,[115] it does not survive the rejection of the doctrine of fundamental breach by the House of Lords. As will be seen below, *as a matter of construction*, where a serious breach has been committed the courts will look closely at the wording of any exemption clause to determine whether it was the intention of the parties to have excluded or limited liability, even in the circumstances of such a breach. The importance of the term broken will be *a* factor in assessing the seriousness of the breach and the likelihood that the parties intended to include it within the scope of the relevant exemption clause. Since, however, each case will depend on its own particular circumstances, it is submitted, with respect,[116] that there is nothing to be gained by any longer seeking to identify a category of fundamental terms.

(ii) *Seriousness of breach*

Seriousness of breach as a rule of construction. Although the doctrine of fundamental breach may have been abrogated, it is still the case, *as a matter of construction*, that the more serious the breach the more closely the courts will look at any exemption clause to determine if it was the intention of the parties to exclude or restrict liability. This is simply the application of the principle of *contra proferentem* to the interpretation of exemption clauses:

7–026

"the degree of strictness appropriate to be applied to their construction may properly depend upon *the extent to which* they involve departure from the implied obligations."[117]

Thus, general words which at first sight appear to cover even the most serious breach may not be construed in this sense, if to give them this effect "would lead to an absurdity, or because it would defeat the main object of the contract or perhaps for some other reason".[118] For example, a carrier who had undertaken to deliver goods to one person could not rely on such general words if he deliberately delivered the goods to another person, or threw them into the sea.[119] That this is, however, only a matter of construction is confirmed by the decisions of the House of Lords in the two cases which heralded the demise of the doctrine of fundamental breach. In the *Suisse Atlantique*[120] case, the liability of charterers for delays was limited to $1,000 per day by a demurrage clause even though it was accepted[121] that the delays which had taken place were so long as to amount to a

[115] *Karsales (Harrow) Ltd v Wallis* [1956] 1 W.L.R. 936 at 943.
[116] This is a departure from previous editions of this book, and see: Treitel, *Some Landmarks of Twentieth Century Contract Law*, Ch.3. cf. *China Shipbuilding Corp v Nippon Yusen Kabukishi Kaisha* [2000] 1 Lloyd's Rep. 367 at 376.
[117] *Photo Production Ltd v Securicor Transport Ltd* [1980] A.C. 827 at 850 per Lord Diplock (emphasis added).
[118] *Suisse Atlantique* case [1967] 1 A.C. 361 at 398; below, para.7–031.
[119] *Sze Hai Tong Bank Ltd v Rambler Cycle Co Ltd* [1959] A.C. 576 at 587. cf. in a different context, *Kenyon Son & Craven Ltd v Baxter Hoare & Co Ltd* [1971] 1 W.L.R. 519 (warehouseman's "gross and culpable" failure to take care to prevent damage to nuts covered by an exemption clause, but Donaldson J. said (at 532) that the clause would not have protected him if he had stored the nuts in the open or in an area which was prohibited by the contract); *Mediterranean Shipping Co SA v Trafigura Beheer BV* [2007] EWCA Civ 794; [2007] 2 Lloyd's Rep. 622 at [30]–[32].
[120] [1967] 1 A.C. 371; Drake 30 M.L.R. 531; Fridman 7 Alberta L.Rev. 281; Treitel 29 M.L.R. 546.
[121] [1967] 1 A.C. 371 at 419, 430.

"fundamental breach".[122] In the *Photo Production*[123] case a security firm which had been engaged to safeguard a factory was protected by an exemption clause which was "clearly and fairly susceptible of one meaning only",[124] even though the firm's breach resulted in the total destruction of the factory by fire. Similarly, in the *Ailsa Craig*[125] case, a security firm was protected by a clause limiting its liability to £1,000, even though the firm had committed a "total" breach of its undertaking to provide a continuous security service for fishing boats, leading to a loss valued at £55,000. As the potential loss which might be caused by the breach was very great in proportion to the sums that could be charged for the service, and as the loss suffered was likely to have been covered by insurance, it was not inherently improbable that the owners of the boats should have agreed to the limitation of liability.

What follows is merely an indication of the sort of considerations which the courts may take into account in construing an exemption clause; in particular, where the breach may be regarded as a serious one. While it will be evident that the court's reluctance to construe a clause so as to apply to a particular breach will, in general, be directly proportioned to the gravity of that breach, each case turns on its own circumstances, including the precise form of words used by the parties.

7–027   **The status of earlier authorities on fundamental breach.** In the course of the developments which led to the rejection of fundamental breach as a substantive rule, the House of Lords overruled a small number of cases that were consistent only with the substantive doctrine[126]; but it did not cast doubt on many other decisions in which the seriousness of the breach had been a ground for holding that an exemption clause afforded no protection. It seems that these earlier cases are to be reinterpreted rather than rejected or ignored. In support of this view, it can be said that some of the earlier judgments explicitly proceeded on the basis that the rule applied was one of construction,[127] while others, though originally based on the substantive doctrine, were later explained as illustrations of the rule of construction,[128] or on other special grounds.[129] Consequently, some of them feature below as illustrations of the courts' approach to the construction of exemption clauses in cases of serious breach.

7–028   **Non-performance and defective performance: "peas and beans".** If a clause exempts the defendant from liability for "defective" performance, it will not protect him if, in fact, he is guilty of "non-performance". For example, if the defendant agrees to supply peas, but sends beans instead, he cannot rely upon a

---

[122] ibid. at 433.

[123] [1980] A.C. 827; below, para.7–032.

[124] ibid. at 851; *Swiss Bank Corp v Brink's-Mat Ltd* [1986] 2 Lloyd's Rep. 79 at 92.

[125] [1983] 1 W.L.R. 964; Palmer 45 M.L.R. 322.

[126] i.e. *Charterhouse Credit Co Ltd v Tolly* [1963] 2 Q.B. 683 ("though the result might have been reached on construction of the contract": *Photo Production* case, above, at 845); *Harbutt's "Plasticine" Ltd v Wayne Tank Co Ltd* [1970] 1 Q.B. 477; *Wathes (Western) Ltd v Austins (Menswear) Ltd* [1976] 1 Lloyd's Rep. 14.

[127] *Gibaud v GE Ry* [1921] 2 K.B. 426: see the *Suisse Atlantique* case [1967] 1 A.C. 361 at 412; and see the judgment of Pearson L.J. in *UGS Finance Ltd v National Mortgage Bank of Greece* [1964] 1 Lloyd's Rep. 446 at 453.

[128] e.g. *Levison v Patent Steam Cleaning Co* [1978] Q.B. 69: see the *Photo Production* case [1980] A.C. 827 at 845, 846; and cf. the *Charterhouse* case, above, fn.126.

[129] i.e. the deviation cases: see below para.7–033.

clause which protects him from liability for "defective" peas, because what he has delivered are not peas at all.[130] This approach first requires the courts to establish precisely what it is for which the parties have contracted. In *George Mitchell (Chesterhall) Ltd v Finney Lock Seeds*, the defendant agreed to supply the claimant with winter cabbage seed, but mistakenly supplied autumn cabbage seed instead. The defendant relied upon an exemption clause which limited its liability for defective "seeds". Parker J.[131] and a majority of the Court of Appeal[132] held that the defendant was unable to rely on the clause. It began by referring to the "seeds or plants sold or *agreed to be sold* by us"[133] and it was held that any other reference to "seeds" should be construed accordingly. On that basis, the defendant had agreed to supply winter cabbage seed and had only limited its liability for the supply of defective winter cabbage seed. The delivery of autumn cabbage seed amounted to non-performance and was not affected by the clause. The House of Lords,[134] and Lord Denning in the Court of Appeal,[135] rejected this construction and held that the defendant had simply agreed to supply "seed". Accordingly, the supply of autumn cabbage seed fell within the clause, but it would not have applied if the defendant had supplied something which did not amount to seeds at all.[136]

Manner of breach. The courts are reluctant to construe exemption clauses so as to apply to acts amounting to a *deliberate* disregard of the main purpose of the contract. They assume that "the parties never contemplated that such a breach should be excused or limited."[137] In accordance with this assumption, it has been held that a tug-owner could not rely on a clause which protected him from liability for "omission" and "default," where he had deliberately abandoned the tow[138]; and that a carrier of goods by sea could not rely on a clause, which protected him from liability after the goods were "discharged", where he had delivered the goods to a person who, as the carrier knew, had no authority to receive them.[139]

The former substantive doctrine of fundamental breach was often invoked in cases in which a bailee of goods had delivered them to the wrong person. It was

7–029

---

[130] *Chanter v Hopkins* (1834) 4 M. & W. 399 at 404; *Nicol v Godts* (1854) 10 Ex. 191; *Pinnock Bros v Lewis & Peat Ltd* [1923] 1 K.B. 690; *Smeaton Hanscomb & Co Ltd v Sassoon I Setty & Co (No.1)* [1953] 1 W.L.R. 1468 at 1470; *Yeoman Credit v Apps* [1962] 2 Q.B. 508; Melville 19 M.L.R. 26; Unger [1957] J.B.L. 30.

[131] [1981] 1 Lloyd's Rep. 476 at 480.

[132] [1983] Q.B. 284 at 305.

[133] Emphasis added.

[134] [1983] 2 A.C. 803; Clarke [1983] C.L.J. 32; Adams 46 M.L.R. 147.

[135] [1983] Q.B. 284 at 296.

[136] There is no doubt that Lord Denning and the House of Lords were encouraged to reject what might be viewed as the strained construction of the majority in the Court of Appeal, since they were able to decide that the clause was, in any event, ineffective because it was unreasonable under s.55 of Sale of Goods Act 1893 (as amended by Supply of Goods (Implied Terms) Act 1973, a forerunner of UCTA)). According to Lord Bridge (at 813), the adoption of such a "strained construction" would come "dangerously near to reintroducing by the back door the doctrine of 'fundamental breach' which this House in the *Photo Production* case had so forcibly evicted from the front".

[137] *Suisse Atlantique* case [1967] 1 A.C. 361 at 435; cf. [1967] 1 A.C. 361 at 394, 397.

[138] *The Cap Palos* [1921] P. 458. cf. *A Turtle Offshore SA v Superior Trading Inc* [2008] EWHC 3034; [2009] 1 Lloyd's Rep. 177.

[139] *Sze Hai Tong Bank Ltd v Rambler Cycle Co Ltd* [1959] A.C. 576; so far as *contra*, *Chartered Bank of India v British India Steam Navigation Co Ltd* [1909] A.C. 369 would no longer be followed: see Guest 77 L.Q.R. 98, 116–118; Wedderburn [1990] C.L.J. 11; *The Ines* [1995] 2 Lloyd's Rep. 144 at 152; *Motis Exports Ltd v Dampskibsselskapet AF 1912* [2000] 1 Lloyd's Rep. 211.

held that exemption clauses did not apply where the misdelivery was deliberate[140] or reckless,[141] but could apply where it was merely negligent.[142] Thus the manner of breach was the crucial point, since the term broken and the consequences of the breach were (in these misdelivery cases) always the same: because of delivery to the wrong person, the goods were lost to the owner. The cases in which the decisive factor was the manner of breach gave rise to much difficulty. For one thing, a "deliberate" breach was hard to define[143]; for another it was puzzlingly held that a deliberate misdelivery by an employee did not deprive the employer of the protection of an exemption clause where the employee had acted with the intention of defrauding his employer.[144] The need for "reconciling" the cases has largely disappeared now that each must be explained as turning on the construction of the clause. The fact that the breach was deliberate would be a ground[145] for holding that the clause was not intended to cover the breach; but it would no longer be a decisive ground. Thus an exemption clause may apply to a breach in spite of the fact that it is deliberate if it is of only trivial importance: "for example, a deliberate delay of one day in unloading."[146] This may be so even where a deliberate but trivial breach gives rise to unexpectedly serious consequences.[147] Where, however, a breach is from the outset both deliberate and repudiatory, only the most explicit form of wording may suffice to exclude liability.[148] Conversely, the parties may expressly agree that any exclusion or limitation of liability does *not* extend to certain degrees of fault,[149] e.g. "wilful misconduct",[150] "deliberate default",[151] or "gross negligence".[152]

7–030   **Consequences of breach.** A breach may be serious by reason of its practical consequences. Failure to perform at the agreed time is always a breach of the same

---

[140] *Alexander v Railway Executive* [1951] 2 K.B. 882.

[141] *J Spurling Ltd v Bradshaw* [1956] 1 W.L.R. 461 at 466; cf. *United Fresh Meat Co Ltd v Charterhouse Cold Storage Ltd* [1974] 2 Lloyd's Rep. 286 at 291.

[142] *Hollins v J Davy Ltd* [1963] 1 Q.B. 844; Guest 26 M.L.R. 301; cf. *The New York Star* [1981] 1 W.L.R. 138.

[143] Probably it meant delivery "to someone known to have no right" to the goods: *Hollins v J Davy Ltd* (above) at 856; see below, fn.150.

[144] *John Carter (Fine Worsteds) Ltd v Hanson Haulage (Leeds) Ltd* [1965] 2 Q.B. 495—a case now to be "treated with caution": *W & J Lane v Spratt* [1970] 1 All E.R. 162 at 172. cf. also *Levison v Patent Steam Carpet Cleaning Co Ltd* [1978] Q.B. 82 (where, on such facts, there is said to be a fundamental breach).

[145] e.g. *The Cap Palos* [1921] P. 458; *Sze Hai Tong Bank Ltd v Rambler Cycle Co Ltd* [1959] A.C. 576; above, at fn.139.

[146] *Suisse Atlantique* case [1967] 1 A.C. 361 at 435.

[147] e.g. *Photo Production Ltd v Securicor Transport Ltd* [1980] A.C. 827 at 840 (fire started deliberately but without the intention of burning down the factory: see below, para.7–032).

[148] *Internet Broadcasting Corporation Ltd v MAR LLC* [2009] EWHC 84 (Ch); [2009] 2 Lloyd's Rep 295; cf. *Astrazeneca UK Ltd v Albemarle International Corporation* [2011] EWHC 1574 (Comm) at [288]–[301].

[149] In the context of liability for misrepresentation, it is customary to carve out any liability for "fraudulent misrepresentation" since otherwise the clause may fail as a whole: see below, para.9–125.

[150] Defined as "conduct by a person who knows that he is committing, and intends to commit a breach of duty, or is reckless in the sense of not caring whether or not he commits a breach of duty", *De Beers UK Ltd v Atos Origin IT Services UK Ltd* [2010] EWHC 3276 (TCC) at [206], citing Romer J. in *Re City Equitable Fire Insurance Company Ltd* [1925] 1 Ch 407.

[151] Defined as "deliberate, in the sense that the person committing the relevant act knew that it was a default (i.e. in this case a breach of contract) . . . it does not extend to recklessness and is therefore narrower than wilful misconduct (although the latter will embrace deliberate default)", *De Beers UK Ltd v Atos Origin IT Services UK Ltd* [2010] EWHC 3276 (TCC) at [206].

[152] See below, para.7–038.

term; but an exemption clause may be construed so as to cover only slight delays and not those that are so prolonged as to cause serious prejudice to the injured party.[153] Again, goods supplied under a contract of sale or hire-purchase may not be fit for the particular purpose for which the customer has acquired them and in a number of cases it has been held that the supplier was not protected by an exemption clause because the defect was so serious as to make the thing practically useless for the customer's purposes.[154] The same result was reached where the proprietor of a parking garage had undertaken to keep a car which had been parked there locked, but left it unlocked, so that the customer's luggage was stolen.[155]

"Total" breach. If the literal effect of a clause is to exempt one party from liability for *any* breach, this would seem to be inconsistent with the main purpose of the contract and may negate the idea that the parties were in a contractual relationship in the first place.[156] Since, by their conduct, it may be clear that the parties intended to create a legal relationship, the court will give the clause a restricted meaning.[157] In *The TFL Prosperity*[158] the claimant charterer suffered a financial loss because the defendant owner's ship was unable to carry the required load, in breach of warranty. The defendant sought to rely on an exemption clause, the potential effect of which was summed up by Lord Roskill as follows:

> "the charter virtually ceases to be a contract . . . and becomes no more than a statement of intent by the owners in return for which the charterers are obliged to pay large sums of hire, though if the owners fail to carry out their promises as to description or delivery, [the charterers] are entitled to nothing in lieu"[159]

and he rejected that construction on the ground that it did not accord with "the true common intention of the parties".[160] The obvious danger with any approach which relies upon an inherent limitation upon the wording employed by the parties is that it comes close to the reintroduction of a substantive rule that the parties cannot agree to exempt liability for serious (i.e. fundamental) breach.[161]

7–031

---

[153] See, e.g. *Bontex Knitting Works Ltd v St John's Garage* [1943] 2 All E.R. 690; [1944] 1 All E.R. 381; *Suisse Atlantique* case [1967] 1 A.C. 361; cf. *Brandt v Liverpool, etc. SN Co Ltd* [1924] 1 K.B. 575 at 597, 601.

[154] *Yeoman Credit Ltd v Apps* [1962] 2 Q.B. 508; *Farnsworth Finance Facilities Ltd v Attryde* [1970] 1 W.L.R. 1053.

[155] *Mendelssohn v Normand Ltd* [1970] 1 Q.B. 177; Treitel 32 M.L.R. 685.

[156] *Suisse Atlantique* case, above, at 432. cf. *Firestone Tyre & Rubber Co Ltd v Vokins & Co Ltd* [1951] 1 Lloyd's Rep. 32 at 39: "It is illusory to say—'we promise to do a thing but we are not liable if we do not do it.' "

[157] ibid.; *The Cap Palos* [1921] P. 458; *Sze Hai Tong Bank Ltd v Rambler Cycle Co Ltd* [1959] A.C. 576; *Glynn v Margetson & Co* [1893] A.C. 351; *J Evans & Son (Portsmouth) Ltd v Andrea Merzario Ltd* [1976] 1 W.L.R. 1078; *Mitsubishi Corp v Eastwind Transport Ltd* [2004] EWHC 2924; [2005] 1 Lloyd's Rep. 383; *A Turtle Offshore SA v Superior Trading Inc* [2008] EWHC 3034; [2009] 1 Lloyd's Rep. 177.

[158] [1984] 1 W.L.R. 48.

[159] ibid. at 58–59.

[160] ibid. at 58. In fact, the defendant was unable to rely on the exemption clause on the narrower ground that references to "loss" in the exemption clause referred only to physical damage to goods and not the purely financial loss which the charterer had suffered through the carrying of a smaller load than anticipated. cf. *The Chanda* [1989] 2 Lloyd's Rep. 494.

[161] See the *George Mitchell* case, above at 814, per Lord Bridge. In a number of the cases which appear to support the substantive doctrine of fundamental breach, one can also find passages which are consistent with the principle of construction advocated by Lord Roskill in the *Tor Line* case. Indeed, that is the basis upon which many of them have subsequently been interpreted.

Thus, when it has been said that an exemption clause "cannot be taken to refer" to "total breach",[162] the best interpretation is, perhaps, that the courts will "lean against"[163] such a construction, while not wholly ruling out the possibility of its being achieved by sufficiently clear words.[164]

7–032   **Effect of termination.**[165] It is clear from the decision in the *Suisse Atlantique* case, where the shipowners were found to have affirmed the charterparty,[166] that affirmation after a serious breach does not affect the operation of an exemption clause which is expressed so as to exclude or restrict only *the right to damages* for that breach[167]: that right continues, after affirmation, to depend on the construction of the clause. The position was formerly thought to be different if the injured party did not affirm the contract but terminated it on account of the serious breach. It was argued that, by terminating, the injured party could bring the whole contract to an end; and that in this way he could get rid of an exemption clause even though the clause, on its true construction, excluded or restricted his right to damages for the breach.[168] But this view was rejected in *Photo Production Ltd v Securicor Transport Ltd*,[169] where defendants had agreed to provide a "night patrol service" for the claimants' factory for a weekly charge of £8 15s. One of their employees started a small fire which got out of control so that the factory, worth £650,000, was destroyed. The contract contained an exemption clause which, on its true construction, applied to this breach, in spite of the seriousness of its effects.[170] The House of Lords held that the claimants could not get rid of the clause by electing to terminate the contract; for to allow their claim on this ground would have amounted to a reintroduction of the "substantive doctrine" after its rejection in the *Suisse Atlantique* case. The effect of the claimants' election to terminate was to put an end to obligations of further performance *after* that election.[171] But it did not operate retrospectively so as to deprive the defendants of the protection of the clause with respect to loss suffered *before* that election had been made.

Where a party exercises his right to terminate for breach, he may, however, be prima facie entitled to damages not only in respect of past loss but also in respect of prospective loss, i.e. loss which he will suffer after termination, as a result of the other party's wrongful repudiation.[172] Suppose, for example, that in the *Suisse Atlantique* case the shipowners had justifiably terminated when only half the period of the charter had expired, and that they had found alternative employment for the ship for the rest of that period. They would then, but for any exemption

---

[162] *Suisse Atlantique* case [1967] 1 A.C. 361 at 432.

[163] *Motis Exports Ltd v Dampskibsselskapet AF 1912* [2000] 1 Lloyd's Rep. 211 at 216.

[164] [2000] 1 Lloyd's Rep. 211 at 217. See also: *The Kapitan Petko Voivoda* [2003] EWCA Civ 451; [2003] 2 Lloyd's Rep. 1 at [23], [29].

[165] For the requirements and effects of termination and affirmation generally, see Ch.18.

[166] [1967] 1 A.C. 361 at 395, 398, 409, 410, 437.

[167] This view is also supported by *Chandris v Isbrandtsen-Moller Inc* [1951] 2 K.B. 240, reversed on another ground [1951] 1 K.B. at 256. For the apparently contrary decision in *Charterhouse Credit Ltd v Tolly* [1963] 2 Q.B. 683, see above, fn.126. cf. Unfair Contract Terms Act 1977, s.9(2); below, para.7–085.

[168] e.g. *Harbutt's "Plasticine" Ltd v Wayne Tank Co Ltd* [1970] 1 Q.B. 447, overruled in *Photo Production Ltd v Securicor Transport Ltd* [1980] A.C. 827.

[169] [1980] A.C. 827. Guest 96 L.Q.R. 324; Sealy [1980] C.L.J. 252; Palmer and Yates [1981] C.L.J. 108; Nicol and Rawlings 43 M.L.R. 567.

[170] See above, para.7–026.

[171] [1980] A.C. 827 at 844–845, 849–850.

[172] See below, para.18–015.

clauses, have been entitled to damages in respect of (i) detention of the ship before termination and (ii) loss suffered thereafter if the alternative employment of the ship was less profitable than that under the original contract. When Lord Reid said that the shipowners would have been entitled to damages over and above the agreed demurrage if, instead of affirming the charterparty, they had justifiably terminated it,[173] he was (it is submitted) referring to this prospective loss. This assumes that the demurrage clause did not cover this type of loss, but only damages for detention under the first head.[174] If an exemption clause on its true construction did cover prospective loss under the second head, it is submitted that the injured party could not, by simply terminating the contract on account of the breach, get rid of the clause so as to recover full damages in respect of loss of this kind. To allow him to do so would not, indeed, infringe the general principle that termination for breach has no retrospective effect on the operation of exemption clauses; but it would be inconsistent with the rejection of the substantive doctrine of fundamental breach. This submission is supported by a dictum of Lord Diplock in the *Photo Production* case that liability for such loss can be "excluded or modified by express words".[175] Clauses which regulate "the manner in which liability . . . is to be established",[176] e.g. by limiting the time within which a claim must be made, similarly continue to govern the future relations of the parties even after termination for serious breach.[177] Arbitration clauses likewise survive such termination.[178]

A surviving rule of law? Deviation and analogous rules. In a contract for   7–033
the carriage of goods by sea, the benefit of an exemption clause is normally lost by a carrier who has without justification[179] deviated, i.e. departed from the agreed or usual route.[180] The same is true where a warehouseman has stored the goods in a place other than that agreed[181]; and where a bailee such as a cleaner or carrier has in the course of unauthorised subcontracting parted with the possession of goods entrusted to him.[182] On the other hand, such a person will not lose the protection of an exemption clause merely because he has broken some other term such as a

---

[173] [1967] 1 A.C. 361 at 398, cf. [1967] 1 A.C. 361 at 419 and 437. It does not seem that Lord Wilberforce intended to cast doubt on this dictum when in the *Photo Production* case at 842 he criticised a different passage of Lord Reid's speech.
[174] See further: *A/S Reidar v Arcos* [1927] 1 K.B. 352; *Chandris v Isbrandtsen-Moller* [1951] 1 K.B. 240 at 248–255; *The Bonde* [1991] 1 Lloyd's Rep. 136 at 139–142; Gay [2004] L.M.C.L.Q. 72.
[175] [1980] A.C. 827 at 849.
[176] *The New York Star* [1981] 1 W.L.R. 138 at 145.
[177] ibid.; cf. the discussion of "ancillary" obligations at para.18–014, below.
[178] *Heyman v Darwins Ltd* [1942] A.C. 356.
[179] See *Kish v Taylor* [1912] A.C. 604 at 617; Carriage of Goods by Sea Act 1971, Sch., Art.IV 4: deviation may be justified for the purpose of saving life or property at sea, or if it is "reasonable".
[180] *Joseph Thorley Ltd v Orchis SS Co Ltd* [1907] 1 K.B. 660; *James Morrison & Co Ltd v Shaw Savill & Albion Co Ltd* [1916] 2 K.B. 783; *Stag Line Ltd v Foscolo, Mango & Co Ltd* [1932] A.C. 328. A strict approach is taken to the construction of any clause in the contract said to confer a liberty to deviate: *Glynn v Margetson & Co* [1893] A.C. 351; cf. *G H Renton & Co v Palmyra Trading Corporation of Panama* [1957] A.C. 149.
[181] *Woolf v Collis Removal Services* [1948] 1 K.B. 11 at 15; cf. *United Fresh Meat Co Ltd v Charterhouse Cold Storage Ltd* [1974] 2 Lloyd's Rep. 286; *The OOCL Bravery* [2000] 1 Lloyd's Rep. 394 at 401 (parking container lorry in street instead of in secured depot).
[182] *Davies v Collins* [1945] 1 All E.R. 247; *Garnham, Harris & Elton Ltd v Alfred W Ellis (Transport) Ltd* [1967] 1 W.L.R. 940.

carrier's undertaking to supply a seaworthy ship[183]; or a warehouseman's undertaking to exercise reasonable care in looking after the goods.[184] The reason for the
distinction is sometimes said to be that the terms as to the route and as to the place
where the goods are to be stored are fundamental,[185] while the other terms
mentioned are not. Thus, in the deviation cases, the courts are not concerned with
the effect of the breach: *any* departure from the agreed route "however for
practical purposes irrelevant"[186] normally deprives the shipowner of the benefit of
the exemption clause. Furthermore, the deviation cases appear to represent an
exception to the general rule that termination does not retrospectively deprive a
party of the benefit of exemption clauses. It is commonly held that the carrier is
deprived of the benefit of exemption clauses in respect of loss which has occurred
before the owner of the goods elected to terminate the contract.[187] One possible
explanation for this state of the law is that it follows from the special considerations
which affect deviation. One reason for classifying deviation as a breach of a
"fundamental term" is that it deprives the cargo-owner of his insurance cover[188];
and since it so deprives him automatically and "as from the time of the deviation",[189] the same reasoning would seem to support the view that deviation
deprives the carrier of the benefit of exemption clauses in the contract of carriage
from the same time and with the same retrospective effect.

The special rule as to the effects of deviation has been criticised.[190] It has been
explained as a rule which, on account of its historical and commercial background,
must be treated as sui generis,[191] but the preferable view is that it should be
"assimilated into the ordinary law of contract".[192] On that basis, both the questions of whether an exemption clause applies and, if so, from when, are to be
decided simply as a matter of the proper construction of the clause in question.[193]
This view is supported by developments in relation to stowage on deck which has
been equated with deviation. In *The Kapitan Petko Voivoda*,[194] the question of

---

[183] *The Europa* [1908] P. 84; *Kish v Taylor* [1912] A.C. 604. But if the unseaworthiness *causes* the loss,
the carrier cannot rely on the exceptions provided under Carriage of Goods by Sea Act 1971: see
Maxine Footwear Ltd v Canadian Government Merchant Marine Ltd [1959] A.C. 589; but he can rely
on the *limitation* so provided: *The Happy Ranger* [2002] EWCA Civ 694; [2002] 2 Lloyd's Rep. 357 at
[38].
[184] *J Spurling Ltd v Bradshaw* [1956] 1 W.L.R. 461; *Kenyon Son & Craven Ltd v Baxter Hoare &
Co Ltd* [1971] 1 W.L.R. 519.
[185] See *Smeaton Hanscomb & Co v Sassoon I Setty* [1953] 1 W.L.R. 1468 at 1470, describing
deviation as a breach of a fundamental term.
[186] *Suisse Atlantique* case [1967] 1 A.C. 361 at 423, e.g. it is irrelevant that the deviation did not cause,
or increase the risk of, loss: *Joseph Thorley Ltd v Orchis SS Co Ltd* [1907] 1 K.B. 660; *James Morrison
& Co v Shaw, Savill & Albion Co Ltd* [1916] 2 K.B. 783.
[187] See the authorities cited at fnn.180–182, above.
[188] *Hain SS Co v Tate & Lyle Ltd* (1936) 41 Com.Cas. 350 at 354. In fact the goods-owner may not
suffer the hardship on which the rule is based, since his insurance policy may provide that he is to be
"held covered" in case of deviation at a premium to be arranged: see *State Trading Corp of India v S
M Golodetz Ltd* [1989] 2 Lloyd's Rep. 277 at 289.
[189] Marine Insurance Act 1906, s.46(1); *The Good Luck* [1992] A.C. 233; below, para.18–007 (dealing
with the corresponding wording in s.33(3)).
[190] *Farr v Hain SS Co (The Tregenna)* 121 F 2d. 940 at 944 (1941). This case arose from the same
facts as *Hain SS Co v Tate & Lyle Ltd*, above; cf. Livermore 2 J.C.L. 241; Reynolds, *Butterworth
Lectures* 1990–91, pp.29–52.
[191] *Photo Production Ltd v Securicor Transport Ltd* [1980] A.C. 827 at 845, per Lord Wilberforce.
[192] *The Antares (Nos 1 and 2)* [1987] 1 Lloyd's Rep. 424 at 430; *The Kapitan Petko Voivoda* [2003]
EWCA Civ 451; [2003] 2 Lloyd's Rep. 1 at [14].
[193] Whether all of the previous decisions on the effect of deviation can be interpreted in this way is
open to debate.
[194] [2003] EWCA Civ 451; [2003] 2 Lloyd's Rep. 1.

whether a carrier which was guilty of unauthorised deck stowage could rely on the package limitation laid down in the Hague Rules was regarded purely as a question of construction. Since the relevant limitation was expressed to apply "in any event",[195] the carrier was entitled to rely upon it.[196]

(iii) *Negligence*

Clear words needed. Legislation has severely restricted the effectiveness of   7–034
clauses purporting to exempt a party from liability for negligence[197]; and the negligence of the party in breach may also support the conclusion that the statutory requirement of reasonableness has not been satisfied.[198] But even where it remains possible to exclude liability for negligence, "clear words" must be used for this purpose, since the courts regard it as "inherently improbable that one party to a contract should intend to absolve the other party from the consequence of his own negligence".[199] The requirement is most obviously satisfied where the exemption clause expressly refers to negligence: i.e. uses the word "negligence"[200] or some synonym for it.[201] It *may* be satisfied, even though there is no such express reference to negligence, if the words are nevertheless wide enough to cover negligence: e.g. if the clause exempts a party from "all liability whatsoever".[202] But whether such general words *actually are* effective to exclude liability for negligence may depend on a further distinction: namely that between cases in which, but for the clause, the party relying on it may be liable irrespective of negligence, and those in which his only possible liability is for negligence.[203] It has also been suggested that where parties have drawn up a series of detailed agreements and the draftsmen have expressly dealt with negligence, a "more significant canon of construction" is that where it has not been expressly referred to that would indicate a deliberate decision by the draftsman to exclude negligence.[204]

---

[195] Art.IV(5). The same wording is included in the limitation provided by the Hague-Visby Rules, Art.IV(5).

[196] The earlier decision in *The Chanda* [1989] 2 Lloyd's Rep. 494 was overruled. *Royal Exchange Shipping Co v Dixon* (1886) 12 App. Cas. 11 and *J Evans & Sons Ltd v Andrea Merzario Ltd* [1976] 1 W.L.R. 1078 where the carrier was unable to rely on a limitation were found to turn on the proper construction of the contract and did not support a wider rule, equivalent to the effect of deviation. See also: *The Antares (No.2)* [1987] 1 Lloyd's Rep. 424; *The Pembroke* [1995] 2 Lloyd's Rep. 290 (*The Chanda* followed in New Zealand); *The Happy Ranger* [2002] EWCA Civ 694; [2002] 2 Lloyd's Rep. 357.

[197] Unfair Contract Terms Act 1977, s.2; below, paras 7–057, 7–065; cf. Unfair Terms in Consumer Contracts Regulations 1999, Sch.2, para.1(a) and (b).

[198] *George Mitchell (Chesterhall) Ltd v Finney Lock Seeds Ltd* [1983] 2 A.C. 803; below, para.7–028.

[199] *Gillespie Bros Ltd v Roy Bowles Transport Ltd* [1973] Q.B. 400 at 419; cf. *Sonat Offshore SA v Amerada Hess Development Ltd* [1988] 1 Lloyd's Rep. 145 at 157.

[200] e.g. *Spriggs v Sotheby Parke Bernet & Co* [1986] 1 Lloyd's Rep. 487; *Henderson v Merrett Syndicates Ltd* [1995] 2 A.C. 145 at 183; *Monarch Airlines Ltd v Luton Airport* [1998] 1 Lloyd's Rep. 403.

[201] *Canada SS Lines Ltd v The King* [1952] A.C. 192 at 208.

[202] ibid.; such general words do not amount to an *express* reference to negligence: see *Smith v South Wales Switchgear Ltd* [1978] W.L.R. 165 at 173 and *Smith v UMB Chrysler (Scotland)* 1978 S.C.(H.L.) 1 at 12, disapproving dicta in *Gillespie v Roy Bowles Transport Ltd* [1973] Q.B. 400 at 420, 421; *The Raphael* [1982] 2 Lloyd's Rep. 42. By contrast, it seems that the words loss or injury "however caused" do amount to such an *express* reference: *Brown v Drake International Ltd* [2004] EWCA Civ 1629 at [21]. This must be open to doubt.

[203] ibid.

[204] *Shell UK Ltd v Total UK Ltd* [2010] EWCA Civ 180; [2010] 3 W.L.R. 1192 at [15].

7–035   **Party liable irrespective of negligence.** If there is a realistic possibility (as opposed to a merely fanciful one[205]) that a party can be made liable irrespective of negligence, an exemption clause in general terms will not normally be construed so as to cover liability for negligence.[206] For example, a common carrier of goods is strictly liable if they are lost or damaged. A clause exempting him from liability "for loss or damage"[207] would be construed to refer to his strict liability only. The position is the same where it is doubtful in law whether the party relying on the clause is liable irrespective of negligence: here again a clause which does not refer to negligence will not prima facie be construed to exempt him from liability for negligence.[208] But in all the situations just described it is not absolutely necessary to refer expressly to negligence; for the rule is one of construction only and "should not be applied rigidly or mechanically so as to defeat [the] intentions [of the parties]".[209] Thus, in the *HIH* case,[210] a clause in an insurance policy excluded the insurer's right to avoid the policy for "any" misrepresentation or non-disclosure by an agent of the insured. Such general wording could have been confined to the right to avoid for innocent misrepresentation, or non-disclosure, but it was clear from all the circumstances that the intention of the parties was to "distance" the insured from any misconduct of the agent,[211] including negligence.[212] It was stressed that the rules applicable to negligence are not rules as such, but rather "helpful guidance" on the proper approach to interpretation.[213]

7–036   **Clauses limiting liability.** The fact that the clause only *limits* (and does not wholly *exclude*) liability is also relevant to the issue of construction. Thus a seller is strictly liable for defects in goods; so that prima facie general words would not exclude liability for defects due to his negligence. But where a seller of seeds undertook to replace defective seeds or to refund the price paid for them, it was

---

[205] See *Hair & Skin Trading Co Ltd v Norman Airfreight Carriers Ltd* [1974] 1 Lloyd's Rep. 442; *Smith v South Wales Switchgear Ltd* [1978] 1 W.L.R. 165 at 178; *The Raphael*, above, fn.202.

[206] *Canada SS Lines Ltd v The King* [1952] A.C. 192, esp. at 208; *White v J Warwick & Co Ltd* [1953] 1 W.L.R. 1285; Gower 17 M.L.R. 155; cf. *EE Caledonia Ltd v Orbit Valve Co Europe* [1994] 1 W.L.R. 221; *Casson v Ostley PJ Ltd* [2002] 18 Const.L.J. 145; *The Socol 3* [2010] EWHC 777 (Comm); [2010] 2 Lloyd's Rep. 221.

[207] See *Rutter v Palmer* [1922] 2 K.B. 87; cf. *The Fantasy* [1991] 2 Lloyd's Rep. 391, affirmed [1992] 1 Lloyd's Rep. 235, without reference to this point.

[208] *The Emmanuel C* [1983] 1 Lloyd's Rep. 310; *The Oceanic Amity* [1984] 2 All E.R. 140 at 151.

[209] *The Golden Leader* [1980] 2 Lloyd's Rep. 573 at 574.

[210] *HIH Casualty & General Ins v Chase Manhattan Bank* [2003] UKHL 6; [2003] 2 Lloyd's Rep 61. See also: *Joseph Travers & Sons Ltd v Cooper* [1915] K.B. 73; cf. *A E Farr Ltd v Admiralty* [1953] 1 W.L.R. 965; *Trident Turboprop(Dublin) Ltd v First Flight Couriers Ltd* [2008] EWHC 1686 (Comm); [2009] 2 Lloyd's Rep. 581, affirmed [2009] EWCA Civ 290; [2010] Q.B. 86 without reference to this point; *Robinson v P E Jones (Contractors) Ltd* [2011] EWCA Civ 9 at [85].

[211] The policy was for film insurance and the insured, a syndicate of banks financing the film production, was "not in the usual position of an insured" (at [48]) being in no better a position than the insurer to estimate the risk.

[212] So far as "pure non-disclosure" was concerned (i.e. non-disclosure not amounting to an implicit misrepresentation) the House of Lords, unlike the Court of Appeal ([2001] EWCA Civ 1250; [2001] 2 Lloyd's Rep. 483), did not rely on the "unitary and absolute" nature of the duty of disclosure which makes no distinction between the ways in which it may be broken, i.e. innocently, negligently, or fraudulently; there "is no reason why the parties should not make such distinctions in a contractual provision which limits its scope": at [74]. The House then held that the clause did not exclude the right to avoid the policy for the fraudulent misrepresentation *or* non-disclosure of the agent: see below, para.7–042.

[213] [2003] UKHL 6; [2003] 2 Lloyd's Rep 61 at [11]. See, to the same effect: *Macquarie International Investments Ltd v Glencore UK Ltd* [2008] EWHC 2716 (Comm); [2008] 2 B.C.L.C. 565.

held that a clause excluding "all [further] liability" did, as a matter of construction, apply where the seller was negligent in supplying seeds which were defective. One reason given for this conclusion was that the rules limiting the scope of exemption clauses in cases of negligent breach "cannot be applied in their full rigour to limitation clauses".[214] The question in all the above cases is whether the intention of one party to exclude liability for negligence has been made sufficiently clear to the other. An express reference to negligence is the safest, but not the only, way of achieving this result.

Party liable only for negligence. Where a contracting party is liable only for 7–037
negligence, the rule of construction discussed above obviously does not apply. It follows that in such cases an exemption clause in general terms (i.e. one not specifically referring to negligence) *can* cover negligence.[215] It used, moreover, to be thought that, in cases of this kind, a clause in general terms necessarily *did* cover negligence, since "it would otherwise lack subject-matter"[216]: it would have no effect if it did not exclude the only liability which the defendant could incur. But this reasoning no longer prevails. Even where the defendant's only liability is for negligence, the clause must make it clear that *liability* is to be excluded. It may do so by general words not containing any express reference to negligence.[217] But in *Hollier v Rambler Motors (AMC) Ltd*[218] a customer's car had been left with the defendants for repair and was damaged in a fire caused by their negligence. It was held that they could not rely on a provision[219] that they were "not responsible for damage caused by fire to customer's cars on the premises". This was so even though they were liable for such damage only if the fire was due to their negligence: the provision merely operated as a warning to the customer that the garage proprietors were not liable for loss caused by a fire which was *not* due to their negligence. Obviously, however, a clause cannot be construed merely as such a warning if it expressly exempts a party from liability for negligence.[220]

Even where a defendant is liable only for negligence and clearly intends to exclude that liability, general words may fail to protect him. In *Re Polemis*[221] a clause in a charterparty provided that liability for fire should be *mutually* excepted, i.e. that neither shipowner nor charterer should be liable for fire. The shipowner was a common carrier and therefore liable without negligence. Thus the clause

---

[214] *George Mitchell (Chesterhall) Ltd v Finney Lock Seeds Ltd* [1983] 2 A.C. 803 at 814; but the fact that the seller was negligent was relevant for the purpose of the statutory reasonableness test: below, para.7–083; cf. *Tradigrain SA v Intertek Testing Services Canada Ltd* [2007] EWCA Civ 154 at [49].

[215] e.g. *White v Blackmore* [1972] 2 Q.B. 651; *Scottish Special Housing Association v Wimpey Construction UK Ltd* [1986] 1 W.L.R. 995; *Rutter v Palmer* [1922] 2 K.B. 87; cf. *Levison v Patent Steam Carpet Cleaning Co Ltd* [1978] Q.B. 69 at 83–84; *BHP Petroleum Ltd v British Steel Ltd* [2000] 2 All E.R. (Comm) 133 (where the duties of the party in breach were partly strict and partly duties of diligence); *Co-operative Retail Services Ltd v Taylor Young Partnerships Ltd* [2002] UKHL 17; [2002] 1 W.L.R. 1419 at [42]–[44].

[216] *Alderslade v Hendon Laundry* [1945] K.B. 189 at 192; cf. *Gibaud v Great Eastern Ry* [1921] 2 K.B. 426; *The Ballyalton* [1961] 1 W.L.R. 929.

[217] *Alderslade v Hendon Laundry Ltd* [1945] K.B. 189, as explained in *Hollier v Rambler Motors (AMC) Ltd* [1972] 2 Q.B. 71; *Hair & Skin Trading Co Ltd v Norman Airfreight Carriers Ltd* [1974] 1 Lloyd's Rep. 442. For similar construction of indemnity clauses, see *Gillespie Bros & Co Ltd v Roy Bowles Transport Ltd* [1973] Q.B. 400; *Arthur White (Contractors) Ltd v Tarmac Civil Engineering Ltd* [1967] 1 W.L.R. 1506 and *Thompson v T Lohan (Plant Hire) Ltd* [1987] 1 W.L.R. 649; cf. *The Super Servant Two* [1990] 1 Lloyd's Rep. 1 at 8 (similar construction of cancellation clause).

[218] [1972] 2 Q.B. 71; cf. *Olley v Marlborough Court* [1949] 1 K.B. 532.

[219] Which was actually not incorporated in the contract: above, fn.51.

[220] *Spriggs v Sotheby Parke Bernet & Co* [1986] 1 Lloyd's Rep. 487.

[221] [1921] 3 K.B. 560.

would not exempt him from liability for negligence, but only from strict liability. In view of this, it was held that the clause did not exempt the charterer from liability for negligence either, although he was liable only for negligence.

7–038   **Gross Negligence.** It has been said that, although often found in commercial documents, the term "gross negligence" has "never been accepted by English civil law as a concept distinct from civil negligence".[222] But in the context of an exclusion clause it has also been said that the issue is not whether, generally, gross negligence is a familiar concept in English civil law, but the meaning of the expression in the relevant clause.[223] In that context, it has been held that "gross negligence" differs from "mere" negligence and embraces "not only conduct undertaken with actual appreciation of the risks involved, but also serious disregard of or indifference to an obvious risk".[224]

(c) Other Common Law Limitations

7–039   Even if an exemption clause on its true construction covers the breach that has occurred, its effectiveness is subject to a number of further common law limitations. These are much reduced in importance by the legislative limitations to be discussed later in this chapter[225]; but they retain their practical importance in cases to which those limitations do not apply.[226]

7–040   **Misrepresentation as to contents.** In *Curtis v Chemical Cleaning & Dyeing Co Ltd*,[227] the claimant took a dress to the defendants to be cleaned. She signed a receipt after being told that it exempted the defendants from liability for certain specified kinds of damage, when it actually exempted them for liability "for any damage, however arising". It was held that the defendants could not rely on the clause as they had induced the claimant to sign the receipt by misrepresenting its contents.[228] Denning L.J. said[229] that mere failure to draw attention to the existence or extent of the exemption clause might in some circumstances amount to misrepresentation.[230]

---

[222] *Tradigrain SA v Internek Testing Services* [2007] EWCA Civ 154 at [23]; cf. *Sucden Financial v Fluxo-CaneOverseas Ltd*, [2010] EWHC 2133 (Comm) at [54]; and *Marex Financial Ltd v Fluxo-Cane Overseas Ltd*, [2010] EWHC 2690 (Comm) at [93].

[223] *Camarata Property Incorporated v Credit Suisse Securities (Europe) Ltd* [2011] EWHC 479 (Comm) at [161].

[224] ibid., citing *The Hellespont Ardent* [1997] 2 Lloyd's Rep. 547 at 586.

[225] See below, paras 7–049—7–126.

[226] See below, paras 7–088—7–094, 7–117. Theoretically, the common law limitations could be used to impugn a clause which satisfied the legislative tests of reasonableness (below, paras 7–064—7–073) and fairness (below, paras 7–103—7–114); but in practice it is unlikely that these tests could be satisfied where one of the common law limitations applied.

[227] [1951] 1 K.B. 805; cf. *Horry v Tate & Lyle Refineries Ltd* [1982] 2 Lloyd's Rep. 416 at 422.

[228] The decision is said to rest on a finding that the clause had not been incorporated into the contract: *Axa Sun Life Services Plc v Campbell Martin Ltd* [2011] EWCA Civ 133 at [105], per Rix L.J. (doubting the reasons given by Denning L.J.).

[229] [1951] 1 K.B. 805 at 809.

[230] cf. *Peekay Intermark Ltd v ANZ Banking Group Ltd* [2006] EWCA Civ 386; [2006] 2 Lloyd's Rep 511 at [47] suggesting that the principle in the *Curtis* case requires a positive representation that the claimant "need not bother to read the documents".

Overriding undertaking. An exemption clause in a document with reference   7-041
to which the parties contract can be overridden by an express inconsistent
undertaking given at or before the time of contracting. Thus a buyer of goods by
auction can recover damages for breach of an oral undertaking given at the time
of sale although the printed conditions of sale exempt the seller from all liability
for defects.[231] To bring this rule into operation, there must be an "express specific
oral promise"[232] which is inconsistent with the exemption clause: a party is not
prevented from relying on a clause merely because no reference was made to it at
the time of contracting, so that (in this sense) it can be said to be inconsistent with
the terms expressly agreed. Where a series of contracts is made under a master
agreement, an obligation imposed by that agreement may similarly override an
exemption clause contained in a written document evidencing the terms of the
particular contract in question.[233]

Excluding liability for fraud. A party cannot contract that he shall not be   7-042
liable for his own fraud.[234] It remains an open question whether this rule of law,
which is based on public policy, extends to the fraud of an agent.[235] There is some
support for the view that it may be possible to exclude liability for the fraud of an
agent in the *performance* of the contract, but not in its *making*.[236] That there is no
direct authority on the point is explained by the fact that, as a matter of
construction, the intention to exclude such liability "must be expressed in clear
and unmistakeable terms on the face of the contract"; general words will not
suffice.[237] It is unlikely that the parties will agree to a term which excludes liability
for the fraud of an agent with sufficient clarity to raise the issue whether it should
be lawful to do so.[238]

Excluding liability for breach of certain fiduciary duties. The promoter   7-043
of a company is under a fiduciary duty to the company not to make a profit out of
the promotion without disclosing it to the company. He cannot contract out of this
duty.[239] It is submitted that any contract term by which a person who was under

---

[231] *Couchman v Hill* [1947] K.B. 554; *Harling v Eddy* [1951] 2 K.B 739; cf. *Brikom Investments Ltd v Carr* [1979] Q.B. 467 at 480; *BCT Software Solutions Ltd v Arnold Laver & Co Ltd* [2002] EWHC 1298 (Ch); [2002] 2 All E.R. (Comm) 85.

[232] *George Mitchell (Chesterhall) Ltd v Finney Lock Seeds Ltd* [1983] Q.B. 284 at 309, affirmed [1983] 2 A.C. 803, without reference to this point.

[233] *Gallaher v BRS Ltd and Containerway & Roadferry* [1974] 2 Lloyd's Rep. 440; *J Evans & Son (Portsmouth) Ltd v Andrea Merzario* [1976] 1 W.L.R. 1078; cf. *Mendelssohn v Normand Ltd* [1970] 1 Q.B. 177.

[234] *HIH Casualty & General Ins v Chase Manhattan Bank* [2003] UKHL 6; [2003] 2 Lloyd's Rep 61; *S Pearson & Son Ltd v Dublin Corp* [1907] A.C. 351 at 353, 362; *Shipskreditforeningen v Emperor Navigation* [1998] 1 Lloyd's Rep. 67 at 76; cf. *Garden Neptune Shipping Ltd v Occidental Worldwide Investment Corp* [1990] 1 Lloyd's Rep. 330 at 335.

[235] ibid. Of the majority in the *HIH* case only Lord Hobhouse held that it does so extend (a view endorsed by Handley 119 L.Q.R. 537); cf. Lord Scott (dissenting) at [122].

[236] ibid. at [77]. See also *Tullis v Jacson* [1892] 3 Ch. 441, which was criticised in *Czarnikow v Roth, Schmidt & Co* [1922] 2 K.B. 478 at 488.

[237] ibid. at [16]. General words may suffice for fraud in the *performance* of the contract by an agent or employee: *Frans Maas (UK) Ltd v Samsung Electronics (UK) Ltd* [2004] EWHC 1502; [2004] 2 Lloyd's Rep. 251 at [152] ("liability howsoever arising" held to limit liability for employee's wilful default).

[238] ibid. at [81].

[239] *Gluckstein v Barnes* [1900] A.C. 240. This rule is quite independent of the statutory provisions referred to at para.9–149, below.

a fiduciary duty attempted to exempt himself from liability for a deliberate breach of that duty would be similarly ineffective.[240]

7–044   **Unreasonableness.** It is sometimes said that exemption clauses may be held invalid on the ground that they are "unreasonable in themselves or irrelevant to the main purpose of the contract"[241] or "so unreasonable that no-one could contemplate that they exist".[242] Unreasonableness of the latter kind can certainly be relevant to the process of incorporation of a clause in a contract, in the sense that the degree of notice required for this purpose increases in proportion to the unusualness of the clause.[243] Some dicta go further and suggest that even a properly incorporated clause can be invalid on the ground of unreasonableness[244] or unfairness.[245] But no decision squarely supports this view, which is also rejected in other dicta.[246]

Many exemption clauses are now subject to a requirement of reasonableness under the Unfair Contract Terms Act 1977 or to one of fairness under the Unfair Terms in Consumer Contracts Regulations 1999.[247] One possible view is that the courts might rely by way of analogy on these requirements so as to develop similar requirements at common law. But such a development would be open to the objection that it would extend the requirements precisely to cases from which the legislator had deliberately excluded them; and it is submitted that the better view is that the existence of the legislative requirements has reduced both the need for, and the likelihood of, the recognition of unreasonableness or unfairness as grounds for the invalidity of exemption clauses[248] at common law.[249]

7–045   **Third parties.** The question whether exemption clauses can protect or prejudice third parties is discussed in Ch.14.[250]

2. OTHER STANDARD TERMS AT COMMON LAW

7–046   **Terms defining the parties' rights.** The problem raised by standard terms is by no means confined to exemption clauses. It can arise also where such terms confer rights on the party relying on them, or where they restrictively define the

---

[240] Contrast *Bogg v Raper, The Times*, April 22, 1998 (liability for *negligence* of a solicitor as a trustee of a will drawn up by himself effectively excluded). See also: *Armitage v Nurse* [1998] Ch. 241; *Spread Trustee Co Ltd v Hutcheson* [2011] UKPC 13 (liability of trustee for *gross negligence* excluded); McCormack [1998] Conv. 100.

[241] *Watkins v Rymill* (1883) 10 Q.B.D. 178 at 189.

[242] *Thompson v London, Midland & Scottish Ry* [1930] 1 K.B. 41 at 56.

[243] See above, para.7–009; cf. (in relation to terms *other* than exemption clauses) below, para.7–047.

[244] See, e.g. Lord Denning M.R. in *Thornton v Shoe Lane Parking Ltd* [1971] 2 Q.B. 163 at 170; *Levison v Patent Steam Carpet Cleaning Co Ltd* [1978] Q.B. 68 at 69.

[245] *Laceys Footwear (Wholesale) Ltd v Bowler International Ltd* [1997] 2 Lloyd's Rep. 369 at 384–385, per Brooke L.J.; the majority based their decision on the construction of the clause.

[246] *Van Toll v South Eastern Ry* (1862) 12 C.B.N.S. 75 at 85; *Grand Trunk Ry of Canada v Robinson* [1915] A.C. 740 at 747; *Luddit v Ginger Coote Airways Ltd* [1947] A.C. 233 at 242.

[247] See below, paras 7–064—7–073, paras 7–103—7–114.

[248] For other standard terms, see below, para.7–046 et seq.

[249] *Clark v West Ham Corp* [1909] 2 K.B. 858 is best explained as turning on the construction of the relevant statute.

[250] See below, para.14–057 et seq.

other party's rights under the contract (other than those based on the former party's breach).

Incorporation and construction. To a limited extent the courts have been   7–047
able to protect the weaker contracting party in some such situations. They have, for example, held that the rules which govern the incorporation of exemption clauses[251] and some of the rules which govern their construction[252] also apply to certain standard terms[253] which purport to confer rights on the party relying on those terms. Such reasoning forms one basis of *Interfoto Picture Library Ltd v Stiletto Visual Programmes Ltd.*[254] In that case, the defendants (an advertising agency) had hired photographic transparencies from the claimants under a contract allegedly incorporating the terms of the claimants' delivery note, which had been sent with the goods. One of these terms purported to make the defendants liable for a "holding charge" of £5 per day (an unusually high rate)[255] for each transparency retained for more than 14 days. In holding that the defendants were not liable to pay this charge, both members of the Court of Appeal regarded it as crucial that the claimants had failed to take reasonable steps to bring the term to the attention of the defendants. But while Dillon L.J. drew from this failure the orthodox conclusion that the term had not been incorporated in the contract,[256] it is less clear exactly why Bingham L.J. regarded the failure as vital. It seems that he so regarded it (even on the assumption that the terms of the delivery note *had* been incorporated into the contract[257]), because, on account of the failure, it would not be "fair to hold [the defendants] bound by the condition in question".[258] He went on to suggest that

"this may yield a result not very different from the civil law principle of good faith, at any rate so far as the formation of the contract is concerned".[259]

The reference here to "formation" seems to indicate that Bingham L.J. was, after all, concerned with the incorporation of the clause and perhaps intended to make the point that "this unreasonable and extortionate clause"[260] was not incorporated *merely* because the formal requirements of offer and acceptance had been satisfied[261]: there must, in addition, be "fair" notice, and the degree of notice

---

[251] See above, paras 7–004—7–013.
[252] See above, para.7–014 et seq.
[253] e.g. indemnity clauses: above, fn.33 and some clauses conferring rights to be paid: *Sonat Offshore SA v Amerada Hess Development Ltd* [1988] 1 Lloyd's Rep. 191.
[254] [1989] Q.B. 433.
[255] ibid. at 436: the "normal" rate would have been £3.50 per transparency per week.
[256] See above, para.7–009.
[257] [1989] Q.B. 433 at 445: "I do not think that the defendants could successfully contend that [the conditions] were not incorporated in the contract."
[258] ibid.; cf. *Timeload Ltd v British Telecommunications Plc* [1995] E.M.L.R. 459 at 468; contrast *Nutting v Baldwin* [1995] 1 W.L.R. 201 at 211, where the term was "neither onerous nor unusual;" cf. above, fn.45.
[259] ibid.; this approach was favoured by Brooke L.J. in *Laceys Footwear (Wholesale) Ltd v Bowler International Ltd* [1997] 2 Lloyd's Rep. 369 at 384 (where the clause in question was a limitation clause).
[260] ibid. *Semble*, it does not for this purpose suffice merely that the clause was *unusual*: *HIH Casualty & General Ins Ltd v New Hampshire Ins Co* [2001] EWCA Civ 735; [2001] 2 All E.R. (Comm) 39 at [211].
[261] cf. above, para.2–075.

required increases with the unusualness or unreasonableness of the clause.[262] But once the requisite degree of notice has been given, the English common law does not, as a general rule, control the *substance* of the clause; it does not impose any further requirement that contracts must be reasonable or that contractual rights must be exercised reasonably.[263] The rejection by the courts of the substantive doctrine of fundamental breach[264] can be said to support this general common law rule. In a number of situations to be discussed later in this chapter, standard terms other than exemption clauses are now subject to legislative control; and the need for such legislation seems to be based on the assumption that, at common law, the principle of freedom of contract as a general rule applies[265] to cases of the kind discussed in this section.

7–048   **Exceptional cases.** There may, however, be highly exceptional cases in which the common law is prepared to recognise exceptions to its general rule. It has, for example, been said that a term in a contract for the deposit of goods at a railway station would be void for unreasonableness if it provided that £1,000 was to be forfeited if the goods were not collected within 48 hours.[266] The far-fetched nature of the example suggests that this common law exception to the general rule is not likely to have much practical importance. The invalidity of penalty clauses[267] could be regarded as another common law exception to the general rule; but this exception is limited in scope, as a clause is penal only if it requires a payment to be made *on breach*: not if it specifies some other event on which the payment is to be made.[268]

3. LEGISLATIVE LIMITATIONS

7–049   The most important legislative limitations on the effectiveness of exemption clauses and unfair terms are now contained in the Unfair Contract Terms Act 1977 and in the Unfair Terms in Consumer Contracts Regulations 1999. These two sets of provisions overlap, so that some types of terms are governed by both of them and others by one though not by the other.[269] The resulting structure is complex and proposals have been made to simplify it by combining the two sets of rules into a single modified legislative scheme.[270] In the present section, we shall deal only with one technique of control (used by this and other legislation), which is to deprive certain exemption clauses and unfair terms of their legal force. Other legislative techniques will be considered in outline in the last section of this chapter.

---

[262] See above, para.7–009.
[263] See, e.g. *Margaronis Navigation Agency Ltd v Henry W Peabody of London Ltd* [1965] 1 Q.B. 300; *Innisfail Laundry v Dawe* (1963) 107 S.J. 437; for exceptions, see above, para.4–017 and below, paras 20–152—2–153; and cf. *Paula Lee Ltd v Robert Zehil & Co Ltd* [1983] 2 All E.R. 390; *Walkinshaw v Diniz* [2001] 1 Lloyd's Rep. 632 at 649, affirmed [2002] 2 Lloyd's Rep. 165.
[264] See above, para.7–024.
[265] cf. below, para.10–049.
[266] *Parker v South Eastern Ry* (1876) 2 C.P.D. 416 at 428.
[267] See below, para.20–130 et seq.
[268] See below, paras 20–144—20–146; in the example in *Parker*'s case, above, at fn.266, it seems that failure to collect the goods is not a breach, so that the clause is not a penalty.
[269] See further para.7–096, below.
[270] *Unfair Terms in Contracts* (Law Com. No.292, Scot Law Com. No.199, 2005).

(a) The Unfair Contract Terms Act 1977[271]

The Act deals almost exclusively with exemption clauses in contracts[272]; it   **7–050**
makes some such clauses ineffective in all circumstances and others ineffective
unless they comply with a requirement of reasonableness.

(i) *Preliminary definitions*

The application and effect of some of the provisions of the Act depends on the   **7–051**
meaning given to certain terms such as "business liability", and "dealing as
consumer". These terms are assessed here at the outset so that their meaning is
understood when describing the controls imposed by the Act below.

"Business liability". The Act defines "business liability" as: "liability for   **7–052**
breach of obligations or duties arising (a) from things done or to be done by a
person in the course of a business (whether his own business or another's); or (b)
from the occupation of premises used for business purposes of the occupier".[273]
Such a person will in the following discussion be called B. "In the course of a
business" has been defined by the courts when defining "deals as consumer".[274]

"Dealing as consumer". A person "deals as consumer"[275] if he does not   **7–053**
make (or hold himself out as making) the contract in the course of a business *and*
the other party does make the contract in the course of a business.[276] For this
purpose, a contract is made "in the course of" a business only if it is "integral"

---

[271] Thompson, *Unfair Contract Terms Act 1977*; Coote (1978) 41 M.L.R. 312; Sealy [1978] C.L.J. 15;
Reynolds [1978] 1 L.M.C.L.Q. 201; Adams and Brownsword 104 L.Q.R. 94.
[272] The Act also deals with certain notices not having contractual effect, e.g. in ss.2 and 11(3).
Attempts by such notices to exclude or restrict tort liability are beyond the scope of this book.
[273] s.1(3). "Business" includes a profession and activities of government departments or local or
public authorities: s.14. Liability to persons gaining access to premises for recreational or educational
purposes is excepted, in certain circumstances, by Occupiers' Liability Act 1984, s.2.
[274] See below, para.7–053.
[275] There is no definition of "consumer", but it has been taken to imply an element of consumption
of goods or services: see *Commerzbank AG v Keen* [2006] EWCA Civ 1536; [2007] I.C.R. 623.
[276] s.12(1)(a) and (b). The EC Directive on the Sale of Consumer Goods and Associated Guarantees
(Dir.1999/44) defines "consumer" more narrowly to mean "any natural person who, in the contracts
covered by this Directive, is acting for purposes not related to his trade, business or profession". The
Regulations which implement this Directive in the UK use similar language in defining "consumer"
as "any natural person who, in contracts covered by these Regulations, is acting for purposes which are
outside his trade, business or profession" (Sale and Supply of Goods to Consumers Regulations 2002
(SI 2002/3045), reg.2). But the techniques adopted by these Regulations to give effect to the new rights
specified in the Directive are (1) to widen the scope of the statutorily implied terms as to quality, where
the person to whom the goods are supplied "deals as consumer" (regs 3, 7, 9, 10 and 13) and (2) to
give certain additional remedies or rights to such persons where the supplier is in breach of certain
statutorily implied terms or of an express term (regs 5 and 9). The expression "dealing as consumer"
is defined in the relevant statutes by cross-reference to Unfair Contract Terms Act 1977: see Sale of
Goods Act 1979, s.61(5A), Supply of Goods and Services Act 1982, s.18(4), Supply of Goods (Implied
Terms) Act 1973, s.11A(4). The reference is to s.12 of the 1977 Act, which is amended by the 2002
Regulations but not so as to restrict the definition of consumer, even in contracts for the supply of
goods, to natural persons: see text at fnn.279 and 280, below. Hence "dealing as consumer" in the Acts
referred to above seems to have a wider meaning than that of "consumer" in the Regulations.

to that business or it forms part of the regular course of dealing of that business.[277] One consequence of this test is that a company may deal as a consumer for the purpose of the Act.[278] In the case of contracts for the supply of goods, it is also necessary (except where the goods are supplied to an individual[279]) for the goods to be of a type ordinarily supplied for private use or consumption.[280] A buyer of goods is not to be regarded as dealing as consumer, (a) if he is an individual and the goods are second hand goods sold at public auction which individuals have the opportunity of attending in person; or (b) if he is not an individual and the goods are sold by auction or competitive tender.[281] In the following discussion a person who deals as consumer will be called C.

Generally, contracts will be made between B and C, or between B1 and B2. It is, however, impossible to have a contract between two persons each of whom deals as consumer, since it is part of the definition of dealing as consumer that one party does, while the other does not, make the contract in the course of a business. If, for example, a car were sold "privately" (neither buyer nor seller acting in the course of a business) there would be no dealing as consumer. However, a person can deal as consumer in disposing of goods, no less than in acquiring goods or services: e.g. if the "private" (non-business) owner of a car transferred it to a car dealer in part-exchange for a new car, he would deal as consumer in relation to the first as well as to the second vehicle.

7–054 **Types of clause covered.** Many sections of the Act limit the effectiveness of clauses that "exclude or restrict" liability. To the same extent these sections also prevent a party from doing certain analogous things: e.g. from imposing a short time-limit within which claims must be brought,[282] or from excluding a particular remedy (such as rejection[283] or set-off[284]) without affecting another (such as damages),[285] or excluding or restricting rules of evidence or procedure.[286] Other clauses which do not in terms exclude or restrict liability may nevertheless have

---

[277] *R & B Customs Brokers Ltd v United Dominions Trust Ltd* [1988] 1 W.L.R. 321; Price 52 M.L.R. 245; Jones and Harland 2 J.C.L. 266; *Feldaroll Foundry Plc v Hermes Leasing (London) Ltd* [2004] EWCA Civ 747. Contrast the more literal interpretation in *Stevenson v Rogers* [1999] Q.B. 1028 of "course of business" in Sale of Goods Act 1979, s.14(2); cf. *GE Capital Bank Ltd v Rushton* [2005] EWCA Civ 1556; [2006] 1 W.L.R. 899 (whether purchaser "carries on business" for the purpose of s.27(2) of the Hire Purchase Act 1964).

[278] ibid. (company held to have dealt as consumer in buying a car for use of one of its directors, having only made two or three such purchases in the past). In the *Unfair Contract Terms Bill* drafted by the Law Commission (above, fn.270) a consumer is defined as an "individual", which is intended to confine the definition to natural persons: para.3.24.

[279] s.12(1A).

[280] s.12(1)(c).

[281] s.12(2).

[282] s.13(1)(a); *Granville Oil & Chemicals Ltd v Davis Turner & Co Ltd* [2003] EWCA Civ 570; [2003] 2 Lloyd's Rep. 356.

[283] But the Act may not apply to the postponement of the right to reject: *Mitchell v BJ Marine* [2005] N.I.Q.B. 72 at [30].

[284] *Stewart Gill Ltd v Horatio Myer & Co Ltd* [1992] Q.B. 600; *Esso Petroleum Ltd v Milton* [1997] 1 W.L.R. 938; *Schenkers Ltd v Overland Shoes Ltd* [1998] 1 Lloyd's Rep. 499; *Axa Sun Life Services Plc v Campbell Martin Ltd* [2011] EWCA Civ 133; cf. *BOC Group Plc v Centeon Plc* [1999] 1 All E.R. (Comm) 970.

[285] s.13(1)(b). In *Axa Sun Life Services Plc v Campbell Martin Ltd* [2011] EWCA Civ 133 it was said to be "common ground" that a clause giving conclusive effect to a certificate of sums due (save for manifest error) was subject to the Act because its effect was to "exclude" the right of set off in relation to the sum due.

[286] s.13(1)(c).

this effect in substance. For example, a provision in a contract between X and Y that Y will indemnify X for any liability which X may incur to Y is in substance a clause excluding X's liability to Y and will be treated as such for the purposes of the Act.[287] A clause requiring an employee to work such long hours as would lead to injury to his health could likewise be regarded as one which exempted the employer from liability which, but for the clause, he would incur in respect of the injury.[288] On the other hand, a valid agreed damages clause[289] is probably not subject to the Act, for such a clause may extend as well as restrict liability. An agreement in writing to submit present or future differences to arbitration is not to be treated as excluding or restricting liability.[290]

Excluding or restricting duties. In two cases, the Act explicitly[291] prevents a party from excluding or restricting *duties* (as opposed to *liabilities*): namely where a provision purports to exclude (i) the duty of care giving rise to liability in negligence[292] or (ii) the duties arising out of terms implied by statute in contracts for the supply of goods.[293] Thus a provision purporting to exclude or restrict a seller's duty as to the fitness of goods for a particular purpose would only be effective to the extent permitted by the Act.[294]

7–055

At common law a distinction is sometimes drawn between clauses which exclude or restrict liability and those which prevent it from arising[295] and in some cases this distinction is no doubt relevant for the purposes of the Act. For example, if a seller of goods expressly warned the buyer *not* to use goods for a specified purpose, any implied term of fitness for that particular purpose would be neg- atived, and the warning would not be subject to the Act.[296] But to give such effect to all provisions which might at common law prevent liability from arising would, it has been said, "emasculate"[297] the Act. In *Smith v Eric S Bush*[298] the House of Lords has therefore held that a clause purporting to exclude responsibility for negligence on the part of the valuer of a house was subject to the test of reasonableness under the Act. The decision was based on s.13(1) of the Act, by which a term purporting to exclude the duty of care giving rise to liability in negligence is to be treated as a term excluding or restricting liability. In order to determine whether such a duty existed, the court must disregard the term purporting to exclude it, and ask itself whether, but for the existence of the term, there would have been such a duty; if so, the effectiveness of the term is then

---

[287] *Phillips Products Ltd v Hyland* [1987] 1 W.L.R. 659; below, para.7–073.

[288] *Johnstone v Bloomsbury Health Authority* [1992] Q.B. 333.

[289] See above, para.7–019; below, para.20–130. For the position under Unfair Terms in Consumer Contracts Regulations 1999, see below, para.7–099.

[290] s.13(2). Contrast the position under Unfair Terms in Consumer Contracts Regulations 1999, below, para.7–112. A jurisdiction agreement may fall within s.13(1)(a) (making enforcement subject to "restrictive or onerous conditions"): *Snookes v Jani-King (GB) Ltd* [2006] EWHC 289).

[291] The practical effect of s.3(2)(b)(i) (below, para.7–068) may also be to prevent a party from excluding or restricting duties which were "reasonably expected".

[292] See the reference to ss.2 and 5 in s.13(1).

[293] See the reference to ss.6 and 7 in s.13(1).

[294] See s.6(1) and (2).

[295] cf. above, para.7–021.

[296] *Wormell v RHM Agriculture (East) Ltd* [1987] 1 W.L.R. 1091; cf. *Harlingdon & Leinster Enterprises Ltd v Christopher Hull Fine Art Ltd* [1990] 1 All E.R. 737 at 753, and the examples given at para.7–021, above.

[297] *Smith v Eric S Bush* [1990] 1 A.C. 831 at 848.

[298] See above, fn.297; cf. *Davies v Parry* [1988] 1 E.G.L.R. 147.

subject to the restrictions imposed by the Act.[299] It seems likely that the courts will also "look behind" certain other clauses which are similarly being used in an obvious attempt to evade the Act.[300]

(ii) *Ineffective terms*

7–056   In the following cases, attempts to exclude or restrict liability are wholly ineffective under the 1977 Act or under other legislation.

7–057   **Negligence liability: death or personal injury.** By s.2(1) of the 1977 Act, B[301] cannot by any contract term or notice exclude or restrict his[302] liability for death or personal injury[303] resulting from negligence[304] to any person (whether C or not). Provisions excluding *strict* liability for death or personal injury are not affected by s.2(1). Under other legislation, any provision in a contract for the carriage of passengers in a public service vehicle[305] is void if it purports to negative or limit the liability of the carrier in respect of the death or personal injury of the passenger.[306] The Act in question does not expressly refer to negligence, but since the carrier is not liable in the absence of negligence[307] its scope is restricted to negligence liability.

Section 2(1) does not apply where death or personal injury results from a breach of contract or duty which can be, and is, committed without negligence: e.g. where a seller supplies defective goods to a buyer, where a producer incurs "product liability" in respect of defective products, or where a person who does work for the provision of a dwelling fits defective components.[308] Clauses purporting to exclude liability for such breaches may, however, be ineffective under other provisions of the Act,[309] or under other Acts.[310]

---

[299] The possible application of s.13(1) would appear to have been overlooked in *Galliford Try Infrastructure Ltd v Mott Macdonald Ltd* [2008] EWHC 1570 (TCC); 120 Con. L.R. 1 at [332].

[300] cf. below, para.9–117—9–118. *Smith v Eric S Bush*, above, deals only with clauses purporting to exclude the duty of care giving rise to liability in negligence. It seems that the "but for" test there formulated would not apply to sale of goods cases such as *Wormell v RHM Agriculture (East) Ltd*, above, fn.296: in order to determine for what "particular purpose" goods had been bought, a warning such as the one given in that case would, it is submitted, have to be taken into account. For possible application of Unfair Terms in Consumer Contracts Regulations 1999, see below, para.7–110.

[301] See above, paras 7–052—7–053.

[302] s.2 does not prevent a contracting party from excluding or restricting the liability of a *third* party: *The Chevalier Roze* [1983] 2 Lloyd's Rep. 438 at 442. For the effect of the section on indemnity clauses, see below, para.7–072.

[303] As defined by s.14.

[304] As defined by s.1(1). "Negligence" is there stated to include "breach . . . of any obligation, arising from the . . . terms . . . of a contract, to take reasonable care . . . "; for the purpose of this definition the court must apply the "but for" test (above, para.7–055): i.e. it must disregard a clause the effect of which is (or would be, if the clause were valid) to exclude liability for such a breach: *Phillips Products Ltd v Hyland* [1987] 1 W.L.R. 659.

[305] As defined by s.1 Public Passenger Vehicles Act 1981.

[306] ibid., s.29; cf. Financial Services and Markets Act 2000, s.253 (dealing with purely financial loss).

[307] *Barkway v South Wales Transport Co Ltd* [1950] 1 All E.R. 392 at 403–404.

[308] For strict liability in such cases, see below, para.17–065.

[309] e.g. ss.6, 7.

[310] Defective Premises Act 1972, s.1(1) ("proper materials") and s.6(3). Consumer Protection Act, 1987, ss.5 and 7(1); below, para.7–061.

"Guarantees" of consumer goods. Section 5 deals with provisions in "guar-   7–058
antees" of goods of a type ordinarily supplied for private use or consumption. It
does not apply between the parties to the contract for the supply of the goods[311]:
exemption clauses in such contracts are regulated by ss.6 and 7. It is aimed at the
relations between manufacturer and customer under so-called manufacturers'
guarantees.[312]

The section defines a "guarantee" as a written promise or assurance that defects
will be made good.[313] It provides that B[314] cannot by means of such a guarantee
exclude or restrict liability for loss or damage that arises from defects in the goods
while in "consumer use" and results from the negligence of a person concerned
in the manufacture or distribution of the goods.[315] Goods are in "consumer use"
when a person is using them or has them in his possession otherwise than
exclusively for the purpose of a business. Thus generally s.5 will apply only
between B and C. But it may also apply in certain other circumstances: e.g. where
a car is bought in the course of a business (so that the buyer does not deal as
consumer) and used partly for business and partly for private purposes.

Under the Sale and Supply of Goods to Consumers Regulations 2002, a
"consumer guarantee" relating to goods supplied to a consumer "takes effect . . .
as a contractual obligation owed by the guarantor."[316] The Regulations do not
themselves[317] prohibit exclusion or restriction of liability *under the guarantee*: e.g.
by terms imposing a short time-limit, or a low financial limit, on claims under the
guarantee; but it seems that, if the "consumer guarantee" were also a "guarantee"
within s.5 of the 1977 Act, then the validity of such terms would be open to attack
under that section.[318] Terms limiting the "duration" of the guarantee itself,[319] or
restricting the consumer's right under it to one to the return of the price,[320] seem,
however, to be authorised under the Regulations, so that their validity is not open
to attack under the Act.[321] The definition of a "consumer guarantee" in the
Regulations differs significantly from that of a "guarantee" in the Act: in particular, the "consumer" under the Regulations must be a "natural person"[322]; the
"guarantor" may be the other party to the contract for the supply of the goods to
the consumer[323]; and there is no requirement of "consumer use" in the Regulations.

Sale of goods and hire-purchase. Section 6(1) provides that liability for   7–059
breach of the undertakings as to title implied by statute[324] into contracts for the
sale or hire-purchase of goods cannot be excluded or restricted by reference to any

---

[311] s.5(3).
[312] See below, para.14–006.
[313] s.5(2)(b); making good is defined so as to include payment of compensation.
[314] See above, paras 7–052—7–053.
[315] s.5(1). Consumer Protection Act 1987, s.7 (below, para.7–061) could also apply to such a
guarantee.
[316] SI 2002/3045 (implementing Dir.1999/44), reg.15(1).
[317] For such a prohibition, see Dir.1999/44, Art.7.
[318] Thus securing compliance with Art.7, above.
[319] SI 2002/3045, reg.15(2) ("duration").
[320] ibid., reg.2 (definition of "consumer guarantee").
[321] Unfair Contract Terms Act 1977, s.29; below, para.7–093.
[322] reg.2 (definition of "consumer").
[323] reg.2 (definition of "guarantor").
[324] By Sale of Goods Act 1979, s.12 and Supply of Goods (Implied Terms) Act 1973, s.8 as
substituted by Consumer Credit Act 1974, s.192 and Sch.4, para.35. For amendments of the 1979 and
1973 Acts, see Sale and Supply of Goods Act 1994, s.7 and Sch.2.

contract term. Section 6(2) lays down the same rule, but only "as against a person dealing as consumer", in relation to the statutorily implied terms as to correspondence of the goods with description or sample, and as to their quality or fitness for a particular purpose.[325]

As a general principle the only types of terms made completely ineffective by the Act are those purporting to exclude or restrict "business liability".[326] Section 6(4), however, provides that the liabilities referred to "in this section" are not only "business liabilities . . . but include those arising under any contract of sale of goods or hire-purchase agreement". It follows that a private (non-business) seller cannot exclude or restrict liability for breach of the implied undertakings as to title. At first sight, s.6(4) suggests that an attempt by a private seller to exclude or restrict liability for breach of the implied undertakings as to correspondence with description, etc. (referred to in s.6(2)) is equally ineffective. But s.6(2) applies only "as against a person dealing as consumer", and a person can so deal only if "the other party does make the contract in the course of a business".[327] Since a private seller does not contract "in the course of a business", it seems that a person who buys from such a seller does not "deal as consumer" and is not protected by s.6(2); he is protected only by the requirement of reasonableness.[328] In some cases, indeed, the statutorily implied term only arises at all where the supplier acts in the course of a business. This is true of the implied terms as to satisfactory quality and fitness for a particular purpose.[329] Here the private supplier is never subject to the statutorily implied term at all, and so the issue of the validity of a clause excluding liability for breach of it cannot arise.[330]

7–060   **Other contracts for the supply of goods.** Section 7 deals with contracts for the supply of goods other than contracts of sale and hire-purchase: e.g. contracts of exchange, pledge or hire. By statute, such contracts contain implied terms as to title, correspondence with description or sample, quality and fitness for a particular purpose.[331] As against C, B[332] cannot, in such contracts, exclude or restrict liability in respect of the failure of the goods to correspond with their description or with a sample, or in respect of their quality or fitness for a particular purpose.[333] So far as liability for breach of the implied terms as to title is concerned, a

---

[325] By Sale of Goods Act 1979, ss.13–15 and Supply of Goods (Implied Terms) Act 1973, ss.9–11 as substituted by Consumer Credit Act 1974, s.192 and Sch.4, para.35; for amendments see above, fn.324; *Hughes v Hall and Hall* [1981] R.T.R. 430. The Regulations referred to in fn.316, above make further amendments to s.14 of the 1979 Act (reg.3) and confer additional rights or remedies on buyers who deal as consumers (Sale of Goods Act 1979, ss.48A–48D, as inserted by reg.5 of those Regulations). It seems that these new provisions are subject to s.6(2) of Unfair Contract Terms Act 1977. For the meaning of the phrase "dealing as consumer" for this purpose see above, fn.276. Similar amendments are made by the same Regulations to Sale of Goods (Implied Terms) Act 1973, below, fn.329) and to Supply of Goods and Services Act 1982 (below, fn.331; see regs 7, 9, 10 and 13).

[326] See above, para.7–052.

[327] s.12(1)(b).

[328] s.6(3); below, para.7–070.

[329] Sale of Goods Act 1979, s.14(2) (as substituted by Sale and Supply of Goods Act 1994, s.1(1)); Supply of Goods (Implied Terms) Act 1973, s.10(2) and (3) as substituted by Consumer Credit Act 1974, s.192 and Sch.4, para.35. For further amendments of the 1979 and 1973 Acts, see above, fn.325.

[330] See further, below, para.7–070.

[331] Supply of Goods and Services Act 1982, ss.2–5, 7–10, as amended by Sale and Supply of Goods Act 1994, s.7 and Sch.2. For further amendments of the 1982 Act, see above, fn.325.

[332] See above, paras 7–052—7–053.

[333] Supply of Goods and Services Act 1982, s.7(2).

distinction must be drawn. Such liability cannot be excluded by B[334] where the contract is one by which he transfers or agrees to transfer the property in the goods to another (not necessarily C): this rule would, for example, apply to a contract of exchange. But where the contract is not one by which property is transferred or to be transferred (e.g. where it is one of pledge or hire) attempts by B[335] to exclude or restrict such liability are subject only to the test of reasonableness.[336]

Product liability. Under Pt I of the Consumer Protection Act 1987, producers and certain other persons engaged in the distribution of products which are defective, in the sense of being unsafe, are liable if the defect causes death or personal injury or certain kinds of damage to property.[337] Section 7 of the 1987 Act provides that such "product liability" (which arises without proof of negligence and irrespective of contract) cannot be limited or excluded by any contract term, notice or other provision.　　　**7–061**

Dangerous goods. Under Pt II of the Consumer Protection Act 1987, it is an offence to supply goods which do not comply with a general safety requirement laid down by the Act and in safety regulations made under the Act. Failure to perform an obligation imposed by such a regulation gives a civil remedy to any person who may be affected by a contravention of the obligation; and the resulting liability cannot be excluded by any contract term, notice or other provision.[338]　　　**7–062**

Distance selling. The Consumer Protection (Distance Selling) Regulations 2000[339] provide, that in "distance contracts" between a commercial supplier of goods or services and a consumer, the consumer must be given specified information and is to have a right to cancel within a specified period and with specified consequences.[340] The Regulations also specify the time within which such contracts must be performed by the supplier, as well as certain legal consequences of his failure to perform it.[341] A term in such a contract is void if and to the extent it is inconsistent with a provision for the protection of the consumer contained in the Regulations.[342]　　　**7–063**

(iii) *Terms subject to the requirement of reasonableness*[343]

In the following cases, exemption clauses are, under the 1977 Act, subject to the requirement of reasonableness. Where the requirement applies, the burden of showing (and of pleading[344]) that it is satisfied lies on the party so claiming.[345]　　　**7–064**

---

[334] ss.1(3) and 7(3A), as inserted by Supply of Goods and Services Act 1982, s.17(2).
[335] Unfair Contract Terms Act 1977, s.1(3).
[336] ibid., s.7(4), as amended by Supply of Goods and Services Act 1982, s.17(3).
[337] See *Winfield & Jolowicz on Tort* (18th edn), para.10–12 et seq.
[338] Consumer Protection Act 1987, s.41(4).
[339] SI 2000/2334, as amended by Consumer Protection (Distance Selling) (Amendment) Regulations 2005 (SI 2005/689), implementing Dir.97/7.
[340] regs 7–18.
[341] regs 19, 20. "Consumer" is defined in reg.3(1).
[342] reg.25.
[343] Brown and Chandler 109 L.Q.R. 41.
[344] *Sheffield v Pickfords Ltd* [1997] C.L.C. 648.
[345] Unfair Contract Terms Act 1977, s.11(5).

7–065   **Negligence liability: harm other than death or personal injury.** By s.2(2) the requirement applies to a contract term or notice[346] by which B[347] seeks to exclude or restrict his[348] liability for negligence[349] giving rise to loss or damage other than death or personal injury. The subsection does not apply to provisions excluding or restricting *strict* liability[350]; on the other hand it is not confined to cases where the other party deals as consumer. In both these respects, it resembles s.2(1).

7–066   **Consumer contracts and standard form contracts.** Section 3 applies to two situations: to any contract between B[351] and C; and to a contract in which a party (not necessarily C) deals with B on the latter's "written standard terms of business".[352] In such cases B cannot "by reference to any contract term", except insofar as it satisfies the requirement of reasonableness, exclude or restrict any liability in respect of his own breach.[353] "Any liability" here includes strict liability[354] for breach of contract.

7–067   **Written standard terms of business.** There is no statutory definition of "written standard terms of business". In almost every contract there will be some negotiation, about the subject matter and the price if nothing else, but if other terms are introduced by one party and are not the subject of negotiation, it is likely that the contract has been made on that party's written standard terms.[355] It is not essential that the defendant has previously used the same terms on numerous occasions, but it may be necessary in some cases to establish by discovery whether a "one-off" contract is, in fact, simply one party's standard terms of business.[356] It is, inevitably, a question of degree and there is some evidence that the courts take into account the underlying mischief towards which the reference to "standard" terms is aimed, i.e. the relative bargaining power of the parties.[357] Where a party makes use of a standard form drafted by a trade association or similar body, the terms of that form are that party's "standard terms" only if he "invariably or at least usually" contracted on those terms.[358] An employee does not deal on the

---

[346] A trustee exemption clause is neither a term nor a notice and is not, therefore, subject to s.2(2), nor to the Act generally: *Baker v JE Clark & Co* [2006] EWCA Civ 464.

[347] See above, paras 7–052—7–053.

[348] See above, fn.302. For the effect of the section on indemnity clauses, see below, para.7–073.

[349] As defined by s.1(1).

[350] But see above, para.7–057.

[351] See above, paras 7–052—7–053.

[352] For an exception to the requirement that, between parties acting in the course of a business, the contract must be on written standard terms, see Late Payment of Commercial Debts (Interest) Act 1998, s.14(2); below, para.20–064.

[353] s.3(2)(a).

[354] See below, para.17–064.

[355] *St. Alban's City and District Council v International Computers Ltd* [1995] F.S.R. 686 at 706; *Pegler v Wang (UK) Ltd* [2000] B.L.R. 218; *Hadley Design Associates Ltd v Westminster London Borough Council* [2003] All ER (D) 164; *Ferryways NV v ABP* [2008] EWHC 225 (Comm); [2008] 1 Lloyd's Rep 639 at [92] ("although a large part of the final agreement was negotiated and was not part of the standard terms, the latter were untouched by the negotiation and remained a sufficiently significant and important part of the agreement to enable it fairly to be said that the parties dealt on the Defendant's standard terms and conditions.")

[356] *Oval (717) Ltd v Aegon Insurance (UK) Ltd* (1997) 54 Con L.R. 74; *The Chester Grosvenor Hotel Company Ltd v Alfred McAlpine Management Ltd* (1991) 56 B.L.R. 115; *South West Water Services Ltd v ICL* [1999] B.L.R. 420.

[357] *Salvage Association v CAP Financial Services*, [1995] F.S.R. 654 at 672.

[358] *British Fermentation Products Ltd v Compair Reavell Ltd* [1999] 2 All E.R. (Comm) 389 at 401.

employer's written standard terms of business, in relation to terms which regulate the work he does for the employer, and the payment he receives for it.[359]

Section 3(2)(b)(i): performance different from that reasonably expected.   7–068
Section 3(2)(b)(i) also applies the test of reasonableness to any term by reference to which B[360] claims "to be entitled . . . to render a contractual performance substantially different from that which was reasonably expected of him".[361] It has been held that a clause giving a lender power to vary interest rates did not fall within s.3(2)(b)(i) since the exercise of that power was not a "contractual performance."[362] Where a term in a contract for services entitles the provider to change those services, the questions what the recipient reasonably expected and whether the change is substantial can obviously give rise to difficult questions of fact and degree.[363] It seems that s.3(2)(b)(i) could apply to provisions in a contract between a carrier and a tour operator purporting to entitle the carrier to change the advertised route, accommodations or means of transport.[364] B could not rely on the provision even though he was not actually obliged to render the performance expected: the criterion is the reasonable expectation of the other party, not the obligation of B under the contract. There would, however, be no such reasonable expectation where the contract made it clear that, while B would endeavour to provide a particular service, he also reserved the right to substitute a reasonable alternative.[365] Section 3(2)(b)(i) may also apply to an "entire agreement" clause.[366]

Section 3(2)(b)(ii): no performance at all. Under s.3(2)(b)(ii) B[367] cannot by   7–069
reference to any contract term "claim to be entitled . . . in respect of the whole or any part of his contractual obligation to render no performance at all". This would apply where an agreement is on its true construction held to impose a contractual obligation but gives or purports to give B a wide discretion whether to perform at all or to the full extent promised. The criterion is not (as it is under s.3(2)(b)(i)) what the other party reasonably expects: it is the obligation undertaken by B. If the "contract term" gave B a totally free discretion whether to perform

---

[359] *Commerzbank AG v Keen* [2006] EWCA Civ 1536; [2007] I.C.R. 623 (leaving open that there may be some terms which are covered, i.e. where the employee is the recipient of the goods or services which are the business of the employer).

[360] See above, paras 7–052—7–053.

[361] In addition to the cases cited below, see also: *Brigden v American Express Bank* [2000] I.R.L.R. 94; *Peninsula Business Services Ltd v Sweeney* [2004] I.R.L.R. 49; *City Index Ltd v Stevenson*, November 6, 2001; *Durabella Ltd v J Jarvis & Sons Ltd* 83 Con. L.R. 145; *Lalji v Post Office Ltd* [2003] EWCA Civ 1873; *Rolls Royce Power Engineering Plc v Ricardo Consulting Engineers Ltd* [2003] EWHC 2871 (TCC); [2004] 2 All E.R. (Comm) 129 at [75]–[76].

[362] *Paragon Finance Ltd v Nash* [2001] EWCA Civ 1466; [2002] 1 W.L.R. 685 at [75].

[363] Contrast *Timeload Ltd v British Telecommunications Plc* [1995] E.M.L.R. 459 with *Zockoll Group Ltd v Mercury Communications Ltd (No.2)* [1999] E.M.L.R. 385.

[364] e.g. it would apply to a situation such as that which arose in *Anglo-Continental Holidays Ltd v Typaldos Lines (London) Ltd* [1967] 2 Lloyd's Rep. 61. A contract of this kind between the tour operator and consumer would be governed by Package Travel, Package Holidays and Package Tours Regulations 1992 (SI 1992/3288): under reg.12, where the "organiser" is "constrained" to alter "an essential term" of the contract, the consumer is entitled to cancel the contract. For the relationship between such legislation and the Unfair Terms in Consumer Contracts Regulations 1999, see below, para.7–116.

[365] *Duffy v Newcastle United Football Club Ltd*, *The Times*, July 7, 2000.

[366] *Axa Sun Life Services Plc v Campbell Martin Ltd* [2011] EWCA Civ 133 at [50]; cf. *SAM Business Systems Ltd v Hedley & Co* [2002] EWHC 2733 (TCC); [2003] 1 All E.R. (Comm) 465 at [62].

[367] See above, paras 7–052—7–053.

or not, there might be no "contractual obligation" on B at all; and in such a case the requirement of reasonableness need not be satisfied.[368] Section 3(2)(b)(ii) would also not apply to a clause defining B's duty[369] in such a way that in the circumstances which have occurred no duty arose; e.g. where B promised to perform "subject to strikes" and strikes have prevented performance.

In a number of other situations, the scope of s.3(2)(b)(ii) is harder to determine. A contract may provide that B is entitled to cancel it by giving notice, or on the occurrence of specified events: e.g. on the other party's failure to perform (whether or not it amounts to a breach) or on some other event, such as the other party's death.[370] Or it may require B to perform only when the other party's performance has been rendered in full, or when some prescribed part of the performance has been rendered.[371] For example, a building contract may provide that nothing is to be paid till the work is completed, or that instalments of the price are to be paid only when specific parts of the work have been done. Such provisions might at first sight appear to be literally within s.3(2)(b)(ii); but it does not seem to have been the purpose of that enactment to alter the law as to cancellation clauses of the kind mentioned above,[372] or as to the effect of the other party's breach on the obligations of B. It is submitted that the scope of the enactment must be narrowed by a restrictive interpretation of the opening words of s.3(2), according to which B cannot do the three things specified in the subsection "by reference to any contract term". These words should be taken to mean "by reference *only* to such a term"—not by reference to it combined with other circumstances justifying B's refusal, such as a failure by the other party to perform his part.[373]

7–070   **Supply of goods.** By s.6(3), the requirement of reasonableness applies to a term in a contract for the sale or hire-purchase of goods purporting to exclude or restrict liability for breach of the statutorily implied terms[374] as to correspondence of the goods with description or sample, or as to their quality or fitness for a particular purpose, where the buyer or hire-purchaser deals otherwise than as consumer.[375] A similar rule is laid down by s.7(3) with regard to terms in other contracts for the supply of goods (such as contracts of hire or exchange) purporting to exclude liability for breach of similar terms implied by law in such contracts.[376] Section 7 applies only to terms purporting to exclude or restrict "business liability"[377] so that s.7(3) is restricted to the case where the supplier acts in the course of a business and the acquirer does not deal as consumer.[378] Section 6 is however not restricted to the case where the supplier acts in the course of a

---

[368] For the position under Unfair Terms in Consumer Contracts Regulations 1999, Sch.2 para.1(c), see below, para.7–113.

[369] See above, para.7–055; s.3 is *not* referred to in s.13(1).

[370] See below, para.18–061.

[371] See below, paras 17–031—17–040.

[372] The view that s.3(2)(b)(ii) does not apply to such cancellation clauses is supported by the *Paragon Finance* case, above, fn.362 at [76]–[77]; the question was left open in *Timeload Ltd v British Telecommunications Plc* [1995] E.M.L.R. 459 at 468. cf. *Hadley Design Associates v Westminster CC* [2003] EWHC 1617; [2004] T.C.L.R. 1.

[373] For the position under Unfair Terms in Consumer Contracts Regulations 1999, Sch.2, para.1(o), see below, para.7–113.

[374] See above, fn.325.

[375] See above, para.7–059 for the position where he deals as consumer.

[376] See above, fn.331.

[377] s.1(3).

[378] e.g. *Stewart Gill Ltd v Horatio Myer & Co Ltd* [1992] Q.B. 600.

business.[379] A term by which a private seller seeks to exclude or restrict liability for breach of the statutorily implied terms (even against a buyer who acts in the course of a business) is therefore under s.6(3) subject to the requirement of reasonableness. However, the statutorily implied terms as to satisfactory quality or fitness for a particular purpose arise only where the supplier acts in the course of a business.[380] A private supplier is under no liability in respect of such matters unless he gives an express undertaking. There is nothing in the Act to prevent him from restricting his liability for breach of such an *express* undertaking, e.g. by limiting his liability to a specified sum. In this respect he is in a better position than a business supplier, whose right so to limit his liability for breach of an express term may be subject to the requirement of reasonableness under s.3, e.g. if he deals on his "written standard terms of business".[381]

We have seen that B cannot exclude or restrict his liability for breach of the implied terms as to title in contracts of sale and hire-purchase, and in certain other contracts under which he transfers or agrees to transfer the property in goods[382] (such as contracts of exchange). In contracts for the transfer or supply of goods which fall outside this group, s.7(4)[383] applies the requirement of reasonableness to terms by which B seeks to exclude or restrict such liability: this would, for example, be the position in contracts of pledge,[384] or hire. As s.7 applies only to "business liability",[385] a private supplier's right to exclude or restrict liability in respect of defects of title in contracts of this kind is in no way affected by the Act. This is also true where a private supplier enters into a contract (other than one of sale or hire-purchase) by which he transfers or agrees to transfer the property in goods: e.g. where the contract is one of exchange.[386] Where, on the other hand, the contract is one of sale or hire-purchase, a term by which even a private supplier seeks to exclude or restrict liability for breach of the implied undertakings as to title is simply ineffective,[387] without regard to its reasonableness.

Indemnity clauses. A contract may provide that if one party incurs a liability   7–071
under it, whether to the other party or to a third party, then the other party shall indemnify the first against such liability. For example, a contract for the hire of a vehicle with a driver may contain a clause by which the hirer promises to indemnify the owner for any injury, loss or damage caused by the negligence of the driver.

Section 4 of the Act applies the requirement of reasonableness to a contract term by which C undertakes to indemnify another person in respect of a business liability[388] incurred by the other for negligence or breach of contract. The

---

[379] s.6(4).

[380] Sale of Goods Act 1979, s.14(2) and (3); Supply of Goods (Implied Terms) Act 1973, s.10(2) and (3), as substituted by Consumer Credit Act 1974, s.192 and Sch.4, para.35. For amendments, see Sale and Supply of Goods Act 1994, s.7 and Sch.2 and Sale and Supply of Goods to Consumers Regulations 2002 (SI 2002/3045), above, fn.325.

[381] See above, para.7–067.

[382] See above, paras 7–059—7–060.

[383] As amended by Supply of Goods and Services Act 1982, s.17(3).

[384] See Supply of Goods and Services Act 1982, s.1(2)(e).

[385] Unfair Contract Terms Act 1977, s.1(3).

[386] The restriction on the effectiveness of terms excluding liability for breach of the implied terms as to title in such contracts is imposed by Unfair Contract Terms Act 1977, s.7(3A) (above, fn.334) which, like the rest of s.7 only applies to "business liability": s.1(3).

[387] s.6(1); above, para.7–059.

[388] s.1(3).

operation of the section, and its relationship to other provisions of the Act, can best be explained by distinguishing between two situations, based on the example just given.

7–072   **Indemnity for injury, loss or damage caused to a third party.** Where the driver negligently injures, or causes loss or damage to, a third party, s.4 subjects the indemnity clause to the requirement of reasonableness, but only if the hirer dealt as consumer. The clause is therefore not subject to the requirement of reasonableness, under s.4, if the contract of hire was between B1 and B2. Nor is the clause treated as an exemption clause for the purposes of the Act, since it does not "exclude or restrict" the liability of the owner to the third party: it simply determines by whom (as between owner and hirer) that liability is to be borne.[389] It follows that s.2 does not apply and that the clause is neither ineffective (in the case of personal injury[390]) nor subject to the requirement of reasonableness (in the case of other loss or damage).[391] Section 4 likewise does not apply to an indemnity clause in a contract between two parties neither of whom acts in the course of a business, since neither party to such a contract "deals as consumer".[392] Here again the clause is not subject to s.2, both because it is not an exemption clause and because s.2 is restricted to "business liability".[393] The clause is likewise not an exemption clause for the purpose of other restrictions (already discussed[394]) imposed by the Act on the operation of exemption clauses.

7–073   **Indemnity for injury, loss or damage caused to indemnifier.** Where (in our example) the driver negligently injures, or causes loss or damage to, the hirer himself, s.4 again subjects the indemnity clause to the requirement of reasonableness if the hirer dealt as consumer. In addition, the clause is regarded as an exemption clause for the purposes of the Act since there is no difference of substance between the owner's saying to the hirer "I am not liable to you" and his saying "you must indemnify me against any damages which I may have to pay to you".[395] The clause is therefore subject not only to s.4 but also to other provisions of the Act, e.g. to s.2. This point is significant for two reasons. First, in cases of personal injury the clause is not merely subject to the requirement of reasonableness, as it would be if s.4 alone applied: the clause is simply ineffective under s.2(1). Secondly, in cases of other loss or damage the requirement of reasonableness must be satisfied, not only in contracts between B and C, as would be the case if s.4 alone applied: it must be satisfied also in contracts between B1 and B2, since s.2 applies even in favour of a person who does not deal as consumer. An indemnity clause in the present type of case will likewise be treated as an exemption clause for the purpose of other restrictions (already discussed[396]) imposed by the Act on the operation of exemption clauses.

---

[389] *Thompson v T Lohan (Plant Hire) Ltd* [1987] 1 W.L.R. 649; Sealy [1988] C.L.J. 6; Adams and Brownsword [1988] J.B.L. 146; cf. *The Caspar Trader* [1991] 2 Lloyd's Rep. 550.
[390] Unfair Contract Terms Act 1977, s.2(1); above, para.7–057.
[391] ibid., s.2(2); above, para.7–065.
[392] See above, para.7–053.
[393] Unfair Contract Terms Act 1977, s.1(3).
[394] e.g. those imposed by ss.6 and 7; above, paras 7–059—7–060, 7–070.
[395] *Phillips Products Ltd v Hyland* [1987] 1 W.L.R. 659.
[396] See fn.394, above.

Misrepresentation. The 1977 Act[397] amends s.3 of the Misrepresentation Act   7–074
1967, which had originally applied a requirement of reasonableness to terms
excluding or restricting liability for misrepresentation. Such terms are now subject
to the requirement of reasonableness as newly defined by the 1977 Act. The
requirement applies to all contracts, and is not restricted to "business liabilities"
or to contracts in which one party "deals as consumer". It is further discussed in
Ch.9.[398]

(iv) *Partly effective terms*

The extent to which, under the 1977 Act, a term may be partly effective and   7–075
partly ineffective is not entirely clear. There are two types of situation in which
this may be the position.

Severability under the reasonableness test. Where a clause is held to be   7–076
unreasonable, the court will not modify it so as to make it reasonable: e.g. by
allowing a limitation of liability where the contract had provided for total exclusion,[399] or by striking out an unreasonably low limitation in the contract and
substituting a higher one that the court regarded as reasonable. In some cases the
courts have also held that it is not possible to sever a clause, only part of which fails
the reasonableness test. For example, where a clause excluded a customer's right
to withhold payment of any amount due from him to a supplier by reason of "any
payment credit set off (or) counterclaim" it was held that it was unreasonable to
exclude his right to rely on payment already made, or any credit and that, as a
consequence, the clause as a whole was unreasonable. It could not be severed so as
to confine it to excluding the right of set-off based on a breach of contract by the
supplier.[400–401] To do any of these things it was said would be inconsistent with the
wording of s.11(1) of the 1977 Act, under which the requirement of reasonableness, which is to be applied when the contract is made, "is that the *term* shall have
been a fair and reasonable one to be included." However, the Act also provides that
terms subject to the requirement of reasonableness are ineffective "except in so far
as",[402] or effective "only in so far as",[403] they satisfy the requirement of reasonableness. The words "in so far as" would seem to make it possible for the court
to hold one part of a term valid and another invalid. Thus, in an earlier case, where
a clause in a contract for the sale of goods imposed a short time-limit on all claims
and also limited the seller's liability to the amount of the contract price, it was held
that the first part of the clause was reasonable, and the second unreasonable.[404]
These cases may be reconciled to some extent on the basis that, in the earlier case,

---

[397] s.8.

[398] See below, para.9–115.

[399] *George Mitchell (Chesterhall) Ltd v Finney Lock Seeds Ltd* [1983] 2 A.C. 803 at 816; cf. *Esso Petroleum Ltd v Milton* [1997] 1 W.L.R. 938.

[400–401] *Stewart Gill Ltd v Horatio Myer & Co Ltd* [1992] Q.B. 600; Hedley [1992] C.L.J. 418; cf. *Skipskreditforeningen v Emperor Navigation* [1998] 1 Lloyd's Rep. 67 at 75 (applying the same principle for the purpose of Misrepresentation Act 1967, s.3, but expressing doubt as to the weight given to the phrase "except in so far as").

[402] ss.2(2), 3(2), 4(1), and 7(4).

[403] ss.6(3) and 7(3).

[404] *R W Green Ltd v Cade Bros Farms* [1978] 1 Lloyd's Rep. 602, decided under s.55 of Sale of Goods Act 1893 (now superseded) under which a term was "enforceable . . . to the extent that" it satisfied the requirement of reasonableness.

the court was willing to regard the clause in question as amounting to two separate terms.[405]

7-077   **Clause covering both non-excludable and excludable liability.** A clause may be drafted so as to exclude or restrict both a liability which cannot be excluded or restricted at all, and one which can be excluded by a provision which satisfies the requirement of reasonableness or by one which is effective subject only to common law restrictions. A clause may, for example, purport to limit the liability of a seller of goods for *any* breach to the return of the contract price. Such a provision is wholly ineffective to protect him from liability for breach of the implied undertaking as to title.[406] But this does not make the clause entirely void.[407] Thus the seller could rely on it to limit his liability for some other breach: e.g. for breach of the statutorily implied terms as to quality if the buyer was not dealing as consumer and the clause satisfied the requirement of reasonableness.[408] He could similarly rely on it to limit liability for late delivery (or simple non-delivery) subject only to common law restrictions.[409] These conclusions follow from the fact that the Act nowhere invalidates contractual provisions as such: it simply says that specified liabilities cannot be excluded or restricted "by reference" to them.

This situation is not the same as that considered in para.7–073 since it is concerned with one term purporting to exclude or restrict two or more different types of liability. But where one type of liability cannot be excluded at all and the other is subject to the test of reasonableness, the requirement to consider the term as a whole would seem to lead to the conclusion that the term must be unreasonable precisely because it purports to exclude or restrict a non-excludable liability. For example, in the context of misrepresentation, it has been held[410] that a term which purports to exclude liability for *any* pre-contractual misrepresentation is unreasonable[411] even if it is only relied upon to exclude liability for non-fraudulent misrepresentation,[412] precisely because it purports also to exclude liability for fraud,[413] i.e. a different liability which cannot be excluded at all.[414] This sort of

---

[405] See to similar effect: *Watford Electronics Ltd v Sanderson Ltd* [2001] EWCA Civ 317; [2001] B.L.R. 143; *Regus (UK) Ltd v Epcot Solutions Ltd* [2008] EWCA Civ 361, [2008] All ER D 199 at [44]–[46]; *J Murphy & Sons Ltd v Johnston Precast Ltd* [2008] EWHC 3024 (TCC) at [137] where the view is expressed that *Gill v Myer* is "not concerned with severance at all" and is "not inconsistent" with *Watford Electronics* and *Regus v Epcot* (the word "not" appears to have been mistakenly omitted from the transcript). Contrast *Lobster Group Ltd v Heidelberg Graphic Equipment Ltd* [2009] EWHC 1919 (TCC) at [131] where the court was not prepared to sub-divide the separate parts of a clause all of which were concerned with the same function of excluding liability.

[406] s.6(1).

[407] cf. *George Mitchell (Chesterhall) Ltd v Finney Lock Seeds Ltd* [1983] Q.B. 284 at 303, 309 decided under an earlier and now superseded statutory requirement of reasonableness and affirmed without reference to this point in [1983] 2 A.C. 803.

[408] s.6(3).

[409] Such breaches are not covered by s.6. If the buyer was not dealing as consumer and the seller was not dealing on his written standard terms of business, the Act would not apply to such a case: see below, para.7–088.

[410] *Witter Ltd v TBP Industries Ltd* [1996] 2 All E.R. 573; below, para.9–125.

[411] Under s.3 of Misrepresentation Act 1967 which applies the test of reasonableness as set out in s.11(1) of Unfair Contract Terms Act 1977.

[412] e.g. under s.2(1) of the Misrepresentation Act 1967, or in negligence: see para.9–033 et seq..

[413] One way in which such a term may be reasonable is by finding first that, as a matter of construction, the general wording employed by the parties was not intended to exclude liability for fraud: *Zanzibar v British Aerospace (Lancaster House) Ltd* [2001] 1 W.L.R. 2333; *Regus (UK) Ltd v Epcot Solutions Ltd* [2008] EWCA Civ 361; [2008] All ER D 199. Below, para.9–125.

[414] In the case of fraud, as a matter of the common law: see above, para.7–042.

result may suggest that the current approach to the question of "severance"[415] may need to be reconsidered. As it is, it seems that draftsmen should seek to avoid the use of one broad general, or compendious, term in favour of separate and more precise terms.[416]

(v) *The test of reasonableness*

A judicially administered requirement of reasonableness is open to the objection 7–078 that it is a source of uncertainty.[417] To meet this objection, the Act lays down a rule as to the time for determining reasonableness and it also provides guidelines for this purpose. In addition, the Act lays down two rules as to the effects of breach on the requirement; their object is to prevent undue restrictions on its scope. Although the 1977 Act is primarily concerned with consumer protection, the vast majority of reported cases in which the reasonableness test has been considered have been concerned with contracts[418] between B1 and B2.[419] In such cases there is an evident judicial awareness that a finding of unreasonableness should not be reached easily in case it interferes with the parties' freedom of contract[420] and their own allocation of risk.[421]

Time for determining reasonableness. The question whether a contract 7–079 term satisfies the requirement of reasonableness is determined by reference to the time at which the contract was made.[422] If the term was a fair and reasonable one

---

[415] It is often not strictly a question of "severance" since a single phrase like "any breach", or "any misrepresentation" could not be subjected to the "blue pencil test" (below, para.11–161). The real difficulty is how an assessment of the reasonableness of the particular exclusion or limitation in issue can be reconciled with the requirement to assess the reasonableness of the "term".

[416] In the example based on misrepresentation, by adding a proviso that "any misrepresentation" is *not* intended to include fraud. There is an obvious overlap here with *contra proferentem*: see above, para.7–022.

[417] Treitel, *Doctrine and Discretion in the Law of Contract*, pp.13–19. For the American experience under UCC ss.2–302, see Leff 115 U. of Pa L.Rev. 485; Ellinghaus 78 Y.L.J. 757.

[418] This is hardly surprising since, where consumers are involved, a term may simply be ineffective, e.g. ss.6(2), 7(2) (above paras 7–059—7–060) and even if the test of reasonableness applies, a term will often more obviously be regarded as unreasonable when relied upon against a consumer, so that litigation is not contested.

[419] Either under provisions which apply to such contracts without more, e.g. ss.2(2), 6(3), 7(3) or because the contract was made on one party's written standard terms of business: s.3; above, paras 7–065—7–070.

[420] For observations to this effect, see: *Watford Electronics Ltd v Sanderson Ltd* [2001] EWCA Civ 317; [2001] B.L.R. 143 at [55]; *Granville Oil & Chemicals Ltd v Davis Turner & Co Ltd* [2003] EWCA Civ 570; [2003] 2 Lloyd's Rep. 356 at [31]. They echo the sentiments expressed by Lord Diplock at the outset of the 1977 Act: *Photo Production Ltd v Securicor Transport Ltd* [1980] A.C. 827 at 851. The courts have even felt it appropriate to make a finding of reasonableness in support of an application for summary judgment: *Macquarie International Investments Ltd v Glencore UK Ltd* [2008] EWHC 2716 (Comm); [2008] 2 B.C.L.C. 565.

[421] Many of the cases in which the relevant term has been found to be unreasonable might be explained on the basis that it did not involve a *conscious and deliberate* allocation of risk, i.e. there was an element of "unfair surprise". For an argument that this should be the principal criterion for a finding of unreasonableness, see Beale, in Burrows & Peel (eds), *Contract Terms*.

[422] 1977 Act, s.11(1). In the case of a non-contractual notice (above, paras 7–057, 7–065) the relevant time is the time when the liability arose or but for the notice would have arisen: s.11(3): see *Monarch Airlines Ltd v London Luton Airport* [1998] 1 Lloyd's Rep. 403; *First National Commercial Bank v Loxleys, The Times*, November 14, 1996.

to be included having regard to the circumstances which were or should reasonably have been known to or in the contemplation of the parties *at that time*, its effectiveness will not be impaired by subsequent events.

7–080   **Guidelines: resources and insurance.** Section 11(4) of the Act lays down two guidelines for determining the reasonableness of provisions limiting a person's liability to a specific sum of money: regard is to be had to (a) the resources which that person could expect to be available to him for the purpose of meeting the liability, and (b) how far it was open to him to cover himself by insurance.[423] Under the second of these guidelines, a clause limiting the liability of a manufacturer for defects would not be reasonable if he could have insured against the liability without materially raising the price of his product (particularly if it would have been difficult or virtually impossible for the customer to have insured against the loss[424]) or if he actually had so insured.[425] On the other hand, a clause limiting the liability of a person engaged in the storage or carriage of goods would be reasonable if he had little knowledge of the nature or value of the goods, and if the goods could be more cheaply insured by their owner than by the bailee.[426] In applying the second guideline, the court considers the *availability* of insurance to the defendant, rather than his *actual* insurance position.[427] The two guidelines stated in s.11(4) do not contain an exhaustive list of factors to be taken into account in deciding whether a limitation clause satisfies a reasonableness test. A negative answer to this question may, for example, be given because of the "insufficient clarity"[428] of the clause.

7–081   **Guidelines: Schedule 2.** Where a term in a contract for the supply of goods is subject to the requirement of reasonableness under ss.6 or 7,[429] the Act provides five further guidelines.[430] These include the strength of the bargaining positions of the parties relative to each other,[431] whether the customer "received an inducement to agree to the term" (e.g. in the form of a lower price), whether he could have bought elsewhere without being subjected to a similar term, and the customer's knowledge or means of knowledge of the existence and extent of the terms.[432] Under these guidelines, the fact that the contract was in a standard form settled

---

[423] s.11(4). The subsection is in terms applicable only to terms which *limit* (as opposed to those which wholly *exclude*) liability: *The Flammar Pride* [1990] 1 Lloyd's Rep. 434 at 438; but the guidelines in question can be applied by analogy to clauses of the latter kind: see below, para.7–082.

[424] *Salvage Association v CAP Services* [1995] F.S.R. 654.

[425] *George Mitchell (Chesterhall) Ltd v Finney Lock Seeds Ltd* [1983] A.C. 803 at 817, decided under earlier and now superseded legislation not containing this guideline; *St Albans City and District Council v International Computers Ltd* [1995] F.S.R. 686, reversed but not on the application of the reasonableness test [1996] 4 All E.R. 481.

[426] *Singer (UK) Ltd v Tees & Hartlepool Port Authority* [1988] 2 Lloyd's Rep. 164.

[427] ibid. at 169; *The Flammar Pride* [1990] 1 Lloyd's Rep. 434 at 439; *Monarch Airlines Ltd v London Luton Airport* [1998] 1 Lloyd's Rep. 403 at 413; sometimes it appears as if it is the *actual* insurance position of the parties which has been considered, but this may be explained as the best evidence of what was available: *Balmoral Group Ltd v Borealis (UK) Ltd* [2006] EWHC 1900 (Comm) at [422]; cf. *St Albans City and District Council v International Computers Ltd*, above, fn.425.

[428] *Overseas Medical Supplier Ltd v Orient Transport Services Ltd* [1999] 2 Lloyd's Rep. 273 at 280. This lack of clarity may, alternatively, be a ground for holding that, as a matter of construction, the clause does not cover the breach: see above, para.7–015.

[429] See above, para.7–070.

[430] s.11(2) and Sch.2.

[431] cf. *Thames Tideway Properties Ltd v Serafty* [1999] 2 Lloyd's Rep. 110 at 110.

[432] The question whether a term has been incorporated in the contract is, however, a separate question, as is recognised by the concluding words of s.11(2).

after negotiations between trade associations to which both parties belonged is relevant to the issue of reasonableness; for it helps to show that its terms were "not imposed by the strong upon the weak".[433] A fortiori, terms are unlikely to be struck down for unreasonableness under the Act where the contract in which they are contained was made between commercial companies "of equal bargaining power"[434] after negotiations in which each party had made concession to the other.[435] In the interests of certainty, an "entire agreement" clause in such a contract is also like to satisfy the test of reasonableness.[436] But where the term has *not* been the subject of negotiation it may be struck down, even in a contract between such parties, if its effect is to "contradict a fundamental assumption that all parties have made in this respect"[437]: e.g. where a seller of ingredients to a manufacturer of beverages supplied a defective ingredient which made the resulting product unsaleable.

Statutory guidelines applied by analogy. These statutory guidelines no doubt help to reduce the uncertainty to which the requirement of reasonableness gives rise; but the restrictions on their scope are hard to understand. Thus it is not easy to see why the strength of the bargaining positions of the parties is relevant only in contracts for the supply of goods; nor why the five guidelines[438] which can apply where a seller delivers goods of the wrong *quality*[439] do not also apply where he delivers goods of the wrong *quantity*.[440] The courts have remedied this defect in the wording of the Act by treating the guidelines as being of general application, so that they may be applied by analogy to other types of contracts and other types of clauses.[441]   7–082

Other factors. Even in relation to the situations covered by them, the statutory guidelines are by no means exhaustive; indeed it has been said that it is "impossible to draw up an exhaustive list of factors to be taken into account when a judge   7–083

---

[433] *R W Green Ltd v Cade Bros Farms Ltd* [1978] 1 Lloyd's Rep. 602 at 607; *Granville Oil & Chemicals Ltd v Davis Turner & Co Ltd* [2003] EWCA Civ 570; [2003] 2 Lloyd's Rep. 356; contrast *George Mitchell (Chesterhall) Ltd v Finney Lock Seeds Ltd* where the conditions were not negotiated by the National Farmers Union but simply introduced by seed merchants without objection from farmers: see [1983] 2 A.C. 803 at 817, but where terms are produced by one of the parties, and not by a trade association, some weight may still be given to the fact they are "normal in the trade": *Expo Fabrics UK Ltd v Naughty Clothing Co Ltd* [2003] EWCA Civ 1165 at [27].

[434] *Watford Electronics Ltd v Sanderson Ltd* [2001] EWCA Civ 317; [2001] B.L.R. 143 at [55]; *Granville Oil & Chemicals Ltd v Davis Turner & Co Ltd* [2003] EWCA Civ 570; [2003] 2 Lloyd's Rep. 356 at [31]. cf. below, para.9–124 for the same approach to the test of reasonableness under Misrepresentation Act 1967, s.3. Equality of bargaining need not be confined to contracts between two commercial parties: *Marplace Ltd v Chaffe Street* [2006] EWHC 1919 (Ch) at [484] ("sophisticated and wealthy consumer").

[435] *Watford Electronics* case, above; *Axa Sun Life Services Plc v Campbell Martin Ltd* [2011] EWCA Civ 133.

[436] ibid. at [39].

[437] *Britvic Soft Drinks Ltd v Messer UK Ltd* [2002] EWCA Civ 548; [2002] 2 Lloyd's Rep. 368 at [26]; *Bacardi Martini Beverages Ltd v Thomas Hardy Packaging Ltd* [2002] EWCA Civ 549; [2002] 2 Lloyd's Rep. 379 at [26].

[438] See above, fn.430.

[439] The requirement of reasonableness applies to terms purporting to exclude or restrict B's liability in such cases if the buyer does not deal as consumer: s.6(3).

[440] The requirement of reasonableness applies to terms purporting to exclude or restrict B's liability in such cases if the contract is made on his "written standard terms of business": s.3.

[441] *Singer (UK) Ltd v Tees & Hartlepool Port Authority* [1988] 2 Lloyd's Rep. 164 at 169; *The Flammar Pride* [1990] 1 Lloyd's Rep. 434 at 439; *Overseas Medical Supplies Ltd v Orient Transport Services Ltd* [1999] 2 Lloyd's Rep. 273 at 276–277; cf. *Monarch Airlines Ltd v London Luton Airport* [1998] 1 Lloyd's Rep. 403; *Schenkers Ltd v Overland Shoes Ltd* [1998] 1 Lloyd's Rep. 499 at 500.

is faced with this very difficult question".[442] In *Smith v Eric S Bush*[443] the House of Lords held that a term purporting to exclude the liability for negligence of surveyors (engaged by a building society) to buyers of dwelling houses did not satisfy the reasonableness test. The principal factors leading to this conclusion were that there was no equality of bargaining power, that the houses were of modest value so that it was not reasonable to expect the buyers to commission their own structural survey, and that the surveyors could easily have insured against the risk without unduly increasing their charges.[444] On the other hand, a disclaimer might be reasonable if the task undertaken had been one of great difficulty and complexity; if the value of the subject-matter had been very high, so that insurance against professional liability would have been very expensive or impossible to obtain[445]; or if it would have been reasonable for the injured party to have taken steps to discover the truth. Thus the requirement of reasonableness was held to have been satisfied where an estate agent disclaimed liability in respect of representations as to area made to the prospective purchaser who later contracted to buy the property in question for £875,000[446]: in such a transaction the purchaser could be expected to make his own investigations before exchanging contracts. The availability to the *other* party of an opportunity of discovering the defect in respect of which he is seeking to exclude liability can likewise be relevant to the issue of reasonableness. Thus where the seller of a car was a company which had been brought into the transaction purely to provide finance, it was said that the test of reasonableness would have been satisfied (if the buyer had not dealt as consumer[447]) because the company had never seen the car.[448] It has also been said that the courts should not be "too ready" to hold a term unreasonable by reference to "remote contingencies" to which the term, if taken literally, might apply but which the parties had not in fact intended to cover.[449]

7–084   **Nature of decision on reasonableness.** A decision on the issue of reasonableness is not merely an exercise of judicial discretion[450]; for it involves the application of statutory and judge-made guidelines. Nevertheless in the *George Mitchell* case Lord Bridge described such a decision as one on which there "will sometimes be room for a legitimate difference of judicial opinion"; and as one with which an appellate court should not interfere "unless satisfied that it proceeded on some erroneous principle or was plainly and obviously wrong".[451] These remarks are

---

[442] *Smith v Eric S Bush* [1990] 1 A.C. 831 at 858.

[443] [1990] 1 A.C. 831; Kaye 52 M.L.R. 841; for other factors relevant to the issue of reasonableness, see *George Mitchell (Chesterhall) Ltd v Finney Lock Seeds Ltd* [1983] 2 A.C. 803, decided under an earlier (now superseded) statutory reasonableness test; *Overseas Medical* case, above, fn.441, at 280.

[444] ibid. at 851–854, 858–859.

[445] ibid. at 859.

[446] *McCullagh v Lane Fox & Partners Ltd* [1996] 1 E.G.L.R. 35.

[447] See above, para.7–053.

[448] *R & B Customs Brokers Ltd v United Dominions Trust Ltd* [1988] 1 W.L.R. 321 at 332. But contrast *Lease Management Services v Purnell Secretarial Services* [1994] Tr. L.R. 337; *Sovereign Finance v Silver Crest Furniture* [1997] C.C.L.R. 76; *Danka Rentals Ltd v Xi Software Ltd* [1998] 17 Tr. L.R. 74.

[449] *Shipkreditforeningen v Emperor Navigation* [1998] 1 Lloyd's Rep. 67 at 75–77 (where the question of reasonableness arose under Misrepresentation Act 1967, s.3; below, para.9–115).

[450] *George Mitchell (Chesterhall) Ltd v Finney Lock Seeds Ltd* [1983] 2 A.C. 803 at 816. cf. *Comemsco Ltd v Contrapol* (unrep.), referred to by Kerr L.J. in [1983] Q.B. 284 at 315.

[451] [1983] 2 A.C. 803 at 810; *Phillips Products Ltd v Hyland* [1987] 1 W.L.R. 659 at 669; *St Albans City & District Council v International Computers Ltd* [1996] 4 All E.R. 481; *Schenkers Ltd v Overland Shoes Ltd* [1998] 1 Lloyd's Rep. 499; *Overseas Medical Supplies Ltd v Orient Transport Services Ltd* [1999] 2 Lloyd's Rep. 273 at 276.

intended to restrict, but not to rule out, the possibility of successful appeals on the issue of reasonableness. An appeal may, for example, succeed where the trial judge has held the clause to be unreasonable by attributing to it a wider meaning than that which, in the view of the appellate court, it could, on its true construction, bear.[452]

Effects of rescission or affirmation. Section 9(1) of the Act provides that   **7–085** effect may be given to a term which satisfies the requirement of reasonableness even though the contract has been terminated; while s.9(2) provides that the requirement of reasonableness is not excluded by affirmation of the contract.[453]

(vi) *Restrictions on evasions*

Secondary contract. A term restricting or excluding liability may be con-   **7–086** tained, not in the principal contract itself, but in another (secondary) contract. To meet the possibility that this would allow for the evasion of the Act, s.10 provides that

> "A person is not bound by any contract term prejudicing or taking away rights of his which arise under, or in connection with the performance of, another contract,[454] so far as those rights extend to the enforcement of another's liability which this Part of this Act[455] prevents[456] that other from excluding or restricting."

Unfortunately, the terminology of s.10 differs from that used elsewhere in the Act,[457] and this fact gives rise to a number of difficulties of interpretation. For example, s.10 refers to a contract term "prejudicing or taking away rights", not to one "excluding or restricting liability". The statutory explanation of the latter phrase[458] therefore does not apply to s.10. In particular, it is by no means clear whether the section would cover a secondary contract excluding a particular *remedy*, or one imposing onerous conditions (such as short time-limits) on the enforcement of a liability; or whether it would apply to a subsequent agreement to submit disputes under the original contract to arbitration.[459]

The exact scope of s.10 is also in doubt in relation to consumer contracts and contracts on written standard terms. Section 3(2) applies the requirement of reasonableness to terms in such contracts which (a) exclude or restrict liability for breach, or (b) purport to entitle a party to render a performance substantially different from that reasonably expected of him, or to render no performance at all.

---

[452] *Watford Electronics Ltd v Sanderson Ltd* [2001] EWCA Civ 317; [2001] B.L.R. 143.

[453] cf. the common law position, above, paras 7–024, 7–032.

[454] s.10 does not apply where a contract between A and B takes away A's right to sue a third party, C, *in tort*, since A's right against C does not arise "under . . . another contract": *The Chevalier Roze* [1983] 2 Lloyd's Rep. 438 at 422.

[455] i.e. Pt I, which extends to England and Wales and to Northern Ireland.

[456] i.e. (*semble*) not only by making it totally ineffective but also by subjecting it to the requirement of reasonableness.

[457] Perhaps because s.10 was introduced at a late stage in the Parliamentary proceedings on the Act.

[458] s.13(1), above, para.7–054.

[459] See s.13(2) which, unlike s.10, uses the standard terminology of the Act—"excluding or restricting liability".

Clearly, a secondary contract seeking to achieve result (a) is within s.10 and thus ineffective. But is the same true of a secondary contract seeking to achieve result (b)? The concluding words of s.10 give rise to a difficulty because the rights affected by the secondary contract must "extend to the enforcement of another's *liability* which ... this Act prevents the other from excluding or restricting". Section 3(2) appears to contrast terms *excluding or restricting liability* with terms purporting to *entitle a party to render a performance substantially different*, etc. It is at least doubtful whether s.10 is apt to cover a secondary agreement having the latter effect.

Section 10 does not apply to a contract by which the parties to an earlier contract, containing terms which would be subject to the Act, reach a settlement of disputes which have arisen between them under the original contract. The argument that such a settlement was a secondary contract within s.10 has been rejected on the ground that there was no hint in the legislative history that the section was intended to strike at such genuine out of court settlements.[460] On the contrary, the legislative history indicates that, in using the phrase "another's liability", s.10 refers to the liability of a third party,[461] so that the section "does not apply where the parties to both contracts are the same".[462] The point of the section is to deal with the case in which a contract between X and Y provides that Y is not to exercise rights against Z under a separate contract between Y and Z.[463] The latter contract may not contain any exemption clause but be of such a kind that, if it did contain such a clause, that clause would be subject to the Act. At common law, Z could not as a general rule rely on the clause in the contract between X and Y as he was not a party to it[464]; and the statutory right to rely on it, which Z may have under the Contracts (Rights of Third Parties) Act 1999, will be of no avail to him where the clause is ineffective under the Unfair Contract Terms Act 1977.[465] The purpose of s.10 of the 1977 Act is to prevent X from enforcing against Y a clause in the contract between X and Y which provides that Y is not to sue Z under the contract between Y and Z and which would have been ineffective under that Act if it had been contained in the contract between Y and Z. Even apart from s.10 such a proceeding might not be open to X unless X could show that he had a sufficient interest[466] in Z's immunity from being sued by Y. The view that s.10 does not apply where the parties to both contracts are the same (even though it is acknowledged that the words of the section are capable of covering such a case[467]) has also been supported by the argument that, between the parties to the original contract, s.10 would be unnecessary since the secondary contract, no less than the original one, would be subject to the requirement of reasonableness under ss.2 and 3 of the Act.[468] But this reasoning seems to overlook

---

[460] *Tudor Grange Holdings Ltd v Citibank NA* [1992] Ch. 53 at 65–67; Brown 108 L.Q.R. 233; Cumberbatch 55 M.L.R. 866; cf. *In the matter of Cape Plc* [2006] EWHC 1316 (Ch); [2006] 3 All E.R. 1222 (1977 Act not applicable to scheme of arrangement under s.425 of Companies Act 1985 in any event (now Companies Act 2006, Pt 26)).

[461] *Hansard*, HL Vol.385, cols 57–59, 511–514 (1977).

[462] *Tudor Grange* case, above, at 66.

[463] See the example given in *Hansard*, HL Vol.385, col.57, on which the discussion in the *Tudor Grange* case above at 66 seems to have been based; reference to the Parliamentary report would now be authorised by *Pepper v Hart* [1993] A.C. 593.

[464] See below, para.14–058.

[465] See below, para.14–112.

[466] See below, para.14–038.

[467] *Tudor Grange* case, above, at 66.

[468] ibid. at 67.

the possibility that the secondary contract may be subject only to the requirement of reasonableness (e.g. under s.3), while the original contract might be one in which the exemption clause was simply ineffective: e.g. under s.6(2) where it excluded or restricted liability for defects in goods sold to a consumer. In such a case to give effect to the secondary contract, even between the parties to the original contract, could significantly reduce the protection which the Act intends to give to the consumer under the original contract.

The view that s.10 does not apply where the parties to both contracts are the same would also help to solve the problem of the renegotiation of a contract before any dispute under it has arisen. A contract may, for example, contain a term limiting the liability of a party to it, and that term may be subject to, and satisfy, the requirement of reasonableness. The parties may later agree on a lower limit of liability which would also (had it been originally incorporated in the contract) have satisfied that requirement. If that later agreement were within s.10, it would be totally ineffective and incapable of being validated by being shown to be reasonable. This—surely undesirable—result can be avoided by arguing *either* that s.10 does not apply between the parties to the original contract *or* that the later agreement is a variation of the original contract, so that the terms of that later agreement do not prejudice rights which "arise under *another* contract." The new limit of the defaulting party's liability would thus be subject to the same requirement of reasonableness as the term which originally limited that liability.

Choice of law clauses. A second possible way of evading the Act is to provide   **7–087** that a contract which would otherwise be subject to its provisions shall be governed by the law of a foreign country (which imposes no such restriction on the effectiveness of contract terms). By s.27(2), the Act applies, even though the contract contains such a clause, where the clause was "imposed" wholly or mainly to evade the Act; or where one of the parties dealt as consumer, was habitually resident in the UK, and the essential steps necessary for the making of the contract were taken there. The effect of such provisions is to confer on the controls in the Act and the Regulations the status of mandatory rules. These are recognised and given effect by the EC Regulation on the law applicable to contractual obligations ('Rome I').[469]

(vii) *Situations not covered by the Act*[470]

Cases not within the scope of the Act. Contract terms excluding or restrict-   **7–088** ing the liability of a person not acting in the course of a business are generally unaffected by the Act. The Act only limits such a person's right to exclude or restrict certain liabilities arising out of contracts for the sale and hire-purchase of goods[471] and for misrepresentation.[472] Even terms excluding or restricting business liability may be outside the scope of the Act: this is the position where a

---

[469] Reg.(EC) 593/2008. Rome I replaces the Rome Convention (Contracts (Applicable Law) Act 1990, s.2 and Sch.1, as amended by SI 1994/1900) for contracts entered into on or after December 17, 2009. There are several bases in the Regulation upon which the mandatory nature of the rules in the Act could be invoked, e.g. Art.6(2) (consumer contracts), 8(1) (employment contracts) and 9(2) (mandatory rules of the forum).

[470] In addition to those set out in the text, Sch.1, para.5 excepts from s.2(1) of the Act the validity of a discharge and indemnity given on or in connection with an award of compensation for pneumoconiosis.

[471] s.6(1) and (4); above, paras 7–059, 7–070.

[472] s.8; below, paras 9–115—9–125.

contract between B1 and B2, not made on written standard terms of business,[473] excludes or restricts a liability other than one for breach of the implied terms in contracts for the supply of goods dealt with in ss.6 and 7 of the Act,[474] or breach of a contractual duty of care.[475] For example, a clause by which B1 excluded or limited liability to B2 for delay in delivering goods, or for short delivery or for an express undertaking as to quality going beyond those implied by law, would not be affected by the Act.

7–089   **Insurance, land, intellectual property, companies and securities.** The principal group of contracts excepted[476] from some of the provisions of the Act is listed in Sch.1. Paragraph 1 of the Schedule lists a number of contracts to which ss.2, 3 and 4 do not apply. In the excepted cases, contract terms[477] excluding or restricting liability for negligence, terms in consumer contracts and provisions in written standard terms of business excluding or restricting liability for breach of contract and indemnity clauses are not subject to the provisions of those sections. The contracts within para.1 of the Schedule are contracts of insurance and any contract "so far as it relates to" the creation, transfer or termination of an interest in land or in any patent, trade mark,[478] copyright or other intellectual property; the formation, dissolution or constitution of a company or the rights or obligations of its members; and the creation or transfer of securities or any right or interest in securities. Contracts of insurance are *wholly* excepted, but a contract falling within the other categories is only excepted "*so far as* it relates to" the matter specified.[479] Where a contract relates to such matters and also to others, the specified sections are excluded with regard to the former: e.g. they do not apply to a share option[480] contained in a contract of employment.[481] In the case of a contract for the transfer of an interest in land, it has been held that a clause in a lease by which rent was payable "without any deduction or set-off whatsoever" was excepted from ss.2, 3 and 4 since the tenant's covenant to pay rent was "an integral part of the creation of the interest in land".[482] This reasoning gives some support to the view that provisions in the lease which do not "relate to" the transfer would not be so excepted.

7–090   **Marine salvage or towage, charterparties and carriage of goods by sea.** Paragraph 2 of the Schedule lists three contracts: contracts of marine salvage or

---

[473] See s.3(1).

[474] See above, paras 7–059, 7–070; it is assumed that there is no "product liability" (above, para.7–051).

[475] ss.1(1)(a), 2.

[476] By s.1(2).

[477] s.2 also deals with certain notices not having contractual effect, but the wording of s.1(2) ("in relation to contracts") indicates that the exclusions in Sch.1 only apply to contract terms.

[478] See Trade Marks Act 1994, s.106(1) and Sch.4, para.1.

[479] *Salvage Association v CAP Financial Services* [1995] F.S.R. 654 (s.2 applicable to a clause in a software licence limiting liability for breach of the implied term that the software would be developed with reasonable skill and care).

[480] *Micklefield v SAC Technology* [1990] 1 W.L.R. 1002.

[481] As to which see Sch.1, para.4, below. For the restricted application of the Act to employment contracts generally, see above, para.7–067, fn.359.

[482] *Electricity Supply Nominees Ltd v IAF Group Ltd* [1993] 1 W.L.R. 1059 at 1063; cf. *Unchained Growth III Plc v Granby Village (Manchester) Management Co* [2000] 1 W.L.R. 739; *Connaught Restaurants Ltd v Indoors Leisure Ltd* [1994] 1 W.L.R. 501 where no attempt was made to rely on the Act, perhaps because the conditions for the applicability of s.3 (above, paras 7–066—7–067) were not satisfied; for the treatment of provisions excluding set-off as exemption clauses under the Act, see above, para.7–054.

towage, charterparties of ships or hovercraft, and contracts for the carriage of goods by ship or hovercraft.[483] These contracts are subject to s.2(1), which provides that B[484] cannot by any contract term exclude or restrict his liability for death or personal injury resulting from negligence. But they are excepted from the remainder of s.2, as well as from ss.3 and 4, except in favour of C. Since some contracts within this group may involve the hire of a chattel[485] they are also excepted from s.7 which limits the extent to which liability for breach of certain implied terms in such contracts can be excluded or restricted.[486]

Paragraph 3 of the Schedule deals with the case where goods are carried by ship or hovercraft under a contract which either specifies that means of carriage only for part of the journey[487] or makes no provision for the means of carriage. Such contracts may not be contracts *for* the carriage of goods by ship or hovercraft, but are nevertheless excepted from the operation of ss.2(2), 3 and 4 in the same way as such contracts.

Employment. By para.4 of the Schedule, ss.2(1) and (2) do not apply to contracts of employment "except in favour of the employee". The liability of the employee for negligence can therefore be restricted or excluded; but the employer cannot exclude or restrict such liability as against the employee. Since s.2 applies only to "business liability" the need for para.4 may not at first sight be apparent. But "business liability" includes liability for breach of a duty arising from things done in the course of *another* person's business[488] so that liability incurred by an employee (whether to his employer or to a third party) can be a "business liability". Moreover, "business" includes profession[489] so that an employee who in the course of his employment exercises a profession could incur a "business liability" which, but for para.4, would attract the operation of s.2(1) and (2).

7–091

Contracts for the international supply of goods. In such contracts,[490] none of the limits "imposed by this Act" on contract terms which exclude or restrict liability apply.[491] It seems that this includes the limits contained in s.3 of the Misrepresentation Act 1967.[492]

7–092

Under the 1977 Act, the requirement of reasonableness sometimes applies to terms which do not "exclude or restrict" liability; e.g. it applies to terms entitling a party to render a performance substantially different from that reasonably expected of him, or to render no performance at all,[493] and to indemnity clauses.[494]

---

[483] See, e.g. *The European Enterprise* [1989] 2 Lloyd's Rep. 185. Certain contracts for the carriage of goods by sea also come within the excepting provisions of s.29; below, para.7–093.

[484] See above, paras 7–052—7–053.

[485] e.g. a demise charterparty.

[486] See above, paras 7–060, 7–070.

[487] This situation commonly arises where the goods are carried in a container from one inland destination to another in an overseas country.

[488] s.1(3).

[489] s.14.

[490] As defined by s.26(3) and (4); see *Ocean Chemical Transport Inc v Exnor Craggs* [2000] 1 Lloyd's Rep. 446 at 451; *Amiri Flight Authority v BAE Systems Plc* [2003] EWCA Civ 1447; [2003] 2 Lloyd's Rep. 767; *Balmoral Group Ltd v Borealis (UK) Ltd* [2006] EWHC 1900 (Comm) at [436]–[450]; *Trident Turboprop (Dublin) Ltd v First Flight Couriers Ltd* [2009] EWCA Civ 290; [2010] Q.B. 86.

[491] s.26(1).

[492] *Trident Turboprop (Dublin) Ltd v First Flight Couriers Ltd* [2009] EWCA Civ 290; [2010] Q.B. 86.

[493] See s.3(2)(b); above, paras 7–068—7–069.

[494] See s.4; above, para.7–071.

Where such terms or clauses are contained in a contract for the international supply of goods, the requirement of reasonableness does not apply.[495]

7–093   **Contractual provisions authorised or required under legislation or international agreements.** An increasingly common technique for controlling exemption clauses (and other contract terms) is found in international conventions, for example those regulating the international carriage of goods and passengers. Many such conventions have been given the force of law by statute.[496] These conventions often lay down a limitation of liability and then provide that any attempt at further reduction in the contract is void. This position is preserved by the 1977 Act.[497]

7–094   **Choice of law clauses.** The Act is intended to deal with contracts having some substantial connection with some part of the UK. A contract may be governed by English law though its connection with England is tenuous (or even non-existent); this can happen if it contains an express term that it is to be governed by English law. Section 27(1)[498] accordingly provides that ss.2 to 7 do not apply where a contract is governed by the law of a part of the UK only by choice of the parties and would apart from that choice have been governed by the law of some country outside the UK. The point is of considerable commercial importance as contracts having no substantial connection with England are quite commonly made subject to English law by choice of the parties.[499]

(b) The Unfair Terms in Consumer Contracts Regulations 1999

7–095   These Regulations[500] give effect to an EC Council Directive[501] which is intended to promote the harmonisation of the laws of Member States so as to ensure that contracts with consumers do not include terms which are unfair to the consumer.[502] They supersede earlier Regulations made in 1994.[503] The 1999 Regulations apply in relation to "unfair terms" which have not been "individually negotiated" in contracts concluded between a "seller" or a "supplier" and a "consumer". Their central provision is that if such terms are "unfair", then they shall not be binding on the consumer.[504]

---

[495] s.26(2).

[496] e.g. Carriage by Air Act 1961, Sch.1, Arts 22, 23(1) and 32; Carriage of Goods by Road Act 1965, Sch., Arts 23, 41; Carriage of Goods by Sea Act 1971, Sch., Arts III. 8 and IV. 5; Merchant Shipping Act 1995, ss.183 and 184 and Sch.6, Pt I, Arts 7, 8, 18 and Pt III (not yet fully in force: for transitional provisions, see Unfair Contract Terms Act 1977, s.28).

[497] s.29. Certain contracts for the carriage of goods by sea are within both this exception and the somewhat more restricted exception of Sch.1, para.2(c); above, para.7–090.

[498] As amended by Contracts (Applicable Law) Act 1990, s.5 and Sch.4.

[499] See *Shipskreditforeningen v Emperor Navigation* [1998] 1 Lloyd's Rep. 67 at 78.

[500] SI 1999/2083, as amended by Unfair Terms in Consumer Contracts (Amendment) Regulations 2001 (SI 2001/1186).

[501] 93/13/EEC. See Brandner and Ulmer (1991) 29 C.M.L.R. 647; Collins (1994) 14 O.J.L.S. 229. For the construction of legislation based on such Directives, see *Litster v Forth Dry Dock & Engineering Co Ltd* [1990] 1 A.C. 546 at 559, adopting a "purposive" construction, "even though perhaps it may involve some departure from the strict and literal application of the words which the legislature has elected to use." And, in the context of Dir. 93/13 itself, see: *R. (Khatun) v Newham LBC* [2004] EWCA Civ 55; [2005] Q.B. 37; discussed below, para.7–098.

[502] 93/13/EEC, Recital 4.

[503] SI 1994/3159.

[504] SI 1999/2083, reg.8(1).

(i) *Relation with Unfair Contract Terms Act 1977*

Need to satisfy both sets of controls, if applicable. The Regulations 7–096
operate side by side with the Unfair Contract Terms Act, so that it is possible for
a term to be valid under the Regulations and not under the Act, and conversely.
Or, to put the same point in another way, a party wishing to rely on a contract term
will have to satisfy the requirements of both sets of rules. The scope of the
Regulations, however, differs significantly from that of the Act, so that often only
one set of rules will apply.

Respects in which Regulations narrower than Act. In some respects, the 7–097
Regulations are or may be narrower in scope than the Act. First, the Regulations
strike only at contract terms,[505] while some of the provisions of the Act apply also
to notices (not forming part of any contract) purporting to exclude or restrict
liability.[506] Secondly, the Regulations apply only to any terms which have "not
been individually negotiated".[507] Only one provision of the Act is restricted to the
situation in which a party deals on the other party's "written standard terms of
business".[508] The other provisions of the Act can apply to individually negotiated
contracts (or to notices given to individuals), though in practice they will no doubt
most commonly apply to terms or notices in standard form. Thirdly, the Regulations apply only where one party acts for purposes relating to his business and the
other is a consumer[509] while some of the provisions of the Act apply where both
parties act, or where neither party acts, in the course of a business.

Respects in which Regulations wider than Act: types of contract cov- 7–098
ered. While both the Regulations[510] and the Act[511] contain a list of contracts
specifically excepted, the list of exceptions in the Act is more extensive so that in
this regard the scope of the Regulations is wider than that of the Act. This is on
the basis, however, that the Regulations otherwise apply to all forms of consumer
contract, since they maintain an enigmatic silence on the subject-matter of the
contracts which are *included* within its provisions. In *R. (Khatun) v Newham
LBC*[512] the Court of Appeal held that the Directive, and therefore the Regulations,
applies to contracts for the grant or transfer of an interest in land. It did so by
adopting a broad purposive interpretation of the Directive which aims at providing
a "high level" of consumer protection. It also emphasised that the numerous
references in the Directive to "goods and services"[513] (in particular, "goods")
should not simply be interpreted in accordance with English law, so as to narrow
its scope. For example, the French term *biens* and its cognates in Italian, Spanish

---

[505] ibid., regs 4(1) and 8(1).
[506] ss.2(1), 5(1), 11(3) and 11(4).
[507] reg.5(1).
[508] s.3(1).
[509] regs 8(1), 3(1).
[510] See below, para.7–117.
[511] See above, para.7–089.
[512] [2004] EWCA Civ 55; [2005] Q.B. 37; cf. *Peabody Trust Governors v Reeve* [2008] EWHC 1432
(Ch) at [30]; *Shaftsbury House (Developments) Ltd v Lee* [2010] EWHC 1484 (Ch) at [54]. See also:
Case C–237/02 *Freiburger Kommunalbauten GmbH Baugesellschaft & Co KG v Hofstetter* [2004] 2
C.M.L.R. 13.
[513] There are two such references in the Regulations themselves: reg.6(1) and 6(2).

and Portuguese, for which the term "goods" is employed as the English equivalent, refers to both immovables and movables.[514] According to the Court of Appeal this "effectively demolished" any argument as to the scope of the Regulations based on the English language version of the Directive. Once that argument is demolished, most of the arguments against the inclusion of other types of contract fall away[515] and a broad purposive interpretation leads almost inevitably to the conclusion that all types of consumer contracts[516] are included, unless expressly excluded. For example, it seems that the Regulations must apply to the most common type of contract for the "sale" of intellectual property to a consumer, i.e. to one licensing him to use computer software, whether or not this also involves the transfer of a moveable physical object.[517] The extended sense in which references in the Directive to "goods" are to be understood probably also means that the Regulations apply to contracts for things in action or money, notwithstanding their exclusion from the definition of goods in statutes concerned to some extent with consumer protection.[518] Some of the illustrations of prima facie unfair terms are evidently based on the assumption that certain transactions in securities could fall within the scope of the Regulations,[519] as well as contracts for the purchase or sale of foreign currency.[520]

7–099   **Respects in which Regulations wider than Act: types of term covered.** In one significant respect, the scope of the Regulations is clearly wider than that of the Act. With the exception of s.4, which deals with indemnity clauses, the Act is concerned only with exemption clauses, that is, with clauses which have the effect of excluding or restricting liability or of excluding or restricting an obligation or a duty. The scope of the Regulations includes such clauses but also extends beyond them to clauses which can confer rights on the party relying on them. This is clear not only from the operative parts of the Regulations, which refer generally to "an unfair term in a contract",[521] but also from the list of illustrations given in the Regulations of terms which may (though they will not necessarily) be regarded as unfair.[522] The list includes terms which allow the seller to retain sums paid by the consumer if the latter decides not to conclude or perform the contract; terms which require the consumer to pay a disproportionately high amount of compensation if he fails to perform his obligations; terms which automatically extend a fixed-term contract if the consumer does not give notice of termination; and terms which enable sellers or suppliers to increase their charges.[523] None of these

---

[514] Where the narrower concept of "goods" is intended, a different term is employed: *merchandises* (French), *merci* (Italian), *marcadorias* (Spanish): Directive, Recital 1.

[515] The view that in the Directive "goods" bears a wider meaning is also supported by some of the items in the list of prima facie unfair terms annexed to the Directive and reproduced in Sch.2 to the Regulations.

[516] i.e. those between a seller or supplier and a consumer containing terms which have not been individually negotiated.

[517] Which it seems is necessary for the contract to qualify as the sale of goods for the purpose of the Sale of Goods Act 1979 and therefore s.6 of the 1977 Act: *St Albans City & District Council v International Computers* [1996] 4 All E.R. 481, per Sir Iain Glidewell; cf. *Southwark LBC v IBM UK Ltd* [2011] EWHC 549 (TCC).

[518] Sale of Goods Act 1979, s.62(1); Consumer Credit Act 1974, s.189(1); Unfair Contract Terms Act 1977, ss.14, 25; Supply of Goods and Services Act 1982, s.18.

[519] Sch.2, para.2(c).

[520] Sch.2, para.2(c)

[521] reg.5(1); cf. reg.4(1).

[522] 1999 Regs, Sch.2.

[523] 1999 Regs, Sch.2, para.1(d), (e), (h), (l); below, para.7–110 et seq.

provisions would fall within the 1977 Act since they are all terms which confer rights on the supplier and not terms which exclude or restrict his liability.

(ii) *Preliminary definitions*

"Seller" or "supplier". The Regulations define this expression to mean "any   **7–100** natural or legal person who, in contracts covered by these Regulations, is acting for purposes relating to his trade, business or profession . . . "[524] The words "contracts covered by these Regulations" here refer to contracts[525] between such a seller or supplier and a consumer, containing terms which have not been "individually negotiated".[526] The requirement of purposes "relating to" his business etc. appears broader than the requirement under the Act of acting "in the course of a business" which has led to a test of regularity of dealing.[527]

"Consumer". This expression is defined[528] to mean "any natural person who,   **7–101** in contracts covered by these Regulations, is acting for purposes which are outside his trade, business or profession".[529] The definition differs in various ways from the definition of "dealing as consumer" in the 1977 Act. First, it is not part of the definition under the Regulations (as it is under the Act) that the other party must make the contract in the course of a business; but this is a point of no significance as the Regulations have no effect on the contract unless the other party[530] acts for purposes relating to his trade, business or profession.[531] Secondly, the Regulations as a general rule[532] include only natural persons in the definition of consumer, while under the Act a corporation can deal as consumer in relation to a contract

---

[524] reg.3(1). This includes a local authority in circumstances where it is carrying out "an activity which could . . . be carried on by a private undertaking in order to make profits": *R. (Khatun) v Newham LBC* [2004] EWCA Civ 55; [2005] Q.B. 37.

[525] See above, para.7–098 for the types of contract covered.

[526] See regs 3(1), 4(1); for exceptions, see below, para.7–117. It seems that the Regulations may apply even where it is the consumer who is the supplier, e.g. as a guarantor: *Barclays Bank Plc v Kufner* [2008] EWHC 2319; [2009] 1 All E.R. (Comm) 1 at [29]; *Royal Bank of Scotland v Chandra* [2010] EWHC 105 (Ch) at [102] (Regulations applied to a bank guarantee where the guarantor *and* the principal debtor each entered into their respective contracts as natural persons and were not acting in the course of their trade or profession), not following earlier decisions that the Regulations do not apply to guarantees at all: *Manches LLP v Freer* [2006] EWHC 991; *Williamson v Bank of Scotland* [2006] EWHC 1289.

[527] See above, para.7–053. The test of "relating to" his business etc. appears closer to the test applied in *Stevenson v Rogers* [1999] Q.B. 1028, above para.7–053, fn.277.

[528] reg.3(1).

[529] For the meaning given to "consumer" by the European Court of Justice in the context of other European instruments, see: Case C-361/89 *France v Di Pinto* [1991] E.C.R. I-1189; Case C-269/95 *Benincasa v Dentalkit* [1997] E.C.R. I-3767; Case C-464/01 *Gruber v Bay Wa AG* [2005] E.C.R. I-439. See *Office of Fair Trading v Foxtons Ltd* [2009] EWHC 1681 (Ch); [2009] 29 E.G. 98 at [28] (distinction drawn between professional or commercial landlords and other owners of property who entered into letting agency contracts); cf. *Barclays Bank Plc v Kufner* [2008] EWHC 2319; [2009] 1 All E.R. (Comm) 1; *Turner & Co (GB) Ltd v Abi* [2010] EWHC 2078 (QB). In *Evans v Cherry Tree Financial Ltd* [2008] EWCA Civ 331, in the context of a loan agreement, it was conceded that if *any* of the purposes for which the claimant borrowed the money were outside his trade or business, he was a consumer as defined by the regulations.

[530] i.e. the seller or supplier: see reg.4(1).

[531] See the definitions of "seller or supplier", above.

[532] Exceptionally, for the purposes of Arbitration Act 1996 the Regulations are extended by ss.89–91 to consumer arbitration agreements and a 'consumer' may include a legal person (s.90): *Heifer International Inc v Christiansen* [2007] EWHC 3015 (TCC).

not made in the course of a business.[533] Thirdly, a person is not to be regarded as dealing as a consumer for the purposes of the Act if he is an "individual"[534] and the goods are second hand goods sold at public auction which individuals have the opportunity of attending in person,[535] but a person who buys in this way may be a "consumer" within the Regulations. Finally, under the Act a person deals as consumer only if "he neither makes the contract in the course of a business nor holds himself out as doing so",[536] while under the Regulations a person is a consumer if in making the contract he "is acting for purposes which are outside his trade, business or profession".[537] These differences between the definitions in the Regulations and the Act should, however, be considered against the background of the relative scope of the two legislative regimes. The Regulations have effect only on contracts with consumers while many of the Act's provisions apply even where both parties act in the course of a business. It is often only the *degree* of control which is affected under the Act by the distinction between such a transaction and one in which one party deals as consumer, so that, for example, an exemption clause in a consumer transaction will be simply ineffective, while one in a business transaction will be subject to the requirement of reasonableness.

A person may be a consumer for the purposes of the Regulations even in relation to a transaction of considerable value: e.g. in one case, to a contract to acquire foreign currency worth $7 million.[538] The value of the transaction appears likewise to be no bar to a person's dealing as consumer for the purposes of the 1977 Act.

7–102   **Term not individually negotiated.** The Regulations apply only to terms which have not been individually negotiated; and reg.5(2) provides that a term

> "shall always be regarded as not having been individually negotiated where it has been drafted in advance *and* the consumer has therefore not been able to influence the substance of the term".[539]

It has been said that it "does not follow from the existence of the *ability to influence* the substance of a term", e.g. because the consumer has instructed a lawyer who has considered the terms "that the term has, in fact, been individually negotiated". It is "still a matter for the supplier to prove".[540] The requirement that the term must have been drafted "in advance" prompts the question: in advance of what? The most obvious answer appears to be "in advance of the conclusion of the contract"; but this is unsatisfactory because all the terms of a contract will normally be drafted before the contract is made. "In advance" is therefore perhaps more appropriately taken to mean "in advance of the negotiations leading to the

---

[533] See above, para.7–053.

[534] There seems to be no significant distinction between "an individual" and a "natural person" within the definition of "consumer": reg.3(1); above, after fn.528.

[535] 1977 Act, s.12(2).

[536] s.12(1)(a).

[537] reg.3(1).

[538] *Standard Bank of London Ltd v Apostolakis* [2000] I.L.Pr. 766. The result and approach of Longmore J. is questioned in *Maple Leaf Macro Volatility Master Fund v Rouvroy* [2009] EWHC 257 (Comm); [2009] 1 Lloyd's Rep. 475 at [208], [270] (affirmed [2009] EWCA Civ 1334 without reference to this point).

[539] Emphasis added.

[540] *UK Housing Alliance Ltd v Francis* [2010] EWCA Civ 117; [2010] 3 All E.R. 519 at [19] (emphasis added)

conclusion of the contract," so that it is *because* of the time at which the term was drafted that the consumer could not influence its substance.[541] The term does not have to have been drafted by the seller or supplier: it may have been drafted by a trade association for use by its members. Where a term has been negotiated between organisations representing on the one hand sellers or suppliers and on the other hand consumers, it would appear not to be "individually" negotiated but the fact that the term has been negotiated between such organisations will no doubt be relevant to the issue of its fairness. Where the terms have been imposed by the consumer rather than the supplier, it may be argued that the consumer had the opportunity to influence the substance of them so they should be regarded as having been individually negotiated,[542] but the better view is that this too should go to the question of fairness.

Where one or more terms (or aspects of a particular term) have been individually negotiated, but the rest of the contract has not been so negotiated, the Regulations will apply to the rest of the contract if, viewed as a whole, it is a "preformulated standard contract".[543] The burden of proof on the issue whether a term was individually negotiated is on the seller or supplier who seeks to rely on the term.[544]

(iii) *The test of unfairness*

The definition of an "unfair term"[545] is the aspect of the Regulations which is   7–103
likely to give rise to the greatest difficulty in their practical operation. A term is unfair "if, contrary to the requirement of good faith, it causes a significant imbalance in the parties' rights and obligations arising under the contract to the detriment of the consumer." The "twin requirements"[546] of "contrary to good faith" and "significant imbalance" standing alone[547] would clearly be a source of considerable uncertainty, and the courts and the Regulations have sought in the ways dealt with below to reduce this uncertainty.

Factors to be taken into account. The Regulations direct the court to take   7–104
into account or to refer to a number of factors.[548] One such factor is "the nature of the goods or services for which the contract was concluded" so that, for example, a term which was not fair in a contract for the sale of new goods might

---

[541] See the word "therefore" in the definition quoted at fn.539, above.

[542] *Bryen & Langley Ltd v Boston* [2005] EWCA Civ 973; [2005] C.I.L.L. 2261 at [46], where the point was left open.

[543] reg.5(3).

[544] reg.5(4).

[545] In regs 5(1) and 6(1).

[546] *Director General of Fair Trading v First National Bank Plc* [2001] UKHL 52; [2002] 1 A.C. 481 at [12]; cf. [2002] 1 A.C. 481 at [36] per Lord Steyn.

[547] They are separate requirements, both of which must be met: *Director General of Fair Trading v First National Bank Plc* [2001] UKHL 52; [2002] 1 A.C. 481 at [17], [36]; *Bryen & Langley Ltd v Boston* [2005] EWCA Civ 973; [2005] C.I.L.L. 2261 at [44]; *UK Housing Alliance Ltd v Francis* [2010] EWCA Civ 117; [2010] 3 All E.R. 519 at [21]–[22]; cf. *Munkenbeck & Marshall v Harold* [2005] EWHC 356 (TCC) at [15] where it appears that the finding of unfairness was based on significant imbalance alone, and see the doubt expressed in *Maple Leaf Macro Volatility Master Fund v Rouvroy* [2009] EWHC 257 (Comm); [2009] 1 Lloyd's Rep. 475, at [273] (affirmed without reference to this point [2009] EWCA Civ 1334). It may be that the level of unfairness under one is sufficient to satisfy the other: see Bright, in Burrows & Peel (eds), *Contract Terms*.

[548] regs 5(1) and 6(1).

be fair if the goods were sold as being second hand. The court is also directed to refer "to all the circumstances attending the conclusion of the contract" as at the time of its conclusion: here the fact that the consumer had examined goods before deciding to buy them would be relevant; and in a contract for the supply of services it would be relevant that, when the contract was made, the consumer was in a position to appreciate the risk that the services might fail to achieve the desired purpose. It is significant that the Regulations refer at this point to the time of the conclusion of the contract, thus supporting the view that the issue of fairness (like that of reasonableness under the 1977 Act[549]) is to be determined by reference to the time of contracting.[550] Finally, the court is directed to take into account "all the other terms of the contract or of another contract on which it is dependent".[551] The point here is that a term which might, standing alone, appear to be unfair could be fair having regard to the structure or system of rights and immunities created by the contract as a whole. It might, for example, be fair for a supplier who undertook liabilities beyond those imposed under a particular type of contract at common law to require notice of claims in respect of such liabilities to be given within a period shorter than the normal period of limitation for claims of the kind in question. The words "or of another contract on which it is dependent" would apply similar reasoning to the case in which the particular contract in question was made under a "master contract" governing a series of transactions between the parties.

7–105   Exclusion of "main subject-matter" and "adequacy of price". Regulation 6(2) provides that

> "In so far as it is in plain intelligible language, the assessment of fairness of a term shall not relate (a) to the definition of the main subject-matter of the contract, or (b) to the adequacy of the price or remuneration, as against the goods or services supplied in exchange."

This provision may be compared with a number of common law principles discussed elsewhere in this book. The most important of these principles is that the court will not, as a general rule, investigate the adequacy of consideration.[552] A term is not unfair for the purposes of the Regulations merely because it fixes a price or remuneration which may be regarded as "excessive" by the application of some objective standard of valuation.[553] Conversely, the Regulations leave it open to the parties to define the subject-matter of the contract: in this respect, they resemble the common law rules discussed earlier in this chapter,[554] under which there would be no breach at all, even though the subject-matter was in some objective sense defective, if what was supplied was what the parties had contracted about: e.g. where the contract was simply to supply "seed" rather than "cabbage seed" and the seed, when planted, disappointed the buyer's expectation of yielding a crop of cabbages.[555] Similarly, in the case of the hostess who asked a supplier to "send me peas or if you haven't got peas send me beans, but for heaven's sake send

---

[549] s.11(1).
[550] *UK Housing Alliance Ltd v Francis* [2010] EWCA Civ 117; [2010] 3 All E.R. 519 at [27].
[551] See *Domsalla v Dyason* [2007] EWHC 1174 (TCC) at [77].
[552] See above, para.3–013.
[553] cf. below, para.10–049.
[554] See above, para.7–028.
[555] Example based on the *George Mitchell* case [1983] 2 A.C. 803; above, para.7–028.

something",[556] the term allowing the supplier to make such a choice would not appear to fall within the Regulations.[557]

A further group of terms excluded from control on the principle of reg.6(2) consists of terms in insurance contracts which "clearly define or circumscribe the insured risk and the insurer's liability".[558] This exclusion is, however, narrower in scope than the exclusion of "any contract of insurance" from the 1977 Act.[559] Terms in an insurance contract, other than those which define its subject-matter,[560] would be within the Regulations, though not within the Act. This would, for example, be true of a clause requiring the consumer to give notice of claims within an unreasonably short period: such a clause could be prima facie unfair on the ground that it "hindered" the consumer's right to take legal action.[561]

"Core" and "ancillary" provisions. Regulation 6(2) is of crucial importance   **7–106** in recognising the parties' freedom of contract with respect to the essential features of their bargain. It is limited by the words of the regulation to cases in which the term in question is "expressed in plain, intelligible language". Hence an obscurely expressed price term which, on its true construction unexpectedly entitled the supplier to make additions to a price prominently stated elsewhere in the contractual document could, by reason of its obscurity, be an "unfair" term. The courts are reluctant to give too wide a scope to reg. 6(2) since the effect of doing this would be to except too great a range of contract terms from the scope of the Regulations so that their object would be "plainly frustrated".[562] A term which specifies payments to be made by the consumer is not necessarily one which relates to "the adequacy of the price or remuneration" within reg.6(2)(b).[563] It depends upon the construction of the contract. The point may be illustrated by reference to a consumer credit agreement, in which a term specifying the rate of interest would no doubt fall within these words; but in *Director General of Fair Trading v First National Bank Plc*[564] the House of Lords held that they did not cover a term requiring the borrower to pay interest on outstanding amounts, even after judgment had been given against him for the principal sum, since this term was "ancillary"[565] to his principal obligation (it was not a "core provision"). The term was therefore subject to the Regulations, though it was found not to be unfair, for the reasons which are explained below.[566]

The requirement of considering the adequacy of the price or remuneration "as against"[567] the subject-matter of the contract could similarly restrict the concept

---

[556] See above, para.7–028.

[557] The term would not be even prima facie unfair (as one enabling the seller unilaterally to alter the characteristics of the product to be provided (within reg.5(2) and Sch.2, para.1(k)) since this product was defined by the contract not as "peas" but as "peas or beans or something".

[558] See Dir.93/13, Recital 19.

[559] 1977 Act, Sch.1, para.1(a).

[560] cf. *Bankers Ins Co v South* [2004] EWHC 380 (QB); [2004] Lloyd's Rep I.R. 1 (exclusion of jet ski injury part of definition of main subject-matter and written in plain and intelligible language).

[561] 1999 Regs, Sch.2, para.1(q).

[562] *Director General of Fair Trading v First National Bank Plc* [2001] UKHL 52; [2002] 1 A.C. 481 at [12]; cf. 2002] 1 A.C. 481 at [34].

[563] Formerly reg.3(2)(b) of the 1994 Regs considered in the case cited in fn.562, above.

[564] [2001] UKHL 52; [2002] 1 A.C. 481; Macdonald (2002) 65 M.L.R. 763; Whittaker (2004) ZEuP 75.

[565] ibid. at [12].

[566] See below, para.7–108.

[567] reg.6(2)(b).

of a "core provision" and hence of reg.6(2)(b). The point may be illustrated by reference to the case in which a contract for the hire of goods for a fixed period provides that the hirer is to pay a "holding charge" if he retains the goods after the end of the stipulated period.[568] Although such a provision could be described as the "price" of an option to extend the period of hire,[569] it could also be regarded as "ancillary"[570] to the main object of the contract; or as fixing the "price", not of what was to be supplied, but of the option described above.[571] The provision would then be subject to the Regulations and, if the charge were unusually high, the term requiring it to be paid could be regarded as "unfair" within them. Indeed, the example comes very close to one of the illustrations given in Sch.2 of prima facie unfair terms.[572]

7–107   **Bank charges case.** While accepting that reg.6(2)(b) should be construed restrictively, in *Office of Fair Trading v Abbey National Plc*[573] the Supreme Court did not think that the distinction between "core bargain" and "ancillary provisions" should be pressed too far. In particular, it rejected the view of the courts below[574] that the distinction between the two should be determined from the perspective of the typical consumer. In that case, a challenge was made to the fairness of the terms under which banks charge a customer for services provided when the customer's account exceeds an authorised borrowing limit. The Court of Appeal had held that such charges were not part of the price for the services provided because they would not have been viewed by the customer as part of the "core bargain". To draw an analogy with the example given in the preceding paragraph, from the typical consumer's perspective the main object of the contract with the bank was to run an account in credit for which the price was the foregoing of interest on the sums in the account, or the payment of a low rate of interest; the charges levied on unauthorised borrowing were the "price" for the option of the services provided when the account was overdrawn. That view was rejected on the basis that it departed from the "natural"[575] or "objective"[576] meaning of the text of reg.6(2). Viewed objectively, what the banks provided was a package of services, including unauthorised borrowing, for which a price was payable. It was irrelevant that the charges for services provided when an account exceeded its authorised borrowing limit were contingent and might not ever *be paid* by the majority of customers. The banks' charging structures had to be in "plain intelligible language", but since it had been found that they were,[577] there could

---

[568] See *Interfoto Picture Library Ltd v Stiletto Visual Programmes Ltd* [1989] Q.B. 433; above, para.7–047.

[569] cf. below, para.20–144.

[570] Above, at fn.565.

[571] cf. *Bairstow Eves London Central Ltd v Darlingtons* [2004] EWHC 263; [2004] 2 E.G.L.R. 25 (term allowing for estate agent's commission of 1.5 per cent if payment made early, or of 3 per cent plus interest if payment made late held not to fall within reg.6(2)).

[572] Sch.2, para.1(l); above, fn.523.

[573] [2009] UKSC 6; [2010] 1 A.C. 696; Whittaker 74 M.L.R. 106; Chen-Wishart 126 L.Q.R. 157.

[574] [2008] EWHC 875 (Comm); [2008] 2 All ER (Comm) 625 (Andrew Smith J.); [2009] EWCA Civ 116; [2009] 2 W.L.R. 1286 (the decision of the Court of Appeal was followed by Mann J. in *Office of Fair Trading v Foxtons Ltd* [2009] EWHC 1681 (Ch); [2009] 29 E.G. 98).

[575] [2009] UKSC 6; [2010] 1 A.C. 696 at [45]

[576] ibid. at [113].

[577] At first instance by Andrew Smith J., save in "relatively minor respects" (at [293]): [2008] EWHC 875 (Comm); [2008] 2 All ER (Comm) 625). There was no appeal from his finding in this regard, nor that this is to be assessed from the perspective of the typical consumer: at [103], [119].

be no challenge to the fairness of the terms, at least on grounds of the appropriateness of the amount of the charges themselves.[578]

In reaching its decision, the Supreme Court did not cast any doubt on the correctness of the decision of the House of Lords in the *First National Bank* case (nor that of Gross J. in *Bairstow Eves London Central Ltd v Darlingtons*[579]). It seems that they can be distinguished on the basis that they both concerned "default" provisions.[580] This seems to introduce into the scope of reg.6(2)(b) the same sort of limit which determines the scope of the rule against penalties, i.e. that it only applies to payments to be made upon breach of the contract and not to analogous provisions where no breach is involved, e.g. price variation clauses.[581] But this limit to the scope of the rule against penalties is vulnerable to manipulation by a skilled draftsman and it has been said that the courts will be alive to the possibility of a disguised penalty clause.[582] A similar sentiment can be detected in the view of the Court of Appeal in the *Abbey National* case that the banks' charges were "akin to default charges".[583] That view was rejected by the Supreme Court[584] and it is this which explains the decision to allow the banks' appeal. Nonetheless, the distinction between default provisions, or those which are "akin to default", and those which are genuinely part of the "price" may be no easier to draw than (or very different from) the distinction between "core" and "ancillary" provisions.[585]

Significant imbalance. In the *First National Bank* case, Lord Bingham stated that:[586]   7–108

---

[578] This is on the basis that what is excluded by reg. 6(2)(b) is any assessment of a price term for fairness by reference to its adequacy as payment for the goods or services provided in exchange and not any assessment of the term itself. This distinction between "excluded assessment" and "excluded term" which was drawn by Andrew Smith J. at first instance was accepted by both parties in the appeal courts. For criticism, see Whittaker 74 M.L.R. 1, based, in part, on the apparently contradictory reasoning of the European Court of Justice in Case 484/08 *Caja de Ahorros y Monte de Piedad de Madrid v Asociación de Usuarios de Servicios Bancarios (Ausbanc)*, June 3, 2010. It is difficult to see what other challenge was left open even on the basis of the "excluded assessment" approach; but see *Office of Fair Trading v Ashbourne Management Services Ltd* [2011] EWHC 1237 (Ch) (dealing with reg.6(2)(a)).

[579] See above, fn.571.

[580] [2009] UKSC 6; [2010] 1 A.C. 696 at [32], [43], [102], [113] (and see the *First National Bank* case, above fn.562, at [12] per Lord Bingham, [34] per Lord Steyn).

[581] See below, para.20–144. In this sense, the material decision in the bank charges case may have been that of Andrew Smith J. at first instance ([2008] EWHC 875 (Comm), [2008] 2 All ER (Comm) 625, from which there was no appeal), who found that the rule against penalties did not apply because there was no breach by a customer who exceeded the authorised borrowing limit; note the observation by counsel for the banks which is picked up by Lord Phillips, at [83].

[582] Most notably by Bingham L.J. in the *Interfoto* case, above fn.568 and it is Lord Bingham in the *First National Bank* case who makes the distinction between "core provisions" and "ancillary provisions".

[583] [2009] EWCA Civ 116 at [107].

[584] "When the relevant facts are viewed as a whole, it seems clear that the Relevant Charges are not concealed default charges designed to discourage customers from overdrawing on their accounts without prior arrangement", at [88] per Lord Phillips; cf. *Ashbourne* case, above fn.578 at [152].

[585] There was a difference of opinion between the Law Lords on whether the interpretation of reg.6(2) was acte clair but no reference to the European Court of Justice was found to be necessary on the basis that, even if the interpretation of the Court of Appeal was correct, the charges were still part of the "core bargain", i.e. the decision was one based on the *application* of reg.6(2)(b) which is a matter for the national court: at [50], [117], [120].

[586] [2001] UKHL 52; [2002] 1 A.C. 481 at [17]

> "The requirement of significant imbalance is met if a term is so weighted in favour of the supplier as to tilt the parties' rights and obligations under the contract significantly in his favour. This may be by the granting to the supplier of a beneficial option or discretion or power, or by the imposing on the consumer of a disadvantageous burden or risk or duty."

The emphasis is on the "substantive fairness of the contract",[587] but the proposition that "significant imbalance" is concerned with "substantive fairness" and "good faith" with "procedural fairness", and any distinction between the two, should not be over-stated: "there is a large area of overlap between the concepts of good faith and significant imbalance."[588]

In the *First National Bank* case itself there was no significant imbalance in the term requiring the borrower to pay interest on outstanding amounts, even after judgment had been given against him for the principal sum. Neither party could have supposed that the bank would willingly forgo any part of its principal or interest and the borrower's obligation to repay the principal in full with interest, was very clearly and unambiguously expressed in the conditions of contract; the absence of such a term would have unbalanced the contract to the detriment of the lender.[589] The obligation to pay interest after judgment could catch out borrowers who failed to appreciate its significance when they agreed to pay the judgment debt over a period of time by instalments. Any "unfairness" in this respect was the result not of the term in question, but of borrowers not being aware of the statutory procedures available under which they might apply for the underlying agreement to be amended, including the obligation to pay post-judgment interest, at least in relation to "regulated agreements".[590]

7–109   **Good faith.** The requirement of good faith has been described in the *First National Bank* case as "one of fair and open dealing".[591] Openness here refers to the way in which terms are set out: they must be "expressed fully, clearly and legibly, containing no concealed pitfalls or traps" and giving due "prominence to terms which might operate disadvantageously to the customer".[592] Fairness requires the supplier not

> "whether deliberately or unconsciously, [to] take advantage of the consumer's necessity, indigence, lack of experience, unfamiliarity with the subject-matter of the contract, [or] weak bargaining position. Good faith in this context looks to . . . good standards of commercial morality and practice."[593]

The Directive on which the Regulations are based further lists, among factors relevant to good faith,

---

[587] Collins 14 O.J.L.S. 229 at 249.
[588] *First National Bank* case, above fn.586 at [37]
[589] ibid. at [20]
[590] Consumer Credit Act 1974, ss.129, 136.
[591] [2001] UKHL 52; [2002] 1 A.C. 481 at [17].
[592] ibid.
[593] ibid.; *Bryen & Langley Ltd v Boston* [2005] EWCA Civ 973; [2005] C.I.L.L. 2261 at [46]; *UK Housing Alliance Ltd v Francis* [2010] EWCA Civ 117; [2010] 3 All E.R. 519 at [28]; *Turner & Co (GB) Ltd v Abi* [2010] EWHC 2078 (QB) at [45].

"the strength of the bargaining positions of the parties, whether the consumer had an inducement to agree to the term and whether the goods or services were supplied to the special order of the consumer".[594]

It is probably impossible, and inappropriate,[595] to achieve greater precision in formulating such an essentially flexible requirement.

(iv) *Examples of unfair terms*

The Regulations contain (in Sch.2) a long and elaborate list of terms "which   **7–110** *may* be regarded as unfair"[596]; this list in effect provides further guidelines. It is "indicative and non-exhaustive",[597] so that, on the one hand, a term is not unfair merely because it is of a type included in the list; and, on the other hand, a term may be unfair even though it does not fall within, or closely resemble, any such type of term.

Terms also amounting to exemption clauses within the 1977 Act. It will   **7–111** be convenient to refer to terms included in the list as "prima facie unfair terms". Some of the prima facie unfair terms listed in Sch.2 would also be classified as exemption clauses within the 1977 Act. Like the Act, Sch.2 distinguishes between clauses which exclude or limit liability for death or personal injury and other clauses excluding or limiting rights: any term of the former kind is prima facie unfair,[598] while in the case of a term of the latter kind there is the additional requirement that it must "inappropriately" exclude or limit the consumer's rights.[599] The list in Sch.2 also includes terms "limiting" the seller's or supplier's obligation to respect commitments undertaken by his agents[600]: such terms would clearly be regarded as an exemption clause under the Act. The fact that the Schedule at this point refers only to terms "limiting" the obligation would not preclude a clause which *excluded* it from being also regarded as prima facie unfair: this follows from the fact that the list is not exhaustive.

Other types of terms listed in Sch.2, which would also be governed by the 1977 Act, are clauses entitling the seller or supplier to dissolve the contract at his discretion where the same facility is not granted to the consumer,[601] to terminate a contract of indeterminate duration without reasonable notice (except on serious grounds),[602] to alter the terms of the contract unilaterally without a valid reason which is specified in the contract[603] or to alter unilaterally without a valid reason

---

[594] Dir.93/13, Recital 16. These guidelines were formerly contained in Sch.2 to the 1994 Regulations (above, para.7–092) but they are not reproduced in the 1999 Regulations. They are clearly equally applicable to both: *UK Housing Alliance Ltd v Francis* [2010] EWCA Civ 117; [2010] 3 All E.R. 519 at [22].

[595] *Director General of Fair Trading v First National Bank Plc* [2001] UKHL 52; [2002] 1 A.C. 481 at [45] per Lord Hope; *Domsalla v Dyason* [2007] EWHC 1174 (TCC) at [78]; *Maple Leaf Macro Volatility Master Fund v Rouvroy* [2009] EWHC 257 (Comm); [2009] 1 Lloyd's Rep. 475 at [272]–[275].

[596] reg.5(5), emphasis added.

[597] ibid.

[598] Sch.2, para.1(a).

[599] Sch.2, para.1(b). There is no reference to negligence in these illustrations.

[600] Sch.2, para.1(n).

[601] Sch.2, para.1(f); cf. 1977 Act, s.3(2)(b)(ii).

[602] Sch.2, para.1(g), subject to Sch.2, para.2(a) and (c); cf. 1977 Act, s.3(2)(b)(ii).

[603] Sch.2, para.1(k); cf. 1977 Act, s.3(2)(b)(i).

any characteristic of the product or service to be provided[604]: all such terms could be subject to the requirement of reasonableness under s.3 of the 1977 Act.[605] Yet other terms listed in Sch.2 which would be classified as exemption clauses under the Act are terms which make the seller's or supplier's commitments subject to compliance with a particular formality,[606] and terms giving him the right to determine whether the goods or services supplied are in conformity with the contract, or giving him the exclusive right to interpret the contract[607]: all such terms could be treated, for the purpose of the 1977 Act, as exemption clauses on the ground that they made the enforcement of the seller's or supplier's liability "subject to restrictive or onerous conditions" within s.13 of that Act.

7–112   **Arbitration and adjudication clauses.** Terms "excluding or hindering"[608] the consumer's right to take legal action or exercise any other legal remedy are included in the list of prima facie unfair terms.[609] In this context, the list refers, in particular, to terms "requiring the consumer to take disputes exclusively to arbitration not covered by legal provisions."[610] At first sight, this goes beyond the Act, which, while recognising that a term excluding or restricting a remedy may be an exemption clause,[611] expressly excepts arbitration agreements from this category.[612] The reference to arbitration clauses in Sch.2 is, however, restricted by the words "not covered by legal provisions" and the purpose of this restriction may be to narrow the category of prima facie unfair arbitration clauses to those in which the parties have agreed to exclude the powers of the courts to control the arbitrator's decision. In English law, the effectiveness of such a stipulation is subject to limitations which, in the case of a "domestic arbitration agreement", make the stipulation ineffective if it is contained in the original contract between the seller or supplier and the consumer.[613]

7–113   **Terms not amounting to exemption clauses.** Schedule 2 also refers to many varieties of terms which would not be regarded as exemption clauses under the Act or at common law, and it is this aspect of the Schedule which is significant in indicating the potentially wide scope of the Regulations. The list in Sch.2 in particular includes many types of terms which confer rights (other than rights of cancellation) on the seller or supplier.

Some such clauses might, indeed, be ineffective at common law on grounds discussed elsewhere in this book. This might, for example, be true of a term making an agreement binding on the consumer while making performance by the

---

[604] Sch.2, para.1(j), subject to Sch.2, para.2(b) and (c); cf. 1977 Act, s.3(2)(b)(i).

[605] See above, paras 7–068—7–069.

[606] Sch.2, para.1(n); it is not clear whether the concluding words of this illustration are limited to commitments undertaken by agents.

[607] Sch.2, para.1(m).

[608] Sch.2, para.1(q).

[609] For the application of the Regulations to adjudication clauses in construction contracts: see *Picardi v Cuniberti* [2002] EWHC 2923; *Zealander v Laing Homes Ltd* (2003) 19 Const. L.J. 350; *Bryen & Langley Ltd v Boston* [2005] EWCA Civ 973; [2005] C.I.L.L. 2261.

[610] Sch.2, para.1(q); the Arbitration Act 1996, s.91 and the Unfair Arbitration Agreements (Specified Amounts) Order 1999 (SI 1999/2167), makes any arbitration agreement with a consumer unfair where less than £5,000 is claimed. For agreements not deemed unfair under these provisions, but assessed for fairness under the Regulations, see: *Heifer International Inc v Christiansen* [2007] EWHC 3015 (TCC); *Mylcrist Builders Ltd v Buck* [2008] EWHC 2172 (TCC)

[611] 1977 Act, s.13(1)(b).

[612] 1977 Act, s.13(2).

[613] Arbitration Act 1996, s.87; below, para.11–050.

seller or supplier subject to a condition depending on his own will alone[614]: at common law there might in such a case be no consideration for the consumer's promise so long as the seller's or supplier's promise remained executory.[615] Similarly, the list includes a term requiring the consumer, when in breach, to pay a disproportionately high sum in compensation[616]: at common law, such a term is likely to be invalid as a penalty.[617] The same might be true of terms entitling the seller to forfeit a deposit paid by the consumer[618]: these again might in certain circumstances be invalid as penalties at common law.[619]

Terms not subject to any other form of legal control. A significant   7–114 number of prima facie unfair terms listed in Sch.2 are, however, of a kind that has not, apart from the Regulations, been subjected to legal control, at least as a matter of general principle, either at common law or by legislation (other than legislation applying to specific types of contract). One type of term within this group is automatically extending a contract of fixed duration unless the consumer gives notice to terminate it, where the time for giving such notice is unreasonably early[620]: in contracts outside the scope of the Regulations, there appears to be no ground on which the validity of such a term could be called into question at common law or under the 1977 Act. The same is true of another type of prima facie invalid term listed in Sch.2, i.e. one "providing for the price of goods to be determined at the time of delivery"[621] or one providing for the price of goods or services to be increased without giving the consumer the right to cancel if the final price is too high in relation to the originally agreed price.[622] There is no reason to suppose that such a clause is open to attack at common law and even its prima facie invalidity under the Regulations is extensively qualified in relation to transactions in which the price is linked to stock exchange fluctuations or which contain other indexation clauses; and in relation to contracts for the purchase of foreign currency or instruments expressed in foreign currency.[623] Yet another type of prima facie unfair term is that obliging the consumer "to fulfil all his obligations where the seller or supplier does not perform his".[624] A clause excluding the consumer's right of set-off would no doubt be regarded as an exemption clause for the purposes of the 1977 Act[625]; but the same would not be true of a clause which so defined the consumer's obligation that he had *no* right of set-off but only a cross-claim for damages in respect of the other party's default.[626] Again, a term is prima facie invalid within Sch.2 if it gives the seller or supplier "the possibility of transferring his rights and obligations under the contract where this may serve to reduce the guarantees for the consumer without the latter's agreement".[627] At

---

[614] Sch.2, para.1(c). Some terms conferring such rights can be exemption clauses under s.3 of the 1977 Act: see text at fn.601, above.

[615] See above, para.3–030.

[616] Sch.2, para.1(e).

[617] See below, para.20–130. But see: *Munkenbeck & Marshall v Harold* [2005] EWHC 356 (TCC) (term not a penalty, but found to be unfair).

[618] Sch.2, para.1(d).

[619] See below, para.20–149.

[620] Sch.2, para.1(h).

[621] Sch.2, para.1(l).

[622] Sch.2, para.1(l)

[623] Sch.2, para.2(c) and (d).

[624] Sch.2, para.1(o).

[625] See above, para.7–054.

[626] See below, para.17–019.

[627] Sch.2, para.1(p).

common law the seller or supplier could not strictly transfer his obligations, though he might arrange for them to be vicariously performed,[628] and he could certainly transfer his rights by assignment[629]; and these powers would not seem at common law to be limited by the possibility that this would impair the consumer's guarantees. A term expressly limiting the effectiveness of guarantees given by the seller or supplier would no doubt be subject to control as an exemption clause, but that is not the type of term here under consideration. Yet another prima facie invalid term is one which has the object or effect of "irrevocably binding the consumer to terms with which he had no real opportunity of becoming acquainted before the conclusion of the contract".[630] This may already represent the common law position with regard to the incorporation of standard terms by notice[631]; but at first sight, it differs strikingly from the common law rule governing the incorporation of such terms by signature. The latter common law rule is, however, concerned with the effect of *signature*,[632] rather than with *terms specifying that effect*. If a consumer signed a document containing a term incorporating by reference conditions set out in another document, then *that term* could be prima facie unfair under the Regulations if the other document was not readily accessible to the consumer.

(v) *Excluded terms*

7–115   **Statutory or regulatory provisions.** The Regulations do not apply to contractual terms which reflect "mandatory statutory or regulatory provisions".[633] The effect of these words is that the Regulations do not apply to terms which a contract is by other legislation required to contain.[634] The 1977 Act is subject to a similar, but more broadly expressed, limitation: it does not apply to contractual provisions "*authorised or* required"[635] by legislation. The use of the word "mandatory"[636] in the Regulations seems to mean that the exception in them does not extend to provisions which are merely authorised but not required by other legislation; though the fact that they are so authorised would no doubt be taken into account in determining whether they were "unfair". For example, the Consumer Credit Act 1974 at least by implication authorises a term in a regulated hire-purchase agreement requiring the hirer on exercising his right to cancel to make a minimum payment not exceeding one half of the hire-purchase price.[637] If that sum is excessive, the hirer can seek relief by way of reduction of the minimum payment under the 1974 Act[638]; and an undesirable conflict would be created

---

[628] See below, para.17–008.
[629] See below, Ch.15.
[630] Sch.2, para.1(i).
[631] See above, paras 7–005—7–010.
[632] See above, para.7–004.
[633] reg.4(2)(a).
[634] e.g. below, para.7–126. This will cover terms implied by statute. So far as terms implied at common law are concerned, since they must be reasonable it is hard to see how they could ever be found to be unfair, but the view has been expressed that the Regulations do not apply at all to such terms: *Office of Fair Trading v Abbey National Plc* [2008] EWHC 875 (Comm); [2008] 2 All ER (Comm) 625 at [102]; *Baybut v Eccle Riggs Country Park Ltd, The Times*, November 13, 2006.
[635] s.29(1)(a).
[636] Above, at fn.633.
[637] s.100(1).
[638] s.100(3); below, para.20–145.

between that Act and the Regulations if, under them, such a term were held to be "unfair" (and so not binding at all on the hirer).

International conventions. The Regulations also do not apply to contractual 7–116 terms which reflect "the provisions or principles of international conventions to which the Member States or the Community are party".[639] Again this exclusion resembles a similar limitation on the scope of the 1977 Act.[640] The exclusion is, however, wider than that contained in the Act in two respects. First, it refers to international conventions to which the Member States or the Community are party (while the Act refers only to international agreements to which the UK is a party). Secondly, the Regulations refer to "the provisions *or principles*" of such conventions, so that a term based on the principles of a relevant convention would not be governed by the Regulations even though the contract in which the term was contained was not governed by the convention: e.g. where a term in a contract for the domestic carriage of goods was based on the principles of a convention which in terms governed only international carriage.

Unlike the 1977 Act,[641] the Regulations contain no exception for international supply contracts; but it seems that contracts governed by the Vienna Convention on Contracts for the International Sale of Goods[642] would fall within the present exception. The point is not likely to be of major importance since the Regulations apply only to consumer contracts, and these will only rarely (if ever) be governed by the Convention.[643] But where the Convention does govern such contracts, the parties are allowed by it to "derogate" from or vary its provisions,[644] and thus a seller can exclude or restrict liability which, but for such derogation, would be imposed on him by the Convention. This appears to be one of the "principles" of the Convention, so that the Regulations would not apply to a term of this kind in such a contract.

(vi) *Excluded contracts*

The Directive on which the Regulations are based lists a number of contracts 7–117 which "must be *excluded* from this Directive".[645] The most important of the contracts excluded by the Directive are contracts "relating to employment".[646] This exclusion differs from the corresponding provision of the 1977 Act, some of the provisions of which do not extend to contracts of employment "except in favour of the employee".[647] Under the Directive, even the employee cannot rely on the unfairness of a term against the employer: the problems arising from such terms are left to be dealt with by employment law or perhaps by collective bargaining. The Directive also excludes "contracts relating to succession rights"

---

[639] reg.4(2)(b); for definitions of "Member States" and "the Community," see reg.3(1).
[640] s.29(1)(b).
[641] 1977 Act, s.26.
[642] The Convention has not yet been ratified by the UK.
[643] Art.2(a) of the Vienna Convention; Art.1, referring to "places of business," may suggest that the Convention does not apply to consumer contracts at all.
[644] Art.6 of the Vienna Convention.
[645] Dir.93/13, Recital 10. Unlike the 1994 Regulations this list is not reproduced in the 1999 Regulations, but it is "uncontentious" that the scope of the Regulations is to be determined by the scope of the Directive: *R. (Khatun) v Newham LBC* [2004] EWCA Civ 55; [2005] Q.B. 37 at [56].
[646] ibid.
[647] 1977 Act, Sch.1, para.4. And see *Commerzbank AG v Keen* [2006] EWCA Civ 1536; [2007] I.C.R. 623; above, para.7–067, fn.359, restricting the scope of s.3.

or to "any contract relating to rights under family law"[648]; but these exceptions are unlikely to be of great practical importance in English law, which seems to provide no examples of such contracts being made between a seller or supplier acting in the course of business and a consumer. The Directive finally excludes "contracts relating to the incorporation and organisation of companies or partnership agreements".[649] This resembles a similar exclusion from the operation of the 1977 Act.[650]

(vii) Drafting and interpretation

7–118   **Plain and intelligible language.** Regulation 7 provides that "(1) A seller or supplier shall ensure that any written term of a contract is expressed in plain, intelligible language" and "(2) If there is doubt about the meaning of a written term, the interpretation most favourable to the consumer shall prevail . . . ".[651] The restriction of these requirements to terms in writing indicates that oral contracts are covered by the Regulations[652] but (curiously) they are not required to be in plain or intelligible language. Failure to express a written term "in plain, intelligible language" does not of itself make the term even prima facie unfair. In this respect the present requirement is weaker than that already noted, by which a term defining the price or subject-matter of the contract must be in "plain intelligible language"[653]: here the sanction for failure to comply with the requirement is that the term may be considered unfair. The words of reg.7(2), quoted above, appear to be no more than a legislative formulation of the *contra proferentem* principle.[654] No doubt this will most commonly apply to terms which are not drafted in plain, intelligible language; but it does not appear to be restricted to such terms. Language which is plain and intelligible may nevertheless be ambiguous; the fascination of oracular statements lies precisely in the fact that they combine these qualities.

(viii) Effects of unfairness

7–119   **Unfair term not binding on consumer.** Regulation 8(1) provides that "an unfair term in a contract concluded with a consumer by a seller or supplier shall not be binding on the consumer". The exact legal consequence of this regulation will depend on the nature of the unfair term. If that term is one excluding or limiting the liability of the seller or supplier, or the rights of the consumer,[655] the latter will be able to enforce those rights as if the term had not been included in the contract. If the unfair term is one conferring rights on the seller or supplier (such as one extending a contract of fixed duration without giving the consumer a reasonable opportunity of cancelling it[656]) these rights will not arise. If effect has been given to such rights, reg.8(1) may require those effects to be undone: e.g.

---

[648] Dir.93/13, Recital 10.
[649] ibid.
[650] 1977 Act, Sch.1, para.1(d).
[651] The concluding words of reg.7(2) make this provision inapplicable to proceedings for injunctions under reg.12 to prevent the continued use of unfair terms.
[652] cf. Dir.93/13, Recital 11.
[653] reg.3(2); above, para.7–105.
[654] See above, para.7–015.
[655] Under Sch.2, para.1(a) and (b).
[656] Under Sch.2, para.1(h).

where the term was unfair because it permitted the seller or supplier to retain sums paid by the consumer,[657] any such sums, if paid, would have to be restored. It is only the consumer who is not bound by the unfair term.[658] The other party is so bound: e.g. he may be bound by a term extending a contract of fixed duration[659] if the consumer should wish to enforce that term.

Rest of contract generally unaffected. In general, the fact that the unfair **7–120** term does not bind the consumer does not affect the binding force, even on the consumer, of the rest of the contract: e.g. the fact that he is not bound by an exemption clause does not relieve him from liability for the price (though such liability may be reduced to the extent that a breach covered by the ineffective clause has caused him loss). The point is put beyond doubt by reg.8(2), which provides that "the contract shall continue to bind the parties if it is capable of continuing in existence without the unfair term". The reason for the concluding words of this provision is that sometimes an invalid term goes so much to the heart of the contract that the effect of its not being binding on the consumer is likely to be that the consumer is not bound by the contract at all. This would, for example, be the position where the term was unfair because it irrevocably bound the consumer "to terms with which he had no real opportunity of becoming acquainted before the conclusion of the contract".[660] If that term was not binding on the consumer, it would seem to follow that the terms to which it referred[661] were not binding on him either; and if those terms contained the whole or the essential part of the contract he would not be bound by any part of that contract. The other party would, however, be so bound if the consumer wished to enforce the contract: the argument that the consumer had provided no consideration because his own promises were not binding would probably be rejected on the ground that it was not the policy of the Regulations to protect the other party.[662] The question whether a term goes so much to the heart of the contract that the effect of its not being binding on the consumer is to relieve him of all obligations under the contract is obviously in borderline cases one of degree. The point may be illustrated by reference to a term which is prima facie unfair because it provides for the price of goods to be determined at the time of delivery without giving the consumer the right to cancel if that price is "too high in relation to the price agreed [if any?] when the contract was concluded".[663] One possible consequence of the consumer's taking the point that the term is not binding is that the contract contains no price term and is therefore not binding on him at all; another is that the contract contains no price term but remains in being as one under which a reasonable price must be paid; and a third is that the contract remains in being as one under which the originally agreed price (if any) must be paid. No doubt the result will depend on the exact wording of the price term; but, subject to this point, it is submitted that the "reasonable price" solution will normally achieve the most satisfactory balance between the interests of the parties. There is, of course, nothing to prevent the consumer from enforcing the contract according to its terms where it is in his interest to do so.

---

[657] Under Sch.2, para.1(d).
[658] Case C-243/08 *Pannon GSM Zrt v Erzsébet Sustikné Györfi* June 4, 2009.
[659] See Sch.2, para.3(g).
[660] See Sch.2, para.1(i).
[661] See above, para.7–114.
[662] See above, para.3–154.
[663] See Sch.2, para.1(l); above, para.7–114.

7–121   **Comparison of effects of unfairness with 1977 Act.** The 1999 Regulations differ from the 1977 Act in that they lay down a single criterion (that of fairness[664]) on which the effectiveness of a term depends. Under that Act, by contrast, there are two possibilities: a term may be simply ineffective, or effective only insofar as it complies with the requirement of reasonableness. No difficulty arises from this difference in the situations (already discussed[665]) in which a term falls only within the scope of the Regulations or only within the scope of the Act. But where the same term falls within both legislative schemes there is the possibility that it may satisfy the requirements of the one but not those of the other. For example, a contract for the sale of goods to a consumer may contain a term limiting the seller's liability for breach of the terms implied by the Sale of Goods Act 1979 as to the quality of the goods. Such a term may be fair under the Regulations (which list among prima facie unfair terms those *"inappropriately* excluding or limit-ing"[666] the consumer's rights in respect of such terms) but it is simply ineffective under the Act.[667] Again, under the Regulations a term excluding or limiting liability for death or personal injury is only prima facie unfair,[668] while under the Act such a term is (if the defendant was negligent) simply ineffective.[669] The two schemes may also lead to different results where the same term is subject to a requirement of reasonableness under the Act and to one of fairness under the Regulations. No doubt in most cases a term which satisfied one of these require-ments would also satisfy the other; but it is possible to imagine situations in which this might not be true, particularly where the guidelines for determining reason-ableness under that Act differ from those for determining fairness under the Regulations.[670] A contract for the supply of services to a consumer might, for example, contain a term limiting the supplier's liability for breach to a specified sum of money, and this term might satisfy the requirement of reasonableness[671] under one of the guidelines applicable under the 1977 Act to such terms: e.g. on the ground that the supplier could not have insured against the breach without materially raising his charges.[672] But this guideline has no counterpart in the Regulations so that under them the term in question could nevertheless be an unfair one. In all such cases, in which the term falls within both the Act and the Regulations, the party relying on the term will have to show that the term satisfies the requirements of both these legislative schemes.

(ix) *Restriction on evasion*

7–122   **Choice of law.** Like the 1977 Act,[673] the Regulations protect the consumer against the risk of being deprived of his protection under them by means of a choice of law clause: they apply "notwithstanding any contract term which applies

---

[664] reg.8.
[665] See above, para.7–096 et seq.
[666] Sch.2, para.1(b).
[667] s.6(2).
[668] Sch.2, para.1(a).
[669] s.2(1).
[670] See above, para.7–103 et seq.
[671] Imposed by s.3 of the 1977 Act, or s.2(2) if the liability is for breach of a contractual duty of care (s.1(1)(a)).
[672] Imposed by s.3 of the 1977 Act, or s.2(2) if the liability is for breach of a contractual duty of care (s.1(1)(a)), s.11(4); above, para.7–080.
[673] s.27(2); above, para.7–087.

or purports to apply the law of a non–Member State, if the contract has a close connection with the territory of the Member States". Thus the Regulations cannot be excluded by a term specifying a law applicable *only* by virtue of being so specified, but they can be excluded by a term specifying a law which would or might have applied even in absence of the term. Certain of the provisions of the Rome I Regulation (which has already been discussed[674]) give similar protection to the consumer. The Regulations differ from the Act in that they do not except from their operation contracts governed by the law of a part of the UK only by virtue of the choice of the parties[675]; a consumer contract is perhaps thought unlikely to contain such a choice of law clause.

4. OTHER LEGISLATIVE TECHNIQUES

Simply to deprive an exemption clause of legal validity might be a wholly ineffective means of control, particularly in cases between consumers on the one hand and commercial suppliers of goods and services on the other. If, for example, a contract contained an invalid exemption clause the consumer might believe that he was bound by it and so not pursue his claim. Even if he did make a claim, the supplier might settle it so as to avoid a judicial declaration of invalidity, and then continue to use the clause. To remedy this situation other legislative techniques have been devised.

7–123

Supervised bargaining. This technique requires the bargain to be made under the supervision of the court or some administrative body. For example, the Landlord and Tenant Act 1985 provides that in certain leases covenants by the landlord to repair are implied.[676] These can be excluded but only by a court order made with the consent of both parties.[677] The court's supervision ensures that no unfair advantage is taken of the tenant.

7–124

Administrative control. This technique involves the intervention of a public authority with powers to enforce certain legislation.[678] It is a technique used by the Unfair Terms in Consumer Contracts Regulations 1999, which impose on the Office of Fair Trading[679] ("OFT") a duty to consider any complaint made to it that any contract term drawn up for general use is unfair[680]; a similar duty is imposed on certain "qualifying bodies" (listed in the Regulations) which have agreed to consider such complaints.[681] If it appears to the OFT (or to the qualifying body) that the term is unfair, the OFT (or that body after due notice to it) may apply to the court for an injunction to restrain the use of the term, and the court may grant the injunction on such terms as it thinks fit,[682] both to prevent

7–125

---

[674] See above, para.7–087.

[675] 1977 Act, s.27(1); above, para.7–094.

[676] s.11.

[677] Landlord and Tenant Act 1985, s.12.

[678] cf. National Minimum Wage Act 1998, s.19D.

[679] See Enterprise Act 2002, s.2(3), substituting the OFT for the reference in the Regulations to the Director General of Fair Trading, an office which is abolished by s.2(2) of that Act.

[680] reg.10.

[681] reg.11; "qualifying bodies" include a number of public bodies whose functions include the protection of consumers (Sch.1, Pt 1) and the Consumers' Association (Sch.1, Pt 2).

[682] reg.12. cf. Consumer Protection (Distance Selling) Regulations 2000 (SI 2000/2334), reg.27, implementing Dir.97/7; Late Payment of Commercial Debts Regulations 2002 (SI 2002/1674), reg.3, implementing Dir.2000/35.

the enforcement of the term in existing contracts, as well as future contracts.[683] The OFT and most of the qualifying bodies are also empowered to obtain information about the terms and use of any "pre-formulated contract in dealings with consumers",[684] and it is envisaged that the OFT and qualifying bodies may obtain undertakings from or on behalf of any person (such as a seller or supplier) as to the continued use of terms which it or the qualifying body considers to be unfair in contracts with consumers.[685] These provisions appear to be intended to promote negotiations between, on the one hand, the OFT and qualifying bodies, and, on the other, commercial sellers and suppliers or their trade associations. Such "pre-emptive challenges"[686] may well have greater practical effect than private litigation, initiated by consumers, in controlling unfair standard terms in consumer contracts.[687] A similar system of control is applied more generally as a consequence of Pt 8 of the Enterprise Act 2002,[688] under which the OFT and other bodies[689] are given powers to enforce certain consumer legislation.[690] An application for an "enforcement order" may be made in certain circumstances,[691] but it is envisaged that compliance will be secured by negotiation and, if necessary, by appropriate undertakings from the person or body under investigation.[692] The OFT and other enforcers are given considerable powers to request information and collect evidence.[693]

7–126   **Prescribing the contents of a contract.** This is another common method of controlling contracts of a particular type. It is well illustrated by the elaborate system of legislative control which exists in relation to regulated consumer credit agreements. To a considerable extent, the contents of such agreements are pre-scribed by the Consumer Credit Act 1974 and by delegated legislation[694]: the debtor is given a cooling-off period[695]; the creditor's power to terminate on the death of the debtor is restricted[696] and he can terminate for default only after giving a notice calling on the debtor to make good the default[697]; the debtor has the right to make early payment and thereby to earn certain rebates[698]; and in the

---

[683] *Office of Fair Trading v Foxtons Ltd* [2009] EWCA Civ 288; [2010] 1 W.L.R. 663.

[684] reg.13(3); the Consumers' Association is not given this power: see reg.13(2).

[685] regs 10(3) and 11(2).

[686] *Director General of Fair Trading v First National Bank Plc* [2001] UKHL 52; [2002] 1 A.C. 481 at [33].

[687] Under the 1999 Regulations, there are no criminal sanctions for the use of such terms.

[688] See also: the Consumer Protection from Unfair Trading Regulations 2008 (SI 2008/1277) breach of which may constitute a criminal offence, but will not render a contract void or unenforceable: above, para.9–001, fn.1; and the Regulatory Enforcement and Sanctions Act 2008, Pt.3.

[689] The OFT, and certain other bodies, are regarded as a "general enforcer"; the Secretary of State may also confer the status of "designated enforcer" on other persons or bodies: s.213, e.g. the Financial Services Authority (SI 2004/935).

[690] The 2002 Act differentiates between the infringement of domestic legislation (s.211) which could include the Unfair Contract Terms Act 1977 and of European Community legislation (s.212) which could include the 1999 Regulations.

[691] ss.212, 214.

[692] s.219.

[693] ss.224–227F.

[694] See above, para.5–007.

[695] s.67.

[696] s.86.

[697] s.87.

[698] ss.94, 95.

case of a regulated hire-purchase agreement he can terminate in certain circumstances on making prescribed payments.[699] Any term in such an agreement is void to the extent of its inconsistency with any such legislative provision for the protection of the debtor.[700] A number of other types of contracts are subject to similar detailed legislative control. These include contracts for the provision of package travel and similar facilities to consumers,[701] contracts with consumers concluded away from the trader's business premises,[702] and "distance contracts" with consumers.[703] A similar principle has been laid down by legislation regulating electronic commerce.[704] Where the customer places his order by "technological means"[705] (e.g. on a website) the service provider must make available to him "accessible"[706] means allowing the customer to identify and correct input errors before placing the order. Failure to comply with this requirement gives the customer the right to rescind the contract unless the court orders otherwise.[707]

---

[699] ss.99, 100.

[700] s.173. See *Wilson v Robertsons (London) Ltd* [2005] EWHC 1425; [2006] 1 W.L.R. 1248.

[701] Package Travel, Package Holidays and Package Tours Regulations 1992 (SI 1992/3288) (which compulsorily imply terms into such contracts and restrict the other party's ability to exclude his liability to the consumer).

[702] Cancellation of Contracts made in a Consumer's Home or Place of Work etc. Regulations (SI 2008/1816)

[703] Consumer Protection (Distance Selling) Regulations 2000 (SI 2000/2334), reg.10, implementing Dir.97/7. *cf.* Financial Services (Distant Marketing) Regulations 2004 (SI 2004/2095) (implementing Dir.2002/65 ([2002] O.J. L271/16).

[704] Electronic Commerce (EC Directive) Regulations 2002 (SI 2002/2013), implementing most of Dir.2000/31.

[705] SI 2002/2013, reg.11(1); contrast use of the phrase "electronic means" in reg.9(1).

[706] ibid., reg.11(1)(b).

[707] ibid., reg.15.

CHAPTER EIGHT

MISTAKE[1]

1. INTRODUCTION

8–001   In *Bell v Lever Bros Ltd*,[2] Lord Atkin said: "If mistake operates at all, it operates so as to negative or in some cases to nullify consent." Mistake *negatives* consent where it puts the parties at cross-purposes so as to prevent them from reaching agreement, e.g. because they intend to contract about different things. The cases which fall into this category are often referred to as cases of "unilateral mistake", though as we will see, in a few cases it is not possible to say which of the parties

---

[1] Champness, *Mistakes in the Law of Contract*; Palmer, *Mistake and Unjust Enrichment*; Stoljar, *Mistake and Misrepresentation*; Cartwright, *Misrepresentation, Mistake and Non-Disclosure* (2nd edn). Lawson 52 L.Q.R. 79; Tylor 11 M.L.R. 257; Wade 7 C.L.J. 361; Grunfeld 13 M.L.R. 50; 15 M.L.R. 297; Slade 70 L.Q.R. 385; Atiyah 73 L.Q.R. 340; Atiyah and Bennion 24 M.L.R. 421; Shatwell 33 Can. Bar Rev. 164; Bamford 72 S.A.L.J. 166, 282; Stoljar 28 M.L.R. 265; Sutton 7 N.Z.U.L.R. 40 (discussing possible reforms); Cartwright 103 L.Q.R. 594; Smith 110 L.Q.R. 400; other articles dealing specifically with mistakes as to identity are cited below, fn.178.

[2] [1932] A.C. 161 at 217.

is the "mistaken" party.[3] Mistake *nullifies* consent where the parties reach an agreement which is based on a fundamental mistaken assumption made by both of them, e.g. where a contract is made to paint a portrait of someone who, unknown to either party, has just died. The cases which fall into this category are usually referred to as cases of "common mistake".[4] At law, the effect of mistake is to make a contract void[5]; but this rule is confined within very narrow limits. It is thought to be in the interests of commercial convenience that, in general, apparent contracts should be enforced. Equity sometimes gives relief for mistakes which have no effect at common law; but the scope of such relief is restricted.[6] Certain special rules apply to documents mistakenly signed.

The effects of unilateral mistake go to the question of whether the parties have reached agreement and may be analysed as part of the rules on offer and acceptance.[7] The effects of common mistake go to the question of whether a contract has been formed where the parties have reached agreement, but have done so on the basis of a shared false premise and share some similarities with frustration.[8] In some respects therefore they are not that closely related to each other and might have been assessed separately in other parts of this book. They are assessed here because the cases raising the issues considered in this chapter are most naturally regarded as cases of "mistake" and it is preferable to begin by considering them from that perspective.

2. COMMON MISTAKE

(a) Common Law

(i) *In general*

Effect and techniques. In some cases, the courts have held that a contract entered into between the parties on the basis of a shared mistaken assumption is void. The conclusion reached in such cases is that the extreme injustice of holding one of the parties[9] to the contract outweighs the general principle that apparent contracts should be enforced.[10] The types of mistake which will render a contract void are sometimes referred to as "fundamental" mistakes and different techniques may be used to identify them. First, it may be asked whether there was an implied term that the validity of the contract depended on the existence of the state of affairs assumed to exist.[11] At one time, the implied term theory was used to explain the closely related doctrine of frustration,[12] but it fell out of favour and

8–002

---

[3] See below, para.8–042.

[4] They are also sometimes referred to as cases of "mutual mistake", but this is liable to confuse them with a particular category of unilateral mistake which is also referred to as mutual mistake, or mutual misunderstanding: see below, para.8–042.

[5] *Associated Japanese Bank (International) Ltd v Crédit du Nord SA* [1989] 1 W.L.R. 255 at 268.

[6] See below, para.8–029.

[7] See below, para.8–054.

[8] Though those similarities should not be pressed too far: see below, para.19–121.

[9] The mistake may have been shared but when discovered it will usually be to the advantage of one of the parties who will seek to enforce the contract.

[10] A further injustice can result in that any loss incurred by the parties in attempting to perform the contract before the mistake comes to light is left to lie where it falls. It is left to the law of unjust enrichment to curb the worst excesses of this potential situation. There is no equivalent of the Law Reform (Frustrated Contracts) Act 1943: below, paras 19–095, 19–100.

[11] Smith 110 L.Q.R. 400 at p.401.

[12] See below, para.19–115.

it has also been rejected as the best explanation of those cases where the contract is void for common mistake. Instead, but still pursuing the analogy with frustration:

> "the avoidance of a contract on the ground of common mistake results from a rule of law under which, if it transpires that one or both of the parties have agreed to do something which it is impossible to perform, no obligation arises out of that agreement."[13]

8–003   **Performance 'impossible'.** The test of whether performance of the contract is impossible depends upon first determining precisely what it is that the parties agreed would be performed.[14] For example, in *Griffith v Brymer*[15] a contract was made for the hire of a room on June 26, 1902, the day fixed for the coronation of King Edward VII, for the purpose of viewing the coronation procession. At the time the contract was made, but unknown to the parties, the decision to postpone the coronation had already been taken.[16] If the contract was merely for the hire of the room on June 26, performance was perfectly possible. If, however, the contract was for the hire of the room on June 26 *to view the coronation procession*, performance was impossible. The contract in this case was, in fact, held void. In many cases, in determining what it is that the parties agreed, it will not be possible to rely solely upon the express provisions of the contract, since they may very well be silent about a situation which neither of the parties had foreseen.[17] It is also necessary to consider "any implications that may arise out of the surrounding circumstances".[18] The parties in *Griffith v Brymer* did not spell out in the contract that the booking was for the purpose of viewing the coronation procession, but in all the circumstances this was found to be the true nature of the "contractual adventure".

8–004   **Whether one party has taken responsibility for the mistake.** The process of determining precisely what it is that the parties have agreed is a question of the proper construction of the contract. The answer to that question may be that, while performance is impossible, one of the parties had taken responsibility for the existence of the assumed state of affairs, i.e. it had taken the risk of the mistake.[19] This was the position in *McRae v Commonwealth Disposals Commission*,[20] where the defendants purported to sell the wreck of an oil tanker, said to be lying on the Jourmand Reef, and to contain oil. The claimants sent out an expedition to salvage

---

[13] *The Great Peace* [2002] EWCA Civ 1407; [2003] Q.B. 679 at [73].

[14] cf. *Kyle Bay Ltd v Underwriters Subscribing Under Policy No.019057/08/01* [2007] EWCA Civ 57; [2007] 1 C.L.C. 164 at [25], where, because of the potential for confusion in a literal interpretation of the test of impossibility, Neuberger L.J. preferred the test of whether the mistake rendered the subject-matter of the contract "radically and essentially different" from the subject-matter which the parties believed to exist (which he considered amounted to the same thing): *Associated Japanese Bank (International) Ltd v Crédit du Nord SA* [1989] 1 W.L.R. 255 at 268F.

[15] (1903) 19 T.L.R. 434; cf. below, para.19–041.

[16] cf. similar cases in frustration where the contract was made before the decision to postpone: see below, para.19–042.

[17] One exception is a "lost or not lost" clause which may be found in a contract of marine insurance: the effect of this is that both parties are bound although the thing insured had (unknown to them) perished at the time of the contract. cf. Marine Insurance Act 1906, Sch.1, r.1.

[18] *The Great Peace* [2002] EWCA Civ 1407; [2003] Q.B. 679 at [74].

[19] *Butters v BBC Worldwide Ltd* [2009] EWHC 1954 (Ch) at [68]–[69].

[20] (1951) 84 C.L.R. 377 and see below, para.20–032.

the tanker but found that there was not and never had been any such tanker. The High Court of Australia held that the defendants had impliedly undertaken that there was a tanker there[21]; and that, being in breach of this undertaking, they were liable in damages.

In other cases, the construction of the contract will lead to the conclusion that one party has taken the risk of the mistake, but without making them liable for breach of contract, as in *McRae*. Instead the contract remains valid and the party in question is simply required to perform it in a way which is disadvantageous.[22] For example, in one case the tenant of a coal mine agreed to raise a minimum quantity of coal and to pay a minimum rent *in any event*. He was held liable to pay this rent, though there was not so much coal in the mine, because the parties had appreciated the risk and had thrown it on the tenant.[23] Indeed, in all cases where the contract remains valid and performable, the risk of the mistake is, in effect, allocated to one of the parties. In the leading case of *Bell v Lever Bros*,[24] the decision that the settlement with the directors was not void for mistake had the effect of throwing on the company the risk of the mistaken assumption that they had enforceable service contracts.

Whether mistake was the fault of one of the parties. A party may be liable, even where he did not expressly or impliedly take the risk of the mistake, if he was at fault in inducing the mistake in the mind of the other party. This was a further ground for the decision in *McRae*'s case,[25] where it was said that a party could not rely on a mistake consisting "of a belief which is . . . entertained without any reasonable ground, and . . . deliberately induced by him in the mind of the other party."[26] In most cases the answer to the question whether the mistake was the fault of one of the parties will be the same as the answer to the question whether one party has taken responsibility for the mistake.[27]   8–005

The limits of construction. The decision in *McRae*, above, is explained on the basis of an implied term; in that case an implied warranty as to the existence of the tanker. The implied term theory which has been used to explain when a contract may be void[28] merely takes this process of construction one stage further, in cases where responsibility for the mistake is allocated to neither of the parties, by implying a term that the validity of the contract depends on the existence of the state of affairs assumed to exist.[29] However, the approach most recently advocated by the Court of Appeal in *The Great Peace*[30] confines the process of construction   8–006

---

[21] cf. the explanation of *McRae*'s case in *The Great Peace* [2002] EWCA Civ 1407; [2003] Q.B. 679 at [76]–[77].

[22] *Standard Chartered Bank v Banque Marocaine du Commerce Exterieur* [2006] EWHC 413.

[23] *Bute v Thompson* (1844) 13 M. & W. 487; cf. *Clifford v Watts* (1870) L.R. 5 C.P. 577.

[24] [1932] A.C. 161. See below, para.8–017.

[25] (1951) 84 C.L.R. 377.

[26] ibid. at 408; cf. *The Great Peace* [2002] EWCA Civ 1407; [2003] Q.B. 679 at [76]–[77]. In *Associated Japanese Bank (International) Ltd v Crédit du Nord SA* [1989] 1 W.L.R. 255 at 268 Steyn J. carries the principle further by omitting the second requirement (i.e. that of inducement) stated in the passage quoted in the text above from *McRae*'s case.

[27] *The Great Peace* [2002] EWCA Civ 1407; [2003] Q.B. 679 at [84]. One party may rely simply on the fault of the other in cases where his concern is to show only that he should not be bound, e.g. if the Commission had sought payment from the salvors in *McRae*, but not that the other party should be held liable in damages.

[28] See above, para.8–002.

[29] Used in the sense of a contingent condition: see above, para.2–104.

[30] [2002] EWCA Civ 1407; [2003] Q.B. 679.

to determining what it is the parties have agreed, including whether they have allocated responsibility for the mistake to one party or the other. Thereafter, and in the absence of any such allocation of responsibility, it is a question of whether the mistake has rendered performance "impossible". It is submitted, with respect, that this is simply a different way of reaching the same result and whether one technique or the other is preferred should not affect the outcome in any case.[31] That it may have done so in some cases seems to have been due to the application of a separate doctrine of common mistake in equity, now rejected after *The Great Peace*,[32] without considering the proper construction of the contract at all.[33]

8–007   **Summary.** In *The Great Peace*[34] the Court of Appeal summed up the elements which must be present if a contract is to be held void for common mistake as follows[35]: (i) there must be a common assumption as to the existence of a state of affairs; (ii) there must be no warranty by either party that that state of affairs exists; (iii) the non-existence of the state of affairs must not be attributable to the fault of either party; (iv) the non-existence of the state of affairs must render performance of the contract impossible; (v) the state of affairs may be the existence, or a vital attribute, of the consideration to be provided or circumstances which must subsist if performance of the contractual adventure is to be possible. In the last of these elements the Court of Appeal gives some indication of the difficulty of applying this test to different types of mistake and it is to the types of mistake which may be relied upon that we must now turn. In one sense the only type of mistake which is "fundamental", or makes performance impossible, is a mistake as to the existence of the subject-matter,[36] e.g. in *Griffiths v Brymer*[37], the "subject matter" of the contract was identified as "a room to view the coronation procession". In the sections which follow the types of mistake which have been considered by the courts are organised *factually*, but the issue in each case was whether, *legally*, they amounted to a mistake as to the existence of the subject-matter of the contract.

(ii) *Mistake as to the existence of the subject-matter*

8–008   Performance is impossible, and the contract void, where both parties are mistaken as to the existence of the subject-matter. Thus it has been held that a separation deed between a man and a woman, who mistakenly thought that they were married to each other, was void, because it purported to deal with a marriage

---

[31] Smith 110 L.Q.R. 400. cf. *Associated Japanese Bank (International) Ltd v Crédit du Nord SA* [1989] 1 W.L.R. 255 where Steyn J. applied the implied term theory to find that the contract was void, but then also went on to ask if the mistake was fundamental; it is perhaps not surprising that he reached the same conclusion that the contract was void. The same approach was applied in *Graves v Graves* [2007] EWCA Civ 660; [2008] H.L.R. 10, but the court found it "not necessary" to consider whether the contract was void for mistake.

[32] See below, para.8–029.

[33] See, e.g. *Grist v Bailey* [1967] Ch. 532; *Laurence v Lexcourt Holdings Ltd* [1978] 1 W.L.R. 1128, both of which were doubted in *William Sindall Plc v Cambridgeshire CC* [1994] 1 W.L.R. 1016 at 1035 on the ground that the risk of the mistake had been allocated by the contract.

[34] [2002] EWCA Civ 1407; [2003] Q.B. 679 at [76].

[35] This is an adaptation of the elements identified by Lord Alverstone C.J. in *Blakeley v Muller & Co* (1903) 19 T.L.R. 186 as necessary for a contract to be discharged for frustration.

[36] *Perpetual Trustee Co Ltd v BNY Corporate Trustee Services Ltd* [2009] EWCA Civ 1160; [2010] Ch 347 at [108].

[37] See above, para.8–003.

which did not exist[38]; and that a contract to buy an annuity was void where, at the time of the contract, the annuitant had died, so that the annuity no longer existed.[39]

Sale of goods. Contracts for the sale of non-existent goods illustrate the same point, but give rise to further difficulties. In *Couturier v Hastie*[40] a contract was made for the sale of a cargo of corn with payment due on the handing over of the shipping documents. Before the contract was made, the cargo had, unknown to the parties, become overheated and been sold at Tunis to prevent further deterioration. The seller argued that the buyer was nevertheless liable for the price: what he had bought was an interest in a maritime adventure, or such rights as the seller had under the shipping documents, against which payment was to be made.[41] But the House of Lords rejected this argument and held that the buyer was not liable. Lord Cranworth L.C. said:

8–009

> "The whole question turns upon the construction of the contract . . . Looking to the contract . . . alone it appears to me clearly that what the parties contemplated . . . was that there was an existing something to be sold and bought."[42]

The contract was for the sale of existing goods—not for the sale of the goods *or* the documents representing them. A similar issue may arise in relation to an accessory contract. In *Associated Japanese Bank* (*International*) *Ltd v Crédit du Nord SA*[43] a guarantee of the lease of certain machinery was found to contain an express or implied undertaking in favour of the guarantor that the machinery was in existence; and as the machinery did not exist the guarantor was not liable.

In each of these cases the non-existence of the underlying subject-matter merely absolved the party prejudiced by that fact from liability, but it may as a matter of construction also impose a liability on the other party, as in *McRae*.[44] Thus there may be a good contract about a non-existent subject-matter if on the true construction of the contract the risk of non-existence is thrown on one party.[45] In *Couturier v Hastie* the risk was not thrown on the buyer: he was not liable for the price. It is more doubtful whether the risk was thrown on the seller, i.e. whether the buyer could have claimed damages for non-delivery. In *McRae*'s case the court thought that prima facie the seller in *Couturier v Hastie* had promised that the goods were in existence[46]: on this view, the contract in that case was not void and the seller could have been held liable on it. But in *Barrow, Lane & Ballard Ltd v Phillips & Co Ltd*,[47] Wright J. said:

---

[38] *Galloway v Galloway* (1914) 30 T.L.R. 531.

[39] *Strickland v Turner* (1852) 7 Ex. 208.

[40] (1856) 5 H.L.C. 673; Atiyah 73 L.Q.R. 487.

[41] This would normally have satisfied the buyer, as he could have claimed the insurance money. But if the contract was indeed void the buyer would not have acquired any rights by virtue of it under the "shipping documents," including the insurance policy.

[42] (1856) 5 H.L.C. 673 at 681.

[43] [1989] 1 W.L.R. 255; below, para.8–018.

[44] See above, para.8–004.

[45] cf. *Kalsep Ltd v X-Flow BV*, *The Times*, May 3, 2001.

[46] (1951) 84 C.L.R. 377 at 407.

[47] [1929] 1 K.B. 574 at 582; below, para.8–021; cf. *Bell v Lever Bros* [1932] A.C. 161 at 217, per Lord Atkin: "void if in fact the article had perished before the date of the sale".

"Where a contract relates to specific goods which do not exist, the case is not to be treated as one in which the seller warrants the existence of those specific goods, but as one in which there has been failure of consideration and mistake."

The English courts would probably adopt this approach. Prima facie a seller would not be held to undertake that the goods existed, any more than the buyer would bind himself to pay for them in any event. Thus, neither party is bound and the contract can properly be called void. This explains why the contract in *Couturier v Hastie* has long been regarded as void for mistake, although the words "void" and "mistake" do not occur in any of the judgments.

8–010   **Sale of Goods Act 1979, section 6.** In *McRae*'s case the tanker never existed; in *Couturier v Hastie* the goods originally existed but had, before the contract was made, "perished" as a commercial entity. This distinction, unimportant in principle, gives rise to difficulty because s.6 of the Sale of Goods Act 1979 provides that:

"Where there is a contract for the sale of specific goods, and the goods without the knowledge of the seller have perished at the time when the contract is made, the contract is void."

At first sight this section prevents the buyer from recovering damages even though the seller has expressly guaranteed that the goods exist, and the seller from recovering the price or damages even though the buyer has expressly promised to pay whether or not the goods exist. The problem may be of more theoretical than practical interest, for it does not seem that contracts on such terms are at all common. In practice the more important question is whether s.6 would apply where the contract was *either* a sale of alternatives (e.g. of the goods *or* the shipping documents representing them[48]) *or* simply one of the documents. Probably s.6 would not apply as such transactions would, in the events which had happened, be sales of things in action and not of goods at all.[49]

If the parties are conscious of a doubt as to the existence of the goods, and one of them expressly undertakes to bear the risk that they may not exist, there seems to be no strong reason against upholding the contract. But in view of s.6 some ingenuity is required to reach this result. One possible argument is that s.6 is only a rule of construction which can be ousted by proof of contrary intention.[50] But many other sections of the Act expressly provide that they are subject to contrary agreement and there is no such provision in s.6. Another possibility is to say that the main contract is void but that the seller can be held liable on a collateral

---

[48] But for this possibility, *Couturier v Hastie* would scarcely have reached the House of Lords. There does not seem to be any English case in which the court was called upon to consider a simple *sale* of goods "lost or not lost" at the time of the contract unless the buyer was entitled under the contract to documents giving him rights against the carrier or insurer in respect of the loss of the goods in certain events.

[49] See the definition of "goods" given in s.61(1) of Sale of Goods Act 1979. The normal contract for the sale of goods on c.i.f. terms is not regarded as a sale of documents but as a sale of goods to be performed by the delivery of documents: see *Arnhold Karberg & Co v Blythe, Green Jourdain & Co* [1916] 1 K.B. 495 at 510, 514; and other authorities cited in *Benjamin's Sale of Goods* (8th edn), §19–008. *Couturier v Hastie* provides an early illustration of a c.i.f. contract.

[50] Atiyah 73 L.Q.R. 340.

contract that the goods do exist. But if nothing had been done under the main contract it would be hard to find any consideration for the seller's promise under the collateral contract. It is just possible that such consideration could be found in the buyer's act of purporting to enter into the main contract, especially if it involved the execution of a document.[51] There is even more difficulty in seeing how the buyer's promise to pay can be expressed as a collateral contract, for it seems to be merely a reiteration of his principal obligation under the main contract. It is finally possible that a seller who warrants that goods exist may be liable in damages for negligent misrepresentation[52]; but the damages on such a claim would be differently assessed from those for breach of contract,[53] and the claim would fail if the seller was wholly innocent.[54]

(iii) *Mistake as to the identity of the subject-matter*

Such a mistake usually arises where one party intends to deal with one thing and the other with a different thing, i.e. in cases of "unilateral mistake".[55] A case of common mistake which makes performance impossible could arise if *both* parties thought that they were dealing with one thing when they were in fact dealing with another.[56] Mistake as to a fundamental quality of the subject-matter may sometimes be regarded as affecting the identity of the subject-matter; this possibility is discussed below.[57]   8–011

(iv) *Mistake as to the possibility of performing the contract*

Physical impossibility. In *Sheikh Bros Ltd v Ochsner*[58] a contract was made for the exploitation of sisal, growing on land belonging to A. The contract provided that B was to cut and process the sisal and to deliver an average of 50 tons of sisal fibre per month to A. It was held that the contract was void because (contrary to the parties' belief) the land was not capable of producing 50 tons of fibre per month.   8–012

Legal impossibility. A contract may be void if it provides for something to be done which cannot, as a matter of law, be done. For example, a person cannot acquire property which he already owns, and Lords Atkin and Wright have said that, if he purports to do so in the mistaken belief that the property belongs to the   8–013

---

[51] cf. above, para.3–029. Such a consideration would be blatantly invented (above, para.3–009).

[52] At common law, if there was a "special relationship" (below, para.9–033); and possibly under s.2(1) of the Misrepresentation Act 1967 (below, para.9–039). But that subsection only applies "Where a person has entered into a contract . . . " and it is not clear whether these words cover the case where the "contract" is wholly void.

[53] See below, para.9–059. cf. the damages recovered in *McRae*'s case (below, para.20–027).

[54] See below, paras 9–071, 9–073—9–076.

[55] See below, paras 8–042—8–043.

[56] cf. *Diamond v British Columbia Thoroughbred Breeders' Society* (1966) 52 D.L.R. (2d) 146, where two horses at an auction were confused by the auctioneer *and* by the bidders; but the court held that the difference was one of quality only: sed quaere. See also *Grains & Fourrages SA v Huyton* [1997] 1 Lloyd's Rep. 628.

[57] See below, para.8–015 et seq.

[58] [1957] A.C. 136.

other contracting party, the contract is void.[59] On the other hand, a contract is not void merely because it purports to dispose of property which belongs to a third party,[60] for in such a case the vendor might be able to acquire the property and then make a proper transfer.

One special case of legal impossibility is illegality. A contract involving the commission of a crime is often illegal.[61] The contract may be illegal even though both parties believe it to be lawful, so that in a sense they were under a mistake as to the legal possibility of performing it. Persons may, moreover, agree to do what is the actus reus of crime, but may not commit a crime if they do the act because they lack mens rea. Such an agreement might not be illegal, but would probably be void for legal impossibility.

8–014   **Commercial impossibility.** In *Griffith v Brymer*,[62] considered above, performance may have been physically and legally possible, but its commercial object was defeated. It could also be said that the parties had made a mistake about a quality of the subject-matter. On this view, the present status of the decision[63] depends on the discussion that follows.

(v) *Mistake as to quality*

8–015   **Whether sale by description.** Where the subject-matter of the contract lacks some quality which it is believed to have, the first question is whether the quality forms part of the contractual description of the thing. If it does and "the article does not answer the description of that which is sold",[64] the contract is valid and the party who gave the description is in breach.[65]

8–016   **Contract generally valid.** If there is no contractual misdescription, the general rule is that mistake as to quality does not make performance impossible and the contract remains valid. This is so whether the mistake prejudices the buyer (so that he pays "too much") or the seller (so that he charges "too little"). In *Scott v Littledale*[66] a contract for the sale of tea was held valid in spite of a mistake as to its quality and hence as to its value. The same rule applies where the mistake affects, not the value of the subject-matter, but its utility. In *The Great Peace*[67] a ship had been chartered for a minimum period of five days to provide

---

[59] *Bell v Lever Bros Ltd* [1932] A.C. 161 at 218; *Norwich Union Fire Ins Society Ltd v Price* [1934] A.C. 455 at 463. The proposition supported by these dicta remains valid even though, to the extent that they are based on *Cooper v Phibbs* (1867) L.R. 2 H.L. 149, they may involve a misinterpretation of that case: see Matthews 105 L.Q.R. 599. For the view that the contract in that case should now be regarded as void, see also *The Great Peace* [2002] EWCA Civ 1407; [2003] Q.B. 679 at [126]–[128] (though it may not have been so regarded at the time: see [2003] Q.B. 679 at [110]).

[60] *Bell v Lever Bros Ltd*, above; *Clare v Lamb* (1875) L.R. 10 C.P. 334.

[61] See below, para.11–011 et seq.

[62] (1903) 19 T.L.R. 434.

[63] The case is cited with apparent approval in *The Great Peace* [2002] EWCA Civ 1407; [2003] Q.B. 679 at [67].

[64] *Gompertz v Bartlett* (1853) 2 E. & B. 849 at 853; cf. *Gurney v Womersley* (1854) 4 E. & B. 133. Contrast *Harlingdon and Leinster Enterprises Ltd v Christopher Hull Fine Art Ltd* [1991] 1 Q.B. 564.

[65] *Gompertz v Bartlett*, above; Sale of Goods Act 1979, s.13.

[66] (1858) 8 E. & B. 815; cf. *Pope & Pearson v Buenos Ayres New Gas Co* (1892) 8 T.L.R. 758; *William Sindall Plc v Cambridgeshire CC* [1994] 1 W.L.R. 1016.

[67] *The Great Peace* [2002] EWCA Civ 1407; [2003] Q.B. 679; cf. *Harrison & Jones v Bunten & Lancaster* [1953] 1 Q.B. 646.

escort services to another ship which was in distress at sea, in the mistaken belief, apparently shared by charterer and shipowner,[68] that the chartered ship was "in close proximity" to the one in distress or that the former was "the closest vessel" to the latter.[69] This mistake did not make the contract void since the chartered ship could, in spite of it, have reached the scene of the casualty to "provide several days of escort service".[70]

It does not follow from these illustrations of the general rule that a mistake as to quality can *never* make a contract void at law. In *Kennedy v Panama, etc. Royal Mail Co*,[71] the claimant applied for shares in a company on the faith of an untrue statement (made in good faith) that the company had secured a contract to carry mail for the New Zealand Government. The shares were allotted to him, and the actual decision was that the resulting contract between him and the company was valid.[72] But in reaching this conclusion Blackburn J. referred to the Roman doctrine of *error in substantia*, by which mistakes as to quality may make a contract void if they relate to the "substance" of the subject-matter, e.g. to the metal of which a thing is made.[73] He added that:

> "the principle of our law is the same as that of the civil law; and the difficulty in every case is to determine whether the mistake or misapprehension is as to the substance of the whole consideration, going, as it were, to the root of the matter, or only to some point, even though a material point, an error as to which does not affect the substance of the whole consideration".[74]

This principle did not help the claimant as he got the very shares he bargained for and as his mistake did not affect the substance of the whole transaction. But it may be possible[75] to infer from Blackburn J.'s approval of the Roman texts that, in his view, mistake as to quality could in some cases make a contract void in English law.

Bell v Lever Bros. Whether this view is correct depends on the decision of the House of Lords in *Bell v Lever Bros Ltd*.[76] Bell and Snelling had agreed with Lever Bros to serve for five years as chairman and vice-chairman of a company controlled by Lever Bros. Before the end of this period Lever Bros wished to terminate these service contracts, and the parties entered into compensation agreements under which Bell and Snelling received between them £50,000 for loss

8–017

---

[68] See [2003] Q.B. 679, above, at [162] ("common assumption of both parties"); from the statement of facts at [8], [9], the exact state of the shipowner's mind is less clear.

[69] ibid. at [8], [9]. The two ships were believed to have been 35 miles apart when, in fact, the distance between them was 410 miles.

[70] ibid. at [165]. This conclusion was supported by the fact that the charterers themselves did not seek to cancel the contract immediately on discovery of the truth, but only when a third ship came on the scene (which happened also to be under charter to the charterers) and was able to provide the escort services.

[71] (1867) L.R. 2 Q.B. 580. Contrast *Emmerson's Case* (1866) L.R. 1 Ch. App. 433 (where special statutory provisions affected the result).

[72] There being then no remedy for innocent misrepresentation at common law: below, paras 9–073, 9–079.

[73] Lawson 52 L.Q.R. 79; De Zulueta, *The Roman Law of Sale*, p.26. The Romans did not call such an error one of "quality" but an English lawyer could so describe it.

[74] *Kennedy v Panama, etc. Royal Mail Co*, above, at 588.

[75] The point is not clear: see *The Great Peace* [2002] EWCA Civ 1407; [2003] Q.B. 679 at [59].

[76] [1932] A.C. 161; MacMillan 119 L.Q.R. 625.

of office. Lever Bros then discovered that Bell and Snelling had broken their service contracts in a way which would have justified their summary dismissal without compensation.[77] It was found that Bell and Snelling had forgotten about these breaches of the service contracts when the compensation agreements were made, so that they were not guilty of fraudulent concealment.[78] The remaining issue was whether the compensation agreements were void for mistake, so as to entitle Lever Bros to recover back the £50,000 which they had paid under those agreements.[79] They had made the compensation agreements in the belief that the service contracts still bound them when in fact they were terminable. They had paid £50,000 to get rid of Bell and Snelling, when they might have got rid of them for nothing. Wright J. and a unanimous Court of Appeal held that the compensation agreements were void as Lever Bros had made them under a fundamental mistake. But the House of Lords, by a narrow majority, reversed this decision. The mistake related only to a quality of the service contracts (which were the subject-matter of the compensation agreements), and was not fundamental. Lord Atkin said: "The contract released is the identical contract in both cases,[80] and the party paying for release gets exactly what he bargained for".[81] Lord Thankerton stressed that mistake even as to a fundamental quality was of no effect unless it related to some assumption which *both* parties regarded as essential. In his view there was nothing to show that Bell and Snelling regarded the binding force of the service contracts as vital: only Lever Bros did so.[82]

The mistake in this case gave rise to a belief that subject-matter which was actually worthless had a value of £50,000. It might be thought that if such a mistake is not fundamental, no mistake as to quality can ever have this effect; but once one accepts the principle that a mere mistake as to value is not fundamental, the size of that difference cannot be decisive. *Bell v Lever Bros Ltd* has indeed been described as "a quite exceptional case"[83]; and dicta in it do recognise that some mistakes as to quality may be fundamental. Lord Atkin said that mistake as to quality

"will not affect assent unless it is the mistake of both parties, and is as to the existence of some quality which makes the thing without the quality essentially different from the thing as it was believed to be".[84]

Lord Thankerton said that a mistake as to subject-matter must relate to "something which both must necessarily have accepted in their minds as an essential and integral element of the subject-matter".[85]

---

[77] See below, para.16–096; the harshness of this rule may account for the eventual decision in the case; cf. Treitel 104 L.Q.R. 501 at 505.

[78] Nor were they under any duty to disclose their breaches of duty: cf. below, para.9–151.

[79] See below, para.22–015.

[80] i.e. whether the service contracts were binding on Lever Bros or terminable by them; cf. *Robert A Munro & Co Ltd v Meyer* [1930] 2 K.B. 312.

[81] *Bell v Lever Bros Ltd*, above, at 223. It was particularly important for Lever Bros to get rid of Bell and Snelling by May 1, 1929, but this fact is not stressed in the speeches of Lords Atkin and Thankerton.

[82] At 235.

[83] *Associated Japanese Bank (International) Ltd v Crédit du Nord SA* [1989] 1 W.L.R. 255 at 267.

[84] [1932] A.C. 161 at 218.

[85] ibid. at 256.

Quality mistakes affecting the subject-matter. These are stringent   8–018
requirements, which make the common law doctrine of mistake "markedly narrower in scope than the civilian doctrine"[86] referred to by Blackburn J. in the
dictum cited above.[87] It follows that generally a mistake as to quality will not make
a contract void. According to Lord Atkin, it would not have this effect if a man
bought a horse mistakenly believed to be sound; if he bought a dwelling-house
mistakenly believed to be inhabitable; if he bought a garage on a road which was
about to be starved of all traffic by the construction of a by-pass; and (most
difficult of all): "A buys a picture from B; both A and B believe it to be the work
of an old master and a high price is paid. It turns out to be a modern copy. A has
no remedy in the absence of representation or warranty"[88]: i.e. the contract is
valid. The same view was taken in *Leaf v International Galleries*,[89] where it was
said[90] that a contract for the sale of a picture would not be void if the parties
mistakenly believed that it was by Constable. Similarly it was held in *Solle v
Butcher*[91] that a lease was not void because the parties mistakenly believed the
premises to be free from rent control; and in *Oscar Chess Ltd v Williams* it was said
that a contract for the sale of a car would not be void because the parties made a
mistake as to its age, so that the buyer paid more than he would have done, had
he known the truth.[92]

But according to other dicta and decisions a mistake as to quality can sometimes
make a contract void.[93] Thus it has been said that a contract for the sale of land
believed to be freehold could be avoided if it turned out to be leasehold.[94] In *Bell
v Lever Bros Ltd* Greer L.J. said in the Court of Appeal that a contract for the sale
of a horse, believed to be a racehorse, would be void if it turned out to be a
carthorse[95]: it may be significant that Lord Atkin, in his example of the *unsound*
horse,[96] did not contradict this suggestion. Similarly, in *Scott v Coulson*[97] a policy
on the life of one Death was sold for £460 on the assumption that Death was alive.
The price paid was therefore fixed in relation to the surrender value of the policy.
In fact Death was dead, so that the policy had matured and was worth £777. The
vendor successfully claimed to have the contract set aside and Vaughan Williams

---

[86] *Associated Japanese Bank* case, above, fn.83 at 268, approved in *The Great Peace* [2002] EWCA Civ
1407; [2003] Q.B. 679 at [90]–[91].
[87] See above, at fn.74.
[88] [1932] A.C. 161 at 224. Contrast *Smith v Zimbalist*, 2 Cal.App. 2d 234; 38 P.2d 170 (1934) (violins
mistakenly believed to be by Stradivarius and Guarnerius: held buyer not liable for the price on
grounds of mistake *and* breach of warranty).
[89] [1950] 2 K.B. 86.
[90] ibid. at 89; below, para.8–020. cf. *Harlingdon and Leinster Enterprise Ltd v Christopher Hull Fine Art
Ltd* [1991] 1 Q.B. 564, where the buyer's claim (which failed) was based solely on breach; no attempt
was made to base it on mistake as to the authenticity of the picture; Lawrenson 54 M.L.R. 122.
[91] [1950] 1 K.B. 671. cf. *Magee v Pennine Ins Co Ltd* [1969] 2 Q.B. 507; 85 L.Q.R. 454; Harris 32
M.L.R. 688. For the relief given in these two cases on equitable grounds see below, paras
8–027—8–028.
[92] [1957] 1 W.L.R. 370 at 373; cf. *F E Rose (London) Ltd v W H Pim Jnr & Co Ltd* [1953] 2 Q.B.
450 at 459. Contrast Restatement, *Contracts*, para.503, Ill. 3, but see Restatement 2d, *Contracts* para.154
Ill. 3.
[93] In addition to those referred to in the text, see: *Nutt v Read* (2000) 32 H.L.R. 761
[94] *Durham v Legard* (1835) 34 Beav. 611 at 613, possibly expressing a purely equitable view.
[95] [1931] 1 K.B. 557, 597; cf. *Naughton v O'Callaghan* [1990] 3 All E.R. 191 (horse sold by auction
with a false pedigree said to be "a different animal altogether" (at 197) but it was not suggested that
the contract was void).
[96] [1932] A.C. 161 at 224; above, fn.88.
[97] [1903] 2 Ch. 249.

L.J. said[98] that it was void at law. Again, in the *Associated Japanese Bank*[99] case payments to be made by the lessee under a purported sale and lease-back of machinery were guaranteed by the defendant. In fact no such machinery existed, so that the lease was voidable for fraud; and it was said that the guarantee was void for mistake. And in *Nicholson & Venn v Smith-Marriott*[100] the defendants put up for auction table napkins "with the crest of Charles I and the authentic property of that monarch". On the faith of this description the lot was bought for £787 10s., but the napkins were Georgian and worth £105 only. The buyer recovered damages for breach of contract but Hallett J. also said that the contract might have been treated *by the buyer*[101] as void for mistake. The transaction could be regarded in two ways. The parties may have intended to buy and sell antique table linen: in this case a mistake as to its exact age, provenance or value would not be fundamental; performance would not have been "impossible". Alternatively, the parties may have intended to buy and sell a Carolean relic; in this case their mistake would be fundamental; performance would be impossible and the contract would be void. This is just another example of the need, first, to identify precisely what was the subject-matter of the contract.

8–019   **A general principle?** The cases and examples concerning mistakes as to quality cannot be perfectly reconciled; but there is a principle which runs through them. A thing has many qualities. A car may be black, old, fast and so forth. For any particular purpose one or more of these qualities may be uppermost in the minds of the persons dealing with the thing. Some particular quality may be so important to them that they actually use it to *identify* the thing. If the thing lacks that quality, it is suggested that the parties have made a fundamental mistake, even though they have not mistaken one thing for another, or made a mistake as to the existence of the thing, as such. The matter may be tested by imagining that one can ask the parties, immediately after they made the contract, what its subject-matter was. If, in spite of the mistake, they would give the right answer the contract is valid at law. Thus in *Bell v Lever Bros Ltd*, the parties would have said, quite rightly: "We are contracting about a service agreement". In *Nicholson & Venn v Smith-Marriott* they might have said, rightly, "We are contracting about antique table linen", in which case the contract would be valid; or they might have said, wrongly, "We are contracting about a Carolean relic", in which case the contract would be void.

This suggested test for determining whether a mistake is fundamental, presupposes that both parties would give the same answer to the question "what are you contracting about?" If they would give different answers, the mistake, whatever else its effect may be, will not *nullify* consent. A seller may intend to sell antique table linen and the buyer to buy a Carolean relic. If the parties are thus at cross-purposes consent may be *negatived*. The question whether the buyer could rely on the mistake as making the contract void at law would then depend on factors discussed later in this chapter.[102]

---

[98] [1903] 2 Ch. 249 at 252; cf. *Gloyne v Richardson* [2001] EWCA Civ 716; [2001] B.C.L.C. 669 at [41] (agreement made in mistaken belief that option had been exercised).

[99] *Associated Japanese Bank (International) Ltd v Crédit du Nord SA* [1989] 1 W.L.R. 255; Treitel 104 L.Q.R. 501; Cartwright [1988] L.M.C.L.Q. 300; Marston [1989] C.L.J. 173.

[100] (1947) 177 L.T. 189.

[101] Above, para.8–009.

[102] See below, para.8–033 et seq.

Difficult cases. Most of the cases and illustrations given above can be   8–020
explained in accordance with the principle suggested above, but three of them give
rise to particular difficulty. The first is *Scott v Coulson*, where the subject-matter
of the contract would no doubt have been described as "an insurance policy" so
that the contract ought to have been valid at law. The view that the contract was
void is also very hard to reconcile[103] with *Bell v Lever Bros Ltd*. If the difference
between a binding and a terminable contract is not fundamental, why is there a
fundamental difference between a contingent and an accrued debt?[104]

A second source of difficulty is that the contract of guarantee in the *Associated
Japanese Bank* case was held to be *void*. The subject-matter of that contract was
not the machinery, but the lease *of* the machinery, and this contract was not void
but only voidable for fraud. Yet the compensation agreements in *Bell v Lever Bros
Ltd* were held *valid* even though their subject-matter, too, consisted of the earlier
service contracts which were also terminable but not void. One possible way of
distinguishing the cases is to say that the lease in the *Associated Japanese Bank* case
was voidable for fraud, so that it was liable to be rescinded *ab initio*,[105] while the
factor vitiating the service agreements in *Bell v Lever Bros Ltd* was breach, which
entitled the employers to terminate them by dismissing the employees, but not
with retrospective effect[106]: hence the mistake in the former case could be said to
be more serious than that in the latter case. Another is that in the *Associated
Japanese Bank* case the guarantee was part of a composite transaction intended to
raise money on the security of the alleged machinery, so that "the analogy of the
classic *res extincta* cases . . . [was] fairly close".[107] Hence the crucial fact was that
guarantor and lessor both mistakenly believed that *the machinery* existed: this was
more important than their state of mind as to the legal effect of the fraud on *the
lease*.

The third source of difficulty is Lord Atkin's example of a modern copy bought
for a high price in the belief that it is an old master, supported by dicta in *Leaf v
International Galleries*.[108] The assumption behind these statements seems to be
that the parties would identify the subject-matter simply as "a picture"; but this
seems to be a questionable assumption. Suppose that A has just paid B £10 million
for what both believe to be a painting by Rembrandt. If A were asked "what have
you just bought?" he would almost certainly reply "a Rembrandt"—not "a
picture." With the greatest respect, this type of case stands on a different level
from Lord Atkin's other examples.[109] Nor are the dicta in *Leaf v International
Galleries* conclusive, for the buyer there sought only to rescind the contract for
misrepresentation and did not claim that it was void for mistake.[110] It is submitted

---

[103] *The Great Peace* [2002] EWCA Civ 1407; [2003] Q.B. 679 at [87].

[104] In *Bell v Lever Bros Ltd* [1932] A.C. 161 at 236 Lord Thankerton regards the contract in *Scott
v Coulson* as one for the sale of a non-existent subject matter.

[105] See below, para.9–078 et seq.

[106] See below, paras 18–010—18–011; cf. above, para.7–032.

[107] *Associated Japanese Bank (International) Ltd v Crédit du Nord SA* [1989] 1 W.L.R. 255 at 269.

[108] [1950] 2 K.B. 86; cf. also *Hindle v Brown* (1907) 98 L.T. 44, where only misrepresentation was
discussed.

[109] See above, para.8–018. The answer to the question "what have you just bought?" would in those
cases be: "a horse", "a house", and "a garage."

[110] Nor did he claim damages for breach of warranty, though Denning and Jenkins L.JJ. thought that
this remedy was open to him; cf. *Harlingdon and Leinster Enterprises Ltd v Christopher Hull Fine Art Ltd*
[1991] 1 Q.B. 564 at 578, stating that, at least between art dealers, the principle of *caveat emptor*
applied.

that, on the bare facts given by Lord Atkin, the contract should be held void. Of course in practice the facts of cases of this kind are likely to be more complex. On the one hand, it may be a term of the contract that the picture is authentic, in which case the seller is liable for breach of contract[111] so that no question of mistake will arise. On the other hand, a picture may be sold speculatively, in which case the contract will be valid and the seller will not be in breach, even though the buyer's belief in the authenticity of the picture turns out to be incorrect. Between these extremes lies the large group of cases in which both parties may believe the picture to be authentic but in which there can be no certainty on the point; scholarly or expert opinion as to the authenticity of a picture may vary from time to time.[112] In cases within this group, it has been held that the seller does not impliedly undertake that the picture is genuine (at least where the sale is by one dealer to another, and the seller indicates that he is not an expert on the work of the artist in question)[113]; and it is submitted that the element of uncertainty would make it equally inappropriate to regard such a case as one in which the contract was void for mistake.

(vi) *Mistake as to quantity*

8–021   Mistake as to quantity may be capable of invalidating a contract at law. In *Cox v Prentice*[114] a silver bar was sold under a mistake as to its weight. The buyer (who was the party prejudiced by the mistake) obtained a verdict for damages for the difference in value between the weight of the bar as it was, and as it was believed to be. The court added that the buyer could have recovered back the price he paid for the bar, which may suggest that he had the option of treating the contract as void for mistake. Similarly, Lord Atkin in *Bell v Lever Bros Ltd* said: "I agree that an agreement to take an assignment of a lease for five years is not the same thing as to take an assignment of a lease for three years, still less a term for a few months,"[115] though it is not clear from the context whether Lord Atkin thought that such a mistake could make a contract void. And in *Barrow, Lane & Ballard Ltd v Phillips & Co Ltd*[116] a contract for the sale of an "indivisible parcel" of 700 bags of nuts was held to be void because, unknown to the parties, only 591 bags were in existence.

(vii) *Mistake of law*

8–022   **Contract may be void for mistake of law.** At common law, the traditional view was that a mistake could affect the validity of a contract only if it was one of "fact" as opposed to one of "law". That view has been rejected by the Court of

---

[111] As in *Peco Arts Inc v Hazlitt Gallery Ltd* [1983] 1 W.L.R. 1315.

[112] See *Firestone & Parson Inc v Union League of Philadelphia* 672 F. Supp. 819 (1987), affirmed 833 F. 2d. 304; cf. *Luxmoore-May v Messenger May Baverstock* [1990] 1 W.L.R. 1009 at 1028; *Thomson v Christie Manson & Woods Ltd* [2005] EWCA Civ 555; [2005] P.N.L.R. 38.

[113] *Harlingdon and Leinster Enterprises Ltd v Christopher Hull Fine Art Ltd* [1991] 1 Q.B. 564.

[114] (1815) 3 M. & S. 344; cf. *Devaux v Connolly* (1849) 8 C.B. 640 at 659

[115] [1932] A.C. 161 at 223.

[116] [1929] 1 K.B. 574.

Appeal in *Brennan v Bolt Burdon*.[117] In that case, litigation was settled after a ruling that the claim form had been served out of time. The mistaken assumption of the parties was that, on the basis of the law as it then stood, this ruling could not be challenged successfully. Shortly afterwards, the Court of Appeal[118] reversed the earlier decision upon which the ruling had been based. The issue to which this gave rise was whether the settlement was void by reason of the parties' common mistake of law. The earlier decision of the House of Lords in *Kleinwort Benson Ltd v Lincoln City Council*[119] had removed the bar preventing recovery of payments made under a mistake of law, the mistake there being that contracts under which moneys had been paid to local authorities were valid when they were later ruled to be void because the authorities concerned had gone beyond their powers.[120] According to Kay L.J., in *Brennan v Bolt Burdon*, it could not be doubted that the effect of that decision "now permeates the law of contract",[121] a view which was shared by the other members of the court.[122] It is now possible therefore for a contract to be void for a common mistake of law.[123] This decision is to be welcomed, if only because the distinction between mistakes of fact and mistakes of law was not always easy to draw[124] or to justify.[125] However, it raises the difficult question of *when* a contract will be void for a mistake of law.

The nature of a mistake of law. The principal difficulty faced by the House of Lords in deciding whether to remove the mistake of law bar in *Kleinwort Benson v Lincoln City Council* was how to deal with the effect of "changes" in the law; in particular where the law as it is understood at the relevant time is held to be otherwise by a later decision of the courts. The majority accepted the "declaratory theory" under which the later decision does not change the law, but merely declares what it has always been.[126] The effect is that where parties act on the basis that the law is X, including when it has been declared to be X by an earlier judicial decision, they will be found to have been mistaken if the law is later declared to be Y. In *Kleinwort Benson v Lincoln City Council* the House of Lords was concerned with the effect of such "retrospective" mistake[127] on the security of payments. In *Brennan v Bolt Burdon*, the Court of Appeal was concerned with its effect on the certainty of contract.

8–023

---

[117] [2004] EWCA Civ 1017; [2005] Q.B. 303.

[118] *Anderton v Clwyd CC* [2002] EWCA Civ 933; [2002] 3 All E.R. 813.

[119] [1999] 2 A.C. 349; below, para.22–016.

[120] *Hazell v Hammersmith and Fulham LBC* [1992] 2 A.C. 1.

[121] [2005] Q.B. 303 at [10]. Contrast *S v S* [2002] EWHC 223; [2003] Fam. 1 at [70]. For the possible effect in the law of misrepresentation, see below, para.9–013.

[122] Contrast *BP v Aon Ltd* [2006] EWHC 424 (Comm); [2006] 1 C.L.C. 881 at [274]: "substantial area of doubt" whether the *Kleinwort Benson* decision applies to a contract entered into under a mistake of law. The decision in the *Brennan* case is not referred to in the judgment of Colman J.

[123] *Graves v Graves* [2007] EWCA Civ 660; [2008] H.L.R. 10 at [32].

[124] See *Friendly Provident Life Office v Hilliers Parker May & Rowden* [1997] Q.B. 85.

[125] cf. *Avon CC v Howlett* [1983] 1 W.L.R. 605 at 620; *Woolwich Equitable Building Society v IRC (No.2)* [1993] A.C. 70 at 154, 199.

[126] Finnis 115 L.Q.R. 170. See Beatson, in Burrows & Rodger (eds), *Mapping the Law* and the comments, in response, of Lord Hoffmann in *Deutsche Morgan Grenfell Group Plc v IRC* [2006] UKHL 49; [2007] 1 A.C. 558 at [23].

[127] A change in legislation will only have this effect where the legislation itself is intended to apply retrospectively—a rare occurrence—and even then, two of the Law Lords in the majority in the *Kleinwort Benson* case (Lord Goff, at 381; Lord Hope, at 410) did not think it would lead to a finding of mistake based on the earlier legislation.

8–024   **Contracts of compromise.** The settlement in *Brennan v Bolt Burdon* amounted to a compromise of extant litigation, enshrined in a consent order.[128] All three members of the Court of Appeal indicated that there may have been a very short answer to the appeal if it had been argued that, as a matter of public policy, a compromise of extant litigation should never be vitiated for mistake[129] because of the need for finality.[130] As it was, the case was decided on the basis that a compromise *may* be vitiated by a common mistake of law. The Court of Appeal found that the earlier decision supporting the ruling that the claim form was served out of time was open to challenge, even if an opinion had been obtained that it would be difficult. It ought also to have been known that an appeal from that very decision was shortly to be heard. This fell short of the unequivocal but mistaken view of the law in *Kleinwort Benson v Lincoln City Council*. The compromise was not therefore void for mistake.

8–025   **Other contracts.** The likely impact of the decision in *Brennan v Bolt Burdon* for contracts generally is a little difficult to assess because the observations made by the Court of Appeal were so obviously made in the context of a contract of compromise. For example, a certain emphasis was placed on the observation of Lord Hope in *Kleinwort Benson* that "a state of doubt is different from that of mistake".[131] This should not be applied too literally since, even in cases of the most fundamental mistake of fact, there can always be said to have been an element of doubt about the assumptions made by the parties. What matters is the degree of doubt and whether this can be taken to imply that the risk of the mistake had been allocated by the contract.[132] In other words, the mistake of law bar having been lifted, future cases should be decided simply by applying the tests hitherto applied to mistakes of fact.[133] As Sedley L.J. observed[134] those tests may have to be adapted a little before the effect of a mistake of law "can be equiparated with the impossibility of a contractual venture". In *Brennan v Bolt Burdon*, the answer was clearly that the risk of the mistake had been allocated to the claimant, or was the fault of those advising her, so that she was left with a valid, but disadvantageous, contract. That will be the usual outcome in contracts of compromise of

---

[128] Orders made by consent have the effect of contracts: *Huddersfield Banking Co Ltd v Henry Lister & Son Ltd* [1895] 2 Ch. 273; *Allcard v Walker* [1896] 2 Ch. 369 (order set aside in equity, on terms, for a mistake of law). But a "consent" order may be merely one to which a party submits without objection in which case it does not have the effect of a contract: *Siebe Gorman & Co Ltd v Pneupac Ltd* [1982] 1 W.L.R. 185; and in matrimonial proceedings consent orders are not now regarded as contracts: *Thwaite v Thwaite* [1982] Fam. 1; *Jenkins v Livesey* [1985] A.C. 424.
[129] Kay L.J. expressed the rule in terms of vitiation by a subsequent judicial decision, but the policy of finality should exclude vitiation for any mistake, whether of law, or fact.
[130] [2005] Q.B. 303 at [23], [31], [62]; cf. *BCCI v Ali* [2002] 1 A.C. 251 which concerned a general release of a prospective dispute. The case was argued on the basis of construction and the finding of the majority was that an employee had not given up a claim of which he could not have been aware. The principal "mistake", if the case is considered in such terms, was a mistake of fact, i.e. as to the corrupt way in which the employers had been running the business (though that may only have been a unilateral mistake of the employee); this only became significant as a matter of law when the House of Lords later recognised the availability of damages for the "stigma" of having worked for such an employer: *Malik v BCCI* [1998] A.C. 20. See below, para.20–092.
[131] [1999] 2 A.C. 349 at 410B; *In the matter of Kaupthing Singer & Friedlander Ltd* [2010] EWCA Civ 561; [2010] 2 B.C.L.C. 259 at [90].
[132] *Deutsche Morgan Grenfell Group Plc v IRC* [2006] UKHL 49; [2007] 1 A.C. 558 at [22], per Lord Hoffmann; cf. Lord Simon Brown, at [175].
[133] See above, para.8–007.
[134] [2005] Q.B. 303 at [59].

whatever hue.[135] For other contracts it may be found that the effect of the mistake is to make performance of the contract something fundamentally different from that which the parties had contemplated, in circumstances where the risk of the mistake had not been allocated to one of them.[136] In such cases the contract will be void for a mistake of law.

Even though the bar against mistakes of law has been lifted, it may be thought relevant still to give some account of the cases which had previously distinguished between mistakes of law and mistakes of fact.[137] A mistake of *law* will usually only be made on the basis of the declaratory theory[138] and it might be thought more appropriate to allocate the risk of such a mistake to one of the parties (as opposed to a mistake of *fact*), i.e. the parties will, or should, be aware that the law may be "changed" with retrospective effect. This may be true for those in receipt of legal advice, though even here it may be open to doubt,[139] but it is far too broad a generalisation. Furthermore, it would only serve to perpetuate the unsatisfactory and tenuous distinction which it has been necessary to draw in the past between mistakes of fact and mistakes of law.[140] Each case, whether concerned with a mistake of fact, or of law, and without any real concern as to which in borderline cases, should depend on its own circumstances and the application of the tests referred to in para.8–007, above.

(b) Equity

(i) *General*

The extent to which it is necessary to take account of a different approach in equity to the effect of a common mistake has been greatly reduced as a result of two developments. First, the Court of Appeal has held that there is no separate doctrine of common mistake in equity under which a contract might be rescinded in circumstances where it is valid at law.[141] Secondly, the lifting of the bar on mistakes of law[142] means that it is no longer necessary to take account of cases in which relief had been given in equity for certain types of mistake which would not have affected the validity of the contract under the common law as it then stood because they were mistakes of law.[143] It is still possible for equity to give relief by refusing specific performance of a contract entered into on the basis of a common mistake which is not sufficient to make the contract void at common law, but this

8–026

---

[135] See *Kyle Bay Ltd v Underwriters Subscribing Under Policy No.019057/08/01* [2007] EWCA Civ 57.

[136] e.g. the sort of mistake made in *Kleinwort Benson v Lincoln City Council* itself, where it was not necessary to rely on a mistake of law to set aside the contract; it was void simply because it was ultra vires.

[137] See the 11th edn, pp.314–316.

[138] In *Brennan v Bolt Burdon* Sedley L.J. considered that the prospect of "a mistake as to the *current* state of the law which is both mutual and non-negligent is not great" (emphasis added): [2005] Q.B. 303 at [63].

[139] And it would be "strange if a party whose lawyer had raised a doubt on the question ... should be in a worse position than a party who had no doubts because he had never taken any advice": *Deutsche Morgan Grenfell Group Plc v IRC* above, fn.132 at [27], per Lord Hoffmann.

[140] *Nurdin & Peacock Plc v DDB Ramsden & Co Ltd* [1999] 1 W.L.R. 1249 at 1272.

[141] *The Great Peace* [2002] EWCA Civ 1407; [2003] Q.B. 679. See below, para.8–029.

[142] See above, para.8–022.

[143] e.g. *Allcard v Walker* [1896] 2 Ch. 369. See the 11th edn, pp.314–316.

form of relief is largely confined to cases of unilateral mistake.[144] The other form of equitable relief still available, rectification, is specifically concerned with mistakes in reducing the parties' agreement to writing and is considered separately.[145]

(ii) *No separate doctrine of common mistake in equity*

8–027   **The separate doctrine.** A line of twentieth-century cases supported the view that a contract could be rescinded (on terms, if appropriate) on the ground that it was made under a mistake, even though the mistake was not fundamental in the narrow common law sense and so did not affect the validity of the contract at law. The leading case was *Solle v Butcher*[146] where a flat had been let for £250 per annum, both parties mistakenly believing that it was free from rent control, when in fact it was subject to the Rent Acts and to a standard rent of £140 per annum. Had the landlord realised this, he could, before granting the lease, have increased the rent to about £250 per annum, on account of the work done by him to the flat; but he had no right to make such an increase during the currency of a lease already granted. The tenant claimed a declaration that the standard rent was £140 per annum and repayment of the excess; the landlord claimed rescission of the lease. It was held that the lease could be rescinded, though it was valid at law.[147] As it would have caused considerable hardship to the tenant to turn him out of the flat, the court gave him the option of staying on if he paid the standard rent plus the amount by which the landlord could have increased it, had he been aware of the true position when he granted the lease.

8–028   **Criticism.** In the 50 years after *Solle v Butcher*, the equitable power to rescind contracts for mistakes which did not invalidate them at law was exercised in a number of first instance and Court of Appeal decisions.[148] In one of these cases[149] Winn L.J. dissented on the ground that the majority view (that the contract should be rescinded) was inconsistent with the refusal of the House of Lords in *Bell v Lever Bros Ltd*[150] to grant relief for mistake; and no satisfactory way was ever found of explaining the relationship between that leading case and the equitable jurisdiction to rescind.[151] One view was that the equitable jurisdiction could have been exercised in *Bell v Lever Bros Ltd* if an attempt had been made to invoke it; but some of the relevant equity cases were cited to,[152] and equitable principles were discussed by, the House of Lords.[153] A second view was that the exercise of

---

[144] See below, para.8–031, 8–056.

[145] See below, para.8–059 et seq.

[146] [1950] 1 K.B. 671.

[147] The mistake was variously described as one of fact, of private rights, or of law (at 685, 693, 705 (Jenkins L.J.)), but it seems to have been assumed by all members of the court that relief for a mistake of pure law was not available even in equity: see now, para.8–022.

[148] See, e.g. *Laurence v Lexcourt Holdings Ltd* [1978] 1 W.L.R. 1128; *Grist v Bailey* [1967] Ch. 532 (both of which were doubted in *William Sindall Plc v Cambridgeshire CC* [1994] 1 W.L.R. 1016 at 1035); *Magee v Pennine Ins Co Ltd* [1969] 2 Q.B. 507.

[149] *Magee*'s case, above.

[150] [1932] A.C. 161.

[151] A.L.G. 66 L.Q.R. 169; Atiyah & Bennion 24 M.L.R. 421 at 439.

[152] e.g. *Paget v Marshall* (1884) 28 Ch.D. 255; cf. *Associated Japanese Bank International Ltd v Crédit du Nord SA* [1989] 1 W.L.R. 255 at 256.

[153] See the discussion in *Bell v Lever Bros Ltd*, above, of *Cooper v Phibbs* (1872) L.R. 2 H.L. 149 and the discussion of the latter case in *The Great Peace* [2002] EWCA Civ 1407; [2003] Q.B. 679 at [100] et seq.

the equitable jurisdiction depended on relative degrees of "fault" so that rescission would not be ordered in favour of a party who was himself at fault,[154] while conversely it could be ordered against one who had acted improperly in inducing the mistake,[155] or whose insistence on his legal rights after becoming aware of the mistake was unconscientious.[156] The difficulty with this view was that, since there was no definition of "fault" for this purpose, it did little to clarify the scope of the jurisdiction. A third view was that the common law rules laid down in *Bell v Lever Bros Ltd* determined the rights of the parties, while the equitable jurisdiction entitled the court to vary these at its discretion, so that equity "supplemented"[157] the common law; but the difficulty with this view lay in the failure of the relevant cases to formulate any principles governing the equitable discretion.

The Great Peace. At one time it seemed that, in spite of the criticisms   8–029
summarised in the preceding paragraph, the courts had accepted the existence of the equitable jurisdiction, though without giving any clear answer to the question just when a contract which was valid at law could be rescinded in equity. The issue arose again in *The Great Peace*[158] where, as will be recalled, it was held that a charterparty was not void at law[159] by reason of a mistake as to the "proximity" of the chartered ship to the vessel to which she was to render escort services. The Court of Appeal further held that there was no power to rescind the charterparty in equity. It did so on the ground that *Solle v Butcher* was inconsistent with *Bell v Lever Bros Ltd*[160] and that there was, therefore, no equitable power to rescind a contract which, in spite of the mistake, was "valid and enforceable on ordinary principles of contract law".[161] Only by taking this view could "coherence . . . be restored to this area of our law" which had been thrown into "confusion" by *Solle v Butcher* and later cases which had exercised the jurisdiction to rescind.[162]

Effect. To the extent that equity had allowed rescission for mistakes which do   8–030
not make a contract void at law, it sacrificed the requirement of certainty which is emphasised by the common law. It may be, however, that the need for certainty is over-stressed.[163] This is suggested by the fact that the American rules on this subject are much closer to those of English equity than to those of the English common law,[164] and do not seem to have caused widespread inconvenience. Nor has such inconvenience resulted from the rule that a contract can be set aside for even a wholly innocent misrepresentation.[165] Yet from the representor's point of view this rule creates almost as much uncertainty as would a broad doctrine of mistake. In *The Great Peace* Lord Phillips M.R. merely hints that there is "scope

---

[154] [1950] 1 K.B. at 693; cf. *Laurence v Lexcourt Holdings Ltd* [1978] 1 W.L.R. 1128; *Associated Japanese Bank International Ltd v Crédit du Nord SA* [1989] 1 W.L.R. 255 at 270.

[155] e.g. *Cocking v Pratt* (1749) 1 Ves.Sen. 400; *Torrance v Bolton* (1872) L.R. 8 Ch. App. 118; cf. *Beauchamp v Winn* (1873) L.R. 6 H.L. 223 at 233.

[156] e.g. *Hitchcock v Giddings* (1817) 4 Price 135; but see *Riverlate Properties Ltd v Paul* [1975] Ch. 133 at 140–141.

[157] *Associated Japanese Bank (International) Ltd v Crédit du Nord SA* [1989] 1 W.L.R. 255 at 267.

[158] [2002] EWCA Civ 1407; [2003] Q.B. 679.

[159] Above, para.8–016.

[160] *The Great Peace*, above, fn.141, at [157], [160].

[161] ibid. at [161].

[162] ibid. at [157].

[163] What lies at the heart of the reasoning in *The Great Peace* is the need for doctrinal consistency, rather than any attempt to evaluate past exercises of the equitable jurisdiction on their merits.

[164] Restatement 2d, *Contracts*, paras.152, 153.

[165] See below, para.9–078.

for legislation to give greater flexibility to our law of mistake than the common law allows".[166] Two further possibilities cannot be ruled out. The first is that the House of Lords might yet disagree with the Court of Appeal on the issue of discretionary relief for mistake, and the second (no doubt more remote) one is that the House might even review the narrowness of the scope of mistake at common law as laid down in *Bell v Lever Bros Ltd*.[167] With regard to *The Great Peace* itself, it may be relevant to note that the question of equitable relief arose in the context of a charterparty, that this is a type of contract in which certainty (which would be subverted by the exercise of a discretion to rescind) is of paramount importance, and that on the facts there was said to be "no injustice in the result".[168]

(iii) *Refusal of specific performance*

8–031   A mistake which is not sufficient to make a contract void at common law may be used as a defence to an action for specific performance.[169] Most of the cases in which specific performance has been refused have been concerned with unilateral mistake,[170] but one possible effect of the decision in *The Great Peace* may be to lead to more widespread use of this form of relief in cases of common mistake, where appropriate.[171] Since it leaves the contract enforceable at law,[172] it does not seriously prejudice the interests of certainty.

8–032   **No relief for mistake as to expectation.** Equity may grant relief for a mistake which is not fundamental in the narrow common law sense, but not for a mistake "which related to the expectation of the parties".[173] This is illustrated by *Amalgamated Investment & Property Co Ltd v John Walker & Sons Ltd*[174] where a

---

[166] Above fn.141, at [161]. His reference to the analogy of the Law Reform (Frustrated Contracts) Act 1943 is puzzling since that Act deals with the consequences of discharge for frustration and says nothing about *when* a contract is discharged for frustration. There may be scope for something similar to the 1943 Act to deal with the consequences of a finding that a contract is void for mistake (see below, para.19–123), but that was not the issue Lord Phillips was addressing.

[167] [1932] A.C. 161. For doubts about the merits of the case, see also above, at fn.164 and (perhaps) at n.81; cf. Treitel 104 L.Q.R. 501 at 505.

[168] *The Great Peace* [2002] EWCA Civ 1407; [2003] Q.B. 679 at [166]; cf. above, fn.70. The outcome was that the owners recovered five days' hire even though the charterers had cancelled only about two hours after the chartered ship had changed course towards the stricken vessel: see [15], [21]; it is arguable that, on receipt of the charterer's cancellation, the owners should have mitigated by resuming their original course: see below, para.20–116.

[169] Specific performance will clearly be refused where the contract is *void* at law, e.g. where a person contracts to buy his own property: *Jones v Clifford* (1876) 3 Ch.D. 779.

[170] See below, para.8–056.

[171] *Heath v Heath* [2009] EWHC 1908 (Ch); [2010] F.L.R. 610 at [26], where the mistake was induced by the party seeking specific performance and was "practically indistinguishable" from misrepresentation. Earlier cases in which equitable relief was given by way of (or amounting to) rescission may still serve to illustrate the types of mistake for which relief will be given by way of refusing specific performance: e.g. *Hitchcock v Giddings* (1817) 4 Price 135; *Colyer v Clay* (1843) 7 Beav. 188; *Cocking v Pratt* (1750) 1 Ves. Snr. 400 (better viewed as a case of undue influence: see below, para.10–022, fn.127); *Re Garnett* (1885) 31 Ch.D. 1 (where it is unclear whether the "mistake" was a common or unilateral one). It has been noted that "no coherent equitable doctrine of mistake can be spelt" out from these and other earlier cases: Goff & Jones, *The Law of Restituion* (7th edn), para.9–044); *The Great Peace*, above, fn.168, at [100], but this comment is directed at the question of when a contract might be rescinded in equity, not what type of mistake may be sufficient for some form of equitable relief.

[172] By way of an action for damages.

[173] *Amalgamated Investment & Property Co Ltd v Walker & Sons Ltd* [1977] 1 W.L.R. 164 at 172.

[174] See above; Brownsword 40 M.L.R. 467.

contract was made for the sale of a London warehouse which the purchaser (to the vendor's knowledge) intended to redevelop. Before the contract was made, a government official had decided that the warehouse ought to be listed as a building of special architectural or historic interest. But the actual listing took place only after the conclusion of the contract; its effect was to make it harder to obtain permission to redevelop. If such permission were refused the value of the property would be reduced by some £1,500,000 below the contract price of £1,710,000. The Court of Appeal held that equity could not intervene, whether by rescission or by refusal of specific performance,[175] merely because the purchaser mistakenly believed that the property was "suitable for and capable of being developed".[176] No doubt the official's decision, if known, would have affected the negotiations; but that decision did not amount to a listing, and therefore did not affect the quality of the subject-matter at the time of contracting. It only affected the extent of the risk that permission to redevelop might be refused—a risk which would have existed, though to a lesser extent, quite apart from any question of listing. It follows, a fortiori, that relief will not be given for a mistake which relates neither to subject-matter nor to the terms of contract, but only to "the commercial advantage which the contract gave"[177] to the mistaken party.

3. UNILATERAL MISTAKE

Mistake *negatives* consent where the parties are so much at cross-purposes that they do not reach agreement. This may happen where one party is mistaken about the identity of the other, where one party intends to deal with one thing and the other with something different, or where one party intends to deal on one set of terms and the other on a different set of terms. A mistake as to the other party or as to the subject-matter of the contract has no effect unless it is "fundamental", but this alone does not make a contract void. The mistake must also induce the contract, and be operative. In many cases, the last requirement will not be satisfied, so that there will often be a contract in spite of the fact that the consent of one of the parties was negatived.

8–033

(a) Types of Mistake

(i) *Mistake as to the person*[178]

The context in which mistaken identity will usually arise. It will be seen that in the vast majority of the cases which follow, the dispute was between two innocent parties. A seller is induced to sell his goods to a buyer, on credit, in the belief that the buyer is someone, or something, else.[179] Before the buyer has paid for the goods, he sells them on to a sub-buyer for full value. When the seller discovers that he is not going to be paid and the goods are now in the possession of the sub-buyer he may bring an action in conversion against the sub-buyer. The outcome of this claim will turn on which of the seller or sub-buyer has the better

8–034

---

[175] Rescission is now ruled out by the development described at para.8–029, above.
[176] [1977] 1 W.L.R. 164 at 171.
[177] *Clarion Ltd v National Provident Association* [2000] 1 W.L.R. 1888 at 1905.
[178] Goodhart 57 L.Q.R. 228; Williams 23 Can.Bar Rev. 271 at 380; Wilson 17 M.L.R. 515; Unger 18 M.L.R. 259; Smith & Thomas 20 M.L.R. 38; MacMillan [2005] C.L.J. 711.
[179] The "one" and the "thing" matter: see below, para.8–036.

title to the goods. This, in turn, will depend on the effect on the first contract of the seller's "mistake" when selling to the intermediate buyer. Where, as is usually the case, the seller's mistake was induced by the fraudulent misrepresentation of the buyer, the contract will be voidable. If the seller has not taken steps to set aside the contract before the goods are sold to the sub-buyer, title will pass to the buyer, assuming he has bought them in good faith[180]; in particular, in this context, without notice of the fraud. If the seller is to prevail, he must prove that the contract with the buyer was not merely voidable, but was void. He may do this by proving that he did not intend to sell to the buyer at all, i.e. that he made a fundamental mistake as to the identity of the party to whom he was selling.[181] If the initial contract of sale is void, no title will pass to the buyer, nor to the sub-buyer as a result, in accordance with the general rule of *nemo dat quod non habet*.[182] A recommendation by the Law Reform Committee to reverse this result so as to protect the sub-buyer[183] has not been implemented by legislation and it has been left to the courts to determine whether and when, in this type of case, a contract is void, or voidable.[184] Some cases may perhaps be explained quite simply on the basis of the court's preference for one innocent party over another.[185]

8–035   **Fundamental mistake of identity.** A mistake as to the person is fundamental, so that consent is negatived, if one party is mistaken as to the *identity* of the other. In *Cundy v Lindsay*[186] the claimants received an order for handkerchiefs from a dishonest person called Blenkarn, who gave his address as 37, Wood Street, Cheapside. He signed his name to make it look like "Blenkiron & Co", a respectable firm known by reputation to the claimants and carrying on business at 123, Wood Street. The claimants sent the goods to "Blenkiron & Co, 37, Wood Street," where Blenkarn took possession of them. He did not pay for the goods and he later sold them to the defendants. It was held that there was no contract between the claimants and Blenkarn, as the claimants did not intend to deal with him but with someone else. Thus no property in the handkerchiefs passed to Blenkarn,[187] so that he could pass none to the defendants, who were accordingly liable for conversion.

8–036   **Mistake as to attribute.** By contrast, a mistake by one party as to an *attribute* of the other will not as a general rule put the parties so seriously at cross-purposes as to negative consent. In *King's Norton Metal Co Ltd v Edridge, Merrett & Co Ltd*[188] the claimants received an order for wire from "Hallam & Co" which was made on the letter-head to appear as a substantial firm having a large factory in Sheffield and depôts in various other places. In fact "Hallam & Co" consisted solely of an impecunious rogue called Wallis. The claimants sent the goods to "Hallam & Co" on credit. Wallis took possession of them, failed to pay, and sold

---

[180] See below, para.9–107.
[181] He must also show that the mistake induced the contract (para.8–045) and that it was operative (para.8–048), both of which will almost certainly be satisfied in this type of case.
[182] "No one gives who possesses not".
[183] 12th Report Cmnd.2958 (1966), para.15.
[184] Or entirely valid, in the rare case where the mistake is not fundamental and has not been induced by a misrepresentation.
[185] *Ingram v Little* [1961] 1 Q.B. 31 would seem to be a prime example and, as a consequence, its authority is in serious doubt after the decision in the *Shogun* case: see below, para.8–038.
[186] (1878) 3 App.Cas. 459; cf. *Baillie's Case* [1898] 1 Ch. 110.
[187] cf. above, para.8–034.
[188] (1897) 14 T.L.R. 98.

them to the defendants. It was held that the claimants had contracted with "the writer of the letters".[189] Thus property in the goods passed to Wallis, so that he could pass it to the defendants, who were accordingly not liable for conversion. As Wallis and "Hallam & Co" were one and the same person, the claimants had not made any mistake as to the identity, but only one as to the credit-worthiness, of the other contracting party, whom they identified as the writer of the letter. The essential point is that "Hallam & Co" *was* Wallis, just as much as "Currer Bell"[190] *was* Charlotte Brontë.

Whether mistake one of identity or attribute. In cases involving mistake as   8–037
to the person, it may be difficult to say precisely what mistake has been made: i.e. whether B thought that A was C, as opposed to merely thinking that A was not A or making a mistake about A's credit-worthiness. In other cases, it may be clear what mistake has been made, but disputed whether it should be described as one of identity or attribute. It is submitted that the test formulated for the purpose of defining fundamental mistakes as to the subject-matter in cases of common mistake[191] should also (with appropriate modifications) be applied in the present context. A person may be identified by reference to any one of his attributes. If a mistake is made as to that attribute,[192] there can be said to be a mistake as to identity. It is supported by a dictum of Greene L.J. in *Craven-Ellis v Canons Ltd*,[193] where a director's service agreement was held "void ab initio" as neither he nor those who appointed him had the necessary qualification shares. One reason for this conclusion was that the agreement was made "under a mistake as to the present existence of an essential fact recognised by the law as the foundation of the contract".[194] Other hypothetical cases can be imagined which would come within the same principle. A college may hold a private dance and intend to sell tickets only to past or present members. In such a case, for the purpose of the contract to sell a ticket, the identifying attribute of an applicant might be his or her membership of the college.

The principle, then, is that a mistake as to *the* attribute by which a person is identified is in law regarded as a mistake of identity. But one attribute on which the mistaken party cannot in law rely for this purpose is that of the credit-worthiness of the other party, about whom no other mistake is made.[195] In deciding whether the other party is credit-worthy, the mistaken party takes a business risk. It would be undesirable to allow an error of judgment on such a point to negative consent. In applying this principle, the law makes certain prima facie assumptions about the way in which a person is identified, two of which now fall to be considered.

Mistake *inter praesentes*. The difficulty of deciding whether the mistake is one   8–038
of attribute or of identity is particularly acute where the parties who are alleged to have contracted have come physically face to face. In *Phillips v Brooks Ltd*,[196] a rogue called North entered a shop and asked to see pearls and rings. He selected

---

[189] (1897) 14 T.L.R. 98 at 99.
[190] The pseudonym under which Charlotte Brontë wrote *Jane Eyre*.
[191] See above, para.8–019.
[192] Contrast *Sunderland Association FC v Uruguay Montevideo FC* [2001] 2 All E.R. (Comm) 828 at 830 (mistake as to the division in which a football club competed not one of identity).
[193] [1936] 2 K.B. 403.
[194] ibid. at 413.
[195] e.g. *King's Norton Metal Co Ltd v Edridge Merrett & Co* (1897) 14 T.L.R. 98; above, para.8–036.
[196] [1919] 2 K.B. 243; cf. *Dennant v Skinner* [1948] 2 K.B. 164.

(inter alia) a ring worth £450, produced a chequebook, claimed to be Sir George Bullough (a wealthy man known by name to the shopkeeper) and gave Sir George's address. The shopkeeper checked this address in a directory, and then allowed North to take away the ring in exchange for a cheque, which was dishonoured. North later pledged the ring with the defendant. The shopkeeper claimed that there was never any contract between him and North, so that the latter had no title to the ring which he could pass to the defendant. But Horridge J. held that the shopkeeper had

> "contracted to sell and deliver [the ring] to the person who came into his shop . . . who obtained the sale and delivery by means of the false pretence that he was Sir George Bullough".[197]

The shopkeeper's mistake was not one of identity: "His intention was to sell to the person present and identified by sight and hearing."[198] Lord Haldane has explained the decision on the alternative ground that the sale was concluded before any mention was made of Sir George Bullough, and that the mistake only induced the shopkeeper to let North take the ring away on credit.[199] But this explanation was rejected in a later judicial discussion of the case[200]; and it is only doubtfully consistent with the reported facts. North made an offer to buy when he selected the ring[201]; and it is not clear whether he said that he was Sir George Bullough before or after the offer was accepted.[202]

The same result was reached in *Lewis v Averay*,[203] where a person had advertised his car for sale and was visited by a rogue who falsely claimed to be a well-known actor called Richard Greene. By this pretence the rogue induced the seller to sell the car to him on credit and to let him take it away in exchange for a cheque, which was dishonoured. The seller claimed the car from the defendant, who had bought it in good faith from the rogue; but the claim failed as the contract between the seller and the rogue was not void for mistake. The presumption that the seller intended to contract with the person physically before him had not been overcome[204]: his mistake was not one of identity[205] but as to the credit-worthiness of the other party.[206]

The presumption that the seller intends to contract with the person before him is clearly a strong one,[207] but it does not follow from *Phillips v Brooks* or *Lewis v Averay* that there can be no fundamental mistake as to the person merely because

---

[197] ibid. at 246.
[198] ibid. at 247.
[199] *Lake v Simmons* [1927] A.C. 487 at 501.
[200] *Lewis v Averay* [1972] 1 Q.B. 198 at 206.
[201] See above, para.2–009.
[202] See the inconsistent accounts in 88 L.J.K.B. 952; 35 T.L.R. 470; 24 Com.Cas. 263; [1919] 2 K.B. 243; and 121 L.T. 249.
[203] [1972] 1 Q.B. 198; A.L.G. 88 L.Q.R. 161; Turpin [1972] C.L.J. 19.
[204] ibid. at 208, 209.
[205] Lord Denning M.R. said at 207 that there *was* a mistake of identity but that it did not make the contract void. With respect, this approach cannot be reconciled with *Cundy v Lindsay* (1878) 3 App.Cas. 459; above, para.8–035.
[206] [1972] 1 Q.B. at 209.
[207] In *Shogun Finance Ltd v Hudson* [2003] UKHL 62; [2004] 1 A.C. 919, considered below at para.8–039, Lord Millett (at [67]) went so far as to suggest that it is more like a rule of law; cf. Lord Walker (at [187]) for whom it remained a presumption, exceptions to which would be rare.

the parties alleged to have contracted were in each other's presence. There may be such a mistake where A induces B to deal with him by pretending to act as agent for C, while in fact intending to contract on his own behalf.[208] In such a case it could be said that there was no mistake as to the identity of A, but rather one as to the capacity in which he purported to contract.[209] Beyond the example of agency, however, it is difficult to see the exceptional circumstances which would allow the presumption to be rebutted.[210] In *Ingram v Little*[211] the owners of a car had advertised it for sale and been visited by a rogue who falsely claimed to be "P. G. M. Hutchinson of Stanstead House, Stanstead Road, Caterham." They agreed to sell the car to him on credit, but only after one of them had checked in a telephone directory that there was a person of that name living at that address. The rogue later sold the car to the defendants from whom the owners claimed it when the rogue's cheque was dishonoured. A majority of the Court of Appeal upheld the claim on the ground that the owners had intended to deal with the Hutchinson of Stanstead House and not with the person before them *as such*. The case was doubted in *Lewis v Averay*,[212] and by members of both the majority and the minority in *Shogun Finance Ltd v Hudson*,[213] and it should, with respect, be regarded as wrongly decided.

Contracts made in writing. Where a contract is in writing, the parties to that   8–039
contract are prima facie the persons described as such in the writing. This view was endorsed in *Shogun Finance Ltd v Hudson*[214] in which the House of Lords reviewed the leading cases on the effect of a mistake as to the person. A rogue obtained possession of a car by pretending to be Mr Durlabh Patel, producing a driving licence in Mr Patel's name and forging his signature to a hire-purchase agreement purporting to be between the claimant finance company selling the car and Mr Patel. The rogue then sold the car to the defendant who bought it in good faith and for full value. All of their Lordships agreed that the validity of the hire-purchase agreement depended on the intention of the claimant, objectively ascertained, i.e. on the basis that the "hirer" made the offer by completing the application form, whose offer did the claimant purport to accept: the rogue's or Mr Patel's?[215] For the majority, in cases where a "contract" is in writing this is simply a question of construction which, "making appropriate use of extrinsic

---

[208] *Hardman v Booth* (1863) 1 H. & C. 803; cf. *Higgons v Burton* (1857) 26 L.J.Ex. 342. Contrast *Citibank NA v Brown Shipley & Co Ltd* [1991] 2 All E.R. 690 (identity of person acting as mere messenger not fundamental).

[209] This may be the only explanation of Lord Haldane's remark in *Lake v Simmons* [1927] A.C. 487 that there was no contract when a jeweller gave possession of a necklace on approval to a woman called Esmé Ellison having been told by her that she was married to one Van der Borgh. In the *Shogun* case, above, fn.207, Lord Phillips (at [141]) found his approach inconsistent with *Phillips v Brooks*, above, fn.196; cf. *Ingram v Little* [1961] 1 Q.B. 31 at 50, 66.

[210] *Shogun* case, above, fn.207, at [37], per Lord Nicholls.

[211] [1961] 1 Q.B. 31.

[212] [1972] 1 Q.B. 198 at 206, 208 (Megaw L.J.).

[213] [2003] UKHL 62; [2004] 1 A.C. 919; at [87], per Lord Millett; at [185], per Lord Walker: considered below, para.8–039.

[214] [2003] UKHL 62; [2004] 1 A.C. 919; Elliott [2004] J.B.L. 381; Phang, Lee and Koh [2004] C.L.J. 24; Scott [2004] L.M.C.L.Q. 292; McLauchlan [2005] J.C.L. 1; *The Sibohelle* [2011] EWHC 1150 (Comm).

[215] Clearly, there could be no contract with Mr Patel since he had not given the rogue authority to make the contract on his behalf.

evidence,[216] will normally enable the court to reach a firm conclusion as to the person with whom a party intends to contract."[217] In some cases, it may be found that the party named is a mere alias for the rogue, as in the *King's Norton* case,[218] but where the putative agreement refers to an "unequivocally identifiable" individual, as in *Cundy v Lindsay*,[219] this precludes any other finding; the process of construction leads "inexorably" to the conclusion that the person with whom it was intended to contract was the person thus described.[220] In *Shogun*, the application form filled in by the rogue and accepted by the claimant fell into this category. Accordingly, the rogue was not a party to the agreement, so that the defendant acquired no title to the car.[221]

At the very least then, when the named party is "unequivocally identifiable" there is a strong presumption that the other party intended to contract with the named party and with no one else. As with the presumption in the "face-to-face" cases, it is difficult to see the exceptional circumstances which would allow this presumption to be rebutted,[222] agency apart.[223] The consequence is that most cases will be conclusively determined, and with very different outcomes, on the basis of what may be fine distinctions as to the type of contract involved, i.e. whether "face to face" or "in writing", which will in turn depend on what particular form of deception was practised by the rogue involved.

It was this which persuaded the minority that the law in this area had developed in an unacceptable way. For a number of reasons, their preference was to apply the presumption applicable to face-to-face dealings more generally, i.e. it is presumed that the seller intended to sell his goods to the person *with whom he was dealing*.[224] To say that with written contracts it is simply a matter of construction "begs the

---

[216] Lord Hobhouse applied the parol evidence rule to exclude any evidence which sought to *contradict* that Mr Patel was the contracting party, and Lord Phillips' approval (at [155]) of the use of the rule in *Young v Schuler* 11 Q.B.D. 651 at 654–655 implies that this is how one should understand his reference to the "appropriate use of extrinsic evidence". But since the issue in *Shogun* was one of contract formation, this application of the rule is open to doubt: *The Starsin* [2004] 1 A.C. 715 at [175], per Lord Millett; McLauchlan 121 L.Q.R. 9; Stevens, in Burrows & Peel (eds), *Contract Terms*.

[217] [2004] 1 A.C. 919 at [154], per Lord Phillips (emphasis added).

[218] Above, para.8–036.

[219] Above, para.8–035, though it may be noted that the rogue did not give the correct address for Blenkiron & Co.

[220] [2004] 1 A.C. 919 at [161], per Lord Phillips.

[221] Under Hire-Purchase Act 1964, s.27.

[222] One possible example (hinted at by Lord Phillips ([2004] 1 A.C. 919 at [166]) and Lord Walker (ibid. at [192])) might have been *Hector v Lyons* (1989) 58 P. & C.R. 156 where a father conducted negotiations for the purchase of a house, and, when these were successfully concluded, instructed his solicitors to draw up the contract in the name of his son (who was a minor) as purchaser. The decision not to award the father specific performance is readily understandable on the basis of ample evidence that he did not come to court with "clean hands" (see below, para.21–032), but the conclusion that there was no contract at all with the father does perhaps support the view that such cases are based on the parol evidence rule, or something similar to it, i.e. the *non-admissibility* of evidence to *contradict* the written contract, which named the son as purchaser. See also: *Dumford Trading AG v OAO Atlantryb-flot* [2005] EWCA Civ 24; [2005] 1 Lloyd's Rep. 289 at [37].

[223] *Doncaster M.B.C. v Racing (UK) Ltd* [2005] EWCA Civ 999; *The Sibohelle* [2011] EWHC 1150 (Comm); cf. *Young v Schuler* 11 Q.B.D. 651 (where the issue was reversed: did the agent also sign as principal?); cf. below, para.16–056.

[224] [2004] 1 A.C. 919 at [28], per Lord Nicholls; at [81], per Lord Millett. Lord Nicholls (at [36]) thought it not easy to think of practical circumstances where "once in point", the presumption would be displaced: *Boulton v Jones* (1857) 2 H & N 564 (para.8–045, below) might be thought to represent an exception, but it is perhaps better explained as a case where the presumption that the buyer intended to buy from the person "with whom he was dealing" pointed to the named party Brocklehurst and not Boulton, to whom Brocklehurst had transferred his business earlier the same day.

crucial question"[225]: to whom was the offer made, or, as in *Shogun*, to whom was the acceptance directed? In cases said to involve a mistake of identity, the identity of the other party was merely incidental[226]: the seller sold to the rogue Hallam in the *King's Norton* case in the mistaken belief that he was credit-worthy, but the seller only sold to the rogue in *Cundy* in the mistaken belief that he was Blenkiron and was, *therefore*, credit-worthy, just as the seller did in the face-to-face cases of *Lewis v Averay* and *Phillips v Brooks*. In each case, the mistake made by the seller may explain *why* he sold to the party with whom he was dealing but does not negate his intention to sell *to that person*, i.e. the rogue. As a matter of legal policy the loss is more appropriately borne by the person who takes the risk in parting with his goods without receiving payment.[227] Finally, it is difficult to see how, as has been suggested,[228] the rogue in these cases could have been sued by the seller under what is a supposedly non-existent contract.[229] This is a formidable array of argument. As it is, in the unlikely event that the House of Lords is persuaded to re-visit this issue so soon after having given it the fullest consideration, the law can only be rescued from what Lord Nicholls regarded as its "unsatisfactory and unprincipled state" by the intervention of Parliament.[230]

Whether contract is "in writing"? Such is the almost conclusive nature of 8–040 the presumptions at work in this area, it is crucial to the outcome of any given case which of them applies, e.g. whether the contract is "in writing" so as to attract the presumption upheld by the majority in the *Shogun* case. There are indications from the majority that this category is to be construed narrowly.[231] According to Lord Phillips it should be confined to dealings which are "exclusively conducted in writing"[232]; where there is "*some* form of personal contact",[233] the presumption in the "face-to-face" cases should be applied.[234] Similarly, Lord Walker thought that the presumption in the "face-to-face" cases was not applicable where the "*only* contract[235] was by written communication sent by post or by e-mail".[236]

---

[225] ibid. at [30], per Lord Nicholls; at [103], per Lord Millett.

[226] ibid. at [35], per Lord Nicholls.

[227] ibid. at [35], per Lord Nicholls; at [82], per Lord Millett. In the context of *Shogun* the buyer from the rogue could have asked for a search to be done (via the Hire Purchase Index) to determine whether the car was subject to an outstanding hire-purchase agreement, though since the sale to him took place on the day after the rogue had obtained possession of the car it is unlikely that the agreement would yet have been registered. The fact that the seller has failed to register the agreement, or failed to do so with immediate effect, might be thought to support Lord Nicholls' assessment of which party should bear the risk.

[228] See below, para.8–053.

[229] [2004] 1 A.C. 919 at [93], per Lord Millett. It has been suggested (Stevens, above, fn.216) that this may be explained by a process of "ratification" analogous to the ratification of a contract entered into by an agent without the authority of the principal (see below, para.16–042), but it is the conferral of an "option" on the part of the seller which has such potentially harsh effects on a *third party* that makes this analogy inapposite (cf. below, para.16–051).

[230] Possibly by reconsidering the proposals for reform in the 12th Report of the Law Reform Committee, Cmnd.2958 (1966), para.15.

[231] Perhaps, in part, to allay the concerns of the minority about "fine" and "unprincipled" distinctions.

[232] [2004] 1 A.C. 919 at [170].

[233] ibid. (emphasis added).

[234] There was considerable personal contact in *Hector v Lyons*, above, fn.222, a case which is relied on by the majority to support the presumption for contracts made in writing. This may explain why the decision in that case is queried by Lord Phillips (at [166]), and Lord Walker (at [192]).

[235] Perhaps this should read "contact".

[236] [2004] 1 A.C. 919 at [188].

They would probably therefore agree with Lord Nicholls' observation that, if some form of writing had been introduced in *Phillips v Brooks*,[237] such as an invoice or receipt made out in favour of Sir George Bullough, it would "be neither here nor there"[238] and amount to no more than "stark contemporary confirmation that the misrepresentation was made and that the seller believed it".[239] By contrast, in *Cundy v Lindsay*,[240] the rogue sent a written order to the seller which simply despatched the goods to the address supplied. There will, inevitably, be more difficult cases. In *Shogun* itself, the application form was faxed to the finance house which never met the rogue, but there were telephone communications between the finance house and the dealer making the car available, creating the prospect that it was a face-to-face case if the dealer was acting as agent of the finance house,[241] which clearly he was not.[242] When a fraudster purchases goods over the counter of a shop with the aid of a stolen credit card, the "face-to-face" presumption must apply, but if he does so over the internet by giving the details from a stolen card, that would seem closer, by analogy, to Lord Walker's example of communication only by email, so as to attract the presumption that the seller only intended to sell to the cardholder.[243]

8-041   **Undisclosed principals.** A person who knows that another is unwilling to contract with him may employ an agent to make the contract without disclosing the existence of the principal. In some such cases the undisclosed principal is not allowed to intervene and take the benefit of the contract. But the contract is not void since the agent can (fraud apart) enforce it. These cases are discussed in Ch.16.[244]

(ii) Mistake as to the subject-matter

8-042   **Subject-matter.** Consent is negatived if one party intends to deal with one thing, and the other with a different one. This principle may have been applied in *Raffles v Wichelhaus*,[245] where a seller of cotton "to arrive *ex Peerless* from Bombay" tendered cotton from a ship called *Peerless* which had sailed from Bombay in December. The buyer refused to accept the goods, alleging that he had intended to buy the cotton shipped on another *Peerless* which had sailed from Bombay in October: thus it was argued that there was no agreement between the parties. On a claim by the seller, judgment was given for the buyer but, as no reasons were stated, it is hard to tell whether the ground of decision was that there

---

[237] See above, para.8–038.
[238] According to Lord Phillips (at [176]), the written agreement would have been "no more than peripheral to the dealings".
[239] [2004] 1 A.C. 919 at [25].
[240] See above, para.8–035.
[241] Described by Lord Nicholls (at [41]) as a "singularly sterile argument" which only served to underline the "practical absurdity" of the distinctions in play.
[242] For the reasons explained by Lord Hobhouse, at [51].
[243] The customary security check seems to be to ask for the card number, the date of expiry, any additional security number and the *name of the cardholder* as it appears on the card. This sort of fine distinction might be thought to add to the minority's criticism of the current state of the law.
[244] See below, paras 16–056—16–060.
[245] (1864) 2 H. & C. 906.

was *no* contract,[246] or that there *was* a contract to deliver cotton from the October *Peerless* which could not be performed by delivering cotton from the December *Peerless*.[247]

Consent was clearly negatived in *Falck v Williams*.[248] A and B were negotiating about two charterparties: one to carry shale from Sydney to Barcelona, and one to carry copra from Fiji to Barcelona. B's agent sent a coded telegram intending to confirm the copra charter, but the telegram was ambiguous and was understood by A to refer to the shale charter. It was held that there was no contract. Similarly, consent is negatived if a buyer at an auction thinks that the lot for which he is bidding consists of hemp when it consists of hemp and tow.[249]

Quality. On the other hand, consent is not generally negatived by a mere   8–043 mistake as to quality: thus it was held in *Smith v Hughes*[250] that if a person buys oats, thinking that they are old, from a seller who knows that they are new, there is a good contract. Similarly, a contract for the sale of goods is not void merely because the seller, under a mistake as to the quality of the goods, charges a lower price than he would have done, had he known the truth.[251] In such cases, the parties are at cross-purposes, but not to such an extent that they are not in agreement at all. A mistake as to quality can negative consent only if it is a mistake as to a fundamental quality by which the thing is identified.[252]

(iii) *Mistake as to the terms of the contract*

Consent is negatived if the parties intend to contract on different terms, e.g. if   8–044 A sells goods to B for so many "pounds" intended by A to mean sterling and by B to mean a different currency[253]; or if A intends to sell rabbit skins at a fixed price per piece when B intends to buy at the same price per pound, there being about three pieces to the pound.[254]

Mistakes as to the person and mistakes as to the subject-matter negative consent only if they are fundamental. There seems to be no such requirement where the mistake is as to the terms of the contract. A sale of oats is not void merely because they are believed by one party to be old but known by the other to be new. The mistake is as to a quality of the subject-matter and is not fundamental.[255] But according to *Smith v Hughes*[256] a sale of oats believed by the buyer to be *warranted*

---

[246] *Smith v Hughes* (1871) L.R. 6 Q.B. 597 at 609; *O T Africa Line Ltd v Vickers Plc* [1996] 1 Lloyd's Rep. 700 at 703. There was no allegation that the seller intended to deal with the cargo of the December rather than the October *Peerless*. The case was decided on a demurrer so that the facts were never proved.

[247] *Van Praagh v Everidge* [1902] 2 Ch. 266 at 269. On this view the buyer could have got damages for the seller's failure to deliver cotton from the October *Peerless*.

[248] [1900] A.C. 176.

[249] *Scriven Bros & Co v Hindley & Co* [1913] 3 K.B. 564.

[250] (1871) L.R. 6 Q.B. 597.

[251] *Dip Kaur v Chief Constable of Hampshire* [1981] 1 W.L.R. 578.

[252] As defined above, para.8–019.

[253] See *Woodhouse AC Israel Cocoa Ltd v Nigerian Produce Marketing Co* [1972] A.C. 741 at 768; cf. *Felthouse v Bindley* (1862) 11 C.B.(N.S.) 869 ("30" intended to mean pounds by buyer but guineas by seller); *Smidt v Tiden* (1874) L.R. 9 Q.B. 446.

[254] *Hartog v Colin & Shields* [1939] 3 All E.R. 566.

[255] See above, after fn.250.

[256] (1871) L.R. 6 Q.B. 597; cf. *London Holeproof Hosiery Co Ltd v Padmore* (1928) 44 T.L.R. 499; *Sullivan v Constable* (1932) 49 T.L.R. 369.

to be old and not intended by the seller to be so warranted may be void for mistake. The mistake is as to a term of the contract and negatives consent although the term relates to a quality of the subject-matter which is not fundamental. This distinction seems to be generally accepted, but the reason for it is not easy to see. If a quality is not fundamental, a mistake as to its existence does not destroy consent. Why should consent be destroyed by mistake as to a warranty of that same quality? Is it really true, in the latter case, that the parties have not agreed at all?[257] An alternative explanation for this aspect of *Smith v Hughes* will be put forward later in this chapter.[258]

(b) Mistake must Induce the Contract

8–045   **Mistake as to the person.** A mistake negatives consent only if it induced the mistaken party to enter into the contract. If that party takes the risk that the facts are not as he supposed them to be,[259] or if he is simply indifferent as to the matter to which the mistake relates, the validity of the contract is not affected. For example, in *Mackie v European Assurance Society*[260] the claimant took out an insurance policy through an agent, believing that the agent was acting for one company when in fact he was acting for another. It was held that the policy with the latter company was not void for mistake. The claimant's intention "was not to remain uninsured for one hour and in what office it was was a secondary consideration, provided it would meet its engagements and was able to do so".[261]

This case should be contrasted with *Boulton v Jones*.[262] Boulton had just bought a shop from one Brocklehurst when the defendant sent his servant to the shop with an order, addressed to Brocklehurst, for a quantity of pipe hose. Boulton supplied the goods, no doubt thinking that the defendant did not care from whom he obtained them. The defendant was apparently satisfied with the goods and used them. He had clearly made a fundamental mistake, in that he thought he was dealing with Brocklehurst when he dealt with Boulton. Ordinarily, that mistake would have had no effect, since it would not matter to the defendant whether the goods were supplied by Boulton or by Brocklehurst. But Brocklehurst owed money to the defendant, who had intended to set off this debt against the price of the goods. He could thus show that it was important for him to contract with Brocklehurst rather than with Boulton. It was therefore held that there was no contract so that the defendant was not liable for the price of the goods.[263] To have

---

[257] *The Harriette N* [2008] EWHC 2257; [2008] 2 Lloyd's Rep. 685 at [87] (a compromise over the demurrage due from a buyer used a lower figure because of the seller's mistake about the date when the ship completed its unloading. The buyer knew of the mistake but as the date for completion of unloading was "not a term of the contract of compromise" the mistake did not affect the objective agreement of the parties. No submission appears to have been made that the amount of demurrage mistakenly stated by the seller was a term, i.e. the "price" for the agreement to discharge the buyer from its obligation to pay the demurrage actually due, but this may be thought to be something of a circular argument).

[258] See below, para.8–051.

[259] *Wales v Wadham* [1977] 1 W.L.R. 199 at 220; (approved on the issue of mistake in *Jenkins v Livesey* [1985] A.C. 424); cf. above, paras 8–004, 8–010.

[260] (1869) 21 L.T. 102; cf. *Fellowes v Gwydyr* (1829) 1 Russ. & My. 83.

[261] ibid. at 105.

[262] (1857) 2 H. & N. 564; L.J.Ex. 117; 6 W.R. 107.

[263] cf. *Westminster CC v Reema Construction (No.2)* (1992) 24 Con.L.R. 26 (no *liability* of successor in business under contract with predecessor).

held him liable would have been unjust as it would have deprived him of the benefit of his set-off against Brocklehurst. But the result of holding him not liable was almost equally unjust. The defendant got the goods for nothing but retained his right to sue Brocklehurst for the amount which the latter owed him. It seems that on such facts the defendant should be under some liability for unjust enrichment,[264] or that he should at least be bound to transfer his claim against Brocklehurst to the supplier.[265]

Other types of mistake. The requirement that the mistake must induce the contract applies not only to mistake as to the person but also to other types of mistake. If in *Raffles v Wichelhaus*[266] both ships *Peerless* had sailed from Bombay on the same day and had arrived at the same time, it might not have mattered to the buyer which cargo he got. In that case he could not have escaped liability by saying that he intended to buy the cargo in the one ship while the seller intended to sell the cargo in the other.   8-046

(c) When Mistake is Operative

(i) *Contract generally valid*

Objective principle. A mistake which negatives consent does not necessarily make the contract void. On the contrary, the general rule is that a party is bound, in spite of his mistake: this follows from the objective principle,[267] under which one party (A) is often bound if his words or conduct are such as to induce the other party (B) reasonably to believe that A was assenting to the terms proposed by B.[268]   8-047

The operation of the objective principle is most easily illustrated by the case of a person who by mistake bids for the wrong lot at an auction. Although the parties may not be *ad idem*,[269] (as they intended to deal with different things), the bidder is prevented by the objective principle from relying on the mistake and so from saying that the contract is void.[270] The same principle applies to mistakes as to the person[271] and as to the terms of the contract. Thus a seller who, as a result of some miscalculation, offers goods at a price lower than that which he would have asked but for the mistake cannot, after the offer has been accepted, generally rely on the mistake to make the contract void.[272] Similarly, where a landlord as a result of a clerical error offers to grant a tenancy at a rent of £1,000 per month, he cannot, after the offer has been accepted, escape from the transaction merely by showing

---

[264] cf. below, para.22–024.

[265] Goff and Jones, *The Law of Restitution* (7th edn), para.23–006.

[266] (1864) 2 H. & C. 906; cf. *Ind's Case* (1872) L.R. 7 Ch.App. 485 (validity of share transfer not affected by which shares the transferee gets, so long as he gets the quantity contracted for).

[267] See above, paras 1–002, 2–002.

[268] *Smith v Hughes* (1871) L.R. 6 Q.B. 597, 607; *OT Africa Line Ltd v Vickers Plc* [1996] 1 Lloyd's Rep. 700.

[269] *Van Praagh v Everidge* [1903] 1 Ch. 434.

[270] *Robinson, Fisher & Harding v Behar* [1927] 1 K.B. 513.

[271] *Cornish v Abington* (1859) 4 H. & N. 549; *Re Reed* (1876) 3 Ch.D. 123, so far as *contra*, seems wrong.

[272] This would have been the position in *Hartog v Colin & Shields* [1939] 3 All E.R. 566 (below, para.8–053) if the court had not taken the view that the claimant must have known of the defendant's mistake.

that his real intention was to make the offer at a rent of £2,000 per month.[273] The position is the same where a person signs a document under some other mistake about its terms or legal effects: he cannot, in general, say that the contract is void because of his mistake.[274]

(ii) *Exceptional cases in which mistake is operative*

8-048   Where the objective principle applies, the contract is valid in spite of the existence of a mistake, so that it is unnecessary to go into the difficult question whether the mistake is fundamental. That question need only be answered in the following three exceptional situations, in which the objective principle does not apply, so that the mistake is *operative*.

8-049   **Ambiguity.** There may be such ambiguity in the circumstances that a reasonable person could not draw any relevant inference from them at all. In *Raffles v Wichelhaus*[275] a reasonable person could not have deduced with which cargo the parties intended to deal. Similarly, if parties stipulate for the payment of freight "per charterparty" but there are two charterparties in the case, providing for payment of different rates of freight, the reasonable person cannot put any definite interpretation on the promises.[276] In these cases, therefore, the mistake is operative and makes the contract void.

8-050   **Mistake known to other party.** The objective principle applies where A's words or conduct induce B reasonably to believe that A is contracting with him; but it does not apply where B actually knows that (in spite of the objective appearance) A has no such intention.[277] It follows that the objective principle will not apply, and that the mistake will be operative, if A's mistake is known to B.[278] This is the reason why the contract in *Cundy v Lindsay*[279] was void. The claimants may have behaved so as to induce a reasonable person to believe that they were dealing with Blenkarn, but the mistake was operative as Blenkarn knew that they had no such intention. The case would have been different if Blenkarn had written to the claimants in good faith and they had misread his signature for "Blenkiron & Co." In such a case, the claimants could not have relied on their mistake, had they simply sent the goods to Blenkarn's address, unless it had been clear to

---

[273] *Centrovincial Estates Plc v Merchant Investors Assurance Co Ltd* [1983] Com.L.R. 158.

[274] *Blay v Pollard & Morris* [1930] 1 K.B. 628; cf. *L'Estrange v F Graucob Ltd* [1934] 2 K.B. 394, a case of ignorance rather than mistake, discussed in Spencer [1973] C.L.J. 104.

[275] (1864) 2 H. & C. 906 ("a case of latent ambiguity": *The Great Peace* [2002] EWCA Civ 1407; [2003] Q.B. 679 at [29]); cf. *Hickman v Berens* [1895] 2 Ch. 638; *NBTY Europe Ltd v Nutricia International BV* [2005] EWHC 734; [2005] 2 Lloyd's Rep. 350.

[276] *Smidt v Tiden* (1874) L.R. 9 Q.B. 446.

[277] See above, para.2–003.

[278] There is no clear authority on the question of whether a mistake is operative where it *ought to* have been known to the non-mistaken party: see *Centrovincial Estates Plc v Merchant Investors Assurance Co Ltd* [1983] Com. L.R. 158; *OT Africa Line Ltd v Vickers Plc* [1996] 1 Lloyd's Rep. 700, but there is obviously a fine line between a finding that it ought to have been known and that it must have been known, which was sufficient in *Hartog v Colin & Shields* [1939] 3 All E.R. 566, below, para.8–053; cf. *Chwee Kin Keong v Digilandmall.com Pte Ltd* [2005] SGCA 2; [2005] 1 S.L.R. 502 (Sing. Ct. of Appeal); cases on rectification and the meaning given to "knowledge": below, para.8–067.

[279] (1878) 3 App.Cas. 459.

Blenkarn from the contractual documents that they did not intend to deal with him but with Blenkiron & Co.[280]

In *Boulton v Jones*[281] the defendant's order was addressed to Brocklehurst, so that Boulton knew it was not meant for him. It is not clear whether he also knew *why* the order was not meant for him, i.e. whether he knew that Brocklehurst owed money to Jones. Probably such knowledge is not essential to make the contract void. A person who accepts an offer knowing that it is addressed to another must take the risk that the mistake may turn out to be material.

Smith v Hughes. The rule that a mistake of one party is operative if known to the other is further illustrated by *Smith v Hughes.*[282] Oats were bought by sample, the buyer thinking that they were old when, in fact, they were new. He refused to accept them, as he had no use for new oats. In an action for the price, the trial judge told the jury to find for the buyer (1) if the word "old" had been used in the negotiations, i.e. if the oats had been *expressly described* as old; or (2) if "the [seller] believed the [buyer] to believe, or to be under the impression, that he was *contracting for the purchase of old oats*". The jury found for the buyer, but did not say which of these two questions they had answered in his favour. If they thought that the word "old" had been used, their verdict was clearly correct. But they might have based their verdict on their answer to the second question, so that the court had to decide whether this question was correctly formulated.

8–051

If the buyer's mistake had been *as to the subject-matter*, it could not in law negative consent at all because it was not fundamental; it was only a mistake as to quality.[283] The seller's knowledge of the buyer's mistake would not alter this.[284] But if the mistake had been *as to the terms of the contract* it could negative consent.[285] There would have been such a mistake if the buyer believed that the seller had *warranted* the oats to be old, while the seller intended to sell without warranty. Prima facie this mistake would not be operative: the objective principle would apply, the buyer having behaved so as to induce the seller reasonably to believe that the buyer was buying oats of the same quality as those in the sample. The mistake would be operative only if the seller knew of the buyer's mistake—i.e. if he knew that the buyer believed he was buying the oats with a warranty that they were old.[286] Thus if the buyer thought the oats *were old* there was a good contract even if the seller knew of this mistake; but if the buyer thought the oats were *warranted to be old* and the seller knew of this, quite different, mistake the contract was void. The court ordered a new trial because the direction to the jury did not clearly distinguish between the two mistakes which the buyer might have made.

It has been suggested above[287] that it is hard to see why a mistake as to a warranty of quality should negative consent when a mistake as to the existence of the quality itself does not have this effect. The distinction is based on *Smith v Hughes*; and it is submitted that if the buyer did believe the oats to have been warranted old, and the seller knew this, the buyer could have been absolved from

---

[280] cf. *The Unique Mariner* [1978] 1 Lloyd's Rep. 438 at 451–452.
[281] (1857) 2 H. & N. 564; L.J.Ex. 117; 6 W.R. 107, above, para.8–045.
[282] (1871) L.R. 6 Q.B. 597.
[283] See above, para.8–043.
[284] cf. *The Harriette N* [2008] EWHC 2257; [2008] 2 Lloyd's Rep. 685, above fn.257.
[285] See above, para.8–044.
[286] cf. *Hartog v Colin & Shields* [1939] 3 All E.R. 566 (below, para.8–053).
[287] See above, para.8–044.

liability on an alternative ground. In such a case it could be said that there *was* a contract under which the seller was bound by the warranty that the oats were old, because he had behaved so as to induce the buyer reasonably to believe that he was contracting on those terms.[288] Breach of the warranty that the oats were old could have justified the buyer's refusal to accept new oats.[289]

8–052   **Mistake negligently induced.** A mistake is operative where one party has negligently led the other to make it. In *Scriven Bros v Hindley & Co*[290] the defendant at an auction bid for two lots believing that both were lots of hemp, whereas one was a lot of hemp and tow. Normally, he could not have relied on this mistake,[291] but he was able to do so in this case because the mistake was caused by the misleading nature of the catalogue and by the conduct of one of the seller's servants. This principle is distinct from that which applies in cases of ambiguity.[292] Where a mistake is negligently induced, the circumstances need not be so perfectly ambiguous as to make each party's view of the contract equally tenable. If auction particulars are so obscure as to lead a purchaser to make a mistake, the mistake will be operative even though the particulars, properly interpreted, can only bear the meaning intended by the vendor.[293]

(iii) *Mistake may operate against one party only*

8–053   If A's mistake is deliberately induced by B, then A can treat the contract as void, but it does not follow that B can do so. It seems probable that in *Cundy v Lindsay* Blenkarn could have been sued for the price of the handkerchiefs.[294] The same may be true even where B does not in any way bring about A's mistake. In *Hartog v Colin & Shields*[295] the defendants intended to offer hare skins for sale at a stated price "per piece", but inadvertently offered to sell at that price "per pound". A pound contained, on average, three pieces. The claimant purported to accept this offer. It was held that there was "no contract"[296] as the claimant must have known of the defendants' mistake in expressing their offer.[297] But it is possible that the defendants could have held the claimant liable on his acceptance if a fall in the market had made them wish to do so.

---

[288] This is the argument of counsel for the buyer as reported in 40 L.J.Q.B. at 223. But in the *Law Reports*, counsel is reported as saying: "The parties were not *ad idem*" (at 600); cf. below, para.8–054.

[289] It is true that under Sale of Goods Act 1979, s.11 refusal to accept is (as a general rule) justified only by a breach of *condition* and not by one of *warranty* (below, para.18–039 et seq.). But in 1871 these words were probably not used in their present sense: see below, para.18–041; cf. *Hardwick Game Farm v Suffolk Agricultural, etc. Association* [1969] 2 A.C. 31 at 83.

[290] [1913] 3 K.B. 564.

[291] See above, para.8–047; cf. *Lloyds Bank v Waterhouse* [1993] 2 F.L.R. 97 at 123.

[292] See above, para.8–049.

[293] cf. *Swaisland v Dearsley* (1861) Beav. 430, in equity, but *Scriven Bros & Co v Hindley & Co* [1913] 3 K.B. 564 shows that the common law is the same.

[294] So in the agency situation discussed at para.8–038, above, the agent might have been liable: cf. *Bell v Balls* [1897] 1 Ch. 663 at 669.

[295] [1939] 3 All E.R. 566.

[296] ibid. at 567.

[297] cf. *Watkin v Watson-Smith, The Times*, July 3, 1986.

(d) Theoretical Basis

The offer and acceptance theory. It has been suggested[298] that the cases   8–054
discussed in this section do not depend on mistake at all, but on the rule that there
is no contract if offer and acceptance do not correspond. If, for example, contract
notes are exchanged by which A agrees to sell "St. Petersburgh clean hemp ex
Annetta" but B agrees to buy "Riga Rhine hemp ex *Annetta*",[299] then it is as
plausible to say that there is no contract because offer and acceptance do not
correspond as it is to say that there is no contract because the parties intended to
deal with different things.[300]

But there are also difficulties in the way of this "offer and acceptance" theory.[301]
It clearly does not mean that there is a good contract merely because the express
words of the offer correspond with those of the acceptance. In *Raffles v Wichelhaus*,[302] there was, so far as appears from the report, no lack of verbal correspondence between offer and acceptance, and yet (on one view of the case) there was
no contract.

Another version of the same theory is that the full terms of the offer, as
intended by the offeror, must correspond with the full terms of the acceptance, as
intended by the offeree. But on this view it is hard to see why some discrepancies
prevent the formation of a contract, while others do not. Two cases may be
contrasted. In the first, A intends to sell oats which are new; B intends to buy oats
which are old. In the second, A intends to sell cotton ex *Peerless* (December); B
intends to buy cotton ex *Peerless* (October). The contract in the first case is
expressed to be for "oats" and in the second for "cotton ex *Peerless*". In both cases
offer and acceptance correspond verbally. In neither case would they correspond
if each party expressed his full intention. Yet in the first case there is a good
contract, while in the second there is none. This version of the "offer and
acceptance" theory makes no allowance for the crucial distinction between mistakes which are fundamental and those which are not.

A third version of the theory is that the required correspondence is between
offer and acceptance *as construed by the court*. On this view *Raffles v Wichelhaus* can
be explained on the ground that offer and acceptance were so ambiguous that the
court could not, in the context, determine their meaning at all. But this version of
the theory makes it hard to explain the distinction drawn in *Smith v Hughes*
between a mistake as to the age of the oats and a mistake as to a warranty as to their
age; and, more generally, to say why offer and acceptance should have been held
to correspond in some of the cases discussed in this section, but not in others. It
seems that this version of the "offer and acceptance" theory still raises the same
difficulties as those which arise under the doctrine of mistake. If the offer and
acceptance correspond verbally, the court is unlikely to hold that they do not
correspond on their true construction unless the parties are very seriously at

---

[298] Slade 70 L.Q.R. 385; Shatwell 33 Can.Bar Rev. 164; Atiyah 2 Ottawa L.Rev. 337, esp. at
pp.344–350 and *Essays in Contract*, pp.253–260; cf. *Whittaker v Campbell* [1984] Q.B. 319 at 327—but
in that case the mistake was as to attribute only, and so not fundamental: see [1984] Q.B. 319 at
329.
[299] As in *Thornton v Kempster* (1814) 5 Taunt. 786.
[300] cf. *The Harriette N* [2008] EWHC 2257; [2008] 2 Lloyd's Rep. 685 at [87] per Aikens J ("Some
of the cases talk of such a contract being void, but I think it is clearer to say that there never was a
contract at all").
[301] cf. Devlin L.J. (dissenting) in *Ingram v Little* [1961] 1 Q.B. 31.
[302] (1864) 2 H. & C. 906; above, para.8–042.

cross-purposes; and such a process of construction would not appear to differ substantially from the application of the principle of fundamental mistake.[303]

(e) Equity

8–055   The common law of unilateral mistake can be a source of hardship. A contract may be valid, in spite of the existence of a fundamental mistake, because of the objective principle. Here the mistaken party can suffer hardship through being held to a contract which he did not intend to make, though this hardship must be weighed against that which the other party might suffer if the contract were held invalid.[304] Conversely, an innocent third party may suffer hardship where the contract is void, as in *Shogun Finance v Hudson*.[305] Equity provides no relief against the hardship to third parties that can arise when the contract is void at law,[306] and deals only to a limited extent with the hardship which the mistaken party can suffer when the contract is valid.

8–056   **Refusal of specific performance.** Specific performance will clearly be refused where the contract is *void* at law, e.g. where one party, to the knowledge of the other, makes a mistake as to the terms of the contract[307]; or as to its binding force.[308]

Specific performance may be refused where the contract is *valid* at law because the mistake is not fundamental,[309] or not operative[310] by reason of the objective principle.[311] Thus in *Day v Wells*[312] the defendant instructed an auctioneer to sell cottages thinking that he had told the auctioneer to put a reserve price on them. The auctioneer sold without reserve, at a lower price, and it was held that the defendant could not be compelled to perform specifically.

In exercising its discretion, the court must weigh the hardship of granting the remedy against the uncertainty caused by refusing it. Two cases may be contrasted. In *Malins v Freeman*[313] the defendant at an auction bid for one lot under

---

[303] Atiyah, above, fn.298 at 350 and 260, suggests that the courts are "in fact using" the construction technique and not the mistake technique, citing *Sullivan v Constable* (1932) 48 T.L.R. 369. On the other hand, it seems that the mistake technique was used in *Dennant v Skinner* [1948] 2 K.B. 164 and in *Lewis v Averay* [1972] 1 Q.B. 198. It is also accepted in the Law Reform Committee's 12th Report, Cmnd.2958 (1966), para.15. The difficulty of determining which technique was used by the majority in *Ingram v Little* [1961] 1 Q.B. 31 may support the view expressed in the text that there is little (if any) practical difference between them.

[304] The other party can, however, invoke the objective principle even though he has not suffered any detriment by relying on the appearance of agreement induced by the conduct of the mistaken party: above, para.8–047.

[305] [2003] UKHL 62; [2004] 1 A.C. 919; above, para.8–039.

[306] cf. a number of statements by Lord Denning to the effect that the contract in cases such as *Cundy v Lindsay* (1878) 3 App.Cas. 459 would now be voidable in equity: *Solle v Butcher* [1950] 1 K.B. 671 at 692; *Lewis v Averay* [1972] 1 Q.B. 198 at 207. The attraction of this view is that it would enable the court in such cases to protect innocent third parties. But he has also said that there was "no contract at all" in *Cundy v Lindsay* (*Gallie v Lee* [1969] 2 Ch. 17 at 33 (affirmed [1971] A.C. 1004)); and this view is certainly more consistent with the decision; cf. below, para.8–058.

[307] *Webster v Cecil* (1861) 30 Beav. 62. It seems reasonable to deduce from the report that the claimant knew of the defendant's mistake; but this fact is not actually stated.

[308] *Pateman v Pay* (1974) 232 E.G. 457.

[309] e.g. *Jones v Rimmer* (1880) 14 Ch.D. 588.

[310] See above, para.8–047.

[311] *Manser v Back* (1848) 6 Hare 433.

[312] (1861) 30 Beav. 220; cf. *Wood v Scarth* (1855) 2 K. & J. 33.

[313] (1837) 2 Keen 25.

the mistaken impression that he was bidding for another. Although he was clearly liable at law,[314] it was held that specific performance should not be ordered against him. But in *Tamplin v James*[315] the defendant at an auction bid for an inn and a shop mistakenly believing that the lot included a certain garden. The Court of Appeal ordered specific performance, stressing the uncertainty which would result from allowing the defendant to rely on his own mistake. James L.J. said that a defendant could rely on a mistake to which the claimant had not contributed only "where a hardship amounting to injustice would have been inflicted upon him by holding him to his bargain, and it was unreasonable to hold him to it".[316] The two cases may be reconciled by saying that it is a "hardship amounting to injustice" to force a person to take one property when he thinks he has bought another, but not to force a person to take a property which is less extensive than he thought.

Since the object of refusing specific performance is to avoid hardship to the party prejudiced by the mistake, it follows that, where the contract is valid at law, only that party can rely on the mistake. Thus if A thinks that he is buying more than B intends to sell, A can specifically enforce the contract for the smaller quantity intended by B.[317] But where the contract is void at law, neither party can specifically enforce it[318] unless the circumstances are such that, even at law, one party, but not the other, can rely on the mistake.[319]

Specific performance on terms. Equity can take a middle course between refusing specific performance and granting it in spite of the mistake: it can, where the contract is valid at law, grant specific performance on terms. Thus in *Baskcomb v Beckwith*[320] an estate was sold in lots, on the terms that the purchaser of each lot should covenant not to build a public house on it. The vendor kept one of the lots himself, and proposed to build a public house there, but the plan of the lots did not make this clear. It was held that the vendor could specifically enforce the contract but only if he covenanted not to build a public house on the land retained by him. Similarly, equity can order specific performance with compensation, i.e. abatement or increase of the purchase price, where the value of the property sold is less or greater than supposed because of some misdescription of the property.[321]

8–057

No rescission in equity. Where a contract is valid because the mistake of one of the parties is not operative, equity may refuse specific performance against the mistaken party, but it will not rescind[322] and so deprive the other party of his remedy at law on the contract; for to take this step would subvert the certainty which the objective principle is intended to promote. Accordingly, equity will, in general, follow the common law rule that a mistake is not operative if the mistaken

8–058

---

[314] See above, para.8–047.

[315] (1880) 15 Ch.D. 215; cf. *Calverley v Williams* (1790) 1 Ves.Jun. 209.

[316] *Tamplin v James*, above, at 221; cf. *Manser v Back* (1848) 6 Hare 433; *Stewart v Kennedy* (1890) 15 App.Cas. 75 at 105.

[317] *Preston v Luck* (1884) 27 Ch.D. 497.

[318] *Higginson v Clowes* (1808) 15 Ves. 516 (vendor's claim); *Clowes v Higginson* (1813) 1 Ves & B. 524 (purchaser's claim).

[319] See above, para.8–053.

[320] (1869) L.R. 8 Eq. 100.

[321] See below, para.18–029.

[322] *The Harriette N* [2008] EWHC 2257; [2008] 2 Lloyd's Rep. 685 at [105] disagreeing with *Huyton SA v Distribuidora Internacional de Productos Agricolas SA* [2002] EWHC 2088 (Comm); [2003] 2 Lloyd's Rep. 780 at [455].

party, A, has so conducted himself as to induce the other party, B, reasonably to believe that A has agreed to the terms proposed by B. In particular, a person cannot have a contract set aside because of a mistake which he made because he failed to act with due diligence.[323]

4. RECTIFICATION[324]

(a) In General

8–059   Contracting parties may execute a document purporting to contain the terms previously agreed between them. If, as a result of a mistake, the document fails to contain all those terms, or contains different terms, the court may rectify it by ordering its wording to be changed so as to bring it into line with the earlier agreement[325]; alternatively, the court may treat the document as having been so rectified without making a formal order for its rectification.[326] Having been developed in equity, rectification is a discretionary remedy.[327] It is available where there has been a mistake, not in the *making*, but in the *recording*, of a contract: "Courts of equity do not rectify contracts; they may and do rectify instruments."[328] Rectification can be ordered although the contract is one which must be in, or evidenced in, writing.[329] An entire agreement clause in the executed document does not preclude a claim in rectification.[330] The requirements to be met differ according to whether the mistake is made by both parties,[331] or only one.[332]

8–060   **Types of mistake.** Rectification is most frequently ordered where the terms of a document do not correspond with those of the agreement between the parties, e.g. where the rent is misstated in a lease, or the area of land to be conveyed is misstated in a conveyance.[333] For this purpose, "the agreement" refers to the terms actually agreed between the parties. Thus where those terms were accurately recorded in a lease it was held that rectification was not available merely because they had not been correctly stated in the earlier written agreement for the

---

[323] *Attorney-General v Tomline* (1877) 7 Ch.D. 388; *Soper v Arnold* (1877) 37 Ch.D. 96; 14 App.Cas. 429; cf. *The Harriette N* [2008] EWHC 2257; [2008] 2 Lloyd's Rep. 685. For the common law position, cf. above, para.8–004.

[324] Burrows, in Burrows & Peel (eds) *Contract Terms*; Buxton 69 C.L.J. 253.

[325] *Murray v Parker* (1854) 19 Beav. 305; *The Rhodian River* [1984] 1 Lloyd's Rep. 373.

[326] *The Nile Rhapsody* [1994] 1 Lloyd's Rep. 382; *OTV Birwelco Ltd v Technical & General Guarantee Co Ltd* [2002] EWHC 2240 (TCC); [2002] 4 All E.R. 668 at [39].

[327] *Re Butlin's Settlement Trusts* [1976] Ch. 251 at 263. Rectification may be ordered by consent, but it remains a matter for the discretion of the court: *Burford (Fareham) Ltd v Christian Vision* [2005] EWHC 2533.

[328] *Mackenzie v Coulson* (1869) L.R. 8 Eq. 369 at 375; *The Olympic Pride* [1980] 2 Lloyd's Rep. 67 at 72.

[329] *Olley v Fisher* (1886) 34 Ch.D. 367; *Johnson v Bragge* [1901] 1 Ch. 28; *USA v Motor Trucks Ltd* [1924] A.C. 196; *May v Platt* [1900] 1 Ch. 616, if *contra*, is not law: *Craddock Bros v Hunt* [1923] 2 Ch. 136; Law Com. No.164, paras 5, 6.

[330] *JJ Huber Ltd v The Private DIY Company Ltd* (1995) 70 P. & C.R. 33 (unilateral mistake); *Surgicraft Ltd v Paradigm Biovices Inc* [2010] EWHC 1291 (Comm).

[331] See below, para.8–062.

[332] See below, para.8–067.

[333] e.g. *Beale v Kyte* [1907] 1 Ch. 564; *Blacklocks v J B Developments (Godalming) Ltd* [1982] Ch. 183.

lease.[334] The only "mistake" of the parties was as to the effect of that written agreement, and to rectify the lease would have defeated, rather than given effect to, the intention of the parties.

Rectification is also available where a person who intends to sign a document in one capacity does so in another, e.g. where the name of a person to whom a bill of exchange is meant to be payable is put in as drawer instead of as payee.[335] The court may also rectify a document executed under a mistake as to its meaning or legal effect[336]; but such a mistake will not be a ground for rectification if the true legal effect of the document was fully explained to the party claiming to have made the mistake,[337] or if the mistake is not as to the legal effect of the document but as to the fiscal effect of making payments pursuant to it.[338]

An obvious drafting mistake may be corrected as a matter of construction, provided there was a clear mistake on the face of the instrument and it is also clear what correction ought to be made in order to cure the mistake.[339] If the "mistaken" party's claim for construction succeeds, rectification is strictly unnecessary[340] though it may be convenient, e.g. if the contract is likely to come into the hands of a third party. If it fails, rectification may still be available. For example, A may believe that the document relates to X alone, so far as its subject-matter is concerned, and B alleges that it relates to X and Y. Even if B succeeds on the issue of construction, rectification will be available to A if the case is one of the exceptional ones (described below[341-342]) in which the remedy can be granted in spite of the fact that the mistake was that of one party only.[343]

Clear evidence. When rectification is claimed, the court has to guard against two dangers. The first is that the remedy may result in imposing on a party terms to which he might not in fact have agreed. The second is that the "certainty and ready enforceability [of written agreements] would be hindered by constant attempts to cloud the issue by reference to pre-contract negotiations".[344] For these reasons, the burden of proof falls on the party seeking rectification and it will be ordered only if there is strong and convincing evidence that the document failed   **8–061**

---

[334] *London Regional Transport v Wimpey Group Services* (1987) 53 P. & C.R. 356.

[335] *Druiff v Parker* (1868) L.R. 5 Eq. 131 cf. *Co-operative Bank Plc v Tipper* [1996] 4 All E.R. 366 (guarantor's name mistakenly inserted as borrower's).

[336] *Re Colebrook's Conveyances* [1973] 1 W.L.R. 1379; cf. *Jervis v Howle & Talke Colliery Ltd* [1937] Ch. 67, following *Burroughes v Abbott* [1922] 1 Ch. 86; *Re Butlin's Settlement Trusts* [1976] Ch. 251. No claim for rectification was made in *Keen v Holland* [1984] 1 W.L.R. 251 (where a mistake as to legal effect was held not sufficient to give rise to an estoppel by convention: above, para.3–099).

[337] *Constantinidi v Ralli* [1953] Ch. 427.

[338] *Allnutt v Wilding* [2007] EWCA Civ 412.

[339] *East v Pantiles (Plant Hire)* [1982] 2 E.G.L.R. 111 at 112. The mistake "on the face" may emerge only when the document is read with regard to the "background or context": *Chartbrook Ltd v Persimmon Homes Ltd* [2009] UKHL 38; [2009] 1 A.C. 1101 at [24]. For the law relating to misnomer, see: *Nittan UK Ltd v Solent Steel Fabrications Ltd* [1981] 1 Lloyd's Rep. 633; *Dumford Trading AG v OAO Atlantrybflot* [2005] EWCA Civ 24; [2005] 1 Lloyd's Rep. 289 at [27]–[34]; cf. *Gastronome (UK) Ltd v Anglo-Dutch Meats (UK) Ltd* [2006] EWCA Civ 1233; [2006] 2 Lloyd's Rep. 587 at [16]–[17].

[340] cf. *Mangistaumunaigaz Oil Production Association v United World Trade Inc* [1995] 1 Lloyd's Rep. 617; *Alliance v Tishby* [2011] EWHC 1015 (Ch) at [42]. In *Woodford Land Ltd v Persimmon Homes Ltd* [2011] EWHC 984 (Ch) this produced a very odd result.

[341-342] See below, para.8–067.

[343] *QRS Sciences Ltd v BTG International Ltd* [2005] EWHC 670 (Ch); [2005] F.S.R. 43.

[344] *The Olympic Pride* [1980] 2 Lloyd's Rep. 67 at 73.

accurately to record the intention of the parties.[345] The court is, in particular, reluctant to rectify a contract solely on the oral evidence of the party claiming rectification[346] but there is no absolute rule against rectification on such evidence.[347] In ordinary commercial contracts, there is no room for a duty of care on the parties to point out, or not take advantage of mistakes that would not be sufficient for rectification.[348]

(b) Common Mistake[349]

8–062   **Mistake of both parties.** A contractual document[350] can, in general, be rectified only if it fails to record the intention of *both* parties.[351] Thus if A lets a house to B and both agree that the rent is to be £200 per month, the lease can be rectified if by mistake it states the monthly rent to be only £100. But if all the time A intended to charge £200 while B intended to pay only £100 the lease could not be rectified to conform with A's intention,[352] for this would force on B a contract to which he had never agreed. In such circumstances, a contractual document will only be rectified where B is guilty of some form of unconscionable conduct.[353] What matters for the purposes of determining whether both parties were mistaken is their *objective* intention, i.e. in the example above, whether what A and B said or did would convey to a reasonable observer that they intended the rent to be £200 per month.[354] If a prior consensus is established on this basis, it is no bar to rectification for B to prove that, subjectively, he only intended to pay £100.[355]

---

[345] *Joscelyne v Nissen* [1970] 2 Q.B. 86; *Ernest Scragg & Sons Ltd v Perseverence Banking & Trust Co* [1973] 2 Lloyd's Rep. 101; *The Olympic Pride*, above, fn.344, at 73; *Thomas Bates & Son Ltd v Wyndham's (Lingerie) Ltd* [1981] 1 W.L.R. 505 at 521. On the question whether the evidence must come up to the standard required in criminal cases contrast *Earl v Hector Whaling* [1961] 1 Lloyd's Rep. 459 at 468, 470; and *Mangistaumunaigaz Oil Production Association v United Trade Inc* [1995] 1 Lloyd's Rep. 617 at 621 with *The Pina* [1991] 1 Lloyd's Rep. 246 at 250, affirmed on other grounds [1992] 2 Lloyd's Rep. 103; *Luk Leamington Ltd v Whitmarch Plc* [2002] 1 Lloyd's Rep. 6 at 18–19. See below, para.8–065.

[346] *Tucker v Bennett* (1887) 38 Ch.D. 1; *Fredensen v Rothschild* [1941] 1 All E.R. 430; *Thomas Bates & Son Ltd v Wyndham's (Lingerie) Ltd*, above, at 514, 521.

[347] *Cook v Fearn* (1878) 48 L.J.Ch. 63.

[348] *Daventry District Council v Daventry & District Housing Ltd* [2010] EWHC 1935 (Ch).

[349] Smith 123 L.Q.R. 116.

[350] A voluntary settlement can be rectified on account of a mistake of the settlor alone: *Re Butlin's Settlement Trusts* [1976] Ch. 251.

[351] Where a term is implied into the *contract* between the parties by custom (see above, para.6–046), it may also be convenient to rectify any written version. Since it is based on custom there may be no evidence that the parties actually intended the term to be incorporated: *Caraman, Rowley & May v Aperghis* (1923) 40 T.L.R. 124.

[352] *Faraday v Tamworth Union* (1917) 86 L.J.Ch. 436; *W Higgins Ltd v Northampton Corp* [1927] 1 Ch. 128; cf. *Lloyd v Stanbury* [1971] 1 W.L.R. 535; *The Nai Genova* [1984] 1 Lloyd's Rep. 353; *Thomas Witter Ltd v TBP Industries Ltd* [1996] 2 All E.R. 573 at 601.

[353] See below, para.8–067.

[354] *Frederick E Rose (London) Ltd v William H Pim Jnr & Co Ld* [1953] 2 QB 450 at 461; *Olympic Pride (Etablissements Georges et Paul Levy v Adderley Navigation Co Panama SA* [1980] 2 Lloyd's Rep 67 at 72; *Britoil plc v Hunt Overseas Oil Inc* [1994] C.L.C. 561 at 578; *Chartbrook Ltd v Persimmon Homes Ltd* [2009] UKHL 38; [2009] 1 A.C. 1101 at [57]–[66]; McLauchlan 126 L.Q.R. 8; *The Aktor* [2008] EWHC 1330 (Comm); [2008] 2 Lloyd's Rep. 246 at [38]–[48].

[355] The parties' *shared* subjective and mistaken understanding as to the legal effect of a document may form the basis of rectification, e.g. where both parties purposely use the words in question but they have ascribed the wrong interpretation to them: *Re Butlin's Settlement Trusts* [1976] 1 Ch. 251 at 261.

One party indifferent. In *Van der Linde v Van der Linde*[356] the court refused   **8-063**
to rectify a covenant so as to achieve the tax advantage which the covenantor had
intended (but failed) to secure. One reason for the refusal was that there was not
sufficient evidence of mistake; another was that the covenantee had no view as to
"the intention of the document".[357] In *Whiteside v Whiteside*[358] the court likewise
refused to rectify a covenant made for (but failing to achieve) the same purpose,
partly because there was no evidence of the *common* intention of the parties, and
partly because there was no issue between them: the covenantor went on paying
the covenantee (his wife) as if the covenant had been rectified. But such an issue
can be manufactured by simply refusing to make a single payment. If the document in fact fails to express the intention of the parties, rectification can be
ordered even though there is no dispute between them *inter se*, but only one
between them and the Revenue authorities.[359]

A continuing common intention. The court can rectify a document which   **8-064**
was preceded by a concluded agreement or a "continuing common intention"[360]
(objectively ascertained[361]) even though there was no prior binding contract,[362] for
example, because the prior agreement was binding in honour only.[363] In *Joscelyne
v Nissen*[364] an agreement for the transfer of a business and premises was negotiated
between a father and daughter, it being understood that the father should continue
to live in the premises and that the daughter should pay his gas and electricity
bills. No provision for such payments was made in the formal contract finally
executed. Rectification was ordered even though, before execution of the document, the agreement between the parties had no contractual force. It was enough
that there was "some outward expression of accord"[365] and that this was "adhered
to in intention by the parties to the subsequent written contract".[366] On the other
hand, a document cannot be rectified to bring it into line with mere steps in the
antecedent negotiations,[367] for these may not have led to a concluded agreement
on the particular point, or, if they did, that agreement may not have been
maintained till the execution of the document.[368]

---

[356] [1947] Ch. 306.

[357] ibid. at 312.

[358] [1950] Ch. 65; cf. *Rabin v Gerson Berger Assocation Ltd* [1986] 1 W.L.R. 526 at 534 (where no claim for rectification was made).

[359] *Re Colebrook's Conveyances* [1973] 1 W.L.R. 1379; cf. *Re Slocock's Will Trust* [1979] 1 All E.R. 359; *Lake v Lake* [1989] S.T.C. 865.

[360] *The Olympic Pride* [1980] 2 Lloyd's Rep. 67 at 72; *Grand Metropolitan Plc v William Hill Group Plc* [1997] 1 B.C.L.C. 390; *Swainland Builders Ltd v Freehold Properties Ltd* [2002] 2 E.G.L.R. 71 at [33].

[361] See the cases cited at fn.354 above.

[362] For the now rejected contrary view, see *Mackenzie v Coulson* (1869) L.R. 8 Eq. 369 at 375.

[363] *Eagle Star, etc., Insurance Co v Reiner* (1927) 43 T.L.R. 259; cf. *Symington & Co v Union Ins Society of Canton* (1928) 34 Comm.Cas. 233.

[364] [1970] 2 Q.B. 86; Bromley 87 L.Q.R. 532; Kavanagh 34 M.L.R. 102; cf. *Wilson v Wilson* [1969] 1 W.L.R. 1470; *Michael Richards Properties v St Saviour's Parish* [1975] 3 All E.R. 416 at 423; *The Olympic Pride*, above, fn.360, at 72.

[365] See below, para.8–065.

[366] [1970] 2 Q.B. 86 at 99; *Shipley Urban DC v Bradford Corp* [1936] Ch. 375 at 396; cf. *Crane v Hegeman-Harris Co Inc* [1939] 1 All E.R. 662 at 664–665; criticised in *F E Rose (London) Ltd v W H Pim, Jnr & Co Ltd* [1953] 2 Q.B. 450 at 461; distinguished in *Ashville Investments Ltd v Elmer Contractors Ltd* [1989] Q.B. 488 at 516, and in *Ethiopian Oilseeds & Pulses Corp v Rio del Mar Foods Inc* [1990] 1 Lloyd's Rep. 86; approved in *Joscelyne v Nissen* [1970] 2 Q.B. 86.

[367] *Lovell & Christmas Ltd v Wall* (1911) 104 L.T. 85 at 88.

[368] *The Aktor* [2008] EWHC 1330 (Comm); [2008] 2 Lloyd's Rep. 246 at [60].

8–065   **Outward expression of accord.** The need for an "outward expression of accord" should be seen "more as an evidential factor, rather than a strict legal requirement in all cases of rectification."[369] It does not require that the term in question must have been expressly mentioned. It can have been implied: "there must be *some material* upon which it can be said that the instrument does not reflect what the parties agreed . . . ",[370] bearing in mind at all times that clear evidence will be needed for rectification.[371]

8–066   **Document accurately recording prior agreement.** It follows from the principle that equity rectifies instruments and not contracts[372] that a document which accurately records a prior agreement cannot be rectified merely because that agreement was made under some mistake. In *F E Rose (London) Ltd v W H Pim, Jnr & Co Ltd*[373] the claimants had received an order from a customer for "Moroccan horsebeans described here as feveroles" and asked the defendants (their suppliers) what "feveroles" were. The defendants replied that feveroles were just horsebeans and orally agreed to sell "horsebeans" to the claimants. When this contract was reduced to writing, the goods were again described as "horsebeans". In fact there were three types of Moroccan horsebeans: feves, feveroles and fevettes. The defendants supplied feves, which were less valuable than feveroles. It was held that the written contract could not be rectified by inserting "feveroles" after "horsebeans", as it accurately recorded the previous oral agreement.[374]

(c) Unilateral Mistake[375]

8–067   **Requirement of unconscionable conduct.** Where only one party makes a mistake in the recording of a contract, the relevant document may be rectified if, in addition, the non-mistaken party was guilty of fraud,[376] or misrepresentation,[377] or the requirements for an estoppel have been met.[378] Rectification will also be ordered if the non-mistaken party knew of the mistake.[379] For these purposes, knowledge refers not only to actual knowledge, but also includes wilfully shutting one's eyes to an obvious mistake, or wilfully and recklessly failing to make such

---

[369] *Munt v Beasley* [2006] EWCA Civ 370 at [36]; cf. *JIS (1974) Ltd v MCP Investment Nominees Ltd* [2003] EWCA Civ 721 at [34].

[370] *Britoil plc v Hunt Overseas Oil Inc* [1994] C.L.C. 561, at 578, per Hoffmann L.J.

[371] See above, para.8–061.

[372] See above, para.8–059.

[373] [1953] 2 Q.B. 450; cf. *The Ypatia Halcoussi* [1985] 2 Lloyd's Rep. 364 at 371.

[374] The contract was not void for mistake: above, para.8–016. Nor could the claimants rescind for misrepresentation as they had resold the horsebeans: cf. below, para.9–097, but they might now be able to claim damages under Misrepresentation Act 1967, s.2(1) (below, para.9–039). They might also (as Denning L.J. suggested) be able to claim damages for breach of a collateral warranty, if the necessary *animus contrahendi* on the part of the seller could be shown (below, paras 9–051—9–052).

[375] McLauchlan 124 L.Q.R. 608.

[376] *Blay v Pollard & Morris* [1930] 1 K.B. 628 at 633.

[377] See Ch.9; *Wimpey (UK) Ltd v VI Construction Ltd* [2005] EWCA Civ 77; [2005] B.L.R. 135 at [54].

[378] *A Roberts & Co Ltd v Leicestershire CC* [1961] Ch. 555; *The Nai Genova* [1984] 1 Lloyd's Rep. 353 at 363.

[379] ibid.; *Commission for the New Towns v Cooper (Great Britain) Ltd* [1995] Ch. 259; *Thomas Bates & Son Ltd v Wyndham's (Lingerie) Ltd* [1981] 1 W.L.R. 505; *Wimpey (UK) Ltd v VI Construction Ltd* [2005] EWCA Civ 77; [2005] B.L.R. 135.

inquiries as an honest[380] and reasonable man would make.[381] It has been said that the non-mistaken party must have been guilty of "sharp practice",[382] but the preferable view is that his conduct must be such as to make it inequitable that he should be allowed to object to the rectification of the document.[383] Other forms of unconscionable conduct may therefore suffice,[384] e.g. it is not enough that the non-mistaken party merely suspects that a mistake has been made,[385] but if he intended the other party to be mistaken as to the construction of the document and prevented him from discovering the mistake by making "false and misleading statements" during the negotiations then rectification may be ordered.[386] In all of these cases, the remedy would cause no injustice to B.

No antecedent agreement necessary. In *Littmann v Aspen Oil (Broking)*   8–068
Ltd,[387] had it been necessary, the Court of Appeal would have ordered rectification of a lease for unilateral mistake where there was no antecedent agreement about the content of the clause to be rectified[388] and all three judges observed that this would be the first such case of its kind. This is open to doubt and rather depends on what is meant by an "antecedent agreement". In the *Roberts* case,[389] the parties were negotiating for different completion dates: the claimant, in 1955; the defendant, in 1956. The defendant knew *before* the contract was drawn up to include the date in 1956 that the claimant was assuming that it would be 1955. The court ordered rectification, when it may be said that there was no common intention as to the completion date. But it has already been noted that where a mistake as to terms is known by the non-mistaken party to have been made he may be bound by the contract which the other party had intended.[390] In that sense there was a prior common intention in the *Roberts* case which was mistakenly recorded.[391] In the *Littmann* case, the landlord put forward a break clause to which the tenant would have objected, but because it included the word "landlord", where "tenant" had really been meant, and therefore caused no harm to the tenant as worded, no objection was raised. There was no common intention because there were other aspects of the clause, apart from the "mistaken" element, to which the tenant had not assented, and would not have assented had the clause correctly referred to "tenant". But even here, it seems that where the non-mistaken party is guilty of

---

[380] Since a failure to make such enquiries is not necessarily equated with personal dishonesty, Sedley L.J. preferred to substitute "honourable" for "honest": *Wimpey (UK) Ltd v VI Construction Ltd* [2005] EWCA Civ 77; [2005] B.L.R. 135 at [56].

[381] *Thomas Bates & Son Ltd v Wyndham's (Lingerie) Ltd* [1981] 1 W.L.R. 505; *Wimpey (UK) Ltd v VI Construction Ltd* [2005] EWCA Civ 77; [2005] B.L.R. 135, based on the analysis of various forms of knowledge made by Peter Gibson J. in *Baden v Société Générale pour Favoriser le Développement du Commerce et de l'Industrie en France SA (Note)* [1993] 1 W.L.R. 509.

[382] *Riverlate Properties Ltd v Paul* [1975] Ch. 133 at 140.

[383] *Thomas Bates & Son Ltd v Wyndham's (Lingerie) Ltd* [1981] 1 W.L.R. 505 at 515.

[384] As well as the situations referred to in the text, rectification may be ordered if there was "undue influence or a fiduciary relationship between the parties": *The Nai Genova* [1984] 1 Lloyd's Rep. 353 at 365.

[385] *The Ypatia Halcoussi* [1985] 2 Lloyd's Rep. 364 at 371.

[386] *Commission for the New Towns v Cooper (Great Britain) Ltd* [1995] Ch. 259 at 280; *Hurst Stores and Interiors Ltd v ML Europe Property Ltd* [2004] EWCA Civ 490; [2004] B.L.R. 249 at [19].

[387] [2005] EWCA Civ 1579; [2006] 2 P. & C.R. 2.

[388] The appeal was determined on the basis that an obvious mistake had been made which could be corrected as a matter of construction: see above, para.8–060.

[389] Above, fn.378.

[390] See above, para.8–051 and the discussion of *Smith v Hughes*.

[391] And similarly in *Commission for the New Towns v Cooper (Great Britain) Ltd*, above, fn.386; cf. *QRS Sciences Ltd v BTG International Ltd* [2005] EWHC 670 (Ch); [2005] F.S.R. 43.

trying to take advantage of an error, the court will proceed on the basis that there was the necessary antecedent agreement. According to Jacob L.J., in reality the tenant's conduct "amounted to an agreement—by accepting the clause knowing what the other side thought it meant, he was accepting just that and equity should not allow him to resile".[392]

(d) Limitations on the Remedy

8–069   **Executed contracts.** Although the contrary has been suggested[393] execution (i.e. performance) of a contract is no bar to rectification. Thus leases and conveyances can be rectified on the ground that they are inconsistent with the contracts which preceded them.[394] Any other view would conflict with the whole concept of rectification, for the formal document which it is sought to rectify often *is* the execution of the prior contract.

8–070   **Restitutio in integrum impossible.** Impossibility of restoring the parties to the position in which they were before the contract is, in general, no bar to rectification. For example, a marriage settlement can be rectified after the marriage has taken place.[395]

8–071   **Lapse of time.** A claim for rectification is barred by lapse of time. It is not clear whether time begins to run when the contract was made[396] or when the mistake is discovered[397] or when it should by the exercise of reasonable diligence have been discovered. The last view probably applies in cases of innocent misrepresentation[398]; and there seems to be no good reason for applying a different rule where rectification is claimed.

8–072   **Third party rights.** The right to claim rectification, like the other equitable rights, can be asserted against a purchaser with notice of the mistake,[399] but not against a bona fide purchaser for value without notice, at least in circumstances where the third party has acquired a proprietary interest in the subject matter, e.g. a tenant cannot claim rectification of the tenancy agreement against any bona fide purchaser of the reversion.[400] In the case of purely contractual rights, an assignee takes "subject to equities"[401] and that may include the equity of rectification even as against an assignee without notice.[402]

---

[392] [2006] 2 P. & C.R. 2 at [24].
[393] e.g. in *May v Platt* [1900] 1 Ch. 616, criticised in *Thompson v Hickman* [1907] 1 Ch. 550.
[394] e.g. *Murray v Parker* (1854) 19 Beav. 305; *Cowen v Truefitt Ltd* [1899] 2 Ch. 309; *Stait v Fenner* [1912] 2 Ch. 504.
[395] *Cook v Fearn* (1878) 48 L.J. Ch. 63; *Johnson v Bragge* [1901] 1 Ch. 28.
[396] *Bloomer v Spittle* (1872) L.R. 13 Eq. 427.
[397] *Beale v Kyte* [1907] 1 Ch. 564.
[398] See below, para.9–114.
[399] *Craddock Bros v Hunt* [1923] 2 Ch. 136; *Blacklocks v J B Developments (Godalming) Ltd* [1982] Ch. 183.
[400] *Smith v Jones* [1954] 1 W.L.R. 1089; cf. *Garrard. v Frankel* (1862) 30 Beav. 445.
[401] See below, para.15–037.
[402] Berg 124 L.Q.R. 6 at 12, commenting on the decision at first instance in *Chartbrook Ltd v Persimmon Homes Ltd* [2007] EWHC 409; (2007) 11 EG 160 (affirmed: [2009] UKHL 38; [2009] 1 A.C. 1101); see above, para.6–022, fn.119. For the right to rectify *of the assignee*, see below, para.8–074.

Judgment. A claim for rectification is barred by a judgment in proceedings in   8–073
which the issue of rectification could have been (though it was not) raised.[403] But
judgment in proceedings in which the question of rectification could *not* have been
raised is no bar to a later claim for rectification.[404]

Assignment. It has been suggested that, even where a contracting party can   8–074
claim rectification, a person to whom he assigns his rights cannot do so.[405] The
basis for this suggestion seems to be that in such circumstances rectification might
produce an undeserved windfall for the assignee.

Instruments which cannot be rectified. The articles of association of a   8–075
company cannot be rectified once they have been registered, even if they contain
a simple clerical error.[406] To allow rectification would cut across the scheme laid
down by the Companies Acts for the registration and alteration of such documents.

In *Phillipson v Kerry*[407] it was held that a deed poll cannot be rectified, though,
if executed under a mistake, it can be set aside. One possible reason for this rule,
given in the judgment, is that a voluntary gift cannot be rectified. But as it is now
clear that a voluntary deed *inter partes* can be rectified,[408] there does not seem to
be any convincing reason for the rule.

The court cannot rectify a settlement which is binding, not as a contract, but
by virtue of a court order.[409] If a mistake is made in drawing up such an order, it
is more appropriate to ask the court which made the order to vary it than to ask
another court to rectify it.

5. DOCUMENTS MISTAKENLY SIGNED

(a) Development

Recognition of non est factum. As a general rule, a person is bound by his   8–076
signature to a document whether he reads it or understands it, or not. But at the
end of the sixteenth century an exception to this rule was established. It was held
in *Thoroughgood's* Case[410] that if a person who could not read executed a deed after
it had been incorrectly read over to him, he was not bound by it. He could plead
non est factum: it is not my deed.

Extension of the doctrine. In the nineteenth century, it was settled that this   8–077
doctrine was no longer confined to persons who were unable to read. The reason
for this extension of the doctrine was the insistence on the requirement of

---

[403] *Caird v Moss* (1886) 33 Ch.D. 22.

[404] *Crane v Hegeman-Harris Co Inc* [1939] 4 All E.R. 68.

[405] *Napier v Williams* [1911] 1 Ch. 361; the actual decision would now be different because of Law
of Property Act 1925, s.82. Where the assignment forms part of a conveyance, the assignee can claim
rectification by virtue of Law of Property Act 1925, s.63(1): *Boots the Chemist v Street* (1983) 268 E.G.
817; *Berkley Leisure Group Ltd v Williamson* [1996] E.G.C.S. 18.

[406] *Scott v Frank F Scott (London) Ltd* [1904] Ch. 794.

[407] (1863) 32 Beav. 628.

[408] *Bonhote v Henderson* [1895] 1 Ch. 742; *Re Butlin's Settlement Trusts* [1976] Ch. 251; *Re Slocock's
Will Trust* [1979] 1 All E.R. 359.

[409] *Mills v Fox* (1887) 37 Ch.D. 153.

[410] (1584) 2 Co.Rep. 9a; cf. *Hitchman v Avery* (1892) 8 T.L.R. 698; *Lloyds Bank Plc v Waterhouse*
[1993] 2 F.L.R. 97 at 108.

consensus ad idem in contract. A person who signed a document without being aware of its nature was not bound because "the mind of the signer did not accompany the signature".[411] But if too wide a scope were given to this reasoning, it could lead to results that were inconsistent with the objective principle[412] and with the general common law requirement that a mistake must be fundamental if it is to negative consent.[413]

The objective principle does not operate in favour of a person who *knows* of the mistake of the signer[414]; and if that person has induced the mistake by some misrepresentation about the document which is alleged to contain the contract between him and the signer, then the signer will be entitled to avoid the contract on that ground.[415] Often, however, the document purports to be a contract between the signer and someone other than the fraudulent party. For example, A may induce B to sign a guarantee of A's bank overdraft by representing that it is an insurance proposal. Here the document is an apparent contract, not between A and B, but between B and *the bank*, which may reasonably believe that B has assented to the terms of the document. As the bank is not responsible for the fraud of A, B's only hope is to plead *non est factum*;[416] but success of the plea would deprive the bank of the protection of the objective principle.

Even if the document is an apparent contract only between A and B, the latter may try to invoke the doctrine of *non est factum* because it may provide a better remedy for him than rescission on the ground of A's fraud. This will be the position where B has under the contract parted with property and an innocent third party has later acquired an interest in that property for value.[417] If the doctrine of *non est factum* applies, the contract will be void so that B will be entitled to the return of the property; while if the contract is only voidable for A's fraud the third party will be protected. In cases of mistaken identity, the courts have in many cases protected such innocent third parties by a strict insistence on the requirement that the mistake must be fundamental[418]; and a similar requirement has restricted the scope of the *non est factum* defence.[419]

(b) Scope of the Doctrine

8–078   **Persons to whom the plea is available.** The nineteenth-century extension of the doctrine to persons who could read has been called "one of the less happy developments in our law"[420] and it has been suggested that the doctrine should not apply in favour of such persons if they were of full age and capacity.[421] But this very narrow view has not prevailed. In *Gallie v Lee* Lord Reid said that the doctrine may apply to

---

[411] *Foster v Mackinnon* (1869) L.R. 4 C.P. 704 at 711.
[412] See above, para.8–047.
[413] See above, para.8–033, but see para.8–044.
[414] See above, para.8–050.
[415] See below, para.9–084; *Lloyds Bank Plc v Waterhouse* (above, fn.410) at 111.
[416] Unless he can fix the bank with the fraud, or other wrongdoing of A: see below, 10–037.
[417] As in *Gallie v Lee* [1971] A.C. 1004; below, para.8–080.
[418] See above, para.8–034 et seq.
[419] *Norwich and Peterborough BS v Steeds (No.2)* [1993] 1 All E.R. 330 at 337.
[420] *Gallie v Lee* [1969] 2 Ch. 17 at 43, per Salmon L.J.
[421] ibid. at 36–37.

"those who are permanently or temporarily unable through no fault of their own to have without explanation any real understanding of the purport of a particular document, whether that be from defective education, illness or innate incapacity",[422]

and to these must be added persons who have been tricked into signing the document.[423] The doctrine may thus apply not only to the blind or illiterate but also to persons who are senile, of very low intelligence or ignorant of the language in which the document is expressed. But it will not normally protect literate persons of full capacity.[424]

Serious mistake required. In their desire to restrict the scope of the doctrine,   8–079
the courts have insisted that the plea of *non est factum* is available only where the mistake of the signer was a serious one. Formerly, they gave effect to this policy by drawing a distinction between the "character"[425] of a document and its "contents".[426] But in *Gallie v Lee*[427] the House of Lords rejected this distinction as unworkable,[428] and put in its place the requirement that the difference between the document as it was and as it was believed to be must be radical or substantial or fundamental.[429] Under this test, the seriousness of the mistake is to be judged by "difference in practical result" rather than by "difference in legal character".[430] The facts of the case were that a widow of 78 wanted to help her nephew Parkin to raise money on the security of her leasehold house, provided that she could continue to live there rent free for the rest of her life. Parkin did not want the loan to be in his own name, or to become owner of the house as he feared that this would enable his wife (from whom he was separated) to enforce her claim for maintenance against him. He therefore arranged that the money should be raised through an intermediary called Lee on a mortgage of the house; and as a first step in this scheme a document was prepared which was in fact an assignment on sale of the lease to Lee for £3,000. The widow did not read this document as her glasses were broken, but she signed it after being told by Lee that it was a deed of gift to Parkin (who witnessed the document). Lee mortgaged the house to a building society, but did not pay over the money so raised either to Parkin or to the widow. It was held that the widow was not protected by the doctrine of *non est factum* as her mistake was not sufficiently serious. She believed that the document would enable her nephew to raise money on the security of the house, and the document was in fact designed to achieve this purpose, though by a different process from that contemplated by her.[431]

---

[422] [1971] A.C. 1004 at 1016.

[423] ibid. at 1025.

[424] ibid. at 1016, 1025.

[425] e.g. *Foster v Mackinnon* (1869) L.R. C.P. 704.

[426] e.g. *Howatson v Webb* [1907] 1 Ch. 537, affirmed [1908] 1 Ch. 1.

[427] [1971] A.C. 1004.

[428] *Muskham Finance Ltd v Howard* [1963] 1 Q.B. 904 is, for example, hard to reconcile with *Howatson v Webb*, above. See also *Gallie v Lee* [1969] 2 Ch. 17 at 31–32, per Lord Denning M.R.

[429] [1971] A.C. 1004 at 1017, 1019, 1021, 1026, 1034.

[430] ibid. at 1017.

[431] cf. *Mercantile Credit Ltd v Hamblin* [1965] 2 Q.B. 242; *Avon Finance Co v Bridger* [1985] 2 All E.R. 281. For a difference of judicial opinion on a similar point, see *Lloyds Bank Plc v Waterhouse* [1993] 2 F.L.R. 97.

8–080   **Mistake as to identity.** We have seen that consent may be negatived, so as to make a contract void, where A deals with B in the mistaken belief that B is C.[432] But if A signs a document expressed to be in favour of B, the defence of *non est factum* is not open to A merely because A thought that the party named in the document was C. Thus in *Gallie v Lee*[433] the defence failed even though the widow thought that she was making a gift to Parkin when in fact she was making a conveyance to Lee. The reason for this rule may be that the mistaken party can discover the mistake by reading the document.

8–081   **Ignorance.** The plea of *non est factum* is not normally open to a person who is merely ignorant of (as opposed to mistaken about) what he is signing[434]: e.g. to one who signs a document in the belief that it is "only a form" without having any precise idea as to its nature.[435] Similarly, in *Gillman v Gillman*[436] a wife, shortly before her husband left her, signed a document which was in fact a separation deed. She did not know this when she signed it, but neither had she any definite idea as to what it was that she was signing. It was held that she was bound by the deed.

8–082   **Mistake as to capacity.** The rule just stated is subject to an exception where a person signs a document under a mistaken belief as to the capacity in which he signs. Thus in *Lewis v Clay*[437] the defendant was induced to sign two promissory notes by the fraudulent representation that his signature was required as a witness and that the documents were of a private nature. The plea of *non est factum* succeeded even though the defendant could not say precisely what type of document he thought he had signed.

8–083   **Carelessness.** Carelessness of the signer excludes the doctrine of *non est factum*. This was a second ground for the decision in *Gallie v Lee*[438]: the widow could not rely on the doctrine as she had been careless in signing the document without reading it. For the same reason, a person cannot rely on the doctrine if he signs a document containing blanks which are later filled in otherwise than in accordance with his instructions.[439]

In this context, the standard of care cannot be that of the reasonable person, for such a person will not normally be able to rely on the doctrine of *non est factum* at all.[440] One has to assume that the person relying on the doctrine falls within the class of persons to whom it is available, and then to ask whether that person took such care as one so disadvantaged could have been expected to take. In *Gallie v Lee*

---

[432] e.g. *Cundy v Lindsay* (1873) 3 App.Cas. 459; *Shogun Finance v Hudson* [2003] UKHL 62; [2004] 1 A.C. 919; above, paras 8–035, 8–039.

[433] [1971] A.C. 1004; cf. *Howatson v Webb* [1907] 1 Ch. 535, affirmed [1908] 1 Ch. 1. For discussion of the mistaken identity point, see *Gallie v Lee* [1969] 2 Ch. 17 at 44.

[434] *Norwich and Peterborough BS v Steeds (No.2)* [1993] 1 All E.R. 330 at 338–339.

[435] *Hunter v Walters* (1871) L.R. 7 Ch.App. 75; cf. *National Provincial Bank of England v Jackson* (1886) 33 Ch.D. 1.

[436] (1946) 174 L.T. 272; cf. *Mercantile Credit Co Ltd v Hamblin* [1965] 2 Q.B. 242 (but in that case the signer escaped liability on another ground).

[437] (1897) 67 L.J.Q.B. 224.

[438] [1971] A.C. 1004, overruling *Carlisle & Cumberland Banking Co v Bragg* [1911] 1 K.B. 489. See also *Lewis v Clay* (1897) 67 L.J.Q.B. 224 at 226; *Howatson v Webb* [1908] 1 Ch. 1; *Avon Finance Co v Bridger* [1985] 2 All E.R. 281.

[439] *United Dominion's Trust Ltd v Western* [1976] Q.B. 513; Marston [1976] C.L.J. 218.

[440] See above, para.8–079.

itself, this test was not satisfied; for, although the widow could not be expected to follow the intricacies of conveyancing, she could at least be expected to make sure that the person named in the document as transferee was the person intended by her. It does not follow that failure to read the document will exclude the plea of *non est factum* in all cases: the plea might, for example, still be available if reading the document would not have revealed its true character to a person of the signer's limited capabilities.[441]

---

[441] [1971] A.C. 1004 at 1023; cf. *Lloyds Bank Plc v Waterhouse* [1993] 2 F.L.R. 97.

MISREPRESENTION[1]

---

[1] Cartwright, *Misrepresentation, Mistake and Non-Disclosure* (2nd edn). The Unfair Commercial Practices Directive 2005/29, [2005] O.J. L149/22, implemented by the Consumer Protection from Unfair Trading Regulations 2008 (SI 2008/1277) and the Business Protection from Misleading Marketing Regulations 2008 (SI 2008/1276) includes, among the specific prohibitions, the provision of "false information" (Art.6), or the omission of "material information" (Art.7). The Directive does not confer individual rights on consumers and is "without prejudice to contract law, and, in particular, the rules on the validity, formation and effect of a contract" (Art.3(2)). As a result an agreement is not void or unenforceable by reason only of a breach of the Regulations. See Twigg-Fleisner 121 L.Q.R. 386; Law Commission Consultation Paper No.199: *Consumer Redress for Misrepresentation and Aggressive Practices.*

Our concern in this chapter is with the remedies available to a person who has **9–001** been induced to enter into a contract by a statement which is misleading. These remedies are available only if the statement is of a kind which the law recognises as giving rise to liability, and if certain general conditions of liability are satisfied. The representee may then be able to claim damages or to rescind the contract or to do both these things. Similar remedies may also in certain cases be available where there has been mere non-disclosure of material facts, as opposed to active misrepresentation.

1. GENERAL CONDITIONS OF LIABILITY

Where a representation does not have contractual force, it will give rise to the **9–002** remedies discussed in sections 2 and 3 of this chapter only if it is a false statement of fact (or law), material and if the representee has relied on it.

(a) False statement of fact or law

General rule. The general rule is that no relief will be given for a mis- **9–003** representation as such unless it is a statement of existing fact or, it now seems, of law.[2]

Objective meaning. Whether any and if so what representation has been made **9–004** is to be "judged objectively according to the impact that whatever is said may be expected to have on a reasonable representee in the position and with the known characteristics of the actual representee."[3] In the case of an express statement, "the court has to understand what a reasonable person would have understood from the words used in the context in which they were used."[4] In the case of an implied representation, whether implied from an express statement of fact or from an opinion,[5] the court has to "consider what a reasonable person would have inferred was being implicitly represented by the representor's words and conduct in their context."[6] The same objective approach is taken to determine the falsity of any statement. It will be treated as true if it is substantially correct and the difference between what is represented and what is actually correct would not have

---

[2] See para.9–013, below.

[3] *MCI WorldCom International Inc v Primus Telecommunications Inc* [2004] EWCA Civ 957 at [30]; cf. *Raiffeisen Zentralbank Osterreich AG v Royal Bank of Scotland Plc* [2010] EWHC 1392 (Comm) at [81]; *Springwell Navigation Corporation v JP Morgan Chase Bank* [2010] EWCA Civ 1221 at [121]

[4] *IFE Fund SA v Goldman Sachs International* [2006] EWHC 2887 (Comm); [2007] 1 Lloyd's Rep. 264 at [50], affirmed [2007] EWCA Civ 811; [2007] 2 Lloyd's Rep. 449; cf. *Raiffeisen Zentralbank Osterreich AG v Royal Bank of* Scotland *Plc* [2010] EWHC 1392 (Comm) at [82].

[5] See below, para.9–008. For representations implied by conduct, see below para.9–128.

[6] *IFE Fund SA v Goldman Sachs International* [2006] EWHC 2887 (Comm); [2007] 1 Lloyd's Rep. 264 at [50], affirmed [2007] EWCA Civ 811; [2007] 2 Lloyd's Rep. 449.

been likely to induce a reasonable person in the position of the claimant to enter into the contract.[7]

9–005   **Implied representation.** The terms, if any, upon which the parties have exchanged information will be a material factor in determining whether any implied representation has been made.[8] Thus, in *IFE Fund SA v Goldman Sachs International*[9] the defendant arranger of a syndicated loan supplied to the claimant, as a potential lender, pre-acquisition reports on the target company which had been purchased but failed to pass on post-acquisition reports which it was claimed cast doubt on the reliability of the earlier reports. It did so pursuant to an information memorandum in which it was stated that no representation, express or implied, was made as to the "accuracy or completeness" of the information supplied[10] or that the information supplied "will be updated." The claimants argued that that still left room for an implied and continuing representation that the defendant knew nothing which showed that the information supplied was *or might be* materially incorrect. According to Toulson J. this went too far and would "open up wide and uncertain territory".[11] The only implied representation was that in supplying the information the defendant was acting in good faith, i.e. it did not actually know of anything which made the information given misleading.[12] The claimant in the *Goldman Sachs* case was a sophisticated commercial entity. In light of the statement above that the courts will take into account the known characteristics of the actual representee, a consumer who is told that no representations are being made to him may be treated quite differently.[13]

9–006   **Ambiguous representation.** A statement may be intended by the representor to bear a meaning which is true, but be so obscure that the representee understands it in another sense, in which it is untrue. In such a case the representor is not liable if his interpretation is the correct one[14]; and even if the court holds that the representee's interpretation was the correct one, the representor is not guilty of fraud.[15] This is so in spite of the fact that the representor's interpretation was an unreasonable one, so long as he honestly believed in it.[16] A fortiori the representee has no remedy in deceit if the representation is ambiguous and he did not in fact understand it in a different sense from that intended by the representor.[17]

---

[7] *Avon Ins Plc v Swire Fraser Ltd* [2000] 1 All E.R. (Comm) 573 at [17]; cf. *Raiffeisen Zentralbank Osterreich AG v Royal Bank of Scotland Plc* [2010] EWHC 1392 (Comm) at [149]. This is consistent with the test for materiality: below, para.9–016.

[8] *Raiffeisen Zentralbank Osterreich AG v Royal Bank of Scotland Plc* [2010] EWHC 1392 (Comm) at [97].

[9] [2006] EWHC 2887 (Comm); [2007] 1 Lloyd's Rep. 264; [2007] EWCA Civ 811; [2007] 2 Lloyd's Rep. 449.

[10] The principal significance of this type of provision is the effect that it can have on excluding liability for representations that *have been made*: see below, para.9–117.

[11] [2007] 1 Lloyd's Rep. 264 at [58].

[12] ibid. at [60].

[13] *Raiffeisen Zentralbank Osterreich AG v Royal Bank of Scotland Plc* [2010] EWHC 1392 (Comm) at [81].

[14] *McInerny v Lloyds Bank Ltd* [1974] 1 Lloyd's Rep. 246 at 254; contrast *Spice Girls Ltd v Aprilia World Service BV* [2002] EWCA Civ 15; [2002] E.M.L.R. 27 at [67], where there was held to be *no* ambiguity in the representation.

[15] *Akerhielm v De Mare* [1959] A.C. 789; *Gross v Lewis Hillman Ltd* [1970] Ch. 445; and cf. below, para.9–134.

[16] See below, para.9–030.

[17] *Smith v Chadwick* (1884) 9 App.Cas. 187.

A representor is guilty of fraud if he makes an ambiguous statement intending it to bear a meaning which is to his knowledge untrue,[18] and if the statement is reasonably understood in that sense by the representee. In such a case it is no defence for the representor to show that, on its true construction, the statement bore a meaning that was in fact true.[19]

Mere puffs. Mere puffs are statements which are so vague that they have no effect at law or in equity. To describe land as "fertile and improvable" is mere sales talk which affords no ground for relief.[20] But there is a liability for more precise claims, e.g. that use of a carbolic smoke-ball will give immunity from influenza.[21] The distinction is between indiscriminate praise, and specific promises or assertions of verifiable facts.   **9–007**

Statements of opinion or belief. Even where a statement is not so vague as to be a mere puff, it may nevertheless have no legal effect because it is not a positive assertion that the fact stated is true, but only a statement of the maker's opinion or belief.[22] Assertions that an anchorage was safe and that a piece of land had the capacity to support 2,000 sheep have been held to be of this character[23]; for in each case, the party making the statement had (as the other party knew) no personal knowledge of the facts on which it was based: it was understood that he could only state his belief.   **9–008**

A statement may, in terms, be one of opinion or belief, but by implication involve a statement of fact: "All depends upon the particular statement in its particular context",[24] including the terms, if any, under which it has been provided.[25] Thus, an incorrect forecast may amount to a misrepresentation, not because the forecast is incorrect, but because of the implied, but false, statement that reasonable care has been taken in making it.[26] It is also a misrepresentation of fact for a person to say that he holds an opinion which he does not hold, e.g. to say that he thinks a picture is a Rembrandt when he thinks it is a copy.[27] If that party has or professes to have some special knowledge or skill as to the matter stated, the statement is also likely to be treated as one of fact.[28] And if the facts on which an opinion is based are particularly within the knowledge of the person stating the opinion, he may be taken to have represented that those facts exist. For example, where the vendor of a house describes it as "let to a most desirable

---

[18] *Henry Ansbacher& Co Ltd v Binks Stern, The Times,* June 26, 1997.

[19] *The Siboen and the Sibotre* [1976] 1 Lloyd's Rep. 293 at 318.

[20] *Dimmock v Hallett* (1866) L.R. 2 Ch.App. 21; cf. above, para.4–002.

[21] *Carlill v Carbolic Smoke Ball Co* [1893] 1 Q.B. 256.

[22] Or a contention, or statement of position, e.g. as to the meaning of a prior contract between parties: *Kyle Bay Ltd v Underwriters Subscribing Under Policy No.019057/08/01* [2007] EWCA Civ 57 at [29]–[37]; cf. *Royal Bank of Scotland v Chandra* [2011] EWCA Civ 192 at [39] (no misrepresentation in an "over-optimistic" forecast).

[23] *Anderson v Pacific Fire & Marine Ins Co* (1872) L.R. 7 C.P. 65; *Bissett v Wilkinson* [1927] A.C. 177.

[24] *Jaffray v Society of Lloyds* [2002] EWCA Civ 1101 at [59]; *Foodco UK LLP v Henry Boot Developments Ltd* [2010] EWHC 358 (Ch) at [197].

[25] See above, para.9–005.

[26] *Foodco UK LLP v Henry Boot Developments Ltd,* above at [207]

[27] *Jendwine v Slade* (1797) 2 Esp. 571 at 573; *Brown v Raphael* [1958] Ch. 636 at 641; contrast *Harlingdon and Leinster Enterprises Ltd v Christopher Hull Fine Art Ltd* [1991] 1 Q.B. 564.

[28] e.g. *Esso Petroleum Co Ltd v Mardon* [1976] Q.B. 801; below, para.9–038; *Box v Midland Bank Ltd* [1979] 2 Lloyd's Rep. 391 (reversed as to costs only [1981] 1 Lloyd's Rep. 434); *Thomas Witter Ltd v TBP Industries Ltd* [1996] 2 All E.R. 573 at 594–595.

tenant", when the tenant has for long been in arrears with his rent, he mis-represents a fact, "for he impliedly states that he knows facts which justify his opinion".[29] The same principle applies where a person honestly makes a statement of belief but fails to check the facts on which it appears to be based, when he could easily have done so and therefore impliedly represents that he had reasonable grounds for his opinion.[30] A statement that the representor had been informed of a particular fact has also been held to be a representation, not merely that the representor had been so informed, but that the fact existed.[31]

9–009   **Representations as to the future.** A representation as to the future does not, of itself, give rise to any cause of action[32] unless it is binding as a contract. Thus if A induces B to lend him money by representing that he will not borrow from anybody else, and then does borrow elsewhere, he is not liable to B unless the representation is a term of the contract of loan or amounts to a collateral con-tract.[33]

9–010   **Statement of present intention as a statement of fact.** A person who promises to do something may simply be making a statement as to his future conduct; if so, he does not misrepresent a fact merely because he fails to do what he said he would do.[34] But he may also be making a statement of his present intention; if so, he does misrepresent a fact if, when he made the statement, he had no such intention. The courts tend to construe statements as to the future in the second of these two ways in order to protect the interests of persons deceived by them. In *Edgington v Fitzmaurice*[35] the directors of a company procured a loan of money to their company by representing that the money would be used to improve the company's buildings and to expand its business. In fact the directors intended to use the money to pay off the company's existing debts. They were held liable to the lender in deceit. Bowen L.J. said:

> "There must be a mis-statement of an existing fact; but the state of a man's mind is as much a fact as the state of his digestion. . . . A misrepresentation as to the state of a man's mind is, therefore, a mis-statement of fact".[36]

9–011   **Statement of present expectation or belief as statement of fact.** The principle stated above is not restricted to statements of intention. A person may

---

[29] *Smith v Land & House Property Corp* (1884) 28 Ch.D. 7 at 15.

[30] *Brown v Raphael* [1958] Ch. 636; *Thomson v Christie Manson & Woods Ltd* [2004] EWHC 1101 (QB); [2004] P.N.L.R. 42 at [199] (decision reversed [2005] EWCA Civ 555; [2005] P.N.L.R. 38, without reference to this point)). Contrast *Humming Bird Motors v Hobbs* [1986] R.T.R. 276; *William Sindall Plc v Cambridgeshire CC* [1994] 1 W.L.R. 1016.

[31] *Sirius International Ins Corp v Oriental Assurance Corp* [1999] 1 All E.R. (Comm) 699; presumably the latter representation arose by implication from the former.

[32] It may be a ground for refusing specific performance: below, para.21–030. It may also, in combination with other circumstances, give rise to a proprietary estoppel: see above, para.3–118 et seq.

[33] cf. *Ex p. Burrell* (1876) 1 Ch.D. 537 at 552; *Strachan & Henshaw Ltd v Stein Industrie (UK) Ltd (No.2)* (1998) 87 B.L.R. 52.

[34] *The Seaflower* [2000] 2 Lloyd's Rep. 37 at 42; but the eventual outcome was that the representee was entitled to rescind *for breach*: *The Seaflower* [2001] 1 Lloyd's Rep. 341; below, para.18–050.

[35] (1885) 29 Ch.D. 459.

[36] ibid. at 482; cf. *Smith Kline & French Laboratories Ltd v Long* [1988] 1 W.L.R. 1; *Kleinwort Benson Ltd v Malaysian Mining Corp* [1989] 1 W.L.R. 379 at 396; *East v Maurer* [1991] 1 W.L.R. 461 at 463; *Tudor Grange Holdings Ltd v Citibank NA* [1992] Ch. 53 at 67–68.

misrepresent a fact if he states an *expectation* or a *belief* which he does not hold as to some future event. The Marine Insurance Act 1906 provides that a marine policy can be avoided for an untrue representation of expectation or belief[37]; but that such a representation "is true if it be made in good faith".[38] These rules apply also to other types of insurance and under them a person would be guilty of misrepresentation if he stated a belief which he did not in fact hold. But the standard imposed by them is no more than one of honesty, so that where a representor made an honest statement of his knowledge and belief (which turned out to be wrong) as to the value of the contents of a house it was held that he was not guilty of misrepresentation: he was not required to show that he had reasonable grounds for making the statement.[39] In contexts other than that of insurance, however, a statement of expectation or belief may be held to contain an implied assertion that the representor did have reasonable grounds for making it. For example, a shipowner who in a charterparty says that his ship is "expected ready to load" at a particular port on or about a specified date impliedly represents that he honestly holds that belief, and that he does so on reasonable grounds. If he has no reasonable grounds for holding the belief, he misrepresents a fact.[40]

Statement of intention coupled with statement of fact. A statement of intention may also be coupled with an *express* statement of existing fact. Thus a statement by A that he *had* sold flour and *would* pay over the proceeds to B is a misrepresentation of fact if A had made no such sale.[41]   9–012

Statements of law. The traditional view, at common law, was that no right to rescind nor any right to damages could be based on a misrepresentation of law, and the same was probably true of claims for damages under the Misrepresentation Act 1967.[42] In equity, too, a money claim could not be based on a misrepresentation of law,[43] though it was more doubtful whether it was a ground for rescission in equity.[44] It has been said that *wilful* misrepresentation of law was ground for equitable relief.[45] And equity gave relief for misrepresentation as to private rights[46] whether or not these were rightly called misrepresentation of fact.   9–013

In *Kleinwort Benson Ltd v Lincoln City Council*[47] the House of Lords removed the bar preventing recovery of payments made under a *mistake* of law. This has led the Court of Appeal to remove the bar which prevents a mistake of law from rendering a contract void[48] and, in so doing, the view was expressed that the effect

---

[37] s.20(1) and (3).

[38] s.20(1) and (3), s.20(5); *The Zephyr* [1985] 2 Lloyd's Rep. 529 at 538.

[39] *Economides v Commercial Union Assurance Plc* [1998] Q.B. 587 rejecting (at 599, 606) so far as *contra*, dicta in *Highlands Ins Co v Continental Ins Co* [1987] 1 Lloyd's Rep. 109.

[40] *The Mihalis Angelos* [1971] 1 Q.B. 164 at 194, 205; *Foodco UK LLP v Henry Boot Developments Ltd* [2010] EWHC 358 (Ch) at [207].

[41] *Babcock v Lawson* (1880) 5 Q.B.D. 284; cf. *Ismail v Polish Ocean Lines Ltd* [1976] Q.B. 893: statement that goods *were* so packed that they *would* withstand the voyage.

[42] *André &Cie SA v Ets Michel Blanc &Fils* [1979] 2 Lloyd's Rep. 427 at 432, 434–435.

[43] See *Rashdall v Ford* (1866) L.R. 2 Eq. 750; *Eaglesfield v Londonderry* (1876) 4 Ch.D. 693.

[44] e.g. in *Wauton v Coppard* [1899] 1 Ch. 92 and *Mackenzie v Royal Bank of Canada* [1934] A.C. 468. But in each of these cases the representation was held to be one of fact.

[45] *West London Commercial Bank v Kitson* (1884) 13 Q.B.D. 360 at 362–363.

[46] *André &Cie SA v Ets Michel Blanc &Fils*, above, fn.42, at 431, 432.

[47] [1999] 2 A.C. 349; below, para.22–016.

[48] *Brennan v Bolt Burdon* [2004] EWCA Civ 1017; [2005] Q.B. 303; below, para.8–022.

of the decision in the *Kleinwort Benson* case "now permeates the law of con-tract".[49] Furthermore, in *Pankhania v Hackney LBC*,[50] it has been held that the "misrepresentation of law" rule "has not survived" the decision in the *Kleinwort Benson* case. A degree of caution is perhaps still needed before it can finally be concluded that the distinction between fact and law is no longer relevant to misrepresentation.[51] It is submitted, however, that the decision in *Pankhania* is highly likely to be followed by the higher courts.[52] The distinction between representations of fact and representations of law was sometimes hard to draw and its effects were hard to justify,[53] and a person who has acted to his prejudice in reliance on a misrepresentation of law has at least as strong a claim for relief as one who is entitled to relief because he has spontaneously made a mistake of law.

On the assumption that the misrepresentation of law rule has been removed, the same principles may be employed to determine whether the representor has made a representation of law, as are employed to determine whether he has made a representation of fact. For example, a statement of opinion about the law may be a mere opinion and, therefore, not actionable, or it may amount to an implicit representation of law.[54]

9–014   **Representation made by another.** As a general rule the representation must have been made by the party against whom relief is sought, or by his agent. In some cases relief may be available even where the representation was made by another party who was not acting as agent, e.g. where A, by a misrepresentation addressed to B, induces B to guarantee A's overdraft with the C bank. The bank's ability to enforce such a transaction depends on whether it is "put on enquiry"[55] as to the circumstances in which it was concluded. As in most of the recent cases of this kind the alleged vitiating factor has been undue influence (sometimes together with misrepresentation[56]), a full discussion of the effect of such factors on the rights of the third party will be found in Ch.10.[57]

9–015   **Non-disclosure amounting to representation.** As a general rule, a person who is about to enter into a contract is under no duty to disclose material facts known to him but not to the other party. There are a number of exceptions to this rule and in relation to some the true nature of the non-disclosure is that a representation can be inferred from conduct or from the surrounding circum-stances, e.g. where a representation is falsified by later events,[58] or where a

---

[49] *Brennan v Bolt Burdon* [2004] EWCA Civ 1017; [2005] Q.B. 303 at [10].

[50] [2002] EWHC 2441 (Ch) at [57].

[51] The decision in *Pankhania* departs from higher authority on the basis that any earlier cases which support the misrepresentation of law rule cannot be followed after the House of Lords' decision in the *Kleinwort Benson* case: *Young v Bristol Aeroplane Co Ltd* [1944] 1 K.B. 718.

[52] For this reason, no account is given of earlier cases which were decided on the assumption that the representee's remedies are more restricted where the representation is one of law than where it is one of fact. If the prediction that *Pankhania* will be followed proves to be incorrect, readers are referred to the 11th edn, pp.333–335.

[53] See *André & Cie SA v Ets Michel Blanc* [1997] 2 Lloyd's Rep. 427 at 431; *Brikom Investments Ltd v Seaford* [1981] 1 W.L.R. 863 at 869; cf. *Amalgamated Investment & Property Co Ltd v Texas Commerce International Bank Ltd* [1982] Q.B. 84 at 122.

[54] See para.9–008.

[55] *Royal Bank of Scotland v Etridge (No.2)* [2001] UKHL 44; [2002] 2 A.C. 773 at [44].

[56] The same test applies to both: *Annulment Funding Company Ltd v Cowey* [2010] EWCA Civ 711 at [64].

[57] Below, paras 10–035—10–041.

[58] See below, para.9–132.

statement is literally true but misleading,[59] or where disclosure is required by custom.[60] They are dealt with in more detail below along with other exceptions to the general rule.[61]

(b) Material

General rule. A misrepresentation generally has no legal effect unless it is material.[62] That is, it must be one which would affect the judgment of a reasonable person in deciding whether, or on what terms, to enter into the contract; or one that would induce him to enter into the contract without making such inquiries as he would otherwise make.[63] Thus in a contract of insurance it is material that the subject-matter has been grossly overvalued[64] or that a previous proposal for insuring it has been declined[65]; and in a contract for a loan of money it is material that the lender is a notoriously ruthless money-lender.[66] Conversely, a representation as to the identity of the purchaser may be material where the vendor is willing to sell to X but not to Y. In such a case the vendor can rescind if the purchaser knows that the representation is material, even though he does not know why it is so regarded by the vendor.[67] A misrepresentation may be material although the representor in good faith thinks that it is not material.[68]

9–016

Exceptions: fraud and express contractual provision. There are two exceptions to the requirement of materiality. First, a person who has successfully perpetrated a fraud cannot be heard to say that the representation which he used to achieve this end was immaterial.[69] Secondly, every representation is material if the contract so provides. Thus if a policy of insurance provides that statements by the assured in the proposal form shall be the basis of the contract, or are warranted to be true, such statements are material,[70] however unimportant they may be in themselves.

9–017

---

[59] See below, para.9–134.
[60] See below, para.9–135.
[61] See below, para.9–130 et seq.
[62] *McDowell v Fraser* (1779) 1 Dougl. 247 at 248, per Lord Mansfield; *Lonrho Plc v Fayed (No.2)* [1992] 1 W.L.R. 1 at 6; cf. (in cases of non-disclosure) below, para.9–138.
[63] *Traill v Baring* (1864) 4 D.J. & S. 318 at 326; *Whurr v Devenish* (1904) 20 T.L.R. 385; Marine Insurance Act 1906, s.20(2), expressing the general law: *Industrial Properties Ltd v A E I Ltd* [1977] Q.B. 580 at 597, 601; *Highland Ins Co v Continental Ins Co* [1987] 1 Lloyd's Rep. 109; *Pan Atlantic Ins Co Ltd v Pine Top Ins Co Ltd* [1995] 2 A.C. 501; cf. *Walker v Boyle* [1982] 1 W.L.R. 495 at 503; *Raiffeisen Zentralbank Osterreich AG v Royal Bank of Scotland Plc* [2010] EWHC 1392 (Comm) at [149].
[64] *Ionides v Pender* (1874) L.R. 9 Q.B. 531.
[65] *Locker & Woolf Ltd v W Australian Insurance Co Ltd*.
[66] *Gordon v Street* [1899] 2 Q.B. 641.
[67] *Lonrho Plc v Fayed (No.2)* [1992] 1 W.L.R. 1 at 5–6.
[68] *Lindenau v Desborough* (1828) 8 B. & C. 586; *Joel v Law Union & Crown Ins Co* [1908] 2 K.B. 863 at 883.
[69] *Smith v Kay* (1859) 7 H.L.C. 750; cf. *Rafsanjan Pistachio Producers Co-operative v Bank Leumi (UK) Plc* [1992] 1 Lloyd's Rep. 514 at 542; *Agapitos v Agnew* [2002] EWCA Civ 247; [2003] Q.B. 556 at [32]–[33]; *Dadourian Group International Inc v Simms* [2009] EWCA Civ 169; [2009] 1 Lloyd's Rep. 601 at [101]. A dictum in *Downs v Chappell* [1997] 1 W.L.R. 345 at 351 applies the requirement of materiality even in a case of fraud, but is *obiter* since it was not there suggested that the representation was not material.
[70] *Andersen v Fitzgerald* (1853) 4 H.L.C. 484; and see below, para.9–140. Such clauses are not affected by Unfair Contract Terms Act 1977: above, para.7–089; nor (*semble*) by Unfair Terms in Consumer Contracts Regulations 1999: above, para.7–105.

9–018   **Negligence.** It has also been said that materiality was not relevant where the claim was "not for misrepresentation" but for "negligence only".[71] This distinction was drawn in a case in which solicitors were held liable for failure to provide accurate information to a client who, in consequence, made a mortgage loan on a security which turned out to be inadequate. What the distinction seems to mean is that the client's claim was for breach of a contractual duty of care[72] and not for inducing the claimant by misrepresentation to enter into a contract with the defendant; and that materiality is not relevant to a claim of the former kind. It should not be taken to mean that "misrepresentation" and "negligence" are mutually exclusive categories[73] or that materiality is irrelevant to claims for negligent misrepresentation inducing a contract, at least where the contract is made with the representor.

9–019   **Requirement of materiality doubted.** The requirement of materiality has been doubted,[74] but it is consistent with the objective assessment of whether any representation has been made and its falsity.[75] In evaluating any doubts about a requirement of materiality a distinction should, it is submitted, be drawn between two reasons why the misrepresentation would not affect the judgment of a reasonable person. This may be the position either because of the *circumstances in which the representation was made*, or because of its *contents*. The first possibility is illustrated by *Museprime Properties Ltd v Adhill Properties Ltd*,[76] where a purchaser by auction of commercial property was allowed to rescind for a representation by the auctioneer that higher rents could still be negotiated, when in fact the rents had been fixed for the next rent review period. The court held that it was sufficient for the purchaser to show that his bid had actually been affected by the representation: he did not have to show that a reasonable bidder would have allowed it to affect his bid. The representation could certainly have affected the value of the property and was in this sense material. The only sense in which it was not material was that the representee had (and did not take) the opportunity of discovering the truth; but even though a reasonable person might have made use of such an opportunity, it is settled that a representee's failure to do so is no bar to relief for misrepresentation.[77] The case is, in other words, concerned with the question whether the representee could be taken to have *relied* on the representation (or had been *induced* by it to enter it into the contract); and this is distinct from the question of materiality.[78] The second of the two possibilities mentioned above arises where the matter misrepresented is not "material" because it had little (or only a trivial) effect on the value of the subject-matter. What is an "immaterial" representation (in this sense) can be illustrated by supposing that the auctioneer in the *Museprime* case had represented the tenant to be 40 years old when actually he was 39 or 41, that this representation had (for some reason) been a factor inducing the representee's successful bid, and that its falsity had caused no, or no substantial, loss to the representee. If the representor has made such a

---

[71] *Bristol & West B S v Mothew* [1998] Ch. 1 at 10–11.
[72] See below, para.17–066.
[73] See *Hedley Byrne & Co Ltd v Heller & Partners Ltd* [1964] A.C. 465; below para.9–033.
[74] *Chitty on Contracts* (30th edn), Vol.I, para.6–037; cf. *Primus Telecommunications Plc v MCI Worldcom International Inc* [2004] EWCA Civ 957 at [31] (doubts expressed in previous edition of *Chitty* said to "put the position too cautiously")
[75] See above para.9–004.
[76] [1990] 2 E.G.L.R. 196.
[77] See below, para.9–023 where this settled position is nonetheless called into question.
[78] *The Mercadian Continent* [2001] EWCA Civ 1275; [2001] 2 Lloyd's Rep. 563 at [26].

representation in good faith it is hard to see why a representee should be entitled to any relief when, by definition, the representation would not have influenced a reasonable person. Damages would be no more than nominal, and a claim to rescind for such a misrepresentation has been rejected as totally unmeritorious.[79]

(c) Reliance

Inducement. The person to whom the representation was made must have relied on it in the sense that it must have induced him to enter into the contract.[80] Various formulations have been used for the test of inducement, e.g. that the representation must have been an "effective cause",[81] a "material inducement",[82] "materially contributed",[83] or played a "real and substantial part".[84] The essential test is "but for" causation, i.e. in the present context, had the representation not been made to him,[85] the representee would not have contracted or would not have done so on the same terms,[86] or would not have abstained "from doing something bearing on his material interests."[87] He therefore cannot rescind, or claim damages, for misrepresentation if he would have entered into the contract in any event,[88] if the representation did not come to his notice,[89] if he knew the

9–020

---

[79] *Industrial Properties Ltd v A E I Ltd* [1977] Q.B. 580; *Re a Company (No.001946 of 1991) Ex p. Fin Soft Holdings SA* [1991] B.C.L.C. 737 at 748; cf. Restatement 2d., *Contracts* §162, Ill. 4. This conclusion could also be justified on the analogous ground that the representation was "substantially correct": see above, text to fn.7.

[80] Our concern in this chapter is with representations inducing contracts. For some types of claim, e.g. a claim under Misrepresentation Act 1967, s.2(1) (see para.9–039 et seq.), that is the only type of reliance which will suffice; for others, e.g. negligence at common law, the necessary reliance may take some other form, including an inducement not to enter into a contract.

[81] *Assicurazioni Generali SpA v Arab Insurance Group* [2002] EWCA Civ 1642; [2003] 1 W.L.R. 577 at [59].

[82] *Spice Girls Ltd v Aprilia World Service BV* [2002] EWCA Civ 15; [2002] E.M.L.R. 27 at [68]–[72]

[83] *Edgington v Fitzmaurice* (1882) 29 Ch. D 459 at 482.

[84] *J E B Fasteners Ltd v Marks Bloom & Co* [1983] 1 All E.R. 583 at 590; *Dadourian Group International Inc v Simms* [2009] EWCA Civ 169; [2009] 1 Lloyd's Rep. 601 at [100].

[85] The relevant question is what would the representee have done if there had been no representation at all; not what would he have done if he had been told the truth, though in practice, in the majority of cases, this will produce the same answer: *Raiffeisen*case, below at [174]–[191]; cf. *Bank of Tokyo-Mitsubishi UFJ Ltd v Baskan Gida Sanayi Ve Pazarlama AS* [2009] EWHC 1276 (Ch) at [1005].

[86] *Raiffeisen Zentralbank Osterreich AG v Royal Bank of Scotland Plc* [2010] EWHC 1392 (Comm) at [171] per Christopher Clarke L.J. who regarded this as consistent with the decision of the House of Lords in *Pan Atlantic Ins Co Ltd v Pine Top Ins Co Ltd* [1995] 2 A.C. 501 which was an application to marine insurance of the common law as to inducement: [2010] EWHC 1392 (Comm) at [172]; cf. *Assicurazioni Generali SpA v Arab Insurance Group* [2002] EWCA Civ 1642; [2003] 1 W.L.R. 577 at [62].

[87] *Parabola Investments Ltd v Browallia Cal Ltd* [2009] EWHC 901 (Comm) at [107], affirmed [2010] EWCA Civ 486; [2010] 3 W.L.R. 1266 without reference to this point (claimant continued with financially disastrous trading because of the defendant's continuous misrepresentation when otherwise he would have ceased).

[88] *JEB Fasteners Ltd v Marks Bloom & Co* [1983] 1 All E.R. 583, affirming [1981] 3 All E.R. 289, discussed below, para.9–026.

[89] *Ex p. Biggs* (1859) 28 L.J.Ch. 50. It need not come to his attention personally; the automatic processing of a statement by a computer may suffice: *Renault UK Ltd v Fleetpro Technical Services Ltd* [2007] EWHC 2541 (QB).

representation was false,[90] if he relied on his own information,[91] or if he took a deliberate risk as to the truth of the matter stated.[92] If, however, the representee enters into the contract after a *fraudulent* misrepresentation has been made to him, it is no bar to a claim for rescission[93] that he would have acted in the same way even if the misrepresentation had not been made,[94] provided it had some influence, i.e. it was still *a* reason for his decision.[95] This appears to be one of a number of harsher rules applied in an attempt to deter fraud.[96]

9–021   **Other inducements.** It is no bar to relief that the claimant entered into the contract on the basis of a number of inducements, including misrepresentation. Thus in *Edgington v Fitzmaurice*[97] a lender was induced to lend money to a company by (i) the misrepresentations which have already been discussed,[98] and (ii) his mistaken belief that he would have a charge on the assets of the company. He was entitled to damages for deceit[99] even though he admitted that he would not have lent the money, had he not held this mistaken belief. But if two statements are made to a person, one true and one untrue, and he relies exclusively on the true one, he has no right to relief. Thus in *Heilbut, Symons & Co v Buckleton*[100] a person bought shares in a company after being told (i) that it was a rubber company (which was untrue), and (ii) that the defendants were "bringing it out" (which was true). One reason given by Lord Atkinson for dismissing the buyer's claim for damages was that he had relied on the second statement to the exclusion of the first.

9–022   **Truth known to agent.** A person cannot get relief for misrepresentation if the truth, though not known to him, was known to his agent while acting within the scope of his authority.[101] But the principal may get such relief if the agent found

---

[90] *Cooper v Tamms* [1988] 1 E.G.L.R. 257; *Eurocopy v Teesdale* [1992] B.C.L.C. 1067; *Rushmer v Smith* [2009] EWHC 94 at [65]–[66].

[91] *Jennings v Broughton* (1854) 5 D.M. & G. 126; cf. *The Morning Watch* [1990] 1 Lloyd's Rep. 547 at 556.

[92] *Kyle Bay Ltd v Underwriters Subscribing Under Policy No.019057/08/01* [2007] EWCA Civ 57 at [42], where the circumstances of the case were regarded as "very unusual".

[93] A claim for damages will not succeed unless the claimant can show that the loss in question was caused by the fraud: *Smith New Court Securities Ltd v Scrimgeour Vickers (Asset Management) Ltd* [1997] A.C. 254 at 284; *Barings Plc v Coopers & Lybrand* [2002] EWHC 461 (Ch); [2002] 2 B.C.L.C. 410 at [127]–[130]; cf. *South Australia Asset Management Corp v York Montague Ltd* [1997] A.C. 191 at 216.

[94] *Barton v Armstrong* [1976] A.C. 104 (a case of duress to the person: below para.10–003) in which an analogy is drawn with fraudulent misrepresentation, based on *Reynell v Sprye* (1852) 1 De G.M. & G. 660 at 678; cf. *UCB Corporate Services Ltd v Williams* [2002] EWCA Civ 555; [2002] 3 F.C.R. 448 at [86], [89] (a case of actual undue influence, which is regarded as a "species of fraud").

[95] In *Barton v Armstrong*, above, the Privy Council placed the burden of proving that the fraud (duress) contributed nothing on the defendant.

[96] See further below paras 9–065, 9–113.

[97] (1885) 29 Ch.D. 459; *The Siboen and the Sibotre* [1976] 1 Lloyd's Rep. 293 at 324; *BP Operating Co Ltd v Chevron Transport (Scotland)* [2001] UKHL 50; [2001] 3 W.L.R. 949 at [105]; *Spice Girls Ltd v Aprilia World Service BV* [2002] EWCA Civ 15; [2002] E.M.L.R. 27 at [70]; *UCB Corporate Services Ltd v Williams* [2002] EWCA Civ 555; [2002] 3 F.C.R. 448; cf. (in cases of duress) *Barton v Armstrong* [1976] A.C. 104; and above, para.3–083.

[98] See above, para.9–010.

[99] See *Standard Chartered Bank v Pakistan National Shipping Co* [2002] UKHL 43; [2003] 1 A.C. 959 at [17] for the view that the rule is "probably restricted" to cases of fraud.

[100] [1913] A.C. 30; above, para.4–003.

[101] *Bawden v London Assurance* [1892] 2 Q.B. 534; *Strover v Harrington* [1988] Ch. 390; contrast *El Ajou v Dollar Holdings Plc* [1994] 2 All E.R. 685 at 689, 702–705.

out the truth while acting for the other party,[102] or in fraud of the principal,[103] or in any way outside the scope of his authority.

Testing accuracy. A person who himself tests the accuracy of the representa- 9–023 tion can be said to rely on his own judgment, rather than on the representation. Accordingly, he cannot obtain relief for innocent[104] (or probably for negligent[105]) misrepresentation. But this rule does not apply in cases of fraud. In *S Pearson & Son Ltd v Dublin Corp.*[106] the claimants undertook to execute works for the corporation on the faith of plans supplied by it. The contract provided that the claimants should satisfy themselves of the accuracy of the plans.[107] It was held that this provision would not protect the corporation if the plans were fraudulent. It is not clear what steps, if any, the claimants took to test the accuracy of the plans. But it is submitted that if, in spite of taking some such steps, they had failed to discover the truth, the corporation should still have been liable on proof of fraud.

Opportunity to find out the truth. A person may be entitled to relief even 9–024 though he had, but did not take, the opportunity to test the accuracy of the representation.[108] This rule is most frequently applied to cases of fraud,[109] but in *Redgrave v Hurd*[110] it was held that such an opportunity to discover the truth was no bar to relief even where the misrepresentation was innocent and in *Peekay Intermark Ltd v ANZ Banking Group Ltd,*[111] in the context of a claim under s.2(1) of the Misrepresentation Act 1967, Moore-Bick L.J. concluded that, once a misrepresentation has been made, "it is not enough to show that the claimant *could have* discovered the truth, but that he *did* discover it".[112] However, he distinguished the case before him and held that there had not been the necessary inducement on the basis that the misrepresentation was corrected "by the express terms of the very contract to which the claimant put his signature", but which he

---

[102] *Newsholme v Road Transport Ins Co Ltd* [1929] 2 K.B. 356; *The Hellespont Ardent* [1997] 2 Lloyd's Rep. 547 at 596.
[103] *Wells v Smith* [1914] 3 K.B. 722; *Group Josi Re v Wallbrook Ins Co Ltd* [1996] 1 W.L.R. 1152; *Renault UK Ltd v Fleetpro Technical Services Ltd* [2007] EWHC 2541 (QB).
[104] *Clarke v Mackintosh* (1862) 4 Giff.134; *Redgrave v Hurd* (1881) 20 Ch.D. 1 at 14, discussing *Attwood v Small* (1838) 6 Cl. & F. 232.
[105] *McInerny v Lloyds Bank Ltd* [1974] 1 Lloyd's Rep. 246 at 254.
[106] [1907] A.C. 351.
[107] For the effect of such provisions under Misrepresentation Act 1967, s.3, see below, para.9–117.
[108] *Dobell v Stevens* (1825) 3 B. & C. 623; *Reynell v Sprye* (1852) 1 D.M. & G. 660; *Central Ry of Venezuela v Kisch* (1867) L.R. 2 H.L. 99; *Redgrave v Hurd* (1881) 20 Ch.D. 1; *Smith v Land & House Property Corp* (1884) 28 Ch.D. 7; *Aaron's Reefs Ltd v Twiss* [1896] A.C. 273; cf. *Rignal Developments Ltd v Halil* [1988] Ch. 190 at 199, *aliter*, if a person reads a document revealing the truth, but simply fails to understand it: *Ex p. Briggs* (1866) L.R. 1 Eq. 483.
[109] e.g. *Gordon v Selico Ltd* (1986) 278 E.G. 53 at 61; *Strover v Harrington* [1988] Ch. 390 at 410; cf. *Commission for the New Towns v Cooper (Great Britain) Ltd* [1995] Ch. 259 at 282. *Horsfall v Thomas* (1862) 1 H. & C. 90, so far as *contra*, was doubted in *Smith v Hughes* (1871) L.R. 6 Q.B. 597 at 605.
[110] (1881) 20 Ch.D. 1; *Laurence v Lexcourt Holdings Ltd* [1978] 1 W.L.R. 1128.
[111] [2006] EWCA Civ 386; [2006] 2 Lloyd's Rep 511; cf. *Assicurazioni Generali SpA v Arab Ins Group* [2002] EWCA Civ 1642; [2003] 1 All E.R. (Comm) 140; *Flack v Pattinson* [2002] EWCA Civ 1862; [2002] All E.R. (D) 31 (Dec).
[112] ibid. at [40].

failed to read.[113] It is submitted that a preferable explanation for this decision is simply that a claim for misrepresentation, *other than for fraud*, may be defeated where it is reasonable to expect the representee to make use of the opportunity to discover the truth,[114] and to this extent it is submitted that the rule in *Redgrave v Hurd* no longer applies.[115] Support for this principle can be derived from the decision in *Smith v Eric S Bush*.[116] The claimants in that case had bought a house with the aid of a mortgage, relying on a valuation which had been negligently conducted by a surveyor engaged by the lender. Their claim against the surveyor succeeded in spite of the fact that they might have discovered the truth if they had conducted their own independent survey; for it was neither reasonable to expect them to take this step, nor likely that they would do so, since the house in question was one of modest value. But the House of Lords indicated[117] that the position might be different on the purchase of commercial or industrial premises, or even of residential property of high value.[118]

9–025　　**Representation addressed to another.** A person may rely on a representation even though it was not made directly to him: e.g. where A makes a misrepresentation to B which later comes to the notice of C and induces C to contract with A. If A intended to bring about this result he is liable to C.[119]

A representation made by A to B may also make A liable to C where it was reasonable for A to anticipate that the representation would be passed on to C and that C would act on it in some way other than by entering into a contract with

---

[113] ibid. at [40].

[114] Thus, in the *Peekay* case, the claimant, as a sophisticated investor, was careless to rely on the "rough and ready" representation made to him by an employee of the defendant about the nature of the investment to be made and then to sign, without reading, the contractual documentation which "contained the only formal description he would receive" of the true nature of the investment (at [52]).

[115] cf. *Archer v Brown* [1985] Q.B. 401 at 416 (doubting *Redgrave v Hurd* on another point).

[116] [1990] 1 A.C. 831. And see the analogous approach taken in the context of an agent's apparent authority: below, para.16–026.

[117] ibid. at 854, 872 (dealing with the issue of reasonableness under Unfair Contract Terms Act 1977).

[118] It has been suggested that the rule in *Redgrave v Hurd* should continue to apply to claims for rescission, on the basis that the misrepresentor should not retain the advantage of the contract entered into, notwithstanding the carelessness of the representee, and that the observations of the House of Lords in *Smith v Eric S Bush* should be confined to claims for damages against a third party: *Chitty*, above, fn.74, para.6–039. The carelessness of the representee may be a ground for reducing damages for negligent misrepresentation (or under the Misrepresentation Act 1967 (*Gran Gelato Ltd v Richcliff (Group) Ltd* [1992] Ch. 560 at 573–574)) under Law Reform (Contributory Negligence) Act 1945. The 1945 Act does not apply where the misrepresentation was fraudulent: *Alliance & Leicester BS v Edgestrop* [1993] 1 W.L.R. 1462; *Standard Chartered Bank v Pakistan National Shipping Co* [2002] UKHL 43; [2003] 1 A.C. 959. Nor would the 1945 Act affect a right to *rescind* for misrepresentation.

[119] *Pilmore v Hood* (1838) 5 Bing.N.C. 97; cf. *Langridge v Levy* (1837) 2 M. & W. 519; *Tackey v McBain* [1912] A.C. 186; *Brikom Investments Ltd v Carr* [1979] Q.B. 467 at 485; *Standard Chartered Bank v Pakistan National Shipping Corp* [1995] 2 Lloyd's Rep. 365 at 378 (as to which see above, fn.118); *Possfund Custodian Trustees Ltd v Diamond* [1996] 1 W.L.R. 1351. Contrast *Peek v Gurney* (1873) L.R. 6. H.L. 377 (but see Financial Services and Markets Act 2000, s.90, as amended by the Prospectus Regulations 2005 (SI 2005/1433)). It is sometimes said more generally that the representor must have intended the representee to act on the representation, but this is only a "live issue" in the present context, i.e. where it is contested that the representation was not addressed to the claimant or to a class of persons of whom the claimant was one: *Raiffeisen Zentralbank Osterreich AG v Royal Bank of Scotland Plc* [2010] EWHC 1392 (Comm) at [226].

A.[120] This possibility is illustrated by cases such as *Smith v Eric S Bush*,[121] where a representation in a report as to the value or condition of a house was made by A to B, was then passed on by B to C, and induced C to buy the house from X. Where the contract induced by the misrepresentation is not made between A and C, it may be difficult to determine whether A owed any duty of care to C. This question is discussed later in this chapter[122]; the present point is simply that the requirement of reliance on the representation may be satisfied even though the representation is not made directly by the representor to the representee.

Where A by misrepresentation induces B to buy something from him, he will not be liable to C merely because B repeats the misrepresentation when later reselling the subject-matter to C. In one such case it was held that the mis-representation was "spent"[123] when the contract was made between A and B, so that C could not rely on it against A. He might, however, be able to do so if he could show that A knew that B intended to resell and was likely to repeat the misrepresentation on the occasion of the sale to C.[124]

Reliance distinguished from materiality. The rule that the representee must rely on the representation is distinct from the requirement of materiality. Whether a representation is material depends, in general,[125] on the significance which a reasonable person would have attached to it. Whether the representee has relied on the representation depends on his actual state of mind. The mere fact that a representation is material gives rise to no "inference of law" that the representation was relied on.[126] For example, in *JEB Fasteners Ltd v Marks Bloom & Co*[127] the claimants took over a company after seeing its accounts, which were inaccurate, having been negligently prepared by the defendants (a firm of account-ants). A duty of care seems to have arisen because the accounts had been "impliedly confirmed directly to the [claimant] . . . with a particular transaction in contemplation",[128] and the misrepresentation was clearly material; but the claim-ants' claim for damages was dismissed as they had placed no reliance on the accounts. Their object in taking over the company was to secure the services of two of its directors and they would have proceeded with the transaction even if the accounts had shown the company's true financial state. 9–026

Burden of proof. For the purpose of the requirement of reliance, the repre-sentee need only show that the representation was made and that it was capable of inducing the contract, i.e. that it was material. The burden then passes to the 9–027

---

[120] But not in the absence of such circumstances: *The Zephyr* [1985] 2 Lloyd's Rep. 529 at 539; cf. *Goodwill v National Pregnancy Advisory Service* [1996] 1 W.L.R. 1397.

[121] [1990] 1 A.C. 831; *Yianni v Edwin Evans & Sons* [1982] Q.B. 438.

[122] See below, para.9–033 et seq.

[123] *Gross v Lewis Hillman Ltd* [1970] Ch. 445 at 461.

[124] ibid. at 461; cf. *The Sennar (No.2)* [1985] 1 W.L.R. 490; cf. *Clef Aquitaine SARL v Laporte Materials (Barrow) Ltd* [2001] Q.B. 485, where the subject-matter was transferred by B to C by novation. A was a necessary party to this transaction (below, para.15–003) and knew that his representa-tion would be passed on by B to C, those entities being under the same control.

[125] See above, para.9–016.

[126] *Smith v Land & House Property Corp* (1884) 28 Ch.D. 7 at 16.

[127] [1983] 1 All E.R. 583, affirming [1981] 3 All E.R. 289. The question whether the defendants owed any duty to the claimants was only discussed at first instance; on this point see below, para.9–035.

[128] *Al Saudi Banque v Clark Pixley* [1990] Ch. 313 at 335.

representor to show that the representee would have entered into the contract anyway, even if the misrepresentation had not been made.[129]

2. DAMAGES FOR MISREPRESENTATION[130]

9–028   In this section, we shall discuss the five grounds on which damages can be recovered for misrepresentation and consider the relationship between them; and refer, in the context of misrepresentation, to the power of criminal courts to make compensation orders in criminal cases. We shall first consider the requirements for liability on each of the five grounds and then the basis upon which damages are assessed, including the rules of remoteness which are applied.

(a) Liability

(i) Fraud

9–029   At common law a person who suffers loss as a result of acting in reliance on a fraudulent statement can recover damages in an action of deceit.[131] He can generally do this whether he rescinds the contract or not[132] though he cannot pursue both remedies if this results in his recovering twice over for the same loss.[133]

9–030   **The fraudulent state of mind.** In *Derry v Peek*[134] the House of Lords held that a statement is fraudulent only if made (i) with knowledge of its falsity,[135] or (ii) without belief in its truth,[136] or (iii) recklessly,[137] not caring whether it is true

---

[129] *Smith v Chadwick* (1884) 9 App.Cas. 187 at 196; *Barton v County NatWest Ltd* [1999] Lloyds Rep. Banking 408 at [58]; *Dadourian Group International Inc v Simms* [2009] EWCA Civ 169; [2009] 1 Lloyd's Rep. 601 at [100]. The cases cited were concerned with fraud and it has been said that the inference of reliance is confined to fraudulent misrepresentation: *Fitzroy Robinson Ltd v Mentmore Towers Ltd* [2009] EWHC 1552 (TCC); [2009] B.L.R. 555. It is respectfully submitted that the preferable view may be that the inference is particularly strong in a case of fraud: *Ross River Ltd v Cambridge City Football Club* [2007] EWHC 2115 (Ch); 117 Con L.R. 129 at [241].

[130] Greig 87 L.Q.R. 179.

[131] It is doubtful whether the remedy of an account of profits is available: *Murad v Al-Saraj* [2005] EWCA Civ 959; [2005] W.T.L.R. 1573; *Renault UK Ltd v Fleetpro Technical Services Ltd* [2007] EWHC 2541 (QB) at [152]–[158].

[132] *Newbigging v Adam* (1886) 34 Ch.D. 582 at 592; *Archer v Brown* [1985] Q.B. 401 at 415; *Tang Man Sit v Capacious Investments Ltd* [1996] A.C. 514 at 521; cf. Companies Act 2006, s.655 overriding the former rule in *Houldsworth v City of Glasgow Bank* (1880) 5 App.Cas. 317 "at least in part": *Soden v British & Commonwealth Holdings Plc* [1998] A.C. 298 at 327.

[133] *Archer v Brown*, above, at 415.

[134] (1889) 14 App.Cas. 337 (actual decision was reversed by Directors Liability Act 1890; see now Financial Services and Markets Act 2000, s.90, as amended by Prospectus Regulations 2005 (SI 2005/1433)); *The Kriti Palm* [2006] EWCA Civ 1601; [2007] 1 Lloyd's Rep. 555 at [256]–[258]; and see fn.142, below.

[135] Including knowingly failing to correct a representation which has become false: *Fitzroy Robinson Ltd v Mentmore Towers Ltd* [2009] EWHC 1552 (TCC); [2009] B.L.R. 555; below para.9–132.

[136] Quaere whether this state of mind is sufficient for the personal liability of a mere employee of a company acting under the instructions of a director: *GE Commerce Finance Ltd v Gee* [2005] EWHC 2056 (QB); [2006] 1 Lloyd's Rep. 337 at [111].

[137] Recklessness goes beyond mere carelessness: *The Kriti Palm* [2006] EWCA Civ 1601; [2007] 1 Lloyd's Rep. 555 at [257].

or false. Fraud is a serious charge which must be clearly and distinctly proved.[138] A person who negligently makes a false statement will now often be liable in damages, but it may still be important that he is not guilty of fraud at common law. One reason for this is that the damages for fraud may not be the same as damages for negligence.[139] Another is that certain special rules may apply to rescission for fraud.[140]

Motive irrelevant. It must be shown that the representor intended the repre- 9–031 sentee to rely on the false statement,[141] but a statement may be fraudulent although it was made without bad motive and without intention to cause loss: an "intention to deceive" suffices even though there is no "intention to defraud".[142] Thus in *Polhill v Walter*[143] an agent purported to accept a bill of exchange on behalf of his principal, knowing that he had no authority to do so but believing that his principal would ratify. He was held liable in deceit. This case should be contrasted with *Angus v Clifford*.[144] The directors of a company which had bought a gold mine issued a prospectus containing extracts from an engineer's report said to have been "prepared for the directors". It had in fact been prepared for the sellers of the mine. The directors knew this, but were held not liable for fraud as they did not at the time of issuing the prospectus appreciate the importance of the words "prepared for the directors". Thus it seems that a person is not guilty of fraud if he knows that his statement is false but does not appreciate its materiality.[145]

Principal and agent. Responsibility for a statement may be divided between 9–032 principal and agent or between several agents of the same principal. If an agent within the scope of his authority makes a statement which he knows to be false, the principal is liable for the fraud of the agent[146]; the agent is also liable for his own fraud.[147] If the agent who made the statement did not know that it was false, but

---

[138] *The Kriti Palm*, above at [259]; *Dadourian Group International Inc v Simms* [2009] EWCA Civ 169; [2009] 1 Lloyd's Rep. 601 at [31]–[32]; *Raiffeisen Zentralbank Osterreich AG v Royal Bank of Scotland Plc* [2010] EWHC 1392 (Comm) at [341].

[139] See below, para.9–066.

[140] See above, para.9–020; below, paras 9–088, 9–100, 9–113; cf. para.9–055.

[141] See above, para.9–025; *Abu Dhabi Investment Company Ltd v H Clarkson & Co* [2008] EWCA Civ 699 at [33]; *Clef Aquitaine Sarl v Laporte Materials (Barrow) Ltd* [2001] 1 Q.B. 488 at 503, 506, 513.

[142] *Standard Chartered Bank v Pakistan National Shipping Corp* [1995] 2 Lloyd's Rep. 365 at 375; see further [1998] 1 Lloyd's Rep. 656; *Standard Chartered Bank v Pakistan National Shipping Co (No.2)* [2000] 1 Lloyd's Rep. 218 at 221, 224 (reversed on another point [2002] UKHL 43; [2003] 1 A.C. 959). "Dishonesty" seems to be used to mean no more than "intention to deceive" in *Armitage v Nurse* [1998] Ch. 241 at 251.

[143] (1832) 3 B. & Ad. 114; cf. *Edgington v Fitzmaurice* (1885) 29 Ch.D. 459 at 481; *Watts v Spence* [1976] Ch. 165 at 176 (where fraud was not alleged).

[144] [1891] 2 Ch. 449.

[145] But such failure may give rise to liability in negligence (not recognised at the time of *Angus v Clifford*): *Bank of Tokyo-Mitsubishi UFJ Ltd v BaskanGidaSanayiVePazarlama AS* [2009] EWHC 1276 (Comm) at [1002].

[146] *S Pearson & Son Ltd v Dublin Corp* [1907] A.C. 351; *Briess v Woolley* [1954] A.C. 333; cf. *Man Nutzfahrzeuge AG v Freightliner Ltd* [2005] EWHC 2347; *Clapp v Enron (Thrace) Exploration & Production BV* [2005] EWCA Civ 1511; [2006] 1 C.L.C. 94 at [29].

[147] *Standard Chartered Bank v Pakistan National Shipping Co* [2002] UKHL 43; [2003] 1 A.C. 959; *Renault UK Ltd v Fleetpro Technical Services Ltd* [2007] EWHC 2541 (QB). But see the doubts expressed by Tugenhadt J. in *GE Commercial Finance Ltd v Gee* [2005] EWHC 2056 (QB); [2006] 1 Lloyd's Rep 337 at [103]–[104]; above, fn.136.

the principal, or another agent did know this, the principal is in general not liable for fraud.[148] The mens rea required for fraud cannot be established by adding together the states of mind of several persons, each of whom is innocent. But if the principal or the second agent stood by, knowing that the representation was being made and that it was false, the principal would be guilty of fraud or liable for the fraud of the second agent.[149] In such a case the principal or second agent has mens rea, though he made no representation. The same rule should apply where the representation is innocently made by the principal, and the agent, acting within his authority, stands by knowing that the representation is going to be made and that it is false.[150]

(ii) *Negligence at common law*[151]

9-033   **Duty of care.** A misrepresentation is negligent if it is made carelessly and in breach of a duty owed by the representor to the representee to take reasonable care that the representation is accurate. It used to be thought that such a duty could arise only where the relationship between representor and representee arose out of a pre-existing contract between them, or where it was "fiduciary".[152] But this narrow view was rejected in *Hedley Byrne & Co Ltd v Heller & Partners Ltd*.[153] The claimants in that case suffered loss as a result of having given credit to a firm called Easipower Ltd, in reliance on a reference carelessly given by Easipower's bank, who knew of the purpose for which the reference was required. The actual decision was that the bank was not liable because the reference had been given "without responsibility".[154] But the House of Lords made it clear that, had there been no such disclaimer, the bank would have owed to the claimants a duty to take reasonable care in the making of the statements contained in the reference. A duty of the kind just described can arise at common law if there is a "special relationship" between the parties. The crucial question, therefore, is when such a relationship will come into existence; and two approaches to this question are taken by the authorities.

---

[148] *Cornfoot v Fowke* (1840) 6 M. & W. 358; *Gordon Hill Trust Ltd v Segall* [1941] 2 All E.R. 379; *Armstrong v Strain* [1952] 1 K.B. 232; Devlin 53 L.Q.R. 344; Gower 15 M.L.R. 232. For liability in negligence, see below.

[149] *London County Freehold v Berkeley Property Co Ltd* [1936] 2 All E.R. 1039; *The Siboen and the Sibotre* [1976] 1 Lloyd's Rep. 293 at 321; cf. *GG 132 Ltd v Hampson Industries Plc* [2011] EWHC (Comm) at [42].

[150] Whether the *principal* could be made liable for fraud in such circumstances will depend on the rules for the attribution to one person of the state of mind of another: *Man Nutzfahrzeuge AG v Freightliner Ltd* [2005] EWHC 2347 (no attribution where the agent was neither a director, nor an employee of the defendant company).

[151] The principal concern of this chapter is with misrepresentation which induces the representee to contract *with the representor*. In such cases, s.2(1) of the Misrepresentation Act 1967 is the more likely cause of action: below, para.9–039 et seq. But a claim in negligence, or for "negligent mis-statement" as it is sometimes called in this context, is also available between the contracting parties: below, para.9–038. Claims in negligence generally, including for negligent misrepresentation are beyond the scope of this book. What follows therefore is an outline account. For a more detailed account, see *Clerk & Lindsell on Torts* (20th edn), Chs.8, 10.

[152] *Nocton v Ashburton* [1914] A.C. 932.

[153] [1964] A.C. 465; Stevens 27 M.L.R. 121; Honoré 8 J.S.P.T.L. 284; Craig 92 L.Q.R. 213.

[154] Such a provision would now be subject to the requirement of reasonableness by virtue of Unfair Contract Terms Act 1977, ss.2(1) and 13(1): see *Smith v Eric S Bush* [1990] 1 A.C. 831 at 875–876; above, para.7–055.

The "threefold test". Under this test, there is a "special relationship" when **9–034** three conditions are satisfied: it must be reasonably foreseeable by the representor that the representee will rely on the statement; there must be sufficient "proximity" between the parties; and it must be fair just and reasonable for the law to impose the duty.[155] It is obvious that these requirements are closely related, so much so that it has been said that they are "at least in most cases, merely facets of the same thing".[156] In the context of misrepresentation, foreseeable reliance by the representee on the representor's statement or advice is the single most important requirement of the special relationship.[157] But while it is a necessary condition of liability in tort for misrepresentation inducing a contract,[158] it is not a sufficient one. Thus a purely social relationship will not normally suffice to give rise to a duty, so that no action normally lies at common law where a person suffers loss as a result of acting on careless friendly advice,[159] even if it is given by a professional person.[160] In such a case, it would not normally be just and reasonable to impose a duty.

On the other hand, there was a "special relationship" between the claimants and the bank in *Hedley Byrne*'s case,[161] and it is clear from dicta in that case, from earlier decisions which were overruled[162] or rehabilitated[163] by it, and from later cases, that a duty of care will often arise where the representor makes the representation while acting in some professional capacity. If he makes the representation to his own client, his duty of care with respect to its accuracy will generally be imposed by his contract with that client,[164] though a duty of care imposed by the general law (and giving rise to liability in tort) may exist side by side with such a contractual duty.[165] The more important point to be made here is that such a duty of care may also arise under the law of tort even though there is *no* contract between representor and representee. Thus the duty may be owed by accountants,[166] surveyors and valuers[167] even to persons other than their immediate clients who rely on their statements, where the conditions (stated above) which give rise to a duty of care are satisfied.

Representations made for a particular purpose. A duty is more likely to **9–035** arise in cases of this kind where the statement was made for the purpose of the transaction which it induced than where it was not so made. There was accordingly sufficient proximity between a surveyor and the prospective purchaser of a

---

[155] *Smith v Eric S Bush* [1990] 1 A.C. 831 at 865; *Caparo Industries Plc v Dickman* [1990] 2 A.C. 605 at 617–618; cf. *Yuen Kun Yeu v Attorney-General of Hong Kong* [1988] A.C. 175.
[156] *Caparo Industries Plc v Dickman* [1900] 2 A.C. 605 at 632.
[157] *Murphy v Brentwood DC* [1991] 1 A.C. 398 at 480, 486–487.
[158] Though not of liability for negligence arising in other ways: see *White v Jones* [1995] 2 A.C. 207 at 268, 275; *Spring v Guardian Royal Insurance Plc* [1995] 2 A.C. 296 at 344.
[159] [1964] A.C. 465 at 482; see [1964] A.C. 465 at 531 for possible exceptions. In *Chaudhry v Prabakhar* [1989] 1 W.L.R. 29 (above, para.3–169) the existence of a duty was conceded; this concession was approved by two members of the court, who, however, also recognised (at 36 and 34) that advice given in "family, domestic or social relationships" would not normally be actionable.
[160] *Mutual Life and Citizens' Assurance Co Ltd v Evatt* [1971] A.C. 793 at 806.
[161] [1964] A.C. 465 at 494, 502, 538, 539.
[162] *Candler v Crane, Christmas & Co* [1951] 2 K.B. 164.
[163] *Cann v Willson* (1883) 39 Ch.D. 39.
[164] See below, para.17–066.
[165] cf. *Henderson v Merrett Syndicates Ltd* [1995] 2 A.C. 145; and see below, paras 14–045, 20–124. This case was one of liability, not for negligent *statements*, but for negligently rendered *services*.
[166] See generally *Jackson & Powell on Professional Liability* (6th edn), Ch.17.
[167] ibid. Ch.10.

house, where the surveyor had been commissioned by a building society to report on the value of that house, knowing that his report would be passed on to the purchaser, where it was so passed on, and the house was bought in reliance on it.[168] Similarly, an accountant's report on the financial state of a company can give rise to liability to an intending lender to, or investor in, the company if it was made for the purpose of providing such a person with the information on which his decision whether to make the loan or investment is likely to be, and is in fact, based.[169] But the position is different where auditors are appointed by a company to enable the company to perform its statutory obligation to produce audited annual accounts. In such a case there is no sufficient proximity between those auditors and prospective lenders to, or investors in, the company, or even between the auditors and shareholders in the company who, in reliance on the accounts, buy additional shares.[170] The reason why no duty is owed to these persons is that the audited accounts are produced simply for the purpose of satisfying the statutory obligation described above, and not to induce the transactions in question. The same principle may limit the scope of the duty to the particular transaction for the purpose of which the statement was made. Thus where auditors employed by a company produced accounts which, as they knew, were to determine the price at which the claimants were to acquire a substantial shareholding in the company, the auditors were held to owe a duty to the claimants in respect of that purchase but not in respect of loans of money made to the company nor in respect of a further purchase of shares in the company made by the claimants over three years after the original transaction.[171]

9–036   **"Assumption of responsibility".** A second test which may be used to determine whether a special relationship exists, and which now applies more generally in the law of negligence, is to ask whether the defendant "assumed responsibility for what he said and did vis-à-vis the claimant, or is to be treated by the law as having done so".[172] As is clear from this dictum of Lord Bingham the

---

[168] e.g. *Smith v Eric S Bush* [1990] 1 A.C. 831.

[169] *Caparo Industries Plc v Dickman* [1990] 2 A.C. 605 at 625, 647–648; *Morgan Crucible Co Plc v Hill Samuel Bank Ltd* [1991] 1 All E.R. 148; *Barings Plc v Coopers & Lybrand* [1997] 1 B.C.L.C. 427; *Law Society v KPMG Peat Marwick* [2000] 1 W.L.R. 1921; *So v HSBC* [2009] EWCA Civ 296; [2009] C.L.C. 503. Contrast *James McNaughton Paper Group v Hicks Anderson & Co* [1991] 1 All E.R. 134.

[170] e.g. *Al Saudi Banque v Clark Pixley* [1990] Ch. 313; *Caparo Industries Plc v Dickman* [1990] 2 A.C. 605; Fleming 106 L.Q.R. 349; *Esanda Finance Corp Ltd v Peat Marwick Hungerfords* (1997) 71 A.J.L.R. 448 (High Court of Australia); *The Morning Watch* [1990] 1 Lloyd's Rep. 547. Contrast *Law Society v KPMG Peat Marwick*, above, fn.169, where the duty was owed to, and the loss suffered by, the very body to which the defendants' report was, by the statute, required to be made.

[171] *Galoo Ltd v Bright Grahame Murray* [1994] 1 W.L.R. 1360; cf. in relation to false statements in a company prospectus, *Al Nakib Investments (Jersey) Ltd v Longcroft* [1990] 1 W.L.R. 1390; contrast *Possfund Custodian Trustees Ltd v Diamond* [1996] 1 W.L.R. 1351, where it was arguable such statements were intended to induce "after-market" purchases. These cases concerned common law liability, as opposed to liability under the statutory provisions now contained in Financial Services and Markets Act 2000, s.90, as amended by the Prospectus Regulations 2005 (SI 2005/1433); Financial Services and Markets Act 2000, s.90A, as amended by the Financial Services and Markets Act 2000 (Liability of Issuers) Regulations 2010 (SI 2010/1192).

[172] *Customs and Excise Commissioners v Barclays Bank Plc* [2006] UKHL 28; [2007] 1 A.C. 181 at [4], per Lord Bingham (no liability for negligent misrepresentation: see below fn.173). See earlier: *Hedley Byrne & Co Ltd v Heller & Partners Ltd* [1964] A.C. 494 at 529; *Simaan General Contracting Co v Pilkington Glass Ltd (No.2)* [1988] Q.B. 758 at 784; *Henderson v Merrett Syndicates Ltd* [1995] 2 A.C. 145 at 180, 181, 205; *White v Jones* [1995] 2 A.C. 207 at 256, 268–269; *Spring v Guardian Ins Plc* [1995] 2 A.C. 296 at 324.

test of assumption of responsibility is applied objectively; it is not a case of what the defendant intended but, "as in the case of contractual liability", what would reasonably be inferred from his conduct against the background of all the circumstances of the case.[173] As far as the relationship with the threefold test is concerned, it seems that an assumption of responsibility is to be regarded as a sufficient, but not a necessary, condition of liability: if it is satisfied, it is unnecessary to ask whether it would be fair, just and reasonable to impose liability; if not, further consideration is called for under the threefold test.[174] As for the tests themselves, there is candid recognition that they are of doubtful utility.[175] While decisions have been reached by applying one test or the other, of far greater relevance has been the circumstances of the case and the relationship between the parties in the context of their legal and factual situation.[176] Two factors of particular relevance are the purpose for which any representations were made,[177] and whether to impose liability in negligence would unduly interfere with any contractual arrangements made by the parties.[178]

Professional skill. One feature of the relationships discussed above, in which the representor was held to owe a duty of care, was that he made the statement in the exercise of some professional skill. The absence of this factor was held to negative liability in *Mutual Life and Citizen's Ins Co Ltd v Evatt*,[179] where a company carelessly gave misleading information about an associated company to a prospective investor in the latter company. As a result the investor suffered loss, but the majority of the Privy Council held that the first company was not liable in negligence as it was not and did not purport to be engaged in the business of giving skilled advice on investments.[180] The majority regarded this as an essential ingredient of liability[181]; but the prevailing view is that, so long as other conditions of liability are satisfied, the representor may be liable even though he was not in the business of giving advice[182] and even though the representee did not seek his advice (but only asked for information).[183]

9–037

---

[173] ibid. at [35], per Lord Hoffmann. There must however have been an element of voluntariness in the conduct of the defendant upon which the assumption of responsibility can be imposed. Thus, in the *Customs* case no duty of care was owed by a bank served with a freezing order to the judgment creditor in whose favour the order had been granted.

[174] ibid. at [4], [35]; *Henderson v Merrett Syndicates Ltd* [1995] 2 A.C. 145 at 181. Contrast *McCullagh v Lane Fox & Partners Ltd* [1996] 1 E.G.L.R. 35 at 41, where assumption of responsibility was seen as an essential ingredient of liability for negligent misrepresentation. The weight of authority, much of it cited in the *Customs and Excise* case, is against such a view.

[175] ibid. at [36]; *Caparo v Dickman* [1990] 2 A.C. 617 at 628; *Merrett v Babb* [2001] EWCA Civ 214; [2001] Q.B. 1174 at [41].

[176] *Precis (521) v William Mercer Ltd* [2005] EWCA Civ 114; [2005] P.N.L.R. 28.

[177] See para.9–035, above.

[178] See discussion at para.14–045 et seq.

[179] [1971] A.C. 793; A.L.G. 87 L.Q.R. 147; Rickford 34 M.L.R. 328.

[180] ibid. at 809.

[181] ibid. at 805, 809.

[182] The views of the minority in *Evatt*'s case were preferred to those of the majority by Ormrod L.J. in *Esso Petroleum Co Ltd v Mardon* [1976] Q.B. 801 at 827 and by Lord Denning M.R. (dissenting) and Shaw L.J. in *Howard Marine & Dredging Co Ltd v A Ogden & Sons (Excavations) Ltd* [1978] Q.B. 574 at 591, 600. The point was left open in *Caparo Industries Plc v Dickman* [1990] 2 A.C. 605 at 637, but the case is viewed with some scepticism in *Spring v Guardian Insurance Plc* [1995] 2 A.C. 296 at 320.

[183] *Box v Midland Bank Ltd* [1979] 2 Lloyd's Rep. 391. Contrast *Royal Bank Trust Co (Trinidad) v John Robert Pampellone* [1987] 1 Lloyd's Rep. 218; *Civic Structures v Clark Quinney & Co* [1991] 2 E.G.L.R. 165: no liability for merely *passing on* information.

9-038   **Commercial relationships.** A duty of care may exist at common law even in a purely commercial relationship, such as that of buyer and seller or landlord and tenant. For example, in *Esso Petroleum Co Ltd v Mardon*[184] a tenant was induced to take a lease of a petrol station from an oil company by a statement made by an experienced salesman on the company's behalf, as to the potential future turnover of the premises. As the tenant had relied on the salesman's superior knowledge and experience, it was held that the company was under a duty of care at common law. On the other hand there are many commercial relationships in which each party consciously relies on his own skill or judgment[185] or where it is reasonable for the representor to assume that the representee will be advised by his own experts.[186] In such cases there would be no duty of care at common law; though, even in the absence of a "special relationship", there can be liability in damages under the Misrepresentation Act.[187]

(iii) *Misrepresentation Act 1967, section 2(1)*

9-039   This subsection creates a statutory liability for misrepresentation. It provides:

"Where a person has entered into a contract after[188] a misrepresentation has been made to him by another party thereto and as a result thereof he has suffered loss, then, if the person making the misrepresentation would be liable to damages in respect thereof had the misrepresentation been made fraudulently, that person shall be so liable notwithstanding that the mis-representation was not made fraudulently, unless he proves that he had reasonable ground to believe and did believe up to the time the contract was made that the facts represented were true".

9-040   **Scope.** Unlike negligence, it is not necessary under the subsection to ask whether there was a "special relationship", giving rise to a duty of care, between the parties[189]: it is enough if the representation is made by one contracting party to the other. For this reason, it has been said that the subsection imposes an "absolute obligation"[190]; but these words cannot be taken to refer to the *standard* of liability. This is far from "absolute", for under the concluding words of s.2(1), the representor can escape liability by proving that his belief in the truth of the

---

[184] [1976] Q.B. 801; Gravells 39 M.L.R. 462; cf. dicta in *Hedley Byrne's* case [1964] A.C. 465 at 486, 514, 528–529; *Gran Gelato Ltd v Richcliff (Group) Ltd* [1992] Ch. 560 (claim against first defendant); *McCullagh v Lane Fox & Partners* [1996] 1 E.G.L.R. 35 at 42.

[185] *Oleificio Zucchi SA v Northern Sales Ltd* [1965] 2 Lloyd's Rep. 496 at 519; cf. *Amalgamated Metal Trading Ltd v DTI, The Times,* March 31, 1989.

[186] *McInerny v Lloyds Bank Ltd* [1974] 1 Lloyd's Rep. 246.

[187] s.2(1), below; on the facts of *Esso Petroleum Co Ltd v Mardon,* above, fn.184, there would now be liability under this provision, as well as at common law.

[188] Where the misrepresentation is made in the contract itself, it may be difficult to argue that it was a *pre*-contractual representation which induced the very contract in which it now appears: *Senate Electrical Wholesalers Ltd v STC Submarine Systems Ltd,* unreported, May 26, 1994; it may, however, be sufficient to point to its having been made earlier in the pre-contractual negotiations, including earlier drafts of the contract: *Eurovideo Bildprogramm GmbH v Pulse Entertainment Ltd* [2002] EWCA Civ 1235 at [19].

[189] *Howard Marine & Dredging Co Ltd v A Ogden & Sons (Excavations) Ltd* [1978] Q.B. 574 at 596; Sills 96 L.Q.R. 15; Sealy [1978] C.L.J. 229; *Cemp Properties (UK) v Dentsply Research & Developments Corp* [1991] 2 E.G.L.R. 197.

[190] *The Skopas* [1983] 1 W.L.R. 857 at 861; cf. the *Howard Marine* case, above, at 647.

facts stated was not formed carelessly. Liability under the subsection is in this respect "essentially founded on negligence".[191] There are two situations in which the subsection does not apply, though there may be liability in negligence at common law: namely, where (as in *Hedley Byrne's*[192] case) the representation is made by a stranger to the contract; and where the negotiations between representor and representee do not reach the stage of a concluded contract.

Burden of proof. At common law, the representee must prove negligence, while under the subsection the representor is liable "unless he proves that he had reasonable ground to believe and did believe up to the time the contract was made that the facts represented were true". The difficulty of discharging this burden is illustrated by a case in which, during negotiations for the hire of barges, the owner's agent mis-stated their deadweight capacity, relying on an erroneous statement in Lloyd's Register. It was held that the burden had not been discharged since the owner could have discovered the true state of affairs by looking at documents in his possession.[193] But where the representor had no such means of discovering the truth, the burden would probably be discharged if he could show that he was himself the victim of an earlier fraud and that he had innocently repeated a representation previously made to him,[194] or that he had reasonably relied on an expert's report on the point in question,[195] or that he had made due enquiries before making the statement.[196] The subsection requires him to prove only that he had reasonable ground for his belief, so that his actual means of knowledge are relevant: accordingly, a layman may succeed in discharging the burden where an expert would fail. **9–041**

Agents. Under the subsection, a contracting party can be held liable for a representation made on his behalf by his agent.[197] But the agent himself is not liable under the subsection,[198] though he will be liable in negligence at common law if the representee can establish that there was a "special relationship" between himself and the agent, and that the agent was in breach of the resulting duty of care; but the agent would not be so liable where the only special relationship was between his *principal* and the representee.[199] **9–042**

The fiction of fraud. Section 2(1) has the effect of imposing liability in damages for careless misrepresentation; but instead of simply providing that the representor shall be liable in damages[200] it says that he shall be so liable if he "would be liable to damages . . . had the misrepresentation been made fraudulently". This fiction of fraud seems to be quite unnecessary; and it may lead the **9–043**

---

[191] *Gran Gelato Ltd v Richcliff Group Ltd* [1992] Ch. 560 at 573; cf. *South Australia Asset Management Corp v York Montague Ltd* [1997] A.C. 191 at 216.

[192] See above, para.9–033; *Kleinwort Benson Ltd v Malaysian Mining Corp* [1989] 1 W.L.R. 379 at 386.

[193] *Howard Marine* case, above; cf. *Walker v Boyle* [1982] 1 W.L.R. 495 at 509.

[194] As in *Oscar Chess Ltd v Williams* [1957] 1 W.L.R. 370; below, para.9–048; cf. *Humming Bird Motors v Hobbs* [1986] R.T.R. 276; below, para.9–050.

[195] *Cooper v Tamms* [1988] 1 E.G.L.R. 257.

[196] *William Sindall Plc v Cambridgeshire CC* [1994] 1 W.L.R. 1016.

[197] *Gosling v Anderson* (1972) 223 E.G. 1743; *Howard Marine* case, above.

[198] *The Skopas* [1983] 1 W.L.R. 857; Owen [1984] C.L.J. 27.

[199] *Williams v Natural Life Health Foods Ltd* [1998] 1 W.L.R. 835; *J Jarvis & Sons Ltd v Castle Wharf Development Ltd* [2001] EWCA Civ 19; [2001] Lloyd's Rep. P.N. 308.

[200] cf. Financial Services and Markets Act 2000, s.90 ("is liable to pay compensation").

courts to extend to cases within s.2(1) rules which have been developed in the context of fraudulent misrepresentation and which are wholly inappropriate where there is no actual fraud.[201] In the Parliamentary debates on the Act, Lord Reid suggested that the effect of the fiction might be to apply to the new cause of action the extended period of limitation which applies where an action is "based upon"[202] fraud. But he added that this result would be "rather unreasonable"[203] and a more recent dictum indicates that the fiction of fraud would not be applied to this situation.[204] Further support for the view that the fiction is not to be literally applied is provided by a case in which the Court of Appeal has held[205] that a principal may be liable under the subsection for his agent's misrepresentation even though there is no such shared responsibility for the statement as is required to make the principal liable in cases of fraud.[206] It is to be hoped that the courts will similarly reject certain other consequences[207] which could be deduced from the fiction of fraud.

9–044   **Effect of affirmation.** The right to *rescind* a contract for misrepresentation can be lost by affirmation[208]; but affirmation does not deprive the representee of his right to damages under s.2(1). Such damages can therefore in principle be recovered if, after having entered into the contract, the representee discovers the truth and nevertheless performs the contract.[209] Of course the right to damages may be limited in such cases: e.g. if the matter to which the misrepresentation relates was so serious that the representee's performance with knowledge of the truth amounts to failure by him to mitigate his loss.[210]

(iv) *Contractual statements*

9–045   So far, in this section, we have assumed that the misrepresentation induces the representee to enter into the contract, but that it has not become a term of the

---

[201] See *Royscot Trust Ltd v Rogerson* [1991] 2 Q.B. 297 (below, para.9–066), where the court seems to have viewed such a result with equanimity.

[202] See now Limitation Act 1980, s.32(1).

[203] 274 H.L. 936.

[204] *Garden Neptune Shipping Ltd v Occidental Worldwide Investment Corp* [1990] 1 Lloyd's Rep. 330 at 335; cf. (in another context) *Mander v Evans* [2001] 1 W.L.R. 2378. A claim under s.2(1) is not an action for negligence within the meaning of s.14A of Limitation Act 1980; quaere whether it is a claim in tort for the purposes of s.2 of the 1980 Act: *Laws v Society of Lloyds* [2003] EWCA Civ 1887; *The Times*, January 23, 2004.

[205] *Gosling v Anderson* (1972) 223 E.G. 1743.

[206] See above, para.9–032.

[207] e.g. the rule that a fraudulent statement need not be material (above, para.9–017), the rule in *S Pearson Ltd v Dublin Corp* [1907] A.C. 351 (above, para.9–023), and the rule that a person cannot exclude liability for his own fraud (above, para.7–042): see the *Garden Neptune* case, above, fn.204. On the other hand the rule that a representation as to a third person's credit must be in writing to give rise to liability under Statute of Frauds Amendment Act 1828, s.6 applies only to *fraudulent* misrepresentation: *Banbury v Bank of Montreal* [1918] A.C. 626; *Contex Drouzhba Ltd v Wiseman* [2007] EWCA Civ 1201; [2008] 1 B.C.L.C. 631; and in *The Pacific Colocotronis* [1984] Q.B. 713 at 718–719 it seems to have been thought that the fiction of fraud applied in this context, for it was "common ground" that the requirement of writing equally applied for the purpose of an action under Misrepresentation Act 1967, s.2(1). And see below, para.9–066 as to damages under s.2(1).

[208] See below, para.9–108.

[209] *Production Technology Consultants v Bartlett* [1986] 1 E.G.L.R. 82; cf. at common law *Arnison v Smith* (1889) 41 Ch.D. 348 (where, however, the claimants did not have full knowledge of their right to rescind and so could not be said to have affirmed).

[210] See below, para.20–116.

contract or otherwise acquired contractual force. If the misrepresentation does have contractual force, the representee is entitled to recover damages for breach of contract. He may also be entitled to terminate the contract for breach or rescind for misrepresentation. The relation between these various rights will be considered below[211]; our only concern here is with the right to damages. This differs in two ways from the rights to damages previously considered in this section: it can arise without fraud or negligence, and it is governed by different rules as to assessment of damages and remoteness.[212] It also differs in a number of ways from the power of the court to award damages in lieu of rescission, which will be considered below.[213] That power is discretionary, while damages for breach of contract can be recovered as of right; a representee cannot rescind for misrepresentation *and* claim damages in lieu of rescission, while (if the misrepresentation has become a term of the contract) he may be able to terminate and claim damages for breach of contract[214]; a party who once had the right to rescind, but has lost it, may not be able to recover damages in lieu of rescission,[215] though he can clearly recover damages for breach of contract.

For all these reasons it is still necessary to distinguish between contractual statements and "mere" representations inducing a contract,[216] though the provisions of the Misrepresentation Act as to damages will probably reduce the practical importance of the distinction. A contractual statement may either be a term of the main contract or a collateral contract.

Term of main contract. Where a contract is in writing, a descriptive statement may actually be made in the contractual document. Such a statement will clearly be a contractual term if it is said to be the basis of the contract.[217] Subject to such express provisions, the question whether the statement is a term or a mere representation is one of construction.[218] The same is true where the statement is contained in a written offer, the acceptance of which concludes the contract.[219] Where a descriptive statement is contained in a contractual document it may[220] be a term even though it did not induce the party complaining of its untruth to enter into the contract,[221] and, indeed, even though he was at the time of contracting unaware of its existence.[222]

Often a statement inducing a contract will not be set out in the contractual document, but will be made during the negotiations leading up to the contract. The question whether such a statement was a mere representation or a term of the contract depends on the intention with which the statement was made,[223] objectively ascertained.[224] It is impossible to lay down any strict rules for determining

9–046

---

[211] See below, paras 9–059—9–062, 9–092.
[212] See below, paras 9–059—9–066.
[213] See below, paras 9–054—9–057.
[214] See below, para.9–092.
[215] See below, para.9–056.
[216] Atiyah 1971 Alberta L.Rev. 347, and *Essays in Contract*, p.275.
[217] e.g. *London Assurance v Mansel* (1879) 11 Ch.D. 363.
[218] *Behn v Burness* (1863) 1 B. & S. 751 at 754 (statement in charterparty as to position of ship).
[219] *The Larissa* [1983] 2 Lloyd's Rep. 325 at 330.
[220] Though reliance may be relevant in determining whether the statement was intended as a term: see *Harlingdon & Leinster Enterprises Ltd v Christopher Hull Fine Art Ltd* [1991] 1 Q.B. 564.
[221] [1991] 1 Q.B. 564, above, at 574, 579, 584.
[222] cf. above, para.7–004: the principle of incorporation by signature can here work *in favour* of the signer.
[223] *Howard Marine & Dredging Co Ltd v A Ogden & Son (Excavations) Ltd* [1978] Q.B. 574 at 595.
[224] See above, paras 1–002, 2–002.

when the intention to treat the statement as a term can be said to exist. But a number of guiding principles can be deduced from the cases.

9–047   **Verification.** A statement is unlikely to be a term of the contract if the person making it expressly asks the other party to verify its truth. In *Ecay v Godfrey*[225] the seller of a boat said that it was sound but advised the buyer to have it surveyed. This advice negatived any intention to warrant the soundness of the boat. The same principle applies where the circumstances are such that the person to whom the statement was made would normally be expected to verify it. This is the reason traditionally given for the view that statements made by sellers of houses in pre-contract negotiations do not normally have contractual force: the buyer is expected to rely on a survey, commissioned by himself or his building society, for information with regard to the state of the premises.[226] It has indeed been held that, if the buyer relies on a survey negligently conducted by a surveyor commissioned by the building society he may have a right of action in tort against that surveyor, in spite of the fact that he might have discovered the truth by commissioning his own survey.[227] But that does not affect the present point, which is that the buyer normally has no cause of action *in contract* against the seller in respect of statements made by the latter about the condition of the property.

On the other hand, a statement is likely to be a term of the contract if it is intended to prevent the other party from finding out the truth, has this effect, and induces him to contract in reliance on it. This was, for example, said to be the position[228] where a buyer of a horse was about to examine it but was induced to buy without examination by the seller's statement that "You need not look for anything; the horse is perfectly sound. If there was anything the matter with the horse I should tell you". An earlier case,[229] in which a similar statement by a seller was held not to have contractual force, turns on the special facts that the sale was at Tattersall's and that sales there were known by both parties to be without warranty unless the contrary was expressly stated in the catalogue.

9–048   **Importance.** A statement is likely to be a term of the contract where its importance is such that, if it had not been made, the representee would not have entered into the contract at all.[230] Such a statement can be a term of the contract even though it conflicts with a previous written statement. Thus in *Couchman v Hill*[231] a heifer was put up for auction under printed conditions of sale which provided that no warranty was given. A bidder asked whether the heifer was in calf, adding that, if she were, he would not bid. He bought the heifer after being assured that she was not in calf, and it was held that this assurance was a term of the contract. On the other hand, in *Oscar Chess Ltd v Williams*,[232] where the defendant sold a car for £280 honestly describing it as a 1948 Morris 10 when it was in fact a 1939 model worth £175, the statement that the car was a 1948 model

---

[225] (1947) 80 Ll.L.R. 286; cf. *Mahon v Ainscough* [1952] 1 All E.R. 337; *Eustace v Kempe-Roberts* [1964] C.L.Y. 3280.

[226] See *Longman v Blount* (1896) 12 T.L.R. 520; cf. *Terence Ltd v Nelson* (1937) 157 L.T. 254.

[227] *Smith v Eric S Bush* [1990] 1 A.C. 831; above, para.9–024.

[228] *Schawawel v Reade* [1913] 2 I.R. 64, HL.

[229] *Hopkins v Tanqueray* (1854) 15 C.B. 130.

[230] *Bannerman v White* (1861) 10 C.B.(N.S.) 844.

[231] [1947] K.B. 554. Alternatively, the statement was said to be a collateral contract: below, para.9–051; see also *Otto v Bolton* [1936] 2 K.B. 46.

[232] [1957] 1 W.L.R. 370.

was held not to be a term of the contract. If in this case, the buyers had known the truth, they might still have bought the car (though for less money)[233] but if the buyer in *Couchman v Hill* had known the truth, he would not have bought at all.

Special knowledge. The question whether a statement is a contractual term or a mere representation may turn on the relative abilities of the parties to ascertain the truth of what was stated.[234] In *Oscar Chess Ltd v Williams* the seller was a private person to whom the car had been previously sold as a 1948 model, with a forged logbook. The main reason why his statement as to the age of the car was not a term of the contract was that he had no special knowledge as to the age of the car, while the buyers were car dealers, and so in at least as good a position as the seller to know whether the statement was true.[235] The case may be contrasted with *Dick Bentley Productions Ltd v Harold Smith (Motors) Ltd*[236] where a dealer sold a Bentley car, representing that it had only done 20,000 miles since being fitted with a replacement engine, when in fact it had done nearly 100,000 miles since then. He was clearly in a better position than the buyer to know whether the representation was true, and it was held to be a warranty. Salmon L.J. based this conclusion on the orthodox test of contractual intention,[237] while Lord Denning M.R. took the different view, that any inducing representation was prima facie a warranty, though the representor could "rebut this inference if he can show that it really was an innocent misrepresentation, in that he was in fact innocent of fault in making it, and that it would not be reasonable for him in the circumstances to be bound by it".[238] But the view that an inducing misrepresentation has contractual force unless the misrepresenter can disprove "fault" is hard to reconcile with cases in which representors have escaped liability for breach of contract without having disproved "fault"; and in some of these the representors were clearly careless.[239] The representor will often be careless where he is in a better position than the representee to know the truth, but *Gilchester Properties Ltd v Gomm*[240] shows that this fact is not, for the present purpose, decisive.[241] In that case, a statement by the vendor of a block of flats as to the rent at which the flats were let was held to have no contractual force, though obviously the vendor was in a better position than the purchaser to know the truth. Of course a representor who is guilty of "fault" may be liable for damages in tort at common law or under

9–049

---

[233] cf. *Moore v Khan Ghauri* [1991] 2 E.G.L.R. 9.

[234] cf. *Esso Petroleum Co Ltd v Mardon* [1976] Q.B. 801, where this test was applied to determine the existence of a collateral contract (below, para.9–051).

[235] cf. *Routledge v McKay* [1954] 1 W.L.R. 615; *Hummingbird Motors v Hobbs* [1986] R.T.R. 276 (below, para.9–047), where the seller was not a dealer, though he occasionally sold cars; and see *Harrison v Knowles & Foster* [1918] 1 K.B. 608; Contrast *Beale v Taylor* [1967] 1 W.L.R. 1193; Koh [1968] C.L.J. 11; this case is hard to reconcile with the *Oscar Chess* case, which was not cited to the court (the seller conducted his own case).

[236] [1965] 1 W.L.R. 623.

[237] ibid. at 629.

[238] ibid. at 627–628. Contrast his dissenting judgment in *Howard Marine & Dredging Co Ltd v A Ogden & Son (Excavations) Ltd* [1978] Q.B. 574 at 591, applying the test of whether the statement was "intended to be binding".

[239] e.g. *Redgrave v Hurd* (1881) 20 Ch.D. 1; above, para.9–024.

[240] [1948] 1 All E.R. 493.

[241] See criticisms in *Heilbut, Symons & Co v Buckleton* [1913] A.C. 30 at 50 of *De Lassalle v Guildford* [1901] 2 K.B. 215 on this point.

the Misrepresentation Act[242]; but such liability may differ in extent from liability for breach of contract.[243]

9–050   **Opinion.** Statements of opinion which are so vague that they cannot be verified are mere puffs and have no legal effect.[244] But a statement which is one of opinion in the sense that it states a fact which is difficult, but not impossible, to verify may be a term of the contract. In *Jendwine v Slade*[245] Lord Kenyon held that statements that two pictures were respectively by Claude Lorrain and Teniers were not warranties: the authenticity of pictures painted "some centuries back" could only be a matter of opinion. But later cases show that this is not an inflexible rule. In *Power v Barham*[246] it was held that a statement that certain pictures were by Canaletto could be a warranty, *Jendwine v Slade* being distinguished on the ground that Canaletto was "not a very old painter".[247] Similarly, in *Leaf v International Galleries*[248] the Court of Appeal indicated that a representation made in 1945 that a picture was a Constable could be a warranty; though the position will be different where the seller of a picture makes an attribution but expressly disclaims expert knowledge.[249] Nor will a statement be a warranty as to a quality if the statement is *expressly* one of opinion or belief. Thus where the seller of a car said that, to the best of his knowledge and belief, the odometer reading was correct, it was held that he had not given a warranty of such correctness, and that he was not liable merely because, unknown to him, the odometer had been tampered with before he had acquired the car.[250]

9–051   **Collateral contract.**[251] It may not be possible for a statement made during the negotiations leading up to the contract to take effect as one of its terms. The contract may be in writing, so that extrinsic evidence cannot be used to add to it, or to vary it[252]; or the statement may be oral and the contract one which the law requires to be in, or evidenced in, writing.[253] In such cases[254] the oral statement may nevertheless be enforceable as a "collateral contract". There are then two contracts between the parties: the main (written) contract and the collateral (oral) contract, both relating to the same subject-matter. Thus in *De Lassalle v Guildford*[255] the intending lessee of a house refused to execute the lease unless the landlord first assured him that the drains were in good order. The landlord gave

---

[242] See above, paras 9–033—9–044.

[243] See below, paras 9–059—9–066; the claim in the *Dick Bentley* case was limited to £400.

[244] See above, para.9–007.

[245] (1797) 2 Esp. 571; cf. *Gee v Lucas* (1867) 16 L.T. 357.

[246] (1836) 4 A. & E. 473.

[247] ibid. at 476. He had died in 1768.

[248] [1950] 2 K.B. 86. Quaere, however, whether there was such a warranty; above, para.8–020, fn.110.

[249] *Harlingdon and Leinster Enterprises Ltd v Christopher Hull Fine Art Ltd* [1991] 1 Q.B. 564.

[250] *Humming Bird Motors v Hobbs* [1986] R.T.R. 276. Liability in negligence was also excluded; and the seller had not misrepresented his knowledge or belief: cf. above, para.9–010, and the example given by Toulson J. in *IFE Fund SA v Goldman Sachs International* [2006] EWHC 2887 (Comm); [2007] 1 Lloyd's Rep. 264 at [68]–[69], affirmed [2007] EWCA Civ 811; [2007] 2 Lloyd's Rep. 449.

[251] Wedderburn [1959] C.L.J. 58. The question whether evidence of a collateral contract is admissible if it actually *contradicts* the main written contract has been discussed in Ch.6.

[252] See above, para.6–013 et seq., especially para.6–029.

[253] *Angell v Duke* (1875) L.R. 10 Q.B. 174; *Hill v Harris* [1965] 2 Q.B. 601; Law Com. No.164, paras 5.7–5.8; above, paras 5–006—5–012.

[254] See *J Evans & Son (Portsmouth) Ltd v Andrew Merzario Ltd* [1976] 1 W.L.R. 1078 at 1083.

[255] [1901] 2 K.B. 215.

this assurance, which was not incorporated in the lease. He was nonetheless held liable, when the drains were found to be defective, for breach of a collateral contract. The statement made on behalf of the landlord in *Esso Petroleum Co Ltd v Mardon*,[256] was similarly held to amount to a collateral contract.

A test of intention. A statement can, it seems, take effect as a collateral **9–052** contract only if two conditions are satisfied. First, it must have been intended to have contractual effect; and secondly, there must be some indication that the parties intended it to take effect as a collateral contract and not simply as a term in the main contract. These requirements have already been discussed[257] and it will suffice here to recall the statement of principle by Lord Moulton in *Heilbut, Symons & Co v Buckleton*[258]:

> "There may be a contract the consideration for which is the making of some other contract. . . . Such collateral contracts, the sole effect of which is to vary or add to the terms of the principal contract, are therefore viewed with suspicion by the law . . . Not only the terms of such contracts but the existence of an *animus contrahendi* on the part of all the parties to them must be clearly shown".[259]

It follows that statements made during negotiations leading up to the contract will not amount to a collateral contract if the main contract provides that they are *not* to have this effect.[260] Contractual intention may also be negatived by the fact that there was a considerable interval of time between the making of the statement alleged to constitute the collateral contract and the conclusion of the main contract.[261]

Consideration. In one respect a person who relies on a statement as a collateral **9–053** contract is at first sight in a worse position than one who relies on it as a term of the main contract: since a collateral contract exists apart from the main contract, it must be supported by *separate* consideration. But this requirement would usually be satisfied by entering into the main contract. The only cases in which this analysis could give rise to difficulty are those in which the party relying on the collateral contract was already bound to enter into the main contract, e.g. where a lease was executed in performance of an agreement to enter into it.[262] Even in such cases, however, the act of entering into the main contract (i.e. the execution

---

[256] [1976] Q.B. 801; above, para.9–038.

[257] See above, paras 5–009, 6–029.

[258] [1913] A.C. 30 at 47; above, para.4–003. In *J Evans & Son (Portsmouth) Ltd v Andrea Merzario Ltd* [1967] W.L.R. 1078 at 1081 Lord Denning M.R. described "much of what was said in that case as entirely out of date". But, though damages may be recoverable under Misrepresentation Act 1967, s.2 for statements which do not satisfy Lord Moulton's test, that test remains good law so far as *contractual* liability is concerned: *IBA v EMI (Electronics) Ltd* (1980) 14 B.L.R. 1 (below, para.14–008).

[259] cf. *Hill v Harris* [1965] 2 Q.B. 601.

[260] *Inntrepreneur Pub Co (GL) v East Crown Ltd* [2000] 2 Lloyd's Rep. 611 at 614 ("entire agreement" clause). Contrast *Cheverny Consulting Ltd v Whitehead Mann Ltd* [2005] EWHC 2431 (side letter executed contemporaneously with the main contract not excluded by entire agreement clause; for further proceedings, see [2006] EWCA Civ 1303).

[261] [2000] 2 Lloyd's Rep. 611, above, at 617 (five years); cf. the *Cheverny* case, above, fn.260 and the emphasis placed on the phrase "preceding the date" of the main contract.

[262] See the discussion of *Brikom Investments Ltd v Carr* [1979] Q.B. 467; above, para.3–065.

of the lease) would constitute consideration for the collateral contract if that act in fact conferred a benefit on the other party.[263]

(v) Damages in lieu of rescission

9–054   **Misrepresentation Act 1967, section 2(2).** Before the Misrepresentation Act, damages could not be awarded for a wholly innocent misrepresentation (i.e. for one that was neither fraudulent nor negligent[264]) if it did not have contractual force.[265] The principal remedy for innocent misrepresentation was rescission, though when a contract was rescinded, the court could make some form of monetary adjustment by granting an "indemnity".[266] This position was unsatisfactory since, in cases of wholly innocent misrepresentation, the entire transaction would have to be set aside (even though the misrepresentation related to a matter of relatively minor importance), if any remedy at all were to be given to the representee. Section 2(2) of the Misrepresentation Act partly cures this defect by giving the court a discretionary power to declare the contract subsisting and to award damages in lieu of rescission. It provides:

> "Where a person has entered into a contract after a misrepresentation has been made to him otherwise than fraudulently,[267] and he would be entitled, by reason of the misrepresentation, to rescind the contract, then, if it is claimed, in any proceedings arising out of the contract, that the contract ought to be or has been rescinded, the court or arbitrator may declare the contract subsisting and award damages in lieu of rescission, if of opinion that it would be equitable to do so, having regard to the nature of the misrepresentation and the loss that would be caused by it if the contract were upheld, as well as to the loss that rescission would cause to the other party".

9–055   **Discretionary award.** The power to uphold the contract and to award damages in lieu of rescission is discretionary: neither party has a right to require its exercise. The concluding words of the subsection specify the factors which the court is to consider in deciding whether to exercise the power. It seems that the court can balance the interests of the parties in on the one hand seeking and on the other resisting rescission. The court is likely to confine the representee to damages in lieu if the representation related to a relatively minor[268] matter and if the representor was not guilty of fault,[269] though it may also do so even if the representation is just short of fraudulent, or if the loss caused to the representee by rescission would grossly exceed the loss caused to the representor by upholding the contract.[270] On the other hand, the "policing function"[271] of the remedy of

---

[263] *Williams v Roffey Bros & Nicholls (Contractors) Ltd* [1991] 1 Q.B. 1; above, para.3–050.

[264] See above, paras 9–029, 9–033.

[265] *Redgrave v Hurd* (1881) 20 Ch.D. 1; *Archer v Brown* [1985] Q.B. 401 at 416; cf. above, para.9–024.

[266] See below, paras 9–074—9–075.

[267] i.e. it is not confined to wholly innocent misrepresentation.

[268] *William Sindall Plc v Cambridgeshire CC* [1994] 1 W.L.R. 1016 at 1036, 1043.

[269] See *The Lucy* [1983] 1 Lloyd's Rep. 188 at 202.

[270] *UCB Corporate Services v Thomason* [2005] EWCA Civ 225 (where fraud was not pleaded, but the representations were described as "multiple, intentional . . . and fundamental").

[271] *Highlands Ins Co v Continental Ins Co* [1987] 1 Lloyd's Rep. 109 at 118.

rescission may also be taken into account: this was the ground on which the court refused to uphold a contract of reinsurance which had been induced by a broker's material misrepresentation.[272]

In lieu of rescission. Damages under the subsection can be awarded only "in   9–056
lieu of rescission", so that the representee cannot rescind *and* claim such damages.[273] If he rescinds on account of a wholly innocent misrepresentation[274] which has no contractual force,[275] any claim for monetary compensation will continue to be governed by the principles which determine the extent of an indemnity.[276] The misrepresentee can, however, still rescind *and* claim damages for fraud, since fraudulent misrepresentation is expressly excepted from the subsection; and there is nothing in the subsection to prevent him from rescinding *and* claiming damages for negligence at common law or under s.2(1). The suggestion that the victim of an "innocent" misrepresentation can now rescind and claim damages under "section 2"[277] cannot, it is submitted, be interpreted to mean that the representee can rescind *and* claim damages under s.2(2) in spite of the fact that the representor was not negligent and has succeeded in discharging the burden of proof under s.2(1). Such an interpretation would be plainly inconsistent with the words of s.2(2), that the damages which can be awarded under it are "in lieu of rescission".

A further consequence of the rule that damages under the subsection are "in lieu of rescission" is more controversial. Such damages are available where a person "would be entitled, by reason of the misrepresentation, to rescind the contract". It is not clear from these words whether the court can award damages if the representee once had the right to rescind but has lost it[278] before the court can consider any award under s.2(2); and conflicting views on the point have been expressed in decisions at first instance. On the one hand, the fact that the court's power is to award damages "in lieu of rescission", and the description of the factors to which the court is to have regard in determining whether to exercise its discretion, suggest that the court must have some real choice in the matter and therefore support the view that damages in lieu cannot be awarded where the right to rescind has been lost.[279] On the other hand it is hard, as a matter of policy, to see why the factors which bar the right to rescind should limit the discretion to award damages. The intervention of third party rights, for instance, may make it highly inappropriate to rescind the contract,[280] but it does not follow that it should prevent the court from awarding monetary compensation to the representee.[281]

Incorporated misrepresentation. A representation originally made to induce   9–057
a contract may become a term of the contract by being subsequently incorporated

---

[272] ibid.; cf. *TSB v Camfield* [1995] 1 W.L.R. 430 at 439.
[273] ibid.; cf. *TSB v Camfield* [1995] 1 W.L.R. 430 at 439.
[274] See above, at fn.264.
[275] For "incorporated misrepresentations" see below, paras 9–057, 9–091.
[276] See below, paras 9–074—9–075.
[277] *Archer v Brown* [1985] Q.B. 401 at 415; the suggestion is obiter as the case was one of fraud, and "innocent" may have been intended simply to mean "not fraudulent".
[278] See below, paras 9–097—9–114.
[279] *Zanzibar v British Aerospace (Lancaster House) Ltd* [2001] 1 W.L.R. 2333; *Floods of Queensferry Ltd v Shand Construction Ltd (No.3)* [2000] B.L.R. 81 at 93; *Pankhania v Hackney LBC* [2002] EWHC 2441 (Ch) at [76].
[280] The *third party* cannot invoke s.2(2): see *TSB Bank Plc v Camfield* [1995] 1 W.L.R. 430.
[281] See *Thomas Witter Ltd v TBP Industries Ltd* [1996] 2 All E.R. 573 at 589–590.

in it; and this does not affect the right to rescind for misrepresentation.[282] In such cases the representee is entitled as of right to *damages* for breach of contract; this right is not subject to the discretion of the court. The question whether his right to "*rescind*" for breach of contract is affected by s.2(2) will be discussed below.[283]

(b) Basis of Assessment and Remoteness

9–058   Where a representee claims damages, questions may arise as to the basis of assessment and remoteness. These questions are discussed generally in Ch.20,[284] but some special factors relating to misrepresentation must be considered here.

(i) *Basis of assessment*

9–059   **Tort and contract distinguished.** Liability for misrepresentation may arise in tort (where the representation is made fraudulently or negligently) or in contract (where the representation has contractual force). This distinction affects the assessment of damages in the most common case of misrepresentation: namely, where a seller represents that the subject-matter of a contract has a quality which in fact it lacks. The general principle is that in tort the claimant is entitled to such damages as will put him into the position in which he would have been if the tort had not been committed; while in contract he is entitled to be put into the position in which he would have been if the contract had been performed.[285] It is thought to follow that in tort the claimant is entitled to be put into the position in which he would have been if the representation *had not been made*, while in contract he is entitled to be put into the position in which he would have been if the representation *had been true.*[286] If the representation induces the claimant to buy something which, but for the misrepresentation, he would not have bought at all, it follows that the damages in tort are prima facie the amount by which the actual value of the thing bought is less than *the price* paid for it.[287] In contract, on the other hand, the damages are prima facie the amount by which the actual value of the thing bought is less than *the value which it would have had if the representation had been true*[288]; and this value is not relevant to the assessment of damages in tort for deceit.[289]

---

[282] See below, para.9–091.

[283] See below, para.9–093.

[284] See below, paras 20–038 et seq.

[285] *McGregor on Damages* (18th edn), para.1–023.

[286] *Smith Kline French Laboratories Ltd v Long* [1989] 1 W.L.R. 1 at 6; *East v Maurer* [1991] 1 W.L.R. 461 at 464, 467, 468 (below, para.20–022); *Gran Gelato Ltd v Richcliff (Group) Ltd* [1992] Ch. 570 at 575; *South Australia Asset Management Corp v York Montague Ltd* [1997] A.C. 191 at 216.

[287] This rule is stated in many cases: see, e.g. *Peek v Derry* (1887) 37 Ch.D. 541 at 578 (reversed on liability 14 App.Cas. 337); *Twycross v Grant* (1877) 2 C.P.D. 496 at 504; *Smith v Eric S Bush* [1990] 1 A.C. 831 at 851; *Hussey v Eels* [1990] 2 Q.B. 227 at 241; the assessment in *Roberts v J Hampson & Co* [1990] 1 W.L.R. 94 is (if correctly reported) hard to reconcile with the normal basis of assessment.

[288] See, e.g. Sale of Goods Act 1979, s.53(3); an alternative measure is the cost of making the defect good (below, para.20–040). For the measure of a price reduction under s.48C of the Act, as inserted by Sale and Supply of Goods to Consumers Regulations 2002 (SI 2002/3045), reg.5, see below, para.20–054.

[289] *Smith New Court Securities Ltd v Scrimgeour Vickers (Asset Management) Ltd* [1997] A.C. 254 at 267 (per Lord Browne-Wilkinson) and 283 (per Lord Steyn) disapproving *Downs v Chappell* [1997] 1 W.L.R. 426 at 444 on this point; see also *South Australia Asset Management Corp v York Montague Ltd* [1997] A.C. 191 at 215–216 (per Lord Hoffmann) expressing no concluded view on the point.

Misrepresentation Act 1967, section 2(1). The generally held view is that   9–060
damages under subs.2(1) of the 1967 Act are "the same as in an action of
deceit",[290] i.e. that they are to be assessed on a tortious basis. It is submitted that
this is correct since the reference to fraud in s.2(1) indicates that the statutory
cause of action is tortious in nature. Accordingly, the tortious basis of assessment
applies where the representee has received something which lacked a quality that
it was represented to have.

Breach of contractual duty of care. A representation may have contractual   9–061
force, but the contract may be to the effect, not that the representation is true, but
that the representor has taken due care in making it. This was the position in *Esso
Petroleum Co Ltd v Mardon*[291] where a tenant was induced to take a lease of a petrol
station by a statement made on behalf of the landlord that the future annual
turnover could be estimated at 200,000 gallons. The estimate had been carelessly
made and the actual turnover was much lower. The landlord was held liable both
for negligence at common law and for breach of collateral warranty.[292] But even on
the latter basis the tenant did not recover damages for loss of his bargain[293] (i.e. for
loss of the profit that he would have made if the turnover had been 200,000
gallons); for the warranty was not that 200,000 gallons would be sold but only that
the estimate had been prepared with due care.[294]

Loss of opportunity. In tort, the claimant cannot recover damages for loss of   9–062
bargain, i.e. he cannot normally recover any element of lost profit. He may,
however, be entitled to damages for loss of the chance of making profits out of
another business in which he would have invested his money, had he not been
induced by the misrepresentation to enter into the contract with the defendant.[295]
When one takes into account damages for this sort of "loss of opportunity" the
distinction between the bases of assessment in tort and contract can be hard to
draw. In the *Clef Aquitaine* case[296] the claimant was induced by fraudulent
misrepresentation to purchase the defendant's product at a higher price than he
would have, as part of a 20-year distribution agreement. The claimant still sold the
product to customers at a profit, but claimed that, if it had not been for the
defendant's misrepresentation, he would have been able to sell at an even higher
profit and this difference in profit was recoverable in a claim for misrepresentation.
The Court of Appeal found that the difference in profit levels was recoverable,
though on slightly differing grounds. According to Simon Brown L.J.[297] it was
appropriate to extend the loss of opportunity reasoning employed in the earlier

---

[290] See, e.g. *André &Cie SA v Ets Michel Blanc &Fils* [1977] 2 Lloyd's Rep. 166 at 181 (affirmed
[1979] 2 Lloyd's Rep. 427, without reference to this point); *Archer v Brown* [1985] Q.B. 401 at 426–427
(denying an item of loss of bargain damages); contrast *Davis & Co (Wines) Ltd v Afa Minerva (EMI)
Ltd* [1974] 2 Lloyd's Rep. 27 at 32; Taylor 45 M.L.R. 139; Cartwright [1987] Conv. 423; Wadsley 54
M.L.R. 698.
[291] [1976] Q.B. 801.
[292] See above, paras 9–038, 9–051.
[293] [1976] Q.B. 801 at 820.
[294] Contrast *Lion Nathan v CC Bottlers Ltd* [1996] 1 W.L.R. 1438 where the price of a business was
based on the vendor's warranty that its achievable *profits* had been "calculated in good faith and on a
proper basis".
[295] *East v Maurer* [1991] 1 W.L.R. 461; below para.20–022.
[296] *Clef Aquitaine Sarl v Laporte Materials (Barrow) Ltd* [2001] Q.B. 488.
[297] With whom Sedley L.J. agreed.

case of *East v Maurer*[298] by awarding as damages the *higher* profits which the claimant would have generated under the contract he would have made with the defendant (and not a third party) had the truth been known. According to Ward L.J. it was possible to employ the conventional measure of the difference between the price paid and the actual value. Where, as here, there was no market, the actual value was the price which the claimant would have paid had the true state of affairs been known.[299] The fact that the claimant was still able to sell the goods for a sum in excess of that value was disregarded since it was concerned with events occurring after the date of the transaction.[300] Whichever approach is adopted, it is submitted that the decisions in both *East v Maurer* and the *Clef Aquitaine* case are correct.[301] They are consistent with the aim, in tort, of putting the claimant into the position in which he would have been if the tort had not been committed i.e. as if the misrepresentation had not been made. Indeed, in another case of fraudulent misrepresentation the principle applied in *East v Maurer* has been taken further to allow the claimant to recover not only the profits he would have made under an alternative investment, but also the further profits he would have made from re-investing those profits up until the date of trial ("profits on profits").[302] It was however emphasised that there was clear evidence of the claimant's remarkable track record as a successful investor.[303] Furthermore, the duty to mitigate may require the claimant to borrow the money lost so as to make the alternative investment and damages will be limited to the cost of borrowing.[304]

9–063   **Claims by seller.** In the cases so far discussed, the misrepresentations were made *by* the seller and affected the price paid by the buyer. They may also be made *to* the seller and affect his willingness to contract with a particular buyer. In one case,[305] manufacturers of pharmaceuticals were induced to sell tablets to a company by the defendant's representation that the company intended to resell them in Central Africa; in fact they were resold in Holland. If the sellers had known the truth, they would not have sold to the company; but that sale did not affect their capacity to supply other customers. In these circumstances, the proper way of putting the sellers into the position in which they would have been, if the representation had not been made, was to ensure that they should receive the market value of the tablets. As this value was not shown to exceed the contract price, the defendant was liable for no more than the contract price, less that part of it which had already been paid by the company.

---

[298] Above, fn.296. See also: *4 Eng Ltd v Harper* [2008] EWHC 915 (Ch); [2009] Ch. 91 where damages were discounted to reflect the fact that the owner of the alternative business may not have agreed to sell.

[299] Based on the principles expounded by Devlin J. in the context of the sale of defective goods: *Biggin & Co Ltd v Permanite Ltd* [1951] 1 K.B. 422 at 437–440. See below, para.20–048 et seq.

[300] *Jamal v Moolla Dawood Sons & Co* [1916] 1 A.C. 175. For the significance of the date of transaction, see below, para.9–067; cf. below, para.20–121.

[301] Both are cases of fraud. In principle, the same "loss of opportunity" claim may be made in negligence (and under subs.2(1) of Misrepresentation Act 1967, especially if the "fiction of fraud" is applied in full: see below, para.9–066), but where the loss in question is a consequential loss (as it was in *East v Maurer*) the opportunity said to have been lost may be considered too remote.

[302] *Parabola Investments Ltd v Browallia Cal Ltd* [2010] EWCA Civ 486; [2010] 3 W.L.R. 1266.

[303] ibid. at [57].

[304] ibid. at [58].

[305] *Smith Kline & French Laboratories Ltd v Long* [1989] 1 W.L.R. 1

Valuation by third party. There is, finally, the possibility that a misrep-   9–064
resentation relating to the value of the subject-matter may be made by a third
party. For example, A may lend money to B on the security of B's property in
reliance on a valuation of that property negligently made by C. Here the damages
for which C is liable to A are based, not on the interest which B should have paid
on the loan, but on the position in which A would have been if C had made the
valuation with due care.[306] If on that assumption A would not have made the loan
to B, he can recover from C not only loss of principal but also damages for loss of
use of the money: i.e. what he would have earned by putting the money on deposit
elsewhere, or by using it to enter into other transactions.[307] But C is not liable for
any interest above normal market rates which B may have undertaken to pay to
A.[308] This is so whether A's claim is brought in contract[309] or in tort since C in
such case undertakes only to make the valuation with due care: he makes no
promise or representation that B will perform his contractual obligations to
A.[310]

(ii) *Remoteness*

Fraud. The fact that the subject-matter lacks a quality which it was represented   9–065
to have may, apart from affecting its value, also cause the representee to suffer
consequential loss. For example, where diseased cows are sold under representations of soundness and infect the buyer's other animals, he may be able to recover
for the loss of those animals[311]; and where a business is sold under misrepresentations as to its profitability the buyer may be able to recover damages for losses
suffered in the course of running the business.[312] Consequential losses can,
however, be recovered only if they are not too remote[313]; and the rules as to
remoteness are more favourable to the claimant in actions of deceit than they are
in actions for breach of contract.[314] Lord Denning M.R. has said that

> "In contract the damages are limited to what may reasonably be supposed to
> have been in the contemplation of the parties. In fraud they are not so
> limited. The defendant is bound to make reparation for all the actual damage
> directly flowing from the fraudulent inducement. . . . It does not lie in the
> mouth of the fraudulent person to say that they could not reasonably have
> been foreseen".[315]

---

[306] Not on the position in which A would have been had C's valuation been correct: cf. above, at
fn.294.

[307] *First National Commercial Bank Plc v Humberts* [1995] 2 All E.R. 673 at 677.

[308] *Swingcastle Ltd v Gibson* [1991] 2 A.C. 223.

[309] See below, paras 20–022—20–025, for the scope of C's duty where this arises under a contract
between A and C.

[310] *Swingcastle v Gibson*, above, at 238. For the time at which the loss is suffered, see *First National
Commercial Bank Plc v Humberts* [1995] 2 All E.R. 673.

[311] *Mullett v Mason* (1866) L.R. 1 C.P. 559 (fraud); *Smith v Green* (1875) 1 C.P.D. 92 (breach of
contract).

[312] *Doyle v Olby (Ironmongers) Ltd* [1969] 2 Q.B. 158; Treitel 32 M.L.R. 526; *Hornal v Neuberger
Products* [1957] 1 Q.B. 247 at 259; *Man Nutzfahrzeuge AG v Freightliner Ltd* [2005] EWHC 2347; cf.
Naughton v O'Callaghan [1990] 3 All E.R. 191. As to punitive damages, see below, para.20–020.

[313] See below, paras 20–099—20–114.

[314] Especially after *The Heron II* [1969] 1 A.C. 350; below, para.20–102. In *Archer v Brown* [1985]
Q.B. 401 at 417–418 both tests were satisfied.

[315] [1969] 2 Q.B. 158 at 167.

A number of later dicta in the House of Lords similarly regard foreseeability as irrelevant in actions for deceit.[316] The key to understanding the absence of any test of remoteness in fraud lies in the requirement that the defendant will be liable only for all loss "directly flowing" from the fraudulent inducement, e.g. the defendant will not be liable for loss which may be due to the claimant's own unreasonable actions.[317] Thus, the requirements of causation (and mitigation) apply, but there is no additional requirement of foreseeability[318]; dicta which appear to suggest that *some* test of remoteness applies even in fraud should be understood to refer to the requirement of causation.[319]

9–066   **Negligence and Misrepresentation Act 1967, section 2(1).** In an action based on negligent misrepresentation at common law, the loss must be reasonably foreseeable, that being the general rule applied in actions for negligence.[320] This rule may be less favourable to the claimant than the rule in fraud but it is probably more favourable than the rule in a contractual action.[321] Where the action is brought under s.2(1) of the Misrepresentation Act, one possible view is that the fraud rule applies by virtue of the fiction of fraud.[322] Support for this view is provided by *Royscot Trust Ltd v Rogerson*,[323] where a car-dealer induced a finance company to enter into a hire-purchase agreement by misrepresenting the amount of the deposit paid by the customer, who later defaulted and sold the car to a third party.[324] The dealer was held liable to the finance company under s.2(1) for the balance due under the agreement on the ground that "the plain words"[325] of the subsection required the court to apply the fraud rule, under which the dealer was liable for "all the losses" suffered by the finance company "even if those losses were unforeseeable, provided that they were not otherwise too remote".[326] Later discussions of the *Royscot* case in the House of Lords somewhat pointedly refrain from expressing any concluded view as to its correctness[327]; and in one of these discussions the question whether the fraud rule should be to applied to cases of "innocent misrepresentation under the Misrepresentation Act 1967"[328] is expressly left open by Lord Browne-Wilkinson. It is submitted that the words of

---

[316] *Smith New Court Securities Ltd v Scrimgeour Vickers (Asset Management) Ltd* [1997] A.C. 254 at 265, 267, 269; cf. also *South Australia Asset Management Corp v York Montague Ltd* [1997] A.C. 191 at 215; *Kuwait Airways Corp v Iraqi Airways Corp* [2002] UKHL 19; [2002] 2 A.C. 883 at [100].

[317] *Doyle v Olby (Ironmongers) Ltd* [1969] 2 Q.B. 158 at 171.

[318] *Downs v Chappell* [1997] 1 W.L.R. 426 at 434.

[319] *Mullen v Mason* (1866) L.R. 1 C.P. 559 at 564; *Doyle v Olby (Ironmongers) Ltd* [1969] 2 Q.B. 158 at 169; *Smith New Court* case, above, at 285; cf. *Man Nutzfahrzeuge AG v Freightliner Ltd* [2005] EWHC 2347 at [213]; cf. below, para.9–067 et seq.

[320] *The Wagon Mound* [1961] A.C. 388; cf. *Esso Petroleum Co Ltd v Mardon* [1976] Q.B. 801 at 822. For a possible alternative explanation of the rule, see below, para.20–024.

[321] See *The Heron II* [1969] 1 A.C. 350; below, paras 20–102 and 20–113.

[322] See above, para.9–043.

[323] [1991] 2 Q.B. 297; Hooley 107 L.Q.R. 547; cf. *William Sindall Plc v Cambridgeshire CC* [1994] 1 W.L.R. 1016 at 1037, 1043.

[324] Who obtained good title to the car.

[325] [1991] 2 Q.B. 297 at 306; cf. p.309.

[326] ibid. at 307. For the likely interpretation of the concluding words, see text to fn.319, above.

[327] *Smith New Court Securities Ltd v Scrimgeour Vickers (Asset Management) Ltd* [1997] A.C. 254 at 267, 283; *South Australia Asset Management Corp v York Montague Ltd* [1997] A.C. 191 at 216. See also: *Avon Ins Plc v Swire Fraser Ltd* [2000] 1 All E.R. (Comm) 573 at 576; *Raiffeisen Zentralbank Osterreich AG v Royal Bank of Scotland Plc* [2010] EWHC 1392 (Comm) at [386].

[328] ibid. at 267; the reference seems from the context to be to s.2(1), which imposes a species of liability for negligence (above, para.9–040).

the subsection are not so "plain"[329] as to compel the court to apply the fraud rule in the present context. We have seen that there are other contexts[330] in which the courts have not given a similar literal effect to the fiction of fraud, which could be interpreted to refer to the *existence* of liability, rather than to its extent. This view derives some support from the legislative history of the subsection.[331] It can also be supported on the policy ground that the severity of a rule which is justified in cases of actual fraud will often be inappropriate where the defendant is merely negligent.[332]

(iii) *Fluctuations in value*

Date of transaction rule. Some of the earlier cases which had established the principle that damages in tort for misrepresentation were based on the difference between the price paid by the injured party and the actual value of the subject-matter[333] also supported the so-called "date of transaction"[334] rule, by which for this purpose the relevant value of the subject-matter was its value at the time of its acquisition.[335] Thus if the claimant had been induced by fraud to pay £15 each for shares which at that time were worth no more than £10, the defendant was liable for £5 per share, but not for further loss suffered by reason of any later fall in the market value of the shares. Such further loss was irrecoverable because it was assumed either that it had not been caused by the wrong, or that the claimant's retention of the shares on a falling market amounted to a failure on his part to take reasonable steps to mitigate his loss.[336]

9–067

Exceptions. The "date of transaction" rule continues to be recognised as the general rule[337]; but its inflexible application could lead to injustice where the defrauded party had acted reasonably in retaining the subject-matter after that date. Recent cases have therefore created exceptions to the general rule where the assumptions on which it is based are not in fact true. This may be so for a variety of reasons:[338] the subject-matter may suffer from some hidden flaw, not known to the market,[339] so that its market value at the time of the transaction does not reflect its true value[340]; or the claimant may "by reason of the fraud, [be] locked into the property"[341]; or the decline in value may have taken place before the claimant

9–068

---

[329] [1997] A.C. 254 at 283, referring to "the rather loose wording" of the 1967 Act.

[330] See above, para.9–043.

[331] ibid.

[332] cf. *Shepheard v Broome* [1904] A.C. 342 at 345, 346.

[333] See above, para.9–059.

[334] *Smith New Court Securities Ltd v Scrimgeour Vickers (Asset Management) Ltd* [1997] A.C. 254 at 283.

[335] e.g. *Twycross v Grant* (1877) 2 C.P.D. 469; *Peek v Derry* (1887) 37 Ch.D. 541; *McConnell v Wright* [1903] 1 Ch. 546.

[336] cf. see below, para.20–117 (mitigation by means of a substitute transaction).

[337] *Smith New Court* case, above, fn.334, at 267, 284.

[338] The instances provided by Lord Browne-Wilkinson in the *Smith New Court* case, at 267, were described by him as not amounting to a comprehensive statement; they are "illustrative rather than exclusive", *Parabola Investments Ltd v Browallia Cal Ltd* [2010] EWCA Civ 486; [2010] 3 W.L.R. 1266 at [34].

[339] ibid. ("pregnant with disaster").

[340] This is not so much an exception as an application of the rule; what it is really concerned with is the correct method of valuation as at the transaction date.

[341] *Smith New Court* case, above, at 267, per Lord Browne-Wilkinson; *Standard Chartered Bank v Pakistan National Shipping Co (No.3)* [2001] EWCA Civ 55; [2001] 1 All E.R. (Comm) 822 at [37].

discovered the truth, so that the misrepresentation "continued to operate . . . so as to induce the (claimant) to retain"[342] the subject-matter. In such cases, his damages for deceit will be based on the difference between the price which he paid for the subject-matter and *either* the proceeds of his actual disposal of it,[343]*or* the proceeds which would have been realised by an earlier disposal of it which he should, acting reasonably, have made.[344] In a case of the latter kind, he will be compensated for loss due to the fall in the value of the subject-matter up to the time when it was reasonable for such a disposal to have been made, but not for loss due to any further fall in its market value after that time.[345]

9–069   **Negligence.** When the general "date of transaction" rule was first developed, liability in damages for misrepresentation existed only in cases of fraud,[346] and that rule must therefore have been restricted to such cases. The recent cases which have established exceptions to the general rule have likewise been cases in which the purchase of assets was induced by fraud; and they do not settle the question how damages are to be assessed where the inducing representation is merely negligent.[347] There is no doubt that the general "date of transaction" rule applies to such cases and it is submitted that so too should the exceptions to it. The rule is applied on the presumption that it gives effect to the overriding compensatory rule,[348] i.e. that it fulfils the aim of putting the claimant in the same position as if there had been no tort (in this case, misrepresentation). The overriding compensatory rule must itself take account of the requirements of causation and mitigation.[349] Where the normal operation of these requirements indicates that the date of transaction rule will under-compensate,[350] or over-compensate[351] it is not applied. The same overriding compensatory rule applies to claims in negligence.

Support for the submission that the date of transaction rule and its exceptions applies equally to claims in negligence can be derived from *Downs v Chappell*.[352] In that case, the representee alleged fraud against the seller of a business but only negligence against his accountants, and *both* these defendants were held liable for an amount by which the value of the business had fallen by reason of a general market decline between the time of the sale induced by the misrepresentation and

---

[342] ibid.; *Man Nutzfahrzeuge AG v Freightliner Ltd* [2005] EWHC 2347.

[343] As in the *Smith New Court* case, above, fn.334.

[344] *Downs v Chappell* [1997] 1 W.L.R. 426.

[345] ibid.

[346] See above, para.9–029.

[347] In *Thomson v Christie Manson & Woods Ltd* [2005] EWCA Civ 555; [2005] P.N.L.R. 38 at [138] May L.J. emphasised that "(this) is not a fraud" case, but found that the exceptions laid down in the *Smith New Court* case did not apply in any event.

[348] *Smith New Court* case, above, at 284B; *County Personnel (Employment) Agency Ltd v Alan Pulver& Co* [1987] 1 W.L.R. 916 at 925–926; *Potts v Miller* 64 C.L.R. 282 at 299.

[349] Support for the view that the date of transaction rule should be understood generally as a default rule of causation (and mitigation) is provided by another fraud case in which the exception based on the continuing effect of the misrepresentation was applied not to determine damages for the value of the business acquired, but to allow for the recovery of consequential losses in running it: *Man Nutzfahrzeuge AG v Freightliner Ltd* [2005] EWHC 2347.

[350] As in the cases considered in para.9–068.

[351] *Pankhania v Hackney LBC* [2004] EWHC 323; [2004] 1 E.G.L.R. 135 (where it was not found to result in over-compensation); below, para.9–070.

[352] [1997] 1 W.L.R. 426. Further support may be derived from *Naughton v O'Callaghan* [1990] 3 All E.R. 191, though the case is a difficult one and is probably best explained by the "exception" that the market value on acquisition did not reflect the true value which, it is submitted, is not an exception at all: see above, fn.340.

the time when the representee, acting reasonably, should have disposed of the business. If *Downs v Chappell* does not provide direct authority it is because the accountants were "recklessly negligent"[353]; and recklessness suffices to give rise to liability in deceit even though it does not amount to actual dishonesty.[354]

Misrepresentation Act 1967, section 2(1). It is also submitted that the date **9–070** of transaction rule and the exceptions to it apply to claims under s.2(1) of the 1967 Act. Support for this submission can be derived from *Pankhania v Hackney LBC*[355] where the issue was whether the "normal measure" produced by the date of transaction rule would over-compensate the claimant when compared to the level of recovery if the principles of causation and mitigation were applied in the ordinary way. Indeed, this case explains very clearly the relationship between the ordinary requirements of the overriding compensatory rule and the date of transaction rule. The court is required to take a "general view" of what heads of loss would be recoverable on the basis of the ordinary requirements and then determine whether the sum to be awarded under the date of transaction rule "broadly represents" the claimant's loss.[356] If it does not, the court should not apply that rule and must seek to establish in more detail the loss which may be recovered by the claimant.[357]

(iv) *Misrepresentation Act 1967, section 2(2)*

Basis of assessment. Under this subsection "damages" may be awarded in **9–071** lieu of rescission even though the misrepresentation is wholly innocent[358] and even though it has no contractual force. There is, therefore, no reason for regarding these damages as being either tortious or contractual. They are really sui generis, and the subsection gives no clue as to the basis of assessment or as to the rules as to remoteness that govern an award under it.[359] The legislative history gives some slight support to the view that the contractual basis was not to be applied[360]; and indeed it seems unreasonable to make a person who has not guaranteed the truth of his representations liable as if he had. On the other hand, a person should not actually profit from even a wholly innocent non-contractual misrepresentation; and accordingly he should be liable for the amount by which the actual value of what he has transferred is less than the price received by him.[361]

---

[353] [1997] 1 W.L.R. 426 at 431, 445.

[354] See above, para.9–030.

[355] [2004] EWHC 323; [2004] 1 E.G.L.R. 135. The application of the rule and its exceptions could be explained by the fiction of fraud and the *Royscot* decision was, of course, binding on the court. It has been submitted above that this fiction should not be applied literally: see above, para.9–043.

[356] ibid. at [37].

[357] In that sense, it may not be entirely accurate to say that "the transaction date ... avoids any question of causation": *Smith New Court* case, at 266C-F, per Lord Browne-Wilkinson.

[358] i.e. even though it is neither fraudulent nor negligent and even though the representor has discharged the burden of proof under s.2(1).

[359] See Birks [1997] R.L.R. 72 for the argument that it is intended to reverse any unjust enrichment.

[360] At one stage an amendment was introduced to apply the contractual basis to actions under s.2(2): Standing Committee G, February 23, 1966. But it was withdrawn without discussion.

[361] In *UCB Corporate Services v Thomason* [2005] EWCA Civ 225 the court declined to rescind an agreement waiving the representee's entitlement under a guarantee; damages in lieu were confined to the extent that the representee was worse off as a result of the misrepresentation, rather than the sum due under the guarantee, because there was no evidence that the representee would have recovered any more than the sum paid under the waiver agreement even if it had known the truth.

9–072   **Remoteness.** So far as remoteness is concerned, there is nothing in the wording of the subsection[362] to suggest that the strict fraud rule applies, nor (as a matter of policy) should it apply against a misrepresentor who is wholly innocent; and it may be doubted whether he should be liable for consequential loss at all.[363] The view that he should not be so liable can perhaps be supported by reference to s.2(3) which provides that damages may be awarded under subs.(2) against a person who is also liable under subs.(1), "but where he is so liable any award under the said subsection (2) shall be taken into account in assessing his liability under the said subsection (1)". It can be inferred from these words that damages under subs.(2) are meant to be less than damages under subs.(1). One possible explanation for this may be that remoteness is governed by the fraud rule under subs.(1) while under subs.(2) damages are limited by the contract rule of remoteness, which is more restrictive even than that applicable in tort to cases of negligence.[364] Dicta which support this view of the damages recoverable under s.2(2)[365] do not, however, rule out the possibility that such damages may be *less* than those recoverable in contract,[366] and they could be less if, under the subsection, consequential loss were not recoverable at all. If this view were to be accepted, a wholly innocent misrepresentor would be liable *only* for the amount by which the actual value was less than the price; while a negligent misrepresentor could be made liable for this amount under subss.(1) or (2), and, in addition, for consequential loss under subs.(1).[367]

(v) *Limit of the right to damages*

9–073   **Cases in which damages cannot be recovered: innocent misrepresentation.** Although the availability of damages for misrepresentation has been greatly extended by *Hedley Byrne*'s case and the Misrepresentation Act, there is still no *right* to damages for a wholly innocent misrepresentation which has no contractual force. In the case of such a misrepresentation, the court has a discretionary power to award damages in lieu of rescission; but it cannot rescind the contract, or regard it as rescinded *and* award damages. If the representee wishes to rescind for a wholly innocent non-contractual misrepresentation, and if the court does not think it equitable to declare the contract subsisting and award damages in lieu of rescission, the old rule that damages cannot be recovered for innocent misrepresentation[368] will continue to apply. In such a case the representee may, however, have a remedy by way of an indemnity.

9–074   **Indemnity.** In rescinding a contract, equity will so far as possible order each party to restore benefits received under the contract from the other. In the simplest case, the seller will have to restore the price and the buyer the thing sold.

---

[362] i.e. there is no fiction of fraud so that the reasoning of the *Royscot* case [1991] 2 Q.B. 297; above, para.9–066, (even if sound) does not apply.

[363] It has been assumed that s.2(2) extends to consequential loss: *Davis & Co (Wines) Ltd v Afa-Minerva (EMI) Ltd* [1974] 2 Lloyd's Rep. 27; *William Sindall v Cambridgeshire CC* [1994] 1 W.L.R. 1016 at 1044.

[364] See below, paras 20–113.

[365] *William Sindall v Cambridgeshire CC* [1994] 1 W.L.R. 1016 at 1038, 1044.

[366] [1994] 1 W.L.R. 1016, above, at 1038 ("not necessary . . . to discuss the circumstances in which they may be less").

[367] See *Thomas Witter Ltd v TBP Industries Ltd* [1996] 2 All E.R. 573 at 591.

[368] See above, para.9–054.

It is sometimes necessary, as part of the process of rescission, to go further and to order one party to "restore" a benefit not received directly by him. Suppose, for example, that a buyer rescinds after having, under the terms of the contract, paid the price to a third party. There is little doubt that in such a case rescission would entitle the buyer to recover the money so paid from the seller.[369]

On the same principle, the buyer can sometimes recover an "indemnity" in respect of certain expenses; while other expenses are regarded as damages and may therefore be irrecoverable in cases of wholly innocent non-contractual misrepresentation. The distinction can be illustrated by reference to *Whittington v Seale-Hayne*.[370] A tenant had taken a lease of premises for the purpose of breeding poultry; he had done so in reliance on a representation that the premises were in good sanitary condition. In fact the water supply was poisoned so that the tenant's manager became ill and most of the birds died. The landlord submitted to rescission and agreed to repay £20 in respect of rent and rates paid, and repairs done, by the tenant under the lease. On the other hand, claims for loss of profits and loss of stock were disallowed as they were clearly claims for damages. Further claims for removal expenses[371] and medical expenses were rejected on the same ground: they were not claims for an indemnity, since such claims could be allowed only in respect of expenses incurred in discharging obligations *created* by the contract.[372] The important distinction is that between the money spent on rates and repairs on the one hand, and the removal and medical expenses on the other. It is that the lease obliged the tenant to pay rates and to do repairs, but not to move in and employ a manager. The tenant's undertaking to pay rates and to do repairs was really *part of the price* for the lease of the premises. If the lease had provided that the landlord should do these things, he would no doubt have charged a higher rent, which he would clearly have had to restore. He was under a similar liability in respect of part of the price not paid directly to him, or not paid in cash. The tenant's removal and medical expenses could not be regarded in this way. On the facts of the case a claim for damages under s.2(1) of the Misrepresentation Act would now almost certainly succeed[373]; but if the defendant could discharge the burden of proof under that subsection[374] the representee would still be restricted to a claim for an indemnity. He could not rescind *and* get damages under s.2(2) of the Act.

Indemnity and damages. The distinction between indemnity and damages, 9–075 it is submitted, is that stated in the preceding paragraph, but there is thought to be some conflict of opinion on the point in *Newbigging v Adam*.[375] The representee was induced by the defendants' fraud to enter into a partnership with them and another person. On rescinding the contract of partnership he was clearly entitled to get back the money which he had paid for his share. The Court of Appeal held that he was also entitled to be indemnified against his liability to pay debts incurred by the partnership.[376] The crucial point is that it is a term of a contract

---

[369] Any question between seller and third party would not be the concern of the buyer.

[370] (1900) 82 L.T. 49; 16 T.L.R. 181; 44 S.J. 229.

[371] On this point, cf. *Redgrave v Hurd* (1881) 20 Ch.D. 1.

[372] For a possible extension of the right to necessary maintenance costs, see *Lagunas Nitrate Co v Lagunas Syndicate* [1899] 2 Ch. 392.

[373] cf. above, fn.258.

[374] See above, para.9–041.

[375] (1886) 34 Ch.D. 582.

[376] In the House of Lords it was held that the question of indemnity did not arise because the debt in question was not enforceable against the firm: *Adam v Newbigging* (1888) 13 App.Cas. 308.

of partnership, or a legal incident of it,[377] that each partner is liable for the partnership debts. Hence any partner who pays such debts performs an obligation *under that contract*, though it is also true that the debts arise under another contract (i.e. that with the creditor of the partnership). Accordingly Cotton L.J. said that the representee was entitled to an indemnity "against the obligations which he has *contracted under the contract which is set aside*".[378] Bowen L.J. similarly said that he was entitled to be restored to his original position "so far as regards the rights and obligations *created by the contract into which he has been induced to enter*".[379] Only Fry L.J. appears to state a broader view when he says that the representee is entitled to an indemnity not only against obligations "created by" the contract but also against such "obligations *entered into under the contract* as are within the reasonable expectation of the parties to the contract".[380] What seems to have troubled Fry L.J. is that the *debts of the partnership* were not "created by" the contract of partnership. But the representee's *liability to contribute to the payment of those debts* clearly was "created by" or "contracted under" that contract. In the context of *Newbigging v Adam*, it is submitted that Fry L.J.'s statement does not conflict with the distinction drawn above between indemnity and damages. The point can be illustrated by supposing that the tenant in *Whittington v Seale-Hayne*[381] had employed a builder to do the repairs and a furniture remover to move in his furniture. The debt to the builder would not of course have been "created by" the lease, but the tenant's obligation to repair was so created, thus entitling him to an indemnity against the cost of its performance: this would amount, prima facie, to the sum due to the builder. The debt to the furniture remover would simply have been incurred *in reliance* on the lease: it would obviously not have been "created by" the lease; nor even would it have been "entered into under" the lease within Fry L.J.'s formulation.

9–076   **No indemnity if right to rescind is barred.** The grant of an indemnity amounts only to "working out the proper result of setting aside a contract in consequence of misrepresentation".[382] It is ancillary to rescission. It follows that, if the right to rescind is barred, the court cannot grant an indemnity unless the misrepresentor consents to rescission.[383] Where the right to rescind is barred, the court may[384] have no power to award damages in lieu of rescission; and if this is the position the victim of a wholly innocent misrepresentation might still be left, in such a case, without any remedy.

(vi) *Compensation orders in criminal cases*

9–077   Misrepresentation may involve criminal liability, for example, where a person dishonestly makes a false representation, and intends, by making the representation to make a gain for himself or another, or to cause loss to another or to expose

---

[377] cf. Partnership Act 1890, s.41.
[378] (1886) 34 Ch. 582 at 589 (emphasis added).
[379] ibid. at 592–593 (emphasis added).
[380] ibid. at 596 (emphasis added).
[381] See above, para.9–074.
[382] *Newbigging v Adam*, above, at 589.
[383] As in *Whittington v Seale-Hayne* (1900) 16 T.L.R. 181, where the right to rescind was probably barred by the execution of the lease; see now below, para.9–095.
[384] See above, para.9–056.

another to a risk of loss,[385] or he obtains services dishonestly,[386] or he "engages in a commercial practice which is a misleading action" under the Consumer Protection from Unfair Trading Regulations 2008.[387] The court by or before which such a person is convicted may order the offender to pay compensation "for any . . . loss or damage resulting from that offence . . . ".[388] Such an order may be made even though the conduct constituting the offence does not give rise to any civil liability in damages.[389] In the more common case where the criminal conduct also involves civil liability, the making of a compensation order is no bar to later civil proceedings. The damages in those proceedings will be *assessed* on normal principles, without reference to the order; but, to prevent double recovery, the sum so assessed will be reduced by the amount paid under the compensation order.[390]

3. RESCISSION

(a) Introduction

It is impossible to understand the authorities on this subject without referring to the difference between the rules of common law and equity before the Judicature Acts 1873–1875.

9–078

Common law. At common law the general rule was that a contract could be rescinded *for misrepresentation* only on the ground of fraud; but this requirement of fraud was subject to several qualifications. If an innocent misrepresentation became a term of the contract, it might give rise to a right to "rescind" the contract *for breach*.[391] If it led to a fundamental *mistake* it might make the contract void so that each party could, on returning what he had got under the contract, recover back what he had given. This was sometimes called "rescinding" the contract, though strictly there was no need to rescind since the contract was void ab initio.[392] Rescission was also available at common law in certain cases of *non-disclosure*.[393]

9–079

Equity. In equity, on the other hand, there was a general rule that a contract could be rescinded for "innocent misrepresentation"[394]; this phrase covered every misrepresentation which was not fraudulent, and so included negligent misrepresentation.[395] Now that the equitable rule prevails, the distinction between rescission at common law and in equity is of small (if any) importance; but the fact that the distinction once existed may account for some of the surviving differences between rescission for fraudulent and for "innocent" misrepresentation.

9–080

---

[385] Fraud Act 2006, s.2.
[386] ibid. s.11
[387] SI 2008/1277, regs 5, 9.
[388] Powers of Criminal Courts (Sentencing) Act 2000, s.130(1)(a). See also Financial Services and Markets Act 2000, s.397.
[389] *R. v Chappell*, The Times, May 26, 1986.
[390] Powers of Criminal Courts (Sentencing) Act 2000, s.134.
[391] See below, para.18–023 et seq.
[392] See *Kennedy v Panama, etc. Royal Mail Co Ltd* (1867) L.R. 2 Q.B. 580 at 587, stating the common law position before the Judicature Acts.
[393] See below, para.9–152; see, e.g. *Ionides v Pender* (1874) L.R. 9 Q.B. 531.
[394] See *Redgrave v Hurd* (1881) 20 Ch.D. 1.
[395] See above, para.9–039.

9–081   **Various meanings of "rescission".** Bowen L.J. once said that "A fallacy may possibly lurk in the use of the word 'rescission'"[396]; and it is a great pity that subsequent lawmakers have not taken this observation to heart. The Misrepresentation Act, in particular, uses the expressions "rescind", "rescinded" and "rescission" without attempting to define them. They have in the past been used in a number of senses, and it is impossible to say that one of these rather than another is the "correct" one: "there is no primary meaning".[397] The following distinctions, in particular, are relevant in this chapter.

9–082   **Rescission for misrepresentation and "rescission" for breach.** Where a misrepresentation is not a term of the contract, the process which may be referred to as "rescission for misrepresentation" amounts to setting the contract aside for all purposes,[398] so as to restore, as far as possible, the state of things which existed before the contract.[399] Where, on the other hand, a misrepresentation has become a term of the contract[400] the victim of the misrepresentation may seek "rescission for breach", and this may also result in a restoration of the state of things which existed before the contract.[401] But there is a crucial difference between the two processes.[402] Rescission for misrepresentation involves an allegation that there was a defect in the *formation* of the contract; and if this allegation is substantiated it follows that the contract is avoided ab initio. "Rescission" for breach, on the other hand, involves an allegation that there was a defect in the *performance* of the contract; and the existence of such a defect does not lead to the conclusion that the contract should be treated as if it had never existed. It follows that a party who "rescinds" for breach can also claim damages for breach of the contract[403]; while one who rescinds for misrepresentation has, by treating the contract as if it never existed, prima facie lost the right to claim damages for its breach.[404] If such a conclusion were to cause hardship to the representee the court could exercise its discretion under s.2(2) of the Misrepresentation Act to declare the contract subsisting.[405] Since at least some of the potential for confusion between two quite different processes may arise from referring to them both as "rescission", this book throughout now refers instead to "termination" for breach.[406]

9–083   **Rescinding and pleading misrepresentation as a defence.** A party who "rescinds" a contract (whether for misrepresentation or for breach) may take active steps to this end: e.g. by seeking the cancellation of the contract, or a declaration of its invalidity, or the return of money or property with which he has

---

[396] *Mersey Steel and Iron Co v Naylor Benzon& Co* (1882) 9 Q.B.D. 648 at 671.

[397] *Buckland v Farmar & Moody* [1979] 1 W.L.R. 221 at 232.

[398] *The Kanchenjunga* [1990] 1 Lloyd's Rep. 391 at 398 ("wipe it out altogether"); cf. *TSB Bank Plc v Camfield* [1995] 1 W.L.R. 430 (no partial rescission); contrast *Bank Melli Iran v Samadi-Rad* [1995] 1 F.C.R. 465.

[399] A duty to restore a loan of money obtained by fraud may arise even before rescission: *Stanlake Holdings Ltd v Tropical Capital Investments Ltd*, *Financial Times*, June 25, 1991.

[400] See below, para.9–091.

[401] See below, para.22–005.

[402] *Johnson v Agnew* [1980] A.C. 367 at 392–393; cf. *Eagle Star Ins Co Ltd v Provincial Ins Plc* [1994] 1 A.C. 130 at 140; and, in cases of non-disclsoure, *The Star Sea* [2001] UKHL 1; [2003] 1 A.C. 469 at [52].

[403] See below, para.18–015.

[404] cf. the rule that a party cannot rescind in part while affirming some particular term of the contract: below, para.9–110.

[405] See above, para.9–054. See further below, para.9–092.

[406] See below, para.18–001.

parted under the contract, on restoring what he obtained under it. Alternatively he may simply rely on the misrepresentation (or breach) as a defence to an action on the contract; and this process is not necessarily governed by the same rules as the active process of rescission.[407]

(b) Rescission for Misrepresentation

(i) *Contract voidable*

The general rule is that misrepresentation makes the contract voidable at the option of the representee.[408] In *Redgrave v Hurd*,[409] for instance, the defendant was induced to buy a solicitor's house and practice by an innocent misrepresentation as to the value of the practice. It was held that he could rescind the contract and so get back the deposit he had paid.   **9–084**

Effect on property rights. Misrepresentation makes a contract voidable but not void[410]; and this has important effects on property rights in the subject-matter,[411] both as between the parties and between one of them and a third party. When the contract is one involving the transfer of property in its subject-matter, then between the parties such property is transferred to the representor to the extent that the representee intended it to be so transferred[412]; and if the entire property has been so transferred, then it remains in the representor until rescission.[413] So far as third parties are concerned, we have seen that if a person obtains goods under a contract which is void for mistake, property in the goods may not pass to him so that the goods can be recovered by the owner from a third person into whose hands they have come.[414] But if a person obtains goods under a contract which is only voidable for misrepresentation, a voidable title passes to him and the former owner's right to avoid it is lost when an innocent third party for value acquires an interest in the goods.[415]   **9–085**

Effect on assignment. The position of the third party in such cases should be contrasted with that of a third party to whom a chose in action[416] is assigned. The assignee takes "subject to equities"[417] and one such "equity" is the possibility of rescission for misrepresentation. Thus if A induces B to sell him a gold watch on   **9–086**

---

[407] See below, paras 9–087—9–089.

[408] *Clough v L & NW Ry* (1871) L.R. 7 Ex. 26 at 34; *Urquhart v Macpherson* (1878) 3 App.Cas. 831 at 838; cf. *Whittaker v Campbell* [1984] Q.B. 319; *Killick v Roberts* [1991] 1 W.L.R. 1146.

[409] (1881) 20 Ch.D. 1.

[410] See the authorities cited in fn.415, below; for a contrary dictum, see *Pilgrim v Rice-Smith* [1977] 1 W.L.R. 671 at 675; Phillips 93 L.Q.R. 497; *Lonrho Plc v Fayed (No.2)* [1992] 1 W.L.R. 1 at 7.

[411] *Lonrho Plc v Fayed (No.2)*, above.

[412] See *Collings v Lee* [2001] 2 All E.R. 332 (legal title, but not equitable interest, transferred by house-owners to their agent who had fraudulently claimed to have found a purchaser for the house).

[413] Before rescission, the representor therefore does not hold the property as trustee for the injured party: *Bristol & West BS v Mothew* [1998] Ch. 1 at 22–23.

[414] e.g. *Shogun Finance Ltd v Hudson* [2003] UKHL 62; [2004] 1 A.C. 919; above, para.8–039.

[415] *White v Garden* (1851) 10 C.B. 919; *Stevenson v Newnham* (1853) 13 C.B. 285; the third party must give value: *Scholefield v Templer* (1859) 4 D. & J. 429; and see generally above, para.8–034 et seq.

[416] For the meaning of "chose in action", see below, para.15–002.

[417] See below, para.15–037; cf. Marine Insurance Act 1906, s.50(2); *William Pickersgill & Sons Ltd v London & Provincial Marine, etc. Ins Co Ltd* [1912] 3 K.B. 614 (non-disclosure).

credit by some fraud (not giving rise to a fundamental mistake) and pledges the watch to C, C's right to retain the watch is not affected by A's fraud. But if A by fraud induces B to buy a worthless watch, said to be of gold, and assigns the benefit of B's promise to pay for it to C as security for a loan, C's right to sue B is affected by A's fraud.[418] It looks at first sight strange that the third party's position should depend on whether the fraudulent person was buyer or seller. One reason for treating the two cases differently may be that the law gives greater protection to proprietary than to contractual rights; and this distinction could be justified by saying that the assignee of a chose in action takes a greater business risk than the pledgee of a chattel. But some cases will still cause difficulty. For example, a person may fraudulently induce a company to allot shares to him and then sell them to an innocent third party. It is disputed whether shares are to be regarded as choses in action or as property in possession,[419] and it is therefore not clear whether the third party would take subject to the company's "equity" of rescission, or whether the company's right to rescind would be barred by the third party's acquisition of a proprietary interest.

(ii) *Mode of rescission*

9–087   **Legal proceedings not always necessary.** A contract may be rescinded by bringing legal proceedings, or simply by giving notice to the other party, though, even in the latter case, legal proceedings may be necessary to work out the consequences of rescission. This is most obviously true where, as a result of rescission, a sum of money becomes due to the representee and the representor refuses to pay it. It may also be desirable to have a court order stating that a formal transaction (such as a lease or a transfer of shares) has been or ought to be set aside. Even in such a case rescission is the act of the representee and not that of the court, so that the time at which it takes effect is when the representee gives the notice or commences legal proceedings—not the time of the court's order.[420] In other cases no legal proceedings are necessary to give effect to the consequences of rescission[421]: thus where goods have been obtained by fraud rescission can be effected by simply taking them back.[422]

9–088   **Notice not always necessary.** All these modes of rescission involve some degree of notice to the representor; but it has been held that this is not always necessary. In *Car & Universal Finance Co Ltd v Caldwell*[423] the owner of a car was induced by fraud to sell it to a rogue who absconded and could not be traced. On discovering the fraud, the owner notified the police and the Automobile Association and asked them for help in recovering the car. It was held that these acts were

---

[418] Good faith on the part of C is assumed in both examples.

[419] See Gower, *Modern Company Law* (8th edn), paras 23–1—23–2. In *MCC Proceeds Inc v Lehman Bros International Europe* [1998] 4 All E.R. 675 at 686 share *certificates* were treated as chattels for the purpose of a claim in conversion (which failed) but Hobhouse L.J. said at 699 that the shares themselves were, for that purpose, choses in action.

[420] *Reese Silver Mining Co v Smith* (1869) L.R. 4 H.L. 64.

[421] A court order may be necessary by way of statute, e.g. Housing Act 1985, s.82: see *Islington LBC v UCKAC* [2006] EWCA Civ 340; [2006] 1 W.L.R. 1303 (Dyson L.J.'s suggestion that, for misrepresentation generally, a court order is necessary (at [26]) is inconsistent with the cases referred to in this para and para.9–088).

[422] *Re Eastgate* [1905] 1 K.B. 465, doubted but *semble* not on this point in *Re Goldcorp Exchange Ltd* [1995] 1 A.C. 74 at 103.

[423] [1965] 1 Q.B. 525.

enough to rescind the contract, so that an innocent third party who later bought the car got no title to it. It would no doubt be hard on the owner to hold that he could only rescind by communicating with the rogue, for this would deprive him of the right to rescind whenever the rogue disappears. But the actual decision is equally hard on the third party[424]; and the Law Reform Committee has recommended that it should be reversed.[425] It applies only where the representor has disappeared or for some other reason cannot be reached.[426]

The general principles governing the mode of rescission apply whether the representation is fraudulent or negligent or innocent. But in *Caldwell*'s case the Court of Appeal left open the question whether the rule there laid down applies where the misrepresentation is negligent. The question is perhaps academic since negligent representors are not likely to go into hiding; but it is submitted that the rule can be justified, if at all, only by the strong need to protect victims of fraud and that it should not be applied in cases of negligent or wholly innocent misrepresentation. It is also questionable whether the rule that a contract can be rescinded by simply taking back goods delivered under it should be applied except in cases of fraud.

(iii) *Misrepresentation as a defence*

The operation of misrepresentation as a defence to an action to enforce the contract is illustrated by further reference to *Redgrave v Hurd*.[427] The purchaser there successfully relied on the misrepresentations as to the value of the practice by way of defence to the vendor's claim for specific performance. Since this process of pleading misrepresentation as a defence is a form of "rescission"[428] it is, in general, subject to the requirement that the representee must return what he got under the contract.[429] But this requirement does not always apply where the representor is guilty of actual fraud. For example, where a ship was insured after she had, to the knowledge of the assured, been lost, it was held that the insurer could repudiate liability under the policy on the ground of fraud, and also keep the premiums.[430] The result is to leave the insurer with a windfall; but the rule may perhaps be justified by the strong need to discourage fraud.[431] Even this justification is, however, hard to square with the further rule that, if the insurer takes the

9–089

---

[424] Such a third party may, in appropriate circumstances, be protected by s.25 of the Sale of Goods Act 1979: *Newtons of Wembley Ltd v Williams* [1965] 1 Q.B. 560; but the scope of this protection is limited: see Thornley [1965] C.L.J. 24.

[425] 12th Report, Cmnd.2958 (1996), para.16.

[426] *Empresa Cubana de Fletes v Lagonisi Shipping Co Ltd* [1971] 1 Q.B. 488 at 505 (actual decision overruled in *The Laconia* [1977] A.C. 850).

[427] (1881) 20 Ch.D. 1.

[428] See above, para.9–083.

[429] See above, para.9–082; below, para.9–097.

[430] *Feise v Parkinson* (1812) 4 Taunt. 639 at 641; *Anderson v Thornton* (1853) 8 Exch. 425 at 428. *Contra, Fowkes v Manchester, etc. Assurance* (1863) 3 B. & S. 917 at 929, where Blackburn J. is reported to have said that in cases of *fraudulent* misrepresentation the premiums could be recovered back. But the corresponding passages in 11 W.R. 622 at 623 and 8 L.T. 309 at 311 refer to *innocent* misrepresentation; and these reports are to be preferred as they make the statement consistent with the earlier authorities, from which Blackburn J. showed no intention of departing. See also Marine Insurance Act 1906, s.84(1) and (3), restating the common law rule.

[431] If the assured could recover back the premiums, the only risk to which he would be exposed under the civil law would be that of not being able to sue on the policy; and where he had already lost the property this would be no risk at all.

initiative by suing for rescission, he does have to return the premiums.[432] This is also the position where he relies on a negligent or wholly innocent misrepresentation as a defence[433]; unless the policy provides for forfeiture of premiums if *any* false statement is made in the proposal form.[434]

A further situation in which a person can plead fraud as a defence without restoring what he has obtained under the contract is illustrated by *Berg v Sadler & Moore*.[435] The claimant was a retail tobacconist, and knew that the defendants (who were wholesalers) would not supply him as he had been put on a stop-list[436] for price-cutting. He therefore sent one Reece to the defendants to buy cigarettes, ostensibly in his own name. Reece paid with money supplied by the claimant but when the defendants discovered the true facts they refused to deliver the cigarettes or to pay back the price. It was held that the claimant was not entitled to the return of the price, so that (as in the insurance cases discussed above) the defendants were left with a windfall. The court justified this result on the ground that the claimant had been engaged in an attempt to perpetrate a *criminal* fraud; and the rule seems to be based on the supposed need to deter such fraud,[437] though it is far from clear why adequate deterrence is not provided by the criminal law.[438] The rule would probably not apply where the fraud was not criminal: e.g. where a statement was made with knowledge of its falsity but without dishonest intent.[439] The rule should certainly not apply where the misrepresentation was only negligent or where it was innocent.

(iv) *Application to sale of goods*

9–090   It has been doubted whether the equitable remedy of rescission for innocent misrepresentation applies at all to a contract for sale of goods[440] on the basis that it is not mentioned in the Sale of Goods Act 1979.[441] However, a number of cases support the view that a contract for the sale of goods can be rescinded for innocent misrepresentation. In *Leaf v International Galleries*[442] and *Long v Lloyd*[443] the right to rescind such contracts for innocent misrepresentation was held to be

---

[432] *Barker v Walters* (1844) 8 Beav. 92 at 96; *London Assurance v Mansel* (1879) 11 Ch.D. 363; cf. *The Litsian Pride* [1985] 1 Lloyd's Rep. 437 at 515 (disapproved on another point in *The Star Sea* [2001] UKHL 1; [2003] 1 A.C. 469 at [71]). Quaere whether an insurer who only claims a *declaration* that he is entitled to avoid the policy on the ground of fraud (as in *Fire, etc., Insurance v Greene* [1964] 2 Q.B. 687) must return the premiums.

[433] *Feise v Parkinson* (1812) 4 Taunt.639; *Anderson v Thornton* (1853) 8 Exch. 425.

[434] *Kumar v Life Ins Corp of India* [1974] 1 Lloyd's Rep. 147. If the insured was a consumer, such a term might not bind the consumer if it was "unfair" within Unfair Terms in Consumer Contracts Regulations 1999, above, para.7–110 et seq.

[435] [1937] 2 K.B. 158; Allen 54 L.Q.R. 201; Goodhart 54 L.Q.R. 216; Treitel in *Essays in Memory of Sir Rupert Cross*, pp.107–108.

[436] This practice was made unlawful by Resale Prices Act 1976, Pt I, but that Act has (subject to transitional provisions) been repealed by Competition Act 1998, s.1.

[437] *South Australia Asset Management Corp v York Montague Ltd* [1997] A.C. 191 at 215; *Smith New Court Securities Ltd v Scrimgeour Vickers (Asset Management) Ltd* [1997] A.C. 254 at 279.

[438] It has been pointed out (*Chitty on Contracts* (30th edn), para.6–109 at fn.459) that *Berg v Sadler & Moore* is contrary to dicta of the Exchequer Chamber in *Clough v L.&N.W.Ry.* (1871) L.R. 7 Ex. 26 at 37 which appear not to have been cited and that the refusal of the claim for return of the money may be better explained on the basis of illegality: below, para.11–129.

[439] See *Polhill v Walter* (1832) 3 B. & Ad. 114; above, para.9–030.

[440] Atiyah 22 M.L.R. 76.

[441] *Re Wait* [1927] 1 Ch. 606 at 635.

[442] [1950] 2 K.B. 86.

[443] [1958] 1 W.L.R. 753.

barred—in the first case by lapse of time and in the second by acceptance.[444] The decision in each case was that the right to rescind had been lost: not that it never existed. In *Goldsmith v Rodger*[445] a contract for the sale of a boat was induced by an innocent[446] misrepresentation of the buyer; and it was held that the seller could "rescind" in the sense of being able to rely on the misrepresentation as a defence. If a contract for the sale of goods could not be rescinded for innocent misrepresentation the injured party would have no remedy at all for an innocent misrepresentation not incorporated in the contract. Such an unjust result ought not to be reached in the absence of a clear statutory provision to that effect.

(c) Incorporated Misrepresentation

Right to rescind for misrepresentation survives incorporation. Section 1(a) of the Misrepresentation Act 1967 provides that a person who has entered into a contract after a misrepresentation has been made to him shall be entitled to rescind notwithstanding that "the misrepresentation has become a term of the contract" if he would otherwise be entitled to rescind without alleging fraud. This right to rescind therefore survives when a statement of fact (as opposed to a promise[447]) is made to induce a contract and later becomes one of its terms. But s.1(a) does not take away any remedies for breach of contract; and the relation between these remedies and the statutory right to rescind is obscure.

9–091

Effect of rescission for misrepresentation on damages for breach. Apart from the Misrepresentation Act, breach of contract gives rise sometimes to a right to damages for breach only, and sometimes to a right to damages and also to a right to terminate for breach.[448] Where an incorporated misrepresentation gives rise to both these rights, they can presumably still be exercised independently of s.1 (and the right to terminate for breach is probably unaffected by s.2(2)).[449] Where the incorporated misrepresentation gives rise (apart from the Act) to a right to damages for breach only, the representee can ignore his right to rescind under the Act and claim damages for breach of contract. But it is not clear whether he can still claim such damages if he does "rescind" under s.1(a). It is arguable that rescission for misrepresentation destroys all outstanding liabilities under the contract, including liability in damages for its breach. This view might cause hardship where a representee had rescinded out of court (e.g. by returning defective goods) but the court could probably come to his rescue by declaring the contract subsisting under s.2(2) of the Act. It is true that damages in lieu of rescission under that subsection may be less than damages for breach of contract[450]; but one effect of declaring the contract subsisting might be to revive the right to damages for breach of contract, i.e. for the untruth of the incorporated misrepresentation.[451]

9–092

---

[444] cf. below, paras 9–108, 9–113.
[445] [1962] 2 Lloyd's Rep. 249.
[446] i.e. not fraudulent: cf. above, para.9–079.
[447] See above, para.9–009.
[448] See above, para.9–082; below, para.18–023 et seq. For further remedies in consumer sales, see Sale of Goods Act 1979, s.48A to 48F, as inserted by Sale and Supply of Goods to Consumers Regulations 2002 (SI 2002/3045), reg.5.
[449] See the discussion in para.9–093, below.
[450] See above, para.9–071.
[451] A possibility which was overlooked in 30 M.L.R. at 372.

9–093   **Possible limiting effect of Misrepresentation Act 1967, section 2(2).** This subsection, which gives the court a discretion to declare the contract subsisting, and award damages in lieu of rescission,[452] may limit the right to rescind for an incorporated misrepresentation. Where the representee does not rescind but simply claims damages for breach of contract, the subsection clearly has no effect, for the court's discretion depends on a claim having been made "that the contract ought to be or has been rescinded". Where the representee does claim "rescission" it is first necessary to ask what would be the effect of the incorporated misrepresentation viewed purely as a breach of contract. If its only effect as a breach would be to give rise to a right to damages, any claim to "rescind" must be a claim to "rescind for misrepresentation" which is subject to the discretion of the court, so that the court could refuse to allow rescission and confine the claimant to a claim for damages. If on the other hand, the effect of the incorporated misrepresentation as a breach would be to give rise to a right to damages and also to a right to terminate for breach, the position is less clear. While the process now referred to in this book as "termination" for breach may also be referred to as "rescission", there is no hint in the legislative history of the Act that s.2(2) was intended to apply to that process, whatever the correct terminology. If such a change in the law has been made it would be an extraordinarily partial one, for it would apply only to breaches resulting from representations *of fact* made before the contract (and not to breaches of *promises*). The better view seems to be that "rescinded" in s.2(2) refers only to "rescission for misrepresentation" as the subsection deals with the case of a person "who is entitled, *by reason of the misrepresentation* to rescind the contract"; and that, accordingly, the right to "rescind for breach" is not subject to the discretion of that court.

4. LIMITS TO THE RIGHT TO RESCIND

9–094   The right to rescind a contract may be barred by a number of factors. Before these are considered, two points must be made with regard to the effects of the Misrepresentation Act 1967.

(a) Effects of Misrepresentation Act 1967

9–095   **No bar to rescission of executed contract.** First, the Act has abrogated one restriction on the right to rescind. Before the Act, it had been held that certain contracts could not be rescinded for innocent misrepresentation after they had been "executed" (i.e. performed). This rule applied, in particular, where a contract for the disposition of an interest in land was performed by execution of the conveyance or lease[453]; and where a contract for the sale of shares was performed by transfer of the shares.[454] Many applications[455] of the rule were hard to justify, and its scope was uncertain. It was reversed by s.1(b) of the Act, which provides that a person who would otherwise be entitled to rescind a contract for misrepresentation without alleging fraud[456] shall be so entitled notwithstanding that

---

[452] See above, para.9–054.

[453] *Angel v Jay* [1911] 1 K.B. 666 (lease).

[454] *Seddon v North Eastern Salt Co* [1905] 1 Ch. 326.

[455] e.g. in the cases cited in the last two notes.

[456] The rule that an executed contract could not be rescinded never applied to cases of fraudulent misrepresentation, so that it was not necessary to change the law in such cases.

"the contract has been performed". The buyer of a house can therefore rescind for misrepresentation even after conveyance and even though the misrepresentation was wholly innocent.

Discretion of court under section 2(2). Secondly, the right to rescind a   9–096
contract for misrepresentation is now subject to the discretion of the court under s.2(2) of the Act.[457] In the case just put, of a house-purchaser claiming rescission for wholly innocent misrepresentation, the court might prefer to declare the contract subsisting and to award damages in lieu of rescission. For if (as would often be the case) the vendor had used the purchase-money to buy another house, rescission might cause him severe hardship. This would be a factor which the court could take into account under s.2(2), so that rescission would probably be allowed only where the buyer had suffered serious prejudice as a result of the misrepresentation. Section 2(2) may, similarly, operate in cases which are not precisely covered by the bars to rescission but in which the court nevertheless considers that damages would be a more appropriate remedy than rescission. It is, however, still necessary to define the bars to rescission because if one of them has arisen the court has *no* discretion to allow rescission and, on one possible interpretation of s.2(2),[458] cannot award damages either.

(b) Bars to Rescission

(i) *Restitution impossible*

Normally, a party who wishes to rescind a contract for misrepresentation is   9–097
required to restore to the other any benefits which he has obtained under the contract: e.g., a buyer who wants to rescind with a view to getting back the price must give back the goods. If the benefit obtained is a sum of money[459] there is never any difficulty in complying with this requirement: the representee restores an equivalent sum. But, where he has obtained a benefit other than money, he may for some reason be unable to restore it; and this inability will sometimes bar his right to rescind.

Changes made by misrepresentee. Where a contract of sale has been   9–098
induced by a misrepresentation of the seller, the buyer may lose the right to rescind if he has so changed the subject-matter that he can no longer restore what he obtained under the contract: e.g., the buyer of an animal who has slaughtered it cannot rescind on returning the corpse.[460] Similarly, the purchaser of a business cannot get back his purchase-money after carrying on the business for four months and disposing of some of its assets,[461] or after changing a partnership into

---

[457] See above, para.9–054. Rescission was said to be a discretionary remedy even before the 1967 Act: see *Spence v Crawford* [1939] 3 All E.R. 271 at 288; but this principle would be hard to apply to rescission by some extra-judicial act of the representee (above, paras 9–087—9–088); cf. *TSB Bank Plc v Camfield* [1995] 1 W.L.R. 430 at 438.

[458] See above, para.9–056.

[459] Or the release of an obligation to pay money, as in *The Siboen and the Sibotre* [1976] 1 Lloyd's Rep. 293; see esp. at 337.

[460] *Clarke v Dickson* (1858) E.B. & E. 148 at 155.

[461] *Sheffield Nickel Co Ltd v Unwin* (1877) 2 Q.B.D. 215; cf. *Thomas Witter Ltd v BTP Industries Ltd* [1996] 2 All E.R. 573 at 588.

a limited company[462]; nor can the purchaser of a mine rescind after he has worked it out.[463] On the same principle a person cannot rescind after he has disposed of the subject–matter of the contract unless, perhaps, he has been able to get back that subject–matter or its substantial equivalent.[464]

9–099   **Other deterioration or decline in value.** In the cases discussed above, deterioration or decline in value barred the right to rescind because it was due to the acts of the representee. Where it is due to other causes, different rules apply. The right to rescind is clearly not barred where the subject–matter deteriorates precisely because it lacks a quality that it was represented to possess. Thus a person who is induced to enter into a partnership by a misrepresentation as to its solvency can still rescind after the bankruptcy of the firm.[465] The position is the same where the deterioration or decline in value is not related to the mis-representation but is due to some external cause. In *Armstrong v Jackson*[466] a broker purported to buy shares for a client, but in fact sold his own shares to the client. Five years later, when the shares had fallen in value from nearly £3 to 5s., it was held that the client could rescind on account of the broker's breach of duty.[467] He still had the identical shares and was able to return them, together with the dividends he had received. McCardie J. said:

> "It is only . . . where the (claimant) has sustained loss by the inferiority of the subject–matter or a substantial fall in its value that he will desire to exert his power of rescission. . . . If mere deterioration of the subject–matter negatived the right to rescind, the doctrine of rescission would become a vain thing".[468]

Similarly, a contractual right to reject is not lost simply because the subject–matter deteriorates without the fault of the party claiming to reject.[469] It is submitted that these rules also apply where the buyer is induced to buy by a misrepresentation which has been incorporated in the contract.[470]

9–100   **Changes made by misrepresentor.** Where the misrepresentation is that of the seller, the question is whether the buyer (i.e. misrepresent*ee*) can rescind even though he cannot restore the subject–matter in its original state. A sale may also be induced by a misrepresentation on the part of the buyer, e.g. as to his solvency

---

[462] *Clarke v Dickson* (1858) E.B. & E. 148; quaere whether this is per se decisive; *Western Bank of Scotland v Addie* (1867) L.R. 1 Sc. & Div. 145 at 159.

[463] ibid.; *Lagunas Nitrate Co v Lagunas Syndicate* [1899] 2 Ch. 392.

[464] e.g. where a buyer of shares has sold them but can reacquire an equivalent quantity in the market. In *Smith New Court Securities Ltd v Scrimgeour Vickers (Asset Management) Ltd* the Court of Appeal seems to have taken the view that the buyer could not rescind in such a case: [1994] 1 W.L.R. 1271 at 1280; but on appeal Lord Browne-Wilkinson said that the law on the point would have to be "closely looked at hereafter": [1997] A.C. 254 at 264. Some difficulty might arise where the representee had bought the subject-matter back for less than the amount for which he had previously sold it, so that he would make an actual profit out of rescission: see *Marr v Tumulty* 175 N.E. 356 (1931). Perhaps he could be required to account for any such profit as part of the process of rescission.

[465] *Adam v Newbigging* (1886) 34 Ch.D. 582; (1888) 13 App.Cas. 308.

[466] [1917] 2 K.B. 822.

[467] See below, para.16–095.

[468] [1917] 2 K.B. 822 at 829.

[469] *Head v Tattersall* (1871) L.R. Ex. 7.

[470] cf. *Long v Lloyd* [1958] 1 W.L.R. 753 at 760.

or as to the value of the subject-matter. The question then arises whether the seller's right to rescind is affected by some dealing with the subject-matter by the buyer (who in such a case is the misrepresent*or*). Obviously, the right may be so affected in a practical sense where the buyer consumes the property or so alters it that the seller has no interest in getting it back. As a matter of law, however, a buyer who is guilty of fraud cannot rely on his own dealings[471] with the subject-matter as a bar to the seller's right to rescind. In *Spence v Crawford*[472] A was induced by the fraud of B to enter into a contract by which (i) A sold to B shares in a company, and (ii) B undertook to relieve A of his liability under a guarantee of the company's bank overdraft, and to procure the release of securities deposited by A with the bank. A duly transferred the shares, while B relieved A of his liability to the bank and freed the securities by giving his own personal guarantee to the bank. The constitution of the company was later altered and some of the shares in it were sold. It was held that this dealing with the shares did not bar A's right to rescind. The question whether it would have had this effect if B's misrepresentation had been innocent was left open.[473]

Benefit to misrepresentee. The mere fact that the misrepresentee has received a benefit under the contract does not bar his right to rescind, if the misrepresentor has not been put to any expense in conferring that benefit. Thus in *Spence v Crawford* the fact that B had relieved A of his liability to the bank and freed his securities did not bar A's right to rescind. B was not put to any expense *by merely giving* the guarantee to the bank, nor was he ever asked to pay anything under it, as the company prospered. We shall see that B did suffer some loss as a result of giving his guarantee, but this did not bar A's claim to rescind as he was able to make allowance for it.[474] **9–101**

Conversely, if no benefit has been received by the representee, the right to rescind is not lost *merely* because the representor has acted on the contract to his prejudice. In *Mackenzie v Royal Bank of Canada*[475] a wife was induced by misrepresentation to deposit share certificates with a bank as security for the overdraft of a company controlled by her husband. She was able to rescind although the bank had, after the deposit, advanced further money to the company, for she had received no benefit from this payment. It is sometimes said that the object of rescission is to restore the parties to the situation in which they would have been if the contract had never been made,[476] but in the light of *Mackenzie's* case such statements are not quite accurate. The essential point is that the representee should not be unjustly enriched at the representor's expense[477]; that the representor should not be prejudiced is a secondary consideration.[478]

Precise restitution impossible. The general rule requiring restoration of what had been obtained under the contract was very strictly applied at common law where a person sought the return of his money on termination for breach,[479] **9–102**

---

[471] Nor on the other party's dealings at his request: cf. *Hulton v Hulton* [1917] 1 K.B. 813 (destruction of letters).

[472] [1939] 3 All E.R. 271.

[473] ibid. at 281. The effect of negligence in such a situation is also unclear.

[474] See below, para.9–102.

[475] [1934] A.C. 468; cf. *TSB Bank v Camfield* [1995] 1 W.L.R. 430.

[476] e.g. *Gillett v Peppercorne* (1840) 3 Beav. 78 at 81.

[477] *Bouygues Offshore v Ultisol Transport Contractors* [1996] 2 Lloyd's Rep. 153 at 159.

[478] *Halpern v Halpern* [2007] EWCA Civ 291; [2008] Q.B. 195 at [74].

[479] *Hunt v Silk* (1804) 5 East 449; *Blackburn v Smith* (1848) 2 Ex. 783; below, para.22–005.

but a more flexible rule was developed by equity in cases of misrepresentation.[480] A representee who is able to make substantial, though not precise, restitution can rescind if he returns the subject-matter of the contract in its altered state, accounts for any profits derived from it and makes allowance for deterioration caused by his dealing with it. Thus a person who has gone into possession under a contract to buy, or take a lease of, land can rescind[481] on terms of paying rent for the period of his occupation.[482] The court can also set off benefits received by one party against those received by the other.[483] Similarly, in *Erlanger v New Sombrero Phosphate Co*[484] a company bought and worked a phosphate mine, but did not so work it out as to make restitution utterly impossible. It was held that the company could rescind the sale for breach of fiduciary duty by one of its promoters on terms of returning the mine and accounting for the profits of working it. Lord Blackburn said that equity could

> "take account of profits and make allowance for deterioration.[485] And I think the practice has always been for a court of equity to give this relief whenever, by the exercise of its powers, it can do what is practically just, though it cannot restore the parties precisely to the state they were in before the contract".[486]

These powers of adjustment are normally exercised where the misrepresentee is a buyer who claims back his money. They may also be available in the converse case where the misrepresentee is a seller who claims back his property, as in *Spence v Crawford*.[487] The fraudulent buyer in that case had performed his contractual undertaking to relieve the seller of certain obligations to a bank. He was asked by the bank to sell some stock to maintain his liquidity, and the sale resulted in a loss to him of £1,000. The final order made in that case was that the seller should recover back his shares plus the dividends received by the buyer; but that he should repay the purchase price plus interest, and make allowance in respect of part[488] of the £1,000 lost by the buyer on the sale of his stock.

9–103   **Nature of subject-matter.** Restitution by the representee may be possible but the court may be unwilling to order it on account of the nature of the property. This was the position in *The Siben*[489] where a contract for the sale of property included an escort agency, the employees of which provided "sexual favours" for its clients. The sale had been induced by the vendor's fraudulent misrepresentations unrelated to this point; and a claim to rescind the contract was rejected on

---

[480] cf. *Halpern v Halpern (No.2)* [2007] EWCA Civ 291; [2008] Q.B. 195 (a case of duress); below, para.10–011.

[481] *Redgrave v Hurd* (1881) 20 Ch.D. 1.

[482] *Hulton v Hulton* [1917] 1 K.B. 813 at 826. It seems that no such terms were imposed in *Redgrave v Hurd*, above, where the buyer got back the whole of his deposit in spite of having been in possession for a short time.

[483] *Hulton v Hulton* [1917] 1 K.B. 813.

[484] (1878) 3 App.Cas. 1218; cf. *The Lucy* [1983] 1 Lloyd's Rep. 188 at 202.

[485] cf. *Cheese v Thomas* [1994] 1 W.L.R. 129 (undue influence; below, para.10–030).

[486] (1878) 3 App.Cas. 1218 at 1278–1279; approved in *Guiness Plc v Saunders* [1990] 2 A.C. 663 at 698, but distinguished as the agreement in the latter case was not voidable but void.

[487] [1939] 3 All E.R. 271; above, para.9–100.

[488] This seems to have been a compromise, adopted to avoid the need to take complicated cross-accounts.

[489] [1996] 1 Lloyd's Rep. 35; for further proceedings see [1996] 2 Lloyd's Rep. 667.

the ground that the court should not "make an order which would in principle have the effect of transferring an illegal business from one party to another".[490] This reasoning is not easy to reconcile with the principle that rescission is the act of the representee, not that of the court[491]; and the return of the illegal business would, moreover, be merely a condition of any judgment which might have been given for the return of the price, so that there would have been no need to make an actual order for the return of that business.

Improvements in the subject-matter. Two problems arise where dealings   9–104
with the subject-matter have not decreased its value, but have improved it. The first is whether such dealings bar the right to rescind; the second is what allowance (if any) is to be awarded in respect of the improvements. These may be made either by the misrepresentee or by the misrepresentor.

Improvements made by the misrepresentee. One illustration of this possi-   9–105
bility is provided by *Boyd & Forrest v Glasgow & SW Ry*.[492] Contractors alleged that they had been induced to enter into a contract to build a railway by misrepresentations as to the strata. After the railway had been built, they claimed to rescind, with a view to recovering a quantum meruit (exceeding the contract price) for the cost of the work. The claim failed on a number of grounds, one of which was that the right to rescind was barred since it was no longer possible to restore the railway company to its original position. This is an unusual application of the requirement of restoration, which normally prevents the representee from rescinding unless he can *give back* benefits that he has *received*. In this case, the requirement prevented rescission because the representee could not *take back* benefits that he had *conferred*.[493] The decision can be explained on the ground that it was not practicable to restore the parties to their pre-contract position, so that "rescission" made no practical sense. The more convenient remedy is damages and on such facts this would now generally be available under s.2(1) of the Misrepresentation Act.[494]

A second, and perhaps more common, illustration of this situation is provided by the case of a person who is induced by misrepresentation to buy something which he improves before discovering the truth. In such a case, the improvements probably do not bar the right to rescind; and their cost can often be claimed as damages.[495] Where the representation is wholly innocent and the contract has been rescinded, there will be no such claim[496]; but the representee might be able to set off the cost of the improvements against his liability[497] to make allowance for benefits received by him under the contract.[498]

Improvements made by the misrepresentor. In *Spence v Crawford*[499] the   9–106
fraudulent buyer was granted an allowance in respect of his loss on sale of stock.

---

[490] ibid. at 62.

[491] See above, para.9–087.

[492] 1915 S.C.(H.L.) 20.

[493] For the suggestion that, in such cases, the representee may be able to "waive restitution due to him", see *Bouygues Offshore v Ultisol Transport Contractors* [1996] 2 Lloyd's Rep. 153 at 159.

[494] See above, para.9–039.

[495] See above, para.9–065 et seq.

[496] See above, para.9–073 et seq.

[497] See above, para.9–102.

[498] cf. *Cooper v Phibbs* (1867) L.R. 2 H.L. 149.

[499] [1939] 3 All E.R. 271; above, paras 9–100, 9–102.

This loss did not produce any directly corresponding increase in the value of what he had bought; and it was incurred in consequence of something that he was *obliged* under the contract to do. It does not follow from the decision that a buyer who obtains property by misrepresentation can, if the seller claims rescission, insist on an allowance for improvements which he has made *without* being contractually bound to do so. It can be argued on the one hand that the seller would get a windfall if he did not have to pay anything for the improvements[500]; and on the other that he should not be forced to pay for improvements (which he may not want or be able to afford) as a condition of getting back his property. The better view, probably, is that if the seller claims rescission, he should have to make some allowance (based on increase in value rather than the cost of work to the buyer).[501] If the seller is unwilling or unable to pay the allowance he can generally fall back on his alternative remedy of damages.[502]

(ii) *Third party rights*

9–107   The right to rescind a contract may be barred by the intervention of third party rights.[503] For example, a person who has been induced by fraud to sell goods cannot rescind after the goods have been bought by an innocent third party, that is, by one without notice of the fraud.[504] On the same principle, a person cannot rescind an allotment of shares in a company after the company has gone into liquidation. At that point the rights of third parties intervene in that the assets of the company have to be collected for distribution among the company's creditors.[505] This should be contrasted with the rule in the bankruptcy of an individual that the trustee in bankruptcy takes the property "subject to equities", including the right of rescission. Thus in *Load v Green*[506] a seller was by fraud induced to sell goods to one Bannister, who became bankrupt. It was held that the seller could disaffirm the contract and recover the value of his goods from Bannister's trustee in bankruptcy. It is difficult to find any convincing reason for this distinction between winding up of insolvent companies and individual bankruptcy. It seems to be based on the assumption that third parties place greater reliance on a company's nominal share capital (especially if the company is a new one, or has just raised new capital) than on an individual's appearance of wealth.

(iii) *Affirmation*

9–108   **No rescission if contract affirmed.** A contract cannot be rescinded for misrepresentation if the representee expressly or by conduct affirms it after

---

[500] e.g. *Williams v Logue* 122 So. 490 (1929).

[501] cf. *Walker v Galt* 171 F. 2d 613 (1948); *Cheese v Thomas* [1994] 1 W.L.R. 129 at 137.

[502] See above, para.9–028 et seq.

[503] In some cases, the effect of rescission on a third party may be taken into account in assessing the requirement to make counter-restitution: *Crystal Palace FC Ltd v Dowie* [2007] EWHC 1392 (QB); [2007] I.R.L.R. 682 at [216].

[504] See above, para.9–085; and see below, para.10–035; cf. *Society of Lloyds v Lyon, The Times,* August 11, 1997.

[505] *Re Scottish Petroleum Co* (1883) 23 Ch.D. 413.

[506] (1846) 15 M. & W. 216.

discovering the truth, i.e. with knowledge of the facts and of his right to rescind.[507] To hear rumours that the representation may be untrue is not, for this purpose, discovery of the truth.[508] But if the representee knows all the facts from which a reasonable person would deduce the truth, he may be taken to know it.[509] Thus a person who is induced by misrepresentation to buy goods cannot rescind if, after discovering the truth, he uses them[510]; a person who is induced by misrepresentation to subscribe for shares in a company cannot rescind if, after discovering the truth, he accepts dividends, votes at meetings or tries to sell the shares[511]; a person who is induced by misrepresentation to take a lease cannot rescind if, after discovering the truth, he stays on and pays rent[512]; a fortiori a mining lease cannot be rescinded if, after discovering the truth, the lessee continues to work the mine.[513] Use of the subject-matter for the sole purpose of testing the accuracy of the representation does not, however, amount to affirmation.[514]

Affirmation inferred from failure to rescind. Affirmation may be inferred even from failure to rescind: e.g. where a person wishes to rescind an allotment of shares in a company on the ground of misrepresentation. Such a person is not allowed to wait and see whether the company will prosper: he must not only tell the company that he rescinds but must also take steps to remove his name from the register of shareholders.[515]   9–109

No partial rescission. On a principle analogous to affirmation[516] a person cannot set aside one term of a contract on the ground of misrepresentation while affirming the rest. For example, a person who has been induced to enter into an agreement to take a lease by a misrepresentation relating to one of its terms cannot repudiate that term while affirming the rest of the lease.[517] Similarly, an insurance company can rescind a policy for non-disclosure, but it cannot repudiate a particular claim while purporting to recognise that the policy is still in force.[518] Nor is it open to the court at the request of the representor to restrict rescission to the part of the contract to which the representation relates. If, for example, a guarantee is procured by a representation that it relates only to future debts, when   9–110

---

[507] *Habib Bank Ltd v Tufail* [2006] EWCA Civ 374 at [20] ("it is undoubtedly the law that knowledge of the right to rescind is essential"); *Donegal International Ltd v Zambia* [2007] EWHC 197; [2007] 1 Lloyd's Rep. 397 at [467]; cf. the loss of the right to terminate *for breach*: para.18–080. Where the representee does not have the requisite knowledge, he may lose the right to rescind by promissory estoppel, but only if the misrepresentor can demonstrate the necessary reliance: *Habib Bank* above; cf. para.3–083, 18–078, 18–081.

[508] *Central Ry of Venezuela v Kisch* (1867) L.R. 2 H.L. 99.

[509] *Scholey v Central Ry of Venezuela* (1870) L.R. 9 Eq. 266n.; *Long v Lloyd* [1958] 1 W.L.R. 753 at 760.

[510] *United Shoe Machinery Co of Canada v Brunet* [1909] A.C. 330; cf. *Long v Lloyd* [1958] 1 W.L.R. 753; *Skipskreditforeningen v Emperor Navigation* [1998] 1 Lloyd's Rep. 67 at 73–74.

[511] *Western Bank of Scotland v Addie* (1867) L.R. 1 Sc. & Div. 145; *Scholey v Central Ry of Venezuela* (1870) L.R. 9 Eq. 266n.; *Ex p. Briggs* (1866) L.R. 1 Eq. 483.

[512] *Kennard v Ashman* (1894) 10 T.L.R. 213.

[513] *Vigers v Pike* (1842) 8 Cl. & F. 562.

[514] *Long v Lloyd* [1958] 1 W.L.R. 753 (first trip); cf. *Lindsay Petroleum Co v Hurd* (1874) L.R. 5 P.C. 221 (sinking exploratory well no bar to rescission).

[515] *First National Reinsurance Co Ltd v Greenfield* [1921] 2 K.B. 260; for a qualification of this principle, see *Pawle's Case* (1869) L.R. 4 Ch.App. 487.

[516] *Urquhart v Macpherson* (1878) 3 App.Cas. 831.

[517] *Inntrepreneur Pub Co v Sweeney* [2002] EWHC 1060; [2002] E.G.L.R. 132.

[518] *West v National Motors & Accident Ins Union Ltd* [1955] 1 W.L.R. 343. The result might have been different had fraud been alleged; above, para.9–089.

in fact it relates to past and future debts, then the guarantee cannot be rescinded with regard to the past, but upheld with regard to the future debts: such a course would amount to remaking, not to rescinding the contract.[519]

9–111   **Acceptance?** In *Leaf v International Galleries*[520] Denning L.J. said:

> "An innocent misrepresentation is much less potent than a breach of condition; and a claim to rescission for innocent misrepresentation must at any rate be barred when the right to reject for breach of condition is barred".

The right to reject for breach of condition[521] is barred by (inter alia) "acceptance", and this takes place (a) when the buyer intimates that he accepts the goods; or (b) when the goods have been delivered to him and he does any act inconsistent with the ownership of the seller; or (c) when after lapse of a reasonable time he retains the goods without intimating that he has rejected them.[522] In the first two cases, the buyer is not deemed to have accepted the goods until he has had a reasonable opportunity of examining them, and in the third the question whether he has had such an opportunity is material in determining whether a reasonable time has elapsed.[523] But in all three cases it is the opportunity of discovering the defect, rather than its actual discovery, which is the crucial factor, so that a buyer may "accept" without discovering the truth,[524] and a literal reading of Denning L.J.'s dictum would suggest that acceptance will always deprive him of the right to rescind for innocent misrepresentation. But it is submitted that the dictum must be read, according to its context, to refer to cases in which a claim to rescission is resisted on the ground of lapse of time. In other words, it means only that, where lapse of time amounts to acceptance, then it will also bar the right to rescind for misrepresentation. If the buyer, in ignorance of the true facts, "accepts" in some other way he may nevertheless be able to rescind for misrepresentation; and he may, by virtue of s.1(a) of the Misrepresentation Act, be able to do this even where the misrepresentation had been incorporated in the contract.

9–112   **Effect of affirmation on a claim for damages.** The primary effect of affirmation is that the representee will have lost the right to rescind the contract. But if the representee then claims damages to put him in the same position as if no misrepresentation had been made, that may produce a result which is the functional equivalent of rescission, e.g. if A is induced by B's misrepresentation to pay £100 for goods which are, in fact, worth £70, the result of rescinding the contract is that A will recover the price and return the goods, i.e. he will be better off by £30. If he has affirmed the contract he must keep the goods and cannot recover the price, but an award of damages would result in him receiving the difference between the price paid and the actual value of the goods (on the basis that, if no misrepresentation had been made, A would not have entered into the contract), i.e. he will be better off by £30. On this basis, it may be that affirmation

[519] *TSB Plc v Camfield* [1995] 1 W.L.R. 430, citing *Barclays Bank Plc v O'Brien* [1994] 1 A.C. 180 at 199; *De Molestina v Ponton* [2002] 1 Lloyd's Rep. 271 at 286–288.
[520] [1950] 2 K.B. 86, 90.
[521] See below, para.18–083.
[522] Sale of Goods Act 1979, s.35(1) and (2).
[523] ibid., s.35(4) and (5).
[524] e.g. where he has a reasonable opportunity of examining the goods but does not discover the truth. See below, para.18–083.

should also act as a bar to damages which are "equivalent to the benefit (A) would have received from avoidance."[525]Affirmation would not affect any claim for consequential loss.

(iv) *Lapse of time*

Fraud and breach of fiduciary duty. In cases of fraud or breach of fiduciary duty, lapse of time does not itself bar rescission. It is simply evidence of affirmation.[526] This view is supported by the rule that time begins to run only from the discovery of the truth[527]; and by the rule that time spent in negotiations to settle the dispute does not bar rescission.[528]   **9–113**

Innocent and negligent misrepresentation. In *Leaf v International Galleries*[529] the claimant was induced to buy a picture by the innocent misrepresentation that it was "by J. Constable".[530] Five years later he sought to rescind but it was held that his right to do so was barred by lapse of time. As rescission was sought promptly on discovery of the truth, the lapse of time was not evidence of affirmation, so that, even in the absence of such evidence, lapse of time is a bar to the right to rescind for *innocent* misrepresentation. The length of time required for this purpose seems to be such as would enable a reasonably diligent inquirer to discover the truth. This rule probably applies to a negligent misrepresentation in the same way as to a wholly innocent one.   **9–114**

5. EXCLUDING LIABILITY FOR MISREPRESENTATION

The common law starts with the principle that contract terms which exclude liability for misrepresentation (including those which exclude the right to rescind)[531] are valid. Their effectiveness may be limited by the general rules relating to exemption clauses, discussed elsewhere in this book.[532] In addition, s.3 of the Misrepresentation Act 1967 provides: **9–115**

> "If a contract contains a term[533] which would exclude or restrict (*a*) any liability to which a party to a contract may be subject by reason of any misrepresentation made by him before the contract was made; or (*b*) any remedy available to another party to the contract by reason of such a misrepresentation, that term shall be of no effect except in so far as it satisfies the requirement of reasonableness as stated in section 11(1) of the Unfair

---

[525] *Argo Systems FZE v Liberty Insurance (PTE)* [2011] EWHC 301 (Comm) at [46].

[526] *Clough v LNW Ry* (1871) L.R. 7 Ex. 26, 35; cf. (in cases of breach) below, para.18–080.

[527] *Gillett v Peppercorne* (1840) 3 Beav. 78; *Armstrong v Jackson* [1917] 2 K.B. 822; *Aaron's Reefs Ltd v Twiss* [1896] A.C. 273 at 287.

[528] *Erlanger v New Sombrero Phosphate Co* (1878) 3 App.Cas. 1218 at 1252.

[529] [1950] 2 K.B. 86.

[530] See above, para.8–020.

[531] *Toomey v Eagle Star Ins Co* [1995] 2 Lloyd's Rep. 89.

[532] See especially above, para.7–042.

[533] S.3 does not apply to non-contractual notices, but it has been suggested that, as a result, such notices are entirely ineffective: *IFE Fund SA v Goldman Sachs International* [2006] EWHC 2887 (Comm); [2007] 1 Lloyd's Rep. 264 at [65], affirmed [2007] EWCA Civ 811; [2007] 2 Lloyd's Rep. 449 without further reference to this point.

Contract Terms Act 1977; and it is for those claiming that the term satisfies that requirement to show that it does".

(a) Scope of the Misrepresentation Act 1967, section 3

9–116   **Excluding or restricting liabilities or remedies.** The section covers not only clauses excluding or limiting a party's liability but also certain analogous terms: e.g. clauses which impose a short time-limit within which claims must be brought, or which exclude a particular remedy (such as rescission or set-off[534]) without affecting another (such as damages).[535] On the other hand, it probably does not cover a valid agreed damages clause, since this might in some circumstances extend rather than restrict liability.[536] The section applies to terms excluding or restricting "*any* remedy". This phrase obviously covers the normal remedies of damages and rescission.[537] It probably also covers terms restricting or excluding the right to plead misrepresentation as a defence,[538] for this could be described as a "remedy" in a broad sense. Similarly, a term excluding or restricting the right to retake goods obtained by fraud[539] would be within the section. The section does not apply if the contract is an international supply contract within the meaning of s.26 of the Unfair Contract Terms Act.[540]

9–117   **"No representation" or "non-reliance" clauses.**[541] Some terms purport not to exclude or restrict liability, or any remedy, but rather to prevent liability from arising. The most common instance of this type of provision is a clause in which the parties agree, or acknowledge[542] that no representations have been made, or that they have not relied on any representations that have been made, either at all or save for those that are set out in the contract. The precise effect of such provisions has been considered in rather a large number of recent cases;[543] in particular, in the context of what may be referred to as the mis-selling of financial

---

[534] *Skipskreditforeningen v Emperor Navigation* [1998] 1 Lloyd's Rep. 67 at 74.

[535] cf. above, para.7–055 for a similar definition in s.13 of Unfair Contract Terms Act 1977. That definition only applies in terms for the purposes of Pt I of 1977 Act, which is not considered to include (though it amends) s.3 of the Misrepresentation Act 1967: see s.11(1) of the 1977 Act. An arbitration clause is excluded from the definition in s.13 of the 1977 Act, but may be covered by s.3 of the Misrepresentation Act.

[536] cf. above, para.7–054; below, para.20–130 et seq.

[537] And has been held to cover a clause under which the representee gives up "any rights" as a result of any misrepresentation: *Trident Turboprop (Dublin) Ltd v First Flight Couriers Ltd* [2008] EWHC 1686 (Comm); [2008] 2 Lloyd's Rep. 581, affirmed [2009] EWCA Civ 290; [2009] 3 W.L.R. 361 without reference to this point.

[538] See above, para.9–089.

[539] See above, para.9–087.

[540] *Trident Turboprop (Dublin) Ltd v First Flight Couriers Ltd* [2009] EWCA Civ 290; [2009] 3 W.L.R. 361.

[541] Trukhtanov 125 L.Q.R. 648.

[542] "Agree", "acknowledge" or "represent" is not significant: *Springwell Navigation Corporation v JP Morgan Chase Bank* [2010] EWCA Civ 1221 at [170], but *what* has been agreed, or acknowledged, or represented, may be significant: see below, text to fn.557.

[543] In addition to those cited below, see also: *Six Continents Hotels Inc v Event Hotels GmbH* [2006] EWHC 2317 (QB); *Donegal International Ltd v Zambia* [2007] EWHC 197 (Comm); [2007] 1 Lloyd's Rep 397; *Titan Steel Wheels Ltd v Royal Bank of Scotland* [2010] EWHC 211 (Comm); [2010] 2 Lloyd's Rep. 92; *Camarata Property Inc v Credit Suisse Securities (Europe) Ltd* [2011] EWHC 479; *Bank Leumi (UK) Plc v Wachner* [2011] EWHC 656 (Comm); *Casa di Risparmio Della Repubblica di San Marino SpA v Barclays Bank Ltd* [2011] EWHC 484 (Comm).

products. The position which appears to have been reached may be reduced to three propositions.

First, as noted above, such provisions may have a role to play in determining whether any respresentation has been made at all,[544] or whether a statement was intended to be understood and acted on as a representation, i.e. that no representation was impliedly being made may be "underscored" by a "no representation" clause.[545]

Secondly, where a representation has in fact been made, or has been relied upon, the effect of the type of provision under consideration may be to create an estoppel preventing the representee from basing his claim on the representation in question. In the case of estoppel by representation, the representor is required to show that he relied on the representee's counter-representation, in the form of the no representation, or non-reliance clause,[546] and he may not be able to do so if it is clear that he did make a representation and it was intended that the representee should rely upon it.[547] More recently, the courts have recognised that such clauses may create a contractual estoppel,[548] in relation to which it seems[549] that the only requirement is that the clause is appropriately drafted;[550] there is no requirement of reliance by the representor,[551] nor any need to show, as is required for estoppel by convention,[552] that it would be unconscionable for the representee to resile from his own representation that no representation was made to him or that he did not rely on any that was made.[553] Furthermore, it is no bar to a finding of contractual estoppel that it is invoked in such cases to deny a past fact,[554] i.e. that a representation was made.[555]

It has been noted above that in order to provide the basis for contractual estoppel, the clause in question must have been appropriately drafted. It must

---

[544] See above, para.9–005.

[545] *Raiffeisen Zentralbank Osterreich AG v Royal Bank of Scotland Plc* [2010] EWHC 1392 (Comm) at [110]; cf. *Springwell Navigation Corporation v JP Morgan Chase Bank* [2008] EWHC 1973 (Comm) at [669]–[670], [674]–[675], affirmed [2010] EWCA Civ 1221 at [171], [180].

[546] *Lowe v Lombank* [1960] 1 W.L.R. 196; *Grimstead v McGarrigan* [1999] All E.R. (D) 1163; *Watford Electronics Ltd v Sanderson CFL Ltd* [2001] EWCA Civ 317; [2001] B.L.R. 143 at [39]–[40].

[547] As in *Quest 4 Finance Ltd v Maxfield* [2007] EWHC 2313; [2007] 2 C.L.C. 706.

[548] *Peekay Intermark Ltd v ANZ Banking Group Ltd* [2006] EWCA Civ 386; *Foodco UK Ltd v Henry Boot Developments Ltd* [2010] EWHC 358 (Ch); *Raiffeisen Zentralbank Osterreich AG v Royal Bank of Scotland Plc* [2010] EWHC 1392 (Comm); *Springwell Navigation Corporation v JP Morgan Chase Bank* [2010] EWCA Civ 1221. In the *Foodco* case (at [171]), the court rejected the submission that contractual estoppel is confined to "no representation" clauses and only estoppel by representation may be invoked in relation to "non-reliance" clauses.

[549] In *Morgan v Pooley* [2010] EWHC 2447 (QB) at [114] it is said that if the clause is not one of which it may be reasonable to expect the representee to be aware, it cannot be invoked on the basis that it is contained in the very contract which is to be set aside for misrepresentation. But in the *Peekay* case, this argument was acknowledged by Moore-Bick L.J. (at [57]) who seemed then to suggest that the whole point of contractual estoppel is to prevent it from being made without any distinction based on the reasonable awareness of the term. Any lack of awareness might be reflected in the test of reasonableness under s.3 of the 1967 Act.

[550] It must of course take effect *as a contract*, but this may be assumed if the clause is set out in what is a binding contract.

[551] The basis of the "estoppel" is agreement, not reliance: *Springwell Navigation Corporation v JP Morgan Chase Bank* [2010] EWCA Civ 1221 at [144].

[552] See above, para.3–094.

[553] *Springwell Navigation Corporation v JP Morgan Chase Bank* [2010] EWCA Civ 1221 at [177].

[554] ibid. at [144].

[555] Comments from Diplock J. in *Lowe v Lombank*, above fn.546 in apparent support of such a submission have been found either to be not on point: *Springwell*, above fn.553 at [150], or, to the extent necessary, wrong: *Raiffeisen*, above fn.545 at [255].

make clear that any representations that may have been made are "withdrawn, overridden or of no legal effect so far as any liability for misrepresentation may be concerned".[556] It is not sufficient to point to wording that may be typical of an entire agreement clause that any representations made shall not take effect *as terms of the contract*; it is necessary to convey the parties' agreement that they shall not take effect *as representations.*[557]

Thirdly, whether taking effect by way of estoppel by representation or contractual estoppel, a no representation or non-reliance clause prevents the representee from seeking relief for misrepresentation. So far as the application of s.3 of the Misrepresentation Act 1967 is concerned, a potential problem arises in that the wording of the section is limited to terms which "exclude or restrict" liability or any remedy and, strictly speaking, terms of the type under consideration do not exclude or restrict any anterior liability; they prevent it from arising in the first place.[558] The courts have not allowed this type of submission to dictate the scope of s.3[559] and, in the present context, it has been said that it is a question of "substance, and not form" whether a term amounts to an exclusion or restriction of liability for the purpose of s.3 of the 1967 Act. Put at its simplest, although it does not matter for a finding of contractual estoppel that a clause may deny a past fact, or seek to "re-write history", it is precisely when it does so that it will, in substance, be regarded as a term which excludes or restricts liability[560] and therefore subject to the test of reasonableness under section 3.[561] Where, however, there is some doubt as to the representation being made, or whether any representation is made at all, e.g. an implied representation, and the clause is relied upon to assist in resolving that doubt in favour of the representor,[562] it will not be

---

[556] *BSkyB Ltd v HP Enterprise Services UK Ltd* [2010] EWHC 86 (TCC); [2010] B.L.R. 267 at [382].

[557] ibid.; cf. *Deepak v. ICI* [1999] 1 Lloyd's Rep 387; *Axa Sun Life Services Plc v Campbell Martin Ltd* [2011] EWCA Civ 133 at [92] ("no language to the effect that the parties were agreed that no representations had been made or relied upon").

[558] This problem does not arise where the relevant statutory control is s.2 UCTA which will apply to any claim for negligent misrepresentation where the misrepresentor is not the other party to the contract: below, para.9–040. Section 2 must be read subject to s.13(1) which extends it to any term which excludes or restricts the "relevant obligation or duty". That still, of course, leaves the problem of determining whether a term does exclude or restrict a duty or simply establish what that duty is in the first place, i.e. determine the scope of the contract: *Springwell Navigation Corporation v JP Morgan Chase Bank* [2010] EWCA Civ 1221 at [181].

[559] See especially, the colourful view of Scarman L.J. in *Cremdean Properties v Nash* (1977) 244 E.G. 547 at 550: "Humpty Dumpty would have fallen for this argument. If we were to fall for it, the Misrepresentation Act would be dashed to pieces which not all the King's lawyers could put together again". But contrast the view of Chadwick L.J. in the *Watford Electronics case*, above fn. 546 (at [41]) that it would be "bizarre" to attribute to the parties an intention to exclude a liability which they thought would never arise.

[560] There may also be an element of timing to take into account in applying this distinction. Where the term only appears in the contract which is entered into at the end of the negotiations, it is more likely to have "rewritten history" and therefore amount to an exclusion clause. That may not be the finding if it is introduced at the start of any negotiations as part of other contractual documentation, e.g. in an information memorandum, or a confidentiality agreement: *Raiffeisen Zentralbank Osterreich AG v Royal Bank of Scotland Plc* [2010] EWHC 1392 (Comm) at [318]

[561] Where a representation has been made fraudulently, the clause is of no effect: *Raiffeisen Zentralbank Osterreich AG v Royal Bank of Scotland Plc* [2010] EWHC 1392 (Comm) at [325]; cf. *Peart Stevenson Associates v Holland* [2008] EWHC 1868 (QB); *Foodco UK Ltd v Henry Boot Developments Ltd* [2010] EWHC 358 (Ch).

[562] See above, para.9–005.

subject to statutory control. This somewhat elusive distinction[563] has been best summed up by Toulson J. in *IFE Fund SA v Goldman Sachs International*:[564]

"The question is one of substance and not form. If a seller of a car said to a buyer "I have serviced the car since it was new, it has had only one owner and the clock reading is accurate", those statements would be representations, and they would still have that character even if the seller added the words "but those statements are not representations on which you can rely". *Cremdean Properties Ltd v Nash*,[565] which Mr Nash cited, is authority for the principle that a party cannot by a carefully chosen form of wording circumvent the statutory controls on exclusion of liability for a representation which has on proper analysis been made.

If, however, the seller of the car said "The clock reading is 20,000 miles, but I have no knowledge whether the reading is true or false", the position would be different, because the qualifying words could not fairly be regarded as an attempt to exclude liability for a false representation arising from the first half of the sentence."

Other terms preventing liability from arising. In a similar vein to no representation or non-reliance clauses, a clause in an auctioneer's catalogue might provide that all representations in it were statements of opinion only. If the court, on applying the tests stated earlier in this chapter,[566] concluded that such a representation would, but for the clause, be one of fact, it might well hold that the clause was within s.3. By contrast, it seems that the section would not apply to a term in a contract made through an agent negativing his ostensible authority to make representation as to the subject-matter,[567] nor to statements by a carrier in a bill of lading as to the weight or quantity of goods shipped which are qualified by the words "weight unknown", or "said to contain".[568]   9–118

"Party to a contract". The section applies only to provisions excluding or restricting the liability of a "party to a contract", and the subsequent words of the section show that this means *the* contract induced by the misrepresentation. The   9–119

---

[563] "Everything must depend on the facts": *Raiffeisen Zentralbank Osterreich AG v Royal Bank of Scotland Plc* [2010] EWHC 1392 (Comm) at [311].

[564] [2006] EWHC 2887 (Comm); [2007] 1 Lloyd's Rep. 264 at [67]–[68], affirmed [2007] EWCA Civ 811; [2007] 2 Lloyd's Rep. 449; cf. *Thomas Witter v TBP Industries* [1996] 2 All ER 573; *Government of Zanzibar v British Aerospace (Lancaster House) Ltd* [2000] 1 W.L.R. 2333; *Trident Turboprop (Dublin) Ltd v First Flight Couriers Ltd* [2008] EWHC 1686 (Comm); [2008] 2 Lloyd's Rep. 581 (in which Aikens J. applies a "but for" test reminiscent of that used in *Smith v Eric S Bush* [1990] 1 A.C. 831 (above, para.7–055)), affirmed [2009] EWCA Civ 290; [2009] 3 W.L.R. 361; *Raiffeisen Zentralbank Osterreich AG v Royal Bank of Scotland Plc* [2010] EWHC 1392 (Comm) at [310]–[316]. Contrast *William Sindall Plc v Cambridgeshire CC* [1994] 1 W.L.R. 1016 at 1034E. A statement can take effect as a misrepresentation in spite of the fact that it is made in a document expressly warning the representee to make his own enquiries into its accuracy: *Walker v Boyle* [1982] 1 W.L.R. 495; cf. *South Western General Property Co Ltd v Marton* (1982) 263 E.G. 1090.

[565] (1977) 244 E.G. 547

[566] See above, para.9–008.

[567] See *Overbrooke Estates Ltd v Glencombe Properties Ltd* [1974] 1 W.L.R. 1335; Coote [1975] C.L.J. 17; the amendments to s.3 made by Unfair Contract Terms Act 1977, s.8(1) appear not to affect the point; cf. *Museprime Properties Ltd v Adhill Properties Ltd* [1990] 2 E.G.L.R. 196 at 200.

[568] *The Mata K* [1998] 2 Lloyd's Rep. 614 (discussing earlier authorities on such "weight unknown" provisions). See *Carver on Bills of Lading* (2nd edn), §2–004.

section therefore would not apply to disclaimers of liability in cases such as *Hedley Byrne & Co Ltd v Heller & Partners Ltd*[569] and *Smith v Eric S Bush*[570] since the contracts induced by the misrepresentations in those cases were not made with the representor but with a third person. Such disclaimers of liability for negligence in giving advice in the course of a business would, however, be subject to the test of reasonableness under the Unfair Contract Terms Act 1977.[571] The scope of that test is, however, as will be seen below, in several ways significantly narrower than that of s.3 of the Misrepresentation Act 1967.

9–120 **"By reason of any misrepresentation made".** Where a misrepresentation has been made, s.3 clearly applies to terms excluding or restricting liability for mere misrepresentations.[572] It equally clearly does not apply to terms which exclude or restrict liability only for breaches of pure promises (as opposed to statements of fact) or for breaches of implied terms not dependent on statements of fact. Terms which exclude or restrict liability only for such breaches may be subject to the test of reasonableness under the Unfair Contract Terms Act 1977. But the scope of the test under that Act is limited[573]: it does not, for example, generally apply where the party relying on the clause has made the contract otherwise than in the course of a business, nor does it apply to certain specified contracts, such as contracts for the sale of land.[574] The scope of s.3 of the Misrepresentation Act is not so limited; and the difference in the scope of the two Acts gives rise to two problems. In discussing these, we shall assume that the case is one in which the reasonableness test under the 1977 Act does not apply.

9–121 **Incorporated misrepresentation.** Where a misrepresentation is incorporated in the contract, the right to rescind for misrepresentation is preserved by s.1(a), and a term purporting to exclude or restrict that right would be within s.3. But a term may purport to exclude or restrict liabilities or remedies available only because the representation has been incorporated in the contract: e.g. it may provide that the representee is to recover no more than out-of-pocket expenses and is not to have damages for loss of his bargain.[575] It seems that such a term would not be within s.3, for the liability which it purported to exclude would arise, not by reason of the *making* of the representation, but by reason of its *incorporation* into the contract. This conclusion is, however, subject to the point next to be discussed.

9–122 **Provision applicable to misrepresentation and breach.** A single term may exclude liability for misrepresentation *and* for breach of contract. A clause excluding liability "for all defects" would have this effect where some defects were merely represented not to exist while others amounted to breaches of contract. Section 3 provides that where a term would exclude or restrict any liability for misrepresentation "*that term* shall be of no effect except in so far as" the test of reasonableness is satisfied. It seems to follow that the *whole* term may be subject to the reasonableness test and not only the part of it which excludes liability for

---

[569] [1964] A.C. 465; above, para.9–033.
[570] [1990] 1 A.C. 831; above, para.7–055.
[571] i.e. under s.2(2) (above, para.7–065) and possibly under s.3(2) (above, paras 7–066—7–069).
[572] For the possible application of the section to cases of non-disclosure, see below, para.9–155.
[573] See above, paras 7–088—7–094.
[574] See above, para.7–089.
[575] cf. above, paras 9–059—9–064.

misrepresentation, unless that part is severable,[576] in which case the reasonableness of the part relating to breach would, if it fell within relevant provisions of the Unfair Contract Terms Act 1977,[577] have to be determined under that Act.[578] An unseverable term excluding liability for "misrepresentation" generally could be ineffective (if unreasonable[579]) to exclude contractual liability for an incorporated misrepresentation.[580]

"Before the contract was made". Section 3 applies to terms excluding or   9–123 restricting liability for misrepresentations made before the conclusion of the contract. It does not apply to terms excluding or restricting liability for mis-representations made in the course of *performing* a contract. However, in general[581] such liability is likely to be incurred only by a person who acts in the course of a business and is negligent: e.g. by a negligent surveyor or valuer. In such a case, a term excluding or restricting liability is subject to the test of reasonableness under the Unfair Contract Terms Act 1977.[582] If the representation was fraudulent, a clause excluding liability for it is probably void at common law.[583]

(b) The Reasonableness Test

Guidelines. Section 3 applies "the test of reasonableness *as stated in s.11(1)* of   9–124 the Unfair Contract Terms Act 1977" to terms excluding or restricting liability for misrepresentation. Section 11(1) provides that, in order to determine whether the test of reasonableness is satisfied, regard is to be had to the time of contracting; this rule is expressly stated in s.11(1) to apply for the purposes of s.3 of the Misrepresentation Act 1967. The 1977 Act also lays down guidelines for deter-mining reasonableness; these take effect under s.11(2) and 11(4) of that Act.[584] At first sight, none of these guidelines apply for the purpose of s.3 of the Mis-representation Act, since s.3 of that Act refers only to s.11(1) of the 1977 Act, while s.11(2) of that Act contains no words that could be taken to refer to s.3 of the 1967 Act. However, the guidelines contained in s.11(4) are there said to apply where "the question arises (under this *or any other* Act) whether the term . . . satisfies the test of reasonableness". In view of the italicised words, those guide-lines[585] are, it is submitted, applicable for the purpose of s.3 of the Misrepresenta-tion Act. Even the guidelines referred to in s.11(2) apply by analogy to contracts which are not literally within the wording of the subsection[586]; and they could by a process of further analogous extension be applied to cases in which the reason-ableness test applies by virtue only of s.3 of the 1967 Act. The statutory guidelines are, moreover, not exhaustive for the purpose of s.3: in this respect their position under this section is indistinguishable from that under the 1977 Act.[587]

---

[576] cf. above, paras 7–076—7–077.
[577] See above, paras 7–064—7–074.
[578] *Skipskreditforeningen v Emperor Navigation* [1998] 1 Lloyd's Rep. 67 at 75.
[579] See below, para.9–125.
[580] Above, fn.578. Mance J. expressed doubt as to the correctness of the rule of "non-severance"; see above, para.7–076, and below, para.9–125.
[581] For an exception, see *Chaudhry v Prabhakar* [1989] 1 W.L.R. 29.
[582] i.e. s.2(2) (above, para.7–065) and possibly s.3(2) (above, paras 7–066—7–069).
[583] See above, para.7–042.
[584] See above, paras 7–080—7–081.
[585] See above, para.7–080.
[586] See above, para.7–081.
[587] See above, para.7–082.

9–125   **Severability.** A term which purports to exclude liability "for misrepresentation" may be taken to extend to liability for fraudulent misrepresentation, which
cannot be excluded as a matter of public policy.[588] Since, on one interpretation, the
test of reasonableness must be applied to the whole of a term which falls within its
scope,[589] it would seem that such a term cannot be enforced.[590] An alternative and,
it is submitted, preferable view is that, as a matter of construction, when a term
purporting to exclude liability refers simply to "misrepresentation" the parties
cannot have intended to exclude liability in fraud in the absence of an express
provision to this effect.[591] This issue has been most commonly encountered in
connection with "non-reliance clauses",[592] and such a clause, so construed as not
to cover fraud, will often be regarded as reasonable in the type of commercial
contract where it is usually to be found.[593]

(c) Unfair Terms in Consumer Contracts Regulations 1999[594]

9–126   These Regulations have in some respects a narrower scope than s.3 of the
Misrepresentation Act, 1967. They apply only where the party relying on the term
is acting for purposes relating to his trade, business or profession, where the other
party is a consumer, and where the term in question is not individually negotiated.
None of these limitations applies to s.3 of the 1967 Act. For example, an individually negotiated term by which a private seller of land to a property developer
excluded liability for misrepresentation could fall within s.3; but it would not fall
within the Regulations because (i) the seller did not act for purposes relating to any
trade, etc.; (ii) the buyer did so act; and (iii) the term was individually negotiated.
On the other hand, s.3 applies only to terms "which would exclude or restrict"
liability for misrepresentation,[595] while under the Regulations terms other than
exemption clauses may be struck down as unfair.

6. NON-DISCLOSURE[596]

(a) General Rule

(i) *No duty of disclosure*

9–127   As a general rule, a person who is about to enter into a contract is under no duty
to disclose material facts known to him but not to the other party.[597] Thus it has

---

[588] See above, para.7–042.

[589] See above, para.9–122.

[590] *Thomas Witter Ltd v TBP Industries Ltd* [1996] 2 All E.R. 573 at 598; *South West Water Services Ltd v International Computers Ltd* [1999] B.L.R. 420.

[591] *Zanzibar v British Aerospace (Lancaster House) Ltd* [2001] 1 W.L.R. 2333; *Six Continents Hotels Inc v Event Hotels GmbH* [2006] EWHC 2317 (QB) at [53]; *Raiffeisen Zentralbank Osterreich AG v Royal Bank of Scotland Plc* [2010] EWHC 1392 (Comm) at [325].

[592] About which there is some doubt whether they fall within the scope of s.3 at all: see above, para.9–117.

[593] See generally the cases discussed at para.9–117 above; cf. *National Westminster Bank Plc v Utrecht-America Finance Co* [2001] EWCA Civ 658; [2001] 3 All E.R. 733 at [6]–[61]. Contrast: *Walker v Boyle* [1982] 1 W.L.R. 495 (residential purchase, where clause held unreasonable).

[594] See above, para.7–095 et seq.

[595] Though that may be given an extended meaning (see above, para.9–116, above), it is still narrower than the range of terms covered by the Regulations.

[596] Cartwright, *Misrepresentation, Mistake and Non-Disclosure* (2nd edn), Pt III; Duggan, Bryan and Hanks, *Contractual Non-Disclosure* (1994).

[597] *Norwich Union Life Ins Co Ltd v Qureshi* [1999] 2 All E.R. (Comm) 707 at 717.

been held that a landlord is not liable in deceit if before letting his house he fails to tell the tenant that it is in a ruinous condition[598]; and that a person who applies for the post of governess is not bound to divulge the fact that she is a divorcee.[599] Sometimes the rule may appear to operate harshly; but if a general duty of disclosure did exist it would be very hard to say exactly what must be disclosed in any particular case.

(ii) *Representation by conduct*

A person may make a representation by conduct[600] and, if he fails to correct the impression given by his conduct, he cannot rely on the general rule that there is no duty of disclosure.[601] Active concealment of a defect amounts to misrepresentation[602]; and even conduct falling short of this may suffice.[603] In the words of Blackburn J.:   **9–128**

"The defendant, by taking the cow to a public market to be sold . . . thereby furnishes evidence of a representation that, so far as his knowledge goes, the animal is not suffering from any infectious disease. . . . The case might be different where the sale takes place privately".[604]

(iii) *Latent defects*

It has been said that a person must disclose latent defects in the subject-matter of the contract which are known to him.[605] But cases which may appear to support this view are best explained on the ground of active misrepresentation[606] by words or by conduct and the preferable view is that English law does not recognise any general duty to disclose known latent defects. In the dictum quoted above,[607] Blackburn J. based liability, not on any general duty to disclose latent defects, but on the defendant's conduct in taking the cow to market. The dictum was cited without comment in *Ward v Hobbs*[608] where pigs were taken to Newbury market and sold there "with all faults". The seller knew that the pigs were diseased but he did not disclose this fact to the buyer. It was held that the buyer had no remedy as there was no general duty to disclose known latent defects and any representation which might be inferred from the seller's conduct in taking the pigs to market was negatived by the words "with all faults". These words might, on such facts,   **9–129**

---

[598] *Keates v Cadogan* (1851) 10 C.B. 591.

[599] *Fletcher v Krell* (1872) 42 L.J.Q.B. 55; cf. *The Unique Mariner* [1978] 1 Lloyd's Rep. 438 at 449; *Lloyds Bank v Egremont* [1990] 2 FLR 351.

[600] *Curtis v Chemical Cleaning & Dyeing Co Ltd* [1951] 1 K.B. 805 at 808; contrast *Geest Plc v Fyffes Plc* [1999] 1 All E.R. (Comm) 672 at 686 (where the conduct gave rise to no such inference).

[601] *Walters v Morgan* (1861) 3 D.F. & J. 718 at 723; *Spice Girls Ltd v Aprilia World Service BV* [2002] EWCA Civ 15; [2002] E.M.L.R. 27 at [61]–[63].

[602] *Schneider v Heath* (1813) 3 Camp. 506; *Sybron Corp v Rochem Ltd* [1984] Ch. 112 at 130 ("covering up and deliberately concealing"); *Gordon v Selico Ltd* (1986) 278 E.G. 53.

[603] There is, however, no misrepresentation in tacitly acquiescing in another's self-deception: *Donegal International Ltd v Zambia* [2007] EWHC 197 (Comm); [2007] 1 Lloyd's Rep 397 at [465].

[604] *Bodger v Nicholls* (1873) 28 L.T. 441 at 445.

[605] *Horsfall v Thomas* (1862) 1 H. & C. 90 at 100.

[606] e.g. *Hill v Gray* (1816) 1 Stark. 434, as explained in *Keates v Cadogan* (1851) 10 C.B. at 600.

[607] See above, at fn.604.

[608] (1878) 4 App.Cas. 13.

now protect the seller only if they satisfied the legislative requirements of reasonableness or fairness.[609] Moreover, if the thing sold suffers from a latent defect of which the seller knows, and if that defect causes injury to the buyer, or harm to other property belonging to him, then the seller's failure to warn the buyer of the defect may make him liable in negligence; and it has been suggested that *Ward v Hobbs* may require reconsideration in the light of this possibility.[610] But there is generally no such liability where the defect caused no loss to the buyer except in making the thing sold less valuable than he had supposed it to be.[611] Cases of this kind continue to be governed by the general rule that there is no duty of disclosure.

The general rule has been applied where land sold was subject to a latent physical defect[612]; and it has similarly been held that a vendor of a leasehold interest was not bound to disclose the fact that the organisation to which the premises were let had only a limited "life".[613] There is some support for the view that on a sale of land latent defects of title must be disclosed[614] but even here it seems that there is no general duty of disclosure,[615] and that an undisclosed defect of this kind is a ground for relief only if it is unusual,[616] or if it leads to a breach of contract[617] or to an operative mistake.[618] It can also, if known to the vendor, prevent him from relying on a term of the contract under which the purchaser is deemed to have made enquiries relating to the matter in question and to have knowledge of it.[619]

The general rule that there is no duty of disclosure also applies where the buyer knows (but the seller does not) of some latent quality which makes the subject-matter of the contract *more* valuable. Thus a contract for the sale of land is binding even though the buyer, but not the seller, knew that it contained valuable minerals.[620]

---

[609] See above, paras 7–065, 9–116 et seq.

[610] *Hurley v Dyke* [1979] R.T.R. 265 at 303. For a similar duty to disclose one's own *breach* where it may lead to danger, see below, para.9–151.

[611] cf. below, para.14–045. There is no such liability in tort even where (exceptionally) there *is* a duty of disclosure because the contract is uberrimae fidei (below, para.9–136): *Banque Keyser Ullmann SA v Skandia (UK) Ins Co Ltd* [1990] 1 Q.B. 665 at 798–800; [1991] 2 A.C. 249 at 282 (where the decision was affirmed on other grounds).

[612] *Shepherd v Croft* [1911] 1 Ch. 521.

[613] *Safehaven Investments Ltd v Springbok Ltd* (1996) 71 P. & C.R. 59.

[614] *Selkirk v Romar Investments Ltd* [1963] 1 W.L.R. 1415 at 1423; *Faruqi v English Real Estates* [1979] 1 W.L.R. 963; *William Sindall Plc v Cambridgeshire CC* [1994] 1 W.L.R. 1016 at 1023.

[615] Megarry and Wade, *The Law of Real Property* (7th edn), para.15–070.

[616] *Molyneux v Hawtrey* [1903] 2 K.B. 487; cf. *Carlish v Salt* [1906] 1 Ch. 335; *Celsteel Ltd v Alton House Holdings Ltd (No.2)* [1986] 1 All E.R. 598 at 607 (not reported on this point in [1986] 1 W.L.R. 666).

[617] e.g. *Flight v Booth* (1834) 1 Bing. N.C. 370; *Peyman v Lanjani* [1985] Ch. 457 at 496. Certain covenants for title are implied under Law of Property (Miscellaneous Provisions) Act 1994, Pt I.

[618] See above, para.8–047.

[619] *Rignall Developments Ltd v Halil* [1988] Ch. 190.

[620] *Smith v Hughes* (1871) L.R. 6 Q.B. 587 at 604; quaere whether the contract would be specifically enforced: below, para.21–032; cf. also *Phillips v Homfray* (1871) L.R. 7 Ch.App. 770. For a statutory exception, see Criminal Justice Act 1993, Pt V, giving effect to EC Council Directive 89/592, and imposing criminal penalties on "insider dealing"; and see Insider Dealing (Securities and Regulated Markets) Amendment Order 1996 (SI 1996/1561). But the validity or enforceability of the resulting transaction is not affected: 1993 Act, s.63(2), the wording of which appears to reverse this aspect of *Chase Manhattan Equities Ltd v Goodman* [1991] B.C.L.C. 897. See also the powers to impose penalties for "market abuse" under Financial Services and Markets Act 2000, ss.118–118C (as substituted by Prospectus Regulations 2005 (SI 2005/1433)) and 123.

(b) Exceptions

Extent of duty of disclosure. There are many important exceptions to the   9–130
rule that there is no liability for non-disclosure. In these exceptional cases, a
person is, in general, bound to disclose only facts which he knew (or which he
would have known if he had not "wilfully shut his eyes" to them).[621] A person
may, however, be under a duty to disclose facts which, though not known to him,
were known to his agent, if that knowledge had been acquired within the scope of
the agent's authority and if it was the agent's duty to communicate it to the
principal.[622] He may also be under a duty to disclose facts which he ought to have
known, if there is a "special relationship" between the parties within *Hedley Byrne
& Co Ltd v Heller & Partners Ltd*.[623]

A continuing duty. Where a duty of disclosure exists, it generally continues   9–131
until the contract becomes legally binding.[624] But where a contract is regarded as
binding as a matter of business the duty to disclose may cease at that point even
though the contract is not yet binding in law. Thus in contracts of insurance the
duty ceases when the insurer initials a slip saying that he will accept the risk, even
where there is no legally binding contract until a policy is executed.[625] Conversely
the duty may in a sense continue even after the conclusion of the contract. For
example, a person who takes a fidelity bond for the honesty of one of his servants
is under a continuing duty to disclose to the surety any acts of dishonesty on the
part of the servant[626]; and the express or implied terms of a contract may impose
a contractual duty of disclosure to be further discussed below.[627] Once the parties
become engaged in hostile litigation, however, any continuing duties of disclosure
are superseded by the rules of procedure which govern such litigation.[628] Failure
to perform a continuing (post-contractual) duty of disclosure does not, moreover,
vitiate the *formation* of the contract but amounts to a *breach* of one of its express
or implied terms[629]; and this distinction has significant effects, to be discussed
below,[630] on the remedies for this type of non-disclosure. In insurance contracts,
the duty of disclosure also continues after the making of the original contract in
the sense that its performance is a prerequisite to any renewal of the insurance.

---

[621] *Blackburn, Low & Co v Vigors* (1887) 12 App.Cas. 531; *Economides v Commercial Union Assurance
Co Plc* [1998] Q.B. 587 at 602; *Zeller v British Caymanian Insurance Company Ltd* [2008] UKPC 4 at
[18]; cf. *William Sindall Plc v Cambridgeshire CC* [1994] 1 W.L.R. 1016, (where the contract expressly
restricted the duty in this way); Marine Insurance Act 1906, s.18(1).
[622] *Proudfoot v Montefiore* (1867) L.R. 2 Q.B. 511; *Joel v Law Union and Crown Ins Co* [1908] 2 K.B.
863.
[623] [1964] A.C. 465; above, para.9–033.
[624] *Container Transport International Inc v Oceanus Mutual, etc., Association* [1984] 1 Lloyd's Rep. 476
at 486, disapproved on another point in *Pan Atlantic Ins Co v Pine Top Incs Co* [1995] 2 A.C. 501 (below,
para.9–138; above, para.9–026).
[625] *Cory v Patton* (1872) L.R. 7 Q.B. 304; *Citadel Ins Co v Atlantic Union Ins Co* [1982] 2 Lloyd's
Rep. 543 at 548. S.2(1) of the Misrepresentation Act (requiring belief in the truth of the "facts
represented" up to the time that the contract was made) would not apply to pure non-disclosure: cf.
below, para.9–155.
[626] *Phillips v Foxall* (1872) L.R. 7 Q.B. 666; cf. *Roadworks (1952) Ltd v Charman* [1994] 2 Lloyd's
Rep. 99 at 107–108.
[627] Below, para.9–151.
[628] *The Star Sea* [2001] UKHL 1; [2003] 1 A.C. 469 at [73]–[78]; *Agapitos v Agnew* [2002] EWCA
Civ 247; [2003] Q.B. 556 at [52].
[629] cf. above, para.9–082.
[630] See below, para.9–154.

(i) *Representation falsified by later events*

9–132   **Duty to correct representation later made false.** A person may have to disclose material facts which come to his notice[631] before the conclusion of a contract if they falsify a representation previously made[632] by him.[633] In *With v O'Flanagan*[634] negotiations for the sale of a medical practice were begun in January, when the practice was said to be worth £2,000. A contract of sale was made on May 1, by which time the practice had become worthless because of the intervening illness of the vendor. The contract was set aside on the ground that the vendor ought to have communicated this change of circumstances to the purchasers. But there would probably be no need to disclose minor variations in the income of the practice.[635] And there are obvious limitations on the scope of any duty of disclosure which may arise from a statement such as one as to a person's financial position, which can influence a series of transactions extending, perhaps, over many years. A time must come when the representation loses its force and the representee begins to rely rather on his own judgment.[636]

9–133   **Change of mind.** There are conflicting decisions on the question whether a duty of disclosure arises where during negotiations a party makes a representation as to his present intention but changes his mind before the conclusion of the contract. In *Traill v Baring*[637] an insurance company made a proposal for reinsurance to a second company, stating that it would retain part of the risk. This was its intention when it made the representation but before the proposal was accepted it disposed of that part of the risk. It was held that the "change of intention"[638] of the first company should have been disclosed to the second company. On the other hand, in *Wales v Wadham*[639] a husband who had left his wife made her an offer of financial provision after she had declared her intention of not remarrying. She accepted the offer after having decided to marry again. If the husband had known this, he would have made a lower offer; but it was held that the wife was not bound to disclose her change of mind. The duty of disclosing changed circumstances was said only to apply where the original representation was one of *fact*: not where it was one of *intention*.[640] The view that the wife was not bound to disclose her decision to remarry was disapproved by the House of Lords in *Jenkins*

---

[631] Or, which, if there is a "special relationship", should have come to his notice, had he exercised reasonable care.

[632] For this requirement, see *English v Dedham Vale Properties Ltd* [1978] 1 W.L.R. 93 at 104.

[633] The obligation to correct any falsehood applies only to the misrepresentor: *The Kriti Palm* [2006] EWCA Civ 1601; [2007] 1 Lloyd's Rep. 555 at [296].

[634] [1936] Ch. 575; cf.*Traill v Baring* (1864) 4 D.J. & S. 318; *Brownlie v Campbell* (1880) 5 App.Cas. 925 at 950; *Zamir v S of S for the Home Dept* [1980] A.C. 730 at 750; *Spice Girls Ltd v Aprilia World Service BV* [2002] EWCA Civ 15; [2002] E.M.L.R. 27 at [51], [58]. If the defendant knows of the change which has falsified any earlier statement and of its significance he will be liable in fraud: *Foodco UK LLP v Henry Boot Developments Ltd* [2010] EWHC 358 (Ch) at [214]; cf. *Fitzroy Robinson Ltd v Mentmore Towers Ltd* [2009] EWHC 1552 (TCC); [2009] B.L.R. 555. Contrast *Thomas Witter Ltd v TBP Industries Ltd* [1994] Tr.L.R. 145. And see Financial Services and Markets Act 2000, ss.81, 87G (as inserted by the Prospectus Regulations 2005 (SI 2005/1433)).

[635] For the possible application of the Misrepresentation Act 1967, see below, para.9–155.

[636] cf. *Argy Trading Development Co Ltd v Lapid Developments Ltd* [1977] 1 W.L.R. 444 at 461–462; *Limit (No.2) Ltd v Axa Versicherung AG* [2008] EWCA Civ 1231; [2008] 2 C.L.C. 673 at [26].

[637] (1864) 4 D.J. & S. 318.

[638] ibid. at 326, 330.

[639] [1977] 1 W.L.R. 199.

[640] ibid. at 211.

v Livesey,[641] but only on the ground that the agreement for financial provision had been embodied in a consent order made in matrimonial proceedings; and that parties seeking such an order were, by statute,[642] under a duty to make full and frank disclosure to the court which made the order. So far as common law liability for fraud and non-disclosure was concerned, *Wales v Wadham* was approved, though without any reference to *Traill v Baring*. It may be possible to reconcile these two decisions by saying that in *Traill v Baring* the first company had, before acceptance of its offer, not merely changed its mind but acted accordingly, while the wife in *Wales v Wadham* had not actually remarried when she accepted the husband's offer; or by saying that the wife's statement in the latter case was as to an intention so intrinsically likely to be changed that the husband should not have relied on the statement. Subject to these possible distinctions, it is submitted that the principle in *Traill v Baring* is to be preferred; for, in cases of this kind, what was originally a misrepresentation of intention becomes by the time of contracting one of fact, *viz.* as to the representor's state of mind at that time.[643] And there is no difficulty in specifying exactly what should be disclosed, so that the reason for the general rule against imposing a duty of disclosure does not apply.

(ii) *Statement literally true, but misleading*

A person is guilty of misrepresentation, though all the facts stated by him are true, if his statement is misleading as a whole because it does not refer to other facts affecting the weight of those stated. In *Notts Patent Brick and Tile Co v Butler*[644] a purchaser of land asked the vendor's solicitor whether the land was subject to restrictive covenants. The solicitor replied that he was not aware of any, but failed to add that this was because he had not troubled to read the relevant documents. The solicitor's reply, though literally true, amounted to a misrepresentation entitling the purchaser to rescind.

9–134

The duty of disclosure in cases of this kind is narrower than that which exists in contracts uberrimae fidei.[645] The maker of a statement which is literally true but on the whole misleading is required to disclose only such facts as affect the weight of those stated[646]; he need not disclose further facts merely because they might reasonably be regarded by the representee as material.[647]

(iii) *Custom*

In *Jones v Bowden*[648] pimento was sold after having been damaged by sea water. It was usual in the trade, when pimento had been so damaged, to declare this, but

9–135

---

[641] [1985] A.C. 424.

[642] Matrimonial Causes Act 1973, ss.23–25.

[643] See above, para.9–010.

[644] (1886) 16 Q.B.D. 778; cf. *R. v Kylsant* [1932] 1 K.B. 442; *Faruqi v English Real Estates* [1979] 1 W.L.R. 963; *The Lucy* [1983] 1 Lloyd's Rep. 188 (where relief was denied as the requirement of reliance was not satisfied: above, para.9–020); *Cemp Properties (UK) Ltd v Dentsply Research & Development Corp* [1991] 2 E.G.L.R. 197.

[645] See below, paras 9–136—9–143.

[646] See the common law position with regard to company prospectuses, as stated in *New Brunswick and Canada Ry v Muggeridge* (1860) 1 Dr. & Sm. 363 at 381; approved in *Central Ry of Venezuela v Kisch* (1867) L.R. 2. H.L. 99; cf. *Oakes v Turquand* (1867) L.R. 2 H.L. 325. For statutory duties of disclosure in such cases, see below, para.9–149.

[647] *Aaron's Reefs Ltd v Twiss* [1896] A.C. 273 at 287.

[648] (1813) 4 Taunt. 847.

the seller failed to make such a declaration. He was held liable in deceit as, in view of the custom, his silence amounted to misrepresentation.

(iv) *Contracts uberrimae fidei*

9–136　　There is a duty to disclose material facts in contracts uberrimae fidei (i.e. of "utmost good faith"[649]), in which one party is in a particularly strong position, and the other in a particularly weak one, to know the material facts.

9–137　　**Insurance.** "It has been for centuries in England the law in connection with insurance of all sorts, marine, fire, life, guarantee and every kind of policy, that, as the underwriter knows nothing and the man who comes to him to ask him to insure knows everything, it is the duty of the assured . . . to make a full disclosure to the underwriters, without being asked, of all the material circumstances".[650]

9–138　　**Materiality and reliance.** The assured must disclose all such facts as a prudent insurer would take into account in deciding whether or at what premium or on what conditions he would take the risk.[651] A fact may be material even though its disclosure would not necessarily have an effect on the decision whether to take the risk, or at what premium[652]; but as for misrepresentation generally[653] the non-disclosure must have induced the contract.[654] A policy of marine insurance can therefore be avoided if the assured conceals the real value of the cargo[655]; or if he fails to declare that it may be carried on deck (thus increasing the risk),[656] that the ship carrying the cargo had already been stranded,[657] or that she had been engaged in smuggling, so that those operating her faced criminal charges.[658] Similarly a policy of life insurance can be avoided if the assured fails to disclose a medical condition material to the risk,[659] or the fact that a number of other insurance offices had declined proposals to insure his life[660]; a policy of insurance on jewellery can be avoided if the insurer is not told that jewellery had on several occasions been stolen from the assured[661]; and a home contents insurance policy can be avoided by reason of the insured's failure to disclose that he had been

---

[649] Marine Insurance Act 1906, s.17.

[650] *Rozanes v Bowen* (1928) 32 Ll.L.R. 98 at 102.

[651] *Lambert v Co-operative Ins Society Ltd* [1975] 2 Lloyd's Rep. 485; Marine Insurance Act 1906, s.18(2); *Woolcott v Sun Alliance, etc., Ins Ltd* [1978] 1 W.L.R. 493 at 498; *Woolcott v Excess Ins Co Ltd* [1979] 1 Lloyd's Rep. 231; [1979] 2 Lloyd's Rep. 210; *Container Transport International v Oceanus Mutual, etc., Association* [1984] 1 Lloyd's Rep. 476, disapproved on the point stated at fn.654 in *Pan Atlantic Ins Co Ltd v Pine Top Ins Co Ltd* [1995] 1 A.C. 501. For criticism and proposals for reform, see Law Com. No.104, paras 3.17–3.19, 4.43–4.53; *Pan Atlantic* case, above, at 528.

[652] *Pan Atlantic Ins Co Ltd v Pine Top Ins Co* [1995] 1 A.C. 501; *Aneco Reinsurance Underwriting v Johnson & Higgins* [1998] 1 Lloyd's Rep. 565 at 589.

[653] See above, para.9–016.

[654] [1995] 1 A.C. 501 at 517–518, 549, 570, 571; *Aneco Reinsurance Underwriting v Johnson & Higgins* [1998] 1 Lloyd's Rep. 565 at 589; *St Paul Fire & Marine Ins Co (UK) Ltd v McConnell Dowell Contractors Ltd* [1995] 2 Lloyd's Rep. 116.

[655] *Ionides v Pender* (1874) L.R. 9 Q.B. 531.

[656] *Hood v West End Motor Car Packing Co* [1917] 2 K.B. 38.

[657] *Proudfoot v Montefiore* (1867) L.R. 2 Q.B. 511.

[658] *Inversiones Mannia SA v Sphere Drake Ins Co Plc* [1989] 1 Lloyd's Rep. 69.

[659] *Winter v Irish Life Assurance Plc* [1995] 2 Lloyd's Rep. 274.

[660] *London Assurance v Mansel* (1879) 11 Ch.D. 363.

[661] *Rozanes v Bowen* (1928) 32 Ll.L.R. 98; cf. *Pan Atlantic* case, above, fn.652 and *Marc Rich & Co AG v Portman* [1997] 1 Lloyd's Rep. 225.

convicted of obtaining money by deception.[662] A policy can also be avoided on the ground of non-disclosure of facts material to the risk[663] by the insurer,[664] e.g. if he accepts a premium for insuring a voyage which he knows to have been safely accomplished.

Facts which need not be disclosed. The assured need not disclose facts   9–139 which the insurer himself knows or ought to know,[665] facts which diminish the risk, facts which both parties have equal means of knowing, "general topics of speculation",[666] and facts the disclosure of which is waived by the insurer.[667]

Basis of the contract clauses. The duty of disclosure gives a generous   9–140 measure of protection to insurers, but they often add that the accuracy and completeness of the answers given by the assured to questions in the proposal form shall be the basis of the contract.[668] The result is that quite unimportant misstatements or failure to disclose some quite trivial matter can vitiate a policy.[669] This position has drawn strong judicial criticism[670] and the Law Commission has recommended that basis of the contract clauses should cease to have this effect.[671] Meanwhile, the courts do their best to protect policyholders by construing the basis of the contract clauses strictly against insurers.[672]

Insurance distinguished from suretyship or guarantee. A contract of   9–141 insurance must be distinguished from a contract of suretyship or guarantee, since it is disputed whether the latter type of contract is uberrimae fidei.[673]

A promise to pay another person's debt if he fails to pay it is normally a contract of guarantee, but it is possible to insure against non-payment of a debt, or against some other breach of contract. In *Seaton v Heath*[674] A guaranteed a loan of £15,000 made by B to X. B then obtained a promise from C "in consideration of

---

[662] *Galloway v Guardian Royal Exchange (UK) Ltd* [1999] L.R.L.R. 209.

[663] *Banque Keyser Ullmann SA v Skandia (UK) Ins Co Ltd* [1991] 2 A.C. 249.

[664] *Carter v Boehm* (1766) 3 Burr. 1905 at 1909 and Marine Insurance Act 1906, s.17 ("either party"). No such duty is owed to, or by, an assignee of the policy: *The Good Luck* [1989] 2 Lloyd's Rep. 238 (reversed on other grounds [1992] 1 A.C. 233) or by a third party entitled to the benefit of the policy under the principle stated at para.14–130, below: *Sumitomo Bank Ltd v Banque Bruxelles Lambert SA* [1997] 1 Lloyd's Rep. 487.

[665] Not facts coming to the notice of his agent while acting in fraud of the principal: *PCW Syndicates v PCW Reinsurers* [1996] 1 W.L.R. 1136.

[666] *Carter v Boehm*, above, at 1910.

[667] *Roberts v Plaisted* [1989] 2 Lloyd's Rep. 341; "waiver" here refers to failure to enquire into circumstances material to the risk when a reasonable insurer would make such enquiries: see *Container Transport International v Oceanus Mutual, etc., Association* [1984] 1 Lloyd's Rep. 476; *Marc Rich & Co AG v Portman* [1996] 1 Lloyd's Rep. 430 at 442, affirmed [1997] 1 Lloyd's Rep. 225; *WISE Ltd (Underwriting Agency) Ltd v Grupo Nacional Provincial SA* [2004] EWCA Civ 962; [2004] 2 Lloyd's Rep 483.

[668] Hasson (1971) 34 M.L.R. 29.

[669] *Dawsons Ltd v Bonnin* [1922] 2 A.C. 413.

[670] *Joel v Law Union & Crown Ins Co* [1908] 2 K.B. 863 at 885; cf. *West v National Motor & Accident Ins Union Ltd* [1955] 1 W.L.R. 343 at 348; *The Star Sea* [2001] UKHL 1; [2003] 1 A.C. 469 at [50], quoted below, at fn.712.

[671] Law Com. No.104, para.7.4; cf. Law Reform Committee Fifth Report, Cmnd.63 (1957). Contracts of insurance are excepted from the relevant provisions of Unfair Contract Terms Act 1977: above, para.7–089. They may be open to challenge under Unfair Terms in Consumer Contracts Regulations 1999 (see above, para.7–098), but the Regulations are confined to consumer contracts.

[672] *Joel's* case, above, fn.670.

[673] See below, para.9–144.

[674] [1899] 1 Q.B. 782, reversed on another ground [1900] A.C. 135.

a premium of 50s. per cent" to "guarantee" A's solvency. The contract between B and C was held to be one of insurance. But in *Trade Indemnity Co Ltd v Workington Harbour Board*[675] A agreed to build a dock for B. C gave B a "guarantee" of £50,000 that A would complete the work, and it was held that this was not a contract of insurance.

The distinction between the two types of contract is that a guarantor is usually provided by the debtor,[676] while an insurer is usually sought out by the creditor. Thus the creditworthiness of the debtor is a matter about which a guarantor is likely to know at least as much as the creditor[677]; while an insurer is likely to know less about it than the creditor, having probably had no previous dealings with the debtor. Hence a higher duty of disclosure is owed to the insurer.[678]

9–142   Source of duty of disclosure in insurance contracts. In *William Pickersgill & Sons Ltd v London, etc., Insurance Co*[679] Hamilton J. said:

> "The rule imposing an obligation to disclose upon the intending assured does not rest upon a general principle of common law, but arises out of an implied condition, contained in the contract itself, precedent to the liability of the underwriter to pay".

One possible interpretation of this dictum is that, in contracts of insurance, there is a *contractual* duty of disclosure based on an implied term in the contract. This duty, being mutual,[680] would rest on the underwriter no less than on the insured; and failure to perform it would amount to a breach of contract, giving rise to a right, not only to terminate the contract, but also to recover damages for its breach. But the prevailing view is that the duty "derives from a rule of law, not from the parties' agreement",[681] and that the "condition precedent" to which it gives rise is contingent only and not promissory.[682] That is, the party who fails to make the disclosure required of him cannot enforce the contract, but is not, merely on account of the non–disclosure, liable in damages for breach of the contract.[683] Nor does the non-disclosure give the other party a right to claim damages in tort for negligence, or fraud.[684] It has been said that the effect of allowing such a claim would be to undermine the general common law principle that there is no duty of disclosure in the negotiations leading to the conclusion of a contract.[685] That

---

[675] [1937] A.C. 1; *Trafalgar House Construction (Regions) Ltd v General Surety & Guarantee Co Ltd* [1996] A.C. 199.

[676] *The Zuhal K* [1987] 1 Lloyd's Rep. 151 at 155.

[677] e.g. where the debtor is a company and the guarantor is one of its directors.

[678] cf. *Re Denton's Estate* [1904] 2 Ch. 178 at 188.

[679] [1912] 3 K.B. 614 at 621.

[680] See above, para.9–137.

[681] *The Star Sea* [2001] UKHL 1; [2003] 1 A.C. 469 at [46]; *Banque Keyser Ullmann SA v Skandia (UK) Ins Ltd* [1988] 2 Lloyd's Rep. 513 at 549, affirmed [1991] 2 A.C. 249; *The Grecia Express* [2002] 2 Lloyd's Rep. 88.

[682] See above, para.2–104 for the distinction between contingent and promissory conditions.

[683] *Banque Keyser Ullmann SA v Skandia (UK) Ins Co Ltd* [1990] 1 Q.B. 665 at 779–781, approved on this point [1991] 2 A.C. 249 at 288, where the case was affirmed on other grounds; cf. *The Good Luck* [1990] 1 Q.B. 818 at 888, reversed on other grounds [1992] 1 A.C. 233; Clarke [1989] C.L.J. 363; Davenport [1989] L.M.C.L.Q. 251; *Agnew v Landsförsäkringsbolagens AB* [2001] A.C. 223 at 246.

[684] *HIH Casualty & General Ins v Chase Manhattan Bank* [2003] UKHL 6; [2003] 2 Lloyd's Rep. 61 at [23], [75]: see below, fn.723.

[685] *Banque Keyser Ullmann SA v Skandia (UK) Ins Co Ltd* [1990] 1 Q.B. 665 at 801–802, as to which see above, fn.683.

general principle is attenuated in insurance contracts only to the extent that the law provides a remedy by way of rescission for non-disclosure of material facts.

Family arrangements. There is a duty to make full disclosure in certain family arrangements, e.g. in agreements between members of a family for settling disputes as to the family property. Thus parties to an agreement for the division of the property of a deceased member of the family must disclose to each other all facts known to them which bear on their rights to the estate, or on its value.[686]   9–143

(v) *Contracts in which there is a limited duty of disclosure*

Suretyship or guarantee. Contracts of suretyship or guarantee are sometimes said to be uberrimae fidei[687]; but the better view is that they do not fall into this category.[688] The creditor is bound only to disclose unusual circumstances, which the surety would not commonly expect.[689] An employer who takes a fidelity bond, by which the honesty of one of his employees is guaranteed, is under a somewhat higher duty: he must disclose to the surety any acts of dishonesty by the employee of which he has notice[690]; even if such acts occur after the execution of the bond.   9–144

Sale of land. Contracts for the sale of land are not uberrimae fidei,[691] so that there is in general no duty on a seller of land to disclose latent physical defects, but there may be a duty to disclose *unusual* defects of title which a reasonably prudent purchaser could not be expected to discover.[692]   9–145

Compromises & releases. It has been said that parties negotiating a contractual compromise of a disputed claim do not in general owe each other duties to disclose information relating to the claim,[693] but there are dicta which may suggest otherwise.[694] In the context of a release, failure by one party to disclose   9–146

---

[686] *Gordon v Gordon* (1817) 3 Swan.400; *Greenwood v Greenwood* (1863) 1 D.J. & S. 28; cf. *Tennent v Tennents* (1870) L.R. 2 Sc. & Div. 6. Contrast *Wales v Wadham* [1977] 1 W.L.R. 199 at 218; above, para.9–133, where the rule did not apply as the parties bargained at arm's length, and *Crowden v Aldridge* [1993] 1 W.L.R. 433 at 442–443, where no dispute between members of a family existed before execution of the document in question.

[687] *Railton v Matthews* (1844) 10 Cl. & F. 934, 943; *March Cabaret Club & Casino Ltd v London Assurance* [1975] 1 Lloyd's Rep. 169 at 175; *Wales v Wadham* [1977] 1 W.L.R. 199 at 214.

[688] *Davies v London & Provincial Marine Ins Co* (1878) 8 Ch.D. 469 at 475; *LGOC Ltd v Holloway* [1912] 2 K.B. 72 at 81, 83; *Royal Bank of Scotland v Edridge (No.2)* [2001] UKHL 44; [2002] 2 A.C. 773 at [114]. The point was left open in *Mackenzie v Royal Bank of Canada* [1934] A.C. 468 at 475 and in *Trade Indemnity Co Ltd v Workington Harbour & Dock Board* [1937] A.C. 1 at 18.

[689] *National Provincial Bank of England Ltd v Glanusk* [1913] 3 K.B. 335 at 338; *Cooper v National Provincial Bank* [1946] K.B. 1 at 7; *Levett v Barclays Bank Plc* [1995] 1 W.L.R. 1260; *Estate of Imorette Palmer v Cornerstone Investments and Finance Co* [2007] UKPC 49 at [40]–[41]; *North Shore Ventures Ltd v Anstead Holdings Inc* [2011] EWCA Civ 230.

[690] *LGOC Ltd v Holloway*, above.

[691] *Safehaven Investments Ltd v Springbok Ltd* (1996) 71 P. & C.R. 59 at 66.

[692] See above, para.9–129.

[693] Cartwright, *Misrepresentation, Mistake and Non-Disclosure*, (2nd edn) at 17.26, citing *Turner v Green* and see *Silver Queen Maritime Ltd v Persia Petroleum Services Ltd* [2010] EWHC 2867 (QB) at [130].

[694] *Colchester BC v Smith* [1992] Ch.421 at 435 ("without concealment of essential information"); cf. *Miles v New Zealand Alford Estate Co* (1886) 32 Ch.D. 267 at 284.

that the other party had or might have a claim of which the latter party was ignorant may be a ground on which the latter party can set the release aside.[695]

9–147   **Exemption clauses.** In some cases failure to disclose or draw attention to the terms of a contractual document may (without affecting the validity of the contract as a whole) deprive one party of the benefit of an exemption clause.[696]

(vi) *Fiduciary relationship*

9–148   A duty of disclosure may arise from the relationship of the parties, but "will not lightly be implied, in particular in commercial contracts negotiated at arms' length between parties with comparable bargaining power, and all the more so where the contract in question sets out in detail the extent . . . of a party's disclosure obligations".[697] There is clearly such a duty where the relationship is one to which the equitable doctrine of undue influence applies.[698] The duty in such cases is indeed not discharged by mere disclosure; more stringent conditions must be satisfied before a person who is under the duty can take the benefit of a transaction with the person to whom the duty is owed.[699] But there are other cases in which a person is under a fiduciary duty which he can discharge merely by making full disclosure. This is the position between principal and agent,[700] partners,[701] and between a company and its promoters.[702] A company promoter owes no such common law duty to persons who subscribe for shares in the company on the faith of a prospectus or listing particulars issued by him,[703] but he does owe them an extensive statutory duty of disclosure.[704]

(vii) *Legislation*

9–149   Under the Financial Services and Markets Act 2000, extensive duties of disclosure are imposed on persons who apply for an official listing of securities on the Stock Exchange, and on those who issue a prospectus inviting subscriptions for unlisted securities,[705] and in relation to information which is required in order to comply with the Transparency Obligations Directive.[706]

---

[695] *Bank of Credit and Commerce International SA v Ali* [2001] UKHL 8; [2002] 1 A.C. 251; above, para.3–035.

[696] See above, para.7–040.

[697] *Ross River Ltd v Cambridge City Football Club Ltd* [2007] EWHC 2115 (Ch); [2008] 1 All E.R. 1004 at [197] (Briggs J. preferred to find that there was an obligation of good faith, falling short of a "strict duty of disclosure").

[698] See below, para.10–012 et seq.

[699] See below, para.10–026.

[700] e.g. *Armstrong v Jackson* [1917] 2 K.B. 822.

[701] Lindley and Banks, *Partnership* (18th edn), para.16–01, which duty extends to persons negotiating their entry into partnership: *Simms v Conlon* [2006] EWCA Civ 1749; [2008] 1 W.L.R. 484 at [128].

[702] Gower, *Modern Company Law* (8th edn), paras.5–2-5–3; *Erlanger v New Sombrero Phosphate Co* (1879) 3 App.Cas. 1218.

[703] *Heyman v European Central Ry* (1868) L.R. 7 Eq. 154.

[704] Below, para.9–149. Breach of this duty gives rise to a right to damages against those responsible for the prospectus, but not to a right to rescind an allotment of shares: *Re South of England Natural Gas Co* [1911] 1 Ch. 573. This position seems to be unaffected by Financial Services and Markets Act 2000, s.90, as amended by Prospectus Regulations 2005 (SI 2005/1433).

[705] ss.80, 87A-B, as inserted by Prospectus Regulations 2005 (SI 2005/1433).

[706] 2004/109/EC.; s.90A, as amended by Financial Services and Markets Act 2000 (Liability of Issuers) Regulations 2010 (SI 2010/1192).

Parties to matrimonial proceedings who seek a consent order from the Family Division for the settlement of their financial and proprietary arrangements must make full and frank disclosure of relevant circumstances to the court that is asked to make the order.[707]

(viii) *Duty to clarify legal relationship*

A duty of disclosure may arise where A sees B acting in reliance on a view of a legal relationship between them which is to A's knowledge false.[708] In the authorities which support the existence of such a duty, the effect of its breach has simply been to give rise to an estoppel[709]; but it is conceivable that such a breach might also invalidate a contract. **9–150**

(ix) *Duty of disclosure in performance of contract*

So far, our main concern has been with the exceptional cases in which a duty of disclosure may exist in the negotiations leading to the conclusion of a contract. The further question is whether a duty of disclosure can arise in the *performance* of an already concluded contract. At common law, there is no general duty of disclosure in cases of this kind: e.g. a bank which has entered into a contract to provide banking services is under no duty to disclose to its customer (A) that it has made later contracts with other customers for the provision of substantially similar services on terms more favourable to the customers than those of its contract with A.[710–711] But there are many situations (which may be regarded as exceptions to the general principle) in which such a duty of disclosure does arise.[712] For example, an employee may be bound to disclose breaches of duty of fellow-employees who have defrauded the employer[713]; though he is not normally bound to disclose his own breaches of duty,[714] let alone his intention to commit breaches of duty in the future.[715] A contracting party may, however, be under a duty to disclose his own breaches of the contract on the ground that they may lead to danger of physical injury to persons or to property.[716] A professional person may be under certain duties of disclosure towards the person who has engaged his services; but again these duties arise out of the contract (or relationship giving rise **9–151**

---

[707] *Jenkins v Livesey* [1985] A.C. 424.

[708] *Bell v Marsh* [1903] 1 Ch. 528 at 541; *Spiro v Lintern* [1973] 1 W.L.R. 1002 at 1010–1011, quoted above, para.2–045; *The Henrik Sif* [1982] 1 Lloyd's Rep. 456; *The Stolt Loyalty* [1993] 2 Lloyd's Rep. 281 at 289 (affirmed [1995] 1 Lloyd's Rep. 599, without reference to this point); *ING Bank NV v Ros Roca* SA [2011] EWCA Civ 353 at [87]–[96]. Contrast *The Tatra* [1990] 2 Lloyd's Rep. 51 (where A had no such knowledge); *Rafsanjan Pistachio Producers Co-operative v Bank Leumi (UK) Plc* [1991] 1 Lloyd's Rep. 513 at 542.

[709] See below, para.9–156; cf. also the cases of "estoppel by convention" discussed at para.3–094, above.

[710–711] *Suriya & Douglas v Midland Bank Plc* [1999] 1 All E.R. (Comm) 612.

[712] *The Star Sea* [2001] UKHL 1; [2003] 1 A.C. 469 at [50].

[713] *Sybron Corp v Rochem Ltd* [1984] Ch. 112 at 126–127, 129; Kerr L.J. treated the case as one of "covering up and deliberately concealing": [1984] Ch. 112 at 130.

[714] *Bell v Lever Bros* [1932] A.C. 161; *Nottingham University v Fischel* [2000] I.C.R. 1462; *Lonmar Global Risks Ltd v West* [2010] EWHC 2878 (QB) at [150]–[152]; cf. *Fassihi v Item Software (UK) Ltd* [2004] EWCA Civ 1244; [2004] I.R.L.R. 928; *Brandeaux Advisers Ltd v Chadwick* [2010] EWHC 3241 (QB); [2011] I.R.L.R. 224 at [47] (fiduciary obligation to report).

[715] *Horcal v Gatland* [1984] I.R.L.R. 288; cf. *Balston v Headline Filters* [1990] F.S.R. 385.

[716] *The Zinnia* [1984] 2 Lloyd's Rep. 211 at 218.

to liability in tort[717]) between them: their performance is not a prerequisite for its creation. Sometimes, failure to perform a duty of disclosure imposed by one contract may vitiate a second contract between the same parties: thus in one case it was held that an employee's failure to perform his duty under his contract of employment to disclose frauds being perpetrated by his subordinates on his employers entitled the employers to rescind an arrangement with the employee under which he had obtained considerable benefits on "early retirement".[718] Similarly, it has been suggested that, where a bank lends money on a mortgage to one of its customers, it is under a duty "to proffer to her some adequate explanation of the nature and effect of the document which she had come to sign".[719]

(c) Effects of Non-disclosure

(i) *In general*

9–152   In discussing the effects of non-disclosure two preliminary distinctions must be drawn. The first relates to what may be called the nature of the non-disclosure; the second relates to the time when the facts which were not disclosed should have been disclosed.

9–153   **Nature of non-disclosure.** Cases of liability for non-disclosure can be divided into two kinds. First, there are cases in which no misrepresentation has been made in so many words, but one can be inferred from conduct or from the surrounding circumstances, e.g. where a representation is falsified by later events, or where a statement is literally true but misleading, or where disclosure is required by custom.[720] Secondly, there are cases of what may be called "pure" non-disclosure, in which no such inference can be drawn, but the law nevertheless gives a remedy for non-disclosure, e.g. in contracts of insurance, or by statute.[721]

In the first of the above groups of cases, non-disclosure can give rise to the same remedies as active misrepresentation, that is, to a right to rescind the contract (in the sense of setting it aside ab initio for all purposes[722]) and to a common law right to damages for deceit, or for negligence (but not for breach of the rescinded contract). The position is more complex in the second group of cases, i.e. in those of "pure" non-disclosure. We have seen that failure to perform the duty of disclosure in contracts uberrimae fidei gives rise to a right to rescind, but not to

---

[717] See the discussion of the extent of a surgeon's duty of disclosure before carrying out an operation: *Sidaway v Bethlehem Royal Hospital* [1985] A.C. 871; and the duty of a doctor carrying out a vasectomy to warn the patient that sterility might not be permanent: *Thake v Maurice* [1986] Q.B. 644. Cases in which solicitors acting both for mortgage lender and borrowers were held liable to the lender for failing to disclose facts coming to their notice in the course of the transaction fall into the present category: see, e.g., *Bristol & West Building Society v May, May & Merrimans* [1996] 2 All E.R. 801; *Mortgage Express Ltd v Bowerman* [1996] 2 All E.R. 836; contrast *National Home Loans Corp v Giffen Couch & Archer* [1997] 3 All E.R. 808 (where no duty of disclosure arose).
[718] *Sybron Corp v Rochem Ltd* [1984] Ch. 112; Honeyball [1983] C.L.J. 218.
[719] *Cornish v Midland Bank Plc* [1985] 3 All E.R. 513 at 523, where the bank was found to be guilty of active misrepresentation. Contrast *Barclays Bank Plc v Khaira, The Times*, December 19, 1991 (no such duty owed to a person who was not a customer of the bank).
[720] See above, paras 9–132—9–135.
[721] See above, paras 9–137, 9–149.
[722] See above, fn.398; the contract is voidable, not void: Marine Insurance Act 1906, s.17 ("may be avoided"); *The Grecia Express* [2002] 2 Lloyd's Rep. 88 at 127–128.

one to damages either for breach of contract, or for negligence, or fraud.[723] Conversely, breach of the statutory duty of disclosure imposed on persons issuing a company prospectus has been held to give rise to a right to damages, but not to one to rescind.[724] General statements about the effects of "pure" non-disclosure are best avoided: the effects depend on the purpose of the rule of law by which the duty of disclosure is imposed.

Pre- and post-contract non-disclosure. The remedy of rescission for non-disclosure, in the sense of setting the contract aside ab initio,[725] sometimes operates harshly: e.g. where this remedy is available to an insurer in respect of non-disclosure by the insured, which may be quite innocent. The courts have therefore mitigated the severity of the remedy by distinguishing between cases in which the non-disclosure occurred before, and induced the formation of, the contract, and those in which it occurred after the contract had been made and amounted to a breach of one of its terms.[726] Rescission ab initio (as for misrepresentation) is available (if at all[727]) only in cases of the former kind. Where the non-disclosure is post-contractual and amounts to a breach of the contract, the drastic effects of rescission ab initio would be "disproportionate" and "penal"[728]; and the injured party's remedies in respect of it depend on the rules relating to the effects of breach,[729] to be discussed later in this book.[730] These remedies are in one respect more extensive than those for pre-contractual non-disclosure: termination for breach does not deprive the injured party of the right to damages for breach of the contract.[731] On the other hand, while the effect of rescission for pre-contractual non-disclosure is to "wipe [the contract] out altogether",[732] with retrospective effect, termination for breach operates only with *prospective* effect[733]; and the remedy is, as a general rule,[734] available only in respect of a breach which causes serious prejudice to the injured party.[735] The rule that post-contractual non-disclosure has no retrospective effect is, however, subject to an exception in cases of fraud: if an insured person makes a fraudulent claim,[736] the insurer is entitled

9-154

---

[723] See above, para.9–142. Statements to the effect that a fraudulent non-disclosure may give rise to a claim in damages must be treated with care: see, e.g. *Simms v Conlon* [2006] EWCA Civ 1749; [2008] 1 W.L.R. 484 at [130]. Non-disclosure does not "as such" give rise to a claim for damages: *HIH Casualty & General Ins v Chase Manhattan Bank* [2003] UKHL 6; [2003] 2 Lloyd's Rep. 61 at [75]; but a fraudulent breach of the duty to disclose may also, in the circumstances, lead to a finding of fraudulent misrepresentation: "it cannot be easy to conceal material facts in the course of negotiating insurance contracts . . . without falsifying something which has been expressly or impliedly stated": [2003] 2 Lloyd's Rep. 61 at [71]; cf. *The Star Sea* [2001] UKHL 1; [2003] 1 A.C. 469 at [46]; Cartwright in Burrows & Peel (eds.), *Contract Formation and Parties*.
[724] See above, fn.704.
[725] See above, fn.722.
[726] See above, para.9–151.
[727] It may not be available even in such cases: see above, fn.725.
[728] *The Star Sea* [2001] UKHL 1; [2003] 1 A.C. 469 at [51].
[729] [2003] 1 A.C. 469 at [50], [52].
[730] See below, para.18–005 et seq.
[731] See below, para.18–015.
[732] *The Kanchenjunga* [1990] 1 Lloyd's Rep. 391 at 398; above, para.9–082.
[733] See below, para.18–011, *The Star Sea*, above, fn.728, at [50].
[734] See below, para.18–037 et seq. for exceptions.
[735] See below, para.18–025, *The Mercadian Continent* [2001] EWCA Civ 1275; [2001] 2 Lloyd's Rep. 563 at [14].
[736] i.e. one the *validity* of which depends on the false statement. The exception does not apply to false statements relating to other, and relatively minor, matters; e.g. in *The Mercadian Continent*, above, fn.735 it did not apply to a false statement affecting only the jurisdiction of the court called on to determine the validity of the claim, rather than that validity itself.

to reject not only that claim but also any lesser claim which the insured might honestly have made.[737] The exception has been explained on the ground that, if it did not exist, the insured would have nothing to lose (though he would incur the risk of a criminal penalty[738]) by putting forward a fraudulent claim.[739]

(ii) *Effects of Misrepresentation Act 1967*

9–155   The Misrepresentation Act repeatedly uses the expression "misrepresentation made". This refers primarily to active misrepresentation and not to "pure" non-disclosure,[740] as described above. The Act therefore does not impose liability for such non-disclosure where none existed before.[741] Nor does it affect any liability for, or defence based on, such non-disclosure which did exist before the Act. It follows that liability in damages for "pure" non-disclosure could not arise under s.2(1); that the court has no discretion in cases of such non-disclosure to award damages in lieu of rescission under s.2(2); and that a term whose sole effect was to exclude or restrict liability for such non-disclosure is not affected by s.3.

On the other hand, the distinction between cases of "pure" non-disclosure, and those in which a misrepresentation, though not made in so many words, can be inferred from conduct, probably applies for the purposes of the Act. It is submitted that the Act would apply to cases of the latter kind,[742] e.g. where a representation had been made by conduct,[743] and where a representation had been made which was literally true but misleading because it was obscure or only told part of the truth.[744] It seems probable that the Act would also apply where the representation was true when it was made but was falsified by later events.[745] Section 2(1) in particular might be thought to apply to such a case as it requires the representor to show that he believed "up to the time the contract was made that the facts represented were true". It could be said that there was no "misrepresentation made" if the facts originally stated were then true; but the answer to this point may be that the representation can be treated as a continuing one and that it would become a *mis*representation when the falsifying event occurred. Section 3 could also apply to a term which by general words excluded liability for all non-disclosure, since such words could cover cases in which a representation was inferred from conduct or the surrounding circumstances. In one case[746] a term containing such general words was assumed to be covered by s.3 but was held to satisfy the requirement of reasonableness. The question whether the section

---

[737] *The Star Sea*, above, fn.728, at [62]; *Axa General Ins v Gottlieb* [2005] EWCA Civ 112; [2005] 1 C.L.C. 62 (interim payments already made are also recoverable).
[738] cf. above, para.9–089.
[739] *The Star Sea*, above, fn.728, at [62].
[740] *HIH Casualty & General Ins v Chase Manhattan Bank* [2001] EWCA Civ 1250; [2001] 2 Lloyd's Rep. 483 at [51] (affirmed in part, [2003] UKHL 6; [2003] 2 Lloyd's Rep. 61). The 1967 Act has not altered the common law meaning of "misrepresentation": *André & Cie SA v Ets Michel Blanc & Fils* [1979] 2 Lloyd's Rep. 427 at 435.
[741] *Banque Keyser Ullmann SA v Skandia (UK) Ins Co Ltd* [1990] 1 Q.B. 665 at 789–790, affirmed [1991] 2 A.C. 249; Cartwright in Burrows & Peel (eds.), *Contract Formation and Parties*.
[742] See Hudson 85 L.Q.R. 524.
[743] See above, para.9–128.
[744] See above, para.9–134.
[745] See above, para.9–132.
[746] *National Westminster Bank v Utrecht-American Finance Co* [2001] EWCA Civ 658; [2001] 3 All ER 733 at [59].

would apply to a term excluding liability only for "pure" non–disclosure was not discussed.

7. MISREPRESENTATION AND ESTOPPEL

Estoppel as defence. Under the doctrine of estoppel by representation,[747] a   9–156
person who makes a precise and unambiguous[748] representation[749] of fact[750] may
be prevented from denying the truth of the statement if the person to whom it was
made was intended to act on it, and did act on it to his detriment.[751] It is generally
said that the doctrine does not give rise to a cause of action[752] but only to a
defence. Thus if A agrees to let a house to B, representing that the drains are
sound when they are not, B cannot rely on the doctrine of estoppel to found a
claim for damages against A.[753] But the doctrine could provide B with a defence:
e.g. if A, immediately after the execution of the lease, brought an action for breach
of covenant to repair.[754] Such a defence would be available even though B had
affirmed (and not rescinded) the lease.

Estoppel to remove a defence. In addition to providing a defence to the   9–157
representee, estoppel may remove one that would otherwise be available to the
representor. Thus it may help a claimant no less than a defendant.[755] In *Burrowes
v Lock*[756] a beneficiary under a trust fund proposed to assign his share for value
to a prospective lender, who, before advancing any money, asked the trustee
whether the beneficiary had previously encumbered his share. The trustee replied
that there was no encumbrance, having forgotten that 10 years earlier the beneficiary had in fact encumbered his share. It was held that the trustee was estopped
from denying the truth of his statement. Thus he was liable to pay the assigned
share to the assignee, free from the earlier encumbrance. The assignee here had an
independent cause of action against the trustee based on the assignment; and the
trustee was, by his representation, deprived of the defence that he was already
bound to pay part of the fund to the previous encumbrancer. Similarly, a warehouseman may make a contractual promise to deliver goods out of his warehouse;
and if the promise is coupled with an untrue statement about the goods (e.g. that
they are in good condition, or in the warehouse, when they are not), he may be

---

[747] In this chapter our only concern is with this kind of estoppel. Estoppel by negligence (or
acquiescence) is beyond the scope of this book. For the distinction, see *Moorgate Mercantile Co v
Twitchings* [1977] A.C. 890. For promissory estoppel, estoppel by convention and proprietary estoppel,
see above, paras 3–076—3–099, 3–118—3–152.

[748] See above, para.3–081.

[749] Non–disclosure or inaction will not normally suffice: see above para.3–082.

[750] As distinct from one of law: see *Territorial & Auxiliary Forces Association v Nichols* [1949] 1 K.B.
35; *The Argo Hellas* [1984] 1 Lloyd's Rep. 296 at 304; (but see above, para.9–013); and from a
representation as to the future (or a promise): see above, paras 3–092, 9–009.

[751] See above, para.3–090.

[752] *Low v Bouverie* [1891] 3 Ch. 82; *The Anemone* [1987] 1 Lloyd's Rep. 546 at 557.

[753] Of course, there might be a claim for damages under one of the five heads discussed at paras
9–028—9–057, above.

[754] cf. *Oades v Spafford* [1949] 1 K.B. 74.

[755] e.g. *Cotterell v Leeds Day* [2001] W.T.L.R. 435 (estoppel depriving defendant of defence that
claim was time-barred); *Shah v Shah* [2001] EWCA Civ 537; [2002] Q.B. 35 at [31] (defendant
estopped from relying on fact that witness to a deed had not signed in his presence); *Aker Oil & Gas
Technology UK Plc v Sovereign Corporate Ltd* [2002] C.L.C. 557; Jackson 81 L.Q.R. 223; cf. above,
para.3–089.

[756] (1805) 10 Ves. 470, as explained in *Low v Bouverie*, above.

estopped from denying the truth of the statement.[757] The cause of action is based on the contractual promise, and the effect of the estoppel is simply to remove a defence.[758] And a person who has entered into a voidable contract may indicate that he is not going to exercise his power to avoid it. The effect of such a representation will be that he is bound by the contract without any power of avoidance[759]; and this result may be explained on the ground of either affirmation or estoppel. If the second explanation is adopted, it is again not the estoppel, but the contract, which constitutes the cause of action: the effect of the estoppel is simply to remove the power of avoidance.

---

[757] See *Coventry Shepherd & Co v GE Ry* (1883) 11 Q.B.D. 76; cf. *Alicia Hosiery Ltd v Brown Shipley & Co Ltd* [1970] 1 Q.B. 195, 206; *Griswold v Haven*, 25 N.Y. 595 (1862).

[758] e.g. *European Asian Bank v Punjab & Sind Bank* [1983] 2 All E.R. 508; *The Uhenbels* [1986] 2 Lloyd's Rep. 294 at 300.

[759] *Janred Properties Ltd v Ente Nazionale Italiano per il Turismo* [1989] 2 All E.R. 444.

CHAPTER TEN

DURESS, UNDUE INFLUENCE AND UNCONSCIONABLE BARGAINS[1]

The consent of a contracting party may have been obtained by some form of pressure which the law regards as improper. The victim of such pressure may be entitled to relief under the common law of duress, and under the equitable rules of undue influence. In some circumstances he may be protected against an unconscionable bargain. He is also protected by certain special statutory provisions. **10–001**

1. DURESS

(a) In General

A contract is voidable[2] at common law if it was made under duress.[3] At one time the common law concept of duress was a very narrow one. It was restricted to actual or threatened physical violence to the person. This view was open to the objection that it failed to give due weight to the coercive effect of other illegitimate conduct or threats.[4] It was therefore rejected in *The Siboen and the Sibotre*[5] by Kerr **10–002**

---

[1] See the comment in Ch.9, fn.1 in relation to The Unfair Commercial Practices Directive which is equally applicable to this chapter.

[2] In *Barton v Armstrong* [1976] A.C. 104 certain deeds were declared "void" for duress; cf. Lanham 29 M.L.R. 615. But the general view is that a contract procured by duress is only voidable: *Pao On v Lau Yiu Long* [1980] A.C. 614 at 634; *The Universe Sentinel* [1983] 1 A.C. 366 at 383, 400; *The Evia Luck (No.2)* [1992] 2 A.C. 152 at 168.

[3] For the effect of duress by a third party, see below, para.10–035 et seq.

[4] Equity's solution was to set aside the contract on the grounds of undue influence. Many of the cases in which it did so would, and should, now be regarded as cases of duress: see below, para. 10–014.

[5] [1976] 1 Lloyd's Rep. 293. Beatson 92 L.Q.R. 496.

J. and his views have been accepted in later cases.[6] The question is no longer what was threatened, but whether the threat amounts to a form of illegitimate pressure.[7] A threat may be illegitimate either because what is threatened is a legal wrong,[8] or because the threat itself is wrongful (as in the case of the blackmailer's threat to disclose his victim's conduct to third parties[9]), or because it is contrary to public policy,[10] or because it amounts to "unconscionable conduct".[11] Whether illegitimate pressure actually gives rise to duress must then be considered by reference to its causal effect in each case. It has been said that it must have brought about a "coercion of the will, which vitiates consent".[12] If this is interpreted to mean the absence of consent, it is open to criticism.[13] In cases of duress, it is not that consent is negatived, but that it has been improperly obtained.[14]

In practice, the cases divide into three categories of duress: duress of the person, duress of goods and "economic duress". These categories are relevant not only for ease of exposition, but also because the requirements may vary between them; in particular, the necessary causal link may differ depending upon the type of illegitimate pressure involved.

The burden of proving that a contract was procured by duress falls generally on the party seeking relief,[15] but it seems that it may be reversed in cases of duress of the person.[16]

(b) Duress of the Person

10–003   Duress of the person involves actual or threatened physical violence, or unlawful constraint.[17] It will normally be directed at the person of the contracting party,

---

[6] *The Atlantic Baron* [1979] Q.B. 705; *Pao On v Lau Yiu Long* [1980] A.C. 614; *The Evia Luck (No.2)* [1992] 2 A.C. 152 at 165.

[7] The terminology of a "threat" is employed because most of the cases involve a threat of future conduct, but the illegitimate pressure may be based on actual conduct, albeit in such cases it is probably the implicit threat of the same conduct in the future which is material: *Borrelli v Ting* [2010] UKPC 21; [2010] Bus. L.R. 1718, where the Privy Council laid stress on the actual conduct of the defendant in obstructing the liquidators of a company, but the pressure lay in the implicit threat to maintain that obstruction.

[8] Hence a threat merely to exercise one's rights under a contract is not illegitimate: *The Olib* [1991] 2 Lloyd's Rep. 108, but see text to fn.33.

[9] *Thorne v Motor Trade Association* [1937] A.C. 797 at 806; *The Universe Sentinel* [1983] 1 A.C. 366 at 401.

[10] *The Evia Luck (No.2)* [1990] 1 Lloyd's Rep. 319 at 329, affirmed [1992] 2 A.C. 152 (where the illegitimacy of the threat was no longer in dispute); cf. *The Evia Luck* [1986] 2 Lloyd's Rep. 165 at 178.

[11] *Borrelli v Ting* [2010] UKPC 21; [2010] Bus. L.R. 1718.

[12] *Pao On v Lau Yiu Long* [1980] A.C. 614 at 636; cf. *The Atlantic Baron* [1979] Q.B. 705; *The Proodos C* [1980] 2 Lloyd's Rep. 390 at 393; Coote [1980] C.L.J. 40; *Re T* [1993] Fam. 95 at 115–116.

[13] Atiyah 98 L.Q.R. 197; Beatson, *The Use and Abuse of Unjust Enrichment* at 113 et seq.; *Crescendo Management Pty Ltd v Westpac Banking Corp* (1989–1990) 19 N.S.W.L.R. 40; *The Evia Luck (No.2)* [1992] 2 A.C. 152, 166; cf. *Lynch v DPP of Northern Ireland* [1975] A.C. 653.

[14] *The Universe Sentinel* [1983] 1 A.C. 366 at 384, 400; *Huyton SA v Peter Cremer GmbH* [1999] 1 Lloyd's Rep. 620 at 638 (will "deflected"); [1999] 1 Lloyd's Rep. 620 at 642.

[15] *Huyton SA v Peter Cremer GmbH* [1999] 1 Lloyd's Rep. 620 at 639.

[16] *Barton v Armstrong* [1976] A.C. 104.

[17] *Cumming v Ince* (1847) 11 Q.B. 112 at 120; the violence threatened had to be unlawful: *Biffin v Bignell* (1862) 7 H. & N. 877; *Smith v Monteith* (1844) 13 M. & W. 427. cf. *Latter v Bradell* (1880) 50 L.J.C.P. 166; (1881) 50 L.J.Q.B. 448. It may extend to the threat of requiring conduct contrary to one party's religious belief: *Halpern v Halpern* [2006] EWHC 603 (Comm); [2006] 2 Lloyd's Rep. 83 at [87], appeal allowed in part [2007] EWCA Civ 291; [2008] Q.B. 195.

but it also includes threats directed at employees for whom he is responsible.[18] In *Barton v Armstrong*,[19] the Privy Council drew an analogy with fraudulent misrepresentation and held that it is not necessary to show that the threat was the sole inducement of the contract, or that it would not have been entered "but for" the threat.[20] It is enough that it was *a* factor and it seems that, once the threat has been established, the burden is on the defendant to prove that it "contributed nothing" to the decision to enter the contract.[21]

(c) Duress of Goods

The view that unlawful violence to the person was necessary to constitute duress had led in a number of nineteenth-century cases to the conclusion that a contract could not be invalidated by "duress of goods". This meant that an agreement to pay money for the release of goods unlawfully detained, or to prevent their unlawful seizure, was valid.[22] But it had also been held that money which had actually been paid for such a purpose could be recovered back.[23] The authorities now support the view that the "duress of goods" cases are governed by the modern, flexible, test of duress, so that the question in each case is whether there has in fact been illegitimate pressure with the necessary causal effect and that this test governs both the validity of the contract and the right to recover back money paid under it.[24] Duress of goods may now be seen as a particular instance of the broader concept of economic duress,[25] so that the test is the same for both. It is considered in the next paragraph.   **10–004**

(d) Economic Duress

In *The Evia Luck*[26] Lord Goff held that: **10–005**

> "it is now accepted[27] that economic pressure may be sufficient to amount to duress . . . provided at least that the economic pressure may be characterised as illegitimate and has constituted a significant cause inducing the [claimant] to enter into the relevant contract."[28]

While not confined to one particular type of economic pressure, the most common instance of economic duress is the threat by one party to break a contract unless

---

[18] cf. *Gulf Azov Shipping Co Ltd v Idisi* [2001] 1 Lloyd's Rep. 727.

[19] [1976] A.C. 104.

[20] See above, para.9–020.

[21] [1976] A.C. 104 at 120.

[22] *Skeate v Beale* (1841) 11 A. & E. 983.

[23] *Astley v Reynolds* (1731) 2 Str. 915; *Maskell v Horner* [1915] 3 K.B. 106; cf. Beatson [1974] C.L.J. 97, *The Use and Abuse of Unjust Enrichment*, Ch.5, suggesting that the cases of valid agreements should be explained as compromises (above, paras 3–036—3–038) or on similar grounds.

[24] *The Universe Sentinel* [1983] 1 A.C. 366; cf. *The Atlantic Baron* [1979] Q.B. 705 (where the claim there failed on the ground of affirmation); *The Alev* [1989] 1 Lloyd's Rep. 138.

[25] See: *The Alev* [1989] 1 Lloyd's Rep. 138; *The Olib* [1991] 2 Lloyd's Rep. 108; *Alf Vaughan & Co Ltd v Royscot Trust Ltd* [1999] 1 All E.R. (Comm) 856.

[26] [1992] 2 A.C. 152 at 165.

[27] Primarily on the basis of the earlier decisions in: *The Siboen and the Sibotre* [1976] 1 Lloyd's Rep. 293; *The Atlantic Baron* [1979] Q.B. 705; *Pao On v Lau Yiu Long* [1980] A.C. 614.

[28] See also: *The Universe Sentinel* [1983] 1 A.C. 366 at 400; *R. v HM Attorney General for England and Wales* [2003] UKPC 22; [2003] E.M.L.R. 24 at [15].

the other party agrees to its variation, or compromise.[29] Such a variation or compromise may be unenforceable for want of consideration, but recent developments mean that is less likely,[30] and the question then is whether the varied contract, or compromise, is voidable for duress.

10–006   **Illegitimate pressure and causation.** The aim of the courts is to distinguish between agreements which are the result of mere "commercial pressure",[31] and those which are the consequence of unfair exploitation. This is not an easy distinction to apply in practice and it is, perhaps, for this reason that the passage from Lord Goff has been said to "leave room for flexibility in the characterisation of illegitimate pressure and of the relevant causal link".[32] Thus, some cases in which duress has not been established may be best explained on the basis that the threat to break the original contract was not illegitimate in the circumstances,[33] while in others the illegitimate pressure created by the threat may not have amounted to "a significant cause"[34] of the decision to enter into the further, or varied, contract. Indeed, the two factors may also be said to be interdependent in the sense that the more illegitimate the pressure the lower the causal threshold. This may explain why, for duress of the person, it need only be proved that the threat was one reason why the contract was entered into,[35] whereas for economic duress[36] the "minimum" requirement before it can be said that the threat was a significant cause is to satisfy the "but for" test, i.e. that the agreement would not have been made at all or on the terms it was made.[37] In principle, it is submitted that the "but for" test should apply to cases of economic duress and duress of goods, without qualification, and that any departure from this requirement should be confined to duress of the person.[38]

10–007   **Cases where duress has been established.** The emphasis on flexibility above may be reproached for the introduction of a judicial "discretion",[39] but it recognises that the question whether a threat amounts to duress depends on its coercive

---

[29] It is sometimes said that an agreement cannot be set aside if it is "in submission to an honest claim" (*Maskell v Horner* [1915] 3 K.B. 106) but this should not be interpreted to mean that "a compromise" *cannot* be set aside for duress; it depends upon whether it was made "voluntarily to close the transaction", or "under compulsion of urgent and compelling necessity" (*Maskell v Horner* [1915] 3 K.B. 106 at 118).

[30] See above, para.3–050; *Williams v Roffey Bros & Nicholls (Contractors) Ltd* [1991] 1 Q.B. 1; *Adam Opel GmbH v Mitras Automotive (UK) Ltd* [2008] EWHC 3205 (QB); [2088] C.I.L.L. 2561.

[31] *The Siboen and the Sibotre* [1976] 1 Lloyd's Rep. 293 at 336.

[32] *Huyton SA v Peter Cremer GmbH* [1999] 1 Lloyd's Rep. 620 at 637.

[33] ibid.; *DSND Subsea Ltd v Petroleum Geo-Services ASA* [2000] B.L.R. 530 at [134]. The cases tend to proceed on the basis that a threatened breach of contract is, by definition, illegitimate. In *CTN Cash & Carry Ltd v Gallaher Ltd* [1994] 4 All E.R. 714 Steyn L.J. did not rule out the possibility of "lawful act duress" (e.g. a threat not to enter into a future contract) which, conversely, would break the link between lawfulness and legitimacy; cf. in the context of salvage: *The Port Caledonia and the Anna* [1903] P. 184. See now: Merchant Shipping Act 1995, s.224 giving effect to the Salvage Convention 1989; *Daniel v Drew* [2005] EWCA Civ 507; [2005] 2 F.C.R. 365; below, para.10–015, fn.85.

[34] *The Evia Luck (No.2)* [1992] 2 A.C. 152 at 165.

[35] *Barton v Armstrong* [1976] A.C. 104; above, para.10–003.

[36] Including duress of goods.

[37] *Huyton SA v Peter Cremer GmbH* [1999] 1 Lloyd's Rep. 620 at 636; *Kolmar Group AG v Traxpo Enterprises Pvt Ltd* [2010] EWHC 113 (Comm); [2010] 2 Lloyd's Rep. 653 at [92].

[38] This would bring economic duress and duress of goods in line with non-fraudulent misrepresentation and duress of the person in line with fraudulent misrepresentation: above, paras 9–021—9–022.

[39] *Huyton SA v Peter Cremer GmbH* [1999] 1 Lloyd's Rep. 620 at 637.

effect in each case.[40] Thus cases such as *D & C Builders v Rees*[41] have been explained[42] on the ground that the creditor's promise to accept part payment in full settlement had been obtained by duress. Similarly, in *B & S Contracts and Designs Ltd v Victor Green Publications Ltd*[43] a contractor who had undertaken to erect stands for an exhibition told his client, less than a week before the exhibition was due to open, that the contract would be cancelled unless the client paid an additional sum to meet claims which were being made against the contractor by his workforce. The consequence of not having the stands available in time would have been disastrous for the client in that it would have gravely damaged his reputation and might have exposed him to heavy claims for damages from exhibitors to whom space on the stands had been let. In these circumstances it was held that the payment had been made under duress and that the client was entitled to recover it back.

Cases where duress has not been established. The cases just referred to **10–008** must be contrasted with *Pao On v Lau Yiu Long*,[44] where the claimants threatened to break a contract with a company unless the defendants, who were shareholders in the company, gave them a guarantee against loss resulting from the performance of that contract. The defendants, thinking that the risk of such loss was small, gave the guarantee in order to avoid the adverse publicity which the company might suffer if the contract were not performed. In these circumstances, it was held that there was no "coercion of the will", so that the guarantee was not voidable for duress. The relevant causal link would not now be described as a coercion of the will;[45] instead in the *Pao On* case it could not be said that, but for the claimant's threat, the defendants would not have given the guarantee. Alternatively, it may be better to regard *Pao On* as a case where the threat did not amount to illegitimate pressure.[46]

The availability of an alternative course of action. In assessing whether **10–009** causation is established, the court will take into account[47] what courses of action (other than submission to the threat) were reasonably available to that person[48]: e.g. whether it would have been reasonable for him to have resisted the threatened

---

[40] *CTN Cash & Carry Ltd v Gallaher Ltd* [1994] 4 All E.R. 714 at 717; *XS Racing & Event Marketing Ltd v Sunseeker Europe* [2005] EWHC 3023 (QB) at [28].

[41] [1966] 2 Q.B. 617; above, para.3–117; cf. *The Atlantic Baron* [1979] Q.B. 705; above, para.3–052; *Nixon v Furphy* (1925) 25 S.R. (N.S.W.) 151; contrast *Smith v Charlick* (1923–4) 34 C.L.R. 38 (payment to avoid threat not to enter into *future* contracts); *Williams v Roffey Bros & Nicholls (Contractors) Ltd* [1991] 1 Q.B. 1 (where no threat was made and duress was not pleaded).

[42] In *The Siboen and The Sibotre*, above, at 335.

[43] [1984] I.C.R. 419; Palmer and Catchpole 48 M.L.R. 102; cf. *The Alev* [1989] 1 Lloyd's Rep. 138; *Atlas Express Ltd v Kafco (Importers & Distributors) Ltd* [1989] Q.B. 833; Chandler [1989] L.M.C.L.Q. 270; Fleming [1989] C.L.J. 362; Phang 53 M.L.R. 107; *Adam Opel GmbH v Mitras Automotive (UK) Ltd* [2008] EWHC 3205 (QB); [2088] C.I.L.L. 2561.

[44] [1980] A.C. 614; cf. *Alec Lobb (Garages) Ltd v Total Oil (Great Britain) Ltd* [1983] 1 W.L.R. 87.

[45] See above, fn.14.

[46] See above, fn.33; Birks [1990] L.M.C.L.Q. 342.

[47] i.e. as a matter of evidence, not an "inflexible third ingredient" in addition to illegitimate pressure and causation: *Huyton SA v Peter Cremer GmbH* [1999] 1 Lloyd's Rep. 620 at 638

[48] *The Universe Sentinel* [1983] 1 A.C. 366 at 400; *B & S Contracts and Designs Ltd v Victor Green Publications Ltd* [1984] I.C.R. 419 at 426, 428; *Huyton SA v Peter Cremer GmbH* [1999] 1 Lloyd's Rep. 620 at 638; *Kolmar Group AG v Traxpo Enterprises Pvt Ltd* [2010] EWHC 113 (Comm); [2010] 2 Lloyd's Rep. 653 at [92], [95].

wrong by taking legal proceedings.[49] An evidential role may also be given to the degree of protest by the party claiming duress, though this may not be given much weight depending on the circumstances.[50]

(e) Unlawful Demands for Payment

10–010   The rule that money extorted by duress can be recovered also applies where an unlawful charge is levied by unlawful threats, e.g. where a carrier refuses to carry goods unless he is paid more than he is legally entitled to charge.[51] Money paid by a citizen under an ultra vires demand for a tax or similar levy is also recoverable by the payor, irrespective of whether the demand amounts to duress[52]: this rule can be explained as resting either on the general principles of unjust enrichment[53] or on "common justice"[54] or on the ground that a payment made in response to such an invalid demand is analogous to one made for a consideration which has failed,[55] or on a mistake of law.[56] But where the demand is not of this kind, so that the only ground for recovery is duress, the claim for the return of the money will fail if the demand for the payment was not backed by any threat[57]; or where it is backed only by a threat to take legal proceedings[58]: if such a payment could be recovered back, no compromise would be secure.

(f) Remedies

10–011   A contract which has been made under duress is voidable.[59] The right to rescind is subject to the usual bars against relief: affirmation,[60] lapse of time, third party rights, and, it seems, the impossibility of making counter-restitution.[61] In many cases, the contract obtained by duress is a variation of an earlier contract. It is only the varied contract which may be rescinded, leaving the parties to their respective entitlements under the original contract.

According to Lord Dipock, duress is not a tort *per se* for which damages may be awarded,[62] but in the same case Lord Scarman held that it "is actionable as a

---

[49] e.g. *Hennessy v Craigmyle & Co* [1986] I.C.R. 461; cf. *Adam Opel GmbH v Mitras Automotive (UK) Ltd* [2008] EWHC 3205 (QB); [2088] C.I.L.L. 2561 (where an application for an injunction was not a realistic alternative); *Astley v Reynolds* (1731) 2 Stra. 915 at 916.

[50] *Pao On v Lau Yiu Long* [1980] A.C. 614; *Maskell v Horner* [1915] 3 K.B. 106 at 120.

[51] *Great Western Ry v Sutton* (1869) L.R. 4 H.L. 226; Winfield 60 L.Q.R. 341.

[52] *Woolwich Equitable BS v IRC (No.2)* [1993] A.C. 70.

[53] ibid. at 197.

[54] ibid. at 172.

[55] ibid. at 197, 198.

[56] *Deutsche Morgan Grenfell Group Plc v IRC* [2006] UKHL 49; [2007] 1 A.C. 558.

[57] *Twyford v Manchester Corp* [1946] Ch. 236; discussed by Marsh 62 L.Q.R. 333, and see next note.

[58] *Brown v M'Kinally* (1795) 1 Esp. 279; *William Whiteley Ltd v R.* (1910) 101 L.T. 741. The *Twyford* and *William Whiteley* cases were doubted in the *Woolwich Equitable* case [1993] A.C. 70, but only in so far as they concerned unlawful demands for taxes and similar levies by public officials.

[59] See above, para.10–002.

[60] *The Atlantic Baron* [1979] Q.B. 705; *DSND Subsea Ltd v Petroleum Geo-Services* ASA [2000] B.L.R. 530; *Antonio v Antonio* [2010] EWHC 1199 (QB) at [74] where the court took into account that the duress continued after the contract had been entered; *Borrelli v Ting* [2010] UKPC 21; [2010] Bus. L.R. 1718 at [37].

[61] *Halpern v Halpern* [2007] EWCA Civ 291; [2008] Q.B. 195 at [74–75]; *Borrelli v Ting* [2010] UKPC 21; [2010] Bus. L.R. 1718 at [38].

[62] *The Universe Sentinel* [1983] 1 A.C. 366 at 385. Lord Diplock's views on this issue are cited with apparent approval in *The Evia Luck (No.2)* [1992] 2 A.C. 152 at 166–167.

tort, if it causes damage or loss".[63] These differing views may be reconciled on the basis that they both require the duress to take the form of a *separate* tort before damages may be awarded, but Lord Scarman's view may reflect the fact that the sort of threatened conduct which amounts to duress will also amount to the tort of intimidation. In *Kolmar Group AG v Traxpo Enterprises Pvt Ltd*,[64] damages were awarded for the tort of intimidation, but the same sum was also awarded by way of restitution, either on the grounds of duress, or failure of consideration.

2. UNDUE INFLUENCE[65]

A transaction can be set aside in equity if, because it has been procured by undue influence exerted by one party (A) on the other (B), it cannot "fairly be treated as the expression of [B's] free will."[66] The cases in which such relief is given are commonly divided into so-called "actual" and "presumed" undue influence, but as will be seen below, this distinction can be misleading. Relief can be given on the ground of undue influence even though the person to whom the gift or promise was made obtained no personal benefit from it. Thus the rule applies where the head of a religious order uses a gift wholly for the purposes of the order and where a trustee extracts a promise from one beneficiary solely for the benefit of another.[67]

10–012

When is influence "undue"? Whether actually proved,[68] or as a result of the failure to rebut its presumption,[69] a transaction will be set aside when it was procured by undue influence; not when it was procured by influence. This begs the obvious question, therefore, of when influence is "undue"? Is the concern to protect B from an inability to express his own free will, or to prevent A from improperly taking advantage of that inability, whether or not he benefits personally?[70] One can find clear statements which would suggest that it is the latter:

10–013

> "However great the influence which one person may be able to wield over another equity does not intervene unless that influence has been abused. Equity does not save people from the consequence of their own folly; it acts to save them from being victimised by other people."[71]

But this and similar statements which refer to the "unconscionable conduct" of A[72] are somewhat circular in that what is being said is no more than that equity will not intervene to protect against the exercise of influence, only the exercise of *undue* influence, or the abuse of influence. That still leaves the question of when influence is "undue", or when it is that the weaker party has been "victimised".

---

[63] ibid. at 400. In *R. v HM Attorney-General for England and Wales* [2003] UKPC 22 at [15] Lord Hoffmann refers to the "wrong of duress".

[64] [2010] EWHC 113 (Comm); [2010] 2 Lloyd's Rep. 653 at [118]–[121].

[65] Lewison, Chancery Bar Association Conference Lecture 2011.

[66] *Royal Bank of Scotland v Etridge (No.2)* [2001] UKHL 44; [2002] 2 A.C. 773 at [7].

[67] *Allcard v Skinner* (1887) L.R. 36 Ch. D 145; *Ellis v Barker* (1871) L.R. 7 Ch.App. 104; cf. *Bullock v Lloyds Bank* [1955] Ch. 317.

[68] See below, para.10–014.

[69] See below, para. 10–017 et seq.

[70] See text to fn.67 above.

[71] *National Commercial Bank of Jamaica v Hew* [2003] UKPC 51 at [33] per Lord Millett;

[72] *Dunbar Bank v Nadeem* [1998] 3 All E.R. 876 at 883–884; *Etridge* case, above fn.66 at [8]–[10]

It has been said that it is not necessary to prove any misconduct by A,[73] and transactions have been set aside on the ground of undue influence when it is clear that A had been attempting to act in the best interests of B.[74] It is submitted therefore that *undue* influence is exercised by A whenever, through his influence, the transaction was not entered into as a result of B's own free[75] will.[76] It is not necessary that the transaction should have been to B's disadvantage or one that calls for explanation,[77] but this will often be the case and the latter will have to be proved in order to raise a presumption that undue influence was exercised.[78] As for the conduct of A, it will only be "improper" or "unconscionable" in the sense that he seeks to uphold the transaction, which *ex hypothesi* will always be the case where there is a dispute between the parties, or their representatives (e.g. B's executors). If the court finds that the transaction was entered into as a result of B's own free will, A's conduct in seeking to uphold the transaction is not improper or unconscionable and vice versa, but what matters is the finding as to the exercise of B's free will. In this sense, it is probably most apt to say only that undue influence has a "connotation of impropriety".[79]

(a) Actual Undue Influence

10–014   **"Actual" undue influence and "presumed" undue influence.** The traditional distinction between "actual" undue influence and "presumed" undue influence is employed in this part, but it is potentially misleading. As will be seen below, any claimant seeking to set aside a transaction on the ground that it was procured by undue influence must prove his case, i.e. he must prove that undue influence was exercised. In cases of so-called presumed undue influence, the transaction will only be set aside if the court is satisfied on the "totality of the evidence"[80] that there was undue influence, albeit it may make that finding with the aid of a presumption. The real distinction therefore is between those cases where the exercise of undue influence is actually proved and those where it is presumed and cannot be rebutted.[81]

---

[73] *Jennings v Cairns* [2003] EWCA 1935; [2004] W.T.L.R. 361 at [34]–[35], [40]; *Macklin v Dowsett* [2004] EWCA Civ 904; (2004) 34 E.G. 68 at [10]; *Niersmans v Pesticcio* [2004] EWCA Civ 372; [2004] W.T.L.R. 699 at [20]; *Turkey v Awadh* [2005] EWCA Civ 382; [2005] 2 F.C.R. 7 at [11]; *Hackett v Crown Prosecution Service* [2011] EWHC 1170 (Admin) at [64].

[74] E.g. *Cheese v Thomas* [1994] 1 W.L.R. 173.

[75] The emphasis should be on "free" will: "a finding of undue influence does not depend, as a necessary pre-requisite, upon a conclusion that the victim made no decision of her own, or that her will and intention was completely overborne", *Hewett v First Plus Financial Group Plc* [2010] EWCA Civ 312; [2010] 2 F.L.R. 177 at [25]. Thus, deliberate suppression of information which would have deterred B from entering into the transaction may constitute undue influence: *Hewett*, above; *Royal Bank of Scotland Plc v Chandra* [2010] EWHC 105 (Ch); [2010] 1 Lloyd's Rep. 677 at [140].

[76] Birks and Chin in Beatson and Friedmann (eds.), *Good Faith and Fault in Contract Law.* Contrast Enonchong, *Duress, Undue Influence and Unconscionable Dealing* at para.7–006; Chen-Wishart 59 C.L.P. 231.

[77] *Thompson v Foy* [2009] EWHC 1076 (Ch); [2010] 1 P. & C.R. 16 at [99].

[78] See below, para.10–019.

[79] *Etridge* case, above, fn.66, at [32]; *Abbey National Bank Plc v Stringer* [2006] EWCA Civ 338 at [46].

[80] See below, para.10–027.

[81] *Etridge* case, above, fn.66 at [92]; *Annulment Funding Company Ltd v Cowey* [2010] EWCA Civ 711 at [50].

Actual pressure. The first group of cases in which equity gave relief on the ground of undue influence are those in which one party had induced the other to enter into the transaction by actual pressure which equity regarded as improper but which was formerly thought not to amount to duress at common law because no element of violence to the person was involved.[82] For example, a promise to pay money could be set aside if obtained by a threat to prosecute the promisor,[83] or his close relative, or his spouse, for a criminal offence.[84] Such threats would now constitute duress,[85] but the equitable concept of "pressure" is still wider than that of duress at common law, for undue influence can be exercised without making illegitimate threats[86] or indeed any threats at all.[87] The party who claims relief on the ground of actual undue influence must show that such influence existed and had been exercised,[88] i.e. that he had no "means of forming an independent judgment",[89] and that the transaction resulted from that influence. There is no further requirement in cases of this kind that the transaction must be shown to be to the manifest disadvantage of the party seeking to set it aside[90] or that the transaction must be one that "calls for explanation"[91] by the other party.

10–015

Causation. In *Bank of Credit and Commerce International SA v Aboody*,[92] the Court of Appeal had applied the "but-for" test of causation, i.e. the transaction would not be set aside, even where undue influence had actually been proved, if the evidence established "on balance of probabilities" that the victim of the influence would have entered into it in any event. The *Aboody* case has been overruled on other grounds,[93] and in *UCB Corporate Services v Williams*[94] the Court of Appeal rejected its earlier "but for" test as inconsistent with Lord Browne-Wilkinson's statement of principle in the *Pitt* case that the victim of undue influence is entitled to have the transaction set aside "as of right".[95] Once it is established that the victim's consent was vitiated, there is no further requirement to prove that, "absent the equitable fraud", the victim would not have executed the transaction in question.[96] In this sense, it need only be proved that the undue influence was *a* factor. This brings the test for causation in cases of

10–016

---

[82] *Turnbull & Co v Duvall* [1902] A.C. 429 at 434; *Barclays Bank v O'Brien* [1994] 1 A.C. 180 at 191–192; *Avon Finance Co v Bridger* [1985] 2 All E.R. 281 at 285.

[83] Such a threat was formerly thought to be incapable of giving rise to duress at common law: *Flower v Sadler* (1882) 10 Q.B.D. 572.

[84] *Williams v Bayley* (1866) L.R. 1 H.L. 200; *Kaufman v Gerson* [1904] 1 K.B. 591; *Mutual Finance Ltd v Wetton* [1937] 2 K.B. 389.

[85] cf. *Daniel v Drew* [2005] EWCA Civ 507; [2005] 2 F.C.R. 365 which is decided as a case of actual undue influence; the improper pressure, in "the rare and exceptional" circumstances of the case, was a lawful "threat" to institute civil proceedings.

[86] Though see the apparent absence of a threat in the finding of duress in *Borrelli v Ting* [2010] UKPC 21; [2010] Bus. L.R. 1718, above fn.7.

[87] e.g. *CIBC Mortgages v Pitt* [1994] 1 A.C. 200, where the claim failed for reasons stated below, para.10–038.

[88] *Howes v Bishop* [1909] 2 K.B. 390; *Bank of Montreal v Stuart* [1911] A.C. 120 at 127.

[89] *Bank of Montreal v Stuart* [1911] A.C. 120 at 136.

[90] *CIBC Mortgages v Pitt* [1994] 1 A.C. 200, disapproving *Bank of Credit & Commerce International SA v Aboody* [1990] 1 Q.B. 923 on this point; Cretney 105 L.Q.R. 169; Dixon [1989] C.L.J. 359.

[91] See below, para.10–019.

[92] [1990] 1 Q.B. 923.

[93] See below, para.10–019.

[94] [2002] EWCA Civ 555; [2003] 1 P. & C.R. 12.

[95] Above, fn.90, at 209.

[96] [2003] 1 P. & C.R. 12 at [91].

actual undue influence in line with the test for fraudulent misrepresentation,[97] and duress to the person[98] and if this analogy is pursued to its conclusion, it seems that the burden is on the stronger party to show that any undue influence played no part at all.

(b) Presumed Undue Influence

10–017   The second group of cases in which equity gives relief for undue influence is that in which the relationship between the parties is such as to give rise to what has been called a "presumption of undue influence".[99] This phrase contains an unfortunate element of ambiguity: it can mean either that such influence is presumed to *exist* or that it is presumed to have been *exercised*. It might be better if use of the phrase were abandoned; but as there is little prospect of such a development, we shall here continue to use it, drawing attention from time to time to its different shades of meaning.[100] At this stage, it suffices to say that, where the presumption applies, it is not necessary for the party claiming relief actually to prove that the impugned transaction was procured by undue influence.

(i) *Types of presumptions*

10–018   For the purpose of explaining when a contract may be set aside for "presumed" undue influence, it is first necessary to explain the different types of presumption which may be in play. A presumption is a rule of law by which, on proof of a specified fact or facts (the basic fact(s)), another fact (the presumed fact) is taken to exist. There are many classifications of presumptions; for the present purposes it suffices to distinguish between so-called irrebuttable presumptions and rebuttable ones. Irrebuttable (or conclusive) presumptions are rules of substantive law which have nothing to do with ways of proving facts.[101] If the law says that, on proof of the basic fact, the presumed fact is irrebuttably taken to exist, this means that proof of the basic fact produces the same legal consequence as proof of the presumed fact, even though the latter fact may be shown not to exist. A rebuttable presumption, by contrast, is a rule of law by which, on proof of the basic fact(s), the presumed fact is assumed to exist in the absence of evidence negativing (or "rebutting") its existence. Such presumptions may be subdivided into (i) those which require the person against whom the presumption operates to show (on a balance of probabilities) that the presumed fact does *not* exist; and (ii) those which merely require that person to introduce some evidence to that effect, leaving it up to the proponent of the presumption to show that (on a balance of probabilities) that fact does exist. Presumptions of the latter kind are sometimes called "evidential presumptions,"[102] though this phrase has no generally accepted technical meaning.

---

[97] See below, para.9–020.
[98] See above, para.10–003.
[99] *Barclays Bank Plc v O'Brien* [1994] 1 A.C. 180 at 189; *Etridge* case, above, fn.66, at [16].
[100] See further below, fnn.153 and 154.
[101] *Cross and Tapper on Evidence* (12th edn), at 131.
[102] This usage is adopted in the *Etridge* case, fn.66 above, e.g. at [16]; cf. *Abbey National Bank Plc v Stringer* [2006] EWCA Civ 338 at [39]

(ii) *The presumption of undue influence*

Requirements. To give rise to the "presumption of undue influence",[103] two **10–019** basic facts must be established by the party claiming relief.[104] The first is the existence of a relationship between A and B by virtue of which B either in fact reposed trust and confidence in A or is taken as a matter of law to have done so; the kinds of relationship which are capable of producing these effects are discussed below.[105] The second basic fact relates to the nature of the impugned transactions; and conflicting views have been expressed on the question whether it was necessary for B to show that the transaction was "disadvantageous" or "manifestly disadvantageous" to him. The original view appears to have been that there was no such requirement and that, once a relationship of trust and confidence was established, the transaction could be set aside on grounds of public policy, even though it was not in fact disadvantageous to B.[106] Later it was said that the ground for relief was "not a vague 'public policy' but specifically the victimization of one party [B] by the other [A]" and that B had to show that the transaction was to his "manifest disadvantage".[107] But this view was later doubted,[108] especially on the ground that, where A stood in a fiduciary position to B, the impugned transaction would (on grounds of public policy) not be allowed to stand unless its fairness was affirmatively proved by A[109]; the requirement of "manifest disadvantage" also does not apply in cases of actual undue influence.[110] In the *Etridge* case, the use of the words "manifest disadvantage" to describe the second requirement of the presumption was therefore discouraged and the requirement was restated in the form that the transaction must be one which "calls for explanation"[111] or that it must be one which "is not readily explicable by the relationship between the parties."[112] This formulation of the requirement differs from that in terms of "manifest disadvantage" since a substantial transaction may call for an explanation from A even though B may benefit from it indirectly (so that the disadvantage, if any, to B would not be "manifest"[113]). On the other hand, an ordinary (or moderate) Christmas or birthday gift from B to A would not (even where there was a relationship of trust and confidence between them) "call for explanation" and so could not be set aside for presumed undue influence.[114]

---

[103] See above, at fn.99.

[104] *Etridge* case, above, fn.66, at [13].

[105] See below, para.10–021.

[106] *Allcard v Skinner* (1887) 36 Ch.D. 145 at 171; *Lloyds Bank Ltd v Bundy* [1975] Q.B. 326 at 342; cf. *Hylton v Hylton* (1745) 2 Ves. Sen. 547 at 549.

[107] *National Westminster Bank Plc v Morgan* [1985] A.C. 686 at 706; cf. *Hart v O'Connor* [1985] A.C. 1000 at 1024.

[108] *CIBC Mortgages Plc v Pitt* [1994] 1 A.C. 200 at 209.

[109] ibid.; see the authorities cited in fn.131, below, and the reference to "public policy" in *Hammond v Osborn* [2002] EWCA Civ 885; [2002] W.T.L.R. 1125.

[110] ibid.; disapproving *Bank of Credit & Commerce International SA v Aboody* [1990] 1 Q.B. 923 on this point.

[111] [2001] UKHL 44; [2002] 2 A.C. 773 at [14], per Lord Nicholls, with whose speech Lords Bingham and Clyde agreed. See: *Mortgage Agency Services Number Two Ltd v Chater* [2003] EWCA Civ 490; [2004] 1 P. & C.R. 4 at [30]. Contrast *Turkey v Awadh* [2005] EWCA Civ 382; [2005] 2 F.C.R. 7 at [20]–[22], [220], preferring the requirement of Lord Scott that the transaction must be one that cannot be explained by ordinary motives.

[112] ibid. at [21].

[113] *Macklin v Dowsett* [2004] EWCA Civ 904; (2004) 34 E.G. 68 at [10].

[114] *Etridge* case above at [24], [156]; cf. ibid. at [104] (reasonable fee paid to solicitor). Small sums which, considered individually, may not call for explanation, may do so when taken in the aggregate: *Aldridge v Turner* [2004] EWHC 2768.

10–020   **Effect and nature.** Once the basic facts of the presumption (i.e. a relationship between A and B of trust and confidence, and a transaction calling for explanation) are established, then the presumed fact is that "the transaction can only have been procured by undue influence."[115] This presumption has been described as "a rebuttable evidential presumption of undue influence".[116] As the first of the phrases just quoted shows, the presumed fact is that such influence has been *exercised* (or that the trust and confidence has been abused). In this respect, the present presumption differs from another presumption, to be discussed below,[117] which merely establishes (or dispenses with the need to establish) that a relationship of trust and confidence *exists*. The statement that the presumption with which we are here concerned is "rebuttable" refers to the point that it can be displaced in one of the ways to be more fully discussed below[118]: e.g. that B took independent legal advice before entering into the transaction; or by other evidence that the transaction was the "expression of [B's] free will".[119] The meaning of the statement that the presumption is "evidential"[120] seems to be that, after proof by B of the basic facts giving rise to the presumption that the transaction was procured by undue influence, the onus shifts to A to prove that it was not so procured.[121]

10–021   **Relationships of trust and confidence.** These relationships have traditionally been divided into two categories which became known as "class 2A" and "class 2B" cases.[122] Some difficulty arises in determining whether this classification has survived after the *Etridge* case. It will be convenient first to describe the traditional categories and then to consider the effect on the classification of that case. It should be emphasised that this discussion is concerned with only *one* of the basic facts which must be established before it can be presumed that the transaction "can only have been procured by undue influence".[123] Even if the requisite relationship is established, this presumption will arise only if it is *also* shown that the impugned transaction is one "which calls for explanation".[124]

10–022   **Relationships of presumed trust and confidence (class 2A).** Where one of the types of relationship to be listed below exists, it is settled by law or (what amounts to the same thing),[125] "the law presumes, irrebuttably, that [A] had influence over [B]".[126] This presumption has been held to apply where the relationship between A and B is that of parent and child,[127] guardian and ward,[128]

---

[115] ibid. at [14].
[116] ibid. at [16], [153], [194].
[117] See below, para.10–022.
[118] See below, para.10–026.
[119] *Etridge* case [2002] 2 A.C. 773 at [7].
[120] See above, at fn.116.
[121] See *Etridge* case, above, fn.119 at [158].
[122] This terminology goes back to *Bank of Credit & Commerce International SA v Aboody* [1990] 1 Q.B. 923 at 953 and was approved in *Barclays Bank Plc v O'Brien* [1994] 1 A.C. 180 at 189–190. "Class 1" (not relevant to the present discussion) comprises cases of *actual* undue influence (above, para. 10–009; *Etridge* case, above, fn.119, at [14]).
[123] *Etridge* case, above, fn.119, at [14].
[124] ibid.
[125] See above, para.10–018.
[126] ibid. at [18]; cf. ibid. at [104].
[127] *Bullock v Lloyds Bank*, above; *Cocking v Pratt* (1749) 1 Ves.Sen. 400; cf. *Re T* [1993] Fam. 95.
[128] *Hylton v Hylton* (1754) 2 Ves.Sen. 547; the de facto relation of guardian and ward suffices: *Archer v Hudson* (1846) 15 L.J.Ch. 211.

religious adviser and disciple,[129] doctor and patient,[130] solicitor and client,[131] trustee and cestui que trust[132] and fiancé and fiancée.[133] The present presumption does not apply between husband and wife,[134] or between employer and employee.[135] Nor does it apply to all relationships which are fiduciary in the sense that they give rise to a duty of disclosure: thus it does not apply between agent and principal.[136] The presumption may apply even after the relationship has ceased if the influence continues, for example, between solicitor and ex-client[137]; and between parent and child for a "short" time[138] after the child has come of age, but not once the child is "emancipated" from parental control.[139] Even the marriage of a child does not invariably have this effect.[140]

The present presumption must be "distinguished sharply"[141] from the "evidential presumption"[142] described above. The first distinction between them is that the present presumption is said to be irrebuttable, while the "evidential presumption" is rebuttable. Since an irrebuttable presumption is (as was pointed out above[143]) a rule of substantive law, rather than a means of establishing facts, the effect of the present presumption is that proof of the relationship (e.g. of parent and child) becomes, in cases of alleged undue influence, a *substitute* for the need to prove that B reposed trust and confidence in A. It is then, on the one hand, unnecessary for B to show that (s)he actually reposed trust and confidence in A and, on the other,[144] irrelevant for A to show that this was not the case.[145] The second is that the presumed fact of the "irrebuttable" presumption is quite different from that of the "evidential" presumption: the former is that A "had influence over"[146] B; the latter is that "the transaction can only have been procured *by* undue influence".[147] The third difference relates to the respective legal consequences of the two presumptions. The "irrebuttable" presumption is

---

[129] *Allcard v Skinner*, above, fn.106; cf. *Tufton v Sperni* [1952] 2 T.L.R. 516; *Roche v Sherrington* [1982] 1 W.L.R. 599 at 606.

[130] *Dent v Bennett* (1839) 4 My. & Cr. 269; cf. *Re CMG* [1970] Ch. 574 (authorities in charge of mental hospital and patient residing there); *Claughton v Price* [1997] E.G.C.S. 51.

[131] *Wright v Carter* [1903] 1 Ch. 27; cf. *Wintle v Nye* [1959] 1 W.L.R. 284.

[132] *Ellis v Barker* (1871) L.R. 7 Ch.App. 104; *Thomson v Eastwood* (1877) 2 App.Cas. 215.

[133] *Re Lloyds Bank Ltd* [1931] 1 Ch. 289; *Leeder v Stevens* [2005] EWCA Civ 50; cf. *Zamet v Hyman* [1961] 1 W.L.R. 1442 at 1445 where the view expressed that a "presumption" only "may" arise should be understood to refer to the presumption that undue influence was *exercised* and not whether a relationship of influence *existed*.

[134] *Bank of Montreal v Stuart* [1911] A.C. 120; *Mackenzie v Royal Bank of Canada* [1934] A.C. 468; *National Westminster Bank Plc v Morgan* [1985] A.C. 686 at 703; *Kings North Trust Ltd v Bell* [1986] 1 W.L.R. 119 at 127; Andrews [1986] C.L.J. 195.

[135] *Mathew v Bobbins* (1980) 256 E.G. 603.

[136] *Re Coomber* [1911] 1 Ch. 723.

[137] *McMaster v Byrne* [1952] 1 All E.R. 1362; cf. *Longstaff v Birtles* [2002] EWCA Civ 1219; [2002] 1 W.L.R. 470 (a case, not of presumed undue influence, but of breach of fiduciary duty: see at [40]); *Allison v Clayhills* (1907) 97 L.T. 709 at 711.

[138] See *Re Pauling's Settlement Trusts* [1964] Ch. 303 at 337.

[139] *Bainbrigge v Browne* (1881) 18 Ch.D. 188.

[140] *Lancashire Loans Ltd v Black* [1934] 1 K.B. 380.

[141] *Etridge* case [2002] 2 A.C. 773 at [18].

[142] ibid. at [16], [18].

[143] See above, fn.101.

[144] *Etridge* case, above, fn.141 at [18].

[145] It is only irrelevant to the question of whether there was a relationship of influence; evidence that A did not, in fact, have any influence over B may be relied upon to rebut the presumption that undue influence was exercised: below, para.10–026.

[146] *Etridge* case, above, at [18].

[147] ibid. at [14] (emphasis added).

not itself a ground for relief[148]: it is merely a way of establishing *one* of the basic facts of the "evidential" presumption. An ordinary or moderate Christmas or birthday present can no more be set aside where it is made by a child to a parent or by a client to his solicitor than where it is made by a wife to her husband.[149] It follows that even where the "irrebuttable" presumption applies, B will be entitled to relief only if he shows that the transaction was *also* one that called for explanation; and if this further fact is established, then the "evidential" presumption comes into operation. Thus the two presumptions will operate in the same case and the "evidential" presumption remains rebuttable[150] (e.g. by evidence that B was independently advised) even where the relationship between A and B was such as to give rise to the "irrebuttable" presumption. There is, therefore, no inconsistency between saying, on the one hand, that, in the special relationship cases, "the law presumes, *irrebuttably*, that [A] had influence over [B]"[151] and, on the other, that if B in addition showed that the impugned transaction called for explanation, then a "*rebuttable* evidential presumption"[152] arises that the transaction was "procured by" that influence. The irrebuttable presumption relates to the *existence*[153] of the influence, the rebuttable evidential presumption to its *exercise*.[154] The distinction is obscured by the unfortunate use of the ambiguous phrase "presumption *of* undue influence",[155] which is capable of referring to either or both of these operations.

10–023   **Relationships of actual confidence (class 2B).** In this group of cases, i.e. all those falling outside class 2A, the relationship between A and B must be one in which B has in fact reposed trust and confidence in A. The paradigm case is one in which B has reposed trust and confidence in A in relation to the management of B's *financial* affairs,[156] but more generally it is necessary for B to establish that A has acquired influence over B "in relation to some general aspect of (B's) affairs".[157] If B shows this, and that the transaction which B seeks to avoid was such as to call for explanation, then the rebuttable presumption will arise that the transaction was procured by undue influence.[158]

It follows from the nature of the present group of cases that the question in each such case will be whether the party seeking to set the transaction aside has reposed sufficient trust and confidence in the other, rather than whether the relationship

---

[148] ibid. at [104] ("no presumption properly so called that the confidence has been abused").

[149] ibid. at [24], [156]; cf. [104].

[150] This point accounts for the discussion by Lord Nicholls (ibid. at [15]) of *Bainbrigge v Brown* (1881) 18 Ch.D. 188 in the context of the "evidential" presumption, even though the relationship of the parties was that of father and "unemancipated" children (above, fn.139) so that the "irrebuttable presumption"; would *also* have operated between them.

[151] *Etridge* case, above, fn.141 at [18] (emphasis added).

[152] ibid. at [219] (emphasis added).

[153] ibid. at [18].

[154] ibid. at [14].

[155] See above, at fnn.99 and100.

[156] *Etridge* case, above, fn.141, at [14].

[157] *Morley v Elmaleh* [2009] EWHC 1196 (Ch) at [598]; *Thompson v Foy* [2009] EWHC 1076 (Ch); [2010] 1 P. & C.R. 16 at 100; *Hewett v First Plus Financial Group Plc* [2010] EWCA Civ 312; [2010] 2 F.L.R. 177 at [27]; cf. *Goldsworthy v Brickell* [1987] Ch. 378 at 404. It may be established, in part, by the execution of a power of attorney by B in favour of A: *Hackett v Crown Prosecution Service* [2011] EWHC 1170 (Admin) at [54].

[158] *Barclays Bank Plc v O'Brien* [1994] A.C. 180 at 189–190; *Etridge* case [2002] 2 A.C. 773 at [14].

between the parties belongs to a particular type.[159] For example, the relation of banker and customer will not normally amount to a relationship of trust and confidence in the sense which is required,[160] but it can do so in exceptional cases if the customer has placed himself entirely in the hands of the bank.[161]

The flexible character of the present group of cases is illustrated by *Tate v Williamson*,[162] where the defendant became financial adviser to an extravagant Oxford undergraduate who sold him his estate for half its value and then drank himself to death at the age of 24. His executors successfully claimed that the sale should be set aside. Lord Chelmsford said: "The courts have always been careful not to fetter this jurisdiction by defining the exact limits of its exercise."[163] A more modern illustration of the principle is provided by *O'Sullivan v Management Agency & Music Ltd*[164] where the relationship between the claimant (then a young and unknown composer and performer of music) and his manager was held to be such as to give rise to a presumption of undue influence; and transactions which turned out to be unfair to the claimant when he later became a celebrity were accordingly set aside.

Effects of the *Etridge* case. This classification of cases just described was adopted by the House of Lords in *Barclays Bank Plc v O'Brien* where Lord Browne-Wilkinson, giving the leading speech, said that, where the relationship between A and B was such as to fall into class 2A, then a presumption arose "that undue influence had been exercised",[165] while if that relationship fell into class 2B, then proof of it raised "the presumption of undue influence".[166] Reference has already been made to the ambiguity of the latter phrase,[167] but, from the context, the two phrases (quoted above) in Lord Browne-Wilkinson's speech seem to mean the same thing—i.e. that, on proof of the relationship, it was presumed that undue influence had been exercised. If the phrases mean this, they must be qualified in the light of the *Etridge* case: as already noted,[168] the existence of the relationship between the parties (whether in a class 2A or class 2B case) is only *one* of the basic facts of the presumption that undue influence has been *exercised*. That presumption arises only if it is also shown that the transaction is one which "calls for explanation".[169]

10–024

---

[159] Cited with approval in the *Etridge* case above at [10]; cf. ibid. at [80] ("cannot be exhaustively classified").

[160] *National Westminster Bank Plc v Morgan* [1985] A.C. 686; Andrews [1985] C.L.J. 192; Tiplady 48 M.L.R. 579; *Bank of Baroda v Panessar* [1987] Ch. 335.

[161] *Lloyd's Bank Ltd v Bundy* [1955] Q.B. 326, esp. at 342; Carr 38 M.L.R. 463; Sealy [1975] C.L.J. 17. The case was said in *National Westminster Bank Plc v Morgan* [1985] A.C. 686 at 698 to turn on its "very special facts." cf. *Cornish v Midland Bank Plc* [1985] 3 All E.R. 513 at 518.

[162] (1866) L.R. 2 Ch.App. 55. For similar relationships between the aged and their advisors or companions, see *Inche Noriah v Shaik Allie bin Omar* [1929] A.C. 127; *Re Craig* [1971] Ch. 95; contrast *Re Brocklehurst* [1978] 1 Ch. 14.

[163] ibid. at 60; cf. *Tufton v Sperni* [1952] 2 T.L.R. 516; *National Westminster Bank Plc v Morgan* [1985] A.C. 686 at 708–709; *Goldsworthy v Brickell* [1987] Ch. 378; *Cheese v Thomas* [1994] W.L.R. 129.

[164] [1985] Q.B. 428; cf. also *Mahoney v Purnell* [1996] 3 All E.R. 61; *Credit Lyonnais Bank Nederland NV v Burch* [1997] 1 All E.R. 144 (employer and employee) (approved in the *Etridge* case [2002] 2 A.C. 773 at [83], [86]).

[165] [1994] 1 A.C. 180 at 489.

[166] ibid.

[167] See above, fnn. 99, 100 and 155.

[168] See above, at fnn.146–148.

[169] *Etridge* case, above, fn.158 at [14].

In the *Etridge* case, the leading speech was given by Lord Nicholls. Lords Bingham and Clyde expressed their agreement with this speech. At the same time, Lord Clyde questioned "the wisdom . . . of attempting to make classifications of cases of undue influence"[170] while Lords Hobhouse and Scott appeared, at least at first sight, to reject or doubt the "class 2B" category.[171] The question thus arises whether that category has survived the *Etridge* case.

Lord Nicholls' speech in that case does not make any express reference to the distinction between class 2A and class 2B cases. But he does distinguish between cases in which there is "[p]roof that [B] has placed trust and confidence in [A]"[172] and those in which B "need not prove he actually reposed trust and confidence in" A because their relationship is such that "the law presumes, irrebuttably, that [A] had influence over [B]"[173]: e.g. where their relationship is that of parent and child. This distinction appears to resemble the substance (though not the nomenclature) of the distinction between class 2A and class 2B cases. Lord Hobhouse, on the other hand, says that "the so-called class 2B presumption ought not to be adopted"[174] while Lord Scott says that he "doubt[s] the utility of the class 2B classification".[175] The question arises how these statements are to be reconciled with the distinction drawn by Lord Nicholls in the terms just quoted.[176]

One possible answer is that if the distinction between class 2A and 2B is confined to the question of whether there is the necessary relationship of trust and confidence, it makes no sense to speak in terms of a class 2B *presumption*. By definition, relationships falling within class 2B are all those which do not fall within class 2A and in which it is necessary to *prove* that a relationship of trust and confidence existed. However, in the context in which they cast doubt on the utility of the class 2B presumption, it seems clear that Lords Hobhouse and Scott are referring to the presumption that undue influence has been exercised. It is submitted therefore that a preferable way of reconciling the apparent conflict of opinion is to have regard to the exact context in which it arose in the *Etridge* case.

10–025   **Surety spouses.** The appeals before the House of Lords in the *Etridge* case concerned a group of cases in which wives had provided security for their husbands' business debts, usually by means of a guarantee by the wife of those debts, supported by a charge on the matrimonial home owned either by the wife alone or by her and the husband jointly. On the principal debtor's default, the lender (usually a bank) would seek to enforce the security, typically by sale of the house. The question to what extent and in what circumstances such a third party is adversely affected by actual or presumed undue influence between husband and wife will be discussed later in this chapter.[177] Our present concern is with the question to what extent the presumption of undue influence operates in such cases between husband and wife. This way of putting the question assumes that the interests of these parties are opposed to each other; but in practice this may well

---

[170] ibid. at [92].

[171] See below, at fnn.174 and 175.

[172] *Etridge* case, above, fn.158 at [14].

[173] ibid. at [18].

[174] ibid. at [107].

[175] ibid. at [161]; cf. *McGregor v Taylor* [2002] 2 Lloyd's Rep. 468 at [16] (but see also *Etridge* case at [93]).

[176] At fnn.172 and 173, above.

[177] See below, para.10–037. One of the cases under appeal concerned a different kind of dispute, i.e. one between the wife and her solicitor.

not be true in the present context. In a realistic sense, husband and wife in the situations under discussion may well make common cause against the bank since, if the wife's case of undue influence succeeds against the husband, then the bank may not be able to evict the couple from their home. There is little doubt that this aspect of such cases has influenced the development of the branch of the law.

It is against this background that Lord Nicholls observed that "in the ordinary course" a guarantee by a wife of her husband's business debts is not "to be regarded as a transaction which, failing proof to the contrary, is explicable only on the basis that it has been procured by the exercise of undue influence"[178]; similarly, Lord Scott observed that undue influence is a "relatively unlikely" explanation of such a guarantee.[179] This may be because there is nothing out of the ordinary in the relationship between the husband and wife beyond the normal trust and confidence to be found between a "mutually loyal married couple",[180] or because the transaction is not one which "calls for an explanation",[181] such as, e.g. the guarantee of a loan for the sole and exclusive use of the husband in his personal capacity. In this context, the statements of Lord Hobhouse and Lord Scott,[182] rejecting, or doubting the utility of, the class 2B presumption are therefore, with respect, entirely appropriate (and are indeed reflected in the speech of Lord Nicholls[183]). In "spouse surety" cases, it would normally be inappropriate to apply the class 2B presumption; and the same is probably true of the closely analogous situation of parties living together in a quasi-marital relationship without being married.[184] But it is submitted that the same reasoning does not apply to other situations in which there is a relationship of trust and confidence, a transaction calling for explanation, and *no* explanation more plausible than that it was procured by undue influence: e.g. in cases such as *Tate v Williamson*.[185] In such cases, there is still scope for the presumption that the transaction was procured by undue influence, even though the relationship of the parties is not one in which (in Lord Nicholls' words) "the law presumes, irrebuttably, that one party had influence over the other".[186]

(iii) *Rebutting the presumption*

The free exercise of independent will. The presumption of undue influence **10–026** is rebutted if the party benefiting from the transaction (A) shows that it was "the free exercise of independent will".[187] The most usual way of doing this is to show

---

[178] *Etridge* case, above, fn.158 at [30].

[179] ibid. at [162].

[180] ibid. at [159]. See also Lord Scott's assessment of the facts in the *Harris* appeal, at [224]. cf. *Barclays Bank v Coleman* in which it was found that the wife was "in a position of subservience and obedience to the wishes of her husband" (at [283]) and could therefore have set the transaction aside "against" her husband; her claim for relief against the bank whose loan to him she had guaranteed failed on grounds to be discussed later in this chapter: below, para.10–037.

[181] ibid. at [31].

[182] See above, fnn.174 and 175.

[183] *Etridge* case above, fn.158, at [30].

[184] cf. ibid. at [47].

[185] (1866) L.R. 2 Ch.App. 55; above, para.10–023 and other cases there cited.

[186] *Etridge* case above, fn.158, at [18].

[187] *Inche Noriah v Shaik Allie bin Omar* [1929] A.C. 127 at 136; *Mahoney v Purnell* [1996] 3 All E.R. 61 at 85; *Royal Bank of Scotland v Etridge (No.2)* [2001] UKHL 44; [2002] 2 A.C. 773; [2001] 4 All E.R. 44 at [7]; *Hammond v Osborn* [2002] EWCA Civ 865; [2002] W.T.L.R. 1125.

that the other party (B) had independent advice before entering into the transaction.[188] But the mere fact that independent advice was given will not of itself save the transaction.[189] The advice must be competent and based on knowledge of all the relevant facts.[190] It has been suggested that the independent adviser must also approve the transaction, and that his advice must be followed.[191] This may be necessary where the influence is particularly strong, or where a very large gift is made; but it is not necessary in every case.[192] There is indeed no invariable rule that independent advice is necessary to save the transaction[193]; but A would lack elementary prudence if he did not ensure that such advice was given.

10–027   **The totality of the evidence.** Although the provision of independent advice is the most usual way of rebutting the presumption of undue influence, it is clear from the above that it is not decisive in every case and the reality is that the "kind of evidence needed to rebut the presumption is entirely at large".[194] As it has been said, even where the requirements for the presumption have been met "when the principal participants have given oral evidence, the issue for the Court is whether on the totality of the evidence, including any appropriate inference, it finds that the transaction was in fact brought about by undue influence."[195] It is primarily for this reason that the distinction between actual and presumed undue influence is misleading; they are not "alternatives to each other".[196] It follows that if the court finds as a fact that B was *not* the victim of actual undue influence,[197] then B cannot succeed on the ground of presumed undue influence; for the former finding rebuts the presumed fact.[198]

10–028   **Successive agreements.** A and B may enter into an initial agreement which is voidable for undue influence, but then replace it with a further agreement which

---

[188] *Allcard v Skinner* (1887) 36 Ch.D. 145 at 190; *Bullock v Lloyds Bank* [1955] Ch. 317; *Claughton v Price* [1997] E.G.C.S. 51.

[189] Particularly stringent rules apply where a solicitor buys from or sells to his client: *Wright v Carter* [1903] 1 Ch, or where a trustee buys from his cestui que trust: *Thomson v Eastwood* (1877) 2 App.Cas. 215.

[190] *Inche Noriah v Shaik Allie bin Omar* [1929] A.C. 127.

[191] *Powell v Powell* [1900] 1 Ch. 243 at 246; *Wright v Carter* [1903] 1 Ch. 27; *Credit Lyonnais Bank Nederland v Burch* [1997] 1 All E.R. 144 at 155–156.

[192] *Re Coomber* [1911] 1 Ch. 723 at 730; *Banco Exterior Industrial SA v Thomas* [1997] 1 All E.R. 46.

[193] *Inche Noriah v Shaik Allie bin Omar* [1929] A.C. 127 at 135; *Re Brocklehurst* [1978] Ch. 14; *R. v HM Attorney General for England and Wales* [2003] UKPC 22 at [23].

[194] Lewison, above fn.65.

[195] *Royal Bank of Scotland Plc v Chandra* [2010] EWHC 105 (Ch); [2010] 1 Lloyd's Rep. 677 at [121]; *Hackett v Crown Prosecution Service* [2011] EWHC 1170 (Admin) at [72]–[74] advocating the need for special care where B is suffering from a mental impairment or a learning difficulty cf. *Etridge* case above, fn.158 at [219].

[196] *Etridge* case above, fn.158, at [291].

[197] There is no inconsistency in the court finding it to have been proved that B *was* the victim of undue influence, but relying in the alternative on the presumption: *Annulment Funding Company Ltd v Cowey* [2010] EWCA Civ 711 at [70].

[198] *Etridge* case above, fn.158, at [281]. In this regard. see Lewison, above fn.65 ("Where ... the judge is satisfied on the totality of the evidence that there was no undue influence then absence of undue influence is proved. One must not confuse absence of evidence with evidence of absence") and his criticism on this basis of the following decisions of the Court of Appeal: *Hammond v Osborn* [2002] EWCA Civ 865; [2002] W.T.L.R. 1125; *Jennings v Cairns* [2003] EWCA 1935; [2004] W.T.L.R. 361; *Niersmans v Pesticcio* [2004] EWCA Civ 372; [2004] W.T.L.R. 699; *Goodchild v Bradbury* [2006] EWCA Civ 1868; [2007] W.T.L.R. 463.

is not, in itself, voidable. If the undue influence which procured the first agreement is still "operative", i.e. B is unaware that the first agreement could have been set aside, the voidability of the first agreement may be "transferred" to the second. Thus, in one case where a first mortgage granted by B was procured by the undue influence of A, B was entitled to set aside a second mortgage entered into to discharge the first, notwithstanding that the second mortgage itself was not procured by undue influence, on the basis that the second mortgage was granted before B became aware that she had a right to avoid the first.[199] By contrast, in another case B was not entitled to set aside a settlement agreement which had been entered into to terminate an earlier management agreement. The management agreement was found to have been procured by undue influence, but B had received independent advice before entering the settlement agreement which would have made him aware of the right to set aside the management agreement.[200]

(c) Remedies

Rescission. The normal remedy in cases of undue influence is to set aside the impugned transaction.[201] The right to rescind for undue influence is barred on grounds similar to those which limit the right to rescind for misrepresentation.

10–029

Impossibility of restitution. The party seeking rescission must restore benefits that he has obtained under the contract. He may be allowed to rescind in spite of the fact that he cannot make *precise* restitution, so long as equity can achieve a result that is "practically just".[202] The point is illustrated by *O'Sullivan v Management Agency & Music Ltd*[203] where the claimant sought to set aside for undue influence a number of management, sole agency, recording and publishing agreements and transfers of copyrights. On the one hand the defendants argued that rescission should not be allowed as they could no longer be restored to their pre-contract position in view of the work which they had done to promote the claimant's success; on the other hand the claimant argued that rescission for undue influence was (unlike rescission for misrepresentation) not subject to any requirement of restitution at all. The court rejected both arguments, holding that, even though precise restitution was not possible, rescission could be ordered so long as the court could do substantial justice. This could be done by upholding the claim for rescission while allowing the defendants a reasonable remuneration for their work on behalf of the claimant.[204]

10–030

The pursuit of practical justice may also require a sharing of loss, as well as the restoration of benefits received. In *Allcard v Skinner*[205] where the right to rescind a gift was lost through delay,[206] it was held that, in any event, the claimant would only have been entitled to recover so much of the gift as remained in the

---

[199] *Yorkshire Bank Plc v Tinsley* [2004] EWCA Civ 816; [2004] 1 W.L.R. 2380.
[200] *Wadlow v Samuel* [2007] EWCA Civ 155.
[201] It may be set aside in part, if severable: *Barclays Bank Plc v Caplan* [1998] 1 F.L.R. 532.
[202] *Erlanger v New Sombrero Phosphate Co* (1878) 3 App.Cas. 1218 at 1279; above, para.9–102; *Cheese v Thomas* [1994] 1 W.L.R. 129 (cf. *Dunbar Bank Plc v Nadeem* [1998] 3 All E.R. 876 (where the claim based on undue influence failed)).
[203] [1985] Q.B. 428; above, para.10–023.
[204] cf. above, para.9–102 for similar relief in cases of misrepresentation.
[205] (1887) 36 Ch.D. 145.
[206] See below, para.10–032.

defendant's hands after some of it had been spent in accordance with the claimant's wishes.[207] Similarly, where the purchase of a house jointly by the claimant
and defendant was set aside for undue influence after the value of the house had
fallen, the claimant was not entitled to recover in full the sum he had invested, but
only that sum which represented the same proportion as his contribution to the
purchase price.[208] In neither case is the right to rescind lost, but the claimant is
expected to bear some or all of a subsequent reduction in the value of the property
in question.

10–031   **Affirmation & estoppel.** The right to rescind on the ground of undue
influence may be lost by affirmation of the transaction, acquiescence, or estoppel,[209] but only after the influence (or the relationship giving rise to a presumption
of influence) has ceased.[210] It has been held that affirmation is effective though
made without independent advice and in ignorance of the right to have the
transaction set aside.[211] It is submitted that the law on this point should (as in
cases of misrepresentation and breach) require the injured party to know, or to
have obvious means of knowing, of the right to rescind.[212]

Where a wife had, under her husband's undue influence, joined him in charging
the matrimonial home to a bank and later affirmed the transaction as against the
husband, it was held that she had also lost the secondary right of avoidance against
the bank[213] which would, but for the affirmation, have been available to her under
the rules stated later in this chapter.[214]

10–032   **Delay.** The victim of undue influence must "seek relief within a reasonable
time after the removal of the influence under which the gift was made".[215] If with
knowledge or obvious means of knowledge of his rights he fails to seek relief, he
is assumed to have affirmed the transaction.

10–033   **Third party rights.** The right to rescind may be lost by the intervention of
third party rights. In one common type of case[216] this has given rise to a number
of problems, so that this issue is discussed separately below.

10–034   **Damages.** Damages as such are not available for undue influence. Where,
however, rescission is no longer possible, the court may make an award in the
nature of damages giving the victim of the undue influence the difference between
the amount for which he parted with the subject-matter and its fair value at the
time of the transaction.[217]

---

[207] (1887) 36 Ch.D. 145 at 164, 171, 180, 186.
[208] *Cheese v Thomas* [1994] W.L.R. 129, Chen-Wishart 110 L.Q.R. 173; *Smith v Cooper* [2010]
EWCA Civ 722; [2010] 2 F.C.R. 551.
[209] *Goldsworthy v Brickell* [1987] Ch. 378 at 410–411.
[210] *Moxon v Payne* (1873) L.R. 8 Ch. App. 881 at 885.
[211] *Mitchell v Homfray* (1882) 8 Q.B.D. 587. See also: *Goldsworthy v Brickell* [1987] Ch. 378 at 412,
416.
[212] See above, para.9–108; below, para.18–080.
[213] *First National Bank Plc v Walker* [2001] 1 F.L.R. 505.
[214] See below, para.10–037.
[215] *Allcard v Skinner* (1887) 36 Ch.D. 145 at 187.
[216] The second of those explained in para.10–035, below.
[217] *Mahoney v Purnell* [1996] 3 All E.R. 61; Birks [1997] R.L.R. 72.

(d) Undue Influence and Third Parties

Two types of cases call for discussion. In the first, A acquires property from B   **10–035**
under a transaction procured, or presumed to have been procured, by undue
influence; and A then transfers that property to C. In the second, A by undue
influence, or in circumstances in which undue influence may be presumed,
induces B to enter into a contract with C. The question in each case is to what
extent C is adversely affected by the undue influence exerted, or presumed to have
been exerted, by A on B. The principles which have emerged from cases concerned mainly with undue influence also apply where B's consent has been
"vitiated" in other ways, e.g. misrepresentation,[218] or duress.[219]

Property acquired by undue influence transferred to third party. In this   **10–036**
type of case, B can set the transaction aside if C did not give value for the transfer
from A or if he took it "with notice of the equity . . . or with notice of the
circumstances from which the court infers the equity".[220] In this context, "notice"
refers not only to actual knowledge of those circumstances but also to cases in
which it is alleged that C ought to have known of them, or (in other words) where
he had constructive notice of them. The "circumstances," notice of which will
prejudicially affect C, are those that would, but for the transfer to him, have
entitled B to relief against A on the ground of undue influence.[221] But B will not
be entitled to set the transaction aside against C on this ground if C has in good
faith (i.e. without notice, actual or constructive) and for value acquired an interest
for value in the subject-matter. For example, in *O'Sullivan v Management Agency
& Music Ltd*[222] relief was not available against a company which had acquired
some of the claimant's copyrights and tapes in good faith and for value.

Undue influence inducing contract with third party. Our concern here is   **10–037**
with the situation in which A is alleged to have induced B to deal directly with C.
The most common (though not the only[223]) illustration of this situation is
provided by a large group of cases in which a loan was made by C (a bank or
building society) to A for the purposes of A's business[224] and B (usually A's wife)
guaranteed the loan and provided security for it, e.g. by a charge on the matrimonial home owned by B or by A and B jointly. On A's default, the question would
arise whether C was adversely affected by undue influence exerted or presumed to
have been exerted by A on B (or by some other vitiating factor, such as misrepresentation, that would have operated between A and B, had the impugned
transaction been between them).

Whether third party "put on inquiry". Before the *Etridge* case, the answer   **10–038**
to this question had been said to depend on whether C had "constructive

---

[218] As in *Barclays Bank Plc v O'Brien* [1994] 1 A.C. 180; cf. *Annulment Funding Company Ltd v Cowey* [2010] EWCA Civ 711 at [64].
[219] *Halpern v Halpern* [2006] EWHC 603 (Comm); [2006] 2 Lloyd's Rep. 83 at [96]; appeal allowed in part [2007] EWCA Civ 291; [2008] Q.B. 195.
[220] *Bainbrigge v Browne* (1881) 18 Ch.D. 188 at 197.
[221] See above, paras 10–012—10–028.
[222] [1985] Q.B. 428 at 459–460.
[223] See *Naidoo v Naidu, The Times,* November 1, 2000.
[224] *Bank of Cyprus v Markou* [1999] 2 All E.R. 707; *Royal Bank of Scotland v Etridge (No.2)* [2001] UKHL 44, [2002] 2 A.C. 773 at [49].

notice"[225] of the circumstances that would (or would be presumed to have) vitiated the transaction between A and B.[226] In the *Etridge* case,[227] however, the House of Lords discouraged this use, in the present context, of the concept of "constructive notice" (which normally operates in the context of transfers of *property* by persons with a defective title[228]). Instead, the test is whether C, the bank, is "put on inquiry."[229] Even this is "strictly a misnomer"[230] since C is not bound to investigate the state of the relationship between A and B[231]; but the phrase is a convenient one to indicate that C must take reasonable steps to reduce the risk of B's entering into the transaction as a result of undue influence (or other similar vitiating factor) exerted by A on B.[232] The circumstances in which such steps must be taken go far beyond those in which the vitiating factor actually exists or is presumed to exist. Thus "a bank is put on inquiry whenever a wife offers to stand surety for her husband's debts"[233] even though (as the discussion in an earlier part of this chapter shows) in many such cases the wife will not be able to show that the guarantee was actually procured by undue influence or to rely on the presumption that it was so procured.[234] The law as to when C is "put on inquiry" or (in other words) required to take steps to protect B against the risk of B's consent having been improperly obtained) was extensively reviewed in the *Etridge* case, from which it appears that C's duty in this respect depends primarily on two factors.

10–039   **The nature of the impugned transaction.** The first factor which may put C on inquiry is the nature of the impugned transaction. Thus C's duty will arise where B guarantees business debts incurred by A or by a company through which A runs his business.[235] But a bank is not "put on inquiry" where it makes a joint loan to a husband and wife (even if the loan is secured on their matrimonial home) "unless the bank is aware that the loan is being made for the husband's purposes, as distinct from their joint purposes."[236] The reason for the distinction is that a wife's guarantee of her husband's business debts is, on its face, disadvantageous to her (in the sense of her not deriving any direct benefit from it), while this is not true of a joint loan to her and her husband.[237]

---

[225] *Barclays Bank Plc v O'Brien* [1994] 1 A.C. 180 at 186.
[226] An alternative ground for allowing B to set the transaction aside was that C had constituted A as his agent for the purpose of concluding the transaction with B. But the reasoning has been described as "artificial" (*Barclays Bank Plc v O'Brien* [1994] 1 A.C. 180 at 195) and is now unlikely to be followed unless A had acted as C's agent "in a real sense": *CIBC Mortgages Plc v Pitt* [1994] 1 A.C. 200 at 211.
[227] *Royal Bank of Scotland v Etridge (No.2)* [2001] UKHL 44; [2002] 2 A.C. 773.
[228] ibid. at [39].
[229] ibid. at [44].
[230] ibid.
[231] *Mortgage Agency Services Number Two Ltd v Chater* [2003] EWCA Civ 490; [2004] 1 P. & C.R. 4 at [67].
[232] *Etridge* case, above fn.227, at [41].
[233] ibid. at [44], [46]. The burden of proof is on B to show that C knew her to be A's wife living with him (or that there was an analogous relationship between them) and that the transaction was one calling for an explanation; it is then up to C to show that it took reasonable steps to ensure that B's consent was properly obtained: *Barclays Bank Plc v Boulter* [1999] 1 W.L.R. 1919.
[234] See above, para.10–025.
[235] *Etridge* case, above, fn.227, at [48].
[236] ibid. citing *CIBC Mortgages v Pitt* [1994] 1 A.C. 200; contrast *Goode Durrant Administration v Biddulph* [1995] F.C.R. 196; *Allied Irish Bank v Byrne* [1995] 2 F.L.R. 325.
[237] Nor of a joint loan to mother and son: *Mortgage Agency Services Number Two Ltd v Chater* [2003] EWCA Civ 490; [2004] 1 P. & C.R. 4.

The relationship between the parties. The second factor which may put C   **10–040**
on inquiry is the relationship between A and B. In most of the reported cases, B
was A's wife; but C's duty applies equally in the converse case where "the husband
stands surety for his wife's debts"[238] and to "the case of unmarried couples,
whether heterosexual or homosexual".[239] It can apply even where the relationship
is neither a marital nor a quasi-marital one but is one in which trust and
confidence is in fact reposed by B in A.[240] According to a "wider principle"
approved by Lord Nicholls in the *Etridge* case,[241] the bank's duty extends to all
cases in which the relationship between the surety (B) and the principal debtor is
a non-commercial one.[242] The advantage of this formulation of the principle is that
it promotes certainty in the sense that the creditor's duty to take steps to protect
the surety against the risks described above will arise in all such suretyship cases
and will not depend on any investigation by the bank of the actual state of the
relationship between A and B. The principle would not, on the other hand, apply
where the relationship between A and B was a commercial one: e.g. where they
were associated companies or where A paid B a fee for acting as surety.[243]

Steps to be taken by a third party put on inquiry. The steps that C (the   **10–041**
bank) is required to take in performance of its duty were also reviewed in the
Etridge case. As the duty is no more than one to take reasonable care to protect B
(the surety) against the risk of undue influence, C is not required itself to
investigate the question whether B was in fact subjected to such influence.[244] Nor
is it necessary[245] for C to arrange for one of its representatives to hold a personal
meeting with B.[246] It will (in future cases[247]) suffice for C to communicate
directly[248] with B to the effect that C will require a solicitor acting for B[249] (who
may also act for A or C (or both of them) in the transaction[250] to confirm to C in
writing that the solicitor has explained to B the nature and effects of the documents to be signed by B, containing the transaction[251]; this explanation must be
given in a face-to-face meeting between the solicitor and B, conducted in the
absence of A.[252] The solicitor must also be supplied by C with the financial
information that he needs for the purpose of this explanation.[253] If these steps are
taken, C will normally be entitled to rely on the solicitor's confirmation that he has

---

[238] *Etridge* case, above, fn.227, at [47].

[239] ibid.; *Barclays Bank Plc v O'Brien* [1994] A.C. 180 at 198; *Massey v Midland Bank Plc* [1995] 1
All E.R. 929 at 933.

[240] e.g. *Avon Finance Co v Bridger* [1985] 2 All E.R. 281, approved in *Barclays Bank Plc v O'Brien*,
above; *Credit Lyonnais Bank Nederland NV v Burch* [1997] 1 All E.R. 144.

[241] *Etridge* case, above, fn.227, at [82], citing Birks in Rose (ed.), *Restitution and Banking Law*,
p.185.

[242] ibid. at [87].

[243] ibid. at [88].

[244] ibid. at [53].

[245] Though such a step may be sufficient if the required explanation and recommendation to seek
independent legal advice are given: ibid. at [50].

[246] ibid. at [55].

[247] See the reference in ibid. at [50] to "the future".

[248] ibid. at [79].

[249] See *National Westminster Bank Plc v Amin* [2002] UKHL 9; [2002] 1 F.L.R. 735, where it was not
clear that this requirement had been satisfied.

[250] *Etridge* case, above, fn.227, at [74].

[251] ibid. at [79].

[252] ibid. at [76].

[253] ibid. at [79].

"advised the wife [B] appropriately".[254] The word "advised" here refers to the solicitor's duty to *explain* the transaction: it is no part of his duty "to veto the transaction"[255] merely because he thinks it is not in B's best interests.[256] If, indeed, it is "*glaringly* obvious that the wife (B) is being *grievously* wronged"[257] he should decline to act further; and it seems that, if he did not so decline, his confirmation would not protect C. But in cases falling outside this extreme range, C is not precluded from relying on the solicitor's confirmation merely because the solicitor is not satisfied that the transaction was one into which [B] "could sensibly be advised to enter",[258] nor even because the transaction was "one into which no competent solicitor could have advised the wife [B] to enter".[259] If C takes the required steps (outlined above), it will normally[260] be entitled to rely on the solicitor's confirmation that the solicitor has "advised the wife [B] appropriately."[261] If C fails to take the required steps, C runs the risk of not being able to enforce the transaction against B.[262]

The above steps are designed to protect B against the *risk* of undue influence (or similar vitiating factors). The mere fact that they were not taken does not therefore provide grounds on which B will be entitled to set the transaction aside for undue influence. B will be so entitled, even if C has not taken the required steps, only if B can also establish either that the transaction was procured by undue influence or that the basic facts of the "evidential presumption"[263] that it was so procured exist and if the presumption is not otherwise rebutted.

3. UNCONSCIONABLE BARGAINS[264]

10–042   Equity can give relief against unconscionable bargains[265] in certain cases in which one party is in a position to exploit a particular weakness of the other. The burden of justifying such a transaction is on the former party.[266]

(a) Catching Bargains[267]

10–043   Equity can set aside or modify an agreement with an "expectant heir" made in anticipation of his expectations. The transaction need not amount to a sale of or charge on the expectation.[268] Thus equity can relieve against a post-obit bond, by

---

[254] ibid. at [56]; *Barclays Bank Plc v Goff* [2001] EWCA Civ 635; [2001] 2 All E.R. (Comm) 847.
[255] ibid. at [61].
[256] ibid.
[257] ibid. at [62] (emphasis added).
[258] ibid. at [58]–[59].
[259] ibid. at [63].
[260] ibid. at [61]; but not if C knows that the solicitor "has not duly advised" B: *Etridge* case, above, fn.227, at [57]; cf. *National Westminster Bank Plc v Breeds* [2001] N.L.J. 170.
[261] ibid. at [56]; cf. ibid. at [292] where this requirement was held to have been complied with in *Barclays Bank Plc v Coleman*, one of the cases under consideration in the *Etridge* case.
[262] But only against B; if the property against which the loan is secured is jointly owned by A and B, the court may order its sale so as to realise A's share: *First National Bank Plc v Achampong* [2003] EWCA Civ 487; [2004] 1 F.C.R. 18.
[263] See above, para.10–019.
[264] Capper 126 L.Q.R. 403.
[265] Not against *gifts*, though these can be set aside for undue influence: *Langton v Langton* [1995] F.L.R. 890.
[266] *Aylesford v Morris* (1873) L.R. 8 Ch.App. 484.
[267] Dawson 45 Mich.L.Rev. 267–279.
[268] *Aylesford v Morris* (1873) L.R. 8 Ch.App. 484.

which a debtor promises his creditor a certain sum if the debtor survives a named person and becomes entitled to a share in his estate.[269] Nor is the equitable jurisdiction confined to "heirs": relief can be given to a young man whose sole expectation of wealth is from his father, who is still alive.[270]

A person who sold a reversionary interest could at one time obtain relief by proving only that the sale was at an undervalue. The law was changed by the Sales of Reversions Act 1867, now re-enacted in s.174 of the Law of Property Act 1925. This provides that no sale of a "reversionary interest" (which includes a mere expectancy) shall be opened or set aside merely on the ground of undervalue; but the section expressly preserves the jurisdiction of the court to set aside or modify unconscionable bargains. Undervalue remains "a material element in cases in which it is not the sole equitable ground for relief",[271] and may form the sole ground for relief if it is "so gross as to amount of itself to evidence of fraud".[272] Fraud is not here used in its common law sense[273] but means "an unconscientious use of the power arising out of" the relative positions of the parties.[274]

(b) Dealing with "Poor and Ignorant" Persons

In *Evans v Llewellin*[275] a poor man became entitled to a share of an estate worth £1,700. He sold it for 200 guineas cash, and was later able to set the transaction aside as it was "improvidently obtained". A modern illustration of the principle may be provided by a case in which an employee of modest financial means guaranteed her employer's overdraft for up to £270,000. The transaction was described as "harsh and unconscionable"[276] and set aside; but the actual ground for the decision was that the relationship between employer and employee was such as to give rise to a presumption of undue influence. It seems that equity may, even in the absence of such influence, give such relief when unfair advantage is taken of a person who is poor, ignorant or weak-minded, or is for some other reason in need of special protection.[277] Specific performance may be refused on similar grounds.[278] The equitable rule is based on unconscientious conduct by the stronger party:[279] relief will not be granted merely because the transaction is unfair[280] or improvident.[281] A fortiori, mere inadequacy of consideration is not a ground for relief where the parties have bargained on equal terms.[282]

10–044

---

[269] See *Chesterfield v Janssen* (1750) 2 Ves.Sen. 125.
[270] *Nevill v Snelling* (1880) 15 Ch.D. 679.
[271] *O'Rorke v Bolingbroke* (1877) 2 App.Cas. 814 at 833.
[272] *Fry v Lane* (1888) 40 Ch.D. 312 at 321.
[273] See above, para.9–029.
[274] *Aylesford v Morris* (1873) L.R. 8 Ch.App. 484 at 491.
[275] (1787) 1 Cox C.C. 333; mentioned with approval in *Fry v Lane*, above; *Clark v Malpas* (1862) 4 D.F. & J. 401; *Lloyds Bank Ltd v Bundy* [1975] Q.B. 326 at 337.
[276] *Credit Lyonnais Bank Nederland NV v Burch* [1997] 1 All E.R. 144 at 151.
[277] e.g. *Cresswell v Potter* [1978] 1 W.L.R 255n. (wife in course of divorce proceedings transferring her share in the matrimonial home to husband without getting independent advice and for inadequate consideration); cf. *Backhouse v Backhouse* [1978] 1 W.L.R. 243. Mere unfamiliarity with the English language is not a ground for relief: *Barclays Bank Plc v Schwartz, The Times*, August 2, 1995.
[278] e.g. *Falcke v Gray* (1859) 4 Drew. 651: see below, para.21–031.
[279] *Strydom v Vendside Ltd* [2009] EWHC 2130 (QB) at [36].
[280] *Alec Lobb (Garages) Ltd v Total Oil (Great Britain) Ltd* [1985] 1 W.L.R. 173; *Hart v O'Connor* [1985] A.C. 1000; *Boustany v Pigott* (1995) 69 P.& C.R. 298. *Irvani v Irvani* [2000] 1 Lloyd's Rep. 412 at 425.
[281] *Fineland Investments Ltd v Pritchard* [2011] EWHC 113 (Ch).
[282] See *Collier v Brown* (1788) 1 Cox C.C. 428; *Western v Russell* (1814) 3 Ves. & B. 187.

4. MONEYLENDING AND CONSUMER PROTECTION

(a) Unfair Credit Relationships

10–045   Statutory powers to control moneylending contracts are now contained in the Consumer Credit Act 1974 (as amended by the Consumer Credit Act 2006). Under that Act, the court has wide powers in relation to any "unfair relationship".[283] It may exercise those powers where the relationship between the creditor and the debtor is unfair because of any of the following: any of the terms of the agreement or of any related agreement; the way in which the creditor has exercised or enforced any of his rights under the agreement or any related agreement; and any other thing done (or not done) by, or on behalf of, the creditor (either before or after the making of the agreement or any related agreement).[284] In deciding whether to make a determination that a relationship is unfair, the court shall have regard to all matters it thinks relevant.[285] Earlier authorities which were concerned with whether an agreement amounted to an "extortionate credit bargain" regarded the requirements to be met as stringent: e.g. a bargain was not "extortionate" merely because it was harsh or even unconscionable.[286] The amendments introduced by the 2006 Act represent a potential widening of the powers of the court.[287]

(b) Consumer Trade Practices

10–046   Reference has been made in Chapter 7 to legislation which provides for administrative control of exemption clauses and of other unfair terms in consumer contracts.[288] It can also be argued that much legislation protects the consumer against a form of economic duress.[289] A similar policy against such duress appears to underlie the statutory provisions giving consumers a "cooling-off" period in certain cases. For example, a person who is induced to sign a regulated consumer credit agreement[290] at home is entitled to cancel it within such a period.[291] And the policy of protecting consumers against certain exemption clauses and unfair terms

---

[283] Consumer Credit Act 1974, s.140(A)–(C). These powers do not extend to consumer credit agreements secured on land that are regulated by the Financial Services Authority under Financial Services and Markets Act 2000: 1974 Act, s.140(A)(5), 16(C). See generally: *Maple Leaf Macro Volatility Master Fund v Rouvroy* [2009] EWHC 257 (Comm); [2009] 1 Lloyd's Rep. 475, at [276]–[290], affirmed without reference to this point [2009] EWCA Civ 1334).

[284] ibid. s.140(A)(1).

[285] ibid. s.140(A)(2).

[286] *Davies v Directloans Ltd* [1986] 1 W.L.R. 823; *Ketley v Scott* [1981] I.C.R. 241; *Paragon Finance Plc v Nash* [2001] EWCA Civ 1466; [2002] 1 W.L.R. 685; *Paragon Finance Plc v Pender* [2005] EWCA Civ 760; [2005] 1 W.L.R. 3412. Nor does it seem that such a term would be affected by Unfair Terms in Consumer Contracts Regulations 1999: see reg.4(2)(a) and reg.6(2)(a), above, para.7–106.

[287] *Patel v Patel* [2009] EWHC 3264; contrast *Khodari v Tamimi* [2009] EWCA 1109; *Maple Leaf Macro Volatility Master Fund v Rouvroy* [2009] EWHC 257 (Comm); [2009] 1 Lloyd's Rep. 475 at [283]–[290], affirmed without consideration of this point [2009] EWCA Civ 1334.

[288] Above, para.7–125.

[289] e.g. The Unfair Commercial Practices Directive 2005/29, [2005] O.J. L149/22, implemented by the Consumer Protection from Unfair Trading Regulations 2008 (SI 2008/1277).

[290] See above, para.5–007.

[291] Consumer Credit Act 1974, ss.67–68; cf. Consumer Protection (Distance Selling) Regulations 2000 (SI 2000/2334) reg.10; Cancellation of Contracts made in a Consumer's Home or Place of Work etc. Regulations 2008 (SI 2008/1816).

has been an important influence on the legislative controls of such terms which have been discussed in Ch.7.[292]

5. INEQUALITY OF BARGAINING POWER[293]

A number of judicial statements give some support to the view that one party to a contract may be entitled to relief if the other has taken unfair advantage of the fact that there is a marked inequality of bargaining power between them. **10–047**

Restraint of trade. One group of such statements is concerned with the special problem of the validity of covenants in restraint of trade.[294] This depends on whether the covenant is "reasonable", and the adequacy of consideration is taken into account in determining the issue of reasonableness.[295] The fairness of the bargain (which to some extent depends on the relative bargaining positions of the parties) is therefore relevant to the validity of the restraint; but the fact that it is taken into account for this purpose does not support a general principle of relief against harsh bargains on the ground of inequality of bargaining power. **10–048**

A general principle? Such a principle was stated (as an alternative ground of decision) by Lord Denning M.R. in *Lloyds Bank Ltd v Bundy.*[296] He referred to a number of rules (discussed earlier[297] in this chapter) under which relief was given against harsh or unfair contracts; and he derived from them the generalisation that **10–049**

" . . . English law gives relief to one who, without independent advice, enters into a contract upon terms which are very unfair or transfers property for a consideration which is grossly inadequate, when his bargaining power is grievously impaired by reason of his own needs or desires, or by his own ignorance or infirmity, coupled with undue influence or pressures brought to bear on him by or for the benefit of the other".[298]

The other members of the Court of Appeal based their decision solely on the equitable doctrine of undue influence.[299] Thus, while expressing "some sympathy"[300] for Lord Denning's principle, they did not find it necessary to express a concluded opinion on it. It follows that the principle does not form the ground for the decision.[301]

---

[292] See above, paras 7–049—7–122.

[293] Cartwright, *Unequal Bargaining*; Thal 8 O.J.L.S. 17.

[294] *A Schroeder Music Publishing Co v Macaulay* [1974] 1 W.L.R. 1308 at 1315; cf. *Clifford Davis Management v WEA Records* [1975] 1 W.L.R. 61; *Shell UK Ltd v Lostock Garages Ltd* [1976] 1 W.L.R. 1187 at 1197; Wooldridge [1977] J.B.L. 312.

[295] See below, para.11–079.

[296] [1975] Q.B. 326; above, para.10–023.

[297] See above, paras 10–012—10–044.

[298] [1975] Q.B. 326 at 339; Beatson 1 O.J.L.S. 426.

[299] See above, para.10–017; cf. *Horry v Tate & Lyle Refineries Ltd* [1982] 2 Lloyd's Rep. 417 at 422.

[300] [1975] Q.B. 326 at 347 (Sir Eric Sachs, with whom Cairns L.J. agreed); cf. *Backhouse v Backhouse* [1978] 1 W.L.R. 243 at 251; *Credit Lyonnais Bank Nederland NV v Burch* [1997] 1 All E.R. 144.

[301] *National Westminster Bank Ltd v Morgan* [1985] A.C. 686 at 708–709.

In a number of later cases, Lord Denning has nevertheless repeated his view that the law recognised a principle of "inequality of bargaining power".[302] The scope of the alleged principle seems to be very wide: it can apparently apply to such disparate transactions or terms as the contract in *Lloyds Bank Ltd v Bundy*,[303] the renegotiation of a contract,[304] the settlement of a tort claim,[305] and the inclusion of an exemption clause in a cleaning contract made in standard form.[306] No clear limit to the principle is stated except that a bargain will not be upset if it is "the result of the ordinary interplay of forces".[307] Reference by Lord Denning to "the American policy of inadequate bargaining power"[308] is from this point of view scarcely reassuring; for the lengths to which American courts have gone in implementing this policy would hardly be acceptable in England without express legislative authority. It is, for example, hard to imagine an English court holding that a consumer could keep goods after paying only part of the price simply because the seller's profit on the full contract price would be excessive.[309] The regulation of these and similar matters is in England, by general consent, left to legislation.[310]

For these reasons, Lord Denning's principle has little judicial[311] support in England. On the contrary, in *Pao On v Lau Yiu Long*[312] the Privy Council, having held that the contract was not voidable for duress,[313] also rejected the argument that it was invalid as having been procured by "an unfair use of a dominant bargaining position".[314] To treat this as a ground of invalidity distinct from duress would, in Lord Scarman's words, "be unhelpful because it would render the law uncertain".[315] In *National Westminster Bank Plc v Morgan* Lord Scarman again expressed similar views when questioning "whether there is any need in the modern law to erect a general principle of relief against inequality of bargaining power".[316] Legislation having dealt with a number of specific instances in which superior bargaining power might be abused,[317] he doubted "whether the courts should assume the burden of formulating further restrictions"[318]; and the need for them to do so has also been reduced by the widening of the scope of duress.[319]

---

[302] *Arrale v Costain Civil Engineering Ltd* [1976] 1 Lloyd's Rep. 98 at 102; *Levison v Patent Steam Carpet Cleaning Co Ltd* [1978] Q.B. 69 at 78.

[303] [1975] Q.B. 326; above, para.10–023.

[304] *D & C Builders v Rees* [1966] 2 Q.B. 617.

[305] *Arrale v Costain Civil Engineering Ltd* [1976] 1 Lloyd's Rep. 98.

[306] *Levison v Patent Steam Carpet Cleaning Co Ltd* [1978] Q.B. 69.

[307] *Lloyds Bank Ltd v Bundy* [1975] Q.B. 326 at 336.

[308] ibid. at 333 (during argument).

[309] *Jones v Star Credit Corp* 298 N.Y.S. 2d 264 (1969).

[310] See *Lloyds Bank Ltd v Bundy* [1975] Q.B. 326 at 336.

[311] Inequality of bargaining power may also be relevant to the exercise of discretions conferred *by legislation* to control contract terms: see, e.g. Unfair Contract Terms Act 1977, Sch.2 para.(a) (above, para.7–081); Consumer Credit Act 1974, s.140A(2) (as inserted by Consumer Credit Act 2006, s.190); Unfair Terms in Consumer Contracts Regulations 1999 (above, para.7–109). But such discretions do not seem to provide any basis for a general *common law* principle: see below, at fn.318.

[312] [1980] A.C. 614.

[313] See above, para.10–008.

[314] [1980] A.C. 614 at 634.

[315] ibid.

[316] ibid. at 708.

[317] See fn.311, above.

[318] [1985] A.C. 686 at 708; cf. *Lloyds Bank Ltd v Bundy* [1975] Q.B. 326 at 336.

[319] See above, para.10–002.

Decisions of the lower courts have similarly rejected the argument that inequality of bargaining power is, of itself, a ground of invalidity[320]; and this is true even in the restraint of trade cases, in which the courts have traditionally taken the "fairness" of the bargain into account.[321]

---

[320] *Horry v Tate & Lyle Refineries Ltd* [1982] 2 Lloyd's Rep. 417 at 422; *Alec Lobb (Garages) Ltd v Total Oil (Great Britain) Ltd* [1985] 1 W.L.R. 173; *CTN Cash & Carry Ltd v Gallaher Ltd* [1994] 4 All E.R. 714 at 717.

[321] The *Alec Lobb* case, above, concerned restraint of trade.

CHAPTER ELEVEN

ILLEGALITY[1]

[1] Buckley, *Illegality and Public Policy*; Furmston (1966) U. of Tor.L.J. 267.

The law may refuse to give full effect to a contract on the ground of illegality, **11–001** i.e. because the contract involves the commission of a legal wrong or is in some other way contrary to public policy.

1. THE PROBLEM OF CLASSIFICATION

Purpose of classification. English writers commonly divide the cases in **11–002** which contracts are affected by illegality into a number of classes. One object of this classification is to make it possible to generalise about the *effects* of illegality; but it is doubtful whether any of the suggested classifications achieve this object to any considerable extent. Another object of classification is purely expository, and this does no harm so long as it is not actually misleading.

Source of the rule infringed. One classification is based on the source of the **11–003** rule infringed. Thus it is sometimes said that a contract is more likely to be invalid for violation of a statute than for violation of a rule of common law. The distinction is appropriate where a statute expressly prohibits or invalidates a contract.[2] But it is not decisive where the statute contains no such express prohibition and the illegality consists only in the method of making or performing the contract.[3] In *St John Shipping Corp v Joseph Rank Ltd*[4] a shipowner committed a statutory offence by overloading his ship while performing a number of contracts for the carriage of goods. Devlin J. held that he was nonetheless entitled to freight, because the object of the statute was to prevent overloading and not to prohibit contracts. This object was to be achieved by imposing a fine, and not by subjecting the shipowner to the additional financial loss which would result from invalidating the contracts of carriage. It is submitted that this approach should not be confined to cases in which the offence is statutory.[5] It would have been just as appropriate, and would probably have led to the same result, had the shipowner been convicted of manslaughter committed in the course of the voyage.

---

[2] e.g. Fair Trading Act 1973, Pt XI, as extended by Trading Schemes Act 1996 (pyramid selling). cf. below, para.11–121.

[3] See *Shaw v Groom* [1970] 2 Q.B. 540; *London & Harrogate Securities Ltd v Pitts* [1976] 1 W.L.R. 1063.

[4] [1957] 1 Q.B. 267.

[5] *Wetherell v Jones* (1832) 3 B. & Ad. 221 at 225–226; *Coral Leisure Group v Barnett* [1981] I.C.R. 503 at 509. For a similar approach in case of a civil wrong, see *The Ypatianna* [1988] Q.B. 345 at 369–370.

11–004   **Legal consequences.** Classification may proceed, alternatively, by the legal consequences of the contracts concerned. Thus, an attempt may be made to distinguish between "illegal" and "void" contracts. This classification cannot, of course, lead to any deductions about the legal effects of the contracts in question as it assumes that those consequences are already known. Moreover, the classification tries to do the impossible. The nature of the illegality which may affect a contract varies almost infinitely in seriousness. To classify these contracts by their effects into only two groups is likely to result in a misleading degree of over-simplification.

11–005   **Legal wrongs and public policy.** In section 2 of this chapter, for purposes of exposition, illegal contracts are divided into two groups, namely contracts involving the commission of a legal wrong and contracts contrary to public policy. The second group includes one particularly important type of contracts, those in restraint of trade. Because of the complexity of the law relating to such contracts, they will be discussed under an independent heading, in section 3. The exact effects of illegality should ideally be discussed separately in relation to each type of contract, but such treatment would be inordinately long. An attempt will therefore be made in section 4 of this chapter to provide a general discussion of the effects of illegality. This approach can be justified on the ground that many of the relevant rules apply to all types of illegal contracts; but it is also often true that the effects vary with the type of illegality. Where this is the case, the general propositions in section 4 will be qualified accordingly.

11–006   **Statutory invalidity.** Where a statute prohibits or regulates the making or performance of a contract, breach of the statute may make the contract illegal, void or unenforceable, or leave it perfectly valid. If the breach of the statute amounts to a crime, the effects of its breach depend on the principles discussed in section 2, part 1.[6] Apart from these principles, the effect of a breach of a statute depends primarily on its express provisions, which may, for example, make the contract (or the offending term[7]) void,[8] voidable[9] or unenforceable[10]; or state that the breach is not to affect the validity of the contract.[11] The difficult cases are those in which the statute gives no clear lead. They may be divided into three groups.

11–007   **"Void" contracts held to be illegal.** Section 1 of the Life Assurance Act 1774 provides that "no insurance shall be made" by any person on the life of another, or on certain other risks, unless the assured has an interest in the subject-matter

---

[6] See below, paras 11–011—11–031.

[7] e.g. the former Sex Discrimination Act 1975, s.77(1) and (2); Race Relations Act 1977, s.72(1) and (2) (now repealed by the Equality Act 2010)—"void" but only "unenforceable against" the victim of unlawful discrimination or harassment: *Orphanos v Queen Mary College* [1985] A.C. 761; similarly, Disability Discrimination Act 1995, s.26(1) (also now repealed by the Equality Act 2010). The Equality Act 2010, s.142(1) provides only that the offending term is "unenforceable against" the person in question; and below, para.11–121.

[8] e.g. Matrimonial Causes Act 1973, s.34 (below, para.11–048); Pension Schemes Act 1993, s.160(1)(a) ("void"); Competition Act 1998, s.2(4) (making agreements prohibited by s.2(1) "void").

[9] Companies Act 2006, s.213(2); *Re Ciro Citterio Menswear Plc* [2002] EWHC 662; [2002] 2 All E.R. 717.

[10] Either in so many words (e.g. Equality Act 2010, s.142(1); Consumer Credit Act 1974, s.40(1); Financial Services and Markets Act 2000, ss.26(1), 27(1) (unenforceable against one party only)) or by saying that "no action shall be brought", or by use of similar expressions: e.g. Statute of Frauds 1677, s.4; above para.5–013; Pension Schemes Act 1993, s.160(1)(b) ("unenforceable").

[11] e.g. Financial Services and Markets Act 2000, s.20(2)(b).

of the insurance. Contracts of insurance made in breach of this section are declared to be "void" but have repeatedly been held illegal.[12] Similarly, s.1 of the Marine Insurance Act 1745 provided that "no assurance shall be made" on the terms that no further proof of interest than the policy should be required and declared that policies made in breach of the section were to be "void"; and again such policies were held illegal.[13] But when the section was replaced by s.4(1) of the Marine Insurance Act 1906, which simply made such policies void, it was held that they were no longer illegal.[14] The reason for this distinction seems to be that the older Acts first prohibited the contracts (though without penalty) and then declared them void, while the Act of 1906 contains no prohibition but only a declaration of nullity.

Consequences of breach not specified. A statute may prohibit the making of a contract without imposing a criminal penalty or specifying all the civil consequences of breach. Contracts which violated such a prohibition were held illegal[15] if such a consequence was, in the court's view, necessary to give effect to the purpose of the prohibition.[16]   11–008

Formalities required by statute. A statute may require some formalities to be observed in making a contract, or require some specific terms to be inserted into the contract, and again fail to specify the consequences of failure to comply with the requirement.[17] The question then is whether the statutory requirement is to be construed as being "directory only or obligatory".[18] Failure to comply with the statute makes the contract void if the requirement is obligatory, but not if it is only directory. In the case in which the distinction was drawn, statutory requirements as to the execution of a mortgage of a ship were held to be obligatory. Failure to comply with them accordingly invalidated the transaction though this effect of the failure was not specified in the legislation.[19] It seems that in applying the distinction the court will ask whether it is necessary, to promote the object of the statute, to hold that failure to comply with its requirements should invalidate transactions.[20] In the absence of any express provision in the statute concerned, a failure to comply with the formalities required does not make the contract illegal so as to trigger the effects discussed in Part 4 of this Chapter.   11–009

Gaming and wagering, or "gambling" contracts. Previously, a contract that fell into the category of a gaming or wagering contract was unenforceable   11–010

---

[12] *Hughes v Liverpool Victoria Legal Friendly Society* [1916] 2 K.B. 482; *Re London County Commercial Reinsurance Office* [1922] 2 Ch. 67. cf. *Fuji Finance Inc v Aetna Life Ins Co Ltd* [1997] Ch. 173.
[13] *Gedge v Royal Exchange Assurance* [1900] 2 Q.B. 214; *contra, Tasker v Scott* (1815) 6 Taunt. 234.
[14] *Re London County Commercial Reinsurance Office* [1922] 2 Ch. 67.
[15] *Sykes v Beadon* (1897) 11 Ch.D. 170; disapproved in *Smith v Anderson* (1880) 15 Ch.D. 247, but not on this point: *Shaw v Benson* (1883) 11 Q.B.D. 563; cf. *Greenberg v Cooperstein* [1926] Ch. 657. The prohibition with which these cases were concerned is repealed by the Regulatory Reform (Removal of 20 Member Limit in Partnerships, etc.) Order 2002 (SI 2002/3203).
[16] For conflicting views on the purpose of a statutory provision which failed to specify the civil consequences of a prohibition, see *Fuji Finance Ltd v Aetna Life Ins Co Ltd* [1997] Ch. 173; cf. below, para.11–122.
[17] See above, paras 5–007—5–010 for cases in which the statute does specify the effects of non-compliance.
[18] *Liverpool Borough Bank v Turner* (1860) 2 D.F. & J. 502 at 508.
[19] ibid. (actual decision reversed by Merchant Shipping Act 1894, s.57).
[20] cf. *St. John Shipping Corp v Joseph Rank Ltd* [1957] 1 Q.B. 267; above, para.11–003.

because it was "null and void".[21] As a result of Pt 17 of the Gambling Act 2005[22] "the fact that a contract relates to gambling[23] shall not prevent its enforcement".[24] This wording deliberately leaves open the possibility that such a contract may be unenforceable on some other ground,[25] including illegality.[26] The 2005 Act may itself be the source of such illegality, e.g. in the case of a gambling contract entered into pursuant to unlicensed commercial gambling.[27] The effect of the reforms contained in Pt 17 is that the "special" unenforceability of gambling contracts has been removed. Their unenforceability on grounds of illegality will turn on the principles to be considered in the rest of this chapter.

2. TYPES OF ILLEGALITY

(a) Contracts Involving the Commission of a Legal Wrong

(i) *Contracts amounting to a legal wrong*

11–011   A contract is illegal[28] if the mere making of it is a legal wrong: e.g. if legislation prohibits the making of the contract.[29] At common law, a contract to "rig the market" by offering inflated prices for shares in a particular company is similarly illegal as it is a criminal conspiracy.[30]

A contract to stifle a prosecution for treason is illegal as it amounts to compounding. It is also an offence for a person who knows that a "relevant offence" has been committed, and that he has information which may help to secure the conviction of the offender, to accept or agree to accept any consideration (other than the making good of the loss or injury caused by the offence) for not disclosing the information.[31] The mere making of some contracts is expressly made criminal

---

[21] Gaming Act 1845, s.18.

[22] Which came into force on September 1, 2007: SI 2006/3272.

[23] Defined as gaming, betting and participating in a lottery: 2005 Act, s.3. These terms are further defined by ss.6, 9, 10 (which excludes from "betting" regulated activity within the meaning of s.22 of Financial Services and Markets Act 2000), 12(1), 14 and 15.

[24] Gambling Act 2005, s.335(1). For the impact of this on other effects of the previous non-enforceability of such contracts, see paras 3–032, 3–157. One consequence of the wording of s.335(1) is that the parties may expressly reassert the status of a gaming contract prior to the 2005 reforms by ensuring, through appropriate drafting, that there is no "contract" between them, save in honour only; cf. below, para.11–055. In addition to s.18 of the 1845 Act, the following are also repealed (by s.334(1) of the 2005 Act): Gaming Act 1710, s.1 (voiding of security for winnings or for repayment of gaming loan, etc.); Gaming Act 1835 (security deemed given for illegal consideration); Gaming Act 1892, s.1 (voiding of promise to repay); Financial Services and Markets Act 2000, s.412 (gaming contracts), though not with retrospective effect (s.334(2)). Nothing in the 2005 Act appears intended to affect Marine Insurance Act 1906, s.4 under which insurance without an insurable interest is void, but the technique used to achieve this is to deem it to be a "gaming or wagering contract" (s.4(2)).

[25] In addition to the grounds on which any other contract may be unenforceable, the Gambling Commission has the power, in certain cases, to make an order that any contract in relation to a bet is void: s.336. If such an order is made any money paid in relation to the bet must be repaid to the payor: s.336(2).

[26] s.335(2) states: "Subsection (1) is without prejudice to any rule of law preventing the enforcement of a contract on the grounds of unlawfulness (other than a rule relating specifically to gambling)."

[27] ss.33, 37.

[28] Except to the extent that a statute provides the contrary: e.g. Equality Act 2010, s.142(1).

[29] See *Mohamed v Alaga & Co* [2000] 1 W.L.R. 1815; *Hughes v Kingston upon Hull CC* [1999] Q.B. 1193; see now para.11–013, below.

[30] *Scott v Brown* [1892] 2 Q.B. 724; cf. *Harry Parker Ltd v Mason* [1940] 2 K.B. 590.

[31] Criminal Law Act 1967, s.5(1); "relevant offence" is defined by s.4(1A), as inserted by Serious Organised Crime and Police Act 2005, Sch.7, Pt 3.

by statute: it is, for example, an offence to agree to indemnify a surety in criminal proceedings against liability to forfeit a recognisance,[32] and to deal for payment in human material.[33] Such contracts are no doubt illegal, as is one which causes or permits a child or young person to gamble with the holder of an operating licence under the Gambling Act 2005.[34] And where the making or variation of a contract is prohibited by a court order, disobedience of the order amounts to contempt of court; and the prohibited contract, or variation, is illegal.[35]

Champerty. A contract by which one person agrees to finance another's litigation in return for a share in the proceeds, the former having no genuine or substantial interest in the outcome,[36] used to amount to the crime and tort of champerty; and accordingly the contract was illegal. Although criminal and tortious liability for champerty have been abolished[37] a champertous agreement remains, as a general rule, illegal.[38] It has been said that, to be champertous, the agreement must amount to "wanton or officious intermeddling with the disputes of others", to which "must be added the notion of a division of the spoils."[39] The former requirement is a description of maintenance[40] so that champerty may be seen as a sub-species thereof. More recently, and in the light of the statutory developments which are described in the next paragraph, it has been acknowledged that there may be champerty without maintenance and that what is "in play" is the policy "against a person who is in a position to influence the outcome of litigation having an interest in that outcome."[41]   11–012

Contingency or conditional fees. At common law agreements between a client and his legal advisers in litigation for the payment of either a "contingency" or a "conditional" fee are champertous and illegal.[42] Conditional fee agreements are those which provide that the legal adviser is to be paid his fee if he wins the case but not if he loses it. With respect to such agreements, legislation now provides[43] that, in most cases,[44] an agreement in writing can validly be made[45] by which a client promises to pay a "conditional fee" to a person who provides him   11–013

---

[32] Bail Act 1976, s.9.

[33] Human Tissue Act 2004, s.32.

[34] s.46.

[35] *Clarke v Chadburn* [1985] 1 W.L.R. 78.

[36] See below, paras 15–062—15–065.

[37] Criminal Law Act 1967, ss.13(1), 14(1).

[38] Criminal Law Act 1967, s.14(2); *Trendtex Trading Corp v Crédit Suisse* [1982] A.C. 679; *McFarlane v EE Caledonia (No.2)* [1995] 1 W.L.R. 366 at 372.

[39] *Giles v Thompson* [1994] 1 A.C. 142 at 164, citing *British Cash and Parcel Conveyors Ltd v Lamson Store Service Co Ltd* [1908] 1 K.B. 1006, at 1014.

[40] See below, para.15–058.

[41] *Sibthorpe v Southwark L.B.C.* [2011] EWCA Civ 25 at [54], citing *R. (Factortame Ltd) v Secretary of State for Transport, Local Government and the Regions (No.8)* [2002] EWCA Civ 932; [2003] Q.B. 381 at [76].

[42] *Wallersteiner v Moir (No.2)* [1975] Q.B. 373; *Awwad v Geraghty & Co* [2001] Q.B. 570; *Westlaw Services Ltd v Boddy* [2009] EWCA Civ 929; [2011] P.N.L.R. 4; *Sibthorpe v Southwark L.B.C.* [2011] EWCA Civ 25.

[43] Courts and Legal Services Act 1990, s.58 and 58A, as substituted by Access to Justice Act 1999, s.27; and see fnn.45 and 46, below.

[44] Criminal proceedings and most family proceedings are excluded by s.58A(1) of the 1990 Act.

[45] Courts and Legal Services Act 1990, s.58(3). And see: Conditional Fee Agreements (Revocation) Regulations 2005, SI 2005/2305

with advocacy or litigation services in legal proceedings.[46] The condition may be that the litigation ends in the client's favour; and the fee may be a "success fee", that is, one which provides that, in that event, the provider's fee is to be increased above the amount of normal fee[47] by a percentage (not exceeding that specified by the Lord Chancellor[48]). Conditional fee agreements which are not in terms validated by this legislation are declared by it to be unenforceable,[49] and are also illegal at common law,[50] though it has been suggested that it may be right "to step back and consider the matter afresh in the light of modern conditions."[51] This has led to the view that there is at least no requirement to *expand* the scope of champerty in this area, so that a conditional fee agreement which was otherwise lawful was not illegal because the legal advisers also provided an indemnity to their client against the costs which would have to be paid if the claim was unsuccessful.[52] It has not, as yet, led to the view that agreements which are champertous under the existing law should be regarded as lawful.[53] Thus, for example, contingency fee agreements under which the legal adviser is remunerated by a share in the amount recovered remain illegal. So far as agreements with parties who are not legal advisers are concerned, e.g. accountants[54] and surveyors,[55] the modern approach is to make an assessment on a case by case basis and only to regard as illegal those agreements which "would corrupt public justice".[56]

(ii) *Contracts to commit a crime*

11–014   A contract for the deliberate commission of a crime is obviously illegal.[57] Such a contract would also amount to conspiracy. But many statutory crimes can be committed without criminal intent; and there are cases in which only one of the parties to a contract has any criminal intent. The exact effects of illegality on such contracts, where one or both parties act in good faith, will be considered later in this chapter.[58]

---

[46] These need not be court proceedings: Courts and Legal Services Act 1990, s.58A(4).

[47] Courts and Legal Services Act 1990, s.58(2)(a): i.e. the amount to which he would have been entitled if his right to payment had not been conditional on the success of the client's claim.

[48] ibid., s.58(4)(c); Conditional Fee Agreements Order 2000 (SI 2000/823), reg.4.

[49] ibid., s.58(1).

[50] See the cases cited in fn.42, above. The point is significant in relation to restitutionary remedies: below, para.11–128 et seq.

[51] *Thai Trading Co v Taylor* [1998] Q.B. 785 at 790; *Kellar v Williams* [2004] UKPC 30 at [21]; *R. (Factortame Ltd) v Secretary of State for Transport, Local Government and the Regions (No.8)* [2002] EWCA Civ 932; [2003] Q.B. 381 at [32].

[52] *Sibthorpe v Southwark L.B.C.* [2011] EWCA Civ 25.

[53] ibid. at [54]. Any view to the contrary expressed in *Thai Trading Co v Taylor* [1998] Q.B. 785 is to be regarded as *per incuriam* and treated with caution: ibid. at [24], [39]; The *Thai Trading* case was also doubted in *Westlaw Services Ltd v Boddy* [2009] EWCA Civ 929; [2011] P.N.L.R. 4 (agreement to share fees with a non-qualified consultant in breach of the Solicitors Practice Rules).

[54] *R. (Factortame Ltd) v Secretary of State for Transport, Local Government and the Regions (No.8)* [2002] EWCA Civ 932; [2003] Q.B. 381, cf. *Giles v Thompson* [1994] 1 A.C. 142.

[55] *Picton Jones & Co v Arcadia Developments* [1989] 1 E.G.L.R. 43.

[56] *Sibthorpe v Southwark L.B.C.* [2011] EWCA Civ 25 at [35].

[57] e.g. *Bigos v Bousted* [1951] 1 All E.R. 92; cf. *Ashton v Turner* [1981] Q.B. 137; *Pitts v Hunt* [1991] 1 Q.B. 24. Ignorance of the law makes no difference: see *Belvoir Finance Co Ltd v Stapleton* [1971] 1 Q.B. 210.

[58] See below, paras 11–116—11–127.

(iii) *Contracts to commit a civil wrong*

Deliberate commission of a civil wrong. A contract is illegal where its 11–015
object is the *deliberate* commission of a civil wrong. Thus contracts to assault[59] or
defraud[60] a third party are illegal: and the same is true of a contract by an insolvent
debtor to pay one of his creditors in fraud of the others.[61] Similarly a contract may
be illegal if its object is to procure one party to break a contract known by both
to be binding on him.[62] Where a contract involves the *unintentional* commission of
a civil wrong two types of cases call for discussion.

Unintentional commission: one party innocent. One party may know that 11–016
the performance of the contract will involve the commission of a civil wrong, while
the other is innocent. In *Clay v Yates*[63] the claimant agreed with the defendant to
print a book with a dedication. He refused to print the dedication on discovering
that it was libellous, but claimed the cost of printing the book. The defendant did
not plead illegality but argued that the obligation to print the book with the
dedication was "entire",[64] and that the claimant could not recover anything as he
had performed only in part. In rejecting this argument, Pollock C.B. said that
there was an implied undertaking to pay "for so much of the work *as is lawful*"[65];
while Martin B. said that the defendant was liable "to pay the [claimant] for that
part *which he has performed*".[66] If the claimant had printed the dedication without
knowing the facts which made it libellous, it seems that he could not have
recovered his charges on Pollock C.B.'s test but that he could have done so under
Martin B.'s test; and it is submitted that the latter is the preferable view.[67]

Unintentional commission: both parties innocent. If neither party knows 11–017
that performance of the contract involves the commission of a civil wrong the
contract is not illegal.[68] A contract for the sale of goods belonging to a third party
may make buyer and seller liable to that third party in tort[69] even though they
believed that the goods belonged to the seller; but such a contract has never been
held illegal.[70]

(iv) *Use of subject-matter for unlawful purpose*

A contract which is in itself lawful may be illegal if its subject-matter is to be 11–018
used for an unlawful purpose. In *Langton v Hughes*[71] Spanish juice, isinglass and

---

[59] *Allen v Rescous* (1676) 2 Lev. 174.
[60] *Begbie v Phosphate Sewage Co Ltd* (1875) L.R. 10 Q.B. 491; cf. *Customs & Excise Commissioners v Oliver* [1980] 1 All E.R. 355; *Taylor v Bhail* [1995] C.L.C. 337.
[61] *Mallalieu v Hodgson* (1851) 16 Q.B. 689; cf. *Cadbury Schweppes Plc v Somji* [2001] 1 W.L.R. 615.
[62] Lauterpacht 52 L.Q.R. 494.
[63] (1856) 1 H. & N. 73.
[64] See below, para.17–031.
[65] *Clay v Yates*, above, at 79 (emphasis added).
[66] ibid. at 80.
[67] Williams 8 C.L.J. at 54; Martin B.'s view may be reconciled with *Frank W Clifford Ltd v Garth* [1956] 1 W.L.R. 570; below, para.11–157, on the ground that the builder in that case took a conscious risk of illegality. cf. *ZYX Music GmbH v King* [1995] 3 All E.R. 1 at 10.
[68] *Clarion Ltd v National Power Association* [2000] 1 W.L.R. 1888 at 1908.
[69] See below, para.22–011.
[70] Sale of Goods Act 1979, s.12 (as amended by Sale and Supply of Goods Act 1994, s.7(1) and Sch.2) assumes that the contract is valid.
[71] (1813) 1 M. & S. 593; cf. *Gas Light & Coke Co v Turner* (1839) 6 Bing.N.C. 324.

ginger were sold to a brewer who, as the seller knew, intended to put them into his beer. The contract was held to be illegal because an Act of 1802 made it an offence to use anything except malt and hops to flavour beer. Later cases suggest that this rule applies only if the seller to some extent "participates" in the illegal purpose.[72] Where the line is to be drawn in any particular case is a question of fact and degree, but the more the subject-matter has been "tailored" for the unlawful purpose, the more readily can the inference of participation be made.[73]

(v) *Unlawful method of performance*

11–019   **Breach of statute.** A contract which is lawful in itself may be performed in a way which involves one or both parties in criminal liability. It used to be thought that the contract was illegal[74] if its performance involved breach of a statute passed for the protection of the public; but that, if the statute was passed only for the protection of the revenue, the contract was not illegal.[75] But the distinction between these two types of statutes is by no means decisive.[76] Even where the object of the statute is to protect the public (or a section of it) a contract involving a breach of it is not invariably illegal. Thus a contract to grant (or to transfer) a lease is not illegal merely because the landlord has committed a statutory offence by receiving or demanding an illegal premium. The tenant can accordingly enforce the contract, though without having to pay the premium.[77] Similarly, a tenancy is not illegal merely because the landlord has committed a statutory offence by failing to give his tenant a rent-book. Here the illegality relates to a merely collateral matter, so that the contract can be enforced even by the offender: i.e. the landlord can sue for the rent.[78] On the other hand, a contract may be illegal although the statute which it violates was passed for the protection of the revenue.[79] The test for determining whether an otherwise lawful contract is illegal because its performance involved the breach of a statute is that laid down in *St John Shipping Corp v Joseph Rank Ltd*[80]: did the statute intend only to penalise *conduct* or also to prohibit *contracts*? Some statutes expressly solve this problem: a contract for the supply of goods is not, for example, to be void or unenforceable

---

[72] *J M Allan (Merchandising) Ltd v Cloke* [1963] 2 Q.B. 340, at 348; cf. *Ashmore, Benson Pease & Co Ltd v A V Dawson Ltd* [1973] 1 W.L.R. 828, below, para.11–114.

[73] *Anglo Petroleum Ltd v TFB (Mortgages) Ltd* [2007] EWCA Civ 456; [2008] 1 B.C.L.C. 185 at [79].

[74] *Little v Poole* (1829) 9 B. & C. 192; *Victorian Daylesford Syndicate v Dott* [1905] 2 Ch. 624; *Brightman & Co v Tate* [1919] 1 K.B. 463.

[75] *Johnson v Hudson* (1805) 11 East 180; *Learoyd v Bracken* [1894] 1 Q.B. 114; cf. *Wetherell v Jones* (1832) 3 B. & Ad. 221.

[76] *Cope v Rowlands* (1836) 2 M. & W. 149 at 157.

[77] *Ailion v Spiekermann* [1976] Ch. 158; for enforceability of a contract by an innocent third party (in spite of a formal defect making one of the parties liable to a fine) see *OTV Birwelco Ltd v Technical & General Guarantee Co Ltd* [2002] EWHC 2240; [2002] 4 All E.R. 668 at [55].

[78] *Shaw v Groom* [1970] 2 Q.B. 504; cf. *London & Harrogate Securities Ltd v Pitts* [1976] 1 W.L.R. 1063; *P & B (Run Off) Ltd v Woolley* [2002] EWCA Civ 65; [2002] 1 All E.R. (Comm) 577.

[79] e.g. where the object of the contract is to evade or to delay the payment of income tax: *Napier v National Business Agency Ltd* [1951] 2 All E.R. 264; cf. *Miller v Karlinski* (1945) 62 T.L.R. 85; below, para.11–056.

[80] [1957] 1 Q.B. 267; above, para.11–003; *Crédit Lyonnais v P T Barnard & Associates* [1976] 1 Lloyd's Rep. 557; cf. *Curragh Investments Ltd v Cook* [1974] 1 W.L.R. 1559; *Mohammed v Alaga & Co* [2000] 1 W.L.R. 1815 at 1824, applying the same test to legislation which prohibited the *making* of a contract.

merely because, in performing it, the seller has committed an offence under the Trade Descriptions Act 1968.[81]

Licensing requirements. A statute may subject contracts to a licensing or similar requirement, so that they can be lawfully performed only with the consent of some public body. Such a statute may expressly prohibit (and so render illegal) a contract made in breach of its provisions[82]; and even where the statute does not expressly prohibit the contract, it may do so by implication. Such an implication is most likely to arise where *both* parties are prohibited from making or performing the contract; but the implication may arise even where the statutory prohibition is directed at only one of the parties. At common law, this was the position where an insurer committed a statutory offence by engaging in certain types of insurance business without government authorisation[83]; by statute, such contracts are no longer illegal, but only unenforceable against the other party.[84]

11–020

A licensing or similar requirement may also apply merely to the performance of a particular contract (as opposed to the carrying on of a business): e.g. where a licence is required for the erection of a building or for the export or import of goods. Such a contract is not illegal if it is expressly or by implication made subject to the relevant consent.[85] It will be illegal only if it is performed without such licence or consent[86] or if the parties intend to perform it even though no licence or consent is obtained.[87] A party may, however, guarantee that the licence will be obtained; if so, the undertaking can be enforced against him as a collateral contract, even though the main contract is illegal.[88] He may also be liable in damages for failing to perform an express or implied promise to make reasonable efforts to obtain the licence.[89]

Subsequent commission of a civil wrong. A contract which is initially lawful may become illegal if, in the course of performing it, the parties agree deliberately to commit a civil wrong: e.g. to defraud a third person who had undertaken to provide the finance necessary for its performance.[90] But a contract which is in itself lawful does not become illegal merely because in the course of performing it one party commits a fraud on the other.[91] That fraud is, however, likely to be a repudiatory breach, so that the victim of the fraud will be entitled to terminate the contract and so to avoid further liability under it.[92]

11–021

---

[81] s.35; and see below, para.11–120. Such a legislative provision may also be implied: see *Currencies Direct Ltd v Ellis* [2002] EWCA Civ 779; [2002] 2 B.C.L.C. 482 (Companies Act 1985, s.341 (now Companies Act 2006, s.213(2)), by making a prohibited loan *voidable by the company*, by implication entitled company to enforce it).

[82] cf. *Re Mahmoud and Ispahani* [1921] 2 K.B. 716; below, para.11–119.

[83] *Bedford Ins Co Ltd v Instituto de Resseguros do Brazil* [1985] 1 Q.B. 966; *Phoenix General Ins Co of Greece v Halvanon Ins Co Ltd* [1988] Q.B. 216.

[84] Financial Services and Markets Act 2000, ss.26(1), 27(1).

[85] *Michael Richards Properties Ltd v St Saviour's Parish* [1975] 3 All E.R. 416.

[86] e.g. *J Dennis & Co Ltd v Munn* [1949] 2 K.B. 327. For an exception, see *SA Ancien Maison Marcel Bauche v Woodhouse Drake & Carey (Sugar) Ltd* [1982] 2 Lloyd's Rep. 516.

[87] e.g. *Bigos v Bousted* [1951] 1 All E.R. 92.

[88] *Peter Cassidy Seed Co Ltd v Osuustukkukauppa* [1957] 1 W.L.R. 273, as explained in *Walton (Grain and Shipping) Ltd v British Trading Co* [1959] 1 Lloyd's Rep. 223 at 236; cf. below, para.11–123. Both cases concerned foreign licensing requirements.

[89] See above, para.2–110; below, para.17–070.

[90] *Birkett v Acorn Business Machines Ltd* [1999] 2 All E.R. (Comm) 429.

[91] *Broaders v Kalhare Property Maintenance* [1990] I.R.L.R. 421.

[92] See below, para.18–025 et seq.

(vi) *Contracts to indemnify against liability for unlawful acts*

11–022   **Criminal liability.** A contract to indemnify a person against criminal liability
is illegal if the crime is one which can only be, or in fact is, committed with guilty
intent.[93] But the position is less clear where the crime is one of strict liability. In
Cointat v Myham & Sons[94] the defendants sold to a butcher the carcass of a pig,
which was unfit for food. The butcher innocently exposed it for sale and was
consequently convicted and fined £20. It was held that he could recover this sum
from the defendants; but the legality of their implied promise to indemnify him
was not discussed. The case has been criticised on the ground that "punishment
inflicted by a criminal court is personal to the offender" and is fixed "having
regard to the personal responsibility of the offender in respect of the offence".[95]
One object of imposing strict criminal liability is to make a person take care not
to commit the offence; and this object might be defeated by allowing him to
recover the fine from a third party. Nonetheless it seems that the courts will allow
a person to recover an indemnity against criminal liability if they are satisfied that
he is wholly innocent. For example, in *Osman v J Ralph Moss Ltd*[96] a motorist had
been convicted of driving while uninsured. He was morally innocent, having been
told by his insurance agent that he was properly insured, and it was held that his
fine could be included in the damages recoverable from the agent for breach of
contract.

11–023   **Guilty intent.** That the guilty intent of the person claiming an indemnity is to
be taken into account is supported by a number of recent cases. In *Gray v Thames
Trains Ltd,*[97] the claimant was convicted of manslaughter by diminished responsibility as a result of his suffering from a mental illness after an accident caused by
the negligence of the defendant. The House of Lords was concerned not with a
contract to indemnify the claimant, but with the question of whether the defendant's liability in negligence to the claimant extended to the losses incurred by him
as a consequence of his criminal act.[98] A distinction was drawn between cases
where the claimant seeks compensation for loss which flows from a *sentence*
imposed in consequence of his unlawful act[99] and those where he seeks compensation for loss which flows from the criminal act itself,[100] but in either instance in

---

[93] *Colburn v Patmore* (1834) 1 C.M. & R. 73; *Fitzgerald v Leonard* (1893) L.R. 33 Ir. 675; *Safeway Stores Ltd v Twigger* [2010] EWCA Civ 1472; [2011] 1 Lloyd's Rep 462.

[94] [1913] 2 K.B. 220, reversed on another ground [1914] W.N. 46.

[95] *Askey v Golden Wine Co* (1948) 64 T.L.R. 379 at 380; cf. *R Leslie Ltd v Reliable Advertising, etc. Agency Ltd* [1915] 1 K.B. 652.

[96] [1970] 1 Lloyd's Rep. 313; cf. *Griffin v UHY Hacker Young & Partners* [2010] EWHC 146 (Ch) (claim in tort).

[97] [2009] UKHL 33; [2009] 1 A.C. 1339. See also earlier cases in tort: *Clunis v Camden and Islington Health Authority* [1998] Q.B. 978; *Vellino v Chief Constable of the Greater Manchester Police* [2001] EWCA Civ 1249; [2002] 1 W.L.R. 218.

[98] Though one of the heads of loss was an indemnity against any claims made against him by the representatives of the deceased.

[99] cf. Lord Denning's emphasis on "punishment" in the passage quoted from the *Askey* case above, fn.95.

[100] *Gray v Thames Trains Ltd* [2009] UKHL 33; [2009] 1 A.C. 1339 at [29]. The former ("narrower") instance is based on the "inconsistency" of requiring the law to compensate for damage imposed by the law as a matter of penal policy. The latter ("wider") instance is based on a broader policy which, in the context of the negligence claim in *Gray*, was described in terms similar to the "public conscience" test which is considered below (para.11–112): "the wider rule has to be justified on the ground that it is offensive to public notions of the fair distribution of resources that a claimant should be compensated . . . for the consequences of his own criminal conduct", [2009] 1 A.C. 1339 at [51].

Gray the claimant was found guilty of an offence where mens rea was an essential element. In a later case[101] where the claimant sought damages from his accountant for failing to advise him that his conduct in winding up a company might lead to a fine and other consequential losses as a result of his conviction for what was a strict liability offence,[102] the claim was not struck out on the basis that "it could at least be argued that negligence [of the claimant] would not be sufficient to deprive a claimant guilty of some, at least, strict liability offences of a remedy against a defendant guilty of professional negligence."[103] It has also been said that, before the claimant can be prevented from claiming an indemnity there must have been "moral turpitude or moral reprehensibility involved in the relevant conduct".[104]

Company acting through its agents. The requirement of a guilty intent may   11–024
be problematic where the claimant is a company which is said to have committed an offence through the actions of its agents or its employees and it claims an indemnity either from a third party, or from the agents or employees themselves. The former case is demonstrated by the facts of *Stone & Rolls Ltd v Moore Stephens*[105] where a company perpetrated frauds on a number of banks and then sought damages from their auditors for failing to detect the dishonest activities of the director responsible, S. The company was prevented from doing so on the basis of illegality, but a key feature of the case is that the company was entirely owned, controlled and managed by S and, as his was the "directing mind and will" of the company, the liability of the company was direct and personal.[106] As a general rule, a company will not be prevented from claiming an indemnity where the liability of the company arises because of vicarious liability, or because the acts of its agents are attributed to the company, at least where there are "independent" shareholders who have been "hijacked by a fraudulent but dominant managing director".[107]

The latter type of case is demonstrated by *Safeway Stores Ltd v Twigger*.[108] A company admitted its liability for breach of certain of the provisions of the Competition Act 1998 and the principal element of the loss it suffered as a result was the fine imposed. It sought to recover this loss from the former directors and employees who were, for the purpose of an application to strike out the claim, assumed to have been responsible for the infringements. The trial judge had refused to strike out the claim because it had not been shown that the company was

---

[101] *Griffin v UHY Hacker Young & Partners* [2010] EWHC 146 (Ch).
[102] Of becoming a director of another company using a trade name of the liquidated company without obtaining leave of the court: Insolvency Act 1986 s.216(3).
[103] *Griffin v UHY Hacker Young & Partners* [2010] EWHC 146 (Ch) at [60].
[104] *Safeway Stores Ltd v Twigger* [2010] EWHC 11 (Comm) at [26] (reversed on appeal [2010] EWCA Civ 1472; [2011] 1 Lloyd's Rep 462, below]; cf. *Stone & Rolls Ltd v Moore Stephens* [2009] UKHL 39; [2009] 1 A.C. 1391 at [24]; contrast *Les Laboratoires Servier v Apotex Inc* [2011] EWHC 730 (Pat) at [71].
[105] [2009] UKHL 39; [2009] 1 A.C. 1391.
[106] This was the primary reasoning of Lord Walker and Lord Brown, but the other Law Lord in the majority, Lord Phillips, based his reasoning on the scope of the duty owed by the auditors, holding that it did not extend to the creditors of the company, who were not tainted by illegality. As a result, it has been said that "it is difficult to understand what the precise ratio of the decision in *Stone & Rolls* is", *Lexi Holdings Plc v Pannone & Partners* [2009] EWHC 3507 (Ch) at [13].
[107] [2009] UKHL 39; [2009] 1 A.C. 1391 at [32].
[108] [2010] EWCA Civ 1472; [2011] 1 Lloyd's Rep 462.

"personally" at fault,[109] but it was said by Longmore L.J. that it was simply not possible for the company to make such a submission when it had admitted its liability, albeit via the actions of its employees and agents, for an offence for which a penalty could only be imposed if the infringement was committed "intentionally or negligently."[110] As Longmore L.J. commented:[111] "It is more in accordance with principle to say that if the liability of the company is personal (rather than merely vicarious) then there is no impediment to the application of the maxim,[112] save (perhaps) in cases of strict liability where there has been no intention or negligence on the part of any person, which is not something that needs decision now".[113]

11–025   **Civil liability arising out of criminal acts.** Where an act amounts both to a crime and to a civil wrong, a promise to indemnify the wrongdoer against civil liability incurred as a result of the act is often illegal. For example, in *Gray v Barr*[114] a husband shot and killed his wife's lover in circumstances amounting in the view of the Court of Appeal to manslaughter (though in the criminal proceedings he had been acquitted). It was held that the husband could not recover under an insurance policy (even if it covered the occurrence) the damages which he had had to pay to the lover's estate. The decision was based on the public interest in deterring armed violence; but it does not follow that promises to indemnify against civil liability are necessarily invalid merely because the act giving rise to that liability also amounts to a crime. There are, in particular, three situations in which they may be upheld.

First, a promise to indemnify a person against civil liability can be enforced, even though the act giving rise to that liability is criminal, if the crime is one of strict liability or is in fact committed without mens rea. Thus in *Gray v Barr* the possibility was left open that a person who committed manslaughter in circumstances amounting to little more than an error of judgment might be able to recover an indemnity from his insurance company.[115] The view that such an indemnity is recoverable is supported by a dictum in a later case, according to which the test "is not the label which the law applies to the crime which has been committed, but the nature of the crime itself".[116] Similarly, if the butcher in *Cointat v Myham & Son*[117] had had to pay damages for breach of contract to a customer who was poisoned by the pork, he should have been able to claim an indemnity against this loss from the defendant.

---

[109] [2010] EWHC 11 (Comm) based on the decision of the House of Lords in the *Stone & Rolls* case, above at fn.105.

[110] Competition Act 1998, s.31(3); [2010] EWCA Civ 1472; [2011] 1 Lloyd's Rep 462 at [18], [25], [37], [43].

[111] [2011] 1 Lloyd's Rep 462 at [26].

[112] Ex turpi causa non oritur actio.

[113] Under the Bribery Act 2010, s.14, a company is guilty of the offence of bribery if the offence is proved to have been committed with the consent or connivance of "a senior officer" of the company or a person purporting to act in such a capacity. For the definition of a senior officer, see s.14(3), (4).

[114] [1971] 2 Q.B. 554; Fleming 34 M.L.R. 177; cf. *Haseldine v Hosken* [1933] 1 K.B. 822.

[115] ibid. at 581; cf. *Gregory v Ford* [1951] 1 All E.R. 121 (employment contract).

[116] *R. v National Insurance Commissioner Ex p. Connor* [1981] Q.B. 758, 765 (where a claim for widow's benefit under Social Security Act 1975 was rejected as the claimant had been convicted of manslaughter by *deliberately* stabbing her husband to death); cf. *Gray v Thames Trains Ltd* above, where mens rea was an essential element of the offence committed leading to a potential civil liability to the representatives of the deceased.

[117] [1913] 2 K.B. 220; above, para.11–022.

The second situation arises in the law of motor insurance. In *Tinline v White Cross Insurance*[118] a motorist, who was insured against liability for "accidental personal injury" to third parties, killed a pedestrian by driving with criminal negligence, and was convicted of manslaughter. He successfully sued the insurers for the damages which he had had to pay to the deceased. The motorist has this right only where the crime is committed negligently—not where it is committed deliberately.[119] But even in the latter case the position of the innocent victim of the motorist's crime is protected by being given rights in certain circumstances against the insurer or against the Motor Insurers' Bureau.[120] The existence of such rights is obviously necessary to maintain the effectiveness of the scheme of compulsory motor insurance.

Thirdly, the principle stated in *Gray v Barr* applies only to contracts to indemnify the wrongdoer *himself* against civil liability arising out of criminal conduct. That conduct may also make the wrongdoer's *employer* civilly liable to the victim; and the employer can validly insure against such liability, even to the extent that the wrong gives rise to a claim against him for exemplary (or punitive) damages.[121]

Civil liability. A contract to indemnify a person against civil liability may be illegal if the wrong is intentionally and knowingly committed: e.g. a contract to indemnify a person against liability for deceit is illegal.[122] Similarly, a person who publishes what he knows to be a libel cannot recover an indemnity from the person who instigated the publication,[123] for the tendency of such an agreement might be to increase the circulation of the libel. On the other hand, a contract to keep a communication confidential, and to indemnify the maker against any liability resulting from its disclosure, has been held valid even where the communication contained a malicious libel[124]—apparently because the tendency of such an agreement is to restrict the circulation of the libel.

A contract to indemnify a person against civil liability is perfectly valid if the liability was incurred innocently or negligently.[125] Indeed, in many such cases promises to indemnify, far from being illegal, are actually implied in law. The general principle is that where A at B's request does an act which is not "manifestly tortious", B must indemnify A for any liability incurred by A if the act turns out to be injurious to C.[126] The cases provide many illustrations of the validity of such express or implied promises to indemnify. Thus the innocent publisher of a libel can recover an indemnity from the person who instigated the

11–026

---

[118] [1921] 3 K.B. 327; followed in *James v British General Ins Co Ltd* [1927] 2 K.B. 311; doubted in *Haseldine v Hosken* [1933] 1 K.B. 822 but approved in *Marles v Philip Trant & Sons Ltd* [1954] 1 Q.B. 29 at 40, and in *Gray v Barr* [1971] 2 Q.B. 544 at 568, 581.

[119] *Gardner v Moore* [1984] A.C. 548 at 560; *Pitts v Hunt* [1991] 1 Q.B. 24 at 30; *Charlton v Fisher* [2001] EWCA Civ 112; [2002] Q.B. 578.

[120] See below, para.14–130; *Hardy v MIB* [1964] 2 Q.B. 743; *Gardner v Moore* [1984] A.C. 548 at 560–561.

[121] *Lancashire CC v Municipal Mutual Ins Ltd* [1997] Q.B. 897.

[122] *Brown Jenkinson & Co Ltd v Percy Dalton (London) Ltd* [1957] 2 Q.B. 621; contrast *The Jag Ravi* [2011] EWHC 1372 (Comm).

[123] *W H Smith & Sons v Clinton* (1909) 99 L.T. 840.

[124] *Weld-Blundell v Stephens* [1919] 1 K.B. 520; *Bradstreets British Ltd v Mitchell and Carpanayoti & Co Ltd* [1933] Ch. 190; contrast *Howard v Odham's Press Ltd* [1938] 1 K.B. 1. And see *Distillers Co Ltd v Times Newspapers Ltd* [1975] Q.B. 613.

[125] *Betts v Gibbins* (1834) 2 A. & E. 57; cf. *Yeung v Hong Kong & Shanghai Banking Corp* [1981] A.C. 787.

[126] *The Nogar Marin* [1988] 1 Lloyd's Rep. 412 at 417.

publication.[127] An agent can recover an indemnity from his principal if he is made liable in conversion for selling a third person's property on the principal's instructions.[128] An employer can insure himself against civil liability for the tort of his employee; and he may also be entitled to an indemnity against such liability from the employee under the contract of employment.[129] And where A holds property which is claimed by B and C, a promise by one of them to indemnify A against liability to the other if he delivers the property to the promisor is perfectly valid.[130]

(vii) *Promises to pay money on the commission of an unlawful act*

11–027   A contract may be illegal if it provides for the payment of money to a person in the event of his doing an unlawful act, e.g. if A promises B £5 if B breaks the speed limit. A life insurance policy was never wholly illegal merely because it provided that the sum insured was to be paid even if the assured committed suicide (which was formerly a crime). It could clearly be enforced if he died in some other way. But in *Beresford v Royal Exchange Assurance*[131] it was, however, held that such a policy could not be enforced by the personal representatives of the assured if he did commit suicide; to allow a man, or his estate, to benefit from his own crime was said to be against public policy.[132] But if the assured assigned the policy and then committed suicide, the assignees were entitled to the policy moneys since it was they, and not the assured, who benefited from the crime.[133] It is hard to see the force of this distinction where, as in *Beresford*'s case, the assured was bankrupt, so that the only people who could benefit were his creditors. The actual decision can now be regarded as resting on the alternative ground that, under ordinary principles of insurance law, the assured cannot recover if he by his own deliberate act causes the event on which the insurance money is payable.[134]

(viii) *Effect of changes in the law*

11–028   In relation to contracts which involve the commission of a legal wrong it is necessary to consider the effect of changes in the law, both on contracts in existence at the time of the change and on contracts made after the change.

11–029   **Conduct made unlawful.** The law may change so that previously lawful conduct becomes a legal wrong. The effect of such a change may be to frustrate

---

[127] *Daily Mirror Newspapers Ltd v Exclusive News Agency* (1937) 81 S.J. 924; Defamation Act 1952, s.11.

[128] *Adamson v Jarvis* (1827) 4 Bing. 66; *Betts v Gibbins* (1834) 2 A. & E. 57.

[129] *Lister v Romford Ice & Cold Storage Co Ltd* [1957] A.C. 555; above, para.6–044.

[130] e.g. *Betts v Gibbins* (1834) 2 A. & E. 57.

[131] [1938] A.C. 586; Goodhart 52 L.Q.R. 575.

[132] This principle applies even though the contract is not illegal: *Davitt v Titcumb* [1989] 3 All E.R. 417 (murderer not allowed to benefit indirectly from policy on joint lives of victim and himself); *Geismar v Sun Alliance* [1978] Q.B. 383 (insurer not liable to pay for loss of goods smuggled into this country; liability for loss of *other* goods covered by the policies seems not to have been disputed); contrast *Euro-Diam Ltd v Bathurst* [1990] Q.B. 1; below, para.11–166.

[133] *White v British Empire, etc. Assurance Co* (1868) L.R. 7 Eq. 394; *Charlton v Fisher* [2001] EWCA Civ 112; [2002] Q.B. 518 at [13].

[134] [1938] A.C. 586 at 595; *Reeves v Commissioner of Police of the Metropolis* [2000] 1 A.C. 360 at 388 (per Lord Hobhouse, dissenting).

existing contracts[135] and to make future contracts illegal. Whether it actually has this effect will depend on principles stated in *St John Shipping Corp v Joseph Rank Ltd.*[136]

Conduct made lawful: future contracts. A second kind of change is one by which conduct previously amounting to a legal wrong ceases to be so; and prima facie the effect of such a change in the law is that future contracts involving such conduct will be valid. This would be the case where the conduct in question had been criminal under some regulatory statute (e.g. one requiring certain work to be licensed) which was then repealed. But there are exceptions to this general rule. First, a statute abrogating a rule of law under which certain conduct was unlawful may expressly preserve a rule under which a contract involving such conduct was previously illegal: this is the position (in general[137]) with regard to champertous agreements.[138] Secondly, it is possible that, even after the conduct in question has ceased to be a legal wrong, a contract involving such conduct would still be contrary to public policy. But contracts should not generally be regarded as contrary to public policy merely because they involve conduct which was formerly criminal. Thus it is submitted that a contract to render services in connection with a lawful abortion is valid even though it would have been a contract to commit a crime before the Abortion Act 1967. Similarly it is submitted that the reasoning of *Beresford*'s case is obsolete now that suicide is no longer a crime.[139]

11–030

Conduct made lawful: existing contracts. The effect of this second kind of change in the law on contracts already in existence when the law was changed is more problematical. Changes in the law made after action is brought are generally disregarded[140] but there seems to be no authority on the effect of changes in the law between the making of the contract and the commencement of the action. One possible view is that the validity of the contract must be determined, once for all, when it is made. But it is submitted that, so long as the act in question is lawful *when it is done*, no useful purpose is served by holding the contract invalid. The statute may itself solve the problem by specifying whether, and if so to what extent, the change in the law has retrospective effect.

11–031

(b) Contracts Contrary to Public Policy[141]

A contract which does not involve the commission of a legal wrong may be illegal because its tendency is to bring about a state of affairs of which the law disapproves on grounds of public policy. A contract is illegal for this reason only if its harmful tendency is clear, that is, if injury to the public is its probable and not merely its possible consequence.[142] Such contracts are often called "illegal".[143]

11–032

---

[135] See below, para.19–044.
[136] [1957] 1 Q.B. 267; above, para.11–003.
[137] For an exception, see Courts and Legal Services Act 1990, s.58 and 58A; above, para.11–013.
[138] Criminal Law Act 1967, s.14(2); above, para.11–012.
[139] Suicide Act 1961; cf. *Gray v Barr* [1971] 2 Q.B. 544 at 582. In practice, insurers may pay in such circumstances: see *Foskett v McKeown* [2001] 1 A.C. 102.
[140] *Hitchcock v Way* (1837) 6 A. & E. 943.
[141] Lloyd, *Public Policy*; Winfield 42 Harv.L.R. 76.
[142] *Fender v St John Mildmay* [1938] A.C. 1, 13; cf. *Multiservice Bookbinding Ltd v Marden* [1979] Ch. 84 at 104.
[143] e.g. *McEllistrim's Case* [1919] A.C. 548 at 571; cf. Criminal Law Act 1967, s.14(2) ("contrary to public policy or otherwise illegal").

It is sometimes said that they are only "void" or "unenforceable"[144]; but these statements only emphasise that no specific legal wrong is involved. So long as this point is borne in mind, no harm is done by using the traditional terminology in which these contracts are "illegal".[145] Perhaps the most important type of contracts of which the law disapproves on grounds of public policy are those in restraint of trade. They are made the subject of separate consideration after first considering other examples.

11–033   **Scope of the doctrine of public policy.**[146] Public policy is a variable notion, depending on changing manners, morals and economic conditions. In theory, this flexibility of the doctrine of public policy could provide a judge with an excuse for invalidating any contract which he violently disliked. With this danger in mind, judges have sometimes criticised the doctrine of public policy. In 1824 Burroughs J. described it as "a very unruly horse, and when once you get astride it you never know where it will carry you. It may lead you from the sound law".[147] And Lord Halsbury has denied that any court could "invent a new head of public policy".[148] On the other hand, the law does adapt itself to changes in economic and social conditions, as can be seen particularly from the development of the rules as to contracts in restraint of trade. This point has often been recognised judicially. Thus Lord Haldane has said: "What the law recognises as contrary to public policy turns out to vary greatly from time to time".[149] And Lord Denning has put a similar point of view: "With a good man in the saddle, the unruly horse can be kept in control. It can jump over obstacles".[150] The present attitude of the courts represents a compromise between the flexibility inherent in the notion of public policy and the need for certainty in commercial affairs.

11–034   **A general reluctance to extend.** In the interests of certainty the courts will in general refuse to apply the doctrine of public policy to contracts of a kind to which the doctrine has never been applied before. In *Printing & Numerical Registering Co v Sampson*,[151] for instance, an inventor assigned a patent to a company and also agreed to assign to the company any patent of a like nature thereafter to be acquired by him. He argued that this agreement was contrary to public policy as it tended to discourage inventors. In rejecting the argument, Jessel M.R. said: "You are not to extend arbitrarily those rules which say that a given contract is void as being against public policy".[152] The reason why the courts are

---

[144] e.g. *Bennett v Bennett* [1952] 1 K.B. 249 at 260; *Pau On v Lau Yiu Long* [1980] A.C. 614 at 634–635; *O'Sullivan v Management Agency & Music Ltd* [1985] Q.B. 428 at 447, 448, 469.
[145] cf. *Mogul SS Co Ltd v McGregor Gow & Co* [1892] A.C. 25 at 46.
[146] Shand [1972] C.L.J. 144.
[147] *Richardson v Mellish* (1824) 2 Bing. 229 at 252.
[148] *Janson v Driefontein Consolidated Mines Ltd* [1902] A.C. 484 at 491; cf. *Geismar v Sun Alliance & London Ins* [1978] Q.B. 383 at 389; *Nickerson v Barraclough* [1981] Ch. 426; *Deutsche Schachtbau-und Tiefbohrgesellschaft mbH v Ras Al Khaima National Oil Co* [1990] 1 A.C. 295 at 316 (reversed on other grounds [1990] 1 A.C. 295 at 329 et seq.).
[149] *Rodriguez v Speyer Bros* [1919] A.C. 59 at 79; cf. *Nordenfelt v Maxim Nordenfelt Guns & Ammunition Co* [1894] A.C. 535 at 553; *Gray v Barr* [1971] 2 Q.B. 554 at 582; *Thai Trading Co v Taylor* [1998] Q.B. 781 at 786 (as to which see above, para.11–013); *Kellar v Williams* [2004] UKPC 30 at [21].
[150] *Enderby Town FC Ltd v The Football Association Ltd* [1971] Ch. 591 at 606.
[151] (1875) L.R. 19 Eq. 462.
[152] ibid. at 465.

less ready to apply the doctrine of public policy to new classes of contracts is that Parliament and its delegates have become more active in this field.[153]

Novel applications. In some cases (particularly "where the subject–matter is 'lawyers' law'"[154]) judicial intervention may still as a last resort be desirable.[155] The courts may occasionally invalidate a contract even though it is of a kind to which the doctrine of public policy has not been applied before. Such novel applications of the doctrine of public policy are illustrated by decisions to the effect that a moneylending contract is illegal if it imposes quasi-servile obligations on the borrower[156]; that a contract by which a trade journal promises not to comment on the affairs of a company is illegal as it may prevent the journal from exposing frauds perpetrated by the company[157]; that an attempt to contract out of certain statutory provisions governing the liquidation of companies is contrary to public policy[158]; and that the same is true of an attempt to deprive an agricultural tenant of security of tenure where he is entitled to it by statute.[159] There are also cases in which attempts to impeach agreements by reference to new heads of public policy have been rejected on the ground that the agreement in question did not in fact have any injurious tendency.[160] It may be possible to infer from this reasoning that, if such a tendency had been established, the attempt would not have failed merely because the alleged head of public policy was a novel one.

11–035

Disguised applications. There are, finally, cases in which the courts may invalidate contracts or contractual provisions on what are essentially grounds of public policy without, as a general rule, making express reference to the doctrine of public policy, or to some established "head" of public policy. Some of the limitations on contractual capacity could be based on public policy: and indeed the former "incapacity"[161] of a barrister to make a contract with his client,[162] has been explained on this ground. At one time the invalidity of promises to pay extra wages to seamen who were already bound to serve[163] and of promises not to enforce claims which were known to be invalid[164] was explained on grounds of public

11–036

---

[153] See *D v NSPCC* [1978] A.C. 171 at 235; *Johnson v Moreton* [1980] A.C. 37 at 67; *Cheall v APEX* [1983] 2 A.C. 180 at 191; *Johnstone v Bloomsbury Health Authority* [1992] Q.B. 333 at 347, 349; cf. *Multiservice Bookbinding Ltd v Marden* [1979] Ch. 84 (Swiss franc uplift clause in mortgage); *Nationwide BS v Registry of Friendly Societies* [1983] 1 W.L.R. 1226 (index-linked mortgage).

[154] ibid.

[155] cf. *Monkland v Jack Barclay Ltd* [1951] 2 K.B. 252 at 265.

[156] *Horwood v Millar's Timber & Trading Co* [1917] 1 K.B. 305; above, para.11–061.

[157] *Neville v Dominion of Canada News Co Ltd* [1915] 3 K.B. 556; cf. *Initial Services Ltd v Putterill* [1968] 1 Q.B. 396 at 410; *Slater v Raw, The Times*, October 15, 1977.

[158] *British Eagle International Airlines Ltd v Cie Nationale Air France* [1975] 1 W.L.R. 758; *Folgate London Market Ltd v Chaucer Insurance Plc* [2011] EWCA Civ 328.

[159] *Johnson v Moreton* [1980] A.C. 37; *Featherstone v Staples* [1986] 1 W.L.R. 861; *Gisborne v Burton* [1989] Q.B. 390. The statute in question did not specify the legal effects of attempts to "contract out" of its provisions: contrast the provisions of Rent Act 1977 cited in para.1–005, fn.19, above.

[160] e.g. *Giles v Thompson* [1994] 1 A.C. 142 at 165 rejecting the argument that allegedly champertous car-hire agreements created "a risk of exploitation" of motorists, since no such risk was created.

[161] *Kennedy v Broun* (1863) 13 C.B.(N.S.) 667 at 736.

[162] *Rondel v Worsley* [1969] 1 A.C. 191 at 264. See now Courts and Legal Services Act 1990, s.61. The disapproval of *Rondel v Worsley* in *Arthur JS Hall Ltd v Simons* [2002] 1 A.C. 615 does not affect the present point.

[163] *Harris v Watson* (1791) Peake 102; above, para.3–048.

[164] *Wade v Simeon* (1846) 2 C.B. 548 at 564 ("almost *contra bonos mores*"); *Edwards v Baugh* (1843) 11 M. & W. 641 at 646.

policy; though it is now more common to base these rules on lack of consideration.[165] The rule against the assignment of "mere rights of action"[166] was not usually discussed under the heading of public policy, though it might well be considered to belong there.[167] The same is true of the rules under which penalty clauses are invalid,[168] and of some of the common law rules which limit the operation of exemption clauses.[169] All these rules could be regarded as disguised extensions or applications of the doctrine of public policy.

11-037   **Categories.** What follows is discussion of contracts which, in the past, the courts have not enforced because they have been found to be contrary to public policy, organised into certain categories. It should be borne in mind that the scope of these categories has been, and will continue to be, affected by changes in prevailing attitudes and, in some cases, the very existence of a particular category may be called into question.[170]

(i) *Agreements by married persons to marry*

11-038   An agreement to marry was formerly regarded as a contract, the breach of which gave rise to an action for damages. It was, however, thought to be against public policy to allow such actions to be brought on a promise by a married person to marry.[171] Actions for breach of promise of marriage were abolished by s.1 of the Law Reform (Miscellaneous Provisions) Act 1970,[172] but s.2 of the Act provides that "where an agreement to marry is terminated" the formerly engaged couple is to be treated for the purpose of certain rights[173] in, and disputes about, property as if they had been married. Difficult problems with regard to rights in property can obviously arise when an ex-fiancée makes a claim under s.2 against a man who, when he promised to marry her, was already married to someone else. It has been held that a party to an agreement to marry which is later brought to an end can take the benefit of s.2 even though that party was already married and so before the Act could not have claimed damages for breach of the promise.[174] It seems, a fortiori, to follow that the other (unmarried) party to the dissolved engagement should also be entitled to rely on the section. In such a case care must, however, be taken to safeguard the rights of the other party to the marriage: e.g. where the

---

[165] *Stilk v Myrick* (1809) as reported in 2 Camp. 317; *Poteliakhoff v Teakle* [1938] 2 K.B. 816; above, paras 3–036, 3–048.

[166] See below, para.15–058.

[167] *Trendtex Trading Corp v Crédit Suisse* [1982] A.C. 679 at 694.

[168] See below, para.20–130 et seq.; *Robophone Facilities Ltd v Blank* [1966] 1 W.L.R. 1428 at 1446; *The Angelic Star* [1988] 1 Lloyd's Rep. 122 at 127; *Azimut-Benetti SpA v Healey* [2010] EWHC 2234 (Comm); 132 Con L.R. 113 at [24] ("The rule against penalties is ultimately based on public policy").

[169] e.g. above, paras 7–039—7–044: see the reference to "public policy" in *HIH Casualty & General Ins v Chase Manhattan Bank* [2000] EWCA Civ 1250; [2001] 2 Lloyd's Rep. 483 at [103], reversed in part [2003] UKHL 6; [2003] 2 Lloyd's Rep. 61.

[170] See the former category of agreements between spouses for future separation (12th edn, para 11–103) which has been "swept away": below, para.11–049.

[171] *Spiers v Hunt* [1908] 1 K.B. 720; *Wilson v Carnley* [1908] 1 K.B. 729; *Fender v St John Mildmay* [1938] A.C. 1.

[172] Cretney 33 M.L.R. 534.

[173] Not all: *Mossop v Mossop* [1989] Fam. 77.

[174] *Shaw v Fitzgerald* [1992] 1 F.L.R. 357.

property in question was a house in which a man had lived first with his wife and then with a fiancée from whom he had later parted.[175]

(ii) *Agreements in contemplation of divorce*

At common law, an arrangement or agreement between parties to divorce proceedings (about such matters as the wife's maintenance) was invalid if it was made with a corrupt intention, e.g. if it amounted to a bribe to institute, or carry on, the proceedings,[176] or to a conspiracy to deceive the court. But it was valid if it was an honest attempt to minimise the difficulties which had arisen between the parties.[177] The law on this topic was formerly influenced by the rule that collusion was a bar to divorce; but the abolition of this rule "completely alters the public policy on this point",[178] so that an agreement is no longer invalid merely because it is collusive.

11–039

(iii) *Agreements inconsistent with parental responsibility*

At common law a father had the custody of his legitimate child and a contract by which he purported to assign that custody to any person was contrary to public policy as it was "repugnant entirely to his parental duty".[179] By statute, both parents have "parental responsibility"[180] for their child if they were married to each other at the time of the child's birth; if they were not, the mother has parental responsibility.[181] In the latter case, the parents may enter into a "parental responsibility agreement" providing for the father to have parental responsibility for the child[182]; but freedom of contract in making such an agreement, and in bringing it to an end, is severely restricted so as to protect the interests of the child.[183] The effect of such an agreement seems to be that parental responsibility is vested in both parents: the mother does not lose such responsibility since "a person who has parental responsibility for a child may not surrender or transfer such responsibility to another".[184] This statutory provision resembles the common law principle stated above and seems to be based on similar grounds of public policy. The person with parental responsibility may "arrange for some or all of it to be met by one or more persons acting on his behalf".[185] In such a case the responsibility is not transferred but vicariously performed.[186]

11–040

---

[175] cf. Family Law Act 1996, s.33(1)(b)(i) permitting the court to make an order relating to a "matrimonial home" in favour of an "associated" person; persons are "associated" if "they have agreed to marry one another (whether or not that agreement has been terminated)" (s.62(3)(e)). The 1996 Act does not deal with the question whether the validity of the agreement is affected by the fact that one of the parties to it was married when it was made.

[176] *Hope v Hope* (1857) 8 D.M. & G. 731; *Churchward v Churchward* [1895] P. 7.

[177] *Scott v Scott* [1913] P. 52.

[178] *Sutton v Sutton* [1984] Ch. 184 at 194; cf. *N v N* [1992] 1 F.L.R. 266.

[179] *Vansittart v Vansittart* (1858) D. & J. 249 at 259; cf. *Cole v Gower* (1805) 6 East 110. cf. Adoption and Children Act 2002, ss.92, 95, 96.

[180] As defined by Children Act 1989, s.3.

[181] ibid., s.2(1); and see s.2(4), abolishing the former common law rule.

[182] ibid., s.4(1)(b).

[183] ibid., ss.4(1) and (3), 1(1) (though see changes pending to s.4(1)(a) pursuant to the Welfare Reform Act 2009, Sch.6(2)).

[184] ibid., s.2(9).

[185] ibid., s.2(9); cf. also Child Support Act 1991, s.9, providing for the legal effects of certain maintenance agreements in favour of children.

[186] cf. below, para.17–007.

(iv) *Agreements in restraint of marriage*

11–041   A contract may be invalid on the ground that it unjustifiably restricts a person's freedom to marry. This is, for example, true of a promise by a widow to pay £100 if she remarries,[187] and of a promise not to marry anyone except a specified person (not amounting to a promise to marry that person[188]). It may be that such promises are valid if they are limited in duration or otherwise reasonable: e.g. if a limited restraint is imposed for the sake of a person's health or (conceivably) of his moral well-being.[189] It is also possible that a promise not to marry anyone except a member of a fairly large group (e.g. some religious denomination) might be valid.

The above cases concern actual promises not to marry, or to pay a sum of money on marriage. It seems that a contract is not invalid merely because it may in some other way deter one of the parties from marrying. Thus a promise to pay an allowance, or to permit a person to occupy a house, until the promisee's marriage, is valid.[190] Such promises may tend to discourage marriage, but they do not impose any contractual liability on a person as a result of marriage.[191]

(v) *Marriage brokage contracts*[192]

11–042   A marriage brokage contract is one by which a person promises in return for a money consideration to procure the marriage of another. Until the eighteenth century such contracts were valid at common law, thus making it possible for servants of young heiresses to obtain payment for assisting their charges to elope with fortune-hunters.[193] Equity therefore prevented the enforcement of these contracts[194]; and this equitable principle is not restricted to contracts to procure a marriage between one of the contracting parties and a *particular* third person. Thus a contract by which a marriage bureau simply undertakes to make efforts to find a spouse for a client has been held invalid, because it involved "the introduction of the consideration of a money payment into that which should be free from any such taint".[195] The harmful tendencies of such contracts seem to be no greater than those of contracts between "computer dating" agencies and their clients; and it has not been suggested that such contracts are contrary to public policy.

(vi) *Contracts promoting sexual immorality*

11–043   A contract may be illegal if its object is sexually immoral. The common law originally applied this principle to all cases in which a contract could be said to promote such an object. But a distinction is now drawn between contracts with

---

[187] *Baker v White* (1690) 2 Vern. 215; cf. *Hartley v Rice* (1808) 10 East 22.
[188] *Lowe v Peers* (1768) 2 Burr. 2225.
[189] cf. *Denny v Denny* [1919] 1 K.B. 583; below, para.11–061.
[190] *Gibson v Dickie* (1815) 3 M. & S. 463; the same point was assumed in *Thomas v Thomas* (1842) 2 Q.B. 851.
[191] Contrast the position in the restraint of trade cases, below, para.11–083. It is perhaps thought that stipulations which deter persons from trading are more likely to prejudice the public than those which deter them from marrying.
[192] Powell 6 C.L.P. 254.
[193] e.g. *Goldsmith v Bruning* (1700) 1 Eq.Ca.Abr. 89, pl. 4.
[194] *Cole v Gibson* (1750) 1 Ves.Sen. 503 at 506.
[195] *Hermann v Charlesworth* [1905] 2 K.B. 123 at 130; below, para.11–130.

purely meretricious purposes and those which are intended to regulate stable extra-marital relationships.

Meretricious purposes. A promise by a man to pay a woman money if she will become his mistress is illegal.[196] A promise to pay money to a woman with whom the promisor had illicitly cohabited in the past is not contrary to public policy since it does not *promote* immorality. It is simply void because the consideration for it is past,[197] and it will be valid if made in a deed.[198] The validity of a promise in a deed made *during* cohabitation depends on its purpose. If it is simply a gift,[199] or voluntary bond, it is as valid as one given after cohabitation.[200] But if its object is to secure the continuance of cohabitation, it is illegal.[201] A bond given after cohabitation would also be invalid if it were merely given to secure the performance of a promise of payment made before cohabitation.

11–044

A contract is also illegal if it indirectly promotes sexual immorality. Thus in *Pearce v Brooks*[202] a contract to hire out a brougham to a prostitute for the purposes of her profession was held to be illegal. The same would be true of a contract of employment by which the employee undertook to procure prostitutes for the employer's clients.[203] On the other hand, a contract to let a room to a prostitute who practises her profession elsewhere is valid "because persons of that description must have a place to lay their heads".[204] In *Lloyd v Johnson*[205] a contract to wash a prostitute's linen was held valid even though the linen included a quantity of gentlemen's nightcaps.

In the cases on this subject "immorality" always means extra-marital sexual intercourse. A contract might promote some other form of activity that could be described as immoral and sexual. For example, a contract might be made to publish an indecent book whose publication did not amount to a crime. Such a contract might formerly have been regarded as invalid on account of its "grossly immoral" tendency[206]; "But at the present day the difficulty is to identify what sexual conduct is to be treated as grossly immoral"[207]—so that it is less likely that such a contract would now be struck down on this ground.

---

[196] *Benyon v Nettlefold* (1850) 3 Mac. & G. 94.

[197] *Beaumont v Reeve* (1846) 8 Q.B. 483.

[198] *Annadale v Harris* (1727) 2 P.Wms. 432, affirmed 1 Bro.P.C. 250; *Turner v Vaughan* (1767) 2 Wils.K.B. 339; *Knye v Moore* (1822) 1 S. & S. 61. It is stressed in some of the old cases that the promisor was the seducer and that the payment was promised as "*praemium pudicitiae*". Thus it was doubtful whether the rule applied in favour of a common prostitute: *Bainham v Manning* (1691) 2 Vern. 242; *Whaley v Norton* (1687) 1 Vern. 483; *contra*, *Hill v Spencer* (1767) Amb. 641, 836.

[199] A promise to pay must also be distinguished from a completed gift: *Ayerst v Jenkins* (1873) L.R. 16 Eq. 275.

[200] *Gray v Mathias* (1800) 5 Ves. 286; *Hall v Palmer* (1844) 3 Hare 532.

[201] *The Lady Cox's Case* (1734) 3 P.Wms. 339; *Walker v Perkins* (1764) 3 Burr. 1568.

[202] (1866) L.R. 1 Ex. 213; cf. *Upfill v Wright* [1911] 1 K.B. 506, a case viewed with some scepticism in *Heglibiston Establishment v Heyman* (1977) 36 P. & C.R. 351.

[203] See *Coral Leisure Group v Barnett* [1981] I.C.R. 503 at 508 (where no such undertaking had, on the facts, been established); cf. *The Siben* [1996] 1 Lloyd's Rep. 35 at 62.

[204] *Appleton v Campbell* (1826) 2 C. & P. 347; cf. *Bowry v Bennett* (1808) 1 Camp. 348.

[205] (1798) 1 B. & P. 340.

[206] cf. *Glyn v Weston Feature Film Co* [1916] 1 Ch. 261 approved in *Attorney-General v Guardian Newspapers (No.2)* [1990] A.C. 109 at 262, 276; contrast *ZYX Music GmbH v King* [1995] 3 All E.R. 1 at 10; *A v B* [2000] E.M.L.R. 1007.

[207] *Stephens v Avery* [1988] Ch. 449 at 453; *Armhouse Lee Ltd v Chappel, The Times*, August 7, 1996.

11–045   **Stable relationships.** The traditional common law approach to immoral
contracts no longer applies to persons who live together in a common household
as husband and wife without being married. It has for example been held that a
licence under which such a couple occupied furnished accommodation was not
contrary to public policy.[208] The law also recognises that legal effects can flow from
agreements between such persons with respect to the house in which they live.
Where the house is owned by one of them, the agreement can confer legally
enforceable rights on the other, such as a contractual licence to remain there,[209] or
a share in the value of the house in respect of the contribution made by the other
to its acquisition, maintenance or improvement.[210] The opening of a bank account
by one party to such a relationship with funds intended to belong to both jointly
has been held (on proof of the appropriate intention) to amount to a declaration
of trust in favour of the other.[211] And "when an illegitimate child has been born,
there is certainly nothing contrary to public policy in the parents coming to an
agreement which they intend to be binding in law, for the maintenance of the child
and mother".[212]

These illustrations[213] show that the law now recognises that "unmarried cohabitation, whether heterosexual or homosexual, is widespread"[214]; and they suggest
that the old common law rule governing immoral contracts will in future be
confined to meretricious relationships (of whatever sexual orientation). Where
domestic arrangements between parties to the present group of stable relationships satisfy the requirement of contractual intention,[215] they will no longer be
struck down on grounds of public policy.[216]

(vii) *Contracts interfering with the course of justice*

11–046   A contract may be illegal because the mere making of it amounts to a conspiracy
to pervert the course of justice: e.g. where a person promises another money for
giving false evidence on his behalf in criminal proceedings[217] or where two men
agree to bribe a prosecution witness to withdraw a charge of rape.[218] A contract
may also (even though it does not amount to a criminal conspiracy) be illegal if its
object is to interfere with the course of justice. Before the distinction between
felonies and misdemeanours was abolished, a contract to stifle a prosecution for a
misdemeanour was not itself an offence but such contracts were often held illegal.
Thus contracts to stifle prosecutions for perjury, riot, assault on a police officer,

---

[208] *Somma v Hazelhurst* [1979] 1 W.L.R. 1014 (disapproved on another point in *Street v Mountford*
[1985] A.C. 809); cf. also *Watson v Lucas* [1980] 1 W.L.R. 1493.

[209] *Tanner v Tanner* [1975] 1 W.L.R. 1346; cf. *Fitzpatrick v Sterling Housing Association* [2001] 1 A.C.
27 (homosexual partner part of "family" for purposes of Rent Act 1977); and see the court's power
under Family Law Act 1996, ss.36 and 38 to exclude a "cohabitant" (as defined by s.62(1)(a)) from a
dwelling-house.

[210] *Eves v Eves* [1975] 1 W.L.R. 1338.

[211] *Paul v Constance* [1977] 1 W.L.R. 527.

[212] *Horrocks v Forray* [1976] 1 W.L.R. 230 at 239.

[213] cf. *Heglibiston Establishment v Heyman* (1977) 36 P. & C.R. 351.

[214] *Barclays Bank Plc v O'Brien* [1994] 1 A.C. 180 at 198; *Royal Bank of Scotland v Etridge (No.2)*
[2001] UKHL 44; [2002] 2 A.C. 773 at [47].

[215] See above, para.4–016.

[216] Devlin 39 M.L.R. 1 at 12; Dwyer 93 L.Q.R. 386.

[217] *R. v Andrews* [1973] Q.B. 422.

[218] *R. v Panayiotou* [1973] 3 All E.R. 112; cf. *R. v Ali* [1993] Crim.L.R. 396.

interfering with a public road, and obtaining by false pretences were held illegal.[219] But this rule was not applied where the misdemeanour was said to be of a "private" nature. Thus in *McGregor v McGregor*[220] it was held that a husband and wife who had taken out cross-summonses for assault against each other could validly compromise them in a separation agreement. It has similarly been held that a prosecution for trade-mark offences could be compromised by agreement between the owner and the offender[221]; and it has been said that the same principle applies to criminal libel.[222]

The old cases must now be read in the light of the abolition of the distinction between felonies and misdemeanours and of the creation of the offence of concealing a "relevant offence".[223] A person does not, however, commit this offence if he withholds information which may lead to the conviction of the offender in consideration only of the making good of the loss or injury caused by the offence[224]; and it is doubtful whether an agreement to this effect should now be held illegal.[225] One view is that the agreement may still be illegal, even though it does not itself amount to an offence, for this was precisely the position under the old law where an agreement was made to stifle a prosecution for a misdemeanour. A second view is that, where the only consideration is the making good of the loss, no public interest is harmed by upholding the agreement; and this view can be supported by reference to the old cases concerning misdemeanours of a "private" nature. A third view is that the legality of an agreement to stifle a prosecution (not amounting to a conspiracy to pervert the course of justice or to the offence of concealing a relevant offence) should depend on the question whether it was in the public interest that the prosecution should be brought; and it is submitted that this is the best view.

The principle of public policy is not confined to contracts to stifle a prosecution: thus a contract to indemnify a surety in criminal proceedings is illegal.[226] Nor is the principle restricted to contracts affecting criminal proceedings. Thus agreements to obstruct bankruptcy proceedings[227] and corrupt agreements relating to matrimonial proceedings[228] are illegal. It has also been said that a contract by which a witness promised one party to a civil dispute not to give evidence for the other would be contrary to public policy.[229] On the other hand, it has been held not to be contrary to public policy for one party to an agreement to undertake

---

[219] *Collins v Blantern* (1767) 2 Wils.K.B. 341; *Keir v Leeman* (1846) 9 Q.B. 371; *Windhill Local Board of Health v Vint* (1890) 45 Ch.D. 351; *Clubb v Huston* (1865) 18 C.B.(N.S.) 414 (embezzlement); cf. *Howard v Odham's Press Ltd* [1938] 1 K.B. 42 (contract not to disclose confession of fraud); and cf. below, fn.342. Contracts to stifle a prosecution for a felony were sometimes held illegal on this ground (e.g. *Rawlings v Coal Consumers' Association* (1874) 43 L.J.M.C. 111; *Whitmore v Farley* (1881) 45 L.T. 99), but were also illegal as they formerly amounted to compounding.

[220] (1888) 21 Q.B.D. 424.

[221] *Fisher & Co v Apollinaris Co* (1875) L.R. 10 Ch.App. 297.

[222] ibid. at 303.

[223] Criminal Law Act 1967, ss.1, 5(1). A "relevant offence" is defined by s.4(1A), as inserted by Serious Organised Crime and Police Act 2005, Sch.7, Pt 3.

[224] Criminal Law Act 1967, s.5(1).

[225] Hudson 43 M.L.R. 532.

[226] *Herman v Jeuchner* (1885) 15 Q.B.D. 561. It is now an offence to make such an agreement: Bail Act 1976, s.9.

[227] *Elliott v Richardson* (1870) L.R. 5 C.P. 744; cf. *Kearley v Thomson* (1890) 24 Q.B.D. 742; *Coppock v Bower* (1838) 4 M. & W. 361 (agreement to abandon election petition on ground of bribery illegal); *Norman v Cole* (1800) 3 Esp. 253 (money paid for help in procuring a pardon).

[228] See above, para.11–039.

[229] *Harmony Shipping Co SA v Saudi Europe Line Ltd* [1979] 1 W.L.R. 1380 at 1386.

that he would not oppose the other's application for planning applications and not give evidence in support of a compulsory purchase order relating to the land in question.[230] An ordinary civil claim can, of course, be validly compromised,[231] even though the facts giving rise to the claim also amount to a crime. But in such a case an agreement to abandon "any legal proceedings" may be illegal, as this phrase is wide enough to refer to possible civil *and* criminal proceedings.[232]

(viii) *Contracts purporting to oust the jurisdiction of the courts*

11–047   A contract is at common law contrary to public policy if it purports to deprive the courts of a jurisdiction which they would otherwise have. For example, a clause in an insurance policy which provides that the policy is in certain events to become "incontestable"[233] does not prevent the court from deciding whether the assured had any insurable interest.[234] Such agreements are contrary to public policy because they would, if valid, make it possible to evade or contravene many peremptory rules of law. It follows that they are invalid only so far as they purport to exclude the jurisdiction of the courts on a point of *law*. An agreement is not invalid to the extent that it gives a non-judicial body power to make final and binding decisions on questions of *fact*.[235] Such a provision does not, moreover, normally[236] rule out the possibility of a legal challenge to the decision on the ground of "unfairness, bad faith or perversity",[237] so that the provision does not wholly exclude the jurisdiction of the courts even on questions of fact. Whether a power conferred on the courts by statute is one which the parties are entitled to exclude depends upon the proper construction of the statute.[238] The rule against allowing parties by contract to oust the jurisdiction of the courts is further illustrated by the following cases.

11–048   **Agreements for maintenance.** One spouse may, as part of a separation agreement or in the course of matrimonial proceedings, promise to pay the other an allowance in return for a promise not to apply to the court for maintenance. In *Hyman v Hyman*[239] the House of Lords held that such an agreement did not prevent the other spouse from applying to the court for maintenance. The contract was illegal, since the "The wife's right to future maintenance is a matter of public concern which she cannot barter away".[240] But this rule had one unfortunate result: if the first spouse failed to pay the promised allowance, the other could not sue for it, since a promise cannot be enforced if the sole or main consideration for

---

[230] *Fulham Football Club Ltd v Cabra Estates* (1992) 56 P. & C.R. 284.

[231] *Australia & New Zealand Banking Group Ltd v Compagnie Noga d'Importation et d'Exportation SA* [2007] EWHC 293 (Comm); [2007] 1 Lloyd's Rep. 487 at [31].

[232] *Lound v Grimwade* (1888) 39 Ch.D. 605.

[233] *Anctil v Manufacturers' Life Ins Co* [1899] A.C. 604.

[234] But such clauses are effective to prevent the insurer from contesting certain matters of *fact*, e.g. that statements in the proposal form were true: cf. below, at fn.235.

[235] *The Glacier Bay* [1996] 1 Lloyd's Rep. 370 and see below, fn.283.

[236] For a common law exception, see below at fn.284.

[237] *The Glacier Bay*, above, at 379.

[238] *Aribisala v St James Homes (Grosvenor) Dock Ltd* [2007] EWHC 1694 (Ch); [2007] 37 E.G. 234 (contract to exclude s.49(2) Law of Property Act 1925 contrary to public policy).

[239] [1929] A.C. 601.

[240] ibid. at 629. But such an agreement is not contrary to public policy if it only ousts the jurisdiction of a foreign court: *Addison v Brown* [1954] 1 W.L.R. 779; nor if it is sanctioned by order of the court: *L v L* [1962] P. 101; *Minton v Minton* [1979] A.C. 594.

it is illegal.[241] By statute, if the agreement is in writing, an action may be brought for the promised allowance, in spite of the fact that the promise not to apply to the court is void.[242] The court can also take the agreement into account when exercising its power to grant ancillary relief.[243]

Nuptial agreements Ante- and post-nuptial agreements were at one time unenforceable because of the rule that agreements providing for *future* separation were contrary to public policy. That rule is now obsolete and has been "swept away".[244] Such agreements are still contrary to public policy to the extent that they oust the jurisdiction of the courts, but they may be taken into account by the courts in the exercise of their power under Pt II of the Matrimonial Causes Act 1973 to order ancillary relief when granting a decree of divorce, nullity, or judicial separation.[245] In this sense, at least as a matter of English law,[246] their enforceability is a "red herring" since "in ancillary relief proceedings the court is not bound to give effect to nuptial agreements, and is bound to have regard to them, whether or not they are contracts."[247]   11–049

Arbitration clauses. There is no doubt about the validity of such clauses if they merely provide that the parties are to resort to arbitration before going to court. In *Scott v Avery*[248] a clause of this kind was upheld as it did not purport to oust the jurisdiction of the court,[249] but simply to lay down at what stage the cause of action arose upon which that jurisdiction might be exercised. At common law such a clause did not prevent the courts from nevertheless determining the dispute, though the party who disregarded the clause and in breach of it brought an action was liable in damages.[250] The courts have, however, an inherent jurisdiction to stay an action brought in breach of an agreement to decide disputes in some way other than by bringing an action.[251] Moreover, the Arbitration Act 1996 provides that, where an arbitration agreement is in writing,[252] the court must stay   11–050

---

[241] *Bennett v Bennett* [1952] 1 K.B. 249; cf. *Sutton v Sutton* [1984] Ch. 184 (where *each* party promised not to invoke the jurisdiction of the court); and see below, para.11–154.

[242] Matrimonial Causes Act 1973, s.34. In *Sutton v Sutton*, above, the agreement was oral, so that s.34 did not apply. Under Child Support Act 1991, s.9 (as amended by Child Support Act 1995, s.18), similar rules apply to certain maintenance agreements in respect of children.

[243] *Edgar v Edgar* [1980] 1 W.L.R. 1410.

[244] *Radmacher v Granatino* [2010] UKSC 42, [2011] 1 A.C. 534 at [52].

[245] ibid.

[246] The fact that such agreements might be enforced in a foreign court which lacks the jurisdiction under Pt II of the 1973 Act led Lord Mance (ibid. at [128]) to express no view on the binding nature of an ante-nuptial agreement and was one of the reasons for the dissenting speech of Baroness Hale.

[247] ibid. at [62]. The decision of the Supreme Court that *ante*-nuptial agreements are not otherwise contrary to public policy and are enforceable is therefore "mercifully *obiter*" (Baroness Hale, at [138]). The Privy Council had earlier decided that *post*-nuptial agreements are not contrary to public policy in *MacLeod v MacLeod* [2008] UKPC 64; [2010] 1 A.C. 298.

[248] (1855) 5 H.L.C. 811; cf. *Atlantic Shipping & Trading Co Ltd v Louis Dreyfus & Co* [1922] 2 A.C. 250; *Persson v London County Buses* [1974] 1 W.L.R. 569.

[249] See *Halifax Financial Services v Intuitive Systems Ltd* [1999] 1 All E.R. (Comm) 303 at 310, where the clause in question was a "dispute resolution" clause which failed for lack of certainty: above, para.2–100.

[250] *Doleman & Sons v Ossett Corp* [1912] 3 K.B. 257 at 267.

[251] *Channel Tunnel Group Ltd v Balfour Beatty Construction Ltd* [1993] A.C. 334; cf. *Cott UK Ltd v F E Barber Ltd* [1997] 3 All E.R. 540; and *T & N Ltd & Sun Alliance Plc* [2002] EWHC 2420; [2002] C.L.C. 1342 where a stay was refused.

[252] For this requirement, see s.5(1).

an action brought in breach of the agreement[253] unless the agreement is "null and void, inoperative or incapable of being performed". Where the agreement is made between a party acting in the course of a business and a consumer, it does not bind the consumer if the amount claimed is less than £5,000[254]; but it binds the other party.

11–051   **Potential grounds of invalidity.** The fact that an arbitration clause excluded the jurisdiction of the court might at common law make the clause invalid on one of two grounds. First, such a clause was invalid to the extent that it purported to deprive the parties of the right to go to court to sue on a completed cause of action, or to exclude the power granted to the courts by statute to control the decisions of arbitrators on points of law.[255] This rule was justified by the argument that, if such a clause were valid, an arbitrator who decided a dispute on principles at variance with the general law would be subject to no control at all[256]; and this would be particularly undesirable if he made an award enforcing a wholly illegal agreement.[257] A substantially similar risk could arise where the clause, though not in terms restricting the parties' right to ask the court to control the arbitrator's decision, laid down standards which made such control nugatory. This is a second ground of invalidity at common law, so that "a clause which purported to free arbitrators to decide without regard to law and according, for example, to their own notions of what would be fair would not be a valid arbitration clause".[258] But the parties can validly specify standards which, at least to some extent, guard against the risk of invalidity on this ground: it is, for example, not contrary to public policy to enforce an arbitration award based on "internationally accepted principles of law governing contractual relations".[259] An arbitration clause can also free arbitrators from the need to apply strict legal rules of construction, e.g. by empowering them to interpret a contract "as an honourable engagement rather than in accordance with a literal interpretation of the language".[260] And the courts can to some extent save an arbitration clause which transgresses such limits by striking out such parts of the clause as go "further than the law permits in freeing arbitrators from strict rules of law".[261] The Arbitration Act 1996 provides more generally that "the parties should be free to agree how their disputes are to be resolved",[262] but this general principle is expressly made "subject to such safe-guards as are necessary in the public interest".[263] These words seem to leave it open to the courts to continue to apply standards of public policy to such

---

[253] s.9(4); *Halki Shipping Corp v Sopex Oils Ltd* [1998] 1 W.L.R. 726; this rule cannot be excluded by contract: see s.4 and Sch.1.

[254] s.91; Unfair Arbitration Agreements (Specified Amounts) Order 1999 (SI 1999/2167).

[255] *Czarnikow v Roth Schmidt & Co* [1922] 2 K.B. 478. For a different approach in New Zealand, see *CBI NZ Ltd v Badger Chiyoda* [1989] N.Z.L.R. 669.

[256] Clauses making an arbitrator's decision "final" do not have this effect: see *Ford v Clarkson's Holidays Ltd* [1971] 1 W.L.R. 1412; cf. *Jones v Sherwood Computer Services* [1992] 1 W.L.R. 227 ("final and conclusive" valuation reviewable for error of law).

[257] cf. *Soleimany v Soleimany* [1999] Q.B. 785 at 799. See now below, after fn.265.

[258] *Home and Overseas Ins Co Ltd v Mentor Ins Co (UK) Ltd* [1989] 1 Lloyd's Rep. 473 at 485; and see below, fn.261.

[259] *Deutsche Schachtbau-und Tiefbohrgesellschaft mbH v Ras Al Khaimah National Oil Co* [1990] 1 A.C. 295 at 315 (reversed on other grounds [1990] 1 A.C. 295, pp.329 et seq.).

[260] *Overseas Union Ins Ltd v AA Mutual International Ins Ltd* [1988] 2 Lloyd's Rep. 63; *Home and Overseas Ins Co Ltd v Mentor Ins Co (UK) Ltd*, above, fn.258.

[261] *Home Ins Co v Administrata Asigurarilor* [1983] 2 Lloyd's Rep. 674 at 677.

[262] s.1(b).

[263] s.1(b).

agreements. The Act also provides that the court may refuse to recognise or enforce an arbitral award on grounds of public policy,[264] and this provision could be applied where such an award purported to enforce an illegal agreement.

The effect of the Arbitration Act 1996. The invalidity, at common law, of **11–052** arbitration clauses which purported to exclude the powers of the court to control an arbitrator's decision on points of law was open to a practical objection: the resulting impossibility of excluding judicial control tended to erode the virtues of speed and cheapness that were supposed to be characteristics of arbitration as a method of settling disputes. The Arbitration Act 1996 therefore, while retaining a degree of judicial control over arbitration proceedings,[265] reduces the scope of such control in two important respects. First, the parties to a written arbitration agreement[266] can exclude such judicial control by agreement.[267] Secondly, the Act imposes strict limits on the scope of judicial control. This will generally be exercised by way of appeal to the court on a question of law.[268] Such an appeal can be brought either with the consent of the parties or with the leave of the court,[269] and such leave can be given only if a number of statutory requirements[270] are satisfied. The point of law must be one which substantially affects the rights of one or more of the parties and which the arbitral tribunal was asked to determine; the decision of that tribunal must *either* be "obviously wrong" *or* raise a question of "general public importance" and be "at least open to serious doubt"; and it must, in spite of the parties' agreement to resolve the dispute by arbitration be "just and proper for the court to determine the question". These requirements are based on (but go slightly beyond[271]) tests which had been developed by the courts under earlier legislation.[272] The overriding consideration remains that stated in the course of this judicial development: i.e. whether the decision of the court "would add significantly to the clarity and certainty of English commercial law".[273] Thus the court is more likely to grant leave if the issue is as to the true construction of a standard form commercial contract in common use,[274] or if it raises an important general question of law,[275] than if it relates merely to the construction of a "one-off" contract specially drafted for a particular transaction.[276] A similar distinction has been drawn in relation to *events* giving rise to the dispute, or interfering with the performance of a contract. Thus leave is more likely to be given where the event is one that may affect many contracts (such as the hostilities in the Persian

---

[264] s.81(1)(c); cf. above, after fn.256.

[265] See below, at fn.268.

[266] Arbitration Act 1996, s.5(1).

[267] See the opening words of ss.45(1) and 69(1).

[268] s.69; under s.45 the court also has powers to determine preliminary questions of law, i.e. of the law of England and Wales: s.82(1); *Reliance Industries Ltd v Enron Oil & Gas Co* [2002] 1 Lloyd's Rep. 645.

[269] s.69(2).

[270] s.69(3).

[271] *CMA CGM SA v Beteilingungs-Kommanditgesellschaft mbH & Co* [2002] EWCA Civ 1878; [2003] 1 W.L.R. 1015.

[272] *The Nema* [1982] A.C. 724 and other cases; for full citations of these cases, see the 9th edn of this book at pp.408–409.

[273] ibid. at 743. For other grounds of public interest that may lead the court to give leave, see *Bulk Oil (Zug) AG v Sun International* [1984] 1 W.L.R. 147.

[274] *The Rio Sun* [1981] 2 Lloyd's Rep. 489; see also [1982] 1 Lloyd's Rep. 404.

[275] *The Alaskan Trader* [1983] 1 Lloyd's Rep. 315.

[276] *The Nema*, above, at 743.

Gulf, preventing the movement of shipping there,[277] or an embargo on the export of some commodity from a major exporting country) than where the event is not likely to have this effect (e.g. where it is a strike that affects only the export of goods from a particular port[278]).

11-053   **Other grounds of invalidity.** An arbitration agreement may, finally, be invalid for illegality at common law on grounds other than its tendency to exclude the jurisdiction of the courts. Such invalidity could arise by reason of the nature of the underlying transaction: e.g. the court "would not recognise an agreement between highwayman to arbitrate their differences any more than it would recognise the original agreement to split the proceeds"[279]; and even if an arbitrator made an award in such a case, the court would not enforce it.[280] Under statute, an arbitration agreement may be unenforceable in relation to particular types of claim.[281] An arbitration agreement stipulating that the arbitrators are to be drawn from members of a particular religious group is not contrary to rules against religious discrimination.[282]

11-054   **Construction of rules of associations.** A clause in the rules of an association such as a trade union may purport to give to the committee of the association exclusive jurisdiction to construe the rules. But, as the construction of the rules is a question of law, it has been held that any attempt to deprive the courts of their jurisdiction over it is invalid.[283] By contrast, the jurisdiction of the Visitor of a University to decide matters governed by the "internal laws" of the University is at common law[284] exclusive, so that his decisions on points of this kind cannot be challenged in the ordinary courts.[285]

11-055   **Scope of the rule.** Contracts purporting to exclude the jurisdiction of the courts must be distinguished from promises in honour only.[286] A provision that a

---

[277] *The Wenjiang* [1982] 1 Lloyd's Rep. 128.

[278] As in *The Nema*, above.

[279] *Soleimany v Soleimany* [1999] Q.B. 785 at 797; [1999] 3 All E.R. at 857; contrast *Westacre Investments Inc v Jugoimport-SDPR Holdings Co Ltd* [1999] 2 Lloyd's Rep. 65; [1999] 3 All E.R. 864; [2000] Q.B. 288 and *Omnium de Traitment et de Valorisation SA v Hilmarton Ltd* [1999] 2 Lloyd's Rep. 222 (contract not illegal by its proper law nor enforcement contrary to English public policy).

[280] *Soleimany v Soleimany*, above, at 799; and see Arbitration Act 1996, s.81(1)(c).

[281] See, e.g. Employment Rights Act 1996, s.203; Equality Act 2010, s.144; *Clyde & Co LLP v van Winkelhof* [2011] EWHC 668 (QB).

[282] *Jivraj v Hashwani* [2011] UKSC 40, on the basis that an arbitrator is not a person employed "personally to do any work" under the Employment Equality (Religion or Belief) Regulations 2003 (SI 2003/1660).

[283] *Lee v Showmen's Guild of Great Britain* [1952] 2 Q.B. 329; cf. *Edwards v Aberayron Ins Society Ltd* (1876) 1 Q.B.D. 563; *Re Davstone Estate Ltd's Leases* [1969] 2 Ch. 378; *Edwards v SOGAT* [1971] Ch. 354. There is no objection to leaving questions of *fact* to the final determination of a private tribunal: *Brown v Overbury* (1856) 11 Exch. 715; *Cipriani v Burnett* [1933] A.C. 83. See also Trade Union and Labour Relations (Consolidation) Act 1992, s.63 (right of union members to go to court after six months).

[284] The jurisdiction of the Visitor is now drastically reduced: Higher Education Act 2004, ss.20, 46.

[285] *Thomas v University of Bradford* [1987] A.C. 795 (for subsequent proceedings before the Visitor, see *Thomas v University of Bradford* [1992] 1 All E.R. 964); *R. v Lord President of the Privy Council Ex p. Page* [1993] A.C. 682. Contrast *Clark v University of Lincolnshire and Humberside* [2000] 1 W.L.R. 1985.

[286] See above, para.4–005.

promise "shall not be enforced in any court" makes the promise legally unenforce-able, but does not purport to oust the jurisdiction of the court to say so. Similar reasoning applies to the compromise of a genuine dispute as to legal rights. Such a compromise may vary or supersede the legal rights of the parties; but it does not prevent the courts from determining what those rights are. It is therefore not contrary to public policy[287]; and this is true even though the public can be said to have some interest in the dispute, e.g. because it relates to the performance of duties under a charitable trust.[288]

(ix) *Contracts to deceive public authorities*

In *Alexander v Rayson*[289] a landlord let a service flat to the defendant for £1,200. **11–056** Two documents were executed: in the first the defendant agreed to pay £450 for the flat and certain services; in the second she agreed to pay £750 for the same services, plus the use of a refrigerator. The landlord's object in splitting up the contract in this way was to defraud the rating authorities by showing them the first document only. The contract was therefore held to be illegal. A contract by which an employee gets an expense allowance grossly in excess of the expenses he actually incurs is similarly illegal as a fraud on the Revenue.[290] But where the contract is in itself lawful and is merely the "setting for an act contrary to public policy"[291] it is not illegal if it is too remote from the intention to defraud.[292] Furthermore, the contract is illegal only if the scheme that it furthers is a fraudulent one. Thus it is perfectly lawful for a contract of employment to provide that the employee is to receive a specified amount "free of tax", so long as the employer accounts to the revenue authorities for the tax due.[293] And where a seller sent out a false invoice with the intention of merely postponing the payment of VAT, it was held that this did not turn an originally lawful sale into an illegal contract, it having been found as a fact that the seller had acted without dishonest intent.[294]

(x) *Sale of offices and honours*

Certain contracts for the sale of public offices are prohibited by statute[295] while **11–057** others are illegal at common law.[296] Contracts of this kind are contrary to public policy because of their tendency to lead to corruption and inefficiency. Similarly,

---

[287] See above, para.3–034. For compromise of a claim known by the claimant to be invalid, see above, para.3–036; below, para.11–110.

[288] *Bradshaw v University College of Wales* [1988] 1 W.L.R. 190.

[289] [1936] 1 K.B. 169; cf. *Palaniappa Chettiar v Arunasalam Chettiar* [1962] A.C. 294.

[290] *Miller v Karlinski* (1945) 62 T.L.R. 85; cf. *Hyland v J Barber (North West)* [1985] I.C.R. 861; *Corby v Morrison* [1980] I.C.R. 564.

[291] Furmston (1966) University of Toronto L.J. 267 at 287.

[292] *21st Century Logistic Solutions Ltd v Madysen Ltd* [2004] EWHC 231; [2004] 2 Lloyd's Rep. 92 (contract not unenforceable as a consequence of the seller's intention not to account to the Revenue for the VAT element of the price).

[293] See *Newland v Simmons & Willer (Hairdressers) Ltd* [1981] I.C.R. 521.

[294] *Skilton v Sullivan*, The Times, March 25, 1994; see further para.11–114, below.

[295] Sale of Offices Act 1551, extended by Sale of Offices Act 1809, as amended by Criminal Law Act 1967, s.10 and Sch.3.

[296] e.g. *Garforth v Fearon* (1787) 1 H.B.L. 327; *Law v Law* (1735) 3 P.Wms. 391; *Parsons v Thompson* (1790) 1 H.B. 322. cf. the rule against assignment of a public officer's salary: below, para.15–066.

it was held in *Parkinson v College of Ambulance Ltd*[297] that a contract to procure a knighthood was illegal as it might lead to corruption and as it was "derogatory to the dignity of the Sovereign".[298] It is now an offence to make such a contract.[299] And a contract by a Member of Parliament to vote in accordance with the direction of some body outside Parliament is invalid.[300]

(xi) *Lobbying & Bribery*

11–058   Similar problems about the potential to corrupt can arise from the practice of "lobbying" for government contracts. While in some cases the practice has been said to be "recognised and respectable",[301] it is in others contrary to public policy. This was, for example, held to be the case where the defendant promised large commissions to the claimant for using its influence to secure the renewal of contracts between the defendant and a foreign government. It was essential to the success of the scheme that the government should be kept in ignorance of the claimant's financial interest in the matter, while the claimant knew that the original contract provided that no commissions should be paid to third parties. The claim for the commission was therefore rejected on grounds of public policy.[302]

Under the Bribery Act 2010,[303] it is now an offence to promise or give a financial or other advantage to a person if it is intended to induce that person, or another, to perform improperly a relevant function or activity, or if it is intended to reward that person, or another, for the improper performance of such a function or activity, or the person conferring the advantage knows or believes that the acceptance of it would itself constitute the improper performance of a relevant function or activity.[304] A relevant function or activity includes "any function of a public nature", as well as any activity connected with a business, any activity performed in the course of a person's employment, and any activity performed by or on behalf of a body of persons (whether corporate or unincorporate),[305] if the person performing it is either in a position of trust by virtue of its performance or is expected to perform it in good faith, or impartially.[306] A relevant function or activity is improperly performed if performance, or the failure to perform, is in breach of a "relevant expectation[307]", i.e. that it will be performed in good faith, impartially or in a manner consistent with the position of trust bestowed on the

---

[297] [1925] 2 K.B. 1.
[298] ibid. at 14.
[299] Honours (Prevention of Abuses) Act 1925.
[300] *ASRS v Osborne* [1910] A.C. 87.
[301] *Lemenda Trading Co Ltd v African Middle East Petroleum Co* [1988] Q.B. 448 at 458; Collier [1988] C.L.J. 169.
[302] ibid. Contrast *Tekron Resources Ltd v Guinea Investment Co Ltd* [2003] EWHC 2577; [2004] 2 Lloyd's Rep. 26. See now the Bribery Act 2010, s.6.
[303] In force from July 1, 2011: SI 2011/1418.
[304] s.1. Under s.2 similar provisions deal with the offence of being bribed.
[305] s.3(2).
[306] s.3(3).
[307] i.e. "what a reasonable person in the United Kingdom would expect in relation to the performance of the type of function or activity concerned" (s.5(1)). Where the performance is not subject to the law of any part of the United Kingdom, any local custom or practice is to be disregarded unless it is permitted or required by the written law applicable to the country or territory concerned (s.5(2)).

person in question.[308] Special provision is made for the bribery of foreign public officials.[309]

(xii) *Trading with the enemy*

A contract made during a war to which this country is a party is illegal if it involves commercial intercourse with an enemy.[310] An enemy, for this purpose, is a person voluntarily resident or carrying on business in enemy-occupied territory.[311] Such contracts are illegal as they tend to aid the economy of the enemy country. A contract is not illegal if one of the parties to it is an "enemy" but its performance involves no further commercial intercourse with the enemy[312] and it can be enforced if this does not benefit the enemy.[313] It is a statutory offence to trade or to attempt to trade with an enemy.[314]

11–059

(xiii) *Contracts which involve doing an illegal act in a friendly foreign country*

In the interests of good foreign relations, the courts will not enforce a contract which is lawful on its face if it is entered for a purpose which is unlawful under the law of a friendly foreign state.[315] For example, contracts which had as their objective the smuggling of whisky into the USA during the Prohibition period have been held unenforceable.[316] And in *Regazzoni v KC Sethia Ltd*[317] a contract was made for the export of Indian jute to Italy, with a view to re-export to South Africa. The House of Lords refused to enforce the contract as it contravened an Indian law prohibiting the export of goods produced in India to South Africa, and as it could be performed only by making false declarations in India.

11–060

(xiv) *Contracts restricting personal liberty*

A contract may be illegal if it so severely restricts the liberty of an individual as to reduce him to a quasi-servile condition. In *Horwood v Millar's Timber and*

11–061

---

[308] s.4.

[309] s.6.

[310] *Sovfracht (V/O) v Van Udens Scheepvaart en Agentuur Maatschappij (NV Gebr.)* [1943] A.C. 203.

[311] *Porter v Freudenberg* [1915] 1 K.B. 857.

[312] *Tingley v Muller* [1917] 2 Ch. 144.

[313] *Rodriguez v Speyer Bros* [1919] A.C. 59.

[314] Trading with the Enemy Act 1939.

[315] Since the coming into force of the Rome I Regulation ((EC) 593/2008), it seems that this rule must be accommodated within Art.21 (formerly Rome Convention (Contracts (Applicable Law) Act 1990, s.2(1), Sch.1, Art.16): *Dicey, Morris & Collins, The Conflict of Laws* (14th edn), r.210.

[316] *Foster v Driscoll* [1929] 1 K.B. 470; *Mahonia Ltd v JP Morgan Chase Bank* [2003] EWHC 1927; [2003] 2 Lloyd's Rep. 911; *Soleimany v Soleimany* [1999] Q.B. 785 at 797; contrast *Libyan Arab Foreign Bank v Bankers Trust Co* [1989] Q.B. 728 at 744–745 (where there was no intention to do or procure an illegal act abroad); *Bangladesh Export & Import Co Ltd v Sucden Kerry SA* [1995] 2 Lloyd's Rep. 1 at 6 (where there was no obligation to do such an act); *Royal Boskalis Westminster NV v Mountain* [1997] 2 All E.R. 929; *Emeraldian Partnership Ltd v Wellmix Shipping Ltd* [2010] EWHC 1411 (Comm) at [175]–[179]; cf. *Ralli Bros v Compañia Naviera Sota y Aznar* [1920] 2 K.B. 287 (*supervening* illegality of payment and therefore probably best seen as a case of frustration).

[317] [1958] A.C. 301. Contrast *Fox v Henderson Investment Fund Ltd* [1999] 2 Lloyd's Rep. 303 (no illegality merely because acts to be done *in England* in performance of the contract would involve breach of an order made by a *foreign* court).

Trading Co[318] a clerk borrowed money from a moneylender and agreed that he would not without the lender's written consent leave his job, borrow money, dispose of his property or move house. The contract was held to be illegal as it unduly restricted the liberty of the borrower.

But a case has to be extreme to fall within this principle. In *Denny v Denny*[319] a father promised to pay his son's debts and to make him an allowance if the son did not become a bankrupt; became and remained a reformed character; gave up some named associates (who were swindlers); did not go within 80 miles of Piccadilly Circus without his father's previous consent; did not borrow money, or bet or directly or indirectly have any business or personal relations with any moneylenders, bookmakers or turf accountants or their servants. This contract was upheld even though, taken literally, it prevented the son from having personal relations with a bookmaker's clerk, who might be perfectly honest. The court was mainly influenced by the fact that the father had imposed the restrictions for the son's benefit, while the moneylender in *Horwood*'s case had acted from selfish motives.

3. CONTRACTS IN RESTRAINT OF TRADE[320]

(a) Introduction

11-062   Contracts which prevent or regulate business competition were at one time regarded as invariably void[321]; and persons who made them were even threatened with imprisonment.[322] But it came to be recognised that this inflexible attitude might defeat its own ends. A master might be reluctant to employ and train apprentices if he could not to some extent restrain them from competing with him after the end of their apprenticeship. And a trader might be unable to sell the business he had built up if he could not bind himself not to compete with the purchaser. The courts therefore began to uphold contracts in restraint of trade, and in 1711 the subject was reviewed in *Mitchel v Reynolds*.[323] The effect of that case, as interpreted in later decisions, was that a restraint was prima facie valid if it was supported by adequate consideration and was not general—i.e. did not extend over the whole Kingdom.

11-063   **Summary of the present position.** Since then, the law has changed in three respects. First, restraints are no longer prima facie valid; they are prima facie void,[324] but can be justified if they are reasonable and not contrary to the public

---

[318] [1917] 3 K.B. 305; cf. *Hepworth Manufacturing Co v Ryott* [1920] 1 Ch. 1; *Gaumont-British Picture Corp v Alexander* [1936] 2 All E.R. 1686. See also *Tailby v Official Receiver* (1888) 13 App.Cas. 533; *King v Michael Faraday & Partners Ltd* [1939] 2 K.B. 753 (assignment of salary depriving assignor of his sole means of support invalid), and *Syrett v Egerton* [1957] 1 W.L.R. 1130 (whether assignment of *all* an individual's property is contrary to public policy). Under Human Rights Act 1998, s.1 and Sch.1, Pt I, Art.5, contractual restrictions on personal liberty of the kind described in the text above could be unlawful if imposed by a "public authority": see s.6. Such restrictions do not appear to fall within Art.1 of Sch.1, Pt I.

[319] [1919] 1 K.B. 583; cf. *Upton v Henderson* (1912) 28 T.L.R. 398.

[320] Heydon, *The Restraint of Trade Doctrine* (3rd edn) and 50 A.L.J. 290; Trebilcock, *The Common Law of Restraint of Trade*.

[321] *Claygate v Batchelor* (1602) Owen 143.

[322] *Dyer's Case* (1414) Y.B. 2 Hen. V, Pasch. pl. 26.

[323] (1711) 1 P.Wms. 181.

[324] As the basis of the rule is public policy the contract cannot be affirmed: *Proactive Sports Management Ltd v Rooney* [2010] EWHC 1807 (QB), not following *Panayiotou v Sony Music Entertainment (UK) Ltd*, The Times, June 30, 1994.

interest.[325] Secondly, it is no longer essential that the consideration should be adequate,[326] "though ... the quantum of consideration may enter into the question of the reasonableness of the agreement".[327] Thirdly, the rule that a restraint must not be general no longer applies. In *Nordenfelt v Maxim Nordenfelt Guns & Ammunition Co*[328] the owner of an armaments business sold it to a company and covenanted not to carry on such a business for 25 years except on behalf of the company. The covenant was held valid although it prevented competition anywhere in the world.

Time for determining validity. Most authorities support the view that the 11–064 question whether a restraint is valid must be determined once for all by reference to the circumstances in existence when the contract was made.[329] The view that a restraint which satisfies the tests of validity at that time may become invalid or unenforceable in the light of subsequent events[330] has been generally rejected as it would give rise to an unacceptable degree of uncertainty.

Categories. Agreements which have been held to be within the doctrine of 11–065 restraint of trade can be divided into a number of groups or categories which will be discussed below. We shall see that some agreements which are, or may be, within the doctrine do not fall readily within any of these categories; and that other agreements which can in a sense be said to restrain trade are not within the doctrine at all, and are therefore not subject to the conditions on which the validity of covenants in restraint of trade depends.[331] Our main concern will be with the common law rules on this topic. After discussing these rules, we shall consider the relationship between them and the legislation which governs EC and UK competition law.[332]

(b) Sale of a Business and Employment

In this group of cases, a covenant in restraint of trade is invalid unless three 11–066 conditions are satisfied: there must be an interest meriting protection; the restraint must be reasonable; and it must not be contrary to the public interest.

(i) *Interest*

The interest must arise from the relationship of the parties as buyer and seller 11–067 or as employer and employee. In the absence of such a relationship, freedom from ordinary trade competition is not, of itself, an interest meriting protection.[333]

---

[325] See below, paras 11–074—11–079.

[326] *Tallis v Tallis* (1853) 1 E. & B. 391.

[327] *Nordenfelt v Maxim Nordenfelt Guns and Ammunition Co* [1894] A.C. 535 at 565; *Esso Petroleum Ltd v Harper's Garage (Stourport) Ltd* [1968] A.C. 300 at 318, 323; *Amoco Australia Pty Ltd v Rocca Bros Motor Engineering Pty Ltd* (1973) 47 A.L.J.R. 681 (affirmed [1975] A.C. 561, without reference to this point); *Alec Lobb (Garages) Ltd v Total Oil (Great Britain) Ltd* [1985] 1 W.L.R. 173 at 179.

[328] [1894] A.C. 535.

[329] *Commercial Plastics Ltd v Vincent* [1965] 1 Q.B. 623 at 644 (citing earlier authorities); *A Schroeder Music Publishing Co Ltd v Macaulay* [1974] 1 W.L.R. 1308 at 1309; *Shell UK Ltd v Lostock Garages Ltd* [1976] 1 W.L.R. 1187 at 1203; *Watson v Prager* [1991] 1 W.L.R. 726 at 738; *Symbian Ltd v Christensen* [2001] I.R.L.R. 77.

[330] *Shell UK Ltd v Lostock Garages Ltd* [1976] W.L.R. 1187 at 1198.

[331] See below, para.11–102.

[332] See below, para.11–105.

[333] cf. *Vancouver Malt & Sake Brewing Co v Vancouver Breweries Ltd* [1934] A.C. 181.

Thus a bare promise to a shopkeeper not to open (or work for) a competing business would be void; such a promise is known as a covenant in gross. Normally the covenant must be contained in a contract of sale or employment, but this is not absolutely necessary. It is enough if the covenant is closely related to such a contract; e.g. if it is contained in a contract made (shortly after the termination of an employment contract) to settle outstanding differences.[334]

11–068   **Sale of a business.** Even in the absence of a covenant in restraint of trade, the purchaser of the goodwill of a business can restrain the vendor from canvassing the old customers of the business.[335] This rule would not prevent the vendor from competing in other ways (e.g. from dealing with his old customers if they spontaneously came to him); but the purchaser can validly stipulate against such competition by a covenant in restraint of trade. His right to do so is said to depend on his "proprietary interest" in the goodwill of the business which he has bought.[336]

It follows that the purchaser is entitled to protection only in respect of the business which he has bought, and not in respect of some other business which he already carries on or may carry on in the future. If a company which owns shops in all parts of the country buys a village shop it can restrain the seller from competing in or near that village, but not at other places where it happens to carry on business.[337] Similarly, in the *Nordenfelt* case[338] the covenant restrained the seller from engaging not only in the manufacture of armaments but also "in any other business competing or liable to compete with that for the time being carried on by" the buyer. The latter part of the covenant was invalid. Its effect would be to restrain the seller from competing with the company if it started to make ploughshares; and he had sold no such business.[339] But a person who buys a business which is about to expand may be able to take a covenant against competition covering the area of the proposed expansion.[340] And the rule that the buyer can restrain the seller from competing only with the business formerly carried on by the seller is subject to a common-sense exception. A person who sells shares in a company which he controls may covenant not to compete in respect of the business carried on by *the company.* Such a covenant may be valid if it was in substance the seller who, through his control of the company, carried on the business[341]; and even a seller of a minority shareholding can validly covenant with the buyer not to use confidential information which relates to the business of the company.[342] If, however, the *business* carried on by a company (as opposed to the *shares* in it) is sold, it may be hard to frame a suitable covenant to protect the buyer from competition by associated companies.[343]

---

[334] *Stenhouse Australia Ltd v Phillips* [1974] A.C. 391.

[335] *Trego v Hunt* [1896] A.C. 7.

[336] There can be such an interest even though the goodwill is inalienable: see *Whitehill v Bradford* [1952] Ch. 236; *Kerr v Morris* [1987] Ch. 90; and even though the interest is not purely financial: cf. in an analogous context, *Young v Evans-Jones* [2001] EWCA Civ 732; [2001] 1 P. & C.R. 176.

[337] cf. *British Reinforced Concrete Engineering Co Ltd v Schelff* [1921] 2 Ch. 563.

[338] [1894] A.C. 535.

[339] cf. (between employer and employee) *Scully UK Ltd v Lee* [1998] I.R.L.R. 259.

[340] *Lamson Pneumatic Tube Co v Phillips* (1904) 91 L.T. 363; *TSC Europe (UK) Ltd v Massey* [1999] I.R.L.R. 22 at 27–28.

[341] *Connors Bros v Connors Ltd* [1940] 4 All E.R. 179; cf. *Kirby (Inspector of Taxes) v Thorn EMI* [1988] 1 W.L.R. 445 (covenant on sale by company of shares in its subsidiary).

[342] *Systems Reliability Holdings v Smith* [1990] I.R.L.R. 377.

[343] See *Doyle v Olby (Ironmongers) Ltd* [1969] 2 Q.B. 158.

Employment.[344] Even in the absence of a covenant in restraint of trade, the   **11–069**
law gives an employer some degree of protection against his employee.[345] He can
restrain the employee from (i) using or disclosing trade secrets; (ii) using or
disclosing confidential information[346] falling short of a trade secret[347]; and (iii)
soliciting the employer's customers. The restriction on the use or disclosure of
trade secrets applies at any time[348]; that on the solicitation of customers applies
only to solicitation during the period of employment[349]; while that relating to
confidential information occupies an intermediate position. It is normally limited
to the employee's conduct during employment[350]; but it can extend beyond that
period: e.g. where, on leaving his job, the employee takes away, copies or memo-
rises lists of the employer's trade connections.[351] He can then be restrained from
using such information for his own benefit (or for that of a third party) for so long
as such use would give him (or the third party) an unfair competitive advantage
over the employer.[352] A similar restriction may be imposed where the employee
sells such information, as opposed to using it to earn his living.[353] Certain
confidential information acquired by employees in the public service is also subject
to a lifelong duty of confidentiality.[354] All these rights of the employer are once
again said to constitute "proprietary interests" which the employer is entitled to
protect by a covenant in restraint of trade; and such a covenant may (as in the cases

---

[344] The following principles may also be applied, by analogy, to the restraint of an agent, against
whom it has been said to be "unlikely" that he should have more onerous covenants upheld: *BCM
Group Plc v Visualmark Ltd* [2006] EWHC 1831 (QB).

[345] The fiduciary duty of a director not to place himself in a position where his interests conflict with
those of the company may be breached if the director promotes a competing business before resigning
from the company concerned: *Shepherds Investments Ltd v Walters* [2006] EWHC 836 (Ch); [2007]
I.R.L.R. 110.

[346] Except where disclosure would be in the public interest, e.g. where the employer has been guilty
of misconduct which ought to be disclosed: *Initial Services Ltd v Putterill* [1968] 1 Q.B. 396; North
[1968] J.B.L. 32; cf. *Malone v Metropolitan Police Commissioner* [1979] Ch. 344 at 361–362; *British Steel
Corp v Granada Television Ltd* [1981] A.C. 1096 at 1168, 1177, 1201; *Attorney-General v Guardian
Newspapers Ltd (No.2)* [1990] A.C. 109 at 268. Contrast *Distillers Co Ltd v Times Newspapers Ltd*
[1976] Q.B. 613; *Schering Chemicals Ltd v Falkman Ltd* [1982] Q.B. 1; *Stephens v Avery* [1988] Ch. 449;
Re Barlow Clowes Gilt Managers Ltd [1992] Ch. 208. For proposals to widen the scope of the "public
interest" exception, see Law Com. No.110, paras 6.84(i) and 6.134(iii).

[347] See below, at fn.351.

[348] *Printers & Finishers Ltd v Holloway* [1965] 1 W.L.R. 1; *Faccenda Chicken Ltd v Fowler* [1987] Ch.
117 at 136; *Berkley Administration v McClelland* [1990] F.S.R. 565. cf. *Attorney-General v Barker* [1990]
3 All E.R. 257 (express covenant by employee of Royal Household); *Poly Lina Ltd v Finch* [1995] F.S.R.
751.

[349] *Wessex Dairies Ltd v Smith* [1935] 2 K.B. 60; cf. *Wallace Bogan & Co v Cove* [1997] I.R.L.R. 453.
If the solicitation occurs during employment it is irrelevant that the actual contract with the customers
is made thereafter: *Sanders v Parry* [1967] 1 W.L.R. 753.

[350] cf. *Murray v Yorkshire Food Managers Ltd* [1998] 1 W.L.R. 951.

[351] *Faccenda Chicken Ltd v Fowler* [1987] Ch. 117 at 139; Miller 102 L.Q.R. 359; cf. *Johnson & Blay
(Holdings) Ltd v Wolstenholme Rink Plc* [1989] F.S.R. 135; *Universal Thermosensors Ltd v Hibden* [1992]
1 W.L.R. 840 at 850.

[352] *Roger Bullivant Ltd v Ellis* [1987] I.C.R. 464. The "springboard relief" provided by this decision
is not confined to the misuse of confidential information: *UBS Wealth Management UK Ltd v Vestra
Wealth LLP* [2008] EWHC 1974 (QB); [2008] I.R.L.R. 965.

[353] *Faccenda Chicken Ltd v Fowler* [1987] Ch. 117 at 139.

[354] *Attorney-General v Guardian Newspapers (No.2)* [1990] A.C. 109 at 264, 284; *Lord Advocate v
Scotsman Publications Ltd* [1990] 1 A.C. 812 at 821. Contrast *Attorney-General v Blake* [1998] Ch. 439
at 454–455 where the information was no longer confidential and an injunction to restrain its use was
said to be an unjustifiable restraint of trade; in the House of Lords, the defendant was held liable for
breach of his *express* promise not to disclose the information: [2001] 1 A.C. 268; below,
para.20–012.

between vendor and purchaser) afford somewhat greater protection[355] than that provided by law in the absence of a covenant. But the employer cannot justify a covenant in restraint of trade simply on the ground that the covenant would protect the business in which the employee has worked.

11–070   **Sale of business and employment contrasted.** Thus the interest meriting protection is more narrowly defined between employer and employee than between buyer and seller,[356] and two reasons have been given for this distinction. First, buyer and seller may bargain on a more equal footing than employer and employee. The courts certainly attach importance to disparity of bargaining power in restraint of trade cases.[357] But this factor would scarcely be significant where the terms of employment were settled between an employer and a powerful trade union, or where the restraint was undertaken by a company director who, though technically an employee, was by no means in a weak bargaining position.[358] In such cases, it is better to fall back on the second justification for the distinction between the two types of contract. The buyer of a business pays for freedom from competition and would lose part of what he paid for if the seller began to compete with him.[359] An employer pays for his employee's services and would not be deprived of what he paid for if the employee competed with him after leaving his service.

11–071   **Trade secrets and influence.** Unlike the purchaser of a business, an employer cannot protect himself by a covenant in restraint of trade against his former employee's competition as such. He cannot restrain the employee from using his own skill even though that skill was learnt from the employer.[360] To establish that he has an interest meriting protection, the employer must show *either* that the employee has learnt the employer's trade secrets, *or* that he has acquired influence over the employer's clients or customers.[361] Trade secrets include secret formulae or processes, and certain other similar kinds of highly confidential information[362] (but not information which is merely confidential in the sense that the employee must not disclose it during employment[363]). It used to be thought that "know-

---

[355] See *Attorney-General v Blake*, fn.354, above and below, para.11–074.

[356] *Mason v Provident Clothing & Supply Co* [1913] A.C. 724; *Bridge v Deacons* [1984] A.C. 705 at 713; *Systems Reliability Holdings v Smith* [1990] I.R.L.R. 377.

[357] *A Schroeder Music Publishing Co Ltd v Macaulay* [1974] 1 W.L.R. 1308; *Clifford Davies Management v WEA Records Ltd* [1975] 1 W.L.R. 61; below, para.11–079.

[358] "A managing director can look after himself": *M & S Drapers v Reynolds* [1957] 1 W.L.R. 9 at 19.

[359] *Attwood v Lamont* [1920] 3 K.B. 571 at 590; cf. *Herbert Morris Ltd v Saxelby* [1916] 1 A.C. 688 at 701.

[360] *Herbert Morris Ltd v Saxelby* [1916] 1 A.C. 688; cf. *Eastes v Russ* [1914] 1 Ch. 468; *Faccenda Chicken Ltd v Fowler* [1987] Ch. 117 at 137; For a proposal to extend this principle to certain persons other than employees, see Law Com. No.110, para.6.75.

[361] Where the employer is a holding company with no clients of its own, it may still have the necessary interest as a result of the business carried out by its subsidiaries: *Beckett Investment Management Group Ltd v Hall* [2007] EWCA Civ 613; [2007] I.C.R. 1539 at [23].

[362] *Caribonum Co Ltd v Le Couch* (1913) 109 L.T. 587; cf. *The Littlewoods Organisation Ltd v Harris* [1977] 1 W.L.R. 1472. And see *Lansing Linde Ltd v Kerr* [1991] 1 W.L.R. 251 at 259, 268, 270; *Balston v Headline Filters* [1990] F.S.R. 385 at 417; *Pennell Publishing (UK) Ltd v Ornstein* [2008] 2 B.C.L.C. 246. Trade secrets do not need to be disclosed by public authorities under the Freedom of Information Act 2000: see ss.2 and 43.

[363] *Faccenda Chicken Ltd v Fowler* [1987] Ch. 117 at 136; *Brooks v Olyslager Oms (UK) Ltd* [1998] I.R.L.R. 590; *Intelsec Systems Ltd v Grech-Cini* [2000] 1 W.L.R. 1190.

how" could not be protected[364] but now that such expertise has become a saleable commodity[365] it is likely that the courts will recognise it as an interest meriting protection.[366] In respect of clients or customers, the employer is entitled to protection only if the nature of the employment was such as to enable the employee to acquire influence over them,[367] e.g. where the employee was a solicitor's managing clerk,[368] or a hairdresser's assistant[369] but not where he was a factory worker who never came into contact with customers. If the employee comes into contact with some customers, the employer may be able to protect himself also in respect of some others.[370]

Commercial interests. The question whether there is any other interest which an employer can protect by a covenant in restraint of trade was raised in *Eastham v Newcastle United Football Club Ltd.*[371] The defendant club employed a professional footballer subject to the "retain and transfer" system.[372] Under that system, a player who was "retained"[373] by one club could not be employed by another; nor could he be transferred to another club without the consent of both clubs. The defendant club could not claim that this system protected either of the two traditional interests. But Wilberforce J. said that "it would be wrong to pass straight to the conclusion that no ... interest ... exists".[374] He considered other possible interests, such as the danger that, but for the "retain and transfer" system, all the best players might go to the richest clubs. He found that such consequences would not in fact follow if the system were abandoned[375]; that there was thus no interest to be protected; and that the system was invalid. But his approach suggests that interests other than the traditional ones might be entitled to protection. A covenant by a film actor not to appear on the stage for three months, made with the object of furthering the success of a new film,[376] might be enforceable even though it did not protect either of the orthodox interests. Such new interests would differ from the traditional ones in that they would be protected *only* if there was a covenant, while the traditional ones are to some extent protected even if there is no covenant. For this reason the new interests may be called "commercial" rather than "proprietary" ones; and we shall see that in some categories of contracts in restraint of trade the law now recognises that such commercial interests may be protected by covenants.[377] It is possible that this recognition will help to modify the strict insistence on the need for a "proprietary" interest in cases between vendor and purchaser, and between employer and

11–072

---

[364] *Herbert Morris Ltd v Saxelby*, above; *Sir W C Leng & Co v Andrews* [1909] 1 Ch. 763 at 768.
[365] Blanco White 15 Conv. 89; 26 Conv. 366.
[366] In *Commercial Plastics Ltd v Vincent* [1965] 1 Q.B. 623 at 642 Pearson L.J. hints at this possibility.
[367] *Faccenda Chicken Ltd v Fowler* [1987] Ch. 117 at 137.
[368] *Fitch v Dewes* [1921] 2 A.C. 158; below, para.11–076.
[369] *Marion White Ltd v Francis* [1972] 1 W.L.R. 1423.
[370] *G W Plowman & Son Ltd v Ash* [1964] 1 W.L.R. 568; and see para.11–075, below.
[371] [1964] Ch. 413; cf. *Greig v Insole* [1978] 1 W.L.R. 302.
[372] See further below, at fn.478.
[373] A player could be "retained" by giving him notice and paying him a reasonable wage (determined, in case of dispute, by the Football Association).
[374] *Eastham v Newcastle United Football Club Ltd*, above, at 432.
[375] Subsequent events would appear to have proved him wrong.
[376] For this practice, see *Higgs v Olivier* [1951] Ch. 899; cf. *Vaughan-Neil v IRC* [1979] 1 W.L.R. 1283 (covenant by a barrister, on becoming an employee of a company, not to practise at the Bar).
[377] See below, paras 11–087, 11–096.

employee. The mere goodwill of a company, however, is not a legitimate interest capable of protection by a restriction on a former employee.[378]

11–073   **Other cases.** The distinction between vendor-purchaser and employer-employee covenants is by no means exhaustive. Thus a covenant by a retiring doctor or solicitor not to compete with his former partners does not fall precisely into either category[379]; but the courts do not subject it to the strict tests of validity that they apply to employer-employee covenants.[380] A covenant by a writer or composer not to dispose of his work except to a particular publisher may for present purposes be treated in the same way as an employer-employee covenant, even though there was never any contract of employment between the parties.[381]

A person may sell his business to a company of which he then becomes managing director. It seems that a covenant by such a person not to compete should be treated in the same way as a vendor-purchaser covenant, whether it is contained in the sale agreement or in the service agreement[382] or in both.[383] Similarly, the restraints on an ex-franchisee are assessed in much the same ways as those on a vendor, in order to protect the goodwill of the business to be made available to the new franchisee.[384]

(ii) *Reasonableness*

11–074   A restraint is valid only if it goes no further than is reasonably necessary for the protection of the covenantee's interest. Reasonableness is determined by looking at the relationship between that interest and the covenant.[385]

11–075   **Area covenants and solicitation covenants.** To be reasonable, the restraint need not be precisely co-terminous with the interest.[386] If there were such a requirement, there would be little point in taking a covenant, since a "proprietary interest" is (by definition) protected even in the absence of a covenant.[387] So long as the employer has trade secrets he can take a covenant which to some extent prevents the employee from using his own skill by restraining him from working in competition with the employer. And an employer who has a "proprietary" interest in his relations with clients or customers can restrain his employee from

---

[378] *Countrywide Assured Financial Services Ltd v Smart* [2004] EWHC 1214.

[379] *Bridge v Deacons* [1984] A.C. 705 at 714.

[380] *Whitehill v Bradford* [1952] Ch. 236; *Espley v Williams* [1997] 1 E.G.L.R. 9; *contra, Jenkins v Reid* [1948] 1 All E.R. 471—but the defendant's covenant seems to have been "in gross".

[381] See *A Schroeder Music Publishing Co Ltd v Macaulay* [1974] 1 W.L.R. 1308.

[382] See *Silverman Ltd v Silverman, The Times*, July 7, 1969. cf. *Blake v Blake* (1967) 111 S.J. 715 (restraints imposed, on dissolution of a company, on its major shareholders: these were treated in the same way as vendor-purchaser covenants); *Allied Dunbar (Frank Weisinger) Ltd v Frank Weisinger* [1988] I.R.L.R. 60; *Alliance Property Group Plc v Prestwich* [1995] I.R.L.R. 25; *Dawnay Day & Co v D'Alphen* [1997] I.R.L.R. 442 (so far as it relates to the service agreement).

[383] *T & C Europe (UK) Ltd v Massey* [1999] I.R.L.R. 22 at 26.

[384] *Kall Kwik Printing (UK) Ltd v Rush* [1996] F.S.R. 114; *Dymond Plc v Reeve* [1999] F.S.R. 148, at 153; *Convenience Co Ltd v Roberts* [2001] F.S.R. 35; *Chipsaway International Ltd v Kerr* [2009] EWCA Civ 320.

[385] *Allied Dunbar (Frank Weisinger) Ltd v Frank Weisinger* [1988] I.R.L.R. 60 at 65.

[386] cf. *Systems Reliability Holdings v Smith* [1990] I.R.L.R. 377 at 384; *Marshall v NM Financial Management Ltd* [1997] 1 W.L.R. 1527 at 1533.

[387] See above, paras 11–068, 11–069.

working in the *area* in which those clients or customers live, even though most of the inhabitants of the area have never dealt with the employer.[388] Such restraints may be necessary for the protection of the employer as the actual infringement of his proprietary interests could be very hard to establish: in particular it would, if the employee were allowed to work for a competitor, be hard to tell whether he was disclosing trade secrets.[389] The covenant may, moreover, be enforced even though the "proprietary interest" infringed is of little value to the employer. Thus a former employee can be restrained from dealing with a client who has decided to deal with the ex-employee, rather than with the employer, since it is precisely this type of competition "against which the covenant is designed to give protection".[390]

On the other hand, such "area covenants" may operate to some extent as pure restraints on competition; and in a number of cases[391] the courts have distinguished them from "solicitation covenants" (against soliciting the employer's old clients or customers). On the facts of those cases the courts have held or said that only "solicitation covenants" would be regarded as reasonable. The cases do not absolutely rule out the possibility that an "area covenant" may be valid between employer and employee[392]; but such a covenant will be void if it covers a much larger area than is needed for the protection of the employer's interest. Thus in *Mason v Provident Clothing & Supply Co Ltd*,[393] a canvasser who was employed to sell clothes in Islington covenanted not to enter into similar business within 25 miles of London. The covenant was held void because the area of the restraint was about 1,000 times as large as that in which the canvasser had been employed. It was said that the employer could have protected himself by a covenant restricted to the area in which the canvasser had worked. But if that area is very large and the employee has only dealt with a small number of customers within it, an area covenant will not,[394] though a solicitation covenant might,[395] be upheld.

Between vendor and purchaser (and in analogous cases[396]) area covenants are commonly enforced; and a restraint may be reasonable even though it is *unlimited* as to area. In the *Nordenfelt* case[397] such a restraint was enforced against the vendor of an armaments business since that business extended over the whole world; and where an employer is entitled to protect trade secrets of a business

---

[388] *Fitch v Dewes* [1921] 2 A.C. 158; *Scorer v Seymour-Johns* [1966] 1 W.L.R. 1419; contrast *Fellowes v Fisher* [1976] Q.B. 122.

[389] *Poly Lina Ltd v Finch* [1995] F.S.R. 751; *Thomas v Farr Plc* [2007] EWCA Civ 118; [2007] I.C.R. 932; cf. *Kall Kwik Printing (UK) Ltd v Rush* [1996] F.S.R. 114 (franchise agreement).

[390] *John Michael Design Plc v Cooke* [1987] I.C.R. 445 at 446.

[391] *S W Strange Ltd v Mann* [1965] 1 W.L.R. 629; *Gledhow Autoparts Ltd v Delaney* [1965] 1 W.L.R. 1366; *T Lucas & Co Ltd v Mitchell* [1974] Ch. 129; *Stenhouse Australia Ltd v Phillips* [1974] A.C. 391; *Dairy Crest Ltd v Pigott* [1989] I.C.R. 92; cf. *Bridge v Deacons* [1984] A.C. 705 (solicitation covenant in partnership agreement between solicitors upheld); *Hanover Ins Brokers v Schapiro* [1994] I.R.L.R. 82.

[392] e.g. *Anscombe & Ringland v Butchoff* (1984) 134 N.L.J. 37.

[393] [1913] A.C. 724; cf. *Empire Meat Co Ltd v Patrick* [1939] 2 All E.R. 85; *Spencer v Marchington* [1988] I.R.L.R. 392; *Office Angels Ltd v Rainer-Thomas* [1991] I.R.L.R. 214; for conflicting dicta in a borderline case, see *Lyne-Pirkis v Jones* [1969] 1 W.L.R. 1293.

[394] *Marley Tile Co Ltd v Johnson* [1982] I.R.L.R. 75.

[395] *Gledhow Autoparts Ltd v Delaney* [1965] 1 W.L.R. 1366. Contrast *Office Angels Ltd v Rainer-Thomas*, above, fn.393 and *Lapthorne v Eurofi Ltd* [2001] EWCA Civ 999; [2001] U.K.C.L.R. 999.

[396] e.g. *Kerr v Morris* [1987] Ch. 90; cf. *Kall Kwik Printing (UK) Ltd v Bell* [1994] F.S.R. 674 (franchisee); *Alliance Property Group Plc v Prestwich* [1996] I.R.L.R. 25.

[397] [1894] A.C. 535; cf. *Systems Reliability Holdings v Smith* [1990] I.R.L.R. 377 at 382; *Dawnay Day & Co v D'Alphen* [1997] I.R.L.R. 442. Contrast *Convenience Co Ltd v Roberts* [2001] F.S.R. 35 (one-year covenant in franchise agreement not to compete in UK too wide in area).

which has no clear geographical limits, a covenant which is unlimited as to area may similarly be enforced against the employee.[398] A "solicitation covenant" in a contract of employment may likewise be enforced though it contains no express limitations as to area,[399] particularly if it is limited to customers with whom the employee came into contact in the course of his employment[400]; but such a limitation is not essential to the validity of the covenant.[401] A worldwide restraint against disclosing confidential information is unlikely to be upheld if the information in question relates only to business done by the employer in a limited geographical area (e.g. to customers in one country).[402]

11–076   **Duration of the restraint.** The question whether a restraint is invalid for excessive duration depends on the nature of the business to be protected.[403] If it is one to which customers or clients are likely to resort for a long time, a restraint for the lifetime of the covenantor may be valid. Thus in *Fitch v Dewes*[404] a lifelong restraint on a solicitor's managing clerk not to practise within seven miles of his principal's office was upheld. But in view of the distinction between "area" and "solicitation" covenants, it is unlikely that a *lifelong* restraint in an "area" covenant would now be regarded as valid.[405] A more lenient view was taken of a "solicitation" covenant for a *fixed period* in *Bridge v Deacons*[406]: the Privy Council there upheld a covenant by a partner in a firm of solicitors not to act as solicitor in Hong Kong for any client of the firm for five years after ceasing to be a partner; and a one-year "area" covenant operating within a 10-mile radius has likewise been enforced against an assistant solicitor.[407] Where the business to be protected is of a more fluctuating nature, long restraints are unlikely to be upheld whether they are contained in "area" or in "solicitation" covenants.[408] A maximum duration of two years is prescribed by legislation in the case of a restraint on a "commercial agent".[409]

An employee's covenant not to disclose confidential information relating to the employer need not be limited as to time: such a covenant has, for example, been upheld where an employee of the Royal Household undertook that he would not either during or after service disclose information concerning any member of the Royal Family (and certain other persons) without written authority.[410] Such a

---

[398] *Poly Lina Ltd v Finch* [1995] F.S.R. 751.

[399] *G W Plowman & Son Ltd v Ash* [1964] 1 W.L.R. 568; cf. *Morris Angel & Son Ltd v Hollande* [1993] I.C.R. 71.

[400] As in *Stenhouse Australia Ltd v Phillips* [1974] A.C. 391; contrast *Austin Knight (UK) v Hinds* [1994] F.S.R. 52 (covenant invalid as not so limited).

[401] *Plowman & Son Ltd v Ash*, above, fn.399.

[402] *Lansing Linde Ltd v Kerr* [1991] 1 W.L.R. 251 at 259.

[403] *Janes v Johal* [2006] EWHC 286 (Ch); [2006] I.C.R. 742 at [32]; *Beckett Investment Management Group Ltd v Hall* [2007] EWCA Civ 613; [2007] I.C.R. 1539 at [25]–[26] (12 months reasonable for a senior employee of a financial services company).

[404] [1921] 2 A.C. 158.

[405] See *Fellowes v Fisher* [1976] Q.B. 122.

[406] [1984] A.C. 705; the suggestion made, [1984] A.C. 705 at 717 that a covenant which is otherwise reasonable will not be struck down "solely because of its duration" is, with respect, hard to reconcile with *Esso Petroleum Co Ltd v Harper's Garage (Stourport) Ltd* [1968] A.C. 269 (below, para.11–093), so far as that case related to the 21-year tie; and with *Eastes v Russ* [1914] 1 Ch. 468. See further Spowart-Taylor and Hough 47 M.L.R. 745.

[407] *Hollis & Co v Stocks* [2000] U.K.C.L.R. 685.

[408] e.g. *M & S Drapers v Reynolds* [1957] 1 W.L.R. 9; cf. *Eastes v Russ* [1914] 1 Ch. 468.

[409] See below, para.16–011; SI 1993/3053, reg.20(2).

[410] *Attorney-General v Barker* [1990] 3 All E.R. 257.

limited restraint does not prevent the former employee from working for others, and is therefore not objectionable on grounds of public policy.

Scope of restraint. A restraint must not extend to an activity which is 11–077 irrelevant to the interest to be protected. Thus a restraint in a tailor's service contract against working as a hatter is unreasonable.[411] Nor can an employer use his proprietary interest in trade secrets and confidential information to support a covenant restraining an employee from disclosing any information whatsoever "relating to the company [i.e. the employer] or its customers of which [the employee] becomes possessed while acting as sales director"[412]; for much information of this kind will have nothing to do with the employer's proprietary interest.

Drafting problems. So long as there is an interest meriting protection, some 11–078 restraint can be validly imposed, but the draftsman may, by drawing the restraint too widely, wholly fail to achieve his purpose.[413] An attempt to evade this difficulty was made in *Davies v Davies*,[414] where the covenant simply restrained competition "so far as the law allows"; but this was held void for uncertainty.[415] The draftsman is therefore forced to use more precise language and this may impose an excessive restraint even though the parties may not have intended that meaning. The same principles are applied to the construction of a covenant in restraint of trade as are applied to the construction of any other written term,[416] and the apparent width of a restraint cannot be cut down by an "*artificially* implied term."[417] For example, in *Lyne-Pirkis v Jones*[418] a covenant in a partnership agreement between doctors in *general practice* provided that a retiring partner should not (within certain limits of time and space) "engage in medical practice". The court here refused to construe these words so as to refer only to general practice and held the covenant invalid as it prohibited practice even as a *consultant*. On the other hand, in *Home Counties Dairies Ltd v Skilton*[419] a covenant in a milk roundsman's contract provided that he should not serve or sell "milk or dairy produce". It was argued that this would prevent him from serving cheese as a grocer's assistant, but the court refused to invalidate the covenant as the parties clearly did not intend it to bear this meaning.[420] A similar approach was adopted in *Rock Refrigeration Ltd v*

---

[411] *Attwood v Lamont* [1920] 3 K.B. 571; cf. *Scully UK Ltd v Lee* [1998] I.R.L.R. 259.
[412] *Lawrence David v Ashton* [1989] I.C.R. 123; cf. *Intelsec Systems Ltd v Grech-Cini* [2000] 1 W.L.R. 1190.
[413] cf. below, para.11–162.
[414] (1887) 36 Ch.D. 359.
[415] cf. *Days Medical Aids Ltd v Pihsiang Machinery Manufacturing Co Ltd* [2004] EWHC 44 (Comm); [2004] 1 All E.R. (Comm) 991.
[416] *Beckett Investment Management Group Ltd v Hall* [2007] EWCA Civ 613; [2007] I.C.R. 1539 at [11].
[417] *Townends Group Ltd v Cobb* [2004] EWHC 3432 (Ch); *The Times*, December 1, 2004 at [53].
[418] [1969] 1 W.L.R. 1293; cf. *Peyton v Mindham* [1972] 1 W.L.R. 8; *J A Mont (UK) Ltd v Mills* [1993] I.R.L.R. 172; *Advantage Business Systems Ltd v Hopley* [2007] EWHC (QB) 1783.
[419] [1970] 1 W.L.R. 526; cf. *G W Plowman Ltd v Ash* [1964] 1 W.L.R. 568; *Marion White Ltd v Francis* [1972] 1 W.L.R. 1423; *The Littlewoods Organisation Ltd v Harris* [1977] 1 W.L.R. 1472; (doubting *Commercial Plastics Ltd v Vincent* [1961] 1 Q.B. 623 on the issue of construction); *Edwards v Worboys* [1984] A.C. 724n.; *Turner v Commonwealth Minerals Ltd* [2000] I.R.L.R. 114; *TFS Derivatives Ltd v Morgan* [2004] EWHC 2809; [2005] I.R.L.R. 246.
[420] A result which is consistent with the more "purposive" approach to be taken to the interpretation of contracts (see para.6–011), which may call into doubt some of the decisions in the cases referred to in fn.418. See also: *Kynixa Ltd v Hynes* [2008] EWHC 1495 (QB) at [179]–[180] ("very little weight" to be given to "remote possibilities").

Jones[421] where a sales director's contract of employment contained a covenant which was to take effect on termination of the contract "however occasioned". The contract was in fact terminated as a result of his resignation; but he argued that the words just quoted made the covenant unreasonable as they would also cover the case in which termination occurred as a result of his wrongful dismissal.[422] The argument was rejected, the majority of the Court of Appeal taking the view that the covenant would not as a matter of law operate in such a case since the effect of the employee's acceptance of the employer's repudiation would be to release the employee from further performance of the covenant.[423]

11–079   **Reasonableness and fairness.** The law of restraint of trade has long recognised two principles: that adequacy of consideration is relevant to the validity of a restraint[424] and that the law has regard to the relative bargaining strengths of the parties.[425] This does not mean that a restraint is invalid merely because it was undertaken by the weaker party; for the transaction may be a perfectly fair one, having regard to the benefits obtained by that party under it.[426] It is only where the stronger party makes unconscionable use of his superior bargaining power that the resulting bargain may be struck down on account of its unfairness.[427] To this extent, the fairness of the bargain is a *necessary* condition of the validity of the restraint; but it is submitted that it is not a *sufficient* condition. It has indeed been said that a restraint cannot be unreasonable if the parties have freely agreed to it[428] or if it is to their mutual advantage. This is true in the sense that the agreement of the parties may determine how much the covenantee has bought, and hence how much he can protect. But once the interest has been defined, the restraint will be upheld only if it is necessary for the protection of that interest.[429] This will generally depend on the relation between the restraint and the interest.[430] A world wide restraint in a contract for the sale of a village shop would not satisfy this test however much both parties wanted to enter into it and even if the buyer had paid a greatly enhanced price to secure the restraint. The same point can be made in

---

[421] [1997] I.C.R. 938; cf. also *Kall Kwik Printing (UK) Ltd v Rush* [1996] F.S.R. 114.
[422] For the invalidity of a covenant operating in such circumstances, see *D v M* [1996] I.R.L.R. 192.
[423] On the principle of *General Billposting Co Ltd v Atkinson* [1909] A.C. 118, see below para.18–009; Phillips L.J. based the same conclusion on the different ground that the possibility of the employer's repudiating the contract was no more than a "remote" one (at 960).
[424] See above, para.11–063.
[425] See above, para.11–070.
[426] *Alec Lobb (Garages) Ltd v Total Oil (Great Britain) Ltd* [1985] 1 W.L.R. 173; this case, and those cited in the next note, were concerned with the type of restraint discussed below, para.11–092 et seq.
[427] *A Schroeder Music Publishing Co v Macaulay* [1974] 1 W.L.R. 1308 at 1315–1316 (where Lord Diplock did not distinguish between unfairness and unconscionability); *Clifford Davis Management Ltd v WEA Records Ltd* [1975] 1 W.L.R. 61. Quaere whether it is up to the stronger party to establish the fairness of the restraint or to the weaker party to establish its unfairness. The latter view perhaps derives some support from the comparison in *Barclays Bank Plc v Caplan* [1998] F.L.R. 532 at 546 of restraint of trade with undue influence cases: see below, para.10–012 et seq.
[428] *NW Salt Co v Electrolytic Alkali Co Ltd* [1914] A.C. 461 at 471; *English Hop Growers Ltd v Dering* [1928] 2 K.B. 174 at 185. cf. *World Wide Fund for Nature v World Wrestling Federation* [2002] EWCA Civ 196; [2002] U.K.C.L.R. 388 at [42], as to which see further below, para.11–085.
[429] cf. *A Schroeder Music Publishing Co Ltd v Macaulay*, above at 1316 ("reasonably necessary for the protection of the legitimate interests of the promisee").
[430] See above, para.11–074; *Allied Dunbar (Frank Weisinger) Ltd v Frank Weisinger* [1988] I.R.L.R. 60 at 65.

relation to a partnership agreement. Thus in *Bridge v Deacons* one factor emphasised by the Privy Council was "the mutuality of the contract", by which the five-year restraint "applied equally to all partners".[431] But while this was relevant to the validity of a five-year solicitation covenant it would not, it is submitted, have justified a life time area covenant covering the whole of Hong Kong since that would have been wholly disproportionate to the interest recognised as meriting protection. The rule that the restraint must not go further than necessary for the protection of the recognised interest of the covenantee is one of public policy and accordingly cannot be excluded merely by the agreement of the parties.

(iii) *Public interest*

Employment. In one sense, the requirement of reasonableness can be said to raise issues of public interest. But even if the restraint is "reasonable" in relation to the interest which the covenantee is entitled to protect, it may still be invalid if it is likely to prejudice the public. Many dicta state this rule,[432] but there is little direct authority to support it. In *Wyatt v Kreglinger & Fernau*[433] the employers of a wool broker promised to pay him a pension on his retirement provided that he did not re-enter the wool trade and did nothing to their detriment (fair business competition excepted). Nine years later the Court of Appeal rejected his claim for arrears of pension. Three reasons can be found in the judgments: that the employers' promise to pay the pension was simply a gratuitous promise; that the stipulation against competition was void because it was unreasonable; and that the stipulation against competition was void because it was contrary to the public interest. The view that a restraint imposed on an elderly wool broker at the time of his retirement was likely to injure the public may be regarded with some scepticism,[434] especially in view of the countervailing public interest of encouraging young recruits to the profession.[435] Reaction against it has gone so far that it has sometimes been said that public interest was not an independent ground of invalidity at all.[436] But *Wyatt*'s case was followed in a later similar case[437]; and it is arguable that a restraint on persons whose services are in short supply may be contrary to the public interest, even though it is reasonable in relation to the interest which the covenantee is entitled to protect.[438] This argument is not, it is submitted, inconsistent with cases holding that it was not contrary to the public interest to restrain a solicitor from acting for a particular client or group of clients *merely* because of the fiduciary relationship between solicitor and client.[439] For the present purpose, the decisive factor is not the nature of the services but the

11–080

---

[431] [1984] A.C. 705 at 716.

[432] e.g. *Attorney-General for Australia v Adelaide SS Co* [1913] A.C. 781 at 796; *Herbert Morris Ltd v Saxelby* [1916] A.C. 688 at 700; *McEllistrim's Case* [1919] A.C. 548 at 562; *Bridge v Deacons* [1984] A.C. 705 at 713; cf. *Kerr v Morris* [1987] Ch. 90, where the covenant was admitted to be reasonable in area and duration and public interest was discussed as a *separate* issue.

[433] [1933] 1 K.B. 793.

[434] 49 L.Q.R. 465.

[435] cf. *Bridge v Deacons* [1984] A.C. 705 at 718.

[436] *Routh v Jones* [1947] 1 All E.R. 179 at 182; cf. *Systems Reliability Holdings v Smith* [1990] I.R.L.R. 377 at 382; but at 384 reasonableness *and* public interest are stated as separate requirements of validity.

[437] *Bull v Pitney-Bowes Ltd* [1967] 1 W.L.R. 273; Koh 30 M.L.R. 587.

[438] cf. *Dranez Anstalt v Hayetz* [2002] EWCA Civ 1729; [2003] F.S.R. 32 at [25].

[439] *Edwards v Worboys* [1984] A.C. 724n.; *Bridge v Deacons* [1984] A.C. 705 at 720; disapproving contrary dicta in *Oswald Hickson Collier & Co v Carter-Ruck* [1984] A.C. 720n.

availability of alternative sources of supply: the public interest lies in their general availability and not in their being rendered by a particular individual. Thus a restraint on a former partner in a general medical practice would not be invalid merely because patients wished to continue to be treated by that partner,[440] but such restraint might be contrary to the public interest if there was a shortage of doctors in the area in question.

11–081   **Sale of business.** The principle of public interest may, equally, apply to covenants for the sale of a business. In the *Nordenfelt*[441] case it was said that, as the business sold was a foreign one, a restraint on the vendor would not injure "the public policy of this country"; and more recently the promotion of export sales has been mentioned as a head of public interest.[442] The principle of public interest has, moreover, become increasingly important in relation to other categories of contracts in restraint of trade[443]; and it now seems to be clear that it can be an independent ground of invalidity.

11–082   **Scope of "public interest".** In the common law relating to restraint of trade, the "public interest" refers to legally recognised interests, and in particular to the interest of the public that a person should not be subjected to unreasonable restrictions on his freedom to work or trade. An agreement is unlikely to be invalidated by a common law court because it is alleged to infringe some wider public interest, e.g. because it might lead to an improper allocation of economic resources, or prove inflationary. Such allegations often lack precision, and courts of law are not well equipped to evaluate them.[444]

(iv) *No actual covenant against competition*

11–083   The restraint of trade doctrine may apply where the terms of the contract provide a party with a financial incentive not to compete, even though he makes no actual promise not to do so: this was the position in *Wyatt v Kreglinger & Fernau* where the employee made no promise not to compete, but his right to his pension was conditional on his not doing so.[445] Similarly, in *Stenhouse Australia Ltd v Phillips*[446] the defendant undertook to pay to his former employers half the gross commission which he might receive in respect of business done with their clients. This was held to be in restraint of trade (though there was no covenant) since it was "in effect . . . likely to cause the employee to refuse business which

---

[440] *Kerr v Morris* [1987] Ch. 90, overruling *Hensman v Traill* (1980) 124 S.J. 776; cf. *Araci v Fallon* [2011] EWCA Civ 668 at [60].

[441] [1894] A.C. 535 at 550; cf. [1894] A.C. 535 at 574.

[442] *Bull v Pitney-Bowes Ltd* [1967] 1 W.L.R. 273 at 276.

[443] See below, paras 11–092—11–101.

[444] *Texaco Ltd v Mulberry Filling Station Ltd* [1972] 1 W.L.R. 814 at 827, a case concerned with the type of restraint discussed at para.11–092 et seq., below; contrast *Bull v Pitney-Bowes Ltd*, above, fn.442.

[445] [1933] 1 K.B. 793, per Scrutton and Slesser L.JJ.; Greer L.J. interpreted the correspondence to mean that there *was* a covenant not to complete. cf. *Sadler v Imperial Life Assurance of Canada* [1988] I.R.L.R. 388, where the stipulation by the agent not to compete after the end of his agency was similarly not a promise but his entitlement to future commissions was conditional on his not doing so; cf. *Marshall v NM Financial Management Ltd* [1997] 1 W.L.R. 1527 at 1533.

[446] [1974] A.C. 391.

otherwise he would take ... ".[447] On the other hand, in *Alder v Moore*[448] a professional footballer was paid £500 for "permanent total disability". He made a "declaration" not to play professional football again "and in the event of infringing this condition I will be subject to a penalty of £500". He did infringe the "condition" and a majority of the Court of Appeal held that he was liable to repay the £500. The sole question discussed was whether the stipulation to repay was a penalty[449]; and no reference was made to the restraint of trade doctrine. Prima facie, the stipulation appears to fall within that doctrine, though it may have been perfectly reasonable and not contrary to the public interest.

(v) *Restraint operating during employment*

In the employment cases so far discussed, the issue has been as to the validity of covenants operating *after* the end of the period of service.[450] Restrictions on competition *during* that period are normally valid,[451] and indeed may be implied by law by virtue of the servant's duty of fidelity.[452] In such cases the restriction is generally reasonable, having regard to the interests of the employer, and does not cause any undue hardship to the employee, who will receive a wage or salary for the period in question. But the contract may be a long-term one, and the main purpose of the restraint may be, not to secure faithful service, but to protect the employer from competition by sterilising the employee's working capacity. In such a case the restraint may be invalid even though it operates only during the period in which the employee can be required to serve,[453] and even if it is valid, the court may refuse the remedy of an injunction to the employer.[454] An increasingly common form of restraint operating during employment is "gardening leave", where the employee is paid during a period of notice, but not required to work for the employer. If the restraints imposed during that period are valid, any additional *post-termination* restraint may be challenged on the basis that it could more reasonably have been achieved by extending the period of gardening leave.[455]

11–084

(vi) *Establishing validity of restraint*

The reasonableness of the restraint must be established by the person who seeks to enforce the contract; it is then up to the party resisting enforcement to establish

11–085

---

[447] ibid. at 402–403.

[448] [1961] 2 Q.B. 57.

[449] See below, para.20–130.

[450] The restraint of trade doctrine may apply to an option entitling the employer to *re-employ* the employee at some time in the future: *Leeds Rugby Ltd v Harris* [2005] EWHC 1591 (QB).

[451] cf. *GFI Group v Eaglestone*, The Times, October 29, 1993; *Crédit Suisse Asset Management Ltd v Armstrong* [1996] I.C.R. 882 covenant operating during "garden leave" (below, para.17–054) valid; but see below, at fn.454.

[452] See above, para.6–041. *Faccenda Chicken Ltd v Fowler* [1987] Ch. 117 at 135–136; cf. *Evening Standard Co Ltd v Henderson* [1987] I.C.R. 588; *Provident Financial Group Plc v Hayward* [1989] I.C.R. 160.

[453] *A Schroeder Music Publishing Co Ltd v Macaulay* [1974] 1 W.L.R. 1308; *Clifford Davis Management Ltd v WEA Records* [1975] 1 W.L.R. 61. Contrast *Greig v Insole* [1978] 1 W.L.R. 302 at 326; *Panayiotou v Sony Music Entertainment (UK) Ltd*, The Times, June 30, 1994. cf. *Proactive Sports Management Ltd v Rooney* [2010] EWHC 1807 (QB) (image rights representation agreement).

[454] *William Hill Organisation Ltd v Tucker* [1998] I.R.L.R. 313; *Symbian Ltd v Christenson* [2001] I.R.L.R. 37; below, para.21–058.

[455] See *TFS Derivatives Ltd v Morgan* [2004] EWHC 2809; [2005] I.R.L.R. 246, where Cox. J declined to express any general view.

that the restraint is contrary to the public interest.[456] Thus in the normal case, in
which the covenantee sues to enforce the restraint, he must establish its reasonableness and the covenantor its tendency to injure the public. But where, as in
Wyatt v Kreglinger & Fernau[457] the action is brought by the covenantor to enforce
the promise for which the restraint constitutes the consideration, the roles are
reversed: the person under the restraint must show that it is reasonable and the
other party that it is contrary to the public interest. It has further been held that
where a stipulation in restraint of trade is contained in an agreement for the
settlement of a genuine dispute relating to intellectual property rights, then it is
not up to the party seeking to enforce the settlement to show that it is "reasonable".[458] The public policy against restraint of trade here appears to come into
conflict with that in favour of bona fide compromises and the latter prevails so that
it is up to the party resisting enforcement of the compromise to show that there
was no genuine dispute or claim. It seems that "reasonableness" here refers to the
genuineness of the underlying dispute[459]; and this is a different issue from the
"reasonableness" which is a requirement of the validity of covenants in restraint
of trade.[460]

The questions of reasonableness and public interest are questions of law[461] so
that it is strictly inaccurate to say that the party claiming enforcement has the *onus
of proving* that the covenant is reasonable. What he must do is to prove the
circumstances from which the court may conclude that the ratio between the
restraint and the interest is reasonable.[462] The same principle applies to the
question of public interest.

(c) Restrictive Trading and Similar Agreements

11–086   Agreements between suppliers of goods or services restricting competition
between them are at common law[463] subject to the restraint of trade doctrine, so
that they are prima facie void, but valid if reasonable and not contrary to the public
interest. They also give rise to a number of special problems.

11–087   **The interest.** In *McEllistrim*'s case Lord Birkenhead said that "in this class of
case the covenantee is not entitled to be protected against competition *per se*".[464]
But he evidently regarded "stability in their lists of customers"[465] as an interest
which producers were entitled to protect; and it is not clear how this differs from
protection against "competition per se". It seems that in this group of cases, as in

---

[456] See *Herbert Morris Ltd v Saxelby* [1916] A.C. 589 at 700, 706–707; *Attwood v Lamont* [1920] 3
K.B. 571 at 587–588; *Kores v Kolok Manufacturing Co Ltd* [1959] Ch. 108 at 120.
[457] [1933] 1 K.B. 793; above, para.11–080.
[458] *World Wide Fund for Nature v World Wrestling Foundation* [2002] EWCA Civ 196; [2002]
U.K.C.L.R. 388 at [42].
[459] cf. above, paras 3–037—3–038.
[460] This difference may account for the fact that none of the authorities cited at fnn.456 and 457,
above is referred to in the *World Wide* case, above, fn.458.
[461] *Dowden & Pook Ltd v Pook* [1904] 1 K.B. 45.
[462] *Herbert Morris Ltd v Saxelby* [1916] 1 A.C. 688 at 707 ("no question of onus either way").
[463] For the effect of competition law on some such agreements, see below, paras 11–105—11–109.
[464] [1919] A.C. 548 at 564.
[465] ibid.

another to be discussed below,[466] a "commercial" as opposed to a "proprietary" interest[467] may support a covenant.

Conditions of validity. The broad definition of the interest meriting protec- **11–088** tion by agreements of the present kind made it relatively easier to establish their validity than that of restraints between vendor and purchaser or between employer and employee. In *English Hop Growers v Dering*,[468] for example, the court upheld an agreement by which hop growers undertook to deliver their crops to a central selling agency in order to avoid cut-throat competition at a time when it was feared that there would be a glut of hops on the market. But even agreements of this kind were held invalid if they were plainly unreasonable or contrary to the public interest: e.g. where the effect of the agreement was to force one of the parties to close down his business altogether.[469]

Hardship to a particular group. An agreement may cause hardship to a **11–089** particular group of persons, without being contrary to the interests of the public at large. In *Kores Manufacturing Co Ltd v Kolok Manufacturing Co Ltd*[470] two manufacturers of carbon paper and typewriter ribbons agreed not to employ each others' former employees for five years after they had left their original employer. The Court of Appeal held that, although the parties were entitled to protect their trade secrets, the covenant was invalid, as it covered all employees, whether they knew trade secrets or not, and as it was of excessive duration. It was further argued that the parties were entitled to protect their labour supplies, but the court doubted whether "labour supplies" were an interest meriting protection. If they were, employers could, by contracting with each other, achieve what they could not do by contracting directly with the employees themselves. An undertaking by an employee not to work for another employer would be invalid for lack of a proper interest[471] if he knew no trade secrets and had no influence over customers. The same principle should apply where the restraint was contained in a contract between employers and indirectly prejudiced their employees' opportunities of finding work.[472] It seems that the court can take hardship to third parties into account and hold that it invalidates a contract of this kind by making it contrary to the public interest,[473] so that a covenant by which A promised B not to employ or to offer to employ B's employees would be invalid[474] (though one by which A merely promised "not to solicit or entice away" B's employees could be upheld since it would not preclude A from employing them if they came to him of their own accord[475]).

---

[466] i.e. at para.11–092, below.

[467] See above, para.11–067.

[468] [1928] 2 K.B. 174; cf. *NW Salt Co v Electrolytic Alkali Co Ltd* [1914] A.C. 461.

[469] cf. *Joseph Evans & Co v Heathcote* [1918] 1 K.B. 418; *McEllistrim's* case, above; *Collins v Locke* (1879) 4 App.Cas. 674

[470] [1959] Ch. 108; cf. *Mineral Water, etc. Trade Protection Society v Booth* (1887) 36 Ch.D. 465; Sales 104 L.Q.R. 600.

[471] See above, para.11–071.

[472] See *TSC Europe (UK) Ltd v Massey* [1999] I.R.L.R. 22 at 29; cf. below, at fn.480.

[473] See *Esso Petroleum Ltd v Harper's Garage (Stourport) Ltd* [1968] A.C. 269 at 300, 319.

[474] *Hanover Ins Brokers v Shapiro* [1994] I.R.L.R. 82; *Dawnay Day & Co Ltd v D'Alphen* [1997] I.R.L.R. 442, so far as it relates to cl.12.1.2 of the service contract: see [1997] I.R.L.R. 285 at 296 (contrast *Alliance Paper Group Plc v Prestwich* [1996] I.R.L.R. 25, where the "no poaching" covenant referred only to *senior* employees).

[475] See the *Dawnay Day* case [1997] I.R.L.R. 442 at 448 (above at fn.474) so far as it relates to cl.12.1.1. of the contract.

11-090   **Remedies of third parties.** Reasoning of the kind just considered can help a
third party only where one of the parties to the agreement has challenged its
validity. In practice, these restrictive agreements were rarely broken, because they
were usually beneficial to the contracting parties, however much third parties
might suffer from them; and at common law the contracting parties are at liberty
to give effect to the agreement.[476] If they did so, the third parties could not claim
damages for conspiracy at common law[477]; and it used to be thought that they had
no standing at all to challenge such agreements. But in *Eastham v Newcastle United
Football Club Ltd*[478] a professional footballer sought a declaration that the "retain
and transfer" system was invalid. The remedy was granted, not only against his
club, but also against the Football Association and the Football League, with whom
the claimant had never been in any contractual relationship; and it was said to be
available "whether or not the (claimant) has a legal cause of action against the
defendants".[479] The weakness of this remedy by way of declaration is that it has
no coercive effect: it would not prevent the parties to the invalid agreement from
continuing to act in accordance with it. The declaration could help the third party
only by giving one of the contracting parties grounds for thinking that he could
break the agreement with impunity if it suited him to do so.

Sometimes a third party may, even at common law, have a more effective
remedy. There is some support for the view that a person can obtain an injunction
against a professional association to restrain it from applying a rule under which
he is excluded from membership, and so prevented from exercising the profession,[480] on grounds not relevant to his capacity to do so.[481] Whether such a
remedy is available in cases of this kind to a claimant who has no "cause of action
against the defendants"[482] is, however, open to doubt,[483] for normally an injunction will be granted only where there is such a cause of action.[484] In one case[485]
it was held that this requirement was satisfied where football clubs claimed a
declaration that a resolution passed by an association from which they had
resigned was in restraint of trade. The mere availability of a declaration was said
to be a "cause of action", so that an interlocutory injunction could be granted to
the clubs to restrain the association from acting on the resolution until the action
for a declaration came to trial. This conclusion is, however, hard to reconcile with
that part of the reasoning of the *Eastham* case (quoted above[486]) which assumes
that a declaration is available even though the claimant has *no* cause of action
against the third party. The possibility of the third party's obtaining injunctive
relief appears, in any event, to be restricted to cases in which the right to work (or

---

[476] *Boddington v Lawton* [1994] I.C.R. 478.

[477] *Mogul SS Co v McGregor, Gow & Co* [1892] A.C. 25 at 39, 42, 46, 51, 57, 58.

[478] [1964] Ch. 413; above, para.11–072; cf. *Greig v Insole* [1978] 1 W.L.R. 302; *Newport Association
Football Club Ltd v Football Association of Wales Ltd* [1995] 2 All E.R. 87.

[479] [1964] Ch. 413 at 426; cf. *R. v Jockey Club Ex p. RAM Racecourses Ltd* [1993] 2 All E.R. 225 at
243.

[480] The rule would not be contrary to public policy unless it had this effect: cf. *Cheall v APEX*
[1983] 2 A.C. 180 at 191 (expulsion from a trade union).

[481] See *Nagle v Feilden* [1966] 2 Q.B. 633; A.L.G. (1966) 82 L.Q.R. 319; Rideout (1966) 29 M.L.R.
424. That case concerned discrimination now unlawful under the Equality Act 2010.

[482] See above, at fn.479.

[483] *R. v Disciplinary Committee of the Jockey Club Ex p. Aga Khan* [1993] 1 W.L.R. 909 at 933, where
the applicant did have a cause of action in contract.

[484] See below, para.21–061.

[485] *Newport Association FC v Football Association of Wales Ltd* [1995] 2 All E.R. 87.

[486] At fn.479, above.

perhaps the right to trade[487]) is arbitrarily restricted by a contract between others. It seems unlikely that a buyer of goods or services could at common law get an injunction against a price-ring merely because it operated to his prejudice.

(d) Trade Unions and Employers' Associations

At common law the validity of the rules of a trade union depended nominally on the principles which governed other contracts in restraint of trade. But in practice there was at one time a strong judicial tendency to hold such rules illegal. The courts relied in particular on the fact that the rules of a trade union might require an employee to stop work against his will; and they were no doubt also influenced by the fear that they might be called on to enforce a strike by injunction. The common law position was changed by legislation as long ago as 1871[488]; and the matter is now dealt with by the Trade Union and Labour Relations (Consolidation) Act 1992. A detailed analysis of this complicated Act cannot be attempted in this book; but the main point is that under s.11 the purposes of a trade union[489] are not, by reason only of the fact that they are in restraint of trade, to be unlawful so as to make void or voidable any agreement; nor is any rule of a union to be unenforceable by reason only of its being in restraint of trade.[490] The Act contains similar provisions with regard to the purposes and rules of employers' associations,[491] which are to the same extent excepted from the scope of the restraint of trade doctrine.[492] But an agreement or rule of a trade union may still be invalid for some other reason. In particular, an employee (or person seeking employment) has a statutory right not to be excluded or expelled from a trade union[493] except in certain specified circumstances; and union rules which restrict membership are unenforceable unless they satisfy one or more of a number of criteria laid down by the legislation: e.g. they may validly restrict membership by reference to qualifications for the type of work in question.[494]

11–091

(e) Exclusive Dealing

(i) *In general*

Originally regarded as valid. The original tendency of the common law was to regard exclusive dealing arrangements as valid. This attitude is illustrated by decisions upholding sole agency and exclusive service agreements,[495] agreements not to buy or sell goods except from or to a particular person,[496] and agreements

11–092

---

[487] It was this right which was at stake in the *Newport* case, above, fn.485.

[488] Trade Union Act 1871, s.3.

[489] As defined by s.1.

[490] The exact scope of s.11 depends on whether or not the union is a "special register body" as defined by s.117.

[491] As defined by s.122(1).

[492] s.128: the exact scope of this section depends on whether the association is incorporated.

[493] Trade Union and Labour Relations (Consolidation) Act 1992, ss.174 to 177 (as substituted by Trade Union Reform and Employment Rights Act 1993, s.14); cf. also Equality Act 2010, s.57.

[494] 1992 Act, above, s.174(3).

[495] See *Esso Petroleum Co Ltd v Harper's Garage (Stourport) Ltd* [1968] A.C. 269 at 294, 307, 336; the last dictum excepts restrictions which are "purely limitative or sterilising" as in *Young v Timmins* (1831) 1 C. & J. 331; cf. above, para.11–083.

[496] *Metropolitan Electric Supply Co v Ginder* [1901] 2 Ch. 799; *Monkland v Jack Barclay Ltd* [1951] 2 K.B. 252.

not to use goods except with others made by the same manufacturer.[497] In other cases, the courts have upheld a contract by which the owner of a restaurant agreed to buy all the burgundy sold there from the claimants[498]; and a contract by a purchaser of garage premises to buy from the vendor all petrol used in the business carried on there.[499] Where the agreements were upheld, the rules relating to restraint of trade were in some cases simply not mentioned, while in others the rules were mentioned but the contracts were nevertheless held valid. In these cases, it was not always clear whether the contracts were valid because the restraint of trade doctrine did not apply to them at all or because its requirements were satisfied. The distinction is crucial because if the doctrine did not apply at all it would be unnecessary for the person seeking to enforce the agreement to establish its reasonableness.

11–093   **The effect of decisions on "solus agreements".** The older authorities must now be read subject to a line of cases concerned with the validity of "solus agreements" between oil companies and garage proprietors. These agreements were usually made when an oil company advanced money to help with the purchase or development of garage premises; in return, the garage proprietor would give three undertakings: a "tying covenant", to buy all petrol (and some-times certain other products) from the oil company; a "compulsory trading covenant", to keep his garage open at all reasonable times for the sale of petrol; and a "continuity covenant", to extract similar undertakings from any person to whom he might sell the garage during the subsistence of the solus agreement. The leading *Esso* case[500] concerned solus agreements made in respect of two garages. One agreement was to last for about four and a half years, and the other for 21 years. The House of Lords held that the solus agreements were within the restraint of trade doctrine; that the four-and-a-half year agreement was valid; but that the 21-year agreement was invalid as it was unreasonable and contrary to the public interest. Undertakings with regard to solus petrol agreements were later given to the Government by oil companies in consequence of a report by the Monopolies Commission[501]; but the decision in the *Esso* case gives rise to a number of general problems which still require discussion.

(ii) *Whether such agreements are within the restraint of trade doctrine*

11–094   In the *Esso* case Lord Pearce distinguished between

> "those contracts which are in restraint of trade and . . . those which merely regulate the normal commercial relations between the parties and which are therefore free from the doctrine".[502]

---

[497] *United Shoe Machinery Co of Canada v Brunet* [1909] A.C. 330, criticised in the *Esso* case, above, at 297.
[498] *Bouchard Servais v Prince's Hall Restaurant Ltd* (1904) 20 T.L.R. 574; *Greenall's Management Ltd v Canavan, The Times*, August 20, 1997.
[499] *Foley v Classique Coaches* [1934] 2 K.B. 1.
[500] *Esso Petroleum Co Ltd v Harper's Garage (Stourport) Ltd* [1968] A.C. 269; Heydon 85 L.Q.R. 229; P.V.B. 83 L.Q.R. 478; Koh [1967] C.L.J. 151; and see Whiteman 29 M.L.R. 507.
[501] 1965, House of Commons Paper 264; further undertakings have been given subsequently.
[502] [1968] A.C. 269 at 327.

He regarded solus agreements as falling within the former class, principally on the ground that the oil company gave no assurance that it would provide a supply of petrol at a reasonable price.[503] Lord Wilberforce said that contracts were not within the doctrine of restraint of trade if they were "such ... as, under contemporary conditions, may be found to have passed into the accepted and normal currency of contractual or conveyancing relations".[504] The agreements in the *Esso* case were not of a kind which had in this way "passed into acceptance . . . ; the solus system is both too recent and too variable for this to be said".[505] However, Lord Wilberforce reserved the powers of the court to subject even "accepted" contracts to scrutiny in the light of changing social or economic conditions or of special features in individual transactions.[506] Later decisions have, in particular, made it clear that a contract is not taken out of the restraint of trade doctrine merely because it is in standard form and contains only terms which are usual in that type of transaction.[507] This factor may take contracts out of the restraint of trade doctrine if they have been freely negotiated,[508] but the position is different where there is great disparity of bargaining power and the terms are imposed by the stronger on the weaker party. In *A Schroeder Music Publishing Co v Macaulay*[509] it was accordingly held that a contract by which an unknown song-writer undertook to give his exclusive services to a publisher who made no promise to publish his work was subject to the doctrine. Lord Reid said:

> "Normally the doctrine of restraint of trade has no application to such restrictions: they require no justification. But if contractual restrictions appear to be unnecessary or to be reasonably capable of enforcement in an oppressive manner, then they must be justified before they can be enforced".[510]

This may be the position even where the contract is made on terms settled by a professional association for the purpose of protecting the party subject to the restraint, and where both parties have no alternative but to make use of such terms.[511]

The tests proposed by Lords Pearce and Wilberforce in the *Esso* case, and by Lord Reid in the *Schroeder* case continue to recognise the possibility that some exclusive dealing and exclusive service agreements will not be subject to the doctrine of restraint of trade. Many of the earlier cases which support this view[512] were cited, and none was overruled, in the *Esso* case. At the same time, the tests are very vague and leave much discretion to the courts in defining the scope of the doctrine in relation to such contracts. It seems probable that in future the doctrine

---

[503] ibid. at 329.
[504] ibid. at 332–333.
[505] ibid. at 337.
[506] ibid. at 333; *Watson v Prager* [1991] 1 W.L.R. 726 at 744.
[507] *Watson v Prager*, above.
[508] *A Schroeder Music Publishing Co Ltd v Macaulay* [1974] 1 W.L.R. 1308 at 1314.
[509] See above; cf. *O'Sullivan v Management Agency & Music Ltd* [1985] Q.B. 428; *Watson v Prager*, above.
[510] [1974] 1 W.L.R. 1308 at 1314; *Watson v Prager*, above, at 747.
[511] *Watson v Prager* [1991] 1 W.L.R. 726.
[512] See above, para.11-092.

will apply to contracts of this kind if they present any novel or unusual features,[513] or if they contain terms which are likely to operate harshly on a party of weak bargaining power.

(iii) *Requirements of validity*

11–095   Where an exclusive dealing or service contract is subject to the doctrine of restraint of trade, the usual requirements must be satisfied before it can be enforced.

11–096   **Interest.** We have distinguished elsewhere between "proprietary" and "commercial" interests[514]; and the *Esso* case shows that a "commercial" interest will suffice in the present group of cases. Lord Reid there said that the statement "that a person is not to be protected against mere competition" was "not ... very helpful in a case like the present"[515] and Lord Pearce, after expressing substantially the same view, seems to have regarded the oil company's "network of outlets"[516] as the interest which they sought to protect. Some difficulty arises from Lord Morris' description of the covenants as "naked covenants or covenants in gross"[517]; but he obviously regarded this, not as a ground of invalidity[518] (for he upheld one of the covenants), but merely as a ground for subjecting the covenants to the doctrine of restraint of trade.

11–097   **Reasonableness.** To satisfy the test of reasonableness, the party seeking to enforce the restrictions must show that they were "no more than what was reasonably required to protect his legitimate interest".[519] Here, as elsewhere,[520] relevant factors include the length of the restraint[521] and the adequacy of the consideration provided for it.[522] The reasonableness of the length of restraint may depend upon the type of contract concerned:

> "A period of 9½ years is not a long one in the context of a defence project using and developing cutting edge technology ... A decade in the pop music business, by contrast, is a very long time indeed".[523]

We have seen that in the *Esso* case a four-and-a-half year tie was upheld and a 21-year one struck down.[524] But in a later case a 21-year tie in a solus agreement contained in a lease was upheld since the premises were already, before the lease, subject to a valid three-year tie, since the tenant had the right to break the lease

---

[513] *Days Medical Aids Ltd v Pihsiang Machinery Manufacturing Co Ltd* [2004] EWHC 44 (Comm); [2004] 1 All E.R. (Comm) 991 at [224] (doctrine applied and restraint unreasonable if 10-year term also included right of perpetual renewal); cf. below, fn.599.

[514] See above, para.11–072.

[515] [1968] A.C. 269 at 301.

[516] ibid. at 329.

[517] ibid. at 309.

[518] cf. above, para.11–067.

[519] *A Schroeder Music Publishing Co Ltd v Macaulay* [1974] 1 W.L.R. 1308 at 1310.

[520] See above, paras 11–074—11–077.

[521] *Watson v Prager* [1991] 1 W.L.R. 726 at 748.

[522] *Societa Esplosivi Industriali SpA v Ordnance Technologies (UK) Ltd* [2004] EWHC 48 (Ch); [2004] 1 All E.R. (Comm) 619 at [145].

[523] ibid. at [146].

[524] See above, para.11–093.

after seven and 14 years, and since the landlord had paid the tenant £35,000 under a previous transaction leading to the execution of the lease.[525]

Fairness. The fairness of the contract is also a relevant factor, particularly where the restrictions are imposed on the weaker party to a relationship of unequal bargaining power. The point is well illustrated by agreements between musical performers and recording companies. In one case,[526] a long-term (though not exclusive) contract of this kind was made to settle differences which had arisen under an earlier contract between the parties; when the new contract was made, the performer's reputation was well established and he had the benefit of expert legal advice. In these circumstances, the new contract was regarded as reasonable in view of the benefits which the performer had received under it. By contrast, the restriction imposed on the composer in *A Schroeder Music Publishing Co Ltd v Macaulay*[527] was neither necessary nor fair. It extended over a period of five years, during which he had to submit all his compositions to the publishers, while they were under no obligation to promote his work and had to make no more than minimal payments if they failed to do so. The restriction was accordingly invalid as it went beyond the protection of the publishers' legitimate interests and operated harshly on the other party: "his work will be sterilised and he can earn nothing from his abilities as a composer".[528]

Terms may also be unfair because the party claiming the benefit of the restriction is under the contract put into a position where his interest conflicts with the duty that he owes to the other party. This was the position in *Watson v Prager*[529] where a professional boxer agreed to be "managed and directed exclusively" by the defendant, who was both a manager and a boxing promoter and who undertook to negotiate terms "as advantageous as possible" for the boxer; the agreement was for an initial period of three years, renewable for a further period of equal length. The main reason why the agreement was held to be contrary to public policy was that it was not fair to hold the boxer to an agreement of such long duration since under it the defendant's duty as manager was to negotiate the highest possible fees for the boxer, and this conflicted with his interest as promoter, since in that capacity he would have to meet the cost of these fees.

Public interest. Lord Reid in the *Schroeder* case based his decision partly on the ground that

> "The public interest requires in the interests both of the public and of the individual that everyone should be free so far as practicable to earn a livelihood and give to the public the fruits of his particular abilities".[530]

The *Esso* case, too, is noteworthy for the stress placed on the element of public interest; indeed Lord Hodson bases the invalidity of the 21-year agreement "on

11–098

11–099

---

[525] *Alec Lobb (Garages) Ltd v Total Oil (Great Britain) Ltd* [1985] 1 W.L.R. 173.
[526] *Panayiotou v Sony Music Entertainment (UK) Ltd, The Times*, June 30, 1994; cf. *Proactive Sports Management Ltd v Rooney* [2010] EWHC 1807 (QB) (image rights representation agreement); the *Alec Lobb* case, above.
[527] [1974] 1 W.L.R. 1308; above, para.11–094.
[528] ibid. at 1314.
[529] [1991] 1 W.L.R. 726.
[530] [1974] 1 W.L.R. 1308 at 1313; Lord Diplock at 1315 seems to view this point with some scepticism.

the public interest rather than on that of the parties"[531]; Lord Pearce says that the ultimate ground for interference in all cases is public policy so that there is no real separation between "what is reasonable on grounds of public policy and what is reasonable as between the parties".[532] Lord Wilberforce appears to take the same view but adds that it is "important that the vitality of the second limb . . . of the wider aspects of a single public policy rule should continue to be recognised".[533] These statements show that the courts would in these cases reject the once fashionable argument[534] that, if an agreement was shown to be reasonable between the parties, the public interest would also be satisfied.

(f) Covenants Affecting the Use of Land

11–100   **No restraint of trade if giving up no right?** Covenants affecting the use of land are commonly enforced although they no doubt restrain trade, e.g. by imposing restrictions on building, or on the carrying on of some particular business or trade, or by providing that the land shall be used for residential purposes only. In the *Esso* case a majority of the House of Lords explained these cases on the ground that

> "A person buying or leasing land had no previous right to be there at all, let alone to trade there, and when he takes possession of that land subject to a negative restrictive covenant he gives up no right or freedom which he previously had".[535]

It has therefore been held that where a person enters into a solus agreement when he acquires land, and that agreement is a term of the conveyance by which the land is transferred, the doctrine of restraint of trade does not apply at all.[536] Nevertheless, it is submitted that the reasoning is hard to reconcile with the emphasis placed in the *Esso* case itself on the element of public interest[537]; for restrictions on the use of land may cause harm to the public where they are imposed at the time when the land is acquired, no less than where they are imposed later. Of course, generally speaking, the object of a restrictive covenant affecting land is to preserve amenities and not to restrain trade or to prevent competition; and in most cases such a covenant would in any event pass the test of reasonableness because it would affect only a small area. But sometimes covenants of this kind do expressly restrain the carrying on of a particular business on the land acquired[538]; and cases of this kind can be imagined in which the covenant would not be reasonable.

A person who owned a garage business on a 1,000-acre estate might sell all the land except for the garage and take a covenant that the purchaser would not carry

---

[531] [1968] A.C. 269 at 321; cf. above, para.11–081.

[532] ibid. at 324.

[533] ibid. at 341.

[534] See above, para.11–080.

[535] [1968] A.C. 269 at 298; cf. ibid. at 309, 316–317, 325.

[536] *Cleveland Petroleum Ltd v Dartstone Ltd* [1969] 1 W.L.R. 116; Korah 32 M.L.R. 323; below, fn.541. See also *Re Ravenseft Properties Ltd's Application* [1978] Q.B. 52 (where exceptions are envisaged at 67–68).

[537] See above, at fn.531.

[538] See, e.g. *Holloway Bros v Hill* [1902] 2 Ch. 612; *Newton Abbott Co-operative Society Ltd v Williamson & Treadgold Ltd* [1952] Ch. 286; cf. *Rother v Colchester Corp* [1969] 1 W.L.R. 720.

on a garage business on any part of the land bought. Such a covenant could offend public policy just as much as a covenant not to compete within a given radius of the garage. Moreover, we may vary the example by supposing the original owner sells the garage but keeps the rest of the land, and covenants not to carry on a garage business on it. This covenant would, according to the reasoning of the *Esso* case, be subject to the doctrine of restraint of trade, for the landowner would be giving up a right which he previously had, to carry on a garage business on the land which he kept.[539] It is hard to see why the doctrine of restraint of trade should not apply to the first as well as to the second of these hypothetical cases. Suppose, further that the owner of a garage sells or leases it to an oil company and then *leases it back* on terms that include a solus agreement. Here it would seem that he did have a "previous right to be there" so that the doctrine of restraint of trade would apply.[540] Attempts have, indeed, been made to evade this result by interposing a company controlled by the garage owner into such an agreement. Thus there is some support for the view that, if the land is leased from a garage owner and leased back to a company controlled by him, then the restraint of trade doctrine should not apply because *the company* had no "previous right to be there".[541] But the distinction between this situation and that in which the two leases are between the same parties can hardly be justified in terms of public policy. Accordingly, it has been held that the restraint of trade doctrine did apply where garage premises were owned by a company controlled by a mother and son, leased by that company to an oil company and then leased back to the mother and son personally.[542] It was said that the court should "pierce the corporate veil" and not give effect to such a "palpable device"[543] for evading the restraint of trade doctrine.

Situations in which the restraint of trade doctrine applies. In three further situations the restraint of trade doctrine applies to covenants affecting land. First, it applies where the covenant is given by A to B on the acquisition of land by A, not from B, but from a third party C, e.g. where (as in the *Esso* case itself) the oil company (B) takes the covenant as one of the terms of a loan to A to enable him to buy a garage from C.[544] Secondly, it applies where the owner of a garage mortgages his existing premises and the mortgage contains a solus agreement.[545] Thirdly, it applies where the restriction is imposed not in the conveyance itself but in a separate contemporaneous agreement: this was the position in *Foley*

11–101

---

[539] cf. *Kerrick v Schoenberg* 328 S.W. 2d 595, 602 (1959).

[540] e.g. *Amoco Australia Pty Ltd v Rocca Bros Motor Engineering Co Pty Ltd* [1975] A.C. 561; Bowman, 38 M.L.R. 571.

[541] *Cleveland Petroleum Ltd v Dartstone Ltd* [1969] 1 W.L.R. 116, where the claim to enforce the restraint was actually made against an assignee of the company's leasehold interest in the garage.

[542] *Alec Lobb (Garages) Ltd v Total Oil (Great Britain) Ltd* [1985] 1 W.L.R. 173 (where the restraint was held reasonable).

[543] ibid. at 178.

[544] Heydon 85 L.Q.R. 229 at 233 (and *The Restraint of Trade Doctrine*, pp.58–59) argues that this makes the reasoning in the *Esso* case inconsistent with the decision: as A had "no previous right to be there", the restraint of trade doctrine should not have applied. But it is submitted that this part of the reasoning was intended only to apply where the agreement imposing the restriction was between the same parties as the disposition of the land; cf. also *Petrofina (Great Britain) Ltd v Martin* [1966] Ch. 146, where a solus agreement with an oil company on the purchase of a garage from a third party was also held invalid for restraint of trade.

[545] *Texaco Ltd v Mulberry Filling Station Ltd* [1972] 1 W.L.R. 814; *semble* the mortgage in the *Esso* case was similarly executed after the defendant company had acquired the Corner Garage (though it was executed in pursuance of an earlier agreement).

v Classique Coaches[546] where it was assumed that the doctrine did apply and this assumption seems to have been accepted in the *Esso* case.[547] But it is once again by no means clear why, if the doctrine of restraint of trade can apply in these cases, it should not apply to a restrictive covenant forming part of a conveyance between the parties to the covenant. Perhaps similar principles can be applied, if not at common law, then by virtue of s.84 of the Law of Property Act 1925.[548] That section gives the Lands Tribunal a statutory power in certain cases to discharge or modify restrictive covenants affecting land if they have become obsolete by reason of changes in the character of the neighbourhood or because their continued existence "would impede some reasonable user of the land for private or public purposes". This enactment is, in effect, a statutory extension of the doctrine of public policy to these covenants.[549]

(g) Other Agreements

11–102   **Categories "never closed".** In the past the courts were reluctant to apply the doctrine of restraint of trade to new classes of contracts. Thus at common law price-maintenance agreements are valid,[550] though some such agreements may be void under the rules (to be discussed later in this chapter) which prohibit certain anti-competitive agreements.[551] So, too, at common law an agreement between two persons not to bid against each other at an auction is not illegal[552] but if at least one of them is a dealer they may be guilty of a statutory offence under the Auctions (Bidding Agreements) Act 1927.[553] This Act also provides that the contract can be set aside by the owner of the property auctioned; and, although it does not explicitly invalidate the agreement not to bid as between the parties to it, such invalidity probably follows at common law from the criminality of the agreement.[554] In these cases legislative intervention has been necessary to extend the scope of the doctrine of restraint of trade, but there are signs that the courts are prepared to resume a more creative role in this field. In the *Esso* case Lord Wilberforce said that no exhaustive tests could be stated for defining or identifying contracts in restraint of trade[555]; and that, although such contracts might "be listed, provisionally, in categories . . . the classification must remain fluid and the categories can never be closed".[556]

11–103   **New departures.** Subsequent cases illustrate a number of new departures. It has, for example, been held that covenants in a joint venture agreement (not amounting to a partnership) were subject to the restraint of trade doctrine and so

---

[546] [1934] 2 K.B. 1; above, para.11–092.

[547] See [1968] A.C. 269 at 296, 311, 316, 327, 339.

[548] As amended by s.28 of Law of Property Act 1969.

[549] Under the section, the person seeking modification may be ordered to pay compensation. It is arguable that this practice should be extended to some other cases where a person seeks relief from a promise in restraint of trade for which he has received consideration.

[550] *Palmolive Co (of England) v Freedman* [1928] Ch. 264. cf. *Re Dott's Lease* [1920] 1 Ch. 281 (covenant to maintain price of tickets at the Garrick Theatre).

[551] See below, para.11–106, esp. at fn.580.

[552] *Rawlings v General Trading Co Ltd* [1921] 1 K.B. 635; *Harrop v Thompson* [1975] 1 W.L.R. 545.

[553] As amended by Auctions (Bidding Agreement) Act 1969.

[554] See above, para.11–011.

[555] [1968] A.C. 269 at 332.

[556] ibid. at 337; cf. *Petrofina (Great Britain) Ltd v Martin* [1966] Ch. 146 at 169.

enforceable only to the extent to which they were reasonable, having regard to the covenantee's interest.[557] It seems that, where a dispute about intellectual property is settled, the doctrine can apply to terms of the settlement which restrict a party's right to make use of the property.[558] It also applies to the assignment of a patent which entitles the assignee to any improvements.[559] A further novel application of the doctrine is illustrated by *Pharmaceutical Society of Great Britain v Dickson*,[560] where the House of Lords held that a rule of the Society restricting the trading activities of chemists was invalid. One ground for the decision was that the rule was ultra vires[561]; but a majority of the House of Lords also held that it was invalid for restraint of trade.[562] The rule was held invalid on this ground even though it was no more than part of a professional code of ethics which was not legally binding (whether as a contract or otherwise). A fortiori, a rule of a professional association may be in restraint of trade if it *is* intended to have contractual force. It has, for example, been said that the rule of the International Tennis Federation by which its members are subject to disqualification for taking prohibited drugs is in restraint of trade, though reasonable and hence valid at common law.[563]

Essential feature of contracts within the doctrine. The doctrine of restraint of trade does not apply merely because a contract restricts a party's freedom to deal with its particular subject-matter, for every contract "necessarily limits the freedom to enter into another contract".[564] The essential feature of contracts within the doctrine is that of "fettering a person's freedom in the future to carry on his trade, business or profession".[565] Various further kinds of agreements or arrangements can be imagined which might have this effect: e.g. an agreement by A not to manufacture a certain product in competition with B[566]; an agreement on the sale of a ship not to operate her on certain routes; an agreement by a buyer not to export goods to a particular country[567]; or an agreement, on the lease of a hall for an exhibition, not to hold a similar exhibition there for six months.[568] It is not suggested that all or any of such agreements will be held invalid; but they may require justification under the doctrine of restraint of trade. **11–104**

(h) Competition Law

Competition Act 1998. Earlier in this chapter, we saw that the common law relating to restrictive trading agreements[569] gave only limited protection to third **11–105**

---

[557] *Dawnay Day & Co Ltd v D'Alphen* [1997] I.R.L.R. 422.
[558] *World Wide Fund for Nature v World Wrestling Federation* [2002] EWCA Civ 196; [2002] U.K.C.L.R. 388 at [40]–[42] (agreement held valid).
[559] *Buchanan v Alba Diagnostics Ltd* [2004] UKHL 5; [2004] R.P.C. 34 (agreement held valid)
[560] [1970] A.C. 403; Koh 31 M.L.R. 70.
[561] See below, para.12–064 et seq.
[562] Contrast *R. v General Medical Council Ex p. Coleman* [1990] 1 All E.R. 489 (refusal to allow advertising of holistic medical practice held not to be open to challenge for restraint of trade as the refusal was authorised by statute).
[563] *Wilander and Novacek v Tobin & Jude* [1997] 2 Lloyd's Rep. 295 at 297.
[564] *Shearson Lehman Hutton Inc v Maclaine Watson & Co* [1989] 2 Lloyd's Rep. 570 at 615.
[565] ibid.
[566] *International Pediatric Products Ltd v Cuddle-King Products Ltd* (1964) 46 D.L.R. (2d) 581.
[567] As in *National Panasonic (UK) Ltd v Commission of the European Communities* [1981] I.C.R. 51.
[568] cf. *Modern Exhibition Services v Cardiff Corp* (1965) 63 L.G.R. 316, where restraint of trade was not discussed.
[569] See above, para.11–090.

parties who might be adversely affected by the willingness of the parties to such agreements to give effect to them. A more comprehensive attack on this problem has, since 1956,[570] been made by legislation. The relevant rules are now contained in the Competition Act 1998.

11–106   **Chapter I prohibition.** Chapter I of Pt I of this Act prohibits a number of anti-competitive practices; it does so in words which closely follow those of Art.101[571] of the Treaty on the Functioning of the European Union ("TFEU").[572] This prohibition (called "the Chapter 1 prohibition"[573]) is to be interpreted in accordance with the extensive case law on the interpretation and effects of that Article[574]; the main difference between the two sets of provisions lies in their geographical scope. The prohibitions apply to agreements[575] between undertakings,[576] decisions by associations of undertakings or concerted practices which (a) may affect trade (under Ch.I) within the UK or (under Art.101 TFEU (ex Art.81 EC) between Member States, and (b) have as their object or effect the prevention, restriction or distortion of competition within (under Ch.I) the UK or (under Art.101 TFEU) the common market.[577] Prohibited agreements (etc.) are void[578] unless they then satisfy the criteria laid down in s.9(1) of the 1998 Act or Art.101(3) TFEU and thus benefit from the legal exception regime set out in the current enforcement Regulation.[579] Examples of agreements covered by the prohibition include those which "directly or indirectly fix purchase or selling prices or any other trading conditions".[580] Under Art.101 TFEU, this prohibition applies, not only to so-called "horizontal" agreements (i.e. to those between parties operating at the same level of production or supply, such as agreements between manufacturers as to the prices which they will charge for their products), but also to so-called "vertical" agreements (i.e. to those between parties operating at different levels of supply, such as exclusive dealing agreements between producers and dealers[581]). Under the 1998 Act, its provisions (including the Ch.I prohibition) can be made to apply to "vertical" and to "land" agreements by delegated legislation[582] defining these terms[583]; alternatively, such legislation may exclude the application of these prohibitions to such agreements.[584] The latter power was exercised in relation to "land" agreements,[585] but this exclusion has now been

---

[570] When the first of the Restrictive Trade Practices Acts (now repealed) was passed.

[571] Formerly Art.85 EEC and then Art.81 EC.

[572] Which has the force of law in the UK by virtue of the European Communities Act 1972, s.2. The European Communities (Amendment) Act 1993 does not affect the rules stated in the text.

[573] Competition Act 1998, s.2(8).

[574] This is the effect of s.60 of the 1998 Act.

[575] It has been held under what is now Art.101 that the agreement need not be legally binding: *Italian Flat Glass* case [1990] 4 C.M.L.R. 535; *Re Northern Europe-USA Freight Lines Agreement* [1990] 4 C.M.L.R. 518.

[576] An individual engaged in economic activity can for the purposes of what is now Art.101 be an "undertaking" *Re Unitel* [1978] 3 C.M.L.R. 306 (opera singers).

[577] Competition Act 1998 s.2(1); Art.101(1) TFEU.

[578] 1998 Act, s.2(4); Art.101(2) TFEU.

[579] 1998 Act, ss.4, 6; Art.101(3) TFEU; Council Regulation 1/2003 [2003] O.J. L1/1.

[580] 1998 Act, s.2(2)(a); Art.101(1)(a) TFEU.

[581] *Consten & Grundig v Commission* [1966] E.C.R. 299; *Guidelines on Vertical Restraints* [2010] O.J. C 130/1.

[582] s.50(1).

[583] s.50(5).

[584] s.50(2).

[585] Competition Act 1998 (Land Agreements Exclusion and Revocation) Order 2004 (SI 2004/1260).

repealed,[586] making both vertical and land agreements prohibited by the 1998 Act.[587] The Act further makes claims for monetary compensation available to persons who have suffered loss or damage as a result of an infringement of these prohibitions.[588] Where such persons are consumers, such claims can be brought on their behalf by bodies to be specified for this purpose by the Secretary of State.[589] Such claims could, for example, have been brought on behalf of consumers who had paid prices inflated by price-fixing agreements between suppliers.

Relationship with the common law. No attempt can be made in a book of this nature even to summarise the extremely complex rules which govern the scope of the above prohibitions and of the exemptions from them which have been granted under EU law[590]; but a number of points must be made about the relationship between the prohibitions and the common law rules relating to restraint of trade. First, competition law does not apply to individuals as such, but to "undertakings". Whilst individuals may act as undertakings,[591] an employee is not an "undertaking" within Art.101 TFEU,[592] so that the prohibitions would not affect the common law rules relating to restraints in employment contracts.[593] Secondly, the Art.101 TFEU prohibitions apply only where the agreement (etc.) in question has an "appreciable" effect on trade between Member States.[594] The Commission has issued extensive guidelines on the application of this jurisdictional concept.[595] Though there is no single determinative factor the percentage of the share of the market affected by the agreement is an important consideration: e.g. the prohibitions have been held not to apply where that share was no more than 0.02 per cent[596]; and it seems that a share of less than 5 per cent would be treated in the same way.[597] If an agreement between undertakings has an appreciable effect on trade between Member States, Art.3(1) of Regulation 1/2003 requires national courts and competition authorities to apply Art.101 TFEU and Art.3(2) of Regulation 1/2003 provides that national competition law may not

11–107

---

[586] Competition Act 1998 (Land Agreements Exclusion Revocation) Order (SI 2010/1709); Office of Fair Trading *Land Agreements: The application of competition law following the revocation of the Land Agreements Exclusion Order* March 2011, OFT1280a.

[587] i.e. by s.2 of the 1998 Act; see above, after fn.573.

[588] s.47A, as inserted by Enterprise Act 2002, s.18. Case C-453/99 *Courage Ltd v Bernard Crehan and Bernard Crehan v Courage Ltd* [2001] ECR I-6297 establishes the right to damages for breach of Community competition law.

[589] s.47B, as inserted by Enterprise Act 2002, s.19.

[590] See, e.g. Bellamy and Child, *European Community Law of Competition* (6th edn).

[591] See *Re Unitel* [1978] 3 C.M.L.R. 306

[592] See *Suiker Unie v Commission* [1975] E.C.R. 1663 at 2007, para.539; Case C-67/96 *Albany International BV v Stichting Bedrijfspenioensfonds Textielindustrie* [1999] E.C.R. I-5751, para.215.

[593] See above, para.11–069 et seq.

[594] *Völk v Etablissements J Vervaecke SPRL* [1969] C.M.L.R. 273.

[595] Guidelines on the effect on trade concept contained in Arts101 and 102 TFEU [2004] O.J. C101/81.

[596] *Völk v Vervaeke* [1969] C.M.L.R. 273; cf. *Passmore v Morland Plc* [1998] 4 All E.R. 468, affirmed [1999] 3 All E.R. 1005; *Inntrepreneur Pub Co (CPC) Ltd v Price, The Times*, December 4, 1998. The question of "appreciable" effect is judged at the time, not of the agreement, but of the proceedings: *Passmore v Morland Plc* [1999] 3 All E.R. 1005, so that an agreement which was invalid under Art.101 TFEU when made may become valid in the light of later events, and conversely. cf. Korah (1998) 19 E.C.L.R. N135–136; Preece (2000) 21 E.C.L.R. 433–436. Contrast the position under the common law of restraint of trade: above, para.11–064.

[597] See, e.g. *Miller v Commission* [1978] E.C.R. 131; *AEG v Commission* [1983] E.C.R. 3151. cf. Competition Act 1998 s.39, relating to "small" agreements and *Commission Notice on agreements of minor importance which do not appreciably restrict competition under Article 81(1) of the Treaty establishing the European Community (de minimis)* [2001] O.J C 368/13, para. 3.

prohibit agreements permissible under Art.101 TFEU nor may it permit that which is prohibited under Art.101 TFEU.[598] The common law rules of restraint of trade have been considered to be competition law within the meaning of Art.3(2).[599] Those rules may be applied when the agreement is not between one or more undertakings; or does not have a sufficiently "appreciable" effect on trade between Member States to fall within the scope of Art.101 TFEU. Chapter I of the Act is silent on whether it prevents the application of the common law rules on restraint of trade when the agreement is within the scope and permitted by the Ch.I prohibition. The common law rules therefore continue to operate alongside the Art.101 and Ch.I prohibitions, so that it is perfectly possible for an agreement to fall outside those prohibitions but nevertheless to be invalid for restraint of trade at common law. The same may also be true of agreements which fall outside Art.101 and Ch.I because of their geographical scope as described above[600]; e.g. of an agreement which affected trade only in South America. The point appears to be that the purpose of the two sets of rules is different: the Art.101 and Ch.I prohibitions are concerned with the effect of agreements (etc.) on the economy as a whole, while under the common law rules an agreement may be void by reason of its adverse effect merely on the party restrained by it.[601]

11–108   **Abuse of a "dominant position".** Contracts in restraint of trade can also be affected by the prohibition contained in Ch.II of Pt I of the Competition Act 1998 and Art.102 TFEU[602] against abuse by an undertaking of a "dominant position".[603] Such an abuse can of course occur without any contract being made to give effect to it; but it could also invalidate certain types of contracts,[604] such as contracts obliging a buyer of goods to secure supplies of other goods or services from the same supplier.[605]

(i) Other Aspects of European Union Law

11–109   Other provisions of the EU Treaties which may be relevant in the context of contracts in restraint of trade include those which relate to the free movement of goods,[606] the free movement of workers,[607] freedom of establishment[608] and

---

[598] Council Regulation 1/2003 [2003] O.J. L1/1.

[599] *Days Medical Aids Ltd v Pihsiang Machinery Manufacturing Co Ltd* [2004] EWHC 44 (Comm); [2004] 1 All E.R. (Comm) 991: common law rules not applicable to an agreement which falls within the *scope* of Art.101 TFEU but is not prohibited either because it is subject to an exemption, or is found not to have an anti-competitive effect; cf. *Jones v Ricoh UK Ltd* [2010] EWHC 1743 (Ch) at [49].

[600] See above, at fn.577.

[601] cf. above, at fn.427.

[602] Formerly Art.86.

[603] Competition Act 1998, s.18.

[604] It could also give rise to a remedy for refusal to enter into a contract: see above, para.1–007.

[605] e.g. *Hilti v Commission* [1991] E.C.R. II-1439; *Elopak Italia Srl v Tetra Pak (No.2)* [1992] 4 C.M.L.R. 551.

[606] e.g. Art.34 TFEU (formerly Art.28 EC), prohibiting quantitative restrictions on imports; this was held not to have been contravened in *R. v Royal Pharmaceutical Society of GB* [1989] 2 All E.R. 758.

[607] Art.45 TFEU (formerly Art.39 EC); see *Union Royale Belge des Sociétés de Football Association ASBL v Bosman* [1996] All E.R. (EC) 97.

[608] Art.49 TFEU (formerly Art.43 EC).

freedom to provide services.[609] Discussion of these provisions is beyond the scope of this book; reference should be made to works on EU law.[610]

4. EFFECTS OF ILLEGALITY

(a) Enforcement

A contract affected by illegality is sometimes unenforceable by one party and sometimes unenforceable by both. Where it is "wholly unenforceable because it is contrary to English law, it may . . . accurately be said to be void as a contract, that is, not to be a contract at all"[611]; or to be "illegal and void".[612] In the restraint of trade cases, the illegality often affects only the term which imposes the restraint, and generally its effect is not to make the contract wholly void: it only makes *the stipulation in restraint of trade* unenforceable or "void"[613] in so far as it has not been performed.[614] It follows that, where one party voluntarily performs[615] another term of such a contract by paying money to the other, the payment cannot be recovered back from the payee; nor, if the contract is between more than two parties, can any other party to it prevent the payor from voluntarily making the payment to the payee.[616] A contract in restraint of trade would only be "wholly unenforceable" and "void" (in accordance with the statements quoted above) where the restraint formed the sole or principal subject-matter of the contract[617]; and it would also be appropriate to describe it as void where the law provided a third party with a remedy to prevent the parties to the contract from acting in accordance with it.[618]

A court will never "enforce" an illegal contract in the sense of ordering a party actually to do something that is unlawful or contrary to public policy.[619] But if A promises B £10 in return for B's promise to do such an act the court may sometimes award damages to A if B fails to do the act, or allow B to claim the £10 if he has actually done it. The law on this question is complex and not very satisfactory.[620]

Where, under the rules to be discussed below, the contract is unenforceable by one or both parties, the court "may refuse to enforce it even if illegality is not

11–110

---

[609] Art. 56 TFEU (formerly Art.49 EC); this was held not to have been contravened in *Wilander and Novacek v Tobin and Jude* [1997] 2 Lloyd's Rep. 295 or in *Edwards v British Athletics Federation, The Times*, June 30, 1997.

[610] e.g. *Wyatt and Dashwood's European Union Law* (5th edn).

[611] *Mackender v Feldia* [1967] 2 Q.B. 590 at 601; cf. *Arnhold Karberg & Co v Blythe, Green, Jourdain & Co* [1915] 2 K.B. 379 at 388 ("illegal and void"), affirmed [1916] 1 K.B. 49; *Clarke v Chadburn* [1985] 1 W.L.R. 78 at 81 ("void for illegality").

[612] *Phoenix General Ins Co of Greece SA v Halvanon General Ins Co* [1988] Q.B. 216 at 249, 267, 268 (as to which see above, para.11–020); *Harbour Assurance (UK) Ltd v Kansa General International Ins* [1993] Q.B. 701 at 703, 724.

[613] *Rock Refrigeration Ltd v Jones* [1997] I.C.R. 938 at 948, 953.

[614] *O'Sullivan v Management Agency & Music Ltd* [1985] Q.B. 428 at 469 at least "where, as here, the restriction is during the pendency of the agreement": [1985] Q.B. 428 at 447.

[615] See below, para.11–157.

[616] *Boddington v Lawton* [1994] I.C.R. 478.

[617] As in *Amoco Australia Pty v Rocca Bros Motor Engineering Pty Ltd* [1975] A.C. 561, where acts done under the agreement were accordingly annulled with retrospective effect: below, para.11–164.

[618] See *Newport Association FC v Football Association of Wales Ltd* [1995] 2 All E.R. 87; above, para.11–090.

[619] e.g. to perform a contract if to do so would amount to a criminal offence: cf. above, paras 11–014, 11–019.

[620] See below, para.11–168.

pleaded or alleged".[621] The unenforceability of illegal contracts rests on overriding grounds of public interest[622] and the present rule ensures that these cannot be circumvented by the litigation tactics of the parties to such transactions.

(i) *Position of guilty party*

11–111   **No enforcement by guilty party.** An illegal contract cannot be enforced by a guilty party. Thus a person who hires a hall to deliver blasphemous lectures cannot sue for possession[623]; a landlord who lets premises with guilty intent cannot sue for rent[624]; and the owner of a brougham knowingly let to a prostitute for the purpose of her profession cannot sue for hire.[625] A guilty party cannot evade the rule by enforcing the contract indirectly.[626] Thus the court will set aside or refuse to enforce an arbitration award enforcing an illegal contract,[627] and will not administer the funds of an illegal association.[628] Nor, where an illegal contract purports to release rights under an earlier valid contract, will a guilty party be allowed to rely on the illegal contract by way of defence to a claim to enforce those rights.[629]

11–112   **Rejection of the "public conscience" test.** The traditional justification for the rule is that it exists, "not for the sake of the defendant, but because the courts will not lend their aid to such a (claimant)".[630] Thus it applies even though the defendant shares the claimant's guilt and even though its effect may be to allow the defendant to keep a substantial benefit for nothing. For example, where money has been lent under an illegal loan, a guilty lender cannot recover it from the borrower.[631] The rule is capable of producing harsh results,[632] particularly as a

---

[621] *Birkett v Acorn Business Machines Ltd* [1999] 2 All E.R. (Comm) 429 at 433; *Snell v Unity Finance Co Ltd* [1964] Q.B. 203; *Charlton v Fisher* [2001] EWCA Civ 112; [2002] Q.B. 518 at [80]. But facts giving rise to illegality must be pleaded where the contract is not *ex facie* illegal: *Bank of India v Transcontinental Merchants Ltd* [1982] 1 Lloyd's Rep. 427.

[622] *Birkett's* case, above, at 435; *Awwad v Geraghty & Co* [2001] Q.B. 570 at 596.

[623] *Cowan v Milbourn* (1867) L.R. 2 Ex. 230.

[624] cf. *Alexander v Rayson* [1936] 1 K.B. 169; *Edler v Auerbach* [1950] 1 K.B. 359.

[625] *Pearce v Brooks* (1866) L.R. 1 Ex. 213; the court stressed that the owner knew of the use to which the brougham was to be put; cf. below, para.11–114.

[626] *The Angel Bell* [1981] Q.B. 65 at 72–73.

[627] *David Taylor & Sons Ltd v Barnett Trading Co* [1953] 1 W.L.R. 562; *Soleimany v Soleimany* [1999] Q.B. 785; and see above, at fn.279. But this principle does not apply to findings of *fact* on which the legality of the contract depend: *Binder v Alachouzos* [1972] 2 Q.B. 151; nor does an arbitrator necessarily lack jurisdiction to determine whether a contract is illegal: *Harbour Assurance (UK) Ltd v Kansa General International Ins Co Ltd* [1993] Q.B. 701; Arbitration Act 1996, s.30(1)(a); nor is he deprived of such jurisdiction merely because it is alleged that performance of an originally lawful contract subsequently became illegal: *Prodexport v E D & F Man Ltd* [1973] 1 Q.B. 389; *Soleimany v Soleimany*, above, at 804.

[628] *Sykes v Beadon* (1879) 11 Ch.D. 170; disapproved in *Smith v Anderson* (1880) 15 Ch.D. 247, but not on this point; *Shaw v Benson* (1883) 11 Q.B.D. 563. The court can order repayment of such funds to the members or contributors: *Barclay v Pearson* [1893] 2 Ch. 154; *Greenberg v Cooperstein* [1926] Ch. 657.

[629] *Royal Boskalis Westminster NV v Mountain* [1997] 2 All E.R. 929 (Phillips L.J. dissenting on this point).

[630] *Holman v Johnson* (1775) 1 Cowp. 341 at 343; *Soleimany v Soleimany* [1999] Q.B. 785 at 800.

[631] *Boissevain v Weil* [1950] A.C. 372; *Spector v Ageda* [1973] Ch. 30; cf. *Shanshal v Al Kishtaini* [2001] EWCA Civ 264; [2001] 2 All E.R. (Comm) 601, also holding that his position is not affected by Human Rights Act 1998, Sch.1, Pt II.

[632] *Birkett v Avon Business Machines Ltd* [1999] 2 All E.R. (Comm) 429 at 434.

party may be "guilty" without being morally to blame[633]; and it has therefore been suggested that the rule should be displaced by a general principle that the courts will refuse to assist the claimant only where to do so "would be an affront to the public conscience."[634] This approach, and the difficulties inherent in it, are illustrated by *Howard v Shirlstar Container Transport Ltd*[635] where the defendants, who owned two aircraft which had been detained in Nigeria after a *coup d'état*, promised to pay $25,000 to the claimant if he flew the aircraft out of that country. The claimant did fly the aircraft out of Nigeria and in doing so he committed breaches of Nigerian air traffic control regulations; he did so in order to make good his escape, after he had been warned that his life and that of his wireless operator (who was also his fiancée) would be in danger if they stayed in Nigeria. It was held that the claimant's claim under the contract was not barred by illegality since "in the perilous and life-threatening circumstances ... it would not amount to an affront to the public conscience to afford the (claimant) the relief he sought".[636] It has been said that such a test is "very difficult to apply"[637]; and the House of Lords has rejected the "public conscience" test as one which can determine whether a guilty party should be allowed to enforce an illegal contract.[638] *Howard v Shirlstar Container Transport Ltd* has been explained[639] instead as an illustration of the principle of *St John SS Corp v Joseph Rank Ltd*,[640] i.e. on the ground that the purpose of the legislation was not to invalidate contracts but only to prohibit conduct. In applying this principle, it may be relevant that in *Howard*'s case there were no passengers on board the aircraft, and that it made its escape by flying low over the sea. A different view might have been taken if an aircraft with passengers on board had (in breach of air traffic regulations) been flown low over a densely populated area. To have allowed the pilot in such circumstances to enforce the contract might well have been thought to contravene the purpose of the legislation. The rule that a guilty party cannot enforce an illegal contract therefore survives; but its severity is mitigated in two ways.

Other remedies. First, the rule only prevents a guilty party from enforcing *the contract*: it does not necessarily prevent him from recovering damages in tort where the other party's conduct constitutes, not merely a breach of the illegal contract, but also an independent tort.[641] This was the position in *Saunders v Edwards*,[642] where a contract had been made for the sale of a flat and the furniture in it; the

11–113

---

[633] See below, para.11–114.

[634] *Euro-Diam Ltd v Bathurst* [1990] Q.B. 1 at 35. cf. (in the context of recovery of property obtained illegally) *Thackwell v Barclays Bank Plc* [1986] 1 All E.R. 676 at 687.

[635] [1990] 1 W.L.R. 1292.

[636] ibid. at 1301.

[637] *Pitts v Hunt* [1991] 1 Q.B. 24 at 56.

[638] *Tinsley v Milligan* [1994] 1 A.C. 340 at 358–361 and 363–364, per Lord Goff, who dissented in the result but with whose views on the present point all the other members of the House of Lords directly or indirectly expressed their agreement; *Webb v Chief Constable of Merseyside Police* [2000] Q.B. 427 at 445.

[639] ibid. at 360.

[640] [1957] 1 Q.B. 267; above, para.11–019.

[641] For a similar principle governing claims for the recovery of money paid or property transferred under an illegal contract, see below, para.11–134; cf. *Hall v Woolston Hall Leisure Ltd* [2001] 1 W.L.R. 225 (illegality of employment contract no bar to claim for unlawful sex discrimination); *Sweetman v Nathan* [2003] EWCA Civ 1115; [2004] P.N.L.R. 7; contrast *Vakante v Addey & Stanhope School* [2004] EWCA Civ 1065; [2005] I.C.R. 231 (claim for racial discrimination barred where employee responsible for illegality of contract).

[642] [1987] 1 W.L.R. 1116; cf. *The Siben* [1996] 1 Lloyd's Rep. 35 at 63.

purchasers had been induced to enter into the contract by the vendor's fraudulent misrepresentation that the premises included a roof-garden. The contract was also illegal[643] in that £5,000 of the agreed price of £45,000 was attributed to the furniture, which was worth no more than £1,000: this was apparently done at the suggestion of the purchasers, with a view to saving them the relatively small sum of £300 in stamp duty. Their claim for damages of over £7,000 for the vendor's deceit was nevertheless upheld. One reason for this result was that the purchasers were "not seeking to enforce the contract"[644] but only to claim damages in tort.[645] Another was that, in deciding whether to allow the tort claim, the court could, and should, have regard to the "relative moral culpability"[646] of the parties: the purchasers' fairly moderate tax evasion was outweighed by the vendor's more serious fraud. It is an open question whether this reasoning can survive the rejection of the "public conscience" test[647]; and, even if it can, there will still be situations in which a guilty party to an illegal contract will not be able to succeed merely by formulating his claim in tort. Thus in *Ashton v Turner*[648] one of two persons who had agreed (when drunk) to commit burglary together sued the other for injuries inflicted by the latter when negligently driving the get-away car. The action failed as it would have been obviously contrary to public policy to allow such a claim.

11–114	**Determining the "guilty" party.** A second form of mitigation is that there is some latitude in determining who is a "guilty" party where the illegality lies in the method of performance. For the present purpose, a party is not guilty merely because he performs a contract in an unlawful manner. Thus the shipowner in *St John Shipping Corp v Joseph Rank Ltd*[649] succeeded in his claim for freight although he had overloaded his ship; but he could not have enforced the contract if he had at the time of contracting intended to overload his ship.[650] Similarly, a seller of fish succeeded in his claim for the price even though, after the contract was made, he committed an offence by sending a false invoice to the buyer with the intention of postponing the payment of VAT on the sale[651]; but it seems that his claim would have failed if at the time of the sale he had already formed the intention of issuing the false invoice. The same rules apply where the offending conduct is not contrary to law, but (for example) immoral. Thus an employee

---

[643] On the principle of *Alexander v Rayson* [1936] 1 K.B. 169; above, para.11–056.

[644] [1987] 1 W.L.R. 1116 at 1125.

[645] cf. the successful tort claim in *Edler v Auerbach* [1950] 1 K.B. 359 in respect of a bath wrongfully removed by the tenant of premises let under an illegal lease.

[646] [1987] 1 W.L.R. 1116 at 1127.

[647] See above, para.11–112. In *Tinsley v Milligan* [1994] 1 A.C. 340 the House of Lords do not refer to *Saunders v Edwards*, above; while Ralph Gibson L.J. (whose views on this issue eventually prevailed) explained that case as turning on the first of the two reasons stated in the text above: [1992] Ch. 310 at 332. After *Tinsley v Milligan* dicta in *Saunders v Edwards* at 1134 cannot stand so far as they relate to the claim in contract.

[648] [1981] Q.B. 137; *semble* there was no *animus contrahendi* and hence no contract; cf. *Pitts v Hunt* [1991] 1 Q.B. 24; *Gala v Preston* (1991) 172 C.L.R. 243.

[649] [1957] 1 Q.B. 267; cf. *Shaw v Groom* [1970] 2 Q.B. 504; *Yango Pastoral Co Pty Ltd v First National Chicago Australia Ltd* (1978) 139 C.L.R. 410, as explained in *Phoenix General Ins Co of Greece SA v Halvanon General Ins Co Ltd* [1988] Q.B. 216 (as to which see above, para.11–020); *Euro–Diam Ltd v Bathurst* [1990] Q.B. 1.

[650] ibid. at 283; cf. *Fielding & Platt Ltd v Najjar* [1969] 1 W.L.R. 357. Quaere whether in the *St John Shipping* case the test of intention would have been strictly subjective. If the shipowner had made a single contract for so much cargo that his ship would inevitably be overloaded, would the court have said that he "must have" intended at the time of contracting to break the law?

[651] *Skilton v Sullivan, The Times*, March 25, 1994.

would not be precluded from enforcing a contract of employment which was lawful in itself merely because he had, in the course of performing it, procured prostitutes for his employer's clients[652]; but if he had agreed to do this when entering into the contract he could not have enforced it.[653] Where the intention that one party should do an unlawful (or immoral) act exists at the time of contracting, even the other party may be unable to sue on the contract. In *Ashmore, Benson, Pease & Co Ltd v A V Dawson Ltd*[654] a contract to carry two 25-ton loads was performed by using lorries which could not lawfully carry loads of more than 20 tons. This was known both to the carrier and to the owner of the goods, whose claim for damage done to them in the course of transit was rejected as he not only knew of the illegality but "participated" in it. "Participation" here means that he assented to a method of performance which he knew to be illegal,[655] and that he hoped to benefit from it by saving the extra expense of having the goods carried on different vehicles.

Purpose of the statute, or the relevant rule of the common law. It is submitted below that, so far as a claim by an innocent party is concerned, it is appropriate to ask whether the avoidance of the contract would further the purpose of the statute, or the relevant rule of law under which the illegality has arisen.[656] The same test may be applied to a claim by a guilty party. Some support for this is provided by *Hill v Secretary of State for the Environment, Food and Rural Affairs*.[657] The defendant entered into a contract with the claimant company for the cleaning and disinfection of a farm suspected of being infected with foot and mouth disease. The defendant refused to pay for the work done because the contract had been brought about by H, an undischarged bankrupt, in breach of s.1 of the Company Directors Disqualification Act 1986. The court accepted the defendant's contention that the policy underlying the section was the protection of the public from individuals not regarded as trustworthy persons to be involved in the management of a limited liability company, but found that it was primarily aimed at the protection of creditors and, on that basis, it was more consistent with the underlying policy to enforce the contract so as to avoid "the destruction of the company's debtor book".[658]   11–115

(ii) *Position of innocent party*

Party "innocent" because of ignorance or mistake of law. In general ignorance of the law, or a mistake of law, does not give a party the right to enforce   11–116

---

[652] *Coral Leisure Group v Barnett* [1981] I.C.R. 503.

[653] ibid. at 509.

[654] [1973] 1 W.L.R. 828; Hamson [1973] C.L.J. 199.

[655] *Hall v Woolston Hall Leisure Ltd* [2001] 1 W.L.R. 225 at 234 ("knowingly participated ... "); *Wheeler v Quality Deep Ltd* [2004] EWCA Civ 1085; [2005] I.C.R. 265; cf. *Enfield Technical Services v Payne* [2008] EWCA Civ 393; [2008] I.R.L.R. 500 at [38]: "The requirement of knowing participation does not require that the employee should realise that what is being done is illegal, but it is necessary that he or she should know of the facts which make it illegal".

[656] See below, para.11–122.

[657] [2005] EWHC 696 (Ch); [2006] 1 B.C.L.C. 601.

[658] It might have been argued that the company was not a "guilty party", but it was regarded as the "mere proxy" of H; cf. *Stone & Rolls Ltd v Moore Stephens* [2009] UKHL 39; [2009] 1 A.C. 1391, discussed above para.11–024.

a contract which is affected by illegality. In *Nash v Stevenson Transport Ltd*[659] A agreed to allow B to use goods vehicle licences taken out by A in his own name. This arrangement was made in good faith, but by statute it involved both parties in criminal liability. It was held that A could not sue for the money promised to him under the contract. Similarly a person could not enforce a contract in restraint of trade merely because he thought that such contracts were valid.

In these cases the performance or enforcement of the contract *necessarily* involves a breach of the law, or a result which is contrary to public policy. Where this is not the position, the effect of mistake of law is harder to determine. In *Waugh v Morris*[660] a ship was chartered to carry hay from a French port to London. The cargo was to be taken from the ship "alongside," and the master was orally instructed to deliver it to a wharf in Deptford Creek. This could not lawfully be done because, before the time of contracting, an order had, unknown to the parties, been made prohibiting the landing of hay from French ports in the UK. The hay was therefore trans-shipped and exported. It was held that the shipowner could sue on the charterparty as it could have been, and in fact had been, performed lawfully. But in *J M Allan (Merchandising) Ltd v Cloke*[661] a roulette wheel was let on hire for the purpose of enabling the hirer to play roulette royale at a country club. Both parties honestly thought that this game was lawful when it was not. It was held that the owner of the wheel could not sue for payment of the agreed hire. One reason for the decision was that the parties had a "common design to use the subject-matter for an unlawful purpose".[662] But it is equally true that in *Waugh v Morris* the parties had a common design to land the hay in Deptford, and that this was an unlawful purpose. Alternatively, there was in *Cloke*'s case an actual contract that the wheel should be used for playing roulette royale[663]: the position was as it would have been in *Waugh v Morris*, had the contract there been to *land* the hay at Deptford and not deliver it "alongside". It is, of course, possible that the hirer could, without committing a breach of contract, have used the wheel to play some other game; but this would not alter the fact that the owner had contracted to provide facilities for playing roulette royale. Thus if one party cannot perform his obligations without committing or abetting a breach of the law he cannot enforce the contract even though he was "innocent" in the sense that he made a mistake of law.

11–117   **Party "innocent" because of ignorance or mistake of fact.** A party may be innocent in the sense of being unaware of, or mistaken about, the *facts* which give rise to the illegality. The right of such a party to enforce the contract has been upheld in some cases but denied in others; even where it has been denied, other remedies may be available to the innocent party.

11–118   **Cases upholding the innocent party's claim.** A decision in favour of the innocent party is *Bloxsome v Williams*[664] where a person sold a horse on a Sunday

---

[659] [1936] 2 K.B. 128; cf. *Corby v Morrison* [1980] I.C.R. 218; *Mohamed v Alaga & Co* [2000] 1 W.L.R. 1815 at 1820, 1824, 1827.

[660] (1873) L.R. 8 Q.B. 202; cf. *Hindley & Co Ltd v General Fibre Co Ltd* [1940] 2 K.B. 517.

[661] [1963] 2 Q.B. 340.

[662] ibid. at 348.

[663] ibid. at 351.

[664] (1824) 3 B. & C. 232; cf. *Newland v Simons & Willer* [1981] I.C.R. 521. See also: *Clay v Yates* (1856) 1 H. & N. 73; above, para.11–016.

and thereby committed an offence under the Sunday Observance Act 1677,[665] as he was a dealer. The buyer did not know that the seller was a dealer and recovered the money he had paid for the horse as damages for breach of warranty. *Bloxsome v Williams* was doubted in the *Bedford Insurance*[666] case, where a company issued insurance policies in violation of a statutory prohibition against "the effecting and carrying out of [certain] contracts of insurance" without government authorisation. The policies were described as "illegal and void ab initio"; and it was said that the insured person, though innocent, acquired no rights under the policies "for it would be an offence for the insurer to pay him."[667] In the case of such contracts, this result has been reversed by statute,[668] and, even if the reasoning is sound as a matter of common law, it does not follow that *Bloxsome v Williams* was wrongly decided; for the buyer in that case was claiming, not delivery of the horse, but the return of his money. In upholding this claim, the court was not ordering the defendant to do an act prohibited by statute. This was also the position in *Archbolds (Freightage) Ltd v Spanglett Ltd*,[669] where the defendants contracted to carry the claimants' whisky in a van which was not licensed to carry goods belonging to third parties. In carrying the whisky in this van, the defendants committed a statutory offence. The whisky was stolen and the claimants, who did not know that the van was not properly licensed, recovered the value of the whisky as damages for breach of the contract.

Cases rejecting the innocent party's claim. The leading case in this group is *Re Mahmoud and Ispahani*,[670] where a contract was made to sell linseed oil at a time when it was (under delegated legislation) an offence to buy or sell such oil without licence. The seller had a licence to sell to other licensed dealers and was induced to enter into the contract by the buyer's fraudulent representation that he also had a licence. The buyer later refused to accept the oil, and it was held that the seller could not claim damages for non-acceptance, even if his lack of mens rea would exonerate him from criminal liability. Similarly, it has been held that builders who did work in the bona fide but mistaken belief that the necessary licences had been obtained could not enforce the contracts under which the work was done.[671] And, although the point has not been decided, it seems that mistake of fact would not entitle an innocent person to enforce a contract in restraint of trade or one to trade with the enemy. Thus the buyer of a shop whose customers all lived within one mile of it could not enforce a covenant against competition within 20 miles merely because he believed that the customers lived within the larger area. And a person who made a contract with a resident of an enemy

11–119

---

[665] Now repealed.

[666] [1985] Q.B. 966.

[667] ibid. at 982; approved in *Phoenix General Ins Co of Greece SA v Halvanon Ins Co Ltd* [1988] Q.B. 216: see above, para.11–020; see also *Fuji Finance Inc v Aetna Life Ins Co Ltd* [1997] Ch. 173 (where conflicting views were expressed on the effects on contracts of the breach of a statute which did *not* amount to an offence) and *Parks v Esso Petroleum Co Ltd* [1999] 1 C.M.L.R. 445 (where on appeal it was held that there was no illegality: [2000] Eu.L.R. 25).

[668] See now Financial Services and Markets Act 2000, ss.26(1) and 32; above, para.11–020; below, para.11–121.

[669] [1961] 1 Q.B. 374. cf. *Fielding & Platt Ltd v Najjar* [1969] 1 W.L.R. 357.

[670] [1921] 2 K.B. 716; cf. *Yin v San* [1962] A.C. 304; Williams 8 C.L.J. 51; Buckley 38 M.L.R. 535; Treitel, in (ed. Tapper) *Essays in Memory of Sir Rupert Cross*, pp.96–99.

[671] *J Dennis & Co Ltd v Munn* [1949] 2 K.B. 327; and see below, para.11–123.

country could not enforce it merely because he did not know that war had just broken out between the UK and that country.[672]

11-120   **Tests for distinguishing the two groups of cases.** Various tests have been suggested for distinguishing between the cases in which the innocent party can, and those in which he cannot, enforce the contract. One is to say that the contract can be enforced by the innocent party so long as it is not ex facie illegal. But if the contract is ex facie illegal and one party is innocent his mistake is almost always one of law; and the mere fact that the contract is *ex facie* legal is certainly not enough to enable the innocent party to sue.[673] Another suggestion is that the innocent party can enforce the contract where it is illegal as performed but not where it is illegal as formed. But in *Bloxsome v Williams* the innocent party's claim was upheld even though the contract was illegal as formed. Moreover, in *Archbolds (Freightage) Ltd v S Spanglett Ltd* the Court of Appeal regarded it as irrelevant whether the contract was to carry the whisky in the particular van, and yet this fact would be crucial if enforceability depended on whether the contract was illegal as formed or as performed. A third suggestion is that the innocent party's claim will succeed in cases of common law but not of statutory illegality. But this again does not fit the cases: in *Bloxsome v Williams* and *Archbolds (Freightage) Ltd v S Spanglett Ltd* the innocent party succeeded although the illegality was statutory. And if the suggestions made at the end of the last paragraph are sound there are cases in which the innocent party will fail although the illegality is brought about by common law. It is, moreover, hard to see why the innocent party's rights should depend on the distinction between statutory and common law illegality.

11-121   **Express or implied statutory provision.** The distinction between statutory and common law illegality can, of course, be decisive where the illegality is statutory and the statute expressly or by implication specifies its effect on con- tracts. On the one hand, the statute may expressly provide that the validity of the contract is not to be affected. It is, for example, an offence under s.65(1) of the Road Traffic Act 1988 to supply certain vehicles which do not comply with specified safety requirements; and s.65(4) provides that "nothing in subsection (1) . . . shall affect the validity of any contract or any rights arising under or in relation to a contract".[674] On the other hand, the statute may expressly or impliedly provide that even an innocent party is not to be entitled to enforce the contract. This possibility was formerly illustrated by the cases, already men- tioned,[675] in which insurance policies were issued in the course of a business carried on without government authorisation, thus making the insurers who had issued them guilty of a statutory offence; the general view was that such policies could not be enforced even by an insured person who was quite innocent of the illegality. This result was thought to follow from the wording of the statute, which was considered to have impliedly invalidated the contract by prohibiting the

---

[672] For discharge by *supervening* illegality in such cases see below, para.19–044 et seq.

[673] e.g. *Re Mahmoud and Ispahani* [1921] 2 K.B. 716.

[674] cf. Road Traffic Act 1988, s.75(7); Property Misdescriptions Act 1991, s.1(4); Criminal Justice Act 1993, s.63(2), the effect of which appears to be to reverse this aspect of *Chase Manhattan Equities Ltd v Goodman* [1991] B.C.L.C. 897.

[675] *viz.*, the *Bedford* case [1985] 1 Q.B. 966 and the *Phoenix* case [1988] Q.B. 216; above, para.11–020. The statements were strictly obiter since in the *Bedford* case the action was by a *guilty* insurer against an innocent reinsurer while in the *Phoenix* case no offence had been committed. For cases following or approving reasoning of these cases see *Re Cavalier Ins Co Ltd* [1989] 2 Lloyd's Rep. 430; *DR Ins Co v Seguros America Banamex* [1993] 1 Lloyd's Rep. 120.

"carrying out" of the policies. But to deny a remedy to the innocent party certainly did not promote the policy of the statutory requirement,[676] which had been imposed on insurers for the protection of insured persons; and the law in cases of this kind has been changed by the Financial Services and Markets Act 2000. This lays down the general principle that, where A provides specified financial services to B without A's having the requisite authorisation, then the contract is unenforceable against (not by) B,[677] who is also entitled to the return of money paid or property transferred by him under it, and to compensation for loss suffered by him as a result of having parted with the money or property.[678] However, if A (no less than B) is innocent of the illegality, then the court may exceptionally allow the contract to be enforced and money or property transferred under it to be retained.[679] Similarly, under the Gambling Act 2005, it is an offence for the holder of an operating licence to permit a child or young person to gamble[680] and any contract will not be enforced in the sense that the licence holder may not give a prize to the child or young person.[681] Any money paid by the latter must, however, be repaid.[682]

Test of the purpose of the statute, or the relevant rule of the common law. Where the statute does not expressly or by implication specify the effects of the illegality on contracts, those effects are, it is submitted, to be determined by reference to the purpose of the statute. This approach is suggested by Devlin L.J. in *Archbolds (Freightage) Ltd v S Spanglett Ltd*, where he said: **11–122**

"I think that the purpose of this statute is sufficiently served by the penalties prescribed for the offender; the avoidance of the contract would cause grave inconvenience and injury to members of the public *without furthering the object of the statute.*"[683]

Although Devlin L.J. refers only to statutory illegality, it is submitted that the same approach would be appropriate where the illegality was due to a rule of common law[684]: the court has to consider how it would further the object of the relevant rule of law to invalidate the contract. Where the rule exists for the protection of a class of persons, its object will obviously not be promoted by rejecting a claim to enforce the contract made by an innocent member of that class.[685] In other cases, it is more difficult to strike a balance between the interests

---

[676] From this point of view, the result in *Stewart v Oriental Fire & Marine Ins Co Ltd* [1985] 1 Q.B. 988 (giving the innocent party a remedy on the contract against the guilty party) was preferable to the reasoning of the authorities cited in fn.675, above; cf. Clarke [1987] L.M.C.L.Q. 201; *DR Ins Co Ltd v Central National Ins Co* [1996] 1 Lloyd's Rep. 74.

[677] Financial Services and Markets Act 2000, ss.26(1), 27(1).

[678] ibid., ss.26(2), 27(2); if B elects not to perform or claims restitution he must in turn restore benefits received by him under the contract: s.28(7).

[679] ibid., s.28(3)–(6).

[680] Gambling Act 2005, s.46.

[681] ibid., s.83(1)(b).

[682] See below, para.11–131.

[683] [1961] 1 Q.B. 374 at 390 (italics added).

[684] cf. *Cope v Rowlands* (1836) 2 M. & W. 149 at 157 ("expressly forbidden by the common law or statute law"), cited in *Hughes v Asset Managers Plc* [1995] 3 All E.R. 669 at 674.

[685] See *Nash v Halifax Building Society* [1979] Ch. 584, so far as it relates to the enforcement of the security; cf. *Hughes v Asset Management Plc* [1995] 3 All E.R. 669 at 674, 675. The contract cannot of course be enforced *against* a member of the protected class: *Johnson v Moreton* [1980] A.C. 37.

of the public (which the invalidating rule is meant to protect) and those of the innocent party. Of course specific performance of a promise to do an act that is unlawful or against public policy will not be ordered. The questions are whether, if the guilty party has failed to perform such a promise, the innocent party should be entitled to damages; and whether, if the latter party has innocently done such an act, he should be entitled to enforce the guilty party's counter-promise (typically, one to pay the agreed sum[686]). In what way does it ever "further the object" of the invalidating rule to deny the innocent party such a remedy?

One possible answer to this question is that the denial of a remedy may induce the innocent party to take greater care not to enter into an illegal transaction. Another is that a remedy should be refused whenever the contract is executory, since the availability of such a remedy might induce the other (guilty) party to perform. But where these arguments are sound, the innocent party should have no remedy at all, or at least no remedy as good as the action on the contract. In fact the innocent party who cannot enforce the contract may have other remedies, and one of these seems to be no worse than an action on the contract. There are three such remedies.

11–123   **Collateral warranty.** First, the innocent party may be able to recover damages for breach of "collateral warranty". In *Strongman (1945) Ltd v Sincock*[687] the defendant employed a firm of builders to modernise his house. He promised to get the necessary licences (without which it was illegal to do the work), but he got licences for only part of the work and refused to pay for the rest on the ground that the contract to do it was illegal. The builders could not enforce the contract although they had acted in good faith. But they recovered damages (amounting to the value of the unlicensed work) for breach of the defendant's collateral under-taking to get the necessary licences. This is a useful device for doing justice to the innocent party, and in *Strongman (1945) Ltd v Sincock* little harm was done to the public interest. For in that case the defendant was an architect so that the builders were not careless[688] in failing to ask to see the licence. And the work had been completed, so that it would have been futile to deny a remedy on the ground that to grant it might induce the performance of an illegal act. But to allow the innocent party to sue on a "collateral warranty" in a case like *Re Mahmoud and Ispahani*[689] would be quite inconsistent with the rationale of the rule denying him a remedy on the contract. It would be mere sophistry to say: we will protect the public interest by denying a remedy on the contract, but we will also protect the innocent claimant by giving him as good a remedy on a collateral warranty. This remedy should be granted only where it will provide no incentive to do the illegal act and where the innocent party was not careless. But if these conditions are satisfied there seems to be no reason why the innocent party should not be able to enforce on the contract itself. Alternatively, the innocent party could be given a restitutionary claim for the reasonable value of his services. This follows a fortiori from the suggestion (to be discussed later in this chapter[690]) that such a remedy may sometimes be available even to the guilty party.

---

[686] It is assumed that the making of the payment is not prohibited.
[687] [1955] 2 Q.B. 525.
[688] ibid. at 536.
[689] [1921] 2 K.B. 716; above, para.11–119.
[690] See below, para.11–151.

Misrepresentation. Secondly, the innocent party may be able to recover   **11–124**
damages in tort for misrepresentation. In *Shelley v Paddock*[691] the claimant was by
the fraud of the defendant induced to enter into a contract to buy a house in Spain
and to make payments under it which were illegal as they violated exchange
control regulations. Since the claimant's breach of the law was innocent and
resulted from the defendant's fraud, she was entitled to damages for that fraud.
Even where the misrepresentation was *not* fraudulent, a person who had, as a
result of it, innocently entered into an illegal contract might similarly be entitled
to damages, either for negligence at common law[692] or under the Misrepresentation Act 1967; and he might also be able to rescind the contract. But these
remedies could be less advantageous than an action on the contract as they would
not give the innocent party damages for loss of his bargain.[693]

Restitution. Thirdly, innocence may be material in an action for the recovery   **11–125**
of money paid or property transferred under an illegal contract.[694] The object of
the invalidating rule is less likely to be defeated by this remedy than by an award
of damages for breach of contract since it amounts rather to an undoing[695] than to
an enforcement[696] of the contract. The remedy may, however, be less advantageous
than any of those so far discussed, for under it the claimant can only get back what
he gave: he cannot recover in respect of other losses incurred in reliance on the
contract, or for loss of his bargain.

(iii) *De facto enforcement*

Remedy for enforced performance. A contract which is illegal may be   **11–126**
enforced de facto in the sense that one party may secure compliance with its terms
by using or threatening to use some form of economic pressure. Such measures
may be taken in good faith, and the question then arises whether the party who is
thus induced to perform a contract that was not binding on him has any remedy
in respect of loss suffered in consequence. In *Shell UK Ltd v Lostock Garages
Ltd*[697] a garage proprietor was in effect compelled to observe the terms of a solus
agreement by the oil company's threats that, if other suppliers were to sell petrol
to him, it would sue them for inducing a breach of the solus agreement. Lord
Denning M.R. held that the solus agreement was unenforceable and that the
garage proprietor was entitled to damages in respect of the loss he had suffered

---

[691] [1980] Q.B. 348; cf. *Burrows v Rhodes* [1899] 1 Q.B. 816 and *Saunders v Edwards* [1987] 1 W.L.R.
1116 (above, para.11–113), where even a "guilty" party recovered damages for a fraud unconnected
with the illegality.

[692] *Mohammed v Alaga & Co* [2000] 1 W.L.R. 1815 at 1826.

[693] cf. above, para.9–059. In *Shelley v Paddock*, above, the damages did not include any element of
compensation for loss of the claimant's bargain: see [1979] Q.B. 120. In *Mohamed v Alaga & Co* [2000]
1 W.L.R. 1815 at 1826 Lord Bingham C.J. said that he could not "conceive that the (claimant) could
be regarded as recovering anything under this head [i.e. in tort] as damages which he would be
debarred from recovering under the contract".

[694] cf. below, para.11–134.

[695] This was the outcome of *Bloxsome v Williams* (1824) 3 B. & C. 232 (above, para.11–118) where
the buyer's claim was for "damages" but the amount that he recovered was the price paid by him.

[696] This was the nature of the claim unsuccessfully made by the seller in *Re Mahmoud and Ispahani*
[1921] 2 K.B. 716 (above, para.11–119); if he had actually delivered the oil to the buyer he could no
doubt have recovered it back: below, para.11–134.

[697] [1977] 1 W.L.R. 1187.

through being nevertheless compelled to observe it.[698] Ormrod L.J. held that no such damages were available,[699] while Bridge L.J. awarded them on the different ground that the oil company was in breach of an implied term of its contract with the garage proprietor.[700] Lord Denning held that no such term could be implied,[701] so that the damages awarded by him cannot have been for breach of contract. His award seems rather to have been based on the novel principle, that the de facto enforcement of an illegal contract can, if it causes loss, give rise to a claim for damages.

11–127   **Prevention of de facto enforcement.** The above discussion is based on the assumption that performance of the illegal contract has actually been secured. Before this has happened, the court may be able to intervene to prevent such performance: e.g. by an injunction to restrain a party from drawing on a letter of credit issued to secure payment under an illegal contract. Since the effect of such a remedy is to prevent illegality, it may be granted even to the guilty party.[702]

(b) Restitution

11–128   A person who cannot enforce an illegal contract may instead claim restitution in respect of money paid, property transferred or services rendered by him under the contract.

(i) *General rule*

11–129   The general rule is that money paid or property transferred under an illegal contract cannot be recovered back.[703] At one time the rule could be justified by saying that the courts should not give any help to a willing party to an illegal transaction; and by the argument that, by leaving one party at the mercy of the other, the rule had a deterrent effect. The first of these arguments is no longer wholly convincing now that a person may in all innocence make a contract that is technically illegal; and the second overlooks the possibility that sometimes illegality may be more effectively discouraged by allowing than by denying recovery. If, for example, a person receives money in the course of conducting an illegal business, the illegality is more likely to be deterred by making him pay the money back, than by allowing him to rely on the rule of non-recovery.[704] It would be better if the law did not adopt a "general rule" but asked in relation to each type of illegality whether it was recovery or non-recovery that was the more likely to promote the purpose of the invalidating rule.

---

[698] [1977] 1 W.L.R. 1187 at 1200; cf. under Art.101 TFEU, *Courage Ltd v Crehan* [2002] Q.B. 507 (European Court of Justice); *Crehan v Inntrepreneur Pub Co CPC* [2004] EWCA Civ 637; [2004] C.L.C. 803 (CA) (reversed on other grounds [2006] UKHL 38; [2006] 3 W.L.R. 148).

[699] ibid. at 1200–1201.

[700] ibid. at 1204.

[701] See above, para.6–034; Ormrod L.J. agreed with Lord Denning on this point.

[702] *Group Josi Re v Walbrook Ins Co Ltd* [1996] 1 W.L.R. 1152 at 1164, where the actual decision was that the performance of the contracts was saved from illegality by legislation of the kind described at para.11–121, above after fn.676, so that no injunction was available.

[703] e.g. *Scott v Brown* [1892] 2 Q.B. 724; *Edler v Auerbach* [1950] 1 K.B. 359; cf. *Shaw v Shaw* [1965] 1 W.L.R. 537. See generally Grodecki 71 L.Q.R. 254; Higgins 25 M.L.R. 598; Rose in (Rose ed.) *Consensus ad Idem, Essays in the Law of Contract in Honour of Guenter Treitel*, p.202.

[704] cf. *Hermann v Charlesworth* [1905] 2 K.B. 123.

Scope of the general rule. The general rule was not settled without a good   **11–130**
deal of hesitation; and in particular equity at one time inclined to the opposite
view.[705] It is subject to many exceptions and it is to those exceptions that we must
now turn. In paras 11–131—11–150 we consider the exceptional cases in which
the recovery of money or property is possible, before considering, in para.11–151,
restitution in respect of services.

(ii) *Class-protecting statutes*

Recovery by member of the protected class. If a contract is made illegal by   **11–131**
a statute passed for the protection of a class of persons, a member of that class can
recover back money paid or property transferred by him under the contract.[706]
Some statutes expressly provide that a member of a protected class shall be
entitled to recover back money paid or property transferred under an illegal
contract.[707] For example, the Rent Act 1977 contains various provisions entitling
a tenant to recover back money which he could not lawfully have been required to
pay.[708] The Financial Services and Markets Act 2000 similarly provides that,
where A provides specified financial services to B without A's having the required
authorisation, B is prima facie entitled to the return of money paid or property
transferred by him under the contract[709]; he is so entitled even though he also has
the option of enforcing the contract.[710]

There was at one time some support for the view that the prevalence of such
statutory provisions had made the old class-protecting rules obsolete.[711] But this
view was rejected in *Kiriri Cotton Ltd v Dewani*,[712] where a landlord had, by
accepting an illegal premium from his tenant, committed an offence under a Rent
Restriction Ordinance which did not expressly say that such premiums could be
recovered back. The Privy Council held that the tenant could recover back the
premium under the old rules relating to class-protecting statutes. Similarly,
premiums paid under an illegal insurance policy of the kind described above could
be recovered back by the innocent policy-holder at common law,[713] even before

---

[705] *Morris v McCullock* (1763) Amb. 432; *Neville v Wilkinson* (1782) 1 Bro.C.C. 547 at 548; *Hermann v Charlesworth* [1905] 2 K.B. 123. The same view was sometimes taken at common law; e.g. *Munt v Stokes* (1792) 4 T.R. 561.

[706] *Browning v Morris* (1778) 2 Cowp. 790; *Barclay v Pearson* [1893] 2 Ch. 154; *Bonnard v Dott* [1906] 1 Ch. 740 (unlicensed moneylender); *One Life Ltd v Roy* [1996] 2 B.C.L.C. 608 (unlawful lottery); *Kasumu v Baba-Egbe* [1956] A.C. 539; cf. *Barclay v Prospect Mortgages* [1974] 1 W.L.R. 837. Under Consumer Credit Act 1974, s.40(1) (as amended by Consumer Credit Act 2006, s.26(1)), a regulated agreement with an unlicensed moneylender is not illegal but only unenforceable against the debtor unless the Office of Fair Trading orders otherwise.

[707] In addition to the examples given in the text, see Gambling Act 2005, ss.58, 83 under which a licence holder must return any money paid by a child or young person (even, it seems, where the young person is himself guilty of an offence by gambling: s.48).

[708] e.g. ss.57, 95, 125.

[709] Financial Services Markets Act 2000, ss.26(2), 27(2); above, para.11–121; and see Financial Services Markets Act 2000 for the courts power under s.28(3)–(6) to deny B's claim for restitution.

[710] Under ss.26(1) and 27(1) of the 2000 Act, the contract is only "unenforceable *against*" (not by) B.

[711] *Green v Portsmouth Stadium* [1953] 2 K.B. 190, esp. at 195.

[712] [1960] A.C. 192; cf. *Nash v Halifax BS* [1979] Ch. 584, so far as it relates to the money lent; and see above, para.11–122.

[713] *Re Cavalier Ins Co Ltd* [1989] 2 Lloyd's Rep. 430 at 450 (and see above, para.11–020).

such a right of recovery was expressly conferred on him by legislation of the kind described in the preceding paragraph.[714]

(iii) *Oppression*

11–132   **Meaning of oppression.** A person can recover back money paid or property transferred under an illegal contract if he was forced by the other party to enter into that contract. "Oppression" is here used in a somewhat broad sense. In *Atkinson v Denby*[715] an insolvent debtor offered to pay his creditors a dividend of 5s. in the £. All the creditors were willing to accept the dividend in full settlement of their claims, except the defendant, who said he would accept it only if the debtor first paid him £50. The debtor did so, but was later allowed to recover back the £50 on the ground that he had been forced to agree to defraud the other creditors. To say that the debtor was oppressed may not be very convincing; but it was a convenient way of avoiding the general rule of non-recovery where that rule would have led to the undesirable result of enabling one creditor to keep more than his fair share of the insolvent debtor's assets.

11–133   **Oppression due to extraneous circumstances.** The "oppression" may be due, not to the conduct of the other party, but to extraneous circumstances, and such "oppression" has been recognised as a ground of recovery where the contract is made illegal by a statute passed for the protection of a class. Thus in *Kiriri Cotton Co Ltd v Dewani* Lord Denning said that the tenant was not "so much to blame" for evading the Rent Restriction Ordinance as the landlord, who was "using his property rights so as to exploit those in need of a roof over their heads".[716] In an American case oppression not caused by the defendant was recognised as a ground of recovery where a person had paid a bribe to escape from the danger of being imprisoned and put to death by the Nazis.[717] Less extreme forms of pressure have in England not been regarded as a ground for recovery. In *Bigos v Bousted*[718] a father made an illegal contract to acquire foreign currency in order to send his daughter to Italy as a cure for her recurrent attacks of pleurisy. This "pressure" did not entitle him to recover back property transferred under the contract.

(iv) *Misrepresentation*

11–134   A person can recover back money paid or property transferred under an illegal contract if he entered into the contract as a result of the other party's fraudulent misrepresentation that the contract was lawful. Thus in *Hughes v Liverpool Victoria Legal Friendly Society*[719] the claimant effected a policy of insurance with the defendants on a life in which he had no insurable interest. The contract was illegal,[720] but the claimant was able to recover back the premiums he had paid as

---

[714] See above, at fn.709.
[715] (1862) 7 H. & N. 934; cf. *Smith v Cuff* (1817) 6 M. & S. 160; *Davies v London & Provincial Marine Ins Co* (1878) 8 Ch.D. 469.
[716] [1960] A.C. 190 at 205.
[717] *Liebman v Rosenthal* 57 N.Y.S. 2d 875 (1945).
[718] [1951] 1 All E.R. 92.
[719] [1916] 2 K.B. 482; cf. *Reynell v Sprye* (1852) 1 D.M. & G. 660.
[720] Life Assurance Act 1774, s.1.

he had been induced to make the contract by the fraudulent representation of the defendants' agent that the policy was valid. The decisive factor in such cases is the fraud of the defendant, and not the innocence of the claimant. The claimant would have failed if the representation that the policy was valid had been innocently made.[721] Similarly, where a tenant was induced by the landlord's misrepresentation to enter into an illegal lease, it was held that he could not recover back a payment of rent without alleging and proving fraud.[722]

Basis of recovery. The cases on this subject suggest that, where recovery is allowed, the basis for it is the invalidity of the contract on the ground of illegality, and not misrepresentation as such. It follows that the right of recovery is not necessarily limited by the bars to rescission for misrepresentation.[723] If no such bar has arisen, it seems that a person who has been induced by even an *innocent* misrepresentation[724] to enter into an illegal contract can rescind it for misrepresentation and so recover back his money or property.[725] The bars to rescission for misrepresentation will also be relevant where the misrepresentation relates to matters other than those which are the source of the illegality: e.g. where a contract for the sale of property is induced by the vendor's misrepresentations as to his title, and the contract is also illegal by reason of its including an immoral business.[726]

11–135

(v) *Mistake*

A party who enters into a contract under a mistake of fact as to its legality can sometimes enforce the contract.[727] In such a situation he should be equally entitled to recover back money paid or property transferred under the contract; for it is inconceivable that this remedy will defeat the object of the invalidating rule where enforcement of the contract is allowed because it will not have this effect. Mistake[728] can also be a ground for recovery of money or property even where it does not give the mistaken party the right to enforce the contract.[729] In *Oom v Bruce*[730] the claimant, as agent for the Russian owner of goods in Russia, took out a policy of insurance on the goods with the defendant. Neither party knew (or could have known) that Russia had declared war on this country before the contract was made. It was held that the claimant could get back his premium as he was not guilty of any fault or blame in entering into the illegal contract. Here

11–136

---

[721] *Harse v Pearl Life Assurance Co* [1904] 1 K.B. 558. *Semble*, that in such a case the object of the invalidating rule would have been better served by allowing recovery: cf. above, para.11–129.

[722] *Edler v Auerbach* [1950] 1 K.B. 359.

[723] See above, para.9–097 et seq.

[724] In *Harse v Pearl Life Assurance Co*, above, the misrepresentation was one of law, and (for the reasons given at para.9–013, above) it seems that such a representation now gives rise to a right to rescind for misrepresentation and so to recover back premiums.

[725] This was assumed in *Edler v Auerbach* [1950] 1 K.B. 359, but in that case the right to rescind for innocent misrepresentation was barred by execution of the lease. This would no longer be a bar: above, para.9–095.

[726] *The Siben* [1996] 1 Lloyd's Rep. 35 at 62; above, para.9–103. The purchaser was not left entirely without remedy since his claim for damages succeeded on the ground stated at fn.642 above.

[727] See above, para.11–117.

[728] For mistake of law, see *Harse v Pearl Life Assurance Co*, and above, fn.724.

[729] e.g. on facts such as those of *Re Mahmoud and Ispahani* [1921] 2 K.B. 716; above, fn.670.

[730] (1810) 12 East 225; cf. *Edler v Auerbach* [1950] 1 K.B. 359 at 374–375, where mistake of the payor alone was said to be insufficient; sed quaere.

again no useful purpose would be served by applying the general rule of non-recovery.

(vi) *Repudiation of illegal purpose*[731]

11–137   A person may be able to reclaim money paid or property transferred under an illegal contract if he repudiates the illegal purpose in time.[732] By giving a party this right, the law tries to encourage him to give up the illegal purpose. Two conditions must be satisfied to bring the rule into operation.

11–138   **Repudiation in time.** A party who repudiates before anything has been done to perform the illegal purpose can recover back his money or property, while one who repudiates after the illegal purpose has been fully carried out cannot recover.[733] The difficult cases are those in which the repudiation takes place after steps have been taken towards the performance of the illegal purpose, but before it has been fully carried out.

One such case was *Taylor v Bowers*,[734] where a debtor was being pressed by his creditors. To prevent certain machinery from falling into their hands, he transferred it to one Alcock. He then called two meetings of creditors in an attempt to reach a settlement with them, but none was reached. The debtor successfully claimed the machinery back from the defendant, who was one of the creditors and had obtained the machinery from Alcock with notice of the fraudulent scheme and in the hope of benefiting from it. The decision is based on the fact that the illegal purpose had not been carried out: no creditor had been defrauded. A similar result was reached in *Tribe v Tribe*[735] where a father transferred shares in a company to his son in order to "safeguard his interests"[736] against claims for dilapidations by the lessors of shops of which the father was tenant and in which the company carried on business. The issue of dilapidations was later resolved without the father's having shown the share transfer to the lessors or to any other creditor. It was held that the father was entitled to the return of the shares since the illegal purpose had "not been carried into effect in any way".[737]

In the contrasting case of *Kearley v Thomson*[738] the friend of a bankrupt paid £40 to the defendants in return for their undertaking not to appear at the bankrupt's public examination and not to oppose his discharge. The defendants duly absented themselves from the public examination, but before any application had been made for the bankrupt's discharge the payor claimed back the £40. His claim failed. Fry L.J. said, first, that the rule permitting recovery on repudiation of the illegal transaction did not exist before *Taylor v Bowers* and he doubted the correctness of that decision. But the principle was at least twice stated in earlier

---

[731] Beatson 91 L.Q.R. 313; Merkin 97 L.Q.R. 420.

[732] *Harry Parker Ltd v Mason* [1940] 2 K.B. 590 at 608.

[733] *Palaniappa Chettiar v Arunasalam Chettiar* [1962] A.C. 294.

[734] (1876) 1 Q.B.D. 291: now a case of "frustration"? cf. below, at fn.746; *Symes v Hughes* (1870) L.R. 9 Eq. 475.

[735] [1996] Ch. 107.

[736] ibid. at 113.

[737] ibid. at 121. For further problems which arose in this case because the relationship of transferor and transferee was that of father and son, see below, para.11–147.

[738] (1890) 24 Q.B.D. 742.

cases[739] and has since been accepted as good law.[740] Secondly, he said that *Taylor v Bowers* was distinguishable from *Kearley v Thomson*, since in the latter case there had been "a partial carrying into effect of an illegal purpose in a substantial manner".[741] This distinction looks at first sight tenuous, but it must be remembered that it is not the *transaction* but "the [illegal] *purpose* which has to be carried into effect"[742] to preclude recovery, and that the illegal purposes in the two cases were quite different. The illegal purpose in *Taylor v Bowers* was to defraud creditors, and no creditor was defrauded; this was also true in *Tribe v Tribe*. The illegal purpose in *Kearley v Thomson* was to interfere with the course of public justice,[743] and some such interference took place when the defendants stayed away from the bankrupt's public examination. Thus it seems that the repudiation is in time if it takes place after mere preparation to achieve the illegal purpose, but that it is too late if it takes place after performance of the illegal purpose has actually begun.[744]

There is also the more practical point that in *Taylor v Bowers* the success of the debtor's claim promoted the equal distribution of his property among his creditors; for if the claim had failed, one of the creditors (the defendant) would have benefited at the expense of the others.[745] In *Kearley v Thomson*, on the other hand, the creditors would not have benefited at all if the claim for repayment had succeeded; for the £40 would then have gone back to the payor, and not to the bankrupt's estate.

Voluntariness. Repudiation must be voluntary: it must not be forced on the party claiming recovery by the intervention of the police, or of a third person, or by the other party's breach of the contract.[746] This requirement follows from the justification for the present exception to the general rule of non-recovery, which is its tendency to encourage a party to give up the illegal purpose.

11–139

(vii) *No reliance on illegal transaction*

A person may be entitled to recover money or property which has been transferred under an illegal contract,[747] if he can establish his right or title to it without relying *on the contract* or *on its illegality*.[748] It follows that there are two situations in which the claim may succeed: those in which the claimant does not rely on the illegal contract at all, but claims the property simply because he was

11–140

---

[739] *Hastelow v Jackson* (1828) 8 B. & C. 221 at 226; *Bone v Eckless* (1860) 5 H. & N. 925 at 928.

[740] See *Hermann v Charlesworth* [1905] 2 K.B. 123; *Bigos v Bousted* [1951] 1 All E.R. 92. In *Tribe v Tribe* [1996] Ch. 107 at 125 Millett L.J. doubted part of the *reasoning*, but not the *result*, in *Taylor v Bowers*.

[741] (1890) 24 Q.B.D. at 747.

[742] See *Tribe v Tribe* [1996] Ch. 107 at 122, italics supplied.

[743] cf. above, para.11–046.

[744] cf. in criminal law, the test for whether a defendant has embarked upon an attempt: Herring, *Criminal Law* (6th edn), para.18.4.4.

[745] cf. above, para.11–132.

[746] As in *Bigos v Bousted* [1951] 1 All E.R. 92.

[747] The collateral rights with which the following principles are concerned normally refer to proprietary rights and do not include a right of action on the contract itself: *Mahonia Ltd v JP Morgan Chase Bank* [2003] EWHC 1927; [2003] 2 Lloyd's Rep. 911 at [27].

[748] For the application of a similar principle to a claim for damages for deceit, see *Standard Chartered Bank v Pakistan National Shipping Co (No.2)* [2000] 1 Lloyd's Rep. 218 at 232 (reversed on another point [2002] UKHL 43; [2003] 1 A.C. 959).

already owner of it before that contract was made; and those in which he does rely on the contract (since it was by virtue of that contract that he acquired title) but does not have to rely on the illegality to establish his claim for the recovery of the property.[749] Some judicial statements of the rule refer to both these possibilities[750]; while others refer only to one[751] but should not, it is submitted, be read as excluding the other.

11–141   **Recovering back goods transferred under an illegal contract.** Where goods are sold under an illegal contract, the property in them can pass (in accordance with the usual rules as to passing of property) notwithstanding the illegality[752]; and it may do so even though the goods have not been delivered to the buyer.[753] If the property has passed and the goods have been delivered to the buyer, the seller will not be entitled to their return—a point of special importance where the sale is on credit and the price has not been paid. Similarly, if property has passed to the buyer and the goods have been delivered to a third party, the seller cannot get them back from the third party, having no longer any title on which he can rely. The extent to which the *buyer* can rely on the passing of property in goods which have not been delivered to him is discussed below.[754]

If a thing is pledged, hired or lent under an illegal contract, a "special property" (or right to retain possession) passes when possession is transferred. So long as that special property endures, the subject-matter cannot be recovered back by the transferor. Thus in *Taylor v Chester*[755] half of a £50 Bank of England note was pledged as security for the expenses of a debauch in a brothel. The effect of the pledge was to transfer a special property in the note to the pledgee, with the result that the pledgor could not recover back the note without tendering the amount due. It seems that the effect of such tender would have been to put an end to the pledgee's special property and to entitle the pledgor to recover back the note on the strength of his title; but before the tender the pledgee would be entitled to take the usual steps to enforce his security against the pledged property.[756] The same principles would apply where a thing is hired under an illegal contract: the owner cannot recover it back while the hirer's special property lasts, but he can do so after that special property has come to an end, e.g. because the period of hire has run out.

In *Bowmakers Ltd v Barnet Instruments Ltd*[757] machine tools had been let out under hire-purchase agreements which were illegal[758] as they contravened war

---

[749] *Tinsley v Milligan* [1994] 1 A.C. 340 at 370 ("does not need to rely on the illegal contract for any purpose other than providing the basis of his claim to a property right"); Enonchong 111 L.Q.R. 135.

[750] e.g. the statement in *Bowmakers Ltd v Barnet Instruments Ltd* [1945] K.B. 65 at 71; quoted below, at fn.759.

[751] e.g. *Tinsley v Milligan*, above, at 366 ("provided he does not require to found on the unlawful agreement"); *Tinsley v Milligan*, above, at 369 ("provided that the [claimant] can establish such title without pleading or leading evidence of the illegality").

[752] *Scarfe v Morgan* (1838) 4 M. & W. 270 at 281; *Elder v Kelly* [1919] 2 K.B. 179; *Singh v Ali* [1960] A.C. 167.

[753] *Belvoir Finance Co Ltd v Stapleton* [1971] 1 Q.B. 210; cf. *Kingsley v Sterling Industrial Securities Ltd* [1967] 2 Q.B. 747 at 738; below, para.11–150.

[754] See below, para.11–150.

[755] (1869) L.R. 4 Q.B. 309; the same principle would apply to a pledge of *goods*.

[756] *Norwich Union Life Ins Co Ltd v Qureshi* [1999] 2 All E.R. (Comm) 707 at 709, where no offence had in fact been committed by the pledgee.

[757] [1945] K.B. 65; Hamson 10 C.L.J. 249; Coote 35 M.L.R. 38; Stewart 1 J.C.L. 134.

[758] The owners had acquired the goods from one Smith under a contract which was also illegal; for this aspect of the case, see below, fn.801.

time maximum price and licensing regulations. The hirers failed to pay the instalments due under the agreements, sold some of the goods and kept the rest. The owners successfully claimed damages for the conversion of all the goods. They did not have to "found [their] claim on the illegal contract or . . . plead its illegality in order to support [their] claim",[759] but relied simply on their title. As the period of hire had not run out, it is at first sight hard to see why the hirers could not resist the owners' claim by relying on their special property under the hire-purchase agreements. The reason why they could not do so seems to be that a hirer's right to possession may come to an end otherwise than by lapse of time. First, it can come to an end as a result of a repudiatory breach on the part of the hirer.[760] Since a hirer is guilty of such a breach if he sells the thing hired, the defendants' special property in the goods which they had *sold* had therefore come to an end.[761] But this does not explain why their special property in the goods which they *simply kept* had come to an end. Failure to pay instalments is a breach of contract, but it is not normally of itself a repudiatory one. A possible solution of the difficulty is that a hirer's special property may come to an end as a result of *any* breach *because the contract expressly so provides*; i.e. because it provides that, on failure by the hirer to pay instalments, the agreement should ipso facto determine and that the owner should be entitled to take back the goods. If the agreements in *Bowmakers'* case contained some such clause,[762] the hirers' right to possess the goods ceased as soon as they defaulted in paying instalments. The case can be reconciled with *Taylor v Chester* by assuming that the agreements did contain such a clause.

Whether recovery consistent with the purpose of the rule of law concerned. The preceding discussion of *Taylor v Chester* and *Bowmakers Ltd v Barnett Instruments Ltd* attempts to analyse these cases in the light of the rules governing the transfer of property (general or special) in the subject-matter of illegal contracts. This approach is, however, open to the objection that it ignores the crucial question: whether to allow the owner to recover his property would tend to promote or to defeat the purpose of the rule of law which makes the contract illegal.[763] In *Taylor v Chester* that purpose was presumably to discourage the keeping of brothels; and the decision can perhaps be explained on the ground that it created a stalemate position: the pledge being of *half* a bank note, neither pledgor nor pledgee could enforce any rights under the note until its two halves were reunited. On the other hand, it can be argued that, by giving the pledgor an incentive to redeem his pledge, the decision made it more, rather than less, likely that the brothel-keeper would be paid, and so tended to defeat the purpose of the invalidating rule. In *Bowmakers'* case the purpose of the regulations was presumably to prevent profiteering and to regulate the allocation of scarce resources in time of war; and it is unlikely that these purposes were defeated by upholding

11–142

---

[759] At 71.

[760] *N Central Wagon & Finance Co v Graham* [1950] 2 K.B. 7. Election by the owners to terminate on account of the breach seems to be assumed (cf. below, para.18–005 et seq).

[761] cf. *Belvoir Finance Co v Harold G Cole Co* [1969] 1 W.L.R. 1877 (where the hirer had sold the entire subject-matter); *Union Transport Finance Ltd v British Car Auctions Ltd* [1978] 2 All E.R. 385.

[762] The terms of the agreements are not set out in any of the reports of the case, but such provisions were certainly common.

[763] Treitel in *Essays in Memory of Sir Rupert Cross* (Tapper, ed.), pp.99–104.

the owners' claims, particularly in view of the fact that "their error was involuntary".[764] The position would have been different if the owners had been guilty of a deliberate violation of a regulation made for the purpose of protecting hirers. It is submitted that, if this had been the position, the rule in *Bowmakers'* case should not have been applied; for if it were applied one of the owners' most important remedies for non-payment (that of retaking the goods) would be available irrespective of the legality of the agreement. In the example just given, such a result would defeat, rather than promote, the policy of the invalidating rule.

Where goods are let out under a regulated agreement,[765] the owner cannot retake them unless he first serves a default notice; and in certain cases he must in addition obtain a court order.[766] Such steps seem to amount to a reliance on the agreement and thus not to be available if the agreement is illegal.

11–143   **Recovering back money paid under an illegal contract.** A person who pays money under an illegal contract cannot generally recover it back by relying on his title, since the effect of the payment is almost always to transfer the entire property in the notes or coins to the payee. Money can be recovered back under the present rule only in the rare cases in which it is not paid out-and-out, but is paid as a deposit. Thus a person who deposits money with a stakeholder under an illegal wager can recover it back, so long as the stakeholder has not paid it over, in accordance with his instructions, to the other party to the wager.[767]

11–144   **Illegal leases.** An illegal lease generally vests a term of years in the tenant.[768] Thus if the tenant has gone into possession the landlord cannot rely on his title so as to turn the tenant out during the currency of the lease[769]; but he can do so once the lease has expired. The further question arises whether the landlord could recover possession if the tenant failed to pay rent. If this were possible the rule that a tenant under an illegal lease is not liable for rent[770] would be of small practical importance, for such a tenant, like any other, could be turned out for non-payment of rent. It might be argued that the tenant's right to possession comes to an end if he fails to pay rent, just as the hirers' right to possession in *Bowmakers'* case came to an end when they failed to pay instalments. But the analogy between illegal leases and *Bowmakers'* case is imperfect if the explanation of that case was that the hirers' right to possession determined ipso facto on the hirers' breach of contract.[771] For a lease cannot determine ipso facto on the tenant's breach as the

---

[764] *Bowmakers'* case [1945] K.B. 65 at 68. The owners themselves had not attempted to make "excess" profits out of the transactions, having been brought in only to provide finance after the hirers had decided to acquire the goods from their former owners.

[765] See above, para.5–007.

[766] Consumer Credit Act 1974, ss.87, 90.

[767] cf. *O'Sullivan v Thomas* [1895] 1 Q.B. 698; *Close v Wilson* [2011] EWCA Civ 5 at [31].

[768] The general rule does not apply if on the true construction of the relevant legislation no interest is intended to pass to a person who takes a lease in contravention of it, e.g. where occupation of the land is meant to be restricted to a particular class: *Amar Singh v Kulubya* [1964] A.C. 142; Hamson [1964] C.L.J. 20; Cornish 27 M.L.R. 225. No legal interest vests in a person occupying land under an agreement amounting, not to a lease, but to a licence: *Parks v Esso Petroleum Co Ltd* [1999] 1 C.M.L.R. 455, affirmed [2000] Eu. L.R. 25, where it was held that there was no illegality.

[769] *Feret v Hill* (1854) 15 C.B. 207; *semble* that this case would now be differently decided on the ground of fraud; and see *Grace Rymer Investments Ltd v Waite* [1958] Ch. 831.

[770] See above, para.11–111.

[771] See above, at fn.762.

law does not recognise such a thing as a lease for an uncertain period.[772] It is possible to have a lease "for five years, subject to forfeiture if the tenant fails to pay rent", but not "for five years, or for so long as the tenant pays rent, whichever is the shorter period". If the tenant fails to pay rent the landlord's right to possession does not automatically revive. He can only attempt to enforce the forfeiture clause. Such an attempt will fail, as it is an attempt to enforce a term of an illegal contract. Hence a landlord cannot recover possession of premises let under an illegal lease simply because the tenant fails to pay rent. A tenancy may also be terminable by notice, quite irrespective of default. If it is determined in this way, it seems that the landlord can recover possession on the strength of his title when the period of notice has expired.[773]

Equitable title. In the cases so far discussed, the claimant succeeded where he **11–145** was able to establish legal title to the property in question without relying on the illegality. There was formerly some authority for the view that the position was different where the claimant relied on an equitable, rather than a legal title, and that in such cases the claim would be rejected once it appeared, or was admitted, that the equitable title had been acquired under an illegal transaction.[774] But this view was rejected by a majority of the House of Lords in *Tinsley v Milligan*, where Lord Browne-Wilkinson said that, as a result of later developments in the law relating to illegal contracts, the former equitable principle had "become elided into the common law rule".[775] The dispute in that case arose out of an agreement between the claimant and the defendant relating to a house in which they lived as lovers and which they jointly ran as a lodging house. The house had been purchased with money provided by both parties; and, although the parties accepted that the house was to be owned by them jointly, it was conveyed into the sole name of the claimant. This was done to enable the defendant to make false claims for social security benefits on the footing that she did not own her home; and such claims were in fact made. The parties later quarrelled and it was held that the defendant was entitled to an order for the sale of the house and to a declaration that it was owned by the parties in equal shares. The defendant was entitled in equity to a half share in the house by virtue of the presumption which normally arises in equity where one party transfers property to another, or provides money for the acquisition of property by another, that the property is held by the latter party (to the appropriate extent) on a resulting trust for the former party. It was this presumption of resulting trust which gave rise to the defendant's equitable title.[776] To establish that title, she had no need to impeach the transaction by relying on its illegality. It was, on the contrary, the claimant who sought to impeach the transaction by relying on its illegality in order to deprive it of its normal effect of giving the defendant an equitable title. The defendant's

---

[772] *Lace v Chandler* [1944] K.B. 368; but see Validation of Wartime Leases Act 1944 (now repealed); *Prudential Assurance Co Ltd v London Residuary Body* [1992] 2 A.C. 386, where Lord Browne-Wilkinson said at 396 that there was no "satisfactory rationale" for the rule.

[773] The contrary assumption seems to have been made in *Amar Singh v Kulubya* [1964] A.C. 142, but was not necessary for the decision.

[774] See *Curtis v Perry* (1802) 2 Ves. 739 at 744 and other authorities on the point discussed in *Tinsley v Milligan* [1994] 1 A.C. 340.

[775] [1994] 1 A.C. 340 at 376; Buckley 110 L.Q.R. 3; Thornton [1993] C.L.J. 394; Stowe 56 M.L.R. 441.

[776] cf. *Silverwood v Silverwood* (1997) 74 P. & C.R. 9; *Mortgage Express v McDonnell* [2001] EWCA Civ 887; [2001] 2 All E.R. (Comm) 886 (equitable title acquired under earlier fraudulent transaction).

position was in substance the same as that of the buyer of goods under an illegal contract: she had acquired her equitable title, just as such a buyer can acquire a legal title,[777] in spite of the illegality. It was, moreover, undesirable for the present purpose to treat equitable title differently from legal title, since to do so would lead to some entirely capricious distinctions: e.g. to the conclusion that the cases on illegal leases[778] would have been differently decided if the contracts had been agreements for leases (which give rise only to an equitable interest[779]) as opposed to executed leases (which give rise to a legal term of years[780]).

11–146   **Whether presumption is of resulting trust, or gift.** The crucial factor in *Tinsley v Milligan* was that the defendant was able to rely on the normal presumption that property bought in part with her money was to that extent, or to the extent agreed upon by the parties, held in trust for her. That presumption could, of course, have been rebutted by proof that the defendant had intended to make a gift; and if the claimant had proved this, then the defendant's claim to a share in the property would have failed for it would then have been the defendant who would have relied on the illegality to defeat the gift.[781] In the case of certain relationships between the parties to the transaction, such an intention to make a gift is, moreover, presumed, thus reversing the normal presumption of resulting trust. This is, for example, the position where a father transfers property (or pays for property to be transferred) to his child: in such cases there is said to be a "presumption of advancement",[782] or, in other words, a presumption that the transfer was intended as a gift to the child. It follows that, if the transfer in such a case is alleged to have been made for an illegal purpose, then the general rule will be that the father will not be able to claim the property by relying on his title; and that he will not be able to do so by impeaching the transfer by reference to the illegal purpose, for this would require him to rely on the illegality. This was the position in *Chettiar v Chettiar*,[783] where a father transferred land to his son by an instrument recording a payment by the son which was not in fact made. The object of the transfer was to deceive the public authorities into thinking that the father held less land than he did, and so to enable the father to evade certain legislative restrictions on the production of rubber. The Privy Council dismissed the father's claim that the son was trustee of the land for him; for in order to rebut the presumption of advancement the father would have had to disclose and to rely on his illegal purpose.

11–147   **Reliance on other exceptions.** The result in *Chettiar v Chettiar*[784] amounted to an application of the general rule that property transferred under an illegal contract cannot be recovered back by the transferor.[785] But we have seen that this rule is subject to a number of *other* exceptions[786] than the one here under discussion (i.e. the one under which the claimant does not need to rely on the

---

[777] See above, para.11–140.
[778] e.g. *Feret v Hill* (1854) 15 C.B. 207; above, para.11–144.
[779] *Walsh v Lonsdale* (1882) 21 Ch.D. 9; above, para.5–005.
[780] See the discussion of *Feret v Hill*, above, in *Tinsley v Milligan* [1994] 1 A.C. 340 at 370.
[781] *Tribe v Tribe* [1996] Ch. 107 at 128–129.
[782] A discussion of the relationships giving rise to the presumption of advancement is beyond the scope of this book. For such a discussion, see *Snell's Equity* (31st edn) paras 9–11 to 9–14.
[783] [1962] A.C. 294.
[784] See above.
[785] See above, para.11–129.
[786] See above, paras 11–131—11–139.

illegal transaction); and where one of those other exceptions applied, a claim for the recovery of property was upheld even though the property was transferred in circumstances giving rise to the presumption of advancement. This was the position in *Tribe v Tribe*,[787] the facts of which have been stated earlier in this chapter.[788] The shares in that case were transferred from father to son, so that there was a presumption of advancement; but a claim for their return was made before the illegal purpose for which they had been transferred had been "carried into effect in any way".[789] Hence the case fell within the exception to the general rule of non-recovery which applies where the illegal purpose is repudiated[790]; and it was held that the father could invoke this exception so as to recover the shares even though the process of rebutting the presumption of advancement involved his relying on the illegality of the transaction to show that it was not intended to be by way of gift. It is submitted that the same result should have followed if that father had been able to invoke one of the other exceptions, considered earlier in this chapter, to the general rule of non-recovery: i.e. if the transfer had been procured by oppression or by misrepresentation or made under a mistake,[791] or if the father had been a member of a protected class.[792]

Whether recovery consistent with the purpose of the rule of law concerned. It was suggested above that the analysis of cases involving the transfer of property in goods under illegal contracts was open to the objection that it could lead to results which failed to promote (and might defeat) the purpose of the prohibition giving rise to the illegality[793]; and the same danger arises in the present group of cases. Suppose, for example, that the transfer in *Chettiar v Chettiar* had not been from father to son, but from son to father to enable the son to evade the legislative restrictions. There would then have been no presumption of advancement but, on the contrary, a presumption of resulting trust; and it would seem to follow from the reasoning of *Tinsley v Milligan* that the son could have recovered the land on the strength of his equitable title. Such a conclusion would scarcely have promoted the purpose of the rule of law which was infringed in that case. Reasoning which is based on proprietary concepts no doubt has the advantage of predictability; its disadvantage in the present context is that it pays insufficient regard to the policy considerations with which the courts are normally concerned in working out the effects of illegality on contracts. *Tribe v Tribe*[794] is, with respect, to be welcomed in allowing a policy-based exception to the general rule of non-recovery to prevail over the more abstract application of purely proprietary reasoning.[795]

11–148

Special cases. There may be special cases in which a person cannot recover back money or property although his right or title to it can be established without reference to the contract or its illegality. It has been suggested that if the property is such that it is unlawful to deal with it at all (e.g. an obscene book) it cannot be

11–149

---

[787] [1996] Ch. 107.
[788] See above, para.11–138.
[789] [1996] Ch. 107 at 121.
[790] See above, para.11–137.
[791] See above, paras 11–134—11–136.
[792] See above, para.11–131—a perhaps unlikely but not impossible situation.
[793] See above, para.11–122.
[794] [1996] Ch. 107; above, para.11–147.
[795] cf. in Australia, *Nelson v Nelson* (1995) 132 A.L.R. 132.

recovered back.[796] There is also some support for the view that the price paid for such a book cannot be recovered back by the buyer,[797] though this is scarcely the best way of discouraging the trade in such things. A further suggestion is that there is no right of recovery if the object of the contract is to enable one party to commit a serious crime,[798] e.g. if a dagger is lent to commit murder. On the other hand, a person who undertakes the safe-keeping of a burglar's house-breaking tools is apparently bound to give them up to the burglar on demand.[799]

11–150   **Remedies available for the protection of money or property obtained under an illegal contract.** The mere fact that something has been obtained under an illegal contract does not deprive the recipient of the usual remedies for its recovery or protection. Thus if goods are sold and delivered under an illegal contract, and the property in them has passed to the buyer, he can recover them or their value if they are later taken away from him by the seller.[800] Such remedies are also available against third parties,[801] and even (subject to statutory exceptions) against the police.[802] They may, moreover, be available to a buyer who has acquired the property in goods under an illegal sale, even though the goods have never been in his possession. In *Belvoir Finance Co Ltd v Stapleton*,[803] Belgravia wanted to acquire cars from Francis, finance being provided by Belvoir. In relation to each car, two contracts were made: a sale by Francis to Belvoir and a letting on hire-purchase by Belvoir to Belgravia. All these contracts were illegal. Belvoir never acquired possession of the cars, which were delivered by Francis straight to Belgravia. It was held that Belgravia's assistant manager was liable to Belvoir for conversion of the cars, since the property in them had passed to Belvoir as soon as the contracts of sale between them and Francis were "executed".[804] The decision is, however, concerned only with the relative rights of the buyer and a third person. *The seller* had no further interest in the cars and was not in possession of them. The case therefore does not support the proposition that a buyer to whom property in goods has passed under an illegal contract can claim them, or damages for their conversion, *from a seller who has never delivered them at all*. Such a claim would not differ in substance from a claim for the delivery, or for damages for the non-delivery, of the goods under the illegal contract. Its success

---

[796] *Bowmakers Ltd v Barnet Instruments Ltd* [1945] K.B. 65 at 72; *Costello v Chief Constable of Derbyshire Constabulary* [2001] EWCA Civ 381; [2001] 1 W.L.R. 1437 at [33]. *Aliter* if the book is seditious? See *Elias v Pasmore* [1934] 2 K.B. 164 at 174.

[797] *The Siben* [1996] 1 Lloyd's Rep. 35, 62; above, para.9–103.

[798] Williams 8 C.L.J. 62, fn.54. *After* conviction of the offender, an order to deprive him of "his rights, if any, in the property" may be made by the court under Powers of Criminal Courts (Sentencing) Act 2000, s.143.

[799] *R. v Lomas* (1913) 110 L.T. 239, as explained in *R. v Bullock* [1955] 1 W.L.R. 1.

[800] *Singh v Ali* [1960] A.C. 167.

[801] See the discussion of *Bowmakers Ltd v Barnet Instruments Ltd* [1945] K.B. 65 in *Tinsley v Milligan* [1994] 1 A.C. 340 at 369: the owners succeeded in spite of the illegality not only of the hire-purchase agreements, but also of the contracts under which they had acquired the goods from their former owner. Contrast *Halley v Law Society* [2003] EWCA Civ 97 (no claim in equity to funds held by trustee where the funds had been obtained fraudulently).

[802] *Gordon v Chief Commr of Metropolitan Police* [1910] 2 K.B. 1080; *Porter v Chief Constable of Merseyside Police* [2000] Q.B. 427. Many statutes confer powers on the courts to make forfeiture, confiscation or similar orders; a complete discussion or even list of such provisions is beyond the scope of this book. Recent examples include Powers of Criminal Courts (Sentencing) Act 2000, s.143 and Anti-terrorism, Crime and Security Act 2001, s.1 and Sch.1; Proceeds of Crime Act 2002, Pt 2; Serious Organised Crime and Police Act 2005, Pt 2, Ch.6.

[803] [1971] 1 Q.B. 210; cf. *Kingsley v Sterling Industrial Securities Ltd* [1967] 2 Q.B. 747 at 783.

[804] ibid. at 220.

would thus defeat the object of the rule against the enforcement of such a contract.

The right to recover money or property obtained under an illegal contract has been extended, sometimes with surprising results, to make an agent employed in an illegal transaction liable to account for its proceeds to his principal. Thus in *Tenant v Elliott*[805] a broker who effected an illegal insurance and later received the policy moneys was held accountable for them to his principal. The same principle was applied in *Bone v Eckless*,[806] where the captain of a ship was instructed to sell it to the Turkish Government, and told the owner that this could be done only if he paid bribes of £500 to Turkish officials. The owner agreed that the bribes should be paid, and the ship was duly sold for £6,500, of which the captain kept £500 to pay the bribes. He paid away only £300 in bribes, and it was held that the owner could recover the remaining £200 from the captain because he "makes out his title to recover £6,500 by proving the sale of his ship for that sum, and it is the [captain] who is relying on the illegal agreement to justify the non-payment of the money".

In these cases the illegality was in the transaction which the agent was employed to effect. The principle would probably not apply where the agency itself was illegal[807] and more recent authority casts some doubt on its validity in suggesting that a claimant could not recover damages from a third party for conversion of property obtained by fraud where the property was "the very proceeds of the fraudulent conduct".[808] Protection will not be denied to property rights merely because their acquisition involves the innocent commission of a civil wrong. For example, the copyright in a musical work may be protected even though its creation involved the innocent infringement of copyright in a previous work.[809]

(viii) *Restitution in respect of services*

Work done under an illegal contract may (no less than money paid or property transferred) give rise to a restitutionary claim, that is, to one for a reasonable remuneration on a quantum meruit basis. This possibility is illustrated by a case[810] in which the claimant had done work under a contract signed by him on behalf of a company. The contract was void because the company no longer existed[811]; and by trading in the name of a company which no longer existed the claimant had also committed an offence under s.34 of the Companies Act 1985.[812] It was held that his claim was "maintainable on a quantum meruit though not under a supposed contract".[813] One possible reason for this result is that the policy of s.34 was not contravened by allowing such a claim.[814] Another is that (as in the cases allowing recovery of property) the claimant did "not need to rely on any illegality to found

11–151

---

[805] (1791) 1 B. & P. 3. cf. *Farmer v Russell* (1798) 1 B. & P. 296 (approved in *Sykes v Beadon* (1879) 11 Ch.D. 170); cf. *Bousfield v Wilson* (1846) 16 L.J.Ex. 44; *Pye v BG Transport Service* [1966] 2 Lloyd's Rep. 300; *Close v Wilson* [2011] EWCA Civ 5; contrast *Griffith v Young* (1810) 12 East 513 at 514.

[806] (1860) 5 H. & N. 925.

[807] See *Booth v Hodgson* (1795) 6 T.R 405; *Harry Parker Ltd v Mason* [1940] 2 K.B. 590.

[808] *Thackwell v Barclays Bank Plc* [1986] 1 All E.R. 676 at 689.

[809] *ZYX Music GmbH v King* [1995] 3 All E.R. 1.

[810] *Cotronic (UK) Ltd v Dezonie (t/a Wendaland Builders Ltd)* [1991] B.C.L.C. 721.

[811] See below, para.16–072.

[812] Now repealed by Companies Act 2006, s.1295, Sch.16.

[813] [1991] B.C.L.C. 721 at 726.

[814] This is suggested by the reference, ibid., to *Shaw v Groom* [1970] 2 Q.B. 504; above, para.11–003.

a claim in that form".[815] The reason why he had no such need was that the contract was void for some *other* reason than the illegality, i.e. on account of the non-existence of the company. Where the *only* ground of invalidity is illegality, a guilty party who had done work under the contract should not, it is submitted, have a quantum meruit claim merely because of that invalidity. To allow such a claim merely on the ground that the contract was invalid for illegality would, at least in most cases[816] be inconsistent with the policy of the invalidating rule.[817] It follows that a solicitor who cannot enforce a conditional fee agreement, because it is illegal under the rules stated earlier in this chapter,[818] is also precluded from recovering the reasonable value of services rendered under it on a quantum meruit basis.[819] The same is not, however, necessarily true of a quantum meruit claim made against a guilty party by a party who is innocent of the illegality (in the sense of being unaware of the rule of law making the contract illegal) in respect of services not affected by the illegality. In one case of this kind, the claimant agreed to introduce clients to solicitors who, in return, promised to pay him a share of the fees paid by those clients; he did not know that such an arrangement was prohibited[820] and that the fee-sharing contract was therefore illegal. It was held that he could neither enforce that contract nor bring a quantum meruit claim in respect of the work of introducing clients[821]; but that such a claim was available in respect of other services rendered by him in acting as interpreter between the clients in question and the solicitors.[822]

(c) Severance[823]

11–152   Where a contract is illegal only in part, two problems can arise. The first is the problem of severance of consideration: can a promise be enforced if it is lawful in itself but is in part supported by illegal consideration? The second is the problem of severance of promises: can a promise be enforced if it is lawful in itself but is coupled with an illegal promise?

(i) *Severance of consideration*

11–153   **Where illegal consideration is substantial.** A promise cannot be enforced if the whole or substantially the whole[824] of the consideration for it is illegal. In

---

[815] [1991] B.C.L.C. 721 at 726, relying on the analogy of *Bowmakers'* case [1945] K.B. 65; above, para.11–141; *AL Barnes Ltd v Time Talk (UK) Ltd* [2003] EWCA Civ 402; [2003] B.L.R. 331 at [14].

[816] e.g. in cases such as *Ashmore Benson Pease & Co Ltd v AV Dawson Ltd* [1973] 1 W.L.R. 828; above, para.11–114; and cf. the situation discussed below, at fn.838.

[817] cf. *Taylor v Bhail* (1995) 50 Con. L.R. 70. Contrast *AL Barnes Ltd v Time Talk (UK) Ltd* [2003] EWCA Civ 402; [2003] B.L.R. 331 (where the claim was for a contractual quantum meruit and *Taylor* was distinguished as applying to contracts illegal on their face or intended by the parties to be illegally performed).

[818] See above, para.11–013.

[819] *Awwad v Geraghty & Co* [2001] Q.B. 570 at 596.

[820] By the Solicitors' Practice Rules, which have the force of law: *Swain v Law Society* [1983] A.C. 598 at 608.

[821] *Mohamed v Alaga & Co* [2000] 1 W.L.R. 1815 at 1824–1825.

[822] ibid. at 1825–1827 as explained in *Awwad v Geraghty & Co*, above, fn.819.

[823] Marsh 64 L.Q.R. 230 at 347.

[824] *Marshall v NM Financial Management Ltd* [1997] 1 W.L.R. 1527 at 1532.

Lound v Grimwade[825] A, who had committed a fraud making him civilly and criminally liable, promised to pay B £3,000 in return for B's promise not to take "any legal proceedings" in respect of the fraud. B's claim for the £3,000 failed as a substantial part of the consideration for A's promise to pay it was B's own illegal promise to stifle a criminal prosecution.[826]

Where illegal consideration is subsidiary. On the other hand, a promise can   **11–154**
be enforced if the main consideration for it is lawful, although it is also supported by a subsidiary illegal consideration.[827] For example, an employee who enters into too wide a contract in restraint of trade can recover his wages.[828] The main consideration for the employer's promise to pay is the employee's promise to serve, or the performance of it; his promise not to compete is only subsidiary. The position is similar where an employee as a term of his contract of service enters into a pension scheme which contains an invalid stipulation in restraint of trade. That stipulation forms only a subsidiary part of the consideration which the employee provides for the various promises made by the employer under the contract as a whole; and if the stipulation is invalid it can be severed, so that the pension will be payable although the stipulation is not complied with.[829] But if the sole consideration for the promise to pay the pension is an invalid stipulation in restraint of trade the employee cannot recover the pension. This was the position in *Wyatt v Kreglinger & Fernau*[830] where the promise was made on the lawful termination of the contract of service and the employee provided no consideration for the promise except his assent to, or performance of, the invalid stipulation in restraint of trade.

Sale of business. Similar principles apply where the vendor of a business   **11–155**
enters into too wide a contract in restraint of trade. If the price is promised mainly for the business premises and stock-in-trade, the illegal promise not to compete is only a subsidiary part of the consideration for the promise to pay, so that the vendor can recover the price. But if the purpose of the transaction, viewed objectively,[831] was the elimination of a competitor, rather than the purchase of a business, it might be held that the vendor's promise not to compete formed a substantial part of the consideration for the purchaser's promise to pay; and that accordingly the vendor would not be entitled to the price.

Primacy of fulfilling the policy of the invalidating rule. The distinction   **11–156**
so far drawn may, however, be displaced by the policy of the invalidating rule. In

---

[825] (1888) 39 Ch.D. 605; cf. *Walrond v Walrond* (1858) Johns. 18.

[826] See above, para.11–046. For rejection on similar grounds of a claim to rescind a contract, see *The Siben* [1996] 1 Lloyd's Rep. 35 at 62.

[827] See *Goodinson v Goodinson* [1954] 2 Q.B. 118 (the actual decision is obsolete: Matrimonial Causes Act 1973, s.34; above, para.11–048); cf. *Kearney v Whitehaven Colliery Co* [1893] 1 Q.B. 700; *Fielding & Platt Ltd v Najjar* [1969] 1 W.L.R. 357 at 362.

[828] *McFarlane v Daniell* (1938) S.R.(N.S.W.) 337, approved in *Carney v Herbert* [1985] A.C. 301 at 311; cf. *Sadler v Imperial Life Assurance Co of Canada* [1988] I.R.L.R. 388 and *Marshall v NM Financial Management Ltd* [1997] 1 W.L.R. 1527 (similar principle applied to agent's claim for commission).

[829] *Bull v Pitney-Bowes Ltd* [1967] 1 W.L.R. 273; *semble* the stipulation was not a mere condition but formed part of the consideration for the employer's promise since it was entered into at the employer's request: see above, para.3–010.

[830] [1933] 1 K.B. 793; above, para.11–080.

[831] *Triggs v Staines Urban DC* [1969] 1 Ch. 10; above, para.11–080.

Ailion v Spiekermann[832] the vendor of a leasehold interest required the purchasers to pay an illegal premium. He thereby committed a statutory offence, but the purchasers (who were "unwilling victims"[833]) committed none by promising to pay the premium. It was held that they could specifically enforce the vendor's obligations without having to pay the premium. They were able to do this, whether or not their promise to pay the premium constituted a substantial part of the consideration; for such enforcement by them was the most effective way of promoting the legislative policy against illegal premiums.

11–157   **Apportionment of promise to legal part of consideration.** In the cases so far discussed, the claimant has either failed or succeeded in full. The claimant in *Lound v Grimwade*[834] got nothing, though part of the consideration provided by him was lawful; while an employee who enters into too wide a restraint of trade can recover his entire wages, though the employer loses one of the advantages for which he bargained. It might be thought fairer to make the defendant liable in proportion to the legal part of the consideration. The objection to such a rule is that it would often be hard to apply as the court cannot easily tell what value the parties attributed to the legal and illegal parts of the consideration respectively. But it seems that where the legal and illegal parts can be precisely valued, the claimant can recover so much of the promised payment as can be attributed to the lawful part of the consideration. In *Frank W Clifford Ltd v Garth*[835] a builder agreed to do building work for the defendant on a "cost plus" basis, so that the total cost of the work could not be known in advance. The bill for the completed work came to £1,911. The defendant refused to pay anything because work costing more than £1,000 was illegal unless licensed, and no licence had been obtained. But he was held liable to pay £1,000: his promise to pay was enforced to the extent to which it was supported by lawful consideration. A person who has done work under a contract which is only partly illegal may also be awarded a reasonable sum in respect of the lawful part of the work.[836] Such an award is based on restitutionary principles and does not strictly speaking amount to partial enforcement *of the contract*, but in practical terms the outcome will often quite closely resemble such enforcement.

11–158   **Special cases.** It has been said that the doctrine of severance does not apply where part of the consideration is criminal or immoral,[837] e.g. where it is a promise to commit robbery or adultery, or the performance of such a promise. But the fact that part of the consideration is criminal prevents severance only if the party who provides it is guilty of a deliberate violation of the law. Thus in *Frank W Clifford Ltd v Garth* the builder recovered £1,000 in spite of the fact that he had committed an offence by doing unlicensed work worth more than £1,000. He would, however, have recovered nothing if he had agreed to do the work without a licence, knowing from the start that it would cost over £1,000.[838]

---

[832] [1979] Ch. 158.
[833] ibid. at 165.
[834] (1888) 39 Ch.D. 605.
[835] [1956] 1 W.L.R. 570; cf. *Ex p. Mather* (1797) 3 Ves. 373; *J Dennis & Co v Munn* [1949] 2 K.B. 327; *Blue Chip Trading v Helbawi* [2009] I.R.L.R. 128; and see *The American Accord* [1983] 1 A.C. 168.
[836] *Mohamed v Alaga & Co* [1999] 3 All E.R. 699 at 707, 710; above, para.11–151.
[837] *Bennett v Bennett* [1952] 1 K.B. 249 at 254.
[838] *Frank W Clifford v Garth* [1956] 1 W.L.R. at 572; cf. above, para.11–114.

(ii) *Severance of promises*

Where the promises of one party to a contract are partly lawful and partly illegal, the court may cut out the illegal promises and enforce the lawful ones alone. It will do this only if three conditions are satisfied: the promise must be of such a kind as can be severed;[839] it must not be necessary to redraft the contract;[840] and severance must not alter the whole nature of the covenant.[841]

11–159

The promise must be of such a kind as can be severed. It has been said that there can be no severance of a criminal or immoral promise.[842] But although this may be generally true, it seems that a criminal promise could be severed if it was made without guilty intent.[843] It has also been said that there can be no severance of a promise to trade with the enemy[844] or of a promise to defraud the Revenue.[845] Promises are most frequently severed in contracts in restraint of trade; and it has been assumed that promises excluding the jurisdiction of the courts can be severed.[846] The question whether other illegal promises can be severed at all is still an open one.

11–160

The "blue pencil" test. Under this test, the court will sever only where this can be done by cutting words out of the contract (or by running a blue pencil through the offending words). The court will not redraft the contract by adding or rearranging words, or by substituting one word for another.[847] Thus in *Mason v Provident Clothing & Supply Co Ltd*[848] the House of Lords refused to strike out of the contract the words "within 25 miles of London" and to substitute "in Islington"; to do so would be, not to sever, but to redraft the contract. The test does little to protect the party subject to the restraint since it can easily be satisfied by skilful draftsmanship, while on the other hand it may entirely prevent enforcement of a restraint drawn up by laymen where some degree of enforcement would be reasonable.[849] Where this is the case, the courts will apply the test with some latitude. In *T Lucas & Co Ltd v Mitchell*[850] a contract provided that a sales representative should not within a certain *area* "deal in any goods similar to" those allocated to him for sale; or "*solicit orders* for . . . any *such* goods". It was held that

11–161

---

[839] See below, para.11–160.

[840] See below, para.11–161.

[841] See below, para.11–162.

[842] *Bennett v Bennett* [1951] 1 K.B. 249 at 254.

[843] As in the case of severance of consideration: above, at fnn.837, 838.

[844] *Kuenigl v Donnersmarck* [1955] 1 Q.B. 515; cf. *Royal Boskalis Westminster NV v Mountain* [1999] Q.B. 674 at 693.

[845] *Miller v Karlinski* (1945) 62 T.L.R. 85; *Corby v Morrison* [1980] I.C.R. 564; the contrary was assumed in *Napier v National Business Agency* [1951] 2 All E.R. 265 but it was held that the contract was not severable as there was only one promise in substance; cf. *Lincoln v CB Richard Ellis Hotels Ltd* [2009] EWHC 2344 (TCC). In the case of long-term employment, the contract is wholly invalid during the period in respect of which the illegal payments are made, but not in respect of the rest of its duration; *Hyland v J H Barber (North-West) Ltd* [1985] I.C.R. 861.

[846] *Re Davstone Estate Ltd's Leases* [1969] 2 Ch. 378; but severance failed because the "blue pencil" test (below) was not satisfied; *Home Ins Co v Administratia Asigurarilor* [1983] 2 Lloyd's Rep. 674 at 677.

[847] And will not give effect to an express provision calling for the same: *Townends Group Ltd v Cobb* [2004] EWHC 3432 (Ch); *The Times*, December 1, 2004 at [60]. Contrast the court's statutory power to revise contracts: in the cases described at para.11–165, below.

[848] [1913] A.C. 724 (above, para.11–075).

[849] See *Commercial Plastics Ltd v Vincent* [1965] 1 Q.B. 623 at 647.

[850] [1974] Ch. 129.

the area covenant was invalid while the solicitation covenant was valid; and that the area covenant could be severed. Strictly speaking, this left no point of reference for the word "such" in the solicitation covenant, but the deleted area covenant could be looked at to give the word meaning.

It used to be thought that promises could be severed merely because the "blue pencil" test was satisfied[851]; but this view no longer prevails. The test may restrict, but it does not determine, the scope of the doctrine of severance. Even if the legal and illegal promises are actually contained in separate documents,[852] the court will sever only if the third requirement is also satisfied.

11–162   **Severance must not alter the nature of the covenant.** The court will not sever if to do so alters the whole nature of the covenant.[853] In *Goldsoll v Goldman*[854] the seller of an imitation jewellery business in New Bond Street undertook that he would not for two years deal in real or imitation jewellery in the UK or certain named places abroad. The covenant was too wide in *area* as the seller had not traded abroad, and in respect of *subject-matter* as he had scarcely dealt in real jewellery. But it was held that the references to the foreign places and to real jewellery could be severed, and that the restraint on dealing in imitation jewellery in the UK could be enforced. The only question discussed by the court was whether the "blue pencil" test was satisfied; but it can be argued that the object of the original covenant was to protect the business which the buyer had bought; that the object of the covenant after severance remained the same; and that severance had thus not altered the nature of the original covenant.

In the contrasting case of *Attwood v Lamont*[855] the claimants had a general outfitters' business at Kidderminster. It was divided into several departments, each of which was supervised by one of their employees. The head of each department undertook that he would not after leaving the claimants' service "be concerned in any of the following trades or businesses: that is to say, the trade or business of a tailor, dressmaker, general draper, milliner, hatter, haberdasher, gentlemen's, ladies' or children's outfitter" within 10 miles of Kidderminster. In an action to enforce this covenant against the head of the tailoring department, the claimants admitted that the covenant was too wide in point of subject-matter, but they argued that everything except the reference to tailoring should be severed, and that part alone enforced. This argument was rejected as severance would have altered the whole nature of the covenant. After severance, the covenant would protect only that part of the business in which the defendant had worked, whereas the original covenant was "part of a scheme by which every head of a department was to be restrained from competition with the (claimants), even in the business of departments with which he had no connection".[856] The valid and invalid covenants were thus interdependent and, where this is the relationship between them, the court will not sever the invalid ones.[857]

---

[851] *Putsman v Taylor* [1927] 1 K.B. 637 at 640; the Court of Appeal held the covenant valid *in toto*, so that severance was not necessary: [1927] 1 K.B. 741.

[852] As in *Kenyon v Darwen Cotton Manufacturing Co Ltd* [1936] 2 K.B. 193.

[853] *Putsman v Taylor* [1927] 1 K.B. 637 at 646; cf. *Spector v Ageda* [1973] Ch. 30 at 45; *Royal Boskalis Westminster NV v Mountain* [1999] Q.B. 674 at 693. This requirement does not apply to an agreement partly invalid under the rules of competition law stated at paras 11–105—11–108, above: *Barrett v Inntrepreneur Pub Co (GL) Ltd* [1999] E.G.C.S. 93.

[854] [1915] 1 Ch. 292.

[855] [1920] 3 K.B. 571.

[856] ibid. at 579–580.

[857] *Scully UK Ltd v Lee* [1998] I.R.L.R. 259; *James E McCabe Ltd v Scottish Courage Ltd* [2006] EWHC 538 (Comm).

It was at one time thought that *Goldsoll v Goldman* and *Attwood v Lamont* could be reconciled simply on the ground that the covenant in the first case was between vendor and purchaser while that in the second was between employer and employee.[858] This view was supported by a dictum in *Mason v Provident Clothing & Supply Co Ltd* that in employment cases the courts should only sever where the excess was trivial,[859] and by the view expressed in *Attwood v Lamont* that in such cases the courts should be reluctant to sever at all.[860] But if the court is satisfied that there are, as a matter of construction, separate covenants, and that one of them can be removed without altering the nature of the covenant, it can sever a restraint in an employment contract,[861] and it may do so even though the excess was not merely trivial.[862] On the other hand, the court will not sever a covenant between vendor and purchaser merely because the "blue pencil" test is satisfied. Even between such parties, severance will not be allowed where its effect would be to alter the nature of the covenant.[863]

Alleged necessity for separate consideration. It is sometimes said that a promise can be severed only if it is supported by separate consideration.[864] But this view is inconsistent with the cases just considered. In *Goldsoll v Goldman*, for instance, no separate consideration was provided for the valid and the invalid parts of the covenant. Yet the invalid parts were severed.   11–163

Whether other promises affected. In the restraint of trade cases discussed above, the covenant not to compete has formed part of a larger transaction; and the effect of holding that excessive parts of the restraint could not be severed was simply that *that covenant* was wholly void. *Other* promises or obligations of the covenantor under the contract as a whole may nevertheless be enforceable. For example, an employee who has entered into a wholly void covenant in restraint of trade may still be restrained from breaking his duty of fidelity.[865] And a person to whom money has been lent on terms which include an invalid covenant in restraint of trade is nevertheless liable to repay the loan and to pay interest.[866] In such cases, it can be said that the main purpose of the contract is to create the relationship of employer and employee or of lender and borrower; and the fact that the contract seeks to impose an invalid restraint on the employee or borrower does not vitiate the entire relationship.   11–164

---

[858] *Ronbar Enterprises Ltd v Green* [1954] 1 W.L.R. 814 at 820.

[859] [1913] A.C. 724 at 745.

[860] [1920] 3 K.B. 571 at 593–596. Contrast the attitude of the court in *Commercial Plastics Ltd v Vincent* [1965] 1 Q.B. 623 at 647 (above, para.11–161) and in *The Littlewoods Organisation Ltd v Harris* [1977] 1 W.L.R. 1472 (where no question of severance arose).

[861] *T Lucas & Co Ltd v Mitchell* [1974] Ch. 129; *Stenhouse Australia Ltd v Phillips* [1975] A.C. 391; *Business Seating (Renovations) Ltd v Broad* [1989] I.C.R. 729 at 734–735; *Dawnay Day & Co Ltd v D'Alphen* [1997] I.R.L.R. 285 at 296, 422. cf. *Commercial Plastics Ltd v Vincent* [1965] 1 Q.B. 623 at 647; *Anscombe & Ringland v Butchoff* (1984) 134 New L.J. 37.

[862] *Putsman v Taylor* [1927] 1 K.B. 637; *Scorer v Seymour-Johns* [1966] 1 W.L.R. 1419; and see fn.861, above.

[863] *British Reinforced Concrete Engineering Co Ltd v Schelff* [1921] 2 Ch. 563, a vendor and purchaser case in which *Attwood v Lamont* [1920] 3 K.B. 571 was followed on this point.

[864] e.g. in *Putsman v Taylor*, above, fn.862, at 640; *Kuenigl v Donnersmarck* [1955] 1 Q.B. 515 at 538.

[865] See above, para.6–041; *Commercial Plastics Ltd v Vincent* [1965] 1 Q.B. 623; *Royal Boskalis Westminster NV v Mountain* [1999] Q.B. 674 at 693.

[866] cf. *Cleveland Petroleum Co v Trinity Garage (Bexleyheath)*, *The Times*, September 8, 1965.

On the other hand, where the main purpose of the contract is to impose the restraint, the invalidity of that restraint can lead to the nullity of the whole contract. In such cases, the issue is not whether one part of the restraint can be severed from another without altering the nature *of the covenant* in restraint of trade; it is, rather, whether the invalidity of the restraint has left *the contract as a whole* without subject-matter. Two cases which raise the latter question may be contrasted. Both were concerned with solus petrol agreements; in each case the garage proprietor had leased his garage to the oil company which had then leased it back by granting an underlease to the garage proprietor, the solus agreement being contained in the underlease.[867] In the *Amoco*[868] case, the underlease was at a nominal rent for a period just one day shorter than the original lease: in these circumstances it was held that the solus agreement "constituted the heart and soul of the underlease".[869] As the solus agreement was invalid, it followed that neither the underlease nor the original lease (which was part of the same arrangement) could remain in force. On the other hand, in the *Alec Lobb*[870] case the original lease was for a period of 51 years; the oil company had paid a premium of £35,000 (the fair market value) for it; the underlease was for only 21 years and yielded a rent of £2,250 per annum. The solus agreement was held valid[871]; but it was said that, even if it had been invalid, the lease and underlease would have remained in force since the transaction as a whole would not, merely because of the invalidity of that one term, have "so changed its character as not to be the sort of contract that the parties intended to enter into at all".[872] The contract would have remained one "for letting a petrol station . . . at a rent which was not nominal. It was therefore the sort of contract which the parties intended to enter into".[873]

The principle just stated is not restricted to cases in which the source of illegality is restraint of trade. In *Carney v Herbert*[874] a contract was made for the sale of shares by instalments; the sellers asked for security for the payment of these instalments, and the form of security agreed on and given was illegal. It was held that the contract as a whole was not vitiated, so that the buyer remained liable for the price since the illegal security "did not go to the heart of the transaction".[875] The sellers had only wanted *some* security and the invalidity of the particular security given did not change the essential character of the contract as one for the sale of the shares.

(iii) *Statutory severance*

11–165   Acts of Parliament which make specific terms in certain contracts unlawful sometimes contain provisions which give rise to a kind of statutory severance.

---

[867] See above, para.11–093.
[868] *Amoco Australia Pty v Rocca Bros Motor Engineering Pty Ltd* [1975] A.C. 561.
[869] ibid. at 578.
[870] *Alec Lobb (Garages) Ltd v Total Oil (Great Britain) Ltd* [1985] 1 W.L.R. 173; cf. the *Amoco* case, above, at 579.
[871] See above, para.11–097.
[872] [1985] 1 W.L.R. 173 at 192, applying the test stated by Buckley L.J. in *Chemidus Wavin Ltd v Soc. pour la Transformation et l'Exploitation des Resines Industrielles* [1978] 3 C.M.L.R. 514 at 520.
[873] ibid. An alternative ground for the decision in the *Alec Lobb* case is suggested by the statement there made at 181 that "The tie provisions . . . were not *either* the sole consideration for the tie *or* the sole object of the transaction" (italics supplied). While the second alternative here stated is (with respect) plainly correct, the first is hard to follow: it seems to suggest that the tie could in part be consideration for itself.
[874] [1985] A.C. 301; cf. below, para.11–166.
[875] ibid. at 316.

Under the Equality Act 2010, for example, the court may make orders for offending terms to be "removed or modified".[876] Similarly the inclusion of certain terms in a contract may be an offence[877]; but a contract for the supply of goods or services is not to be void or unenforceable "by reason only" of the commission of the offence.[878]

(d) Collateral Transactions

Collateral transactions may be infected with the illegality of a principal contract if they help a person to perform an illegal contract, or if they would, if valid, make possible the indirect enforcement of an illegal contract.[879] Thus a loan of money is illegal if it is made to enable the borrower to make or to perform an illegal contract,[880] or to make an illegal payment,[881] or to pay a debt contracted under an illegal contract.[882] Similarly, a policy of insurance on an illegal venture is illegal[883]; a bond, bill of exchange or pledge given to secure an illegal debt is illegal[884]; a bank is not liable on a letter of credit[885] to the extent that[886] the underlying contract of sale is prohibited by statute;[887] and an attempted civil law bribe prevents enforcement of the contract via which the bribe was attempted.[888] But if it is the collateral transaction which is illegal, it does not follow that this illegality infects the otherwise lawful principal contract. Thus where an illegal security was in good faith taken to secure the performance of a legal agreement that agreement was not thereby invalidated.[889] By contrast, under the Gambling Act 2005, it is an offence to provide credit in breach of any conditions attached to an operating licence,[890] or a premises licence[891] and it is arguable that the illegality of the loan would also taint the gambling transaction itself given the closeness of the connection between them.

A contract is not necessarily illegal merely because one of the parties to it is also a party to an illegal contract which is remotely connected with the first. Thus a policy of marine insurance on a voyage is not illegal merely because the master has

11–166

---

[876] Equality Act 2010, s.143.

[877] See above, para.7–126.

[878] Consumer Protection from Unfair Trading Regulations (SI 2008/1277), reg.29.

[879] But not simply where the legal contract happens to coincide with the illegal: *Sutton v Hutchinson* [2005] EWCA Civ 1773 (true loan repayable despite having been made to a prostitute whom the claimant also paid for her services).

[880] *De Begnis v Armistead* (1833) 10 Bing. 107; *M'Kinnell v Robinson* (1838) 3 M. & W. 434.

[881] *Cannan v Bryce* (1819) 3 B. & Ald. 179, as explained in *Spector v Ageda* [1973] Ch. 30.

[882] *Spector v Ageda*, above.

[883] *Toulmin v Anderson* (1808) 1 Taunt. 227.

[884] *Fisher v Bridges* (1854) 3 E. & B. 642 (bond); *Clugas v Penaluna* (1791) 4 T.R. 466 (bill of exchange; as to the rights of a holder in due course, see below, para.15–046); *Taylor v Chester* (1869) L.R. 4 Q.B. 309 (pledge). Contrast *Sharif v Azad* [1967] 1 Q.B. 605 as explained in *Mansouri v Singh* [1986] 1 W.L.R. 1393.

[885] See above, para.3–159.

[886] See above, para.11–157.

[887] *The American Accord* [1983] 1 A.C. 168 (where the sale was not illegal but only unenforceable under the Bretton Woods Agreement Act 1945); *Group Josi Re v Walbrook Ins Co Ltd* [1996] 1 Lloyd's Rep. 345 at 363–364. A cheque given in pursuance of such a transaction is likewise unenforceable between the parties to the transaction: *Mansouri v Singh* [1986] 1 W.L.R. 1393.

[888] *Nayyar v Denton Wilde Sapte* [2009] EWHC 3218 (QB); [2010] P.N.L.R. 15.

[889] *South Western Mineral Water Co Ltd v Ashmore* [1967] 1 W.L.R. 1110; cf. *Carney v Herbert* [1985] A.C. 301; above, para.11–164.

[890] ss.33(1), (2) and 81(2)(a).

[891] ss.37(1), (2) and 177(2)(a).

incurred statutory penalties through failing to make the service contracts with his crew in proper form[892]; a policy of insurance on goods is not illegal merely because, in the course of acquiring the goods, the insured had committed a violation of a foreign revenue law[893]; nor is a promise by one solicitor to pay another's charges in respect of a particular transaction illegal merely because the latter solicitor's client intended (without that solicitor's knowledge) to use the transaction in question as a vehicle of fraud.[894] In such cases, the first contract is illegal only if its object was to assist one of the parties in achieving the unlawful purpose under the second contract.[895]

11–167   **Damages for breach of collateral warranty.** An innocent party to an illegal contract can sometimes recover damages for breach of a "collateral warranty" that the contract was lawful.[896] Such a collateral warranty is not really a separate collateral transaction, but a device invented by law for the protection of an innocent party to an illegal contract.

(e) Criticism

11–168   The law relating to the effects of illegality on contracts is open to a number of criticisms. The most important of these relate to the question of the enforceability of such contracts by, and to other remedies available to, an innocent party,[897] and to the rules governing the right to restitution of benefits conferred under such contracts. In particular, the rules allowing a party to claim restitution of money or property if he can do so without reliance on the contract or its illegality can lead to results which, though explicable on technical grounds, appear to do little to further the policies underlying the legal prohibitions which are the cause of the illegality of the contract.[898]

11–169   In this chapter, it has been suggested that the overriding concern of the courts should be to determine whether their decision would further the purpose of the statute, or the relevant rule of the common law which has rendered the contract illegal or contrary to public policy. That alone will not suffice because it does not necessarily take into account the fact that illegality can involve varying degrees of impropriety and responsibility. As has been said by Lord Hoffmann the maxim ex turpi causa "expresses not so much a principle as a policy" and that "policy is not based upon a single justification but on a group of reasons, which vary in different situations."[899] The difficulty of the task facing the courts is in no small part due to the need to resolve a conflict of policies: the need to do justice between the parties has to be balanced against the wider considerations of public interest which underlie the law's refusal to give effect to illegal contracts. The need to take

---

[892] *Redmond v Smith* (1844) 7 Man. & G. 457.
[893] *Euro-Diam Ltd v Bathurst* [1990] Q.B. 1; the violation of the foreign law did not benefit the insured but only benefited his supplier; Clarke [1988] L.M.C.L.Q. 124; Tan 104 L.Q.R. 523; Tettenborn [1988] C.L.J. 338.
[894] *Rooks Rider v Steel* [1994] 1 W.L.R. 818.
[895] See *Re Trepca Mines Ltd* [1963] Ch. 199; A.L.G. 79 L.Q.R. 49; cf. [1974] 6 C.L. 266.
[896] See above, para.11–123.
[897] See above, paras 11–116—11–127.
[898] See above, paras 11–142, 11–148.
[899] *Gray v Thames Trains Ltd* [2009] UKHL 33; [2009] 1 A.C. 1339 at [30] (a tort case above, para.11–023).

account of the varying reasons referred to by Lord Hoffmann and to strike the balance required between them lends support to the need for a flexible test and, for that reason, the rejection of the "public conscience" test on the grounds of vagueness may be open to criticism. It is notable that, having reviewed this area of the law, the Law Commission has concluded that there should be no legislation on the basis that, notwithstanding the rejection of the "public conscience" test: "(t)he recent case law[900] shows that the courts have become more open in explaining the policy reasons behind the illegality defence. Therefore, in most areas of law, we think that the illegality defence should be left to developments in the common law".[901]

---

[900] Specific reference is made to: *Gray* above; *Stone & Rolls Ltd v Moore Stephens* [2009] UKHL 39; [2009] 1 A.C. 1391; *Nayyar v Denton Wilde Sapte* [2009] EWHC 3218 (QB); [2010] P.N.L.R. 15; and *Lincoln v CB Richard Ellis Hotels Ltd* [2009] EWHC 2344 (TCC).

[901] Law Com No. 328 ("The Illegality Defence") at 1.8.

CHAPTER TWELVE

CAPACITY

1. MINORS[1]

12–001   In the law of contract, persons below the age of majority were formerly called
infants; and this expression is used in many of the older cases which deal with their
contractual capacity. They are now more generally called minors; and, as this term
is used in modern legislation on the subject, it will also be used in this chapter.
When the age of majority was reduced from 21 to 18,[2] the practical importance of
the rules which determine the extent to which minors are bound by their contracts
was greatly reduced. If the decided cases are any guide, many of the legal problems
in this area have in the past concerned the contracts of persons between 18 and 21,
whose contractual capacity is now normal. But the question whether persons
under 18 are bound by contracts can still arise today: e.g. out of the contracts of
young professional entertainers[3] or athletes,[4] or out of hire–purchase agreements
or contracts of employment involving minors. Legal problems can also arise where
a claim is made by the minor against the other party, either to enforce the contract
or to reclaim money or property with which the minor has parted under it.

---

[1] For a comparative study, see Hartwig 15 I.C.L.Q. 780.
[2] Family Law Reform Act 1969, s.1; s.9 provides that a person attains 18 "at the commencement of
the [18th] anniversary of his birth."
[3] e.g. *Mills v IRC* [1975] A.C. 38 at 53.
[4] *Proform Sports Management Ltd v Proactive Sports Management Ltd* [2006] EWHC 2903 (Ch);
[2007] Bus. L.R. 93.

General principles. The law on this topic is based on two principles. The 12–002
first, and more important, is that the law must protect the minor against his
inexperience, which may enable an adult to take unfair advantage of him, or to
induce him to enter into a contract which, though in itself fair, is simply
improvident.[5] This principle is the basis of the general rule that a minor is not
bound by his contracts. The second principle is that the law should not cause
unnecessary hardship to adults who deal fairly with minors. Under this principle
certain contracts with minors are valid; others are voidable in the sense that they
bind the minor unless he repudiates; and a minor may be under some liability in
tort and in restitution.

(a) Valid Contracts

(i) Necessaries

A contract for necessaries is binding "not for the benefit of the tradesman who 12–003
may trust the infant, but for the benefit of the infant himself".[6] It is assumed,
rightly or wrongly,[7] that the tradesman would not give credit to the minor unless
the law imposed liability. In this connection it should be noted that parents are not
liable on their child's contract unless the child acts as their agent[8]; and that in
English law a minor's contract cannot be validated by the consent or authorisation
of his parent or guardian.

Necessaries include goods supplied and services rendered to a minor. He is
bound by a contract for necessaries only if it is on the whole for his benefit: not
if it contains harsh and onerous terms.[9] Nor is he bound by an indivisible contract
comprising necessaries and non-necessaries.[10]

Necessary goods. Necessary goods are not confined to necessities: they 12–004
include "such articles as are fit to maintain the particular person in the state,
station and degree ... in which he is".[11] In one case[12] a livery for a minor's
servant was held to be a necessary; and in another[13] the court refused to disturb
a verdict that rings, pins and a watch-chain supplied to the son of a rich man were
necessaries. These "quaint examples of a bygone age"[14] are hardly cases in which
liability was imposed "for the benefit of the infant himself".[15] The wide definition
of necessaries was adopted rather for the protection of suppliers who reasonably
gave credit to young men from wealthy families.

"Mere luxuries". On the other hand the definition of necessaries was limited 12–005
so as to exclude "mere luxuries". These were distinguished from "luxurious

---

[5] e.g. if the minor for a fair price agrees to buy something that he cannot afford.
[6] *Ryder v Wombwell* (1868) L.R. 4 Ex. 32 at 38; *Zouch v Parsons* (1763) 3 Burr. 1794.
[7] cf. below, para.12–006.
[8] *Blackburn v Mackey* (1823) 1 C. & P. 1; *Law v Wilkin* (1837) 6 A. & E. 718; *Mortimore v Wright*
(1840) 6 M. & W. 482.
[9] *Fawcett v Smethurst* (1914) 84 L.J.Ch. 473.
[10] *Stocks v Wilson* [1913] 2 K.B. 235.
[11] *Peters v Fleming* (1840) 6 M. & W. 42 at 46; *Bryant v Richardson* (1866) 14 L.T. 24 at 26.
[12] *Hands v Slaney* (1800) 8 T.R. 578. But a claim for the price of cockades for soldiers under the
minor's command was disallowed.
[13] *Peters v Fleming*, above, fn.11.
[14] *Allen v Bloomsbury Health Authority* [1993] 1 All E.R. 651 at 661.
[15] See above, para.12–003.

articles of utility",[16] which could be necessaries. Since few articles are so luxurious that they cannot be used at all, the real question was whether it was reasonable for the minor, however rich, to be supplied with articles of the kind in question. Thus it was said that if the son of the richest man in the kingdom bought a racehorse, it could not be a necessary[17] but where an apprentice bought a racing bicycle (which was no more expensive than an ordinary one) it was held to be a necessary.[18] It is doubtful whether goods bought by a minor to be given away can normally be necessaries.[19] But an engagement ring bought to be given to the minor's fiancée, whom he later marries, can be a necessary.[20]

12–006   **Proof.** Much difficulty was caused in the nineteenth century by the tendency of juries (consisting of 12 shopkeepers) to stretch the definition of necessaries beyond its legitimate limits. In one case "an Oxford jury held that champagne and wild ducks were necessaries to an infant undergraduate".[21] To counteract this tendency, the courts first distinguished between articles which could, and those which could not, as a matter of law, be necessaries.[22] They held, secondly, that the question whether goods were necessaries was

> "one of mixed law and fact; in so far as it is a question of fact it must be determined by the jury . . . ; but there is in every case . . . a preliminary question which is one of law, namely whether there is any evidence on which the jury could properly find the question for the party on whom the onus of proof lies".[23]

The onus of proving that the goods are necessaries lies on the supplier. Thus in *Ryder v Wombwell*[24] the son of a deceased baronet bought jewelled cufflinks for £12 10s. apiece and an antique goblet to give to a friend. The jury found that these articles were necessaries. But the court set the verdict aside as there was no evidence on which it could properly be based.

The supplier must show both that the goods are capable of being necessaries and that they actually are necessaries. Thus in *Nash v Inman*[25] a tailor sued a minor for the price of clothes, including 11 fancy waistcoats. The action failed because the tailor had not adduced any evidence fit to be left to the jury that the clothes were suitable to the condition in life of the minor, *and* that the minor was not already adequately supplied with clothes. The courts have put on the claimant the burden of proving the difficult negative proposition that the minor was not adequately supplied. As a general rule a person is only required to prove a negative if such proof depends on facts peculiarly within his own knowledge; here the proof required of the supplier depends on facts peculiarly within the knowledge of the minor.

---

[16] *Chapple v Cooper* (1844) 13 M. & W. 252 at 258.
[17] *Wharton v Mackenzie* (1844) 5 Q.B. 606 at 612. Contrast *Barber v Vincent* (1680) Free.K.B. 581 (horse sold to a minor to carry him about his necessary business held a necessary).
[18] *Clyde Cycle Co v Hargreaves* (1898) 78 L.T. 296.
[19] *Ryder v Wombwell* (1868) L.R. 4 Ex. 32; *Hewlings v Graham* (1901) 84 L.T. 497.
[20] *Jenner v Walker* (1869) 19 L.T. 398.
[21] (1874) *Hansard*, Vol.219, ser.3, col.1225.
[22] *Ryder v Wombwell* (1868) L.R. 4 Ex. 32.
[23] ibid. at 38.
[24] ibid.; cf. *Wharton v Mackenzie* (1844) 5 Q.B. 606.
[25] [1908] 2 K.B. 1.

It was further held that the minor is not liable if he already had an adequate supply, even though the supplier did not know this.[26] Such a rule may help to protect minors; but it is difficult to reconcile with the view that minors are liable for necessaries because, if they were not, traders would not give them credit. For the rule makes it impossible for the supplier to tell, when the contract is made, whether the minor will indeed be bound by it.

Services rendered to a minor. Certain services rendered to a minor may be   12–007
necessaries. These include education (whether liberal or vocational[27]) and medical and legal advice.[28] The provision of a funeral for her deceased husband has been held a necessary for his widow, who was a minor.[29] It seems that any service can be a necessary if it satisfies the tests already stated in relation to necessary goods.

Executory contracts.[30] It is disputed whether a minor is bound by an execu-   12–008
tory contract for necessary goods. Is he liable only if the goods have actually been delivered, or also if he wrongfully repudiates before delivery? Three main arguments have been used to support the view that the minor is liable only if the goods have been delivered.

First: in *Nash v Inman* Fletcher Moulton L.J. said that the minor was liable because he had been supplied, and not because he had contracted.

> "An infant, like a lunatic,[31] is incapable of making a contract . . . in the strict sense of the word: but if a man satisfies the need of the infant or lunatic by supplying to him necessaries, the law will imply an obligation to repay him for the services so rendered, and will enforce that obligation against the estate of the infant or lunatic".[32]

But Buckley L.J. said that a contract for necessaries was "such as the infant, notwithstanding infancy, could make" and that "an infant had a limited capacity to contract".[33] And the analogy of the "lunatic" is, with respect, imperfect. Sometimes the reason why such a person is "incapable of making a contract" may be that he cannot consent; and if he is then supplied with necessaries there is not even the shadow of an agreement to accept and pay for the goods. This may also be true when necessaries are supplied to a very young child.[34] But it is not true when a young man of 17 orders clothes and promises to pay for them. He can and does consent: the only question is whether he ought as a matter of legal policy to be held to the agreement.

---

[26] *Foster v Redgrave* (1867) L.R. 4 Ex. 35n.; *Barnes v Toye* (1884) 13 Q.B.D. 410.
[27] *Walter v Everard* [1891] 2 Q.B. 369; *Roberts v Gray* [1913] 1 K.B. 520. For contracts to pay school fees, see *Practice Direction* [1980] 1 W.L.R. 1441; *Practice Direction* [1983] 1 W.L.R. 800; *Sherdley v Sherdley* [1988] A.C. 213 at 225.
[28] *Huggins v Wiseman* (1690) Carth. 110; *Helps v Clayton* (1864) 17 C.B.(N.S.) 553.
[29] *Chapple v Cooper* (1844) 13 M. & W. 252.
[30] Miles (1927) 43 L.Q.R. 389; Winfield (1942) 58 L.Q.R. 83.
[31] Now called a person lacking mental capacity: see below, para.12–052 et seq.
[32] [1908] 2 K.B. 1 at 8; cf. *Re J* [1909] 1 Ch. 574.
[33] ibid. at 12.
[34] See *Sherdley v Sherdley* [1988] A.C. 213 at 225. *R. v Oldham MBC Ex p. Garlick* [1993] A.C. 509 at 517.

Secondly: the minor is liable only for a reasonable price, which may not be the same as the contract price. "That does not imply a consensual contract."[35] But the law often interferes with one or more of the terms of a transaction and this does not necessarily deprive it of its essential character as a contract.[36]

Thirdly: s.3(2) of the Sale of Goods Act 1979 provides that "Where necessaries are sold and delivered to a minor . . . he must pay a reasonable price for them". Section 3(3) then defines "'necessaries' in subsection (2) above" to mean "goods suitable to the condition in life of the minor . . . and to his actual requirements *at the time of sale and delivery.*" The words here italicised may seem to suggest that goods cannot be necessaries unless they have actually been delivered. But the definition is of necessaries "in subsection (2) above", and that subsection deals only with necessaries sold and delivered. The definition does not apply to goods sold but not yet delivered.

Thus the arguments in support of the view that the minor is not liable on an executory contract are inconclusive; and the contrary view is supported by *Roberts v Gray.*[37] The claimant, a famous billiards player, agreed to take a minor on a world billiards tour, and to pay for his board and lodging and travelling expenses. This was a contract for necessaries, mainly because its object was to teach the minor the profession of a billiards player. The minor repudiated the contract while it was still partly executory; and he was held liable in damages. Hamilton L.J. said: "I am unable to appreciate why a contract which is in itself binding . . . can cease to be binding merely because it is still executory".[38] It has been said that *Roberts v Gray* can be explained on the ground that contracts for education are more closely analogous to beneficial contracts of service[39] than to contracts for the supply of necessary goods.[40] But it is hard to see why any distinction should for this purpose be drawn between necessary goods and education; or between necessaries of either kind and beneficial contracts of service. The reasons for holding a minor liable, and for limiting his liability, are the same in all these cases. It is thought that the minor's overall position might be prejudiced if he could not bind himself, and also that liability should be imposed to protect the legitimate interests of the adult. These considerations have to be balanced against the need to protect the minor. If a balancing of all these factors justifies the view that the minor should be bound by an executory contract for education or of service, it is submitted that it can equally justify the view that he should be bound by an executory contract for the supply of necessary goods.[41]

12–009   **Legislation affecting the maintenance of children.** The common law rules relating to liability for necessaries are not directly affected by legislation imposing on an absent parent the duty to maintain a child[42] or empowering courts to make orders against parents for financial relief in respect of children.[43] Such legislation may, however, indirectly affect a minor's contractual liabilities for necessaries, in

---

[35] *Pontypridd Union v Drew* [1927] 1 K.B. 214 at 220.
[36] See above, para.1–006.
[37] [1913] 1 K.B. 520.
[38] ibid. at 530.
[39] See below, paras 12–011—12–016.
[40] Cheshire, Fifoot and Furmston, *Law of Contract* (15th edn), p.552.
[41] The difficulties discussed above would be diminished if parents were liable for necessaries, or at least for necessities, supplied to a child. For an American case in which such liability was imposed, see *Greenspan v Slate* 12 N.J. 426; 97 A. 2d. 390 (1953).
[42] Child Support Act 1991, s.1(1).
[43] Children Act 1989, s.15.

the sense that if, as a result of its operation, the minor is already adequately supplied with the goods or services in question, they will not fall within the common law definition of necessaries.

Loans for necessaries. At common law a person who spends money in buying   **12–010**
necessaries for a minor is entitled to recover it from the minor.[44] One who lends money to a minor to enable him to buy necessaries cannot recover it at law, but can in equity recover such part of the loan as was actually used by the minor to discharge his liability for necessaries supplied to him.[45] A promise in a mortgage deed to repay such a loan is ineffective since the minor is not bound by his deed.[46] The law leaves the lender for necessaries in a somewhat precarious position— perhaps because a loan of money can more easily be misapplied than an actual supply of necessaries.

(ii) *Service contracts*

Binding if for minor's benefit. A minor[47] is bound by a service contract if it   **12–011**
is on the whole for his benefit. He may be bound even though some of the terms of the contract are to his disadvantage. Thus in *Clements v L & NW Ry*[48] a minor who was a railway porter agreed to join an insurance scheme, to which his employers contributed, and to give up any claim for personal injury under the Employers' Liability Act 1880. His rights under the scheme were in some ways more, and in other ways less, beneficial than those under the Act; and it was held that the contract was on the whole beneficial, so that the minor was bound by it. But a term which simply limits or excludes the liability of the employer without giving the minor any rights in return is unlikely to be upheld.[49] A minor is, a fortiori, not bound by a service contract which is on the whole harsh and oppressive to the minor.[50]

Whether contract is for minor's benefit. In deciding whether a service   **12–012**
contract is on the whole beneficial the court is entitled to look at surrounding circumstances. For example, a service contract with a minor may contain a covenant in restraint of trade. Such a covenant, if otherwise valid,[51] does not invalidate the contract if the minor could not have got similar work on any other

---

[44] *Ellis v Ellis* (1689) Comb. 482; *Earle v Peale* (1712) 10 Mod. 67.

[45] *Marlow v Pitfeild* (1719) 1 P.Wms. 558; *Re National Permanent Benefit Building Society* (1869) L.R. 5 Ch.App. 309 at 313.

[46] *Martin v Gale* (1876) 4 Ch.D. 428.

[47] Contracts of service with children are to some extent regulated by statute: see, e.g. Children and Young Persons Acts 1933, s.18; 1963, s.37.

[48] [1894] 2 Q.B. 482; *Slade v Metrodent* [1953] 2 Q.B. 112; *Mills v IRC* [1975] A.C. 38 at 53.

[49] *Olsen v Corry and Gravesend Aviation Ltd* [1936] 3 All E.R. 241. Even if valid at common law, the term may be ineffective, or subject to the requirement of reasonableness, under Unfair Contracts Terms Act 1977, s.2 (above, paras 7–057, 7–065), and see Sch.1, para.4 ("except in favour of the employee"). The Unfair Terms in Consumer Contracts Regulations 1999 do not apply to contracts relating to employment (above, para.7–117) and nor, in most cases, does s.3 of the 1977 Act (above, para.7–067).

[50] *De Francesco v Barnum* (1889) 43 Ch.D. 165; (1890) 45 Ch.D. 430.

[51] See above, para.11–062 et seq. The fact that the employee was a minor may be relevant to the issue of the reasonableness of the covenant: see *Sir W C Leng & Co Ltd v Andrews* [1909] 1 Ch. 763 at 771–772.

terms.[52] But it would invalidate a service contract with a minor if it was of a kind that was not usually found in service contracts in that trade and locality.[53] These principles also apply to contracts connected with service contracts. Thus they determine the validity of contracts to carry minors to work,[54] of compromises of industrial injury claims,[55] and of agreements to dissolve service contracts.[56]

12–013 **Professions.** The principles evolved in relation to service contracts also determine the validity of contracts under which a minor makes a living by the exercise of some profession, e.g. as an entertainer or author or athlete. In *Doyle v White City Stadium Ltd*[57] a professional boxer who was a minor made a contract to fight for £3,000, win, draw or lose, subject to the rules of the British Boxing Board of Control, under which a boxer who was disqualified forfeited his "purse". The minor was disqualified for hitting below the belt and his claim for the £3,000 was dismissed. Although in the circumstances the rules operated against him, he was bound by them: they were, on the whole, for his benefit as a professional boxer since they encouraged clean fighting. This case was followed in *Chaplin v Leslie Frewin (Publishers) Ltd*[58] where a minor contracted to give a firm of publishers the exclusive right to publish his memoirs. The Court of Appeal unanimously held that this was the sort of contract which could bind the minor if it was on the whole for his benefit.[59] Applying this test Lord Denning M.R. thought that, having regard to the contents of the memoirs, the contract was not binding, as it was not for the minor's good "that he should exploit his discreditable conduct for money".[60] But Danckwerts and Winn L.JJ. took the more materialistic view that "the mud may cling but the profits will be secured": thus the contract was on the whole beneficial, and bound the minor as it enabled him to "make a start as an author".[61]

12–014 **Validity of "beneficial contract" limited to service or analogous contracts.** The rule that a minor is bound by "beneficial" contracts is restricted to service or analogous contracts.[62] There is no general principle that a minor is bound by a contract merely because it is for his benefit. For example, a minor would not be contractually liable to repay[63] a loan without interest. And it has long been settled that a minor is not bound by a trading contract. Thus he is not liable for goods supplied to him for the purpose of trade, nor for damages if he fails to

---

[52] *Bromley v Smith* [1909] 2 K.B. 235; cf. *Leslie v Fitzpatrick* (1877) 3 Q.B.D. 229.

[53] *Sir W C Leng & Co Ltd v Andrews* [1909] 1 Ch. 763.

[54] *Flower v London and North Western Ry* [1894] 2 Q.B. 65; in *Buckpitt v Oates* [1968] 1 All E.R. 1145 it seems to have been assumed that any contract to carry the minor (though not connected with his work) would be binding if on the whole for his benefit; sed quaere. The actual decision would now go the other way: Road Traffic Act 1988, ss.145, 149.

[55] *Stephens v Dudbridge Ironworks Co* [1904] 2 K.B. 225.

[56] *Waterman v Fryer* [1922] 1 K.B. 499.

[57] [1935] 1 K.B. 110. cf. also *Lumley v Wagner* (1852) 1 D.M. & G. 604, where a famous soprano was under age, as appears from 5 De G. & Sm. 485.

[58] [1966] Ch. 71; the case was later compromised: *The Times*, February 16, 1966.

[59] The same rule seems to apply to a contract between an entertainer who is under age and his agent: see *Denmark Productions Ltd v Boscobel Productions Ltd* (1967) 111 S.J. 715, reversed on other grounds [1969] 1 Q.B. 699; below, paras 16–103, 21–010.

[60] [1966] Ch. 71 at 88.

[61] ibid. at 88, 95.

[62] *Proform Sports Management Ltd v Proactive Sports Management Ltd* [2006] EWHC 2903 (Ch); [2007] Bus. L.R. 93 at [35].

[63] For liability to make restitution, see below, para.12–036 et seq.

deliver goods which he has sold as a trader.[64] Nor can he be made bankrupt for trade debts.[65]

Trading contracts. It may be asked: why does the law distinguish between a minor who earns his living by the exercise of a profession and one who earns his living by trading? The traditional answer is that "the law will not suffer him to trade, which may be his undoing".[66] A minor who trades thereby necessarily risks his capital. If he exercises some profession or calling he may incur expense, but putting his capital at risk is not of the essence of the matter. Of course there are difficult borderline cases. A minor who is a haulage contractor is a trader,[67] but probably one who was a racing driver would not be so regarded. Similarly, it is probable that a minor who was a house painter would, while one who was a portrait painter would not, be regarded as a trader.[68] There is no precise definition of "trade" for this purpose.

12–015

Apprenticeship. Contracts of apprenticeship were governed by special rules. It was held in the seventeenth century that an apprentice who was under age was not liable in damages if, in breach of contract, he departed from service.[69] This rule was originally based on the fact that the master had other remedies such as having the minor ordered by a justice of the peace to return to work. These remedies no longer exist[70] and it seems that contracts of apprenticeship will now be governed by the normal rules. A minor is not bound by an apprenticeship deed as such, but he is bound by it as a simple contract. Thus he is liable to pay any premium which he has agreed to pay.[71] Similarly, a covenant in restraint of trade (if otherwise valid[72]) or an arbitration clause contained in the apprenticeship deed can be enforced against him so long as the deed is on the whole for his benefit.[73]

12–016

(b) Voidable Contracts

(i) *Cases of voidable contracts*

In four cases a minor's contract is voidable: that is, it binds both parties but the minor can avoid liability by repudiating before majority or within a reasonable time thereafter. The other party cannot repudiate.[74]

12–017

---

[64] *Mercantile Union Guarantee Corp Ltd v Ball* [1937] 2 K.B. 498; *Cowern v Nield* [1912] 2 K.B. 491; below, para.12–051.
[65] *Ex p. Jones* (1881) 18 Ch.D. 109; but he can be made bankrupt in respect of tax liability incurred in the course of trade: *Re a Debtor* [1950] Ch. 282.
[66] *Whywall v Campion* (1738) 2 Stra. 1083.
[67] *Mercantile Union Guarantee Corp Ltd v Ball*, above, fn.64.
[68] Quaere what the position would be if a minor agreed to sell a picture which he had painted without having been commissioned to paint it.
[69] *Gylbert v Fletcher* (1630) Cro.Car. 179.
[70] Family Law Reform Act 1969, s.11.
[71] *Walter v Everard* [1891] 2 Q.B. 369.
[72] See above, fn.51.
[73] *Gadd v Thompson* [1911] 1 K.B. 304; *Slade v Metrodent* [1953] 2 Q.B. 112.
[74] *Clayton v Ashdown* (1714) 2 Eq.Ca.Abr. 516.

12–018   **Contracts concerning land.** A lessee who is under age is liable for rent unless he repudiates.[75] A minor who agrees to purchase freehold land is similarly bound unless he repudiates.[76] It seems that the same principle applies where a minor lets or agrees to sell land.[77] Actual conveyances to and by minors give rise to special problems which are outside the scope of this book.

According to one case[78] a lessee who is under age is liable for rent only if the subject-matter of the lease is a necessary, but if this were so he could presumably not repudiate. The requirement is not elsewhere stated and is probably not law. On the contrary, it seems that a lessee who is under age is liable unless he repudiates even though the lease is disadvantageous to him.[79]

12–019   **Shares in companies.** A minor who agrees to subscribe for shares in a company, or buys shares which are not fully paid, is liable for calls unless he repudiates. A mere plea that he has not ratified the transaction does not relieve him from liability.[80] If he repudiates he ceases to be liable and can have his name removed from the company's register.[81] If the minor buys shares from a previous owner and fails to repudiate liability for calls on them, *the company* cannot generally avoid the transaction and so make the transferor liable for the calls.[82] But if the company is being wound-up while the buyer is still a minor, the liquidator can exercise the minor's right of repudiation for him and so make the transferor again liable for calls.[83]

The cases on this subject all concern the relations between the minor and the company or between the company and the person who has transferred shares to a minor. There appears to be no authority on the effect between buyer and seller of a sale of shares by or to a minor. Suppose that a minor buys shares, fails to pay for them when due, and then repudiates after majority. If the contract is voidable this repudiation may be too late,[84] so that the minor will be liable to pay. But he would not be liable if the contract had never been binding on him at all.[85]

12–020   **Partnership.** A minor can become a partner and is to some extent bound by the partnership agreement. He cannot be sued during minority by persons who give credit to the firm,[86] or be made liable for its losses.[87] But he is liable if after majority he fails to put an end to the partnership.[88] And he is not entitled to any

---

[75] *Davies v Benyon-Harris* (1931) 47 T.L.R. 424. A minor can no longer hold a legal estate in land: Law of Property Act 1925, s.1(6); cf. Trusts of Land and Appointment of Trustees Act 1996, s.2(6) and Sch.2; but these enactments do not affect the proposition in the text.

[76] *Whittingham v Murdy* (1889) 60 L.T. 956; *Orakpo v Manson Investments Ltd* [1978] A.C. 95 at 106, 113.

[77] *Slator v Trimble* (1861) 14 Ir.C.L.R. 342.

[78] *Lowe v Griffith* (1835) 4 L.J.C.P. 94.

[79] *North Western Ry v M'Michael* (1850) 5 Ex. 114 at 128.

[80] ibid.; *Ebbett's Case* (1870) L.R. 5 Ch.App. 302. The rule was originally thought to be based simply on the provisions of the Act incorporating the company: *Cork & Bandon Ry v Cazenove* (1847) 10 Q.B. 935; but this reasoning was disapproved in *M'Michael's* case, above. Thus the rule applies to shares in all companies, however incorporated.

[81] *Dublin & Wicklow Ry v Black*, above; *Steinberg v Scala (Leeds) Ltd* [1923] 2 Ch. 452.

[82] *Lumsden's Case* (1868) L.R. 4 Ch.App. 31; *Gooch's Case* (1872) L.R. 8 Ch.App. 266.

[83] *Capper's Case* (1868) L.R. 3 Ch.App. 458; *Symon's Case* (1870) L.R. 5 Ch.App. 298.

[84] See below, para.12–023.

[85] i.e. if it fell within the general rule stated at para.12–027, below.

[86] *Goode v Harrison* (1821) 5 B. & Ald. 147 at 157; *Lovell & Christmas v Beauchamp* [1894] A.C. 607.

[87] ibid. at 159.

[88] ibid.

share in the profits or assets of the partnership until its liabilities have been discharged.[89]

Marriage settlements. It was once thought that a marriage settlement by a   12–021
minor was binding to the extent to which it benefited him; but was otherwise not binding unless ratified after majority.[90] But the prevailing view is that such a settlement binds the minor unless he repudiates.[91]

(ii) *Loans for voidable contracts*

Rights of the lender. A minor may borrow money to enable him to make a   12–022
payment due from him under a voidable contract, and actually use the money borrowed to make the payment. The minor is not for this reason bound by the contract for the loan of the money[92]; but the lender has rights similar to those of a lender for necessaries.[93] In *Nottingham Permanent Benefit Building Society v Thurstan*[94] a minor borrowed money from a building society to buy land. She paid the money to the vendor and executed a mortgage to the society. The mortgage was void,[95] but the society was entitled to stand in the shoes of the vendor and to exercise the lien that he would have had over the property, if he had not been paid.

(iii) *Rules relating to repudiation*

Time of repudiation. A voidable contract can be repudiated during minority,   12–023
but such a repudiation can be withdrawn by the minor before, or within reasonable time of, majority.[96] If the minor repudiates during minority he need take no further steps to avoid liability on reaching full age.[97]

If the minor does not repudiate during minority, he must do so within a reasonable time of reaching full age. This is so even though he did not know of his right to repudiate, and even though his obligation under the contract had not yet matured. Thus a covenant by a minor in a marriage settlement to settle after-acquired property may not become operative for many years after the settlor comes of age. But it binds him unless he repudiates it within a reasonable time of majority. In *Edwards v Carter*[98] it was held that a settlement could not be

---

[89] *Lovell & Christmas v Beauchamp* [1894] A.C. 607 at 611. *Semble*, the rules stated in this paragraph would apply to the relations between persons who became members of a limited liability partnership (below, para.12–070) if one or more of them were a minor: ss.4 and 5 of the Limited Liability Partnerships Act 2000 contain no reference to minority. Since under s.1 of the Act such a partnership is a body corporate, a minor would not (any more than a person of full age) be liable on its contracts; but his liability to contribute to the assets of the partnership would seem to be governed by the principles stated at fnn.79 and 80, above.
[90] See *Simson v Jones* (1831) 2 Russ & My. 365.
[91] *Duncan v Dixon* (1890) 44 Ch.D. 211; *Edwards v Carter* [1893] A.C. 360; [1892] 2 Ch. 278.
[92] It falls within the general rule stated at para.12–027, below.
[93] See above, para.12–010.
[94] [1903] A.C. 6.
[95] See above, at fn.46.
[96] *North Western Ry v M'Michael* (1850) 5 Ex. 114 at 127; *Slator v Trimble* (1861) 14 Ir.C.L.R. 342.
[97] *Newry and Enniskillen Ry v Combe* (1849) 3 Ex. 565 at 575.
[98] [1893] A.C. 360.

repudiated nearly five years after the majority of the settlor, although he was for most of that time ignorant of his right to repudiate.

12–024   **Effects of repudiation.** Repudiation relieves the minor from liabilities which would, but for the repudiation, have accrued after its date. There are conflicting dicta[99] on the question whether liabilities which have already accrued are extinguished by repudiation. According to an Irish case repudiation has no retrospective effect[100]; thus a lessee who is under age is liable for rent which has become payable before repudiation.

A minor cannot recover back money paid under a voidable contract unless there has been a "total failure of consideration".[101] In *Steinberg v Scala (Leeds) Ltd,*[102] a minor applied for shares in a company but repudiated after allotment. She thus avoided liability for future calls, but her claim for the return of money already paid was rejected as there was no total failure of consideration: she had got the very shares she bargained for. Property transferred under a marriage settlement would similarly be irrecoverable once the marriage had taken place. On the other hand, in *Corpe v Overton*[103] a minor agreed to enter into a partnership and paid a deposit of £100, to be forfeited if he failed to execute the partnership deed. No partnership deed was ever executed because the minor repudiated, and it was held that he could get his deposit back as there had been a total failure of consideration. An adult, too, can recover back money if there has been a total failure of consideration; but a minor (unlike an adult) can do so even though the failure of consideration is due to his own act in repudiating the contract.

(iv) *Why are these contracts voidable?*

12–025   **The orthodox view.** In general a minor is not bound by his contracts.[104] He need not repudiate to escape liability. Why must he do so in the four cases discussed above?[105] The orthodox view is that the minor must repudiate because he has acquired an interest in a subject-matter of a permanent nature to which continuing obligations are attached: it would be unjust to allow him to retain the interest without fulfilling the obligations.[106] But this explanation is not wholly satisfactory. First, it is vague: what is meant by "permanent" here? Is a lease for one year permanent because land is virtually indestructible? Partnerships and shares in companies do not necessarily confer an interest in property which is permanent even in this sense. And marriage settlements can be brought within the explanation only by arguing that the marriage is permanent, whether the settled property is permanent or not. Secondly, the explanation does not cover all cases within the rule. It has been held that a minor's contract to buy freehold land to be paid for in instalments is voidable.[107] Nothing in the judgment suggests that it

---

[99] *North Western Ry v M'Michael*, above, fn.96 at 125 (retrospective); *Keteley's Case* (1613) 1 Brownl. 120 (not retrospective); dicta in *Steinberg v Scala (Leeds) Ltd* [1923] 2 Ch. 452 at 463 can be cited on both sides.
[100] *Blake v Concannon* (1870) I.R. 4 C.L. 323.
[101] See below, para.22–003.
[102] [1923] 2 Ch. 452.
[103] (1833) 10 Bing. 252; *Everett v Wilkins* (1874) 29 L.T. 846.
[104] See below, para.12–027.
[105] See above, paras 12–018—12–021.
[106] See, e.g. *Davies v Benyon Harris* (1931) 47 T.L.R. 424.
[107] *Whittingham v Murdy* (1889) 60 L.T. 956.

would have made any difference, had the price been payable in one lump sum. Yet in such a case the contract would not have created any "continuing" obligation between the parties. Thirdly, the explanation proves too much. It is admittedly unjust to allow a tenant who is a minor to retain possession of land without paying rent. But it is equally unjust to allow a minor to keep a car obtained under a hire purchase agreement without paying instalments. Yet the hire-purchase agreement does not bind the minor[108]: he need not repudiate.

No satisfactory explanation. There seems to be no satisfactory explanation **12–026** for the existence of this separate class of voidable contracts. It perhaps provides the clearest illustration of the dilemma in which the law sometimes finds itself when it tries at the same time to protect minors and not to cause undue hardship to adults who deal with them. But this dilemma exists in all cases of contracts with minors and scarcely justifies special treatment of the four classes of voidable contracts. Perhaps this is based on social and economic factors which have long since passed away.

(c) Other contracts

Minor not bound. Contracts which are neither valid, nor voidable in the sense **12–027** just discussed, do not bind the minor but have a number of legal effects.

Other party bound. Contracts in this group bind the other party.[109] However, **12–028** the remedies available to the minor are somewhat restricted in that he cannot claim *specific* performance of the contract.[110]

Ratification. The minor as a general rule[111] becomes liable on the contract if **12–029** he ratifies it after reaching full age.[112] Ratification may be express, or implied from conduct: the latter possibility is illustrated by the case in which the former minor continues after majority to act on the contract in such a way as to show that he regards it as binding on himself.[113] Because contracts in this group became binding as a result of ratification, they were sometimes called "voidable". But this is misleading as "voidable" normally means binding unless repudiated, whereas these contracts do not bind the minor unless he ratifies.

Executed contracts. Once the minor has actually performed the contract he **12–030** cannot recover back money paid or property transferred by him under it merely on the ground that the contract did not bind him by reason of his minority.[114] He can recover back such money or property only in the same circumstances in which this remedy is available to an adult: e.g. he can recover back money paid under the contract if there has been a total failure of consideration.[115] There is, indeed, some

---

[108] e.g. *Mercantile Union Guarantee Corp Ltd v Ball* [1937] 2 K.B. 498.

[109] *Farnham v Atkins* (1670) 1 Sid. 446; *Bruce v Warwick* (1815) 6 Taunt. 118.

[110] *Flight v Boland* (1828) 4 Russ. 298; *Lumley v Ravenscroft* [1895] 1 Q.B. 683; below, para.21–046.

[111] Exceptionally, a penal bond is void so that it cannot be ratified: *Baylis v Dinely* (1815) 3 M. & S. 477.

[112] See *Williams v Moor* (1843) 11 M. & W. 256.

[113] e.g. *Brown v Harper* (1893) 68 L.T. 488.

[114] *Wilson v Kearse* (1800) Peake Add. Cas. 196; *Ex p. Taylor* (1856) 8 D.M. & G. 254 at 256.

[115] See below, para.22–003.

doubt as to the scope of the rule that property transferred in pursuance of contracts in this category cannot be recovered back. In *Chaplin v Leslie Frewin (Publishers) Ltd*[116] a majority of the Court of Appeal accepted the view that the minor would not be able to recover the copyright which he had transferred under the contract even if (contrary to the view of that majority) the contract did not bind him.[117] Lord Denning M.R., on the other hand, said that the rule, by which property could not be recovered back, applied only to transfers by delivery and not to those which require a written document: it would be "absurd to hold that a contract to make a disposition is voidable and that the disposition is not".[118] But it is, with respect, hard to see why this is more absurd when the disposition has to be in writing than when it can, and does, take effect by delivery.[119]

12–031   **Passing of property from minor.** It was said by Lush J. in *Stocks v Wilson*[120] that, where goods were delivered to a minor under a contract of sale, the property in them passed to him "by the delivery". The view that property can pass to a minor under a contract which does not bind him seems to be supported by s.3(1) of the Minors' Contracts Act 1987: this subsection[121] refers to "property acquired" by the minor under such a contract, and to the power of the court to order him to "transfer" such property.[122] The property, in the case put, seems to pass by delivery with intention to pass property. It may indeed be argued that the seller's intention to pass property is based on the assumption that the contract binds the minor and is nullified if this assumption is untrue, just as (in cases not involving minors) a seller's intention to pass property is nullified if the contract is void for mistake as to the identity of the buyer.[123] But delivery to the wrong person may well differ in legal effect from delivery for the wrong reason. In the first case there is no intention to pass the property to the person to whom the delivery is made; in the second there is such an intention, though possibly based on a mistaken assumption. Thus it is submitted that delivery of the goods to the minor can pass property to him. The attraction of this view is that it enables the law to protect an innocent third party who later buys the goods from the minor. It is an open question whether property can pass to the minor without delivery,[124] simply by virtue of the contract. The question is of small practical importance since property is unlikely to pass in this way until the price has been paid[125]; and in that case the seller generally has no interest in claiming that he still has the property in the goods.

---

[116] [1966] Ch. 71; above, para.12–013.

[117] This view was based "on the authorities cited to us" (at 94). But these were not strictly in point as the contract in one of them (*Steinberg v Scala (Leeds) Ltd* [1923] 2 Ch. 452) was truly voidable, while in the other two (*Valentini v Canali* (1889) 24 Q.B.D. 166; *Pearce v Brain* [1929] 2 K.B. 310) the contracts were "absolutely void" within s.1 of Infants Relief Act 1874 (repealed by Minors' Contracts Act 1987, ss.1(a) and 4(2)). The majority's view is more appropriately supported by the authorities cited in fn.17, above.

[118] [1966] Ch. 71 at 90; cf. *G (A) v G (T)* [1970] 2 Q.B. 643 at 652.

[119] No such distinction is drawn where the contract is voidable for misrepresentation above, para.9–078 et seq.

[120] [1913] 2 K.B. 235 at 246; cf. *Watts v Seymour* [1967] 2 Q.B. 647.

[121] See below, para.12–037; a similar assumption seems to underlie Criminal Justice Act 1988, s.141A(1), as inserted by Offensive Weapons Act 1996, s.6(1).

[122] See further below, paras 12–037—12–042.

[123] *Shogun Finance v Hudson* [2003] UKHL 62; [2004] 1 A.C. 919; above, para.8–039.

[124] e.g. under Sale of Goods Act 1979, s.18, r.1.

[125] See *R V Ward Ltd v Bignall* [1967] 1 Q.B. 534 at 545.

Passing of property from minor. Cases such as *Chaplin v Leslie Frewin* 12–032
(Publishers) Ltd[126] show that property can pass *from* the minor under a contract
which does not bind him.[127] The same principle would apply where the minor
made a pledge to secure a debt incurred under such a contract. The person taking
the pledge would normally be guilty of an offence,[128] but this does not affect the
civil consequences of the transaction.[129] Thus it seems that a special property in
the thing pledged would pass to the pledgee and that the minor could not get the
thing back without paying off the loan. This conclusion may be disadvantageous
to the minor, but the argument that property passes by delivery seems to apply as
much where the delivery is made *by*, as where it is made *to*, the minor.

(d) Liability in Tort

Cause of action arising out of non-binding contract. The general rule is 12–033
that minors are liable in tort in the same way as adults. One possible exception to
this rule exists in the case of very young children. Our concern here, however, is
with another exception, which exists where a cause of action in tort arises out of,
or in connection with, a contract which does not bind the minor.

Wrongful and forbidden conduct. Conduct amounting to a breach of con- 12–034
tract may also be a tort.[130] If a minor engages in such conduct and is sued in tort,
he can sometimes set up the invalidity of the contract as a defence to the tort
claim. He can do so where the tort consists of wrongfully doing an act authorised
by the contract,[131] but not where it consists of doing an act forbidden by the
contract.[132] The distinction between these two types of cases can be explained as
the product of the law's two conflicting desires: to protect minors, but without
causing unnecessary hardship to adults who deal with them.

Tortious procurement of the contract. The minor may be immune from 12–035
liability in tort, not only where he commits a tort in breaking the invalid contract,
but also where he commits a tort in procuring it. Thus it was held in *R Leslie Ltd
v Sheill*[133] that a minor could not be sued in deceit for inducing an adult to lend
him money by fraudulent misrepresentations as to his age. Similarly it was held in
Stocks v Wilson[134] that a minor could not be sued in deceit for inducing an adult
by such misrepresentations to sell and deliver goods to him. The practical effect
of a judgment in tort in such cases would be to force the minor to repay the money
lent or to pay the value of the goods obtained; and this would once again
undermine the protection which the law gives to the minor by holding the contract
invalid.

---

[126] [1966] Ch. 71; above, para.12–013.

[127] Even Lord Denning accepted this view where the property was alleged to have passed by *delivery*:
see above, at fn.118.

[128] Consumer Credit Act 1974, s.114(2).

[129] ibid., s.170(1); quaere whether this excludes the rules stated at para.11–131, above; cf. also
paras 11–140—11–150, above. cf. *Wilson v Robertsons (London) Ltd* [2006] EWCA Civ 1088 (claim for
conversion available alongside sanctions imposed for breach of the Act).

[130] See below, para.20–127.

[131] *Jennings v Rundall* (1799) 8 T.R. 335; cf. *Fawcett v Smethurst* (1914) 84 L.J.K.B. 473.

[132] *Burnard v Haggis* (1863) 14 C.B.(N.S.) 45; cf. *Ballett Mingay* [1943] K.B. 281 (under-age bailee
wrongfully disposing of the goods).

[133] [1914] 3 K.B. 607; *Johnson v Pye* (1665) 1 Sid. 258.

[134] [1913] 2 K.B. 235.

(e) Liability in Restitution

12–036   Before the Minors' Contracts Act 1987, a minor could be held liable to restore certain benefits received by him under a contract which did not bind him. Such liability was imposed in equity if the minor was guilty of fraud,[135] and (probably) in certain other cases at common law.[136] Section 3(1) of the 1987 Act now gives the court a discretion to order the minor to transfer to the adult party any property acquired by the minor under such a contract, or any property representing it. Section 3(2) goes on to provide that nothing in s.3 "shall be taken to prejudice any other remedy available to the" adult party to the contract: thus in cases which fall outside s.3(1), or in which the court declines to exercise its discretion under that subsection, it remains open to the adult to seek restitution under the old rules of equity or common law. These therefore still call for discussion, even though generally claims for restitution are now likely to be made under s.3(1), since the conditions imposed by the subsection are less onerous than those imposed by the equitable or the common law rules.

(i) *Minors' Contracts Act 1987, section 3(1)*

12–037   **Scope.** This subsection deals with the case where a contract has been made with a minor and the contract "is unenforceable against [the minor] (or he repudiates it)[137] because he was a minor when the contract was made". In such a case the court

> "may, if it is just and equitable to do so, require [the minor] to transfer to the [other party] any property acquired by the [minor] under the contract, or any property representing it".

12–038   **Restoration of property acquired.** The subsection would most obviously apply to a case like *Nash v Inman*[138]: the minor could be ordered to return the fancy waistcoats to the seller. Such an order could be made even though the minor was not guilty of fraud, which is essential to liability in equity[139]; and even though there would, in the case put, be no liability in restitution at common law.[140]

12–039   **Proceeds of property acquired.** Section 3(1) goes beyond the simple case just put, in that the court can order the minor to transfer either the "property acquired ... under the contract" or "any property representing it". Thus if the minor were to exchange the fancy waistcoats for a set of silver candlesticks, he could be ordered to transfer those to the seller of the fancy waistcoats. On the other hand, s.3(1) would not apply where the minor had dissipated the property acquired under the contract or its proceeds: e.g. where he had bought champagne and

---

[135] See below, para.12–043.

[136] See below, para.12–048.

[137] This phrase refers to the "voidable" contracts discussed above, at paras 12–017—12–021.

[138] [1908] 2 K.B. 1; above, para.12–006.

[139] See below, para.12–043.

[140] This is on the basis that English law does not recognise any common law restitutionary claim for the recovery of chattels (as distinct from money): see *Power v Wells* (1778) 2 Cowp. 818 and the only possible claim for chattels is in tort for wrongful interference with possession or with an immediate right to possession; and in the case put there would be no such claim as property in the goods would have passed to the minor.

consumed it, or where he had sold property acquired under the contract for cash and had used the money to pay for a holiday. Section 3(1) only empowers the court to order the minor to transfer either the property acquired under the contract or property representing it: the court cannot order him to pay either the price or the reasonable value of what he has obtained out of his other assets. The underlying principle seems to be that the minor should not be enriched by retaining "property" obtained under the contract. But his general assets (other than that "property") are not to be diminished as a result of the exercise of the court's discretion under the section.

Property "representing" the property acquired. The discretion will pre-   **12–040** sent few problems where the "property acquired . . . under the contract" is still in the minor's possession; but difficulty can obviously arise where the discretion is invoked in respect of "property representing it". The case in which the minor simply exchanges the "property acquired" for something else will be relatively uncommon. More usually, he will sell the "property acquired" and use the money to buy something else; that other thing may have been paid for wholly or in part with the money obtained from the sale of the property originally acquired. Further problems can arise where that money is paid by the minor into a bank account which is in credit and from which money is then drawn out to pay for the substitute purchase. In such a case it may be very hard to tell whether that substitute is indeed "property representing" the property acquired under the original contract. Even greater difficulties could arise if the substitute had been bought under another contract which was unenforceable against the minor, and if only part of the price due under that contract had been paid by the minor; in such a case claims under s.3 for the transfer of the same thing might be made by two sellers.

Meaning of "property." A final difficulty is to determine what is meant by   **12–041** "property" in the section; and in particular whether "property" includes money.[141] The difficulty arises because the cases decided before the Act displayed a somewhat greater reluctance to make a minor "restore" a sum of money than to return goods obtained by him under the contract[142]—apparently because a judgment against him to pay a sum of money was more likely than one for the return of goods to present the appearance of indirectly enforcing the contract. But those cases do not rule out the possibility of making the minor restore money,[143] at least where he was guilty of fraud, and s.3(1) seems to be intended to extend such liability to cases in which there was no fraud.[144] Moreover, it appears from the legislative history of the Act that s.3(1) is intended to produce the result that "the minor can be compelled to hand over the proceeds if he has sold the property"[145]; and, in the case of goods at least, the proceeds of a *sale*, by definition, consist of

---

[141] The Act contains no definition of property; contrast Theft Act 1968, s.4(1), expressly providing that "property" includes money. The 1987 Act refers to "property", not to "goods", so that the definitions referred to at para.7–099, above are not relevant in the present context.
[142] See *R Leslie Ltd v Sheill* [1914] 3 K.B. 607 (below, para.12–046); *Cowern v Neild* [1912] 2 K.B. 419 (below, para.12–051).
[143] See *Stocks v Wilson* [1913] 2 K.B. 235; below, para.12–046, and below, paras 12–048—12–051.
[144] See Law Com. No.134, para.4.21.
[145] ibid.

money.[146] This supports the view that the "property representing" the "property acquired" includes money; and if this is so, then it is submitted that the "property acquired" also includes money, since the word "property" must prima facie bear the same meaning in both the places in which it occurs in the subsection. Thus it is submitted that where a minor buys goods under a contract which is unenforceable against him by reason of his minority, and then sells them, he can be ordered to transfer the money to the seller; while if the minor borrows money under such a contract, and uses it to buy goods, he can be ordered to transfer those goods to the lender.

12–042   **Discretion of the court.** Section 3(1) does not entitle the other party to the transfer of the property as of right: it only provides that the court "may, if it is just and equitable to do so," order the transfer. Of the factors which the court can take into account in exercising this discretion, two call for comment. The first is the difficulty, where the minor has disposed of the property acquired, of determining whether assets still owned by him are indeed "property representing" what he originally acquired. The process of "tracing" assets into their product can be complex[147]; and the court may restrict the operation of s.3(1) to cases in which it is relatively clear that the property which the minor is ordered to restore does indeed represent that acquired under the contract. To extend the operation of the subsection beyond this point would increase the danger that an order to transfer property (especially in the form of money) would amount to indirect enforcement of the contract against the minor. The operation of the equitable doctrine of restitution in cases of the minor's fraud gave rise to a similar danger, and it was to avert this danger that the courts restricted the scope of that doctrine. The relevant equity cases are discussed below[148] (even though the equitable doctrine has lost much of its former practical importance) because it is submitted that they now provide guidance for the exercise of the statutory discretion. The second factor which the court might take into account is the fairness of the original contract: thus if the court regarded the price payable under the contract as too high it might order the minor to return the property unless he paid a reasonable price fixed by the court.[149] In failing to specify the circumstances and manner in which the discretion is to be exercised, the subsection no doubt gives rise to some uncertainty; but it avoids complexity. In the context, the balance that it thus strikes seems to be satisfactory, since the rules which govern a minor's liability in restitution are not of a kind on which either party to the contract relies (or should be encouraged to rely) in conducting his business affairs.

(ii) *Effects of fraud*

12–043   **Common law.** At common law, a minor cannot be made liable on a contract merely because he has committed a fraud on the other party in inducing him to

---

[146] Sale of Goods Act 1979, s.2(1) ("for a money consideration").
[147] See Goff and Jones, *The Law of Restitution* (7th edn), paras 2–021 to 2–053.
[148] See below, paras 12–044—12–047.
[149] See the reference in para.4.21 of the Law Commission's Report (above, fn.144) to para.6.10 of the Commission's earlier Working Paper No.81 on Minors' Contracts.

enter into the contract.[150] The other party can at most rely on the fraud as a
defence or as a ground of rescission.[151]

Equity. The common law rules just stated unduly favoured a class of minors   **12–044**
that least deserved protection. Hence equity gave further relief against minors on
the ground of fraud. For this purpose, it seems that fraud meant some misrepresentation by the minor as to his age, so that his mere failure to declare that
he was under age did not amount to fraud[152]; nor was it fraud for him to keep,
without paying, goods obtained by him under a contract which did not bind
him.[153] Equitable relief on the ground of fraud took a number of forms.

Restoration of benefits. Our principal concern is with the power of equity to   **12–045**
order the fraudulent minor to restore benefits obtained under the contract.[154] The
remedy, being equitable, was presumably discretionary,[155] and in this respect it
resembles the statutory remedy now available under s.3(1) of the Minors' Contracts Act 1987.[156] On the other hand, the statutory remedy is in two respects
more favourable to the adult than the old equitable remedy. First, the statutory
remedy is available even though the minor was not guilty of fraud. Secondly, there
is no doubt that the statutory remedy extends to the proceeds of the thing obtained
under the contract,[157] while it was disputed whether the equitable remedy was
available in respect of such proceeds.[158] Thus although the equitable remedy is one
of those expressly preserved by the 1987 Act,[159] there seems to be no reason why
the other party should wish to resort to it. It follows that questions as to the exact
scope and extent of the equitable remedy no longer have any practical importance.
The cases concerned with such questions are now useful only as providing
illustrations of the factors that the courts may take into account in deciding
whether to exercise their statutory discretion to order the minor to transfer
property acquired under the contract, or property representing it.

Examples of the courts' discretion. In *Stocks v Wilson*[160] a minor had   **12–046**
obtained goods under a contract induced by fraud and had disposed of some of

---

[150] *Bartlett v Wells* (1862) 1 B. & S. 836; *Miller v Blankley* (1878) 38 L.T. 527; *Levene v Brougham*
(1909) 25 T.L.R. 265; exceptionally a debt incurred by fraud can be proved in an uncontested
bankruptcy: *Re King* (1858) 3 D. & J. 63.
[151] e.g. *Lemprière v Lange* (1879) 12 Ch.D. 675. No attempt seems to have been made in the cases
to argue that the adult could, by rescinding the contract for fraud, avoid the minor's title *at law* (cf.
above, para.9–079). Quaere whether the court could award damages in lieu of rescission against a minor
under s.2(2) of Misrepresentation Act 1967 (above, para.9–054). To do this might amount to indirect
enforcement of the contract in the sense discussed at para.12–046, below.
[152] For the definition of fraud, see above, para.9–030. In equity a person could be guilty of fraud even
though he had no "actual intention to cheat": *Nocton v Ashburton* [1914] A.C. 932 at 954; but in the
present context a number of cases state the requirement of a misrepresentation as to age: *Stikeman v
Dawson* (1847) 1 De G. & Sm. 90 at 103; *Ex p. Jones* (1881) 18 CL.D. 109 at 120; *Re Hodson* [1894]
2 Ch. 421 at 427.
[153] This must have been assumed in *Nash v Inman* [1908] 2 K.B. 1; for the contrary view, see Atiyah
22 M.L.R. 273 at p.275. Because of the Minors' Contracts Act 1987, s.3(1), the point no longer has any
practical importance: see below, after fn.159.
[154] e.g. *Clarke v Cobley* (1789) 2 Cox 173.
[155] cf. above, para.8–027 and see para.9–097 et seq.; below, paras 21–028, 21–051.
[156] See above, para.12–037.
[157] See the words "any property representing it" in s.3(1): above, para.12–040.
[158] See below, at fnn.160 to 167.
[159] s.3(2).
[160] [1913] 2 K.B. 235.

those goods. He was held liable to account[161] to the original seller for the proceeds of the goods. By contrast, in *R Leslie Ltd v Sheill*[162] a minor had by fraud obtained a loan of £400 and was held not liable in equity to restore the money. Lord Sumner said:

> "the money was paid over to be used as the defendant's own and he has so used it, and, I suppose, spent it. There is no question of tracing it, no possibility of restoring the very thing got by fraud, nothing but compulsion through a personal judgment to pay an equivalent sum out of his present or future resources . . . ".[163]

The crucial point in *R Leslie Ltd v Sheill* was that there was no question of tracing the money, that is of showing that it, or some asset representing it, was still in the hands of the minor. If he had still got the £400 he could have been made to restore it in equity[164]; and if he had used the £400 to buy a car he could have been ordered to hand the car over to the lender.[165] An order to "transfer . . . property" could now be made in such circumstances under s.3(1) of the 1987 Act, even in the absence of fraud.[166] Conversely, in a case like *Stocks v Wilson* the minor could, under the subsection, be ordered to transfer the proceeds of sale if they could be identified as "property representing" the goods.[167] It is submitted that such an order could be made even if the minor had happened to resell the goods for the exact equivalent of the contract price. It is no objection to a claim for restitution that it leads to the same *measure* of recovery as an action on the contract. To order a minor to pay such an amount (or any amount) becomes objectionable only on account of the *nature* of the judgment: that is, if the judgment is, in Lord Sumner's words, "a personal judgment to pay an equivalent sum out of his present or future resources". The only type of order that can be made against the minor is one to *restore* the property acquired, or its proceeds, in equity, or to *transfer* it under s.3(1). He cannot be made liable to *pay* for the property acquired or to *account* for its proceeds by a personal judgment enforceable against his general assets. This point seems to have been overlooked in *Stocks v Wilson* where the court ordered the minor to *account for* the proceeds of sale without enquiring whether those proceeds were still in the hands of the minor.[168] The purpose of the equitable and statutory remedies is to ensure that the minor is not enriched as a result of the transaction which is not binding on him; but the remedy should not diminish such general resources as he had apart from the transaction. It follows that the remedies are limited by the value of the property in the hands of the minor at the time of judgment. If by then the minor has dissipated part of the property (or its proceeds) the remedy is available only in respect of the remainder.

---

[161] [1913] 2 K.B. 235 at 247—a passage criticised in *R Leslie Ltd v Sheill* [1914] 3 K.B. 607.

[162] See above.

[163] [1914] 3 K.B. 607 at 619.

[164] There would have been, in Lord Sumner's words (above, at fn.163), a "possibility of restoring the very thing got by fraud."

[165] It is assumed that the money lent could be "traced" into the car, within Lord Sumner's words (above, at fn.163).

[166] See above, paras 12–037—12–040.

[167] See above, para.12–040.

[168] In *Westdeutsche Landesbank Girozentrale v Islington BC* [1996] A.C. 669 at 716 Lord Browne-Wilkinson refers with evident approval to *Stocks v Wilson* but treats it as a case in which the minor was "bound in equity to *restore*" property obtained by fraud.

Other forms of relief. Equity gives relief against fraudulent minors in a 12–047
number of other ways. It has, for example, been held that a minor who obtained
payment of a share in a trust fund by fraudulently pretending to be of age could
not claim a second payment on reaching full age[169]; and that a minor remainder-
man who by fraud enabled the tenant for life to mortgage the estate could not,
when the estate vested in him, deny the validity of the charge.[170] These cases do
not call for extended discussion here as they are not directly connected with the
law of contract. It has been further suggested that equity recognised a broad
principle of relief: *viz.* that if a minor sued without offering to pay he would be
guilty of "fraud" which would give the adult an equitable defence,[171] even
(apparently) where, under the contract, payment from the minor was not due until
after the adult's performance. But the authorities do not support such a broad
definition of "fraud": on the contrary, they support the view that, even in equity,
relief is available to the other party only where the minor's "fraud" takes the form
of a misrepresentation by him as to his age.[172]

(iii) *Liability in restitution at common law*

In certain circumstances a minor who has obtained benefits at the expense of an 12–048
adult may be liable to make restitution to the adult at common law. This remedy
is available as of right, and it is expressly preserved by s.3(2) of the Minors'
Contracts Act 1987.

Waiver of tort. It is illustrated by cases of so-called waiver of tort, in which the 12–049
victim of a fraud (and of certain other torts) can claim restitution in respect of
certain benefits obtained by the tortfeasor. Such an action lies against a minor if
he would have been liable to the direct action in tort. Thus it was available in
Bristow v Eastman,[173] where an apprentice, while under age, had embezzled[174] his
master's property.

Non-circumvention of lack of capacity. But the courts will not allow a 12–050
minor's lack of contractual capacity to be circumvented by means of such a
restitutionary action. Thus in *R Leslie Ltd v Sheill* the lenders made an alternative
claim that the minor was liable to repay the money lent as money had and received
to their use. This claim also failed as

> "the cause of action is in substance *ex contractu* and is so directly connected
> with the contract of loan that the action would be an indirect way of enforcing
> that contract".[175]

Here again the decisive objection is not that the measure of liability may be the
same in a restitutionary action as in one for breach of contract: the crucial point

---

[169] *Cory v Gertcken* (1816) 2 Madd. 40.
[170] *Watts v Cresswell* (1714) 2 Eq.Ca.Abr. 515.
[171] Atiyah 22 M.L.R. 273.
[172] See above, para.12–044.
[173] (1794) 1 Esp. 172. "Even this has been doubted": per Lord Sumner in *R Leslie Ltd v Sheill* [1914]
3 K.B. 607 at 613.
[174] Such conduct would now be an offence under Fraud Act 2006, s.4.
[175] [1914] 3 K.B. 607 at 621; cf. 613.

is that, where the money had been spent, the only possible effect of the judgment in either kind of action would be to impose personal liability on the minor, enforceable against his assets generally.[176]

12–051   *Cowern v Nield.* Much difficulty is caused by *Cowern v Nield.*[177] A minor who was a trader sold hay and clover, and was paid in advance. He failed to deliver any hay, and the clover which he delivered was defective, so that the buyer justifiably rejected it. As the contract was a trading contract, the buyer's claim for damages failed; and his claim for the return of the money that he had paid was also rejected. The court took the view that such a claim could have succeeded if the minor had obtained the money by fraud, and therefore ordered a new trial on the issue of fraud. But this view is, with respect, open to doubt. A minor cannot be made liable in restitution if "the action would be an indirect way of enforcing [the invalid] contract".[178] If (contrary to the submission made above) this means that the judgment must not impose the same *measure* of liability as a judgment in action for breach of contract, then the action for the return of the price should have succeeded in *Cowern v Nield* irrespective of fraud. For the minor's duty under the contract was to deliver the goods, and the damages for their non–delivery might have been quite different from the price. But if (as seems more probable) indirect enforcement refers to the imposition of *personal* liability on the minor, the action should not have succeeded merely on proof of fraud. The minor should have been liable only to the extent that the money or its identifiable proceeds were still in his hands. Under s.3(1) of the Minors' Contracts Act 1987 the court could now order the minor to transfer such money, or property representing it, to the buyer, irrespective of fraud; but that remedy is discretionary, so that the buyer might prefer to pursue his restitutionary remedy at common law, as this is available as of right.

2. MENTAL INCAPACITY

12–052   The law relating to contracts with persons "who lack capacity" represents a compromise between two principles. The first is that such a person should not be liable on his contracts if he did not have the capacity to consent. The second is that it might cause hardship to one contracting party to allow the other to "stultify himself".[179]

12–053   **Lack of capacity.** For the purposes of the Mental Capacity Act 2005, a person

> "lacks capacity in relation to a matter if at the material time he is unable to make a decision for himself in relation to the matter because of an impairment of, or a disturbance in the functioning of, the mind or brain."[180]

---

[176] cf. above, para.12–046.
[177] [1912] 2 K.B. 419.
[178] *R Leslie Ltd v Sheill* [1914] 3 K.B. 607 at 621.
[179] *Beverley's Case* (1603) 4 Co.Rep. 123b.
[180] s.2(1).

Section 3 goes on to state that a person is unable to make a decision for himself if he is

> "unable (a) to understand the information relevant to the decision, (b) to retain that information, (c) to use or weigh that information as part of the process of making the decision, or (d) to communicate his decision (whether by talking, using sign language or any other means)".[181]

This is broadly consistent with the test applied by the courts at common law which has been to ask whether a person had an understanding of what "was going on and what was involved in the transaction involved".[182] Since it would seem to make little sense to have two broadly similar, but potentially different, tests in operation, it is submitted that the test laid down in the 2005 Act should be applied even in cases which are not governed by the Act, e.g. the enforceability of a contract other than for necessaries.[183] A person who lacks capacity, whether under the common law test, or that stated in the 2005 Act, will be referred to in this part as M.

(a) In General

A contract with M is valid, except in the two cases dealt with below.   12–054

(i) *Incapacity known to other party*

If the other contracting party knows of M's incapacity, the contract is voidable   12–055
at M's option.[184] The burden is on M to show that his incapacity prevented him from understanding the transaction,[185] and that the other party knew this. It seems that M becomes absolutely bound if he ratifies the contract after he is no longer suffering from the incapacity.[186] There is also some support for the view that the contract is binding so long as it was a fair one, even though the incapacity of M was known to the other party.[187]

Where the other party does not know of M's incapacity, the contract is valid: it cannot be attacked merely on the ground that it was "unfair" in the sense that its terms were more favourable to the other party than they were to M.[188] The contract can be attacked on the ground of "unfairness" only (if at all) where the circumstances are such that M can rely, like a person of normal capacity, on the equitable rules relating to undue influence or unconscionable bargains.[189]

---

[181] For other factors which should, and should not, be taken into account, see ss.2(2)–(4) and 3(2)–(4).

[182] Fridman 79 L.Q.R. 502, 518–519. See: *Manches v Trimborn* (1946) 115 L.J.K.B. 305; *In the Estate of Park* [1954] P. 112; *Gibbons v Wright* (1954) 91 C.L.R. 423; *Re Beaney* [1978] 1 W.L.R. 770.

[183] See below, para.12–054 et seq. In *Local Authority X v MM (an adult)* [2007] EWHC 2003 (Fam); [2009] 1 F.L.R. 443 at [79]–[80] it is said that the courts may adopt the new definition in cases not covered by the Act, if "appropriate"; cf. *Saulle v Nouvet* [2007] EWHC 2902 (QB).

[184] *Molton v Camroux* (1849) 4 Ex. 17; *Imperial Loan Co v Stone* [1892] 1 Q.B. 599.

[185] *Re K* [1988] Ch. 310.

[186] *Birkin v Wing* (1890) 63 L.T. 80; *Manches v Trimborn* (1946) 115 L.J.K.B. 305.

[187] *Dane v Kirkwall* (1838) 8 C. & P. 679.

[188] *Hart v O'Connor* [1985] A.C. 1000; *Irvani v Irvani* [2000] 1 Lloyd's Rep. 412 at 420.

[189] See above, para.10–012 et seq.

(ii) *Property and affairs subject to control of the court*

12–056   **Contract only binding on other party.** If M's property is subject to the control of the court[190] an attempt by him to dispose of the property does not bind him, since, if it did bind him, it would interfere with the court's control over the property.[191] But the contract binds the other party.[192]

12–057   **Scope of the rule.** The rule that the contract does not bind M clearly applies to any contract which purports to dispose of M's property. But it is not clear whether the rule applies *only* to such contracts, or whether it extends to *all* contracts with those whose property is subject to the control of the court. On the one hand it can be argued that every contract creates a potential liability to pay money and thus interferes with the court's control over the property. On the other hand there are some negative contracts which can be enforced by injunction against M's person which need not interfere with his property. There is no reason, on principle, why such contracts should not be enforced in this way. The question is largely academic as the court only exercises control over the property and affairs of M in cases of serious incapacity. The other party will generally know of such incapacity and his claim will fail on this ground.

(b) Necessaries

12–058   Section 7 of the 2005 Act[193] provides that: "If necessary goods or services[194] are supplied to a person who lacks capacity to contract for the supply, he must pay a reasonable price for them." For this purpose, "'necessary' means suitable to a person's condition in life and to his actual requirements at the time when the goods or services are supplied."[195]

12–059   **No effect on binding contract.** If M would be bound by the contract under the rules stated above, his liability for necessaries is not affected by s.7. Thus a person who supplies necessaries to M without knowing of his incapacity can enforce the contract[196]: he is not limited to an action for a reasonable price.

12–060   **Effect on non-binding contract.** If M would not be bound by the contract under the rules stated above, he is liable under s.7. Thus a person who supplies

---

[190] Under ss.15–19 and Pt II of the 2005 Act (replacing Pt VII of Mental Health Act 1983). Under s.15 the court may make a declaration about whether M lacks capacity to make decisions on such matters as are specified, but the court's own powers are limited to matters concerning M's "personal welfare", or his "property and affairs"; s.18(1) provides a non-exhaustive, indicative list of the matters within the powers of the court relating to property and affairs which largely reproduces the list previously set out in s.96 of the 1983 Act. An innovation of the 2005 Act is to allow the court to appoint a "deputy" to act on behalf of M, who shall be treated as M's agent in relation to anything done within the scope of his appointment (s.19(6)), but the court is required to have regard to the principle that "a decision by the court is to be preferred to the appointment of a deputy to make a decision" (s.16(4)(a)).

[191] *Re Walker* [1905] 1 Ch. 160; *Re Marshall* [1920] 1 Ch. 284.

[192] cf. *Baldwyn v Smith* [1900] 1 Ch. 588.

[193] Superseding s.3(2) of Sale of Goods Act 1979 which no longer refers to mental incapacity.

[194] Services were not covered by s.3(2) of the 1979 Act, but as illustrated in the case of minors, it was supplemented in this regard by the common law: above, para.12–011.

[195] s.7(2).

[196] *Baxter v Portsmouth* (1826) 5 B. & C. 170.

necessaries to M knowing of his incapacity cannot enforce the contract: he can only recover a reasonable price. Section 3(2) of the Sale of Goods Act 1979, which s.7 replaces,[197] had applied where necessaries were "sold and delivered" to M. Those words were scarcely appropriate where necessaries are simply supplied to a patient whose incapacity is so serious that he is incapable of rational thought; or where a patient in this condition is simply maintained at the expense of another person.[198] In such cases the person who supplied or paid for the necessaries had a remedy at common law under the doctrine of agency of necessity[199] unless he acted gratuitously, without thought of recompense.[200] Since s.7 now refers simply to goods or services which are "supplied", it may be that the "supplier" will be entitled to a reasonable price; alternatively, the proper construction of the provision may be to confine it to the supply of necessaries under a purported contract for the supply which is found not to be binding, in which case the position will be unaltered.

Loans. A person who lends money to M knowing of his incapacity cannot enforce the contract, but can recover so much of the money as has actually been spent on necessaries.[201]   **12–061**

3. DRINK AND DRUGS

Drink. Extreme drunkenness is a defence to an action on a contract if it prevents the defendant from understanding the transaction, and if the claimant knows this.[202] The drunkard is liable if he ratifies the contract when he becomes sober.[203] He is also liable for necessaries.[204]   **12–062**

A defendant cannot rely at law on drunkenness which merely blurred his business sense: but such drunkenness is a ground on which equity may refuse to order specific performance.[205] Nor does a party's habitual drunkenness deprive him of contractual capacity[206] but it could be a ground for relief if the other party had taken over the position of guardian or adviser to the drunkard so as to give rise to a presumption of undue influence between them.[207]

Drugs. The rules relating to drunkenness could perhaps be applied by analogy to the case of a person whose ability to understand the transaction was impaired by drugs.[208] Such impairment may, indeed, have been brought about by the illegal conduct of that party but this fact should not preclude reliance on the impairment (if known to the other party) since this course of action would not amount either   **12–063**

---

[197] See above, fn.193.

[198] If that other person is a "deputy", they will have binding authority to enter the contract on M's behalf, if it falls within the scope of their appointment: see above, fn.190.

[199] *Brockwell v Bullock* (1889) 22 Q.B.D. 567; *Pontypridd Union v Drew* [1927] 1 K.B. 214 at 220; see also *Re Rhodes* (1889) 44 Ch.D. 94 and below, para.16–040.

[200] *Re Rhodes*, above.

[201] *Re Beavan* [1912] 1 Ch. 196.

[202] *Gore v Gibson* (1843) 13 M. & W. 623.

[203] *Matthews v Baxter* (1873) L.R. 8 Ex. 132.

[204] *Gore v Gibson*, above, at 626; Sale of Goods Act 1979, s.3(2).

[205] See below, para.21–030.

[206] *Irvani v Irvani* [2000] 1 Lloyd's Rep. 412 at 425.

[207] ibid.; above, para.10–117 et seq.

[208] The mere fact that a person was a habitual drug addict does not suffice for this purpose: see *Irvani v Irvani*, above, at 425.

to reliance on the illegality or to enforcement of the contract. Nor is there any good reason for denying a remedy to a supplier of necessaries to such a person, at least where (as will often be the case) the supplier has no connection with the illegality and seeks merely to alleviate the effect of the drugs.

4. CORPORATIONS

(a) Common Law Corporations

12–064   Corporations are created at common law by Royal Charter. The orthodox view is that a common law corporation has the same contractual capacity as a natural person of full age and capacity. Although this view is based only on dicta,[209] which have been doubted,[210] it is probably good law. Thus a contract with such a corporation is binding although it is forbidden, or not authorised, by its charter. But if the corporation makes such a contract the Attorney-General can take proceedings for the revocation of its charter; and any member of the corporation can restrain it by injunction from carrying on a forbidden activity which may lead to the revocation of its charter,[211] or claim a declaration that the activity is ultra vires.[212]

(b) Statutory Corporations

12–065   **Creation of statutory corporations.** Statutory corporations can be created in two ways: first, by complying with the formalities required by statute; and secondly, by special statute, passed to create the particular corporation in question. Since 1862, most trading companies have been created in the first of these two ways; the relevant Act in this regard is now the Companies Act 2006.[213]

(i) *Companies created under the Companies Act 2006*

12–066   **Introduction.** The contractual capacity of a company created under the Companies Acts was formerly limited by the ultra vires doctrine, under which any act which was not authorised by the memorandum of association was void in law; and, being a nullity, it could not be ratified even by a unanimous vote of the company's shareholders.[214] It followed that the company was not liable on a contract which was not authorised by its memorandum. The primary purpose of the doctrine was to protect investors in the company by giving them some assurance that the assets of the company would not be used in some wholly unexpected way. On the other

---

[209] *British S Africa Co v De Beers Consolidated Mines* [1910] 1 Ch. 354 at 374; *Jenkin v Pharmaceutical Society* [1921] 1 Ch. 392 at 398; *Institution of Mechanical Engineers v Cane* [1961] A.C. 696 at 724; *Hazell v Hammersmith & Fulham LBC* [1992] 2 A.C. 1 at 39; Furmston 24 M.L.R. 518. The point is left open in *Crédit Suisse v Allerdale BC* [1997] Q.B. 306 at 336. For the possibility that the powers of a charter corporation may be restricted by special legislation, see below, para.12–072.

[210] e.g. Holdsworth, *History of English Law*, Vol.9, pp.55–66; Street, *Ultra Vires*, at 18–22; Carden 26 L.Q.R. 320.

[211] *Jenkin v Pharmaceutical Society* [1921] 1 Ch. 392.

[212] *Pharmaceutical Society of Great Britain v Dickson* [1970] A.C. 403.

[213] The 2006 Act restates almost all of the provisions of the Companies Act 1985, together with the company law provisions of the Companies Act 1989 ("the 1989 Act") and the Companies (Audit, Investigations and Community Enterprise) Act 2004.

[214] *Ashbury Ry Carriage & Iron Co v Riche* (1875) L.R. 7 H.L. 653.

hand, a person who made a contract with the company was liable to be prejudiced by the doctrine, since he was unlikely to have read the company's memorandum, or (if he had read it) to have understood it. The doctrine could also prejudice the company itself by preventing it from taking advantage of business opportunities which (perhaps as a result of a defect in drafting) fell technically outside its objects. The company could to some extent avoid this prejudice by altering its objects, but its power to make such alterations could be exercised only for seven specified purposes.[215] It could also draw its objects clause in very wide terms, enabling it to do almost any act which could be done by a company[216]; but such very widely drawn clauses tended to be restrictively interpreted by the courts,[217] since they made the protection which the ultra vires doctrine was intended to give to shareholders quite illusory.

The effects of the ultra vires doctrine, as described above, were subjected to much criticism[218] and significant reforms were introduced by the Companies Act 1989,[219] which have now been taken further by the Companies Act 2006.

A company's constitution. Under s.17 of the 2006 Act a company's constitution includes the articles of association, and any resolutions and agreements to which Ch.3 of Pt II of the Act applies. While this is intended to be a non-exhaustive[220] definition,[221] it does not include the memorandum of association which will no longer state the objects of the company and is now confined to a role in its formation.[222] Unless specifically restricted by its articles of association, the objects of a company are unrestricted.[223] In the absence of any such restrictions the ultra vires doctrine can have no application. Where any restrictions have been included in the articles of association, it is necessary to distinguish between the *capacity* of the company and the *powers* of the board of directors to bind it.[224]   12–067

The company's capacity. Under s.39(1) of the 2006 Act the validity of an act done by a company shall not be called into question on the ground of lack of capacity by reason of anything in the company's constitution.[225] The argument that a contract is void for lack of capacity if it is not authorised by the company's   12–068

---

[215] Companies Act 1985, s.4 (original version, now repealed).

[216] *Cotman v Brougham* [1918] A.C. 514; *Brady v Brady* [1989] A.C. 755 at 772.

[217] e.g. *Rolled Steel (Holdings) Ltd v BSC* [1986] Ch. 246, drawing the distinction referred to at fn.224, below.

[218] See especially Prentice, *Reform of the Ultra Vires Rule*, a consultative paper issued by the Department of Trade and Industry in 1986.

[219] Which inserted a number of new sections into the Companies Act 1985.

[220] Other documents will have constitutional relevance for certain purposes, e.g. the certificate of incorporation summarises key information pertaining to the company such as whether it is public or private: s.15.

[221] This definition applies throughout the 2006 Act unless the context requires a wider or more restricted meaning, e.g. s.257 expands the definition of a company's constitution for the purposes of Pt X: see below, para.12–069.

[222] Companies Act 2006, s.8. In the case of companies already in existence, provisions that are contained in the memorandum but are not of the kind now required by s.8 are to be treated as provisions of the company's articles: s.28, though the company in question may also alter its articles to this effect.

[223] ibid., s.31(1).

[224] This is a distinction which was recognised in the previous English case law (*Rolled Steel (Holdings) Ltd v BSC* [1986] Ch. 246 and which was also drawn in an EC Council Directive (Dir.68/151, Art.9) implemented by the Companies Act 1989.

[225] This rule is modified if the company is a charity, by s.42, under which such acts will be ultra vires unless the person dealing with the charity can satisfy one of the requirements set out.

constitution is thus no longer available, either to the company or to the person dealing with the company.[226]

12–069   **The powers of the directors.** The directors of a company must act in accordance with the company's constitution[227] and only exercise powers for the purposes for which they are conferred.[228] But this duty may be breached and, where a contract is not authorised by the company's constitution, the mere fact that it cannot be called into question on the ground of lack of capacity will not enable a person who deals with the company to enforce it; for the making of such an unauthorised contract is necessarily beyond the powers of the directors. Further protection to such a person is therefore given by s.40 of the Act.[229] This provides that,

> "in favour of a person dealing with[230] a company in good faith, the power of the directors to bind the company, or authorise others to do so, is deemed to be free of any limitation under the company's constitution."[231]

The person who deals with the company is not bound to enquire as to any limitation on the powers of the directors to bind the company or authorise others to do so.[232] He is presumed to have acted in good faith until the contrary is proved[233]; and he is not to be regarded as acting in bad faith "by reason *only* of his knowing that an act is beyond the powers of the directors under the company's constitution."[234] This provision allows for the possibility that it may be in the

---

[226] Subs.39(1) of the 2006 Act replaces subs.35(1) of the Companies Act 1985, but there is no replacement for subss.35(2) or (3) which are simply repealed. Those two provisions were intended to protect the members of the company by giving them the right to bring proceedings to restrain the doing of an act which would be beyond the company's capacity but for s.35(1) and relieving the directors from their liability for transgressing any limit on their powers by special resolution, separate from any special resolution to ratify their actions. They were considered unnecessary in the 2006 Act on the basis of the duties of the directors and the restrictions on their powers now imposed under the 2006 Act and which are dealt with in para.12–069.

[227] For this purpose the "company's constitution" is given a wider definition than in s.17 (above, para.12–067) and includes decisions taken in accordance with the company's articles, and other decisions taken by the members (or a class of them) if they are to be treated by virtue of any enactment or rule of law as decisions of the company: s.257.

[228] Companies Act 2006, s.171, codifying the principle of law to this effect: Davies, *Gower and Davies' Principles of Modern Company Law* (7th edn), p.381; Payne and Prentice [2005] L.M.C.L.Q. 447.

[229] The rules set out in s.40 are modified for transactions involving directors or their associates (see s.41), and companies that are charities (see s.42; above, fn.225).

[230] A person "deals with" a company if he is a party to any transaction or other act to which the company is a party (s.40(2)(a)), but this does not apply to "an internal arrangement with no diminution or increase in the assets or liabilities of the company": *EIC Services Ltd v Phipps* [2004] EWCA Civ 1069; [2005] 1 W.L.R. 1377 at [35] (s.40(1) (formerly, s.35A of the 1985 Act) not applicable to shareholder receiving bonus share issue). On whether a director of the company can fall within s.40(1), see *Smith v Henniker-Major & Co* [2002] EWCA Civ 762; [2002] BCLC 655.

[231] Companies Act 2006, s.40(1). For this purpose "limitations on the directors' powers under the company's constitution" include limitations deriving from a resolution of the company or of any class of shareholders, or from any agreement between the members of the company or of any class of shareholders: s.40(3).

[232] ibid., s.40(2)(b)(i). But if there are circumstances which should have "put him on enquiry" and he does not so enquire he may be found not to have dealt in good faith: *Wrexham Association Football Club Ltd v Crucialmove Ltd* [2006] EWCA Civ 237; [2007] B.C.C. 139 at [47].

[233] ibid., s.40(2)(b)(ii).

[234] ibid., s.40(2)(b)(iii) (italics supplied).

interests of the company to take advantage of a commercial opportunity by entering into a contract which is technically not authorised by its constitution. On the other hand, a person would presumably not be dealing with the company in good faith if the transaction in question was not only beyond the powers of the directors but also constituted a breach of their fiduciary duty to it, or was otherwise a collusive attempt on the part of the directors and the person dealing with the company to act in a way that was contrary to the interests of the company. In such a case the fact that a contract was not authorised by the company's constitution would not, indeed, make it open to challenge on the ground of lack of capacity; but by reason of the element of bad faith the contract would be unenforceable as it was beyond the directors' powers, and it would not be saved by s.40(1).

Persons who deal with the company are further protected by s.40(5) which provides that s.40 does not affect any liability incurred by the directors, or any other person, by reason of the directors' exceeding their powers. Where the company *is* liable by virtue of s.40(1), such liability is unlikely to be incurred by the directors[235]; though it is possible for a director to undertake additional personal liability under a collateral contract. Where the company is *not* liable because the person dealing with it did so in bad faith, a claim against the directors is unlikely to succeed: it would probably be dismissed on the analogy of the rule that a contract to defraud a third party (i.e. the company) is illegal and void.[236]

Members of the company are protected in that they can bring proceedings to restrain the doing of an act which is beyond the powers of the directors.[237] But no such proceedings lie "in respect of an act to be done in fulfilment of a legal obligation arising from a previous act of the company".[238] Presumably it follows that proceedings cannot be brought to restrain a company from performing a contract which a person dealing with the company could enforce against it under s.40(1). It seems that such a contract will, by virtue of that subsection, be deemed to be an "act of the company" even though the directors actually had no power to enter into it on the company's behalf.

Section 40(1) only operates "in favour of a person dealing with" the company. It therefore does not confer rights on the company. The company can however acquire such rights by ratifying the transaction.[239]

(ii) *Limited Liability Partnerships*

Limited Liability Partnerships Act 2000. The Limited Liability Partner- 12–070
ships Act 2000 makes provision[240] for the incorporation of limited liability partnerships by registration of specified documents. Such a partnership is "a body corporate (with legal personality separate from its members)"[241] and "has unlimited capacity".[242] The ultra vires doctrine therefore does not apply to it.

---

[235] e.g. the remedy for breach of warranty of authority (below, para.12–079) would not be available if the contract bound the company under s.35A(1): see below, para.16–081.

[236] See above, para.11–015.

[237] s.40(4).

[238] s.40(4).

[239] *Grant v UK Switchback Ry* (1888) 40 Ch.D. 135.

[240] Limited Liability Partnerships Act, s.2.

[241] ibid., s.1(2). The general law relating to other partnerships (which do not have legal personality separate from their members) does not apply to limited liability partnerships: ibid., s.1(5).

[242] ibid., s.1(3).

(iii) *Corporations incorporated by special statute*

12–071   The ultra vires doctrine was originally established in relation to such corporations.[243] With respect to them, it is not affected by the reforms which have been described above,[244] though it has been mitigated with respect to certain contracts made by local authorities.[245] Before any of these reforms came into force, many of the rules which determine the scope and effects of the doctrine were laid down in cases arising out of contracts with companies incorporated under the Companies Acts (or with local authorities). These cases are obsolete now that the common law doctrine no longer invalidates such contracts (or has been mitigated with respect to them). But the principles stated in them can still (where appropriate) apply to transactions with other corporations which are created, or whose capacity is limited, by special statute. For this reason, the following account is to some extent based on such cases.

12–072   **The ultra vires doctrine.** The contractual capacity of a corporation created by special statute continues, in general,[246] to be restricted by the ultra vires doctrine. The objects of such a corporation are set out in the statute by which it was created (or in rules made in pursuance of that statute). Any act done by or on behalf of the corporation which is not authorised by (or under) the incorporating statute is ultra vires and ineffective. It follows that an ultra vires contract made by such a corporation does not bind the corporation. The corporation can also be restrained from doing ultra vires acts.[247] The same rules apply where the corporation has been created in some other way (e.g. by Royal Charter) but its capacity is nevertheless defined or limited by statute.[248]

12–073   **Whether transaction is ultra vires.** The question whether a particular transaction falls within the powers of the corporation turns in the first place on the construction of the statute[249] by which it is incorporated, or which otherwise defines or limits its capacity. Particular difficulty can arise where the statute, after setting out the specific objects for which the corporation is created, goes on to confer a general power to do other acts which it is necessary or desirable for the company to do in order to achieve these objects. When the ultra vires doctrine applied to companies incorporated under the Companies Acts, the courts were faced with similar difficulties arising from analogous, broadly drafted, provisions in memoranda of association.[250] In deciding questions of this kind, they distinguished between the *objects* of a company and its *powers*. They went on to hold that, although powers could be exercised only for the purpose of the objects, their exercise for other purposes was not ultra vires but only beyond the powers of the directors; and that their exercise for other purposes could not confer rights on the other party to the transaction if he had notice of the fact that the powers had been

---

[243] See *Eastern Counties Ry v Hawkes* (1855) 5 H.L.C. 331 at 347–348 (citing earlier cases).
[244] See above, para.12–067 et seq; *Crédit Suisse v Allerdale BC* [1997] Q.B. 306.
[245] Local Government (Contracts) Act 1997.
[246] For a statutory exception, see fn.245, above.
[247] e.g. *LCC v Attorney-General* [1902] A.C. 165.
[248] e.g. *Hazell v Hammersmith and Fulham LBC* [1992] 2 A.C. 1.
[249] *Den Norske Creditbank v The Sarawak Economic Development Corp* [1988] 2 Lloyd's Rep. 616.
[250] See above, fn.216.

so exercised.[251] It is arguable that the same distinction between objects and powers may apply where the officers of a corporation, whose capacity is defined by the incorporating statute, purport to exercise a general power (conferred by the statute) but do so for the purpose of achieving unauthorised objects: e.g. where they give a guarantee and it is alleged that the transaction in respect of which it is given is not an authorised object.[252] In the last resort, however, the question in cases of the present kind turns simply on the construction of the relevant legislation. Thus where the corporation was empowered to do "anything . . . which in its opinion is calculated to facilitate the proper discharge of its functions or is incidental or conducive thereto," it was held that a guarantee given by the corporation could not be challenged on the ground that it was ultra vires.[253]

Incidental objects. Even in the absence of widely drafted provisions of the kind just discussed, a corporation can do acts which it is not expressly authorised to do, if they are fairly incidental to the objects for which it was established. For example, in *Foster v London, Dover & Chatham Ry*[254] it was held that a railway company could validly grant short leases of the spaces under the arches of a viaduct, so long as those leases did not disable it from carrying on its railway business. But this rule does not enable the corporation to carry on activities substantially distinct from those authorised: thus a corporation authorised to run trams could not "incidentally" run buses.[255]   **12–074**

Contracts ex facie intra vires. A contract which is *ex facie* within the capacity of the corporation is not invalid merely because the corporation uses its proceeds for an ultra vires purpose: e.g. where an *intra vires* loan is spent on an ultra vires purpose.[256] But the corporation would not be bound by the contract if the lender knew that it intended to use the loan for such a purpose, or if he knew facts from which he could reasonably have deduced that the corporation had such an intention.[257]   **12–075**

Alternative remedies. Where a transaction with a corporation is ultra vires, its invalidity can be a source of hardship to the other party: that party will, for example, have no remedy against the corporation if the corporation defaults on a transaction which has, by reason of market fluctuations, turned out to be disadvantageous to the corporation.[258] In theory, the other party can protect himself against this risk, before entering into the transaction, by reading the statute which defines or limits the corporation's powers. But in practice the other party is   **12–076**

---

[251] *Rolled Steel Products (Holdings) Ltd v BSC* [1986] Ch. 246; cf. above, at fn.224. See also *Introductions Ltd v National Provincial Bank Ltd* [1970] Ch. 199; Wedderburn 32 M.L.R. 563; 46 M.L.R. 204; Gregory 48 M.L.R. 109.

[252] *Crédit Suisse v Allerdale BC* [1997] Q.B. 306; *Crédit Suisse v Waltham Forest LBC* [1997] Q.B. 362; *Sutton LBC v Morgan Grenfell & Co* (1997) 29 H.L.R. 608; in all these cases, the guarantees were held void.

[253] *Den Norske Creditbank v The Sarawak Economic Development Corp* [1988] 2 Lloyd's Rep. 616 (where the incorporating legislation was a Malaysian Ordinance).

[254] [1895] 1 Q.B. 711; cf. *Charles Roberts & Co v British Railways Board* [1965] 1 W.L.R. 396.

[255] *LCC v Attorney-General* [1902] A.C. 165; cf. *Hazell v Hammersmith & Fulham LBC* [1992] 2 A.C. 1.

[256] *Re David Payne & Co Ltd* [1904] 2 Ch. 608.

[257] *Re Jon Beauforte Ltd* [1953] Ch. 131; cf. *Introductions Ltd v National Provincial Bank Ltd* [1970] Ch. 199.

[258] e.g. *Hazell v Hammersmith and Fulham BC* [1992] 2 A.C. 1.

unlikely to take this step; and, even if he does take it, he runs the risk that his interpretation of the statute may, in legal proceedings on the contract, be held to have been erroneous. The law to some extent mitigates this hardship by making a number of alternative remedies available to the other party to the transaction.

12–077   **Subrogation.** An ultra vires lender can recover so much of his loan as is used by the company to pay debts incurred under *intra vires* contracts.[259]

12–078   **Return of money.** Money paid under an ultra vires contract is normally recoverable as money paid under a void contract.[260] This remedy is more fully discussed in Ch.22.[261]

12–079   **Remedy against officers.** A person who is induced to contract with a corporation by the false representation of a director that the contract is *intra vires* may be able to sue the director in tort for deceit or negligence,[262] or in contract for breach of implied warranty of authority.[263] The contractual action lies even though the representation was made innocently and in good faith.[264] It has been held that this remedy is not available if the misrepresentation is one of law[265]; though for reasons given in Ch.9 the present status of this restriction on the scope of the remedy is open to question.[266] The construction of the company's incorporating statute is a matter of law,[267] so that a director who represents that, on the true construction of the statute, a contract is *intra vires*, makes a representation of law.

An ultra vires contractor may, finally, be able to show that the director is personally liable on the contract itself. Intention on the part of an agent to assume personal liability is readily inferred when the principal is non-existent.[268] Such an inference might also be drawn where the principal exists but lacks capacity to make the contract.

12–080   **Enforcement by the corporation.**[269] The ultra vires doctrine normally operates so as to prevent a contract from being enforced *against* the corporation. The authorities provide no clear answer to the question whether the doctrine also precludes enforcement of the contract *by* the corporation.

A similar problem used to arise where a contract with a corporation should have been, but was not, made under its common seal.[270] If such a contract was executory, the company could not enforce it because its own promise, being

---

[259] *Blackburn BS v Cunliffe, Brooks & Co* (1882) 22 Ch.D. 61; on appeal it was not necessary to decide this point: 9 App.Cas. 857.

[260] *Westdeutsche Landesbank Girozentrale v Islington LBC* [1996] A.C. 669 disagreeing with *Sinclair v Brougham* [1914] A.C. 398 so far as *contra*.

[261] See below, para.22–013.

[262] At common law, but not under s.2(1) of Misrepresentation Act 1967; see above, para.9–042 at fn.198.

[263] See below, para.16–077.

[264] *Firbank's Executors v Humphreys* (1886) 18 Q.B.D. 54; cf. *Weeks v Propert* (1873) L.R. 8 C.P. 427; *Cherry v Colonial Bank of Australia* (1869) L.R. 3 P.C. 24.

[265] See below, para.16–080.

[266] See above, para.9–013.

[267] *Rashdall v Ford* (1866) L.R. 2 Eq. 750; cf. *Beattie v Ebury* (1872) L.R. 7 Ch.App. 777, affirmed L.R. 7 H.L. 102.

[268] *Kelner v Baxter* (1866) L.R. 2 C.P. 174; below, para.16–047.

[269] Furmston 24 M.L.R. 215.

[270] This formal requirement was abolished by Corporate Bodies Contracts Act 1960.

invalid, was no consideration for that of the other party[271]; but if the corporation actually performed its own invalid promise it thereby provided consideration and so became entitled to enforce the contract.[272] It can be argued that a similar distinction should be applied to ultra vires contracts; but it is submitted that the better approach is to ask whether the object of the statutory limitation on the corporation's capacity would be subverted by allowing it to enforce the contract (rather than to ask whether the corporation had provided consideration).[273] Where the corporation wishes to enforce the contract but has *not* yet performed its part, that object is likely to be subverted by allowing such enforcement, at least if enforcement by the corporation were (as would often be the case[274]) conditional on performance by it. In such cases the corporation would be encouraged to engage in ultra vires activity so as to satisfy the condition; and since it should not be given any incentive to engage in such activity, the contract should not be enforceable by it.[275] Where, on the other hand, the corporation *has* performed its part, this argument has no force: enforceability by the corporation could not encourage it to engage in future ultra vires activity since (at least in relation to the transaction in question[276]) the ultra vires activity has already taken place; and this reasoning gives some support to the view that a corporation which has performed its part of the contract should be able to enforce that contract. But it is submitted that this result should not necessarily follow and that a distinction should be drawn between cases in which the nature of the performance is such that it cannot, and those in which it is such that it can, be restored to the corporation. The first possibility is illustrated by the case in which the corporation has rendered services under an ultra vires contract. In such a case, the object of the rule making the contract ultra vires is hardly likely to be defeated by allowing the corporation to sue for the agreed price of the services so that there is no strong argument against allowing it to enforce the contract; though the injustice of denying it such a remedy would at least be mitigated by allowing it to claim a reasonable remuneration in respect of services rendered by it under a void contract.[277] The second possibility can be illustrated by supposing that the corporation has purported to sell an article which it was by its incorporating statute prohibited from selling,[278] and that it had actually delivered that article to the buyer. The object of the statute would, it is submitted, be more effectively promoted by allowing the corporation to sue for the return of the article than by allowing it to sue for the price, or for damages for non-acceptance of the subject-matter of the sale.[279] This argument is

---

[271] *Kidderminster Corp v Harwick* (1873) L.R. 9 Ex. 13; above, para.3–155.

[272] *Fishmongers' Co v Robertson* (1843) 5 Man. & G. 131.

[273] This approach would make it inappropriate to apply to ultra vires cases the further rule, laid down in *Ecclesiastical Commissioners v Merral* (1869) L.R. 4 Ex. 162, that a corporation could enforce a contract which should have been (but was not) under seal if the *other* party had done such acts of part performance as made the contract enforceable against the corporation.

[274] See below, para.17–014; exceptions would be cases of independent promises (below, para.17–019) and of accepted anticipatory breach (below, paras 17–027, 17–088, 18–009).

[275] See *Pellatt's Case* (1867) L.R. 2 Ch.App. 527; *Triggs v Staines Urban DC* [1969] Ch. 10; *Bell Houses Ltd v City Wall Properties Ltd* [1966] 1 Q.B. 207 (reversed [1966] 2 Q.B. 656 on the ground that the contract was *intra vires*).

[276] *Bell Houses Ltd v City Wall Properties Ltd* [1966] 2 Q.B. 656 at 694.

[277] On the principle of *Craven-Ellis v Cannons Ltd* [1936] 2 K.B. 403; below para.22–024.

[278] e.g. British Museum Act 1963, s.3(4), as amended by Museums and Galleries Act 1992, s.11(2) and Sch.8, para.5.

[279] cf. the suggestion in the *Bell Houses* case, above, at first instance that the corporation's remedy should be in restitution (though this would not be a possible remedy for the recovery of goods in specie).

supported by a group of cases in which moneys had been paid both by and to corporations under ultra vires contracts and it was held that the payments must be returned to the corporation where it was the payor[280] and by the corporation where it was the payee.[281] It must follow from these cases that the corporation could not have enforced the contracts by claiming the money or damages for failure to pay it; and emphatic statements in them that the contracts were "wholly void"[282] and "devoid of any legal contractual effects"[283] lend further support to the view that an ultra vires contract cannot be enforced by, any more than against the corporation.

---

[280] *South Tyneside MBC v Svenska International Plc* [1995] 1 All E.R. 545; *Kleinwort Benson Ltd v Lincoln CC* [1999] 2 A.C. 349 at 416.

[281] e.g. *Westdeutsche Landesbank Girozentrale v Islington LBC* [1996] A.C. 669; *Guinness Mahon & Co Ltd v Kensington & Chelsea Royal BC* [1999] Q.B. 215; *Kleinwort Benson Ltd v Lincoln CC* [1999] 2 A.C. 349; below, para.22–016.

[282] *Morgan Grenfell & Co Ltd v Welwyn Hatfield DC* [1995] 1 All E.R. 1 at 4.

[283] *Guinness Mahon* case, above, fn.281, at 284.

CHAPTER THIRTEEN

PLURALITY OF PARTIES

A promise may be made by or to more than one person. Such a promise must **13–001** be distinguished from a multilateral contract.[1] If three persons agree to run a race subject to certain rules, there are three sides to the contract, but each side consists of only one person.[2] If two persons promise to pay a third £10, or if one person promises to pay £10 to two others, there may only be two sides to the contract, one consisting of two persons and the other of one person. This chapter is concerned with promises of this kind.

1. PLURALITY OF DEBTORS[3]

(a) Definitions

Independent promises. If A and B *each separately* promise to pay C £10 this **13–002** does not amount to one promise by several to one, but to two independent promises. Thus C is entitled to £10 from A and a further £10 from B. This was, for example, the position where C granted licences to A and B under agreements providing for payment of a weekly sum by each of them,[4] and where a group of Lloyd's underwriters issued an insurance policy to an assured by which they bound themselves "each for his own part and not one for another".[5] There may be two such separate promises even where both are contained in the same document.[6]

---

[1] See above, para.2–076.
[2] cf. *Rockeagle Ltd v Alsop Wilkinson* [1992] Ch. 47 at 50 ("tripartite agreement").
[3] Williams, *Joint Obligations.*
[4] *Mikeover v Brady* [1989] 3 All E.R. 618.
[5] *Touche Ross & Co v Colin Baker* [1992] 2 Lloyd's Rep. 207 at 209.
[6] *Collins v Prosser* (1823) 1 B. & C. 682; *Gibson v Lupton* (1832) 9 Bing. 297; *Lee v Nixon* (1834) 1 A. & E. 201.

13–003   **Joint or joint and several promises.** If A and B *together* promise to pay £10,
the promise may be joint, or joint and several.[7] It is joint if A and B make only one
promise binding both of them; it is joint and several if they make one promise
binding both of them and if in addition each makes a separate promise binding
him alone. A joint and several promise is distinguishable from two entirely
separate promises in that it does not involve the promisors in cumulative liability.
If A and B jointly and severally promise to pay C £10, C is not entitled to more
than £10 in all. It is a question of construction whether a promise is joint, or joint
and several.[8] A promise by two persons together is deemed to be joint, unless it
is qualified in some way.[9] To make a promise joint and several, it is advisable to say
expressly "we promise jointly and severally," or "we, and each of us, will pay". But
this is not the only way of creating joint and several liability. In *Tippins v Coates*[10]
three persons executed a bond by which they bound themselves "jointly and our
respective heirs". This was held to be a joint and several promise, since that was
evidently the intention of the parties: if it were held to be a joint bond, the
respective heirs of the promisors would not be bound, but only the heir of the
survivor.[11]

13–004   **Express provision by statute.** In some cases the question of whether liability
is joint, or joint and several, is expressly dealt with by statute. For example, s.9 of
the Partnership Act 1890, provides that "every partner in a firm is liable jointly
with the other partners ... for all debts and obligations of the firm incurred
while he is a partner". On the other hand promissory notes made by a number of
persons are deemed to be joint and several.[12]

(b) Differences Between Joint, and Joint and Several, Promises

(i) *Parties to the action*

13–005   **Action on a joint promise.** At common law, an action on a *joint* promise had
to be brought against all the surviving joint debtors.[13] If this was not done the
defendants could plead the non-joinder of their co-debtors in abatement.
Although pleas in abatement no longer exist, it is still the general rule that the
action must be brought against all the joint debtors.[14] But the court has a
discretion to allow the action to proceed against one joint debtor if the other is out

---

[7] In identifying the mutual obligations of the debtors it is unlikely to make any difference whether
their covenant was joint, joint and several or only several: *Stroude v Beazer Homes Ltd* [2005] EWHC
2686; (2005) 48 E.G. 223 (implied term that one landowner had right to enter land of another to fulfil
concurrent obligation to construct bypass).
[8] cf. Bills of Exchange Act 1882, s.85(1) ("according to its tenour").
[9] *Levy v Sale* (1877) 37 L.T. 709; *White v Tyndall* (1888) 13 App.Cas. 263; *The Argo Hellas* [1984]
1 Lloyd's Rep. 296 at 300.
[10] (1853) 18 Beav. 401.
[11] See below, para.13–009.
[12] Bills of Exchange Act 1882, s.85(2); see also Law of Property Act 1925, s.119; Landlord and
Tenant (Covenants) Act 1995, s.13(1).
[13] *Cabell v Vaughan* (1669) 1 Wms.Saund. 291; *Richards v Heather* (1817) 1 B. & Ald. 29.
[14] *Norbury, Natzio & Co Ltd v Griffiths* [1918] 2 K.B. 369; it is up to the defendant to take the point;
Wegg-Prosser v Evans [1895] 1 Q.B. 108. And see CPR, r.19.2(1).

of the jurisdiction, or cannot be traced.[15] If one joint debtor is bankrupt, the other or others may be sued without him.[16]

Action on a joint and several promise. An action on a *joint and several* promise could at common law be brought against one or all the co-debtors but not, it seems, against some (but not all). The creditor could either sue each debtor individually on his several promise or all on their joint promise; but he could not, by suing some, treat the contract as joint without also joining all the others.[17] It seems that in such a case the court now has a discretion to order all the other joint and several debtors to be joined to the action since it may order the names of persons to be joined to an action if their presence is "desirable . . . so that the court can resolve all matters in dispute in the proceedings".[18] The court might order such joinder so that the amount of the debt may be conclusively established for the purpose of the contribution[19] between all the debtors. It seems that the onus is on the debtor who is sued to bring his co-debtors before the court as third parties, with a view to claiming contribution from them.[20]

13–006

(ii) *Judgment*

Judgment against one joint debtor. If one *joint* debtor is sued alone and does not plead non-joinder of the others, judgment may be given against him alone. After the creditor had recovered such a judgment, it was formerly the rule that he could not take further proceedings against any of the other joint debtors (even though the judgment remained unsatisfied) because the original cause of action was merged in the judgment.[21] This rule was, however, likely to cause hardship to the creditor; and it has been abolished by statute,[22] so that a creditor is no longer precluded from suing one joint debtor merely because he has previously obtained a judgment against another.

13–007

Judgment against one joint and several debtor. Where the contract is *joint and several*, judgment against one debtor was never regarded as a bar to proceedings against another. Each is liable on his separate promise, as well as on the joint promise: hence there are several causes of action only some of which are merged in the first judgment.[23] A claim against joint and several debtors is barred only if one of them satisfies it, whether under a judgment or otherwise.

13–008

---

[15] *Wilson, Sons & Co Ltd v Balcarres Brook SS Co Ltd* [1893] 1 Q.B. 422; *Robinson v Geisel* [1894] 2 Q.B. 685.

[16] Insolvency Act 1986, s.345(4).

[17] *Cabell v Vaughan* (1669) 1 Wms.Saund. 291, n.4.

[18] CPR, r.19.2(2)(a).

[19] See below, para.13–017.

[20] cf. *Wilson, Sons & Co Ltd v Balcarres Brook SS Co Ltd*, above, fn.15, at 428 (where the contract was joint).

[21] *Kendall v Hamilton* (1879) 4 App.Cas. 504.

[22] Civil Liability (Contribution) Act 1978, ss.3, 7(1). For a situation not covered by these provisions, see *The Argo Hellas* [1984] 1 Lloyd's Rep. 296 at 304. S.3 also does not apply where a debt is discharged by an accord and satisfaction which is later embodied in a court order: *Morris v Molesworth* [1998] N.L.J. 1551. See also CPR, r.12.8 (default judgment).

[23] *Blyth v Fladgate* [1891] 1 Ch. 337.

(iii) *Survivorship*

13–009   **Common law.** At common law the liability of a *joint* debtor passed on his death to the surviving joint debtors.[24] The creditor therefore had no claim against the estate of the deceased, but only one against the surviving joint debtors. If they paid, they might be able to recover contribution from the estate of the deceased[25]; but the creditor himself had no direct right against the estate. On the death of the last surviving joint debtor, the creditor could recover the debt from his estate.[26]

On the death of a *joint and several* debtor, on the other hand, his several (though not his joint) liability remained enforceable against his estate.[27]

13–010   **Equity.** The rule that joint liability passed to the surviving debtors might be convenient where the debtors were engaged in administering a trust, but it was highly inconvenient in commercial affairs. If only one of a number of joint debtors was solvent, and that one happened to die, the creditor would lose all substantial remedy. The difficulty was particularly acute in partnership cases. Equity therefore treated partnership debts as joint and several to this extent, that they could be enforced against the estate of a deceased partner.[28] This rule is confirmed by s.9 of the Partnership Act 1890.[29]

The equitable right to enforce a joint debt against the estate of a deceased joint contractor was applied mainly in partnership cases, but there is some authority for saying that it was not confined to such cases, nor even to cases involving mercantile transactions.[30] It is therefore arguable that, on the question of survivorship, there was, before the Judicature Act 1873, a conflict between common law and equity, so that equity now prevails.[31] It is also arguable that the principle of survivorship has been abolished by s.1(1) of the Law Reform (Miscellaneous Provisions) Act 1934, which provides that all causes of action subsisting against a person at the time of his death shall (with certain exceptions) survive against the estate. The object of this provision was to abolish the common law rule that actions *in tort* could not be brought against the estate of a deceased tortfeasor; but its words seem apt to abolish the rule that the liability of a joint debtor passed on his death to the surviving joint debtors (so that it could no longer be enforced against his estate).

(c) Similarities Between Joint, and Joint and Several, Promises

(i) *Defence of one*

13–011   **Whether defence of one is a defence for all.** If one of several co-debtors has a defence to the action, the question whether that defence also avails the others

---

[24] *Cabell v Vaughan* (1669) 1 Wms.Saund. 291, n.4(*f*); *Godson v Good* (1816) 6 Taunt. 587 at 594.
[25] *Batard v Hawes* (1853) 2 E. & B. 287; below, para.13–017.
[26] *Calder v Rutherford* (1822) 3 Brod. & B. 302.
[27] *Read v Price* [1909] 1 K.B. 577.
[28] See *Kendall v Hamilton* (1879) 4 App.Cas. 504 at 517. Lord Mansfield had anticipated the equitable rule: *Rice v Shute* (1770) 5 Burr. 2611 at 2613.
[29] But under this section separate debts of a deceased partner must be paid in priority to the partnership debts.
[30] *Thorpe v Jackson* (1837) 2 Y. & C. Ex. 553.
[31] Judicature Act 1873, s.25(11); now Senior Courts Act 1981, s.49(1).

depends on its nature. If it goes to the root of the claim, and wholly destroys it, the other debtors can take advantage of it. Thus they can do so if one co-debtor can prove that the debt has been paid, or that the creditor is not entitled to payment because of his own breach of contract, or that a written contract is a forgery, or that the creditor was guilty of fraud.[32] But if the defence is personal to one co-debtor, e.g. that he was a minor or that he had been discharged as a result of bankruptcy proceedings, it does not avail the others as co-debtors.[33]

Contracts of guarantee. Special rules apply to contracts of guarantee, under which the guarantor generally undertakes joint and several liability with the principal debtor.[34] It has been held that the guarantor is not liable if the principal debt is illegal,[35] or if the principal debtor has been discharged as a result of the creditor's breach,[36] or if the principal debt is unenforceable under the rule against penalties.[37] A guarantor of a debt that was unenforceable under the Moneylenders Acts was not liable on the guarantee[38]; and the Consumer Credit Act 1974 (which repeals those Acts) lays down a similar rule in the case of a guarantee given in respect of a regulated agreement.[39] These rules cannot be deduced from the general principles governing joint and several contracts, but appear to be based on considerations of policy.[40] It is obviously undesirable to allow a person who lends for an illegal purpose, or a lender who tries to evade the Consumer Credit Act, to recover his loan from any person whatsoever.

13–012

On the other hand, a guarantee may be valid where the principal debtor is a corporation acting ultra vires. Whether it is actually valid depends on its construction: did the guarantor undertake to pay only what the corporation could lawfully be required to pay, or what it had in fact promised to pay?[41] Where the principal debt is incurred by a company incorporated under the Companies Act 2006, the validity of that debt can no longer (as a general rule) be called into question on the ground of lack of the company's capacity by reason of anything in its constitution[42]; it follows that the guarantee cannot be called into question on this ground. The position is the same where the principal debt arises out of a contract which is made by a person dealing with the company in good faith, but which is, under the company's constitution, beyond the power of the board of directors: in favour of the other contracting party, the power of the board is (as a general rule) deemed

---

[32] *Porter v Harris* (1663) 1 Lev. 63; *Gardner v Walsh* (1855) 5 E. & B. 83; *Pirie v Richardson* [1927] 1 K.B. 448.

[33] *Burgess v Merrill* (1812) 4 Taunt. 468; *Lovell & Christmas v Beauchamp* [1894] A.C. 607; *Pirie v Richardson* [1927] 1 K.B. 448, cf. *Chaplin v Leslie Frewin (Publishers) Ltd* [1966] Ch. 71.

[34] e.g. *Anderson v Martindale* (1801) 1 East 497; *Read v Price* [1909] 1 K.B. 577.

[35] *Swan v Bank of Scotland* (1836) 10 Bli.(N.S.) 627; *Heald v O'Connor* [1971] 1 W.L.R. 497.

[36] *Unity Finance Ltd v Woodcock* [1963] 1 W.L.R. 455, explained on another ground in *Goulston Discount Co Ltd v Clark* [1967] 2 Q.B. 493.

[37] *Azimut-Benetti SpA v Healey* [2010] EWHC 2234 (Comm); 132 Con L.R. 113 (where the debt did not amount to a penalty).

[38] *Eldridge & Morris v Taylor* [1931] 2 K.B. 416; *Temperance Loan Fund Ltd v Rose* [1932] 2 K.B. 522.

[39] s.113(1) and (2); see above, para.5–007 for the meaning of "regulated" agreement.

[40] Mitchell 63 L.Q.R. 354.

[41] *Yorks Ry & Wagon Co v Maclure* (1882) 21 Ch.D. 309; *Garrard v James* [1925] Ch. 616, as explained in *Heald v O'Connor* [1971] 1 W.L.R. 497.

[42] Companies Act 2006, s.39(1) (modified rules apply to companies which are charities: ss.39(2), 42); above, para.12–068.

to be free from any limitation under the company's constitution,[43] so that the contract giving rise to the debt, and consequently also the guarantee, cannot be challenged on the ground that it was beyond the powers of the board. The general rule is that the principal contract will be invalid only if the other party to it dealt with the company in bad faith; and mere knowledge of the fact that the contract was beyond the powers of the directors is not sufficient to constitute bad faith.[44] It seems that some kind of actual dishonesty is required to constitute bad faith; and if the principal transaction is invalid on this ground, then it is submitted that the guarantee should also be invalid. This submission is based on the analogy of the rule relating to illegal contracts,[45] for the principal contract in our last example would be, or would come close to being, one to defraud the company.[46] The only other situations in which the principal contract is now likely to be invalid on the ground that it is *ultra vires* are (i) those in which a statutory corporation was not incorporated under the Companies Act, so that the common law doctrine of *ultra vires* still applied to it,[47] and (ii) those in which, though the company was incorporated under the Act, the statutory modifications of the *ultra vires* doctrine, described above, exceptionally do not apply.[48] If in such cases the creditor is induced to enter into the contract in reliance on a guarantee given by one of the corporation's directors or officers, it is submitted that the guarantor should be liable on the guarantee: there seems to be no ground of policy for allowing him to rely on the invalidity of the principal debt.

Similar policy considerations apply where the principal debtor is a minor: it would be wrong to allow the guarantor on this ground to escape from a liability deliberately undertaken since such a result would not be necessary for the protection of minors. It has therefore been provided by statute that the guarantee shall not be unenforceable against the guarantor merely because the principal obligation was unenforceable against the debtor because he was a minor when he incurred it.[49]

(ii) *Release of one*

13–013   **Release of one debtor by the creditor is a release of all.** If the creditor releases one co-debtor, the release is available for the benefit of all the others since it wholly destroys the cause of action.[50] At first sight, the application of this rule to joint and several debtors looks illogical, since there are several causes of action against them; but it may be justified on the ground that it would make the release partly futile to hold that only one of the co-debtors was released. If the others could still be sued, they could claim contribution from the one who had been released, who would thus indirectly be made liable, notwithstanding the release.[51]

---

[43] ibid., s.40(1) (modified rules apply to companies which are charities: ss.40(6), 42; and transactions with directors and their associates: ss.40(6), 41); above, para.12–069.
[44] ibid., s.40(2)(b)(iii).
[45] See above, at fn.35.
[46] cf. above, para.11–015.
[47] See above, para.12–071; subject to the exceptions there stated relating to local authorities.
[48] i.e. charitable companies and transactions with directors or their associates; above, fnn.42, 43.
[49] Minors' Contracts Act 1987, s.2 (reversing *Coutts & Co v Browne-Lecky* [1947] K.B. 104); and see s.4, amending Consumer Credit Act 1974, s.113(7).
[50] *Nicholson v Revill* (1836) 4 A. & E. 675; *Re EWA* [1901] 2 K.B. 642; *Morris v Molesworth* [1998] N.L.J. 1551. In tort, the rule applies where the liability is joint: *New Zealand Guardian Trust Ltd v Brooks* [1995] 1 W.L.R. 96; and where it is concurrent: *Jameson v CEGB* [2000] 1 A.C. 455.
[51] *Jenkins v Jenkins* [1928] 2 K.B. 501 at 508.

But in spite of this argument, a covenant not to sue a single co-debtor releases him alone and does not release the other co-debtors.[52]

Reservation of right to sue co-debtors. It used to be thought that a release **13–014** granted to one co-debtor released the others even though it reserved the creditor's rights against them.[53] But the courts originally evaded this rule by distinguishing between a release and a covenant not to sue. The former released all the co-debtors; the latter released only the debtor with whom it was made.[54] The distinction turned on the construction of the document and the present approach is to go directly to the question of construction without first distinguishing between "release" and "covenant not to sue".[55] Accordingly, if the document releases one co-debtor but reserves the creditor's rights against the other or others, the courts will give effect to the intention of the parties as so expressed.[56] But a document which simply released one co-debtor without expressly or impliedly[57] reserving the creditor's rights against the others would still wholly extinguish those rights.[58]

Release of one debtor by operation of law is no release of co-debtors. **13–015** The rules discussed above apply only to release by act of the parties. Where one co-debtor is released by operation of law (e.g. by an order of discharge in bankruptcy) the others are not released.[59] If the creditor appoints one co-debtor his executor, both the co-debtor and the others are released when probate is obtained. The reason for this rule is that "the debt is deemed to have been paid by the debtor [*qua* debtor] to himself as executor" and thus discharged.[60] In equity the executor is then deemed to have the amount of the debt in his hands as assets of the testator, and is thus accountable for it to the estate.[61]

Release of one debtor under an independent promise. Problems similar to **13–016** those discussed above can arise where A and B are not joint, or joint and several, debtors but are persons who have entered into, and then broken, two entirely separate contracts with C.[62] The losses suffered by C in consequence of these

---

[52] See the authorities cited in fn.54, below.

[53] *Nicholson v Revill* (1836) 4 A. & E. 675 at 683.

[54] *Hutton v Eyre* (1815) 6 Taunt. 289; *Webb v Hewitt* (1857) 3 K. & J. 438; *Ex p. Good* (1876) 5 Ch.D. 46. In *Duck v Mayeu* [1892] 2 Q.B. 511 and *Gardiner v Moore* [1969] 1 Q.B. 55 the same rule was applied in tort; the latter case also shows that reservation of the rights against one of the persons liable may be implied; for such an implied reservation, see also *Finley v Connell Associates* [1999] Lloyd's Rep. P.N. 895.

[55] *Johnson v Davies* [1999] Ch. 117 at 127–128, following *Watts v Aldington, The Times*, December 16, 1993.

[56] *Johnson v Davies*, above; for earlier cases reaching the same conclusion, see *Price v Barker* (1855) 4 E. & B. 760; *Appleby Estates Co v De Bernales* [1947] Ch. 217 (tort); cf. *Banco Santander SA v Bayfern Ltd* [2000] 1 All E.R. (Comm) 776 at 780 (release of one joint and several debtor by assignment of the creditor's right to that one). If payments made by the co-debtors who have been released extinguish the debt in full, there can be no surviving cause of action against any remaining co-debtor notwithstanding a reservation of rights against him: *Crooks v Newdigate Properties Ltd* [2009] EWCA Civ 283.

[57] See *Gardiner v Moore*, above, fn.54.

[58] cf. *Cutler v McPhail* [1962] 2 Q.B. 292; cf. *Deanplan Ltd v Mahmoud* [1993] Ch. 151 (where the liability of successive assignees of a lease was cumulative).

[59] Insolvency Act 1986, s.281(7); *Re Garner's Motors Ltd* [1937] Ch. 594.

[60] *Jenkins v Jenkins* [1928] 2 K.B. 501 at 509; Limitation (Amendment) Act 1980, s.10.

[61] ibid. at 509; *Commissioner of Stamp Duties v Bone* [1977] A.C. 511.

[62] For the distinction between the two types of promises, see above, para.13–002.

breaches may be related: e.g. where A and B are associated companies and A's wrongful termination of an agency contract with C on the ground of C's alleged but unsubstantiated misconduct leads B wrongfully to terminate a similar (but not identical) contract, also with C.[63] An agreement by which C settles his claim against A may be expressed to release C's claim against A in respect of loss suffered by C by reason, not only of A's, but also of B's, wrongful termination of the contracts with C[64]; and the effect, if any, of this agreement on C's claim against B depends on its construction.[65] If it meant that the sum paid in pursuance of it were intended to represent the full amount of C's loss, resulting from both breaches, then C, having been fully compensated for that loss by A, would have no further claim in respect of it against B.[66] But such an agreement to release A from liability for A's breach will not bar C's claim against B in respect of other causes of action (than B's breach of contract) which C may have against B or in respect of loss caused by B's breach to the extent to which that loss was attributable to B's (rather than to A's) breach.[67] The only effect of C's settlement with A on such a claim results from the principle that C cannot recover twice over the same loss: that is, C must give credit to B for sums paid by A under the settlement so far as they represent the loss suffered by C as a result of B's breach[68] for which A nevertheless accepted liability on the ground that this breach was a consequence of A's prior breach.

(iii) *Contribution*

13–017   If one co-debtor, being liable to pay the entire debt,[69] has paid it in full, he is entitled to recover contribution from the others.[70] Prima facie, he is entitled to recover from each co-debtor the amount of the debt divided by the number of co-debtors. If one of the co-debtors has died, his estate is liable to contribute, even if he was a joint debtor. The general rule may be varied by the terms of the contract or by the bankruptcy of one co-debtor.

13–018   **Terms of the contract.** The co-debtors can make any provision they like as to contribution. Where the co-debtors are principal debtor and surety, it is implied that the surety, if called on to pay, is entitled to be wholly indemnified by the principal debtor. Conversely, if the principal debtor pays the whole debt, he has no right of contribution against the surety. Several sureties for the same debt are prima facie entitled *inter se* to contribution in proportion to their number; but

---

[63] As in *Heaton v Axa Equity and Law Life Assurance Society Plc* [2002] UKHL 15; [2002] 2 A.C. 329.

[64] ibid., where A's (unsubstantiated) allegations of misconduct may also have influenced B.

[65] ibid. at [8], [9], [27], [41].

[66] ibid. at [8].

[67] This was the outcome in the *Heaton* case, above.

[68] In the *Heaton* case, C accepted the need to give credit for such sums (paid by A) in their claim against B and this concesssion was evidently regarded as correct by Lord Mackay at [47], with whose reasoning Lords Bingham, Steyn and Hutton agreed.

[69] For this requirement, see *Legal & General Assurance Society v Drake Ins Co Ltd* [1992] Q.B. 887 where a debtor who was liable for only part of the debt, but had paid it in full, was held not to be entitled to contribution. Where a guarantee provided for payment on demand and one guarantor paid more than his share before any such demand had been made, he was nevertheless held entitled to contribution as the payment had not been made "officiously" and the making of the demand was said not to be a "condition precedent" of his liability: *Stimpson v Smith* [1999] 2 All E.R. 833.

[70] e.g. *Davitt v Titcumb* [1990] Ch. 110 at 117.

where one surety (A) promises to pay only if neither the debtor nor another surety (B) does so, and B pays on the debtor's default, then B will not be entitled to contribution from A.[71]

Bankruptcy. At common law, the rule that the amount of contribution was the amount of the debt divided by the number of co-debtors prevailed even though some of the co-debtors were insolvent.[72] Equity adopted the fairer rule that the amount of contribution was the amount of the debt divided by the number of sureties who were *solvent* when the right to contribution arose.[73] This equitable rule now prevails.[74]   13–019

2. PLURALITY OF CREDITORS

(a) Definitions

If X promises to pay A and B £10, he may make two separate promises, under which A and B are entitled to £10 *each*, so that X's total liability is to pay £20. No special problems arise out of such promises. But if X makes only one promise to A and B, so that he is liable to pay only £10 in all, it becomes important to determine whether his promise to A and B is made to them jointly, or whether it is made to them severally. At common law, the question whether a contract was made with two persons jointly or with them severally depended on the wording of the contract, and on the interests of the parties in enforcing it.   13–020

If the contract was made with a number of persons "jointly" and their interests were joint, it was a joint contract[75]; if it was made with a number of persons severally, i.e. "with them and each of them" and their interests were several, it was a several contract.[76] If the contract was ambiguous, or did not state whether it was joint and several, then it was joint if the interests of the creditors were joint, and otherwise several.[77] The interests of the creditors were joint if each had the same interest in the performance of the contract, even though they had separate interests in the property affected. Hence a covenant to repair made with a number of lessors jointly was joint, though they did not hold the land jointly, but in common, so that their interests in it were several.[78] On the other hand, where land was sold by tenants in common and the purchaser promised to pay them the price in fixed proportions corresponding with their shares in the land, the promise was regarded as several.[79] The position was less clear where the contract was expressly joint and the interests several, or conversely; but the prevailing view appears to be that the court would give effect to the intention of the parties, as expressed in the

---

[71] *Scholefield Goodman & Sons Ltd v Zyngier* [1986] A.C. 562.

[72] *Lowe v Dixon* (1885) 16 Q.B.D. 455 at 458.

[73] *Hitchman v Stewart* (1855) 3 Drew. 271.

[74] *Lowe v Dixon*, above. The rules as to assessment of contribution laid down in Civil Liability (Contribution) Act 1978, s.2 do not alter this position: they apply to *damages* but not to *debts*; for this distinction, cf. below, para.21–001.

[75] cf. *Sorsbie v Park* (1843) 12 M. & W. 146 at 158.

[76] *James v Emery* (1818) 5 Price 529.

[77] e.g. *Anderson v Martindale* (1801) 1 East 487; *Palmer v Mallett* (1887) 36 Ch.D. 411.

[78] *Bradburne v Botfield* (1845) 14 M. & W. 559; *Thompson v Hakewill* (1865) 19 C.B.(N.S.) 713. For the position between the tenants in common *inter se*, see *Beer v Beer* (1852) 12 C.B. 60.

[79] *James v Emery* (1818) 5 Price 529.

agreement.[80] The common law did not originally recognise the possibility that a promise *to* a number of persons could be joint *and* several.[81] The possibility was, however, recognised in the late nineteenth century[82]; and the question is now of little importance as s.81 of the Law and Property Act 1925 provides that a covenant, and a contract made under seal[83] and a bond or obligation under seal made with two or more persons jointly, shall, if made after 1925, "be construed as being also made with each of them"[84] unless a contrary intention is expressed; where the instrument is executed by an individual, s.1 of the Law of Property (Miscellaneous Provisions) Act 1989 provides that it need no longer be sealed: execution as a deed in accordance with the requirements of that section is sufficient.[85] Such covenants, etc., are now prima facie joint and several.[86] Section 81 of the 1925 Act applies only to promises in deeds[87]; its object seems to have been to avoid in relation to such promises the common law rule that on the death of a joint creditor his rights passed by survivorship[88] to the other or others. In this respect, it resembles the rule under which a contract for the repayment of money lent by a number of lenders was presumed in equity to create a several right in each lender, even though under the common law rules the contract was joint.[89] The presumption could be rebutted, e.g. if the lenders were trustees[90]; here survivorship was administratively convenient, and created no substantive injustice. It seems that promises regarded as several under s.81 and under the equitable presumption will be so regarded not only for the purpose of limiting the doctrine of survivorship, but also for the other purposes to be discussed below.

(b) Parties to the Action

13–021   Joint promise. Where a promise is made to a number of persons *jointly*, all of them (if living) must be parties to the action.[91] If one joint creditor is unwilling

---

[80] *Sorsbie v Park* (1843) 12 M. & W. 146 at 158; *Keightley v Watson* (1849) 3 Ex. 716; *Beer v Beer* (1852) 12 C.B. 60; for the earlier view that the interest of the parties was always decisive, see *Slingsby's Case* (1588) 5 Co. Rep. 18b. *Withers v Bircham* (1824) 3 B. & C. 254 at 256; *Hopkinson v Lee* (1845) 6 Q.B. 964.

[81] *Slingsby's Case*, above; *Anderson v Martindale*, above; *Bradburne v Botfield* (1854) 14 M. & W. 559 at 573; *Keightley v Watson*, above, at 723 (criticising the rule).

[82] *Thompson v Hakewill* (1865) 19 C.B.(N.S.), 713 at 726; *Palmer v Mallett* (1887) 36 Ch.D. 410 at 421.

[83] See now Law of Property (Miscellaneous Provisions) Act 1989, s.1(7).

[84] Re-enacting, with some changes, Conveyancing Act 1881, s.60. The section does not affect the law relating to joint *debtors*: *Johnson v Davies* [1999] Ch. 117 at 127.

[85] Law of Property (Miscellaneous Provisions) Act 1989, s.1(8) and Sch.1. And see above, para.3–170 for execution of deeds by corporations.

[86] See *Josselson v Borst* [1938] 1 K.B. 723; for a statutory exception, see Law of Property Act 1925, s.119 (covenants with several mortgagees deemed to be joint).

[87] The primary meaning of "covenant" is a promise by deed: see *Rank Xerox Ltd v Lane* (*Inspector of Taxes*) [1981] A.C. 629 at 639. It seems that in Law of Property Act 1925, s.81, "covenant" refers to a promise which would not be binding unless it were under seal, and "contract . . . under seal" to one which would be binding even if it were not sealed.

[88] See below, para.13–023.

[89] *Steeds v Steeds* (1889) 22 Q.B.D. 537.

[90] ibid. at 542.

[91] *Jell v Douglas* (1821) 4 B. & Ald. 374; *Sorsbie v Park* (1843) 12 M. & W. 146; *Thompson v Hakewill* (1865) 19 C.B.(N.S.) 713.

to join, the one wishing to sue must offer him an indemnity as to costs; if he still refuses to join he can then be added as co-defendant.[92]

Several promise. Where a promise is made to two or more persons *severally*   **13–022** an action can be brought by one or more of them: it is not necessary to join them all.[93]

(c) Survivorship

Joint creditor. On the death of a *joint* creditor, his rights pass to his surviving   **13–023** co-creditors.[94]

Several creditor. On the death of a *several* creditor, his rights pass, not to his   **13–024** co-creditors, but to his personal representatives.[95]

(d) Defence Against One

Joint contract. Where a contract is *joint*, a defence available against one   **13–025** creditor can be raised against the others if it goes to the root of the claim. For example,

> "when two persons are jointly insured and their interests are inseparably connected, so that a loss or gain necessarily affects them both, the misconduct of one is sufficient to contaminate the whole insurance".[96]

It seems, although there is no authority precisely in point, that a defence available against one joint creditor does not avail against the other if it is purely personal to the first. Thus, if the debtor can plead ultra vires against one joint creditor,[97] he may remain liable to the others.

Several contract. Where a contract is *several*, a defence available against one   **13–026** creditor cannot be raised against the others. In *Hagedorn v Bazett*[98] an insurance of cargo covered goods some of which belonged to British subjects, some to neutrals and some to an alien enemy. It was held that the policy amounted to a number of separate policies, one with each owner, and was not wholly vitiated by the fact that one of the owners was an alien enemy. "There was no common or joint interest in the whole of the property insured subsisting in the different

---

[92] *Cullen v Knowles* [1898] 2 Q.B. 380; no such indemnity need be offered to one joint creditor who is guilty of a fraud on the other: *Johnson v Stephens & Carter Ltd* [1923] 2 K.B. 857. If a joint creditor is added as co-defendant without being offered such an indemnity, the only person who can object is that joint creditor, and not the debtor; *Burnside v Harrison Marks Productions Ltd* [1968] 1 W.L.R. 728.

[93] *James v Emery* (1818) 5 Price 529; *Keightley v Watson* (1849) 3 Ex. 716; *Palmer v Mallett* (1887) 36 Ch.D. 411.

[94] *Anderson v Martindale* (1801) 1 East 497.

[95] *Withers v Bircham* (1824) 3 B. & C. 254.

[96] *P Samuel & Co v Dumas* [1924] A.C. 432 at 445; *Arab Bank Plc v Zurich Insurance Co* [1999] 1 Lloyd's Rep. 263 at 272.

[97] See above, para.12–071.

[98] (1813) 2 M. & S. 100; *State of the Netherlands v Youell and Hayward* [1997] 2 Lloyd's Rep. 440, affirmed on other grounds [1998] 1 Lloyd's Rep. 236.

individuals, nor was there any fraud".[99] The reason why fraud would have vitiated the whole insurance is that the fraud referred to was that of the common agent of all the parties, and thus imputable to them all. It does not follow that the fraud of one several creditor is a defence against others to whom it cannot be imputed. Had the policy been joint (as it might have been if a single item jointly owned by the promisees had been its subject-matter), the fact that one of the owners was an alien enemy would have made it wholly illegal since it seems that this kind of illegal promise cannot be severed.[100]

13–027   **Joint bank accounts.** Where a joint bank account is opened in the names of two persons, the amount standing to the credit of the account is owed to them jointly, so that neither of them can enforce the debt against the bank without joining the other.[101] But a promise by the bank to honour only instructions given by both account holders is made separately to each of them, so that, if the bank allows one of them to draw on the account without the knowledge or authority of the other, the latter can sue alone and recover damage from the bank for breach of this promise.[102]

(e) Release by One

13–028   **Joint creditor.** A release granted by one *joint* creditor discharges the debt. Unless this were so, the one who granted the release might be able, after the death of his co-creditor, to recover the debt in spite of his own release, under the rule of survivorship.[103] But if the release is given by one creditor in fraud of another, the latter can have it set aside.[104]

13–029   **Several creditor.** A release granted by one of a number of creditors entitled *severally* (whether at law or in equity) releases only the share of the grantor.[105]

(f) Payment to One

13–030   **Joint creditor.** The general rule is that payment to one of two *joint* creditors discharges the debt.[106] But this rule may be varied by the contract, and such variation may be implied from a course of dealing. Thus where persons have a joint account with a bank, and the usual course of dealing is to make payments only with the authority of them all, a payment made to one without the authority of the others does not discharge the bank.[107] Even where payment to one discharges the debt, it does not discharge any security which may have been given for the debt except to the extent of the payee's beneficial interest in the debt.[108]

---

[99] (1813) 2 M. & S. 100 at 105.
[100] See above, para.11–160.
[101] *Brewer v Westminster Bank Ltd* [1952] 2 T.L.R. 568 (as to which, see next note).
[102] *Catlin v Cyprus Finance Corp (London) Ltd* [1983] Q.B. 759 not following *Brewer*'s case, above, on this point; Vroegop 100 L.Q.R. 25.
[103] *Wallace v Kelsall* (1840) 7 M. & W. 264 at 274.
[104] *Jones v Herbert* (1817) 7 Taunt. 421.
[105] *Steeds v Steeds* (1889) 22 Q.B.D. 537.
[106] *Husband v Davis* (1851) 10 C.B. 645; *Powell v Broadhurst* [1901] 2 Ch. 160 at 164; *Barrett v Universal Island Records Ltd* [2006] EWHC 1009 (Ch); [2006] E.M.L.R. 21 at [214].
[107] *Husband v Davis* (1851) 10 C.B. 645 at 650.
[108] *Powell v Broadhurst* [1901] 2 Ch. 160 at 166.

Several creditor. Payment to one of a number of *several* creditors clearly does   **13–031**
not discharge the whole debt since each is separately entitled to his share.

(g) Consideration Moving from One[109]

Joint promise. Where a promise is made to A and B *jointly*, it can be enforced   **13–032**
by both of them, even though the whole consideration was provided by A.[110] If
this were not so, the promise could not be enforced at all; for, if A tried to sue
alone, he would be defeated by the rule that all the promisees must be parties to
the action.[111] It follows from the doctrine of survivorship[112] that B would be
entitled to the entire benefit of the promise after A's death.

Several promise. None of the above reasoning applies where a promise is   **13–033**
made to A and B *severally*. Hence each promisee must provide consideration for
the separate promise made to him.

Joint and several promise. It is, however, uncertain which of the above rules   **13–034**
applies to the intermediate case of a promise made to two persons *jointly and
severally*.[113] In *McEvoy v Belfast Banking Co*,[114] a father (A) deposited £10,000 in
a bank; the deposit receipt stated that the money had been received from him and
his son (B) and that it was payable "to either or the survivor". Lord Atkin said
obiter that the contract was not by the bank with A for the benefit of B[115] but
"with A and B, and I think with them jointly and severally. A purports to make
a contract on behalf of B as well as himself, and the consideration supports such
a contract."[116] Of course after A's death (which in *McEvoy*'s case had occurred),
B would be entitled to enforce any joint promise under the doctrine of survivorship.[117] But it is harder to see how he could sue on any several promise, for this
is *ex hypothesi* an independent promise, and on the facts stated no consideration
for it moved from B.[118] Indeed, the more probable view of such facts is that the
bank makes no promise to B but only has authority to pay him. Hence it is
discharged by a payment to B, but is not liable to him.[119] The bank would not,
however, be discharged by such payment if it was *not* authorised by its contract
with A to pay B. This possibility is illustrated by *Thavorn v Bank of Credit &
Commerce SA*,[120] where A opened a bank account in the name of her nephew B
(who was under age), stipulating that only A should operate the account. It was

---

[109] Cullity 85 L.Q.R. 530; Winterton 47 Can.Bar Rev. 483; Coote [1978] C.L.J. 301.

[110] This proposition seems to have been accepted in *Coulls v Bagot's Executor and Trustee Co Ltd*
[1967] A.L.R. 385; although the majority of the court held that no joint promise had in fact been made;
below, para.14–041.

[111] See above, para.13–021.

[112] See above, para.13–023.

[113] For this type of promise, see above, para.13–003.

[114] [1935] A.C. 24.

[115] On this view, B would not be a "third party" for the purposes of the discussion in Ch.14.

[116] At 43.

[117] cf. *Aroso v Coutts & Co* [2002] 1 All E.R. 241, where the contract expressly so provided.

[118] S.J.B. 51 L.Q.R. 419.

[119] See *Coulls v Bagot's Executor and Trustee Co Ltd* [1967] A.L.R. 385; below, para.14–041.

[120] [1985] 1 Lloyd's Rep. 259. The Contracts (Rights of Third Parties) Act 1999 (below, para.14–090)
would not apply to such a case since it was not the intention of the contracting parties that B should
be entitled to enforce the contract: see subs.1(2) of the Act.

held that B was a mere nominee and that the bank was not discharged by (or was liable in damages for) paying B at the sole request of B and without any instructions from A. As no promise to (or in favour of) B had been made by the bank, it follows that B could not have sued the bank on its promise to A.

THIRD PARTIES

1. INTRODUCTION

Our concern in this chapter is with the extent to which persons can either take 14–001
the benefit of, or be bound by, contracts to which they are not parties. At common
law, the doctrine of privity states first, that a contract cannot confer rights and
secondly that it cannot impose liabilities, on anyone except a party to it. The
second of these propositions is generally regarded as just and sensible and for that
reason has generated far less controversy. It is not affected by the reform referred
to below. The limited exceptions or modifications to this aspect of privity are dealt

with primarily at the end of this chapter,[1] although the extent to which an exemption clause may bind a non-party is deal with separately.[2]

14–002   **1999 Reform.** The bulk of this chapter is concerned with the first aspect of privity, i.e. that a contract cannot confer rights on a non-party. It has been subjected to much criticism,[3] which culminated in a Report, issued by the Law Commission in 1996, on *Privity of Contract: Contracts for the Benefit of Third Parties.*[4] The recommendations of this Report have been implemented by the Contracts (Rights of Third Parties) Act 1999,[5] and where appropriate references will be made to the Report. It is important at the outset to make a point about the nature of the reforms made by the 1999 Act, since this determines the present structure of the subject. A crucial passage in the Report states that

> "it is important to emphasise that, while our proposed reform will give some third parties the right to enforce contracts, there will remain many contracts where a third party stands to benefit and yet will not have a right of enforceability. Our proposed statute carves out a general and wide-ranging exception to the third party rule, but it leaves that rule intact for cases not covered by the statute".[6]

The rights conferred on third parties by the 1999 Act therefore have the character of a new statutory exception[7] to the common law doctrine of privity; and the Act is therefore treated as such an exception in this chapter, though because of its importance a separate section is devoted to it.[8]

14–003   **The limits of the 1999 reform.** The new exception created by the 1999 Act is limited in two ways. First, a number of situations which have in the past been perceived as giving rise to problems resulting from the doctrine of privity are simply outside the scope of the exception and so are not affected by the provisions of the 1999 Act at all: this is, for example, true of cases in which third parties who have suffered loss in consequence of the breach of a contract between others have sought a remedy in tort against the party in breach.[9] Secondly, the exception created by the 1999 Act is, in turn, under that Act subject to exceptions[10] to which the third party's new statutory rights do not extend; and the effect of this is that

---

[1] See below, para.14–134 et seq.

[2] See below, paras 14–072—14–076.

[3] See para.14–015, below.

[4] Law Com. No.242 (hereafter "Report"). For an earlier proposal, see Law Revision Committee, sixth Interim Report, Cmd.5449 (1937), Section D.

[5] The Act does not precisely follow the Act in all respects, but the only major departure from the Report's recommendations is s.8 of the Act, subjecting the third party's rights to arbitration agreements, contrary to the views expressed in the Report, above, paras 14.14 to 14.19.

[6] Report, para.5.16; and see para.13.2.

[7] *Heaton v Axa Equity & Law Life Assurance Plc* [2002] UKHL 15; [2002] 2 A.C. 329 at [9]; cf. *Alfred McAlpine Construction Ltd v Panatown Ltd* [2001] 1 A.C. 518 at 535, per Lord Clyde, and at 575, per Lord Browne-Wilkinson. It is respectfully submitted that Lord Goff is not quite right when he refers to the "abolition" by the Act of the doctrine of privity: *Alfred McAlpine Construction Ltd v Panatown Ltd* [2001] 1 A.C. 518 at 544, repeated in *Johnson v Gore Wood & Co* [2002] 2 A.C. 1 at 40.

[8] See below, para.14–090 et seq.

[9] For further discussion of this point, see below, para.14–045 et seq.

[10] See s.6 of the Act, discussed at para.14–114, below.

in some[11] of these cases the common law doctrine of privity continues to apply. The Act also does not affect any rights which the third party has apart from its provisions[12]: thus it does not deprive the third party of rights which he has because the case falls either outside the *scope* of the common law doctrine[13] or within one of the *exceptions* to it recognised either at common law, or in equity or under other legislation.[14]

The scope of the doctrine and these other exceptions therefore continue to call for discussion, particularly because the content of rights available apart from the 1999 Act in some ways differs from that of the rights available under it.[15] The Act also does not affect any rights of the promisee to enforce any term of the contract[16]: such questions as whether the promisee can recover damages in respect of the third party's loss will therefore continue to be governed by the rules which have been (and no doubt will further be) developed as a matter of common law.[17] There is finally the point that the 1999 Act does not apply to contracts made before the end of the period of six months beginning on the day on which it was passed and came into force,[18] except where a contract made within that period expressly provides that the Act is to apply to it.[19] It is still therefore possible for the courts to be concerned with contracts subject to the rules of law established before the Act came into force. These rules will also, in a significant number of the situations described above, continue to apply even to contracts made after that date. They therefore still require discussion, even though a considerable number of the cases on which they are based would if their facts occurred now be decided differently (where they had denied the third party the right to enforce the contract) or be decided on different grounds (where they had given the third party such a right). The result of all these points is that the 1999 Act may have improved, but it has scarcely simplified, the law on this topic.

2. THE COMMON LAW DOCTRINE[20]

General rule. The common law doctrine of privity means that a contract   14–004
cannot, as a general rule, confer rights or impose obligations arising under it on any person except the parties to it. Two questions arise from this statement: who are the parties to the agreement, and has the claimant provided consideration for the promise which he is seeking to enforce?

(a) Parties to the Agreement

Normally, the parties to the agreement are the persons from whose communica-   14–005
tions with each other the agreement has resulted. There may, indeed, be factual

---

[11] e.g. s.6(2) and 6(3); under some of the other exceptions, the third party will be able to get rights by another legal route: e.g. under those stated in s.6(1) and (5): see below, para.14–114.

[12] s.7(1), below paras 14–116—14–117; Report, para.12.12.

[13] See below, paras 14–044—14–054.

[14] See below, paras 14–077—14–089, 14–123—14–133.

[15] e.g. ss.2 and 3 of the 1999 Act do not apply where the third party has rights apart from the Act; below, paras 14–116—14–117.

[16] s.4; below, para.14–121.

[17] See below, para.14–022 et seq.

[18] On November 11, 1999, when the Act received Royal Assent: see s.10(2).

[19] See s.10(3).

[20] Finlay, *Contracts for the Benefit of Third Persons*; Dold, *Stipulations for a Third Party*; Wilson 11 Sydney L.Rev. 300; Flannigan 105 L.Q.R. 564; Kincaid [1989] C.L.J. 454; Andrews 8 *Legal Studies* 14.

difficulties in identifying these persons[21]; but such difficulties do not generally[22] raise any questions of legal principle. Problems as to the legal analysis of clearly established facts can, however, arise in situations in which there is clearly an agreement, while it is doubtful exactly who the parties to it are, or in which there are several contracts which affect the same subject-matter and involve more than two parties. The rights of all the parties to such contracts arise independently of the Contracts (Rights of Third Parties) Act 1999, and are not limited by its provisions.[23]

(i) *Collateral contracts*[24]

14–006   **Illustrations.** A contract between two persons may be accompanied by a collateral contract between one of them and a third person relating to the same subject-matter. In *Shanklin Pier v Detel Products Ltd*,[25] the claimants employed contractors to paint a pier and instructed them for this purpose to buy and use paint made by the defendants. The instruction was given in reliance on a representation made by the defendants to the claimants that the paint would last for seven years. In fact it lasted for only three months. The main contract for the sale of the paint was between the contractors and the defendants, but it was held that there was also a collateral contract between the claimants and the defendants that the paint would last for seven years.[26]

The same reasoning can apply where a person buys goods from a dealer and is given a guarantee issued by the manufacturer. The main contract of sale is between the dealer and the customer, but it seems that the guarantee is a collateral contract between the manufacturer and the customer.[27] Special legislation applies to certain guarantees given to consumers in respect of goods sold or supplied to them. Where the requirements specified in this legislation are satisfied, such guarantees are to take effect as contractual obligations[28] whether or not the requirements of a collateral contract[29] are satisfied; but these requirements continue to apply to manufacturers' guarantees not covered by this legislation: e.g. where the person to whom the guarantee is given is not a "consumer".[30] A collateral contract may also arise in the context of building work between a

---

[21] e.g. *The Zinnia* [1984] 2 Lloyd's Rep. 211; *Uddin v Ahmed* [2001] EWCA Civ 240; [2001] 3 F.C.R. 300; *The Starsin* [2003] UKHL 12; [2004] 1 A.C. 715 at [175].

[22] A highly specialised group of cases (beyond the scope of this book) concerns bills of lading issued in respect of goods shipped on a chartered ship: see *Carver on Bills of Lading* (2nd edn), paras 4–028 to 4–055; *The Starsin*, above, fn.21.

[23] Contracts (Rights of Third Parties) Act 1999, s.7(1).

[24] Wedderburn [1959] C.L.J. 58.

[25] [1951] 2 K.B. 854; followed in *Wells (Merstham) Ltd v Buckland Sand & Silica Co Ltd* [1965] 2 Q.B. 170; cf. *Moody v Condor Ins Ltd* [2006] EWHC 100 (Ch); [2006] 1 W.L.R. 1847 at [39]; also below, para.16–076.

[26] cf. *Fuji Seal Europe Ltd v Catalytic Combustion Corp* [2005] EWHC 1659; 102 Con. L.R. 47 (no collateral contract between a parent company and a customer of one of its subsidiaries (though the parent was found liable in negligence: see para.14–045, below); it was an "important feature" of the *Shanklin Pier* case that the claimants and the contractors were "at arms' length": at [157]).

[27] cf. above, para.3–017.

[28] Sale and Supply of Goods to Consumers Regulations 2002 (SI 2002/3045), reg.15, implementing Dir.1999/44, Arts 2(e) and 6; for the meaning of "consumer" in this context, see reg.2.

[29] i.e. those of consideration and contractual intention (below, paras 14–007, 14–008).

[30] e.g. on facts such as those of the *Shanklin Pier* case, above, fn.25.

developer and a nominated sub-contractor[31]; in the use of a cheque card or credit card for the purchase of goods between the supplier and the issuer of the card[32]; and in the context of employment between an agency worker and the party for whom work is carried out.[33]

The collateral contract device has also been used in the context of hire-purchase agreements. The customer may think of himself as "buying on hire-purchase" from the dealer on whose premises he selects the goods. Actually, the transaction may involve a sale of the goods by the dealer to a finance company which then hires them out to the customer and grants him an option to purchase them. Thus the main contract of hire-purchase is between the customer and the finance company. A representation by the dealer as to the quality of the goods used not to bind the finance company,[34] but it could be enforced against the dealer as a collateral contract.[35] If the transaction is a regulated agreement within the Consumer Credit Act 1974,[36] a dealer who conducts antecedent negotiations is deemed to do so as agent of the finance company as well as in his actual capacity.[37] His representations can therefore make the company liable under the main contract, while he himself may still be liable under a collateral contract.[38]

Consideration for collateral contracts. To be enforceable as a collateral contract, a promise must be supported by consideration,[39] and in the cases so far discussed this requirement was clearly satisfied. In the *Shanklin Pier* case the consideration was the instruction given by the claimants to their contractors[40]; in the guarantee case it is the purchase by the customer of the goods from the dealer[41]; in the building sub-contractor case, it is similarly the nomination of the sub-contractor by the client; in the cheque or credit card case it is the supply of goods by the supplier to the customer and the discount allowed by the supplier to the issuer of the card[42]; and in the hire-purchase case it is the entering by the customer into a hire-purchase agreement with the finance company. A case in

14–007

---

[31] *Holland Hannen & Cubitts (Northern) v Welsh Health Technical Services Ltd* (1987) 7 Con.L.R. 14; cf. *Greater Nottingham Co-operative Soc Ltd v Cementation Ltd* [1989] Q.B. 71; for the sub-contractor's possible liability in tort, see below, para.14–049.

[32] *Re Charge Card Services* [1987] Ch. 150, affirmed [1989] Ch. 497; Tiplady [1989] L.M.C.L.Q. 22; Jones [1988] J.B.L. 457; cf. *Customs & Excise Commissioners v Diners Club Ltd* [1989] 1 W.L.R. 1196; *First Sport Ltd v Barclays Bank Plc* [1993] 1 W.L.R. 1229; a different analysis probably applies where the card is issued by *the supplier*, as is the practice of some department stores: *Richardson v Worral* [1985] S.T.C. 693 at 720.

[33] *Brook Street Bureau Ltd v Dacas* [2004] EWCA Civ 217; [2004] I.C.R. 1437; *Cable & Wireless Plc v Muscat* [2006] EWCA Civ 220; [2006] I.C.R. 975; *James v Greenwich LBC* [2008] EWCA Civ 35; [2008] I.C.R. 545; *Tilson v Alstom Transport* [2010] EWCA Civ 1308.

[34] *Campbell Discount Co Ltd v Gall* [1961] 1 Q.B. 431, reversed on other points in *Branwhite v Worcester Works Finance Ltd* [1969] 1 A.C. 552 and *United Dominions Trust Ltd v Western* [1976] Q.B. 513.

[35] *Brown v Sheen & Richmond Car Sales* [1950] 1 All E.R. 1102; *Andrews v Hopkinson* [1957] 1 Q.B. 229; cf. *Astley Industrial Trust Ltd v Grimley* [1963] 1 W.L.R. 584; as to damages, see *Yeoman Credit Ltd v Odgers* [1962] 1 W.L.R. 215.

[36] See above, para.5–007.

[37] s.56(2); cf. also s.75, under which the finance company is liable for any breach of contract by the supplier, but entitled to an indemnity from him in respect of such liability.

[38] This follows from s.56(2), above.

[39] cf. *Brikom Investments Ltd v Carr* [1979] Q.B. 467 (above, para.3–065), where no third party problem arose.

[40] [1951] 2 K.B. 854 at 856.

[41] cf. (in a different context) *Penn v Bristol & West BS* [1997] 1 W.L.R. 1356 at 1363 ("entering into some transaction with a third party").

[42] *Customs & Excise Commissioners v Diners Club Ltd* [1989] 1 W.L.R. 1196.

which the problem of consideration gives rise to more difficulty is *Charnock v Liverpool Corp*,[43] where a car was damaged and repaired under a contract between the owner's insurance company and a garage. It was held that there was also a collateral contract by which the garage promised the owner to do the repairs reasonably quickly. Although the owner did not pay or promise to pay the garage anything,[44] he had provided consideration by "leaving his car with the garage for repair".[45] This might not be a detriment to the owner, at least in the factual sense.[46] But it benefited the garage in giving it the opportunity of making a contract for the repair of the car with the insurance company; and this benefit constituted the consideration for the garage's promise to the owner.[47]

14–008   **Contractual intention.** In the present context, as in others,[48] a promise will not amount to a collateral contract if it was made without contractual intention. For example, in *Independent Broadcasting Authority v EMI Electronics*[49] EMI had contracted to erect a television mast for the IBA, on the terms that the actual work was to be done by a sub-contractor, who was not a party to the main contract. The sub-contractor wrote to the IBA, saying: "We are well satisfied that the structure will not oscillate dangerously". The mast having later collapsed, it was held that this letter did not have contractual force as there was no *animus contrahendi*[50] (though the sub-contractor was held liable in negligence).

(ii) *Agency*

14–009   Where an agent negotiates a contract with a third party on behalf of his principal, that contract will generally be between the principal and the third party.[51] But it is sometimes doubtful whether a person acted as agent or on his own behalf.[52] Thus where a husband booked tickets on a cross-Channel ferry for himself, his wife and children, there was said to be a "contract of carriage between the [wife] and the [carriers]",[53] presumably made by the husband as agent of the wife. Where a husband and wife lunched together at a restaurant, it was again held that there was a contract between the wife and the proprietor, though on the different ground that husband and wife each made a separate contract with the

---

[43] [1968] 1 W.L.R. 1498.

[44] cf. *Godfrey Davies Ltd v Culling and Hecht* [1962] 2 Lloyd's Rep. 349; *Brown & Davies v Galbraith* [1972] 1 W.L.R. 997.

[45] [1968] 1 W.L.R. 1498 at 1505.

[46] See above, para.3–006.

[47] cf. above, para.3–050. For similar reasoning, see *International Petroleum Refining & Supply Sociedad v Caleb Brett & Son Ltd* [1980] 1 Lloyd's Rep. 569 at 594.

[48] See above, paras 4–003, 5–009, 6–029, 9–051.

[49] (1980) 14 Build.L.R. 1; cf. *Alicia Hosiery Ltd v Brown Shipley Ltd* [1970] 1 Q.B. 195; *Lambert v Lewis* [1982] A.C. 225; *Law Debenture Trust Corp v Ural Caspian Oil Corp Ltd* [1993] 1 W.L.R. 138 at 142; for a successful appeal on another point, see [1995] Ch. 152; below, para.14–140.

[50] cf. also *Hannam v Bradford CC* [1970] 1 W.L.R. 937; *Construction Industry Training Board v Labour Force Ltd* [1970] 3 All E.R. 220.

[51] See below, para.16–054 et seq.

[52] See below, paras 16–004—16–008; *P Samuel & Co Ltd v Dumas* [1923] 1 K.B. 593; [1924] A.C. 431. Similar problems commonly arise in relation to "forwarding agents": see, e.g. *Jones v European General Express* (1920) 25 Com.Cas. 296; *Elektronska, etc. v Transped, etc.* [1986] 1 Lloyd's Rep. 49.

[53] *The Dragon* [1979] 1 Lloyd's Rep. 257 at 262, affirmed [1980] 2 Lloyd's Rep. 415; cf. *Bowerman v Association of British Travel Agents* [1995] N.L.J. 1815 (holiday booked for pupil by teacher).

proprietor.[54] But if there were no such separate contracts and the host on such an occasion did not act as agent it has been said that there would be a contract only between him and the restaurant proprietor.[55]

Similar problems arise where an agent employs a sub-agent. In some such cases there is a direct contract between principal and sub-agent; while in others the sub-agent is in a contractual relationship only with the agent who employed him.[56] In these cases it is again clear that there is a contract, but doubtful who the parties to it are.[57]

(iii) *Multilateral contracts*

Clubs or other unincorporated associations. When a person joins a club or other unincorporated association he may be in direct communication only with the secretary and be unaware of the identity of the other members. But his contract of membership is likely to be with them,[58] and not with the secretary.[59] It has similarly been held that an insurance policy, which was expressed to be between the assured and a syndicate of underwriters at Lloyd's, nevertheless constituted a number of separate contracts between the assured and each member of the syndicate.[60]   14–010

Competitions. Problems of this kind can also arise where a number of persons agree to enter into a competition subject to rules laid down by the organising club. In *The Satanita*[61] it was held that the competitors in a regatta had contracted not only with the committee of the club but also with each other. But in *Ellesmere v Wallace*[62] it was held that persons who entered horses for races organised by the Jockey Club had contracted with the club, and not with each other.   14–011

(iv) *Corporations*

Companies. Under the Companies Act 2006, the provisions of a company's constitution[63] bind the company and its members to the same extent as if there   14–012

---

[54] *Lockett v A M Charles Ltd* [1938] 4 All E.R. 170.

[55] *Jackson v Horizon Holidays Ltd* [1975] 1 W.L.R. 1468 at 1473 (where *Lockett v A M Charles Ltd*, *supra*, was not cited).

[56] See below, para.16–098; contrast *Robbins v Fennell* (1847) 11 Q.B. 248 with *Collins v Brook* (1860) 5 H. & N. 700; cf. also *The Antama* [1982] 2 Lloyd's Rep. 112.

[57] *Henderson v Merrett Syndicates Ltd* [1995] 2 A.C. 145, at 202D–G; *Grosvenor Casinos Ltd v National Bank of Abu Dhabi* [2008] EWHC 511 (Comm); [2008] 1 Lloyd's Rep. at [147]–[149].

[58] *Lee v Showmen's Guild* [1952] 2 Q.B. 329 at 341.

[59] *Gray v Pearson* (1870) L.R. 5 C.P. 568; *Evans v Hooper* (1875) 1 Q.B.D. 45; *Nutting v Baldwin* [1995] 1 W.L.R. 201. But where a club was *owned by a company* of which the club's members were shareholders, the rules of the club were held to constitute contracts between each member and the company, and not between the members *inter se*: *Peskin v Anderson* [2000] 2 B.C.L.C. 1.

[60] *Touche Ross & Co v Colin Bank* [1992] 2 Lloyd's Rep. 207 at 209–210.

[61] [1895] P. 248; affirmed sub nom. *Clarke v Dunraven* [1897] A.C. 59, where only Lord Herschell dealt with the point here discussed; cf. *Meggeson v Burns* [1972] 1 Lloyd's Rep. 223; *White v Blackmore* [1972] 2 Q.B. 651 (where there was no contractual intention).

[62] [1929] 2 Ch. 1.

[63] As defined by the 2006 Act, s.17.

were covenants on the part of the company and of each member to observe those provisions.[64] This has been said to amount to a "statutory contract"[65] between each member and the company[66]; and also to one between the members *inter se*.[67] But they only have the latter effect between the members in their capacity as members[68]; a director is not liable or entitled under them in his capacity as director simply because he happens also to be a member.[69]

14–013   **Limited liability partnerships.** In the case of a limited liability partnership (which is a body corporate),[70] the mutual rights and liabilities of the members *inter se* and between the members and the partnership are governed by agreement between the members or between them and the partnership[71]; or, in the absence of such agreement, by regulations made under the Act governing such partnerships.[72]

(b) Party to the Consideration

14–014   **Two distinct rules.** The common law rule that only a party to the agreement can enforce it will often lead to the same result as the rule that consideration must move from the promisee[73]; but the two rules appear to be distinct. They require the claimant to show (1) that the promise was made to him *and* (2) that the consideration for it moved from him. The statement that consideration must move *from the promisee* simply assumes that the first requirement has been satisfied. If the rule were stated to be that consideration must move *from the party seeking to enforce the promise* it would clearly be distinct from the common law rule that only a party to the agreement can sue. A father might, for example, promise his daughter to pay £1,000 to anyone who married her. A man who married the daughter with knowledge of and in reliance on such a promise might provide consideration for it, but could not enforce it, as it was not addressed to him.[74]

---

[64] Companies Act 2006, s.33(1).
[65] *Soden v British Commonwealth Holdings* [1998] A.C. 298 at 323 (based on the former Companies Act 1985, s.14 which referred to the memorandum and articles of association, rather than the "constitution").
[66] *Hickman v Kent or Romney Marsh Sheepbreeders Association* [1915] 1 Ch. 881; cf. *Cumbrian Newspaper Group v Cumberland and Westmorland Herald Ltd* [1987] Ch. 1.
[67] *Rayfield v Hands* [1960] Ch. 1; *J H Rayner (Mincing Lane) Ltd v DTI* [1989] Ch. 72 at 190 (approved on this point [1990] 2 A.C. 418 at 515); cf. *Russell v Northern Bank Development Corp Ltd* [1992] B.C.L.C. 1016. But there is no contract between members on the one hand and third parties on the other: *Eley v Positive, etc., Assurance Co* (1876) 1 Ex.D. 88.
[68] For limitations on the scope of this contract, see *Soden v British and Commonwealth Holdings* [1998] A.C. 298. They are not affected by Contracts (Rights of Third Parties) Act 1999: see s.6(2), below, para.14–115.
[69] *Beattie v E & F Beattie Ltd* [1938] Ch. 708; *Rayfield v Hands*, above, is difficult to reconcile with this principle: L.C.B.G. 21 M.L.R. 401.
[70] See above, para.12–070.
[71] Limited Liability Partnership Act 2000, s.5(1)(a).
[72] ibid., s.5(1)(c).
[73] See *Price v Easton* (1833) B. & Ad. 433; *Tweddle v Atkinson* (1861) B. & S. 393; Furmston 23 M.L.R. 373.
[74] cf. *Uddin v Ahmed* [2001] EWCA Civ 204, [2001] 3 F.C.R. 300 at [20]. Support for the view that the two rules are distinct may be provided by the decision of the Privy Council in *Kepong Prospecting Ltd v Schmidt* [1968] A.C. 810.

(c) Reasons for the Doctrine

There are two aspects of the common law doctrine of privity: no one except a   **14–015**
party to a contract can acquire rights under it; and no one except a party can be
subjected to liabilities under it. The reason for the second aspect of the doctrine
is obvious: a person should not, as a general rule, have contractual obligations
imposed on him without his consent. The first aspect of the doctrine is harder to
explain; indeed, Steyn L.J. has gone so far as to say that there is "no doctrinal,
logical or policy reason"[75] for it. The rule that a third party cannot acquire rights
under a contract can scarcely be justified by saying that a contract is, or gives rise,
to a personal relationship, affecting only the parties to it; for this is rather a
restatement of the rule than a reason for its existence. Nor is it satisfactory to say
that it would be unjust to allow a person to sue on a contract on which he could
not be sued[76]; for the law enforces unilateral contracts, to which the same
argument applies.[77] A further possible reason is that, if third parties could enforce
contracts made for their benefit, the rights of contracting parties to rescind or vary
such contracts would be unduly hampered: this reasoning has certainly been
influential in limiting the development of one of the judge-made exceptions to the
doctrine,[78] and also is reflected in the reform introduced by the 1999 Act.[79] Yet
another possible reason is that the third party is often a mere donee. A system of
law which does not give a right to enforce a gratuitous promise to the promisee
may well be reluctant to give such a right to a gratuitous beneficiary who is not
even a promisee. None of these reasons for the common law doctrine takes account
of the inconvenience that can result from its practical operation. This factor
accounts for the many exceptions to the doctrine which will be discussed later in
this chapter.[80]

(d) Development

Early development. In the early authorities, there was considerable conflict on   **14–016**
the question whether a person could enforce a contract to which he was not a
party.[81] A negative answer to this question was given in 1861 in *Tweddle v
Atkinson*,[82] where A promised B to pay a marriage portion to B's son C on C's
marriage to A's daughter. It was held that C could not enforce this promise against

---

[75] *Darlington BC v Wiltshier Northern Ltd* [1995] 1 W.L.R. 68 at 76.
[76] *Tweddle v Atkinson* (1861) 1 B. & S. 393 at 398.
[77] See above, paras 2–051—2–057, 3–158.
[78] See below, para.14–084.
[79] In s.2: below, para.14–100.
[80] See below, para.14–090 et seq; see also paras 14–077—14–089.
[81] In *Crow v Rogers* (1724) 1 Str. 592; *Bourne v Mason* (1669) 1 Ventr. 6 and *Price v Easton* (1833)
4 B. & Ad. 433 the third party's claim failed; but it was upheld in *Thomas v ——* (1655) Sty. 461;
Dutton v Poole (1678) 2 Lev. 210, affirmed T. Raym. 302 and approved in *Martyn v Hind* (1776) Cowp.
437 at 443; *Green v Horn* (1693) Comb. 219 (reversed (1694) 1 Salk. 197 on the ground that the third
party must at least be mentioned in the deed) and *Marchington v Vernon* (1786) 1 B. & P. 101n.(*c*); E.J.P.
70 L.Q.R. 467; Scammel 8 C.L.P. 134–135; Palmer 33 Am. Jl. of Legal History 3; Ibbetson in (ed.)
Barton, *Towards a General Law of Contract*, pp.67, 96–99; Palmer *The Paths to Privity: the History of
Third Party Beneficiaries in English Law*; Andrews 69 Tulane L.Rev. 69.
[82] (1861) 1 B. & S. 393.

A. This case was generally considered to have established the common law doctrine,[83] which was approved by the House of Lords in 1915, when the principle that "only a person who is a party to the contract can sue on it" was said to be a "fundamental"[84] one in English law. This view was, indeed, judicially doubted in a number of cases.[85] But in 1961 the House of Lords once again affirmed the existence of the doctrine,[86] and this view of the law has been accepted in many later cases.[87]

14–017   *Beswick v Beswick.* The leading modern case is *Beswick v Beswick*.[88] A coal merchant transferred his business to his nephew who made various promises in return. One of these was that he would, after the uncle's death, pay £5 per week to the uncle's widow. The uncle died and the widow became his administratrix. She brought an action to enforce the nephew's promise, suing both in her own right and as administratrix. The House of Lords held that the widow could enforce the nephew's promise in her capacity as administratrix of the promisee and that she was entitled to an order of specific performance against the nephew, obliging him to make the payments to her for her personal benefit. In the Court of Appeal Lord Denning M.R. had said that the widow could also sue in her own right at common law,[89] because the doctrine of privity was "at bottom . . . only a rule of procedure"[90] and could be overcome by simply joining the promisee as a party to the action. The House of Lords found it unnecessary to express a concluded view on this point. But the speeches all assume the correctness of the generally accepted view that a contract can at common law be enforced only by the parties to it[91]; though the House of Lords has on a number of occasions indicated its willingness to reconsider this position.[92] Such reconsideration has indeed been undertaken by a majority of the High Court of Australia, but in a decision in which so many divergent views were expressed, that it provides no firm guidance for the

---

[83] *Gandy v Gandy* (1884) 30 Ch.D. 57 at 69.

[84] *Dunlop Pneumatic Tyre Co Ltd v Selfridge & Co Ltd* [1915] A.C. 847 at 853; for a similar, earlier, statement, see *Keighley Maxsted & Co v Durant* [1901] A.C. 240 at 246.

[85] In *Smith and Snipes Hall Farm Ltd v River Douglas Catchment Board* [1949] 2 K.B. 500 at 519; *Drive Yourself Hire Co (London) Ltd v Strutt* [1954] 1 Q.B. 250 at 274; *Pyrene Co Ltd v Scindia Steam Navigation Co Ltd* [1954] 2 Q.B. 402 at 426; *Rayfield v Hands* [1960] Ch. 1; Dowrick 19 M.L.R. 375; cf. Andrews 8 Legal Studies 14; Flannigan 105 L.Q.R. 564.

[86] *Scruttons Ltd v Midland Silicones Ltd* [1962] A.C. 446; below, para.14–060; see also *Green v Russell* [1959] 2 Q.B. 226.

[87] *Rookes v Barnard* [1964] A.C. 1129 (below, para.14–055); *Hepburn v A Tomlinson (Hauliers) Ltd* [1966] A.C. 451; *The Eurymedon* [1975] A.C. 154 at 166; *The New York Star* [1981] 1 W.L.R. 138; *Woodar Investments & Development Ltd v Wimpey Construction UK Ltd* [1980] 1 W.L.R. 277; *Balsamo v Medici* [1984] 1 W.L.R. 951 at 959–960; *Siu Yin Kwan v Eastern Insurance* [1994] 2 A.C. 199 at 207; *Rhone v Stephens* [1994] 2 A.C. 310 at 321; *The Pioneer Container* [1994] 2 A.C. 324 at 335; *White v Jones* [1995] 2 A.C. 207 at 252, 266; *The Mahkutai* [1996] A.C. 650 at 658; *The Starsin* [2003] UKHL 12; [2003] 1 A.C. 715; the point is perhaps left open in *Esso Petroleum Ltd v Hall Russell & Co* [1989] A.C. 643 at 662.

[88] [1965] 2 All E.R. 858; [1966] Ch. 538; [1968] A.C. 58; Goodhart 83 L.Q.R. 465; Fairest [1967] C.L.J. 149; Treitel 29 M.L.R. 657; 30 M.L.R. 687.

[89] For the effect of Law of Property Act 1925, s.56, see below, para.14–131.

[90] [1966] Ch. 538 at 557.

[91] [1968] A.C. 58 at 72, 81, 83, 92–93, 95.

[92] ibid. at 72; *Woodar Investment Development Ltd v Wimpey Construction UK Ltd* [1980] 1 W.L.R. 277 at 291, 297–298, 300; *Swain v Law Society* [1983] 1 A.C. 598 at 611; cf. *Williams v Natural Life Health Foods* [1998] 1 W.L.R. 830 at 837.

development of the law.[93] The difficulties of reaching satisfactory results in this area through purely judicial reconsideration are formidable:[94] they arise, particularly, in defining exactly what classes of third parties can acquire rights under the contract, and in determining how those rights are to be affected by attempts by the contracting parties to rescind the contract or to vary it, and by defences available between the contracting parties.[95] A satisfactory solution of such difficulties is more likely to be achieved by legislative reform,[96] such as that contained in the Contracts (Rights of Third Parties) Act 1999.[97] In a significant number of situations, however, third parties will not acquire rights by virtue of this Act[98]; and in many such situations the common law doctrine of privity will continue (at least for the time being[99]) to apply.

(e) Operation of the Doctrine

Although at common law a third party cannot generally assert rights under a contract made for his benefit, the contract remains nevertheless binding between promisor and promisee. The fact that the contract was made for the benefit of a third party does, however, give rise to special problems so far as the promisee's remedies against the promisor are concerned. Actual performance of the contract may also lead to disputes between promisee and third party.

14–018

(i) *Promisee's remedies*

Specific performance. The promisee (or those acting for his estate) may seek specific performance. If, as in *Beswick v Beswick*,[100] this remedy is granted, the third party will in fact receive the benefit contracted for. But the scope of the remedy of specific performance is limited in various ways; these limitations, and their applicability to cases involving third parties, will be discussed in detail in

14–019

---

[93] *Trident Ins Co Ltd v McNiece Bros Pty Ltd* (1988) 165 C.L.R. 107, where a claim under a liability insurance policy by a person who was not a party to it was upheld by a majority of five to two. But one member of the majority (Deane J.) was only prepared to allow the third party's claim under the well-established trust exception to the doctrine of privity (below, para.14–081), while another (Gaudron J.) based her decision in favour of the third party, not on contract, but on unjust enrichment (below, para.14–056), and said that this was "not an abrogation of the doctrine of privity of contract" (at 177). Only three of the seven members of the court can be said to have countenanced such an abrogation, and even their view may be restricted to the special insurance context with which the case was concerned; Edgell [1989] L.M.C.L.Q. 139.

[94] Kincaid 2 J.C.L. 160. For a different judicial approach in Canada, proceeding by means of the creation of an exception to the doctrine in the context of exemption clauses, see *London Drugs Ltd v Kuehne & Nagel International Ltd* [1992] 3 S.C.R. 299 (below, para.14–060); Waddams 109 L.Q.R. 349; Adams and Brownsword 56 M.L.R. 722. cf. *Fraser River Pile and Dredge Ltd v Can-Drive Services Ltd* [2000] 1 Lloyds Rep. 199, where the Supreme Court of Canada, while refusing to engage in "wholesale abolition" of the doctrine of privity, continued to make "incremental changes" by holding that a third party could take the benefit of a "waiver of subrogation" clause in an insurance policy.

[95] See the elaborate discussion of these problems in American law (which in principle recognises the rights of third party beneficiaries) in *Corbin on Contracts*, Chs 41–44. The effect of rescission or variation by the contracting parties gives rise to particular difficulties: cf. below, para.14–084.

[96] See Treitel 29 M.L.R. 657, 665; Reynolds 105 L.Q.R. 1, 3; contrast *Darlington BC v Wiltshier Northern Ltd* [1995] 1 W.L.R. 68 at 76, favouring judicial reform.

[97] See below, para.14–090 et seq.

[98] See below, paras 14–094, 14–113—14–115.

[99] The passing of the 1999 Act will probably reduce the pressure for judicial reform.

[100] [1968] A.C. 58; above, para.14–017.

Ch.21.[101] It is therefore necessary to consider what other remedies may be available to the promisee if the contract is broken.

14–020   **Restitution.** The promisee may claim restitution of the consideration provided by him. But part performance by the promisor[102] might defeat this remedy,[103] and it might also be unjust to restrict the promisee to such a claim: e.g. return of premiums could be a quite inadequate remedy where a policy of life insurance had been taken out for the benefit of a third party and had matured.

14–021   **Agreed sum.** The promisee may claim payment to himself of the agreed sum. It can be objected that to allow such a claim would force the promisor to do something which he never contracted to do, *viz.* to pay the promisee when he contracted to pay the third party; and one view is therefore that the promisee cannot sue for the agreed sum,[104] save in the exceptional circumstances to be described later in this chapter.[105] But the objection to allowing the promisee to claim payment to himself loses most of its force where the promisor would not in fact be prejudiced by having to pay the promisee rather than the third party (so long as by such payment gave him a good discharge). In such a case, the contract may, on its true construction, be one to pay the third party or as the promisee shall direct,[106] so that it would not be inconsistent with its terms to allow the promisee to claim payment for himself. The promisee is a fortiori so entitled where the contract is one to pay him (the promisee) as nominee for the third party[107]: such a contract is not one for the benefit of a third party[108] in the sense of one purporting to give that party a right against the promisor.

14–022   **Damages in respect of promisee's loss.** The promisee may claim damages where he has suffered loss as a result of the promisor's failure to perform in favour of the third party.[109] But in *Beswick v Beswick* the majority of the House of Lords evidently thought that no such loss had been or would be suffered and that the damages recoverable by the estate for breach of the nephew's promise would be merely nominal.[110] Lord Upjohn explained that this would be the case because the promisee "died *without any assets* save and except the agreement which he hoped would keep him and then his widow for their lives".[111] It seems from this that damages might have been substantial if the promisee had had other assets—either because the widow might then have had a claim against those assets if the promise

---

[101] See below, paras 21–048—21–050.
[102] As in *Beswick v Beswick* [1968] A.C. 58.
[103] As there would be no "total failure of consideration"; and as termination for breach could probably not be allowed unless the third party was willing to restore any performance received: below, para.22–005. For the suggestion that *the third party* may have a claim in restitution, see below, para.14–056.
[104] See *Coulls v Bagot's Executor and Trustee Co Ltd* [1967] A.L.R. 385 at 409–411; cf. *Beswick v Beswick* [1968] A.C. at 88, 101 (dealing with the remedy of damages).
[105] See *Cleaver v Mutual Reserve Fund Life Association* [1892] 1 Q.B. 147; cf. below, para.14–085.
[106] *The Spiros C* [2000] 2 Lloyd's Rep. 319 at 331; below, para.14–040.
[107] *The Turiddu* [1999] 2 Lloyd's Rep. 401 at 407.
[108] ibid.
[109] *De Jongh Weill v Mean Fiddler Holdings* [2005] All E.R. (D) 331 (share warrants not granted to nominee, but loss found to have been suffered by promisee).
[110] Lord Pearce, however, thought that damages would be substantial: [1968] A.C. 58 at 88. It is not entirely clear whether he had in mind an action for *damages* or one for the *agreed sum*: see his reference at 87 to "separate actions as each sum falls due".
[111] [1968] A.C. 58 at 102 (italics supplied).

was not performed[112] or because the promisee or his estate would in fact, even if not legally obliged to do so, have made some other, wholly voluntary, provision for the widow. The loss suffered by the promisee would be the cost of making an alternative provision, and there is some authority to support the view that damages for breach of contract may be recovered to compensate for such loss even though the provision is wholly voluntary.[113] A fortiori the promisee can recover substantial damages where he is under a legal obligation to make a payment to the third party and where this obligation would have been discharged if the promisor had paid in accordance with the contract. Where loss *is* in fact suffered by the promisee, substantial damages can be recovered even though the promisee is under a legal duty to pay those damages to a third party.[114]

Damages in respect of third party's loss: general rule. The starting point 14–023
of the following discussion is the general principle that, in an action for damages, a claimant cannot recover more than the amount required to compensate him for his loss,[115] so that he cannot, in general, recover damages for breach of a contract made for the benefit of a third party in respect of loss suffered, not by the promisee, but by that third party.[116] That principle was indeed doubted by Lord Denning M.R. in *Jackson v Horizon Holidays Ltd*,[117] where the defendants contracted with the claimant to provide holiday accommodation for the claimant, his wife and their two three-year-old children.[118] The accommodation fell far short of the promised standard, and the claimant recovered damages, including £500 for "mental distress".[119] Lord Denning M.R. said that this sum would have been excessive compensation for the claimant's own distress.[120] He nevertheless upheld the award on the ground that the claimant had made a contract for the benefit both of himself and of his wife and children[121]; and that he could recover damages in respect of their loss as well as in respect of his own. But the authorities cited in support of this conclusion seem to contradict rather than to favour it. Moreover, in *Beswick v Beswick* the majority of the House of Lords said that the promisee's estate could have recovered no more than nominal damages as it had suffered no loss.[122] This is scarcely consistent with the view that the promisee under a contract for the benefit of a third party is, as a general rule, entitled to

---

[112] e.g. under Inheritance (Family Provision) Act 1938, now Inheritance (Provision for Family and Dependants) Act 1975.

[113] *Admiralty Commissioners v SS Amerika* [1917] A.C. 38 at 61 (the actual decision was that payments voluntarily made to the victim of an alleged *tort* could not be recovered: on this point see also *Esso Petroleum Co Ltd v Hall Russell & Co Ltd* [1989] A.C. 643). For the possibility of recovering, as damages for breach of contract, voluntary payments to or benefits conferred on third parties, see also *Banco de Portugal v Waterlow & Sons Ltd* [1932] A.C. 452; below, para.20–119. And see the discussion at paras 14–025, 14–029, below of *Linden Gardens Trust Ltd v Lenesta Sludge Disposals Ltd* [1994] 1 A.C. 85 and of *Alfred McAlpine Construction Ltd v Panatown Ltd* [2001] 1 A.C. 518.

[114] *Chappell v Somers & Blake* [2003] EWHC 1644; [2004] Ch. 19; discussed below, para.14–052.

[115] See below, para.20–004; cf. *White v Jones* [1995] 2 A.C. 207; below, para.14–052, where the damages recoverable by the estate of the other party to the contract would have been no more than nominal.

[116] *The Albazero* [1977] A.C. 774 at 846; *Linden Gardens* case, above, fn.113 at 114; *Alfred McAlpine Construction Co Ltd v Panatown Ltd* [2001] 1 A.C. 518; below, at fnn.163 and 164.

[117] [1975] 1 W.L.R. 1468; Yates 39 M.L.R. 202.

[118] It was assumed that the wife and children were not parties to the contract. Contrast, as to this, above, at fn.53.

[119] [1975] 1 W.L.R. 1468 at 1472.

[120] ibid. 1474.

[121] ibid.; cf. *McCall v Abelesz* [1976] Q.B. 585 at 594.

[122] See above, para.14–022.

damages in respect of the third party's loss. James L.J. in *Jackson*'s case seems to have regarded the £500 as compensation for the claimant's own distress.[123] No doubt this was increased by his witnessing the distress suffered by his wife and children, and if the promisee himself suffers loss he should not be prevented from recovering it in full merely because the contract was made partly for the benefit of third parties[124] who also suffered loss. In *Woodar Investment Development Ltd v Wimpey Construction Co Ltd*[125] the House of Lords disapproved Lord Denning's approach to the question of damages in *Jackson*'s case, though the actual decision in the latter case was supported on the ground that the damages were awarded in respect of the claimant's own loss[126]; or alternatively on the ground that cases such as the booking of family holidays or ordering meals in restaurants[127] might "call for special treatment".[128] In the *Woodar* case itself a contract for the sale of land provided that, on completion, the purchaser should pay £850,000 to the vendor and also £150,000 to a third party. The vendor claimed damages on the footing that the purchaser had wrongfully repudiated the contract and the actual decision was that there had been no such repudiation,[129] so that the issue of damages did not arise. But the question of what damages would have been recoverable in the *Woodar* case itself if there had been a wrongful repudiation was there described as "one of great doubt and difficulty"[130]: presumably it would turn on such factors as whether the vendor was under a legal obligation to ensure that the third party received the payment, or whether, on the purchaser's failure to make the payment, the vendor had himself made it, or procured it to be made, from other resources available to him.

The assumption underlying the *Woodar* case thus seems to be that, where a contract for the benefit of a third party has been broken, the promisee cannot generally recover damages in respect of a loss suffered only by the third party. But this position was there described as "most unsatisfactory"[131] and said to be in need of reconsideration, either by the legislature or by the House of Lords itself.[132] It is unsatisfactory because it can give rise to what has been called a "legal black hole"[133]; that is, to a situation in which the promisor has committed a plain breach which has caused loss to the third party whom the contracting parties intended to

---

[123] At 1474.

[124] cf. *Radford v De Froberville* [1977] 1 W.L.R. 1262 (damages for failure to build a wall not reduced merely because claimant had entered into the contract, not only for his own benefit alone, but also for that of his tenants).

[125] [1980] 1 W.L.R. 277.

[126] ibid. at 283, 293, 297. Where a contract is made with a company and the breach causes loss to its subsidiary, damages may be recovered by the company since the value of its holding in the subsidiary will be reduced in consequence of the loss: *George Fischer (Great Britain) Ltd v Multi Construction Ltd* [1995] 1 B.C.L.C. 260.

[127] cf. *Lockett v AM Charles Ltd* [1938] 4 All E.R. 170, where agency reasoning was used in such a situation.

[128] [1980] 1 W.L.R. 277 at 283. cf. *Calabar Properties Ltd v Stitcher* [1984] 1 W.L.R. 287 at 290 where it was not disputed that a tenant's damages for her landlord's breach of his covenant to repair should include compensation for ill-health suffered by her husband.

[129] See below, para.18–035.

[130] [1980] 1 W.L.R. 277 at 284. See also below, fn.231.

[131] ibid. at 291; cf. ibid. at 297–298, 300–301.

[132] cf. *Beswick v Beswick* [1968] A.C. 58 at 72.

[133] *Darlington BC v Wiltshier (Northern) Ltd* [1995] 1 W.L.R. 68 at 79; for the origins of this metaphor, see *Alfred McAlpine Construction Ltd v Panatown Ltd* [2001] A.C. 518 at 529. For the limits, see *Tele 2 International Card Co SA v Post Office Ltd* [2009] EWCA Civ 9 at [87].

benefit but none to the promisee, and in which no other remedy[134-135] (than damages for the third party's loss) is available against the promisor.

Damages in respect of third party's loss: exceptions in general. Judicial awareness of the unsatisfactory results which can flow from the general rule that a promisee can recover damages only for his own loss has led to the creation of exceptions to that rule. For example, substantial damages for breach of contract can be recovered by a trustee even though the loss is suffered by his cestui que trust[136]; by an agent even though the loss is suffered by his undisclosed principal[137]; by a local authority even though the loss is suffered (ultimately) by its inhabitants[138]; and by the shipper of goods for breach of the contract of carriage with the shipowner even though the loss is suffered by a person to whom he has sold the goods, and to whom the risk and property in them had passed, but who has not himself acquired any rights to sue the shipowner under the contract of carriage[139]: it will be convenient to refer to this rule as "the *Albazero* exception", after the leading modern case in which it is recognised.[140] In all these exceptional cases a person recovers substantial damages for breach of contract even though the breach caused loss, not to him, but to a third party.

14–024

Further exceptions: building contracts. The list of exceptions just stated should not be regarded as closed and the possibility of extending them or of creating further exceptions is illustrated by a line of cases beginning with *Linden Gardens Trust v Lenesta Sludge Disposals Ltd.*[141] In that case, a building contract between parties described in it as employer and contractor provided for work to be done by the contractor by way of developing a site owned by the employer as shops, offices and flats. The site (but not the benefit of the contract) was later transferred by the employer to a third party, and it was assumed[142] for the purpose of the proceedings that the third party had suffered financial loss as a result of having to remedy breaches of the building contract committed after the transfer. In an action for breach of the building contract brought by the employer, the contractor argued that no loss had been suffered by the employer as he was no longer owner of the land when the alleged breaches occurred, and that the employer was therefore entitled to no more than nominal damages. In the House

14–025

[134-135] e.g. by way of specific performance, as in *Beswick v Beswick* [1968] A.C. 58.

[136] *Rolls Royce Power Engineering Plc v Ricardo Consulting Engineers Ltd* [2003] EWHC 2871 (TCC); [2004] 2 All E.R. (Comm) 129 at [116]; *Shell UK Ltd v Total UK Ltd* [2010] EWCA Civ 180; [2010] 3 W.L.R. 1192 at [144].

[137] See, e.g. below, para.16–070.

[138] cf. *St Albans' CC v International Computers Ltd* [1996] 4 All E.R. 481.

[139] *Dunlop v Lambert* (1839) 2 Cl. & F. 626 at 627 (as to which see *Alfred McAlpine Construction Ltd v Panatown Ltd* [2001] 1 A.C. 518 at 523 et seq.); *The Sanix Ace* [1987] 1 Lloyd's Rep. 465; *The Chanda* [1989] 2 Lloyd's Rep. 494. The rule was recognised in *The Albazero* [1977] A.C. 774, but held inapplicable as the buyer had acquired his own contractual rights against the shipowner under s.1 of the Bills of Lading Act 1855 (now repealed and replaced by Carriage of Goods by Sea Act 1992); Weir [1977] C.L.J. 24. In the case of contracts to which Carriage of Goods by Sea Act 1992 applies, a special statutory exception is created by s.2(4) of the Act to the general rule that a person can recover damages only in respect of his own loss; for a full discussion of this subsection, see *Carver on Bills of Lading* (2nd edn), paras 5–075 to 5–082.

[140] *The Albazero*, above, fn.139.

[141] [1994] 1 A.C. 85; Duncan Wallace 110 L.Q.R. 42.

[142] The case is reported on a preliminary issue of law, so that the alleged facts had not been proved.

of Lords, this argument was rejected, and the employer's claim upheld,[143] on two distinct grounds.

14–026   **The "broader ground": promisee's loss.** Lord Griffiths upheld the employer's claim on what has become known as the "broader ground"[144] that the employer "ha[d] suffered financial loss because he ha[d] to spend money to give him the benefit of the bargain which the defendant had promised but failed to deliver".[145] He added that "the court will of course wish to be satisfied that the repairs have been or are likely to be carried out".[146] This approach is, it is submitted, consistent with the explanation given in *Beswick v Beswick*[147] of the fact that the damages there were regarded as no more than nominal: the court there could not be satisfied that the substitute provision for the widow was likely to be made, precisely because the promisee lacked the means to make it.[148] The essence of Lord Griffiths' reasoning is that the promisee recovers damages in respect of the loss which he himself has suffered in ensuring that the third party receives the intended benefit. On this basis, the "broader ground" cannot apply where there is no practical possibility of curing the breach and so of securing the intended benefit to the third party, as in the "family holiday" cases discussed above.[149]

14–027   **The "narrower" ground: recovery of third party loss.** Although Lord Keith had "much sympathy"[150] with, and Lord Bridge was "much attracted by",[151] Lord Griffiths' reasoning, they (as well as Lord Ackner) preferred to base their decision on the narrower ground stated by Lord Browne-Wilkinson. This treats the loss as having been suffered by the third party rather than by the employer, but concludes that the employer could nevertheless recover substantial damages as the case fell within the rationale of the *Albazero* exception[152] to the general rule that a party can recover damages only in respect of his own loss. The rationale of this exception was that, in the carriage of goods cases to which it applies, the shipper and carrier must have contemplated that property in the goods might be transferred to third parties after the contract had been made, and that the shipper must therefore be treated in law as having made the contract of carriage for the benefit of all persons who might after the time of contracting acquire

---

[143] cf. *IMI Cornelius (UK) v Alan J Bloor* (1993) 57 Build. L.R. 108.

[144] *Linden Gardens* case, above, at 96–97 (per Lord Griffiths); *Alfred McAlpine Construction Ltd v Panatown Ltd* [2001] 1 A.C. 518, e.g. at 532.

[145] [1994] 1 A.C. 85 at 97. In fact the third party had reimbursed the employer in respect of this expenditure: see ibid.; but this did not affect the question of liability.

[146] ibid. This requirement has been doubted on the ground that, in general, the court is "not concerned with what the (claimant) proposes to do with his damages": *Darlington BC v Wiltshier Northern Ltd* [1995] 1 W.L.R. 68 at 80; and see below, para.20–044. But it seems, with respect, that Lord Griffiths' requirement is concerned, not with the question what the claimant proposes to do with the damages, but with the question whether he has suffered *any loss*. In *Alfred McAlpine Construction Ltd v Panatown Ltd* [2001] 1 A.C. 518 at 592, Lord Millett (dissenting) rejects the above reasoning, apparently on the ground that the promisee is "bound to mitigate his loss" and "cannot increase it by entering into other arrangements". But, with respect, the mitigation rules only require the injured party to act reasonably (below, para.20–116 et seq.) and in cases of the present kind this requirement would normally be satisfied where he made alternative provision to secure for the third party the benefit which the promisor has, in breach of the contract, failed to provide.

[147] [1968] A.C. 58.

[148] ibid. at 102; above, para.14–022.

[149] But see further discussion of *Beswick v Beswick*, below, para.14–030.

[150] [1994] 1 A.C. 85 at 95.

[151] ibid. at 96.

[152] See above, at fn.139.

interests in the goods.[153] This rationale applied equally to the facts of the *Linden Gardens* case since the contractor could foresee that parts of the new development were going to be "occupied and possibly purchased by third parties" so that "it could be foreseen that damage caused by a breach would cause loss to later owners".[154] The contractor could also foresee that a later owner would not have acquired rights under the building contract against the contractor since that contract expressly prohibited assignment by the employer without the contractor's written consent, which had not been sought. The effect of the *Linden Gardens* case was thus to extend the *Albazero* exception to other contracts,[155] but it was consistent with two factors which had restricted the scope of that exception: namely that (a) the loss or damage was caused to property which had been transferred by one of the contracting parties to the third party; and (b) the third party had not acquired any rights under the building contract[156] and it was foreseeable (by reason of the prohibition against assignment) that he would not do so. The significance of these factors is further considered in the later cases discussed below.

No transfer of the subject-matter to third party. In *Darlington BC v Wiltshier Northern Ltd*[157] a local authority (the council) wished to develop land which it already owned. The building work was to be done by the defendant; finance was to be provided by a bank but this could not be done in the most obvious way, by a loan to the council from the bank, since such an arrangement would have violated government restrictions on local authority borrowing. The transaction was therefore cast in the form of two contracts: (1) a building contract in which the bank was the employer and the defendant the building contractor; and (2) a contract between the council and the bank, by which the bank undertook to procure the erection of the buildings on the site, to pay all sums due under the building contract and to assign to the council the benefit of any rights against the defendant to which the bank might be entitled at the time of the assignment. Clause 4(5) of this second contract provided that the bank was not to be liable to the council "for any incompleteness or defect in the building work"; and it was this provision which was the principal source of the difficulties in the case. The bank duly assigned its rights against the defendant to the council which claimed damages as such assignee from the defendant in respect of defects in the work. Since an assignee cannot recover more than the assignor could have been done,[158] the question arose what the bank could have recovered; and it was argued that it could have recovered no more than nominal damages since it had suffered no loss, having no interest in the land (or buildings) on which the work had been done and

14–028

---

[153] *The Albazero* [1977] A.C. 744 at 847; *HSBC Rail (UK) Ltd v Network Rail Infrastructure Ltd* [2005] EWCA Civ 1437; [2006] 1 W.L.R. 643 at [23].

[154] [1994] 1 A.C. 85 at 114.

[155] cf. *JP Morgan Chase Bank v Springwell Navigation Corp* [2005] EWHC 1044 (Comm) at [45] in which the exception is described simply as "*a contract* rule"; *Smithkline Beecham Plc v Apotex Europe Ltd* [2006] EWCA Civ 658; [2007] Ch. 71; *DRC Distribution Ltd v Ulva* [2007] EWHC 1716 (QB) at [68]–[75]; *Mirant Asia-Pacific (Hong Kong) Ltd v Ove Arup and Partners International Ltd* [2007] EWHC 918 (TCC); [2007] C.I.L.L. 2840 (below, fn.188). The underlying concern "to see that justice is done between the parties" has also been reflected in the assessment of damages after assignment: *Offer-Hoar v Larkstore Ltd* [2006] EWCA Civ 1079; [2006] 1 W.L.R. 2926, below para.15–045.

[156] cf. above, at fn.139.

[157] [1995] 1 W.L.R. 68.

[158] See below, para.15–045, especially the discussion of *Offer-Hoar v Larkstore Ltd* [2006] EWCA Civ 1079; [2006] 1 W.L.R. 2926.

being protected by cl.4(5) from any liability to the council for defects in the work. But the Court of Appeal rejected this argument and held that the bank could have recovered substantial damages from the defendant in respect of the council's loss and that it was this right which had been assigned to the council. This amounted to an extension[159] of the *Linden Gardens* case to a situation in which there was *no* transfer of the property affected by the breach from the promisee to the third party. This extension was later approved by the House of Lords,[160] so that, at least in the context of defective performance of building contracts,[161] such a transfer is no longer a necessary condition of the promisee's right to recover damages in respect of the third party's loss.

14–029   **Third party with independent contractual right against promisor.** In *Alfred McAlpine Construction Ltd v Panatown Ltd*[162] the facts resembled those of the *Darlington* case in that a building contract was again made, not between the building contractor and the company which owned the site (the owner), but between that contractor and another company (the employer) associated with the owners; the object of adopting this tripartite structure was to avoid VAT. On the same day on which this building contract was made, a separate contract (the "Duty of Care Deed") was made between the owner and the contractor; the obligations imposed on the contractor by this deed were not precisely co-terminous with those imposed on him by the building contract; and the Deed did not, while the contract did, contain an arbitration clause. The employer alleged that the building work was seriously defective and in arbitration proceedings claimed damages from the contractor, who argued that the employer should recover no more than nominal damages since any loss resulting from the alleged defects in the work had been suffered, not by the employer (as the employer had never owned the property), but by the owner. The House of Lords, by a majority, upheld the contractor's argument and so rejected the employer's claim for substantial damages in respect of the owner's loss. It was accepted by the majority[163] and by one of the dissentients[164] that, as a general rule, a contracting party could not recover damages in respect of loss suffered, not by himself, but by a third party; and the question therefore arose whether the case could be brought within an exception to that general rule. This raised, in turn, the question whether either of the grounds for the decision in the *Linden Gardens* case[165] supported the employer's claim.

It will be recalled that the "narrow" ground for that decision was derived from the "*Albazero* exception" under which a shipper of goods can sometimes recover

---

[159] [1995] 1 W.L.R. 68 at 79, per Steyn L.J. Dillon L.J. regarded the result in the *Darlington* case as a "direct application" of the *Linden Gardens* case: [1995] 1 W.L.R. 68 at 75. These two views may be reconciled if the facts are approached *as if* the property had first been owned by the bank and then transferred to the council. See also *John Harris Partnership v Groveworld Ltd* [1999] P.N.L.R. 697 (developer entitled to recover from architect retained by him loss suffered in part by a third party who had financed the building project).

[160] *Alfred McAlpine Construction Ltd v Panatown Ltd* [2001] A.C. 518 at 531, 566, per Lords Clyde and Jauncey; ibid. at 545, 584, per Lords Goff and Millett (dissenting).

[161] Quaere whether this extension will be applied in the carriage by sea context in which the exception originated: see *Carver on Bills of Lading* (2nd edn), para.5–062.

[162] [2001] 1 A.C. 518; Coote 117 L.Q.R. 81, McKendrick (2003) O.U.C.L.J. 145 (reversing (1998) 58 Con. L.R. 58; Treitel 114 L.Q.R. 572; for further proceedings see (2001) 76 Con.L.R. 222).

[163] ibid. at 522, 563, 575.

[164] Lord Millett, ibid. at 580–581; Lord Goff is more sceptical: ibid. at 538–539.

[165] [1994] 1 A.C. 85; above, para.14–025; referred to as the *St Martin* case throughout the speeches in the *Panatown* case.

damages in respect of a third party's loss.[166] That exception is, however, subject to the restriction that it does not apply where the third party had himself acquired contractual rights against the carrier, usually by transfer to the third party of a bill of lading.[167] In the *Panatown* case, the majority held (and the dissentients accepted) that the case fell within this restriction, so that the *Albazero* exception (and hence the "narrow ground" in the *Linden Gardens* case) did not apply because the Duty of Care Deed gave the owner an independent contractual right against the contractor. This point was, moreover, decisive even though that right did not arise under a *building* contract, so that, in this respect the restriction was somewhat expanded: in the carriage by sea cases, the restriction normally[168] came into operation because the third party had acquired rights under a contract of *carriage*. Nevertheless it is respectfully submitted that this aspect of the *Panatown* case is consistent with the rationale of the restriction. In the carriage by sea cases, this could and did apply even though the *content* of the third party's contractual right against the carrier was not the same as that of the shipper's right[169]; and it was based on the reasoning that, where the third party had his own contractual rights against the carrier, the exception did not apply "because it was not needed".[170] It was not needed because, where the third party had his own contractual rights against the party in breach there was no risk of the "legal black hole" which had driven judges to create exceptions to the general rule that a contracting party can recover damages only in respect of his own loss.[171]

The majority in the *Panatown* case further held that the existence of the third party's rights against the contractor under the Duty of Care Deed also precluded the employer from recovering damages under the "broader ground" given by Lord Griffiths in the *Linden Gardens* case. In view of the existence of those rights, the employer had no pecuniary interest in curing the defects in the contractor's work.[172] Hence he neither had suffered nor would suffer any loss of his own, in consequence of the contractor's breach,[173] and under the "broad ground" it is in respect of his *own* (not of the third party's) loss that the promisee recovers damages. This conclusion can, on the facts of the *Panatown* case, be supported for two further reasons. First, the creation or extension of exceptions to the general rule that a party can recover damages only in respect of his own loss is and should be driven and limited by necessity[174]: that is, by the need to guard against the risk of "legal black holes" of the kind described above; and in the *Panatown* case there was no such risk.[175] Secondly, the decision gives effect to the "contractual

---

[166] *The Albazero* [1977] A.C. 774; above, para.14–024.

[167] See above, fn.139.

[168] The restriction could also apply where the third party's contractual rights against the carrier were under an implied contract of the kind illustrated by *Brandt v Liverpool, etc., SN Co* [1924] 1 K.B. 575; see *The Albazero* [1977] A.C. 774 at 847.

[169] As in *The Albazero* [1977] A.C. 774.

[170] *Panatown* case [2001] 1 A.C. 518 at 575; *The Albazero*, above, at 847–848. cf. *Catlin Estates Ltd v Carter Jonas* [2005] EWHC 2315; [2006] P.N.L.R. 15 at [304] (*Albazero* exception not excluded unless the third party has a claim which can be brought "on the same conditions"; in that case, a potential claim under Defective Premises Act 1972 (not established) would not have prevented the application of the exception).

[171] *Darlington BC v Wiltshier Northern Ltd* [1975] 1 W.L.R. 68 at 79.

[172] *Panatown* case [2001] 1 A.C. 518 at 574 and 577 (per Lords Jauncey and Browne-Wilkinson).

[173] cf. below, para.20–009.

[174] See the references given in fn.170, above.

[175] *Panatown* case [2001] 1 A.C. 518 at 574, per Lord Jauncey; cf. *Smithkline Beecham Plc v Apotex Europe Ltd* [2006] EWCA Civ 658; [2007] Ch. 71 at [94].

scheme"[176] created by the parties; and this point, so far from being undermined by the fact that the contractor's obligations to the owner under the Duty of Care Deed were not precisely co-terminous with his obligations to the employer under the building contract, is reinforced by this fact. As the parties had taken the "plain and deliberate course"[177] of giving the owner a "distinct entitlement"[178] against the contractor in respect of defects in the work, and as this entitlement was to be governed by the terms of one contract (the Duty of Care Deed), it followed that there was no good practical reason for holding the contractor liable in respect of the same defects on the terms of another contract (the building contract) for substantial damages to the employer, to whom these defects had caused no loss of his own. The fact that the "general rule" has been the subject of frequent judicial disapproval no doubt gives rise to the temptation to continue the process of eroding it by creating new or extending existing exceptions to it. But that criticism has occurred mainly in cases in which the third party problem was an inescapable consequence of normal commercial factors such as those which existed in the *Linden Gardens* case. The pressure for eroding the unpopular general rule is much less strong where the third party problem is, so to speak, manufactured by the parties for an ulterior motive, such as government restrictions on borrowing, as in the *Darlington* case, or avoiding tax,[179] as in the *Panatown* case, where, in the view of the majority any such pressure was eliminated for the further reason that the third party had his own contractual remedy against the party in breach under a separate contract between these parties.

14–030   **Status of the "broader ground", or "performance interest".** The *Panatown* case is significant not only for the points it decides, but also for some of those which it leaves open. The first such point relates to the effect of the case on the status of Lord Griffiths' "broader ground" in the *Linden Gardens* case. This ground forms the basis of the two dissenting speeches[180] in the *Panatown* case, in which it is referred to as the "performance interest", and it is not the subject of any adverse comment from the majority,[181] whose speeches do not rule out the possibility of its being applied in the, perhaps more common, situation in which the third party has *no* contractual rights of his own against the promisor in respect of loss suffered by him in consequence of the defective services rendered under the contract between promisor and promisee. It seems that, even in such a situation, the majority would deny the employer's right to recover substantial damages under the "performance interest" unless *either* the condition stated by Lord Griffiths is satisfied, i.e. "the repairs have been or are likely to be carried out",[182] or the employer has entered into a separate contract with the owner

---

[176] ibid. at 577, per Lord Browne-Wilkinson; and see 76 Con.L.R. 224 at [38] ("made their contractual bed"); cf. *Henderson v Merrett Syndicates Ltd* [1992] 2 A.C. 145 at 195, using the phrase "contractual structure" in the context of the question whether a contract between A and B can impose on a duty of care to C: see below, para.14–045 et seq.; cf. *Greater Nottingham Co-operative Society Ltd v Cementation Piling and Foundation Ltd* [1989] Q.B. 71 (tort duty excluded by tripartite contractual structure); and *R M Turton & Co Ltd v Kerslake & Partners* [2000] Lloyd's Rep. P.N. 967 (New Zealand Court of Appeal).
[177] ibid. at 536, per Lord Clyde.
[178] ibid.
[179] For the contrary view, see Lord Goff, dissenting, in the *Panatown* case, above, at 556–557.
[180] Of Lords Goff and Millett.
[181] Lords Clyde, Jauncey and Browne-Wilkinson.
[182] *Linden Gardens* case [1994] 1 A.C. 85 at 97; see further, below at fn.218.

undertaking liability in respect of defects in the contractor's work.[183] Where neither of these requirements is satisfied, the result of allowing the promisee to recover the cost of repairs as damages for his own loss would be "unattractive" in that it would enable him to "put the money in his own pocket"[184] without carrying out or paying for repairs: the technique of requiring him to hold the damages for the third party applies, on the authorities,[185] only where damages are recovered (under one of the exceptions to the general rule) in respect of the *third party's*, not in respect of the promisee's *own* loss. It follows that the requirements stated above[186] do not apply where the promisee's claim can succeed on the "narrow ground": in this respect, that ground is, paradoxically, broader than the "broader ground", or "performance interest".

Scope of the "performance interest". If the "performance interest" is 14–031 accepted for cases in which the third party has no contractual rights of his own against the promisor, then a further problem arises as to its scope. It need not be confined to building contracts, but it clearly does not apply merely because a third party has been adversely affected by a breach of contract.[187] The example given by Lord Griffiths in support of this ground is one in which loss is caused by reason of the *defective* performance of a contract to render *services*.[188] The case put by him[189] is that of a husband who contracts with a builder to have his wife's house repaired; if the builder does the work defectively the husband is (so long as the other requirements of the "broader ground" are satisfied) entitled (in the example) to substantial damages, i.e. to the cost of putting the defects right. Two questions then arise. The first is whether the rationale of the "broader ground" applies to cases in which the breach consists of a simple *failure* or *refusal* to perform. And the second is whether it applies where the obligation which is not performed is one to do something other than to render services.

The two questions come together in a case where, for a consideration provided or to be provided by A, a promise is made by B to A to pay a sum of money to C and B fails or refuses, wholly or in part, to perform that promise. Those were, in substance, the facts of *Beswick v Beswick*[190] where the majority of the House of Lords took the view that the damages recoverable by the estate would be no more than nominal. That may not, indeed, amount to a direct rejection of the "broader ground" in such cases. The reason given in *Beswick v Beswick* for the view that the promisee's damages would there have been merely nominal was that the estate had

---

[183] No such separate contract was established in the *Panatown* case: see 76 Con.L.R. 224 at [35].

[184] *Panatown* case [2001] 1 A.C. 518 at 571. This possible restriction on the scope of the broader ground is not considered in the discussion of that ground in the further proceedings in that case (76 Con.L.R. 244 at [20]) being unnecessary to the decision at this stage.

[185] See below, para.14–040.

[186] See above, at fnn.182 and 183.

[187] *Smithkline Beecham Plc v Apotex Europe Ltd* [2006] EWCA Civ 658; [2007] Ch. 71 at [95].

[188] Lord Millett's dissent is restricted to this situation: [2001] 1 A.C. 518 at 591; Lord Goff's dissent does not appear to be so restricted: ibid. at 545, 552–553; cf. *Rolls Royce Power Engineering Plc v Ricardo Consulting Engineers Ltd* [2003] EWHC 2871 (TCC); [2004] 2 All E.R. (Comm) 129 at [128]. In *Mirant Asia-Pacific (Hong Kong) Ltd v Ove Arup and Partners International Ltd* [2007] EWHC 918 (TCC); [2007] C.I.L.L. 2840, the court held (at [628]) that "in principle" the claimant was entitled to recover damages for loss that may have been incurred by a sister company as a result of the breach of an engineering design contract on the basis that "*it* did not receive from the defendants the performance of the bargain which it contracted for". It is not entirely clear whether "it" refers to the claimant (broad ground) or the sister company (narrow ground).

[189] *Linden Gardens* case [1994] 1 A.C. 85 at 97.

[190] [1968] A.C. 58; above, para.14–017.

no assets out of which it could make the payments to C which B had promised, but failed, to make.[191] But it is not clear whether in substance that reasoning is inconsistent with the "broader ground"; for, if the cost to A of securing the benefit intended for C is to be defrayed *out of the damages*, then it should not matter that A cannot provide that benefit out of his *other* assets, at least so long as A is solvent. The views expressed in *Beswick v Beswick* on the question of damages recoverable by the estate should, it is submitted, now be read subject to developments of the law as to damages in respect of a third party's loss in a number of later cases.

14–032   **The need to avoid the "black hole".** The most directly relevant of the later cases is the *Woodar* case[192] where it appears to be assumed that, as a general rule,[193] A cannot recover substantial damages from B for B's failure to perform his promise to A to pay a sum of money to C. This conclusion seems to be based on the assumptions that the loss is C's and that A cannot generally recover damages in respect of C's loss. It does not seem to preclude the possibility of A's recovering damages in respect of any loss which he himself might have suffered in consequence of B's breach: e.g. because A was under a contractual obligation to procure the payment to C or because A, acting reasonably, has made alternative provision for C.[194] Even in the absence of such factors, it is submitted that, in the light of the developments since the *Woodar* case,[195] the law should take account of the possibility that, unless B were held liable for substantial damages to A, then he might be under no substantial liability at all: in other words, that there would be a "legal black hole". In *Beswick v Beswick* and the *Panatown* case there were no such "black holes": in the former case, because of the availability of a satisfactory remedy for A against B by way of specific performance in favour of C[196]; in the latter because of the availability of a satisfactory remedy for C against B in damages under the separate contract between these parties.[197] If there is no such remedy and if the conditions in which A can (under the "broader ground") recover damages in respect of his *own* loss are not satisfied,[198] then the lack of any such remedy should, it is submitted be a ground for allowing A to claim damages in respect of C's loss. The need to avoid the "black hole" should generate this remedy;[199] and, where A has suffered no loss himself, the result of allowing him to recover damages in respect of C's loss (rather than in respect of A's own loss) would also have the advantage of ensuring that these damages were to be held for C,[200] thus avoiding the "unattractive" result of allowing A to "put the money in his own pocket".[201]

---

[191] [1968] A.C. 58 at 102; above, para.14–022.

[192] [1980] 1 W.L.R. 277; above, para.14–023.

[193] i.e. unless A can show that B's breach caused loss *to* A *himself*.

[194] See above, para.14–024.

[195] i.e. in the *Linden Gardens* case [1994] A.C. 85; the *Darlington* case [1995] 1 W.L.R. 68; and the *Panatown* case [2001] 1 A.C. 518.

[196] See above, para.14–017.

[197] See above, para.14–029.

[198] See below, after fn.218.

[199] That the need to avoid the "black hole" should determine the scope of the broad ground, and its relationship with the narrow ground, is supported by the decision of the Court of Appeal in *Offer-Hoar v Larkstore Ltd* [2006] EWCA Civ 1079; [2006] 1 W.L.R. 2926 in the context of assignment, which is discussed below para.15–045. According to Rix L.J. (at [83]): "where a real loss has been caused by a real breach of contract, then there should if at all possible be a real remedy which directs recovery from the defendant towards the party which has suffered the loss."

[200] See below, para.14–043.

[201] *Panatown* case [2001] 1 A.C. 518 at 571.

A developing and difficult area of law. In *Helmsley Acceptances Ltd v*   **14–033**
Lambert Smith Hampton[202] A commissioned a valuation report from B in support
of a decision to make a loan secured by a mortgage which A then syndicated to
other lenders (C). The borrower defaulted and there was insufficient security in
the property which was alleged to be due to the negligent over-valuation of the
property by B, in breach of the contract with A. Because the loan had been
syndicated the loss was divided between A and C, but nonetheless A sued B for
the full loss and C was also subsequently joined to the action on the basis that C
had potential claims against B in negligence.[203] Summary judgment was given at
first instance against A's claim to recover the full loss, including the losses
incurred by C, on the basis of the *Albazero* exception. It was overturned by the
Court of Appeal who found that it was a matter for full trial to determine whether
the exception applied. Longmore L.J. referred to this as "a developing and
difficult area of the law"[204] and some of the difficulty, which is reflected in the
points made above,[205] can be seen in the *Helmsley* case itself. For example, A may
have had a claim to the full loss in its own right on the basis that it acquired the
"defective asset" as mortgagee and thereby suffered "the relevant loss",[206] it
making no difference that it assigned part of the loan to C and constituted itself
trustee of the loan and the securities for the loan.[207] If A could not recover
damages for his *own* loss, then in accordance with the approach suggested above,
it is a question of whether A should recover in respect of C's loss. That would raise
the question of whether there really was a "black hole" in a case where A allegedly
made known to B its plan to syndicate the loan and the need for C to be able to
rely on the valuation, but B provided the report subject to a disclaimer that it was
for the sole use of A and B "accepted no responsibility whatsoever to any other
person". If such a disclaimer was effective to defeat C's claim in negligence, one
analysis may be not that C had a direct right against A (which had nonetheless
failed), thus ruling out the *Albazero* exception, but rather that C had no direct
right; in other words, that the facts in a case like *Helmsley* more closely resemble
those in *Linden Gardens* where C could not sue A because of a prohibition against
assignment, than they resemble those in *Panatown* where C could sue A under the
duty of care deed. The contrary argument is that C's claim under the duty of care
deed in *Panatown* was not guaranteed to succeed, if for example C could not
establish that B's breach of the building contract amounted to negligence, but the
parties were still held to the contractual structure which they had put in place.
Similarly, in *Helmsley* the contractual structure was such that B's only potential
liability to C was in negligence, but B had negotiated for a disclaimer of such
liability. Longmore L.J. noted that there was "much to be said" for the latter
argument,[208] but earlier he had described B's position as "not an attractive one",
on the assumption that they had been negligent and had caused a substantial
loss.[209]

---

[202] [2010] EWCA Civ 356.

[203] See below, para.14–045 et seq.

[204] [2010] EWCA Civ 356 at [13].

[205] See above, paras 14–030—14–032.

[206] [2010] EWCA Civ 356 at [10].

[207] It was also a matter to be resolved at trial whether A could recover as trustee of the rights
associated with the securities in accordance with the exception referred to above, fn.136.

[208] [2010] EWCA Civ 356 at [13].

[209] ibid. at [8].

14–034   **Non-performance.** It is submitted that the approach advocated in para.14–032 above is also appropriate to the case where the contract between A and B is one for services for the benefit of C which B simply fails or refuses to perform, instead of performing them defectively, as in Lord Griffiths' example,[210] in which it seems to be assumed that A has paid for the work. Lord Griffiths does not discuss the case of total non-performance by B, presumably assuming that in such a case B would not have been paid.[211] If A then gets another builder to do the work and that other builder charges no more than B would have done, A will (subject to questions of mitigation[212] and remoteness) be able to recover the difference as damages for his *own* loss. The position will be substantially the same where A has paid B in advance and B has done no part of the work: in that case A will be entitled to claim restitution of his payment[213] together with damages for his own loss in respect of any extra cost of employing a substitute builder.[214] So in none of these cases of total non-performance is there any "black hole" and hence no need to generate a new remedy at the suit of A in respect of C's loss. The most difficult case is that of an advance payment by A followed by *part* performance by B in circumstances in which A himself has suffered no loss: e.g. because A was under no obligation to C to secure completion of the performance that B was to render and has neither himself taken any steps to secure that completion nor is likely to do so.[215] In such a case of partial performance there might be considerable difficulty in holding B liable for partial restitution[216]; and if, in addition, the remedy of specific performance were not available (e.g. because the contract was one for personal services to be rendered by B[217]) then there would be at least a partial "black hole" and this fact should (it is again submitted) be a ground for allowing A to recover substantial damages from B in respect of C's loss.

14–035   **Use to which damages are put.** It will be recalled that, in his statement of the "broader ground" in the *Linden Gardens* case, Lord Griffiths said that the court would wish to be "satisfied that the repairs have been or are likely to be carried out".[218] In later cases, conflicting views have been expressed on the question whether this is an essential requirement for the operation of the "broader ground".

One view is that it is not, since (at least as a general rule[219]) a court in awarding damages is not concerned with the question of what the claimant intends to do with these damages[220]; that question is said to be relevant only to the issue of "reasonableness". This issue, however, arises, not for the purpose of determining the *existence* of a claim for substantial damages, but its *extent*: it may be relevant

---

[210] See above, at fn.189.

[211] Performance of the work is in contracts of this kind prima facie a condition precedent of the right to be paid: below, para.17–015.

[212] e.g. damages on a "cost of cure" basis are not recoverable if the cost of cure is wholly disproportionate to the benefit to be derived from cure: below, para.20–042.

[213] There will be a "total failure of consideration": below, para.22–003.

[214] See below, para.20–037.

[215] As in *Beswick v Beswick* [1968] A.C. 58; above, para.14–017.

[216] The "failure of consideration" would be only "partial": see below, para.22–004.

[217] See below, paras 21–035—21–037.

[218] [1994] 1 A.C. 85 at 97.

[219] For a possible exception, see the discussion at para.20–044 of the question whether cost of cure is recoverable where cure is not undertaken.

[220] See the *Darlington* case [1995] 1 W.L.R. 68 at 80; the *Panatown* case [2001] 1 A.C. 518 at 556, 592, per Lords Goff and Millett, dissenting; *Ruxley Electronics and Construction Co v Forsyth* [1966] A.C. 344 at 357 and 359; above, fn.146.

in determining whether damages in a two-party case are to be assessed on a difference in value or on a cost of cure basis,[221] or whether the claimant has failed to mitigate his loss[222]; but such questions arise only on the assumption that a claim for substantial damages does exist. A related argument in favour of the view that the claimant's intention with regard to the disposal of the damages is irrelevant is that he has been deprived by the defendant's breach of the benefit of his bargain, and this fact is, of itself, enough to support a claim for substantial damages.[223] This line of reasoning is, however, with respect, hard to reconcile with the principle that the victim of a breach has no claim to substantial damages if the breach has no adverse effect.[224] The assumption underlying this principle is that the mere failure to perform a contract does not suffice to sustain a claim for substantial damages: as Lord Clyde said in the *Panatown* case, "A breach of contract may cause a loss but is not in itself a loss in any meaningful sense".[225] In the cases here under consideration, the breach will have no adverse effect *on the claimant* (the prom-isee[226]) unless he has carried out or intends to carry out cure; and the argument that he has been deprived of his bargain cannot answer the question whether it must be shown that this deprivation has had an adverse effect *on him*: it merely pushes this question back one stage.

The alternative view is that damages in respect of the cost of curing the breach (and so of securing the intended benefit for the third party) can be recovered only if cure has been, or is likely to be, carried out. The main practical argument in favour of this view is that (as noted above) it would be "unattractive" to allow the promisee to recover the cost of cure as damages in respect of his own loss and then to "put the money in his own pocket".[227] It is respectfully submitted that this is the preferable view. In a two-party case it is indeed generally[228] no concern of the court's what the claimant intends to do with the damages; but the rationale of this rule does not necessarily apply in a three-party case. That rationale in a two-party case is that the defendant has, by reason of the breach, inflicted injury, loss or damage on the person or property *of the claimant* (or has failed to improve, or to transfer, an asset belonging to, or to be vested in, the claimant) who should therefore be able to deal in whatever way he pleases with the damages awarded to him in substitution of the interest *of his own* of which he has been deprived by the breach. For example, in the case of a contract to repair the claimant's own house, he could, but for the breach, have sold the house at a price reflecting the value of the repairs, had they been properly carried out, and then have disposed of the proceeds of the sale in any way he pleased; and so he should be able to dispose in the same way of the damages due to him for failure to carry out the repairs. Obviously, this reasoning cannot apply where the house is owned, not by the claimant, but by a third party. There is also the further point that, although in Lord Griffith's example the claimant as a matter of legal principle recovers damages in respect of his *own* loss, as a practical matter the purpose of the award

---

[221] See below, para.20–040.

[222] See below, para.20–115 et seq.

[223] See the references to the *Darlington* and *Panatown* cases in fn.220, above.

[224] See below, para.20–009.

[225] [2001] 1 A.C. 518 at 534.

[226] Our concern here is with adverse *financial* effect on the claimant. A claim for damages for "loss of amenity" will generally be one for loss suffered by the claimant, though in the family holiday cases (above, para.14–023) this loss may be increased by the claimaint's witnessing the sufferings of his family in comfortless hotels; cf. also below, para.20–088.

[227] *Panatown* case [2001] 1 A.C. 158 at 571.

[228] See fn.219, above.

in such a case is to protect the interests of the third party. Where damages are awarded in respect of a third party's loss (under one of the exceptions to the general rule) the court requires the promisee to hold these damages for the third party.[229] No such machinery is available where the damages are awarded in respect of the promisee's own loss; but a practical way of ensuring that the damages are in fact destined for the benefit of the third party is to require the promisee to show (as a condition of his entitlement to substantial damages) that they will be so used.

14-036   **Relation to third party's right.** Even where, in one of the exceptional situations discussed above, the promisee can recover damages in respect of the third party's loss, no right to enforce the contract is conferred directly on the third party, whose only claim will be to the fruits of any action which the promisee may decide to bring.[230] The third party will have a direct right against the promisor only under one of the exceptions to the doctrine of privity. On the facts of some[231] (though not of all[232]) of the cases discussed above, the third party would probably, if those facts recurred now, have such a right under the Contracts (Rights of Third Parties) Act 1999.[233] If the third party has such a right, then this very fact may restrict the number of situations in which the promisee can recover damages in respect of the third party's loss[234]; and it will probably reduce the pressure on the courts to extend the range of such situations.[235] Section 4 of the 1999 Act, however, preserves the promisee's rights under the contract.[236] The question of his right to recover damages in respect of the third party's loss will therefore continue to arise and to be of practical importance: e.g. where the promisor has a defence against the third party which is not available against the promisee.[237]

14-037   **Negative promise.** Where the promise is negative in nature, the promisee's most obvious remedy is an injunction to restrain the promisor's breach. This remedy would, for example, be available where A validly promised B not to compete with C.

14-038   **Promise not to sue third party.** One type of negative promise which gives rise to special difficulty is a promise by A to B *not to sue* C, e.g. for a debt owed by C to A. If, in breach of such a promise, A nevertheless did sue C, it would not be appropriate for B to start a second action for an injunction to restrain A from proceeding with the first action; for such a step would lead to undesirable

---

[229] See below, para.14–043.
[230] ibid.
[231] e.g. the *Woodar* case [1980] 1 W.L.R. 277 (above para.14–023); see Law Com. No.242, para.7.49.
[232] e.g. probably the *Linden Gardens* case [1994] 1 A.C. 85 (above, para.14–025): see below, para.14–094.
[233] See below, para.14–090 et seq. Subss.1(1)(a) and (3) of the 1999 Act will make it possible to draw up contracts, on facts similar to those of the *Linden Gardens* case, above, so as to confer a right of enforcement directly on the third party: see below, para.14–091.
[234] On the reasoning of *The Albazero* [1977] A.C. 774; above, para.14–024 and of *Alfred McAlpine Construction Ltd v Panatown Ltd* [2001] 1 A.C. 518; above, para.14–029.
[235] The "legal black hole" referred to in the *Darlington* case [1995] 1 W.L.R. 68 at 79 would be much reduced in significance.
[236] See below, para.14–121.
[237] 1999 Act, s.3(4); below, para.14–111.

multiplicity of legal proceedings.[238] B's remedy is to ask the court to exercise its discretion[239] to stay A's action against C. In *Gore v Van der Lann*[240] the Court of Appeal held that B could obtain a stay of A's action against C only if two conditions were satisfied: there must be a definite promise by A to B not to sue C, and B must have a sufficient interest[241] in the enforcement of A's promise. This last requirement would not be satisfied unless, as a result of A's breach, B were exposed to the risk of incurring legal liability to C: e.g. where B had *contracted with* C to procure his release from a debt or a liability to A, and would be put in breach of that contract by A's action against C.

Snelling v John G Snelling Ltd[242] goes even further in giving effect to a promise of this kind. Three brothers had lent money to a family company of which they were directors. They agreed that if one of them resigned he should "forfeit" any money due to him from the company. One of them did resign and sued the company for the amounts due to him. By way of defence the company relied on the agreement between the brothers, and, if matters had rested there, the defence would have failed as the company was not a party to the agreement.[243] But the other two brothers applied to be joined as defendants to the action, adopted the company's defence and counterclaimed for a declaration that the third brother's loan was forfeited. It was held that they were entitled to such a declaration by virtue of the contract between them and that brother.[244] Ormrod J. further held that they could obtain a stay of the action against the company and that the most convenient way of disposing of the action against the company was to dismiss it. So far as the granting of the stay is concerned, the judgment is hard to reconcile with the requirement of a sufficient interest as defined in *Gore v Van der Lann*[245]; but it is submitted that Ormrod J.'s decision is consistent with the spirit of *Beswick v Beswick*.[246] If *the promisee* takes steps specifically to enforce the contract the court should, wherever possible, grant such remedy as is most appropriate for that purpose. Normally this will be an order of specific performance or an injunction. The fact that the latter remedy is not appropriate to enforce a promise not to sue should not deter the court from granting other remedies that serve substantially to enforce the promise. Such a remedy is, again, available only if it is sought *by the promisee*.[247] If the two brothers in the *Snelling* case had not applied to be joined to the action, the company could not have relied on the agreement between them and the third brother by way of defence.[248]

---

[238] Senior Courts Act 1981, s.49(2).

[239] ibid., s.49(3).

[240] [1967] 2 Q.B. 31; Davies 1 *Legal Studies* 287; *European Asian Bank AG v Punjab and Sind Bank* [1982] 2 Lloyd's Rep. 356; *The Chevalier Roze* [1983] 2 Lloyd's Rep. 438; and see below, para.14–069.

[241] *The Elbe Maru* [1978] 1 Lloyd's Rep. 206 at 209–210l; *Deepak Fertilisers & Petrochemical Corp v ICI Chemicals & Polymers Ltd* [1999] 1 Lloyd's Rep. 378 at 401; *The Marielle Bolten* [2009] EWHC 2552 (Comm); [2010] 1 Lloyd's Rep. 648.

[242] [1973] Q.B. 87; Wilkie 36 M.L.R. 214.

[243] ibid. at 95.

[244] ibid. at 96.

[245] [1967] 2 Q.B. 31.

[246] [1968] A.C. 58; above, para.14–017.

[247] cf. *Heaton v Axa Equity and Law Life Assurance Society Plc* [2002] UKHL 15; [2002] 2 A.C. 329 at [9] ("is enforceable by B", i.e. the promisee. No such promise had been made: see above, para.13–016).

[248] *Snelling v John G Snelling Ltd* [1973] Q.B. 87 at 95.

(ii) *Position between promisee and third party*

14-039   The promisor may be willing to perform, and may actually perform, in favour of the third party, e.g. by paying him the agreed sum. These possibilities give rise to further problems between the third party and the promisee. In discussing these problems we shall at this stage assume that the case does not fall within any of the exceptions to the doctrine of privity which will be considered later in this chapter.[249]

14-040   **Promisor pays or is willing to pay.** The first problem arises where the promisor has actually paid the third party or is willing to pay him, and the promisee claims that the third party is not entitled to keep the money for his own benefit but must hold it on behalf of the promisee. Such a claim is not likely to be made by the promisee himself, as he wants to benefit the third party. But it might be made by the promisee's trustee in bankruptcy, or by his personal representative on death. In *Beswick v Beswick* the House of Lords held that the third party (the widow) was entitled to keep the money which the promisor (the nephew) was ordered to pay her, simply because it appeared from the true construction of the contract that this was the intention of the contracting parties.[250] It seems that the position would be the same where payments were made willingly, i.e. without any order of the court.[251] Payments actually received by the third party can be claimed by the promisee only if, on the true construction of the contract, they were made to the third party as nominee for the promisee. Where the money has not yet been paid, the promisor and the promisee can agree to rescind or vary the contract; and if they vary it so as to provide for payment to the promisee, the third party has no claim under the contract. But the question whether the promisee can unilaterally (i.e. without the consent of the promisor) demand that payment should be made to himself depends once again on the construction of the contract. If the contract can be construed as one to pay the third party "or as the promisee shall direct", then the promisee is entitled to demand payment to himself.[252] But the contract is not likely to be construed in this way where it is a matter of concern to the promisor that payment should be made to the third party, e.g. because the third party is a close relative of the promisor and it matters to the promisor that the third party should be provided for.[253]

14-041   *Coulls v Bagot's Executor and Trustee Co.* The rules just stated apply only if there is indeed a promise to pay the third party. In *Coulls v Bagot's Executor and Trustee Co Ltd*[254] an agreement between A and B provided for payment of royalties by B to A and concluded: "I [A] authorise . . . [B] to pay all money connected

---

[249] See below, para.14–077 et seq.

[250] *Beswick v Beswick* [1968] A.C. 58 at 71, 96, on this point overruling *Re Engelbach's Estate* [1924] 2 Ch. 348 and doubting *Re Sinclair's Life Policy* [1938] Ch. 799. Earlier cases supporting the view stated in the text include *Ashby v Costin* (1888) 21 Q.B.D. 401; *Harris v United Kingdom, etc. Society* (1889) 87 L.T.J. 272; *Re Davies* [1892] 3 Ch. 63.

[251] This appears from the treatment in *Beswick v Beswick* of *Re Engelbach's Estate* (above), where the money had in fact been paid to the third party: see 93 L.J.Ch. 616 at 617.

[252] *The Spiros C* [2000] 2 Lloyd's Rep. 319 at 331; cf. *Mitchell v Ede* (1840) 11 Ad. & El. 888; *The Lycaon* [1983] 2 Lloyd's Rep. 548.

[253] As in *Re Stapleton-Bretherton* [1941] Ch. 482.

[254] [1967] A.L.R. 385; for a similar distinction, see below, para.15–017.

with this agreement to my wife [W] … and myself … as joint tenants". The document was signed by A, B and W. A majority of the High Court of Australia held that there was no *promise* by B to A to pay W but only a *mandate* by A authorising B to pay W (so that such payment would discharge B). This mandate was revocable and had been revoked by A's death. Consequently, the money (which B was willing to pay) belonged to A's estate and not to W. The third party would, a fortiori, not be entitled to the money if he were mentioned in the contract as a mere nominee in such a way as to indicate that no beneficial interest was intended to pass to him, and that payment to him without the request of the promisee should not discharge the promisor.[255]

Promisee refuses to sue. The second problem arises where the promisee fails **14–042** or refuses to take any action to enforce the promise. Lord Denning has suggested that, even at common law the third party could in such a case circumvent the doctrine of privity by suing the promisor and joining the promisee as co-defendant.[256] But Diplock and Salmon L.JJ. have said that the action can (in cases not falling within any of the exceptions to the doctrine of privity[257]) be brought only by the promisee[258]; and it is submitted that this is the correct view. Lord Denning's view is inconsistent with the common law doctrine of privity which was recognised in *Beswick v Beswick* and in later cases.[259] It is also inconsistent with the reasoning of the cases on trusts of promises to be discussed below,[260] for if the third party could always sue by joining the promisee to the action, it would be pointless to insist that he must in addition show the existence of a trust.

Promisee sues for damages or restitution. The final problem arises where **14–043** the promisee sues but claims some form of relief other than specific performance in favour of the third party: i.e. where he claims damages or recovery of the consideration provided by him. If such a claim succeeded, it would seem to lead to a judgment for payment to the promisee and not to the third party; and the question would arise whether the promisee could keep the payment for his own benefit or whether he would be bound to hold it for the third party. In tort, a person can sometimes recover damages for a loss suffered, not by himself, but by another: e.g. a husband may get damages for loss of earnings suffered by his wife in giving up her job to nurse him after an accident and such damages must then be held on trust for the other person.[261] Similarly, damages for breach of contract can in the exceptional situations discussed above be recovered in respect of loss suffered by another[262]; such damages must be held for that other person.[263] This

---

[255] *Thavorn v Bank of Credit & Commerce SA* [1985] 1 Lloyd's Rep. 259, as to which see above, para.13–034, fn.119; *The Turridu* [1999] 2 Lloyd's Rep. 401.
[256] *Beswick v Beswick* [1966] Ch. 538 at 557; *Gurtner v Circuit* [1968] 2 Q.B. 587 at 596.
[257] *Gurtner v Circuit*, above at 599, 606.
[258] See above, at fn.249.
[259] See above, paras 14–016—14–017.
[260] See below, paras 14–081—14–088.
[261] *Hunt v Severs* [1994] 2 A.C. 350 at 363, following *Cunningham v Harrison* [1973] Q.B. 942 at 952 and rejecting the contrary view in *Donnelly v Joyce* [1974] Q.B. 454 at 461–462.
[262] See above, paras 14–024—14–025.
[263] *The Albazero* [1977] A.C. 774 at 845; *O'Sullivan v Williams* [1992] 3 All E.R. 385 at 387, discussing *The Winkfield* [1902] P. 42; *Linden Gardens* case [1994] 1 A.C. 85 (above, para.14–025); *John Harris Partnership v Groveland Ltd* [1999] P.N.L.R. 697; Carriage of Goods by Sea Act 1992, s.2(4).

may also be the position in the cases which call "for special treatment",[264] such as the booking of family holidays or ordering meals in restaurants; if, in such cases, the promisee can recover damages in respect of the third party's loss, it may be that those damages, when recovered, would be held by the promisee as money had and received for the use of the third party.[265] But apart from these exceptional or special cases there does not appear to be any similar possibility where the promisee claims damages for breach of a contract merely because the contract was made for the benefit of a third party. The general rule in such a case is that damages will be awarded only to compensate the promisee for his *own* loss[266]; and where that general rule applies, it does not seem that he can be under any obligation to pay those damages (or any part of them) over to the third party.[267]

3. SCOPE

(a) General

14–044   The common law doctrine of privity means that a person cannot acquire rights or be subjected to liabilities *arising under* a contract to which he is not a party. It does not mean that a contract between A and B cannot affect the legal rights of C indirectly. For example, an agreement between A and B under which A accepts from B part payment of a debt owed by C to A in full settlement of that debt can benefit C by precluding A from suing C for the balance of the debt[268]; and a fortiori full performance by B of C's obligation to A can discharge that obligation.[269] Conversely, a building contract between A and B may benefit C by defining his rights: e.g. by specifying the time at which payment becomes due to C under a sub-contract between B and C for the execution of part of the work.[270] It is also possible for a contract between A and B to affect C adversely.[271] The circumstances in which this may happen are discussed in the last part of this chapter. In this part, we are concerned with the circumstances in which a contract between A and B may *benefit* C without C acquiring any right to enforce the contract itself, or relying on the remedies available to A.[272]

(b) Liability in Negligence to Third Parties

14–045   While the primary effect of a contract between A and B is to oblige them to perform their respective promises to each other, the contract may also impose on

---

[264] *Woodar Investment Development Ltd v Wimpey Construction UK Ltd* [1980] 1 W.L.R. 277 at 283; above, para.14–023.

[265] This was the view of Lord Denning M.R. in *Jackson v Horizon Holidays Ltd* [1975] 1 W.L.R. 1468 at 1473.

[266] See above, para.14–030.

[267] cf. *Coulls v Bagot's Executor and Trustee Co Ltd* [1967] A.L.R. 385 at 411.

[268] *Hirachand Punamchand v Temple* [1911] 2 K.B. 330; above, para.3–108 (where the effects on such facts of Contracts (Rights of Third Parties) Act 1999 are also discussed); cf. *Johnson v Davies* [1999] Ch. 117 at 130.

[269] For the conditions to be satisfied for such discharge, see below, para.17–007 et seq.

[270] *Co-operative Wholesale Society Ltd v Birse Construction Ltd* (1997) 84 B.L.R. 58.

[271] e.g. *The Glacier Bay* [1996] 1 Lloyd's Rep. 370; *Banque Financière de la Cité v Parc (Battersea) Ltd* [1999] 1 A.C. 221; cf. below, paras 14–071—14–076.

[272] As discussed above, para.14–019 et seq.

A a duty of care to C, the breach of which will enable C to sue A in tort for negligence. The contract may have this effect because it gives rise to a relationship in which A owes a duty of care to C: e.g. to the relationship of passenger (or cargo-owner) and carrier,[273] of occupier of premises and visitor,[274] or of bailor and sub-bailee,[275] or of building owner and sub-contractor.[276] In a number of cases persons providing professional services, such as solicitors,[277] insurance brokers[278] and safety consultants[279] have been held liable in tort to persons other than their immediate clients for negligence in the performance of contracts with those clients. Surveyors, valuers, accountants and auditors can similarly be liable for negligent misrepresentation to third parties: the basis, and limits, of such liability have been discussed in Ch.9.[280] Sometimes the provider of the services is liable in tort because his negligence in performing the contract with his client of itself causes loss to the third party: e.g. where a solicitor's negligence in failing to carry out his client's testamentary instructions causes an intended gift to a prospective beneficiary to fail.[281] Sometimes the defendant's negligence results in his making a misrepresentation to the third party and the loss is suffered by the latter in consequence of his acting in reliance on the representation: e.g. where a valuer (A) employed by B negligently makes a report on the structure of a house and the report is communicated to C and induces him to buy the house for more than its true value.[282]

Policy factors. As will be apparent from the paragraph above one can point to a significant body of case law in which A's defective performance of his contract with B has led to a liability in negligence to C. Ever since the decision in *Donoghue v Stevenson*,[283] this has been largely uncontroversial where the loss suffered by C is some form of personal injury, or damage to C's property. The fact that A, the manufacturer of the ginger beer alleged to contain a decomposed snail, had supplied it under his contract with a distributor (B) did not amount to an

14–046

---

[273] *Austin v GW Ry* (1867) L.R. 2 Q.B. 442; *The Antonis P Lemos* [1985] A.C. 711.

[274] Occupiers' Liability Act 1957, s.3; Defective Premises Act 1972, ss.1(1)(b), 4.

[275] *Moukataff v BOAC* [1967] 1 Lloyd's Rep. 396; *Bart v BWIA* [1967] 1 Lloyd's Rep. 239. A sub-bailment may also operate to the disadvantage of C (the head bailor) in that he may be *bound* by an exemption clause in the contract between A (the head bailee) and B (the sub-bailee): see *Morris v CW Martin Ltd* [1996] 1 Q.B. 716 at 729 and *The Pioneer Container* [1994] 2 A.C. 324; below, para.14–073. But this principle does not enable B to take the *benefit* of a term in the contract between A and C: see *The Mahkutai* [1996] A.C. 650 at 667–668; it merely enables B to rely on the terms of B's *own* contract with A against C where C has authorised the relevant terms of the sub-bailment. No "sub-bailment" arises merely because a sub-agent has received the proceeds of sale of the principal's property: *Balsamo v Medici* [1984] 1 W.L.R. 951.

[276] See para.14–049, below.

[277] See para.14–052, below.

[278] *Punjab National Bank v de Boinville* [1992] 1 W.L.R. 1138 at 1152; cf. *Henderson v Merrett Syndicates Ltd* [1995] 2 A.C. 145 (discussed below, para.14–051); *BP v AON Ltd* [2006] EWHC 424; [2006] 1 C.L.C. 881.

[279] *Driver v William Willett (Contractors) Ltd* [1969] 1 All E.R. 655; cf. *Dove v Banham's Patent Locks Ltd* [1983] 1 W.L.R. 1436; Contrast *The Nicholas H* [1996] 1 A.C. 211; below, para.14–050.

[280] See above, paras 9–033—9–038.

[281] See below, para.14–052.

[282] e.g. *Smith v Eric S Bush* [1990] 1 A.C. 831; above, para.9–024; cf. *Niru Battery Manufacturing Co v Milestone Trading Ltd* [2003] EWCA Civ 1446; [2004] 1 Lloyd's Rep. 344 (liability of certification company to third party).

[283] [1932] A.C. 562.

automatic bar against liability in negligence when it was later consumed by Mrs Donoghue (C) and made her ill. But, as will be seen,[284] even in cases of personal injury or damage to C's property, the circumstances of the case may be such as to negate the existence of any duty of care and one of those circumstances *may* be the contract which existed between A and B. The courts are concerned, in particular, to ensure that a claim in tort does not have the effect of upsetting the contractual allocation of the risk of injury or damage which the parties, including C,[285] may deliberately have put in place, and which privity operates to keep intact.

A second problem is that in a number of the cases in which C has sued A in negligence, he has done so for pure economic loss, i.e. financial loss which is not the consequence of injury to C, or damage to his property. For example, where A sells defective goods to B who, in turn, sells them to C, C's claim may simply be for the reduction in the value of the goods and the loss caused by his inability to use them in their defective state. Such a claim may be made by C in an action for breach of contract *against B*. The aim of contract is the guaranteed performance of B's promise and, as a general rule, the remedies for breach seek to put the promisee (C) into the same position *as if the contract had been performed*.[286] This type of claim is not normally available in the tort of negligence,[287] where damages are awarded to put C into the position in which he was *before the tort was committed*, i.e. to ensure that C *is no worse off*; hence the usual requirement that C must point to some personal injury or damage to property other than that supplied.[288] In fact, this problem may be overstated.[289] In the example just given, the position C was in before A supplied defective goods was one in which he had the anticipated benefit of a valid performance from B; the "loss of opportunity" to C, caused by A's negligence, is one which has been recognised in other claims in tort.[290] For this reason, it is submitted that the first problem, namely interference with the parties' contractual allocation of the risk of loss, provides a securer basis for explaining the cases in which liability in negligence has been imposed on A for pure economic loss, and those in which it has not.

The examples considered thus far have been concerned with claims by C for losses caused by A's *defective performance* of his contract with B and not for any *failure to perform*. As a general rule, there is no action in negligence for a failure to act[291] and the same is true when A's failure constitutes a breach of his contract with B. A claim for failure to perform may be brought in contract, e.g. C may sue B in contract for any non-performance by B brought about by A's non-performance of his contract with B, but, as a general rule, C may not sue A in negligence.

---

[284] See below, para.14–050.

[285] This could not apply to *Donoghue v Stevenson* since the ginger beer consumed by Mrs Donoghue was purchased not by her, but by a friend.

[286] See below, para.20–022.

[287] There may be an exception to this general rule where the defect is a source of danger in respect of which the claimant could become liable to third parties, so that money has to be spent in averting this danger: *The Orjula* [1995] 2 Lloyd's Rep. 395 at 402, where it was also arguable that the defective thing supplied by the defendant had caused physical harm to *other* property in which the claimant had a prior interest as lessee.

[288] This also serves to put a limit on the claims which may be made against A so as to avoid the problem of "opening the floodgates".

[289] *White v Jones* [1995] 2 A.C. 207 at 269.

[290] e.g. *East v Maurer* [1991] 1 W.L.R. 461; see above, para.9–062.

[291] *Smith v Littlewoods Organisation Ltd* [1987] A.C. 241.

In some cases, however, the courts seem to have been able to overcome even this problem.[292]

The general rule remains that A is not liable in negligence to C for pure economic loss caused by A's defective performance of his contract with B,[293] nor for any failure to perform. There are exceptions, but the limited nature of those exceptions and the restrictions imposed on the duty of care which A may owe to C are largely explained[294] by the presence of some, or all, of the factors outlined above.

General principles. In claims for pure economic loss, and now more generally in the law of negligence,[295] two tests have emerged to determine when a duty of care may be owed by the defendant (A) to the claimant (C). The first is to ask whether A "assumed responsibility for what he said and did vis-à-vis [C], or is to be treated by the law as having done so".[296] The second may be referred to as the "threefold test": whether loss to C was a reasonably foreseeable consequence of what A did or failed to do; whether the relationship between the parties was sufficiently proximate; and whether in all the circumstances it is fair, just and reasonable to impose a duty of care on A towards C.[297] It seems that the first test of "assumption of responsibility" is to be regarded as a sufficient, but not a necessary, condition of liability: if it is satisfied, it is unnecessary to ask whether it would be fair, just and reasonable to impose liability; if not, further consideration is called for under the threefold test.[298]

As for the tests themselves, there is candid recognition that they are of doubtful utility.[299] It is clear from the dictum of Lord Bingham above[300] that the test of assumption of responsibility is applied objectively; it is not a case of what A intended but, "as in the case of contractual liability", what would reasonably be inferred from his conduct against the background of all the circumstances of the

14-047

---

[292] See below, para.14–052.

[293] *Tate & Lyle Industries Ltd v GLC* [1983] 2 A.C. 509 at 530–531; cf. *Greater Nottingham Co-operative Soc Ltd v Cementation Piling & Foundation Ltd* [1989] Q.B. 71 at 94. In *European Gas Turbines Ltd v MSAS Cargo International Ltd* [2001] C.L.C. 880 a cargo-owner (C) recovered damages from a sub-contracting carrier (A) for purely economic loss resulting from breach of A's sub-contract with the contracting carrier (B) as to the mode of carriage. There was no contract between A and C so that this conclusion is at first sight hard to reconcile with the other authorities cited in this note. The case may be explicable on the ground that C's agent had notified A of the importance to C of carriage by the stipulated mode and that A had accepted this position so as to give rise to an "assumption of responsibility" to A to observe that stipulation.

[294] In addition to the floodgates problem (above, fn.288), it has been said in some cases that there may be a constitutional problem where Parliament has indicated the limits of liability in a given area (see, e.g. *Murphy v Brentwood DC* [1991] 1 A.C. 398 at 480), though the relevance of this factor in the *Murphy* case is open to doubt: Stapleton 107 L.Q.R. 249, 268–269.

[295] See, e.g. *The Nicholas H* [1996] A.C. 211; *Phelps v Hillingdon LBC* [2001] 2 A.C. 619; *Watson v British Boxing Board of Control Ltd* [2001] Q.B. 1134.

[296] *Customs and Excise Commissioners v Barclays Bank Plc* [2006] UKHL 28; [2007] 1 A.C. 181 at [4], per Lord Bingham.

[297] ibid.; cf. *Caparo Industries Plc v Dickman* [1990] 2 A.C. 605 at 617–618; *Murphy v Brentwood DC* [1991] 1 A.C. 398 at 480, 486; *X (minors) v Bedfordshire CC* [1995] 2 A.C. 633 at 739.

[298] ibid. at [4], [35]; *Henderson v Merrett Syndicates Ltd* [1995] 2 A.C. 145 at 181. Contrast *BP v AON Ltd* [2006] EWHC 424; [2006] 1 C.L.C. 881 at [79]: "the extended assumption of responsibility principle is the *only* available coherent and rational methodology by the application of which damages can be recovered in the tort of negligence for pure economic loss caused by the negligent conduct of services."

[299] ibid. at [36]; *Caparo v Dickman* [1990] 2 A.C. 617 at 628; *Merrett v Babb* [2001] EWCA Civ 214; [2001] Q.B. 1174 at [41].

[300] See above, at fn.296.

case.[301] A notable feature of the test of assumption of responsibility is that it requires the court to identify a relationship "equivalent to contract".[302] Furthermore, it has been said that one of its functions is to make up for the apparent shortcomings of contract, in cases where no claim is available because of the absence of consideration,[303] or because of the operation of the doctrine of privity.[304] Under the threefold test, it is the third element which will usually be determinative and which inevitably raises questions of fairness and policy.

While, therefore, in the cases which follow, decisions have been reached by applying one test or the other, of far greater relevance have been the circumstances of the case and the relationship between the parties in the context of their legal and factual situation, with particular emphasis on the three factors outlined above.[305] This is an area of the law which to some extent resists categorisation, but for present purposes the cases may be considered under the following broad and non-exhaustive headings. By so dividing the cases it is not suggested that the arguments of principle which are applied are confined to the particular type of case under consideration.

14–048		**Supply of goods.** We have already seen that where A sells goods to B, who in turn sells or supplies them to C, A owes a duty of care to C not to cause personal injury, or damage to property other than the goods supplied. However, as a general rule, A owes no duty of care to avoid pure economic loss, including any loss which flows simply from the defect in the goods supplied.[306] In *Simaan General Contracting Co v Pilkington Glass Ltd (No.2)*[307] the defendants (A) had been nominated as suppliers of glass for incorporation in a building which was being erected by the claimants (C) as main contractors for a client in Abu Dhabi. The glass had been sold by the defendants to a sub-contractor (B) engaged by C, so that there was no contract between C and A; the glass was perfectly sound but was not of the colour specified in the contract of sale or in the main building contract. In consequence of this shortcoming, C was not paid by the employer and so suffered financial loss; but it was held that A's breach of the contract with B did not give C any right of action in tort against A merely because that breach had caused C to suffer financial loss.

The distinction between recoverable property damage and irrecoverable economic loss is well illustrated by *Muirhead v Industrial Tank Specialities Ltd*[308] where C, who owned a lobster farm, had entered into a contract for the installation of pumps which failed because of a defect in their electric motors. There was no contract between C and the supplier of the motors (A) but his claim against A

---

[301] *Customs and Excise Commissioners v Barclays Bank Plc* [2006] UKHL 28; [2007] 1 A.C. 181 at [35], per Lord Hoffmann. There must however have been an element of voluntariness in the conduct of A upon which an assumption of responsibility can be established. Thus, in the *Customs* case no duty of care was owed by a bank served with a freezing order to the judgment creditor in whose favour the order had been granted.

[302] *Hedley Byrne & Co Ltd v Heller & Partners Ltd* [1964] A.C. 465 at 530.

[303] See above para.3–169.

[304] *Williams v Natural Life Health Foods Ltd* [1998] 1 W.L.R. 830 at 837.

[305] See above, para.14–046.

[306] *Aswan Engineering Establishment Co v Lupine Ltd* [1987] 1 W.L.R. 1; *The Rebecca Elaine* [1999] 2 Lloyd's Rep. 1 at 8; cf. *Bacardi-Martini Beverages Ltd v Thomas Hardy Packaging Ltd* [2002] EWCA Civ 549; [2002] 2 Lloyd's Rep. 379 at [18] (contaminated ingredient used in manufacturing making finished product useless).

[307] [1988] Q.B. 758.

[308] [1986] Q.B. 507; Whittaker 49 M.L.R. 369; Oughton [1987] J.B.L. 370.

succeeded in tort in respect of the physical damage caused by the failure (i.e. the value of the lobsters which had died); and in respect of "any financial loss suffered by (C) in consequence of that physical damage"[309] (i.e. the loss of profits on the sale of the lobsters which had died). But a further claim "in respect of the whole economic loss suffered"[310] by C (i.e. for loss of the profits that he would have made from the installation, had it not been defective) was rejected: such damages might have been recoverable from the installer of the pumps (B) in contract but they could not be claimed from A, as supplier to B, in tort.

In *Henderson v Merrett Syndicates Ltd* Lord Goff observed that, in the type of case exemplified by the *Simaan* case, there is generally no assumption of responsibility by the supplier (A), "the parties[311] having so structured their relationship that it is inconsistent with any such assumption of responsibility."[312] For example, A may have supplied the goods to B with the benefit of certain exclusions or limitations on his liability which are reflected in the price paid by B; B in turn may have sold to C either with no such exclusions or limitations, or with the benefit of different exclusions or limitations which are reflected in the price paid by C. If C sues A in negligence for pure economic loss, he is able, in effect, to secure the benefit of a bargain which none of the parties had envisaged, i.e. between A and C. Since none of the exclusions and limitations for which A negotiated with B will ordinarily affect C's claim,[313] A will be left with the burden of a "contract" which is not reflected in the price received by him and C may enjoy the benefit of a "contract" for which he has not paid in full. C is entitled to sue in negligence only where A's breach of his contract with B has caused damage to C or his property.[314] The parties themselves may create a direct contractual relationship (e.g. in the form of a manufacturer's guarantee,[315]) but it is not for the courts to create such a relationship.

Building contracts. Similarly, in *Henderson v Merrett Syndicates Ltd* Lord   **14–049**
Goff was also of the opinion that a sub-contractor (A) will not generally be found to have assumed responsibility to a developer, or building owner (C).[316] It is certainly true that, as a general rule, A is under no liability for defects in the property constructed or economic loss flowing therefrom to anyone other than the main contractor (B),[317] or any other parties[318] with whom he is in a direct

---

[309] ibid. at 533.

[310] ibid.

[311] i.e. A, B and C.

[312] [1995] 2 A.C. 145 at 196; cf. the *Simaan* case, above, fn.307 at 781, per Lord Bingham.

[313] cf. below, fn.348. For possible exceptions, see below, para.14–070 and para.14–073.

[314] Where C is a consumer he may also have the benefit of strict liability for any injury or damage caused by a "defective" product under Consumer Protection Act 1987. Claims under the Act are not available for the defect itself (s.5(2)), i.e. not for pure economic loss. Indeed, the position of a consumer is instructive in this regard: his claim in tort against A is bolstered by the 1987 Act and any claim under a manufacturer's guarantee has been strengthened by the Sale and Supply of Goods to Consumers Regulations 2002 (SI 2002/3045), reg.15 (see above, para.14–006). His claim in contract against B (if B sold in the course of business) is enhanced by the terms implied by Sale of Goods Act 1979, ss.13–15 and the ineffectiveness of any attempt to exclude them (Unfair Contract Terms Act 1977, s.6(2): see above, para.7–059). But this is thought to represent the limit of the protection appropriate even for a consumer.

[315] See above, fn.314.

[316] See above, at fn.312.

[317] As a general rule, his liability for pure economic loss will be limited to breach of contract; it seems he owes no concurrent duty of care in tort *even to B*: *Robinson v P E Jones (Contractors) Ltd* [2011] EWCA Civ 9.

[318] See the discusssion of collateral warranties, below, at fn.323.

contractual relationship.[319] His liability in negligence is limited to personal injury or damage to "other" property.[320] Again, the principal reason is the effect that such liability would have on the parties' contractual allocation of risk. In the *D & F Estates* case,[321] a lessee (C) claimed damages in tort for the cost of remedying defects alleged to be due to the negligence of a building contractor (A) in the performance of a contract to which the lessee was not a party. A was held not liable in tort, even if he was negligent, since the defects had been discovered before they had caused any personal injury, or damage to other property belonging to C. To make A liable for the purely economic loss suffered by C in remedying the defect would "impose upon [A] for the benefit of those with whom he had no contractual relationship the obligation of one who warranted the quality of"[322] his work. That this now seems to be the accepted position is reflected in the practice of the parties concerned. In commercial developments, if the developer (or owner) (C) wishes to secure the benefit of a claim for pure economic loss against a party (A) with whom he is not already in a direct contractual relationship, he is expected to negotiate for it, usually in the form of a collateral warranty, and pay a price.[323] In the case of a residential purchase, which will often take place long after the building work, a collateral warranty from the builder (A) is unrealistic, but the purchaser (C) is expected to protect his interest[324] by obtaining a survey.[325]

In the context of building contracts, there is one notable exception to the general rule. In *Junior Books Ltd v Veitchi Co Ltd*[326] B was to build a factory for C under a contract which entitled C to nominate sub-contractors. C nominated A as flooring sub-contractor; B in consequence entered into a contract with A by which A undertook to lay the floor; but no contract came into existence between A and C.[327] The floor later cracked and, on the assumption that this was due to A's negligence in doing the work defectively, it was held that A was liable to C for the loss suffered by C in consequence of the fact that the work had to be done again, i.e. for defects in the floor itself. Later authorities have emphasised the exceptional nature of the circumstances of the *Junior Books* case.[328] It has been said

---

[319] *D & F Estates Ltd v Church Commissioners for England* [1989] A.C. 177; *Department of the Environment v Thomas Bates & Son Ltd* [1991] 1 A.C. 499; *Murphy v Brentwood DC* [1991] 1 A.C. 398. cf. *Galliford Try Infrastructure Ltd v Mott Macdonald Ltd* [2008] EWHC 1570 (TCC); 120 Con. L.R. 1.

[320] *Nitrigin Eirann Teoranta v Inco Alloys Ltd* [1992] 1 W.L.R. 498; *Targett v Torfaen BC* [1992] 3 All E.R. 27; *British Telecommunications Plc v James Thomson & Sons (Engineers) Ltd* [1999] 1 W.L.R. 9; *Bellefield Computer Services Ltd v E Turner & Sons* [2000] B.L.R. 97.

[321] *D & F Estates Ltd v Church Commissioners for England* [1989] A.C. 177. cf. *Department of the Environment v Thomas Bates & Son Ltd* [1991] 1 A.C. 499.

[322] [1989] A.C. 177 at 207; cf. ibid. at 211–212.

[323] See, e.g. *Safeway Stores Ltd v Interserve Projects Ltd* [2005] EWHC 3085 (TCC); 105 Con.L.R. 60 (C's claim against A limited to the extent of A's liability to B).

[324] The incentive to protect his interest in this way is all the greater since his claim in contract against the vendor (B) may be of little value, subject as it is to the principle of caveat emptor.

[325] Or by relying on a survey prepared for the lender from whom he borrows the funds to purchase the property: *Smith v Eric S Bush* [1990] 1 A.C. 831: see above, para.9–024. In one sense, it is because the purchaser may sue the surveyor in negligence for pure economic loss that he is prevented from so suing the builder.

[326] [1983] 1 A.C. 520; Jaffey [1983] C.L.J. 37; Palmer and Murdoch 46 M.L.R. 213. See further Jaffey 5 Legal Studies 77; Reynolds (1985) 11 N.Z.U.L.R. 215; Stapleton 104 L.Q.R. 213 and 389; Huxley 53 M.L.R. 361; Beyleveld and Brownsword 54 M.L.R. 48. The Contracts (Rights of Third Parties) Act 1999 probably does not apply on such facts: below, para.14–094.

[327] Quaere whether a collateral contract might have been found to exist: see above, para.14–006.

[328] It may be noted that, in *Henderson v Merrett*, above, fn.312, Lord Goff (at 196A) considered the nomination of the sub-contractor to be a common feature in building contracts.

that those circumstances were "unique"[329]; that the case "cannot now be regarded as a useful pointer to the development of the law"[330] or "as laying down any principle of general application in the law of tort"[331]; and that the statement of principle in Lord Brandon's dissenting speech is to be preferred to that of the majority.[332] The authority of the case is further undermined by the fact that the reasoning of the majority is to a considerable extent based on earlier decisions[333] which (so far as they hold the defendants liable for economic loss) have since been overruled by the House of Lords.[334] In consequence of these developments, the decision in the *Junior Books* case has been described as "discredited"[335], "virtually extinguished"[336] and "aberrant (and) heretical".[337]

Carriage of goods by sea. The rights and liabilities of carriers and cargo-owners are regulated by international Conventions which have the force of law and claims in negligence by cargo-owners which have attempted to bypass them have not met with success. In *The Aliakmon*[338] A, a carrier, had contracted with B for the carriage of a quantity of steel coils which B had sold to C. The coils were damaged, as a result of A's negligent breach of the contract of carriage, after the risk in them had passed to C under the contract of sale, but while B remained owner. C had no claim under the contract of carriage as he was not a party to it[339]; and the House of Lords held that he also had no cause of action against A in tort in respect of the loss which he had suffered as a result of remaining liable for the full price of the coils in spite of the fact that they had been damaged in transit. This conclusion was based on a long line of authority[340] which had established the "principle of law that, in order to enable a person to claim in negligence for loss caused to him by reason of loss or damage to property, he must have had either the legal ownership of or a possessory title[341] to the property concerned at the time

14–050

---

[329] *D & F Estates Ltd v Church Commissioners for England* [1989] A.C. 177 at 202; cf. *Van Oppen v Clerk to the Bedford Charity Trustees* [1989] 1 All E.R. 273 at 289, affirmed [1990] 1 W.L.R. 235; *Nitrigin Eirann Teoranta v Inco Alloys Ltd* [1992] 1 W.L.R. 498 at 504.

[330] *Simaan General Contracting Co v Pilkington Glass Ltd (No.2)* [1988] Q.B. 758 at 784.

[331] *D & F Estates Ltd v Church Commissioners for England* [1989] A.C. 177 at 202; cf. ibid. at 215.

[332] ibid. at 202, 215; cf. *Murphy v Brentwood DC* [1991] 2 A.C. 398 at 466, 469.

[333] i.e. *Anns v Merton LBC* [1978] A.C. 728; *Dutton v Bognor Regis Urban DC* [1972] 1 Q.B. 373.

[334] *Murphy v Brentwood DC* [1991] 2 A.C. 398.

[335] *Société Commerciale de Réassurance v ERAS International Ltd* [1992] 1 Lloyd's Rep. 570 at 599.

[336] *The Volvox Hollandia (No.2)* [1993] 2 Lloyd's Rep. 315 at 322; *The Orjula* [1995] 2 Lloyd's Rep. 395 at 401.

[337] *Robinson v P E Jones (Contractors) Ltd* [2011] EWCA Civ 9 at [92].

[338] [1986] A.C. 785; Treitel [1986] L.M.C.L.Q. 294; Markesinis 103 L.Q.R. 354 at 384–390; Tettenborn [1987] J.B.L. 12; cf. *The Ciudad de Pasto* [1988] 1 W.L.R. 1145; *The Filiatra Legacy* [1991] 2 Lloyd's Rep. 337 at 339; *The Gudermes* [1993] 1 Lloyd's Rep. 311 at 326; *The Seven Pioneer* [2001] 2 Lloyd's Rep. 57 (High Court of New Zealand). For a possible qualification, see *The Kapetan Georgis* [1988] 1 Lloyd's Rep. 352, where A in breach of his contract with B caused physical harm to B in respect of which C became liable to indemnify B, and C was held to have an arguable case against A.

[339] On the facts of *The Aliakmon* rights under the contract of carriage would now be transferred to C by virtue of Carriage of Goods by Sea Act 1992, s.2: see *White v Jones* [1995] 2 A.C. 207 at 265. But cases can still be imagined where this would not be the position: see *Carver on Bills of Lading* (2nd edn) para.5–108.

[340] Stretching from *Cattle v Stockton Waterworks Co* (1875) L.R. 10 Q.B. 453 through *The Wear Breeze* [1969] 1 Q.B. 219 to *The Mineral Transporter* [1986] A.C. 1.

[341] A bailor may retain an immediate possessory interest in goods even after transferring his contractual rights to the bailee: *Scottish & Newcastle International Ltd v Othon Ghalanos Ltd* [2008] UKHL 11; [2008] 1 Lloyd's Rep. 462 at [46].

when the loss or damage occurred"[342] or, where the loss is caused by a continuing process, at the time when the cause of action in respect of it first accrued.[343] It is not enough for him "to have only had contractual rights in relation to such property"[344] when the loss or damage occurred.[345] The House of Lords refused to create an exception to this principle where (as in the present case) the contractual right, which C had under his contract of sale with B, was one to have property and possession of the goods transferred to him at a later date. The main reason for this refusal was that the contract of carriage between A and B was expressed to be subject to the Hague Rules[346] which gave A (as carrier) the benefit of certain immunities from, and limitations of, liability; and to have held A liable in tort to C would have produced the undesirable result of depriving A of the protection of that contract,[347] since C (being a stranger to it) was no more bound by its terms than entitled to assert rights under it.[348]

Such is the concern to ensure that the internationally accepted regimes operating in this area should not be bypassed, a claim in negligence may fail even where C has suffered damage to goods in which he has the proprietary interest required by the decision in *The Aliakmon*. In *The Nicholas H*[349] a ship classification society (A) had, in breach of its contract with shipowners (B), advised them that their ship could proceed on her current voyage until the cargo which she was then carrying had been discharged. In the course of that voyage the ship sank, and it was held that the owners of the cargo (C) had no cause of action in tort against A in respect of the loss of their cargo. The main reason given by the House of Lords for this conclusion was that B was, as a result of the loss of the cargo, in breach of the contract of carriage with C; and that it was not fair, just or reasonable to impose

---

[342] [1986] A.C. 785 at 809.

[343] *The Starsin* [2001] EWCA Civ 56; [2001] 1 Lloyd's Rep. 437 at [96] (per Rix L.J., whose judgment was on this point affirmed on appeal: [2003] UKHL 12; [2004] 1 A.C. 715 at [40], [64], [90], [139].

[344] [1986] A.C 785 at 809. Griew (1986) 136 N.L.J. 1201 suggests that the principle may have been qualified by Latent Damage Act 1986, s.3; but there is no hint in the legislative history of s.3 that such a qualification was intended. It can in any event only apply where the damage was still latent when the claimant became owner: this was not the position in *The Aliakmon*. The point was left open in *The Starsin* [2001] EWCA Civ 56; [2001] 1 Lloyd's Rep. 437 at [119]–[128] (per Rix L.J., dissenting but not on this point), [134], [202], [203] and not discussed in the House of Lords (above, fn.343).

[345] Beneficial ownership will suffice if the legal owner is joined as a party to the action: *The Aliakmon* [1986] A.C. 785 at 812; *Shell UK Ltd v Total UK Ltd* [2010] EWCA Civ 180; [2010] 3 W.L.R. 1192 at [119].

[346] As set out in the Schedule to the Carriage of Goods by Sea Act 1924, now superseded in England by Carriage of Goods by Sea Act 1971 (the Hague-Visby Rules). The Hague-Visby Rules may, in turn, be replaced by the Rotterdam Rules which have been approved by the United Nations, but do not yet have the force of law in the United Kingdom.

[347] cf. below, para.14–074; *Simaan General Contracting Co v Pilkington Glass Ltd (No.2)* [1988] Q.B. 758 at 782–783. For the suggestion that the position may be different where the potential tortfeasor has no such protection, see *Triangle Steel & Supply Co v Korean United Lines Inc* (1985) 63 B.C.L.R. 66 at 80 (the reasoning of which is in other respects inconsistent with that of *The Aliakmon*). For further discussion of this aspect of *The Aliakmon* see below, para.519.

[348] In the Court of Appeal ([1985] Q.B. 350 at 399), Robert Goff L.J. proposed that any duty owed to C might be modified by the terms of the contract between A and B, but his theory of "transferred loss" was rejected by the House of Lords; cf. *White v Jones* [1995] 2 A.C. 207 at 268 where, as Lord Goff, he achieved something similar in his use of an "extended" assumption of responsibility; cf. Markesinis 103 L.Q.R. 354; below, para.14–076.

[349] [1996] A.C. 211; cf. *Reeman v Dept of Transport* [1997] 2 Lloyd's Rep. 648; *R M Turton & Co Ltd v Kerslake & Partners* [2000] Lloyd's Rep. P.N. 967 (New Zealand CA).

on A a liability to C in tort[350] since this would not be subject to the limitations of liability available to B under the international Conventions[351] which are intended to regulate liability. The effect of holding classification societies liable in tort to cargo-owners in this situation would be to deprive shipowners of the benefits of these Conventions since the societies would pass on their unlimited liability to shipowners; and this would be an undesirable conclusion,[352] particularly as loss suffered by cargo-owners in excess of the Convention limits was "readily insurable".[353]

Financial services. In the context of what may be referred to as financial services there are two notable exceptions to the general rule that A owes no duty of care where the negligent performance of those services causes pure economic loss to a third party, C.[354] The first is *Henderson v Merrett Syndicates Ltd*[355] which involved claims in negligence by underwriting members at Lloyd's (C), known as Names, against managing agents (A) who were alleged to have been negligent in the conduct of the Names' underwriting affairs, leading to excessive losses. In some cases, the managing agents were in a direct contractual relationship with the Names, but in others the Names dealt with members' agents (B), so that the underwriting was conducted by the managing agents as sub-agents. Unlike cases such as the *Simaan* case,[356] which was considered by analogy by Lord Goff, in the cases in *Henderson v Merrett* where a sub-agency was involved, the parties were not found to have "structured their relationship so as to exclude any duty of care owed."[357] Lord Goff emphasised that the situation in *Henderson v Merrett* was "most unusual".[358] One possible distinguishing feature is that the Names had "no choice",[359] or control, over the internal organisation of the agents involved which determined whether or not they were in a direct contractual relationship with the managing agents, as opposed to the *Simaan* case where the contractual structure was deliberately and consciously put in place by all of the parties involved. This may be a relevant factor but it is not necessarily determinative, such that, if it is absent, no duty of care is owed by A to C. Rather, the question with which the courts are concerned is whether the contractual structure, *and the circumstances in which it was put in place by the parties,* is inconsistent with the existence of a duty of care owed by A to C which cuts across that structure.

14–051

---

[350] Nor had there been an "assumption of responsibility" (above, para.14–047) since the cargo-owners were "not even aware of [the classification society's] examination of the ship": [1996] A.C. 211 at 242.

[351] In *The Nicholas H* the Convention in question related to tonnage limitations; effect was given to it by Merchant Shipping Act 1979, s.17 and Sch.4, now superseded by Merchant Shipping Act 1995, s.185 and Sch.7, Pt I. In *Perrett v Collins* [1998] 2 Lloyd's Rep. 255 no such policy reasons were held to exist for protecting an aircraft inspection society from liability for *personal* injury to a passenger; cf. *Watson v British Boxing Board of Control Ltd* [2001] Q.B. 1134

[352] cf. above, at fnn.346 and 347.

[353] *The Nicholas H* [1996] A.C. 211 at 242.

[354] Many of the cases in the area of financial services have been concerned with liability for negligent misrepresentation and are considered earlier: see above, paras 9–033—9–038. It has been suggested the relevant distinction in determining whether a duty of care is owed is whether services were provided under a "professional retainer": *Robinson v P E Jones (Contractors) Ltd* [2011] EWCA Civ 9 at [75]–[76].

[355] [1995] 2 A.C. 145.

[356] [1988] Q.B. 758: see above, para.14–048.

[357] Above, fn.355, at 195. The duty owed was based on the test of assumption of responsibility: see above, para.14–047.

[358] ibid.

[359] This was counsel for the defendant's argument in the *Riyad* bank case: see below, fn.360.

This is evident from the second of the notable exceptions to the general rule. In *Riyad Bank v Ahli United Bank (UK) Plc*[360] an investment fund (C) was set up by the Riyad bank, and an entity within the Riyad bank (B) acted as C's general adviser. The defendant (A), a Kuwaiti bank, provided advice on the investments under a contract with B, but had no contract with C; it was, in formal terms, a sub-adviser. C suffered losses as a result of A's negligent advice as to the value of the investments made. The contractual structure had been deliberately adopted by the parties, in contrast to *Henderson v Merrett*, but the background made it clear that this was not inconsistent with an assumption of responsibility by A to C. In reality, C was the creation of A which had operated similar funds in the past and it was A which acted as principal adviser. It had only been necessary to set up a separate fund and interpose B because of objections to the Riyad bank's customers investing in a Kuwaiti-administered fund and dealing with a Kuwaiti bank. In those circumstances, A was found to owe a duty of care to C.

14–052   **Disappointed beneficiaries.** The courts appear to have gone furthest in imposing a duty of care on A not to cause pure economic loss to C in a number of cases concerned principally with the failure of solicitors to fulfil their client (B)'s testamentary instructions in the drawing up of the will, or the administration of the estate. In *White v Jones*,[361] B had instructed his solicitor (A) to draw up a will containing bequests in favour of his daughters C and D, but A negligently and in breach of his contract with B had done nothing to carry out these instructions by the time of B's death. The House of Lords by a majority held that A was liable in tort to C and D, and that the damages to which they were entitled consisted of the amounts which they would have obtained under B's will, if A had duly carried out B's instructions. The case presented certain special features, namely that C had discussed B's testamentary intentions with A, and that the letter setting out B's wishes had been drafted by D's husband. The majority do not seem to restrict the principle of liability to such special circumstances[362] though they accept that there must be "boundaries to the availability of the remedy" which "will have to be worked out . . . as practical problems come before the courts".[363] It is, for example, an open question whether such a remedy would be available to a prospective beneficiary who had no previous connection with the testator or knowledge of his intentions; and it seems that the solicitor would not be liable for the amount of the intended benefit where it would have been reasonable for the beneficiary to have secured this benefit by taking proceedings against the estate for rectification of the will.[364]

---

[360] [2006] EWCA Civ 780; [2006] 2 Lloyd's Rep. 292; cf. *BP v AON Ltd* [2006] EWHC 424 (Comm); [2006] 1 C.L.C. 881 (liability of insurance sub-broker to insured).

[361] [1995] 2 A.C. 207 (Lords Keith and Mustill dissenting), approving the result (though not the reasoning) in *Ross v Caunters* [1980] Ch. 287, where B's negligence took the form, not of simply failing to carry out A's instructions, but of carrying them out ineffectively; cf. *Esterhuizen v Allied Dunbar Assurance Plc* [1998] 2 F.L.R. 668 (similar liability of company offering will-making services); and, in Australia, *Hill v van Erp* (1997) 142 A.L.R. 687 (also a case of actual misfeasance by the solicitor); *Martin v Triggs Turner Bartons* [2009] EWHC 1920 (Ch); [2010] P.N.L.R. 3. Contrast *Clark v Bruce Lance* [1988] 1 All E.R. 364 (solicitor acting for testator in a different transaction held to owe no duty to beneficiary).

[362] ibid. at 295.

[363] ibid. at 269. The alleged beneficiary's claim clearly cannot succeed without proof of the requisite testamentary intention in his favour: see *Gibbons v Nelsons* [2000] Lloyd's Rep. P.N. 603.

[364] Contrast *Walker v Geo H Medlicott & Son* [1999] 1 W.L.R. 727, with *Horsfall v Hayward* [1999] 1 F.L.R. 1182.

Where the principle (whatever its precise scope may turn out to be) does apply, its effect is to put C into the position in which he would have been if the contract between A and B had been properly performed. One distinguishing feature of the cases in this category, compared to those considered above, is that there is no chain of contracts involved, i.e. a contract between A and B, and between B and C. C does not therefore have even the protection of a claim in contract against B for any breach brought about by A's defective performance of his contract with B. All that C has is the expectation that B wished to bestow the legacy upon him, and this cannot be fulfilled where, as in *White v Jones*, B has died. Where, however, a defect in the will is discovered when cure is still possible, the solicitor owes no duty to the beneficiary, since C can request B to execute a new will and it is entirely a matter for B whether he chooses to do so.[365] There are also the points that, if any duty is to be imposed on the solicitor to the disappointed beneficiary, the only realistic measure of damages is the value of the lost benefit; and that no more than nominal damages could be recovered from the solicitor by the client's estate, since it would have suffered no loss. The negligent solicitor would thus escape all substantial liability if he were not held liable to the disappointed beneficiary for the value of the lost benefit.

An important feature of *White v Jones* is that the estate had suffered no loss. Where it has done so as a result of the solicitor's negligence, a claim may be made by the estate[366] which will then be under a duty to account to the intended legatee for any damages received.[367] The result achieved is similar to that seen in the building contract cases where damages are recovered on behalf of a third party,[368] but the duty to account is here derived from the terms of the will. As a consequence, where any recovery by the estate will benefit not the intended legatee, but instead the person entitled under the will to the residuary estate, thus defeating the intention of the testatrix, a claim[369] may still be made by the intended legatee.[370]

Disappointed beneficiaries: analogous cases. The principle of the "disappointed beneficiary" cases has been extended to the situation in which the benefit of which the claimant was deprived as a result of the defendant's negligence was one which would have arisen otherwise than under a will. In *Gorham v British Telecommunications Plc*[371] an insurance company (A) sold a policy to a customer (B) who had made it clear to the company that he was buying the policy to provide for his wife and dependent children (C) in the event of his predeceasing them. A negligently failed to advise B that C would have been better off if B had joined his employers' pension scheme; and it was held that A was liable to C for loss of benefits under the employers' scheme up to (but not beyond) the time when A had

14–053

---

[365] *Hemmens v Wilson Browne* [1995] Ch. 223; cf. *Hughes v Richards* [2004] EWCA Civ 266; [2004] P.N.L.R. 35.

[366] In contract and in tort.

[367] *Chappell v Somers & Blake* [2003] EWHC 1644; [2004] Ch. 19.

[368] See above, para.14–027.

[369] In tort alone.

[370] *Carr-Glynn v Frearsons* [1998] 4 All E.R. 225. Whether the claim is brought by the estate, or the intended legatee, the court will seek to ensure there is no prospect of double recovery: *Corbett v Bond Pearce* [2001] EWCA Civ 531; [2001] 3 All E.R. 769; *Chappell v Somers & Blake* [2003] EWHC 1644; [2004] Ch. 19 at [17]; cf. *Daniels v Thompson* [2004] EWCA Civ 307; [2004] P.N.L.R. 33; *Rind v Theodore Goddard* [2008] EWHC 459 (Ch); [2008] P.N.L.R. 24.

[371] [2000] 1 W.L.R. 2129.

corrected its original advice. The principle of *White v Jones*[372] applied because (as in that case) B had not himself suffered any loss, so that, if C's claims had been rejected, then neither the persons who had suffered loss nor anyone else would have any claim for established negligence; and because the advice had been given "in a context in which the interests of [C] were fundamental to the transaction".[373] In both these respects, the case was closely analogous to that of a disappointed testamentary beneficiary.[374]

The "disappointed beneficiary" cases go further than any other group of negligence cases in encroaching on the common law doctrine of privity of contract.[375] Perhaps for this reason, they were described as "an unusual class of case" in *Goodwill v Pregnancy Advisory Service*.[376] In that case, the defendant (A) had arranged for B to have a vasectomy and, after the operation had been carried out, told B that it had been successful and that he no longer needed to use any other method of contraception. Some three years later, B formed a sexual relationship with C, to whom he communicated the information given to him by A relating to the vasectomy; C ceased to use any method of contraception after having consulted her own general practitioner who told her that there was only a minute chance of her becoming pregnant. The vasectomy having undergone a spontaneous reversal, C became pregnant by B and one reason given for holding that A was not liable to C in damages[377] was that a doctor performing a vasectomy could not realistically be described as having been employed to confer a benefit on his patient's future sexual partners. The case was also said to be unlike the "disappointed beneficiary" cases in that dismissal of the claim would not produce the "rank injustice"[378] that would arise in those cases if in them the only person with a claim against the negligent solicitor were the testator's estate, and that estate had suffered no loss. In a sterilisation case, a substantial remedy for negligence (if established) would normally be available to the patient him (or her) self.[379]

14–054 **Conclusion.** The categories of case considered above are not exhaustive of the circumstances in which A may owe a duty of care to C arising from the performance of his contract with B.[380] Nothing is to be gained, however, by considering further examples since, in each case, the existence and scope of any duty will be determined by the courts' assessment of the policy factors outlined in para.14–046 and illustrated by the cases above. The point to be stressed, by way of conclusion,

---

[372] [1995] 2 A.C. 207; above, para.14–052.

[373] *Gorham*'s case, above, fn.371, at 2142.

[374] cf. the reference in *Dean v Allin & Watts* [2001] EWCA Civ 758; [2001] 2 Lloyd's Rep. 249 at [69] by Robert Walker L.J. to the "very special problems" which had arisen in *White v Jones* and *Gorham*'s case, evidently not sharing the view of Lightman J. in *Dean v Allin & Watts*, above, at [40] that the decision there represented a further extension of the principle in *White v Jones*.

[375] Liability is imposed in some cases (e.g. *White v Jones*) for A's failure to perform, rather than his defective performance, and while liability is said to be based on the test of assumption of responsibility, there is no reliance by C, which had previously been thought to be a necessary element of that test.

[376] [1996] 1 W.L.R. 1397 at 1403.

[377] Damages are now limited to a conventional sum in such cases, in any event: *Rees v Darlington Memorial Hospital NHS Trust* [2003] UKHL 52; [2004] 1 A.C. 309.

[378] [1996] 1 W.L.R. 1397 at 1403.

[379] But see above, fn.377.

[380] In addition to those considered above, and earlier in paras 9–033—9–038, see also: *Al Kandari v JR Brown & Co* [1988] Q.B. 665; *Dean v Allin & Watts* [2001] EWCA Civ 758; [2001] 2 Lloyd's Rep. 249 at [33] (whether lawyer (A) under duty of care to party (C) other than his client (B)); *Barex Brothers Ltd v Morris Dean & Co* [1999] P.N.L.R. 344 (Valuer (A) engaged by borrower (B) owed duty to prospective lender (C), but not to C's assignee).

is that the majority of cases involve a chain of contracts which link A and C, but under which C is normally expected to rely on his claims against the party (B) with whom he has a contractual relationship within the chain. This, of course, is the very essence of privity. The difficulty for the courts is that

> "there cannot be a general proposition that, just because a chain exists, no responsibility . . . is ever assumed to a non-contractual party. It all depends on the facts."[381]

Where C is not at the end of a chain and does not have the benefit of a claim against B in contract, the courts have gone further and, in exceptional cases, have been prepared to impose liability in negligence in order to produce a just outcome.[382]

For the most part, where A is liable in negligence to C, such claims do not represent an exception to the doctrine of privity. In cases where C sues for personal injury or damage to "other" property, any claim in negligence protects a different interest from that protected in contract.[383] Even in cases where A is liable to C in negligence for pure economic loss, there will normally be important differences in the claims which may be made by C, when compared to a claim for the direct enforcement of the contract between A and B. With the exception of the disappointed beneficiary cases, A is only liable in negligence if he has been guilty of defective performance of his contract with B, and not merely a failure to perform.[384] C must also prove that such defective performance amounted to, or was the consequence of, negligence, whereas A's liability under his contract with B may, and often will, be strict.[385] Furthermore, in contract, B has a cause of action against A as soon as the breach occurs, but in tort C's cause of action accrues only when the resulting loss is suffered.[386]

(c) Intimidation

The tort of intimidation is committed where A induces B to act to the detriment **14–055** of C by threatening B with some unlawful course of conduct. In *Rookes v Barnard*[387] the House of Lords decided that a threat by A to break his contract with B is for this purpose a threat to do an unlawful act. Such a threat may therefore entitle C to sue A for intimidation. It has been said that this view outflanks the common law doctrine of privity.[388] No doubt in such a case C bases

---

[381] *Riyad Bank v Ahli Bank (UK) Plc* [2006] EWCA Civ 780; [2006] 2 Lloyd's Rep. 292 at [32], per Longmore L.J.

[382] See above, paras 14–052—14–053.

[383] See para.14–046, above.

[384] The duty owed by A to C in tort may also be less extensive than that owed by A to the other contracting party: e.g. *Woodward v Wolferstans, The Times*, April 8, 1997.

[385] This difference between tort and contract liability in some cases is reduced in importance by Consumer Protection Act 1987, Pt I, introducing strict "product liability" to the ultimate consumer, but such liability does not extend to pure economic loss: see above, fn.314.

[386] *Dove v Banham's Safety Locks Ltd* [1983] 1 W.L.R. 1463; cf. *Bell v Peter Browne & Co* [1990] 2 Q.B. 495.

[387] [1964] A.C. 1129. The scope of such liability is restricted where the unlawful conduct takes the form of acts done in the contemplation of furtherance of a trade dispute: see Winfield & Jolowicz, *Tort* (18th edn), paras 18–36—18–43.

[388] Wedderburn 24 M.L.R. 572 at 577; in *Rookes v Barnard* the argument was accepted in the Court of Appeal: [1963] 1 Q.B. 623 at 695, but rejected by the House of Lords; below, at fn.389.

his cause of action on the threat to break a contract to which he is not a party. But the doctrine of privity only prevents C from enforcing A's promise to B; and in cases of intimidation C is certainly not doing that. If A induces B to dismiss C by threatening to defame B, C may be able to sue A for intimidation, but not for defamation. So, if A induces B to dismiss C by threatening to break A's contract with B, C may be able to sue A for intimidation, but not for breach of contract. In such a case C is not trying to enforce A's promise to B: "his ground of action is quite different".[389] C's complaint is not that A has broken his promise to B but that he has coerced B into acting to C's detriment.[390] The House of Lords has therefore rejected the argument that the doctrine of privity would be outflanked by holding that the tort of intimidation could be committed by threatening to commit a breach of contract.[391]

(e) Restitution?

14–056   It has been suggested in Australia that the third party may have a claim in restitution where the promisor has received payment (or some other performance) from the promisee and has then failed or refused to perform the promise in favour of the third party; and that the measure of recovery on such a claim is the amount promised.[392] The suggestion was made where premiums under a policy of liability insurance for the benefit of a third party had been paid by the promisee to the promisor (the insurance company) which had then refused to pay the third party. The promisor's liability in restitution was said to be based on his unjust enrichment, and to arise in spite of the fact that there was no correlative impoverishment of the third party. But while it is true that liability in restitution is not based on loss to the claimant, it is (in the case put) based on gain to the defendant and it is hard to see what justification there can be for wholly disregarding this *basis* of restitutionary liability in determining its *measure*. And the argument that, to hold the promisor liable to the third party was "not an abrogation of the doctrine of privity of contract",[393] merely because the liability was said to arise in restitution, is, it is submitted, inconsistent with the practical result of making the promisor so liable. In England, as a general rule, the promisor is not liable in tort where the practical effect of imposing such liability would be to abrogate the doctrine of privity[394]; and there seems to be no reason why the position should be different merely because the alleged basis of liability is restitution rather than tort. The suggestion that the promisor is liable in restitution to the third party for the amount promised, merely because the promisor has received performance from the promisee is also inconsistent with the reasoning of *Beswick v Beswick*,[395] where it was assumed that the third party had no common law right to sue the promisor

---

[389] *Rookes v Barnard* [1964] A.C. 1129 at 1168; cf. at 1208; if C were trying to enforce the contract, the damages might be quite different.
[390] ibid. at 1208.
[391] ibid. at 1168, 1200, 1208, 1235; Hamson [1961] C.L.J. 189; [1964] C.L.J. 159; Hoffmann 81 L.Q.R. 116 at 124–128. This proposition is not affected by the attempt to re-state the principles of the so-called economic torts in *OBG Ltd v Allan* [2007] UKHL 21; [2008] 1 A.C. 1 in which intimidation is described (at [7]) as a "variant" of the tort of causing loss by unlawful means.
[392] *Trident Ins Co Ltd v McNiece Bros Pty Ltd* (1988) 165 C.L.R. 107, per Gaudron J.; this view does not seem to be shared by any other member of the court; Soh 105 L.Q.R. 4.
[393] (1988) 165 C.L.R. 107 at 177.
[394] *Balsamo v Medici* [1984] 1 W.L.R. 951, 959–960; cf. above, para.14–049, at fn.322.
[395] [1968] A.C. 58; above, para.14–017.

in her own name, in spite of the fact that the promisor had received performance in full from the promisee. The view that claims of the kind here discussed fall outside the scope of the doctrine of privity of contract must therefore be regarded with scepticism. The argument based on restitution would in any event be of no avail to the third party where the promisor was willing to pay and the issue was merely whether it should pay the third party or the promisee[396]: in such cases the promisor would not be unjustly enriched so that there would be no basis for restitutionary liability.

The above discussion is based on the assumption that the promisor would be unjustly enriched if he were allowed to retain a payment received *from the promisee* in spite of his failure to perform his promise to pay the third party. There is the further possibility that the promisor may have received a benefit *from a third party*: e.g. where A contracts to grant a development lease to B, a company controlled by C, and C incurs expense in improving A's land in anticipation of the development, which then fails to take place because of A's failure to perform his contract with B. In such a case, it is arguable that C may have a restitution claim against A.[397] To allow such a claim would not be inconsistent with the doctrine of privity since in such a case C's claim is not based on any promise made by A to B for the benefit of C; no such promise has been made. The basis and measure of any restitution claim which C may have against A is more closely analogous to cases in which restitution is granted in respect of benefits conferred under anticipated contracts which fail to come into existence.[398]

4. EXEMPTION CLAUSES AND THIRD PARTIES

Where an exemption clause purports to affect a third party,[399] two questions   **14–057** arise. Can the third party take the benefit of the clause? Can he be bound by it? For the purpose of this discussion, it will be assumed that the clause is valid under the rules stated in Ch.7.[400]

(a) The Benefit

(i) *Privity and exceptions*

Originally, the courts held that a person could only take the benefit of an   **14–058** exemption clause in a contract which he did not make himself if one of the recognised exceptions to the doctrine of privity could be invoked in his favour: e.g. if the contract was made through an agent acting either for him or for the other

---

[396] See above, para.14–040; cf. such cases as *Re Schebsman* [1944] Ch. 83 (below, para.14–082) and *Re Sinclair's Life Policy* [1938] Ch. 799 (below, para.14–084).

[397] *Brennan v Brighton BC, The Times*, May 15, 1997, where B was a company which had been wound-up and so could no longer sue A for breach of the contract between them.

[398] See below, para.22–021.

[399] A contract between A and B may by reference incorporate an exemption clause contained in a contract between B and C. If so, A is not for the present purpose a third party: see, e.g. *The Coral* [1993] 1 Lloyd's Rep. 1.

[400] Many of the cases discussed in this section concern contracts for the international carriage of goods by sea and would not be affected by Unfair Contract Terms Act 1977 or by Unfair Terms in Consumer Contracts Regulations 1999; above, paras 7–093, 7–116. Others (e.g. those in which the claim was for personal injuries) would now often be differently decided, or decided on other grounds, under the Act or the Regulations; above, paras 7–057, 7–111.

party.[401] Such agency reasoning might sometimes be artificial, but it at any rate saved the face of the doctrine of privity. A further exception has been created by the Contracts (Rights of Third Parties) Act 1999, under which third parties are, if the requirements of the Act are satisfied,[402] entitled to the benefit of exemption clauses in contracts between others.[403] But some of the cases with which the following discussion is concerned are[404] or may[405] not be covered by that legislation; and in others it may be to the third party's advantage to rely, not on the new statutory exception, but on a common law exception,[406] since this is not limited by the provisions of the Act.[407]

14–059   **Vicarious immunity rejected.** The principle of vicarious immunity, as a means of extending the benefit of an exemption clause to a non-party, was introduced by the decision of the House of Lords in *Elder, Dempster & Co v Paterson, Zochonis & Co*.[408] A company agreed to carry the claimant's palm-oil from West Africa to Hull and time-chartered a ship for this purpose. The contract of carriage was evidenced by a bill of lading, the parties to which were the claimants and the company; this bill exempted "the shipowners, hereinafter called the company",[409] from liability for bad stowage. The oil was damaged by bad stowage and it was held that the shipowners were protected by the exemption clause, although there was no express contract directly made between them and the claimants. One possible ground for this decision was that the company had acted as the shipowners' agent for the purpose of making a contract between them and the claimants.[410] The inference that the company had so acted appears to have been based on the ground that the exemption clause expressly referred to, and purported to protect, the shipowners[411]; and, although this fact would no longer of itself support such an inference,[412] the agency reasoning is consistent with the doctrine of privity in that it gives rise to a contract between the claimants and the shipowners. A second possible ground for the decision was that the act of the

---

[401] *Hall v NE Ry* (1875) L.R. 10 Q.B. 437; cf. *Barrett v Great Northern Ry* (1904) 20 T.L.R. 175; *The Kirknes* [1957] P. 51.

[402] See especially s.1(1), (2) and (3); below, paras 14–090—14–096.

[403] s.1(6).

[404] e.g. *Adler v Dickson* [1955] 1 Q.B. 158; *Scruttons Ltd v Midland Silicones Ltd* [1962] A.C. 446; see below, para.14–095.

[405] For the question whether *Elder, Dempster & Co v Paterson Zochonis & Co* [1924] A.C. 522 would be covered by the 1999 Act, see below, fn.696.

[406] s.7(1) of the Act preserves the third party's right to rely on such an exception.

[407] e.g. by ss.2 or 3: below, paras 14–100—14–112.

[408] [1924] A.C. 522; distinguished in *Gadsden Pty Ltd v Australian Coastal Shipping Commission* [1977] 1 N.S.W.L.R. 575; *The Golden Lake* [1982] 2 Lloyd's Rep. 632; *The Forum Craftsman* [1985] 1 Lloyd's Rep. 291 (especially at 295); and in *The Kapetan Markos NL (No.2)* [1987] 2 Lloyd's Rep. 321 at 331.

[409] It was admitted that these words were apt to protect the company: [1923] 1 K.B. 422.

[410] [1924] A.C. 522 at 534 (first sentence); cf. *Norfolk Southern Railway Co v James N Kirby Ltd* 543 U.S. 14 (2004) where the concept of agency "for a *single limited* purpose" (at 31) was used not to extend the benefit of a limitation in the contract between the cargo-owner and the "agent" to a third party, but to find that the cargo-owner was bound by limitations to which the "agent" had agreed in a sub-contract with the third party for the transport of the goods (by sea and by rail): see below, fn.417 and para.14–065.

[411] Quaere whether the inference was realistic. The company usually carried goods in its *own* ships and may simply, as a result of an oversight, have used a form of bill of lading designed for this situation in the different one in which the carrying ship had been chartered from a third party.

[412] *Cosgrove v Horsfall* (1946) 62 T.L.R. 140; *Genys v Matthews* [1965] 3 All E.R. 24; *Gore v Van der Lann* [1967] 2 Q.B. 31; for the effect of Contracts (Rights of Third Parties) Act 1999, see below, para.14–091.

claimants in presenting the goods for carriage, followed by that of the captain in accepting them for this purpose on behalf of the shipowners,[413] gave rise to what Lord Sumner called a "bailment on terms"[414] between the claimants and the shipowners, that is, to one which incorporated the exemption clause by tacit reference.[415] "Bailment on terms" is, however, unfortunately an expression with more than one possible meaning. It has been judicially interpreted to refer *either* to a bailment into which terms were incorporated by virtue of an implied contract[416] arising from the conduct of the parties, *or* to a bailment operating irrespective of contract.[417] On the former view, the requirement of privity would be satisfied, while on the latter there would be no need to satisfy it, bailment being a relationship which can come into existence without any contract.[418] The bailment reasoning is thus again consistent with the doctrine of privity. But a third possible reason for the decision in the *Elder, Dempster* case is the so-called principle of vicarious immunity: this states that, where a person employs an agent to perform a contract, that agent is entitled, in performing the contract, to any immunity from liability which the contract confers on the principal.[419] Under this principle, the shipowners were protected by the exemption clause because, in carrying out the carriage *operation*, they had acted as agents for the company, even though the *contract* to perform that operation was between the company and the claimants. This reasoning is inconsistent with the doctrine of privity in the sense that it would enable an agent to rely by way of defence on the terms of a contract to which he was not a party; and it was rejected by the House of Lords in *Scruttons Ltd v Midland Silicones Ltd*.[420]

The *Midland Silicones* case. In that case a drum of chemicals had been shipped under a contract between shipper and carrier evidenced by a bill of lading which limited the liability of "the carrier" to $500. After the rights and duties under this contract had passed to the claimants by transfer of the bill of lading,[421]

14–060

---

[413] The charter being a time charter, the captain remained the shipowners' employee and took possession of the goods on the shipowners' behalf: cf. the authorities cited in fn.884, below. This point is not affected by the fact that he signed the bill of lading (see *Scruttons Ltd v Midland Silicones Ltd* [1962] A.C. 446 at 455) on behalf of the charterers (see [1923] 1 K.B. 420 at 424).

[414] [1924] A.C. 522 at 564.

[415] Exactly how the exemption clause in the contract between the claimant and the company came to be incorporated into the bailment between the claimant and the shipowner is not made clear. Lord Sumner's reference ([1924] A.C. 522 and 564) to "the known and contemplated form of bill of lading" suggests the analogy of incorporation by custom or usage: above, para.6–046.

[416] *Adler v Dickson* [1955] 1 Q.B. 158 at 189, per Morris L.J.; *Pyrene Co Ltd v Scindia Navigation Co Ltd* [1954] 2 Q.B. 402 at 406, per Devlin J.; *Scruttons Ltd v Midland Silicones Ltd* [1959] 2 Q.B. 171 at 187, per Diplock J.; cf. also *Sandeman Coprimar SA v Transitos y Transportes Integrales* [2003] EWCA Civ 113; [2003] 2 Lloyd's Rep. 172 at [62], [63]; below, fn.539.

[417] *The Pioneer Container* [1994] 2 A.C. 324 at 335, 339–340, per Lord Goff ("notwithstanding the *absence of any contract*"); the question in this case was not whether a third party could take the *benefit* of a contract between others but whether he could be *bound* by such a contract: below, para.14–073. Lord Goff's reference in *The Mahkutai* [1996] A.C. 650 at 661 to the claimants in the *Elder, Dempster* case having "impliedly agreed that the goods were received by the shipowners, as bailees, subject to" the exemption clause could be read as supporting either the contractual or the non-contractual view. The latter view is supported by *The Starsin* [2003] UKHL 12; [2003] 1 A.C. 715 at [136].

[418] See above, para.3–166.

[419] [1924] A.C. 522 at 534 (second sentence), approving the view of Scrutton L.J. in the Court of Appeal [1923] 1 K.B. 420 at 441–442; cf. *Mersey Shipping & Transport Co v Rea* (1925) 21 Ll.L.R. 375 at 378.

[420] [1962] A.C. 446.

[421] See now Carriage of Goods by Sea Act 1992, ss.2 and 3; below, paras 15–009, 15–084.

the drum was damaged by the negligence of a firm of stevedores who had been employed by the carrier to unload the ship. The House of Lords[422] held that the stevedores could not rely on the $500 limitation of liability as they were not parties to the contract of carriage; and that the principle of vicarious immunity was not the ratio decidendi of the *Elder, Dempster* case. Nor did any of the other reasons for that decision help the stevedores. It was not possible to infer that the carrier had intended to act as agent of the stevedores for the purpose of making a contract between them and the claimants so as to give the stevedores the benefit of the limitation clause in the bill of lading, for that term limited the liability only of *the carrier* and made no reference to the stevedores,[423] nor were there any circumstances extrinsic to the bill on which an inference of agency could be based.[424] Nor did any implied contract arise between the claimants and the stevedores since the claimants had not asked the stevedores to render any services that would normally be governed by contractual terms between them.[425] The claimants had merely applied to the carrier for delivery of the drum, which had been stored in a shed rented by the carrier from the port authority; and when the process of moving the drum from that shed into the lorry sent by the claimants to collect it was carried out through the instrumentality of the stevedores, the latter regarded this as no more than "the performance of their own obligations under the contract which they had made with"[426] the carrier. The implied contract argument thus failed for want of contractual intention.[427] Nor could the stevedores invoke the "bailment on terms" reasoning since, in the circumstances just described, they had not been entrusted with possession of the drum so as to become bailees of it.[428] Even if they had been such bailees (e.g. if the drum had been stored in a shed owned by them) it is far from clear that the mental element requisite for the incorporation of the limitation clause into the supposed bailment would have been satisfied. There would obviously be no requirement of *contractual* intention where the bailment was a non-contractual one, but it would appear that the *consent* of the claimants and of the stevedores was a necessary condition for the incorporation of the terms

---

[422] Lord Denning dissenting; his dissent was based, not on the ground that the stevedores were entitled to the *benefit* of the limitation provision in the contract of carriage, but on the ground that the cargo-owners were *bound* by a similar term (below, para.14–071) in the contract between carrier and stevedores: see [1962] A.C. 446 at 489 ("I must be wrong about all this"), 491. See also his judgments in *Adler v Dickson*, above, fn.416; *White v Warwick (John) & Co Ltd* [1953] 1 W.L.R. 1285 and *Morris v C W Martin & Sons Ltd* [1966] 1 Q.B. 716.

[423] [1962] A.C. 446 at 466, rejecting the argument that "carrier" could be construed so as to mean or include stevedores. For this reason, the stevedores would not, under Contracts (Rights of Third Parties) Act 1999, be entitled to the benefit of a clause protecting only the carrier: below, para.14–095. cf. *Robert C Herd & Co v Krawill Machinery Corp* 359 U.S. 297 (1959); below, fn.433. Contrast *South Australia Management Corp v Sheahan* [1995] A.L.M. 3577 where, in another context "carrier" was construed to include sub-contractors of the carrier.

[424] For such extrinsic circumstances, see, e.g. *The Kirknes* [1957] P. 51 at 66; *Raymond Burke Motors Ltd v Mersey Docks & Harbour Co* [1986] 1 Lloyd's Rep. 155; *Texas Instruments Ltd v Nason (Europe) Ltd* [1991] 1 Lloyd's Rep. 146 at 149.

[425] Diplock J. may have gone too far in saying that the claimants had not asked the stevedores to "do anything to their goods": [1959] 2 K.B. 171 at 188–189; but the mere moving of the goods from a store to a waiting lorry would not by itself normally be governed by contractual terms. See also [1962] 1 Q.B. 102 at 136.

[426] [1962] A.C. 446 at 496.

[427] For other cases in which contractual intention was negatived by a party's belief that he was merely performing a previously existing contract, see above, para.4–021.

[428] [1962] A.C. 446 at 470; *The Starsin* [2003] UKHL 12; [2004] 1 A.C. 715 at [146]. Contrast *The Rigoletto* [2000] 2 Lloyd's Rep. 532 at 540 (goods in stevedores' possession for six days before loss).

of the contract of carriage into the supposed bailment[429]; and though the stevedores may be assumed to have consented to a limitation clause which could operate
only in their favour,[430] there would have been nothing to show that the claimants
had consented, not only to the hypothetical sub-bailment, but also to the inclusion
of that clause in the sub-bailment so as to protect the stevedores.[431]

Criticism. The reasoning of the *Midland Silicones* case may give the appear-   **14–061**
ance of being merely a technical application of the doctrine of privity[432]; but the
decision also reflects a conflict of policies. On one hand, there is the view that a
"self-confessed tortfeasor" should not be allowed to "shelter behind a document
that is no concern of his",[433] particularly where it is not clear that the injured party
has agreed to the third party's having the benefit of the contractual exemptions
from and limitations of liability. On the other hand, there is force in the argument
that, if the third party were not protected, there would often be an "easy way
round"[434] exemption and limitation clauses; it was this argument which was
originally used to support the principle of vicarious immunity.[435] In rejecting that
principle, the *Midland Silicones* case severely limited the effectiveness of such
clauses. A person who suffered loss or injury as a result of a negligent breach of
contract generally had a remedy against someone, if only against the workman who
was negligent. In practice the employer would often feel morally obliged to pay the
damages awarded against his employee,[436] and might be legally liable to do so.[437]
Hence employers tried to protect their servants or agents by differently worded
exemption clauses, and the cases to be discussed below make it clear that they can
now do so by using appropriate words. There is no objection to this on policy
grounds where the clause is itself valid[438] and constitutes a legitimate device for
allocating contractual risks and the burden of insurance. The Contracts (Rights of
Third Parties) Act 1999 now provides a relatively simple drafting mechanism for

---

[429] See *The Pioneer Container* [1994] 2 A.C. 324 at 339–340 where Lord Goff, in discussing the
"bailment on terms" explanation of the *Elder, Dempster* case refers in turn to the state of mind of the
shipowners ("the terms upon which the shipowners implicitly received the goods") and of the shippers
("the shippers . . . [having] impliedly consented" to the terms of the sub-bailment); cf. his use of the
phrase "impliedly agreed" in the *The Mahkutai* [1996] A.C. 650 at 661.

[430] The requirement of the third party's consent is nevertheless significant, particularly where the
term alleged to be incorporated in the bailment is one that can operate against him: e.g. an exclusive
jurisdiction clause which the third party wished to contest: see *The Forum Craftsman* [1984] 2 Lloyd's
Rep. 102 at 107.

[431] [1962] A.C. 446 at 474.

[432] ibid. at 463, 473 and 494.

[433] *Wilson v Darling Island Stevedoring Co* [1956] 1 Lloyd's Rep. 349 at 359; cf. *Adler v Dickson* [1955]
1 Q.B. 158 at 187; in *Robert C Herd & Co v Krawill Machinery Corp* 359 U.S. 297 (1959) at 303 this
reasoning prevailed even in the US, where the law *rejects* the doctrine of privity, so that the third party
could have been protected by making him a "beneficiary" of the contract, even though he was not a
"party" to it: ibid. at 308. Contrast *Norfolk Southern Railway Co v James N Kirby Ltd* 543 U.S. 14
(2004) where the wording employed was sufficient to make the third party an intended beneficiary.

[434] *Elder, Dempster & Co v Paterson, Zochonis & Co* [1923] 1 K.B. 420 at 441, approved [1924] A.C.
522 at 534.

[435] The same argument continues to be used in support of that principle: see the *London Drugs* case
[1992] 3 S.C.R. 299 (below, at fn.441) at 499.

[436] In *Adler v Dickson* [1955] 1 Q.B. 158, the employers said that they would satisfy any judgment
which might be given against their servants.

[437] i.e. under an express contract to indemnify the servant or agent.

[438] See *The Starsin* [2003] UKHL 12; [2003] 2 W.L.R. 711; below para.14–066, where this
requirement was not complied with.

giving third parties the benefit of exemption and limitation clauses[439]; and some statutes which limit the liability of carriers expressly extend these limitations to the carriers' servants or agents.[440] This position is generally regarded as acceptable; and in Canada the courts have recognised an exception to the doctrine of privity precisely to protect employees of a contracting party by enabling them to rely on an exemption clause which is clearly intended to protect them, even though it does not expressly refer to them.[441] The doctrine of privity was never a satisfactory instrument for controlling undesirable exemption clauses,[442] and should no longer be used for this purpose now that the ability of a contracting party to exclude or restrict liability by means of such clauses is directly controlled by legislation.[443] Direct control of exemption clauses between the contracting parties is clearly preferable to indirect evasion by means of a claim against a third party whom the words of the clause seek to protect.

(ii) Himalaya clauses

14–062 Granted, then, that on balance policy considerations support the view that a third party should, in appropriate cases, be able to take advantage of an exemption clause, the remaining question is how this result may be achieved. The most obvious possibility is by drafting the clause in such a way as to extend its protection to the third party; for the decision in the *Midland Silicones* case was partly based on the fact that the clause there did not refer to the stevedores at all, but only to the carrier. At common law it would not suffice simply to say that the third party was to be protected,[444] or that he was to be deemed to be a party to the contract.[445] But a much more elaborate clause (known as a "Himalaya" clause[446]) was considered in *The Eurymedon*,[447] where it was held to be capable of protecting the third party. Our present concern is with the common law rules relating to such clauses: the effect on them of the Contracts (Rights of Third Parties) Act 1999 is considered later in this chapter.[448]

14–063 **Nature and effect.** In *The Eurymedon* a contract was made between a shipper and a carrier for the carriage of machinery from England to New Zealand. The

---

[439] See ss.1(1)(a) and (b) and 6(5) ("tailpiece"); below, para.14–090 et seq., esp. 14–091, 14–114; *Precis (521) v William Mercer Ltd* [2005] EWCA Civ 114; [2005] P.N.L.R. 28. A clause taking effect by virtue of these provisions will, however, do so only subject to the restrictions imposed by other provisions of the Act: above, para.14–058, below, paras 14–116—14–118; and these restrictions differ from those which may arise at common law by reason of defects in the main contract: see below, para.14–068.

[440] e.g. Carriage by Air Act 1961, Sch.1, art.25A; Carriage of Goods by Sea Act 1971, Sch., art.4 *bis* (stevedores, being independent contractors rather than agents, would not be protected under this provision); Merchant Shipping Act 1995, s.183 and Sch.6, Pt I, art.11, and s.186(2) and (3).

[441] *London Drugs Ltd v Kuehne & Nagel International Ltd* [1992] 3 S.C.R. 299.

[442] cf. *Mason v Uxbridge Boat Centre* [1980] 2 Lloyd's Rep. 593 at 598.

[443] See above, para.7–049 et seq.

[444] *Cosgrove v Horsfall* (1946) 62 T.L.R. 140; *Genys v Matthews* [1965] 3 All E.R. 24. Contrast the position in the US: see above, fn.433 and *The Hellespont Ardent* [1997] 2 Lloyd's Rep. 547 at 579, 592.

[445] cf. in another context, *Taddy v Sterious* [1904] 1 Ch. 354.

[446] So named after the cruise ship in *Adler v Dickson* [1955] 1 Q.B. 155. For a fuller discussion of such clauses, see *Carver on Bills of Lading* (2nd edn) paras 7–046 to 7–065.

[447] [1975] A.C. 154; Reynolds 90 L.Q.R. 301; Coote 37 M.L.R. 453; Palmer [1974] J.B.L. 101, 220; Powles [1979] L.M.C.L.Q. 331; Davies & Palmer [1979] J.B.L. 337. And see below, para.14–072.

[448] See below, para.14–091.

machinery was damaged by employees of the stevedore while it was being unloaded; and the question was whether the stevedore was protected by the bill of lading issued by the carrier to the shipper as evidence of the contract. The relevant clause of the bill provided that no servant or agent (including independent contractor) of the carrier was to be liable for any act or default in the course of his employment[449]; that every limitation applicable to the carrier should be available to such persons; that for the purpose of the clause the carrier should be deemed to be acting as agent or trustee for such persons; and that they should to this extent be or be deemed to be parties to the contract. All the members of the Privy Council agreed that such third persons could be protected by an appropriately drawn clause; and a majority held that the clause in question did protect the stevedore. Lord Wilberforce said that the bill of lading

"brought into existence a bargain initially unilateral but capable of becoming mutual, between the shipper and the [stevedore], made through the carrier as agent. This became a full contract when the [stevedore] performed the services by discharging the goods".[450]

At this stage, a new contract arose[451] between the cargo–owner and the stevedore, separate from or collateral to the main contract of carriage, to which the stevedore was not a party.

Analysis. A possible objection to this analysis is that stevedores (unlike carriers) might not be aware of the terms of bills of lading under which goods were carried, so that these could not amount to offers to them which they could accept by performing the services. On the facts of *The Eurymedon* this objection has little substance as the carrier was a subsidiary of the stevedore who probably did know of the terms of the bill of lading.[452] But the more important point is that it is by no means unknown for contracts to come into existence by a process which cannot be strictly analysed in terms of offer and acceptance.[453] The decision should therefore be evaluated, not in terms of such analysis, but by asking two questions: (1) was there any objection on grounds of policy to extending the protection of the clause to third parties such as the stevedores? and (2) did that extension give effect to the intention of the parties? It has already been suggested[454] that the first question should be answered in the negative, and this must have been the view even of the dissentients in *The Eurymedon*, for they accepted that a third party could be protected by an appropriately-worded clause. The second question is

14–064

---

[449] At common law, this part of the clause was crucial for the purpose of creating privity of contract between the cargo–owner and the third party; without it, the doctrine of privity would have prevented that party from relying of the clause: see above, fn.444.

[450] At 167–168. More recently, it has been suggested that the contract would be regarded as "nowadays bilateral": *The Mahkutai* [1996] A.C. 650 at 664; but this description should not be understood as meaning that the contract granting the third party the limitation of or exemption from liability imposed executory obligations on the third party: see *Starsin* [2003] UKHL 12; [2003] 1 A.C. 715 at [34], [93], [152], [153] and [196], where the contract is described as "unilateral".

[451] See below, at fn.473.

[452] He at least had means of knowledge since one original of the bill of lading had been delivered to him before the goods were unloaded, though only in his capacity as agent of the carrier; see [1975] A.C. 154 at 164.

[453] See *The Satanita* [1895] P. 248, affirmed sub nom. *Clarke v Dunraven* [1897] A.C. 59; above, para.2–076.

[454] See above, para.14–060.

THIRD PARTIES

harder to answer but it seems unlikely that the parties at the time of contracting made any conscious distinction between the shipper's rights against the carrier and against persons employed by the carrier in the performance of the contract of carriage; while it was no doubt the stevedore's intention to perform the work of unloading the goods only under the protective terms of the bill of lading. It is submitted that the majority's interpretation of an admittedly obscure clause did give effect to the intentions and commercial expectations of the parties; and that the decision is therefore to be welcomed.

14–065   **Agency requirements.** Difficulty with regard to Himalaya clauses arises from a much-quoted passage in Lord Reid's speech in the *Midland Silicones* case. This states a number of requirements which must be satisfied before a third party, such as a stevedore, can at common law claim the protection of terms in the contract between shipper and carrier. Our present concern is with two of these requirements: first, the clause must make it clear that the carrier had contracted as agent of the stevedore for the purpose of securing the benefit of such terms for him; and secondly, the carrier must have had "authority from the stevedore to do so, or perhaps later ratification would suffice".[455] The first of these requirements is a question of the construction of the relevant term[456] and is normally satisfied simply by a declaration of agency in the Himalaya clause; but the second refers to factors extrinsic to the contract in which that clause is contained. In *The Eurymedon*, the relevant extrinsic factor was the previous connection between carrier and stevedore (as associated companies); and the reasoning of the case leaves open the possibility that, in the absence of some such previous connection, the requirement of "authority from the stevedore" would not be satisfied. In one case it was indeed held that the lack of any such connection made it impossible to regard the carrier as the stevedore's agent for the purpose of making a contract between him and the owner of the goods, so that the stevedore was not protected by virtue of the Himalaya clause.[457] But in *The New York Star*[458] the Privy Council followed *The Eurymedon* in unanimously holding that stevedores (who were regularly employed and partly owned by the carriers) were protected by virtue of a similarly-worded clause. Lord Wilberforce said that stevedores would "normally and typically" be protected by such a clause and that "their Lordships would not encourage a search for fine distinctions which would diminish the general applicability, in the light of established commercial practice, of the principle".[459] In the later Privy Council case of *The Mahkutai* Lord Goff did, indeed, say that it was "inevitable that technical points of contract and agency law will continue to be invoked" and that counsel had acted "legitimately"[460] in raising such points. But he evidently did not regard the requirement of the third party's having authorised

---

[455] [1962] A.C. 446 at 474.

[456] *The Borvigilant* [2003] EWCA Civ 935; [2003] 2 Lloyd's Rep. 520 at [17]–[33].

[457] *The Suleyman Stalskiy* [1976] 2 Lloyd's Rep. 609; cf. *Southern Water Authority v Carey* [1985] 2 All E.R. 1077 at 1085, a building case where the sub-contractor could not for this reason take the benefit of an exemption clause in the main contract, but succeeded on another ground stated at fn.504.

[458] *The New York Star* [1981] 1 W.L.R. 138; Reynolds 96 L.Q.R. 506; Coote [1981] C.L.J. 13; Clarke [1981] C.L.J. 17; Rose 44 M.L.R. 336. The reasoning of *The Eurymedon* was also approved in *The Starsin* [2003] UKHL 12; [2003] 1 A.C. 715, though in that case the third party was, for the reason given at para.14–066, below, not protected by the clause.

[459] [1981] 1 W.L.R. 138 at 144; cf. *The Borvigilant* [2003] EWCA Civ 935; [2003] 2 Lloyd's Rep. 520 at [57].

[460] [1996] A.C. 650 at 664.

the carrier to act on his behalf as an obstacle to the enforceability of the Himalaya clause in that case, though reliance on it failed on grounds to be discussed below.[461] Similarly, in *The Pioneer Container* the actual decision was that a third party was protected by the terms of his *own* sub-bailment from the carrier, so that he did not have to rely on the Himalaya clause[462]; but it was also said that he could have relied on that clause.[463] In both these cases, *The Eurymedon* and *The New York Star* were discussed with evident approval and with no direct reference to or emphasis on the special circumstances[464] of those cases; nor was there evidence of extrinsic circumstances from which previous authorisation could be inferred in *The Pioneer Container* and *The Mahkutai*. Moreover, while there are no doubt good reasons for requiring such previous authorisation where the contract arising by virtue of the Himalaya clause[465] can impose obligations[466] on the third party,[467] it is hard to see what practical grounds there are for such a requirement where the only effect of that contract can be to *benefit* that party (by excluding his liability) and where that contract cannot, by reason of its nature as a unilateral contract,[468] impose any obligations on him. And even where the common law requirement of previous authorisation is not satisfied, the stevedore or other third party will "in the majority of cases"[469] be able to ratify the carrier's act and so by virtue of the Himalaya clause gain the protection of the exemptions from and limitations of liability available under the main contract of carriage to the carrier.

Scope. The scope of the Himalaya clause depends on its construction; and since typically such a clause is expressed to protect the third party only while he is engaged in the performance of the contract in which the clause is contained, he will not be protected by the clause in such terms, if he damages the goods before performance of that contract has begun[470] or after such performance has been completed.[471]   **14–066**

At common law, the part of the typical Himalaya clause which purports to exclude or limit the third party's liability cannot *itself* produce the desired effect.[472] This can follow only from the separate contract[473] which arises or may

---

[461] See below, para.14–066.

[462] See below, para.14–073.

[463] [1994] 2 A.C. 324 at 344.

[464] i.e. to the fact that stevedores and carriers were associated companies; cf. *Godina v Patrick Operations Ltd* [1984] 2 Lloyd's Rep. 333; *The Zinnia* [1984] 2 Lloyd's Rep. 211 at 217; for express authorisation by the third party of the carrier, see *Raymond Burke Motors Ltd v Mersey Docks & Harbour Co* [1986] 1 Lloyd's Rep. 155.

[465] i.e. the new or separate contract referred to at fn.473.

[466] e.g. where it purports to be on the terms of an exclusive jurisdiction clause. Such a clause is not normally within the scope of a Himalaya clause: below, at fn.475; but could be brought within it by express words to that effect.

[467] The "third party" to the main contract is of course an immediate party to the separate contract referred to in fn.465, above.

[468] See above, at fn.450.

[469] *The Mahkutai* [1996] A.C. 650 at 664, per Lord Goff. The phrase "in the majority of cases" is not amplified. It could refer to the requirement in the law relating to ratification that the stevedoring company must have been in *existence* when the carrier purported to act as its agent by issuing the bill of lading containing the Himalaya clause: for this requirement see below, para.16–047.

[470] *Raymond Burke Motors Ltd v Mersey Docks & Harbour Co* [1986] 1 Lloyd's Rep. 155; cf. *The Rigoletto* [2000] 2 Lloyd's Rep. 532 at 545, 547.

[471] This is implicit in the reasoning of *The New York Star* [1981] 1 W.L.R. 138, where the actual decision was that at the relevant time such performance had *not* been completed.

[472] See above, at fn.451.

[473] *The Starsin* [2003] UKHC 12; [2003] 1 A.C. 715 at [59] (dissenting, but not on this point), [93].

arise from the agency provision of such a clause followed by the conduct of the third party and the injured party in relation to each other; the effect of this contract may be to extend to the third party the protection of, not only the Himalaya clause itself, but also *other* terms of the contract in which that clause is contained. Two further questions can therefore arise. The first is whether the provision which the third party seeks to invoke is covered by the wording of the Himalaya clause. This question arose in *The Mahkutai*[474] where such a clause in a bill of lading provided that sub-contracting carriers were to have the benefit of "all exceptions, limitations, provisions and liberties herein". It was held that these words did not entitle the sub-contractors to rely on an exclusive jurisdiction clause in the bill of lading, since they referred only to those provisions in it which benefited *one* of the parties to it, while the exclusive jurisdiction clause was a "mutual agreement" creating "mutual obligations".[475] The second question is whether the terms of the clause, or of other provisions in the main contract to which it refers, do indeed protect the third party. The answer to this question depends on the rules relating to the construction and effectiveness of exemption clauses generally. These are discussed in Ch.7; here it is necessary only to make the point that the third party would not be protected by a clause which, on its true construction, would not apply in the events which have happened or cover the loss which has occurred, or by a clause which was legally invalid.[476] The latter possibility is illustrated by *The Starsin*,[477] where goods were damaged whilst being carried in a chartered ship under a bill of lading constituting a contract between charterer and shipper.[478] The benefit of a Himalaya clause in the bill of lading was claimed by the shipowner who was not a party to the contract of carriage and who relied on words in the clause exempting him from "any liability whatsoever to the shipper" for loss resulting from acts done by the shipowner in the course of his employment by the carrier.[479] The clause also provided that the shipowner was (to the extent to which it protected him) to be deemed to be a party to the bill of lading contract[480]; and another term of that contract[481] incorporated into it an international convention known as the Hague Rules. These rules specify certain obligations of a carrier of goods by sea, make available to him certain exemptions from and limitations of liability, and provide that any clause in the contract "lessening such liability otherwise than as provided in this convention shall be null and void."[482] The House of Lords held[483] that this provision of the Rules

---

[474] [1996] A.C. 650.

[475] ibid. at 666; followed on this point in *Bougoyes Offshore SA v Caspian Shipping Co (No.2)* [1997] 2 Lloyd's Rep. 485 at 490.

[476] e.g. *Eisen and Metall AG v Ceres Stevedoring Co Ltd* [1977] 1 Lloyd's Rep. 665.

[477] [2003] UKHL 12; [2004] 1 A.C. 715.

[478] In this respect, the case resembles the *Elder, Dempster* case [1924] A.C. 522; above, para.14–059.

[479] cl.5(1) of the bill of lading, in the numbering given by Lord Bingham in *The Starsin*, above, fn.477, at [20].

[480] cl.5(3), in the same numbering.

[481] cl.2: see *The Starsin*, above, fn.477, at [31].

[482] Art.III.8: see now the Hague Visby Rules, Art.III.8, which have the force of law by virtue of Carriage of Goods by Sea Act 1971, s.1 and Sch.

[483] Lord Steyn dissenting, Lord Hobhouse took the view that the contract between shipper and shipowner created by virtue of the Himalaya clause was a "contract of carriage within the Rules": see at [153], [156]; but this view is rejected by Lord Millett at [203] and does not seem to be adopted by Lord Bingham or Lord Hoffmann: Peel 120 L.Q.R. 11. See also: *The Marielle Bolten* [2009] EWHC 2552 (Comm); [2010] 1 Lloyd's Rep. 648 at [32]–[42].

invalidated the wide words of the Himalaya clause quoted above, so that the shipowner was not protected by them.

Terms of any express contract will prevail. The cases on Himalaya clauses   14–067
assume that the third party seeking to invoke them is not in any contractual relationship with the claimant except for the collateral contract which may arise by virtue of such a clause. Where there is also an express contract between these parties on terms inconsistent with those of any such a collateral contract, then the terms of that express contract will prevail: e.g. where a stevedore enters into an express contract with the cargo–owner making him liable to the cargo–owner for negligence but the bill of lading contains a Himalaya clause the effect of which would (if there were no such express contract) be to exonerate the stevedore from such liability.[484]

Defect in the main contract. In *The Eurymedon*[485] the Himalaya clause in the   14–068
contract between shipper and carrier gave rise to a separate contract between shipper and stevedore collateral to the main contract of carriage.[486] This contract has what may be called certain parasitic qualities so that it may fail to protect the third party, at least in certain cases, where the main contract suffers from some legal defect. Thus in a South African case,[487] in which the relations of the parties were governed by English law,[488] the main contract between A and B contained a Himalaya clause by virtue of which C was prima facie entitled to the benefits of the exemptions from liability which the main contract conferred on A. The main contract was rescinded by B on account of A's misrepresentations and it was held that the Himalaya clause did not entitle C to the protection of the exemption clauses in the main contract since "once those . . . exemptions . . . fall away on rescission of the [main contract], nothing remains to exempt [C]".[489] This was so even though the Himalaya clause had given rise to a "separate contract" between A and C, since under the terms of that contract C took only "the benefits of the same exemptions which the carrier [A] receives, no more and no less".[490]

It is an essential part of this reasoning that the effect of misrepresentation on a contract is to "wipe it out altogether"[491] with retrospective effect. The position would be the same where the main contract was void for mistake at common law. On the other hand, the reasoning would not apply where the main contract was terminated for A's breach, since this process brings the contract to an end only from the time of termination[492] and therefore does not deprive the guilty party of the protection of exemption and limitation clauses in respect of breaches occurring before such termination[493]; consequently, it would not deprive the third party of this benefit where he was otherwise entitled to it by virtue of a Himalaya clause.[494]

---

[484] *The Rigoletto* [2000] 2 Lloyd's Rep. 532.

[485] [1975] A.C. 154.

[486] See above, at fnn.451, 473.

[487] *Bougoyes Offshore v Ultisol Transport Contractors* [1996] 2 Lloyd's Rep. 153, Note.

[488] ibid. at 154, 155.

[489] ibid. at 165.

[490] ibid. For a similar restriction on the third party's right to rely on exemption clauses under Contracts (Rights of Third Parties) Act 1999, see s.3(6) of that Act (below, para.14–112).

[491] *The Kanchenjunga* [1990] 1 Lloyd's Rep. 391 at 398; above, para.9–082.

[492] See below, para.18–011.

[493] See above, para.7–032.

[494] Contracts (Rights of Third Parties) Act 1999, s.3(2) (below, para.14–109) would not apply to such a case: it deals with a different situation in which C sues A and A seeks to rely, against C, on B's repudiatory breach.

If the main contract were frustrated, the third party would likewise be deprived of its protection by virtue of such a clause only in respect of breaches of duty which had occurred after, and not in respect of those which had occurred before, the frustrating event: this follows from the principle that frustration discharges the contract only from the time of the frustrating event.[495] The most difficult cases would be those in which the main contract was affected by illegality. The source of the difficulty is that the effects of illegality vary widely[496]; and that the illegality of the main contract does not necessarily affect the validity of a collateral contract.[497] The guiding principle, it is submitted, should be that the illegality which affects the main contract should deprive the third party of the protection of the collateral contract which arises by virtue of the Himalaya clause only where such a result would in some way promote the policy of the rule of law, the violation of which had given rise to the illegality.[498] No doubt in applying this principle the court would have regard not only to the nature of the illegality but also to the third party's knowledge of or participation in the illegal purpose.

(iii) *Other drafting devices*

14–069   **Promise not to sue, etc.** The third party could also be protected by a form of words other than that used in *The Eurymedon*. For example, an exemption clause in a contract between A and B may contain an express promise by A to B not to sue C. Under the rules already considered, B can, even at common law,[499] enforce that promise by getting a stay of any action by A against C,[500] e.g. if there is a contract between B and C under which B is bound to indemnify C against liability to third parties incurred in the performance of his duties under that contract.[501] Alternatively, the contract between A and B might provide that A should be liable to pay over to B any sum that A might recover from C.[502]

(iv) *Clauses defining duties*

14–070   **Restricting the duty of care.** The preceding discussion is based on the assumptions that C is under a prima facie liability in tort to A and that C seeks to rely on a provision in a contract between A and B in order to exclude or restrict the liability. But it is arguable that the terms of that contract can be relevant at an

---

[495] See below, para.19–090.

[496] See above, paras 11–110—11–127.

[497] See above, para.11–166.

[498] cf. above, para.11–115.

[499] For the position under Contracts (Rights of Third Parties) Act 1999, see below, para.14–002. C's rights at common law would not be subject to the provisions of the Act: cf. above, para.14–058; below, paras 14–116—14–118.

[500] *Snelling v John G Snelling Ltd* [1973] 1 Q.B. 87; above, para.14–038.

[501] See *Gore v Van der Lann* [1967] 2 Q.B. 31; above, para.14–038; *The Elbe Maru* [1978] 1 Lloyds's Rep. 206; contrast *The Starsin* [2004] 1 A.C. 715, where the House of Lords rejected the view that the words of the Himalaya clause quoted (at fn.479) amounted only to a covenant not to sue. For the purpose of enforcement of such a covenant, it suffices that C has a claim for such an indemnity which is not "obviously bad": *Deepak Fertilisers & Petrochemicals Corp v ICI Chemicals & Polymers Ltd* [1999] 1 Lloyd's Rep. 378 at 401. Contrast *The Chevalier Roze* [1983] 2 Lloyd's Rep. 438 (where the contract between A and B had been fully performed before A's cause of action against C arose, and so did not protect C).

[502] Quaere whether this would be a penalty; see below, para.20–130 et seq. For further possible devices, see the *Midland Silicones* case [1962] A.C. 446 at 473 and Hamson [1959] C.L.J. 150.

earlier stage, namely in determining the extent of any duty of care owed to A by C. For example, work under a building contract between A and B may be done by a sub-contractor (C), who is a party to the sub-contract between himself and B, but not a party to B's main contract with A. If C does the work negligently and so causes harm to A (e.g. by damaging other property belonging to A[503]), then C may be liable in tort to A, and an exemption clause in the main contract between A and B will not, as such, at common law protect C. But in the *Junior Books* case, Lord Roskill suggested that a "relevant exclusion clause in the main contract" might "limit the duty of care"[504] of C and so indirectly provide him with a defence to a claim in tort by A. In *The Aliakmon*, this suggestion was doubted by Lord Brandon on the ground that the exemption clause in the example was contained "in a contract to which the (claimant) [was] a party but the defendant [was] not"[505]: in other words, because there was no privity of contract between them. *The Aliakmon* was, however, concerned with the converse of the situation discussed by Lord Roskill, namely with the case in which the exemption clause was contained in a contract to which the defendant was a party but the claimant was not.[506] Both situations raise issues of privity of contract but they are concerned with different aspects of that doctrine: the first with the question whether C can take the *benefit* of an exemption clause in a contract between A and B, and the second with the question whether A can be *bound* by an exemption clause in a contract between B and C. As a matter of policy, there is less objection to giving an affirmative answer to the first question than to the second; for in the first situation A has assented to the clause while in the second no inference of such assent can be drawn merely from the presence of the clause in the contract between B and C. Lord Roskill's suggestion has therefore been followed in a number of later cases in which exemption clauses in the main contract between A and B have been held to negative any duty of care which C might (but for such clauses) have owed to A.[507] It has, however, been held that not only must A have assented to the clause, but C must also have known about it, before commencing work.[508] In such cases, C is protected, in spite of the absence of privity of contract,[509] because the clause "destroys the duty of [C] if duty there ever was".[510] It follows that the clause may be available not only to C, but also to any other person whose hypothetical duty is in this way affected. It may thus protect C's employees as well as C himself: in one case of this kind it was said that if C owed no duty "then neither can any of their employees have done so".[511] Whether a clause affects the duty of persons other than C depends simply on its construction and not on the doctrine of privity.

---

[503] In this respect the facts of the example given in the text differ from those of the *Junior Books* case [1983] 1 A.C. 520 and so do not give rise to the difficulties occasioned by that case (see above, para.14–049).

[504] [1983] 1 A.C. 520 at 546, applied in *Southern Water Authority v Carey* [1985] 2 All E.R. 1077 at 1086.

[505] [1986] A.C. 785 at 817.

[506] See below, para.14–071. Lord Brandon's view (above, fn.504) was accordingly questioned in *Pacific Associates Inc v Baxter* [1990] 1 Q.B. 993 at 1022.

[507] *Southern Water Authority v Carey* [1985] 2 All E.R. 1077; *Norwich CC v Harvey* [1989] 1 W.L.R. 828; *Pacific Associates Inc v Baxter* [1990] 1 Q.B. 993; Adams and Brownsword [1990] J.B.L. 23.

[508] *Precis (521) v William Mercer Ltd* [2005] EWCA Civ 114; [2005] P.N.L.R. 28 at [25].

[509] *Norwich CC v Harvey* [1989] 1 W.L.R. 828 at 837.

[510] *Pacific Associates Inc v Baxter* [1990] 1 Q.B. 993 at 1038.

[511] *Norwich CC v Harvey* [1989] 1 W.L.R. 828 at 834.

Lord Roskill's statement refers only to "a *relevant* exclusion clause": that is, to one which can "limit *the duty of care*". A clause which merely imposed a financial limit on the *amount recoverable* would not be of this kind since such a clause would come into operation only on the assumption that a duty was owed and had been broken.[512] Similarly, the clause must refer to the duty of the person relying on it: thus if a contract between a building owner and a contractor contained a provision restricting the duty of sub-contractors *nominated* by the owner, that provision would not protect *other* sub-contractors (who had not been so nominated).[513]

(b) The Burden

(i) *General rule*

14–071   **Non-party to contract not bound by exemption clause.** The law starts with the principle that a person is not bound by an exemption clause in a contract to which he is not a party, unless one of the recognised exceptions to the doctrine of privity (such as agency) can be invoked against him.[514] In the *Midland Silicones* case[515] the contract between the carrier and the stevedores provided that the stevedores should have "such protection as is afforded by the terms of the bill of lading". The owners of the drum nonetheless recovered full damages from the stevedores. They were not bound by what was, in effect, a limitation clause in the contract between the stevedores and the carrier.[516] Similarly, in *The Aliakmon*[517] the buyers were not bound by exemption provisions in the contract of carriage since the only parties to that contract were the sellers and the shipowners.[518] The general rule may be unsatisfactory in practice,[519] and is therefore subject to a number of exceptions.

(ii) *Exceptions*

14–072   **Agency and implied contract.** The first such exception is illustrated by *Pyrene Co Ltd v Scindia Navigation Co Ltd*,[520] where a fire tender which had been sold for export was to be shipped under a contract between buyer and carrier,

---

[512] cf. below, para.14–074.

[513] *British Telecommunications Plc v James Thomson & Sons (Engineering) Ltd* [1999] 2 All E.R. 241.

[514] *Delaurier v Wyllie* (1889) 17 R. (Ct. of Sess.) 167: cf. *The Kite* [1933] P. 164; *White v Warwick (John) & Co Ltd* [1953] 2 W.L.R. 1285 at 1294. This rule applies even in systems of law under which a third party can take the *benefit* of a contract, as in the US (see *The OOCL Bravery* [2000] 1 Lloyd's Rep. 394 at 399), but see the concept of a "limited agency" under which a third party may become bound: *Norfolk Southern Railway Co v James N Kirby Ltd* 543 U.S. 14 (2004), above, fn.410. It follows that in England the rule survives the Contracts (Rights of Third Parties) Act 1999, s.1(6).

[515] [1962] A.C. 446; above, para.14–060.

[516] ibid.

[517] [1986] A.C. 785; above, para.14–050.

[518] Paradoxically, it was the buyers who argued (unsuccessfully) that they *were* bound, their object being to establish that the undesirable consequence of depriving the shipowners of the benefit of those provisions (see above, para.14–050) would not follow if the shipowners were held liable to them in tort.

[519] e.g. if the buyers in *The Aliakmon*, above had been owners of the goods when they were damaged their tort claim would then have succeeded on the reasoning given at para.14–050, above, but they might still not have been parties to the contract of carriage, so that the carriers would have been deprived of the protection of the international Convention known as the Hague Rules.

[520] [1954] 2 Q.B. 402.

which limited the latter's liability.[521] The seller presented the tender for loading to the carrier who, in carrying out this operation, damaged the tender while it was still at the seller's risk. It was held that the seller was bound by the limitation clause. The decision was partly based on the doubts which had been expressed in earlier cases as to the existence of the doctrine of privity.[522] It can no longer be supported on this ground; nor is the seller's tort claim against the carrier in such a case adversely affected by the Contracts (Rights of Third Parties) Act 1999, since under this Act a person will not, in general, be *bound* by terms of a contract to which he is not a party.[523] But the *Pyrene* case can still be justified either on the ground that the buyer was the seller's agent in making the contract with the carrier, at least so far as it concerned the seller[524]; or on the ground that an implied contract incorporating the limitation clause arose between seller and carrier when the tender was presented by the seller and accepted by the carrier for loading. The latter explanation is the one now generally accepted[525] though it is not entirely free from difficulty since the carrier may at this stage have intended merely to perform his contract of carriage with the buyer and so have lacked the contractual intention necessary for the creation of a new contract.[526]

Implied contract reasoning was also used in *The Eurymedon*,[527] to deal with the point that the action against the stevedore was brought, not by the shipper, but by the consignee, who (it was assumed) was not a party to the contract of carriage contained or evidenced in the bill of lading.[528] It was held that the consignee was nevertheless bound by the exclusion clause in that contract since an implied contract arose[529] between stevedore and consignee, as a result of the consignee's "acceptance of [the bill of lading] and request for delivery of the goods thereunder"[530]; and this implied contract incorporated the terms of the bill of lading (which protected the stevedore[531]). In the *Midland Silicones* case,[532] by contrast, there was no implied contract between the claimants and the stevedores incorporating the terms of the contract between the carrier and the stevedores. The case differs from *The Eurymedon* in that there the consignees had possession of the bill of lading and so knew, or at least had means of knowing, its terms, while in the *Midland Silicones* case there was nothing to indicate that the claimants knew anything about the contract between the carrier and the stevedores.[533] The implied contract argument may also fail on other grounds. In *The Aliakmon* the buyers had presented a bill of lading to which they were not parties, and took delivery of the

---

[521] Under what is now Carriage of Goods by Sea Act 1971, Sch., art.IV.5.

[522] At 426; and see above, para.14–015.

[523] See above, para.14–001; for a qualification, not relevant in the present context of a third party's claim brought apart from the Act, see below, para.14–075.

[524] See [1954] 2 Q.B. 402 at 423–425; *The Kite* [1933] P. 164 at 181 ("limited authority": cf. *Norfolk Southern Railway Co v James N Kirby Ltd* 543 U.S. 14 (2004), above, fn.410).

[525] *Scruttons Ltd v Midland Silicones Ltd* [1962] A.C. 446 at 471; *The Kapetan Markos NL (No.2)* [1987] 2 Lloyd's Rep. 321 at 331; *The Captain Gregos (No.2)* [1990] 2 Lloyd's Rep. 395 (claim by B.P.).

[526] cf. above, para.4–021.

[527] [1975] A.C. 154.

[528] It was assumed that the consignee had not become a party to the contract under Bills of Lading Act 1855, s.1 since it was not clear that the requirements of the section had been satisfied. See now Carriage of Goods by Sea Act 1992, s.2; below, paras 15–009, 15–084.

[529] On the analogy of *Brandt v Liverpool, etc. SN Co Ltd* [1924] 1 K.B. 575.

[530] [1975] A.C. 154 at 168.

[531] See above, para.14–063.

[532] [1962] A.C. 446; above, para.14–060.

[533] ibid. at 467, 493.

goods; but no implied contract arose since they had done these acts purely as agents of the sellers.[534]

Where an injured party is bound by the exemption clause in a contract between two others by virtue of agency or implied contract reasoning, the legal basis for his being so bound is not in doubt: it is that he is brought into a contractual relationship with the party relying on the clause. There are, however, a number of further grounds on which the injured party may be bound by an exemption clause in a contract to which he is not a party in spite of the fact that he has not come into any contractual relationship with the person relying on the clause; and it is with these grounds that the following discussion is concerned.

14–073   **Bailment on terms.** One such ground is that the injured party is so bound by virtue of a bailment on terms. Earlier in this chapter, we saw that this concept could be invoked to enable a person to get the *benefit* of an exemption clause in a contract to which he was not a party.[535] Our present concern is with the use of the concept for the converse purpose of *binding* a person by such a clause in a contract between others. This possibility is illustrated by the case in which a customer sends goods to a cleaner or repairer and allows him to send the work out to a sub-contractor. If the sub-contract contains an exemption clause, the owner may be bound by it on the ground that he has "expressly or impliedly consented to the bailee making a sub-bailment containing those conditions, but not otherwise".[536] The same principle was applied in *The Pioneer Container*[537] where C had entered into a contract with B for the carriage of C's goods on terms which authorised B to sub-contract "on any terms". B did enter into a sub-contract with A (another carrier) on terms containing an exclusive jurisdiction clause and it was held that C was bound by this clause. Lord Goff said that the effect of the clause on C did "not depend for its efficacy either on the doctrine of privity of contract or on the doctrine of consideration"[538]; in other words, C was bound by it irrespective of contract.[539] He was bound under the law of bailment, because he had consented

---

[534] [1986] A.C. 785 at 808; this fact was known to the carrier: see [1985] Q.B. 350 at 364.

[535] *Elder, Dempster & Co v Paterson, Zochonis & Co* [1924] A.C. 522 at 564; above, para.14–059.

[536] *Morris v C W Martin & Sons Ltd* [1966] 1 Q.B. 716 at 729; cf. [1966] 1 Q.B. 716 at 741; *Port Swettenham Authority v T W Wu & Co* [1979] A.C. 580; *The Captain Gregos (No.2)* [1990] 2 Lloyd's Rep. 395 at 405; Palmer [1988] L.M.C.L.Q. 466; Phang 8 O.J.L.S. 418. Carnegie 3 Adelaide L.Rev 7; cf. also Occupiers' Liability Act 1957, s.3; Defective Premises Act 1972, ss.4 and 11(b); *White v Blackmore* [1972] 2 Q.B. 651 at 676.

[537] [1994] 2 A.C. 324; *Johnson Matthey & Co v Constantine Terminals Ltd* [1976] 2 Lloyd's Rep. 215; *Dresser UK Ltd v Falconbridge Management Ltd* [1992] Q.B. 502; *The Gudermes* [1993] 1 Lloyd's Rep. 311 at 328; *Sonicare International Ltd v EAFT Ltd* [1997] 2 Lloyd's Rep. 48; Coote [1977] C.L.J. 177; *East West Corp v DKBS 1912* [2003] EWCA Civ 83; [2003] Q.B. 1509 at [30], [69]; *The Starsin* [2003] UKHL 12; [2004] 1 A.C. 715 at [133]–[136]; *Scottish & Newcastle International Ltd v Othon Ghalanos Ltd* [2008] UKHL 11; [2008] 1 Lloyd's Rep. 462 at [47]; cf. *The Agia Skepi* [1992] 2 Lloyd's Rep. 467 at 472; *The Termagent* (1914) 1 Com. Cas. 239, where no consent to the sub-bailment had been given.

[538] ibid. at 339.

[539] C may be bound by reason *both* of a bailment on terms *and* of a contract between C and A made through the agency of B: see *Sandeman Coprimar SA v Transitos y Transportes Integrales SL* [2003] EWCA Civ 113; [2003] 2 Lloyd's Rep. 172 at [62], [63]. See also *East West Corp v DKBS 1912* [2003] EWCA Civ 83; [2003] Q.B. 1509 at [24], [69], holding the same principle to be applicable to the case where the bailor was originally in a contractual relationship with the bailee and had lost his rights under the contract by transfer of the bill of lading which evidenced or contained the contract; but concluding that there were no relevant terms in that contract which protected the bailee: see [2003] EWCA Civ 83; [2003] Q.B. 1509 at [81], [85].

to the making of the sub-bailment by B to A and to the terms of that sub-bailment. C's consent to those terms was thus essential[540]; though no doubt the law will here (as elsewhere) apply an objective test, so that C may be bound by terms of the sub-bailment, even though he has not actually consented to them, if he has so conducted himself as to induce A to believe that he has so consented.[541] The principle of such cases is, however, confined to situations in which there is a relationship of bailor and bailee (or sub-bailee) between the claimant and the defendant. In *The Aliakmon*, the exception did not apply as no such relationship there existed between the *buyers* and the shipowners: "The only bailment of the goods was one by the sellers to the shipowners".[542] Similarly, in the *Midland Silicones* case the present exception did not apply since, for the reasons given earlier in this chapter,[543] the stevedores were not bailees of the drum.[544]

Where the present exception does apply, the head bailor, C, is bound by an exemption clause in the sub-bailment between the head bailee, B, and the sub-bailee, A, in spite of the fact that there is no contract between A and C. Some legal basis other than contract must therefore be found to explain this result. One view is that C is bound simply because he consented to the inclusion of the term in the contract between B and A.[545] But if this were the reason for the exception, then it would not be restricted, as on the authorities it is,[546] to cases of bailment. The reason for the restriction appears to be that (in cases of the present kind) C has consented, not only to the terms of the contract between B and A, but also to the creation of the very relationship of bailor and sub-bailee between C and A which is the sole source of the duty alleged to be owed by A to C and to have been broken.[547] It follows that the exception does not apply where C does not need to rely on the bailment to establish that A owed him a duty of care. This would be the position, not only where A was never a bailee of C's goods at all (as in the *Midland Silicones* case), but also where A was such a bailee and C's loss resulted, not from A's breach of his custodial duty as bailee, but from A's conduct causing

---

[540] [1994] 2 A.C. 324 at 340–342, rejecting the view that no such consent was necessary, which had been expressed by Donaldson J. in *Johnson Matthey & Co v Constantine Terminals Ltd* [1976] 2 Lloyd's Rep. 215 at 221.
[541] See Lord Goff's reference in *The Pioneer Container* [1994] 2 A.C. 324 at 342 to ostensible authority; cf. *Norfolk Southern Railway Co v James N Kirby Ltd* 543 U.S. 14 (2004); above, fn.410 (which is decided on the basis of contract, and not bailment).
[542] [1986] A.C. 785 at 818; cf. *Swiss Bank Corp v Brink's-Mat Ltd* [1986] 2 Lloyd's Rep. 79 at 98; *The Captain Gregos (No.2)* [1990] 2 Lloyd's Rep. 395 (claim by PEAG), but the same case shows that a bailment incorporating the terms of the contract can arise by subsequent attornment of the carrier to the buyer (claim by B.P.). On the question whether a bailment relationship can arise between a carrier and a buyer of goods who is not an original party to the contract of carriage, see also *The Kapetan Markos NL (No.2)* [1987] 2 Lloyd's Rep. 321, where it was said at 332 that the existence of such a relationship was "not seriously disputed"; and *Sonicare International Ltd v EAFT* [1997] 2 Lloyd's Rep. 48 at 53.
[543] See above, para.14–060.
[544] [1962] A.C. 446 at 470.
[545] This appears to have been the view of Denning L.J. in *Morris v CW Martin Ltd* [1966] 1 Q.B. 716 at 729 and in his dissenting speech in the *Midland Silicones* case [1962] A.C. 446 at 491.
[546] See the *Midland Silicones* case, above, at fnn.543 and 544 and the authorities cited in fn.536, above and *The Mahkutai* [1996] A.C. 650 and fn.547, below.
[547] See *The Pioneer Container* [1994] 2 A.C. 324 at 336; *The Starsin* [2003] UKHL 12; [2004] 1 A.C. 715 at [136]. The view that the exception may extend beyond cases of bailment derives some support from an obiter dictum in *Henderson v Merrett Syndicates Ltd* [1995] 2 A.C. 145 at 196 and is also supported by Toulson J. in *Lukoil-Kalingradmorneft Plc v Tata Ltd* [1999] 1 Lloyd's Rep. 365 at 375, affirmed [1999] 2 Lloyd's Rep. 129, without reference to this point.

damage to C's goods in breach of a duty which had arisen quite apart from the bailment, "simply by virtue of A's proximity to the goods".[548]

14–074 **Clauses defining duties.** A distinction must here (as elsewhere[549]) be drawn between exemption clauses and clauses which define a party's duty. Clauses of the latter kind can adversely affect a claimant even though they are contained in a contract to which he is not a party. Breach of that contract may amount also to breach of a duty of care owed to a third party, giving that third party a remedy in tort[550] and the terms of the contract can be relevant to the scope of that duty of care. For example, where work in pursuance of a building contract between C and B is done by A under a roofing sub-contract between B and A, the terms of the latter contract would clearly determine the type of work to be done by A.[551] If the sub-contract merely required A to tile the roof he would not be liable in tort to C on the ground that the main contract required the roof to be tiled and felted, or even on the ground that tiling and felting was standard practice for the type of building in question. It would not, in such a case, be "unfair"[552] to C to deprive him of a right in tort against A by a term in a contract over which C had no control; for C would not (even if B were authorised to sub-contract the work) be precluded from recovering damages for breach of contract from B if the work done by A was not in conformity with the contract between C and B.[553] Different reasoning would apply to a clause in the sub-contract which merely limited A's liability (e.g. to the cost of replacing defective tiles). Such a clause would not be relevant to the definition of A's duty to C in tort since it would not define what A had to do, but merely specify the legal consequences of failing to do it.[554] Hence such a clause would as a general rule not bind C contractually, since he was not a party to the contract in which it was contained.

14–075 **Comparison with the 1999 Act.** Under the Contracts (Rights of Third Parties) Act 1999 a third party C is, in circumstances to be discussed later in this chapter,[555] entitled to enforce a term in a contract between two others; but his right to do so is, in general, subject to defences which would have been available to the promisor A if the proceedings to enforce the term had been brought by the promisee B.[556] If, for example, a contract between A and B contained (1) a promise by A to B to render some service to C and (2) a term excluding or limiting A's liability for specified breaches, then, in an action by C under the 1999 Act to enforce the first of these terms, A would be entitled to rely on the second. In such a case, C's right, being derived from B's right, is subject to the restrictions which

---

[548] *The Kapetan Markos NL (No.2)* [1987] 2 Lloyd's Rep. 321 at 340; cf. *Johnson Matthey & Co v Constantine Terminals Ltd* [1976] 2 Lloyd's Rep. 215 at 222; this point is not affected by the disapproval of the case on another point, referred to in fn.540, above.

[549] See above, paras 7–021, 14–070.

[550] See above, paras 14–045—14–054.

[551] *Junior Books* case [1983] 1 A.C. 520 at 534; cf. *Simaan General Contracting Co v Pilkington Glass Ltd (No.2)* [1988] Q.B. 758 at 782–783.

[552] ibid., discussing a sale of goods example.

[553] See below, para.17–012.

[554] See *The Aliakmon* where the contract incorporated the Hague Rules which contained an intricate set of provisions, some of which defined duties while others provided immunities and limitations; taken together, these could not be "synthesised into a standard of care": [1985] Q.B. 350 at 368, approved [1986] A.C. 785 at 818; cf. *Twins Transport Ltd v Patrick Brocklehurst* (1983) 25 Build.L.R. 65.

[555] See below, para.14–090 et seq.

[556] 1996 Act, s.3(2); below, para.14–109.

govern the latter right.[557] This statutory rule, however, applies only where C's claim against A is one to enforce a term of the contract between A and B under the 1999 Act. It does not apply where C's claim is not derived from that contract but arises independently of it and is made apart from the Act. This was the position in most of the cases with which the preceding discussion has been concerned. In them, the claim made by C against A was typically one in tort, and it was argued that C's right to sue A in tort was excluded or limited by the terms of a contract between A and B. That contract was not, in such cases, the basis of C's claim against A, but (at most) part of the history or chain of events giving rise to the circumstances in which A owed (or was alleged to owe) a duty of care to C. The 1999 Act expressly states that such common law claims are not to be affected by its provisions.[558]

Transferred loss. A more controversial way in which a person might, at common law, be adversely affected by an exemption clause in a contract to which he is not a party has been said to arise under the so-called "principle of transferred loss".[559] The principle was, so far as English law is concerned, first stated by Robert Goff L.J. (as he then was) in *The Aliakmon*. It is said to apply where A, in breach of a duty of care in tort, causes physical damage to B's property but can reasonably foresee that the loss will fall on C, e.g. because B has sold the property to C and the risk under that contract has passed to C. The effect of the doctrine is then said to be that "C will be entitled, *subject to the terms of any contract restricting A's liability to B*, to bring an action in tort against A in respect of such loss or damage to the extent to which it falls upon him".[560] In *The Aliakmon* itself[561] the effect of the principle, on the assumption that the damage was due to the negligence of A,[562] would, in Robert Goff L.J.'s view, have been that C would have acquired a tort claim against A, and that this claim would have been subject to any terms in the bill of lading contract between A and B which restricted or excluded A's liability to B under that contract. But when the case reached the House of Lords, Lord Brandon[563] described the principle as "not only unsupported by authority, but . . . on the contrary inconsistent with it"[564] and declared himself unwilling to introduce it into English law. A more favourable view of the principle of transferred loss was, however, taken by Lord Goff in *White v Jones*,[565] the "disappointed beneficiary" case discussed earlier in this chapter.[566] The actual decision in that case could not, indeed, be based on the principle since the solicitor's breach of duty had not caused any loss to his client[567]; but the analogy

14–076

---

[557] cf. Law Com. No.242, para.10.24.

[558] 1999 Act, s.7(1); below, para.14–116.

[559] *The Aliakmon* [1986] A.C. 785 at 820; *White v Jones* [1995] 2 A.C. 207 at 264; Unberath, *Transferred Loss*.

[560] [1985] Q.B. 350 at 399 (italics supplied).

[561] See above, para.14–049.

[562] Robert Goff L.J.'s conclusion was that A (the shipowner) was not liable since the person responsible for the damage was not A but the time charterer. Lord Donaldson M.R. and Oliver L.J. also held that A was not liable, but on the different ground that A owed no duty of care to C; this was also the view of the House of Lords: see above, para.14–049.

[563] With whom all the other members of the House agreed.

[564] [1986] A.C. 785 at 820; see further para.14–049, above.

[565] [1995] 2 A.C. 207 at 264–265. In *Alfred McAlpine Construction Ltd v Panatown Ltd* [2001] 1 A.C. 518 at 529, the principle is referred to with apparent approval and, with some misgivings, by Lord Goff (dissenting) at 557, citing Unberath 115 L.Q.R. 535.

[566] See above, para.14–052.

[567] [1995] 2 A.C. 207 at 265.

between cases covered by the principle and the facts of *White v Jones* was said to be "very close".[568] One point of resemblance between them is that, in Lord Goff's view, the solicitor's tort liability to an intended beneficiary would be "subject to any term of the contract between the solicitor and the testator which may exclude or restrict the solicitor's liability to the testator … ".[569] The fact that there is no support in the speeches of other members of the majority in *White v Jones* for this restriction on the beneficiary's tort claim[570] may be explicable on the ground that the restriction would be based on terms of a contract to which the beneficiary was not a party, to which he had not consented and which he had not authorised; for the principle of transferred loss, as formulated above,[571] does not contain any requirement that C should have consented to or authorised the exemption or limitation clauses in the contract between A and B. This position may be contrasted with the requirement of such consent which has been stated in a number of other contexts in which a person is or may be bound at common law by an exemption clause in a contract to which he is not a party: for example, in the sub-bailment cases discussed above.[572] If the principle of transferred loss were to be accepted in English law, and if rights of a third party arising under it could be excluded or restricted by the terms of a contract between others, further judicial consideration would have to be given to the question whether there should, for the purpose of binding the third party by such terms, be a requirement of his authorisation of or consent to them. One possible view is that the bailment and other cases, in which such a requirement seems now to be firmly established, should be followed by analogy in cases in which the third party's right (if any) arose under the principle of transferred loss. The alternative view is that in those other cases the third party has an independent tort claim, of which he should not be deprived by terms of a contract over which he had no control, while a third party who relied on the principle of transferred loss would assert what is, in effect, a derivative claim which, in its nature, should not be more extensive than the claim of the person from whom it is derived.

5. EXCEPTIONS

14–077   The doctrine of privity would, if inflexibly applied, give rise to considerable injustice and inconvenience. Many exceptions to it have therefore been developed by the courts and the legislature. The most important of these is the "general and wide ranging"[573] one which has been created by the Contracts (Rights of Third Parties) Act 1999. This Act preserves any right or remedy which the third party may have apart from its provisions.[574] The exceptions which were established before the Act came into force therefore still call for discussion, particularly because situations may arise in which it will be to the third parties' advantage to rely on one of these exceptions, rather than on the new one which has been created by the Act.[575]

---

[568] ibid.

[569] ibid. at 268; cf. *Trusted v Clifford Chance* [2000] W.T.L.R. 1219.

[570] There is no reference to the point in the speech of Lord Browne-Wilkinson, while Lord Nolan at 294 left the point open.

[571] At fn.560.

[572] See especially *The Pioneer Container* [1994] 2 A.C. 324; cf. also Lord Goff's dictum in *Henderson v Merrett Syndicates Ltd* [1995] 2 A.C. 145 at 196; above, fn.547.

[573] Law Com. No.242, para.5.16.

[574] s.7(1); this can apply not only to existing, but also to future, exceptions.

[575] See above, para.14–003; below, paras 14–091, 14–116—14–118.

(a) Judge-made Exceptions

(i) *Covenants concerning land*

Covenants in a lease can benefit or bind persons, other than the original parties   **14–078**
to the lease, who later acquire an interest in the property or the reversion; a person
may be able to enforce a covenant affecting land made by his predecessor in title,
and one who acquires land with notice that it is burdened by a restrictive covenant
may be bound by it although he was not a party to the covenant. Detailed
discussion of these topics will be found in works on land law.[576]

(ii) *Agency*

Agency is the relationship which arises when one person (the principal) author-   **14–079**
ises another (the agent) to act on his behalf and the agent agrees to do so. One legal
consequence of this relationship is that the principal acquires rights and incurs
liabilities under contracts made by the agent on his behalf with third parties. It is
sometimes said that this is only an apparent exception to the doctrine of privity,
since in such cases the agent is only the instrument of the principal, who is the real
contracting party.[577] This may be true where the agent acts within his actual
authority. But it is only doubtfully true where the principal is liable under the
doctrine of apparent authority although the agent's act is unauthorised, or where
the principal ratifies.[578] And the principles of agency would seem to constitute a
clear exception to the doctrine of privity where the agent acts without actual but
within his "usual" authority,[579] where the principal is undisclosed,[580] and in
certain cases of agency of necessity.[581] These matters are discussed in Ch.16.

(iii) *Assignment*

Assignment is a process whereby a contractual right is transferred to someone   **14–080**
other than the original creditor without the consent of the original debtor. It is a
clear exception to the doctrine of privity and is discussed in Ch.15.

(iv) *Trusts of promises*[582]

Equity developed a more general exception to the doctrine of privity by use of   **14–081**
the concept of trust. A trust is an equitable obligation to hold property on behalf
of another. It may be express or implied; and a person may be trustee not only of
a physical thing or of a sum of money, but also of a *chose in action*,[583] such as a debt
owed to him. In equity, a person could, moreover, be trustee of a promise to pay
money, not to himself, but to a third party; and where such a trust was established,

---

[576] e.g. Megarry and Wade, *The Law of Real Property* (7th edn), Ch.32.
[577] cf. Pollock, *Principles of Contract* (13th edn), p.163.
[578] See below, paras 16–020—16–028, 16–042—16–052.
[579] *Watteau v Fenwick* [1893] 1 Q.B. 346; below, paras 16–029—16–030.
[580] See below, paras 16–056—16–060.
[581] See below, paras 16–031—16–041.
[582] Corbin 46 L.Q.R. 12; *Contracts*, Ch.46; Jaconelli [1998] Conv. 88.
[583] See below, para.15–002.

the third party could enforce the promise against the promisor.[584] This device was applied in a number of eighteenth- and nineteenth-century cases[585] and was even recognised by the common law courts, who sometimes allowed the promisee to recover more than he had lost on the ground that he was bound to hold the surplus for a third party.[586] It was approved by the House of Lords in *Walford's* case,[587] where a broker (C) negotiated a charterparty by which the shipowner (A) promised the charterer (B) to pay the broker a commission. It was held that B was trustee of this promise for C, who could thus enforce it against A.[588] Many problems arise in determining the scope and effects of this trust device.

14–082   **Intention to create a trust.** A promisee will not be regarded as trustee for a third party unless he has the intention to create a trust.[589] Such an intention can be made clear by using the word "trust" or "trustee",[590] but a trust may be created without using any particular form of words, and where the word "trust" or "trustee" is not used, the question of intention gives rise to great difficulty. Two cases may be contrasted. In *Re Flavell*[591] a partner retired and the continuing partners promised him that they would, after his death, pay an annuity to his widow. It was held that there was a trust in favour of the widow. But in *Re Schebsman*[592] a company promised one of its employees on his retirement that it would, after his death, pay annuities to his widow for a specified period, or (if she should die within that period) to his daughter. It was held that there was no trust in favour of the widow or daughter.

Similarly, a life insurance policy expressed to be for the benefit of a third party has in some cases been held to create a trust in his favour,[593] but in others to confer no rights on him.[594] And in some cases concerning other types of insurance[595] the courts have held that a third party could take advantage of the policy under the

---

[584] *Tomlinson v Gill* (1756) Amb. 330. For the effectiveness of directions (not of a contractual nature) to executors in favour of a third party, see *Crowden v Aldridge* [1993] 1 W.L.R. 433.

[585] e.g. above, fn.584; *Lloyd's v Harper* (1880) 16 Ch.D. 290.

[586] e.g. *Robertson v Wait* (1853) 8 Ex. 299; *Prudential Staff Union v Hall* [1947] K.B. 685.

[587] *Les Affréteurs Réunis, SA v Leopold Walford (London) Ltd* [1919] A.C. 801; *Atlas Shipping Agency (UK) Ltd v Suisse Atlantique Société d'Armement SA* [1995] 2 Lloyd's Rep. 188. Contrast *The Manifest Lipkowy* [1989] 2 Lloyd's Rep. 138, where an agreement for the sale of a ship provided for deduction of the broker's commission from the price, but seems to have contained no *promise* by the seller to pay the broker.

[588] Lord Finlay seems to have regarded the broker as a party to the contract.

[589] *Swain v Law Society* [1983] 1 A.C. 598 at 620; Feltham 98 L.Q.R. 17. For the purpose of the present discussion, it is assumed that formal requirements, such as that imposed by Law of Property Act 1925, s.53(1)(b), have been satisfied. As to the effect on the rights of third parties of failure to satisfy such requirements, see Feltham [1987] Conv. 246.

[590] *Fletcher v Fletcher* (1844) 4 Hare 67; *Bowskill v Dawson* [1955] 1 Q.B. 13.

[591] (1883) 25 Ch.D. 89; see further, cf. *Re Gordon* [1940] Ch. 851; *Drimmie v Davies* [1899] 1 I.R. 176.

[592] [1944] Ch. 83; see further, below, fn.611; cf. *Re Stapleton-Bretherton* [1941] Ch. 482. In *Re Miller's Agreement* [1947] Ch. 615 and *Beswick v Beswick* [1968] A.C. 58 it was conceded that there was no trust.

[593] *Royal Exchange Assurance v Hope* [1928] Ch. 179; *Re Webb* [1941] Ch. 225; *Re Foster's Policy* [1966] 1 W.L.R. 222.

[594] *Re Burgess' Policy* (1915) 113 L.T. 443; *Re Sinclair's Life Policy* [1938] Ch. 799; *Re Engelbach's Estate* [1924] 2 Ch. 348.

[595] For statutory exceptions to the doctrine of privity in cases of insurance, see below, paras 14–124—14–129.

trust device[596] while in others they have held that the third party had no rights because of the doctrine of privity.[597] These cases cannot be reconciled. They represent different stages of development and show that the courts became reluctant to apply the trust device because, once a trust was held to have been created, the parties to the contract lost their right to rescind or vary that contract by mutual consent.[598] The most that can be done is to try to extract from them a number of principles which will at any rate serve as guides to the solution of future problems.

There must be an intention to benefit the third party. If the promisee   14-083
intends the promise to be for his own benefit, there will be no trust in favour of the third party.[599] The same result may follow if it is as consistent with the facts that the promisee took the promise for his own benefit as for that of a third party.[600] Conversely, the fact that the promisee had *not* intended to take the promise for his own benefit can be relied on to support the argument that there was a trust in favour of the third party.[601]

The intention to benefit the third party must be irrevocable. It is now[602]   14-084
settled that a contract will not normally[603] give rise to a trust in favour of a third party if, under the terms of the contract, the promisee is entitled to deprive the third party of the intended benefit by diverting it to himself. Thus in *Re Sinclair's Life Policy*[604] a policy of life insurance, taken out by the assured for the benefit of his godson, contained an option enabling the assured to surrender the policy for his own benefit.[605] This fact negatived the intention to create a trust. On the other hand, the existence of such a power to divert the benefit was held not to negative the intention to create the trust where the power was expressed to be exercisable only for a limited period and was not exercised within that period.[606] Nor will the existence of a trust necessarily be negatived where the contract names a group of beneficiaries but reserves to the promisee the power to alter the nature or destination of the benefit as between those beneficiaries.[607] And where a contract

---

[596] *Williams v Baltic Ins Co* [1924] 2 K.B. 282; cf. *Waters v Monarch Assurance Co* (1856) 5 E. & B. 870 at 881. See also Deane J. in *Trident General Ins Co Ltd v McNiece Bros Pty Ltd* (1988) 165 C.L.R. 107 (above, para.14–017).

[597] *Vandepitte v Preferred Accident Ins Corp* [1933] A.C. 70; *Green v Russell* [1959] 2 Q.B. 226, cited with approval in *McCamley v Cammell Laird Shipbuilders* [1990] 1 W.L.R. 963 at 969.

[598] See above, para.14–015; below, para.14–084.

[599] See *West v Houghton* (1879) 4 C.P.D. 197; criticised in *Re Flavell* (1883) 25 Ch.D. 89 at 98 and in *Lloyd's v Harper* (1880) 16 Ch.D. 290 at 311.

[600] *Vandepitte v Preferred Accident Ins Corp* [1993] A.C. 70, where one relevant factor for denying that a motor insurance policy created a trust in favour of a person authorised to drive the insured's car was that the insured was himself liable for the torts of that person. Contrast *Williams v Baltic Ins Co* [1920] 2 K.B. 283; for the statutory position relating to such policies, see below, para.14–126.

[601] *Lyus v Prowsa Developments Ltd* [1982] 1 W.L.R. 1044.

[602] Contrast the earlier decisions in *Hill v Gomme* (1839) 5 My. & Cr. 250; *Page v Cox* (1852) 10 Hare 163.

[603] For exceptions, see below, at fnn.606 to 609.

[604] [1938] Ch. 799; criticised on another ground in *Beswick v Beswick* [1968] A.C. 58 at 96; above, fn.250.

[605] A provision of this kind would not fall within Contracts (Rights of Third Parties) Act 1999, s.2 since this applies only to rescission or variation by *agreement*: see below, para.14–106.

[606] *Re Foster's Policy* [1966] 1 W.L.R. 432.

[607] *Re Webb* [1941] Ch. 225; *Re Flavell* (1883) 25 Ch.D. 89.

by statute creates a trust[608] a general provision in the contract entitling the promisee to divert the benefit to whom he pleases will not defeat the trust: on the contrary such power can be exercised only for the benefit of objects of the trust.[609] The court may conclude that there was no intention irrevocably to benefit the third party even though the contract contains no express provision entitling the promisee to divert the benefit away from the third party. It may do so on the ground that the contract would, if it were held to give rise to a trust, unduly limit the freedom of action of the parties or of one of them, e.g. by restricting the promisee's freedom of movement[610] or by depriving the parties to the contract of their rights to vary it by mutual consent.[611]

14–085   **Intention to benefit third party is not sufficient.** An intention to create a trust must be distinguished from an intention to make a gift.[612] There are also many cases in which the courts have refused to apply the trust device although the promisee clearly and without qualification intended to benefit the third party.[613] It seems that the necessary intention to create a trust will readily be found where the contract for the benefit of the third party is made in performance of a previous contract between promisee and third party, e.g. where an employer promises to insure his employee against accident and then does so.[614] An intention to create a trust should, on principle, involve an intention on the part of the promisee to assume fiduciary responsibilities towards the third party.[615] But there is no clear definition of "fiduciary" for this purpose; and the courts did not at one time insist very strictly on proof of the intention to create a trust. The fact that they later came to do so is largely responsible for the present, more restricted, scope of the trust device.

The intention to create a trust may, finally, be negatived on the ground that a trust is not necessary to give rights to the third party because he is entitled to

---

[608] See below, para.14–125.

[609] *Re a Policy of the Equitable Life Assurance of the United States and Mitchell* (1911) 27 T.L.R. 213; *Re Fleetwood's Policy* [1926] Ch. 48.

[610] e.g. *Re Burgess' Policy* (1915) 113 L.T. 43 (policy to become void if insured went "beyond the boundaries of Europe" without previously notifying insurers).

[611] e.g. *Re Schebsman* [1944] Ch. 83 at 104 (parties "intended to keep alive their common law right consensually to vary the terms of the obligation"). The mere existence of such a right does not negative the statutory right of enforcement which a third party has under Contracts (Rights of Third Parties) Act 1999: this is clear from s.2 of that Act, below, paras 14–100—14–106.

[612] See *Richards v Delbridge* (1874) L.R. 18 Eq. 11.

[613] *Re Engelbach's Estate* [1924] 2 Ch. 348 (overruled on another point in *Beswick v Beswick* [1968] A.C. 58); *Re Clay's Policy of Assurance* [1937] 2 All E.R. 548; *Re Stapleton-Bretherton* [1941] Ch. 482; *Green v Russell* [1959] 1 Q.B. 28; *Re Cook's Settlement Trusts* [1965] Ch. 902; cf. *Cleaver v Mutual Reserve Fund Life Association* [1892] 1 Q.B. 147 at 152. Under Contracts (Rights of Third Parties) Act 1999, s.1(1)(b) and (2) (below, paras 14–092—14–093) it will suffice for the term to purport to confer a benefit on the third party, so long as it is not shown that the contracting parties did not intend the term to be enforceable by the third party. For the reasons given at para.14–002, above and paras 14–091, 14–116—14–118, below, however, it may be in the third party's interest to establish an intention to create a trust, so that he can rely on the trust exception rather than on the statutory right.

[614] See *Re Independent Air Travel Ltd, The Times*, May 20, 1961, where counsel, with the approval of the court, conceded this point.

[615] See *Harmer v Armstrong* [1934] Ch. 65, where the fact that the promisee was the third party's agent, and so under a fiduciary duty (below, para.16–095), helped to establish the necessary intention.

enforce the contract, even in the absence of a trust, under a statutory exception to the doctrine of privity.[616]

Effects of the trust. The third party is entitled to sue the promisor for the money or property which the promisor had promised to pay or to transfer to him,[617] but only where that is consistent with the terms of the promise.[618] He must join the promisee as a party to the action[619] since if this were not done the promisor might be sued a second time by the promisee. As this rule as to joinder of parties exists for the benefit of the promisor, it can be waived by him. The third party is (as a general rule[620]) also beneficially entitled to any money paid or payable under the contract; the promisee has no right to such money.[621] After *Beswick v Beswick*[622] the third party can generally keep money paid to him even if there is no trust.

14–086

There are exceptional cases in which the promisee may be entitled to the money even though there was a trust. In *Cleaver v Mutual Reserve Fund Life Association*[623] a husband insured his life for the benefit of his wife by a policy which, by statute, created a trust in her favour.[624] The wife was convicted of murdering the husband and was therefore disqualified from enforcing the trust. It was held that the executors of the husband were entitled to the policy moneys. It can be argued that the promisor should not have been held liable to pay the promisee when its promise was one to pay the third party.[625] But it seems that the destination of the payments was a matter of indifference to the insurance company and that there was nothing to show that the company would (even if there had been no conviction) have been in any way prejudiced by paying the husband's executors rather than the wife.[626] The actual decision may also turn on the interpretation of the statute creating the trust.[627]

Kinds of promises which can be held on trust. The trust device has so far been applied only to promises to pay money or to transfer property.[628] It is sometimes suggested that it might be applied to other kinds of promises, e.g. that

14–087

---

[616] *Swain v Law Society* [1983] 1 A.C. 598, esp. at 621.

[617] But where a trustee engages a professional adviser for the purpose of administering the trust, a claim for negligence against that adviser cannot be brought by the beneficiary since such a claim is not part of the trust property (though any damages recovered by the trustee would be): *Bradstock Trustee Services Ltd v Nabarro Nathanson* [1995] 1 W.L.R. 1405.

[618] e.g. not where a prohibition on assignment also prohibits a declaration of trust; cf. *Barbados Trust Co Ltd v Bank of Zambia* [2007] EWCA Civ 148; [2007] 1 Lloyd's Rep. 495; below, para.15–050.

[619] cf. *Performing Right Society Ltd v London Theatre of Varieties* [1924] A.C. 1; *Atlas Shipping Agency (UK) Ltd v Suisse Atlantique Société d'Armement* [1995] 2 Lloyd's Rep. 188 at 193; and below, para.15–007.

[620] i.e. subject to the exception stated at fn.623, below.

[621] *Re Flavell* (1883) 25 Ch.D. 89; *Re Gordon* [1940] Ch. 851; cf. *Paul v Constance* [1977] 1 W.L.R. 52.

[622] [1968] A.C. 58; see above, para.14–038.

[623] [1892] 1 Q.B. 147.

[624] Married Women's Property Act 1882, s.11; below, para.14–125.

[625] Ames, *Lectures*, at p.320; *Coulls v Bagot's Executor & Trustee Co Ltd* [1967] A.L.R. 385 at 410–411, per Windeyer J. (dissenting).

[626] cf. above, para.14–022.

[627] See [1892] 1 Q.B. 147 at 157.

[628] For a possible extension, see *Swain v Law Society* [1982] 1 A.C. 598, where a promise to provide indemnity insurance was evidently regarded as a possible subject-matter of a trust; though for the reason given at para.14–085 at fn.616, above, there was no intention to create a trust.

an employer might hold the benefit of an exemption clause on trust for his employee.[629] But the present judicial tendency is to restrict the scope of the trust device; and the suggestion has therefore been rejected on the ground that "the conception of a trust attaching to a benefit under an exclusion clause extends far beyond conventional limits".[630] Other techniques for making the benefit of such clauses available to third parties have been discussed earlier in this chapter.[631]

14–088   **Relation between trust device and privity.** The trust device has here been treated as an exception to the doctrine of privity,[632] of limited if uncertain scope. It has, however, been argued that where a third party was enabled by this device to enforce a contract made for his benefit there was, before the Judicature Act 1873, a conflict between the rules of equity and those of common law; that the rules of equity now prevail[633]; and that therefore the third party generally has a right of action.[634] But this view has not been accepted.[635] Even in equity the third party did not succeed merely because the contract was expressed to have been made for his benefit: he had to show, in addition, that a trust had been created in his favour.[636] And the argument that third parties were entitled to enforce contracts made for their benefit has been rejected in many cases after the Judicature Act 1873. Some of these were admittedly argued entirely on common law principles,[637] but in others the equitable argument was considered and rejected.[638]

(v) *Covenants in marriage settlements*

14–089   A covenant to settle after-acquired property contained in a marriage settlement can be enforced by all persons "within the marriage consideration", i.e. the spouses and issue of the marriage, but not by anyone else.[639] For example, it cannot be enforced by either spouse's next-of-kin, who are regarded as volunteers.[640]

---

[629] See the clause in *The Eurymedon* [1975] A.C. 154; above, para.14–063.

[630] *Southern Water Authority v Carey* [1985] 2 All E.R. 1077 at 1083.

[631] See above, paras 14–059—14–070.

[632] *Barbados Trust Co Ltd v Bank of Zambia* [2007] EWCA Civ 148; [2007] 1 Lloyd's Rep. 495 at [99].

[633] Judicature Act 1873, s.25(11); now Senior Courts Act 1981, s.49(1).

[634] *Drimmie v Davies* [1899] 1 I.R. 176 at 182 (the actual decision was that specific performance could be obtained by the executors of the promisee); Corbin 46 L.Q.R. 12 at p.36; cf. Langbein 105 Yale L.J. 625 at 646–647.

[635] *Re Schebsman* [1943] 1 Ch. 366 at 370, approved [1944] Ch. 83 at 104.

[636] *Colyear v Mulgrave* (1836) 2 Keen 81; the actual decision has been criticised, but the principle remains unimpaired. See *Page v Cox* (1852) 10 Hare 163; *Kekewich v Manning* (1851) 1 D.M. & G. 176.

[637] e.g. *Dunlop Pneumatic Tyre Co Ltd v Selfridge & Co Ltd* [1915] A.C. 847.

[638] *Re Burgess' Policy* (1915) 113 L.T. 443; *Re Sinclair's Life Policy* [1938] Ch. 799; *Re Schebsman* [1944] Ch. 83; *Green v Russell* [1959] 1 Q.B. 28.

[639] *Hill v Gomme* (1839) 5 My. & Cr. 250 at 254; *Re D'Angibau* (1880) 15 Ch.D. 228 at 242; *Re Plumptre's Marriage Settlement* [1910] 1 Ch. 609 at 619. These cases, apart from constituting an exception to the doctrine of privity, are also hard to reconcile with the modern definition of consideration: above, para.3–021.

[640] *Re Cook's Settlement Trusts* [1965] Ch. 902 at 915–918; Lee 85 L.Q.R. 213; Barton 91 L.Q.R. 326; Meagher and Lehane 92 L.Q.R. 427.

(b) Contracts (Rights of Third Parties) Act 1999[641]

(i) *Third party's right of enforcement*

"A general and wide-ranging exception to"[642] the doctrine of privity is created 14–090
by this Act, the central purpose of which is to enable a third party to acquire rights
under a contract[643] if, and to the extent that, the parties to the contract so intend.
Subsection 1(1) provides that a person who is not a party to the contract may in
his own right enforce a term of the contract in the two situations to be described
below. In discussing these situations and other provisions of the Act, it will be
convenient to refer to the person who makes the promise which the third party is
claiming to enforce (the promisor) as A, to the person to whom that promise is
made (the promisee) as B[644] and to the third party as C.

Express provision. Under subs.1(1)(a) of the 1999 Act, C can enforce a term 14–091
of the contract if "the contract expressly provides that he may": e.g. where a
contract contains a promise by A to B to pay £1,000 to C and also provides that
C is to be entitled to enforce the term which contains this promise. If the contract
contains such a provision, there is no further requirement (as there is under
subs.1(1)(b), to be discussed below) that the promise must have been made for C's
own benefit: e.g. he can enforce the term even though the payment is to be made
to him as trustee for D.[645] Express provisions in contracts of the kind just
described, to the effect that C is to be entitled to enforce the term containing the
promise made by A to B, have hitherto been rare, presumably because under the
doctrine of privity they would at common law have been ineffective.[646] The 1999
Act provides a new drafting device to enable the contracting parties to give effect
to their intention that C is to acquire an enforceable right against A. Apart from
the Act, a similar result can be achieved by creating a trust of A's promise in
favour of C[647] or by making him a joint promisee.[648] There is a procedural
advantage in making use of the machinery of subs.1(1)(a) in that, if C sues under
this provision, he will not (it seems) need to join B as a party to the action[649];
though the court could order B to be so joined where claims against A were made
by both B and C, or where A relied against C on a defence available to A against
B,[650] since in such cases B's presence before the court is likely to be "desirable ...
so that the court can resolve all the matters in dispute in the proceedings".[651] If
C does have a claim apart from the Act as the beneficiary of a trust of A's promise
or as joint promisee, it may, in spite of the need to join B to the action, be in C's

---

[641] Andrews 60 C.L.J. 353; Burrows [2000] L.M.C.L.Q. 540; MacMillan 63 M.L.R. 721; Stevens
120 L.Q.R. 292; Beale in Burrows and Peel (eds), *Contract Formation and Parties.*
[642] Law Commission Report on *Privity of Contract: Contracts for the Benefit of Third Parties,* Law
Com. No.242 (1996), hereafter "Report"; Merkin & Faber (eds), *Privity—the Impact of the Contracts
(Rights of Third Parties) Act 1999.*
[643] In *Prudential Assurance Co Ltd v Ayres* [2007] EWHC 775 (Ch); [2007] 3 All ER 946, no
argument was made that the Act did not apply to a supplemental *deed* (appeal allowed without
consideration of the Act: [2008] EWCA Civ 52; [2008] 1 All ER 1266).
[644] cf. the definitions of "promisor" and "promisee" in s.1(7) of the 1999 Act.
[645] Report, para.7.5.
[646] As in *Tweddle v Atkinson* (1861) 1 B. & S. 393; above, para.14–016.
[647] See above, para.14–081.
[648] See *McEvoy v Belfast Banking Co* [1935] A.C. 24; above, para.13–034.
[649] This appears to follow from the words "in his own right" in subs.1(1); cf. Report, para.14.3.
[650] Under s.3 of the 1999 Act: see below, para.14–108.
[651] CPR, r.19.2(2)(a); cf. above, para.13–006.

interest to pursue that claim since it would not be subject to other provisions of the Act which may restrict his rights under it: e.g. to those relating to the rescission or variation of the contract between A and B, or to defences available to A against B.[652]

Section 1(1)(a) is also likely to apply to terms such as Himalaya clauses,[653] by which A promises B that exemptions from or limitations of liability contained in a contract between A and B shall be available for the benefit of C, who typically will be an employee, agent or sub-contractor employed by B for the purpose of performing some or all of B's obligations under the contract. This follows from subs.1(6) of the 1999 Act, by which references to C's "enforcing" a term which "excludes or limits liability"[654] are to be "construed as references to his availing himself of the exclusion or limitation". Words in the contract to the effect that C is to be protected by the exemption or limitation clause therefore amount in themselves to an express provision that C may enforce the clause[655]; no further words will be necessary. C's protection under the Act will, however, be based on a theory different from that which accounts for the effectiveness of Himalaya clauses at common law. The common law theory is that such clauses, and the conduct of the relevant parties, can give rise to a separate or collateral contract between A and C.[656] Under the Act, by contrast, C enforces a term of a contract to which he is *not* a party.[657] It follows that the agency requirements which exist at common law[658] are irrelevant for the purposes of the Act. On the other hand, under the Act C's right to "enforce" a Himalaya clause is subject to the provisions of the Act[659] while at common law the operation of such a clause is subject only to the common law rules discussed earlier in this chapter[660]; and if C wishes to rely on his common law rights, in preference to those under the Act, it is open to him to do so.[661] For these (among other[662]) reasons, what may be called the old law relating to Himalaya clauses retains a considerable degree of practical importance, so that it would not be safe to rely exclusively on the simpler forms of words that can protect third parties under the Act.

14–092   **Term conferring benefit on third party.** Under subs.1(1)(b) of the 1999 Act, C may enforce a term of the contract if "the term purports to confer a benefit on him"; but his right to do so in such a case is subject to subs.1(2), by which C has no such right "if on a proper construction of the contract it appears that [A and B] did not intend the term to be enforceable by" C. These will probably be the

---

[652] See ss.2 and 3 (below, paras 14–100—14–112) and s.7(1) of the Act (below, para.14–116). For the effect on one co-promisee of a defence available against, or of a release granted by, another, see above, paras 13–011—13–012.

[653] See above, para.14–062. For the effect of the Act on such clauses, see further *Carver on Bills of Lading* (2nd edn), paras 7.073 to 7.079.

[654] This phrase would not include *other* terms in the contract on which C might wish to rely: e.g. not choice of forum clauses: see Report, para.14.9; cf. at common law, *The Mahkutai* [1996] A.C. 650; above, para.14–066.

[655] Report, para.7.10.

[656] See above, para.14–063.

[657] s.1(1) ("a person who is not a party . . . ").

[658] See above, para.14–065.

[659] s.1(1); see especially ss.2 and 3; below paras 14–100—14–112.

[660] See above, paras 14–068—14–070.

[661] 1999 Act, s.7(1).

[662] See fn.654, above.

most significant provisions of the 1999 Act and their interpretation is likely to give rise to a number of difficulties. It seems that a "benefit" within subs.1(1)(b) can include any performance due under the contract between A and B: thus it can include a payment of money, a transfer of property, or the rendering of a service; it can also (by virtue of subs.1(6)) include the benefit of an exemption or limitation clause. The term must, moreover, purport to *confer* the benefit on C, so that it is not enough for C to show that he would happen to benefit from its performance.[663] The question whether the term purports to confer a benefit on C is one of construction.[664] For example, a term requiring payment to be made by A to B by making payment into C's account might result in a benefit to C, e.g. by allowing him to deduct his commission before accounting to B, but the term itself does not purport to confer a benefit on C.[665]

Rebutting the presumption created under section 1(1)(b). A further and different question of construction arises (with regard to the intention of A and B) under subs.1(2) (quoted above) and it appears from the wording of this subsection that the burden of proof under it rests on A, or (in other words) that if the term purports to confer a benefit on C, then there is a rebuttable presumption that the term is intended by A and B to be enforceable by C.[666] To rebut the presumption, A must (in the words of subs.1(2)) show that "the parties" did not intend the term to be enforceable by C. This seems to mean that it is not enough for A to show that he did not so intend; he must show that neither he nor B had this intention. Nor is the presumption rebutted merely because in the contract A and B had reserved the right to rescind or vary the contract: this follows from the provisions with regard to such rescission or variation made in s.2 of the Act and discussed below.[667] A standard clause which states that *the agreement* is not "intended to benefit or be enforceable by" anyone other than the parties may be insufficient to rebut the presumption created by a particular *term* which contains an undertaking in favour of the third party personally.[668] As the question of intention put in subs.1(2) is there described as one of construction, it seems that the evidence which A will be allowed to adduce for this purpose will, in general, be limited by the rules which restrict the types of evidence admissible on other questions of construction, and what the courts must establish is the objective intention of the parties.[669]

It seems that it will not be sufficient to rebut the presumption created under s.1(1)(b) for A to point to another means by which the term might be enforced by, or on behalf of, C. In the *Nisshin Shipping*[670] case a term for the payment of commission to a shipbroker was included in the charterparty which the broker had

14–093

---

[663] *Dolphin Maritime & Aviation Services Ltd v Sveriges Angfartygs Assurans Forening* [2009] EWHC 716 (Comm); [2009] 2 Lloyd's Rep. 123 at [74].

[664] *The Laemthong Glory (No.2)* [2005] EWCA Civ 519; [2005] 1 Lloyd's Rep. 688, esp. at [40]; *Prudential Assurance Co Ltd v Ayres* [2007] EWHC 775 (Ch); [2007] 3 All ER 946 at [28] (appeal allowed without consideration of the Act: [2008] EWCA Civ 52; [2008] 1 All ER 1266).

[665] *Dolphin Maritime & Aviation Services Ltd v Sveriges Angfartygs Assurans Forening* [2009] EWHC 716 (Comm); [2009] 2 Lloyd's Rep. 123.

[666] Report, paras 7.5, 7.17; *Nisshin Shipping Co Ltd v Cleaves & Co Ltd* [2003] EWHC 2602; [2004] 1 Lloyd's Rep. 38 at [23].

[667] See below, paras 14–100—14–107. If, of course, A and B have the right to vary the contract they may be able to do so to the prejudice of any right of enforcement in favour of C: *Dolphin Maritime & Aviation Services Ltd v Sveriges Angfartygs Assurans Forening* above, fn.665 at [79].

[668] *Mentmore International Ltd v Abbey Healthcare (Festival) Ltd* [2010] EWCA Civ 761 at [33].

[669] See above, paras 6–021—6–024.

[670] *Nisshin Shipping Co Ltd v Cleaves & Co Ltd* [2003] EWHC 2602; [2004] 1 Lloyd's Rep. 38.

negotiated between the shipowners and the charterers. This is the normal practice and, in the past, a trust of the promise was found to have been created.[671] The existence of such a trust is unaffected by the Act,[672] but in the absence of any indication in the contract there was no evidence of the parties' intention that it should be the *only* means for enforcing the broker's right to payment.[673] Nor does the mere existence of a chain of contracts rebut the presumption that C is entitled to enforce a term direct against A, e.g. where A is under contract with B and B is under contract with C.[674] In some well-known situations, however, the commercial practice may be sufficient to rebut the presumption that C is entitled to enforce a term in a way which cuts across the legal framework customarily employed:[675] possible examples[676] are claims by a developer (C) against a sub-contractor (A) which attempt to bypass the developer's contract with the head-contractor (B),[677] and claims by a purchaser of goods (C) against a manufacturer (A) which attempt to bypass the purchaser's contract with the retailer (B).[678]

14–094   **Other illustrations.** There is not, as yet, a lot of case law on the application of the Act. It is tempting therefore to speculate how its provisions would apply to some of the leading cases in which the doctrine of privity was applied. To some extent, such an exercise is likely to be fruitless since the courts have not in the past directed their attention to the issues which will arise under the Act. In *Beswick v Beswick*,[679] for example, the contract no doubt purported to confer a benefit on C; but no finding of fact was made (because such a finding would have been irrelevant) as to the intention of A and B on the issue of legal enforceability by C: it is conceivable that A could succeed on this issue if, for example, he could show that A and B had, when the contract was made, instructed the solicitor who drafted it to do so in such a way as *not* to confer legally enforceable rights on C.[680] On the facts (if they now recurred) of a number of other cases, the position under the 1999 Act would, it is submitted, be clearer. Thus in the "disappointed beneficiary" cases such as *White v Jones*[681] C would not get a right under the Act against A, the negligent solicitor, since the terms of the solicitor's retainer (even if they identified C[682]) would not purport to confer a benefit on C: the intended benefit was to come, not from A, but from B.[683] It is similarly unlikely that cases

---

[671] *Les Affréteurs Réunis, SA v Leopold Walford (London) Ltd* [1919] A.C. 801; above, para.14–081.

[672] s.7(1).

[673] [2004] 1 Lloyd's Rep. 38 at [31].

[674] *The Laemthong Glory (No.2)* [2005] EWCA Civ 519; [2005] 1 Lloyd's Rep. 688 at [53].

[675] In *Dolphin Maritime & Aviation Services Ltd v Sveriges Angfartygs Assurans Forening* above, fn.665, *if* the term requiring payment to B to be made via C had raised the presumption created by s.1(1)(b) (see text to fn.665), it would have been rebutted; on a proper construction of the contract, it was (at [84]) "in the same category as that of A who agrees to pay B at B's bankers, C".

[676] Report, para.7.18.

[677] The expectation is probably still that the developer must negotiate for a direct right against the sub-contractor under a collateral warranty: see below, para.14–049.

[678] The purchaser may have a direct right under a manufacturer's guarantee, the binding effect of which has been put beyond any doubt for consumers by Sale and Supply of Goods to Consumers Regulations 2002 (SI 2002/3045), reg.15; above, para.14–006.

[679] [1968] A.C. 58; above, para.14–017.

[680] It would have been easy for the solicitor to have drafted the contract so as to make it enforceable by C: e.g. by expressly making B trustee for C (above, para.14–082) or by making C a joint promisee with B (above, paras 13–032—13–034). We do not know whether the solicitor explained these possibilities to A and B or whether he received any instructions from them on the point.

[681] [1995] 2 A.C. 207; above, para.14–052.

[682] See below, para.14–095.

[683] Report, para.7.25.

such as the *Junior Books* case,[684] in which A is a sub-contractor employed by B to enable B to perform his contract with C, would be covered, even if the sub-contract named C, either because the purpose of such a sub-contract would prima facie be to regulate the relations between A and B rather than to confer a benefit on C, or any presumption created by s.1(1)(b) would be rebutted by the legal framework adopted by the parties.[685] Cases such as the *Linden Gardens* case[686] would likewise not be affected by s.1 of the Act, since the mere possibility that land on which work is done by a building contractor might be transferred to purchasers from the owner would not be sufficient to show that the term relating to the quality of the work purported to "confer a benefit" on such purchasers; nor would the contract, without more, adequately "identify"[687] such purchasers as third parties for the purpose of subs.1(1)(b). Nor, in circumstances such as those in the *Panatown* case,[688] would the mere fact that the building contractor (A) knew that the property on which he was working in pursuance of his contract with B belonged to someone other than B suffice to show that a benefit was to be conferred on that other person (C): the answer to the question whether the work was being done for the benefit of C or of B would depend on the contractual relations between B and C, of the details of which A might be wholly unaware. In the "family holiday" cases[689] the outcome under the Act would depend on the nature of the transaction. If the person making the booking supplied the names of other members of the family when the contract was made, those other members would probably acquire rights under subs.1(1); but no such rights are likely to be acquired if a person simply rented a holiday cottage without giving any information as to the number or names of the persons with whom he proposed to share the accommodation. In many of the situations which have here been discussed, the question whether the contract purports to confer a benefit on C will be closely related to the question, to be discussed in the following paragraph, whether C is adequately "identified" in the contract between A and B.

Identification of third party. Under subs.1(3) of the 1999 Act, it is a **14–095** requirement of C's right to enforce A's promise that C must have been "*expressly identified*" in the contract between A and B, either "by name, as a member of a class or as answering a particular description";[690] it follows from this requirement that C cannot rely for the purpose of subs.1(1) on the argument that the contract refers to him by implication, or by a process of construction.[691] So long as C is identified in accordance with these requirements, there is no need for C to be in existence when the contract was made: e.g. a promise in favour of an unborn child, a future spouse or an unformed company could be enforced by[692] such a third

---

[684] [1983] 1 A.C. 520; above, para.14–049.

[685] See above, para.14–093.

[686] [1994] 1 A.C. 85; above, para.14–025.

[687] Within subs.1(3), below.

[688] *Alfred McAlpine Construction Ltd v Panatown Ltd* [2001] 1 A.C. 518; above, para.14–029.

[689] See above, para.14–023.

[690] *Prudential Assurance Co Ltd v Ayres*, above fn.664 ('any previous tenant'); *Crowson v HSBC Insurance Brokers Ltd* [2010] Lloyd's Rep. I.R. 441 at [12] (director of company).

[691] *Avraamides v Colwill* [2006] EWCA Civ 1533; [2006] N.P.C. 120 at [19].

[692] A company which did not at the time of the contract exist could, on coming into existence, by virtue of subs.1(3) enforce a term made for its benefit (within subs.1(2)); but the rules relating to contracts made on behalf of such a company stated at para.16–072, below would continue to govern the extent to which such a company could be *bound* by a contract made on its behalf: Report, paras 8.9 to 8.16.

party when it came into existence. The requirements of subs.1(3) are additional to those of subss.1(1) and 1(2), but very often the question of whether C has been identified will be closely related to the question of whether it was the parties' intention to entitle C to enforce a term of the contract. For example, on the facts of the *Midland Silicones*[693] case, C would not be able to enforce the limitation clause since the contract between A and B contained no express reference to C (whether by name, by description or as a member of a class): C would not have been identified and this very fact would indicate that the contract did not purport to confer a benefit on him under subs.1(1)(b). Where a contract is contained in or evidenced by a bill of lading, it is now likely to contain a Himalaya clause,[694] which would be likely adequately to identify C and confer a right on him to "enforce"[695] the limitation clause under subss.1(1)(b) and 1(2). The question whether C is identified in such a way as to give him an enforceable right may itself raise a question of construction: e.g. where the words of the term are literally adequate to identify C but the term does not purport (or A and B do not intend) to confer a benefit on him.[696]

14–096   **Conditional benefit.** The 1999 Act does not affect the principle that C cannot be bound by a contract between A and B. However, the effect of subs.1(4) is that the term *benefiting* C can only be enforced "subject to and in accordance with any other relevant terms of the contract". In this sense, C may have to comply with the burden of certain terms as a condition to acquiring the benefit of others, but the burden cannot be imposed on him independently of the benefit to which it is attached, e.g. if A, under a contract with B, grants a right of way over his land to C subject to C keeping it in repair, A may withdraw the right of way if C fails to keep it in repair, but C cannot be sued for breach of the repairing obligation.[697]

14–097   **Remedies.** Where C has a right to enforce a term of the contract by virtue of subs.1(1) of the 1999 Act, he has this right in spite of the fact that he is not a party to the contract: the Act does not, in general, adopt the technique of transferring rights from B to C or of treating C as having acquired rights by means of the fiction that he has become a party to the contract.[698] It does, however, make use of such a fiction so far as C's *remedies* are concerned.[699] Subsection 1(5) provides that

> "For the purpose of exercising his right to enforce a term of the contract, there shall be available to the third party any remedy that would have been available to him in an action for breach of contract if he had been a party to

---

[693] [1962] A.C. 446; above, para.14–060.

[694] See above, para.14–061.

[695] See s.1(6); above, para.14–091.

[696] See the argument of counsel to this effect, which was rejected by the Court of Appeal, in *The Laemthong Glory (No.2)* [2005] EWCA Civ 519; [2005] 1 Lloyd's Rep. 688 at [37]–[48]. A similar argument might have been raised on the facts in *Elder, Dempster* [1924] A.C. 522, above, para.14–059; cf. *Broughton v Capital Quality Ltd* [2008] EWHC 3457 (QB) at [27]–[28].

[697] Report, para.10.26.

[698] 1999 Act, s.7(4). This refers only to other *legislation*, but the principle that C is not to be treated as a party to the contract appears also to apply for the purpose of rules of common law: see below at fn.710.

[699] Also for a number of other purposes relating to defences available to A against C: see s.3(4) and (6); below, paras 14–108—14–112; and to arbitration provisions: see s.8; below, para.14–098.

the contract (and the rules relating to damages, injunctions, specific performance and other relief shall apply accordingly)".

It follows from this provision that C can invoke the same kinds of judicial remedies as would be available to B if no third party were involved, and that C can recover damages for loss of bargain (or "expectation" loss[700]) even though the bargain was made, not with him, but with B. It also follows that the same principles which would limit B's remedies in a two-party case apply to an action brought by C: e.g. the principles of remoteness[701] and mitigation[702] and those which restrict the availability of specific relief.[703] The application of these principles may, however, lead to different practical results where the action is brought by C from those which would follow from them in an action brought by B. For example, in an action brought by C, the test of remoteness would be whether it was C's (not B's) loss which A ought reasonably have contemplated; the principles of mitigation would require the court to ask what steps C (not B) ought reasonably have taken to mitigate his loss; and the question whether specific relief should be refused on account of the conduct of the claimant could receive one answer where the action was brought by C and another if it were brought by B.

Arbitration agreements. The contract containing the term which C seeks to enforce against A may also contain an arbitration clause amounting to a written arbitration agreement within the Arbitration Act 1996.[704] The 1999 Act provides that, if C seeks to enforce the former term against A, then C is to be treated as a party to the arbitration agreement.[705] It follows that, if C attempted to enforce that term *by action*, A could obtain a stay of that action under the 1996 Act and so secure compliance by C with the arbitration agreement.[706] A contract between A and B may also provide that C is to be entitled to submit to arbitration some dispute between himself and A *other* than one concerning the enforcement by C against A of one of the other terms of the contract. Such an arbitration provision cannot compel C to resort to arbitration of (for example) a tort claim between himself and A.[707] But if the provision is a term which C is entitled to enforce under s.1 of the 1999 Act and is also a written arbitration agreement within the Arbitration Act 1996 and C *chooses* to submit the dispute with A to arbitration, then C is treated for the purpose of the 1996 Act as a party to the arbitration agreement so that the arbitration proceedings will be governed by that Act.[708]

14–098

No requirement of consideration moving from third party. The 1999 Act does not impose any requirement that consideration for A's promise must move

14–099

---

[700] See below, para.20–022.
[701] See below, para.20–099.
[702] See below, para.20–115.
[703] See below, para.21–017; and cf. below, para.21–001. Report, paras 3.32, 3.33.
[704] See above, para.11–052.
[705] 1999 Act, s.8(1). Some difficulty is created in this regard by the wording "is subject to a term providing for" arbitration. If the arbitration agreement refers only to A and B, and not C, C will nonetheless be "subject to" it because he occupies a position equivalent to that of a statutory assignee: *Nisshin Shipping Co Ltd v Cleaves & Co Ltd* [2003] EWHC 2602; [2004] 1 Lloyd's Rep. 38 at [42].
[706] This is a further example of a "conditional benefit": see above, para.14–096.
[707] Since it would represent the imposition of a "pure burden" rather than the enforcement of a conditional benefit: above, para.14–096.
[708] 1999 Act, s.8(2).

from C. It does not contain any express provision to this effect[709]; but the consequence follows from the fact that the Act gives C the right to enforce the term and is further supported by the general principle that C is not to be treated as a party to the contract between A and B.[710] Since the promise in contracts of the kind in question is made to B, the fact that C need not provide any consideration for it is not strictly an exception to the rule that consideration must move *from the promisee*, but it can be regarded as a quasi-exception to that rule in the sense that C is a person in whose favour a promise is made and who can enforce it even though he may be no more than a gratuitous beneficiary.

(ii) *Right to rescind or vary the contract*

14–100   Under the judge-made rules relating to contracts for the benefit of third parties, one objection to the creation of such rights has been that it would deprive the contracting parties of their right to rescind or vary the contract by mutual consent.[711] The 1999 Act deals with this problem by means of a compromise: it specifies the circumstances in which A and B prima facie lose this right, while it at the same time enables them so to draw up their contract so as to retain the right, or to change the prima facie rules laid down in the Act which specify when it is lost.

14–101   **General rule: C's consent required.** The general rule, stated in subs.2(1) of the 1999 Act, is that, once C has acquired the right to enforce a term of the contract between A and B "under section 1", then, if one of the circumstances to be described below has arisen, A and B may not, without C's consent, by agreement rescind or vary the contract, or vary it so as to "extinguish or alter" C's entitlement. Rescission calls for no further comment here; but with regard to variation it should be noted that A and B are, under the general rule, precluded from varying the contract not only so as to *extinguish* but also *so as to alter* C's rights. An alteration may of course operate, not only to C's prejudice, but also to his advantage: e.g. where it purports to increase payments to be made to C under the term in question. Such a variation is unlikely to give rise to any problems between A and C, since C will presumably consent to it as soon as he hears of it. But the argument that C is entitled to enforce a term of a contract between A and B can also give rise to problems between one of these parties and outside interests: e.g. creditors of B in the event of B's insolvency.[712] Such persons may seek to invoke subs.2(1) where the variation increases C's rights but where, on the crucial date for the assertion of their rights, C has either not yet acquired any knowledge of the variation or has not yet made any communication to A or done any other act from which his assent to the variation can be inferred.

14–102   **Exception: C's assent to the term.** The first of the circumstances in which A and B may not, without C's consent, agree to rescind the contract, or vary it in the ways described above, arises where C has communicated his assent to the term

---

[709] Report, para. 6.8, fn.8.
[710] See above, at fn.698.
[711] This has been one reason for the restrictions on the scope of the equitable exception to the doctrine of privity by way of trusts of promises: above, para.14–083.
[712] As, for example, in *Re Schebsman* [1944] Ch. 83; above, para.14–082.

to A[713]; communication to B does not suffice for this purpose.[714] C must have communicated his assent before A and B purport to vary or rescind the contract.[715] The assent may be by words or conduct[716]; and if it is "sent" to A by post or other means, it is not regarded as communicated to him "until received by him".[717] In other words, the "posting" rule, as developed in cases of contract formation[718] does not apply in the present context. "Sent" here seems to refer to some act done by C in order to communicate *words* of assent to A. The rule relating to an assent "sent" to A by post or other means is negative in nature: it states that the assent is not communicated to A until received by him. It thus leaves open the question whether an assent which has been so sent can take effect before it has actually come to A's notice: e.g. where it has been delivered to his address but not yet been read by him. If the overriding requirement is one of communication, it may not be satisfied in such a case. The expression "sent" also does not seem to be appropriate to refer to an assent by *conduct*; but it seems that such an assent must come to A's notice: this seems to follow from the general requirement that C's assent must be "communicated"[719] to A. No formality (such as writing) is required even for an assent in words,[720] so that an oral communication suffices.

Exception: C's reliance. The right to rescind or vary the contract is also   **14–103** barred where A is aware of C's having relied on the term,[721] or where A could reasonably have foreseen such reliance and it has actually taken place.[722] It would seem that, in such cases, C may be entitled, not merely to the promised performance, but also to damages in respect of his reliance loss: e.g. where he has travelled to the place specified in the contract for the receipt by him of the promised performance. This follows from the rule laid down by the 1999 Act with respect to C's remedies[723]; it also follows from this rule that C could not claim under both heads to the extent to which such a combination of claims would result in double recovery or in his being placed in a better position than that in which he would have been if A had performed his promise in accordance with its original terms.[724]

Consequences of attempted rescission or variation without C's consent.   **14–104** The general rule in subs.2(1) is that A and B "may not" by agreement rescind the contract, or vary it in the ways described above, without C's consent. The most obvious consequence of this provision is that a purported rescission or variation

---

[713] s.2(1)(a).

[714] This follows from the words "to the promisor" in s.2(1)(a).

[715] *Precis (521) v William Mercer Ltd* [2005] EWCA Civ 114; [2005] P.N.L.R. 28 at [30] (where the benefit to C is in the form of an exemption clause, there is no further requirement on C to communicate his assent before committing the acts in relation to which the contract between A and B excluded liability).

[716] s.2(2)(a).

[717] s.2(2)(b).

[718] See above, para.2–029.

[719] s.2(1)(a).

[720] Contrast Law of Property Act 1925, s.136(1) (below, para.15–010), requiring written notice of an assignment.

[721] s.2(1)(b).

[722] s.2(1)(c).

[723] s.1(5); above, para.14–097.

[724] e.g. where it would have been necessary for C to incur the reliance expenditure in order to secure the benefit—perhaps by travelling to the place where it was to be conferred. cf. below, para.20–035.

without C's consent is simply *ineffective*, so that C can, in spite of it, enforce the term in question *against A*. But such enforcement may, because of the rescission, become a practical impossibility (e.g. because A has in consequence of the rescission put it out of his power to perform); and it is arguable that the purported rescission is also *wrongful* so as to give C a remedy in damages *against B*, perhaps on the analogy of liability for wrongful interference with contractual rights.[725] This possibility could have practical significance in the event of A's insolvency.

14–105 **Contract conferring choices on promisee.** Subsection 2(1) of the 1999 Act deals with the situation in which C has become entitled to enforce a term of the contract "under section 1" and A and B then attempt by agreement to rescind or vary the contract. This situation must be distinguished from that in which A promises B to perform in favour of C *or as B shall direct*. If, in such a case, B directs A to perform in favour of D (or of B himself) the contract is not varied. On the contrary, it is performed in accordance with its original terms, under which B has a choice as to the person to whom performance is to be rendered. The case therefore does not fall within subs.2(1), so that the requirement of C's consent, as there stated, does not apply.[726] Another way of explaining this conclusion is to say that, in the case put, the mere making of the promise was not intended to confer an indefeasible right on C; for the fact that B had power to divert the benefit away from C would indicate that A and B did not at this stage intend[727] the term to be enforceable by C if B exercised that power. A term of the present kind might, however, also limit B's power to divert the benefit away from C: e.g. by providing that the power was to be exercisable only for a specified period. After the end of the period, C could no longer be deprived of the benefit of A's promise by the unilateral act of B since the consent of A and B would then as a matter of common law be necessary to vary the contract; and any *such* variation would then be subject to the requirement of C's consent under subs.2(1).

14–106 **Contrary provision in the contract.** The general requirement of C's consent, imposed by subs.2(1), may be displaced by an express term of the contract. Two possibilities are envisaged. The first, stated in subs.2(3)(a), is for such an express term to state that A and B may by agreement rescind or vary the contract without the consent of C. A and B can then rescind or vary the contract by agreement in spite of the fact that C has acquired a right under subs.1(1) and in spite of the fact that the circumstances specified in subs.2(1) have occurred: that is, even after communication of assent by C to A, or after reliance by C of which A is aware or which he could reasonably have been expected to foresee. It is not entirely clear whether it is enough for the express term to provide that A and B may by agreement rescind or vary the contract or whether it must go on to say in so many words that they may do so without the consent of C; but to be sure of achieving the desired result, A and B would be well advised to use the latter form of words.

The second possibility, stated in subs.2(3)(b), is for the express term to provide that the consent of C is required in circumstances other than those specified in subs.2(1). For example, the term might provide that such consent was required only for a specified period or that it must be given in a specified form (e.g. by

---

[725] See below, para.14–135.
[726] cf. Report, para.10.30.
[727] Within s.1(2).

registered letter). Again effect would be given to such provisions, so that in the first of our two examples C's consent would no longer be needed (even after the circumstances described in subs.2(1) had occurred) after the end of the period; and in the second it would be ineffective if not given in the specified form.

Judicial discretion to dispense with consent. Subsection 2(4) gives the   **14–107** court power, on the application of A and B, to dispense with the requirement of C's consent to a rescission or variation of the contract in two situations: (a) where C's consent cannot be obtained because "his whereabouts cannot reasonably be ascertained"; or (b) where he is mentally incapable of giving his consent.[728] On a similar principle, the court has under subs.2(5) the same power where it is alleged that C's consent is required because A could reasonably have foreseen that C would rely on the term[729] but it cannot reasonably be ascertained whether he has in fact relied on it. Where the court under these provisions dispenses with C's consent, it may order compensation to be paid to him[730]; such an order may presumably be made against either A or B or both of them.

(iii) *Promisor's defences against third party*

Section 3 of the 1999 Act contains an elaborate set of provisions which specify   **14–108** matters on which A can rely by way of defence, set-off or counterclaim against C in an action by C for the enforcement, "in reliance on section 1",[731] of a term of the contract between A and B.

General principle. The starting principle, stated in subs.3(2), is that A can   **14–109** rely by way of defence or set-off on any matter that "arises from or in connection with the contract [between A and B] and is relevant to the term" and would have been available to A if the proceedings (to enforce the term) had been brought by B. Under this principle, A could, for example, rely against C on a valid exemption clause in the contract between A and B[732]; and on the fact that the contract was void for mistake or voidable for misrepresentation,[733] or that it had been frustrated or that A was justified in refusing to perform it on account of B's repudiatory breach.

Contrary provision. This general principle can, however, be excluded by a   **14–110** contrary provision in the contract: i.e. by a term in the contract between A and B that A is not to be entitled to rely on such matters against C[734]; though where the contract between A and B was wholly void such a term would appear to be of no more effect than the rest of the purported contract. The general principle can, conversely, be extended by an express term in the contract. Subsection 3(3) provides that A can (in addition to the matters referred to in subs.3(2)) rely by way

---

[728] The Mental Capacity Act 2005 sets out a test of mental incapacity "for the purposes of the Act" (s.2(1)) and, as yet, no consequential amendment has been made to s.2(4)(b) of the 1999 Act; in the absence of any such amendment it is submitted, nonetheless, that the test in the 2005 Act should be applied: above, para.12–053.

[729] See s.2(1)(c).

[730] s.2(6).

[731] s.3(1).

[732] cf. Report, para.10.31.

[733] *Moody v Condor Ins Ltd* [2006] EWHC 100; [2006] 1 W.L.R. 1847 at [30].

[734] s.3(5).

of defence or set-off against C on any matter if "an express term of the contract provides for it to be available to him in proceedings brought by" C and it would have been so available to A in proceedings brought by B. Under this provision, A could rely against C on debts owed by B to A even though the debts arose out of other transactions, if the contract containing the term which C was seeking to enforce contained an express term that A was to be entitled to rely on those debts also against C.

14–111   **Defences against C only.** There is the further possibility that A may have defences or counterclaims against C which he would not have against B: e.g. where A had been induced to enter into the contract by C's misrepresentation, or where C was indebted to A under another transaction. Subsection 3(4) enables A to rely on such matters against C if they could have been so relied on if C had been a party to the contract; though this rule, like the general principle stated in subs.3(2), can be modified or excluded by an express term of the contract between A and B.[735]

14–112   **Reliance on exemption clauses.** A rule analogous to the general principle of subs.3(2) applies where the "enforcement" of the term by C takes the form of his availing himself of an exemption or limitation clause in his favour in the contract between A and B.[736] Subsection 3(6) provides that C cannot in this way "enforce" the term if he could not have done so, had he been a party to the contract. This restriction on C's right to enforce the term would, for example, apply if, by reason of the Unfair Contract Terms Act 1977[737] the clause had been invalid or if it had not satisfied the requirement of reasonableness as imposed by that Act; or if C was guilty of a fraud on A and so could not have relied on the term (even though B might have been able to do so) by reason of the common law rule that an exemption clause does not protect a party from liability for his own fraud.[738]

(iv) *Exceptions to third party's entitlement*

14–113   A number of situations which prima facie fall within s.1 of the 1999 Act are excepted by s.6 from the operation of s.1. These exceptions fall into two groups. In cases which fall within the first group, C has, or can acquire, rights under the contract between A and B by virtue of some other rule of law; and the purpose of excepting these cases from the operation of s.1 is to preserve the conditions under which C's rights arise or may arise under those other rules of law. In cases which fall within the second group, by contrast, C has prima facie no rights under other rules of law; and the purpose of excepting these cases from the operation of s.1 is to preserve in them the general rule of common law by which C acquires no rights under the contract between A and B. Such cases, in other words, continue to be governed by the common law doctrine of privity, subject to any limitations on its scope and to any exceptions to it that may exist at common law or under other legislation.

---

[735] s.3(5) applies to subs.3(4) as well as to subs.3(2).
[736] See s.1(6); above, para.14–091.
[737] See above, para.7–050 et seq.; Report, para.10.22.
[738] See above, para.7–042.

Where C can acquire rights under some other rule of law. The first of the   **14–114**
above group of exceptions includes contracts on bills of exchange, promissory
notes and other negotiable instruments[739]: third parties can acquire rights under
such contracts under the rules relating to negotiability, discussed elsewhere in this
book, and it is not the purpose of the 1999 Act to extend these rights.[740] It also
includes contracts for the carriage of goods by sea which are governed by the
Carriage of Goods by Sea Act 1992, and corresponding electronic transactions to
which that Act may be applied by Order.[741] The carefully regulated scheme of the
1992 Act[742] for the acquisition of rights under such contracts by third parties
(such as transferees of bills of lading) would be seriously disrupted if such third
parties could acquire rights under the 1999 Act in circumstances in which no such
rights would be acquired under the 1992 Act. The same is (mutatis mutandis) true
of contracts for the international carriage of goods by rail, road and air, which are
governed by international Conventions having the force of law in the UK,[743] so
that these contracts are likewise excepted from the operation of s.1 of the 1999
Act.[744] The exception is, however, in turn, subject to an exception: C is not
precluded from taking the benefit of an exemption or limitation clause in a
contract for the carriage of goods governed by the 1992 Act or by the international
Conventions referred to above merely because such legislation applies to the
contract.[745] Before the 1999 Act, C could in many cases take the benefit of an
exemption or limitation clause in the contract of carriage, e.g. where that contract
contained a Himalaya clause.[746] The legal reasoning on which this result was based
was that a separate or collateral contract arose by virtue of such a clause between
A and C.[747] Since C is a *party* to this contract, his right to "enforce" it does not
depend (in the words of the present exception) on any "reliance on . . . section"
1.[748] The effectiveness of Himalaya clauses would therefore not be directly
affected by the present exception[749] to a *third party's* entitlement under s.1 to
"enforce" an exemption or limitation clause. But one of the objects of the 1999 Act
appears to have been to simplify the drafting of Himalaya clauses and to remove
obstacles to their efficacy which might be encountered in establishing the separate
contract between A and C[750]; and it is for this reason that the present exception
to the operation of s.1 does not apply to exemption and limitation clauses in
contracts of carriage which, for other purposes, fall within that exception.

Where C acquires no rights. The second of the groups of exceptions   **14–115**
described above includes the contract which binds a company and its members on
the terms of the company's constitution, by virtue of s.33 of the Companies Act
2006. The purpose of this exception is presumably to preserve the established

---

[739] s.6(1).
[740] See below, para.15–046; Report, para.12.16.
[741] s.6(5).
[742] For details of this scheme, see *Carver on Bills of Lading* (2nd edn), paras 5–012 et seq.
[743] See *Chitty on Contracts* (30th edn), Vol.II, Chs 35 and 36.
[744] ss.6(5)(b) and 8.
[745] s.6(5), "tailpiece".
[746] See above, para.14–062.
[747] See above, para.14–063.
[748] s.1(1) confers a right of enforcement only on a "person who is *not* a party" to the contract.
[749] i.e. that contained in s.6(5) of the 1999 Act.
[750] See Report, paras 2.35, 12.10; for the complexity of the drafting of Himalaya clauses and the
difficulties which arise, or are thought to arise, in satisfying the common law requirement of a separate
contract between A and C, see above, paras 14–062—14–068.

limitations of the scope of this "statutory contract"[751]: e.g. the rule that this contract confers no rights on a director of the company as such.[752] The second group also includes contracts of employment and certain analogous contracts to the extent that such a contract will not give the employer's customer any right under s.1 of the 1999 Act to enforce any term of the contract against the employee.[753]

(v) *Third party's other rights unaffected*

14–116   **Rights or remedies available apart from the 1999 Act.** Subsection 7(1) of the 1999 Act provides that "Section 1 does not affect any right or remedy of a third party that exists or is available apart from this Act". It follows that C will continue, after the coming into force of the Act, to be able to enforce rights and to rely on defences arising under a contract between A and B, if before then he could have done so under exceptions to the doctrine of privity established at common law, in equity or under other legislation, or if he could have done so because the case fell outside the scope of the doctrine of privity of contract: these possibilities are discussed elsewhere in this chapter.[754] C will, for example, continue to be able to enforce a promise made by A to B if there is a trust of the promise in his favour[755]; he will be able to rely on Himalaya clauses and on other common law and statutory rules under which the benefit of an exemption clause in a contract between A and B is available to him[756]; and he will continue to be able to enforce collateral contracts between himself and A.[757] Indeed, in some such cases the person seeking to enforce the term is not truly a "third party" within the 1999 Act.[758] The whole point of the collateral contract device is to establish a direct contractual relationship between the parties that have here been called A and C; and the legal basis for the efficacy of Himalaya clauses is similarly that a contract of some kind comes into existence between A and C, though this is not the same as "the contract" (i.e. that between A and B) containing the term which C is seeking to enforce.[759] Subsection 7(1) also preserves any rights which C may have to sue A in tort in respect of loss suffered by C in consequence of A's breach of his contract with B; we have seen that in such cases C will often have no rights under the 1999 Act.[760] The subsection also leaves it open to the courts to develop new exceptions at common law to the doctrine of privity of contract.[761]

14–117   **Scope of the saving in subsection 7(1).** Although subs.7(1) in terms states only that "Section 1" does not affect other rights and remedies available to C, it follows from the structure of the 1999 Act that many of its other provisions will likewise not apply where C's rights against A arise apart from the Act. Of

---

[751] *Soden v British & Commonwealth Holdings* [1998] A.C. 298 at 323.
[752] See above, para.14–012.
[753] s.6(3) and (4).
[754] See above, para.14–045 et seq.; below, para.14–123 et seq.
[755] See above, para.14–081 et seq., but this alone will not affect his right to enforce a term of the contract under the 1999 Act: *Nisshin Shipping Co Ltd v Cleaves & Co Ltd* [2003] EWHC 2602; [2004] 1 Lloyd's Rep. 38; see above, para.14–093.
[756] See above, para.14–061 et seq.
[757] See above, para.14–006 et seq.
[758] s.1(1) ("not a party ... ").
[759] See para.14–066, above.
[760] See above, para.14–094.
[761] See below, at fn.767

particular significance are the points that the rules as to rescission and variation, contained in s.2, and the rules as to defences and related matters, contained in s.3, will not so apply, since s.2 applies only "where a third party has a right *under section 1* to enforce a term of the contract"[762] and s.3 applies only "where, *in reliance on section 1*, proceedings for the enforcement of a term of a contract are brought by a third party".[763]

The interaction of C's rights under, and apart from, the Act. The structure resulting from the above distinctions is therefore a complex one. Four types of cases call for consideration. The first is that in which C has rights under the 1999 Act but none at common law because the case falls within the scope of the doctrine of privity of contract but not within any of the judge-made or other legislative exceptions to it. Here C's rights and remedies are clearly subject to the provisions of the Act. The second is the case in which C has no rights under the Act (either because the requirements of its s.1 are not satisfied or because one of the exceptions listed in its s.6 applies) but in which he does have rights apart from the Act, because the case falls either outside the scope of the doctrine of privity of contract or within one of the judge-made or other legislative exceptions to it. Here the rights and remedies to which C is entitled are clearly not subject to the provisions of the Act.[764] The third is the case in which C has rights both under the Act and apart from it (because the case falls outside the scope of the doctrine of privity of contract or within one of the judge-made or other legislative exceptions to it). It would seem that in such a case C can choose between making his claim under the Act (and so subject to its provisions) and apart from the Act (and so not subject to its provisions).[765] If, for example, C has a cause of action against A in tort at common law, it may be to C's advantage to pursue that claim (rather than one which may also be prima facie available to him under s.1) since in making such a common law claim he would not, in general, be bound by an exemption clause in the contract between A and B, while he would be so bound if he made a claim under the Act.[766] The fourth is the case in which C has no rights under the Act and none under the existing rules of common law or under other legislative exceptions to the doctrine of privity of contract. Here, C's only hope is to induce the court to create a new exception to the doctrine of privity[767] or (in the Supreme Court) to reject that doctrine altogether. If C's claim were upheld on one of these grounds, it would plainly not be subject to the provisions of the 1999 Act.

14–118

(vi) *Nature of the third party's rights*

Although the 1999 Act for a number of purposes[768] makes use of the fiction of treating C as if he were a party to the contract, it in general treats C's rights and

14–119

---

[762] s.2(1).

[763] s.3(1). See: *Moody v Condor Ins Ltd* [2006] EWHC 100; [2006] 1 W.L.R. 1847 at [30].

[764] *White v Jones* [1995] 2 A.C. 207 (above, para.14–052) illustrates this possibility.

[765] *Nisshin Shipping Co Ltd v Cleaves & Co Ltd* [2003] EWHC 2602; [2004] 1 Lloyd's Rep. 38.

[766] s.3(2); above, para.14–109.

[767] e.g. perhaps, to follow the Supreme Court of Canada's decision in *London Drugs Ltd v Kuehne & Nagel International Ltd* [1992] 3 S.C.R. 299 in recognising, at least to a limited extent, the principle of vicarious immunity: see above, para.14–060.

[768] See s.1(5), relating to C's remedies: above, para.14–097; s.3(4), relating to certain defences and s.3(6), relating to restrictions on the availability of exemption clauses: above, para.14–112; for a different technique, see s.7(3), relating to limitation of actions and s.8, relating to arbitration agreements (above, para.14–098).

defences as being sui generis. It does not, in other words, except for those purposes treat C as if he were or were deemed to be, or to have become, a party to the contract. In particular, the Act provides that C is not to be treated as a party to the contract between A and B for the purposes of other legislation.[769] For example, the references to a party or to the parties to a contract in the Law Reform (Frustrated Contracts) Act 1943[770] and in the Misrepresentation Act 1967[771] do not, under the Act, include references to C. The same is true of the Unfair Contract Terms Act 1977. The point can be illustrated by supposing that a contract was made between A and B on A's standard terms of business, that a term of this contract conferred a benefit on C, that this term was enforceable by C by virtue of s.1 of the Act, and that the contract contained a term excluding or restricting A's liability for defects in the performance rendered to C. The requirement of reasonableness under s.3 of the 1977 Act[772] would not apply in favour of C since he was not one of the parties to the contract between A and B, or a party who had dealt on A's standard terms: the requirement would apply only in favour of B.[773] The justification given by the Law Commission for this position is that to apply the 1977 Act in a three-party case would raise complex policy issues going beyond those involved in reforming the doctrine of privity.[774]

(vii) Effect on Unfair Contract Terms Act 1977, section 2

14–120   The relationship between the 1999 Act and the Unfair Contract Terms Act 1977 gives rise to the further difficulty that, under s.2(1) of the 1977 Act,[775] contract terms may be void if they purport to exclude or restrict liability for death or personal injury resulting from negligence; and that under s.2(2)[776] contract terms may be subject to the requirement of reasonableness if they purport to exclude or restrict liability for negligence in respect of other loss. Negligence here can include the breach of a contractual duty of care,[777] so that a claim by C affected by s.2 of the 1977 Act could be brought either under the 1999 Act or in tort, apart from the Act. Where it is brought under the 1999 Act, a compromise solution is adopted for cases of the kind here under discussion, i.e. for those in which C sues A for breach of a duty of care arising out of a contract between A and B, and A seeks to rely on a term of that contract as excluding or restricting his liability for negligence.[778] Where C in consequence of the breach suffers death or personal injury, the strong policy considerations against contract terms exclud-ing or restricting A's liability for such harm are to prevail, so that nothing in the 1999 Act will affect C's right to impugn the validity of a term excluding or restricting A's liability for such harm under s.2(1) of the 1977 Act. But where C suffers other loss, the case is regarded as more closely analogous to the situation

---

[769] 1999 Act, s.7(4). This provides that C is not to be so treated "by virtue of section 1(5) or 3(4) or 3(6)", above, fn.827. No reference is made in s.7(4) to s.8, above, fn.768, by virtue of which C *is* treated as a party to an arbitration agreement for the purposes of Arbitration Act 1996: see above, para.14–098.

[770] See below, para.19–095 et seq.

[771] See above, para.9–039 et seq.

[772] See above, para.7–064.

[773] Report, para.13.10; for B's right of enforcement, see below, para.14–121.

[774] Report, para.13.10(vii) and (viii).

[775] See above, para.7–057.

[776] See above, para.7–065.

[777] Unfair Contract Terms Act 1977, s.1(1)(a).

[778] See Report, para.13.12.

(described above) that can arise under s.3 of the 1977 Act. Subsection 7(2) of the 1999 Act therefore provides that s.2(2) of the 1977 Act is not to apply where A's alleged negligence consists of the breach of an obligation arising from a term of a contract (between A and B) and the claim by C is brought in reliance on s.1 of the 1999 Act. In such an action, therefore, a term in that contract excluding or restricting A's liability for loss other than death or personal injury is not subject to the requirement of reasonableness under the 1977 Act.

(viii) *Promisee's rights*

In general. At common law, the doctrine of privity of contract does not preclude the promisee from enforcing the contract[779] and this position is preserved by s.4 of the 1999 Act, by which "Section 1 does not affect any right of the promisee to enforce any term of the contract". The contract between A and B can thus be enforced by B even where the 1999 Act also gives C the right to enforce one of its terms against A. On A's failure to perform that term in favour of C, B can therefore make any claims for the agreed sum, for other specific relief or for damages that would have been available to him at common law apart from the Act. There is also nothing in the Act that affects B's right to restitution[780] against A in the event of the latter's non-performance of the term in favour of C, even though B's right to restitution would not normally be a "right of [B] to *enforce* a term of the contract" within s.4: it would have this character only where the contract provided for the return by A of the consideration provided by B to A in the event of A's failure to perform in favour of C. The 1999 Act also contains nothing to affect the common law rules which govern the relative rights of B and C where A has performed, or is willing to perform, in favour of C.[781]

14–121

Provision against double liability. At common law, A's failure to perform in favour of C may, in circumstances discussed earlier in this chapter,[782] give B a right to recover damages in respect of C's loss or in respect of expenses incurred by B in making good A's default: e.g. in completing A's unfinished, or in repairing A's defective, work. If, after B had recovered such damages, C were to make a claim against A under s.1 of the 1999 Act, there would be a risk of A's being made liable twice over for the same loss. Section 5 of the Act therefore directs the court in such circumstances "to reduce any award to [C] to such extent as it thinks appropriate to take account of the sum recovered by" B. Such a reduction would not prejudice C since, where damages had been recovered by B in respect of C's loss, these would have to be held by B for C[783]; and where B had incurred expense in curing A's breach, C's loss would be reduced in fact by his receipt of the intended benefit,[784] though by a route other than that envisaged by the contract. Section 5 of the Act applies only where B has recovered "a sum" (i.e. of money) in respect of C's loss or B's expense in making good A's default. Thus it will normally apply where B has recovered *damages*, though the possibility of its also applying where B has recovered *the agreed sum* or where he has made a successful

14–122

---

[779] See above, para.14–019.
[780] See above, para.14–020.
[781] See above, para.14–039 et seq.
[782] See above, para.14–024 et seq.
[783] See above, para.14–043.
[784] cf. below, para.20–121.

claim for *restitution* does not appear to be excluded. It will not, however, apply where B has obtained an order for the specific performance of an obligation by A to render some performance to C other than the payment of money, or where B has obtained an injunction to enforce a negative promise made by A for the benefit of C. In such cases, C will obtain the performance due to him under the term made enforceable by him by virtue of s.1 and so will not have any right to damages for its non-performance. But C might, in addition to the receipt of the performance, claim damages from A, e.g. in respect of delay in rendering the performance. Such a claim is not, and should not be, affected by s.5 of the 1999 Act since its success would not make A liable twice over for the *same* loss.

(c) Other Statutory Exceptions

14–123   A number of other exceptions to the doctrine of privity have been created by statute[785] and continue to be available to the third party after the Contracts (Rights of Third Parties) Act 1999.[786] The most important of these are the following.

(i) *Insurance*

14–124   The doctrine of privity applies to contracts of insurance.[787] It was in practice much modified in this field by the trust device and by agency; but the inadequacy of these exceptions has led to the creation of further exceptions to the doctrine by statute.

14–125   **Life insurance.** Section 11 of the Married Women's Property Act 1882 provides that where a man insures his life for the benefit of his wife or children, or a woman insures her life for the benefit of her husband or children,[788] the policy "shall create a trust in favour of the objects therein named". This provision also now applies where a civil partner insures his life for the benefit of his civil partner or children.[789] It is a good provision so far as it goes, but it is subject to some odd limitations. It applies only where a person insures his or her own life, and not where the policy is on the life of the third party[790]; and it is restricted to policies for the benefit of spouses and children, so that it does not apply in favour of other dependants, such as informally adopted children.[791] These restrictions will not be affected by the 1999 Act[792]; but persons who have no rights under s.11 of the 1882 Act may, if the requirements of the 1999 Act are satisfied, acquire the more

---

[785] A statutory exception to the doctrine enabling price maintenance agreements to be enforced against third parties formerly existed by virtue of Resale Prices Act 1976, s.26; but that Act has been repealed by s.1 of the Competition Act 1998 which makes no similar provision where such agreements are exempted (under ss.4 to 9) from prima facie invalidity under s.2.

[786] s.7(1).

[787] See *Boston Fruit Co v British & Foreign Marine Ins Co* [1906] A.C. 336; *Yangtsze Ins Association v Lukmanjee* [1918] A.C. 585. Contrast, in Australia, *Trident General Ins Co Ltd v McNiece Bros Pty Ltd* (1988) 165 C.L.R. 107 (above, para.14–017).

[788] Illegitimate children are included: Family Law Reform Act 1969, s.19(1).

[789] Civil Partnership Act 2004, s.70.

[790] *Re Engelbach's Estate* [1924] 2 Ch. 348, overruled on another point in *Beswick v Beswick* [1968] A.C. 58.

[791] *Re Clay's Policy of Assurance* [1937] 2 All E.R. 548.

[792] Law Com. No.242, para.12.27.

restricted[793] rights conferred on third parties by that Act. They may also have rights under the trust exception to the doctrine of privity.[794]

Motor insurance. A person driving a car with the owner's consent can take the **14–126** benefit of the owner's insurance policy (provided the policy so allows) without having to prove that the owner intended to constitute himself trustee.[795]

Fire insurance. Where a house which is insured is destroyed by fire, "any **14–127** person . . . interested" may require the insurance money to be laid out towards reinstating the house[796]; thus a tenant may claim under his landlord's insurance,[797] and a landlord under his tenant's insurance.

Insurance by persons with limited interests. A person may insure property **14–128** for its full value although he has only a limited interest in it. He may then be able to recover its full value from the insurers but be liable to pay over to the other persons interested any sum exceeding his own loss.[798] A number of real or supposed limitations on this principle have been removed by statute.[799] Thus it has been provided that any person who has an interest in the subject-matter of a policy of marine insurance can insure "on behalf of and for the benefit of other persons interested as well as for his own benefit".[800] On a somewhat similar principle, where property is sold and suffers damage before the sale is completed, any insurance money to which the vendor is entitled in respect of the damage must be held by him for the purchaser, and be paid over to the purchaser on completion.[801]

Solicitors' indemnity insurance. Under s.37 of the Solicitors Act 1974, a **14–129** scheme has been established by the Law Society for the compulsory insurance of

---

[793] e.g. powers of rescission or variation under s.2 of the 1999 Act do not apply where a trust has arisen under s.11 of the 1882 Act; cf. above, para.14–119.

[794] *Re Foster's Policy* [1966] 1 W.L.R. 222; above, para.14–082.

[795] Road Traffic Act 1988, s.148(7), replacing Road Traffic Act 1930, s.36(4), discussed in *Tattersal v Drysdale* [1935] 2 K.B. 174; *Austin v Zurich, etc., Ins Co* [1944] 2 All E.R. 243 at 248.

[796] Fires Prevention (Metropolis) Act 1774, s.83.

[797] *Portavon Cinema Co Ltd v Price and Century Ins Co* [1939] 4 All E.R. 601; *Mark Rowlands Ltd v Berni Inns Ltd* [1986] Q.B. 211; *Lonsdale & Thompson Ltd v Black Arrow Group Plc* [1993] Ch. 361.

[798] *Waters v Monarch Ins Co* (1856) 5 E. & B. 870; *Hepburn v Tomlinson (Hauliers) Ltd* [1966] A.C. 451; *Lonsdale Thompson Ltd v Black Arrow Group Plc*, above, fn.797; cf. *Petrofina (UK) Ltd v Magnaload Ltd* [1984] Q.B. 127 (head contractor insuring for the benefit of himself and sub-contractors); contrast *Stone Vickers Ltd v Appledore Ferguson Shipbuilders Ltd* [1992] 2 Lloyd's Rep. 578, where the main contractor had no authority or intention to contract on behalf of the sub-contractors; cf. *Colonia Versicherung AG v Amoco Oil Co* [1997] 1 Lloyd's Rep. 261 at 270–272; and see *Simon Container Machinery Ltd v Emba Machinery AB* [1998] 2 Lloyd's Rep. 428 at 437.

[799] The principle may be displaced by the wording of the policy: *Ramco (UK) Ltd v International Ins Co of Hanover* [2004] EWCA Civ 675; [2004] 2 Lloyd's Rep 595; *Ramco Ltd v Weller Russell and Laws Insurance Brokers Ltd* [2008] EWHC 2202 (QB); [2009] Lloyd's Rep. I.R. at [12].

[800] Marine Insurance Act 1906, s.14(2).

[801] Law of Property Act 1925, s.47. For the definition of "property" see Law of Property Act 1925, s.205(1)(xx). In contracts for the sale of land, s.47 appears to be commonly excluded: see Law Com. No.191, para.3.2; cf. also Law of Property Act 1925, s.108 as to the application of insurance money where property is mortgaged.

solicitors against liability for professional negligence or breach of duty. The scheme takes the form of a contract between the Society and insurers whereby the insurers undertake, on being paid the appropriate premiums, to provide indemnity insurance to solicitors. It has been held that the scheme gives rise to reciprocal rights and duties between the insurers and solicitors.[802] This result follows "by virtue of public law, not the ordinary English private law of contract"[803]; for in operating the scheme the Society acts, not in its private capacity as a professional association, but in its public capacity as a body, one of whose functions is to protect members of the public against loss which they may suffer from dealings with solicitors.

14–130   **Third parties' rights against insurers.** Our concern here is not with insurance contracts which purport to confer benefits on third parties, but with those which insure the policy-holder against liability to third parties. By statute[804] such a third party may in certain circumstances[805] enforce the rights of the insured under the policy by proceeding directly against the insurance company. In the case of victims of motor accidents, these rights are supplemented by an agreement originally made between the Motor Insurers' Bureau and the Minister of Transport.[806] This provides that the Bureau will pay any judgment (to the extent to which it remains unsatisfied) "in respect of any liability which is required to be covered by a policy of insurance" under the statutory scheme of compulsory motor insurance. A person who is injured in a road accident cannot technically enforce the agreement as he is not a party to it. But the agreement may be specifically enforced by the Minister,[807] and, although "the foundations in jurisprudence" of the agreement "are better not questioned",[808] the Bureau's practice is not to rely on the doctrine of privity as a defence to claims by the injured parties themselves.[809]

---

[802] *Swain v Law Society* [1983] 1 A.C. 598.

[803] ibid. at 611.

[804] Third Parties (Rights Against Insurers) Act 1930, s.1 (due to be repealed by the Third Parties (Rights against Insurers) Act 2010). See also: Road Traffic Act 1988, ss.151–153, as amended by Road Traffic Act 1991, s.48 and Sch.4; Michel [1987] L.M.C.L.Q. 228.

[805] For the circumstances under which the 1930 Act (not in force at time of writing) transferred the rights of the insured to the third party, see the 12th edn, para.14–135, n.864. The 2010 Act maintains the same basic principle that rights are transferred on the "insolvency" of the insured, but introduces some important changes: (i) the insured must qualify as a "relevant person" and this is defined to include circumstances which do not amount to insolvency as such (see the list in ss.4–7); (ii) the liability of the insured to the third party must still be established, but it can be established in the proceedings brought by the third party against the insurer (ss.1(3), 2); (iii) the transfer is "not subject to a condition requiring the prior discharge by the insured of the insured's liability to the third party" (s.9(5)), even if the policy contains a provision to that effect (thus reversing the effect of the decision in *The Fanti and Padre Island* [1991] 2 A.C. 1).

[806] *Hardy v MIB* [1964] 2 Q.B. 745 at 770; *White v London Transport* [1971] 2 Q.B. 721 at 729; *White v White* [2001] UKHL 9; [2001] 1 W.L.R. 481.

[807] See *Gurtner v Circuit* [1968] 2 Q.B. 587.

[808] *Gardner v Moore* [1984] A.C. 548 at 556.

[809] *Persson v London County Buses* [1974] 1 W.L.R. 569; and see *Hardy v MIB*, above, fn.806, at 757; *Randall v MIB* [1968] 1 W.L.R. 1900; for enforceability of the agreement by third parties, see also *Charlton v Fisher* [2001] EWCA Civ 112; [2002] Q.B. 578 at [25], [82]. As the Bureau is, therefore, interested in the outcome of litigation between the injured party and the driver, it may, at the court's discretion, be added as a party to such litigation: see *Gurtner v Circuit* [1968] 2 Q.B. 587; contrast *White v London Transport* [1971] 2 Q.B. 721.

(ii) *Law of Property Act 1925, section 56*[810]

Common law background. At common law a person could not take an **14–131** immediate interest in property, or the benefit of any covenant, under an indenture purporting to be inter partes, unless he was named as a party to the indenture.[811] An indenture was a deed whose top was indented to match with a counterpart, as a precaution against fraud. It was said to be "*inter partes*" if it was expressed to be "between A of the first part, B of the second part . . . ", etc. The common law rule did not apply to deeds poll (deeds with a smooth top) or to indentures not inter partes.[812] In the case of such deeds the grantee never had to be named *as a party*; and it was eventually settled that he need not be named at all, so long as he was sufficiently designated.[813] Deeds no longer have to be indented for any purposes,[814] but the law still distinguishes between deeds inter partes and other deeds and the distinction seems to retain some practical significance.[815]

Section 56. The common law rule with regard to indentures *inter partes* was **14–132** modified by s.5 of the Real Property Act 1845,[816] which was in turn replaced by s.56(1) of the Law of Property Act 1925, which provides:

> "A person may take an immediate or other interest in land or other property, or the benefit of any condition, right of entry, covenant or agreement over or respecting land or other property, although he may not be named as a party to the conveyance or other instrument".

The 1925 Act further defines "property" to include "any thing in action".[817] In *Beswick v Beswick* Lord Denning M.R. and Danckwerts L.J. held that a promise in writing by A to B to pay a sum of money to C would, by virtue of this definition of "property", be within s.56(1) and so give C a right to sue A.[818] In their view, s.56(1) was a "clear" provision to this effect, doing away with the doctrine of privity where the contract is written. But the words "although he may not be *named as a party*" are far from clear. They could refer to a number of things: to

---

[810] Elliot 20 Conv. 43 at 114; Andrews 23 Conv. 179; Wade [1964] C.L.J. 66; Furmston 23 M.L.R. 380–385; Ellinger 26 M.L.R. 396; all these comments on s.56(1) must now be read in the light of the decision of the House of Lords, in *Beswick v Beswick* [1968] A.C. 58.

[811] *Scudamore v Vandenstene* (1587) 2 CoInst. 673; *Southampton v Brown* (1827) 6 B. & C. 718.

[812] *Cooker v Child* (1673) 2 Lev. 74; *Chelsea & Waltham Green Building Soc v Armstrong* [1951] Ch. 853; *Moody v Condor Ins Ltd* [2006] EWHC 100; [2006] 1 W.L.R. 1847.

[813] *Sunderland Marine Ins Co v Kearney* (1851) 16 Q.B. 925; qualifying *Green v Horn* (1694) 1 Salk. 197. The old rule relating to indentures *inter partes* appears still to apply to deeds *inter partes* in cases falling outside s.56(1) of the Law of Property Act 1925; see *Beswick v Beswick* [1968] A.C. 58 at 104.

[814] Law of Property Act 1925, s.56(2).

[815] See fn.813, above; *Moody v Condor Ins Ltd* [2006] EWHC 100; [2006] 1 W.L.R. 1847 (deed of guarantee of instalments due on the sale of a company held to amount to a deed poll and enforceable by the seller, though it was not a party to the deed).

[816] S.5 of the 1845 Act applied only to real property: *Beswick v Beswick* [1968] A.C. 58 at 87, 104, and, in the case of covenants, to those which ran with the land: *Forster v Elvett Colliery Co Ltd* [1908] 1 K.B. 629 (in the House of Lords, Lord Macnaghten reserved the point: *Dyson v Forster* [1909] A.C. 98 at 102); *Grant v Edmondson* [1931] 1 Ch. 1.

[817] s.205(1)(xx).

[818] [1966] Ch. 538; see also *Smith and Snipes Hall Farm Ltd v River Douglas Catchment Board Ltd* [1949] 2 K.B. 500 and *Drive Yourself Hire Co (London) Ltd v Strutt* [1954] 1 Q.B. 250; criticised on this point by Wade [1954] C.L.J. 66.

a party who is not named but only described; to a person who is named but not as a party; and to a person who is neither named nor a party[819] (e.g. where A promises B to pay a pension "to any of your employees who is injured at work"). The House of Lords in *Beswick v Beswick* rejected the view of Lord Denning M.R. and Danckwerts L.J., principally on the ground that the definition of "property" in the Act was stated to apply "unless the context otherwise requires". The context in s.56(1) did otherwise require, since s.56(1) was part of a consolidating Act and was designed to reproduce s.5 of the 1845 Act, which admittedly did not have the wide effect suggested for s.56(1).[820] There was, moreover, nothing in the legislative history of s.56(1) to support the view that the subsection was intended to abolish the doctrine of privity in relation to written contracts.[821]

14–133   **The scope of subsection 56(1).** Section 56(1) therefore does not apply to a bare promise in writing by A to B to pay a sum of money to C; and the correctness of a number of previous decisions to this effect[822] is reaffirmed by *Beswick v Beswick*. But the question, to what other cases the subsection does apply, remains one of great difficulty. There is support in *Beswick v Beswick* for four limitations on its scope: namely, that it applies only (1) to real property[823]; (2) to covenants running with the land[824]; (3) to cases where the instrument is not merely for the benefit of the third party but purports to contain a grant to or covenant with him[825]; and (4) to deeds strictly inter partes.[826] But there is no clear majority in the speeches in favour of all, some or even one of these limitations, so that the scope of the subsection remains obscure. There appear to be only three reported cases in which s.56(1) has actually been applied. The first[827] is consistent with all four of the above limitations, the second[828] is consistent only with the last two and it is not clear whether the third is consistent with any of them.[829] The third limitation was regarded as the operative one in both of the first two cases and also in a number of others in which the courts have refused to apply the subsection.[830] It seems probable that the subsection will be applied only where this limitation is satisfied. There is also much to be said on historical grounds for the fourth limitation, which is consistent with all the cases, though it does not form a ground of decision in any of them. The scope of s.56(1) is further limited by a rule which it was not necessary to consider in *Beswick v Beswick*, namely, that a person cannot take the benefit of a covenant under the subsection unless he, or his predecessor

---

[819] cf. the side-note to s.56: "Persons taking who are not parties."

[820] [1968] A.C. 58 at 77, 81, 87.

[821] ibid. at 77, 81, 104; cf. Treitel 29 M.L.R. 657 at 661.

[822] *Re Sinclair's Life Policy* [1938] Ch. 799 (criticised on another ground in *Beswick v Beswick* [1968] A.C. 58 at 90); *Re Foster* [1938] 3 All E.R. 357; *Re Miller's Agreement* [1947] Ch. 615.

[823] See [1968] A.C. 58 at 87 and 76; contrast 105. See also *Southern Water Authority v Carey* [1985] 2 All E.R. 1077 at 1083.

[824] ibid. at 87; contrast 77, 93, 105.

[825] ibid. at 94, 106; cf. 74–75 and 87.

[826] ibid. at 94, 106; cf. 76–77. See above, para.14–131.

[827] *Re Ecclesiastical Commissioners' Conveyance* [1936] Ch. 430; cf. *Re Windle* [1975] 1 W.L.R. 1628 at 1631 (not affected on this point by doubts expressed in *Re Kumar* [1993] 1 W.L.R. 224 at 235).

[828] *Stromdale and Ball Ltd v Burden* [1952] Ch. 223.

[829] *OTV Birwelco Ltd v Technical & General Guarantee Co Ltd* [2002] EWHC 2240; [2002] 4 All E.R. 686 at [12]; the statement of facts leaves the point in doubt.

[830] See the cases cited in fn.822, above; *White v Bijou Mansions* [1937] Ch. 610, affirmed [1938] Ch. 351; *Lyus v Prowsa Developments Ltd* [1982] 1 W.L.R. 1044 at 1049; *Amsprop Trading Ltd v Harris Distribution Ltd* [1997] 1 W.L.R. 1025. This is a more stringent requirement than those contained in Contracts (Rights of Third Parties) Act 1999, s.1(1) and (2); above, paras 14–093—14–095.

in title, was in existence[831] and identifiable in accordance with the terms of the instrument at the time when it was made.[832]

6. IMPOSING LIABILITY ON THIRD PARTIES

General rule. The general rule is that what may sometimes be referred to as the "burden" of the contract cannot be imposed on a third party: A and B cannot by a contract between them impose an obligation on C to perform duties arising under the contract. This aspect of the doctrine of privity is so obvious that it scarcely needs to be stated: if A and B agreed that C was to pay £100 to A, no one would suppose that this agreement could oblige C to make the payment. Similarly, as a general rule, A and B cannot by a contract between them seek to impose on C an exclusion clause. The circumstances under which C may nevertheless be bound by such a clause have been dealt with earlier.[833] We have also seen that the 1999 Act does not affect the general rule, but there are circumstances in which C may have to fulfil an obligation under the contract between A and B as a condition of enforcing a term against A.[834]

14–134

If a contract between A and B cannot directly impose an obligation on C, it may in some other way restrict C's freedom of action: e.g. it may create rights in or over property, such as a lien[835] or a lease[836] or an equitable interest, or give rise to a constructive trust affecting property[837]; and such interests can affect the rights of third parties who later acquire the property. In this part, we are concerned with other ways in which C's freedom of action may be restricted by a contract to which he is not a party.

Inducing breach of contract.[838] Although a contract primarily creates rights and duties enforceable by the contracting parties against each other, it also incidentally imposes on third parties the duty not to interfere with the contracting parties in performing the contract and if they do so they may be liable for the tort of inducing breach. The requirements of the tort have been re-stated by the House of Lords in *OBG Ltd v Allan*.[839] It is quite separate from the tort of causing loss

14–135

---

[831] There is no such requirement under Contracts (Rights of Third Parties) Act 1999: see s.1(3); above, para.14–095.

[832] *Kelsey v Dodd* (1883) 52 L.J.Ch. 34; *Westhoughton Urban DC v Wigan Coal Co* [1919] 1 Ch. 159 (both these cases were decided under s.5 of Real Property Act 1845, but the position under s.56(1) of the 1925 Act seems to be the same); *White v Bijou Mansions*, above.

[833] See above, para.14–071 et seq.

[834] See above, para.14–096.

[835] See *Faith v EIC* (1821) 4 B. & Ald. 630; *Tappenden v Artus* [1964] 2 Q.B. 185; *T Comedy (UK) Ltd v Easy Managed Transport Ltd* [2007] EWHC 611 (Comm); [2007] 2 Lloyd's Rep. 397; contrast *Chellaram & Sons (London) Ltd v Butler's Warehousing & Distribution Ltd* [1978] 2 Lloyd's Rep. 412.

[836] As in *Ashburn Anstalt v Arnold* [1989] Ch. 1, overruled on another point in *Prudential Assurance Co Ltd v London Residuary Body* [1992] A.C. 386.

[837] See *Ashburn Anstalt v Arnold*, above, where the mere fact that C had notice of an earlier contract between A and B was said at 25–26 to be insufficient to give rise to a constructive trust on C's acquisition of the land affected by that contract; and where Fox L.J. (delivering the judgment of the court) at 17 disapproved dicta in *Errington v Errington* [1952] 1 K.B. 290 (which had been followed in *Re Sharpe* [1980] 1 W.L.R. 219) to the effect that a contractual licence granted by A to B gave rise to an equitable interest binding third parties; Hill 51 M.L.R. 226; Oakley [1988] C.L.J. 353; cf. also *Binions v Evans* [1972] Ch. 359; Smith [1973] C.L.J. 81; Hornby 93 L.Q.R. 568; *Pritchard v Briggs* [1980] Ch. 338 (option to purchase); *Lyus v Prowsa Developments Ltd* [1982] 1 W.L.R. 1044.

[838] For a detailed analysis, see *Winfield & Jolowicz on Tort* (18th edn) at paras 18.2–18.8.

[839] [2007] UKHL 21; [2008] 1 A.C. 1; cf. *Lumley v Gye* (1853) 2 E. & B. 216.

by unlawful means.[840] The tort of inducing breach is a form of "accessory" liability, i.e. C is an accessory to B's breach of the contract between A and B, whereas causing loss by unlawful means is a tort of "primary" liability, even if the two torts might sometimes overlap on the same set of facts.[841] As a tort of accessory liability, C is liable for inducing breach only if there has, in fact, been a breach of the contract between A and B[842] and C's acts "of encouragement, threat, persuasion and so forth [had] a sufficient causal connection with the breach by [B]."[843] C must have known that he was inducing a breach, where knowledge includes "turning a blind eye", i.e. a reckless indifference to whether there is a breach of contract, but not negligence.[844] C must also have intended to cause the breach as an end in itself or as the means to another end, but mere foresight of a breach as a possible consequence of his acts is not sufficient.[845]

14–136   **Contracts affecting property.** The tort of inducing breach may help to solve the problem which arises when C acquires property with notice of a contract concerning it, previously made between A and B. The problem is: to what extent is C restricted by the contract in the use which he is entitled to make of the property? Such contracts may be divided into four groups.[846] The first consists of contracts restricting the use or disposition of goods, e.g. contracts that goods shall be sold only in packets sealed by the manufacturer, or after a certain time has elapsed. The second group of contracts consists of those requiring the use of *particular* chattels for their performance, without creating any proprietary or possessory interest in those chattels; e.g. a contract to carry cargo in a particular ship. The third group consists of contracts for the hire of a chattel, and the fourth of options to purchase a chattel. These last two groups are now very common; a hire-purchase agreement is a contract for the hire of a chattel, coupled with an option to purchase it.

14–137   **Protection against third parties in special cases.** In a number of special cases, the courts protect the rights arising under such contracts against third parties with notice of them: e.g. where an option to purchase a chattel is specifically enforceable, it may be enforced against third parties who acquire the chattel

---

[840] The House of Lords rejected a unified theory of the "economic torts" supported in *D.C. Thompson & Co v Deakin* [1952] Ch. 646

[841] [2008] 1 A.C. 1 at [21], e.g. where C uses unlawful means to cause loss to A and that loss is caused by B having breached a contract with A. The difference between the two torts is that C may be liable to A for inducing the breach where he meets the requirements for that tort, even if his actions do not constitute "unlawful means" or he did not intended to cause loss.

[842] *Torquay Hotel Co Ltd v. Cousins* [1969] 2 Ch. 106 at 138 and *Merkur Island Shipping Corpn v Laughton* [1983] 2 A.C. 570 at 607–608 are disapproved in this regard.

[843] [2008] 1 A.C. 1 at [36].

[844] ibid. at [40]; cf. *Emerald Construction Co Ltd v Lowthian* [1966] 1 W.L.R. 691, at 700–701. Thus, in one of the conjoined appeals heard by the House of Lords in *OBG v Allan* (*Mainstream Properties Ltd v Young*) C provided finance to B to exploit an opportunity which B should have made available to A, a company of which B was a director. C honestly believed B's assurance that B was free to exploit the opportunity himself and was not therefore liable for inducing B's breach. It was perhaps another instance where the court "vindicated [C's] honesty... at the expense of his intelligence": *British Industrial Plastics Ltd v Ferguson* [1938] 4 All E.R. 504 at 513 per McKinnon L.J., affirmed [1940] 1 All E.R. 479; cf. *Meretz Investments NV v ACP Ltd* [2007] EWCA Civ 1303; [2008] Ch. 244.

[845] ibid. at [42]–[43]. The earlier decision of the Court of Appeal in *Miller v Bassey* [1994] E.M.L.R. 44 is disapproved in this regard.

[846] See Chafee 41 H.L.R. 945; cf. Wade 44 L.Q.R. 51; Gardner 98 L.Q.R. 278; Tettenborn [1982] C.L.J. 58; Cohen-Grabelsky 45 M.L.R. 241.

with notice of the option.[847] The same would be true where money was lent on the terms that the loan was to be repaid out of specific property. Since such an undertaking to repay is specifically enforceable, it would create a charge in equity over the property in favour of the lender, and this would prevail against a third party who later acquired an interest in it, unless he was a bona fide purchaser for value without notice.[848]

General principle of protection against third parties rejected. A more   **14–138** general principle was formulated in *De Mattos v Gibson*,[849] where Knight Bruce L.J. said:

> "Reason and justice seem to prescribe that, at least as a general rule, where a man, by gift or purchase, acquires property from another, with knowledge of a previous contract, lawfully and for valuable consideration made . . . with a third person, to use and employ the property . . . in a specified manner, the acquirer shall not, to the material damage of the third person, in opposition to the contract and inconsistently with it, use and employ the property in a manner not allowable to the giver or seller".

This principle came to be associated with the rule in *Tulk v Moxhay*[850] under which third parties are bound by restrictive covenants concerning land. That rule was later confined to cases in which the claimant's interest in enforcing the covenant consisted in the ownership of land capable of being benefited by the covenant. This usually meant adjacent land[851]; and since adjacency is hardly a satisfactory criterion of interest in the case of things that can be moved, the tendency of these developments of the rule in *Tulk v Moxhay* was to undermine the suggested general principle.[852] Nevertheless, in *Lord Strathcona SS Co v Dominion Coal Co*[853] the Privy Council relied on that principle to hold that the time charterer of a ship had an interest in the ship which he could enforce against a purchaser of the ship with notice of the charterparty; the purchaser was also said to be "in the position of a constructive trustee, with obligations which a court of equity would not allow him to violate".[854] The decision provoked adverse criticism,[855] particularly because the land law analogies and the constructive trust reasoning on which it was based might lead to the third party's being made liable where he had only constructive notice of the earlier contract. Where that contract concerned the use or disposition of a chattel, such a conclusion was open to the objection that it might have the undesirable effect of introducing the doctrine of

---

[847] *Falcke v Gray* (1859) 4 Drew. 651, as explained in *Erskine Macdonald Ltd v Eyles* [1921] 1 Ch. 631 at 641.

[848] *Swiss Bank Corp v Lloyds Bank Ltd* [1982] A.C. 548 at 598, 613; the actual decision was that the contract of loan did *not* create an obligation to repay out of specific property so that there was no specifically enforceable agreement affecting it: see below, para.21–020, fn.92; cf. *MacJordan Construction Ltd v Brookmount Erostin* [1992] B.C.L.C. 350.

[849] (1858) 4 D. & J. 276 at 282.

[850] (1848) 2 Ph. 774.

[851] *LCC v Allen* [1914] 3 K.B. 642; the actual decision was reversed by statute, but the principle stated in the text remains unimpaired.

[852] See *Barker v Stickney* [1919] 1 K.B. 121 at 131; for criticism, see *Tito v Waddell (No.2)* [1977] Ch. 106 at 300.

[853] [1926] A.C. 108.

[854] ibid. at 125.

[855] e.g. *Greenhalgh v Mallard* [1943] 2 All E.R. 234.

constructive notice into commercial affairs. When a similar problem arose in *Port Line Ltd v Ben Line Steamers Ltd*,[856] Diplock J. therefore refused to follow the Privy Council's decision. Alternatively, he was prepared to distinguish it: the buyer of the ship in the *Port Line* case knew that she was under charter to the claimant, but he did not have actual notice of the precise extent of the claimant's rights under the charterparty.[857] Thus the *Port Line* case rejects the principle stated by Knight Bruce L.J. so far as it relates to contracts concerning chattels; but it does not decide that a third party can always disregard such a contract. A number of possibilities must be considered.

14–139   **Remedy available.** Later authorities have restricted the principle stated in *De Mattos v Gibson*[858] by emphasising that the remedy there sought was simply an injunction to restrain the acquirer, C, from using the property inconsistently with the terms of the contract between A and B, known to C.[859] The principle therefore cannot impose any positive obligation on C to perform the terms of the contract between A and B. Thus where A acquired shares from B, promising to make payments to B on the occurrence of specific events, which later happened, it was held that that promise could not be enforced against C who later acquired the shares from A with knowledge of the contract between A and B, nor against D who acquired them from C with such knowledge.[860] An injunction on the principle of *De Mattos v Gibson* was not available against C or D as they were not proposing to act inconsistently with the contract between A and B: "they [were] merely proposing . . . to do nothing whatever".[861]

14–140   **Third party's liability in tort.** A third party who acquires a chattel with knowledge[862] of a contract affecting it may, if his acquisition or use of the chattel is inconsistent with that contract, be liable in tort for inducing a breach of contract.[863] Thus in *BMTA v Salvadori*[864] B bought a car and covenanted with A that he would not resell it for one year without first offering it to A. During the year, C bought the car from B with notice of the covenant, and was held liable to A for inducing a breach of the contract between A and B. It has been suggested that the decision of the Privy Council in the *Lord Strathcona* case[865] can be explained on the ground that the purchaser of the ship had committed this tort

---

[856] [1958] Q.B. 146. The cases cited above, at fn.837 all apply the constructive trust reasoning to contracts concerning land and do not, it is submitted, undermine the rejection of that reasoning in the *Port Line* case so far as contracts affecting the use or disposition of chattels are concerned.

[857] Hence the buyer was not liable in tort: see below, fn.862.

[858] See above, at fn.849

[859] *Swiss Bank Corp v Lloyds Bank Ltd* [1979] Ch. 581 at 574 (as to which see also below, fn.866).

[860] *Law Debenture Trust Corp v Ural Caspian Oil Corp Ltd* [1993] 1 W.L.R. 138; Tettenborn [1993] C.L.J. 382; for a successful appeal on another point see [1995] Ch. 152; below, fn.872.

[861] [1993] 1 W.L.R. 138 at 146.

[862] As now defined after *OBG v Allan*: see above, fn.844. In the *Port Line* case (above, para.14–138) the defendant was not liable in tort as he honestly believed that the terms of the charterparty were such that it would not be breached.

[863] See above para.14–135.

[864] [1949] Ch. 556; *Rickless v United Artists Corp* [1988] Q.B. 40 at 58–59; cf. *Law Debenture Corp v Ural Caspian Oil Corp Ltd* [1993] 1 W.L.R. 138, where the fifth defendant admitted liability on this ground; for a successful appeal on another point, see [1995] Ch. 152.

[865] [1926] A.C. 108.

against the charterer.[866] The tort may be committed even though B was quite willing to break his contract with A. Thus it is immaterial whether B or C began the negotiations leading to the contract between them[867]; indeed, C's tort liability may arise precisely because he has colluded with B in an effort to get rid of a restriction imposed in favour of A by the contract between A and B.[868] The merit of this approach is that it avoids the danger of importing the doctrine of constructive notice into this branch of the law. On the other hand, it is subject to two limitations.

First, the tort is not committed if the defendant's interference was not the cause of the claimant's loss. In the *Lord Strathcona* case,[869] the purchasers of the ship (who were the defendants in the Privy Council proceedings) mortgaged her, but were too poor to put her to sea. The mortgage gave the mortgagees the right to sell the ship, and it was held that they were entitled to sell her free from the charterer's rights, though they had notice of those rights. The cause of the failure to perform the charterparty was the shipowners' poverty, and not the mortgagees' sale of the ship.[870] Similarly, where breach of the contract has already been induced by C's acquisition of the property from B, there will be no tort liability for inducing breach of contract on D, who subsequently buys the property from C, even with knowledge of the contract between A and B, for D's conduct will not have played any part in inducing the original breach.[871] Nor is D in such a case liable for interference with the remedies arising out of the broken contract between A and B.[872]

Secondly, tort liability for interference with contractual rights is based on intentional wrongdoing.[873] It follows that, if a defendant negligently damaged a ship which was subject to a time charterparty, he would not commit this tort against the charterer; nor would he be liable to the charterer in negligence for pecuniary loss, such as hire wasted or profits lost while the ship was, by reason of the damage, out of service.[874]

So far, in discussing the third party's liability for inducing a breach of contract, it has been assumed that C either knew, or that he did not know, of the contract between A and B. In the former situation, he could, but in the latter he could not, be liable for the tort.[875] There is also an intermediate situation, in which C at the time of his contract with B had no more than constructive notice of B's earlier contract with A, but then acquired actual knowledge of that contract before calling

---

[866] *Swiss Bank Corp v Lloyds Bank Ltd* [1979] Ch. 548 at 574; in the Court of Appeal it was conceded that there was "no substance" in the point in that case: see [1982] A.C. 584 at 598 and below, fn.880.

[867] *Sefton v Tophams Ltd* [1965] Ch. 1140 at 1161, 1167, reversed [1967] A.C. 50, without reference to this point.

[868] *Esso Petroleum Co Ltd v Kingswood Motors (Addlestone) Ltd* [1974] Q.B. 142.

[869] [1926] A.C. 108; above, para.14–138.

[870] *The Lord Strathcona* [1925] P. 143; judgment in this case was given four months before judgment in the Privy Council proceedings so that the injunction issued by the Privy Council never took effect. *De Mattos v Gibson* suffered a similar fate: (1858) 4 D. & J. 276. cf. *The Myrto* [1977] 2 Lloyd's Rep. 243; *Lyus v Prowsa Developments Ltd* [1982] 1 W.L.R. 1044 at 1049; *Anton Durbeck GmbH v Den Norske Bank ASA* [2005] EWHC 2497 (Comm); [2006] 1 Lloyd's Rep. 93 at [50]–[64].

[871] *Law Debenture Trust Corp v Ural Caspian Oil Corp Ltd* [1993] 1 W.L.R. 138; and see next note.

[872] *Law Debenture Trust Corp v Ural Caspian Oil Corp Ltd* [1995] Ch. 152, reversing the decision at first instance (above) on this point.

[873] See above, para.14–135.

[874] On the principle stated at para.14–050, above: *The Mineral Transporter* [1986] A.C. 1.

[875] See above, para.14–135.

for (or receiving) performance of his own contract with B.[876] The question then arises whether, on such facts, C is liable to A for the tort of inducing a breach of the contract between A and B. That tort is subject to the defence of "justification",[877] which is certainly available to C where he had contracted with B *before* A had done so.[878] The defence is a flexible one,[879] and the principle on which it is based appears to be equally applicable where C's contract with B was made *after* A's but in ignorance of it. The exercise by C of rights thus acquired in good faith against B should not, it is submitted, make C liable for the tort to A.[880] Even in such a situation, however, C may be liable to A (under the rules relating to special cases stated above[881]) if A's contract with B is specifically enforceable. Where the specific enforceability of this contract gives rise to an equitable interest, this can be asserted against C even though he had, when he contracted with B, only constructive notice of B's contract with A. In such a case, the tort claim would be "of no value"[882] if, as has been submitted above, it arises only where C, when he contracted with B, had actual knowledge of A's rights; but it would equally be unnecessary to rely on it,[883] since A could succeed against C on the different ground that A's contract with B was specifically enforceable and therefore conferred an equitable interest on A.

14–141   **Protection of "possessory rights".** A final possibility relates to contracts under which possession of a chattel is, or is to be, transferred. The contracts in the *Strathcona* and *Port Line* cases were not of this kind: they were time charters, under which a shipowner undertakes to render services by the use of a particular ship, which remains in his possession.[884] Such charters must be contrasted with demise charters, which are contracts for the hire of a ship under which the shipowner does transfer, or undertake to transfer, possession of the ship to the charterer.[885] The nearest analogy in land law to a contract for the hire of a chattel is a lease,[886] and not a restrictive covenant. Hence the development of the doctrine of *Tulk v Moxhay*, discussed above,[887] need not affect cases concerning such contracts. One reason given by Diplock J. for his decision in the *Port Line* case was

---

[876] This was the position in *Swiss Bank Corp v Lloyds Bank Ltd* [1982] A.C. 584: see [1979] Ch. 548 at 568–569, and see below, fn.880.

[877] *OBG Ltd v Allan* [2007] UKHL 21; [2008] 1 A.C. 1 at [193]. See *Winfield & Jolowicz on Tort* (18th edn), para.18–7.

[878] *Smithies v National Association of Operative Plasterers* [1909] 1 K.B. 310 at 337; *Edwin Hill & Partners v First National Finance Corp Plc* [1989] 1 W.L.R. 225 at 230; *Meretz Investments NV v ACP Ltd* [2007] EWCA Civ 1303; [2008] Ch. 244 at [142]. For terms which may be imposed on C as a condition of obtaining relief against A, see *Guiness Peat Aviation (Belgium) NV v Hispania Lineas Aereas SA* [1992] 1 Lloyd's Rep. 190.

[879] *Glamorgan Coal Co v South Wales Miners' Federation* [1903] 2 K.B. 545 at 574–575.

[880] This was admitted in *Swiss Bank Corp v Lloyds Bank Ltd*, above, fn.876: see [1979] Ch. 548 at 569–573; cf. *Anton Durbeck GmbH v Den Norske Bank ASA* [2005] EWHC 2497 (Comm); [2006] 1 Lloyd's Rep. 93.

[881] See above, para.14–137.

[882] *Swiss Bank Corp v Lloyds Bank Ltd* [1982] A.C. 584 at 598, where it was held, on construction, that the contract was *not* specifically enforceable; see below, para.21–020, fn.92.

[883] [1982] A.C. 584 at 598.

[884] *The Lancaster* [1980] 2 Lloyd's Rep. 497 at 500; *The Scaptrade* [1983] A.C. 694 at 702; *The Niizura* [1996] 2 Lloyd's Rep. 66 at 72; *The Starsin* [2003] UKHL 12; [2004] 1 A.C. 715 at [119].

[885] *Baumwoll Manufactur v Furness* [1893] A.C. 8; *The Giuseppe di Vittorio* [1998] 1 Lloyd's Rep. 136 at 156; *BP Operating Co Ltd v Chevron Transport (Scotland) Ltd* [2001] UKHL 50; [2003] A.C. 197 at [78], [79].

[886] cf. above, at fn.836.

[887] See above, para.14–138.

that a time charterer had "no proprietary *or possessory* rights in the ship".[888] It can be inferred that a "possessory right" might have been protected. Where the hirer of a chattel is in actual possession of it he should certainly be protected against a third party who acquires the chattel with notice of the hirer's interest.

It is less clear whether, in this context, the words "possessory rights" refer only to rights *of* possession, or extend also to rights *to* possession, i.e. whether a person who has a contractual right to the *future* possession of a chattel would similarly be protected against the third party. In *The Stena Nautica (No.2)*[889] B had demise-chartered his ship to A under a contract which also gave A an option to purchase her. Later, while B was in possession of the ship, he granted a second demise charter of her to C who had no knowledge of the earlier contract. A exercised his option to purchase and it was held that his only remedy was by way of damages against B: since A's option to purchase was not specifically enforceable,[890] he could not assert rights to the ship against C. The question whether A could assert a *right to future possession as demise charterer* against C did not, strictly speaking, arise since A was suing to enforce, not that right, but rather his right as a person who had exercised an option to purchase. But it seems from the reasoning of the Court of Appeal that A's right to possession as demise charterer would have been protected only if the contract under which the right arose was one in respect of which the court was willing to make an order of specific performance. The argument of commercial convenience which justifies the decision in the *Port Line* case[891] would seem to apply as much where a contract creates a right to the future possession of a chattel as where it creates the right to have some particular use made of the chattel. In each case the right is hard to discover and should not be enforced against a third party *without* actual knowledge of it; and adequate protection against a third party *with* such knowledge is provided by the rules relating to the tort of inducing a breach of contract.

---

[888] [1958] 2 Q.B. 146 at 166 (italics supplied).

[889] [1982] 2 Lloyd's Rep. 336.

[890] See below, para.21–023. A licence to occupy *land* can be enforced against a trespasser even by a licensee not yet in possession: *Dutton v Manchester Airport Plc* [1999] 2 All E.R. 675.

[891] See above, para.14–138.

CHAPTER FIFTEEN

ASSIGNMENT[1]

15–001   The benefit of a contract may be transferred to a third party by a process called assignment. This is a transaction between the person entitled to the benefit of the contract (called the creditor or assignor) and the third party (called the assignee) as a result of which the assignee becomes entitled to sue the person liable under the contract (called the debtor). The debtor is not a party to the transaction and his consent is not necessary for its validity.

1. AT COMMON LAW

15–002   The common law refused to give effect to assignments of "choses in action", that is, of rights which could be asserted only by bringing an action and not by taking possession of a physical thing. The early lawyers found it hard to think of a transfer of something intangible like a contractual right.[2] Later the rule was

---

[1] Marshall, *The Assignment of Choses in Action*; Smith, *The Law of Assignment*; Tolhurst, *The Assignment of Contractual Rights*.
[2] Pollock and Maitland, *History of English Law*, Vol.II, p.226.

based on the fear that assignments of choses in action might lead to maintenance,[3] that is, to "intermeddling in litigation in which the intermeddler has no concern."[4] Such conduct was formerly a crime and a tort.[5]

Exceptionally, debts due to and by the Crown[6] and negotiable instruments[7] could be assigned at law. The common law also recognised that assignments were effective in equity: thus a promise by the assignee not to sue the debtor was good consideration for a promise by the debtor to pay the assignee.[8] And although an assignment did not at law entitle the assignee to sue the debtor, it might be binding as a contract between assignor and assignee, for breach of which the assignee could recover damages.[9]

The common law did give effect to three kinds of transactions which to some extent did the work of assignment.

Novation. Novation is a contract between debtor, creditor and a third party **15–003** that the debt owed by the debtor shall henceforth be owed to the third party. This is not assignment because the consent of all three parties,[10] including that of the debtor,[11] is necessary, and because the original debt is not, strictly, transferred. The third party's right against the debtor is based on the new contract between him and debtor,[12] the consideration for the debtor's promise typically taking the form of some benefit (such as a payment of money) provided by the third party to the original creditor.[13] As the "third party" is thus a party to the tripartite contract of novation, it follows that he would not acquire any rights under the Contracts (Rights of Third Parties) Act 1999.[14] At common law, the third party's claim under the novation would fail if no consideration moved from him for the debtor's promise to pay him[15]; and this position is probably not affected by the 1999 Act.[16]

---

[3] *Johnson v Collings* (1880) 1 East 98; *Liversidge v Broadbent* (1859) 4 H. & N. 603; *Fitzroy v Cave* [1905] 2 K.B. 364 at 372.

[4] *Neville v London Express Newspaper Ltd* [1919] A.C. 368 at 385.

[5] Criminal and tortious liability for maintenance and champerty (bargaining for a share in the proceeds of the litigation) were abolished by Criminal Law Act 1967, ss.13(1) and 14(1), but under s.14(2) this has (in general) no effect on the validity of contracts: see para.11–012, above. For possible effects on the validity of certain assignments, see below, para.15–058 et seq.

[6] *Miles v Williams* (1714) 1 P.Wms. 249 at 259.

[7] *Ryall v Rowles* (1750) 1 Ves.Sen. 348; below, para.15–046.

[8] *Forth v Stanton* (1681) 1 Wms.Saund. 210; cf. *Moulsdale v Birchall* (1772) 2 W.Bl. 820; *Master v Miller* (1791) 4 T.R. 320 at 341 (for another explanation, see *Israel v Douglas* (1789) 1 H.Bl. 239). For other instances of recognition of assignment at common law, see *Winch v Keely* (1787) 1 T.R. 619; *Carpenter v Marnell* (1802) 3 B. & P. 40; *Crowfoot v Gurney* (1832) 9 Bing. 372.

[9] *Gerrard v Lewis* (1867) L.R. 2 C.P. 305.

[10] See *The Aktion* [1987] 1 Lloyd's Rep. 283 at 309.

[11] Such consent may be given in advance, in the initial contract with the creditor: *Habibsons Bank Ltd v Standard Chartered Bank (Hong Kong) Ltd* [2010] EWCA Civ 1335 at [22].

[12] e.g. *Rasbora Ltd v JCL Marine Ltd* [1977] 1 Lloyd's Rep. 645.

[13] Consideration need not move to the promisor (the original debtor): above, para.3–024.

[14] Rights are conferred by virtue of this Act only on "a person who is *not* a party" to the contract (s.1(1)).

[15] *Tatlock v Harris* (1789) 3 T.R. 174 at 180; *Cuxon v Chadley* (1824) 3 B. & C. 591; *Wharton v Walker* (1825) 4 B. & C. 163.

[16] A third party can make a claim under the Act even though he provided no consideration (above, para.14–099); but in the case put in the text the "third party" is a person to whom a promise has been made and the Act does not make it clear whether, if that promise is not enforceable, the person to whom it was made is to be regarded as a promisee or as a third party. Prima facie "promisee" in the Act means a "party to the contract by whom the term is enforceable against the promisor" (s.1(7)); but the Act also envisages the possibility of a person's being the promisee even though the term is *not* so enforceable because a "defence" is available to the promisor (s.3(2)(b)).

15–004   **Acknowledgment.**[17] If a creditor asks his debtor to pay a third party, and the debtor agrees to do so, and notifies the third party of his agreement, then the third party may be entitled to sue the debtor.[18] It was for long doubtful whether such a transaction had to be supported by consideration. In the second half of the nineteenth century, the following distinction was established: that consideration was, in general, necessary; but that it was not necessary where the debtor actually had in his hands (e.g. as banker) a fund belonging to the creditor.[19] But this distinction, which seems to have little merit, was disregarded in the later case of *Shamia v Joory*.[20] The defendant owed some £1,200 to his agent Youssuf, who asked him to pay £500 of this sum to the claimant, Youssuf's brother. The defendant agreed to do so and notified the claimant of this agreement. It was held that the claimant could sue the defendant for the £500, though no consideration moved from him. If this decision is right,[21] acknowledgment is in one respect more advantageous than assignment, since certain types of assignment have to be supported by consideration.[22] On facts such as those of *Shamia v Joory*, it is probable that the defendant's promise to Youssuf to pay the £500 to the claimant could now be enforced by the claimant against the defendant by virtue of the Contracts (Right of Third Parties) Act 1999[23]; and such a claim could succeed even though the claimant had not provided any consideration for that promise.[24]

15–005   **Power of attorney.** A creditor can give a third party a power of attorney, authorising him to sue for the debt in the creditor's name, without any liability to account to creditor. But this device had many disadvantages from the third party's point of view. The most important of these was that a power of attorney could generally be revoked by the creditor, and was often revoked automatically by his death.[25]

2. EQUITABLE ASSIGNMENTS

15–006   Equity regarded the common law's fear of maintenance as unrealistic[26] and took the view that choses in action were property[27] which ought, in the interest of commercial convenience, to be transferable, e.g. to provide security for a loan. Choses in action were therefore assignable in equity.[28] The phrase "choses in

---

[17] Davies 75 L.Q.R. 220; cf. Yates 41 Conv. 49.
[18] *Wilson v Coupland* (1821) 5 B. & Ald. 228; *Hamilton v Spottiswoode* (1842) 4 Ex. 200; *Griffin v Weatherby* (1868) L.R. 3 Q.B. 753.
[19] *Liversidge v Broadbent* (1859) 4 H. & N. 603 at 612.
[20] [1958] 1 Q.B. 448.
[21] For criticism, see Goff and Jones, *The Law of Restitution* (7th edn), para.28–003.
[22] See below, para.15–024 et seq.
[23] This would depend on whether (a) the agreement between the defendant and Youssuf had contractual force; and (b) the requirements of ss.1(1)(a) or (b) and (2) were satisfied: see above, paras 14–091—14–093 the reasoning in nn.13 and 16 above would not apply since the claimant was clearly not a party to the agreement between those parties nor a promisee in it.
[24] See above, para.14–099. Any such claim would not affect the claimant's common law rights as described in the text above: see 1999 Act, s7(1).
[25] See below, para.16–106.
[26] *Wright v Wright* (1750) 1 Ves.Sen. 409 at 411 ("very refined").
[27] cf. *Alloway v Phillips (Inspector of Taxes)* [1980] 1 W.L.R. 888 at 893.
[28] *Crouch v Martin* (1707) 2 Vern. 595; *Ryall v Rowles* (1750) 1 Ves.Sen. 348; *Ex p. South* (1818) 3 Swanst. 392.

action" here refers to claims for the enforcement of a contract (e.g. for the sum due under it or for damages for its breach). These must be distinguished from *remedies* that are sometimes provided by law for purposes other than enforcement: e.g. where a person who has entered into a transaction as a result of misrepresentation or undue influence is entitled to rescind it. It has been held that this remedy is not itself a chose in action and therefore cannot be assigned; but it is possible for the person to whom the remedy is available to agree to account to another person for any financial benefit which he may derive from its exercise.[29]

Where a chose in action is assigned, the machinery used for enforcing the assignment varied with the nature of the chose in action, which might be legal or equitable. A legal chose is one which could be sued for only in a common law court, e.g. a contract debt. An equitable chose is one which could be sued for only in the Court of Chancery, e.g. an interest in a trust fund.

Legal choses. There were four reasons why equity could not simply allow the assignee of a legal chose to sue the debtor in the Court of Chancery. First, equity did not in general enforce purely legal debts. Secondly, the debtor might suffer hardship if he were later sued for a second payment at common law by the original creditor (the assignor): he would have to take separate proceedings in Chancery to make good his defence. Thirdly, the assignor might retain some interest in the debt, e.g. he might assign only part of it: in such a case, it was desirable to have him (as well as the assignee) before the court, so that the relative rights of all the parties could be determined in a single action. Fourthly, the assignor might wish to dispute the validity of the assignment: this possibility again made it desirable to have him before the court at some stage.   **15–007**

These difficulties were solved by allowing the assignee to sue the debtor at common law in the name of the assignor. If the assignor refused to co-operate, equity could compel him to do so. In the resulting proceedings in Chancery, the rights of the assignor could be adequately safeguarded. Now that common law and equity are administered in the same courts, the first of the above two reasons for the original method of enforcing equitable assignments are of purely historical interest, but the third and fourth reasons may retain their force and sometimes make it important to have all the parties before the court.[30] But the action against the debtor need no longer be brought in the name of the assignor[31]: he is simply joined as co-claimant if he is willing to co-operate with the assignee, and as co-defendant if he is not,[32] i.e. if he wishes to dispute the validity of the assignment. The machinery of joining the assignor as a party to the action may, however, break down if the assignor has ceased to exist, e.g. because the assignor is a company which has been dissolved.[33] Where the assignor is a natural person

---

[29] *Investors Compensation Scheme Ltd v West Bromwich BC* [1998] 1 W.L.R. 896; for contrary dicta, see below, para.15–063.

[30] *The Aiolos* [1983] 2 Lloyd's Rep. 25 at 33; cf. *Deposit Protection Board v Dalia* [1994] 2 A.C. 367 at 387, reversed on other grounds, [1994] 2 A.C. 367 at 391. See generally, Tolhurst 118 L.Q.R. 98.

[31] *Weddell v J A Pearce & Major* [1988] Ch. 26 at 40.

[32] Conversely, if the assignor sues the debtor, the assignee must be joined as a party to the action: *Three Rivers DC v Bank of England* [1996] Q.B. 292.

[33] See *M H Smith (Plant Hire) Ltd v D L Mainwaring (T/A Onshore) Ltd* [1986] 2 Lloyd's Rep. 244, where subrogation (below, fn.239) was said at 246 in this respect to resemble equitable assignment.

and has died, it would seem to be possible for the assignee to sue, joining the assignor's legal personal representatives.

15–008   **Equitable choses.** The assignee of an equitable chose could in his own name sue the trustee in the Court of Chancery.[34] The chose being equitable, the trustee was not exposed to the danger of a subsequent action in a different (common law) court by the assignor. It was necessary to make the assignor a party to the proceedings only if he retained some interest in the subject-matter. If he wished to dispute the validity of the assignment, he could take separate proceedings for that purpose.[35]

3. STATUTORY ASSIGNMENTS

15–009   Certain specific contracts, such as life and marine insurance policies and bills of lading, were made assignable by statute during the nineteenth century.[36] A more general provision was made by the Judicature Act 1873, which fused the courts of common law and equity, and so made obsolete some of the reasons for the original method for enforcing equitable assignments of legal choses. There was no longer any difficulty in allowing the assignee to sue in any Division of the High Court; and a debtor who was successfully sued by the assignee no longer had to take separate proceedings if he were sued again by the assignor: he could simply rely on his payment to the assignee as a defence in the second action. Thus it was no longer necessary to have the assignor before the court unless he retained an interest in the subject-matter[37] or wished to dispute the validity of the assignment.

15–010   **Law of Property Act 1925, section 136(1).** Section 136(1) of the Law of Property Act 1925 (re-enacting s.25(6) of the Judicature Act 1873), provides that an absolute assignment by writing under the hand of the assignor (not purporting to be by way of charge only) of any debt or other legal thing in action, of which express notice in writing has been given to the debtor or trustee, is effectual in law to pass the legal right to the debt or thing in action to the assignee. The effect of such an assignment is to enable the assignee to sue the debtor in his own name, and to sue alone, i.e. without joining the assignor as a party to the action. The subsection finally makes provision for enabling the assignor to dispute the validity of the assignment; if he does so, the debtor can drop out of the proceedings and leave the dispute to be fought out between assignor and assignee.

(a) Absolute Assignment

15–011   Under s.136(1), the assignee can sue alone only if the assignment is *absolute*; this requirement excludes cases in which the assignor retains an interest in the subject-

---

[34] *Cator v Croydon Canal Co* (1841) 4 Y. & C. Ex. 405 at 593; *Donaldson v Donaldson* (1854) Kay 711.

[35] e.g. *Bridge v Bridge* (1852) 16 Beav. 315.

[36] e.g. Bills of Lading Act 1855, s.1 (now repealed and superseded by Carriage of Goods by Sea Act 1992); Policies of Assurance Act 1867 (life insurance); Marine Insurance Act 1868 (see now 1906 Act, s.50(1)).

[37] *The Mount I* [2001] EWCA Civ 68; [2001] 1 Lloyd's Rep. 597 at [60].

matter so that it is still desirable to have him before the court. Absolute assignments are for this purpose contrasted with the following.

Assignment by way of charge. In *Durham Bros v Robertson*[38] a builder to whom £1,080 was due under a building contract borrowed money and assigned the £1,080 to the lender as security for the loan "until the money [lent] . . . be repaid." This was held to be an assignment by way of charge. The builder had not assigned the £1,080 absolutely to the lender; he had only charged that sum with the repayment of the money he had borrowed. But an assignment may be absolute although it is made by way of mortgage, and does not transfer the subject-matter out-and-out. Thus in *Tancred v Delagoa Bay, etc., Ry*[39] a debt was assigned as security for a loan of money, with the proviso that, if the assignor repaid the loan, the debt should be reassigned to him. This was held to be an absolute assignment.

15–012

The distinction between these two cases can best be understood by taking the point of view of the debtor, and assuming that he wants to pay the debt. In *Tancred*'s case, he can find out from documents in his own possession whether he ought to pay the assignor or the assignee; for even if the debt is reassigned to the assignor, the debtor can safely pay the assignee until he gets notice of the reassignment.[40] But in *Durham Bros v Robertson* the debtor does not know whether to pay the assignee until it is settled whether the assignor still owes anything to the assignee. The debtor cannot find this out from documents in his own possession: he would have to investigate the state of accounts between the assignor and assignee. Similarly, if the assignee sued the debtor, the court could not determine whom the debtor should pay without investigating the state of accounts between assignor and assignee; and it cannot satisfactorily do this if the assignor is not before the court. For similar reasons, an assignment of a debt to a bank was held to be by way of charge only where it was expressed to be made as security for a loan from the bank and was to become operative only on the assignor's failing to perform his obligations under the original contract which had given rise to the debt or under the loan agreement with the bank.[41]

In *Bank of Liverpool v Holland*[42] a creditor assigned a debt of £285 to a bank "to hold the same absolutely. And it is hereby agreed and declared that the amount recoverable by these presents shall not at any time exceed" £150. This was held to be an absolute assignment of the whole debt, with the proviso that, if the bank recovered more than £150, it was to hold the excess on trust for the assignor. This part of the arrangement did not concern the debtor: he could get a good discharge by paying the bank at any time.

Assignment of part of a debt. An assignment of part of a debt (e.g. of £500 out of the £1,000 which X owes me; or of half of what X owes me) is not

15–013

---

[38] [1898] 1 Q.B. 765; cf. *Jones v Humphreys* [1902] 1 K.B. 10; *Mercantile Bank of London Ltd v Evans* [1899] 2 Q.B. 613; *Colonial Mutual General Ins Co v ANZ Banking Group (New Zealand)* [1995] 1 W.L.R. 1140 at 1144.

[39] (1889) 23 Q.B.D. 239; cf. *Hughes v Pump House Hotel Co Ltd* [1902] 2 K.B. 190; *The Cebu* [1983] Q.B. 1005 at 1016 (where nothing seems to have turned on the distinction between equitable and statutory assignments).

[40] See below, para.15–023.

[41] *The Halcyon the Great* [1984] 1 Lloyd's Rep. 283.

[42] (1926) 43 T.L.R. 29; cf. *Comfort v Betts* [1891] 1 Q.B. 737; *Fitzroy v Cave* [1905] 2 K.B. 364; *Ramsay v Hartley* [1977] 1 W.L.R. 686.

absolute.[43] In such a case a debtor who wants to pay may know perfectly well how much to pay to whom. But to hold such an assignment absolute might cause hardship to a debtor who wished to dispute the debt. If the assignment were absolute, the assignee would be able to sue alone. In this action, the debtor might be able to show that there was no debt. But he would have to prove this over again if he were later sued by the assignor for the balance of the alleged debt. And if the assignor split the debt up into a large number of small parts, the debtor might have to defend many actions arising out of the same transaction. Hence it is necessary, for the protection of the debtor, to have all the interested parties before the court. For the same reason, an assign*or* of part of a debt cannot sue for the part he retains without joining the assignee as a party to the action.[44]

The above reasoning does not apply to an assignment of the *balance* of a debt. Suppose A owes B £100 and pays off £25 of the debt. An assignment of the remaining £75 would be absolute since it would be an assignment of B's entire remaining interest in the debt.[45]

15–014   **Conditional assignment.** Section 136(1) of the Law of Property Act 1925 contrasts absolute assignments with assignments by way of charge; but some judgments also distinguish between absolute and conditional assignments.[46] Many assignments by way of charge are, in fact, assignments subject to the condition subsequent that they will cease to have effect when the assignor pays off the debt which he owes to the assignee. Assignments which are subject to some other condition (whether precedent or subsequent) should be treated in the same way.[47] Whatever the condition may be, the assignor retains a contingent interest in the debt, and is thus a desirable party to an action to recover it. Suppose that A assigns rent due under a lease "to my daughter until she marries". The assignment should not be absolute since it is desirable that A should be a party to an action brought by his daughter against the tenant for rent. If the daughter could sue alone, she might be able to prove that she was unmarried, and so entitled to the rent. But this would not prevent A, in a subsequent action against the tenant, from proving that the court in the first action had made a mistake in finding that the daughter was unmarried, so that the tenant would have to pay over again. What matters to the tenant is not whether the daughter is married but that the question should be decided, one way or the other, so as to bind both A and the daughter.[48]

(b) Debt or Other Legal Thing in Action

15–015   A "debt" in s.136(1) is a sum certain due under contract or otherwise.[49] The phrase "other legal thing in action" has been broadly interpreted: it means any

---

[43] *Forster v Baker* [1910] 2 K.B. 636; *Re Steel Wing Co* [1921] 1 Ch. 349; *Williams v Atlantic Assurance Co Ltd* [1933] 1 K.B. 81 at 100 (the actual decision seems to turn on Marine Insurance Act 1906, s.50(2)); *Deposit Protection Board v Dalia* [1994] 2 A.C. 367 at 392; *The Mount I* [2001] EWCA Civ 68; [2001] 1 Lloyd's Rep. 597 at [74].
[44] *Walter & Sullivan Ltd v J Murphy & Sons Ltd* [1955] 2 Q.B. 584.
[45] e.g. *Harding v Harding* (1886) 17 Q.B.D. 442.
[46] e.g. *Durham Bros v Robertson* [1898] 1 Q.B. 765 at 773; cf. *The Balder London* [1980] 2 Lloyd's Rep. 489 at 495.
[47] e.g. *The Halcyon the Great* [1984] 1 Lloyd's Rep. 283; *Herkules Piling v Tilbury Construction* (1992) 61 Build.L.R. 107 at 117.
[48] cf. *The Aiolos* [1983] 2 Lloyd's Rep. 25 at 33.
[49] e.g. under statute: *Dawson v Great Northern & City Ry* [1905] 1 K.B. 260.

"debt or right which the common law looks on as not assignable by reason of its being a chose in action, but which a court of equity deals with as being assignable".[50]

The phrase includes equitable choses in action,[51] though this point is of little practical importance since an assignment of an equitable chose is no more effective under the statute than it is in equity. The phrase also includes a debt not yet due but accruing due,[52] and the benefit of an obligation to do something other than to pay cash,[53] or of one to forbear from doing something.[54] It does not include choses in action which can be transferred *only*[55] by complying with some other statute; thus shares in a company cannot be assigned by statutory assignment under s.136, but only in the manner prescribed by the articles of association of the company.[56]

4. GENERAL REQUIREMENTS

(a) Formalities

A statutory assignment must be "by writing under the hand of the assignor". An assignment which for some reason fails to take effect as a statutory assignment may still be a good equitable assignment. Thus although an oral assignment cannot take effect under the statute, it may be valid in equity.[57] The statute merely provides an alternative method of making assignments; it does not destroy the earlier method.

15–016

A disposition of an equitable interest "must be in writing signed by the person disposing of the same or by his agent thereunto lawfully authorised".[58] This rule is mandatory: an oral assignment of an equitable chose is therefore void.[59]

As a general rule, writing is not necessary for an equitable assignment of a legal chose in action. But a contract may provide that rights under it shall be assigned only by use of a specified form, such as writing. An attempt to assign such rights without using the stipulated form is probably not effective as an assignment, though it may amount to a contract to assign.[60]

---

[50] *Torkington v Magee* [1902] 2 K.B. 427 at 430 (actual decision reversed on another ground: [1903] 1 K.B. 644); cf. *King v Victoria Ins Co* [1896] A.C. 250 at 254; *Manchester Brewery v Coombs* [1901] 2 Ch. 608 at 619.

[51] *Re Pain* [1919] 1 Ch. 38 at 44.

[52] *Brice v Bannister* (1878) 3 Q.B.D. 569 at 574; *Walker v Bradford Old Bank* (1884) 12 Q.B.D. 511; *Re Green* [1979] 1 W.L.R. 1211 at 1219–1224. Contrast *Law v Coburn* [1972] 1 W.L.R. 1238, where the date on which the debt became due was crucial under the relevant legislation.

[53] *Torkington v Magee*, above.

[54] *Jacoby v Whitmore* (1883) 49 L.T. 335.

[55] s.136 may apply to a policy of marine insurance though such a policy is *also* assignable under Marine Insurance Act 1906, s.50: see *The Mount I* [2001] EWCA Civ 68; [2001] 1 Lloyd's Rep. 597, at [74].

[56] Companies Act 2006, s.544(1).

[57] cf. below, para.15–035.

[58] Law of Property Act 1925, s.53(1)(c), formerly Statute of Frauds 1677, s.9. Unlike the statute of frauds, s.53(1)(c) applies to all "dispositions", whether they are assignments or not. But it does not apply to a transfer of the legal title which is intended to operate as a transfer of the equitable interest, even though before the transfer the legal title and the equitable interest were in different hands; *Vandervell v IRC* [1967] 2 A.C. 291. Nor does it apply to resulting, implied or constructive trusts: see s.53(2) and *Neville v Wilson* [1997] Ch. 144. As to joinder of documents, see above, para.5–024.

[59] *Oughtred v IRC* [1960] A.C. 206; cf. *Grey v IRC* [1960] A.C. 1.

[60] cf. below, para.15–025.

For the protection of the assignor's creditors, provision has been made by various statutes for the registration of certain assignments. Section 344 of the Insolvency Act 1986,[61] for example, requires general assignments of book debts (or any class of them) made by a person engaged in any business to be registered; if they are not registered they are void as against the trustee in bankruptcy to the extent specified in the section.

(b) Intention to Assign

15–017   Although assignments must sometimes be in writing, no particular form of words has to be used to effect an assignment. The document need not on its face purport to be an assignment.[62] As Lord Macnaghten said in *William Brandt's Sons & Co v Dunlop Rubber Co*[63]:

> "An equitable assignment does not always take that form. It may be addressed to the debtor. It may be couched in the language of command. It may be a courteous request. It may assume the form of mere permission. The language is immaterial if the meaning is plain. All that is necessary is that the debtor should be given to understand that the debt has been made over by the creditor to some third person."[64]

An assignment is not itself a contract between assignor and debtor: its legal nature is that of a direction amounting to the transfer of a right. It follows that an assignment does not confer rights on the assignee, under the Contracts (Rights of Third Parties) Act 1999.[65]

15–018   **Assignment distinguished from mandate.** A creditor does not necessarily assign a debt by asking his debtor to pay a third party. The request may be intended only as a mandate (or instruction) to the debtor to pay the third party.[66] Such a mandate does not give the third party any rights against the debtor, and can be revoked by the creditor. Similarly, a person who draws a cheque on his bank in favour of a third person does not thereby assign part of his bank balance.[67] The bank is not liable to the third party, though if it fails to pay him it may be liable in damages to its own customer. The position is the same where the customer gives a standing order or direct debit instruction to his bank in favour of the third party.[68]

---

[61] See also Companies Act 2006, ss.860, 861.

[62] But an ineffective transfer (i.e. a novation, see para.15–003) may not suffice as an intention to assign: *Essar Steel Ltd v The Argo Fund* [2006] EWCA Civ 241; [2006] 2 Lloyd's Rep 134 at [63].

[63] [1905] A.C. 454.

[64] At 462; cf. also *Spellman v Spellman* [1961] 1 W.L.R. 921; *Palmer v Carey* [1926] A.C. 703; *Re Marwalt* [1992] BCC 32 at 37; *Colonial Mutual General Ins Co Ltd v ANZ Banking Group (New Zealand) Ltd* [1995] 1 W.L.R. 1140; *Coulter v Chief of Dorset Police* [2003] EWHC 3391 (Ch); [2004] 1 W.L.R. 1425; and see *Swiss Bank Corp v Lloyds Bank Ltd* [1982] A.C. 584 at 613 and *Kijowski v New Capital Properties* (1990) 15 Con.L.R. 1 (where there was no assignment).

[65] See above, para.14–090 et seq.

[66] *Ex p. Hall* (1878) 10 Ch.D. 615; cf. *Re Williams* [1917] 1 Ch. 1; *Timpson's Executors v Yerbury* [1936] 1 K.B. 645; *Dalton v IRC* [1958] T.R. 45. For a similar distinction between a contract for the benefit of a third party and a mandate to pay a third party, see above, para.14–041.

[67] Bills of Exchange Act 1882, s.53(1); *Schroeder v Central Bank of London Ltd* (1876) 34 L.T. 735; *Deposit Protection Board v Dalia* [1994] 2 A.C. 367 at 400.

[68] cf., in Scotland, *Mercedes-Benz Finance Ltd v Clydesdale Bank Plc* 1997 S.L.T. 905.

(c) Communication to Assignee

An assignment has no effect unless it is communicated[69] to the assignee by the   **15–019**
assignor, or by someone with his authority[70]; or unless it is made in pursuance of
a prior agreement between assignor and assignee. The reason for the requirement
is not immediately obvious since a person can have property transferred to him
without his knowledge, subject to a right to repudiate the transfer when he
becomes aware of it.[71] One possible reason for the requirement is that communication to the assignee is evidence of intention to assign[72]; but such an intention could
equally well be proved by other evidence. Alternatively, communication to the
assignee may be regarded as the equivalent of the delivery which is necessary to
perfect a gift of a chattel made otherwise than by deed.[73] A final possible
explanation of the requirement is that it is based on the nature of assignment as
a transaction between assignor and assignee.

(d) Notice to Debtor

(i) *How to give notice*

Notice of an equitable assignment may be oral,[74] but if the chose assigned is   **15–020**
equitable, oral notice will seldom be effective between successive assignees.[75]
Notice of a statutory assignment under s.136 of the Law of Property Act 1925
must be in writing.[76] It need not be given by the assignor, nor at the time of the
assignment: it may be given by the assignee and is effective so long as it is given
before action is brought.[77] There must, however, be a *notice* of assignment given
by assignor or assignee: it is not enough to show that the debtor came to know of
the assignment in some other way: e.g. as a result of discovery in legal or arbitral
proceedings.[78] No particular form of words is necessary[79]; but the notice must
clearly and unconditionally[80] tell the debtor to pay a third party *as assignee*, and not
merely as agent for the creditor.[81] A notice which incorrectly states the date of the
assignment or, it seems, the amount of the debt, is invalid.[82] But a notice which

---

[69] According to *Alexander v Steinhardt, Walker & Co* [1903] 2 K.B. 208 posting is sufficient
communication, but that case was doubted in *Timpson's Executors v Yerbury* [1936] 1 K.B. 645 at
657.
[70] e.g. by the debtor: *Burn v Carvalho* (1839) 4 My. & Cr. 690.
[71] *Standing v Bowring* (1885) 31 Ch.D. 282.
[72] See *Re Hamilton* (1921) 124 L.T. 737.
[73] See below, para.15–029.
[74] *Ex p. Agra Bank* (1868) L.R. 3 Ch.App. 555.
[75] See below, para.15–023.
[76] See above, para.15–016; there is no requirement of notice for an assignment under Marine
Insurance Act 1906, s.50: *The Mount I* [2001] EWCA Civ 68; [2001] 1 Lloyd's Rep. 597.
[77] *Walker v Bradford Old Bank* (1884) 12 Q.B.D. 511; *Bateman v Hunt* [1904] 2 K.B. 530; *Re
Westerton* [1919] 2 Ch. 104; *Holt v Heatherfield Trust Ltd* [1942] 2 K.B. 1.
[78] *Herkules Piling Ltd v Tilbury Construction Ltd* (1992) 61 Build.L.R. 107.
[79] *Smith v SS "Zigurds" Owners* [1934] A.C. 209.
[80] *The Balder London* [1980] 2 Lloyd's Rep. 489 at 495.
[81] *James Talcott Ltd v John Lewis & Co Ltd* [1940] 3 All E.R. 592.
[82] *Stanley v English Fibres Industries Ltd* (1889) 68 L.J.Q.B. 839; *W F Harrison & Co Ltd v Burke*
[1956] 1 W.L.R. 419; criticised by R.E.M. 72 L.Q.R. 321 and quaere whether a different result might
obtain in the light of the current more "purposive" approach to interpretation (see above, para.6–011),
especially as applied to notices: *Mannai Investment Co Ltd v Eagle Star Life Assurance Co Ltd* [1997]
A.C. 749.

says nothing at all about these particulars appears to be valid, so long as it describes the debt with sufficient certainty. A notice is valid although it inaccurately states that another notice had been previously given.[83]

A notice sent through the post has been said to take effect when it is received by the debtor.[84] This is clearly right where a dispute arises between assignee and debtor, for it is unreasonable to make the debtor suffer for failing to act on a notice of which he is not yet aware. But where the dispute is between successive assignees, it is at least arguable that the first to post his notice should have priority over any other assignee who has not yet posted his notice (or otherwise communicated with the debtor) when the first notice was posted.[85]

(ii) Effects of notice

15–021   **Between assignor and assignee.** The rights of these parties may depend on whether the assignment is statutory[86]; and it can only have this character if notice is given.[87] If no notice is given, the assignment may still be effective in equity.[88] Notice to the debtor is not necessary to perfect the rights of an equitable assignee against the assignor.[89]

15–022   **Between assignee and debtor.** Notice is, however, necessary to perfect the title of an equitable assignee against the debtor,[90] since without such notice the debtor is entitled to assume that he remains liable to his original creditor (the assignor) and that he will get a good discharge by paying the assignor.[91] Notice may[92] also turn the assignment into a statutory assignment, in which case the debtor is liable to be sued by the assignee alone: he can no longer insist that the assignor be made a party to the action. Where the assignment is statutory, the debtor ceases, as soon as notice has been given, to be liable to the assignor[93] and becomes liable to the assignee. It is submitted that the same is true, where an assignment of part of a debt is valid in equity, to the extent of the amount assigned[94]; for it has been held that if the debtor in such a case ignores the notice and pays the assignor he is not discharged and will have to make a second payment

---

[83] *Van Lynn Developments Ltd v Pelias Construction Ltd* [1969] 1 Q.B. 607.

[84] *Holt v Heatherfield Trust Ltd* [1942] 2 K.B. 1 at 6.

[85] *Holt v Heatherfield Trust Ltd*, above is not inconsistent with this suggestion since the order in which the two claimants communicated with the debtor is not stated in the report.

[86] See below, para.15–026.

[87] Law of Property Act 1925, s.136(1).

[88] *Holt v Heatherfield Trust Ltd* [1942] 2 K.B. 1.

[89] *Gorringe v Irwell India Rubber, etc., Works* (1886) 34 Ch.D. 128; *Re Trytel* [1952] 2 T.L.R. 32. Other aspects of the latter case are discussed in *Performing Rights Society v Rowland* [1997] 3 All E.R. 336.

[90] *Warner Bros Records Inc v Rollgreen Ltd* [1976] Q.B. 430; Kloss 39 Conv.(N.S.) 261; *Herkules Piling v Tilbury Construction* (1992) 61 Build.L.R. 107 at 119.

[91] See *Stocks v Dobson* (1853) 4 D.M. & G. 11.

[92] i.e. if the assignment is in writing and is "absolute" (above, paras 15–011—15–014).

[93] *Cottage Club Estates Ltd v Woodside Estates (Amersham) Ltd* [1928] 2 Q.B. 463 at 467; *The Halcyon the Great* [1984] 1 Lloyd's Rep. 283 at 289.

[94] The contrary view was, indeed, taken by Simon Brown L.J. in *Deposit Protection Board v Dalia* [1994] 2 A.C. 367 at 382, but in a dissenting judgment; actual decision reversed but on other grounds [1994] 2 A.C. 391.

to the assignee.[95] Nor, once notice of an equitable assignment had been given, could the assignor sue the debtor without joining the assignee[96]; and if he does join the assignee his claim will fail to the extent of the amount assigned.[97]

Between successive assignees. A chose in action may be successively **15–023** assigned by an insolvent assignor to several persons for more than it is worth. It is then necessary to decide in what order the assignees are to be paid. The rule is that successive assignments taken in good faith rank in the order in which notice is given to the debtor. Thus a later assignee may gain priority over an earlier one by giving notice first.[98] Notice of the assignment of an equitable chose should be given in writing, since oral notice of an assignment of such a chose does not give priority over later assignees in good faith and for value.[99]

5. CONSIDERATION[100]

The question whether an assignment must be supported by consideration is one **15–024** of great complexity. Two points must be made to clear the ground for the discussion. First, the dispute concerns only the relative rights of assignor and assignee. The debtor cannot refuse to pay the assignee on the ground that the assignment was gratuitous[101]; he is liable to pay the debt in any event and his only interest is to see that all possible claimants are before the court, so that he does not run the risk of having to pay twice over. So long as this possibility of prejudice to the debtor is removed by the joinder of all appropriate parties, it is only the assignor who can raise an issue as to the validity of the assignment on the ground that no consideration was given for it; indeed the only purpose of taking the point

---

[95] *Jones v Farrell* (1857) 1 D. & J. 208; *Brice v Bannister* (1878) 3 Q.B.D. 569 (where the assignment was equitable: see *Durham Bros v Robertson* [1898] 1 Q.B. 765 at 774); *Ex p. Nichols* (1883) 22 Ch.D. 782 at 787. In view of these authorities it is hard to accept the suggestion in *Warner Bros Records Inc v Rollgreen Ltd* [1976] Q.B. 430 at 443, 445 that an equitable assignment (of a legal chose) gives the assignee rights only against the assignor but none against the debtor. This suggestion may be true of an agreement to assign a chose in action in the future; but any historical support which may once have existed for it in the case of an actual present assignment seems to have been made obsolete by the developments outlined at paras 15–006—15–008, above. The suggestion seems, with respect, to be based on failure to distinguish between the substantive rights arising in equity out of assignments and the procedure for their enforcement: see *Three Rivers DC v Bank of England* [1996] Q.B. 292 at 315 and [1996] Q.B. 292 at 312, describing the requirement of joinder of the assignor to the action as "procedural and not substantive".
[96] See above, para.15–013.
[97] *Deposit Protection Board v Dalia* [1994] 2 A.C. 367 at 386, 387, reversed on other grounds [1994] 2 A.C. 367 at 391.
[98] *Dearle v Hall*, (1828) 3 Russ. 1; cf. *Stocks v Dobson* (1853) 4 D.M. & G. 11; *Mutual Life Assurance Society v Langley* (1886) 32 Ch.D. 460; *Pfeiffer Weinkellerei-Weineinkauf GmbH & Co v Arbuthnot Factors* [1988] 1 W.L.R. 150. See also Goode 92 L.Q.R. 554–559; Donaldson 93 L.Q.R. 324; Goode 93 L.Q.R.487.
[99] Law of Property Act 1925, s.137(3).
[100] Megarry 59 L.Q.R. 58; Hollond 59 L.Q.R. 129; Hall [1959] C.L.J. 99; Sheridan 33 Can. Bar Rev. 284.
[101] *Walker v Bradford Old Bank* (1884) 12 Q.B.D. 511; the question of consideration may also be relevant for revenue purposes, but the question in cases of this kind is always whether the assignor could have denied the validity of the assignment, as against the assignee: e.g. *Re Rose* [1952] Ch. 499; *Letts v IRC* [1957] 1 W.L.R. 201. Nor is the assignor precluded from relying on want of consideration moving from the assignee by Contracts (Rights of Third Parties) Act 1999 since in the relations between assignor and assignee the latter will not be a "third party" within subs.1(1).

is to enable the assignor to claim payment of the debt for himself. In practice this most frequently happens if the assignor has died or become bankrupt: his representatives may, for the benefit of his estate or of his creditors, wish to challenge the validity of the assignment. Secondly, the discussion concerns all gratuitous assignments, even those made by deed or for a nominal consideration.[102] The fact that an assignment is so made may make an assignor who disputes it liable in damages for breach of contract,[103] or make an agreement to assign binding contractually. But it does not, of itself, make the assignment effective as a transfer of the debt.

(a) Assignments of Future Property

15–025   An assignment is the transfer of an existing right. There can be no assignment of rights which do not yet exist or belong to the assignor. Such rights are sometimes called "future property". An attempt to assign future property may operate as an agreement to assign which must be supported by consideration if it is to be binding.[104]

Money payable in the future under an existing contract is not necessarily future property, and a disposition of the right to receive such money may be an assignment and not an agreement to assign.[105] If the contingency on which the money is payable is within the control of the creditor, there is no difficulty in holding that the disposition is an assignment: thus a builder can assign instalments to become due to him under a building contract as the work progresses, for here the contingency on which the money will become due is simply his own performance.[106] If, however, the contingency is not within his control, the disposition is prima facie an agreement to assign: this would be the position where a person purported to assign future dividends in a company which was not under any obligation to him to declare any dividends.[107] But even where the rights of the assignor depend on a contingency outside his control, he may purport to assign *either* his present right to future income from a specified source *or* the future income itself. A disposition of the first kind may be regarded as an assignment[108] and a disposition of the second kind as an agreement to assign.[109] The question into which category it falls turns on the construction of the document purporting to effect the disposition.

---

[102] *Kekewich v Manning* (1851) 1 D.M. & G. 176 (deed); *Dillon v Coppin* (1839) 4 My. & Cr. 647 (nominal consideration).

[103] *Gerrard v Lewis* (1867) L.R. 2 C.P. 305; *Cannon v Hartley* [1949] Ch. 213.

[104] *Tailby v Official Receiver* (1888) 13 App.Cas. 523; *Glegg v Bromley* [1912] 3 K.B. 474; *Cotton v Heyl* [1930] 1 Ch. 510; cf. *Meek v Kettlewell* (1843) 1 Ph. 342; *The Attika Hope* [1988] 1 Lloyd's Rep. 439 at 442 (where "*or* future chose" seems to be a misprint for "*of a* future chose"); *Wu Koon Tai v Wy Yau Loi* [1997] A.C. 179 at 189; *The Cebu (No.2)* [1993] Q.B. 1 (where it was not necessary to distinguish between an assignment and an agreement to assign); *The Mount I* [2001] EWCA Civ 68; [2001] 1 Lloyd's Rep. 597 at [80] ("for value"); *Smith v Smith* [2001] 1 W.L.R. 1937 at [11].

[105] cf. *Performing Rights Society v Rowland* [1997] 3 All E.R. 336 at 348.

[106] e.g. *Hughes v Pump House Hotel Co Ltd* [1902] 2 K.B. 190.

[107] *Norman v Commissioner of Taxation* (1963) 109 C.L.R. 9.

[108] *Shepherd v Commissioner of Taxation* [1966] A.L.R. 969; *The Mount I* [2001] EWCA Civ 68; [2001] 1 Lloyd's Rep. 597 at [80].

[109] *Williams v Commissioner of Inland Revenue* [1965] N.Z.L.R. 395.

(b) Statutory Assignments

A statutory assignment, whether of a legal or of an equitable chose in action, is **15–026**
effective although it is made without consideration.[110] The reasons for this rule are
discussed below.[111]

(c) Equitable Assignments

The effects of a "voluntary" equitable assignment (i.e. one which is not **15–027**
supported by consideration) must be discussed historically.

(i) *Before the Judicature Act 1873*

Procedural view. There are two main views as to the position in equity before **15–028**
1873. According to one view, the need for consideration depended on the procedure for enforcing the assignment. In *Re Westerton*[112] Sargant J. gave the following
reason for holding that a statutory assignment was effective without consideration:

> "Apart from the Judicature Act . . . the want of consideration would have
> been fatal to [the assignee's] claim. Prior to the Judicature Act . . . a legal
> chose in action such as this debt could not be transferred at law, and the
> assignee of the debt could only have sued in the name of the assignor, and in
> the absence of consent . . . or of a binding contract by the assignor . . . the
> use of the assignor's name could only have been enforced by filing a bill in
> equity . . . and equity would not have granted that relief unless the
> assignment had been for valuable consideration".[113]

Since a statutory assignee can now sue the debtor without the co-operation of the
assignor, "there is no reason for continuing against the assignee those terms which
were imposed by equity as a condition of granting relief".[114] In other words,
consideration is necessary if the assignee needs the co-operation of the assignor to
recover the debt, but is not necessary if the assignee does not need such co-operation. If this were true three things would follow.

First: consideration should not have been necessary in the rare cases in which
the assignee could sue alone at law.[115] This assumption is to some extent supported
by the rule that the voluntary transferee of a negotiable instrument could sue all
the parties liable on it, except the transferor.[116] But this rule was based on
commercial practice, and not on the fact that the transferee did not need the
co-operation of the transferor. It is not clear whether assignments of debts due to
and from the Crown had to be supported by consideration.

---

[110] *Harding v Harding* (1886) 17 Q.B.D. 442; *Re Westerton* [1919] 2 Ch. 104.
[111] See below, after fn.113 and below, at fn.126.
[112] [1919] 2 Ch. 104.
[113] ibid. at 111.
[114] ibid. at 114.
[115] See above, para.15–002.
[116] *Easton v Pratchett* (1835) 1 Cr.M. & R. 798 at 808. There is no reference to consideration in
Carriage of Goods by Sea Act 1992, s.2, which deals with the transfer of rights arising under a contract
contained in or evidenced by a bill of lading.

Secondly: consideration should not have been necessary for absolute assignments of equitable choses, since the assignee could sue without the co-operation of the assignor.[117] This assumption, too, is borne out by cases in which such assignments were upheld, though they were voluntary. But in most of these cases the fact that the assignee could sue alone is not even mentioned, let alone relied on.[118] The decisions were based on the view that the assignor had made a completed gift.[119] And in some cases voluntary assignments of equitable choses were held invalid as incomplete gifts[120]; these are hard to explain on the procedural view.

Thirdly: consideration should have been generally[121] necessary for the assignment of a legal chose, since the assignee could not sue the debtor without the co-operation of the assignor. Here the procedural view breaks down. Although some voluntary assignments of legal choses were held invalid, others were upheld.[122] The distinction between valid and invalid assignments was not based on procedural requirements. It depended on the question whether the assignor had made a completed gift.

15–029   **Completed gift view.** A person may enter into a contract to dispose of his property, or make a gift of it, or create a trust of the property in favour of another. Consideration (or a deed) is clearly necessary for the validity of a contract to dispose of property, including a contract to assign a chose in action. It is equally clear that consideration is not necessary for the validity of a trust of a chose in action.[123] All that is necessary is that the settlor should clearly have expressed his intention to create a trust. As in the case of trusts of promises for the benefit of a third party,[124] a mere intention to benefit is not enough: there must be an intention to create a trust. The settlor must intend to undertake a legally binding obligation to hold the subject-matter for the beneficiary, or to persuade someone else to undertake such an obligation.[125]

Consideration is also unnecessary for the validity of a completed gift. Thus in *Harding v Harding*[126] a voluntary statutory assignment was held binding on the ground that it was a completed gift. In many cases, the law requires a gift to be

---

[117] See above, para.15–008.

[118] Exceptionally, the argument is mentioned in *Ward v Audland* (1845) 8 Beav. 201 (the actual decision was doubted in *Kekewich v Manning* (1851) 1 D.M. & G. 176).

[119] *Kekewich v Manning*, above; *Bentley v Mackay* (1851) 15 Beav. 12; *Voyle v Hughes* (1854) 2 Sm. & G. 18; *Donaldson v Donaldson* (1854) Kay 711; *Nanney v Morgan* (1887) 37 Ch.D. 346; *Re Way's Trust* (1864) 2 D.J. & S. 365.

[120] e.g. *Bridge v Bridge* (1852) 16 Beav. 315 (doubted but distinguished in *T Choithram International v Pagarani* [2001] 1 W.L.R. 1 at 12); *Beech v Keep* (1854) 18 Beav. 285.

[121] Except where the legal chose was, even before the Judicature Act, assignable by some special statute (above, para.15–009) or at common law (above, para.15–002).

[122] *Ex p. Pye* (1811) Ves. 140; *Fortescue v Barnett* (1834) 3 My. & K. 36; *Paterson v Murphy* (1853) 11 Hare 88; *Richardson v Richardson* (1867) L.R. 3 Eq. 686; *Re King* (1879) 14 Ch.D. 179 (where the assignment was made before the Judicature Act); cf. *Re Patrick* [1891] 1 Ch. 82 and *Re Griffin* [1899] 1 Ch. 408, in which the provisions of the Judicature Act relating to assignment were not mentioned.

[123] *Ex p. Pye*, above; *Bentley v Mackay* (1851) 15 Beav. 12; *Paterson v Murphy*, above; *Richardson v Richardson*, above; *Paul v Constance* [1977] 1 W.L.R. 527. A declaration of trust is not, strictly, an assignment: see *Grey v IRC* [1958] Ch. 690, affirmed on other grounds: [1960] A.C. 1; cf. *Barbados Trust Co Ltd v Bank of Zambia* [2007] EWCA Civ 148; [2007] 1 Lloyd's Rep. 495.

[124] See above, paras 14–081—14–082.

[125] *Bayley v Boulcott* (1828) 4 Russ. 345; *Smith v Warde* (1845) 15 Sim. 56; *Re Caplen's Estate* (1876) 45 L.J.Ch. 280.

[126] (1886) 17 Q.B.D. 442.

made in a prescribed way: e.g. the gift of a chattel must be made by delivery with intention to pass the property, or by deed of gift.[127] If a purported gift of a chattel is not made in one of these two ways, it is incomplete or imperfect; and equity refuses to complete an imperfect gift by ordering the donor to make it in the proper legal manner.[128] In the same way, a voluntary assignment of a chose in action did not bind the assignor unless it was made in the manner, if any, required by law. In *Milroy v Lord*[129] the owner of shares in a company voluntarily assigned them by deed poll. This was held to be an imperfect gift since the legal title to the shares could not be transferred except by the execution of a proper instrument of transfer. Turner L.J. said:

> "In order to render a voluntary settlement valid and effectual, the settlor must have done everything which, according to the nature of the property comprised in the settlement, was necessary to be done in order to transfer the property and render the settlement binding upon him."[130]

The assignment thus failed as a gift but the assignees argued that it could still take effect as a declaration of trust. This argument, too, was rejected, as the donor had no intention to create a trust, but only an intention to make a gift.

Mitigation of the rule in *Milroy v Lord*. A gift is only incomplete under the rule in *Milroy v Lord* if something more has to be done *by the donor* to transfer the property. If the donor has done all that he needs to do to transfer the property, the gift is complete even though further steps to vest the property in the donee have to be taken by a third party,[131] or by the donee himself.[132] The rigour of the rule has, moreover, been mitigated in a number of ways. It has been held that, where the gift takes the form of a declaration of trust, the vesting of its subject-matter in *one* of a number of trustees suffices to complete the gift[133]; and that a gift of shares in a company may be completed by the execution of a proper instrument of transfer (coupled with evidence of intention that this was to take effect as a gift and with circumstances making it unconscionable for the donor to resile from the gift) even without delivery of the instrument of transfer to either the donee or to the company.[134] Where further steps to complete the gift are capable of being taken by the donee, the donor may constitute himself the agent for the donee to take those steps: e.g., by telling the donee that nothing more needs to be done by the donee to perfect the gift. Failure by the donor to take those steps will not then vitiate the

15–030

---

[127] *Re Breton's Estate* (1881) 17 Ch.D. 416; *Cochrane v Moore* (1890) 25 Q.B.D. 57; *Re Cole* [1964] Ch. 175.

[128] *Ellison v Ellison* (1802) 6 Ves. 656 at 662. For a special exception in cases of so-called *donatio mortis causa* see *Sen v Headley* [1991] Ch. 425 (land); *Woodard v Woodard* [1995] 3 All E.R. 980 (chattel).

[129] (1862) 4 D.F. & J. 264; cf. *Antrobus v Smith* (1805) 12 Ves. 39; *Jones v Lock* (1865) L.R. 1 Ch.App. 25; *Richards v Delbridge* (1874) L.R. 18 Eq. 11; *Heartley v Nicholson* (1875) L.R. 19 Eq. 233; *Macedo v Stroud* [1922] 2 A.C. 330; *Re Wale* [1956] 1 W.L.R. 1346; *Pappadakis v Pappadakis* [2000] 1 W.L.R. 79; McKay 40 Conv. 139.

[130] (1862) 4 D.F. & J. 264 at 274.

[131] *Re Rose* [1952] Ch. 499; following *Re Rose* [1949] Ch. 78; cf. *Mascall v Mascall* (1985) P. & C.R. 119 (transfer of a house); contrast *Re Fry* [1946] Ch. 312.

[132] cf. *Re Paradise Motor Co Ltd* [1968] 1 W.L.R. 1125 (defective execution by transferee did not invalidate gift of shares).

[133] *T Choithram International SA v Pagarani* [2001] 1 W.L.R. 1.

[134] *Pennington v Waine* [2002] EWCA Civ 227; [2002] 1 W.L.R. 2075; the *execution* of the instrument of transfer by donor is essential for this purpose: [2002] EWCA Civ 227 at [69].

gift if the donee has relied on the donor's statement so as to make it unconsciona-ble for the donor to invoke that failure as a ground of invalidity.[135]

The rule in *Milroy v Lord* applied only to gifts which had, by law, to be made in a certain form. The only formal requirement for the assignment of an *equitable* chose was that it must be in writing.[136] Hence in *Kekewich v Manning*[137] a voluntary settlement in writing of an equitable interest in property was held binding on the settlor, since there was nothing more that he could have done to transfer the property. Again, in the absence of special rules, such as those governing the transfer of shares in companies, equity did not lay down any formal requirements for the transfer of *legal* choses. Thus in *Fortescue v Barnett*[138] a voluntary assignment by deed[139] of a life insurance policy[140] was held binding on the assignor, as there was nothing more that he could do to complete the trans-fer.

15–031   **Other forms of incomplete gift.** A gift may be imperfect for some reason other than failure to use the proper form. The donor may only have said that he would make a gift in the future, or subject to some condition which can only be satisfied by his doing some further act. Thus a gift "to my daughter when she marries a man of whom I approve" is imperfect until the donor gives his approval.

15–032   **Completed gift view to be preferred.** The "completed gift" view seems to be preferable to the "procedural" view in two respects. It is more consistent with the reasoning of the cases decided before the Judicature Act. And it explains why voluntary assignments of legal choses were sometimes upheld.

(ii) *After the Judicature Act 1873*

15–033   An assignment may now fail to be statutory, and so take effect (if at all) in equity, for one of three reasons.

15–034   **No written notice.** An assignment which fails to be statutory merely because written notice has not yet been given to the debtor is effective although it is not supported by consideration.[141] The assignor has done all that need be done *by him* to transfer the property, as notice can be given by the assignee. It would be futile to insist that the assignee must give consideration, since he could evade the requirement by simply writing to the debtor and so making the assignment statutory.

---

[135] *Pennington v Waine* [2002] EWCA Civ 227 at [67].
[136] See above, para.15–016; cf. *Chinn v Collins* [1981] A.C. 533 at 548.
[137] (1851) 1 D.M. & G. 176; cf. *Re Way's Trusts* (1864) 2 D.J. & S. 365; *Nanney v Morgan* (1887) 37 Ch.D. 346, decided after the Judicature Act, but without reference to its provisions regarding assignments.
[138] (1834) 3 My. & K. 36; cf. *Edwards v Jones* (1836) 1 My. & Cr. 226; *Re King* (1879) 14 Ch.D. 179; *Re Patrick* [1891] 1 Ch. 82.
[139] This would not cure the want of consideration for the present purpose: above, para.15–024.
[140] See above, para.15–009: for assignment of life insurance policies.
[141] *Holt v Heatherfield Trust Ltd* [1942] 2 K.B. 1.

No writing. An oral assignment of an equitable chose is void, quite apart from   **15–035**
the question of consideration.[142] It is more doubtful whether a voluntary oral
assignment of a legal chose can be valid as a gift.

One view is that consideration is not now necessary in cases of this kind because
the assignee no longer needs the co-operation of the assignor to sue the debtor: if
the assignor refuses to join as co-claimant, he can simply be joined as co-defendant. But this argument is based on the untenable "procedural" view of the old
rules of equity and it would fail even if that view were sound. It can make no
difference whether the assignor is joined as co-claimant or as co-defendant. The
important point is that he is joined at all. He is joined, not out of respect for
history, but "to allow him to dispute the assignment."[143] One reason for disputing
it might be that it was voluntary. If the assignor disputed the assignment on this
ground, the debtor would in practice leave the assignor and assignee to fight out
the dispute in which the debtor would have no interest. Thus in substance the
assignor would be the sole defendant.[144] To argue that he will lose simply because
he has been made defendant is to assume the very point in issue.

Another view is that an oral voluntary assignment of a legal chose in action fails
as an imperfect gift under the rule in *Milroy v Lord*.[145] On this view, the proper
way to transfer a debt is by making a statutory assignment. If the assignor does not
put the assignment into writing, he has not done "everything which, according to
the nature of the property . . . was necessary to be done [by him] to transfer the
property". This view was adopted in the Australian case of *Olsson v Dyson*[146]
where a voluntary oral assignment of a debt was accordingly held ineffective.

Under the first of the above views, all oral voluntary assignments of legal choses
would be valid; under the second they would all be invalid. Neither of these
conclusions can be accepted. The law may recognise two ways of making a gift of
a chose in action, just as it recognises two ways of making a gift of a chattel.[147]
Before the Judicature Act a gift of a chose in action could be made by equitable
assignment and equity laid down no formal requirements for this purpose. The
Act provided a second method of making such a gift, without necessarily affecting
the first. Thus in *German v Yates*[148] a voluntary oral assignment of a debt was held
binding on the personal representatives of the assignor. Lush J. rejected the
argument that the gift was imperfect, and said that the Judicature Act had not
"destroyed equitable assignments or impaired their validity in any way".[149]

The true position seems to be that oral voluntary assignments of legal choses
can be valid so long as they are perfect gifts. They are not imperfect *merely* for
want of writing, but they may be imperfect for some other reason. In particular,
there may be room for doubt whether an oral statement was a completed gift,
rather than a promise to make a gift in the future.

---

[142] See above, para.15–016.
[143] *Durham Bros v Robertson* [1898] 1 Q.B. 765 at 770.
[144] cf. above, para.15–007.
[145] (1862) 4 D.F. & J. 264; above, para.15–029.
[146] (1969) 120 C.L.R. 365.
[147] See above, para.15–029.
[148] (1915) 32 T.L.R. 52.
[149] ibid. at 53. He also said that the assignor might have been able to revoke the assignment but that
his personal representative could not do so; and that there might have been consideration for the
agreement because the parties thought there was. No reasons were given for these puzzling statements.
The decision is, however, consistent with the mitigations of the rule in *Milroy v Lord* described above,
at fnn.133 and 134.

15–036   **Not absolute.**[150] An assignment of part of a debt may be effective without consideration. This can be deduced from *Re McArdle*.[151] A testator left his estate in equal shares to his five children. The wife of one of them, at her own expense, made improvements to a farm belonging to the estate. Thereafter, the children wrote to the wife: "In consideration of your carrying out certain alterations . . . we . . . hereby agree that the executors shall repay you [£488] from the estate." This promise was supported only by past consideration[152] and was held to be ineffective because it purported to be a contract and not a gift. It was further said that, even if the letter could be construed as a gift, it was not perfect, because something more had to be done by the donors; the executors could not have paid the wife without referring back to the children to find out whether the work had been done to their satisfaction.[153] On this reasoning, the result would have been different if the letter had on its face been a gift and had involved no reference back to the children. A letter simply saying "We hereby agree that the executors shall pay you £488 out of the estate" would have been a valid equitable assignment.

The question whether an assignment by way of charge must be supported by consideration is not likely to arise. Such an assignment is almost always made to secure a debt, so that there will generally be consideration for it in the shape of the assignee's advancing money or promising not to sue or actually forbearing to sue.[154] Moreover, such an assignment is usually intended to operate as a disposition by way of contract, and cannot be construed as a gift merely because, for some technical reason, there is no consideration. Even if the assignment were intended to operate as a gift, the fact that the amount assigned would fluctuate from time to time as the assignor increased or decreased his indebtedness to the assignee would show that the gift was not perfect.

The validity of a voluntary conditional assignment depends on the nature of the condition. An assignment of rent due under a lease "to A until she marries" might well be a perfect gift, and so might an assignment "to A when she marries", unless it is construed as a promise to make a gift in the future. But a gift "to A when she marries a man of whom I approve"[155] would be imperfect as it could not take effect until some further act had been done by the donor.

6. SUBJECT TO EQUITIES

15–037   An assignee takes "subject to equities",[156] i.e. subject to any defects in the assignor's title and subject to certain claims which the debtor has against the assignor. He takes subject to such defects and claims whether they arise at law or in equity, and whether or not he knew of their existence when he took his assignment.[157] And he cannot recover more than the assignor could have recovered. The object of these rules is to ensure that the debtor is not prejudiced by the assignment.[158]

---

[150] See above, paras 15–011—15–014.

[151] [1951] Ch. 669; Stone 14 M.L.R. 356.

[152] See above, para.3–017.

[153] For criticism of this reasoning, see R.E.M. 67 L.Q.R. 295.

[154] See above, paras 3–034—3–042.

[155] It is assumed that this is a condition and not consideration (cf. above, para.3–011).

[156] *Ord v White* (1840) 3 Beav. 357; *Mangles v Dixon* (1852) 3 H.L.C. 702 at 731; Law of Property Act 1925, s.136(1).

[157] *Athenaeum Soc v Pooley* (1853) 3 D. & J. 294.

[158] cf. *Sinclair v British Telecommunications Plc* [2001] 1 W.L.R. 38 (action by assignee stayed till an order for costs against assignor on an earlier action on the same contract had been satisfied).

(a) Defects of Title

An assignor cannot confer any title if he had none himself. Thus if a builder   15–038
assigns money to become due to him under a building contract, and then fails to
perform the contract so that the money never becomes due, the assignee takes
nothing.[159] Similarly, the assignee of a contract which is affected by mistake or
illegality generally[160] takes no greater rights than the assignor would have had.
And the assignee of a contract which is voidable for a misrepresentation made by
the assignor takes subject to the right of the debtor to set the contract aside.[161]
Defences available by the terms of the contract to the debtor against the assignor
can similarly be raised against the assignee.[162] On the other hand payment of the
debt to the assignor is a defence against the assignee only if made before notice of
the assignment was given to the debtor[163] and the same is presumably true of
rescission of the contract assigned by subsequent agreement between debtor and
assignor.

(b) Claims by Debtor against Assignor

The debtor may have claims[164] against the assignor which he could set up, if he   15–039
were sued by the assignor, to diminish or extinguish his liability. Whether he can
rely on such claims against the assignee depends on the way in which they
arose.

(i) *Claims arising out of the contract assigned*

Defence or set off. If the debtor has claims *arising out of the contract assigned*,   15–040
on which he could have relied by way of defence or set off against the assignor, he
can also rely on those claims against the assignee, and he can do so whether the
claims have arisen before or after notice of the assignment is given to him.[165] Thus
if a builder assigns money due to him under a building contract, and then commits
a breach of that contract, the debtor can set off against the assignee the amount of
any damages which he could have recovered from the assignor.[166] If this amount
exceeds the sum assigned, the assignee will not be entitled to anything; but he is
not liable to the debtor for the excess[167] as he is not himself in breach of the
contract. Nor, once the assignee has been paid, is he liable to return the payment

---

[159] *Tooth v Hallett* (1869) L.R. 4 Ch.App. 242.

[160] An assignee for value may be able to enforce a life insurance policy though the estate of the assured could not do so because he died by his own hand: above, para.11–027.

[161] See above, para.9–084 et seq.

[162] *The League* [1984] 2 Lloyd's Rep. 259 (arbitration clause); *Glencore International AG v Metro Trading International Inc* [1999] 2 All E.R. (Comm) 899 at 917 (exclusive jurisdiction clause).

[163] See above, para.15–022.

[164] For this purpose *legal* (as opposed to *equitable*) claims can be "equities": *Roxburghe v Cox* (1881) 17 Ch.D. 520; *Glencore Grain Ltd v Argos Trading Co* [1999] 2 Lloyd's Rep. 410 at 420.

[165] *Graham v Johnson* (1869) L.R. 8 Eq. 36; *William Pickersgill & Sons Ltd v London & Provincial Marine, etc., Ins Co Ltd* [1912] 3 K.B. 614; *The Raven* [1980] 2 Lloyd's Rep. 266; contrast *The Dominique* [1987] 1 Lloyd's Rep. 239 at 251 (approved [1989] A.C. 1056 at 1109–1101), where the debtor's claim could *not* have been set up against the assignor and was therefore not available against the assignee.

[166] cf. *Govt of Newfoundland v Newfoundland Ry* (1888) 13 App.Cas. 199.

[167] *Young v Kitchin* (1878) 3 Ex.D. 127.

merely because events later happen which make the assignor liable to return it to the debtor.[168]

15–041   **Rescission for misrepresentation.** If the debtor has been induced to enter into the contract by a misrepresentation on the part of the assignor, he can rely against the assignee on the right to rescind the contract on that ground[169]; but a further problem arises where that right has been lost. In *Stoddart v Union Trust Ltd*,[170] the defendants were induced by the fraud of one Price to buy a business from him. Price made an assignment of £800, part of the agreed price, and the assignees now claimed this sum from the defendants. Two defences were raised. First, the defendants counterclaimed for damages for Price's fraud, but such a claim could not be made against the assignees, as they were not themselves guilty of fraud, nor responsible for the fraud of Price. Secondly, the defendants pleaded that by reason of Price's fraud they had suffered loss exceeding £800, so that no money was due from them. This defence would have succeeded against Price; but it failed against the assignees as the claim for damages did not "arise out of the contract in question at all"[171] but was "something *dehors* the contract".[172] The decision seems to lead to the regrettable result that a contract may be worth more in the hands of the assignee than in the hands of the assignor, and so to defeat the purpose of the rule that an assignee takes "subject to equities". No attempt was made by the defendants to rely simply on their right to rescind the contract. They had disposed of the subject-matter and seem to have assumed that they could not rescind as they were unable to make restitution.[173] But the victim of a criminal fraud can rely on it by way of defence without making restitution.[174] This defence would seem to be an "equity" and should have been available against the assignee.

(ii) *Claims arising out of other transactions*

15–042   **Claims against assignor.** The debtor may have a claim against the assignor arising out of some transaction other than the contract assigned: e.g. a debtor may owe money under a building contract and in turn have a claim against the builder for the price of goods sold and delivered. Such a claim can only be set up against an assignee of the debt due under the building contract if it arose before notice of the assignment was given to the debtor.[175] If the claim arises later, the debtor is not prejudiced by being unable to raise it against the assignee. He knows that the assignor is no longer his creditor in respect of the debt assigned and cannot therefore expect to set off against it any claims which he may later acquire against the assignor.

---

[168] *The Trident Beauty* [1994] 1 W.L.R. 161.
[169] See *Banco Santander SA v Bayfern Ltd* [2000] 1 All E.R. (Comm) 766.
[170] [1912] 1 K.B. 181; the decision is viewed with scepticism in the *Banco Santander* case, above, fn.169.
[171] ibid. at 193.
[172] ibid. at 194.
[173] See above, para.9–097 et seq.
[174] See above, para.9–089.
[175] *Stephens v Venables* (1862) 30 Beav. 625; cf. *Watson v Mid Wales Ry* (1867) L.R. 2 C.P. 593; *Roxburghe v Cox* (1881) 17 Ch.D. 520; *Business Computers Ltd v Anglo-African Leasing Ltd* [1977] 1 W.L.R. 578.

Claims against intermediate assignee. Where a debt which has been   **15–043**
assigned to one person is then assigned by him to another, the question may arise
whether a claim or defence which the debtor has against the first assignee can be
set up against the second assignee. Such a claim or defence should be available
against the second assignee, if it arose after the first assignment,[176] but before
notice of the second assignment had been given to the debtor. If the debtor *paid*
the first assignee before the notice of the second assignment, he would clearly not
have to make a second payment to the second assignee. The same rule should
apply if the debtor supplied goods to the first assignee on the terms that the price
was to be set off against the debt assigned.[177]

Provisions of the contract. The rule that claims arising before notice of the   **15–044**
assignment can be set-off against the assignee may be excluded by the express
provisions of the contract creating the debt. Such provisions are often found in
debentures issued by companies to secure loans, since the rule that an assignee
takes subject to equities unduly restricts the transferability of such instruments.[178]

(iii) Assignee cannot recover more than assignor

The assignee cannot recover more from the debtor than the assignor could have   **15–045**
done. Thus in *Dawson v GN & City Ry*[179] a landowner had a statutory claim
against a railway company for injuriously affecting his land. He sold the land and
assigned the statutory claim to the buyer. It was held that the railway company's
liability to the buyer must be measured by the loss which would have been suffered
by the assignor and that any *extra* loss suffered by the buyer by reason of a trade
carried on by him, but not by the assignor, must be disregarded.

An attempt to distort the rather limited purpose of this principle was made in
Technotrade Ltd v Larkstore Ltd.[180] The defendant produced a soil inspection
report for the assignor in connection with the development of a site which the
assignor then sold to the assignee. During the course of development by the
assignee, a landslip occurred, after which the assignor assigned the benefit of the
soil report to the assignee. The defendant argued that the assignee was unable to
recover for the loss caused by the landslip since the assignor had parted with the
site for full value and, having suffered no loss as a result of any breach by the
defendant, could not itself have recovered damages from the defendant. This

---

[176] Not if it arose *before* then, since in that case the debtor can have had no expectation of being able
to set it up in diminution of the debt assigned: *The Raven* [1980] 2 Lloyd's Rep. 266.

[177] According to a dictum in *Re Milan Tramways Co* (1884) 25 Ch.D. 587 at 593 an ultimate assignee
takes "free from any equities which only attach on the intermediate assignee"; but this view could cause
injustice to the debtor, and the actual decision can be explained on the ground that the intermediate
assignee's liability to the debtor was not established until *after* the *second* assignment had been made
(see ibid. at 637). The actual decision in the *Milan Tramways* case was approved in *Fryer v Ewart* [1902]
A.C. 187 at 192.

[178] Pennington, *Company Law* (8th edn), pp.612–613.

[179] [1905] 1 K.B. 260; cf. *Crooks v Newdigate Properties Ltd* [2009] EWCA Civ 283 (payments made
by co-debtors who had subsequently been released from a debt had extinguished the debt in full, so
that there was no surviving cause of action against the remaining co-debtor notwithstanding a
reservation of rights against him and an assignee of those "rights" could be in no better a position).

[180] [2006] EWCA Civ 1079; [2006] 1 W.L.R. 2926; cf. *Prescott v Dunwoody Sports Marketing* [2007]
EWCA Civ 461; [2007] 1 W.L.R. 2343 at [33]–[39].

argument was rejected by the Court of Appeal as contrary to "legal principle and good sense".[181] The principle that the assignee cannot recover more than the assignor is intended to ensure that the debtor is no worse off as a consequence of the assignment, as in the *Dawson* case; it is not intended to enable the debtor to rely on the fact of the assignment in order to escape all legal liability for his breach of contract.[182] In the context of what was the transfer of land with the benefit of an assignment, the Court of Appeal approved of the following dictum of Staughton L.J. in the *Linden Gardens* case:

> "the assignee can recover no more than the assignor could have recovered if there had been no assignment, *and if the building had not been transferred to the assignee*".[183]

More generally, the assignee recovers to the same extent that the assignor could have done on the hypothesis that there had been no assignment and the assignor had not disposed of the subject-matter of the contract.[184] On this basis, so far as assigning the benefit of a contract is concerned,[185] it makes no difference, for the purpose of the present rule,[186] whether the breach, or the loss, occurs before or after the transfer of the subject-matter, or the assignment.[187]

7. NEGOTIABILITY

15–046   Special rules apply to the assignment of certain written contracts, called negotiable instruments, such as bills of exchange, cheques and promissory notes. A bill of exchange is a written order made by one person (the drawer) requiring another (the drawee) to pay a sum of money either to, or to the order of, the drawer or a named third person, or simply to the bearer.[188] If the drawee accepts the bill, he becomes liable as acceptor of a bill. A cheque is a bill of exchange drawn on a banker payable on demand[189]; cheques are now usually deprived of negotiability by

---

[181] ibid. at [44]. The decision reached by the Court of Appeal was said to be supported by decisions which have extended the recovery of damages for third party losses: *Linden Gardens Trust v Lenesta Sludge Disposals* [1994] A.C. 85; *Darlington BC v Wiltshier Northern Ltd* [1975] 1 W.L.R. 68; *Alfred McAlpine Construction Ltd v Panatown Ltd* [2001] 1 A.C. 518 (discussed above, para.14–025 et seq.), the aim of which is to ensure "that where a real loss has been caused by a real breach of contract, then there should if at all possible be a real remedy which directs recovery from the defendant towards the party which has suffered the loss" (ibid. at [83]).

[182] ibid. at [42].

[183] *Linden Gardens Trust v Lenesta Sludge Disposals* 57 B.L.R. 57 at 80–81 (emphasis added) (in the House of Lords, a prohibition against assignment was found to be valid (below, at fn.205) and the decision of the Court of Appeal was varied on other grounds: [1994] A.C. 85; see above, para.14–025).

[184] cf. *Landfast (Anglia) Ltd v Cameron Taylor One Ltd* [2008] EWHC 343 (TCC); 117 Con L.R. 53 at [29].

[185] For the purpose of assigning a claim in tort, the damage must have occurred prior to any sale so as to constitute the chose in action the benefit of which is then assigned, as in *GUS Property Management Ltd v Littlewoods Mail Order Stores Ltd* 1982 S.L.T. 583 (but claims in tort are generally non-assignable: see below, para.15–059).

[186] cf. para.15–063 below.

[187] In the *Technotrade* case, the breach occurred before the sale of the site and the loss occurred after the sale, but before the assignment; in the *Linden Gardens* case (above, fn.181), the breach and the loss (though not the financial cost of remedying it) both occurred before the sale and assignment. This difference was regarded as "not crucial", above, fn.180 at [75]. *Darlington BC v Wiltshier Northern Ltd* [1975] 1 W.L.R. 68 (see above, para.14–028) was the equivalent of a case where breach and loss occurred after the "sale" and assignment since the assignor never owned the site to be developed.

[188] Bills of Exchange Act 1882, s.3.

[189] ibid., s.73.

being crossed "a/c payee" or "a/c payee only".[190] A promissory note is an unconditional promise in writing to pay a person a sum of money.[191] The categories of negotiable instruments are not closed, so that instruments can still become negotiable by mercantile custom, that is, by being regularly so treated by businessmen.[192] The transfer of a negotiable instrument differs from the assignment of an ordinary chose in action in the following ways.

Transfer. A negotiable instrument is actually or potentially transferable by   15–047
delivery. A bill of exchange payable to bearer can be transferred by simply handing
it to the transferee. If a bill of exchange is payable to the order of A, he can transfer
it by indorsing it, i.e. by signing his name on it, and then handing it to the
transferee. Notice of the transfer need not be given to the person or persons liable
on the instrument.

Defects of title. An ordinary assignee takes "subject to equities".[193] But   15–048
negotiable instruments pass from hand to hand like cash, so that it is particularly
important that those who deal with them should be able to rely on their apparent
validity. The transferee of a negotiable instrument therefore takes it free from
certain defects in the title of prior parties[194] and from defences available among
them, if he is a "holder in due course".[195] Such a holder is a person in possession
of the instrument who has in good faith given value for it, provided that it is
complete and regular on its face, not overdue and that it has not, to his knowledge,
been dishonoured.[196] Every holder is prima facie deemed to be a holder in due
course[197] unless the instrument is affected by fraud, duress or illegality[198]; but
even in such a case the holder can still enforce the instrument if he can prove that
he in fact gave value for the instrument in good faith. The only cases in which his
title is no better than that of the transferor are those in which a party's signature
to the instrument is wholly void, i.e. for mistake or under statute.[199]

Consideration. The holder of a bill of exchange is deemed to be a holder for   15–049
value if value[200] has at any time[201] been given for the bill. Thus he can enforce it
against (for example) the acceptor even though he himself gave no consideration
for it. This rule should be distinguished from the further rule that consideration
is not necessary for the validity of a transfer of a negotiable instrument.[202] Suppose

---

[190] ibid., s.81A, as inserted by Cheques Act 1992; *Esso Petroleum Ltd v Milton* [1997] 1 W.L.R. 938 at 946, 954.
[191] ibid., s.83(1). A promissory note must be distinguished from an IOU, which is only evidence of a debt.
[192] *Crouch v Crédit Foncier of England Ltd* (1873) L.R. 8 Q.B. 374.
[193] See above, para.15–037.
[194] Bills of Exchange Act 1882, s.38(2).
[195] ibid., s.29. And see Consumer Credit Act 1974, s.125, for special provisions designed to prevent evasions of that Act.
[196] ibid., s.29(1).
[197] ibid., s.30(2).
[198] ibid., s.30(2).
[199] *Foster v Mackinnon* (1869) L.R. 4 C.P. 704; for contracts declared to be "void" by statute, see above, para.11–007.
[200] An antecedent debt or liability is sufficient by way of exception to the rule that consideration must not be past: Bills of Exchange Act 1882, s.27(1)(b); above, para.3–022.
[201] Bills of Exchange Act 1882, s.30(2), s.27(2).
[202] *Easton v Pratchett* (1835) 1 Cr.M. & R. 798 at 808. The transferee could not *sue* the transferor, but the transferor could not prevent the transferee from collecting the amount due from the other parties liable.

that A draws a bill of exchange on B who accepts it. If A transfers the bill to C, neither A nor B can deny the validity of the transfer on the ground that it was gratuitous. But B can escape liability by showing that his acceptance was gratuitous, and that C gave no consideration for the transfer. Want of consideration may enable the acceptor to resist an action *on the bill*. But it does not entitle the transferor to deny the validity of the *transfer*.

8. RIGHTS WHICH ARE NOT ASSIGNABLE[203]

(a) Contracts Expressed to be Not Assignable[204]

15–050　　If a contract provides that the rights arising under it shall not be assigned, a purported assignment of such rights is not only a breach of that contract but is also ineffective, in the sense that it does not give the assignee any rights against the debtor.[205] For example, a hire-purchase agreement may provide that the rights of the hirer shall not be assignable; and if he nevertheless purports to assign them, the assignee cannot enforce them against the owner.[206] An assignment of the benefit of a contract which is expressed to be not assignable may be binding as a contract or as a declaration of trust between assignor and assignee. Thus it has been held that a settlement of an insurance policy, expressed to be not assignable, could be enforced by the beneficiaries against the settlor.[207] The beneficiary may even be able to enforce the contract against the debtor, albeit indirectly, by joining the trustee as a party to the action.[208]

Where assignment is prohibited without the prior consent of the debtor and it is not sought, it seems to be no answer to say that, if it had been sought, it could not have been unreasonably withheld.[209] Where the contract states that consent will be deemed to have been given within a certain period of the request, it only

---

[203] Tettenborn [2007] L.M.C.L.Q. 392; Tettenborn, in Burrows & Peel (eds.), *Contract Formation and Parties*; Turner [2008] L.M.C.L.Q. 306.

[204] Goode [2009] L.M.C.L.Q. 300.

[205] *Helstan Securities Ltd v Hertfordshire CC* [1978] 3 All E.R. 262; Munday [1979] C.L.J. 50; *Linden Gardens Trust Ltd v Lenesta Sludge Disposals Ltd* [1994] 1 A.C. 85 (rejecting the argument that such a prohibition is contrary to public policy); cf. *Hendry v Chartsearch Ltd* [1998] C.L.C. 1382 (assignment invalid where contract required debtor's consent and that consent had not been sought); see generally Goode 42 M.L.R. 453; Alcock [1983] C.L.J. 328. For the construction of clauses prohibiting assignment, see *Flood v Shand Construction Ltd* (1987) 81 B.L.R. 31.

[206] *United Dominion Trust Ltd v Parkway Motors* [1955] 1 W.L.R. 719 (disapproved as to the effect of such a provision on measure of damages in *Wickham Holdings Ltd v Brooke House Motors Ltd* [1967] 1 W.L.R. 295). Apart from such clauses prohibiting assignment, hire-purchase agreements are assignable: *Whiteley Ltd v Hilt* [1918] 2 K.B. 808.

[207] *Re Turcan* (1888) 40 Ch.D. 5; cf. *Don King Productions Inc v Warren* [2000] Ch. 291; *Spellman v Spellman* [1961] 1 W.L.R. 921.

[208] *Barbados Trust Co Ltd v Bank of Zambia* [2007] EWCA Civ 148; [2007] 1 Lloyd's Rep. 495 at [47], [119]; contrast, [2007] 1 Lloyd's Rep. 495 at [139]; above, para.14–086, at fn.619; Smith 124 L.Q.R. 517; Turner (2004) 20 J.C.L. 97.

[209] *Hendry v Chartsearch Ltd* [1998] C.L.C. 1382 (per Henry and Millett L.JJ; Evans L.J. preferred not to express a concluded view); cf. *CEP Holdings Ltd v Steni AS* [2009] EWHC 2447 (QB). In *Hendry* the contract stated expressly that consent was not to be unreasonably withheld. Where there is no qualification to the debtor's consent, it may be subject to the requirement that it shall be exercised in good faith and must not be withheld "arbitrarily" or "capriciously": *Lymington Marina Ltd v McNamara* [2007] EWCA Civ 151 (see above, para.2–096, fn.479). Quaere whether, where assignment is made subject to the "absolute discretion" of the debtor, there is no restriction or whether the test just referred to represents the minimum criteria (as conceded in a different context in *Do–Buy 95 Ltd v National Westminster Bank Plc* [2010] EWHC 2862 (QB) at [37]).

takes effect at the end of that period and any earlier assignment will be ineffective.[210]

(b) Personal Contracts

The benefit of a contract cannot be assigned if it is clear that the debtor is willing to perform only in favour of one particular creditor, and if it would be unjust to force him to perform in favour of another. In such cases it is sometimes said that the "personal" nature of the contract prevents assignment. **15–051**

Employment contracts. An important application of this principle is that an employer cannot assign the benefit of his employee's promise to serve. It has been said that the right of the employee to choose whom he would serve "constituted the main difference between a servant and a serf".[211] But in the case of an employee of a company, this right of choice will often depend on distinctions which are somewhat technical. If *the shares* in the company are sold, and its directors are replaced by others in the course of a take-over bid, the employee is, it seems, bound to go on serving the company. In law he still has the same employer[212] but his right of choice is in such cases of more theoretical than real importance. If, on the other hand, the company sells its *business*, then at common law the effect of the sale is to terminate the contracts of employment.[213] This common law rule has in turn been modified by delegated legislation by which certain transfers of undertakings do not terminate the contracts of their employees. Each contract of employment is kept in being as if it had originally been made between the employee and the transferee of the undertaking.[214] It follows that the contract can be enforced by the transferee against the employee,[215] but the employee can avoid this consequence by giving notice to the transferor or to the transferee that he objects to becoming employed by the transferee[216]: hence his legal right to choose his employer is preserved. **15–052**

Contracts involving personal confidence. The common law principle applies to all contracts involving personal confidence. Thus a publisher cannot assign the benefit of an author's contract to write a book if the author relied on the publisher's skill and judgment as a publisher.[217] And the holder of a motor insurance policy cannot assign it since the insurer relies on the holder's skill and **15–053**

---

[210] *Barbados Trust Co Ltd v Bank of Zambia* [2007] EWCA Civ 148; [2007] 1 Lloyd's Rep. 495.

[211] *Nokes v Doncaster Amalgamated Collieries Ltd* [1940] A.C. 1014 at 1026; cf. *Denman v Midland Employer's Mutual Assurance Soc Ltd* [1955] 2 Q.B. 437; *O'Brien (Inspector of Taxes) v Benson's Hosiery (Holdings) Ltd* [1980] A.C. 562 at 572; *Don King* case, above, fn.207.

[212] cf. *Re Mack Trucks (Britain) Ltd* [1967] 1 W.L.R. 780; *Griffiths v S of S for Social Services* [1974] Q.B. 468; *Nicholl v Cutts* 1985 P.C.C. 311 (service contracts not determined by appointment of receiver); cf. *Gill & Duffus SA v Rionda Futures Ltd* [1994] 2 Lloyd's Rep. 67 at 83, 84 (guarantee not terminated by change of ownership of guarantor company).

[213] *Re Foster Clark Ltd's Indenture Trusts* [1966] 1 W.L.R. 125.

[214] Transfer of Undertakings (Protection of Employment) Regulations 2006 (SI 2006/246), reg.4(1); cf. also Learning & Skills Act 2000, s.95.

[215] *Morris Angel & Son Ltd v Hollande* [1993] I.C.R. 71; cf. *Newns v British Airways* [1992] I.R.L.R. 575. For enforcement by the employee against the transferee, see below, para.15–084.

[216] Above, fn.214, reg.4(7); *Humphreys v Oxford University* [2000] I.C.R. 405.

[217] *Stevens v Benning* (1854) 1 K. & J. 168; 6 D.M. & G. 223; *Hole v Bradbury* (1879) 12 Ch.D. 886; *Griffith v Tower Publishing Co* [1897] 1 Ch. 21.

record as a driver.[218] It may be that even the benefit of a builder's promise under a building contract cannot be assigned, since such contracts are "pregnant with disputes" so that the builder may intend to deal only "with the particular employer with whom he has chosen to enter into a contract."[219] However, these comments have to be seen in context. They were put forward as one of the reasons why the builder may wish to insert into the contract an express prohibition against assignment and the implication is that, in the absence of such a prohibition, the builder's promise is assignable. Thus, it has been held that the benefit to the employer of a lump sum building contract is assignable.[220]

15–054   **Sale of goods.** In some circumstances, the principle may apply to contracts for the sale of goods. In *Kemp v Baerselman*[221] a farmer agreed to supply to a baker all the eggs which the latter should need in his business for one year; and the baker agreed not to buy eggs elsewhere during that period. The baker sold his business to a large company, to whom he purported to assign the benefit of his contract with the farmer. It was held that the farmer was justified in refusing to supply eggs to the company. One reason for the decision was that the baker's promise to deal exclusively with the farmer could not be enforced against the company.[222] Thus if the farmer were compelled to supply eggs to the company he would be subject to all the burdens of the original contract, but would lose the privilege of exclusive trading for which he had originally bargained.

But the benefit of a long-term contract for the sale of goods can be assigned if it was expressly or impliedly made with the buyer *or his assigns*. In *Tolhurst v Associated Portland Cement Co*[223] Tolhurst agreed that he would for 50 years supply to Imperial so much chalk as it should require for the manufacture of cement on certain land which was described in the contract. Imperial sold its business to Associated (a much larger concern), to which it purported to assign the benefit of its contract with Tolhurst. It was held that Tolhurst was not justified in refusing to supply chalk to Associated, since the contract was impliedly made between the parties and their respective assigns. The fact that Associated was a larger concern than Imperial did not increase Tolhurst's burden, since the contract obliged him only to supply so much chalk as was needed on the land originally occupied by Imperial.

15–055   **Accrued right to a fixed sum of money.** It seems that the rule against the assignment of "personal" contracts does not apply where the creditor has an accrued right to a fixed sum of money. A person who is indebted to an indulgent

---

[218] *Peters v GAFLAC* [1937] 4 All E.R. 628.

[219] *Linden Gardens Trust Ltd v Lenesta Sludge Disposals Ltd* [1994] 1 A.C. 85 at 105.

[220] *Charlotte Thirty Ltd and Bison Ltd v Croker Ltd* (1990) Con LR 46 (QBD).

[221] [1906] 2 K.B. 604; cf. *Cooper v Micklefield Coal & Lime Co Ltd* (1912) 107 L.T. 457.

[222] For the validity of such exclusive dealing arrangements, see above, paras 11–092—11–099. Where a *lease* contains such a covenant by the tenant (e.g. one to buy all the petrol that he needs for his business on the premises) it may "run with the land". If so, the principle in *Kemp v Baerselman* does not apply and the covenant is at common law enforceable against an assignee of the landlord's interest in the land by virtue of the rules referred to in para.14–078, above: *Clegg v Hands* (1890) 44 Ch.D. 503; *Caerns Motor Services Ltd v Texaco Ltd* [1994] 1 W.L.R. 1249. For the effect of the Competition Act 1998, see s.50; above, para.11–106.

[223] [1903] A.C. 414; cf. *Shayler v Woolf* [1946] Ch. 320.

creditor cannot apparently complain if the creditor assigns the debt to the debtor's trade rival (who may make him bankrupt), or to a debt-collecting agency.[224]

Benefit assignable by one party. In cases of "personal contracts", one party   15–056
may be able to assign the benefit of the contract while the other cannot do so. Thus
in *Kemp v Baerselman*[225] the farmer could no doubt have assigned the benefit of
the baker's promise to pay for the eggs.

Effect between assignor and assignee. Where a purported assignment fails   15–057
because of the "personal" nature of the debtor's obligation, the transaction may
nevertheless take effect between assignor and assignee by way of contract between
them or by way of trust.[226]

(c) Mere Rights of Action

Maintenance and champerty. Maintenance involves the "wanton and offi-   15–058
cious intermeddling with the disputes of others in which the [maintainer] has no
interest whatever, and where the assistance he renders to the one or the other party
is without justification or excuse."[227] Champerty involves maintenance with the
"added[228] notion of a division of the spoils."[229] Equity in general[230] regarded the
common law's fear that assignments would lead to maintenance as exaggerated.
But where assignments in fact savoured of maintenance[231] or champerty,[232] equity
refused to enforce them. The Criminal Law Act 1967 abolishes criminal and
tortious liability for maintenance and champerty[233] but goes on to provide that this
"shall not affect any rule of law as to the cases in which a contract is to be treated
as contrary to public policy or otherwise illegal".[234] Although reference is made to
"a contract", it seems that this saving is not confined to contracts to assign, but
extends to assignment itself. The rule against the assignment of certain rights
known as "mere rights of action" has therefore survived the 1967 Act.[235] But,
partly as a result of the Act, and partly as a result of the current "more liberal
attitude"[236] towards maintenance and champerty, the courts have considerably
restricted the scope of the rule.

---

[224] cf. *Fitzroy v Cave* [1905] 2 K.B. 364. But the "personality" of the creditor may be material to the debtor: see *Gordon v Street* [1899] 2 Q.B. 641.

[225] [1906] 2 K.B. 604; above, para.15–054.

[226] *Don King Productions Inc v Warren* [2000] Ch. 291; Tettenborn [1998] L.M.C.L.Q. 498; [1999] L.M.C.L.Q. 353; cf. above, at fn.207.

[227] *Giles v Thompson* [1994] 1 A.C. 142 at 164, citing *British Cash and Parcel Conveyors Ltd v Lamson Store Service Co Ltd* [1908] 1 K.B. 1006, at 1014.

[228] In some contexts (see above para.11–012) there may be champerty without maintenance: *Sibthorpe v Southwark L.B.C.* [2011] EWCA Civ 25 at [54].

[229] ibid.

[230] See above, para.15–006.

[231] *Rees v De Bernardy* [1896] 2 Ch. 437.

[232] *Laurent v Sale & Co* [1963] 1 W.L.R. 829; *Trendtex Trading Co v Crédit Suisse* [1982] A.C. 679 at 694–695; *Camdex International Ltd v Bank of Zambia* [1998] Q.B. 22 at 37.

[233] s.13(1) and (2).

[234] s.14(2).

[235] *Trendtex Trading Corp v Crédit Suisse* [1982] A.C. 679.

[236] ibid. at 702. cf. *Giles v Thompson* [1994] 1 A.C. 142; see above, para.11–013.

(i) *Claims in tort*

15–059   **Assignment generally ineffective.** A right of action in tort cannot generally be assigned.[237] A person who is defamed or assaulted cannot sell his right to sue the tortfeasor. He can, however, sue the tortfeasor and agree to assign any damages he may recover; this is unobjectionable as it does not give the assignee any right to interfere with the conduct of the action.[238] Exceptionally, a right of action in tort can be assigned to an insurance company which has compensated the victim of the tort[239] and by a trustee in bankruptcy or the liquidator of an insolvent company who is, by statute, entitled to sell all rights of action for the benefit of the bankrupt's or of the company's creditors.[240]

15–060   **Criticism.** The generality of the rule against assignment of claims in tort is open to criticism. Such claims may be brought to assert rights of property;[241] and it is hard to see why the assignment of a right of action in (for example) conversion is more likely to lead to maintenance than the assignment of a debt.[242] Some tort claims can be enforced by restitutionary actions,[243] and it is arguable that the assignment of these, at least, should be allowed.[244]

(ii) *Liquidated claims*

15–061   **Assignment allowed whether or not liability of the debtor denied.** A liquidated sum due under contract (e.g. for money lent, goods supplied, or services rendered) or otherwise[245] can be assigned in spite of the fact that the debtor denies liability. A debtor cannot destroy the assignability of a debt by refusing to pay it.[246] Nor is it relevant that such an assignment is made or taken

---

[237] *Defries v Milne* [1913] 1 Ch. 98.

[238] *Glegg v Bromley* [1912] 3 K.B. 474; *Trendtex Trading Corp v Crédit Suisse* [1982] A.C. 679 at 702.

[239] *King v Victoria Ins Co* [1896] A.C. 250; *Compania Colombiana de Seguros v Pacific Steam Navigation Co* [1965] 1 Q.B. 101. Even if there is no assignment, the insurer is, to the extent that he has compensated the victim, entitled to be subrogated to the latter's rights against the tortfeasor: Mitchell and Watterson, *Subrogation: Law and Practice*, para.10.40.

[240] *Norglen Ltd v Reeds Rains Prudential Ltd* [1999] 2 A.C. 1 at 11–12. But see *Ruttle Plant Ltd v Secretary of State for Environment, Food and Rural Affairs (No.3)* [2008] EWHC 238 (TCC); [2009] 1 All E.R. 448 where the liquidator purported to assign the fruits of the cause of action *and* the rights which he had to commence and conduct those proceedings. The latter are not assets of the company but powers conferred on the liquidator by statute and not therefore assignable, so that the purported assignment was champertous. The insolvent company could be joined as a party and continue the proceedings and it seems that the problem would not arise on an assignment of the bare cause of action since in that case "the liquidator is thereby exercising the power of sale granted to him and an intrinsic part of that sale is the right to commence or continue those proceedings": [2009] 1 All E.R. 448 at [44].

[241] *Dawson v Great Northern and City Ry.* [1905] 1 K.B. 260; *Ellis v Torrington* [1920] 1 K.B. 399; *GUS Property Management Ltd v Littlewoods Mail Order Stores Ltd* 1982 S.L.T. 583.

[242] In *Three Rivers DC v Bank of England (No.1)* [1996] Q.B. 292 no objection seems to have been raised to the assignment on the ground that its subject-matter was described at 305 as a claim "for a tortious wrong"; cf. in Australia, *South Australian Management Corp v Sheehan* [1995] A.L.M. 3577.

[243] i.e. in cases of so-called "waiver" of tort where the tort benefits the defendant, e.g. where he converts the claimant's property. See Burrows, *The Law of Restitution* (3rd edn), ch.24.

[244] cf. *Re Berkeley Securities (Property) Ltd* [1980] 1 W.L.R. 1589 at 1611.

[245] *Dawson v Great Northern and City Ry* [1905] 1 K.B. 260.

[246] *County Hotel & Wine Co v London and North Western Ry* [1918] 2 K.B. 251 at 258; *Camdex International Ltd v Bank of Zambia* [1998] Q.B. 22.

with an oblique motive. An assignment of a debt is not invalid merely because its object is to enable the assignee to make the debtor bankrupt.[247]

(iii) *Unliquidated claims*

If the benefit of a contract, e.g. to deliver goods, is assigned before breach, the   **15–062** assignee can claim damages for the seller's subsequent refusal to deliver the goods. But it is less clear whether the right to claim unliquidated damages for breach of contract can be assigned after the contract has already been broken.

Assignment after breach. One view is that such a right is a "mere" right of   **15–063** action and cannot be assigned.[248] But this view causes difficulty where the contract provides for the payment of a fixed sum in the event of its breach. Such a provision may be (i) invalid as a penalty, in which case no more than the actual loss is recoverable; or (ii) valid as a liquidated damages clause, in which case the fixed sum (no more and no less) is recoverable.[249] According to the present view, the assignment would be valid if the contractual provision were a liquidated damages clause, and invalid if the contractual provision were penal. But this distinction has no relevance to the tendency of the assignment to maintenance.

Another view is that a right to claim unliquidated damages for breach of contract can, generally,[250] be assigned. But this view in turn gives rise to difficulty where the claim which has been assigned could be framed in contract or in tort.[251] The assignability of the right to damages can hardly depend on the way in which it is described.

Whether in fact assignment savours of maintenance or champerty. As   **15–064** both the views so far discussed are unsatisfactory, the law has adopted the intermediate view that a right to unliquidated damages for breach of contract may be validly assigned, so long as the assignment does not in fact savour of maintenance or champerty. If, for example, the assignee has a *proprietary* interest in the subject-matter, the assignment is valid since maintenance is committed only where a person interferes in another's litigation without having a genuine or substantial interest[252] in the outcome. Thus a vendor of land can assign to the purchaser the right to claim damages for breaches of covenant committed by the vendor's tenants before the sale[253]; and a buyer of goods which turn out to be defective can assign his claim in respect of the defect to a sub-buyer to whom he has resold the goods.[254] Similarly, "a conveyance of land can include the right to set aside an

---

[247] *Fitzroy v Cave* [1905] 2 K.B. 364; *Camdex* case, above, at 32; for a different oblique motive, see *Deposit Protection Board v Dalia* [1994] 2 A.C. 367 and see below, at fn.270.

[248] *May v Lane* (1894) 64 L.J.Q.B. 236 at 237, 238.

[249] See below, para.20–130 et seq.

[250] In *County Hotel & Wine Co v London and North Western Ry*, above, at 259, an exception is made for contracts which are "personal" in the sense discussed at paras 15–051—15–057, above.

[251] e.g. *Matthews v Kuwait Bechtel Corp* [1959] 2 Q.B. 57 at 77.

[252] *Martell v Consett Iron Co Ltd* [1955] Ch. 363.

[253] *Williams v Protheroe* (1829) 5 Bing 309; *Defries v Milne* [1913] 1 Ch. 98; *Ellis v Torrington* [1920] 1 K.B. 399.

[254] *Total Liban SA v Vitol Energy SA* [2001] Q.B. 643.

earlier transaction relating to it".[255] And a person can assign the benefit of a specifically enforceable contract, though the assignee elects, or is forced, to claim damages.[256]

15–065 **Whether assignee has a "genuine commercial interest".** Even where the assignee has no proprietary interest, the assignment may be valid if he has a "genuine commercial interest"[257] in the subject-matter of the action. Thus in *Trendtex Trading Ltd v Crédit Suisse*[258] a bank had financed a sale of cement by one of its customers. It was held that the bank could validly have taken an assignment from the customer of his claim for damages for wrongful failure to pay for the cement.[259] But the assignment actually made was held to be champertous and invalid because it was expressed to have been taken for the purpose of enabling the bank to resell the customer's right of action to a third party, so that the profit resulting from its enforcement (which was considerable[260]) could be divided between the third party and the bank. The crucial fact was that the assignee contemplated a further sale of the right, as opposed to its enforcement by himself. If he intends to pursue the latter course, the assignment is not champertous merely because he expects to improve his position by taking the assignment: unless this were so, few assignments would be valid.[261]

(iv) *Public policy*

15–066 **Wages or salary.** In English law, an assignment of wages or salary is generally valid,[262] so long as it does not deprive the employee of his sole means of support.[263] But a public officer cannot assign his salary.[264] This rule was originally based on

---

[255] *Defries v Milne* [1913] 1 Ch. 98 at 110, citing *Dickinson v Burrell* (1866) L.R. 1 Eq. 337 (see especially at 342). The only point of these dicta is that such an assignment is not champertous. On the issue of the assignability of a right to rescind, they are hard to reconcile with *Investors Compensation Scheme Ltd v West Bromwich BC* [1998] W.L.R. 896 (above, para.15–006) where they were not cited.
[256] *Torkington v Magee* [1902] 2 K.B. 427, reversed on another ground: [1903] 1 K.B. 644.
[257] *Trendtex Trading Ltd v Crédit Suisse* [1982] A.C. 679 at 703; cf. *The Aiolos* [1983] 2 Lloyd's Rep. 25; *Brownton Ltd v Edward Moore Inbucon Ltd* [1985] 3 All E.R. 499 (where the same result could now be reached without assignment under Civil Liability (Contribution) Act 1978, ss.1(1), 2(1)); *The Kelo* [1985] 2 Lloyd's Rep. 85; *Weddell v J A Pearce & Major* [1988] Ch. 26 at 43; *Murray v Young & Co's Brewery Co* [1997] 1 Lloyd's Rep. 236; *Tharros Shipping Co v Den Norske Bank Plc* [1997] 1 Lloyd's Rep. 541; *Stocznia Gdanska v Latvian Shipping Co (No.2)* [1999] 3 All E.R. 822; *Massai Aviation Services v Att-Gen of the Bahamas* [2007] UKPC 12.
[258] See above; Thornely [1982] C.L.J. 29. For the requirement that the maintainer must accept liability for costs to the other party to the litigation, see *McFarlane v EE Caledonia Ltd* [1995] 1 W.L.R. 366.
[259] The claim was not against the buyer for the price but against a bank for damages for failing to honour a letter of credit: cf. below, para.20–063.
[260] The bank paid $800,000 for the claim and sold it for $1,100,000 to the third party who settled it for $8,000,000.
[261] *Brownton Ltd v Edward Moore Inbucon Ltd* [1985] 3 All E.R. 499 at 506, 509; cf. *Massai Aviation Services v Att-Gen of the Bahamas* [2007] UKPC 12 (shareholders retained the benefit of a lawsuit by assigning it to a new company and sold existing business at a reduced price because it did not include the lawsuit).
[262] For a statutory exception, see Merchant Shipping Act 1995, s.34(1)(c). See also Employment Rights Act 1996, s.14(4) for formal requirements to be satisfied before the amount assigned can be deducted from wages.
[263] *King v Michael Faraday & Partners Ltd* [1939] 2 K.B. 753.
[264] *Methwold v Walbank* (1750) 2 Ves.Sen. 238; *Liverpool Corp v Wright* (1859) 28 L.J.Ch. 868.

two considerations of public policy.[265] First, it was thought that a public officer must not be deprived of the means to maintain the dignity of his office; but this argument now has little force, except, perhaps, in the case of ambassadors. Secondly, it was thought that public officers must have the means to pay damages for wrongs committed by them or by their order; but this is no longer important since the injured party can now sue the Crown.[266] It could perhaps be argued that to allow such assignments might lead to corruption. But this seems to be a remote contingency; and the argument proves too much. Officers who are paid out of local funds can assign their salaries,[267] but are presumably just as corruptible as officers paid out of national funds.

Maintenance. Maintenance and other similar payments to which a wife may   15–067
become entitled as a result of matrimonial proceedings are inalienable, since to allow the wife to assign them might leave her destitute.[268]

Statutory restrictions. There are many other statutory restrictions on assign-   15–068
ment, based on various considerations of public policy.[269]

Oblique motive. An assignment is not contrary to public policy merely   15–069
because it was made and taken with an oblique motive: e.g. if its purpose was to enable the assignee to obtain legal aid when this would not have been available in an action brought by the assignor against the debtor.[270]

9. ASSIGNMENT BY OPERATION OF LAW

(a) Death

Rights generally pass to personal representatives. On the death of a   15–070
contracting party, his rights generally pass to his personal representatives, who can recover any sums due under the contract or damages for its breach. The representatives may sometimes recover less than the deceased would have done, and sometimes more. Thus, personal representatives cannot recover exemplary damages.[271] On the other hand, in *Otter v Church, Adams, Tatham & Co*[272] solicitors negligently advised a client that he had an absolute interest in property, when in fact he had an entailed interest. Had the mistake been discovered while the client was alive, he could have barred the entail, so that the solicitors would only have been liable for nominal damages. But the mistake was not discovered until after the client's death, with the result that the solicitors had to pay substantial damages as the entailed property was through their negligence lost to the client's estate.

---

[265] Logan 61 L.Q.R. 240.
[266] Under the Crown Proceedings Act 1947.
[267] *Re Mirams* [1891] 1 Q.B. 594.
[268] *Watkins v Watkins* [1896] P. 222.
[269] e.g. Superannuation Act 1972, s.5(1); Police Pensions Act 1976, s.9; Social Security Administration Act 1992, s.187; Pension Schemes Act 1993, s.159; Pensions Act 1995, s.91. For statutory restrictions aimed at the protection of the assignor's creditors, see *Chitty on Contracts* (30th edn), paras 19–062–19–067.
[270] See *Norglen Ltd v Reeds Rains Prudential Ltd* [1999] 2 A.C. 1; cf. above, at fn.247.
[271] Law Reform (Miscellaneous Provisions) Act 1934, s.1(2)(a)(i), as amended by Administration of Justice Act 1982, s.4. Such damages are hardly ever (if at all) recoverable on a breach of contract: below, para.20–020.
[272] [1953] Ch. 280.

15–071   **Personal contracts.** Where at time of death the contract is still partly executory, the personal representatives are generally entitled to complete its performance and to claim the agreed remuneration. But they cannot do so if the contract
is "personal" in the sense that one party places confidence in the skill, judgment
or integrity of the other. Thus if either party to a contract of employment dies, his
right to go on serving, or to be served (as the case may be), does not pass to his
representatives: they can enforce only rights which had accrued before,[273] or which
accrue on,[274] death. It is possible for one party, but not the other, to rely on such
personal considerations. If a painter contracted to paint a house and died when the
work was half-done, his representatives might not be entitled to finish the work
and claim the contract price; but if the houseowner died, his representatives might
well be able to demand further performance from the painter.

(b) Bankruptcy

15–072   **Deemed assignment to trustee in bankruptcy.** When a person is adjudged
bankrupt, things in action forming part of his estate at the commencement of the
bankruptcy[275] are "deemed to have been assigned" to his trustee in bankruptcy.[276]
Thus the trustee can recover debts due to the bankrupt and claim damages for
breach of any contract with the bankrupt. Where the contract is executory, the
trustee may be entitled to perform it and claim payment from the other party.

15–073   **Personal contracts.** Certain "personal" rights do not pass to the trustee. The
word "personal" is here used in two senses. First: rights do not pass to the trustee
if they are concerned with the person or personal affairs of the bankrupt. Thus a
right to claim damages for injury to reputation does not pass,[277] nor does the
benefit of a contract "to carry him [the bankrupt] in safety, [or] to cure his person
of a wound or disease . . . ."[278] Such rights do not pass to the trustee, even though
they have accrued before bankruptcy. The rule is based on the view that only the
bankrupt's property is divisible between his creditors: they are not entitled to
benefit from injuries to his person. The "property"[279] of the bankrupt that vests
in his trustee[280] includes "things in action"[281] without qualification; it includes
contractual rights even though the contract giving rise to them in terms prohibits
their assignment.[282] But the definition has not changed the previous rules relating
to "personal" rights of the kind just described.[283] The bankrupt may have a single
cause of action giving rise to a right to damages in respect both of personal loss
(such as pain and suffering resulting from personal injury) and economic loss
(such as loss of earnings resulting from the same injury). The cause of action is

---

[273] *Stubbs v Holywell Ry* (1867) L.R. 2 Ex. 311.
[274] e.g. death benefits payable under a contract of employment.
[275] For after-acquired property, see Insolvency Act 1986, s.307.
[276] Insolvency Act 1986, s.311.
[277] *Wilson v United Counties Bank* [1920] A.C. 102.
[278] *Beckham v Drake* (1849) 2 H.L.C. 579 at 627.
[279] Insolvency Act 1986, s.283(1).
[280] ibid., s.306.
[281] ibid., s.436; *Re Landau* [1998] Ch. 223; *Performing Rights Society v Rowland* [1997] 3 All E.R. 336
at 348.
[282] See *Re Landau* above; *Krasner v Dennison* [2001] Ch. 76; and see fn.286.
[283] *Heath v Tang* [1993] 1 W.L.R. 1421 at 1423; *Ord v Upton* [2000] Ch. 352 at 360; *Haigh v Aitken*
[2001] Ch. 110 (bankrupt's personal correspondence not "property" for present purpose); *Cork v
Rawlings* [2001] EWCA Civ 202; [2001] Ch. 792 at [21].

then vested in his trustee but the trustee must account to the bankrupt for such part of the amount recovered as relates to the bankrupt's personal loss, and to earnings lost after the bankrupt's discharge.[284] The proceeds of insurance against permanent disability, on the other hand, do pass to the trustee since the purpose of such a policy is to protect the insured against economic loss by the payment of premiums which, had they not been used for this purpose, would have been available for the payment of his debts.[285] By statute, rights under certain pension schemes are excluded from the bankrupt's estate.[286]

Secondly: the benefit of an *executory* contract does not pass to the trustee if it was "personal" in the sense that the other contracting party relied on the skill and judgment of the bankrupt. In such a case the other party cannot be required to accept performance from the trustee or someone employed by him. Thus where a contract to build a house was "personal" in this sense, the trustee was not entitled to finish the house and then to demand payment.[287] But the trustee may employ the bankrupt to finish the work, and if the other party in this way gets precisely what he bargained for, the trustee can enforce the contract against him.[288]

Income to which the bankrupt is from time to time entitled. Special   15–074
rules apply to payments in the nature of income to which the bankrupt is from time to time entitled.[289] Such entitlement may not vest in the trustee because the bankrupt's right to the payment may not arise until after the commencement of the bankruptcy,[290] typically where the income consists of the bankrupt's earnings after the date of the bankruptcy. In respect of such earnings,[291] the trustee may apply to the court for an "income payments order"[292] requiring either the bankrupt or the person from whom the payments are due[293] to pay to the trustee so much of the income as may be specified in the order. In deciding what part (if any) of the income is to be paid over to the trustee, the court takes account of "what appears . . . to be necessary for meeting the reasonable domestic needs of the bankrupt and his family"[294]: an income payments order must not be made if its effect would be to reduce the income of the bankrupt below this level. These provisions are not based on the "personal" nature of the contract under which the income is earned (for *ex hypothesi* the bankrupt is himself still rendering the services) but on the need to allow the bankrupt to work to maintain himself and his family.[295]

---

[284] *Ord v Upton* [2000] Ch. 352.

[285] *Cork v Rawlings* [2001] EWCA Civ 202; [2001] Ch. 792.

[286] Welfare Reform and Pensions Act 1999, s.11 (as amended by the Taxation of Pension Schemes (Consequential Amendments) Order 2006 (SI 2006/745), art.15(1), (3)), dealing with situations such as those in the cases cited in fn.282, above.

[287] *Knight v Burgess* (1864) 33 L.J.Ch. 727; cf. *Lucas v Moncrieff* (1905) 21 T.L.R. 683.

[288] *Oliphant v Wadling* (1875) 1 Q.B.D. 145; *Re Shine* [1892] 1 Q.B. 522. To the extent that the right to the money had not yet vested in the bankrupt at the commencement of the bankruptcy, the trustee could claim it as after-acquired property under Insolvency Act 1986, s.307.

[289] Insolvency Act 1986, s.310(7).

[290] ibid., s.283(1)(a).

[291] See *Krasner v Dennison* [2001] Ch. 76 at [33] (on such facts see now above, at fn.284).

[292] Insolvency Act 1986, s.310(1).

[293] ibid., s.310(3).

[294] ibid., s.310(2).

[295] cf. *Re Roberts* [1900] 1 Q.B. 122, commenting on the position under earlier legislation.

15–075 **Priority.** A trustee in bankruptcy is in a less favourable position than an ordinary assignee in that he cannot gain priority over a previous assignee for value by being the first to give notice to the debtor.[296]

10. ASSIGNMENT DISTINGUISHED FROM TRANSFER OF LIABILITIES

15–076 Assignment is the transfer of a *right* without the consent of the debtor. The common law does not recognise the converse process of the transfer of a contractual *liability* without the consent of the creditor: "the burden of a contract can never be assigned without the consent of the other party to the contract . . . ".[297] If A has a contractual right against X, he cannot be deprived of that right merely because X and Y agree that X's duty under his contract with A is to be performed by Y and not by X.[298] The phrase "assignment of liabilities" is highly misleading and should be avoided.

It is of course possible for Y to perform X's obligation. The question whether the creditor is bound to accept such vicarious performance (so as to discharge X) will be considered in Ch.17.[299] It is also possible, in the situations to be discussed below, for Y to become liable to perform the obligation originally undertaken by X; but in these situations there is generally[300] no true transfer of liability.

(a) Novation

15–077 We have seen that it is possible by novation to substitute one creditor for another.[301] Similarly, one debtor may by novation be substituted for another. In *Miller*'s case[302] the claimant insured his life with the X Co, which was later amalgamated with the Y Co, which agreed to become liable on the policy if the claimant paid future premiums to it. The claimant did so, and it was held that he could enforce the policy against the Y Co. It has been suggested that a similar analysis may apply where a customer pays by credit card[303] for goods supplied by a retailer: the customer's liability to the retailer is discharged and a new liability to the retailer is undertaken by the company issuing the card.[304] Such arrangements are binding only if they are made with the appropriate contractual intention,[305] and if they are supported by consideration. Usually the creditor provides

---

[296] *Re Wallis* [1902] 1 K.B. 719. This rule does not seem to be affected by Insolvency Act 1986, s.311(4).

[297] *Linden Gardens Trust Ltd v Lenesta Sludge Disposals Ltd* [1994] 1 A.C. 85 at 103; *Don King Productions Inc v Warren* [1998] 1 All E.R. 609 at 631, affirmed [2000] Ch. 291; cf. *Société Commerciale de Réassurance v ERAS International Ltd* [1992] 1 Lloyd's Rep. 570 at 595–596; *Weldon v GRE Linked Life Assurance Ltd* [2000] 2 All E.R. (Comm) 914 at 922.

[298] For statutory exceptions to this principle, by which either party to a lease may be released from liabilities under it in consequence of the assignment of his interest, see Landlord and Tenant (Covenants) Act 1995, ss.5, 6.

[299] See below, paras 17–007—17–013.

[300] For what seems to be an exception, see below, para.15–084.

[301] See above, para.15–003.

[302] (1876) 3 Ch.D. 391; cf. *Société Commerciale de Réassurance v ERAS International Ltd* [1992] 1 Lloyd's Rep. 570 at 596. Contrast *Re a Company (No.0032314 of 1992), Duckwari Plc v Offerventure Ltd* [1995] B.C.C. 89.

[303] See below, para.17–005.

[304] *Customs & Excise Commissioners v Diners Club Ltd* [1989] 1 W.L.R. 1196, citing *Re Charge Card Services* [1989] Ch. 497 at 513 ("quasi-novation").

[305] A requirement not satisfied in *Tito v Waddell (No.2)* [1977] Ch. 106: see at 287.

consideration for the new debtor's promise to pay him by agreeing to release the original debtor or to accept a discount[306]; and the original debtor provides consideration for the creditor's promise to release him by providing a new debtor.[307] The effect of novation is not, in strict theory, to *transfer* a liability, but to extinguish it and put a new one in its place.[308]

(b) Benefit and Burden

Generally, a person to whom the benefit of a contract is assigned makes no   **15–078**
promise to perform the obligations of the assignor; and in the ordinary case such an assignee does not become liable under the contract. Suppose, for example, that a builder assigns to a bank moneys due or to become due under a building contract. The bank is under no liability to the builder's client for any breach of contract by the builder; the most that the client can do is to rely on the builder's breach in diminution or extinction of the bank's claim.[309]

Conditional benefit. There are, however, exceptions, or apparent exceptions,   **15–079**
to this general rule.[310] In particular, the discharge of a burden may be a condition of the enjoyment of the benefit, so that the burden can be said to be annexed to the benefit, or to the subject-matter of the contract. Where this is the case, a person (other than one of the original contracting parties) to whom the benefit is transferred must perform the burden, or at least forego the benefit if he fails to do so. If, for example, a right to extract minerals is subject to the duty to pay compensation if the surface of the land is let down, such compensation may have to be paid by the assignee of the mining right.[311] This exception, however, does not apply if the burden, though imposed in the same instrument which creates the right, is not a condition of its exercise but an independent obligation undertaken by the original grantee of the right.[312]

"Pure principle of benefit and burden". But even the burden of such   **15–080**
independent obligations may have to be performed by an assignee under a second, and broader, exception to the general rule. This has been called by Megarry V.C. the "pure principle of benefit and burden"[313]; it is "distinct from the conditional benefit cases, and cases of burdens annexed to property."[314] In *Tito v Waddell*

---

[306] *Customs & Excise Commissioners v Diners Club Ltd* [1988] 2 All E.R. 1016 at 1023, affirmed [1989] 1 W.L.R. 1196.

[307] See above, para.3–163.

[308] The substitution of a party to one particular obligation does not necessarily mean that the rest of a large and complex contract which contains other obligations has been terminated and replaced by an entirely new one: *Langston Group Corporation v Cardiff City Football Club Ltd* [2008] EWHC 535 (Ch) at [42].

[309] See *Young v Kitchin* (1878) 3 Ex.D. 127; *The Trident Beauty* [1994] 1 W.L.R. 161 at 165, 170; Tettenborn [1993] C.L.J. 220; above, para.15–040.

[310] For a statutory exception relating to covenants in leases, see Landlord and Tenant (Covenants) Act 1995, s.3.

[311] e.g. *Aspden v Seddon (No.2)* (1876) 1 Ex.D. 496 (for earlier proceedings see (1875) L.R. 10 Ch.App. 394); cf. *Chamber Colliery Co Ltd v Twyerould* (1893) [1915] 1 Ch. 268n; *Werderman v Société Générale d'Electricité* (1881) 19 Ch.D. 246; *Schiffahrtsgesellschaft Detlev von Appen GmbH v Voest Alpine Intertrading GmbH* [1997] 2 Lloyd's Rep. 279 at 286, 291.

[312] *Radstock Co-operative and Industrial Society v Norton-Radstock UDC* [1967] Ch. 1094; [1968] Ch. 605. For independent obligations, cf. below, para.17–019.

[313] *Tito v Waddell (No.2)* [1977] Ch. 106 at 302.

[314] ibid.

(No.2)[315] a company that was engaged in mining phosphates on a Pacific island had acquired land there under contracts obliging it to return any worked out land to its former owners and to replant it. The rights under these contracts were transferred to commissioners "subject to ... the covenants ... therein contained"; and the commissioners undertook to keep the company indemnified against claims by the landowners under the original contracts. Many years after the company had been wound-up, it was held that the commissioners were liable to the landowners for failing to perform the covenant to replant. Their liability was based on the "pure principle of benefit and burden".[316]

That principle had been recognised in a number of earlier cases[317]; but its existence does give rise to the problem of how it is to be reconciled with the rule "that in general contractual burdens are not assignable, though contractual benefits are".[318] A person is certainly not subject to the burdens of a contract merely because he has taken benefits under it: it has, for example, been held that the equitable assignee of a licence to use a patent was not subject to the burdens imposed by the licence on the original licensee.[319] The "pure principle" is best regarded as a limited exception to this rule, restricted in scope by two factors. The first is that "the condition [which gives rise to the burden] must be relevant to the exercise of the right".[320] This limitation is illustrated by *Rhone v Stephens*[321] where the owner of a house covenanted to keep the common roof of the house and an adjoining cottage in repair and both properties were then sold. It was held that the "pure principle" did not entitle the purchaser of the cottage to enforce the repairing covenant against the purchaser of the house: the duty to repair the roof was not a "relevant" condition of the right to occupy the house as there was no necessary connection between them. The second factor which restricts the operation of the "pure principle" is the intention of the parties to the assignment.[322] An intention to subject the assignee of contractual rights to liabilities arising under the contract will not normally be inferred.[323] In particular, any such inference will be displaced where it is the assignor who has undertaken (in the contract between assignor and assignee) to discharge the burden[324]; where it is plainly the intention of both parties to the assignment that the assignee is *not* to be subject to the obligations imposed by the original contract on the assignor[325]; and where the assignment is of benefits acquired by the assignor under one instrument but the burden is imposed by another, recording a separate transaction.[326] Even where the

---

[315] ibid.

[316] ibid. at 307; the original contracts between the company and the landowners had not made the benefits conditional on discharge of the burdens.

[317] *Elliston v Reacher* [1908] 2 Ch. 665 at 669 (in argument); *Halsall v Brizell* [1957] Ch. 169 at 182 (but the point was conceded—see 180—and not necessary for the decision); *E R Ives Investment Ltd v High* [1967] 2 Q.B. 379 at 394, 399, 400 (where estoppel was another ground of decision).

[318] [1977] Ch. 106 at 291; cf. at 299; above, para.15–076.

[319] *Bagot Pneumatic Tyre Co v Clipper Pneumatic Tyre Co* [1902] 1 Ch. 146; cf. *Cox v Bishop* (1857) 8 D.M. & G. 815; *Barker v Stickney* [1919] 1 K.B. 121.

[320] *Rhone v Stephens* [1994] 2 A.C. 310 at 322.

[321] See above; see also *Amsprop Trading Ltd v Harris Distribution Ltd* [1997] 1 W.L.R. 1025 at 1034–1035.

[322] *Tito v Waddell (No.2)* [1977] Ch. 106 at 302; *Davies v Jones* [2009] EWCA Civ 1164; [2010] 5 E.G. 114.

[323] ibid. at 291; cf. at 299.

[324] ibid. at 302.

[325] *Law Debenture Trust Corp v Ural Caspian Oil Corp Ltd* [1993] 1 W.L.R. 138 at 146–147; for a successful appeal on another point see [1995] Ch. 152.

[326] ibid. at 146; and see previous note.

"pure principle" does apply, its effect is not strictly to transfer a liability; for the assignor remains liable to the other contracting party.

(c) Operation of Law

In the following cases, a creditor may by operation of law be entitled to sue **15–081** someone (other than the original debtor) who has not voluntarily undertaken such liability.

Death. Contractual liabilities pass to the personal representatives of a deceased **15–082** person in the sense that they must apply his assets in discharging those liabilities. They are not personally liable, so that there is no true transfer of liability.

Bankruptcy and insolvency. Contractual liabilities of a bankrupt pass to his **15–083** trustee in bankruptcy in the sense that the latter must distribute the bankrupt's assets among his creditors. Again there is no true transfer of liability as the trustee is not personally liable. He can also disclaim a contract which is wholly or partly executory if it is onerous or unprofitable, e.g. a lease at too high a rent.[327] Such disclaimer puts an end to the contract but does not relieve the bankrupt's estate from liability for breach of it.[328] An administrative receiver of a company may become liable on contracts by "adopting" them[329]; but this liability arises from a new contract taking effect on such adoption, rather than under a transfer of the company's liability, incurred before adoption, under the old contract.

Legislation. Under legislation referred to earlier in this chapter,[330] not only the **15–084** benefit but also the burden of a contract of employment may be transferred as a result of the transfer of the undertaking. The transferor thus ceases to be liable on the contract,[331] while liabilities under it are imposed on the transferee, though the employee can take steps to avoid being bound to serve the transferee.[332] In this sense, the consent of all three parties to the transfer is necessary; and, perhaps for this reason, the process has been described as a "statutory novation"[333] of the contract.

Under the Carriage of Goods by Sea Act 1992, a person may acquire rights under a contract for the carriage of goods by sea to which he was not an original party: e.g. by becoming the lawful holder of the bill of lading which contains or evidences the contract.[334] Such a person may also become subject to liabilities under the contract: e.g. if he takes or demands delivery of the goods.[335] But the original party to the contract of carriage remains liable under it, so that there is no *transfer* of liability.[336]

---

[327] Insolvency Act 1986, s.315; cf. Insolvency Act 1986, s.178. For exceptions, see Companies Act 1989, s.164.

[328] For the measure of such liability, see *Re Park Air Services Plc* [2000] 2 A.C. 172.

[329] Insolvency Act 1986, s.44, as amended by Insolvency Act 1994; *Powdrill v Watson* [1995] 2 A.C. 394.

[330] Transfer of Undertakings (Protection of Employment) Regulations 2006 (SI 2006/246), reg.4(1).

[331] reg.4(2); *Wilson v St Helens BC* [1999] 2 A.C. 52 at 76, 83.

[332] See above, at fn.216.

[333] *Newns v British Airways* [1992] I.R.L.R. 575 at 577.

[334] s.2(1)(a).

[335] s.3(1)(a); see *The Berge Sisar* [2001] UKHL 17; [2002] 2 A.C. 205.

[336] Carriage of Goods by Sea Act 1992, s.3(3).

CHAPTER SIXTEEN

AGENCY[1]

1. DEFINITION

16–001   Agency is a relationship which arises when one person, called the principal,
authorises another, called the agent, to act on his behalf, and the other agrees to
do so. Generally, the relationship arises out of an agreement[2] between principal
and agent. Its most important effect, for the purpose of this book, is that it enables
the agent to make a contract between his principal and a third party.

(a) Agreement

16–002   **Agreement need not be enforceable as a contract.** The agreement between
principal and agent is often a contract. But agency may also arise out of an
agreement which does not amount to a contract because one of the parties lacks

---

[1] *Bowstead and Reynolds on Agency* (19th edn); Krebs in Burrows & Peel (eds.), *Contract Formation and Parties.*
[2] *Garnac Grain Co Inc v Faure & Fairclough Ltd* [1968] A.C. 1130 at 1137; Fridman 84 L.Q.R. 224.

contractual capacity[3] or because there is no consideration. Thus the committee of a club, though they act gratuitously, may be agents of the members.[4]

Agency without agreement. The law may attribute an agent to a person: e.g. **16–003** when a company is first formed, its original directors are its agents by operation of law.[5] Public corporations created by statute are sometimes regarded as agents of the Crown[6]: such agency arises simply by virtue of the incorporating statute. Moreover, by statute, one person, or the court, may have power to appoint an agent to act on behalf of another: thus a mortgagee can in certain circumstances appoint an agent of the mortgagor[7]; an administrative receiver appointed by debenture holders is deemed to be the agent of the company[8]; and a "deputy" may be appointed by the court to manage the affairs of a person lacking mental capacity by acting as that person's agent.[9] At common law, one person may be regarded as the agent of another, even against the latter's will, under the doctrine of agency of necessity.[10]

Under the doctrines of apparent and usual authority[11] a principal is liable on contracts made by his agent although he has not authorised the agent to make them.

(b) Intention to Act on Behalf of Principal

Whether a person intends to act on behalf of another is a question of fact. Thus **16–004** a person who agrees out of friendship to ferry another's car from one place to another can be regarded as the owner's agent,[12] so that his negligent driving may make the owner liable in tort; but a person who borrows another's car for his own purposes would not be so regarded.[13] Even where the owner is liable for the driver's torts, it does not follow that the driver is his agent for other purposes, such as pledging his credit for fuel or repairs. Where a person does intend to act on behalf of another, agency may arise although a contract between the parties declares that there is no such relationship[14]; conversely the mere fact that a person says he is an agent does not make him one if he intends to act on his own behalf and not on behalf of his alleged principal.[15]

The rule that an agent must intend to act on behalf of his principal distinguishes agency from other analogous relationships, and is helpful in cases where it is clear that a person acted as agent, but not clear whose agent he was.

---

[3] See below, para.16–012.

[4] cf. *Flemyng v Hector* (1836) 2 M. & W. 172.

[5] cf. Companies Act 2006, s.154. But English law does not regard the company as agent for its shareholders: *J H Rayner (Mincing Lane) Ltd v DTI* [1989] Ch. 72 at 188 (approved on this point [1990] 2 A.C. 418 at 515). See also Limited Liability Partnerships Act 2000, s.6(1): members of a limited liability partnership (which is a body corporate: s.1(2)) are agents of the partnership.

[6] e.g. *Bank voor Handel en Scheepvaart NV v Administrator of Hungarian Property* [1954] A.C. 584.

[7] Law of Property Act 1925, s.109; see *Medforth v Blake* [2000] Ch. 86.

[8] Insolvency Act 1986, s.44(1)(a); cf. s.8, Sch.B1, as substituted by the Enterprise Act 2002, s.248(1), (2).

[9] Mental Capacity Act 2005, s.19(6); above, para.12–056, fn.190.

[10] See below, para.16–031 et seq.

[11] See below, paras 16–020—16–030.

[12] e.g. *Ormrod v Crosville Motor Services Ltd* [1953] 1 W.L.R. 1120; *Vandyke v Fender* [1970] 2 Q.B. 292.

[13] e.g. *Hewitt v Bonvin* [1940] 1 K.B. 188; *Morgans v Launchbury* [1973] A.C. 127.

[14] *McLaughlin v Gentles* (1919) 51 D.L.R. 383.

[15] *Kennedy v De Trafford* [1897] A.C. 180 at 188.

(i) *Agency distinguished from other relationships*

16–005   **Buyer and seller.** A retailer or distributor may describe himself as the "agent" of the manufacturer whose products he sells. This description is legally accurate if he negotiates a contract between manufacturer and customer, accounts to the manufacturer for the price paid by the customer, and is remunerated by a commission or salary paid by the manufacturer; it may be accurate even if he is remunerated by a "mark-up" on the price that he pays to the manufacturer.[16] But generally the retailer acts, not in this capacity,[17] but as a middleman who buys and resells on his own behalf. He is the manufacturer's "agent" only in a commercial, and not in the legal sense.[18] Thus if the goods are defective the customer can sue only the retailer, and not the manufacturer, on the contract of sale. The manufacturer may be liable to the customer on a separate contract if he gives a guarantee[19]; he may also be liable in tort[20] if the customer suffers loss or injury because of a defect in the goods. Again a manufacturer who contracts to make something for a customer is not the agent of the customer. Although he makes the thing at the customer's request, he acts primarily for his own profit and on his own behalf.[21]

16–006   **Hire-purchase.** A dealer who negotiates a hire–purchase agreement between a customer and a finance company is considered at common law to act primarily on his own behalf.[22] But he may be the agent of the company for some purposes, e.g. to accept offers on the terms of the company's proposal form.[23] And under the Consumer Credit Act 1974 he may be treated as the agent of the company when he makes any representation in the course of negotiations as to the quality of the goods,[24] and when he receives notice from the customer that the agreement has been cancelled or rescinded, or that the customer's offer has been withdrawn.[25]

16–007   **Banker and customer.** The relation of banker and customer is primarily that of debtor and creditor but may for certain purposes be that of agent and principal: e.g. where a bank on the instructions of its customer makes a transfer of funds out of the customer's account.[26] Conversely, an ordinary agency agreement does not give rise to the relationship of banker and customer merely because funds belong-

---

[16] cf. *Mercantile International Group Plc v Chuan Soon Huat International Group Ltd* [2002] EWCA Civ 288; [2002] 1 All E.R. (Comm) 788.

[17] cf. whether a person who is asked to procure goods for another is his agent or a seller to him: see *Kloeckner & Co AG v Gatoil Overseas Inc* [1990] 1 Lloyd's Rep. 177; cf. *The Coral Rose* [1991] 1 Lloyd's Rep. 563.

[18] cf. *AMB Imballaggi Plastici SRL v Pacflex Ltd* [1999] 2 All E.R. (Comm) 249.

[19] See above, paras 3–017, 4–003 (at fn.6), 14–006.

[20] For negligence at common law or under Consumer Protection Act 1987.

[21] *Dixon v London Small Arms Co* (1876) 1 App.Cas. 632; *State of the Netherlands v Youell* [1998] 1 Lloyd's Rep. 236.

[22] *Mercantile Credit Co Ltd v Hamblin* [1965] 2 Q.B. 242 at 269; cf. *Shogun Finance Ltd v Hudson* [2003] UKHL 62; [2004] 1 A.C. 919 at [51]. In *Branwhite v Worcester Works Finance Ltd* [1969] 1 A.C. 552 Lords Morris, Guest and Upjohn took the view stated in the text, but Lords Reid and Wilberforce said that the dealer would normally be the finance company's agent.

[23] *Northgran Finance Ltd v Ashley* [1963] 1 Q.B. 476.

[24] s.56(2); by s.56(3) a provision in a regulated agreement purporting to make the dealer the *customer's* agent is void.

[25] ss.69(6), 102(1), 57(3). See also s.175 for the "agent's" duty to transmit such notices.

[26] *Barclays Bank Plc v Quinecare Ltd* [1992] 4 All E.R. 363.

ing to or destined for the principal are held (and used to make payments under the agreement) by the agent.[27]

Provision of services. Persons who are engaged in the business or profession 16-008 of supplying services may be described as "agents" in the commercial sense, without being agents in the legal sense: "To carry on the business of an 'agent' is not the same thing as saying that you are contracting as agent."[28] For example, where a "forwarding agent" is engaged to arrange for goods to be transported to a foreign destination, he may act as agent (in the legal sense) in making a contract between the exporter and a carrier[29]; but he may equally well act as principal in undertaking to get the goods to the specified destination.[30] Whether such persons act in the legal sense as agents depends on the responsibilities that they undertake in relation to the particular transaction.[31] An estate agent who is instructed to negotiate the sale of a house by private treaty has normally[32] no power to make a contract between his client and a prospective purchaser.[33] He may for certain purposes act on behalf of the client, e.g. for the purpose of making representations about the property[34]; and he also owes the client certain duties similar to those owed by an agent to his principal.[35] But "an estate agent, despite the style, is an independent person"[36] who for most purposes does not normally act in the legal sense as the vendor's agent. In particular, he does not so act when he receives a deposit from a person who has agreed, subject to contract, to buy the property.[37] So long as no contract of sale has been concluded, he must not pay the deposit over to his client. He holds the money in trust for the prospective purchaser,[38] and must return it to him on demand; but if he fails to do so the client is not liable for the deposit unless he had expressly authorised the estate agent to receive it on his behalf.[39]

(ii) *Whose agent?*

It may be clear that a person is an agent, but doubtful whose agent he is.[40] Thus 16-009 it has been held that a London agent employed by a country solicitor was the

---

[27] *Kingscroft Ins Co Ltd v HS Weaver (Underwriting) Agencies Ltd* [1993] 1 Lloyd's Rep. 187 at 191.

[28] *Elektronska etc. v Transped etc.* [1986] 1 Lloyd's Rep. 49 at 52.

[29] *Lukoil-Kalingradmorneft Plc v Tata Ltd* [1999] 2 Lloyd's Rep. 129 at 138.

[30] See *Jones v European General Express* (1920) 25 Com.Cas. 296; cf. *Poseidon Freight Forwarding Co Ltd* [1996] 2 Lloyd's Rep. 388 at 389.

[31] See, for example: *Leicestershire CC v Michael Faraday & Partners Ltd* [1941] 2 K.B. 205 at 216 (valuer); *Tudor v Hamid* [1988] 1 E.G.L.R. 251, contrast *Hastingwood Property Ltd v Sanders Bearman Anselm* [1991] Ch. 114 (solicitor); *Gibbon v Pease* [1905] 1 K.B. 810 (architect).

[32] i.e. unless specifically so authorised, as seems to have been the case in *Spiro v Lintern* [1973] 1 W.L.R. 1002 at 1006; cf. *Jawara v Gambia Airways* [1992] E.G.C.S. 54, where such authority was held to have been conferred on a solicitor.

[33] *Wragg v Lovett* [1948] 2 All E.R. 968.

[34] *Sorrell v Finch* [1977] A.C. 728 at 753.

[35] e.g. *Regier v Campbell-Stuart* [1939] Ch. 766 (agent engaged to *find* a property for the client); cf. in the case of a commodity broker, *Brandeis (Brokers) Ltd v Black* [2001] 2 Lloyd's Rep. 359.

[36] *Sorrell v Finch* [1977] A.C. 728 at 753.

[37] *Sorrell v Finch*, above; *John McCann & Co v Pow* [1974] 1 W.L.R. 1643 at 1647; Reynolds 92 L.Q.R. 484.

[38] Estate Agents Act 1979, s.13(1)(a).

[39] *Ryan v Pilkington* [1959] 1 W.L.R. 403, as explained in *Sorrell v Finch*, above, at 750.

[40] Where an agent is acting for two separate principals under two separate contracts and the question is which contract he has *performed*, see: *Albright & Wilson (UK) Ltd v Biachem Ltd* [2002] UKHL 37; [2002] 2 All E.R. (Comm) 753.

agent, not of the lay client, but of the country solicitor.[41] On the other hand counsel, though briefed by the solicitor, may be the client's agent.[42]

16–010   **Agent of another for some purposes.** In other cases the question is whether a person who is undoubtedly the agent of P may not also for some purposes be the agent of Q. Thus persons employed by an insurance company to solicit proposals for insurance are generally the company's agents,[43] but may become the agents of the proposer when helping him to complete the proposal form.[44] On the other hand insurance brokers are for most purposes agents of the insured persons and not of the insurers.[45] But they may be agents of the insurers for some purposes, such as the provision of interim insurance cover until the policy is issued.[46] Again, directors of a company are primarily the agents of the company, and not of the shareholders; but they may for some purposes become agents of the shareholders, e.g. for the purpose of negotiating a sale of their shares.[47]

(c) Commercial Agents

16–011   **Commercial Agents Regulations.** Our main concern in this chapter is with the common law principles of agency. Some of these are in effect restated, but others are modified, by regulations which give effect to an EC Council Directive[48] governing the relations between "commercial agents" and their principals.[49] The Regulations define "commercial agent" to mean "a self-employed intermediary who has continuing authority to negotiate the sale or purchase of goods on behalf of another person (the 'principal'), or to negotiate and conclude the sale or purchase of goods on behalf of and in the name of the principal".[50] A detailed discussion of these Regulations is beyond the scope of this book,[51] but their effect on the rules here under discussion will be noted at appropriate points in this chapter.

2. CAPACITY

16–012   **Capacity to act as agent.** As agency is a consensual but not necessarily a contractual relationship, any person who is capable of consenting can act as agent, although his contractual capacity may be limited, e.g. because he is a minor. But to say that a person of limited contractual capacity can act as agent does not mean

---

[41] *Robbins v Fennell* (1847) 11 Q.B. 248.

[42] *Grindell v Bass* [1920] 2 Ch. 487.

[43] *Bawden v London Assurance* [1892] 2 Q.B. 534; *Stone v Reliance Mutual Ins Soc Ltd* [1972] 1 Lloyd's Rep. 469; Reynolds 88 L.Q.R. 462.

[44] *Biggar v Rock Life Assurance Co* [1902] 1 K.B. 516; *Newsholme v Road Transport Ins Co* [1929] 2 K.B. 356; cf. above, para.9–022.

[45] *Anglo-African Merchants v Bayley* [1970] 1 Q.B. 311 at 322; *McNealy v Pennine Ins Co* [1978] 2 Lloyd's Rep. 18; For criticism, see *Roberts v Plaisted* [1989] 2 Lloyd's Rep. 341 at 345.

[46] *Stockton v Mason* [1978] 2 Lloyd's Rep. 430 (except in cases of marine insurance: cf. above, para.5–012).

[47] *Briess v Woolley* [1954] A.C. 333.

[48] Dir.86/653.

[49] Commercial Agents (Council Directive) Regulations 1993 (SI 1993/3053), as amended by Commercial Agents (Council Directive) (Amendment) Regulations 1993 and 1998 (SI 1993/3173 and SI 1998/2868).

[50] reg.2(1); for excepted cases, see reg.2(1)(i)–(iii) and 2(2).

[51] See *Bowstead & Reynolds on Agency* (19th edn), ch.11.

that his agreement to do so gives rise to all the legal consequences that usually result from the relationship of principal and agent. It means that he can make a contract between his principal and a third party, but not that he acquires all the rights or is subject to all the liabilities of an agent towards his principal or the third party. The agent could not be made liable if to hold him liable would defeat the protection which the law means to give him by limiting his capacity. Thus he could not be made liable on the contract between principal and third party, even though the circumstances were such that an agent of full capacity would be so liable.[52] On the other hand, there is no reason to suppose that he would be denied the ordinary agent's right of indemnity[53] against his principal.

Capacity to act as principal. Capacity to act as principal is determined by the rules governing contractual capacity generally. Thus a minor cannot make himself liable for luxuries merely by employing an agent; but he can appoint an agent to make a contract which would have bound him if he had made it personally.[54] This rule again applies primarily to determine the reciprocal rights and liabilities of principal and third party. It might also protect the principal from liability to the agent. Thus a principal who was under age would not be liable to indemnify an agent employed to buy luxuries. But the rule would not necessarily protect the agent: thus an under-age principal might well have a remedy against the agent if the latter accepted a bribe[55] from the third party.   **16–013**

3. CREATION OF AGENCY

Agency may arise by express or implied agreement, or without agreement under the doctrines of apparent and usual authority, and where a person has authority of necessity. Finally, agency may arise ex post facto by ratification.   **16–014**

(a) Agency by Agreement

(i) *Express authority*

No formality required. An agent's authority is commonly conferred by express appointment. At common law, no formality is required.[56] Oral appointment suffices even where the agent is appointed to make a contract which has to be in writing, or evidenced in writing.[57]   **16–015**

Scope of authority. The extent of an agent's express authority depends on the true construction of the words of the appointment. If these are vague or ambiguous, the principal may be bound even though the agent, in good faith, interprets   **16–016**

---

[52] See below, para.16–066 et seq.
[53] See below, para.16–091.
[54] *G (A) v G (T)* [1970] 2 Q.B. 644 at 651–652; Webb 18 M.L.R. 861; R.E.M. 69 L.Q.R. 446.
[55] See below, para.16–097.
[56] For a statutory exception, see Law of Property Act 1925, s.53(1)(a). Under the Commercial Agents (Council Directive) Regulations 1993 (SI 1993/3053), reg.13(1) (above, para.16–011) agent and principal are entitled, on request, to receive from the other a signed written document setting out the terms of the agency contract.
[57] *Heard v Pilley* (1869) L.R. 4 Ch. 548; *McLaughlin v Duffill* [2008] EWCA Civ 1627; [2010] Ch. 1, distinguishing s.53(1)(a) above and Law of Property Miscellaneous Provisions Act 1989, s.2. For further discussion, see *Bowstead and Reynolds on Agency*, (19th edn), paras 8–003—8–004.

them in a sense not intended by the principal.[58] But in such cases the speed of modern communications will often make it reasonable for the agent to seek clarification of his instructions, and if he fails to do so he will not be able to rely on his own mistaken interpretation of his instructions.[59] Where the agent's instructions are clear, it makes no difference that the principal acted under a mistake in giving them: e.g. if he instructed the agent to insure a ship for £3 million he is liable to indemnify the agent for the premium even though his actual intention was to insure her for only £2 million.[60]

It has been said that "an act of an agent within the scope of his actual or apparent authority does not cease to bind his principal merely because the agent was acting fraudulently and in furtherance of his own interests",[61] but this statement of the law should be limited to apparent authority, i.e. acting fraudulently or in furtherance of the agent's own interests will by its very nature nullify actual authority (both express and implied), but not apparent authority.[62]

(ii) *Implied authority*

16–017   **Existence of authority implied.** A number of earlier cases deal with the extent to which a husband who lives with his wife, or an unmarried partner,[63] impliedly authorises her to pledge his credit for necessary household expenses,[64] but they are unlikely to be of much significance in modern conditions when household supplies are generally paid for either on delivery or on credit terms requiring the signature of the debtor personally. More generally, the authority to act as agent may be "inferred from the conduct of the parties and the circumstances of the case."[65] For this purpose, the conduct of the parties is assessed objectively but it is not necessary to meet the test of "necessity" laid down for implied terms since "implied authority depends on consent not contract."[66]

16–018   **Incidental authority.** An agent who is appointed for a particular purpose may have implied authority to do acts incidental to the execution of that authority. For example, a solicitor, or counsel engaged to conduct litigation, may have implied

---

[58] *Weigall v Runciman* (1916) 85 L.J.K.B. 1187; cf. *Ireland v Livingston* (1871) L.R. 5 H.L. 395, as explained in *Woodhouse AC Israel Cocoa Ltd SA v Nigerian Produce Marketing Co* [1972] A.C. 741 at 757, 771–772; *Credit Agricole Indosuez v Muslim Commercial Bank Ltd* [2000] 1 Lloyd's Rep. 275 at 280.

[59] *European Asian Bank v Punjab & Sind Bank (No.2)* [1983] 1 W.L.R. 642 at 656 (where the claim succeeded on another ground).

[60] *The Tzelepi* [1991] 2 Lloyd's Rep. 265.

[61] *Macmillan Inc v Bishopgate Trust (No 3)* [1995] 1 W.L.R. 978 at 984.

[62] *Hopkins v TL Dallas Group Ltd* [2004] EWHC 1379; [2005] 1 B.C.L.C. 543 at [89].

[63] *Blades v Free* (1829) 9 B. & C. 167. For the implied authority of a child to pledge his parents' credit, see *Law v Wilkin* (1837) 6 A. & E. 718; some dicta in this case are too sweeping: *Mortimore v Wright* (1840) 6 M. & W. 487

[64] *Jewsbury v Newbold* (1857) 26 L.J.Ex. 247; *Jolly v Rees* (1864) 15 C.B.(N.S.) 628; *Phillipson v Hayter* (1870) L.R. 6 C.P. 38 at 42; *Debenham v Mellon* (1880) 6 App.Cas. 24; *Morel Bros v Westmorland* [1903] 1 K.B. 63, affirmed [1904] A.C. 11; *Miss Gray Ltd v Cathcart* (1922) 38 T.L.R. 562.

[65] *Hely-Hutchinson v Brayhead Ltd* [1968] 1 Q.B. 549 at 583; *Branwhite v Worcester Works Finance Ltd* [1969] 1 A.C. 552 at 587.

[66] *Targe Towing Ltd v Marine Blast Ltd* [2004] EWCA Civ 346; [2004] 1 Lloyd's Rep. 721 at [19]–[22]; cf. *Hudson Bay Apparel Brands Inc LLC v Umbro International Ltd* [2010] EWCA Civ 949; [2011] 1 B.C.L.C. 259 at [50] ("powerful argument" that, principal "would have been bound (whether through an implied term, implied agency, or, possibly, on some other basis)").

authority to compromise the suit.[67] On the other hand, an agent employed to sell a thing has generally no authority to receive payment for it.[68] The question whether he has authority to warrant its quality is one of fact, depending on the circumstances of each case.[69]

Customary authority.[70] A principal who employs an agent to act for him in a particular market impliedly authorises the agent to act in accordance with the custom of that market.[71] He is bound by the custom even if he is not aware of it.[72] But the inference that the principal authorises the agent to act in accordance with the custom cannot be drawn if the custom is inconsistent with the instructions given by the principal to the agent, or with the very relationship of principal and agent. The custom is then said to be "unreasonable" and the principal is not bound by it unless he knows of it.[73] Thus in *Robinson v Mollett*[74] there was a custom in the tallow market by which an agent employed by several principals was allowed to buy in bulk to satisfy the needs of all. The custom was held unreasonable since its effect was to turn an agent into a seller. This was inconsistent with the relationship of principal and agent since an agent must buy for his principal as cheaply as he can, while a seller sells at the highest price he can get. But in *Scott v Godfrey*[75] a custom of the Stock Exchange permitting stockbrokers to buy enough shares for several principals from a single seller was held reasonable because all the parties intended that contracts should be made between the seller and the various buyers.

16–019

(b) Agency without Agreement

(i) *Apparent authority*

Where a person represents to a third party that he has authorised an agent to act on his behalf, he may, as against the third party, not be allowed to deny the truth of the representation, and be bound by the agent's act whether he in fact had authorised it or not.[76] The following conditions must be satisfied before apparent authority arises.

16–020

---

[67] *Waugh v H B Clifford & Sons* [1982] Ch. 374.
[68] *Butwick v Grant* [1924] 2 K.B. 483; cf. above, para.16–008 as to deposits received by estate agents.
[69] Such authority was implied in *Alexander v Gibson* (1811) 2 Camp. 555; *Howard v Sheward* (1866) L.R. 2 C.P. 148; and *Baldry v Bates* (1885) 52 L.T. 620; contrast *Brady v Todd* (1861) 9 C.B.(N.S.) 592.
[70] cf. above, para.6–046, for the view that it is artificial to base such authority on actual agreement.
[71] *Graves v Legg* (1857) 2 H. & N. 210.
[72] *Pollock v Stables* (1848) 12 Q.B. 765; *Reynolds v Smith* (1893) 9 T.L.R. 494.
[73] e.g. *Perry v Barnett* (1885) 15 Q.B.D. 388 (custom to make contract without complying with statutory formalities and hence void); contrast *Seymour v Bridge* (1885) 14 Q.B.D. 460, where the principal knew of the custom.
[74] (1875) L.R. 7 H.L. 802; cf. *North & South Trust Co v Berkeley* [1971] 1 W.L.R. 471.
[75] [1901] 2 Q.B. 726.
[76] *Summers v Solomon* (1857) 7 E. & B. 879; cf. *Pole v Leask* (1862) 33 L.J.Ch. 155; *The Unique Mariner* [1978] 1 Lloyd's Rep. 438; *Waugh v H B Clifford & Sons* [1982] Ch. 374; *First Sport Ltd v Barclays Bank Plc* [1993] 1 W.L.R. 1229. The following discussion deals only with the extent to which the principal can as a result of the representation be held liable on an unauthorised contract. It is not concerned with any other form of liability for misrepresentation.

16–021   **Representation of authority.** This may be express[77] but it is more frequently implied: e.g. from a course of dealing, or from placing the agent in such a position that it is reasonable for third parties to assume that he has the principal's authority to make a contract of the kind in question[78]; or from the known relationship of the parties, so that where a partner has retired he continues to be liable to those who deal with the firm and know that he had been a partner but not that he had retired[79]; and conversely the firm will be liable to such third parties on contracts made by him, ostensibly on its behalf.[80] In such cases, the apparent authority is said to be *general* in character since it extends generally to all transactions which a person, in the position in which the principal has placed the agent, is normally regarded as having authority to conclude.[81] Even where the agent has no such apparent authority by virtue of his position, he may have *specific* apparent author-ity to enter into a particular transaction; but since in such cases it is (*ex hypothesi*) clear to the third party that the agent does not *normally* have authority to conclude a transaction of that kind, the principal will be liable on the basis of specific apparent authority only if the third party can show that the principal expressly represented that the agent had authority to enter into the particular contract on his behalf.[82]

16–022   **Must the representation be one of fact?** The view that a representation of law does not give rise to apparent authority[83] predates the decision of the House of Lords in *Kleinwort Benson Ltd v Lincoln CC*[84] removing the bar preventing recovery of payments made under a mistake of law, and may therefore need to be reconsidered. Furthermore, it is a decision which it has been said "now permeates the law of contract",[85] so that a contract may be *void* for a mistake of law,[86] or (it seems) *rescinded* for a misrepresentation of law.[87] It may be, however, that the present rule is unaffected, since it is concerned with the *creation* of contractual rights.

16–023   **The representation must be that the "agent" is authorised to act as agent.** Apparent authority does not arise if a person is represented to be the *owner* of a business or other property. In such cases the representor may be bound under the doctrine of usual authority, or under some analogous doctrine.[88] But the scope of these doctrines is limited, and where they do not apply, the representee can fall back on the more general doctrine of apparent authority only if the representation is one of *agency*.

---

[77] e.g. *Gurtner v Beaton* [1993] 2 Lloyd's Rep. 369.
[78] *Panorama Developments (Guildford) Ltd v Fidelis Furnishing Fabrics Ltd* [1971] 2 Q.B. 711; *The Ocean Frost* [1986] A.C. 717 at 777; cf. *Strover v Harrington* [1988] Ch. 390 at 409–410; contrast *Cleveland Manufacturing Co v Muslim Commercial Bank Ltd* [1981] 2 Lloyd's Rep. 646.
[79] Partnership Act 1890, s.14(1); and cf. *Scarf v Jardine* (1882) 7 App.Cas. 345.
[80] cf. Limited Liability Partnerships Act 2000, s.6(3)(a).
[81] *The Ocean Frost* [1986] A.C. 717 at 777. The relevant "transactions" for which it is said that the agent has apparent authority may have to be quite specific: *Sea Emerald SA v Prominvestbank* [2008] EWHC 1979 (Comm) at [107], distinguishing between "guarantees" and the particular refund guarantee which the third party was seeking to enforce.
[82] *The Ocean Frost*, above, where the third party's claim on this basis failed.
[83] *Chapleo v Brunswick PBBS* (1881) 6 Q.B.D. 696.
[84] [1999] 2 A.C. 349.
[85] *Brennan v Bolt Burdon* [2004] EWCA Civ 1017; [2005] Q.B. 303 at [10].
[86] ibid.; below, para.8–022.
[87] See below, para.9–013.
[88] See below, paras 16–029—16–030.

The representation must be made by the principal. Apparent authority   16–024
can arise only out of a representation made by the principal: it cannot arise out of
a representation made by some other person[89] or out of one made by the agent
himself.[90] Of course, a principal may represent that the agent has authority to
make further representations on his behalf; and the principal may make such a
representation by conduct, e.g. by placing the agent in a position in which he
would normally have authority to enter into a transaction of the type in question[91]
or to communicate what purports to be the principal's approval of it[92] (even
though the principal's instructions had negatived the agent's *actual* authority to
take such steps[93]). In such a case, the agent may by his own representation enlarge
an existing authority,[94] or confer authority on another agent,[95] but such a representation cannot create an apparent authority out of nothing.[96]

The representation must be made to the third party. The representation   16–025
must be made to a third person or group of persons. The old notion of holding a
person out as agent "to the world"[97] has long been discredited.[98] Nor can a
representation made by principal to agent give rise to apparent authority.

The third party must have relied on the representation. The third party   16–026
must have been induced by the representation to deal with the agent in the belief
that the principal had authorised the agent to enter into the transaction.[99] Two
consequences flow from this requirement. First, the representation must actually
be known to the third party; and this requirement cannot be satisfied if the
representation is contained in a document which has not actually come to his
attention.[100] Secondly, the third party is not allowed to say that he relied on the
representation if he knew that it was untrue,[101] or if he had, but did not take, a

---

[89] *The Rhodian River* [1984] 1 Lloyd's Rep. 373; *First Sport Ltd v Barclays Bank Plc* [1993] 1 W.L.R.
1229 at 1240; cf. American Restatement Third, at paras. 2.03, 3.03 and the requirement that the third
party's belief in apparent authority "is traceable to the principal's manifestations" (viewed as "not
uncontentious" as a matter of English law: *Sea Emerald SA v Prominvestbank* [2008] EWHC 1979
(Comm) at [114].
[90] *Attorney-General for Ceylon v Silva* [1953] A.C. 461; *The Raffaella* [1985] 2 Lloyd's Rep. 36 at 43;
The Ocean Frost [1986] A.C. 717 at 778; *Re Selectmove* [1995] 1 W.L.R. 474 at 478.
[91] cf. *Pacific Carriers Ltd v BNP Paribas* (2004) 218 C.L.R. 451; Reynolds 121 L.Q.R. 55.
[92] *First Energy (UK) Ltd v Hungarian International Bank Ltd* [1993] 2 Lloyd's Rep. 195.
[93] *United Bank of Kuwait v Hamoud* [1988] 1 W.L.R. 1051.
[94] *The Raffaella* [1985] 2 Lloyd's Rep. 36 at 43.
[95] *British Bank of the Middle East v Sun Life Assurance Co of Canada (UK) Ltd* [1983] 2 Lloyd's Rep.
9 at 17; *ING Re (UK) Ltd v R&V Versicherung AG* [2006] EWHC 1544 (Comm); [2007] 1 B.C.L.C.
108 at [100].
[96] *The Ocean Frost* [1986] A.C. 717 at 778; *United Bank of Kuwait v Hamoud* [1988] 1 W.L.R. 1051
at 1064 ("cannot hold himself out"); cf. *Hirst v Etherington* [1999] Lloyd's Rep. P.N. 938.
[97] *Whitehead v Tuckett* (1812) 15 East 400 at 411.
[98] *Dickinson v Valpy* (1829) 10 B. & C. 128 at 140.
[99] *Kooragang Investments Pty Ltd v Richardson & Wrench Ltd* [1982] A.C. 462; *Bedford Ins Co Ltd
v Instituto de Ressaguros do Brasil* [1985] Q.B. 966; cf. *Nationwide BS v Lewis* [1998] Ch. 482.
[100] *The Ocean Frost* [1986] A.C. 717 at 778.
[101] See: *Hopkins v TL Dallas Group Ltd* [2004] EWHC 1379; [2005] 1 B.C.L.C. 543 at [95] (where
actual knowledge was "plainly to be inferred"). If a third party knows that the contract is contrary to
the commercial interests of the principal, it is "likely to be very difficult . . . to assert . . . that he
believed the agent did have actual authority. Lack of such belief would be fatal to a claim that the agent
had apparent authority": *Criterion Properties Plc v Stratford UK Properties LLC* [2004] UKHL 28;
[2004] 1 W.L.R. 1846 at [31]; cf. *Lexi Holdings v Pannone & Partners* [2009] EWHC 2590 (Ch) at [99]
where it is said that, beyond actual knowledge, nothing less than "Nelsonian knowledge" (wilful
blindness) or "bad faith" will do; Limited Liability Partnerships Act 2000, s.6(2).

reasonable chance of reading the agent's instructions and so of discovering the truth.[102]

These requirements have given rise to particular difficulties in cases in which a third party dealt with a corporation through an agent who had no actual authority to enter into the transaction. In the case of a company incorporated under the Companies Acts, these difficulties arose largely because the authority of such an agent might be set out in, or limited by, the company's memorandum or articles of association; and the rule was that the third party had constructive notice of these documents.[103] Furthermore, this doctrine of constructive notice operated in favour of the company but not against it.[104] This state of the law could cause considerable hardship to third parties, and important changes were made which can now be found in the Companies Act 2006.

A provision which would have abolished the doctrine of constructive or deemed notice of the company's registered documents was never brought into force.[105] It may be that this was thought to be unnecessary because of a further provision under which "a person dealing with a company is not bound to enquire as to any limitation on the powers of the directors to bind the company or authorise others to do so."[106] The third party is thus not bound to inquire whether the directors actually had the power to authorise the agent, with whom he dealt, to enter into the transaction on behalf of the company. In addition, in favour of a person dealing in good faith with the company, the power of the board of directors to bind the company is "deemed to be free of any limitation under the company's constitution".[107] This provision has already been discussed[108]; here it is only necessary to repeat that a person does not act in bad faith merely because he knows that an act is beyond the powers of the directors under the company's constitution.[109] Liability under this provision may therefore arise even though the requirements of the doctrine of apparent authority are *not* satisfied because the third party knows of the limitation on the directors' authority.

The common law principles governing apparent authority can, however, still apply where the third party relies, not on the apparent *existence* of powers, but on their *exercise*. The point may be illustrated by supposing that the board of directors of a company has power under the company's constitution[110] to appoint a managing director, but that the person with whom the third party has dealt as such has

---

[102] *Jacobs v Morris* [1902] 1 Ch. 816; *Overbrooke Estates Ltd v Glencombe Properties Ltd* [1974] 1 W.L.R. 1335; Coote [1975] C.L.J. 17; *Rolled Steel (Holdings) Ltd v BSC* [1986] Ch. 246 at 295–296. The principle seems to have been overlooked in *Mendelssohn v Normand Ltd* [1970] 1 Q.B. 177 and cf. *Quinn v CC Automotive Group Ltd* [2010] EWCA Civ 1412 at [23] doubting the "room for any consideration of whether the third party was 'put on enquiry' ".

[103] *Mahony v East Holyford Mining Co Ltd* (1875) L.R. 7 H.L. 869.

[104] See *Rama Corp v Proved Tin & General Investments Ltd* [1952] 2 Q.B. 147, discussing earlier authorities; for further discussion, see *Freeman & Lockyer v Buckhurst Properties (Mangal) Ltd* [1964] 2 Q.B. 480.

[105] Companies Act 1985, s.711A(1) (as inserted by Companies Act 1989, s.142); repealed by Companies Act 2006, s.1295, Sch.16. Under Limited Liability Partnerships Act 2000, s.6(3)(b) the apparent authority of a member of such a body can be terminated by giving notice that he has ceased to be a member to the Registrar of Companies.

[106] Companies Act 2006, s.40(2)(b)(i) (formerly Companies Act 1985, s.35B (as inserted by Companies Act 1989, s.108(1))).

[107] ibid., s.40(1).

[108] See above, para.12–069.

[109] Companies Act 2006, s.40(2)(b)(iii).

[110] For the definition of what constitutes the "company's constitution" for this purpose, see Companies Act 2006, ss.17, 257; above, para.12–069 at fn.227.

not actually been appointed to the post. The third party cannot then rely simply on the fact that the board had power to make the appointment. But the third party's claim will be upheld if he can show that there has been a representation by the persons entitled to make the appointment, to the effect that it has in fact been made. Such a representation need not be express but may be implied from conduct: e.g. from the action of the board in allowing the person with whom the third party dealt to act as managing director. The company will then be bound by contracts made by him (even though he has not actually been appointed managing director) so long as those contracts are within the scope of the authority normally conferred on managing directors.[111] A company may also be bound by contracts made by its officers on the ground that they were impliedly authorised to make them; but here the liability is based on actual (implied) and not on apparent authority.[112]

Forgeries by agent. In two cases, company secretaries affixed the common seals of their companies to documents which they had forged. It was held that third parties who were taken in by the forgeries could not, against the companies, rely on them.[113] But in *Uxbridge PBS v Pickard*[114] a solicitor's clerk obtained money by way of mortgage on the strength of forged title deeds alleged to belong to a fictitious client. His principal was held liable. In the former cases, the secretaries had not been held out as having authority to execute the documents (respectively a power of attorney and a share transfer). In the latter case, the clerk had been held out as having authority to conclude mortgage transactions. Alternatively, the first two cases can be regarded as cases in which the agent had, in effect, forged the principal's signature. When this happens, the third party is induced to believe, not that the agent has his principal's authority, but that the signature is the act of the principal himself. Such a belief does not give rise to apparent authority.[115] The person whose signature is forged is, however, liable if he knew of the forgery and acquiesced in it.[116]

16–027

Subsequent conduct of "principal". A person may be bound by a contract, even though the requirements of apparent authority are not satisfied, if he is precluded by his subsequent conduct from denying that the contract was made on his behalf. In *Spiro v Lintern*[117] a wife purported to enter into a contract for the sale of her husband's house. She had no actual authority to do so, nor had the husband before the transaction led the purchaser to believe that she was his agent for the purpose. But afterwards the husband met the purchaser, gave him the impression that there was a binding contract and allowed him to incur expenses in connection with the property. It was held that the husband was estopped[118] from denying his wife's authority to make the contract on his behalf.

16–028

---

[111] *Freeman & Lockyer v Buckhurst Properties (Mangal) Ltd*, above, fn.104.

[112] *Hely-Hutchinson v Brayhead Ltd* [1968] 1 Q.B. 549 at 573; Nock 30 M.L.R. 705.

[113] *Bank of Ireland v Evan's Trustees* (1855) 5 H.L.C. 389; *Ruben v Great Fingall Consolidated* [1906] A.C. 439.

[114] [1939] 2 K.B. 248.

[115] cf. *Kooragang Investments Pty Ltd v Richardson & Wrench Ltd* [1982] A.C. 462.

[116] *Greenwood v Martins Bank Ltd* [1933] A.C. 51.

[117] [1973] 1 W.L.R. 1002; followed in *Worboys v Carter* [1987] 2 E.G.L.R. 1; cf. *Janred Properties Ltd v Ente Nazionale Italiano per il Turismo* [1989] 2 All E.R. 444; *Geniki Investments International Ltd v Ellis Stockbrokers Ltd* [2008] EWHC 549 (QB); [2008] 1 B.C.L.C. 662.

[118] Detrimental reliance by the third party is necessary for this type of estoppel (above, para.9–156); while for the purposes of apparent authority, "the only detriment that has to be shown . . . is the entering into the contract": *The Tatra* [1990] 2 Lloyd's Rep. 51 at 59.

(ii) *Usual authority*

16–029   **Meaning.** The phrase "usual authority" is used in a number of senses. First, it may mean implied authority, and, in particular, incidental authority.[119] Secondly, it may refer to cases in which an agent has apparent authority because he has been placed by his principal in a situation in which he would have had incidental authority, if this had not been expressly negatived by instructions given to him by the principal (and not communicated to the third party[120]). But the phrase will here be used in a third sense, to refer to cases in which a principal is bound by his agent's contracts although there is no express, implied or apparent authority. This usage is based on *Watteau v Fenwick*,[121] where the owner of a public house was sued for the price of cigars bought without his authority by his manager for the purposes of the business. The manager had bought the cigars in his own name. Thus the seller could not rely on any appearance of authority since he believed, at the time of the contract, that the manager was contracting on his own behalf. But the defendant was nonetheless held liable. Wills J. said:

> "The principal is liable for all the acts of the agent which are within the authority usually confided to an agent of that character, notwithstanding limitations, as between the principal and the agent, put upon that authority. It is said that this is only so where there has been a holding out of authority . . . But I do not think so."[122]

This decision has been criticised,[123] and has been more often distinguished than followed, but later courts which have thought it necessary to distinguish it must have regarded it as still good law.[124] There are, moreover, other cases in which a principal is bound by his agent's acts done outside the scope of his express, implied or apparent authority. Thus if a principal gives his agent documents and authorises him to borrow a fixed sum on the security of them, he may be liable to a third party from whom the agent borrows more, even though the third party did not think that the agent had any authority to borrow.[125] Similarly, at common law a person was bound by an unauthorised sale of his goods by a factor, though the factor sold in his own name.[126] At common law, he was not bound by an unauthorised pledge, but under the Factors Act 1889, he is bound, if certain conditions are satisfied, by any disposition (though unauthorised) made by such an

---

[119] See above, para.16–018.
[120] *The Raffaella* [1985] 2 Lloyd's Rep. 36 at 41; *First Energy (UK) Ltd v Hungarian International Bank Ltd* [1993] 2 Lloyd's Rep. 195 at 201.
[121] [1893] 1 Q.B. 346.
[122] ibid. at 348–349; cf. *The Ocean Frost* [1986] A.C. 717 at 734 (affirmed, *The Ocean Frost* [1986] A.C. 717 at 773), where there was no holding out for the different reason stated at para.16–024, above.
[123] See Montrose 17 Can.Bar Rev. 693; Hornby [1961] C.L.J. 239; *The Rhodian River* [1984] 1 Lloyd's Rep. 373 at 379.
[124] See *Johnston v Reading* (1893) 9 T.L.R. 200; *Lloyds Bank v Swiss Bankverein* (1912) 107 L.T. 309; 108 L.T. 143; *Jerome v Bentley & Co* [1952] 2 T.L.R. 58. Two Privy Council decisions can be said to be inconsistent with the principle of usual authority, in that they simply did not consider it as a possible basis of liability where the requirements of apparent authority were not satisfied: *Miles v McIlwraith* (1883) 8 App.Cas. 120; *Attorney-General for Ceylon v Silva* [1953] A.C. 461; above, para.16–024, at fn.90.
[125] *Brocklesby v Temperance PBS* [1895] A.C. 173; *Fry v Smellie* [1912] 3 K.B. 282. For criticism of the reasoning of these cases, see *Bowstead and Reynolds on Agency* (19th edn), para.8–135.
[126] *Coles v NW Bank* (1875) L.R. 10 C.P. 354 at 362.

agent. These rules are, it is submitted, based on the same principle as *Watteau v Fenwick*. That principle seems to be more closely analogous to the doctrine of vicarious liability in tort (under which an employer may be liable even for forbidden acts if done by an employee in the course of employment[127]) than to the doctrine of apparent authority.

Scope. The extent of an agent's usual authority depends on the class of agent to which he belongs and on the common understanding of the trade concerning such agents. *Watteau v Fenwick* should from this point of view be contrasted with *Daun v Simmins*,[128] where it was held that the manager of a tied public house had no usual authority to order spirits from any person he chose. And where the agent does not belong to a well-known class of agents, but is simply appointed for an isolated transaction, the doctrine of usual authority does not apply. Thus in *Jerome v Bentley & Co*[129] a retired army officer to whom jewellery had been entrusted for sale was held not to have the usual authority which a mercantile agent would have had in the same circumstances.   **16–030**

A principal is liable under the doctrine of usual authority only if there is some dealing between the third party and the agent: the doctrine does not apply if the agent's involvement in the transaction has been concealed so that the third party thinks that he is dealing directly with the principal.[130] The contract must also be made in the course of the principal's business: in *Kinahan v Parry*[131] it was accordingly held that a hotel owner was not liable for whisky bought without his authority by his manager, since it was not proved that the manager had bought it for use in the hotel rather than for his personal use. Similarly, where the manager of a tied house bought beer from outside suppliers and resold it on the premises on his own account, it was said that his employers could not have been sued for the price of the beer.[132] A person is, a fortiori, not liable under the doctrine of usual authority if the business in the course of which the contract was made was not his business at all. Thus in *MacFisheries Ltd v Harrison*[133] the owner of a public house sold it as a going concern, but forgot to transfer the licence to the buyer. He was not liable for food supplied to his successor for consumption on the premises, since the latter was carrying on the business entirely on his own behalf.

(iii) *Authority of necessity*[134]

Under this heading, we shall first discuss a number of situations in which one person acts to protect some interest of another without any previous authorisation from that other person.[135] We shall then consider whether any useful purpose is served by attempting to bring all these, somewhat disparate, cases within the scope of a single doctrine.   **16–031**

---

[127] *Limpus v LGOC* (1862) 1 H. & C. 526; *Rose v Plenty* [1976] 1 W.L.R. 141.

[128] (1879) 41 L.T. 783.

[129] [1952] 2 T.L.R. 58.

[130] *Kooragang Investments Pty Ltd v Richardson & Wrench Ltd* [1982] A.C. 462.

[131] [1911] 1 K.B. 459.

[132] *Attorney-General's Reference (No.1 of 1985)* [1986] Q.B. 491 at 506.

[133] (1924) 93 L.J.K.B. 811.

[134] Treitel 3 W.A.A.L. Rev. 1; Wade 19 Vanderbilt L.Rev. 1183; Birks 10 C.L.P. 110; Matthews [1981] C.L.J. 340.

[135] In addition to the situations discussed in the text, see also: Mental Capacity Act 2005, ss.5–8; cf. above, para.12–058.

16–032   **Acceptance of a bill of exchange for the honour of the drawer.** When a
bill is not accepted by the person on whom it is drawn, a stranger may, with the
consent of the holder, accept the bill for the honour of the drawer. If the stranger
has to pay on this acceptance, he becomes entitled to the rights of the holder to
sue the drawer on the bill.[136]

16–033   **Shipmasters.** Where it is necessary[137] to do so for the further prosecution of
the voyage, the master of a ship has authority of necessity to borrow on the
shipowner's credit, to hypothecate the ship, cargo and freight, or the cargo alone,
to sell part of the cargo,[138] and to enter into a salvage agreement on behalf of the
cargo–owner.[139]

16–034   **Salvage.** A person who goes to the aid of a ship in distress at sea[140] and saves
life or property is entitled to a reward the amount of which is (subject to certain
limitations), at the discretion of the court.

16–035   **Other cases.** The courts have been reluctant to extend the doctrine of agency
of necessity, because it may deprive a person of his property, or subject him to an
obligation, without his consent.[141] But the doctrine is not confined to the three
situations described above. It extends to a number of other situations, in some (but
not in all) of which the authority is based on some prior relationship between the
parties.[142]

16–036   **Powers of sale.** It has been held that land carriers can have authority of
necessity to sell.[143] At common law, the courts were reluctant to hold that a bailee
with whom goods had been left for storage or repair was entitled to sell them
merely because the owner had failed to collect them and could not be traced. By
statute, the bailee is now entitled to sell in a number of situations if he has given
notice to the bailor of his intention to sell or if he has failed to trace the bailor after
having taken reasonable steps to do so.[144] This statutory power extends to cases in
which there was, at common law, no authority of necessity to sell.[145] There may
also be cases in which, though the statutory requirements are not satisfied, a sale
can be justified under the common law doctrine of agency of necessity. For
example, a buyer of goods may justifiably reject them on the ground that they are
not in conformity with the contract of sale; and if the seller refuses to accept their

---

[136] See Bills of Exchange Act 1882, ss.65–68.
[137] See below, para.16–039.
[138] See *Notara v Henderson* (1872) L.R. 7 Q.B. 225.
[139] *The Winson* [1982] A.C. 939. But where the conditions stated at para.16–039, below, are not
satisfied, the master has no *implied* authority to enter into such an agreement: *The Choko Star* [1990]
1 Lloyd's Rep. 516; cf. *The Kos* [2010] EWCA Civ 772; [2010] 2 Lloyd's Rep. 409.
[140] For this restriction, see *The Goring* [1988] A.C. 831.
[141] *Falcke v Scottish Imperial Assurance Co* (1886) 34 Ch.D. 234 at 248; *The Winson* [1982] A.C. 939
at 962.
[142] *Re F* [1990] 2 A.C. 1 at 75; cf. *Crantrave Ltd v Lloyds Bank Plc* [2000] Q.B. 917 at 922–923, where
there was no "necessity".
[143] *Sims & Co v Midland Ry* [1913] 1 K.B. 103 at 112; *Springer v Great Western Ry* [1921] 1 K.B.
257 at 265, 267; cf. Carriage of Goods by Road Act 1965, Sch., arts 14(2), 16(3), for statutory provisions
in case of international carriage.
[144] Torts (Interference with Goods) Act 1977, ss.12, 13 and Sch.1.
[145] e.g. *Munro v Wilmott* [1949] 1 K.B. 295.

return, the buyer may then have authority of necessity to sell them for the account of the seller.[146]

Preservation of another's property. A number of cases raise the question   16–037
whether a person who preserves another's property has any claim against the owner. Two eighteenth-century cases decided that such a person has no lien on the property saved[147]; but it does not necessarily follow that he has no claim for reimbursement. In *Tetley v British Trade Corp*[148] an agent who, contrary to his principal's express instruction, removed goods from Batum to Constantinople (to save them from seizure by an invading army) recovered the expense of the removal from his principal. In *The Winson*[149] a salvor of goods from a stranded ship took them to a place of safety and (to prevent them from deteriorating) had them stored in a warehouse there. It was held that the owner was liable to the salvor for the cost of warehousing the goods.

Improvement of another's property. A person who improves another's   16–038
property may do so in the mistaken but honest belief that it is his own. In such a case there is no agency of necessity since the improver's intention is to act on his own behalf, and not on behalf of the owner. If the subject-matter is goods and the owner sues the improver for wrongful interference, the improver is by statute entitled to an allowance (against the owner's claim) in respect of the improvements.[150] A similar rule existed at common law, and presumably applies in relation to property other than goods.[151] It is more doubtful whether the improver has an independent claim in respect of the improvements,[152] i.e. one that he can assert even though no action has been brought against him by the owner.

If the improver knows that he has no title to the property he may again have certain limited rights in respect of the improvements. In *Munro v Wilmott*[153] the claimant with the defendant's permission left his car in the defendant's yard. Some years later, the defendant wanted to have the car moved, and, after trying unsuccessfully to contact the claimant, spent some £85 on making the car saleable, and sold it. He was held liable for conversion, but the damages were reduced by £85 "not from the point of view of payment for what he has done, but in order to arrive at . . . the true value of the property which the [claimant] had lost".[154] The case would now come within the statutory provisions authorising sales of uncollected goods,[155] so that the defendant would no longer be liable in conversion. Under the statutory provisions the bailee must account for the proceeds of sale to the bailor and is entitled to deduct items such as the costs of sale and sums due to him under the terms of the bailment[156]; but nothing is said about the value of

---

[146] *Graanhandel T Vink BW v European Grain & Shipping Co* [1989] 2 Lloyd's Rep. 531 at 533 (where there was no such agency as the buyer had lost his right to reject); cf. *The Olib* [1991] 2 Lloyd's Rep. 108 at 114.

[147] *Binstead v Buck* (1776) 2 Wm.Bl. 1117; *Nicholson v Chapman* (1793) 2 H.Bl. 254.

[148] Cited in (1922) 10 Ll.L.R. at 678.

[149] [1982] A.C. 939; Samuel 98 L.Q.R. 362; cf. *GN Ry v Swaffield* (1874) L.R. 9 Ex. 132

[150] Torts (Interference with Goods) Act 1977, ss.6(1), 3(7).

[151] *Peruvian Guano Co v Dreyfus Bros* [1892] A.C. 166 at 176.

[152] For a suggestion that there is such a claim, see *Greenwood v Bennett* [1973] Q.B. 195 at 201 (but see at 203); Jones 93 L.Q.R. 273.

[153] [1949] 1 K.B. 295.

[154] ibid. at 299.

[155] Torts (Interference with Goods) Act 1977, ss.12, 13 and Sch.1; Palmer [1987] L.M.C.L.Q. 43.

[156] ibid., s.12(5).

improvements.[157] However, the bailee can apply to the court for an order authorising the sale "subject to such terms . . . as may be specified in the order".[158] These could perhaps give him the right to make a deduction in respect of improvements. Even this possibility would not be open to the bailee if he did not sell the goods but simply returned them to the bailor. In such a case he could perhaps invoke the doctrine of agency of necessity.

16–039   **Conditions to be satisfied.** In the sale, preservation and improvement cases just discussed, the common law doctrine of agency of necessity will apply only if certain conditions are satisfied.[159] It must be impossible to communicate with the owner of the goods in time to get his instructions or impossible to obtain such instructions because the owner (though he can be reached) fails to give them[160]; the agent must act reasonably, in good faith and in the interests of the owner; and his acts must have been commercially necessary. It is not "necessary" to sell goods merely because they are causing inconvenience,[161] for there may be a reasonable opportunity of storing them.[162]

16–040   **Preservation of life or health.** The doctrine of agency of necessity may apply where one person preserves the life or health of another. Thus it is the basis on which a person can sue for the value of necessaries supplied to a person lacking mental capacity.[163] A doctor who gives medical attention to an unconscious person might recover a fee on the same ground[164]; the case for allowing him to do so would be particularly strong where the doctor's acts are not merely lawful but are done in the performance of a legal duty to render the services in question.[165] A right to payment would of course be negatived if the circumstances were such that the services would not normally be paid for: this would be the position where emergency treatment is given under the National Health Service. Special statutory provisions entitle the doctor to a fee where he gives emergency treatment to the victim of a road accident[166] and require National Health Service charges to be paid to the Secretary of State in respect of treatment given by the Service to an "injured person" if a "compensation payment" is made (normally by an insurer) by or on behalf of a person who is, or is alleged to be, liable to any extent in respect of the injury, or in pursuance of a compensation scheme for motor accidents.[167]

---

[157] s.6 of the Torts (Interference with Goods) Act 1977 would not apply as the defendant knew that he had no title to the car.

[158] Torts (Interference with Goods) Act 1977, s.13(1)(a).

[159] See *Springer v GW Ry* [1921] 1 K.B. 257; *Prager v Blatspiel, Stamp & Heacock Ltd* [1924] 1 K.B. 566. These principles also apply to a shipmaster's authority of necessity: above, para.16–033; cf. *The Winson* [1982] A.C. 939.

[160] *The Winson*, above, at 962; *The Olib* [1991] 2 Lloyd's Rep. 108 at 104; the possibility that the owner may fail to give the instructions shows that the difficulty of obtaining them is not invariably "overcome today by modern means of communication" (*Re F* [1990] 2 A.C. 1 at 75); cf. *The Choko Star* [1990] 1 Lloyd's Rep. 516 at 524); it may also be impracticable for a shipmaster to obtain instructions from *all* the cargo-owners.

[161] *Sachs v Miklos* [1948] 2 K.B. 23.

[162] As in *Prager v Blatspiel, Stamp & Heacock Ltd* [1924] 1 K.B. 566. *Semble* the statutory power of sale referred to at para.16–036, above, would not extend to the facts of this case.

[163] See above, paras 12–058—12–061.

[164] *Cotnam v Wisdom* 83 Ark. 601; 104 S.W. 164 (1907); *Re Crisan's Estate* 102 N.W. 2d 907 (1961).

[165] *Re F* [1990] 2 A.C. 1 at 55, where the issue was whether the treatment was *lawful*.

[166] Road Traffic Act 1988, ss.158, 159, as amended by Road Traffic (NHS Charges) Act 1999, s.18(2).

[167] Health and Social Care (Community Health and Standards) Act 2003, s.150.

Scope of the doctrine. It will be seen from the situations discussed above that 16–041
"agency of necessity" can produce three quite different results. First, it may
enable the agent to create a contract between the principal and a third party[168];
secondly it may entitle the agent to dispose of the principal's property[169]; and
thirdly it may entitle the agent to recompense or reimbursement in respect of the
efforts that he has made, or the expense that he has incurred, to protect the
interests of the principal.[170] It has been suggested that the expression "agency of
necessity" should no longer be used in its traditional broad sense, to refer to all
these consequences, but that it should be used in a narrower sense, to refer only
to cases in which the question is whether the agent has, by reason of the necessity,
the power to create a contract between his principal and a third party.[171]

The purpose of this suggested departure from the traditional terminology is to
make the point that the three consequences described above do not necessarily
depend on the same requirements.[172] Thus a person who, to prevent another's
goods from deteriorating, arranges for them to be stored in a warehouse, may have
a claim against the owner for reimbursement of the charges that he has paid to the
warehouseman. It does not follow from this that he also has the power to make a
contract between the owner and the warehouseman, so that the warehouseman can
sue the owner directly for his charges.[173] On the other hand, the fact that both
consequences depend on necessity makes it at least likely that similar factors will
often be relevant to each of them. Similarly, it is relevant for the purpose of both
consequences to ask whether the agent acted in the interests of the owner or out
of self-interest.[174]

Thus it is submitted that the question whether the label "agency of necessity"
should be used in its traditional broad, or in a new narrow, sense is largely one of
emphasis, or, as has been said, a "purely terminological"[175] one. It is part of the
wider question as to the effects of non-consensual agency, to be discussed later in
this chapter.[176] Such agency scarcely ever produces *all* of the effects of agency
based on agreement, but it generally does produce *some* of those effects. This is
true of all forms of non-consensual agency; and it is submitted that, so long as the
relationships discussed under the present heading produce at least some of the
consequences that normally flow from agency by agreement, it is not inappropriate
to say that they give rise to "agency of necessity".

(c) Ratification

(i) *What amounts to ratification*

Express or implied. Ratification may be express or implied. It can be implied 16–042
if the principal by conduct unequivocally affirms the agent's acts, even though he

---

[168] e.g. above, at fn.139.
[169] e.g. above, at fn.143.
[170] e.g. above, at fnn.148–149.
[171] *The Winson* [1982] A.C. 939 at 958.
[172] ibid.
[173] ibid.
[174] ibid. at 962.
[175] ibid. at 965; cf. *Re F* [1990] 2 A.C. 1 at 75 (using the expression to refer to the intervenor's right
to reimbursement).
[176] See below, para.16–100.

purports to repudiate them.[177] Mere passive acquiescence does not of itself amount to ratification,[178] but it may, when combined with other circumstances, have this effect: e.g. where the principal knows that the third party believes him to have accepted the agent's act as having been authorised and takes no steps within a reasonable time to repudiate the transaction.[179]

16-043   **Knowledge of the principal.** Ratification will not generally be implied from conduct unless the principal has full knowledge of the agent's unauthorised act.[180] Where the question of ratification arises in the context of a claim by the third party against the principal, as opposed to a claim by the principal against the agent for breach of authority, it may be sufficient that the principal has knowledge of what the agent has done, but not that the agent lacked the authority to do it.[181] But whatever the context, a principal may be held to have ratified if he indicates that he will support whatever the agent has done on his behalf, even though he does not know exactly what the agent has agreed to: in such a case the principal takes the risk of the agent's having exceeded his authority.[182]

16-044   **Need for a free choice.** An act will be regarded as a ratification only if the principal had a free choice whether to do it or not. Merely taking back one's own property after a third party has, in reliance on unauthorised instructions, done work on it is not ratification.[183]

(ii) *When ratification possible*

16-045   **The agent must purport to act on behalf of the principal.** A principal can only ratify acts which the agent purported to do on his behalf.[184] The most important consequence of this rule is that if the agent purports to act on his own behalf the principal cannot ratify; or, in other words, that an undisclosed principal[185] cannot ratify. Thus in *Keighley, Maxsted & Co v Durant*[186] an agent bought corn at a price above that at which he had been instructed to buy. He intended to buy for his principal, but did not disclose this fact to the seller. The undisclosed principal purported to ratify the purchase, but later refused to accept delivery. It was held that the ratification was ineffective and that the principal was not liable. Lord Macnaghten said that "Civil obligations are not to be created by or founded

---

[177] *Cornwall v Henson* (1750) 1 Ves.Sen. 509.

[178] *Moon v Towers* (1860) 8 C.B.(N.S.) 611, reversed on other grounds: (1860) 9 H.L.C. 78. Contrast the now doubtful case of *Waithman v Wakefield* (1807) 1 Camp. 120; and *Michael Elliott & Partners v UK Land* [1991] 1 E.G.L.R. 39.

[179] *Suncorp Ins & Finance v Milano Assicurazioni SpA* [1993] 2 Lloyd's Rep. 225 at 241.

[180] *Lewis v Read* (1845) 13 M. & W. 834; *Sea Emerald SA v Prominvestbank* [2008] EWHC 1979 (Comm) at [102]. "Ignorance of the law" is no defence: *AMB Generali Holding AG v SEB Trygg Liv Holding Aktiebolag* [2005] EWCA Civ 1237; [2006] 1 W.L.R. 2276 at [43] ("a party cannot meet a claim of ratification by saying that if he had properly understood the effect of a legal document he would not have acted as he did").

[181] *ING Re (UK) Ltd v R&V Versicherung AG* [2006] EWHC 1544 (Comm) at [155]–[157];

[182] *Fitzmaurice v Bayley* (1856) 6 E. & B. 868; cf. *Haseler v Lemoyne* (1858) 5 C.B.(N.S.) 530; *Suncorp* case, above, fn.179, at 234.

[183] *Foreman & Co Pty Ltd v The Liddesdale* [1900] A.C. 190.

[184] *Wilson v Tumman* (1843) 6 Man. & G. 236.

[185] For the definition of "undisclosed principal", see below, para.16–054.

[186] [1901] A.C. 240; cf. *The Astyanax* [1985] 2 Lloyd's Rep. 109; *Welsh Development Agency v Export Finance Co* [1992] B.C.L.C. 148; *Siu Yin Kwan v Eastern Ins* [1994] 2 A.C. 199 at 207.

upon undisclosed intentions."[187] It could be objected that this reasoning would destroy the whole law relating to undisclosed principals. But the decision is nonetheless intelligible, having regard to the common law doctrine of privity of contract. Ratification and the undisclosed principal are two important exceptions to that doctrine. To allow both exceptions to operate on the same set of facts would go far towards overthrowing the doctrine of privity altogether.[188]

On the other hand, an unnamed principal[189] can ratify. Policies of marine insurance may be taken out "for and on behalf of any person interested"; and such persons can ratify although they are not named in the policy.[190]

The rule that the agent must *purport* to act on behalf of the principal does not mean that he must *intend* to do so. Thus the principal may ratify although the agent intended to defraud him.[191]

In *Brook v Hook*[192] an agent forged his principal's signature to a promissory note. The principal's later ratification was held to be ineffective. This case has given rise to a dispute on the question whether a forgery can ever be ratified. But it does not seem that this question arises in a case of this kind. If an agent forges his principal's signature he does not say "I am signing for my principal" but "this is my principal's signature". The principal cannot ratify because the agent did not purport to act on his behalf.[193] But if the principal stands by knowing that his agent will forge his signature he may be estopped from denying its genuineness.[194]

The principal's capacity. At common law, a corporation cannot ratify the **16–046** unauthorised act of its agent in entering into an ultra vires contract.[195] There are two reasons why, in general,[196] this rule no longer applies in relation to companies incorporated under the Companies Act 2006. First, the validity of an act done by such a company can no longer be called into question on the ground of lack of capacity by reason of anything in the company's constitution.[197] Secondly, in favour of a person dealing with the company in good faith, the power of the board of directors to bind the company, or to authorise others to do so, is deemed to be free of any limitation under the company's constitution.[198] Entering into a contract

---

[187] [1901] A.C. 240 at 247.

[188] Since an undisclosed principal is, by definition, not identified in the contract, the present rule is not affected by Contracts (Rights of Third Parties) Act 1999: see s.1(3); above, para.14–095. A further reason why the Act would not apply on facts such as those of the *Keighley Maxsted* case, above, is that the issue there was whether the ratifier was *liable* under the contract; and the rule that a contract does not *bind* a third party is generally unaffected by the Act: above, para.14–001.

[189] For the definition of "unnamed principal," see below, para.16–054.

[190] *Hagedorn v Oliverson* (1814) 2 M. & S. 485. Quaere whether the requirement stated in *Watson v Swann* (1862) 11 C.B.(N.S.) 756 at 771, that the person seeking to ratify must be described at the time of the contract in such a way as to be ascertainable at that time is generally accepted: see *Boston Fruit Co v British & Foreign Marine Ins Co* [1906] A.C. 336 at 338–339 (a case apparently overlooked in *Southern Water Authority v Carey* [1985] 2 All E.R. 1077 at 1085).

[191] *Re Tiedemann & Ledermann Frères* [1899] 2 Q.B. 66.

[192] (1871) L.R. 6 Ex. 89.

[193] *Imperial Bank of Canada v Begley* [1936] 2 All E.R. 367.

[194] *Greenwood v Martins Bank Ltd* [1933] A.C. 51.

[195] *Ashbury Ry Carriage & Iron Co v Riche* (1875) L.R. 7 H.L. 653; *Mann v Edinburgh N Tramways* [1893] A.C. 69; *Rolled Steel Products (Holdings) Ltd v BSC* [1986] Ch. 246 at 304.

[196] For exceptions, see below, fnn.197, 198.

[197] Companies Act 2006, s.39(1) (modified rules apply to companies which are charities: ss.39(2), 42); above, para.12–068.

[198] ibid., s.40(1) (modified rules apply to companies which are charities: ss.40(6), 42; and transactions with directors and their associates: ss.40(6), 41); above, para.12–069.

which is outside the company's objects constitutes a breach of duty by a director.[199] Section 239 of the 2006 Act permits ratification of a breach of duty by a director by ordinary resolution, but what is being ratified is the breach of duty and not the contract, as this is made binding by the operation of the provisions mentioned earlier.[200]

A person can become liable on a contract made by him while he was a minor if he "ratifies" it after reaching full age.[201] "Ratification" here seems to refer to confirmation by a person of a contract made by himself; but there seems to be no reason why a person should not be similarly liable on a ratification after full age of a contract made on his behalf, but without his authority, while he was a minor. There are, however, cases in which a person is not liable on a ratification in the sense of a confirmation of a contract made during minority by himself[202]; and it is submitted that he would equally not be liable if, after full age, he ratified a contract of this kind which had during his minority been made on his behalf but without his authority.[203]

16–047   **The principal must have been in existence when the act was done.** This rule can give rise to inconvenience when promoters contract on behalf of a projected company. It was held in *Kelner v Baxter*[204] that the company could not, after its formation, ratify the promoters' contracts, since it was not in existence when those contracts were made. One way of evading this rule is for the promoter to enter into a draft agreement providing that the company, when formed, shall enter into a similar agreement with the third party and that the liability of the promoter shall thereupon cease. But the draft agreement creates no binding contract between company and third party, so that each can, with the collusion of the promoter, deprive the other of the expected benefit of the contract. The position is somewhat better in equity. The company may be able to enforce the contract against the third party by showing that the promoter acted as trustee for it,[205] and the third party may be able to claim a reasonable remuneration out of any sum which the company has paid, or bound itself to pay, to the promoter for initial expenses.[206] But the third party has no such right if the company has neither made nor promised any payment to the promoter[207]; nor has he any claim against the company on a purely executory contract. By statute, a contract which purports to be made by or on behalf of a company before it is formed has effect (subject to contrary agreement) as a contract between the third party and the person purporting to act for the company or as agent for it.[208] But it is still impossible to create

---

[199] ibid., s.171(a).

[200] In the exceptional cases where the contract is not binding on the company, there is no provision in the 2006 Act for ratification *of the contract* (cf. s.41(6)); furthermore, s.239 does not affect "any rule of law as to acts that are incapable of being ratified by the company" (s.239(7)), which would suggest that the common law rule stated at the outset of this paragraph continues to apply in such cases.

[201] See above, para.12–029.

[202] A penal bond could not be ratified as it was considered to be wholly void: *Baylis v Dineley* (1815) 3 M. & S. 477.

[203] On the principle that a nullity cannot be ratified: below, para.16–049.

[204] (1866) L.R. 2 C.P. 174; cf. *Melhado v Porto Alegre Ry* (1874) L.R. 9 C.P. 503.

[205] See above, para.14–081 et seq.

[206] *Touche v Metropolitan Ry* (1871) L.R. 6 Ch.App. 671; cf. *Re Hereford, etc., Engineering Co* (1876) 2 Ch.D. 621 (where the third party lost his rights because of the promoter's fraud); *Re Empress Engineering Co* (1880) 16 Ch.D. 125. *Spiller v Paris Skating Rink Co* (1878) 7 Ch.D. 368 states the equitable principle too widely.

[207] *Re Rotherham Alum & Chemical Co* (1883) 25 Ch.D. 103.

[208] Companies Act 2006, s.51; below, para.16–072.

a direct contract between the company and the third party by ratification after incorporation. It would be better if the rule in *Kelner v Baxter* were wholly repealed by legislation.[209] We shall see that legislation to some extent solves the problems which arise out of pre-incorporation contracts; but it does so by techniques other than ratification.[210]

The principal must ratify in time. A contract cannot be ratified after the time fixed for its performance[211]; if no such time is fixed, it must be ratified within a reasonable time of the principal's acquiring notice of the unauthorised act.[212] Nor can a contract be ratified at a time when the principal could not validly have made it.[213] Thus it has been held that, where an agent, without authority, insures his principal's property, the latter cannot ratify the insurance after the destruction of the property,[214] since he could not at that time have insured it. But exceptionally a policy of marine insurance can be ratified after the destruction of the property insured[215] and it has been suggested that this rule should also be applied to other kinds of insurance.[216]   16–048

A nullity cannot be ratified.[217] Although ratification is not confined to lawful acts, an act which is simply void in law cannot be validated by ratification. Similarly, a principal cannot become liable if the unauthorised contract was prohibited by statute: "life cannot be given by ratification to prohibited transactions".[218] This is an additional reason for saying that a forgery cannot be ratified.[219]   16–049

(iii) *Effect of ratification*

Ratification relates back to time of unauthorised act. The effect of ratification is to put principal, agent and third party into the position in which they would have been, if the agent's acts had been authorised from the start: his authority is said to relate back to the time of the unauthorised act. Thus in *Bolton Partners v Lambert*[220] an agent without authority purported to buy a house for his principal from the defendant, who later repudiated the contract. The principal   16–050

---

[209] Given that this opportunity was not taken in the recent Companies Act 2006 (s.51; above, fn.208) merely restates the rule previously set out in Companies Act 1985, s.36C), it must be thought an unlikely development in the near future. The Explanatory Notes to the 2006 Act (at para.141) suggest novation as a possible solution, which "may be express or implied": above, para.15–003.

[210] See below, paras 16–061, 16–065, 16–072.

[211] *Metropolitan Asylums Board v Kingham* (1890) 6 T.L.R. 217; *Dibbins v Dibbins* [1896] 2 Ch. 348.

[212] *Re Portuguese Consolidated Copper Mines* (1890) 45 Ch.D. 16; cf. *Bedford Ins Co Ltd v Instituto de Ressaguros do Brasil* [1985] Q.B. 966 at 987 (and see above, para.11–020).

[213] cf. *Bird v Brown* (1850) 4 Ex. 786 at 789, quoted with approval by Dillon L.J. in *Presentaciones Musicales SA v Secunda* [1994] Ch. 271; for another explanation of *Bird v Brown*, see below, fn.225.

[214] *Grover & Grover Ltd v Matthews* [1910] 2 K.B. 401.

[215] *Williams v N China Ins Co* (1876) 1 C.P.D. 757; Marine Insurance Act 1906, s.86.

[216] *NOW v DOL* [1993] 2 Lloyd's Rep. 582 at 607–608.

[217] For a discussion of this rule, see *Danish Mercantile Co v Beaumont* [1951] Ch. 680 (where the act was held not to be a nullity).

[218] *Bedford Ins Co Ltd v Instituto de Ressaguros do Brasil* [1985] Q.B. 966 at 986 (and see above, para.11–020).

[219] See above, para.16–045.

[220] (1888) 41 Ch.D. 295; cf. *Maclean v Dunn* (1828) 4 Bing. 722; *Koenigsblatt v Sweet* [1923] 2 Ch. 314.

then ratified. It was held that the defendant was bound by the contract. His repudiation was ineffective as the principal's ratification related back to the time of the agent's unauthorised purchase. The same rule applies where the agent does some act other than the making of a contract. Where, for example, he without authority, begins legal proceedings on behalf of his principal, the principal can ratify even after the expiry of the period of limitation.[221] For the purpose of the doctrine of relation back, it is assumed that the unauthorised act is not a nullity: if it were, ratification would be ineffective either because a nullity cannot be ratified or on the ground that, when it took place, the principal could not himself have validly or effectively done the act in question.[222]

The rule that ratification relates back does not apply where the agent contracts "subject to ratification": in such a case the third party can withdraw at any time before ratification.[223] Nor does the rule apply where before ratification the agent and the third party have cancelled the unauthorised transaction by mutual consent.[224]

16–051   **Not effective where would cause unfair prejudice to the third party.** It has been held that the retrospective effect of ratification will not be permitted to defeat a "vested property right". That may be true in the sense that it will not be allowed to deprive a stranger to the contract of a property right which had vested in him before ratification,[225] but beyond that any interference with a property right should simply be seen as a possible example of a broader principle that ratification is not effective where to permit it would unfairly prejudice the third party.[226] In accordance with this principle, it has been held that ratification was effective to prevent time running for the purpose of limitation, even though it took place after the expiry of the relevant period,[227] and it was also effective to confer an immunity even though it took place after the casualty in relation to which the immunity was conferred.[228] By contrast, it has been held that ratification of the assignment of a cause of action three years after its execution was not effective in circumstances where the delay in bringing proceedings had caused unfair prejudice to the defendant.[229]

16–052   **Criticism.** The rule in *Bolton Partners v Lambert* has been criticised on the ground that it puts the third party at the mercy of the principal, who is free to

---

[221] *Presentaciones Musicales SA v Secunda* [1994] Ch. 271.

[222] ibid. at 280.

[223] *Watson v Davies* [1931] 1 Ch. 455; *Warehousing & Forwarding Co of East Africa Ltd v Jafferali & Sons Ltd* [1964] A.C. 1.

[224] *Walter v James* (1871) L.R. 6 Ex. 124; *Pacific & General Ins Co Ltd v Hazell* [1997] L.R.L.R. 65.

[225] *Bird v Brown* (1850) 4 Ex. 786, as explained in *Presentaciones Musicales SA v Secunda* [1994] Ch. 271 at 285; Tan Cheng Han 117 L.Q.R. 626.

[226] *Smith v Henniker-Major* [2002] EWCA Civ 762; [2003] Ch. 182 at [71], [73]; *The Borvigilant* [2003] EWCA Civ 935; [2003] 2 Lloyd's Rep. 520 at [70] et seq., approving the principle to this effect in *Bowstead and Reynolds on Agency* (18th edn), Art.19. In *The Borvigilant* Clarke L.J. stressed (at [87]) that "in the vast majority of cases it would be unjust to the third party to give effect to a ratification if to do so would divest a vested property right."

[227] *Presentaciones Musicales SA v Secunda* [1994] Ch. 271; cf. *Nottinghamshire Health Care Trust v Prison Officers Association* [2003] I.C.R. 1192.

[228] *The Borvigilant*, above, fn.226.

[229] *Smith v Henniker-Major* [2002] EWCA Civ 762; [2003] Ch. 182 (this aspect of the decision was obiter).

ratify or not as he pleases.[230] But the hardship to the third party should not be exaggerated. If the principal does not ratify, the third party has his remedy against the agent for breach of implied warranty of authority.[231] If the principal does ratify, the third party will be liable to him; but since this is precisely what he expected, he cannot complain.[232] The only hardship is that the principal may be able to keep the third party waiting while he decides whether to ratify, but the recognition of the broad principle referred to in the last paragraph does much to address any real prejudice caused by such delay. In any event, the principal must ratify within a reasonable time; and the extent of such time is considerably abridged if the third party tells the principal that he wishes to withdraw from the contract.[233] Moreover, a principal cannot ratify after he has, by words or conduct, intimated to the third party that he does not intend to do so[234]; and such an intention could probably be inferred from his remaining silent for more than a comparatively short time after notice of the third party's intention to withdraw. Thus the third party need not be kept indefinitely in suspense. He can, in effect, say to the principal: ratify quickly or not at all.

4. EFFECTS OF AGENCY

When an agent makes a contract on behalf of his principal with a third party, the transaction can give rise to legal effects between principal and third party, between agent and third party, and between principal and agent. In discussing these effects, we shall first assume that the agency has arisen by consent, and then consider to what extent the same effects result from non-consensual agency.   16–053

(a) Between Principal and Third Party

(i) *Rights of principal against third party*

Whether principal disclosed or undisclosed. The rights of principal against third party depend in part on the distinction between disclosed and undisclosed principals. A *disclosed principal* is one of whose existence the third party is aware at the time of contracting. He is called a named principal if the third party also knew his name, and an unnamed principal if the third party did not know his name.[235] An *undisclosed principal* is one of whose existence the third party is unaware at the time of contracting. Where a person makes a contract "as agent" or "on behalf of my client" the principal will generally be disclosed. But such words may not make it clear that that person is acting as agent *in the legal sense*[236]; they may merely indicate that he is acting as agent in a commercial sense. If that is the position and the person described as "agent" actually has a principal in the legal sense, that principal may be undisclosed.[237]   16–054

---

[230] Wambaugh 9 Harv.L.R. 60; and see *Fleming v Bank of New Zealand* [1900] A.C. 577.

[231] See below, paras 16–077—16–082.

[232] *The Borvigilant*, above, fn.226, at [88].

[233] *Re Portuguese Consolidated Copper Mines* (1890) 45 Ch.D. 16.

[234] *McEvoy v Belfast Banking Co* [1935] A.C. 24.

[235] Reynolds in (Rose, ed.) *Consensus ad Idem, Essays in the Law of Contract in Honour of Guenter Treitel*, p.77.

[236] See above, para.16–005.

[237] See a difference of opinion on this point in *Teheran-Europe Co Ltd v S T Belton (Tractors) Ltd* [1968] 2 Q.B. 545 at 552, 556, 561.

16–055   **Disclosed principal.** The general rule is that a disclosed principal can enforce the contract against the third party.[238] The third party is not discharged by settling with the agent unless the principal by his conduct induced the third party to do so, or unless the agent had authority to receive payment.[239] The third party cannot set off against the principal any debt which the agent may owe to the third party[240]; and a custom enabling the agent to receive payment by such set-off is unreasonable.[241]

16–056   **Undisclosed principal.**[242] An undisclosed principal can also, in general, enforce the contract against the third party. Attempts have been made to reconcile this rule with the doctrine of privity. One view is that the contract is "in truth" made with the undisclosed principal,[243] but this is scarcely consistent with the rule that the agent is fully entitled and liable under the contract.[244] Other views recognise that the contract is between agent and third party but say that the principal can intervene because his contract with the agent entitles him to do so, or because he is a cestui que trust or a quasi-assignee.[245] But the better view seems to be that the undisclosed principal's right is not based on the theory that he has somehow acquired the agent's right. His right is an independent right,[246] established by way of exception to the common law doctrine of privity,[247] in the interests of commercial convenience.[248]

The undisclosed principal's right could prejudice a third party, who necessarily thought that he was dealing only with the agent. To avoid such prejudice, the undisclosed principal's right is limited in the following ways.

16–057   **Consistency with the terms of the contract.** An undisclosed principal is not allowed to intervene where this would be inconsistent with the terms of the contract. In *Humble v Hunter*[249] a person signed a charterparty as "owner". This was held to mean that he and he alone was owner,[250] so that his undisclosed

---

[238] *Langton v Waite* (1868) L.R. 6 Eq. 165. The principal's right arises because he *is* a party, so that it is not governed by Contracts (Rights of Third Parties) Act 1999: this creates rights only in favour of "a person who is *not* a party" (s.1(1)).

[239] *Yates v Freckleton* (1781) 2 Dougl. 623; *Linck, Moeller & Co v Jameson & Co* (1885) 2 T.L.R. 206; *Butwick v Grant* [1924] 2 K.B. 483.

[240] *Pratt v Willey* (1826) 2 C. & P. 350; *Cooke v Eshelby* (1887) 12 App.Cas. 271; unless the agent has authority to receive payment in this way: *Stewart v Aberdein* (1838) 4 M. & W. 211 at 228.

[241] *Pearson v Scott* (1878) 9 Ch.D. 198.

[242] Tettenborn [1998] C.L.J. 274; Tan Cheng-Han 120 L.Q.R. 480.

[243] *Keighley Maxsted & Co v Durant* [1901] A.C. 240 at 261.

[244] See below, para.16–070.

[245] For discussions of the basis of the doctrine, see Ames, *Essays*, p.453; Seavey 29 Y.L.J. 859; Goodhart and Hamson 4 C.L.J. 320; Montrose 16 Can.Bar Rev. 757; Dowrick 17 M.L.R. 25; Higgins 28 M.L.R. 167; Reynolds above, fn.41, at 89–90.

[246] *Pople v Evans* [1969] 2 Ch. 255; *The Havprins* [1983] 2 Lloyd's Rep. 356 at 362.

[247] *Welsh Development Agency v Export Finance Co Ltd* [1992] B.C.L.C. 148 at 182, describing the exception as "anomalous".

[248] *Siu Yin Kwan v Eastern Ins Co Ltd* [1994] 2 A.C. 199 at 207. The Contracts (Rights of Third Parties) Act 1999 does not confer any rights on the undisclosed principal both for the reason given in fn.238, above and because he is, by definition, not "expressly identified" within s.1(3) (above, para.14–095).

[249] (1842) 12 Q.B. 316; *Formby Bros v Formby* (1910) 102 L.T. 116; cf. *The Astyanax* [1985] 2 Lloyd's Rep. 109.

[250] For the construction in this context of phrases such as "disponent owner" or "operating owner", see *The Yanxilas* [1982] 2 Lloyd's Rep. 444. In the context of a bill of lading, "[ship]owner" can refer to the person with whom the shipper enters into the contract of carriage and so include a charterer: *The Stolt Loyalty* [1995] 1 Lloyd's Rep. 598.

principal was not allowed to intervene. But in *F Drughorn Ltd v Rederiaktiebolaget Transatlantic*[251] the fact that an agent signed a charterparty as "charterer" did not exclude his undisclosed principal's right to enforce the contract; and in *Siu Yin Kwan v Eastern Ins Co Ltd*[252] the fact that the agent was described in an employer's liability policy as the employer did not exclude the right of the undisclosed principal (who was in fact the employer) to intervene. It seems that the courts have become reluctant to hold that this right has been excluded by descriptive words in the contract, since such a conclusion would tend to defeat the considerations of commercial convenience on which the doctrine of the undisclosed principal is based.[253]

Personal considerations relating to the agent. If the third party can show that he wanted to deal with the agent *and with no one else*, the undisclosed principal cannot intervene. This will, for example, be the position where the third party wished to contract only with the agent because the nature of the contract was such as to show that the third party relied on the agent's business reputation or integrity[254]; or because the agent owed him money which was to be set off against the amount due from the third party under the contract which the principal sought to enforce.[255] But the third party will not be prejudiced by the undisclosed principal's right to intervene if (as may be the case in many commercial contexts) it is a matter of indifference to him whether his contract is with the agent or with the undisclosed principal.[256] This was held to be the position in the *Siu Yin Kwan*[257] case, where the Privy Council also rejected the argument that the undisclosed principal's right should be excluded merely because the contract was one of indemnity insurance. While in some such contracts the insurer may rely on personal considerations relating to the insured,[258] he had not done so here since the proposal form had given him all the information relating to the principal that was relevant to the risk.[259] Presumably, however, the principal could not have intervened if the insurer had proved that, in entering into the contract, he had in fact relied on personal considerations relating to the agent.

16-058

Personal considerations relating to the principal. A third party who has no particular reason for wanting to deal with the agent may nevertheless *not want to* deal with the principal. If the agent expressly says that he is not acting for the

16-059

---

[251] [1919] A.C. 203; *Danziger v Thompson* [1944] K.B. 654. Contrast *The Starsin* [2003] UKHL 12; [2004] 1 A.C. 715 at [84], [85].

[252] [1994] 2 A.C. 199; *Rolls Royce Power Engineering Plc v Ricardo Consulting Engineers Ltd* [2004] EWHC 2871; 98 Con. L.R. 169; *Ferryways NV v Associated British Ports* [2008] EWHC 225; [2008] 1 Lloyd's Rep. 639.

[253] ibid. at 210; cf. *Epps v Rothnie* [1945] K.B. 562 at 565, doubting *Humble v Hunter*, above. But see: *Talbot Underwriting Ltd v Nausch Hogan & Mirray Inc* [2006] EWCA Civ 889; [2006] 2 Lloyd's Rep. 195 at [35]–[36] (inclusion of undisclosed principal as a co-assured of too significant an effect on insurer's rights of subrogation).

[254] *Collins v Associated Greyhound Racecourses Ltd* [1930] Ch. 1 (underwriting contract).

[255] *Greer v Downs Supply Co* [1927] 2 K.B. 28; quaere whether this decision was necessary for the protection of the third party since an undisclosed principal can intervene only subject to the third party's right of set-off against the agent: below, para.16–060.

[256] *Siu Yin Kwan v Eastern Ins Co Ltd* [1994] 2 A.C. 199 at 210.

[257] ibid. The claim was by employees of the principal under the equivalent of Third Parties (Rights Against Insurers) Act 1930; above, para.14–130.

[258] cf. above, para.15–053 for restrictions on the assignment of such policies on this ground.

[259] [1984] 2 A.C. 199 at 208.

principal, the third party can avoid the contract for fraud.[260] If he makes no such misrepresentation, the law is less clear.

In *Nash v Dix*[261] a committee of Roman Catholics wanted to buy a Congregational chapel from the defendants and to turn it into a place of Roman Catholic worship. The defendants refused to deal with the committee as they disapproved of the proposed user. The committee then told the claimant that if he could buy the chapel from the defendants they would buy it from him for £100 more than he had paid for it. The defendants sold the chapel to the claimant but repudiated the contract on discovering that he intended to resell to the committee. North J. held that the defendants were bound (1) because the claimant was not an agent, but simply a person who had bought for resale; and (2) because the claimant had not been guilty of any misrepresentation. It appears from the judgment that the claimant would have failed if he *had* been the agent of the committee.

In *Said v Butt*[262] the claimant wanted to go to the first night of a play, but knew that the proprietors of the theatre would not sell him a ticket as he had in the past strongly criticised their conduct. He therefore sent a friend to the box office to buy a ticket for him without disclosing his name, but he was later refused admission by the manager of the theatre. In an action against the manager for inducing a breach of contract, McCardie J. held that there was no contract between the proprietors and the claimant: since the proprietors reserved the right to sell first-night tickets to specially selected persons, the "personality" of the other contracting party was a material element in the contract.

Both these cases were distinguished in *Dyster v Randall & Sons*.[263] The claimant wanted to buy land from the defendants, who, to his knowledge, would not deal with him as they distrusted him. He employed an agent to buy the land in the agent's own name, and then claimed that he was entitled to intervene as undisclosed principal. Lawrence J. upheld the claim: he said that it would be futile to deny the claimant's right to sue since the agent could have assigned the benefit of the contract to him. But this reasoning does not satisfactorily distinguish *Said v Butt*: theatre tickets can (unless they expressly provide the contrary) be assigned no less than contracts to buy land. Again it was said that "personal" consideration entered into the two earlier cases but not into *Dyster v Randall & Sons*. While this may distinguish *Said v Butt*, it does not satisfactorily explain why the action in *Nash v Dix* would have failed if the claimant had been an agent; for it is hard to see why an objection based on religious grounds is more "personal" than one based on distrust.

It is submitted that an undisclosed principal should not be allowed to intervene if he knows that the third party does not want to deal with him. If the principal directly concealed his identity, the contract would be void for mistake, or voidable for fraud; and the principal should not be able to improve his position by simply employing an agent. The position is the same where the agent knows, or should know, that the third party wanted to contract *only* with him.[264]

---

[260] *Archer v Stone* (1898) 78 L.T. 34; cf. *Berg v Sadler & Moore* [1937] 2 K.B. 158; above, para.9–089.
[261] (1898) 78 L.T. 445.
[262] [1920] 3 K.B. 497.
[263] [1926] Ch. 932; cf. *Smith v Wheatcroft* (1878) 9 Ch.D. 223; for a discussion of these cases, see Williams 23 Can.Bar Rev. 397.
[264] *Siu Yin Kwan v Eastern Ins Co Ltd* [1994] 2 A.C. 199 at 207.

Other safeguards. The rights of the undisclosed principal against the third **16–060** party are subject to any defences which the third party has against the agent.[265] This rule is necessary for the protection of the third party, who thinks that he is dealing with the agent alone. Thus if the agent owes money to the third party, the debt can be set off by the third party against the principal, and if the third party pays the agent he can rely on the payment against the principal.[266] This rule is based on the third party's belief that he is dealing with the agent alone: it therefore does not apply where the third party has no such belief. In *Cooke v Eshelby*[267] the third party had no belief one way or the other whether the person with whom he was dealing was principal or agent. He was in fact an agent. The third party was not allowed to set off against the principal a debt which the agent owed to the third party.

The principal may intend the agent to disclose his existence, but the agent may fail to do so because he wants to misappropriate the proceeds of the contract, or to induce the third party to accept the principal's property in discharge of a debt which the agent owes to the third party. In such cases the third party can only rely on his settlement with, or set-off against, the agent, in an action brought by the principal, if the latter has so conducted himself as to enable the agent to appear as principal in the transaction.[268]

Non-existent principal. At common law, a principal cannot become a party to **16–061** a contract made on his or its behalf before the principal came into existence. This is, for example, the position where a contract purports to be made on behalf of a corporation before its incorporation: such a contract is a nullity because one party to it does not exist.[269] The Contracts (Rights of Third Parties) Act 1999, however, makes it possible so to draw up the contract as to make the corporation a third party beneficiary; it will then, in the circumstances specified in the Act,[270] be entitled to enforce the relevant terms of the contract.[271] The Act expressly provides that, for this purpose, the third party "need not be in existence when the contract is entered into."[272] Statutory provisions which deal with the contractual relations between the *agent* and the third party under pre-incorporation contracts are discussed later in this chapter.[273]

(ii) *Liability of principal to third party*

General rule. The general rule is that a principal, whether disclosed or **16–062** undisclosed, is liable to the third party.[274] The limitations on the right of an undisclosed principal to intervene exist mainly for the protection of the third party. Hence they do not necessarily apply where the third party sues the principal. But a person who is alleged to have contracted on behalf of another may,

---

[265] *Browning v Provincial Ins Co of Canada* (1873) L.R. 5 P.C. 263 at 272.
[266] *George v Clagett* (1797) 7 T.R. 359; *Mann v Forrester* (1814) 4 Camp. 60; *Montague v Forwood* [1893] 2 Q.B. 350; Derham [1986] C.L.J. 384.
[267] (1887) 12 App.Cas. 271; Reynolds [1983] C.L.P. 119.
[268] *Drakeford v Piercey* (1866) 14 L.T. 403.
[269] See below, fn.327.
[270] See especially ss.1(1) and (2); above, paras 14–091—14–093.
[271] s.1(1).
[272] s.1(3).
[273] See below, para.16–072.
[274] See *Boyter v Thomson* [1995] 2 A.C. 629 at 632.

on the true construction of the contract, have contracted solely on his own behalf. In that case he alone is liable on the contract[275]: the reason why the other is not liable is not that he is an undisclosed principal whose liability is excluded, but that he is not a principal in the transaction at all.

16–063   **Set-off.** The principal cannot set off against the third party any money owed to the principal by the agent.[276] If the principal gives the agent the money with which to pay the third party, but the agent fails to pay it over, the principal remains liable to the third party: he must seek out his creditor and see that he is paid.[277] The principal is discharged by payment to the agent only if such payment is made at the third party's request,[278] or if the third party looked to the agent for payment and so induced the principal to settle with the agent.[279]

16–064   **Undisclosed principal settling with agent.** In *Heald v Kenworthy*[280] it was assumed that an undisclosed principal is not (any more than one who is disclosed) discharged by settling with his agent. But in *Armstrong v Stokes*[281] the court said that this rule produced "intolerable hardship",[282] and refused to follow it. Thus it was held that an undisclosed principal who settled with his agent was not liable to make a second payment to the third party if the agent failed to pay over the money. Of course, it is hard for the principal to have to pay twice over; but it is equally hard for the third party not to be paid at all. It could be argued that the law should, in this situation, have no sympathy for the third party since he did not rely on the credit of a principal of whose existence he was unaware at the time of contracting. But this proves too much: whenever an undisclosed principal is sued the third party gets a windfall of this kind. Thus the case for applying a special rule to undisclosed principals in this context is weak. *Armstrong v Stokes* was doubted by the Court of Appeal in *Irvine v Watson*[283]; and it is submitted that an undisclosed principal who settles with his agent should remain liable to the third party.

16–065   **Contracts (Rights of Third Parties) Act 1999.** At common law, a contract purporting to be made with a non-existent principal, e.g. with a corporation before its incorporation, is a nullity[284] and so cannot impose liabilities, any more than it can confer rights, on the corporation. This position is not directly affected by the Contracts (Rights of Third Parties) Act 1999; for although a third party can by virtue of this Act acquire *rights* under a contract, the Act does not impose any *liabilities* on the third party.[285] However, the third party's right to enforce the term conferring a benefit on that party is "subject to . . . any other terms of the contract".[286] Thus it is possible to draw up a pre-incorporation contract so as to

---

[275] *J H Rayner (Mincing Lane) Ltd v DTI* [1989] Ch. 72 at 190–191, approved on this point [1990] 2 A.C. 418 at 515.
[276] *Waring v Favenck* (1807) 2 Camp. 85.
[277] *Irvine v Watson* (1880) 5 Q.B.D. 414.
[278] *Smyth v Anderson* (1849) 7 C.B. 21.
[279] See *Wyatt v Hertford* (1802) 3 East 147.
[280] (1855) 10 Ex. 739; Reynolds (1983) C.L.P. 119.
[281] (1872) L.R. 7 Q.B. 598.
[282] ibid. at 610.
[283] See above, fn.277.
[284] See below, at fn.327.
[285] See above, para.14–001.
[286] Contracts (Rights of Third Parties) Act 1999, s.1(4).

make the corporation's right of enforcement (once it has come into existence) subject to its discharging liabilities undertaken by its agents on its behalf. Even if this is not done, the corporation's right of enforcement is under the Act subject to defences available against the promisee (i.e. in the present context, the agent[287]). The result is that the corporation cannot enforce rights under the contract unless it discharges the relevant liabilities. But if it chooses not to enforce the rights, then the liabilities cannot be enforced against it merely because it is named as a third party beneficiary in the contract. By statute, this problem is now in part resolved in the case of an agreement made before the incorporation of a limited liability partnership between the persons who subscribe their names to the incorporation document.[288] Such an agreement "may impose obligations"[289] on the partnership to take effect after its incorporation. But even this provision does not extend to agreements made with *other* persons before the incorporation of the partnership and purporting to impose liabilities on it.[290]

(b) Between Agent and Third Party

Agent and third party may incur reciprocal rights and liabilities either under the contract which the agent makes on behalf of his principal, or under a collateral contract. The agent may also be liable for breach of implied warranty of authority and for other misrepresentation.   16–066

(i) *Under the contract*

General rule. The general rule is that an agent is neither liable under,[291] nor entitled to enforce,[292] a contract he makes on behalf of his principal. An agent may enter into a contract on his own behalf as well as on behalf of the principal and so be liable or entitled under the contract. This possibility is illustrated by the following cases.   16–067

Agent contracting personally. An agent is liable under the contract if he intended to undertake personal liability. Where the contract is in writing, the question whether he had this intention is one of construction.[293] An agent who is described in a written contract as a party to it and signs it without qualification is liable under it although the third party knew that he was acting as agent.[294] He may be liable even though such a contract also provides that it is signed on behalf   16–068

---

[287] Contracts (Rights of Third Parties) Act 1999, s.3(2); cf. above, para.14–075, fn.557.
[288] For the status of such a partnership as a body corporate, see Limited Liability Partnerships Act 2000, s.1(2).
[289] ibid., s.5(2).
[290] The rule contained in Companies Act 2006, s.51 (above, para.16–047) applies to limited liability partnerships by virtue of Limited Liability Partnership (Application of Companies Act 2006) Regulations 2009 (SI 2009/1804), reg.7, but does not impose liabilities on the principal.
[291] *Robins v Bridge* (1837) 3 M. & W. 114; *N & J Vlassopulos v Ney Shipping Ltd* [1977] 2 Lloyd's Rep. 478; *Boyter v Thomson* [1995] 2 A.C. 629 at 632.
[292] *Lucas v Beale* (1851) 10 C.B. 739; *Fairlie v Fenton* (1870) L.R. 5 Ex. 169.
[293] *Punjab National Bank v de Boinville* [1992] 1 W.L.R. 1138 at 1155; cf. *Ignazio Messina & Co v Polskie Linie Oceaniczne* [1995] 2 Lloyd's Rep. 566 at 571; *Internaut Shipping GmbH v Fercometal SARL* [2003] EWCA Civ 812; [2003] 2 Lloyd's Rep. 430; *Foxtons Ltd v Thesleff* [2005] EWCA Civ 514; (2005) 21 E.G. 140.
[294] *Basma v Weekes* [1950] A.C. 441; cf. *Davies v Sweet* [1962] 2 Q.B. 300; *Sika Contracts v Gill* (1978) 9 Build.L.R. 11; *Kai Yung v Hong Kong & Shanghai Banking Corp* [1981] A.C. 787 at 795.

of a third person, for such a provision may merely be intended to mean that that person is to be a party to the contract and not that the agent is to be absolved from liability under it.[295] At the other extreme, an agent who is described as agent in the contract and signs as agent is not liable.[296] But an agent may be described as agent in the body of the contract and sign without qualification; or he may be described as a party in the body of the contract and sign as agent.[297] A distinction has been drawn in such cases between words which merely describe the agent's profession, and words of representation, which show that he is acting as agent. The former do not, while the latter do, exonerate him from liability. Thus the words "we, as solicitors, undertake . . . " were held in *Burrell v Jones*[298] to be merely descriptive; and even the words "as agent" when used in their commercial, rather than their legal, sense have been held to be descriptive.[299] The words "on behalf of" or "*per procurationem*" are generally representative. But no particular formula is conclusive; and where the description is equivocal the court will rely on other relevant circumstances in order to determine, on an objective standard, whether an undertaking of personal liability may be inferred.[300] An agent is no longer personally liable merely because he acts on behalf of a foreign principal.[301]

Just as the agent may on the true construction of the contract, be liable, so he may be entitled.[302] The courts will, if possible, hold that "the existence of the liability on the one hand involves the existence of the correlative right on the other"[303]; but words which indicate that the agent is not to be liable are not necessarily construed to mean that he is not to be entitled. Thus where an agent had contracted "on account of" his principal, it was held that the agent was not personally liable on the contract[304]; but where a policy of insurance described the assured as a bank "a/c [a named customer]" it was held to confer rights on the bank (the agent), the reference to the customer being merely intended to remind the bank which of its customers was concerned with the transaction in question.[305] It follows that the agent can be entitled without being liable or liable without being entitled, if that is the true meaning of the contract. In the first of these situations, there may indeed be some difficulty in seeing what consideration has been provided by the agent so long as the contract remains wholly executory, but there would be no such difficulty where the agent has actually performed, e.g. by making a payment under the contract on behalf of the principal. In the second situation

---

[295] *The Sun Happiness* [1984] 1 Lloyd's Rep. 381.

[296] *Mahony v Kekulé* (1854) 14 C.B. 390; *The Rialto (No.2)* [1998] 1 Lloyd's Rep. 322 at 328.

[297] As in *Gadd v Houghton* (1876) 1 Ex.D. 357; *Universal Steam Navigation Co Ltd v James McKelvie & Co* [1923] A.C. 492 (in these cases the agents were held not liable); *The Maria D* [1992] 1 A.C. 21.

[298] (1819) 3 B. & Ald. 47.

[299] *Parker v Winlow* (1857) 7 E. & B. 942; cf. above, para.16–005.

[300] *The Swan* [1968] 1 Lloyd's Rep. 5; Reynolds 85 L.Q.R. 92; Legh-Jones 32 M.L.R. 325; cf. *Tudor Marine Ltd v Tradax Export SA* [1976] 2 Lloyd's Rep. 135; *The Primorje* [1980] 2 Lloyd's Rep. 74; *The Riza Sun* [1997] 2 Lloyd's Rep. 314; *British Energy Power & Trading Ltd v Credit Suisse* [2008] EWCA Civ 53; [2008] 1 Lloyd's Rep. 413; contrast *Astilleros Canarios SA v Cape Hatteras Shipping Co SA* [1982] 1 Lloyd's Rep. 518.

[301] *Miller, Gibb & Co v Smith & Tyrer Ltd* [1917] 2 K.B. 141; Hudson 23 M.L.R. 695; 29 M.L.R. 353; 35 Can.Bar Rev. 336.

[302] *Short v Spackman* (1831) 2 B. & Ad. 962; *H O Brandt & Co v H N Morris & Co Ltd* [1917] 2 K.B. 784; cf. *The Yanxilas* [1982] 2 Lloyd's Rep. 444; *Fraser v Thames Television* [1984] Q.B. 44; *Transcontinental Underwriting Agency SRL v Grand Union Ins Co Ltd* [1987] 2 Lloyd's Rep. 409.

[303] *Repetto v Millar's Karri & Jarrah Forests Ltd* [1901] 2 K.B. 306 at 310.

[304] *Gadd v Houghton* (1876) 1 Ex. D. 357.

[305] *Punjab National Bank v de Boinville* [1992] 1 W.L.R. 1138.

there is no similar difficulty even if the contract is still executory; the third party provides consideration for the agent's promise by undertaking liability towards the principal and it is immaterial that the consideration does not move to the agent: consideration must move from the promisee (the third party) but need not move to the promisor (the agent).[306]

Trade usage or custom. An agent may be personally liable or entitled if that is the usual course of business either between particular parties or in relation to a particular class of agents.[307] For example, "where one attorney does work for another, it is common practice for him to give credit to that other and not to the client".[308] A local or trade custom can have the same effect.[309]   16–069

Principal undisclosed. Where the principal is undisclosed the agent is both entitled and liable[310]; but this rule does not apply where the agent uses words of representation and the principal is only unnamed.[311] The agent's failure to name the principal may make it easy to infer that he intended to contract personally; but there is no general rule to that effect.[312]   16–070

Agent in fact principal. An agent may purport to act on behalf of a principal when he is in fact acting on his own behalf. If he purports to act for an unnamed principal, he can enforce the contract for his own benefit.[313] But if he purports to act for a named principal, he can enforce the contract only after giving due notice to the third party that he acted on his own behalf.[314] Even then the agent will not be allowed to enforce the contract if this would prejudice the third party.[315] These safeguards are necessary as the third party may have relied on the principal's solvency or other attributes when he made the contract. It follows that the agent cannot enforce the contract if he knew that, for some "personal" reason, the third party was unwilling to contract with him either at all, or on the same terms as those on which he was willing to contract with the principal.[316] If the claimant in *Said v Butt*[317] had gone in person to buy a ticket, pretending that it was not for him but for a friend, he could not later have said that his friend was in fact himself.   16–071

---

[306] See above, para.3–024.

[307] This may be the best explanation of the decision that a collecting bank acts as an "agent with an interest" and is entitled to sue the buyer under an irrevocable payment undertaking: *Raiffeisen Zentralbank Osterreich Attorney-General v China Marine Bunker (Petrochina) Co Ltd* [2006] EWHC 212; [2006] All E.R. (D) 37 at [33].

[308] *Scrace v Whittington* (1823) 2 B. & C. 11. The above dictum makes the agent *exclusively* liable: cf. below, para.16–075.

[309] *Fleet v Murton* (1871) L.R. 7 Q.B. 126; cf. *Cory Brothers Shipping Ltd v Baldan Ltd* [1997] 2 Lloyd's Rep. 58 (forwarding agent acting for unnamed principal liable, by custom, for freight).

[310] *Sims v Bond* (1833) 5 B. & Ad. 389 at 393; *Siu Yin Kwan v Eastern Ins Co Ltd* [1994] 2 A.C. 199 at 207; *Boyter v Thomson* [1995] 2 A.C. 629 at 632.

[311] e.g. *Universal Steam Navigation Co v James McKelvie & Co* [1923] A.C. 492; *Benton v Campbell, Parker & Co Ltd* [1925] 2 K.B. 410.

[312] *N & J Vlassopulos v Ney Shipping Ltd* [1977] 2 Lloyd's Rep. 478; cf. *Pershore Produce (Fruit & Vegetables) Ltd v Reed* [2010] EWCA Civ 795.

[313] *Schmaltz v Avery* (1851) 16 Q.B. 655; *Harper & Co v Vigers Bros* [1909] 2 K.B. 549. In *Bowstead and Reynolds on Agency* (19th edn), para.9–096 this rule is regarded as doubtful.

[314] *Bickerton v Burrell* (1816) 5 M. & S. 383; *aliter* if the other party knows that the "agent" is the real principal: *Rayner v Grote* (1846) 15 M. & W. 359.

[315] See *Fellowes v Gwydyr* (1829) 1 Russ. & M. 83.

[316] *The Remco* [1984] 2 Lloyd's Rep. 205.

[317] [1920] 3 K.B. 497; above, para.16–059.

The present exception to the general rule, that an agent acquires no rights under the contract, is based on the assumptions that he has (i) purported to contract as agent and (ii) in fact contracted as principal. The exception therefore did not apply where a father conducted negotiations for the purchase of a house and the resulting contract was drawn up in the name of his son (who was a minor). It was held that the father could not enforce the contract since the contract did not say that he had entered into it on behalf of the son, or indeed mention the father's name at all.[318]

16–072   **Principal non-existent.** Where the alleged principal does not exist, it may be easy to infer that the agent intended to assume personal liability. At common law this inference was drawn in *Kelner v Baxter*[319] with the result that promoters were held personally liable on a contract made by them on behalf of a company which had not yet been formed. But such an inference is not necessarily drawn merely because the agent purports to act for a non-existent principal[320]: the question is one of intention in each case.[321] The agent was accordingly held not liable where the contract was with a non-existent company which was believed to form part of a group of companies, the third party's intention being merely to contract with a company within that group, and one such company having accepted responsibility under the contract.[322] Similarly, it is arguable that the agent should not be personally liable where, under the rules discussed earlier in this chapter,[323] the principal can be held liable under the contract in spite of not having been in existence when the contract was made.

Section 51(1) of the Companies Act 2006 provides that "a contract that purports to be made . . . on behalf of a company[324] at a time when the company has not been formed has effect, subject to any agreement to the contrary, as one made with the person purporting to act . . . as agent for" the company. Under this subsection, the agent can no longer escape liability merely on the ground that he entered into the contract "as agent"[325]; it is up to him to establish that there was an "agreement to the contrary" exonerating him from liability. The subsection puzzlingly concludes with the words "and he [i.e. the agent, in our examples] is personally liable on the contract accordingly". It seems these words merely spell out *one* consequence of the previous words and do not limit their operation: i.e. the agent may be *entitled* as well as liable.

At common law, a distinction was drawn between the cases so far considered where the agent purported to *act on behalf* of the unformed company, and those in which he said that the contract *actually was that* of the company[326] and purported

---

[318] *Hector v Lyons* (1989) 58 P. & C.R. 156. No such point arose in *Shogun Finance Ltd v Hudson* [2003] UKHL 62; [2004] 1 A.C. 919 (above, para.8–039) where any attempt by the rogue to enforce the contract would have failed by reason of his fraud.

[319] (1886) L.R. 2 C.P. 174; cf. *Phonogram Ltd v Lane* [1982] Q.B. 938; Green 47 M.L.R. 671.

[320] *Holman v Pullin* (1884) Cab. & El. 254.

[321] *Black v Smallwood* [1966] A.L.R. 744; Baxt 30 M.L.R. 328; Lücke 3 Adelaide L.Rev. 102.

[322] *Coral (UK) Ltd v Rechtman* [1996] 1 Lloyd's Rep. 235.

[323] See above, at fn.289.

[324] i.e. one incorporated in the UK: *Rover International Ltd v Cannon Film Sales Ltd (No.3)* (1987) 3 B.C.C. 369, reversed in part on other grounds [1989] 1 W.L.R. 912. The same rule applies to limited liability partnerships: see above, fn.290.

[325] *Phonogram Ltd v Lane* [1982] Q.B. 938 at 944; McMullen [1982] C.L.J. 47. Contrast *Badgerhill Properties v Cottrell* [1991] B.C.L.C. 805 (agent not liable merely because existing company's name was incorrectly stated in the contract).

[326] For the concept of an act done by the company itself, see *Meridian Global Funds Management Asia Ltd v Securities Commission* [1995] 2 A.C. 500 at 506–507.

to affix the company's signature. In the latter case it was held that the resulting transaction was a complete nullity,[327] and that the agent could not acquire any rights under it.[328] But the distinction between the two situations was criticised as highly technical[329] and one which businessmen were unlikely to appreciate. The provisions of s.51(1) of the Companies Act 2006 therefore extend also to "a contract which purports to be made by a company" before it is formed. Such a contract has effect (subject to contrary agreement) "as one made with the person purporting to act for the company"; e.g. by the officer purporting to affix the company's signature. The concluding words of the subsection again refer only to the *liability* of such a person, but it has been held that he is also *entitled* to enforce the contract, subject only to restrictions which may be imposed on his right to do so at common law[330]: e.g. on the ground that, for "personal" reasons of the kind described above, the third party was willing to contract only with the company, or unwilling to contract with the person purporting to act on its behalf.[331] But the subsection does not apply where the contract purports to have been made by a company which had once existed and later been dissolved before the time of the putative contract. That contract is then a nullity and cannot be enforced either by the person purporting to have acted for the company or by a new company formed after the date of contracting to carry on the business of the former company. The reason why such a case is not within s.51(1) is that the agent purported to act for the old company rather than on behalf of the new company before it was formed.[332]

Deeds. At common law, an agent who executed a deed was personally liable on   16–073
it even though the deed said that he had executed it on behalf of his principal.[333]
It seems, however, that this rule has been reversed by statute.[334]

Statute. An agent may be personally liable by statute: e.g. an administrative   16–074
receiver appointed by debenture holders, who is deemed to be the agent of the company,[335] is nevertheless personally liable on a contract into which he enters in carrying out his functions, except in so far as the contract or legislation otherwise provides.[336]

Election.[337] Where an agent is liable on the contract, one possible inter-   16–075
pretation of the transaction is that he is solely liable, or, in other words, that the contract is simply between him and the third party and not between the third

---

[327] cf. *Rover International Ltd v Cannon Film Sales Ltd (No.3)* [1989] 1 W.L.R. 912—a position described in earlier proceedings in the same case as "a blot on English jurisprudence": [1987] 1 W.L.R. 670 at 679.

[328] *Newborne v Sensolid (Great Britain) Ltd* [1954] 1 Q.B. 45.

[329] *Phonogram Ltd v Lane* [1982] Q.B. 938 at 944.

[330] *Braymist Ltd v Wise Finance Co Ltd* [2002] EWCA Civ 127; [2002] Ch. 273 (applying s.36C(1) of the Companies Act 1985).

[331] ibid. at [63], [83]. The *Braymist* case itself was not of this kind.

[332] *Cotronic (UK) Ltd v Dezonie (t/a Wendaland Builders Ltd)* [1991] B.C.L.C. 721.

[333] *Appleton v Binks* (1804) 5 East 148.

[334] Powers of Attorney Act 1971, s.7(1), as amended by Law of Property (Miscellaneous Provisions) Act 1989, ss.1(8) and 4 and Schs 1 and 2.

[335] Insolvency Act 1986, s.44(1)(a).

[336] ibid., s.44(1)(b) as amended by Insolvency Act 1994, s.2; cf. *Powdrill v Watson* [1995] 2 A.C. 394 (personal liability on "adopted" contracts of employment); for his right of indemnity, see 1986 Act, s.45.

[337] Reynolds 86 L.Q.R. 318.

party and the principal at all.[338] Another possibility is that the agent and the principal are both liable under the contract.[339] This is certainly the position where the principal is undisclosed[340] and it may also be true where an agent incurs personal responsibility under a contract made on behalf of a disclosed principal.[341]

Where both principal and agent are liable on the contract, the third party may lose his right to sue one of them on the ground that he has "elected" to hold the other liable. This doctrine is most commonly discussed in relation to cases involving undisclosed principals, though there is some authority for applying it in all cases in which both principal and agent are liable on the contract.[342] The reasons for the doctrine are obscure: it is hard to see why a principal should be released merely because the third party has "elected" to hold the agent liable. It might be more satisfactory to hold that the principal should be released only if he had relied on the third party's conduct in such a way that he would be prejudiced by being subsequently held liable: e.g. if the principal had adjusted his accounts with the agent in reliance on the third party's conduct.[343] Election to hold the principal liable may similarly be a ground for releasing the agent if it has led to action in reliance by the agent: e.g. to his giving up rights against the principal. Where there has been no action in reliance on the third party's conduct, the courts do not often apply the doctrine of election. What amounts to election is a question of fact; and in the decided cases the courts have been somewhat reluctant to find an election. Merely sending a bill to one of two parties liable has been held not to be an election[344]; and even the commencement of legal proceedings, though strong evidence of election,[345] is not necessarily conclusive.[346] The mere obtaining of a judgment against principal or agent will no longer bar proceedings against the other[347]; though it might, presumably, still amount to an "election".

(ii) *Under a collateral contract*

16–076   There may be a collateral contract between agent and third party, quite distinct from the main contract between principal and third party. Thus when goods are sold by auction, the auctioneer undertakes certain obligations towards the buyer,[348] but they are not co-extensive with those of the seller. The seller undertakes that he has the right to sell, but the auctioneer only undertakes to give the buyer possession[349] so that he is not liable for the seller's lack of title.[350] The collateral

---

[338] e.g. above, at fn.308; below, fn.342.

[339] See Reynolds 85 L.Q.R. 92.

[340] See above, paras 16–056, 16–070.

[341] See *The Swan* [1968] 1 Lloyd's Rep. 5 at 12; *Teheran-Europe Co v S T Belton (Tractors) Ltd* [1968] 2 Q.B. 545 at 558; *The Kurnia Dewi* [1997] 1 Lloyd's Rep. 553 at 559.

[342] *Debenham v Perkins* (1925) 113 L.T. 252 at 254. Other cases which have been cited to support the doctrine of election where the principal was disclosed may turn rather on the point that he was never liable under the contract at all because it was made solely with the agent: e.g. *Thomson v Davenport* (1829) 9 B. & C. 78; *Calder v Dobell* (1871) L.R. 6 C.P. 486.

[343] *Smethurst v Mitchell* (1859) 1 E. & E. 622; *Davison v Donaldson* (1882) 9 Q.B.D. 623.

[344] *Chesterton v Barone* [1987] 1 E.G.L.R. 15.

[345] See *Scarf v Jardine* (1882) 7 App.Cas. 345.

[346] *Curtis v Williamson* (1874) L.R. 10 Q.B. 57; *Clarkson Booker Ltd v Andjel* [1964] 2 Q.B. 775; cf. *The Scaplake* [1978] 2 Lloyd's Rep. 380.

[347] Civil Liability (Contribution) Act 1978, s.3.

[348] *Woolfe v Horne* (1877) 2 Q.B.D. 355.

[349] *Wood v Baxter* (1883) 49 L.T. 45.

[350] *Benton v Campbell, Parker & Co* [1925] 2 K.B. 410.

contract may confer rights, as well as impose liabilities, on the agent. Thus an auctioneer can sue the buyer for the price of the goods sold.[351] The liability of an auctioneer who refuses to knock goods down to the highest bidder at an auction sale without reserve[352] has also been explained on the ground of a "collateral agreement existing between the auctioneer and the bidder."[353]

(iii) *Implied warranty of authority*

Nature of liability. An agent who purports to act for a principal, knowing that he has no authority to do so, is liable to the third party in deceit, even if he believed that the principal would ratify.[354] It was at one time thought that if the agent honestly believed that he had authority when in fact he had none, he was under no liability.[355] But it was settled in *Collen v Wright*[356] that the agent was in such circumstances liable for breach of an implied warranty that he had the authority which he purported to have. It makes no difference that the agent has acted in good faith and with due diligence.[357]

16–077

The rule sometimes operates harshly on the agent, and it might be more reasonable to imply a warranty that the agent should not negligently exceed his authority.[358] The agent's position has been alleviated by legislation, so that an agent who acts under a power of attorney incurs no liability if the power of attorney has without his knowledge been revoked.[359]

The agent does not impliedly[360] warrant that the contract which he makes between principal and third party will be performed, but only that he has authority to make it.[361] This has an important bearing on damages. If the third party could have obtained full satisfaction from the principal, had the contract been binding on him, the agent is liable to the same extent.[362] But if the principal is insolvent, the third party cannot recover more from the agent than he would have got from the principal, had the agent had authority; and this may be very little, or nothing, according to the degree of the principal's insolvency.[363]

---

[351] *Coppin v Walker* (1816) 7 Taunt. 237; cf. *Wilson v Pike* [1949] 1 K.B. 176; *Chelmsford Auctions Ltd v Poole* [1973] Q.B. 542.
[352] See above, paras 2–008, 3–162.
[353] *Barry v Davies* [2000] 1 W.L.R. 1962 at 1968.
[354] *Polhill v Walter* (1832) 3 B. & Ad. 114.
[355] This was one basis of *Smout v Ilbery* (1842) 10 M. & W. 1; see also below, para.16–079.
[356] (1857) 8 E. & B. 647, approved by the House of Lords in *Starkey v Bank of England* [1903] A.C. 114 and followed in *V/O Rasnoimport v Guthrie & Co Ltd* [1966] 1 Lloyd's Rep. 1; Reynolds 83 L.Q.R. 189.
[357] *Yonge v Toynbee* [1910] 1 K.B. 215; see below, para.16–105, for survival of apparent authority in cases of the principal's insanity.
[358] Negligence may lead to liability in damages at common law or under Misrepresentation Act 1967; but the measure of such damages could differ from that for breach of implied warranty of authority: cf. above, para.9–058 et seq.
[359] Powers of Attorney Act 1971, s.5(1), which is also extended to apply to lasting powers of attorney (see below, para.16–113): Mental Capacity Act 2005, s.14(5).
[360] He may expressly do so as (for example) in *The Maria D* [1992] 1 A.C. 21.
[361] *Nelson v Nelson* [1997] 1 W.L.R. 233; *AMB Generali Holding AG v SEB Trygg Liv Holding Aktiebolag* [2005] EWCA Civ 1237; [2006] 1 W.L.R. 2276 at [63]; cf. *Knight Frank LLP v Haney* [2011] EWCA Civ 404; [2011] N.P.C. 40 (agent not liable where name of principal had been misrepresented but was capable of being established).
[362] cf. *Habton Farms v Nimmo* [2003] EWCA Civ 68; [2004] Q.B. 1.
[363] See below, para.20–095.

Normally, the effect of the warranty is to induce the third party to enter into a contract with the principal or supposed principal. But liability may also be incurred if the third party acts in reliance on the warranty in some other way: e.g. where the agent falsely represents to a building society that he is authorised to act for a vendor of property and the society in consequence makes a loan to the purchaser.[364]

16–078   **Restrictions on liability.** An agent is not, or may not be, liable for breach of implied warranty of authority in the following cases.

16–079   **Want of authority known to third party.** The agent is not liable where the third party knew, or must be taken to have known, that the agent had no authority.[365] The agent may also not be liable where he and the third party had equal means of knowing that the agent had no authority; though the claim in the case[366] which supports this view was actually one for goods sold and delivered, i.e. on the main contract of sale. Thus the case may not be authoritative on an agent's liability for breach of implied warranty.[367]

16–080   **Representation of law.** The traditional view (which is now open to serious doubt[368]) is that the agent is not liable where the representation is one of law.[369] Accordingly, it has been held that, since the construction of a document is a matter of law, an agent who misrepresents its meaning is not liable for breach of implied warranty. Thus if the director of a statutory corporation[370] which has, on the true construction of its incorporating statute, no borrowing powers, purports to borrow on its behalf, he is not liable for breach of implied warranty.[371] But if such a corporation has a limited power to borrow up to, say, £10 million, and the director purports to borrow on its behalf above that limit, he is liable for breach of implied warranty, for he has misrepresented a fact: namely, that the company has not yet borrowed £10 million.[372] If a loan is made to a company incorporated under the Companies Act 2006 by a lender dealing with the company in good faith, the contract of loan will normally be enforceable against the company even though the directors had, under the company's constitution, no power to enter into the contract.[373] The lender's claim for breach of warranty against the directors will therefore fail on the principle stated in the following paragraph. If the lender had *no* claim against the company because he had acted in bad faith, he would know that the loan was unauthorised. His claim for breach of warranty of authority would fail on the ground that he knew of the agent's want of authority.[374]

16–081   **Principal liable on main contract.** An agent who has no actual authority is probably not liable for breach of implied warranty if the principal is liable to the

---

[364] *Penn v Bristol & West BS* [1997] 1 W.L.R. 1356.

[365] *Lilly, Wilson & Co v Smales, Eeles & Co* [1892] 1 Q.B. 456; *Halbot v Lens* [1901] 1 Ch. 344.

[366] *Smout v Ilberry* (1842) 10 M. & W. 1.

[367] See *Oliver v Bank of England* [1901] 1 Ch. 652 at 660.

[368] See the discussion of *Kleinwort Benson Ltd v Lincoln CC* [1999] 2 A.C. 349, above para.16–022.

[369] *Saffron Walden, etc. BS v Rayner* (1880) 14 Ch.D. 406.

[370] Such corporations remain subject to the ultra vires doctrine: above, para.12–072.

[371] *Rashdall v Ford* (1866) L.R. 2 Eq. 750.

[372] *Cherry v Colonial Bank of Australasia* (1869) L.R. 3 P.C. 24; *Weeks v Propert* (1873) L.R. 8 C.P. 427.

[373] Companies Act 2006, s.40(1); see above, para.12–069 for certain exceptions.

[374] See above, at fn.365.

third party on the ground of apparent or usual authority. In *Rainbow v Howkins*[375] an auctioneer who had authority to sell a horse, subject to a reserve price, sold it without reserve. It was held that he was not liable for breach of implied warranty, as the buyer could have enforced the main contract against the seller on the ground that the auctioneer had apparent authority to sell without reserve.[376] Similarly, an agent would not be liable for breach of implied warranty if he did an unauthorised act which the principal later ratified.

Crown agent. An agent of the Crown is probably not liable for breach of implied warranty of authority. The assumption that such an agent impliedly warrants his authority is "utterly inconsistent with the facts".[377] In view of the enormous value of some government contracts, it would be extremely harsh to impose liability on a civil servant who in good faith and without negligence had misrepresented his authority.   **16–082**

(iv) *Other liability for misrepresentation*

The agent's liability for breach of warranty of authority arises where he   **16–083** misrepresents his authority; but he may also be liable to the third party in tort for other misrepresentations. This was, for example, held to be the case where an estate agent who had been engaged by the vendor of property negligently made misrepresentations about it to a prospective purchaser who, in reliance on those representations, entered into a contract with the vendor for the purchase of the property.[378] Under the Property Misdescriptions Act 1991, an agent who makes such a misrepresentation may also incur criminal liability. The Act provides that no right of action in civil proceedings is to arise "by reason *only*" of the commission of such an offence[379]; but this provision would not seem to preclude the agent's being held liable to the third party for negligence at common law.

(c) Between Principal and Agent

(i) *Rights of agent*

Whether commission is payable. Whether an agent is entitled to any com-   **16–084** mission at all depends on the terms of the agreement between principal and agent. In *Taylor v Bremer*[380] an agent was to receive "such commission . . . as should be deemed right" by the principal. It was held that he had no legal right to commission. But where the agency is a commercial relationship the courts are reluctant to send the agent away empty-handed.[381] Thus if the agreement merely provides that the *amount* of commission is to be left to the principal's discretion,

---

[375] [1904] 2 K.B. 322; criticised in *McManus v Fortescue* [1907] 2 K.B. 1 at 6, but that case can be explained on the ground that the third party knew of the agent's want of authority.
[376] cf. *Mitsui & Co Ltd v Marpo Industrial Ltd* [1974] 1 Lloyd's Rep. 386 at 393. Quaere whether this reasoning might have been applied in *Yonge v Toynbee* [1910] 1 K.B. 215; cf. below, fn.509.
[377] *Dunn v Macdonald* [1897] 1 Q.B. 555 at 558.
[378] *McCullagh v Lane Fox & Partners Ltd* [1994] 1 E.G.L.R. 48.
[379] Property Misdescriptions Act 1991, s.1(4).
[380] (1813) 1 M. & S. 290.
[381] See *Kofi Sunkersette Obu v A Strauss & Co Ltd* [1951] A.C. 243.

and he refuses to fix the amount, he may be liable to pay a reasonable sum.[382] On the other hand, the director of a company may agree to work for it "for such remuneration as the other directors may determine" on the understanding that he will receive nothing until the company has "got on its feet". If this never happens, he cannot claim a reasonable remuneration for his work.[383]

16–085   **When commission is earned.** Commission is payable only in respect of a transaction which the agent was employed to bring about. In *Toulmin v Millar*[384] the owner of a house employed an agent to find a tenant. The agent found a tenant, who later bought the house. His claim for commission on the sale failed, since he was only employed to let the house.

The transaction must also be caused by the agent's efforts.[385] In *Tribe v Taylor*[386] a principal employed an agent to raise a loan of money. The lender later entered into partnership with the principal and on this occasion made a further loan. The agent's claim for commission on this second loan failed, since it was not brought about by his efforts.

Unless otherwise agreed,[387] the agent is not entitled to commission in respect of transactions which take place after the termination of the agency.[388] A contract may, however, provide that commission is *earned* when the agent secures the order (so that nothing more need be done by him to perfect his entitlement to it) but that it is only to *become payable* at some later stage, e.g. when the order is executed. In such a case the agent is entitled to commission on orders obtained before, though not executed till after, the termination of the agency.[389] Under the Regulations which apply to "commercial agents",[390] such an agent has somewhat more extensive rights in respect of transactions concluded after the termination of the

---

[382] *Bryant v Flight* (1839) 5 M. & W. 114; *British Bank for Foreign Trade Ltd v Novinex Ltd* [1949] 1 K.B. 623; *Powell v Braun* [1954] 1 W.L.R. 401.

[383] *Re Richmond Gate Property Co Ltd* [1965] 1 W.L.R. 335.

[384] (1887) 12 App.Cas. 746; cf. *Millar v Radford* (1903) 19 T.L.R. 575; *Charania v Harbour Estates* [2009] EWCA Civ 1123; [2009] N.P.C. 119.

[385] In the absence of any contrary provision, it is usually implied that the agent must have been "the effective cause" of the transaction; whether he is or not will depend on all the circumstances, including of course what is meant by the "transaction" (see, in relation to estate agents, below para.16–087). See, only by way of recent examples: *Foxtons Ltd v Bicknell* [2008] EWCA Civ 419; [2008] 24 E.G. 142 and the summary of the propositions to be derived from the decided cases set out at [20]; *County Homesearch Co (Thames and Chilterns) Ltd v Cowham* [2008] EWCA Civ 26; [2008] 1 W.L.R. 909; *MSM Consulting Ltd v Tanzania* [2009] EWHC 121 (QB); 123 Con L.R. 154; Contrast *Glentree Estates Ltd v Favermead Ltd* [2010] EWCA Civ 1473; [2011] 11 E.G. 104 (no such implication where the contract was not in standard form, the property was unusual and the parties were commercial entities with access to sophisticated advice); cf. *Watersheds Ltd v Simms* [2009] EWHC 713 (QB).

[386] (1876) 1 C.P.D. 505; cf. *Debenham, Tewson & Chinnocks Plc v Rimington* [1989] 2 E.G.L.R. 26 (where, however, the agents were awarded a reasonable remuneration for their efforts); *Harwood v Smith, The Times,* December 8, 1997; contrast *Nahun v Royal Holloway and Bedford New Colleges Ltd, The Times,* November 19, 1998.

[387] *Levy v Goldhill* [1917] 2 Ch. 297; cf. *Brian Cooper & Co v Fairview Estates (Investments) Ltd* [1987] 1 E.G.L.R. 18; *Robert Bruce & Partners v Wynyard Developments* [1987] 1 E.G.L.R. 20; *Barnard Marcus & Co v Ashraf* [1988] 1 E.G.L.R. 7; *Marshall v N M Financial Management Ltd* [1997] 1 W.L.R. 1527 (so far as it relates to the "renewal commission").

[388] *Crocker-Horlock v B Lang & Co Ltd* [1949] 1 All E.R. 526; *Bronester Ltd v Priddle* [1961] 1 W.L.R. 1294.

[389] *Sellers v London Counties Newspapers* [1951] 1 K.B. 784; *Explora Group Plc v Hesco Bastion Ltd* [2005] EWCA Civ 646.

[390] See above, para.16–011.

agency[391] and in respect of transactions not brought about by his efforts but concluded in breach of an exclusive agency agreement.[392]

More than one agent engaged. A principal may engage more than one agent: e.g. where an owner instructs two estate agents to find a purchaser for his house.[393] Commission will then be due to the agent whose efforts have brought about the sale[394]; and where the efforts of both have contributed to this result, each may[395] be entitled to commission.[396] Where two "commercial agents" appointed in succession claim commission on the same transaction, the first agent is not normally entitled to commission, but the court may, if it is equitable to do so, order the commission to be shared between the two agents.[397]

16–086

Estate agents' commission: common law.[398] The precise stage at which the agent becomes entitled to commission depends on the terms of the contract between principal and agent.[399] This question has given rise to much litigation in cases concerning estate agents' commission.[400] In *Luxor (Eastbourne) Ltd v Cooper*[401] the landowner undertook to pay the estate agent his commission "on completion of sale". No sale took place because the owner refused to deal with the prospective purchaser introduced by the agent. It was held that the agent was not entitled to commission.[402] Again, a contract for the payment of commission on the agent's "introducing a person ready, willing and able to purchase" does not entitle him to commission if the prospective purchaser makes a conditional offer subject to contract and satisfactory survey; or if he makes an offer and withdraws it before the vendor accepts[403]; or if he signs a contract which cannot be completed because of a defect in the vendor's title[404]; or if, before the prospective purchaser is introduced, the owner has entered into a binding contract to sell the property to

16–087

---

[391] SI 1993/3053, regs 7(1)(b), 8.

[392] ibid., reg.7(2); at common law, the agent's remedy in such a case would be by way of damages: cf. *Alpha Trading Ltd v Dunshaw-Patten* [1981] Q.B. 290; below, para.16–090. For exclusive dealing agreements, see above, para.11–092 et seq.

[393] Although estate agents are not "agents" for the purpose of enabling them to conclude contracts between their clients and third parties (above, para.16–008), they are treated in the same way as agents for the purpose of their right to commission.

[394] *John D Wood & Co v Dantata* (1985) 275 E.G. 1278; *Chasen Rider v Hedges* [1993] 1 E.G.L.R. 47.

[395] Depending on the terms of the contract: see the authorities cited at fnn.401–408, below.

[396] *Lordgate Properties v Balcombe* (1985) 274 E.G. 493; *Anscombe & Ringland v Watson* [1991] 2 E.G.L.R. 28.

[397] SI 1993/3053, reg.9.

[398] In addition to the cases discussed in this para, see the authorities referred to above in fn.385.

[399] See, e.g. *Fairvale v Sabharwall* [1992] 2 E.G.L.R. 27.

[400] Gower 13 M.L.R. 490; Hardy-Ivamy (1951) C.L.P. 305.

[401] [1941] A.C. 108; *Foxtons Ltd v Thesleff* [2005] EWCA Civ 514; (2005) 21 E.G. 140.

[402] The award of a quantum meruit will be rare "in the face of the express provision for remuneration which the contract contains. This must necessarily exclude such a claim, unless it can (upon the facts of a particular case) be based upon a contract subsequent to the original contract, and arising from some conduct on the part of the principal", [1941] A.C. 108 at 125; *Adler v Ananhall Advisory & Consultancy Services Ltd* [2009] EWCA Civ 586; [2009] N.P.C. 80.

[403] *Dennis Reed Ltd v Goody* [1950] 2 K.B. 277; *Graham & Scott (Southgate) Ltd v Oxlade* [1950] 2 K.B. 257. Contrast *Christie Owen & Davies Ltd v Rapacioli* [1974] Q.B. 781 (where a vendor who withdrew after a firm offer had been made by the prospective purchaser was held liable for commission).

[404] *Dellafiora v Lester* [1962] 1 W.L.R. 1208; cf. *Blake & Co v Sohn* [1969] 1 W.L.R. 1412.

a purchaser introduced by another agent.[405] Nor does a promise to pay commission "in the event of your introducing ... a person prepared to enter into a contract" entitle the agent to commission where the person introduced only agrees to sign a contract which is subject to conditions.[406] Even a contract for the payment of commission "in the event of securing for you an offer" does not entitle the agent to commission unless a firm, unconditional offer is made.[407] But where the contract was to pay commission as soon as "any person introduced by us enters into a legally binding contract to purchase" it was held that the agent was entitled when such a contract was made although the vendor later terminated it on account of the purchaser's breach.[408]

16–088   **Estate agents' commission: statutory provisions.** The common law on this topic is far from satisfactory. On the one hand it is hard for the estate agent, who may have gone to much trouble and expense in advertising[409] a house and securing offers, to be deprived of all reward through the caprice of his client. On the other hand it is hard for the client to have to pay commission where it is not his fault that no sale takes place: the common understanding is that the commission should come out of the proceeds of sale. In this conflict of interests, the estate agents usually have the advantage of being able to submit a standard form of contract[410] to the client, who may accept its terms without question. The courts have to some extent redressed the balance in favour of the client. They have (as the above cases show) construed stipulations for commission strictly against the agents,[411] or held them to be ineffective for uncertainty or for misrepresentation.[412] But it remains possible for commission to be payable even though there is no sale. It would perhaps be better if the question when an estate agent was entitled to commission ceased to be regarded purely as one of construction. Only legislation could now achieve this result; but the Estate Agents Act 1979 (which regulates the activities of estate agents) does not lay down any rules for this purpose. It merely requires the agent, before a client enters into an agency contract with him, to give the client particulars of the circumstances in which the commission will become due.[413] Nor are the estate agency cases affected by the Regulations which apply to "commercial agents" since these Regulations apply only to agents who have continuing authority and who negotiate sales or purchases of *goods*.[414] If an agent acts for purposes

---

[405] *A A Dickinson & Co v O'Leary* (1979) 254 E.G. 731.
[406] *A L Wilkinson Ltd v Brown* [1966] 1 W.L.R. 1914.
[407] *Bennett, Walden & Co v Wood* [1950] 2 All E.R. 134; cf. *Christie, Owen & Davies Ltd v Stockton* [1953] 1 W.L.R. 1353.
[408] *Scheggia v Gradwell* [1963] 1 W.L.R. 1049; cf. *Midgeley Estates Ltd v Hand* [1952] 2 Q.B. 432; *Drewery & Drewery v Ware-Lane* [1960] 1 W.L.R. 1204; *aliter* if the contract goes off because of the agent's misrepresentation: *Peter Long & Partners v Burns* [1956] 1 W.L.R. 413 at 1083.
[409] The agent can expressly stipulate for reimbursement of advertising expenses, as in *Bernard Thorpe & Partners v Flannery* (1977) 244 E.G. 129.
[410] The Unfair Contract Terms Act 1977 does not affect the validity of the provisions discussed: they confer *rights* on the agent and do not exclude or restrict his liability. For possible application of Unfair Terms in Consumer Contracts Regulations 1999, see below, at fn.415.
[411] See above, at fnn.401–408.
[412] See *Jaques v Lloyd D George & Partners* [1968] 1 W.L.R. 625.
[413] s.18(2)(a); supplemented by Estate Agents (Provision of Information) Regulations 1991 (SI 1991/859). In *Foxtons Ltd v Bicknell* [2008] EWCA Civ 419; [2008] 24 E.G. 142 the estate agent's term for the payment of commission closely followed the prescribed provisions of the Regulations ("purchaser introduced by us") but this still raised an issue of construction which was resolved in favour of the purchaser.
[414] See above, para.16–011.

relating to his trade, business or profession, the client is a consumer and the term in question is not individually negotiated, that term might not be binding on the consumer under the Unfair Terms in Consumer Contracts Regulations 1999[415]: e.g. if it provided for payment of the full commission even if no sale took place. Even where the agent is not entitled to commission, he may have other rights against the client. He may be entitled to damages[416] where the sale goes off as a result of the client's fault.[417] If the sale goes off as a result of the purchaser's default, and the purchaser's deposit is forfeited to the client, it has been suggested that the agent should be entitled to a quantum meruit out of the sum so forfeited.[418]

Commercial Agents Regulations. Under the Regulations which apply to "commercial agents", commission becomes due when the principal has executed the transaction or when he should have done so or when the third party has done so[419]; and it becomes due at the latest when the third party has executed the transaction or would have done so if the principal had duly executed his part of it.[420] Where "execution" fails the Regulations give the agent the right to commission only if the failure is due to the principal's breach of his contract with the third party.[421] Except in this situation, the question whether the agent can become entitled to commission before "execution" of that contract is (under the Regulations, no less than at common law) one of construction of the agency agreement.   16–089

Opportunity to earn commission. If a principal employs an agent for a fixed period he is not, in general, bound to stay in business merely to enable the agent to earn his commission.[422] But if, on the true construction of the agency contract, the principal has undertaken to stay in business so as to enable the agent to earn his commission, then the principal is liable in damages if he fails to do so. This was the effect of the contract in *Turner v Goldsmith*,[423] where the principal employed the agent for five years to obtain orders for shirts "manufactured or sold" by the principal. It was held that he was not justified in putting an end to the agency   16–090

---

[415] See above, para.7–095 et seq.

[416] Unless the contractual provision for commission is intended to be his *only* remedy, as in *Property Choice v Fronda* [1991] 2 E.G.L.R. 249.

[417] *Dennis Reed Ltd v Goody* [1950] 2 K.B. 277 at 285; for this purpose the default must be wilful, and not merely inability to complete on account of a defect of title: *Blake & Co v Sohn* [1969] 1 W.L.R. 1412.

[418] *Boots v E Christopher & Co* [1952] 1 K.B. 89 at 99; cf. *Debenham Tewson & Chinnock Plc v Rimington* [1989] 2 E.G.L.R. 26. In the US, there is authority for holding the prospective *purchaser* liable to the agent for commission where he defaults: *Ellsworth Dobbs Inc v Johnson* 236 A. 2d. 843 (1967). Contrast *The Manifest Lipkowy* [1989] 2 Lloyd's Rep. 138 (buyer's agent held to have no right to commission against defaulting seller).

[419] SI 1993/3053, reg.10(1); above, para.16–011.

[420] reg.10(2). This rule cannot be excluded to the detriment of the agent: reg.10(4).

[421] ibid.; this would seem to apply in a situation analogous to that in those estate agency cases in which completion was prevented by a defect in the vendor's title: above, at fn.404. The actual estate agency cases fall outside the scope of the 1993 Regulations for the reason stated at fn.414, above.

[422] *Rhodes v Forwood* (1876) 1 App.Cas. 256; cf. *L French & Co Ltd v Leeston Shipping Co Ltd* [1922] 1 A.C. 451; Burrows 31 M.L.R. 390. Contrast the position of "commercial agents" (above, para.16–011), SI 1993/3053, reg.17(7): *Page v Combined Shipping & Trading Co* [1997] 3 All E.R. 656.

[423] [1891] 1 Q.B. 544; cf. *Re Patent Floor Cloth Co* (1872) 26 L.T. 467; *Standard Life Healthcare Ltd v Gorman* [2009] EWCA Civ 1292; [2010] I.R.L.R. 233.

agreement simply because the factory in which he manufactured shirts was burnt down. An agency agreement may, moreover, relate to a specific contract which is actually concluded between principal and third party. In such a case, a term may be implied into the agency agreement that the principal will not break *that contract* so as to deprive the agent of his commission.[424]

A client who employs an estate agent to sell a house is, in general, under no liability if he sells it himself or through a second agent.[425] If the agent is appointed "sole agent" the client cannot sell through another agent, but he can still sell the house himself unless he gives the agent "the sole and exclusive right to sell".[426] A manufacturer's "sole agent" may simply be a buyer and not an agent at all.[427] The manufacturer's undertaking to sell all his output to such a "sole agent" would bind him not to dispose of any of it himself,[428] so long as it was not invalid for restraint of trade.[429]

16–091   **Indemnity.** A principal must indemnify his agent against all liabilities reasonably incurred or discharged by him in the execution of his authority.[430] This right of indemnity exists not only where the agent incurs contractual liability, but also where he incurs tortious liability, e.g. as a result of selling a third person's property under the instructions of his principal.[431] The agent is not entitled to any indemnity in respect of an obviously illegal transaction,[432] nor in respect of a liability due to his own breach of duty.[433]

An agent may even be entitled to an indemnity in respect of payments which he was not legally obliged to make[434] so long as the payment, though not legally due, was made in the usual course of business, or possibly if it was made under a strong moral obligation.

16–092   **Lien.** An agent is (unless otherwise agreed[435]) entitled to a lien on all property of the principal which has come into his possession in the course of the agency. Every agent has a *particular* lien: that is, he can hold the property until the principal satisfies all claims of the agent arising out of the agency. An agent may by custom or by special contract also have a *general* lien, entitling him to hold the property until the principal satisfies all claims of the agent, whether they have arisen out of the agency or not.

---

[424] *Alpha Trading Ltd v Dunshaw-Patten* [1981] Q.B. 290; Carter 45 M.L.R. 220; cf. above, paras 2–106—2–109 and at fn.409; *George Moundreas & Co SA v Navimpex Centrala Navala* [1985] 2 Lloyd's Rep. 515; *The Energy Progress* [1993] 1 Lloyd's Rep. 355; *Explora Group Plc v Hesco Bastion Ltd* [2005] EWCA Civ 646 at [86].

[425] *Luxor (Eastbourne) Ltd v Cooper* [1941] A.C. 108.

[426] *Bentall Horsley & Baldry v Vicary* [1931] 1 K.B. 253; *Hampton & Sons Ltd v George* [1939] 3 All.E.R. 627; cf. in the case of "commercial agents", SI 1993/3053, reg.7(2): above, para.16–085.

[427] See above, para.16–005.

[428] *W T Lamb & Sons v Goring Brick Co Ltd* [1932] 1 K.B. 710.

[429] See above, para.11–092 et seq.

[430] *Thacker v Hardy* (1878) 4 Q.B.D. 685; *Reynolds v Smith* (1893) 9 T.L.R. 494; cf. Insolvency Act 1986, s.44(1)(c) and (3); contrast *Wilson v Avec Audio Visual Equipment Ltd* [1974] 1 Lloyd's Rep. 80 (payment made after termination of authority).

[431] *Adamson v Jarvis* (1827) 4 Bing. 66.

[432] *Thacker v Hardy*, above, at 687.

[433] cf. *Lister v Romford Ice & Cold Storage Co Ltd* [1957] A.C. 555; above, para.6–044.

[434] *Read v Anderson* (1884) 13 Q.B.D. 779; cf. *Adams v Morgan* [1924] 1 K.B. 751.

[435] *Rolls Razor Ltd v Cox* [1967] 1 Q.B. 552.

(ii) *Duties of agent*

To carry out his instructions. An agent who is appointed under a contract 16–093
binding him to carry out his instructions is obviously obliged to carry them out.[436]
He may be liable for failing to do so even if the contract which he was instructed
to make would not, if made, have been a binding one.[437] He will also be in breach
of the contract if he acts in a way not authorised by the terms of his appointment.[438] An agent who acts gratuitously or under a unilateral contract[439] is not
bound to do anything, but may be liable if he starts to perform and then leaves the
task unfinished.

To act with due care and skill. The degree of care and skill expected of an 16–094
agent depends on the circumstances. A person who holds himself out as being
skilled in some profession or trade[440] must show greater care and skill than one
who merely offers to give what help he can as a friend. There is probably no rigid
distinction between paid and gratuitous agents for this purpose. The fact that the
agent is paid is taken into account, along with other circumstances, in determining
the degree of the care and skill to be expected of him; but even a gratuitous agent
may be liable in tort for acting negligently.[441]

Fiduciary duty. Although the position of an agent in various respects differs 16–095
from that of a trustee,[442] an agent does, because the principal places confidence in
him, owe a fiduciary duty to the principal.[443] This duty is distinct from his duty
to act with due care and skill: its breach "connotes disloyalty or infidelity" and not
merely failure by the agent to do his "incompetent best".[444] Its most important
consequences are dealt with in paras 16–096—16–097.

Conflict of interest and duty. The agent must not put himself into a position 16–096
where his interest and duty conflict.[445] He must not, for instance, sell his own
goods to the principal when he is employed to buy: his interest as a seller would
be to get the highest possible price, whereas his duty as agent is to buy at the lowest

---

[436] cf. in the case of "commercial agents" (above, para.16–011), SI 1993/3053, reg.3(2)(a).

[437] *Fraser v BN Furman (Productions) Ltd* [1967] 1 W.L.R. 898; *Dunbar v A & B Painters Ltd* [1986] 2 Lloyd's Rep. 38.

[438] *County Ltd v Girozentrale Securities* [1996] 3 All E.R. 834.

[439] See above, paras 2–051, 3–158, 3–169; *The Zephyr* [1985] 2 Lloyd's Rep. 529 at 538.

[440] See above, para.6–041.

[441] *Hedley Byrne & Co Ltd v Heller & Partners Ltd* [1964] A.C. 465 at 495, 510, 526–527, 530, 538, approving *Wilkinson v Coverdale* (1793) 1 Esp. 75; above, para.3–169.

[442] See, e.g. above, para.10–022; *Kingscroft Ins Co Ltd v H S Weaver (Underwriting) Ltd* [1993] 1 Lloyd's Rep. 187 at 191.

[443] *Attorney-General of Hong Kong v Reid* [1994] 1 A.C. 324; below at fn.454 and para.16–097; cf. in the case of "commercial agents" (above, para.16–011), SI 1993/3053, reg.3(1) (duty of good faith).

[444] *Bristol & West BS v Mothew* [1998] Ch. 1 at 18; cf. *Coulthard v Disco Mix Club* [2000] 1 W.L.R. 707: claim in respect of under-accounting by agent held (for limitation purposes) to be a simple contract claim and not one for breach of fiduciary duty.

[445] *Lamb v Evans* [1893] 1 Ch. 218; cf. *Reading v Attorney-General* [1951] A.C. 507. An agent's duty of loyalty may also require him to disclose his own wrongdoing to the principal: *Fassihi v Item Software Ltd* [2004] EWCA Civ 1244; [2004] I.R.L.R. 928 at [44]; cf. *G Attwood Holdings Ltd v Woodward* [2009] EWHC 1083 (Ch); *Brandeaux Advisers Ltd v Chadwick* [2010] EWHC 3241 (QB); [2011] I.R.L.R. 224 at [47]. Contrast *P & V Industries Pty Ltd v Porto* [2005] V.S.C. 131. For potential criminal liability under s.4 Fraud Act 2006, see *Cavell USA Inc v Seaton Insurance Co* [2009] EWCA Civ 1363; [2009] 2 C.L.C. 991 at [25]–[30].

possible price.[446] Similarly, he must not, if employed to sell, buy the principal's property for himself.[447] Again, he must not subject himself to conflicting duties by acting as agent for both principal and third party,[448] unless he fully discloses the position to each of these persons.[449] But where the nature of the agent's business is such that he will normally act for more than one principal it is an implied term of the contract of agency that he should be free to do so, even though the interests of the various principals are likely to conflict. Thus an estate agent is entitled to accept instructions for the sale of properties from several principals, and where he does so he is both entitled and bound not to disclose confidential information received from any one of his clients to the other or others.[450]

A contract made in breach of this fiduciary duty is voidable at the option of the principal. The agent himself cannot avoid a transaction on the ground that it may conflict with his duties to his principal.[451]

16–097   **Bribes and secret profits.**[452] The agent must not without the principal's consent[453] accept a commission from a third party. Such a secret commission is called a "bribe" if the third party, at the time of paying it, knew that the payee was acting as agent for another: the payment is then regarded as "a gift accepted by a fiduciary as an inducement to betray his trust".[454] It is immaterial that the third party had no corrupt motive in making the payment.[455] The promise or payment of a bribe has drastic effects. The agent can (even if he has been appointed for a fixed period) be summarily dismissed[456]; he loses his right to commission on the tainted transaction[457]; and he must account to the principal for any profit made, whether or not the principal has suffered loss.[458] A decision of the Privy Council has held that the principal is entitled to a proprietary remedy so that he may claim

---

[446] *Armstrong v Jackson* [1917] 2 K.B. 822; *Tetley v Shand* (1871) 25 L.T. 658; *Guiness Plc v Saunders* [1990] 2 A.C 663; cf. Companies Act 2006, ss.182–187.

[447] *McPherson v Watt* (1877) 3 App.Cas. 254.

[448] *Fullwood v Hurley* [1928] 1 K.B. 498 at 502; *Anglo-African Merchants v Bayley* [1970] 1 Q.B. 311 at 322–323; *North & South Trust Co v Berkeley* [1971] 1 W.L.R. 470.

[449] See *Harrods Ltd v Lemon* [1931] 2 K.B. 157 and *Clark v Boyce Mouat* [1994] 1 A.C. 428 (where full disclosure was made); cf. Estate Agents Act 1979, s.21 (imposing a statutory duty of disclosure on estate agents: the remedy is disqualification under s.3 of the Act).

[450] *Kelly v Cooper* [1993] A.C. 205. Where the agent is not known normally to act for multiple principals, see: *Prince Jefri Bolkiah v KPMG* [1999] 2 A.C. 222; *Hilton v Barker Booth & Eastwood* [2005] UKHL 8; [2005] 1 W.L.R. 567; Getzler 122 L.Q.R. 1.

[451] *Boulting v ACCT* [1963] 2 Q.B. 606.

[452] Needham 95 L.Q.R. 536. For the potential criminal liability of the agent, see Bribery Act 2010, ss.1, 2 and of the principal for bribery committed by the agent, see ibid., ss. 7, 8.

[453] See *Anangel Atlas Compania Naviera SA v Ishikawajima-Harima Heavy Industries Co* [1990] 1 Lloyd's Rep. 167 (where the principal knew of the payments).

[454] *Attorney-General of Hong Kong v Reid* [1994] 1 A.C. 324 at 330; *Allwood v Clifford* [2002] E.M.L.R. 3 (where there was no such knowledge).

[455] *Industries & General Mortgage Co v Lewis* [1949] 2 All E.R. 573.

[456] *Boston Deep Sea Fishing & Ice Co v Ansell* (1888) 39 Ch.D. 339. For the effect of such dismissal on the agent's rights to salary (or recompense for work actually done), see below, paras 17–035—17–036. In the case of "commercial agents", (above, para.16–011) this right of dismissal is preserved by SI 1993/3053, reg.16.

[457] *Solomon v Pender* (1865) 3 H. & C. 639; *Andrews v Ramsey* [1903] 2 K.B. 635 (but commission on other transactions remains payable if they are severable: *Nitedals Taenstickfabrik v Bruster* [1906] 2 Ch. 671 (doubted in *Imageview Management Ltd v Jack* [2009] EWCA Civ 63; [2009] 1 Lloyd's Rep. 436 and said to be limited to cases of "harmless collaterality").

[458] *Reading v Attorney-General* [1951] A.C. 507; *Phipps v Boardman* [1967] 2 A.C. 46.

any increase in the value of the bribe or of its product.[459] This has subsequently been held not to be binding on the domestic courts on the basis that it is contrary to earlier decisions.[460] They establish that the principal cannot claim proprietary ownership of an asset purchased by the defaulting fiduciary with funds which, although they could not have been obtained by him if he had not enjoyed his fiduciary status, were not beneficially owned by the principal or derived from opportunities beneficially owned by the principal; in the absence of those requirements the principal is confined to a personal claim by way of an equitable account.[461] If the bribe has not yet been paid, the agent cannot recover it from the third party, but the principal can do so.[462] The principal can further set the tainted transaction aside and retain the bribe, if it has been paid over to him by the agent[463]; whether or not the bribe has been paid, the principal can, as an alternative to claiming the bribe,[464] claim damages from the agent and the third party for the loss suffered as a result of the bribery.[465] These claims are available even though the payment of the bribe did not induce the principal to enter into any contract with the third party.[466] If the principal was induced to enter into such a contract with the third party, that party is also liable to the principal for an account of the profits made by the third party from that contract, but only to the extent that these exceed the profits that he would have made if the contract had not been induced by bribery and provided that the third party has not already been required to pay such amounts to the principal by way of damages.[467] Where the secret profit is not a bribe, the third party is under no contractual or tortious liability. The agent can be summarily dismissed[468] and is civilly liable to account for the payment to the principal.[469]

Personal performance. The general rule is that an agent cannot delegate the performance of his duties, unless the principal expressly or impliedly authorises him to appoint a sub-agent.[470] But an agent does not "delegate" by instructing his own employees to do various necessary acts in connection with the execution of his duty.

An agent may have authority to appoint a sub-agent and to make a contract between the sub-agent and the principal.[471] He may, alternatively, have authority

16–098

[459] *Attorney-General of Hong Kong v Reid* [1994] 1 A.C. 324; followed in *Daraydan Holdings Ltd v Solland International Ltd* [2004] EWHC 622 (Ch); [2005] Ch. 119.

[460] Most notably, *Lister v Stubbs* (1890) 45 Ch.D. 1.

[461] *Sinclair Investments (UK) Ltd v Versailles Trade Finance Ltd* [2011] EWCA Civ 347 at [89].

[462] *Harrington v Victoria Graving Dock Co* (1878) 3 Q.B.D. 549; *Industries & General Mortgage Co v Lewis*, above, fn.455.

[463] *Logicrose v Southend United FC* [1988] 1 W.L.R. 1256; Jones [1989] C.L.J. 22.

[464] *T Mahesan S/O Thambiah v Malaysian Government Officers' Housing Society* [1979] A.C. 374; disapproving dicta in *Salford Corp v Lever* [1891] 1 Q.B. 168; Tettenborn 95 L.Q.R. 68; *Arab Monetary Fund v Hashim* [1993] 1 Lloyd's Rep. 543; *Island Records Ltd v Tring International Plc* [1996] 1 W.L.R. 1256 at 1257; *Fyffes Group Ltd v Templeman* [2000] 2 Lloyd's Rep. 643.

[465] *Salford Corp v Lever* [1891] 1 Q.B. 168.

[466] *Petrotrade Inc v Smith* [2000] 1 Lloyd's Rep. 486, where the "third party" had itself been appointed as agent but the bribes were paid by its employees to *another* of the principal's agents, i.e. to one of the latter's employees.

[467] *Fyffes Group Ltd v Templeman* [2000] 2 Lloyd's Rep. 643 at 672.

[468] *Neary v Dean of Westminster* [1999] I.R.L.R. 288.

[469] *Imageview Management Ltd v Jack* [2009] EWCA Civ 63; [2009] 1 Lloyd's Rep. 436; Watts 129 L.Q.R. 369; Oram [2010] L.M.C.L.Q. 95; *Accidia Foundation v Simon C Dickinson Ltd* [2010] EWHC 3058 (Ch).

[470] e.g. *John McCann & Co v Pow* [1974] 1 W.L.R. 1643.

[471] *De Bussche v Alt* (1878) 8 Ch.D. 286.

to delegate (in the sense that he commits no breach of duty by performing through another) but have no authority to make a contract between principal and sub-agent.[472] In such a case the agent remains contractually liable to the principal if the sub-agent performs defectively,[473] while the sub-agent is under no contractual duty to the principal.[474] The sub-agent may, however, be liable on other grounds, e.g. for breach of fiduciary duty[475] or in tort if he negligently causes damage to the principal's property.[476] But the sub-agent is not liable in tort merely because he has negligently paid over the proceeds of the principal's property to an impostor (so that the principal suffers financial loss[477]); for such liability would be in practice indistinguishable from contractual liability and so be inconsistent with the absence of a contractual relationship between principal and sub-agent. The contract between agent and sub-agent could also be drawn up in such a way as to confer rights on the principal under the Contracts (Rights of Third Parties) Act 1999.[478]

16–099   **Indemnity.** It is an implied term in a contract of employment that the employee will indemnify the employer against any liability to third parties incurred by reason of the employee's negligence in doing what he was employed to do.[479] A contract of agency will generally give rise to a similar liability to indemnify the principal.

(d) Effects of Non-consensual Agency

16–100   **Dependent upon the underlying policy.** It is a difficult and largely unsolved problem to what extent the effects of agency which have so far been discussed arise where the agency is not created by agreement between principal and agent, e.g. in cases of apparent and usual authority, and in cases of agency of necessity.

One effect of apparent or usual authority is to make the principal liable to the third party. But is the third party liable to the principal? When an agent acts within his apparent authority, the principal is liable because he is estopped from denying the agent's authority; but no similar estoppel need arise against the third party. If the principal wants to enforce the contract, he will usually ratify. But there may be some reason why he cannot do so,[480] and, if this is the case, it is far from clear that he could sue the third party simply because the third party can sue

[472] *New Zealand & Australian Land Co v Watson* (1881) 7 Q.B.D. 374; *Royal Products Ltd v Midland Bank Ltd* [1981] 2 Lloyd's Rep. 194 at 198; *Henderson v Merrett Syndicates Ltd* [1995] 2 A.C. 145 at 202; *Prentis Donegan & Partners v Leeds & Leeds Plc* [1998] 2 Lloyd's Rep. 326; Tettenborn 115 L.Q.R. 655.
[473] *Powell & Thomas v Evan Jones & Co* [1905] 1 K.B. 11 apparently disapproved, but on another point, in *Attorney-General of Hong Kong v Reid* [1994] 1 A.C. 324 at 337.
[474] *Calico Printers Association v Barclays Bank* (1931) 145 L.T. 51.
[475] *Markel International Insurance Co Ltd v Surety Guarantee Consultants Ltd* [2008] EWHC 1135 (Comm)
[476] *Meyerstein v Eastern Agency* (1885) 1 T.L.R. 595; cf. *Stewart v Reavell's Garage* [1952] 2 Q.B. 545.
[477] *Balsamo v Medici* [1984] 1 W.L.R. 951; contrast *Henderson v Merrett Syndicates Ltd* [1995] 2 A.C. 145, where in a "most unusual" (at 195) situation a sub-agent was held liable in tort to the principal for negligently inflicted financial loss. See also *Aiken v Stewart Wrightson Members Agency* [1995] 1 W.L.R. 1281.
[478] See above, para.14–090 et seq.
[479] *Lister v Romford Ice & Cold Storage Co Ltd* [1957] A.C. 555; contrast *Harvey v R G O'Dell Ltd* [1958] 2 Q.B. 78.
[480] See above, para.16–042 et seq.; e.g. it may be too late to ratify.

him. An agent who does an unauthorised act which binds his principal is clearly not entitled to commission, but is probably subject to the usual liabilities if he accepts a bribe or makes a secret profit.[481] An agent of necessity often acquires rights of recompense or reimbursement against his principal, but it is less common for him to be able to create a contract between principal and third party. Thus it is impossible to make any general statement about the effects of non-consensual agency. The problems which may arise must be considered in the light of the considerations of policy which underlie each type of non-consensual agency.

5. TERMINATION

Agency as a contract is determined by any event which terminates a contract,[482] and also in certain special ways. After discussing these, we shall discuss the effects of termination and finally consider some cases of irrevocable agency.   **16–101**

(a) Modes of Termination

(i) *Consensual agency*

It will be convenient first to consider modes of termination at common law and then to deal with special rules applicable to "commercial agents".[483]   **16–102**

Notice. An agent's authority can be determined by giving him notice. Where   **16–103**
the agency is contractual it may be for a fixed term or specify a period of notice. If no term or period of notice is specified, the contract is determinable on reasonable notice.[484] A notice given in breach of contract is, in general,[485] nonetheless *effective*. It determines the agent's actual authority[486] and the relationship of principal and agent. Thus the agent cannot restrain the breach by injunction or obtain a declaration that his dismissal was void or claim his agreed remuneration in respect of periods after the wrongful termination.[487] His normal remedies are by way of damages for wrongful dismissal and a declaration that the dismissal was wrongful.[488] He may also be able to restrain by injunction the breach of a negative

---

[481] *English v Dedham Vale Properties Ltd* [1978] 1 W.L.R. 93.

[482] e.g. by performance, termination for breach, or frustration.

[483] See above, para.16–011.

[484] *Martin–Baker Aircraft Co Ltd v Canadian Flight Equipment Ltd* [1955] 2 Q.B. 556; cf. *Re Spenborough UDC's Agreement* [1968] Ch. 139; *Richardson v Koefod* [1969] 1 W.L.R. 1812 at 1814. The "presumption of perpetual duration" in contracts specifying no time-limit, stated in *Llanelly Ry & Dock Co v L & NW Ry* (1875) L.R. 7 H.L. 550 (discussed by Carnegie 85 L.Q.R. 392) does not apply to contracts of agency.

[485] For exceptions, see below, para.21–036.

[486] i.e. the authority based on the wrongfully repudiated contract; as to apparent authority, usual authority and authority of necessity, see below, para.16–109.

[487] *Denmark Productions Ltd v Boscobel Productions Ltd* [1969] 1 Q.B. 699; *Roberts v Elwells Engineering Co Ltd* [1972] 2 Q.B. 586; *Gunton v Richmond upon Thames LBC* [1981] Ch. 448; *Delaney v Staples* [1992] 1 A.C. 687 at 692; below, para.21–010; Freedland 32 M.L.R. 314; Drake [1969] J.B.L. 113. Remuneration earned before the dismissal but payable thereafter could be claimed on the principle of *Sellers v London County Newspapers* [1951] 1 K.B. 784. Remuneration can also be claimed where the termination is lawful because it is authorised by a contractual provision for notice or payment in lieu: *Abrahams v Performing Rights Society* [1995] I.C.R. 1028.

[488] As to damages, see *Denmark Productions Ltd v Boscobel Productions Ltd*, above; *Marsh v National Autistic Society* [1993] I.C.R. 453 and *Boyo v Lambeth LBC* [1994] I.C.R. 727; as to declaration, see *Taylor v NUS* [1967] 1 W.L.R. 532.

stipulation in the agency contract,[489] such as an undertaking by the principal not to appoint another agent to conduct the business in question.[490]

16–104   **Inconsistent conduct.** It seems that agency can be determined without notice by conduct inconsistent with its continuance, e.g. if the principal sells the subject-matter of the agency.[491] Such conduct may again be a breach of contract but nevertheless puts an end to the agency.

16–105   **Insanity.** At common law,[492] agency is determined by the supervening insanity of principal or agent if the insanity is inconsistent with the consensual nature of agency. The principal's insanity terminates agency even though the agent has no notice of it.[493]

16–106   **Death.** Death of principal or agent terminates agency, whether the survivor has notice of death or not.[494] Dissolution of a company has the same effect, and so has dissolution of a partnership, unless the contract is, on its true construction, with the partners constituting the firm from time to time.[495] However, in such a case dissolution may be a repudiatory breach, justifying termination of the contract by the agent.[496]

16–107   **Bankruptcy.** The principal's bankruptcy terminates the agent's authority.[497] The bankruptcy of the agent terminates his authority if it makes him unfit to perform his duties.[498]

16–108   **Commercial agents.** The Regulations governing "commercial agents"[499] specify minimum periods of notice (depending on the duration of the agency contract) which must be given to terminate the agency contract.[500] The relevant rules appear to apply only to the relationship of the parties to that contract. They do not seem to apply to the agent's authority: in other words, the position under the Regulations appears to resemble the common law position that failure to give proper notice makes the termination wrongful, but not ineffective. Even where proper notice is given, the agent is entitled under the Regulations to compensation or to an indemnity in respect of the termination.[501] The object of this rule appears to be to provide the agent with a sort of redundancy or severance payment, reflecting the loss of the agency business, including whatever goodwill attaches to

---

[489] See below, paras 21–056—21–057.
[490] *Decro-Wall International SA v Practitioners in Marketing Ltd* [1971] 1 W.L.R. 361.
[491] *E P Nelson & Co v Rolfe* [1950] 1 K.B. 139.
[492] For a statutory exception, see below, paras 16–112—16–113.
[493] *Yonge v Toynbee* [1910] 1 K.B. 215; above, at fn.357.
[494] *Campanari v Woodburn* (1854) 15 C.B. 400; *Pool v Pool* (1889) 58 L.J.P. 67; *Lodgepower Ltd v Taylor* [2004] EWCA Civ 1367; [2005] 1 E.G.L.R. 1.
[495] *Salton v New Beeston Cycle Co* [1900] 1 Ch. 43. And see *Brace v Calder* [1895] 2 Q.B. 253; *Tunstall v Condon* [1980] I.C.R. 786; *Briggs v Oates* [1990] I.C.R. 473. Dissolution of a limited liability partnership incorporated under the Limited Liability Partnership Act 2000 (above, para.12–070) seems for the present purpose to have the same effect as dissolution of a company.
[496] *Briggs v Oates*, above.
[497] *Elliott v Turquand* (1881) 7 App.Cas. 79.
[498] *McCall v Australian Meat Co Ltd* (1870) 19 W.R. 188.
[499] See above, para.16–011.
[500] SI 1993/3053, reg.15.
[501] ibid., reg.17.

it.[502] The rights of compensation and indemnity can also apply where the agency contract is terminated by the death of the agent[503] or by notice given by himself on the ground of his age, illness or infirmity,[504] or on account of the principal's breach,[505] or by effluxion of time.[506] But the agent has no such rights where termination is justified by his own breach.[507]

(ii) *Non-consensual agency*

The events listed above terminate an agent's express or implied authority, but do not necessarily terminate apparent or usual authority, or authority of necessity. Notice to the agent obviously does not terminate apparent or usual authority: notice must be given to the third party to have this effect.[508] Again, a principal's insanity terminates his agent's actual authority; but a third party who goes on dealing with the agent without notice of the principal's insanity may be able to hold the principal liable on the ground that the agent still had apparent authority.[509] It is submitted that the position should be the same where (unknown to the third party) the agent's actual authority has been terminated by the principal's death.[510] Agency of necessity can sometimes be terminated by notice, e.g. a shipmaster's authority would be terminated, just as it could be prevented from arising, in this way. But notice would not terminate such authority where the need to encourage the agent to act was particularly strong.[511]

(b) Irrevocable Agency

In the following cases agency is irrevocable in the sense that any attempt to revoke it is not merely a breach of contract but also ineffective. The agent's authority continues in spite of the attempt to revoke it.

Authority coupled with an interest. An authority coupled with an interest is irrevocable. This does not mean that an authority is irrevocable simply because the agent can, by executing it, earn commission. The authority must be given for valuable consideration or by deed to secure some interest of the agent which exists

16–109

16–110

16–111

---

[502] *Lonsdale v Howard & Hallam* [2007] UKHL 32; [2007] 1 W.L.R. 2055; Saintier 128 L.Q.R. 31; *Nigel Fryer Joinery Services Ltd v Ian Firth Hardware Ltd* [2008] EWHC 767 (Ch); [2008] 2 Lloyd's Rep. 108.

[503] SI 1993/3053, reg.17(8).

[504] cf. *Abbott v Condici Ltd* [2005] 2 Lloyd's Rep. 450.

[505] Above, fn.503, reg.18(b) (as amended by SI 1993/3173).

[506] *Tigana v Decoro Ltd* [2003] EWHC 23.

[507] Above, fn.503, reg.18(a). Termination by notice will not preclude the application of reg.18(a) so as to prevent the agent from claiming compensation if it is "because of" a breach which would have justified termination for that reason: *Crane v Sky In-Home Service Ltd* [2007] EWHC 66 (Ch); [2007] 1 C.L.C. 389 at [90]–[91]; contrast *Cooper v Pure Fishing (UK) Ltd* [2004] EWCA Civ 375; [2004] 2 Lloyd's Rep. 518 where the agency terminated through effluxion of time and the principal chose not to renew and the agent was entitled to compensation even though the principal believed he had grounds to terminate for breach.

[508] *AMB Generali Holding AG v SEB Trygg Liv Holding Aktiebolag* [2005] EWCA Civ 1237; [2006] 1 W.L.R. 2276 at [30]–[32].

[509] *Drew v Nunn* (1879) 4 Q.B.D. 661; cf. *Yonge v Toynbee* [1910] 1 K.B. 215 where the court did not consider the possibility that the principal might have been held liable on the footing of apparent authority.

[510] As in *Blades v Free* (1829) 9 B. & C. 167, where apparent authority was not discussed.

[511] *GN Ry v Swaffield* (1874) L.R. 9 Ex. 142; above, para.16–037.

independently of the agency. Thus in *Carmichael's* Case[512] one Phillips promoted a company to buy a mine from him. Carmichael agreed to underwrite 1,000 shares in this company—i.e. to take up so many of these shares as could not be sold to the public—and authorised Phillips to apply for the shares on his behalf. This authority was held to be irrevocable; it was coupled with an "interest" because, if the shares were not taken up, Phillips would not get the purchase-money for the mine.

This rule only applies if the authority was intended for the protection of the interest.[513] It therefore cannot apply where the interest arises after the creation of the authority.[514]

16–112　　　**Powers of attorney.** At common law a power of attorney, even though coupled with an interest, was revoked by the death of the donor, i.e. of the principal.[515]

This rule might cause hardship both to the agent and to a person who bought from him in ignorance of the principal's death. The Powers of Attorney Act 1971 therefore provides that a power of attorney which is expressed to be irrevocable and is given to secure a proprietary interest of, or the performance of an obligation owed to, the donee shall not be revoked by the donor without the consent of the donee, or by the donor's death, incapacity or bankruptcy, so long as the interest or obligation secured by it remains in being.[516] The Act also protects third parties who deal in good faith with the donee of a power which is expressed to be irrevocable and to be given by way of security. Such persons are entitled to assume (unless they know the contrary) that the power cannot be revoked except by the donor acting with the consent of the donee, and that it has not been revoked in this way.[517]

16–113　　　**Lasting powers of attorney.** Under the Mental Capacity Act 2005,[518] a lasting power of attorney is one under which the donee has authority to make decisions about the donor's personal welfare,[519] as well as his property or financial affairs.[520] It includes authority to make such decisions in circumstances where the donor no longer has capacity.[521] In addition to a number of other requirements laid down by the Act,[522] the donor must have reached the age of 18 and must have had capacity to execute the instrument creating the power of attorney. He may revoke a lasting power of attorney at any time when he has the capacity to do so[523] and it will also be revoked in the following circumstances if the donee is not replaced or, in the case of joint donees, there is no remaining donee[524]: disclaimer of the appointment

---

[512] [1896] 2 Ch. 643; cf. *Walsh v Whitcomb* (1797) 2 Esp. 565; *Re Olympic Fire & General Reinsurance Co Ltd* [1920] 2 Ch. 341.

[513] *Frith v Frith* [1906] A.C. 254.

[514] *Smart v Sandars* (1848) 5 C.B. 895.

[515] *Watson v King* (1815) 4 Camp. 272.

[516] s.4.

[517] s.5(3); special protection is provided for transferees under stock exchange transactions by s.6.

[518] The Enduring Powers of Attorney Act 1979 is repealed, but existing enduring powers are unaffected: 2005 Act, s.66, Sch.4.

[519] Such decisions are subject to the restrictions set out in s.11.

[520] s.9(1).

[521] s.9(1).

[522] ss.9(2), 10, Sch.1. See also: Lasting Powers of Attorney, Enduring Powers of Attorney and Public Guardian Relations 2007 (SI 2007/1953).

[523] s.13(2).

[524] s.13(7).

by the donee[525]; the death or winding-up of the donee[526]; the dissolution or annulment of a marriage or civil partnership between the donor and the donee, unless the instrument provides otherwise[527]; and the lack of capacity of the donee. In addition, the bankruptcy of the donor or the donee will revoke the power in so far as it gives authority to deal with the donee's property and affairs, but not his personal welfare.[528] The operation of a lasting power of attorney is subject to the powers of the court laid down in the Act.[529]

---

[525] s.13(6)(a).
[526] s.13(6)(b).
[527] ss.13(6)(c), (11).
[528] ss.13(3), (4), 6(b), (8), (9).
[529] See s.23.

CHAPTER SEVENTEEN

PERFORMANCE & BREACH

17–001   A party who performs a contract in accordance with its terms is thereby discharged from his obligations under it. Such performance also normally entitles him to enforce the other party's undertakings. It is often possible to perform a contract vicariously, i.e. by procuring performance by a third party. In the vast majority of cases (but not all[1]), a failure to perform will amount to a breach of contract. The consequences of such a finding are dealt with in Chapters 18 (termination for breach), 20 (damages) and 21 (specific remedies).

1. METHOD OF PERFORMANCE

17–002   **When performance is due.** The general rule is that performance is due without demand: a debtor must seek his creditor.[2] This rule can be varied by

---

[1] See below, para.17–059.
[2] *Walton v Mascall* (1844) 13 M. & W. 452; cf. *Carne v Debono* [1988] 1 W.L.R. 1107.

contrary agreement, by mercantile usage or by other rules of law. The first possibility is illustrated by a contract which provides for payment to be made "on demand". The effect of these words is that the debtor is not bound to pay before the demand is made,[3] and that normally he must pay within a reasonable time of receiving the demand.[4] The second possibility is illustrated by the rule that the holder of a bill of exchange is not entitled to payment unless he first presents the bill for payment.[5] A demand or notice of default may also have to be given where the party from whom performance is claimed cannot, without notice, reasonably be expected to know that performance is due. Thus "a landlord is not in breach of his covenant to repair [the demised premises[6]] until he has been given notice of the want of repair and a reasonable time has elapsed in which repair could have been carried out."[7] The third possibility is illustrated by a legislative provision by which a tenant under a long lease of a dwelling is not liable to make payment of rent under the lease unless the landlord has given him a notice relating to the payment.[8] In certain other cases, a demand or notice of default is also necessary to entitle the injured party to terminate,[9] though not to establish breach.

Time of the essence. Stipulations as to time and, in particular, whether time is "of the essence" are principally relevant in the context of the injured party's right to terminate for breach and are dealt with in Ch.18.[10]   17–003

Tender. A tender of money is ineffective unless the money is actually produced, or unless production is dispensed with by the creditor.[11] Tender of part of a debt is bad.[12] Conversely, tender of too large a sum, *requiring change*, is bad, as this might put an unreasonable burden on the creditor.[13]   17–004

Tender of goods due under a contract of sale must be made at a reasonable hour; what is a reasonable hour is a question of fact.[14]

Where a bad tender is rejected and is, within the time fixed for performance, followed by a good tender, the latter must generally be accepted.[15] But if the first tender amounts to a repudiation of the contract, the injured party is entitled to

---

[3] *Esso Petroleum Co Ltd v Alstonbridge Properties Ltd* [1975] 1 W.L.R. 1474; *Libyan Arab Foreign Bank v Bankers Trust Co* [1989] Q.B. 728 at 748–749. The requirement of a "demand" may be waived: see *Stimson v Smith* [1999] Ch. 340; above, para.13–017.

[4] *Bank of Baroda v Panessar* [1987] Ch. 335. If the debtor has made it clear that he cannot or will not pay, he will be in default as soon as the demand is made: *Sheppard & Cooper Ltd v TSB Bank* [1996] 2 All E.R. 654.

[5] Bills of Exchange Act 1882, ss.41(1)(a), 40(1).

[6] *British Telecommunications Plc v Sun Life Assurance Society Plc* [1996] Ch. 69 at 74 (where the landlord was in immediate breach as soon as the want of repair occurred in *another* part of the building).

[7] *Calabar Properties Ltd v Stitcher* [1984] 1 W.L.R. 287 at 298.

[8] Commonhold and Leasehold Reform Act 2002, s.166.

[9] See below, paras 18–061—18–062, 18–097.

[10] Below, para.18–089 et seq.

[11] *Finch v Brook* (1834) 1 Bing.N.C. 253; *Farquharson v Pearl Ins Co Ltd* [1937] 3 All E.R. 124.

[12] *Dixon v Clark* (1847) 5 C.B. 365.

[13] *Betterbee v Davis* (1811) 3 Camp. 70; *Robinson v Cook* (1815) 6 Taunt. 336.

[14] Sale of Goods Act 1979, s.29(5).

[15] *Tetley v Shand* (1871) 25 L.T. 658; cf. *Borrowman Phillips & Co v Free & Hollis* (1878) 4 Q.B.D. 500; *Agricultores Federados Argentinos v Ampro SA* [1965] 2 Lloyd's Rep. 157; *Bremer Handelsgesellschaft mbH v J H Rayner & Co* [1979] 2 Lloyd's Rep. 216 at 224–229; *The Playa Larga* [1983] 2 Lloyd's Rep. 171 at 186; Apps [1994] L.M.C.L.Q. 525.

terminate the contract,[16] and if he does so he will not be bound to accept the second tender.

17–005   **Payment by cheque or credit card.** There is a presumption that payment by cheque or negotiable[17] security operates only as conditional payment: that is, the payer is not discharged until the cheque or security is honoured.[18] During the currency of the security, the creditor impliedly undertakes not to sue on the original debt.[19] But the presumption of conditional payment can be rebutted by proof of contrary intention, i.e. by showing that the creditor had accepted the security unconditionally in payment of the debt.[20] The presumption that payment is merely conditional does not apply where a customer pays for goods or services by use of a charge or credit card. Use by the customer of such a card discharges his obligations under the contract with the supplier and makes the customer liable to reimburse the card issuing company in accordance with the contract between these two parties. If the company should fail to pay the supplier (e.g. because it has become insolvent) the supplier's sole remedy is against the company.[21] He cannot claim the price from the customer; for to allow him to do so would make the customer liable to immediate full payment in cash for the goods or services supplied and so impose on him an obligation substantially more onerous than that to which he agreed when contracting with the supplier on the terms that payment was to be made by means of the card.

17–006   **Alternatives.**[22] A contract may provide for performance in one of several ways without stating which party is to have the power of choosing between them. In *Reed v Kilburn Co-operative Society*[23] the claimant lent £50 to the defendants at 6 per cent per annum "for six or nine months". The period of the loan was held to depend on the choice of the borrower. One reason given was that "the alternative was put in for the benefit of the borrower".[24] On this view the result could vary with the state of the market: the alternative might be for the benefit of the borrower if interest rates were thought likely to rise and for that of the lender if they were thought likely to fall. But this is not the law: the choice is always the borrower's, unless the contract expressly provides the contrary. Another reason given was that "the option is in the party who is to do the first act; here the

---

[16] See below, para.17–082.

[17] Cheques are now rarely negotiable: above, para.15–046.

[18] Once it is honoured, payment is taken to have been made when the cheque was received: *Homes v Smith* [2000] Lloyd's Rep. Bank. 139.

[19] *Sayer v Wagstaff* (1844) 14 L.J.Ch. 116; *Re Romer & Haslam* [1893] 2 Q.B. 286; cf. *Maran Road Saw Mill v Austin Taylor & Co Ltd* [1975] 1 Lloyd's Rep. 156 and *EDF Man v Nigerian Sweets & Confectionery Co* [1977] 2 Lloyd's Rep. 50 (payment by letter of credit). Payment by direct debit has been treated as equivalent to payment by cheque, at least for the purpose of set-off: *Esso Petroleum Ltd v Milton* [1997] 1 W.L.R. 938. In *DPP v Turner* [1974] A.C. 357 at 367–368, and *Jameson v CEGB* [2000] 1 A.C. 455 at 478 it is suggested that giving a cheque amounts to payment but that the debt revives if the cheque is not met. However, in *Sayer v Wagstaff* (above) "payment" was held to have taken place when the promissory note was *paid*, not when it was *given*.

[20] *Sard v Rhodes* (1836) 1 M. & W. 153.

[21] *Re Charge Card Services Ltd* [1989] Ch. 497; cf. *Richardson v Worrall* [1985] S.T.C. 693 at 717, 720; *Customs & Excise Commissioners v Diners Club Ltd* [1989] 1 W.L.R. 1196 at 1205–1206 rejecting the argument that the debt is not extinguished but assigned to the card-issuing company.

[22] cf. below, para.19–053.

[23] (1875) L.R. 10 Q.B. 264; cf. *Price v Nixon* (1813) 5 Taunt. 338.

[24] ibid. at 265.

borrower is to do the first act by paying".[25] But this test would not satisfactorily solve all cases. Quain J. during the argument said: "A lease for seven, fourteen, or twenty-one years, without saying at whose option, is at the option of the lessee."[26] Yet before one knows whose the option is, it is impossible to tell who is to do the first act, i.e. whether landlord or tenant must give notice of termination. No general rule is satisfactory where parties make such obscure contracts. It is a matter to be resolved by the construction of the contract, though the "natural meaning" is likely to be that it is for the promisor to choose.[27]

2. VICARIOUS PERFORMANCE

A contract may be performed by a third party on behalf of the debtor. The legal effects of such performance depend on whether it is made (or tendered) with or without the creditor's consent.

17–007

(a) With the Creditor's Consent

Vicarious performance will generally discharge the contract. If the creditor agrees to accept[28] performance by a third party, such performance can discharge the contract, even though it is not the same as that stipulated for in the contract. In *Hirachand Punamchand v Temple*[29] a debt was held to have been discharged when the creditor accepted a smaller sum from the debtor's father in full settlement. Payment by a third party will, however, discharge the debtor only if it was made by the third party on behalf of the debtor and with the intention of discharging him. These requirements are illustrated by a case[30] in which a company made an ex gratia payment to a person who had been defrauded by its secretary. The victim of the fraud was nevertheless entitled to claim the whole of his loss from the secretary, since the company's payment was not made on the secretary's behalf. Similarly, part-payment by one of two persons who are both liable for a debt will not discharge the other, since it will be presumed to have been made on account of his own and not of his co-debtor's liability.[31] It is an open question whether the debt is discharged if payment by a third party is made without the knowledge or consent of the debtor.[32] Some dicta support the view that the debt is discharged[33]; and this consequence clearly results if the debtor adopts or ratifies the payment.[34] But if, before he has done so, the transaction

17–008

---

[25] ibid.

[26] ibid. at 265.

[27] *Mora Shipping Inc v Axa Corporate Solutions Assurance SA* [2005] EWCA Civ 1069; [2005] 2 Lloyd's Rep. 769 at [44].

[28] See *Customs & Excise Commissioners v National Westminister Bank Plc* [2002] EWHC 2204; [2003] 1 All E.R. (Comm) 327.

[29] [1911] 2 K.B. 330; above, para.3–108.

[30] *Re Rowe* [1904] 2 K.B. 483; *Pacific Associates Inc v Baxter* [1990] 1 Q.B. 993 at 1033–1034.

[31] *Jones v Broadhurst* (1850) 9 C.B. 173; *Cook v Lister* (1863) 13 C.B.(N.S.) 543 at 594; *Kemp v Balls* (1854) 10 Ex. 607.

[32] See generally Beatson, *The Use and Abuse of Unjust Enrichment*, Ch.7.

[33] *Cook v Lister* (1863) 13 C.B.(N.S.) 543 at 594; contrast *Guardian Ocean Cargoes Ltd v Banco do Brasil SA* [1991] 2 Lloyd's Rep. 68 at 88, affirmed [1994] 2 Lloyd's Rep. 152. A theoretical objection might be based on the doctrine of privity but it is submitted that cases of the present kind fall outside the scope of that doctrine as properly understood: see above, para.14–044. For the possible application of Contracts (Rights of Third Parties) Act 1999 to cases of this kind, see above, para.3–108.

[34] See *Walter v James* (1871) L.R. 6 Ex. 124 at 127.

between creditor and third party is cancelled and the payment is returned to the third party, there is no discharge[35]; nor will the payment discharge the debt if the third party made it in the mistaken belief (however genuine[36]) that he was authorised by the debtor to pay the debt on his behalf.[37] It follows that, where a bank without its customer's authority or ratification pays the customer's debt, then the debt is not discharged; nor is the bank entitled to debit the customer's account with the amount of the payment.[38]

The cases on this subject all concern the payment of debts; but presumably the same principles apply where a creditor agrees to accept vicarious performance of some other obligation.[39]

(b) Without the Creditor's Consent

17–009   A creditor cannot object to vicarious performance where he is not prejudiced by the fact that the debtor does not perform personally. Thus a tradesman, to whom money is owed for goods, cannot object if the debtor procures full payment in cash to be made on his behalf by a third party. The same is often true of obligations to do something other than pay cash. Thus in *British Waggon Co v Lea & Co*[40] it was held that a contract to let out railway wagons and to keep them in repair for seven years could be vicariously performed: it did not matter to the hirer who kept the wagons in repair so long as the work was efficiently done by someone.

But a creditor may be entitled to object to vicarious performance either on account of the nature of the contract or because of its terms.

17–010   **Nature of the contract.** When a contract is "personal" in the sense that one party relies on the skill and judgment of the other, the latter must perform personally. Thus duties under a contract of service cannot be vicariously performed;[41] an estate agent who has been instructed to find a purchaser for a house cannot perform vicariously, since he "holds a position of discretion and trust"[42]; a person who agrees to store another's goods must perform personally, since the owner of the goods relies on his skill and integrity[43]; and a shipowner must perform a charterparty personally in the sense that he cannot require the charterer to accept performance from a third party to whom the ship has been sold.[44] There are cases in which even a contract for the sale of goods must be personally performed by the seller, e.g. if the goods are to be manufactured by the seller and

---

[35] This was the position in *Walter v James* itself; cf. above, para.16–050.

[36] *Crantrave Ltd v Lloyds Bank Plc* [2000] Q.B. 917.

[37] *Barclays Bank Ltd v W J Simms Son & Co (Southern) Ltd* [1980] Q.B. 677. Contrast *Lloyds Bank Plc v Independent Ins Ltd* [2000] Q.B. 110, where the payment was authorised.

[38] *Crantrave Ltd v Lloyds Bank Plc* [2000] Q.B. 917.

[39] *William Page & Co Ltd v BNP Paribas Securities Services Customer Bank Ltd* [2008] EWHC 3077; [2009] L & T.R. 8.

[40] (1880) 5 Q.B.D. 149; cf. *Phillips v Alhambra Palace Co* [1901] 1 Q.B. 59.

[41] *Robson v Drummond* (1831) 2 B. & Ad. 303 would seem an extreme example.

[42] *John McCann & Co v Pow* [1974] 1 W.L.R. 1643 at 1647; cf. above, para.16–098; *Southway Group v Wolff* (1991) 57 Build L.R. 33 (supervision by architect).

[43] *Edwards v Newland* [1950] 2 K.B. 534.

[44] *Fratelli Sorrentino v Buerger* [1915] 3 K.B. 367 at 370, but that case shows that the charterer cannot object if, notwithstanding the sale, the shipowner can still perform personally, i.e. if he retains the control and management of the ship during the chartered period or voyage; cf. *Humble v Hunter* (1842) 12 Q.B. 310; above, para.16–057.

the buyer has relied on the seller's skill as a manufacturer[45] or if the buyer has in some other way relied on the personal integrity of the seller.[46]

Terms of the contract. It is obvious that a contract must be personally performed if it expressly so provides. A contract may also contain terms which impliedly rule out vicarious performance. In *Davies v Collins*[47] the defendant accepted a uniform for cleaning under a contract which provided: "Whilst every care is exercised in cleaning . . . garments, all orders are accepted at owners' risk." It was held that the defendant had broken the contract by sending the uniform to be cleaned by a sub-contractor (who had lost it); for the words "whilst every care is exercised in cleaning . . . " were inconsistent with the right to perform the cleaning operation vicariously. If, however, the uniform had been properly cleaned, and returned, by the sub-contractor, the owner would not have been prejudiced by the fact of vicarious performance, and it is submitted that he should have been liable to make at any rate some payment.[48] Lord Greene M.R. said that the clause did not preclude every kind of sub-contracting: the cleaner might have employed a sub-contractor to perform some purely ancillary service, such as returning the uniform to the customer. It is arguable that the clause precluded only vicarious performance of the duty to take care of the goods, and that, so long as that duty remained unbroken, the owner was liable to pay the cleaning charges.

17–011

(c) Vicarious Performance Distinguished from Assignment

No transfer of liability. The factors which determine whether a contract can be vicariously performed closely resemble those which determine whether the benefit of a "personal" contract is assignable.[49] For this reason, vicarious performance is sometimes called *assignment of liabilities*; but this is (as already noted) a concept which is not recognised by the common law.[50] Where vicarious performance is permitted no liability is *transferred*; the original debtor remains liable for the due performance of his obligations under the contract; and the sub-contractor does not at common law become liable in contract to the creditor.[51] In *Stewart v Reavell's Garage*[52] the owner of a 1929 Bentley motorcar took it to the defendants' garage to have the brakes relined. At the defendants' suggestion, the owner agreed that the work should be done by a sub-contractor, who did it so badly that the brakes failed, and the owner was injured. The defendants were clearly entitled to perform vicariously, as the owner had agreed to their doing so. But they were nonetheless held liable for the sub-contractor's defective workmanship: their liability was not transferred. Nor did the sub-contractor incur any contractual

17–012

---

[45] *Johnson v Raylton, Dixon & Co* (1881) 7 Q.B.D. 438.

[46] *Dr Jaeger's Sanitary Woollen System Co Ltd v Walker & Sons* (1897) 77 L.T. 180.

[47] [1945] 1 All E.R. 247; cf. *Kollerich & Cie SA v The State Trading Co of India* [1980] 2 Lloyd's Rep. 32.

[48] cf. below, para.17–043.

[49] See, e.g. *Don King Productions Inc v Warren* [2000] Ch. 291 at 335–336; above, paras 15–051—15–057.

[50] See above, para.15–076.

[51] Unless the main contractor is the other party's agent for the purpose of making a contract between him and the sub-contractor; above, para.16–098.

[52] [1952] 2 Q.B. 545; cf. *Basildon DC v J E Lesser (Properties) Ltd* [1985] Q.B. 839; *Wong Mee Wan v Kwan Kin Travel Services Ltd* [1996] 1 W.L.R. 38.

liability to the owner. He might have been liable to the owner in tort for doing the work negligently[53] but he would not have been liable to the owner in contract, had he failed to do the work at all. The Contracts (Rights of Third Parties) Act 1999[54] makes it possible to draw up the sub-contract in such a way as to confer rights against the sub-contractor on the creditor; but even if this is done, the debtor will not be relieved from his liability to the creditor under the main contract.

17–013   **Contracts to arrange a service.** The above discussion is based on the assumption that a contract contains an undertaking by A to B for the provision of some service and that the contract permits A to delegate the performance of the service to C. It is, however, also possible for A's undertaking to be, not one that he will *render* the service, but one that he will *arrange* for it to be rendered by another person (C) as his agent.[55] In that case, A's duty is merely to exercise reasonable care and skill in selecting the agent[56]; and if he performs that duty he will not be liable to B for defects in C's performance. Such a case is not one of *vicarious* performance at all: A will have *personally* performed the only duty which the contract imposed on him.

3. ORDER OF PERFORMANCE

17–014   The order in which contracting parties must perform their respective obligations depends on the distinction between conditions precedent, concurrent conditions, and independent promises. Somewhat confusingly, English law also uses the expression "condition" in rules which deal with the *conformity* of one party's performance with that promised (as opposed to the *order* in which the two performances must be rendered). This usage, and the distinction between these two senses of "condition," are discussed in Ch.18.[57]

(a) Condition Precedent

17–015   Performance by one party, A, is a condition precedent to the liability of the other, B, when A has to perform before B's liability accrues. This will most obviously be the case if the contract expressly provides that A's act is to be done before B's.[58] Thus if A agrees to work for B at a weekly wage payable in arrear, B

---

[53] cf. *Learoyd Bros v Pope & Sons* [1966] 2 Lloyd's Rep. 142; *British Telecommunications Plc v James Thomson & Sons (Engineers) Ltd* [1999] 1 W.L.R. 9.

[54] See above, para.14–090 et seq.

[55] *Wong Mee Wan v Kwan Kim Travel Services* [1996] 1 W.L.R. 38, where the contract was not of this kind, and A was held liable for C's defective performance.

[56] ibid.; *Raflatec Ltd v Eade* [1999] 1 Lloyd's Rep. 507 at 509. The same conclusion has been drawn where performance required specialist skills which A could not reasonably be expected to have: see *Investors in Industry Commercial Property Ltd v Bedfordshire CC* [1986] 1 All E.R. 787 at 807 (not reported on this point in [1986] Q.B. 1034); for a similar rule where the defendant's only liability to the claimant is in tort for negligence, see *D & F Estates Ltd v Church Commissioners for England* [1989] A.C. 177 at 209 (the claim for the "trivial sum" of £50 in respect of damage to carpets); cf. *Aiken v Stewart Wrightson Members Agency Ltd* [1995] 1 W.L.R. 1281.

[57] See below, para.18–039 et seq.

[58] *Société Générale de Paris v Milders* (1883) 49 L.T. 55 at 59; cf. *Pioneer Concrete (UK) Ltd v National Employers Mutual, etc.* [1985] 2 All E.R. 395; *Kazakstan Wool Processors (Europe) Ltd v Nederlandsche Credietverzekering Maatschappij NV* [2000] C.L.C. 822.

need not pay A until A has done a week's work.[59] Performance by A may also be a condition precedent to the liability of B even though the contract does not expressly state the order in which the two acts are to be done. In *Trans Trust SPRL v Danubian Trading Co*[60] A bought steel from B to be paid for by "cash against shipping documents from a confirmed credit to be opened by" an American company (to whom A had resold) in favour of B. A undertook that the credit would be opened "forthwith". Performance by A of his undertaking to procure the letter of credit was regarded as a condition precedent to the liability of B although the order in which their acts were to be done was not expressly laid down in the contract. A knew that B could not get supplies of steel unless the credit was made available. Hence the nature of the contract made it clear that A was to perform before B became liable.

Condition precedent in the promissory sense. In Chapter 2 we distinguished between contingent and promissory conditions, and noted that "condition" was used to refer either to an event or to a term of a contract.[61] Our present concern is with conditions as events. In this sense, a contingent condition is an event which neither party undertakes to bring about and on which the existence of a contract, or the binding force of its principal obligations, depends. A promissory condition, on the other hand, refers to an event which one party is obliged by the contract to bring about. In the *Trans Trust* case, A argued that the opening of the credit was a condition of the former kind, so that A was not liable when his sub-buyer failed to open the credit. But the court rejected the argument and held A liable on the ground that the opening of the credit was not a condition precedent to the existence of the contract, but only a condition precedent to the liability of B. In other words, it was not a contingent, but a promissory condition. In its contingent sense, condition precedent is contrasted with condition subsequent. In its promissory sense (with which we are here concerned), condition precedent is contrasted with concurrent condition and independent promise: these concepts are discussed below.   17–016

Whether condition precedent is contingent or promissory. The distinction between a contingent and a promissory condition turns on the question whether the agreement purports to impose on A an obligation to bring about the stipulated event.[62] For example, in one case A undertook to erect buildings on B's land, and B undertook, when A had done so, to grant a lease of the land to A. This was held not to be a (contingently) "conditional contract", but a case in which performance by A was a (promissory) condition precedent to the liability of B.[63] The position is similar where A contracts to buy a house from B and to pay a deposit. As A promised to pay the deposit, that payment is not a contingent   17–017

---

[59] *Morton v Lamb* (1797) 7 T.R. 125; *Cresswell v Board of Inland Revenue* [1984] I.C.R. 508; *Miles v Wakefield MDC* [1987] A.C. 539 at 561, 574; *Wiluszynski v Tower Hamlets LBC* [1989] I.C.R. 493 at 498; see further para.17–045, below.

[60] [1952] 2 Q.B. 297. For a similar argument in a different context, see *Films Rover International v Cannon Film Sales Ltd* [1987] 1 W.L.R. 670 at 684; for further proceedings see [1989] 1 W.L.R. 912. Contrast *Clowes Development (UK) Ltd v Mulchinock* [1998] 1 W.L.R. 42.

[61] See above, para.2–103; cf. below, para.18–039.

[62] cf. *Albion Sugar Co Ltd v Williams Tankers Ltd* [1977] 2 Lloyd's Rep. 457 at 464; *The Fanti and the Padre Island* [1991] 2 A.C. 1 at 31; *UR Power GmbH v Kuok Oils and Grains Pte Ltd* [2009] EWHC 1940 (Comm); [2009] 2 Lloyd's Rep. 495 at [15].

[63] *Eastham v Leigh, London & Provincial Properties Ltd* [1971] 1 Ch. 871; cf. *Michaels v Harley House (Marylebone) Ltd* [1997] 1 W.L.R. 967.

condition precedent to the existence of the contract[64] but a promissory condition precedent to the liability of B. If the deposit is not paid, B is, moreover, entitled to terminate the contract,[65] while A can be sued for the unpaid deposit, or for damages for failing to pay it.[66]

(b) Concurrent Condition

17–018   The two performances are said to be concurrent conditions when the parties undertake to perform concurrently (or simultaneously). Thus in the case of a contract for the sale of goods delivery and payment are concurrent conditions: this means that the buyer cannot claim delivery unless he is ready and willing to pay, and the seller cannot claim the price unless he is ready and willing to deliver.[67] Of course this rule can be varied by contrary agreement: the seller may agree to give credit or the buyer to pay in advance. Similarly, under a charterparty, delivery of the goods by the shipowner and payment of the freight are (unless otherwise agreed[68]) concurrent conditions.[69]

(c) Independent Promises

17–019   If promises are "independent" each party can enforce the other's promise although he has not performed his own. The remedy of the party sued is not to withhold performance, but to make a counterclaim to enforce the promise of the party suing. A contract for the sale of land would now generally require conveyance and payment to take place concurrently. But a tenant's covenant to pay rent and a landlord's covenant to repair are still regarded as independent, so that the landlord is not entitled to refuse to perform his covenant to repair merely because the tenant is in arrears with his rent.[70] Similarly, where goods carried on a chartered ship are damaged as a result of the shipowner's breach of the charterparty, before the time fixed for payment of freight, the charterer must nevertheless make the payment when that time comes: his remedy is by way of a cross-action for damages.[71]

---

[64] *Michael Richards Properties Ltd v St Saviour's Parish* [1975] 3 All E.R. 416 at 420; *Millichamp v Jones* [1982] 1 W.L.R. 1422; *The Blankenstein* [1985] 1 W.L.R. 435. These authorities reject the contrary view stated in *Myton Ltd v Schwab-Morris* [1974] 1 W.L.R. 331 at 336.

[65] *Myton Ltd v Schwab-Morris* [1974] 1 W.L.R. 331 at 337; below, para.18–032. The contract may require B to give notice of termination before he is entitled to terminate, as in *Millichamp v Jones* [1982] 1 W.L.R. 1422 (where this requirement was not satisfied).

[66] See below, paras 18–017, 20–155.

[67] Sale of Goods Act 1979, s.28; *Morton v Lamb* (1797) 7 T.R. 125; *The Aktor* [2008] EWHC 1330 (Comm); [2008] 2 Lloyd's Rep. 246 at [66].

[68] e.g. *The Karin Vatis* [1988] 2 Lloyd's Rep. 330.

[69] *Paynter v James* (1867) L.R. 2 C.P. 348 at 355; cf. *Stanton v Richardson* (1872) L.R. 7 C.P. 421 at 433 (affirmed 45 L.J.Q.B. 78); *The Poseidon* [2001] 1 Lloyd's Rep. 697.

[70] *Taylor v Webb* [1937] 2 K.B. 283 at 290 (reversed, [1937] 2 K.B. 283 at 290, on another ground which was disapproved in *Regis Property Co Ltd v Dudley* [1959] A.C. 370); cf. *Johnstone v Milling* (1886) 16 Q.B.D. 460 at 468; *Tito v Waddell (No.2)* [1977] Ch. 106 at 290; *Yorbrook Investments Ltd v Batten* (1986) P. & C.R. 51.

[71] See below, paras 17–036, 18–039, fn.235; the rule applies even though the shipowner's breach was repudiatory: see *The Dominique* [1989] A.C. 1056 (not a case of damage but of delay).

(d) Criteria for Drawing the Distinction

The distinction between conditions precedent, concurrent conditions and inde-   **17–020**
pendent promises is easily illustrated by reference to stereotyped situations, such
as the employment, sale of goods and tenancy cases referred to in the preceding
discussion. In those cases, the distinction is governed by well-settled rules, though
these can be excluded by express or implied[72] agreement. But more difficulty
arises in drawing the distinction in cases of first impression which fall outside
these stereotyped situations. For this purpose the courts have regard to certain
policy considerations, though these can be displaced by evidence of the intention
of the parties.

Presumption in favour of concurrent conditions if simultaneous per-   **17–021**
formance is possible. The effect of holding promises to be independent is to
expose each party to the risk of having to perform without any security for the
performance of the other; the effect of holding performance by one party to be a
condition precedent is to expose that party to the same risk. To reduce the first of
these risks, the courts have long been reluctant to classify promises as independent[73] unless the intention of the parties to that effect was clear. Both risks would
be eliminated if the two performances were held to be concurrent conditions; and
for this reason the law should, in doubtful cases, favour such a classification
whenever simultaneous performance by both parties is possible.[74] In a contract
between a commercial seller or supplier and a consumer, a term which has not
been individually negotiated and which makes the consumer's undertaking (e.g. to
pay the agreed price or charge) independent of the due performance of the other
party's obligations is prima facie unfair under the Unfair Terms in Consumer
Contracts Regulations 1999,[75] and if it is actually unfair it will not bind the
consumer.[76]

Where simultaneous performance is not possible. Where simultaneous   **17–022**
performance is not possible (as in the case of contracts to do work over a period
of time) performance by one party must necessarily be a condition precedent to
the liability of the other. Which party has to perform first depends on their relative
bargaining power and on the court's view (right or wrong) as to which of them is
more likely to default after the other has performed. These factors no doubt
account for the general rule that work must precede pay.[77] The position of the
person doing the work is in practice safeguarded by stipulating for interim
payments, such as weekly or monthly remuneration under contracts of employment, or progress payments under building contracts.

Simultaneous performance possible, but promises classified as inde-   **17–023**
pendent. Even where it is possible for the two performances to be rendered
simultaneously, it does not follow that they should invariably be classified as

---

[72] As in the *Trans Trust* case [1952] 2 Q.B. 297; above, para.17–015.
[73] See *Kingston v Preston* (1773) Lofft. 194; and *Jones v Barkley* (1781) 2 Dougl. 648 at 689.
[74] This is the view taken by the Restatement 2d, *Contracts*, para.234(1).
[75] See above, para.7–095 et seq.; SI 1999/2083, reg.5(5) and Sch.2, para.1(o).
[76] reg.8(1).
[77] See above, para.17–015.

concurrent conditions. It may be appropriate to classify a promise as independent where it is only of minor importance,[78] or where the circumstances show that this was the intention of the parties.[79] Promises may also be classified as independent because of their commercial setting. This possibility arises where goods are sold for export on "c.i.f." terms, that is, for an inclusive price covering their cost, insurance and freight. Under such a contract the seller must ship goods that are in conformity with the contract and tender certain shipping documents to the buyer, while the buyer must pay the price on tender of the documents.[80] So long as the documents are in accordance with the contract, the buyer cannot refuse to pay against tender of those documents merely because the goods were not, when shipped, in conformity with the contract.[81] This is true even if the non-conformity of the goods is such that it would justify their rejection when the goods themselves (as opposed to the documents) later reach the buyer. The seller's undertaking with respect to the conformity of *the goods* can therefore be described as an independent promise in the sense that his failure to perform it does not prevent the buyer's duty to pay the price from arising on tender of *documents*. The buyer's remedies, in the case put, are to claim damages for the defects in the goods, or to reject them and reclaim the price if, on their arrival at the agreed destination, it turns out that they suffered, when they were shipped, from defects of a kind that justify their rejection.[82]

(e) Effects of the Distinction

17-024　　**Whether failure to perform justifies termination of the contract.** In Chapter 18 we will see that a failure to perform by one party (A) may entitle the other (B) to "terminate" the contract, in the sense that B is released from his obligation to perform. It follows from the nature of an independent promise that failure by A to perform such a promise does not justify termination by B. The position where A fails to perform a condition precedent or a concurrent condition is more complex: such a failure justifies B's refusal to perform for so long as the failure continues, but it does not, of itself, justify termination in the sense of an outright refusal by B to perform, or to accept further performance from A. If A, a buyer of goods, fails to perform the concurrent condition of paying or tendering the price when due, the seller, B, is prima facie justified in withholding delivery; but it does not follow that B is, merely on account of the failure, entitled to terminate the contract:[83] he may, for example, still be bound to deliver if A tenders the price on the day after that fixed by the contract. A's failure to perform will only justify termination if it is (in accordance with the principles to be discussed in Ch.18[84]) *either* sufficiently serious *or* such that it falls within one of the exceptions to the requirement of serious failure.

[78] *Huntoon Co v Kolynos (Inc)* [1930] 1 Ch. 528 at 558.
[79] *The Odenfeld* [1978] 2 Lloyd's Rep. 357.
[80] See generally *Benjamin's Sale of Goods* (8th edn), paras 19–076 to 19–078.
[81] *Gill & Duffus SA v Berger & Co Inc* [1984] A.C. 382, more fully discussed in *Benjamin's Sale of Goods* (8th edn), paras 19–164 to 19–165.
[82] e.g. from defects amounting to a breach of condition: see below, para.18–039 et seq.
[83] cf. Sale of Goods Act 1979, s.10(1); below, para.18–093.
[84] See below, paras 18–023—18–074.

(f) Wrongful Refusal to Accept Performance

(i) *As a ground of termination*

In general, A's failure to perform a condition precedent or a concurrent   **17–025**
condition justifies a refusal by B to perform. But this rule is displaced if, before
performance from A has become due, B has repudiated the contract by wrongfully
refusing to accept performance (or indicating that he would do so) and A has
terminated the contract on account of that repudiation.[85] The effect of this
displacement may differ depending upon whether A's failure to perform was
induced by B's repudiation.

Where failure to perform induced by other party's repudiation. Suppose   **17–026**
that a contract for the sale of goods provides that the goods are to be manufactured
by A to B's order. If, before anything has, or should have been, done by A, B
wrongfully repudiates the contract, A is entitled to terminate the contract; and, if
he does so, two things follow: A need no longer manufacture the goods, and he can
claim damages from B.[86] It would be pointless to require A to manufacture and
tender the goods when the tender was virtually certain to be rejected. His inability
to deliver the goods at the agreed time is not allowed to prejudice his rights against
B as it was induced by B's wrongful repudiation; another way of putting the point
is to say that B is estopped from relying on A's inability to perform.[87] A buyer is
similarly not entitled to rely on the seller's failure to deliver where that failure was
induced by the buyer's insistence on delivery at a place other than that specified
by the contract.[88]

Where failure to perform not induced by other party's repudiation. In   **17–027**
the situations just described, it has been assumed that A could have performed,
and would have done so, if B had not repudiated. But sometimes A can recover
damages even though he cannot show that he would, but for B's repudiation, have
been able to perform his part. In *British and Beningtons Ltd v NW Cachar Tea Co
Ltd*[89] A sold tea to B who, before delivery was due, without justification stated that
they would refuse to accept it. It was held that A was entitled to damages even
though he could not show that he could have delivered the tea at the agreed time
and place. B's wrongful refusal to accept was an anticipatory breach,[90] and, once
this had been "accepted" by A so as to terminate the contract, later events
affecting A's ability to perform did not deprive A of his right of action[91]; for, by

---

[85] See, generally, Ch.18.
[86] e.g. *Glencore Grain Rotterdam BV v LORICO* [1997] 2 Lloyd's Rep. 386, where a seller's refusal
to load goods was justified by the buyer's refusal to operate the contractual payment mechanism unless
unjustified demands by the buyer were met; cf. *Grant v Cigman* [1996] B.C.L.C. 24 (A's inability to
perform induced by B's failure to co-operate). As to A's remedy in such cases, see *The Odenfeld* [1978]
2 Lloyd's Rep. 357; below, para.21–013.
[87] *The Simona* [1989] A.C. 788 at 805–806. *Foran v Wight* (1989) 168 C.L.R. 385 is explicable on this
relatively simple ground.
[88] *Bulk Oil (Zug) AG v Sun International Ltd* [1984] 1 Lloyd's Rep. 531 at 546.
[89] [1923] A.C. 48; cf. *Cort v Ambergate Ry* (1851) 7 Q.B. 127; *Rightside Properties Ltd v Gray* [1975]
Ch. 72 at 87; *Texaxo Ltd v Eurogolf Shipping Co Ltd* [1987] 2 Lloyd's Rep. 541.
[90] See below, paras 17–073—17–090.
[91] See below, para.17–088; *Braithwaite v Foreign Hardwood Co* [1905] 2 K.B. 543, as explained in *The
Simona* [1989] A.C. 788 at 805.

terminating the contract, A had been liberated from his duty of further perform-ance.[92] The position would have been different if, at the time of B's refusal to accept, A had himself already committed a repudiatory breach,[93] for such a breach would have justified B's refusal. It is therefore crucial to determine which party committed the first breach,[94] whether that breach was repudiatory, and whether it was accepted by the other party so as to terminate the contract.

These questions are easy enough to formulate but they can raise difficult issues of fact and law where each party to a commercial dispute in good faith believes that he is acting in accordance with the contract, and that the other is not. The issue is further complicated by two rules. The first is that A is not necessarily in breach merely because he makes a defective tender; for it may be open to him to cure the defect by making a second (and good) tender within the time allowed for perform-ance.[95] The second is that B is not necessarily in breach merely because, at the time of his refusal to accept A's performance, he gives an inadequate reason for the refusal, or none at all; for if he actually had a lawful excuse he can (in general) rely on it later even though he did not state it, or even know of it, at the time of his refusal to accept performance.[96]

17–028   **Pre-termination non-repudiatory breach by injured party.** Before termi-nating the contract on account of B's repudiation, A may himself have committed a breach, but one which did not justify B's repudiation, e.g. a breach of an independent promise.[97] Termination by A does not affect his liability for that pre-termination breach[98]; so that the damages to which A is entitled on account of B's wrongful repudiation will be reduced by those for which he is liable in respect of

---

[92] *Gill & Duffus SA v Berger & Co Inc* [1984] A.C. 382 at 390; cf. *MSC Mediterranean Shipping Co SA v BRE Metro Ltd* [1985] 2 Lloyd's Rep. 239 at 240; *Glencore Grain Rotterdam BV v LORICO* [1997] 2 Lloyd's Rep. 386 at 394–395; *North Sea Energy Holdings NV v Petroleum Authority of Thailand* [1997] 2 Lloyd's Rep. 418 at 432, where the principle stated in the text above was held at first instance not to apply because the contract had become ineffective by reason of failure of a condition precedent, without default of the allegedly repudiating party, *before* acceptance of any repudiation by the other party; the decision was affirmed on appeal without further reference to the present point: [1999] 1 Lloyd's Rep. 483. Dawson 96 L.Q.R. 239 argues that *Universal Cargo Carriers Corp v Citati* [1957] 2 Q.B. 401 is inconsistent with the explanation of the *British and Beningtons* case given in the text above. But the claim in the *Citati* case was made *against* the party alleged to be unable to perform (the charterer) while in the *British and Beningtons* case it was made *by* that party. Moreover, in the *Citati* case the charterer was already in breach (actual and anticipatory) at the time of the shipowner's refusal to perform while in the *British and Beningtons* case the sellers were not in breach at the time of the buyer's refusal. The crucial issue in the *Citati* case was simply whether the charterer's breach was sufficiently serious to justify the shipowner's termination.

[93] i.e. one that satisfied the requirement of "substantial failure" (below, paras 18–025—18–036) or fell within an exception to that requirement (below, paras 18–039—18–074). In *Braithwaite*'s case (above, fn.91) A had already shipped non-conforming goods before B's repudiation; but there are at least three possible reasons why this did not justify that repudiation: (1) A had not yet tendered the goods: *Taylor v Oakes Roncoroni & Co* (1922) 38 T.L.R. 349 at 351 (affirmed (1922) 38 T.L.R. 349 at 517); (2) A still had the opportunity to cure the breach (below, at fn.95) and was induced by B's repudiation not to make use of it: cf. below, at fn.113; (3) as the contract was on c.i.f. terms (see 74 L.J.K.B. 688 at 694) A's shipment of non-conforming goods was a breach only of an independent covenant and hence did not justify B's repudiation: above, para.17–023. See further Benjamin's *Sale of Goods* (8th edn), paras 19–176 to 19–180.

[94] *Glencore Grain* case, above, fn.92; cf. *The Energy Progress* [1993] 1 Lloyd's Rep. 355 at 358.

[95] See above, para.17–004.

[96] See below, para.17–062.

[97] See above, para.17–019.

[98] See below, para.18–015.

his own pre-termination breach.[99] Those damages will prima facie be the amount by which A's breach reduces the value of his performance.[100]

(ii) *Where injured party does not terminate*

The reason for the rule that A may be entitled to damages for B's repudiation, without having to show that he could have performed, is that, when A accepts B's repudiation, he is liberated from his own duty to perform.[101] That reasoning obviously cannot apply where A does not accept the repudiation. In such a case, A continues to be bound by his own duties under the contract, so that his failure to perform these duties, even after B's repudiation, can (if not induced by B's repudiation[102]) amount to a breach by A. Such a breach will make A liable in damages,[103] and, if it is repudiatory,[104] it will also justify B's refusal to perform and so absolve B from liability in damages to A.[105] These principles were applied, by analogy, in *Acre 1127 Ltd v De Montfort Fine Art Ltd*.[106] B was found to have repudiated the contract, but A did not accept the repudiation until sometime later. Nonetheless, A was found to have its own "settled intention" not to perform which pre-dated B's repudiation. In the unusual circumstances of the case, that did not make A guilty of an earlier repudiation, but it indicated clearly that A was not willing to perform its own obligations where that unwillingness was not a consequence of B's repudiation. B was therefore absolved from any liability in damages.

Where A does not accept B's repudiation and then commits a breach which does *not* justify B's refusal to perform (e.g. because it is a breach of an independent promise[107]), A's breach will nevertheless be relevant to the damages to which A is entitled on account of B's repudiation. At the least, those damages will (as in the case where A has terminated) be reduced by the damages for which A is liable by reason of his own breach, e.g. by the amount by which the value of goods delivered by A is reduced by reason of a defect in them. There are, moreover, circumstances in which, if A has not terminated the contract, B can rely on A's breach so as to reduce still further the damages for which B is liable by reason of his repudiation. This possibility arises where A's breach, though not originally of such a kind as to justify B's repudiation, later acquires that character. Where goods are sold on c.i.f. terms, the buyer is not justified in refusing to pay against *documents* merely because the *goods* were not, when shipped, in conformity with the contract; but such non-conformity may give him the right to reject the goods, a right that he will usually exercise when the goods arrive at the contractual destination and are actually delivered to him.[108] That stage is never reached if the seller terminates the

17–029

---

[99] *Gill & Duffus SA v Berger & Co Inc* [1984] A.C. 382 at 390 (where a "certification clause" in the contract excluded such liability).

[100] See below, para.20–051.

[101] See above, para.17–027.

[102] ibid.

[103] *Regent OHG Aisenstadt und Barig v Francesco of Jermyn Street* [1983] 3 All E.R. 327 at 335.

[104] In the sense described in fn.93, above.

[105] See *The Simona* [1989] A.C. 788, where A's failure was not a breach but justified cancellation under an express cancelling clause in the contract; Marston [1988] C.L.J. 340; Carter [1989] L.M.C.L.Q. 81.

[106] [2011] EWCA Civ 87 (for further proceedings, see: [2011] EWCA Civ 130).

[107] See above, para.17–019.

[108] See above, para.17–023.

contract on the buyer's wrongful refusal to pay against documents[109]; but if the seller does *not* terminate the contract, and the defect in the goods is such as to give the buyer the right to reject them on arrival, then the buyer will be able to argue that he would, even if he had duly paid against documents, have rejected the goods on arrival and so have become entitled to the return of the money that he ought to have paid at the earlier stage of tender of documents.[110] The effect of this argument is that the seller's damages will be merely nominal: he will have lost nothing but the worthless right to be paid a sum of money which he would (had it been paid) have later become liable to repay.[111] Such an argument is not, however, available to the buyer where it was still open to the seller to have cured his breach[112] and his failure to do so was induced by the buyer's wrongful repudiation.[113] If the seller's failure to cure was induced in this way, the buyer cannot rely on it in reduction of damages, any more than he can rely on the seller's original failure to perform (when so induced) on the issue of liability.[114]

(iii) *Evaluation*

17–030   The rule that A is entitled to terminate the contract and to recover damages where his own inability to perform is induced by B's repudiation is generally regarded as uncontroversial. But there is dispute about the merit of the rule that A has the same rights where he could not have performed even if B had not repudiated and where his inability to perform was not in any way induced by B's conduct. This aspect of the rule can be criticised by saying that B is made liable in damages for merely saying that he will not perform, even though he may not thereby cause any prejudice to A. On the other hand, B can avoid this hardship by simply waiting till A's performance is due: if it is not forthcoming at that time it is A, not B, who will be liable in damages; and any hardship that the rule may cause to B if he repudiates before that time is mitigated by the qualifications on its scope that have been stated above.[115] For these reasons, it does not seem that the rule causes undue prejudice to B. It can be justified on the ground that it promotes certainty by discouraging premature repudiation.

4. ENTIRE AND SEVERABLE OBLIGATIONS

(a) Entire Obligations

17–031   **Definition.** A contractual obligation is said to be "entire" when the contract requires it to be *completely* performed by one party (A) before the other (B) is to

---

[109] As in *Gill & Duffus SA v Berger & Co Inc* [1984] A.C. 382.

[110] See *Henry Dean & Sons (Sydney) Ltd v O'Day Pty Ltd* (1929) 39 C.L.R. 330 at 340, so far as it relates to the *seller's* claim; the disapproval of that decision in *Gill & Duffus SA v Berger & Co Inc*, above, relates to the *buyer's* claim only; and in the *Gill & Duffus* case itself the House of Lords treated the seller's termination as crucial to the success of his claim.

[111] cf. *The Mihalis Angelos* [1971] 1 Q.B. 641; below, para.18–062. An alternative view is that the seller's damages are nominal only if the defect makes the goods worthless: see *Bunge Corp v Vegetable Vitamin Foods (Private) Ltd* [1985] 1 Lloyd's Rep. 613 at 620; but the buyer's case is not that *the goods* are worthless: it is that the seller's *right to have them accepted* is worthless because the buyer's option to reject them would certainly have been exercised.

[112] See above, at fn.95.

[113] This is one possible explanation of *Braithwaite v Foreign Hardwood Co* [1905] 2 K.B. 543; above, fn.91; cf. *Sheffield v Conran* (1987) 22 Con L.R. 108.

[114] cf. above, para.17–026.

[115] i.e. at fnn.96–112, above.

pay, or to render such other counter-performance as may have been agreed.[116] Complete performance by A is sometimes said to be a "condition precedent" to B's liability; but the cases are not necessarily concerned with disputes as to the *order* of performance.[117] Often the dispute arises because A's purported performance, though rendered in the stipulated order, is in some way incomplete or defective.

No recovery for partial performance. Where A fails to complete performance of an entire obligation, B is entitled to refuse to pay even though the deficiency in A's performance causes him little prejudice or none at all.[118] At common law A is not even generally entitled to any other recompense for the partial performance which he has rendered. In *Cutter v Powell*[119] a seaman agreed to serve on a ship bound from Jamaica for Liverpool; he was to be paid 30 guineas "ten days after the ship arrives at Liverpool . . . provided he proceeds, continues and does his duty . . . from hence to the port of Liverpool." On August 2 the ship sailed from Jamaica; she arrived at Liverpool on October 9, but the seaman had died on September 20. It was held that his administratrix could not recover for the work he had done before his death; for the contract meant that nothing was to be paid unless and until he had served for the whole voyage. At the ordinary rates of pay then prevailing, he would have earned only £8 for such a voyage. The higher rate of pay seems to have been intended to throw the risk of his completing the voyage on him. Lord Kenyon C.J. said: "It was a kind of insurance".[120] The result was that the administratrix recovered neither the 30 guineas, nor a proportionate part of it, nor a reasonable sum for the six or seven weeks' service which the deceased had rendered. According to one case, the same rule applies even where a contract of employment is terminated by mutual consent.[121]

Similarly, where a contract for the carriage of goods by sea provides that freight is to become due on arrival of the goods at the agreed destination, the shipowner cannot recover either the stipulated freight, or freight pro rata, if he is compelled to abandon the voyage by perils of the sea and to discharge the cargo at an intermediate port.[122] The rule can be excluded by contrary provision in the contract, e.g. by one to the effect that freight is to be deemed to have been *earned*

17–032

---

[116] Such a term is not affected by Unfair Contract Terms Act 1977, s.3(2)(b)(ii) for the reason stated at para.7–069, above; and also because B is not claiming to be entitled to render no performance "in respect of his contractual obligation": his case is rather that, before A's performance, he is not under any relevant obligation. Nor are the Unfair Terms in Consumer Contracts Regulations 1999 (above, para.7–095 et seq.) likely to affect the effectiveness of such a term. Reg.8(1) applies to contracts between a commercial seller or supplier and a consumer and provides that unfair standard terms in such contracts do not bind *the consumer*. Any entire obligation which may be imposed by such a contract is likely to be that of the *supplier*. The Regulations do not apply to contracts relating to employment: see Dir.93/13, Recital 10, above, para.7–117, so that they would not apply to cases such as *Cutter v Powell*, below, fn.119.

[117] cf. above, para.17–014.

[118] Where, however, the partial performance confers a benefit on him which he voluntarily accepts, he may be under an obligation to pay a reasonable sum for it: see below, para.17–041 et seq.

[119] (1795) 6 T.R. 320; Stoljar 34 Can.Bar.Rev. 288; Dockray 117 L.Q.R. 626.

[120] ibid. at 324. Quaere whether it was really insurance against the death of members of the crew, or against their desertion. For possible effects of the Apportionment Act 1870 and of the Law Reform (Frustrated Contracts) Act 1943 in a case like *Cutter v Powell*, see below, paras 17–047, 19–102.

[121] *Lambourn v Cruden* (1841) 2 M. & G. 253.

[122] *Vlierboom v Chapman* (1844) 13 M. & W. 230; *St Enoch Shipping Co Ltd v Phosphate Mining Co* [1916] 2 K.B. 624; cf. *The Fort Kip* [1985] 2 Lloyd's Rep. 168. See, similarly, where the a ship is abandoned at sea and later saved by third parties: *The Kathleen* (1874) L.R. 4 A. & E. 269; contrast *Bradley v H Newsom, Sons & Co* [1919] A.C. 16 (where there was no abandonment).

on loading.[123] In such a case, the shipowner can recover the freight even though the contract provides that it is to be *paid* on or after unloading: that provision affects only the *time* of payment, not the creation of the obligation to pay.[124]

The same principle is again illustrated by *Sumpter v Hedges*[125] where a builder agreed to build two houses for the defendant on the latter's land for a lump sum of £565. When the houses were still unfinished the builder told the defendant that he had run out of money and could not finish the work; and the defendant later completed the houses himself. It was held that the builder could not recover the agreed sum; nor could he recover a reasonable remuneration for his work as there was no evidence of a "new contract" to pay such a sum.[126]

17–033   **Sale of goods.** As a general rule, a contract for the sale of goods is considered to impose an entire obligation with regard to the quantity contracted for.[127] If the seller fails to deliver the correct quantity the buyer is not bound to accept and pay (though if he does accept he must pay at the contract rate[128]). The rule applies where the seller delivers *more* than the quantity contracted for just as much as where he delivers less.[129] The rule is, however, subject to a number of qualifications. First, it can be varied by the provisions of the contract, e.g. by one calling for delivery of "about" the stipulated quantity, or for "five per cent more or less"[130] (though such a margin must not be exceeded[131]). Secondly, the rule does not permit rejection for a wholly trivial discrepancy, e.g. for an excess of 55lbs, in a contract calling for delivery of 4,950 tons of wheat.[132] Thirdly, the rule is subject to a statutory exception which applies where the buyer does *not* deal as a consumer: in such a case he may not reject the whole of the quantity actually delivered on account of a shortfall or excess which is "so slight that it would be unreasonable for him to do so".[133] It seems that a defect may be "slight" for the purpose of this exception even though it is not wholly trivial within the common law exception stated above. The statutory exception applies only where the discrepancy is slight *and* it would be unreasonable for the buyer to reject. Thus it does not apply merely because the discrepancy is "slight", for it may nevertheless be commercially reasonable for the buyer to reject[134]; nor, where the discrepancy is *not* "slight", does the exception apply merely because it would be unreasonable for the buyer to reject (e.g. where his sole motive for rejection was to escape from

---

[123] *The Dominique* [1989] A.C. 1056; Crabtree [1989] L.M.C.L.Q. 289; *The Karin Vatis* [1988] 2 Lloyd's Rep. 330.

[124] See the authorities cited in fn.123; contrast *The Lorna I* [1983] 1 Lloyd's Rep. 373 (where there was no stipulation as to when the freight was *earned*, but only one as to when it was to be *paid*).

[125] [1898] 1 Q.B. 673; cf. *Munro v Butt* (1858) 8 E. & B. 738; *Bolton v Mahadeva* [1972] 1 W.L.R. 1009.

[126] For this requirement, see below, para.17–042.

[127] See *Oxendale v Wetherell* (1829) 9 B. & C. 386–387; *Reuter v Sala* (1879) 4 C.P.D. 239; cf. *Cobec Brazilian Trading & Warehousing Corp v Alfred C Toepfer* [1983] 2 Lloyd's Rep. 386.

[128] Sale of Goods Act 1979, s.30(1). Conversely, the buyer cannot insist on delivery of less than he agreed to accept: *Honck v Muller* (1881) 7 Q.B.D. 92.

[129] Sale of Goods Act 1979, s.30(2).

[130] e.g. *Re Thornett and Fehr and Yuills* [1921] 1 K.B. 219; Sale of Goods Act 1979, s.30(5).

[131] *Tamvaco v Lucas* (1859) 1 E. & E. 581.

[132] *Shipton Anderson & Co v Weil Bros* [1912] 1 K.B. 574.

[133] Sale of Goods Act 1979, s.30(2A). Where *too much* is delivered, the buyer can in any event reject *the excess*.

[134] e.g. because he has resold under a contract from which s.30(2A) is excluded: see below, at fn.136.

a bad bargain[135]). The uncertainty caused by the vagueness of the statutory exception is mitigated by the fact that the exception can be excluded by contrary agreement[136]; and it is submitted that it would be so excluded where the contract had expressly stipulated for a margin and that margin had been exceeded. Finally, the rule entitling the buyer to reject merely on account of quantitative defects does not apply where the contract provides for delivery by instalments, so that, where short delivery is made of one instalment the buyer is not entitled to refuse to accept either future deliveries, or even the instalment in question.[137]

Complete performance justifiably prevented by other party. The rule   17–034
that a party cannot recover anything for partial performance of an entire obligation also applies where that party was willing to complete performance but was justifiably prevented from completing by the other party, e.g. where an employee is dismissed for misconduct.

(b) Severable Obligations

Definition. A contract imposes severable obligations if payment under it is due   17–035
from time to time as performance of a specified part of the contract is rendered. This is the situation under contracts of employment, which typically provide for payment to be made at weekly or monthly intervals, even though the contract may be expressed to continue for longer periods. Similarly, in building contracts the rule in *Sumpter v Hedges*[138] is often excluded by provision for "progress payments", to be made as specified as stages of the work are completed. The principle can be further illustrated by contrasting *Cutter v Powell*[139] with the case in which a seaman agrees to serve at a fixed rate *per month*; under such a contract, he can recover his pay for each completed month although he fails to complete the voyage for which he was engaged.[140] This would be so even though no money was actually to be *paid over* until the end of the voyage. On the same principle, a piece-rate worker does not forfeit wages already earned simply because it was agreed that nothing should actually be paid out to him till the end of each working week and he left or was lawfully dismissed before the end of the week.[141] Similarly, a contract for the sale of goods may be made severable by providing for delivery and payment in instalments. In all these cases, no more than the specified part of the performance need be rendered before the corresponding payment can be claimed. It is also true that, as a general rule, the specified part must be rendered in full. Thus an employee cannot at common law[142] recover his current pay if he is

---

[135] As in *Cunliffe v Harrison* (1851) 6 Ex. 901; below, para.17–039, where the excess (of 50 per cent) was far from "slight".

[136] Sale of Goods Act 1989, s.30(5).

[137] *Regent OHG Aisenstadt und Barig v Francesco of Jermyn Street* [1981] 3 All E.R. 327: such a case is governed by s.31(2) of the Sale of Goods Act 1979. For the contrast between s.31(2) and s.30(1), see below, para.18–031, fn.172. Quaere whether s.30(1) should not apply to the short-delivered instalment itself.

[138] [1898] 1 Q.B. 673; above, para.17–032.

[139] (1795) 6 T.R. 320; above, para.17–032.

[140] *Taylor v Laird* (1856) 25 L.J.Ex. 329; *Button v Thompson* (1869) L.R. 4 C.P. 330.

[141] *Warburton v Heyworth* (1880) 6 Q.B.D. 1.

[142] For the position under the Apportionment Act 1870, s.2, see below, para.17–047.

justifiably dismissed for misconduct during the period at the end of which he is to be paid.[143]

17–036   **Recovery for partial performance.** Where a contract imposes severable obligations, a party who has fully performed the specified part can recover the corresponding payment even though his failure to complete the whole of the promised performance is a breach of contract. In *Ritchie v Atkinson*[144] a shipowner agreed to carry a cargo at a stipulated rate *per ton*. He carried only part of the cargo, and was entitled to recover a corresponding proportion of the freight. But he was later held liable in damages for failing to carry the rest of the cargo.[145] There is a similar liability in damages where performance of one of the specified parts is completed but is defective because it in some way falls short of the performance promised. For example, an employee may serve for the full payment period but fail or refuse, in the course of that period, to carry out some task which he was contractually obliged to perform. The employer is then entitled to damages in respect of that failure or refusal even though he may be bound to pay the agreed remuneration.[146] Whether he is so bound, and what other remedies may be available to him, are matters to be discussed later in this chapter.[147]

(c) Distinction Between Entire and Severable Obligations

17–037   **Obligations, and not contracts, are entire or severable.** In discussions of the cases so far considered, it is sometimes said that the *contracts* are entire or severable. But this is misleading: what is entire or severable is a particular *obligation*[148] arising under the contract. The point is most easily illustrated by reference to contracts for the carriage of goods by sea. Suppose a shipowner agrees to carry 1,000 tons at a stated rate, due on delivery, for each ton carried to London. If he carries 1,000 tons to Southampton he is not entitled to any freight[149]; if he carries 750 tons to London he is prima facie entitled to three quarters of the freight[150]; and if he carries 1,000 tons to London but the goods arrive damaged,

---

[143] *Ridgway v Hungerford Market Co* (1835) 3 A. & E. 171; *Boston Deep Sea Fishing & Ice Co v Ansell* (1888) 39 Ch.D. 339. *Semble* that he can recover remuneration which became due before dismissal though it was earned after a breach of duty justifying dismissal: *Healey v SA Française Rubastic* [1917] 1 K.B. 947; the employer's claim for damages in the form of the salary paid may be offset by the value of the work done: *Brandeaux Advisers Ltd v Chadwick* [2010] EWHC 3241 (QB); [2011] I.R.L.R. 224 at [56]. As to commission on transactions tainted by bribes, see above, para.16–097. For the position where the employee is *not* dismissed see below, para.17–045.

[144] (1808) 10 East 295.

[145] ibid. at 530.

[146] *Sim v Rotherham Metropolitan BC* [1987] Ch. 216; *Miles v Wakefield Metropolitan DC* [1987] A.C. 539 (where the measure of damages was said to be, *obiter*, the wages for the "lost hours of work". Strictly speaking the measure of damages should be the loss suffered by the employer, which is not necessarily the same. cf. below, paras 20–040, 22–012.

[147] See below, paras 17–038, 17–045.

[148] cf. *Cobec Brazilian Trading & Warehousing Corp v Alfred C Toepfer* [1982] 1 Lloyd's Rep. 528 at 531 ("indivisible obligation"), affirmed [1983] 2 Lloyd's Rep. 386; *Baltic Shipping Co Ltd v Dillon* (1993) 176 C.L.R. 344 at 350.

[149] See above, para.17–032, below, para.17–044.

[150] *Ritchie v Atkinson* (1808) 10 East 295. If the contract provides for a "lump sum" freight, the shipowner will, in such a situation, be entitled to the entire freight: *Merchant Shipping Co v Armitage* (1873) L.R. 9 Q.B. 99; *Thomas v Harrowing SS Co* [1915] A.C. 58. He will also be entitled to the whole freight if the contract provides for freight to be computed by reference to the quantity taken on board though it is only payable after discharge of the cargo: see *The Aries* [1977] 1 W.L.R. 185; *The Metula* [1978] 2 Lloyd's Rep. 5; unless the contract provides for a deduction to be made if the quantity delivered is less than that taken on board, as in *The Olympic Brilliance* [1982] 2 Lloyd's Rep. 205.

he will be entitled to full freight[151] unless the damage is so serious that the description under which the goods have been shipped ceases to apply to them: e.g. where cement solidifies as a result of being damaged by water.[152]

A building contract may provide for payments as the work progresses, subject to a "retention fund" to be paid over on completion. There is then a series of severable obligations to complete each stage as well as an entire obligation to complete the whole.[153] In *Sumpter v Hedges*[154] the builder's obligation was entire with respect to the quantity of work to be done; but his claim would not have been dismissed merely because he had failed in some other way to comply with the contract, e.g. by completing a week late[155] or (unless the contract had expressly made his right to payment subject to his doing the work strictly in accordance with the contract[156]) by completing the buildings with minor defects. Thus in *Hoenig v Isaacs*[157] the claimant contracted to redecorate and furnish the defendant's flat for £750. There were minor defects in the furniture, which could have been made good for £55. The defendant argued that the claimant was entitled to no more than a reasonable remuneration for work done in accordance with the contract. But the court held that he was entitled to be paid at the full contract rate (less the cost of making the defects good), as he had substantially completed the work. The obligation of a seller of goods is, again, generally entire as to quantity, but if the correct quantity is delivered he may be able to enforce the contract in spite of the fact that the goods are defective in quality.[158] Of course failure to perform an obligation which is not entire may give the other party a right to terminate the contract on some other ground, e.g. that the failure is substantial[159]; but it does not release him from liability under the present rule.

A question of construction. In the cases so far discussed the distinction   17–038
between entire and severable obligations is clearly settled either by the express terms of the contract or by commercial practice recognised by law. But there may be no rule of law on the point and the contract may be silent or self-contradictory, e.g. where A employs B to paint A's house for £1,000 but fails to say when it is to be paid; or where the contract provides for payment of "£200 per room payable on completion". In such cases the question whether a particular obligation is entire or severable is one of construction; and where a party agrees to do work under a contract, the courts are reluctant to construe the contract so as to require complete performance before any payment becomes due. "Contracts may be so made; but they require plain words to shew that such a bargain was really

---

[151] *Dakin v Oxley* (1864) 15 C.B.(N.S.) 646; *The Brede* [1974] Q.B. 233 (no freight allowed in respect of a part of the goods that was *lost:* see [1972] 2 Lloyd's Rep. at 514, 519; but the Court of Appeal was concerned only with the part of the goods that was *damaged:* [1974] Q.B. at 245).

[152] *Duthie v Hilton* (1868) L.R. 4 C.P. 138; cf. *The Caspian Sea* [1980] 1 W.L.R. 48; *Dakin v Oxley*, above, at 664; contrast *Britannia Distribution Co Ltd v Factor Pace Ltd* [1998] 2 Lloyd's Rep. 420 at 423.

[153] *Hoenig v Isaacs* [1952] 2 All E.R. 176 at 181.

[154] [1898] 1 Q.B. 673.

[155] ibid. at 676.

[156] *Eshelby v Federated European Bank* [1932] 1 K.B. 423.

[157] [1952] 2 All E.R. 176; approving *Dakin & Co Ltd v Lee* [1916] 1 K.B. 566, which had been doubted in *Eshelby v Federated European Bank* [1932] 1 K.B. 423; *Williams v Roffey Bros & Nicholls (Contractors) Ltd* [1991] 1 Q.B. 1; below, fn.173.

[158] e.g. as in *The Hansa Nord* [1976] Q.B. 44; below, para.18–047, fn.300.

[159] See below, para.18–025.

intended".[160] If the contract contains contradictory provisions the courts tend to give greater weight to those making the obligation to work a severable one. Thus where a contract provided (1) for payment at a fixed rate per month, but (2) that nothing was to be paid till performance was complete, the first clause prevailed over the second, i.e. the contract was construed as imposing severable obligations.[161] In one type of case this hostility towards entire obligations has been reinforced by statute: an agreement by a seaman to abandon his right to wages in case the ship is lost is void.[162]

17–039   **Sale of goods.** The reason why the courts are reluctant to construe obligations to do work as entire is that such a construction will often lead to the unjust enrichment of the party receiving the partial or defective performance.[163] There is no such reluctance in contracts for the sale of goods: we have seen that the buyer is not generally bound to accept a different quantity from that contracted for[164]; nor is he bound, unless the contract so provides,[165] to accept delivery in instalments.[166] This state of the law does not give rise to any danger of unjust enrichment: if a buyer of goods rejects delivery of the wrong quantity, the goods will be returned to the seller. But even in this type of case rejection may cause a different type of hardship to the seller, namely that of throwing back on him the risk of market fluctuations. In *Cunliffe v Harrison*[167] a seller of wine delivered more than the agreed quantity. It was held that the buyer was not bound to accept any part of the wine, "although it may be that the refusal to take the wine was not bona fide but grounded upon the fact that the wine had fallen in price".[168]

(d) So-called Doctrine of Substantial Performance[169]

17–040   Cases such as *Hoenig v Isaacs*[170] are sometimes explained on the ground that the claimant had "substantially" performed an "entire contract".[171] It is submitted that the explanation is unsatisfactory since it is based on the error that *contracts*, as opposed to particular *obligations*, can be entire.[172] The basis of *Hoenig v Isaacs* is that the builder, even if he was under an entire obligation as to the quantity of

---

[160] *Button v Thompson* (1869) L.R. 4 C.P. 330 at 342; cf. *Roberts v Havelock* (1832) 3 B. & Ad. 404; *Davidson v Jones-Fenleigh* (1980) 124 S.J. 204.

[161] See *The Juliana* (1822) 2 Dods. 504.

[162] Merchant Shipping Act 1995, s.38(1) (reversing the common law rule that freight was the "mother of wages").

[163] See below, para.17–042.

[164] See above, para.17–033.

[165] On this question of construction, contrast *Reuter v Sala* (1879) 4 C.P.D. 239 with *Brandt v Lawrence* (1876) 1 Q.B.D. 344.

[166] Sale of Goods Act 1979, s.31(1).

[167] (1851) 6 Ex. 901.

[168] ibid. at 907; of course it is possible that the seller was not acting bona fide either but that he was trying to unload an excessive quantity on a falling market.

[169] Beck 38 M.L.R. 413.

[170] [1952] 2 All E.R. 176; above, para.17–037.

[171] *Geipel v Smith* (1872) L.R. 7 Q.B. 404 at 411; cf. *Dakin v Lee* [1916] 1 K.B. 566 at 598; *Sim v Rotherham MBC* [1987] Ch. 216 at 253; *Williams v Roffey Bros & Nicholls (Contractors) Ltd* [1991] 1 Q.B. 1 at 8–10; no such view is in terms stated by the court in *Hoenig v Isaacs*, above.

[172] See above, para.17–037.

work to be done, was under no such obligation as to its quality.[173] Defects of quality therefore fell to be considered under the general requirement of substantial failure, and on the facts there was no such failure.[174] To say that an obligation is entire *means* that it must be completely performed before payment becomes due. Suppose a contract is made to carry goods from Melbourne to London and the freight is payable on delivery in London. If the goods are carried only to Southampton, the carrier may have "substantially" performed; but he is not entitled to the freight.[175] In relation to "entire" obligations, there is no scope for any doctrine of "substantial performance".[176]

(e) Voluntary Acceptance of Benefit

Where a party terminates for breach of an entire obligation[177] but "voluntarily"   **17–041**
accepts the partial or defective[178] performance he must make some payment for it.

The present principle applies only if the benefit is accepted "voluntarily".[179] A person is not considered to accept a benefit "voluntarily" if he merely takes possession of his own property. Thus a shipowner who discharges cargo at an intermediate port cannot recover freight pro rata merely because the cargo-owner has under protest taken possession of his own goods there.[180] In *Sumpter v Hedges*[181] the builder's claim for the reasonable value of his work was dismissed on similar grounds. Such a claim would succeed only if a "new contract"[182] to pay a reasonable sum could be inferred. No such inference could be drawn from the mere fact that the defendant had reoccupied his own land with the partly completed buildings on it; he had no real "option whether he will take the benefit of the work done or not."[183] He did, however, "voluntarily" make use of certain loose materials left by the builder on the site and was held liable for the reasonable value of these materials.

---

[173] *Williams v Roffey Bros & Nicholls (Contractors) Ltd* [1991] 1 Q.B. 1 (where a sub-contractor recovered instalments subject to a "small deduction for defective and *incomplete* items" ([1991] 1 Q.B. 1 at 17) purports to follow *Hoenig v Isaacs*, but that case was concerned only with defective, not with incomplete, items.

[174] Contrast *Lawson v Supasink* (1984) Tr.L. 37 (where qualitative defects in kitchen installations were sufficiently serious to justify rescission).

[175] See above, para.17–032; cf. *Metcalfe v Britannia Ironworks* (1877) 2 Q.B.D. 423.

[176] Even when correctly understood, it has no application at all where the defendant is not in breach, e.g. where a builder has done less than the work anticipated in a fixed-price contract: *SWI Ltd v P & I Data Services Ltd* [2007] EWCA Civ 663; [2007] B.L.R. 430.

[177] In the absence of termination, the parties' rights and obligations continue to be governed by the contract, as opposed to the law of restitution, but see the employment cases discussed at para.17–045 below where the contract had not been terminated.

[178] i.e. where the defect prevents complete performance of the obligation in question: see above, para.17–037; cf. *Bolton v Mahadeva*, below, para.17–042.

[179] *Christy v Row* (1808) 1 Taunt. 300; cf. *Lambourn v Cruden* (1841) 2 M. & G. 253 at 256.

[180] *Metcalfe v Britannia Ironworks Co* (1877) 2 Q.B.D. 423; cf. above, para.17–032.

[181] [1898] 1 Q.B. 673; above, para.17–032.

[182] The language of a "new contract" may no longer be entirely apt given the rejection of "quasi-contract" as the basis of a common law restitutionary claim (*Westdeutsche Landesbank Girozentrale v Islington LBC* [1996] A.C. 669 at 710; *Cleveland Bridge UK Ltd v Multiplex Constructions UK Ltd* [2010] EWCA Civ 139 at [118]–[138]). It is retained either on the basis that it is confined to a "genuine" implied contract (*Chitty on Contracts* (30th edn) at 21–021, 21–073) or, as exemplifying the need in the present group of cases for a voluntary acceptance of the benefit.

[183] *Westdeutsche Landesbank Girozentrale v Islington LBC* [1996] A.C. 669 at 676.

17–042   **Unjust enrichment.** The object of the requirement of a "new contract" is, no doubt, to protect the party receiving the partial or defective performance, who may be prejudiced by having to pay pro rata or a reasonable sum. He may have suffered loss in consequence of the failure in performance, and, if the failure does not amount to a breach,[184] termination of the contract may be his only remedy.[185] Even if there has been a breach, the damages legally recoverable for it may fall short of the actual loss suffered. The victim may have stipulated for complete performance before payment precisely in order to protect himself against these risks. On the other hand, the failure in performance may not cause any loss at all,[186] or it may cause a loss worth much less than the value of the partial performance. In such cases the requirement of a "new contract" may lead to the unjust enrichment of the party by whom such performance has been received. Under the rule in *Sumpter v Hedges* a landowner may get nearly completed buildings for nothing. This did not actually happen in the leading case itself, in which considerable payments had been made to the builder on account of the work.[187] But in *Bolton v Mahadeva*[188] a builder recovered nothing for his defective performance of a contract to install a central heating system for £560, even though no part of this sum had been paid to him, the defects in his work cost only £170 to put right, and the house-owner's other damages were assessed at £15. Again, where a shipowner discharges goods at an intermediate port, the cargo-owner may get the benefit of having them carried a considerable distance for nothing. This possibility is strikingly illustrated by a case in which it was held that the cargo-owner was not bound to pay anything even though the failure to carry the goods to their destination apparently benefited him, the goods having been sold for *more* at the intermediate port than they were worth at the agreed destination.[189] At the same time the requirement of a "new" contract may bear very harshly on the party conferring the benefit; and therefore the requirement that acceptance of the benefit must be "voluntary" so as to support the inference of a new contract is, or may be, modified in a number of situations.

17–043   **Sale of goods.** The clearest modification of the requirement of voluntary acceptance can be seen in cases in which a seller of goods delivers the wrong quantity, e.g. a quantity less than that contracted for. In such a case the buyer can generally reject the goods[190] but if he "accepts" them he "must pay for them at the contract rate."[191] This acceptance need not be "voluntary" in the full sense, for the buyer may do acts amounting to "acceptance" before he knows of the defect in delivery.[192]

---

[184] e.g. because it is the subject of some lawful excuse: see below, para.17–059.

[185] See, generally, Ch.18. Termination is available for a sufficiently serious failure to perform, which may not (but often will) amount to a breach (below, para.18–001).

[186] See below, at fn.189.

[187] The value of the work done is stated to be "about £333" and the builder had received £219 (67 L.J.Q.B. 545) or £119 plus two horses worth £100 (46 W.R. 464). Hence the total enrichment of the defendant appears to have been at the most £114, against which any loss suffered by him should be set off. The actual result may not have been unjust; certainly the builder's claim for £230 (78 L.T. 378) or £222 (46 W.R. 464) seems excessive.

[188] [1972] 1 W.L.R. 1009.

[189] *Hopper v Burness* (1876) 1 C.P.D. 137; it was said that there was no hardship to the shipowner as "the proper remedy is by insurance of freight" (at 141).

[190] See above, para.17–033.

[191] Sale of Goods Act 1979, s.30(1).

[192] See below, para.18–083.

Deviation. A second situation in which the requirement of "voluntary" accep-   **17–044**
tance may be modified arises where a carrier by sea deviates.[193] This undoubtedly
gives the cargo–owner the right to terminate the contract[194]; but he may not
exercise this right and may accept the goods after the carrier has carried them to
their agreed destination. This acceptance of the goods is no more "voluntary"
than taking possession of goods which have been discharged without their owner's
consent at an intermediate port; but dicta in the House of Lords in *Hain SS Co
Ltd v Tate & Lyle Ltd*[195] support the view that the shipowner may in such a case
be entitled to a reasonable freight. This is not necessarily the same as the
stipulated freight, so that the risk of any fall in freight rates would be on the
carrier; but it seems most unlikely that he would be allowed to rely on the
deviation to secure the benefit of any rise in freight rates.

Contracts of employment. A third modification of the requirement that   **17–045**
acceptance of the benefit must be "voluntary" may exist where breaches of a
contract of employment are committed in the course of an industrial dispute. Such
a breach may take the form, not only of an outright refusal to work, but also of a
refusal merely to carry out certain specified tasks. If (as will often be the case) the
refusal amounts to a breach giving rise to the right to terminate,[196] the employer
is at common law entitled to dismiss the employee. But he may not exercise that
power and instead follow one of three other courses of action. First, he may
voluntarily accept such services as the employee is willing to render. In that case,
he can at the very least deduct from the employee's wages, by way of damages, any
loss which he has suffered as a result of the breach.[197] Even if he has not suffered
any loss, he can deduct from the employee's pay such part of the agreed wages as
is attributable to the work which the employee has refused to perform[198]: that
amount (at least) will not have been earned by reason of the employee's failure to
perform a condition precedent.[199] Secondly, he may tell the employee that he
declines to accept the services (falling short of those due under the contract) which
the employee is prepared to render, and actually does render. In that event, the
employee is not entitled to pay for any period during which no services are
rendered[200]; nor is he entitled to any pay for rendering services falling short of
those due, even if the employer has not physically prevented him from rendering
them.[201] Thirdly, the employer may accept the services which the employee is

---

[193] For deviation, see para.7–033.

[194] See above, para.7–033.

[195] (1936) 41 Com.Cas. 350 at 358, 367, doubting contrary dicta in the Court of Appeal 34 Com.Cas.
259 at 285. The dicta in the House of Lords are accepted in *Scrutton on Charterparties* (20th edn),
p.260, and in Carver, *Carriage of Goods by Sea* (13th edn), para.1197; for the basis of liability, see *Carver
on Bills of Lading* (2nd edn), paras 9–036—9–059; cf. *Bornman v Tooke* (1808) 1 Camp. 376. Contrast
Pilbrow v Pearless De Rougement & Co [1999] 3 All E.R. 355 at 360 (no claim for the reasonable value
of the services rendered was made in that case).

[196] See below, para.17–072.

[197] *Sim v Rotherham Metropolitan BC* [1987] Ch. 216, where the action was not for the agreed wages,
but for a declaration that the employer was not entitled to deduct damages: see *Miles v Wakefield
Metropolitan DC* [1987] A.C. 539 at 574–575; Napier [1987] C.L.J. 44.

[198] *Miles v Wakefield Metropolitan DC*, above; McMullen 51 M.L.R. 234; the contrary assumption
made in *Sim v Rotherham Metropolitan BC*, above, at 255) is no longer maintainable.

[199] See above, para.17–015.

[200] *Ticehurst & Thompson v British Telecommunications* [1992] I.C.R. 383.

[201] *Wiluszynski v Tower Hamlets LBC* [1989] I.C.R. 493; McLean [1990] C.L.J. 28; Mead 106 L.Q.R.
192; *Macpherson v Lambeth LBC* [1988] I.R.L.R. 470.

prepared to render, and do so, not voluntarily, but "of necessity"[202]: he may do this either because he has no practical choice (where he cannot in fact prevent the employee from gaining access to his place of work), or because he is required to accept the services offered in order to mitigate his loss.[203] In such a case there has been no "voluntary" acceptance of a benefit; but there is nevertheless some support for the view that the employer must pay a reasonable remuneration for the services actually rendered.[204] This view seems to be based on unjust enrichment rather than on a "new contract": the employer is liable because he has received a benefit, not because he has impliedly agreed to pay for it. The difficulty in accepting this view, however, arises precisely because in the case put the employer has *not* terminated the contract, so that prima facie the rights and duties of the parties continue to be governed by that contract.[205]

17–046   **Wrongful Prevention of Performance.** In the cases just discussed, the courts were concerned with the reasonable remuneration of the party in breach. If, in a contract under which one party (A) is not to be paid until he completes performance, A begins to perform but the other party (B) wrongfully refuses to let him complete, A can, no doubt, claim damages for breach of contract.[206] Alternatively, he can claim a quantum meruit for the work he has done. In *Planché v Colburn*[207] A agreed to write a book on costume and ancient armour which was to appear in serial form in B's periodical. B stopped publishing the periodical when A had written the greater part of the work, and it was held that A was entitled to a quantum meruit. No benefit appears to have been received by B which may suggest that this rule differs from those applicable when the claim is made by the party in breach.[208] Alternatively, it has been suggested[209] that the award in *Planché v Colburn* is better viewed as being the equivalent of damages and that for claims by the innocent party, just as much as for claims by the party in breach, it is necessary to establish that the defendant has been benefited.[210]

(f) Apportionment Act 1870

17–047   Section 2 of this Act provides that

> "All rents, annuities, dividends and other periodical payments in the nature of income ... shall ... be considered as accruing from day to day, and shall be apportionable in respect of time accordingly."

By s.5 "annuities" includes "salaries and pensions"; and by s.7 the Act does not apply where it is "expressly stipulated that no apportionment shall take place."

---

[202] *Miles v Wakefield Metropolitan DC* [1987] A.C. 539 at 553.

[203] ibid. at 561; cf. below, para.20–118.

[204] ibid. at 553 (per Lord Brightman) and 561 (per Lord Templeman). The point is left open by Lord Brandon (at 552) and Lord Oliver (at 576).

[205] ibid. at 552 (per Lord Bridge), and cf. below, para.22–023.

[206] It is assumed here that A could have completed but for B's wrongful refusal, so that the problem discussed at paras 17–025—17–030, above does not arise.

[207] (1831) 8 Bing. 14.

[208] See paras 17–041—17–045.

[209] Burrows, *The Law of Restitution* (3rd edn) at 346.

[210] As appears to have been the case in *De Bernardy v Harding* (1853) 8 Exch. 822.

It seems that a "periodical" payment refers to a sum or sums payable under a contract at the end of a stipulated time, or at fixed intervals of time. A single lump sum payable for a specific piece of work would not be a periodical payment; and this is one reason why the Act would not apply to a case like *Cutter v Powell*.[211] Nor would the payment be periodical merely because the contract stipulated the time within which the piece of work was to be done: thus the Act would not apply to a case like *Sumpter v Hedges*[212] even though the contract in that case contained a completion date.[213] A bonus, the payment and level of which is dependent upon an uncertain factor, such as the level of profits made by an employer does not qualify as a "salary", nor as a "periodical payment".[214]

In *Fassihi v Item Software (UK) Ltd*[215] the Court of Appeal held that the Act entitles a person whose salary is payable at the end of a stipulated period to recover on a proportionate basis if he works for only part of the period. This brought to an end a considerable period of uncertainty about the application of the Act to "part-earned" salary,[216] but it did not entirely resolve a further question which is whether the Act can be invoked where the party in question is in breach of contract. This was, in fact, the situation in the *Fassihi* case, but while it was decided at first instance that the Act could be invoked where the employee was guilty of misconduct, this further issue was not the subject of any appeal. Nonetheless, Holman J. felt that the issue "demands an answer" and observed that there was nothing in the Act to exclude its application. This interpretation of the Act is to be welcomed.[217] Earlier authorities which at least appeared to suggest that the Act cannot be invoked by a party in breach were considered by the Court of Appeal in relation to the question of "part-earned" salary and found not to stand as authority on the interpretation of the Act at all.[218]

Criticism. Notwithstanding the mitigations of the rule in *Sumpter v Hedges*,[219] a party who has failed to complete performance of an entire obligation may have no rights at all against the other party. This can plainly lead to the unjust enrichment of the latter party, and seems to go further than necessary for his protection.[220] He should normally be liable to make some payment for benefits received, though he should be entitled to a deduction in respect of any loss that he has suffered as result of the failure in performance.[221]

17–048

---

[211] (1795) 6 T.R. 320; apportionment would also on such facts be excluded by the express terms of the contract: see above, para.17–032.

[212] [1898] 1 Q.B. 673.

[213] See 67 L.J.Q.B. 545; 78 L.T. 378; 46 W.R. 464.

[214] *Vaught v Tel Sell UK Ltd* [2005] EWHC 2404 at [152].

[215] [2004] EWCA Civ 1244; [2004] I.R.L.R. 928.

[216] Earlier authorities providing implicit support for the application of the Act (see the cases to follow) were preferred to those seemingly against (see below, fn.218): *Moriarty v Regent's Garage Co* [1921] 1 K.B. 423 (reversed on procedural grounds: [1921] 2 K.B. 766, where the issue was left open); *Sim v Rotherham Metropolitan BC* [1987] Ch. 216, at 255; *Treacy v Corcoran* (1874) I.R. 8 C.L. 40. See also: *Thames Water Utilities v Reynolds* [1996] I.R.L.R. 186.

[217] Williams 57 L.Q.R. 381–383; cf. Matthews 2 Legal Studies 302 whose more restricted interpretation of the Act was rejected by the Court in the *Fassihi* case.

[218] *Boston Deep Sea Fishing and Ice Co v Ansell* (1888) 39 Ch.D. 339; *Re Central de Kaap Gold Mines* (1899) 69 L.J.Ch. 18; *McConnell's Claim* [1901] 1 Ch. 728; *Healey v SA Française Rubastic* [1917] 1 K.B. 947; *Miles v Wakefield* [1987] A.C. 539 at 570.

[219] See above, paras 17–041—17–047.

[220] Burrows, *The Law of Restitution* (3rd edn) at 356–358; *Cleveland Bridge UK Ltd v Multiplex Constructions UK Ltd* [2010] EWCA Civ 139 at [118]–[138].

[221] See Law Com. No.121; not to be implemented: Law Commission, 19th Annual Report, para.2.11; Burrows 47 M.L.R. 76. See also McFarlane and Stevens 118 L.Q.R. 596.

5. BREACH

17–049   A breach of contract is committed when a party without lawful excuse fails or refuses to perform what is due from him under the contract, or performs defectively or incapacitates himself from performing. A breach of contract may entitle the injured party to claim damages, the agreed sum, specific performance or an injunction, in accordance with the principles discussed in Chs 20 and 21. In appropriate circumstances he may be entitled to more than one of these remedies: e.g. to an injunction and damages. Breach may also give the injured party the right to "terminate" the contract in the circumstances which are discussed in Ch.18.[222] An "anticipatory breach" may occur before performance is due and is considered separately below.[223]

(a) Failure or Refusal to Perform

17–050   Failure or refusal to perform a contractual promise when performance has fallen due is prima facie a breach. This point looks obvious enough, but it does raise a number of problems.

17–051   **Whether stipulation is a promise or a condition.** It must be determined whether the stipulation which has not been complied with is indeed a promise, or only a condition. In the standard case of a unilateral contract, where A promises B £100 if B will walk to York,[224] B has not promised to do anything: his walking to York is merely a condition[225] of A's liability. Hence B commits no breach if he does not start the walk, or if, having started, he fails to complete it. But the distinction between the two types of stipulations is sometimes hard to draw.[226] It is, for example, not clearly settled whether an estate agent who is engaged to find a buyer for a house makes any promise to do anything[227]; and it is also possible for a person to commit a breach by failing to complete performance of an act which he was not originally bound to do if, by beginning performance, he impliedly promised to complete it.[228]

17–052   **Whether performance has become due.** Obviously performance is not due before the stipulated time: a promise to pay £100 tomorrow is not broken by failing to pay today. But greater difficulty arises where the contract, or the liability of one party, is subject to a condition. Where the contract is subject to a *contingent* condition precedent,[229] failure to perform is not a breach if the condition has not occurred; nor does the principal obligation of either party become due if one of them fails to bring about the condition on which the binding force of that obligation depends. At most, that party may be liable for breach of some subsidiary duty: e.g. he is often under a duty not actively to prevent the occurrence of the condition; and he may be under a duty to make reasonable efforts to bring about

---

[222] See below, para.18–025 et seq.
[223] See below, para.17–073.
[224] See above, para.2–051.
[225] i.e. in the contingent sense (above, para.2–104) as B makes no promise.
[226] cf. above, para.2–051; and see below, paras 18–072—18–074.
[227] See above, para.2–056.
[228] See above, para.2–051.
[229] See above, para.2–104.

its occurrence.[230] On the other hand, where the liability of A is subject to a *promissory* condition[231] to be performed by B, failure by B to perform that promise not only puts B in breach[232] of his principal obligation, but also prevents A's obligation to perform his counter-promise from becoming due.

Whether party under any obligation. A contract may contain a promise by   17–053
one party, but fail to make it clear exactly what (if anything) has been promised in return by the other. In *Churchward v R.*[233] a contractor agreed with the Admiralty that he would for 11 years carry from Dover to Calais such mail as he should from time to time be asked to carry by the Admiralty or the Postmaster-General. He was not given any mail to carry and claimed damages. One reason why his claim failed was that the agreement did not oblige the Admiralty to employ him: it only obliged him to carry mail if the Admiralty asked him to do so. The agreement thus resembled a tender by the contractor and amounted to no more than an offer, which might be accepted by the Admiralty from time to time.[234] A document which in terms imposes an obligation on only one party may, indeed, by implication also oblige the other to do something which is not expressly stated. Thus it was said in *Churchward v R.* that

> "Where there is an engagement to manufacture some article [for a customer] a corresponding engagement on the other party is implied to take it, for otherwise it would be impossible that the party bestowing his services could claim any remuneration."[235]

Similarly, where a document is headed "contract of sale" and in terms only imposes an obligation on the seller to sell, the court might imply an obligation on the buyer to buy.[236] But no such implication will be made where the terms of the document or the surrounding circumstances negative any intention on the prospective buyer's part to give such an undertaking.[237]

Specifying the obligation. A contract may clearly oblige a party to do   17–054
something but fail to specify exactly what. The question sometimes arises, for example, whether an employer is bound only to pay the agreed wages, or whether he must actually give the employee work. The traditional view is that generally the employer need only pay wages,[238] though this rule does not apply where one of the objects of the contract is to enable the employee to gain, or retain, a skill, or to keep his name before the public. Thus a person who employs a well-known actor must actually give him a part in the play for which he was engaged.[239] It has also

---

[230] See above, paras 2–105—2–111.
[231] See above, paras 17–015—17–017.
[232] e.g. *Trans Trust SPRL v Danubian Trading Co* [1952] 2 Q.B. 297; above, para.17–015.
[233] (1865) L.R. 1 Q.B. 173; cf. *R. v Demers* [1900] A.C. 103.
[234] cf. above, para.2–022.
[235] *Churchward v R.*, above, at 195; cf. *The Unique Mariner (No.2)* [1979] 1 Lloyd's Rep. 37 at 51–52.
[236] *Firstpost Homes Ltd v Johnson* [1995] 1 W.L.R. 1567 at 1574.
[237] ibid.
[238] *Turner v Sawdon* [1901] 2 K.B. 653; cf. *Delaney v Staples* [1992] 1 A.C. 687 at 692 (discussing so called "garden leave"); *Marshall (Cambridge) Ltd v Hamblin* [1994] I.R.L.R. 260; *Abrahams v Performing Rights Society* [1995] I.C.R. 1028.
[239] *Herbert Clayton & Jack Waller Ltd v Oliver* [1930] A.C. 209.

been said that the law in some cases recognises a "right to work"[240] and that the question whether the contract gives rise to such a right depends on its express or implied terms.[241] If the employee needs to work to acquire or retain a skill or reputation, this fact is likely to support an implication that the employer must actually give him work. It does not follow that this duty can be specifically enforced[242]; but an employer who breaks a duty to provide work may be liable in damages on that account.

17–055   **Failure to perform in substance.** There may be a breach if a party *in substance* refuses to perform, and paradoxically he may do this by insisting with too great literalness on the terms of the contract. "Working to rule" in order to disrupt the employer's business may therefore be a breach of a contract of employment.[243]

(b) Defective Performance

17–056   The phrase "defective performance" arguably contains an element of self-contradiction, in the sense that a person who promises to do one thing does not perform if he does another. Where the "defect" in performance is of a particularly serious kind, the acts done by the party in breach may indeed amount or lead to non-performance rather than defective performance, as in the case of the seller who promises beans but delivers peas.[244] But where the performance rendered is of the same kind as that promised, differing from it only in point of time, quantity or quality, it is reasonable to refer to it as defective performance.[245] It undoubtedly amounts to a breach; but the effects of such a breach often differ from those of a complete failure or refusal to perform.[246]

(c) Incapacitating Oneself

17–057   A person may break a contract by incapacitating himself from performing it. Thus a seller commits a breach of contract for the sale of a specific thing if he sells it to a third party[247]; and a shipowner commits a breach of a charterparty if he sells the ship to a third party "free from any . . . charter engagement".[248] But a person who is entitled to make a choice as to the method of performance does not incapacitate himself merely by declaring that he will perform in a way that is impossible. For example, a seller of generic goods does not put himself in breach

[240] *Langston v AUEW* [1974] 1 W.L.R. 185; cf. *Gunton v Richmond-upon-Thames LBC* [1981] Ch. 448 at 472 (exclusion from place of work an "immediate breach" though salary was paid for a further month). Even if the employer is not in breach by failing to provide work, he may be unable to restrain such an employee from working for others in breach of another term of the contract of employment: see *Provident Financial Group Plc v Hayward* [1989] I.C.R. 160; below, para.21–056.

[241] *William Hill Organisation Ltd v Tucker* [1998] I.R.L.R. 313.

[242] *Langston v AUEW (No.2)* [1974] I.C.R. 510; below, para.21–035.

[243] *Secretary of State v ASLEF (No.2)* [1972] 2 Q.B. 455; contrast *Power Packing Casemakers Ltd v Faust* [1983] Q.B. 471 (ban on overtime not a breach).

[244] *Chanter v Hopkins* (1838) 4 M. & W. 399 at 404; *Pilbrow v Pearless De Rougemont & Co* [1999] 3 All E.R. 355.

[245] *The Stork* [1955] 2 Q.B. 68 at 76; *Leeds Shipping Co Ltd v Soc Française Bunge* [1958] 2 Lloyd's Rep. 124 at 145; *Pilbrow v Pearless De Rougemont & Co*, above, at 360.

[246] See below, para.18–025 et seq., paras 22–001—22–012.

[247] *Bowdell v Parsons* (1808) 10 East 359; *Lovelock v Franklyn* (1846) 8 Q.B. 371.

[248] *Omnium D'Entreprises v Sutherland* [1919] 1 K.B. 618.

merely by telling the buyer that he will make delivery from a source which does not exist.[249] He is normally[250] entitled and bound to deliver from another source, and is in breach only if he fails or refuses to do so.

Insolvency. A person is not incapacitated from performing a contract under   **17–058** which he is obliged to pay money, merely because he is insolvent.[251] If the contract is profitable, his trustee in bankruptcy will probably wish to enforce it and provide funds to discharge his obligations under it. Insolvency incapacitates a contracting party only if no assets are set aside out of his estate for the performance of the contract.[252] Where, after a contract has been made, one party to it is adjudged bankrupt, the other party may apply to the court for an order discharging obligations under the contract; and the court may make such an order on such terms as to payment of damages by the bankrupt or by the other party as appear to the court to be equitable.[253]

(d) Without Lawful Excuse

Illustrations. There is no breach when non-performance of a contract is   **17–059** justified by some lawful excuse. In one sense, such an excuse for non-performance exists where one party is entitled to refuse to perform because the other has failed to perform a promissory condition precedent or a concurrent condition. In such cases, performance of the former party's obligation has never become due. This topic has already been discussed[254]; our present concern is with cases in which *after* an obligation has accrued, an extraneous event occurs which interferes with its performance. The event may interfere so seriously with performance that both parties are discharged under the doctrine of frustration (to be discussed in Ch.19). But even where its effects are less drastic, it may still provide a party with an excuse for non-performance. Thus an employee who does not go to work because he is ill is not in breach,[255] even though the illness is not so serious as to frustrate the contract (so that performance must be resumed when the illness is over). Other extraneous circumstances may similarly justify refusal to perform, or to accept performance, at least in part. In one case it was, for example, held that the owner of a London café, who had engaged the claimants to give cabaret performances there, was justified in refusing to allow such performances to take place on the day on which King George V died, and on the following day, but not on the four days after that.[256] Again, if a farmer agrees to sell 500 tons of wheat to be grown on his farm and, through no fault of his, only 200 are produced, he is not liable for failing

---

[249] *The Vladimir Ilich* [1975] 1 Lloyd's Rep. 322 at 329.

[250] In *The Vladimir Ilich*, above, the seller would not have been entitled to do this under the contract, since this provided that he was to give a "notice of appropriation" and that a valid notice of appropriation, once given, could not be withdrawn. But by treating the notice as *invalid* the buyer had precluded himself from relying on this provision.

[251] *Re Agra Bank* (1867) L.R. 5 Eq. 160.

[252] *Ex p. Chalmers* (1873) L.R. 8 Ch.App. 289; cf. *Sale Continuation Ltd v Austin Taylor & Co* [1968] 2 Q.B. 849.

[253] Insolvency Act 1986, s.345(1) and (2).

[254] See above, paras 17–015—17–017.

[255] *Poussard v Spiers* (1875–76) L.R. 1 Q.B.D. 410 at 414; below, para.19–023, but contrast *Bettini v Gye* (1875–76) L.R. 1 Q.B.D. 183 at 189. The excuse may extend to prevention by other causes: see *Sim v Rotherham Metropolitan BC* [1987] Ch. 216 at 254 (teacher locked in school lavatory "through no fault of his own").

[256] *Minnevitch v Café de Paris (Londres) Ltd* [1936] 1 All E.R. 884.

to produce the other 300 tons, though he will be liable in damages if he fails to deliver the 200 tons.[257] And a tenant is not in breach of a covenant to redevelop a site by a specified date if such redevelopment is prevented by an order listing a building on the site as of special architectural interest.[258]

17–060   **Express provision.** Excuses for non-performance may be provided by the contract itself, which may contain "exceptions" absolving a party from his duty to perform if he is prevented from doing so by specified circumstances, such as strikes or similar delays. Failure to perform, if brought about by such events, is not a breach at all. The function of the "exception" is not to exclude liability for an assumed breach but rather to define the scope of the contracting party's obligations.[259]

17–061   **Time.** A party relying on an excuse for non-performance must show that the excuse existed at the time of his refusal to perform: it is not enough for him to show that it arose or would (if the other party had not discharged the contract on account of the refusal) have arisen at some later time.[260] Suppose, for example, that a seller of wheat of a certain description is about to deliver wheat of a different description. The buyer cannot at this stage rely on the non-conformity as a ground for discharging the contract, for the seller is not actually in breach until he tenders non-conforming goods.[261] Once a defective tender has been made, the buyer is indeed entitled to reject it, but it still does not follow that he is entitled to terminate the contract; for if, within the time allowed for delivery, the seller can make a further good tender, the buyer is normally bound to accept it.[262]

17–062   **Whether excuse must be stated.** The general rule is that a refusal to perform by a party who has an excuse for non-performance is not a breach, even though he did not state the excuse, or even know of it, at the time of the refusal. Thus an employer can lawfully dismiss an employee who has committed a breach of duty justifying dismissal, though he did not at the time of the dismissal know of the breach, and though at that time he gave some other, insufficient, reason, or no reason at all.[263] Similarly a buyer can reject goods, if there has been a breach of condition, even though he did not know of the breach; and the rejection will not be wrongful merely because at the time he mistakenly alleged breach of some other condition.[264]

---

[257] *Howell v Coupland* (1876) 1 Q.B.D. 258; *H R and S Sainsbury Ltd v Street* [1972] 1 W.L.R. 834; Thornely [1973] C.L.J. 15; Goldberg 88 L.Q.R. 464.

[258] *John Lewis Properties v Viscount Chelsea* [1993] 2 E.G.L.R. 77.

[259] *The Angelia* [1973] 1 W.L.R. 210; above, para.7–021.

[260] *British & Beningtons Ltd v NW Cachar Tea Co* [1923] A.C. 48; above, para.17–027; cf. *The Siboen and the Sibotre* [1976] 1 Lloyd's Rep. 293.

[261] *Braithwaite v Foreign Hardwood Co Ltd* [1905] 2 K.B. 543, as explained in *Taylor v Oakes, Roncoroni & Co* (1922) 38 T.L.R. 349 at 351; and see above, para.17–027.

[262] See above, para.17–004.

[263] *Ridgway v Hungerford Market Co* (1835) 3 A. & E. 171; *Baillie v Kell* (1838) 4 Bing.N.C. 638; *Boston Deep Sea Fishing & Ice Co v Ansell* (1888) 39 Ch.D. 339; *Cyril Leonard & Co v Simo Securities Trust Ltd* [1972] 1 W.L.R. 80; *Glencore Grain Rotterdam BV v LORICO* [1997] 2 Lloyd's Rep. 386 at 394; *Stocznia Gdanska SA v Latvian Shipping Co* [2002] EWCA Civ 889; [2002] 2 Lloyd's Rep 436 at [32]; *South Caribbean Trading Ltd v Trafigura Beheer BV* [2004] EWHC 2676 (Comm); [2005] 1 Lloyd's Rep. 128 at [133]–[134]; *Reinwood Ltd v L Brown & Sons Ltd* [2008] EWCA Civ 1090; 121 Con L.R. 1, below para.18–009, fn.59.

[264] e.g. *Arcos Ltd v E A Ronaasen & Sons* [1933] A.C. 470.

The rule may sometimes be justifiable on the ground that it prevents the party in breach from benefiting from the concealment of his own wrong. But it can also cause surprise and even hardship to the party in breach, and it has therefore been limited in a number of ways.[265] A party cannot rely on an excuse which he did not specify at the time of his refusal to perform "if the point which was not taken is one which if taken could have been put right."[266] This might be the position if the effect of a buyer's failure to state the ground which justified rejection was to deprive the seller of the opportunity of curing the defect and making a second good tender[267] within the time allowed for performance.[268] The case is even stronger if the buyer makes some groundless objection to the seller's tender and the seller incurs trouble or expense in investigating or seeking to cure that objection.[269] In such circumstances, an estoppel can arise, precluding the buyer from alleging the existence of another, sufficient, reason for his refusal to perform.

The *Panchaud Frères* case. One controversial case goes further in holding that a buyer who failed to specify a defect in existence at the time of rejection could not later rely on it, even though the defect was one which the seller could *not* have cured and even though the seller did not in any way change his position in consequence of the buyer's original failure to specify it. This is the *Panchaud Frères* case,[270] where maize was sold under a contract which provided for shipment to be made in "June/July". The goods were shipped in August and the buyers could have rejected them on this ground. But they paid against documents which would, if carefully examined, have revealed the fact of late shipment; and when the goods arrived the buyers rejected them for defects of quality. This was a bad ground as the goods were sound when shipped and the sellers were not responsible for their subsequent deterioration. The buyers claimed their money back, and, three years after their rejection of the goods, they relied for the first time on the fact of late shipment. Their claim failed, no doubt because the court was impressed by the possibly harsh consequences of allowing the buyers at such a late stage to rely on an originally unstated excuse for non-performance. To allow the buyers to do this would, it was said, be inconsistent with a "requirement of fair conduct."[271] But the vagueness of this requirement makes it virtually impossible to tell which cases will be governed by it and which by the general rule that a party

17–063

---

[265] It has been said, obiter, that it cannot apply where the earlier repudiatory breach is in the form of renunciation since "no amount of 'deemed knowledge' . . . can remedy the complete absence of the essential ingredient of renunciation, namely communication to or knowledge of [the claimant] at the time of what are said to have been renunciatory words or conduct": *The Ekha* [2009] EWHC 1530 (Comm); [2010] 1 Lloyd's Rep. 543 at [267] (affirmed, without reference to this point: [2010] EWCA Civ 691; 131 Con.L.R. 9). Quaere, if the claimant has heard the words, or knows of the conduct in question, but has failed to appreciate its significance until it is later relied upon to excuse non-performance.

[266] *Heisler v Anglo-Dal Ltd* [1954] 1 W.L.R. 1273 at 1278; *André & Cie v Cook Industries Inc* [1987] 2 Lloyd's Rep. 463.

[267] See above, para.17–004.

[268] Hence the present exception does not apply where that time has expired by the time of the refusal: see *Glencore Grain Rotterdam BV v LORICO* [1997] 2 Lloyd's Rep. 386 at 395, where it was the buyer who was guilty of the wrongful repudiation.

[269] cf. *The Lena* [1981] 1 Lloyd's Rep. 68 at 79; *The Eurometal* [1981] 1 Lloyd's Rep. 337 at 341.

[270] *Panchaud Frères SA v Établissement General Grain Co* [1970] 1 Lloyd's Rep. 53.

[271] [1970] 1 Lloyd's Rep. 53 at 59.

can rely on an originally unstated excuse for non-performance.[272] Hence other attempts have been made to explain the *Panchaud Frères* case. One suggestion is that the case was one of waiver[273] (in the sense of election[274]); but this was rejected in the case itself on the ground that the buyers did not know of the late shipment when they accepted the documents.[275] Another view is that the buyers' conduct gave rise to an estoppel or equitable estoppel.[276] These doctrines, however, operate only if two requirements are satisfied: an unequivocal representation made by one party and reliance on it by the other.[277] In one later case[278] the argument based on estoppel accordingly failed on the ground that no such representation had been made; and in the *Panchaud Frères* case, even if the inference of a representation could be drawn from the buyers' acceptance of the documents, it is hard to see in what way the sellers had relied on that representation.[279] They certainly lost no chance of curing the defect in their tender, for when that tender was made such a cure was no longer possible. Probably the safest explanation of the case is that the buyers had lost their right to reject by acceptance[280] when they paid against documents which disclosed the fact of late shipment.[281] It follows that the buyers could have relied on the fact of late shipment if they had *rejected* the documents, even though they had, at the time of such rejection, given an inadequate reason, or none at all.[282]

(e) Standard of Duty[283]

(i) *Strict liability*

17–064   **Non-performance.** Many contractual duties are strict.[284] The most obvious illustration of this principle is provided by the case of a buyer who cannot pay the price because his bank has failed or because his expectation of raising a loan has not been fulfilled, or because he is prevented by exchange control regulations from remitting money to the place where he has agreed to pay,[285] or because his supply of the currency in which he has agreed to pay has become exhausted and cannot

---

[272] Perhaps for this reason, the decision is treated with some reserve in *The Proodos C* [1980] 2 Lloyd's Rep. 390 at 392.

[273] *V Berg & Son Ltd v Vanden Avenne-Izegem PVBA* [1977] 1 Lloyd's Rep. 499 at 502–503; *Bremer Handelsgesellschaft mbH v C Mackprang Jr* [1979] 1 Lloyd's Rep. 221 at 225.

[274] See below, para.18–076.

[275] For the requirement of such knowledge, see below, para.18–080.

[276] This was the view of Lord Denning M.R. in the *Panchaud Frères* case itself: [1970] 1 Lloyd's Rep. 53 at 56; cf. *V Berg & Son Ltd v Vanden Avenne-Izegem PVBA*, above, fn.273, at 502–503; *The Manila* [1988] 3 All E.R. 843 at 852.

[277] See above, paras 9–156, 3–081—3–085.

[278] *Glencore Grain Rotterdam BV v LORICO* [1997] 2 Lloyd's Rep. 386.

[279] cf. *Raiffeisen Hauptgenossenschaft v Louis Dreyfuss & Co* [1981] 1 Lloyd's Rep. 345 at 352, where the *Panchaud Frères* case was held inapplicable precisely because the requirement of reliance was not satisfied.

[280] *BP Exploration Co (Libya) Ltd v Hunt* [1979] 1 W.L.R. 783 at 810–811 affirmed [1983] 2 A.C. 352, without reference to this point; *Glencore Grain Rotterdam BV v LORICO* [1997] 2 Lloyd's Rep. 386 at 396.

[281] The defect in the goods must be apparent on the face of the documents and the only relevant documents for this purpose are the *shipping* documents, i.e. those the seller is obliged to tender in fulfilment of the contract: *The Manila* [1988] 3 All E.R. 843.

[282] cf. *V Berg & Son Ltd v Vanden Avenne-Izegem PVBA* [1977] 1 Lloyd's Rep. 499.

[283] Treitel, in Bos and Brownlie (eds), *Liber Amicorum for Lord Wilberforce*, p.185.

[284] *Raineri v Miles* [1981] A.C. 1050 at 1086.

[285] *Universal Corp v Five Ways Properties Ltd* [1979] 1 All E.R. 552.

be replenished.[286] In such cases there is no doubt that he is liable[287]: inability to pay money, even if it occurs entirely without the fault of the party who was to make the payment, is not an excuse for failing to make the payment. The same principle of strict liability applies to the duty of a seller of generic goods to make delivery. It is no defence for him to say that he was prevented from making delivery because he was let down by his supplier[288] or because no shipping space was available to get the goods to their agreed destination.[289] A charterparty similarly imposes a strict duty on the charterer to provide a cargo, so that inability to find one is no excuse.[290] In all these cases, the principle of strict liability may be modified by the terms of the contract (e.g. by a "*force majeure*" clause), but unless this is done liability is quite independent of fault.

Defective performance. The principle of strict liability also applies to certain cases of defective performance. At common law, a carrier of goods by sea was held to give an "absolute" warranty of seaworthiness[291]: it was not enough for him to show that he had taken reasonable care to make the ship seaworthy. In practice, sea carriers often contracted out of this strict liability; and in many cases the duty is now reduced by statute to one of due diligence.[292]   **17–065**

Liability is, again, strict where goods delivered under a contract of sale are defective: e.g. because they do not comply with the seller's undertakings as to quality.[293] It is no defence for the seller to show that he took all reasonable care to see that there were no defects,[294] or that he could not have discovered the defects because he was a retailer selling goods in packages sealed by the manufacturer.[295] The position appears to be the same where goods are supplied under a contract for the supply of goods other than one of sale, e.g. under one of hire or hire-purchase.[296]

A contractor who executes repairs or building work is also strictly liable for defects in components fitted by him. He is not exonerated by showing that the

---

[286] *Congimex SARL (Lisbon) v Continental Grain Export Corp (New York)* [1979] 2 Lloyd's Rep. 346.

[287] cf. *Francis v Cowcliffe* (1977) 33 P. & C.R. 368; *Christy v Pilkington* 273 S.W. 2d 533 (1954).

[288] *Barnett v Javeri & Co* [1916] 2 K.B. 390; *P J van der Zijden Wildhandel v Tucker & Cross Ltd* [1975] 2 Lloyd's Rep. 240; cf. *The Al Tawfiq* [1984] 2 Lloyd's Rep. 598 (late delivery).

[289] *Lewis Emanuel & Son Ltd v Sammut* [1952] 2 Lloyd's Rep. 629.

[290] *The Aello* [1961] A.C. 135 (overruled on another point in *The Johanna Oldendorff* [1974] A.C. 479); *The Zuiho Maru* [1977] 2 Lloyd's Rep. 552; cf. *Hills v Sughrue* (1846) 15 M. & W. 252 (where it was the shipowner who undertook to find the cargo); *The World Navigator* [1991] 2 Lloyd's Rep. 23 at 30, 31 (time of loading); *The Athenasia Comninos* [1990] 1 Lloyd's Rep. 277 at 282 and *The Giannis K* [1998] A.C. 605 at 619, 624 (shipper's "warranty" that cargo is not dangerous).

[291] *Steel v State Line SS Co* (1877) 3 App.Cas. 72 at 86.

[292] Carriage of Goods by Sea Act 1971, s.3.

[293] e.g. with those implied under Sale of Goods Act 1979, s.14; an element of fault enters into these provisions by virtue of s.14(2E)(a) by which a seller is not liable in respect of a "public statement" about specific characteristics of the goods if he "was not, and could not reasonably have been, aware of the statement".

[294] *Frost v Aylesbury Dairy Co Ltd* [1905] 1 K.B. 608; cf. *Lockett v AM Charles Ltd* [1938] 4 All E.R. 170; *H Parsons (Livestock) Ltd v Uttley Ingham & Co Ltd* [1978] Q.B. 791 at 799–800.

[295] *Daniels v White & Son* [1938] 4 All E.R. 258.

[296] See Supply of Goods (Implied Terms) Act 1973, s.10; Supply of Goods and Services Act 1982, ss.4 and 9, as substituted by Sale and Supply of Goods Act 1994, s.7(1) and Sch.2, para.6. An element of fault enters into them for reasons *mutatis mutandis* the same as those given in relation to sale of goods in fn.293, above; cf. *Wettern Electric Ltd v Welsh Development Agency* [1983] Q.B. 796 (strict liability for breach of implied undertaking in licence to occupy factory that premises are fit for occupier's purpose).

components were supplied by a reputable manufacturer and that the defects were latent so that they could not have been discovered by the exercise of reasonable care.[297] Contracts of this kind contain both a supply of goods, and a service, element. Strict liability with regard to the supply element can be justified on the ground that this is closely analogous to sale; and also on the ground that it is the first link in a chain of contractual liability which will stretch back to the manufacturer, on whom the liability should properly rest. The customer has no rights against the manufacturer in contract, as there is no contract between them[298]; and, by making the contractor strictly liable to the customer, the law gives the contractor an incentive[299] to recoup the loss so incurred by claiming damages for breach of contract from the manufacturer from whom he had bought the components. The introduction of the manufacturer's strict "product liability"[300] directly to the customer weakens this argument for the contractor's strict liability in contract to the customer, but does not wholly deprive it of its force since "product liability" is subject to many important qualifications.[301] The "chain of liability" argument is also open to the objection that the chain may be broken by a valid exemption clause. It has therefore been suggested that, if the manufacturer is willing to sell the components only on terms that exclude his liability, and this fact was known both to the contractor and to his customer, then the contractor would not be strictly liable to his customer for defects in those components.[302]

(ii) Liability based on fault

17–066   **Supply of services.** Under the Supply of Goods and Services Act 1982, a person who supplies a service in the course of a business impliedly undertakes to "carry out the service with reasonable care and skill".[303] Such liability is clearly based on fault; but the Act also preserves "any rule of law which imposes on the supplier a stricter duty".[304] Hence the question whether the supplier's liability is strict or is based on fault will continue to depend on distinctions drawn at common law.

---

[297] G H Myers & Co v Brent Cross Service Co [1934] 1 K.B. 46; Young & Marten Ltd v McManus Childs Ltd [1969] 1 A.C. 454; cf. Hancock v Brazier [1966] 1 W.L.R. 1317; Barclays Bank Plc v Fairclough Builders Ltd [1995] Q.B. 214. In The Zinnia [1984] 2 Lloyd's Rep. 211 at 218 the repairer's duty was said to be one to ensure that reasonable care in buying the components was exercised; but as he was found not to have taken such care the further question whether he might be strictly liable did not arise. It is not clear what standard of liability is imposed by Defective Premises Act 1972, s.1(1)(a).

[298] This position appears not to be affected by Contracts (Rights of Third Parties) Act 1999 (above, para.14–003, at fn.9) and para.14–095, at fn.691). A direct contractual relationship may be created through the use of a manufacturer's guarantee: see above, para.14–006.

[299] Even if the contractor were not liable to the customer, he might be able to claim damages in respect of the customer's loss under the principle applied in Linden Gardens Trust Ltd v Lenesta Sludge Disposals Ltd [1994] A.C. 85: above, para.14–025; but the customer would have no legal right to require him to make such a claim.

[300] Consumer Protection Act 1987, Pt I.

[301] e.g. those arising from the meaning given to "defect" by s.3 of the 1987 Act, the defences made available by s.4, and the definition of "damage" in s.5.

[302] In Young & Marten Ltd v McManus Childs Ltd [1969] 1 A.C. 454 at 467; the suggestion is perhaps based on the fact that the building contract specified tiles which could be obtained only from a single manufacturer.

[303] s.13; Wilson v Best Travel Ltd [1993] 1 All E.R. 353.

[304] s.16(3)(a).

Supply of services and components. Where the contract is one for the   **17–067**
supply of *services and components*, liability for defects in the components is (as we
have just seen) generally strict[305]; but the contractor's liability with regard to other
phases of his operation is often based on fault. For example, a car repairer's duty
with regard to the safe-keeping of a customer's car is one of care only.[306] The
standard of a building or repairing contractor's duty with regard to the actual
carrying out of the work that he is employed to do is less clear. In one of the
relevant cases,[307] a sharp distinction was drawn between the "supply of goods"
and "service" elements of the contract, and it seems to have been accepted that,
in respect of the "service" element, the contractor's duty was one of care only.[308]
Similarly, a contract for the supply of goods may impose on the supplier a duty not
only to supply the goods but also to service, or to repair defects in, them after they
have been supplied. He will then be strictly liable in respect of defects in the goods
when supplied, but his service or repair undertakings will impose duties of
diligence only.[309]

Supply of services alone. Where the contract is one for the supply of *services*   **17–068**
alone, liability is often based on fault. Thus the general rule is that contracts under
which services are rendered by professional persons (such as solicitors, architects,
accountants or doctors) impose duties of care only.[310] In some at least of such
cases, the person rendering the services obviously does not guarantee to produce
a result: this is particularly clear in the case of the lawyer engaged to conduct
litigation since one party must inevitably lose, and of the doctor since a person who
provides medical treatment is not normally understood to guarantee its success.[311]
All that such persons undertake is to perform the promised services with reasonable care and skill. The same is true of the architect to the extent that he
undertakes to supervise the work of others, or the supply of materials by them: in
performing this function he cannot be expected to do more than exercise a
reasonable degree of professional care and skill.

But the position is different where an architect commits an error, not of
supervision, but of design: there is considerable support for the view that, where

---

[305] See above, para.17–065. S.12(3)(a) of Supply of Goods and Services Act 1982 provides that such
contracts are contracts for the supply of services for the purposes of the Act; but it does not specify
the standard of liability.

[306] See *Hollier v Rambler Motors (AMC) Ltd* [1972] 2 Q.B. 71; cf. *Alderslade v Hendon Laundry Ltd*
[1945] 1 K.B. 189; *Smith v Eric S Bush* [1990] 1 A.C. 831 at 843.

[307] *Young & Marten Ltd v McManus Childs Ltd* [1969] 1 A.C. 454.

[308] ibid. at 465; cf. *H Parsons (Livestock) Ltd v Uttley Ingham & Co Ltd* [1978] Q.B. 791 at 800; *The
Raphael* [1981] 2 Lloyd's Rep. 659 at 665. See also *BP Exploration (Libya) Ltd v Hunt* [1979] 1 W.L.R.
783 at 796 (affirmed [1983] 2 A.C. 352).

[309] *BHP Petroleum Ltd v British Steel Plc* [1999] 2 Lloyd's Rep. 583, affirmed [2000] 2 Lloyd's Rep.
277.

[310] e.g. *Clark v Kirby-Smith* [1964] Ch. 506 (solicitor); *Bagot v Stevens, Scanlan & Co Ltd* [1966] 1
Q.B. 197 (architect); *O'Connor v Kirby* [1972] 1 Q.B. 90 (insurance broker); *Stafford v Conti Commodity
Services* [1981] 1 All E.R. 691 (commodities broker); *Perry v Sidney Phillips & Son* [1982] 1 All E.R.
1005 at 1010, varied [1982] 1 W.L.R. 1287 (surveyor); *Luxmoore-May v Messenger May Baverstock*
[1990] 1 W.L.R. 1009; *Henderson v Merrett Syndicates Ltd* [1995] 2 A.C. 145 (underwriting agent);
Hone v Going Places Leisure Travel Ltd [2001] EWCA Civ 947; *The Times*, August 6, 2001 (package
holiday).

[311] See *Eyre v Measday* [1986] 1 All E.R. 488 and *Thake v Maurice* [1986] Q.B. 644. There may be
a duty to warn of the risk of an unsuccessful outcome, in contract (*Thake v Maurice*), or in tort
(*Goodwill v Pregnancy Advisory Service* [1996] 1 W.L.R. 1379); above, para.14–053.

he designs a structure, he gives an "absolute warranty"[312] that it will be fit for his client's purposes. Similarly, a person who in the course of a profession or business undertakes to *design and supply* an article has been held strictly liable for defects in that article.[313] Some dicta, indeed, suggest that liability is strict *only* where the contract contains a "supply" as well as a "service" element[314]; but this limitation on the incidence of strict liability may, with respect, be doubted. In some of the relevant authorities no defect in the components or raw materials was alleged[315]; and where a defendant is thus held liable for defects in services alone it would be strange if the standard of that liability depended on the existence of another obligation (i.e. to supply materials) in respect of which he was not in breach.

(iii) *Fault and excuses for non-performance*

17–069   Failure to perform is not a breach where a supervening event either discharges a contract under the doctrine of frustration[316] or provides a party with an excuse for non-performance.[317] An event has this effect only if it occurs without the fault of the party relying on it. In cases of frustration, this requirement is expressed by saying that frustration must not be "self-induced".[318] Similarly, a party generally[319] cannot rely as an excuse for non-performance on an event that is due to his fault e.g. a farmer who agreed to sell a quantity of wheat to be grown on his land could not rely on the fact that less was produced if this was due to want of proper cultivation.[320]

Excuses for non-performance may be provided by "exceptions" in the contract itself, and such provisions must be distinguished from exemption clauses. Where performance is prevented by an event specified in an "exception", there is no breach at all, while an exemption clause excludes or restricts liability once a breach has been established. One factor tending to put a provision into the category of "exceptions" is that the specified event was beyond the control of the party relying on the provision, and occurred without fault.[321] Here again fault is relevant in determining whether non-performance is excused or amounts to a breach.

---

[312] *Greaves & Co (Contractors) Ltd v Baynham Meikle & Partners* [1975] 1 W.L.R. 1095 at 1101; *IBA v EMI (Electronics) Ltd* (1980) 14 Build.L.R. 1, especially at 47–48 (where the contract contained a supply of goods element but no defect in the goods was alleged); *CFW Architects v Cowlin Construction Ltd* [2006] EWHC 6 (TCC); 105 Con. L.R. 116 at [46].

[313] *Samuels v Davies* [1943] K.B. 526 (dentist supplying false teeth: here the "supply" element predominated and du Parq L.J. regarded the contract as one of sale); *IBA v EMI (Electronics) Ltd* (1980) 14 Build.L.R. 1 (contract to design and erect a television mast).

[314] *Basildon DC v J E Lesser Properties* [1985] 1 All E.R. 20 at 26 (not reported on this point in [1985] Q.B. 839); cf. *Cynat Properties Ltd v Landbuild (Investments & Property) Ltd* [1984] 3 All E.R. 513 at 523; *Wimpey Construction UK Ltd v DV Poole* [1984] 2 Lloyd's Rep. 499 at 514 (no undertaking by *designer* as to quality and *execution* of the work); *George Hawkins v Chrysler (UK)* (1986) 38 Build.L.R. 36 (where the contract contained no supply element).

[315] There was no such allegation in the cases cited in fn.313, above.

[316] See below, Ch.19.

[317] See above, para.17–059.

[318] See below, para.19–082.

[319] Illness preventing performance of a contract of personal service may be an exception: cf. below, para.19–085.

[320] Lack of fault is mentioned, apparently as an essential ingredient of the excuse, in the cases discussed at para.17–059, above.

[321] *The Angelia* [1973] 1 W.L.R. 210 at 230; above, para.7–021; cf. *The Xantho* (1877) 2 App.Cas. 503.

(iv) *Conditional contracts*

Where a contract is subject to a contingent condition,[322] two rules apply which to some extent make fault relevant to the issue of contractual liability. First, a party may be in breach if he deliberately prevents the occurrence of the condition.[323] Secondly, a party may be under some degree of duty to bring about the occurrence of the condition: e.g. where goods are sold "subject to" export or import licence. In such a case the duty of the party who is to obtain the licence is normally one of diligence only,[324] so that fault is again relevant to the question whether a breach of contract has been committed.

17–070

(f) Breach Distinguished from Lawful Termination

A contract may give a party the right lawfully to terminate it by notice. If that party says to the other that he no longer intends to perform, it may be hard to tell whether he has broken or terminated the contract. In *Bridge v Campbell Discount Co Ltd*[325] a hire-purchase agreement gave the hirer the right to terminate it by notice. He wrote to the owners: "Owing to unforeseen circumstances I am sorry but I will not be able to pay any more payments . . . Will you please let me know when and where I will have to return the car. I am very sorry regarding this, but I have no alternative." The House of Lords held (by a majority) that he had not terminated but broken the contract, apparently because that was his intention. "Why should the hirer apologise so humbly, twice, if *he thought* that he was merely exercising an option given to him by the agreement?"[326]

17–071

Industrial action. The analogous question has been raised whether a strike or other "industrial action" amounts to a breach of a contract of employment.[327] This depends in the first place on the exact form taken by the conduct in question. While "working to rule" may be a breach,[328] no breach is committed merely because employees who usually work overtime (without being under any contractual obligation to do so) refuse to continue the practice.[329] In the more common case of a refusal by employees to perform their contractual obligation to work, there is clearly a breach if the contract contains a "no strikes" clause.[330] The same is true if an employee stops work (whether in the course of a strike or not) without giving the notice required by the terms of the contract. If the contract does not contain a "no strikes" clause and if due notice of the strike has been

17–072

---

[322] See above, paras 2–104—2–111.

[323] See above, para.2–108.

[324] See above, para.2–110.

[325] [1962] A.C. 600; cf. *United Dominions Trust (Commercial) Ltd v Ennis* [1968] 1 Q.B. 54; *Marriott v Oxford & District Co-operative Society Ltd* [1970] Q.B. 186; *Comet Group v British Sky Broadcasting*, *The Times*, April 26, 1991.

[326] ibid. at 615 (italics supplied); cf. ibid. at 674. Another (and probably most likely) reason for the decision is that it was in the hirer's interest to establish that he was in breach: see below, para.20–145.

[327] Foster 34 M.L.R. 274.

[328] See above, para.17–055.

[329] *Tramp Shipping Corp v Greenwich Marine Inc* [1975] 1 W.L.R. 1042; cf. *Power Packing Casemakers v Faust* [1983] Q.B. 471.

[330] As in *Rookes v Barnard* [1964] A.C. 1129.

given, one view is that the notice terminates the contract; but this is said[331] to be unrealistic since both parties would expect a return to work under the old contract (suitably modified) after the strike was over. A second view is that a strike notice operates as a lawful suspension of the contract, at least if the notice is no shorter than that required for lawful termination of the contract.[332] This view in turn gives rise to difficulties, particularly as the notion of "suspending" a contract is one with which English law is unfamiliar[333] and which the courts have not favoured.[334] The prevailing view, therefore, is[335] that generally a strike is a breach of contract and that it is, moreover, a "repudiatory breach",[336] i.e. one which at common law[337] entitles the employer to dismiss the employee. The employer's other remedies by way of damages and withholding pay have already been discussed.[338]

6. ANTICIPATORY BREACH[339]

(a) The Doctrine of Anticipatory Breach

17-073   An "anticipatory breach"[340] is said to occur when, before performance is due, a party *either* renounces the contract *or* disables himself from performing it.[341]

17-074   **Renunciation.** Renunciation requires a "clear" and "absolute"[342] refusal to perform; this need not be express but can take the form of conduct indicating that the party is unwilling, even though he may be able, to perform. A renunciation may even be inferred from silence where it is a "speaking silence"[343]: e.g. the previous conduct of a party in refusing to perform another related contract may give rise to the inference that he will refuse to perform the contract in question. His silence or inactivity can then be a renunciation of that contract unless he takes

[331] By Donovan L.J. in *Rookes v Barnard* [1963] 1 Q.B. 623 at 682. The statement was approved in the House of Lords by Lord Devlin: [1964] A.C. 1129 at 1204, though the decision of the Court of Appeal was reversed. See also Wedderburn 25 M.L.R. 258; 27 M.L.R. 268.

[332] *Morgan v Fry* [1968] 2 Q.B. 710 at 728, per Lord Denning M.R.; cf. [1968] 2 Q.B. 710 at 733, per Davies L.J.; O'Higgins [1968] C.L.J. 223. Trade Union and Labour Relations (Consolidation) Act 1992, s.234A requires at least seven days' notice to be given.

[333] See *Daily Mirror Newspapers Ltd v Gardner* [1968] 2 Q.B. 762; *Gorse v Durham CC* [1971] 1 W.L.R. 775. A contract can only be "suspended" if it contains a provision to that effect, as, for example, in *Bird v British Celanese Ltd* [1945] K.B. 336.

[334] *Shell UK Ltd v Lostock Garages Ltd* [1976] 1 W.L.R. 1187.

[335] *Simmons v Hoover Ltd* [1977] Q.B. 284; Napier [1977] C.L.J. 34; cf. *Rookes v Barnard* [1963] 1 Q.B. 623 at 682, per Donovan L.J.; *Chappell v Times Newspapers Ltd* [1975] 1 W.L.R. 482 at 502.

[336] *Miles v Wakefield Metropolitan DC* [1987] A.C. 539 at 562; *Wiluszynski v Tower Hamlets LBC* [1989] I.C.R. 493 at 503.

[337] By statute, the dismissal may be *unfair*, even where it is not *wrongful* at common law: see Employment Rights Act 1996, s.94.

[338] See above, para.17–045.

[339] Liu [2007] C.L.J. 574.

[340] For criticism of this terminology, see *Bradley v H Newsom, Sons & Co* [1919] A.C. 16 at 53; *The Mihalis Angelos* [1971] 1 Q.B. 164 at 196. And see Dawson [1981] C.L.J. 83; Mustill, *Butterworth Lectures, 1989–1990,* p.1.

[341] *Universal Cargo Carriers Corp v Citati* [1957] 2 Q.B. 401 at 438; cf. *The Angelia* [1973] 1 W.L.R. 210; Tiplady 89 L.Q.R. 465.

[342] *The Hermosa* [1982] 1 Lloyd's Rep. 570 at 572; cf. *The Gregos* [1994] 1 W.L.R. 1465; *Jaks (UK) Ltd v Cera Investment Bank SA* [1998] 2 Lloyd's Rep. 89 at 93.

[343] *Stocznia Gdanska SA v Latvian Shipping Co* [2002] EWCA Civ 889; [2002] 2 Lloyd's Rep 436 at [96].

positive steps to dispel that inference.[344] The conduct must indicate to the other party that the party alleged to have renounced the contract is about to commit a breach of it: an indication given to a third party of an intention to commit a breach at an unspecified time in the future has been held not to amount to a renunciation.[345]

Disablement. Disablement need not be "deliberate",[346] in the sense that there **17–075** may be an anticipatory breach even though it was not the party's intention to disable himself from performing; but the disablement must be due to the party's "own act or default".[347] Such disablement is most clearly illustrated by cases in which a party does a positive act which is certain to prevent performance, such as disposing elsewhere of the specific thing[348] which forms the subject-matter of the contract.

Omission as disablement. Disablement may, however, also take the form of **17–076** an omission. For example, a contract may be made for the sale of goods for future delivery, to be manufactured by the seller, or to be acquired by him from a third party, and the seller may fail to take any steps to manufacture the goods or to acquire them from the supplier. The failure will then amount to his "own ... default" in the sense that he will have failed to do something that he was obliged by the contract to do in order to put himself into the position of being able to perform on the due date. But if a seller of goods to be acquired from a third party had duly contracted with that third party to acquire the goods, he would not be in anticipatory breach merely because it became highly unlikely that the third party would deliver them under his contract with the seller, so that the seller himself would, in turn, be unable to perform his contract with the buyer. A fortiori a seller is not in anticipatory breach merely because the buyer *fears* that the subject-matter of the sale, when delivered, will turn out to be defective.[349] Nor would a buyer be in anticipatory breach merely because, before the time fixed for payment, some external cause (such as exchange control, or the failure of a bank) made it virtually certain that he would be unable to pay on the due date. In the last three examples there is no disablement by the party's "own ... default": hence the prospective inability does not amount to an anticipatory breach,[350] even though it would, if it persisted up to the time when performance was due, then amount to an actual breach.[351] Difficulties can obviously arise in deciding whether a prospective inability resulting from an omission is due to the party's "own ... default." The difficulty is illustrated by the very case in which this requirement is stated, *Universal Cargo Carriers Corp v Citati*.[352] In that case, a charterer was

[344] ibid.
[345] *Laughton and Hawley v BAPP Industrial Supplies* [1986] I.C.R. 245.
[346] *Universal Cargo Carriers Corp v Citati*, above, at 438; contrast *The Super Servant Two* [1989] 1 Lloyd's Rep. 149 at 155 ("deliberate or at least voluntary"), affirmed [1990] 1 Lloyd's Rep. 1.
[347] ibid. at 441; or (as in that case) from the act or default of another person to whom he had delegated performance of his contractual duty.
[348] Disposing of a thing which is *not* specific does not amount to disablement, for the seller may be able to perform, by supplying another thing of the contract description out of stock or from another source: *Texaco Ltd v Eurogulf Shipping Co Ltd* [1987] 2 Lloyd's Rep. 541; cf. *Alfred C Toepfer International GmbH v Itex Itagrani Export SA* [1993] 1 Lloyd's Rep. 360.
[349] *The Veracruz I* [1992] 1 Lloyd's Rep. 356; *The P* [1992] 1 Lloyd's Rep. 470.
[350] *F C Shepherd & Co Ltd v Jerrom* [1987] Q.B. 301 at 327–328.
[351] This may be so even though the party in breach is in no way at fault, e.g. where his source of funds fails: see above, para.17–064.
[352] [1957] 2 Q.B. 401 and see below, para.17–086.

held to be in anticipatory breach of his obligation to provide a cargo, at the time fixed for loading, because of the prospective failure of a third party, with whom he had contracted for the supply of the goods, to deliver them within that time. This aspect of the case has been judicially described as "debatable"[353]; it can perhaps be explained on the ground that the charterer had failed to ensure that his supply contract was effective for the purpose of the performance of his own obligations under the charterparty.

17–077   **Effect.** Where one party has committed an anticipatory breach, the other has a choice. He can try to keep the contract alive by continuing to press for performance,[354] in which case the anticipatory breach will have the same effects as an actual breach. Alternatively, he can "accept" the breach, in which case his rights to damages and termination are governed by the special rules to be discussed below.

(b) Acceptance of the Breach

17–078   A breach can be accepted by bringing an action for damages; or by giving notice of intention to accept it to the party in breach. Conduct known to the party in breach will suffice even if no notice of it is given by the injured party.[355] Conversely, once the injured party has made it plain that he is treating the contract as at an end, he "does not need to *do* anything more".[356] Mere acquiescence or inactivity will often be equivocal and so fail to constitute an acceptance for this purpose.[357] But there is no absolute rule of law to this effect: e.g. the fact of the injured party's having failed, in response to the breach, to take the steps which he would normally have been expected to take in the further performance of the contract may unequivocally indicate his acceptance of the breach.[358]

Acceptance of the breach must be complete and unequivocal.[359] A party cannot accept an anticipatory breach of one term in a contract while treating the contract as still in existence for other purposes.[360]

(c) Effects of Accepting the Breach

(i) *Damages for anticipatory breach*

17–079   **Damages available at once.** The most striking feature of the doctrine of anticipatory breach is that acceptance of the breach entitles the victim to claim

---

[353] *F C Shepherd & Co Ltd v Jerrom*, above, at 323.

[354] *Michael v Hart & Co* [1902] 1 K.B. 482; *Harvela Investments Ltd v Royal Trust of Canada (CI) Ltd* [1986] A.C. 207 at 227.

[355] *Vitol SA v Norelf Ltd* [1996] A.C. 800, as to which see also fn.358, below.

[356] *Lefevre v White* [1990] 1 Lloyd's Rep. 569 at 574; statements in *Société Génerale de Paris v Milders* (1883) 49 L.T. 55 at 57, which refer to the need to act on the notice of acceptance, can be explained as merely descriptive of the usual course of events.

[357] *Cranleigh Precision Engineering Ltd v Bryant* [1965] 1 W.L.R. 1293; *State Trading Corp of India v M Golodetz Ltd* [1989] 2 Lloyd's Rep. 277 at 286; *Lefevre v White* [1990] 1 Lloyd's Rep. 569 at 574, 576–577.

[358] *Vitol SA v Norelf Ltd*, above, fn.355. The case was treated in the lower courts as one of anticipatory breach, but, except in quotations from the judgments of those courts, no reference to this aspect of the case was made in the House of Lords.

[359] *Harrison v Northwest Holt Group Administration* [1985] I.C.R. 668; *Jaks (UK) Ltd v Cera Investment Bank Ltd* [1998] 2 Lloyd's Rep. 89 at 94.

[360] This was one reason for the decision in *Johnstone v Milling* (1886) 16 Q.B.D. 460.

damages *at once*, before the time fixed for performance. This rule was established in *Hochster v De la Tour*[361] where the defendant had agreed to employ the claimant as courier for three months from June 1, and repudiated the contract on May 11. The claimant was able to claim damages at once: he did not have to wait until June 1 before beginning his action. The main reason for the decision was that

> "if the claimant has no remedy for breach of contract unless he treats the contract as in force and acts upon it down to the 1st of June 1852, it follows that, till then, he must enter into no employment".[362]

This reasoning has been justly criticised,[363] for the court could have held that the defendant's repudiation gave the claimant *the option to terminate* at once but did not *entitle him to damages* until June 1: there is no necessary connection between these two consequences of the repudiation.

Practical problems. Where the interval between repudiation and the time fixed for performance is a long one, there are also practical objections to the rule in *Hochster v De la Tour*, and these are particularly strong where the trial takes place well before the time fixed for performance.[364] One such objection is that the rule may lead to a wrong quantification of damages. If a seller of goods to be delivered in three years' time repudiates and the buyer claims damages at once, the quantification of those damages may depend on the market price at the time fixed for delivery[365]; but if the case is tried before that time the court can only guess what that price will be. Another objection to the rule is that it results in an acceleration of the defendant's obligation; he will have to pay damages now, even though under the contract he was not to perform until some future time.[366] Thus if a debtor repudiates liability to repay future instalments of a debt, the creditor can claim damages at once, even though the instalments, or some of them, are not payable until a future day. Of course in assessing those damages the court will allow the debtor "a discount for accelerated payment".[367] Even more strikingly, the defendant will have to pay damages at once although at the time of the action his liability is still contingent and might never mature at all. Thus damages have been recovered for anticipatory breach of a husband's promise to make a will leaving a life interest in property to his wife, although it was uncertain at the time of the action whether the wife would survive the husband.[368]

17–080

---

[361] (1853) 2 E. & B. 678.

[362] ibid. at 689.

[363] See Williston, *Contracts* (3rd edn), paras 1300 et seq.; Corbin, *Contracts*, paras 959 et seq.; Vold 41 Harv.L.Rev. 340 suggests that anticipatory breach might be regarded as a tort; cf. Weir [1964] C.L.J. 231; but see Hoffmann 81 L.Q.R. 116.

[364] Where it takes place *after* the time fixed for performance, the court may take into account events which are now known to have happened and which reduce the value of the contract to the injured party: *The Golden Victory* [2007] UKHL 12; [2007] 2 A.C. 353; below, para.20–080.

[365] See below, para.20–072.

[366] If the injured party affirms the contract and sues for specific performance, the court may give judgment in his favour at once, but the judgment will not order the defendant to perform until the time fixed for performance arrives: see *Hasham v Zenab* [1960] A.C. 316.

[367] *Lep Air Services Ltd v Rolloswin Investments Ltd* [1973] A.C. 331 at 356; *Re Park Air Services* [1999] 1 All E.R. 673 at 676.

[368] *Synge v Synge* [1894] 1 Q.B. 466.

17–081   **Defence of the rule.** In spite of these objections, the rule in *Hochster v De la Tour* is well established[369] and at least two points can be made in its favour. First, the rule may help to minimise loss. In a case like *Hochster v De la Tour*, the injured party might in fact be more *likely* (whether or not he was *bound*) to keep himself ready to perform if he had no right to sue at once. The rule giving him that right provides at any rate some incentive for him to abandon the contract, and so to avoid this extra loss. Secondly, the rule may sometimes be necessary to protect the injured party: e.g. if he has paid in advance for a promise of future performance which is then repudiated. In such a case the injured party could be seriously prejudiced if he had no claim against the other party until the time fixed for performance had arrived; for, having made the advance payment, he might lack the means to procure a substitute contract.

Acceptance of the breach affects not only the claimant's entitlement to damages, but also the way in which those damages are assessed. The latter point is discussed in Ch.20.[370]

(ii) *Termination for anticipatory breach*

17–082   **General requirement of substantial failure.** An "anticipatory breach", like an actual breach, can give rise to a right to terminate and that right arises immediately, i.e. before performance is due. Whether it does give rise to such a right depends on the factors discussed in Ch.18.[371] Generally, the right to terminate will arise only if the prospective effects of the anticipatory breach are such as to satisfy the requirement of substantial failure in performance.[372] Thus a charterer's advance announcement of a deliberate delay of one day in loading would not (any more than an actual delay of this kind[373]) justify termination.

17–083   **Exceptions.** In relation to actual breach the requirement of substantial failure is subject to exceptions[374]; and the question arises whether the right to termination for anticipatory breach extends to cases falling within those exceptions. There is one type of case in which a negative answer must clearly be given to this question, namely that in which the right to terminate exists by reason only of an express provision in the contract for determination.[375] Under such provisions in charter-parties charterers cannot exercise their rights to cancel for late arrival of the ship, nor owners withdraw for non-payment of hire, merely because it has become certain that the ship *will not* arrive, or that the hire *will not* be paid in time: they are only entitled to terminate when the specified day has gone by without performance being rendered.[376] In *The Afovos* a shipowner gave notice (under such an express provision) of his intention to terminate on account of the charterer's failure to pay hire in time, but he did so while the charterer's breach was merely anticipatory; and Lord Diplock, in holding the purported termination to be

---

[369] See *Lep Air Services Ltd v Rolloswin Investments Ltd* [1973] A.C. 331 at 356, 358; *Woodar Investments Development Ltd v Wimpey Construction UK Ltd* [1980] 1 W.L.R. 277 at 297; *Gunton v Richmond-upon-Thames LBC* [1981] Ch. 448 at 467; *The Hazelmoor* [1980] 2 Lloyd's Rep. 351.
[370] See below, paras 20–077—20–082.
[371] See below, paras 18–025—18–074.
[372] See below, paras 18–025—18–036.
[373] See below, para.18–034.
[374] See below, paras 18–037—18–074.
[375] See below, paras 18–061—18–071.
[376] See below, para.18–062.

wrongful, said: "it is to fundamental breaches alone that the doctrine of anticipatory breach is applicable".[377] On the facts, the conclusion that the notice of termination was premature cannot be doubted, for it is clear that the right to terminate for anticipatory breach does not apply to *the particular* exception to the requirement of substantial failure with which *The Afovos* was concerned, i.e. the exception under which termination for actual breach is allowed because of an express provision for determination. But the mere fact that the right to terminate for anticipatory breach does not apply to *one* such exception does not support the conclusion that it cannot apply to *any* of them. In this regard, Lord Diplock's suggestion in *The Afovos*,[378] that there can be no right to terminate for an anticipatory breach of condition may, with respect, be doubted. In part, the question whether there can be such a right is one of terminology. Lord Diplock has elsewhere defined "conditions" as terms the breach of which gives rise to the right to terminate because the parties have so "agreed, whether by express words or by implication of law".[379] Under this definition, express provisions for determination on non-performance *are* "conditions"; but a term is often classified as a "condition" by statute or by judicial decision[380] even though the parties have not expressly agreed that *any* breach of it is to give rise to the right to terminate. This group of conditions is in practice the more important group of such terms[381]: and it is submitted that the right to terminate for anticipatory breach does extend to conditions of this kind.[382] Thus in one leading case[383] on anticipatory breach the court asked *first* whether the prospective breaches were breaches of condition and (having reached the conclusion that they were not[384]) proceeded *secondly* to the question whether they were sufficiently serious to justify termination for anticipatory breach.[385] The first enquiry would have been unnecessary if the doctrine of anticipatory breach could never apply to breaches of condition.

Prospective effect of breach. In cases of anticipatory breach, the right to terminate may depend on the prospective effects of the breach. A question therefore arises as to what the injured party has to show to justify termination. Is it enough for him to show that, at the time of termination, he *reasonably believed* that the breach would, by the time fixed for performance, have acquired the character of a breach giving rise to the right to terminate? Or must he show that, at the time of termination, it was *already certain* that the breach was going to be of this kind? This depends on the form taken by the anticipatory breach.　**17–084**

Renunciation. The first form of anticipatory breach is by renunciation, i.e. by a "clear" and "absolute"[386] refusal to perform. This may be inferred from conduct　**17–085**

---

[377] [1983] 1 W.L.R. 195 at 203.
[378] ibid.
[379] *Photo Production Ltd v Securicor Transport Ltd* [1980] A.C. 827 at 849; cf. below, paras 18–039—18–042.
[380] See below, paras 18–043—18–044.
[381] ibid.
[382] See *The Aktor* [2008] EWHC 1330 (Comm); [2008] 2 Lloyd's Rep. 246, where the analysis appears to be that the contract for sale of a vessel was validly terminated for an anticipatory breach of condition; the reference to the right of cancellation at [69] is not thought to cast doubt on the decision in *The Afovos*.
[383] *Universal Cargo Carriers Corp v Citati* [1957] 2 Q.B. 401.
[384] See below, fnn.392, 393.
[385] See below at fn.395.
[386] *The Hermosa* [1982] 1 Lloyd's Rep. 570 at 572.

where the party in breach has "acted in such a way as to lead a reasonable man to conclude that [he] did not intend to fulfil [his] part of the contract".[387] Whether conduct has this effect "is to be considered as at the time when it is treated as terminating the contract, in the light of the then existing circumstances".[388] The court therefore looks to the time of termination to determine whether the injured party reasonably took the view that the refusal was sufficiently clear and absolute to give him the right to terminate.[389] The assessment is an objective one, but the motive of the party in breach is not irrelevant "if it reflects something of which the innocent party was, or a reasonable person in his or her position would have been, aware and throws light on the way the alleged repudiatory act would be viewed as such by a reasonable person."[390]

17–086   **Prospective inability.** Where a party is alleged to have committed an anticipatory breach by disabling himself from performing, the question whether the other party is entitled to terminate will generally depend on the seriousness of the resulting failure in performance. That failure being wholly prospective, its seriousness is more than usually a matter of speculation; but the injured party may nevertheless seek to terminate before the time fixed for performance. The problem arose in *Universal Cargo Carriers Corp v Citati*[391] where a charterparty obliged the charterer to provide a cargo of 6,000 tons of scrap iron, to load it at the rate of 1,000 tons a day, and to complete the loading by July 21. He had failed to provide any cargo by July 18 and on that day the shipowners purported to terminate. The charterer's failure to provide a cargo was an actual breach, though not one which of itself justified termination.[392] It seems that the charterer was also in breach of his obligation to load, for if loading were to be completed at the rate of 1,000 tons a day by July 21 it ought to have begun before July 18. However, perhaps because the obligation to complete loading still lay in the future, the breach was at least in part anticipatory[393]; and the question discussed[394] was whether this breach by the charterer, assuming it to be anticipatory, justified termination by the shipowners on July 18. This depended on the seriousness of the breach: the shipowners had to show "that on July 18 the charterer was unable to load a cargo within such a time as would not have frustrated the venture".[395] It was not sufficient for them to show that on July 18 they had reasonable grounds for believing that such a frustrating delay would occur; they were justified in terminating only if they could prove that a delay of this kind would actually have occurred.[396]

This rule is likely to prove inconvenient in practice. It does not apply where the contract is alleged to be frustrated.[397] In one such case Scrutton J. said that

---

[387] ibid. at 580.

[388] ibid. at 572.

[389] ibid. at 573; *Universal Cargo Carriers Corp v Citati* [1957] 2 Q.B. 401 at 439–440; *The Sanko Iris* [1987] 1 Lloyd's Rep. 487; Carter [1988] L.M.C.L.Q. 21.

[390] *Eminence Property Developments v Heaney Ltd* [2010] EWCA Civ 1168; (2010) 43 E.G. 99 at [63]; *Tullett Prebon Plc v BGC Partners LP* [2011] EWCA Civ 131; [2011] I.R.L.R. 420 at [22]–[29].

[391] [1957] 2 Q.B. 401; *Re Simoco Digital UK Ltd* [2004] EWHC 209 (Ch); [2004] 1 B.C.L.C. 541 at [22]–[23].

[392] ibid. at 429. He was also in breach of his obligation to nominate a berth. Neither breach was one of condition: ibid. at 429 and cf. below, para.18–047.

[393] Devlin J. at 429 discusses whether *this* breach (which was also not one of condition) was actual or anticipatory and concludes that "it must be one or the other".

[394] See [1957] 2 Q.B. 401 at 436.

[395] ibid. at 450.

[396] ibid. at 449. The point appears to have been conceded.

[397] See below, paras 19–051—19–052.

"Commercial men must not be asked to wait till the end of a long delay to find out from what in fact happens whether they are bound by a contract or not; they must be entitled to act on reasonable commercial probabilities at the time when they are called upon to make up their minds."[398]

In the *Citati* case Devlin J. held that this principle did not apply to "questions of breach of contract"[399]; and he added that "An anticipatory breach must be proved in fact and not in supposition."[400] One can to some extent justify the distinction between the two types of cases. Frustration leads only to discharge of the contract, while anticipatory breach can lead both to termination and to liability in damages. It seems obviously unfair to hold one party (A) liable *in damages*, merely because the other (B) reasonably believed that A would be unable to perform, if it turns out that A is in fact able to perform at the appointed time. But it does not follow that B should not in these circumstances be entitled to terminate. On this point the reasoning of the *Citati* case is open to the same objection as that of *Hochster v De la Tour*[401]: it assumes that, in cases of anticipatory breach, the right to damages and the right to terminate necessarily arise at the same time. This is, however, no criticism of the actual decision in the *Citati* case, which appears to be consistent with the view here put forward; for the issue in the case was not whether the shipowners were liable for wrongful repudiation, but whether the charterer was liable in damages for an anticipatory breach of his obligation to load.

Prospective effects of actual breach. A reasonable belief that a substantial   17–087
failure will occur is also sufficient to justify termination where there has at the time of termination been an actual breach which gives rise to uncertainty as to future performance. For example, where a ship is unseaworthy, "the charterer may rightly terminate . . . if the delay in remedying any breach is so long in fact, *or likely to be so long in reasonable anticipation*, that the commercial purpose of the contract would be frustrated".[402] In such a case the court need not fear that the shipowner will be held liable in damages merely because it was reasonably anticipated that he could not perform. His liability in damages is already established by reason of the actual breach; all that is in issue is the right of the injured party to terminate. *That right* should, it is submitted, depend on "reasonable anticipation" in cases of anticipatory, no less than of actual[403] breach.

Consequences of termination. Where the injured party is entitled to, and   17–088
does, terminate for anticipatory breach, two results follow. First, he is released from future obligations under the contract: this is so even though between acceptance of the anticipatory breach and the time fixed for performance the party

---

[398] *Embiricos v Sydney Reid & Co* [1914] 3 K.B. 45 at 54.

[399] [1957] 2 Q.B. 401 at 449.

[400] ibid. at 450; Carter 47 M.L.R. 422; cf. *BV Oliehandel Jongkind v Coastal International Ltd* [1983] 2 Lloyd's Rep. 463 where the contract to some extent modified the English rule stated by Devlin J. in the *Citati* case. Contrast the American doctrine of "adequate assurance of performance" contained in U.C.C. s.2–609.

[401] (1853) 2 E. & B. 678 at 679; above, para.17–079.

[402] *Hongkong Fir Shipping Co Ltd v Kawasaki Kisen Kaisha Ltd* [1962] 2 Q.B. 26 at 57 (italics supplied); *Snia v Suzuki & Co* (1929) 29 Com.Cas. 284 (the *Citati* case itself may have been of this kind: see above, para.17–086); cf. *The Hermosa* [1982] 1 Lloyd's Rep. 570 at 580 (where a mere reasonable *suspicion*, as opposed to a reasonable *conclusion*, of future inability was held insufficient to justify termination).

[403] See below, para.18–032.

in breach changes his mind and offers after all to perform.[404] Secondly, the injured party is no longer bound to perform in order to establish his right of action on the contract; indeed he need not even show that he could at the time fixed for performance have performed a condition precedent to the other party's liability or a concurrent condition.[405]

(d) Effects of Not Accepting the Breach

17–089   **Contract remains in force.** If the injured party does not accept the breach, he remains liable to perform,[406] and he retains the right to enforce the other party's primary obligations.[407] As a practical matter, he also keeps alive the possibility of securing actual performance of the contract without legal action.

17–090   **Whether affirmation irrevocable.** The fact that the injured party initially calls for performance does not prevent him from terminating the contract on account of a later *actual* breach[408]; but there is a conflict of judicial opinion on the question whether, after the injured party has affirmed the contract, he can then change his mind while the breach remains anticipatory and still continues at the time of the injured party's later termination. One view is that the injured party should not be allowed to change course in this way[409] since, if the guilty party has acted in reliance on the affirmation by making continued efforts to perform the contract, he will be prejudiced by that change of course.[410] But where no such prejudice is suffered,[411] it is hard to see why effect should not be given to the change of course in cases of anticipatory (as it is in cases of actual[412]) breach. Refusal to give it such effect could unduly prejudice the injured party. For one thing, such refusal could require that party to "engage in performance that is entirely pointless and wasteful"[413] while the other party's anticipatory breach continued. For another, the injured party's initial reaction to the anticipatory breach might well be to call on the guilty party to perform and this might be regarded as an affirmation of the contract. One way of protecting the injured party in such cases would be to hold that the demand did not of itself amount to an affirmation,[414] but this possibility might be ruled out on the facts: e.g. by the terms of the demand. In such cases the possible hardship to the guilty party has to be set

---

[404] *Danube, etc., Ry v Xenos* (1863) 13 C.B.(N.S.) 825; cf. *Decro-Wall International SA v Practitioners in Marketing Ltd* [1971] 1 W.L.R. 361 at 382.

[405] See above, paras 17–025—17–030.

[406] See below, para.18–019.

[407] ibid.

[408] *Stocznia Gdanska SA v Latvian Shipping Co* [1997] 2 Lloyd's Rep. 228 at 236; cf. below, paras 18–021—18–022.

[409] This was the point actually decided in the *Stocznia* case, above; Treitel 114 L.Q.R. 22. The decision was later set aside by the House of Lords: [1998] 1 W.L.R. 574 at 594 but without final resolution of the point here under discussion and see below, fn.415.

[410] *Stocznia* case [1997] 2 Lloyd's Rep. 228 at 235–236.

[411] No such prejudice could have been suffered in the *Stocznia* case, above, since the injured party had originally served notices of termination; but as these were served *under* express provisions of the contract they formed (perhaps somewhat paradoxically) part of the process of affirmation.

[412] See below, paras 18–021—18–022.

[413] *Stocznia Gdanska SA v Latvian Shipping Co* [2001] 1 Lloyd's Rep. 537 at 565, affirmed [2002] EWCA Civ 889; [2002] 2 Lloyd's Rep. 436.

[414] See *Yukong Line Ltd of Korea v Rendsburg Investments Co of Liberia* [1996] 2 Lloyd's Rep. 604; *Stocznia Gdanska SA v Latvian Shipping Co* [2001] 1 Lloyd's Rep. 537 at 563–564, affirmed on this ground, above, fn.413, at [87]–[92].

against that to the injured party and it is submitted that, on balance, the preferable view[415] is that the injured party should not, as a general rule, be precluded by his initial affirmation from terminating the contract, even while the breach remains anticipatory, if after the affirmation the guilty party persists in his refusal. Any hardship which this view might cause to the guilty party would be removed by holding that there could be no such change of course where the original demand for performance induced the guilty party to continue, in response to the demand, to make efforts to perform the contract.

Damages. A party who does not accept the breach cannot at common law get damages before the time fixed for performance[416]; and meanwhile he runs the risk of losing his right of action altogether. This could, for example, happen if the contract created a contingent right and events occurred to defeat that right between the time of the anticipatory breach and that fixed for performance.[417] The injured party will similarly lose his rights in respect of the anticipatory breach if he does not accept it and if, before performance from the guilty party has become due, that party withdraws his repudiation,[418] or lawfully puts an end to the contract, e.g. under an express cancelling clause.[419] The position is the same if, before that time, the contract was discharged by operation of law under the doctrine of frustration[420]; it would, in such a case, make no difference if the repudiating party had been unable to perform even if the frustrating event had not occurred.[421]   **17–091**

---

[415] Expressed in the *Stocznia* case, above, fn.413, affirmed [2002] EWCA Civ 889; [2002] 2 Lloyd's Rep. 436, leaving the present point open at [97]–[100] but inclining towards the view stated in the text above.

[416] For a possible statutory power to award damages in such a case, if the contract was of a kind that is specifically enforceable, see below, para.21–060.

[417] e.g. if in *Synge v Synge* [1894] 1 Q.B. 466; above, para.17–080, the wife had died before the husband without accepting the breach.

[418] *Harrison v Northwest Holt Group Administration* [1985] I.C.R. 668.

[419] *The Simona* [1989] A.C. 788; cf. below, para.18–061.

[420] *Avery v Bowden* (1855) 5 E. & B. 714; (1856) 6 E. & B. 953; cf. *The Playa Larga* [1983] 2 Lloyd's Rep. 171 at 186; for frustration, see below, Ch.19.

[421] *Continental Grain Export Corp v STM Grain Ltd* [1979] 2 Lloyd's Rep. 460 at 470.

CHAPTER EIGHTEEN

TERMINATION FOR BREACH[1]

1. INTRODUCTION

18–001   **Terminology.** In previous editions the bulk of the material in this chapter can be found in a chapter on "Performance" and was considered under the heading of "Rescission for failure to perform". That was an entirely accurate acknowledgement that a failure to perform may be sufficient for the contract to be terminated, but without amounting to a breach so as to give rise to a right to damages, e.g. because the failure to perform is covered by some lawful excuse.[2] But in the vast majority of cases failure to perform will amount to a breach of contract and it seems natural therefore to assess the availability of termination as a consequence of breach, while acknowledging that in a few cases it may be available without any breach as such.

Termination in the present context is used to describe the remedy by which one party (the "injured party") is released from his obligation to perform because of the other party's defective or non-performance. It differs from other remedies such as damages or specific performance which seek to put the injured party into the position in which he would have been if the contract had been performed. It may, and often will, be used in combination with a claim for damages.[3] In some circumstances, the injured party may wish not only to be released from his own

---

[1] Devlin [1966] C.L.J. 192; Reynolds 79 L.Q.R. 534; Treitel 30 M.L.R. 139; Shea 42 M.L.R. 623; Beatson 97 L.Q.R. 389.

[2] See e.g. *Poussard v Speirs & Pond* (1876) 1 Q.B.D. 410 at 414; below, para.18–032, fn.177. On lawful excuse generally, see above, para.17–059.

[3] For the effect of termination (and the mode thereof) on the level of recovery in damages, see below, para.18–068.

obligation to perform, but to "undo" the transaction by returning the defective performance and claiming back the consideration which he provided for it, e.g. he may return defective goods and sue for recovery of the price which he had paid for them.[4]

In earlier editions, the term "rescission" was employed to describe the remedy discussed in this chapter, rather than "termination". No term seems ideally suited.[5] In the *Photo Production* case, Lord Diplock described the use of either "determination" or "rescission" as "misleading" unless it was borne in mind that such rescission did not deprive the injured party of his right to claim damages for breach.[6] The chief source of this possible confusion seems, however, to lie with the word "rescission"[7] and the contrast with rescission *for misrepresentation*, the effect of which is to deprive the injured party of his claim in damages *for breach*. Therefore, while the courts[8] (including Lord Diplock[9]) and Parliament[10] may sometimes continue to use the term "rescission", "termination" is preferred here so as to distinguish clearly the remedy available specifically for breach.

Policy considerations. The law governing the right to terminate for breach is complex and difficult; and in this it reflects the difficulty which the courts have experienced in balancing or reconciling the conflicting interests of the parties in respectively seeking, and resisting, the remedy of termination.[11]   18–002

Interests of the injured party. The interests of the injured party in seeking termination may be grouped under three heads. First, termination will be his only remedy where the failure in performance is not, in fact, a breach.[12] Secondly, termination may, even where the failure is a breach, lead to a result which is more favourable to the injured party in monetary terms than a claim for damages. This will be true where the contract would have been a bad bargain for the injured party even if it had been duly performed[13]; and also where the loss or injury which he suffers is one for which he might not recover damages in an action for breach of   18–003

---

[4] This remedy is more fully discussed below, paras 22–002—22–012.

[5] It is also now quite common to see it described as "discharge by breach". "Discharge" may be appropriate to describe the effect of the remedy on the obligations of the parties, but is not ideal vis-à-vis the contract itself: "[T]he aggrieved party is *discharged* from his obligations and can *rescind* the contract": Devlin [1966] C.L.J. 192. Even the word "by" may not be thought entirely appropriate since it tends to suggest an automatic process rather than one which depends on the election of the injured party; below, para.18–005.

[6] [1980] A.C. 827 at 851; below, para.18–015; cf. *Federal Commissioner of Taxation v Reliance Carpet Co Pty Ltd* (2008) 236 C.L.R. 342.

[7] *Photo Production Ltd v Securicor Transport Ltd* [1980] A.C. 827 at 844, per Lord Wilberforce; cf. an earlier criticism in *Heyman v Darwins Ltd* [1942] A.C. 356 at 399.

[8] See, e.g. *Bunge Corp v Tradax Export SA* [1981] 1 W.L.R. 711 at 719, 723, 724; *Stocznia Gdanska SA v Latvian Shipping Co* [1998] 1 W.L.R. 574 at 584.

[9] *The Scaptrade* [1983] 2 A.C. 694 at 702; *Gill & Duffus SA v Berger Co Inc* [1984] A.C. 382 at 390, 391.

[10] The Sale of Goods Act 1979 refers to a contract of sale as being "rescinded" by the seller on account of the buyer's breach; and it meets the point made by Lord Diplock by going on to provide that the rescission is "without prejudice to any claim the seller may have for damages": s.48(4). The same terminology is retained by recent amendments to the Act: s.48A(2)(b)(ii), 48C and 48F, as inserted by Sale and Supply of Goods to Consumers Regulations 2002, (SI 2002/3045), reg.5.

[11] Honnold 97 U. of Pa.L.Rev. 457.

[12] See above, fn.2.

[13] e.g. if he has agreed to pay £100 for something which would, because of a later fall in the market, be worth only £50 on delivery even if there had been no breach. This is a constantly recurring problem: see above, para.17–039; below, paras 18–033, 18–045, 18–046.

contract: e.g., if his loss (or part of it) is irrecoverable because it is too remote.[14] Thirdly, the injured party may, by terminating, get a quicker and more efficacious remedy. A buyer who has not yet paid for defective goods will often prefer to "terminate" (in the sense of rejecting the goods and refusing to pay) than to perform his side of the bargain and be left to pursue a claim for damages. By terminating he avoids the delays of litigation, and the risk that the seller's credit may fail.

18–004   **Interests of the defaulting party.** The party who fails to perform in accordance with the contract may have equally strong interests in resisting terminating. He may have incurred expenses in the course of performance, e.g. by paying commission on a sale or by transporting goods to a distant place; and these expenses will be thrown away if the contract is terminated. He may, in addition, have conferred benefits on the injured party who may be unjustly enriched by being allowed to terminate: termination of partly performed building contracts may, for example, produce this result.[15] And he may suffer hardship if the injured party is allowed to terminate on a falling market: he may be left with goods whose value has diminished by an amount far in excess of the loss which the defect in his performance would have caused to the injured party.

In balancing these conflicting interests, the courts have developed a number of rules and distinctions which prima facie determine the availability of termination as a remedy for breach. Further rules specify that the right to terminate, even where it is prima facie available, may be limited or barred by certain supervening factors. Before they are considered it is necessary to understand the nature and effect of termination.

2. NATURE AND EFFECT OF TERMINATION

(a) Nature

18–005   **No automatic termination.** A breach which justifies termination (sometimes referred to as a "repudiatory breach") does not automatically determine the contract.[16] It only gives the injured party the option either to terminate the contract or to affirm it and to claim further performance. This is generally the case, even if the contract says that it is to become "void" on breach.[17] Normally such a stipulation is construed[18] restrictively so as to prevent one party from

---

[14] See below, para.20–099 et seq.

[15] See above, para.17–042.

[16] *Heyman v Darwins Ltd* [1942] A.C. 356 at 361; *Decro-Wall International SA v Practitioners in Marketing Ltd* [1971] 1 W.L.R. 361 at 368, 375, 381; *The Simona* [1989] A.C. 788 at 800; cf. the overruling in *Photo Production Ltd v Securicor Transport Ltd* [1980] A.C. 827 of *Harbutt's "Plasticine" Ltd v Wayne Tank & Pump Co Ltd* [1970] 1 Q.B. 447. See Thompson 41 M.L.R. 137, suggesting a possible reconsideration of the rule stated in the text.

[17] cf. *Davenport v R.* (1877) 3 App.Cas. 115; *New Zealand Shipping Co v Société des Ateliers, etc., de France* [1919] A.C. 1. Automatic termination results only if the event on which the contract is expressed to come to an end occurs without breach of duty, as in *Brown v Knowsley BC* [1986] I.R.L.R. 102.

[18] e.g. *Alghussein Establishment v Eton College* [1988] 1 W.L.R. 587; for the status of the rule as one of construction, capable of being excluded by contrary provision, see *Cheall v Apex* [1983] 2 A.C. 180 at 189; cf. *The Bonde* [1991] 1 Lloyd's Rep. 136 at 144; *Decoma (UK) Ltd v Haden Drysys International Ltd* [2006] EWCA Civ 723 at [41]; *BDW Trading Ltd v JM Rowe Investments Ltd* [2011] EWCA Civ 548 at [31]; but it may be more accurate to regard it as an implied term: see below, para.6–045.

relying on his own breach of duty to the other party.[19] The reason for the rule that termination depends on the injured party's election is that the guilty party should not be allowed to rely on his own wrong so as to obtain a benefit under the contract,[20] or to excuse his own failure of further performance, or in some other way to prejudice the injured party's legal position under the contract.[21] Thus the guilty party is not allowed to take advantage of the breach by arguing that the original contract is discharged, so as to be entitled to a quantum meruit for work done by him,[22] or that he need pay only at the market rate (below that fixed by the contract) for services rendered to him.[23] Nor is he allowed to rely on the breach so as to prevent the injured party from enforcing provisions in the contract which are advantageous to that party and which may operate after the breach (such as a valid exclusive dealing clause[24]); or so as to deprive the injured party of the chance of claiming specific relief,[25] or of obtaining a lien on the guilty party's property.[26]

Employment contracts. In some situations, the general rule that a repudiatory breach does not of itself terminate the contract clearly applies to employment contracts. For example, in *Rigby v Ferodo Ltd*[27] an employer had committed such a breach by imposing a wage-cut. The employee nevertheless continued to work and it was held that the contract had not been terminated by the employer's unaccepted repudiation. It followed that the employee was entitled to recover the difference between the wages paid and those due under the contract. 18–006

But there is some support for the view that the position is different where the employee does *not* continue to work for the employer after the repudiatory breach,[28] either because he has been wrongfully dismissed or because he has left in breach of contract. In such cases, it is sometimes said that wrongful repudiation by one party automatically terminates the contract, without any need for the injured party to exercise the option to terminate. One argument in support of this

---

[19] For the requirement that the duty must be owed to the other party, see *Thompson v ASDA-MFI Group Plc* [1988] Ch. 241; contrast *Cheall v Apex*, above (breach of duty to third party).

[20] See the *Alghussein* case, above, fn.18.

[21] ibid.; contrast *Cheall v APEX* [1983] 2 A.C. 180 (breach of agreement with third party).

[22] *Boston Deep Sea Fishing & Ice Co v Ansell* (1888) 39 Ch.D. 339 at 364. The circumstances in which the injured party may terminate for breach and claim a quantum meruit are discussed below: para.22–023 et seq.; cf. above, para.17–046.

[23] Example based on *Timber Shipping Co SA v London & Overseas Freighters Ltd* [1972] A.C. 1 (where there was no breach).

[24] e.g. *Decro-Wall International v Practitioners in Marketing Ltd* [1971] 1 W.L.R. 361; cf. *Thomas Marshall (Exports) Ltd v Guinle* [1979] Ch. 227; *WPM Retail v Laing* [1978] I.C.R. 787 (employee preserving right to bonus after wrongful dismissal); *Lusograin Commercio Internacional de Cereas Ltda v Bunge AG* [1986] 2 Lloyd's Rep. 654 (seller's right to "carrying charges" (below, para.20–144) after repudiation by buyer). For exclusion of the rule by contrary agreement, see above, fn.18.

[25] See *Decro-Wall International SA v Practitioners in Marketing Ltd* [1971] 1 W.L.R. 361 (where it was held that there was no automatic termination); *Evening Standard Co Ltd v Henderson* [1987] I.C.R. 588.

[26] *G Barker v Eynon* [1974] 1 W.L.R. 462 (where again the view that termination is automatic was implicitly rejected).

[27] [1988] I.C.R. 29.

[28] *Sanders v Ernest A Neale* [1974] I.C.R. 565; *Gannon v Firth* [1976] I.R.L.R. 415; cf. *Hare v Murphy Bros Ltd* [1974] I.C.R. 603 (where the contract seems to have been frustrated on the ground stated at para.19–084, below); *R. v East Berkshire Health Authority Ex p. Walsh* [1985] Q.B. 152 at 161; Thomson 38 M.L.R. 347; Napier [1975] C.L.J. 36.

view is that, where the employee is no longer working for the employer (in consequence of the repudiation), the employment *relationship* has plainly come to an end,[29] even against the wishes of the injured party. But it does not follow from this that the *contract* of employment is similarly terminated[30]: the argument that the repudiating party should not be allowed to rely on his own wrong to deprive the injured party of valuable rights under the contract has as much force where the contract is one of employment as it has in relation to other contracts. A further argument for the view that a contract of employment is automatically terminated by repudiatory breach is that, if the contract were not so terminated, a wrongfully dismissed employee would be entitled to sue for his wages until the time of his election to terminate; whereas it is settled that his remedy is in damages and not by action for the agreed wages.[31] But this argument fails to distinguish between the continued existence of the *contract*, and the *remedies* for its breach.[32] This point is by no means restricted to contracts of employment. Suppose, for example, that a buyer wrongfully repudiates an instalment contract for the sale of goods by refusing to accept further instalments. If the seller elects to treat the contract as remaining in existence, it does not follow that he can sue for *the price* of the undelivered instalments. His remedy is normally in damages, though the amount recoverable may depend on whether he elects to terminate.[33] Similarly, where a time charter is wrongfully repudiated by the charterer, the shipowner is not bound to accept the repudiation; but even if he elects to affirm his remedy may be in damages rather than for the agreed hire[34]: "It is ... the range of remedies which is limited, not the right to elect."[35] The same is true of contracts of employment: it does not follow from the continued existence of the *contract* that a wrongfully dismissed employee's *remedy* is by action for the agreed sum.[36] Thus it is submitted that the general rule applies to such contracts, i.e., that a repudiatory breach by either party does not lead to automatic termination, but only gives the injured party an option to terminate the contract.[37] An employment contract may confer an express power to terminate the contract[38] and may dispense with the

---

[29] *Micklefield v SAC Technology* [1990] 1 W.L.R. 1002 at 1006; *Delaney v Staples* [1992] 1 A.C. 687 at 692; *Wilson v St Helens BC* [1998] I.C.R. 1141 at 1152.

[30] *Gunton v Richmond-upon-Thames LBC* [1981] Ch. 448 at 474 (doubted on this point in *Ex p. Walsh*, above); followed, though with reluctance, in *Boyo v Lambeth LBC* [1995] I.C.R. 727; cf. above, para.15–052; *Micklefield v SAC Technology* [1990] 1 W.L.R. 1002; *Litster v Forth Dry Dock & Engineering Co Ltd* [1990] 1 A.C. 546 at 568; *Villella v MFI Furniture Centres Ltd* [1999] I.R.L.R. 468 at 474. Conversely, the *relationship* may continue after the *contract* has come to an end: *Eastbourne BC v Foster* [2001] EWCA Civ 1091; [2002] I.C.R. 234.

[31] ibid.; *Marsh v National Autistic Society* [1993] I.C.R. 453; cf. *Delaney v Staples* [1992] 1 A.C. 687 at 693; *Cerberus Software Ltd v Rowley* [2001] EWCA Civ 78; [2001] I.C.R. 376.

[32] See below, para.21–010, fn.28.

[33] See below, para.20–077.

[34] See below, para.21–013.

[35] *The Alaskan Trader (No.2)* [1983] 2 Lloyd's Rep. 645 at 651.

[36] e.g. *Silvey v Pendragon Plc* [2001] EWCA Civ 784; [2001] I.R.L.R. 685.

[37] *Simmons v Hoover Ltd* [1977] Q.B. 284; *Western Excavating (EEC) Ltd v Sharp* [1978] Q.B. 761 at 769; *Gunton v Richmond-upon-Thames LBC* [1981] 1 Ch. 448; *Burdett-Coutts v Hertfordshire CC* [1984] I.R.L.R. 91; *Evening Standard Co Ltd v Henderson* [1987] I.C.R. 586 at 593, 595; cf. also *Decro-Wall International SA v Practitioners in Marketing Ltd* [1971] 1 W.L.R. 361 at 369–370, 375–376, 380–381; the same assumption seems to underlie *Miles v Wakefield MDC* [1987] A.C. 539; below, para.18–019; Thompson 97 L.Q.R. 8 at 235; 98 L.Q.R. 423; 42 M.L.R. 91; McMullen [1982] C.L.J. 110; *Visscher v Honourable President Justice Giudice* (2009) 239 C.L.R. 361.

[38] See below, para.18–061 et seq.

need to give formal notice if some other mechanism is provided, e.g. making payment in lieu of notice.[39]

Insurance Contracts. In the law of insurance, "warranty" is used in a sense similar to that now more usually given to "condition": i.e. to refer to a term, the breach of which justifies the injured party's refusal to perform.[40] But the exact legal effects of a breach of "warranty" in insurance law are not identical with those elsewhere given to a breach of "condition": in particular, there is no requirement in insurance law that an insurer who is the victim of a breach of "warranty" must take any steps to exercise his option to avoid liability. A statutory statement of this position is given in s.33(3) of the Marine Insurance Act 1906, which provides that:

18–007

> "A warranty is a condition which must be exactly complied with. If it be not so complied with, then . . . the insurer is discharged from liability as from the date of the breach of warranty."

The effect of these words was considered in *The Good Luck*,[41] where a ship had been insured under a policy entitling the insurers to declare certain areas as prohibited and containing a "warranty" that the shipowner would comply with any such prohibition. The policy was assigned to a bank (to which the ship had been mortgaged) and the insurers undertook to notify the bank "promptly" if they "ceased to insure" the ship. Some months later the ship was struck by an Iraqi missile while trading in the Persian Gulf (which had been declared by the insurers to be a prohibited area) and became a constructive total loss. A claim on the policy having been rejected, it was held that the insurers were liable on their undertaking to the bank. They had "ceased to insure" the ship as soon as she had entered the prohibited area: this breach of "warranty" released the insurers automatically,[42] without any election on their part.[43] This followed from the wording of s.33(3), by which the insurer "is discharged from liability as from the date of the breach of warranty". These words should be contrasted with those of the Sale of Goods Act 1979, giving a buyer, in cases of breach of condition, "a right to treat the contract as repudiated".[44] The principle of automatic discharge for breach of "warranty" in insurance law was explained by Lord Goff in *The Good Luck* on the ground that "fulfilment of the warranty is a condition precedent to the liability [or further liability] of the insurer".[45] At first sight this gives rise to some difficulty, for if performance of the warranty were a condition precedent it would follow that the

---

[39] *Société Générale v Geys* [2011] EWCA Civ 307; [2011] I.R.L.R. 482, but if the employee is not aware that the contract has been terminated, some further notice may be necessary to determine the effective date of termination for the purpose of claims under the Employment Rights Act 1996: see. s.97(1); cf. *Gisda Cyf v Barratt* [2010] UKSC 41; [2010] I.R.L.R. 1073.

[40] See below, para.18–039.

[41] [1992] 1 A.C. 233.

[42] cf. *Hussain v Brown* [1996] 1 Lloyd's Rep. 627 at 630, where, because of this "draconian" consequence of breach, the court refused to hold the "warranty" to be a *continuing* one.

[43] It follows that an insurer setting up breach of warranty as a defence does not thereby "rescind" the contract within the meaning of an exemption clause in the policy: *HIH Casualty & General Insurance Ltd v New Hampshire Insurance Co* [2001] EWCA Civ 735; [2001] 2 Lloyd's Rep. 161 at [122].

[44] Sale of Goods Act 1979, s.11(3).

[45] [1992] 1 A.C. 233 at 263; the words in square brackets do not occur in this report but do occur in [1991] 3 All E.R. 1 at 16 and in [1991] 2 Lloyd's Rep. 191 at 202.

insurer never became liable at all; while s.33(3) says that he is "discharged", thus suggesting that a pre-existing liability has been brought to an end. It may be that this difficulty can be resolved by reference to the special nature of an insurance contract. Such a contract differs from a more typical contract (such as one of sale) in which the parties bargain for an exchange of performances (i.e. of the goods for the price). In a contract of indemnity insurance the position is that the performance of one party (i.e. payment of the premium by the assured) is exchanged for the promise of the other[46] (i.e., that of the insurer to indemnify against the loss), and in the great majority of cases this promise does not have to be performed at all because the event insured against does not occur. The occurrence of this event is thus a contingent condition precedent[47] of the insurer's liability *to pay*, while on breach of the "warranty" he is "discharged" from his conditional promise even before the event occurs.

18–008   **Restrictions on injured party's choice.** Although termination depends (except in the insurance situation just discussed) on the election of the injured party, that party's option is to some extent curtailed by the rule that the damages to which he is entitled may be reduced if he fails to take reasonable steps to mitigate his loss.[48] This rule will sometimes put pressure on the injured party to terminate, for one common way of mitigating loss is to make a substitute contract; and the effect of doing this will often be to put it out of the injured party's power to perform the old contract. Where this is the case, the making of the substitute contract will involve the termination of the original one. Thus if a wrongfully dismissed employee mitigates his loss by taking another job he will thereby be "taken to have accepted his wrongful dismissal as a repudiatory breach leading to a determination of the contract of service".[49] The same would be true where a seller, on the buyer's repudiation, disposed elsewhere of the subject-matter. In these cases the injured party is not under any legal obligation to make the substitute contract[50]; so that in this sense he remains free to choose between affirmation and termination. But his freedom of choice is limited in that, if he acts unreasonably in failing to make such a contract, he will suffer a reduction in the damages to which he is entitled by reason of breach of the original contract.

Conversely, the mitigation rules may require the injured party to accept performance from the party in breach even though it is not in accordance with the contract: e.g. they may require a buyer to accept late delivery.[51] In such a case, the mitigation rules again do not, strictly speaking, restrict the injured party's right to terminate, but they do require him, having terminated, to enter into a new contract for late performance at the original price (subject to damages for delay[52]). The injured party does not commit any breach of duty by failing to enter into such

---

[46] cf. below, para.22–003.

[47] See above, para.2–104.

[48] See below, para.20–115.

[49] *Gunton v Richmond-upon-Thames LBC* [1981] Ch. 448 at 468. The same result can follow where the employee continues to work for the employer "on an entirely different basis" from that of the repudiated contract: *Eastbourne BC v Foster* [2001] EWCA Civ 1091; [2002] I.C.R. 234.

[50] See below, para.20–115.

[51] *The Solholt* [1981] 2 Lloyd's Rep. 574 (affirmed [1983] 1 Lloyd's Rep. 605).

[52] *The Solholt* [1983] 1 Lloyd's Rep. 605, criticising *Strutt v Whitnell* [1975] 1 W.L.R. 870 for failing to observe the distinction drawn in the text.

a new contract, but his failure to do so will reduce the damages to which he is entitled for breach of the original contract. Hence his freedom of choice will, as a practical matter, be restricted, this time in the direction of putting him under pressure to accept performance, though subject to relatively minor modifications.

Exercise of the option to terminate. The question whether the option to 18–009 terminate has been exercised has been described as one of fact[53]; but this description assumes that a number of legal requirements have been satisfied. The prime requirement is that the behaviour of the injured party must unequivocally indicate his intention to exercise the option.[54] A notice which purports to terminate the contract, but stipulates *unilaterally* that it shall continue to be performed on a without prejudice basis is not effective.[55]

Normally mere "silence and inactivity"[56] will not suffice for this purpose, but there is no absolute rule to this effect. Thus in *Vitol SA v Norelf Ltd*[57] a contract for the sale of propane was wrongfully repudiated by the buyer and, after receiving the repudiation, the seller made no attempt to take any of the steps which he would have been expected to take for the purpose of performing the contract,[58] if he were treating it as still in force. The House of Lords held that an arbitrator's finding that the seller had accepted the repudiation was not wrong in law; for, even if the seller's reaction to the breach could be described as "inactivity", it was in the circumstances not equivocal since it clearly conveyed to the buyer that the seller was treating the contract as at an end. The option will commonly be exercised by giving notice to this effect to the party in breach,[59] and sometimes such notice must be given: e.g. where the injured party seeks the return of property with which he has parted under the contract.[60] But there is plainly no such requirement where "inactivity" suffices for the exercise of the option; nor does notice seem to be necessary where the injured party has put it out of his power to perform the original contract by making a substitute contract to satisfy the mitigation requirement.[61] The option can also be exercised by the commencement of proceedings

---

[53] *Kish v Taylor* [1912] A.C. 604 at 617; *Agrokor AG v Tradigrain SA* [2000] 1 Lloyd's Rep. 497 at 500.

[54] *Sookraj v Samaroo* [2004] UKPC 50 at [17].

[55] *Leofelis SA v Lonsdale Sports Ltd* [2008] EWCA Civ 680; *The Times*, July 23, 2008. After termination, the parties may *agree* to the continued performance of the contract on a without prejudice basis, which *may* avoid a finding of repudiation by the party serving the notice if it is later found to be invalid (cf. *Federal Commerce Navigation Co Ltd v Molena Alpha Inc* [1979] A.C. 757), and will serve to mitigate any loss if there is a finding of repudiation.

[56] *State Trading Corp of India v M Golodetz Ltd* [1989] 2 Lloyd's Rep. 277 at 286; *Glencore Grain Rotterdam BV v LORICO* [1997] 2 Lloyd's Rep. 386 at 394. cf. below, para.17–078.

[57] [1996] A.C. 800.

[58] Such as tendering shipping documents as "a precondition to payment of the price": 1996] A.C. 800 at 811. Contrast *Jaks (UK) Ltd v Cera Investment Bank SA* [1998] 2 Lloyd's Rep. 89 at 96 (failure to take steps to perform another contract with a third party not sufficient).

[59] Notice to a third party may suffice where the defendant cannot be traced: *Bell Electric Ltd v Aweco Appliance Systems GmbH & Co KG* [2002] C.L.C. 1246 at [30]. A notice of termination is valid notwithstanding that it refers to a notice of default which is found to be invalid, in circumstances where it is possible to rely instead on an earlier valid notice of default: *Reinwood Ltd v L Brown & Sons Ltd* [2008] EWCA Civ 1090; 121 Con L.R. 1 (based on the general rule referred to in para.17–062).

[60] *Lakshmijit v Sherani* [1974] A.C. 605.

[61] *Gunton v Richmond-upon-Thames LBC* [1981] Ch. 448 at 468.

brought on the contract.[62] A notice of intended termination at a later date if certain conditions are not fulfilled is not effective unless the threatened termination is then implemented.[63]

Obviously the injured party affirms the contract by claiming specific performance, though he may later terminate on the basis of the guilty party's continued failure to perform,[64] and a "decision not to pursue a remedy of specific performance does not commit the innocent party to accept a repudiatory or anticipatory breach."[65] There is no inconsistency between claiming damages for a prior breach, or for the breach in question, and exercising the option to terminate.[66] There are, moreover, cases in which the victim merely refuses to perform until the other party either cures his breach or (in the case of contracts calling for continuing performance) resumes performance in conformity with the contract. For example, an employer may refuse to pay wages, or to pay them in full, for so long as his employee refuses (in the course of "industrial action") to perform his duties under the contract of employment. Such a temporary refusal on the employer's part does not amount to an exercise by him of the option to terminate.[67]

If the injured party accepts further performance after breach, he may be held to have affirmed, so that he cannot later terminate the contract.[68] He must, moreover, terminate the contract as a whole: e.g. a tenant cannot remain on premises and ignore a particular term of the lease on the ground that the landlord had, in the past, failed to perform his obligations under that term.[69]

(b) Effects of Termination or Affirmation

(i) *Termination*

18–010 **On obligations of the injured party.** After termination, the injured party is no longer bound to accept or pay for further performance.[70] He is also entitled to refuse to make payments which had not yet fallen due at the time of termination, e.g. because the other party's performance was incomplete or defective[71]; and he

---

[62] *Downing v Al Tameer Establishment* [2002] EWCA Civ 721; [2002] C.L.C. 1291 (proceedings amounted to acceptance of repudiation of an arbitration agreement). It can be exercised even after beginning of the proceedings: *Tilcons Ltd v Land & Real Estate Investments Ltd* [1987] 1 W.L.R. 46. The mere issue of a claim form in which the claimant purports to terminate the contract is too unequivocal an act; acceptance of the defendant's repudiation occurs upon service (unless some other form of notice is given before then): *Bell Electric Ltd v Aweco Appliance Systems GmbH & Co KG* [2002] C.L.C. 1246 at [28].

[63] *Standard Bank Plc v Agrinvest International Inc* [2010] EWCA Civ 1400; [2010] 2 C.L.C. 886. The wording of the relevant letter in that case ("we will close out . . . ") does not rule out an effective "conditional" termination without the need to take any additional steps.

[64] See para.18–022.

[65] *Bear Stearns Bank Plc v Forum Global Equity Ltd* [2007] EWHC 1576 (Comm) at [127].

[66] *General Billposting Co Ltd v Atkinson* [1909] A.C. 118. Contrast *United Dominions Trust (Commercial) Ltd v Ennis* [1968] 1 Q.B. 54 at 65 (below, para.18–071).

[67] *Wiluszynski v Tower Hamlets LBC* [1989] I.C.R. 493; it is assumed that the breach justified termination. For the different question whether failure to perform a condition precedent of itself *entitles* the injured party to terminate, see above, para.17–024.

[68] cf. below, para.18–076 et seq.; an *unsatisfied demand* for performance does not have the same effect: below, para.18–021.

[69] *Total Oil Great Britain Ltd v Thompson Garages (Biggin Hill) Ltd* [1972] 1 Q.B. 318.

[70] *Photo Production Ltd v Securicor Transport Ltd* [1980] A.C. 827 at 849.

[71] e.g. above, para.17–032; *SCI (Sales Curve Interactive) v Titus SARL* [2001] EWCA Civ 591; [2001] 2 All E.R. (Comm) 416 at [28]–[33], [65].

is released from other obligations which, under the contract, were to be performed in the future: e.g. a wrongfully dismissed employee is no longer bound by covenants in restraint of trade in his contract of employment.[72]

Limited retrospective effect. Termination does not operate retrospectively,[73] in the sense of liberating the injured party from his duty to perform obligations which had accrued before termination.[74] For example, where freight under a charterparty is deemed earned on loading, the charterer remains liable to pay it even though he later justifiably terminates on account of the shipowner's repudiatory breach.[75] The injured party may also himself have been in breach at the time of the other party's repudiation, but not in such a way as to justify that repudiation.[76] In such a case, the injured party is, in spite of his own breach, entitled to terminate, but he remains liable in damages for the breach which he had himself committed before terminating.[77] The injured party also continues to be bound, after termination, by ancillary obligations of the kind to be described below,[78] and even by primary obligations where the contract expressly so provides.[79] **18–011**

If, at the time of termination, the injured party has already performed, he may be entitled to recover back that performance. For example, a buyer who justifiably rejects goods for breach of condition is normally entitled to the return of the price.[80] To this extent, termination has a retrospective effect.[81] It is submitted that, where the injured party would thus be entitled, after he has terminated, to recover back money paid before termination, he should also be relieved from liability to pay sums which had become due (but had not been paid) before termination; for it would make no practical sense to hold him liable in one action for a payment which he could then claim back in another.[82]

On the obligations of the party in breach. For the purpose of stating the effects of termination on the obligations of the party in breach, it is necessary to distinguish between primary and secondary obligations.[83] The primary obligation **18–012**

---

[72] *General Billposting Co Ltd v Atkinson* [1909] A.C. 118; *Briggs v Oates* [1990] I.C.R. 473; cf. *Thompson v Corroon* (1993) 66 P. & C.R. 445; contrast *Lawrence David Ltd v Ashton* [1991] 1 All E.R. 384 (where it was not clear that the employer was in repudiatory breach).

[73] *Hurst v Bryk* [2002] 1 A.C. 185.

[74] *The Bow Cedar* [2004] EWHC 2929; [2005] 1 Lloyd's Rep. 275 at [34]–[35].

[75] *The Dominique* [1989] A.C. 1056; cf. *Hurst v Bryk* [2002] 1 A.C. 185 for a special application of this principle to a partner's obligation to pay his share of the partnership liabilities incurred before, but falling due after, termination.

[76] e.g. where the injured party's own breach is a breach of an independent covenant (above, para.17–019); or one which is not sufficiently serious to justify termination (above, para.18–025 et seq.); or one which occurs simultaneously with the other party's breach, as in *State Trading Corp of India v M Golodetz* [1989] 2 Lloyd's Rep. 277 at 288.

[77] *Gill & Duffus SA v Berger & Co Inc* [1984] A.C. 382 at 390.

[78] See below, after fn.90.

[79] See below, at fn.88.

[80] See below, para.22–005.

[81] In *Taylor v Motability Finance* Ltd [2004] EWHC 2619 (Comm), Cooke J.'s observations that termination cannot have a retrospective effect must be understood in the context of the claim made in that case: see paras 22–005 and 22–022 below.

[82] cf. *McDonald v Denys Lascelles Ltd* (1933) 48 C.L.R. 457 (see below, para.20–155) where a claim against the party in breach failed on similar reasoning, which should a fortiori protect the *injured party*; and below, para.19–093.

[83] A distinction drawn by Lord Diplock in a number of cases, e.g. in *Lep Air Services v Rolloswin Investments Ltd* [1973] A.C. 331 at 354–355 and *Photo Production Ltd v Securicor Transport Ltd* [1980] A.C. 827 at 848–849; cf. also below, para.21–003.

is one to render the actual performance promised; the secondary obligation is one to pay damages for failure to perform the primary obligation.

18–013   **Effect on primary obligations.** The effect of termination on the primary obligations of the party in breach is exactly the same as its effect on those of the injured party: normally the party in breach is released from primary obligations which had not yet fallen due at the time of termination,[84] but he remains liable to perform those which had already fallen due at that time,[85] except where a payment which he should have made before termination was one which he could, if he had so made it, have recovered back, even on termination for his own breach,[86] e.g. where there has been a total failure of consideration.[87]

The rules stated in the preceding paragraph can be excluded by contrary provision in the contract or by other evidence of contrary intention.[88] Thus even a primary obligation which has not yet fallen due can survive termination if the contract so provides,[89] while liability for one which had fallen due will not survive if the contract validly provides that termination is to be the sole remedy.[90]

18–014   **Ancillary obligations.** Primary obligations must be distinguished from ancillary ones, i.e. those imposed by provisions which deal not with the performance to be rendered, but with such matters as the resolution of disputes arising out of the contract,[91] or the inspection by one party of records to be kept by the other for the purpose of ascertaining what rights and duties have come into existence under the contract.[92] Normally, such ancillary obligations are intended to survive termination and are accordingly not released by it.[93]

18–015   **Secondary obligation to pay damages.** The important difference between the effects of termination on the obligations of the two parties is that the party in breach (unlike the injured party) comes, as a result of termination, under a

---

[84] cf. above, para.18–010. It follows that there can be no specific enforcement of those primary obligations: see *Walker v Standard Chartered Bank* [1992] B.C.L.C. 535.

[85] *Stocznia Gdanska SA v Latvian Shipping Co* [1998] 1 W.L.R. 574; cf. *Fielding & Platt Ltd v Najjar* [1969] 1 W.L.R. 357 at 361; *Lep Air Services v Rolloswin Investments Ltd* [1973] A.C. 331 at 354–355; *Photo Production Ltd v Securicor Transport Ltd* [1980] A.C. 827 at 844, 849; *Hyundai Heavy Industries Ltd v Papadopoulos* [1980] 1 W.L.R. 1129; below, para.20–155; *The Trident Beauty* [1994] 1 W.L.R. 161 at 164.

[86] *McDonald v Denys Lascelles Ltd*, above, fn.82.

[87] *Mirimskaya v Evans* [2007] EWHC 2073 (TCC); (2007) 114 Con. L.R. 131.

[88] *Yasuda Fire & Marine Ins Co of Europe v Orion Marine Ins Underwriting Agency Ltd* [1995] 1 Lloyd's Rep. 525.

[89] *Harbinger UK Ltd v GE Information Services Ltd* [2000] 1 All E.R. (Comm) 166 (a case of lawful termination by notice; but there seems to be no reason why a similar express provision should not take effect after termination for breach).

[90] *Malcolm-Ellis (Liverpool) v American Electronics Laboratory* (1984) N.L.J. 500.

[91] *Heyman v Darwins Ltd* [1942] A.C. 356 (arbitration); *Connex South Eastern Ltd v MJ Building Services Group Plc* [2004] EWHC 1518 (TCC); [2004] B.L.R. 333 at [25] (affirmed [2005] EWCA Civ 193; [2005] 1 W.L.R. 3323, without consideration of this issue); cf. Arbitration Act 1996, s.7.

[92] *The Yasuda Fire & Marine Ins Co of Europe Ltd v Orion Marine Ins Underwriting Agency Ltd* [1995] 1 Lloyd's Rep. 525.

[93] See the authorities cited in fnn.91 and 92 above. The same view was taken by Phillips L.J. in *Rock Refrigeration Ltd v Jones* [1997] I.C.R. 938 of covenants in restraint of trade in an employment contract which had been wrongfully repudiated by the employer; but this is hard to reconcile with *General Billposting Ltd v Atkinson* [1908] A.C. 118 (above, para.18–010), on which the other two members of the court based their decision in the *Rock Refrigeration* case. For the different position where the contract is wrongfully repudiated *by* the person subject to the restraint, see *Kall Kwick Printing (UK) Ltd v Rush* [1996] F.S.R. 114.

secondary obligation to pay damages,[94] and that his liability in damages may relate both to breaches committed before termination and to losses suffered by the injured party as a result of the non-performance of future obligations brought about by termination.[95] Suppose, for example, that a hirer under a hire-purchase agreement fails to make the agreed payments in circumstances amounting to a wrongful repudiation and therefore gives the owner the right to terminate. If the owner does terminate, the hirer remains liable for instalments which had fallen due *before* termination, his primary obligation to pay these being unaffected[96]; but he is not liable for *subsequent* instalments, having been released by termination from his primary obligation to make these payments. On the other hand, the hirer is liable in damages for wrongful repudiation[97] and these may include compensation for loss suffered by the owner after, and as a result of, the premature termination of the agreement: e.g. where he has to dispose of the goods elsewhere for less than the amount which would have been paid by the defaulting hirer if the agreement with him had run its full course. Damages for the non-performance of future obligations brought about by termination are not available where the injured party terminates under an express contractual provision in circumstances which would not entitle him to terminate under the general law.[98]

Claims for agreed sum. For the purpose of these rules, it is important to distinguish between claims for *damages* (which can be brought in respect of future losses) and claims for *agreed sums*[99] (which can be brought only in respect of sums that have become due at the time of termination). The distinction is sometimes overlooked because there is a tendency to describe any claim for money as one for damages, even when it is actually a claim for the enforcement of a primary obligation to pay an agreed sum. The point can be illustrated by taking the common case of a contract of sale which requires the buyer to pay a deposit and which is terminated by the seller after, and on account of, the buyer's breach in failing to pay that deposit. In such a case, the seller will be entitled to (i) the deposit as an agreed sum due at the time of termination; and (ii) damages for the buyer's repudiatory breach,[100] e.g. for loss suffered because the seller can resell the property only for an amount which falls short of the contract price by more than the amount of the deposit. In such a case, it is not strictly accurate to say that the seller can "sue for damages *including* the amount of the unpaid deposit."[101] This statement is accurate only where the seller has terminated on account of some *other* breach by the buyer *before* the buyer's primary obligation to pay the deposit

18–016

---

[94] *R V Ward Ltd v Bignall* [1967] 1 Q.B. 534 at 548; Thornely [1967] C.L.J. 168; *Lep Air Services Ltd v Rolloswin Investments Ltd* [1973] A.C. 331, esp. at 350; *State Trading Corp of India v M Golodetz Ltd* [1989] 2 Lloyd's Rep. 277 at 286; Carter 1 J.C.L. 113 and 249.

[95] *R Leslie Shipping Co v Welstead* [1921] 3 K.B. 420; *Bridge v Campbell Discount Co Ltd* [1962] A.C. 600; *Hyundai Heavy Industries Ltd v Papadopoulos* [1980] 1 W.L.R. 1129 at 1141; *Photo Production Ltd v Securicor Transport Ltd* [1980] A.C. 827 at 849 ("anticipatory secondary obligation"); *Gill & Duffus SA v Berger Co Inc* [1984] A.C. 382 at 390.

[96] *Brooks v Beirnstein* [1909] 1 K.B. 98; *Chatterton v Maclean* [1951] 1 All E.R. 761; cf. *The Almare Seconda* [1981] 2 Lloyd's Rep. 443; and see below, para.20–155, fn.956.

[97] cf. *Stocznia Gdanska SA v Latvian Shipping Co* [2002] EWCA Civ 889; [2002] 2 Lloyd's Rep 436 at [83] (damages in respect of failure to pay instalments which would have become due after termination).

[98] Discussed further at para.18–068 et seq.

[99] See below, para.21–001 et seq.

[100] See above, para.18–015.

[101] *Millichamp v Jones* [1982] 1 W.L.R. 1422 at 1430.

had accrued. This was the position in *The Blankenstein*,[102] where a contract for the sale of three ships provided for the signing of a formal memorandum and for the payment of a deposit of $236,500 on such signing. The seller terminated on account of the buyer's wrongful refusal to sign and resold the ships for $60,000 less than the original contract price. As the deposit was to be paid only on signing, the primary obligation to pay it never accrued. But it was held that the seller was entitled to $236,500 as damages for the buyer's repudiation in wrongfully refusing to sign the memorandum. The majority of the Court of Appeal rejected the argument that the seller's damages should be no more than $60,000; and their view seems, with respect, to be correct. At the time of termination, the seller had been deprived, by the buyer's breach, of his right to receive the full amount of the deposit. He thus became entitled to damages of a precisely ascertainable amount, and later events (i.e. the relatively favourable resale of the ships) should not be allowed to deprive him of that accrued right. Such events should be relevant to the assessment of damages only where, at the time of termination, it is *not* possible to put an exact value on the injured party's loss.

18–017   **No inconsistency in terminating for breach and claiming damages.** It follows from the preceding discussion that there is no inconsistency between terminating a contract for breach and at the same time claiming damages for that breach. Accordingly it has been held that damages can be recovered by a buyer who rejects goods because they are defective,[103] or delivered late[104]; by a wrongfully dismissed employee who has terminated so as to free himself from a covenant in restraint of trade[105]; by a vendor of land who has terminated because of the purchaser's failure to comply with a notice to complete[106]; and by a purchaser of land who has terminated on account of the vendor's breach.[107] Termination for breach differs in this respect from rescission for misrepresentation, the effect of which is to treat the contract as if it had never existed.[108]

18–018   **Insurance contracts.** The rules stated above assume that the injured party has, and has exercised, an option to terminate. We have seen that in the law of insurance an insurer may be discharged from liability automatically, without any such election on his part[109]; and where he is so discharged it does not follow that even the *primary* obligations of the other party are similarly discharged. Thus the assured can remain liable for premiums even though his breach of "warranty" has discharged the insurer.[110]

---

[102] [1985] 1 W.L.R. 435; Carter 104 L.Q.R. 207.

[103] *Millar's Machinery Co Ltd v David Way & Son* (1935) 40 Com.Cas. 204. cf. also the right of an unpaid *seller* to terminate (by exercising his right of resale) and claim damages: Sale of Goods Act 1979, s.48(4).

[104] *The Al Tawfiq* [1984] 2 Lloyd's Rep. 598.

[105] *General Billposting Co Ltd v Atkinson* [1909] A.C. 118.

[106] *Buckland v Farmar & Moody* [1979] 1 W.L.R. 221; *Johnson v Agnew* [1980] A.C. 367.

[107] The contrary was held in *Horsler v Zorro* [1975] Ch. 302 but that decision was disapproved in *Buckland v Farmar & Moody*, above, and overruled in *Johnson v Agnew*, above; Alberry 91 L.Q.R. 337; cf. Gummow 92 L.Q.R. 5; Oakley [1980] C.L.J. 58; Dawson 39 M.L.R. 241; Hetherington 96 L.Q.R. 401; Jackson 97 L.Q.R. 26.

[108] See above, para.9–084 and cf. *Johnson v Agnew* [1980] A.C. 367 at 395, 398, also disapproving the reasoning of *Barber v Wolfe* [1945] Ch. 187.

[109] See above, para.18–007.

[110] *The Good Luck* [1992] A.C. 233 at 263.

(ii) *Affirmation or failure to terminate*

Contract remains in force. The injured party may positively affirm the   18–019
contract,[111] or simply fail to exercise his option to terminate.[112] In either of these
cases, the contract remains in force,[113] so that each party is bound to perform his
primary obligations when that performance falls due.[114] It must, however, be
recalled that, under the rules relating to the order of performance,[115] the effect of
one party's breach may be to prevent performance of the other's obligations from
falling due. For example, an employee may, in breach of contract, refuse to
perform his duty to work and so give the employer a right to dismiss him.[116] The
mere fact that the employer does not exercise that right does not lead to the result
that the employer must continue to pay the agreed wages. On the contrary, he is
under no such liability since performance of the employee's duty to work is a
condition precedent of the employer's duty to pay.[117] The position is more
complex where the employee's breach takes the form, not of an outright refusal to
work, but of a refusal merely to perform specified tasks while continuing to
perform the remaining duties of his employment. This situation has already been
discussed[118]; the only point which needs to be made here is that, if the employer
voluntarily accepts such partial performance, he must pay for it at the contract
rate,[119] while the employee is liable in damages for loss caused by his breach.[120] It
is in this sense that the obligations of both parties "remain in force".

Remedies. The statement just made relates only to the *obligations* of the   18–020
parties, and not to the *remedies* for their enforcement. To say that a party remains
bound under the contract to do or to abstain from doing some act does not mean
that these obligations can be enforced by an order of specific performance or by an
injunction; and similarly to say that a party remains bound to make certain
payments does not mean that an action for the agreed sum can be brought against
him.[121] The circumstances in which these remedies are available are discussed in
Ch.21[122]; here it is necessary only to say that, in any of the cases just mentioned,
the injured party's only remedy may be an action for damages.

(iii) *Change of course*

Injured party pressing for performance before terminating. Once the   18–021
injured party has terminated, he cannot later affirm and demand performance: this

---

[111] See below, para.18–076 et seq.

[112] Mere inaction does not necessarily amount to such failure: see this situation discussed above,
after fn.56.

[113] e.g. *Segap Garages Ltd v Gulf Oil (Great Britain) Ltd*, *The Times*, October 24, 1989; *BMBF
(No.12) v Harland & Wolff Shipbuilding & Heavy Industries Ltd* [2001] EWCA Civ 862; [2001] 2
Lloyd's Rep. 227. These were cases of *actual* breach. The same rule applies in cases of *anticipatory*
breach: below, para.17–089.

[114] For certain effects of the injured party's inability to perform, see above, para.17–026 et seq.

[115] See above, para.17–014 et seq.

[116] See below, para.18–034.

[117] See above, para.17–015.

[118] See above, para.17–045.

[119] i.e. he can make a pro rata deduction in respect of the unperformed services: *Miles v Wakefield
Metropolitan DC* [1987] A.C. 539.

[120] *Sim v Rotherham Metropolitan BC* [1987] Ch. 216.

[121] *Telephone Rentals v Burgess Salmon*, *The Independent*, April 22, 1987.

[122] See especially below, paras 21–001—21–015.

follows from the rule that termination releases the defaulting party from his primary obligation to perform.[123] On the other hand, where the injured party's original reaction to the breach is to press for performance, he plainly does not release the guilty party from any obligation; nor does he, by demanding performance after breach,[124] necessarily waive his right to terminate, since such a demand is not of itself a "clear and unequivocal" representation[125] that that right will not be exercised.[126] So long as there are no other circumstances from which such a representation can be inferred, the injured party can therefore still terminate if the other party does not comply with the demand for performance.[127]

18–022   **Order for specific performance and termination.** A special application of the rule just stated is to cases in which the injured party has actually obtained an order of specific performance. If the defendant fails to comply with the order, one possible course of action open to the injured party is to apply to the court for enforcement of the order. There was formerly some support for the view that this was the only remedy available to him, and that he could not, after having obtained an order of specific performance, then terminate and claim damages.[128] But this view was rejected by the House of Lords in *Johnson v Agnew*.[129] In that case, vendors of land were (as the purchaser knew) relying on the proceeds of the sale to pay off a mortgage on the land. The purchaser failed to complete, even after specific performance had been ordered against her, with the result that the land was sold by the mortgagee. The vendors were therefore no longer able to enforce the order of specific performance (since they could no longer convey the land) and it was held that they were entitled to damages, not only under the special statutory power to award damages in lieu of specific performance,[130] but also at common law.[131] The reasoning of *Johnson v Agnew* is not, moreover, restricted to the situation in which failure to comply with the order of specific performance has disabled the party who had obtained it from performing his side of the bargain. It is based on the general rules relating to the effects of repudiatory breach and therefore applies even where no such disability results. The right to damages is subject only to the qualification that, where an order of specific performance has

---

[123] See above, para.18–013; *Johnson v Agnew* [1980] A.C. 367 at 393; cf. *Meng Leong Developments Pte Ltd v Jip Hong Trading Co* [1985] A.C. 511. The position may be different where the party in breach denies the breach and maintains the continued existence of the contract: see *Systems Control Plc v Munro Corporate Plc* [1990] B.C.L.C. 659 at 666.

[124] Our concern here is with the injured party's reaction to an *actual* breach. For the position in cases of *anticipatory* breach, see below, para.17–089.

[125] See below, para.18–079; e.g. *Yukong Line Ltd of Korea v Rendsburg Investments Co of Liberia* [1996] 2 Lloyd's Rep. 604.

[126] Even in cases where the injured party has affirmed the contract, he may still terminate if the guilty party commits a further breach, or persists in the initial breach: see below, para.18–078.

[127] cf. *Tilcon Ltd v Land and Real Estate Investments Ltd* [1987] 1 All E.R. 615; *Safehaven Investments Inc v Springbok Ltd* (1995) 71 P. & C.R. 59 at [68]; *Stocznia Gdanska SA v Latvian Shipping Co* [2002] EWCA Civ 889; [2002] 2 Lloyd's Rep 436 at [100].

[128] See *Capital & Suburban Properties Ltd v Swycher* [1976] Ch. 319 and the authorities there cited; Dawson 93 L.Q.R. 232; Oakley [1977] C.L.J. 20.

[129] [1980] A.C. 367.

[130] See below, para.21–060; such damages had been awarded in *Biggin v Minton* [1977] 1 W.L.R. 701.

[131] *Singh v Nazeer* [1979] Ch. 474 is contrary, but that case followed *Capital & Suburban Properties v Swycher*, above, which is now disapproved: above, fn.128.

not been complied with, the party who had obtained the order and now wishes to claim damages must apply to the court for the dissolution of the order "and ask the court to put an end to the contract".[132]

3. AVAILABILITY OF THE RIGHT TO TERMINATE

As a matter of general law, the right to terminate for breach arises in three situations: renunciation, impossibility and substantial failure to perform. A party is guilty of renunciation where, by words or conduct, he has "clearly shown an intention to abandon and altogether refuse to perform the contract."[133] Impossibility refers to the situation where one party has by his "own act or default" disabled himself from performing. Both renunciation and impossibility may occur at or during the time fixed for performance[134] but, in such cases, the court will assess whether that which one party is refusing to do, or cannot now do, is sufficiently serious to justify termination,[135] i.e. whether it amounts to a substantial failure to perform[136] (or one of the exceptions thereto in the form of breach of condition[137]). For this reason, renunciation and impossibility are usually relied upon "independently" of the test of substantial failure to perform in cases of anticipatory breach, i.e. where one party has renounced the contract, or disabled himself from performing it, *before* the time fixed for performance.[138] It is in this context that they are given further consideration.[139] In the case of termination for actual breach, the general requirement is that the party in default must have been guilty of a substantial failure to perform.

18–023

Order of performance. We saw in Chapter 17 that there is no right to terminate for breach of an independent promise.[140] In the case of "dependent" promises (whether condition precedent or concurrent condition), a breach justifies the injured party's refusal to perform for as long as the breach continues; but it does not, of itself, justify termination. It has the latter effect only where the failure is (in accordance with the principles to follow) either sufficiently serious to justify termination or such that it falls within one of the exceptions to the requirement of substantial failure.[141]

18–024

---

[132] [1980] A.C. 367 at 394; *GKN Distributors v Tyne Tees Fabrication* (1985) 50 P. & C.R. 403; *Hillel v Christoforides* (1991) 63 P. & C.R. 301.

[133] *Eminence Property Developments v Heaney Ltd* [2010] EWCA Civ 1168; (2010) 43 E.G. 99 at [61]

[134] *Withers v Reynolds* (1831) 2 B. & Ad. 882; *Cort v Ambergate, etc., Ry* (1851) 17 Q.B. 127.

[135] *Dalkia Utilities Services Plc v Celtech International Ltd* [2006] EWHC 63; [2006] 1 Lloyd's Rep 599 at [133].

[136] This requirement will obviously be satisfied where one party refuses, or is unable, to perform at all.

[137] See below, para.18–039 et seq.

[138] But again the two tests do not operate entirely independently since, short of an intention not to, or an inability to, perform *at all*, the court will need to be satisfied that that which one party intends not to do, or is unable to do, would have been sufficiently serious to justify termination at the time performance was due: *The Afovos* [1983] 1 W.L.R. 195 at 203

[139] See above, para.17–085 et seq.

[140] See above, para.17–024.

[141] See, above, para.17–025 et seq. for the effect on one party's obligation to perform of the wrongful refusal of the other to accept performance and the difference in effect depending upon whether the contract has, or has not, been terminated in accordance with the principles set out in this chapter.

(a) General Requirement of Substantial Failure

18–025   One party's performance may be deficient in quality or quantity or it may be late, i.e. after the agreed time. The general principle is that any such defect in performance must attain a certain minimum degree of seriousness to entitle the injured party to terminate.[142] In the following discussion we shall refer to this principle as the requirement of "substantial failure" in performance. Our present concern is with the general principle; it is subject to important exceptions which will be considered later in this chapter.[143]

18–026   **When failure is substantial.** The question when a failure in performance is sufficiently serious to entitle the injured party to terminate gives rise to very great difficulty. The frequent references in the cases to breaches which "substantially" deprive a party of what he bargained for, or "go to the root" of a contract, or which "frustrate" his purpose in making the contract are not particularly helpful in analysing the law or in predicting the course of future decisions. It is submitted that the courts, in applying the general requirement of substantial failure,[144] generally classify a failure in performance with an eye on the consequences. On the one hand, they consider whether termination (as opposed to damages) is necessary to protect the injured party and, on the other hand, they take into account the prejudice which termination will cause to the other party. If, on balancing these factors, they conclude that the injured party should be allowed to terminate, they will classify the failure in performance as "substantial" in order to produce the desired result; and conversely.[145] An attempt will be made in the following pages to illustrate this approach. The decisions are for the most part soundly based on practical considerations; though it must be admitted that these do not always appear very clearly from the judgments.

18–027   **Unjust enrichment.** Where the requirement of substantial failure applies,[146] the courts are reluctant to allow a party to refuse to perform if he has received a benefit from the other party's partial or defective performance and cannot, or will not, restore that benefit.[147]

18–028   **Adequacy of damages.** Sometimes the main reason for allowing termination is that damages would not adequately compensate the injured party. In *Vigers v Cook*[148] an undertaker had contracted to make arrangements for the funeral of the defendant's son, but so negligently constructed the coffin that it could not be taken into the church where the funeral service was held. He was not entitled to recover any part of his charges as it was "an essential part of the funeral that the body

---

[142] This may be traced back to the decision in *Boone v Eyre* (1777) 1 Hy.Bl. 273n.; 2 W.Bl. 1312, or, to be more accurate, the discussion of it in a number of later cases: *Duke of St Albans v Shore* (1789) 1 Hy.Bl. 270; *Glazebrook v Woodrow* (1799) 8 T.R. 366 at 374; *Ellen v Topp* (1851) 6 Ex. 424 at 442.

[143] See below, para.18–037 et seq.

[144] Different factors govern the exceptions discussed below, para.18–037 et seq.

[145] *Decro-Wall International SA v Practitioners in Marketing Ltd* [1971] 1 W.L.R. 361 at 380.

[146] In some cases, termination often does lead to unjust enrichment, e.g. where one party's refusal to pay is justified by the other's failure to perform an "entire" obligation; above, para.17–032.

[147] This factor may explain, in part, the different outcomes in *Boone v Eyre* and *Duke of St Albans v Shore*: above, fn.142.

[148] [1919] 2 K.B. 475; cf. *Sinclair v Bowles* (1829) 9 B. & C. 92.

should be taken into the church so that the service might be read in its presence".[149] The breach was one for which a money payment could not compensate.[150] But where the loss suffered in consequence of the breach can be valued with relative certainty, an award or allowance of the sum so assessed will be regarded as an adequate remedy, more suitable than termination.[151] For example, in one case the fact that a party was persistently late in making payments under a long-term contract was held not to be a ground of termination, since the other party suffered no prejudice except in having to pay a relatively small amount of interest on the outstanding sums, and this loss could easily have been recovered from the party in breach.[152]

Sale of land. The principle that the courts will consider the adequacy of **18–029** compensation is illustrated by the equitable jurisdiction to order specific performance of contracts for the sale of land with "compensation"—i.e. at a price reduced to take account of a deficiency or defect.[153] The jurisdiction will not be exercised (so that specific performance will not be ordered) where the defect is "substantial"[154]; and the test for determining whether the defect is of this character appears to be whether adequate compensation can be made for it by a monetary adjustment.[155] The same test applies where the contract itself provides that errors and misdescriptions shall not annul the sale but shall give rise to a claim for compensation.[156] Such a clause can (unlike the equitable jurisdiction) be invoked even after the contract has been performed[157]; but (like the equitable jurisdiction) it is normally inapplicable where the defect is "substantial".[158] Cases concerning such clauses can be regarded as illustrating what later became known as the doctrine of fundamental breach. They would therefore now turn on the construction of the clause in question, rather than on any rule of substantive law making it impossible to exclude the right to terminate.[159] On the other hand, a clause of this kind is not subject to the test of reasonableness under ss.2 to 4 of the Unfair Contract Terms Act 1977 since those sections do not apply to any contract so far as it relates to the creation or transfer of an interest in land.[160] This could be an important point where a developer entered into a contract for the sale of a house

---

[149] [1919] 2 K.B. 475 at 479.

[150] Had the defendant claimed damages he would (at least as the law then stood) have recovered nothing for injury to his feelings: below, para.20–083 et seq.

[151] cf. the rule that specific relief may be refused where the more appropriate remedy is in damages: below, para.21–017 et seq.

[152] *Decro-Wall International SA v Practitioners in Marketing Ltd* [1971] 1 W.L.R. 361. See also: *The Angelia* [1973] 1 W.L.R. 210. cf. also below, para.18–093.

[153] e.g. *Aspinalls to Powell and Scholefield* (1889) 60 L.T. 595; Harpum [1981] C.L.J. 47.

[154] *Re Fawcett and Holmes' Contract* (1889) 42 Ch.D. 150; *Jacobs v Revell* [1900] 2 Ch. 858; *Strover v Harrington* [1988] Ch. 390 at 411; *Rutherford; Frasers Islington Ltd v Hanover Trustee Co Ltd* [2010] EWHC 1514 (Ch); [2010] 27 E.G. 85 at [16]–[19].

[155] *Cato v Thomson* (1882) 9 Q.B.D. 616 at 618; *Rudd v Lascelles* [1900] 1 Ch. 815; if the defect is substantial the party prejudiced by it may, instead of terminating, claim specific performance, but only without compensation: *Durham v Legard* (1865) 34 Beav. 611.

[156] Harpum [1992] C.L.J. 263.

[157] *Bos v Helsham* (1866) L.R. 2 Ex. 72; *Re Turner and Skelton* (1879) 13 Ch.D. 130; *Palmer v Johnson* (1884) 13 Q.B.D. 351.

[158] *Flight v Booth* (1834) 1 Bing.N.C. 370; cf. *Walker v Boyle* [1982] 1 W.L.R. 495 (above, para.9–114).

[159] See above, para.7–024.

[160] Unfair Contract Terms Act 1977, Sch.1, para.1(c). The Unfair Terms in Consumer Contracts Regulations 1999 would apply: para.7–098. For attempts to exclude liability for misrepresentation, see above, para.9–115; below, at fn.165.

on written standard terms which would otherwise be subject to the requirement of reasonableness under s.3 of the Act.[161]

A misdescription may not form part of the contract but be a misrepresentation inducing it; or it may originate as such a misrepresentation and be later incorporated in the contract. Under the Misrepresentation Act 1967, there is, in such a case, a right to rescind for misrepresentation,[162] but this is subject to the discretion of the court to declare the contract subsisting and to award damages in lieu of rescission.[163] Where the defect is not "substantial" the court will probably uphold the contract and award "damages"; and it seems likely that these will be assessed in much the same way as that in which "compensation" for misdescription was assessed in equity. The main difference between the old equitable and the new statutory powers is that the latter can be exercised even after conveyance.[164] The further question then arises whether, in cases of the present kind, a contract term restricting remedies for misdescription would be ineffective on the ground that it failed to satisfy the test of reasonableness imposed by s.3 of the Misrepresentation Act 1967.[165] Before that Act, it was held that a term which excluded the right to rescind *and* the right to compensation entitled the vendor to enforce the contract without compensation.[166] Now such a term might be regarded as unreasonable in so far as it excluded the purchaser's right to compensation, or his right to rescind for a misrepresentation relating to a matter of substantial importance.[167] But if that matter was of only minor importance and the term, while excluding the right to rescind, *provided* for compensation, it is submitted that the requirement of reasonableness would normally be satisfied; for in such a case the term would not prejudice the purchaser. It would merely give contractual effect to the right that the vendor would have had, even in the absence of the term, to specific performance with compensation, or to the result that the court would be likely to reach in the exercise of its discretion to declare the contract subsisting and to award damages in lieu of rescission.[168]

18–030   **Sale of goods.** These rules as to "compensation" in sales of land should be contrasted with the rule that a quantitative defect in delivery under a contract for the sale of goods generally justifies termination,[169] even though it causes little prejudice to the buyer, and even though compensation for it may be quite easy to assess. It is, however, unlikely that the latter rule applies where a specific parcel of goods is sold and is said to contain a different quantity from that which it in fact contains,[170] e.g. where the sale is of "a cargo of 1,000 tons" in a named ship which actually contains only 950 tons. Such cases constitute the closest analogy to the land cases, so that the treatment of the two types of contract is not so radically different as might at first sight appear.

---

[161] See above, para.7–066.
[162] s.1(a); above, para.9–091.
[163] s.2(2); above, para.9–093.
[164] s.1(b); above, para.9–095.
[165] Above, para.9–124.
[166] *Re Courcier and Harrold's Contract* [1923] 1 Ch. 565.
[167] *Walker v Boyle* [1982] 1 W.L.R. 495; *Cremdean Properties Ltd v Nash* (1977) 244 E.G. 547; *South Western General Property Co v Marton* (1982) 263 E.G. 1090.
[168] See above, after fn.163.
[169] See above, para.17–033.
[170] See *Levi v Berk* (1886) 2 T.L.R. 898 at 899; *Benjamin's Sale of Goods* (8th edn), para.21–034; *Ellis v Hodder & Tolley Ltd* (1914) 33 N.Z.L.R. 362.

Ratio of failure to the performance undertaken. The higher the ratio of   18–031
the failure is to the performance undertaken, the more likely it is that the court
will regard the failure as substantial. Thus where a buyer of oil deliverable in two
instalments without justification refused to accept one of them (and added that he
would not accept any other delivery) it was held that the seller was entitled to
terminate.[171] On the other hand, in the *Maple Flock* case[172] a contract provided for
delivery of 100 tons of rag flock in instalments of 1.5 tons at the rate of three
instalments a week. The sixteenth instalment contained an excessive amount of
chlorine and one reason why the court held that this breach did not entitle the
buyers to terminate was that it related to a single instalment which bore only a
small quantitative ratio to the contract as a whole.[173] Similarly, in the *Hongkong Fir*
case,[174] a ship began service under a 24-month time charterparty. She was later
found to be unseaworthy and to need extensive repairs which took altogether 20
weeks to complete. The charterers purported to terminate on a number of
grounds,[175] one of which was that the delay caused by the unseaworthiness was
such as to "frustrate" their purpose in entering into the contract. One reason why
this argument was rejected was that the ship was still available, after the completion of repairs, for 17 out of the original 24 months of the charterparty.[176]

Uncertainty as to future performance. In the case of continuing contracts,   18–032
calling for repeated acts of performance over a period of time, the courts are
influenced by the need to remove the uncertainty which may result from failure to
perform some of those acts.[177] In *Bradford v Williams*,[178] for example, the defendant's ship was chartered for one year from May to May; but in September the
charterers wrongfully refused to provide a cargo. This refusal justified the defendant in putting an end to the contract as "no cross-action for damages would have
fully compensated him".[179] In such a cross-action it might be alleged that he had
failed to mitigate[180] by finding substitute employment for the ship. It would be
hard for him to know for how long such employment should be sought, since, if
the original charterparty had remained in force, the charterers might later have
demanded further performance, and the shipowner would have been bound to
have his ship available in response to such a demand. Again, the failure of a house-
buyer to pay a deposit as required by the contract gives rise to uncertainty in

---

[171] *Warinco AG v Samor SpA* [1979] 1 Lloyd's Rep. 450.

[172] *Maple Flock Co Ltd v Universal Furniture Products (Wembley) Ltd* [1934] 1 K.B. 148; cf. *Simpson
v Crippin* (1872) L.R. 8 Q.B. 14 (failure by buyer to take delivery). For such instalment contracts, the
vague language of Sale of Goods Act 1979, s.31(2) gives virtually no guidance on the question when
a breach justifies termination. Contrast the very rigid rule laid down by s.30(1) with respect to short
delivery (modified, in the case of non-consumer sales, by s.30(2A) as inserted by Sale and Supply of
Goods Act 1994, s.4(2)); above, para.17–033.

[173] cf. *Financings Ltd v Baldock* [1963] 2 Q.B. 104; *The Seaflower* [2000] 2 Lloyd's Rep. 37 at 41 (in
further proceedings ([2001] 1 Lloyd's Rep. 341) the term in question was held to be a condition).

[174] *Hongkong Fir Shipping Co Ltd v Kawasaki Kisen Kaisha Ltd* [1962] 2 Q.B. 26.

[175] See also below, paras 18–032, 18–033, 18–047.

[176] [1962] 2 Q.B. 26 at 40, per Salmon J., whose judgment on this issue was simply approved by the
Court of Appeal: see [1962] 2 Q.B. 26 at 61, 73.

[177] The need to remove uncertainty as to future performance is one factor which helps to explain the
distinction between *Poussard v Speirs & Pond* (1876) 1 Q.B.D. 410 and *Bettini v Gye* (1876) 1 Q.B.D.
183.

[178] (1872) L.R. 7 Ex. 259; *The Sanko Iris* [1987] 1 Lloyd's Rep. 487.

[179] ibid. at 269.

[180] See below, para.20–115.

depriving the vendor of an important safeguard against eventual default; and accordingly it justifies termination by the vendor.[181]

By way of contrast, further reference may be made to the *Hongkong Fir*[182] case, where it was said that, once major repairs were begun, there was no reasonable ground for believing that the ship would not be available for service within a fairly short and predictable time.[183] In the *Maple Flock* case[184] the court similarly stressed that the sellers' business was well conducted, that the source of the defect could easily be tracked down, and that the likelihood of its recurrence was small. Such likelihood has also been stressed where a seller has sought to terminate an instalment contract because of the buyer's refusal to pay in accordance with its terms.[185] Similarly, the insolvency of a buyer who has failed to pay may justify the seller's refusal to perform (at least in the sense that he need no longer deliver *on credit*) if it is unlikely that the buyer or his trustee in bankruptcy will eventually be able to pay in accordance with the contract.[186] On the other hand, mere delay in payment will not of itself justify termination. In the *Decro-Wall* case[187] an English company had been appointed "sole concessionaires" for the sale in the UK of decorative tiles manufactured by a French company. The English company was persistently (though only slightly) late in making payments under the contract. One reason[188] why this did not justify termination by the French company was that the delays did not give it any reason to doubt that payment would be made as soon as the English company had disposed of the goods.

Even where a breach does create uncertainty as to future performance, the need to remove it may be overcome by the desire to prevent unjust enrichment. Thus in one case[189] it was held that long delay in payment of the *final* instalment due on a sale of land did not justify termination by the vendor.

18–033   **Ulterior motives for termination.** It sometimes happens that a party's real motive for wishing to terminate is not that there has been some failure in performance, but that the contract was, or has because of market movements become, a bad bargain for him.[190] In such circumstances the courts will often (if the case is one to which the general requirement of substantial failure applies[191]) hold that the failure in performance is not sufficiently serious and so refuse to allow termination. The underlying policy has been stated by Roskill L.J.: "Contracts are made to be performed and not to be avoided according to the whims of

---

[181] *Myton Ltd v Schwab-Morris* [1974] 1 W.L.R. 331; *The Blankenstein* [1985] 1 W.L.R. 435 at 446.

[182] [1962] 2 Q.B. 26.

[183] ibid. at 40. cf. *The Hermosa* [1982] 1 Lloyd's Rep. 570, where it was held that a charterer was not entitled to terminate even though his "demand for reassurance" (at 580) was not met. The case seems near the line; the American principle of "adequate assurance of performance" (U.C.C. ss.2–609, Restatement 2d, *Contracts* §251) would be useful in such a situation. See also *Rice v Great Yarmouth BC, The Times,* July 26, 2000.

[184] [1934] 1 K.B. 148.

[185] Contrast *Withers v Reynolds* (1831) 2 B. & Ad. 882 with *Mersey Steel and Iron Co v Naylor Benzon and Co* (1884) 9 App.Cas. 434 and *Freeth v Burr* (1874) L.R. 9 C.P. 208; below, para.18–035.

[186] *Bloomer v Bernstein* (1874) L.R. 9 C.P. 588; Insolvency Act 1986, s.345(1) and (2); *Leyland Daf Ltd v Automotive Products Plc, The Times,* April 6, 1993, affirmed *The Times,* April 9, 1993.

[187] *Decro-Wall International SA v Practitioners in Marketing Ltd* [1971] 1 W.L.R. 361.

[188] For another see above, para.18–028.

[189] *Cornwall v Henson* [1900] 2 Ch. 298.

[190] cf. above, para.18–003.

[191] Where exceptions to the requirement apply, refusal to perform has often been allowed even though the motive for it fairly clearly was to escape from a bad bargain, e.g. *Cunliffe v Harrison* (1851) 6 Exch. 901; above, para.17–039; *Arcos v Ronaasen* [1933] A.C. 470; below, para.18–045.

market fluctuation."[192] Such considerations may have influenced the decision in the *Hongkong Fir* case.[193] By the time the ship had been repaired, there had been a "catastrophic fall in the freight market"[194] to 13s. 6d. per ton, as against the 47s. per ton reserved in the charterparty.[195] In a 24-month charterparty the risk of such a fall in the freight market would normally be on the charterer; and the court was probably reluctant to allow him to throw it back on the shipowner by putting an end to the charterparty. It may also be relevant that the shipowner's breaches did not (so far as appears from the report) cause the charterer any loss at all.[196] But if a charterer can show that the owner's breach *was* a source of serious prejudice to him, he will not be prevented from terminating merely because there has been a steep fall in the freight market. This is particularly true if his conduct shows that his real motive for terminating was to avoid the prejudice caused by the breach, and not to escape from what has turned out to be a bad bargain.[197]

Deliberate breach. A breach will not justify termination merely because it is deliberate.[198] The fact that the breach is deliberate may justify termination on the ground that it is evidence of "an intention no longer to be bound by the contract"[199] so far as any *future* performance is concerned, and so also amounts to an anticipatory breach in the form of renunciation.[200] But termination for the *actual* breach itself will depend on whether it was sufficiently serious,[201] whether or not it was committed deliberately.[202] For example, in the *Hongkong Fir* case[203]

18–034

---

[192] *The Hansa Nord* [1976] Q.B. 44 at 71; cf. *Dakin v Oxley* (1864) 15 C.B.(N.S.) 647 at 667–668; *The Gregos* [1994] 1 W.L.R. 1465 at 1475.

[193] [1962] 2 Q.B. 26; above, para.18–031.

[194] ibid. at 39.

[195] [1961] 2 All E.R. at 261.

[196] The shipowner's breaches can be said to have benefited the charterer by relieving him for 20 weeks from the obligation to pay the high rate of hire reserved by the charterparty, since, while the ship was under repair, she was "off hire".

[197] cf. *Federal Commerce Navigation Co Ltd v Molena Alpha Inc* [1979] A.C. 757.

[198] *Suisse Atlantique* case [1967] 1 A.C. 361 at 435; cf. *Decro-Wall International SA v Practitioners in Marketing Ltd* [1971] 1 W.L.R. 361 at 369. There was formerly some support for a special rule in contracts of employment that "wilful disobedience of any lawful order is . . . a good ground of discharge." *Turner v Mason* (1845) 14 M. & W. 112 at 117; the courts now apply in employment cases the same rules as are outlined in this paragraph: *Gorse v Durham CC* (above); cf. *Miles v Wakefield MDC* [1987] A.C. 539 at 559–560; *Wiluszynshki v Tower Hamlets LBC* [1989] I.C.R. 493; *Laws v London Chronicle (Indicator Newspapers) Ltd* [1959] 1 W.L.R. 698; *Pepper v Webb* [1969] 1 W.L.R. 514; P.V.B. 85 L.Q.R. 325.

[199] *Freeth v Burr* (1874) L.R. 9 C.P. 208 at 213; cf. *Bradley v H Newsom, Sons & Co* [1919] A.C. 16 at 52; *Suisse Atlantique* case [1967] 1 A.C. 361 at 394, 429, 435; *Warinco AG v Samor SpA* [1979] 1 Lloyd's Rep. 450; *The Product Star (No.2)* [1993] 1 Lloyd's Rep. 397 at 407; *Cantor Fitzgerald International v Callaghan* [1999] 2 All E.R. 411 at 420. Contrast *The Aktion* [1987] 1 Lloyd's Rep. 283.

[200] *Withers v Reynolds* (1831) 2 B. & Ad. 882; *Total Oil Great Britain Ltd v Thompson Garages (Biggin Hill) Ltd* [1972] 1 Q.B. 318 at 322; *Alan Auld Associates Ltd v Rick Pollard Associates* [2008] EWCA Civ 655; [2008] B.L.R. 419.

[201] Or whether termination was available on the basis of one of the exceptions considered below, para.18–037 et seq.

[202] *Millar's Karri & Jarrah Co (1902) v Weddell, Turner & Co* (1909) 100 L.T. 128; cf. *Robert A Munro & Co Ltd v Meyer* [1930] 2 K.B. 312; *Federal Commerce and Navigation v Molena Alpha* [1979] A.C. 757. Similarly, for dishonest breach: *The Mercandian Continent* [2001] EWCA Civ 1275; [2001] 2 Lloyd's Rep. 563 at [35]; *Acre 1127 Ltd v De Montfort Fine Art Ltd* [2011] EWCA Civ 87 at [43]: "dishonesty will be material only if it is of itself destructive of a necessary relationship of trust or if it is of itself indicative of an intention no longer to be bound by the contract."

[203] [1962] 2 Q.B. 26.

it was held that unseaworthiness is not of itself a ground on which a charterer is entitled to terminate a charterparty; it has this effect only if it produces a substantial failure in performance. But in the *Hongkong Fir* case it was also said that the charterer could have refused to accept the ship if the unseaworthiness had been discovered on or before her delivery and the shipowner had refused to comply with a request to put the matter right within the time allowed for delivery. Such refusal would have been evidence of the shipowner's intention no longer to be bound by the contract.[204] Conversely, the giving by time charterers of an order for a voyage which is illegitimate because the voyage cannot be completed within the period of the charter will not of itself entitle the owner to terminate,[205] but he will become entitled to do so if the charterers' "persistence in it ... showed that they did not intend to perform the charter."[206] It should be stressed that where a breach is deliberate, or is persisted in, and this is taken as evidence of intention not to perform, the intention must go to a matter which is itself sufficiently serious to justify termination[207]; in the *Hongkong Fir* case it would have been the delivery on time of a vessel in accordance with the charterparty, the time of delivery being regarded as a condition of the contract.[208] In some cases, it may not be that the party in breach has no intention of remedying the breach, but rather that "it *cannot* be remedied within such a time as not to frustrate the object of the (contract)" so that the injured party is entitled to terminate for this reason.[209]

18–035   **Honest mistaken belief.** The distinction drawn in the previous paragraph between actual breach and anticipatory breach[210] may help to explain the circumstances when a party may rely on his honest, but mistaken, belief that the terms of the contract justified his refusal to perform so as to deny the injured party's right to terminate.[211] In the case of an actual breach which would justify termination, it is no defence that the party in breach was acting on the advice of his lawyers, or that he was under an honest misapprehension.[212] By contrast, in the case of termination for anticipatory breach by way of renunciation the honest mistake of the party in breach, and any legal advice he has received, may be

---

[204] ibid. at 56.
[205] See below, para.18–047.
[206] *The Gregos* [1994] 1 W.L.R. 1465 at 1476.
[207] The deliberate or persistent nature of the breach may also create uncertainty as to future performance and justify termination on this ground: *Alan Auld Associates Ltd v Rick Pollard Associates* [2008] EWCA Civ 655; [2008] B.L.R. 419; see above, para.18–032.
[208] [1962] 2 Q.B. 26 at 56 (Sellers L.J.).
[209] *Stanton v Richardson* (1872) L.R. 7 C.P. 421 at 437 (Brett J.), affirmed (1875) 45 L.J.C.P. 78. An important feature of the *Hongkong Fir* case (*ex hypothesi*) and *Stanton v Richardson* is that the charterer was entitled not to perform until the shipowner's breach had been remedied: in *Hongkong Fir* by not accepting delivery of an unseaworthy vessel and in *Stanton v Richardson* by not loading on an uncargoworthy vessel; cf. *Mantovani v Carapelli SpA* [1978] 2 Lloyd's Rep. 63 at 72 (affirmed [1980] 1 Lloyd's Rep. 375).
[210] For criticism of the term "anticipatory breach" see para.17–073, fn.340.
[211] *Spettabile Consorzio Veneziano, etc. v Northern Ireland Shipbuilding Co Ltd* (1919) 121 L.T. 628 at 635; *James Shaffer Ltd v Findlay Durham & Brodie* [1953] 1 W.L.R. 106.
[212] *Federal Commerce and Navigation v Molena Alpha* [1978] Q.B. 927 at 929 (Lord Denning), affirmed [1979] A.C. 757; Carter [1979] C.L.J. 270; cf. *Dalkia Utilities Services Plc v Celtech International Ltd* [2006] EWHC 63; [2006] 1 Lloyd's Rep 599 at [150]; *James Shaffer Ltd v Findlay Durham & Brodie* [1953] 1 W.L.R. 106 where the mistaken party's performance was due, at least in part, but it must be assumed (since it appears not to have been argued) that the actual breaches committed were not sufficiently serious to justify termination.

relevant. In *Mersey Steel & Iron Co v Naylor Benzon & Co*[213] a buyer of steel under an instalment contract refused to pay for one instalment. The refusal to pay at the time due amounted to an actual breach, but this was not sufficiently serious to justify the seller in withholding delivery[214]; nor did it justify termination by the seller on the basis of renunciation since the buyer's refusal to pay on this occasion was not evidence of his intention no longer to be bound by the contract. The buyer wished to fulfil the contract,[215] but had been advised, incorrectly, that it could not safely pay the instalment due without the sanction of a court order, the seller having been made the subject of a winding up petition. Similarly,[216] in *Woodar Investment Development Ltd v Wimpey Construction UK Ltd*[217] a purchaser of land purported to withdraw on a ground which, on the true construction of a somewhat obscure term in the contract, did not justify his withdrawal; but the House of Lords held that he had not repudiated, for he had acted in the bona fide belief[218] that he was entitled to withdraw and had indicated throughout that he would perform if it should be decided that his interpretation of the contract was wrong.[219] The same principle can apply where a party makes a demand which goes beyond his rights: e.g. where a seller in good faith claims a price higher than that to which he is under the contract entitled,[220] or where a minor and obvious error

---

[213] (1884) 9 App.Cas. 434; cf. *Payzu Ltd v Saunders* [1919] 2 K.B. 581; *Peter Dumenil & Co Ltd v James Ruddin Ltd* [1953] 1 W.L.R. 815; *Sweet & Maxwell Ltd v Universal News Ltd* [1964] 2 Q.B. 699; *Toepfer v Cremer* [1975] 2 Lloyd's Rep. 118; *Bunge GmbH v CCV Landbouwbeland* [1980] 1 Lloyd's Rep. 458.

[214] ibid. at 439. Contrast *Dymocks Franchise Systems (NSW) Pty Ltd v Todd* [2002] UKPC 50; [2002] 2 All E.R. (Comm) 849 where non-payment of a fee was expressly stated in the contract to be a "fundamental breach".

[215] Lord Blackburn refers (9 App.Cas. 434 at 443) to the fact that the market price of the steel bought "had risen above the contract price". cf. above, paras 18–003, 18–033.

[216] Unlike the *Mersey Steel* case, in *Woodar v Wimpey* the purchaser was guilty of no actual breach at all; the case turned entirely on whether it had evinced an intention not to perform when required to do so (the contract contained a number of alternative dates for completion, of which the latest was some seven years from the date of the contract); cf. *Concord Trust v Law Debenture Trust Corp Plc* [2005] UKHL 27; [2005] 1 W.L.R. 1591 (no breach in serving an invalid notice of event of default where only relied on to accelerate the redemption of a bond); Peel 122 L.Q.R. 179.

[217] [1980] 1 W.L.R. 277; Carter [1980] C.L.J. 256; Nicol and Rawlings (1980) 43 M.L.R. 696; cf. *The Hazelmoor* [1980] 2 Lloyd's Rep. 351; *Spencer v Marchington* [1988] I.R.L.R. 392; *Nottingham BS v Eurodynamics Systems* [1995] F.S.R. 605; *Gulf Agri Trade FZCO v Aston Agro Industrial AG* [2008] EWHC 1252 (Comm); [2008] 2 Lloyd's Rep. 376 at [44]; Contrast *Agrokor AG v Tradigrain* [2000] 1 Lloyd's Rep. 497 (unfounded assertion that performance was impossible said to amount to a repudiation).

[218] Lord Wilberforce does indicate (at 280H) that a different result would flow if the invocation of the provision in question "were totally abusive or lacking in good faith", but if the finding of the court is that a party is willing to abide by whatever is, in fact, the correct interpretation of the contract, it is not entirely clear why the additional element of bad faith should make any difference. Perhaps it may be said that there is an implied term that the parties will not test the interpretation of the contract other than in good faith and it is the breach of this provision which justifies termination.

[219] Lord Salmon and Lord Russell of Killowen dissented. One of the factors which persuaded Lord Russell that Wimpey had been guilty of repudiation was its failure to take out a construction summons to test its interpretation of the contract. While this may be taken into account, it is respectfully submitted that, on the facts of the case as a whole, the view of the majority is to be preferred. It is no repudiation of a building contract to make an interim valuation, which later turns out to be incorrect, if the valuation is referred to an adjudicator in accordance with the terms of the contract and the contractor agrees to abide by the adjudication: *Multiplex Constructions UK Ltd v Cleveland Bridge UK Ltd* [2006] EWHC 1341 (TCC); 107 Con L.R. 1.

[220] *Vaswani v Italian Motors (Sales and Services) Ltd* [1996] 1 W.L.R. 270; Peel [1996] L.M.C.L.Q. 309.

is made in the calculation of the date for completion under a notice to complete.[221]

18–036   **Other factors.** The factors influencing decisions as to the availability of termination by reason of the effects of a failure in performance cannot be exhaustively classified. Even where none of the factors discussed above is present, termination may nevertheless be justified. In *Aerial Advertising Co v Batchelor's Peas Ltd*,[222] for example, the claimants agreed to conduct an advertising campaign for the defendants. On Armistice Day 1937 one of the claimants' aeroplanes set out with a banner bearing the message "Eat Batchelor's Peas". Unfortunately the aeroplane towed the banner over the main square of Salford, Lancashire, at the precise time when a large crowd was gathered there observing the two-minute silence. The effect of this breach of contract was described as "disastrous",[223] and it was held that the defendants were justified in refusing to accept further performance of the contract. Again, where a contract presupposes the continuation of a relationship involving personal confidence, it is possible for some isolated act of one party to destroy that confidence and so to justify termination by the other.[224] In some of the cases, termination was held to be justified because the nature or effects of the breach were regarded as sufficiently "serious" in ways that are hard to explain or even to articulate.[225] Such a vague notion has its dangers, but it cannot be altogether eliminated from a discussion of this branch of the law.

(b) Exceptions to the Requirement of Substantial Failure

18–037   The preceding discussion attempts to identify factors that influence decisions on the issue of substantial failure in performance; but it must be admitted that their practical operation is not easy to predict. In the interests of greater certainty, the law therefore recognises a number of exceptions[226] to the requirement of substantial failure. Inevitably, the resulting certainty has sometimes been achieved only at the expense of justice, so that these exceptions have attracted an increasing weight of criticism.

18–038   **Entire obligations.** One exception, in the form of the distinction between entire and severable obligations, has been dealt with earlier.[227] In the case of an entire obligation, it is not so much that the injured party is entitled to terminate the contract for incomplete performance, but rather that he is released from his own obligation to perform until the obligation of the other party is completed in full.[228]

---

[221] *Eminence Property Developments v Heaney Ltd* [2010] EWCA Civ 1168; (2010) 43 E.G. 99; *Oates v Hooper* [2010] EWCA Civ 1346; (2010) 48 E.G. 85.

[222] [1938] 2 All E.R. 788.

[223] ibid. at 792.

[224] See *Denmark Productions Ltd v Boscobel Productions Ltd* [1969] 1 Q.B. 699, where it was held by a majority that termination was not justified on the facts; cf. also the employers' right to terminate the original service agreement in *Bell v Lever Bros Ltd* [1932] A.C. 161 (above, para.8–017).

[225] See *Bright v Ganas* 189 A. 427 (1936), where a servant forfeited all rights to pay for four-and-a-half years' service by writing a love-letter to his employer's wife.

[226] For a further special exception in the law of agency, see above, paras 16–095—16–097.

[227] See above, para.17–031 et seq.

[228] On the question of what is meant by complete performance and the so-called doctrine of "substantial performance", see above, para.17–040.

(i) Conditions, warranties and intermediate terms

Statement of the distinction. English law has for some considerable time   18–039
recognised a distinction between two classes of contractual terms: conditions and
warranties. "Condition" is here used (in its promissory sense[229]) to refer to a
contractual term, the breach of which gives the injured party the right to
terminate the contract. Of course he need not terminate but may instead affirm;
and he can claim damages whether he affirms[230] or terminates.[231] A warranty, on
the other hand, is a term "the breach of which gives rise to a claim for damages
but not to a right . . . to treat the contract as repudiated,"[232] so that the injured
party is not entitled to terminate merely[233] on account of such a breach.[234] The
injured party can generally set up the damages to which he is entitled by reason
of a breach of warranty in diminution or extinction of the price[235] and if they are
equal to, or exceed, the price he will not have to pay anything. Such an outcome
may seem to resemble termination (in the sense of refusal to pay); but the process
differs from termination in that it requires the injured party to prove both the
breach and his loss, while termination requires him to prove no more than the
breach.

Nature of the distinction. In Chapter 17 we saw that the phrases "condition   18–040
precedent" and "concurrent condition" were used to make a point about the *order*
of performance.[236] At this stage, the word "condition" is used to make a different
point, namely, one about the *conformity* of the performance rendered with that
promised. In the first of these two senses, the *performance* by one party may be a
"condition precedent" to the liability of the other; in the second it is a *term* of the
contract which is described as the "condition". It is perfectly possible for a party
to comply with a condition in one of these senses but not in the other: e.g. a seller
of goods by sample who has agreed to give credit may deliver the goods before
being paid and so perform a "condition precedent", but if the goods turn out not
to correspond with the sample he will be in breach of "condition".[237] The

---

[229] See above, para.2–104.

[230] e.g. *Aruna Mills Ltd v Dhanrajmal Gobindram* [1968] 1 Q.B. 655.

[231] See, e.g. *Millar's Machinery Co Ltd v David Way & Son* (1935) 40 Com.Cas. 204; *New India Assurance Co Ltd v Yeo Beng Chao* [1972] 1 W.L.R. 786; *Microbeads AG v Vinshurst Road Markings Ltd* [1975] 1 W.L.R. 218 at 225; cf. *General Billposting Co v Atkinson* [1909] A.C. 118; *Kwei Tek Chao v British Traders & Shippers Ltd* [1954] 2 Q.B. 459 at 473 (but see [1954] 2 Q.B. 459 at 477); and cf. above, para.18–015.

[232] Sale of Goods Act 1979, s.61(1) (definition of "warranty").

[233] See below, paras 18–057—18–059.

[234] cf. *United Scientific Holdings Ltd v Burnley BC* [1978] A.C. 904 at 945; and see below, fn.324. For a possible statutory exception, see below, para.18–060.

[235] Sale of Goods Act 1979, s.53(1)(a); cf. the right of a buyer who "deals as consumer" (see s.61(5A) of the 1979 Act) in certain cases to "require the seller to reduce the price", as an alternative to termination for breach of condition, under s.48C(1)(a) of the 1979 Act. The measure of such price reduction is not, however, necessarily the same as the measure of damages under s.53(3): see below, para.20–054. For the right to set off damages against agreed sums to be paid under other types of contracts, see *Gilbert-Ash (Northern) Ltd v Modern Engineering (Bristol) Ltd* [1974] A.C. 689; *Sim v Rotherham MBC* [1987] Ch. 216; *Connaught Restaurants Ltd v Indoor Leisure Ltd* [1994] 1 W.L.R. 501; *Eller v Grovecrest Investments Ltd* [1995] Q.B. 272; cf. *Miles v Wakefield MDC* [1987] A.C. 539; for statutory restrictions, see Employment Rights Act 1996, Pt. II. The process is not available against a claim for freight under a voyage charterparty: *The Brede* [1974] Q.B. 233; *The Aries* [1977] 1 W.L.R. 185.

[236] See above, para.17–014 et seq.

[237] See below, para.18–044.

distinction was formerly obscured by use of the phrase "condition precedent" in cases concerned with conformity, rather than with order of performance[238]: thus "condition precedent" was used to refer both to a term of a contract and to an event, i.e. the prior or concurrent performance by one party before that of the other became due. The use of the same phrase in these two senses is, however, confusing since the effects of one party's failure to perform a "condition precedent" or a "concurrent condition" differ in two ways from those of breach of "condition" (as opposed to warranty). First, a failure of the former kind only justifies refusal by the injured party to perform for so long as the failure continues[239]; while breach of condition justifies termination in the sense of an outright refusal[240] to perform and to accept further performance from the party in breach. Secondly, the injured party's right to refuse to perform so long as a condition precedent or concurrent condition remains unperformed can be exercised without any previous election by the injured party (whose position is simply that his performance is not yet due[241]); while such an election is required for the purpose of the more drastic remedy of termination (in the sense of an outright refusal of the kind just described) for breach of condition.[242] Modern authority accordingly recognises the distinction between the two concepts[243] and tends[244] to use the phrase "condition" when discussing conformity, and "condition precedent" when discussing the order of performance. That usage is adopted in this chapter so that "condition precedent" is contrasted with "concurrent condition" and "independent covenant"; while "condition" (without any qualifying adjective) is contrasted with "warranty" and "intermediate term".[245]

18–041   **Bases of the distinction.** The distinction between conditions and warranties was originally based on two factors. One was the intention of the parties, as expressed in the contract: hence the question into which category a stipulation fell was treated as one of construction.[246] But often the intention of the parties in this respect was not discoverable from the words used; and so the courts relied secondly on the general requirement of substantial failure in performance. If

---

[238] e.g. *Glaholm v Hays* (1841) 2 Man. & G. 257 at 267; *Behn v Burness* (1863) 3 B. & S. 751 at 755: *Bentsen v Taylor* [1893] 2 Q.B. 274 at 281.

[239] See above, para.17–024.

[240] It is assumed that the time for "curing" the breach, under the rule stated at para.17–027, at fn.95 above, has expired.

[241] See *The Good Luck* [1992] 1 A.C. 233 at 262.

[242] See above, para.18–039.

[243] e.g. *State Trading Corp of India v M Golodetz Ltd* [1989] 2 Lloyd's Rep. 277 at 284 treating "condition" and "condition precedent" as distinct concepts; Treitel 106 L.Q.R. 185.

[244] But not invariably: see, e.g. *The Aktion* [1989] 1 Lloyd's Rep. 283 at 285; *Soon Hua Seng Co Ltd v Glencore Grain Ltd* [1996] 1 Lloyd's Rep. 398 at 402; *The Niizura* [1996] 2 Lloyd's Rep. 66 at 70. For failure to recognise the distinction, see also *Alfred McAlpine Plc v BAI (Run-off) Ltd* [2000] 1 Lloyd's Rep. 437 at 441, 444; requirement that insured must give notice of claim "as soon as possible" held not to be a "condition precedent" so that *delay* in giving such notice was no bar to a claim; but clearly notice had to be given *before* the insurer could be held liable. The real issue in the *BAI* case was whether, in addition to being a condition precedent, the notice clause was also a "condition". Waller L.J.'s view that such a clause is not a condition, but may be an innominate term any serious breach of which would entitle the insurer to reject *the particular claim*, rather than terminate the policy, was followed in the *Mercandian Continent* [2001] EWCA Civ 1275; [2001] 2 Lloyd's Rep. 563; *Bankers Ins Co Ltd v South* [2003] EWHC 380; [2004] Lloyd's Rep. I.R. 1, but disapproved in *Friends Provident Life & Pensions Ltd v Sirius International Ins* [2005] EWCA Civ 601; [2005] 2 Lloyd's Rep. 517.

[245] See below, para.18–047.

[246] *Glaholm v Hays* (1841) 2 Man. & G. 257 at 266; Sale of Goods Act 1979, s.11(3); cf. *Tradax Export SA v European Grain & Shipping Co* [1983] 2 Lloyd's Rep. 100.

"performance of the stipulation [went] to the very root . . . of the contract",[247] then the stipulation was treated as a condition. We shall see that a term may also be treated as a condition on other grounds[248]; but the actually or potentially serious effects of breach are still taken into account in deciding, in cases of first impression, whether the term broken is to be classified as a condition.[249] If a contractual term[250] relates to "a substantial ingredient in the identity of the thing sold",[251] it will be classified as a condition, and its breach will entitle the victim to terminate, on the basis that it would be unjust to require him to accept and pay for something which differed in an important way from that for which he had contracted. A warranty, on the other hand, concerns some less important or subsidiary element of the contract. Its breach does not entitle the victim to terminate, on the basis that a minor breach can be adequately remedied by the payment of money.

This approach can be seen in a number of cases in which decisions were based on the commercial importance of the term to the injured party: e.g. if a buyer said that he would not buy goods at all unless they had a certain quality, then this fact would tend to support the view that an undertaking with respect to that quality was a condition.[252] Where there is no such evidence of intention, the court will base its decision on its own view of the commercial importance of the term. The older authorities on this question must be treated with caution, because in them the word "warranty" was sometimes used to refer to what would now be called a "condition".[253] But the cases do establish that there are certain terms the breach of which prima facie gives rise to a right to terminate and which are therefore "conditions" in the terminology now current. In *Behn v Burness*[254] a ship was described in a charterparty as "now in the port of Amsterdam" when in fact she was elsewhere. It was held that the charterer was entitled to terminate: the statement was a condition because of the commercial importance which charterers usually attach to such descriptive statements. Similarly, a statement that a ship will sail on a certain day has been treated as a condition in a charterparty.[255] The same is true of a statement in a charterparty that the ship is "expected ready to load" on or about a certain day.[256] The commercial importance of such a statement is, indeed, reduced by the rule that the shipowner will not be in breach merely

---

[247] ibid., at 268; cf. *Bentsen v Taylor* [1893] 2 Q.B. 274 at 281.

[248] See below, para.18–043.

[249] Thus the fact that the breach is *not* likely to cause serious prejudice can support the view that the term is not a condition: see *State Trading Corp of India v M Golodetz Ltd* [1989] 2 Lloyd's Rep. 277; below, para.18–051, fn.327.

[250] See *Harlingdon & Leinster Enterprises Ltd v Christopher Hull Fine Art Ltd* [1991] 1 Q.B. 564 at 586 (where the statement was held *not* to be a contractual term: above, para.9–050).

[251] *Couchman v Hill* [1947] K.B. 544 at 559.

[252] cf. *Bannerman v White* (1861) 10 C.B.(N.S.) 844; above, para.9–048.

[253] e.g. in *Behn v Burness* (1863) 3 B. & S. 751 at 755: "a warranty, that is to say a condition . . . ". A similar (though not identical) usage has survived in insurance law: see above, para.18–007; cf. *Hadenfayre Ltd v British National Ins Society* [1984] 2 Lloyd's Rep. 393 at 401. See also *Lambert v Lewis* [1982] A.C. 225 at 273, 276, where Lord Diplock refers to the implied terms classified as *conditions* in s.14 of Sale of Goods Act 1979 as "warranties"; and see *The Evia (No.2)* [1983] 1 A.C. 736 at 765.

[254] (1863) 3 B. & S. 751; cf. *The New Prosper* [1991] 2 Lloyd's Rep. 93 (statement as to ship's ability to comply with load port regulations); *The Aegean Dolphin* [1992] 2 Lloyd's Rep. 178 (statement as to speed of cruise ship).

[255] *Glaholm v Hays* (1841) 2 Man. & G. 257; cf. *Bentsen v Taylor* [1893] 2 Q.B. 274 (statement that ship "now sailed or about to sail" held to be a condition).

[256] *The Mihalis Angelos* [1971] 1 Q.B. 164; Rogers 34 M.L.R. 190; Greig 89 L.Q.R. 93; cf. *The Mavro Vetranic* [1985] 1 Lloyd's Rep. 580 at 584 (estimated time of ship's arrival); *The Baleares* [1993] 1 Lloyd's Rep. 215 at 225.

878 TERMINATION FOR BREACH

because the ship is not ready on or about the day named. The term is broken only if the statement was made dishonestly or without reasonable grounds,[257] so that it does not give the charterer any firm assurance as to the date of readiness. The classification of the statement as a condition can, however, be justified on the ground that a shipowner who has made such a statement dishonestly or without reasonable grounds, is in a poor position to complain of any prejudice which he may suffer as a result of termination.[258]

18–042   **Breach of condition need not, in fact, amount to substantial failure to perform.** The reasoning of the cases discussed above is based on the requirement of serious failure in performance; and emphasis on this requirement gave rise at one time to the view that a term could be a condition *only* if

> "every breach . . . [of it would] . . . deprive the party not in breach of substantially the whole benefit which it was intended that he should obtain from the contract".[259]

But this view was rejected by the House of Lords in *Bunge Corp v Tradax Export SA*, where Lord Roskill said that there were

> "many cases . . . where terms the breaches of which do not deprive the innocent party of substantially the whole benefit which he was intended to receive from the contract were nonetheless held to be conditions any breach of which entitled the innocent party to rescind".[260]

The statement that "conditions . . . have the property that any breach of them is treated as going to the root of the contract"[261] must similarly be viewed with caution. It is accurate only in the sense that a breach of condition, like one going to the root of the contract, gives rise to a right to terminate; but that right arises, in the two cases, for different reasons. Where the breach *actually* "goes to the root of the contract", the right to terminate is intended to protect the injured party from serious prejudice; where the breach is one of condition, that right is intended to promote certainty, "without regard to the magnitude of the breach".[262] For this reason, breach of condition is here treated as an exception to, and not as an application of, the requirement of substantial failure in performance.

18–043   **Express classification by the parties.** One basis for distinguishing conditions from warranties is the intention of the parties[263]; and the courts continue to

---

[257] *Scrutton on Charterparties and Bills of Lading* (20th edn), pp.92–94.
[258] *The Mihalis Angelos*, above, at 205. The charterer could also rescind for misrepresentation: ibid. at 194.
[259] *Hongkong Fir Shipping Co Ltd v Kawasaki Kisen Kaisha Ltd* [1962] 2 Q.B. 26 at 69, per Diplock L.J.; cf. *United Scientific Holdings v Burnley BC* [1978] A.C. 904 at 928.
[260] [1981] 1 W.L.R. 711 at 724; cf. [1981] 1 W.L.R. 711 at 715–716, 718. On this point the House of Lords followed the reasoning of Megaw L.J. in the Court of Appeal: see [1980] 1 Lloyd's Rep. 294 at 305. Lord Diplock himself took a similar view in *Photo Production Ltd v Securicor Transport Ltd* [1980] A.C. 827 at 849.
[261] *Lombard North Central Plc v Butterworth* [1987] Q.B. 527 at 535.
[262] ibid. (referring, apparently, to terms which are conditions by express classification of the parties).
[263] See above, para.18–041.

rely on this factor where that intention can be ascertained.[264] Thus if a contract expressly says that a particular term is a condition,[265] that term will generally be so regarded; and the same is true where the contract expressly states that termination will be available on breach of the term.[266] But if a term can be broken in a way which will cause only trifling (if any) loss, the court may hold that such a breach will not justify termination even though the term is called a "condition" in the contract. In *Wickman Ltd v Schuler AG*[267] it was a "condition" of a four-year distributorship agreement that the distributor should visit six named customers once a week. The House of Lords held that the contract could not be terminated *merely* because this term had been broken. The parties could not have intended the agreement to mean that a failure to make only one out of an obligatory total of some 1,400 visits should have such drastic results. More probably they had used "condition" in a non-technical sense, to mean simply a term of the contract (as in the phrase "conditions of sale"). This view was supported by the fact that another clause in the contract conferred an express power of "determination" for any "material" breach: the exercise of such a power may not require the proof of a "serious" breach,[268] in the sense discussed earlier in this chapter, but it clearly implied the need for something more than the minor breach committed by the distributor.

Statutory classification. In some cases the question whether a particular term is a condition or a warranty is determined by statute. The outstanding example of statutory classification is to be found in ss.12 to 15 of the Sale of Goods Act 1979,[269] which lay down in some detail which of the implied terms in a contract for the sale of goods are conditions and which are warranties. A full discussion of these provisions will be found in works on the sale of goods; but it is interesting to note that most of them are implied *conditions* (thus favouring the buyer's right to reject[270]); and a few of them may be mentioned here to illustrate the distinction between conditions and warranties. It is an implied condition that goods sold by description shall correspond with the contractual description,[271] that goods sold by sample shall correspond with the sample,[272] and (in certain cases) that goods shall be of satisfactory quality and fit for a particular purpose.[273] The right to terminate for breach of these implied conditions is subject to a statutory restriction to be discussed later in this chapter.[274] There is an implied condition that the

18–044

---

[264] *Astley Industrial Trust Ltd v Grimley* [1963] 1 W.L.R. 584 at 590; *Bunge Corp v Tradax Export SA* [1981] 1 W.L.R. 711 at 716.

[265] e.g. *Dawson's Ltd v Bonnin* [1922] 2 A.C. 413.

[266] *Harling v Eddy* [1951] 2 K.B. 739; *George Hunt Cranes Ltd v Scottish Boiler & General Ins Ltd* [2001] EWCA Civ 1964; [2002] 1 All E.R. (Comm) 366. It is important to distinguish between wording which converts a term into a condition and wording which amounts to an express provision to terminate: below, para.18–061.

[267] [1974] A.C. 235; Baker [1973] C.L.J. 196; Brownsword 37 M.L.R. 104.

[268] See the authorities referred to below, at fn.416.

[269] As amended by Sale and Supply of Goods Act 1994, ss.1, 7(1) and Sch.2, para.5 and by Sale and Supply of Goods to Consumers Regulations 2002 (SI 2002/3045), reg.3.

[270] This is also true of the similar terms implied in other contracts for the supply of goods: Supply of Goods (Implied Terms) Act 1973, ss.8–11; Supply of Goods and Services Act 1982, ss.2–5, 7–10.

[271] Sale of Goods Act 1979, s.13.

[272] ibid., s.15.

[273] ibid., s.14.

[274] See below, para.18–053.

seller has the right to sell the goods,[275] but only an implied warranty that they are free from charges or incumbrances in favour of third parties.[276] To allow the seller to enforce the contract, when he had no right to sell, would generally[277] cause hardship to the buyer, as he would have to give the goods up to the true owner. But there is less hardship if the goods are subject to third party charges; these can simply be paid off so that the buyer can adequately and conveniently be compensated by damages. The distinction between conditions and warranties does not apply to *quantitative* defects in the performance of a contract for the sale of goods. Subject to restrictions already discussed,[278] such defects justify termination even though they cause little or no prejudice to the buyer.[279]

18–045   **Technical applications of the distinction.** In some cases, termination is allowed simply because the term broken has previously been classified as a condition, either by statute or a previous decision of the courts. It is allowed even though there is no indication in the contract that the parties intended the remedy to be available, and even though the breach causes little prejudice, or none at all, to the injured party. Cases of this kind give rise to the question why the injured party should, in such circumstances, be entitled to terminate.

Sometimes, this result is justified by an argument based on hypothetical hardship. Termination is allowed because the breach *might* have caused serious prejudice, irrespective of the question whether it *actually* did so.[280] In other cases, no attempt is made to justify the result even by reference to such hypothetical hardship. Thus in *Arcos Ltd v Ronaasen*[281] timber was bought for the purpose of making cement barrels and was described in the contract as half an inch thick. Most of the timber delivered was in fact 9/16 of an inch thick, but this did not in the least impair its usefulness for making cement barrels. It was held that the buyers were nevertheless entitled to reject for breach of the condition that the timber would correspond with its description.[282] It seems probable that their motive for wishing to do so was not that the timber did not comply with the description but that the market price of the timber had fallen. Similarly, goods may be sold on the terms that they will be (or have been) shipped within a particular month. Such a term is part of the description of the goods and if they are shipped by so much as a day before or after the stipulated period the buyer can reject.[283] He can do this even though the early or late shipment does not in the least affect the value of the goods or prejudice him in any way; and even though his motive for rejection is simply to escape from a bad bargain on a falling market.

Such decisions can perhaps be explained on the ground that they promote certainty. Once a term has been classified as a "condition", the injured party can safely terminate for breach of it, without having to consider the often difficult

---

[275] Sale of Goods Act 1979, s.12(1); an *express* term to this effect is likewise a condition: *Barber v NSW Bank Ltd* [1996] 1 W.L.R. 641.

[276] ibid., s.12(2).

[277] For an exception, see Sale of Goods Act 1979, s.12(3) (agreement to transfer only such title as seller or third party may have).

[278] See above, para.17–033.

[279] Sale of Goods Act 1979, s.30(1) and (2).

[280] *Re Moore & Co Ltd and Landauer Co* [1921] 2 K.B. 519 at 525.

[281] [1933] A.C. 470.

[282] Then under Sale of Goods Act 1893, s.13.

[283] *Bowes v Shand* (1877) 2 App.Cas. 455. The duty to tender conforming shipping documents (*e.g.* in performance of a c.i.f. contract) is similarly a condition: *The Hansa Nord* [1976] Q.B. 44 at 70; *Soon Hua Seng Co v Glencore Grain Ltd* [1996] 1 Lloyd's Rep. 398.

question whether the breach amounted to a "substantial" failure in performance. On the other hand, in some of the examples given above, the exercise of the right to terminate can occasion obvious hardship to the party in breach: it results in his having to bear a loss that was not caused by the breach at all, but by market movements. For this reason, there has been some judicial reaction against the authorities which give a wide scope to the right to terminate; and in contracts for the supply of goods that right has also been limited by legislation.

Restrictions of technical applications. In *Reardon Smith Line Ltd v Hansen Tangen*[284] Lord Wilberforce[285] said that some of the authorities just discussed were "excessively technical and due for fresh examination in this House"[286]; and that generally, where goods are sold by description, the court should   **18–046**

> "ask whether a particular item in a description constitutes a substantial ingredient in the identity of the thing sold, and only if it does ... treat it as a condition".[287]

However, he recognised a possible exception in the case of "unascertained future goods (e.g. commodities) as to which each detail of the description must be assumed to be vital".[288] Since such goods often pass rapidly through many hands, the argument of commercial certainty is in such cases particularly strong: it is important for each buyer to be able to tell at once whether some defect or misdescription justifies rejection.

The judicial reaction against the excessively technical use of the right to terminate is illustrated by *Reardon Smith Line Ltd v Hansen Tangen* itself. The case arose out of the sub-charter of a tanker then under construction and therefore not yet named. In the contract, she was accordingly described as "Yard No. 354 at Osaka ... " (the name of the shipbuilder). She was built elsewhere, but by a company under Osaka's control and in accordance with the physical specifications in the sub-charter. The tanker market fell and the sub-charterers sought to reject, but it was held that they were not entitled to do so. The phrase "Yard No. 354 at Osaka" was not part of the description but a mere substitute for a name: it was a means of identification, which, in the circumstances, had not failed. The effect of the case is to reintroduce the requirement of substantial failure into this branch of the law by making it part of the definition of a "description"[289]; and by thus narrowing the scope of an implied term which is undoubtedly a condition, i.e. the term requiring the goods to correspond with the contractual description.

Intermediate or innominate terms. The courts have also achieved a result similar to that just described by reducing the number of terms which are to be classified as conditions. They have done so by recognising that the distinction between conditions and warranties is not exhaustive. As Diplock L.J. has said: **18–047**

---

[284] [1976] 1 W.L.R. 989; cf. *Sanko SS Co Ltd v Kano Trading Co Ltd* [1978] 1 Lloyd's Rep. 156.
[285] With whom Lords Simon and Kilbrandon agreed.
[286] [1976] 1 W.L.R. 989 at 998; cf. the criticism of the effects of breach of "warranty" in insurance law (above, fn.253) in *Forsikringsaktieselskapet Vesta v Butcher* [1989] A.C. 852 at 893–894.
[287] ibid.
[288] ibid.
[289] See above, at fn.287.

"There are many ... contractual undertakings ... which cannot be categorised as being 'conditions' or 'warranties' ... Of such undertakings, all that can be predicated is that some breaches will and others will not give rise to an event which will deprive the party not in default of substantially the whole benefit which it was intended that he should obtain."[290]

These "intermediate or innominate terms"[291] differ from conditions, in that their breach does not of itself give rise to a right to terminate; and from warranties in that the injured party's remedy is not even prima facie restricted to damages. He can terminate for breach of an intermediate term if, but only if, the requirement of substantial failure is satisfied.[292] Thus it has been held that a shipowner's undertakings in a charterparty to provide a seaworthy ship[293] and to use reasonable despatch[294] are not conditions, so that the *mere* fact that they are not performed will not entitle the charterer to terminate. The same is true of the charterer's obligation to load within the time stipulated in the charterparty, so that the mere fact of delay will not justify termination by the shipowner.[295] Similarly, it has been held that a time-charterer's obligation to repair the ship before redelivery is not a condition, so that his failure to repair does not, of itself, justify the shipowner's refusal to accept redelivery[296]; and it is probable that his breach ordering the ship to embark on a voyage which is illegitimate (because it cannot be completed within the period of the charter) will not of itself entitle the shipowner to terminate.[297] Some terms implied by statute seem also to fall into the category of intermediate terms. This seems to be true of the terms implied by the Supply of Goods and Services Act 1982 into contracts for the supply of services, that the services will be carried out with due care and skill and in a reasonable time; for the Act describes them simply as "terms"[298] (as opposed to the "conditions" and "warranties" implied into contracts for the supply of goods by the same Act[299]). The category of intermediate terms is thus established and is of general application.[300] Its existence does, however, give rise to two further problems.

---

[290] *Hongkong Fir Shipping Co Ltd v Kawasaki Kisen Kaisha Ltd* [1962] 2 Q.B. 26 at 70.

[291] *Bunge Corp v Tradax Export SA* [1981] 1 W.L.R. 711 at 714.

[292] e.g. *Freeman v Taylor* (1831) 8 Bing. 124; cf. *The Antaios* [1985] A.C. 191 at 200; *Federal Commerce & Navigation v Molena Alpha* [1979] A.C. 757, esp. at 779. In insurance breach by the insured of an intermediate term relating to a claim may entitle the insurer to reject that claim but not to avoid the whole policy: see *Alfred McAlpine Plc v BAI (Run-off) Ltd* [2000] 1 Lloyd's Rep. 437 at 444, disapproved in *Friends Provident Life & Pensions Ltd v Sirius International Ins* [2005] EWCA Civ 601; [2005] 2 Lloyd's Rep. 517; see below, fn.304.

[293] *Hongkong Fir* case, above; cf. *The Ymnos* [1982] 2 Lloyd's Rep. 574; *The Torenia* [1983] 2 Lloyd's Rep. 210 at 217.

[294] *Clipsham v Vertue* (1843) 5 Q.B. 265; *MacAndrew v Chapple* (1886) L.R. 1 C.P. 643.

[295] *Universal Cargo Carriers Corp v Citati* [1957] 2 Q.B. 401; *The Angelia* [1973] 1 W.L.R. 210.

[296] *Attica Sea Carriers Corp v Ferrostaal Poseidon Bulk Reederei GmbH* [1976] 1 Lloyd's Rep. 250 at 253, 256.

[297] *The Gregos* [1994] 1 W.L.R. 1465 at 1476, where it was not necessary to decide the point as the owner was entitled to terminate on the ground stated at para.18–034, above.

[298] Supply of Goods and Services Act 1982, ss.13, 14.

[299] ibid., ss.2–5 and 7–10.

[300] There was formerly some doubt on the question whether the category of intermediate terms existed in relation to contracts for the sale of goods, but this was removed by the decision of the Court of Appeal in *The Hansa Nord* [1976] Q.B. 44; Reynolds 92 L.Q.R. 17; Weir [1976] C.L.J. 33; cf. *The Aktion* [1987] 1 Lloyd's Rep. 283; below, para.18–059.

Are there three categories of terms? This is a largely terminological prob-   18–048
lem.[301] The general view is that there are three classes of contractual terms:
conditions, the breach of which at common law[302] invariably gives rise to a right
to terminate; warranties, the breach of which gives rise only to a right to damages;
and intermediate terms, the breach of which gives rise to a right to terminate if it
is sufficiently serious, but otherwise sounds only in damages. There is, however,
support for the alternative view that there are only two categories: conditions and
other terms.[303] This view is based on the argument that the injured party may be
entitled to terminate even for a breach of warranty, if the effect of the breach is
sufficiently serious.[304] There is considerable force in this argument[305] and if it is
correct a warranty may be said to resemble an intermediate term, in that the
availability of termination as a remedy for breach of either type of term depends
on the seriousness of the breach. Nevertheless, the weight of authority supports
the continued existence of the threefold division of contractual terms.[306] It is
respectfully submitted that this is the preferable view since the distinction
between warranties and intermediate terms remains for practical purposes an
important one. Even if, in extreme cases, termination is available for breach of
warranty, there is at least a prima facie rule that the normal remedy for such a
breach is by way of damages. In relation to intermediate terms, there is no such
prima facie rule; so that (to put the matter at its lowest) there is a greater likelihood
that termination will be available for breach of an intermediate term than for
breach of warranty.

Scope of the category of intermediate terms. Granted that the threefold   18–049
classification of terms does exist, the question then arises into which category
particular terms should be placed. In discussing this question we shall assume that
the parties have not expressly classified the term in the contract itself; and that the
court will generally apply a previous judicial classification of the term.[307] Our
concern here is therefore with previously unclassified terms. Since judicial classification of a term as a warranty is rare,[308] the important issue is whether a
previously unclassified term is to be classified as a condition or as an intermediate

---

[301] *The Ymnos* [1982] 2 Lloyd's Rep. 574 at 583.

[302] For statutory exceptions see below, para.18–053.

[303] e.g. in *The Hansa Nord* [1976] Q.B. 44 at 60; cf. *Koompahtoo Local Aboriginal Land Council v
Sanpine Pty Ltd* [2007] H.C.A. 61, 233 C.L.R. 115 at [109].

[304] In *Friends Provident Life & Pensions Ltd v Sirius International Ins* [2005] EWCA Civ 601; [2005]
2 Lloyd's Rep. 517 at [32], Mance L.J. held that breach of a claims notification clause in an insurance
policy sounds in damages (i.e. it is a warranty), but appeared to rule out treating it as an innominate
term if the breach was serious. However, this was said in the context of a debate about whether an
insurer might reject the particular claim, rather than terminate the policy: cf. above, para.17–015.

[305] See above, para.18–034.

[306] *Bunge Corp v Tradax Export SA* [1981] 1 W.L.R. 711 at 725 (where Lord Roskill, with whom
three of the other members of the House of Lords agreed, referred to a "third class of term"); *Regent
OHG Aisenstadt und Barig v Francesco of Jermyn Street* [1981] 3 All E.R. 327 at 334; *The Mercandian
Continent* [2001] EWCA Civ 1275; [2001] 1 Lloyd's Rep. 563 at [13]; cf. Lord Diplock's division of
stipulations as to time into three categories in *United Scientific Holdings Ltd v Burnley BC* [1978] A.C.
904 at 943. His statement in *Photo Production Ltd v Securicor Transport Ltd* [1980] A.C. 827 at 849 of
a general rule subject to two exceptions similarly amounts to a three fold classification.

[307] Occasionally the court may wish to reconsider such a classification: cf. Lord Wilberforce's
suggestion in *Reardon-Smith Line Ltd v Hansen Tangen* [1976] 1 W.L.R. 989 at 998; above,
para.18–046.

[308] For an example of such a classification, see *The Captain George K* [1970] 2 Lloyd's Rep. 21.

term. This issue is a difficult one because it gives rise to a conflict between two policies.

18–050 **Policy considerations.** The first of these policies is to restrict the right to terminate to cases in which the breach causes serious prejudice to the injured party, and so to prevent a party from terminating for ulterior motives (such as his wish "of escaping from an unwelcome bargain"[309]) or on grounds that have been criticised as "excessively technical."[310] This policy favours the classification of terms as intermediate. It is illustrated by the *Hongkong Fir*[311] case, the *Hansa Nord*[312] and by a number of later decisions.[313] It can be displaced by evidence of contrary intention,[314] but where there is no such evidence of the intention of the parties, the policy of "leaning in favour"[315] of classifying stipulations as intermediate terms can be said to promote the interests of justice by preventing the injured party from terminating on grounds that are technical or unmeritorious.

The second policy, by contrast, emphasises the requirement of commercial certainty; and it in turn favours the classification of terms as conditions. Such a classification makes it unnecessary to go into the difficult questions of fact and degree which arise in determining whether a breach is "serious and substantial."[316] And once a term has been classified as a condition, the breach of such a term will, in a future case, enable the injured party to know, as soon as the breach has been committed, that he is entitled to terminate: he will not need to show anything about its effects. These considerations prevailed in *Bunge Corp v Tradax Export SA*.[317] A contract for the sale of soya bean meal provided that the goods were to be delivered during June. Delivery was to begin on a day in that month to be chosen by the buyers and was to be made free on board on a ship provided by the buyers at a US Gulf port to be selected by the sellers. The contract went on to require the buyers to give at least 15 days' notice of the ship's readiness to load the goods. It was held that this term was a condition, so that the sellers were entitled to terminate on the ground that the notice reached them five days too late. Two justifications for this classification were given. First, the sellers could not, as a practical matter, perform their own obligation of nominating a port until the buyers had given them notice of the ship's readiness to load[318]; but later cases show that, though this factor is relevant to the classification of the term,[319] it is not decisive, so that terms have been classified as conditions even where there was no such interdependence between the obligations of the parties.[320] The second, and

[309] *The Gregos* [1994] 1 W.L.R. 1465 at 1475.
[310] *Reardon-Smith Line Ltd v Hansen Tangen* [1976] 1 W.L.R. 989 at 998.
[311] [1962] 2 Q.B. 26; above, para.18–047.
[312] [1976] Q.B. 44; above, fn.300.
[313] *Tradax Internacional SA v Goldschmidt SA* [1977] 2 Lloyd's Rep. 604; *Bremer Handelsgesellschaft mbH v Vanden Avenne-Izegem PVBA* [1978] 2 Lloyd's Rep. 109 at 113; *Federal Commerce & Navigation v Molena Alpha* [1979] A.C. 757.
[314] The fact that there was evidence of such intention appears to be the best ground for distinguishing *Tradax Internacional SA v Goldschmidt SA*, above, from *Tradax Export SA v European Grain & Shipping Co* [1983] 2 Lloyd's Rep. 100: see also *The Zeus V* [2002] 2 Lloyd's Rep. 587.
[315] *Tradax Internacional SA v Goldschmidt SA* above, at 612.
[316] ibid.
[317] [1981] 1 W.L.R. 711.
[318] cf. *Gill & Duffus SA v Société pour l'Exportation des Sucres SA* [1986] 1 Lloyd's Rep. 322.
[319] *Universal Bulk Carriers Ltd v Andre & Cie* [2001] EWCA Civ 588; [2001] 2 Lloyd's Rep. 65 at [40].
[320] *The Mavro Vetranic* [1985] 1 Lloyd's Rep. 580 at 583; *Michael J Warde v Feedex International Inc* [1985] 2 Lloyd's Rep. 289 at 298; *The Niizura* [1996] 2 Lloyd's Rep. 66 at 71; *The Seaflower* [2001] 1 Lloyd's Rep. 341.

more important, point was that the classification promoted certainty, for it enabled the sellers to tell, immediately on receipt of the notice of the ship's readiness to load, whether they were bound to deliver.

Time clauses.[321-322] Failure to adhere to similar timetables laid down by **18-051** commodity contracts and charterparties has, in a number of other cases, likewise been held to amount to a breach of condition.[323] One explanation for this special treatment of time clauses is that "as to such a clause there is only one kind of breach possible, namely to be late"[324]; while terms that have been classified as intermediate are typically such as might be broken in various ways, some trivial and some serious.[325] This is, for example, true of the shipowner's undertaking of seaworthiness in a charterparty; but it is equally true that delay may be trivial or serious; and the law does not always give the injured party the right to terminate for delay which is not serious: we have, for example, seen that a charterer is not in breach of condition merely because he has failed to load within the time stipulated in the charterparty.[326] Stipulations as to the time of performance can, however, be put into a separate category on the ground that breach by delay is particularly easy to establish: if the injured party has received no performance by the due day, there can be no doubt about the fact of delay; while qualitative breaches (such as unseaworthiness) can give rise to many disputed issues of fact. Delay is also of obvious commercial importance in dealings with commodities, which can fluctuate rapidly in value. It is this combination of the ease of establishing the breach without legal proceedings and of its likely commercial importance which accounts for the readiness of the courts to treat stipulations as to the time of performance in contracts for the sale of commodities as conditions, so that *any* breach of them will justify termination.

It follows from the above reasoning that a stipulation as to the time of performance will not invariably be treated as a condition. It may, for example, not be so treated precisely because the context shows that its due performance is *not* of vital importance[327]; or because of the effect of other provisions;[328] or because to give the injured party the right to terminate for *any* breach of it would make the contract unworkable[329]; or because the contract provides that damages are to be the sole

---

[321-322] See further, para.18–089 et seq.

[323] e.g. *Krohn & Co v Mitsui & Co Europe GmbH* [1978] 2 Lloyd's Rep. 419; *Toepfer v Lenersan-Poortman NV* [1980] 1 Lloyd's Rep. 143; cf. *Nichimen Corp v Gatoil Overseas Inc* [1987] 2 Lloyd's Rep. 46; *The Naxos* [1990] 1 W.L.R. 1337; *The Aktor* [2008] EWHC 1330 (Comm); [2008] 2 Lloyd's Rep. 246; Treitel [1991] L.M.C.L.Q. 147; for time stipulations in charterparties, see *The Niizura* [1996] 2 Lloyd's Rep. 66 (distinguished in the *Universal Bulk* case, above, fn.319) and *The Seaflower*, above, fn.320. And see the authorities cited in fnn.318 and 320, above.

[324] *Bunge Corp v Tradax Export SA* [1981] 1 W.L.R. 711 at 715.

[325] ibid.; cf. *The Ymnos* [1982] 2 Lloyd's Rep. 574 at 584.

[326] See above, at fn.295; cf. Lord Wilberforce's statement that a charterer's deliberate delay in loading of only one day "can appropriately be sanctioned by damages": *Suisse Atlantique* case [1967] 1 A.C. 361 at 423 (above, para.18–034).

[327] *State Trading Corp of India v M Golodetz Ltd* [1989] 2 Lloyd's Rep. 277 (where the stipulation was contained in one contract but related to a different contract between the same parties which was not to be performed for six months and was relatively unimportant in terms of money); *The Ballenita* [1992] 2 Lloyd's Rep. 445 at 464–465; *The Gregos* [1994] 1 W.L.R. 1465 at 1475.

[328] *ERG Raffinerie Mediterranée SpA v Chevron USA Inc* [2007] EWCA Civ 494; [2007] 2 Lloyd's Rep. 542 (time of loading normally a condition in an fob contract, but not where laycan provision also included).

[329] As in *The Honam Jade* [1991] 1 Lloyd's Rep. 39 (where strict compliance with the timetable was impossible in chain contracts).

remedy for failure to comply with the stipulation[330]; or because failure by one party to perform the stipulation did not create any uncertainty as to the time at which the other party would have to perform[331]; or because the stipulation did not specify a *precise* time for performance, or enable that time to be precisely ascertained in the light of later events,[332] so that its classification as a condition would not promote certainty. Thus the House of Lords has held that a stipulation requiring a seller to give notice "without delay" of the occurrence of circumstances entitling him to invoke a prohibition of export clause was an intermediate term only.[333] In a later decision at first instance, on the other hand, a term in a contract of sale required the seller to give the buyer a notice appropriating goods to the contract "as soon as possible after vessel's sailing".[334] This term was held to be a condition and the earlier decision[335] was distinguished on the ground that in it the House of Lords had been concerned with a stipulation governing the machinery of *termination* while the later case was concerned with a stipulation governing the machinery of *performance*.[336] But the explanation is not entirely convincing[337] since an important question in relation to either kind of term is whether the breach of it entitles the injured party to treat the contract as at an end. The main justification for classifying the term as a condition is that this will significantly promote certainty by enabling the buyer to know exactly when delay on the seller's part in giving the notice will justify him (the buyer) in terminating the contract.[338] Vague expressions such as "without delay", or "as soon as possible" do not enable him to know this, and stipulations containing such words should not be classified as conditions[339] in the absence of express provisions to that effect[340] or of other evidence that the parties clearly intended them to take effect as such.

18–052　　**"Leaning in favour" of intermediate terms.** The foregoing discussion shows that there is considerable support both for the view that the court should "lean in favour"[341] of classifying contractual stipulations as intermediate terms, and for the view that commercial certainty sometimes requires their classification as conditions. The second of these views was applied in *Bunge Corp v Tradax*

---

[330] As in *The Aragon* [1991] 1 Lloyd's Rep. 61.

[331] *Universal Bulk Carriers Ltd v Andre & Cie* [2001] EWCA Civ 588; [2001] 2 Lloyd's Rep. 65 at [40].

[332] For terms enabling the time so to be ascertained, see *Toepfer v Lenersan-Poortman NV* [1980] 1 Lloyd's Rep. 143; *The Naxos* [1990] 1 W.L.R. 1337.

[333] *Bremer Handelsgellschaft mbH v Vanden Avenne-Izegem PVBA*, above, fn.313, so far as it relates to the notice under cl.21 of the contract; cf. *Tradax Export SA v Italgrani di Francesco Ambrosio* [1986] 1 Lloyd's Rep. 112 at 120.

[334] *The Post Chaser* [1981] 2 Lloyd's Rep. 695.

[335] See above, at fn.333.

[336] [1981] 2 Lloyd's Rep. 695 at 700; cf. *McDougall v Aeromarine of Emsworth Ltd* [1958] 1 W.L.R. 1126 (duty to deliver within a *reasonable time*).

[337] For the difficulty of reconciling the two cases here under discussion, see *Concordia Trading BV v Richco International Ltd* [1991] 1 Lloyd's Rep. 475 at 481.

[338] See *Tradax Export SA v Italgrani di Francesco Ambrosio* [1986] 1 Lloyd's Rep. 112 at 120.

[339] *Alfred McAlpine Ltd v BAI (Run-off) Ltd* [2001] 1 Lloyd's Rep. 437; *The Beursgracht* [2001] EWCA Civ 2051; [2002] 1 Lloyd's Rep. 574 at [43], [44] (but see above, fn.304 for the further issue of whether the term in question was an innominate one).

[340] As in *George Hunt Cranes Ltd v Scottish Boilers & General Ins Co Ltd* [2001] 2 Lloyd's Rep. 65 at [28].

[341] In addition to those referred to in fn.333 above, see *State Trading Corp of India v M Golodetz Ltd* [1989] 2 Lloyd's Rep. 277 at 283; *The Gregos* [1994] 1 W.L.R. 1465 at 1475; *Universal Bulk Carriers Ltd v Andre & Cie* [2001] 2 Lloyd's Rep. 65 at [28].

Export SA[342]; but the first was not rejected: on the contrary, Lord Wilberforce said that "the courts should not be too ready to interpret contractual clauses as conditions"[343]; while Lord Roskill recognised "the modern approach of not being over-ready to construe terms as conditions unless the contract clearly requires the court to do so."[344] The effect of the decision is not to discard, but rather to qualify, that approach by emphasising the importance traditionally attached in certain commercial contracts to exact compliance with stipulations as to the time of performance.[345] Stipulations of this kind are now likely to be classified as conditions if they are sufficiently precise; and other terms may also be so classified if exact performance of them is regarded as commercially vital[346] or if there is evidence either from the commercial setting or from the course of negotiations that the parties intended them to have the force of conditions.[347] Where a term does not fall within any of these three categories, the judicial attitude continues to be one of not being "too ready" to classify it as a condition. Such other terms are therefore likely to be classified as intermediate, so that termination will be allowed only where the breach causes serious prejudice to the injured party.

Statutory restriction on right to terminate for breach of condition. As a result of amendments to the Sale of Goods Act 1979 made in 1994,[348] the buyer's right to reject the goods for breach of condition is restricted where the buyer does *not* deal as consumer; further restrictions on that right where the buyer *does* deal as consumer are imposed by amendments of the 1979 Act made in 2002.[349] Similar restrictions apply to other contracts for the supply of goods; but for the sake of brevity the following discussion will deal only with cases of sale.   18–053

Buyer not dealing as consumer. Section 15A[350] of the Sale of Goods Act 1979 applies where the buyer does not deal as consumer and where he would be entitled to reject by reason of a breach of condition implied into the contract under the Sale of Goods Act 1979 as to correspondence with description or sample and as to quality.[351] Section 15A provides that if, in such cases, the seller can   18–054

---

[342] [1981] 1 W.L.R. 714; above, para.18–050.

[343] ibid. at 715.

[344] ibid. at 727; cf. also *Toepfer v Lenersan Poortman NV* [1980] 1 Lloyd's Rep. 143 at 147; *The Ymnos* [1982] 1 Lloyd's Rep. 574 at 583; *The Gregos* [1994] 1 W.L.R. 1465 at 1475.

[345] cf. *Bowes v Shand* (1877) 2 App.Cas. 455; above, para.18–045.

[346] *The Post Chaser* [1981] 2 Lloyd's Rep. 695 may be explicable on this ground: see at 700; or on the ground of concessions made in that case, see *British & Commonwealth Holdings Plc v Quadrex Holdings Inc* [1989] Q.B. 842 at 857. The arbitrators' finding as to the commercial importance of compliance with the stipulation was a second ground for the decision in *The Naxos* [1990] 1 W.L.R. 1337; cf. *The New Prosper* [1991] 2 Lloyd's Rep. 93 at 99; *Petrotrade Inc v Stinnes Handel GmbH* [1995] 1 Lloyd's Rep. 142 (place of delivery in f.o.b. contract vital to buyers as they had to provide a ship there).

[347] e.g. *Tradax Export SA v European Grain & Shipping Co* [1983] 2 Lloyd's Rep. 100; *Bergerco USA v Vegoil Ltd* [1984] 1 Lloyd's Rep. 440; cf. also *Michael J Warde v Feedex International Inc* [1985] 2 Lloyd's Rep. 284 at 288.

[348] By the Sale and Supply of Goods Act 1994.

[349] By the Sale and Supply of Goods to Consumers Regulations 2002 (SI 2002/3045).

[350] Inserted by Sale and Supply of Goods Act 1994, s.4(1) giving effect to recommendations of the Law Commission in Law Com. No.160 (1987), para.4.21. For similar provisions relating to other contracts for the supply of goods, see Supply of Goods (Implied Terms) Act 1973, s.11A and Supply of Goods and Services Act 1982, s.5A, as inserted by Sale and Supply of Goods Act 1994, s.7(1) and Sch.2, paras 4 and 6.

[351] i.e. the terms implied by ss.13, 14 and 15 of the 1979 Act: above, para.18–044.

show[352] that the breach is "so slight that it would be unreasonable"[353] for the buyer to reject the goods, then the breach is "not to be treated as a breach of condition but may be treated as a breach of warranty"[354]; when it is so treated the buyer's remedy will therefore be in damages. This exception to the general common law rule that breach of condition automatically justifies termination is "not intended as a major alteration in the law".[355] Its scope is, in particular, limited in the following ways.

First, it applies only to contracts for the supply of goods: the law relating to breach of condition in, for example, time or voyage charterparties,[356] is unaffected. Secondly, it applies only to breaches by the supplier: a case such as *Bunge Corp v Tradax Export SA*[357] would not be affected since the breach was committed by the buyer. Thirdly, it applies only to breach of certain *implied* terms: the right to reject for breach of an *express* condition[358] is not affected. Fourthly, it applies only to breach of the statutorily implied terms listed above.[359] It does not apply to any other terms which may be implied by statute,[360] nor to terms implied as a matter of common law. Fifthly, the exception is excluded where "a contrary intention appears in, or is to be implied from, the contract".[361] Such an implication may arise from the nature of the contract or from its commercial setting. It is, for example, envisaged that the exception will for this reason not apply to breaches of such time clauses in commercial contracts as have been classified as conditions[362] (though the wording of the new s.15A can scarcely be said to make this point clear). Sixthly, the exception does not apply where the buyer deals as consumer: such a buyer is not well placed to dispose of defective goods on the market, so that it is important to preserve his unqualified right to reject for breach of the statutorily implied conditions.[363]

Where a case falls within s.15A, two requirements must be satisfied[364] before the buyer is deprived of his right to reject for breach of condition: the breach must be "slight" and it must be "unreasonable for [the buyer] to reject" the goods. The policy underlying these requirements is similar to that on which the development of the category of intermediate terms is based[365]: it is to prevent the buyer from rejecting on unmeritorious grounds (though his motives for rejection are said not to be relevant[366]). But it should not be thought that, where the section applies, it has the effect of turning the implied conditions to which it refers into intermediate terms. The section only precludes the buyer from rejecting where the breach is "slight"; and a breach which is too serious to be "slight" may nevertheless not be serious enough to deprive the buyer of substantially the whole benefit which it was

---

[352] Sale of Goods Act 1979, s.15A(3).

[353] ibid., s.15A(1)(b).

[354] ibid., s.15A(1).

[355] Law Com. No.160, para.4.21.

[356] See above, para.18–041.

[357] [1981] 1 W.L.R. 711; above, para.18–050.

[358] As, for example, in *Bremer Handelsgesellschaft mbH v Vanden Avenne-Izegem PVBA* [1978] 2 Lloyd's Rep. 109 (so far as it relates to cl.22).

[359] See above, at fn.351.

[360] e.g. by Sale of Goods Act 1979, s.12(1) (such a breach might be "slight" if it affected only part of the goods sold).

[361] Sale of Goods Act 1979, s.15A(2).

[362] Law Com. No.160, para.4.24; e.g. *Bowes v Shand* (1877) 2 App. Cas. 455; above, para.18–045.

[363] See Law Com. No.160, Scot. Law Com. No.104, paras 4.09–4.15.

[364] Law Com. No.160, para.4.21 ("slight *and* it is unreasonable . . . ").

[365] See above, para.18–047.

[366] Law Com. No.160, paras 4.18 and 4.19.

intended that he should obtain from the contract.[367] Where the breach falls between these extremes, the buyer's right to reject for breach of condition is not affected by s.15A, even though a similar breach would not give him a right to reject for breach of an intermediate term. The question just when a breach is so slight as to make it unreasonable for the buyer to reject the goods remains to be settled by judicial decision; and the vagueness of s.15A on this point is a source of regrettable uncertainty. It is, for example, far from clear how a case such as *Arcos Ltd v Ronaasen*[368] would now be decided. The difference between half an inch and 9/16 of an inch is by no means obviously "slight" (at least as a proportion); and if it were not slight the buyer would not be deprived of his right to reject merely because it was unreasonable for him to reject or because his motive for rejection was to escape from what had turned out to be a bad bargain because of a fall in the market.[369]

Section 15A is, it is submitted, an unfortunate provision which manages to fall between two stools. On the one hand, the section undermines the certainty which classification of the implied terms in question as conditions was intended to provide. It is no answer to this argument to say that the limitation on the right to reject which the section imposes will not often apply: the point is that it is hard to predict when it will apply, so that a buyer's legal adviser will not be able to answer that question with certainty.[370] Nor is it an answer to say that the limitation can be excluded by implied agreement[371]: it is, again, impossible to predict with certainty when such an implication will be made. On the other hand, the section scarcely goes far enough to promote justice: for this purpose, the right to reject should be restricted to serious breaches and not merely excluded if the breach is slight. If a case like *Arcos Ltd v Ronaasen*[372] would not be affected by s.15A, the right to reject could still be exercised so as to cause injustice. Even if the section did cover all cases in which it would be unjust to allow the buyer to reject, it would be extraordinarily partial in its operation. Termination by a seller can lead to just as much injustice as rejection by the buyer; but the section does nothing to limit the exercise by a seller of a right to terminate. It is submitted that the section has sacrificed certainty without attaining justice.

Buyer dealing as consumer. Sections 48A to 48C[373] of the Sale of Goods Act 1979 specify a number of "additional rights"[374] available to a buyer who "deals as consumer"[375] where the goods[376] do not conform to the contract of sale at the time of delivery.[377] For this purpose goods do not conform to the contract where the

18–055

---

[367] This is the test for determining when a breach of an intermediate term gives rise to a right to terminate: *Hongkong Fir Shipping Co Ltd v Kawasaki Kisen Kaisha Ltd* [1962] 2 Q.B. 26 at 70.

[368] [1933] A.C. 470; above, para.18–045.

[369] See above, at fn.366.

[370] For a similar view in an analogous context, see *Union Eagle Ltd v Golden Achievement Ltd* [1997] A.C. 514 at 519. The Law Commission does not explain its statement that "the uncertainty will be more apparent than real": Law Com. No.160, para.4.23.

[371] *Union Eagle Ltd v Golden Achievement Ltd* [1997] A.C. 514 at 519.

[372] [1933] A.C. 470; above, at fn.368.

[373] Inserted into the Act by Sale and Supply of Goods to Consumers Regulations 2002 (SI 2002/3045), reg.5, implementing Directive 1999/44.

[374] Heading to new Pt 5A of the 1979 Act.

[375] Sale of Goods Act 1979, s.61(5A), cross-referring to the definition in Unfair Contract Terms Act 1977, discussed at para.7–053, above.

[376] Second-hand goods and certain auction sales are excepted by amendments to s.12(2) of the 1977 Act made by reg.14; above, para.7–053.

[377] Sale of Goods Act 1979, s.48A(1)(b).

seller is in breach of the conditions implied into the contract under the Act as to correspondence with description or sample, or as to quality[378]; or where he is in breach of an express term.[379] The first of these "additional rights" (conferred by s.48B) is one to require the seller to repair or replace the goods,[380] subject to specified limitations.[381] Where these limitations apply, so that the right is not available, or where the seller has failed to comply with the buyer's requirement to repair or replace the goods within a reasonable time,[382] then the buyer has the right (under these sections) to terminate the contract with regard to the non-conforming goods.[383] The buyer's right to reject goods for breach of condition is also limited in that, if he requires the seller to repair or replace the non-conforming goods under the above provisions, then he must not reject the goods for breach of condition[384] until he has given the seller a reasonable time to repair or replace the goods.[385] The right of the buyer who deals as consumer to terminate the contract under s.48A and 48C is also, in effect, subject to the discretion of the court. Section 48E provides (inter alia) that, where the buyer has claimed to terminate under s.48C, then if the court decides that another remedy under s.48B or 48C (e.g. price reduction) is appropriate, the court may give effect to that other remedy.[386] These restrictions on the buyer's right to reject and to terminate the contract at first sight come into conflict with the policy underlying s.15A, of preserving the consumer's unqualified right to reject for breach of condition. The conflict is, however, more apparent than real since the rights here under discussion are "additional" to his right to reject for breach of condition under the provisions of the Act which governed that right before the "additional rights" were created.[387] There is nothing in s.48A to 48C to compel the consumer to require repair or replacement or to seek to terminate under these new sections; and the restrictions here discussed on his remedies do not extend to cases in which the buyer simply rejects for breach of condition under the rules stated earlier in this chapter,[388] without seeking to assert any of the "additional rights" given to him by those sections.

18–056   **Other restrictions on termination for breach of condition.** The right to terminate for breach of condition may be limited in the following further ways.

The contract may contain a term purporting to exclude the right to terminate.[389] Such a clause is subject to the rules discussed in Ch.7, which limit the

---

[378] ibid., s.48F, referring to ss.13–15.

[379] ibid., s.48F ("express term").

[380] ibid., ss.48A(2)(a) and 48B.

[381] ibid., s.48B(3) and (4).

[382] ibid., s.48C(2).

[383] ibid., s.48C(1)(b). The statutory provisions use the terminology of "rescission", but for consistency with the rest of this chapter "termination" is retained: see above, para.18–001 for the debate as to terminology.

[384] ibid., s.48D(1), (2)(a).

[385] ibid., s.48D(1), (2)(a).

[386] ibid., s.48E(3), (4).

[387] ibid., s.48E, which in effect enables the court to override the buyer's choice of remedies provided by s.48B and 48C, does not apply where the buyer's choice is to pursue a remedy other than any of these specified in those sections.

[388] See para.18–039, above.

[389] e.g. a "non-rejection" or "non-cancellation" clause which bars the right to terminate without affecting the right to damages: *The Aegean Dolphin* [1992] 2 Lloyd's Rep. 178.

effectiveness of exemption clauses.[390] It is submitted that, in applying the tests of reasonableness[391] and fairness[392] found in the statutory controls to clauses excluding the right to terminate for breach of condition, the courts may be influenced by the likely effects of the breach (as viewed at the time of contracting), and so take into account the factors which determine whether a failure in performance is sufficiently "substantial" to give rise to a right to terminate. A similar point can be made with regard to the process of construction which is applied to exemption clauses in certain cases of particularly serious breach.[393]

Where a person has been induced to enter into a contract by a false statement of *fact*, his right to rescind for misrepresentation is subject to the discretion of the court under s.2(2) of the Misrepresentation Act 1967,[394] to declare the contract subsisting and to award damages in lieu of rescission. It is arguable that this discretion can be exercised even where the misrepresentation which induced the contract is later incorporated in it as a condition. But the better view seems to be that the subsection applies only to the right to rescind a contract *for misrepresentation*, and that it has not affected the right to terminate for breach.[395]

Termination for breach of warranty? Once a term is classified as a "condition" any breach of it at common law gives right to a right to terminate. It might be thought, conversely, to follow from the definition of "warranty"[396] that, once a term had been classified as a warranty, then a claim for damages was the only remedy for its breach. But there are three situations in which the injured party may be able to terminate for breach of warranty.   18–057

Misrepresentation incorporated as warranty. A statement of *fact* made before the contract may give rise to a right to rescind the contract for misrepresentation, and this right will survive the subsequent incorporation of the statement in the contract as a warranty.[397] It is not that the contract may be terminated *for breach of warranty*, but rather the injured party is entitled to invoke the surviving right to rescind for misrepresentation. Furthermore, if the breach (and, with it, the misrepresentation) is of relatively small importance, it seems likely that the court will exercise its discretion under s.2(2) of the Misrepresentation Act 1967[398] to declare the contract subsisting and to award damages in lieu of rescission.   18–058

Breach of warranty amounting to substantial failure. It has been suggested[399] that breach of warranty may justify termination where it leads (or   18–059

---

[390] A clause which excludes only the right to terminate and not all liability is still caught by Unfair Contract Terms Act, under s.13(1)(b): see above, para.7–054.

[391] Under Unfair Contract Terms Act 1977: see above, para.7–050 et seq.

[392] Under Unfair Terms in Consumer Contracts Regulations 1999: see above, para.7–095 et seq.

[393] See *J Aron & Co (Inc) v Comptoir Wegimont* [1921] 3 K.B. 435 for the application of these principles to non-rejection clauses.

[394] See para.9–054, above.

[395] See above, para.9–096.

[396] Sale of Goods Act 1979, s.61(1) (below, at fn.400); cf. Sale of Goods Act 1979, s.11(3); above, para.18–039.

[397] Misrepresentation Act 1967, s.1(a); above, para.9–091.

[398] See above, para.9–054.

[399] *Astley Industrial Trust Ltd v Grimley* [1963] 1 W.L.R. 584 at 599. The term broken in this example would now be a condition under Supply of Goods and Services Act 1982, s.9(4) if the party in breach acted in the course of a business.

amounts) to a substantial failure in performance. There is at first sight some difficulty in applying this suggestion to contracts for the sale of goods. The difficulty arises because "warranty" is defined in the Sale of Goods Act 1979 as an agreement

> "collateral to the main purpose of [the] contract, the breach of which gives rise to a claim for damages but not to a right to reject the goods . . . ."[400]

On the other hand, it is arguable that the rule allowing termination for a "substantial" failure in performance is a rule of common law, preserved by s.62(2) of the Act "except in so far as . . . inconsistent with the express provisions of this Act". In *The Hansa Nord*[401] this subsection was invoked in support of the view that the statutory classification of terms into conditions and warranties was not exhaustive. It can similarly be used to support the view that the Act does not exhaustively state the effects of breach of warranty.[402] If in particular circumstances such a breach leads to a substantial failure in performance, the prima facie rule[403] that damages are the only remedy for breach of warranty should be displaced and termination should be allowed.

18–060   **Consumer sales.** Under s.48A and 48C of the Sale of Goods Act 1979, a buyer who deals as consumer has, in circumstances described earlier in this chapter,[404] a right to terminate the contract with regard to non-conforming goods.[405] Goods which do not conform to the contract are those in relation to which there is a breach of *either* the terms implied by ss.13 to 14 of the 1979 Act *or* of "an express term".[406] The former are necessarily breaches of condition, but the latter may be a breach of warranty. Under these sections, the buyer may therefore have a right to terminate for breach of warranty. This right is, however, subject to the power of the court to proceed as if the buyer had instead sought another remedy (such as price reduction) made available by those sections.[407]

(ii) *Express provision for determination*

18–061   **Literal enforcement in general.** A contract may expressly provide that one party shall be entitled to terminate in the event of some specified failure by the other to perform.[408] For example, a voyage charterparty may stipulate that the ship is expected to be ready to load at a named port on (or about) a specified date, and that if she fails to arrive there within (say) 10 days of that date the charterer shall be entitled to cancel; and a time charterparty may provide either that the owner

---

[400] s.61(1).

[401] [1976] Q.B. 44.

[402] ibid. at 83.

[403] See above, para.18–039.

[404] Above, para.18–055.

[405] Sale of Goods Act 1979, s.48A(2)(b)(ii) and 48C(1)(b). The statutory provisions use the terminology of "rescission", but for consistency with the rest of this chapter "termination" is retained: see above, para.18–001 for the debate as to terminology.

[406] ibid., s.48F.

[407] ibid., s.48E(3) and (4).

[408] As with termination under the general law, the event in question need not be a breach; indeed, it need not even amount to a failure to perform (e.g. termination upon the appointment of a receiver), but in most cases the relevant event will be such a failure, which will often also amount to a breach.

shall be entitled to withdraw the ship if hire is not punctually paid, or that the charterer shall be entitled to cancel if the ship becomes unavailable for service for more than a specified number of days.[409] The purpose of such clauses is to prevent disputes from arising as to the often difficult question whether the failure in performance is sufficiently serious to justify termination; and they take effect even though there is no substantial failure.[410] For example, under a clause in a time charterparty entitling the shipowner to withdraw the ship if the charter fails to pay hire by a specified day, the shipowner can exercise his right of withdrawal immediately on such failure[411]; and he can do this even though the charterer tenders payment very soon after it was due, even though the short delay in payment causes the shipowner little prejudice, and even though his motive for withdrawal is simply that the freight market has risen. Such clauses are literally enforced because, in cases of this kind, "certainty is of primary importance"[412]; while the charterer can mitigate the severity of the clause by insisting (if his bargaining position permits) on the inclusion of a so-called "anti-technicality" provision allowing days of grace or requiring notice of default before withdrawal.[413] The principle of literal enforcement similarly applies where a contract for the sale of land specifies a completion date and provides that, on the purchaser's failure to comply with any of the terms of the contract, the vendor is to be entitled to terminate. In one such case[414] the vendor declared the contract terminated one minute after the time fixed for completion and the termination was held to be effective, so that the purchaser was not entitled to specific performance on tendering the purchase price a mere 10 minutes after that time. Again this conclusion was supported on the ground that "the parties should know with certainty that the terms of the contract will be enforced".[415]

Strict compliance required. Although, for the reasons just given, the law normally gives literal effect to express provisions for determination, it does insist on compliance with three requirements. First, the party who relies on the express term as justifying termination for a breach which is not serious must show that the term does, as a matter of construction, apply to that breach. Thus where a term in a four-year maintenance contract allowed one party to terminate in the event of the other's breach of "*any* of its obligations under the contract", it was held that

18–062

---

[409] *The Span Terza (No.2)* [1984] 1 W.L.R. 27; such a clause avoids the difficulties that arose in the *Hongkong Fir* case [1962] 2 Q.B. 26; above, para.18–031. See also: *The Solholt* [1983] 1 Lloyd's Rep. 605; *The Oro Chef* [1983] 2 Lloyd's Rep. 509; cf. *Bettini v Gye* (1876) 1 Q.B.D. 183 at 187.

[410] Such clauses are probably not within s.3(2)(b)(ii) of the Unfair Contract Terms Act 1977 for the reasons given at para.7–069, above, and because termination under such clauses terminates the primary obligations of *both* parties; cf. *The Super Servant Two* [1990] 1 Lloyd's Rep. 1 at 7, distinguishing between cancellation and exemption clauses.

[411] *The Brimnes* [1975] Q.B. 929; *The Laconia* [1977] A.C. 850; Rose 30 C.L.P. 213; cf. *The Chikuma* [1981] 1 W.L.R. 314; Mann 97 L.Q.R. 379–382.

[412] *The Laconia* [1977] A.C. 850 at 878; *The Lutetian* [1982] 2 Lloyd's Rep. 140 at 159; cf. *The Chikuma*, above, at 322.

[413] As in *Libyaville* [1975] 1 Lloyd's Rep. 537; and in *Federal Commerce and Navigation Co Ltd v Molena Alpha Inc* [1979] A.C. 757. cf. *The Laconia*, above, at 878; *The Afovos* [1983] 1 W.L.R. 195; *Artpower Ltd v Bespoke Couture Ltd* [2006] EWCA Civ 1696 (notice of default not sufficient to effect termination which also required election of injured party).

[414] *Union Eagle Ltd v Golden Achievement Ltd* [1997] A.C. 514.

[415] ibid. at 519; cf. ibid. at 523; *Kazakstan Wool Processors (Europe) Ltd v Nederlandsche Credietverzekering Maatschappij NV* [2000] C.L.C. 822.

even this emphatic language did not have this effect.[416] Secondly, the party seeking to terminate must act strictly in accordance with the terms of the clause. For example, a voyage charterparty may provide that the charterer can cancel if the ship is not at the port of loading by September 30. The charterer would not be entitled to cancel on September 29, even though at that time the ship was so far away from the port that she could not possibly get there the next day.[417] Conversely where a time charterparty gives the shipowner the right to give notice of withdrawal, if hire is not paid on the due day, he is not entitled to exercise that right before the end of that day, even though the bank at which payment was to be made had already closed so that the charterer could not possibly have made the payment in accordance with the contract.[418] The willingness of the courts to adopt a "purposive" approach to interpretation[419] may mean that strict compliance with this particular requirement can be relaxed a little.[420] Thirdly, the party relying on the express provision must terminate without undue delay. Thus, in cases of non-payment of hire by a time charterer it has been said that the shipowner must exercise his right to withdraw the ship "within a reasonable time after default".[421]

18–063   **Relief against forfeiture in certain cases.**[422] The willingness of the courts to give effect to express provisions for determination is, in the cases so far discussed, based on the assumption that the parties have bargained on more or less equal terms.[423] Where this is not the case, the law has developed restrictions on the right of a party to rely on an express provision for determination. This is the position where a lease entitles the landlord to forfeit if the tenant breaks *any* covenant; and where a regulated hire-purchase agreement[424] entitles the owner to terminate it if the hirer defaults in the payment of even a single instalment. In

---

[416] *Rice v Great Yarmouth BC, The Times*, July 26, 2000; it was admitted that the clause did not allow termination for a "trivial" breach, but it is open to doubt whether the court was correct to conclude that the term added nothing to the general law such that the only breaches covered were those which would have amounted to a repudiatory breach in any event; cf. *Dominion Corporate Trustees Ltd v Debenhams Properties Ltd* [2010] EWHC 1193 (Ch); [2010] 23 E.G. 106 at [32]; *Wickman Ltd v Schuler AG* [1974] A.C. 235; below, para.18–043, and a number of authorities dealing with the meaning of "material breach": *Glolite Ltd v Jasper Conran Ltd, The Times*, January 28, 1998; *Fortman Holdings v Modem Holdings* [2001] EWCA Civ 1235; *Dalkia Utilities Services Plc v Celtech International Ltd* [2006] EWHC 63; [2006] 1 Lloyd's Rep 599. For the interpretation of breaches "not capable of remedy", see the discussion in *Force India Formula One Team Ltd v Etihad Airways PJSC* [2010] EWCA Civ 1051 at [100]–[110].
[417] *The Mihalis Angelos* [1971] 1 Q.B. 164; cf. *The Madeleine* [1967] 2 Lloyd's Rep. 224 at 243.
[418] *The Afovos* [1983] 1 W.L.R. 195; cf. *The Pamela* [1995] 2 Lloyd's Rep. 249,
[419] See above, para.6–011.
[420] *Ellis Tylin Ltd v Co-operative Retail Services Ltd* [1999] B.L.R. 205 (validity of notice of termination); cf. *ED&F Man Commodity Advisers Ltd v Fluxo-Cane Overseas Ltd* [2010] EWHC 212 Comm) at [58]; *Sucden Financial Ltd v Fluxo-Cane Overseas Ltd* [2010] EWHC 2133 (Comm), [2010] 2 C.L.C. 216 at [45], in both of which notice of liquidation was stated to be based on an event of default which had not occurred, but there was "nothing to inhibit reliance on any other event of default" .
[421] *The Laconia* [1977] A.C. 850 at 872; *The Scaptrade* [1981] 2 Lloyd's Rep. 425 at 430, affirmed [1983] 2 A.C. 699, without reference to this point; cf. *The Great Marine* [1990] 2 Lloyd's Rep. 245 at 249. The rule is based either on waiver or on an implied term that the right to withdraw must be exercised within a reasonable time: see *The Antaios* [1985] A.C. 191. It seems to be restricted to cases of termination under an express term: see *Nichimen Corp v Gatoil Inc* [1987] 2 Lloyd's Rep. 46 at 54.
[422] Smith [2001] C.L.J. 178 (written before the decision of the House of Lords in the *On Demand Information* case, below, fn.436).
[423] See *The Scaptrade* [1983] Q.B. 529 at 539–540, approved [1983] 2 A.C. 699.
[424] See above, para.5–007.

such cases the provision for determination would deprive a party who committed some quite minor breach of the benefit of a contract which he has for a long period performed satisfactorily; and the court may allow him a period of grace within which to make good his default.[425] Normally such "relief against forfeiture" only gives the party in breach extra time to perform[426]; but sometimes such relief is allowed even though the breach cannot be remedied at all. Thus where a tenant had innocently broken a covenant against subletting it was held that the landlord could not enforce a forfeiture clause, as the breach had not prejudiced him in any way.[427] Further statutory restrictions apply to a landlord's right to forfeit certain long leases of dwelling-houses for non-payment by the tenant of rent or certain other charges.[428]

Relief confined to proprietary or possessory rights. In some of the time charterparty cases discussed above, it was suggested that relief against forfeiture should be granted to a charterer who failed to pay hire on time, and that the exercise by the shipowner of his right to withdraw the ship under a withdrawal clause should be restricted accordingly.[429] But the House of Lords rejected these suggestions[430] for two reasons. First, the courts should give effect to commercial agreements concluded (as time charters usually are) between parties who had bargained on equal terms. Secondly, the principle of relief against forfeiture was restricted to cases where the party in breach would, if the contract were literally enforced, be deprived of "proprietary or possessory rights",[431] while a time charter conferred only contractual rights, being merely a contract for services to be rendered by the shipowner.[432]

    18–064

The distinction between terms which deprive a party of "proprietary or possessory rights" and those which deprive him only of contractual rights can be a fine one. The point can be illustrated by contrasting two cases. In the *Sport International* case[433] it was held that relief against forfeiture was not available where A granted B a licence to use certain trade-marks and the contract provided that the licence was to determine on B's default. But in *BICC Plc v Burndy Corp*[434] such relief was held to be available where an agreement by which certain patents were vested in A and B provided that, on B's default, he should assign his rights in the patents to A. No doubt the cases are technically distinguishable on the ground that the actual *assignment* of a patent involves a transfer of "property", while the *termination of a contractual licence* to use a trade mark does not. But from a commercial point of view a licence to use such forms of "intellectual property"

---

[425] See Consumer Credit Act 1974, ss.88, 89; requiring formal notice of termination and giving the hirer at least 14 days to make good his default; and the rules relating to relief against forfeiture of leases: Law of Property Act 1925, s.146; cf. also the rules as to damages, discussed at paras 18–068—18–070, below.

[426] See *Nutting v Baldwin* [1995] 1 W.L.R. 201 at 208.

[427] *Scala House & District Property Co Ltd v Forbes* [1974] Q.B. 575; cf. *Akici v LR Butlin Ltd* [2005] EWCA Civ 1296; [2006] 1 W.L.R. 201.

[428] Commonhold and Leasehold Reform Act 2002, ss.167–170.

[429] *The Afovos* [1980] 2 Lloyd's Rep. 477 at 479, reversed on other grounds [1983] 1 W.L.R. 195; *The Tropwind* [1982] 1 Lloyd's Rep. 232 at 234.

[430] *The Scaptrade* [1983] 2 A.C. 694 and see the authorities cited above, fn.412.

[431] ibid. at 702; cf. *SCI (Sales Curve Interactive) v Titus SARL* [2001] EWCA Civ 591; [2001] 2 All E.R. (Comm) 416 at [47].

[432] ibid.; *Jones v Society of Lloyd's*, The Times, February 2, 2000.

[433] *Sport International Bussum BV v Inter-Footwear Ltd* [1984] 1 W.L.R. 776; Harpum 100 L.Q.R. 369.

[434] [1985] Ch. 232.

often serves the same purpose as an actual transfer; and the practical effect of the clause in each case was to deprive the party in default of the right to make use of the "property".

In the charterparty cases both lines of the reasoning employed supported the conclusion that there should be no relief against forfeiture. But a contract of a "commercial" nature may confer "proprietary or possessory rights" on the party in breach. That will be sufficient to determine the *existence* of the court's jurisdiction to grant relief,[435] but the policy of giving effect to commercial contracts militates against its *exercise*. It is, with respect, open to question whether some of the decisions in which the courts have exercised their jurisdiction in favour of the party in breach of a commercial contract[436] are consistent with the emphasis on the requirements of commercial certainty in a number of House of Lords and Privy Council decisions concerned with express provisions for determination.[437] A more consistent approach can be seen in *The Jotunheim*[438] in which the possessory right conferred by a demise charterparty was sufficient to confer jurisdiction to grant relief, but it was not granted principally because of the need for certainty in the commercial context.

18–065   **Sale of land.** By virtue of the conclusion of a contract for the sale of land, the purchaser acquires an equitable interest in the land which might be considered sufficient, in the light of the cases considered above, to allow for relief in the event of late payment by the purchaser. In *Union Eagle Ltd v Golden Achievement Ltd*,[439] however, Lord Hoffmann confirmed that the courts are "unwilling to grant relief by way of specific performance against breach of an essential condition as to time."[440] At most, the purchaser may be able to obtain "restitutionary . . . relief against forfeiture" by securing the return of a penal deposit.[441] It is not entirely clear whether, in such cases, the courts have no jurisdiction to grant relief, or that they will very rarely exercise it. There is rather more support for the former interpretation. Lord Hoffmann endorsed the principle that the courts *never* exercise the jurisdiction "where the parties have expressly intimated in their agreement that it is not to apply by providing that time is to be the essence of their bargain."[442] He also stressed that the mere *existence* of the power to grant relief is

---

[435] Provided also that the right of forfeiture is to secure the payment of money or is security for the attainment of a specific result which can be achieved through the courts: *Shiloh Spinners Ltd v Harding* [1973] A.C. 691; *On Demand Information Plc v Michael Gerson (Finance) Plc* [2001] 1 W.L.R. 155, CA (this aspect of the decision was not challenged in the appeal to the House of Lords, below, fn.436); *Celestial Aviation Trading 71 Ltd v Paramount Airways Private Ltd* [2010] EWHC 185 (Comm); [2011] 1 Lloyd's Rep. 9.

[436] In addition to the *Burndy* case, see: *Transag Haulage Ltd v Leyland DAF Finance Plc* [1994] 2 B.C.L.C. 88; *On Demand Information Plc v Michael Gerson (Finance) Plc* [2002] UKHL 13; [2003] 1 A.C. 368 (relief against termination of a finance lease for video and editing equipment; relief was granted notwithstanding that the equipment had been sold by the lessee's receiver, under court order, and the parties were really disputing their contractual entitlement to the proceeds of sale which had been paid into an escrow account. By obtaining relief, the receiver was entitled to 95 per cent of the proceeds in accordance with the provisions of the lease).

[437] See *The Laconia* [1977] A.C. 850; *The Chikuma* [1981] 1 W.L.R. 314; *The Scaptrade* [1983] 2 A.C. 694; *Union Eagle Ltd v Golden Achievement Ltd* [1997] A.C. 514.

[438] [2004] EWHC 671 (Comm); [2005] 1 Lloyd's Rep. 181; cf. *Celestial Aviation Trading 71 Ltd v Paramount Airways Private Ltd* [2010] EWHC 185 (Comm); [2011] 1 Lloyd's Rep. 9 at [122].

[439] [1997] A.C. 514.

[440] ibid. at 520.

[441] See below, para.20–149.

[442] *Steedman v Drinkle* [1916] 1 A.C. 275 at 279. Where time is "of the essence", the contract may be terminated for breach of condition (see below, para.18–089), for which there is no jurisdiction to grant relief.

sufficient to create the uncertainty to be avoided and held that the purpose of the express term is to "restore to the vendor his freedom to deal with the land as he pleases."[443] The mere *availability* of relief by way of specific performance would (while restitutionary relief would not) make it impossible for the vendor to know with certainty when that freedom had been restored. While he acknowledged the existence of cases where relief by way of specific performance had been granted,[444] they might be explained on the basis that in the state of English law at the time they were decided it would not have been easy to find a restitutionary remedy which provided adequate relief against forfeiture.[445]

Consumer protection. An express cancellation clause in a standard form contract between a commercial seller or supplier and a consumer may also be open to challenge under the Unfair Terms in Consumer Contracts Regulations 1999 on the ground that it is "unfair" to the consumer and hence not binding on him.[446] The list of prima facie invalid terms given in the Regulations indeed refers only to cancellation clauses in contracts "of indeterminate duration"[447]; but as the list is "non-exhaustive" this restriction would not preclude the court from holding that a cancellation clause in a fixed-term contract was also unfair.   18–066

Invalidity on other grounds. It is arguable that in exceptional circumstances an "oppressive" cancellation clause may be open to attack at common law in accordance with the principles discussed in Ch.7, or at least restricted in its operation so that the power to cancel can be exercised only on reasonable grounds.[448] Provisions entitling a party to refuse to make payments under a contract in default of exact performance by the other may also be invalid as penalties.[449]   18–067

Damages. We saw earlier that the effect of termination for a repudiatory breach is that both parties are released from their primary obligations to perform and the guilty party comes under a secondary obligation to pay damages.[450] So far as the guilty party's *primary* obligations to perform are concerned, the exercise of a right to terminate which has arisen under an express contractual provision has exactly the same effect: in general accrued obligations remain due, while future ones (other than "ancillary" ones[451]) are released.[452] But there is an important difference between the effects of termination under the general law, and termination under an express contractual provision, on the guilty party's *secondary* obligation to pay damages. Where the injured party terminates under the general   18–068

---

[443] *Union Eagle* case, above, at 520; cf. the conditions laid down by the *Shiloh Spinners* case, above, fn.435.

[444] e.g. *In Re Dagenham (Thames) Dock Co Ex p. Hulse* (1872–73) L.R. 8 Ch. App. 1022 (the purchaser had been in possession of the land pending completion for five years, during which time it had constructed a dock at its own expense).

[445] [1997] A.C. 514 at 521.

[446] SI 1999/2083, reg.8(1); above, para.7–095 et seq.

[447] reg.5(5) and Sch.2, para.1(g).

[448] *Timeload Ltd v British Telecommunications Plc* [1995] E.M.L.R. 459 at 467; cf. *Hadley Design Associates v Westminster CC* [2003] EWHC 1617; [2004] T.C.L.R. 1; *Looney v Trafigura Beheer NV* [2011] EWHC 125 (Ch).

[449] See *Gilbert-Ash (Northern) Ltd v Modern Engineeering (Bristol) Ltd* [1974] A.C. 689; below, para.20–146.

[450] See above, paras 18–010, 18–013, 18–015.

[451] See above, para.18–014.

[452] See above, at fnn.84–85; for exceptions, see above at fnn.86–93.

law, he can recover damages in respect of any loss suffered by reason of the premature determination of the contract[453] but he has (unless the contract otherwise provides[454]) no such right where he terminates for a non-repudiatory breach[455] under an express contractual provision entitling him to do so. Suppose, for example, that a hire-purchase agreement expressly provides that the owner can terminate for any failure by the hirer to pay an instalment. If the owner terminates for the hirer's failure to pay two out of 24 instalments, he can sue for the two unpaid instalments, but not for any further ones which would have accrued later if he had not terminated the agreement.[456] Moreover, it was held in *Financings Ltd v Baldock*[457] that he cannot recover damages in respect of loss suffered by reason of the premature termination of the agreement, i.e. the remaining sum due under the outstanding rentals, less any sums recovered in mitigation.[458] The reason for this is that, in the case put, the hirer's *only* breach is his failure to pay the two instalments. He is not, in addition, guilty of a repudiation of the whole contract. This restriction on the right to damages can, it is submitted, be supported on the policy ground that it alleviates the sometimes harsh operation of express provisions which allow a party to terminate even for a minor breach.[459]

18–069   **Distinguishing termination under the general law and under an express contractual provision.** The distinction between cases in which the right to terminate arises under the general law, and those in which it arises under an express contractual provision may, however, itself give rise to difficulty. The source of this difficulty is the willingness of the courts to regard any termination for a breach of condition as a "repudiatory breach" and, in that sense, the equivalent of a substantial failure to perform, even where the breach in question is a minor one.[460] Moreover, a term may be a condition on the sole ground that the parties have expressly classified it as such in their contract.[461] Where such a term is broken, it is just as plausible to say that the right to terminate has arisen under a general rule of law (i.e. the rule that breach of condition gives rise to a right to terminate) as to say that it has arisen under an express provision of the contract (i.e. the express classification by the parties of the term as a condition). A similar point can be made about stipulations as to the time of performance. Breach of such a stipulation justifies termination if time is "of the essence" of the contract and this will be the position if (a) delay causes, or is likely to cause, serious prejudice to the injured party,[462] or (b) the contract expressly provides that time is to be of

---

[453] See above, at fn.100.

[454] As in *The Solholt* [1981] 2 Lloyd's Rep. 574 at 579 (affirmed [1983] 1 Lloyd's Rep. 605, without reference to this point).

[455] Assuming there is a breach: see above, fn.408.

[456] *Financings Ltd v Baldock* [1963] 2 Q.B. 104 at 110; *Brady v St Margaret's Trust* [1963] 2 Q.B. 494; *Charterhouse Credit Corp v Tolly* [1963] Q.B. 683; *UCB Leasing Ltd v Holtom* [1987] R.T.R. 362.

[457] See above; *Amer-UDC Finance Ltd v Austin* (1986) 162 C.L.R. 170 (discussing earlier Australian cases); Goode 104 L.Q.R. 25; Beale 104 L.Q.R. 355; Opeskin 106 L.Q.R. 293.

[458] In the case of a hire-purchase agreement, this will usually consist of the sale proceeds of the repossessed item, or the proceeds of any re-hiring. A discount will normally also be applied to the outstanding rentals since they will have included an element of interest to cover credit.

[459] See above, para.18–062.

[460] See above, para.18–039 et seq.; *SCI (Sales Curve Interactive) v Titus SARL* [2001] EWCA Civ 591; [2001] 2 All E.R. (Comm) 416 at [19]; *Stocznia Gdanska SA v Latvian Shipping Co (No.3)* [2002] EWCA Civ 889; [2002] 2 Lloyd's Rep 436 at [76] (where there was, in fact, also an actual repudiation).

[461] See above, para.18–043.

[462] See below, at fnn.630–637.

the essence.[463] In the latter case it is, again, possible to say *either* that the right to terminate for breach at the agreed time has arisen under a general rule of law (i.e. the rule giving rise to a right to terminate where time is of the essence) *or* that the right has arisen under an express provision of the contract (i.e. the provision making time of the essence).

Financings Ltd v Baldock[464] may from this point of view be contrasted with *Lombard North Central Plc v Butterworth*,[465] where a contract of hire provided (1) that the owner could terminate for any failure to pay instalments when due; and (2) that the time of payment was of the essence of the contract. It was held that the second of these provisions made the stipulation as to the time of payment a condition of the contract so that its breach entitled the owners not only to terminate but also to damages for the premature termination of the agreement. But the decision was reached with evident reluctance[466] since there was no substantial distinction between the facts of this case and those of *Financings Ltd v Baldock*.[467] In the *Lombard* case the two provisions summarised above were simply two ways of saying the same thing and the policy consideration of alleviating the harsh operation of express provisions for determination is no weaker where the contract contains two such provisions than where it contains only one. For this reason it is submitted that the earlier decision in *Financings Ltd v Baldock* is to be preferred[468]: i.e. that damages for premature determination should not be available merely[469] because the injured party has terminated under express provisions giving him the right to do so. On that basis, damages for premature determination should only be available where there has been a substantial failure to perform, or the term broken amounted to a condition other than as a consequence of the parties' express classification. One might go further and confine such damages for premature determination to the former, but not the latter. The principal function of both conditions and express contractual provisions is to ensure certainty so far as the right to terminate is concerned. That can be retained without also conferring what may be an unmerited claim to damages.

Relationship between express provisions and the general law. The fact   18–070
that a contract contains an express contractual provision for termination upon breach does not necessarily exclude the right to terminate under the general law for a repudiatory breach. It is a question of construction[470] and the courts are unlikely to find that this was the intention of the parties in the absence of "clear

---

[463] See below, para.18–092.

[464] See above, fn.456.

[465] [1987] Q.B. 527; Treitel [1987] L.M.C.L.Q. 143; Bojczuk [1987] J.B.L. 353; Nicholson 1 J.C.L. 64; cf. also *The Afovos* [1983] 1 W.L.R. 195 at 203; *BNP Paribas v Wockhardt EU Operations (Swiss) AG* [2009] EWHC 3116 (Comm); 132 Con L.R. 177.

[466] ibid. at 546 ("with considerable dissatisfaction") and at 540 ("not a result which I view with much satisfaction").

[467] [1963] 2 Q.B. 683; above, para.18–068.

[468] For the same reason, *Financings Ltd v Baldock*, above, is (it is submitted) to be preferred to the reasoning of the Supreme Court of Canada in *Keneric Tractor Sales Ltd v Langille* [1987] 2 S.C.R. 440; Ziegel [1988] L.M.C.L.Q. 277 and 104 L.Q.R. 513.

[469] The injured party may be entitled to such damages by virtue of an express term giving him *this* right, even on termination for a minor breach; but such a term runs the risk of being void as a penalty (below, para.20–130), as would have been in the *Lombard* case, above, fn.466.

[470] *Leslie Shipping v Welstead* [1921] 3 K.B. 420; *The Mihalis Angelos* [1971] 1 Q.B. 164

words".[471] Nonetheless, the terms of an express provision may give guidance on whether a particular breach is to be treated as repudiatory.[472] Where an express provision only allows for termination if the breach reaches a certain level of seriousness, or makes it subject to a period of notice to remedy the breach, a breach falling below that level or without the opportunity to remedy is "unlikely" to amount to a repudiatory breach.[473]

18-071 **Whether contract terminated under the general law, or under an express contractual provision.**[474] As a consequence of decisions such as that in *Lombard*, damages for premature determination are available where the contract is terminated under the general law, including for breach of condition. Does it matter, however, whether that is the reason given for termination? For example, if the injured party purports to terminate under an express contractual provision, may he later rely on the fact that he also had the right to terminate under the general law and claim damages for premature determination? Some cases seem to proceed on the basis that the only question is whether the injured party has a right to terminate under the general law. If he has such a right, he can recover damages for premature determination even though, in terminating the contract, he relies on an expressly conferred contractual right.[475] In others, it is suggested that if the injured party terminates under an express contractual provision it may be too late to accept the repudiatory breach in support of the claim for damages.[476] The explanation for this latter approach is that by relying on the express provision, the injured party has affirmed the contract,[477] so far as any repudiatory breach is concerned, albeit in a way which, paradoxically, brings about its early termination.[478] Where the contractual right to terminate under an express provision is itself based on a repudiatory breach (i.e. the parties have agreed that the breach in question amounts to a breach of condition), no question of affirmation can arise from its exercise since the injured party is not required to "elect" between "alternative rights which have different consequences",[479] and he is not prevented from claiming damages for the premature determination of the contract. Where the contractual right to terminate under an express provision is not itself based on repudiatory breach (e.g. a "material breach"[480]), but the breach committed might

---

[471] *Dalkia Utilities Services Plc v Celtech International Ltd* [2006] EWHC 63; [2006] 1 Lloyd's Rep 599 at [21].

[472] *Lockland Builders v Rickwood* (1995) 46 Con L.R. 92.

[473] *BSkyB Ltd v HP Enterprise Services UK Ltd* [2010] EWHC 86 (TCC); [2010] B.L.R. 267 at [1366].

[474] Carter and Goh 26 J.C.L. 103.

[475] *Yeoman Credit Ltd v Waragowski* [1961] 1 W.L.R. 1124; *Hyundai Heavy Industries Ltd v Pournaras* [1980] 1 W.L.R. 1129; *The Almare Seconda* [1981] 2 Lloyd's Rep. 433

[476] *United Dominions Trust (Commercial) Ltd v Ennis* (1968) 1 Q.B. 54 at 65–66; *UCB Leasing Ltd v Holtom* [1987] R.T.R. 362 at 368. This may also be the best interpretation of the decision in *Laing Management Ltd v Aegon Ins Co (UK) Ltd* (1998) 86 Build. L.R. 70.

[477] See below, para.18–076 et seq.

[478] Peel 125 L.Q.R. 378.

[479] *Stocznia Gdynia SA v Gearbulk Holdings Ltd* [2009] EWCA Civ 75; [2010] Q.B. 27 at [44]. It is only in this particular context that the following dictum of Moore-Bick L.J. (at [20]) can be explained: "it is wrong to treat the right to terminate in accordance with the terms of the contract as different in substance from the right to treat the contract as discharged by reason of repudiation at common law." It is clear from the discussion in para.18–068 that they are different in substance, at least when it comes to any additional claim for damages.

[480] As in *Dalkia Utilities Services Plc v Celtech International Ltd* [2006] EWHC 63; [2006] 1 Lloyd's Rep 599.

also *in fact* have amounted to a repudiatory breach (i.e. a substantial failure to perform[481]), the termination of the contract by reference to the express provision will not, it seems, amount to affirmation,[482] but any claim to additional contractual rights which are "inconsistent" with termination for repudiatory breach may do so, e.g. a claim under a minimum payment clause,[483] or under a refund guarantee,[484] or for a "termination sum" set out in the contract.[485]

Even in cases where the injured party is put to his election because the two modes of termination invoke inconsistent rights, it may be possible for him to give notice that the contract is terminated for repudiatory breach, thereby ensuring that a claim for damages for premature determination may be brought if there was, in fact, a repudiatory breach, while taking the precaution of giving notice in the alternative that, if there was no repudiatory breach, the contract is terminated pursuant to the express contractual provision.[486] Whatever the validity or effectiveness of such a notice,[487] it seems that it could not be used if the contractual right to terminate under an express provision is not one which can be exercised immediately, e.g. because it requires the other party to be given a period of time in which to remedy the breach in question. He must be entitled to know whether there is any point in him embarking on such a process. Where the contractual right to terminate is an "immediate" one, it may in fact be necessary to do no more than ensure that the notice which is given is notice of termination for repudiatory breach. If that is challenged and it is later found that there was no repudiatory breach, it is the injured party who may have been guilty of a repudiatory breach for his wrongful termination, but he may at that point invoke the right to terminate under the express contractual provision (assuming it is available) by reference to the principle that a refusal to perform by a party who has an excuse for non-performance is not a breach, even though he did not state the excuse, or even know of it, at the time of the refusal.[488] There is no reason to confine that principle to cases where the excuse is a (or another) repudiatory breach, but where the excuse is in the form of the right to have terminated the contract under an express contractual provision, it may be said that the injured party has failed to

---

[481] Or perhaps the breach of another term of the contract which amounts to a condition.

[482] *Dalkia Utilities Services Plc v Celtech International Ltd* [2006] EWHC 63; [2006] 1 Lloyd's Rep 599 at [143]; *Force India Formula One v Etihad* [2010] EWCA Civ 1051 at [117]–[118]; *Gold Group Properties Ltd v BDW Trading Ltd* [2010] EWHC 1632 (TCC) at [110]; cf. *Bolton MBC v Municipal Mutual Ins Ltd* [2006] EWCA Civ 50; [2006] 1 W.L.R. 1493, below, fn.541; *Kris Motor Spares Ltd v Fox Williams LLP* [2009] EWHC 2813 (QB) at [99].

[483] *United Dominions Trust (Commercial) Ltd v Ennis* (1968) 1 Q.B. 54.

[484] This was the decision of Burton J. at first instance in the *Gearbulk* case, above ([2008] EWHC 944 (Comm); [2008] 2 Lloyd's Rep. 202) but an appeal was allowed for the different reasons explained in the text to fn.479; cf. *Shell Egypt West Manzala GmbH v Dana Gas Egypt Ltd* [2010] EWHC 465 (Comm).

[485] *Dalkia Utilities Services Plc v Celtech International Ltd*, above at [144] where the dictum of Christopher Clarke J. in this respect is obiter in that he found that there had been no repudiatory breach.

[486] *Shell Egypt West Manzala GmbH v Dana Gas Egypt Ltd* [2010] EWHC 465 (Comm) at [34]; Liu [2011] L.M.C.L.Q. 4.

[487] In the *Shell* case, above, Tomlinson J. could see "no reason" why such a notice may not be given, but it may run the risk that it is too equivocal to be effective as a notice of either mode of termination (cf. *Leofelis SA v Lonsdale Sports Ltd* [2008] EWCA Civ 680; *The Times*, July 23, 2008, above, para.18–009), or that it is invalid as an attempt to approbate and reprobate the contract at the same time (*Suisse Atlantique* case [1967] 1 A.C. 361, at 398).

[488] See above, para.17–027.

meet the requirement of strict compliance.[489] It is for this reason that a notice in the alternative may be the safer course of action.[490]

(iii) *Unilateral contracts and options*

18–072   **Contingent conditions: unilateral contracts.** A party may fail to perform some act which he has not promised to perform, but the performance of which is a contingent condition[491] of the other party's liability. Such a condition must be strictly complied with. The rule may be illustrated by the case of a unilateral contract.[492] If A promises B £100 if B walks from London to York, B must walk all the way to York before he is entitled to the £100.[493] The requirement of strict performance can be explained on the ground that A has no other remedy than to withhold performance. He cannot recover damages if B fails to complete the walk, since B has made no promise.

18–073   **Contingent conditions: bilateral contracts.** The distinction between promises and conditions can apply also in relation to particular terms in bilateral contracts and has, in relation to such terms, given rise to differences of judicial opinion.[494] The question in each case is whether the term, on its true construction, imposes an obligation on one of the parties to do an act (e.g. to give a specified notice to the other) or whether its effect is merely to make the performance of the act a prerequisite of the accrual of the other party's liability. The authorities give little guidance on this question of construction, but at least the effect of the resulting distinction is clear. If the term in question is construed as a condition, the party seeking to terminate need not show that the other's failure to comply with the term prejudiced him seriously or at all. Yet where a term is construed as a *promise* such prejudice must, as a general rule,[495] be shown by a party who seeks to terminate.

18–074   **Options.** The requirement that conditions which are not promises must be strictly complied with also applies to options to purchase. If the grantee fails to comply in any respect with a condition to which the exercise of the option is subject, he cannot enforce the option.[496] It makes no difference that the failure

---

[489] *Decro-Wall International SA v Practitioners in Marketing Ltd* [1971] 1 W.L.R. 361 at 371, 378, 382.

[490] Whether an acceptance of repudiatory breach is given first, in the alternative, or on its own, if it is effective (i.e. there was a repudiatory breach and it has been accepted), the innocent party may then, of course, be deprived of the additional benefits of the contractual termination, such as a refund guarantee, since the premise of the reasoning employed in some of the cases above is that it was necessary to affirm to obtain those contractual benefits.

[491] See above, para.2–104.

[492] See above, para.2–051.

[493] It is assumed that A has not attempted to withdraw before B reaches York: see above, para.2–054.

[494] e.g. *Shires v Brock* (1977) 247 E.G. 127 where the disputed term appears to have been treated by Goff and Buckley L.JJ. at 131 and 133 as a condition, but by Scarman L.J. at 133 as a promise; cf. *United Dominion Trust Ltd v Eagle Aircraft Ltd* [1968] 1 W.L.R. 74, criticised by Atiyah 31 M.L.R. 332 but approved in *United Scientific Holdings Ltd v Burnley BC* [1978] A.C. 904 at 928, 945, 951.

[495] i.e. in cases falling within the general rule discussed at paras 18–025—18–036, above, as opposed to the exceptions discussed at paras 18–037—18–070.

[496] *Hare v Nicholl* [1966] 2 Q.B. 160; *Allardyce v Roebuck* [2004] EWHC 1538 (Ch); (2005) 1 W.L.R. 815 at [25]. The rule may be excluded by the terms of the option: see *Millichamp v Jones* [1982] 1 W.L.R. 1422, where the term which the grantee failed to perform was not a condition of the exercise of the option, but a promissory condition of the contract resulting from that exercise: cf. above, para.17–016.

causes only insignificant prejudice, or none at all, to the grantor. Moreover, in the case of an option the rule applies even though the condition is the performance by the grantee of an obligation under another term of the agreement in which the option is contained. Thus in *West Country Cleaners (Falmouth) Ltd v Saly*[497] a lease gave a tenant an option to renew "providing all covenants herein contained have been duly observed and performed." The tenant had committed minor breaches of his covenant to paint the interior of his premises; and it was held that he was not entitled to exercise the option, even though it did not appear that the landlord was seriously prejudiced by the breaches. This application of the rule has been explained on the ground that

> "an option of this character is a privilege—a right which has always been treated by the law as requiring complete compliance with the terms and conditions upon which the option is to be exercised".[498]

The severity of the rule is, however, mitigated in a number of ways. Thus the rule does not apply where a tenant was at one time in breach but has cured that breach by the time of the exercise of the option: e.g. if by that time he has paid off rent which had at an earlier stage been overdue.[499] The rule may also be displaced by a strict construction of the term imposing the condition, leading to the conclusion that there has been no failure to comply with it.[500]

4. LIMITATIONS ON THE RIGHT TO TERMINATE

The right to terminate may be excluded by the terms of the contract, e.g. by a   **18–075** clause which, in accordance with the rules discussed in Ch.7, is valid and on its true construction covers the breach which has occurred.[501] Our present concern is with cases in which a right to terminate[502] has at one stage arisen but it is later lost or limited. Where there are several breaches, each giving rise to a right to terminate, the fact that one such right has been lost does not necessarily bar the other or others.[503]

(a) Affirmation, Waiver & Estoppel

Waiver in the sense of election: affirmation. Waiver is used in a number of   **18–076** senses, of which two (or possibly three[504]) are relevant to the present discussion. First, a party who is entitled to terminate may indicate that he will nevertheless perform his part of the contract. He is then said to have waived his right to terminate, or to have elected[505] to affirm the contract. For example, in *Bentsen v Taylor*[506] a charterparty falsely described the ship as "now sailed or about to sail"

---

[497] [1966] 1 W.L.R. 1485.

[498] ibid. at 1486.

[499] *Bass Holdings Ltd v Morton Music Ltd* [1988] Ch. 493.

[500] *Little v Courage Ltd* (1995) 70 P. & C.R. 469.

[501] See above, para.7–014 et seq.

[502] Whether under the general requirement of substantial failure, or under one of the exceptions thereto.

[503] See *Kwei Tek Chao v British Traders & Shippers Ltd* [1954] 2 Q.B. 459.

[504] What are referred to below as "total waiver" and "estoppel" are both just forms of equitable estoppel. For other senses of waiver, see above, para.3–066 et seq.

[505] *The Kanchenjunga* [1990] 1 Lloyd's Rep. 391 at 397–398.

[506] [1893] 2 Q.B. 274.

from a specified port. This was a breach of condition[507] on account of which the charterer could have refused to load; but he said that he would nevertheless load, and then refused to do so. It was held that he was liable for failure to load as he had waived his right to terminate.[508] Conversely, in *The Kanchenjunga*[509] a charterer in breach of contract nominated a port which was unsafe because of the Gulf war between Iran and Iraq, but the shipowner nevertheless pressed him to load there, and then sailed away. It was held that the shipowner had waived the charterer's breach and that he would have been liable in damages, if he had not been protected from such liability by a "war clause" in the charterparty. On the same principle, a shipowner loses his right to put an end to a charterparty under an express term entitling him to withdraw the ship for late payment of hire if he accepts such a payment knowing that the time for making it has passed[510]; a landlord loses the right to forfeit a lease for breach of covenant by the tenant if, knowing of the breach, he makes a demand for rent[511]; and a buyer of goods may lose the right to reject for breach of *one* implied condition if he has agreed with the seller that he will reject *only* for a breach of a *different* implied condition.[512] These examples all depend on the innocent party having been put to an "immediate election"; if, under the contract, he acquires the right to terminate "at any time" after a specified event has occurred, his continued performance will not amount to an election because it is not inconsistent with his right to terminate at a later date, unless his conduct also indicates an intention to abandon that right in clear and unequivocal terms.[513] An important characteristic of waiver in the sense of election is that it bars only the injured party's right to terminate: it does not deprive him of his right to damages for the breach. Thus the shipowner in *The Kanchenjunga* would have been entitled to damages if his ship had entered the port and suffered damage there as a result of the charterer's breach.[514]

18–077   **Distinguished from total waiver.** The expression "total waiver" refers to the situation in which a contracting party purports wholly to abandon rights under the contract.[515] It differs from waiver in the sense of election in that the injured party

---

[507] See above, para.18–041.

[508] [1893] 2 Q.B. 274 at 283, 285.

[509] [1990] 1 Lloyd's Rep. 391.

[510] *The Brimnes* [1975] Q.B. 929 at 954–956; *The Libyaville* [1975] 1 Lloyd's Rep. 537 at 554; cf. *Modern Transport Co Ltd v Duneric SS Co* [1917] 1 K.B. 370 (submission of question whether hire was due to arbitration held to be a waiver of the right to withdraw). But there is no waiver if the late payment is made into the owner's bank and rejected by him as soon as he learns of the payment: *The Laconia* [1977] A.C. 850; cf. *John Lewis Properties v Viscount Chelsea* [1993] 2 E.G.L.R. 77; and acceptance of an underpayment does not amount to waiver if there is still a reasonable possibility that the balance may be paid in time: *The Mihalios Xilas* [1979] 1 W.L.R. 1018.

[511] *David Blackstone Ltd v Burnetts* [1973] 1 W.L.R. 1487; *Expert Clothing Service & Sales Ltd v Hillgate House Ltd* [1986] Ch. 340 at 359; *Thomas v Ken Thomas Ltd* [2006] EWCA Civ 1504; [2007] 1 E.G. 94. For an illustration of waiver by a purchaser of leasehold land see *Aquis Estates Ltd v Minton* [1975] 1 W.L.R. 1452 at 1596. Contrast *Re a Debtor (No.13A–10–1995)* [1995] 1 W.L.R. 1127 (no waiver where rent is demanded before or on the breach in question).

[512] *S N Kurkjan (Commodity) Brokers Ltd v Marketing Exchange for Africa Ltd* [1986] 2 Lloyd's Rep. 614.

[513] *BDW Trading Ltd v JM Rowe Investments Ltd* [2011] EWCA Civ 548 where the right to terminate arose not on breach by the other party but upon the failure to fulfil a condition precedent. At first instance ([2010] EWHC 1987 (Ch) at [136]), Peter Smith J. doubted whether this was a case "involving election at all".

[514] [1990] 1 Lloyd's Rep. 391 at 393, 397, 401.

[515] cf. *Tufton Associates Ltd v Dilmun Shipping* [1992] 1 Lloyd's Rep. 71, where the requirement of full performance of an entire obligation (above, para.17–031) was displaced by waiver.

indicates that he is giving up, not merely his right to terminate, but also his right to damages[516] or to performance. Section 11(2) of the Sale of Goods Act 1979 recognises both types of waiver in providing that

> "where a contract of sale is subject to a condition to be fulfilled by the seller, the buyer may *waive* the condition, *or* may *elect* to treat the breach of condition as a breach of warranty and not as a ground for treating the contract as repudiated."[517]

Here "waive" is used to refer to total waiver (i.e. an abandonment by the buyer of his rights to terminate *and* to claim damages); while "elect" refers to waiver in the sense of election (i.e. to the buyer's abandonment of the right to terminate, while keeping alive his right to damages). It might be better if the courts were to use "waiver" only to refer to total waiver, and to use some other term, such as "election" or "affirmation" to refer to waiver in the sense of election.[518] They have in fact used "waiver" to refer to them both, perhaps because of an important similarity between the two processes[519]; but unfortunately this usage also obscures an equally important difference between them.[520] It will be convenient, to refer to the two processes respectively as "total waiver" and "affirmation" (meaning waiver in the sense of election).

Distinguished from estoppel. Affirmation, as a type of waiver, must also be   **18–078**
distinguished from estoppel, or "waiver by estoppel".[521] The latter may arise where the injured party has by his words or conduct led the party in breach to believe that the right to terminate will not be exercised and the party in breach has relied upon this representation. As will be seen,[522] total waiver is also a form of estoppel. In this context, "estoppel" refers to the effect of the injured party's representation only that he will not exercise the right to terminate; "total waiver" refers to the effect of a representation that he will forgo performance altogether, including the right to damages.[523] In principle, affirmation and estoppel have a different effect. Affirmation is irrevocable[524] and, in that sense, final; once the

---

[516] *Ets Soules & Cie v International Trade Development Co Ltd* [1980] 1 Lloyd's Rep. 129 at 137–138; cf. *Banning v Wright* [1972] 1 W.L.R. 972; *The Happy Day* [2002] EWCA Civ 1068; [2002] 2 Lloyd's Rep. 487 at [64]–[65], [67].

[517] Italics supplied.

[518] cf. *Kammins Ballroom Ltd v Zenith Investments (Torquay) Ltd* [1971] A.C. 850 at 882–883; *State Trading Corp of India v Cie Française d'Importation et de Distribution* [1983] 2 Lloyd's Rep. 679 at 681.

[519] See below, para.18–079.

[520] See below, paras 18–080, 18–081.

[521] *Kosmar Villa Holidays Plc v Trustees of Syndicate 1243* [2008] EWCA Civ 147; [2008] Bus L.R. 931 (only estoppel applicable in the context of breach of a procedural condition precedent in an insurance contract).

[522] See below, para.18–081.

[523] In the case of a representation by words it will be a matter of construction whether the innocent party represented that he would forego the right to terminate, or forego performance altogether; in the case of representation by conduct, it will be a matter of what can reasonably be inferred from such conduct and in this case it is likely that, if any clear and unequivocal representation can be inferred *at all*, it will be a representation to forego performance altogether. Since a representation by words is only likely to be made in circumstances where the injured party knows of the right to terminate and so will amount to an election, cases of estoppel will usually be based on conduct and will, for the reasons just stated, amount to a "total waiver", but a more limited estoppel in which the injured party is only estopped from exercising his right to terminate cannot be ruled out.

[524] *Hain SS Co Ltd v Tate & Lyle Ltd* (1936) 41 Com.Cas. 350 at 355; *Peyman v Lanjani* [1985] Ch. 457; *Yukong Line of Korea v Rendsburg Investments Co of Liberia* [1996] 2 Lloyd's Rep. 604 at 607.

injured party's decision to affirm the contract has been communicated to the party in breach, he cannot later change his mind and terminate the contract. By contrast, we have already seen that estoppel only has a suspensory effect[525] so that the injured party might, upon giving reasonable notice, retract his waiver and terminate the contract. In practice, the difference in effect is less marked. Affirmation is only irrevocable in relation to the particular breach which gave rise to the right to terminate. The injured party may later terminate either on the basis that a further separate breach has occurred,[526] or that the other party has continued to persist in the same breach.[527] Estoppel will have a permanent effect in cases where it would be inequitable to allow the injured party to retract his waiver.[528] This is perhaps most likely to occur in the context of waiver of breach because the injured party's failure to exercise the right to terminate may have deprived the other party of the opportunity to tender a substitute performance.[529] Since affirmation and estoppel will, therefore, often have the same effect in practice, the more important differences between them lie in the requirements to be met; in some cases both may be applicable, but in others it will only be possible to invoke one or the other.

18-079   **Requirement of representation.** The operation of affirmation, estoppel and total waiver each depend on a "clear and unequivocal representation".[530] In relation to estoppel and total waiver, this requirement is discussed in Ch.3.[531] Affirmation also requires "an unequivocal act or statement"[532] by which the injured party clearly indicates that he intends, not to terminate, but to affirm, the contract. The reference to an "unequivocal act" shows that the injured party need not make an express statement of his intention to affirm: it is enough if he does some positive act from which that intention can be inferred. If the intention does not clearly appear from his words or conduct, there is no affirmation. This may be the position where the injured party accepts defective performance subject to an express reservation of his rights,[533] or against the background of a "no waiver" clause,[534] but since the question of whether he has elected to affirm is ultimately

---

[525] See above, para.3–086.

[526] *Yukong Line of Korea v Rendsburg Investments Co of Liberia* [1996] 2 Lloyd's Rep. 604 at 607. In *Bell Electric Ltd v Aweco Appliance Systems Gmbh & Co KG* [2002] C.L.C. 1246 at [37] it is said that a further breach can be regarded as repudiatory "when seen against" earlier breaches, even though those earlier breaches can no longer be relied upon themselves because of the injured party's affirmation.

[527] *Johnson v Agnew* [1908] A.C. 367; *Stocznia Gdanska SA v Latvian Shipping Co* [2002] EWCA Civ 889; [2002] 2 Lloyd's Rep 436 at [94]–[100]. Whether a breach is a continuing one will depend on all the circumstances: *Automotive Latch Systems Ltd v Honeywell International Inc* [2008] EWHC 2171 (Comm) at [660] ("The correct analysis is that this is not a case of continuing breach which remained unremedied, but of past breaches which, in the light of the subsequent good progress with the project, were simply not continuing.")

[528] See above, para.3–087.

[529] e.g. *Toepfer v Warinco AG* [1978] 2 Lloyd's Rep 569 at 576.

[530] *Peyman v Lanjani* [1985] Ch. 457 at 501; *The Kanchenjunga* [1990] 1 Lloyd's Rep. 391 at 399; *The Great Marine (No.1)* [1990] 2 Lloyd's Rep. 245 at 249.

[531] See above, para.3–081.

[532] *The Mihalios Xilas* [1979] 1 W.L.R. 1018 at 1024; cf. *Bremer Handelsgesellschaft mbH v Finagrain (etc.) SA* [1981] 2 Lloyd's Rep. 259 at 266.

[533] *Bremer Handelsgesellschaft mbH v Deutsche Conti Handelsgesellschaft mbH* [1983] 2 Lloyd's Rep. 45; cf. *Nova Petroleum International Establishment v Trican Trading Ltd* [1989] 1 Lloyd's Rep. 312. Where several grounds of termination exist and the reservation refers to only some of these, it will not preclude affirmation in respect of the others: *The Wise* [1989] 2 Lloyd's Rep.

[534] *State Securities Plc v Initial Industry Ltd* [2004] All E.R. (D) 317 (Jan) at [57].

a question of fact, his conduct may imply the necessary intention notwithstanding such a reservation.[535] It has, similarly, been held that the right to terminate was not lost by affirmation where a vendor of land, after the purchaser should have performed, said that he would consider a request for an extension of time[536]; where a buyer to whom short delivery had been made called for a "full tender"[537]; where a landlord, after the tenant had committed a breach of covenant, sent him a "negotiating document" designed to resolve the dispute[538]; where an employee continued, after the employer's breach, to accept wages for such time as was reasonably necessary for him to consider his position[539]; and where the injured party merely called on the guilty party to reconsider his position and to withdraw his repudiation.[540] An intention to affirm the contract cannot be inferred because the injured party has taken one of several alternative courses of action; the action taken must have been *inconsistent* with termination of the contract.[541] The right to terminate is not lost by mere failure to exercise it: such failure is not normally a sufficiently clear indication that the right will not be exercised.[542] But where, as a matter of business, it is reasonable to expect the injured party to act promptly, unreasonable delay in exercising the right to terminate may give rise to the inference that the contract has been affirmed.[543] In the period when he "is making up his mind what to do" in the face of anticipatory repudiatory breach the injured party runs the risk that, while he may not have affirmed the contract, the guilty party may resume performance and thus end the right to terminate.[544] It seems that this does not extend to an actual repudiatory breach so that it cannot be "cured" and thereby take away the injured party's option of acceptance or affirmation.[545]

Whether knowledge[546] required. There is some conflict in the authorities on the question whether a party can be said to have affirmed the contract if he does   **18–080**

---

[535] *Tele 2 International Card Co SA v Post Office Ltd* [2009] EWCA Civ 9.

[536] *Prosper Homes v Hambros Bank Executor & Trustee Co* (1979) 39 P. & C.R. 395.

[537] *Cobec Brazilian Trading & Warehousing Corp v Alfred C Toepfer* [1983] 2 Lloyd's Rep. 386.

[538] *Expert Clothing Services & Sales Ltd v Hillgate House Ltd* [1986] Ch. 340.

[539] *Bliss v SE Thames Regional Health Authority* [1987] I.C.R. 700.

[540] *Yukong Line of Korea v Rendsburg Investments Co of Liberia* [1996] 2 Lloyd's Rep. 604; for further proceedings, see *The Times*, October 30, 1997.

[541] *Bolton MBC v Municipal Mutual Ins Ltd* [2006] EWCA Civ 50; [2006] 1 W.L.R. 149. In the employment context if the employer is complying with "disciplinary investigations and procedures leading to dismissal", it will "rarely be capable of being said that the employer has at the same time somehow affirmed the contract": *Cook v MSHK Ltd* [2009] EWCA Civ 624; [2009] I.R.L.R. 838 at [56]. For the circumstances in which the injured party may have elected to affirm, somewhat paradoxically, by exercising a contractual right to terminate, see above, para.18–071.

[542] See *Allen v Robles* [1969] 1 W.L.R. 1193; cf. *Bremer Handelsgesellschaft mbH v Deutsche Conti Handelsgesellschaft mbH*, above, fn.533; *The Scaptrade* [1981] 2 Lloyd's Rep. 425 at 430 (affirmed [1983] 2 A.C. 694, without reference to this point); *Cantor Fitzgerald International v Callaghan* [1999] 2 All E.R. 411 at 423.

[543] *The Scaptrade* (above, fn.542) [1981] 2 Lloyd's Rep. 425 at 430; *The Laconia* [1977] A.C. 850 at 872; *Stocznia Gdanska SA v Latvian Shipping Co* [2002] EWCA Civ 889; [2002] 2 Lloyd's Rep 436 at [87]; *Force India Formula One Team Ltd v Etihad Airways PJSC* [2010] EWCA Civ 1051 at [113], [122].

[544] *Stocznia Gdanska SA v Latvian Shipping Co* [2002] EWCA Civ 889; [2002] 2 Lloyd's Rep 436 at [87].

[545] *Buckland v Bournemouth University Higher Education Corporation* [2010] EWCA Civ 121; [2010] I.R.L.R. 445.

[546] i.e. "actual knowledge or knowledge which a person deliberately refrains from acquiring": *Transcatalana de Commercio SA v Incrobasa Industrial e Commercio Brazileira SA* [1995] 1 Lloyd's Rep. 215 at 219.

not actually know of the existence of the right to terminate. At the very least, the idea that the injured party must be "taken to have affirmed"[547] the contract requires an "informed choice, made with knowledge of the facts giving rise to the right" to terminate.[548] There is also some support for the view that the injured party must not only know the facts giving rise to the right to terminate, but must also know that he has the right.[549] In *Peyman v Lanjani*[550] the defendant had obtained a leasehold interest in a restaurant by means of a fraudulent impersonation, and later agreed to sell that interest. By reason of the fraud, the defendant's title was defective and the buyer, with knowledge of the fraud but not of the fact that it gave him the right to terminate, paid £10,000 and went into possession of the restaurant as the defendant's manager. It was held that the buyer had not lost the right to terminate; and one reason[551] for this conclusion was that he could not have elected to affirm the contract until he had become aware, not merely of the *facts* giving rise to the right to terminate, but of the *existence of the right* itself.[552] By contrast, in cases of estoppel, no knowledge of the existence of the right, nor of the facts giving rise to it, is necessary. Statements to the effect that a person can "waive" rights without being aware of their existence are best regarded as referring to one or other of these two forms of waiver,[553] which are based on action in reliance by the party *to* whom the representation is made rather than on the subjective intention of the (allegedly affirming) party *by* whom it is made.

18–081   **Reliance.** We saw in Chapter 3 that waiver by estoppel operated only where the party, to whom the representation giving rise to the waiver was made, had acted in reliance on that representation.[554] There is no such requirement for the operation of affirmation. The distinction is recognised in a number of cases,[555] though in some it is obscured by the use of "waiver" to describe the different processes involved in affirmation, estoppel and total waiver.[556] In the case of total

---

[547] *Kwei Tek Chao v British Traders & Shippers Ltd* [1954] 2 Q.B. 459 at 477.

[548] *The Kanchenjunga* [1990] 1 Lloyd's Rep. 391 at 399; *Cobec Brazilian Trading & Warehousing Corp v Alfred C Toepfer* [1983] 2 Lloyd's Rep. 386 at 392; *The Happy Day* [2002] EWCA Civ 1068; [2002] 2 Lloyd's Rep. 487 at [68].

[549] cf. Handley 122 L.Q.R. 82.

[550] [1985] Ch. 457; applied in *Transcatalana de Commercio SA v Incrobasa Industrial e Commercio Brazileira SA* [1995] 1 Lloyd's Rep. 215, discussing both "waiver in the sense of election" (219) and estoppel (220); cf. in another context, *Banner Industrial & Commercial Properties v Clark Paterson* [1990] 2 E.G.L.R. 139; and, in the context of misrepresentation, *Habib Bank Ltd v Tufail* [2006] EWCA Civ 374 at [20] ("it is undoubtedly the law that knowledge of the right to rescind is essential").

[551] A second was that there had been no unequivocal representation: [1985] Ch. 457 at 501–502.

[552] cf. *Yukong Line of Korea v Rendsburg Investments Corp* [1996] 2 Lloyd's Rep. 604 at 608, 609; *Donegal International Ltd v Zambia* [2007] EWHC 197; [2007] 1 Lloyd's Rep. 397 at [467]; *Hudson Bay Apparel Brands LLC v Umbro International Ltd* [2010] EWCA Civ 949 at [60]; *Argo Systems FZE v Liberty Insurance (PTE)* [2011] EWHC 301 (Comm) at [38]; *BDW Trading Ltd v JM Rowe Investments Ltd* [2011] EWCA Civ 548 at [75] ("Unequivocal conduct coupled with knowledge of the right to elect is enough"). In *The Kanchenjunga* [1990] 1 Lloyd's Rep. 391 at 398 it was not necessary to discuss the conflict on this point since the injured party knew of the facts giving rise to the right to rescind *and* of the existence of the right.

[553] See *Bremer Handelsgesellschaft mbH v C Mackprang Jr* [1979] 1 Lloyd's Rep. 221 at 230; contrast [1979] 1 Lloyd's Rep. 221 at 229.

[554] See above, para.3–083.

[555] *The Scaptrade* [1981] 2 Lloyd's Rep. 425 at 430, affirmed [1983] A.C. 694; *Peyman v Lanjani* [1985] Ch. 457 at 493, 500–501; *The Kanchenjunga* [1990] 1 Lloyd's Rep. 391 at 399; *The Happy Day* [2002] EWCA Civ 1068; [2002] 2 Lloyd's Rep. 487 at [67].

[556] e.g. *The Eurometal* [1981] 1 Lloyd's Rep. 337 at 341; cf. *Bremer Handelsgesellschaft mbH v Finagrain (etc.) SA* [1981] 2 Lloyd's Rep. 259 at 265.

waiver, one explanation for the requirement of reliance is that the injured party makes a promise wholly to give up his right to some or all of the performance due to him under the contract. Prima facie, this cannot be any benefit to him or any detriment to the party in breach, so that the promise is unsupported by consideration.[557] Action in reliance on the promise is necessary as a substitute for, or alternative to, consideration so as to give at least some legal effect to the promise.[558] In the case of affirmation, the injured party has indicated that he is giving up only one of his remedies (i.e. termination) but not any of his other remedies (by way of enforced performance or damages). Even if such an indication can be said to amount to a promise not to terminate, the process has never been considered to give rise to any problems of consideration.[559] The injured party is not *necessarily* in a worse position if he elects, instead of terminating, to keep the contract in being and to claim damages. This *may* be more beneficial to him than termination; and this possibility is sufficient to satisfy the requirement of consideration.[560]

On the basis of this explanation, however, it would not seem necessary to establish reliance for estoppel, i.e. where the injured party is taken to have represented only that he will not exercise his right to terminate. Since he retains the benefit of the contract and his right to damages he too *may* be better off than he would be if the contract was terminated. The requirement of reliance for estoppel in this context might be explained on the basis that the representation is "different in character in the two cases" of affirmation and estoppel.[561] In the case of affirmation, the injured party is communicating his choice whether or not to exercise the right to terminate. In the case of estoppel, he is representing that he will not *in future* enforce his legal rights; his representation is therefore in the nature of a promise which requires some element of reliance for any legal consequences because it is not supported by consideration.[562] But it has been noted in the previous paragraph that an election to affirm can be viewed as a promise not to terminate, so that this explanation may appear somewhat formalistic. It is submitted that the better explanation for the distinction between affirmation and estoppel, so far as reliance is concerned, lies in the role played in each of them by the knowledge of the representor; he may only unknowingly lose his right to terminate[563] if the other party has relied upon it to such an extent that it would be inequitable still to exercise it.[564]

(b) Acceptance

Part performance generally no bar. The fact that the party in breach has **18–082** partly performed the contract does not of itself bar the right to terminate. For example, express provisions for termination often operate after part performance of the contract.[565] That illustration concerns an *exception* to the requirement of serious failure in performance. In cases to which that requirement *applies*, the

---

[557] See above, paras 3–057—3–065.
[558] See above, paras 3–066—3–093.
[559] *The Kanchenjunga* [1990] 1 Lloyd's Rep. 391 at 398.
[560] cf. above, paras 3–063, 3–102—3–110.
[561] *The Kanchenjunga* [1990] 1 Lloyd's Rep. 391 at 399.
[562] ibid.
[563] And then perhaps only temporarily if the estoppel has only suspensory effect: para.3–086.
[564] In cases of total waiver this provides an additional explanation to that advanced in the previous paragraph.
[565] e.g. above, para.18–061.

courts do sometimes take the fact of part performance into account so as to conclude that the failure is not sufficiently serious to give rise to a right to terminate at all.[566] But once the failure is found to be of the required degree of seriousness, the injured party will not lose the right to refuse to perform or to accept further performance[567] merely because the other party has partly performed the contract: e.g. in *Aerial Advertising Co v Batchelor's Peas Ltd*[568] termination was allowed after such part performance.

18-083   **Effect of acceptance on breach of condition.** Although part performance does not usually bar the right to terminate, there is a rule that, where this right is based on a breach of condition, it may be lost by conduct of the injured party consequent on the other party's defective performance of the contract. This rule is most clearly illustrated by s.11(4) of the Sale of Goods Act 1979,[569] which provides that where a buyer has "accepted"[570] goods under a contract which is not severable[571] "the breach of a condition to be fulfilled by the seller can only be treated as a breach of warranty, and not as a ground for rejecting the goods and treating the contract as repudiated."[572] This rule differs from affirmation[573] in that it can apply even though the injured party has no knowledge of the breach.[574] A buyer of defective goods is, for example, deemed to have accepted them if he retains them after the lapse of a reasonable time without intimating to the seller that he has rejected them.[575] In determining what is, for this purpose, a reasonable time, the court will consider whether the buyer has had a reasonable *opportunity* of examining the goods[576]; but he may have accepted them, and so have lost the right to reject, even though he has not actually discovered the defect.[577] The general rule, then, is clear: "acceptance" bars the right to terminate a contract for breach of condition. But the rule is subject to three qualifications.

---

[566] e.g. in *Boone v Eyre* (1777) 1 Hy.Bl. 273n.

[567] For the effect of part performance on his right to recover back money paid, or to return payments received, see below, ch 22.

[568] [1938] 2 All E.R. 786; above, para.18–036. *Thorpe v Fasey* [1949] Ch. 649 may at first sight suggest that there cannot be termination after part performance; but the case is best explained on the ground that termination was not available as the breach was not a serious one and time was not of the essence of the contract: below, para.18–090.

[569] As amended by Sale and Supply of Goods Act 1994, s.3(2).

[570] See above, para.9–111.

[571] See above, para.17–035.

[572] Where the goods have nonetheless been returned the seller may have waived the right to argue that they had been accepted, and be confined to a claim in damages for non-acceptance: *Whitecap Leisure Ltd v John H Rundle Ltd* [2008] EWCA Civ 429; [2008] 2 Lloyd's Rep. 216 at [48].

[573] In this respect, it also differs from voluntary acceptance of a benefit: see above, para.17–041.

[574] *The Kanchenjunga* [1990] 1 Lloyd's Rep. 391 at 398; *Transcatalana de Commercio SA v Incrobasa Industrial e Commercio Brazileira SA* [1995] 1 Lloyd's Rep. 215 at 220.

[575] Sale of Goods Act 1979, s.35(4) (as substituted by Sale and Supply of Goods Act 1994, s.2(1)).

[576] ibid., s.35(5).

[577] e.g. *Bernstein v Pamson Motors (Golders Green) Ltd* [1987] 2 All E.R. 220; Reynolds 104 L.Q.R. 16. It has been said that, in the light of amendments to s.35, the decision in Bernstein "does not represent the law now": *Clegg v Olle Andersson (T/A Nordic Marine)* [2003] EWCA Civ 320; [2003] 2 Lloyd's Rep 32 at [63]; cf. *Jones v Gallagher* [2004] EWCA Civ 10; [2005] 1 Lloyd's Rep 377; Bradgate 120 L.Q.R. 558; *Mitchell v BJ Marine* [2005] N.I.Q.B. 72; *Kingsway Hall Hotel Ltd v Red Sky IT (Hounslow) Ltd* [2010] EWHC 965 (TCC). A more generous approach may now be taken, but what is a reasonable time remains a question of fact and a buyer may still lose the right to reject before he has discovered the defect.

Partial rejection. A buyer of goods may have the right to reject all the goods 18–084
even though only some of them are not in conformity with the contract. If he
accepts some of the goods, he does not thereby lose his right to reject the
rest.[578]

Incorporated misrepresentation. If a misrepresentation made before the 18–085
contract is incorporated in the contract as a condition, the right to rescind the
contract *for misrepresentation* survives and may be exercised in spite of the fact that
the contract has been performed.[579] A buyer of goods might be able to exercise this
right even though his right to terminate *for breach*[580] was barred by "acceptance".
But the right to rescind for misrepresentation is subject to the court's discretion[581]
to declare the contract subsisting and to award damages in lieu of rescission. It
seems probable that the court will generally follow this course where the right to
terminate for breach has been lost by "acceptance", though there may be cases of
hardship to a buyer in which the court would not wish to confine him to a remedy
in damages.

Consumer sales. A buyer who deals as a consumer may (subject to certain 18–086
restrictions) require the seller to repair or to replace goods which do not conform
to the contract by reason of the seller's breach of certain implied conditions or of
an express term.[582] The seller then has a reasonable time within which to comply
with the buyer's requirement.[583] During that time the buyer may not reject the
goods for breach of condition[584]; but if by the end of the reasonable time the seller
has failed so to comply, then the buyer may terminate the contract.[585] Nothing in
these provisions precludes the application of the rule that the right to terminate
for breach of condition is lost by acceptance; but their structure makes it clear that
a buyer does not accept goods merely by exercising his statutory right to require
the seller to repair or replace them.

(c) Both Parties in Breach

Non-simultaneous breaches. Where both parties are alleged to have com- 18–087
mitted breaches, each of which is claimed to be a ground for termination, the first
question to be considered is the order in which the alleged breaches have
occurred. If A's breach occurred before B's, the normal position is that A's breach
gives B a right to terminate, and, if B exercises that right, his subsequent failure
to perform does not amount to a breach at all (even though it would have done so,
if A had not committed the earlier breach[586]). If B has not exercised the right to
terminate, A remains free to terminate for B's breach, provided the performance
of the obligation which A has earlier breached was not a condition precedent to

---

[578] Sale of Goods Act 1979, s.35A.
[579] Misrepresentation Act 1967, s.1(a); above, para.9–121.
[580] For the distinction between this right and the right to rescind for misrepresentation, see above, paras 9–084, 9–092.
[581] Misrepresentation Act 1967, s.2(2); above, para.9–093.
[582] Sale of Goods Act 1979, s.48A, 48B and 48F; above, para.18–055.
[583] ibid., s.48B(2)(a).
[584] ibid., s.48D(1) and (2)(a).
[585] ibid., s.48C(1)(b) and (2)(b).
[586] See above, para.17–027.

performance of the obligation which B is alleged to have breached.[587] In *DRC Distribution Ltd v Ulva*[588] A served a 30 day notice of termination on the basis of B's later breach but during that 30 day period B exercised its right to terminate with immediate effect. B's termination was valid, but any damages payable by A were confined to the period when the contract would have terminated in accordance with A's notice.

18–088   **Simultaneous breaches.** The normal rule where both parties simultaneously commit breaches, each of which, standing alone, would justify termination is that each party is entitled to terminate on account of the other's breach.[589] There is, however, some support for a different conclusion where the two breaches are interrelated in the sense that the second consists of failure to perform a duty to avoid the consequences of the first. This was said to be the position in a line of cases concerning agreements to submit claims to arbitration. Where a claimant had committed a breach of such an agreement by undue delay in prosecuting his claim after it had been brought, it was held to be the duty of the respondent to apply to the arbitrator for directions to put an end to that delay. It was said to follow that

> "both claimant and respondent were in breach of their contractual obligations to each other[590]; and neither can rely on the other's breach as giving him a right to treat the primary obligations of each to proceed with the reference as at an end".[591]

This reasoning had the unfortunate practical consequence that an arbitration might be allowed to continue after so long a delay that a satisfactory hearing was no longer possible. This problem has been discussed in Ch.2, where a number of common law and statutory solutions to it were considered.[592] The present point is that the reasoning just quoted is, with respect, open to question; for if both parties are in breach it is by no means clear why it should follow that neither can terminate; it is equally possible to conclude that each party has the option to do so. Now that the reasoning of the arbitration cases has been made largely obsolete by statute,[593] it should no longer be regarded as justifying an exception to the general rule[594] that, where both parties are guilty of breaches justifying termination, each should be entitled to terminate the contract. The justification for that general rule is, it is submitted, that no good purpose is served by holding parties

---

[587] *State Trading Corp of India v M Golodetz Ltd* [1989] 2 Lloyd's Rep. 277 at 286. The position *may* be different in the context of employment contracts: see *Brandeaux Advisors UK Ltd v Chadwick* [2010] EWHC 2370 (QB) and the conflicting authorities referred to therein.

[588] [2007] EWHC 1716 (QB).

[589] *State Trading Corp of India v M Golodetz Ltd* [1989] 2 Lloyd's Rep. 277 at 286.

[590] cf. Arbitration Act 1996, s.40(2)(b), stating a more restricted duty.

[591] *Bremer Vulkan u Maschinenfabrik v South India Shipping Co* [1981] A.C. 909 at 987; this reasoning was affirmed, and the decision followed, in *The Hannah Blumenthal* [1983] 1 A.C. 854; cf. *The Matja Gubec* [1981] 1 Lloyd's Rep. 31; *The Boucraa* [1944] 1 A.C. 486 at 521–522; *The Frotanorte* [1996] 2 Lloyd's Rep. 461, referring to criticisms of the rule.

[592] See above, paras 2–005, 2–047.

[593] Arbitration Act 1996, s.41.

[594] Stated at fn.587, above.

to a contract after each of them has committed a breach justifying its termination.[595]

5. STIPULATIONS AS TO TIME[596]

Failure to perform a stipulation as to time does not differ intrinsically from any other failure to perform; indeed a number of cases already discussed in this chapter concern stipulations of this kind. But the subject has a history and terminology of its own; and for this, perhaps not very satisfactory, reason it is usually discussed separately. Certain stipulations as to time are said to be "of the essence" of a contract.[597] Any failure to perform such a stipulation justifies termination; it makes no difference that the failure is trivial and causes little or no prejudice to the injured party; in that sense, a time provision which is found to be "of the essence" amounts to a condition.[598] Where, on the other hand, a stipulation as to time is *not* of the essence, only a substantial or serious failure to comply with it will justify termination.[599]

18–089

Where no period of time is specified for performance which is to be rendered by one party,[600] a term is implied that it must take place within a reasonable time.[601] What is a reasonable time for this purpose is a "broad consideration" and is assessed by taking into account all of the circumstances, including the benefit of hindsight, i.e. it is not confined to what the parties contemplated at the time of the contract.[602]

Where a contract provides that money is to be paid on, or by, a specified day, the debtor has the whole of that day to make the payment. The creditor cannot treat him as in default before the end of that day (i.e. before midnight) merely because the bank at which payment was, under the contract, to be made had already closed.[603] As a practical matter, the debtor therefore cannot be treated as in default until the day following that specified in the contract.

Law of Property Act 1925, section 41. This section, re-enacting s.25(7) of the Judicature Act 1873, provides:

18–090

"Stipulations in a contract, as to time or otherwise, which according to rules of equity, are not deemed to be or to have become of the essence of the contract, are also construed and have effect at law in accordance with the same rules".

---

[595] Unless, of course, they both elect to affirm the contract: see above, para.18–076 et seq.

[596] Stannard, *Delay in the Performance of Contractual Obligations*. For the principles determining *when* performance is due, see above, para.17–014 et seq.

[597] See below, para.18–091.

[598] In the sense in which that term is used above: para.18–039 et seq.

[599] See below, para.18–090.

[600] Joint acts of the parties are subject to an implied term that each will use reasonable diligence in performing his part: *Ford v Cotesworth* (1868) L.R. 4 Q.B. 127; (1870) L.R. 5 Q.B. 544.

[601] *Postlethwaite v Freeland* (1880) 5 App. Cas 599; *Hick v Raymond & Reid* [1893] A.C. 22; *Hulthen v Stewart & Co* [1903] A.C. 389; cf. *Orchard Developments (Holdings) Ltd v Reuter Ltd* [2009] EWCA Civ 6; [2009] 16 E.G. 140 at [30] (no room for implication without underlying obligation to act (in that case to acknowledge informal break notice)).

[602] *Peregrine Systems Ltd v Steria Ltd* [2005] EWCA Civ 239 at [15]; *Astea (UK) Ltd v Time Group Ltd* [2003] EWHC 725 (TCC) at [144]; cf. *Hick v Raymond & Reid* [1893] A.C. 22.

[603] *The Lutetian* [1982] 2 Lloyd's Rep. 140; *The Afovos* [1983] 1 W.L.R. 195.

It follows from the section that the equitable rules now prevail.[604]

At common law, stipulations which specified[605] the time of performance were normally regarded as "of the essence".[606] Equity did not follow the common law rule but took the view that stipulations as to time were not generally "of the essence".[607] The equitable rule which now prevails is an application of the general requirement of substantial failure in performance. It is based on the view that delay does not normally deprive the injured party of the substance of his bargain, damages being an adequate remedy.[608] Hence the general rule is that delay will justify termination only where it does cause serious prejudice to the other party.[609]

18-091   **Whether time "of the essence".** The effect of s.41 is that a delay in performance will amount to a breach[610] giving rise to liability in damages,[611] but it will only entitle the injured party to terminate the contract if the delay amounts to a substantial failure to perform, or time is regarded as "of the essence" under one of the exceptions to the general rule in equity. A time stipulation will be regarded as "of the essence" if it is made so expressly by the parties, or by implication from the circumstances of the contract, or the nature of the subject-matter. For these exceptions to apply, the stipulation must specify a date or time for performance: they cannot apply where a contract merely provides for performance "as soon as practicable."[612] Where a time stipulation is not initially regarded as "of the essence", it may be made so by notice of one of the parties.[613]

18-092   **Time "of the essence" by express agreement.** Time will obviously be of the essence if the contract expressly so provides.[614] The contract may provide that, in the event of one party's failure to perform within the stipulated time, the other is to be entitled to terminate[615]; or that the stipulation as to time is to be a

---

[604] The section is not restricted to cases in which equity would have intervened before the Judicature Acts; it enables the courts also to take into account the subsequent development of equitable principles: *United Scientific Holdings Ltd v Burnley BC* [1978] A.C. 904 at 925, 957; Baker 93 L.Q.R. 529. The equitable rule was developed in cases for the sale of land, but is not so confined.

[605] cf. below, para.18–091.

[606] *Parkin v Thorold* (1852) 16 Beav. 59 at 65; unless the contract, on its true construction, provided otherwise: *Rightside Properties Ltd v Gray* [1975] Ch. 72 at 89.

[607] *Parkin v Thorold* (1852) 16 Beav. 59; cf. *Cole v Rose* [1978] 3 All E.R. 1121; *Graham v Pitkin* [1992] 1 W.L.R. 403.

[608] See above, para.18–028; *Chancery Land Development v Wade's Development Stores* (1987) 53 P. & C.R. 306.

[609] *United Scientific Holdings Ltd v Burnley BC* [1978] A.C. 904 at 942; *Peregrine Systems Ltd v Steria Ltd* [2005] EWCA Civ 239 at [15]; *Shawton Engineering v DGP International Ltd* [2005] EWCA Civ 1359; [2006] B.L.R. 1 at [33] ("where time is not of the essence and where the party said to be in breach by delay is nevertheless making an effort to perform the contract, it is intrinsically difficult for the other party to establish a fundamental breach"); cf. *Amherst v James Walker Goldsmith & Silversmith Ltd* [1983] Ch. 305; *Metrolands Investments Ltd v J H Dewhurst Ltd* [1986] 3 All E.R. 659.

[610] Unless there is some lawful excuse for non-performance: above, para.17–059.

[611] *Raineri v Miles* [1981] A.C. 1050 (rejecting the view that the right to damages was restricted to cases of negligent or wilful default); Samuels 44 M.L.R. 100.

[612] *British & Commonwealth Holdings Plc v Quadrex Holdings Inc* [1989] Q.B. 842 (not followed, on another point, in *Behzadi v Shaftsbury Hotels Ltd* [1992] Ch. 1).

[613] See below, para.18–097.

[614] e.g. *Steedman v Drinkle* [1916] 1 A.C. 275; cf. *Country & Metropolitan Homes Surrey Ltd v Topclaim Ltd* [1996] Ch. 307 at 313; *Union Eagle Ltd v Golden Achievement Ltd* [1997] A.C. 514; above, para.18–064.

[615] e.g. above, para.18–061.

condition.[616] That time is expressed to be "of the essence" is itself a form of words which the courts have accepted as sufficient to create a condition.[617]

Time "of the essence" by implication. In the absence of any contractual   18–093
provisions on the point, the question of whether time is of the essence is often determined by rules of law which have classified certain commonly found stipulations as to time in certain types of contracts as either being, or not being, of the essence. We have, for example, seen that in a charterparty failure by the shipowner to comply with a stipulation as to the time of sailing[618] or as to the ship's expected readiness to load[619] of itself justifies termination; while the charterer's failure to load within the agreed time only has this effect if the delay is so serious as to frustrate the purpose of the contract.[620] Similarly, in a contract for the sale of goods a stipulation as to the time at which the seller is to deliver the goods is treated as of the essence of the contract[621]; while a stipulation as to the time at which the buyer is to pay for them is not normally so regarded (presumably because it is thought, rightly or wrongly, that late payment is unlikely to cause serious prejudice to the seller[622]). To the latter rule there are, however, many exceptions: it will, for example, be displaced if the goods are perishable[623]; if the buyer fails to comply with a stipulation as to the time of paying a deposit under a contract with "a very tight time scale"[624]; or if there are other indications of the intention of the parties to treat the stipulation as of the essence.[625] The position is similar with regard to stipulations as to the time of taking delivery: failure by the buyer to comply with such a stipulation will not normally entitle the seller to terminate[626]; but it will have this effect if the goods are perishable,[627] or if the buyer undertakes to provide the ship on which the goods are to be loaded but fails to do so within the agreed time,[628] or if he fails within the time specified by the contract to notify the seller of the ship's readiness to load.[629]

---

[616] i.e. in the sense discussed at para.18–039 et seq., above; *The Scaptrade* [1983] 2 A.C. 694 at 703.

[617] The element of surprise which this creates for those not aware of their special meaning is, perhaps, what adds to the unease felt at decisions such as that in *Lombard North Central Plc v Butterworth* [1987] Q.B. 527; discussed above: para.18–069. It may also provide the basis for a challenge under Unfair Terms in Consumer Contracts Regulations 1999, where applicable: para.7–095 et seq.

[618] *Glaholm v Hays* (1841) 2 Man. & G. 751; above, para.18–041.

[619] *The Mihalis Angelos* [1971] 1 Q.B. 164; above, para.18–041.

[620] *Universal Cargo Carriers Corp v Citati* [1957] 2 Q.B. 401; above, paras 17–086, 18–047.

[621] *Hartley v Hymans* [1920] 3 K.B. 475 at 484; cf. *Aruna Mills Ltd v Dhanrajmal Gobindram* [1968] 1 Q.B. 655; *Toepfer v Lenersan Poortman NV* [1980] 1 Lloyd's Rep. 143 (time of tender of shipping documents). See also *Bowes v Shand* (1877) 2 App.Cas. 455 (where *early* shipment by the seller justified rejection; above, para.18–045).

[622] *Martindale v Smith* (1841) 1 Q.B. 389; Sale of Goods Act 1979, s.10(1). For a similar rule as to the effect of delay in payment in a distributorship agreement, see *Decro-Wall International SA v Practitioners in Marketing Ltd* [1971] 1 W.L.R. 361; cf. *Figre Ltd v Mander* [1999] Lloyd's Rep. I.R. 193 (time of payment of reinsurance premium not of the essence).

[623] See *Maclean v Dunn* (1828) 4 Bing. 722 at 728; *Ryan v Ridley & Co* (1902) 8 Com.Cas. 105; *R V Ward Ltd v Bignall* [1967] 1 Q.B. 534 at 550; Sale of Goods Act 1979, s.48(3).

[624] *The Selene G* [1981] 2 Lloyd's Rep. 180 at 185. Contrast *Millichamp v Jones* [1982] 1 W.L.R. 1422 at 1431 (deposit paid late by "mere oversight").

[625] e.g. where payment was to be by irrevocable letter of credit to be opened within a stipulated time: see *Bunge Corp v Tradax Export SA* [1981] 1 W.L.R. 711 at 725.

[626] *Woolfe v Horne* (1877) 2 Q.B.D. 355 (rags).

[627] *Sharp v Christmas* (1892) 8 T.L.R. 687 (potatoes).

[628] *The Osterbek* [1973] 2 Lloyd's Rep. 86.

[629] *Bunge Corp v Tradax Export SA* [1981] 1 W.L.R. 711; above, para.18–050.

In contracts for the sale of land, it has been held that time is of the essence in sales of short leaseholds[630] or reversionary interests[631]; since the former will depreciate and the latter appreciate rapidly with the passing of time. Time has also been held to be of the essence of a contract for the sale of a public house as a going concern[632]; of a contract for the sale of land which the buyer wanted to develop quickly for business purposes[633]; and, it seems, of a contract for the sale of a brickfield.[634] On the other hand, it has been held that time was not of the essence of a contract to sell 34 plots of land as and when each was built on.[635] This result may be justified on the ground that the completion date was "only a target."[636] Generally, time will also be regarded as of the essence where the subject-matter of the contract is of a highly speculative nature.[637]

In an insurance contract, it has been doubted whether the time within which the insured must notify the insurer of a claim and provide reasonable particulars should be regarded as of the essence, so as to relieve the insurer of liability.[638]

18–094　　**A general principle of classification.** Attempts have been made to formulate some general principle governing the legal classification of stipulations as to time. Thus it has been said, on the one hand, that "In modern English law time is *prima facie* not of the essence of the contract"[639]; and, on the other hand, that "*Broadly speaking* time will be considered of the essence in mercantile contracts."[640] But the italicised words indicate the tentative nature of these generalisations; and (as a glance at the rules stated in the preceding paragraph shows) they are, with respect, of limited value.[641] The classification of stipulations as to time seems to be based on considerations of commercial convenience applicable in particular contexts, rather than on any general principle or presumption as to time being, or not being, of the essence.

18–095　　**Conditional contracts.** The performance by one party of some stipulated act may be a condition precedent either to the existence of the contract or to the obligation of the other party.[642] Where the very existence of the contract depends on a condition to be performed by one of the parties, that condition must be performed within the time expressly or impliedly fixed by the contract.[643] If no time is expressly fixed, the condition must be performed by the date fixed for

[630] *Hudson v Temple* (1860) 29 Beav. 536.
[631] *Newman v Rogers* (1793) 4 Bro.C.C. 391; unless there is evidence of contrary intention: *Patrick v Milner* (1877) 2 C.P.D. 342.
[632] *Coslake v Till* (1826) 1 Russ. 376; *Lock v Bell* [1931] 1 Ch. 35.
[633] *Bernard v Williams* (1928) 44 T.L.R. 436; cf. *Hargreaves Transport Ltd v Lynch* [1969] 1 W.L.R. 215.
[634] See *Harold Wood Brick Co Ltd v Ferris* [1935] 2 K.B. 198.
[635] *Williams v Greatrex* [1957] 1 W.L.R. 31.
[636] ibid. at 35.
[637] See *Hare v Nicholl* [1966] 2 Q.B. 130.
[638] *Diab v Regent Ins Co Ltd* [2006] UKPC 29; [2007] 1 W.L.R. 797 at [16] (no argument on the point).
[639] *United Scientific Holdings Ltd v Burnley BC* [1978] A.C. 904 at 940; *British and Commonwealth Holdings Plc v Quadrex Holdings Inc* [1989] Q.B. 842 at 857.
[640] *Bunge Corp v Tradax Export SA* [1981] 1 W.L.R. 711 at 716.
[641] cf. ibid. at 729; *The Peter Schmidt* [1998] 2 Lloyd's Rep. 1 at 7; *Peregrine Systems Ltd v Steria Ltd* [2005] EWCA Civ 239 at [15].
[642] See above, para.17–015.
[643] cf. *Hare v Nicholl* [1966] 2 Q.B. 130.

completion[644]; if no date is fixed for completion, it must be performed within a reasonable time.[645] The equitable principle that time is not of the essence of a contract does not apply in these cases, for until the condition is performed the whole existence of the contract remains in doubt. For the same reason, an option can be exercised only within the time laid down in the agreement by which it was granted.[646]

Waiver. The general principle that the right to terminate may be lost by   18–096
affirmation[647] (or estoppel[648]) applies where time is of the essence of a contract.[649]
Accordingly the requirement of punctual performance may be waived by giving the party in breach a further period for performance after the expiry of the period specified in the contract. Such waiver only has the effect of substituting the extended time for the original time; it is "not an utter destruction of the essential character of time."[650] Moreover, the mere fact that the injured party has not accepted the guilty party's failure to perform as a repudiation does not amount to affirmation. The fact that the contract has not been terminated merely entitles the guilty party to "perform the contract according to its terms"[651]; and this is no longer possible after the expiry of the stipulated time.

Notice making time "of the essence".[652] Where time is not of the essence   18–097
under the contract, but there has been a delay and, therefore, a breach, the injured party may serve a notice on the guilty party requiring him to comply. The notice may be served as soon as the other party is in default.[653] It has been noted that such a notice is invariably described as one making time of the essence,[654] but this description is "not quite accurate".[655] Time is not made "of the essence" in the sense that the relevant stipulation is converted into a condition: "one party cannot vary the terms of the contract on his own".[656] What the injured party is entitled

---

[644] *Re Sandwell Park Colliery Co* [1929] 1 Ch. 277; *Aberfoyle Plantations v Cheng* [1960] A.C. 115; *aliter* where the completion date is only a target date subject to the occurrence of the condition; *Hargreaves Transport Ltd v Lynch* [1969] 1 W.L.R. 215 at 220; and where the condition is subsequent (above, para.2–104) and time is expressly stated *not* to be of the essence, as in *29 Equities Ltd v Bank Leumi (UK) Ltd* [1986] 1 W.L.R. 1490.

[645] *Re Longlands Farm* [1968] 3 All E.R. 522.

[646] *Hare v Nicholl* [1966] 2 Q.B. 130; *United Dominions Trust (Commercial) Ltd v Eagle Aircraft Ltd* [1968] 1 W.L.R. 74; *United Scientific Holdings Ltd v Burnley BC* [1978] A.C. 904 at 936.

[647] See above, para.18–076.

[648] See above, paras 18–077—18–078.

[649] In addition to waiver by the injured party, the court may grant equitable relief in cases of late payment: e.g. *Shiloh Spinners Ltd v Harding* [1973] A.C. 691 at 722. See, generally, para.18–063 et seq.

[650] *Barclay v Messenger* (1874) 43 L.J. Ch. 449; *Nichimen Corp v Gatoil Overseas Inc* [1987] 2 Lloyd's Rep. 46.

[651] *Union Eagle Ltd v Golden Achievement Ltd* [1997] A.C. 514 at 518.

[652] Stannard 120 L.Q.R. 137.

[653] *Behzadi v Shaftsbury Hotels Ltd* [1992] Ch. 1, overruling *Smith v Hamilton* [1951] Ch. 174 and the requirement that there must have been an unreasonable delay before the notice can be served. Of course, where the contract is an "open" one, i.e. where no date for performance of the obligation is stipulated, it is only when there has been an unreasonable delay that there will have been a breach in the first place: *Shawton Engineering v DGP International Ltd* [2005] EWCA Civ 1359; [2006] B.L.R. 1 at [72].

[654] That is certainly how it is often worded by the injured party.

[655] *Behzadi v Shaftsbury Hotels Ltd* [1992] Ch. 1 at 12, 24; *Sentinel International Ltd v Cordes* [2008] UKPC 60 at [41].

[656] ibid. See, to similar effect: *Eshun v Moorgate Mercantile Credit Co Ltd* [1971] 1 W.L.R. 722 at 726.

to do is stipulate a reasonable time within which the guilty party must comply. If the time stipulated is reasonable and the guilty party has failed to comply when it expires, the injured party is entitled to terminate.[657] In this sense, it resembles a condition of the contract in that, as soon as the guilty party is in default of the notice, the contract may be terminated. It is for this reason that it is, perhaps, permissible to refer to the notice as having made time of the essence. The reality is that the injured party has a right to terminate because the unreasonable delay of the guilty party amounts to a repudiation of the contract. The questions of whether the notice has stipulated a *reasonable* time, or the guilty party has been guilty of an *unreasonable* delay amounting to a repudiation of the contract amount to the same thing:

> "The result of non-compliance with the notice is that the party in default is guilty of unreasonable delay in complying with a non–essential time stipulation. The unreasonable delay amounts to a repudiation and this justifies rescission."[658]

On this basis, it may be questioned whether anything is to be gained by the injured party by serving a notice, since he may simply wait until an unreasonable delay has occurred.[659] There are, at least, two possible gains. First, the notice is intended, in the first instance, to encourage the party in default to perform and it may have this effect whether the time stipulated is reasonable or not. Secondly, while the court will have to be persuaded that the time allowed was reasonable, the injured party is given the opportunity to convert that into something a little more precise.[660]

What is a reasonable time is a question of fact.[661] If one party has constantly pressed the other to complete, he can rely on this fact to shorten the amount of time which must be allowed by the notice.[662] Where the injured party elects to serve a notice immediately upon breach he must be "cautious" about the time allowed before he reserves the right to terminate. A notice, once given, binds *both* parties. Thus if one of them gives notice to complete within a reasonable time, but is not ready to do so when the notice expires, the other can terminate.[663]

6. CRITICISM[664]

18–098   The law relating to termination for breach is hard to state; and parts of it are still harder to justify. Criticism can, in particular, be directed at some of the

---

[657] Under Sale of Goods Act 1979, s.48(3) an unpaid seller of goods can give the buyer notice of his intention to resell the goods and may resell them if the buyer does not "within a reasonable time" pay or tender the price.

[658] *Louinder v Leis* 149 C.L.R. 509 at 526, per Mason J.

[659] If the notice contains an unreasonable timetable, but the injured party does not elect to terminate when it expires, he may later be entitled to terminate on the basis of further delay.

[660] *Dalkia Utilities Services Plc v Celtech International Ltd* [2006] EWHC 63; [2006] 1 Lloyd's Rep 599 at [131]. In this regard there may also be the benefit of a "margin of appreciation" in that the court may be persuaded to accept as "reasonable" a time-table which is not precisely the one which would they would have applied in assessing whether there had been a repudiatory breach.

[661] *North Eastern Properties Ltd v Coleman* [2010] EWCA Civ 277; [2010] 1 W.L.R. 2715. A notice giving only seven days to deduce title was held in *Behzadi*'s case, above, to be too short so that the purchaser was guilty of a wrongful repudiation by terminating the contract on the strength of the notice.

[662] *Stickney v Keeble* [1915] A.C. 386.

[663] *Quadrangle Development and Construction Co Ltd v Jenner* [1974] 1 W.L.R. 68; *Oakdown Ltd v Bernstein & Co* (1985) 49 P. & C.R. 282.

[664] Treitel 30 M.L.R. 139.

exceptions to the requirement that a failure in performance must be substantial if it is to justify termination. A number of judicial restrictions[665] on the scope of these exceptions may have improved the law; but it is arguable that two major defects remain.

Termination where no prejudice occurs. The first is that a party may still **18–099** be entitled to terminate though the breach does not prejudice him seriously or at all, e.g. where the breach is of a term previously classified as a "condition", or where a seller fails to deliver the correct quantity.[666] In such cases, the right to terminate can simply provide a party with an excuse for escaping from a bad bargain.[667] It would, it is submitted, be more satisfactory as a general principle to focus attention on the question whether damages were an adequate remedy for the breach; and to restrict exceptions to this general principle to cases in which the interests of commercial certainty require a clear recognition of the right to terminate for certain breaches, irrespective of their effects.[668] Some of the legislative limitations on the right to terminate[669] may have mitigated the defect in the law under which that right can be exercised on unmeritorious or technical grounds. But they have failed wholly to remove that defect while they have, on the other hand, undermined the virtue of certainty precisely in those commercial cases in which exceptions to the requirement of substantial failure in performance are intended to promote that virtue.[670]

The rule in *Sumpter v Hedges*. The second main defect in the law is the rule **18–100** in *Sumpter v Hedges*,[671] under which a party who has failed to complete performance may have no rights at all against the other party to the contract, following termination.[672]

---

[665] Especially *Wickman Ltd v Schuler AG* [1974] A.C. 235; *The Hansa Nord* [1976] Q.B. 44 and *Reardon-Smith Line Ltd v Hansen-Tangen* [1976] 1 W.L.R. 989.

[666] See above, paras 18–039, 17–033.

[667] e.g. in *Cunliffe v Harrison* (1851) 6 Ex. 901; *Arcos Ltd v Ronaasen* [1933] A.C. 47; above, paras 17–039, 18–045.

[668] e.g. *Bunge Corp v Tradax Export SA* [1981] 1 W.L.R. 711 (above, para.18–050); cf. also *The Laconia* [1977] A.C. 850; *The Chikuma* [1981] 1 W.L.R. 314 (above, para.18–061).

[669] Sale of Goods Act 1979, ss.15A and 30(2A); and other legislation referred to above, fn.350.

[670] See above, para.18–054.

[671] [1898] 1 Q.B. 673; above, para.17–032.

[672] See above, paras 17–032, 17–048.

19–001   Under the doctrine of frustration a contract may be discharged if after its formation events occur making its performance impossible or illegal, and in certain analogous situations. This chapter will consider first the development of the doctrine and then its applications and effects. In the light of the decided cases, it concludes with an assessment of the theoretical basis of frustration.

1. DEVELOPMENT

19–002   **The doctrine of absolute contracts.** At one time most contractual duties were regarded as absolute, in the sense that supervening events provided no excuse

---

[1] McElroy and Williams, *Impossibility of Performance*; Treitel, *Frustration and Force Majeure* (2nd edn); McKendrick, (ed.), *Force Majeure and Frustration* (2nd edn).

for non-performance. In *Paradine v Jane*[2] a tenant was sued for rent and pleaded that he had for about two years of his tenancy been dispossessed by act of the King's enemies. This plea was held bad.

"When the party by his own contract creates a duty or charge upon himself, he is bound to make it good, if he may,[3] notwithstanding any accident by inevitable necessity, because he might have provided against it by his contract".[4]

This doctrine of absolute contracts works well enough (and continues to apply) where it would be reasonable, having regard to the nature of the contract or the circumstances in which it was made, to expect it to provide for the event.[5] But where this is not the case, the doctrine is no longer regarded as a satisfactory way of allocating the loss that is occasioned by supervening events.

Origins of the doctrine of frustration. The doctrine of absolute contracts probably never applied where a contract called for personal performance by a party who died or was permanently incapacitated[6]; and another early exception to it was recognised in cases of supervening illegality.[7] In *Taylor v Caldwell*[8] Blackburn J. relied on the first of these exceptions, and on a number of others, as bases for formulating the general rule of discharge which has become known as the doctrine of frustration. The defendants in that case had contracted to hire out the Surrey Gardens and Music Hall "for the purpose of giving four grand concerts" on four designated days in the summer of 1861; the defendants were also to provide various side-shows and other entertainments in the gardens. The hirers agreed to pay £100 on the evening of each of the designated days and to provide "all the necessary artistes". Six days before the first concert was to have been given, the hall was destroyed by an accidental fire, so that "it became impossible to give the concerts".[9] It was held that the defendants were not liable in damages for the hirers' wasted advertising and other expenses. The contract had been discharged because, "the parties must from the beginning have known that it could not be fulfilled unless . . . some particular specified thing continued to exist", and in these circumstances it was

19–003

"not to be construed as a positive contract, but as subject to an implied condition that the parties shall be excused in case, before breach, performance becomes impossible from the perishing of the thing without the fault of the contractor".[10]

---

[2] (1647) Aleyn 26; Ibbetson in (Rose, ed.) *Consensus ad Idem, Essays in the Law of Contract in Honour of Guenter Treitel* p.3.

[3] i.e. if performance has not become illegal: below, para.19–044.

[4] At 27.

[5] e.g. in *Lewis Emanuel & Son Ltd v Sammut* [1959] 2 Lloyd's Rep. 629 (where the seller could reasonably have been expected to contract "subject to shipment", but did not do so); *The Zuiho Maru* [1977] 2 Lloyd's Rep. 552.

[6] *Taylor v Caldwell* (1863) 3 B. & S. 826 at 836.

[7] *Brewster v Kitchell* (1691) 1 Salk. 198; *Atkinson v Ritchie* (1809) 10 East 530 at 534–535.

[8] (1863) 3 B. & S. 826.

[9] ibid. at 830.

[10] ibid. at 833.

19–004   **Extension.** After being established in *Taylor v Caldwell*, the doctrine of frustration entered into a period of growth. It was extended to cases in which performance became impossible otherwise than through the perishing of a specific thing;
and even to cases where performance did not become impossible at all but the
commercial object, or purpose, of the contract was frustrated. In *Krell v Henry*[11]
the defendant hired a flat in Pall Mall for the days on which the processions
planned for the coronation of King Edward VII were to take place. His object was
to see the processions, though this was not expressly stated in the contract.[12] The
contract was frustrated when the processions were postponed because of the
illness of the King. Performance was not physically impossible: the defendant
could have used and paid for the flat on the days in question. But frustration was
not restricted to physical impossibility: it also applied

> "to cases where the event which renders the contract incapable of perform-
> ance is the cessation or non-existence of an express condition or state of
> things, going to the root of the contract, and essential to its perform-
> ance".[13]

19–005   **Limits.** It can fairly be said that the defendant in *Krell v Henry* would have
suffered unacceptable hardship if he had been held to the contract in the altered
circumstances. But the courts have refused to extend the doctrine beyond this
point; for to do so might enable a party to claim relief merely because circumstances had changed so as to turn the contract, for him, into a very bad bargain.
In the *British Movietonews* case[14] the House of Lords rejected the view that a mere
"uncontemplated turn of events"[15] (in that case, the cessation of wartime conditions in which the contract had been made) was a ground of frustration. Lord
Simon said:

> "The parties to an executory contract are often faced, in the course of
> carrying it out, with a turn of events which they did not at all anticipate—a
> wholly abnormal rise or fall in prices, a sudden depreciation of currency, an
> unexpected obstacle to the execution, or the like. Yet this does not in itself
> affect the bargain which they have made".[16]

Lord Roskill has similarly said that the doctrine of frustration was "not lightly to
be invoked to relieve contracting parties of the normal consequences of imprudent
commercial bargains".[17]
    A less strict approach appears at first sight to have been taken by Lord Hailsham
in *National Carriers Ltd v Panalpina (Northern) Ltd*, when he described the
"proposition that the doctrine was not to be extended" as "untenable".[18] But the

---

[11] [1903] 2 K.B. 740. See further para.19–041, below.
[12] In this respect *Krell v Henry* is unique among the "coronation seat" cases: the contracts in all the
other reported cases expressly refer to one or both of the two planned processions.
[13] At 748.
[14] *British Movietonews Ltd v London and District Cinemas* [1952] A.C. 166.
[15] [1951] 1 K.B. at 201, per Denning L.J.
[16] [1952] A.C. 166 at 185; cf. *Multiservice Bookbinding Ltd v Marden* [1979] Ch. 84 at 112–113.
[17] *The Nema* [1982] A.C. 724 at 752; cf. *Tsakiroglou & Co Ltd v Noblee Thorl GmbH* [1962] A.C. 93
at 115; *The Super Servant Two* [1990] 1 Lloyd's Rep. 1 at 8; *The Sea Angel* [2007] EWCA Civ 547;
[2007] 2 Lloyd's Rep. 517 at [111].
[18] [1981] A.C. 675 at 689; cf. ibid. at 694, 712.

point of this observation was that the doctrine applied to contracts generally: thus suggestions that it did not apply to particular contracts, such as time charters, demise charters, and leases of land, have from time to time been rejected by the courts.[19] The actual decision in the *National Carriers* case was that events which temporarily prevented one of the parties from putting the subject-matter to its intended use were not sufficiently serious to frustrate the contract. In this respect, the case, so far from departing from, actually illustrates, the approach adopted in the *British Movietonews* case.

A narrowing of the doctrine. Since that case, there seems to have been some   **19–006** narrowing in the scope of the doctrine of frustration. Many factors account for this trend: the reluctance of the courts to allow a party to rely on the doctrine as an excuse for escaping from a bad bargain; the difficulty of drawing the line between cases of frustration and cases where liability for breach of contract is strict; the tendency of businessmen to "draft out" possible causes of frustration by making their own express provisions for obstacles to performance; and the practical difficulties to be discussed in the paragraph that follows. The trend is illustrated by the fact that the Second World War gave rise to few[20] reported cases in which contracts were held to be frustrated otherwise than by supervening illegality.[21] The Suez crisis of 1956 produced only two reported English cases in which frustration was successfully pleaded. Both these cases were later overruled.[22] When the Suez Canal was again closed in 1967, pleas of frustration met with no more success[23]; and the "energy crisis" resulting from further hostilities in the Middle East in 1973 did not lead to any reported cases in England in which frustration was even raised as a defence.[24] All this is not to say that the doctrine will not be applied where performance is actually prevented, as it was in a number of charterparty cases in which ships were trapped for long periods after the outbreak of hostilities between Iran and Iraq in 1980,[25] so that performance of the agreed services became impossible. In the Suez cases there was (with one exception[26]) no such prevention: performance merely became more onerous for the party alleging frustration. There is now a marked reluctance to apply the doctrine in such circumstances.

Practical difficulties. From a practical point of view, the doctrine of frustra-   **19–007** tion gives rise to two related difficulties. The first is that it may scarcely be more satisfactory to hold that the contract is totally discharged than to hold that it remains in full force: often some compromise may be a more reasonable solution.

---

[19] *Bank Line Ltd v Arthur Capel & Co* [1919] A.C. 435 (time charters); *Blane Steamships Ltd v Minister of Transport* [1951] 2 K.B. 965 (demise charters); *National Carriers Ltd v Panalpina (Northern) Ltd* [1981] A.C. 675 (leases of land).

[20] There were some, e.g. *Morgan v Manser* [1948] 1 K.B. 184.

[21] The *Fibrosa* case [1943] A.C. 32; the *Denny, Mott* case [1944] A.C. 265; and the *Cricklewood* case [1945] A.C. 221 were all cases of supervening illegality.

[22] *Carapanayoti & Co Ltd v ET Green Ltd* [1959] 1 Q.B. 131, overruled in the *Tsakiroglou* case [1962] A.C. 93; and *The Massalia* [1961] 2 Q.B. 278, overruled in *The Eugenia* [1964] 2 Q.B. 226.

[23] For the Suez cases, see further para.19–031, below.

[24] cf. *Sky Petroleum Ltd v VIP Petroleum Ltd* [1974] 1 W.L.R. 576, where the only dispute was as to the injured party's remedy; no attempt was made to rely on frustration.

[25] *The Evia (No.2)* [1983] 1 A.C. 736; *The Agathon* [1982] 2 Lloyd's Rep. 211; *The Wenjiang (No.2)* [1983] 1 Lloyd's Rep. 400; *The Chrysalis* [1983] 1 Lloyd's Rep. 503.

[26] i.e. *The Eugenia* [1964] 2 Q.B. 226; but there the fact that the ship was trapped in the Canal did not lead to frustration as it was due to the charterer's prior breach of the contract: see below, para.19–083.

Thus in some of the coronation seat cases the contracts provided that, if the procession were cancelled, the ticket-holder should be entitled to use the ticket on the day on which the procession eventually did take place.[27] Similarly, after 1956, contracts for the carriage or sale of goods began to specify which party was to bear any extra expense that might be incurred, should the Suez Canal again be closed.[28] In the absence of such express provisions, this kind of solution is not open to the courts: they have no power to *modify* contracts in the light of supervening events.

The second difficulty is that the allocation of risks produced at common law by the doctrine of frustration is not always entirely satisfactory. In a case like *Taylor v Caldwell* it may be reasonable that neither party should be liable for loss of the benefit that the other expected to derive from performance, so that the one should not recover his loss of anticipated profits, nor the other the payments promised to him. But it does not follow that loss suffered by one party as a result of acting in reliance on the contract should equally lie where it falls. In *Taylor v Caldwell* the hirers' claim was not one for loss of profits, but only one for expenses thrown away in advertising and preparing for the concerts.[29] No doubt the defendants also incurred expenses on the side-shows and other facilities for entertainment, which the contract obliged them to provide. It might be more satisfactory if such losses could be apportioned. At common law this was possible only where the contract expressly so provided: e.g. in one of the coronation cases the contract provided that, if the procession was cancelled, the ticket-holder was to get his money back, less a percentage to cover the other party's expenses.[30] A more general, but still limited, power of adjustment now exists by statute, but it does not cover all cases in which some form of apportionment would seem to be desirable.[31]

19–008   **A "multi-factorial" approach.** What follows in the next two parts of this chapter are illustrations of the doctrine of frustration in practice, in which, for the purpose of analysis, the relevance of particular factors will fall to be assessed. It is helpful to stress at the outset therefore that the application of the doctrine requires a "multi-factorial" approach.[32] As it has been put:[33]

> Among the factors which have to be considered are the terms of the contract itself, its matrix or context, the parties' knowledge, expectations, assumptions and contemplations, in particular as to risk, as at the time of contract, at any rate so far as these can be ascribed mutually and objectively, and then the nature of the supervening event, and the parties' reasonable and objectively

---

[27] For contracts containing such provisions, see *Clark v Lindsay* (1903) 19 T.L.R. 202 and *Victoria Seats Agency v Paget* (1902) 19 T.L.R. 16 (first contract).

[28] *Achille Laura v Total Societa Italiana per Azioni* [1969] 2 Lloyd's Rep. 65; *D I Henry Ltd v Wilhelm G Clasen* [1973] 1 Lloyd's Rep. 159.

[29] (1863) 3 B. & S. at 827.

[30] *Victoria Seats Agency v Paget*, above, fn.27 (second contract); cf. *Elliott v Crutchley* [1904] 1 K.B. 565, affirmed [1906] A.C. 7. The rule that advance payments could not be recovered back (below, para.19–094) no doubt produced a sort of rough apportionment, but in a way that was quite unrelated to any expenses actually incurred.

[31] See below, para.19–095 et seq.

[32] *The Sea Angel* [2007] EWCA Civ 547; [2007] 2 Lloyd's Rep. 517 at [111]; cf. *The Mary Nour* [2008] EWCA Civ 856; [2008] 1 Lloyd's Rep. 179 at [14]; *Islamic Republic of Iran Shipping Lines v Steamship Mutual Underwriting Association (Bermuda) Ltd* [2010] EWHC 2661 (Comm); [2011] 1 Lloyd's Rep. 195.

[33] ibid.

ascertainable calculations as to the possibilities of future performance in the new circumstances.

Thus, in the case from which this dictum is taken, a vessel used for a salvage operation was detained by the port authorities in the last few days of a 20 day charter. At the date when the contract was said to have been frustrated, it had been detained for five weeks with the prospect of at least a further four to six weeks of delay while legal proceedings for its release were pursued. Nonetheless, the charter was not frustrated because of other factors: the contractual risk of delay was on the charterers,[34] the detention was foreseeable[35] and the purpose for which the vessel had been chartered had been performed.[36]

2. APPLICATIONS

(a) Impossibility

Supervening impossibility of performance is the most obvious ground of frustration. The various ways in which it can arise are discussed below; but it must be emphasised at the outset that such impossibility is by no means invariably a ground of discharge. We shall see that even the destruction of the subject-matter of a contract does not necessarily discharge it[37]; and where liability for breach of contract is strict,[38] a party may be liable for failing to do the impossible. For example, a seller who has undertaken to ship goods to his buyer may be liable for failing to do so, even though the failure was due to lack of shipping space caused by events entirely beyond his control.[39] By contrast, a shipowner may be excused from liability under a charterparty if, after the time of contracting, his ship is disabled by an explosion which is not proved to be due to his fault.[40] The distinction between the two situations is not easy to put into words. In neither of them is the party claiming excuse at fault, so that lack of fault is not sufficient (though it is necessary[41]) to discharge the contract. It could be said that lack of shipping space was a risk undertaken by the seller in our first example, while in the second the explosion was not within the contractual risk taken by the shipowner; but this seems to amount to a restatement of the distinction rather than to an explanation for it. Another way of expressing the distinction is that in the first case the seller *undertook* that shipping space would be available, while in the second the parties merely *assumed* that the particular ship would remain available; and that it is impossibility resulting from the failure of such a common assumption that leads to discharge.

19–009

---

[34] Based both on the terms of the charterparty and the salvage agreement: ibid. at [119].

[35] See further below, para.19–078.

[36] The remaining obligation was the redelivery of the vessel. The parties were therefore disputing on which of them the financial consequences of the detention should fall.

[37] See the discussion of frustration and risk at para.19–013, below.

[38] See above, paras 17–064—17–065.

[39] *Lewis Emanuel & Sons Ltd v Sammut* [1959] 2 Lloyd's Rep. 629.

[40] *Joseph Constantine SS Line v Imperial Smelting Corp Ltd* [1942] A.C. 154; below, para.19–089.

[41] See below, para.19–083.

(i) *Destruction of a particular thing*

19–010   **Illustrations.** The clearest illustration of frustration by the destruction of a particular thing is *Taylor v Caldwell*[42] itself, where it was the subject-matter of the contract which was destroyed. An agreement for the sale of specific goods is similarly avoided if, without the fault of either party, the goods perish before the risk has passed to the buyer.[43] For the present purpose, destruction need not amount to total annihilation. In *Asfar & Co v Blundell*[44] a cargo of dates was sunk and so affected by water and sewage as to become "for business purposes something else",[45] though it was still sold for £2,400. The cargo-owner's liability to pay freight was discharged as the merchantable character of the cargo had been destroyed.

19–011   **Destruction of only part of the subject-matter.** *Taylor v Caldwell* shows that a contract may be frustrated by the destruction of only part of the subject-matter. The contract related to "the Surrey Gardens and Music Hall" and was discharged though only the Hall was destroyed, while the gardens remained in use as a place of entertainment. The contract was frustrated because its main purpose (the giving of the concerts) had been defeated.[46] Partial destruction which does not defeat the main purpose of the contract will not frustrate it, though it may provide one party with an excuse for not performing in full[47] or give the other party the option to terminate.[48]

19–012   **Destruction of something essential for performance.** A contract may be frustrated where what is destroyed is not its subject-matter but something essential for its performance. For example, a contract to install machinery in a particular factory can be frustrated by the destruction of the *factory*,[49] even though its subject-matter is the *machinery*. The question whether something is essential for performance depends on the terms of the contract. Thus where an agency agreement related to goods to be "manufactured *or sold*" by the owner of a factory it was held that destruction of the factory did not frustrate the agreement.[50]

19–013   **Frustration and risk.** Even the destruction of the subject-matter of the contract will not necessarily frustrate it. In certain types of contracts, it will instead be governed by rules which determine when the "risk of loss" passes from one party to the other. Where these rules apply, the contract will not be frustrated by the destruction of the subject-matter, though it may be frustrated by other events (such as delay or illegality[51]). The effects of the risk rules are radically different from those of frustration. The difference can be summed up by saying that where the destruction leads to frustration it discharges all the contractual obligations of both parties, while where it is governed by the rules as to risk it

---

[42] (1863) 3 B. & S. 826; above, para.19–003.
[43] Sale of Goods Act 1979, s.7; for risk, see para.19–013, below.
[44] [1896] 1 Q.B. 123.
[45] At 128; cf. *The Badagry* [1985] 1 Lloyd's Rep. 395 at 399. Contrast *Horn v Minister of Food* [1948] 2 All E.R. 1036.
[46] cf. below, paras 19–020, 19–023, 19–031, 19–043, 19–058, 19–059.
[47] See above, para.17–059.
[48] See below, para.19–023.
[49] *Appleby v Myers* (1867) L.R. 2 C.P. 651.
[50] *Turner v Goldsmith* [1891] 1 Q.B. 544.
[51] See below, paras 19–019, 19–045, 19–062.

discharges only some of the obligations of one party. At this stage,[52] two types of contracts will serve to illustrate the distinction.

Sale of goods. Under a contract for the sale of goods, the general rule is that **19–014** (unless otherwise agreed) risk passes with property.[53] Property may pass before delivery,[54] so that it is possible for the risk in goods to have passed to the buyer while they are still in the hands of the seller.[55] If the goods are destroyed *after* the risk has passed, the contract is not frustrated: on the contrary, the statement that the risk has passed *means* that the buyer must still pay the price, while the seller is discharged from his duty to deliver. But the seller is not necessarily discharged from *all* his obligations: he may, for example, have expressly or impliedly undertaken to transfer the benefit of insurance on the goods to the buyer, and this obligation would survive their destruction.[56] If goods are destroyed *before* the risk has passed, the contract is frustrated if the goods are specific,[57] or if they are to be taken from a particular source and all the goods from that source are destroyed.[58] If, on the other hand, the sale is of unascertained goods by description, the contract is not frustrated merely because the particular goods which the seller intended to supply under the contract were destroyed before the risk had passed. On the contrary, to say that the risk has not passed in this situation means that the seller is bound to deliver other goods of the contract description; and if he does so the buyer must accept and pay.

Building contracts. Under a building contract, the risk of the work is (unless **19–015** otherwise agreed) on the builder until the agreed work is completed. Thus a contract to build a house or a factory would not be frustrated by destruction of the buildings before completion. On the other hand, where a builder agrees to do work on an existing building, e.g. to install new machinery in a factory, a distinction must be drawn. If, before the work is finished, the *factory* is destroyed, the contract is frustrated[59]; but if only the *machinery* is destroyed there is no frustration and the builder will remain bound to complete the installation without extra charge.[60]

(ii) *Death or incapacity*

Certain "personal" contracts, such as contracts of employment, apprenticeship **19–016** or agency, are discharged by the death of either party.[61] Even a commercial contract may involve reliance by one party on the personal skill of the other[62]; in

---

[52] For the passing of risk and related problems in contracts for the sale of land, see below, paras 19–062—19–065.
[53] Sale of Goods Act 1979, s.20(1).
[54] e.g. under Sale of Goods Act 1979, s.18, r.1.
[55] Where the buyer "deals as consumer", risk does not pass until the goods are delivered to the consumer: Sale of Goods Act 1979, s.20(4), as inserted by Sale and Supply of Goods to Consumers Regulations 2002 (SI 2002/3045), reg.4; for the definition of "deals as consumer", see s.61(5A) of the 1979 Act.
[56] e.g. *Manbré Saccharine Co Ltd v Corn Products Co Ltd* [1919] 1 K.B. 198.
[57] Sale of Goods Act 1979, s.7; above, para.19–010.
[58] See below, paras 19–024—19–025.
[59] *Appleby v Myers* (1867) L.R. 2 C.P. 651.
[60] ibid. at 660.
[61] cf. *Cutter v Powell* (1795) 6 T.R. 320; *Whincup v Hughes* (1871) L.R. 6 C.P. 78; above, para.17–032.
[62] cf. above, para.15–053.

which case the death of that party (though not that of the other) can discharge the contract. The same rules apply where a party is permanently incapacitated from performing such a contract. Thus a contract to write a book would be frustrated by the supervening insanity of the author[63]; and a contract to render services would be frustrated if continued performance involved a serious risk to the health of the person who had agreed to render them.[64] A contract may likewise be frustrated where it is the capacity of a party to *receive* performance that is affected by the supervening event: e.g. where a person who had booked a course of dancing lessons was so seriously injured that he could no longer dance[65]; but in contracts governed by the Regulations which apply to package travel it is an implied term that a consumer who is "prevented from proceeding with the package"[66] can transfer the booking to a suitably qualified person, so that the contract is not discharged by the supervening event. A contract may also be frustrated by the death or incapacity of a third party: e.g. a contract between A and B to paint a portrait of C could be frustrated if C died before work on the portrait had begun.

(iii) *Unavailability*

19–017   **In general.** A contract may be frustrated if its subject-matter, or a thing or person essential for the purpose of its performance, though not ceasing to exist or suffering permanent incapacity, becomes unavailable for that purpose. Thus charterparties have been frustrated where the ship was seized, detained[67] or requisitioned,[68] and where cargo was unavailable because of a strike at the port of loading[69]; a contract for the sale of goods has been frustrated where the goods were requisitioned[70]; a contract to operate and share in the profits of an oilfield has been frustrated where the interests of both parties were expropriated by the government of the country in which the oilfield was situated[71]; and contracts for personal services have been frustrated where one of the parties fell ill[72] or was interned or conscripted.[73]

19–018   **Temporary unavailability.** A person or thing essential for performance may, as a result of the supervening event, be unavailable at the time fixed for performance, but become available later. Such temporary unavailability will most obviously frustrate the contract where it is clear from the terms or nature of the contract that it was to be performed only at, or within, the specified time, and that the time of performance was of the essence[74] of the contract. Thus a contract to play in a

---

[63] *Jackson v Union Marine Ins Co Ltd* (1874) L.R. 10 C.P. 125 at 145.

[64] *Condor v The Barron Knights Ltd* [1966] 1 W.L.R. 87.

[65] *Parker v Arthur Murray Inc* 295 N.E. 2d 487 (1973).

[66] Package Travel, Package Holidays and Package Tours Regulations 1992 (SI 1992/3288), reg.10(1).

[67] e.g. in the Gulf War cases (above, para.19–006, below, para.19–052), and in *The Adelfa* [1988] 2 Lloyd's Rep. 466; cf. *The Sea Angel* [2007] EWCA Civ 547; [2007] 2 Lloyd's Rep. 517, above, para.19–008.

[68] e.g. *Bank Line Ltd v Arthur Capel & Co* [1919] A.C. 435.

[69] *The Nema* [1982] A.C. 724.

[70] e.g. *Re Shipton, Anderson & Co* [1915] 3 K.B. 676.

[71] *BP Exploration (Libya) Ltd v Hunt* [1983] 2 A.C. 352; below, para.19–101.

[72] e.g. *Hart v A R Marshall & Sons (Bulwell) Ltd* [1977] 1 W.L.R. 1067.

[73] e.g. *Morgan v Manser* [1948] 1 K.B. 184.

[74] See above, para.18–089.

concert on a particular day is frustrated by the performer's illness on that day.[75] Temporary unavailability may also frustrate a contract even though no fixed date is expressly specified for performance and even though a time is fixed but is not of the essence. In such cases, the contract may be frustrated, not by the mere *fact*, but by the *length*, of the delay in performance.

Delay frustrating purpose of contract. This possibility is illustrated by **19–019** *Jackson v Union Marine Ins Co*,[76] where a charterparty was made in November 1871 for the carriage of rails from Newport to San Francisco; it provided that the ship was to proceed to Newport with all possible despatch. On her way there she went aground in January 1872 and was not repaired until the following August. The contract was held to have been frustrated by the length of the delay, in consequence of which the voyage which the ship was capable of making was substantially different from that envisaged in the contract. It was as if a ship chartered "to go from Newport to St. Michael's . . . in time for the fruit season"[77] did not become available till after the season was over. Contracts in cases of this kind are frustrated because performance at the end of the delay is no longer of any use to the party to whom it was to be rendered, i.e. to the charterer.

Change in conditions. In another group of cases, the contract is frustrated for **19–020** the different reason that, after the delay, the performance to be rendered by one party would be significantly more onerous for that party. This possibility is illustrated by *Metropolitan Water Board v Dick, Kerr & Co*[78] where wartime restrictions imposed an indefinite delay on the performance of a contract to build a reservoir. It was held that the contract was frustrated since it was likely that there would be a total change in conditions by the time that the restrictions might be lifted.

Even where delay does not increase the *costs* of the party whose performance is affected by it, that party may be prejudiced for the different reason that rates of pay for the service which he was to render have increased substantially between the time of contracting and the end of the delay. This sort of reasoning appears to explain *Bank Line Ltd v Arthur Capel & Co*,[79] where a ship was chartered for 12 months; it was contemplated, though not expressly provided, that the period would run from April 1915 to April 1916. She was requisitioned before delivery and the owners did not procure her release till September 1915. In an action by the charterer for damages for non-delivery, the House of Lords held the charterparty frustrated. The contract was, in substance if not in form, an April to April charter; and to hold the parties to a September to September charter would be to hold them to a contract which was "as a matter of business a totally different thing".[80] The reason for this view cannot have been that the delay prejudiced the charterers (for they were claiming performance). It seems rather to have been that the shipowners would have been prejudiced by the delay (if the contract had not been discharged) because freight rates had risen[81] so that by September they could

[75] *Robinson v Davison* (1871) L.R. 6 Ex. 269.
[76] (1874) L.R. 10 C.P. 125.
[77] ibid. at 143.
[78] [1918] A.C. 119; cf. *Acetylene Co of GB v Canada Carbide Co* (1922) 8 Ll.L.Rep. 456
[79] [1919] A.C. 435; cf. *Hirji Mulji v Cheong Yue SS Co Ltd* [1926] A.C. 497; *Autry v Republic Productions* 180 P.2d 888 (1947).
[80] At 460.
[81] cf. *Modern Transport Co Ltd v Duneric SS Co* [1917] 1 K.B. 370 at 376.

have charged considerably more for their services than the amount payable under the original contract.[82]

19–021   **Delay and partly performed contracts.** In the cases so far considered, it was claimed that performance should be rendered *in full* when the temporary unavailability ceased. In other cases, involving long-term contracts, the claim was that *the balance* of the contract should then be performed. Obviously such a claim cannot succeed if the delay lasts, or is likely to last, for so long that *no* part of the agreed performance remains possible. Thus in *Countess of Warwick SS Co v Le Nickel SA*[83] the wartime requisition of a ship was held to frustrate a one-year charter which, at the time of the requisition, still had six months to run, because it was unlikely that the ship would be released in time to render any substantial services under the charter. For the same reason, charterparties were frustrated in a number of cases in which ships became unavailable for service as a result of being trapped for long periods in the course of the Gulf War between Iran and Iraq.[84]

If, on the other hand, performance for some balance of the contract period remains, or is likely to remain, possible, the outcome of claims for that balance depends on the proportion of the interruption, or likely interruption, to the contract period: the greater that proportion is, the more likely it is that the contract will be frustrated. Thus in *The Nema*[85] a charterparty for six or seven voyages to be made from April to December was frustrated when, after the first voyage, a long strike at the loading port made it impossible to accomplish more than a further two voyages within the contract period. By contrast, in *Tamplin SS Co Ltd v Anglo-Mexican Petroleum Co*[86] the wartime requisition of a ship in February 1915 did not frustrate a five-year charter which was not due to expire till December 1917: the majority of the House of Lords took the view that "there may be many months during which the ship will be available before the five years have expired".[87] The effect of such requisition must theoretically be determined at or near the time when it takes place.[88] In practice, the courts no doubt take later events into account, but the *Tamplin* case was decided before the end of the chartered period. Thus the House of Lords had to speculate as to the probable length of the requisition and indirectly as to the probable duration of the war. In the light of later events, the majority may have speculated wrongly. But this is no criticism of the decision, which has also been supported on another ground to be discussed later in this chapter.[89]

19–022   **Contracts involving personal service.** Events such as illness, conscription or internment may interfere temporarily with the performance of long-term contracts involving personal service. Here again one test of frustration is the proportion which the interruption, or likely interruption, bears to the period specified in

---

[82] This appears from the fact that £31,000 would have been awarded to the charterers by way of damages if the contract had not been discharged: see [1919] A.C. 435 at 441.

[83] [1918] 1 K.B. 372.

[84] *The Evia (No.2)* [1983] A.C. 736; *The Agathon* [1982] 2 Lloyd's Rep. 211; *The Wenjiang (No.2)* [1983] 1 Lloyd's Rep. 400; *The Chrysalis* [1983] 1 Lloyd's Rep. 503.

[85] [1982] A.C. 724.

[86] [1916] 2 A.C. 397; cf. *Port Line v Ben Line Steamers Ltd* [1958] 2 Q.B. 146.

[87] ibid. at 405.

[88] See below, para.19–051.

[89] See below, para.19–091.

the contract. Thus in *Morgan v Manser*[90] a music hall artiste employed a manager for 10 years from 1938. He was conscripted in 1940 and demobilised in 1946. The contract was held to be frustrated since in 1940 it was likely that the artiste would remain in the Army for a very long time. On the other hand, in *Nordman v Rayner & Sturgess*[91] a long-term commission agency was not frustrated when the agent (an Alsatian with anti-German sympathies) was interned, since his internment was not likely to last long and in fact only lasted one month.

Employment contracts. A contract of employment may be frustrated by the illness of the employee. This is true, not only where the contract is a long-term one, but also where it provides for determination by relatively short periods of notice, since even such a contract is often intended to give rise to an enduring relationship.[92] But temporary illness will not of itself frustrate a contract of employment[93]: it will have this effect only where it is so serious as to put an end to the possibility of performance "in a business sense",[94] e.g. by making resumption within a reasonable time a practical impossibility.[95] An illness which is not serious enough to frustrate the contract does, however, have a number of other legal effects. It gives the employee a *temporary* excuse for non-performance, and it may also give the employer an *option* to terminate.[96] Unless and until this option is exercised, the employee is prima facie entitled to wages during sickness.[97] This prima facie rule can be displaced by an express contrary provision, or by circumstances from which a contrary provision can be implied. To establish such an implied term, it is not necessary to show that the employee would, at the time of contracting, have agreed that he should not be paid during sickness.[98] The rule can be displaced by other circumstances: e.g. by the practice of the employers not to make such payments and the failure of the employee to claim them.[99]

19–023

(iv) *Failure of a particular source*

A contract may be discharged where the subject-matter was to be obtained from a particular source which without the fault of either party becomes unavailable: e.g. where goods were to be taken from a particular crop which fails as a result of drought or disease; or where they are to be imported from a particular country and such import is prevented by war, natural disasters or prohibition of export. Such

19–024

---

[90] [1948] 1 K.B. 184 (where it is not clear what prejudice the artiste would have suffered by being held to the balance of the contract); cf. *Unger v Preston Corp* [1942] 1 All E.R. 200 (a case very near the line).

[91] (1916) 33 T.L.R. 87.

[92] *Notcutt v Universal Equipment Co (London) Ltd* [1986] 1 W.L.R. 641; Howarth [1987] C.L.J. 47; cf. *R. (Verner) v Derby CC* [2003] EWHC 2708 (Admin); [2004] I.C.R. 535.

[93] *Marshall v Harland & Wolff Ltd* [1972] 1 W.L.R. 899; *Williams v Watson's Luxury Coaches* [1990] I.C.R. 536; cf. *Mount v Oldham Corp* [1973] Q.B. 309.

[94] *Jackson v Union Marine Ins Co Ltd* (1874) L.R. 10 C.P. 124 at 145.

[95] e.g. *Hart v A R Marshall & Sons (Bulwell) Ltd* [1977] 1 W.L.R. 1067; *Notcutt v Universal Equipment Co (London) Ltd* [1986] 1 W.L.R. 641; cf. *Gryf-Lowczowski v Hinchingbrooke Healthcare NHS Trust* [2005] EWHC 2407; [2006] I.C.R. 100 (contract of under-performing surgeon not frustrated because still a realistic possibility of "re-skilling").

[96] See above, paras 17–059, 18–032.

[97] *Marrison v Bell* [1939] 2 K.B. 187; *Mears v Safecar Securities Ltd* [1983] Q.B. 54 at 79; cf. Employment Rights Act 1996, s.64.

[98] *Mears v Safecar Securities Ltd* [1983] Q.B. 54 at 74, disapproving *Orman v Saville Sportswear Ltd* [1960] 1 W.L.R. 1065, and following *O'Grady v Saper* [1940] 2 K.B. 469.

[99] *Mears v Safecar Securities Ltd*, above.

cases raise two questions: whether the failure frustrates the contract; and what is the position where the source only fails in part.

19–025 **Express reference to source.** Where the contract expressly provides that the goods are to be taken from the specified source, the contract is frustrated if that source fails. Thus in *Howell v Coupland*[100] a farmer sold 200 tons of potatoes to be grown on land specified in the contract. That crop largely[101] failed, and it was held that the contract was frustrated so that the farmer was not liable in damages for non-delivery. For this purpose it is assumed that the contract specifies an *exclusive* source of supply. Where it refers to several sources, the contract is not frustrated merely because one of them becomes unavailable.[102]

19–026 **Source intended by one party only.** Where the contract contains no reference to the source and only one of the parties intends to use that source, the failure of that source does not lead to frustration. Thus a contract for the sale of "Finland birch timber" was not frustrated merely because the seller expected to get supplies from Finland and could not do so because of the severing of trade routes after the outbreak of war in 1914. For all the buyer knew, delivery might have been made from stocks kept in England.[103] Nor is a contract frustrated merely because the seller is let down by his supplier.[104] This is so even where that supplier is the sole producer of goods of the contract description, so long, at least, as the buyer was unaware of this fact.[105] The same rule applies where a buyer's source of payment fails. Thus a contract is not frustrated merely because the buyer intends (unknown to the seller) to pay with money to be remitted from a foreign country and the remittance is prevented or delayed by changes in that country's exchange control regulations.[106] A fortiori, a contract is not frustrated merely because the buyer's supply of the currency in which payment was to be made has become exhausted.[107]

19–027 **Source intended by both parties.** The most difficult cases are those in which the contract makes no express reference to the source but *both* parties contemplate that it will be used. Such contracts are sometimes construed as containing an implied reference to the source[108]; but for this purpose it is not enough to show that the parties contemplated the source: they must have intended that that source (and no other), should be used.[109] There is little English authority on the question whether (in the absence of any evidence of such intention) the failure of a source which was merely contemplated by both parties will frustrate a contract. In one case, it was conceded that the partial failure of such a source released the seller in

---

[100] (1876) 1 Q.B.D. 258.

[101] Not entirely: for a discussion of this aspect of the case, see below, para.19–028.

[102] e.g. *Turner v Goldsmith* [1891] 1 Q.B. 544; cf. *The Super Servant Two* [1990] 1 Lloyd's Rep. 1; and see below, para.19–053.

[103] *Blackburn Bobbin Co Ltd v TW Allen Ltd* [1918] 2 K.B. 467.

[104] *The Mary Nour* [2008] EWCA Civ 856; [2008] 1 Lloyd's Rep. 179.

[105] *Intertradex SA v Lesieur Torteaux SARL* [1978] 2 Lloyd's Rep. 509.

[106] *Universal Corp v Five Ways Properties Ltd* [1979] 1 All E.R. 552; cf. above, para.17–064. For an analogous situation, see *Hole & Pugsley v Sumption* [2001] N.L.J. 1851.

[107] *Congimex SARL (Lisbon) v Continental Grain Export Corp (New York)* [1979] 2 Lloyd's Rep. 346 at 353; cf. *Janos Paczy v Haendler & Natermann GmbH* [1981] 1 Lloyd's Rep. 302.

[108] e.g. *Ockerby & Co Ltd v Murdock* (1916) 19 W.A.R. 1, affirmed (1916) 22 C.L.R. 420.

[109] See above, at fn.102.

part.[110] The view that the total failure of a mutually contemplated source will frustrate the contract is sometimes said to be supported by *Re Badische Co*,[111] where a contract for the supply of chemicals was held to be frustrated by illegality on the outbreak of war in 1914 because both parties intended the goods to be obtained from Germany. But this was a special case: it would clearly be contrary to public policy to allow such a contract to subsist; and this would be so whether the parties had specified the source or merely contemplated that it should be used. The problems raised where the supervening event makes the contract illegal differ significantly from those which arise where it makes performance impossible[112]; and there is no clear English decision on the effect of failure of a mutually contemplated (but unspecified) source of supply. Where that source was contemplated by one party only, the courts have sometimes emphasised this fact in rejecting the defence of frustration[113]; and this may give some support to the view that the defence would succeed where the source was contemplated by both. On the other hand, in some such cases the commercial background may now be that it would be usual for the seller to protect himself against the contingency: e.g. by a prohibition of export clause. Where this is the position it is less likely that failure of even a mutually contemplated source would frustrate the contract.

Partial failure. A contract for the sale of goods may specify the source from which the goods are to be taken, so that the total failure of that source would undoubtedly lead to frustration. Further problems can then arise if the source fails only in part. Such partial failure normally has three consequences. First, the seller is excused to the extent of the deficiency. This was the outcome in *Howell v Coupland*,[114] where the seller had delivered the small quantity actually produced, and was held not to be liable for the rest of the quantity sold. Secondly, the seller is bound to deliver the quantity actually produced[115]; unless, perhaps, it is so small that it is uneconomical to harvest it.[116] Thirdly, the buyer is not generally bound to accept the quantity produced if it is less than that contracted for[117]; but as partial crop failures normally lead to a rise in prices this point is of little practical importance.

19–028

More than one contract. Additional complications arise where a seller has made a number of contracts to deliver goods from a specified source, and that source fails in part. For example, a farmer who reasonably expects his land to yield 1,000 tons agrees to sell 200 tons to each of five customers, and as a result of partial crop failure only 600 tons are produced; or a seller of goods to be taken from a foreign source similarly agrees to sell 200 tons to each of five customers, and, as a result of export restrictions, cannot obtain more than 600 tons. If total failure of

19–029

---

[110] *Lipton Ltd v Ford* [1917] 2 K.B. 647.
[111] [1921] 2 Ch. 331.
[112] See below, para.19–044.
[113] *Blackburn Bobbin Co Ltd v TW Allen Ltd* [1918] 2 K.B. 467.
[114] (1876) 1 Q.B.D. 256; above, para.19–025.
[115] *H R and S Sainsbury Ltd v Street* [1972] 1 W.L.R. 834; above, para.17–059.
[116] The contrary seems to have been held in *International Paper Co v Rockefeller* 146 N.Y.S. 371 (1914); sed quaere: such a case could be regarded as being, in substance, one of total failure of the source.
[117] Sale of Goods Act 1979, s.30(1). For qualifications of the buyer's right to reject, see above, para.17–033.

the source would have frustrated the contracts,[118] what difference does it make that the failure was only partial?

One possible view is that it makes no difference, so that all the contracts are frustrated because the seller cannot perform them all in full. But this is unlikely to be accepted because it would enable the seller to keep the available goods and so to make a windfall profit from the rising prices likely to result from the shortage.[119] A second possibility is to say that none of the contracts is frustrated: if the seller delivered 200 tons to each of three buyers, his inability to deliver to the other two would be due to his voluntary act or "election" and would therefore be incapable of frustrating his contracts with these two.[120] This view derives some support from an analogous case[121]; but it will be submitted later in this chapter that there is no true "election" where, after the supervening event, the seller's only choice is whether to perform one contract rather than another.[122] The argument that discharge is due to the seller's "election" could also be met by imposing legal restrictions on his choice. This possibility leads to the third view, that some of the contracts are discharged. If this view were interpreted to mean that the seller must deliver to such buyers as were designated by law (e.g. by reference to the order in which their contracts were made or to the standard of reasonableness) it would not be open to the objection that the seller's failure to deliver to the other buyers resulted from his "election". A fourth view adopts the principle of pro rata division, so that in our examples the contracts would not be frustrated, but each buyer would receive 120 tons.[123] The difficulty with this view is that, under it, the contracts would be modified, rather than discharged[124]; and at common law the doctrine of frustration appears to be capable only of leading to a total discharge of the contract.[125] The principle of pro rata division does, however, have considerable support in cases in which the seller has relied on the partial failure of the source as discharging him, not under the common law doctrine of frustration, but under an express provision of the contract, such as a force majeure or prohibition of export clause. In such cases, there is support for two versions of the pro rata principle. One states negatively that no buyer is entitled to delivery in full[126]; the other states affirmatively that each buyer is entitled to his pro rata share, so that he would be entitled to damages if he received no delivery at all.[127] But there is also

---

[118] See *Bremer Handelsgesellschaft mbH v Continental Grain Co* [1983] 1 Lloyd's Rep. 269, where this requirement was not satisfied.

[119] The view that all the contracts are frustrated may at first sight seem to be supported by *Tennants (Lancashire) Ltd v C S Wilson & Co Ltd* [1917] A.C. 495; but the only point actually decided was that no single buyer was entitled to delivery *in full*; and the seller was a middleman who would himself have had to pay the higher prices and so could not have profited from frustration.

[120] See below, paras 19–086—19–088.

[121] *The Super Servant Two* [1990] 1 Lloyd's Rep. 1; below, para.19–088.

[122] See below, para.19–088.

[123] cf. in the US U.C.C., s.2–615(b). The rule there stated, that the seller can take into account "regular customers not . . . under contract", does not seem to represent English law: see *Pancommerce SA v Veecheema BV* [1983] 2 Lloyd's Rep. 304. Much less are the English courts likely to accept the further rule stated in s.2–615(b) that the seller can take into account "his own requirements for further manufacture": this seems inconsistent with *Maritime National Fish Ltd v Ocean Trawlers Ltd* [1935] A.C. 524; below, para.19–087; see generally Hudson 31 M.L.R. 535.

[124] *The Super Servant Two* [1989] 1 Lloyd's Rep. 148 at 158, affirmed [1990] 1 Lloyd's Rep. 1.

[125] See above, para.19–007; below, para.19–090.

[126] *Bremer Handelsgesellschaft mbH v Vanden Avenne-Izegem P v BA* [1978] 2 Lloyd's Rep. 109 at 115, 128, 131 (where the exact method of division is left open); cf. *Tennants (Lancashire) Ltd v C S Wilson & Co Ltd* [1917] A.C. 495 at 511–512.

[127] *Bremer Handelsgesellschaft mbH v C Mackprang Jr* [1979] 1 Lloyd's Rep. 221 at 224; the point is left open in *Continental Grain Export Corp v STM Grain Ltd* [1979] 2 Lloyd's Rep. 460 at 472.

support for the view that, if the seller allocates all his supplies to earlier buyers, he is not liable if he delivers nothing to later ones.[128] Probably, the overriding test is whether the seller acted reasonably in allocating the available supplies. In applying this test, the court can have regard to circumstances other than the order in which the contracts were made, e.g. to the fact that the available quantity was "too small to be sensibly apportioned among relevant purchasers".[129] Pro rata division is, of course, possible only where the subject-matter is physically divisible. Suppose that a farmer sold to each of five buyers "a calf to be born to my herd", expecting that at least five calves would be so born, and that (for reasons beyond his control) only three calves were born. In such a case, pro rata division would not work,[130] and it is submitted that, if the farmer delivered to the earliest three buyers, his contracts with the later two should be frustrated.[131]

(v) *Method of performance impossible*

In general. A contract may be discharged if it provides for a method of performance which becomes impossible. In *Nickoll & Knight v Ashton Edridge & Co*[132] a contract was made for the sale of cottonseed "to be shipped per steamship *Orlando* from Alexandria during . . . January". The *Orlando* later went aground in the Baltic so that she could not get to Alexandria in January. It was held that the contract was frustrated since, in the view of the majority of the Court of Appeal, it was to be construed as providing for performance *only* in the stipulated manner. If the stipulated method had not been regarded as exclusive, the seller might have been obliged to perform in a different way, e.g. by shipping the goods on a different ship or at a later time.[133] Whether he would actually have been obliged to do this would then have depended on whether the substituted method of performance differed fundamentally from that originally undertaken. This appears from the Suez cases to be discussed below.

19–030

The Suez cases. These cases arose because an agreed or contemplated method of performance became impossible when the Suez Canal was closed as a result of hostilities in the Middle East in 1956 and again in 1967. The first question was whether the parties had actually stipulated for the particular method of performance, or had only expected that it would probably be used. In *Tsakiroglou & Co Ltd v Noblee Thorl GmbH*[134] a contract was made for the sale of Sudanese groundnuts at an inclusive price to cover the cost of the goods, insurance and carriage to Hamburg. When the contract was made both parties expected that shipment would be via Suez, but the contract did not so provide. It was held that the contract was not frustrated by the closure of the Suez Canal, so that the seller

19–031

---

[128] *Intertradex SA v Lesieur Torteaux SARL* [1978] 2 Lloyd's Rep. 509; cf. *Continental Grain Export Corp v STM Grain Ltd*, above, at 473; *The Marine Star* [1993] 1 Lloyd's Rep. 329 at 332–333; and (in another context) *Cox v Bankside* [1995] 2 Lloyd's Rep. 434.

[129] *Bremer Handelsgesellschaft mbH v Continental Grain Co* [1983] 1 Lloyd's Rep. 269 at 293, citing *Westfalische Genossenschaft GmbH v Seabright Ltd*, unreported, per Robert Goff J.

[130] See I Kings 3: 25.

[131] *The Super Servant Two* [1990] 1 Lloyd's Rep. 1 is distinguishable on the ground that the defendant claimed discharge in respect of the *earlier* contract: see below, para.19–088.

[132] [1901] 2 K.B. 126; cf. *Maine Spinning Co v Sutcliffe & Co* (1918) 87 L.J.K.B. 382, discussed in Benjamin's *Sale of Goods* (8th edn), para.20–018.

[133] cf. in the US, *Meyer v Sullivan* 181 P. 847 (1919); U.C.C., s.2–614(1). This rule prevents the seller from making a profit out of frustration on a rising market: cf. below, para.19–091.

[134] [1962] A.C. 93.

ought to have shipped the goods via the Cape of Good Hope. Although this would have taken two and a half times as long as shipment via Suez and would have doubled the cost of carriage, the difference between the two methods of performance was not sufficiently fundamental to frustrate the contract.[135] If the difference had been of this kind, it seems that the contract could have been frustrated even though the method of performance was not specified in the contract but only contemplated by both parties.[136]

Where, on the other hand, there is no such fundamental difference, the contract may stand even if it does provide for performance by the method which becomes impossible. Thus it was suggested in the *Tsakiroglou* case[137] that the contract there would not have been frustrated even if it *had* provided for shipment via Suez. The same view is supported by a number of cases in which shipowners argued that voyage charters were frustrated because of the extra length and expense of the voyage via the Cape of Good Hope. In some of these cases the contracts expressly referred to Suez[138]; and even where there was no such reference it was no doubt an implied term that the ship should go via the Suez Canal as that was the usual and customary route when the contract was made.[139] Nevertheless the contracts were not frustrated,[140] so that the shipowners were bound to carry the goods at no extra charge by the longer, available, route. The difference between the two routes was not sufficiently fundamental, even though in one case[141] the voyage actually accomplished was twice as long as that originally contracted for and in another added nearly a third to the shipowner's anticipated costs.[142] The same principle can, on the other hand, favour the shipowner where the charterparty provides for payment by reference to the time taken to accomplish the voyage. In one such case[143] the charterer pleaded frustration but the plea was rejected: once again the court took the view that the voyage via the Cape was not fundamentally different from that via Suez, though exceeding it in length by about a third. To provide an illustration of frustration resulting from the closure of the Canal it is necessary to put a more extreme case, such as that of a contract to carry perishable goods from Port Sudan to Alexandria.

(vi) *Impossibility and impracticability*

19–032   **Impracticability distinguished from impossibility.** The doctrine of frustration originated in cases where performance was said to have become "impossible". That is, in itself, something of a relative term. What is "impossible"

---

[135] See further below, at fn.420.

[136] cf. in another context, *Florida Power & Light Co v Westinghouse Electric Corp* 826 F.2d 239 (1987), where the contemplated method of performing an obligation to remove irradiated fuel from a nuclear power station was *by reprocessing* and when this became impossible the obligation could be performed only *by storing* the fuel. The difference between these modes was held to be sufficiently fundamental to discharge the obligation since reprocessing would have yielded a profit to the contractor of some $18 million while storing the fuel would have imposed costs on him in the region of $80 million. And see *Codelfa Construction Pty Ltd v State Rail Authority of NSW* (1982) 149 C.L.R. 337.

[137] [1962] A.C. 93 at 112; cf. *Congimex Companhia Geral, etc. v Tradax Export SA* [1981] 2 Lloyd's Rep. 687 at 692 (affirmed [1983] 1 Lloyd's Rep. 250).

[138] e.g. *The Captain George K* [1970] 2 Lloyd's Rep. 21; *The Washington Trader* [1972] 1 Lloyd's Rep. 463; 453 F.2d 939.

[139] *Scrutton on Charterparties* (20th edn), p.256.

[140] See, the authorities cited in fn.138, above, and *Glidden v Hellenic Lines Ltd* 275 F. 2d. 253 (1960); *Transatlantic Finance Corp v USA* 363 F.2d 312 (1966).

[141] *The Captain George K*, above, fn.138.

[142] *The Washington Trader*, above, fn.138.

[143] *The Eugenia* [1964] 2 Q.B. 226.

depends partly on the current state of technology,[144] and partly on the amount of trouble and expense to which one is prepared to go to achieve it. It has been said that even *Taylor v Caldwell* was not a case of literal impossibility since "by the expenditure of huge sums of money" the music hall could probably have been rebuilt "in time for the scheduled concerts"[145]; but no reasonable businessman would have been expected to incur such expenditure. For this reason the trend in the US has been to abandon the very words "impossible" and "impossibility" and to use instead the terms "impracticable" and "impracticability".[146] This seems, moreover, to be intended to widen the scope of the doctrine of discharge by supervening events.[147] "Impracticability" includes "extreme and unreasonable difficulty, expense, injury or loss"[148] to one of the parties. Examples include "A severe shortage of raw materials or of supplies due to war, embargo, local crop failure, unforeseen shutdown of major sources of supply or the like, which . . . causes a marked increase in cost . . . ".[149] The caveat is entered that "Increased cost alone does not excuse performance . . . "[150] but it is suggested that a price increase "well beyond the normal range"[151] could lead to discharge. In England, dicta to the effect that a contract may be discharged if its performance becomes "impracticable" are occasionally found in the cases.[152] But the weight of English authority rejects this view. Thus it has been said in the House of Lords that "a wholly abnormal rise or fall in prices"[153] would not affect the bargain; and that

"The argument that a man can be excused from performance of his contract when it becomes 'commercially' impossible seems to me a dangerous contention which ought not to be admitted unless the parties have plainly contracted to that effect".[154]

Impracticability generally no excuse. A number of cases illustrate the view 19–033 that "impracticability" is not generally sufficient to frustrate a contract in English law. In *Davis Contractors Ltd v Fareham Urban DC*[155] contractors agreed to build 78 houses for a local authority in eight months for £94,000. Because of labour shortages, the work took 22 months and cost the contractors £115,000. They claimed that the contract had been frustrated and that they were therefore entitled

[144] See, e.g., the illustration of "absolute" impossibility given in *Corbin on Contracts* (1962), para.1325: "No-one can go to the moon".
[145] Fuller & Eisenberg, *Basic Contract Law* (3rd edn), p.801.
[146] U.C.C., s.2–615; Restatement 2d, *Contracts*, para.261.
[147] *Neal-Cooper Grain Co v Texas Gulf Sulphur Co*, 508 F.2d 283 at 293 (1974) ("less stringent test of impracticability"); cf. *Nora Springs Co-operative Co v Brandau* 247 N.W.2d 744 at 748 (1976).
[148] Restatement, *Contracts*, §454; Restatement 2d, *Contracts*, §261, Comment d.
[149] ibid.; U.C.C., s.2–615, Comment 4.
[150] U.C.C., s.2–615, Comment 4.
[151] Restatement 2d, *Contracts*, §261, Comment d.
[152] e.g. *Horlock v Beal* [1916] A.C. 486 at 492; *The Furness Bridge* [1977] 2 Lloyd's Rep. 367 at 377; *Nile Co for the Export of Agricultural Crops v H & J M Bennett (Commodities) Ltd* [1986] 1 Lloyd's Rep. 555 at 581; cf. *The Badagry* [1985] 1 Lloyd's Rep. 395 at 399. See further Beatson in (Rose, ed.), *Consensus ad Idem, Essays in the Law of Contract in Honour of Guenter Treitel*, p.123.
[153] *British Movietonews Ltd v London and District Cinemas* [1952] A.C. 166 at 185.
[154] *Tennants (Lancashire) Ltd v C S Wilson & Co Ltd* [1917] A.C. 495 at 510 (where the sellers were excused by the express terms of the contract); cf. *Shearson Lehman Hutton Inc v Maclaine Watson & Co Ltd* [1989] 2 Lloyd's Rep. 570 at 508 (commodity contract not frustrated by closure of market); and see the cases discussed in the next paragraph.
[155] [1956] A.C. 696.

to extra remuneration on a quantum meruit basis.[156] But the House of Lords rejected the claim as the events which caused the delays were within the ordinary range of commercial probability and had not brought about a fundamental change of circumstances. Lord Radcliffe said:

> "It is not hardship or inconvenience or material loss itself which calls the principle of frustration into play. There must be as well such a change in the significance of the obligation that the thing undertaken would, if performed, be a different thing from that contracted for".[157]

The Suez cases[158] similarly reject the argument that the greater expense caused to the party prejudiced by the closure of the Canal was a ground of frustration. In the words of Lord Simonds, "an increase of expense is not a ground of frustration".[159] Where performance would, in view of changed circumstances, cause not merely extra expense but acute personal hardship to one party, it has been said that "equitable relief may . . . be refused because of an unforeseen change of circumstances not amounting to legal frustration".[160] But in such cases the contract is not discharged: the defendant remains liable in damages even though specific performance is refused on the ground of severe hardship.[161]

19–034   **Possible exceptions.** Four types of cases to be discussed below may at first sight seem to give some support to the view that a contract can be frustrated by "impracticability". But it will be submitted that these cases are all explicable on other grounds and that they do not support the view that impracticability (in the sense of great financial or commercial hardship to one of the parties) is of itself sufficient to discharge a contract in English law.

19–035   **Impracticability combined with impossibility or illegality.** First, there are the cases in which discharge is based, not on impracticability alone, but on this factor when it is combined with impossibility or illegality. One group of such cases is that already discussed,[162] in which long delays in performance resulted from wartime restrictions, and it was held that performance need not be resumed in the totally altered conditions which prevailed when those restrictions were removed.

---

[156] See below, para.22–019.
[157] [1956] A.C. 696 at 729; cf. *Multiservice Bookbinding Ltd v Marden* [1979] Ch. 84 at 113; *Chaucer Estates v Fairclough Homes* [1991] E.G.C.S. 65.
[158] See above, para.19–031.
[159] *Tsakiroglou & Co v Noblee Thorl GmbH* [1962] A.C. 93 at 115; cf. *Exportelisa SA v Guiseppe Figli Soc Coll* [1978] 1 Lloyd's Rep. 433; *Finland Steamship Co Ltd v Felixstowe Dock Ry Co* [1980] 2 Lloyd's Rep. 287, where no attempt was made to argue that a contract was frustrated by cost increases described at 288 as "devastating"; and *The Mercedes Envoy* where no attempt was made to rely on frustration on the ground that a ship had been so severely damaged that it was "not commercially viable" to repair her: [1995] 2 Lloyd's Rep. 559 at 563. Extreme cost increases might, however, be relevant where all that a party was bound to do was to take reasonable steps to produce a specified result. For example, in *Brauer & Co (Great Britain) Ltd v James Clark (Brush Materials) Ltd* [1952] 2 All E.R. 497 at 501 it was said that a seller would not be liable for failure to get an export licence if the cost of getting it were 100 times the contract price; the seller's duty in that case would have been limited to one to take reasonable steps (above, para.2–110) even if the contract had not been expressly "subject to export licence".
[160] *Patel v Ali* [1984] Ch. 283 at 288.
[161] See below, para.21–029. In *Patel v Ali*, above, the defendant was required to pay £10,000 into court as a condition of the discharge of the order of specific performance against her.
[162] *Metropolitan Water Board v Dick Kerr & Co* [1918] A.C. 119; *Acetylene Co of GB v Canada Carbide Co* (1922) 8 Ll.L.Rep. 456; above, para.19–020; cf. *Florida Power & Light Co v Westinghouse Electric Corp* 826 F.2d 239 (1987): above, fn.136.

It could be said that performance at the later time was "impracticable"; but this was only one factor leading to discharge, the other being that, for a considerable period, the wartime conditions made performance actually impossible. Similar reasoning can apply where a supervening change in the law makes it illegal to perform a contract to render a service unless (for example) additional safety precautions are taken by the party who is to render it. The extra expense to be incurred by that party in taking those precautions may then be regarded as a kind of "impracticability", leading to discharge[163]; but this result will, more significantly, be based on the special considerations of public policy on which discharge is based in cases of supervening illegality[164]: in other words, it does not follow that the contract would be discharged if the same amount of extra expense were occasioned simply by commercial factors, without any element of supervening illegality.

Express contractual provision. Secondly, there are cases in which contracts   19–036
were discharged, not under the general doctrine of frustration, but under express contractual provisions (such as force majeure or prohibition of export clauses) which excuse one party, or both, if a specified event prevents performance. Such clauses do not protect a party merely because supervening events make performance more difficult or more expensive for him[165]; nor do they normally protect him where he can perform in alternative ways and only one of them becomes impossible: e.g. a seller who cannot obtain the goods that he had undertaken to deliver from the source intended by him (e.g. because of being let down by his supplier or because of an export embargo) must obtain them from other sources that remain available.[166] But this rule is subject to an exception which applies where it would be unreasonable to require the seller to perform in this way, because attempts to do so by him, and by other sellers similarly situated, would drive prices up to "unheard of levels".[167] In one case of this kind, it was said that the seller need not make such an attempt where to require him to do so would be "impracticable and commercially unsuitable".[168] These cases are, however, concerned, not with discharge under the general doctrine of frustration, but with discharge under express contractual provisions for supervening events.[169] Such a

---

[163] It seems to have been so regarded in *William Cory v LCC* [1951] 1 K.B. 8, affirmed [1951] 2 K.B. 476. Similar considerations may in part account for the American decision in *Florida Power & Light Co v Westinghouse Electric Corp* 826 F.2d 239 (1987).

[164] See below, para.19–044.

[165] See, e.g. *Brauer & Co (Great Britain) Ltd v James Clark (Brush Materials) Ltd* [1952] 2 All E.R. 497; *B & S Contracts & Designs Ltd v Victor Green Publications Ltd* [1984] I.C.R. 419; *Thames Valley Power Ltd v Total Gas & Power Ltd* [2005] EWHC 2208; [2006] 1 Lloyd's Rep. 441; *Tandrin Aviation Holdings Ltd v Aero Toy Store LLC* [2010] EWHC 40 (Comm); [2010] 2 Lloyd's Rep. 668 (re financial crisis of late 2008).

[166] e.g. *PJ van der Zijden Wildhandel NV v Tucker & Cross Ltd* [1975] 2 Lloyd's Rep. 240; *Agrokar AG v Tradigrain SA* [2000] 1 Lloyd's Rep. 497. For the possibility of excluding this rule by the terms of the clause, see *The Morning Watch* [1996] 2 Lloyd's Rep. 383.

[167] *Tradax Export SA v André & Cie* [1976] 1 Lloyd's Rep. 416 at 423; cf. *André & Cie SA v Tradax Export SA* [1983] 1 Lloyd's Rep. 254; *Cook Industries v Tradax Export SA* [1983] 1 Lloyd's Rep. 327 at 344, affirmed [1985] 2 Lloyd's Rep. 454, without reference to this point and see generally *Benjamin's Sale of Goods* (8th edn), para.19–141.

[168] *Bremer Handelsgesellschaft mbH v Vanden Avenne-Izegem PV BA* [1978] 2 Lloyd's Rep. 109 at 115. cf. *Owners of Steamship Matheos v Louis Dreyfus* [1925] A.C. 654 at 666 ("commercially impracticable").

[169] The same is true of *Ford & Sons (Oldham) Ltd v Henry Leetham & Sons Ltd* (1915) 21 Com.Cas. 55, which is nevertheless cited in support of the general principle of discharge by "impracticability" in U.C.C., s.2–615, Comment 4.

provision often operates in circumstances falling short of frustration under the general law.[170] Thus the fact that it may, on its true construction, cover "impracticability" does not support the view that the same circumstances would frustrate a contract which contained no such provision.

19–037   **Contracts of indefinite duration.** Thirdly, it is arguable that impracticability may be a ground of discharge where the contract is one of indefinite duration. In *Staffordshire Area Health Authority v South Staffordshire Waterworks Co*[171] a hospital had in 1919 contracted to give up to a waterworks company its right to take water from a well, and the company had in return promised "at all times hereafter" to supply water to the hospital at a fixed price specified in the contract. In 1975 the cost to the company of making the supply had risen to over 18 times that fixed price and the company gave seven months' notice to terminate the agreement. It was held that this notice was effective. Lord Denning M.R. regarded the contract as frustrated by the change of circumstances which had occurred between 1919 and 1975. But this view is, with respect, open to question, as it was based on the very passage of his own judgment in the *British Movietonews* case which had there been disapproved by the House of Lords.[172] The preferable reason for the decision in the *Staffordshire* case is therefore that of the majority, who held that the agreement was, on its true construction, intended to be of indefinite (and not of perpetual) duration[173]: hence the case fell within the general principle under which, in commercial agreements of indefinite duration, a term is often implied entitling either party to terminate by reasonable notice.[174] It follows from this reasoning that the decision would have gone the other way if the agreement had been for a fixed term, e.g. for 10 years. The agreement could then not have been terminated by notice before the end of the 10 years, nor would an increase in the suppliers' costs during that period have been a ground of frustration. This view is supported by later authority[175] and seems also to be correct in principle: if parties enter into a fixed term fixed price contract they must be taken thereby to have allocated the risks of market fluctuations. If the parties are not prepared to accept these risks (or to accept them in full) they can adopt the now common practice of providing in the contract itself for flexible pricing.[176]

---

[170] See below, para.19–075. For the significance of the distinction between discharge by frustration and under an express term, cf. also *The Super Servant Two* [1989] 1 Lloyd's Rep. 148 at 149; [1990] 1 Lloyd's Rep. 1 at 8.

[171] [1978] 1 W.L.R. 1387; Rose 96 L.Q.R. 177.

[172] [1952] A.C. 166 at 185; above, para.19–005.

[173] "At all times hereafter" was (obviously) not to be taken literally, but meant "at all times hereafter during the subsistence of the agreement." The majority view was followed in *Tower Hamlets LBC v British Gas Corp, The Times*, March 23, 1982, affirmed *The Times*, December 14, 1983, and approved in *Watford DC v Watford Rural DC* (1988) 86 L.G.R. 524 at 529.

[174] cf. above, para.16–103; contrast *Watford DC v Watford Rural DC* above, where it was held that no such term could be implied in an agreement to contribute variable amounts towards the maintenance of cemeteries; *Islwyn BC v Newport BC* (1994) 6 Admin. L.R. 386. For exclusion of an implied term permitting termination on reasonable notice by other words in the contract, see also *Harbinger UK Ltd v GE Information Services Ltd* [2000] 1 All E.R. (Comm) 166; *Servicepower Asia Pacific Pty Ltd v Servicepower Business Solutions Ltd* [2009] EWHC 179 (Ch).

[175] *Kirklees MBC v Yorks Woollen District Transport Co* (1978) 77 L.G.R. 448.

[176] See *Superior Overseas Development Corp v British Gas Corp* [1982] 1 Lloyd's Rep. 262; *Wates v GLC* (1983) 25 Build L.R. 1 (below, at fn.180); *Watford DC v Watford Rural DC* (1988) 86 L.G.R. 524 at 548; *Queensland Electricity Generating Board v New Hope Collieries Pty Ltd* [1989] 1 Lloyd's Rep. 205.

The Playa Larga. The three situations so far discussed should be distinguished **19–038** from a fourth which arose in *The Playa Larga.*[177] Sugar had been sold by a Cuban state trading organisation to a buyer controlled by a state trading organisation in Chile. When the contract was made, Cuba and Chile were both ruled by Marxist governments; but before deliveries under the contract had been completed, the Marxist Government in Chile was overthrown; diplomatic relations between the two countries were severed; and there was a complete breakdown of commercial relations between them. It was held that the contract was frustrated even though its performance had not become impossible in any of the senses discussed in this chapter. The decision was, however, based, not on extreme hardship to the seller, but on the fact that, in the altered conditions, there was no possibility of the implementation of the contract on either side[178]; and the court concluded that, in these conditions, the contract was no longer intended to be binding. A breakdown of diplomatic and commercial relations between governments would not normally be a ground of discharge; but in *The Playa Larga* it had this effect because both contracting parties were controlled by the governments in question.

Inflation. In the cases so far discussed, increases in the cost of performing a **19–039** particular contract have made that contract unprofitable to one party. A similar situation may arise where the general process of inflation reduces in real terms the benefit which that party expected to obtain under the contract. In the *British Movietonews* case "a sudden depreciation of currency" is listed as one of the uncontemplated turns of events which do *not* frustrate a contract.[179] The passage continues to make the general point that a contract would cease to bind if a "fundamentally different situation" were to emerge. This may refer back to the illustrations, previously given in the passage, of events (such as currency fluctuations) which are stated *not* to frustrate a contract; but more probably the reference is to *other* (i.e. to frustrating) events. Again, in *Wates Ltd v GLC*[180] a building contract to some extent protected the builder against inflation, by means of a price-escalation clause; and it was said that the fact that "inflation increased not [at] a trot or at a canter but at a gallop . . . was not so radical a difference from the inflation contemplated and provided for as to frustrate the contract".[181] Thus the English authorities do not support the view that inflation is a ground of frustration, though the possibility that extreme (as opposed to merely severe) inflation may be capable of frustrating a contract cannot be wholly ruled out.[182] It is again open to a party who fears that he will be prejudiced by inflation to guard against this risk by an express term, e.g. by providing (if his bargaining position permits) for "index-linked" payments.[183]

Currency fluctuations. A debtor whose obligations are defined by reference to **19–040** a foreign currency cannot avoid liability to pay in full merely because the pound

---

[177] [1983] 2 Lloyd's Rep. 171.
[178] ibid. at 188.
[179] [1952] A.C. 166 at 185.
[180] (1983) 25 Build.L.R. 1.
[181] ibid. at 34.
[182] cf. Lord Roskill's reference in *National Carriers Ltd v Panalpina Northern Ltd* [1981] A.C. 675 at 712 to "inflation" as one of the "circumstances in which the doctrine [of frustration] has been invoked, sometimes with success, *sometimes without*".
[183] See *Nationwide BS v Registry of Friendly Societies* [1983] 1 W.L.R. 1226.

sterling has fallen in value in relation to that currency by an unexpectedly large amount.[184]

(b) Frustration of Purpose

19–041   **Definition.** Frustration of purpose is, in a sense, the converse of impracticability. The two ideas resemble each other in that neither is concerned with cases in which performance has become impossible. Impracticability is normally[185] said to arise when a *supplier* of goods, services or other facilities alleges that supervening events have made performance of his own promise so much more burdensome to him that he should no longer be bound to render it. The argument of frustration of purpose, on the other hand, is normally put forward by the *recipient* of the goods, services or facilities[186]: it is that supervening events have so greatly reduced the value to him of the other party's performance that he should no longer be bound to accept it and to pay the agreed price.

19–042   **Coronation cases.** Such an argument succeeded in some of the cases which arose out of the postponement of the coronation of King Edward VII. We have seen that in *Krell v Henry*[187] the effect of the postponement was to discharge a contract for the hire of a flat overlooking the route of the proposed processions. The obvious danger of such a rule is that it can all too easily be invoked by a party for whom a contract has simply become a very bad bargain. *Krell v Henry* has therefore attracted much criticism[188]; but the decision can be justified[189] on the ground that the contract was, on its true construction, not merely one for the hire of the flat, but one to provide facilities for viewing the coronation processions.[190] The actual decision may be contrasted with an example given in one of the judgments: a contract to take a cab to Epsom on Derby day "at a suitable enhanced price"[191] would not be frustrated if the Derby were cancelled. Here the contract was evidently regarded as one to get the passenger to Epsom—not as one to get him to the Derby.

Similar reasoning distinguishes *Krell v Henry* from *Herne Bay Steamboat Co v Hutton*,[192] another of the coronation cases. A pleasure boat was hired "for the purpose of viewing the naval review and for a day's cruise round the fleet". The review, which formed part of the proposed coronation celebrations, was cancelled

---

[184] *Multiservice Bookbinding Ltd v Marden* [1979] Ch. 84.

[185] See next note.

[186] Occasionally, the normal positions are reversed so that a buyer relies on impracticability where the cost to him of taking delivery has risen sharply (as in *Mineral Park Land Co v Howard*) 156 P. 458 (1916)) or a seller relies on frustration of purpose where supervening events affect his ability to realise the financial instruments by which payment is to be made (as in *Re Comptoir Commercial Anversois and Power Sons & Co* [1920] 1 K.B. 868).

[187] [1903] 2 K.B. 740 (above, para.19–004); McElroy and Williams 4 M.L.R. 241; 5 M.L.R. 1.

[188] *Blackburn Bobbin Co Ltd v T W Allen & Sons Ltd* [1918] 1 K.B. 540 at 542 (affirmed [1918] 2 K.B. 467); cf. *Maritime National Fish Ltd v Ocean Trawlers Ltd* [1935] A.C. 524 at 528; *Scanlan's New Neon Ltd v Toohey's Ltd* (1943) 67 C.L.R. 169 at 191–194; Landon 52 L.Q.R. 168; Gordon 52 L.Q.R. 326.

[189] See *Codelfa Construction Pty Ltd v State Rail Authority of NSW* (1982) 149 C.L.R. 337 at 358.

[190] cf. *The Great Peace* [2002] EWCA Civ 1407; [2003] Q.B. 679 at [66] (contract for "a room with a view").

[191] [1903] 2 K.B. 740 at 750.

[192] [1903] 2 K.B. 683.

when the King fell ill, but the contract was not frustrated. It was construed simply as a contract for the hire of a boat; and it could still be performed although one of the motives of the hirer[193]—to carry passengers at high prices to see the review—was defeated.

Limited application. Although the actual decision in *Krell v Henry* appears   19–043
to be justifiable on the grounds stated above, the case has scarcely ever been followed in England. Normally, a contract is not frustrated merely because supervening events have prevented one party from putting the subject-matter to the use intended by him, even though that use was also contemplated by the other.[194] Thus a contract by which a gas company agreed with a local authority to "provide, maintain and light" street lamps was not frustrated when wartime black-out regulations prohibited the lighting of such lamps,[195] since performance of the maintenance obligation ("which cannot be regarded as . . . trivial"[196]) remained possible.[197] Similarly, a contract for the sale of goods is not frustrated merely because the buyer's purpose to export the goods from, or to import them into, a particular country is defeated by export or import restrictions.[198] Perhaps the most striking illustration of the reluctance of the courts to apply the principle of frustration of purpose is provided by the *Amalgamated Investment & Property*[199] case, where it was held that a contract for the purchase of property for redevelopment was not frustrated when the buildings on the land were listed as being of special architectural or historic interest, so that redevelopment became more difficult or impossible and the property lost most of its value.[200]

Such cases show that "the frustrated expectations and intentions of one party to a contract do not necessarily, or indeed usually, lead to the frustration of that contract".[201] They make it difficult to establish the defence of frustration of purpose; but they do not make it impossible. In *Denny, Mott & Dickson v James B Fraser & Co Ltd*[202] an agreement for the lease of a timber yard was made for the purpose of enabling the parties to carry out a contract between them for the sale of timber. When performance of the contract of sale was prohibited by wartime regulations, the House of Lords held that the agreement for the lease of the yard was also frustrated. The actual decision may to some extent rest on special policy considerations applicable to cases of supervening illegality; but other situations can

---

[193] For the requirement that the purpose of *both* parties must be frustrated, see *The Siboen and the Sibotre* [1976] 1 Lloyd's Rep. 293.

[194] *North Shore Ventures Ltd v Anstead Holdings Inc* [2010] EWHC 1485 (Ch); [2010] 2 Lloyd's Rep. 265 (use to which part of loan could be put partially restricted).

[195] *Leiston Gas Co v Leiston-cum-Sizewell Urban DC* [1916] 2 K.B. 428; on the interpretation of express contractual provisions for such events, see *Williams v Mercer* [1940] 3 All E.R. 293 and contrast *Egham & Staines Electricity Co Ltd v Egham Urban DC* [1944] 1 All E.R. 107.

[196] ibid. at 433.

[197] For contrasting decisions on the effect of black-out regulations on contracts for the hire of electric advertising signs, see *Scanlan's New Neon Ltd v Toohey's Ltd* (1943) 67 C.L.R. 169 (contract not discharged); *20th Century Lites v Goodman* 149 P.2d 88 (1944) (contract discharged).

[198] e.g. *D McMaster & Co v Cox McEwen & Co* 1921 S.C. (HL) 1; *Congimex SARL (Lisbon) v Continental Grain Export Corp (New York)* [1979] 2 Lloyd's Rep. 346; *Bangladesh Export Import Co Ltd v Sucden Kerry SA* [1995] 2 Lloyd's Rep. 1, where an additional ground for rejecting the buyer's plea of frustration was that the contract in terms imposed an obligation to obtain an import licence on the buyer.

[199] *Amalgamated Investment & Property Co Ltd v John Walker & Son Ltd* [1977] 1 W.L.R. 164.

[200] The listing was said to have reduced the value of the property to £200,000—against a contract price of £1,710,000.

[201] *Congimex Companhia Geral, etc., SARL v Tradax Export SA* [1983] 1 Lloyd's Rep. 250 at 253.

[202] [1944] A.C. 265.

be imagined in which the principle of frustration of purpose might also apply. For example, if premises were leased as a warehouse and supervening events made their use as such impossible for the whole period of the lease, it seems that the contract might be frustrated.[203] In such a case, the contract would be discharged, even though performance had not become impossible, because the supervening event had destroyed "some basic, though tacit assumption on which the parties had contracted".[204]

(c) Illegality

19–044   A contract may be discharged by a supervening prohibition if the prohibition would have made the contract illegal, had it been in force when the contract was made.[205]

The object of the doctrine of frustration in cases of supervening impossibility or of frustration of purpose is to provide a satisfactory method of allocating or distributing the loss caused by the supervening event. Where, however, a contract is affected by supervening illegality, the court has to take into account, not only the relative interests of the parties, but also the interests of the public in seeing that the law is observed[206]; and this public interest may sometimes outweigh the importance of achieving a fair distribution of loss. For this reason supervening illegality is a ground of discharge distinct from supervening impossibility, and is to some extent governed by special rules.

(i) *Illustrations*

19–045   **Trading with the enemy.** The public interest considerations just mentioned are particularly strong where a contract becomes illegal as a result of the wartime prohibition against trading with the enemy. In the leading *Fibrosa* case[207] a contract for the sale of machinery to be shipped to Gdynia was frustrated when that port was occupied by the enemy during the Second World War. Although it might have been physically possible to get the goods to the destination,[208] the contract was discharged because of the strong public interest in ensuring that no aid should be given to the enemy economy in time of war. The same principle applies where goods are to be imported from an enemy country: the contract is

---

[203] This seems to be assumed in *National Carriers Ltd v Panalpina (Northern) Ltd* [1981] A.C. 675 (below, paras 19–057—19–061), where the temporary nature of the interruption was stressed in rejecting the plea of frustration.

[204] *Sir Lindsay Parkinson Ltd v Commissioners of Works* [1949] 2 K.B. 632 at 665.

[205] See above, para.11–029.

[206] This book deals only with discharge by supervening illegality which arises under English law. The justification for discharge where the illegality arises under *foreign* law (e.g. under a foreign prohibition of export or import) is somewhat different: see *Benjamin's Sale of Goods* (8th edn), para.18–337.

[207] *Fibrosa Spolka Ackcyjna v Fairbairn, Lawson Combe Barbour Ltd* [1943] A.C. 32.

[208] The mere outbreak of war does not frustrate a contract: see *The Chrysalis* [1983] 1 W.L.R. 1469 (where the war was one to which the UK was not a party, so that no question of trading with the enemy could arise). The suggestion in *Stocznia Gdanska SA v Latvian Shipping Co* [1998] 1 W.L.R. 574 at 600 that in the *Fibrosa* case "the outbreak of war frustrated the contract" is, with respect, open to question: it was not the outbreak of war, but the enemy occupation of the port of destination, which was the ground of frustration.

frustrated even though the enemy source is not specified in the contract but only contemplated by the parties.[209] The public interest principle is so strong in these cases that frustration by or as a result of the prohibition cannot be excluded even by an express provision in the contract.[210]

Other prohibitions. The cases provide many illustrations of frustration by supervening prohibitions other than that against trading with the enemy. In the *Denny, Mott*[211] case, for example, a contract for the sale of timber was frustrated by a wartime prohibition against dealing in goods of the contract description. Contracts can similarly be frustrated by prohibition of export or import, by restrictions on the movement of capital,[212] or by licensing requirements of the kinds to be discussed below. In these cases the public interest in seeing that the prohibition is observed is less strong than in the trading with the enemy cases[213]; and they differ from the trading with the enemy cases in two further ways. First, frustration results only if it is an actual term of the contract that the subsequently prohibited act is to be done. Thus a contract for the sale of goods may be frustrated by prohibition of export if it provides that the goods are to be exported,[214] but not merely because the buyer intended to export them, even though the seller knew this.[215] Secondly, frustration can be excluded by express contractual provisions. Thus provisions suspending performance in the event of prohibition of export are valid[216] since, so far from contravening the policy of the prohibition, they assume that it will be observed. Similar provisions in trading with the enemy cases are contrary to the public interest since they involve continuing relations with an enemy subject, and so may indirectly support the enemy economy.

19–046

(ii) *Supervening and antecedent prohibition*

No frustration for an antecedent prohibition. Under the rules stated above, frustration may result from a supervening prohibition, i.e. from one imposed by a law made after the contract was made.[217] If, at the time of contracting, the prohibition is already in force, the case is one of antecedent

19–047

---

[209] *Re Badische Co* [1921] 2 Ch. 331; above, para.19–027.

[210] *Ertel Bieber & Co v Rio Tinto Co Ltd* [1918] A.C. 260; below, para.19–077.

[211] [1944] A.C. 265; above, para.19–043; cf. *Marsh v Glanvill* [1917] 2 K.B. 87 at 91.

[212] See *Libyan Arab Foreign Bank v Bankers Trust Co* [1989] Q.B. 728 at 749, though in that case there was no frustration: [1989] Q.B. 728 at 771–772; cf. *Wahda Bank v Arab Bank Plc, The Times*, December 23, 1992; for further proceedings in this case, see [1996] 1 Lloyd's Rep. 470.

[213] cf. *Benjamin's Sale of Goods* (8th edn), para.18–376 et seq.

[214] As in *Andrew Miller & Co v Taylor & Co Ltd* [1916] 1 K.B. 402 (see at 403, 417); but in that case the plea of frustration failed as the embargo was not permanent: as to this point see below, para.19–051, fn.237.

[215] See above, para.19–043.

[216] See below, para.19–075.

[217] For the present purpose, a prohibition is supervening if it was imposed after the contract even though the state of affairs on which it is based already existed when the contract was made, as in *Gamerco SA v ICM/Fair Warning (Agency) Ltd* [1995] 1 W.L.R. 1226, where a stadium in which a "rock concert" was to be given suffered *before* the contract was made from an undiscovered structural defect and use of the stadium for giving the concert was prohibited when the defect was discovered *after* the contract was made.

prohibition. This may make the contract void ab initio for illegality,[218] but it will not bring about frustration.

19–048   **An intermediate situation: consent of public authority withheld.** There is an intermediate situation in which at the time of contracting a law is in force under which the contract can be lawfully performed only with the consent of a public authority: e.g. if a licence to build, or to export or import goods, is obtained. Such a licence may be sought but refused *after* the contract is made; and it is then possible to regard the refusal as a supervening event which frustrates the contract.[219] But it is submitted that generally there will be no frustration in cases of this kind. The cases fall into three groups.

In the first, the parties intend to perform, or actually perform, without the required licence. In such cases, the contract is not frustrated but illegal ab initio.[220]

In the second, the parties intend to perform only if the required licence is obtained. Here the principal obligations under the contract are subject to the condition precedent that the licence will be obtained; and normally one of the parties (e.g. a seller of goods for export) will be under a duty to take reasonable steps to obtain the licence.[221] If he takes such steps but the licence is nevertheless refused, he is not liable in damages[222]; but the reason is not that he is prevented from performing (and so discharged) but that he *has* performed by doing all that was required of him. Equally, the buyer is not liable, but again the reason is not that his liability is discharged: it is that he never became liable because the seller was unable to deliver and so failed to perform a condition precedent to, or a concurrent condition of, the buyer's duty to accept and pay.[223] Thus although neither party is liable the contract is not frustrated.[224] An alternative possibility, in cases of this kind, is that the seller has undertaken absolutely to obtain a licence.[225] If he fails, he is liable in damages; and to avoid conflict with the rules as to illegal contracts it has been said that the seller's liability is based on a collateral contract that he will secure the licence.[226]

In the third group of cases the licensing requirement is in existence at the time of the contract and the parties intend to perform only if a licence is obtained; but afterwards there is a change in government policy with regard to the issue of such

---

[218] See above, paras 11–019—11–020.

[219] This is a possible interpretation of a dictum in *A V Pound & Co Ltd v M W Hardy Inc* [1956] A.C. 588 at 604 that "further performance of the contract was excused"; for another interpretation, see fn.224, below.

[220] See above, para.11–014.

[221] See above, para.2–110.

[222] *Benjamin's Sale of Goods* (8th edn), para.18–371.

[223] See above, paras 17–015—17–018.

[224] This is an alternative, and preferable, interpretation of the dictum in *A V Pound & Co Ltd v M W Hardy Inc*, cited above, fn.219; the issue of frustration was specifically left open in that case. cf. *Benjamin's Sale of Goods* (8th edn), paras 18–372—18–374. The question whether the contract is frustrated, or whether the parties escape liability on other grounds, is of more than academic interest: if there is no frustration the Law Reform (Frustrated Contracts) Act 1943 (below, para.19–095 et seq.) does not apply.

[225] *Peter Cassidy Seed Co Ltd v Osuustukkukaupa Ltd* [1957] 1 W.L.R. 273; *Pagnan Spa v Tradax Ocean Transport SA* [1987] 3 All E.R. 565; cf. *Congimex Companhia Geral, etc., SARL v Tradax Export SA* [1983] 1 Lloyd's Rep. 250 (absolute duty to obtain licence undertaken by buyer). "Clear words" are required to impose such an absolute duty, especially where the law prohibiting performance is passed after the time of contracting: *The Playa Larga* [1983] 2 Lloyd's Rep. 171 at 191.

[226] *Walton (Grain and Shipping) Ltd v British Italian Trading Co* [1959] 1 Lloyd's Rep. 223 at 226; *Johnson Matthey Bankers Ltd v State Trading Co of India* [1984] 1 Lloyd's Rep. 427 at 434.

licences. If such a change leads to the refusal of licences which previously had been issued as a matter of course,[227] it is possible that the change of policy may be regarded as a supervening event which is capable of frustrating the contract.[228]

(iii) *Partial and temporary illegality*

Whether contract frustrated. Whether partial or temporary illegality frustrates the contract depends (as in cases of partial impossibility[229]) on whether it defeats the main purpose of the contract. Thus in the *Denny, Mott* case[230] a long-term agreement for the sale of timber provided that "to enable the aforesaid agreement to be carried out" the buyer should let a timber yard to the seller. When dealings in timber under the agreement were prohibited, it was held that the whole contract was frustrated, since its main object, namely trading in timber, had become illegal. Hence the seller could not enforce the part of it that related to the letting of the yard. But in *Cricklewood Property Investment Trust Ltd v Leighton's Investment Trust Ltd*[231] temporary wartime restrictions on building did not frustrate a 99-year building lease; for the illegality did not destroy the main object of the lease as there would probably be ample time for building after the wartime restrictions were removed.

19–049

Whether excuses non-performance. The second question is whether illegality which does not frustrate the contract but affects only some subsidiary obligation excuses non-performance of that obligation. On principle it should have this effect. For example, a charterparty might provide that a ship should call at 10 ports. If one of them became an enemy port, the shipowner could hardly be made liable for failing to call there, even if it were physically possible for him to do so.[232] Where temporary illegality does not discharge the contract,[233] it has similarly been held to provide an excuse for non-performance for so long as the prohibition lasted.[234] But in *Eyre v Johnson*[235] a tenant was held liable in damages for breach of his covenant to repair even though wartime regulations made it illegal for him

19–050

---

[227] cf. the example given in *C Czarnikow Ltd v Centrala Handlu Zagranicznego "Rolimpex"* [1979] A.C. 351 at 372 (dog and television licences); *Johnson Matthey Bankers Ltd v State Trading Corp of India* [1984] 1 Lloyd's Rep. 427 at 429; contrast *Atisa SA v Aztec AG* [1983] 2 Lloyd's Rep. 579 (where the foreign government simply broke its contract to supply the seller).

[228] This was assumed in *Maritime National Fish Ltd v Ocean Trawlers Ltd* [1935] A.C. 524 (where the plea of frustration failed for reasons discussed at para.19–087, below); cf. also *Walton (Grain and Shipping) Ltd v British Trading Co* [1959] 1 Lloyd's Rep. 223 at 236 (where the seller was excused by a *force majeure* clause); *Congimex SARL (Lisbon) v Continental Grain Export Corp (New York)* [1979] 2 Lloyd's Rep. 386; *Nile Co for the Export of Agricultural Produce v H & J M Bennett (Commodities) Ltd* [1986] 1 Lloyd's Rep. 555 at 581–582.

[229] See above, para.19–011.

[230] [1944] A.C. 265; cf. *Nile Co for the Export of Agricultural Crops v H & J M Bennett (Commodities) Ltd* [1986] 1 Lloyd's Rep. 555 at 581 (foreign government imposing change on method of payment).

[231] [1945] A.C. 221; cf. *Islamic Republic of Iran Shipping Lines v Steamship Mutual Underwriting Association (Bermuda) Ltd* [2010] EWHC 2661 (Comm); [2011] 1 Lloyd's Rep. 195 (order preventing continuation of insurance cover allowed for temporary continuation of limited cover which was held still to be in force when the relevant insured event occurred).

[232] cf. *Hindley & Co Ltd v General Fibre Co Ltd* [1940] 2 K.B. 517.

[233] As in the *Cricklewood* case, above, fn.231.

[234] *Libyan Arab Foreign Bank v Bankers Trust Co* [1989] Q.B. 728 at 772 ("suspended but not discharged"); cf. *John Lewis Properties v Viscount Chelsea* [1993] 2 E.G.L.R. 77 (where it was not necessary to distinguish between impossibility and illegality).

[235] [1946] K.B. 481.

to do the work. The better view, however, is that the tenant ought not to be held liable for refusing to do an act which subsequent legislation has made illegal. Though the lease as a whole is not frustrated, the illegality should provide the tenant with an excuse for non-performance of the part that has become illegal.[236]

(d) Prospective Frustration

19–051   **Time for assessment.** A claim that a contract has been discharged may be made before there actually *has* been any (or any sufficiently serious) interference with performance, on the ground that supervening events have made it highly probable that there *will* be such interference. The general rule is that the effect of those events must then be determined, not by waiting to see how they actually affect performance, but by reference to the time when they occur. The point is well illustrated by *Embiricos v Sydney Reid & Co*[237] where a Greek ship had been chartered for a voyage involving passage of the Dardanelles. On the outbreak of war between Greece and Turkey, it was held that the charterer was justified in treating the contract as frustrated, even though later the Turkish authorities unexpectedly announced that Greek ships were to be allowed through the straits during an "escape period" which would have made performance of the contract voyage possible. Similarly, where requisition interferes with performance of a charterparty, the question whether it frustrates the contract is to be determined by reference to the time of requisition.[238] The reason for the rule is that rights should not be left indefinitely in suspense.[239]

19–052   **Qualification.** The rule is based on the assumption that the event is of such a kind that a reasonable view of its probable effect on the contract can be taken as soon as it occurs. Where this cannot be done, because the event is one which may equally well cause slight or serious interference with performance, the rule is necessarily subject to some qualification. This is, for example, the position where a strike of dockworkers interferes with performance of a charterparty.[240] The contract is not frustrated at once, as soon as the strike begins. It is "necessary to wait upon events"[241]—not, indeed, until the strike is over,[242] but until it has gone on for so long that a reasonable person would conclude that it was likely to interfere fundamentally with performance. This test determines not only the question whether the contract is frustrated, but also the date of frustration. The point arose in a number of cases in which ships which had been time-chartered were detained in the Shatt al Arab in the course of the Gulf War between Iran and

---

[236] *Cricklewood* case, above, fn.231, at 233, 244; *Sturcke v S W Edwards Ltd* (1971) 23 P. & C.R. 185 at 190; cf. *Brewster v Kitchell* (1691) 1 Salk. 198 ("the statute repeals the covenant"); *Grimsdick v Sweetman* [1909] 2 K.B. 740.

[237] [1914] 3 K.B. 45; so far as *contra*, *Andrew Miller v Taylor & Co Ltd* [1916] 1 K.B. 402 is criticised in *Watts, Watts & Co Ltd v Mitsui & Co Ltd* [1917] 2 A.C. 227 at 245.

[238] *Bank Line Ltd v Arthur Capel & Co* [1919] A.C. 435; cf. also *National Carriers Ltd v Panalpina (Northern) Ltd* [1981] A.C. 675 at 706; *Wong Lai Ying v Chinachem Investment Co* (1979) 13 Build. L.R. 81.

[239] ibid. at 454; cf. *Embiricos v Sydney Reid & Co* [1914] 3 K.B. 45 at 54, quoted above, para.17–086, at fn.398; *Total Gas Marketing Ltd v Arco British Ltd* [1998] 2 Lloyd's Rep. 209 at 222.

[240] As in *The Nema* [1982] A.C. 724.

[241] ibid. at 753.

[242] ibid. ("businessmen must not be required to await events too long"); cf. *Chakki v United Yeast Ltd* [1982] I.C.R. 140.

Iraq.[243] That war is generally regarded as having begun on September 22, 1980; but at that time commercial opinion was that the war would soon be brought to an end and that foreign vessels would be speedily released. Later events falsified these forecasts and there was no doubt that the length of the detention which occurred was sufficient to frustrate the charterparties. But it was held that the contracts could be frustrated before the detention had *actually* gone on for this length of time, and that they were frustrated as soon as "a sensible prognosis of the commercial probabilities"[244] could be made that the delay *would* continue for so long as to prevent the resumption of substantial services under the charterparties.[245] Similarly, where an employee suffered from a heart attack, his contract of employment was not discharged at once, but only when the effects of his heart attack could be assessed and "both sides accepted that . . . [he] was not going to work again".[246]

(e) Alternatives

A contract is said to impose an alternative obligation when it gives a party the right to choose between two or more specified performances (e.g. to deliver X or Y) or between two or more specified ways of rendering performance (e.g. to deliver X on any day in October[247]). The power of selection between the alternatives may be given to either party: e.g. a contract providing for goods to be delivered during a specified month, or at a range of ports, may give the power to choose the date or place of delivery or shipment to either seller[248] or buyer.[249] The general rule is that if a supervening event makes one of such alternative performances impossible or illegal, the contract is not discharged so long as another remains possible and lawful.[250] For example, if a contract is to deliver goods at X or Y, delivery must be made at X if delivery at Y has become impossible; if shipment is to be made from X or Y, shipment must be made from X if shipment from Y has become impossible.[251] The general rule, and the qualifications of it to be discussed below, apply not only where the contract is alleged to have been frustrated, but also where a party relies on the supervening event as providing him with an excuse under an express term of the contract, such as a force majeure clause.[252]

19–053

---

[243] *The Evia (No.2)* [1983] 1 A.C. 736; *The Wenjiang (No.2)* [1983] 1 Lloyd's Rep. 400; *The Chrysalis* [1983] 1 W.L.R. 1469.

[244] *The Evia (No.2)* [1982] 1 Lloyd's Rep. 334 at 346, affirmed [1983] 1 A.C. 736; *The Wenjiang (No.2)*, above, at 408; cf. *The Adelfa* [1988] 2 Lloyd's Rep. 466 (delay in unloading due to arrest of ship).

[245] Commercial arbitrators had fixed the date of frustration as October 4, 1980 in *The Evia (No.2)*, above, and as November 24, 1980 in *The Wenjiang (No.2)*, above, and in *The Chrysalis*, above. The courts expressed no opinion of their own as to the dates of frustration, merely holding that the arbitrators had applied the correct principle of law in fixing those dates.

[246] *Notcutt v Universal Equipment Co (London) Ltd* [1986] 1 W.L.R. 641 at 644.

[247] e.g. *Ross T Smyth & Co (Liverpool) v W N Lindsay (Leith)* [1953] 1 W.L.R. 1280 at 1283.

[248] ibid.

[249] e.g. *David T Boyd & Co Ltd v Louis Louca* [1973] 1 Lloyd's Rep. 209 (where no issue of discharge arose).

[250] *Barkworth v Young* (1856) 1 Drew. 1 at 25; *Reardon Smith Line Ltd v Ministry of Agriculture Fisheries and Food* [1963] A.C. 691 at 730; cf. *The Super Servant Two* [1989] 1 Lloyd's Rep. 148 at 157, affirmed [1990] 1 Lloyd's Rep. 1; for further difficulties arising from this case, see below, para.19–088.

[251] *The Furness Bridge* [1977] 2 Lloyd's Rep. 367; cf. *Warinco AG v Fritz Mauthner* [1978] 1 Lloyd's Rep. 151; *The Safeer* [1994] 1 Lloyd's Rep. 637 at 642.

[252] See above, para.19–036; cf. *Warinco* case, above, fn.251.

19–054   **Exceptions.** The general rule can be excluded by an express provision in the contract, e.g. by a strike clause which on its true construction excuses a seller if the port from which he intended to ship becomes strikebound, even though shipment from other ports within the contractual range remains possible.[253] Nor does the general rule apply where the contract calls for performance X and gives the party who is to render it a liberty to substitute Y: e.g. where a charterparty names ship X as its subject-matter but entitles the shipowner to substitute another ship. Under such a contract, X is due unless the liberty to substitute another ship (Y) is exercised,[254] while in the case of a true alternative obligation one cannot at the time of contracting tell whether X or Y is due. Hence, in the case of a liberty to substitute, the destruction of X before Y had been substituted, or the destruction of Y after the substitution had been made, would discharge the contract.[255] The distinction is further illustrated by contrasting a case in which a charterparty required the charterer to load a cargo of wheat, and gave him an "option" of instead loading rye,[256] with one in which a charterparty required the charterer to load a cargo of wheat or rye.[257] A contract of the first kind is sometimes said to confer a "contractual option" while one of the second kind is said to give rise to a "performance option".[258] Whatever terminology may be used to express the distinction, its effect (in the context of frustration) is clear. Supervening impossibility of loading wheat will discharge the contract in the first case (if the option to load rye has not been exercised when it became impossible to load wheat[259]); but it will not have this effect in the second case even if the charterer has indicated that he intends to load wheat.[260]

19–055   **Distinguished from contingent obligation.** An alternative obligation must also be distinguished from a contingent obligation: i.e. from one to do X but, if X is not done, to do Y.[261] Under such a contract, the primary obligation is to do X[262] and Y becomes due only if X is not performed and without any notice of election on the debtor's part.[263] Clearly the obligation to do X is not affected if it becomes impossible to do Y. Whether supervening impossibility of doing X is a ground of discharge depends on the construction of the contract: the contract would be discharged if it meant that Y was to become due if the debtor in *breach of contract* failed to do X, but not if it meant that Y was to become due if *for any reason* X was not done.

---

[253] *Sociedad Iberica de Molturacion SA v Tradax Export SA* [1978] 2 Lloyd's Rep. 545.
[254] *The Marine Star* [1993] 1 Lloyd's Rep. 329; *The Fjord Wind* [1999] 1 Lloyd's Rep. 307 at 328, affirmed [2000] 2 Lloyd's Rep. 191.
[255] See *The Badagry* [1985] 1 Lloyd's Rep. 395.
[256] *Reardon Smith Line Ltd v Ministry of Agriculture Fisheries and Food* [1963] A.C. 691.
[257] *Brightman & Co v Bunge y Born Limitada Sociedad* [1924] 2 K.B. 619, affirmed on another ground [1925] A.C. 799.
[258] *The Didymi and the Leon* [1984] 1 Lloyd's Rep. 583 at 587, per Sir John Donaldson M.R. A contractual term may also impose an *obligation* on one party to notify the other as to the way in, or time at, which performance is to be required. Such a term is distinct from one merely giving the former party an *option*: see *Universal Bulk Carriers Ltd v André & Cie* [2001] EWCA Civ 588; [2001] 2 Lloyd's Rep. 65 at [17].
[259] This follows from the reasoning of the *Reardon Smith* case, above, fn.256.
[260] *Brightman* case, above, fn.257 [1924] 2 K.B. 619 at 637; cf. ibid. at 630.
[261] See *Deverill v Burnell* (1873) L.R. 8 C.P. 475.
[262] In this respect it differs from a "performance option" (above, at fn.258).
[263] In this respect it differs from a "contractual option" (above, at fn.258).

(f) Events Affecting Only One Party's Performance

Both parties are discharged. In *Taylor v Caldwell*[264] the court was directly   **19–056**
concerned only with the liability of the defendants, the performance of whose
obligation to supply the music hall was made impossible by the fire. Yet the court
clearly regarded the hirers as also having been discharged,[265] even though their
principal obligation (to pay the agreed hire) had in no way become impossible.
This is a common situation: in a typical bilateral contract one party undertakes to
perform some act or abstention, while the other undertakes to pay for it. Supervening impossibility normally affects only the former undertaking (though illegality may affect either or both[266]). This fact was at one time thought to support the
view that a time charter could not be frustrated by the unavailability of the
ship:

> "if the shipowner's object is to receive the chartered hire . . . he does not care
> how much the charterer's adventures are frustrated, so long as he is able to
> pay".[267]

But the argument was rejected on the ground that the "common object"[268] of the
parties was frustrated; for even the owner's object "is not only to get hire but to
afford services".[269] The "common object" in all these cases is the *exchange* of the
services or facilities to be provided by one party for the payment to be made by
the other. The same reasoning applies to cases of frustration of purpose. In *Krell
v Henry*[270] the common object of the parties was the provision of facilities for
seeing the coronation processions: this was what one party intended to sell and the
other to buy. It made no difference that the one expected to benefit by receiving
a sum of money and the other by seeing the processions. Hence both parties are
discharged even though the supervening event affects only the performance of
one.

(g) Special Factors Affecting Land

(i) *Leases*

It was formerly thought that a lease of land could not be frustrated[271] because,   **19–057**
in giving the tenant the right to exclusive possession for the specified time, it
created a legal estate in the land. This estate was regarded as the subject-matter of
the contract and survived even if later events prevented the tenant from making
any use of the premises. But the commercial reality is that, generally, the tenant
bargains for use and occupation and not simply for a legal estate; and in *National*

---

[264] (1863) 3 B. & S. 826; above, para.19–003.
[265] ibid. at 840 ("both parties are excused").
[266] cf. *Libyan Arab Foreign Bank v Bankers Trust Co* [1989] Q.B. 728 at 749, recognising that "an
obligation to pay money can be frustrated" by illegality.
[267] *Bank Line Ltd v Arthur Capel & Co* [1919] A.C. 435 at 452.
[268] *Hirji Mulji v Cheong Yue SS Co Ltd* [1926] A.C. 497 at 507; contrast *Scanlan's New Neon v
Toohey's Ltd* (1943) 67 C.L.R. 169 at 196–197.
[269] *Bank Line Ltd v Arthur Capel & Co Ltd* [1919] A.C. 435 at 453.
[270] [1903] 2 K.B. 740; above, paras 19–004, 19–042.
[271] See the authorities cited in fnn.279–284, below.

Carriers Ltd v Panalpina (Northern) Ltd[272] the House of Lords held that the doctrine of frustration could apply to leases of land.

19–058   **Frustration a rare event.** At the same time it was emphasised that the frustration of a lease will be a very rare event.[273] One reason for this is that a lease for a long period of years is in the nature of a long-term speculation. Such a transaction is hard to frustrate since the parties must contemplate that circumstances may change radically during its currency, and so to a large extent take the risk of supervening events.[274] Nor would interruption of enjoyment which was likely to last for only a few years frustrate a lease for a long term, such as 99 years, since the ratio of the interruption to the whole would be too small.[275] Even the physical destruction of the premises would not usually frustrate since it would normally be covered by express provisions[276] in the lease, such as covenants to repair and to keep the premises insured. A further reason why frustration of leases is uncommon is that to hold a long-term lease frustrated by the destruction of the buildings on the land could, paradoxically, operate to the prejudice of *tenants*, especially in a period of rising land values. Frustration operates automatically,[277] so that its effect, in the case put, would be to deprive the tenant of a valuable site long before the end of the agreed term.

For these reasons, the House of Lords in the *National Carriers*[278] case did not disapprove any of the earlier decisions to the extent that they held that the leases in question *were not* frustrated.[279] In those cases it had been held that the leases were not discharged by the destruction of the premises by enemy action[280]; by the requisitioning of the premises[281]; by wartime legislation which prevented the tenant from residing on the premises[282] or from developing the land[283]; or by the death of the tenant of furnished rooms.[284] In the *National Carriers* case itself a tenant claimed that a 10-year lease of a warehouse had been frustrated when, four-and-a-half years before the end of the term, the only access road to the premises had been closed by the local authority and had remained closed for 20 months. The claim was rejected on the ground that the interruption was not sufficiently serious to bring about frustration.[285]

19–059   **Short-term leases.** The doctrine of frustration is most likely to apply where the lease is a short-term one for a particular purpose: e.g. where a holiday cottage which has been rented for a month is burnt down without the fault of either party.

---

[272] [1981] A.C. 675.
[273] ibid. at 692, 697.
[274] cf. below, para.19–069.
[275] cf. above, para.19–021.
[276] cf. below, para.19–070.
[277] See below, para.19–090.
[278] [1981] A.C. 675.
[279] Though ibid. at 715 *Matthey v Curling* [1922] 2 A.C. 180 was described as "a singularly harsh decision from the tenant's point of view."
[280] *Redmond v Dainton* [1920] 2 K.B. 256; *Denman v Brise* [1949] 1 K.B. 22; *Cusack-Smith v London Corp* [1956] 1 W.L.R. 1368.
[281] *Whitehall Court Ltd v Ettlinger* [1920] 1 K.B. 680; *Matthey v Curling* [1922] 2 A.C. 180; *Swift v Macbean* [1942] 1 K.B. 375.
[282] *London & Northern Estates Ltd v Schlesinger* [1916] 1 K.B. 20.
[283] *Cricklewood Property and Investment Trust Ltd v Leighton's Investment Trust Ltd* [1945] A.C. 221.
[284] *Youngmin v Heath* [1974] 1 W.L.R. 135.
[285] cf. above, para.19–005.

Similarly, the contracts in cases like *Taylor v Caldwell*[286] and *Krell v Henry*[287] could be frustrated, even if the transactions were expressed as leases and not (as they actually were) as licences.[288] A lease could also be frustrated if "some vast convulsion of nature swallowed up the property altogether, or buried it in the depths of the sea"; or if, in the case of a building lease, "legislation were subsequently passed which permanently prohibited private building in the area or dedicated it as an open space for ever".[289]

Agreement for a lease. The doctrine of frustration can apply to an agreement for a lease, no less than to an executed lease.[290]   **19–060**

Excuse for non-performance. Even where the lease is not frustrated, super-   **19–061**
vening events can nevertheless provide a party with an excuse for not performing a particular obligation imposed by the lease. In *Baily v De Crespigny*[291] a landlord covenanted that neither he nor his assigns would permit building on a paddock adjoining the land let. The paddock was then compulsorily acquired by a railway company, which built a station on it. It was held that the landlord was not liable in damages for breach of his covenant, first because on the true construction of the covenant "assigns" did not include assigns by compulsion of law, and secondly because it was impossible for him to secure performance of the covenant.[292] Similarly, a tenant who covenanted to build would not be liable in damages if wartime conditions or legislation made building impossible or illegal.[293]

(ii) *Sale of land*

The doctrine of frustration applies to contracts for the sale of land,[294] but its   **19–062**
operation in relation to such contracts is restricted by the rule that under such a contract risk of loss passes[295] (unless otherwise agreed) as soon as the contract is made. It follows that the contract is not frustrated if the house or buildings on the land (for the sake of which it was bought) are destroyed or seriously damaged between contract and completion.[296]

---

[286] (1863) 3 B. & S. 826; above, para.19–003.

[287] [1903] 2 K.B. 740; above, paras 19–004, 19–042.

[288] *Tay Salmon Fisheries Co v Speedie* 1929 S.C. 593 (lease of a salmon fishery held to be frustrated when construction of a nearby bombing range prevented the tenant from using the fishery).

[289] *Cricklewood* case [1945] A.C. 221 at 229; cf. at 240.

[290] *Denny, Mott & Dickson v James B Fraser & Co Ltd* [1944] A.C. 265 (a decision not confined to Scots Law: see the *National Carriers* case [1981] A.C. 675 at 704); *Rom Securities Ltd v Rogers (Holdings) Ltd* (1968) 205 E.G. 427; cf. *Property Discount Corp Ltd v Lyon Group Ltd* [1981] 1 W.L.R. 300 at 305.

[291] (1869) L.R. 4 Q.B. 180.

[292] The actual decision seems to be very unjust. The landlord presumably got compensation from the railway company and was able to keep this for himself though the tenant's interests were prejudiced by the erection of the station.

[293] *Cricklewood* case [1945] A.C. 221 at 233; *Eyre v Johnson* [1946] K.B. 481, *contra*, is doubted at para.19–050, above.

[294] This is assumed in *Amalgamated Investment and Property Co Ltd v John Walker & Co Ltd* [1977] 1 W.L.R. 164, where, for reasons stated at para.19–043, above, the contract was not frustrated.

[295] See above, para.19–013.

[296] *Paine v Meller* (1801) 6 Ves. 349; *E Johnson & Co (Barbados) Ltd v NSR Ltd* [1997] A.C. 400 at 406.

19–063   **Express contractual provision.** The rule promoted certainty by making it unnecessary to ask whether partial destruction was sufficiently serious to bring about frustration. On the other hand, it could cause hardship to the purchaser by making him bear the risk of losses occurring before he had possession and hence before he could take steps to safeguard the property. The hardship was mitigated by the fact that the purchaser had the benefit of the vendor's insurance[297]; but as he could not be sure of the adequacy of this insurance he would normally take out his own insurance as soon as contracts were exchanged. This position could lead to double insurance and hence to a windfall for insurers. The rule that risk passes on contract is therefore commonly varied by contract: e.g. by provisions leaving the risk with the seller till completion, and giving a right to rescind the contract *either* to the purchaser if the property has become unusable for its purpose, *or* to the vendor in the event of damage which it is not legally possible for the vendor to make good.[298]

19–064   **Sale of land with buildings to be constructed.** The rule that risk passes on contract applies where the land is sold with buildings already on it. Where a developer sells land with a house *to be built* on it, the risk *of the work* remains (unless otherwise agreed) on the vendor until the work is completed, in accordance with the rules applicable to building contracts.[299] Hence destruction of the partly completed building does not frustrate the contract and the vendor must do the work again at no extra cost. But the contract may be frustrated on other grounds. Thus where a landslip not only destroyed a partly completed block of flats, but also delayed the construction work for two-and-a-half years, it was held that a contract for the sale of one of the flats was frustrated *by the delay*; for in the interval market conditions had changed to such an extent as to make performance at the end of the delay radically different from that originally undertaken.[300]

19–065   **Compulsory purchase.** Specific performance of a contract for the sale of land can be ordered against the purchaser even though, after contract, a compulsory purchase order is made in respect of the land.[301] The contract is not frustrated because the risk of compulsory acquisition is on the purchaser from the time of the contract[302]; and because the court's order will result in the conveyance of the land to him, against payment of the price, so that he will in due course get the compensation payable by the acquiring authority. Where, in pursuance of the compulsory acquisition order, the land is taken over by the acquiring authority *after* completion has become due, but before the hearing, the court will not order *specific* performance, since it cannot order the vendor to convey, but the contract is not frustrated, so that the purchaser's failure to complete on the due day is a breach for which he is liable in damages.[303] The position is different where the land is sold with vacant possession and is actually requisitioned *before* completion is due. In such a case it has been held, not only that the vendor cannot specifically

[297] Law of Property Act 1925, s.47 (above, para.14–128, at fn.801).
[298] Law Society's Standard Conditions of Sale (4th edn), Conditions 5.1.1 to 5.1.4.
[299] See above, para.19–015.
[300] *Wong Lai Ying v Chinachem Investment Co* (1979) 13 Build. L.R. 81.
[301] *Hillingdon Estates Co v Stonefield Estate Co* [1952] Ch. 627. The mere making of such an order does not affect ownership of the land.
[302] See above, para.19–062.
[303] *E Johnson Co (Barbados) Ltd v NSR Ltd* [1997] A.C. 400.

enforce the contract[304] (since he cannot perform his obligation to give possession on the due date), but also that the purchaser can get back his deposit.[305] It must follow from this reasoning that the purchaser will not be liable in damages.

(h) Fact or Law

The question whether frustration is a matter of fact or law used to be important in determining the respective functions of judge and jury. Trial by jury is now rare in civil cases; but the question whether frustration is a matter of fact or law is still important in determining whether a court can control an arbitrator's finding. Such a finding is generally conclusive on matters of fact,[306] but does not bind the court when determining appeals from arbitrators on points of law.   **19–066**

Frustration a question of law. The point is illustrated by the Suez cases where such questions as the greater length and cost of a voyage round the Cape of Good Hope and its physical effect on the ship or the goods were clearly questions of fact. In the *Tsakiroglou* case[307] the arbitrator found, in general terms, that performance of the contract by shipping via the Cape was "not commercially or fundamentally different from" performance by shipping via Suez. The House of Lords agreed with this finding, but added that it did not bind the court as the question whether the difference was fundamental was one of law[308] or one of mixed law and fact.[309]   **19–067**

Limits of review by the courts. It does not follow from the description of the issue of frustration as one of law that the court will substitute its own view for that taken by an arbitrator merely because it disagrees with his conclusion. It will do so only if the arbitrator has applied the wrong legal test or, while purporting to apply the correct test, has reached a conclusion which no reasonable person would have reached on the primary facts as found.[310] That said, the issue of frustration arises in "a wide range of different factual circumstances" ranging from those which call for "the evaluation of a range of factors which a commercial tribunal is particularly well equipped to undertake" to those which call for "the application of established principles to a clearly defined event rendering performance impossible".[311] In the case of the latter, the court must accept the findings of fact made by the arbitrators, but need not "be unduly inhibited by the arbitrators' conclusion that the facts they have found are sufficient to satisfy the legal test for frustration".[312]   **19–068**

---

[304] *Cook v Taylor* [1942] Ch. 349.

[305] *James Macara Ltd v Barclays Bank Ltd* [1945] K.B. 148.

[306] See, e.g. *Universal Petroleum Co Ltd v Handels und Transport Gesellschaft mbH* [1987] 1 Lloyd's Rep. 517.

[307] [1962] A.C. 93.

[308] cf. *Re Comptoir Commercial Anversois and John Power Sons & Co* [1920] 1 K.B. 868; *The Captain George K* [1970] 2 Lloyd's Rep. 21; *The Wenjiang (No.2)* [1983] 1 Lloyd's Rep. 400 at 402.

[309] [1962] A.C. 93 at 116 and 123; *The Chrysalis* [1983] 1 W.L.R. 1469 at 1475.

[310] *The Nema* [1982] A.C. 724 (disapproving on this point *The Angelia* [1973] 1 W.L.R. 210); *The Wenjiang (No.2)* [1983] 1 Lloyd's Rep. 400; *The Chrysalis* [1983] 1 W.L.R. 1469 at 1475; *The Safeer* [1994] 1 Lloyd's Rep. 637.

[311] *The Mary Nour* [2008] EWCA Civ 856; [2008] 2 Lloyd's Rep. 526 at [11], per Moore-Bick L.J.; *The Nema*, above is cited as a prime example of the former category; *The Mary Nour* itself (see above, para.19–026 fn.104) is regarded as an example of the latter.

[312] ibid.

3. LIMITATIONS

19–069   Even if an event occurs which would normally frustrate a contract under the rules so far considered, the doctrine of frustration may be excluded if the contract provides for the event; if the event was foreseen or foreseeable; or if it was due to the "fault" of one of the parties.

(a) Contractual Provision for the Event

(i) *In general*

19–070   **Express exclusion of frustration.** The object of the doctrine of frustration is to find a satisfactory way of allocating the risk of supervening events. There is, however, nothing to prevent the parties from making their own provisions for this purpose. Thus they can expressly provide that the risk of supervening events shall be borne by one of them and not by the other[313] or they can apportion it or deal with it in various other ways.[314] Such provisions exclude frustration[315]; and the same is true of an express term which, though it does not precisely cover the supervening event, shows that the parties had contemplated it and allocated the risk of its occurrence.[316]

19–071   **Implied exclusion of frustration.** A provision that excludes frustration may also be implied: e.g. where the nature of the contract makes it clear that the parties intended the risk of supervening events to lie where it falls. In *Larrinaga & Co v Société Franco-Américaine des Phosphates de Médulla*[317] a contract was made in 1913 for the carriage of six cargoes of phosphates between March 1918 and November 1920. After the end of the First World War, the carriers argued that the contract was frustrated because of the altered shipping conditions then prevailing. The argument was rejected by the House of Lords. A contract of this kind, not to be performed for many years, was essentially speculative,[318] since each party had consciously taken the risk that conditions might alter. An implied agreement to exclude frustration may also be based on other characteristics of a transaction. In *The Maira (No.2)* agents had undertaken to manage a ship which was subsequently lost. It was held that this did not frustrate the management contract since the parties could hardly have intended "that the managers should be entitled to wash their hands of all duties concerning the vessel as soon as [it] was lost"[319]: they would be expected to attend to such matters as the repatriation of the crew and the settlement of claims arising out of the loss. It is finally possible for legislation to provide for the implication of a term which excludes frustration.[320]

---

[313] *Budgett v Binnington & Co* [1891] 1 Q.B. 35 at 41; *Thiis v Byers* (1876) 1 Q.B.D. 244.

[314] e.g. by provisions of the type mentioned at para.19–006 above, or by provisions for flexible pricing (above, para.19–037), as in *Wates Ltd v GLC* (1983) 25 Build. L.R. 1.

[315] *Joseph Constantine SS Line Ltd v Imperial Smelting Corp Ltd* [1942] A.C. 154 at 163; *The Safeer* [1994] 1 Lloyd's Rep. 637.

[316] *Bangladesh Export Import Co Ltd v Sucden Kerry SA* [1995] 2 Lloyd's Rep. 1; cf. *Select Commodities Ltd v Valdo SA* [2006] EWHC 1137 (Comm); [2007] 1 Lloyd's Rep. 1 (liberty clause in charterparty not found to exclude doctrine of frustration).

[317] (1923) 92 L.J.K.B. 455.

[318] cf. above, para.1–003.

[319] [1985] 1 Lloyd's Rep. 300 at 311, affirmed on other grounds [1986] 2 Lloyd's Rep. 12.

[320] See above, at fn.66.

(ii) *Qualifications*

Trading with the enemy. A contract may be frustrated by supervening **19–072** illegality on the ground that it involves trading with the enemy; and such frustration is not excluded by a contrary provision in the contract. In *Ertel Bieber & Co v Rio Tinto Co Ltd*[321] an English company contracted to deliver copper ore to a German company from 1911 to 1919. It was held that the contract was wholly frustrated on the outbreak of war in 1914 even though it provided that, in the event of war, certain obligations should only be suspended; for to give effect to this provision would, for reasons stated earlier in this chapter, be contrary to public policy.[322] The rule is based on the particular strength of the policy against giving aid to the economy of an enemy in time of war. It does not apply to express provisions which deal with other kinds of supervening illegality, such as prohibition of export. If, for example, a contract provides for a payment to be made in the event of such a prohibition,[323] or for suspension of the contract, followed by its termination if the prohibition is not lifted by the end of a specified period,[324] frustration is effectively excluded. Clauses of this kind are not contrary to public policy[325] since they assume that the prohibition is going to be observed, and since the continuation of the contractual relationship in cases of this kind does not have any tendency to subvert the purpose of the prohibition.

Provision narrowly construed. A clause may be literally wide enough to **19–073** cover the event, but be held on its true construction not to have this effect. In *Metropolitan Water Board v Dick, Kerr & Co*[326] contractors agreed in July 1914 to construct a reservoir in six years; in the event of delays "however occasioned", they were to be given an extension of time. In February 1916, the contractors were required by a Government Order to stop work, and to sell their plant. It was held that the contract was frustrated although the events which had happened were literally within the delay clause. That clause was meant to apply to temporary difficulties, such as labour shortages, bad weather, or failure of supplies. It did not

> "cover the case in which the interruption is of such a character and duration that it vitally and fundamentally changes the conditions of the contract, and could not possibly have been in the contemplation of the parties to the contract when it was made".[327]

---

[321] [1918] A.C. 260; such clauses may also be narrowly construed, so as not to refer to war between the countries to which the contracting parties belong: *Re Badische Co Ltd* [1921] 2 Ch. 331 at 379; cf. *Fibrosa* case [1943] A.C. 32.

[322] ibid. at 286; above, para.19–045.

[323] e.g. *Johnson Matthey Bankers Ltd v State Trading Corp of India* [1984] 1 Lloyd's Rep. 427.

[324] e.g. in the *Tsakiroglou* case [1962] A.C. 93 at 95.

[325] *Johnson Matthey* case, above, at 434.

[326] [1918] A.C. 119; *The Penelope* [1928] P. 180 (approved, though with some reservations, in *The Nema* [1982] A.C. 724 at 754); cf. *Fibrosa* case [1943] A.C. 32 at 40; *C Czarnikow Ltd v Centrala Handlu Zagranicznego Rolimpex* [1979] A.C. 351; *Wong Lai Ying v Chinachem Investment Co* (1979) 13 Build. L.R. 81; *The Playa Larga* [1983] 2 Lloyd's Rep. 171 at 189; *Notcutt v Universal Equipment Co (London) Ltd* [1986] 1 W.L.R. 641 at 647; *F C Shepherd & Co Ltd v Jerrom* [1987] Q.B. 301.

[327] [1918] A.C. 119 at 126.

A fortiori, an express provision in a contract for *some* events which might otherwise frustrate it does not exclude the possibility of frustration by *other* events.[328]

19–074   **Provision incomplete.** A clause may make some provision for the event which happens, but fail to make complete provision for it. In *Bank Line Ltd v Arthur Capel & Co*[329] a shipowner was sued for damages for failing to deliver a ship due under a charterparty. He pleaded that the contract was frustrated by the requisition of the ship. The charterer argued that frustration was excluded by two clauses giving him, but not the owner, the option to cancel if the ship was commandeered by the Government or if she was not delivered by April 30, 1915. But the House of Lords held that the charterparty was frustrated. Lord Sumner said that a contract could not be frustrated by a contingency for which it made "full and complete"[330] provision; but he added:

> "A contingency may be provided for, but not in such terms as to show that the provision is meant to be all the provision for it. A contingency may be provided for, but in such a way as shows that it is provided for only for the purpose of dealing with one of its effects and not with all".[331]

Requisition or delay might frustrate the charterparty, but would not necessarily have this effect, e.g. if performance were only delayed by one week. The cancelling clauses entitled the charterer to cancel even if the contract was *not* frustrated. He could *escape* liability in that event. It did not follow that the shipowner should *remain* liable if requisition or delay did amount to frustration.

This principle is further illustrated by *Jackson v Union Marine Ins Co*[332] where a charterparty provided that the ship should proceed with all possible dispatch (dangers and accidents of navigation excepted) to Newport. On the way there she was so badly damaged that she was not ready for service for eight months. The charterparty was held to be frustrated in spite of the provision excepting dangers and accidents of navigation. One possible explanation is that these words were not intended to cover so long a delay as had actually occurred.[333] But the reason given by the court was that the words of the exception "excuse the shipowner, but give him no right".[334] A delay caused by dangers and accidents of navigation might (but for the exception) have amounted either to a breach or to a frustrating event. The effect of the exception was to prevent the delay from constituting a breach. It did not deal with the effect of such delay as a possible frustrating event, and thus did not rule out frustration. To say that the shipowner is not liable for a delay does not lead necessarily to the conclusion that he can enforce the contract in spite of the delay.

---

[328] *Intertradex SA v Lesieur-Torteaux SARL* [1978] 2 Lloyd's Rep. 509 at 515.

[329] [1919] A.C. 435; cf. *BP Exploration (Libya) Ltd v Hunt* [1979] 1 W.L.R. 783 at 830 (affirmed [1983] 2 A.C. 352); *The Evia* [1982] 1 Lloyd's Rep. 334 (affirmed [1983] 1 A.C. 736 at 767).

[330] ibid. at 455.

[331] ibid. at 456.

[332] (1874) L.R. 10 C.P. 125.

[333] *Sir Lindsay Parkinson & Co Ltd v Commissioners of Works* [1949] 2 K.B. 632 at 665.

[334] At 144; cf. *Blane Steamships Ltd v Minister of Transport* [1951] 2 K.B. 965, where the words of the charterparty excused the charterer but were held to give him no rights.

(iii) *Provision for non-frustrating events*

In its practical operation, the doctrine of frustration can give rise to two   **19–075**
problems. It can be a source of *uncertainty* because it is often hard to tell whether
the effect of supervening events on the contract is indeed sufficiently serious to
discharge it. And it can be a source of *hardship* because, as a result of its narrow
scope, a party may remain bound by a contract in spite of the fact that supervening
events have made it substantially more burdensome or less beneficial than he could
reasonably have expected. To avoid these difficulties, the contract may provide for
discharge on the occurrence of specified events, or by other events "beyond the
control" of the parties or of one of them[335] and such a provision may take effect
whether or not the effect of the event is such as to frustrate the contract under the
general law. Such a clause may either give one of the parties the option to cancel
the contract,[336] or provide for its automatic determination.[337] A clause of the latter
kind has been described as a "contractual frustration clause".[338] The point of this
description is, however, simply that the *effect* of the clause resembles that of
frustration, in giving rise to automatic discharge.[339] The question *whether* the
clause operates in the events which have happened depends simply on its construction[340] and not on the tests of frustration developed by the general law; and,
if the clause does come into operation, the contract is discharged under one of its
express terms and not under the general doctrine of frustration.[341]

(b) Foreseen and Foreseeable Events[342]

(i) *In general*

No frustration for foreseen or foreseeable events. Where the parties can at   **19–076**
the time of contracting foresee the risk that a supervening event may interfere with
performance, the normal inference is that their contract was made with reference
to that risk. If, for example, the event would make performance more expensive for
one party, he is likely to increase his charges; if, on the other hand, it would
frustrate the other's purpose, he is likely to reduce the amount that he is willing
to pay. Having thus allocated the risk by their contract, the parties should not be

---

[335] Such a clause is normally construed so as to protect the party relying on it only if he has taken
all reasonable steps to avoid the operation of the event or to mitigate its results: see *Channel Island
Ferries Ltd v Sealink UK Ltd* [1988] 1 Lloyd's Rep. 323; *The Kriti Rex* [1996] 2 Lloyd's Rep. 171 at
196; contrast (on the point of construction) *The Marine Star (No.2)* [1996] 2 Lloyd's Rep. 383.
[336] e.g. *Bank Line Ltd v Arthur Capel & Co* [1918] A.C. 119.
[337] e.g. in the *Tsakiroglou* case: [1962] A.C. 93 at 95.
[338] *Bremer Handelsgesellschaft mbH v Vanden Avenne-Izegem PVBA* [1978] 2 Lloyd's Rep. 109 at
112.
[339] See below, para.19–090.
[340] See, e.g. *Hoecheong Products Ltd v Cargill Hong Kong Ltd* [1995] 1 Lloyd's Rep. 584; *The Kriti
Rex* [1996] 2 Lloyd's Rep. 171.
[341] *Agrokor AG v Tradigrain SA* [2000] 1 Lloyd's Rep. 497 at 504. Hence the Law Reform
(Frustrated Contracts) Act 1943 (below, para.19–095) will not apply. Nor would such clauses be subject
to Unfair Contract Terms Act 1977 since they are clauses defining duties rather than exemption clauses
(above, para.7–055). Nor would they normally be open to attack under Unfair Terms in Consumer
Contracts Regulations 1999 (above, para.7–095 et seq.) since a term operating only in circumstances
beyond control of the party relying on it would not normally be unfair: cf. Sch.2, para.1(g) ("except
where there are serious grounds . . . ").
[342] Hall 4 *Legal Studies* 300.

discharged if the event indeed occurs[343]; the loss caused by the event should lie where it falls. As Vaughan Williams L.J. has said, "The test [of frustration] seems to be whether the event which causes the impossibility was or might have been anticipated . . . ".[344] Many other dicta similarly support the view that a contract cannot be frustrated by foreseen or foreseeable events[345]; and in other jurisdictions pleas of frustration have been rejected on this ground.[346] There is no English case in which this was the sole ground for rejecting the plea; but it has been held that a party cannot rely, as a ground of frustration, on an event which was, or should have been, foreseen by him but not by the other party. In *Walton Harvey Ltd v Walker & Homfrays Ltd*[347] the defendants granted the claimants the right to display an advertising sign on the defendants' hotel for seven years. Within this period the hotel was compulsorily acquired, and demolished, by a local authority acting under statutory powers. The defendants were held liable in damages. The contract was not frustrated because the defendants knew, and the claimants did not, of the risk of compulsory acquisition. "They could have provided against that risk, but they did not".[348]

(ii) *Qualifications*

19–077   **Trading with the enemy.** A contract may be frustrated by supervening illegality resulting from the wartime prohibition against trading with the enemy, in spite of the fact that the war was a foreseeable event. Even an express provision against frustration does not save the contract in such a case[349]; and the policy considerations which justify this rule apply just as strongly where the event was or should have been foreseen. Thus contracts made in the summer of 1939 could be frustrated as a result of the outbreak of war with Germany in September although this event was foreseeable.

19–078   **Degree and extent of foreseeability.** The inference that the parties contracted with reference to the event (and so took the risk of its occurrence) can be drawn only if the event was either actually foreseen or if the degree of foreseeability was a very high one.[350] It is not sufficient for the low degree of foreseeability which constitutes the test of remoteness in tort[351] to be satisfied. In this sense, it was no doubt "foreseeable" that King Edward VII (who was 60 years old at the

---

[343] See *Comptoir Commercial Anversois v Power, Son & Co* [1920] 1 K.B. 868 at 895, 901.

[344] *Krell v Henry* [1903] 2 K.B. 740 at 752.

[345] *Baily v De Crespigny* (1869) L.R. 4 Q.B. 180 at 185; *Tamplin* case [1916] 2 A.C. 397 at 424; *Bank Line* case [1919] A.C. 435 at 458; *Re Badische Co Ltd* [1921] 2 Ch. 331 at 379; *Cricklewood* case [1945] A.C. 221 at 228; *Fareham* case [1956] A.C. 696 at 731; *Denmark Productions Ltd v Boscobel Productions Ltd* [1969] 1 Q.B. 699 at 725; *The Hannah Blumenthal* [1983] 1 A.C. 854 at 909; *Gamerco SA v ICM (Fair Warning) Agency Ltd* [1995] 1 W.L.R. 1226 at 1231; cf. in the context of setting aside consent orders in the light of supervening events, *S v S* [2002] EWHC 223; [2003] Fam. 1.

[346] *Baetjer v New England Alcohol Co* 66 N.E.2d 748 (1946); *Glidden v Hellenic Lines* 275 F.2d 253 at 256 (1960).

[347] [1931] 1 Ch. 274.

[348] ibid. at 282.

[349] See above, para.19–045.

[350] *The Sea Angel* [2007] EWCA Civ 547; [2007] 2 Lloyd's Rep. 517 at [104], [127] where the submissions were described as "over-refined": "the less that an event . . . is foreseeable, the more likely it is to be a factor which, depending on other factors in the case, may lead to frustration".

[351] See below, para.20–113.

time) might fall ill on the day fixed for his coronation.[352] To support the inference of risk-assumption, the event must be one which any person of ordinary intelligence would regard as likely to occur. Moreover, the event or its consequences must be foreseeable in some detail. It is not sufficient that *a* delay or *some* interference with performance can be foreseen if *the* delay or interference which occurs is wholly different in extent. We have seen that this distinction restricts the scope of express provisions for a supervening event[353]; and there is no reason why it should not equally apply in relation to events alleged to have been foreseeable or foreseen. Where the "relevant" risk is foreseeable, it is unnecessary to draw distinctions between what are no more than "variants on a theme".[354] Thus, in *The Sea Angel*,[355] the relevant risk was the unreasonable detention by the port authorities of a vessel used for a salvage operation where there was a risk of pollution; it did not matter whether that detention was for the purpose of ensuring the continuation of the salvage operation, or, as was the case, to secure a claim against a third party responsible for the pollution.

Tatem Ltd v Gamboa. It is submitted that the points made above as to the   **19–079** degree and extent of foreseeability provide the best explanation for cases in which it was said that a contract could be frustrated by foreseen or foreseeable events. One such case is *W J Tatem Ltd v Gamboa*.[356] During the Spanish Civil War, the defendant, as agent for the Republicans, chartered a ship for 30 days from July 1 "for the evacuation of civil population from North Spain". Hire was to be paid at the rate of £250 per day "until her redelivery to the owners", but was to cease if the ship was "missing". On July 14 the ship was seized by the Nationalists, who kept her until September 7, so that she was not redelivered to the owners till September 11. The charterers had paid hire in advance up to July 31, but the owners claimed further hire from August 1 to September 11. Goddard J. rejected the claim on the ground that the charterparty was frustrated. The actual decision can be justified on the ground that it was *not* foreseeable that the ship would be detained "not only for the period of her charter but for a long period thereafter".[357] But Goddard J. added that the contract would have been frustrated even if that risk had been foreseen:

> "If the true foundation of the doctrine [of frustration] is that once the subject-matter of the contract is destroyed or the existence of a certain state of facts has come to an end, the contract is at an end, that result follows whether or not the event causing it was contemplated by the parties".[358]

But it is submitted that a contract is not necessarily at an end if the existence of a certain state of facts has come to an end; for the parties may have been engaged

---

[352] cf. the express provisions made in some of the contracts for the possibility of postponement: e.g. *Victoria Seats Agency v Paget* (1902) 19 T.L.R. 16. According to D.N.B., 2d Supp. p.591, "A few days before the date appointed for the great ceremony rumours of the King's ill-health gained currency and were denied."

[353] See above, para.19–046.

[354] *The Sea Angel* [2007] EWCA Civ 547; [2007] 2 Lloyd's Rep. 517 at [128]

[355] ibid.

[356] [1939] 1 K.B. 132.

[357] ibid. at 135.

[358] ibid. at 138; cf. *The Captain George K* [1970] 2 Lloyd's Rep. 21 at 31.

in a deliberate speculation on this point.[359] A similar objection applies to the suggestion[360] that an event can frustrate a contract, even though it "was or ought to have been foreseen", if it was "outside the scope of the contract on its true construction". It is submitted that it would be wrong first to construe the contract and *then* to have regard to the fact that the event was foreseen; for that fact must be of crucial importance in determining "the scope of the contract", i.e. whether the parties took the risk of the occurrence of the event.[361] Where they actually foresaw the event, the more natural inference is that each of them took that risk unless the contract expressly protected him. In *W J Tatem Ltd v Gamboa* the contract did not expressly protect the defendant from liability if the ship were seized and detained. The inference that he accepted the risk of these events (to the extent to which they were foreseen[362]) is strengthened by the fact that the contract did expressly protect him against another foreseen risk, namely, that the ship might be lost; in that event his liability to pay hire was to cease.[363]

19–080   *The Eugenia.* Another such case is *The Eugenia.*[364] In September 1956, the defendants wished to charter the owners' ship to carry iron goods from Russian Black Sea ports to India. At that time "mercantile men realised that there was a risk that the Suez Canal might be closed"[365] because of the Suez crisis. The agents of the parties appreciated this risk and each made a suggestion for dealing with it.[366] But when the charterparty was concluded on September 19, nothing was expressly said about the risk of closure. The reason may be that before November 16 "mercantile men would not have formed any conclusion as to whether the obstructions in the Canal were other than temporary".[367] The actual decision was that the contract was not frustrated by the closure of the Canal on October 31, resulting in the detention of the ship: the charterers could not rely on the detention as it was due to their prior breach of contract and thus "self-induced"[368]; nor on the extra length of the voyage as the difference between a voyage via the Canal and one via the Cape was not sufficiently fundamental.[369] But Lord Denning M.R. also seemed to reject the further argument that frustration might have been excluded on the ground that at the time of contracting the closure of the Canal was foreseeable. He said:

> "It has often been said that the doctrine of frustration only applies where the new situation is 'unforeseen' or 'unexpected' or 'uncontemplated' as if that were an essential feature. But it is not so. The only thing that is essential is that [the parties] should have made no provision for it in the contract".[370]

---

[359] cf. above, paras 1–003, 19–070.

[360] *Nile Co for the Export of Agriculture Crops v H & J M Bennett (Commodities) Ltd* [1986] 1 Lloyd's Rep. 555 at 582.

[361] *The Sea Angel* [2006] EWHC 1713 (Comm); [2006] 2 C.L.C. 600 at [84iv]; affirmed on appeal [2007] EWCA Civ 547; [2007] 2 Lloyd's Rep. 517.

[362] See above, at fn.357.

[363] The shipowners may have found it easier to insure against loss than against detention and have distinguished for this reason between the effect of the two events.

[364] [1964] 2 Q.B. 226.

[365] [1963] 2 Lloyd's Rep. at 159. The facts are more fully stated in this report.

[366] ibid.

[367] ibid. at 162.

[368] See below, para.19–083.

[369] See above, para.19–030.

[370] [1964] 2 Q.B. 226 at 239.

But these remarks are obiter and it is respectfully submitted that this aspect of the decision can be explained on other grounds. At the time of contracting, the risk of the Canal's being closed for a *very considerable time* was not foreseen; nor was it foreseeable on the high standard of foreseeability[371] required to exclude frustration. To the extent that the parties did foresee the risk, they seem to have allocated it by the terms of the charterparty. This provided that the voyage was to be paid for by the time it took,[372] so indicating an intention to throw the risk of delay on the charterers. There seems to be no reason why the court should, by applying the doctrine of frustration to foreseen events, reverse such an allocation of risks deliberately made by the contracting parties.

Contrary intention. The inference that the parties have assumed the risk of foreseen (or readily foreseeable) events is only a prima facie one and can be excluded by evidence of contrary intention. The parties may foresee an event and intend, if it occurs, "to leave the lawyers to sort it out"[373]; or they may actually provide that if the event occurs they will then determine how it is to affect the contract.[374] If the lawyers cannot "sort it out" or if the parties cannot reach agreement, the contract may then be frustrated even though the event was foreseen. **19–081**

Similar reasoning explains *Bank Line Ltd v Arthur Capel Ltd*[375] where a charterparty was frustrated although the parties foresaw that the ship might be requisitioned and actually made some provision for this event. But it is by no means clear that the parties foresaw a requisition of such long duration as would frustrate the contract. Even if they did foresee this, the very fact that they had made *some* provision for the event complicated the issue. The contract entitled the charterer to cancel on requisition (so that the risk of the event was clearly not meant to be on him); but it made no reference to the effect of requisition on the liability of the owner. One could infer from this silence that the parties had decided to throw the risk of requisition on him, or that they had not thought about its effect on his liability at all. If the latter inference is correct, the contract could be frustrated although requisition was foreseen, and the House of Lords so held. The normal inference that parties take the risk of foreseen events was displaced by the special terms of the contract.

(c) Self-induced Frustration

A party cannot rely on "self-induced frustration",[376] that is, on frustration due to his own conduct or to the conduct of those for whom he is responsible.[377] **19–082**

---

[371] See above, para.19–078.

[372] The contract was in the form of a "time charter trip" which has become common: see *The Cebu* [1983] 1 Lloyd's Rep. 302 at 305.

[373] *The Eugenia* [1964] 2 Q.B. 226 at 234.

[374] *Autry v Republic Productions* 180 P.2d 888 (1947).

[375] [1919] A.C. 435; above, para.19–074.

[376] *Bank Line* case, above, fn.375, at 452; *Sudbrook Trading Estate Ltd v Eggleton* [1983] 1 A.C. 444 at 497; Swanton 2 J.C.L. 699.

[377] Frustration is not self-induced where the cause of the delay is the act of a third party for whom the defendant is *not* responsible: see *The Adelfa* [1988] 2 Lloyd's Rep. 466 at 471; nor merely because one of the parties is an enterprise controlled by a State which has by some legislative or executive act prevented performance of the contract or made it illegal: *C Czarnikow Ltd v Centrala Handlu Zagranicznego "Rolimpex"* [1979] A.C. 351 at 372; *The Playa Larga* [1983] 2 Lloyd's Rep. 171 at 192.

19–083   **No frustration as a consequence of breach.** The doctrine of frustration obviously does not protect a party whose own breach of contract actually is, or brings about, the frustrating event. Nor does it protect him if the breach is only one of the factors leading to frustration. Thus a charterer who in breach of contract orders a ship into a war-zone, so that she is detained, cannot rely on the detention as a ground of frustration.[378] Similarly, unseaworthiness amounting to a breach of contract may cause delays in the prosecution of the voyage; and if war intervenes, so that the voyage cannot be completed, the carrier will be liable in damages[379]; such cases show that even an omission (i.e. failure to make the ship seaworthy) can sometimes exclude frustration.[380] The doctrine likewise does not apply where the circumstances alleged to have brought it into operation result partly from the breach of one party and partly from that of the other, e.g. where both breaches contribute to an allegedly frustrating delay.[381]

19–084   **Deliberate acts.** Where the allegedly frustrating event results from one party's deliberate act, that party cannot rely on it as a ground of frustration, even though the act is not in itself a breach of the contract[382]; but the other party may be able to rely on it for this purpose. Thus where an employee has been prevented from performing the agreed work because he has been imprisoned for a criminal offence, the employer can rely on this circumstance as a ground of frustration, so as to defeat a claim by the employee for unfair dismissal; and he can do this even though the offence had no connection with the employment, so that its mere commission did not amount to a breach of the contract.[383] But an attempt by the employee to set up the imprisonment as a ground of frustration, in an action against him by the employer on the contract, would fail[384] on the ground that the employee could not rely on self-induced frustration.

(ii) *Negligence*

19–085   **No frustration as a consequence of negligence.** Lord Simon has put the case of a prima donna who failed to perform a contract because she had lost her

---

[378] *The Eugenia* [1964] 2 Q.B. 226; *The Lucille* [1984] 1 Lloyd's Rep. 244; cf. *Mertens v Home Freeholds Co* [1921] 2 K.B. 526.

[379] See *Monarch SS Co v A/B Karlshamns Oljefabriker* [1949] A.C. 196. The position is different where the breach has no causal connection with the frustrating event: *The Silver Sky* [1981] 2 Lloyd's Rep. 95 at 98.

[380] cf. *Amalgamated Investment & Property Co Ltd v John Walker & Sons Ltd* [1977] 1 W.L.R. 164 (failure to take any steps to obtain planning permission).

[381] *The Hannah Blumenthal* [1983] 1 A.C. 854, rejecting suggestions in *The Splendid Sun* [1981] Q.B. 694 at 703, *The Argonaut* [1982] 2 Lloyd's Rep. 214 at 221, and *The Kehera* [1983] 1 Lloyd's Rep. 29 that there could be frustration "by mutual default". In *The Hannah Blumenthal* the plea of frustration failed on the further ground that the delay did not produce a radically different state of affairs; cf. on this point, *Stockport MBC v O'Reilly* [1983] 2 Lloyd's Rep. 70. And see above, para.2–005 for a statutory solution of the problem which arose in *The Hannah Blumenthal*.

[382] *Denmark Production Ltd v Boscobel Productions Ltd* [1969] 1 Q.B. 699; *Black Clawson International Ltd v Papierwerke Waldhof-Aschaffenburg AG* [1981] 2 Lloyd's Rep. 446 at 457.

[383] *Harrington v Kent CC* [1980] I.R.L.R. 353; *FC Shepherd & Co Ltd v Jerrom* [1987] Q.B. 301; *contra*, *Norris v Southampton CC* [1982] I.C.R. 177. Whether the imprisonment actually frustrates the contract depends on such circumstances as the length of the sentence and the nature of the employment: see *Chakki v United Yeast Ltd* [1982] I.C.R. 140 and *F C Shepherd & Co Ltd v Jerrom*, above.

[384] cf. *Sumnall v Statt* (1984) 49 P. & C.R. 367 (imprisonment of tenant no excuse for failing to perform covenant to "reside constantly" at farmhouse).

voice through carelessly catching cold. He seemed to incline to the view that she could rely on frustration so long as the incapacity "was not deliberately induced in order to get out of the engagement".[385] This result can perhaps be justified by the difficulty of foreseeing the effect of conduct on one's health.[386] But it is submitted that generally negligence should exclude frustration: e.g. the plea should have failed in *Taylor v Caldwell*[387] if the fire had been due to the negligence of the defendants, for in such a case it would be unjust to make the other party bear the loss. Similarly, a shipowner cannot rely on the loss of his ship as a ground of frustration of a contract to carry goods in her if the loss is due to his negligence.[388] These examples show that "negligence" in this context is not restricted to "breach of an actionable legal duty": it includes "an event which the party relying on it had means and opportunity to prevent but nevertheless caused or permitted to come about".[389]

(iii) *Choosing between several contracts*

Where a party has entered into a number of contracts, supervening events may deprive him of the power of performing them all, without depriving him of the power of performing one or some of them. He may then claim that one or more of the contracts are frustrated because the supervening event was one for which he was not responsible; but in two cases such claims have failed.

19–086

Maritime National Fish v Ocean Trawlers. The first is *Maritime National Fish Ltd v Ocean Trawlers Ltd*,[390] where the defendants operated a fleet of five trawlers for fishing with otter trawls. Three of the trawlers were owned by the defendants through their subsidiaries,[391] while two, of which one was the *St Cuthbert*, were chartered from other owners. The use of otter trawls without licence was illegal, and because of a change in government policy[392] the defendants secured only three out of the five licences for which they had applied. Having allocated two of these to two of their own trawlers and one to the other chartered trawler,[393] they argued that the charter of the *St Cuthbert* had been frustrated. The argument was rejected by the Canadian courts on the ground that the defendants had taken the risk of not getting licences for all five trawlers, the licensing requirement being known both to them and to the owners of the *St Cuthbert* at the time of contracting. The Privy Council, though not dissenting from this view, preferred to base its decision on the ground that frustration was self-induced: "it was the act and election of [the defendants] which prevented the *St Cuthbert* from being licensed for fishing with an otter trawl".[394] On the facts, there clearly was such an election, for the defendants could have allocated one of the three licences to the *St Cuthbert* rather

19–087

---

[385] *Joseph Constantine SS Co v Imperial Smelting Corp Ltd* [1942] A.C. 154 at 166–167.

[386] Restatement 2d, *Contracts*, para.262, Comment (a).

[387] (1863) 3 B. & S. 826. Lack of "fault" is mentioned in the passage at 833 quoted at para.19–003, above.

[388] See *The Super Servant Two* [1990] 1 Lloyd's Rep. 1.

[389] [1990] 1 Lloyd's Rep. 1 at 10; cf. *North Shore Ventures Ltd v Anstead Holdings Inc* [2010] EWHC 1485 (Ch); [2010] 2 Lloyd's Rep. 265 at [316].

[390] [1935] A.C. 524.

[391] See [1934] 1 D.L.R. 621 at 623; [1934] 4 D.L.R. 288 at 299.

[392] See above, para.19–048.

[393] See the references in fn.391, above.

[394] [1935] A.C. 524 at 529.

than to one of their own trawlers. But suppose that the defendants had operated only the two chartered trawlers, had obtained only one licence, and that the licensing requirement had been introduced after both charterparties were concluded. The question would then have arisen whether their choice to allocate their only licence to one of the trawlers would have been an "election", so as to exclude the doctrine of frustration in relation to the charter of the other.

19–088   *The Super Servant Two.* An affirmative answer to a similar question was given in *The Super Servant Two*,[395] where a contract was made to carry the claimants' drilling rig in one of two ships, the *Super Servant One* or the *Super Servant Two*, at the carrier's option. The *Super Servant Two* was lost and the carrier claimed that the contract was frustrated by this event because the *Super Servant One* was the subject of another fixture and hence not available for the purposes of performing the carrier's contract with the claimants. The argument was rejected on the ground that the carrier's decision to use the *Super Servant One* for the purpose of performing the other contract amounted to an "election" by him, thus precluding his reliance on the loss of the *Super Servant Two* as a ground of frustration, even if that loss was in no way due to his fault. Three grounds for the decision appear from the judgments but it is submitted with great respect that none of them is wholly convincing. First, it was said that the *Maritime National Fish* case had established that a party could not rely on frustration where his failure or inability was due to his "election"; and that the court in *The Super Servant Two* should follow that decision.[396] It is, however, submitted that the two cases are readily distinguishable: in the *Maritime National Fish* case it was possible for the charterer to perform *all* the contracts which he had made with the owners of the other trawlers, even though only three licences had been allocated to him; while in *The Super Servant Two* it was no longer possible, after the loss of the ship, for the carrier to perform all the contracts which he had made to carry drilling rigs during the period in question. Secondly, it was said that, if the carrier were given the choice which of the contracts he would perform, frustration of the other or others could come about only as a result of the exercise of that choice, and such a position would be inconsistent with the rule that frustration occurs automatically, *without* any election by either party.[397] Again, it is submitted that this line of reasoning is not conclusive since the rule that frustration operates automatically is subject to qualification precisely in cases of allegedly self-induced frustration[398]: we have seen, for example, that the imprisonment of an employee is a circumstance on which the employer, but not the employee, can rely as a ground of discharge,[399] so that discharge cannot in such cases be described as automatic. Even where the rule that frustration operates automatically does apply, we shall see that this rule forms one of the least attractive aspects of the doctrine of frustration,[400] so that it is one which should not be extended. Moreover, the element of "election" could be eliminated if the question which of the contracts was to be discharged were left to be determined, not by the free choice of the promisor, but by a rule of law: e.g. by a rule to the effect that the various contracts should for this purpose rank in the

---

[395] [1990] 1 Lloyd's Rep. 1, affirming [1989] 1 Lloyd's Rep. 148; McKendrick [1990] L.M.C.L.Q. 153.

[396] ibid. at 10, 13 (rejecting the contrary submission made in earlier editions of this book).

[397] ibid. at 9, 14.

[398] See below, para.19–091.

[399] *Shepherd & Co Ltd v Jerrom* [1987] Q.B. 301; discussed at para.19–084, above.

[400] See below, paras 19–090—19–091.

order in which they were made.[401] It may, from this point of view, be relevant that, in *The Super Servant Two*, some of the contracts which the carrier chose to perform (by the use of his other ship during the relevant period) had not been made "at any rate finally"[402] until *after* the contract with the claimants, and that, even after the loss of the *Super Servant Two*, the carrier had continued to negotiate for extra fees to be paid under one of those contracts, "before finally allocating the *Super Servant One* to the performance of these contracts".[403] The third reason given for the decision is that "It is within the promisor's own control how many contracts he enters into and the risk should be his".[404] But this point seems to undermine the whole basis of the doctrine of frustration: it has just as much force where the promisor enters into a single contract as where he enters into two or more, with different contracting parties. This, indeed, is the fundamental objection to the reasoning of *The Super Servant Two*, and it is submitted that the rationale of the doctrine should lead to discharge of some of the contracts where the supervening event (which makes it impossible to perform them all) occurs without the fault of the party claiming discharge.[405] Consistency with the reasoning of the *Maritime National Fish* case could be preserved by holding that *which* contracts were to be discharged should depend, not on the election of the party who can no longer perform, but on a rule of law. On this view, the actual decision in *The Super Servant Two* could be justified by reference to the order in which the various contracts with the carrier were made.

(iv) *Burden of proof*

Burden on party alleging self-inducement. The onus of proving that 19–089 frustration is self-induced is on the party who alleges that this is the case. In *Joseph Constantine SS Line v Imperial Smelting Corp Ltd*[406] a ship was disabled by an explosion so that her owners were prevented from performing their obligations under a charterparty. The charterers' claim for damages was rejected: the House of Lords held that the shipowners were discharged by frustration without having to disprove fault and in spite of the fact that the cause of the explosion was never explained. A possible objection to the rule is that the charterers were much less likely than the owners to be able to show how the explosion occurred. This reasoning does, indeed, prevail in one group of cases: a person to whom goods have been bailed, and who seeks to rely on their destruction as a ground of frustration of the contract of bailment, must show that the destruction was not due to any breach of his duty as a bailee.[407] But, this special situation excepted, the rule as to burden of proof laid down in the *Joseph Constantine* case, can be defended on

---

[401] cf. above, para.19–029.
[402] [1990] 1 Lloyd's Rep. 1 at 9.
[403] ibid. at 13.
[404] [1989] 1 Lloyd's Rep. 148 at 158 (at first instance); the reasoning of this judgment was approved on appeal in [1990] 1 Lloyd's Rep. 1.
[405] cf. *Bremer Handelsgesellschaft mbH v Continental Grain Co* [1983] 1 Lloyd's Rep. 269 at 292–293; the treatment of the 92 tonnes in *Bremer Handelsgesellschaft mbH v Vanden Avenne-Izegem PVBA* [1978] 2 Lloyd's Rep. 109 at 115; and see above, para.19–029.
[406] [1942] A.C. 154; Stone 60 L.Q.R. 262. A contrary dictum in *F C Shepherd & Co Ltd v Jerrom* [1987] Q.B. 301 at 319 seems to have been made per incuriam.
[407] *The Torrenia* [1983] 2 Lloyd's Rep. 210 at 216.

the ground that, more often than not, catastrophic events which prevent performance do occur without the fault of either party. To impose the burden of disproving fault on the party relying on frustration is therefore less likely than the converse rule to lead to the right result in the majority of cases.

4. EFFECTS OF FRUSTRATION[408]

(a) General

19–090　**Contract automatically terminated at time of frustrating event.** Frustration terminates a contract automatically at the time of the frustrating event.[409] The court may therefore hold that the contract was frustrated even though the parties for some time after the event went on behaving as if the contract still existed.[410]

> "Whatever the consequences of the frustration may be upon the conduct of the parties, its legal effect does not depend on their opinions, or even knowledge, as to the event".[411]

Accordingly, "what the parties may say or do" has been described as "only evidence, and not necessarily weighty evidence, of the view to be taken of the event by informed and experienced minds".[412] This does not mean that the courts disregard the views of the parties as to the effect of the event: thus in one case Lord Sumner said:

> "Both [parties] thought its result was to terminate their contractual relations . . . and as they must have known more about it than I do there is no reason why I should not think so too".[413]

The true position is that "the parties' beliefs are not determinative, but nor are they irrelevant".[414]

19–091　**No requirement of election.** As frustration operates automatically, it is generally thought to terminate the contract without any election by either party: in this respect it differs from breach, which enables the victim to choose whether to treat the contract as discharged.[415] It follows that frustration can be invoked by either party, and not only by the party likely to be adversely affected by the frustrating event. Suppose, for example, that a ship under charter is requisitioned so that the charterer does not receive the promised performance (i.e. the services

---

[408] Williams, *The Law Reform (Frustrated Contracts) Act 1943.*
[409] *Hirji Mulji v Cheong Yue SS Co Ltd* [1926] A.C. 497 at 505; *BP Exploration (Libya) Ltd v Hunt* [1979] 1 W.L.R. 783 at 809 (affirmed [1983] 2 A.C. 352); *The Super Servant Two* [1990] 1 Lloyd's Rep. 1 at 8, 9, 14.
[410] cf. *The Agathon* [1982] 2 Lloyd's Rep. 211 at 213; *G F Sharp & Co v McMillan* [1998] I.R.L.R. 632.
[411] *Hirji Mulji* case, above, at 509; cf. *Morgan v Manser* [1948] 1 K.B. 184 at 191.
[412] *Hirji Mulji* case, above.
[413] *Bank Line Ltd v Arthur Capel & Co* [1919] A.C. 435 at 460. See also *Black Clawson International Ltd v Papierwerke Waldhof-Aschaffenburg AG* [1981] 2 Lloyd's Rep. 446 at 457 where the fact that a party had "affirmed the contract" was said to exclude frustration.
[414] *The Wenjiang (No.2)* [1983] 2 Lloyd's Rep. 400 at 408.
[415] *F C Shepherd Ltd v Jerrom* [1987] Q.B. 301 at 327.

of the ship). Frustration may, paradoxically, be claimed by the shipowner, even though the charterer is perfectly willing to pay the agreed hire[416]; for if the compensation paid by the Government for the requisition exceeds that hire, the shipowner will actually profit from frustration. The courts are understandably reluctant to allow the doctrine of frustration to be used in this way. Thus the rejection of the plea of frustration in the *Tamplin*[417] case has been explained precisely on the ground that the House of Lords saw no good reason why the shipowner should be allowed to make a profit of the kind just described.[418] It seems that the seller in the *Tsakiroglou*[419] case would have made a similar profit if his plea of frustration had been upheld, for the market price of the goods had risen by more than the extra cost of carriage via the Cape of Good Hope[420]; and this fact may have had some influence on the decision that the contract remained in force. But in other cases the rule of automatic termination has, no doubt, enabled a party to profit from frustration.[421] It is doubtful whether such a result is necessary, and it might be better if frustration only gave an option to terminate to any party who is prejudiced by the supervening event in the sense of not receiving the now impossible performance (or, in cases of frustration of purpose, of not being able to use the subject-matter for its intended purpose). There is, indeed, some support for this view in the cases relating to self-induced frustration. Where an event is brought about by the deliberate act of one party (not amounting in itself to a breach), that party cannot rely on it as frustrating the contract; but the other party may be able so to rely on it. This is, for example, the position where an employee is imprisoned for a criminal offence and so unable to perform his part of a contract of employment. The employer can invoke frustration in such circumstances[422]; but the employee cannot do so since a party cannot rely on self-induced frustration.[423]

(b) Problems of Adjustment[424]

The common law starts with the principle that frustration discharges the parties only from duties of "future performance".[425] Rights accrued before frustration therefore remain enforceable while those which would, but for the frustrating event, have accrued after the time of discharge do not become due. These rules sometimes caused hardship which has been mitigated both by common law developments and by statute.   **19–092**

---

[416] e.g. *Bank Line Ltd v Arthur Capel & Co* [1919] A.C. 435.

[417] [1916] 2 A.C. 397; above, para.19–021.

[418] *Metropolitan Water Board v Dick Kerr & Co* [1918] A.C. 119 at 129; cf. also *Port Line Ltd v Ben Line Steamers Ltd* [1958] 2 Q.B. 146.

[419] [1962] A.C. 93; above, para.19–031.

[420] Shortly after the end of the shipment period, the market price of the goods had risen by £18 15s. per ton above the contract price, while the cost of shipment via the Cape was only £7 10s. per ton more than the cost of shipment via Suez.

[421] A striking illustration is *The Isle of Mull* 278 F. 131 (1921); cf. also *Nickoll & Knight v Ashton Edridge & Co* [1901] 2 K.B. 126 (above, para.19–030) where the market price of the goods rose above the contract price so that the seller seems to have made a profit out of frustration.

[422] *F C Shepherd & Co v Jerrom* [1987] Q.B. 301; above, para.19–084.

[423] ibid.

[424] Stewart and Carter [1992] C.L.J. 66.

[425] *Joseph Constantine* case [1942] A.C. 154 at 187; cf. *The Super Servant Two* [1990] 1 Lloyd's Rep. 1 at 18 ("further liability").

(i) Rights accrued before frustration

19–093   **Common law.** The rule that rights which had accrued before frustration remain enforceable can be illustrated by supposing that in *Taylor v Caldwell*[426] the fire had occurred after the first, but before the second, of the four specified days. The rest of the contract would then have been discharged, while each party would have remained liable for any failure to perform obligations which had fallen due on the first day. But the application of this principle could lead to injustice where one party's performance under the contract had become due before the frustrating event while that of the other was only to be rendered thereafter; for in such a case the former party would have still to perform, without getting what he had bargained for in return. For example, in *Chandler v Webster*[427] a contract for the hire of a room overlooking the proposed route of King Edward VII's coronation processions provided for payment of £141 15s. in advance: this was due, and £100 of it had been paid, before the day on which the processions were cancelled. The hirer was held liable to pay the remaining £41 15s. as the payment had fallen due before the contract was frustrated; while his claim to recover back the £100 already paid on the ground of "total failure of consideration"[428] was rejected[429]: it was thought that the failure of consideration was not total as frustration released the parties only from further performance, and did not make the contract void ab initio. But this aspect of *Chandler v Webster* was overruled in the *Fibrosa* case.[430] An English company had agreed to sell machinery to a Polish company for £4,800, of which £1,600 was to be paid in advance. When £1,000 had been paid, the contract was frustrated by the German occupation of Gdynia after the outbreak of war in 1939. The House of Lords held that the Polish company could recover back the £1,000 since the consideration for the payment had wholly failed: no part of the machinery had been delivered. Liability to pay the outstanding £600 must likewise have been discharged, for it would have been futile to require the buyer to make a payment which he would then immediately have been entitled to recover.[431]

19–094   **Defects in the common law.** But this solution was defective in two ways. First, it applied only where the consideration had *wholly* failed.[432] In *Whincup v Hughes*[433] a father apprenticed his son to a watchmaker for six years at a premium of £25. After one year the watchmaker died. The father could not recover back any part of the premium as the failure of consideration was only partial. Secondly, to allow the payor to recover back the whole of his advance payment might in turn cause injustice to the payee, who might (and in the *Fibrosa* case did) use the

---

[426] (1863) 3 B. & S. 826, above, para.19–003.

[427] [1904] 1 K.B. 493; cf. Buckland 46 Harv.L.Rev. 1281.

[428] See below, para.22–003.

[429] cf. *Blakeley v Muller & Co* [1903] 2 K.B. 760n. (referred to in *The Great Peace* [2002] EWCA Civ 1407; [2003] Q.B. 679 at [65], [76] under its alternative name of *Hobson v Pattenden & Co*); *Civil Service Co-operative Society v General Steam Navigation Co* [1903] 2 K.B. 756.

[430] *Fibrosa Spolka Akcyjna v Fairbairn, Lawson, Combe, Barbour Ltd* [1943] A.C. 32; above, para.19–045. This point seems to have been overlooked in *Re Goldcorp Exchange Ltd* [1995] A.C. 74 at 103, where the Privy Council repeats what is in substance the reasoning of *Chandler v Webster*, without referring either to that case or the *Fibrosa* case.

[431] cf. in another context, *McDonald v Denys Lascelles Ltd* (1933) 48 C.L.R. 457; above, para.18–011; *Fibrosa* case [1943] A.C. 32 at 53.

[432] cf. below, paras 22–003—22–004.

[433] (1871) L.R. 6 C.P. 78.

advance payment to finance the initial stages of the contract. If, in consequence of frustration, that expenditure was wasted, the resulting loss would fall entirely on the payee.

Law Reform (Frustrated Contracts) Act 1943, section 1(2). To remedy the defects just described, s.1(2) of the Law Reform (Frustrated Contracts) Act 1943 lays down three rules.

19–095

Sums due before the frustrating event cease to be payable. All sums payable under the contract before the time of discharge cease to be payable on frustration: thus in *Chandler v Webster* the claim for the unpaid £41 15s. would now fail.

19–096

Sums actually paid are prima facie recoverable. All sums actually paid in pursuance of the contract before the time of discharge are recoverable from the payee "as money received by him to the use of the" payor. As the subsection does not refer to "total failure of consideration", this statutory right to recover back money arises even where the failure is only partial, for example, in such cases as *Whincup v Hughes*.

19–097

The payee may retain or recover a sum on account of expenses. If the party to whom sums were paid or payable in pursuance of the contract has before the time of discharge incurred expenses in or for the purpose of the performance of the contract, the court may allow him to retain or recover the whole or any part of the sums so paid or payable; but the court cannot allow him to retain or recover more than the actual amount of his expenses. The court can make an award in respect of expenses under s.1(2) only if the contract contains a stipulation for pre-payment; a party who incurs expenses without asking for a pre-payment, or who incurs greater expenses than the amount of the pre-payment, does so at his own risk.[434]

19–098

The court is not bound to make any award in respect of expenses and has a discretion as to the amount of the award. This discretion is subject to two upper limits: the award must not exceed either the amount of the expenses incurred, or the amount of the stipulated prepayment.[435] No doubt in exercising its discretion the court will be influenced by the degree to which the expenses have been made useless by the frustrating event. If machinery made for one customer can easily be sold to another, very little will be awarded; if it cannot be disposed of except as scrap, the court is likely to make a substantial award. Even in such a case, however, the court will not necessarily award the maximum amount available under the Act. Suppose that in the *Fibrosa* case the seller had received a prepayment of £1,600 and had incurred expenses of exactly that amount. Under the common law rule he would have had to pay back the whole £1,600, and this was unjust because it left him to bear the entire loss of the wasted expenditure. If, under the Act, the court were to allow him to retain the whole £1,600, this could be equally unjust as it would leave the buyer to bear the whole of that loss. In the exercise of its discretion

---

[434] An award in respect of expenses can be made under s.1(2) only where a *sum of money* was paid or payable to the party who has incurred expenses. Where that party has received a "payment in kind" a similar result may be reached under s.1(3)(a): below, para.19–104.

[435] Proceeds of insurance payable to the claimant by reason of the frustrating events must be disregarded: s.1(5).

under s.1(2) the court could split the loss (instead of merely shifting it from one party to the other) in such proportions as it thought just.[436]

In exercising its discretion under s.1(2), the court can also take account of the fact that expenses have been incurred by the *payor*. This was the position in *Gamerco SA v ICM/Fair Warning (Agency) Ltd*,[437] where the promoter of a "rock concert" had made an advance payment to the performers and the contract was then frustrated. Exercising a "broad discretion",[438] the court allowed the promoter to recover the payment in full, without any deduction in respect of expenses incurred by the performers for the purpose of the performance of the contract.[439] It did so on the grounds that the promoter had also incurred expenses which not only exceeded the pre-payment[440] but also amounted to about nine times those incurred by the performers,[441] and that each set of expenses had been wholly wasted.

(ii) *Rights not yet accrued*

19–099   **Common law.** At common law, rights not yet accrued at the time of frustration are unenforceable.[442] If a builder agrees to build a house for £100,000 payable on completion he cannot recover the £100,000 if the contract is frustrated before completion. This rule is perfectly reasonable: it would be unjust to make the building-owner pay the full price for an unfinished house. But, further, at common law the builder could not recover anything at all for partial performance before frustration. He could not recover a quantum meruit as no agreement to pay a proportionate sum for doing part of the work as that would be inconsistent with the express agreement for payment on completion. Thus, in *Appleby v Myers*[443] engineering contractors agreed "to make and erect the whole of the machinery" in the defendant's factory "and to keep the whole in order for two years from the date of completion". After part of the machinery had been erected, an accidental fire destroyed the factory with such of the machinery as was already in it, and frustrated the contract. It was held that the contractors could recover nothing for the machinery which they had erected. The general view is that this result is unsatisfactory[444] and that the builder should get something for his work.

19–100   **Law Reform (Frustrated Contracts) Act 1943, section 1(3).** The common law rule stated above was modified by s.1(3) of the Law Reform (Frustrated Contracts) Act 1943, which provides that "Where any party to the contract has, by reason of anything done by any other party thereto in, or for the purpose of, the performance of the contract, obtained a valuable benefit (other than a payment of money to which [s.1(2)] applies) before the time of discharge, there shall be

---

[436] s.1(2) refers to "the whole *or any part* of the sums so paid or payable."

[437] [1995] 1 W.L.R. 1226.

[438] ibid. at 1236.

[439] s.1(5), above, also required the court to disregard the fact that both parties had insured against cancellation and received payments under those policies.

[440] The promoter's expenses exceeded $450,000; the prepayment amounted to $412,500.

[441] The performers' expenses appear to have been about $50,000.

[442] *The M Vatan* [1987] 2 Lloyd's Rep. 416 at 426.

[443] (1867) L.R. 2 C.P. 651; cf. *Cutter v Powell* (1795) 6 T.R. 320, above para.17–032.

[444] cf. above, paras 17–041—17–042 for criticism of the rule that nothing can be recovered for partial performance of an entire obligation. One practical justification for that rule in cases of *breach* may be that it puts pressure to perform on the party in breach, but that argument cannot apply where performance is prevented by an event for which neither party is responsible.

recoverable from him by the said other party such sum (if any), not exceeding the value of the said benefit to the party obtaining it, as the court considers just, having regard to all the circumstances of the case"[445] and in particular to (a) the amount of any expenses incurred by the benefited party before the time of discharge, and (b) "the effect, in relation to the said benefit, of the circumstances giving rise to the frustration of the contract". Thus if A agrees to decorate B's house for £2,500 payable on completion but dies after decorating half the house, A's estate may recover something.

Measure of recovery. The measure of recovery under s.1(3) was the main issue in *BP (Exploration) Libya Ltd v Hunt*.[446] The case arose out of an elaborate agreement between BP and Mr Hunt for the exploitation of an oil concession in Libya belonging to Mr Hunt. BP were to do all the work of exploration and to provide the necessary finance; they were also to make certain "farm-in" payments in cash and oil. In return, they were to get a half share in the concession; and, as soon as the field began to produce oil, they were to receive "reimbursement oil" (to be taken out of Mr Hunt's share) until they had recouped 125 per cent of their initial expenditure. A large oil field was discovered and oil began to flow from it in 1967; but in 1971 the contract between BP and Mr Hunt was frustrated when their interests in the concession were expropriated by Libyan decrees. At this time, BP had received only about one-third of the "reimbursement oil" to which they were entitled in respect of their initial expenditure; and they brought a claim under s.1(3) of the 1943 Act. The claim was allowed by Robert Goff J., whose decision was (subject to relatively minor modifications[447]) upheld by the Court of Appeal and the House of Lords. The learned judge held that, in considering a claim under s.1(3), the court must proceed in two stages: it must first identify and value the benefit obtained, and then assess the just sum (not exceeding the value of the benefit) which it was proper to award. At the first stage, he held that "benefit", on the true construction of s.1(3), referred, not to the cost of perform-ance incurred by the claimant, but to the end product received by the other party.[448] In the case before him, that end product was the enhancement of the value of Mr Hunt's share in the concession resulting from BP's work; but because s.1(3)(b) required the court to have regard to "the effect, in relation to the said benefit, of the circumstances giving rise to . . . frustration", the value of that benefit had to be reduced to take account of the expropriation. In view of this fact, the total benefit obtained by Mr Hunt was the net amount of oil he had received from the concession, plus the compensation paid to him by the Libyan Govern-ment. Of this total, half was attributed to BP's efforts and half to Mr Hunt's original ownership of the concession. The value of this benefit was quantified at some $85 million. In assessing the "just sum" to be awarded, however, Robert

19–101

---

[445] But not to the proceeds of insurance payable to the claimant by reason of the frustrating event: s.1(5).

[446] [1979] 1 W.L.R. 783, affirmed [1981] 1 W.L.R. 236; [1983] 2 A.C. 352; Baker [1979] C.L.J. 266.

[447] Recovery of a "farm-in" payment of $2 million in *cash* had been allowed under s.1(3) when it plainly should have been allowed under s.1(2): see [1981] 1 W.L.R. 236 at 240; [1983] 2 A.C. 352 at 370; and see below, fn.450.

[448] For this reason a claim for the "time value of money"—i.e. for the use that Mr. Hunt could have made of the proceeds of the sale of the oil—was rejected for it was not shown that he did make such use. But interest on the award from the time of frustration was allowed under Law Reform (Miscella-neous Provisions) Act 1934, s.3; see now Supreme Court Act 1981, s.35A(1); below, para.20–065.

Goff J. adopted a criterion which he had rejected in valuing the benefit, *viz.* the cost to BP of the work to the extent that it was done for Mr Hunt. To this was added the value of the "farm in" oil[449] and the resulting total was then reduced by the amount of the reimbursement oil already received by BP. On this basis, the just sum was some $34.67 million[450] and, as the valuable benefit exceeded this amount, BP recovered the just sum in full.

19–102   **Definition of "valuable benefit".** It follows from the definition of valuable benefit as an "end product" that s.1(3) will not apply merely because the claimant has incurred trouble and expense for the purpose of the performance of the contract.[451] On the other hand, there can be a valuable benefit within s.1(3) even though no physical thing has been transferred by the claimant to the defendant. Thus in *BP Exploration (Libya) Ltd v Hunt* the services rendered by BP to Mr Hunt constituted at least part of the benefit. In the case of a contract to paint a house, there would similarly be a valuable benefit if the contract was frustrated by illegality after half the work had been done.[452] In such cases the improvement to the defendant's property can be said to be an "end product"; but there are other contexts in which the definition of "valuable benefit" as an "end product" would be inappropriate: e.g. where the contract was one of the hire of a chattel. Such a contract is not intended to leave any "end product" in the hands of the hirer, who can nevertheless be said to have benefited if he has had the use of the chattel for part of the agreed period before the contract is frustrated. It would be unfortunate if s.1(3) were held to be inapplicable in such a case merely because of the definition of valuable benefit adopted in the different context of *BP Exploration (Libya) Ltd v Hunt*.[453]

19–103   **Destruction of the benefit.** The machinery of the Act worked satisfactorily in *BP (Exploration) Libya Ltd v Hunt* because the valuable benefit, even when reduced in the light of the frustrating event, exceeded the just sum. But the position would have been different if the expropriation had occurred immediately before oil had begun to flow and if no compensation for expropriation had been paid. On the reasoning of the judgment, there would then have been no valuable benefit (beyond the "farm-in" oil); for that reasoning has regard to "the circumstances giving rise to the frustration" within s.1(3)(b) in *valuing the benefit* rather than in *assessing the just sum*. The same reasoning is adopted in an example which closely resembles *Appleby v Myers*[454]:

---

[449] This value seems also to be relevant to the identification of the benefit.

[450] [1981] 1 W.L.R. 236 at 241; this contrasts with the figure of some $35.40 million in [1979] 1 W.L.R. 783 at 827. The difference is not explained and may be due to the adoption of different currency conversion factors at first instance and in the Court of Appeal.

[451] This was precisely the position in *Taylor v Caldwell* (1863) 3 B. & S. 826: see above, para.19–003. For the court's power to allow the *recipient* of the benefit to deduct expenses, see below, para.19–104.

[452] Illustration given by Lord Simon L.C. when introducing s.1(3): HL Deb., June 29, 1943, Col. 139.

[453] s.1(3) should therefore apply on facts such as those in *Cutter v Powell* (1795) 6 T.R. 320; above, para.17–032 unless the contract was literally one of insurance: see above, para.17–032 and below, para.19–110. The "just sum" should not be based on the exceptionally high rate of pay contracted for, but on current market rates (see above, para.17–032).

[454] (1867) L.R. 2 C.P. 651.

"Suppose that a contract for work on a building is frustrated by a fire which destroys the building and which therefore destroys a substantial amount of the work already done by the [claimant]. Although *it might be thought just* to award the [claimant] a sum assessed on a *quantum meruit* basis, the effect of s.1(3)(b) will be to reduce the award to nil . . . ".[455]

If this is right, *Appleby v Myers* would not be affected by the Act; but in view of the evident reluctance with which the learned judge reached this conclusion it is submitted that an alternative interpretation of s.1(3) is to be preferred. This would make the destruction of the benefit relevant, not to the identification of the benefit, but to the assessment of the just sum. Two points seem to support such an interpretation. First, s.1(3) applies where a valuable benefit has been obtained *before* the time of discharge: thus to identify the benefit in a case like *Appleby v Myers* the court must look at the facts as they were before, and not after, the fire. The partly completed installation would at least prima facie be a benefit, since completion of the installation would be likely to cost less after part of the work had been done. Secondly, there is the structure of the subsection. This begins by setting out the circumstances in which the court has power to make an award (i.e. when a valuable benefit has been obtained) and then provides guidelines for the exercise of that power. The guideline contained in s.1(3)(b) is introduced by the words "such sum as the court thinks just having regard to . . . "; and these words seem to link the guideline to the *exercise* rather than to the *existence* of the court's discretion. This interpretation cannot cause any injustice, for if the court thinks that very little or nothing should be awarded it can exercise its discretion to that effect; and for this purpose the court can take the destruction of the benefit into account so as to split the loss in such proportions as the court thinks just. But if such destruction necessarily led to the conclusion that no valuable benefit had been obtained before frustration, the court would have no discretion to award anything at all. It would be a pity if this useful discretion were restricted in a way that is neither clearly required by the words of the subsection nor necessary to promote justice.

Relationship between section 1(2) and 1(3). The power to make an award in respect of a valuable benefit under s.1(3) is, in theory, additional to the power to make an award in respect of expenses under s.1(2). Thus if a party who has incurred expenses has also both conferred a valuable benefit and received (or stipulated for) a pre-payment he can claim under both subsections. But any amount awarded in respect of expenses will be taken into account in deciding how much should be awarded in respect of valuable benefit, and vice versa.[456] If the party who has incurred expenses has *received* a valuable benefit other than money (e.g. a "pre-payment" in kind) he cannot make any claim in respect of expenses under s.1(2) as that subsection only applies where a *sum of money* is paid or payable. But the court can reach much the same result under s.1(3), for it can take the expenses into account in deciding how much the recipient of the valuable benefit should pay for it.[457]

19–104

---

[455] [1979] 1 W.L.R. 783 at 801 (italics supplied); cf. *Parsons Bros Ltd v Shea* (1966) 53 D.L.R. 2d 36, decided under a Newfoundland Act in similar (but not identical) terms to those of the English Act.

[456] See s.1(3)(a).

[457] ibid.

(iii) Casus omissus?

19–105   **Pre-frustration payments in kind.** Under s.1(2), sums of money payable before frustration cease to be payable on frustration. The subsection is restricted to *payments of money*. Section 1(3), by contrast, provides for restitution claims in respect of *other benefits*, e.g. where A renders services or transfers property to B before frustration. But nothing in s.1(3) in terms releases A where before frustration he ought to have performed an obligation to do something other than to pay cash, has failed to do so, and would, if he had performed, have been entitled to make a claim for restitution under s.1(3). Thus if A has promised to make an advance payment *in cash* and has failed before frustration to do so, he is released by s.1(2); but if the stipulated payment had been *in kind* he would not be released by anything in s.1(2) or s.1(3). Nor can he, in the latter case, neutralise his liability by making a claim under s.1(3), for B has not "by reason of anything done [by A] obtained a valuable benefit . . . *before* the time of discharge". On the contrary, B has failed to obtain an expected benefit by reason of something not done by A. B may *after* the time of discharge obtain a benefit by suing A, but this does not bring the case within s.1(3) as the benefit is obtained too late. Nor would it help A to argue that before the time of discharge B had a valuable benefit, namely, his right to sue A, for this benefit would not have been obtained "by reason of anything done [by A] in or for the purpose of the performance of the contract". It is hard to believe that these consequences were intended. The failure of the Act in these circumstances to provide for the release of obligations other than those to pay money seems to be a *casus omissus*.

(iv) Special cases

19–106   **Severability.** A contract may provide for one party to make payments from time to time in response to specified parts of the other's performance. The common law rule was that, if the contract was frustrated, such payments as were due at the time of frustration could be recovered. In *Stubbs v Holywell Ry*[458] a consulting engineer was appointed for 15 months for £500 payable in five equal quarterly instalments. After two quarters he died. His administrator successfully claimed the £200 due to him at the date of his death. But he could have recovered nothing more had the deceased worked for another two months in the next quarter. Under the 1943 Act he can do so. Section 2(4) provides that if parts of a contract which have been wholly performed can properly be severed from the remainder, they are to be treated as separate contracts; and that the provisions of s.1 (discussed above) shall apply to the remainder of the contract.

Section 2(4) also affects the rights of a person to recover back money paid under such a contract. At common law money could be recovered back if paid for some severable part of the consideration which had wholly failed, even though the consideration for the whole payment had not failed.[459] If in *Stubbs v Holywell Ry* the whole £500 had been paid in advance, £200 could have been recovered back as no work at all was done by the deceased in the last two quarters; but nothing could have been recovered back in respect of the third quarter, if the deceased had

---

[458] (1867) L.R. 2 Ex. 311.
[459] See *Tyrie v Fletcher* (1777) 2 Cowp. 666 at 668; Marine Insurance Act 1906, s.84(2) (divisible insurance policies); below, para.22–004.

done so much as a week's work in it. Now money paid in respect of the third quarter could be recovered back, but the personal representative could claim under s.1(3) in respect of the work done by the deceased in that week. An obligation may also be severable by statute under the provisions of the Apportionment Act 1870.[460]

Contrary agreement. The common law rule that money is recoverable on the ground of total failure of consideration can be excluded by contrary agreement: the money may be paid out-and-out, with the intention that the payee shall keep it in any event.[461] The provisions of the Act can similarly be excluded by contrary agreement[462]; whether a term has this effect depends on its construction. In *BP Exploration (Libya) Ltd v Hunt*[463] the contract provided that the defendant was not to be personally liable to repay any advances and that BP's rights were to be exercisable only against the defendant's share of the oil. This provision did not exclude the Act as, on its true construction, it was not intended to deal with the risk of expropriation but with the different risk that no oil might be found. **19–107**

Commercial agents. Under the Regulations which govern contracts between "commercial agents"[464] and their principals, certain rights to "compensation" or "indemnity" accrue to the agent or to his estate on his death or on his serious disability preventing further performance of the contract.[465] The content of these rights differs significantly from the consequences of frustration under the 1943 Act. They can, for example, take account of the agent's loss of commission and of expenses incurred by him or of loss suffered by him,[466] in circumstances in which no claim in respect of a valuable benefit or allowance in respect of expenses could be made under the Act[467]; and (unlike rights under the Act) they cannot be excluded by the contract.[468] **19–108**

---

[460] See above, para.17–047.

[461] *Fibrosa* case [1943] A.C. 32 at 43, 77. The common law rule could still apply: e.g. to contracts excluded from the operation of the Act by s.2(5)(c): below, para.19–109 et seq.

[462] s.2(3). Contract terms *excluding the common law rule* stated at fn.458, above, would not be subject to the requirement of reasonableness under Unfair Contract Terms Act 1977, s.3(2)(b)(ii) (above, para.7–069) since in the case of a frustrated contract there would be *no* "contractual obligation" to perform. They might, however, in a standard consumer contract be subject to the requirement of fairness under Unfair Terms in Consumer Contracts Regulations 1999 (above, para.7–095 et seq.): see Sch.2, para.1(o). Contract terms *excluding the 1943 Act* would not be subject to Unfair Contract Terms Act 1977, being "authorised" by s.2(3) of the 1943 Act and so excepted from the 1977 Act by virtue of s.29(1)(a) of that Act (above, para.7–093); but they could be subject to Unfair Terms in Consumer Contracts Regulations 1999, for although these Regulations do not apply to "mandatory statutory ... provisions" (reg.4(2)(a)) the provisions of the 1943 Act are (by reasons of s.2(3)) not "mandatory". The fact that s.2(3) permitted the parties to exclude the provisions of the 1943 Act would, however, be relevant to the question whether a term to this effect was "unfair" for the purposes of the 1999 Regulations.

[463] [1983] 2 A.C. 352.

[464] Commercial Agents (Council Directive) Regulations 1993 (SI 1993/3053), as amended by SI 1993/3173 and SI 1998/2868; above, para.16–011.

[465] regs 17 and 18. The effect of frustration by other events is governed under reg.16 by the general law of frustration.

[466] reg.17(3)(a) (subject to a limit of one year's commission under reg.17(4)) and 17(7)).

[467] e.g. because no valuable benefit had been obtained by the principal or no stipulation for prepayment to the agent had been made.

[468] reg.19.

(v) *Contracts excluded from the 1943 Act*

19–109   **Voyage charterparties and other contracts for the carriage of goods by sea.**[469] The 1943 Act does not apply to voyage charterparties and other contracts for the carriage of goods by sea. The object of this exception is to preserve two rules which are well established and known in the trade: first, that freight which has become due or been paid before frustration remains due and (if paid) cannot be recovered back, even though the cargo is lost[470]; and, secondly, that a person who contracts to carry goods by sea to a specified port cannot recover freight pro rata, even if he is forced by events outside his control to discharge them at an intermediate port.[471]

19–110   **Contracts of insurance.** The 1943 Act does not apply to contracts of insurance.[472] This exception preserves the rule that there can, in general, be no apportionment of premiums under an insurance policy once the risk has begun to run. The essence of a contract of insurance is that "the contract is for the whole entire risk, and no part of the consideration shall be returned".[473] Thus if a ship is insured but lost in some way not covered by the policy after part of the period of insurance has run, no part of the premium can be recovered back. This is obviously in accordance with the intention of the parties, for such a contract is essentially speculative. Had the ship been lost by one of the perils insured against on the first day, the insurer would have had to bear the whole loss. Conversely, he can keep the whole premium if the ship is lost by a peril that is not covered by the policy at any time during the period of insurance.

19–111   **Contracts to which section 7 of the Sale of Goods Act 1979 applies.** Section 2(5)(c)[474] provides that the 1943 Act shall not apply to two types of contracts for the sale of goods. First, it does not apply to "any contract to which s.7 of the Sale of Goods Act 1979 . . . applies". Under s.7 of that Act, an agreement to sell specific goods is avoided if the goods perish without any fault on the part of the seller or buyer before the risk[475] has passed to the buyer. That is, the buyer is not liable for the price and neither party is liable in damages. The same result would normally follow from the common law rules of frustration, since the destruction of specific goods would frustrate the contract. The cases in which the 1943 Act would (if it were not excluded by s.2(5)(c)) make a difference are those in which there has been an advance payment or part-delivery.

---

[469] s.2(5)(a) provides that the Act shall not apply "to any charterparty, except a time charterparty or a charterparty by way of demise, or to any contract (other than a charterparty) for the carriage of goods by sea." These words make it clear that the Act does not apply to voyage charterparties, but leave open the question whether it applies to a "time charter trip" (above, fn.372). The answer may depend on the degree of particularity with which the contract describes the voyage.

[470] *Byrne v Schiller* (1871) L.R. 6 Ex. 319; unless the contract provides the contrary, as in *The Oliva* [1972] 1 Lloyd's Rep. 458; contrast *The Lorna I* [1983] 1 Lloyd's Rep. 373 where, on the true construction of the contract, freight was not to become due till after the frustrating event. Freight may be *earned* before it is *payable*: above, para.17–032.

[471] *St Enoch Shipping Co Ltd v Phosphate Mining Co* [1916] 2 K.B. 625; above, para.17–032.

[472] s.2(5)(b).

[473] *Tyrie v Fletcher* (1777) 2 Cowp. 666 at 668. For a contractual provision displacing the normal rule, see *The M Vatan* [1987] 2 Lloyd's Rep. 416.

[474] As amended by Sale of Goods Act 1979, s.63 and Sch.2, para.2.

[475] See above, para.19–013.

If the buyer pays in advance but does not get any of the goods, he can recover back his payment on the ground of total failure of consideration.[476] The exclusion of the Act does not affect this right, but it does prevent the seller from setting off any expenses which he may have incurred, e.g. in putting the goods into a deliverable state.

Part-delivery followed by frustration raises two problems. First, a buyer of a specific parcel of goods may have paid the whole price in advance and received only part-delivery. He probably cannot recover back any part of the payment at common law as the failure of consideration is not total.[477] Nor can he rely on the 1943 Act, as that is excluded. It has been suggested that he may be able to recover back a proportionate part of the advance payment simply on the ground that the undelivered goods are still at the seller's risk,[478] but this suggestion would give rise to difficulty where the price was not readily apportionable between the delivered and the undelivered parts.[479] Secondly, a seller may have delivered part of the goods and been paid nothing. As the 1943 Act is excluded, he cannot rely on it to recover anything in respect of the valuable benefit obtained by the buyer. He may be able to recover something at common law if a new contract can be implied from the buyer's keeping the goods after frustration. But it would be hard to imply such a contract if the buyer no longer had the goods, e.g. because he had used or resold them before frustration.

Where specific goods have perished. The 1943 Act secondly does not appply to "any other contract for the sale, or the sale and delivery, of specific goods, where the contract is frustrated by reason of the fact that the goods have perished". These words seem to refer to a case which would not fall within s.7 of the Sale of Goods Act 1979, because the risk has passed to the buyer. It is difficult to imagine how in such a case the contract could be frustrated by the perishing of the goods. Perhaps the point of excepting such a case from the 1943 Act is to make it clear that the buyer is liable for the whole price and that there is no power to order restitution or to apportion expenses.   19–112

Scope of section 2(5)(c). Section 2(5)(c) can produce some entirely capricious distinctions. The 1943 Act is excluded only where the goods are specific. Suppose that a farmer agrees to sell 200 tons out of a crop to be grown on his land, and the crop is destroyed by events for which he is not responsible.[480] As the goods are not specific,[481] the 1943 Act is not excluded and the farmer can set off his expenses of cultivating the crop[482] against any advance payment made by the buyer. But if an agreement were made to sell an identified parcel of 200 tons after the crop had been lifted, the goods would be specific so that the 1943 Act would be excluded. Hence if the agreement in such a case had provided that the farmer was to put the   19–113

---

[476] *Logan v Le Mesurier* (1846) 6 Moo.P.C. 116.

[477] It is assumed that the value of the part undelivered is not readily apportionable to the whole: see below, para.22–004.

[478] Atiyah, Adams & McQueen, *Sale of Goods* (11th edn), p.367.

[479] e.g. if a contract for the sale of specific machinery to be delivered in sections is frustrated after payment in full and part delivery.

[480] See *Howell v Coupland* (1876) 1 Q.B.D. 258; above, para.19–025.

[481] s.61(1) of Sale of Goods Act 1979 as amended by Sale of Goods (Amendment) Act 1995, s.2(d); *Re Wait* [1927] 1 Ch. 606 at 631.

[482] At least if incurred *after* the contract. In *Howell v Coupland* 25 of the 68 acres of the defendant's land at Whaplode had been sown *before* the contract; quaere whether such expenditure would be recoverable under the Act.

goods into sacks, and if the goods had been destroyed before this operation had been completed, the farmer would have to return the whole of any advance payment made by the buyer,[483] and have no right to deduct any part of the expenses of packaging.

The 1943 Act is also excluded only where the cause of frustration is the perishing of the goods. Thus the Act applies where the contract is frustrated by illegality or requisition.

The reason for these distinctions is far from clear; and one might ask why contracts for the sale of goods were singled out for separate treatment at all. As a matter of abstract justice, there seems to be no reason why the powers of restitution and apportionment provided by the Act should apply to a contract to build a house but not a contract to supply a specific piece of machinery. The main reason for not applying the Act to contracts for the sale of goods is that in such contracts certainty is more important than justice; and the certainty which the rules as to the passing of risk is meant to provide would be disrupted if their effects could be modified by the exercise of the discretionary powers conferred on the courts by the 1943 Act. But on this view contracts for the sale of goods should have been wholly excluded from the operation of the 1943 Act. Their partial exclusion does not satisfy the requirements of either certainty or justice.

5. JURISTIC BASIS[484]

(a) Theories of Frustration

19–114   Much discussion is to be found in the cases as to the so-called theoretical or juristic basis of the doctrine of frustration. The first puzzle is why judges have devoted so much attention to this question. Perhaps the reason is that they have felt the need to justify in some way their departure from the doctrine of absolute contracts. The second puzzle is to know exactly what the discussion is about. Two questions have become, perhaps inevitably, intertwined: *why* are contracts frustrated, and *when*? Thus in *Davis Contractors Ltd v Fareham Urban DC* Lord Radcliffe said that "frustration occurs *whenever*" the changed circumstances make performance "radically different from that which was undertaken."[485] This seems to deal with the second question; but it has also been regarded as providing an answer to the first.[486] Discussions of the juristic basis of the doctrine of frustration attempt sometimes to justify the doctrine, and sometimes to evolve some general formula for describing the conditions in which it operates. The main theories of frustration found in the cases are as follows.

19–115   **Implied term.** The first theory is that the contract is discharged because it impliedly provides that in the events which have happened it shall cease to bind. This theory is put forward by Lord Loreburn in the *Tamplin* case. "No court has absolving power"[487] but the court will not regard an obligation as absolute if the parties themselves did not intend it to be absolute. If they "must have made their

---

[483] Under the rule in the *Fibrosa* case [1943] A.C. 32; above, para.19–093.
[484] McNair 56 L.Q.R. 173; *Legal Effects of War*, pp.143 et seq.; Treitel, *Frustration and Force Majeure* (2nd edn), paras.16–006-16–016.
[485] [1956] A.C. 696 at 729.
[486] e.g. in *National Carriers Ltd v Panalpina (Northern) Ltd* [1981] A.C. 675 at 688, 717.
[487] *Tamplin* case [1916] 2 A.C. 397 at 404.

bargain on the footing that a particular thing or state of things would continue to exist . . . a term to that effect will be implied".[488]

In a purely subjective sense this theory is clearly untenable. The implication would have to arise at the time of contracting and at that time the parties are unlikely to have any view as to the effects on the contract of the supervening event; and after the event has occurred, the parties might well have no *common* view as to its effects: e.g. one party might well take the view that it should, and the other that it should not, discharge the contract. Even if the parties could reach some agreement on the point, they would probably not agree to total, unconditional discharge. As Lord Wright has said, "they would almost certainly on the one side or the other have sought to introduce reservations or qualifications or compensations".[489]

In fact Lord Loreburn did not put forward a purely subjective version of the implied term theory. He said:

"From the nature of the contract it cannot be supposed that the parties *as reasonable men* intended it to be binding on them under such altered conditions. . . . "[490]

The fact that the implied term theory did not seek to give effect to the subjective intention of the parties may explain why it fell out of favour,[491] but as has been noted earlier,[492] the implication of terms in general[493] is an objective process and it is very closely related to, if not the same as, the equally objective process of the interpretation,[494] or construction, of the contract which may provide the most satisfactory explanation for the doctrine of frustration.[495]

Just solution. Lord Sumner once described the doctrine of frustration as "a **19–116** device by which the rules as to absolute contracts are reconciled with a special exception which justice demands".[496] Lord Wright in the *Denny, Mott* case, found "the theory of the basis of the rule"[497] in this statement; he added that the

---

[488] *Tamplin* case [1916] 2 A.C. 397 at 403.

[489] *Denny, Mott* case [1944] A.C. 265 at 275; cf. *Shell UK Ltd v Lostock Garages Ltd* [1976] 1 W.L.R. 1187 at 1196: *Atisa SA v Aztec AG* [1983] 2 Lloyd's Rep. 579 at 586 (describing the implied term theory as "now rejected"); *F C Shepherd & Co Ltd v Jerrom* [1987] Q.B. 301 at 322; *The Super Servant Two* [1989] 1 Lloyd's Rep. 145 at 154, affirmed [1990] 1 Lloyd's Rep. 1; *The Great Peace* [2002] EWCA Civ 1407; [2003] Q.B. 679 at [73] ("not realistic"); cf. Trakman 46 M.L.R. 39. For a possible power of the court to introduce "reservations", etc. by means of an implied term while holding the contract *not* frustrated, see *The Maira (No.2)* [1985] 1 Lloyd's Rep. 300 at 311 (affirmed on other grounds [1986] 2 Lloyd's Rep. 12).

[490] [1916] 2 A.C. 397 at 404; cf. *Davis Contractors Ltd v Fareham Urban DC* [1956] A.C. 696 at 728 per Lord Reid: "By this time it might seem that the parties themselves have become so far disembodied spirits that their actual persons should be allowed to rest in peace. In their place there rises the figure of the fair and reasonable man. And the spokesman of the fair and reasonable man, who represents after all no more than the anthropomorphic conception of justice, is and must be the court itself".

[491] See above fn.489.

[492] See above, para. 6–032.

[493] i.e. terms implied *in fact*.

[494] See above, para.6–032.

[495] See below, para.19–118. There is an obvious analogy here with the doctrine of common mistake where there is a role for the construction of the contract, but the courts have rejected the implied term theory as the best explanation for when a contract is void for mistake: see above, paras. 8–002—8–007. The analogy between frustration and mistake is considered further below: para.19–121.

[496] *Hirji Mulji v Cheong Yue SS Co Ltd* [1926] A.C. 497 at 510.

[497] [1944] A.C. 265 at 275.

doctrine of frustration did not depend on the possibility of implying a term, but was "a substantive and particular rule which the common law has evolved".[498] And in the *Constantine* case he said: "The court is exercising powers, when it decides that a contract is frustrated, in order to achieve a result which is just and reasonable".[499] This "just solution" theory does not purport to explain why the courts sometimes abandon the doctrine of absolute contracts: it simply says that they do so. The theory should not, moreover, be interpreted to mean that the courts can do what they think just whenever a change of circumstances causes hardship to one party: it does not supersede the strict rules which determine the scope of the doctrine of frustration,[500] though the "dictates of justice" are the "ultimate rationale of the doctrine".[501] Nor does it determine the type of relief which can be given. When a contract is frustrated, both parties are at common law discharged, though the "just solution" might be an apportionment of loss.

19–117   **Foundation of the contract.** This theory was stated by Lord Haldane in the *Tamplin* case:

> "When people enter into a contract which is dependent for the possibility of performance on the continued availability of a specific thing, and that availability comes to an end by reason of circumstances beyond the control of the parties, the contract is *prima facie* regarded as dissolved. . . . Although the words of the stipulation may be such that the mere letter would describe what has occurred, the occurrence itself may yet be of a character and extent so sweeping that the foundation of what the parties are deemed to have had in contemplation has disappeared, and the contract itself has vanished with that foundation".[502]

In *W J Tatem Ltd v Gamboa*[503] Goddard J. regarded this as "the surest ground on which to rest the doctrine of frustration".

At first sight this theory has the merit of simplicity as it does not involve speculation as to the intention of the parties. It is particularly appropriate where performance depends on the continued availability of a specific thing. But in other cases the metaphor "foundation" is unhelpful. How can one tell whether passage through the Suez Canal is the "foundation" of a charterparty? What is the "foundation" of a contract in which the parties take a deliberate risk as to the continued availability of a specific thing or existence of some state of affairs? Such questions can, in the last resort, only be resolved by construing the contract. If this is so, there is no real difference between the "foundation" theory and the "implied term" theory in its objective sense. Indeed, exponents of one sometimes use the language of the other. Thus in the *Tamplin* case Lord Loreburn, after stating the implied term theory, said that the court

---

[498] ibid. at 274.
[499] [1942] A.C. 154 at 186; cf. *National Carriers Ltd v Panalpina (Northern) Ltd* [1981] A.C. 675 at 696; *The Super Servant Two* [1990] 1 Lloyd's Rep. 1 at 8.
[500] See above, paras 19–005, 19–033; *The Sea Angel* [2007] EWCA Civ 547; [2007] 2 Lloyd's Rep. 517 at [113].
[501] *The Sea Angel* [2007] EWCA Civ 547; [2007] 2 Lloyd's Rep. 517 at [132].
[502] [1916] 2 A.C. 397 at 406. Lord Haldane's was a dissenting speech.
[503] [1939] 1 K.B. 132 at 137.

"can infer from the nature of the contract and the surrounding circumstances that a condition which is not expressed was a foundation on which the parties contracted".[504]

Construction. All the theories so far stated depend in the last resort on the   **19–118**
construction of the contract: to this extent, they "shade into one another".[505] After stating the implied term theory, Lord Loreburn proposed, as the ultimate test: "what, in fact, is the true meaning of the contract?"[506] Similarly, in *Taylor v Caldwell*, Blackburn J. said:

"the contract is not to be *construed* as a positive contract, but as subject to an *implied condition* that the parties shall be excused in case, before breach, performance becomes impossible. . . . "[507]

Construing the contract and implying a term are in these cases only alternative ways of describing the same process. Similarly, the "foundation" theory raises a question of construction whenever it is at all doubtful what the "foundation" of the contract is. And Lord Wright, in the course of stating the "just solution" theory, said: "What happens is that the contract is held on its true construction not to apply at all from the time when the frustrating circumstances supervene".[508] It seems that this is the most satisfactory explanation of the doctrine of frustration.

Failure of consideration. This theory is sometimes used to explain why *both*   **19–119**
parties are discharged in the situation (discussed earlier in this chapter[509]) in which the supervening event makes the performance of only *one* party impossible. Thus destruction of a specific thing may make performance of the *supplier's* obligation impossible; but it has no such effect on the *recipient's* obligation to pay, and it can be said that the latter is discharged by failure of consideration,[510] i.e. because he does not receive the performance for which he bargained. In England, however, these cases are explained on the ground that the "common object" of the parties is frustrated.[511] Moreover, in so far as the present theory suggests that the failure of consideration must be total[512] it is plainly wrong since frustration can occur in cases of partial destruction or after part performance; and the theory has for this reason been rejected in the House of Lords.[513]

---

[504] [1916] 2 A.C. 397 at 404.

[505] *National Carriers Ltd v Panalpina (Northern) Ltd* [1981] A.C. 675 at 693.

[506] [1916] A.C. 397 at 404. There are obvious echoes here of the question proposed by Lord Hoffmann in *Attorney General of Belize v Belize Telecom Ltd* [2009] UKPC 10; [2009] 1 W.L.R. 1988 to determine whether a term should be implied in fact: "is that what the instrument, read as a whole against the relevant background, would reasonably be understood to mean?" (at [21]): see above, para.6–032.

[507] (1863) 3 B. & S. 826 at 833 (italics supplied).

[508] *Denny, Mott* case [1944] A.C. 265 at 274; cf. *The Eugenia* [1964] 2 Q.B. 226 at 239; *The Siboen and the Sibotre* [1976] 1 Lloyd's Rep. 293 at 235.

[509] See above, para.19–056.

[510] This explanation is commonly given in the US: Corbin, *Contracts*, §§1320, 1322; Restatement 2d, *Contracts*, Introductory Note to Ch.11, p.310.

[511] *Hirji Mulji v Cheong Yue SS Co Ltd* [1926] A.C. 497 at 510; above, para.19–056.

[512] For total failure of consideration, see above, para.19–094; below, para.22–003.

[513] *National Carriers Ltd v Panalpina (Northern) Ltd* [1981] A.C. 675 at 687, 702.

(b) Practical Importance

19–120   It is sometimes asked whether the above theoretical discussion has any practical importance. It seems to have none.[514] A number of possibilities must be discussed.

In *W J Tatem Ltd v Gamboa* Goddard J. said that the contract would be frustrated although the parties foresaw that the ship would be seized and detained. He even said: "If the foundation of the contract goes, it goes whether or not the parties have made a provision for it".[515] These statements could only be made by an adherent of the "foundation" theory. But the first has been doubted earlier in this chapter,[516] while the second was qualified later in the judgment: "*Unless the contrary intention is made plain*, the law imposes this doctrine of frustration".[517]

In the *Davis Contractors* case, Lord Reid said that no review was possible of the arbitrator's decision on the "foundation" theory, as the question whether the "foundation" had disappeared was one of fact; while such review was possible on the "implied term" or "construction" theories, as implication and construction were questions of law.[518] But a question of law would be involved even on the "foundation" theory if the question: what is the "foundation"? is itself one of construction. And after the *Tsakiroglou* case[519] it is difficult to argue that the right to review an arbitrator's decision is restricted by any particular theory.

In the *Davis Contractors* case, Lord Reid said that there might be a further practical difference between the "implied term" and "construction" theories. On the latter theory,

> "there is no need to consider what the parties thought or how they or reasonable men in their shoes would have dealt with the new situation if they had foreseen it. The question is whether the contract which they did make is, on its true construction, wide enough to apply to the new situation: if not, then it is at an end".[520]

But in construing the contract the court does not disregard the intention of the parties. The court may not have to ask: what would the parties have said, had they thought of the frustrating event? But it does have to ask: in what circumstances did the parties intend the contract to operate? In answering this question, the court no doubt applies an objective test[521]; but it is only after the question has been answered that the intention of the parties becomes irrelevant: that is, it is not necessary to go on and ask whether they would have agreed to discharge or to some compromise. But this question does not arise under the implied term theory either, as frustration at common law always results in total discharge of the contract.

---

[514] This seems to be the view of Lords Wilberforce and Roskill in *National Carriers Ltd v Panalpina (Northern) Ltd* [1981] A.C. 675 at 693, 717. Lord Hailsham ([1981] A.C. 675 at 687) regards "the theoretical basis of the doctrine as clearly relevant to the point under discussion"; but he does not specify in what respect it is relevant.

[515] [1939] 1 K.B. 132 at 138.

[516] See above, para.19–079.

[517] [1939] 1 K.B. 132 at 139 (italics supplied).

[518] *Davis Contractors Ltd v Fareham Urban DC* [1956] A.C. 696 at 720.

[519] [1962] A.C. 93; see generally above, para.19–066.

[520] [1956] A.C. 696 at 721.

[521] cf. above, paras 1–002, 2–002.

(c) Frustration and Mistake

Frustration is sometimes compared with common mistake[522] because the sup- **19–121**
posed subject-matter of the contract does not exist or is fundamentally different
from the subject-matter as it was believed to be. Thus in *Krell v Henry*[523] a
contract for the hire of a room overlooking the route of the coronation processions
was frustrated when the processions were *later* cancelled; in *Griffith v Brymer*[524]
a similar contract was held void for mistake when the processions had *already* been
cancelled before the contract was made.

Different juristic concepts. This analogy is interesting and sometimes help- **19–122**
ful; but it should not be pressed too far. Mistake and frustration are "different
juristic concepts",[525] the one relating to the formation and the other to the
discharge of contracts. Their factual bases are different in that mistake requires
the parties to entertain an *affirmative belief* in the existence of the subject-matter,
or of a state of affairs, when it in fact no longer exists. In cases of frustration, the
parties often have no affirmative belief as to the event: they need not *believe* that
it *will not* occur. Moreover, events which frustrate a contract would not necessarily
make it void for mistake if, unknown to the parties, they had already happened
when the contract was made.[526] Again, parties may validly agree on a contractual
term "requiring one of them to do the impossible",[527] e.g. on a term requiring a
seller of goods to deliver them from a named ship at a specified port which the ship
was incapable of entering. The seller would then be liable for failing to deliver in
accordance with that term; but he could be discharged if *after* the time of
contracting an event happened which made it impossible for the ship to get into
the port, e.g. "if a sudden storm had silted up the harbour"[528] there. The law
seems to be less ready to hold a contract void for mistake than discharged by
frustration, perhaps because it is, in general, easier to be sure of present facts than
to foresee future events,[529] or because a contracting party is more likely, on the

---

[522] See above, para.8–002 et seq.; *Associated Japanese Bank (International) Ltd v Crédit du Nord SA*
[1989] 1 W.L.R. 255 at 264 ("related areas"); *William Sindall Plc v Cambridgeshire CC* [1994] 1 W.L.R.
1016 at 1039). See also the reference to *Krell v Henry* [1903] 2 K.B. 740 in *Bell v Lever Bros Ltd* [1932]
A.C. 161 at 226 and the words "whether as to existing or future facts": [1932] A.C. 161 at 226–227;
and the reliance on frustration cases in the mistake case of *The Great Peace* [2002] EWCA Civ 1407;
[2003] Q.B. 679 at [61]–[76]. This view of the relationship between the two doctrines seems not to have
been shared by Blackburn J., whose judgment in *Taylor v Caldwell* (1863) 3 B. & S. 826 is generally
regarded as having established the doctrine of frustration. His judgment, given only four years later,
in the mistake case of *Kennedy v Panama, etc. Royal Mail Co* (1867) L.R. 2 Q.B. 580 contains no
reference to *Taylor v Caldwell* even though that case was cited to the court in *Kennedy*'s case at 581.
The extent to which frustration cases are a safe guide to the solution of problems of mistake was also
qualified in *The Great Peace* itself: see below, fn.526.
[523] [1903] 2 K.B. 740.
[524] (1903) 19 T.L.R. 434.
[525] *Constantine* case [1942] A.C. 154 at 186; cf. *Bell v Lever Bros Ltd* [1932] A.C. 161 at 237; *Fibrosa*
case [1943] A.C. 32 at 77.
[526] The view that the test for common mistake is stricter than that of frustration appears to be
supported by *The Great Peace* [2002] EWCA Civ 1407; [2003] Q.B. 679 at [83] (test of frustration "may
not be adequate in the context of mistake"). Hence the analogy between the two doctrines drawn in that
case in the passages referred to at fn.522, above is, at best, imperfect.
[527] *The Epaphus* [1987] 2 Lloyd's Rep. 215 at 218; *The New Prosper* [1991] 2 Lloyd's Rep. 93 at
99.
[528] ibid. at 220; cf. *Bell v Lever Bros Ltd* [1932] A.C. 161 at 218, per Lord Atkin, approving the
formulation by counsel (Sir John Simon K.C.).
[529] cf. *McAlpine Humberoak Ltd v McDermott International* (1992) 58 Build. L.R. 1.

true construction of the contract, to have undertaken responsibility for an existing, than for an unexpected future, state of affairs.[530]

19–123   **Distinct legal effects.** The legal effects of the two doctrines are also distinct. At common law, mistake makes a contract void ab initio, while frustration discharges it only from the time of the frustrating event.[531] In equity, indeed, the courts at one time claimed a power to set contracts aside for certain kinds of mistake which did not make them void at law.[532] But the Court of Appeal has held that there is no such power,[533] and even if this view were to be rejected by the House of Lords and the equitable jurisdiction were again to be recognised, its operation would still differ from that of frustration in two ways. First, the equitable power in cases of mistake was regarded as discretionary while frustration discharges a contract automatically, by operation of law, without any scope for judicial discretion; frustration moreover results in total discharge, while the equitable jurisdiction was to set the contract aside on terms.[534] It is, finally, clear from the wording[535] of the Law Reform (Frustrated Contracts) Act 1943 that the powers of adjustment conferred by that Act apply only to discharge by supervening (and not to invalidity on the ground of antecedent) events.[536]

---

[530] *The Great Peace* [2002] EWCA Civ 1407; [2003] Q.B. 679 at [85].

[531] See above, paras 8–001, 19–090.

[532] See above, para.8–027.

[533] *The Great Peace* [2002] EWCA Civ 1407; [2003] Q.B. 679.

[534] See above, paras 8–027, 19–090.

[535] s.1(1) ("where a contract ... *has become* impossible of performance or *been* otherwise frustrated").

[536] In *The Great Peace* [2002] EWCA Civ 1407; [2003] Q.B. 679 it was recognised at [161] that the 1943 Act did not apply to cases of mistakes making contracts void.

DAMAGES[1]

Damages and other remedies. A breach of contract is a civil wrong. To break **20–001** a contract can also occasionally be a criminal offence[2]; and some statutes penalise

---

[1] Burrows, *Remedies for Torts and Breach of Contract* (3rd edn); Harris, Campbell and Halson, *Remedies in Contract and Tort* (2nd edn); Treitel, *Remedies for Breach of Contract: a Comparative Account.*

[2] e.g. Protection from Eviction Act 1977, s.1(1); cf. National Minimum Wage Act 1998, s.31. See further, Treitel in *Essays in Memory of Sir Rupert Cross*, pp.82–92.

dangerous or deceptive conduct which may amount[3] to a breach of contract. Conviction in such cases makes the offender liable not only to punishment, but also to an order requiring him to pay compensation for any personal injury, loss or damage resulting from the offence.[4] In most cases, however, a breach of contract will involve only civil liability; and our sole concern in this chapter will be with the remedy of damages. A claim for damages is one for compensation in money for the fact that the claimant has not received the performance for which he bargained. In Ch.21 we will consider claims for specific relief (the action for an agreed sum, specific performance and injunctions). A person who has performed his part of the contract but has not received the agreed counter-performance may also claim back his performance or its reasonable value. These restitutionary remedies are not confined to cases of breach of contract and are considered separately in Ch.22.

20–002   **Damages are available as of right.** The action for damages is always available, as of right, when a contract has been broken. It should, from this point of view, be contrasted with claims for specific relief and for restitution, which are either subject to the discretion of the court or only available if certain conditions (to be discussed in the following chapters) are satisfied. An action for damages can succeed even though the victim has not suffered any loss: in that event, it will result in an award of nominal damages. The effect of such an award may simply be to establish what the rights and liabilities of the parties under a contract are, though for this purpose the action for a declaration now provides a more convenient remedy. Generally the victim will claim damages for a substantial loss; and our concern is with the law governing the award of such damages.

20–003   **A pragmatic subject.** It has been said that the assessment of damages in contract (and tort) is "a pragmatic subject . . . (which) does not lend itself to hard-and-fast rules"[5] and, in a similar vein, that "with so many disputes about damages, the issue is primarily one of fact."[6] This may be a reflection of the fact that, traditionally, the assessment of damages was seen as a matter for the good sense of the jury.[7] Even today, the courts sometimes revert to the language of "commonsense" to explain their decisions,[8] but this is not an area devoid of rules and principles and it is by reference to them that this chapter has been organised.[9] We shall consider, first, the general principles which govern awards of damages;[10] secondly, the way in which damages are assessed or quantified;[11] thirdly, the recovery of damages for non-pecuniary loss;[12] fourthly, certain rules limiting the damages which can be recovered;[13] and finally, contractual provisions purporting

---

[3] e.g. Consumer Protection Act 1987, Pt II: under these provisions, offences may be committed even though no contract is ever made or broken.

[4] Powers of Criminal Courts (Sentencing) Act 2000, s.130; cf. also Consumer Protection Act 1987, s.41 and para.9–077, above.

[5] *Takaro Properties Ltd v Rowling* (1986) 1 N.Z.L.R. 22 at 69; cf. *Johnson v Agnew* [1980] A.C. 367 at 400–401.

[6] *Hussey v Eeels* [1990] 2 Q.B. 227, at 241; below, para.20–122.

[7] See, e.g., *Chaplin v Hicks* [1911] 2 K.B. 786 at 792–793, 796; below, para.20–060.

[8] *Galoo Ltd v Bright Grahame Murray* [1994] 1 W.L.R. 1360 at 1374–1375; below, para.20–095; *The Fanis* [1994] 1 Lloyd's Rep 633 at 636–637.

[9] Recent developments have thrown into sharper focus the conceptual basis of some of these principles; most notably, the rule of remoteness; below, para.20–099.

[10] See below, paras 20–004—20–037.

[11] See below, paras 20–038—20–082.

[12] See below, paras 20–083—20–093.

[13] See below, paras 20–094—20–129.

to establish in advance the amount that can be recovered (or retained) by the victim.[14]

1. GENERAL PRINCIPLES

(a) Damages are Compensatory

(i) *Loss to claimant the criterion*

General rule. As a general rule,[15] damages are based on loss to the claimant[16] and not on gain to the defendant.[17] In a Scottish case,[18] a financier broke a contract to invest £15,000 in the business of a timber merchant and instead invested the same sum in a distillery. It was held that the timber merchant's damages were based on the loss to his business and not on the much larger profits which the financier had derived from the distillery. The same principle applies where a person who has agreed to sell goods for future delivery for £x fails to deliver because he has disposed elsewhere of the goods for £x - 100. If the buyer can in fact get goods of the same description for £x or less at the time fixed for delivery, he will have suffered no loss and will get no (substantial) damages: it is irrelevant that the seller has, in a sense, made a profit of £100 out of the breach.[19] It also follows from the general rule that damages are not awarded merely on the ground that the defendant has by the breach saved himself expense.

20–004

(ii) *What constitutes loss?*

The meaning of "loss".[20] Perhaps as a result of the pragmatic fact-based approach referred to above,[21] the law of damages for breach of contract lacks a clear conceptual basis of what constitutes "loss". This has left room for a number of theories: for example, that a more fundamental distinction should be drawn between what may be referred to as "direct" loss, i.e. the non-receipt of the performance bargained for, and "consequential loss", i.e. the subsequent adverse consequences of such non-receipt,[22] leading to the view that damages for the former should be awarded either as a "substitute" for the right infringed,[23] or as

20–005

---

[14] See below, paras 20–130—20–156.

[15] For possible exceptions, see below, paras 20–010—20–019.

[16] For exceptional cases in which the claimant can recover damages in respect of a third party's loss see above, para.14–024 et seq.

[17] *Tito v Waddell (No.2)* [1977] Ch.106 at 332; *The Solholt* [1983] 1 Lloyd's Rep. 605 at 608; Jones 99 L.Q.R. 443, Friedmann 80 Col.L.Rev. 504; Farnsworth 94 Yale L.J. 1339; Birks [1987] L.M.C.L.Q. 421; Friedmann 104 L.Q.R. 383; Birks 1990–1991 Butterworth Lectures 55; cf. Stoljar 2 J.C.L. 1; Edelman *Gain Based Damages*.

[18] *Teacher v Calder* (1889) 1 F.(H.L.) 39; cf. *The Siboen and the Sibotre* [1976] 1 Lloyd's Rep. 293 at 337; *The Sine Nomine* [2002] 1 Lloyd's Rep. 805 (arbitration award).

[19] *Acmé Mills v Johnson* 133 S.W. 784 (1911); cf. *The Solholt* [1983] 1 Lloyd's Rep. 605, where the buyer's damages were nominal as he had failed to mitigate (below, para.20–118) and it was irrelevant that the seller (who was in breach) had made a profit on resale.

[20] Scott [2007] L.M.C.L.Q. 465.

[21] See above, para.20–003.

[22] e.g. in a contract for the sale of goods where the seller fails to deliver, the direct loss is the difference between the market price and the contract price; the consequential loss would take the form of a loss of use, or the loss of a sub-sale, if any: below, para.20–056.

[23] Stevens, in Neyers, Bronaugh & Pitel (eds.) *Exploring Contract Law* (2009).

the cost of performance.[24] The principal practical effect of such theories is that damages, when awarded as a substitute for the right infringed, or as the cost of performance are not subject to the principles of mitigation or remoteness.[25] These theories, and others,[26] have led to a shift in terminology: traditionally, the claimant was said to be entitled to the protection of his "expectation interest", but increasingly reference is made to the "performance interest". The courts have not gone as far as is advocated by some, but recent developments have shown a willingness to expand the concept of loss beyond the more obvious forms of financial loss which are prevalent in the earlier cases in which the rules and principles for the recovery of damages were formulated.[27] Thus, we have already seen a willingness to embrace the concept of the "performance interest" in claims for losses suffered by a third party,[28] and in this chapter it is perhaps most evident in the award of damages for breach of contracts for services,[29] in the greater recognition of damages to compensate for disappointment, or loss of enjoyment,[30] and in the wider availability in exceptional cases of damages awarded by reference to gains made by the defendant.[31] For the present purpose, loss includes any harm to the person or property of the claimant, and any other injury to his economic position in the wider sense now recognised by the courts.

20–006   **Overall position taken into account.** In determining whether the victim has suffered loss, his overall position is taken into account.[32] Relevant factors include any benefits which he may have obtained under the broken contract, and his release from obligations under it. If, for example, a buyer has not yet paid and is released from his obligation to do so by the seller's wrongful failure to deliver, his loss will prima facie be the value of the goods less the price; and if he has agreed to pay no more than the goods are worth he may have suffered no loss at all.

The court will similarly take the claimant's overall position into account in determining the basis on which damages are to be assessed: it will not generally order the defendant to pay an amount which will actually make the claimant's position better than it would have been if the contract had been performed.[33] The principle is illustrated by *Phillips v Ward*[34] where a surveyor in breach of contract failed to draw his client's attention to the fact that the roof timbers of a house, which the latter was about to buy, were rotten. It was held that the client was not

---

[24] Edelman (2010) 4 *Journal of Equity* 122.

[25] The rule of remoteness probably does not apply to direct loss in any event (*Re National Coffee Palace Co* (1883) 24 Ch. D. 367 at 372); alternatively, it does apply but such loss always arises in "the ordinary course of things" (the "first limb") and is not therefore too remote: see below, para.20–100. Until recently, it did not matter which explanation is offered, but in the light of the decision of the House of Lords in *The Achilleas*, it may now matter since a loss falling within the first limb may nonetheless be found to be too remote: see below, para.20–111.

[26] See, inter alia, Friedmann 111 L.Q.R. 628; Coote [1997] C.L.J. 537; Duncan Wallace 115 L.Q.R. 394; cf. Campbell and Harris 22 J. of L. Studies 208; Campbell [2003] J. Bus. L. 131.

[27] "The law recognises that a party to a contract may have an interest in performance which is not readily measurable in terms of money": *Attorney General v Blake* [2001] 1 A.C. 268 at 282 per Lord Nicholls.

[28] See above, paras 14–024—14–036.

[29] See below, para.20–047.

[30] See below, para.20–088.

[31] See below, para.20–010 et seq.

[32] e.g. *The Baleares* [1990] 2 Lloyd's Rep. 130 (and see [1991] 2 All E.R. 110); cf. below, para.20–121.

[33] See below, para.20–029 (reliance); *Demarco v Perkins* [2006] EWCA Civ 188; [2006] P.N.L.R. at [73].

[34] [1956] 1 W.L.R. 471.

entitled to damages based on the cost of making the defects good. Such an award would put him into a better position than that in which he would have been if the contract had not been broken; for it would enable him to have a new roof with new timbers, which would be less expensive to maintain than an old roof with sound timbers. Hence the client was entitled to recover only the difference between the price that he paid and the value of the house when he bought it[35]; or the difference between the price actually paid and that which would have been paid if the surveyor had made his report with due care.[36]

Qualifications. The principle that the claimant's overall position should not   20–007
be made better than it would have been, if the contract had not been broken, is subject to a number of qualifications. First, it is not inflexibly applied where costs are actually incurred by the claimant in remedying the breach.[37] In *Harbutt's "Plasticine" Ltd v Wayne Tank & Pump Co Ltd*[38] the claimant's factory was burnt down as a result of the defendant's breach of contract. It was held that the claimant could recover the cost of rebuilding the factory without making any allowance for the fact that he would then have a new (and therefore more valuable) factory. The case can be explained on the ground that the claimant had no reasonable alternative but to rebuild, or that he did so in order to mitigate his loss.[39] Secondly, the principle was modified where a client had suffered loss in consequence of bad investment advice given by the defendant and had, before suffering the loss, spent some of the income produced by the investments on living expenses. This expenditure yielded no permanent benefit to the client and did not have to be brought into account since the very object of the contract was to produce an increased income for the client, so that it was foreseeable that he might spend that income, or part of it, in a way that left no product of permanent benefit to him.[40] Thirdly, the principle in *Phillips v Ward* does not require the court to take into account benefits derived by the claimant under some contract with the defendant, other than the one which has been broken. Thus if the claimant makes two contracts with the defendant, any profit made by the claimant in consequence of the performance of one of those contracts will not have to be brought into account in assessing his damages in respect of the breach of the other.[41]

Intended use of subject-matter. It is sometimes argued that a claimant has   20–008
suffered no loss because, even if the contract had been performed, he would not

---

[35] See *Perry v Sidney Phillips & Son* [1982] 1 W.L.R. 1297 at 1305, 1306; Burrows 47 M.L.R. 357; *Watts v Morrow* [1991] 1 W.L.R. 1421; *Gardner v Marsh & Parsons* [1997] 1 W.L.R. 489. Where the client pays *more* than the valuation, such excess may be irrecoverable: see *Lucas v Ogden* [1988] 2 E.G.L.R. 176.

[36] ibid. at 1302 (where the two formulae stated in the text would have yielded the same result). In appropriate circumstances, further damages may be recoverable for such a breach. Thus in *Patel v Hooper & Jackson* [1999] 1 All E.R. 992 the defect which the surveyor's report should have revealed made the house uninhabitable, and the client recovered the reasonable costs of extricating himself from the transaction and damages in respect of discomfort suffered in the course of this process (cf. below, para.20–087).

[37] See further, para.20–042, below.

[38] [1970] 1 Q.B. 447, followed on this point in *Bacon v Cooper Metals Ltd* [1982] 1 All E.R. 397, and *Haysman v Mrs Rogers Films Ltd* [2008] EWHC 2494; cf. *Re-Source America International Ltd v Platt Site Services Ltd* [2005] EWCA Civ 97; [2005] 2 Lloyd's Rep. 50 (full replacement cost reduced by savings made on refurbishment).

[39] See below, para.20–119.

[40] *R. v Investors Compensation Scheme Ex p. Bowden* [1995] Q.B. 107, reversed on other grounds [1996] A.C. 261.

[41] *Brown v KMR Services Ltd* [1995] 4 All E.R. 598 at 640.

have used the subject-matter profitably, or at all. In one case,[42] contractors were sued for agreed damages[43] for delay in delivering warships to the Spanish Government. The delay being prima facie a source of loss, it was held to be no defence that warships are not put to profitable use, or that the ships, if delivered on time, would probably have been sunk in a naval battle in which the fleet which they were to have joined suffered defeat. However, the claimant's intended use of the subject-matter may affect the amount of his loss: this is, for example, the case where a buyer of goods has made a sub-sale of the very goods comprised in the original sale.[44] Similarly, by statute a landlord cannot recover damages for breach of his tenant's obligation to repair if the tenant can prove that the landlord was going to demolish the premises.[45]

(iii) *Breach having no adverse effect*

20–009   A further consequence of the compensatory principle is that the claimant cannot recover substantial damages if the breach has not adversely affected his position;[46] for "damages are designed to compensate for an established loss and not to provide a gratuitous benefit to the aggrieved party".[47] Another way of putting the point is that "A breach of contract may cause a loss but is not itself a loss in any meaningful sense".[48] This aspect of the principle is most readily illustrated by the case in which a seller of goods wrongfully fails to deliver on a falling market. If the buyer has not paid and if, at the time fixed for delivery, he can buy substitute goods more cheaply elsewhere, the breach will prima facie have had no adverse effect on him, so that he will not be entitled to substantial damages. Similarly, a shipowner cannot get substantial damages for breach of the charterer's obligation to load if he finds alternative and more profitable employment for the ship.[49] Nor can a buyer recover substantial damages merely because the seller delivers goods which are not of the contract description if they are in fact no less valuable than goods which are of the contract description.[50] These are all instances where the claimant has suffered no loss at all. He similarly cannot recover in respect of a loss which he does suffer if he would have suffered the same loss, even if there had been no breach. This situation is discussed later in this chapter.[51]

(iv) *Damages based on the gain made by the defendant*[52]

20–010   We have seen above that, as a general rule, damages for breach of contract are based on loss to the claimant and not on gain to the defendant. There is one clear exception to that general rule where the claimant is awarded an account of the

---

[42] *Clydebank Engineering Co v Don Jose Ramos Isquierdo y Castaneda* [1905] A.C. 6.
[43] See below, para.20–130 et seq.
[44] *Re R & H Hall Ltd and W H Pim Jr & Co's Arbitration* (1928) 139 L.T. 50; below, para.20–049.
[45] Landlord and Tenant Act 1927, s.18(1).
[46] See, e.g., *Ford v White* [1964] 1 W.L.R. 885.
[47] *Ruxley Electronics and Construction Co Ltd v Forsyth* [1996] A.C. 344 at 357.
[48] *Alfred McAlpine Construction Ltd v Panatown Ltd* [2001] 1 A.C. 518 at 534.
[49] *Staniforth v Lyall* (1830) 7 Bing. 169.
[50] *Taylor v Bank of Athens* (1922) 27 Com.Cas. 142.
[51] See below, para.20–095.
[52] Edelman, *Gain Based Damages*; Cunnington 71 M.L.R. 559 .

profits made by the defendant as a consequence of the breach.[53] In rather more cases, the claimant has been awarded damages which have been calculated, at least in part, by reference to the profits made by the defendant ("*Wrotham Park* damages").[54] It is not entirely clear whether such damages are best explained as compensation for loss incurred by the claimant, or as restitution of a gain made by the defendant.

Account of profits. In some situations, there is no doubt that a contract 20–011 breaker must hand over to the victim any gain resulting from the breach. If, for example, the subject-matter of a sale is land, the vendor is, after the conclusion of the contract, considered to hold the land as trustee for the purchaser; and if the vendor wrongfully resells the land to a third party, the purchaser is entitled to the proceeds of that sale, even though they may exceed his loss.[55] An account of profits may be ordered against a person who wrongfully uses another's trade secrets or confidential information[56]; and this remedy may also be available where the wrongful use amounts to a breach of a contract of employment,[57] or a confidentiality agreement.[58] Where a breach of contract amounts also to breach of a fiduciary obligation, damages may similarly be based on the defendant's profit.[59] For example, an agent who commits a breach of his fiduciary duty by taking a bribe, or by selling his own property to a principal, when he has been employed to buy for him, is liable to account for any profit made in this way.[60]

Attorney-General v Blake. The wider availability of the remedy of an account 20–012 of profits for breach of contract was recognised by the House of Lords in *Attorney-General v Blake*.[61] While employed as a member of the security services, Blake passed secret information to agents of the Soviet Union, in breach not only of the terms of his employment but also of the Official Secrets Act 1911; he was convicted of offences under that Act and sentenced to 42 years' imprisonment. He escaped from prison and fled to Moscow where, over 20 years later, he entered into an agreement with an English publisher for the publication of his autobiography. Although the information in the book was no longer confidential[62] at the time of the delivery of his manuscript and of the publication of the book, the disclosure of the information amounted to both a further offence under the 1911 Act and a further breach of Blake's contract with the Crown. This breach, however, caused no material loss to the Crown in respect of which compensatory damages could

---

[53] See below, para.20–011.

[54] See below, para.20–015.

[55] See *Lake v Bayliss* [1974] 1 W.L.R. 1073.

[56] *Peter Pan Mfg Corp v Corsets Silhouette Ltd* [1964] 1 W.L.R. 96; *Attorney-General v Guardian Newspapers (No.2)* [1990] A.C. 109 at 262, 288; cf. Law Com. No.110, paras 4.86 and 6.114(2)(b).

[57] cf. *Printers & Finishers Ltd v Holloway* [1965] 1 W.L.R. 1.

[58] *Pell Frischmann Engineering Ltd v Bow Valley Iran Ltd* [2009] UKPC 45; [2010] B.L.R. 73;*Vercoe v Rutland Fund Management Ltd* [2010] EWHC 424 (Ch). In both cases, the claim for breach of contract was confined to *Wrotham Park* damages (see below, para.20–015) and in the *Vercoe* case it was held that the claimant was not entitled to any more extensive relief by way of an account in a claim for breach of confidence: at [334]–[346].

[59] *Mathew v T M Sutton Ltd* [1994] 1 W.L.R. 1455; *Tang Man Sit v Capacious Investments Ltd* [1996] A.C. 514 (where the claimant elected to claim damages for breach of trust rather than an account of profits); cf. *Nottingham University v Fishel* [2000] I.C.R. 1462 at 1489.

[60] See above, para.16–097.

[61] [2001] 1 A.C. 268.

[62] So that the case did not fall directly within the exception (to the general rule that damages are compensatory) referred to, above at fn.56.

have been recovered and, after publication, the remedy by way of injunction, which could have been sought before then, was no longer available; nor could the case be brought within any of the qualifications of the compensatory principle which have been described above.[63] The House of Lords nevertheless held, by a majority, that where (as in *Blake*'s case) damages were not a "sufficient"[64] remedy, the court should "exceptionally" be able to "grant the discretionary remedy of requiring a defendant to account to the [claimant] for benefits derived from his breach of contract".[65] This development was based on the analogy of the discretionary remedies by way of specific relief in equity, which are available also where damages are not an adequate (or the most appropriate[66]) remedy for breach.

20–013 **Scope of the discretionary account of profits.** Two questions arise in relation to the discretion to award an account of profits for breach of contract: when does it *exist* and when will it be *exercised*? In relation to the equitable remedies by way of specific relief, the uncertainty that could arise from their discretionary nature is much reduced by the accumulation of case law which not only indicates which types of contracts can (and which cannot) be specifically enforced[67] but also lists factors to be taken into account in determining when the discretion to order specific relief will be exercised[68]: the overriding principle is that this discretion is "to be governed so far as possible by fixed rules and principles".[69] In relation to the discretion created by *Blake*'s case, there can be no guidance on the first of these points since that discretion applies to breaches of contract generally; and with regard to the second point Lord Nicholls said that "no fixed rules can be prescribed"[70] with regard to the exercise of the discretion. He was prepared only to give the "general guide" that this depends on "whether the [claimant] had a legitimate interest in preventing the defendant's profit-making activity"[71]; but this formula does little to reduce the resulting uncertainty, since every contracting party can be said to have a "legitimate interest" in the performance of a contractual promise made to him.[72] Some further guidance of a negative nature is, however, provided. An account of profits is not to be available *merely because*[73] the defendant is guilty of either "skimped performance"[74] (the difference in value between what was and what should have been provided being the normal measure of damages in such a case[75]) or of breach of a negative obligation "by

---

[63] See above, para.20–011.

[64] [2001] 1 A.C. 268 at 285.

[65] ibid. at 284–285, per Lord Nicholls, who ([2001] 1 A.C. 268 at 284) preferred the phrase "account of profits" to "the unhappy expression 'restitutionary damages' ".

[66] See below, para.21–027; cf. the use by Lord Nicholls in *Blake*'s case of the phrase "most appropriate" at 285.

[67] See below, paras 21–035—21–045.

[68] See below, para.21–016 et seq.

[69] See below, para.21–028.

[70] [2001] 1 A.C. 268 at 285.

[71] ibid.

[72] In this respect, the "legitimate interest" in receiving performance differs from that in continuing performance, referred to in a different context at para.21–012, below.

[73] Lord Nicholls stated that none of the factors which follow "would be, *by itself*, a good reason for ordering an account of profits": [2001] 1 A.C. 268 at 286 (emphasis added); a combination of such factors appears to form the basis of the decision to award *Wrotham Park* damages in the *Experience Hendrix* case, below text to fn.114.

[74] [2001] 1 A.C. 268.

[75] ibid. See below, para.20–047.

doing the very thing he has promised not to do"[76]; nor merely because the breach was "cynical and deliberate" or "enabled the defendant to enter into a more profitable contract elsewhere"[77]; nor merely because, by entering into such a contract "the defendant put it out of his power to perform his contract with the [claimant]".[78] But as no positive indications are given as to when the discretion to order an account of profits *will* be exercised, the creation of that discretion remains a source of considerable uncertainty.[79]

Only in exceptional circumstances. With regard to this uncertainty, a   **20–014** number of points can, however, be made in relation to *Blake*'s case. First, the facts of that case can fairly be described as not merely exceptional, but as extreme; and it is hard to take issue with the outcome on those facts. Secondly, on such facts there would normally be other ways (not available on the special facts) of stripping the wrongdoer of his profits: e.g. by a confiscation order[80] if Blake had at the relevant time been amenable to the jurisdiction of the English criminal courts, or by an injunction if that remedy had been sought in time. Thirdly, in the factual context the argument in favour of certainty lacks its usual force. Certainty in rules of contract law is intended to enable parties to *rely* on such rules in regulating their conduct; and there is little plausibility and even less merit in the argument that, in deciding to break his contract with the Crown, Blake relied (or should have been encouraged to rely) on the rule that damages were compensatory. But although these points may justify the actual decision in *Blake*'s case, they cannot entirely dispel the concern caused by the ill-defined discretionary exception to the compensatory principle that was there created. Lord Hobhouse, in his dissent, referred to the "disruptive"[81] consequences that could follow from attempts "to extend the decision of the present exceptional case to commercial situations so as to introduce restitutionary rights beyond those presently recognised by the law of restitution".[82] Such consequences could, for example, follow where a party to a commercial contract decided to commit a breach of it with a view to making a profit even after he has compensated the other party for his loss. It is hard to see why in such a case the law should "confer a windfall on the injured party"[83] by awarding such profits to him in excess of his loss or, a fortiori, why it should make such an award where he has suffered no loss at all. It seems from the terms of Lord Nicholls' speech that the discretion created in *Blake*'s case is not intended to extend to cases of this kind.[84]

The exceptional nature of the *Blake* case is borne out by the decision of the Court of Appeal in *Experience Hendrix LLC v PPX Enterprises Inc*,[85] where the

---

[76] ibid. at 286. These suggestions, which were approved by the Court of Appeal ([1998] Ch 439 at 458) were doubted in the 10th edition of this book at p.869 and were rejected in the House of Lords not only by Lord Nicholls (above) but also by Lord Steyn at 291.

[77] ibid.; cf. Birks [1987] L.M.C.L.Q. 421.

[78] ibid.

[79] cf. Beatson 118 L.Q.R. 377.

[80] See above, para.11–150.

[81] [2001] 1 A.C. 268 at 299; cf. *Surrey CC v Bredero Homes Ltd* [1993] 1 W.L.R. 1361 at 1370.

[82] ibid.

[83] *Surrey CC v Bredero Homes Ltd*, above, at 1370.

[84] See above, at fn.77; cf. *Luxe Holding Ltd v Midland Resources Holding Ltd* [2010] EWHC 1908 (Ch) at [53]; above fn.19.

[85] [2003] EWCA Civ 323; [2003] E.M.L.R. 515 at [56].

defendant, in breach of an earlier settlement with the claimant, granted licences to others to market certain musical recordings. There, a claim for an account of profits was rejected[86] on the basis of three "obvious" distinctions from the *Blake* case,[87] namely that there was no parallel with: the special interest of the state in maintaining national security and the integrity of its secret service; the fact that the notoriety which accounted for the level of Blake's royalty-earning capacity derived from his prior breaches of secrecy; or the close analogy between Blake's position and that of a fiduciary. On the other hand, and this is indicative of the uncertainty in this area, not all of these factors need to be present. In *Esso Petroleum v Niad*[88] an account of profits was ordered as a remedy for breach of a contractual scheme under which Esso provided financial support to the defendant, in exchange for him agreeing to keep the price at which petrol was sold from his garage at a certain level (the "Pricewatch" scheme). The defendant received the financial support, but did not lower the price as required. Damages were regarded as an inadequate remedy, since it was impossible for Esso to attribute any lost sales of petrol to breach of the scheme by one dealer, but it was equally impossible to assess the claimant's loss in the *Experience Hendrix* case, and the most that could be said of the *Niad* case, when compared to the distinguishing features of the *Blake* case, is that Esso had a "special interest" in maintaining the integrity of the Pricewatch scheme. One possible explanation for the *Niad* case may be that, while the claimant's loss in *Experience Hendrix* was impossible to quantify in normal terms, damages were not an inadequate remedy because they were available in the form of *Wrotham Park* damages which are considered below.[89] It is difficult to see how such an award could have been made in the *Niad* case.

20–015   **Wrotham Park damages.** This award of damages is so named after the-*Wrotham Park*[90] case, in which a developer had acquired land subject to a restrictive covenant which had been imposed for the benefit of an adjoining estate. In breach of the covenant, the developer built houses on the land; this did not diminish the value of the estate, but its owners nevertheless recovered substantial damages for the breach, amounting to 5 per cent of the additional profit made by the defendant. This percentage was said to represent "such sum of money as might reasonably have been demanded by the [claimants] from [the defendant] as a quid pro quo for releasing the covenant".[91] Similarly, in the *Experience Hendrix* case, above,[92] the defendant was ordered to pay the sum that might reasonably have been charged and paid between willing parties for the release of the restriction

---

[86] The defendant was ordered to pay *Wrotham Park* damages: see below at fn.93.

[87] [2003] EWCA Civ 323; [2003] E.M.L.R. 515 at [37].

[88] [2001] All E.R. (D) 324.

[89] See below, para.20–015.

[90] *Wrotham Park Estate Co v Parkside Homes Ltd* [1974] 1 W.L.R. 798; cf. *Amec Developments Ltd v Jury's Hotel Management (UK) Ltd* (2000) 82 P. & C.R. 286; *Lane v O'Brien Homes* [2004] EWHC 303 (QB); Sharpe and Waddams 1 O.J.L.S. 290. In *Surrey CC v Bredero Homes Ltd* [1993] 1 W.L.R. 1361 the Court of Appeal declined to award any damages in a very similar case. The decision is not easy to reconcile with the *Wrotham Park* case and it has been said that "so far as the *Bredero Homes Ltd* decision is inconsistent with the approach adopted in the *Wrotham Park* case, the latter is to be preferred": *Attorney General v Blake* [2001] 1 A.C. 268 at 283.

[91] [1974] 1 W.L.R. 798 at 815; cf. *Lunn Poly Ltd v Liverpool & Lancashire Properties Ltd* (2006) 25 E.G. 210 at [25].

[92] See above at fn.85.

imposed on the commercial exploitation of the recordings in question by the terms of the settlement agreement.[93]

Compensation or restitution? The concept of a quid pro quo for releasing the covenant is equally consistent with a compensatory or restitutionary analysis, i.e. the claimant is either compensated for the loss of the opportunity to bargain for a sum to release the defendant from his contractual obligation,[94] or the defendant is required to restore the gain made by his breach in the form of the opportunity to generate the profits in question. It is openly acknowledged that, in many cases, the claimant would not have been prepared to grant a release at any price so there cannot, in any real sense, have been a "loss" of the opportunity to bargain for a release fee.[95] This artificiality has led to the view that a restitutionary analysis is to be preferred,[96] but while this has some judicial support,[97] the prevailing view is that *Wrotham Park* damages should be regarded as compensation for the claimant's loss.[98] Which is correct may not make any practical difference, but the compensatory analysis appears to be more consistent with the approach taken by the courts to the effect of subsequent events; in particular, the level of profits which the defendant has, in fact, made. Thus, in *Pell Frischmann Engineering Ltd v Bow Valley Iran Ltd*[99] the defendant, in breach of a confidentiality agreement with the claimant, entered into a contract with X which was meant to be obtained by way of a joint venture with the claimant. The actual profits made by the defendant were found to be in the region of $1–1.8m. Nonetheless, the Privy Council awarded damages of $2.5m on the basis that, as *Wrotham Park* damages "*are meant to be compensatory*, and are normally to be assessed or valued at the date of breach, principle and consistency indicate that post-valuation events are normally irrelevant".[100] The fact that the award of damages exceeded the profits made by the defendant is not, however, entirely inconsistent with a restitutionary analysis since the gain made by the defendant may be seen not as the actual profits realised, but the opportunity to generate them, or the commercial

20–016

---

[93] cf. *World Wide Fund for Nature v World Wrestling Federation Entertainment Inc* [2007] EWCA Civ 286; [2008] 1 W.L.R. 445 where the claim was in fact struck out as an abuse of process.

[94] Sharpe and Waddams (1982) 2 O.J.L.S. 290; Stoljar (1989) 2 J.C.L. 1.

[95] *Experience Hendrix LLC v PPX Enterprises Inc* [2003] EWCA Civ 323; [2003] E.M.L.R. 515 at [45]; cf. *Douglas v Hello! Ltd (No.3)* [2005] EWCA Civ 595; [2006] Q.B. 125 at [246].

[96] Rotherham [2008] L.M.C.L.Q. 25; Burrows in Saidov and Cunnington (eds.), *Contract Damages*.

[97] *Surrey CC v Bredero Homes Ltd* [1993] 1 W.L.R. 1361 at 1369–1370.

[98] *Jaggard v Sawyer* [1995] 1 W.L.R. 269; *Attorney-General v Blake* [2001] 1 A.C. 268 at 281; *Lane v O'Brien Homes* [2004] EWHC 303 (QB); *World Wide Fund for Nature v World Wrestling Federation Entertainment Inc* [2007] EWCA Civ 286; [2008] 1 W.L.R. 445 at [59]. The precise basis of the award made in the *Experience Hendrix* case (above, fn.93) is not entirely easy to discern. The emphasis placed on the profits made by the defendant suggests a restitutionary analysis, but this is not inconsistent with an attempt to assess the claimant's loss of opportunity (see below, para.20–019) and there are numerous references to the damages awarded as "compensation".

[99] [2009] UKPC 45; [2010] B.L.R. 73.

[100] *Lunn Poly Ltd v Liverpool & Lancashire Properties Ltd* (2006) 25 E.G. 210 at [29] per Neuberger L.J., approved by the Privy Council, above fn.99 at [50] (emphasis added). Neuberger L.J. also referred to the "quasi-equitable nature" of the damages (see below fn.103) and acknowledged that "the judge may, where there are good reasons, direct a departure from the norm, either by selecting a different valuation date or by directing that a specific post-valuation-date event be taken into account", e.g. in the *Pell Frsichmann* case that there had been an "extraordinary and unexplained delay in bringing proceedings" (at [54]) (the claim was nonetheless not out of time under the law of Jersey).

value of the right infringed,[101] regardless of how well that opportunity or right was or was not exploited.[102]

20–017   **Limits.** Of greater practical significance than the question whether *Wrotham Park* damages are compensatory or restitutionary in nature, is the scope of the courts' power to make such an award. As with the award of an account of profits, the law in this respect is uncertain. Taken to its logical conclusion, the decision in the *Pell Frischmann* case indicates that the courts are not confined to cases where the defendant has made a profit as a consequence of his breach, but a feature of that case and those which preceded it is that the defendant was guilty of the breach of a negative obligation. This has two possible implications. The first is that damages may only be awarded in lieu of an injunction to restrain the defendant's breach,[103] that being the more normal remedy for breach of a negative obligation. While there are references in the cases to this jurisdiction of the courts,[104] it would be artificial to so restrict the award of *Wrotham Park* damages given that the House of Lords has, since the *Wrotham Park* case, held that the principles governing the assessment of damages are the same whether the award is made in equity or at common law[105] and given also the acknowledgement that it is not necessary that an injunction should actually have been claimed in the proceedings, or that there should have been any prospect, on the facts, of it being granted.[106] Secondly, an injunction is often the remedy for breach of a negative obligation, rather than damages, because it is in the nature of such an obligation that the breach of it may not result in any provable loss to the claimant and it has appeared as though a precondition to the award of *Wrotham Park* damages is the "absence of financially measurable loss",[107] or that the claimant "cannot demonstrate identifiable financial loss".[108] Most recently, it has been held that *Wrotham Park* damages are not confined to the breach of a negative obligation,[109] but what is less clear is whether, even though available for breach of a positive obligation, they are nonetheless confined to cases where the claimant would otherwise be entitled to no, or nominal, damages. In the case in question, it was not regarded as a bar that the claimant might have been entitled to modest damages for consequential loss.[110] The difficulty is that, shorn of any of these limitations, it can only be said that an award of *Wrotham Park* damages may be made "in a suitable case"[111] or where

---

[101] *Experience Hendrix LLC v PPX Enterprises Inc* [2003] EWCA Civ 323; [2003] E.M.L.R. 515 at [45]. A restitutionary analysis may also seem most apt where the effect of the defendant's breach is not that he was able to make profits under another contract, but that he saved the expense of performing the contract with the claimant, as in *Guido van der Garde BV v Force India Formula One Ltd* [2010] EWHC 2373 (QB).

[102] Edelman, *Gain-based damages*, ch.3.

[103] i.e. under the jurisdiction created by s.2 of the Chancery Amendment Act 1858 ("Lord Cairns's Act"): below, para.21–060.

[104] See, most recently, the *Pell Frischmann* case, above fn.99 at [48].

[105] *Johnson v Agnew* [1980] A.C. 367; below, para.21–062.

[106] *Jaggard v Sawyer* [1995] 1 W.L.R. 269 at 285; *Attorney-General v Blake* [2001] 1 A.C. 268 at 282; *World Wide Fund for Nature v World Wrestling Federation Entertainment Inc* [2007] EWCA Civ 286; [2008] 1 W.L.R. 445 at [54]; *Pell Frischmann Engineering Ltd v Bow Valley Iran Ltd* [2009] UKPC 45; [2010] B.L.R. 73 at [48]; Smith (1995) 24 Can B.L.J. 121.

[107] *Experience Hendrix LLC v PPX Enterprises Inc* [2003] EWCA Civ 323; [2003] E.M.L.R. 515 at [56].

[108] *World Wide Fund for Nature v World Wrestling Federation Entertainment Inc* [2007] EWHC Civ 286, at [59]; [2007] EWCA Civ 286; [2008] 1 W.L.R. 445 at [34].

[109] *Guido van der Garde BV v Force India Formula One Ltd* [2010] EWHC 2373 (QB) at [533].

[110] ibid. at [539].

[111] ibid. at [532].

necessary to do "practical justice".[112] Notwithstanding the rejection by Lord Nicholls of the factors referred to above as being sufficient *by themselves* to explain when an account of profits may be ordered,[113] some combination of them may suffice to explain when it would be a suitable case to award an account of profits, or *Wrotham Park* damages.[114] Of those listed, the factor which appears to be most consistent with the decisions to date is the cynical and deliberate nature of the breach by the defendant.

Account of profits or *Wrotham Park* damages? The question of when   20–018
Wrotham Park damages might be ordered is bound up with the question of whether the court should award such damages, or an account of profits. Both remedies are discretionary, in that the court will first assess whether damages will provide an "adequate" remedy if assessed on the traditional basis of the claimant's proven loss. Quite what is meant by "inadequate" has yet to be fully explored[115] and further analogies may be drawn in future cases with the test of the inadequacy of damages as a pre-requisite to an order for specific performance.[116]An attempt at "a more principled examination of the circumstances" in which the courts will award either an account of profits or *Wrotham Park* damages was made by Sales J. in *Vercoe v Rutland Fund Management Ltd*.[117] At a "high level of generality" the question is what is a just response to the wrong in question.[118] In this enquiry, there is a role for what has been referred to above as the "performance interest"[119] and in cases where the claimant's "interest in full performance is recognised as being particularly strong" (e.g. the infringement of proprietary rights, or a right of a kind where it would never be reasonable to expect that it could be bought out for some reasonable fee (such as the promise to keep state secrets in *Blake*'s case), or the breach of a fiduciary duty) an account of profits may be the appropriate remedy. Where however "one is not dealing with infringement of a right which is clearly proprietary in nature . . . and there is nothing exceptional to indicate that the defendant should never have been entitled to adopt a commercial approach in deciding how to behave in relation to that right, the appropriate remedy is likely to be an award of damages assessed by reference to a reasonable buy out fee rather than an account of profits."[120]

Assessment. Where it is found that *Wrotham Park* damages is the more   20–019
appropriate remedy it has been held that it is reasonable for the court to look at

---

[112] ibid. at [539].

[113] See above, para.20–013.

[114] *Experience Hendrix LLC v PPX Enterprises Inc* [2003] EWCA Civ 323; [2003] E.M.L.R. 515 at [44], [58].

[115] For example, if both parties are well aware that the defendant's breach is unlikely to occasion any loss to the claimant, that factor itself would allow the defendant to say that any negotiation for a release would only have produced a modest sum, if any. But, as seen (above, at fn.100), the parties' assessment in this regard would have to be made at the date of breach; the defendant cannot rely on subsequent events to argue that he would have negotiated a lower figure.

[116] See, generally, para.21–017 below and, in particular, the discussion of their Lordships in *Beswick v Beswick* [1968] A.C. 58 (are damages "inadequate" because the claimant has suffered no loss and they would therefore be nominal, or is that not "inadequate", but simply a reflection of the principle that damages are only awarded to compensate for loss?).

[117] [2010] EWHC 424 (Ch).

[118] ibid. at [339]; *Attorney General v Blake*, above fn.98 at 284H

[119] See above, para.20–005.

[120] [2010] EWHC 424 (Ch) at [341]; cf. *Jones v Ricoh UK Ltd* [2010] EWHC 1743 (Ch) at [89]–[91]; *Luxe Holding Ltd v Midland Resources Holding Ltd* [2010] EWHC 1908 (Ch) at [55].

the eventual outcome and to consider whether or not that is a useful guide to what the parties would have thought at the time of their hypothetical bargain.[121] But, as made clear by the decision of the Privy Council in the *Pell Frischmann* case to award damages in excess of the profits made by the defendant, the focus is primarily on how the notional negotiation would have proceeded in the light of the information available to the parties and the commercial context at the time that it should have taken place. That negotiation is assumed to be between a willing seller and a willing buyer acting reasonably.[122] It has also been said that the courts should take into account "any additional factors particularly affecting the just balance to be struck between the competing interests of the parties"[123] and should not "provide relief out of proportion to the real extent of the claimant's interest in proper performance judged on an objective basis by reference to the situation which presents itself to the court."[124] Such considerations perhaps serve to emphasise the uncertainty surrounding the scope and extent of this relief, but there are obvious signs here of the recognition of the performance interest.[125]

(v) *Punitive damages*

20–020   **General rule: no punitive damages.** Punitive (or exemplary) damages can be awarded in certain tort cases.[126] The purpose of such damages is not to compensate the claimant, nor even to strip the defendant of his profit, but to express the court's disapproval of the defendant's conduct, e.g. where he has deliberately committed a wrong (such as defamation[127]) with a view to profit.[128]

As a general rule punitive damages cannot be awarded in a purely contractual action,[129] since the object of such an action is not to punish the defendant but to compensate the claimant.[130] Punitive damages are not available even though the breach was committed deliberately and with a view to profit. If the court is particularly outraged by the defendant's conduct, it can sometimes achieve much the same result by awarding damages for injury to the claimant's feelings.[131] In

---

[121] *Pell Frischmann Engineering Ltd v Bow Valley Iran Ltd* [2009] UKPC 45; [2010] B.L.R. 73 at [51].

[122] ibid. at [53].

[123] *Vercoe v Rutland Fund Management Ltd* [2010] EWHC 424 (Ch) at [292].

[124] ibid.

[125] See Sales J. cross-reference (ibid.) to the decision of the House of Lords in *Ruxley v Forsyth* [1996] A.C. 344: below, para.20–046.

[126] See Lord Devlin's speech in *Rookes v Barnard* [1964] A.C. 1129; cf. *Kuddus v Chief Constable of the Leicestershire Constabulary* [2001] UKHL 29; [2002] 2 A.C. 122; *Borders (UK) Ltd v Metropolitan Police Commissioner* [2005] EWCA Civ 197; *The Times*, April 15, 2005.

[127] *Cassell& Co Ltd v Broome* [1972] A.C. 1027.

[128] In *Stoke-on-Trent CC v W & J Wass Ltd* [1988] 1 W.L.R. 1406 at 1414 the damages in the *Wrotham Park* case [1974] 1 W.L.R. 798 were described as "something akin to . . . exemplary damages for breach of contract", and one of the factors that may be taken into account is whether the defendant's breach was deliberate or cynical: above, para.20–017.

[129] *Perera v Vandiyar* [1953] 1 W.L.R. 672; *Reed v Madon* [1989] Ch. 408; *Johnson v Unisys Ltd* [2001] UKHL 13; [2003] 1 A.C. 518 at [15], per Lord Steyn, dissenting on the main issue in that case and see below, fn.131. Law Com. No.247 (1997), para.6.3.19 recognises and recommends no change in the rule that punitive damages are not available for breach of contract. McBride 1995 *Anglo-American Law Review* 369, questions the reasons for the rule.

[130] *Calabar Properties Ltd v Stitcher* [1984] 1 W.L.R. 287 at 297; *Ruxley Electronics and Construction Ltd v Forsyth* [1996] A.C. 344 at 352, 365, 373.

[131] See below, para.20–083 et seq; cf. the suggestion in *McCall v Abelesz* [1976] Q.B. 585 at 594 that damages for injury to feelings could now be awarded in a case like *Perera v Vandiyar*, above; Law Com. No.247, para.6.1.2, preferring the phrase "damages for mental distress" to "aggravated damages" in cases of this kind.

theory such damages are meant to compensate the claimant for mental suffering, rather than to punish the defendant. But in practice the distinction is often hard to draw and—from the defendant's point of view—to perceive.[132] However, where the claimant has a cause of action both in tort and for breach of contract, he may be able to recover punitive damages by framing the claim in tort. For example, a landlord who unlawfully evicts his tenant is guilty both of a breach of contract and of a trespass; and punitive damages have been awarded in such a case.[133] Another type of case in which a defendant seeks to profit from a deliberate wrong which is both a breach of contract and a tort is that in which he gives a fraudulent warranty as to the subject-matter of a contract of sale. In the US, punitive damages have been awarded in such a case[134]; but in England conflicting views have been expressed on the question whether such damages can be awarded in an action based on fraud even if the action is brought in tort.[135] It can be argued, on the one hand that the tort of deceit is generally one from which the defendant seeks to profit, so that it falls into the category of wrongs for which punitive damages are available[136]; and, on the other, that deceit generally involves the wrongdoer in criminal liability and that he should not suffer double punishment by being in addition ordered to pay punitive damages.[137]

(b) Compensation For What?

The principle that, as a general rule, damages are compensatory gives rise to the question: for what is it that the victim of a breach of contract is entitled to be compensated? This question calls for an analysis of the various types of losses for which the victim of a breach of contract can recover damages[138]; and it also gives rise to certain related problems.   **20–021**

(i) Loss of bargain

Contract and tort damages contrasted. The object of damages for breach of contract is to put the victim "so far as money can do it ... in the same situation ... as if the contract had been performed".[139] In other words, the victim is entitled to be compensated for the loss of his bargain, so that his expectations arising out of or created by the contract are protected. This protection of the victim's expectations must be contrasted with the principle on which damages are   **20–022**

---

[132] See, e.g. *Chelini v Nieri* 196 P.2d 915 (1948) where damages of $10,000 for injury to feelings were awarded for breach of contract against a Californian embalmer.

[133] *Drane v Evangelou* [1978] 1 W.L.R. 455; cf. *Guppys (Bridport) v Brookling* (1984) 269 E.G. 846 (nuisance and landlord's breach of covenant to repair); *Millington v Duffy* (1984) 17 H.L.R. 232.

[134] *Grandi v Le Sage* 399 P.2d 285 (1965).

[135] *Mafo v Adams* [1970] 1 Q.B. 548; *Cassell & Co Ltd v Broome*, above, fn.127, at 1076, 1131; *Metall und Rohstoff AG v ACLI Metals (London) Ltd* [1984] 1 Lloyd's Rep. 598 at 612; *Smith Kline & French Laboratories Ltd v Long* [1989] 1 W.L.R. 1; *Kuddus v Chief Constable of the Leicestershire Constabulary* [2001] UKHL 29; [2002] 2 A.C. 122 at [43]; ibid. at [84] leaves the point open.

[136] It is arguable that punitive damages for fraudulent warranties are no longer necessary in view of the recognition in *Attorney-General v Blake* [2001] 1 A.C. 268 (above, para.20–012) of the possibility of awarding an account of profits in certain cases in breach of contract; see *Kuddus v Chief Constable of the Leicestershire Constabulary* [2001] UKHL 29; [2002] 2 A.C. 122 at [109]; but in breach of contract cases the latter remedy is exceptional and discretionary.

[137] *Archer v Brown* [1985] Q.B. 401 at 418–423.

[138] Fuller and Perdue 46 Yale L.J. 52, 373; cf. Burrows 99 L.Q.R. 217; Owen 4 O.J.L.S. 393.

[139] *Robinson v Harman* (1848) 1 Ex. 850 at 855.

awarded in tort: the purpose of such damages is to put the victim into the position in which he would have been, if the tort had not been committed.[140] Of course, in many tort actions the victim can recover damages for loss of expectations: e.g. for loss of expected earnings suffered as a result of personal injury, or for loss of expected profits suffered as a result of damage to a profit-earning thing. But these expectations exist quite independently of the tortious conduct which impairs them[141]: it is the nature of most torts to destroy or impair expectations of this kind, rather than to create new ones. Tortious misrepresentation does, indeed, create new expectations, but the purpose of damages even for that tort is to put the victim into the position in which he would have been, if the misrepresentation had not been made, and not to protect his expectations by putting him into the position in which he would have been, if the representation had been true.[142] Such damages may be awarded in respect of losses which the victim could have avoided if the misrepresentation had not been made, and here again there is a sense in which the victim will recover damages for "loss of a chance",[143] but it is the chance of avoiding loss rather than that of making a profit for which he will be compensated. He may even be compensated for loss of profit if the tort impairs expectations which exist independently of it.[143a] In a contractual action, on the other hand, damages are recoverable as a matter of course for loss of the expectations created *by the very contract for breach of which the action is brought*. That is why damages of this kind are the distinctive feature of a contractual action.

20–023   **What was the bargain: scope of duty broken.** It follows from the principle of compensating the victim for loss of his bargain that the first and crucial question is to determine exactly what had been bargained for, or, in other words, the exact scope of the duty broken by the defendant. This was the question discussed in *South Australia Asset Management Corp v York Montague Ltd*[144] ("the *SAAMCO* case"). Loans of money had been made on the security of properties which had been valued by the defendants who had been engaged by the lender to make these valuations. In breach of their duty to carry out the valuations with due care, the defendants had overvalued the properties, which then also fell in value, in line with the general weakness in the property market. On the borrowers' default, the lenders realised the securities but recovered less than the amounts that they had lent. The House of Lords held that the valuers were liable for loss suffered by the lenders to the extent of the overvaluation but not for any loss beyond this amount which had been suffered by reason of the fall in the market value of the properties after the making of the loan. The point can be illustrated by supposing that a sum of £8 million had been lent on the security of a property valued at £10 million but actually worth only £6 million and that, on the borrower's default, the property (having fallen in value after the loan) yielded no more than £1.5 million. In such a case, the valuers would be liable, not for the £6.5 million lost by the lender,[145] but only to the extent of the £4 million by which they had overvalued the security.

---

[140] cf.above, para.1–010.
[141] This is also true in the "disappointed beneficiary" cases such as *White v Jones* [1995] 2 A.C. 207; above, para.14–051.
[142] See above, para.9–056.
[143] *John W Pryke v Gibbs Hartley Cooper Ltd* [1991] 1 Lloyd's Rep. 602 at 621.
[143a] See below, para.9–062.
[144] [1997] A.C. 191; for subsequent proceedings, see *Nykredit Bank v Edward Erdman Group* [1997] 1 W.L.R. 1627; Peel, in Burrows & Peel (eds), *Commercial Remedies*.
[145] Contrast *Kenny & Good Pty Ltd v MGICA* [2000] Lloyd's Rep. P.N. 25 (High Court of Australia).

This follows from the general principle[146] that a wrongdoer is liable only for "those consequences which are attributable to that which made the act wrongful"[147]; and in the case of a breach of contract the definition of what "made the act wrongful" necessarily depends on the way in which the contractual duty is defined. In the *SAAMCO* case, the duty was merely one to *provide information* (as to the value of the security) on which it was then up to the lenders to decide upon their course of action[148]; and the valuer was held liable for no more than the adverse consequences of his failure to take reasonable care as to the accuracy of that information. Such a duty was distinguished by Lord Hoffmann[149] from a duty to *advise* a client as to a course of action: a defendant who commits a breach of a duty of this kind (by failing to take reasonable care in giving the advice) will be liable for all foreseeable loss suffered in consequence of the client's taking the advice. Liability in such a case could therefore extend to loss suffered by reason of a fall in the market value of the subject-matter acquired in reliance on the advice.[150] The distinction follows from the way in which the defendant's duty is defined; it "has nothing to do with questions of causation[151] or any limit or 'cap' imposed upon damages which would otherwise be recoverable".[152] Those limits cut down liability for losses for which a defendant is prima facie responsible[153]; our present concern is with the extent of his duty and hence of his prima facie responsibility.

Scope of duty and remoteness. The distinction just drawn between limiting damages and defining a duty can give rise to difficulty, particularly in relation to liability in tort for negligence. Here the rule that a defendant is not liable for unforeseeable loss has been explained on the ground that such loss is too remote; but it can equally well be explained on the ground that the defendant is under no duty not to cause unforeseeable loss.[154] In the present group of negligent valuation cases, however, the two issues are clearly distinct: the "scope of the duty" depends on the true meaning of the contract (which clearly imposes *some* duty) while the

20–024

---

[146] A possible exception, applicable where the wrong is a misrepresentation which is, or is to be treated as being, fraudulent is recognised in [1997] A.C. 191 at 215 and discussed at para.9–062, above.

[147] [1997] A.C. 191 at 213.

[148] ibid. at 214; the *extent* of liability for failure to provide accurate information obviously depends on the information that should have been provided: see *Bristol & West BS v Fancy & Jackson* [1997] 4 All E.R. 582 at 621 (distinguishing a solicitor's duty in this respect from that of a valuer).

[149] ibid.; all the other members of the House of Lords agreed with Lord Hoffmann's speech; *Nykredit* case, above, fn.144 at 1638; cf. *Bristol & West BS v Mothew* [1998] Ch. 1 at 11; *Haugesund Kommune v Depfa ACS Bank* [2011] EWCA Civ 33; 134 Con L.R. 51.

[150] cf. *Intervention Board for Agriculture Products v Leidis* [2000] Lloyd's Rep. P.N. 144.

[151] In this respect the case differs from those discussed at paras 9–067—9–070, above and para.20–053, below where the question of recoverability of damages in respect of falls in market value depended on factors other than the definition of the defendant's duty.

[152] *Nykredit Bank v Edward Erdman Group* [1997] 1 W.L.R. 1627 at 1638; *Platform Home Loans Ltd v Oyston Shipways Ltd* [2000] 2 A.C. 190 at 208, 213; though the same case may raise an issue both as to the definition of the duty and as to a "cap" on damages, as in *Bank of Credit & Commerce (Overseas) Ltd v Price Waterhouse (No.3)*, The Times, April 2, 1998.

[153] See below para.20–094 et seq.

[154] See Lord Hobhouse's discussion in *Platform Home Loans Ltd v Oyston Shipways Ltd* [2000] 2 A.C. 190; [1999] 1 All E.R. 835 at 847 of *The Wagon Mound* [1961] A.C. 388; cf. *Aneco Reinsurance Underwriting Ltd v Johnson & Higgins Ltd* [2001] UKHL 51; [2002] 1 Lloyd's Rep 157 at [10]–[12].

test of remoteness depends on what consequences the valuer could have contemplated as likely to result from failure to make the valuation with due care.[155] If that test were applied, the valuer would be liable for the market loss; the effect of the "scope of duty" test is that in the "information" (as opposed to the "advice") cases he is under no prima facie liability for that loss because he has undertaken no duty with regard to the desirability or prudence of the transaction.[156]

20-025   **"Advice" and "information".** Considerable difficulty can also arise in distinguishing, for the present purpose, between "advice" and "information".[157] This difficulty arises, in the first place, from the ambiguity of the word "advise": this may be used to mean either "advise that . . . " or "advise to . . . ". In the former sense, its primary meaning is "to provide information" while in the latter sense it is "to recommend a course of action . . . ". The duty to provide what is commonly called legal "advice" may, for example, be no more than one to provide information: e.g. as to the capacity of a party to contract,[158] or to the existence of restrictions on the use of land. The giving of such information does not involve any recommendation as to the commercial prudence of proceeding with a transaction, e.g. as to the creditworthiness of the other party,[159] or whether to make a loan on the security of the land in question.[160] The second source of the difficulty lies in the fact that a person who expressly undertakes to give information may, by performing that duty, also impliedly give advice.[161] If, for example, A says to B "the girders of this bridge are sound", that statement may well, in the context, mean "you can safely cross", and so amount to advice as well as to information. Similarly, in the *Aneco* case[162] brokers had wrongly told a client that reinsurance against the risk which the client was about to underwrite was available in the market. Their duty was held to be one to "advise on the availability of reinsurance cover in the market, without which the transaction would not have gone ahead"[163] and they were therefore liable for the full loss suffered by the client as a result of having entered into that transaction.

20-026   **Types of expectation.** The above discussion is concerned only with one type of expectation, namely that of receiving the promised performance. A contract can, however, give rise to two quite separate expectations: that of receiving the promised performance and that of being able to put it to some particular use. For example, a buyer of goods (such as machinery or raw materials) may expect not only to receive the goods but also to use them for manufacturing purposes. If the

---

[155] See below, para.20–099. This is an important difference between the "scope of duty" question said to arise in *SAAMCO* and the "scope of duty" question said to arise in *The Achilleas* [2008] UKHL 48; 2009] 1 A.C. 61 where the issue was remoteness; below, para.20–111, fn.675.

[156] cf. Lord Hobhouse's statement in the *Platform Home Loans* case, above, at 848 that the "development" in the *SAAMCO* case (above, fn.144) was to apply the "scope of duty" reasoning to "*quantification* of damages" as opposed to "kinds or categories of damage".

[157] *Thompson v Christie Manson & Woods Ltd* [2005] EWCA Civ 555; [2005] P.N.L.R. 38 at [129]. Referred to as "category 1" and "category 2" cases in *Haugesund Kommune v Depfa ACS Bank* [2011] EWCA Civ 33; 134 Con L.R. 51.

[158] *Haugesund Kommune v Depfa ACS Bank*, above, fn.157.

[159] ibid. at [74].

[160] See *Lloyds Bank Plc v Crosse & Crosse* [2001] EWCA Civ 366; [2001] P.N.L.R. 34; *Dent v Davis Blank Furniss* [2001] Lloyd's Rep. P.N. 534.

[161] See the *Aneco* case, above, fn.154 at [1], [17], [32]; Lord Millett dissented.

[162] See above, fn.154. Contrast *Haugesund Kommune v Depfa ACS Bank* [2011] EWCA Civ 33; 134 Con L.R. 51.

[163] At [1].

seller fails to deliver, the buyer is entitled to damages based on the value of the goods that he should have received ("direct loss") and also to damages for loss of profits ("consequential loss")[164] suffered as a result of not receiving the promised delivery.

(ii) *Reliance loss*

In some cases, the claimant has sought to recover not his loss of bargain, or   **20–027**
expectation loss, but the expenditure which is said to have been wasted as a consequence of the defendant's breach, i.e. his "reliance loss". Sometimes the expenses are of a kind which the claimant *must* incur if he is to perform his part of the contract: e.g. a contract for the sale of goods may provide that the seller is to deliver the goods at the buyer's premises; and if the buyer wrongfully refuses to accept them when they are tendered there, the seller can recover the expenses of delivery as an element of reliance loss. But sometimes wasted expenses may be recoverable as reliance loss even though the claimant was *not*, under the contract, actually obliged to incur them: in *McRae v Commonwealth Disposals Commission*,[165] for example, the defendants were held liable for breach of a contract that there was a wrecked tanker lying in a specified position[166]; and the claimants recovered, inter alia, the £3,000 which it had cost them to send out a salvage expedition to look for the tanker.

Pre-contractual expenditure. In the examples above, the reliance loss is   **20–028**
incurred after the contract was made; but even expenditure incurred before then may be recoverable. In *Anglia Television Ltd v Reed*[167] the defendant broke his contract to take a leading part in the claimants' television play: and he was held liable for £2,750 spent by the claimants on the production before they had entered into the contract with him. Although the claimants had not incurred this expenditure in reliance on their contract with the defendant, it could be said that they had relied on that contract in allowing the expenditure to be wasted: in other words, in forbearing to look for another leading actor to take the part until it was too late. The pre-contract expenditure in such cases is recoverable because it leads to a loss which, after breach, can no longer be avoided.[168]

Pre-contract expenditure may also be recoverable if it was incurred in reliance on an *agreement* before that agreement had become a legally binding *contract*. In *Lloyd v Stanbury*[169] a person who had contracted to sell land was accordingly held liable for certain expenses incurred by the purchaser in reliance on the agreement while it was still subject to contract.[170]

Limit on recovery. While the claimant has the option of claiming damages on   **20–029**
the basis of his reliance loss,[171] this is only on the basis that such loss is presumed

---

[164] Provided that these are not too remote: below, para.20–056 et seq.

[165] (1951) 84 C.L.R. 377, esp. 411.

[166] See above, para.8–004.

[167] [1972] 1 Q.B. 60; A.L.G. 88 L.Q.R. 168; Ogus 35 M.L.R. 423; Clarke [1972] C.L.J. 22.

[168] *CCC Films (London) Ltd v Impact Quadrant Films Ltd* [1985] Q.B. 16; Owen [1985] C.L.J. 24; Burrows 100 L.Q.R. 27.

[169] [1971] 1 W.L.R. 535.

[170] See above, para.2–088.

[171] *Cullinane v British"Rema"Mfg Co* [1954] 1 Q.B. 292 at 303; *Anglia Television Ltd v Reed* [1972] 1 Q.B. 60 at 63–64; *CCC Films (London) Ltd v Impact Quadrant Films Ltd* [1985] Q.B. 16 at 32; cf. *Lloyd v Stanbury* [1971] 1 W.L.R. 535 at 547.

to represent his expectation loss, i.e. that if the contract had been performed, the claimant would, at least, have recouped his expenditure.[172] The claimant is not entitled to claim his reliance loss in order to escape from what was a bad bargain. For example, in *McRae*'s case the claimants should not have been awarded the *whole* of their reliance loss of £3,000 if the tanker, had it existed, would have been worth only £2,000. In such a case the claimant would have lost £1,000, even if there had been no breach; and the court will not shift that loss to the defendant by allowing the claimant to recover the whole of his wasted expenditure.[173] It also follows that where the claimant has suffered no expectation loss because such loss has been mitigated in full, he is not entitled to damages on the basis of his reliance loss.[174] The burden of proof on this issue is on the defendant: in other words, it is not up to the claimant to show that his venture would have been profitable but up to the defendant to show that it would have been unprofitable,[175] or that his expectation loss has been fully mitigated.[176] As much of the relevant information on this issue may be more readily available to the claimant than to the defendant, the defendant may find this burden a hard one to discharge. It may be justified on the basis that it is only because of the defendant's breach that the claimant is prevented from putting to the test whether or not he would have recouped his expenditure.[177] On this basis, it has been held that the shift in the burden of proof does *not* apply where the defendant is sued for breach of a contractual duty of care and the claimant's expectation loss is in the form of the loss of the chance that an acquisition would have been made if the defendant had taken care[178] (as opposed to the loss of bargain involved where the claimant has been deprived of the contracted for subject matter of the contract, such as goods or a warranted performance or outcome). In such a case, the claimant is confined to his expectation loss and there is nothing unfair in requiring him to prove that he lost a substantial chance and the extent of that chance, as would normally be the case.[179]

(iii) *Restitution*[180]

20–030   A claim for restitution is not strictly one for "damages"[181] since its purpose is not to compensate the claimant for a loss, but to deprive the defendant of a benefit. The simplest case of restitution arises where a seller has been paid in advance and then fails to deliver. He is bound to restore the price and the effect of this is to put

---

[172] *The Mamola Challenger* [2010] EWHC 2026 (Comm); [2011] 1 Lloyd's Rep 47, rejecting the view that reliance damages are based on a quite different principle of putting the claimant in the same position as if the contract had not been made: Treitel 108 L.Q.R. 229; cf. Tettenborn [2011] L.M.C.L.Q. 1; McLauchlan 127 L.Q.R. 23.

[173] See *C & P Haulage v Middleton* [1983] 1 W.L.R. 1461; *Bowlay Logging v Domtar* [1978] 4 W.W.R. 105; cf. *CCC Films (London) Ltd v Impact Quadrant Films* [1985] Q.B. 16 at 38; *PJ Spillings Ltd v Bonus Flooring Ltd* [2008] EWHC 1516 (QB).

[174] *The Mamola Challenger*, above fn.172.

[175] *CCC Films (London) Ltd v Impact Quadrant Films* [1985] Q.B. 16; cf. *L. Albert & Son v Armstrong Rubber Co.* (1948) 178 Fed. Rep.182; *Commonwealth of Australia v Amann Aviation Pty Ltd* (1991) 66 A.L.J.R. 123; Treitel 108 L.Q.R. 226.

[176] *The Mamola Challenger*, above fn.172.

[177] *Parker v SJ Berwin & Co* [2008] EWHC 3017 (Comm); [2009] P.N.L.R. 17 at [77].

[178] See below, para.20–060.

[179] *Parker v SJ Berwin & Co* above fn.177.

[180] See further, Ch.22.

[181] *Portman BS v Hamlyn Taylor Neck* [1998] 4 All E.R. 202 at 205; cf. above, fn.65.

both parties into the position in which they would have been if the contract had *not been made*. A restitution claim obviously differs from a loss of bargain claim, which is meant to put the claimant into the position in which he would have been if the contract had been performed. It also differs from a claim for reliance loss since that will leave the defendant in a worse position if he is unable to discharge the burden of proving that the contract would have been unprofitable.[182] In practice there is considerable overlap between reliance and restitution. Performance by the claimant is a form of reliance which often benefits the defendant; and the requirement in restitution claims that the defendant must have "benefited" from that performance is a somewhat elastic one.[183] There may also be an overlap between loss of bargain and restitution where the amount paid by the injured party is the only evidence of the value of what he ought to have received; and in such a case that amount, or an "appropriate proportion"[184] of it will be the prima facie measure of the expectation loss which he suffers as a result of the defendant's failure to perform, or to perform in full.

(iv) *Relationship between loss of bargain, reliance loss and restitution*

Claimant's choice. Where more than one type of claim is available the choice   **20–031** between them (if it has to be made) is the claimant's, who cannot be forced by the defendant to make one of the available claims rather than another. Suppose that a seller has been paid in advance and then fails to deliver. The buyer can choose between claiming the return of his money (restitution) and the value of the goods at the time fixed for delivery (loss of bargain). Obviously he will take the former course if he has made a bad bargain and the latter if he has made a good bargain. If the seller could force him to choose restitution, the buyer could easily be deprived of the benefit of a good bargain.

Loss of bargain. The claim for loss of bargain damages is, in principle, always   **20–032** available. But to make good such a claim the injured party must prove the value of his expectations. If he cannot do so with reasonable certainty, he may be limited to his reliance and restitution claims. The point may be illustrated by further reference to *McRae v Commonwealth Disposals Commission*[185] where the claimants sought damages for loss of their bargain, alleging that the value of the supposed tanker and its contents (for which they had paid £285) would have been £300,000. This basis for quantifying damages was dismissed as "manifestly absurd"[186]; and the claimants recovered their payment of £285 (restitution) plus the £3,000 spent on their fruitless salvage expedition (reliance loss).

Restitution. At the other extreme, the claimant's right to claim restitution is   **20–033** limited, in particular by the rule that he can (in general) recover back money paid under the contract only if there has been a *total* failure of consideration. This rule will be discussed in Ch.22[187]; but a point to be emphasised here is that, if restitution is available, it is no objection to such a claim that it will leave the

---

[182] See above, para.20–029.
[183] See especially para.22–023, below.
[184] *Peninsular & Orient SNCo v Youell* [1997] 2 Lloyd's Rep. 136 at 141; below, para.22–004.
[185] (1951) 84 C.L.R. 377.
[186] ibid. at 411.
[187] See below, paras 22–003—22–012.

claimant better off than he would have been, if the contract had been performed. Indeed, this will be the result of a successful restitution claim whenever the claimant has made a bad bargain, e.g. by paying more for goods than they are worth. There is an obvious contrast here with reliance loss where the claimant is not able to escape from a bad bargain (if proved by the defendant[188]). The reason for this result is that the defendant would otherwise be enriched; and there is no such enrichment merely because a claimant's reliance loss exceeds the value of his bargain.

20–034   **Reliance loss.** It follows from the principles which govern the award of damages for reliance loss[189] that the sort of case in which such a claim is most likely to be pursued is one in which the claimant cannot prove the value of his expectation had the contract been performed.[190] Where he can do so and it exceeds his expenditure he will claim damages for his expectation loss in the normal way. This raises the question whether the claimant can sue for his expectation loss and his reliance loss in the alternative. Dicta in some cases suggest not[191] and that the claimant must elect between the two, but since reliance loss is not in fact an entirely separate basis of assessment to, but rather a presumption of, expectation loss, there is no election needed in the strict sense and it seems that he may therefore sue for them in the alternative.[192] It is nonetheless a slightly curious form of pleading which would require the defendant to prove that the claimant would not at least have recouped his expenditure (or to prove the extent to which he would have failed to do so) while leaving the claimant free, in the first instance, to attempt to prove that he might have gained more than that.[193]

20–035   **Whether claims can be combined.** There is sometimes said to be an inconsistency between combining the various types of claim so far discussed. The courts have not accepted this kind of reasoning and have, in appropriate cases, allowed the claims to be combined. In one case[194] machinery was bought, paid for and installed. The buyer rejected the machinery because it was not in accordance with the contract; and he recovered the price (restitution), installation expenses (reliance loss) and his *net* loss of profits resulting from the breach (loss of bargain).

20–036   **Principle against double recovery.** The true principle is not that there is any logical objection to combining the various types of claim, but that the claimant

---

[188] See above, para.20–029.

[189] ibid.

[190] This is no doubt why reliance loss was claimed in *Anglia Television Ltd v Reed*. But see *Parker v SJ Berwin & Co* [2008] EWHC 3017 (Comm); [2009] P.N.L.R. 17: above, para.20–029, text to fn.179.

[191] *Filobake Ltd v Rondo* Ltd [2005] EWCA Civ 563 at [64]; *Anglia Television Ltd v Reed* [1972] 1 Q.B. 60 at 63–64.

[192] *The Mamola Challenger* [2010] EWHC 2026 (Comm); [2011] 1 Lloyd's Rep 47 at [55]; *Commonwealth of Australia v Amann Aviation Pty Ltd* (1992) 66 A.L.J.R. 123 per Mason C.J. and Dawson J. at [35] ("We do not regard the language of election or the notion that alternative ways are open to a plaintiff in which to frame a claim for relief as appropriate in a discussion of the measure of damages for breach of contract"); cf. Brennan J. at [17] ("These are alternative methods of assessing damages, but the plaintiff does not have an election as to the method").

[193] In *Parker v SJ Berwin & Co* [2008] EWHC 3017 (Comm); [2009] P.N.L.R. 17 at [80] it is described as "a recipe for confusion and uncertainty".

[194] *Millar's Machinery Co Ltd v David Way & Son* (1935) 40 Com.Cas. 204; cf. *Naughton v O'Callaghan* [1990] 3 E.R. 191 at 198; and see above, para.18–017.

cannot combine them so as to recover more than once for the same loss.[195] Suppose that a buyer has paid in advance for goods which are not delivered. He obviously cannot recover both his payment (restitution) and the full value of the goods at the time fixed for delivery (loss of bargain). The point has been well put by Corbin: "*full* damages and *complete* restitution . . . will not both be given for the same breach of contract".[196]

The principle against double recovery also applies where a claimant seeks both reliance loss and damages for the loss of his bargain. If the claimant in *McRae's*[197] case had been able to establish the value of the hypothetical tanker, he should clearly not have been entitled to that amount *and* to the £3,285, for he would have had to spend the latter amount to acquire the former. Similarly, in *Cullinane v British "Rema" Manufacturing Co Ltd*[198] the defendants sold a clay pulverising machine, warranting that it could process clay at 6 tons per hour. The buyer claimed damages for breach of this warranty under two heads: first, the capital cost of the machine and its installation and, secondly, loss of profits. It was held that the buyer could not recover under both of these heads as "a claim for loss of profits could only be founded upon the footing that the capital expenditure had been incurred".[199] To allow the buyer to recover the capital expenditure and also his *full* profit would give him damages twice over for the same loss. It was, however, not established that the profits which would have been derived from the machine over the whole of its useful "life" would have *exceeded* its capital cost. If this had been proved the buyer could, according to a decision of the High Court of Australia, have recovered (a) the capital cost of the machinery less its actual value; plus (b) the excess of the estimated profits over the sum calculated under (a).[200] This alone would put the buyer into as good a financial position as if the contract had been performed.

(v) *Incidental loss*

The victim of a breach of contract can often recover loss which does not fit easily into the categories so far discussed. He may incur expenses after a breach has come to his attention, such as the administrative costs of buying a substitute,[201] or of sending back defective goods, or of wasted staff time.[202] Such

20–037

---

[195] *Peninsular & Orient SN Co v Youell* [1997] 2 Lloyd's Rep. 136 at 141.

[196] Corbin on *Contracts*, para.1221; cf. *The Unique Mariner* [1979] 1 Lloyd's Rep. 37 at 53; *Tang Man Sit v Capacious Investment Ltd* [1996] A.C. 514; *Baltic Shipping Co v Dillon* (1993) 176 C.L.R. 344 at 345.

[197] (1951) 84 C.L.R. 377; *Salvage Association v CAP Financial Services* [1995] F.S.R. 654 at 683.

[198] [1954] 1 Q.B. 292; Macleod [1970] J.B.L. 19; Stoljar 91 L.Q.R. 68; cf. *JP Morgan Chase Bank v Springwell Navigation Corp* [2006] EWCA Civ 161; [2006] P.N.L.R. 28; *4Eng Ltd v Harper* [2008] EWHC 915 (Ch); [2009] Ch. 91 at [49]–[51].

[199] ibid. at 302.

[200] *TC Industrial Plant Pty Ltd v Robert's (Queensland) Ltd* [1964] A.L.R. 1083.

[201] See, e.g. *Robert Stewart & Sons Ltd v Carapanayoti* [1962] 1 W.L.R. 34.

[202] The claimant must show that the relevant breach of contract caused "some significant disruption to the business; in other words that staff have been significantly diverted from their usual activities": *Standard Chartered Bank v Pakistan Shipping Corp.* [2001] EWCA Civ 55; *Verizon UK Ltd v Swiftnet Ltd* [2008] EWHC 551 (Comm) at [56]. When proven, the employment costs are awarded on the basis that employees of a commercial business are taken to generate revenue which is at least equal to the cost of employing them: see *Aerospace Publishing v Thames Water* [2007] EWCA Civ 3 [2007] Bus L.R. 726.

expenses are hardly incurred in reliance *on the contract*; and they will in this chapter be called "incidental" loss.

2. QUANTIFICATION

20–038   Damages always consist of a sum of money, so that the loss has to be quantified in terms of money. This process is variously referred to as "quantifying" or "measuring" or "assessing" damages; it gives rise to a number of problems.

(a) The Bases of Assessment

(i) *Reliance and restitution*

20–039   Relatively little difficulty arises where the injured party claims reliance loss or restitution. In the first case, the basis of assessment is the cost to him of his action in reliance on the contract; and in the second it is generally[203] the benefit obtained by the defendant under the contract. These assessments are particularly straight-forward where the claimant has expended or the defendant received a sum of money. Where the reliance loss or the benefit to be "restored" consists of goods or services, a reasonable value must be placed on them. This may give rise to practical difficulties, but there is no doubt about the principle on which such assessment proceeds.

(ii) *Loss of bargain*

20–040   **"Difference in value" and "cost of cure".** Where the injured party claims to be put into "the same situation . . . as if the contract had been performed",[204] there are two distinct bases of assessment: "difference in value" and "cost of cure". The distinction between these two bases is strikingly illustrated by an American case[205] in which a coal company took a mining lease of farmland, covenanting to restore the land to its original state at the end of the lease. The cost of doing the work would have been $29,000, but the result of not doing it was to reduce the value of the land by only $300. Damages for the company's failure to do the work were assessed at the latter sum. In English law damages for breach of a tenant's covenant to repair are by statute assessed on a "difference in value" basis.[206] Apart from such statutory provisions, the law starts with certain prima facie assumptions for choosing between the two bases[207]; but these assumptions can be displaced. The point can be illustrated principally by reference to contracts for the supply of goods and for the execution of building work, before considering the difficulties which may arise in relation to contracts for services.

---

[203] Not always: see, e.g. *Planché v Colburn* (1831) 8 Bing. 14 (above, para.17–046), where there is no evidence that the defendant benefited at all.

[204] *Robinson v Harman* (1848) 1 Ex. 850 at 855.

[205] *Peevyhouse v Garland Coal Co* 382 P.2d 109 (1962); cf. *Attica Sea Carriers Corp v Ferrostaal Poseidon Bulk Reederei GmbH* [1976] 1 Lloyd's Rep. 250.

[206] Landlord and Tenant Act 1927, s.18; *Culworth Estates Ltd v Society of Licensed Victuallers* (1991) 62 P. & C.R. 211. But in the absence of evidence as to difference in value, cost of repairs is a "starting point": *Drummond v SU Stores* (1980) 258 E.G. 1293 at 1294; cf. below, fn.211.

[207] *Watts v Morrow* [1991] 1 W.L.R. 1421 at 1441.

Supply of goods. Where a seller delivers goods which are not of the contract   **20–041**
quality, the damages are prima facie assessed on a difference in value basis, so that
the buyer can recover "the difference between the value of the goods . . . and the
value they would have had"[208] if they had been in accordance with the contract.
But the rule is only a prima facie one and if the defect in the goods is cured at a
reasonable cost there is little doubt that the cost of such cure can be awarded.[209]
This is the position in analogous hire-purchase cases[210] and there seems to be no
reason for not applying the same rule to sales.[211] Even the cost of an attempted
cure which fails—such as veterinary fees spent on a sick animal which nevertheless dies—can be recovered.[212]

Building work. A defendant who is in breach of an obligation to do building   **20–042**
work is prima facie liable on a "cost of cure" basis: i.e. he must pay for the cost
of putting the defects right or of completing the work.[213] This, again, is only a
prima facie rule, which can be displaced where the cost of putting the defect right
would be out of all proportion to the advantage which cure would confer on the
injured party.[214] This would, for example, be the position where components not
in accordance with the contractual specifications had been built into a structure
which would have to be substantially demolished to effect a cure[215]; where the cost
of cure was greater than the value of the whole building[216]; or where execution of
the promised building work would confer no economic benefit at all on the
claimant.[217] In such cases, difference in value (if any[218]) would form the normal[219]
basis of assessment.[220] This basis of assessment is, in turn, liable to be displaced
by further circumstances. There is some support in the authorities for the view
that the claimant can recover damages on the higher cost of cure basis if he can

---

[208] Sale of Goods Act 1979, s.53(3); below, para.20–051; *The Athenian Harmony* [1998] 2 Lloyd's
Rep. 410 at 419.
[209] Where a buyer who deals as consumer has a "right to reduce the purchase price" under s.48A
and 48C of the 1979 Act (as inserted by Sale and Supply of Goods to Consumers Regulations 2002 (SI
2002/3045), reg.5), the measure of such reduction does not appear to be either difference in value or
cost of cure: see below, para.20–054.
[210] e.g. *Charterhouse Credit Co Ltd v Tolly* [1963] 2 Q.B. 683 at 711–712.
[211] *Jacovides v Constantinou*, *The Times*, October 27, 1986 (a sale of land case where damages were
awarded for misrepresentation apparently having contractual effect). In *Keeley v Guy McDonald* (1984)
134 New L.J. 522 the *cost of repairing* an unmerchantable car was awarded *as the difference in value*
between the car as it was and as it would have been if it had been merchantable.
[212] *Harling v Eddy* [1951] 2 Q.B. 739.
[213] *Mertens v Home Freeholds* [1921] 2 K.B. 526; *Hoenig v Isaacs* [1952] 1 T.L.R. 1360; *William Cory
& Sons v Wingate Investments Ltd* (1978) 248 E.G. 687; cf. *Radford v de Froberville* [1977] 1 W.L.R.
1262 (breach of covenant to build a boundary wall); *Calabar Properties Ltd v Stitcher* [1984] 1 W.L.R.
287.
[214] *Ruxley Electronics and Construction Co Ltd v Forsyth* [1996] A.C. 344; *Birse Construction Ltd v
Eastern Telegraph Co Ltd* [2004] EWHC 2512; (2004) 47 E.G. 164; Contrast *Tabcorp Holdings Ltd v
Bowen Investments Pty Ltd* [2009] H.C.A. 8.
[215] e.g. *Jacob & Youngs v Kent* 129 N.E. 889 (1921).
[216] cf. *Morris v Redland Bricks Ltd* [1970] A.C. 652.
[217] *James v Hutton* [1950] 1 K.B. 9 (where performance of the defendant's promise to restore a shop
front to its pre-contract appearance would not have affected its value).
[218] There being no such difference in *James v Hutton*, above, the damages were held to be nominal.
cf. *Sunrock Aircraft Corporation Ltd v Scandinavian Airlines Systems Denmark-Norway-Sweden* [2007]
EWCA Civ 882; [2007] 2 Lloyd's Rep. 612.
[219] For a possible exception in cases of "deliberate" breach, see *Glaer v Schwartz* 176 N.E. 616
(1913).
[220] See *Jacob & Youngs v Kent*, above; *The Rozel* [1994] 2 Lloyd's Rep. 160 (breach of charterer's
undertaking to repair a ship); *G W Atkins Ltd v Scott* (1996) 46 Con. L.R. 14.

show *either* that he has in fact incurred that cost *or* that he will incur it by getting the work done.[221] He is, however, required to act reasonably to mitigate his loss,[222] and it is submitted that he would have failed to do so if he had insisted on cure even though its cost was wholly disproportionate to the resulting benefit to him. Where this is the position, he should recover only on a difference in value basis.[223] For this purpose, the disproportion would have to be a clear one, since the mitigation rules only require the injured party to act reasonably. Cost of cure which is actually incurred or going to be incurred may therefore be recoverable where the effect of cure on the value of property is speculative[224]; and where the cost of cure, though not resulting in any improvement to the property, is not excessive in relation to the initial value of the property.[225]

20–043   **Surveys.** Damages against a surveyor who fails to draw his client's attention to defects in a house which the client buys in reliance on the surveyor's report are prima facie based on difference in value and not on cost of cure.[226] The reason for this rule is that the surveyor gives no warranty as to the condition of the house: he undertakes only to conduct the survey with reasonable care and skill.[227] The rule may be displaced by special circumstances: e.g. cost of cure may be recoverable if cure is undertaken in a reasonable effort to mitigate loss[228]; and the client may also be able to recover costs reasonably incurred in extricating himself from the transaction.[229]

20–044   **Cases where cure is not undertaken.** Where the claimant is prima facie entitled to damages based on cost of cure, the further question arises whether he can recover this amount (where it exceeds difference in value) even though he does not undertake cure, or propose to do so. There is, at least apparently, some conflict in the authorities on this point. The starting principle is that the cost of cure can be recovered in such cases since, in general, the court is not concerned with the use which the claimant makes of his damages.[230] But this principle is subject to significant qualifications. First, the fact that the injured party has decided not to effect cure is relevant to the issue whether it would have been reasonable for him to do so; if not, cost of cure will be irrecoverable under the mitigation rules already discussed.[231] Secondly, the conduct of the injured party after the breach may affect

---

[221] *Tito v Waddell (No.2)* [1977] Ch. 106 at 332, 335; *Radford v De Froberville* [1977] 1 W.L.R. 1262. For the position in tort, see *Ward v Cannock Chase DC* [1986] Ch. 546; Contrast *Wigsell v School for Indigent Blind* (1882) 8 Q.B.D. 357 (difference in value); and, see Harris, Ogus and Phillips 95 L.Q.R. 581. For the possible relevance of this factor to a claim for damages in respect of a *third party's* loss, see above, paras 14–026, 14–035.

[222] See below, para.20–115 et seq.

[223] cf. e.g. *Darbishire v Warran* [1963] 1 W.L.R. 1067; *The Maersk Colombo* [2001] EWCA Civ 717; [2001] 2 Lloyd's Rep. 275 at [32] (also a tort case).

[224] *Sunshine Exploration Ltd v Dolly Varden Mines Ltd* (1969) 8 D.L.R. (3d) 441.

[225] Corbin on *Contracts*, para.1091. The position may be the same even where the work would actually *reduce* the value of the property: Corbin on *Contracts*, para.1089.

[226] See above, para.20–006.

[227] *Watts v Morrow* [1991] 1 W.L.R. 1421 at 1439.

[228] *Cross v David Martin & Mortimer* [1989] 1 E.G.L.R. 154.

[229] *County Personnel (Employment Agency) Ltd v Alan R Pulver & Co* [1987] 1 W.L.R. 916 (negligent solicitor); contrast *Fulham Leisure Holdings Ltd v Nicholson Graham & Jones* [2006] EWHC 2017 (Ch); [2006] 2 All E.R. 599 at [284] where costs incurred went beyond "extrication".

[230] *Ruxley Electronics and Construction Co Ltd v Forsyth* [1996] A.C. 344 at 359; cf. ibid. at 372; and see the cases discussed at para.20–046, below in which damages are based on market prices.

[231] *Ruxley Electronics* case, above; for this aspect of mitigation, see above, para.20–042.

the basis of assessment: e.g. if he has disposed of the defective or damaged subject-matter without effecting cure, the court is likely to conclude that what he has lost is difference in value rather than cost of cure.[232] In such cases, therefore, difference in value will be the more appropriate basis of assessment.

Both bases may lead to same result. The two bases of assessment will not invariably lead to diverging results. For example, in *Dean v Ainley*[233] a vendor of land broke her contractual undertaking to seal a patio so as to prevent water from leaking into a cellar. The purchaser recovered the cost of doing the promised work, and this sum was variously described as the "cost of the works",[234] or as the extent to which the property was "clearly less valuable"[235] as a result of the vendor's failure to perform her undertaking. Where the only reliable evidence of difference in value is cost of cure,[236] the two methods of assessment will lead to the same practical result.   20–045

Sometimes the process of assessment can with equal plausibility be described as being based on difference in value or cost of cure. This is the position where a buyer is entitled to the difference between the contract and the market price of goods which the seller has failed to deliver.[237] It makes no difference whether such damages are described as the cost of curing the seller's breach or as the difference in value between what the buyer has received (i.e. nothing) and what he should have received (i.e. the goods). The buyer is, moreover, entitled to such damages whether or not he has actually made the substitute purchase.[238]

Other loss. The "difference in value" and "cost of cure" bases are not the only possible ones on which loss of bargain damages may be assessed. The point is well illustrated by *Ruxley Electronics and Construction Ltd v Forsyth*,[239] where a builder had contracted to build a swimming pool in his customer's garden. The contract required the pool to have a maximum depth of 7ft 6in but the pool actually built had a maximum depth of only 6ft 9in. This breach of the contract did not significantly affect the value of the pool; nor, since the pool remained, in spite of the breach, perfectly safe and serviceable, would the cost of rebuilding it to the stipulated depth have been reasonably incurred, being wholly disproportionate to the benefit to be obtained by carrying out these operations. However, the trial judge had awarded him £2,500 for "loss of amenity" and this award was allowed to stand by the House of Lords,[240] even though it was recognised that in most   20–046

---

[232] *Calabar Properties Ltd v Stitcher* [1984] 1 W.L.R. 297 at 229; cf. *Hole & Hole (Sayers Common) Ltd v Harrisons Ltd* [1973] 1 Lloyd's Rep. 345; *Leppard v Excess Ins Co Ltd* [1979] 1 W.L.R. 512; *Charterhouse Credit Ltd v Tolly* [1963] 2 Q.B. 683; *G W Atkins Ltd v Scott* (1996) 46 Con. L.R. 14. In *Perry v Sidney Phillip & Son* [1982] 1 W.L.R. 1297 it was conceded that cost of cure (which was not effected or intended to be effected) was not the appropriate basis for assessing damages against a negligent surveyor; for the proper basis of assessment in such a case, see above, at fnn.35–36.

[233] [1987] 1 W.L.R. 1729; cf. *Watts v Morrow* [1991] 1 W.L.R. 1421 at 1435; *The Rozel* [1994] 2 Lloyd's Rep. 160 at 167.

[234] ibid. at 1736.

[235] ibid. at 1738.

[236] e.g. *Steward v Rapley (t/a RapleyFlatt & Co)* [1989] 1 E.G.L.R. 159.

[237] Sale of Goods Act 1979, s.51(3); below, at fn.261.

[238] cf. *Shearson Lehman Hutton Inc v Maclaine Watson & Co (No.2)* [1990] 1 Lloyd's Rep. 441 at 443 (seller's damages); and (in tort) *Dominion Mosaics & Tile Co Ltd v Trafalgar Trucking Co Ltd* [1990] 2 All E.R. 246.

[239] [1996] A.C. 344; Coote [1997] C.L.J. 537.

[240] At 359; cf. Lord Lloyd's scepticism at 374 as to the amount of the award.

building contract cases no such damages are available to the customer.[241] This aspect of the case is perhaps best explained on the ground that, in contracts for "home improvements",[242] damages can include compensation for the customer's "disappointed expectations"[243] arising from the contractor's failure to provide the degree of comfort or enjoyment which, to the contractor's knowledge, it was the customer's object to obtain.[244]

20–047   **Services.** In the *Ruxley* case, the conclusion that there was no difference in value is the result of focusing on the end product of the builder's services, i.e. the pool. This may also explain the outcome in another case[245] where the defendant contracted with the claimant to provide a firefighting service and was paid the full contract price. At the end of the contract the claimant discovered that the defendant had not provided the stipulated number of firemen or horses or the promised length of hosepipe, but it had not failed to put out any fires in consequence. The court ruled that the claimant had not proved it had suffered any loss and was unable to recover more than nominal damages. But it is clear that in some cases damages may be awarded by reference to the difference in value in the provision of the services themselves, particularly where there is no longer any opportunity for cure,[246] e.g. in the case of the sub-standard holiday,[247] or ruined wedding photographs.[248] Indeed, it is "obvious that in the ordinary way a party who contracts and pays for a superior service or superior goods and receives a substantially inferior service or inferior goods has suffered loss,"[249] and the "obvious measure" of that loss is the diminution in the value of the promised services.[250] The real difficulty in such cases is how to determine the difference in value. This cannot be done by an apportionment of the price as such since that would amount to restitution and undermine the requirement that there must have been a total failure of consideration,[251] though it must be acknowledged that that requirement has been criticised[252] and it has been suggested that a refund of the difference in price would not amount to "a straining of principle in cases where the defendant provided inferior and cheaper services than those contracted for".[253] The difference in price between the performance contacted for and that provided

---

[241] At 374 per Lord Lloyd.

[242] See below, para.20–088, fn.519, 520.

[243] [1996] A.C. 344 at 374.

[244] ibid. at 360–361, per Lord Mustill.

[245] *City of New Orleans v Firemen's Charitable Association* (1891) 9 So. 486.

[246] In accordance with the general rule above (para.20–044), it is no bar to the award of such damages that the claimant has not sought to cure the breach: *Guido van der Garde BV v Force India Formula One Ltd* [2010] EWHC 2373 (QB) at [485], but a failure to do so may be relevant to any question of mitigation.

[247] *Jarvis v Swan Tours Ltd* [1973] Q.B. 233; *Milner v Carnival Plc* [2010] EWCA Civ 389; [2010] 3 All E.R. 701

[248] *Diesen v Samson* 1971 S.L.T. (Sh.Ct.) 49.

[249] *White Arrow Express Ltd v Lamey's Distribution Ltd* [1995] C.L.C. 1251 at 1254.

[250] *Regus (UK) Ltd v Epcot Solutions Ltd* [2008] EWCA Civ 361 at [30].

[251] *White Arrow Express Ltd v Lamey's Distribution Ltd*, above, where the claim for *damages* failed because it was put on that basis.

[252] See below, para.22–003.

[253] *Attorney-General v Blake* [2001] 1 A.C. 268 at 286C (Lord Nicholls referred to a "similar" approach" to a refund in the difference in price which would occur with supply of goods; by "similar" he may have been referring to the evidential role of the price, as discussed in the text); cf. *Experience Hendrix LLC v PPX Enterprises Inc* [2003] EWCA Civ 323; [2003] E.M.L.R. 515 at [28]. In *Samson & Samson v Proctor* [1975] N.Z.L.R. 665 a builder was held liable for expenses saved; no reason is given for this departure from the general rule that damages are based on loss to the claimant.

may be accepted as *evidence* of the difference in value and, in the absence of any other evidence, may well produce a result not very different to a partial, or full refund.[254] It is on this basis that damages have been awarded for the difference in value between the holiday provided to the claimant and that which had been promised,[255] for failing to provide the claimant with a certain number of kilometres of driving in a formula one test car;[256] and, in the context of the interpretation and effect of an exclusion clause, to determine that the claimant was still left with a claim for the difference in value between the air—conditioned office promised and that provided.[257]

(b) Actual and Market Values

Where damages are based on difference in value (or on the cost of a substitute)   20–048
they may be assessed by reference either to actual or to market values. There is said to be a "market" for goods if they can be freely bought or sold at a price fixed by supply and demand,[258] but it has recently also been said that the court "is entitled to infer the existence of a market from any sufficient evidence relevant to that issue."[259] Where there is a market, the loss is prima facie quantified by reference to it; but other factors may also have to be taken into account. Where there is no market, the loss must be quantified in some other, and sometimes more speculative, way.[260]

(i) *Where there is a market*

Non-delivery. If a seller of goods fails to deliver, the buyer can go into the   20–049
market and buy substitute goods at the prevailing price. Thus his damages will prima facie be based on the amount (if any) by which the market price exceeds the contract price.[261] It is irrelevant that the seller has disposed of the goods to a third party for *less* than the market price.[262] Similarly, where breach by a carrier results in a failure of the goods to reach the agreed destination, the injured party's

---

[254] *White Arrow Express Ltd v Lamey's Distribution Ltd* [1995] C.L.C. 1251 at 1256; *Milner v Carnival Plc* [2010] EWCA Civ 389; [2010] 3 All E.R. 701 at [46]; *Guido van der Garde BV v Force India Formula One Ltd* [2010] EWHC 2373 (QB) at [433], [487]; below, para.22–012.

[255] *Jarvis v Swan Tours Ltd* [1973] Q.B. 233; *Milner v Carnival Plc* [2010] EWCA Civ 389; [2010] 3 All E.R. 701; on the distinction between the damages awarded in such cases for diminution in value and those awarded for "mental distress", see below, para.20–090.

[256] *Guido van der Garde BV v Force India Formula One Ltd* [2010] EWHC 2373 (QB).

[257] *Regus (UK) Ltd v Epcot Solutions Ltd* [2008] EWCA Civ 361.

[258] *Dunkirk Colliery Co v Lever* (1878) 9 Ch.D. 20; *W L Thompson Ltd v Robinson (Gunmakers) Ltd* [1955] Ch. 177; *Charter v Sullivan* [1957] 2 Q.B. 117. A "black" market may be taken into account: *Mouatt v Betts Motors Ltd* [1959] A.C. 71; but not a "monopoly market" fixed by a government: *The Texaco Melbourne* [1992] 2 Lloyd's Rep. 303 at 312, reversed on other grounds [1994] 1 Lloyd's Rep. 473.

[259] *Bulkhaul Ltd v RhodiaOrganique Fine Ltd* [2008] EWCA Civ 1452; [2009] 1 Lloyd's Rep 353 at [29].

[260] cf. *Luxmoore-May v Messenger May Baverstock* [1990] 1 W.L.R. 1009 at 1027.

[261] Sale of Goods Act 1979, s.51(3); cf. *The Elena D'Amico* [1980] 1 Lloyd's Rep. 75 (failure to provide a ship under charterparty); *Murray v Lloyd* [1989] 1 W.L.R. 1060 (market cost of substitute accommodation awarded against negligent solicitor).

[262] cf. *Barry v Davies* [2000] 1 W.L.R. 1962 (s.51(3) applied by analogy to auctioneer's wrongful refusal to knock goods down to the highest bidder (above, paras 2–008, 3–162)).

damages are based on the market value of the goods at that destination when they should have been delivered there.[263]

The principle of assessment by reference to the market price normally applies even though the injured party has resold an equivalent quantity of goods at a different price, in the expectation of receiving those due under the contract. Such a sub-sale does not reduce the damages if it is made below the market price[264] for the buyer is nevertheless "entitled to recover the expense of putting himself into the position of having those goods [i.e. those which the seller has failed to deliver], and this he can do by going into the market and purchasing them at the market price".[265] So long as the sub-sale was not of the identical goods bought under the main contract, the buyer might have been able to supply his sub-buyer from some other source before the market rose. He could then have resold the goods bought from the defendant to a third party and made a further profit. Conversely the sub-sale will not increase the damages if it was made above the market price, even if the seller knew that the buyer intended to resell.[266] The buyer's extra loss is either not caused by the seller's breach, but by the buyer's failure to go into the market; or it is irrecoverable as the buyer ought to have mitigated by going into the market to buy a substitute to satisfy his sub-buyer.[267] Once again, however, the position would be different if the sub-sale had been "of the self-same thing"[268]; for in that case the buyer would not have been able to satisfy his sub-buyer with substitute goods. Consequently, he would have lost his profit on the sub-sale and could have recovered that loss, so long as it was not too remote.[269]

20–050   **Late delivery.** Where delay in delivery is a ground of rejection, and the right to reject is exercised, damages are assessed in the same way as for non-delivery.[270] But where late delivery is accepted, damages are assessed on a different basis, the contract price being irrelevant. The buyer's complaint in such a case is not that he has to go into the market to buy a substitute for more than he had originally agreed to pay. It is that he has got the goods at a time that was less advantageous to him than the delivery time fixed by the contract. If he intended, on receipt of the goods, to resell them in the market, he will accordingly have lost the amount by which their market value when they were delivered to him was less than their market value when they should have been delivered; and this amount will be

---

[263] *Rodocanachi Sons & Co v Milburn Bros* (1876) 18 Q.B.D. 67; *The Texaco Melbourne* [1994] 1 Lloyd's Rep. 473 at 479; cf. *Watts, Watts & Co v Mitsui & Co Ltd* [1917] A.C. 227. Expenses saved by the shipper, such as the freight that he would have had to pay if the goods had duly arrived and (in case of failure to ship) insurance premiums are deducted from the amount recoverable on the principle of taking the claimant's overall position into account (above, para.20–006).

[264] *Williams Bros v E T Agius Ltd* [1914] A.C. 510; cf.*Rodocanachi, Sons & Co v Milburn Bros* (1886) 18 Q.B.D. 67; *Brading v F McNeill & Co Ltd* [1946] Ch. 145; *Oxus Gold Plc v Templeton Insurance Ltd* [2007] EWHC 770 (Comm).

[265] *Williams Bros v E T Agius Ltd*, above, at 531.

[266] *KweiTek Chao v British Traders & Shippers Ltd* [1954] 2 Q.B. 459 at 489.

[267] cf. below, para.20–115; *Mobil North Sea Ltd v PJ Pipe & Valve Co* [2001] EWCA Civ 741; [2001] 1 All E.R. (Comm) 289 at [30]. The burden of proof on the issue whether the injured party ought to have mitigated is on the party in breach, whichever of the above rationales of the "market rule" is adopted: see *Standard Chartered Bank v Pakistan National Shipping Co (No.3)* [2001] EWCA Civ 55; [2001] 1 All E.R. (Comm) 822 at [41].

[268] *Williams Bros v E T Agius Ltd* [1914] A.C. 510 at 523; cf. *Seven Seas Properties Ltd v Al-Essa* [1988] 1 W.L.R. 1272.

[269] See below, para.20–099 et seq.; *Re R & H Hall Ltd and W H PimJr* (1928) 139 L.T. 50, where the contract itself expressly provided for resale; *The Honam Jade* [1991] 1 Lloyd's Rep. 38.

[270] e.g. *The Almare Seconda* [1981] 2 Lloyd's Rep. 433; cf. above, para.18–089.

recoverable provided that the chance of resale is not too remote a contingency.[271] It is, however, disputed whether a buyer's damages will be reduced if he has resold the goods for *more* than the market price at the time of actual delivery. In *Wertheim v Chicoutimi Pulp Co*[272] wood pulp was sold for delivery in September/November but not delivered till the following June. The market price per ton was 70s. at the time fixed for delivery and 42s. 6d. at the time of actual delivery. Prima facie the buyers' loss was therefore 27s. 6d. per ton. But they had resold the pulp at 65s. per ton and were able to pass it on to their sub-buyers at that price. The Privy Council held that the sellers could rely on the sub-sale to reduce the damages to 5s. per ton. To allow the buyers to recover 27s. 6d. would, it was said, enable them to make a profit out of the breach. But this is hard to fit in with the principles normally governing the assessment of damages.[273] Two possibilities exist in cases of this kind. First, the buyer has resold the very goods comprised in the main contract.[274] If so he has admittedly not lost 27s. 6d. per ton but it is difficult to see that he has lost anything at all; he would not have been free to sell the pulp in the market at 70s. per ton as he was bound to deliver it to his sub-buyer. Secondly, the buyer has resold an equivalent quantity. If so the sub-sale should be disregarded. Had the pulp been delivered in September/November it could have *then* been sold to a third party, and the sub-buyer could still have been satisfied with an equivalent quantity bought in June at 42s. 6d. per ton. It is improbable that the buyer would have kept the pulp throughout this period on a falling market. On the other hand, if (in view of the delay) the buyer "had bought other goods and used them for the sub-contract he would have been left with the goods delivered at the time when the market price was 42s. 6d. instead of when it was 70s.".[275] Nor is it right to say that the buyer would make a profit *out of the breach* of contract if he were awarded 27s. 6d. a ton. He would make a profit *out of the advantageous sub-sale*.

Defective delivery: in general. Where defective goods are delivered, and are not (or can no longer be) rejected, the buyer's loss is prima facie the difference between the actual value of the goods that he has received and the value that they would have had if they had been in accordance with the contract.[276] As in cases of late delivery, the difference between the contract and the market price is not relevant[277]: the buyer's complaint is not that he will have to buy an equivalent elsewhere, but that he has got something of lower value than that which he should have received. A sub-sale is again ignored[278]; unless it is of the very goods comprised in the original contract.[279]   **20–051**

Bence Graphics. A case of defective delivery which gives rise to much difficulty is *Bence Graphics International Ltd v Fasson UK Ltd*.[280] Vinyl film had been sold for use in the buyers' business of manufacturing decals which their customers   **20–052**

---

[271] See below, para.20–102.

[272] [1911] A.C. 301.

[273] *Slater v Hoyle & Smith* [1920] 2 K.B. 11 at 23.

[274] cf. *Williams Bros v E T Agius Ltd* [1914] A.C. 510 at 530.

[275] *Slater v Hoyle & Smith* [1920] 2 K.B. 11 at 23–24.

[276] Sale of Goods Act 1979, s.53(3). cf. *Vinmar International Ltd v Theresa Navigation SA* [2001] 1 Lloyd's Rep. 1 at [56] (goods damaged as a result of a *carrier's* breach).

[277] cf. *Commercial Fibres (Ireland) Ltd v Zabaida* [1975] 1 Lloyd's Rep. 27.

[278] *Slater v Hoyle & Smith* [1920] 2 K.B. 11.

[279] As in *Champanhac Ltd v Waller Ltd* [1948] 2 All E.R. 724; cf. *Louis Dreyfus Trading Ltd v Reliance Trading Ltd* [2004] EWHC 525; [2004] 2 Lloyd's Rep. 243.

[280] [1998] Q.B. 87; Treitel 113 L.Q.R. 188.

attached to containers used in the carriage of goods. It was a term of the contract of sale that the decals were to have a "life" of five years; and this term was broken so that the film delivered was "worthless".[281] The defect being not immediately apparent, the buyers used the film for making decals; these were in turn defective, so that the buyers were faced with many complaints from their customers, though only with one relatively minor[282] claim; this was settled by the buyers who were compensated in this respect by the sellers. At first instance, the buyers recovered the whole of the price that they had paid since the film delivered had no value and since there was no evidence, other than the price, of the value which it would have had, if it had been in conformity with the contract. On appeal it was held by a majority that the sellers were liable for no more than the price of a small quantity of film which the buyers had returned,[283] plus the amount of the buyers' liability to the ultimate users of the decals; any loss in excess of this amount was regarded as too remote.[284] It may, with respect, be doubted whether the case gave rise to any issue of remoteness. If a seller contracts to deliver an ounce of gold for £210 (its market value) and instead delivers an ounce of base metal worth only £5, there is no doubt that he is liable for £205; and this liability is not subject to any test of remoteness.[285] That test would apply only if he had suffered some *further* loss as a result (for example) of his use of the subject-matter; but no such claim was in issue in the *Bence Graphics* case.[286] A pure "difference in value" claim could, indeed, sometimes be resisted on the ground that the buyer had not lost that difference because he had passed the subject-matter on to a sub-buyer for a price which took no account of the defect. But this would be the position only where the sub-sale was of the very goods comprised in the contract and could be performed only by delivery of those goods.[287] In such a case the goods in the buyer's hands would be worth the amount for which he had resold them; but where the sub-sale is not of those very goods, the buyer does suffer the "difference in value" loss since he could have used *other* goods to satisfy his sub-buyer and would then have been left with the goods bought under the broken contract. If he succeeds in disposing of those goods under an advantageous sub-sale, then it should be "immaterial that by some good fortune with which the [sellers] have nothing to do he has been able to recoup himself what he paid for those goods".[288] This was the position in the *Bence Graphics* case, where the buyers were under no obligation to their customers to use the material supplied by the sellers.[289] From this point of view, the decision is open to the same criticisms as those which have been discussed above in relation to *Wertheim*'s case.[290] It is respectfully submitted that

---

[281] [1998] Q.B. 87 at 108, where it is also said that the sellers "always accepted" this.

[282] Relating to 349 out of over 100,000 decals produced.

[283] Worth £22,000; £564,328 had been paid for the whole amount supplied.

[284] This follows from the reliance by the majority on the rule in *Hadley v Baxendale* (1854) 9 Ex. 341 (below, para.20–100) and Sale of Goods Act 1979, s.53(2), which is thought to embody that rule.

[285] See above, fn.25.

[286] It would have arisen if the buyers' customers had made unexpectedly large claims against them.

[287] See above, at fn.279.

[288] *Slater v Hoyle & Smith* [1920] 2 K.B. 11 at 18.

[289] per Morland J. at first instance, unreported, December 14, 1994, Transcript, p.10.

[290] [1911] A.C. 301; above, para.20–050. It might be argued that both are explained by the overriding nature of the "compensatory principle", which prevents a party from "seeking compensation exceeding the value of the contractual benefits of which they were deprived": *The Golden Victory* [2007] UKHL 12; [2007] 2 A.C. 353 at [38]; below para.20–080; cf. *The Achilleas* [2006] EWHC 3030 (Comm); [2007] 1 Lloyd's Rep. 19 at [88] (reversed [2008] UKHL 48; [2009] 1 A.C. 61 without reference to this point) where the *Bence Graphics* case is cited with apparent approval.

the buyers' claim in the *Bence Graphics* case should have been upheld[291] and that any "windfall" which they might in this way have obtained would have been obtained by the grace of those of their customers who had made no claims against them. There seems to be no reason why this indulgence should benefit the sellers who in breach of contract had delivered goods which they admitted to be worthless and who had received a price based on the warranted quality of those goods.

Defective delivery and loss due to a fall in the market. Where the market value of the goods has fallen between the making of the contract and the defective delivery, the buyer will normally wish to reject; for in this way he will be able to avoid the loss resulting, not from the breach, but from the fall in the market. If, however, he has lost the right to reject, his only remedy will be in damages, and those damages are prima facie recoverable only in respect of the defect, and not in respect of the fall in the market. In one case,[292] a contract for the sale of beans stipulated for shipment by the end of August but the seller delivered a September shipment. By the time of breach the market value of the beans had fallen some £2,000 below the contract price, so that the buyer would certainly have rejected if he had known of the defect in time. But he had "accepted"[293] the goods and it was held that the damages to which he was entitled were no more than nominal as there was no difference between the market value of an August and a September shipment and as the fall in the value of the goods since the time of contracting was not a loss which had resulted[294] from the seller's breach. There may, however, in cases of this kind, be a defect, not only in the goods, but also in the documents which the seller is obliged by the contract to tender[295] and the buyer may have accepted the documents without knowing of the defects in them,[296] paid the price, and so have been deprived (whether as a matter of law or of business[297]) of the chance to reject the goods.[298] In such a case the buyer can get damages on the footing that the defect in the documents was the cause of his losing the chance to reject the goods on a falling market; and he can do so even though the fact that the goods are not of the contract description has in no way affected their value.[299] For this reason it has been rightly said that there is "little merit"[300] in such a claim; and it is available only where there is a defect both in the documents and in the goods, each giving rise to an independent right to reject.[301]

20–053

---

[291] Subject only to a deduction in respect of the claim referred to in fn.283, above.

[292] *Taylor v Bank of Athens* (1922) 27 Com.Cas. 142.

[293] See above, para.18–083.

[294] Within Sale of Goods Act 1979, s.53(2).

[295] Especially under c.i.f. contracts, as to which see above, para.17–029.

[296] For the significance of this point, see *Vargas Pena v Peter Cremer GmbH* [1987] 1 Lloyd's Rep. 392.

[297] This was the position in *Kwei Tek Chao v British Traders & Shippers Ltd* [1954] 2 Q.B. 459.

[298] It is probably more accurate to say that what has been lost by the buyer is the chance to reject *the documents* and *by so doing* reject the goods.

[299] *James Finlay & Co Ltd v NV KwikHoo Tong HM* [1929] 1 K.B. 400; *Kwei Tek Chao v British Traders & Shippers Ltd* [1954] 2 Q.B. 459; *The Kastellon* [1978] 2 Lloyd's Rep. 203. Contrast *Vargas Pena v Peter Cremer GmbH* [1987] 1 Lloyd's Rep. 394 where such damages were not available to a buyer who knew of the defect *in the documents* when he accepted them.

[300] *The Kastellon*, above, at 207 (where the seller was not to blame for the defect in the documents).

[301] *Procter & Gamble Philippine Manufacturing Corp v Kurt A Becher* [1988] 2 Lloyd's Rep. 21; Treitel [1988] L.M.C.L.Q. 457.

20–054   **Defective delivery: consumer sales.** Where non-conforming goods are delivered to a buyer who deals as consumer, the buyer has in certain circumstances the right to require the seller "to reduce the purchase price of the goods in question to the buyer by an appropriate amount".[302] This concept of a price reduction is taken from the civil law, where the price of non-conforming goods is reduced in the proportion which the actual value of the goods bears to the value which they would have had, if they had been in conformity with the contract.[303] Such a reduction is not the same as the "difference in value" measure discussed above[304]: the civil law price reduction would yield *more* than that measure if the buyer had agreed to pay more than the value of the goods if they had been in conformity with the contract, and *less* if the buyer had agreed to pay less than that value. It remains to be seen whether the English courts will, in interpreting the phrase "an appropriate amount", apply the civil law principle of proportionate price reduction. Even if they do apply it, the buyer will not be prejudiced where the price reduction would yield less than difference in value, since the right to a "price reduction" is *additional*[305] to his other rights in respect of the breach. For the same reason, a buyer who claims a price reduction is also not precluded from claiming damages for consequential losses[306] such as personal injury caused by defects in the goods.

20–055   **Refusal to accept and pay.** If a buyer of goods refuses to accept and pay for goods sold to him, the seller can go into the market and sell the goods at the prevailing price. He will then prima facie lose the amount (if any) by which the contract price exceeds the market price[307]; and it is normally[308] irrelevant that the seller has actually resold for a different price.[309] If the market price exceeds the contract price, the seller generally suffers no loss. But this is not always true. The contract may provide for an advance payment without which the seller himself cannot get the goods. If the buyer fails to make this payment, the seller suffers loss even though the market price has risen above the contract price: he loses a good bargain because he is not in a position to take advantage of a rising market. Subject to the rules of remoteness,[310] the buyer will be liable for such a loss.[311] The market may also be relevant where the buyer's breach takes the form of *delay* in taking delivery. If the contract provides that the price is to depend on the market price at the time of taking delivery, and that price falls between the time when delivery should have been, and when it was, taken, the seller will be entitled to damages in respect of that difference.[312]

---

[302] s.48C(1) and (2), as inserted by Sale and Supply of Goods to Consumers Regulations 2002 (SI 2002/3045), reg.5, implementing Dir.1999/44.

[303] Vienna Convention on Contracts for the International Sale of Goods, Art.50 lays down the same formula.

[304] i.e. in Sale of Goods Act 1979, s.53(3); above, para.20–051.

[305] Heading before Sale of Goods Act 1979, s.48A, as inserted by the Regulations referred to at fn.302, above.

[306] See above, para.20–037.

[307] Sale of Goods Act 1979, s.50(3). For administrative expenses, see above, para.20–037.

[308] i.e. subject to the qualifications stated above (in the converse case of breach by the seller), at fnn.268–269.

[309] *Campbell Mostyn Provisions Ltd v Barnett Trading Co* [1954] 1 Lloyd's Rep. 65; *Texaco Ltd v Eurogulf Shipping Co Ltd* [1987] 2 Lloyd's Rep. 541 at 546; cf. *Jamal v Moolla Dawood Son & Co* [1916] 1 A.C. 175 (shares).

[310] See below, para.20–099 et seq.

[311] cf. *Trans Trust SPRL v Danubian Trading Co Ltd* [1952] 2 Q.B. 297.

[312] cf. *Addax Ltd v Arcadia Petroleum Ltd* [2000] 1 Lloyd's Rep. 493.

(ii) *Where there is no market*

Failure to deliver. If a seller or carrier fails to deliver goods which cannot be   **20–056**
replaced by buying in the market, the court must assess the loss as best it can:[313]
relevant factors include the cost of the goods and of their carriage, and a reasonable
profit.[314] Where the goods have actually been resold, the resale price is evidence
of their value, but not conclusive evidence. The weight of the evidence will depend
on such factors as the interval between the wrong and the resale and the extent of
fluctuations in the market price of other similar goods.[315] When the court takes the
latter factor into account, it may be said to have regard to a substitute market; and
a similar process is sometimes adopted where there is no market at the place where
delivery should have been made, but there is a market for goods of the kind in
question elsewhere. It may be reasonable for the injured party to resort to that
other market,[316]and damages may then be based on the cost of doing so at the time
of breach.[317]

Where goods are bought for use, the cost of acquiring a substitute is in principle
the correct measure. In one case this was assessed as the scrap value of the goods,
and this assessment, though described in the Court of Appeal as "surprising"[318]
was held not to be incorrect in principle. At first sight, the scrap value might seem
to be an inappropriate measure where goods were, to the seller's knowledge,
bought for use, since it can hardly represent the cost of acquiring a substitute. But
the case can perhaps be explained on the ground that the goods in question were
a spare part which was not immediately needed by the buyer and might never have
been needed by him. In these circumstances the purchase of a substitute by the
buyer might have been an unreasonable augmentation of his loss[319] which would
be irrecoverable under the mitigation rules.[320]

Failure to accept and pay. If there is no market, the seller's damages for non-   **20–057**
acceptance would prima facie be quantified by reference to the actual proceeds of
a substitute sale,[321] so long as that transaction was in all the circumstances a
reasonable one.[322] As in the case of failure to deliver, the substitute transaction
would be evidence of the value of the goods at the time of breach only if it was
concluded at, or close to, that time. If the seller did not resell, the value of the

---

[313] *Bulkhaul Ltd v Rhodia Organique Fine Ltd* [2008] EWCA Civ 1452; [2009] 1 Lloyd's Rep 353, at
[29]: the court "is entitled to infer the value of goods from any sufficient relevant evidence of
value."

[314] *O'Hanlan v GW Ry* (1865) 6 B. & S. 484; *Schulze v GE Ry* (1887) 19 Q.B.D. 30; *The Texaco
Melbourne* [1994] 1 Lloyd's Rep. 473 at 479; cf. *The Pegase* [1981] 1 Lloyd's Rep. 175 at 183 (late
delivery); *Shearson Lehman Hutton Inc v Maclaine Watson & Co (No.2)* [1990] 1 Lloyd's Rep. 441 at
443; cf. *Quorum A/S v Schramm* [2002] 2 Lloyd's Rep 72 at [100] et seq. (assessment of reduction in
value of work of art as a result of fire damage).

[315] Contrast *France v Gaudet* (1871) L.R. 6 Q.B. 196 and *Stroud v Austin & Co* (1883) Cab. & El.
119 with *The Arpad* [1934] P. 189 and *The Athenian Harmony* [1998] 2 Lloyd's Rep. 410 at 416.

[316] See *Lesters Leather & Skin Co Ltd v Home Overseas Brokers Ltd* (1949) 82 Ll.L.Rep. 203 at
205.

[317] So that loss due to currency fluctuations *after* that time will not be taken into account: see *The
Texaco Melbourne* [1994] 1 Lloyd's Rep. 473.

[318] *The Alecos M* [1991] 1 Lloyd's Rep. 120 at 125; Treitel 107 L.Q.R. 364.

[319] *Ruxley Electronics and Construction Co Ltd v Forsyth* [1996] A.C. 344 at 321–372.

[320] See below, para.20–115.

[321] *Janred Properties Ltd v Ente Nazionale per il Turismo* [1989] 2 All E.R. 444; cf. *The Noel Bay*
[1989] 1 Lloyd's Rep. 361 (damages for charterer's repudiation based on substitute voyage).

[322] *Aercap Partners 1 Ltd v Avia Asset Management AB* [2010] EWHC 2431 (Comm).

goods left on his hands would have to be assessed according to the general criteria stated above[323]; and his damages would prima facie be the amount (if any) by which the contract price exceeded that value.

(iii) *Other loss*

20-058   **Loss of profits, etc. by buyer.** The market and other related rules just stated do not form the limit of recovery. They deal only with the problem of valuing one element of the claimant's loss, namely his expectation of getting either the goods or the price. In addition, the claimant may be able to recover damages for loss of profits. Suppose that a seller has wrongfully failed to deliver goods which the buyer has subsold at a profit. Even if the resale price is *not* good evidence of value,[324] it may nevertheless be taken into consideration in assessing the buyer's damages for loss of profits. Under the rules of remoteness, however, the seller is liable for loss of resale profit only[325] if he knew or could have contemplated[326] that the goods were required for resale,[327] and even then he is not liable for loss of an extraordinary profit unless he is notified of the possibility that such a profit may accrue.[328] If, on the other hand, there is no market and the resale price *is* good evidence of the value of the goods the seller's liability is based on the amount of it, quite irrespective of his state of knowledge.[329] Where the seller is in breach by reason of a defect in the goods, the buyer may similarly (and subject to the rules of remoteness) be able to recover from the seller damages which he has paid, or for which he has become liable, to his sub-buyer in respect of the defect.[330]

20-059   **Loss of profits, etc. by seller.** The possibility of claiming additional damages for loss of profits also exists where a buyer wrongfully refuses to accept and pay for goods. Here the seller may expect both to get the price and to make a profit; and he may lose the profit even though he manages to resell the goods for exactly the same (or even a higher) price to another buyer. The point may be illustrated by cases in which car-dealers have claimed damages for loss of profits from customers who had agreed to buy cars and then in breach of contract refused to accept them. Three situations can be distinguished.[331] First, the sale is of a new car and the supply of cars of the contract description at the dealer's disposal exceeds the demand. Here the dealer's claim will succeed[332]; for he would, if the original customer had not defaulted, have been able to make a sale both to him and

---

[323] At fn.314.

[324] e.g. because the interval between the breach and the resale was too long, as in *The Arpad*, above, fn.315.

[325] *Schulze v GE Ry* (1887) 19 Q.B.D. 30.

[326] See below, para.20–099 et seq.

[327] *Borries v Hutchinson* (1865) 18 C.B.(N.S.) 445; *Patrick v Russo-British Grain Export Co Ltd* [1927] 2 K.B. 535; *Household Machines v Cosmos Exporters Ltd* [1947] 1 K.B. 217; *J Leavey & Co Ltd v G H Hirst & Co Ltd* [1944] K.B. 24.

[328] See below, para.20–108.

[329] See above, fn.25.

[330] *Total Liban SA v Vitol Energy SA* [2001] Q.B. 643.

[331] For the burden of proof in such cases, see: *Sony Computer Entertainment UK Ltd v Cinram Logistics* [2008] EWCA Civ 955; [2009] Bus L.R. 529.

[332] *W L Thompson Ltd v Robinson (Gunmakers) Ltd* [1955] Ch. 177; cf. *Re Vic Mill* [1913] 1 Ch. 465. For the application of similar principles to contracts other than sale, see *Inter-Office Telephones Ltd v Robert Freeman & Co Ltd* [1958] 1 Q.B. 190; *Robophone Facilities Ltd v Blank* [1966] 1 W.L.R. 1428.

to the second customer: hence he would have made two profits,[333] one of which has been lost. Secondly, the sale is of a new car and the demand for cars of the contract description exceeds the supply available to the dealer. Here his claim will fail[334]; for the number of sales that he can make depends on the number of cars that he can get and not on the number of customers that he can find. Hence the default of the original customer does not reduce the number of profits that he can earn. Thirdly, the sale is of a second-hand car. In *Lazenby Garages Ltd v Wright*,[335] it was held that a second-hand BMW car was a "unique" object; and as the car was resold for more than the original price to a second customer, the original customer (who had refused to take it) was not liable for loss of profit. No such loss had been suffered in respect of the car in question; and the possibility that the dealer might have sold a different car to the second customer was dismissed as too remote.[336] Whether it is too remote perhaps depends on the type of car concerned. If the car had been of a kind more commonly sold after use as a "fleet" car, the dealer's chance of selling another (virtually identical) car to a second customer might have been regarded as sufficiently great to satisfy the test of remoteness. Even where the original customer is not liable for loss of profits, any expense of negotiating the second sale can presumably be recovered from him as "incidental" loss.[337]

(c) Speculative Damages

Loss of a chance.[338] A contracting party can recover damages if he can show **20–060** that the breach has caused[339] him to lose the chance of gaining benefit. So long as the contingencies on which that chance depends are not wholly within the control of the party in breach,[340] the injured party can recover damages for loss of such a chance. He need not show that it was certain that he would have got the benefit if the contract had been performed; it is sufficient for the claimant to show that he had a real or substantial chance rather than a speculative one.[341] Thus damages can be recovered for loss of the chance of taking part in a beauty contest,[342] for loss of the chance of future orders from an established customer,[343] for loss of the chance

---

[333] cf. *Jebson v E & W India Dock Co* (1875) L.R. 10 C.P. 300.

[334] *Charter v Sullivan* [1957] 2 Q.B. 117.

[335] [1976] 1 W.L.R. 459.

[336] See below, para.20–099 et seq.

[337] See above, para.20–037.

[338] Poole [2007] L.M.C.L.Q. 63.

[339] For the requirement of causation, see *Allied Maples Group Ltd v Simmons & Simmons* [1995] 1 W.L.R. 1602 at 1623; *Bank of Credit and Commercial International v Ali (No.2)* [2002] EWCA Civ 82; [2002] 3 All E.R. 750, esp. at [42], [65] and [97].

[340] See below, para.20–070. In *Commonwealth of Australia v Amann Aviation Pty Ltd* (1992) 66 A.L.J.R. 123, loss of profits on future contracts which the defendants would probably have awarded to the injured party (without being bound to do so) were taken into account in assessing damages. But the claim was *for reliance loss* and the lost chance was taken into account for the purpose of the rule that such loss is recoverable only to the extent to which it will not leave the injured party better off than he would have been, if the contract had been performed: above, para.20–029. It does not necessarily follow that damages would have been awarded *for loss of the chance*.

[341] *Allied Maples Group Ltd v Simmons & Simmons* [1995] 1 W.L.R. 1602 at 1614; *Normans Bay v Coudert Bros* [2003] EWCA Civ 215 (more than "of no real value at all").

[342] *Chaplin v Hicks* [1911] 2 K.B. 786; cf. *Watson v Ambergate, etc., Ry* (1851) 15 Jur. 448. Contrast *McClory v Post Office* [1992] I.C.R. 758 (no damages for loss of chance to work overtime); Reece 59 M.L.R. 188. Contrast, in tort, *Gregg v Scott* [2005] UKHL 2; [2005] 2 A.C. 176.

[343] *Jackson v Royal Bank of Scotland Plc* [2005] UKHL 3; [2005] 1 W.L.R. 377; discussed below, para.20–107.

of earning tips,[344] for loss of the chance of obtaining pension benefits which depend on the exercise of discretion by a government department[345]; for loss of the chance of appealing against an arbitration award[346]; for loss of the chance of avoiding or of successfully contesting a criminal prosecution[347]; and for loss of the chance (of which clients had been deprived by the negligence of solicitors acting for them in property transactions) of bringing a claim against a third party[348] or of negotiating terms which could have protected the clients from liabilities to third parties.[349] The concept of loss of a chance is also used where the chance is not one of gaining some *specific* benefit or of avoiding some *specific* harm. In this more generalised sense,[350] damages for loss of a chance can be recovered for loss of profits expected to arise from transactions not yet concluded at the time of breach. A carrier of samples who delays in delivering them may thus be liable for loss of profits on contracts which the owner might have made, had he got the samples in time;[351] a person who breaks a contract to deliver a profit-earning thing may be liable for the profits which the other party might have made by using the thing;[352] and a formula one racing team which fails to provide an aspiring driver with the test driving promised may be liable for the harm done to his career prospects.[353]

The quantification of damages in such cases is necessarily speculative.[354] It depends on the value of the expected benefit and the likelihood of the claimant's actually getting it.[355] The chance of winning a beauty contest is obviously worth less than the full prize. In deciding how much the chance is worth the court will consider (1) the number of contingencies on which it depends: "the more contingencies, the lower the value of the chance"[356]; and (2) the likelihood of their being satisfied in the claimant's favour: the greater this likelihood, the higher the value of the chance.[357] Where the chance is assessed as "certain" no discount will be applied, but it is probably more accurate to say that the claim is not then one for loss of a chance.[358]

---

[344] *Manubens v Leon* [1919] 1 K.B. 208.

[345] *Scally v Southern Health and Social Services Board* [1992] 1 A.C. 294.

[346] *Corfield v Bosher & Co* [1992] 1 E.G.L.R. 163.

[347] *Acton v Graham Pearce & Co* [1997] 3 All E.R. 909.

[348] *Harrison v Bloom Camillin (No.2)* [2000] Lloyd's Rep. P.N. 89.

[349] *Allied Maples Group Ltd v Simmons & Simmons* [1995] 1 W.L.R. 1602.

[350] See *Bank of Credit and Commerce International SA v Ali (No.2)* [2002] EWCA Civ 82; [2002] 3 All E.R. 750 at [64]. There is, however, a limit to the "overworked" concept of loss of a chance: *Law Debenture Trust Corp Plc v Elektrim SA* [2010] EWCA Civ 1142 at [46]; cf. *Parabola Investments Ltd v Browallia Cal Ltd* [2010] EWCA Civ 486; [2010] 3 W.L.R. 1266 at [22]–[24]; *Vasiliou v Hajigeorgiou* [2010] EWCA Civ 1475.

[351] e.g. *Simpson v L & NW Ry* (1876) 1 Q.B.D. 274; below, para.20–108.

[352] e.g. *Victoria Laundry (Windsor) Ltd v Newman Industries Ltd* [1949] 2 K.B. 528; below, para.20–101.

[353] *Guido van der Garde BV v Force India Formula One Ltd* [2010] EWHC 2373.

[354] The award of the round figure of $100,000 made in the *van der Garde* case, above,was the result of a "broad brush" approach based on the "totality of the evidence" (at [412]).

[355] *Salford CC v Torkington* [2004] EWCA Civ 1646; (2004) 51 E.G. 89 at [54] (where damages were, in fact, ordered on a different basis).

[356] *Hall v Meyrick* [1957] 2 Q.B. 455 at 471 (actual decision reversed on another ground, [1957] 2 Q.B. 455 at 474); *Obagi v Stanborough (Developments)* (1995) 69 P. & C.R. 573; *Ministry of Defence v Wheeler* [1998] 1 All E.R. 790.

[357] e.g. *Dickinson v Jones Alexander & Co* [1993] 2 F.L.R. 521; cf. *Allied Maples Group Ltd v Simmons & Simmons* [1999] 1 W.L.R. 1602 at 1622–1623; *Maden v Clifford Coppock & Carter* [2004] EWCA Civ 1037; [2005] 2 All E.R. 43 (80 per cent chance of settlement at a certain level); *Football League Ltd v Edge Ellison* [2006] EWHC 1462 (Ch); [2007] P.N.L.R. 2 at [286].

[358] *Nicholas Prestige Homes v Neal* [2010] EWCA Civ 1552 at [33]

The injured party may, as a result of the breach, save the cost of getting the chance. That cost must then be deducted from the damages for loss of the chance, so that no such damages will be recoverable if the cost saved is equal to or greater than the value of the chance.[359]

The court will award speculative damages where no other course is, in the nature of things, open to it. It will not do so where the claimant could have provided evidence as to the value of the bargain that he has lost, and has simply failed to do so.[360]

(d) Interest

Common law. In earlier editions, the extent to which loss of interest might be   20–061
awarded as damages was assessed in the section of this chapter dealing with "methods of limiting damages". That reflected the general rule of the common law that interest could not be recovered as damages for failure to pay a debt when due.[361] To this anomalous rule, the House of Lords had created an anomalous exception,[362] but neither now requires any detailed consideration,[363] thanks to the almost total abolition of the rule by the House of Lords in *Sempra Metals Ltd v Commissioners of Inland Revenue*.[364] What survives is that loss of interest will not be awarded as general damages; the loss must be proved, but, if proved (including compound interest),[365] it is subject only to the same limits as any other claim for damages, e.g. mitigation and remoteness.[366]

Obligations other than to pay money. In the paragraph above the recovery   20–062
of loss of interest has been discussed in the context of the defendant's failure to

---

[359] *Sapwell v Bass* [1910] 2 K.B. 486, as explained in *Chaplin v Hicks* [1911] 2 K.B. 786 at 796; *Demarco v Perkins* [2006] EWCA Civ 188; [2006] P.N.L.R. at [70]. For the effect of a loss of chance claim on the claimant's option to seek "reliance" damages, see *Parker v SJ Berwin& Co* [2008] EWHC 3017 (Comm); [2009] P.N.L.R. 17, discussed above para.20–029.

[360] *Clark v Kirby-Smith* [1964] Ch. 506 at 512.

[361] *London, Chatham & Dover Ry v South Eastern Ry* [1893] A.C. 429; *La Pintada* [1985] A.C. 104; Mann 101 L.Q.R. 30. Interest could be awarded if there was an agreement to pay it in the events which had happened: *Higgins v Sargent* (1823) 2 B. & C. 348; *Janred Properties Ltd v EnteNazionaleItaliano per ilTurismo* [1989] 2 All E.R. 444.

[362] i.e. that damages could be awarded if the loss of interest was proved as special damages falling within the "second limb" of the test of remoteness laid down in *Hadley v Baxendale* (1854) 9 Exch. 341 at 354 (below, para.20–100): *La Pintada* [1985] A.C. 104; *The Lips* [1988] A.C. 395 at 423, 429. The self-evident anomaly is that the more obvious the claim for loss of interest the less likely it could be recovered. One consequence of the rejection of the rule, and therefore the need for the exception, is that the earlier decision of the Court of Appeal in *Wadsworth v Lydall* [1981] 1 W.L.R. 598 may no longer be forced into the second limb when it seems more likely to have been a first limb case: [2007] UKHL 34; [2008] 1 A.C. 561 at [215] per Lord Mance.

[363] For the detail, see the 12th edition, paras.20–113-20–120.

[364] [2007] UKHL 34; [2008] 1 A.C. 561; Mitchell 71 M.L.R. 290. This turn of events was surprising and defied the prediction in the last edition that it was unlikely that the rule would be reversed by judicial decision. The case itself was concerned with claims in restitution and for breach of statutory duty, so that the views of their lordships on the contract rule are obiter dictum. Since, however, four of them revisited the rule in contract (Lord Mance declined to do so) and reached a unanimous view, it would be even more surprising if an attempt was made to argue that this much maligned rule continues to survive.

[365] The claims before the House of Lords proceeded on the basis of conventional rates and periods (for the purpose of compounding). On the degree of particularity of proof needed in general, see Lord Nicholls at [126]–[127].

[366] [2007] UKHL 34; [2008] 1 A.C. 561 at [16]–[17], [94], [100], [132].

pay a debt. That may be the most obvious context in which such a claim may arise, but their Lordships in the *Sempra Metals* case also referred more generally to claims for breach of contract.[367] Thus, if a seller fails to deliver goods, the buyer's normal remedy in damages is the difference between the market price and the contract price, but where there has been a period during which the buyer has had to bear a higher market price, he may also be entitled to an award of interest.[368] And claims may be made in other cases where the consequence of the defendant's breach is to have put the claimant to expense or deprived him of the receipt of money.[369]

20–063   **Other claims for the loss of the use of money.** This part is entitled "interest" because that is the most obvious form in which a loss may be incurred by one party who does not receive, or is deprived of, money as a consequence of the other party's breach of contract. But as Lord Nicholls states in the *Sempra Metals* case, "the loss flowing from the late payment may take some other form."[370] Indeed, the common law rule precluding recovery was said to apply only to claims *for interest* as damages for late payment of money.[371] Thus, subject to other limits on recovery such as mitigation and remoteness, damages other than for loss of interest can be recovered from a banker who wrongfully repudiates liability, or delays in making payments due under a letter of credit,[372] or who wrongfully fails to honour a customer's cheque[373]; from a buyer of goods who fails to provide a confirmed credit in accordance with the terms of the contract of sale[374]; from a person who breaks a contract to subscribe for debentures in a company or who fails to pay calls on shares[375]; from a hire-purchaser or instalment buyer whose wrongful failure to pay instalments amounts to a repudiation of the contract[376]; and probably from any person who breaks a contract to lend or advance money.[377]

20–064   **Late Payments of Commercial Debts (Interest) Act 1998.** Two modifications of the former common law rule against recovery of interest have been made by legislation. The first is the right to "statutory interest" which arises under the Late Payments of Commercial Debts (Interest) Act 1998. The Act applies only to contracts for the supply of goods and services where each party is acting in the

---

[367] See, for example, Lord Nicholls (at [100]): "I consider the court has a common law jurisdiction to award interest, simple and compound, as damages on claims for non-payment of debts as well as on *other claims for breach of contract* and in tort." (emphasis added); cf. at [132] per Lord Scott.

[368] *Panchaud Frères v Pagnan Fratelli* [1974] 1 Lloyd's Rep. 394 at 411.

[369] See. e.g., in the context of services: *Nykreditbank v Edward Erdman Group* [1997] 1 W.L.R. 1627 (the award in that case is described as "doubtful" on the basis of the then state of the law: *McGregor on Damages* (18th edn), para.15–018); and in the context of the sale of land: *Bushwall Properties v Vortex Properties* [1975] 1 W.L.R. 1649, reversed on another ground: [1976] 1 W.L.R 591 ("a case which has not received the attention it deserves", *McGregor*, above, at para.15–016).

[370] [2007] UKHL 34; [2008] 1 A.C. 561 at [95].

[371] *The Lips* [1988] A.C. 395 at 424; cf. *IM Properties Plc v Cape & Dalgleish* [1999] Q.B. 297 at 307 (where no such claim was made).

[372] *Prehn v Royal Bank of Liverpool* (1870) L.R. 5 Ex. 92; *Urquhart Lindsay & Co v Eastern Bank Ltd* [1922] 1 K.B. 318; *Ozalid Group (Export) Ltd v African Continental Bank Ltd* [1979] 2 Lloyd's Rep. 231.

[373] *Rolin v Steward* (1854) 14 C.B. 595.

[374] *Trans Trust SPRL v Danubian Trading Co Ltd* [1952] 2 Q.B. 297; *Urquhart Lindsay & Co v Eastern Bank Ltd* [1922] 1 K.B. 318 at 323; above, para.17–015.

[375] *Wallis Chlorine Syndicate Ltd v American Alkali Co Ltd* (1901) 17 T.L.R. 565.

[376] *Yeoman Credit Ltd v Waragowski* [1961] 1 W.L.R. 1124 at 1128; *Overstone Ltd v Shipway* [1962] 1 W.L.R. 117; cf. para.18–015, above.

[377] See Sedgwick, *Damages* (9th edn), s.622; Corbin, *Contracts*, para.1065.

course of a business.[378] Its central provision is that it is an implied term of a contract to which it applies that "statutory interest" will be payable on any "qualifying debt" created by the contract (i.e. broadly, on the price payable under the contract[379]). Statutory interest starts to run from the day after the date agreed for payment in the contract or, in default of such agreement, 30 days after either the performance of the supplier's obligation or notice of the amount of the debt (whichever is later[380]). Since statutory interest is available by virtue of an implied term, the supplier is in principle entitled to it as of right; but where by reason of his conduct the interests of justice so require, the court can remit such interest wholly or in part.[381] The parties remain free, in general, to make their own contractual provisions with regard to interest and the Act does not place any restrictions on their power to do so after the debt has been created.[382] But their right to contract out of the Act before that time[383] is restricted in that contract terms are, to the extent to which they purport to exclude or restrict the right to statutory interest or to vary it, void unless they provide for a "substantial remedy" for late payment of the debt.[384] Moreover, no reliance can be placed on any contract term purporting to postpone the time at which a qualifying debt would otherwise be created unless that term satisfies the requirement of reasonableness under the Unfair Contract Terms Act 1977[385]; this provision applies whether the contract in which the term is contained was the contract creating the debt or one made before or after that contract.[386] The scope of the Act is restricted in that it applies only to contracts in which *each* party acts in the course of a business and only to contracts for the supply of "goods" and "services".[387] The latter expression may cover financial services; but consumer credit agreements and contracts intended to operate by way of mortgage, pledge, charge or other security are specifically excepted from the provisions of the Act.[388] A person who is entitled to statutory interest under the 1998 Act is, in addition, entitled to a relatively modest fixed sum,[389] intended to compensate him for the cost incurred by reason of the delay in payment

Senior Courts Act 1981, s.35A. The second modification of the former common law rule dates back to 1833, and is now contained in s.35A of the Senior **20–065**

---

[378] s.2(1); for definition of "business", see s.2(7); for definition of "goods and services", see s.2(2) and (3); contracts of service and apprenticeship are excluded by s.2(4).

[379] s.1(1) and (2); "qualifying debt" is defined in s.3; for the treatment of obligations to make an "advance payment", see s.11. For the approach to be taken when the sum payable is in dispute, see: *Ruttle Plant Hire Ltd v Sec of State for Environment, Food & Rural Affairs* [2009] EWCA Civ 97; [2009] B.L.R. 301.

[380] s.4, especially subss.(2), (3) and (5). The rate of statutory interest is 8 per cent above the Bank of England's official dealing rate: Late Payment of Commercial Debts (Rate of Interest) (No.3) Order 2002 (SI 2002/1675).

[381] s.5. See *Banham Marshalls Services Unlimited v Lincolnshire County Council* [2007] EWHC 402 (QB) at [67]–[73].

[382] ss.7(2) and 8(5).

[383] s.7(2).

[384] s.8(1), (3) (4); for the definition of "substantial remedy", see s.9.

[385] s.14, bringing such a term within Unfair Contract Terms Act 1977, s.3(2)(b) even where it is *not* contained in "written standard terms".

[386] This follows from the reference in s.14(3) to the definition of "contract term" in s.10(1).

[387] s.2(1).

[388] s.2(5).

[389] Late Payment of Commercial Debt (Interest) Act 1998, s.5A, inserted by Late Payment of Commercial Debts Regulations 2002 (SI 2002/1674), reg.2(4) implementing Dir.2000/35; the fixed sum ranges from £40 where the debt is less than £1,000 to £100 where the debt is £10,000 or more.

Courts Act 1981. This gives the courts a discretionary power to award interest when giving judgment for a debt or damages[390]; and where proceedings are brought for recovery of a debt and the defendant pays the debt before judgment.[391] The court in exercising this discretion will look at the overall position of the injured party in consequence of the breach. Thus if he retains the income of property sold till payment, the court will not award him interest on the price, since this would amount to allowing double recovery.[392] Unlike the right to "statutory interest" under the 1998 Act, the discretion to award interest under the 1981 Act applies to all contracts; but it is subject to a number of limitations. If the contract has been terminated by the injured party before payment under it from the party in breach has become due, no action for *debt* will be available to the injured party[393]; and in such a case the statutory discretion to award interest will be exercisable only in relation to the *damages* to which that party is entitled.[394] This restriction (which appears to apply also to the right to "statutory interest" under the 1998 Act[395]) is a significant one: the damages suffered on a purchaser's default in completing a contract for the sale of a house are prima facie the difference between the contract price and the proceeds of resale,[396] a much smaller sum than the contract price. The statutory discretion to award interest under the 1981 Act does not, moreover, extend to the case where an overdue debt is paid *before* any proceedings for recovery of the debt have begun.[397]

20–066   **The relationship between the common law and statute.** It will be clear from the limits to the scope of the courts' power to award interest under the statutory regimes that there will be cases where an award of loss of interest may only be made at common law. It is in relation to such cases that the limiting of the common law rule barring recovery will be most welcome. But in many cases, it may be possible to make an award under either the common law, or statute, or both.[398] This possibility does not conflict with the legislation. Section 35(A) of the 1981 Act expressly states that it is not an exhaustive code and does not displace the jurisdiction of the courts themselves to award interest,[399] and a debt does not carry interest under a term implied by the 1998 Act if, or to the extent that, a right to demand interest on it which exists by virtue of any rule of law is exercised.[400] Furthermore, s.35(A) is concerned with interest on debts and damages and "says nothing about the principles to be applied by a court when assessing the amount of damages for which it gives judgment."[401] For a claimant, the principal advantage of the common law is that the courts may award compound interest, but such

---

[390] s.35(A)(1); cf. County Courts Act 1984, s.69.
[391] s.35A(3).
[392] *Janred Properties Ltd v EnteNazionaleItaliano per ilTurismo* [1989] 2 All E.R. 444 at 456.
[393] See above, para.18–013.
[394] *Janred Properties* case, above, fn.392.
[395] Since in the case put there can be no "qualifying *debt*" within ss.1(1) and 3 of the 1998 Act.
[396] See above, para.20–057.
[397] As in *The World Symphony* [1991] 2 Lloyd's Rep. 251, affirmed [1992] 2 Lloyd's Rep. 115, without reference to the point; cf. *IM Properties Plc v Dalgleish* [1999] Q.B. 297 (same principle applied to damages). There is no such restriction on the right to "statutory interest" under the 1998 Act.
[398] It may be assumed that the courts will exercise the powers available to them in a way which will avoid double recovery; cf. *Fletcher v Tayleur* (1855) 17 C.B. 21 at 29; *Jacques v Millar* (1877) 6 Ch D. 153; *Trafigura Beheer BV v Mediterranean Shipping Co SA* [2007] EWCA Civ 794; [2007] 2 Lloyd's Rep. 622 at [42].
[399] s.35(A)(4).
[400] s.3(3).
[401] *Sempra Metals* case [2007] UKHL 34; [2008] 1 A.C. 561 at [99] per Lord Nicholls.

loss must be proved. Under the statutory provisions described above only an award of simple interest is available, but it can be made without proof that any loss of interest has been suffered. It is perhaps for these reasons that it has been observed that, in practice, especially where the period over which interest is sought is short or where the claimant does not have to borrow money to replace the debt, simple interest under s.35A of the 1981 Act is likely to be the more convenient remedy.[402]

(e) Taxation

The rule in *Gourley's* case. The value of the claimant's loss may be affected by the incidence of taxation. In *BTC v Gourley*[403] a person was injured by the negligence of the defendant's servants, and claimed damages for loss of earnings. It was estimated that, but for the accident, the injured party would have earned £37,000. Had he actually earned this sum, it would have been taxed and £6,000 would have been left to him. But had he been awarded damages of £37,000 he could have kept the whole amount, since damages for loss of earnings resulting from personal injury are not taxable. The House of Lords held that the proper measure of damages was £6,000, that being the amount of the injured party's actual loss. *Gourley*'s case was an action in tort, but the same principle can apply where the liability is contractual, e.g. in assessing damages for wrongful dismissal.[404]

20–067

The reason for the rule is that the injured party ought not to make a profit out of the wrong by getting tax-free damages to compensate for loss of a benefit which would have been taxable. Thus the rule applies only if two conditions are satisfied. First, the damages must be compensation for loss of a taxable income or gain, and not simply for loss of a capital asset. Thus the rule would probably not apply if a buyer of goods claimed the amount by which their market value exceeded the contract price. These damages are meant to compensate him for failure to obtain a capital asset (out of which he might make a profit or a loss).[405] Secondly, the damages themselves must not be taxable in the hands of the victim of the breach.[406] Damages for wrongful dismissal are taxable to the extent that they exceed £30,000.[407] Hence such damages must be reduced by reference to the claimant's income-tax liability where his loss of income is less than £30,000[408]; where it is more, the court will assess his net loss and then award such sum as, after tax on the sum so assessed, would be equal to that loss.[409]

---

[402] *Sempra Metals* case [2007] UKHL 34; [2008] 1 A.C. 561 at [17] per Lord Hope.

[403] [1956] A.C. 185; Jolowicz [1959] C.L.J. 85; Tucker [1959] C.L.J. 185; Hall 73 L.Q.R. 212; Baxter 19 M.L.R. 373; Bishop and Kay 103 L.Q.R. 211.

[404] *Beach v Reed Corrugated Cases Ltd* [1956] 1 W.L.R. 807; *Re Houghton Main Colliery* [1956] 1 W.L.R. 1219; *Phipps v Orthodox Unit Trusts Ltd* [1958] 1 Q.B. 314.

[405] cf. *Spencer v MacMillan's Trustees* 1958 S.C. 300; *Lim Foo Yong Ltd v Collector of Land Revenue* [1963] 1 W.L.R. 295. But if goods are *sold* by a trader, damages for non-acceptance are taxable as receipts of his trade and so not subject to reduction in respect of tax: *Deeny v Gooda Walker Ltd (No.2)* [1996] 1 W.L.R. 426 at 432.

[406] *Diamond v Campbell-Jones* [1961] Ch. 22; *Raja's Commercial College v Gian Singh & Co Ltd* [1977] A.C. 312; *Deeny v Gooda Walker Ltd (No.2)* [1996] 1 W.L.R. 426.

[407] Income Tax (Earnings and Pensions) Act 2003, ss.401–404.

[408] *Parsons v BNM Laboratories Ltd* [1964] 1 Q.B. 95.

[409] *Bold v Brough, Nicholson & Hall Ltd* [1964] 1 W.L.R. 201; *Shove v Downs Surgical Plc* [1984] I.C.R. 582; Lee 47 M.L.R. 471.

20–068   **Criticism.** The rule in *Gourley*'s case has been much criticised. It is said to involve a paradox: for revenue purposes damages for loss of earnings are treated as compensation for loss of a capital asset, since otherwise they would be taxable; while in assessing damages they are treated as compensation for loss of income, since otherwise the claimant's tax liability would be irrelevant.[410] A possible solution of this paradox is to say that the damages compensate the claimant for loss of *earning capacity*, which is a capital asset whose value depends on (amongst other things) the incidence of taxation.[411] Other criticisms are concerned with the practical effects of the rule. It is said that the rule enables the defendant to take advantage of wholly extraneous circumstances (e.g. that the claimant has a large private income); that it makes the assessment of damages highly speculative; and that the rule may make it cheaper to break a contract than to perform it. But similar criticisms could be made of other rules relating to damages, which have so far remained immune from them. Thus a seller can sometimes take advantage of an extraneous event, such as a sub-sale made by the buyer, in reducing damages for non-delivery[412]; speculative damages are by no means uncommon[413]; and it may often be cheaper to break a contract than to perform it: e.g. where damages are assessed on a difference in value basis amounting only to a small fraction of the cost of performance.[414] The rule in *Gourley*'s case has therefore survived the criticisms which have been levelled against it; and it can be supported[415] on the ground that it gives effect to the principle that damages are meant only to compensate the claimant for his actual loss.

20–069   **Tax savings.** A breach of contract may actually *reduce* the victim's tax liability. The amount of the reduction is then deducted from the damages for the breach, on the principle that the benefit of having to pay less tax in fact mitigates the victim's loss.[416]

(f) Alternative Modes of Performance

20–070   **General rule.** Where a contract entitles the party in breach to perform in alternative ways, damages are, as a general rule,[417] assessed on the assumption that he would have performed in the way that is least burdensome to himself and least beneficial to the other party.[418] Thus if a voyage charterparty gives the charterer the power to choose between a number of different ports of discharge, damages for

---

[410] Jolowicz, above, fn.403.

[411] Tucker, above, fn.403. Damages for personal injury are not taxable as capital gains: Taxation of Chargeable Gains Act 1992, s.51(2).

[412] See above, para.20–050.

[413] See above, para.20–060.

[414] See above, para.20–040.

[415] See Law Reform Committee, 7th Report (1958) Cmnd. 501.

[416] *Levison v Farin* [1978] 2 All E.R. 1149; below, paras 20–121—20–122.

[417] The rule may be excluded by express contrary stipulation: *Bremer HandelsgesellschaftmbH v Bunge Corp* [1982] 1 Lloyd's Rep. 108, affirmed [1983] 1 Lloyd's Rep. 476, without reference to this point.

[418] *Abrahams v Herbert Reiach Ltd* [1922] 1 K.B. 477; *Withers v General Theatre Corp* [1933] 2 K.B. 536; *The Rijn* [1981] 2 Lloyd's Rep. 267. It has been noted that it is not easy to reconcile all of the dicta in the cases dealing with this principle: *Durham Tees Valley Airport Ltd v Bmibaby Ltd* [2010] EWCA Civ 485; [2011] 1 Lloyd's Rep. 68 at [95]. The rule applies only where the obligation of the defendant is truly alternative: see *Deverill v Burnell* (1873) L.R. 8 C.P. 475.

his failure to load will be assessed on the assumption that he would have chosen the most distant port and so have reduced the shipowner's profit.[419] Similarly, where a supplier of goods has an option as to the exact quantity to be delivered, damages for non-delivery will be based on the assumption that he would have delivered the smallest permissible quantity.[420] The alternative relied upon must, however, constitute a valid performance and may be limited to a mode of performance which could in all the circumstances be regarded as reasonable.[421] Furthermore, performance which is "least burdensome" to the party in breach is not limited strictly to what was the *minimum* level of performance under the contract.[422] It is not to be assumed that he would have acted uncommercially.[423]

Qualifications. The general rule just stated is subject to a number of qualifications. A contract of sale may, for example, give the seller an option as to the time of delivery by allowing him to deliver at any time chosen by him in a stated month. In such a case, damages for non-delivery will prima facie be assessed by reference to the market price at the end of the period. They will not be assessed by reference to the time during it when the market was lowest[424]; for such a rule would give rise to too much uncertainty. Moreover, the party who has the option may declare before breach that he will exercise it in a particular way. Damages will then be assessed on that basis[425] if the effect of the declaration is to bind him contractually to perform in the specified way.[426]   20–071

(g) Time for Assessment

(i) *Time of breach*

The starting principle is, or is generally assumed to be, that damages are assessed by reference to the time of breach. For example, where a buyer of goods fails to accept and pay for them (or a seller fails to deliver) the damages are prima facie the difference between the contract price and the market price   20–072

---

[419] *Kaye SN Co Ltd v W & R Barnett Ltd* (1932) 48 T.L.R. 400; *The Rijn* [1981] 2 Lloyd's Rep. 267 at 270; cf. *The World Navigator* [1991] 2 Lloyd's Rep. 23 at 33.

[420] *Re Thornett & Fehr and Yuills Ltd* [1921] 1 K.B. 219; cf. the statement of the common law position in *Page v Combined Shipping & Trading Co* [1997] 3 All E.R. 656 at 660 (where the rule was displaced by Commercial Agents (Council Directive) Regulations 1993 (SI 1993/3053), reg.17(7)). Where the contract does not clearly specify the supplier's options, these will have to be determined by the court as a matter of construction, as in *Paula Lee Ltd v Robert Zehil Ltd* [1983] 2 All E.R. 390.

[421] *Paula Lee Ltd v Robert Zehil Ltd* [1983] 2 All E.R. 390; *Mulvenna v Royal Bank of Scotland* [2003] EWCA Civ 1112.

[422] *Durham Tees Valley Airport Ltd v Bmibaby Ltd* [2010] EWCA Civ 485; [2011] 1 Lloyd's Rep. 68 at [69]; *Jones v Ricoh UK Ltd* [2010] EWHC 1743 (Ch) at [75].

[423] ibid. at [69]; *Jones v Ricoh UK Ltd* [2010] EWHC 1743 (Ch) at [79]; *Lavarack v Woods of Colchester Ltd* [1967] 1 Q.B. 278 at 294 (to "cut off his nose to spite his face . . . would not be the mode of performing the contract which is 'the least burdensome to the defendant' ", per Diplock L.J.).

[424] cf. *Harlow & Jones Ltd v Panex (International) Ltd* [1967] 2 Lloyd's Rep. 509; *Phoebus D Kyprianou Co v W H Pim Jr* [1977] 2 Lloyd's Rep. 570 (buyer's breach).

[425] See *The Delian Spirit* [1972] 1 Q.B. 103 at 111–112; *Shipping Co of India Ltd v Naviera Letasa SA* [1976] 1 Lloyd's Rep. 132; *Toprak Mahsulleri Ofisi v Finagrain Cie Commerciale* [1979] 2 Lloyd's Rep. 98.

[426] Contrast *The Rijn*, above, fn.418, at 270 (where the declaration was not of this kind).

"at the time or times when the goods ought to have been accepted [or delivered], or (if no time was fixed for acceptance [or delivery]) at the time of the refusal to accept [or deliver]".[427]

The same principle of assessment by reference to the time of breach has been applied where a vendor of land wrongfully refused to convey.[428] The theory behind the rule is that any loss suffered by reason of market movements after the time of breach is not caused by the breach, but rather by the injured party's failure to mitigate[429] by making a substitute contract. Since under the mitigation rules the claimant need only act reasonably, it follows that even the principle of assessment by reference to the time of breach is applied with some latitude. In *C Sharpe & Co Ltd v Nosawa*[430] a contract for the sale of peas required the seller to deliver on "about July 21" but no delivery was made. Goods of the precise contract quality were not available in the market. It was held that the buyers had "a reasonable time to consider their position"[431]; and accordingly the damages were assessed by reference to the market price of similar goods at the end of July.[432]

The principle of assessment by reference to the time of breach is based on two assumptions: that the injured party knows of the breach as soon as it is committed, and that he can at that time take steps to mitigate the loss which is likely to flow from it. Where the facts falsify these assumptions, the courts will depart from the principle, and assess the damages by reference to "such other date as may be appropriate in the circumstances".[433] In particular they will have regard to the time when the breach was, or could have been discovered; and to the question whether it was possible or reasonable for the injured party to make a substitute contract immediately on such discovery.[434]

(ii) *Time of discovery of breach*

20–073   The injured party may not have known of the breach when it was committed and may have been unable, acting with reasonable diligence, to discover it at that

---

[427] Sale of Goods Act 1979, ss.50(3), 51(3); cf. *Jamal v Moolla Dawood Sons & Co* [1916] 1 A.C. 175; *The "Ile aux Moines"* [1974] 1 Lloyd's Rep. 262; *Phillips v Ward* [1956] 1 W.L.R. 471 at 474, 475, 478; *The Texaco Melbourne* [1994] 1 Lloyd's Rep. 473 at 476; and see above, fn.317.

[428] *Diamond v Campbell-Jones* [1961] Ch. 22 at 36; *Janred Properties Ltd v Ente Nazionale Italiano per il Turismo* [1989] 2 All E.R. 444 at 457.

[429] See below, para.20–116.

[430] [1917] 2 K.B. 814; cf. *The Good Friend* [1984] 2 Lloyd's Rep. 586 at 596; *Shearson Lehman Hutton Inc v Maclaine Watson & Co (No.2)* [1990] 2 Lloyd's Rep. 441 at 447.

[431] ibid. at 821; cf. *Techno Land Improvements Ltd v British Leyland (UK) Ltd* (1979) 252 E.G. 805 at 809; *The Playa Larga* [1983] 2 Lloyd's Rep. 171 at 181.

[432] For similar reasons of convenience, the contract itself may provide for assessment by reference to a date other than that of breach: see, e.g. *Bremer HandelsgesellschaftmbH v Vanden Avenne-Izegem PVBA* [1978] 2 Lloyd's Rep. 109 at 117; *Lusograin Comercio Internacional de Cereas Ltda v Bunge AG* [1986] 2 Lloyd's Rep. 654 at 658.

[433] *Johnson v Agnew* [1980] A.C. 367 at 401; *County Personnel (Employment Agency) Ltd v Pulver* [1987] 1 W.L.R. 916; *South Australia Asset Management Corp v York Montague Ltd* [1997] A.C. 191 at 221; quaere, whether time of breach was the appropriate time in *Mahoney v Purnell* [1996] 3 All E.R. 61 at 95–96; cf. *Habton Farms v Nimmo* [2003] EWCA Civ 68; [2004] Q.B. 1.

[434] In addition to the "exceptions" which follow in paras 20–074—20–076, the principle of taking into account events which were contingent at the date of breach but are known at the date of the hearing, applied by the House of Lords in *The Golden Victory* [2007] UKHL 12; [2007] 2 A.C. 353 and discussed below para.20–081 in the context of anticipatory breach, also applies to cases of actual breach.

time. The damages will then prima facie[435] be assessed by reference (at the earliest[436]) to the time when that party, so acting, could have made the discovery. For example, a seller may first "appropriate" goods to the contract by indicating which particular goods he intends to deliver under a contract for the sale of unascertained goods, and then deliver them. If those goods are not in conformity with the contract, the seller will be in breach at the time of appropriation, but the damages are prima facie assessed by reference to the later time of *delivery*.[437] Where goods are sent to the buyer in sealed packages, the damages may be assessed by reference to the even later time, at which it is reasonable to expect the packages to be opened and their contents examined.[438] Similarly, where a builder does defective work and damages are based on cost of cure, they will normally be assessed by reference to the time when the customer, acting with reasonable diligence, could have discovered the defect.[439] Delay in discovering the defect may affect not only the time but also the very basis of assessment; for if at the time of discovery the cost of cure is disproportionately high in relation to the value of a sound building, or if cure has become as a practical matter impossible, the court will award damages on a difference in value basis.[440]

(iii) *Possibility of acting on knowledge of breach*

Even if the injured party knows of the breach, it may be impossible for him to act on that knowledge by making a substitute contract so as to reduce the loss. For example, a buyer might wrongfully refuse to pay for goods after they had been despatched to him, and it might be impossible for the seller to resell them until they had reached their destination. In such a case the damages would be assessed by reference to the time at which the seller could reasonably resell, and not to the time of the buyer's refusal to pay.[441]

20–074

Impossibility of acting on knowledge of the breach may also be due to the fact that the buyer lacks the means to buy a substitute on a rising market. In *Wroth v Tyler*[442] the defendant had contracted to sell his house for £6,000. The sale was to be completed in October 1971, when the value of the house had risen to £7,500; but in July 1971 the defendant had wrongfully repudiated the contract. The buyers started proceedings for specific performance and damages; judgment was given in January 1973, when the house was worth £11,500. It was held that specific

---

[435] The rule will not apply to the extent that delay in discovering the breach had no adverse effect on the injured party's position: cf. above, para.20–009 and see *Re Bell's Indenture* [1980] 1 W.L.R. 1217 (a case of breach of trust).

[436] For assessment by reference to later times, see paras 20–074—20–075.

[437] Sale of Goods Act 1979, s.53(3).

[438] *Van den Hurk v R Martens & Co Ltd* [1920] 1 K.B. 850; cf. *The Hansa Nord* [1976] Q.B. 44 (damages assessed by reference to time of *arrival*, though breach occurred on *shipment*); cf. above, paras 9–067—9–070 for similar principles governing damages in tort for misrepresentation.

[439] *East Ham BC v Bernard Sunley Ltd* [1966] A.C. 406; subsequent increases in cost may be taken into account if it is reasonable to delay the work: see (in tort) *Dodd Properties (Kent) Ltd v Canterbury CC* [1980] 1 W.L.R. 433; Feldman and Libling 75 L.Q.R. 271; Duncan Wallace 96 L.Q.R. 101, 98 L.Q.R. 406; Waddams 97 L.Q.R. 445, 1 O.J.L.S. 134.

[440] *Applegate v Moss* [1971] 1 Q.B. 406; *King v Victor Parsons Ltd* [1972] 1 W.L.R. 801.

[441] cf. *Shearson Lehman Hutton Inc v Maclaine Watson & Co Ltd* [1989] 2 Lloyd's Rep. 570 at 647 (dealings suspended at time of alleged breach).

[442] [1974] Ch. 30; for further discussion see below, at fn.450 and below, para.21–062; cf. *Hulbert v Avens* [2003] EWHC 76 (Ch).

performance should not be ordered[443]; that damages should be awarded in lieu[444] and that these should be assessed by reference to the value of the house at the time, not of breach, but of judgment,[445] i.e. not at £1,500 but at £5,500. Since the buyers had (as the defendant knew[446]) no financial resources beyond the £6,000 they had raised to buy the house, they could not act on their knowledge of the breach by making a substitute purchase on a rapidly rising market.

(iv) *Reasonableness of acting on knowledge of breach*

20–075   Even where it is possible for the injured party to make a substitute contract on discovering the breach, it may not be reasonable to expect him to do so because at that time there is still a reasonable probability that the defendant will make good his default. In such cases damages are prima facie assessed by reference to the time when that probability ceased to exist.[447] Thus if a seller of goods, after the delivery date has gone by, assures the buyer that he will deliver, but then declares his final inability to perform, the damages will be assessed by reference to the market at the date of that declaration.[448] Again, the injured party may continue to press for performance after the agreed time, but finally elect to terminate on account of the breach: in such a case damages are assessed by reference to the date of termination.[449] A similar principle applies where the injured party brings an action for specific performance: thus a further explanation of the decision in *Wroth v Tyler*[450] is that the buyers could not be expected to make a substitute contract so long as their claim for specific performance was being maintained.[451] The same is true where an order of specific performance has actually been made but is not complied with, so that the injured party is eventually driven to abandon his attempt to enforce performance and to seek his remedy in damages: these are then assessed "as at the date when . . . the contract is lost".[452]

(v) *Late performance*

20–076   If the party in default performs late and the other party suffers loss by reason of the delay, the damages for that loss will be assessed by reference to the date when performance actually was (and not by reference to the date when it should have been) rendered.[453]

---

[443] See below, para.21–029.

[444] See below, para.21–062.

[445] For the possibility of assessment by reference to an even later time, see *Grant v Dawkins* [1973] 1 W.L.R. 1406.

[446] *Wroth v Tyler* [1974] Ch. 30 at 57; but for this fact, the loss might (at least in part) have been too remote: below, para.20–104.

[447] *Radford v De Froberville* [1977] 1 W.L.R. 1262; *Johnson Matthey Bankers Ltd v State Trading Corp of India* [1984] 1 Lloyd's Rep. 427 at 437–438; cf. *Habton Farms v Nimmo* [2003] EWCA Civ 68; [2004] Q.B. 1.

[448] *Barnett v Javeri & Co* [1916] 2 K.B. 390.

[449] *Toprak Mahsulleri Ofisi v Finagrain Cie Commerciale* [1979] 2 Lloyd's Rep. 98; *The Aktion* [1987] 1 Lloyd's Rep. 283; cf. *Carpobego-Abastecimento de Combustiveis SA v Amci Export Corp* [2006] EWHC 72 (Comm); [2006] 1 Lloyd's Rep. 736.

[450] [1974] Ch. 30.

[451] *Wroth v Tyler*, above, as explained in *Radford v De Froberville* [1977] 1 W.L.R. 1262 at 1285–1286; *Domb v Isoz* [1980] Ch. 548 at 559; *Meng Leong Development Pty Ltd v Jip Hong Trading Co Pte Ltd* [1985] A.C. 511.

[452] *Johnson v Agnew* [1980] A.C. 367 at 401; cf. *Suleman v Shahsavari* [1988] 1 W.L.R. 1181; *Johnson & Co (Barbados) Ltd v NSR Ltd* [1997] A.C. 400 at 411–412.

[453] *Ozalid Group (Export) Ltd v African Continental Bank Ltd* [1979] 2 Lloyd's Rep. 231.

(vi) *Damages for anticipatory breach*

Breach not accepted. The victim of an anticipatory breach can either con-   20–077
tinue to press for performance, or "accept" the breach.[454] If the injured party does
not accept the breach, the principles (discussed above) as to the time for assessment apply. Assuming that subsequent events have not deprived the injured party
of his right to damages,[455] the general rule is that those damages will be assessed
by reference to the time when the contract ought to have been performed[456] and
not by reference to the time of repudiation. The injured party is under no
obligation to "accept" the breach. It follows that if the market moves so as to
increase his loss between the time of repudiation and the time fixed for performance, he is entitled to damages assessed by reference to the latter time.[457]

Breach accepted. Where the injured party does accept the breach, he can start   20–078
his action before the time fixed for performance; but the principle of assessment
by reference to that time applies even in this type of case.[458] If the action comes
to trial before the time fixed for performance, the damages will therefore necessarily be speculative, as they will be based on forecasts or guesses as to future
market movements.[459] But where the injured party accepts the breach, the principle of assessment by reference to the time fixed for performance is subject to an
important qualification: his damages will be reduced if, after accepting the breach,
he fails to take reasonable steps to mitigate his loss.[460] Under this rule, the injured
party may, and if there is a market generally will, be required to make a substitute
contract; and his damages will be assessed by reference to the time when that
contract should have been made. This will usually be the time of acceptance of the
breach[461] (or such reasonable time thereafter as may be allowed under the rules
stated above[462]). If it is disputed whether a substitute contract could indeed have
been made, the burden of proving that the injured party could have made such a
contract lies on the party in breach. If that burden is not discharged, the damages
will prima facie be assessed by reference to the time fixed for performance.[463]

Effect of probable events after repudiation. Under the rules just stated,   20–079
market movements after acceptance of an anticipatory breach may be relevant to
the assessment of damages; but it is further possible for the right to damages, or
the extent of recovery, to depend on events (other than such a breach) that occur,
or will probably occur, between acceptance of the breach and the time fixed for
performance. This possibility is illustrated by cases in which charterparties gave
charterers a right to cancel if the ship was not ready to load at a named port by

---

[454] See above, para.17–078; *Garnac Grain Co Inc v Faure & Fairclough Ltd* [1968] A.C. 1130 at
1140.
[455] See above, para.17–091 and below, para.20–079.
[456] *Tai Hing Cotton Mill Ltd v Kamsing Knitting Factory* [1979] A.C. 91.
[457] *Tredegar Iron & Coal Co Ltd v Hawthorn Bros & Co* (1902) 18 T.L.R. 716.
[458] *Roper v Johnson* (1873) L.R. 8 C.P. 167; *Melachrino v Nickoll & Knight* [1920] 1 K.B. 693 at
699.
[459] As in *Roper v Johnson*, above.
[460] See below, para.20–116.
[461] *Roth & Co v Taysen Townsend & Co* (1895) 1 Com.Cas.240; (1896) 12 T.L.R. 211.
[462] See *C Sharpe & Co Ltd v Nosawa* [1917] 2 K.B. 814; above, paras 20–073—20–075; *Kaines (UK)
Ltd v Oesterreichische Warenhandelsgesellschaft Autowaren, etc* [1993] 2 Lloyd's Rep. 1.
[463] *Roper v Johnson* (1873) L.R. 8 C.P. 167; cf. in tort, *Geest Plc v Lansiquot* [2002] UKPC 48; [2002]
1 W.L.R. 3111 at [13]–[14].

a specified date, and the charterers then committed anticipatory breaches by purporting to cancel before that date. In *The Mihalis Angelos*[464] it was said that the owner's damages for such a wrongful[465] cancellation would (even if he had so accepted it) have been merely nominal, since in that case it was already clear at the time of that cancellation that the ship could not possibly have reached the port of loading by the specified date. Hence the charterer could have relied on the point that he would have been entitled to cancel on the ship's late arrival; and as it was found that he would certainly have exercised that right, the contract was of no value to the shipowner.[466]

20–080   **Events known to have happened by the time of the hearing.** In *The Mihalis Angelos*[467] it was said by Megaw L.J. that damages should be assessed as "at the date of acceptance of the breach" and that they may be reduced if the relevant events were "inevitable", or "pre-destined" to happen.[468] Lord Denning M.R. referred more generally to the need to "take into account all contingencies which might have reduced . . . the loss",[469] but both approaches adhere to the date of acceptance of the breach and seek to assess, *as at that date*, the likelihood that certain events *might have happened in the future* and the effect this would have on the loss suffered by the injured party as a consequence of the breach. But what is the position if certain events which would not have been anticipated at the date of acceptance of the breach *have happened* in the time between that acceptance and the date on which damages are assessed, and it is clear that they would have affected the performance of the contract had it not been terminated? This was the position in *The Golden Victory*.[470] There, owners accepted the charterer's repudiation on December 17, 2001, when the charterparty was not due to end until December 6, 2005. On March 20, 2003, prior to the award of the arbitrator, the Second Gulf War began, and the charterer argued that damages should not be awarded for the period beyond that date since it would have exercised its right to cancel under a War Clause. By a majority,[471] the House of Lords agreed, on the basis that to award damages for the period after March 20, 2003 "would be inconsistent with the overriding compensatory principle on which awards of contractual damages ought to be based."[472]

It may be said that this is not an exception to the general rule that damages are assessed at the date of breach, or, in the case of anticipatory breach, the date of

---

[464] [1971] 1 Q.B. 164; George [1971] J.B.L. 109.

[465] The actual decision was that the cancellation was justified by the shipowner's breach of condition: above, para.18–041; cf. *Walkinshaw v Diniz* [2002] 2 Lloyd's Rep. 165.

[466] [1971] 1 Q.B. 164 at 209–210; cf. ibid. at 196, 202–203; cf. *The Noel Bay* [1989] 1 Lloyd's Rep. 361 at 365; *The World Navigator* [1991] 2 Lloyd's Rep. 23 at 32; *North Sea Energy Holding NV v Petroleum Authority of Thailand* [1999] 1 Lloyd's Rep. 483 at 496.

[467] ibid. at 210.

[468] cf. *North Sea Energy Holding NV v Petroleum Authority of Thailand* [1999] 1 Lloyd's Rep. 483 at 495.

[469] [1971] 1 Q.B. 164 at 196; cf. *The Seaflower* [2000] 2 Lloyd's Rep. 37 where Lord Denning's formulation was preferred to that of Megaw L.J. but, nevertheless, it was found that the relevant event was "inevitable". See, further, the discussion at fn.479, below.

[470] [2007] UKHL 12; [2007] 2 A.C. 353; Morgan [2007] C.L.J. 263; Reynolds [2008] H.K.L.J. 333; Mustill 124 L.Q.R. 569; Stevens, in Neyers, Bronaugh & Pitel (eds.) *Exploring Contract Law*; Carter and Peden 24 J.C.L. 145; Coote 123 L.Q.R. 503; Treitel 123 L.Q.R. 9, commenting on the decision of the Court of Appeal ([2005] EWCA Civ 1190; [2005] 2 Lloyd's Rep. 747), which was upheld in the House of Lords; cf. *Tele 2 International Card Co SA v Post Office Ltd* [2009] EWCA Civ 99, at [74]–[75].

[471] Lord Scott, Lord Carswell and Lord Brown; Lord Bingham and Lord Walker dissented.

[472] [2007] UKHL 12; [2007] 2 A.C. 353 at [35].

acceptance of the breach. Damages are still assessed at that date,[473] but since their assessment at that date depends upon a contingency, e.g. in *The Golden Victory* the likely remaining length of the charterparty, it is said to make no sense for the courts to confine themselves to what was a matter of guess or estimate if it is now known ("the *Bwllfa* principle"[474]). Nonetheless, this is an approach which makes the date of the hearing a determinative factor in the assessment of damages[475] and the uncertainty which this produces was one of the reasons for the dissenting view of Lord Bingham[476] and Lord Walker.[477]

The scope of the *Bwllfa* principle. This argument from certainty may not be   **20–081** sufficient to prevent any departure from the date of breach rule,[478] but it may limit the scope of that departure. In *The Golden Victory*, by the time of the hearing before the arbitrators the Second Gulf War had begun and the finding was that the charterers would have cancelled under the War Clause, i.e. the requirement that subsequent events must have been "inevitable", or "pre-destined to happen" had been met; in the case of the War itself because it had happened. If the War had not begun and it was still only a possibility, it appears that the arbitrators would have had to take a "snapshot" at the date of the hearing of the stage which events had reached. Where events have moved on in a way which would appear to have reduced the loss suffered by the claimant by the time of the hearing, but they remain unpredictable and could move again in a way which would restore or even increase that loss, it is very debatable whether the courts should do anything other than assess damages as at the date of the breach and on the basis of what was known as at that date.[479] If the war had not started by the time of the hearing in *The Golden Victory* but it had appeared inevitable, it might nonetheless have been averted. By contrast, in *The Mihalis Angelos*, it was quite impossible for the vessel to arrive in time.

One clear limit to the scope of the *Bwllfa* principle is the nature of the damages to be assessed. The *Bwllfa* case was not itself concerned with damages for breach of contract, but with the award of statutory compensation payable under a notice preventing a coal mine from mining a seam. The House of Lords emphasised that compensation was payable for the loss of the use of the coal mine and "not the price on a transaction of sale".[480] Similarly, in *The Golden Victory* damages were

---

[473] *Seatbooker Sales Ltd v Southend United Football Club* [2008] EWHC 157 (QB) at [119].

[474] After *Bwllfa and Merthyr Dare Steam Collieries (1891) Ltd v Pontypridd Waterworks Co* [1903] A.C. 426 which was relied upon by the majority.

[475] The party in breach may be discouraged from entering quickly into a settlement in the hope that events transpire which will reduce the damages payable; Lord Carswell acknowledged this risk, but felt (at [67]) that courts and arbitrators have the ability to prevent such abuse if application is made to them to proceed with dispatch.

[476] [2007] UKHL 12; [2007] 2 A.C. 353 at [35]

[477] Lord Walker described the point about the War Clause as one which was not in either party's mind at the date of breach, but which took on "a life of its own as the litigation has been prolonged" (at [42]).

[478] The same argument was rejected in the *Bwllfa* case, above fn.474.

[479] Even as at that date there appears to be a difference of opinion in *The Golden Victory*. According to Lord Brown (at [77]) this meant no more than that the prospect of war was "less than 50%" but this still represented a contingency which would have to be taken into account even if damages were assessed as at the date of acceptance of the breach. It is debatable whether Lord Brown is right to conclude (at [76]) that Lord Bingham and Lord Walker accepted this as a matter of principle since they were only required to go so far as to approve the test in *The Mihalis Angelos* that one takes account of the "inevitable".

[480] *Bwllfa and Merthyr Dare Steam Collieries (1891) Ltd v Pontypridd Waterworks Co* [1903] A.C. 426 at 432 per Lord Robertson; ibid. at 431 per Lord MacNaghten.

being assessed for the loss to be suffered over a period, i.e. the charter term (subject to the "suspensive condition" of the War Clause),[481] and not the loss of the sale of the vessel with the benefit of the charterparty.[482] In cases of "sale",[483] subject to the qualifications referred to above,[484] damages should be assessed at the date of the breach, or its acceptance.[485]

20-082   **No account taken of the prospect of any future breach by the claimant.** An important feature of the cases just discussed is that a cancelling clause gives the charterer an "independent option" to cancel if the ship is not ready to load by the specified date: it does "not impose any contractual obligation on the owners to commence loading by the cancelling date".[486] In other words, the right to cancel under such a clause is exercisable on the occurrence or non-occurrence of an *event*, and does not depend on any *breach* by the shipowner. The reasoning of *The Mihalis Angelos* would not apply (so as to reduce damages to a nominal amount) where the charterer's case was that he would have been entitled to terminate on account of the shipowner's *future breach*; for once the shipowner had accepted the charterer's earlier repudiation and so terminated the contract for that anticipatory breach,[487] the shipowner would be relieved of any further obligation to perform, so that his failure to perform on the due day could no longer be a breach.[488]

3. NON-PECUNIARY LOSSES

(a) Mental Distress[489]

(i) *General principle*

20-083   *Addis v Gramophone Co Ltd.* In a contractual action,[490] the right to recover damages for injured feelings is restricted by the decision of the House of Lords in

---

[481] [2007] UKHL 12; [2007] 2 A.C. 353 at [82].

[482] In this respect there seems almost to be a difference of opinion between the minority and the majority on a question of *fact*. Lord Bingham stressed that there was an "available market", but in the sense that there was an available market for the re-letting of the vessel that was taken into account by assessing the difference between the charter rate and the market rate at the date of acceptance of the breach and ignoring any subsequent change in the market rate; such a re-letting would have resulted in a charterparty with the same War Clause and therefore the same outcome on the outbreak of the second Gulf War. Lord Bingham (at [22]) appears rather to be concerned with an available market for the sale of the vessel. By contrast Lord Scott (at [37]) stated that "it was accepted in argument before your Lordships that the owners' charterparty rights would not, in practice, have been marketable for a capital sum".

[483] i.e. sale itself and other instances where damages are assessed by reference to a "fixed date": *Joiner v George* [2002] EWCA Civ 160; [2003] B.C.C. 298 at [69]; cf.*Gorne v Scales* [2006] EWCA Civ 311.

[484] See above para.20–072.

[485] cf. *Joiner v George* [2002] EWCA Civ 160; [2003] B.C.C. 298 at [69] (*Bwllfa* decision of "no assistance"); cf. *Greymalkin Ltd v Copleys* [2004] EWHC 1155 (Ch).

[486] *The Simona* [1989] A.C. 788 at 795.

[487] *Gill &Duffus SA v Berger & Co Inc* [1984] A.C. 382 at 391; above, para.17–027. After this case, apparently contrary dicta in *Regent OHG Aisestadt und Barig v Francecso of Jermyn Street* [1981] 3 All E.R. 327 and *Bremer HandelsgesellschaftmbH v JH Rayner& Co* [1979] 2 Lloyd's Rep. 216 at 224, 229 can no longer be supported.

[488] cf. above, at para.17–027.

[489] Jackson 26 I.C.L.Q. 502; Enonchong 16 O.J.L.S. 617.

[490] The same conduct may amount both to a breach of contract and to a tort; and where this is the case the claimant can sometimes recover damages for distress by suing in tort even though such damages would not be available in an action for breach of contract: see, e.g., *Sampson v Floyd* [1989] 2 E.G.L.R. 49 as explained in *Branchett v Beany* [1992] 3 All E.R. 910 at 918.

Addis v Gramophone Co Ltd,[491] where a company wrongfully dismissed its manager in a way that was "harsh and humiliating".[492] He recovered damages for loss of salary and commission, but not for the injury to his feelings caused by the manner of his dismissal. One possible justification for the rule is that such injury is not within the contemplation of the parties and is thus too remote; but an employer considering the effects of *such* a dismissal could surely contemplate injury to the employee's feelings.[493] More probably the rule results from a failure to distinguish between punitive (or exemplary) damages (which are not generally available in a contractual action) and damages for injured feelings (which are meant to compensate the claimant for a loss, though it is not a pecuniary one[494]).

Claims for wrongful dismissal. Whatever may be the basis of the rule in the   20–084
Addis case, it continues to restrict the damages recoverable in an action for wrongful dismissal.[495] Such damages normally consist of the amount which the employee would have earned during the period of notice which the employer was legally obliged to give to bring the contract lawfully to an end. By statute, further compensation may be recoverable for *unfair* dismissal even where such notice is given; and the relevant legislation[496] subjects awards of such compensation to specified financial limits. In *Johnson v Unisys Ltd*,[497] an employee who had recovered the maximum amount available under this legislation (then some £11,600) sought to recover further damages (of some £400,000) at common law, alleging that the manner of his dismissal constituted a separate breach of contract[498] which had caused him to suffer a mental breakdown and consequent loss of earnings. The House of Lords rejected the claim on the ground that it would be wrong to allow the financial limit laid down by the statutory scheme for compensation for unfair dismissal to be evaded by giving the dismissed employee a "parallel remedy[499] [at common law] which is subject to no such limit".[500]

Other claims. It seems that, in cases *not* governed by any such statutory   20–085
scheme, the House of Lords would be prepared to review the principle in *Addis v*

---

[491] [1909] A.C. 488.

[492] At 493.

[493] cf. *Watts v Morrow* [1991] 1 W.L.R. 1421 at 1445.

[494] See above, para.20–020 and *Johnson v Unisys Ltd* [2001] UKHL 13; [2003] 1 A.C. 518 at [15], per Lord Steyn, dissenting on the main issue in that case.

[495] *Shove v Downs Surgical Plc* [1984] I.C.R. 532. The rule is viewed with scepticism, even in the context of wrongful dismissal, in *Johnson v Gore Wood* [2002] 2 A.C. 1 at 50, per Lord Cooke, dissenting on this point. Under the proposals in Law Com. No.247 (1997), para.6.1(2), damages for mental distress to reflect the conduct of the defendant would be available in contractual actions.

[496] Employment Rights Act 1996, Pt X.

[497] See above, fn.494.

[498] In the form of a breach of the implied term that the employer would not, without reasonable and proper cause, conduct itself in a manner calculated and likely to destroy or seriously damage the relationship of trust and confidence: *Malik v BCCI* [1998] A.C. 20; discussed below, para.20–092.

[499] As well as the financial limit, compensation may not be awarded *by way of unfair dismissal* for non-pecuniary loss, including injured feelings: *Dunnachie v Kingston-upon-Hull CC* [2004] UKHL 36; [2005] 1 A.C. 226. On this basis the common law does not merely offer a "parallel" remedy. It has also been doubted whether the statutory award extends to financial loss caused by psychiatric illness: *Eastwood v Magnox Electric Plc* [2004] UKHL 35; [2005] 1 A.C. 503 at [42].

[500] *Johnson v Unisys Ltd*, above, fn.494 at [56], [57]; cf. ibid. at [2], [80], Lord Steyn dissenting on this point.

Gramophone Co Ltd[501]; and this is an important point because that case, though strictly an authority only on damages for wrongful dismissal, has also been regarded as the basis of the wider principle that damages for injured feelings cannot, in general, be recovered in a contractual action.[502] That general principle has been applied so as to preclude the recovery of damages by a company director in respect of mental distress and anxiety suffered by him as a result of alleged breaches of duty by a firm of solicitors engaged by him and the company to carry through the purchase of development land by the company.[503]

(ii) *Exceptions*

20–086   **Pain and suffering, and psychiatric illness.** Damages can be recovered for pain and suffering for a breach of contract which causes personal injury.[504] Such an award takes account of the claimant's mental anguish and to this extent includes damages for injured feelings.[505] Moreover, it seems that personal injury can include physical or mental illness resulting from injury to feelings and that damages for such illness can be recovered,[506] so long as not too remote.[507]

20–087   **Mental distress consequent on physical inconvenience.** Damages can be recovered for physical inconvenience caused by the defendant's breach of contract,[508] and such damages now also extend to any mental suffering "directly

---

[501] See, in *Johnson v Unisys*, apart from criticism of the *Addis* case in Lord Steyn's dissenting speech, the views of Lord Nicholls at [2] and Lord Hoffmann at [43]. In *Eastwood v Magnox Electric Plc* [2004] UKHL 35; [2005] 1 A.C. 503 the House of Lords has held that the "*Johnson* exclusion area" is confined to claims arising *from dismissal*. If before any dismissal the employee has acquired a cause of action for breach of the implied term relied upon in *Johnson v Unisys* (see fn.498, above), that cause of action remains unimpaired (cf. *Edwards v Chesterfield Royal Hospital NHS Foundation Trust* [2010] EWCA Civ 571; [2010] 3 W.L.R. 1285). As in *Johnson v Unisys*, the claims in *Eastwood* were for psychiatric illness and consequent loss of earnings, and outside the "*Johnson* exclusion area" the principle laid down in the *Addis* case is clearly confined to claims for injured feelings: *Gogay v Hertfordshire County Council* [2000] I.R.L.R. 703 at [68] (psychiatric illness); contrast *Bliss v SE Thames Regional Health Authority* [1987] I.C.R. 700 (injured feelings). The complex, and potentially unsatisfactory, interrelation between the common law and statute created by the decisions in *Johnson*, *Dunnachie* (above, fn.499) and *Eastwood* is said to merit the "urgent attention of the Government and the legislature": [2005] 1 A.C. 503 at [33], per Lord Nicholls.
[502] *Watts v Morrow* [1991] 1 W.L.R. 1421 at 1444; *Johnson v Unisys Ltd* [2001] UKHL 13; [2003] 1 A.C. 518 at [69]; *Farley v Skinner* [2001] UKHL 49; [2002] 2 A.C. 732 at [16], [34], [47], [54].
[503] *Johnson v Gore Wood & Co* [2002] 2 A.C. 1; cf. *Groom v Crocker* [1939] 1 K.B. 194; *Hobbs v London and SW Ry Co* (1875) L.R. 10 Q.B. 111 at 122.
[504] e.g. *Godley v Perry* [1960] 1 W.L.R. 9.
[505] See *H West & Sons Ltd v Shephard* [1964] A.C. 326.
[506] e.g. *Cook v Swinfen* [1967] 1 W.L.R. 457; *Esso Petroleum Co Ltd v Mardon* [1976] Q.B. 801 at 822; *Attia v British Gas Plc* [1988] Q.B. 304 (where it is not clear whether the claim was in contract or in tort); *Gogay v Hertfordshire CC* [2000] I.R.L.R. 703.
[507] *Wiseman v Virgin Atlantic Airways* Ltd [2006] EWHC 1566 at [21]. In the employment context, remoteness would depend on the employer's knowledge of the employee's mental state (and so of the likelihood of his suffering mental illness in consequence of the breach) at the time of *contracting*, not at that of *breach*: see below, at fn.611. This point accounts for rejection of the claim in *Johnson v Unisys Ltd* [2001] UKHL 13; [2003] 1 A.C. 518 by Lord Steyn on the ground of remoteness; the same view is taken by Lord Millett, ibid. at [70]. Contrast the test in negligence for determining whether the employer is in breach of his duty of care: *Hatton v Sutherland* [2002] EWCA Civ 76; [2002] I.C.R. 613 (test approved, but appeal allowed on other grounds in *Barber v Somerset CC* [2004] UKHL 13; [2004] 1 W.L.R. 1089).
[508] *Bailey v Bullock* (1950) 66 T.L.R. (Pt. 2) 791; *Mafo v Adams* [1970] 1 Q.B. 548.

related to that inconvenience".[509] Thus, in *Watts v Morrow*,[510] where the defendant omitted certain defects from the survey report upon which the claimants relied in purchasing a house, damages were awarded for the physical inconvenience and directly related mental distress of living in the house while it was being repaired.

Loss of enjoyment, or amenity. Damages for distress or vexation can be awarded in a group of cases in which at least one of the "major and important"[511] objects of the contract was to provide enjoyment, security, comfort or sentimental benefits. Such awards have, for example, been made against a travel agent who broke his contract to provide a couple with accommodation for their honeymoon[512]; against a package-tour operator who provided accommodation falling short of the standard promised and so spoilt his client's holiday[513]; against a carrier for breach of a contract to convey guests to a wedding[514]; against a photographer for breach of a contract to take wedding photographs[515]; against a solicitor who failed to take necessary steps in non-molestation proceedings, so that the molestation of his client continued,[516] or who failed, negligently, to obtain custody of the claimant's children[517]; and against a cemetery for breach of a contract to grant exclusive burial rights.[518]

20–088

The award of damages for "loss of amenity" where a contract to build a swimming pool for the customer's personal use was broken by building the pool to less than the stipulated depth[519] can be explained on the same ground; and this explanation also accounts for the view that an architect who designs a house for his client's personal occupation is liable for failing to incorporate in the design agreed features, such as an impressive entrance hall and wide staircase, thus depriving the client of the pleasure which he expected to derive from these features.[520]

The distinction between cases in which damages are awarded on the present ground and those in which they are awarded for physical inconvenience (under the second exception, discussed above) is sometimes hard to draw.[521] The point is illustrated by *Farley v Skinner*[522] where the claimant had, before buying a house

---

[509] *Watts v Morrow* [1991] 1 W.L.R. 1421 at 1445; cf. *McCall v Abelesz* [1976] Q.B. 585 at 594; *Perry v Sidney Phillips & Son* [1982] 1 W.L.R. 1287; *Patel v Hooper & Jackson* [1999] 1 W.L.R. 1792; *Larkworth Investments Ltd v Temple House Ltd (No.2)* [1999] B.L.R. 297; *English Churches Housing Group v Shine* [2004] EWCA Civ 434; [2005] L & T.R. 7.

[510] ibid.

[511] *Farley v Skinner* [2001] UKHL 49; [2002] 2 A.C. 737 at [24].

[512] *Cook v Spanish Holiday Tours Ltd*, *The Times*, February 6, 1960.

[513] *Jarvis v Swan Tours Ltd* [1973] Q.B. 233; cf. *Jackson v Horizon Holidays Ltd* [1975] 1 W.L.R. 1468; *Wings Ltd v Ellis* [1985] A.C. 272 at 287; *Baltic Shipping Co v Dillon* (1993) 176 C.L.R. 144; *Milner v Carnival Plc* [2010] EWCA Civ 389; [2010] 3 All E.R. 701.

[514] *Chandle v East African Airways Corp* [1964] E.A. 78.

[515] *Diesen v Samson* 1971 S.L.T. (Sh.Ct.) 49.

[516] *Heywood v Wellers* [1976] Q.B. 446; cf. *Dickinson v Jones Alexander & Co* [1993] 2 F.L.R. 521; contrast *Hartle v Laceys* [1997] C.L.Y. 3839 (solicitor employed for conveyancing purposes).

[517] *Hamilton Jones v David & Snape* [2003] EWHC 3147 (Ch); [2004] 1 W.L.R. 924.

[518] *Reed v Madon* [1989] Ch. 408.

[519] *Ruxley Electronics Ltd v Forsyth* [1999] A.C. 344 (above, para.20–046) described in *Johnson v Gore Wood Co* [2002] 2 A.C. 1 at 37 as an "unusual case" but applied in *Farley v Skinner* [2001] UKHL 49; [2002] 2 A.C. 732 where the damages in the *Ruxley* case were said at [21] to have been awarded for "disappointment".

[520] This follows from the overruling in *Farley v Skinner*, above, of *Knott v Bolton* (1995) 45 Con.L.R. 127.

[521] Either ground sufficed in *Haysman v Mrs Rogers Films Ltd* [2008] EWHC 2494.

[522] See above, fn.519.

as his retirement home, engaged a surveyor whom he had specifically instructed to report on the question whether the house would be affected by aircraft noise. The surveyor in breach of contract carelessly failed to provide accurate information on this point and the purchaser recovered damages in respect of the adverse effect which such noise had on the peace and tranquillity of the property, even though the price paid for it by him did not exceed its market value. The main ground for the decision is that one important (though not the sole) object of the contract was to provide "pleasure, relaxation and peace of mind"[523]; but there is also support in the speeches for the view that the award could have been supported on the ground that the claimant had suffered physical inconvenience (and not merely distress or vexation) in having to put up with the unexpected level of noise.[524] On either ground "awards in this area should be restrained and modest."[525]

20–089   **Borderline cases.** The question whether one of the main objects of the contract is to provide "pleasure, relaxation and peace of mind" can give rise to difficulty in borderline cases. Thus in one case damages for distress were awarded against the seller of a new car which broke down and would not restart, so that the buyer suffered "a totally spoilt day comprising nothing but vexation",[526] while in another it was held that no such damages were available for breach of a contract to repair a car.[527] Again, in *Farley v Skinner* it was said that the case was "not 'an ordinary surveyor's contract' "[528] and considerable emphasis was placed on the fact that the contract had specifically referred to aircraft noise. It seems that, but for this fact the surveyor would have been liable only for pecuniary consequences and inconvenience resulting from physical defects in the property itself, as opposed to the vexation caused by adverse environmental factors.[529]

20–090   **Nature of claims for non-pecuniary loss.** Where damages are recoverable for "disappointment" resulting from failure to perform an obligation to provide enjoyment, security or peace of mind, it is sometimes said that the basis of such recovery is that the claimant was, by the breach, "deprived of the contractual benefit to which he was entitled".[530] Such language is, it is submitted, entirely appropriate in the context of such awards, which compensate the claimant in respect of a loss which he has in fact suffered, though the loss is non-pecuniary in nature. But phrases such as that quoted above could, if taken out of that context, be read as supporting the view that the mere fact of breach of contract, even though no loss of any kind had flowed from it, gave rise to a claim for substantial damages; and this view would be inconsistent with a number of the rules or principles on which such claims are based. One such principle is that damages for breach of contract cannot be recovered *merely* in respect of the "anxiety" or

[523] *Farley v Skinner*, above, at [24].
[524] ibid. at [30], [38], [54], [105].
[525] ibid. at [28]; cf. *Eiles v Southwark L.B.C.* [2006] EWHC 1411 (TCC); *Iggleden v Fairview New Homes (Shooters Hill) Ltd* [2007] EWHC 1573 (TCC); *Haysman v Mrs Rogers Films Ltd* [2008] EWHC 2494; *Milner v Carnival Plc* [2010] EWCA Civ 389; [2010] 3 All E.R. 701.
[526] *Bernstein v Pamson Motors (Golders Green) Ltd* [1987] 2 All E.R. 220 at 231; cf. *Jackson v Chrysler Acceptance Ltd* [1978] R.T.R. 474 (defects in car bought for touring holiday).
[527] *Alexander v Rolls Royce Motors Ltd* [1996] R.T.R. 95.
[528] See above, fn.519, at [42], referring to *Watts v Morrow* [1991] 1 W.L.R. 1421 at 1442.
[529] See especially *Farley v Skinner*, above, fn.519, at [44], [54]–[57].
[530] *Farley v Skinner* above at [106]; cf. ibid. at [86].

"disappointment" that may be caused by the breach.[531] Another, discussed earlier in this chapter, is that damages cannot be recovered in respect of a breach which has no adverse effect.[532] In none of these cases are damages recoverable *merely* because the injured party has not received the benefit of the promised performance; and it is submitted that they support the view that "damages should not be awarded, unless perhaps nominally, for the fact of a breach of contract as distinct from the consequences of breach".[533] Of course the adverse consequences need not be of a *financial* kind, as is shown by the many exceptions, discussed above,[534] to the general rule that damages for breach of contract cannot be recovered for injured feelings; but these cases do not negative the requirement that some adverse consequence to the claimant (other than mere "anxiety" or "disappointment") must flow from the breach in order to sustain an award of substantial damages.

Where damages are awarded for non-pecuniary loss, there may be the risk of duplication of damages awarded for pecuniary loss. Thus, in the case of a substandard holiday,[535] it has been said that it is necessary to distinguish "the difference between what the supplier contracted to provide and what was actually provided", which is a pecuniary loss, and "how the client felt about the diminution in the service supplied" which is relevant to an award for non-pecuniary loss in the form of mental distress.[536] It might be said there should be no award for the latter if the claimant has been compensated in full for the former since he has received the equivalent of the holiday, in monetary terms. But the whole point is that the claimant who books a holiday does not want performance in purely monetary terms so that he still has an additional and further loss in the form of his mental distress.[537] This may nonetheless explain why awards under this head should be relatively modest.

(b) Loss of Reputation

No recovery for loss of reputation itself. In *Addis v Gramophone Co Ltd*[538]   **20–091** it was held by the House of Lords that no damages could be awarded for any loss of reputation caused to the claimant by the manner of his dismissal, and the wider principle that damages cannot be awarded for loss of reputation itself has not seriously been questioned in the courts.[539]

---

[531] *Hayes v James & Charles Dodd* [1990] 2 All E.R. 815; *Firsteel Cold Rolled Products v Anaco Precision Products, The Times*, November 21, 1994; *R. v Investors Compensation Scheme Ex p. Bowden* [1994] 1 W.L.R. 17, reversed on other grounds [1995] Q.B. 107, in turn reversed without reference to the present point [1996] A.C. 261.

[532] See above, para.20–009.

[533] *Farley v Skinner*, above, fn.519, at [40], per Lord Clyde. For the application of the same principle to cases where the breach causes loss to a third party but none (beyond the bare fact of breach) to the promisee, see *Alfred McAlpine Construction Ltd v Panatown Ltd* [2001] 1 A.C. 518 at 534, per Lord Clyde; above, para.14–035, at fn.225.

[534] See above, para.20–086 et seq.

[535] *Milner v Carnival Plc* [2010] EWCA Civ 389; [2010] 3 All E.R. 701 in which a clear distinction was drawn between four different heads of loss: (i) diminution in value; (ii) consequential pecuniary loss (e.g. out of pocket expenses); (iii) physical inconvenience and discomfort; and (iv) mental distress.

[536] ibid. at [43].

[537] The award of the diminution in value compensates for direct loss; mental distress is a form of consequential loss, which is consistent with the application to non-pecuniary losses of the limit of remoteness: above, fn.507.

[538] [1909] A.C. 488; above, para.20–083.

[539] *Groom v Crocker* [1939] 1 K.B. 194.

20–092   **Financial loss consequent upon loss of reputation.** In the *Addis* case[540] it was further held that, in an action for wrongful dismissal, the employee could not recover damages for the loss that he might suffer because the dismissal made it more difficult for him to get another job. But the view that damages in such an action cannot be recovered for loss of employment prospects, or for injury to reputation, was hard to justify; and "may no longer be law".[541] In *Malik v BCCI*[542] the House of Lords held that such "stigma damages" were in principle recoverable by former employees of a bank which had collapsed in consequence of corruption and dishonesty in which the employees had not been involved; though the employees' claim ultimately failed as they were unable to establish that the stigma was the cause of the rejection of any job applications which had been made by them; or that any future applications had a sufficiently real chance of success to justify an award for damages for loss of a chance; or that, if such a chance existed, the stigma was the cause of its loss.[543] The damages which they could have recovered if they had been able to establish any of these points would have been recoverable in respect, not of injury to feelings, but in respect of financial loss; and they would have been recoverable, not for wrongful dismissal,[544] but for breach of the employer's implied undertaking not without reasonable cause to conduct itself so as to destroy the relationship of trust and confidence between itself and its employees.[545] According to a further distinction drawn in *Malik*'s case, the employee can recover such damages where the effect of the breach is "positively to damage" his job prospects, but not where its effect is merely a "failure to improve them".[546] It is, however, respectfully submitted that the possibility of the employer's being held liable for loss of the latter kind should not be ruled out, particularly where the employment involves training or similar features intended to enhance the employee's prospects. It was, for example, established even before *Malik*'s case that an apprentice who was wrongfully dismissed before the end of his period of training was entitled to damages for diminution of his future prospects since "the very object of an apprenticeship agreement is to enable the apprentice to fit himself to get better employment".[547]

20–093   **Non-employment cases.** There are many other situations in which damages can be awarded for financial loss consequent upon injury to reputation resulting from a breach of contract. First, a trader can recover damages for injury to his business reputation, e.g. if his reputation suffers because his wholesaler supplies him with defective goods[548]; on the same principle a travel agent can recover damages for loss of "goodwill" from a shipowner who breaks his contract to supply accommodation for passengers on a pleasure cruise.[549] A similar rule applies where

---

[540] [1909] A.C. 488.
[541] *Johnson v Unisys Ltd* [2001] UKHL 13; [2003] 1 A.C. 518 at [70].
[542] [1998] A.C. 20.
[543] *BCCI v Ali (No.2)* [2002] EWCA Civ 82; [2002] I.C.R. 1258.
[544] Where the claim is for loss of reputation caused by dismissal, recovery is ruled out by the reasoning of the House of Lords in the *Unisys* case (though not itself involving loss of reputation): para.20–084, above. This has, in turn, been qualified by the decision in the *Eastwood* case (also not involving loss of reputation): above, fn.501.
[545] See above, para.6–041.
[546] [1998] A.C. 20 at 37.
[547] *Dunk v George Waller & Sons Ltd* [1970] 2 Q.B. 163; cf. the award of damages for loss of a chance in *Guido van der Garde BV v Force India Formula One Ltd* [2010] EWHC 2373 (QB).
[548] *Cointat v Myham & Son* [1913] 2 K.B. 220.
[549] *Anglo-Continental Holidays Ltd v Typaldos Lines (London) Ltd* [1967] 2 Lloyd's Rep. 61.

a bank wrongfully dishonours its customer's cheque. It has long been settled that, if the customer is a trader, he can recover general damages for the resulting injury to his business reputation.[550] A person who was not a trader was formerly thought to be entitled to no more than a nominal amount unless he proved special damages, i.e. particular items of loss resulting from the bank's breach.[551] But this view no longer prevails now that "the credit rating of individuals is as important for their personal transactions . . . as it is for those who are engaged in trade".[552] Hence such persons, too, can now recover general damages in respect of injury to what may be called their financial reputation[553] resulting from the wrongful dishonour of a cheque.[554] Secondly, an actor or author can recover damages for "loss of publicity", that is, for loss of the chance to enhance his reputation,[555] and also for injury to his existing reputation.[556] Thirdly, a person who is wrongfully expelled from a trade union can recover damages for the resulting loss of employment opportunities.[557] Finally, it has been suggested that a claimant should be entitled to damages for injury to reputation where the contract "had as its purpose, or one of its purposes, the protection of the claimant against the sort of damage suffered".[558] Thus damages of this kind were said to be recoverable for breach of a contract not to broadcast a programme concerning the activities of the claimants until after the publication of a report concerning those activities.[559]

4. METHODS OF LIMITING DAMAGES

To compensate the injured party fully for all loss that can, in some sense, be said   20–094
to flow from a breach of contract would often lead to undesirable results. Such complete protection of the injured party's interests would either deter the other party from entering into the contract at all, or lead to an undue raising of charges. The law has therefore developed a number of rules for the purpose of limiting damages for breach of contract.

(a) Causation

General. Our present concern is with cases in which there is a breach, followed   20–095
by a state of affairs clearly disadvantageous to the claimant, but the defendant argues that the breach did not bring about that state of affairs. For example, a shipowner may be technically in breach of contract because his ship was not equipped with a proper medicine chest; but if the ship later foundered in a storm,

---

[550] *Rolin v Steward* (1854) 14 C.B. 595 at 605; *Wilson v United Counties Bank Ltd* [1920] A.C. 102 at 112.

[551] *Gibbons v Westminster Bank* [1939] 2 K.B. 882.

[552] *Kpohraror v Woolwich Building Society* [1996] 4 All E.R. 119 at 124. The claimant in this case was a trader, so that it was not strictly necessary to decide the present point.

[553] Not for "loss of reputation *simpliciter*": *Kpohraror*'s case, above, at 125. The phrase "financial reputation" is used in the text to avoid the awkwardness of referring to the "business reputation" of someone who is not in business.

[554] *Kpohraror*'s case, above, at 124.

[555] *Herbert Clayton & Jack Waller Ltd v Oliver* [1930] A.C. 209; *Joseph v National Magazine Co Ltd* [1959] Ch. 14.

[556] *Malik v BCCI* [1998] A.C. 20, overruling *Withers v General Theatre Corp Ltd* [1933] 2 K.B. 536. For subsequent proceedings in *Malik*'s case, see above, at fn.543.

[557] *Edwards v SOGAT* [1971] Ch. 354 at 378–379.

[558] *Cambridge Nutrition Ltd v BBC* [1990] 3 All E.R. 523 at 540.

[559] ibid.; cf. *McLeish v Amoo-Guttfried & Co, The Times,* October 13, 1993.

the owners of goods on board could not claim that the breach was the cause of their loss.[560] Similarly, the mere fact that a company continues to trade in consequence of its auditor's breach of duty in auditing its accounts does not make the auditor liable for losses incurred in the course of such trading: the auditor's breach is not an effective cause of the loss.[561] Another reason why loss may be held not to have been caused by the breach is that it would have been suffered even if the breach had not been committed. This was, for example, the position where solicitors acting for a mortgage lender committed a breach of contract and a breach of trust by parting with the lender's money before they should have done so; and the lender later suffered loss, not because the money had been paid over too soon, but because the security turned out to be inadequate. It was held that the solicitors were not liable for this loss since the lender had got exactly the charge it had bargained for, and since it would have suffered exactly the same loss, even if the solicitors' breach had not been committed.[562]

20–096   **Concurrent causes.** In all the above cases, the defendant is not liable for a loss which is not caused by the breach at all; but a claimant can often recover damages although the breach is not the *sole* cause of the loss. As Devlin J. has said: "If a breach of contract is one of two causes, both co-operating and both of equal efficacy, . . . it is sufficient to carry a judgment for damages".[563] One such situation is dealt with below: the victim of a breach of contract can recover damages for a loss caused partly by the breach and partly by his own lack of means (so long as the loss is not too remote[564]). Again, unseaworthiness is hardly ever the sole cause of a maritime loss: the shipowner is liable though ordinary sea perils have co-operated with unseaworthiness to produce the loss.[565] But he would not be liable if the unseaworthiness led to a delay and the ship then ran into a typhoon as such a catastrophe may occur anywhere[566] and as the delay would not be causally "of equal efficacy" with the typhoon. Nor is the party in breach liable for a loss in fact wholly caused by an extraneous supervening event, even though, if that event had not occurred, the same loss, or part of it, would have been caused by the breach.[567] Further problems of mitigation and contributory negligence, which arise where the concurrent cause is the victim's own conduct, are discussed below.[568]

---

[560] See *Monarch SS Co v KarlshamnsOljefabriker (A/B)* [1949] A.C. 196 at 226.

[561] *Galoo v Bright Grahame Murray* [1994] 1 W.L.R. 1360; cf. *Bank of Credit & Commerce International (Overseas) Ltd v Price Waterhouse (No.3)*, The Times, April 2, 1998; *Equitable Life Assurance Society v Ernst & Young* [2003] EWCA Civ 1114; [2003] 2 B.C.L.C. 603.

[562] *Target Holdings Ltd v Redferns* [1996] A.C. 421; cf.*Banque Keyser Ullman SA v Skandia (UK) Ins Co Ltd* [1991] 2 A.C. 249; *The World Navigator* [1991] 2 Lloyd's Rep. 23; *Brown v KMR Services Ltd* [1995] 4 All E.R. 598 (the 22 per cent reduction); cf. also *Sykes v Midland Bank Executor & Trustee Co Ltd* [1971] 1 Q.B. 113; A.L.G. 87 L.Q.R. 10; *County Natwest v Pinsent& Co* [1994] 3 Bank. L.R. 4; and *Swindle v Harrison* [1997] 4 All E.R. 705 (where damages were awarded for breach of fiduciary duty); *Freeguard v Rogers* [1999] 1 W.L.R. 375.

[563] *Heskell v Continental Express Ltd* [1950] 1 All E.R. 1033 at 1048, disapproved on another point in *Hedley Byrne & Co Ltd v Heller & Partners Ltd* [1964] A.C. 465 at 532; cf. *Vumar International Ltd v Theresa Navigation SA* [2001] 2 Lloyd's Rep. 1 at [43]; *Supershield Ltd v Siemens Building Technologies FE Ltd* [2010] EWCA Civ 7; [2010] 1 Lloyd's Rep. 349.

[564] See below, para.20–114.

[565] *Smith, Hogg & Co Ltd v Black Sea Ins Co Ltd* [1940] A.C. 997.

[566] *Monarch Steamship* case [1949] A.C. 196 at 215.

[567] *Beoco Ltd v Alfa Laval Co Ltd* [1995] Q.B. 137.

[568] See below, paras 20–115, 20–123.

Intervening acts of the claimant. The chain of causation which leads from 20–097
the breach is only broken by an intervening act of the claimant when it can be
shown[569] that the "true" cause of the loss is the conduct of the claimant.[570] As seen
above,[571] it will not normally be sufficient to show that the breach and the
claimant's subsequent conduct are concurrent causes.[572] The more unreasonable
the conduct of the claimant, the more likely that the chain will have been broken;
conduct which amounts to recklessness is likely to be sufficient, but there is no
rule of law that only this will do.[573] In assessing the reasonableness of his conduct,
the state of knowledge of the claimant is an important factor. In *Lambert v Lewis*[574]
the defendant supplied a defective towing hitch which led to an accident for which
the claimant was held liable to a third party. The defendant was not liable to
indemnify the claimant because the claimant had become aware, or ought to have
been aware,[575] that the coupling mechanism in the hitch was damaged and he had
failed to have it repaired or ascertain whether it was safe to use. By contrast, in
Borealis AB v Geogas Trading SA[576] the defendant supplied butane feedstock
contaminated with fluorides which produced hydrochloric acid and led to extensive damage to the claimant's plant and equipment. A test of the feedstock shortly
after discharge indicated a low pH reading, but the claimant took no further
action. There had been no experience that low pH was harmful to the plant or
equipment and it did not indicate what type of acid might be present; the claimant
did not know and could not reasonably have been expected to know of the kind of
acid introduced into the system by the breach of contract. Although the claimant's
conduct fell below "best practice", it was not sufficiently unreasonable to break
the chain of causation.

Intervening acts of third party. Where loss results partly from the breach 20–098
and partly from the act of a third party, the party in breach is nevertheless liable
for the loss if (but only if[577]) the third party's act was "foreseeable" on the
standard of probability which governs remoteness in contract.[578] Thus a person
who in breach of contract recommends a dishonest stockbroker is liable for loss
caused by the broker's dishonesty[579]; and a house-painter who in breach of
contract leaves his client's house unlocked is liable for the value of goods taken

---

[569] There is an evidential burden on the defendant, but the legal burden of proving his loss remains
on the claimant: *Borealis AB v Geogas Trading SA* [2010] EWHC 2789 (Comm); [2011] 1 Lloyd's Rep
482 at [43]
[570] *Borealis AB v Geogas Trading SA* [2010] EWHC 2789 (Comm); [2011] 1 Lloyd's Rep 482 at [44];
Barings Plc v Coopers & Lybrand [2003] EWHC 1319 (Ch) at [838].
[571] See above, para.20–096.
[572] *County Ltd v Girozentrale* [1996] 3 All E.R. 834, at 849, 857, 858.
[573] ibid. at 857; *Lambert v Lewis* [1982] A.C. 225 at 252; *Borealis AB v Geogas Trading SA* [2010]
EWHC 2789 (Comm); [2011] 1 Lloyd's Rep 482 at [45]
[574] [1982] A.C. 225; cf. *Schering Agrochemicals Ltd v Resibel NV SA* November 26, 1992, CA.
[575] It was "staring him in the face": *Borealis AB v Geogas Trading SA* [2010] EWHC 2789 (Comm);
[2011] 1 Lloyd's Rep 482 at [103].
[576] [2010] EWHC 2789 (Comm); [2011] 1 Lloyd's Rep 482; cf. *County Ltd v Girozentrale*[1996] 3 All
E.R. 834.
[577] *The Silver Sky* [1981] 2 Lloyd's Rep. 95.
[578] See below, para.20–099 et seq.; *Monarch Steamship* case [1949] A.C. 196; *British Racing Drivers'
Club v Hextall Erskine & Co* [1996] 3 All E.R. 667.
[579] *De la Bere v Pearson Ltd* [1908] 1 K.B. 280; cf. *T v Surrey CC* [1994] 4 All E.R. 577 (child-
minder); *Partridge v Morris* [1995] E.G.C.S. 158 (architect recommending builder); *Sasea Finance Ltd
v KPMG* [2000] 1 All E.R. 676 (auditor failing to warn company of senior executives' fraud; cf. *Stone
& Rolls Ltd v Moore Stephens* [2009] UKHL 39; [2009] 1 A.C. 1391, above para.11–024).

from it by thieves.[580] These cases show that, although remoteness and causation are "quite different concepts" (so that a loss may be too remote even though it is clearly caused by the breach[581]) nevertheless "some of the relevant considerations are the same".[582]

In *Weld-Blundell v Stephens*[583] a client employed an accountant to investigate the affairs of a company and wrote him a letter defaming two of the company's directors. The accountant's partner negligently dropped the letter in the company's office, where it was picked up by the manager and shown to the two directors. They recovered heavy damages for libel from the client who, in turn, claimed this amount from the accountant as damages for breach of contract. The House of Lords gave two reasons for dismissing the claim. First, the client's liability for defamation *existed* quite apart from the breach of contract, which simply brought that liability to the directors' attention.[584] Secondly, the loss was not caused by the breach, but by the act of the manager in showing the letter to the directors, and this act was *not* one which the defendant could have foreseen. The view that the manager's act was not foreseeable may be regarded with some scepticism, particularly as the jury found that it was the defendant's duty to keep the letter secret. But it forms one basis of *Weld-Blundell v Stephens*. The case does not support the proposition that a party who breaks a contract can escape liability for loss caused partly by his breach and partly by a *foreseeable* intervening act.

(b) Remoteness

20–099   Even in cases where a loss has been caused to the claimant as a consequence of the defendant's breach, some or all of that loss will not be recovered as damages if it is found to be too remote. In *The Achilleas*[585] the House of Lords has revisited and, in the case of some of their lordships, reformulated the test of remoteness.[586] Since that reformulation appears to have been accepted, and implemented, by the lower courts subsequently, it may seem appropriate to begin with *The Achilleas*. That may follow in later editions, but for now it is thought helpful to begin with an assessment of the law as it was understood prior to *The Achilleas*. There are two reasons for this. First, to aid our understanding of the extent to which, if any, the law has been reformulated and, secondly, because the reformulated approach is said to be confined to the exceptional case:[587] "cases of departure from the ordinary foreseeability rule based on individual circumstances will be unusual."[588]

---

[580] *Stansbie v Troman* [1948] 2 K.B. 48; cf. *Marshall v Rubypoint Ltd* [1997] E.G.C.S. 12.

[581] As in *Bates v Barrow Ltd* [1995] 1 Lloyd's Rep. 680.

[582] *The Yanxilas (No.2)* [1984] 1 Lloyd's Rep. 676 at 682; *The Eurus* [1998] 1 Lloyd's Rep. 351 at 362.

[583] [1920] A.C. 956.

[584] cf. *Clark v Kirby-Smith* [1964] Ch. 506.

[585] [2008] UKHL 48; [2009] 1 A.C. 61.

[586] The term "reformulation" may be challenged; it has been said that the reformulated approach to remoteness which is being referred to is merely a "rationalisation" of the rule of remoteness: *Supershield Ltd v Siemens Building Technologies FE Ltd* [2010] EWCA Civ 7; [2010] 1 Lloyd's Rep. 349 at [43]: below, para.20–112.

[587] *Sylvia Shipping Co Ltd v Progress Bulk Carriers Ltd* [2010] EWHC 542 (Comm); [2010] 2 Lloyd's Rep. 81 at [41]; below, para.20–112.

[588] *The Achilleas* [2008] UKHL 48; [2009] 1 A.C. 61 at [11] per Lord Hoffmann. In fact, in this passage, Lord Hoffmann is really indicating that it will be unusual to depart from the *result* indicated by the "foreseeability rule", but the approach advocated of asking whether the defendant had assumed responsibility for the loss applies in all cases: below, para.20–112.

Nonetheless, in order at the outset to give some sense of the debate which has been provoked by *The Achilleas*, it can be stated by reference to two questions: is the defendant to be held liable for all types of loss which were, or ought to have been, within his reasonable contemplation at the time the contract was made (the "ordinary foreseeability rule"), or is the defendant to be held liable for all types of loss for which he is taken to have "assumed responsibility" in entering into the contract (the "reformulated" approach)? It is the "ordinary foreseeability" rule with which we will begin. Its development can be traced primarily by reference to three leading cases. An assessment will then be made of the impact of *The Achilleas* before attempting to draw some conclusions about the current approach of the courts to remoteness.

Hadley v Baxendale. The general rule on remoteness was formulated in **20–100** *Hadley v Baxendale*.[589] A shaft in the claimants' mill broke and had to be sent to the makers at Greenwich to serve as a pattern for the production of a new one. The defendants agreed to carry the shaft to Greenwich but, as a result of their breach of the contract, its delivery was delayed so that there was a stoppage of several days at the mill. The claimants claimed damages of £300 in respect of their loss of profits during this period. At the trial the case was left generally to the jury, who returned a verdict of £50 for the claimants. The defendants successfully applied for a new trial on the ground of misdirection. Alderson B. stated the principles in accordance with which the jury should have been directed:

> "The damages . . . should be such as may fairly and reasonably be considered *either* arising naturally, i.e. according to the usual course of things, from such breach of contract itself, *or* such as may reasonably be supposed to have been in the contemplation of both parties at the time they made the contract as the probable result of the breach".[590]

Here the stoppage was not the "natural" consequence of the delay: it could not have been contemplated by a carrier that delay in delivering the shaft would keep the mill idle:

> "In the great multitude of cases of millers sending off broken shafts to third persons by a carrier under ordinary circumstances, such consequences would not, in all probability, have occurred".[591]

The claimants might have had a spare shaft[592] or been able to get one.[593] Nor could the stoppage, though it was no doubt anticipated by the *claimants*, have been contemplated by *both* parties at the time of contracting as the probable result of breach.

> "The only circumstances here communicated by the (claimants) to the defendants at the time the contract was made were that the article to be

---

[589] (1854) 9 Exch. 341; Simpson 91 L.Q.R. 272–277; Danzig 4 *Journal of Legal Studies* 249; Pugsley 126 N.L.J. 420; Barton 7 O.J.L.S. 40.

[590] ibid. at 354 (italics supplied).

[591] ibid. at 356.

[592] ibid.

[593] 23 L.J.Ex.at 180.

carried was the broken shaft of a mill, and that the (claimants) were the millers of that mill".[594]

The defendants were not told that any delay by them would keep the mill idle. If they had been told this, they might have attempted to limit their liability "and of this advantage it would be very unjust to deprive them".[595]

20–101   **The *Victoria Laundry* case.** These principles were developed in *Victoria Laundry (Windsor) Ltd v Newman Industries Ltd.*[596] The defendants sold a boiler to buyers who, as the defendants knew, wanted it for immediate use in their laundry business. The boiler was delivered some five months after the agreed date, so that the buyers suffered loss of profits. Asquith L.J. said that the test of remoteness was whether the loss was "reasonably foreseeable as liable to result from the breach".[597] This depended on the state of the defendant's knowledge. Every defendant had imputed to him knowledge of what happens in the ordinary course of things. He might also have actual knowledge of special circumstances, which would enable a reasonable man to foresee extraordinary loss. Here the defendants knew that the buyers wanted the boiler for immediate use in their business: they were thus liable for loss of profits that would ordinarily result from such use. But they were not liable for loss of exceptionally lucrative government contracts, which the buyers would have been able to make if they had received the boiler in time: the defendants knew nothing of these contracts and could not reasonably have foreseen such loss.[598] The same reasoning would apply in the converse case of a buyer's breach, so that the seller could not recover damages in respect of his loss of profit to the extent that this was exceptionally large by reason of his having secured a supply of the goods in question at an unusually low price.[599]

20–102   **The *Heron II*.** The judgment in the *Victoria Laundry* case, and in particular the phrase "reasonably foreseeable as liable to result" gave rise to the view that the same test of "reasonable foreseeability" that governs remoteness in tort applies also in contract.[600] But this view was rejected by the House of Lords in *The Heron II*.[601] In that case a ship was chartered to carry sugar from Constanza to Basrah. At the time of contracting, the charterer intended to sell the sugar as soon as it reached Basrah. The shipowner did not actually know this; but he did know that there was a market for sugar at Basrah, and "if he had thought about the matter he must have realised that at least it was not unlikely that the sugar would be sold in the market at market price on arrival".[602] The shipowner in breach of contract deviated and reached Basrah nine days late. During these nine days the market price of sugar at Basrah fell; and it was held that the charterer was entitled to

---

[594] (1854) 9 Exch. at 355.
[595] ibid.
[596] [1949] 2 K.B. 528.
[597] ibid. at 539.
[598] cf. *Kpohraror v Woolwich BS* [1996] 4 All E.R. 119; *The Mass Glory* [2002] EWHC 27 (Comm); [2002] 2 Lloyd's Rep. 245.
[599] See *North Sea Energy Holdings NV v Petroleum Authority of Thailand* [1997] 2 Lloyd's Rep. 418 at 438, affirmed [1999] 1 Lloyd's Rep. 483.
[600] On the appropriate test of remoteness where the claimant has overlapping claims in contract and tort, see below, para.20–113.
[601] Sub nom. *Koufos v C Czarnikow Ltd* [1969] 1 A.C. 350; Pickering 31 M.L.R. 203.
[602] ibid. at 382.

damages for the loss suffered by reason of the fall in the market. The House of Lords rejected the view that the test of remoteness in contract was "reasonable foreseeability", at least if this phrase referred to the very low degree of probability required to satisfy the test of remoteness in tort.[603] Lord Reid said that the *Victoria Laundry* case was wrong in laying down this test for contract.[604] But when Asquith L.J. there referred to "loss reasonably foreseeable *as liable to result*"[605] he may have had a higher degree of probability in mind; and in this sense his judgment was approved by the other members of the House of Lords. Various expressions are used in *The Heron II* to describe the degree of probability required to satisfy the test of remoteness in contract. There must be a "serious possibility"[606] or a "real danger"[607] or a "very substantial"[608] probability of loss; it must be "not unlikely"[609] or "easily foreseeable"[610] that loss will occur. The result of the decision is that a higher degree of probability is required to satisfy the test of remoteness in contract than in tort. When used in contract cases, the word "foreseeability" refers to this higher degree of probability.

Deduction by the standard of the reasonable person. The test of remote- 20–103
ness to emerge from these cases is whether the loss resulting from the breach was within the reasonable contemplation of the parties at the time they entered into the contract.[611] What the defendant should have deduced from the facts known to him[612] is generally judged by the standard of the reasonable person. Thus in *Hadley v Baxendale* in the absence of any knowledge of the special circumstances the defendants could not reasonably have deduced that their delay would keep the mill idle, as the millers might have had a spare shaft.[613] In the *Victoria Laundry* case, by contrast, it would have been mere fantasy to suppose that the buyers kept a spare boiler.

In deciding what the defendant should reasonably have deduced from the facts known to him, the court can take into account the commercial capacity in which he contracted: "as reasonable businessmen each must be taken to understand the ordinary practices and exigencies of the other's trade or business".[614] Thus a supplier of electricity to a building contractor cannot be expected to foresee the full consequences of a power failure on a complex construction project on which the contractor is engaged.[615] Similarly, in *Hadley v Baxendale* the defendants were

---

[603] ibid.at 385, 411, 425; cf. 413; Cartwright [1996] C.L.J. 488.

[604] ibid. at 389.

[605] A phrase also used in *Farley v Skinner* [2001] UKHL 49; [2002] 2 A.C. 732 at [84].

[606] [1969] 1 A.C. 350 at 414–415; *Malik v BCCI* [1998] A.C. 20 at 37.

[607] ibid. at 425; cf. *Bates v Barrow* [1995] 1 Lloyd's Rep. 680 at 691; *The Kriti Rex* [1996] 2 Lloyd's Rep. 171 at 173.

[608] ibid. at 388.

[609] ibid. at 383; cf. *The Rio Claro* [1987] 2 Lloyd's Rep. 173; *The Achilleas* above fn.585.

[610] ibid.

[611] And not at the date of breach: *Jackson v Royal Bank of Scotland Plc* [2005] UKHL 3; [2005] 1 W.L.R. 377 at [36].

[612] i.e. save for his commercial capacity (see below), no allowance is made for his individual characteristics.

[613] cf. *Gee v Lancs. & Yorks. Ry* (1860) H. & N. 211 (carrier ignorant that manufacturer had no stocks of raw material); *The Pegase* [1981] 1 Lloyd's Rep. 175.

[614] *Monarch SS Co v Karlshamns Oljefabriker (A/B)* [1949] A.C. 196 at 224; cf. *The Arpad* [1934] P. 189 and Scrutton L.J.'s reference (at 201) to "business knowledge"; *The Achilleas* [2008] UKHL 48; [2009] 1 A.C. 61 at [67], per Lord Walker ("The degree of knowledge assumed under the first limb depends on the nature of the business relationship between the contracting parties").

[615] *Balfour Beatty Construction (Scotland) v Scottish Power* 1994 S.L.T. 807 (HL).

general carriers and less well able to foresee the effects of delay than the defendants in the *Victoria Laundry* case, who were qualified engineers and knew more than the uninstructed layman of the purposes for which boilers of the kind in question were likely to be used.[616] But even a carrier can be made liable for loss of the chance of making profits on resale[617] and for loss of profits suffered by a manufacturer through non-delivery of raw materials known to be wanted for manufacturing purposes.[618] Similarly, a carrier who specialises in a particular trade may have imputed to him "a greater knowledge of the relevant market than might have been appropriate in different circumstances",[619] and so be liable for loss suffered by the other contracting party in consequence of movements in that market.

20–104   **What must be "contemplated"?** In tort cases, it is said that the defendant is liable if he could have foreseen the type or kind of loss suffered, even though he could not have foreseen its extent or the precise manner of its happening[620] and there is considerable support for the view that the same is true in contract.[621] As in tort, this is open to the criticism that it allows the courts discretion[622] in the way they divide the claimant's loss into different types, and this can lead to uncertainty. Thus, in *Brown v KMR Services Ltd*[623] a member of Lloyd's recovered "underwriting losses"[624] from his agent as damages for breach of contract committed by the agent in pursuing a "high risk" strategy.[625] The *type* of loss was foreseeable even if its extent was not, due to a series of accidents and events in the relevant period. In the *Victoria Laundry*[626] case by contrast, it seems that the finding that profits lost on the government contracts were too remote must be explained on the basis that they represented a different *type* of lost profits, or the profits lost on a different *type* of contract, to those which a reasonable person would ordinarily have expected of a laundry business.[627]

20–105   **Recovery of loss not in fact suffered.** A defendant is not normally liable for a loss which is likely to occur in the ordinary course of things if it is not

---

[616] [1949] 2 K.B. 528 at 540; cf. *TheAchilleas* [2008] UKHL 48; [2009] 1 A.C. 61 at [67].

[617] e.g. *The Heron II* [1969] 1 A.C. 350; *Panalpina International Transport Ltd v Densil Underwear Ltd* [1981] 1 Lloyd's Rep. 187.

[618] *Monte Video Gas Co v Clan Line Steamers Ltd* (1921) 37 T.L.R. 866; *The Pegase* [1981] 1 Lloyd's Rep. 175; cf. *The Ocean Dynamic* [1982] 2 Lloyd's Rep. 88.

[619] *The Baleares* [1993] 1 Lloyd's Rep. 215 at 227.

[620] e.g. *Smith v Leech Brain & Co Ltd* [1962] 2 Q.B. 405 at 415; cf. *Muirhead v Industrial Tank Specialities Ltd* [1986] Q.B. 507 at 532.

[621] *Wroth v Tyler* [1974] Ch. 30 at 61; above, para.20–074; *GKN Centrax Gears Ltd v Matbro Ltd* [1976] 2 Lloyd's Rep. 555 at 568; *H Parsons (Livestock) Ltd v Uttley Ingham& Co Ltd* [1978] Q.B. 791; below, para.20–113; *Brown v KMR Services Ltd* [1995] 4 All E.R. 598 at 621; *North Sea Energy Holdings NV v Petroleum Authority of Thailand* [1997] 2 Lloyd's Rep. 418 at 438, affirmed [1999] 1 Lloyd's Rep. 483.

[622] Seemingly openly acknowledged by Stuart-Smith L.J. in *Brown v KMR Services Ltd* [1995] 4 All E.R. 598 at 621.

[623] [1995] 4 All E.R. 598.

[624] This was Stuart-Smith's categorisation of the type of loss involved.

[625] This was Hobhouse L.J.'s categorisation of the type of loss involved (Peter Gibson L.J. agreeing with him).

[626] [1949] 2 K.B. 528; above, para.20–101; cf. also *The Forum Craftsman* [1991] 1 Lloyd's Rep. 81 at 85–86; *The Marine Star (No.2)* [1994] 2 Lloyd's Rep. 629 at 636 (reversed on other grounds [1996] 2 Lloyd's Rep. 383).

[627] *Brown v KMR Services Ltd* [1995] 4 All E.R. 598 at 621, per Stuart-Smith L.J. who accepted that "difficulty in practice may arise in categorisation of loss into types or kinds, especially where financial loss is involved."

suffered[628]; nor for a loss which is suffered if it is too remote. But these rules are qualified where the claimant actually suffers a loss which is too remote while the defendant could have anticipated that he would have suffered another, smaller, loss. In *Cory v Thames Ironworks Co*[629] the defendants agreed to sell the hull of a floating boom derrick, but delivered it six months late. The defendants expected the buyers to use the hull as a coal store, and, if it had been so used, the buyers would, as a result of the delay, have lost £420. But, unknown to the defendants, the buyers intended to use the hull for a revolutionary method of transferring coal from colliers to barges, and lost profits of £4,000. The buyers admitted that they could not recover £4,000 and claimed £420. The court held the defendants liable for the latter sum, rejecting their argument that, as the £420 represented a loss not actually suffered, they were not liable even to this extent. There was "no hardship or injustice"[630] in making the sellers liable for the smaller sum when the buyers had lost a larger amount.[631] It is more doubtful whether damages can be recovered if the loss actually suffered is different "in kind" from that which would have occurred in the ordinary course of things. Suppose A sells poisonous cattle-food to B, who eats it himself in the course of an unforeseeable nutritional experiment, and dies. Can his executor sue A for the loss of a cow?

Not solely a test of foresight. Even before the decision in *The Achilleas* it was clear that the test of remoteness is not solely a test of foresight, but in this regard it did seem that a distinction had to be drawn between loss occurring in the ordinary course of things ("first limb") and loss occurring as a result of special circumstances ("second limb").[632]   20–106

Loss occurring in the ordinary course of things. On this ground it has, for example,[633] been held that a person who agrees to supply or repair an obviously profit-earning thing is liable for loss of profits resulting from delay[634]; that a seller of poisonous cattle-food is liable for loss of the cattle to which it is fed[635]; that a merchant who sells defective seed to a farmer is liable for loss of the expected crop[636]; and that a supplier of defective components to a manufacturer is liable for loss of business suffered by the latter when customers, dissatisfied with the end-   20–107

---

[628] *Sunley (B) & Co Ltd v Cunard White Star Ltd* [1940] 1 K.B. 740; *North Sea Energy Holdings NV v Petroleum Authority of Thailand* [1999] 1 Lloyd's Rep. 483.

[629] (1868) L.R. 3 Q.B. 181.

[630] ibid. at 190.

[631] *Building & Civil Engineering Holidays Scheme Management Ltd v Post Office* [1966] 1 Q.B. 247 at 261; the recovery of "ordinary" profits in the *Victoria Laundry* case (above, para.20–101) illustrates the same point.

[632] The boundary between the two has been described as "hazy": *Sempra Metals Ltd v Commissioners of Inland Revenue* [2007] UKHL 34; [2008] 1 A.C. 561 at [215]. One area where it makes a practical difference to determine whether a loss which *is recoverable* falls within one limb or another is in the context of clauses purporting to exclude or limit liability for "consequential loss": see above, para.7–017.

[633] For further examples, see *The Almare Seconda* [1981] 2 Lloyd's Rep. 433; *The Good Luck* [1992] 1 A.C. 233; *The Kriti Rex* [1996] 2 Lloyd's Rep. 171 at 192; *Mason v Burningham* [1949] 2 K.B. 545; cf. *Bunny v Hopkinson* (1859) 27 Beav. 565.

[634] *Fletcher v Tayleur* (1855) 17 C.B. 21; *Wilson v General Iron Screw Colliery Co Ltd* (1887) 47 L.J.Q.B. 239; cf. *Mira v Aylmer Square Investments Ltd* [1990] 1 E.G.L.R. 45.

[635] *Pinnock Bros v Lewis & Peat Ltd* [1923] 1 K.B. 690; *Ashington Piggeries Ltd v Christopher Hill Ltd* [1972] A.C. 441; cf. *Cointat v Myham& Son* [1913] 2 K.B. 220; above, para.11–022.

[636] *George Mitchell (Chesterhall) Ltd v Finney Lock Seeds Ltd* [1983] 2 A.C. 803; and see above, para.20–036.

product, do not place repeat orders.[637] Where a loss is identified as occurring in the ordinary course of things, it appeared that there was no basis, so far as remoteness is concerned, for imposing any further limit to its recovery.[638] It is assumed that the defendant had the opportunity to seek to limit his liability and it is not for the courts to impose a limit which was not bargained for. In *Jackson v Royal Bank of Scotland Plc*,[639] the defendant bank mistakenly disclosed information[640] which led to a loss of future business for the claimant. The Court of Appeal had limited the defendant's liability for such loss to one year of business on the basis of remoteness. This was criticised by the House of Lords as tantamount to the sort of limit upon liability which the defendant might have included in the contract with the claimant, but had not done so.[641] The only limit on the period of liability was the time at which the loss of future business became too speculative to be recovered at all,[642] which was found by the trial judge to be four years.

20–108   **Knowledge of special circumstances.** In *Hadley v Baxendale* it was suggested that the defendants might have been liable for the mill owners' loss of profits if they had known,[643] at the time of contracting, that their delay would keep the mill idle. But mere knowledge of special circumstances is not sufficient.[644] Something more must be shown; and attempts were made in later cases to define that additional requirement. In one case, Blackburn J. said that

> "in order that the notice [of special circumstances] may have any effect, it must be given under such circumstances as that an *actual contract* arises on the part of the defendant to bear the exceptional loss".[645]

But it is clear that there need be no *express* contract to bear the exceptional loss.[646] Liability for loss caused by known special circumstances can perhaps be based on an "implied undertaking . . . to bear it",[647] but the reference seems to be to an undertaking implied in law (and not in fact), and so to mean that the defendant is liable for the exceptional loss, irrespective of any actual agreement to bear it.

---

[637] *GKN Centrax Gears Ltd v Matbro Ltd* [1976] 2 Lloyd's Rep. 555.

[638] This no longer appears to be the case after *The Achilleas*: see below, para.20–110.

[639] [2005] UKHL 3; [2005] 1 W.L.R. 377.

[640] Found to be the breach of an obligation of confidence under the letter of credit provided to the claimant by the bank.

[641] [2005] UKHL 3; [2005] 1 W.L.R. 377 at [37].

[642] In accordance with the principles discussed at above, para.20–060.

[643] Although Alderson B. referred to communication of special circumstances "*by the (claimants) to the defendants*", this is not essential: it is sufficient that the defendant knows of the special circumstances and that the defendant knows the claimant knows that the defendant is aware of them without the need for that knowledge to have been acquired *from the claimant*: *Robophone Facilities Ltd v Blank* [1966] 1 WLR 1428 at 1448; *The Achilleas* [2008] UKHL 48; [2009] 1 A.C. 61 at [68]–[69]; cf. *The Heron II* [1969] 1 A.C. 350 at 385, 411.

[644] e.g. *Mulvenna v Royal Bank of Scotland* [2003] EWCA Civ 1112 at [26].

[645] *Horne v Midland Ry* (1873) L.R. 8 C.P. 131 at 141 (where this requirement was not satisfied); cf. *Coastal International Trading Ltd v Maroil Ltd* [1988] 1 Lloyd's Rep. 92 at 97; contrast *Laceys Footwear (Wholesale) Ltd v Bowler International* [1997] 2 Lloyd's Rep. 369 at 377 (loss of *ordinary* profits within contemplation of parties).

[646] *Robophone Facilities Ltd v Blank* [1966] 1 W.L.R. 1428 at 1448; cf. *The Heron II* [1969] 1 A.C. 350 at 422; *The Pegase* [1981] 1 Lloyd's Rep. 175 at 182; *Panalpina International Transport Ltd v Densil Underwear Ltd* [1981] 1 Lloyd's Rep.187.

[647] ibid.

Simpson v L & NW Ry[648] illustrates the circumstances in which such liability can arise. The defendants had contracted to carry samples of cattle-food from an agricultural show at Bedford to another at Newcastle. They had an agent on the showground at Bedford specifically to attract such custom; the goods were marked "must be at Newcastle by Monday certain" but no express reference was made in the contract of carriage to the Newcastle show. The samples failed to arrive "by Monday" and did not reach Newcastle until after the show there was over. It was held that the defendants were liable for loss of the profits which the owner of the samples would have made, had the samples reached Newcastle in time. This should be contrasted with an example given in a nineteenth-century case: a barrister going to Calcutta, where he had briefs awaiting him, could not sue the carriers for getting him there late, even if they knew why he was going to Calcutta.[649] The distinction between the cases lies in the nature of the two contracts. In the first, the contract was in substance one to carry samples to the Newcastle show—not simply to Newcastle. In the second the contract was one to carry the barrister to Calcutta—not to the Calcutta law sittings. Liability depends on "some knowledge *and acceptance* by one party of the *purpose and intention* of the other in entering the contract".[650]

Partial knowledge. The party in breach may know only some of the circum-   20–109
stances which lead to extra loss. He may then be liable for so much of that loss as he could have anticipated on the basis of the facts known to him, but not for further loss which results from other circumstances of which he was unaware.[651] In such cases, there is no rigid separation between the two limbs of the test in *Hadley v Baxendale*[652] and the defendant's liability increases with his degree of knowledge. Thus one reason why some loss of profits was recovered in the *Victoria Laundry* case, but none in *Hadley v Baxendale*, was that in the former the defendants knew that the boiler was wanted for immediate use, while in the latter case they did not know that want of the shaft would keep the mill idle. In *The Heron II* the defendants' knowledge that there was a sugar market at Basrah sufficed to make them liable for loss due to market movements there. Similarly, delay in the arrival of a chartered ship at a loading port may cause loss to a charterer who intended to *buy* a cargo there, if the market rises during the period of the delay: the shipowner's liability in respect of such loss will depend on the degree of his knowledge of the market and of the charterer's arrangements in relation to the buying of the cargo.[653] And where a bank wrongfully dishonoured

---

[648] (1876) 1 Q.B.D. 274; *Jameson v Midland Ry* (1884) 50 L.T. 426.
[649] *BC Saw-Mill Co Ltd v Nettleship* (1868) L.R. 3 C.P. 499 at 510; cf. *The Panalpina* case, above, fn.646, where a carrier knew that goods were wanted for the Christmas trade but delivered them too late.
[650] *Weld-Blundell v Stephens* [1920] A.C. 956 at 980 (italics supplied); contrast *GKN Centrax Gears Ltd v Matbro Ltd* [1976] 2 Lloyd's Rep. 555 at 580.
[651] *Borries v Hutchinson* (1865) 18 C.B.(N.S.) 445; cf. *International Minerals & Chemicals Corp v Karl O Helm AG* [1986] 1 Lloyd's Rep. 81 at 102 (exchange loss recoverable as damages for late payment in a currency known not to be "the currency of [the seller]"). See also: *Cottrill v Steyning & Littlehampton Building Society* [1966] 1 W.L.R. 753; cf. *G & K Ladenbau (UK) Ltd v Crawley & de Reya* [1978] 1 W.L.R. 266; *Seven Seas Properties Ltd v Al-Essa* [1988] 1 W.L.R. 1272. Contrast, *Diamond v Campbell-Jones* [1961] Ch. 22; cf. *Seven Seas Properties Ltd v Al Essa (No.2)* [1993] 1 W.L.R. 1083; *Strategic Property Ltd v O'Se* [2009] EWHC 3512 (Ch).
[652] *Kpohraror v Woolwich Building Society* [1996] 4 All E.R. 119 at 128; *Hotel Services Ltd v Hilton International (UK) Ltd* [2000] 1 All E.R. (Comm) 750 at 755.
[653] Contrast *The Rio Claro* [1987] 2 Lloyd's Rep. 173 with *The Baleares* [1993] 1 Lloyd's Rep. 215. See also *The Eurus* [1998] 1 Lloyd's Rep. 351.

a customer's cheque, it was held liable to the customer for injury to his business reputation since it knew him to be a trader, but not for the further loss suffered by the customer when the particular transaction in respect of which the cheque had been drawn, and further business opportunities, were lost, since these were circumstances of which the bank neither was, nor could have been, aware on the basis of the facts known to it.[654]

20–110   *The Achilleas*. It is against the background of the understanding of the test of remoteness set out above that we can consider the impact of the decision of the House of Lords in *The Achilleas*.[655] The defendant charterers redelivered a vessel to the claimant owners nine days late. As a consequence the claimants were forced to accept the cancellation of a follow on fixture which they had negotiated at a rate of $39,500 per day and enter into a new fixture at $31,500 per day. The defendants accepted that they were liable for the "overrun period", i.e. the difference between the charter rate which the defendants would continue to pay and the market rate for the nine days of delay, but argued that the losses flowing from the cancellation of the follow on fixture were too remote. This submission was rejected by a majority of the arbitrators and at first instance[656] and in the Court of Appeal.[657] An appeal was allowed unanimously by the House of Lords, but as a result of two different approaches.

Lord Rodger and Baroness Hale found that the loss had not been reasonably contemplated and was, therefore, too remote. An obvious difficulty with this apparently orthodox application of the test of remoteness is that the application of the same test before the arbitrators and in the lower courts produced the opposite result. This is not altogether surprising given that the defendant conceded that it was "not unlikely" that the late redelivery of the vessel would result in the loss of a follow on fixture, i.e. the loss was one which would occur in the ordinary course of things.[658] It seems that the conclusion reached by Lord Rodger and Baroness Hale can only be explained by a different conception of the relevant "loss". Lord Rodger referred to it as the financial consequences of the loss of the fixture which had occurred "only because of the extremely volatile market conditions which produced both the owners' initial (particularly lucrative) transaction . . . and the subsequent pressure on the owners to accept a lower rate for that fixture."[659] This appears to fall into error in requiring reasonable contemplation of the extent of the loss and not the type,[660] and to be inconsistent with earlier dicta that fluctuations in the market are only relevant if they are due to "any unusual or unpredictable factor".[661]

---

[654] *Kpohraror v Woolwich Building Society* [1996] 4 All E.R. 119.

[655] [2008] UKHL 48; [2009] 1 A.C. 61; Peel 125 L.Q.R. 6; Kramer 125 L.Q.R. 408; Wee [2010] L.M.C.L.Q. 150; Hoffmann 14 Edinburgh L.R. 47; Coote 26 J.C.L. 211.

[656] [2006] EWHC 2030 (Comm); [2007] 1 Lloyd's Rep. 19. In the last edition, the decision of Christopher Clarke J. was cited as a straightforward example of loss occurring in the ordinary course of things.

[657] [2007] EWCA Civ 901; [2007] 2 Lloyd's Rep. 555.

[658] See above, text to fn.609.

[659] [2008] UKHL 48; [2009] 1 A.C. 61 at [60].

[660] See above, para.20–104.

[661] *The Heron II* [1969] 1 A.C. 350 at 394, 417. The charter market is ordinarily volatile and Lord Rodger does not appear to suggest that it was *particularly* volatile or distorted by an unusual or unpredictable factor at the relevant time. In *Pindell Ltd v Airasia Berhad* [2010] EWHC 2516 (Comm) at [88] Tomlinson J. considered it to be "axiomatic" that losses due to "extremely volatile market conditions" are too remote, but he was dealing with the unprecedented economic crisis in 2008; the events in *The Achilleas* took place in 2004.

Lord Hoffmann and Lord Hope adopted a different approach in which they gave greater emphasis to what they identified as the underlying basis of remoteness. That basis is that the defendant is only to be held liable for loss which it was the intention of the parties that he should bear, i.e. loss for which he has "assumed responsibility", or which falls within the scope of his duty.[662] As in other areas,[663] the intention of the parties must be objectively ascertained. In most cases it will be determined solely by the test of whether the loss was one which was, or should have been, reasonably contemplated, but in some cases other factors may lead to the conclusion that the parties did not intend that the defendant should be held liable even for a loss that was reasonably contemplated. *The Achilleas* was regarded as such a case. According to both Lord Hoffmann and Lord Hope, one factor was the unpredictable or unquantifiable nature of the loss over which the defendants had no control, i.e. the length and terms of the follow on charter.[664] An additional factor for Lord Hoffmann was market expectation, i.e. the understanding of the shipping industry that the liability of the charterer was confined to the overrun period.[665]

Evaluation. At the outset, it should be stressed that the approach advocated by Lord Hoffmann and Lord Hope does not represent a fundamental departure from the previous understanding of the test of remoteness. First, it has been seen above that, at least in some cases, the test is not merely one of foresight and that "something more" may be required; furthermore, the "something more" has been articulated as some sense that the defendant has accepted, or assented to the risk of the loss.[666] Secondly, the technique of seeking to find an answer in the proper interpretation, or construction, of the contract is used elsewhere, e.g. in determining whether a contract is void for common mistake,[667] or discharged by frustration.[668] Thirdly, if the test of remoteness is not ultimately to be determined by the intention of the parties, the only alternative is to recognise that remoteness is an external rule based on keeping liability within reasonable limits; the distinction between liability based on the intention of the parties, objectively ascertained, and liability based on an externally imposed standard of reasonableness is a fine one.[669]

Nonetheless, the approach advocated by Lord Hoffmann and Lord Hope does appear to go further than the courts have gone before. The requirement of

20–111

---

[662] [2008] UKHL 48; [2009] 1 A.C. 61 at [9], [12], [23] per Lord Hoffmann; at [31] per Lord Hope; Kramer in Cohen and McKendick (eds.), *Comparative Remedies for Breach of Contract*; Hoffmann 14 Edinburgh L.R. 47.

[663] See above, paras 6–009, 6–032.

[664] [2008] UKHL 48; [2009] 1 A.C. 61 at [24], [34].

[665] ibid. at [7], [23].

[666] See, e.g. *BC Saw-Mill Co Ltd v Nettleship* (1868) L.R. 3 C.P. 499 at 510 and in *The Achilleas* itself in the lower courts: [2006] EWHC 2030 (Comm); [2007] 1 Lloyd's Rep. 19 at [65]; [2007] EWCA Civ 901; [2007] 2 Lloyd's Rep. 555 at [115]. See also Lord Hoffmann's explanation that the dividing of loss into different types (above, para.20–104) "reflects what would reasonably have been regarded by the contracting party as significant for the purposes of the risk he was undertaking": [2008] UKHL 48; [2009] 1 A.C. 61 at [22].

[667] See above, para.8–003.

[668] See above, para.19–118.

[669] *Mulvenna v Royal Bank of Scotland* [2003] EWCA Civ 1112 at [33] per Evans L.J.: "the chain of consequences is cut off as a matter of law, *either* because it is regarded as unreasonable to impose liability for that consequence of the breach, *or* because the scope of the duty is limited so as to exclude it." (emphasis added); cf. in tort, "ultimately it is a question of policy for the judges to decide", *Lamb v Camden London Borough Council* [1981] Q.B. 625, at 636 per Lord Denning.

something more than the requisite degree of foresight of the loss has hitherto been confined to losses occurring only as a result of special circumstances ("second limb" losses)[670] whereas *The Achilleas* was concerned with loss which occurred in the ordinary course of things[671] ("first limb" losses). In relation to the latter, it has previously been understood that there is no further limit to recoveryso far as remoteness is concerned.[672] The technique of looking to the proper construction of the contract has been shown to have its limits and has led to the rejection of the implied term theory (i.e. that the answer is to be found by reference to the intention of the parties) to explain when a contract is void for mistake,[673] or is discharged for frustration.[674] There is certainly *a role* for the technique in relation to damages in that the secondary obligation to pay compensation is shaped by the primary obligation which has been breached. It is first necessary to know the scope of the defendant's primary obligation before one can ask what sum would put the claimant in the same position as if the defendant had fulfilled that primary obligation, and the scope of that primary obligation is a question of its proper interpretation. But in *The Achilleas* the primary obligation of the defendant was not in doubt;[675] it was to have returned the vessel before the last date for redelivery and to press into action a search for the intention of the parties, albeit objectively ascertained, so as to determine the scope of the secondary obligation directly seems to border on a fiction.[676]

The sense that Lord Hoffmann and Lord Hope may have gone further than before and, as a result, rendered the law less certain is reinforced by the decision which was reached in *The Achilleas* itself. If the courts are now invited to find that a loss may be too remote even though it occurred in the ordinary course of things one would expect that result only to be reached in very exceptional circumstances. Lord Hoffmann referred to the understanding of the shipping industry that the charterer's liability is confined to the overrun period, but as Rix L.J. demonstrated in the Court of Appeal this issue had not previously been directly before the courts and, when seen in context, there is rather less in the way of indirect support for this view than has been supposed.[677] Both Lord Hoffmann and Lord Hope referred to the unpredictable and unquantifiable nature of the loss, but again as Rix L.J. noted, the follow on fixture was an entirely usual one whereas "an unusual contract is likely to be outside the 'usual course of things' which is the essential

---

[670] See above, para.20–108.

[671] This is on the basis of the rejection of Lord Rodger's conception of the relevant loss: above, para. 20–110.

[672] See above, para.20–107.

[673] See above, para.8–002.

[674] See above, para.19–115.

[675] This is an important difference between *The Achilleas* and *South Australia Asset Management Corp v York Montague Ltd* [1997] A.C. 191 *(SAAMCO)*, from which Lord Hoffmann draws support for his approach to remoteness. As explained above (para.20–023), in *SAAMCO* the defendant valuer was not liable for all loss flowing from the loan entered into by the claimant lender since it did not fall within the scope of his duty (i.e. his primary obligation) to advise generally on the commercial wisdom of the loan; his duty was only to provide information and his liability was limited to the extent to which that information was incorrect.

[676] Robertson (2008) 28 L.S. 172; cf.Tettenborn (2007) 23 J.C.L. 120. One consequence of regarding remoteness as involving a question of the interpretation of the contract is that it involves a question of law: *The Achilleas* [2008] UKHL 48; [2009] 1 A.C. 61 at [25]; the question of whether the loss was foreseeable remains a question of fact: *Monarch Steamship Co Ltd v Karlshamns Oljefabriker (A/B)* [1949] A.C. 196.

[677] [2007] EWCA Civ 901; [2007] 2 Lloyd's Rep. 555 at [30] et seq. discussing, inter alia, dicta in *The Dione* [1975] 1 Lloyd's Rep. 115 at 117–118; *The Johnny* [1977] 2 Lloyd's Rep. 1 at 2; *The Peonia* [1991] 1 Lloyd's Rep. 100 at 118; *The Gregos* [1995] 1 Lloyd's Rep. 1 at 10.

focus of the remoteness rule".[678] In this regard, there is a certain irony in that the typical loss which was actually suffered in *The Achilleas* is held to be too remote because of a hypothetical loss which was not in fact suffered, whereas a typical but hypothetical loss was recovered in the *Victoria Laundry* case after ruling out the unusual loss which was in fact suffered (the loss on the government contracts).[679] This would suggest that the claimants in *The Achilleas* should have been entitled to recover for the loss of what was the usual fixture in that case and this would represent the limit of recovery in any future cases where the owner had entered into an "unusual" fixture. Finally, Lord Hoffmann referred to the control which the owner enjoyed to prevent the loss in the form of his right to refuse to undertake the last voyage if it was bound to overrun and put the follow on fixture at risk.[680] That form of "control" is confined to the particular circumstances of the case before the House of Lords. In most cases, it is not the claimant who will be able to control whether a loss can be avoided; it is the defendant who can control his liability for that loss by the insertion of an appropriately drafted limit on his liability. In one sense, the result reached in *The Achilleas* appears to do what the House of Lords had previously said should not be done,[681] by introducing a limit upon liability which the defendant might have included in the contract with the claimant, but had not done so.[682]

Current approach. The reformulated approach to the test of remoteness in   20–112
The Achilleas is attributed to Lord Hoffmann and Lord Hope whereas Lord Rodger and Baroness Hale appeared to apply the orthodox test, albeit in a way which is open to some doubt.[683] The precise *ratio* of the decision therefore turns on the interpretation of the speech of Lord Walker.[684] He concluded that he would allow the appeal for the reasons given by Lord Rodger *and* Lord Hoffmann and Lord Hope, but it could be argued that he does not go quite as far as the latter in his recognition that the underlying idea of remoteness is "what was the common basis on which the parties were contracting?"[685] Without considering it necessary to establish the *ratio* of the decision in *The Achilleas*, the reformulated approach appears to have been accepted by the Court of Appeal in *Supershield Ltd v Siemens Building Technologies FE Ltd*.[686] In that case, Toulson L.J. referred to *Hadley v Baxendale* as the "standard rule",[687] but recognized that "there may be cases where the court, on examining the contract and the commercial background, decides that the standard approach would not reflect the expectation or intention

---

[678] *The Gregos* [1995] 1 Lloyd's Rep. 1at [112].

[679] See above, para.20–101, and fn.631.

[680] [2008] UKHL 48; [2009] 1 A.C. 61 at [23].

[681] *Jackson v Royal Bank of Scotland Plc* [2005] UKHL 3; [2005] 1 W.L.R. 377; above, para.20–107.

[682] See above, para.20–107.

[683] See above, para.20–110.

[684] Or possibly not: in *The Amer Energy* [2009] 1 Lloyd's Rep. 293 Flaux J. regarded Lord Hoffmann alone as being in the minority in laying down a new test of remoteness; cf. *Sylvia Shipping Co Ltd v Progress Bulk Carriers Ltd* [2010] EWHC 542 (Comm); [2010] 2 Lloyd's Rep. 81 at [39]-40] in which Hamblen J. considered "the *rationale* of assumption of responsibility to have had the support of the majority" (emphasis added); cf. *Classic Maritime v Lion Diversified Holdings* [2009] EWHC 1142; [2010] 1 Lloyd's Rep. 59; *Pindell Ltd v Airasia Berhad* [2010] EWHC 2516 (Comm).

[685] [2008] UKHL 48; [2009] 1 A.C. 61 at [69]; there is a role for this even in the orthodox test: see above, para.20–108.

[686] [2010] EWCA Civ 7; [2010] 1 Lloyd's Rep. 349.

[687] ibid. at [43].

reasonably to be imputed to the parties".[688] Furthermore, taken to its logical conclusion this approach may have an "inclusionary effect" (in contrast to the "exclusionary effect" in *The Achilleas*) in that the loss may be found to be within the scope of the defendant's duty even if it would not have occurred in ordinary circumstances (and, it seems, was not the result of special circumstances made known to the defendant).[689]

Similarly, in *Sylvia Shipping Co Ltd v Progress Bulk Carriers Ltd*[690] Hamblen J. referred to the decision in *The Achilleas* as resulting in "an amalgam of the orthodox and the broader approach".[691] He considered that it would only be in "unusual" cases that it would be necessary "specifically to address the issue of assumption of responsibility".[692] In that case, the defendant shipowner was in breach of a charterparty by delivering the vessel late and was sued by the charterer for the loss of a sub-charter. This was not an "unusual" case in that, unlike *The Achilleas*, there was no relevant understanding of the industry that this was a loss for which the owner would not be held liable and the loss was not "unquantifiable, unpredictable, uncontrollable or disproportionate"[693] since, by definition, the length of the sub-charter could be no longer than the charterparty. But although the test in *Hadley v Baxendale* is described as the "standard rule" or the "orthodox approach" from which the courts should only depart in "unusual cases" the effect of this approach is that, in reality, the test of "assumption of responsibility" is *applied* in all cases; it is only in non-standard, or "unusual", cases that it will produce a different *result* to the test in *Hadley v Baxendale*. Even if the broader, or reformulated, approach is no more than a rationalisation of the test of remoteness, it is the very fact that it was applied in *The Achilleas* to loss which occurred in the ordinary course of things and in circumstances that do not appear to have been particularly exceptional,[694] that may have rendered the law less certain.

20–113   **Contract and Tort.** It has been noted above that the test for remoteness in contract is not the same as the test for remoteness in tort; in particular that a higher degree of foreseeability is needed in contract. The distinction between the two was further considered in *H Parsons (Livestock) Ltd v Uttley Ingham & Co Ltd*.[695] The defendants in that case supplied to the claimants a hopper for storing pig food; they failed, in breach of contract, to provide for proper ventilation, so that the food became mouldy and many of the pigs died from a rare intestinal disease. Swanwick J. ordered damages to be assessed for the value of the pigs which had died, for the claimants' expenses in dealing with the infection, and for "loss of sales and turnover". This judgment was affirmed on appeal, but for divergent reasons which give rise to three main difficulties. The first is to determine exactly what test of remoteness was applied. Lord Denning M.R. said that the higher degree of foreseeability stated in *The Heron II* applied only where

---

[688] ibid.
[689] ibid. This may be logical but one imagines that such an outcome will be rare and it was unnecessary for Toulson L.J to have to go that far in that the issue which he had to resolve was the reasonableness of a settlement of liability entered into by the claimant, including the points it had or had not taken *viz.* remoteness: [2010] EWCA Civ 7; [2010] 1 Lloyd's Rep. 349 at [45].
[690] [2010] EWHC 542 (Comm); [2010] 2 Lloyd's Rep. 81.
[691] ibid. at [40].
[692] ibid. at [41].
[693] ibid. at [73].
[694] See above, para.20–111.
[695] [1978] Q.B. 791.

the claim was for purely financial loss; where it was for physical damage the test of remoteness was the same in contract as in tort. He accordingly found for the claimants on the ground that the tort test was satisfied, even though that laid down in *The Heron II* was not: it was enough that the defendants could have foreseen a "slight possibility"[696] that eating mouldy food might make the pigs ill. Orr and Scarman L.JJ., on the other hand, took the view that there neither was nor should be any distinction between financial loss and physical damage for the purpose of remoteness. Their decision was based on the view that the test of remoteness laid down in *The Heron II* was satisfied as the defendants could have contemplated a "serious possibility"[697] that the pigs might become ill as a result of the defect in the hopper. The second difficulty is to account for the way in which the Court of Appeal dealt with Swanwick J.'s award of damages for "loss of sales and turno-ver".[698] This award was upheld but, in what seems to be a reference to it, Lord Denning M.R. said that the claimants were not entitled to damages "for loss of profit on future sales or future opportunities of gain"[699]; while Orr and Scarman L.JJ. agreed with Lord Denning in the result, but "by a different route".[700] It is not easy to reconcile these positions with each other or with the different ways (discussed above) in which the members of the Court formulated and applied the test of remoteness. Lord Denning's views on these points might seem to lead to the conclusion that there should be no recovery at all for "loss of sales and turnover",[701] while the reasoning of Orr and Scarman L.JJ. makes it hard to understand why they agreed with Lord Denning's conclusion that there should be no recovery "for loss of profit on future sales".[702] The most plausible reconcilia-tion of the apparent conflict is that the claimants recovered damages for loss of the profits that they would have made from the pigs which had died, but not for loss of further profits which they would have been able to make (if the hopper had not been defective) by rearing and selling additional animals.

The third difficulty is to determine whether, in the view of Orr and Scarman L.JJ., the test of remoteness in contract differs from that in tort. At one point, Scarman L.J. said that it was "absurd that the test of remoteness of damage should, in principle, differ according to the legal classification of the cause of action"; and that the law did not "differentiate between contract and tort save in situations where the agreement, or the factual relationship, of the parties with each other requires it in the interests of justice".[703] But he also accepted that

> "the formulation of the remoteness test is not the same in tort and contract because the relationship of the parties in a contract situation differs from that in tort".[704]

---

[696] ibid. at 804.

[697] ibid. at 812; Orr L.J. expressed his agreement with the reasoning of Scarman L.J. In *Saleslease Ltd v Davis* [1999] 1 W.L.R. 1664 the foreseeability test was applied to financial loss resulting from conversion; there was no discussion of any relevant difference between tort and contract rules of remoteness.

[698] ibid. at 793.

[699] ibid. at 804.

[700] ibid. at 806.

[701] Since this loss was financial and the test in *The Heron II* was (in Lord Denning's view) not satisfied.

[702] Since (in their view) the *Heron II* test was satisfied.

[703] [1978] Q.B. 791 at 806; cf. *Bates v Barrow Ltd* [1995] 1 Lloyd's Rep. 680 at 691.

[704] ibid. at 806.

It differs because, as Lord Reid said in *The Heron II*, a contracting party

> "who wishes to protect himself against a risk which to the other party would
> appear to be unusual, ... can direct the other party's attention to it before
> the contract is made. In tort, however, there is no opportunity for the injured
> party to protect himself in that way ... ".[705]

Perhaps one may conclude that the reasoning of Lord Reid should be taken to its
logical conclusion so that the contract test should apply whenever one party has
had the opportunity to alert the other to the type of loss he is at risk of suffering,
regardless of the cause of action pursued. If this is thought a little too uncertain,
it may be preferable to assume that such an opportunity existed when the parties
are in a contractual relationship (as is currently the case for claims made in
contract), but did not exist in the absence of such a relationship. On that basis,
where a claim is made for a tort arising from a contractual relationship, the
contract test should be applied,[706] but where it is made for a tort where there is
no contractual relationship, or which arises entirely independently of any contractual relationship, the tort test should be applied.

20–114   **Extra loss due to claimant's lack of means.** A claimant may suffer extra
loss because his financial position is such that he cannot avoid the adverse
consequences of the breach. Damages can be recovered for such loss if the
defendant knew of the claimant's lack of means and if the extra loss resulting from
it "was such as might reasonably be expected to be in the contemplation of the
parties as likely to flow from a breach of the obligation undertaken".[707]

(c) Mitigation

20–115   Two ideas are usually discussed under this heading. The first is that the
claimant cannot recover damages for a loss that he ought to have avoided. He is
said to be under a *"duty to* mitigate". This expression will be used here even
though it is open to the objection that breach of the "duty" gives rise to no legal
liability[708] but only reduces the amount that the claimant can recover. The second
idea is that the claimant has to give credit for certain benefits accruing to him in
consequence of the breach. Here it can be said that his loss is *in fact* mitigated.

---

[705] [1969] 1 A.C. 350 at 385–386, cited in the *Parsons* case [1978] Q.B. 791 at 806.

[706] Some support for this view may be derived from *Brown v KMR Services Ltd* [1995] 4 All E.R.
598 where the contract test was applied, but the court did not seem to draw any distinction between
the claims which were pursued concurrently in contract and tort. In *Henderson v Merrett Syndicates Ltd*
[1995] 2 A.C. 145, however, it seems to have been assumed (at 185) that the tests would be different.
cf. *Archer v Brown* [1985] Q.B. 401 at 418 (where both tests seem to have been satisfied).

[707] *Muhammed Issa el Sheik Ahmed v Ali* [1947] A.C. 414, as explained in *Monarch SS Co v
Karlshamns Oljefabriker (A/B)* [1949] A.C. 196 at 224; cf. *Trans Trust SPRL v Danubian Trading Co Ltd*
[1952] 2 Q.B. 297; *Wroth v Tyler* [1974] Ch. 30; *Perry v Sidney Phillips & Son* [1982] 1 W.L.R. 1297;
contrast *Pilkington v Wood* [1953] Ch. 770 (where defendant did not know of claimant's overdraft); cf.
in tort, *Lagden v O'Connor* [2003] UKHL 64; [2004] 1 A.C. 1067.

[708] *The Solholt* [1983] 1 Lloyd's Rep. 605 at 608; Lomnicka 99 L.Q.R. 495; *The Alecos M* [1991] 1
Lloyd's Rep. 120 at 124.

(i) *The duty to mitigate*

There are two aspects to the duty to mitigate: first, the claimant must take   **20–116**
reasonable steps to minimise his loss; and secondly he must forbear from taking
unreasonable steps that increase his loss.[709] It follows from the principle on which
the "duty" to mitigate is based that the duty will normally arise only when the
claimant has become aware of the breach.[710] It has been suggested that, where the
claimant has not actually become aware of the breach, the duty will not arise
merely because he was careless in failing to discover it; but that such carelessness
might be relevant for other purposes: e.g. in making the loss (or part of it) too
remote or in reducing the amount recoverable on the ground of contributory
negligence.[711] These techniques would normally lead to much the same result as
the principles of mitigation; but it is submitted that there is no compelling reason
for holding that those principles can never apply where the claimant had, but
failed to take, clear opportunities of discovering the breach: e.g. where a buyer is
warned of the need to test the goods but fails to do so.

Minimising loss.[712] If the claimant fails to take reasonable steps to minimise   **20–117**
his loss, he cannot recover anything in respect of extra loss due to that failure.
Commonly, he is required to make a substitute contract. For example, where a
seller of goods fails to deliver, the buyer must go into the market[713] at the relevant
time[714] to buy substitute goods. If he fails to do so he cannot recover any further
loss that he may suffer because the market continues to rise or because he is
deprived of the opportunity of making a profit out of the use or resale of the
goods.[715] Conversely, a seller of shares who kept them after the buyer's breach
could not recover any extra loss that he might suffer as a result of a later fall in the
market.[716] The injured party is, however, required to mitigate in this way only if
the new transaction would be a true substitute for the old one. Where, for
example, a customer wrongfully repudiates a contract for the provision of services
at a time when the injured party has spare capacity, then the possibility of that
party's making another contract with a new customer will not be taken into
account: such a new contract will not be a true substitute for the broken contract
since the injured party would, but for the breach, have been able to perform both
contracts.[717]

Where the breach has induced the injured party not to claim sums due to him
from third parties, the mitigation rules may require him to assert these claims.[718]
But this is subject to the overriding rule that he need only take such steps as are

---

[709] For the burden of proof on this issue, see below, para.21–013, at fn.53.

[710] *The Superhulls Cover Case (No.2)* [1990] 2 Lloyd's Rep. 431 at 461.

[711] ibid. at 462; below, para.20–123.

[712] Bridge 105 L.Q.R. 398.

[713] If there are several markets, a transaction in any market that it was reasonable for the injured party to use can form the basis of assessment: *Gebruder Metelmann GmbH & Co KG v NBR (London) Ltd* [1984] 1 Lloyd's Rep. 614, a case of buyer's breach.

[714] See above, para.20–072 et seq.

[715] *Hussey v Eels* [1990] 2 Q.B. 227 at 233 ("deemed mitigation"); cf. *The Marine Star (No.2)* [1994] 2 Lloyd's Rep. 629 at 635 (reversed on another ground [1996] 2 Lloyd's Rep. 383); *The Elena D'Amico* [1980] 1 Lloyd's Rep. 75 at 79 (charterparty); and see above, para.20–049.

[716] *Jamal v Moolla Dawood Sons & Co* [1916] 1 A.C. 175 at 179; cf. *Bristol & West BS v Fancy & Jackson* [1997] 4 All E.R. 582 at 623 (delay in realising security).

[717] *Western Web Offset Printers Ltd v Independent Media Ltd*, *The Times*, October 10, 1995; cf. above, para.20–059.

[718] *St Albans City & District Council v International Computers Ltd* [1996] 4 All E.R. 481 (the £484,000 claim).

reasonable: he therefore does not need to take steps which would involve him in complicated litigation[719] or which would ruin his commercial reputation[720] or which would involve him in unreasonable expense or inconvenience.[721]

20–118   **Accepting substitute performance from party in breach.** Sometimes the injured party will be required to mitigate by accepting from the party in breach a performance which differs in some way from that originally bargained for. Thus where a charterer fails to load the agreed cargo, the shipowner may be bound to mitigate by accepting the charterer's reasonable offer of alternative cargo, even at a lower rate[722]; where a seller agrees to give credit and then refuses to deliver except for cash, the buyer may be bound to mitigate by accepting such delivery instead of buying against the seller on a rising market[723]; and where a seller cannot deliver at the agreed time the buyer may be required to mitigate by accepting late delivery.[724] In these cases, any loss suffered by the injured party by reason of the difference between the performance rendered and that originally bargained for can easily and adequately be allowed for in damages. He is not required to mitigate by accepting an offer of modified performance which purports to extinguish his right to such damages.[725] Nor is the injured party bound to mitigate by accepting an offer of modified performance if the modification causes him substantial prejudice: e.g. a buyer of goods need not mitigate by accepting the seller's tender of goods of a lower quality than contracted for, even with an allowance for the inferiority.[726] On a somewhat similar principle, an employee who has been wrongfully dismissed need not accept an offer of re-employment involving a reduction in status,[727] or a lower grade of work[728]; nor need he accept the former employer's offer to take him back, even on the original terms, if the wrongful dismissal occurred in circumstances of personal humiliation, e.g. on a charge of misconduct made before others.[729]

20–119   **Not augmenting loss.** If the claimant acts unreasonably in attempting to mitigate, he cannot recover extra loss which he suffers as a result.[730] Thus in general he should not, for example, spend more on curing a defect in performance

---

[719] *Pilkington v Wood* [1953] Ch. 770; *The Ines* [1995] 2 Lloyd's Rep. 144 at 159; *Markel International Insurance Co Ltd v Surety Guarantee Consultants Ltd* [2008] EWHC 3087 (Comm); cf. *The Greek Fighter* [2006] EWHC 1729 (Comm) at [340] et seq.

[720] *James Finlay & Co Ltd v NV Kwik Hoo Tong HM* [1929] 1 K.B. 400; cf. *London & South of England Building Society v Stone* [1983] 1 W.L.R. 1242 (building society not required to enforce borrower's *personal* covenant).

[721] *The Griparion* [1994] 1 Lloyd's Rep. 533; *Hussey v Eels* [1990] 2 Q.B. 227; *Zodiac Maritime Agencies Ltd v Fortescue Metals Group Ltd* [2010] EWHC 903 (Comm) at [65].

[722] *Harries v Edmonds* (1845) 1 Car. & K. 686.

[723] *Payzu Ltd v Saunders* [1919] 2 K.B. 581; contrast *Harlow & Jones Ltd v Panex International Ltd* [1967] 2 Lloyd's Rep. 509 at 530 (claimant "not bound to nurse the interests of the contract breaker").

[724] *The Solholt* [1983] 1 Lloyd's Rep. 605.

[725] *Shindler v Northern Raincoat Co Ltd* [1960] 1 W.L.R. 1038; *Velmore Estates v Roseberry Homes Ltd* [2005] EWHC 3061; cf. *Strutt v Whitnell* [1975] 1 W.L.R. 870 (said in *The Solholt* [1983] 1 Lloyd's Rep. 605 at 609 to turn "on its own special facts").

[726] *Heaven & Kesterton Ltd v Et François Albiac & Cie* [1956] 2 Lloyd's Rep. 316 at 321.

[727] *Yetton v Eastwood Froy Ltd* [1967] 1 W.L.R. 104.

[728] cf. *Edwards v SOGAT* [1971] 1 Ch. 354.

[729] *Payzu Ltd v Saunders* [1919] 2 K.B. 581 at 589; in the absence of such circumstances it was held in *Brace v Calder* [1895] 2 K.B. 253 that an offer of re-employment should have been accepted.

[730] *The Borag* [1981] 1 W.L.R. 274; *Seven Seas Properties Ltd v Al-Essa* [1988] 1 W.L.R. 1272 at 1276 (the reasoning of the case is obsolete on its facts in view of Law of Property (Miscellaneous Provisions) Act 1989, s.3).

than the subject-matter without the defect would be worth[731]; nor should he continue to incur expense for the purpose of tendering performance after the other party has clearly indicated that he will refuse to accept it. But these are only general rules: the crucial question in each case is whether the claimant has acted reasonably. The point is strikingly illustrated by *Banco de Portugal v Waterlow & Sons Ltd.*[732] The defendants had contracted to print banknotes for the Bank of Portugal, and in breach of contract delivered a large number of these to a criminal, who put them into circulation in Portugal. On discovering this, the Bank withdrew the issue and undertook to exchange all the notes in question for others. The defendants argued that they were liable only for the cost of printing the notes: any further loss was due to the Bank's own act.[733] But the House of Lords, by a majority, held the defendants liable for the full face value of the notes as the conduct of the Bank was reasonable, having regard to its commercial obligations towards the public.[734] A similar result was reached where a manufacturer of soft drinks had been supplied with contaminated ingredients. It was held that, in withdrawing and destroying products containing the ingredient, the manufacturer had acted reasonably to protect its reputation, even though the contamination posed only a negligible risk to health; and that the supplier of the ingredient was liable for the manufacturer's wasted costs.[735]

On the same principle, the claimant may be able to recover amounts paid in reasonable settlement of a liability to a third party incurred in consequence of the breach.[736] Conversely, if the claimant decides to resist a claim brought against him by a third party as a result[737] of the breach, he may be able to recover legal expenses incurred in the proceedings between him and the third party. Thus a buyer can recover from the seller costs reasonably incurred in defending an action brought against him by a sub-buyer on account of a defect for which the seller is liable.[738] Similarly a person who sues an agent for breach of implied warranty of authority can recover costs thrown away in a previous action brought against the principal on the assumption that the agent had the authority he claimed to have.[739] But the costs must be reasonably incurred: the claimant cannot recover them if he persists in litigating when it is clear that he has no chance of success.[740]

---

[731] cf. above, para.20–040; *Darbishire v Warran* [1963] 1 W.L.R. 1067—a tort case; *Grant v Dawkins* [1973] 1 W.L.R. 1406; for an exception see *O'Grady v Westminster Scaffolding Ltd* [1962] 2 Lloyd's Rep. 238—another tort case.

[732] [1932] A.C. 452.

[733] Portuguese currency was not convertible into gold; the bank had a monopoly of issuing notes as legal tender; and, although the amount of notes it could issue was limited by law, the limit had not been reached.

[734] cf. above, at fn.720; and see *Buildings and Civil Engineering Holidays Scheme Management Ltd v Post Office* [1966] 1 Q.B. 247 (where the claim was not in contract).

[735] *Britvic Soft Drinks Ltd v Messer UK Ltd* [2002] 1 Lloyd's Rep 20 at [114], affirmed [2002] EWCA Civ 548; [2002] 2 All E.R. (Comm) 321, without reference to this point.

[736] *Biggin & Co Ltd v Permanite Ltd* [1951] 2 K.B. 314; *Bulk Oil (Zug) AG v Sun International Ltd* [1984] 1 Lloyd's Rep. 531 at 544; *Royal Brompton NHS Trust v Hammond* [1999] N.L.J. 89; *Britvic* case [2002] 1 Lloyd's Rep. 20 at [127]; contrast *Anglian Water Services Ltd v Crawshaw Robbins & Co* [2001] B.L.R. 173 (where loss of this kind was too remote).

[737] See *The Antaios* [1981] 2 Lloyd's Rep. 284 at 299.

[738] *Hammond & Co v Bussey* (1887) 20 Q.B.D. 79; *Lloyds & Scottish Finance Ltd v Modern Cars & Caravans (Kingston) Ltd* [1966] 1 Q.B. 764; *Bowmaker (Commercial) Ltd v Day* [1965] 1 W.L.R. 1396; cf. *The Saragasso* [1994] 1 Lloyd's Rep. 412.

[739] *Hughes v Graeme* (1864) 33 L.J.Q.B. 335; *Godwin v Francis* (1870) L.R. 5 C.P. 295; *Farley Health Products v Babylon Trading Co, The Times,* July 29, 1987.

[740] *Pow v Davies* (1861) 1 B. & S. 220; *Baxendale v London, Chatham & Dover Ry* (1874) L.R. 10 Ex. 38.

20–120   **Recovery of increased loss.** It is possible for steps taken in performance of the duty to mitigate to be reasonable, but actually to increase the loss.[741] For example, a buyer who accepts a seller's anticipatory breach is bound to mitigate by buying a substitute in the market at the time of acceptance. If, when he makes the substitute purchase, the market price exceeds the contract price, he can recover the excess. This is so even though by the time fixed for delivery the market price has fallen below the contract price so that the buyer, if he had not performed the duty to mitigate, would have suffered no loss at all.[742]

(ii) *Mitigation in fact*

20–121   **Benefits accrued as a result of breach.** Loss is sometimes said to be mitigated where some benefit in fact accrues[743] to the claimant as a result of the breach. If, for example, he is released from his own obligation to perform, this fact is taken into account in deciding how much, if anything, he has lost.[744] Or he may benefit from performing his duty to mitigate, e.g. by finding a job comparable to that from which he was wrongfully dismissed.[745] Here again his earnings in the other job will be taken into account in assessing his damages for wrongful dismissal.[746] The principle underlying such cases is that the purpose of an award of damages is "to compensate [the claimant] for his loss, not to enrich him".[747]

There is a further group of cases in which the claimant benefits from doing something that he was *not required* to do in performance of his duty to mitigate: e.g. a wrongfully dismissed employee may take a job involving a reduction in status. His actual earnings in that job are taken into account in assessing damages, even though it was a job that he was not required to take in performance of his duty to mitigate.[748] But some benefits of this kind are not taken into account; and the distinction between the two kinds of benefit is illustrated by *Lavarack v Woods of Colchester Ltd.*[749] The claimant was wrongfully dismissed from his employment with the defendants and so freed from a provision in his contract with them that he should not, without their written consent, be engaged or interested in any other concern (except as a holder of investments quoted on a stock exchange). After his dismissal, he (1) took employment with the X Co at a lower salary than he had earned with the defendants; (2) acquired half the shares in the X Co; and (3) invested money in shares in the Y Co. The value of the shares in both companies

---

[741] *Choil Trading SA v Sahara Energy Resources Ltd* [2010] EWHC 374 (Comm).

[742] *Melachrino v Nickoll& Knight* [1920] 1 K.B. 693 at 697.

[743] e.g. *Platt v London Underground Ltd*, *The Times*, March 13, 2001. "Benefit" here includes avoided loss: *The Kriti Rex* [1996] 2 Lloyd's Rep. 171 at 203.

[744] See above, para.20–006. See also *Levison v Farin* [1978] 2 All E.R. 1149; *C & P Haulage v Middleton* [1983] 1 W.L.R. 1461.

[745] cf. *Evans Marshall & Co v Bertola* [1976] 2 Lloyd's Rep. 17.

[746] e.g. *Cerebus Software Ltd v Rowley* [2001] EWCA Civ 74; [2001] I.C.R. 376; unless the contract otherwise provides, as in *Gregory v Wallace* [1998] I.R.L.R. 387. For the position in cases of unfair dismissal (which generally does not involve any breach of contract) see Employment Rights Act 1996, s.123(4).

[747] *Longden v British Coal Corp* [1998] A.C. 653 at 662; cf. in tort, *Dimond v Lovell* [2002] 1 A.C. 384.

[748] See above, para.20–118; see *Edwards v SOGAT* [1971] Ch. 354; *S of S for Employment v Wilson* [1978] 1 W.L.R. 568; cf. *Techno Land Improvements Ltd v British Leyland (UK) Ltd* (1979) 252 E.G. 805 at 809; *The Concordia C* [1985] 2 Lloyd's Rep. 55; *Dalwood Marine Co v Nordana Line AS* [2009] EWHC 3394 (Comm); [2010] 2 Lloyd's Rep. 315.

[749] [1967] 1 Q.B. 278.

having risen, it was held that the increase in the value of the X Co shares, but not that of the Y Co shares, must be taken into account in reducing the claimant's damages. The former was regarded as a disguised remuneration, while the latter was "not a direct result of his dismissal" but a "collateral benefit".[750]

Whether benefit is "collateral". The question whether a benefit is "col-   20–122 lateral" or a "direct result" of the breach can give rise to difficult problems of causation.[751] In *British Westinghouse Co v Underground Electric Rys Co of London*,[752] A agreed to supply B with turbines of a stated efficiency but supplied less efficient ones, which used more coal. B accepted and used them, reserving his right to claim damages. After some years, and before A's turbines were worn out, B replaced them with others. These were so much more efficient than A's would have been, even had they been in accordance with the contract, that, over the whole period during which A's turbines might have been expected to last, B actually used less coal than he would have done with turbines of the efficiency stated in the contract. The House of Lords held that B was under no duty to mitigate by buying new turbines.[753] But as he had bought the new turbines in consequence of A's breach, the financial advantage he gained by using them had to be set off against the cost of buying them. As B's savings in coal exceeded that cost, he recovered nothing in respect of it. This was so even though it could be argued that the benefit thus obtained by B was only in part the result of the breach; for the turbines originally contracted for had become obsolete so that a reasonable businessman would have replaced them even if they had been in accordance with the contract.[754] On the other hand, B had also, *before* replacing the turbines, suffered loss because the cost of operating them was greater than it would have been if they had been in accordance with the contract. This loss was not diminished as a result of the purchase of the new turbines and was accordingly recoverable.[755]

In the *British Westinghouse* case, it was said that a benefit is taken into account only if it is "one arising from the consequences of the breach".[756] It follows from this requirement that damages will not be reduced by reason of any insurance taken out by the injured party against the consequences of the breach[757] (unless the contract provides that the injured party's sole remedy is to be against the

---

[750] ibid. at 290; cf. *Aruna Mills Ltd v Dhanrajmal Gobindram* [1968] 1 Q.B. 655 at 669; *Hodge v Clifford Cowling & Co* [1990] 2 E.G.L.R. 89; *Mobil North Sea Ltd v P J Pipe & Valve Co* [2001] EWCA Civ 741; [2001] 2 All E.R. (Comm) 289.

[751] It has been said to require a "commonsense overall judgment on the sufficiency of the causal nexus between breach and profit or loss", *The Fanis* [1994] 1 Lloyd's Rep. 633, at 637.

[752] [1912] A.C. 673; cf. *Erie County Natural Gas Co v Carroll* [1911] A.C. 105; *Levison v Farin* [1978] 2 All E.R. 1149; *Merrett v Capitol Indemnity Corp* [1991] 1 Lloyd's Rep. 169.

[753] In this respect the case differs from *Bellingham v Dhillon* [1973] Q.B. 304 (a tort case purporting to follow the *British Westinghouse* case and approved in *Dimond v Lovell* [2002] 1 A.C. 384).

[754] [1912] A.C. 675 at 691.

[755] ibid. at 688.

[756] ibid. at 690.

[757] cf. *Bradburn v Great Western Ry* (1874) L.R. 10 Ex. 1; *The Yasin* [1979] 2 Lloyd's Rep. 45; *Brown v KMR Services* [1994] 4 All E.R. 385 at 399 (varied on other grounds [1995] 4 All E.R. 598); *Bristol & West BS v Christie* [1996] E.G.C.S. 60. Other techniques for avoiding double recovery in such cases are illustrated by *Arab Bank Plc v John D Wood* [2000] 1 W.L.R. 857 and *Amec Civil Engineering Ltd v Cheshire CC* [1999] B.L.R. 303. For other benefits, see generally: *Parry v Cleaver* [1970] A.C. 1; *Pirelli General Plc v Gaca* [2004] EWCA Civ 373; [2004] 1 W.L.R. 2683; Administration of Justice Act 1982, s.5; Social Security (Recovery of Benefits) Act 1997.

insurer[758]); or by reason of the fact that the victim is compensated for the loss under some other contract with a third party,[759] or that gratuitous benefits have been conferred on the victim in respect of the loss by a third party[760] who was under no legal obligation to act in this way.[761] Nor will damages be reduced merely because the injured party has resold the defective subject-matter for more than the contract price. In *Hussey v Eels*[762] the claimants had been induced to buy a house as their home by a misrepresentation[763] that there had been no subsidence. More than two years later, they decided to demolish the house and resold the site for one-and-a-half times the price which they had paid, having obtained planning permission for two dwellings on the site. On the assumption that this resale yielded a profit[764] to the claimants, it was held that this was not to be taken into account: the wrong which had caused their loss had not also caused the gain as the resale was "not . . . part of a continuous transaction of which the purchase . . . was the inception".[765] Similarly, where a buyer is entitled to damages based on the market price, those damages will not normally be reduced on the ground that he has made a good bargain by buying a substitute below the market price. But if a buyer who has rightfully rejected goods then buys *those very same goods* from the seller below the market (and the contract) price, this fact will be taken into account to reduce or extinguish the seller's liability.[766]

(d) Contributory Negligence[767]

20–123   Where the injured party fails to perform the "duty" to mitigate, his damages are reduced because it can be said that he is at fault in failing to avoid loss. He may also be at fault in the sense of actually helping to bring about the loss or the event causing it.[768] In the law of tort, such conduct may lead to a defence of "contributory negligence". At common law, it in some cases totally barred the injured party's claim, while in others it was completely ignored, so that he recovered in

---

[758] *Mark Rowlands Ltd v Berni Inns Ltd* [1986] Q.B. 211; *Bristol & West BS v May, May & Merrimans (No.2)* [1998] 1 W.L.R. 306.

[759] *Gardner v Marsh Parsons* [1997] 1 W.L.R. 489. For a possible qualification of this principle where a settlement agreement between one of two wrongdoers and the victim on its true construction covers the loss resulting from both breaches, see the discussion at para.13–016, above of *Heaton v Axa Equity and Law Life Assurance Society Plc* [2002] UKHL 15; [2002] 2 A.C. 329, where the agreement was held to release the other wrongdoer.

[760] Not where the benefit is conferred by the party in breach: *Williams v BOC Gases Ltd* [2000] I.C.R. 1181; cf. (in tort), *Hunt v Severs* [1994] 2 A.C. 350.

[761] *Merrett v Capitol Indemnity Corp* [1991] 1 Lloyd's Rep. 169; *Linklaters Business Services v Sir Robert McAlpine Ltd* [2010] EWHC 2931 (TCC) at [159]–[163]; cf. (in tort) *Giles v Thompson* [1994] 1 A.C. 142 at 166, where the point is left open.

[762] [1990] 2 Q.B. 227.

[763] Not incorporated in the contract, so that the cause of action was in tort; but the judgment is based on earlier decisions in contract cases; cf. *Komercni Bank AS v Stone & Rolls Ltd* [2002] EWHC 2263; [2003] 1 Lloyd's Rep. 383 at [167] (fraud).

[764] This depended on the cost of comparable accommodation at the time of the resale, as "The [claimants] were not property speculators but residents" [1990] 2 Q.B. 227 at 233; cf. (in tort) *Dominion Mosaics & Tile Co Ltd v Trafalgar Trucking Co Ltd* [1990] 2 All E.R. 246 at 252.

[765] [1990] 2 Q.B. 227 at 241; cf. *Needler Financial Services v Taber* [2002] 3 All E.R. 501; *Primavera v Allied Dunbar Assurance Plc* [2002] EWCA Civ 1327; [2003] P.N.L.R. 12.

[766] *R Pagnan Fratelli v Corbisa Industrial Agropacuaria Ltd* [1970] 1 W.L.R. 1306; this case differs from the *British Westinghouse* case (which it purports to follow) in that the opportunity to buy the goods more cheaply would never have arisen but for the seller's breach.

[767] Williams, *Joint Torts and Contributory Negligence*, para.59; Swanton, 55 A.L.J. 278.

[768] See above, para.20–097.

full. The Law Reform (Contributory Negligence) Act 1945 now provides that, where a person suffers damage as a result partly of his own "fault" and partly of the "fault" of another person, his claim is not to be defeated, but his damages are to be reduced in proportion to his degree of responsibility.

The Law Reform (Contributory Negligence) Act 1945. Whether the 1945   **20–124** Act applies in cases of breach of contract depends on the interpretation of "fault" in the Act which is defined as

> "negligence, breach of statutory duty, or other act or omission which gives rise to liability in tort or would, apart from this Act, give rise to the defence of contributory negligence".[769]

It has been argued that this includes *all* negligence, whether contractual[770] or tortious, and all *other* acts giving rise to liability in tort.[771] But the word "other" supports the view that negligence is here used in its tortious sense.[772]

It does not, however, follow from this interpretation of "fault" that the Act can never apply to cases of breach of contract. Two further distinctions must be drawn. The first is between breaches of contract that are, and those that are not, negligent. Here the phrase "negligent breach of contract" refers to situations in which liability arises for breach of a contractual duty of care[773]—not to cases in which liability for breach of contract is strict,[774] but the breach happens to have been committed negligently.[775] The second distinction is between breaches of contract which amount also to torts and those which do not. The content of a contractual duty of care is often the same as that of the duty of care which the law of tort would impose, even if there were no contract between the parties; and in such cases the same careless conduct prima facie gives rise to liability both for breach of contract and in tort.[776] For example, the liability of many professional persons for breach of the duties of care that they owe to their clients arises both in contract and tort.[777] The same is true of duties arising out of a number of other contractual relationships, such as those between carrier and passenger, employer and

---

[769] s.4. For an extension to include "product liability" see Consumer Protection Act 1987, s.6.
[770] See below, at fnn.773 and 776–778.
[771] Williams, above (fn.767).
[772] *Forsikringsaktieselskapet Vesta v Butcher* [1989] A.C. 852, CA; affirmed ibid. at 880 et seq., without reference to this point; Newman 53 M.L.R. 201; cf. (in another statutory context) *Société Commerciale de Réassurance v ERAS International Ltd* [1992] 1 Lloyd's Rep. 570.
[773] *Quinn v Burch Bros (Builders) Ltd* [1966] 2 Q.B. 370 at 378–379 (affirmed on other grounds; ibid. at 381).
[774] cf. above, paras 17–064—17–065.
[775] *Quinn v Burch Bros (Builders) Ltd*, above, at 378–379.
[776] *Henderson v Merrett Syndicates Ltd* [1995] 2 A.C. 145 at 193.
[777] *Esso Petroleum Co Ltd v Mardon* [1976] Q.B. 801 at 819; *Arenson v Arenson* [1977] A.C. 405 at 420–421; *Forsikringsaktieselskapet Vesta v Butcher* [1989] A.C. 852 at 860 (affirmed on other grounds ibid. at 880 et seq.); *Murphy v Brentwood DC* [1991] 1 A.C. 398 at 465; *The Superhulls Cover Case (No.2)* [1990] 2 Lloyd's Rep. 431; *Henderson v Merrett Syndicates Ltd* [1995] 2 A.C. 145; *South Australia Asset Management Corp v York Montague Ltd* [1997] A.C. 191 at 211; *Nykreditbank v Edward Erdman Group* [1997] 1 W.L.R. 1327 at 1368. After the *Henderson* case, it seems that a solicitor's liability for negligence will prima facie arise in both contract and in tort: see *Bristol & West BS v Mothew* [1998] Ch. 1 at 25, 26; Kaye, 100 L.Q.R. 680.

employee, bailor and bailee, or occupier of premises and visitor.[778] The breach will not, however, amount to a tort where the imposition of a tortious duty would be "so inconsistent with the applicable contract that . . . the parties must be taken to have agreed that the tortious remedy is to be limited or excluded".[779] This possibility is illustrated by a case[780] in which a building subcontractor had entered into a direct contract with the building owner (and not merely into one with the main contractor[781]). The court inferred from the nature of this arrangement that the parties had intended the relationship between owner and sub-contractor to be governed by the contract alone, so that the sub-contractor was not liable to the owner in tort. It follows from these distinctions that three categories of cases must be considered in discussing the application of the 1945 Act to cases involving breach of contract.[782]

20–125   **Breach of strict contractual duty alone.** The first category is where the defendant commits a breach of a strict contractual duty; and the claimant is careless. The Act does not apply: A's conduct, not being an act or omission giving rise to liability in tort falls outside the definition of "fault".[783] Hence at common law the result will depend on which party's conduct caused the loss.[784]

20–126   **Breach of contractual duty of care alone.** In the second category of case, the defendant commits a breach of a contractual duty of care; his conduct does not also amount to a tort, because the relations of the parties are intended to be governed by the contract alone[785]; and the claimant is also careless. Following the decision of the House of Lords in *Henderson v Merrett Syndicates Ltd*,[786] the circumstances in which the defendant is not also liable in tort are likely to be very

---

[778] *Bagot v Stevens, Scanlan & Co Ltd* [1966] 1 Q.B. 197, at 204–205; cf. *Matthews v Kuwait Bechtel Corp* [1959] 2 Q.B. 57; *Sayers v Harlow Urban DC* [1958] 1 W.L.R. 623; *Johnson v Coventry Churchill International Ltd* [1992] 3 All E.R. 14 at 22–23; *The Angelic Grace* [1995] 1 Lloyd's Rep. 87 at 91; *Spring v Guardian Ins Plc* [1995] 2 A.C. 296 at 320; cf. 340. But where the same facts are alleged to give rise to a claim in contract and in tort, the injured party cannot, after failing in contract, succeed by simply reclassifying his claim as one in tort: *Tai Hing Cotton Mill Ltd v Liu Chong Hing Bank* [1986] A.C. 80 at 107; *The Maira (No.3)* [1990] 1 A.C. 637 at 650 (reversed on other grounds 1990] 1 A.C. 637 at 672 et seq.); *Reid v Rush and Tompkins Group Plc* [1990] 1 W.L.R. 212; *The Good Luck* [1990] 1 Q.B. 818 at 900 (reversed on other grounds [1992] 1 A.C. 233).

[779] *Henderson v Merrett Syndicates Ltd* [1995] 2 A.C. 145 at 194.

[780] *Greater Nottingham Co-operative Society Ltd v Cementation Piling & Foundation Ltd* [1989] Q.B. 71; cf. *Tai Hing Cotton Mill Ltd v Liu Chong, Hing Bank* [1986] A.C. 80 at 107; *Johnstone v Bloomsbury Health Authority* [1992] Q.B. 333; *Scally v Southern Health & Social Services Board* [1992] 1 A.C. 294 at 303; *Ashmore v Corp of Lloyd's* [1992] 2 Lloyd's Rep. 563 at 568; *Aiken v Stewart Wrightson Members Agency Ltd* [1995] 1 W.L.R. 1281; *Robinson v PE Jones (Contractors) Ltd* [2011] EWCA Civ 9.

[781] cf. above, para.14–049.

[782] *Forsikringsaktieselskapet Vesta v Butcher* [1986] 2 All E.R. 488 at 508, affirmed [1989] A.C. 852, without reference to this point.

[783] *Basildon DC v J E Lesser Properties* [1985] Q.B. 839 (as explained in *Forsikringsaktieselskapet Vesta v Butcher* [1989] A.C. 852 at 865, affirmed ibid. at 880 et seq., without reference to this point); *The Good Luck* [1990] 1 Q.B. 818 at 904 (reversed on other grounds [1992] 1 A.C. 233); *Barclays Bank Plc v Fairclough Building Ltd* [1995] Q.B. 214; *Anglian Water Services Ltd v Crawshaw Robbins & Co Ltd* [2001] B.L.R. 173.

[784] See above, para.20–095. See also *Young v Purdy* [1996] 2 F.L.R. 795; *Schering Agrochemicals Ltd v Resibel NV SA*, unreported, November 26, 1992; Burrows 109 L.Q.R. 175

[785] See fnn.779 and 780, above.

[786] [1995] 2 A.C. 145.

limited, but for cases falling within this category, the Act does not apply[787]; the defendant's conduct may have been contractually negligent, but for the purpose of the Act it does not amount to "negligence . . . or other act or omission which gives rise to liability in tort."

Breach of contractual duty of care also amounting to a tort. In the third **20–127** category of case, the defendant commits a breach of a contractual duty of care; his conduct also amounts to a tort; and the claimant is also careless. The Act can apply to such a situation: e.g. where the claimant is injured partly through his own carelessness and partly through circumstances amounting both to a breach of contract by the defendant and to a breach of his duties as an occupier of dangerous premises[788]; or where loss is caused partly by the professional negligence of the defendant, amounting both to a breach of contract and to a tort against his client, and partly by that client's own carelessness[789]: e.g. where a mortgage lender suffers loss partly because of the negligence of a valuer engaged by him in overvaluing the security and partly because of the lender's own imprudent lending policy.[790] There was formerly some support for the view that, even in cases in this category, the Act applied only where the claim was framed in tort.[791] But this view has been rightly rejected[792] as it is not supported by the definition of "fault" in the Act, and as it would be unsatisfactory in enabling an injured party to evade the Act by simply suing in contract where he also had a claim in tort. On the other hand the Act would not apply where, though both contracting parties were careless, the court took the view that the loss was entirely caused by the carelessness of one: e.g. that of the client[793] or that of his professional adviser.[794]

---

[787] *Forsikringsaktieselskapet Vesta v Butcher* [1989] A.C. 852 at 866 (affirmed ibid. at 880 et seq., without reference to this point); *Raflatac v Eade* [1999] 1 Lloyd's Rep. 506. The Law Commission recommended that in cases of this kind the claimant's damages should be reduced on account of his contributory negligence, except where the contract expressly or by implication excludes this defence: Law Com. No.219 (1993) paras 4.7–15, 23–25. This may be the effect, in practice, of the decision in *Henderson v Merrett Syndicates Ltd* [1995] 2 A.C. 145, as a consequence of which very few cases will fall in the second category, rather than the third; below, para.20–127.

[788] *Sayers v Harlow Urban DC*, above, fn.778; cf. *Targett v Torfaen BC* [1992] 3 All E.R. 27.

[789] *Forsikringsaktieselskapet Vesta v Butcher* [1989] A.C. 852, affirmed ibid. at 880 et seq., without reference to this point (not followed in Australia: *Astley v Austrust Ltd* [1999] Lloyd's Rep. P.N. 758); *The Superhulls Cover Case (No.2)* [1990] 2 Lloyd's Rep. 431; cf. *Barclays Bank Plc v Fairclough Building Ltd (No.2)* [1995] I.R.L.R. 605 (cf. *Robinson v PE Jones (Contractors) Ltd* [2011] EWCA Civ 9 where the application of the Act was not in issue); *Bristol & West BS v Fancy & Jackson* [1997] 4 All E.R. 582 at 625; *Sumitomo Bank Ltd v Banque Bruxelles Lambert SA* [1997] 1 Lloyd's Rep. 487; *Nationwide BS v J R Jones* [1999] Lloyd's Rep. P.N. 414.

[790] *Platform Home Loans v Oyston Shipways Ltd* [2000] 2 A.C. 190. The reduction of damages on account of the claimant's contributory negligence is in such cases calculated on the loss actually suffered (the "basic loss") and not on the lower amount for which the defendant is responsible under the "scope of duty" test (above, para.20–023).

[791] *Sole v W J Hallt* [1973] Q.B. 574; *The Shinjitsu Maru (No.5)* [1985] 1 W.L.R. 1270; cf. *Basildon DC v J E Lesser (Properties) Ltd* [1985] Q.B. 839 at 849 (as to which see above, fn.783); Andrews [1986] C.L.J. 8; Burrows 101 L.Q.R. 161; Spowart-Taylor 49 M.L.R. 102.

[792] *Forsikringsaktieselskapet Vesta v Butcher* [1989] A.C. 852 (where at 875 in the Court of Appeal, Neill L.J. acknowledged the error of his former contrary view in *The Shinjitsu Maru (No.5)*, above).

[793] *O'Connor v B D Kirby & Co* [1972] 1 Q.B. 90 where the trial court's view that the client should recover *two-thirds* of the loss was described at 99 as "somewhat novel"; cf. *Quinn v Burch Bros (Builders)Ltd* [1966] 2 Q.B. 370; *County Ltd v Girozentrale Securities* [1996] 3 All E.R. 834; *Kapur v J W Francis & Co (No.2)* [1999] Lloyd's Rep. P.N. 834.

[794] *UCB Corporate Services Ltd v Clyde & Co* [2000] 2 All E.R. (Comm) 256 at 265.

20–128   **Wrong committed by injured party.** In the three situations so far discussed, the defendant is guilty of a breach of contract and the claimant's conduct is careless; but that conduct does not amount to a legal wrong against the defendant. Where the loss to each party results in part from a breach of contract committed by one of them (A) against the other (B) and in part by an independent legal wrong committed by B against A, then the losses may be apportioned[795] (quite apart from the Act) on the ground that they resulted from two independent actionable wrongs. Each party can then recover in respect of his own loss to the extent that it was caused by the other's wrongful act. This was, for example, held to be the case where goods belonging to the tenant of part of a warehouse, and the warehouse itself, were damaged as a result partly of the tenant's breach of covenant to repair and partly of omissions of the landlord giving rise to liability in tort. Each party was held liable for the other's loss to the extent that it had been caused by his own wrong.[796] The position would have been the same if the wrongs of both parties had been breaches of contract, e.g. if the tenant had undertaken to do internal and the landlord external repairs and the damage had been due to the failure of both to perform their respective undertakings. But the present line of reasoning cannot apply where only one party (the defendant) was guilty of a legal wrong, while the conduct of the claimant which is alleged to have contributed to his loss did not amount to such a wrong.[797]

20–129   **Where no wrong is committed by the defendant.** All the situations so far discussed must be distinguished from those in which the defendant's contractual undertaking is to compensate the claimant for a loss not brought about by any act or omission on the part of the defendant at all: e.g. where a bank issues travellers' cheques to a customer and promises to compensate him for their face value in the event of his losing them. If the loss is due to the customer's failure to guard against loss, the bank may, if the contract so provides,[798] escape liability for the loss; but such cases raise no issues of contributory negligence as no wrong, leading to the loss, is committed by the bank.

5. LIQUIDATED DAMAGES, DEPOSIT AND PART-PAYMENT[799]

(a) Liquidated Damages[800]

(i) *Distinction between penalty and liquidated damages*

20–130   A contract may provide for the payment of a fixed sum on breach.[801] Such a provision may serve the perfectly proper purpose of enabling a party to know in

---

[795] It is an open question whether there can be such apportionment where B's loss is caused partly by A's legal wrong against B and partly by conduct by B amounting to a legal wrong against a third party (C): see *Standard Chartered Bank v Pakistan National Shipping Co (No.2)* [2000] 1 Lloyd's Rep. 218 at 230, 236 (reversed on another point [2002] UKHL 43; [2003] 1 A.C. 959), where the wrongs committed by A against B and by B against C amounted, not to breach of contract, but to the tort of deceit.

[796] *Tenant Radiant Heat Ltd v Warrington Development Corp* [1988] 1 E.G.L.R. 41; distinguished from contributory negligence cases in *The Good Luck* [1990] 1 Q.B. 818 at 904 (reversed on other grounds [1992] 1 A.C. 233); applied in *W Lamb Ltd v J Jarvis & Sons Plc* [1999] 60 Con. L.R. 1.

[797] *Raflatac Ltd v Eade* [1999] 1 Lloyd's Rep. 507 at 510, where the defendant's wrong was also said at 511 to have been the "dominant cause" of the loss.

[798] *Braithwaite v Thomas Cook Travellers Cheques Ltd* [1989] Q.B. 553; contrast *El Awadi v Bank of Credit and Commerce International SA* [1990] 1 Q.B. 606.

[799] Gullifer, in Burrows & Peel (eds), *Commercial Remedies*.

[800] Carter and Peden 23 J.C.L. 157.

[801] Or some other form of sanction: see below, para.20–138.

advance what his liability will be; and of avoiding difficult questions of quantification. On the other hand the courts are reluctant to allow a party, under such a
provision, to recover a sum which is obviously and considerably greater than his
loss. They have therefore divided such provisions into two categories: penalty
clauses, which are invalid,[802] and liquidated damages clauses, which will generally
be upheld. It will be seen below[803] that while the courts have formulated a number
of rules to determine whether a clause is penal the current approach is to regard
this as "a comparatively broad and simple question, that will not normally call for
detailed analysis of the contractual background."[804]

A question of construction. A clause is penal if it provides for "a payment of   20–131
money stipulated as *in terrorem* of the offending party",[805] or, as it has been put
more recently, if the contractual function of the clause is "deterrent rather than
compensatory".[806] If, on the other hand, the clause is a "genuine"[807] attempt by
the parties to estimate in advance the loss which will result from the breach, it is
a liquidated damages clause. This is so even though the stipulated sum is not
precisely equivalent to the injured party's loss.[808] The question whether a clause
is penal depends on its construction and on the surrounding circumstances at the
time of contracting (not at the time of breach[809]). In answering this question, the
fact that the payment is described in the contract as a "penalty" or as "liquidated
damages" may be relevant,[810] but it is doubtful whether much, if any, weight
should be attached to it.[811] Clauses in identical terms may be held penal or not,
according to the subject-matter of the contracts and to the circumstances in which
the contracts were made.[812] It seems that a clause may be severed so as to exclude
any penal element.[813]

Rules of construction. In *Dunlop Pneumatic Tyre Co Ltd v New Garage &*   20–132
Motor Co Ltd[814] Lord Dunedin formulated four rules for the construction of a
liquidated damages clause:

(a) "It will be held to be a penalty if the sum stipulated for is extravagant
and unconscionable in amount in comparison with the greatest loss that

---

[802] Unless in a form which parties to the kind of contract are, by legislation, required to use: *Golden Bay Realty Pte Ltd v Orchard Twelve Investments Pte Ltd* [1991] 1 W.L.R. 981.

[803] See below, para.20–132.

[804] *Murray v Leisureplay Plc* [2005] EWCA Civ 963; [2005] I.R.L.R. 946 at [113].

[805] *Dunlop Pneumatic Tyre Co Ltd v New Garage & Motor Co Ltd* [1915] A.C. 79 at 86.

[806] *Lordsvale Finance Ltd v Bank of Zambia* [1996] Q.B. 752 at 762G, approved as the "recasting" of the test by Buxton L.J. in *Murray v Leisureplay Plc* [2005] EWCA Civ 963; [2005] I.R.L.R. 946 at [110]; cf. *Cine Bes Filmcilik v United International Pictures* [2003] EWCA Civ 1669; [2004] 1 C.L.C. 401 at [13]; *The Office of Fair Trading v Abbey National Plc* [2008] EWHC 875 (Comm) at [295].

[807] See below, fn.858.

[808] *Murray v Leisureplay Plc* above, fn.804 at [111].

[809] *Dunlop Pneumatic Tyre Co Ltd v New Garage & Motor Co Ltd* [1915] A.C. 79 at 87; *Philips Hong Kong v Attorney-General of Hong Kong* (1993) 61 Build. L.R. 41.

[810] *Willson v Love* [1896] 1 Q.B. 626 at 630; *Alder v Moore* [1961] 2 Q.B. 57 at 65.

[811] *Kemble v Farren* (1829) 6 Bing. 141 ("liquidated damages" held penalty); *Elphinstone v Monkland Iron & Coal Co Ltd* (1886) 11 App.Cas. 332 ("penalty" held liquidated damages); cf. *Pagnan & Fratelli v Coprosol SA* [1981] 1 Lloyd's Rep. 283.

[812] Contrast *Phonographic Equipment* (1958) *Ltd v Muslu* [1961] 1 W.L.R. 1379 with *Lombank Ltd v Excell* [1964] 1 Q.B. 415.

[813] *The Angelic Star* [1988] 1 Lloyd's Rep 122 at 126–127; cf. *Dalkia Utilities Services Plc v Celtech International Ltd* [2006] EWHC 63; [2006] 1 Lloyd's Rep 599 at [123].

[814] [1915] A.C. 79 at 87–88.

could conceivably be proved to have followed from the breach": to quote a rather far-fetched example, a clause in a contract to do building work worth £50 would be penal if it provided that the builder should pay £1 million if he failed to do the work.[815]

(b)   "It will be held to be a penalty if the breach consists only[816] in not paying a sum of money, and the sum stipulated is a sum greater than the sum which ought to have been paid". A clause making a debtor liable to pay £1,000 if he failed to pay £50 on the due day would thus be penal. One explanation formerly given for this rule was that the only amount recoverable, as damages for failure to pay money when due, was interest, and then only when available by statute or by special agreement[817]; but this reasoning is no longer convincing now that damages can be recovered for loss caused by such a breach.[818] Alternatively, it was suggested that the rule was based on an equitable jurisdiction to reform unconscionable bargains.[819] While at the time this explanation may have been suspect because the rule applied even though the contract was fair,[820] it may now carry greater weight in light of the "broader approach" referred to below.[821]

(c)   There is a presumption (but no more than a presumption) that a clause is penal when "a single lump sum is made payable . . . on the occurrence of one or more or all of several events, some of which may occasion serious and others but trifling damage". Under this rule, a sum is not presumed to be penal if it is expressly proportioned to the seriousness of the breach, e.g. if a lease provides for payment of £100 *per acre*[822] of land not restored to its former condition, or if a contractor agrees to pay £500 *per week* for delay.[823] Such stipulations are only penal if extravagant.

On the other hand, a sum payable on one of several events will be treated as penal if one of those events is the non-payment of a smaller sum,[824] or if one event is *bound* to cause greater loss than another.[825] A sum may, therefore, be regarded as penal if it *might* have become due on a trifling breach, even though the breach which *actually* occurred was quite a serious one, and one for which the sum could be regarded as a genuine pre-estimate.[826] In this way, the rule can invalidate perfectly fair

---

[815] *Clydebank Engineering Co v Don Jose Ramos Isquierdo y Castaneda* [1905] A.C. 6 at 10.

[816] See *Thomas P Gonzalez Corp v F R Waring (International) Pty Ltd* [1980] 2 Lloyd's Rep. 160 at 163 (rule inapplicable where breach consists of buyer's failure to *accept and* pay).

[817] [1915] A.C. 79 at 87.

[818] See above, para.20–061.

[819] [1915] A.C. 79 at 87.

[820] As in *Betts v Burch* (1859) 4 H. & N. 506. This case was decided in a common law court before the Judicature Acts 1873–75; but the same rule was recognised, if reluctantly, in the Chancery Division after 1875: *Wallis v Smith* (1882) 21 Ch.D. 243.

[821] See below, para.20–139 and see, in particular, the approach taken to provisions for "default interest": below, para.20–135.

[822] *Elphinstone v Monkland Iron & Coal Co* (1886) 11 App.Cas. 332.

[823] *Clydebank Engineering* case [1905] A.C. 6; *Philips Hong Kong v Attorney-General of Hong Kong* (1993) 61 Build.L.R. 41. Such a provision will not operate where the contract is totally abandoned (since if it did so operate the payments would have to go on forever): *British Glanzstoff Mfg Co v General Accident, etc. Co* [1913] A.C. 143.

[824] As in *Kemble v Farren* (1829) 6 Bing. 141; cf. *Duffen v FRABO SpA* [2000] 1 Lloyd's Rep. 180 at 196.

[825] *Willson v Love* [1896] 1 Q.B. 626; cf. below, para.20–145.

[826] *Ariston SRL v Charly Records Ltd*, *Financial Times*, March 21, 1990.

bargains. The courts will do their best to avoid such results by constru-ing the contract so as to make the sum payable only on major breaches, for which it is a valid pre-estimate.[827] Even where this construction is not possible, it is submitted that the validity of the clause should depend on what is likely to be its normal operation. It should not be struck down merely because, in extraordinary circumstances (which have not in fact occurred), the stipulated sum might greatly exceed the claimant's loss.[828]

(d)   "It is no obstacle to the sum stipulated being a genuine pre-estimate of damage that the consequences of breach are such as to make precise pre-estimation an impossibility. On the contrary, that is just the situation when pre-estimated damage was the true bargain between the parties". Thus in *Dunlop Pneumatic Tyre Co Ltd v New Garage & Motor Co Ltd* itself the defendants bought tyres and agreed with the sellers that they would not (i) tamper with the manufacturer's marks; (ii) sell to the public below list price; (iii) sell to any person "suspended" by the sellers; (iv) exhibit or export the tyres without the seller's written consent. They further agreed to pay £5 to the sellers for every tyre sold or offered in breach of the agreement. The defendants sold to the public below list price. It was held that the provision for payment of £5 per tyre was not penal. The presumption that a sum payable on several events was penal was "rebutted by the very fact that the damage caused by each and every one of those events, however varying in importance, [was] of such an uncertain nature that it cannot be accurately ascertained".[829] But even in such circumstances the sum will be penal if it is extravagant.[830]

Acceleration clauses. The second of Lord Dunedin's rules does not apply   **20–133** merely because a contract under which a sum of money is payable in instalments provides that, on default of any payment, the whole balance is to become imme-diately due.[831] Such a clause is said to accelerate, and not to increase, the liability of the debtor. But early payment in fact is generally more expensive to the debtor; and a provision for an extra payment equal in value to this expense would almost certainly be penal.[832] In strict logic, such acceleration clauses should therefore fall within Lord Dunedin's second rule; the fact that they have been held not to do so is an indication of the courts' reluctance to apply that rule. Cases of real extortion can be dealt with under Lord Dunedin's first rule; and it seems that under this rule an acceleration clause may be penal.[833]

---

[827] *Webster v Bosanquet* [1912] A.C. 394; cf. *Murray v Leisureplay Plc* [2005] EWCA Civ 963; [2005] I.R.L.R. 946, below fn.862.

[828] See *Philips Hong Kong Ltd v Attorney-General of Hong Kong* (1993) 61 Build.L.R. 41; *International Leasing Corp (Vic) Ltd v Aiken* (1966) 85 W.N. (Pt.1) N.S.W. 766.

[829] [1915] A.C. 79 at 96; cf. *Robophone Facilities Ltd v Blank* [1966] 1 W.L.R. 1428.

[830] *Ford Motor Co (England) Ltd v Armstrong* (1915) 31 T.L.R. 267.

[831] *Protector Loan Co v Grice* (1879–80) L.R. 5 Q.B.D. 592; *Wallingford v Mutual Society* (1880) 5 App.Cas. 685; cf. *Sport International Bussum BV v Inter-Footwear Ltd* [1984] 1 W.L.R. 776 at 793, and *White & Carter (Councils) Ltd v McGregor* [1962] A.C. 413, where it was conceded that the acceleration clause was valid; *The Angelic Star* [1988] 1 Lloyd's Rep. 122.

[832] A stipulation for accelerated payment of a loan *plus interest* for the *whole* contractual period was said to be penal in *The Angelic Star* [1988] 1 Lloyd's Rep. 122 at 125; applied in *County Leasing Ltd v East* [2007] EWHC 2907 (QB).

[833] This seems to be the best explanation for *Wadham Stringer Finance Ltd v Meany* [1981] 1 W.L.R. 39 at 48, where such a clause was said to be subject to the rules as to penalties, though it was not penal in effect.

20–134   **Discounts and incentive payments.** As explained below, the rule against penalties only applies to a sum, or sanction, payable on breach.[834] The parties can therefore circumvent the rule by providing that a high sum is to be paid as the contract price, subject to a discount if payment is made by a specified date; or by providing for the payment to be made by a third party under a performance bond.[835] These provisions for acceleration,[836] for discounts, and for payments by third parties may be perfectly fair; and the relative ease with which Lord Dunedin's second rule can, by use of them, be evaded suggests that it serves no useful purpose and should be abandoned.

20–135   **Default interest.** The foregoing submissions derive support from the judicial treatment of clauses which increase the rate of interest payable by a borrower in default. Such clauses are not penal if they operate prospectively only and if the increase is no more than a "modest"[837] one. The reason for this view is that the very fact of the borrower's default makes him a less good credit risk from the time of default and therefore provides a "good commercial reason"[838] for the increase. Even though such a stipulation may not be a genuine estimate of damage, it will therefore not be "*in terrorem*" of the offending party and hence not penal except where the increase is an "exceptionally large"[839] one.[840]

20–136   **Actual loss, or recoverable loss.** It seems that, if the stipulated sum is a genuine pre-estimate of the *actual* loss, the clause is valid even though part of that loss is *irrecoverable* because it is too remote[841]; and that it is similarly not penal if it stipulates for payment to a contracting party of an actual loss that is likely to be suffered, not by him, but by a third party.[842] It may be necessary "to take account" of the duty to mitigate, but this will not be significant in cases where it is difficult to draft a clause which can sensibly do so.[843]

20–137   **Nature of the breach.** The rule against penalties only applies to a sum, or sanction, payable on breach.[844] Where there has been a breach, the rule will therefore apply, and the nature of the breach may be relevant to the question of whether the sum stipulated is penal. Where the defendant is guilty of a non-

---

[834] See below, para.20–144.

[835] ibid.

[836] See above, para.20–133.

[837] *Lordsvale Finance Ltd v Bank of Zambia* [1996] Q.B. 752 at 767.

[838] ibid. at 763.

[839] ibid. at 767.

[840] Cf. *Jeancharm Ltd v Barnet Football Club Ltd* [2003] EWCA Civ 58; 92 Con. L.R. 26 (260 per cent p.a.), not concerned with a loan agreement, but with a failure to pay; see also *Taiwan Scot Co Ltd v The Masters Golf Co Ltd* [2009] EWCA Civ 685 at [17] (15 per cent p.a. not penal); *North Shore Ventures Ltd v Anstead Holdings Inc* [2010] EWHC 1485 (Ch); [2010] 2 Lloyd's Rep. 265 (5 per cent increase with monthly compounding not penal).

[841] *Robophone Facilities Ltd v Blank* [1966] 1 W.L.R. 1428 at 1448. The reasoning of Diplock L.J. would seem, if anything, to be reinforced by the reformulated approach to remoteness taken by some of their lordships in *The Achilleas* [2008] UKHL 48; [2009] 1 A.C. 61 (above, para.20–110) and it is respectfully submitted that the contrary view of Blair J. in *The Paragon* [2009] EWHC 551 (Comm); [2009] 1 Lloyd's Rep. 658 at [22] is open to doubt (affirmed [2009] EWCA Civ 555; [2009] 2 Lloyd's Rep. 688 without explicit reference to this point, but see at [36]).

[842] See *Alfred McAlpine Construction Ltd v Panatown Ltd* (1998) 58 Const. L.R. 58 at 92, reversed, on other grounds [2001] 1 A.C. 518; that payment would have to be held by the payee for the third party, above, para.14–043.

[843] *Murray v Leisureplay Plc* above, fn.804 at [116]

[844] See below, para.20–144.

repudiatory breach, but the contract has been terminated (e.g. under an express provision[845]), he is only liable for the loss which flows from that breach. A clause which stipulated for a sum to be paid on termination which included the loss flowing from the premature determination of the contract (the "full loss of bargain") is likely to be penal. Where, however, the defendant is guilty of a repudiatory breach[846] (e.g. breach of a "condition"[847]) the defendant would be liable for the full loss of bargain and the same clause is therefore unlikely to be penal.[848]

Penalties not confined to payment of money. The penalty clauses with   20–138
which the foregoing discussion is concerned are all stipulations for the payment of *money*. It is equally possible for a clause which requires some other performance from the party in breach to be a penalty.[849] This could, for example, be the position where the clause required that party to make a "payment in kind", or to transfer shares at an undervalue.[850]

A "broader approach". The rule against penalties is difficult to reconcile with   20–139
the principle of freedom of contract.[851] Bearing in mind the protections generally available against "unfair terms",[852] or unfair contracts,[853] it is open to question why there should be a rule, or set of rules, to control one particular type of clause[854] in circumstances where its enforceability is not in doubt under those other protections. This no doubt explains why the courts are "predisposed" to uphold liquidated damages clauses, in particular in the case of commercial contracts between parties of "comparable bargaining power",[855] and why some of the rules of construction set out by Lord Dunedin must now be regarded as of doubtful utility.[856] While the rule against penalties continues to apply, and it is still necessary to ask, at least in the first instance, whether the clause in question amounted to a genuine pre-estimate of loss, the courts have emphasised that they should adopt a "broader approach".[857] It has already been noted that a clause will not necessarily be struck down as a penalty even if it was not a genuine pre-

---

[845] See above, para.18–061.

[846] Whether the contract must have been terminated *for* the repudiatory breach is dealt with above: para.18–071.

[847] See above, para.18–039.

[848] *Lombard North Central Plc v Butterworth* [1987] Q.B. 527; *BNP Paribas v Wockhardt EU Operations (Swiss) AG* [2009] EWHC 3116 (Comm); 132 Con L.R. 177; *Office of Fair Trading v Ashbourne Management Services Ltd* [2011] EWHC 1237 (Ch) at [207].

[849] On the question of whether withholding a payment may amount to a penalty, see below, para. 20–146.

[850] *Jobson v Johnson* [1989] 1 W.L.R. 1026, where it was conceded that such a clause was penal.

[851] *Elsey v J.G. Collins Insurance Agencies Ltd* (1878) 83 D.L.R. (3d.) 1 at 15; cf. *Lehman Brothers Special Financing Inc v Carlton Communications Ltd* [2011] EWHC 718 (Ch) at [46].

[852] See above, ch.7.

[853] See above, chs 9, 10.

[854] In relation to other particular types of provision, such control has been the subject of legislation; most notably the Unfair Contract Terms Act 1977; above, para.7–050.

[855] *Alfred McAlpine Capital Projects Ltd v Tilebox Ltd* [2005] EWHC 281 (TCC); [2005] Build. L.R. 271 at [48] (where it is noted how few cases have resulted in the finding of a penalty); cf. *Philips Hong Kong v Attorney-General of Hong Kong* (1993) 61 Build.L.R. 41 at 59–60.

[856] See above, para.20–134.

[857] *Murray v Leisureplay Plc* [2005] EWCA Civ 963; [2005] I.R.L.R. 946 at [113]; *General Trading Company (Holdings) Ltd v Richmond Corporation Ltd* [2008] EWHC 1479 (Comm); [2008] 2 Lloyd's Rep. 475 at [133]; *Steria Ltd v Sigma Wireless Communications* 118 Con L.R. 177 at [100].

estimate of loss, if its inclusion in the contract was "commercially justifiable",[858] or not "oppressive" and it seems that this leaves room to take account of "market expectations".[859] The broader approach places most, if not all, of the emphasis on the first of the rules set out by Lord Dunedin such that "in most cases it will *only* be where a clause can be shown to be extravagant and unconscionable in relation to the greatest conceivable loss that a clause will properly be found to be a penalty clause."[860] On the basis of this broader approach, it has been held that the following do not amount to a penalty:[861] the payment of 12 months' gross salary and pension contributions to a director for unlawful termination of his service contract;[862] the payment of 50 per cent of net salary and 50 per cent of the agreed signing fee by a finance broker for failing to honour his employment contract;[863] the writing off of 90 per cent of the consideration for the purchase of shares where the seller failed to procure a loan guarantee;[864] and payment on the customer's default of 20 per cent of the purchase price for the construction of a yacht.[865]

(ii) *Effects of the distinction*

20–140   Often the stipulated sum will exceed the claimant's loss. In such a case, the claimant can nevertheless recover that sum if the stipulation is a liquidated damages clause, while if it is a penalty he cannot recover the stipulated sum but only the amount to which he would have been entitled if the contract had not contained the penalty clause.[866] This follows from the nature of the distinction between the two kinds of provision. Two further possibilities, however, require discussion.

20–141   **Stipulated sum intended to be below the estimated loss.** A clause may be intended to provide for payment of a sum below the estimated loss. Such a clause is not invalid as a penalty as its object is not to act *in terrorem*. In *Cellulose Acetate Silk Co Ltd v Widnes Foundry (1925) Ltd*[867] a contract for the construction of an acetone recovery plant provided that if completion was delayed the contractors were to pay "by way of penalty £20 per working week". The plant was completed 30 weeks late, during which period the owners suffered losses of £5,850. It was

---

[858] See above, para.20–135. This begs the question of what is meant by "genuine"; it is clear that the estimate need not prove to be accurate and the parties are allowed "a generous margin" (*Murray v Leisureplay*, above fn.857 at [43]), but it is hard to see how the additional interest imposed in cases like *Lordsvale* (above, fn.837) can even be viewed as a "genuine" estimate since, by definition, any additional interest would provide for recovery of more than the outstanding principal sum and the contract rate of interest; "genuine" may of course just mean anything not penal but that relegates it to the status of an ex post facto label rather than a test in its own right.

[859] *Murray v Leisureplay Plc* above at [70].

[860] *Tullett Prebon Group Ltd v El-Hajjali* [2008] EWHC 1924 (QB); [2008] I.R.L.R. 760 at [38], [74].

[861] In addition to the examples which follow, see the cases referred to at fn.840 above and *M&J Polymers Ltd v Imerys Minerals Ltd* [2008] EWHC 344; [2008] 1 Lloyd's Rep. 541.

[862] *Murray v Leisureplay Plc*, above (where, as a matter of construction, the payment was held to reduce *pro rata* for any notice given, and salary paid, short of 12 months).

[863] *Tullett Prebon Group Ltd v El-Hajjali*, above fn.860.

[864] *General Trading Company (Holdings) Ltd v Richmond Corporation Ltd* [2008] EWHC 1479 (Comm); [2008] 2 Lloyd's Rep. 475: see below, fn.899.

[865] *Azimut-Benetti SpA v Healey* [2010] EWHC 2234 (Comm); [2011] 1 Lloyd's Rep. 473.

[866] *Jobson v Johnson* [1989] 1 W.L.R. 1026 at 1038.

[867] [1933] A.C. 20; cf. *Tullett Prebon Group Ltd v El-Hajjali* [2008] EWHC 1924 (QB); [2008] I.R.L.R. 760 at [83].

held that they could recover £600 only. Both parties must have known that the actual loss would exceed £20 per week, so that one object of the clause was to limit the contractors' liability. But it was not a pure limitation clause, for the contractors would still have had to pay £20 per week even if the owners had lost less.[868] For this reason, liquidated damages clauses are probably not exemption clauses, and so not subject to the Unfair Contract Terms Act 1977,[869] though they may in certain circumstances be subject to the Unfair Terms in Consumer Contracts Regulations 1994.[870]

Effect of penalty where stipulated sum less than actual loss. The clause may be a penalty even though the stipulated sum falls short of the claimant's loss.[871] This apparently paradoxical situation can arise *either* because changing conditions have made an originally extravagant sum inadequate, *or* (though less likely now) because a perfectly reasonable sum is nevertheless penal on technical grounds (i.e. under the second or third rules of construction stated above[872]). The question then arises whether the clause is nevertheless effective to limit the defendant's liability to the amount of the penalty. According to one view, the clause is effective for this purpose; for penalty clauses are struck down to prevent oppression[873] and the party in breach cannot be oppressed by the clause when it actually works in his favour. But this view can cut across the general principle that the validity of contractual provisions should be determined once for all by reference to the time of contracting[874]; for under it a term which was originally invalid as a penalty could become valid as a limitation clause simply by reason of a change of circumstances. Hence in *Wall v Rederiaktiebolaget Lugudde*[875] it was held that a shipowner could disregard a penalty clause in a charterparty and recover his actual loss, which exceeded the amount of the penalty. In the *Cellulose Acetate* case[876] the question whether a penalty clause could always be disregarded in this way was left open as it is possible for a clause on its true construction to be both a penalty and a limitation clause. But this is an implausible construction of a clause which provides for payment of a fixed sum irrespective of proof of loss; and it seems that generally such a clause would be disregarded under the rule in *Wall's* case.

(iii) *Analogous provisions*

Other forms of pressure to perform. A number of other commonly found contractual provisions resemble penalties in their commercial purpose of putting pressure on a party to perform, but are nevertheless valid. This is, for example, true of acceleration clauses,[877] of discounts for punctual payment[878] and of express

20–142

20–143

---

[868] See above, para.7–019.

[869] See above, para.7–054.

[870] See below, para.20–147.

[871] Hudson 90 L.Q.R. 30; Gordon 90 L.Q.R 296; Hudson 91 L.Q.R. 20; Barton 92 L.Q.R. 20.

[872] See above, para.20–132(b) and (c).

[873] *Elsley v J G Collins Ins Agencies* (1978) 3 D.L.R. (3d) 1; cf. *Philips Hong Kong v Attorney-General of Hong Kong* (1993) 61 Build. L.R. 41; Hudson 101 L.Q.R. 480.

[874] See above, paras 7–079, 7–103, 11–064, 20–131.

[875] [1915] 3 K.B. 66 (not cited in the *Elsley* case, above); cf. *Dingwall v Burnett* 1912 S.C. 1097; *W & J Investments Ltd v Bunting* [1984] 1 N.S.W.R. 331.

[876] See above, fn.867.

[877] See above, para.20–133.

[878] See above, para.20–132(b).

provisions for termination on breach[879]; it is also sometimes true of provisions for the forfeiture of deposits and part payments to be discussed below.[880] Two further types of clauses, however, give rise to considerable dispute.

20–144   **Sums payable otherwise than on breach.** The rule against penalties applies only to sums payable *on breach* of the contract in which the stipulation for payment is contained. A clause under which a sum is payable *only* on some other event is therefore not a penalty. In *Alder v Moore*[881] a professional footballer received £500 from an insurance company in respect of an injury which was thought to have disabled him permanently; and he undertook to repay the money in the event of his again playing professional football. This was not a penalty since he committed no breach when he did play again, as he had made no promise not to do so. A "take or pay" clause is subject to the rule against penalties if the buyer is *obliged* to order a minimum quantity and fails to do so,[882] but it may be possible to impose the obligation to *pay* for a minimum quantity without imposing an obligation to order that quantity.[883] Again, a contract for the sale of goods may give the buyer the option of postponing the date on which he is to take delivery, on payment of a "carrying charge". Such a provision is not a penalty since the permitted delay is not a breach and the extra charge is the price which the buyer pays for exercising the option conferred on him by the contract.[884] The ease with which the rule against penalties may be evaded by employing the device of a "price variation" has led to the observation that such a clause may be "challengeable as a disguised penalty",[885] but the courts have, it seems, never gone that far.

Nor it seems is a sum a penalty where the liability to pay it arises, not on the breach itself, but only on an event triggered by the breach. This is the position where a lease provides that, on a tenant's failure to perform his covenant to repair, the landlord is to be entitled to execute the repairs and to recover the cost of so doing from the tenant. A claim for that amount is not a claim for damages but one for the agreed sum,[886] and is not subject to the law relating to penalties.[887] A

---

[879] See above, para.18–061.

[880] See below, para.20–148.

[881] [1961] 2 Q.B. 57; 77 L.Q.R. 300; Goff 24 M.L.R. 637.

[882] *M&J Polymers Ltd v Imerys Minerals Ltd* [2008] EWHC 344; [2008] 1 Lloyd's Rep. 541 (where the clause was not found to amount to a penalty in any event: above, fn.861).

[883] e.g. where the seller agrees to supply as much of the product as the buyer *may* order from time to time, but the buyer agrees to pay a sum which equates to the minimum order; cf. *Associated British Ports v Ferryways NV* [2008] EWHC 1265 (Comm); [2008] 2 Lloyd's Rep. 353, affirmed [2009] EWCA Civ 189; [2009] 1 Lloyd's Rep. without reference to this point.

[884] *Thomas P Gonzalez Corp v F R Waring (International) Pty Ltd* [1980] 2 Lloyd's Rep. 160; *Toepfer v Sosimage SpA* [1980] 2 Lloyd's Rep. 397 at 402; *Fratelli Moretti SpA v Nidera Handelscompagnie BV* [1981] 2 Lloyd's Rep. 47; *Lusograin Commercio Internacional de Cereas Ltda v Bunge AG* [1986] 2 Lloyd's Rep. 654; *The Bonde* [1991] 1 Lloyd's Rep. 136 at 145. But demurrage clauses in charterparties (above, para.7–019) assume that the detention of the ship is a breach and provide for the payment of liquidated damages: *The Lips* [1988] A.C. 395; contrast *The Paragon* [2009] EWCA Civ 555; [2009] 2 Lloyd's Rep. 688 (clause adjusting hire to the market rate not construed as the price for the option of late redelivery); cf. *Jones v Society of Lloyd's, The Times*, February 2, 2000 (revival of original debt on debtor's failure to perform settlement agreement); *The Office of Fair Trading v Abbey National Plc* [2008] EWHC 875 (Comm) (bank charges not payable for breach when overdraft limit exceeded).

[885] *Interfoto Picture Library Ltd v Stiletto Visual Programmes Ltd* [1989] Q.B. 433 at 445–446 ("holding fee" for the failure to return photographic transparencies found to be unenforceable because not incorporated: above, para.7–047).

[886] See below, para.21–001.

[887] *Jervis v Harris* [1996] Ch. 195 at 203; cf. *UK Housing Alliance (North West) Ltd v Francis* [2010] EWCA Civ 117; [2010] 3 All E.R. 519 at [10]; Conte 126 L.Q.R. 529.

stipulation is, similarly, not penal if it provides for the payment of a sum of money on breach of another contract with a third party. In one case A had contracted to build a refinery for B; C had undertaken responsibilities as guarantor for the financing of the project; and A had promised C that, in the event of a breach of A's contract with B, A would pay to C sums equivalent to those which C would have to pay under the guarantee. It was held that the latter stipulation was not a penalty as it "provided for payment of money on a specified event other than a breach of a contractual duty owed by the contemplated payor to the contemplated payee".[888] Similar reasoning seems to apply to performance bonds by which C promises to pay a sum of money to A if B fails to perform his contract with A. Such a promise is independent of the contract between A and B[889] and can be enforced by A against C even if the sum payable exceeds A's true loss; where that is subsequently shown to be the case, however, A must account for any over-payment.[890] Where, however, a clause in a contract between A and B is unenforceable against B because it amounts to a penalty, it is equally unenforceable against C, as guarantor of B's obligations.[891]

Payment triggered by several events, not all of which amount to a breach. It is less clear whether a clause in a contract can be penal if it provides for a payment on several events one of which is a breach of that contract while another is not. The problem has arisen under so-called minimum payment clauses in hire-purchase agreements. Such a clause commonly provides that on premature determination of the agreement the hirer shall bring his payments under it up to a specified proportion of the hire-purchase price (or the whole of it) "by way of agreed compensation for depreciation". It then specifies the events on which the agreement may be determined. The owner is usually given the right to determine if the hirer commits a breach of the agreement, and in certain other events.[892] The hirer also often has a right to return the goods on bringing his payments up to the specified amount.

20–145

The question whether the law as to penalties applies to such clauses has given rise to much dispute. It is said, on the one hand, that only a sum payable on breach can be a penalty; and, on the other, that the whole law as to penalties could be evaded, if it did not apply to these clauses, by simply including, among the events on which the sum was payable, one event which was not a breach. The common law does not fully adopt either of these views. If the agreement is in fact

---

[888] *Export Credit Guarantee Department v Universal Oil Products Co* [1983] 1 W.L.R. 399 at 402; cf. *Euro London Appointments Ltd v Claessens International Ltd* [2006] EWCA Civ 385; [2006] 2 Lloyd's Rep. 437.

[889] *Edward Owen Engineering Ltd v Barclays Bank International* [1978] Q.B. 159.

[890] Usually to B who will have procured and paid for the bond: *Cargill International SA v Bangladesh Sugar & Food Industries Corp* [1998] 1 W.L.R. 461; *Comdel Commodities Ltd v Siporex Trade SA* [1997] 1 Lloyd's Rep. 424 at 431; *Tradigrain v State Trading Corp of India* [2005] EWHC 2206; [2006] 1 Lloyd's Rep. 216.

[891] *Azimut-Benetti SpA v Healey* [2010] EWHC 2234 (Comm); [2011] 1 Lloyd's Rep. 473 where Blair J. (at [24]) based his decision on the public policy which is the basis of the rule, citing *Citicorp Australia Ltd v Hendry* (1985) 4 N.S.W.L.R. 1 at p.21D. An alternative reason (ibid. at [24]) was that B no longer had an "obligation" on which the guarantee could bite, but while that may be avoided by appropriate drafting of the guarantee, the argument from public policy would appear still to apply.

[892] e.g. the hirer's bankruptcy. Provisions for termination on the hirer's death used to be common but are ineffective if the agreement is a regulated agreement (above, para.5–007) within Consumer Credit Act 1974, ss.86, 87.

determined on the ground of the hirer's breach, the law as to penalties applies.[893] If the agreement is determined on some ground other than the hirer's breach, e.g. because the hirer exercises his right to return the goods, the law as to penalties does not apply.[894] This compromise is unsatisfactory; for under it a hirer who wishes to return the goods may be better off if he simply defaults than he would be if he exercised his lawful right to determine the agreement.[895] The hirer's statutory right to determine on payment of one-half of the hire-purchase price and the power of the courts to order payment of a smaller sum under the Consumer Credit Act 1974,[896] if it will adequately compensate the owner, means that this unsatisfactory outcome can at least be avoided for a "regulated agreement".[897]

20–146   **Withholding payments.** Normally, a penalty clause requires the defaulting party to *make* a payment to the victim; but it seems that a provision entitling the injured party to *withhold* a payment can also be penal.[898] Thus, in *General Trading Company (Holdings) Ltd v Richmond Corporation Ltd,*[899] Beatson J. held that the rule against penalties applied to a clause under which the buyer of shares was to be released from the obligation to redeem loan notes which accounted for 90 per cent of the price if the seller failed to procure loan guarantees needed by the buyer to support the business.[900] The contract could have achieved in substance the desired result by providing that the notes were not to be redeemed until the guarantee had been procured, i.e. by making it a condition precedent to the buyer's obligation to redeem, but no breach by the seller if that condition was not fulfilled.[901] Effect has been given to such provisions[902] without any reference to the law as to penalties. Somewhat similar reasoning was used where the rules of an association which had been formed for the enforcement of legal claims by its members provided that members who defaulted in the payment of subscriptions should not share in the proceeds of such claims. Their argument that this provision was a penalty was rejected on the ground that it was "an essential part of the pooling arrangement".[903]

---

[893] *Cooden Engineering Co Ltd v Stanford* [1953] 1 Q.B. 86; *Lamdon Trust Ltd v Hurrell* [1955] 1 W.L.R. 391; cf. *Anglo-Auto Finance Co Ltd v James* [1963] 1 W.L.R. 1042; *United Dominions Trust (Commercial) Ltd v Ennis* [1968] 1 Q.B. 54.

[894] *Associated Distributors Ltd v Hall* [1938] 2 K.B. 83; *Re Apex Supply Co Ltd* [1942] Ch. 108; *Campbell Discount Co Ltd v Bridge* [1961] 1 Q.B. 445, reversed on other grounds [1962] A.C. 600, where the House of Lords was equally divided on the point discussed in the text.

[895] cf. Law Commission Working Paper No.61, para.22.

[896] s.100(1) and (3).

[897] See above, para.5–007.

[898] *Gilbert-Ash (Northern) Ltd v Modern Engineering (Bristol) Ltd* [1974] A.C. 689 at 698, 703, 711, 723. The authoritative status of this decision has been questioned by Bingham L.J. in *The Fanti and the Padre Island (No. 2)* [1989] 1 Lloyd's Rep 239 at 255, but in the same case the majority held that a clause providing for retrospective cesser of cover where a member of a P & I club failed, in breach of contract, to pay a call by the club was a penalty and this was said by Beatson J in the *Richmond Corporation* case (below fn.899) to be binding "whatever may be the position in a higher court"; cf. *The Vainqueur José* [1979] 1 Lloyd's Rep. 557.

[899] [2008] EWHC 1479 (Comm); [2008] 2 Lloyd's Rep. 475.

[900] It was found that the seller had not breached the obligation to procure the guarantee and (*obiter*) that the clause did not amount to a penalty in any event, adopting the "broader approach" referred to above: para.20–139.

[901] Beatson J. rejected this construction of the clause, but it could be achieved with appropriate drafting: above, para.20–144; cf. *Lehman Brothers Special Financing Inc v Carlton Communications Ltd* [2011] EWHC 718 (Ch) at [47].

[902] e.g. *Eshelby v Federated European Bank* [1932] 1 K.B. 423; above, para.17–037.

[903] *Nutting v Baldwin* [1995] 1 W.L.R. 201; cf. *SCI (Sales Curve Interactive) v Titus SARL* [2001] EWCA Civ 591; [2001] 2 All E.R. (Comm) 416 at [66].

(iv) *Unfair Terms in Consumer Contracts Regulations 1999*[904]

An illustration given in the Regulations of a term which is prima facie unfair[905]   **20–147**
and therefore not binding on the consumer, is one requiring "any consumer who
fails to fulfil his obligation to pay a disproportionately high sum in compensation".[906] Such a term is likely also to be invalid as a penalty at common law, so that
normally the common law rules and the Regulations would lead to the same
result.[907] There are, however, significant differences between these two sets of
rules. On the one hand, the scope of the common law rules is perfectly general,
while that of the Regulations is limited in that they apply only to standard terms
in contracts between commercial suppliers and consumers, in that even within
these categories certain types of contract are excepted, and in that certain terms
are excepted even in contracts within the scope of the Regulations.[908] On the other
hand, the scope of the Regulations appears to be wider than that of the common
law rules in that the Regulations may (at least in some cases) apply to sums payable
otherwise than on breach. A consumer who, in the words of the illustration quoted
above, "fails to fulfil his obligations" is not necessarily in breach: he may, for
example, have an excuse for non-performance.[909] The Regulations might also
apply to a term by which a sum of money became payable on an event which was
not a failure in performance at all: e.g. where a buyer agreed to pay a "carrying
charge" if he failed to take delivery on the specified day, or where a hirer agreed
to pay a "holding charge" if he did not return the subject-matter at the end of the
specified period.[910] If the rate at which these charges are fixed is disproportionately high in relation to the amount which would be payable under the contract but
for the delay, the term imposing the charge might be regarded as "unfair" within
the Regulations.[911]

(b) Deposit and Part-payment[912]

A contract may provide that one party shall make an advance payment but fail   **20–148**
to specify what is to happen to the payment if the contract is not performed.
Clearly, the money must be paid back if the *payee*, in breach of contract, fails to
perform.[913] But the more difficult question (with which the following discussion
is concerned) is whether the money must also be paid back where it is the *payor*
who, in breach of contract, fails to perform and the contract is in consequence
terminated by the other party. This depends at common law on the intention with
which the money was paid: it may have been paid as a deposit or as a part-

---

[904] See generally, above para.7–095 et seq.
[905] SI 1999/2083, reg.5(2).
[906] ibid., Sch.2, para.1(e).
[907] But see: *Munkenbeck & Marshall v Harold* [2005] EWHC 356 (TCC) (term unfair, but not a
penalty principally because of the effect of Late Payment of Commercial Debts (Rate of Interest)
(No.3) Order 2002 (SI 2002/1675)).
[908] See above, paras 7–115—7–116.
[909] See above, para.17–059.
[910] See above, at fn.884.
[911] The effect of the decision of the Supreme Court in *Office of Fair Trading v Abbey National Plc*
[2009] UKSC 6; [2010] 1 A.C. 696 is that such terms may have to be regarded as fixing the "price"
of an option, and therefore excluded from the test of fairness by reg.6(2)(a) (above, para.7–107).
[912] Beatson 97 L.Q.R. 389; *The Use and Abuse of Unjust Enrichment*, Ch.3; Milner 42 M.L.R. 508;
Harpum [1984] C.L.J. 134.
[913] *Country & Metropolitan Homes Surrey Ltd v Topclaim Ltd* [1997] 1 All E.R. 254.

payment. A deposit is a sum of money paid as "a guarantee that the contract shall be performed".[914] At common law, it is generally[915] irrecoverable[916] unless the contract otherwise provides,[917] including, if necessary, by a process of implication.[918] A part-payment is simply a payment of part of the contract price: it is generally[919] recoverable[920] unless the contract validly provides the contrary.

20–149 **Deposits and penalties.** A deposit is distinguishable from a penalty on the ground that it is payable before, and not after breach.[921] But the function of the two devices is similar: the only difference between "a guarantee that the contract shall be performed"[922] and "a payment of money stipulated as *in terrorem* of the offending party"[923] lies in the emotive force of the words used. The law as to penalties can therefore apply to deposits. In the *Workers Trust* case,[924] for example, a contract for the sale of land provided for the payment by the purchaser of a deposit of 25 per cent of the price and for forfeiture of that deposit in the event of the purchaser's default. After the purchaser had paid the deposit and then failed to complete on the due day, the vendor terminated the contract and purported to forfeit the deposit; but the Privy Council held that the deposit was not a reasonable pre-estimate of the loss which the vendor was likely to suffer in consequence of the default, that the deposit was therefore penal, and that it must be paid back to the purchaser. On the other hand, where the deposit is reasonable in relation to the loss likely to be suffered, it can be forfeited, particularly if the loss is such that it cannot be accurately assessed in advance.[925]

20–150 **Sale of land.** There is a well-established exception to the general rule that a penal deposit must be paid back. In contracts for the sale of land, it is the normal practice for the purchaser to pay a deposit of 10 per cent of the price and for the contract to provide for forfeiture of that deposit in the event of the purchaser's default. It is generally agreed that such a provision is valid even though it does not, and does not purport to, bear any relation to the vendor's loss. In the *Workers Trust*

---

[914] *Howe v Smith* (1884) 27 Ch.D. 89 at 95; cf. *Public Works Commissioners v Hills* [1906] A.C. 368 (so far as it relates to the retention fund); *The Selene G* [1981] 2 Lloyd's Rep. 180 at 185.

[915] For an exception, see the discussion of deposits and penalties, below, para.20–149.

[916] *Howe v Smith*, above; *Harrison v Holland* [1921] 3 K.B. 297; [1922] 1 K.B. 211; *Union Eagle Ltd v Golden Achievement Ltd* [1997] A.C. 514 at 518; *Omar v El Wakil* [2001] EWCA Civ 1090; [2002] P. & C.R. 3 at [36].

[917] *Palmer v Temple* (1839) 9 A. & E. 508. A *pre-contract* deposit is recoverable if the negotiations fail to lead to the conclusion of the contemplated contract: *Chillingworth v Esche* [1924] 1 Ch. 97; *Guardian Ocean Cargoes Ltd v Banco do Brazil* [1991] 2 Lloyd's Rep. 68; *idem (No.3)* [1992] 2 Lloyd's Rep. 193.

[918] *JSD Corporation Pte Ltd v Al Waha Capital PJSC* [2009] EWHC 3376 (Ch) where a deposit said to be non-refundable in all circumstances was held only to be non-refundable for the buyer's "default".

[919] For a suggested exception, see below, at fn.967.

[920] *Mayson v Clouet* [1924] A.C. 980; *Dies v British International Mining Corp* [1939] 1 K.B. 725.

[921] cf. *Corpe v Overton* (1833) 10 Bing. 252 at 257.

[922] See above, at fn.914.

[923] See above, at fn.805.

[924] *Workers Trust and Merchant Bank Ltd v Dojap Investments Ltd* [1993] A.C. 573; Harpum [1993] C.L.J. 389; cf. *Public Works Commissioners v Hills* [1906] A.C. 368; *Starside Properties Ltd v Mustapha* [1974] 1 W.L.R. 816 at 819; *Jobson v Johnson* [1989] 1 W.L.R. 1026 at 1036, 1041.

[925] *Pye v British Automobile Commercial Syndicate Ltd* [1906] 1 K.B. 425; cf. *Starside Properties Ltd v Mustapha* [1974] 1 W.L.R. 816 at 819.

case, the Privy Council described the exception as anomalous[926] but nevertheless recognised its existence.

Law of Property Act 1925, section 49(2). This subsection gives the court   20–151
power "if it thinks fit" to order the return of a deposit paid under a contract for the sale of land.[927] An earlier and narrow view that the subsection applied only when the vendor could not, for some reason, have obtained specific performance[928] has given way to a broader view that the discretion conferred by it is to be exercised "where justice requires it".[929] This is to be welcomed; but unfortunately the cases give no clear indication of the circumstances in which the courts will exercise their discretion under the subsection.[930] That discretion is no longer needed where the deposit is penal in effect, now that the *Workers Trust* case has held such a deposit to be recoverable at common law. This development may have reduced the need to invoke the statutory discretion and may in part account for the recently expressed view that it will be exercised in favour of a defaulting purchaser only in "exceptional circumstances".[931] Just when circumstances are, for this purpose, exceptional remains obscure; but the requirement is evidently not satisfied merely by the fact that the deposit substantially exceeds the normal 10 per cent of the price[932] or by the fact that the vendor has not established that the breach has caused him any loss.[933]

Forfeiture of instalments. A contract of sale may provide for payment of the   20–152
price in instalments and add that, on default in payment of any one instalment, those already paid shall be forfeited. In such cases equity can sometimes grant certain kinds of relief against forfeiture to the purchaser if he is able and willing to perform after the agreed time,[934] particularly where enforcement of the forfeiture provision would cause him some prejudice (such as the loss of the value of improvements he had made to the land) beyond merely depriving him of the

---

[926] See above, fn.924 at 578; cf. ibid. at 580 ("without logic").

[927] It cannot be excluded by the agreement of the parties: *Aribisala v St James Homes (Grosvenor) Dock Ltd* [2007] EWHC 1694 (Ch); [2007] 37 E.G. 234.

[928] See *James Macara v Barclays Bank Ltd* [1944] 2 All E.R. 31 at 32, affirmed [1945] K.B. 148. See also *Michael Richards Properties Ltd v St Saviour's Parish* [1975] 3 All E.R. 416; *Zieme v Gregory* [1963] V.R. 214.

[929] *Universal Corp v Five Ways Properties Ltd* [1979] 1 All E.R. 552 at 555; Oakley [1980] C.L.J. 24; *Schindler v Pigault* (1975) 30 P. & C.R. 328 at 336. For other examples of the exercise of the discretion, see *Maktoum v South Lodge Flats Ltd, The Times,* April 21, 1980; *Wilson v Kingsgate Mining Industries Ltd* [1973] 2 N.S.W.L.R. 713; *Yammouni v Condidorio* [1975] V.R. 479.

[930] Contrast the authorities cited in fn.929, above with *Carne v De Bono* [1988] 1 W.L.R. 1107, where no attempt was made to rely on the subsection; and *Safehaven Investments Inc v Springbok Ltd* (1996) 71 P. & C.R. 59.

[931] *Omar v El-Wakil* [2001] EWCA Civ 1090 at [37]; [2002] P. & C.R. 3; *Midill (97PL) Ltd v Park Lane Estates Ltd* [2008] EWCA 1227; [2009] 1 W.L.R. 2460.

[932] ibid. at [36]; the deposit was about 31 per cent of the price, but it was not argued that it was penal: *Omar v El-Wakil* [2001] EWCA Civ 1090 at [31]. Perhaps for this reason, no reference was made to the *Workers Trust* case [1993] A.C. 573; above, para.20–149.

[933] ibid. at [37]; *Aribisala v St James Homes (Grosvenor) Dock Ltd* [2008] EWHC 456 (Ch); [2009] 1 W.L.R. 1089; *Midill (97PL) Ltd v Park Lane Estates Ltd* [2008] EWCA 1227; [2009] 1 W.L.R. 2460.

[934] See *Jobson v Johnson* [1989] 1 W.L.R. 1026, where the defendant failed to comply with this requirement; and *Goker v NWS Bank Plc* [1990] C.C.L.R. 34, where relief was denied to a persistent defaulter.

benefit of his bargain[935]; that is, it might be able to extend the time for payment,[936] or order repayment of the forfeited instalments if the purchaser was able and willing to perform, but the vendor was for some reason justified in refusing to accept late performance.[937]

20–153   **Relief against forfeiture where purchaser not able and willing to perform.**[938] It is more doubtful whether equity could order the repayment of forfeited instalments to a purchaser who was *not* able and willing to perform. In *Mussen v Van Diemen's Land Co*[939] land was sold for £321,000 payable in instalments and the contract provided that the vendor was to have the right to terminate, and to forfeit any money paid, in the event of the purchaser's default. Such default occurred after the purchaser had paid £40,200.[940] His claim for the return of the money was rejected as it was not "unconscionable on the part of the vendor, who has contracted to part with his land on agreed terms, to enforce the contract . . . ".[941] This case left open the possibility of ordering repayment when it *was* unconscionable for the vendor to keep the money. In *Stockloser v Johnson*[942] quarrying machinery was sold under a contract which provided for payment in instalments, and, in the event of the buyer's default, for forfeiture of instalments paid. The buyer failed to keep up the agreed payments and the actual decision was that he was not entitled to the return of the forfeited instalments as, in the circumstances, it was not unconscionable for the seller to keep them after terminating the contract: the buyer had speculated on the success of the quarry, and lost. But Somervell and Denning L.JJ.said that repayment could have been ordered if the mere act of keeping the money had been unconscionable.[943] Romer L.J., on the other hand, said that repayment could be ordered only if the vendor was guilty of fraud, sharp practice or other unconscionable conduct; and that there was

---

[935] *Union Eagle Ltd v Golden Achievement Ltd* [1997] A.C. 514 at 520; above, para.18–065.

[936] *Re Dagenham (Thames) Dock Co* (1873) L.R. 8 Ch.App. 1022 and *Kilmer v BC Orchard Lands Ltd* [1913] A.C. 319, as explained in *Union Eagle Ltd v Golden Achievement Ltd* [1997] A.C. 514 at 521; *Starside Properties Ltd v Mustapha* [1974] 1 W.L.R. 816; cf. *Millichamp v Jones* [1982] 1 W.L.R. 1422 (time for payment of deposit extended); Lang 100 L.Q.R. 427. For other applications of, and restrictions on, the principle of relief against forfeiture, see above, paras 18–063—18–065.

[937] *Steedman v Drinkle* [1916] 1 A.C. 275, as explained in *Mussen v Van Diemen's Land Co* [1938] Ch. 253; but see *Stockloser v Johnson* [1954] 1 Q.B. 476.

[938] In addition to the restrictions dealt with below, it is said that the jurisdiction to grant relief is confined to cases depriving a party of proprietary or possessory rights, and not purely contractual rights: *UK Housing Alliance (North West) Ltd v Francis* [2010] EWCA Civ 117; [2010] 3 All E.R. 519; Conte 126 L.Q.R. 529. This requirement, which applies to the forfeiture of the contract itself by way of termination, has been criticised (above, para.18–064) and there is no mention of its requirement in *Stockloser v Johnson* (or in other cases) suggesting that it is not in fact required where relief is sought against the forfeiture of instalments as a consequence of termination: Conte 126 L.Q.R. 529; Smith 60 C.L.J. 178; cf. *Liberty Life Assurance Co v Sheikh, The Times,* June 25, 1985, CA.

[939] See fn.937, above.

[940] Land equal in value to other payments had been conveyed to him.

[941] At 262.

[942] [1954] 1 Q.B. 476; Diamond 19 M.L.R. 498; Price 20 M.L.R. 620; cf. Hodkinson 3 O.J.L.S. 393, discussing *Legione v Hateley* (1983) 152 C.L.R. 406.

[943] ibid. at 483, 485, 489–490. According to *Hyundai Shipbuilding and Heavy Industries Co Ltd v Pournaras* [1978] 2 Lloyd's Rep. 502 at 508 Somervell L.J.'s views are limited to cases of "default" (*sc.* by the buyer), while Denning L.J. went "somewhat further"; but exactly how much further is not made clear, nor is it apparent from the report in *Stockloser's* case.

"nothing inequitable *per se* in a vendor, whose conduct is not open to criticism in other respects, insisting on his contractual right to retain instalments of purchase-money already paid".[944]

Later dicta, as well as a decision at first instance,[945] support Romer L.J.'s view, which is based on the principle that the law should not interfere with contracts freely made. But this principle is discarded in the law as to penalties, and in particular in the law relating to penal deposits. In the *Workers Trust* case[946] the Privy Council left open the question whether relief against forfeiture of instalments should be given to a purchaser who has been let into possession. This fact may, indeed, affect the amount of the vendor's loss; but subject to this practical consideration, it is submitted that, since forfeiture provisions often resemble penalties in their purpose and effect,[947] their validity should depend on the tests that differentiate penalties from liquidated damages clauses. The court should accordingly have power to grant relief where, on these tests, the forfeiture provision is penal in nature.[948] In the cases discussed above, such relief would take the form of ordering repayment of the forfeited instalments; but *Jobson v Johnson*[949] illustrates the possible availability of other forms of relief. In that case a contract for the sale of shares to be paid for by instalments provided that, if the buyer defaulted, he should retransfer the shares for £40,000. It was admitted that this clause was penal in effect[950]; and, on the buyer's default, it was held that the seller was entitled to an order for *either* the sale of the shares and the payment out of the proceeds of sale of the unpaid instalments, *or* the transfer of the shares so long as their value did not exceed the unpaid instalments by more than £40,000. This amounted to putting the seller into the same position as that in which he would have been if the penal element of the clause had been struck out: in this respect it resembled the legal consequence of a penalty clause in the normal sense of that expression.[951]

Contracts for services. The foregoing discussion is concerned with contracts   20–154
of sale, in which, as a result of the buyer's default, the contract is terminated and
the subject-matter remains the property of, or is restored to, the seller. The
position is different where the contract is one for services to be rendered over a
period of time in return for payments to be made at stated intervals. If the
recipient of the services fails to keep up the payments and the contract is
terminated on that ground, he will not be able to recover back payments made

---

[944] ibid. at 501; cf. *Kazakstan Wool Processors (Europe) Ltd v Nederlandsche Credietverzekering Maatschappij NV* [2000] C.L.C. 822 (retention of premium on termination of policy for breach by insured).

[945] *Galbraith v Mitchenall Estates Ltd* [1965] 2 Q.B. 473, citing dicta from *Campbell Discount Co Ltd v Bridge* [1961] 1 Q.B. 445 (reversed on other grounds [1962] A.C. 600); *Else (1982) v Parkland Holdings* [1994] B.C.L.C. 130.

[946] *Workers Trust and Merchant Bank Ltd v Dojap Investments Ltd* [1993] A.C. 573 at 581–582, discussing *Stockloser v Johnson*, above, fn.942.

[947] *Jobson v Johnson* [1989] 1 W.L.R. 1026 at 1041.

[948] cf. *Stockloser v Johnson* [1954] 1 Q.B. 476 at 491; Law Commission Working Paper No.61, paras 65, 66. For a special statutory provision giving the court a discretion to order repayment, see Consumer Credit Act 1974, s.132(1); this would now apply on the facts of *Galbraith*'s case, above, fn.945 and would in a case of this kind displace the Unfair Terms in Consumer Contracts Regulations 1999: above, para.7–115.

[949] [1989] 1 W.L.R. 1026; Harpum [1989] C.L.J. 370.

[950] See above, para.20–138.

[951] See above, para.20–140.

before termination, at least if they "represent the agreed rate of hire [for the services] and not a penny more".[952] In such a case the reasoning even of the majority in *Stockloser v Johnson* cannot apply as the payor will have received (and be unable to restore) pro rata what he bargained for in exchange for his payments.[953] The position might be different if those payments contained a heavy element of "front loading".

20–155   **Failure to pay.** The preceding discussion of deposits and part-payments deals with the situation in which a payment has been made and the contract is *then* broken by the payor. The main issue in such cases is whether the payor can get back the payment that he has made. But the breach may also consist in failing to make the payment; and if the injured party terminates the contract on account of this breach,[954] the question arises whether the payment can be sued for by the prospective payee. The view that it can be sued for is supported by the principle that termination does not retrospectively release the party in breach from accrued obligations[955]; and, after some conflict of judicial opinion, this view has prevailed where the money was to have been paid as a *deposit*[956] which, if it had been duly paid, could not have been claimed back by the payor.[957] But acceptance of the same view in the case of a *part-payment* might lead to the absurdity that the prospective payee could sue for the money because it was due before breach, while the payor could then sue for its return because a part-payment can be recovered back by the payor.[958] Hence in cases involving contracts for the sale of land the position is that a part-payment which was due but remained unpaid at the time of termination cannot be sued for by the prospective payee.[959] It is submitted that the same reasoning should apply even to a claim for an unpaid deposit where the case is one of those exceptional ones in which the deposit would, if paid, have been recoverable by the payor, either at common law[960] or under s.49(2) of the Law of Property Act 1925[961]; and that a claim by the prospective payee for the payment of such a deposit should therefore be rejected.[962]

In the cases just considered, the outcome can be justified on the ground that the seller will, as a result of termination, keep or get back the land, which constituted the entire consideration for the promised part-payment.[963] Hence if liability to make the payments is discharged, each party will be left in, or restored to, his pre-

---

[952] *The Scaptrade* [1983] 2 A.C. 694 at 703; cf. above, para.20–132(b) and below, para.20–156.

[953] See below, para.22–044.

[954] See above, paras 17–017, 18–032.

[955] See above, para.18–011.

[956] *Hinton v Sparkes* (1868) L.R. 3 C.P. 161; *Dewar v Mintoft* [1912] 2 K.B. 373; *Millichamp v Jones* [1982] 1 W.L.R. 1422 at 1428, 1430; Carter 99 L.Q.R. 503; *The Blankenstein* [1985] 1 W.L.R. 435 at 451, disapproving *Lowe v Hope* [1970] 1 Ch. 94, where the court may have been reluctant to enforce what it regarded as in substance a penalty. For a possible way of giving effect to that reluctance, see below, fn.962.

[957] See above, para.20–148.

[958] See above, at fn.920.

[959] *McDonald v Denys Lascelles Ltd* (1933) 48 C.L.R. 457, cited with approval in *Johnson v Agnew* [1980] A.C. 367 at 396 and in *Hyundai Heavy Industries Ltd v Papadopoulos* [1980] 1 W.L.R. 1129 at 1141.

[960] See above, para.20–149.

[961] See above, para.20–151.

[962] In a case like *Lowe v Hope*, above, fn.956, a court could justify its refusal to allow the prospective payee's claim on the ground that it would have ordered the return of the deposit (if paid) under s.49(2) of the 1925 Act.

[963] See below, para.22–004.

contract position (though the buyer will be liable in damages). This is also true where a part-payment is to be made *in advance*, for work to be done in the future, i.e. after the part-payment had become due. In *Rover International Ltd v Cannon Films Ltd (No.3)*[964] it was accordingly held that a payment in respect of services to be rendered in the future under an agreement for the distribution of films on television could not be sued for by the prospective payee, even though the payment had fallen due (but none of the services had been rendered) before termination. But the position was different where part-payments under shipbuilding contracts became due from time to time (as the work progressed) and the builder terminated for the other party's failure to make one of the payments when due.[965] It was held that the builder was entitled to sue for that part-payment since the consideration, for which the part-payment was to be made, was not merely the delivery of the finished product, but also the builder's work. So far as the work which he had done was concerned, he could not be restored to his pre-contract position: hence it was proper to uphold his claim for a part-payment due before termination. For the same reason, instalments due under a hire-purchase agreement before termination can be sued for after termination[966]: their legal character is that of payment for the hire of the subject-matter, and the benefit of possession during each period for which such a payment was due is one that cannot be restored by the hirer to the owner. It is submitted that this reasoning should also apply where the part-payment has actually been made before termination, and that, accordingly, the prima facie rule by which part-payments can be recovered back by the payor[967] should be restricted to cases in which, as a result of termination, each party can be restored to his pre-contract position.

Unfair Terms in Consumer Contracts Regulations 1999. An illustration given in the Regulations[968] of a term which is prima facie unfair[969] is one   **20–156**

> "permitting the seller or supplier to retain sums paid by the consumer where the latter decides not to conclude or perform the contract, without providing for the consumer to receive compensation of an equivalent amount from the seller or supplier where the latter is the party cancelling the contract".[970]

This illustration is based on the civil law institution (which has no counterparty in the common law) by which a contract can, in effect, be dissolved on forfeiture of a deposit or on the return by the payee of double the amount.[971] Thus forfeiture provisions of the kind discussed above do not correspond precisely with the illustration just quoted; but this fact would not prevent the court from holding that such a provision was unfair.[972] It seems to follow not only that the seller or supplier could not sue for the payment, but also that he would have to return the

---

[964] [1989] 1 W.L.R. 912; Beatson 105 L.Q.R. 179; Andrews [1990] C.L.J. 15.
[965] *Hyundai Shipbuilding and Heavy Industries Co Ltd v Pournaras* [1978] 2 Lloyd's Rep. 502; *Hyundai Heavy Industries Ltd v Papadopoulos* [1980] 1 W.L.R. 1129 (Lords Russell and Keith *dubitante* on this point); *Stocznia Gdanska SA v Latvian Shipping Co* [1998] 1 W.L.R. 574.
[966] See above, para.18–015.
[967] See above, at fn.920.
[968] See generally, above para.7–095 et seq.
[969] See above, para.7–110.
[970] SI 1999/2083, Sch.2, para.1(d).
[971] Treitel, *Remedies for Breach of Contract*, para.182.
[972] The list of illustrations in Sch.3 is "non-exhaustive": reg.5(5).

payment, if it had been made.[973] This may now be more important in practice with the recognition that the Regulations can apply to contracts for the sale of land,[974] since it is with such contracts that many of the English cases on deposits and part-payments are concerned. However, the Regulations apply only to contract terms[975] and not to rights of forfeiture conferred by law. Once a payment is classified as a deposit, it can be forfeited even in the absence of a contract term to that effect; and in such a case there would appear to be no relevant contractual term[976] on which the Regulations can operate. The mere description of the payment as a "deposit" would not suffice for this purpose since the question whether a payment has the legal characteristics of a deposit or of a part-payment is one of substance; the use of a particular word or phrase is clearly not decisive.[977]

---

[973] reg.8(1) merely makes the term "not binding on the consumer" but the word "retain" in Sch.2, para.1(d) suggests the availability to the consumer of a remedy for the recovery of the payment.

[974] *R. (Khatun) v Newham LBC* [2004] EWCA Civ 55; [2005] Q.B. 37; above, para.7–098.

[975] See reg.4(1).

[976] See reg.5(1); cf. reg.8(1).

[977] If it were, the law as to part payments could be evaded by simply calling them deposits.

SPECIFIC REMEDIES

1. ACTION FOR AN AGREED SUM

(a) Distinguished from Damages

Nature of relief. A contract commonly provides for the payment by one party **21–001** of an agreed sum in exchange for some performance by the other. Goods are sold for a fixed price; work is done for an agreed remuneration, and so forth. An action for this price or other agreed remuneration is, in its nature, quite different from an action for damages.[1] It is a claim for the *specific* enforcement of the defendant's primary obligation to perform what he has promised[2]; though, as it is simply an action for money, it is not subject to those restrictions which equity imposes on the remedies of specific performance and injunction,[3] on the ground that it would be undesirable actually to force the defendant to perform certain acts (e.g. to render personal service) or that it would be difficult to secure compliance with the court's order. Obviously, these factors have no weight where the claim is simply one for a sum of money. Of the reasons given for refusing specific performance, only one calls for discussion in relation to an action for the agreed sum: this is the possibility that damages may be an "adequate" remedy.[4]

Practical effects. The action for the agreed sum differs from a claim for **21–002** damages not only in its nature, but also in its practical effects. The claimant in an

---

[1] cf. *Re Park Air Services* [1999] 1 All E.R. 673 at 682–683. The distinction is sometimes obscured by the fact that damages may be *equal to* the agreed sum, as in *The Blankenstein* [1985] 1 W.L.R. 435: above, para.18–016; and sometimes by the description of the claim as one for "damages equal to" the agreed sum, when it appears to be one for the agreed sum, e.g. in *UCB Leasing Ltd v Holtom* [1987] R.T.R. 362 at 366.

[2] See above, para.18–013.

[3] See below, paras 21–028—21–047, 21–051—21–059.

[4] See below, paras 21–017—21–027; *Attica Sea Carriers Corp v Ferrostaal Poseidon Bulk Reederei GmbH (The Puerto Buitrago)* [1976] Lloyd's Rep. 250.

action for the agreed sum recovers that sum—neither more nor less; no questions of quantification nor of remoteness can arise.[5] It is irrelevant in an action for the price of goods to ask how much they are worth or how much they cost the seller. The argument that the claimant should have mitigated can, however, arise in an action for the agreed sum.[6] If successful, it will lead to the conclusion that the action is not available at all—not to recovery of a reduced price.

Where the agreed sum is not paid and the claimant also suffers additional loss, he may be entitled to bring *both* the action for the agreed sum *and* an action for damages.[7]

21–003   **Insurance.** Where A (an insurer) promises B (the insured) to pay to B any damages for which B may become liable to C, B's claim against A for the amount of such damages has been described as being itself a claim for damages,[8] so that the action against the insurer is not one to enforce his primary obligation.[9] But in the case put A's only promise is to repay B the damages for which B is liable to C; hence A's primary obligation is to make that payment; and an action to recover it is, it is submitted, one for the specific enforcement of A's promise. It is an action for an agreed sum, in the sense of a sum determined by reference to the agreement, rather than one calculated by reference to the consequences of breach.[10]

21–004   **Contractual indemnity.** In some cases A may agree to indemnify B against any "loss" incurred on the occasion of certain specified events, one of which may include a breach of the contract between them *by A*. This may leave room for a submission that a claim under the indemnity is an action for the agreed sum, and not an action for damages, so that the principles of mitigation and remoteness are inapplicable.[11] The better view, it is submitted, is that while the claim may not be one for damages, the extent of the recovery by B depends upon the construction of the term under which the "indemnity" is provided.[12] Furthermore, a claim under a contractual indemnity which is triggered by a breach by A is presumed to cover no more than the sum which could have been recovered in an action for damages unless the parties have indicated clearly an intention to provide a "full"

---

[5] *Jervis v Harris* [1996] Ch. 195 at 202.

[6] See below, para.21–013.

[7] *Overstone Ltd v Shipway* [1962] 1 W.L.R. 117; cf. *The Halcyon Skies* [1977] Q.B. 14; *Lawlor v Gray* [1984] 3 All E.R. 345; and see above, paras 20–061—20–066.

[8] See *Chandris v Argo Ins Co Ltd* [1963] 2 Lloyd's Rep. 65; cf. *The Fanti and Padre Island* [1991] 2 A.C. 1, 35; *Hong Kong Borneo Services Ltd v Pilcher* [1992] 2 Lloyd's Rep. 593 at 597; *The Kyriaki* [1993] 1 Lloyd's Rep. 137 at 150.

[9] *Phoenix General Ins Co of Greece SA v Halvanon Ins Co Ltd* [1988] Q.B. 216 at 233 (reversed on other grounds [1988] Q.B. 216 at 248 et seq.).

[10] cf. *Jervis v Harris* [1996] Ch. 195, where a lease provided that, on a tenant's breach of his covenant to repair, the landlord could himself execute the repairs and recover the costs of so doing from the tenant. It was held that the landlord's claim to recover these costs "sounds in debt, not damages" (at 202). The action was one for an agreed sum even though that sum was not ascertained when the contract was made: it was enough for it to be ascertained when payment became due. This reasoning is, with respect, preferable to that of the insurance cases referred to above.

[11] As noted in *Jervis v Harris*, above fn.10. it is enough that the sum to be paid can be ascertained when payment is due.

[12] *The Eurus* [1996] 2 Lloyd's Rep 408, affirmed [1998] 1 Lloyd's Rep 351; *The Kos* [2009] EWHC 1843 (Comm); [2010] 1 Lloyd's Rep. 87 at [34]; [2010] EWCA Civ 772; [2010] 2 Lloyd's Rep. 409 at [14]; *Codemasters Software Co Ltd v Automobile Club de L'Ouest* [2009] EWHC 2361 (Ch); [2010] F.S.R. 12 at [20]–[21]; *Pindell Ltd v Airasia Berhad* [2010] EWHC 2516 (Comm) at [94]; cf. *Rust Consulting Ltd v PB Ltd* [2010] EWHC 3423 (TCC) at [45].

indemnity going beyond the obligation to indemnify which is the basis of a claim for damages.[13]

(b) Availability of the Action

(i) *Duty to pay the price*

Obviously an action for the agreed sum cannot be brought if the duty to pay it has not arisen. Whether it has arisen depends primarily on the terms of the contract. Suppose that a contract of employment provides that the employee is to be paid wages after working for a month and that he is wrongfully dismissed after a week. He cannot sue for his wages but only for damages for wrongful dismissal.[14] On the other hand, in *Mount v Oldham Corp*[15] a local authority wrongfully withdrew boys from a school without giving the customary one term's notice. It was held that the headmaster was entitled to bring an action for the term's fees as it was an implied term of the contract that these should be paid in advance. **21–005**

(ii) *Rules of law*

The *action* for the price is not available merely because the *duty* to pay the price has arisen. The contract specifies the *duties* of the parties, but the law determines their *remedies*. This is generally recognised when specific performance is sought,[16] and it is also true of the action for the agreed sum. **21–006**

Sale of Goods Act 1979, section 49. The distinction[17] appears clearly in the Sale of Goods Act 1979. The *duty* to pay the price arises when the seller is ready and willing to deliver the goods (unless, of course, the sale is on credit or stipulates for an advance payment[18]). But s.49 of the Act provides that the *action* for the price is available to the seller if either the property in the goods has passed[19] to the buyer or the price is payable "on a day certain irrespective of delivery".[20] In *Stein Forbes & Co Ltd v County Tailoring Co Ltd*[21] a contract for the sale of sheepskins provided for payment in cash "against documents on arrival of steamer". This provision did not name a "day certain"; and the buyer's wrongful refusal to pay on tender of documents prevented the property in the goods from passing to him. It was held that the seller could not claim the price, but only damages. The effect **21–007**

---

[13] *The Eurus* [1996] 2 Lloyd's Rep 408 at 432; [1998] 1 Lloyd's Rep 351 at 358; *Parbulk AS v Kristen Marine SA* [2010] EWHC 900 (Comm) at [25]–[26]. Quaere whether, in the light of the decision in *The Achilleas* (see para 20–110), a contractual indemnity may be taken as evidence of the parties' intention in satisfaction of remoteness.

[14] See above, paras 17–015, 18–006.

[15] [1973] Q.B. 309; cf. *Denman v Winstanley* (1887) 4 T.L.R. 127.

[16] See below, para.21–028.

[17] The distinction drawn in the text is sometimes overlooked: e.g. in *Huyton SA v Peter Cremer GmbH* [1999] 1 Lloyd's Rep. 620 at 630 and 642.

[18] Sale of Goods Act 1979, ss.27, 28.

[19] s.49(1).

[20] s.49(2) (not applicable where payment dependent upon delivery: *Otis Vehicle Rentals Ltd v Cicely Commercials Ltd* [2002] EWCA Civ 1064; [2002] All E.R. (D) 203 (Jul)).

[21] (1916) 115 L.T. 215; cf. *Tradax Internacional SA v Goldschmidt SA* [1977] 2 Lloyd's Rep. 604; *Regent OHG Aisenstadt und Barig v Francesco of Jermyn Street* [1981] 3 All E.R. 327.

(and probable purpose) of this restriction on the seller's action for the price is to encourage him to dispose of the goods elsewhere and so to mitigate his loss.

The *Stein Forbes* case should be contrasted with *Workman Clark & Co v Lloyd Brasileno*[22] where a contract for the construction and sale of a boat provided for payments in instalments, the first of which was to become due when the keel was laid; and property was not to pass until this payment had been made. After the keel had been laid, the builder successfully sued for the first instalment. The case is hard to reconcile with the wording of s.49; but it nevertheless accurately reflects the underlying policy. At the stage which the work had reached it must have been hard for the builder to mitigate his loss by finding another customer for a boat built to the defendant's order—much harder, probably, than it was for the seller in the *Stein Forbes* case to resell the sheepskins.

(iii) *Conduct of the injured party*

21–008   **If injured party elects to terminate.** If, on wrongful repudiation of a contract, the injured party elects to terminate,[23] he cannot sue for any sum which, under the contract, was to accrue to him only after the date of termination.[24] He can claim damages for wrongful repudiation, and in assessing these the court may take into account any sums which he should have received under the broken contract. For example, if a hire-purchase agreement is wrongfully repudiated by the hirer and terminated by the owner, the owner cannot sue for instalments which were to accrue after the date of termination. But his damages may be based on the difference between the amount which the repudiating hirer was to have paid and the benefits obtained by the owner as a result of termination, e.g. in regaining possession of the goods.[25]

21–009   **If injured party elects to keep the contract alive.** Where the injured party elects to keep the contract alive, he can bring the action for the agreed sum if, at the time of repudiation, he has already done all that is required to make the action available: e.g. if he is a seller of goods and has already transferred the property in them to the buyer.[26] If he has not yet done all that is required to make the action available, the action for an agreed sum will depend on additional factors.

21–010   **Where the co-operation of the guilty party is needed.** No action for the agreed sum is available where it is impossible for the injured party to do the further required acts without the co-operation of the guilty party, who refuses to give it.[27] For example, if a singer wrongfully repudiates his contract with his agent, the latter cannot continue performance without the co-operation of the former;

---

[22] [1908] 1 K.B. 968; this report differs in some significant respects from those in 77 L.J.K.B. 953; 99 L.T. 481; and 11 Asp.M.L.C. 126.

[23] See Ch.18.

[24] See above, paras 18–010—18–012.

[25] See above, para.18–015.

[26] Sale of Goods Act 1979, s.49(1); in *Mackay v Dick* (1881) 6 App.Cas. 251 (where there was no discussion as to the remedy) property had apparently passed to the buyer, so that the action for the price would now be available under s.49(1).

[27] cf. *Ministry of Sound (Ireland) Ltd v World Online Ltd* [2003] EWHC 2178 (Ch); [2003] 2 All E.R. (Comm) 823 (sum due on a "day certain" and not dependent on the performance of the injured party; the action for the price was therefore available notwithstanding the need for co-operation for any further performance, but subject to a "defence" of failure of consideration).

and the agent's only claim is for damages[28]; and where work is to be done by A on the land or goods of B, who wrongfully refuses to allow A to have access to or possession of the property, then A cannot do the work without some co-operation from B and so his only remedy is an action for damages.[29] A could only do the work without B's co-operation if he already had possession of the goods or if he could get them without B's co-operation (e.g. from a warehouseman who had been effectively directed to deliver them to A[30]).

Where no co-operation of the guilty party is required. It is disputed whether the action for the agreed sum is available to the injured party where, at the time of repudiation, that party has not yet done all that was required of him to make the action available,[31] but where he can, and does, continue performance without the co-operation of the other party. In *White & Carter (Councils) Ltd v McGregor*[32] the appellants agreed to advertise the respondents' garage business for three years on plates attached to litterbins. Payment was to be at the rate of 2s. per week per plate, plus 5s. per annum towards the cost of each plate. The respondents repudiated the contract on the very day on which it was made but the appellants nevertheless prepared the plates, displayed them, and claimed the full amount due under the contract: £187 4s. for the space and £9 in respect of the plates. A majority of the House of Lords upheld the claim. The main reason given was that repudiation did not, of itself, bring a contract to an end. It only gave the injured party an option to terminate the contract; and if he chose instead to affirm, the contract remained "in full effect".[33] But this reasoning does not, of itself, lead to any conclusion as to the *particular remedy* available to the injured party. This appears from the cases in which the injured party *cannot* perform without the co-operation of the other party. Even here, repudiation does not of itself bring the contract to an end[34]; but the injured party's only remedy is an action for damages.[35]

21–011

Whether the injured party has a "legitimate interest" in recovering the agreed sum. The problem in cases of this kind is whether an award of the agreed sum is, on the one hand, necessary to protect the injured party, and, on the other, likely to cause undue hardship to the party in breach. In some cases it may make no difference to the injured party whether he (1) incurs the expense of performance and recovers the agreed sum, or (2) saves that expense by not performing and recovers the difference between it and the agreed sum by way of damages. If this is the position, damages are a perfectly adequate remedy. But there are other

21–012

---

[28] *Denmark Productions Ltd v Boscobel Productions Ltd* [1969] 1 Q.B. 699; cf. *Roberts v Ellwells Engineering Ltd* [1972] Q.B. 586; above, para.16–103.

[29] *Hounslow LBC v Twickenham Garden & Builders Ltd* [1971] Ch. 233 at 252–254; cf. *Attica Sea Carriers Corp v Ferrostaal Poseidon Bulk Reederei GmbH* [1976] 1 Lloyd's Rep. 250 at 256.

[30] e.g. *George Barker Transport Ltd v Eynon* [1974] 1 W.L.R. 462 at 468.

[31] The reference to the injured party not yet having done all that is required of him appears to have been misunderstood, or misinterpreted, in counsel's submissions in the *Reichman* case, below fn.39 at [29]; it is not literally a question of whether the injured party has anything *to do*, but whether or not he has *performed* in full so as to be entitled to the price. Thus, in the *Reichman* case, the landlord had granted the lease so that there was no more for him to do, but he had not performed in full in the sense of allowing the lease to run to the end of its term.

[32] [1962] A.C. 413; Goodhart 78 L.Q.R. 263; Nienaber [1962] C.L.J. 213; Liu 74 M.L.R. 171.

[33] ibid. at 427.

[34] See above, para.18–005.

[35] See the authorities cited in fn.28, above; cf. *The Alaskan Trader* [1983] 2 Lloyd's Rep. 645 at 651 (quoted above, para.18–006).

situations in which the injured party would be prejudiced by discontinuing performance and claiming damages: e.g. where this leads to injury to his reputation, for which damages (so far as recoverable at all[36]) could not be accurately assessed; where the injured party has entered into commitments with third parties which he must honour as a matter of business[37]; where part of the loss which the injured party would actually suffer is legally irrecoverable because it is too remote[38]; or where it is unclear that damages could be recovered at all.[39] It is only in cases of this kind that the rule in *McGregor*'s case will be applied, for Lord Reid there said that, if the injured party has "no substantial or legitimate interest"[40] in completing performance, his only remedy will be in damages. "Legitimate interest" here means that "the innocent party must have reasonable grounds for keeping the contract open, bearing in mind also the interests of the wrongdoer",[41] and if these conditions are satisfied, it is hard to see why the injured party should not be entitled to complete his performance and claim the agreed sum. Three contrary arguments must, however, be considered.

21–013   **Mitigation.** The first, and most important, argument is that the injured party should mitigate his loss. It has been said, in reply, that mitigation is relevant only to a claim for damages and not to a claim for an agreed sum[42]; and in many cases this is no doubt true. A seller of goods who claims damages for non-acceptance may be under a duty to mitigate by reselling the goods; but once he has acquired the right to sue for the price[43] there seems, in English law,[44] to be no suggestion that he must mitigate even though he can easily resell and even though he is in a much better position than the buyer to do so. But even if this rule always[45] applies

---

[36] See above, para.20–091; cf. *The Odenfeld* [1978] 2 Lloyd's Rep. 357 (damages very hard to assess).

[37] See *Anglo-African Shipping Co of New York Inc v Mortner* [1962] 1 Lloyd's Rep. 81 at 94, affirmed on other grounds ibid.: at 610; *The Odenfeld* [1978] 2 Lloyd's Rep. 357; below, para.21–013.

[38] See above, para.20–099 et seq.

[39] *Reichman v Beveridge* [2006] EWCA Civ 1659; [2007] 1 P. & C.R. 20 (landlord entitled to maintain lease and recover the rent because it is unclear whether the doctrine of repudiation applies to the English law of landlord and tenant, entitling the landlord to accept the tenant's repudiatory breach and sue for loss of future rent; cf. *Walls v Atcheson* (1826) 3 Bing. 462 (damages not recoverable); the 2000 Blundell Lectures (delivered by Lord Millett and Sir David Neuberger).

[40] [1962] A.C. 413 at 431; *The Alaskan Trader* [1983] 2 Lloyd's Rep. at 651; the legitimate "interest" may be in acquiring a security in the subject-matter: *George Barker Transport Ltd v Eynon* [1974] 1 W.L.R. 462. The requirement of "legitimate interest" brings the English rule close to the American rule, with which it is said to conflict: under Restatement, *Contracts*, s.338, Comment c: the innocent party must not "unreasonably" continue performance after breach; cf. Restatement 2d, *Contracts*, para.350 Comment b.

[41] *Stocznia Gdanska SA v Latvian Shipping Co* [1996] 2 Lloyd's Rep. 132 at 139, reversed on another ground [1998] 1 W.L.R. 574; cf. *Reichman v Beveridge* [2006] EWCA Civ 1659; [2007] 1 P. & C.R. 20 2007] 1 P. & C.R. 20 at [41] (the innocent party's conduct must be "wholly unreasonable").

[42] Scott [1962] C.L.J. 12.

[43] See above, para.21–002.

[44] Contrast U.C.C., s.2–709(1)(b), by which the seller can sue for the price of goods identified to the contract only if he is "unable after reasonable effort to resell them at a reasonable price", or the circumstances indicate that such an effort would be unavailing.

[45] If the seller is "bound to do something to [specific] goods for the purpose of putting them into a deliverable state, the property does not pass until the thing is done and the buyer has notice that it has been done": Sale of Goods Act 1979, s.18, r.2. Thus before the seller does the required act the action for the price is not generally available: s.49(1). It is sometimes assumed that, if the buyer repudiates at this stage, the seller can nevertheless do the act and sue for the price, but there is no actual decision to this effect.

in cases involving sale of goods, it does not follow that it must necessarily apply to cases involving other kinds of contracts. In particular, it is submitted that the policy of the mitigation rules (which is to prevent needless waste) should make those rules applicable, even in an action for the agreed sum, where at the time of repudiation the claimant has not yet done all that is required of him to make that action available. This submission is supported by the *Attica Sea Carriers*[46] case, where a demise charterparty imposed continuing obligations on both parties. The charterer undertook to execute certain repairs before redelivery of the ship and to pay the agreed hire till then; and for the present purpose it was assumed[47] that the contract did not require the owner to accept redelivery until the repairs had been done. On the charterer's refusal to do the repairs, it was nevertheless held that the owner's remedy was not an action for the agreed hire. As the cost of the repairs far exceeded the value of the ship when repaired,[48] the owner had no "legitimate interest" in insisting on continued performance. Hence the mitigation rules required him to accept redelivery of the unrepaired ship and to seek his remedy in damages.

It does not follow that, in cases of this kind, the mitigation rules will always require the injured party to take such a course, since they require him only to act reasonably.[49] In *The Odenfeld*[50] a time charterer wrongfully repudiated the charterparty by refusing to pay the agreed hire. It was held that the shipowners were not bound at once to accept the repudiation and seek their remedy in damages, but that they could sue for the agreed hire until they finally did accept the repudiation. They had acted reasonably in requiring continued performance since the ship remained available for service,[51] and since they had entered into an obligation to third parties (to whom they had assigned hire due under the charterparty) to keep the contract in existence.

The argument that the appellants should have mitigated by discontinuing performance was no doubt open to the respondents in *McGregor*'s case; but it is submitted that the result in that case was consistent with the mitigation rules. There are, as will be recollected,[52] two such rules. The first is that the appellants should have minimised loss by reletting the advertising space. But the burden of proving that they could indeed have done this was on the respondents[53] and does

---

[46] [1976] 1 Lloyd's Rep. 250; Kerr 41 M.L.R. 1 at 20–21; cf. *The Alaskan Trader* [1983] 2 Lloyd's Rep. 645 where a shipowner had no legitimate interest in spending more money than the ship was worth on repairing her so as to keep her available for service; Carter and Marston [1985] C.L.J. 18.

[47] The assumption was in fact regarded as ill-founded: above, para.18–047.

[48] cf. above, paras 20–040, 20–119.

[49] See above, para.20–116.

[50] [1978] 2 Lloyd's Rep. 357.

[51] ibid. at 374; the owners could perform without the charterer's co-operation by simply (in the absence of orders) laying up the ship; contrast, on this point, *The Alaskan Trader* [1983] 2 Lloyd's Rep. 645 at 652.

[52] See above, paras 20–116—20–119.

[53] *Roper v Johnson* (1873) L.R. 8 C.P. 187; *Regent OHG Aisenstadt und Barig v Francesco of Jermyn Street* [1981] 3 All E.R. 327 at 332; *The Kriti Rex* [1996] 2 Lloyd's Rep. 171 at 199; (in these cases, the claims were for damages, but there is no reason to suppose that a different rule as to burden of proof would apply in an action for the agreed sum); and see *Sony Computer Entertainment UK Ltd v Cinram Logistics* [2008] EWCA Civ 955; [2009] Bus L.R. 529. The burden will be particularly difficult to discharge where the defendant could himself have carried out the "act of mitigation", but failed to do so: *Reichman v Beveridge* [2006] EWCA Civ 1659; [2007] 1 P. & C.R. 20 (tenant in default could have found an assignee and asked the landlord not to refuse his consent without reasonable grounds: Landlord and Tenant Act 1988, s.1(3)(a)).

not seem to have been discharged.[54] The argument required proof that the demand for space exceeded the appellants' available supply[55] and no evidence seems to have been directed to this issue. The second rule is that the appellants should not have augmented loss by spending money on the preparation of the plates. This has to be considered on the assumption that the space could not have been re-let, or that it was doubtful whether it could have been re-let. As a matter of strict law, the appellants could (on this assumption) have abandoned the contract and recovered the difference between the agreed rental and any expenses thus saved by way of damages.[56] Hence it could be said that the expense of preparing the plates should not have been incurred as it did not benefit anyone. But the mitigation rules do not require the injured party to act in accordance with the strict law. They only require him to act reasonably[57]; and if there was no possibility of reletting the space, or only a doubtful one, it seems that the appellants did act reasonably in incurring the expense necessary to substantiate their claim for the agreed sum.

21–014   **Indirect specific performance.** The second argument against *McGregor*'s case is that the award of the agreed sum amounted to indirect specific performance,[58] but it does not seem that any of the reasons for refusing direct specific performance of such a contract applied in the circumstances of the case. Possible reasons for such refusal are that enforcement of the decree would require "constant supervision"; that there was no "mutuality"[59]; and that the contract involved "personal" service.[60] But the first two reasons do not apply where the contract has been fully performed by one party and the only outstanding liability of the other is to pay cash.[61] Nor does the third reason seem to apply (even if one makes the doubtful assumption that the services were "personal") where one party has been able to perform *without any co-operation from the other.*[62]

21–015   **Hardship.** A third argument against *McGregor*'s case is that it is hard on the party in breach to have to pay for a performance which he does not want. But the injured party will not be entitled to the agreed sum if he has no "substantial or legitimate interest"[63] in completing performance; and even if he has such an interest, his action for the agreed sum may still fail if he ought to have mitigated by discontinuing performance. When these qualifications are borne in mind, it is

---

[54] Lord Morton [1962] A.C. 413 at 432, says that the appellants "made no effort" to relet the space. But there is nothing to show whether efforts to relet would have succeeded; cf. *Reichman v Beveridge* [2006] EWCA Civ 1659; [2007] 1 P. & C.R. 20 at [15]; Rodger 93 L.Q.R. 168.

[55] Unless this were so, the appellants would be under no duty to re-let the space originally let to the respondents: they would be entitled to let *other* space to other customers, cf. above, para.20–059.

[56] cf. *British and Beningtons Ltd v NW Cachar Tea Co Ltd* [1923] A.C. 48; above, para.17–027.

[57] See above, para.20–116.

[58] [1962] A.C. 413 at 433.

[59] *Ministry of Sound (Ireland) Ltd v World Online Ltd* [2003] EWHC 2178 (Ch); [2003] 2 All E.R. (Comm) 823 at [68].

[60] See below, paras 21–035—21–040, 21–046—21–047.

[61] See below, paras 21–038, 21–046—21–047. The contract in *McGregor*'s case was to display the advertisements for three years from November 1957 and the action was commenced in October 1958, the claim being brought under an acceleration clause (above, paras 20–132(b), 20–133). In view of this clause nothing turned on the fact that performance had not been completed when the action was brought: see [1962] A.C. 413 at 426–427.

[62] [1962] A.C. 413 at 429.

[63] ibid. at 431.

submitted that the rule in *McGregor*'s case represents a reasonable compromise between the interests of the two contracting parties.

2. SPECIFIC RELIEF IN EQUITY[64]

(a) Specific Performance[65]

The common law did not specifically enforce contractual obligations except **21–016** those to pay money. Specific enforcement of other contractual obligations was available only in equity. It was (and is) subject to many restrictions. These are based partly on the drastic character of the remedy,[66] which leads (more readily than an award of damages or of the agreed sum) to attachment of the defendant's person.[67] But this is an important factor only where the contract calls for "personal" performance, i.e. for acts to be done by the defendant himself. Where the contract is not of this kind, it can be specifically enforced without personal constraint: e.g. by sequestration,[68] or by the execution of a formal document by an officer of the court.[69] Other reasons for restricting specific enforcement are that this form of relief may be unnecessary, undesirable or impracticable on various grounds to be considered in the discussion that follows. In a number of later authorities, some of these reasons are no longer regarded as entirely convincing,[70] so that these cases support some expansion in the scope of the remedy.[71] The decision of the House of Lords in *Co-operative Ins Society Ltd v Argyll Stores Ltd*[72] may, however, foreshadow some degree of return to a more restrictive view, though with modern justifications.

(i) *Granted where damages not "adequate"*

The traditional view is that specific performance will not be ordered where **21–017** damages are an "adequate" remedy.[73] After illustrating this requirement, we shall see that it now requires some reformulation.

Availability of satisfactory equivalent. Damages are most obviously an **21–018** adequate remedy where the claimant can get a satisfactory equivalent of what he contracted for from some other source. For this reason specific performance is not generally ordered of contracts for the sale of commodities, or of shares, which are

---

[64] Spry, *Equitable Remedies* (8th edn); Sharpe, *Injunctions and Specific Performance* (3rd edn)

[65] Fry, *Specific Performance* (6th edn); Jones and Goodhart, *Specific Performance* (2nd edn).

[66] cf. *Co-operative Ins Society Ltd v Argyll Stores (Holdings) Ltd* [1998] A.C. 1 at 12.

[67] cf. *Enfield LBC v Mahoney* [1983] 1 W.L.R. 749, where even imprisonment failed to induce compliance with an order for specific restitution. Imprisonment for debt has been abolished (subject to exceptions not here relevant) by Debtors Act 1869, ss.4, 5, and Administration of Justice Act 1970, s.11. "Lawful arrest or detention of a person for non-compliance with the lawful order of a court" is permitted by Human Rights Act 1998, Sch.1, Pt I, Art.5(1)(b).

[68] *Miliangos v George Frank (Textiles) Ltd* [1976] A.C. 443 at 494, 497.

[69] *The Messianiki Tolmi* [1983] 2 A.C. 787.

[70] e.g. below, paras 21–028, 21–035—21–040.

[71] A trend forecast by Lord Justice Fry in his work on *Specific Performance*: see (6th edn), para.47; cf. Burrows 4 Legal Studies 102.

[72] [1998] A.C. 1; below, para.21–040.

[73] ibid. at 11; *Bankers Trust Co v PT Jakarta International Hotels & Development* [1999] 1 Lloyd's Rep. 910 at 911.

readily available in the market.[74] In such cases the claimant can buy in the market and is adequately compensated by recovering the difference between the contract and the market price by way of damages. Indeed, he is required to make the substitute purchase in order to mitigate his loss.[75] If he fails to do so, he cannot recover damages for extra loss suffered because the market has risen after the date when the substitute contract should have been made. To award him specific performance in such a case would, in substance, conflict with the principles of mitigation[76] as well as being oppressive to the defendant.[77] Similar reasoning seems to underlie the rule that a contract to lend money cannot be specifically enforced by either party[78]: it is assumed that damages can easily be assessed by reference to current rates of interest.

21–019   **No satisfactory equivalent available.** Damages will not be regarded as an adequate remedy where the claimant cannot obtain a satisfactory substitute. The law takes the view that a buyer of land or of a house[79] (however ordinary) is not adequately compensated by damages, and that he can therefore get an order of specific performance.[80] Even a contractual licence to occupy land, though creating no interest in the land,[81] may be specifically enforced.[82] A vendor of land, too, can get specific performance, though his only claim is for money.[83] One reason for this

---

[74] *Cud v Rutter* (1719) 1 P.Wms. 570; *Re Schwabacher* (1908) 98 L.T. 127 at 128; cf. *Fothergill v Rowland* (1873) L.R. 17 Eq. 137; *Garden Cottage Foods Ltd v Milk Marketing Board* [1984] A.C. 130; *aliter* if the shares are not readily available: *Langen & Wind Ltd v Bell* [1972] Ch. 685; *Jobson v Johnson* [1989] 1 W.L.R. 1026; *Pena v Dale* [2003] EWHC 1065; [2004] 2 B.C.L.C. 508 at [135], or if the contract is for the sale of shares giving a controlling interest in the company: *Harvela Investments Ltd v Royal Trust C of Canada (CI) Ltd* [1986] A.C. 207.

[75] See above, para.20–116.

[76] See *Buxton v Lister* (1746) 3 Atk. 383 at 384.

[77] See *Re Schwabacher* (1908) 98 L.T. 127, where shares rose in value after breach. In such a case the defendant could be given the option of transferring the shares or paying the difference between contract and market price on the day fixed for performance, as in *Colt v Nettervill* (1725) 2 P.Wms. 301. See also *Whiteley Ltd v Hilt* [1918] 2 K.B. 808; *MEPC v Christian Edwards* [1978] Ch. 281 at 293 (affirmed on other grounds [1981] A.C. 205); *Chinn v Hochstrasser* [1979] Ch. 447 (reversed on other grounds [1981] A.C. 533).

[78] *Rogers v Challis* (1859) 27 Beav. 175 (suit by lender); *Sichel v Mosenthal* (1862) 30 Beav. 371 (suit by borrower: decision based on lack of mutuality (below, para.21–046) rather than adequacy of damages); cf. *Larios v Bonnany y Gurety* (1873) L.R. 5 C.P. 346. By statute the court can specifically enforce a contract to take debentures in a company, that is, to make a secured loan to the company: Companies Act 2006, s.740 reversing *South African Territories Ltd v Wallington* [1898] A.C. 309. A contract to subscribe for shares in a company is also specifically enforceable: *Odessa Tramways Co v Mendel* (1878) 8 Ch.D. 235; *Sri Lanka Omnibus Co v Perera* [1952] A.C. 76.

[79] Fry, *Specific Performance* (6th edn), para.62. Damages are, however, an adequate remedy for breach of a "lock-out" agreement relating to land since such an agreement is intended merely to protect the prospective purchaser from wasting costs and does not give him any right to insist on conveyance of the land: *Tye v House* [1997] 2 E.G.L.R. 171.

[80] Unless he elects to claim damages, as in *Meng Leong Developments Pte Ltd v Jip Hong Trading Co Pte Ltd* [1985] A.C. 511.

[81] See *Ashburn Anstalt v Arnold* [1989] Ch. 1, overruled on another point in *Prudential Assurance Co Ltd v London Residuary Body* [1992] 2 A.C. 386.

[82] *Verrall v Great Yarmouth BC* [1981] Q.B. 202; cf. *Dutton v Manchester Airport Plc* [1999] 2 All E.R. 675, where the licensee's claim was not against the licensor but against a trespasser.

[83] e.g. *Walker v Eastern Counties Ry* (1848) 6 Hare 594; *Miliangos v George Frank (Textiles) Ltd* [1976] A.C. 443 at 496; cf. *Amec Properties v Planning & Research Systems* [1992] 1 E.G.L.R. 70. Where the purchaser has been allowed to go into possession and has then failed to complete, and the vendor has not elected between termination and specific performance, the court may (unless the contract otherwise provides) order the purchaser either to perform or to vacate the premises: see *Greenwood v Turner* [1891] 2 Ch. 144; *Maskell v Ivory* [1970] Ch. 502; *Attfield v DJ Plant Hire & General Contractors* [1987] Ch. 141.

rule is that it is just to allow the remedy *to* him as it is available *against* him. Another is that damages will not adequately compensate him for not getting the whole price, as he may not easily be able to find another purchaser.[84] And he may be anxious to rid himself of burdens attached to the land.[85] But the rule seems to apply though the land is readily saleable to a third party; and it has even been applied where after contract but before completion a compulsory purchase order was made in respect of the land.[86] Yet in such a case damages (consisting of the amount by which the contract price exceeded the compensation payable on compulsory acquisition) would normally be an adequate remedy.

Damages hard to quantify. A second factor which is relevant (though not decisive[87]) in considering the adequacy of damages is the difficulty of assessing and recovering them.[88] This is one reason why specific performance has been ordered of contracts to sell (or to pay) annuities,[89] and of a sale of debts proved in bankruptcy,[90] the value of such rights being uncertain. Similarly, a contract to execute a mortgage in consideration of money lent at, or before, the time of the contract can be specifically enforced,[91] since the value of obtaining security for a debt cannot be precisely quantified. The same is true of the right to have a loan repaid out of specific property; and a term in a contract of loan conferring such a right is therefore specifically enforceable.[92] Even where there is no such difficulty in *quantifying* the loss, damages may be an inadequate remedy because the claimant's loss is difficult to prove,[93] or because certain items of loss[94] may not be legally recoverable, or because damages may be delayed for too long and put the

21–020

---

[84] *Lewis v Lord Lechmere* (1722) 10 Mod. 503.

[85] Fry, *Specific Performance* (6th edn), para.72.

[86] *Hillingdon Estate Co v Stonefield Estates Ltd* [1952] Ch. 627. The contract is not frustrated by the making of the order: above, para.19–065; but after title to the land has vested in the acquiring authority by virtue of the compulsory purchase, the vendor's remedy is in damages and not by way of specific performance: *E Johnson & Co (Barbados) v NSR Ltd* [1997] A.C. 400.

[87] *Soc des Industries Metallurgiques SA v Bronx Engineering Co Ltd* [1975] 1 Lloyd's Rep. 465.

[88] *Thames Valley Power Ltd v Total Gas and Power Ltd* [2005] EWHC 2208 (Comm); [2006] 1 Lloyd's Rep 441 at [64]. The inclusion of a liquidated damages clause in the contract (see above, para.20–130) does not preclude the court from assessing the claimant's actual loss when deciding whether to grant specific relief: *Bath & North East Somerset DC v Mowlem Plc* [2004] EWCA Civ 115; [2004] B.L.R. 153 at [15]. Damages may have been hard to quantify in *The Bremen Max* [2008] EWHC 2755 (Comm); [2009] 1 Lloyd's Rep. 81 where specific performance was ordered of the charterer's undertaking to provide security to prevent the arrest or secure the release of the ship but the reason given was that "the commercial purpose and intention" of the clause was that the Owners should not have to incur the cost themselves at all (at [22]).

[89] *Ball v Coggs* (1710) 1 Bro. P.C. 140; *Kenney v Wexham* (1822) 6 Madd. 355; *Beswick v Beswick* [1968] A.C. 58; see, however, Fry, *Specific Performance* (6th edn), para.65; *Crampton v Varna Ry* (1872) L.R. 7 Ch.App. 562.

[90] *Adderley v Dixon* (1824) 1 C. & S. 607.

[91] *Ashton v Corrigan* (1871) L.R. 13 Eq. 76; *Swiss Bank Corp v Lloyds Bank Ltd* [1982] A.C. 584 at 595, affirmed [1982] A.C. 584 at 610.

[92] *Swiss Bank Corp v Lloyds Bank Ltd* [1979] Ch. 548, reversed [1982] A.C. 584, but on the ground that the contract did not on its true construction contain any such term; cf. *Kingscroft Ins Co Ltd v HS Weaver (Underwriting) Agencies Ltd* [1993] 1 Lloyd's Rep. 187 at 193; *Napier and Ettrick v Hunter* [1993] 1 A.C. 713 at 952.

[93] *Decro-Wall International SA v Practitioners in Marketing Ltd* [1971] 1 W.L.R. 361; *Hollis v Stocks* [2000] U.K.C.L.R. 685.

[94] *Hill v C A Parsons Ltd* [1972] 1 Ch. 305; *Evans Marshall & Co Ltd v Bertola SA* [1973] 1 W.L.R. 349 (injury to employment prospects and reputation; formerly, but no longer, regarded as irrecoverable: see above, para.20–092).

claimant at risk of insolvency,[95] or quite simply because the defendant may not be "good for the money".[96]

21–021   **Damages nominal.** In *Beswick v Beswick*[97] specific performance was ordered of a contract to pay an annuity to a third party. A majority[98] of the House of Lords took the view that damages were an inadequate remedy because they would be purely nominal, the promisee or his estate having suffered no loss. The point here seems to be, not that the promisee would be inadequately compensated, but that the defendant would be unjustly enriched (if damages were the sole remedy) by being allowed to retain the entire benefit of the promisee's performance while performing only a small part of his own promise.

21–022   **Sale of goods.** Section 52 of the Sale of Goods Act 1979 gives the court a discretion to order specific performance in an action for breach of a contract to deliver "specific or ascertained" goods.[99] Although the section deals only with cases in which this remedy is sought by the buyer, the court also has power to order specific performance at the suit of the seller.[100]

21–023   **Whether goods must be "unique".** Section 52 is based on an earlier enactment, which had been passed to broaden the scope of the remedy.[101] This seemed to have been restricted to cases in which the buyer could not get a satisfactory substitute because the goods were "unique". Heirlooms, great works of art and rare antiques are regarded as "unique" for this purpose[102]; and it seems that the courts go some way towards recognising a concept of "commercial uniqueness". Thus they may order specific performance of a contract to supply a ship,[103] or machinery or other industrial plant which cannot readily be obtained elsewhere.[104]

---

[95] *Thames Valley Power Ltd v Total Gas and Power Ltd* [2005] EWHC 2208 (Comm); [2006] 1 Lloyd's Rep 441 at [64].

[96] *Evans Marshall & Co Ltd v Bertola SA*, above, at 380; cf. *The Oakworth* [1975] 1 Lloyd's Rep. 581 at 583; *Themehelp Ltd v West* [1996] Q.B. 84; *Kall-Kwik Printing (UK) v Bell* [1994] F.S.R. 674.

[97] [1968] A.C. 58; above, para.14–017; below, paras 21–048—21–049. For the effects on such facts of the Contracts (Rights of Third Parties) Act 1999, see also above, para.14–094.

[98] For Lord Pearce's view, see below, fn.292.

[99] "Specific" primarily means "identified and agreed on at the time a contract of sale is made": s.61(1); for an extension of the definition, see below, at fn.114. "Ascertained" is not defined in the Act but seems to mean "identified in accordance with the agreement after the time a contract of sale is made": *Re Wait* [1927] 1 Ch. 606 at 630; or identified in any other way: *Thames Sack & Bag Co Ltd v Knowles* (1918) 88 L.J.K.B. 585 at 588.

[100] *The Messiniaki Tolmi* [1982] Q.B. 1248, affirmed [1983] 2 A.C. 787, without reference to this point. For earlier authorities on the availability of the remedy to the seller, contrast *Shell–Mex Ltd v Elton Copy Dyeing Co* (1928) 34 Com Cas. 39 at 47 with *Elliott v Pierson* [1948] 1 All E.R. 939 at 943. The practical effect of ordering specific performance at the suit of the seller is to enable him to get an order for the payment of the price in a case falling outside Sale of Goods Act 1979, s.49 (above, para.21–007).

[101] s.2 of the Mercantile Law Amendment Act 1856; Treitel [1966] J.B.L. 211.

[102] *Pusey v Pusey* (1684) 1 Vern. 273; *Somerset v Cookson* (1735) 3 P.Wms. 390; *Lowther v Lowther* (1806) 3 Ves. 95; *Falcke v Gray* (1859) 4 Drew. 651 at 658.

[103] Which "in some respects the law of contract . . . treats as if she were a piece of realty": *The Laconia* [1977] A.C. 850 at 874.

[104] See *Nutbrown v Thornton* (1804) 10 Ves. 159; *Behnke v Bede Shipping Co* [1927] 1 K.B. 649; *The Star Gazer* [1985] 1 Lloyd's Rep. 370; *Batthyany v Bouch* (1881) 50 L.J.Q.B. 421; cf. *Lingen v Simpson* (1824) 1 S. & S. 600 (pattern books); *Land Rover Group Ltd v UPF (UK) Ltd* [2002] EWHC 3183; [2003] 2 B.C.L.C. 222. Contrast *Soc des Industries Metallurgiques SA v Bronx Engineering Co Ltd* [1975] 1 Lloyd's Rep. 465 (machinery available from another source); *The Stena Nautica (No.2)* [1982] 2 Lloyd's Rep. 336.

Another special factor which may induce the court to order specific performance of a contract for the sale of goods is that the goods form the contents of a house which is being sold by the same seller to the same buyer, either by the same contract or by a separate contemporaneous one.[105] The court is particularly ready to order specific performance in such a case if removal of the goods would damage the land, but the remedy is not limited to such circumstances.[106]

Section 52 does not restrict the discretion to order specific performance to cases in which the goods are "unique"; but the courts nevertheless at one time took the view that the discretion should be sparingly exercised.[107] One reason for this view is that the specific enforceability of a contract for the sale of goods might give the buyer an equitable interest in the goods[108]; and this could adversely affect third parties who had only constructive (but no actual) notice of that interest: e.g. it could give the buyer priority over not only unsecured but also secured creditors if he had paid for the goods and the seller had then become insolvent.[109] But a restrictive view of the scope of specific performance has been taken even where this factor of insolvency was not present. For example, in *Cohen v Roche*[110] the court refused specific performance to a buyer of a set of Hepplewhite chairs, saying they were "ordinary articles of commerce and of no special value or interest".[111] It is hard to see what legitimate interest of the seller was protected by the court's refusal to grant specific performance in this case; nor is the notion that damages are necessarily an adequate remedy for breach of a contract to sell goods unless they are "unique" an easy one to defend. The buyer may not in fact be able to get a substitute; his loss may be hard to assess; and part of it may be irrecoverable (e.g. because it is too remote).

Goods in bulk. Section 52 refers only to goods which are "specific or 21–024 ascertained".[112] The section therefore does not apply where the goods are purely generic (e.g. where the sale is of "1,000 tons of wheat"). Where the goods form an undifferentiated part of an identified bulk, a distinction must, as a result of

---

[105] *Record v Bell* [1991] 1 W.L.R. 853 at 862.

[106] ibid.

[107] A little-noticed exception is *Rawlings v General Trading Co* [1921] 1 K.B. 635, where specific performance was granted without argument as to the remedy.

[108] For the view that specific enforceability does not necessarily give rise to an equitable interest, see *Tailby v Official Receiver* (1888) 13 App. Cas. 523 at 548; *Re London Wine Co (Shippers)* [1986] P.C.C. 121 at 149; cf. also *Leigh & Sillivan Ltd v Aliakmon Shipping Co (The Aliakmon)* [1986] A.C. 785, where it was said at 812–813 that equitable "ownership" or "title" did not pass under a contract for the sale of unascertained goods on "appropriation" of particular goods to the contract; but damages for breach of the contract would clearly have been an adequate remedy (above, para.21–017) so that the question whether an equitable interest in goods can pass under a specifically enforceable contract for the sale of goods remains an open one.

[109] It was the fear of giving the buyer priority over secured creditors that was the main reason why specific performance was refused in *Re Wait* [1927] 1 Ch. 606: see esp. at 640. The buyer's problems in that case arose from the general rule, laid down by Sale of Goods Act 1979, s.16, that property under a contract of sale cannot pass in goods which are unascertained: see *Re Goldcorp Exchange Ltd* [1995] 1 A.C. 74; contrast *Re Stapylton Fletcher* [1994] 1 W.L.R. 1181, where the goods were segregated from the seller's own stock after sale. The buyer's interests are now in turn protected by a statutory exception to the general rule in s.16: see s.20A, discussed after fn.116, below. Insolvency of the defendant is not a ground for refusing specific performance where the remedy is normally available as a matter of course: *Amec Properties v Planning Research and Systems* [1992] 1 E.G.L.R. 70.

[110] [1927] 1 K.B. 169.

[111] ibid. at 181. Contrast *Phillips v Lamdin* [1949] 2 K.B. 33 (Adam-style door).

[112] See fn.99, above.

amendments to the Sale of Goods Act,[113] be drawn between two types of cases. The first consists of cases in which the part sold is expressed as a *fraction or percentage* of the bulk: e.g. half the cotton shipped on the *Peerless*. Such a contract is one for the sale of specific goods so long as the bulk was identified and agreed on when the contract was made[114]; and the court therefore has a discretion to order specific performance of it under s.52 of the 1979 Act. The second consists of cases in which the part sold is expressed as a *specified quantity* of unascertained goods to be taken from an identified bulk[115]: e.g. 5,000 bales out of the cargo of cotton shipped or to be shipped on the *Peerless*, on which 10,000 bales are shipped in bulk. In such a case[116] the buyer can become owner in common of the goods to the extent that he had paid for them[117] and so he would have less need[118] to seek specific performance to secure priority over other creditors in the event of the seller's insolvency. He would, however, acquire such ownership, not because the goods were specific or ascertained, but in spite of the fact they remained unascertained.[119] Cases of this kind are therefore not covered by the words of s.52, under which the court has a discretion to order specific performance of a contract for the delivery of "specific or ascertained" goods.

21–025   **Where goods are not "specific or ascertained".** It is an open question whether the court may not in appropriate circumstances have a discretion to order a seller specifically to perform his undertaking to deliver goods even in cases which fall outside s.52. The section does not in terms say that specific performance can be ordered *only* where the goods are "specific or ascertained"; and it is arguable that the remedy should be available, even where the goods are not of this kind, if to grant it would give effect to the general principle governing its scope. This might, for example, be the position where a contract was made to supply a manufacturer with goods urgently needed by him for the purpose of his business. Damages might be an inadequate remedy in such a case, for they

> "would be a poor consolation if the failure of supplies forces a trader to lay off staff and disappoint his customers (whose affections may be transferred to others) and ultimately forces him towards insolvency . . . ".[120]

The view that specific performance could be ordered on such grounds[121] seemed at one time to have been abandoned[122]; but later cases give it fresh support. During

---

[113] Made by Sale of Goods (Amendment) Act 1995.

[114] Sale of Goods Act 1979, s.61(1), definition of "specific goods" as amended by s.2(a) of the 1995 Act.

[115] As in *Re Wait* [1927] 1 Ch. 606.

[116] Sale of Goods Act 1979, s.20A(1), as inserted by s.1(3) of the 1995 Act.

[117] ibid., s.20A(2).

[118] The buyer's property acquired by virtue of s.20A(2) would not necessarily prevail against a competing interest such as that of a bank to which documents of title representing the goods had been pledged, as in *Re Wait*, above; and where it did not so prevail the court would be unlikely to order specific performance to disturb this state of affairs.

[119] Sale of Goods Act 1979, s.20A(1) refers to the goods (in a case of the present kind) as "a specified quantity of *unascertained* goods."

[120] *Howard E Perry & Co v British Railways Board* [1980] 1 W.L.R. 1375 at 1383.

[121] *Taylor v Neville*, unreported, cited with approval in *Buxton v Lister* (1746) 3 Atk. 383 and in *Adderley v Dixon* (1824) 1 S. & S. 607.

[122] See *Fothergill v Rowland* (1873) L.R. 17 Eq. 137; *Pollard v Clayton* (1885) 1 K. & J. 462; *Dominion Coal Co v Dominion Iron & Steel Co* [1909] A.C. 293. Contrast *Donnell v Bennett* (1883) 23 Ch.D. 835, taking a more liberal view.

a steel strike in 1980 a manufacturer sought an order for the specific delivery of a quantity of steel belonging to him against a rail carrier who (in fear of strike action) refused to allow it to be moved. The court made the order because, during the strike, "steel [was] available only with great difficulty".[123] It is submitted that, in such circumstances, specific performance should similarly be available to a buyer. This view is supported by a case[124] in which, during the "energy crisis" in 1973, an interim injunction was granted to stop an oil company from cutting off supplies of petrol to a garage, since alternative supplies were not available. As the goods were not "specific or ascertained", the case gives some support to the view that an obligation to deliver goods may be specifically enforced in a case falling outside s.52.[125]

Defective goods. The concept of specific performance in s.52 is that of a remedy for *non-delivery* of goods; but there is the further possibility that specific relief may be sought in respect of *defective delivery*, i.e. delivery of goods which are not in conformity with the contract. This possibility is recognised by amendments[126] to the Sale of Goods Act 1979, by which a buyer who deals as a consumer and to whom goods are sold by a commercial seller may, if the goods are not in conformity with the contract, require the seller to repair or replace them.[127] The remedy of specific performance is made available to enforce the seller's duty to comply with such a requirement[128]; and this extension of the remedy is, it is submitted, consistent with the principles governing specific relief in English law. Damages are unlikely to be the most appropriate remedy for a consumer who has bought (for example) an appliance which malfunctions; while hardship to the seller is avoided by a number of restrictions on the remedies described above. Thus repair or replacement cannot be ordered if either remedy is impossible,[129] or disproportionate in comparison to the other remedies available.[130] Specific performance can also be refused where another of the new remedies (such as price reduction) provided by the recent amendments[131] is "appropriate",[132] i.e. more appropriate than specific relief.

21–026

Appropriateness of the remedy. The extension of specific relief (in the cases discussed above[133]) to situations not within s.52, as well as its legislative extension

21–027

---

[123] *Howard E Perry & Co v British Railways Board*, above, at 1383.

[124] *Sky Petroleum Ltd v VIP Petroleum Ltd* [1974] 1 W.L.R. 576; cf. *Total Oil (Great Britain) Ltd v Thompson Garage (Biggin Hill) Ltd* [1972] 1 Q.B. 318 at 324; *Redler Grain Silos Ltd v BICC Ltd* [1982] 1 Lloyd's Rep. 435; *Thames Valley Power Ltd v Total Gas and Power Ltd* [2005] EWHC 2208 (Comm); [2006] 1 Lloyd's Rep 441.

[125] This possibility was doubted in *Re London Wine Co (Shippers)* [1986] P.C.C. 121 at 149 but it was not necessary in that case to reach a final conclusion on the specific enforceability of the contract: see above, fn.108.

[126] Made by Sale and Supply of Goods to Consumers Regulations 2002 (SI 2002/3045) implementing Dir.1999/44. The Regulations provide similar remedies where goods are supplied to a consumer under a contract other than one of sale: for the sake of brevity, the following discussion is confined to cases of sale.

[127] Sale of Goods Act 1979, s.48A(2)(a) and 48B, as inserted by reg.5 of the above Regulations; for dealing as consumer, see Sale of Goods Act 1979, s.61(5A).

[128] ibid., s.48E(2).

[129] ibid., s.48B(3)(a); cf. below, para.21–033

[130] i.e. whichever of repair or replacement is the "other" remedy (s.48B(3)(b)), reduction in the price, or rescission (s.48B(3)(c)); cf. below, para.21–029.

[131] For price reduction, see the new s.48C, inserted by the Regulations referred to in fn.126, above.

[132] Sale of Goods Act 1979, s.48E(3) and (4).

[133] See above, at fnn.117–124.

to certain cases of defective delivery, represents a more satisfactory approach to the scope of the remedy than that of the older authorities according to which the remedy was available to a buyer of goods which were "unique" or in a similar category.[134] The more liberal view of the scope of the remedy is also reflected in dicta to the effect that the availability of specific performance depends on the *appropriateness* of that remedy in the circumstances of each case.[135] The question is not whether damages are an "adequate" remedy, but whether specific performance will "do more perfect and complete justice than an award of damages".[136] The point was well put in a case concerned with the analogous question whether an injunction should be granted:

> "The standard question … , are damages an adequate remedy? might perhaps, in the light of the authorities in recent years, be rewritten: is it just in all circumstances that the [claimant] should be confined to his remedy in damages … ?"[137]

A similar approach has been adopted to the analogous question whether specific performance can be ordered where the action for the agreed sum is also available. At one time a negative answer was given to this question, apparently because the common law remedy was an "adequate" one.[138] The current view, however, is that specific performance can be ordered in such a case if it is, in the circumstances, the most appropriate remedy.[139]

(ii) *Discretion*

21–028   Specific performance is a discretionary remedy: the court is not bound to grant it merely because the contract is valid at law and cannot be impeached on some specific equitable ground such as misrepresentation or undue influence.[140] The discretion is, however, "not an arbitrary … discretion, but one to be governed as far as possible by fixed rules and principles".[141] The court will, in particular, have regard to the grounds to be discussed below. Its discretion to refuse specific performance on such grounds cannot be excluded by the terms of the contract.[142]

21–029   **Severe hardship.** Specific performance can be refused on the ground of severe hardship to the defendant[143] e.g. where the cost of performance to the defendant

---

[134] See above, paras 21–022—21–024, especially at fnn.102, 103, and 110.

[135] *Beswick v Beswick* [1968] A.C. 58 at 88, 90–91, 102; cf. *Coulls v Bagot's Executor & Trustee Co Ltd* [1967] A.L.R. 385 at 412.

[136] *Tito v Waddell (No.2)* [1977] Ch. 106 at 322; *Rainbow Estates Ltd v Tokenhold* [1999] Ch. 64 at 72–73.

[137] *Evans Marshall & Co Ltd v Bertola SA* [1973] 1 W.L.R. 349 at 379.

[138] e.g. *Crampton v Varna Ry* (1872) L.R. 7 Ch.App. 562 at 567 ("a money contract not enforceable in this court").

[139] e.g. *Beswick v Beswick* [1968] A.C. 58. The burden is on the claimant to show that damages are not an adequate remedy: *The Stena Nautica (No.2)* [1982] 2 Lloyd's Rep. 336 at 348.

[140] *Stickney v Keeble* [1915] A.C. 386 at 419.

[141] *Lamare v Dixon* (1873) L.R. 6 H.L. 414 at 423; *Co-operative Ins Society Ltd v Argyll Stores (Holdings) Ltd* [1998] A.C. 1 at 16.

[142] *Quadrant Visual Communications Ltd v Hutchison Telephone (UK)* [1993] B.C.L.C. 442.

[143] *Denne v Light* (1857) 8 D.M. & G. 774; cf. *Wedgwood v Adams* (1843) 6 Beav. 600; *Sullivan v Henderson* [1973] 1 W.L.R. 333; *Jaggard v Sawyer* [1995] 1 W.L.R. 269 (injunction); *Insurance Co v Lloyd's Syndicate* [1995] 1 Lloyd's Rep. 273 at 276 (injunction).

is wholly out of proportion to the benefit which performance will confer on the claimant.[144] The court is also "slow" to order specific performance against a person who can put himself into a position to perform only by taking legal proceedings against a third party, especially where the outcome of such proceedings is in doubt.[145] Severe hardship may be a ground for refusing specific performance even though it results from circumstances which arise after the conclusion of the contract, which affect the person of the defendant rather than the subject-matter of the contract, and for which the claimant is in no way responsible. For example, in *Patel v Ali*[146] specific performance of a contract for the sale of a house was refused after a four-year delay (for which neither party was responsible), the vendor's circumstances having during this time changed disastrously as a result of her husband's bankruptcy and of an illness which had left her disabled. On the other hand, "mere pecuniary difficulties" would "afford no excuse".[147] Thus the purchaser of a house will not be denied specific performance merely because the vendor, on a rising market, finds it difficult to acquire alternative accommodation with the proceeds of the sale.[148] Nor will specific performance be refused merely because compliance with the order exposes the defendant to the risk of a strike by his employees.[149]

Contract obtained by unfair means. The court may refuse specific perform-   21–030
ance of a contract which has been obtained by means that are unfair, even though they do not amount to grounds on which the contract can be invalidated. Thus in *Walters v Morgan*[150] the defendant agreed to grant the claimant a mining lease over land which the defendant had only just bought. Specific performance was refused because the defendant was "surprised and was induced to sign the agreement in ignorance of the value of his property".[151] But specific performance will not be refused merely because the claimant fails to disclose circumstances which affect the value of the property or the defendant's willingness to contract with him.[152] Something more must be shown: e.g. that the claimant has taken unfair advantage of his superior knowledge: in *Walters v Morgan* the court relied on the fact that the claimant had produced a draft lease during the negotiations, and had hurried the defendant into signing it before he could discover the true value of the property. On the same principle specific performance may be refused if the claimant has taken advantage of the defendant's drunkenness, though it was not so extreme as to invalidate the contract at law.[153] The claimant's failure to disclose his own breach of the contract, reducing the value of the subject-matter,[154] has also been

---

[144] *Tito v Waddell (No.2)* [1977] Ch. 106 at 326; cf. *Morris v Redland Bricks Ltd* [1970] A.C. 652.
[145] *Wroth v Tyler* [1974] Ch. 30, where an additional ground for refusing specific performance was that the proceedings would have to be between the defendant and his wife thus tending to split up the family; cf. *Watts v Spence* [1976] Ch. 165 at 173.
[146] [1984] Ch. 283.
[147] ibid. at 288; cf. *Francis v Cowcliffe* (1977) 33 P. & C.R. 368.
[148] *Mountford v Scott* [1975] Ch. 258; cf. *Easton v Brown* [1981] 3 All E.R. 278.
[149] See *Howard E Perry v British Railways Board* [1980] 1 W.L.R. 1375.
[150] (1861) 3 D.F. & J. 718; cf. *Heath v Heath* [2009] EWHC 1908 (Ch); [2010] 1 F.L.R. 610 at [26].
[151] ibid. at 723.
[152] cf. above, paras 9–127, 9–129, 16–058—16–059.
[153] *Malins v Freeman* (1837) 2 Keen 25 at 34; above, para.12–062.
[154] *Quadrant Visual Communications v Hutchison Telephone (UK)* [1993] B.C.L.C. 442.

held to be a ground for refusing specific performance, even though the non-disclosure was not a ground for setting the contract aside at law.[155]

21–031   **Inadequacy of consideration.** The authorities on inadequacy of consideration as a ground for refusing specific performance are not easy to reconcile. On the one hand *mere* inadequacy of consideration is not a ground for refusing specific performance.[156] On the other hand the statement that inadequacy of consideration is not a ground for refusing specific performance unless it is "such as shocks the conscience and amounts in itself to conclusive and decisive evidence of fraud"[157] is probably too narrow, even when allowance is made for the possibility that fraud may have had a wider meaning in equity than at law. The best view seems to be that specific performance may be refused where inadequacy of consideration is coupled with some other factor, not necessarily amounting to fraud or other invalidating cause at law—e.g. mistake that is operative only in equity,[158] surprise[159] or unfair advantage taken by the claimant of his superior knowledge or bargaining position.[160]

21–032   **Conduct of claimant.** "The conduct of the party applying for relief is always an important element for consideration".[161] Thus specific performance can be refused if the claimant fails to perform a promise which induced the defendant to enter into the contract, but which is neither binding contractually, nor (because it relates to the future) operative as a misrepresentation.[162] A similar view may be taken where the claimant has made a misrepresentation but the right to rescind for that misrepresentation has been lost. If the right has been lost by reason of the defendant's affirmation of the contract,[163] he will not be allowed to rely on the misrepresentation as a defence to specific performance since he in turn would be guilty of "unconscionable inconsistency in conduct"[164] in seeking, after *affirmation*, to invoke the misrepresentation for this purpose. But his conduct would not be open to such criticism where the right to rescind had been lost by impossibility of *restitution* arising otherwise than from the defendant's conduct.[165] Hence in a case of this kind the misrepresentation, though no longer a ground for rescission, could be relied on as a defence to the equitable remedy of specific performance.[166] The remedy may similarly be refused if the claimant has acted unfairly in performing the contract, though he has not broken any promise. Specific enforcement of a solus agreement[167] has accordingly been denied to a petrol company on

---

[155] See above, para.9–151.
[156] *Collier v Brown* (1788) 1 Cox C.C. 428; *Western v Russell* (1814) 3 V. & B. 187; *Haywood v Cope* (1858) 25 Beav. 140.
[157] *Coles v Trecothick* (1804) 9 Ves. 234 at 246.
[158] *Webster v Cecil* (1861) 30 Beav. 62; see above, para.8–056.
[159] See above, at fn.151; cf. *Mortlock v Buller* (1804) 10 Ves. 292.
[160] *Falcke v Gray* (1859) 4 Drew. 651.
[161] *Lamare v Dixon* (1873) L.R. 6 H.L. 414 at 423; cf. *Chappell v The Times Newspapers Ltd* [1975] 1 W.L.R. 482; *Wilton Group v Abrams* [1990] B.C.C. 310 at 317 ("commercially disreputable" agreement).
[162] *Lamare v Dixon*, above; and see also above, para.9–009.
[163] See above, para.9–108.
[164] *Geest Plc v Fyffes Plc* [1999] 1 All E.R. (Comm) 672 at 694.
[165] See above, paras 9–097—9–106.
[166] *Geest Plc v Fyffes Plc*, above.
[167] See above, para.11–093.

the ground that it had given discounts to other garages, making it impossible for the defendant garage to trade on the terms of the agreement except at a loss.[168]

An action could formerly be brought on a contract for the sale of land against a party who had provided written evidence of it by one who had not.[169] It had, however, been held that specific performance would not be granted to a purchaser of land if he refused to perform a stipulation to which he had agreed, but which could not be enforced against him for want of written evidence.[170] A contract for the sale of land must now be made (and not merely evidenced) in writing, and the writing must incorporate all the terms on which the parties have expressly agreed.[171] Hence if the stipulation in question was such a term, but was not contained in the documents, specific performance would now be refused on the different ground that no contract had come into existence. An alternative possibility is that the stipulation might have been intended to take effect as a collateral contract.[172] In that event, the main contract would be valid but the reasoning of the cases referred to above might still lead the court to refuse specific performance to the purchaser if it considered that the vendor would not be adequately protected, after being ordered to perform, by his claim for damages for breach of the collateral contract.[173]

Impossibility. Specific performance will not be ordered against a person who   21–033
has agreed to sell land which he does not own and cannot compel the owner to convey to him,[174] or to the claimant,[175] "because the court does not compel a person to do what is impossible".[176] The position is the same where a person has agreed to assign a lease and the landlord withholds his consent, without which the assignment cannot lawfully be effected.[177] Impossibility of enforcing an order of specific performance (e.g. because the defendant is not, and has no assets, within the jurisdiction) may also be a reason for refusing to make such an order.[178]

Other factors. The factors so far discussed operate negatively, as grounds for   21–034
refusing specific performance. Others may operate positively, as grounds for awarding the remedy. Thus specific performance has been ordered of a contract to grant a licence to use a hall for a political meeting, and one reason for making the order was that it would promote freedom of speech and assembly.[179]

---

[168] *Shell UK Ltd v Lostock Garages Ltd* [1976] 1 W.L.R. 1187.

[169] Law of Property Act 1925, s.40, replacing part of Statute of Frauds 1677, s.4, and now repealed by Law of Property (Miscellaneous Provisions) Act 1989, ss.1(8) and 4 and Sch.2; and see above, para.5–008.

[170] See *Martin v Pycroft* (1852) 2 D.M. & G. 785 at 795; *Scott v Bradley* [1971] Ch. 850.

[171] Law of Property (Miscellaneous Provisions) Act 1989, s.2(1); above, para.5–008.

[172] See above, para.5–008.

[173] i.e. on the principle of "mutuality" as now understood: below, paras 21–046—21–047.

[174] See *Castle v Wilkinson* (1870) L.R. 5 Ch.App. 534; *Watts v Spence* [1976] Ch. 165; cf. *Elliot & Elliot (Builders) Ltd v Pierson* [1948] Ch. 453. Contrast *Clark v Lucas Solicitors LLP* [2009] EWHC 1952 (Ch); [2009] 46 E.G. 144 at [57]–[58].

[175] *Jones v Lipman* [1962] 1 W.L.R. 832; *Coles v Samuel Smith Old Brewery Tadcaster* [2007] EWCA Civ 1461.

[176] *Forrer v Nash* (1865) 35 Beav. 167 at 171.

[177] *Wilmott v Barber* (1880) 15 Ch.D. 96; *Warmington v Miller* [1973] Q.B. 877; cf. *Sullivan v Henderson* [1973] 1 W.L.R. 333. Contrast *Rose v Stravrou* [2000] L. & T.R. 133 (where the remedy sought was not specific performance but a declaration).

[178] *The Sea Hawk* [1986] 1 W.L.R. 657 at 665.

[179] *Verrall v Great Yarmouth BC* [1981] Q.B. 202. For the relevance of this factor, see also Human Rights Act 1998, s.12; *Imutran Ltd v Uncaged Campaigns Ltd* [2001] 2 All E.R. 385.

(iii) *Contracts not specifically enforceable*

21–035   **Contracts involving personal service.** It has long been settled that equity will not, as a general rule, enforce a contract of personal service.[180] Specific enforcement against the employee was thought to interfere unduly with his personal liberty; it is this ground of policy which accounts for the rule, so that "questions of the adequacy of damages are irrelevant to this issue".[181] Legislative force is given to the principle by the Trade Union and Labour Relations (Consolidation) Act 1992, s.236 of which provides that no court shall compel an employee to do any work by ordering specific performance of a contract of employment or by restraining the breach of such a contract by injunction.[182] Conversely, an employer could not be forced to employ: it was thought to be difficult or undesirable to enforce the continuance of a "personal" relationship between unwilling parties. This principle is reflected in the provisions of the Employment Rights Act 1996,[183] as to the remedies for "unfair" dismissal (which is not normally a breach of contract at all). Under the Act, a tribunal may order the reinstatement or re-engagement of the employee; but if such an order is not complied with, the employer can, in the last resort, only be made to pay compensation.[184] In practice, reinstatement is "effected in only a tiny proportion of . . . cases"[185] so that it is compensation which is the employee's "primary remedy".[186] The remedy for infringement of the statutory right of a person not to be excluded or expelled from a trade union is likewise by way of declaration and compensation.[187] Where an employee is dismissed in breach of contract, his normal remedy is a claim for damages or a declaration that the dismissal was *wrongful*: not specific enforcement,[188] or a declaration that the dismissal was *invalid*.[189] The statutory right to return to work[190] after maternity, parental or paternity leave appears likewise not to be specifically enforceable.[191]

---

[180] *Johnson v Shrewsbury and Birmingham Ry* (1853) 3 D.M. & G. 358; *Rigby v Connol* (1880) 14 Ch.D. 482 at 487; cf. *Taylor v NUS* [1967] 1 W.L.R. 532; *Chappell v Times Newspapers Ltd* [1975] 1 W.L.R. 482 (injunction); *The Scaptrade* [1983] 2 A.C. 694 at 700–701 (below, para.21–037); *Wishart v National Association of Citizens Advice Bureaux* [1990] I.C.R. 794.

[181] *Young v Robson Rhodes* [1999] 3 All E.R. 524 at 534.

[182] Injunctions in respect of industrial action may lie against the *organisers* of such action, e.g. under Trade Union and Labour Relations (Consolidation) Act 1992, ss.226 or 235A (inserted by Trade Union Reform and Employment Rights Act 1993, s.22), but not against *individual employees*.

[183] Pt X.

[184] Employment Rights Act 1996, ss.113–117. Under ss.129(9) and 130 of the 1996 Act, orders may be made for the continuation of the contract, but these do not give rise to the remedy of specific performance; cf. also Equality Act 2010, s.124; see above, para.1–007.

[185] *Johnson v Unisys Ltd* [2001] UKHL 13; [2003] 1 A.C. 518 at [78], per Lord Millett; Lord Steyn at [23] states the proportion to be "only about three per cent".

[186] See above, fn.488.

[187] Trade Union and Labour Relations (Consolidation) Act 1992, ss.174–177.

[188] See above, para.16–103, fn.488; below, fn.320.

[189] *Francis v Kuala Lumpur Councillors* [1962] 1 W.L.R. 1411; *Vidyodaya University Council v Silva* [1965] 1 W.L.R. 77; *Gunton v Richmond-upon-Thames LBC* [1981] Ch. 448 (declaration that dismissal was "ineffective *lawfully* to determine the contract"); *Marsh v National Autistic Society* [1993] I.C.R. 453. A declaration may also be made that a decision of a disciplinary committee leading to a dismissal is void: *Stevenson v United Road Transport Union* [1977] I.C.R. 893; but this does not amount to a declaration that the *contract* remains in operation: ibid. at 906.

[190] Employment Rights Act 1996, Pt VIII, and see Employment Act 2002, s.7; Maternity and Parental Leave Regulations 1999 (SI 1999/3312), reg.18 (as substituted by SI 2002/2789, regs 3, 12).

[191] The Regulations cited in fn.190, above do not specify civil remedies for infringement of the right.

Exceptions. The arguments usually advanced in support of the equitable   21–036
principle are no longer wholly convincing.[192] It is subject to a growing list of
exceptions. A person who is dismissed from a public office in breach of the terms
of his appointment may be entitled to reinstatement[193]; and the Visitor of a
University has power to order the reinstatement of a wrongfully dismissed lecturer
(even when such a remedy would not be available in the ordinary courts[194]), such
a dismissal being, if it amounts to a violation of the University's Statutes, not
merely wrongful but also invalid.[195] The continuance or creation of a "personal"
relationship may also be enforced where an injunction is granted against expulsion
from a social club,[196] or against the refusal of a professional association to admit
a person to membership.[197] By way of contrast, it has been held that specific relief
was not available against a fee-paying school to reinstate a pupil who had been
excluded for alleged misconduct, since the "breakdown of trust" had made it
undesirable to require the parties "to co-exist in a pastoral and educational
relationship".[198]

More generally, the modern relationship of employer and employee is often
much less personal than the old relationship of master and servant was believed to
be; and there are signs that the courts are prepared to re-examine or qualify the
old equitable principles in the light of this development.[199] Industrial conditions
may in fact force an employer to retain an employee whom he would prefer to
dismiss or to dismiss one whom he is perfectly willing to retain. For example, in
Hill v C A Parsons Ltd[200] employers were forced by union pressure to dismiss an
employee. The dismissal amounted to a breach of contract and the court issued an
injunction to restrain the breach, thus in effect reinstating the employee. As the
employers and the employee were perfectly willing to maintain their relationship,
the decision does not seem to violate the spirit of the general equitable principle
against the specific enforcement of employment contracts. An injunction to
restrain dismissal can also be issued in respect of a period during which no services

---

[192] See Clark 32 M.L.R. 532.
[193] *Ridge v Baldwin* [1964] A.C. 40; *Ganz* 30 M.L.R. 288; *Malloch v Aberdeen Corp* [1971] 1 W.L.R.
1578; *Chief Constable of the North Wales Police v Evans* [1982] 1 W.L.R. 1155; *Jones v Lee* (1979) 78
L.G.R. 213. The line between ordinary and public employment is by no means clear-cut: see criticisms
of the *Vidyodaya University* case, above, in *Malloch v Aberdeen Corp*, above, at 1595.
[194] *Thomas v University of Bradford* [1987] A.C. 795 at 824; for subsequent proceedings, see *Thomas
v University of Bradford* [1992] 1 All E.R. 964.
[195] *Pearce v University of Aston (No.2)* [1991] 2 All E.R. 469.
[196] *Young v Ladies Imperial Club Ltd* [1920] 2 K.B. 522.
[197] cf. *Nagle v Feilden* [1966] 2 Q.B. 633, doubted on the availability of specific relief in *R. v
Disciplinary Committee of the Jockey Club Ex p. Aga Khan* [1993] 1 W.L.R. 909 at 933. In the context
of charitable associations, see *Royal Society for the Prevention of Cruelty to Animals v Attorney-General*
[2002] 1 W.L.R. 448 (society required to invite persons about to be excluded to give reasons why they
should be admitted). See also Equality Act 2010, s.101 (not yet fully in force).
[198] *R. v Incorporated Froebel Educational Institute Ex p. L* [1999] E.L.R. 488 at 493; cf. *R. v Fernhill
Manor School* [1993] F.L.R. 620 (no judicial review of expulsion from private school); *A v Lord Grey's
School* [2004] EWCA Civ 382; [2004] Q.B. 1231 (request for reinstatement at state school denied, but
damages awarded for breach of Human Rights Act 1998, Sch.1, Pt II, Art.2).
[199] See *C H Giles & Co Ltd v Morris* [1972] 1 W.L.R. 307; cf. in Scotland, *Peace v Edinburgh CC*
[1999] I.R.L.R. 417.
[200] [1972] Ch. 305; Hepple [1972] C.L.J. 47; cf. *Irani v Southampton, etc. Health Authority* [1985]
I.C.R. 590 (where the employers retained confidence in an employee but had dismissed him because
of differences between him and another employee); *Powell v Brent LBC* [1988] I.C.R. 176; *Hughes v
Southwark LBC* [1988] I.R.L.R. 55; *Jones v Gwent CC* [1992] I.R.L.R. 521 at 526; *Grady v Prison
Service* [2003] EWCA Civ 527; [2003] I.C.R. 753 at [22].

are to be rendered under the contract. Thus where an employee had been suspended on full pay while disciplinary proceedings against him were in progress, it was held that the employers could be restrained from dismissing him before the disciplinary proceedings had run their full course.[201]

21–037   **Scope of "personal service".** The equitable principle applies to all contracts involving personal service even though they are not strictly contracts of service. Thus an agreement to allow an auctioneer to sell a collection of works of art cannot be specifically enforced[202] by either party, though specific enforcement would hardly be an undue interference with personal liberty, even in a suit against the auctioneer. Again, an agreement to enter into a partnership will not be specifically enforced as "it is impossible to make persons who will not concur carry on a business jointly, for their common advantage".[203] The court can, however, order the execution of a formal partnership agreement, and leave the parties to their remedies on the agreement.[204] Similarly, the court can order the execution of a service contract even though that contract, when made, may not be specifically enforceable.[205]

The equitable principle here under discussion applies only where the services are of a personal nature. There is no general rule against the specific enforcement of a contract merely because one party undertakes to provide services[206] under it. Thus specific performance can be ordered of a contract to publish a piece of music[207] and sometimes of contracts to build.[208] It has been suggested that a time charterparty cannot be specifically enforced against the shipowner because it is a contract for services[209]; but the services that the shipowner undertakes under such a contract will often be no more personal than those to be rendered by a builder

---

[201] *Robb v Hammersmith and Fulham BC* [1991] I.C.R. 514; cf. *Gryf-Lowczowski v Hinchingbrooke Healthcare NHS Trust* [2005] EWHC 2407; [2006] I.C.R. 100; *Lauffer v Barking, Havering and Redbridge University Hospitals NHS Trust* [2009] EWHC 2360 (QB); [2010] Med L.R. 68.

[202] *Chinnock v Sainsbury* (1861) 30 L.J.Ch. 409; cf. *Mortimer v Beckett* [1920] 1 Ch. 571; *Young v Robson Rhodes* [1999] 3 All E.R. 524.

[203] *England v Curling* (1844) 8 Beav. 129 at 137. On the same principle, specific performance has been refused of a house-sharing arrangement which had been made between members of a family who later quarrelled: *Burrows and Burrows v Sharp* (1991) 23 H.L.R. 82, where the basis of liability was not contract but proprietary estoppel (contrast *Stallion v Albert Stallion Holdings Ltd* [2009] EWHC 1950 (Ch); [2010] 2 F.L.R. 78); cf. *Internet Trading Clubs Ltd v Freeserve (Investments) Ltd* [2001] E.B.L.R. 142 at [3] (refusal specifically "to enforce an ongoing business relationship"). Where there is no need for any continuing personal relationship, specific performance may be awarded: *Pena v Dale* [2003] EWHC 1065; [2004] 2 B.C.L.C. 508 (option to acquire minority shareholding in company).

[204] As in *England v Curling* (above), where the object of obtaining such a decree was to ascertain the exact terms that had been agreed, and then to prevent one of the contracting parties from competing in business with the other.

[205] *C H Giles & Co Ltd v Morris* [1972] 1 W.L.R. 307; cf. *Posner v Scott-Lewis* [1987] Ch. 25.

[206] e.g. *Posner v Scott-Lewis* [1987] Ch. 25 (below, at fn.225); *Ferrara Quay Ltd v Carillion Construction Ltd* [2009] B.L.R. 367.

[207] *Barrow v Chappell & Co* (1951), now reported in [1976] R.P.C. 355, and cited in *Joseph v National Magazine Co Ltd* [1959] Ch. 14; contrast *Malcolm v Chancellor Masters and Scholars of the University of Oxford, The Times*, December 19, 1990, where specific performance of a contract to publish a book was refused on the ground that continued co-operation between author and publishers would have been required. For further related proceedings, see [2002] EWHC 10; [2002] E.L.R. 277.

[208] See below, para.21–042.

[209] *The Scaptrade* [1983] 2 A.C. 694 at 700–701; cf. *Lauritzencool AB v Lady Navigation Inc* [2005] EWCA Civ 579; [2005] 1 W.L.R. 3686 at [12] where Mance L.J. accepts "for present purposes" the generality of Lord Diplock's statement in *The Scaptrade*; below, para.21–057.

under a building contract.[210] It is in the nature of some services contracts, even if not of a personal nature, that a "loss of confidence" between the parties will provide another basis upon which to deny specific enforcement.[211]

Contracts requiring constant supervision. Specific performance will not be   21–038 ordered of continuous contractual duties, the proper performance of which might require constant supervision by the court.[212] In *Ryan v Mutual Tontine Association*[213] the lease of a service flat gave the tenant the right to the services of a porter who was to be "constantly in attendance". Specific enforcement of this right was refused on the ground that it would have required "that constant superintendence by the court, which the court in such cases has always declined to give".[214] For the same reason the courts have refused specifically to enforce an undertaking to cultivate a farm in a particular manner[215]; a contract to keep a shop open[216]; a contract to keep an airfield in operation[217]; a contract to deliver goods in instalments[218]; and obligations to operate railway signals[219] and to provide engine power.[220] And it has been held that a voyage charterparty cannot be specifically enforced against the shipowner.[221]

Limits to the difficulty of constant supervision. This "difficulty" of   21–039 supervision should not be exaggerated. In most cases the mere existence of the court's order will suffice to deter a deliberate breach. No practical difficulty seems to have arisen in the cases in which the courts have specifically enforced contracts to do building work.[222] If the defendant were recalcitrant, the court could appoint an expert as its officer to supervise performance. This is no more "difficult" than appointing a person to run the business of a bankrupt or to manage the property of a person lacking mental capacity. The court has appointed a receiver to run a mine in a rescission action[223]; the same thing could be done in an action for specific performance. Alternatively, the claimant could be empowered to appoint a person to act as agent of the defendant to supervise the enforcement of the order:

---

[210] Denial of specific performance in the case of time charters is best explained on other grounds. See below, at fn.221.

[211] *Ericsson AB v EADS Defence and Security Systems Ltd* [2009] EWHC 2598 (TCC); [2010] B.L.R. 131 at [47] (refusal of injunction restraining termination of contract for supply of software and support services).

[212] The principle does not apply to continuous obligations to pay money: thus an agreement to pay an annuity can be specifically enforced (above, para.21–020).

[213] [1893] 1 Ch. 116.

[214] ibid. at 123.

[215] *Rayner v Stone* (1762) 2 Eden 128; *Phipps v Jackson* (1887) 56 L.J.Ch. 350.

[216] *Braddon Towers Ltd v International Stores Ltd* [1987] 1 E.G.L.R. 209 (decided in 1959); *Co-operative Ins Society Ltd v Argyll Stores (Holdings) Ltd* [1998] A.C. 1; below, at fn.226.

[217] *Dowty Boulton Paul Ltd v Wolverhampton Corp* [1971] 1 W.L.R. 204; for later proceedings see [1973] Ch. 94.

[218] *Dominion Coal Co v Dominion Iron & Steel Co* [1900] A.C. 293; but see above, para.21–024.

[219] *Powell Duffryn Steam Coal Co v Taff Vale Ry* (1874) L.R. 9 Ch. 331.

[220] *Blackett v Bates* (1865) L.R. 1 Ch. 177.

[221] *De Mattos v Gibson* (1858) 4 D. & J. 276 (voyage charter). The view expressed in *The Scaptrade* [1983] 2 A.C. 694 at 700–701, that a time charter is not specifically enforceable, is perhaps best explained on the ground that such enforcement would require too much supervision.

[222] See below, para.21–042; cf. *Storer v GW Ry* (1842) 2 Y. & C.C.C. 48 (specific performance ordered of an agreement "for ever . . . to maintain one neat archway"); *Kennard v Cory Bros & Co* [1922] 2 Ch. 1 (mandatory injunction ordering defendant to keep a drain open); *Rainbow Estates Ltd v Tokenhold Ltd* [1999] Ch. 64.

[223] *Gibbs v David* (1870) L.R. 20 Eq. 373.

this would not be radically different from the statutory power of a mortgagee to appoint a receiver to act as agent of the mortgagor.[224] Where the acts to be done under the contract are not to be done by the defendant personally, the court can order him simply to enter into a contract to procure those acts to be done. From this point of view, *Ryan v Mutual Tontine Association* may be contrasted with the later case of *Posner v Scott-Lewis*[225] where the lessor of a block of luxury flats covenanted, so far as lay in his power, to employ a resident porter to perform a number of specified tasks. It was held that the covenant was specifically enforceable in the sense that the lessor could be ordered to appoint a resident porter for the performance of the specified services.

21-040   *Co-operative Insurance Society v Argyll Stores.* This balancing of arguments for and against ordering specific performance in cases of this kind is well illustrated by *Co-operative Ins Society Ltd v Argyll Stores (Holdings) Ltd*,[226] where a 31-year lease of premises for use as a food supermarket in a shopping centre contained a covenant by the tenant to keep the premises "open for retail trade during the usual hours of business". Some six years after the commencement of the lease, the supermarket was running at a loss and the tenant ceased trading there. The main reason given by the House of Lords for refusing to order specific performance was the difficulty of supervising the enforcement of the order since the question whether it was being complied with might require frequent reference to the court. For this purpose, Lord Hoffmann distinguished between orders (such as that sought here) "to carry on an activity" and orders "to achieve a result".[227] In the latter case, "the court . . . only has to examine the finished work"[228] so that compliance with the order could be judged ex post facto: it was on this ground that the cases in which building contracts had been specifically enforced[229] were to be explained. Difficulty of supervision was, however, not the sole ground for the decision. Lord Hoffmann referred also to a number of other factors, such as the "heavy-handed nature of the enforcement mechanism"[230] by proceedings for contempt; the injustice of compelling the tenant to carry on business at a loss which might well exceed the loss which the landlord would be likely to suffer if the covenant were broken; and the fact that it was not "in the public interest for the courts to require someone to carry on business at a loss if there is any plausible alternative by which the other party can be given compensation",[231] i.e. by way of damages. Reliance on such factors suggests that, if the court attaches sufficient importance to the claimant's interest in specific enforcement, it will not be deterred from granting such relief merely on the ground that it will require constant supervision. The outcome in each case will depend on the

---

[224] Law of Property Act 1925, s.101; cf. Insolvency Act 1986, s.44 (as amended by Insolvency Act 1994, s.2).

[225] [1987] Ch. 25.

[226] [1998] A.C. 1.

[227] Also relied on in *Vertex Data Science Ltd v Powergen Retail Ltd* [2006] EWHC 1340; [2006] 2 Lloyd's Rep. 591 at [46] (injunction); *BDW Trading Ltd v JM Rowe Investments Ltd* [2010] EWHC 1987 (Ch) at [163], affirmed [2011] EWCA Civ 548 without reference to this point.

[228] *Vertex Data Science Ltd v Powergen Retail Ltd* [2006] EWHC 1340; [2006] 2 Lloyd's Rep. 591 at 13; all the other members of the House of Lords agreed with Lord Hoffmann's speech.

[229] See below, para.21–042.

[230] [1998] A.C. 1 at 12.

[231] ibid. at 15.

"cumulative effect"[232] of this factor together with any others which favour[233] or (as in the *Co-operative Insurance* case) militate against specific relief.[234]

Contracts which are too vague. An agreement may be so vague that it cannot   21–041
be enforced at all, even by an action for damages.[235] But although an agreement is definite enough to be enforced in some form of legal proceeding, it may still be too vague to be enforced specifically.[236] Thus specific performance has been refused of a contract to publish an article as to the wording of which the parties disagreed.[237] In such a case the court would find it difficult or impossible to state in its order exactly what the defendant was to do; and precision is essential[238] since failure to comply with the court's order may lead to attachment for contempt. An agreement is not, however, too vague to be specifically enforced merely because it is expressed to be subject to such amendments as may reasonably be required by one (or by either) party.[239]

The difficulty of precisely formulating the court's order was at one time thought to prevent the specific enforcement of contracts for the sale of goodwill alone (without business premises): it was considered impossible for the court in its decree to state precisely what the vendor was to do.[240] But in *Beswick v Beswick* it was said that such a contract could be specifically enforced.[241] The older, contrary, authorities were not cited; and it seems that they have been made obsolete by the growing legal and commercial precision of the concept of goodwill.[242]

Building contracts. The general rule is that a contract to erect a building   21–042
cannot be specifically enforced.[243] There seem to be three reasons for this rule. First, damages may be an adequate remedy if the building owner can engage another builder to do the work. Secondly, the contract may be too vague if it fails

---

[232] ibid. at 16.

[233] *Luganda v Service Hotels* [1969] 2 Ch. 209 (mandatory injunction ordering defendants to allow a protected tenant, who had been wrongfully locked out of a room in a residental hotel, to resume his residence in the hotel); cf. *Films Rover International Ltd v Cannon Films Sales Ltd* [1987] 1 W.L.R. 670 at 682 (for further proceedings, see [1989] 1 W.L.R. 912); *Sutton Housing Trust v Lawrence* (1987) 19 H.L.R. 520.

[234] cf. *Shiloh Spinners Ltd v Harding* [1973] A.C. 691 at 724, where difficulty of supervision is said to be no longer a bar to relief against forfeiture (as it had been in *Hill v Barclay* (1810) 16 Ves.Jun. 402); but the possibility is recognised that such difficulty sometimes "explains why specific performance cannot be granted. . . . ". cf. also the interpretation of these remarks in *Co-operative Ins Society Ltd v Argyll Stores (Holdings) Ltd* [1998] A.C. 1 at 14 as relating to relief against forfeiture rather than to the availability of specific performance and doubting their interpretation in *Tito v Waddel (No.2)* [1977] Ch. 106 at 322.

[235] See above, para.2–079; *Waring & Gillow v Thompson* (1912) 29 T.L.R. 154.

[236] *Tito v Waddell (No.2)* [1977] Ch. 106 at 322–323.

[237] *Joseph v National Magazine Co Ltd* [1959] Ch. 14; cf. *Slater v Raw, The Times*, October 15, 1977.

[238] cf. *Lock International Plc v Beswick* [1989] 1 W.L.R. 1268; *Lawrence David Ltd v Ashton* [1989] I.C.R. 123 at 132.

[239] *Sweet & Maxwell Ltd v Universal News Services Ltd* [1964] 2 Q.B. 699; *Alpenstow Ltd v Regalian Properties Plc* [1985] 1 W.L.R. 721.

[240] See, e.g., *Bozon v Farlow* (1816) 1 Mer. 459 at 472; cf. *Darbey v Whitaker* (1857) 4 Drew. 134 at 139.

[241] [1968] A.C. 58 at 89, 97.

[242] *Trego v Hunt* [1896] A.C. 7.

[243] *Flint v Brandon* (1808) 3 Ves. 159; and see *Wolverhampton Corp v Emmons* [1901] 1 Q.B. 515; cf. *Gyllenhammar Partners International v Sour Brodogradevna Industria* [1989] 2 Lloyd's Rep. 403 at 422 (contract to build a ship).

to describe the building with sufficient certainty. Thirdly, specific enforcement of the contract may require more supervision than the court is willing to give.

But where the first two reasons do not apply, the third has not been allowed to prevail. Specific performance of a contract to erect or repair buildings can therefore be ordered if (i) the work is precisely defined with sufficient certainty; (ii) damages will not adequately compensate the claimant; and (iii) the defendant is in possession of the land on which the building is to be done,[244] since in that case the claimant cannot get the work done by employing another builder.

21–043   **Contracts specifically enforceable in part only.** In *Ryan v Mutual Tontine Association*[245] the court refused specifically to enforce a landlord's undertaking to have a porter "constantly in attendance"; and it seems unlikely that the court would, even now, order the landlord to enter into a contract with a porter *on such terms* (though it could make an order of a similar nature where the lease *specified the tasks* to be done by the porter[246]). A further claim that the landlord should be ordered simply to appoint a porter was also rejected on the ground that "when the court cannot grant specific performance of the contract as a whole, it will not interfere to compel specific performance of part of a contract".[247] This does not mean that the court cannot order specific performance of one individual obligation out of a number imposed by a contract[248]: it means only that it will not make such an order in relation to one such obligation if it cannot so enforce the rest of the contract.[249] Even in this restricted sense, the rule is by no means an absolute one. Thus where a monetary adjustment can be made in respect of the unperformable part the court may order specific performance with compensation.[250]

21–044   **Terminable and conditional contracts.** If the party against whom specific performance is sought is entitled to terminate the contract, the order will be refused as the defendant could render it nugatory by exercising his power to terminate.[251] This principle applies whether the contract is terminable under its express terms[252] or on account of the conduct of the party seeking specific

---

[244] *Wolverhampton Corp v Emmons* [1901] 1 Q.B. 515 at 525, as modified by *Carpenters Estates Ltd v Davies* [1940] Ch. 160; cf. *Jeune v Queens Cross Properties Ltd* [1974] Ch. 97; *Calabar Properties Ltd v Stitcher* [1984] 1 W.L.R. 287; Landlord and Tenant Act 1985, s.17; *Barrett v Lounova* [1990] 1 Q.B. 348; *Rainbow Estates Ltd v Tokenhold Ltd* [1999] Ch. 64 at 69, 75, and see *Channel Tunnel Group Ltd v Balfour Beatty Construction Ltd* [1993] A.C. 334, where the House of Lords took the view that it had jurisdiction to restrain a building contractor by injunction from stopping work, but refused such relief as a matter of discretion. For the converse question, whether a builder can, in effect, compel the owner to allow him to complete the work, contrast *Hounslow LBC v Twickenham Garden & Builders Ltd* [1971] Ch. 233 with *Mayfield Holdings v Moana Reef* [1973] 1 N.Z.L.R. 309; and cf. *Finelli v Dee* (1968) 76 D.L.R. (2d.) 393.

[245] [1893] 1 Ch. 116 above, para.21–038.

[246] As in *Posner v Scott-Lewis* [1988] Ch. 25 (above, para.21–039).

[247] [1893] 1 Ch. 116 at 123.

[248] See *Odessa Tramways Co v Mendel* (1878) 8 Ch.D. 235, where such an order was made.

[249] *Rainbow Estates Ltd v Tokenhold Ltd* [1999] Ch. 64 at 65–67; *Odessa Tramways Co v Mendel* (1878) 8 Ch.D. 235 (where contract is severable, specific performance of each part can be separately ordered); *Internet Trading Clubs Ltd v Freeserve (Investments) Ltd* [2001] E.B.L.R. 142 at [30], where specific performance of an unseverable part was refused.

[250] See above, para.18–029.

[251] It perhaps goes without saying that specific performance is not available where the contract *has been* terminated: *Hampshire CC v Supportways Social Services Ltd* [2006] EWCA Civ 1035; [2006] B.L.G.R. 836.

[252] e.g. *Sheffield Gas Co v Harrison* (1853) 17 Beav. 294; but cf. *Allhusen v Borries* (1867) 15 W.R. 739.

performance.[253] On a somewhat similar principle, an obligation which is subject to a condition precedent not within the control of the party seeking the remedy will not be specifically enforced before the condition has occurred[254]; here too the making of the order could turn out to be nugatory if the condition were not satisfied. The occurrence of the condition will remove this obstacle to specific performance.[255]

Promises without consideration. On the principle that equity will not aid a   21–045
volunteer,[256] specific performance will not be ordered of a gratuitous promise even though it is binding at law because it is made by deed or supported by nominal consideration,[257] so that damages or the agreed sum can be recovered by the promisee. Where such a promise is made to a trustee for the benefit of a third party, it has been held that the trustee ought not to enforce the promise at law against the promisor,[258] unless the promise can be regarded as constituting a trust which is "already perfect".[259] Under the Contracts (Rights of Third Parties) Act 1999, promises for the benefit of a third party are (if the statutory requirements are satisfied) enforceable not only by the promisee, but also by the third party,[260] who has the right of enforcement even though he has not provided any consideration for the promise.[261] The third party, moreover, has available to him any remedy, including specific performance, that "would have been available to him in an action for breach of the contract if he had been a party to the contract".[262] Nothing in the Act, however, affects the principle that equity will not aid a volunteer. Hence it is clear that if, between promisor and promisee, the contract is binding at law only because it is contained in a deed or supported by no more than nominal consideration (moving from the promisee), then equity will not order specific performance at the suit of the third party, any more than it will do so at the suit of the promisee. It is less clear what the position would be in the more usual case in which substantial consideration is provided by the promisee but none is provided by the third party. One possible view is that, since the third party is in such a case a volunteer, specific performance will not be ordered in his favour. But this would make the reference to specific performance in the Act, as one of the remedies available to the third party, largely nugatory. The courts may, therefore, prefer to take the view that the equitable principle applies only to gratuitous promises and that specific performance can be ordered at the suit of the third party, even though he has not provided any consideration for the promise, so long as substantial consideration for it has been provided by the promisee.

---

[253] *Gregory v Wilson* (1851) 9 Hare 683.

[254] *Chattey v Farndale Holdings Inc* [1997] 1 E.G.L.R. 153.

[255] cf. *Wu Koon Tai v Wu Yau Loi* [1997] A.C. 179 at 189.

[256] See above, para.3–016.

[257] See *Re Parkin* [1892] 3 Ch. 510; *Cannon v Hartley* [1949] Ch. 213. Contrast *Gurtner v Circuit* [1968] 2 Q.B. 587 at 596 where an agreement by deed between the Minister and the Motor Insurer's Bureau was said to be specifically enforceable by the Minister. The fact that no consideration moved from him was not mentioned by the court; cf. above, para.14–130.

[258] *Re Pryce* [1917] 1 Ch. 234; *Re Kay* [1939] Ch. 239; Elliot 76 L.Q.R. 100; Hornby 78 L.Q.R. 288; Matheson 29 M.L.R. 397; Lee 85 L.Q.R. 213; Barton 91 L.Q.R. 236; Meagher and Lehane 92 L.Q.R. 427; Macnair 8 Legal Studies 172. The rule does not apply where a promise for the benefit of a third party volunteer is made to a promisee who has provided consideration: *Beswick v Beswick* [1968] A.C. 58.

[259] *Fletcher v Fletcher* (1844) 4 Hare 67 at 74.

[260] See above, para.14–090 et seq.

[261] See above, para.14–099.

[262] s.1(5) of the 1999 Act.

The principle that equity will not aid a volunteer does not apply where an option to buy land is granted by deed but without consideration, or for only a nominal consideration. Such an option is for the present purpose regarded as an offer coupled with a legally binding promise not to revoke[263]; and it may therefore be exercised in spite of an attempt to revoke it. The resulting contract of sale can then be specifically enforced[264]—always assuming that it is supported by substantial consideration. The equitable principle likewise does not affect the validity of a *completed gift*: it is concerned with the enforceability of gratuitous *promises*.[265]

(iv) *Mutuality of remedy*

21–046   The court will sometimes refuse to order specific performance at the suit of one party if it cannot order it at the suit of the other. Thus a party who undertakes to render personal services or to perform continuous duties cannot get specific performance as the remedy is not available against him[266]; and for the same reason a minor cannot get specific performance.[267] Such cases were explained on the ground that the remedy of specific performance must be mutual; and it was said that this requirement had to be satisfied at the time when the contract was made.[268]

21–047   **Mutuality required at time of hearing.** There are, however, many cases in which specific performance can be obtained by a party even though it could not at the time of contracting have been ordered against him. Thus, if A agrees to grant a lease of land to B, who agrees to build on it, B cannot normally be forced to build; but if he actually does build he can get specific performance of A's promise to grant the lease.[269] Specific performance cannot be ordered against a person who sells land which he does not own[270] but if he becomes owner before the purchaser repudiates[271] he can get specific performance.[272] Conversely a vendor with defective title may be ordered to convey for a reduced price although he could not himself have obtained specific performance.[273] It seems that a person of full age can get specific performance of a voidable contract made during minority even though he could have elected to repudiate the contract.[274] And a victim of fraudulent or innocent misrepresentation can get specific performance although he may be entitled to rescind the contract so that it could not be enforced against him.[275]

---

[263] For the nature of an option, see above, para.3–160, fn.873.

[264] *Mountford v Scott* [1975] Ch. 258.

[265] *T Choithram International SA v Pagarani* [2001] 1 W.L.R. 1; *Pennington v Waine* [2002] EWCA Civ 227; [2002] 1 W.L.R. 2075.

[266] *Ogden v Fossick* (1862) D. F. & J. 426; *Blackett v Bates* (1865) L.R. 1 Ch.App. 117; cf. *Page One Records Ltd v Britton* [1968] 1 W.L.R. 157 (injunction). A dictum in *Warren v Mendy* [1989] 1 W.L.R. 853 at 866 rejects the requirement of mutuality even in this situation (but specific enforcement was refused for reasons discussed in para.21–056, below).

[267] *Flight v Bolland* (1828) 4 Russ. 298; *Lumley v Ravenscroft* [1895] 1 Q.B. 683.

[268] Fry, *Specific Performance* (6th edn), paras 460, 830.

[269] *Wilkinson v Clements* (1872) L.R. 8 Ch.App. 96.

[270] See above, para.21–033.

[271] *Halkett v Dudley* [1907] 1 Ch. 590 at 596; *Cleadon Trust v Davies* [1940] 1 Ch. 940.

[272] *Hoggart v Scott* (1830) 1 Russ. & My. 293; *Wylson v Dunn* (1887) 34 Ch.D. 569.

[273] *Mortlock v Buller* (1804) 10 Ves. 292 at 315; *Wilson v Wilson* (1857) 3 Jur.(N.S.) 810.

[274] *Clayton v Ashdown* (1714) 9 Vin.Abr. 393 (G.4) 1.

[275] See above, para.9–084 et seq.

Such cases show that the requirement of mutuality does not have to be satisfied at the time of contracting; the crucial time is that of the hearing.[276] The rule was reformulated by Buckley L.J. in *Price v Strange*: the court

> "will not compel a defendant to perform his obligations specifically if it cannot at the same time ensure that any unperformed obligations of the [claimant] will be specifically performed, unless perhaps damages would be an adequate remedy for any default on the [claimant's] part".[277]

The defendant in that case had promised to grant an underlease to the claimant who had in return undertaken to execute certain internal and external repairs. It was admitted that the claimant's undertakings were not specifically enforceable; and it seems clear that he could not have obtained specific performance of the promise to grant the underlease before any of the repairs had been done. For in that case the only remedy available to the defendant for default on the claimant's part might have been in damages, and this might have been inadequate,[278] especially if the claimant was of doubtful solvency. But in fact the claimant had done the internal repairs and was wrongfully prevented from doing the external ones by the defendant, who later had these done at her own expense. As by the time of the hearing all the repairs had been completed, specific enforcement of the defendant's promise to grant the underlease would not expose her to the risk of having no remedy except damages in the event of the claimant's default; and specific performance was ordered on the terms that the claimant make an allowance in respect of the repairs done by the defendant. The principle that mutuality is judged by reference to the time of the hearing similarly accounts for the rule that a person who has been induced to enter into a contract by misrepresentation can specifically enforce it against the other; for by seeking this remedy he affirms the contract[279] and so gives the court power to hold him to it. The court has no such power when specific performance is claimed on behalf of a minor: "the act of filing the bill by his next friend cannot bind him".[280]

(v) *Specific performance and third parties*

Where A promises B to render some performance in favour of C, two problems can arise. The first is whether B can specifically enforce the promise against A; the second is whether C can do so.   21–048

Claim by promisee. In *Beswick v Beswick*[281] A promised B to pay an annuity to C in consideration of B's transferring the goodwill of his business to A. It was   21–049

---

[276] cf. *E Johnson & Co (Barbados) Ltd v NSR Ltd* [1997] A.C. 400 at 410–411.

[277] [1978] Ch. 337 at 367–368; adopting Ames 3 Col.L.Rev. 1; cf. *Lyus v Prowsa Developments Ltd* [1982] 1 W.L.R. 1044 at 1053; *Rainbow Estates Ltd v Tokenhold Ltd* [1999] Ch. 64 at 69, 76. See also *Sutton v Sutton* [1984] Ch. 184 where the argument of lack of mutuality was rejected because one of the claimant's promises had been performed, even though another was not binding. Specific performance was refused on grounds of public policy: above, para.11–048.

[278] cf. *National Provincial BS v British Waterways Board* [1992] E.G.C.S. 149. If the claimant can be ordered to give additional, satisfactory security, he can obtain an order of specific performance even though he has not yet performed and is not ordered immediately to do so: *Langen & Wind Ltd v Bell* [1972] Ch. 685.

[279] See above, para.9–108.

[280] *Flight v Bolland*, above, at 307.

[281] [1968] A.C. 58; above, para.14–017.

held that, although the promise did not give C any right of action, it could be specifically enforced by B's personal representative[282] against A; with the result that A was ordered to make the promised payments to C. Under the Contracts (Rights of Third Parties) Act 1999,[283] C is in many such cases entitled in his own right to enforce against A the term in the contract containing the promise in favour of C; and where C takes this course, the need for B to seek specific performance in favour of C will be much reduced. But it will not be altogether eliminated since there may still be situations in which C will not have any such right against A because the legislative requirements for its acquisition have not been satisfied.[284] The Act also expressly preserves B's right to enforce any term of the contract against A even where C has acquired a right of enforcement against A.[285] The scope of B's remedy by way of specific performance therefore still calls for discussion.

In holding that this remedy was available to B, the House of Lords in *Beswick v Beswick* stressed three points: that B's remedy at law was inadequate as the damages which he could recover would be purely nominal[286]; that A had received the entire consideration for his promise as the business had been transferred to him[287]; and that the contract could have been specifically enforced by A, if B had failed to perform his promise to transfer the business.[288] It is also relevant to the issue of specific enforceability that A's promise, being one to pay an annuity, was of a kind which would have been specifically enforceable if it had been made to B for his own benefit[289]; and that, if the promise had been in these terms, none of the grounds for refusing specific performance which have been discussed in this chapter would have applied.

It does not, however, follow from *Beswick v Beswick* that specific performance in favour of a third party will be granted to the promisee *only* if the circumstances are such that the remedy would have been available in a two-party case. Thus it seems that specific performance could be ordered of a promise to pay a single lump sum to a third party,[290] though in a two-party case such an obligation would more appropriately be enforceable by a common law action for the agreed sum.[291] Again, it seems that specific performance in favour of a third party would not be excluded merely because substantial damages, constituting an "adequate" remedy, were available to the promisee. As Lord Pearce[292] said in *Beswick v Beswick*, such damages "would be a less appropriate remedy since the parties to the agreement were intending an annuity . . . ; and a lump sum of damages does not accord with

---

[282] Who happened to be C.

[283] See above, para.14–090 et seq.

[284] e.g. because the requirements of subss.1(1) and (2) are not satisfied; see above, para.14–094 for the question whether they would be satisfied on the facts of *Beswick v Beswick*, above.

[285] s.4 of the 1999 Act.

[286] [1968] A.C. 58 at 73, 81, 83, 102. Nor did B have any other more satisfactory remedy at law, e.g. he could not have sued for the amount to be paid to C, or for the return of the goodwill (above, paras 14–020—14–021). For the question of whether B could recover damages in respect of C's loss, see above, para.14–031.

[287] [1968] A.C. 58 at 83, 89, 97, 102; cf. above, para.21–021.

[288] ibid. at 89, 97.

[289] See above, para.21–021.

[290] As in *Gurtner v Circuit* [1968] 2 Q.B. 587 (as to which see above, fn.257).

[291] See above, para.21–019.

[292] Who thought that the damages in *Beswick v Beswick* would be substantial: [1968] A.C. 58 at 88.

this".[293] On the other hand specific performance will obviously not be ordered in favour of B where A contracts with B to render personal services to C, for the policy of the rule against the specific enforcement of service contracts applies no less where the services are to be rendered to a third party than where they are to be rendered to the promisee. Again, A may contract with B to pay C £10,000 immediately in return for B's promise to serve A for one year. If A repudiates before B has performed the service, B's claim for specific performance in favour of C should probably be refused on the ground that the grant of the remedy would offend the mutuality requirement[294]: A would have no security for the performance of B's promise to serve except a common law action for damages.

The above examples show that specific performance should not be granted to the promisee merely because the contract provides for performance in favour of a third party, nor refused merely because it would not have been ordered had there been no third party in the case. As a general principle, it is submitted that specific performance in favour of a third party should prima facie be available to the promisee when it is the *most appropriate* remedy for the enforcement of the contract. But it should be open to the defendant to resist specific enforcement by showing that this remedy would lead to one of the undesirable results against which the established limitations on the scope of the remedy are meant to provide protection.

Claim by third party. Under the Contracts (Rights of Third Parties) Act   21–050
1999, C is in many cases entitled in his own right to enforce against A the term in the contract between A and B containing A's promise in favour of C.[295] The Act expressly lists specific performance as one of the remedies available to C where it would have been available to him "if he had been a party to the contract"; and it states that the rules relating to specific performance "shall apply accordingly".[296] Some such rules will apply to a claim by C in the same way as they apply to one by B: e.g. if A's promise is one to render personal service to C, it will not be specifically enforceable at the suit of either B or C. Other rules will obviously apply with some modification: e.g. if A promises B to pay a lump sum to C, then the most appropriate remedy for B might be specific performance in equity, while for C it would be a common law action for the agreed sum. The application to claims by C of the limitations on the scope of specific performance will need to be worked out on a case-by-case basis in the light of the policies which have given rise to these limitations in two-party cases.

(b) Injunction

(i) *General*

Prohibitory injunctions. Where a contract is negative in nature, or contains   21–051
a negative stipulation, breach of it may be restrained by injunction. In such cases, an injunction is normally granted as a matter of course; though, since it is an equitable (and thus in principle a discretionary) remedy, it may be refused on the

---

[293] [1968] A.C. 58 at 88; cf. ibid. at 102 and the citation at 90–91 with approval of a dictum of Windeyer J. in *Coulls v Bagot's Executor & Trustee Co Ltd* [1967] A.L.R. 385 at 412.
[294] See above, paras 21–046—21–047.
[295] See above, para.14–090 et seq.
[296] s.1(5) of the 1999 Act.

ground that its award would cause such "particular hardship"[297] to the defendant as to be oppressive to him.[298] An injunction would not be "oppressive" merely because observance of the contract was burdensome to the defendant[299] or because its breach would cause little or no prejudice to the claimant[300]; for in deciding whether to restrain breach of a negative stipulation, the court is not normally concerned with "the balance of convenience or inconvenience".[301] This rule, however, applies only to a *prohibitory* injunction restraining a defendant from *future* breaches.

21–052   **Mandatory injunctions.** Where the breach lies entirely in the past (e.g. where the defendant has fenced land that he had covenanted to leave open), the claimant may seek a *mandatory* injunction, ordering the breach to be undone. Such an order *is* subject to a "balance of convenience" test and may therefore be refused if the prejudice suffered by the defendant in having to restore the original position heavily outweighs the advantage that will be derived from such restoration by the claimant.[302] In applying the "balance of convenience" test, the court will also take the nature of the breach into account. Thus where the defendant in breach of a restrictive covenant erected a building so as to block the claimant's sea view, a mandatory injunction was granted as the breach had been committed deliberately, with full knowledge of the claimant's rights, and as damages would not be an adequate remedy.[303]

21–053   **Interim injunctions.** The "balance of convenience" test also applies to interim injunctions,[304] (except where there is "a plain and uncontested breach of a clear covenant not to do a particular thing"[305]). If, for example, the grant of an interim injunction would amount in substance to a final resolution of the dispute between the parties, the court will, in considering a claim for interim relief, take into account the likelihood of the claimant's success at the eventual trial.[306] The

---

[297] *Insurance Co v Lloyd's Syndicate* [1995] 1 Lloyd's Rep. 273 at 276 (where there was no such hardship); cf. above, para.21–029.

[298] See below, para.21–053.

[299] cf. above, para.21–029.

[300] *Kemp v Sober* (1851) 1 Sim. (N.S.) 517; *Tipping v Eckersley* (1855) 2 K. & J. 264; *Marco Productions Ltd v Pagola* [1945] K.B. 111; *Hollis & Co v Stocks* [2000] U.K.C.L.R. 685.

[301] *Doherty v Allman* (1878) 3 App.Cas. 709 at 720; cf. *Warner Bros Pictures Inc v Nelson* [1937] 1 K.B. 209 at 217; *Araci v Fallon* [2011] EWCA Civ 668 and (in tort) *Kennaway v Thompson* [1981] Q.B. 88.

[302] *Sharp v Harrison* [1922] 1 Ch. 502; *Shepherd Homes Ltd v Sandham* [1971] Ch. 340; for subsequent proceedings, see [1971] 1 W.L.R. 1062; *Sutton Housing Trust v Lawrence* (1988) 55 P. & C.R. 320 (mandatory and prohibitory injunction); *Reed v Madon* [1989] Ch. 408.

[303] *Wakeham v Wood* (1982) 43 P. & C.R. 40; *Chelsea v Muscut* [1990] 2 E.G.L.R. 48. cf. *Mortimer v Bailey* [2004] EWCA Civ 1514; [2005] 2 E.G. 102.

[304] *Texaco Ltd v Mulberry Filling Station Ltd* [1972] 1 W.L.R. 814; *Evans Marshall & Co v Bertola* [1973] 1 W.L.R. 439; *Clifford Davis Management Ltd v WEA Records Ltd* [1975] 1 W.L.R. 61; *Films Rover International v Cannon Film Sales Ltd* [1987] 1 W.L.R. 670 (for further proceedings, see [1989] 1 W.L.R. 912); *Evening Standard Co Ltd v Henderson* [1987] I.C.R. 588; *Lock International Plc v Beswick* [1989] 1 W.L.R. 1268; *GFI Group Inc v Eaglestone* [1994] I.R.L.R. 119; *Channel Tunnel Group Ltd v Balfour Beatty Construction Ltd* [1993] A.C. 334. For the general principles governing such injunctions, see *American Cyanamid Co v Ethicon* [1975] A.C. 396; *Fellowes v Fisher* [1976] Q.B. 122; *Lawrence David Ltd v Ashton* [1989] I.C.R. 123.

[305] *Hampstead and Suburban Properties Ltd v Diomedous* [1969] 1 Ch. 248 at 259; cf. *Attorney-General v Barker* [1990] 3 All E.R. 257.

[306] *Cambridge Nutrition Ltd v BBC* [1990] 3 All E.R. 523; *Lansing Linde Ltd v Kerr* [1991] 1 W.L.R. 251 at 258; *Imutran v Uncaged Campaigns Ltd* [2001] 2 All E.R. 385.

court can also take into account the financial prejudice which would be likely to be suffered either by the claimant if the injunction were refused,[307] or by the defendant if it were granted,[308] and if at the trial the dispute were resolved in that party's favour. An award of damages to that party might then be an "inadequate" remedy for reasons discussed earlier in this chapter[309]: e.g. because there was an appreciable risk of the other party's not being able to pay the amount of the award.

Oppression. We shall see later in this chapter that the court has power, by statute, to award damages in lieu of specific performance or injunction.[310] This power is likely to be exercised if the injury to the claimant is small, if it can readily be estimated in money, if compensation in money would adequately compensate the claimant, and if the grant of an injunction would be oppressive to the defendant.[311] These conditions were satisfied, and an injunction was refused, in *Jaggard v Sawyer*,[312] where the defendants had built a house on land which could be reached only by committing a breach of covenant and a trespass against neighbouring house-owners, including the claimant. An injunction restraining such access would have rendered the new house "landlocked and incapable of beneficial ownership"[313]; and this would have been oppressive as the defendants had acted "openly and in good faith",[314] and not "in blatant . . . disregard of the [claimant's] rights"[315] in building the house. The test is once again[316] one of oppression rather than one of balance of convenience: if the claimant had sought interlocutory relief before the house had been built, she "would almost certainly have obtained it".[317]

21–054

(ii) *No indirect specific performance*

An injunction will not be granted if its effect is directly or indirectly to compel the defendant to do acts which he could not have been ordered to do by an order of specific performance. Thus an employee cannot be restrained from committing a breach of his positive obligation to work, for that would amount to specific

21–055

---

[307] *Themehelp Ltd v West* [1996] Q.B. 84, doubted on another point in *Group Josi Re v Walbrook Ins Co Ltd* [1996] 1 W.L.R. 1152 at 1162; cf. *British Airways v Unite the Union* [2009] EWHC 3541 (QB); [2010] I.R.L.R. 423.

[308] *Cambridge Nutrition Ltd v BBC* [1990] 3 All E.R. 523; *PI International Ltd v Llewellyn* [2005] EWHC 407 (QB); [2005] U.K.C.L.R. 530.

[309] See above, at fn.96.

[310] See below, para.21–060.

[311] cf. in tort: *Shelfer v City of London Electric Lighting Co* [1895] 1 Ch. 287 at 322–323; *Watson v Croft Promo-Sport Ltd* [2009] EWCA Civ 15; [2009] 3 All E.R. 249. The requirements stated above do not apply where it is the *defendant* who claims that specific relief is the more appropriate remedy since in such a case the grant of the injunction cannot be oppressive to him: *Marcic v Thames Water Utilities (No.2)* [2001] 4 All E.R. 327.

[312] [1995] 1 W.L.R. 269.

[313] ibid. at 288.

[314] ibid. at 289.

[315] ibid. at 283.

[316] cf. above, after fn.298.

[317] [1995] 1 W.L.R. at 289; cf. at 283; and see the similar case of *Gafford v Graham* (1999) 77 P. & C.R. 73.

enforcement of a contract of service.[318] Nor can an employer generally[319] be restrained from dismissing his employee in breach of contract.[320]

21–056   **Contracts of personal service.** A contract of employment may contain negative promises which can be enforced by injunction without indirectly compelling the employee to work, or the employer to employ.[321] Covenants in restraint of trade contained in such contracts are commonly enforced by injunction: this does not compel the employee to work for the employer, as such covenants generally begin to operate after the period of service is over. But some negative stipulations are expressed to operate during that period. These may be enforceable by injunction if the injunction merely provides an inducement to perform the positive obligation, but not if it in effect compels the employee to do the agreed work. Thus in *Lumley v Wagner*[322] Mlle Wagner undertook that for three months she would sing at Mr Lumley's theatre in Drury Lane on two nights a week and that during those three months she would not use her talents at any other theatre without Mr Lumley's written consent. She then agreed, for a larger payment, to sing for Mr Gye at Covent Garden, and to abandon her agreement with Mr Lumley. Mr Lumley was granted an injunction to restrain her from singing for Mr Gye. By contrast, a promise by an employee not to work in *any capacity* except for the employer[323] cannot be enforced by injunction since the effect of the injunction would be "to drive the defendant either to starvation or to specific performance of the positive covenants"[324] to work.

The decision in *Lumley v Wagner* has been much criticised,[325] particularly in relation to contracts of employment. An injunction may put so much economic pressure on the employee as in effect to force him to perform the positive part of the contract. In *Warner Bros Pictures Inc v Nelson*[326] a film actress agreed to act for the claimants for a period of time during which she undertook not to act for anyone else without the claimants' written consent. She was restrained by injunction from breaking this undertaking; and it was said that this would not force her to act for the claimants as she could earn a living by doing other work. But it might be quite unreasonable to expect her to do this; and more recent cases support the view that an injunction should not be granted except where it leaves the employee with some other *reasonable* means of earning a living. They have arisen where professional entertainers or athletes have entered into long-term exclusive contracts with managers, in whom they then lost confidence. It has been held that the managers could not obtain injunctions either against their clients,[327] or against third parties with whom those clients had entered into substitute management

---

[318] *Whitwood Chemical Co v Hardman* [1891] 2 Ch. 416; cf. above, para.21–035.
[319] For an exception to the general rule, see *Hill v C A Parsons & Co Ltd* [1972] 1 Ch. 305; above, para.21–036.
[320] *Chappell v Times Newspapers Ltd* [1975] 1 W.L.R. 482; Hepple [1975] C.L.J. 212; cf. *City & Hackney Health Authority v NUPE* [1985] I.R.L.R. 252; *Alexander v Standard Telephone and Cables Ltd* [1990] I.C.R. 291.
[321] cf. *Evans Marshall & Co Ltd v Bertola SA* [1973] 1 W.L.R. 349.
[322] (1852) 1 D.M. & G. 604.
[323] *Ehrman v Bartholomew* [1898] 1 Ch. 671.
[324] *Warner Bros Pictures Inc v Nelson* [1937] 1 K.B. 209 at 216.
[325] Stevens 6 Cornell L.Q. 235; Ashley 6 Col.L.Rev. 82; Clark 17 Col.L.Rev. 687; and see below, fn.328.
[326] [1937] 1 K.B. 209.
[327] *Page One Records Ltd v Britton* [1968] 1 W.L.R. 157.

contracts,[328] if the effect of the injunction would "as a practical matter"[329] be to force the clients to make use of the services of the original manager; and this would commonly be the case in such contracts given the necessity of maintaining the skill or talent of such persons through their continued display.[330]

An injunction, in cases of this kind, will always put *some* pressure on the defendant to perform his positive obligation to render the agreed services; and the view that this factor is, of itself, a ground for refusing to grant the injunction[331] is, with respect, hard to reconcile with the reasoning of *Lumley v Wagner*.[332] The crucial question, in these cases, is whether the injunction would put *undue* pressure on an employee to perform his positive obligation to work; and this question can give rise to difficult issues of fact and degree. In one case[333] a newspaper reporter undertook during the term of his contract not to work for others; the contract provided for termination by 12 months' notice. The reporter gave only two months' notice of termination, and it was held that he could be restrained by injunction from breach of the negative stipulation. This was said not to subject him to undue pressure since the employers had undertaken to go on paying him, to allow him to go on working for them for the rest of the contract period, and not to claim damages if he should choose simply to draw his pay without doing such work. But the position might have been different if the employers had merely undertaken to go on paying him, without allowing him to work. In such cases, the court can balance the employee's interest in continuing to work (so as to maintain his skill and reputation) against any prejudice likely to be suffered by the employer if the employee works for a third party; and, where the remedy is discretionary,[334] the court may refuse to grant the injunction if it is satisfied that breach of the negative stipulation will not seriously prejudice the employer.[335] A fortiori, such relief will be denied to the employer where his refusal to allow the employee to work amounts to a breach of the contract of employment on the employer's part.[336]

Other services. An injunction to restrain the breach by an employee of a stipulation in a contract of employment will be issued only if the contract contains an *express* negative promise.[337] The remedy has been restricted in this way because,   21–057

---

[328] *Warren v Mendy* [1989] 1 W.L.R. 853, citing criticism of *Warner Bros Inc v Nelson* (above, fn.326) in *Nichols Advance Vehicle Systems Inc v De Angelis*, unreported, 1979; McLean [1990] C.L.J. 15.

[329] *Page One Records Ltd v Britton* [1968] 1 W.L.R. 157 at 166. *Lumley v Wagner* was distinguished at 165 on the ground that Mr Lumley had no obligation except to pay money; but in fact he also made certain promises which were negative in substance: e.g. that certain parts were to "belong exclusively" to Mlle Wagner.

[330] *Warren v Mendy* [1989] 1 W.L.R. 853 at 857.

[331] *Young v Robson Rhodes* [1999] 3 All E.R. 524 at 534 ("to coerce the defendants . . . ").

[332] (1852) 1 D.M. & G 694. *Lumley v Wagner* was cited by counsel, but not referred to in the judgment, in *Young v Robson Rhodes*, above. It seems that the defendant in the former case was not in fact "coerced" into performing her positive obligation to sing at the claimant's theatre: see Waddams 117 L.Q.R. 431 at 440. The two cases may be distinguishable on the ground that there was no express negative covenant in *Young v Robson Rhodes*, above.

[333] *Evening Standard Co Ltd v Henderson* [1987] I.C.R. 588.

[334] See above, at fn.302; cf. *Delaney v Staples* [1992] 1 A.C. 687, 692–693 and *William Hill Organisation Ltd v Tucker* [1998] I.R.L.R. 313, discussing so-called "garden leave".

[335] *Provident Financial Group Plc v Hayward* [1989] I.C.R. 160; cf. *SG & R Valuation Co v Boudrais* [2008] EWHC 1340 (QB); [2008] I.R.L.R. 770.

[336] *William Hill Organisation Ltd v Tucker* [1998] I.R.L.R. 313; above, para.17–054.

[337] *Mortimer v Beckett* [1920] 1 Ch. 571; but breaches of negative obligations *imposed by law* can be restrained by injunction even though there is no express negative stipulation: e.g. *Hivac v Park Royal Scientific Instruments* [1946] Ch. 169.

as has been seen,[338] an injunction may put so much economic pressure on the employee as in effect to force him to perform his positive obligation to work; and this is traditionally regarded as undesirable.[339] But where the defendant's obligation is not one to render personal services, there is less objection to an injunction which puts pressure on him to perform his positive undertaking, even though that undertaking may not be specifically enforceable; and in cases of this kind the courts have implied negative stipulations and restrained their breach by injunction. For example, it has been suggested that a time charterparty cannot be specifically enforced against the shipowner and, on this basis,[340] an injunction will not be granted which is "juristically indistinguishable" from an order for specific performance, e.g. an injunction restraining the shipowner from exercising his right of withdrawal.[341] It is, however, no objection to the grant of injunctive relief that it would "as a matter of practical reality"[342] compel the shipowner to perform, e.g. an injunction restraining him from using a ship under charter inconsistently with the charterparty.[343] Similarly, the practical effect of injunctive relief has not prevented the courts from restraining breach of a promise to give a "first refusal" to purchase land[344] and breaches of various exclusive dealing agreements,[345] or of agreements to submit disputes to arbitration.[346] Furthermore, in such commercial agreements not involving any element of personal service, injunctive relief is not precluded by the fact that the parties will be compelled, in practice, to perform a contract which requires some degree of mutual co-operation or confidence,[347] though this is a factor which the courts will take into account.[348]

In the above cases, a negative stipulation, though not express, can readily be implied. The position would be different where the vagueness of the positive part of the contract made it impossible to say precisely what the defendant had undertaken *not* to do[349]; and also in other cases where an injunction would be "juristically indistinguishable" from an order for specific performance,[350] i.e. where the only negative stipulation which could be implied was one that would embrace the whole positive obligation. For example, if a contract were made for

---

[338] See above, para.21–056.

[339] See above, para.21–035.

[340] The precise reason for this is a matter of debate, and open to challenge: see above, para.21–037 and fn.221.

[341] *The Scaptrade* [1983] 2 A.C. 694 at 701.

[342] *Lauritzencool AB v Lady Navigation Inc* [2005] EWCA Civ 579; [2005] 1 W.L.R. 3686 at [12].

[343] ibid., in which *Warren v Mendy*, above, fn.328, was distinguished (at [24]) on the basis that it was a contract of *personal* service, or a particular sub-category thereof involving special skills, or talent: see above, at fn.330. See also: *Sevin v Deslandes* (1860) 30 L.J. (Ch.) 457; *The Georgos C* [1971] 1 Q.B. 488; *The Oakworth* [1975] 1 Lloyd's Rep. 581.

[344] *Manchester Ship Canal v Manchester Racecourse Co* [1901] 2 Ch. 37.

[345] *Metropolitan Electric Supply Co v Ginder* [1901] 2 Ch. 799; *Decro-Wall International SA v Practitioners in Marketing Ltd* [1971] 1 W.L.R. 361; *Evans Marshall & Co v Bertola SA* [1973] 1 W.L.R. 349; *SAB Miller Africa v Esat African Breweries* [2009] EWHC 2140 (Comm); [2010] 1 Lloyd's Rep. 392. Contrast *Fothergill v Rowland* (1873) L.R. 17 Eq. 132. As to the validity of exclusive dealing agreements, see above, paras 11–092—11–099.

[346] *Bankers Trust Co v PT Jakarta International Development* [1999] 1 Lloyd's Rep. 910 at 911 (injunction against proceedings in foreign court; in respect of English proceedings, the remedy would be by way of a stay: above, para.11–050).

[347] *Evans Marshall & Co v Bertola SA* [1973] 1 W.L.R. 349 at 379; *Lauritzencool AB v Lady Navigation Inc* [2005] EWCA Civ 579; [2005] 1 W.L.R. 3686 at [33].

[348] *Ericsson AB v EADS Defence and Security Systems Ltd* [2009] EWHC 2598 (TCC); [2010] B.L.R. 131 at [47].

[349] *Bower v Bantam Investments Ltd* [1972] 1 W.L.R. 1120.

[350] See above, fn.341.

the sale of unascertained generic goods (such as "100 tons of coal") an injunction "not to break the contract" or "not to withhold delivery" would be indistinguishable from an order of specific performance,[351] and would not normally[352] be granted. And the implication of a narrower negative stipulation (e.g. not to sell to anyone else) would not fairly arise from the contract.

Restraint of trade. A further danger of the rule in *Lumley v Wagner*[353] is that 21–058 the injunction may help to stifle competition. It is arguable that this was the purpose of the negative stipulation, and the effect of the injunction, in the leading case itself; for it might have been physically possible for Mlle Wagner to sing at Drury Lane for two nights a week and to sing elsewhere on other nights. Yet the question whether the contract was invalid for restraint of trade was not discussed at all. It used to be thought that this question arose only where the relevant contractual provisions came into effect *after* the period of employment. A possible reason for this view is that, where the period of employment is fairly short (as in *Lumley v Wagner*), the negative stipulation is reasonable (and therefore valid[354]) because of its limited duration.[355] But this reasoning loses much of its force where the employer has options to extend the term of service, sometimes for very long periods[356] or where long periods of notice have to be given to terminate the contract.[357] The present position is that stipulations which operate during employment (no less than those which operate thereafter) can sometimes have their validity tested under the restraint of trade doctrine[358]; but even where their *validity* is not subject to these tests, the *remedy* of injunction is likely to be granted only where these tests are satisfied.[359] If this were not so, the law as to restraint of trade could, to a considerable extent, be evaded by simply giving the employer options to extend the period of service or by requiring long periods of notice for the termination of the contract.[360] A converse suggestion may also be made. Even where a covenant in restraint of trade takes effect after the period of service and

---

[351] cf. Fry, *Specific Performance* (6th edn), para.857; *Whitwood Chemical Co v Hardman* [1891] 2 Ch. 416 at 426. The granting in *Wake v Renault (UK) Ltd, The Times*, August 1, 1996 of an injunction "not to terminate" a distributorship agreement for some years is, with respect, open to question as it amounted to specific enforcement of an obligation of which specific performance would not normally be ordered since such an order would require "constant supervision" (above, para.21–038).

[352] For exceptions, see above, paras 21–023—21–025.

[353] (1852) 1 D.M. & G. 604.

[354] See above, paras 11–076, 11–084.

[355] Though in *Lumley v Wagner* it was unlimited as to area; cf. *Evening Standard v Henderson* [1987] I.C.R. 588.

[356] As in *Warner Bros Pictures Inc v Nelson* [1937] 1 K.B. 209; cf. the contract in *Riley v Coglan* [1967] 1 W.L.R. 1300, where a rugby league player agreed to serve his club "for the remainder of his football career . . . if the club should so long require." Contrast *Eastham v Newcastle United FC Ltd* [1964] Ch. 413, where the argument that the contract gave the employers a series of options was rejected.

[357] e.g. in cases of "garden leave" (above, para.17–054).

[358] *Esso Petroleum Ltd v Harper's Garage (Stourport) Ltd* [1968] A.C. 269 at 294, 328–329, discussing *Young v Timmins* (1831) 1 Cr. & J. 331; *A Schroeder Music Publishing Co Ltd v Macaulay* [1974] 1 W.L.R. 1308.

[359] *William Hill Organisation Ltd v Tucker* [1998] I.R.L.R. 313; *Symbian Ltd v Christensen* [2001] I.R.L.R. 77 at [52].

[360] It is no answer to an attack on the validity of the clause to say that the employee may get paid since (a) he will not be entitled to any payment if he refuses to work for the employer, unless the contract expressly so provides; and (b) the mere fact that he gets paid does not oust the principles of restraint of trade: cf. *Wyatt v Kreglinger and Fernau* [1933] 1 K.B. 793. If the covenant is valid, the fact that the employee goes on working and gets paid is relevant to the employer's *remedy*: above, at fn.333 and at fn.334.

is valid, it may be appropriate not to enforce it *by injunction* (but only by action for damages) if the injunction would leave the employee with no other reasonable means of making a living: the grant of an injunction in such circumstances might well be regarded as oppressive.[361]

21–059   **Severance.** A negative stipulation which is too widely expressed may be severed and enforced in part. Severance is not here governed by the rules which govern severance of promises in illegal contracts[362]: the question is not (as it is in the restraint of trade cases) whether severance alters the nature of the contract, but simply whether an injunction to enforce such part of the negative stipulation as the claimant specifies amounts to indirect specific performance. Thus in *Warner Bros Pictures Inc v Nelson*[363] the actress undertook, not only that she would not *act* for third parties, but also that she would not "*engage in any other occupation*" without the employers' written consent. She could clearly not be restrained from breach of the latter undertaking as this would force her to choose between idleness and performance of her obligation to work. But as the injunction sought was only one to restrain her from acting for third parties the objection that the whole of her undertaking could not be enforced by injunction was "removed by the restricted form in which the injunction is sought".[364] Of course if the negative stipulation, though operating during employment, is as a whole invalid for restraint of trade, the question of severance will be determined by the principles governing severance of illegal promises in illegal contracts.

(c) Damages and Specific Performance or Injunction[365]

21–060   **Damages in lieu of specific performance or injunction.** Power to award damages in addition to or "in substitution for . . . specific performance" was conferred on the Court of Chancery by s.2 of the Chancery Amendment Act 1858 (also known as Lord Cairns' Act). That power is now vested in the High Court by s.50 of the Senior Courts Act 1981. Under s.49 of the same Act, common law damages can also be awarded where specific performance or an injunction is claimed, even though the case is not one in which specific relief could have been ordered and, as a consequence, it is normally unnecessary to resort to the special power to award damages in lieu of these remedies. But it may sometimes be to the claimant's advantage to invoke that power where he has no completed cause of action at law, and its exercise has also given rise to certain special problems with regard to the assessment of damages.

21–061   **No completed cause of action at law.** Damages may be awarded in lieu of specific performance or injunction even though there is no completed cause of action at law. For example, a court can issue an injunction in respect of a threatened tort which has not yet been committed; and damages can be awarded

---

[361] cf. above, para.21–054.

[362] See above, paras 11–159—11–165.

[363] [1937] 1 K.B. 209.

[364] ibid. at 219; see above, para.21–056 for the question whether an injunction in even these limited terms should be granted; cf. *William Robinson & Co Ltd v Hever* [1898] 2 Ch. 451; *Symbian Ltd v Christensen* [2001] I.R.L.R. 77. Where the contract is illegal, e.g. for restraint of trade, the objection that an unseverable restraint is too wide cannot be met by claiming part-enforcement: contrast *Warner Bros Pictures Inc v Nelson* with *Gledhow Autoparts Ltd v Delaney* [1965] 1 W.L.R. 1366.

[365] Jolowicz [1975] C.L.J. 224; Pettit [1977] C.L.J. 369; [1978] C.L.J. 51.

in lieu of such an injunction.[366] A similar possibility exists where an anticipatory breach of contract has been committed and *not* been accepted. In such a case, an order for specific performance may be made at once[367]; and damages can be awarded in lieu under the Act even though there was (when the proceedings were commenced) no right to damages at common law.[368] However, a party is not in anticipatory breach of contract merely because the other fears that he will commit a breach of it; and where there is neither a present breach nor a wrongful repudiation, an injunction is not available against the former party,[369] so that there can be no award of damages in lieu. Again, an injunction is sometimes available against a refusal to contract; and it may be that damages can be awarded in lieu even though the refusal gives rise to no cause of action at common law.[370] An injunction may also be available to a third party where a contract between two others is in restraint of trade[371]; and in such cases it is arguable that damages may be awarded in lieu even though the third party has no cause of action for breach of contract against the parties to the contract in question.[372]

Assessment of damages. There was formerly some support for the view that the assessment of damages might be more favourable to the claimant under Lord Cairns' Act than at common law, particularly where the value of the subject-matter had risen between the time of breach and the time of judgment. It was assumed that, at common law, damages were necessarily based on the difference between the contract price and the value of the subject-matter *at the time of breach*. In *Wroth v Tyler*[373] one reason given for nevertheless assessing the damages by reference to the *time of judgment*[374] was that they were awarded, not at common law, but under the Act, "in substitution for ... specific performance". Such damages must, it was said, "constitute a true substitute for specific performance",[375] and give "as nearly as may be what specific performance would have given".[376] But even at common law the aim of damages is to put the claimant "in the same position ... *as if* the contract had been *performed*"[377]; and it is hard to see any difference in principle between the two phrases "as if ... performed" and "in substitution for ... specific performance". Both state the same general objective; neither is followed through to its logical conclusion. The judgment in *Wroth v Tyler* itself seems to recognise the possibility that part of the claimant's

21–062

---

[366] *Leeds Industrial Co-operative Society Ltd v Slack* [1924] A.C. 851.
[367] *Hasham v Zenab* [1960] A.C. 316 (but the order will be for performance on the due day).
[368] cf. *Oakacre Ltd v Claire Cleaners (Holdings) Ltd* [1982] Ch. 197.
[369] *The Veracruz I* [1992] 1 Lloyd's Rep. 356; *The P* [1992] 1 Lloyd's Rep. 470; cf. *Zucker v Tyndall Holdings Plc* [1992] 1 W.L.R. 1127; *Mercantile Group (Europe) AG v Aiyela* [1994] Q.B. 366 at 375.
[370] See above, para.1–007; *Garden Cottage Foods Ltd v Milk Marketing Board* [1984] A.C. 130 (where the right to damages was said at 141 to be based on breach of statutory duty); where the refusal is wrongful by statute, the right to damages will often be regulated by that statute, e.g. Equality Act 2010, Pt IX.
[371] See above, para.11–090.
[372] According to *Newport Association FC v Football Association of Wales Ltd* [1995] 2 All E.R. 87, the mere availability to the third party of a declaration that the contract is in restraint of trade is a cause of action; for difficulties arising from this reasoning, see above, para.11–090.
[373] [1974] Ch. 30; above, para.20–065; and see *Grant v Dawkins* [1973] 1 W.L.R. 1406; Pettit, 90 L.Q.R. 297.
[374] See above, para.20–074.
[375] [1974] Ch. 30 at 58.
[376] ibid. at 59.
[377] *Robinson v Harman* (1848) 1 Ex. 850 at 855; above, para.20–022.

loss would have been irrecoverable if it had been too remote[378]; and the mitigation rules can also reduce the amount recoverable as damages in lieu of specific performance.[379] In *Johnson v Agnew*[380] the House of Lords accordingly expressed the view that the assessment of damages was governed by the same principles whether the damages were awarded at common law or in lieu of specific performance.[381] Even at common law, damages are not invariably assessed by reference to the date of breach. This method of assessment is adopted where it would have been reasonable for the claimant, at that date, to have mitigated his loss, e.g. by making a substitute contract; but if, for some reason, this is not the case, the damages will be assessed by reference to some other date.[382] In *Wroth v Tyler* the claimants were not at the time of breach in a position to make a substitute contract; and, so far as the assessment of damages is concerned, the decision must now be explained on that ground.[383]

The general principle that there is no difference between the assessment of damages at common law and damages in lieu of specific performance is based on the assumption that the damages are claimed in respect of the same breach or cause of action. The principle obviously cannot apply where there is no cause of action at common law: e.g. where equitable relief is sought in respect of threatened future breaches.[384]

21–063   **Damages and specific performance or injunction.** Damages may be awarded in addition to specific performance, or an injunction.[385] For example, where a vendor is in breach because his title is subject to an encumbrance, the purchaser can get specific performance ordering the vendor to convey what title he has, plus damages based on the cost of discharging the encumbrance.[386] The court may also award damages for delay in completion in addition to specific performance.[387]

---

[378] [1974] Ch. 30 at 61.

[379] See *Radford v De Froberville* [1977] 1 W.L.R. 1262 at 1286; *Malhotra v Choudhury* [1980] Ch. 52; the point was, in effect, conceded in *Grant v Dawkins*, above.

[380] [1980] A.C. 367 at 400. This decision also makes it hard to accept the suggestion that damages under the Act can, as a general rule, be based on the defendant's gain (rather than, as at common law, on the claimant's loss): see *Surrey CC v Bredero Homes Ltd* [1993] 1 W.L.R. 1361; *Jaggard v Sawyer* [1995] 1 W.L.R. 269. For *other* grounds for basing an award on the defendant's gain and for criticism of the *Bredero* case, see above, para.20–015.

[381] Similarly, where the claimant seeks an account of profits, or damages for loss of the opportunity to negotiate for a fee to release the defendant from the contract: see above, paras 20–010—20–019.

[382] [1980] A.C. at 401; above, para.20–072 et seq.

[383] See above, para.20–074.

[384] *Jaggard v Sawyer* [1995] 1 W.L.R. 269 at 291–292.

[385] *Experience Hendrix LLC v PPX Enterprise Inc* [2003] EWCA Civ 323; [2003] E.M.L.R. 515.

[386] *Grant v Dawkins* [1973] 1 W.L.R. 1406.

[387] *Ford-Hunt v Ragbhir Singh* [1973] 1 W.L.R. 738; cf. *Oakacre Ltd v Claire Cleaners (Holdings) Ltd* [1982] Ch. 197 (damages for delay in substitution for specific performance). For damages for delay see *Raineri v Miles* [1981] A.C. 1050; above, para.18–091.

CHAPTER TWENTY-TWO

UNJUST ENRICHMENT[1]

A party who has wholly or in part performed his side of the contract and has **22–001** not received the agreed counter-performance in full may sometimes be entitled to restitution in respect of his own performance. Where this consists of a payment of money, the payor will simply seek to get it back; where it consists of some other benefit he will claim recompense (or a quantum meruit) in respect of it.

At the outset, it is important to stress that this chapter is not concerned with any aspect of the law of contract as such; it is concerned with a cause of action which may arise when a contract has *failed*.[2] Before any claim for restitution may be allowed, it must first be established that the payments made, or work done, never were, or are no longer, regulated by a contractual obligation,[3] i.e. the contract is void, or incomplete, or unenforceable, or it has been discharged for frustration, or terminated for breach.

(a) Recovery of Money Paid

An action lies, in the cases to be discussed below, to recover back money paid **22–002** under a contract or purported contract.

(i) *"Total failure of consideration"*[4]

Definition. A contracting party can recover back money paid under a contract **22–003** if there is a "total failure of consideration", i.e. if no part of the performance for which he bargained has been rendered.[5] In the *Fibrosa*[6] case, for example, a buyer of goods recovered back an advance payment when frustration had prevented the

---

[1] Beatson 2 J.C.L. 65; Burrows, *The Law of Restitution* (3rd edn), chs 14, 15.

[2] The type of claim considered in this chapter must also be distinguished from what is sometimes referred to as "restitutionary damages" which may be available for breach of a valid and enforceable obligation: see above, para.20–010 et seq.

[3] *Goodman v Pocock* (1850) 15 Q.B. 576; *Thomas v Brown* (1876) 1 Q.B.D. 714; *Kwei Tek Chao v British Traders & Shippers Ltd* [1954] 2 Q.B. 459: *Re Richmond Gate Property Co Ltd* [1965] 1 W.L.R. 335. For an apparent exception to this requirement, see *Miles v Wakefield DC* [1987] A.C. 539 (discussed below, para.22–023); cf. *Roxborough v Rothmans of Pall Mall Australia Ltd* [2001] H.C.A. 68; Tang Hang Wu 23 J.C.L. 201.

[4] Stoljar 75 L.Q.R. 53; Birks in (Rose, ed.) *Consensus ad Idem, Essays in the Law of Contract in Honour of Guenter Treitel*, p.179.

[5] *Stocznia Gdanska SA v Latvian Shipping Co* [1998] 1 W.L.R. 574 at 587, 600; above, para.20–155 (the test is whether performance has been *rendered*, not whether it has been *received*).

[6] [1943] A.C. 32; above, paras 19–045, 19–093.

delivery of any part of the goods. Lord Simon explained the meaning of "consideration" in this context:

> "In the law relating to the formation of contract, the promise to do a thing may often be the consideration, but when one is considering the law of failure of consideration and of the quasi-contractual right to recover money on that ground it is, generally speaking, not the promise which is referred to but the performance of the promise".[7]

This is only "generally speaking" the case[8] because a party may bargain for the promise itself. Thus a person who insures against the destruction of a thing by fire bargains for the insurer's promise. If the thing is then destroyed by water the insured person cannot recover back his premium: there is no total failure of consideration as he had the benefit of the insurer's promise for some time.[9] He could recover back his premium only if the insurer had never been at risk, e.g. if the thing had been destroyed the day before the policy had begun to run.[10]

It is also possible for A to buy the benefit of a promise made to B by C: e.g. where B contracts to assign[11] to A a debt owed by C to B. The actual assignment of the debt by B to A is then the *performance* of B's promise, even though the result of that performance is to confer on A a legal right to the performance of another promise, i.e. of that made by C to B. In such a case there would be a total failure of consideration if the contract between B and C were void in law, so that nothing was transferred from B to A; but this defect was said to have been cured where, as a result of a subsequent novation, A "got the substance of what they were paying for, a valid and enforceable contract with" C, so that "there was no failure of consideration at all".[12] It will be recalled that novation is a transaction involving all three parties,[13] so that B contributed to the end result that A became legally entitled to the benefit of C's promise. If this state of affairs had come about as a result of an independent subsequent transaction involving only A and C, then it would not have cured the defect in B's original performance or prevented the failure of consideration from being total.

22–004   **Partial failure.** In the above cases, there is either a total failure of consideration or no failure at all. There is also an intermediate situation in which there has been a *partial* failure; and in such cases, the traditional view, or general rule, is that there is no right to recover back a proportionate part of the money paid.[14] If, for

---

[7] 1943] A.C. 32 at 48; cf. *Rover International Ltd v Cannon Films Ltd (No.3)* [1989] 1 W.L.R. 912 at 923; *Goss v Chilcott* [1996] A.C. 788 at 797. The point seems to have been overlooked in *Re Goldcorp Exchange Ltd* [1995] 1 A.C. 74 at 103: see above, para.19–093, fn.430.

[8] cf. Lord Goff (dissenting) in *Westdeutsche Landesbank Girozentrale v Islington LBC* [1996] A.C. 669 at 683 ("need not be so narrowly confined").

[9] cf. *Tyrie v Fletcher* (1777) 2 Cowp. 666.

[10] cf. *Stevenson v Snow* (1761) 3 Burr. 1237; and see Marine Insurance Act 1906, s.84.

[11] See above, Ch.15.

[12] *Kleinwort Benson Ltd v South Tyneside MBC* [1994] 4 All E.R. 972 at 989.

[13] See above, para.15–003. In the present case, all three parties were involved: see [1994] 4 All E.R. 972 at 989.

[14] *Whincup v Hughes* (1871) L.R. 6 C.P. 78; the actual decision is no longer law: above, para.19–094; *Salvage Association v CAP Financial Services* [1995] F.S.R. 654 at 682; *Baltic Shipping Co v Dillon* (1993) 176 C.L.R. 344 (no return of part of the price paid for aborted holiday cruise; though the price may be relevant in assessing *damages: Peninsular & Orient SN Co v Youell* [1997] 2 Lloyd's Rep. 136; and see below, para.22–012). In *D O Ferguson & Associates v Sohl* (1992) 62 Build. L.R. 95 an advance payment was made to a builder who failed to do some of the work for which the payment was made. There was said to be a total failure of consideration with regard to the part of the work left undone

example, A employed B for a lump sum paid in advance to paint A's house, and B abandoned the job before it was finished, A could not recover back any part of the payment: the right to recover back money paid on account of failure of consideration is said to be restricted to cases in which the failure is "total". One reason for this requirement is that, in the example just given, A already has his remedy in damages. This is generally governed by the compensatory principle[15] under which A can recover no more than his loss; and to allow him to claim restitution in respect of *any* breach would cut across this principle, particularly where he had made a bad bargain by paying B more than B's performance was worth. If B had simply done nothing after receiving the advance payment, A's right to recover the payment could be justified on the ground that B would be unjustly enriched if he were allowed to keep money paid to him "for nothing but a broken promise".[16] But this reasoning loses much of its force where B has performed in part,[17] particularly where only a small part remains unperformed. A second reason for the general rule is that it may not be easy for the law to apportion the amount of work actually done by B to the whole in respect of which the payment was made; and where this is the case the amount of restitution that he should be required to make is correspondingly hard to assess. But there are also cases in which neither of the above justifications for the general rule applies; and in such cases recovery of money has been allowed even though the failure of consideration is only partial. Thus where apportionment of the unperformed part is in fact easy, the law will allow partial recovery: e.g. a buyer of 100 tons could get back half his money if only 50 tons were delivered.[18]

Apportionment is also easy where the promise which is performed only in part is one by a borrower to pay money, whether by way of interest or of repayment of capital, under a contract for the loan of money. Normally the lender's action in such a case will be one for the recovery of the agreed sum, but where this is for some reason not available,[19] the fact that some payments have been made by the borrower will not deprive the lender of a restitutionary remedy based on failure of consideration.[20] Indeed, the very fact that *no* contractual remedy is available to the promisee will make the court anxious to allow restitution since in such cases this is the *only* way in which unjust enrichment of the promisor can be avoided.[21] This point is also reflected in the statutory provision by which money paid in advance under a contract which is later frustrated can be recovered even though the failure of consideration is only partial.[22] Any difficulty of making an apportionment is again outweighed by the fact that restitution is the payor's only possible remedy, since frustration provides the payee with a defence to any claim for damages.

---

so that the builder was held liable to restore the amount of the payment attributable to that part. But the notion of "total failure of part" is, with respect, quite inconsistent with the requirement of total failure; the case can perhaps be justified on the analogy of the cases discussed at fn.18, below; cf. *Guido van der Garde BV v Force India Formula One Ltd* [2010] EWHC 2373 (QB) at [323].

[15] See above, para.20–004.
[16] Palmer 20 Ohio State L.J. 264, 267; above, para.20–004.
[17] For the position where only a very small part has been performed, see below, para.22–005.
[18] *Whincup v Hughes*, above, at 81; cf. *Ebrahim Dawood Ltd v Heath Ltd* [1961] 2 Lloyd's Rep. 512; *Clough Mill Ltd v Martin* [1985] 1 W.L.R. 111 at 117–118.
[19] See fnn.20 and 21, below for examples.
[20] *Goss v Chilcott* [1996] A.C. 788, where the borrowers had been discharged from their contractual liability by an alteration of the repayment dates in a mortgage made on behalf of the lender.
[21] Hence perhaps the reference in *Kleinwort Benson Ltd v Glasgow CC* [1999] 1 A.C. 153 at 171 to "failure of consideration" (omitting "total") in the context of a claim for the recovery of money paid under a void contract.
[22] See above, para.19–095 et seq.

Partial failure of consideration can also give rise to a right to the return of advance payments where the contract in terms confers such a right.[23] The requirement that the failure must be "total" is, finally, attenuated in the cases, to be discussed below,[24] in which restitution of money has been allowed in spite of the fact that benefits other than those contracted for had been received by the payor; though in some of those cases the grant of the restitutionary remedy is open to criticism precisely on the ground that it has led to the payor's being overcompensated.[25]

The above discussion shows that the requirement of a "total" failure of consideration, though it continues to be stated in the authorities,[26] is now much qualified. These qualifications support the view that it should be restricted to those cases in which the reasons for it, stated above, still have force. It should, in other words, no longer apply where the payor has *no* remedy, or no satisfactory remedy, for breach (e.g. by way of action for damages[27]) in respect of the part left unperformed by the payee, or where there is in fact no difficulty in apportioning that part to the whole in respect of which the payor's advance payment had been made.

22–005   **Returnable and non-returnable benefits.** A party who has received only partial or defective performance may, on that ground, be entitled to terminate the contract.[28] If he does terminate, and restores what he has received under the contract, he brings about a total failure of consideration and can therefore recover any money that he has paid. For example, a buyer who has paid in advance for goods may find, on delivery, that they suffer from a defect amounting to a breach of condition, or that they are not of the agreed quantity. In that case, he can generally reject the goods and get his money back.[29] Normally, he must restore the goods, but this requirement does not apply where his inability to restore them is due to the very defect which has given rise to the right to reject: e.g. if the goods were so defective that they disintegrated; or if they were taken away from the buyer because the seller had no title to them.[30] The position seems to be the same where restoration of the subject-matter is made impossible by some external cause for which neither party was responsible.[31]

Where, on the other hand, the partial or defective performance is of such a nature that it cannot be returned, the mere fact that it has been rendered prevents the failure of consideration from being total: e.g. where work to be done under a lump sum building contract has been paid for in advance, but is left unfinished or is done defectively. In such cases, the client's remedy is in damages: he would be entitled to the return of his payment only if the builder's breach were so serious

---

[23] *The Trident Beauty* [1994] 1 W.L.R. 161 at 164–165.

[24] See below, paras 22–006—22–011.

[25] *Butterworth v Kingsway Motors Ltd* [1954] 1 W.L.R. 1286 and *Barber v NSW Bank Ltd* [1996] 1 W.L.R. 641; below, paras 22–008, 22–009.

[26] e.g. *The Trident Beauty* [1994] 1 W.L.R. 161 at 164–165; *Baltic Shipping Co v Dillon* (1993) 176 C.L.R. 344 at 350–351, 367, 376, 384, 388.

[27] Or, in the case of a loan of money, by way of action for the agreed sum.

[28] See Ch.18.

[29] e.g. *Bragg v Villanova* (1923) 40 T.L.R. 154; *Baldry v Marshall* [1925] 1 Q.B. 260. Contrast *Linz v Electric Wire Co of Palestine* [1948] A.C. 371 (where a buyer of shares forming part of an invalid issue had sold, and was therefore unable to restore, them; in some cases, the claimant may be entitled to return *other* identical shares: *Smith New Court Securities Ltd v Scrimgeour Vickers (Asset Management) Ltd* [1997] A.C. 254 at 262.

[30] e.g. *Rowland v Divall* [1923] 2 K.B. 500.

[31] e.g. *Head v Tattersall* (1871) L.R. 7 Ex. 7.

that the work was wholly useless to the client.[32] Similarly, an employee may commit breaches of duty justifying his dismissal; but if he is not dismissed and is paid his salary or wages, the employer will not, on subsequently discovering the breaches of duty, be able to recover back the payments[33]: his remedy is in damages.

Even if the subject-matter of the contract is returned (or if its return is not required under the rules stated above) the injured party may have derived some benefit from it: e.g. by using or occupying it. Use for the sole purpose of testing is disregarded and so does not impair the right of the injured party to get his money back.[34] But any further use or occupation may prevent the failure of consideration from being total. In *Hunt v Silk*[35] an agreement for a lease provided that possession was to be given immediately; that certain repairs were to be done by the landlord; that the lease was to be executed within 10 days; and that, on execution of the lease, the tenant was to pay £10. The tenant went into possession and paid the £10 before the execution of the lease, but the landlord failed to do the repairs, or to execute the lease within 10 days. After a few more days, the tenant vacated the premises and claimed the return of his £10. The claim was rejected,[36] and (although other explanations are possible[37]) the case has generally been taken to lay down the strict rule that, if a party has received any part of the benefit that he contracted for,[38] there is no total failure of consideration. The rule is open to the objection that it may bar a claim for the recovery of money even though the benefit received is only slight or technical.[39] On the other hand, the actual decision in *Hunt v Silk* does not seem to be unreasonable; for there is nothing in the reported facts to suggest that the tenant did not have a perfectly adequate remedy in damages.

Benefits other than those bargained for. It does not follow from *Hunt v Silk*   22–006
that the receipt of *any* benefit by the injured party will bar his right to get his money back. If the benefit received was *different in kind* from that bargained for,[40] there may be a total failure of consideration even though the benefit cannot be returned in specie: e.g. where a computer is delivered without the software needed

---

[32] *Heywood v Wellers* [1976] Q.B. 446 at 458.
[33] *Horcal v Gatland* [1984] I.R.L.R. 288. For the employer's right to withhold pay, see above, para.17–045.
[34] e.g. *Baldry v Marshall*, above.
[35] (1804) 5 East 449.
[36] Contrast *Wright v Colls* (1848) 8 C.B. 149, where the premium was paid specifically for execution of the lease and was held recoverable when the landlord failed to execute it.
[37] e.g. Goff and Jones, *The Law of Restitution* (7th edn), para.20–013.
[38] The same principle was applied in *Thorpe v Fasey* [1949] Ch. 649 to the converse situation where a vendor claimed termination. But it is hard to see why he should be deprived of this remedy merely because the *purchaser* had had some benefit from the subject-matter. Perhaps the case can be explained on other grounds: cf. above, para.18–082, fn.568.
[39] A kind of statutory modification of the rule in *Hunt v Silk*, above, is contained in Sale of Goods Act 1979, s.48A and 48C, under which a buyer who deals as consumer has in certain circumstances the right to "rescind" the contract on account of non-conformity of the goods. His right to "reimbursement", consequent on the exercise of his right to "rescind", may be reduced "to take account of the use he has had of the goods since they were delivered to him": s.48E(5); but see also fn.50, below.
[40] For this concept, contrast *Wilkinson v Lloyd* (1845) 7 Q.B. 27 with *Stray v Russell* (1859) 1 E. & E. 889 at 916; cf. also *Pilbrow v Pearless De Rougement & Co* [1999] 3 All E.R. 355 where the victim of the breach made no restitution claim; and the question whether such a claim might be available was left open at 361; and see below, para.22–015 for the view (there doubted) that there is a "total failure of consideration" for payments made under a void contract; and *Lipkin Gorman v Karpnale Ltd* [1991] 2 A.C. 548; above, para.3–032.

to make it work,[41] or where it is made useless by the supplier's deliberately activating a disabling device.[42] This idea has made it possible to temper the rigidity of the rule in *Hunt v Silk*, but it has led to rules and distinctions which have in turn attracted criticism.

22–007   *Rowland v Divall.* In *Rowland v Divall*[43] the claimant, who was a car dealer, bought a car from the defendant for £334, repainted it and resold it to a customer for £400. Subsequently the car was seized by the police as it had (unknown to any of the above parties) been stolen. The claimant thereupon repaid his customer the £400 and sued the defendant for the return of the £334. Meanwhile the original owner of the car had been compensated by his insurance company, who "took over the car themselves and then sold it to the (claimant) for £260".[44] The defendant took the position that his liability was limited to this sum and paid it into court.[45] But the Court of Appeal held that there had been a total failure of consideration, so that the claimant could recover back his payment of £334. He had not "received any portion of what he agreed to buy. . . . He did not get what he paid for—namely a car to which he would have title".[46] As the claimant was a dealer, this seems (with respect) to be a reasonable view: he did not want to use, but to resell, the car. For this purpose he needed a marketable title and not mere possession, which was wrongful against the owner. Moreover, the fact that he did not get title caused him serious prejudice beyond having to buy the car a second time; for it resulted in his losing a presumably profitable resale.[47]

22–008   *Butterworth v Kingsway Motors.* The same rule has, however, also been applied in the absence of such circumstances. In *Butterworth v Kingsway Motors Ltd*[48] a car owned by a finance company was let out on hire-purchase to a hirer who wrongfully sold it before she had paid all the instalments. It passed through a number of hands until it was sold for £1,275 by the defendant to a buyer, both of whom acted in good faith. Nearly a year later, the finance company notified the buyer that the car was theirs and asked for its return. Alternatively, they offered to allow the buyer to acquire title for £175, this being all that remained due under the hire-purchase agreement as the hirer had kept up her payments under it. Meanwhile, however, second-hand car prices had fallen, so that the car was worth only £800. Two days after hearing from the finance company, the buyer claimed the return of the £1,275. After another eight days, the original hirer paid off the £175 and acquired a good title which could at that stage have been passed to the buyer. In these circumstances, the court rightly described the buyer's claim as "somewhat lacking in merits"[49]—but nevertheless allowed it in full. The decision represents a regrettable extension of *Rowland v Divall*. It is hardly realistic to say that the buyer did not get any part of what he bargained for: he bought the car for use and did use it for nearly a year. Moreover, any prejudice to the buyer from the

---

[41] *South West Water Services Ltd v International Computers Ltd* [1999] B.L.R. 420.
[42] *Rubicon Computer Systems Ltd v United Paints Ltd* (2000) 2 T.C.L.R. 453.
[43] [1923] 2 K.B. 500.
[44] This fact is stated in the report of the case in 129 L.T. 757.
[45] ibid.
[46] [1923] 2 K.B. 500 at 504.
[47] The eventual fate of the car is not known; cf. above, para.20–059.
[48] [1954] 1 W.L.R. 1286.
[49] ibid. at 1291.

defendant's lack of title was removed when the amount outstanding under the hire-purchase agreement was paid off.

Barber v NSW Bank. The same result was again reached in *Barber v NSW* **22–009** *Bank Plc*,[50] where the buyer entered into a conditional sale agreement with the defendants relating to a car which was (unknown to either party) the subject of an earlier finance agreement and to which the defendant therefore had no title. The buyer became aware of this fact when he attempted, some 20 months after entering into the agreement to resell the car; and after a further three months he terminated the agreement and successfully claimed the return of all the payments he had made under it. Although he had had the use of the car for nearly two years "without let or hinderance",[51] it was said to be "not inequitable in all the circumstances"[52] for him to recover his payments in full. This result was based "on the established authorities"[53] which appear to have included *Rowland v Divall* and *Butterworth v Kingsway Motors*, both of which were cited to the court though neither was referred to in the judgment.[54] It is, with respect, unfortunate that no attempt was made by the Court of Appeal in the *Barber* case to distinguish the former or to evaluate the latter decision. The car had been bought for use (though the breach came to light when the buyer attempted to resell it); and as the buyer had used the car for some 23 months it is hard to accept that he received no part of the benefit for which he had bargained. The court may have attached some weight to the fact that the defendants had become aware of the earlier finance agreement some six months before the buyer terminated[55] and they had made no attempt to settle the third party's claim during that interval.[56] It is, however, not easy to see how even this fact could be said to have deprived the buyer of the whole of what he had bargained for, particularly as he had used the car for more than 16 months before the defendants had acquired any knowledge of the earlier agreement[57] and so had any opportunity of settling the true owner's claim.

Other cases. A line of hire-purchase cases is open to similar criticisms. **22–010** According to these, there is a total failure of consideration if the person letting a car out has no title, so that he cannot give the hirer a valid option to purchase.[58] But once a valid option has been conferred, there is no total failure because the hirer is for some reason prevented from exercising it[59]; or because the car suffers

---

[50] [1996] 1 W.L.R. 641. It seems that the buyer dealt as consumer; and, as the seller's breach was of an *express* term as to title, the new provisions of the Sale of Goods Act 1979 could now apply on such facts: see the reference in s.48F to an "express term". But the buyer could avoid reduction of his restitution claim under s.48E(5) by basing that claim, not on the new "additional rights" conferred on him by Pt 5A of the Act, but on his right to reject for breach of condition under s.11; this right is not affected by s.48E(5); above, fn.39.

[51] ibid. at 647.

[52] ibid.

[53] ibid.

[54] The court relied principally on the authorities cited in fn.58, below, though it accepted, at 646, that it was not bound by these cases.

[55] The defendants became aware of the third party's claim on February 12, 1991; the buyer terminated on August 16, 1991.

[56] They settled it on September 2, 1991.

[57] i.e. from October 10, 1989, when the car was supplied to the buyer, till February 12, 1991.

[58] See *Karflex Ltd v Poole* [1933] 2 K.B. 251; *Warman v Southern Counties Car Finance Corp Ltd* [1959] 2 K.B. 576 (where the point arose on a counterclaim against the hirer).

[59] *Kelly v Lombard Banking Co* [1959] 1 W.L.R. 41; cf. *CCC Films (London) Ltd v Impact Quadrant Films* [1985] Q.B. 16 at 28.

from defects which are so serious that it cannot, for practical purposes, be used at all.[60] It seems unrealistic to say that a hirer who actually uses the car for a substantial period is wholly deprived of what he bargained for merely because there was no valid option, while one who cannot use the car at all because of a physical defect is not so deprived.

22–011   **Criticism.** The view that the buyer in *Rowland v Divall* itself did not get *the* benefit for which he bargained is (as has been suggested above) a perfectly reasonable one. But the decision has nevertheless been criticised on the ground that the buyer recovered the *whole* of the price even though he and his sub-buyer had had the use of the car for some months. One way of meeting this criticism would be to reduce the buyer's claim for the return of the price by giving the seller the right to an allowance in respect of the benefit obtained by the buyer from his use of the subject-matter.[61] But this suggestion in turn gives rise to the problem of valuing that benefit. It would clearly be unfair to the buyer to assess it at a "reasonable rental value" since a person who is buying or hire-purchasing a car would not want to incur the cost of hiring one. An alternative possibility would be to value the buyer's benefit, in general,[62] at the amount by which the cost of replacing the goods when the buyer was deprived of them was less than the contract price.[63]

A further problem arises in cases of this kind because the true owner may have a claim in tort against either the buyer[64] or the seller[65] or both; he may be entitled not only to the return of the property or its value, but also its reasonable rental value.[66] If the owner has already claimed the rental value from the buyer, it seems clear that the seller should restore the *whole* price[67]; for if the buyer also had to give credit to the seller for the use of the goods, he would be required to pay twice over for the same benefit. Similar considerations apply where the true owner has not yet made his claim: if the buyer had to give credit to the seller he could later be sued for a similar sum by the owner. He might be able to claim that second payment back from the seller as damages; but by then the seller may have disappeared or the right to sue him may be barred by lapse of time. Of course the true owner may choose not to assert his claim for rental value; and in that case the buyer would no doubt be enriched by having had the use of the subject-matter and nevertheless being allowed to get back the whole price from the seller. But the enrichment would be at the expense of the *owner* and not at the expense of the seller, who accordingly should not have a claim in respect of it.[68] In view of the

---

[60] *Yeoman Credit Ltd v Apps* [1962] 2 Q.B. 508.

[61] Law Commission Working Paper 65, paras 56–57, for an earlier proposal for reform, see Law Reform Committee, Cmnd.2958 (1966), para.56, discussed by Treitel 30 M.L.R. 139 at 147–149; Law Commission Working Paper 85, paras 6.11–6.13 lists various possible reforms without deciding between them. The Law Commissions (Law Com. No.160, Scot. Law Com. No.104, para.6.5) have concluded that the subject is too complex for legislative reform.

[62] For a suggested exception where the buyer has made a bad bargain, see Law Commission Working Paper 65, paras 74–75; quaere, whether a special provision for this situation is desirable where (*ex hypothesi*) buyer and seller have both acted in good faith.

[63] Law Commission Working Paper 65, para.73.

[64] *Hilberry v Hatton* (1864) 2 H. & C. 822.

[65] *Martindale v Smith* (1841) 1 Q.B. 389.

[66] *Strand Electric & Engineering Co Ltd v Brisford Entertainments Ltd* [1952] 2 K.B. 246.

[67] As in *Newsome v Graham* (1829) 10 B. & C. 234 (where the subject-matter was an interest in land). cf. *Hizzett v Hargreaves* [1987] C.L.Y 1164.

[68] See *Warman v Southern Counties Car Finance Corp Ltd* [1959] 2 K.B. 576 at 582–583.

buyer's possible liability to the true owner, the buyer should only have to make an allowance to the seller for the benefit of the use of the goods if the claim of the true owner has first been satisfied.[69]

Relation to damages. In a number of cases it has been held or said that a claimant may be able to get back money paid under a contract *as damages* for the defendant's breach. For example, in one case a cow had been sold warranted healthy, but in fact she suffered from a disease from which she died; and the buyer recovered the price as one item of damages for breach of warranty.[70] Payments made under hire-purchase agreements by hirers have likewise been recovered by them as damages where the goods were so defective that they were completely useless or rightfully rejected by the hirers.[71] Similar relief has been given to buyers and hire purchasers of stolen goods who elected to claim damages[72]; and to tenants who left premises which had been leased to them in consequence of abusive conduct on the part of their landlord, amounting to breach of his covenant for quiet enjoyment.[73] Strictly speaking, the injured party's damages in such cases should be the *value of the subject-matter* at the relevant date,[74] and not *the price* as such. The cases can perhaps be explained on the ground that in them the price was the best, and indeed the only, evidence of value. It is also possible for the price paid under one contract to be recoverable as reliance loss by way of damages for breach of a second contract between the same parties.[75]

In an action for damages the injured party can often recover more than the money he has paid to the defendant. For example, if in consequence of a breach he is deprived of goods, he may be able to recover, not only what he has paid for them, but also money spent on them[76] or loss of profits (subject to the normal limitations on damages, such as remoteness and mitigation). On the other hand, when the injured party claims damages, benefits obtained by him under the contract are, in principle, taken into account; and he will also recover less than the price if he has paid more for the subject-matter than it was worth, or than it would cost to replace. A claim for damages is also subject to practical difficulties, such as quantification and remoteness, which do not arise on a claim for the recovery of money. The question which action should be brought, where both are available,[77] requires a careful weighing of all these factors. It should certainly not be assumed that the action for the recovery of money is necessarily the better remedy.

22–012

---

[69] Law Commission Working Paper No.65, paras 68–70.

[70] *Harling v Eddy* [1951] 2 K.B. 739; cf. *George Wills & Sons Ltd v Thomas Brown & Sons* (1922) 12 Ll.L.R. 292, where no discussion as to damages is reported.

[71] *Charterhouse Credit Co Ltd v Tolly* [1963] 2 Q.B. 683; *Farnworth Finance Facilities Ltd v Attryde* [1970] 1 W.L.R. 1053; *Doobay v Mohabeer* [1967] 2 A.C. 278.

[72] *Mason v Burningham* [1949] 2 K.B. 545; *Warman v Southern Counties Car Finance Corp Ltd* [1949] 2 K.B. 576.

[73] *Sampson v Floyd* [1989] 2 E.G.L.R. 49.

[74] See above, para.20–022 and 20–048 et seq.; *Greenwood v Bennett* [1973] Q.B. 195 at 201 ("the value of the car as he sold it to them"); *The Rio Sun* [1985] 1 Lloyd's Rep. 351 at 368 ("the value of the oil . . . on the date when [the buyers] received it"; cf. in case of failure to render services, *Miles v Wakefield MDC* [1987] A.C. 539 at 568; above, para.17–036, fn.146; *White Arrow Express Ltd v Lamey's Distribution Ltd* [1995] C.L.C. 1251; above, para.20–047; *Peninsular & Orient SN Co v Youell* [1997] 2 Lloyd's Rep. 136 at 141).

[75] *CCC Films (London) Ltd v Impact Quadrant Films Ltd* [1985] Q.B. 16.

[76] See the authorities cited in fnn.70 and 72, above.

[77] See above, para.20–031.

(ii) *Money paid under a void contract*

22–013   **In general.** The law starts with the assumption that money paid under a void contract can be recovered back.[78] Thus in *Bell v Lever Bros Ltd*[79] it was clearly assumed that the money paid by the claimants under the compensation agreements could have been recovered back, had those agreements been void for mistake. Where a hire-purchase agreement was wholly void for mistake it was accordingly held that the hirer could recover back his deposit[80]; and it does not seem that he was under any liability to pay for the use of the subject-matter of the agreement, which had been in his possession for over three months.[81] Where a contract was void because one of the parties was a company not yet in existence when the contract was made,[82] it was similarly held that instalments paid under it could be recovered back by the payor.[83] The same rule has been applied where money was paid under an *ultra vires* contract[84] and where money was paid under a contract which was void by statute.[85]

22–014   **Bases of the rule.** The general rule that money paid under a void contract can be recovered back is clearly established; but there has been some difference of opinion as to its legal basis. This has arisen in cases[86] involving "interest rate swap" contracts under which A (a bank) had made lump sum payments to B (a local authority) which had in turn made some or all of the payments to A which were expressed under the contracts to be due from B to A. The contracts were found to be ultra vires and void[87] because B had no legal power to enter into them and it was argued that A's claim for the recovery of the balance of its payments[88] was barred *either* on the ground that B had made some of the stipulated counter-payments, so that the failure of consideration for A's payments was no more than partial *or* on the ground that the contracts had been fully performed on both sides, so that there had been no failure of consideration at all. For the reasons to be discussed below, however, these arguments were rejected, so that A's claim was upheld in spite of partial performance by B or even full performance by both parties of the void promises.

---

[78] e.g. *Re London County Commercial Reinsurance Office* [1922] 2 Ch. 67; cf. *Colesworthy v Collmain Services* [1993] C.C.L.R. 4; *aliter* if the contract or relevant term is only unenforceable: *Boddington v Lawton* [1994] I.C.R. 478.

[79] [1932] A.C. 161 (above, para.8–017); Landon 51 L.Q.R. 650; Taylor 52 L.Q.R. 27; Landon 52 L.Q.R. 478; Hamson 53 L.Q.R. 118.

[80] *Branwhite v Worcester Works Finance Ltd* [1969] 1 A.C. 552.

[81] No claim of this kind was made by the finance company in *Branwhite's* case.

[82] See above, para.16–072.

[83] *Rover International Ltd v Cannon Films Ltd (No.3)* [1989] 1 W.L.R. 912; Birks 2 J.C.L. 227.

[84] *Westdeutsche Landesbank Girozentrale v Islington LBC* [1994] 1 W.L.R. 938.

[85] See the discussion in *Westdeutsche Landesbank Girozentrale v Islington LBC* at first instance and in the Court of Appeal [1994] 4 All E.R. 890 at 921–924; [1994] 1 W.L.R. 938 at 946, 952 of the cases on contracts made void by Grants of Life Annuities Act 1777 (17 Geo. 3 c.26), s.1. This is presumably the "annuity bill" to which Sir Peter Teazle refers in Sheridan's *The School for Scandal*, III.1 (first produced in 1777).

[86] See especially *Westdeutsche Landesbank Girozentrale v Islington LBC* [1994] 4 All E.R. 890; [1994] 1 W.L.R. 938; [1996] A.C. 669 (reversing the decision below on the issue of compound interest only); Birks 32 U.W.A.L.R. 195; Burrows [1995] R.L.R. 15.

[87] See *Hazell v Hammersmith & Fulham LBC* [1992] A.C. 1.

[88] i.e. the amount by which A's payments exceeded B's.

Lack or failure of consideration. One reason for allowing A's claim was that the principle on which money paid under a void contract is recoverable differs from that of recovery for "total failure of consideration" under a valid contract. Where the contract is void, the right to recover money paid under it is based, not on failure to perform a contractual obligation (since under a void contract there can be no duty to perform[89]), but on the ground that there is "no legal justification"[90] or "no consideration"[91] for the payment. A second, alternative, reason for upholding A's claim was that there *had* (in the interest rate swap cases) been a total failure of consideration. There are, in turn, two versions of this view. One is that all payments made in pursuance of a void contract are "necessarily made for a consideration which has totally failed".[92] But if there is *necessarily* such a total failure of consideration whenever the contract is void, then there is no *separate* requirement of total failure of consideration: recovery is allowed simply because the contract is void. The other version is that there is a total failure of consideration because A had bargained for B's "*obligation . . .* to make counter-payments"[93] and the benefit of B's having *in fact* made such payments was different in kind from the benefit for which A had bargained.[94] Again this will be true in all cases in which payments are made under void contracts, so that on this view, too, there is no *separate* requirement of total failure of consideration.[95]

Mistake. Where money is paid under a void contract, the payment will often be made in the mistaken belief that the contract was valid. Such a mistake was not formerly a ground on which the payor was entitled to the return of his money since the mistake was one of law and it had been held that there was no right to recover back money paid under a mistake of law (as opposed to one of fact). The authorities which had supported this view[96] were, however, overruled by the House of Lords in *Kleinwort Benson Ltd v Lincoln CC*,[97] where moneys had been paid by a bank to local authorities under interest rate swap contracts which were believed to be valid but which were actually void.[98] It was held that the bank was entitled to recover the moneys on the ground that they had been paid under a

22–015

22–016

---

[89] cf. *Guiness Mahon & Co Ltd v Kensington & Chelsea RLBC* [1999] Q.B. 215 at 236.

[90] *Westdeutsche Landesbank Girozentrale v Islington LBC* [1994] 1 W.L.R. 938 at 953; cf. [1994] 4 All E.R. 890 at 929 ("not contractual payments at all"); *Kleinwort Benson Ltd v Birmingham CC* [1997] Q.B. 380 at 394 ("no justification for the retention of the money").

[91] *South Tyneside MBC v Svenska International Plc* [1995] 1 All E.R. 545 at 577; cf. *Westdeutsche* case, above, fn.86 [1994] 4 All E.R. 890 at 924 ("absence of consideration"); *Kleinwort Benson Ltd v Birmingham CC* [1997] Q.B. 380 at 386–387.

[92] *Guiness Mahon & Co Ltd v Kensington & Chelsea RLBC* [1999] Q.B. 215 at 230.

[93] *Westdeutsche* case, above, fn.86 [1996] A.C. 669 at 711 (italics supplied) approving the reasoning of the Court of Appeal [1994] 1 W.L.R. 938 at 943, per Dillon L.J.; Legatt L.J., [1994] 1 W.L.R. 938 at 951–953 is more equivocal as to the basis of recovery; cf. *Kleinwort Benson Ltd v Glasgow CC* [1999] 1 A.C. 153 at 167, 171.

[94] In this respect these cases can be said to resemble *Rowland v Divall* [1923] 2 K.B. 500; above, para.22–007.

[95] In *Haugesund Kommune v Depfa ACS Bank* [2010] EWCA Civ 579; [2011] 1 All E.R. 190 at [62] Aikens L.J. referred to the distinction between "total failure of consideration" or "absence of consideration" as "a question of which is the more apt terminology; it does not have any legal significance".

[96] *Bilbie v Lumley* 1802) 2 East 469; *Brisbane v Dacres* (1813) 5 Taunt. 143; *Kelly v Solari* (1841) 9 M. & W. 54.

[97] [1999] 2 A.C. 349; *Nurdin & Peacock Plc v D B Ramsden & Co Ltd* [1999] 1 All E.R. 941.

[98] See above, at fn.87.

mistake of law.[99] It was further held that this right was not barred by the fact that the contract had been fully performed by both parties. The cases which supported the latter proposition where the claim was based, not on mistake, but simply on the fact that the contract was void[100] were referred to with approval, thus further supporting the view that money paid under a void contract is recoverable by the payor even though the circumstances are not such as would have given rise, if the contract had been valid, to a total failure of consideration. The reason for this conclusion was that the policy of the rule making the contract void might be defeated if full or partial performance of the contract were a bar to recovery: e.g. if a local authority were precluded by such a bar from recovering ultra vires payments made in the mistaken belief that they were intra vires and hence legally due.[101]

22–017   **Practical considerations.** There are also practical grounds for not applying the "total failure of consideration" requirement to claims for the recovery of payments under void contracts. Where the contract is *valid*, a party who is denied the right to recover back payments because he has received partial performance will normally have a claim for damages in respect of the part left unperformed. Where, on the other hand, the contract is *void*, denial of restitution of money paid on the ground that the payee has partly performed his void promise, would leave the payor without any remedy in respect of the unperformed part.[102] In the interest rate swap cases, there is the further point that there was no difficulty in apportioning the partial performance by B to the total performance for which A had bargained, so that one rationale of the requirement that the failure must be total did not exist and the cases could be brought within the exception to that requirement which exists in cases of such apportionability.[103] Moreover, where the partial or total performance which has taken place consists simply of payments and counter-payments of money under a void contract, there is no difficulty in restoring each party to its pre-contract position and hence no injustice is likely to result from allowing recovery of the balance. It follows from this reasoning that the right to recover might be barred where supervening events do make such mutual restoration impossible.[104] The interest rate swap cases also do not directly touch the problem which would arise where the performance rendered by one party to a void contract is of such a nature that it cannot literally be restored: e.g. where A had paid a sum of money in advance to B in return for B's promise to render services and after some of the services had been rendered it was discovered that B had no power to enter into the contract so that it was ultra vires and void. It is submitted that in such a case A should be entitled to recover its payment on the ground that the contract was void; but that this right should be subject to B's right

---

[99] The bank's reason for relying on mistake was to enable it to take advantage of Limitation Act 1980, s.32(1), under which, in an action "for relief from the consequences of a mistake" the period of limitation did not begin to run until the plaintiff had, or with reasonable diligence could have, discovered the mistake.

[100] e.g. *Westdeutsche Landesbank Girozentrale v Islington LBC*, above, fn.86; *Guiness Mahon & Co v Kensington & Chelsea RLBC*, above, fn.89.

[101] *Kleinwort Benson* case (above, fn.97) [1999] 2 A.C. 349 at 387, 415–416; cf. above, para. 12–080.

[102] cf. above, para.22–004.

[103] See above, para.22–004.

[104] See *Kleinwort Benson Ltd v South Tyneside MBC* [1994] 4 All E.R. 972.

to retain so much of that payment as B could have recovered by way of quantum meruit for work done under a void contract.[105]

Special cases. The rule that money paid under a void contract is recoverable   22–018
is no more than a general one,[106] which may be displaced by the policy considerations underlying the rule of law which makes the contract void. It may, for example, be displaced under the rules (discussed earlier in this book) relating to illegal contracts and minors' contracts.[107] An as yet unresolved question would arise where the contract was void for more than one reason.[108] It may, for example, be both an ultra vires contract and illegal; so that money paid under the contract is prima facie recoverable on the first ground but irrecoverable on the second. The solution in such cases would appear to depend on the reason why the money is thus either recoverable or irrecoverable. Where the contract was both ultra vires and illegal, the policy of the rule making it illegal would normally prevail, so that (for example) a payment made by a local authority for the supply of prostitutes to its members would appear to be irrecoverable. But this can be no more than a general rule: illegality can vary widely in its seriousness so that the answer to the present question would depend in each case on the factors more fully discussed in Ch.11: i.e. on the nature of the illegality and on the states of mind of the parties.

(b) Quantum Meruit[109]

Here we are concerned with cases in which a party claims a reasonable   22–019
recompense for some benefit[110] (other than a payment of money) conferred by him under contract or a purported contract. Many such cases have already been discussed elsewhere in this book and are mentioned here only for the sake of completeness. In those cases where there is a contract between the parties,[111] there may be an express provision for remuneration on specified events[112] and, where that is the case, the general rule is that the court cannot award any other remuneration on those events, nor can it award any remuneration if they do not occur.[113] To allow quantum meruit claims in such cases would contradict the agreement reached by the parties, and the courts will do this only if there are special circumstances justifying such interference.

Contracts not providing for remuneration. A party can claim a quantum   22–020
meruit for work done or goods delivered under a contract which does not expressly provide how much he is to be paid, or which makes some, but not a full,

---

[105] See below, para.22–024.
[106] *Guiness Mahon & Co Ltd v Kensington & Chelsea RLBC* [1999] Q.B. 215 at 231.
[107] See above, paras 11–128—11–150, 12–036—12–042, 12–048—12–051.
[108] See *Morgan Grenfell & Co Ltd v Welwyn Hatfield DC* [1995] 1 All E.R. 1 at 15 where this point was left open.
[109] Birks (1974) C.L.P. 13; Jones (1977) 93 L.Q.R. 273.
[110] Since the basis of liability is the unjust enrichment of the other party, work done which does not benefit that party will not suffice, as in, e.g., *Regalian Properties Plc v London Dockland Development Corp* [1995] 1 W.L.R. 212; below, para.22–021.
[111] See below, paras.22–022, 22–023.
[112] E.g. payment only upon completed performance of an entire obligation: see below, para.22–023.
[113] *Wiluszynski v Tower Hamlets LBC* [1989] I.C.R. 493

provision for payment.[114] This will be the case where the whole agreement is implied from conduct,[115] or where it is simply silent as to the rate of payment. Sometimes it may be clear from the terms of the agreement, or from the circumstances in which it was made, that the claimant was not intended to have any legal right to be paid at all.[116] But if he was intended to have such a right the court will award a reasonable sum. Thus if a contract for the sale of goods does not fix the price, the buyer must pay a reasonable price[117]; and if a contract for services does not fix the remuneration, a reasonable sum must be paid.[118]

22–021 **No concluded contract.**[119] Work may be done and a quantum meruit awarded to the party who has done the work where the parties believe that there is a contract but this is not the case because there was never a clear acceptance of an offer.[120] Such an award may also be made where work is done, under an agreement which lacks contractual force for want of contractual intention,[121] in anticipation of a formal contract which fails to materialise for want of execution of the requisite formal document[122]; and where one party does work at the request of the other during negotiations which are expected to lead to a contract between them but are broken off before its conclusion.[123] But no such award will be made where the party doing the work takes the risk that the negotiations may fail. This was held to be the position where one party to an agreement "subject to contract"[124] incurred expenses without any request from, and without benefiting, the other but solely for the purpose of securing (and then of performing) the contract.[125] An award is made for the market value of the services provided;[126] a figure put forward as a proposed settlement may provide some indication of that value,[127] but should not be taken into account "to the extent of *substituting* it for the market value of the services provided."[128]

---

[114] *Sir Lindsay Parkinson & Co Ltd v Commissioners of Works* [1949] 2 K.B. 632; cf. *Steven v Bromley & Son* [1919] 2 K.B. 722; *The Gregos* [1985] 2 Lloyd's Rep. 347; *The Saronikos* [1986] 2 Lloyd's Rep. 277

[115] See above, paras 2–004, 2–018; *Paynter v Williams* (1833) 1 C. & M. 810; cf. *The Batis* [1990] 1 Lloyd's Rep. 345; *The Kurnia Dewi* [1997] 1 Lloyd's Rep. 553.

[116] See above, paras 4–018, 16–084.

[117] Sale of Goods Act 1979, s.8(2).

[118] Supply of Goods and Services Act 1982, s.15(1); cf. at common law *Way v Latilla* [1937] 3 All E.R. 759; *Berezovsky v Edmiston & Co Ltd* [2011] EWCA Civ 431.

[119] Barker 19 J.C.L. 105; Edelman, in Burrows & Peel (eds.), *Contract Formation and Parties*.

[120] *Peter Lind & Co Ltd v Mersey Docks & Harbour Board* [1972] 2 Lloyd's Rep. 234; above, para. 2–020.

[121] *Galliard Homes Ltd v Jarvis Interiors Ltd* [2000] C.L.C. 411.

[122] ibid. This was accepted by both parties (though doubted by Evans L.J.).

[123] *William Lacey (Hounslow) Ltd v Davis* [1957] 1 W.L.R. 932; *BSC v Cleveland Bridge & Engineering Co Ltd* [1984] 1 All E.R. 504; Ball 99 L.Q.R. 572; *Marston Construction Co v Kigass* (1990) 15 Con.L.R. 116; Key 111 L.Q.R. 576; *Countrywide Communications Ltd v ICL Pathways Ltd* [2000] C.L.C. 324; *Cobbe v Yeoman's Row Management Ltd* [2008] UKHL 55; [2008] 1 W.L.R. 1752; *Whittle Movers Ltd v Hollywood Express Ltd* [2009] EWCA Civ 1189; [2009] 2 C.L.C. 771; Davies 126 L.Q.R. 175; *Benourad v Compass Group Plc* [2010] EWHC 1882 (QB) at [106].

[124] See above, para.2–094.

[125] *Regalian Properties Plc v London Dockland Development Corp* [1995] 1 W.L.R. 212, where the *Marston Construction* case, above, fn.123 was at 229 described as a "surprising decision"; cf. *Blue Haven Enterprises Ltd v Tully* [2006] UKPC 17; *MSM Consulting Ltd v Tanzania* [2009] EWHC 121 (QB); 123 Con L.R. 154 at [171](d).

[126] *Benedetti v Sawiris* [2010] EWCA Civ 1427; *Cobbe v Yeoman's Row Management Ltd* [2008] UKHL 55; [2008] 1 W.L.R. 1752.

[127] As in *Cobbe v Yeoman's Row Management Ltd* [2008] UKHL 55; [2008] 1 W.L.R. 1752

[128] *Benedetti v Sawiris* [2010] EWCA Civ 1427 at [85] (emphasis added).

Contract terminated for breach: claim by innocent party. Termination   22–022
for breach operates prospectively and does not affect obligations and rights which
accrued prior to termination[129]; if, at that time, the claimant has performed his
part of the contract by carrying out work,[130] he will be confined to his action on
the contract, e.g. in debt, or in damages.[131] Where, he has been prevented from
completing performance of an obligation he can claim a quantum meruit at the
contract rate[132] for work done, even though the unperformed obligation is
entire.[133] The party in breach cannot complain of having to pay in circumstances
other than those provided for by the contract.

Contract terminated for breach: claim by party in breach. In Ch.17 we   22–023
saw that, in general, a person who failed to complete performance of an entire
obligation could not recover anything[134]; but that this rule was subject to a number
of exceptions.[135] Under some of these, there is a right to payment of the contract
price or at the contract rate. Under others, there is a right to a quantum meruit
(or reasonable remuneration): e.g. where a benefit conferred by partial performance of services is "voluntarily" accepted by the other party.

In a number of further exceptional cases, a reasonable sum is, or may be, payable
for services rendered by the party in breach even though the services differ from,
or fall short of, those bargained for, there has been no "voluntary" acceptance of
them by the injured party, and the contract remains in force. For example, it has
been said that a carrier by sea who deviates but carries the goods to the agreed
destination can recover a reasonable freight[136]; and conflicting views have been
expressed on the question whether an employer who "of necessity" accepts
services falling short of those bargained for is liable to his employee for a quantum
meruit.[137] Such exceptional cases are controversial precisely because they reveal a
conflict between two policies. One is that the court should not unjustifiably
contradict a subsisting contract by awarding a reasonable sum for services falling
short of those promised; the other is that the court should not allow the injured
party to have the benefit of those services for nothing, since this would lead to his
being unjustly enriched. The exact scope and rationale of the present group of
exceptional cases must therefore remain very much in doubt.

Contract void. In *Craven-Ellis v Canons Ltd*[138] the claimant worked for the   22–024
defendant company as managing director. His service agreement with the company

---

[129] See above, para.18–011.

[130] For payments which have been made, termination may be given a retrospective effect: see below,
para.22–005.

[131] *Taylor v Motability Finance* Ltd [2004] EWHC 2619 (Comm) at [25].

[132] ibid. at [26]; cf. *Lusty v Finsbury Securities* (1991) 58 Build. L.R. 66; *Kehoe v Borough of
Rutherford* 27 A 912 (1893); *Vedatech Corp v Crystal Decisions (UK) Ltd* [2002] EWHC 818 at
[76]–[79]. There is support for the award of the actual value of the work without reference to the
contract price: *Lodder v Slowey* [1904] A.C. 442; *Boomer v Muir* 24 P.2d. 570 (1933) but it seems absurd
that the injured party should recover more for partial, than he could recover for full, performance.
Where one party, after the other's breach, does *extra* work, the reasonable sum recoverable for the work
may exceed the damages recoverable for the breach: *The Batis* [1990] 1 Lloyd's Rep. 345.

[133] See above, para.17–046.

[134] See above, paras 17–031—17–034.

[135] See above, paras 17–041—17–045.

[136] *Hain SS Co Td v Tate & Lyle Ltd* (1936) 41 Com. Cas. 350 at 358, 367; above, para.17–044,
fn.195.

[137] *Miles v Wakefield Metropolitan DC* [1987] A.C. 539 at 552–553, 561; above, para.17–045; cf.
Wiluszynski v Tower Hamlets LBC [1989] I.C.R. 493.

[138] [1936] 2 K.B. 403; Denning 55 L.Q.R. 54.

was void as neither he nor those who appointed him held the necessary qualification shares.[139] Thus he could not recover his agreed pay.[140] But the Court of Appeal held that he was entitled to a quantum meruit. The position is the same where a contract with a company is void because the company was not yet in existence or had been dissolved[141] when the contract was made.[142] A similar principle may apply where goods have been supplied under a contract of sale which is void for a mistake as to the identity of the buyer.[143]

Where the express contract is a nullity, the argument that the court must not interfere with the bargain between the parties loses much of its force.[144] It does not seem that liability in these cases is based on an agreement which can be implied from voluntary acceptance by the defendant of the claimant's services,[145] for the parties usually think that they are acting under an existing valid contract.[146] In *Craven-Ellis v Canons Ltd* Greer L.J. said that the liability to pay a quantum meruit

"is an inference which a rule of law imposes on the parties where work has been done or goods have been delivered under what purports to be a binding contract but is not so in fact".[147]

The principle just stated may, however, be displaced by countervailing policy considerations. In *Guinness Plc v Saunders*[148] a company director did work for the company in the course of negotiations for a take-over bid which was being made by the company. The agreement under which the work was done was void because those who purported to make it on behalf of the company had no authority to do so.[149] It was held that the director was not entitled to quantum meruit since the terms of the agreement (by which his remuneration increased with the amount paid by the company) gave rise to a conflict between his own financial interest and his fiduciary duty to the company as one of its directors.

22–025   **Contract frustrated.** Work done under a contract *before* it is frustrated does not give rise to any quantum meruit claim at common law, though a claim in respect of a valuable benefit conferred by such work can be made under the Law Reform (Frustrated Contracts) Act 1943.[150] But if work is done under the contract *after* frustration, it may be possible to claim a quantum meruit on the principle of

[139] See now Companies Act 2006, ss.40, 41; above. para.12–069.
[140] cf. *Re Bodega Co* [1904] 1 Ch. 276: if he is paid his contractual remuneration he must pay it back.
[141] See above, para.16–072.
[142] *Rover International Ltd v Cannon Films Ltd (No.3)* [1989] 1 W.L.R. 912; *Cotronic (UK) Ltd v Dezonie* [1991] B.C.L.C. 721; above, para.16–072. For pre-incorporation contracts with limited liability partnerships, see Limited Liability Partnerships Act 2000, s.5(2); above, para.16–065.
[143] e.g. on the facts of *Boulton v Jones* (1857) 27 L.J. Ex. 117; for the exact nature of the appropriate remedy in such a situation, see above, para.8–045.
[144] *Rover International Ltd v Cannon Films Ltd (No.3)* [1989] 1 W.L.R. 912 at 927
[145] *Contra*, Denning, above, fn.138.
[146] And, for the same reason that the contract was void in the first place, there was no one qualified to "accept" the benefit; the company is viewed as having obtained the "incontrovertible benefit" of the director's services: Birks 24 C.L.P. 110.
[147] At 410.
[148] [1990] 2 A.C. 663; Beatson and Prentice 106 L.Q.R. 365.
[149] See now Companies Act 2006, ss.40, 41; above, para.12–069.
[150] s.1(3); above, para.19–100; cf. also the rights of "commercial agents" under the legislation discussed at para.19–108, above.

Craven-Ellis v Canons Ltd. The argument that the court must not interfere with the express contract is here met by the fact that the contract has no longer any legal force. A contract for the carriage of goods may be frustrated because the method of performance becomes impossible. The carrier may nonetheless get the goods to their destination in some other way. So long as he acts reasonably in doing so, he can claim a quantum meruit. It is irrelevant that a new contract cannot be implied from the mere fact that the cargo-owner accepts the cargo at its destination.[151]

Contract unenforceable. Work done under a contract which is unenforceable **22–026** for want of formality,[152] or because it is in restraint of trade,[153] may give rise to a quantum meruit at the contract rate,[154] provided such payment does not undermine the policy of the rule which rendered the contract unenforceable.[155]

Incapacity. Where necessaries are sold and delivered to a minor, he need only **22–027** pay a reasonable price for them, although he may have agreed to pay more.[156] There are obvious reasons of policy for interfering with the agreement in such a case. There would be no such reasons where the minor had agreed to pay less than a reasonable price.

---

[151] *The Massalia* [1961] 2 Q.B. 278; overruled in *The Eugenia* [1964] 2 Q.B. 226, but not on this point; cf. *The Kos* [2010] EWCA Civ 772; [2010] 2 Lloyd's Rep. 409.

[152] *Scarisbrick v Pattison* (1869) 20 L.T. 175; cf. *Pulbrook v Lawes* (1876) 1 Q.B.D. 284; *Deglman v Guaranty Trust Co of Canada and Constantineau* [1954] 3 D.L.R. 785; *Pavey & Matthews Ltd v Paul* (1987) 69 A.L.J.R. 577.

[153] *Proactive Sports Management Ltd v Rooney* [2010] EWHC 1807 (QB).

[154] *Scarisbrick v Pattison*, above fn.152; cf. *Benedetti v Sawiris* [2010] EWCA Civ 1427 at [63], [85]; contrast *Proactive Sports Management Ltd v Rooney* above, at [757]–[762].

[155] *Pavey & Matthews Ltd v Paul* (1986) 162 C.L.R. 221 at 584–585; Beatson 104 L.Q.R. 13; cf. *Dimond v Lovell* [2002] 1 A.C. 384 at 398; *Proactive Sports Management Ltd v Rooney* [2010] EWHC 1807 (QB) at [752].

[156] See above, para.12–008; the same is also sometimes true where necessaries are sold and delivered to a person incapacitated by other factors, such as mental illness, drink or drugs: above, paras 12–052—12–068.

INDEX